MacGillivray
on
Insurance Law

relating to all risks other than marine

Tenth Edition

General Editor

NICHOLAS LEGH-JONES, M.A. (Oxon.)
Of Lincoln's Inn and of the Middle Temple,
One of Her Majesty's Counsel

Editors

JOHN BIRDS, LL.M.
Professor of Commercial Law at the University of Sheffield

DAVID OWEN, B.A. (Oxon.)
Of the Middle Temple
Barrister

London
Sweet and Maxwell
2003

First Edition	(1912)	By E. J. MacGillivray
Second Edition	(1937)	By E. J. MacGillivray and Denis Browne
Third Edition	(1947)	By E. J. MacGillivray K.C. and Denis Browne
Fourth Edition	(1953)	By E. J. MacGillivray Q.C. and Denis Browne
Fifth Edition	(1961)	By Denis Browne
Sixth Edition	(1975)	By Michael Parkington, Anthony O'Dowd
Seventh Edition	(1981)	Nicholas Legh-Jones and Andrew Longmore
Eighth Edition	(1988)	By Michael Parkington, Nicholas Legh-Jones Q.C., Andrew Longmore Q.C. and John Birds
Ninth Edition	(1997)	By Nicholas Legh-Jones Q.C., Sir Andrew Longmore, John Birds and David Owen
Tenth Edition	(2002)	By Nicholas Legh-Jones Q.C., John Birds and David Owen

Published by
Sweet and Maxwell Limited of
100 Avenue Road, Swiss Cottage, London NW3 3PF
(http://www.sweetandmaxwell.co.uk)

Printed and bound in Great Britain by
MPG Books Ltd, Bodmin, Cornwall

*No natural forests were destroyed to make this product;
only farmed timber was used and replanted*

A CIP catalogue record for this book is available from the British
Library

ISBN 0 421 70430 6

PREFACE

We note with regret the decision of Sir Andrew Longmore to leave the editorial team in view of the demands made on his time by high judicial office. He was responsible for a large part of the text of the last four editions of MacGillivray. We have greatly missed his valued contribution, especially his unequalled ability to extract the essence of a complex case from a lengthy law report. It is some consolation that we will continue to receive guidance in a different manner from his judgments in insurance cases.

Five years have passed since the publication of the last edition of MacGillivray, and several developments have required amendments to the text. Among these the Financial Services and Markets Act 2000 is perhaps predominant, together with its plethora of regulations and other subordinate legislation, but the new E.C. Council Regulation No. 44/2001, the Contracts (Rights of Third Parties) Act 1999, and the continuing flow of insurance law decisions from the courts, now reported in an increased number of English law reports and insurance law periodicals, have also called for substantial revisions to the book. Among the latter the three recent appellate court decisions on the post-contractual duty of utmost good faith are among the most significant.

While MacGillivray has never aspired to be a textbook on marine insurance law, these decisions in *The Star Sea, The Mercandian Continent* and *The Aegeon* serve to underline the fact that the law laid down in the Marine Insurance Act 1906 is frequently applicable to non-marine insurance, and we therefore continue to cite marine insurance decisions where they illustrate the law relating to non-marine insurance.

We are grateful to Mr Christopher Hancock QC for undertaking the revision of Chapter 10 (Policy terms) and to Miss Sarah Wolffe of the Scottish Bar for reviewing and updating the Scots Law sections of Chapter 9 (Salvage premiums) and Chapter 24 (Life insurance). We would also like to thank our colleagues (too numerous to name here) who, sometimes without realising it, have either drawn our attention to new developments in the law or have contributed to our better understanding of it.

We have endeavoured to state the law as at May 31, 2002, and thank our Publishers for permitting us to include some subsequent English case law as circumstances have allowed.

P.N.L.-J.
J.B.
D.C.O.

v

CONTENTS

CONTENTS

CONTENTS

TABLE OF CASES

[xv]

TABLE OF STATUTES

International Law

TABLE OF STATUTORY INSTRUMENTS

NON-STATUTORY RULES AND REGULATIONS

RULES OF THE SUPREME COURT

SECTION 1

GENERAL PRINCIPLES

CHAPTER 1

DEFINITION OF INSURANCE AND INSURABLE INTEREST

1. INTRODUCTION

1–1 "Contract of insurance"—definition. A satisfactory definition of "contract of insurance" is elusive, but the use of the phrase to define the ambit of fiscal and regulatory legislation has made the task of attempting it inescapable.[1] A useful working definition can be derived from that given by Channell J. in *Prudential Insurance Company v. Inland Revenue Commissioners.*[2] A contract of insurance is one whereby one party (the "insurer") promises in return for a money consideration (the "premium") to pay to the other party (the "assured") a sum of money or provide him with some corresponding benefit, upon the occurrence of one or more specified events. The elements of this definition must be elaborated.

1–2 "Premium." The purpose of a contract of insurance is to organise the sharing among a large number of persons of the cost of losses which are likely to happen only to some of them (or to happen at an earlier time to some than to others). It is therefore characteristic of the contract that the amount of the premium is not intended to be equivalent to the value of the insurer's actual performance (if any) but is calculated in relation to the likelihood that performance will be required (or will be required within a certain time). This characteristic distinguishes contracts of insurance from certain others. Thus a contract by which an engineer undertakes to repair a machine whenever it breaks down is clearly not a contract of insurance if the engineer is to be remunerated in accordance with the amount of work done. If, however, the remuneration is fixed without regard to the amount of work done, it is a consideration of the type of an insurance premium and the contract may be one of insurance.

1–3 "Promises to pay." The insurer must undertake a binding obligation to pay the assured upon the happening of the relevant event. A contract whereby the notional assured has no contractual right to be paid in that eventuality but merely a right to require the notional insurer to give earnest consideration to his claim for an indemnity, and to pay him at its discretion, is

---

[1] The Insurance Companies Act 1982, s.2 and *passim*. For the distinction between insurance and guarantee, see para. 31–40, *post*.
[2] [1904] 2 K.B. 658.

[3]

not a contract of insurance.[3] A contract of insurance is intended to convey security and certainty to the assured, and not merely an expectation of payment, however well founded.[4] A contract in which a part of the cover depends upon the exercise of a discretion in favour of the assured may still be described in general terms as a contract of insurance but the elements of insurance and the discretionary element may have to be separated in certain circumstances.[5]

1–4 "Sum of money or corresponding benefit." It was formerly thought that the only obligation undertaken by the insurer under a contract of insurance was to pay money.[6] However, the decision in *Department of Trade and Industry v. St Christopher Motorists' Association Ltd*[7] widens the definition to include the provision of services to be paid for by the insurer for the benefit of the assured.[8] In that case a company agreed to provide to members of a proprietary club a driver, or a car with driver, in the event of a member being prevented from driving by disqualification or injury. The Department of Trade and Industry sought declarations, *inter alia*, that the company was carrying on an insurance business and was effecting contracts of insurance with members of the club. Templeman J. granted the declarations sought, relying on the part of the judgment of Channell J. in *Prudential Insurance Company v. Inland Revenue Commissioners*,[9] where the learned judge said:

> "A contract of insurance, then, must be a contract for the payment of a sum of money, or for some corresponding benefit such as the rebuilding of a house or the repairing of a ship, to become due on the happening of an event . . ."[10]

Templeman J. thought that the act of the defendant company in paying the driver for the member's benefit fell within the meaning of the phrase "some corresponding benefit",[11] and that it could not logically be distinguished from the alternative of paying the money to the member in order to enable him to engage the chauffeur.[12]

---

[3] *Medical Defence Union Ltd v. Department of Trade* [1980] Ch. 82; *C.V.G. Siderurgica del Orinoco SA v. London Mutual Steamship Owners' Assoc. Ltd* [1979] 1 Lloyd's Rep. 557, 580; *Rafter v. Solicitors Mutual Defence Fund* [1999] 2 I.L.R.M. 305.

[4] *Hampton v. Toxteth Co-op. Provident Soc. Ltd* [1915] 1 Ch. 721

[5] *e.g.* the right to require a claim for indemnity to be considered will not pass to a third party under an Act transferring rights of insurance—*C.V.G. Siderurgica del Orinoco SA v. London Mutual Steamship Owners' Assoc. Ltd* [1979] 1 Lloyd's Rep. 557.

[6] *Rayner v. Preston* (1881) 18 Ch.D. 1, 9; Halsbury's *Laws of England* (4th ed., 1978), Vol. 25, p. 9; *Chitty on Contracts* (23rd ed., 1968), Vol. II, p. 477.

[7] [1974] 1 W.L.R. 99.

[8] *Chitty on Contracts* (28th ed., 1999) para. 41–001; Colinvaux's, *Law of Insurance* (7th ed., 1997), para. 1–055.

[9] [1904] 2 K.B. 658.

[10] [1904] 2 K.B. 658, 664.

[11] [1974] 1 W.L.R. 99, 106.

[12] The extended definition has been accepted by Megarry V.-C. in *Medical Defence Union v. Department of Trade* [1980] Ch. 82, 97; by Nicholls V.-C. in *Fuji Finance Inc. v. Aetna Life Ins. Co.* [1995] Ch. 122, 130, not criticised on appeal—[1997] Ch. 173, and by Rattee J. in *Re Sentinel Securities plc* [1996] 1 W.L.R. 316. Further, the legislature has clearly accepted that a contract of insurance can exist when only benefits in kind are to be provided and it would not appear to

1–5 "Upon a special event." The event must be one involving uncertainty. "There must be either uncertainty whether the event will happen or not, or, if the event is one which must happen at some time, there must be uncertainty as to the time at which it will happen."[13] Channell J. added that the event "must be of a character more or less adverse to the interest of the person effecting the insurance".[14] That is true of indemnity insurance, and of property and liability insurance generally, but it is not the happiest way to describe the achievement of qualifying for payment under a life policy by attaining a given age or surviving for a stated period of years.[15] In this respect the definition given by Channell J. has to be qualified.

1–6 The question was raised in both the *St Christopher Motorists' Association*[16] case and the *Medical Defence Union*[17] case whether the event on which the insurer's liability depends must be one outside the control of the insurer. The point was not decided in either case. It is certainly necessary to distinguish an insurance contract from the express or implied undertaking of a contracting party to pay damages, or to perform some other secondary obligation, such as the repair of a defective article, in the event of his own failure to perform a primary obligation. To admit that a person may offer insurance against the possibility that he himself may commit some voluntary act would be to risk confusing this necessary distinction. It is therefore, submitted that the event upon which a contract of insurance depends must be an event outside the control of the insurer.

1–7 An insurer does not warrant that the relevant event or contingency will not occur.[18] A contract of marine insurance, for instance, is not an assurance that the insured vessel will not sink.[19] Once the specified event happens, however, the insurer on a contingency policy must pay whatever sums are agreed by the policy to be due upon the occurrence of that event.[20] In the case of an indemnity insurance the insurer undertakes to hold the assured harmless against loss caused by an insured peril.[21] Accordingly, once insured property is damaged by fire the insurer is liable in damages to the assured for failing to hold him harmless against loss caused by the fire,[22] while under a liability policy the assured has a right in equity to be indemnified so soon as his liability to a third party is established and

matter whether the insurer pays for benefits to be provided by a third party to the insured (as in the *St Christopher* case) or whether the insurer itself provides the benefits to the insured. Obviously without exemption such contracts require authorisation. The current exemption covers motorists' breakdown assistance contracts: see the Financial Services & Markets Act 2000 Regulated Activities Order, Art. 12 and para. 34–19, *post*.

[13] *Prudential Insurance Co. v. Inland Revenue Commrs* [1904] 2 K.B. 658, 663; *Commercial Union Assurance Co. v. Federal Commissioners of Taxation* (1976–77) 14 A.L.R. 651, 662; *Fuji Finance Inc. v. Aetna Life Ins. Co.* [1995] Ch. 122, 129; [1997] Ch. 173, 198. See also *D.T.I. v. St Christopher's Motorists' Assoc.* [1974] 1 W.L.R. 99, 105; *Lucena v. Craufurd* (1806) 2 Bos. & P. (N.R.) 269, 301; *Scottish Amicable Heritable Secs. v. Northern Ass. Co.* (1883) 11 R. 287, 303.

[14] [1904] 2 K.B. 658, 664.

[15] *Gould v. Curtis* [1913] 3 K.B. 84; *Medical Defence Union v. Department of Trade* [1980] Ch. 82, 93.

[16] [1974] 1 W.L.R. 99.

[17] [1980] Ch. 82.

[18] *Callaghan v. Dominion Ins. Co.* [1997] 2 Lloyd's Rep. 541, 544.

[19] *Grant Smith & Co. v. Seattle Construction Co.* [1920] A.C. 162, 172.

[20] *Virk v. Gan Life Holdings PLC* [2000] Lloyd's Rep. I.R. 159, 162.

[21] *Firma C-Trade SA v. Newcastle P. & I. Assoc.* [1991] 2 A.C. 1.

[22] *Callaghan v. Dominion Ins. Co.* [1997] 2 Lloyd's Rep. 541.

ascertained, and before he has made a payment.[23] These general principles are subject to the provisions of the policy in any given case.[24]

1–8 Problems in Classification. It is sometimes necessary to decide in the context of fiscal or regulatory legislation whether a contract containing insurance and non-insurance elements should be classified wholly or partly as a contract of insurance. The inclusion of indemnity provisions within a contract for the supply of services neither makes the indemnifier an insurer nor justifies describing the contract as wholly or partly one of insurance.[25] When a contract of sale or for services contains elements of insurance it will be regarded as a contract of insurance only if, taking the contract as a whole, it can be said to have as its principal object the provision of insurance. So where a "card protection plan" offered insurance and other facilities to subscribers, it was held to be a contract for the provision of insurance, and so exempt from value added tax, because the dominant objective of the plan was to offer insurance against financial loss and the non-insurance services provided were viewed as minor and ancillary to that aim.[26] The "principal object" test is not, however, appropriate where the contract in question does not have distinct insurance and non-insurance elements, and the question at issue is whether it is properly to be characterised as insurance. In *Fuji Finance Inc. v. Aetna Life Insurance Co.*[27] the question was whether a single premium "capital investment bond" in the form of a life assurance policy was a contract of life assurance, or merely an investment contract. Given that the element of investment is a common feature of modern life assurance policies it was not a case of a contract containing distinct insurance and non-insurance elements, and the Court of Appeal held that the correct approach was to characterise the contract as a whole and then see if it came within the definition of life assurance, which it did.[28]

1–9 One area in which problems of classification have recently arisen is that of after sale warranties and guarantees. When the retailer of a consumer product arranges an insurance under which the purchaser is to be indemnified against the cost of repairing or replacing the product should it break down within a given time span, that is clearly warranty insurance.[29] Where, at the other extreme, the contract of sale itself provides that the retailer will repair or replace the product in that event, or will procure a third party to do so, his undertaking may be regarded as ancillary to the sale of the product and not the provision of breakdown insurance. But where the retailer makes a separate contract with the purchaser as agent for another company, by which the second company promises, for an extra fee, to procure the repair or replacement of a defective product, or to reimburse the purchaser for the cost of having it repaired or replaced elsewhere, then that contract is capable

[23] *Firma C-Trade SA v. Newcastle P. & I. Assoc.* [1991] 2 A.C. 1.
[24] *Virk v. Gan Life Holdings PLC* [2000] Lloyd's Rep. I.R. 159, 164.
[25] *Larrinaga S.S. Co. v. R.* [1945] A.C. 246, 256, 261 (time charterparty); *Caledonia North Sea v. London Bridge Engineering Co.* [2000] Lloyd's Rep. I.R. 249, 263, 287, 291 (specialised service agreement) upheld in H.L. [2002] 1 Lloyd's Rep. 553; *L'Alsacienne Première Soc. v. Unistorebrand Int. Ins. A.S.* [1995] L.R. 333, 348 (business novation agreement).
[26] *Card Protection Plan Ltd v. Customs & Excise Commrs.* [2001] 1 All E.R. (Comm) 438.
[27] [1997] Ch. 173 reversing [1995] Ch. 122.
[28] The decision is the subject of further comment in para. 1–68, *infra*.
[29] An example of extended warranty insurance will be found in *Re. Cavalier Ins. Co.* [1989] 2 Lloyd's Rep. 431.

of being defined as a contract of insurance regardless of the fact that it is not described as such by the parties to the transaction.

1–10 Distinction between insurance and wagers. Both insurance contracts and wagering contracts are aleatory. The risk of loss in a wager, however, is created by the making of the bet itself, and the sole interest of each party consists of the sum or stake he will either win or lose, whereas typically the function of insurance is to protect the assured in respect of the risk of loss to an interest he possesses independently of the conclusion of the insurance contract.[30] This leads to a consideration of the interest required in the subject matter of the insurance.

1–11 Nature of insurable interest. Insurable interest may be described loosely as the assured's pecuniary interest in the subject-matter of the insurance arising from a relationship with it recognised in law.[31] There is nothing in the common law which prohibits contracts of insurance made without interest[32] but a person insured under a contract of insurance is required to possess an insurable interest either because the requirement is inherent in the nature of the particular contract of insurance in order for it to be enforceable or because it is stipulated by statute as a condition of the validity of the policy or for both of these reasons. Insurable interest stipulated by statute must be distinguished at the outset from that required by the character of the contract of insurance itself.

1–12 Interest required by policy of indemnity. If, upon a proper construction of the policy, the insurer has undertaken to indemnify the assured against loss caused by or arising from particular risks, an interest is required by reason of the nature of the contract itself. If the assured has no interest at the time when the event insured against occurs, it is clear that he cannot recover anything on an indemnity policy, because he has suffered no loss against which he can be indemnified.[33] Similarly, if he has an interest limited to something less than the full value of the subject-matter, he can suffer no greater loss than the total value of his actual interest at the time of loss, and his claim for personal indemnity cannot exceed the value of his interest.

1–13 Consequences of lack of contractual interest. The insurer is accordingly entitled to raise the defence that the assured either has no interest at all or an interest insufficient to constitute an insurable interest in law.[34] If so, the

---

[30] *Wilson v. Jones* (1867) L.R. 2 Ex. 139, 146, 150; *Carlill v. Carbolic Smoke Ball Co.* [1892] 2 Q.B. 484, 490–491, aff'd in C.A. [1893] 1 Q.B. 256; *Sharp v. Sphere Drake Ins. plc* [1992] 2 Lloyd's Rep. 501, 510; *The "Maira" (No. 2)* [1984] 1 Lloyd's Rep. 660, 667.

[31] See para. 1–74, *post*, and the definitions attempted in paras. 1–49 and 1–120, *post*.

[32] *Williams v. Baltic Ins. Ass. of London* [1924] 2 K.B. 282, 288. Contrast the approach of the common law in American jurisdictions; see section 3, *infra*.

[33] This was established in the early days of marine insurance. See *Lowry v. Bourdieu* (1780) 2 Dougl. 468, 470; *Kulen Kemp v. Vigne* (1786) 1 T.R. 305, 309.

[34] *Macaura v. Northern Ass. Co.* [1925] A.C. 619, 631–632 in which case the insurance, being on goods, was neither subject to a statutory requirement for insurable interest nor caught by the Gaming Act 1845. A modern example is *Newbury International v. Reliance National Ins. Co. (UK) Ltd* [1994] 1 Lloyd's Rep. 83 (prize indemnity insurance).

policy is not void but merely unenforceable by the assured so that, if the insurer chooses not to deny the assured's insurable interest, the assured will be able to enforce the policy.

1–14 Non-indemnity policies. Not all contracts of insurance are indemnity insurances. Where the contract provides that on the occurrence of an event insured against the insurer will pay a fixed sum, or a sum calculated by the application of a set formula or scale, regardless of whether the assured has suffered a loss and irrespective of the amount of any loss in fact suffered, then it is not an indemnity insurance but what is commonly described as a "contingency insurance". Life and accident insurances are usually drafted in this form.[35]

1–15 Valued policies. These are a special case. The parties may agree a value to be placed on insured property, as is very commonly done in marine insurance, and the agreed value is then conclusive and binding as between both parties. If the property is lost or destroyed the insurer is bound to pay the agreed value and is not permitted to object that this is not the true value.[36] In the case of a partial loss which diminishes the value of the property the assured recovers a proportion of its agreed value corresponding to the depreciation in its actual value.[37] Although a valued insurance is not a contract of perfect indemnity in as much as the assured may recover more or less than the true value of the insured property, it is nonetheless an indemnity insurance in which the value of the subject-matter has been agreed so as indirectly to fix the measure of indemnity payable by consent.[38] The incidents of indemnity insurance apart from proof of loss still apply to it, and interest at the time of loss is still required. Mere overvaluation of the property does not make the insurance void for being a gaming and wagering contract since the definition of contracts by way of gaming and wagering does not apply to a case where the assured possesses a genuine interest in the insured subject matter.[39] Whether a policy is a valued policy depends upon whether, on its true interpretation, it places an agreed value on the subject-matter as opposed to providing a limit to the insurer's liability. This is sometimes difficult to determine.[40]

[35] *Dalby v. India & London Life Ass. Co.* (1854) 15 C.B. 365; *Gerling Konzern General Ins. Co. v. Polygram Holdings Inc.* [1998] 2 Lloyd's Rep. 544, 550–551.

[36] *Maurice v. Goldsbrough Mort & Co.* [1939] A.C. 452, 466–467; M.I.A. 1906, s.27(3).

[37] *Elcock v. Thomson* [1949] 2 K.B. 755; *Cia. Maritima Astra v. Archdale* [1954] A.M.C. 1674.

[38] *Lewis v. Rucker* (1761) 2 Burr. 1167; *Irving v. Manning* (1847) 1 H.L. Cas. 287, 305–308; *Burnand v. Rodacanachi* (1882) 7 App.Cas. 333, 335, 339; *Thames & Mersey Mar. Ins. Co. v. Gunford Ship Co.* [1911] A.C. 529, 548; *Cepheus Shipping Corp. v. Guardian Royal Exchange Ass. PLC* [1995] 1 Lloyd's Rep. 622, 641; *Maurice v. Goldsbrough Mort* [1939] A.C. 452, 466–467.

[39] "*The Maira (No. 2)*" [1984] 1 Lloyd's Rep. 660, 667, referring to M.I.A. 1906 s.4(2) and the classic definition of a contract by way of gaming and wagering in *Carlill v. Carbolic Smoke Ball Co.* [1892] 2 Q.B. 484, 490–491.

[40] *Blascheck v. Bussell* (1916) 33 T.L.R. 74; *Wootton v. Lichfield Brewery Co.* [1916] 1 Ch. 44; *Brunton v. Marshall* (1922) 10 Ll. L. Rep. 689; *Kyzuna Investments v. Ocean Marine Mut. Ins.* [2000] 1 All E.R. (Comm) 557; *Quorum A/S v. Schramm* [2002] 1 Lloyd's Rep. 249.

1–16 Waiver of proof of contractual interest. Where the need for proof of interest arises out of the nature of the insurance and is not statutory, the insurer may waive proof of interest by not denying the assured's interest after a claim is made. Waiver is not lightly to be inferred, and it has been held that neither the initial raising of other defences nor an application to stay court proceedings in order to refer a disputed claim to arbitration constituted a waiver of the insurer's right to demand proof of insurable interest before payment of a claim.[41] An insurer may impliedly waive proof of interest by the assured in advance when he promises by the terms of the policy to pay the assured in circumstances where it is clear that the assured will be unable to show his own interest in the insured subject-matter but will be advancing claims to an indemnity for the benefit of other persons interested in it.[42] In this situation it cannot be suggested that the insurance is void as a wagering contract under the Gaming Act 1845[43] as there is no question of the assured winning or losing on the occurrence of an insured event. Whether proof of interest can be waived in a case not involving third party interests is more debatable. It can be argued that the insurer's promise is not binding on him because it is but one term contained in a contract which is itself unenforceable for want of interest, and that a waiver of proof of interest will result in the contract being void as a contract by way of gaming and wagering. The first objection is most probably ill-founded. The insurance is unenforceable by the assured only if the insurer maintains his contractual right to have interest proved as part of the assured's proof of loss, and the insurer may waive that right by appropriate wording as was permitted by the common law courts[44] in relation to marine insurance policies made on "interest or no interest" terms before the Marine Insurance Act 1745.[45] Whether the insurance was void under the Gaming Act 1845[46] would depend upon the application of the definition of a wagering contract in *Carlill v. Carbolic Smoke Ball Co.*[47] If the assured possessed sufficient interest to take it out of the statute, albeit not to constitute an insurable interest, the insurance would be valid. Additionally, it is hard to describe the assured and insurer as professing different views about the likely occurrence of an event. In a case where the assured possessed an insurable interest but the quantum of that interest was in doubt, there seems no reason why a waiver of proof of interest should not be effective.

1–17 Statutory requirements. Whether the terms of the contract demand an insurable interest or not, an interest of some kind and to some extent is required directly or indirectly by statute in every contract of insurance, and the contract will be void, and in some cases illegal if the requisite interest is absent. Because the contract is void the parties to it will not be able to waive the illegality or nullity by provisions inserted in the policy or otherwise.[48]

---

[41] *Macaura v. Northern Assurance Co.* [1925] A.C. 619, 631.
[42] *Prudential Staff Union v. Hall* [1947] K.B. 685; *Thomas v. N.F.U. Mutual Ins. Co.* [1961] 1 W.L.R. 386. The decisions in *Williams v. Baltic Ins. Co.* [1924] 2 K.B. 282 and *Petrofina (UK) Ltd v. Magnaload Ltd* [1984] 1 Q.B. 127 may also be explained on this basis.
[43] 8 & 9 Vict., c. 109. See s.18.
[44] *Lucena v. Craufurd* (1806) 2 Bos. & Pul. (NR) 269, 321–322.
[45] 19 Geo. 2, c. 37.
[46] *ibid.*
[47] [1892] 2 Q.B. 484, 490–491, cited in para. 1–35, *post.*
[48] *Anctil v. Manufacturers' Life* [1899] A.C. 604; *Royal Exchange Assurance v. Sjoforsakrings* [1902] 2 K.B. 384. The same rule applies in American jurisdictions—*Spare v. Home Mutual*, 15 Fed.Rep. 707 (1883); *Fidelity Phoenix Fire Ins. Co. v. Raper* 6 So. (2d) 513 (Ala. Sup. Ct. 1942).

Where the plaintiff's case discloses, or the evidence shows, that the court is being asked to enforce a contract which is made illegal or void by statute for want of interest, the court must decline to enforce it even if the insurers do not take the point in their defence.[49] Any bargain not to dispute a claim arising under a contract which is illegal and void is itself void.[50] The court will, nonetheless, lean in favour of finding a insurable interest if possible on the principle *ut res magis valeat quam pereat*, and because the plea of want of interest is apt to sound technical and without merit once the insurer has received premiums in respect of the risk covered.[51]

1–18 It is now necessary to consider the nature of the interest prescribed by English statute law. Since enactments concerning insurable interest were made in relation to different types of insurances at different times, a review of the history of the legislation is helpful in order to achieve a clear comprehension of its result. In the next section of this chapter, therefore, the statutes are considered chronologically and their effect upon different categories of insurance contract is then summarised.

2. THE ENGLISH STATUTES

(a) *The Common Law Prior to Legislation*

1–19 Wagers enforceable. In order to understand the impact of these statutes it must be remembered that, until the legislature intervened, gambling and wagering contracts were not prohibited by English law, so that a wager as such was not an illegal agreement and was justiciable in a court. The old reports demonstrate that, although the courts might complain of the waste of valuable judicial time involved, they nonetheless did adjudicate on wagers and bets (albeit with a bad grace), even to the extent of upholding the validity of a wager upon the result of a case being heard by the House of Lords.[52] To this rule there was one exception. The courts refused to adjudicate upon wagers which could be said to involve questions or

---

[49] *Gedge v. Royal Exchange* [1900] 2 K.B. 214; *Griffiths v. Fleming* [1909] 1 K.B. 805, 820; *Newbury International v. Reliance National Ins. Co. (U.K.) Ltd* [1994] 1 Lloyd's Rep. 83, 85; *Cheshire & Co. v. Vaughan & Co.* [1920] 3 K.B. 240, 251, 255–256 (obiter); *Luckett v. Wood* (1908) 26 T.L.R. 617. As to counsel's duty, see *Practice Note* in [1964] 1 All E.R. 680n. The court need not investigate a possible defence of illegality where it is not self-evident and the insurers do not rely upon it—*Petrofina (U.K.) Ltd v. Magnaload Ltd* [1984] Q.B. 127, 136. It is not the duty of the court to search for a possible illegality—*Bank of India v. Trans-Continental Commodity Merchants* [1982] 1 Lloyd's Rep. 427, 434.

[50] *Re London County Commercial Reinsurance Office Ltd* [1922] 2 Ch. 67, 81.

[51] *Stock v. Inglis* (1884) 12 Q.B.D. 564; *Re London County Commercial Reinsurance Office Ltd* [1922] 2 Ch. 67, 79; *Norwich Union Fire Ins. Soc. Ltd v. Traynor* [1972] N.Z.L.R. 504, 505; *Cepheus Shipping Corp. v. Guardian Royal Exchange Ass. PLC* [1995] 1 Lloyd's Rep. 622, 641.

[52] *Jones v. Randall* (1774) Cowp. 37, a case which Kent said "went quite far enough". Comm. III, p. 277 (12th ed.). Other cases illustrating the law on wagering contracts prior to the 1845 Act are: *Pope v. St Leger* (1694) 1 Salk. 344; *Good v. Elliott* (1790) 3 T.R. 693; *Da Costa v. Jones* (1778) Cowp. 729; *Brown v. Leeson* (1792) 2 H.Bl. 43; *March v. Pigot* (1771) 5 Burr. 2802; *Hussey v. Crickett* (1811) 3 Camp. 168.

investigations contrary to the public interest.[53] Apart from that it was never in England considered to be contrary to public policy to adjudicate upon a wager merely because it was a wager, and the furthest the English courts would go in their declared opposition to wagering contracts was to discourage action on wagers by refusing to grant facilities in procedure available to other litigants.[54] The Scottish courts, however, were made of sterner stuff, and from the late eighteenth century held that *sponsiones ludicrae*, as they unsympathetically termed such contracts, were void by the law of Scotland.[55]

1-20 Policies without interest. The same principle which the common law of England applied to wagers in the form of wagers was applied to wagers which were cloaked in the guise of policies of marine insurance. If the parties chose to make a wager in the form of a marine policy, the court enforced the contract.[56] Though in a few early Chancery cases the court did cancel policies on proof of no interest,[57] it is clear from later decisions that wager policies were recognised as valid if it was clear that both parties really intended to wager and not to conclude an insurance contract to indemnify the assured for a real loss.[58] If the contract was expressed in the form of a policy of insurance, the courts tended to interpret it as an indemnity against loss dependent upon an interest possessed by the assured, so that, if the assured were unable to establish an interest, he was unable to recover.

In order to show that a wagering contract in the form of a policy was not intended to be a contract of indemnity, resort was had to such wordings as "interest or no interest" or "without further proof of interest than the policy" ("p.p.i.") in order to make the parties' intention clear and the policy proof against a defence of want of interest. Such terms had been originally introduced in all innocence into bona fide insurances to overcome the difficulty of proving the assured's interest or the amount of it. Later these clauses became to a very great extent an instrument for unchecked wagering because they made it clear that the document containing them were not

[53] *Gilbert v. Sykes* (1812) 16 East 150; *Evans v. Jones* (1839) 5 M. & W. 77; *Atherfold v. Beard* (1788) 2 T.R. 610; *Hartley v. Rice* (1808) 10 East 22; *Henkin v. Gerss* (1810) 2 Camp. 408; *Ditchburn v. Goldsmith* (1815) 4 Camp. 152; *Roebuck v. Hammerton* (1778) 2 Cowp. 737; *Da Costa v. Jones* (1778) 2 Cowp. 729; *Allen v. Hearn* (1785) 1 T.R. 56. A good summary is in *Good v. Elliott* (1790) 3 T.R. 693, 695. The categories of wagers contrary to public policy are analysed in *Chitty on Contracts* (28th ed., 1999) Vol. II, Ch. 40, para. 40–017.

[54] *Jackson v. Colegrave* (1695) Carth. 338; *Gilbert v. Sykes* (1812) 16 East 150, 162.

[55] *Bruce v. Ross* (1787) Mor.Dict. 9523; *Wordsworth v. Pettigrew* (1799) Mor.Dict. 9524; *O'Connell v. Russell* (1864) 3 Macph. 89. See W. W. McBryde, *The Law of Contract in Scotland*, paras 25–15 to 25–25.

[56] *Sharp v. Sphere Drake Insurance PLC* [1992] 2 Lloyd's Rep. 501, 509; *Tomlinson v. Hepburn* [1966] A.C. 451, 477.

[57] *Martin v. Sitwell* (1691) 1 Shaw. 156; *Goddart v. Garrett* (1692) 2 Vern. 269; *Le Pypre v. Farr* (1716) 2 Vern. 716; *Whittingham v. Thornburgh* (1690) 2 Vern. 206.

[58] *Lucena v. Craufurd* (1802) 3 Bos. & Pul. 75, 101; (1806) 2 B. & Pul.N.R. 269; *Cousins v. Nantes* (1811) 3 Taunt. 513; *Assievedo v. Cambridge* (1712) 10 Mod. Rep. 77; *Harman v. Vanhatton* (1716) 2 Vern. 716; *Depaba v. Ludlow* (1720) 1 Com. 360; *Dean v. Dicker* (1746) 2 Stra. 1250; *Dalby v. The India and London Life* (1854) 15 C.B. 365; *British Assurance v. Magee* (1834) Cooke & Al. 182; *Scott v. Roose* (1841) 3 Ir.Eq.R. 170; *Keith v. Protection Marine Insurance Co. of Paris* (1882) 10 L.R.Ir. 51. Bunyon (*Fire Insurance* (3rd ed.), p. 5) stated that a wagering policy of fire insurance would apart from statute be illegal as contrary to public policy. The New York courts once so held (see note 42 to para. 1–44 below) but against English authority, and the latest edition rightly omits that passage.

contracts of strict indemnity but an unabashed promise to pay irrespective of interest. The abuse of these p.p.i. policies became so extensive in marine insurances that it was felt to be against the best interests of sound business to permit them to flourish, and consequently an Act was passed in 1745 which prohibited wagering policies on risks connected with British shipping. That was the first prohibition directed against wager policies.[59]

(b) *The Marine Insurance Acts*

1–21 Acts of 1745 and 1788. The Marine Insurance Act 1745[60] provided that,

> "no assurance or assurances shall be made by any person or persons, bodies corporate or politic on any ship of ships belonging to his Majesty or any of his subjects or on any goods, merchandise, or effects, laden or to be laden on board of any ship or ships, interest or no interest, or without further proof of interest than the policy, or by way of gaming or wagering, or without benefit of salvage to the assurer: and that every such assurance shall be null or void to all intents and purposes."

That was followed by the Marine Insurance Act 1788,[61] which provided

> "that from and after the passing of this Act it shall not be lawful for any person or persons to make or effect, or cause to be made or effected, any policy or policies of assurance upon any ship or ships vessel or vessels, or upon any goods, merchandises, effects or other property whatsoever, without first inserting or causing to be inserted in such policy or policies of assurance the name or names or the usual stile and firm of dealing of one or more of the persons interested in such assurance; or without instead thereof first inserting or causing to be inserted in such policy or policies of assurance the name or names or the usual stile and firm of dealing of the consignor of consignors, consignee or consignees, of the goods, merchandises, effects or property so to be insured; or the name or names, or the usual stile and firm of dealing of the person or persons residing in Great Britain, who shall receive the order for the effect such policy or policies of assurance, or of the person or persons who shall give the order or direction to the agent or agents immediately employed to negotiate or effect such policy or policies of assurance."

1–22 The Act of 1745 was construed as requiring interest to be shown at the time of the loss[62] except in the case of a "lost or not lost" policy, entered

---

[59] Legislation had already been directed against fraudulent and excessive gambling and betting at games or sports (16 Car. 2, c. 7; 9 Anne, c. 19); but neither of these statutes affected the validity of wagering policies of insurance. Bankes and Scrutton L.JJ. have suggested *obiter*, that apart from statute the p.p.i. policy was and is against public policy, and that the statutory enactments were merely the result of its being against public policy: *Thomas Cheshire & Co. v. Vaughan Bros & Co.* [1920] 3 K.B. 240, 251, 256. This takes no account of the wide exemptions in the 1745 Act which permitted their continued use, and the common law's tolerance of such policies before 1745. For the policy behind the Act see Legh Jones (2002) "Elements of Insurable Interest in Marine Insurance" in *The Modern Law of Marine Insurance*, Vol. 2, Ch. 4.

[60] 19 Geo. 2, c. 37; Short Titles Act 1896 (59 & 60 Vict. c. 14).

[61] 28 Geo. 3, c. 56. Short Titles Act 1896 (59 & 60 Vict. c. 14).

[62] *Powles v. Innes* (1843) 11 M. & W. 10; *Barr v. Gibson* (1838) 3 M. & W. 390. The assured having interest at the time of the loss could sue notwithstanding that he had subsequently parted with his interest before action brought: *Sparkes v. Marshall* (1836) 3 Scott 172.

into after a partial loss had occurred in ignorance of such partial loss, in which case it was sufficient to show interest at the time the contract was made.[63] As a general rule it was not necessary to show interest at the time the contract was made.[64] It was sufficient if the contract was to pay on interest at the time of the loss. At one time it was apparently thought to be necessary to aver and prove interest from the time of the commencement of the risk down to the time of the loss,[65] but in practice proof of interest at the time of the loss has always been deemed sufficient, and no doubt for this reason, that the policy being a policy on interest does not attach until interest is acquired, and therefore the acquiring of interest and commencement of the risk are simultaneous. It was never decided whether, if a policy was effected by the assured without any hope or expectation of acquiring interest in the subject matter, such policy would be void as one made by way of gaming or wagering. Under the Marine Insurance Act 1906,[66] a policy made without hope or expectation of interest is declared to be void, but there was probably nothing in the Act of 1745 which made such a policy illegal or void. In the absence of any "p.p.i." or "interest or no interest" clause the policy would be deemed to be made on such interest as might appear, and it would not be competent by extrinsic evidence to show that it was other than a policy to pay only on interest. A contract to pay on interest, if any, at the time of the loss could not be open to objection on the ground of gaming or wagering merely because the assured had no hope or expectation of acquiring an interest at the time the contract was made.

1–23 The Act of 1745 did not apply to foreign vessels or to merchandise carried therein, nor to British privateers, nor to merchandise carried from Spanish and Portuguese possessions in Europe or America. In cases to which the Act did not apply the policy was valid at common law if expressly made irrespective of interest.[67] But where the policy was not p.p.i., or interest or no interest, it was deemed to be made on interest, and therefore interest at the time of the loss had to be averred and proved as in the case of policies within the statute.[68]

1–24 Contract of indemnity not obligatory. Although contracts of marine insurance have always been construed where possible as contracts of strict indemnity, the statute did not require the contract to be confined to a strict indemnity.[69] Thus, valued policies were permitted under the Act, and the assured thereby might recover more than the actual loss which he had sustained.[70] So insurances on freight were by custom deemed to be contracts to pay the gross freight in case of loss, and thus the assured who saved the

---

[63] *Sutherland v. Pratt* (1843) 11 M. & W. 296.

[64] *Rhind v. Wilkinson* (1810) 2 Taunt. 237; applied to non-marine insurance—*Williams v. Baltic Ins. Ass.* [1924] 2 K.B. 282, 291.

[65] *ibid; The Sadlers' Co. v. Badcock* (1743) 2 Atk. 554, *per* Lord Hardwicke L.-C.

[66] 6 Edw. 7, c. 41.

[67] *Thellusson v. Fletcher* (1780) 1 Dougl. 315; *Lucena v. Craufurd* (1806) 2 Bos. & Pul. (NR) 269, 322 (foreign ships and cargoes); *Da Costa v. Firth* (1766) 4 Burr. 1966 (Portuguese bullion).

[68] *Cousins v. Nantes* (1811) 3 Taunt. 513; disapproving on this point *Craufurd v. Hunter* (1798) 8 T.R. 13.

[69] *Page v. Fry* (1800) 2 Bos. & Pul. 240.

[70] If the policy wording dispenses with all proof of interest, it was void under the Act, *Murphy v. Bell* (1828) 4 Bing. 567; if it merely dispensed with proof of the quantum of the assured's interest it was not *Grant v. Parkinson* (1782) 3 Dougl. 16; *Lewis v. Rucker* (1761) 2 Burr. 1167.

expenses of earning the freight recovered more than an indemnity.[71] What the statute therefore required was not that the amount which the insurer contracted to pay should be strictly limited to the amount of the assured's interest at the time of the loss, but merely that the assured should have a substantial interest in the subject-matter at that time.[72] The statute could not be evaded by insurance to a substantial amount on a comparatively trifling or illusory interest.[73]

1–25 The Marine Insurance Act 1906[74] repealed the 1745 Act *in toto* and the 1788 Act in so far as that Act related to marine risks.[75] It enacts in section 4(1) that every contract of marine insurance by way of gaming or wagering is void, and in section 4(2) that contracts of marine insurance made without interest and without expectation of acquiring interest in the subject-matter are deemed to be gaming or wagering contracts, and so also are all p.p.i. policies. The Act does not, however, prohibit such contracts and therefore it does not make them illegal as well as void. "I think," said McCardie J. in one case,[76] "that Parliament has placed a p.p.i. policy on much the same footing as a wager on a horse race." It has been suggested, however, that p.p.i. contracts are, apart from statute, contrary to public policy. A marine insurance policy containing the p.p.i. clause is void even though in fact made on interest.[77]

(c) *The Life Assurance Act 1774*

1–26 Main provisions. Until 1774 policies on other than marine risks were still subject to the rules of the common law and therefore not void merely on the ground that they were wagers made without interest. The Life Assurance Act 1774[78] provided, however, that no insurances should thenceforth be effected on lives or other events[79] wherein the person for whose benefit or on whose account such policy was to be made had no interest, or by way of gaming and wagering.[80] Any "assurance made contrary to the true intent" of

---

[71] *United States Shipping Co. v. Empress Assurance Corp.* [1907] 1 K.G. 259, aff'd. [1908] 1 K.B. 115.

[72] *Robertson v. Hamilton* (1811) 14 East 522.

[73] *Lewis v. Rucker* (1761) 2 Burr. 1167, 1171; *The "Maira" (No. 2)* [1934] 1 Lloyd's Rep. 660, 667.

[74] 6 Edw. 7, c. 41.

[75] Sched. II of the Act. This part of the Act was repealed in the Statute Law Revision Act 1927, but that does not revive the old Acts: Interpretation Act 1978, s.16(1).

[76] *John Edwards & Co. v. Motor Union* [1922] 2 K.B. 249, 255.

[77] *Thomas Cheshire & Co. v. Vaughan Bros Co.* [1920] 3 K.B. 240, 251, 256, and *Re Overseas Marine Ins. Co.* [1930] 36 Ll.L. Rep. 183, where the printing of the p.p.i. clause on a detachable slip removed before claim brought made no difference. See also the Marine Insurance (Gambling Policies) Act 1909 (9 Edw. 7, c. 12), and *Re London County Commercial Re-insurance Office* [1922] 2 Ch. 67, 82. If the policy is additionally one of gambling on loss by maritime perils within s.1 of the 1909 Act it must be not only void but illegal—*Arnould, Law Mar. Ins.* (16th ed., 1982) Vol. 1, para. 389.

[78] 14 Geo. 3, c. 48. Short Titles Act 1896 (59 & 60 Vict. c. 14).

[79] The present title of the Act is clearly misleading. It is also sometimes known as the Gambling Act.

[80] s.1. Section 2 made provision for the insertion in the policy of the names of parties interested in it: see paras 1–107—1–116, *post*. So far as that part of the Act is concerned, there are certain statutory exceptions in the case of particular types of insurances, *e.g.* Road Traffic Act 1988, s.148(7); Local Government Act, 1972, s.140; Married Women's Property Act 1882, s.11; Insurance Companies Amendment Act 1973, s.50(1).

the Act was to be "null and void to all intents and purposes whatsoever".[81] The Act excluded from its application "insurances bona fide made by any person or persons on ships, goods or merchandises".[82] Whatever the real intention of the legislature may have been, the exception was construed as extending to insurances on all chattels whether against marine or non-marine risks,[83] and therefore the passing of this statute still left insurances on chattels against non-marine risks subject only to the common law and accordingly unfettered by any prohibition against wagering transactions.

1–27 It has recently been held that the Act does not apply to indemnity insurances but only to insurances which provide for the payment of a specified sum upon the happening of an insured event.[84]

1–28 The Life Assurance Act 1774 was not intended to prohibit wagering, but only to prohibit wagering under the cloak of a mercantile document which purported to be a contract of insurance.[85] Contracts therefore in the form of an ordinary policy of insurance are within the Act, although not strictly contracts of insurance.[86] A policy made out on a printed form appropriate to marine policies to pay a total loss in the event of peace not being declared between Great Britain and Germany on or before March 31, 1918, was held to be an assurance within the Life Assurance Act 1774, but not within the Marine Insurance Act 1906.[87] Contracts not in the form of a policy are not within the Act, although they may incidentally fulfil some of the objects of a contract of insurance.[88] An advertisement issued by the proprietors of a medical preparation called "The Carbolic Smoke Ball" contained a promise to pay £100 to any person who might contract influenza after having used the ball. Although the acceptance of that offer created a binding contract it was not a policy of insurance and therefore not subject to the provisions of the Life Assurance Act 1774. Lindley L.J. said: "You have only to look at the advertisement to dismiss the suggestion."[89]

1–29 When interest must exist. The Life Assurance Act 1774 is very

---

[81] *ibid.*

[82] s.4.

[83] *Waters v. Monarch Fire and Life Ass. Co.* (1856) 5 E. & B. 870. As to what may be considered insurances on "chattels", see para 1–39 *post.*

[84] *Siu (Yin Kwan) v. Eastern Ins. Co. Ltd* [1994] 2 A.C. 199, 211, preferring the dicta of Kerr L.J. in *Mark Rowlands Ltd v. Berni Inns Ltd* [1986] Q.B. 211, 227 to those of Lord Denning M.R. in *Re King, dec'd.* [1963] Ch. 459, 485. See paras 1–161 to 1–162, *post.*

[85] *Good v. Elliott* (1790) 3 T.R. 693; *Paterson v. Powell* (1832) 9 Bing. 320; *Roebuck v. Hammerton* (1778) 2 Cowp. 737; *Morgan v. Pebrer* (1837) 3 Bing. N.C. 457; *Re London County Commercial Reinsurance Office* [1922] 2 Ch. 67, 78.

[86] *e.g. Roebuck v. Hammerton* (1778) 2 Cowp. 737.

[87] *Re London County Commercial Reinsurance Office Ltd* [1922] 2 Ch. 67.

[88] *Cook v. Field* (1850) 15 Q.B. 460; Bunyon, *Life Insurance* (5th ed.), p. 11; Bunyon, *Fire Insurance* (6th ed.), p. 25. In contrast, the Marine Insurance Act 1745 seems to have been applied to contracts not in the form of a policy, but in substance amounting to an insurance; *Kent v. Bird* (1777) Cowp. 583.

[89] *Carlill v. Carbolic Smoke Ball Co.* [1893] 1 Q.B. 256, 261.

differently worded from the Marine Insurance Act 1745. Both alike prohibit policies made by way of gaming or wagering, but here the similarity ends. The Act of 1745 prohibited policies made "interest or no interest or without further proof of interest than the policy", and that was construed as requiring the contract to be a contract to pay on interest subsisting at the date of the loss, and no other interest was required. The Act of 1774 provides that no insurance shall be made on any event wherein the assured "shall have no interest" and "no greater amount shall be recovered than the amount or value of the interest". Those words have been construed in relation to a life policy as requiring interest to be shown only at the date of the contract and as limiting the amount recoverable to the amount of that interest without any reference to the interest or amount of interest at the date of the loss.[90] The Act deals with all contracts of insurance to which it applies, on exactly the same footing, and the interest required in the case of insurances on lives is the same as the interest required in all other classes of insurance. It seems impossible to give the same words a different construction when applied to fire and other risks from that given to them when applied to life risks.[91] It is submitted therefore that, whatever be the risk to which the statute applies, the statute is satisfied by showing interest at the date of the contract only, and probably the statute will not be satisfied unless the assured had, at the date of the contract, an insurable interest to the extent of the amount claimed. An interest acquired afterwards, although before the loss, does not seem to satisfy the express proviso that no contract shall be made unless the assured shall have an interest.[92]

1–30 If this is a correct inference, a life policy effected by a creditor on the life of his debtor would be void if effected before the debt was legally constituted, and a fire policy effected by the prospective purchaser of a house would be void if effected before he had concluded a binding contract to purchase.[93] The hope or prospect of obtaining an interest during the currency of the policy would not seem to be sufficient even although the hope is realised before the loss. A p.p.i. clause in a policy other than a policy of marine insurance is not fatal to its validity. It is not by itself proof that the policy is made by way of gaming or wagering. It may be inserted on account of the difficulty in proving interest. The p.p.i. clause does not, however, dispense with proof of interest if required by the Act of 1774, and in the absence of such proof may, together with the general character of the risks, lead to the irresistible inference that the policy is an insurance by way of gaming or wagering.[94]

1–31 Interest at date of loss not required. The Act itself does not require interest to be shown at the date of loss. Whether or not that must be shown depends upon the nature of the particular insurance in question. If it is on its proper construction an indemnity insurance, it follows that interest at the

---

[90] *Dalby v. The India and London Life* (1854) 15 C.B. 365.

[91] Bunyon suggested that the Act might be construed differently according to the particular type of insurance to which it was being applied: *Fire Insurance* (3rd ed.), pp. 8–9, but the suggestion was not retained in the latest edition.

[92] In so far as *Barnes v. London, Edinburgh and Glasgow Life Ass. Co.* [1892] 1 Q.B. 864, 867, appears to hold to the contary, it cannot be supported. See para. 1–97, *post*.

[93] This is a reason for holding that indemnity insurances are outside the ambit of the Act—see para. 1–27, *ante*.

[94] *Re London County Commercial Reinsurance Office Ltd* [1922] 2 Ch. 67, 80.

date of loss must be shown quite apart from any legislation on insurable interest, but not necessarily a continuity of interest between time of contract and time of loss.[95] The rule of marine insurance law to construe the contract if possible as a contract of strict indemnity was one so familiar to the judges that (at first) they applied it indiscriminately to all classes of insurance without considering very carefully the peculiar nature of the different contracts with which they were dealing. Thus, in 1807, in the case of *Godsall v. Boldero*,[96] the Court of King's Bench held that a life policy in ordinary form effected by a creditor on the life of his debtor was a contract of indemnity, and that the assured must show interest in the life and consequent loss at the time the life dropped. That decision was received by the insurance world with a chorus of disapprobation, and the companies did not in practice follow it, but paid in full on such policies even although the debt had been paid off when the debtor died.[97] Notwithstanding this, the decision stood unchallenged in the courts for nearly 50 years, and even received judicial approval.[98] Finally, the question was again contested in *Dalby v. The India and London Life Assurance Co.*[99] and carried to the Exchequer Chamber, where *Godsall v. Boldero* was overruled.

1–32 *Dalby*'s case was an action upon a policy of assurance to pay £1,000 on the death of the Duke of Cambridge effected by the Anchor Life Assurance Co. with the India and London Life Assurance Co. as partial cover of the Anchor Life's liability on four policies of assurance amounting to £3,000 on the Duke's life issued to the Rev. John Wright. Before the Duke's death Wright had surrendered his policies to the Anchor Life so that on the Duke's death that company had no further interest in his life. The Exchequer Chamber held that the plaintiff Dalby, acting as trustee for the Anchor Life, was entitled to recover the £1,000 assured by the India and London Life's policy. The Life Assurance Act 1774 required proof of interest only at the date when the policy was effected, and the policy itself, not being a contract of indemnity, required no proof of interest at the time of loss.

Dalby v. The India and London Life[1] is sufficient authority for the proposition that the express words of the statute "shall have interest" refer to interest at the date of the policy and at that date only; but the statute also prohibits policies made "by way of gaming and wagering". It is clear that where the assured has an interest which may last during the whole term of the risk, an absolute promise to pay a sum of money not greater than the assured's interest at the time of the contract is not essentially a gaming or wagering policy. That was *Dalby*'s case, as the interest of the Anchor Life would have lasted until the life dropped if the policies issued by them had not been previously surrendered. But a different case is presented where the assured has at the time the contract is made an interest for a definite period

---

[95] 1 Phil. Ins., s.85; *Crozier v. The Phoenix Insurance* (1870) 13 N.B.R. (2 Han.) 200; *Caldwell v. Stadacona Fire and Life Ins. Co.* (1883) 11 S.C.R. 212. These problems cannot now arise in view of the decision in *Siu Yin Kwan v. Eastern Insurance Co.* [1994] 2 A.C. 199 that all indemnity insurances are outside the scope of the Act of 1774.

[96] (1807) 9 East 72.

[97] *Barber v. Morris* (1831) 1 M. & Rob. 62.

[98] *Henson v. Blackwell* (1845) 4 Hare 434.

[99] (1854) 15 C.B. 365.

[1] *ibid.*; followed in *Chantiam v. Packall Packaging Inc.* (1998) 38 O.R. (3d) 401, and *Feasey v. Sun Life Assurance Co. of Canada* [2002] 2 All E.R. (Comm) 492.

only, after which there is no hope or expectation of the interest being continued or renewed. In such a case a contract containing a promise to pay in the event of loss after the cessation of interest might well be deemed a contract *pro tanto* by way of gaming or wagering.

1–33 Where an insurance was effected by A to pay the amount insured on the death of B within the period of two years from the date of the policy, A's insurable interest was the possible failure of the contingency that B would attain the age of 30 years, upon which event he would succeed to certain property, his interest in which he had assigned to A. B attained the age of 30 years within 20 months of the date of the policy but died within the two years. It was held that, although A took the property when B attained the age of 30 years, he was entitled to recover the amount insured because the insurance was effected bona fide to cover the contingency and was only extended to two years because when it was effected there was some uncertainty as to B's age. Page Wood V.-C. said, however, that it would be very different if, for instance, the risk had been only for one day and the insurance had been for the whole duration of life. That would be a fraud on the statute, and it would be very properly left to the jury to say how such a case should be dealt with.[2] Probably in any case where the insurance is for a longer period than the duration of the interest which supports it, there must be some reasonable expectation of the interest being continued to the date when the loss actually occurs in order to legalise the promise to pay, or else the extension of the term beyond the term of the interest must be bona fide for the purpose of covering some such doubts as to the facts as existed in the above-cited case. Where the interest of the assured is limited to a definite period with no hope or expectation of its being continued beyond such period, an insurance to cover a period substantially longer will probably be void *pro tanto*.

1–34 Section 3 and quantum of interest. Section 3 of the 1774 Act provides that in all cases where the assured has an interest no greater sum shall be recovered or received from the insurer or insurers than the amount of value of the interest of the assured. This means the interest possessed by the assured at the time the insurance is concluded, and not at the time of death or other relevant event.[3] An increase of interest during the running of the risk either in extent or value should, strictly speaking, be the subject of a new contract, but this can be avoided by a generous initial valuation of the assured's interest so long as this is a *bona fide* commercial valuation and not a device for gaming and wagering.[4] Section 3 does not require the court to embark upon a detailed and critical examination of the value of the interest, with or without the benefit of hindsight. The reference in section 3 to "insurer or insurers" embraces recovery on whatever number of insurances the assured has taken out on the life or event in question. In *Hebdon v. West*[5]

---

[2] *Law v. London Indisputable Life Policy* (1855) 1 K. & J. 223; *per contra*, a life insurance policy on the life of an employee taken out by his employer did not become a gaming and wagering policy when the employee resigned from his employment two years after the policy incepted *Chantiam v. Packall Packaging Inc.* (1998) 38 O.R. (3d) 401.
[3] *Dalby v. India & London Life Ass. Co.* (1854) 15 C.B. 365; *Fuji Finance Inc. v. Aetna Life Ins. Co.* [1997] Ch. 173.
[4] *Feasey v. Sun Life Ass. Co. of Canada* [2002] 2 All E.R. (Comm) 492.
[5] (1863) B. & S. 579.

a bank clerk had insured his employer's life in two offices. The first policy was for £5,000 and the second for £2,500. The first policy was taken out to cover a loan of £4,700 which the employer subsequently said would not be called in during his lifetime. The second one was taken out a year later to cover the increased amount of interest accruing on the loan which then totalled £6,000. When the employer died, the assured recovered £5,000 from the first office and used it in repayment of the loan. The refusal of the second office to pay was upheld by the court. The promise not to call in the debt was not a good insurable interest because there was no consideration given for it, and it was unenforceable in law. However, the assured's entitlement to his salary due for the balance of his fixed-term contract of employment was assumed to be a valid source of insurable interest, and at the time of making the second insurance it was about £3,000. The court held that the assured had already recovered more than the value of his interest from the first office, so that section 3 barred further recovery on the second policy. Were the law otherwise, it would be possible to gamble on a life assured by taking out a number of policies for an aggregate sum in excess of the value of the assured's interest in the life.

This decision has been doubted in *Feasey v. Sun Life Assurance Co. of Canada*[6] on the ground that it is inconsistent with that in *Dalby v. India & London Life Assurance*,[7] but it is submitted, with respect, that this is not so. The rule from *Dalby* is simply that the assured must show a pecuniary interest only at the time the insurance was made, and cannot later recover more than its value at that time. The assured in *Hebdon* failed to recover on the second policy not because he no longer possessed an interest worth £2,500 when the life dropped, but because he had already recovered more than his interest was worth when he took out the second policy. The question of multiple insurances did not arise in *Dalby*.

1–35 Absence of statutory penalties. The 1774 Act provides no penalty for its contravention. The legislature must have thought that the refusal of insurers to pay where a policy was effected without interest would be a sufficient deterrent against defiance of the Act, yet it may be doubted whether many insurance companies today would repudiate liability on what is now regarded as a somewhat technical ground.[8] Criminal proceedings in various forms are theoretically competent, in spite of the absence of penalty provisions from the statute.[9] It seems very unlikely, however, that such proceedings will ever be brought to enforce a statute, the necessity for which is nowadays widely doubted.[10]

---

[6] [2002] 2 All E.R. (Comm) 492.

[7] (1854) C.B. 365.

[8] See the attitude of an Australian appellate court in *Carter v. Renouf* (1962) 36 A.L.J.R. 67 and see *Petrofina (U.K.) Ltd v. Magnaload Ltd* [1984] Q.B. 127, 136. In *Worthington v. Curtis* (1875) 1 Ch.D. 419, 424 Mellish J. referred to the practice of not relying upon lack of interest as a defence without making any critcism of it.

[9] The possibilities would seem to be, (i) Prosecution for conspiracy to issue an illegal policy; (ii) commencement of a relator action by the Att.-Gen. to restrain an insurer who persistently flouted the Act; (iii) indictment for issuing policies contrary to the provisions of an Act of Parliament dealing with a public mischief—see *R. v. Hall* [1891] 1 Q.B. 747.

[10] See paras 1–117 to 1–119, *infra*.

(d) *The Gaming Act 1845*[11]

1–36 All wagers void. Section 4 of the Life Assurance Act 1774 left untouched insurances bona fide made on goods or merchandises against land risks. Although there are old decisions[12] which appear to show that in the 18th century, as now, indemnity insurances required proof of interest by reason of their nature, no statute directly or indirectly required interest to be shown in relation to insurances of goods and chattels until 1845 when the Gaming Act was passed. Section 18 provided that, "All contracts or agreements, whether by parole or in writing, by way of gaming or wagering, shall be null and void." The Act applies to Northern Ireland but not to Scotland. Its application to Scotland was unnecessary because the native Scots law regarded all wagering contracts as void.

1–37 Application of Gaming Act to policies of insurance. The Act does not contain a definition of wagering contracts. The classic definition[13] is that of Hawkins J. in *Carlill v. Carbolic Smoke Ball Company*[14]:

> "A wagering contract is one by which two persons professing to hold opposite views touching the issue of a future uncertain event, mutually agree that, dependent on the determination of that event, one shall win from the other ... a sum of money or other stake; neither of the contracting parties having any other interest in that contract other than the sum or stake he will so win or lose."

A policy of indemnity insurance to which the Life Assurance Act 1774 does not apply, whether on goods or otherwise,[15] would be avoided by the section if it was in substance a wager with neither party having any genuine interest in the subject-matter other than that created by the agreement itself.[16] It does not follow, however, that every insurance lacking the strict insurable interest required in English law is by that token avoided by the Gaming Act as a wager. First, a genuine insurance cannot be described as a contract wherein the assured and the insurer profess to hold opposing views about the outcome of a future uncertain event, and it may well have been for this reason that section 4(2)(a) of the Marine Insurance Act 1906 provides that insurances made without interest and expectation of acquiring it are *deemed* to be contracts by way of gaming and wagering.[17] Secondly, the Gaming Act:

> "has no application to a contract upon a matter in which the parties have an interest. It relates to betting upon a mere future event, not to contracts of indemnity."[18]

---

[11] See generally *Chitty on Contracts* (28th ed., 1999) Vol. II, Ch. 40.

[12] *Lynch v. Dalzell* (1729) 4 Bro. Parl. Cas. 431; *Sadlers' Co. v. Badcock* (1743) 2 Atk. 554. At that stage interest was required both at the conclusion of the contract and at the time of loss.

[13] *Ellesmere v. Wallace* [1929] 2 Ch. 1, 48 *per* Russell L.J.; *Tote Investors Ltd v. Smoker* [1968] 1 Q.B. 509, 516 *per* Lord Denning M.R.; *The Maira (No. 2)* [1984] 1 Lloyd's Rep. 660, 667 *per* Hobouse J.

[14] [1892] 2 Q.B. 484, 490–491, affirmed [1893] 1 Q.B. 256.

[15] *Siu Yin Kwan v. Eastern Ins. Co.* [1994] 2 A.C. 199.

[16] *Newbury International v. Reliance National Ins. Co. (UK) Ltd* [1994] 1 Lloyd's Rep. 83 (wager on success of racing driver cloaked in the guise of a liability insurance, but where the assured was not exposed to any genuine liability to third parties).

[17] *Chitty on Contracts* (28th ed., 1999) Vol. II, para. 40–005.

[18] *Wilson v. Jones* [1867] L.R. 2 Ex. 139, 146 *per* Willes J.

It is submitted that the absence of a valid insurable interest in the strict sense does not by itself import the necessary element of gambling. Thus an expectation of future benefit from property does not constitute a valid insurable interest in it,[19] but if the expectation is soundly based an insurance on that property is not a contract by way of gaming or wagering. This is very clear in marine insurance where an expectation of acquiring interest prevents an insurance from being classified as one of gaming or wagering.[20] Conversely, the possession of a sufficient interest to take the insurance out of the Gaming Act 1845 does not necessarily mean that the assured must for that reason possess a valid insurable interest.[21] The plea of want of a valid insurable interest is entirely separate from a defence that the assured is wagering,[22] even though in extreme cases both may be available to the insurer.[23]

(e) *Summary*

1–38 Three classes of insurance. The effect of the various statutory provisions on insurable interest considered in this section is best appreciated if contracts of insurance are divided into three groups for this purpose:—

1–39 (i) *Marine insurances.* These are governed by the Marine Insurance Act 1906.[24] Interest must be proved at the time of loss only, except in the case of "lost or not lost" insurances, when acquisition of interest after loss suffices.[25]

1–40 (ii) *Non-marine indemnity insurances.* Subject to the possibility that the 1788 Act still has an application to non-marine policies on goods,[26] these are governed solely by the Gaming Act 1845. Insurances on goods and chattels are expressly excluded from the 1774 Act by section 4 thereof. The courts interpreted "goods" in a wide sense. In a motor policy case it was held that the 1774 Act had no application even to the insurance against third-party risks which was incidental to the insurance of the car itself.[27]

---

[19] See para. 1–49, *post.*

[20] M.I.A. 1906 s.4(2)(a).

[21] For an argument to the contrary, see Arnould, *Law of Marine Insurance* (16th ed., 1997) Vol. 3, para. 332, following *dicta* of Mr Anthony Colman, Q.C., Deputy Judge, in *The Moonacre* [1992] 2 Lloyd's Rep. 501, 510.

[22] *Macaura v. Northern Ass. Co.* [1925] A.C. 619, 632.

[23] *Newbury International v. Reliance National Ins. Co. (UK) Ltd* [1994] 1 Lloyd's Rep. 83, where the court described the insurance as a bet, lacking insurable interest, but did not treat it as void under the 1845 Act.

[24] s.4, s.5.

[25] s.6(1). It is open to question whether clause 11 of the Institute Cargo Clauses excludes this proviso to s.6(1) Arnould, *Law of Marine Insurance* (16th ed., 1997) Vol. 3, para. 286.

[26] The Marine Insurance Act 1788 was passed to repeal the Marine Insurance Act 1785, both intended to regulate insurances "on ships and on goods, merchandises or effects". The Marine Insurance Act 1906 repealed the 1788 Act in so far as it related to marine insurance. If, as Colinvaux's *Law of Insurance*, (7th ed., 1997) para. 3–04, suggests, the 1788 Act also applied to insurances on goods on land, then it would appear still to require the insertion in a policy on goods of the name of at least one person interested in the insured goods. But this is doubtful. The wording of the Act, with its references to consignors and consignees, suggests that it was solely concerned with policies on cargoes being exported from and imported into the UK. Insertion of the name of the consignor/ee is permitted in place of that of a person interested in the goods.

[27] *Williams v. Baltic Ins. Co. Ltd* [1924] 2 K.B. 282.

Money in a form in which it can be physically burned or asported is "goods" within the meaning of section 4, so that a policy insuring against loss of money by burglary and housebreaking is outside the 1774 Act.[28] It seems that contract works under a building contract are capable of being described as "goods" at least until they become part of the realty.[29] These decisions are now of academic interest following the decision in *Siu Yin Kwan v. Eastern Insurance Co. Ltd*[30] that the Act does not apply to any species of indemnity insurance. However, it must be recalled that the insurers are entitled to require proof of insurable interest at the time of loss in all indemnity insurances irrespective of statutory rules,[31] subject to the express or implied terms of the insurance contract itself.[32]

1–41 (iii) *Life assurances and other insurances not within (i) or (ii) above.* These are governed by the Life Assurance Act 1774 and the Gaming Act 1845. The former Act, but not the latter, requires proof of insurable interest at the time of contract.[33]

1–42 Application of Acts to Ireland. The Life Assurance Act 1774 did not initially apply to Ireland.[34] The provisions of the Act were extended to Ireland by the Life Assurance Act 1866,[35] but only as regards policies of insurance upon lives, and not as regards insurances upon "other events".[36] The Marine Insurance Act 1745 was never in force in Ireland,[37] but the Marine Insurance Act 1906 applies to Northern Ireland as well as to Great Britain.

3. THE AMERICAN LAW

1–43 English statutes not applicable. The decisions of American courts are frequently cited in the course of this chapter, and it is timely to sound a note of caution concerning their usefulness to the English reader. The American authorities upon insurable interest differ in some important respects from English law, and must not be presumed to be identical. Thus, to take one striking example, the American courts have been prepared to

---

[28] *Prudential Staff Union v. Hall* [1947] K.B. 685.
[29] *Petrofina (U.K.) Ltd v. Magnaload Ltd* [1984] Q.B. 127, 136. Lloyd J. declined to decide whether they would remain so thereafter and, if so, for how long. The insurers did not take the point.
[30] [1994] 2 A.C. 199, and see para. 1–27, *ante.*
[31] *Macaura v. Northern Ass. Co.* [1925] A.C. 619, and see paras 1–10—1–11, *ante.*
[32] See, *e.g. Thomas v. National Farmers' Union Mut. Ins. Soc.* [1961] 1 W.L.R. 386, where the wording of a fire policy enabled the assured to succeed in a claim without possession of interest at the time of loss, because the insurers had here waived their contractual right to require proof of his interest. See para. 1–16, *ante.*
[33] *Dalby v. India & London Life Ass. Co.* (1854) 15 C.B. 365.
[34] *British Ass. Co. v. Magee* (1834) 1 Cooke. & Al. 182; *Scott v. Roose* (1841) 3 Ir.Eq.R. 170; *Cook v. Field* (1850) 15 Q.B. 460, 474.
[35] 29 & 30 Vict. c. 42.
[36] *Church & General Ins. Co. v. Connolly*, High Court of Ireland, 7 May 1981, un-rep., in which Costello J. declined to follow para. 30 in the 6th edition of this work, and adopted a construction of the 1866 Act suggested by Bunyon at p. 10 of *Fire Insurance* (3rd ed.), which did not appear in the last edition and which was not cited by the court.
[37] *Keith v. The Protection Marine Ins. Co.* (1882) 10 L.R.Ir. 51.

treat a p.p.i. policy as an ordinary indemnity insurance if interest could in fact be shown and there was no intention to wager.[38]

1–44 These differences stem from the fact that the development of the American law on insurable interest proceeded on a different basis from English law. The eighteenth century English statutes discussed above were not received by the state jurisdictions as part of their own law. After the Revolution it was left to the individual state legislatures to decide the criteria by which English Acts of Parliament were to be judged fit to be adopted as a part of their own law,[39] and the statutes on insurable interest were not adopted. The American judges, however, did not approve of wager policies and determined that the public policy of their own common law required an insurable interest. As Chief Justice Shippen of Pennsylvania expressed it in relation to the 1745 Act: "Certainly the British Act does not bind us *proprio vigore*; but the system of national policy, which dictated the law, has been adopted by our courts."[40]

1–45 The American courts went further in fact than the English law as it stood in 1776, because they soon held in most American jurisdictions that all wagering contracts were against public policy at common law,[41] so that insurances without interest were straightaway unenforceable and void. There was some inconsistency in this approach in so much as the states claimed to adopt the English common law interpreted by the English court which, as we have seen, upheld wager and p.p.i. polices. In New York, the Court of Appeals endeavoured to reinterpret the eighteenth-century English decisions to show that the 1774 Life Assurance Act was in fact only declaratory of the true common law before 1720.[42] Generally, it was realised however, that the American common law's sense of public policy had developed differently from that of the English common law.[43]

1–46 During the course of the nineteenth century, the American states began to pass their own statutes requiring and defining insurable interest. Since they did not adopt a uniform definition, current American insurance law reflects a variety of different definitions of, and criteria for, insurable interest, and further differences in opinion as to the times at which an

---

[38] *Brown v. Merc. Mar. Ins. Co.* 152 Fed.Rep. 411 (C.C.A. 9, 1907); *Hall v. Jefferson Ins. Co.*, 279 F. 893 (S.D.N.Y., D.C., 1921); *Cabaud v. Federal Ins. Co.*, 37 F. 2d 23 (C.C.A. 2, 1930); *The Hai Hsuan (No. 2)* [1958] 2 Lloyd's Rep. 578 (D.C., Md.).

[39] A summary of the dates of these Acts and their general purport is given in Chancellor Kent's *Commentaries*, Vol. I, p.473, 12th ed. by O. W. Holmes Jr.

[40] *Pritchett v. Ins. Co. of N. America*, 3 Yeates 458, 461 (Sup.Ct.Pa., 1803), approved in *Edgell v. M'Laughlin* 6 Whart. 176 (Sup.Ct.Pa., 1840). The Pennsylvania Act concerning recognition of English law had been passed in 1777. See also *Amory v. Gilman*, 2 Mass. 1 (Sup.Ct.Mass. 1806) and *Juhel v. Church*, 2 Johns. 333 (N.Y.Sup.Ct. 1801) for other instances. Vermont chose to ignore all English statutes after 1760, which at once excluded the 1774 Act, and New Jersey chose an adoption date excluding it also.

[41] e.g. *Collamer v. Day*, 2 Vt. 144 (1829); *Perkins v. Eaton*, 3 H.N. 152 (1825); *Lewis v. Littlefield* 15 Me. 233 (1839). "No encouragement should be afforded to the acquisition of property", said the Vermont court, "otherwise than by honest industry". In New York, however, a statute was passed to prohibit the enforcement of wagers: N.Y.Rev.Stat. i, 662, ss.8, 9, 10-innocent wagers having been valid previously.

[42] *Ruse v. Mutual Benefit Life Ins. Co.*, 23 N.Y. 516 (1863), followed in *Freeman v. Fulton Fire Ins. Co.*, 38 Barb. 247 (N.Y.S.C. 1862). The *Ruse* court was applying the common law of New Jersey, which it identified with the English common law.

[43] See note 41, *ante*.

interest should be possessed.[44] For example, in relation to insurances on property, some authorities have followed the English law in requiring the assured to establish a legally recognised relationship with the property insured,[45] whereas other authorities, representing the usual modern view, adopt an "economic" test, whereby, even if the assured possesses no legal or equitable rights over the insured property, he has an insurable interest in it if its destruction would be likely to cause him financial loss.[46]

1–47 Purpose of citation. It is therefore clear that it is no use looking to the American decisions for answers to problems raised by the wording of the English statutes,[47] or to discover whether in a given case an assured will be certain to possess an interest under English law, or, for that matter, to ascertain what "the American law" says. At a time, however, when the rigidity and historical emphasis in the insurable interest rules of English law are open to criticism, and when insurance practice is becoming increasingly impatient of these restrictions, it is useful to bear in mind the American cases as models for comparison. We cite them generally to illustrate how another common law system has contrived to widen the categories of insurable interest in contrast to the narrower approach of the English decisions, and sometimes where they may represent the English law in the absence of English authority. We will also refer to legislation and case-law in Commonwealth jurisdictions which have either adopted the "economic" test of insurable interest or even dispensed with the requirement altogether.

4. General Definition of Insurable Interest

1–48 Statutory definition. Neither the Marine Insurance Act 1745 nor the Life Assurance Act 1774 defines the insurable interest which the assured is required to have in the subject-matter of the insurance, and the first statutory definition appears in the Marine Insurance Act 1906, in relation to marine risks only. It provides by section 5(1) that "every person has an insurable interest who is interested in a marine adventure", and adds in section 5(2): "In particular a person is interested in a marine adventure where he stands in any legal or equitable relation to the adventure or to any

---

[44] See the useful article by Hartnett and Thornton in (1948) 48 Col. L. Rev. 1162 entitled "Insurable Interest in Property: A Socio-Economic Re-evaluation of a Legal Concept", for a survey of the different trends of authority.

[45] *Richards on Insurance*, (5th ed. 1952) para. 69; *Hessen v. Iowa Automobile Mutual Ins. Co.* 195 Iowa 141 (1922); *Basset v. Farmers and Merchants Ins. Co.*, 85 Neb. 85 (1909).

[46] *Fidelity Phoenix and Globe Fire Ins. Co. v. Raper*, 6 So. 2d 513 (Ala., 1942); *Liverpool and London Ins. Co. v. Bolling*, 176 Va. 182 (1940); see generally, Appleman, *Insurance Law and Practice*, para. 2123; Richards, *op. cit.*, para. 87.

[47] Kent's *Commentaries* appropriately warn the American reader against reliance on the English authorities; see (12th ed.), Vol. III, p. 369.

insurable property at risk therein, in consequence of which he may benefit by the safety or due arrival of insurable property, or may be prejudiced by its loss, or by damage thereto, or by the detention thereof, or may incur liability in respect thereof."

It will be seen that the Act does not attempt to formulate an exhaustive definition of insurable interest even in the limited field of marine insurance. Section 5(2) is, however, helpful in that it states in succinct form the principles laid down previously by the courts in relation to marine risks, which are without doubt broadly applicable to non-marine risks. It is important to notice the insistence upon a "legal or equitable relation", because this condition of insurable interest, applied to non-marine risks, has been responsible for the narrower view taken by English courts than by those American and Commonwealth jurisdictions in which a legal relationship is not essential to the existence of a valid interest.

1–49 Working definition. All previous editions of this work have provided the following "good working definition" applicable to all risks under the Life Assurance Act 1774: Where the assured is so situated that the happening of the event on which the insurance money is to become payable would, as a proximate cause, involve the assured in the loss or diminution of any right recognised by law or in any legal liability there is an insurable interest in the happening of that event to the extent of the possible loss or liability. Since that Act now applies for practical purposes only to life, accident and other contingency insurances,[48] it has ceased to provide a useful basis for a general definition, but we have retained the text because it emphasises the general rule of English law that an expectation of benefit from the continued preservation of the subject matter of an insurance does not *per se* create a valid insurable interest in it.

1–50 Right recognised by law. This must be an existing right. One of the main principles laid down by the courts is that the mere hope or expectation of a future benefit is not sufficient to constitute an insurable interest in an event which if it happened would prevent such hope or expectation being realised.[49] This principle was much discussed in the naval prize cases about the beginning of the nineteenth century. The captors of lawful prize became entitled to the proceeds either under the Naval Prize Acts or by a subsequent grant from the Crown, and the captors on making a capture insured the captured vessel against maritime risk until she should be brought into port. In so far as the captors had a vested right under the Prize Acts, it was held that they could insure the vessel,[50] but in cases where they had no such right, but only an expectation of a grant from the Crown, it was held that they had no insurable interest.[51] In one case Lord Mansfield said that where the expectation amounted to a moral certainty which had never been known to be defeated, there was a sufficient interest.[52] But that dictum was disapproved of by Lord Eldon[53] and Lord Ellenborough.[54] Tindal C.J. said in

---

[48] See para. 1–27, *ante* and para. 1–162, *post.*
[49] *Griffiths v. Fleming* [1909] 1 K.B. 805, 820; *Sharp v. Sphere Drake Ins. PLC* [1992] 2 Lloyd's Rep. 501, 510–511.
[50] Park, Mar. Ins. (8th ed., 1842), pp. 568–578.
[51] *Routh v. Thompson* (1809) 11 East 428; *Devaux v. Steele* (1840) 8 Scott 637.
[52] *Le Cras v. Hughes* (1782) 3 Doug. 81.
[53] *Lucena v. Craufurd* (1806) 2 Bos. & Pul. (NR) 269, 323.
[54] *Routh v. Thompson* (1809) 11 East 428, 434.

Devaux v. Steele[55] that if it was still good law it certainly could not be extended beyond cases where the expectation had never been known to fail. It must now be taken as settled on high authority that an expectation of benefit from the preservation of life or property does not of itself create an insurable interest in that life or property.[56]

1–51 The rule that an expectation alone does not constitute an interest is equally applicable to all classes of insurance. For example, a person who has no interest in a house except the hope of possessing it at some date in the future has no insurable interest in the house which entitles him to insure it either against damage by fire, or against a fall in value caused by building developments in the locality, as has been recognised in two decisions in Maine.[57] It has been suggested by a distinguished American author[58] that an expectation may be insured if specifically described, but the detailed description does not overcome the objections to such an interest expressed in the English cases. The event insured against in such a case would be the failure of the expectation owing to certain specified causes or generally owing to any cause. Thus a man might effect an insurance against the chance of his father disinheriting him, or against the diminution of his succession owing to loss by fire of his father's property. It is submitted that such contracts would be contracts made without insurable interest. The assured has undoubtedly, in one sense, a very substantial interest in the event insured against, but he does not stand to lose any legal right nor to suffer any legal liability, and the policy of the law appears to have been to prohibit the insurance of mere visionary or speculative interests.[59] Thus an insurance to pay a total loss in the event of peace between Great Britain and Germany not being declared on or before March 31, 1918, was in the absence of any evidence of actual interest by the insured held to be illegal and void under the Life Assurance Act 1774.[60] The objection taken to the insurance of an interest based on a bare expectation of profit and loss is not that the interest is not sufficiently described, but that such interest is not insurable.

1–52 Moral obligation. Another consequence of the rule that a relationship recognised in law is required is that a mere moral claim affords no insurable interest.[61] The right necessary to support an insurable interest must be one which the law recognises as valid and subsisting whether at law

---

[55] (1840) 8 Scott 637, 660.

[56] *Lucena v. Craufurd* (1806) 2 Bos. & Pul. (N.R.) 269, 321–323 *per* Lord Eldon; *Routh v. Thompson* (1809) 11 East 428, 434 *per* Lord Ellenborough C.J; *Macaura v. Northern Ass. Co.* [1925] A.C. 619, 627 *per* Lord Buckmaster and at 630 *per* Lord Summer. See para. 1–120, *post* (property). As to life, see *Griffiths v. Fleming* [1909] 1 K.B. 805, 820 *per* Kennedy L.J. citing *Halford v. Kymer* (1830) 10 B. & C. 724 and *Hebdon v. West* (1863) 3 B. & S. 579. See para. 1–71, *post*.

[57] *Clark v. Dwelling House Ins. Co.*, 81 Me. 373 (1889); *Trott v. Woolwich Mutual Fire Ins. Co.*, 83 Me. 362 (1891). Maine law required an insurable interest, on public policy grounds, in the nature of a legal or equitable right over the insured property, and these decisions represent English law, it is submitted, although the 1774 Act was not adopted in Maine.

[58] Philips, *Insurance* (3rd ed.), p. 183, described by Brett J. in *Harris v. Scaramanga* as "a book of the highest authority as to English as well as American insurance law" (1872) L.R. 7 C.P. 481, 498.

[59] *Stockdale v. Dunlop* (1840) 6 M. & W. 224; *Knox v. Wood* (1808) 1 Camp. 543; *Lucena v. Craufurd* (1806) 2 Bos. & Pul. (N.R.) 269, 323.

[60] *Re London County Commercial Re-insurance Office Ltd* [1922] 2 Ch. 67.

[61] *Stockdale v. Dunlop, supra*; *Stainbank v. Fenning* (1851) 11 C.B. 51; *Stainbank v. Shepard* (1853) 13 C.B. 418; *Hebdon v. West* (1863) 3 B. & S. 579.

or in equity.[62] A contract which is void, for instance, affords no interest in English law, however likely it may be the promisor will honour his promise as a moral obligation.[63] The interest of the promisee in that case is nothing more than a bare expectation.

1–53 Contingent and defeasible interests. Although a bare expectation of acquiring a right does not ground an insurable interest, a right to property may create an interest notwithstanding that its exercise is contingent upon a future event, even if the chance of its being enjoyed is remote.[64] Similarly a right to property which is defeasible on the happening of a future occurrence creates an insurable interest.[65] These distinctions are important in considering the problem raised by an insurance upon a benefit to which the assured has a claim under a contract which is in some way defective, or to which his right of action is time-barred. In the case of a contract which is void (*e.g.* for want of consideration), the promisee has nothing but an expectation from the outset; it is not founded on any right which the law will enforce even temporarily,[66] and it therefore creates no insurable interest. In the case, however, of a *contract voidable at the option of the promisor*, the promisee has an interest. He has a claim which is enforceable but liable to defeasance if the promisor exercises his option, a thing which he may or may not do. So, where a contract for the sale of land is voidable for fraud or undue influence, the property may be insured by the purchaser even though the vendor might refuse to complete.[67] If, however, the vendor was an infant who could avoid the contract under the Infants Relief Act 1874, then equity would not decree specific performance against him at any stage.[68] In this case, the purchaser never has an enforceable claim, and accordingly he has no insurable interest in the property to be sold.

1–54 Another example of a contract which cannot support an interest is a contract unenforceable for want of written evidence. The principal example[69] of such a contract is one falling within the Law of Property

---

[62] *Smith v. Lascelles* (1788) 2 T.R. 187, 188; *Hill v. Secretan* (1798) 1 Bos. & Pul. 315; *Lucena v. Craufurd* (1802) 3 Bos. & Pul. 75, 103; (1806) 2 Bos. & Pul. (N.R.) 269, 321; *Ex. p. Yallop* (1808) 15 Ves. 60, 67–68; *Samuel v. Dumas* [1924] A.C. 431, 444. The legal right conferred by law may be a statutory right attaching to the assured by reason of his legal status; *Moran, Galloway & Co. v. Uzielli* [1905] 2 K.B. 555. The decision in this case is controversial—see Legh-Jones in *The Modern Law of Marine Insurance* (2002) Vol. 2, Ch. 4.

[63] *Stockdale v. Dunlop* (1840) 6 M. & W. 224.

[64] *Lucena v. Craufurd* (1806) 2 Bos. & Pul. (N.R.) 269, 324–325.

[65] *Boehm v. Bell* (1799) 8 T.R. 154; *Lucena v. Craufurd* (1806) 2 Bos. & Pul. (N.R.) 269; *Stirling v. Vaughan* (1809) 11 East 619, 628, *Geismar v. Sun Alliance Ins. Ltd* [1978] 1 Q.B. 383, 395; Philips, *Insurance* (5th ed.), paras. 176, 183.

[66] *Stockdale v. Dunlop, supra*; *Hebdon v. West* (1863) 3 B. & S. 579.

[67] *Hill v. Secretan* (1798) 1 Bos. & Pul. N.R. 315; *Dwyer v. Edie* (1788) 2 Park; Mar. Ins. (8th ed., 1842), p. 914; *Pettigrew v. Grand River Farmers' Mutual Ins. Co.* (1877) 28 U.C.C.P. 70; *Frierson v. Brenham*, 5 La.Ann. 540 (1850). The Canadian courts have also doubted whether in a case where the assured's title to property has never been disputed by a claimant, the insurers can properly set up the title of a stranger in a plea of no-interest as a defence on their contract: *Stevenson v. London and Lancs. Fire* (1866) 26 U.C.Q.B. 148, 152; *Shaw v. Phoenix Assurance Co.* (1869) 20 U.C.C.P. 170, 181. *Sed quaere* if the insurers have evidence no one else has used?

[68] *Flight v. Bolland* (1828) 4 Russ. 298.

[69] Writing and certain further formalities are essential to the validity of a large number of hire-purchase contracts, but non-compliance does not render the contract void. This case is discussed in para. 1–135, *post*.

(Miscellaneous Provisions) Act 1989 which provides by section 2(1) that a contract for the sale or other disposition of an interest in land can only be made in writing, and only by incorporating all the terms which the parties have expressly agreed in one document or, where contracts are exchanged, in each.

The result of such an enactment is that the purchaser of land, for example, under an unenforceable contract has at no time any legally recognised and protected claim, and he has no insurable interest in the property contracted for. As Parke B. said in *Stockdale v. Dunlop*[70]: "It is an engagement of honour merely. If it is not a contract capable of being enforced at law, it is nothing."

The same principle must apply to an assured's right of action over or in respect of property, whether contractual or otherwise, which has become time-barred under the Limitation Act 1980. In cases where the right of action will soon be barred, the insurable interest arising from the right is unimpeachable, but a person cannot claim an interest in property to which his claim is already time-barred when the insurance cover is requested. In the latter instance, the lack of interest is even clearer if the statute has not only barred the right but actually extinguished it altogether.[71]

1–55 The American decisions on insurable interests in the above situations do not represent the English law, but reflect the prevalent opinion in the United States that an expectancy of future benefit which is likely to be realised does ground a good insurable interest.[72] This avoids the difficulties faced by the English law based on the nature of the assured's title in the property.

1–56 Specific illustrations. The significance of the requirement that the assured must demonstrate a legal right to or over the subject-matter of the insurance may be further illustrated by the following instances:

1–57 *On profits from sale.* It was settled in the early marine insurance decisions that anticipated profits from the sale of a cargo could be insured by its owner so long as they were certain[73] or even pretty certain[74] to be realised. Profits could not be insured when they were entirely speculative, as where the assured had not yet made a binding purchase of the goods which he hoped to resell at a profit.[75] After the decision in *Lucena v. Craufurd*[76] the

---

[70] (1840) 6 M. & W. 224, 233, cited with approval in *Felthouse v. Bindley* (1862) 11 CB(NS) 869, 877 and in *Stock v. Inglis* (1882) 9 Q.B.D. 708, 720. In so far as the decision in *Hebdon v. West* (1863) 3 B. & S. 579 appears to proceed in part on the view that an unenforceable contract *does* afford an interest, this was based on a concession by counsel without reference to the *Stockdale* case, and cannot be correct.

[71] See, *e.g.* Limitation Act 1980, s.3, and *R.B. Policies at Lloyd's v. Butler* [1950] 1 K.B. 76. Time-barred titles to real property are usually extinguished altogether.

[72] *Amsinck v. American Ins. Co.*, 129 Mass. 185 (1880); *Wainer v. Milford Mutual Fire*, 153 Mass. 335 (1891); *Dupuy v. Delaware Ins. Co.*, 63 Fed.Rep. 680 (1894). *Rawls v. American Mutual Life Ins. Co.*, 27 N.Y. 282 (N.Y.C.A. 1863) probably would have been decided similarly on its facts by English law. See notes 45–46, *supra*.

[73] *Grant v. Parkinson* (1781) 3 Doug. 16, 18. Park reports Lord Mansfield as saying that the profits were "pretty certain", Mar. Ins. (8th ed.) p. 562.

[74] *Barclay v. Cousins* (1802) 2 East 544, 550–551; *Henrickson v. Margetson* (1776) 2 East 549 note (a).

[75] *Lucena v. Craufurd* (1806) 2 Bos. & Pul. (N.R.) 269, 321; *Knox v. Wood* (1808) 1 Camp. 543.

[76] (1806) 2 Bos. & Pul. (N.R.) 269.

difficulty of demonstrating a legal right to so intangible a thing as a future profit was met by treating it as an element of additional value which the cargo would possess on its safe arrival at destination, and including it in an agreed valuation of the cargo itself.[77] Although the assured's interest in profits had to be expressly referred to in the policy, the cargo was the subject-matter of the insurance in which an insurable interest was shown, and the profit was merely an "excrescence" upon the cargo.[78] The drawback inherent in this approach was that under the ordinary marine policy the risk attached only on loading of the cargo, and loss of profit due to the loss of the carrying vessel on her approach voyage or delay in loading or on the loaded voyage was not within the cover. Even when the ordinary marine cargo policy was used to insure solely against loss of profits to be made on resale of the cargo the same difficulty could prevent recovery, as happened in *M'Swiney v. Royal Exchange Assurance Company*[79] and *Halhead v. Young.*[80] It was recognised, however, that the assured possessed a "special interest" in profits to be made from the sale of a cargo for which purchase and resale contracts had been concluded, or possibly which he had bought and not yet resold, even if he did not possess a title to it and it was not at his risk. This insurable interest in the expected profits would support an insurance specifically drawn so as to cover those contingencies which could cause them to be lost, such as the loss of or delay to the carrying vessel on her approach voyage.[81] In *Wilson v. Jones*[82] the assured owned shares in a company which was engaged on an important marine project. He was held to have an insurable interest either in the gain which he was certain to realise on the sale of his shares if the project was successful[83] or in the marine adventure on the outcome of which the value of his right of sale depended.[84] The concept of an insurable interest in a non-existent thing, the profit, is nonetheless elusive. It is probably better to analyse the subject-matter of a non-marine insurance on profits as the assured's vested or contingent right of sale, a species of intangible property which is insured against those events liable to defeat it or to diminish its value. The rules concerning proof of loss in such cases are considered in chapter 19.[85]

1–58 *On rent or hire.* The assured may also insure against the loss of other

---

[77] *M'Swiney v. Royal Exchange Assurance Co.* (1849) 14 Q.B. 634, 661.

[78] *Hodgson v. Glover* (1805) 6 East 316, 320; *Eyre v. Glover* (1812) 16 East 218, 220; *Usher v. Noble* (1812) 12 East 639; *Stockdale v. Dunlop* (1840) 6 M & W 224, 232–233; *Halhead v. Young* (1856) 6 E. & B. 312; *Smith v. Reynoulds* (1856) 1 H. & N. 221; *Berridge v. The Man on Sea Ins. Co.* (1887) 18 Q.B.D. 346.

[79] (1849) 14 Q.B. 634.

[80] (1856) 6 E. & B. 312.

[81] (1849) 14 Q.B. 634, 659–661; (1856) 6 E. & B. 312, 324; *Anderson v. Morice* (1875) L.R. 10 C.P. 609, 621–622; *Agra Trading v. McCauslin* [1995] 1 Lloyd's Rep. 182, 184; *Glengate v. Norwich Union* [1996] 1 Lloyd's Rep. 614, 622; *NSW Leather v. Vanguard Ins. Co.* (1991) 25 N.S.W.L.R. 699, 707–708.

[82] (1867) L.R. 2 Ex. 139.

[83] (1867) L.R. 2 Ex. 139, 146; *Macaura v. Northern Assurance Co.* [1925] A.C. 619, 630, *per* Lord Sumner.

[84] (1867) L.R. 2 Ex. 139, 150; [1925] A.C. 619, 628 *per* Lord Buckmaster.

[85] See para. 19–12, *infra*. In *Glengate K-G v. Norwich Union Fire Ins.* [1996] 1 Lloyd's Rep. 614, 624 Auld L.J. stated that a buyer's insurable interest is in "the event insured against", the loss of profits, and not the cargo or goods purchased, citing *Anderson v. Morice* (1876) 1 App.Cas. 713, 723. This is no doubt true, but it is still necessary to identify a legal nexus between the assured and the profits, and that could be the assured's right of sale, dependent upon the successful outcome of the marine adventure.

receipts or benefits which accrue to him by reason of his particular relationship to real or personal property, such as receipts derived from the employment or hiring of property. An early example is a marine insurance on a shipowner's freight which is to be earned under a maritime contract of affreightment.[86] Where the earning of freight or charter hire is endangered by the exposure of the ship to maritime perils, there is a marine adventure,[87] and the insured shipowner's insurable interest therein is established by his legal or equitable relationship to the adventure itself or to the right to the freight or hire itself.[88] Until the beginning of the twentieth century it was incumbent on the assured to show that a binding contract was in existence under which freight was to be earned or else insurable interest in it could not be demonstrated, and it follows that anticipated future freights and hire could not be insured. Later decisions held that a shipowner may insure against the loss of anticipated future earnings from the employment of his ship over a period of time whether or not a contract exists in relation to them either at the inception of the policy or at the time when an insured peril operates.[89] The subject-matter of such insurances is the revenue earning capacity of the ship, in which her owner has an insurable interest. Difficulties in proving the amount of the lost earnings may be met by agreed advance valuation, but proof of loss depends upon the assured proving that the ship would have been deployed in the market as a freight-earning vessel if an insured peril had not operated to prevent it.[90] In similar fashion a landlord may insure against the loss of rent which he may suffer through destruction of or damage to buildings which are demised or let, so long as that interest is insured *eo nomine*. It cannot be recovered on an insurance taken out only against physical loss or damage to the building.[91]

1–59 *On agent's commission.* An agent for the sale of goods, or who manages or sells other property can insure against the loss of his expected commission by an event which destroys or damages the property.[92] He has an interest in the property to the extent of the anticipated commission so long as he has a legal right to be employed and to earn it.[93] A mere expectation of future employment is merely a factual expectation of benefit from the property and will not support a valid insurable interest. The insurance must specify his particular interest in the property in order to cover the commissions.[94]

1–60 *Profits from premises.* If the assured has an insurable interest in premises through ownership or occupancy, he may insure against the loss of trading profits caused by damage to the building which in turn disrupts the

---

[86] *Thompson v. Taylor* (1795) 6 T.R. 478; *Forbes v. Aspinall* (1811) 13 East 323; *Flint v Flemyng* (1830) 1 B. & Ad. 45; *Barber v. Fleming* (1869) L.R. 5 Q.B. 59.

[87] M.I.A. 1906 s.3(2)(b).

[88] M.I.A. 1906 s.5(2).

[89] Manchester Liners v. British & Foreign Mar. Ins. Co. (1901) 7 Com. Cas. 26, 33; *Robertson v. Petros Nomikos Ltd* [1939] A.C. 371, 383; *Papadimitriou v. Henderson* [1939] 64 Ll.L.Rep. 345; *Cepheus Shipping Copr. v. Guardian Royal Exchange Assurance PLC* [1995] 1 Lloyd's Rep. 622.

[90] [1995] 1 Lloyd's Rep. 622, 641–642.

[91] *Re Sun Fire Ass. Co. v. Wright* (1834) 3 N. & M. 819; *Re Wright and Pole* (1834) 1 Ad. & El. 621; *City Tailors v. Evans* (1921) 126 L.T. 439.

[92] *Maurice v. Goldsborough Mort & Co.* [1939] A.C. 452, 463.

[93] *Buchanan v. Faber* (1899) 4 Com.Cas. 223.

[94] *Maurice v. Goldsborough Mort & Co.* [1939] A.C. 452, 463.

business carried on there. The policy must expressly cover that type of loss.[95] It is commonly done by including business interruption or consequential loss cover in an insurance on the buildings, or by obtaining a separate insurance cover.[96] Such insurances commonly exclude cover for loss of profits caused by damage to a building unless the assured has also insured the building against damage to the extent of his personal interest therein.[97]

1–61 *On business profits.* We have already seen that profits expected from the sale of property may be insured as such. A person may also insure against loss of profit attendant upon a named contingency which will frustrate or disrupt an undertaking or adventure, so long as the matter is not merely a visionary project and that contracts are in existence which will supply the necessary interest in the occurrence of the contingency. An early example of such insurance was the insurance against the frustration of a voyage to deliver cargo to, and ship another cargo at, St. Petersburg at the time at which Russia was being pressed by Napoleon to embargo British goods.[98] Today contract frustration insurances and political risk insurances are commonplace. In an American case an agent of an insurance company was remunerated by a certain percentage of the gross receipts and net profits of the company's fire insurance business. He insured "on interest in profits under contract with the X Insurance Co." against loss caused by the company's fire losses exceeding a certain total. It was held that he had an insurable interest and that the risk was sufficiently described.[99] It is submitted that English law would reach the same conclusion, since he had demonstrated a legal nexus with the profits made by the company, and in this kind of case that need not be a proprietary right in the subject-matter.[1]

1–62 *Interest of shareholders.* Analogous to the insurance of the profits from a business or undertaking is the insurance by a shareholder of the shares which he holds in a company. The English courts have adopted the view that a shareholder as such has no insurable interest in the corporate property, or, at any rate, cannot insure simply on the property, but must specify his interest and define the risk as an insurance on his shares or dividends.[2] In other words, he must insure not the property but the capital which he has staked on the adventure and the profits which he expects to derive from the investment. The facts of the *Macaura* case[3] were as follows:

---

[95] *Re Wright & Pole* (1834) 1 Ad. & El. 621.

[96] *Re Wright & Pole, supra; Re Sun Fire Assurance Co. v. Wright* (1834) 3 N. & M. 819; *City Tailors v. Evans* (1922) 38 T.L.R. 230; *Nsubuga v. Comm. Union Assurance Co.* [1998] 2 Lloyd's Rep. 682; *Ins. Corp. of the Channel Islands v. McHugh* [1997] L.R.L.R. 94.

[97] *Glengate-KG Properties v. Norwich Union Fire Ins. Soc.* [1996] 1 Lloyd's Rep. 614.

[98] *Puller v. Stainiforth* (1809) 11 East 232; *Puller v. Glover* (1810) 12 East 124.

[99] *Hayes v. Milford Mutual Fire* 170 Mass. 492 (1898).

[1] *Glengate-KG Properties v. Norwich Union Fire Ins. Soc.* [1996] 1 Lloyd's Rep. 614, 622, 623–624.

[2] *Wilson v. Jones* (1867) L.R. 2 Ex. 139, 144; *Macaura v. Northern Ass. Co.* [1925] A.C. 619. In *Paterson v. Harris* (1861) 1 B. & S. 336, 355 it seems to have been held that a shareholder had an interest in the company's property, but the plea of interest was not traversed by the insurers' and the case is not authoritative [1925] A.C. 619, 628, 630.

[3] [1925] A.C. 619; followed in *Cowan v. Jeffrey Associates* 1999 S.L.T. 757. The same principle has been applied to insurance of a Scottish partnership's property by one of its partners—*Arif v. Excess Ins. Group Ltd* 1987 S.L.T. 473; *Mitchell v. Scottish Eagle Ins. Co.* 1997 S.L.T. 2.

The plaintiff was the owner of the Killymoon estate in the county of Tyrone. In December 1919 he sold to a company the timber on this estate, felled and unfelled, for a total price of £42,000. He received the price in 42,000 fully paid £1 shares and he and his nominees were the only shareholders in the company. Except for some chattels of small value, the only asset of the company was the timber on the plaintiff's estate. The plaintiff advanced money to the company for felling operations, and by August 1921, the whole timber had been felled and sawn and the company owed the plaintiff £19,000. The plaintiff had obtained an overdraft from the Bank of Ireland and had deposited as security therefor the title-deeds of the estate. In these circumstances the plaintiff and the bank took out policies with the defendant in their joint names for the respective interests, insuring them against loss by fire on the felled timber up to £30,000. On February 22, 1922, the greater part of the timber was destroyed. Held, upon a special case stated by an arbitrator, that the plaintiff had no insurable interest in the timber either as shareholder or creditor of the company and that the award must be in favour of the office.

1–63 The decision in *Macaura* has been criticised. In the United States the overwhelming majority of cases hold that a shareholder has an insurable interest in the property of the company in proportion to the amount of his shareholding.[4] In *Constitution Insurance Company of Canada v. Kosmopoulos*[5] the Supreme Court of Canada has held that where there was a "moral certainty" of loss to a shareholder from damage to company property, he possessed an insurable interest in it, and refused to follow the decision in *Macaura*. The Supreme Court adopted what it took to be a broader definition of insurable interest in property enunciated by Lawrence J. when advising the House of Lords in *Lucena v. Crawford*,[6] which was not accepted by the House of Lords.[7] It is difficult to see how, consistent with established principles requiring a legal or equitable relation to insured property, the *Macaura* decision can be reconsidered by any court other than the House of Lords itself. In any event, a shareholder may insure against loss or diminution in the value of his shares generally from any cause or specifically in consequence of the destruction of the company's property by fire or some other specified risk. He may insure his capital and dividends, or the dividends only.[8]

1–64 "Any legal liability". These words in the working definition in

---

[4] See generally Appleman, *Insurance Law and Practice*, para. 2145; *Providence Washington Ins. Co. v. Stanley* 403 F. 2d 844, rehearing denied 406 F. 2d 735 (1968); *American Indemnity Co. v. Southern Missionary College* 260 S.W. 2d 269 (1953).

[5] (1987) 34 D.L.R. (4th) 208, affirming (1983) 149 D.L.R. (3d) 77 (Ontario C.A.). The Supreme Court declined to follow its earlier decisions in *Guarantee Co. of N. America v. Aqua-Land Exploration Co.* (1965) 54 D.L.R. (2d) 229 and *Wandlyn Motels Ltd v. Commerce General Insurance Co.* (1970) 12 D.L.R. (3d) 605, adopting the broad view that insurable interest did not require legally enforceable rights in or over property, but was satisfied by factual expectation of economic gain or loss—see para. 1–117, *post*. A similar result would be arrived at in those Australian jurisdictions in which s.16(1) and 17 of the Insurance Contracts Act 1984 are in force.

[6] (1806) 2 Bos. & Pul. (N.R.) 269, 301. It is submitted that this is a misinterpretation of Lawrence J.'s judgment. See Legh-Jones in *The Modern Law of Marine Insurance* (2002) Vol. 2, Ch. 4.

[7] *ibid.* at p. 321.

[8] *Wilson v. Jones* (1867) L.R. 2 Ex. 139.

paragraph 1–49 above refer to two distinct cases. First, just as an assured has an interest in his own life, so he has an interest in his own assets and is entitled to take out liability insurance to indemnify him against loss in the event of being made liable in damages towards a third party. Secondly, an insurable interest in property is created when the assured's legal relationship to it renders him liable to pay money in the event of it being lost or damaged by an insured peril. Thus a person who has agreed that goods are to be at his risk during transit has an insurable interest in them even when he has neither title to, nor possession of, those goods.[9] A contractual obligation to keep property insured against accidental loss or damage gives the obligor an insurable interest in it.[10] On the same principle all insurers on a valid policy have an insurable interest which entitles them to reinsure or to effect a counter-insurance on the subject matter of the original insurance.[11] An insurer on a void policy has no insurable interest to support a reinsurance, even though in practice underwriters who pay losses on such policies are indemnified by their reinsurers.[12] Wherever a person has assumed a legal obligation to indemnify another against loss of or damage to property,[13] or where the law imposes such obligation on him, he has an insurable interest therein to the extent of his possible liability.[14]

1–65 It has been held that a supplier of goods to be incorporated into a ship or industrial plant acquires an insurable interest in the whole ship or structure by reason of the risk that he might become liable for its loss or damage if caused by defects in the product supplied by him, even though he has not agreed that it shall be at his risk and he has no proprietary interest in it.[15] This represents an extension of the established principle that the assured should normally have proprietary or contractual rights in property to support an insurable interest in it,[16] and appears, with respect, to confuse liability insurance with insurance on property. The risk that a person might become liable for negligently causing damage to another's property does not per se give him an insurable interest in that property, it is submitted, any more than an expectancy of future benefit therefrom would do so. If it did create an insurable interest, then the assureds in *Macaura v. Northern Assurance Co.*[17] and *North British and Mercantile Insurance Co. v. Moffatt*[18] should have succeeded in establishing an insurable interest in goods left on

[9] *e.g.* a buyer of goods on c.i.f. or f.o.b. terms—*Anderson v. Morice* (1876) 1 App.Cas. 713; *Stock v. Inglis* (1884) 12 Q.B.D. 564, aff'd (1885) 10 App.Cas. 263. In this instance the buyer is obliged to pay the price whether the goods come into his possession or are lost.
[10] *Heckman v. Isaac* (1862) 6 L.T. 383; *Lonsdale & Thompson Ltd v. Black Arrow Group plc* [1993] Ch. 361, 368.
[11] *Mackenzie v. Whitworth* (1875) 1 Ex.D. 36.
[12] *Re London County Commercial Reinsurance Office* [1922] 2 Ch. 67; *Bedford Insurance v. Institute de Resseguros do Brasil* [1985] Q.B. 966; *Phoenix General Insurance Co. Greece v. A.D.A.S.* [1988] 1 Q.B. 216, 277.
[13] *Germania Fire Insurance Co. v. Thompson* 95 U.S. 547 (1877).
[14] *Crowley v. Cohen* (1832) 3 B. & Ad. 478. The obligation may be imposed by statute—*British Cash etc. v. Lamson Store Service* [1908] 1 K.B. 1006, 1014–1015.
[15] *Stone Vickers Ltd v. Appledore Ferguson Shipbuilders Ltd* [1991] 1 Lloyd's Rep. 288, 301; *National Oilwell (UK) Ltd v. Davy Offshore Ltd.* [1993] 2 Lloyd's Rep. 582, 611; *Hopewell Project Management v. Ewbank Preece* [1998] 1 Lloyd's Rep. 448, 455. The supplier could of course take out insurance against the risk of that liability.
[16] *Glengate-KG Properties v. Norwich Union Ins. Soc.* [1996] 1 Lloyd's Rep. 614, 623–624 *per* Auld L.J.
[17] [1925] A.C. 619.
[18] (1871) L.R. 7 C.P. 25, 30–31. See para. 1–156, *post.*

their premises in circumstances in which they had no legal or equitable title in or rights over them and when the goods were not at their risk. It is submitted in paragraph 1–157, below, that this reasoning is no longer good law after the decision of the Court of Appeal in *Deepak Fertilisers & Petrochemical Corporation v. ICI Chemicals & Polymers Ltd.*[19]

5. INSURABLE INTEREST IN LIVES

(a) *Principles of the 1774 Act*

1–66 Scope of Act. The statute 14 Geo. 3, c. 48, is the source of the requirement of English law that insurances on lives must be made on interest. As its short title[20] implies, it was indeed primarily directed to check the mischief of effecting insurances on human lives in which the assured had no interest except as the basis of a gaming transaction, although it covered other types of insurances also. The effect of the Act on life assurance is that a claimant on a life policy must show (1) that the person on whose behalf it was made had an insurable interest in the life, (2) that the policy is expressed as having been made on behalf of the person or persons on whose behalf it was in fact made, and (3) that the amount claimed is no greater than the amount of such person's interest.[21]

1–67 It follows from the expressed purpose of the Act that parties are not free to contract out of it. Although the Act does not prescribe penalties in the event of infringement of its provisions, no assured or insurer can dispense with the requirement that an assured shall possess an insurable interest.[22] Therefore a policy which is declared to be made "on honour," or on p.p.i. principles, or which contains an incontestability clause, in no way precludes the insurers from pleading want of interest as a defence to a claim on the policy.[23]

1–68 Application of the Act. Section 1 of the Act provides that:

> "no insurance shall be made by any person … on the life or lives of any person or persons … wherein the person … on whose account such policy … shall be made, shall have no interest…"

The section therefore applies to a contract which is (1) in the nature of an insurance and (2) on the life of a person. The test for the existence of an insurance on life is the existence of an obligation in the insurer to pay a sum of money or other benefit which is payable on an event which is uncertain,

---

[19] [1999] 1 Lloyd's Rep. 387.

[20] Short Titles Act 1896 (59 & 60 Vict. c. 14).

[21] See the preface to the Act, and comment, in Halsbury's *Statutes* (3rd ed.), Vol. 17, p. 827 and R. Merkin, "Gambling by Insurance", in (1980) 9 Anglo-Am.L.R. 331.

[22] See the famous remarks of Scrutton L.J. in *R. v. London County Council* [1931] 2 K.B. 215, 228–229, concerning the attempts of an individual to dispense with the effect of an Act of Parliament, and the discussion in para. 1–35, *supra*, and at note 9 to that paragraph.

[23] *Anctil v. Manufacturers' Life Ins. Co.* [1899] A.C. 604; *Royal Exchange Assurance v. Sjoforsakrings* [1902] 2 K.B. 384. In so far as *Turnbull v. Scottish Provident* (1896) 34 S.L.R. 146 appears to contradict these authorities it should not be followed, but the decision can be upheld on other grounds.

either as to its timing or as to its happening at all, and that event must be dependent on the duration of human life.[24] A whole-life insurance to pay a sum on death is the simplest instance, since although death is certain the timing is uncertain. The contingency upon which money is payable can be the survival of a life to a prescribed age.[25] Where the insurer was liable under a Capital Investment Bond, described as a life assurance policy, to pay the current value of the policy either upon surrender by notice in writing from the corporate policy holder or on the death of the life assured, it was held by the Court of Appeal[26] that the fact that the measure of the benefit payable on surrender was the same as that payable on death did not prevent the bond from being a contract of life insurance within section 1 of the 1774 Act. The right to surrender was related to the duration of life in as much as it could not be exercised by the corporate policy holder after the death of the life assured. Additionally a discontinuance penalty operated upon surrender, but not death, within the first five years of the policy, and an option to postpone payment of benefit for six months was exercisable by the insurers upon surrender but not death.

Under an employees' superannuation scheme the employer funded policies issued to its employees, under which benefits were payable on (1) retirement on or after a specified date, (2) death in employment before the age of seventy and (3) departure from that employment before the retirement date. In each case the benefits payable were measured in the same way, namely, the accumulated contributions made by the employer with interest accrued thereon. Both the Federal Court of Australia[27] and the High Court of New Zealand[28] held that these were policies of life insurance, notwithstanding the identical calculation of benefits payable in the three contingencies mentioned, because each contingency depended upon the duration of human life. These decision were cited with approval in *Fuji Finance Inc. v. Aetna Life Insurance Co. Ltd*,[29] where it was also stated, following earlier authorities in this[30] and other jurisdictions,[31] that a contract under which the insurer runs no real risk of financial loss is nonetheless a contract of life insurance if money is payable on a contingency depending on the duration of human life.

1-69 The width of the definition of insurance upon the life of a person means that endowment policies must be within the 1774 Act. In *Prudential Insurance Co. v. Inland Revenue Commissioners*[32] an "endowment policy" whereby the insurer promised to pay £95 on the life attaining age 65 or £30 on death prior to 65 was held to be "a policy of insurance … upon [a]

---

[24] *Fuji Finance Inc. v. Aetna Life Ins. Co. Ltd* [1995] Ch. 122, 130 (approved as to the test of life insurance in the Court of Appeal [1997] Ch. 173), reviewing and applying *Prudential Ins. Co. v. I.R.C.* [1904] 2 K.B. 658; *Joseph v. Law Integrity Ins. Co.* [1912] 2 Ch. 581 and *Gould v. Curtis* [1913] 3 K.B. 84.

[25] *Gould v. Curtis* [1913] 3 K.B. 84; *NM Superannuation Pty. v. Young* (1993) 113 A.L.R. 39, 54.

[26] *Fuji Finance Inc. v. Aetna Life Ins. Co. Ltd* [1997] Ch. 173, reversing the decision of Nicholls V.-C. at [1995] Ch. 122.

[27] *NM Superannuation Pty Ltd v. Young* (1993) 113 A.L.R. 39

[28] *Jones v. AMP Perpetual Trustee Co.* (1994) 1 N.Z.L.R. 691.

[29] [1997] Ch. 173.

[30] *Flood v. Irish Provident Ass. Co.* [1912] 2 Ch. 597.

[31] *NM Superannuation Pty v. Young* (1993) 113 A.L.R. 39.

[32] [1904] 2 K.B. 658.

contingency depending upon … life" within section 98 of the Stamp Act 1891. Channell J. held *obiter*[33] that the endowment provision on its own came within that definition. In *Gould v. Curtis*[34] a "double endowment assurance" assuring payment of £100 upon death of the life assured within 15 years was held to be an insurance on the life of the policy holder within section 54 of the Income Tax Act 1853. In *Joseph v. Law Integrity Insurance Co. Ltd*[35] "investment policies" under which sums were payable at fixed intervals in return for periodic payments were held to be policies of assurance upon human life, because the insurers contracted to pay given sums upon the occurrence of particular events contingent upon the duration of a life. It is accordingly submitted that the 1774 Act requires an insurable interest in the case of pure endowment policies, and this accords with the validation of such policies in section 1 of the Friendly Societies Act 1929[36] with regard to the lives of certain categories of relatives in whom the member or person assured had no insurable interest.

1–70 Time at which the Act requires interest. Interest must be shown to have subsisted at the date on which the contract was made, but not at death, since the contract is not a contract of indemnity.[37] No doubt a contract to indemnify against loss consequent upon the death of an individual might be made, but the normal life policy taken out on the life of another person is not to be construed as a contract of indemnity unless the intention of the parties that it should be so limited is clearly expressed. How far an insurance made upon interest which is limited to a definite period would be valid in excess of that period has already been considered.[38]

1–71 Nature of interest required. It has been said that the assured must show a pecuniary interest in the life assured,[39] but this is misleading as a general proposition, since in certain important cases an insurable interest is presumed both to be present and to be sufficient, though not pecuniary.

1–72 In three categories of life assurance, an insurable interest is presumed and need not be proved. These are, (i) an insurance by a person on his own life,[40] (ii) insurance by a man on the life of his wife[41] and (iii) insurance by a woman on the life of her husband.[42] In these instances, the law takes the view that the interest of the assured is of higher account than a purely pecuniary interest and is incapable of pecuniary valuation, and accordingly there is no limit upon the amount which may be insured upon such lives or upon the number of policies which may be effected.[43]

[33] [1904] 2 K.B. 658, 664.
[34] [1913] 3 K.B. 84
[35] [1912] 2 Ch. 581, following *Flood v. Irish Provident Ass. Co.* [1912] 2 Ch. 597. See also *Re Ioakimidis' Policy Trusts* [1925] Ch. 403.
[36] 19 & 20 Geo. 5. c.28.
[37] *Dalby v. India and London Life Assurance Co.* (1854) 15 C.B. 365; *Law v. London Indisputable Life Policy* (1855) 1 K. & J. 223. The Act requires interest similarly in the case of insurance against death in an accident policy—*Shilling v. Accidental Death* (1858) 1 F & F. 116.
[38] See para. 1–32 *ante.*
[39] *Halford v. Kymer* (1830) 10 B. & C. 724, 728.
[40] *Wainwright v. Bland* (1835) 1 Moo. & R. 481; (1836) 1 M. & W. 32.
[41] *Griffiths v. Fleming* [1909] 1 K.B. 805; *Wight v. Brown* (1849) 11 D. 459.
[42] *Reed v. Royal Exchange* (1795) Peake Ad.Cas. 70; Married Women's Property Act 1882 (45 & 46 Vict. c. 75), s.11.
[43] *M'Farlane v. The Royal London F.S.* (1886) 2 T.L.R. 755; *Shilling v. Accidental Death* (1857) 2 H. & N. 42.

1-73 There would appear to be no difference in this respect between Scots and English law. The insurable interest of a man in the life of his wife has never been the subject of direct decision in Scotland; but it never seems to have been doubted,[44] and it has been held that when the death of a married woman has been caused by the negligence or misconduct of another, her husband is entitled to recover damages independently of pecuniary loss on the broad ground of solatium for loss of happiness, status and comfort.[45] A woman's insurable interest in the life of her husband is supportable on the same grounds and is implied in the provision of the Married Women's Policies of Assurance (Scotland) Act 1880,[46] that a married woman may effect a policy of life assurance on the life of her husband for her own separate use.

In *Wainwright v. Bland*,[47] which is the leading authority for the proposition that a man has an unlimited insurable interest in his own life, it was argued that, although that may be so on a whole life policy, yet if a man insures his life for a limited period only, he must show that he has some special interest in his life over that period. In rejecting that argument Lord Abinger said that if a party has an interest in his whole life he must surely have an interest in every part of it.

1-74 Apart from the cases mentioned above, cases of industrial assurance and friendly society policies effected to cover funeral expenses, and endowment policies sanctioned by the Industrial Assurance and Friendly Societies Act 1929, the assured must show a pecuniary interest in the life insured. "Pecuniary" really means no more than that the interest must be capable of valuation by a court, and this is necessary inasmuch as section 3 of the Act provides that the assured shall not recover more than the value of his interest at the time the contract was made.[48]

1-75 Besides being capable of valuation, the interest must be of such a nature that the law will take cognisance of it. The assured must show that he will or may lose some legal or equitable right[49] or be placed under the burden of some legal liability[50] in consequence of the death of the person whose life is insured. A mere expectancy or hope of future pecuniary benefit from the prolongation of the life insured or of the fulfilment by him of moral obligations owed to the assured, are insufficient to sustain an insurable interest.[51] If, however, the death of the life insured will involve the assured in a liability, it is no answer for the insurers to show that he will also derive

---

[44] *Champion v. Duncan* (1867) 6 M. 17; *Wight v. Brown* (1849) 11 D. 459.

[45] *Dow v. Brown* (1844) 6 D. 534 (£5,000).

[46] 43 & 44 Vict. c. 26, s.1.

[47] (1835) 1 Moo. & R. 481; (1836) 1 M. & W. 32.

[48] *Simcock v. Scottish Imperial* (1902) 10 S.L.T. 286, 287; *Halford v. Kymer* (1830) 10 B. & C. 724. The assured may insure in more than one company, but his total recovery is limited to the amount of interest he had at the date of the insurance.

[49] *cf.* para. 1–49, *ante.*

[50] *Tidswell v. Ankerstein* (1792) Peake N.P.C. 151; *Feasey v. Sun Life Ass. Co. of Canada* [2002] EWHC 868 (COMM).

[51] *Hebdon v. West* (1863) 3 B. & S. 579; *Simcock v. Scottish Imperial* (1902) 10 S.L.T. 286; *Turnbull v. Scottish Provident Institution* (1896) 34 S.L.T. 146; *Sharma v. Home Ins. Co. of New York* [1966] E.A. 8 (K), where the corresponding passage in the 5th edition of this work was approved. *Contrast* the Aus. Insurance Contracts Act 1984 s.19(3), whereby anyone likely to suffer pecuniary loss as a result of the death of another has an unlimited insurable interest in that person's life.

some compensating benefit, since the contract is not one of indemnity and the insurers may not set off the assured's gain against his loss.[52]

(b) Business and Status Relationships Between the Assured and the Life Assured

1–76 Employer and employee. It has long been established in English law that a contract to employ a person at an ascertained salary and for a term certain gives the employee an insurable interest in the life of his prospective employer to the extent of the actuarial value of the future salary calculated at the date when the insurance is effect.[53] Conversely an employer has an insurable interest in the life of his employee to the extent of the value of the employee's services during such time as he is under a legal obligation to serve his employer.[54] It has been held in two Scottish decisions that, if the employee is employed on the basis of a week's notice, his employer has no insurable interest in his life beyond the value of a week's services.[55]

1–77 So far as the employer's interest is concerned, it may be objected that the narrow degree of recognition afforded to it on the authorities is unrealistic and unacceptable in modern business conditions, and it is true that current insurance practice honours the law more in the breach than in the observance where this class of policy is written. It is nevertheless difficult to see how a different result can be reached consistently with the principles of the 1774 Act.

1–78 In the first place, the employer must not claim an amount greater than the value of his interest in the employee at the start of the policy. It is really impossible to put a precise figure on the financial value of an employee's continued existence to the enterprise which employs him. Even if it were feasible, the valuation would have to be based on his worth at the commencement of the insurance, thereby ignoring any increase in his worth after the attainment of further qualifications, experience or business contacts. The obvious answer to the problem was to accept the assured's own round figure valuation, but at a time when the purpose of the Act as a ban on wagering on lives was more seriously recognised than it is today, the courts presumably would have been reluctant to sanction bargains that seemed to smack of the old forbidden practices outlawed by the Act.[56]

1–79 If the employer were permitted to agree a round-figure valuation with the insurer, there would still remain a second, more intractable, difficulty. The definition of an insurable interest recognised by the courts was arrived at chiefly in the context of marine insurance, and therefore in relation to property concerned in marine ventures. It was established, as we have seen already,[57] that the assured must possess a legal right over the

---

[52] *Branford v. Saunders* (1877) 25 W.R. 650.
[53] *Hebdon v. West* (1863) 3 B. & S. 579. See para. 1–34, *ante,* and note 88 to para. 1–89, *post.*
[54] *Simcock v. Scottish Imperial Insurance Co.* (1902) 10 S.L.T. 286, 288; *Turnbull v. Scottish Provident Institution* (1896) 34 S.L.R. 146.
[55] *ibid.*
[56] For a summary of the situation before the Act was passed, see para. 1–19, *ante.*
[57] See para. 1–49, *ante.*

property or a legal title to benefits accruing from it. The interest of the assured had to be, essentially, that of a person possessing a legal right in or over some thing susceptible of such a title. That "mercantile" definition of insurable interest is frequently inappropriate, however, in the context of lives,[58] and the employment relationship is one such case. An employer has no title or right to the services of an employee beyond the length of a period of notice or, in some cases, a service contract of several years, and a law which assesses his interest solely by reference to his contractual right to insist upon an employee's services ignores the prospect of stable employment for many years, or of the likely renewal of a service contract when it expires. In order to recognise the employer's actual interest, the law needs to recognise a genuine expectation of future gain unsupported by a legal claim, and that it cannot do until the old authorities are challenged in the courts or abrogated by statute.[59]

1–80 American decisions on employer's interest. The American law on insurable interest in lives has developed without the constraint of the 1774 Act. Consequently, it is generally recognised that a reasonable expectation of pecuniary gain or benefit through the continued existence of a person, and of loss consequent upon his death, is sufficient to ground an insurance on that person's life.[60] Therefore, while the relationship of employee and employee is not in every case sufficient to support an interest,[61] it is not difficult for an employer to insure the life of a senior executive or of a manager on whom the successful running of a business depends.[62] The courts accept a valued policy on the life of such a person without questioning the actual sum stated by the parties,[63] but the insurers can always plead want of interest if they can establish that in reality the life assured has no special value to the business.[64] It does not matter if the employee leaves the

---

[58] As is instanced by the three cases, including own life insurance, where an interest is presumed to be present (para. 1–72, *ante*).

[59] For an example of such statutory abrogation, see the Australian Insurance Contracts Act 1984, s.19(4)(b) whereby an employer has an unlimited interest in the life of his employee and vice versa. By s.19(4)(a) a body corporate has an insurable interest in the life of an officer or employee of the company. Note that in the only modern English cases where the point was raised, a round-figure valuation of the amount of the employer's interest was accepted without question: *Marcel Beller Ltd v. Hayden* [1978] Q.B. 694, 697; *Fugi Finance Inc. v. Aetna Life Ins. Co.* [1997] Ch. 173.

[60] *United Security Life Insurance and Trust Co. v. Brown*, 270 Pa. 270 (1921); *Murray v. G. F. Higgins Co.*, 150 A. 2d 629 (Supp.Ct.Pa., 1930); *Sun Life Assurance Co. of Canada v. Allen*, 259 N.W. 281 (Sup.Ct.Mich., 1935); *Turner v. Davidson*, 4 S.E. 2d 814 (Sup.Ct.Ga., 1939) *Warnock v. Davis*, 104 U.S. 775 (1881); *U.S. v. Supplee-Biddle Co.*, 265 U.S. 189 (1923); *Western and Southern Life Ins. Co. v. Webster*, 189 S.W. 429 (Ky Sup.Ct., 1916); *Drane v. Jefferson Standard Life Ins. Co.*, 161 S.W. 2d 1057 (Texas Sup.Ct. 1942).

[61] Insurances on lowly placed and easily replaceable employees will fail on this test; see, *e.g. Turner v. Davidson, supra* (policy on life of truck driver distributing petrol for gasoline distribution company).

[62] *e.g.* president: *U.S. v. Supplee-Biddle Co., supra; Mickleberry's Food Products v. Hauesserman*, 247 S.W. 2d 731 (Mo., 1952); vice president: *Wellhouse v. United Paper Co.*, 29 F. 2d 886 (C.C.A. 1929); general manager: *Sinclair Refining Co. v. Long*, 32 P. 2d 464 (Sup.Ct.Kan., 1934); *Wurzburg v. New York Life Ins. Co.*, 203 S.W. 332 (Sup.Ct.Tenn., 1926).

[63] The sums assured in the above cases range from $1,000 in the *Geisler* case, *supra*, to $250,000 in *Chapman v. Lipscombe-Ellis Co.*, 22 S.E. 2d 393 (Ga.Sup.Ct., 1942), which at that time was a very considerable figure indeed.

[64] *e.g. Sun Life Ass. Co. of Canada v. Allen*, 259 N.W. 281 (Sup.Ct.Mich., 1935), where the evidence of the life assured's landlady helped to convince the court that the life had been a drunkard, of little use, and not worth a fraction of the $250,000 covered on the policy.

assured's employment before the policy matures, because such policies are not strict policies of indemnity, and the interest need not be possessed at the time of the employee's death or retirement.[65]

1–81 The definition of insurable interest by the American courts is apparently broad enough to permit the insurance of the life of someone on whose ability the success of a business depends, even where the assured is not in the business himself but has a vital financial interest in it, such as that of a major shareholder or, possibly, even that of a regular supplier of goods or services to the business. There are no United Kingdom authorities directly dealing with this type of "key man" policy, but it seems, on the authorities already discussed,[66] that such policies do not satisfy the requirements of the 1774 Act.

1–82 Life of testator. In the eighteenth-century case of *Tideswell v. Ankerstein*[67] it was held that a person named as an executor in a will by the terms of which the testator granted an annuity to a named beneficiary had an insurable interest in the life of the testator, inasmuch as on the latter's death he would be able, from the proceeds of a policy on his life, to pay the annuity in full without the risk of incurring a devastavit in the event of an insufficiency of assets to provide for the annuity and pay the testator's creditors. It is submitted that this case cannot be supported inasmuch as the interest claimed was based—(1) on an expectancy, and (2) on a purely moral obligation.

1–83 Joint liability. A joint obligation by A and B to pay a sum of money to a third party gives each of them an insurable interest in the life of the other to the extent of half of the joint liability, inasmuch as the death of one will add that amount to the ultimate liability of the other.[68]

1–84 Contingent proprietary interest. A person who has a proprietary interest contingent on the life of another, has an insurable interest in that other's life,[69] but where there is a mere *spes successionis*, an expectant heir cannot insure the life upon the continuance of which his succession depends.[70]

1–85 Covenant to pay on death. A covenant by A that on the death of B he will repay to C the money he has borrowed from C is not a contract of insurance on the life of B and, therefore, C can recover on such a covenant without proof of any insurable interest in B's life.[71]

[65] *Chapman v. Lipscombe-Ellis Co.*, 22 S.E. 2d 393 (Sup.Ct.G.), *Reilly v. Penn Mutual Life Ins. Co.*, 207 N.W. 583 (Iowa Sup.Ct. 1926); *McMullen v. Lucie County Bank*, 175 So. 721 (Sup.Ct.Fla., 1937); *Wurzburg v. New York Life Ins. Co.*, 203 S.W. 332 (Sup.Ct.Tenn., 1926) *Secor v. Pioneer Foundry Co.* 173 N.W. 2d 780 (Mich. C.A., 1970).

[66] e.g. *Hebdon v. West* (1863) 3 B. & S. 579; *Simcock v. Scottish Imperial Ins. Co.* (1902) 10 S.L.T. 286. In *Chentium v. Packall Packaging Inc.* (1998) 38 O.R. (3d) 401 it was held, following English law, that as keyman insurance on the life of a manager did not become void or contrary to public policy when the life assured left his employment two years after inception.

[67] (1792) Peake N.P.C. 151.

[68] *Branford v. Saunders* (1877) 25 W.R. 650.

[69] *Parson v. Bignold* (1843) 13 Sim. 518; *Henson v. Blackwell* (1845) 4 Hare 434; *Everett v. Desborough* (1829) 5 Bing. 503; *Swete v. Fairlie* (1833) 6 C. & P. 1; *Law v. London Indisputable Life Policy* (1855) 1 K. & J. 223.

[70] *Halford v. Kymer* (1830) 10 B. & C. 724.

[71] *Cook v. Field* (1850) 15 Q.B. 460.

In *Cook v. Field* [72] it was stated as the opinion of the Court of Queen's Bench, that if A, having an expectancy of succession arising on the death of B, borrowed money from C in consideration of a covenant that he would convey to C the estate to which he, A, would succeed if the expectancy were realised, the covenant gave C an insurable interest in the life of B. That opinion has been doubted on the ground that, inasmuch as A's expectancy gave him no insurable interest in the life of B, then C could acquire none on his expectancy of having the estate conveyed to him in satisfaction of A's covenant, Mr Bunyon[73] thought that the decision might be supported on the analogy of the rules of equity to perpetuate testimony to effect that, although one who had a bare expectancy could not file a bill, yet if he had entered into any contract with respect to his expectancy he could do so on the basis of the interest created by his contract. That might give the vendor of an expectancy an interest, but it is not so clear that it would give any interest to a purchaser of the expectancy from him.

1–86 Member of local authority. A local authority has statutory power to insure its members against personal accident while engaged in the business of the authority. Any sum recovered under such insurance is, after deduction of any expenses incurred in the recovery thereof, payable to the member or his personal representative.[74]

1–87 Creditor in life of debtor. A creditor has an insurable interest in the life of his debtor.[75] On the debtor's death he loses his right of action against the debtor, and this loss is sufficient to support the insurance even though the debtor's estate is solvent and there is abundant prospect of the debt being ultimately paid in full. There is no authority in this country which defines the maximum limit of insurable interest which a creditor may have in the life of his debtor. It is clear that a creditor has an interest at least to the amount of the debt and interest due thereon at the time the effects the insurance,[76] but an insurance limited to that amount would not fully protect him because future interest and the costs of maintaining the insurance up to the date of the debtor's death are not provided for.[77]

1–88 The question of the amount which a creditor may recover upon an insurance upon his debtor's life has been much considered in the American courts, without the restrictions imposed by the Life Assurance Act 1774.[78] While there are authorities allowing recovery of the full sum insured even

---

[72] (1850) 15 Q.B. 460.

[73] *Life Assurance* (5th ed.), p. 18. *Dursley v. Fitzhardinge Berkeley* (1801) 6 Ves. 251.

[74] Local Government Act 1972, s.140 as amended by the Local Government (Miscellaneous Provisions) Act 1982, s.39(1).

[75] *Anderson v. Edie* (1795) 2 Park, *Mar. Ins.* (8th ed., 1842); (1798) 1 Bos. & P. 315n., *Von Lindenau v. Desborough* (1828) 3 C. & P. 353; 8 B. & C. 586; *Rawlins v. Desborough* (1840) 2 Moo. & R. 328; *Godsall v. Boldero* (1807) 9 East 72; *Dalby v. India and London Life Ass. Co.* (1845) 15 C.B. 365; *Hebdon v. West* (1863) 3 B. & S. 579. *Macaura v. Northern Ass. Co.* [1925] A.C. 619, 626. For a case where an evil creditor poisoned her debtors after insuring their lives, see *R. v. Flannagan* (1884), 15 Cox C.C. 403, 411 which is modestly selected as an illustration of such abuse by an American author in preference to any American example: Richards, *Law of Insurance* (1952 ed.), p. 398. For further comment see para. 24–255, *post.*

[76] *Law v. London Indisputable Life Insurance Policy* (1885) 1 K. & J. 223; *Hebdon v. West* (1863) 3 B. & S. 579.

[77] *Amick v. Butler*, 12 N.E. 518 (Ind., 1887).

[78] See, generally Appleman, *Insurance Law and Practice* (1981), Vol. 2, para. 851.

though this is substantially in excess of the debt,[79] the majority view now is that the amount of the creditor's interest is the amount of indebtedness at the time of death and the cost of the insurance with interest.[80] Any balance accrues to the deceased debtor's estate.

1–89 This sensible rule cannot correspond with English law since the time at which the creditor's interest must be shown is the inception of the contract, and he may not recover more than the value of that interest at that time. Thus, if A owes B £1,000, payable on January 1, 1970, and on January 1, 1971, B takes out a policy on A's life, his interest at that moment consists of the debt itself, plus a year's interest, plus the first premium. That is the value to be placed on his interest in the debtor's obligation at the date of contract, and section 3 of the 1774 Act prevents him from recovering more.[81] If this is correct it is a good illustration of the unrealistic situation produced by the Act. If a creditor has several joint debtors he may insure the life of any one of them for the whole debt, notwithstanding that each of the others may be able to satisfy his claim in full.[82]

1–90 Irrecoverable debts. Whether or not the creditor's insurable interest in the debtor's life is affected by the fact that the debt is irrecoverable by statute depends upon the nature of the statutory prohibition and the factual circumstances. The requirements of the 1774 Act are satisfied if insurable interest is shown to exist at the time the contract of insurance is made, and it need not subsist until the debtor's death.[83] If, therefore, the creditor's right of action is valid and enforceable at the inception of the risk, but subsequently becomes time-barred under a Limitation Act, his insurable interest is not thereby prejudiced.[84] If, however, the debt was in practice irrecoverable at the commencement of the risk, because, for example, the relevant contract was not in writing where required to be[85] or because the Infants Relief Act 1874[86] provided a defence, then the creditor has no insurable interest. The death of the debtor does not cause the loss or diminution of a right of action recognised and enforceable at law, but only of an expectancy that the debtor will honour his undertaking. Certain American decisions to the contrary[87] were expressly founded on the principle that in the jurisdictions in question an expectancy of future benefit

---

[79] See, *e.g. Ulrich v. Reinoehl*, 143 Pa. 238 (1891), discussed in the 5th edition of this work, para. 83.

[80] See, *e.g. Sachs v. United States*, 412 F. 2d 357 (1969).

[81] *Contra*, Houseman, *Law of Life Assurance* (6th Ed.), p. 17, Since, however, the assured can obtain payment of the debt from the debtor's estate, the position is not so unfavourable in practice.

[82] *Hebdon v. West* (1863) 3 B. & S. 579; *Morrell v. Trenton Mutual Life*, 64 Mass. (10 Cush.) 282 (1864) is to the same effect.

[83] *Dalby v. India and London Life Ass. Co.* (1854) 15 C.B. 365; *Law v. Indisputable Life Ins. Policy Co.* (1855) 1 K. & J. 223.

[84] *Rawls v. American Mutual Life Ins. Co.*, 27 N.Y.App. 282 (1863); *Garner v. Moore* (1855) 3 Drew. 277, indicative of English law.

[85] *e.g.* by the Statute of Frauds 1677, s.4. See *Elpis Maritime Co. v. Marti Chartering Inc.* [1992] 1 A.C. 21.

[86] 37 & 38 Vict c. 62.

[87] *Amsinck v. American Ins. Co.*, 129 Mass. 185 (1880); *Wainer v. Milford Mutual Fire*, 153 Mass. 335 (1891); *Dupuy v. Delaware Ins. Co. of Philadelphia*, 63 Fed.Rep. 680 (Va., 1894); *Rivers. v. Gregg*, 5 Rich.Eq. 274 (S.C.) 1853.

founds an insurable interest if there is a reasonable degree of probability that it will be realised, and that does not represent the English law.[88]

1–91 The same considerations apply to the effect of a discharge in bankruptcy, which extinguishes the debt.[89] If the creditor took out an insurance on the debtor's life while he had a good cause of action for recovery of it, the subsequent discharge does not affect his insurable interest, but he cannot take out a valid insurance after the discharge. In America, however, it has been held that a discharge in bankruptcy, though affording a personal defence to any action against the debtor, does not extinguish the debt, and that the existence of the debt founds an insurable interest after discharge,[90] even where the debtor's moral obligation is the only source of possible repayment.[91] Where no debt subsists in law, a mere moral claim does not provide an insurable interest. Thus a gambling debt,[92] which is not only unenforceable but is absolutely void, or a promise given without good consideration,[93] affords no insurable interest. A creditor has no insurable interest in the life of his debtor's wife, even although the creditor may reasonably expect her to provide the means of payment.[94]

1–92 Debtor on life of creditor. If a creditor is lenient towards his debtor the latter may have a very real interest in the prolongation of his life inasmuch as on his death his personal representative would have a duty to ingather his estate and would not be in a position to extend the same forbearance towards his debtors; but although it may be of the utmost value to him, a debtor's reliance on his creditor's forbearance is in law no more than an expectancy and does not give him any insurable interest in his creditor's life.[95]

1–93 Partners. A partner has an insurable interest in the lives of other members of the partnership to the extent that their deaths would result in his incurring liabilities or losing all or part of their portion of the partnership's capital.[96]

---

[88] In earlier editions of this work *Hebdon v. West* (1863) 3 B. & S. 579 was relied upon as authority for the proposition that an unenforceable legal right could found an insurable interest. It is true that the court took no objection to the fact that the promise of future employment was unenforceable by reason of the Statute of Frauds, s.4, but the court proceeded on a concession by defence counsel: (1863) 3 B. & S. 579, 586–587. This concession was certainly contary to earlier authorities holding that a plaintiff with an unenforceable right possesses in reality only an expectancy of payment which is clearly insufficient, see para. 1–53, *ante. Dwyer v. Edie* (1788) 2 Park, *Mar. Ins.* (8th ed.), p. 914 dates from the time when an expectancy was not yet adjudged to be insufficient, and is clearly wrong on later authorities.

[89] *Heather v. Webb* (1876) 2 C.P.D. 1.

[90] *Fergusson v. Massachussetts Mutual Life Ins. Co.* 39 N.Y. (32 Hun.) 306 (1884); *Manhattan Life v. Hennessy*, 99 Fed.Rep. 64 (1900); *Mutual Reserve Fund Life Association v. Beatty*, 93 Fed.Rep. 747 (C.C.A. 9, 1899).

[91] *Livesay v. First National Bank*, 57 S.W. 2d 86; 91 A.L.R. 873 (Tex., 1933).

[92] *Dwyer v. Edie* (1788) 2 Park, *Mar. Ins.* (8th ed.) p. 914.

[93] *Strong v. Massachussetts Life Ins. Co.*, 27 Mass. (10 Pick.) 40 (1830), indicating the English law.

[94] *Hinton v. Mutual Reserve Fund Life Co.*, 135 N.C. 394 (1904); *Cameron v. Barcus*, 71 S.W. 423 (Tex.Civ.App. 1902), representing English law.

[95] *Hebdon v. West* (1863) 3 B. & S. 579.

[96] See remarks in *Griffiths v. Fleming* [1909] 1 K.B. 805, 815.

(c) *Family Relationships*

1–94 Not *per se* a ground of interest. Relationship other than that of husband and wife does not in itself constitute an insurable interest. Unless there is some pecuniary interest, a parent has no insurable interest in the life of a child, nor the child in the life of its parent, and *a fortiori* no interest arises from any more remote relationship.[97] Inasmuch as an action used to lie for breach of promise of marriage, a person may well have had an insurable interest in the life of his or her fiancé in the past, but the abolition of the action ends any speculation on that score.[98]

1–95 Interest in the life of a child or parent or other relative has been or may be claimed:

(1) on the ground of liability for funeral expenses,
(2) on the ground that there has been expenditure upon the maintenance or education of the person whose life is insured,
(3) on the ground that the person whose life is insured was rendering valuable domestic services to the assured, and that the death of such person would necessitate the payment of a hired servant,
(4) on the ground that the person whose life is insured contributed to a common fund for support of the whole family,
(5) on the ground that the person whose life is insured is under a legal obligation to provide maintenance for the assured in the event of sickness, incapacity, old age and poverty.

These several claims to insurable interest will be considered separately.

1–96 Funeral expenses. If there is a legal obligation to bury a relative, there is an insurable interest in that relative's life to the amount of reasonable funeral expenses, but when the obligation is only a moral one to do that which is right and proper it creates no insurable interest. A man was legally bound to bury his child which died while still a member of his household.[99] This legal liability on the parent has been held to create a good

---

[97] *Halford v. Kymer* (1830) 10 B. & C. 724; *Att.-Gen. v. Murray* [1903] 2 K.B. 64; reversed on appeal without affecting this point [1904] 1 K.B. 165; *Harse v. Pearl Life* [1903] 2 K.B. 92; reversed on another point [1904] 1 K.B. 558. In Scotland a father was formerly deemed to have an insurable interest in the life of his child, but this was based on the common law obligation of a child to aliment his parent. This obligation was abolished by s.1(3) of the Family Law (Scotland) Act 1985. *Carmichael v. Carmichael's Executrix*, 1919 S.C. 636; reversed on another point, 1920 S.C.(H.L.) 195.

The position would no doubt be different if a son validly promised to pay a certain sum of money to a parent or relative at a future date, such as a repayment of university fees, for instance; *Goldstein v. Salvation Army Ass. Society* [1917] 2 K.B. 291, 295. By s.19(2) of the Australian Insurance Contracts Act 1984 a parent of a person under 18, being a guardian of such a person, has an unlimited insurable interest in the young person's life, and by s.19(4)(c) a person has an unlimited interest in the life of someone on whom he depends for maintenance and support.

[98] Law Reform (Misc. Prov.) Act 1970. Abolished in Scotland by s.1(1) of the Law Reform (Husband and Wife) (Scotland) Act 1984. For discussion of the point in jurisdictions where the action lies, see para. 432 of the 5th edition of this work. Another consequence is that co-habitants cannot the lives of insure each other—see *Hemsworth* (1998) 57 Camb.L.J. 65.

[99] According to nineteenth-century decisions, the householder's obligation was to bury not only children who were members of his household (*R. v. Vann* (1851) 5 Cox C.C. 379) but any dead body lying in his house (*R. v. Stewart* (1840) 12 A. & E. 773). These decisions are now obsolete, in view of the provisions of what is now the Public Health (Control of Disease) Act 1984, s.46. Local authorities are obliged to bury the body of any person who has died or is found

insurable interest in the life of a child to the extent of reasonable funeral expenses.[1] An adoption order extinguishes any parental right or duty vested in a parent and vests them in the adopters.[2] It may well be that among those duties is included the duty of burial, and that the adopter has consequently the same insurable interest in the life.[3] A man is under no legal obligation to bury any relative other than his wife or child, and therefore he has no insurable interest on that ground in the life of a parent, grandparent, grandchild uncle or aunt, brother or sister.[4]

1–97 Money expended on maintenance. The fact that a parent or other person in *loco parentis* has expended and will continue to expend money upon the maintenance and education of a child and that there is a reasonable expectation that such expenditure will be reimbursed by the child when he grows up, either in cash or by supporting his parent in his old age, does not constitute a sufficiently definite pecuniary interest in the child's life to give the parent an insurable interest in it.[5] A stranger who received and maintained a child upon the death-bed request of its mother was held by a Divisional Court to have an insurable interest by reason of the expectation that the child would subsequently reimburse the expenditure by services rendered,[6] but that decision can hardly be supported upon principle, and has been doubted in the Court of Appeal.[7] Maintenance of an aged person gives no insurable interest in that person's life to the person who has spent his own money on such maintenance, unless there is a legal obligation on the aged person to repay the money so spent,[8] and even so, if any such obligation were to be created merely for the purpose of acquiring an insurable interest without any reasonable probability of the debtor being able to meet the obligation, the court would probably look upon the transaction as a fraud upon the statute and refuse to recognise it as affording any insurable interest in the aged person's life.[9] A son was held to have no insurable interest in the life of his father who was a pauper but who lived with him and was supported by him under compulsion from the guardians.[10]

---

dead in their area. They recoup their expenses in the first place out of the death grant payable under the Social Security Act 1975, s.32, but have power under s.46(5) of the Act of 1984 to recover any unpaid amount from the estate of the deceased person or from any person who for the purposes of the National Assistance Act 1948 was liable to maintain the deceased person immediately prior to his death. This includes the parent of a deceased child but, since the liability to pay funeral expenses is now an incident of the general duty to maintain, it seems doubtful whether this liability should still be regarded as a separate ground of insurable interest.

[1] *Webber v. Life Insurance Co.*, 172 Pa. 111 (1895), indicating the English law.

[2] Adoption Act 1976, s.12

[3] *Skinner v. Carter* [1948] Ch. 387. Before the cesser of the power to issue such policies he had the same right as a parent to insure the child's life in respect of funeral expenses under the Friendly Societies and Industrial Assurances Acts (Adoption Act 1958, s.14), and was deemed to be the parent for the purposes of those Acts (Friendly Societies Act 1955, s.7).

[4] *Harse v. Pearl Life* [1903] 2 K.B. 92, reversed on another point [1904] 1 K.B. 558; *Shilling v. Accidental Death* (1858) 1 F. & F. 116; *Howard v. Refuge F.S.* (1886) 54 L.T. 644. Insurance for funeral expenses was, however, authorised by the Friendly Societies Act 1896, and the Industrial Assurance Act 1923, in cases to which those Acts applied.

[5] *Halford v. Kymer* (1830) 10 B. & C. 724; *Worthington v. Curtis* (1875) 1 Ch.D. 419, 423.

[6] *Barnes v. London, Edinburgh and Glasgow* [1892] 1 Q.B. 864.

[7] *Griffiths v. Fleming* [1909] 1 K.B. 805.

[8] *Shilling v. Accidental Death* (1858) 1 F. & F. 116. *Cf. Reserve Mutual v. Kane*, 81 Pa. 154 (1876).

[9] See *Seigrist v. Schmoltz*, 113 Pa. 326 (1886).

[10] *Shilling v. Accidental Death* (1858) 1 F. & F. 116.

1–98 Foster-child. A child under 16 years of age who is cared for or maintained by a person who is not a relative, guardian or custodian is known as a foster-child, and any person who maintains such a foster-child for reward is deemed to have no interest in the life of such child for the purposes recover any unpaid amount from the estate of the deceased person or from any person who for the purposes of the National Assistance Act 1948 was liable to maintain the deceased person immediately prior to his death. This includes the parent of a deceased child but, since the liability to pay funeral expenses is now an incident of the general duty to maintain, it seems doubtful whether this liability should still be regarded as a separate ground of insurable interest.
of the Life Assurance Act 1774.[11] It is, however, no longer an offence in Great Britain for such a person to insure or attempt to insure the life of a foster-child, or for a company or society knowingly to issue a policy effecting such insurance.[12] However, there is still such an offence in Northern Ireland in respect of foster-children under 15 years or, in certain cases, 18 years.[13]

1–99 Domestic service. The fact that a child or other relative was rendering valuable domestic service to the assured and that the loss of that service would entail the employment of hired labour in lieu thereof does not create an insurable interest.[14] Pickford J. thought that it was the domestic services rendered by a wife which gave her husband an insurable interest in her life, but the Court of Appeal declined to support his decision on that ground, and it appears to be untenable.[15] A son who lived with and supported his mother who performed in the house the usual domestic duties of a house-keeper was held to have no insurable interest in his mother's life either in respect of the loss of her services or the moral duty to incur the cost of her funeral in the event of her death.[16]

1–100 Child contributing to support of family. A parent may have a legal claim to the earnings of a child under 16 years of age,[17] and, if so, have some insurable interest on that ground,[18] but his insurable interest cannot exceed the value of the term of service for which the child is definitely engaged by some employer, because beyond such term his interest is a mere expectancy. Where the child is engaged by the week or month, the insurable interest must therefore be extremely small.

1–101 Obligation to provide maintenance. Inasmuch as both in English and Scots law the insurable interest of a man in the life of his wife and of a woman in the life of her husband stands on a broader basis than that of pecuniary interest, the legal obligation to provide maintenance or aliment for the assured, as a basis of insurable interest, need only be considered in the case of domestic relationships other than those of husband and wife.

---

[11] Foster Children Act 1980, s.19.
[12] s.214 of the Public Health Act 1936, s.263 of the Public Health (London) Act 1936 and s.7 of the Children and Young Persons (Scotland) Act 1937 were repealed by the Children Act 1958.
[13] See s.7, Children and Young Persons Act (N.I.) 1968. As to the differing age-limits, see ss.10(1) and 19(2).
[14] *Harse v. Pearl Life* [1903] 2 K.B. 92, reversed on another point [1904] 1 K.B. 558.
[15] *Griffiths v. Fleming* [1909] 1 K.B. 805.
[16] *Harse v. Pearl Life* [1903] 2 K.B. 92. *Cf.* Australian Insurance Contracts Act 1984 s.19(3).
[17] Eversley's *Domestic Relations* (6th ed.) pp. 377, 378.
[18] *Wakeman v. Metropolitan Life* (1899) 30 Ont.R. 705.

Apart from statute, the law of England imposes no civil obligation enforceable at law on a parent to support his or her child or grandchild or on a child to support his or her parent or grandparent. In the eye of the common law these obligations are moral only, except that neglect of them in the case of a child in the custody of his or her parent may bring the parent within the reach of the criminal law.[19] The only civil obligation of general application by which a person may be compelled to maintain a relative is that imposed by the National Assistance Act 1948,[20] which provides[21] that a man shall be liable to maintain his wife and his children, and that a woman shall be liable to maintain her husband and her children. For this purpose a man's children include those of whom he has been adjudged to be the putative father, and a woman's children include her illegitimate children.[22] An adoption order extinguishes the liability of the natural parents and substitutes that of the adopter.[23]

1–102 Except as regards husband and wife, these duties of maintenance all date back to the Poor Law Relief Act 1601,[24] and the relevancy of them on a question of insurable interest came under consideration in the case of *Halford v. Kymer*.[25] In that case the plaintiff sought to recover from an insurance company the sum of £5,000 under a policy effected by him on the life of his son. The defendants pleaded no insurable interest, and counsel for the plaintiff, in moving for a rule in the court of King's Bench, argued that the obligation imposed by the statute of Elizabeth I upon a child to maintain his parent in poverty and old age afforded a legal interest sufficient to support the policy. Bayley J. interposing *arguendo*, said: "The parish is bound to maintain him, and it is indifferent to him whether he be maintained by the parish or his son."[26] At the trial of the action Lord Tenterden C.J. non-suited the plaintiff, reserving liberty to him to move to enter a verdict if the court should be of opinion that he had an insurable interest. The Court of King's Bench, consisting of the Chief Justice and Bayley, Littlesdale, and Parke JJ. refused to grant a rule, and so affirmed the judgment of the Chief Justice that the plaintiff had no insurable interest in the life of his son. The authority of that case has not been challenged and the reasoning seems to apply equally to the duty of a parent to maintain his child. The conclusion, however, that on the death of its father a child suffers no such pecuniary loss as is appropriate to be the subject of insurance, is repugnant to common-sense. If any such proposition were generally accepted, the life assurance industry would immediately collapse, for the most usual motive which prompts men to insure their own lives is the desire to safeguard their children against precisely this loss.

1–103 It is, perhaps, only in the case of a broken family that a policy effected by the child might seem to be a preferable way of achieving the same object. In such a case, there may be a maintenance agreement or a court

---

[19] *Bazeley v. Forder* (1868) L.R. 3 Q.B. 559, *per* Cockburn L.C.J. at p. 565.
[20] 1948, 11 & 12 Geo. 6 c. 29.
[21] s.42(1)(a).
[22] s.42(1)(b).
[23] Adoption Act 1976, s.12 as amended by the Children Act 1989, s.88(1). See *Mayor, Aldermen and Citizens of Coventry v. Surrey C.C.* [1935] A.C. 199.
[24] 43 Eliz. 1, c. 2.
[25] (1830) 10 B. & C. 724.
[26] (1830) 10 B. & C. 724, 728.

order[27] by which the father is bound to make periodical payments for the maintenance of the child. There is no authority on the point, but it seems reasonably clear in principle that there is an insurable interest where there is such an agreement or order. The valuation of the interest presents no difficulty, as the obligation is to make payments at a fixed rate for a determinate period of time.

1–104 It is arguable that in view of the comprehensive provision now made by statute for the granting of maintenance orders[28] against parents who fail to maintain their children, the absence of a general common law obligation is of no contemporary importance. There are, however, problems of valuation if it is to be held that a child always has an insurable interest in the life of its parent. A possible solution is to presume an interest of unlimited amount in this case, as in that of husband and wife, but this may be a step too large to be achieved without legislation. In view of the uncertainty which surrounds this topic, we refer below[29] to the American jurisdiction as an example of a legal system affording a much wider recognition of insurable interest between relatives, though for different reasons.[30]

1–105 Scots law. In Scots law a husband has a legal obligation to aliment his wife[31] and a wife has a similar obligation to aliment her husband.[32] Both parents have an obligation to aliment their child,[33] whether or not the parents have ever been married to one another.[34] Persons who adopt a child assume the liability to aliment the child,[35] while the obligation of the natural parents ceases.[36] The obligation is enforceable against either parent[37] and there is no order of priority between the parents.[38] The obligation subsists until the child is 18 or until the child is 25, if the child is being educated or being trained for employment or for a trade, profession or vocation.[39] In addition any person who has accepted a child as a child of his family has a duty to aliment that child, even though the child is not related to him in any way.[40]

[27] Under the Maintenance Orders Act 1950, or the Matrimonial Causes Act 1973, s.23(1) or s.27(1)–(6) to be replaced by section 15 of the Family Law Act 1996 on a date to be appointed, or section 15(1) of the Children Act 1989.

[28] It is particularly noteworthy that the remedy under the Matrimonial Causes Act 1973, s.27, is available even where there are no proceedings for divorce or judicial separation, and that this remedy has none of the quasi-criminal flavour of magistrates' court proceedings under earlier legislation. In view of the availability of this remedy, it is difficult to see why the obligation imposed by the Supplementary Benefits Act 1976, s.17(1), should be considered as anything other than an obligation enforceable at law.

[29] Para. 1–105.

[30] Under the Australian Insurance Contracts Act (Cth) 1984, ss.19(4)(c) and 19(5)(a) a person has an unlimited insurable interest in the life of a person on whom he depends, wholly or partly, for maintenance and support.

[31] Family Law (Scotland) Act 1985 (c. 37), s.1(1)(a). For the law of aliment see J. M. Thomson, *Family Law in Scotland*, pp. 152 *et seq.*

[32] s.1(1)(b). The obligation covers the parties to a valid polygamous marriage: s.1(5).

[33] s.1(1)(c).

[34] s.27(1) as amended by s.10(1) and Sched. 1 of the Law Reform (Parent and Child) (Scotland) Act 1986 (c. 9).

[35] Adoption (Scotland) Act 1978 (c.28), s.12(1).

[36] Adoption (Scotland) Act 1978, s.12(3). For exceptions see s.12(4).

[37] 1985 Act, s.2(1).

[38] s.4(2).

[39] s.1(5).

[40] s.1(1)(d).

The foregoing are now the only cases in which Scots law recognises a legal obligation of aliment and the wider common law obligations have ceased to have effect.[41] Where the obligation exists, it is an obligation to provide such support as is reasonable in the circumstances.[42] It is submitted that the beneficiary of an obligation of support will have an insurable interest in the life of the party under the obligation.[43] An insurable interest in the life of a former spouse[44] will exist where the former spouse has agreed to make alimentary payments or where the court granting the divorce has made an award of periodical allowance[45] against the former spouse, and arguably also in a case where there is a realistic prospect of such an order being made in the future.[46] In all cases the valuation of any insurable interest will depend on the potential extent and duration of any obligation of support.

1–106 American law. American law confers a wider recognition of insurable interest between relatives. This is because it proceeds on a different basis from English law, and indeed Scots law, which limit insurable interest to cases where there is a legal duty to maintain. In American law by contrast the basic rule appears to be[47] that as the requirement of insurable interest exists to avoid the termination of the life insured's life for financial gain, it is automatically satisfied in those cases where the normal ties of love and affection obviate this danger. So interest is presumed as between parent and child,[48] between spouses[49] and fiance(e)s,[50] and between siblings.[51] Otherwise, however, a relationship of dependency must be proved so that the insured has a reasonable expectation of advantage from the continuance of the life insured's life or would lose by his death.[52] On this basis, a granddaughter had been held to have an interest in the life of her grandfather[53] and an adopted daughter in the life of the stranger who adopted her.[54]

(d) *Requirement That Policy Should Name Beneficiary*

1–107 Person interested. The 1774 Act requires by section 1 that the person(s) for whose use, benefit, or on whose account a policy is made shall have an interest. Section 2 complements section 1 by requiring the name(s) of such person(s) to be inserted in the policy, so that no-one should "acquire clandestinely an interest in a policy on the life of another".[55] These are

---

[41] s.1(3). For the common law see the 7th edition of this work, paras. 100–104.

[42] s.1(2) and s.4. For a discussion of s.4, see Thomson, *op. cit.*, pp. 45 *et seq.*

[43] In *Miller v. Pearl Life Ass. Co. Ltd.* (1907) 23 Sh.Ct.Rep. 334, 338, the sheriff said that liability to support "may not be a conclusive test" of insurable interest.

[44] Including a party to a void or voidable marriage. See 1985 Act, s.17.

[45] 1985 Act, s.8(1)(b). For the principles see in particular ss.9, 11 and 13.

[46] *cf.* s.13(1)(b) and (c).

[47] This is a very sketchy description of American Law, which is certainly not settled in all States. For detailed treatment, see Appleman, *Insurance Law and Practice* (1981), Vol. 2, Chapters 45–50.

[48] See, *e.g. Goodwin v. Federal Mutual Ins. Co.*, 180 So. 662 (1938); *Clayton v. Industrial*, 56 A. 2d 292 (1948).

[49] *ibid.*

[50] See *e.g. Chisholm v. National Capitol Life Ins. Co.*, 52 Mo. 213 (1873).

[51] See, *e.g. Mutual Savings Life Ins. Co. v. Noah*, 282 So. 2d 217 (1973).

[52] See especially *Warnock v. Davis*, 104 U.S. 775, 779 (1881).

[53] *Breese v. Metropolitan*, 37 N.Y.App.Div. 152 (1899).

[54] *Carpenter v. U.S. Life*, 161 Pa. 9 (1894).

[55] *Evans v. Bignold* (1869) L.R. 4 Q.B. 622, 625.

cumulative requirements, and if the policy is made for the benefit of someone other than the life assured, and he possesses a valid interest in the life, the policy will nonetheless be unlawful if he is not named therein.[56]

1–108 There is no presumption or rule that the person interested is the named assured. If that were so, nothing would be easier than to evade the Act by taking out a gambling policy in the form of an own-life policy in the name of the life to be insured. The policy may indeed appear on its face to be an own-life policy effected by the assured for his own benefit, and on his death an action may be brought upon it in the name of his personal representative, but the court will go behind the policy and, if satisfied on extrinsic evidence that the insurance was in reality made for the use, benefit or account of someone who possessed no interest in the life or, even if he did, was not named in the policy, will declare the policy void or unlawful under section 1 or 2 of the Act respectively.[57]

1–109 It is easier to show that the policy was made for the benefit or account of a third party where the latter has actively participated in procuring the policy. In *Wainwright v. Bland*[58] an action was brought by the personal representative of a woman who was the nominal assured in an own-life policy. The claim was resisted on the ground that the policy was in fact the policy of the plaintiff who had no interest in the woman's life. At the trial Lord Abinger C.B., in his address to the jury, said:

> "The question in this case is who was the party really and truly effecting the insurance? Was it the policy of Miss Abercromby, or was it substantially the policy of Wainwright, the plaintiff, he using her name for purposes of his own? If you think it was the policy of Miss Abercromby effected by her for her own benefit her representative is entitled to put it in force, and it would be no answer to say that she had no funds of her own to pay premiums. Wainwright might lend her the money for that purpose and the policy still continue her own. But, on the other hand, if, looking at all the strange facts which have been proved before you, you come to the conclusion that the policy was in reality effected by Wainwright, that he merely used her name himself finding the money and meaning (by way of assignment or by bequest, or in some other way) to have the benefit of it himself: then I am of opinion that such a transaction would be a fraudulent evasion of the statute 14 Geo. 3, c. 48, and that your verdict should be for the defendants."

A verdict for the defendants was returned, and on a motion for a new trial it was argued that where a policy was on the face of it an own-life policy and the claim was by the personal representative of the assured, the defendants could not set up as a defence to the claim an intention that a third person

---

[56] *Hodson v. Observer Life Ass. Soc.* (1857) 8 E. & B. 40; *Evans v. Bignold* (1869) L.R. 4 Q.B. 622.

[57] *Wainwright v. Bland* (1835) 1 Moo. & R. 481; *Shilling v. Accidental Death* (1857) 2 H. & N. 42; *McFarlane v. Royal London F.S.* (1886) 2 T.L.R. 755; *Brewster v. National Life Ins. Soc.* (1892) 8 T.L.R. 648; *Holt v. English & Scottish Law, The Times,* August 5, 1899; *Downing v. Marine & General, The Times,* August 7, 1899; *Worthington v. Curtis* (1875) 1 Ch.D. 419, 425; *Harse v. Pearl Life* [1903] 2 K.B. 92 (reversed on another point [1904] 1 K.B. 558); *MacDonald v. National Mutual* (1906) 14 S.L.T. 173; *Wall v. New Ireland Ass. Co.* [1965] I.R. 382, 396; *Brophy v. N. American Life* (1902) 32 Can. S.C.R. 261.

[58] (1835) 1 Moo. & R. 481.

should have the benefit of it. The motion was refused on another ground, and the court expressed some doubt as to the legal position.[59]

1–110 The position was made clear in *Shilling v. Accidental Death*.[60] That case was first argued on demurrer to the defendants' plea that the policy which purported to be a policy by J.S. on his own life

> "was in truth and in fact made and effected by one T.S. in the name and on the pretended behalf of J.S.; but for the use, benefit and on account and behalf of the said T.S. himself, and not for the use, benefit or on account of the said J.S.; and the said T.S. had not any interest in the life of the said J.S."

In support of the demurrer it was argued that parol evidence was not admissible to show that the contract was other than appeared on the face of the policy, or that it was in fact for the benefit of some person other than the assured there named. It was held that the evidence was admissible and that the plea was good. Upon the trial of the case before a jury the evidence established that the policy was effected in the name of a man 77 years old, who was a pauper supported by his son, and that the son had been heard to say that he would insure the old man for £200 as he was a burden to him, and that the proposal was partly in the son's writing, although signed by the father, and that the father 12 days after the policy was issued signed a will bequeathing the policy money to his son. The jury found a verdict for the plaintiff, but on a motion for a new trial the verdict was set aside as being against the weight of evidence, and a new trial was ordered.

1–111 Use of an own-life policy to effect an insurance by and on behalf of one who has no insurable interest in the life insured is sometimes resorted to in the field of industrial assurance. The purpose is usually achieved by procuring the signature of the person whose life is to be insured to a proposal for an own-life policy and then, when the policy is issued, by procuring his signature to a nomination or assignment of the policy money to the party for whose behalf the insurance is intended.[61] Sometimes the same result is obtained by the more simple method of forging the signature of the person whose life is to be insured to the proposal and to the nomination or assignment. As a rule, those illegal transactions are carried out at the instigation of an insurance agent who is anxious to secure new business. Frequently the person for whom the insurance is being effected is a simple person who is unaware that the proposed transaction is illegal and of the criminal methods employed by the agent to effect his purpose. The result as regards illegality for want of insurable interest is the same, although the guilt or innocence of the party for whom the insurance is being effected will have some bearing on his claim for a return of the premiums which he has paid.[62]

1–112 In a case where the Industrial Assurance Commissioner reviewed the leading authorities on this branch of the law, he said: "In my opinion the whole question in every case of alleged illegality under the Life Assurance Act 1774 is one of fact. What was the intention of the parties at the time of

---

[59] (1836) 1 M. & W. 32.
[60] (1857) 2 H. & N. 42; (1858) 1 F. & F. 116.
[61] *Gamble v. City of Glasgow F.S.* [1930] I.A.C.(N.I.) Rep. 35; *Clare v. Co-operative Insurance* [1937] I.A.C.Rep. 5.
[62] *Gamble v. City of Glasgow F.S.* [1930] I.A.C.(N.I.) Rep. 35.

the assurance? Did A intend to take out a policy on B's life for his own benefit without insurable interest? If he did, it is immaterial whether or not his intention was effectively carried out. The cases, in my opinion, decide both under English and Scots law that the court is bound to look at the surrounding circumstances and decide, whether an assignment or a will or a nomination has been executed or not, what the real intention of the parties was."[63] In the case of an industrial assurance policy the society's collector told M.M. that it would be illegal for her to sign a proposal for insurance on the life of her nephew B.H., but that J.H., a brother of B.H., could insure his life for funeral expenses. A proposal for insurance on the life of B.H. was accordingly signed by J.H., but all the premiums were paid by M.M. The Industrial Assurance Commissioner for Northern Ireland held that the policy was effected by M.M., who had no insurable interest in the life of B.H., and that the policy was therefore void.[64]

1–113 Payment of premiums. Prima facie the person who ultimately bears the cost of the premium is the person on whose behalf the policy was effected, but evidence that some person other than the assured paid the premiums is not conclusive to show that the policy was effected on behalf of that person, even although such person does in fact obtain the benefit of the policy.[65]

An own-life policy in respect of which the premiums are paid by some person other than the assured may be intended as a gift from that other person to the assured, and if the assured is the wife or child of the person who pays the premiums there is a presumption that it was so intended; but the presumption may be rebutted by evidence of the real intention of the parties, and if it was in fact intended for the benefit of the person who paid the premiums the policy is illegal, and neither he nor the assured's representative can recover the policy money.[66]

1–114 Mere beneficiaries. The words in the Act "for whose use, benefit, or on whose account" are not to be construed too widely. They do not include all persons whom the assured intends ultimately shall benefit by the insurance through receipt of all or part of the sum insured, although in one sense the policy could be said to have been made for their benefit. An own-life insurance taken out with the intention to provide a sum to be disposed of at the death of the assured is regarded as having been effected for his own benefit and on his own account and not for the benefit of the beneficiaries he has in mind, who, moreover, are not active in procuring the policy. So where the assured effected an own-life insurance intending to benefit the orphaned children of a deceased daughter, and within two years assigned it to his surviving daughters for the benefit of the children, there was no need for the grandchildren to be named in the policy, even though the daughters and not the assured had been paying the premiums.[67] Similarly in

[63] *Fitzsimmons v. City of Glasgow F.S.* [1933] I.A.C.Rep. 24.
[64] *Hamilton v. City of Glasgow F.S.* [1947] I.A.C.(N.I.) Rep. 25.
[65] *Shilling v. Accidental Death* (1858) 1 F. & F. 116; *Wainwright v. Bland* (1835) 1 Moo. & R. 481.
[66] *Jones v. Pearl Assurance* [1937] I.A.C.Rep. 18.
[67] *Brewster v. National Life Ins. Co.* (1892) 8 T.L.R. 648. As reported the reasoning of Lord Esher M.R. and Bowen L.J. is difficult to follow, because it is hard to understand why the insurance company was entitled to repudiate liability. It may be that the assured wished to insure elsewhere and was content with an order for repayment of premium.

Shilling v. Accidental Death the court said that, if TS and JS had agreed that JS should insure his life and TS would keep up the premiums and JS would leave the sum insured to TS in his will, the insurance would not be regarded as made for the use, benefit and on account of TS.[68] The position is more difficult when the assured intends to benefit a third party, takes out an own-life policy, and simultaneously assigns it to the intended beneficiary who has no interest in the life, but has not taken steps to procure the insurance. Is this a veiled evasion of the statute, so that the policy is to be regarded as made for the use and benefit of the third party, or is it merely the transfer of an own-life insurance to an assignee who need not show interest? The answer given by Pollock C.B. in *M'Farlane v. Royal London F.S.*[69] is that if the assignment is at least partly for the benefit of the assured, as when the policy is being assigned as security for a loan, the policy is not solely made for the benefit of the creditor-assignee and is outside the wording of the Act, but it is within the Act if the intention was solely to benefit the assignee and it cannot be said that the insurance was made for the assured's benefit. The decision of the Canadian Supreme Court in *North American Life v. Craigan*[70] proceeded on a different basis. The assured took out an own-life policy, intending it to be for the benefit of another person, and she was nominated as payee of the sum insured by a provision in the policy itself. It was held that because the assured had done nothing to procure the insurance, being ignorant of the assured's intentions, the policy was not to be regarded as within the wording of the 1774 Act, and that the precise timing and method of conferring an interest in the own-life insurance upon her should not be determinative. It is submitted that the decision does not represent English law. The English decisions were not cited by the court and reliance was placed on authorities from New York where the Act was never in force.

1–115 Name to be inserted in policies: group policies. It is important to remember that not only must a life policy be made on behalf of some person who has an interest, but that that person must be named in the policy as the person for whose benefit it is made.[71] Thus, if a policy were effected by a debtor in his own name but solely for the benefit of his creditor, the policy would be void if the creditor's name was not inserted therein.[72] Not only must the person on whose behalf the policy is made be named in the policy, but he must be named as the person on whose behalf it is made.[73] There is no objection, however, to an insurance being effected by a trustee on behalf of the person interested if it is so expressed in the policy.[74]

[68] (1857) 2 H. & N. 42, 43–44.
[69] (1886) 2 T.L.R. 755, 756.
[70] (1880) 13 S.C.R. 278.
[71] *Shilling v. Accidental Death* (1857) 2 H. & N. 42; By contrast, s.20 of the Australian Insurance Contracts Act 1984 provides that the failure to name beneficiaries in the policy does not relieve the insurer of liability.
[72] *Evans v. Bignold* (1869) L.R. 4 Q.B. 622; *Humphrey v. Arabin* (1836) L. & G., *temp.* Plunk. 318, 325. But if the policy was in fact the debtor's policy, made on his own behalf, and merely assigned to the creditor for the purpose of giving him security, it is unnecessary to insert in the policy any other name than that of the debtor: *Downs v. Green* (1844) 12 M. & W. 481; *M'Farlane v. Royal London F.S.* (1886) 2 T.L.R. 755.
[73] *Hodson v. Observer Life* (1857) 8 E. & B. 40; *Evans v. Bignold* (1869) L.R. 4 Q.B. 622; *Forgan v. Pearl Life Ass. Co.* (1907) 51 Sol.J. 230; *Wall v. New Ireland Ass. Co. Ltd* [1965] Ir.R. 382, 386, 396, 405.
[74] *Collett v. Morrison* (1851) 9 Hare 162.

If the name of the person for whose benefit the insurance is intended is inserted as such in the proposal for the policy the omission of his name in the policy is not fatal if the proposal is incorporated into the policy by reference.[75] If the person interested is so referred to in the policy as to be capable of being ascertained at the date when the policy was effected it is probably immaterial that the actual name is not inserted. In the widest sense a person's name is any label which indicates that person as the person who is referred to.

1–116 It was formerly insufficient for the policy to indicate a group or class of beneficiaries, the members of which were not ascertainable at the date when the contract was entered into.[76] Section 50 of the Insurance Companies Amendment Act 1973[77] provides, however, that section 2 of the Act of 1774 does not invalidate a policy for the benefit of unnamed persons from time to time falling within a specified class or description if the class or description is stated in the policy with sufficient particularity to establish the identity of all persons who at any given time are entitled to benefit under the policy.[78]

(e) *Necessity for the Act today*

1–117 The Act was passed over 200 years ago to stamp out the contemporary social evil of employing life assurance as a means to wager on the duration of human life.[79] Subsequently all wagers were rendered void by section 18 of the Gambling Act 1845.[80] The retention of the 1774 Act was justified on the ground that it reduced the temptation to policyholders to do away with the life assured.[81] It is doubtful, however, whether the requirement for interest adds much to the sanctions of the criminal law and the rule that the courts will not assist a criminal to recover the fruits of his wrongdoing.[82] The 1774 Act does not prevent the assignment of own-life policies to assignees who need not show interest in the life, and have the same motive for accelerating its termination. In modern conditions it is probably the insurance companies' invariable practice of requiring medical reports on proposed lives that does much to deter applications by others without the consent of the intended life assured.

1–118 In its present form the Act wholly or partially prevents the provision of adequate life insurance to several classes of assureds including employers seeking to insure key employees, dependent relatives seeking to insure the lives of those maintaining them, and creditors who insure the lives of their debtors as security for their debts.[83] At the same time the ability to enforce these insurances after the original interest of the assured in the life

---

[75] *Wakeman v. Metropolitan Life* (1899) 30 Ont.R. 705.
[76] *Williams v. Baltic Ins. Ass. of London* [1924] 2 K.B. 282, 290.
[77] 1973. c. 58.
[78] This provision applies to policies effected before, as well as after, the commencement of the Act; see s.50(2).
[79] See Merkin, Gambling by Insurance, (1980) 9 Anglo-Am. L.R. 331.
[80] 8 & 9 Vict.
[81] *Evans v. Bignold* (1869) L.R. 4 Q.B. 622, 625; *Worthington v. Curtis* (1875) 1 Ch.D. 419.
[82] See paras 14–30 *et seq.*
[83] See paras 1–76 to 1–79, 1–87 to 1–89, and 1–97 *supra.*

has ceased to exist by, for instance, the resignation of the key employee or the repayment of the debt, has created the opportunity for speculation in a transaction initially intended only to provide security for the assured.[84]

1–119 It is useful to consider reforms adopted in other common law jurisdictions in which the Act was in force. In New Zealand it was repealed.[85] The requirement of interest in the life assured is preserved, although its absence does not render the insurance void or illegal. Wagering policies are void and there is accordingly still a need to preserve the concept of insurable interest in order to differentiate between valid insurances and invalid wagering policies, although interest is not defined in the reforming legislation. In Australia the 1774 Act has been repealed also. While the need for a pecuniary interest in the life assured has been preserved, this need not amount to a legal or equitable interest in the life, and the categories of insurance in which interest is deemed to exist to an unlimited amount have been widened. Neither country has addressed the question whether insurances on the lives of employees, debtors and others should continue to be freely enforceable after the assured's interest in the life has ended, although this has been addressed in certain Canadian provinces, where the consent of an employee is required for the continuation of his employer's insurance on his life after his contract of service has terminated.[86] The Australian statute,[87] it is submitted, would provide a useful model for amending legislation in the United Kingdom.

6. Insurable Interest in Property

(a) *Generally*

1–120 General definition. Insurable interest in property is not confined to absolute legal ownership. Two requirements for the possession of a valid insurable interest may be identified in English law. First, the assured must be so situated to the insured property that he will suffer economic loss as the proximate result of its damage or destruction. In his classic description of an insurable interest in the leading case of *Lucena v. Craufurd* Lawrence J. said[88]:

> "A man is interested in a thing to whom advantage may arise or prejudice happen from the circumstances which may attend it ... and where a man is so circumstanced with respect to matters exposed to certain risks or dangers, as to have a moral certainty of advantage or benefit, but for those risks or dangers, he may be said to be interested in the safety of the thing. To be interested in the preservation of a thing, is to be so circumstanced with respect to it as to have benefit from its existence, prejudice from its destruction."

---

[84] *Dalby v. The India & London Life* (1854) 15 C.B. 365; *Chantiam v. Packall Packaging Inc.* (1998) 38 O.R. (3d) 401.

[85] Insurance Law Reform Act 1985, No. 117, ss.6–7.

[86] *e.g.* Manitoba Insurance Act 1987, s.155(4), (statutory application by life assured to court for order that life policy be terminated).

[87] Insurance Law Act 1984 (Cth.), s.19. See Tarr, Insurable Interest (1986) 60 A.L.J. 613.

[88] (1806) 2 Bos. & Pul. (N.R.) 269, 302.

This passage from his judgment is generally interpreted as recognising an insurable interest in any case where the assured has a "moral certainty" of advantage or benefit from the continued preservation of the insured property, regardless of whether he possesses any legal right in it or pertaining to it,[89] so that in effect Lawrence J. regarded a highly probable factual expectation of benefit from the continuing existence of property as a sufficient ground of insurable interest.[90] When, however, the passage cited above is placed in the overall context of his entire judgment, it appears more probable that he did not intend it to be a complete definition in itself.[91] It lacked a criterion of "moral certainty", something supplied by the remainder of his judgment. From this it seems that the criterion of "moral certainty" in his view was the assured's possession of a legal right to, or legal responsibility for, the insured property, and there is authority for this interpretation also.[92] At all events there is no doubt that the House of Lords did not regard factual expectation, or moral certainty, of benefit as a sufficient basis of insurable interest in property, and added the second requirement of a legal relationship between the assured and the subject-matter of the insurance. Giving the leading speech Lord Eldon said[93]:

> "In order to distinguish that intermediate thing between a strict right, or a right derived under a contract, and a mere expectation or hope, which has been termed an insurable interest, it has been said in many cases to be that which amounts to a moral certainty. I have in vain endeavoured, however, to find a fit definition of that which is between a certainty and an expectation; nor am I able to point out what is an interest unless it be a right in the property or a right derivable out of some contract about the property, which in either case may be lost upon some contingency affecting the possession or enjoyment of the party."

In *Routh v. Thompson*[94] Lord Ellenborough C.J., who had delivered a short speech in *Lucena v. Craufurd* concurring with that of Lord Eldon, described the requirement as possession of a legal or equitable right in property, and Lord Eldon's test was subsequently summarised as requiring a legal or equitable interest in the insured property.[95] If we add the additional ground of insurable interest created by the existence of a legal obligation to bear any

---

[89] *Mark Rowlands v. Berni Inns* [1986] 1 Q.B. 211, 228; *The "Moonacre"* [1992] 2 Lloyd's Rep. 503, 511; *Glengate-KG Properties v. Norwich Union Fire Ins. Soc.* [1996] 1 Lloyd's Rep. 614, 621, 626; *Constitution Ins. Co. of Canada v. Kosmopoulos* (1987) 34 D.L.R. (4th) 208, 216; *Cowan v. Jeffrey Associates* 1999 S.L.T. 757; Merkin, *Insurance Contract Law*, Vol. I, para. A.4.1–19; Bennett, *Law of Marine Insurance* (1996) p. 17; Hartnett & Thornton, "Insurable Interest in Property" 48 Col. L. Rev. 1162 (1948). This view was followed in previous editions of this work (see 9th ed., para. 1–116).

[90] *Macaura v. Northern Assurance Co.* [1925] N.I. 141, 157–158 *per* Andrews L.J., approved by Lord Buckmaster on appeal [1925] A.C. 619, 627. It is unclear precisely what degree of probability is meant by a "moral certainty", which appears to signify something greater than the mere balance of probability and less than complete certainty.

[91] See Legh-Jones (2002) "Elements of Insurable Interest in Marine Insurance" in *The Modern Law of Marine Insurance*, Vol. 2, Ch. 4.

[92] *Ebsworth v. Alliance Marine Ins. Co.* (1873) L.R. 9 C.P. 596, 617, 621, *per* Bovill C.J.; *Moran, Galloway & Co. v. Uzielli* [1905] 2 K.B. 555, 561–562 *per* Walton J.

[93] (1806) 2 Bos. & Pul. (N.R.) 269, 321.

[94] (1809) 11 East 428, 433.

[95] Marine Insurance Act 1906, s.5(2); *Moran, Galloway & Co. v. Uzielli* [1905] 2 K.B. 555, 562; *Macaura v. Northern Ass. Co.* [1925] A.C. 619, 630. The words "a right derivable out of some contract about the property" are apt to cover such cases as the insurable interest possessed by licensees and others with a legal right to occupy and enjoy property—see para. 1–127, *post.*

loss arising from destruction of, or damage to, the insured property, then we have a substantially accurate definition of insurable interest in property.[96]

1–121 Other common law jurisdictions have dispensed with the requirement of a legal or equitable interest. In *Constitution Insurance of Canada v. Kosmopoulos*[97] the Supreme Court of Canada decided not to follow its earlier decision in *Guarantee Co. of North America v. Aqua-Land Exploration Ltd*[98] and held that a moral certainty of economic advantage from property was a sufficient ground of insurable interest therein. The courts in a number of American jurisdictions have adopted a test based upon a factual expectation of benefit from the continuing existence of property, regardless of the existence of a legal or equitable relationship to it.[99] In Australia the legislature has intervened, and section 17 of the Insurance Contracts Act 1984 provides that, when the assured suffers pecuniary or economic loss because insured property has been damaged or destroyed, the absence of an interest at law or in equity in the property at the time of loss does not relieve the insurer from liability. These developments notwithstanding, it is submitted that the English law requirement of a legal interest or obligation regarding the property cannot be dispensed with except by a reforming statute or by restatement of the law by the House of Lords.[1]

1–122 In the sections which follow we examine the different situations

---

[96] *Stock v. Inglis* (1884) 12 Q.B.D. 564, 578 *per* Lindley L.J.; *Glengate-KG Properties Ltd v. Norwich Union Fire Ins. Soc.* [1996] 1 Lloyd's Rep. 614, 623, *per* Auld L.J. This case concerned the interpretation of the word "interest" in a consequential loss policy, but the judgments contain *obiter* observations on the nature of insurable interest required by law in property insurance.

[97] (1987) 34 D.L.R. (4th) 208.

[98] (1965) 54 D.L.R. (2d) 299. See para. 1–59, *ante.* The Supreme Court had approved and followed the statement of the English law in para. 445 of the 5th edition of this work.

[99] See, for instance, cases in which a creditor has been held to have an insurable interest in the property of his debtor after a judgment has been obtained for an un-secured debt, such as *American Equitable Ass. Co. v. Powderly Coal & Lumber Co.*, 128 So. 225 (1930); *Spare v. Home Mutual Ins. Co.* 15 Fed.Rep. 707 (1883); *Rohrbach v. Germania Fire Ins. Co.* 62 N.Y. 47 (1875). See para. 1–149, *post.* So also a person named in the will of a living person as a devisee of property has an insurable interest in the property left to him—*Home Ins. Co. v. Mendenhall*, 45 N.E. 1078 (1897)—*cf.* Lord Eldon's example of the heir at law in *Lucena v. Craufurd* (1806) 2 Bos. & Pul. (N.R.) 269, 324–325. Further illustrations are *Liverpool & London Globe Ins. Co. v. Bolling* 10 S.E. 2d 578 (Va., 1940); *Womble v. Dubuque Fire & Marine Ins. Co.* 37 N.E. 2d 263 (Mass. 1941); *N. British & Mercantile Ins. Co. v. Sciandia*, 54 So. 2d 764 (Ala. 1951); *Putnam v. Mercantile Marine Ins. Co.* 46 Mass. (5 Met.) 386 (1843). For further detail see Hartnett & Thornton (1948) 48 Co.L.Rev. 1162–1188 and Note on *Castle Cars Inc. v. United States Fire Ins. Co.*, 221 Va., 773 (1981) in (1982) 68 Va., L. Rev. 651. Other authorities are cited in *Constitution Ins. Co. v. Kosmopoulos* (1987) 34 D.L.R. (4th) 208.

[1] It is submitted that it is not open to English courts to identify and prefer and allegedly more liberal definition of insurable interest given by Lawrence J. in *Lucena v. Craufurd* (1806) 2 Bos. & Pul. (N.R.) 269 to that approved by the House of Lords in the same case; see para. 1–120, *ante.* The suggestion in *National Oilwell (U.K.) Ltd v. Davy Offshore Ltd* [1993] 2 Lloyd's Rep. 582, 611 that it might be unnecessary to establish a proprietary legal or equitable interest in the insured property is unexceptionable in as much as a contractual right relating to the property, such as a licence to use it, or a contractual obligation to bear loss occasioned by its destruction, will afford a ground of insurable interest. But to say that an insurable interest in property is satisfied by either a close relationship with it, or a certainty of benefit from its preservation, regardless of a legal right to or concerning the property, is incorrect. Observations in *Sharp v. Sphere Drake Ins.* [1992] 2 Lloyd's Rep. 501, 509–512, to that effect are, with respect, in conflict with earlier appellate authority.

which may support an insurable interest in property, indicating where necessary the different rules relating to insurances on real property and insurances on chattels.

1–123 Trustees and beneficiaries. Executors or trustees who hold the legal title to any property and the beneficiaries under a will or trust can insure the property independently, each in respect of their own interests.[2] A trustee as legal owner has an interest to the full value of the trust property, and can therefore insure it in his own name without describing his interest as that of a trustee who has no beneficial interest in it.[3] An executor or administrator may insure the whole estate of the deceased.[4] An executor's interest commences whenever he has accepted the office and before his title has been legally completed by probate,[5] and an executor *de son tort* has an insurable interest because he has made himself responsible for the distribution of assets.[6] A trustee in bankruptcy,[7] an assignee for creditors under a trust deed, and a receiver appointed by the court[8] each has an insurable interest in the property in his hands, but the debtor also retains an insurable interest to the full value since he has an interest in the preservation of the property which is to be applied in satisfying his debts.[9]

1–124 Bare legal title. It is doubtful whether a bare legal title either to land or goods gives its holder an insurable interest[10] although certain dicta of Lord Ellenborough C.J. in *Lucena v. Craufurd*[11] might seem at first sight to indicate that it does. There is no doubt, of course, that a trustee holding a legal estate or title can insure property he is holding for the benefit of beneficiaries under an actual or constructive trust, since the trustee is bound to account to the beneficiaries when he recovers the value of the insured goods or land. A vendor before completion, whose only obligation in respect of the property is to convey it to the purchaser, is not a trustee of the property for the purchaser, so that if he insures the property and it is destroyed by fire before completion, and he recovers the full value, he can prima facie retain it for his own benefit,[12] subject to the provisions of section 47 of the Law of Property Act 1925. This is not merely by reason of his legal title but by reason of his unpaid vendor's lien which gives him an actual pecuniary interest in the property as security for the price.[13] If, however, the vendor has conveyed away the premises before the fire destroys them, then

---

[2] *Lucena v. Craufurd* (1806) 2 Bos. & Pul. (N.R.) 269, 324; *ex p. Yallop* (1808) 15 Ves. 60, 67; *Houghton v. Gribble* (1810) 17 Ves. 251, 253; *Rhind v. Wilkinson* (1810) 2 Taunt. 237.

[3] *L.N.W.R. v. Glyn* (1859) 1 E. & E. 652, 663; *Ebsworth v. Alliance Marine Ins. Co.* (1873) L.R. 8 C.P. 596, 608; *Lonsdale & Thompson Ltd v. Black Arrow Group* [1993] Ch. 361, 369.

[4] *Parry v. Ashley* (1829) 3 Sim. 97; *Re Betty* [1899] 1 Ch. 821.

[5] *Stirling v. Vaughan* (1809) 11 East 619, 628.

[6] *Gill v. Canada Fire and Marine* (1882) 1 Ont.Rep. 341; *Re Hamilton*, 102 Fed.Rep. 683 (1900).

[7] *Lingley v. Queen Insurance* (1868) 12 N.B.R. (1 Han.) 280.

[8] *Thompson v. Phoenix Insurance*, 136 U.S. 287 (1889).

[9] *Marks v. Hamilton* (1852) 7 Ex. 323.

[10] *Kennedy v. Boolarra Butter Factory Pty. Ltd* [1953] V.L.R. 548, 554; *Seagrave v. Union Marine Ins. Co.* (1866) L.R. 1 C.P. 305—see para. 1–138, *post*.

[11] (1806) 2 Bos. & Pul. (N.R.) 269, 324; cited, in *Ebsworth v. Alliance Marine* (1873) L.R. 8 C.P. 596. See also *Commercial Union Assurance Group v. Watson* (1979) 91 D.L.R. (3d) 434.

[12] *Rayner v. Preston* (1881) 18 Ch.D. 1.

[13] *Collingridge v. Royal Exchange Ass. Corp.* (1877) 3 Q.B.D. 173; *Castellain v. Preston* (1883) 11 Q.B.D. 380, 385, 401.

he has no pecuniary interest in them, and he cannot prove the insurable interest at the time of loss that is normally required in any indemnity insurance, a fire policy being of that kind.[14] A mortgagee also has an insurable interest in the mortgaged property,[15] for he has a pecuniary interest in it as security for repayment, quite apart from any legal title.

1–125 Possession. The mere possession of property is probably sufficient to give the person in possession an insurable interest[16] in it. Possession is in English law a root of legal title, and even if a possessory title must be defeated by a claim brought by the true owner, nonetheless it is a legal title good against all others in the absence of special circumstances.[17] It follows that a person who has found a valuable chattel may insure it for its full value.[18] His right is analogous to that of a person with a voidable title to goods. It is also clear that possession entailing legal liability for goods, such as that of a bailee, gives an insurable interest,[19] but possession of property in which there is no right of enjoyment and in respect of which no liability is owed at all would not suffice, should such a situation ever arise.[20]

Whether or not the possessor of property can insure it for its full value must depend upon the circumstances in which he has obtained possession, and his resulting pecuniary interest or legal responsibilities. Even if possession itself is not enough to ground an interest to the full value, possession by an assured is prima facie proof of ownership, so that proof of possession is sufficient in the first instance to establish an interest to the full value.[21]

1–126 Stolen goods. There is a large volume of case-law in the United States concerning whether or not the innocent purchaser of stolen goods has an insurable interest in them. The authorities conflict, although the majority position seems to favour the existence of an interest.[22] A Canadian decision

---

[14] *Collingridge v. Royal Exchange Ass. Corp.* (1877) 3 Q.B.D. 173, 177; *Bank of New South Wales v. The North British and Mercantile Ins. Co.* (1881) 2 N.S.W.L.R. 239; *Ecclesiastical Commrs v. Royal Exch. Ass. Corp.* (1895) 11 T.L.R. 476. If by reason of the contract of by operation of local law the vendor was made trustee of the insurance moneys for the purchaser, then clearly he would have an interest in the property to its full value, *e.g. Insurance Co. v. Updegraff*, 21 Pa. 513 (1853).

[15] *Ebsworth v. Alliance Marine* (1873) L.R. 8 C.P. 596, 608; *Westminster Fire Office v. Glasgow Provident Society* (1888) 13 App.Cas. 699; *Glover v. Black* (1763) 1 Wm.Bl. 396.

[16] *Lucena v. Craufurd* (1806) 2 Bos. & Pul. (N.R.) 269, 323; *Dobson v. Sotheby* (1827) Moo. & M. 90, 93; *Dixon v. Whitworth* (1879) 4 C.P.D. 371, 375.

[17] *Stirling v. Vaughan* (1809) 11 East 619, 628. The American and Canadian courts have not accepted that wrongful possession can ground insurable interest: *Sweeney v. Franklin Fire*, 20 Pa. 337 (1853); *Fidelity Phoenix Fire of New York v. Raper*, 6 So. 2d 513 (Ala., 1942); *Sherboneau v. Beaver Mutual* (1870) 30 U.C.Q.B. 472; *Lingley v. Queen Insurance* (1868) 12 N.B.R. (1 Han.) 280. Possession of goods liable to forfeiture is a root of insurable interest *Zinati v. Canadian Universal Ins. Co.* (1984) 5 D.L.R. (4th) 110; aff'd 12 D.L.R. (4th) 766; *Ardekany v. Dominion General Ins. Co.* (1986) 32 D.L.R. (4th) 23.

[18] *Marks v. Hamilton* (1852) 7 Exch. 323, *per* Pollock C.B., who is more fully reported in (1852) 21 L.J. Ex. 109.

[19] *Boehm v. Bell* (1799) 8 T.R. 154.

[20] *Macaura v. Northern Ass. Co.* [1925] A.C. 619

[21] *Mayor of New York v. Brooklyn Fire*, 61 Barb. 231 (N.Y. 1864); *Stevenson v. London and Lancashire Fire* (1866) 26 U.C.Q.B. 148; *Lingley v. Queen Insurance* (1868) 1 Hann.(N.Br.) 280; *Marks v. Hamilton* (1852) 21 L.J.Ex. 109.

[22] See, *e.g. Scarola v. Ins. Co. of North America*, 292 N.E. 2d 776 (1972); *Reznich v. Home Ins. Co.*, 360 N.E. 2d 461 (1977). Compare, *e.g. Ins. Co. of North America v. Cliff Pettit Motors Inc.*, 513 S.W. 2d 785 (1974).

is to the contrary[23] but this seems to turn upon the assured being under an obligation to surrender the insured car prior to loss, having been told that it had been stolen.

1–127 Licence to use property. Where a person has a licence to use and enjoy any property jointly with the owner, there can be no doubt that he has an insurable interest in it if the licence is contractual, but it is less clear whether this is the case when he has a mere revocable licence. In *Goulstone v. The Royal Insurance Co.*,[24] Pollock C.B. at Nisi Prius held that a husband had an insurable interest and could recover the full value of house property and household furniture which were settled to his wife's separate use, but of which both spouses enjoyed the actual use and occupation. Later American authority supports the reasoning in *Goulstone*. In *Kludt v. German Mutual Fire*[25] a husband living with his wife was held to have an insurable interest, by virtue of occupation, in the matrimonial home, title to which was in his wife; and in *North British and Mercantile v. Sciandia*[26] a husband who owned an undivided moiety in the matrimonial home, which was also his place of business, was held to have an insurable interest in the whole. Where the corporate owner of a yacht executed a power of attorney expressed to be irrevocable for fixed periods of time, and conferring on an individual assured the right to manage, control, charter, use, and dispose of the vessel as he chose, it was held in *Sharp v. Sphere Drake Insurance* that he had an insurable interest in her.[27]

1–128 Vendors and purchasers. A person who has entered into a valid contract for the purchase of any property has an insurable interest in it. The loss of, or damage to, the property may extinguish or diminish the value of his contractual right, and his insurable interest is commensurate with the loss which he may thus suffer. The contract must be valid and subsisting in order to give the purchaser an interest; but the fact that it is voidable does not affect his insurable interest, although it would be otherwise if the contract was unenforceable by action.[28]

In like manner the vendor of any property retains an interest in it for so long as he is in such a legal position with regard to it that any loss or damage to the property might result in loss to him. Vendor and purchaser may in certain circumstances have concurrent interests enabling each to insure and recover the full value of the property.[29] Thus, if the risk has passed to the purchaser but the vendor is unpaid and has a lien on it for the purchase money, the purchaser has an interest to the full value in respect of his risk and of his liability to pay the full price for the property which, when conveyed to him, may have become valueless, and the vendor has an interest to the full value in respect of his lien, because the loss of the property means the loss of his security and the loss of the purchase price if the purchaser is

---

[23] *Chadwick v. Gibraltar Insurance* (1981) 34 O.R. 2d 488. See also *Thompson v. Madill* (1986) 13 C.C.L.I. 242.

[24] (1858) 1 F. & F. 276; *Glengate-KG Properties v. Norwich Union Fire Ins. Soc.* [1996] 1 Lloyd's Rep. 614, 624.

[25] 140 N. W. 321 (Wis. 1914); the divergent case-law is reviewed in the opinion.

[26] 54 So. (2d) 764 (Ala., 1951).

[27] [1992] 2 Lloyd's Rep. 501, 508–513. See also *Williams v. Baltic Ins. Co.* [1924] 2 K.B. 282, 290 (use of car).

[28] For the reasons for this distinction, see para. 1–53, *ante.*

[29] *Andrews v. Patriotic (No. 2)* (1886) 18 L.R.Ir. 355.

insolvent. How far insurers who have paid on either interest may mitigate or extinguish their loss by subrogation to the rights of the assured is another matter, which will be considered later.

1–129 In considering the insurable interests of parties to a contract of sale, it is necessary to give separate consideration to contracts relating to real property and those relating to personal chattels or goods.

1–130 Contracts for the sale of land. A valid contract for the sale of land passes the risk immediately to the purchaser unless the contract is expressed otherwise.[30] The legal title does not pass until there is a formal conveyance by deed, but any loss or damage arising between contract and completion falls upon the purchaser, and he must accept a conveyance of the damaged property and pay the full contract price. The passing of the risk gives the purchaser an insurable interest, and he may at once insure for the full value.[31] The contract may be voidable but the purchaser's interest is not thereby affected so long as the contract subsists, and the insurers cannot rely on the fact that the vendor might have refused to perform the contract.[32] The sale may be subject to a contingency[33] or to the performance of certain conditions by the purchaser[34] but that does not diminish the insurable value of the purchaser's interest. In an American case the vendor had agreed to sell and convey the property on a specified date provided that the purchaser had by then paid the purchase-money by the agreed fixed instalments. The purchaser insured; the payment of the instalments was in arrear, but the vendor had taken no steps to cancel the contract and the purchaser was held to have an insurable interest.[35]

1–131 The vendor of land has an insurable interest to the extent of his lien for the purchase money.[36] It is extremely doubtful whether a vendor who has retained the legal title after payment of the price has any insurable interest in the property,[37] but even if he has, as has been held in other jurisdictions,[38] he would be bound to set off the price received against the claim. Such

---

[30] *Paine v. Meller* (1801) 6 Ves. 349; *Poole v. Adams* (1864) 10 L.T. 287.

[31] *White v. Home Ins. Co.* (1870) 14 Low.Can.Jur. 301; *Milligan v. Equitable Insurance Co.* (1857) 16 U.C.Q.B. 314. For the passing of risk in Scots law see *Sloans Diaries Ltd v. Glasgow Corporation* 1977 S.C. 223. On the sale of heritable property the older practice was to obtain a transfer of the policy to the purchaser upon the completion of the missives of sale, on the footing that the property was then at his risk. The modern practice is for the purchaser to take out a new policy as soon as the sale has been completed. See J. M. Halliday, *Conveyancing Law and Practice in Scotland*, Vol. 2, paras. 15–115 and 15–116.

[32] *Wainer v. Milford Mutual*, 153 Mass. 335 (1891); *Dupuy v. Delaware*, 63 Fed.Rep. 680 (1894); *Carpenter v. German American Ins. Co.*, 135 N.Y. 298 (1892). These cases are not decided on principles akin to those of English law, however, since an expectation of benefit was said of itself to ground an interest.

[33] *Gilbert v. Insurance Co.* 23 Wend. 43 (N.Y.Sup.Ct. 1840).

[34] *Norwich Union Fire Ins. Soc. Ltd v. Traynor* [1972] N.Z.L.R. 505. The grantee of an option to purchase acquires an insurable interest. So does a buyer on a purchase subject to approval—[1972] N.Z.L.R. 505, 507 *per* Woodhouse J., *obiter*.

[35] *Gilman v. Dwelling House Ins. Co.*, 81 Me. 488 (1889).

[36] *Collingridge v. Royal Exchange Ass. Corp.* (1877) 3 Q.B.D. 173; *Castellain v. Preston* (1883) 11 Q.B.D. 380; *Keefer v. Phoenix Ins.* (1898) 26 Ont.A.R. 277; *Ottawa Agricultural Ins. v. Sheridan* (1879) 5 S.C.R. 157; *Weeks v. Cumberland Farmers' Mutual Fire Ins. Co.* (1930) 4 D.L.R. 588.

[37] *Bank of New South Wales v. North British and Mercantile Ins. Co.* (1881) 2 N.S.W.L.R. 239; *Kennedy v. Boolarra Butter Factory Pty. Ltd* [1953] V.L.R. 548, 554.

[38] *Ins. Co. v. Updegraff*, 21 Pa. 513 (1853); *Keefer v. Phoenix Ins.* (1898) 26 Ont.A.R. 277.

insurance would be a contract of personal indemnity, and so he would in practice recover nothing under the policy.[39] If, furthermore, the property has been conveyed and the price paid, it is clear that the assured could not recover on a policy effected before the sale.[40] Where the owner of a house contracted with a housebreaker who, for a specified consideration, agreed to pull it down and take the materials, it was held, notwithstanding such contract, that the owner retained an interest to the full value of the premises and was entitled to recover on his policy the whole damage by fire.[41]

1–132 Contracts for the sale of goods. The acquisition of an insurable interest by the buyer depends principally upon the passing of the risk.[42] The risk usually passes when the property in the goods passes,[43] but the two are not inseparable and it depends upon an interpretation of the terms of the particular contract whether the property passes without the risk or the risk passes prior to the property.[44] If the property passes without the risk, the buyer can insure as owner of the goods.[45] The passing of the risk without the property also gives him an insurable interest because in the event of subsequent loss or damage he must nevertheless pay the contract price, and so the whole loss falls on him.[46] Where either the property or the risk has passed to the buyer, his insurers cannot call upon him to avoid his loss by the exercise of any option which he may have to be released from his contract, *e.g.* to reject for breach of a condition, in order that the insurers may be released from their obligation to indemnify him.[47] If neither property nor risk has passed, payment or part payment of the price will give the buyer an insurable interest, because if the goods were lost or damaged and the seller was insolvent the buyer might not be able to recover the money which he had paid for them.[48]

---

[39] *Castellain v. Preston* (1883) 11 Q.B.D. 380. Taking an assignment of the benefit of the vendor's policy may not, therefore, be of any use to the purchaser—*Ziel Nominees Pty Ltd v. V.A.C.C. Ins. Co. Ltd* (1976) 50 A.L.J.R. 106.

[40] *Sadlers Co. v. Badcock* (1743) 2 Atk. 554; *Ecclesiastical Commissioners v. The Royal Exchange Ass. Co.* (1895) 11 T.L.R. 476.

[41] *Ardill v. Citizens' Ins. Co.* (1893) 20 Ont.A.R. 605.

[42] *Anderson v. Morice* (1875) L.R. 10 C.P. 609; (1876) 1 App.Cas. 713; *Frangano v. Long* (1825) 4 B. & C. 219; *Colonial Ins. v. Adelaide Marine Ins.* (1886) 12 App.Cas. 128. It is debatable whether the cases on marine policies cited below which were decided before the 1906 Act provide an exhaustive test. The language of s.5 of the Act does not in terms require proof that the buyer has acquired property in the goods or that the goods are at his risk in order to establish an interest in the outcome of a marine adventure—*Piper v. Royal Exchange* (1932) 44 Ll.L.Rep. 103, 116.

[43] Sale of Goods Act 1979 s.20; *Rugg v. Minet* (1809) 11 East 210; *Anderson v. Morice* (1875) L.R. 10 C.P. 609, 619; *Comptoir D'Achat et de Vente v. Luis de Ridder Limitada* [1949] A.C. 293, 319. For the position in Scotland when the contract is one of barter rather than sale, see *Widenmeyer v. Burn, Stewart and Co.* 1967 S.C. 85.

[44] *Martineau v. Kitching* (1872) L.R. 7 Q.B. 436, 454.

[45] *Sparkes v. Marshall* (1836) 2 Bing.N.C. 761; *Inglis v. Stock* (1885) 10 App.Cas. 263; *Colonial Ins. v. Adelaide Marine Ins. Co.* (1886) 12 App.Cas. 128.

[46] *Neale v. Reid* (1823) 1 B. & C. 657; *Joyce v. Swann* (1864) 17 C.B.(N.S.) 84, 103–104; *Castle v. Playford* (1872) L.R. 7 Ex. 98; *Anderson v. Morice* (1876) 1 App.Cas. 713; *Colonial Ins. v. Adelaide Marine Ins.* (1886) 12 App.Cas. 128; *Inglis v. Stock* (1884) 12 Q.B.D. 564; (1885) 10 App.Cas. 263.

[47] *Inglis v. Stock* (1885) 10 App.Cas. 263, 274; *Colonial Ins. v. Adelaide Marine Ins.* (1886) 12 App.Cas. 128.

[48] *Cumberland Bone Co. v. Andes Insurance*, 64 Me. 466 (1874), but the insurance in this case is perhaps more appropriately regarded as a guarantee of the seller's contractual liability.

1–133 Immediately a valid agreement for the future sale of goods, or a valid contract of sale, has been effected the buyer has an interest in respect of the profits which he may make on a resale. Profits, however, must be insured *eo nomine* and a purely executory contract for sale probably gives the buyer no interest in respect of which he can insure the goods *simpliciter*.[49] If neither property nor risk has passed to him, and he had neither taken possession, nor paid the price or any part of it, the only loss which can fall upon him is the loss of profit on the transaction. If the goods are lost or damaged, he is not bound to accept them or pay the price, and the whole loss falls upon the seller and none upon the buyer. The unpaid seller of goods who has parted with property in them has no insurable interest in them unless either they remain at his risk or he has a lien, charge or other security interest over them for the price.[50] So long as the risk remains with him, he has an interest whether the property has passed or not,[51] and the measure of his interest is the purchase price or the actual value of the goods, whichever is the greater.[52]

1–134 Even when risk and property have both passed, the seller retains an insurable interest in the goods while he still possesses them because, if he is unpaid in whole or part on account of the buyer's insolvency or for other reasons, he has an interest in respect of his lien[53] for the purchase money.[54] His possession of the goods would also permit him to insure on the buyer's behalf if his intention is clear and the policy does not forbid it.[55] When he has parted with possession, the unpaid seller has a right to regain it in certain instances if the goods are in transit,[56] and this will also support an insurable interest.[57] The buyer's interest in the goods ceases if he rejects them, provided that he is not responsible for their safety during re-delivery.[58] If the seller exercises his right of stoppage in transit, the buyer's interest is determined if the passing of property and risk depends on delivery,[59] but, if property and risk pass independently of delivery, his interest ought not to be affected, since the seller's exercise of the remedy does not without more rescind the contract of sale.[60]

1–135 Hire-purchase agreement. Where by the terms of a hire-purchase

---

[49] *Anderson v. Morice* (1875) L.R. 10 C.P. 609, 622; (1876) 1 App.Cas. 713, 722; *Warder v. Horton*, 4 Binn. 529 (Pa., 1812); *Box v. Provincial Ins.* (1868) 15 Grant Ch.App. 337. See para. 1–57, *ante*.

[50] *United Ins. Co. v. Black* [1940] N.Z.L.R. 377.

[51] *Reed v. Cole* (1764) 3 Burr. 1512.

[52] *Stuart v. Columbia*, 7 U.S. (3 Cranch) 442 (1823).

[53] Sale of Goods Act 1979, s.41.

[54] *L.N.W.R. v. Glyn* (1859) 1 E. & E. 652. By analogy with the position of the vendor of real property he would have to cede to the insurer his rights against the buyer in the event of a loss: *Castellain v. Preston* (1883) 11 Q.B.D. 380.

[55] *North British and Mercantile Ins. Co. v. Moffat* (1871) L.R. 7 C.P. 25, 30–31. The buyer cannot otherwise benefit from an insurance effected by the seller, though in many export contracts the seller must insure for the buyer's benefit in any case, *e.g.* a c.i.f. transaction. Section 47 of the Law of Property Act applies to goods insurances.

[56] See *Kendall v. Marshall Stevens* (1883) 11 Q.B.D. 356; Sale of Goods Act 1979, s.44. The seller's lien and right to stop in transit do not permit him to benefit under the buyer's insurance: *Berndtson v. Strang* (1868) L.R. 3 Ch. App. 588, 591; neither do they affect the buyer's right to insure once risk has passed: *Anderson v. Morice* (1875) L.R. 10 C.P. 609, 619.

[57] *Clay v. Harrison* (1829) 10 B. & C. 99.

[58] *Colonial Insurance v. Adelaide Marine Insurance* (1886) 12 App.Cas. 128.

[59] *Mollison v. Victoria Ins. Co.* (1883) 2 N.Z.(S.C.) 177.

[60] Sale of Goods Act 1979, s.44.

agreement the loss of or damage to the goods relieved the hirer of any obligation to pay the future instalments of the purchase price, the purchaser's interest and right of recovery at the date of the loss were held to be limited to the amount of the instalments paid[61]; but where the whole risk was on the purchaser it was held that he could recover to the full value of the furniture, notwithstanding that the property in it remained with the seller.[62] Such a purchaser, however, is not "sole and unconditional owner", where the policy so requires.[63]

1–136 There is a broad category of hire-purchase and other credit agreements which are required by law to be in writing and to comply in further respects with the Consumer Credit Act 1974. The consequence of non-compliance is not that the contract is void, but merely that it is enforceable by the owner or seller only on an order of the court.[64] If, as will usually be the case, the goods are in the possession of the hirer, the main practical consequence of the restriction on enforceability of the contract will be that the owner loses his right to repossession. Section 65(2) provides that a "retaking of goods" is an enforcement. It seems clear that in this situation the hirer has as good an insurable interest as he could have under a valid contract. The position of the owner is complicated by the fact that under section 127, the court has power to make an enforcement order, despite breach of some of the statutory requirements, if satisfied that non-compliance has not prejudiced the hirer. It is submitted that until a court has been asked to exercise this power and has refused, the owner's insurable interest continues to exist. Once a court has refused to allow recovery, however, the owner's rights would seem to be reduced to a bare legal title which will not support an insurable interest. The same applies in those cases[65] where the court cannot make an enforcement order. When a hire-purchase contract is cancelled by virtue of the statutory right of cancellation,[66] the hirer's insurable interest must continue as long as he retains possession of the goods and is placed by the statute under an obligation to take reasonable care of them.[67]

1–137 Bailee. A bailee has a personal insurable interest in goods bailed with him to the extent of (a) the value of any lien or charge he may have on them for his rent or service charges,[68] and (b) his personal liability to their owner.[69] He may also insure the goods to their full value on behalf of the owner's interest in them; this case is considered below.

1–138 Consignee. A person to whom goods are consigned as agent for the

[61] *Reed v. Williamsburg City Fire*, 74 Me. 537 (1883); *Ryan v. Agricultural*, 188 Mass. 11 (1905); *Bowden v. Bank of America National Trust and Savings Ass.*, 224 P. 2d 713 (Cal., 1950).
   [62] *ibid.*
   [63] *Weaver v. Hartford Fire*, 211 P. 2d 113 (Kan., 1949).
   [64] See s.65.
   [65] See s.127(3)(4).
   [66] See s.69.
   [67] See s.72(4).
   [68] *Dalgleish v. Buchanan & Co.* (1854) 16 D. 332, 337; *Waters v. Monarch Fire and Life Ass. Co.* (1856) 5 E. & B. 870; *Pittsburg Storage Co. v. Scottish Union and National Ins. Co.*, 168 Pa. 522 (1895).
   [69] *Crowley v. Cohen* (1832) 3 B. & Ad. 478; *Stephens v. Australasian Ins. Co.* (1872) L.R. 8 C.P. 18; *Hill v. Scott* (1895) 2 Q.B. 713; *California Ins. Co. v. Union Compress Co.*, 133 U.S. 387 (1889); *Savage v. Corn Exchange Ins. Co.*, 36 N.Y. 655 (1867).

owner has no insurable interest in them if he is a bare consignee. In *Seagrave v. Union Marine Insurance Co.*[70] the plaintiff was a Liverpool broker whose principal shipped goods to an overseas buyer. A bill of lading was obtained made out in his name and it was indorsed over to the buyer. The plaintiff insured the goods in his own name against the risks of the voyage. He had, however, no lien on the goods for advances, commission or otherwise, and he stood to incur no liability in the event of their loss. He could not be considered, on the facts of the case, as an unpaid vendor. It was held by the Court of Common Pleas that his claim on the policy failed for want of insurable interest. It is submitted that a consignee to whom the goods were forwarded, but who had no property in the goods, nor lien for advances or charges or commission fees, would be in no better position assuming the goods not to be at his risk.

1–139 If, however, the consignee has obtained a title to the goods by indorsement to him of the documents of title or by indorsement to bearer, he has probably an interest to the full value.[71] If he has made advances to the owner and is to hold the goods as security for repayment, he has an interest to the extent of his advances although he has not yet obtained either title or possession.[72] Where the owner, being indebted to A, consigned goods to C with instructions to pay the proceeds to A, it was held that A had an insurable interest.[73] If the consignee has obtained possession, that alone may be sufficient to give him an interest to the full value irrespective of title or lien if he is legally responsible for the goods. Although a bare consignee has no interest to insure on the goods themselves, he may insure specifically on his commission or other profits which he expects to make, as agent for sale or otherwise,[74] provided that he has been in fact employed for that purpose and has not merely an expectation of employment.[75] On the same principle, any person who has contracted to render services in connection with any property, whether goods or realty, may insure on his expected profits or benefits therefrom.[76]

1–140 Tenants for life and co-owners. Any owner of a limited interest in land has an insurable interest up to an amount sufficient to compensate him for the loss of his own estate. Thus a tenant for life has an insurable interest up to an amount sufficient to compensate him for the loss of his own life interest.[77] In contrast to a tenant for years, the tenant for life is not liable for permissive waste to the premises occupied by him, so that, subject to the

[70] (1866) L.R. 1 C.P. 305.
[71] *Ebsworth v. Alliance Marine* (1873) L.R. 8 C.P. 596.
[72] *Carruthers v. Sheddon* (1815) 6 Taunt. 14; *Wolff v. Horncastle* (1798) 1 Bos. & Pul. 316; *Robertson v. Hamilton* (1811) 14 East 522; *Parker v. Beasley* (1814) 2 M. & S. 423; *Russell v. Union Insurance*, 1 Wash.C.C. 409 (1806); *Ebsworth v. Alliance Marine* (1873) L.R. 8 C.P. 596; *Aldrich v. The Equitable Safety* (1846) 1 Wood & Min. 272.
[73] *Hill v. Secretan* (1798) 1 Bos. & Pul. 315.
[74] *Maurice v. Goldsbrough Mort & Co.* [1939] A.C. 452, 461; *Lucena v. Craufurd* (1806) 2 Bos. & Pul. (N.R.) 269, 315; *Flint v. Le Messurier* (1796) 2 Park, *Insurance* (8th ed.), p. 563; *Putnam v. Mercantile Marine*, 46 Mass. 386 (1843).
[75] *Buchanan v. Faber* (1899) 4 Com.Cas. 223.
[76] *King v. Glover* (1806) 2 B. & P.(N.R.) 206; *Dalgleish v. Buchanan & Co.* (1854) 16 D. 332, 335, 337; *Cross v. National Fire Ins. Co.*, 132 N.Y. 133 (1892); *Traders' Ins. Co. v. Pacaud*, 150 Ill. 245 (1894); *Robinson v. New York Ins. Co.*, 2 Caine 357 (N.Y. 1805).
[77] *Castellain v. Preston* (1883) 11 Q.B.D. 380, 401; *Beekman v. Fulton*, 66 N.Y.App.Div. 72 (1901).

terms of the settlement under which he is entitled to occupy the settled property, he is not liable for permitting the premises to lapse into disrepair.[78] The value of his own interest is accordingly less than the whole value of the premises.[79]

1–141 Before the coming into force of the 1925 property legislation, a tenant for life could not insure for the recover the full value of the property as trustee of it for the remainderman. He may do this now under a settlement to which the Settled Land Act 1925 applies, since by virtue of the Act the whole fee simple or other estate which is the subject-matter of the settlement is vested in him, and he is trustee of it in respect of his own beneficial interest and the beneficial interests of others under the settlement. If the settlement obliges him to insure buildings contained in it, the insurance will be taken to be for the benefit of successors in title,[80] but, if it does not, it will be a question of construction of the policy whether he has insured for himself alone or to protect other interests as well.[81] In case of doubt, the presumption will be in favour of an insurance sufficient to cover his responsibilities as trustee[82]

Analogous changes are effected by the Law of Property Act 1925 in respect of co-ownership.[83] Before the Act, a partner in a firm who insured the partnership land had only an interest equal to the value of his beneficial share in the property,[84] and a tenant in common had similarly an interest limited to the value of his estate.[85] But now, in the majority of cases of co-ownership, the co-owners are themselves the trustees of the property upon the statutory trusts; the principle stated above will, however, still apply, for example where the property is vested in the Public Trustee under the transitional provisions, or where owing to the number of persons interested exceeding four the particular co-owner who insures is not one of the trustees, or where, owing to a divergence in the devolution of the legal estate on the one hand and the beneficial interest on the other, the same thing has happened.

1–142 Tenant for years. The lessee of premises has an insurable interest in them on one or more grounds:

1–143 (i) *Possession.* Although it is difficult to specify the extent to which enjoyment of premises confers an interest, the tenant must surely have an

---

[78] *Gregg v. Coates* (1856) 23 Beav. 33, 38; *Re Cartwright* (1889) 41 Ch.D. 532. A tenant for life is said to be "impeachable for voluntary waste".
[79] *Castellain v. Preston* (1883) 11 Q.B.D. 380, 401.
[80] *Re Bladon* [1911] 2 Ch. 350, 354.
[81] *Castellain v. Preston* (1883) 11 Q.B.D. 380, 398.
[82] *Gaussen v. Whatman* (1905) 93 L.T. 101 and the older decisions cited in it indicate a presumption that the tenant for life insures for his own benefit only, but at that time he was not a statutory trustee of the other interests.
[83] Law of Property Act 1925, ss.34–36, Sched. 1 Pt. IV.
[84] *Forbes & Co. v. Border Counties Fire Ins. Co.* (1873) 11 M. 278.
[85] Mr. Bunyon was of a contrary opinion (*Fire Insurance* (6th ed.), p. 39), but cited only *Page v. Fry* (1800) 2 Bos. & Pul. 240 in support, and this is not really an authority for the proposition he makes. The case only decided that under 19 Geo. 2, c. 37, a person with a limited interest such as that of a joint owner of goods could insure beyond his interest in his own name and on his own account.

interest on this ground.[86] If his user is for business purposes, he cannot recover for loss of business profits consequent upon the destruction of the premises unless he has specifically insured on such profits.[87]

1–144 (ii) *Liability to pay rent*. Even assuming that possession alone is not sufficient, if the tenant is liable to pay rent during the remainder of the term, notwithstanding the destruction of the premises, his interest in respect of his right of occupation will be greater than it would be if under the lease the liability for rent ceased. In England a tenant, apart from express stipulation in the lease and the provisions of the War Damage Act,[88] remains liable for rent, notwithstanding the accidental demolition of the premises.[89] In Scotland a tenant may abandon his lease and avoid further liability for rent if the fire was not caused by his own fault and has done such damage as to render the premises for a substantial time practically useless for the purpose for which he took them.[90] If a tenant's liability for rent ceases, his interest in respect of his right of occupation is comparatively small and the measure of it would probably be the difference between the rent he was previously paying and the rent which he would have to pay for similar premises elsewhere, calculated for the remainder of the term, and the cost of removal. In *Mark Rowlands Ltd v. Berni Inns Ltd*,[91] it was held, *obiter*, that a tenant had an insurable interest in premises even when under the terms of the lease he was relieved from liability to pay rent if and for so long as the premises were unable to be occupied consequent on the occurrence of an insured peril.[92]

1–145 (iii) *Liability to repair*. A tenant may also have an insurable interest by reason of his liability under the lease.[93] If he has covenanted to repair, he has an interest to the extent to which he may become liable on the covenant,[94] and if he has covenanted to insure he has an interest, because if he does not insure he will be liable for the loss as damages for breach of his

---

[86] *Castellain v. Preston* (1883) 11 Q.B.D. 380, 400; *Schaeffer v. Anchor Mutual*, 113 Iowa 652 (1901). A tenant's claim may well not be limited to the marketable value of his lease: see *Simpson v. Scottish Union Insurance* (1863) 1 H. & M. 618, 628. But possession alone does not confer an interest under Scots law: *Fehilly v. General Accident Fire and Life Ass. Corp. Ltd* 1982 S.C. 163; *Aberdeen Harbour Board v. Heating Enterprises Ltd* 1990 S.L.T. 416.

[87] *Re Wright and Pole* (1834) 1 Ad. & El. 621; *Menzies v. North British Ins. Co.* (1847) 9 D. 694.

[88] War Damage Act 1943 (6 & 7 Geo. 6, c. 21); Landlord and Tenant (War Damage) Acts 1939 and 1941 (2 & 3 Geo. 6, c. 72, and 4 & 5 Geo. 6, c. 41).

[89] *Marshall v. Schofield* (1882) 47 L.T. 406; *Matthey v. Curling* [1992] 2 A.C. 180; *Cricklewood Property v. Leighton* [1945] A.C. 221.

[90] *Duff v. Fleming* (1870) 8 M. 769; *Allan v. Markland* (1882) 10 R. 383; *Fehilly v. General Accident Fire and Life Ass. Corp. Ltd* 1982 S.C. 163, 169.

[91] [1986] 1 Q.B. 211.

[92] Reliance was placed, unusually, on the broader expectation test of insurable interest said to have been propounded by Lawrence J. in *Lucena v. Craufurd* (1806) 2 Bos. & Pul. (N.R.) 269, 302 but it is submitted that the decision is correct because the tenant still retained his legal estate and hence his right of occupation. Of course, as stated above, the measure of his interest would be comparatively small if he were claiming a share of the policy monies, but this was irrelevant on the facts as the landlord was obliged to insure and to reinstate with the policy monies. See *Glengate-KG Properties v. Norwich Union Fire Ins. Soc.* [1996] 1 Lloyd's Rep. 614, 624 *per* Auld L.J. and para. 1–120, *ante*.

[93] Bowen L.J. in *Castellain v. Preston* (1883) 11 Q.B.D. 380, 400.

[94] *Oliver v. Greene*, 3 Mass. 133 (1807); *Berry v. American Central*, 132 N.Y. 49 (1892); *Joyce v. Swann* (1864) 17 C.B.(N.S.) 84, 104.

covenant.[95] Where the lessees of a colliery, having covenanted to keep the premises in repair and to insure, insured "as lessees" on colliery plant "this to insure all their working interest", it was held that they had an interest to the full value and that the risk was sufficiently described.[96] Probably a lessee liable on a covenant to repair could insure generally on the property without specifying his interest unless the conditions of the policy expressly required the interest to be stated.

1–146 Lessor. The landlord has an insurable interest as a reversioner, and this is not diminished by the fact that the premises are not in his occupation and are let for a term of years. In addition, he is obliged to undertake repairs in the case of certain types of dwelling and lease by virtue of statutory regulations[97] and he may in such cases insure to the full value on that ground also. Wherever the landlord is liable for repair, his claim on the policy is not limited to the value of the reversion. Where the tenant is liable to repair, there is a risk that he may nonetheless be insolvent, and the landlord may effect his own insurance to the full value of the premises.[98] In such a case, however, the principle of subrogation may operate to enable the landlord's insurers to pursue the landlord's rights under the lease against the tenant.[99] Where the lessor has covenanted to insure the demised premises for their full reinstatement value and to lay out the insurance proceeds on reinstatement of the building, he has an insurable interest in the premises up to the full reinstatement cost.[1]

1–147 Mortgagor and mortgagee. A mortgagor of land has, as owner of the equity of redemption, an insurable interest to the full value, notwithstanding the mortgage. He may be hopelessly insolvent and have no prospect of ever redeeming the security, but so long as he has the equity of redemption the loss of the property means a reduction of his assets to the full value, and therefore he has interest to that extent.[2]

Even if a mortgagor has sold his equity of redemption, he has by reason of his personal covenant an interest to the extent of the debt charged upon the property because the loss of the property destroys the possibility of the debt

[95] *Heckman v. Isaac* (1862) 6 L.T. 383; *Bartlett v. Walter*, 13 Mass. 267 (1816); *Lawrence v. St Mark's Fire Ins.*, 43 Barb. 479 (N.Y., 1865); *Fehilly v. General Accident Fire & Life Ass. Corp.* 1982 S.C. 163; *Aberdeen Harbour Board v. Heating Enterprises Ltd* 1990 S.L.T. 416. A covenant to insure against loss or damage by fire with a named company or class of companies is a covenant to effect such a policy as was usual at the date of the lease or as might from time to time become usual during the currency of the lease. Prima facie, such a covenant does not oblige the covenantor to insure against war risks: *Enlayde Ltd v. Roberts* [1917] 1 Ch. 109; *Upjohn v. Hitchens* [1918] 2 K.B. 48. A covenant to insure in a named office "or in some other responsible insurance office to be approved by the lessor" does not confer any option on the lessee if the lessor withholds his approval, which he is entitled to do without giving any reason: *Tredegar v. Harwood* [1929] A.C. 72.

[96] *Imperial Fire v. Murray*, 73 Pa. 13 (1873).

[97] Landlord and Tenant Act 1985, s.11.

[98] *Hobbs v. Hannam* (1811) 3 Camp. 93; *Collingridge v. Royal Exchange Ass. Corp.* (1877) 3 Q.B.D. 173.

[99] *Darrell v. Tibbitts* (1880) 5 Q.B.D. 560; *Castellain v. Preston* (1883) 11 Q.B.D. 380, 406. But see para. 22–97, *post*.

[1] *Lonsdale & Thompson Ltd v. Black Arrow Group plc* [1993] Ch. 361, 368.

[2] *Smith v. Lascelles* (1788) 2 T.R. 187; *Smith v. Royal Insurance* (1867) 27 U.C.Q.B. 54; *Ins. Co. v. Stinson*, 103 U.S. 25 (1880).

being satisfied out of it without further recourse to him.[3] On the same principle, where an estate was mortgaged to A to secure a promissory note and A assigned the mortgage to B and indorsed the note to him, it was held that A still retained an insurable interest in the property by reason of his liability on the indorsement.[4]

The fact that the transfer of the property is *ex facie* absolute makes no difference to the mortgagor's interest if in substance the transaction is a mortgage and not a sale.[5]

1–148 Mortgagees, legal and equitable, have an interest in the mortgaged property to the amount of the debt secured on it,[6] and if a mortgagee has covenanted to insure, he has an interest to the full amount in respect of that liability. A mortgagee to whom a title to any property has been conveyed has probably an insurable interest to the full value of the property.[7] A mortgagee has no insurable interest in the rents and profits of the mortgaged property unless he is in possession.[8]

1–149 The insurance of a mortgagee's interest is not a mere guarantee of his debt, but an insurance of his security, and he is entitled to have his security maintained undiminished in value by reason of fire or other risks insured against, so that there may be no chance of his suffering loss in the event of his having recourse to his security.[9] Thus it was held in America that a mortgagee who insured as such on the mortgaged property could recover up to the full amount of his debt, notwithstanding that after the fire the damaged premises were still of sufficient value to satisfy his debt.[10] The mortgagee was entitled to say: "My security, although sufficient, is diminished and I have insured against such diminution."[11] This appears to be undoubtedly sound because property is always liable to unpredictable diminution in market value, and the mortgagee is entitled to have his margin of security maintained as a safeguard against the risk of possible depreciation.

1–150 The interest of a mortgagee is the possible loss which he as an individual may suffer from destruction of or damage to the property insured, and where there are several successive mortgagees they may, in the aggregate, recover more than sufficient to reinstate the premises. Thus, in

---

[3] *Hanover Fire v. Bohn*, 48 Neb. 743 (1868); *Springfield Fire and Marine v. Allen*, 34 N.Y. 389 (1871); *Pettigrew v. The Grand River Farmers' Mutual* (1877), 28 U.C.C.P. 70, 74.

[4] *Williams v. Roger Williams Insurance*, 107 Mass. 377 (1871).

[5] *Alston v. Campbell* (1779) 4 Bro.P.C. 476; *Hibbert v. Carter* (1787) 1 T.R. 745; *Hutchinson v. Wright* (1858) 25 Beav. 444.

[6] *Glover v. Black* (1763) 1 Wm. Bl. 396; *P. Samuel & Co. v. Dumas* [1923] 1 K.B. 592, 615; [1924] A.C., 431, 444; *Westminster Life and Fire Office v. Glasgow Provident Investment Soc.* (1888) 13 App.Cas. 699; *Burton v. Gore District Mutual Fire* (1865) 12 Grant (Ch.App.) 156; *Carpenter v. Providence Washington*, 41 U.S. (16 Pet.) 495 (1842); *Smith v. Columbia Ins. Co.*, 17 Pa. 253 (1851); *Provincial Ins. Co. of Canada v. Leduc* (1874) L.R. 6 P.C. 224, 244.

[7] *Irving v. Richardson* (1831) 2 B. & Ad. 193.

[8] *Westminster Fire Office v. Glasgow Provident Investment Soc.* (1888) 13 App.Cas. 699.

[9] *ibid.*

[10] *Kernochan v. New York Bowery*, 17 N.Y.App. 428, 441 (1858); *Excelsior Fire Ins. Co. v. Royal Ins. Co.*, 55 N.Y.App. 343 (1873). In *Matthewson v. Western Ass. Co.* (1859) 10 Low. Can.R. 8 the mortgagee was held unable to recover on a policy when the mortgagor had reinstated after a fire, since his security was not diminished, and this is no doubt correct.

[11] *Kennedy v. Boolarra Butter Factory Pty Ltd* [1953] V.L.R. 548, 554; *Royal Ins. Co. v. Mylius* (1926) 38 C.L.R. 477.

Westminster Fire v. Glasgow Provident,[12] the premises and site before the fire were sufficient to satisfy all the incumbrancers, who were insured in different offices to the amount of their several debts. On a fire occurring, the offices who insured the prior incumbrancers paid them an amount sufficient to reinstate the premises. These incumbrancers did not reinstate, but retained the insurance money, and the site was no longer of sufficient value to satisfy the remainder of the debts. It was held in the House of Lords on appeal from the Court of Session in Scotland that the postponed incumbrancers had an insurable interest and could recover the amount of their debt. In this case the total of the insurance moneys paid, although more than sufficient to reinstate the premises, was not more than the difference between the market value of the site and premises before the fire and their market value after the fire, and therefore the companies were not, in fact, called upon to pay more than the actual damage which they might have had to pay on a policy issued to an absolute owner where there was no clause entitling them to reinstate in lieu of paying damage. A sole mortgagee would equally have been entitled to recover the difference between the value of the site and premises before, and their value after, the loss. A sole mortgagee could never recover more than such difference in value, but successive mortgagees might possibly in the aggregate recover more.[13] If, for instance, the value of the site and premises before loss was not sufficient to satisfy both the prior and postponed mortgagees, postponed mortgagees would probably still have an insurable interest to the amount of their debt, because if prior mortgagees were paid off their security would then be available. By the fire they would lose their contingent security, and would therefore on general principle be entitled to recover the amount of their debt from the insurers, notwithstanding that the prior mortgagees had already been paid the full amount of the damage.

1–151 Pledgee. On a pledge of chattels, the pledgor parts with possession of them but retains his title therein.[14] The pledgee for his part obtains a possessory title to the chattels pledged so that he can sue in trespass or conversion if third parties interfere with his possession.[15] In addition, he has at common law a right of sale arising on default of payment by the pledgor at the stipulated time.[16] If this right is exercised, the pledgee must account to the pledgor for any surplus remaining after the proceeds of sale have gone to satisfy the debt owed.[17]

It follows that the pledgor retains an insurable interest to the full value of the goods pledged while he has a right to redeem them.[18] The pledgee clearly has an insurable interest to the extent of the debt owed to him, which represents his beneficial interest in the pledged chattels. He is also a person possessing the goods of another with an ultimate responsibility to return

---

[12] (1888) 13 App.Cas. 699.
[13] *Glasgow Provident Investment Society v. Westminster Fire Office* (1887) 14 R. 947, 964.
[14] *Franklin v. Neate* (1844) 13 M. & W. 481.
[15] The nature of his interest is outlined in *The Odessa, The Woolston* [1916] 1 A.C. 145, 158.
[16] *Re Hardwick, ex p. Hubbard* (1886) 17 Q.B.D. 690.
[17] *The Odessa* [1916] 1 A.C. 145, 159.
[18] *Heald v. Builders' Ins. Co.*, 111 Mass. 38 (1872); *Parsons v. Queen Ins. Co.* (1878) 29 U.C.C.P. 18.

them intact, and that liability would give him an interest to their full value. There seems no reason why he should not be considered as a "commercial trustee" of the pledged goods, with the ability to effect one insurance to the full value of the goods covering his own limited interest and the pledgor's also.[19]

1–152 If goods or chattels are mortgaged under a bill of sale, the mortgagee obtains, by contrast, not possession but the legal property in the goods.[20] He may accordingly insure the goods to their full value, since his interest is consonant with full legal ownership.[21] Any equitable charge on personal property which is valid as between grantor and grantee ought to give the grantee an insurable interest to the value of the debt owed, even if the charge be void as against other creditors.[22]

1–153 Creditor in property of debtor. Although a creditor who holds his debtor's property in security for his debt has an insurable interest in such property to the extent of the debt charged on it, he has no insurable interest in his debtor's property merely as such on the ground that the loss of it may diminish his chance of obtaining ultimate satisfaction of his debt.[23] That interest is too remote and too uncertain to make it insurable. A creditor must have a right to have his debt satisfied directly from the proceeds of his debtor's property before he is in a position to insure it.[24] Any legal or equitable lien or right to proceed *in rem* gives the creditor an interest.[25] Where a debtor's property has been seized in execution of a judgment debt his judgment creditor has an insurable interest in such property,[26] but judgment obtained against a debtor does not give the creditor an insurable interest in all the debtor's property which might be seized in execution.[27] In America it has been suggested that, where a debtor's property is insufficient, or barely sufficient, to satisfy a judgment creditor, the latter has an insurable interest in the whole of such property,[28] and it has been held that a creditor of an insolvent deceased has an insurable interest in the whole insolvent estate

---

[19] See the section below relating to commercial trusteeship, para. 1–179, *post*.

[20] *Re Hardwick, ex p. Hubbard* (1886) 17 Q.B.D. 690, 696, 698.

[21] The same considerations must apply to a mortgage of chattels effected by a transfer of a document of title such as a bill of lading or warehouseman's receipt, where it was intended to make the mortgagee the recipient of the general property in the goods: see *Sewell v. Burdick* (1884) 10 App.Cas. 74; *Sutherland v. Pratt* (1843) 11 M. & W. 296; *Todd v. Liverpool, London and Globe Ins. Co.* (1868) 18 U.C.C.P. 192; *Wilson v. Citizens' Ins. Co.* (1875) 19 Low. Can.Jur. 175.

[22] *Wilson v. Martin* (1856) 11 Exch. 684; *Davies v. Home Ins. Co.* (1866) 3 U.C.Err. App. 269; *Clark v. Scottish Imperial Fire Ins.* (1879) 4 S.C.R. 192; *Johnson v. Union Fire Ins. Co. of New Zealand* (1884) 10 Vict.L.R. 154.

[23] *Wilson v. Jones* (1867) L.R. 2 Ex; 139; *Moran, Galloway & Co. v. Uzielli* [1905] 2 K.B. 555; *Macaura v. Northern Ass. Co.* [1925] A.C. 619; *Buchanan v. Ocean Ins. Co.*, 6 Cowen 318 (N.Y., 1826); *Vancouver National Bank v. Land Union*, 153 Fed.Rep. 440 (1907); *Mollison v. Victoria* (1883) 2 N.Z.(S.C.) 177. Likewise a guarantor has no insurable interest in the debtor's property—*General Accident Fire & Life Ass. Co. v. Midland Bank* [1940] 2 K.B. 388, 401.

[24] *Stainbank v. Fenning* (1851) 11 C.B. 51; *Stainbank v. Shepard* (1853) 13 C.B. 418; *Macaura v. Northern Ass. Co.* [1925] A.C. 619.

[25] *Briggs v. Merchant Traders' Ass.* (1849) 13 Q.B. 167; *Moran, Galloway & Co. v. Uzielli* [1905] 2 K.B. 555; *Franklin Fire v. Coates*, 14 Md. 285 (1859).

[26] *Donnell v. Donnell*, 86 Me. 518 (1894); *International Trust v. Boardman*, 149 Mass. 158 (1889).

[27] *Grevemeyer v. Southern Mutual Fire*, 62 Pa. 340 (1849); *Light v. Countryman's Mutual Fire*, 169 Pa. 310 (1895).

[28] *Rohrbach v. Germania Fire*, 62 N.Y.App. 47 (1875).

because the creditor's right is no longer merely *in personam* but *in rem* against the deceased's whole estate.[29] There is no reason why a creditor should not insure against the debtor's insolvency caused by the destruction of the property in question,[30] or against the debtor's failure to pay.[31]

1–154 Contractor. Where a contractor undertakes work and his right to payment is dependent upon the completion of the work, he has an insurable interest in the subject-matter of the contract whether it be in his possession or not, because the destruction of the subject-matter would prevent him from earning his remuneration under the contract.[32] He has an insurable interest up to the value of the work done and materials expended, and on his expected profits if specifically insured. In general, where a contract is to supply a chattel or complete certain work for a price payable on completion, the contractor cannot recover any part of the contract price until completion.[33] If, however, the terms of the contract are such as to entitle the contractor to a *quantum meruit* at any time for the work which he has done and which accident prevents him from completing,[34] he will have no insurable interest except on anticipation of profits from future work in connection with the subject-matter of the contract. A printer who undertakes to print an edition of a book is by the custom of the printing trade not entitled to any remuneration until the whole edition contracted for has been completed.[35] A contractor has an insurable interest upon any property to the full extent of his charges for work done in relation to it if he has a lien upon the property for such charges.[36] A contractor in respect of a chattel may have an insurable interest as a bailee apart from his insurable interest as contractor.

1–155 Sub-contractors. It has been held in cases concerned with the right of an insurer to sue an insured sub-contractor in the name of a co-assured that each sub-contractor engaged under a building or engineering contract is entitled to insure the entire contract works for their full value, and to claim on the policy for damage to a part of the works which is neither his property nor at his risk. In *Petrofina (U.K.) Ltd v. Magnaload Ltd*[37] a sub-contractor who was one of several assureds under a contractor's all risks policy caused damage to the contract works. The insurers indemnified the employers for this damage and brought a subrogated claim for damages for negligence against the sub-contractor responsible, which contended that no claim was maintainable because it was fully insured under the policy in respect of the property damaged. The policy provided that "the insured" were covered "against loss of or damage to the insured property whilst at the contract site". The "insured property" included:

---

[29] *Rohrbach v. Germania Fire (supra)*; *Herkimer v. Rice*, 27 N.Y.App. 163 (1863); *Creed v. Sun Fire*, 101 Ala. 522 (1893). This is not so in English Law—see para. 1–121, *ante*.

[30] *Waterkeyn v. Eagle Star Ins. Co.* (1920) 5 Ll.L.R. 42, 43.

[31] *Anglo-Californian Bank v. London and Provincial Marine* (1904) 10 Com.Cas. 1.

[32] *Deepak Fertilisers & Petrochemicals v. I.C.I.* [1999] 1 Lloyd's Rep. 387, 399.

[33] *Sumpter v. Hedges* [1898] 1 Q.B. 673; *Appleby v. Myers* (1867) L.R. 2 C.P. 651; *Sinclair v. Bowles* (1829) 9 B. & C. 92; *Cook v. Jennings* (1797) 7 T.R. 381; *Metcalfe v. Britannia Iron Works* (1877) 2 Q.B.D. 423.

[34] *Menetone v. Athawes* (1764) 3 Burr. 1592; *Roberts v. Havelock* (1832) 3 B. & Ad. 404.

[35] *Gillet v. Mawman* (1808) 1 Taunt. 137, 140; *Adlard v. Booth* (1835) 7 C. & P. 108.

[36] *Ins. Co. v. Stinson*, 103 U.S. 25 (1880).

[37] [1984] 1 Q.B. 127.

"The works and temporary works erected ... in performance of the insured contract and the materials ... for use in connection therewith belonging to the insured or for which they are responsible...".

Lloyd J. held, first, that as a matter of construction of the policy, each of the insured was insured in respect of the entire contract works, including property belonging to any other of the insured or for which any other of the insured was responsible. This led him to the second question of whether the sub-contractor was entitled to recover the full value of all the property insured despite having an interest in only some of it, namely, the equipment owned by him and being used to perform his sub-contract. Applying the analogy of the bailee entitled to insure goods entrusted to him for their full value, holding the amount in excess of his own interest in trust for their owners, Lloyd J. held that the positions of the bailee and sub-contractor were sufficiently close to entitle the latter to insure the entire contract works and to recover the whole of the insured loss, holding the excess in trust for his co-assured.[38] The result is perhaps commercially convenient, but it is difficult to reconcile the grounds for the decision with earlier authorities. A bailee has a limited insurable interest in all the goods entrusted to him, rooted in his possessory title to them and also invariably in his contractual rights over them arising out of the contract of bailment.[39] These are classic sources of an insurable interest. The sub-contractor in the *Petrofina* case possessed a limited interest in a different sense, because it owned only its own equipment brought into the site to perform the sub-contract, but possessed no legal or equitable rights whatsoever in or over the contract works, so far as one may judge from the report. There was no valid root of insurable interest in the property for which it sought an indemnity. A possible explanation is that the insurers had waived the requirement of contractual insurable interest, which they were free to do because the Life Assurance Act 1774 did not apply to this indemnity insurance on goods.[40] The waiver could be said to have been a necessary implication from the construction of the policy as one insuring each of the assured, including all the sub-contractors, in respect of all the contract works, since no one sub-contractor could be expected to demonstrate a legal interest in the entire works.

1–156 In *Stone Vickers Ltd v. Appledore Ferguson Shipbuilders Ltd*[41] and *National Oilwell (U.K.) Ltd v. Davy Offshore Ltd*[42] the right of a sub-contractor to insure the entire contract works was extended to marine

---

[38] [1984] 1 Q.B. 127, 136. For the decisions on bailees see paras. 1–168 to 1–176, *post*.

[39] *Waters v. Monarch Life Ass. Co.* (1856) 5 E. & B. 870, 882, approved in *Maurice v. Goldsbrough Mort & Co.* [1939] A.C. 452, 464; *Robertson v. Hamilton* (1811) 14 East 522, 532. The bailee's ability to insure goods to their full value does not depend upon a potential liability to their owners for loss or damage—*Tomlinson (Hauliers) v. Hepburn* [1966] A.C. 451, 480–481; *L.N.W.R. v. Glyn* (1859) 1 E. & E. 652, 663–664. In *Petrofina* Lloyd J. recognised this—[1984] 1 Q.B. 127, 135—but he followed the authority of the Canadian Supreme Court in *Commonwealth Construction Co. v. Imperial Oil* (1976) 69 D.L.R. (3d) 558—although the Supreme Court seems to have thought that potential liability was critical—p. 562.

[40] [1984] 1 Q.B. 127, 136. See paras 1–16 and 1–40, *ante*.

[41] [1991] 2 Lloyd's Rep. 288 (supply of propeller to ship). An appeal succeeded on the different point that the supplier was not an assured [1992] 2 Lloyd's Rep. 578. The Court of Appeal did not address the present issue.

[42] [1993] 2 Lloyd's Rep. 582 ("Christmas tree" wellhead system for off-shore oil production facility). An appeal was heard in 1995 but the parties reached a compromise after the hearing and no judgments were delivered. The reasoning in these two cases was followed in *Hopewell Project Management Ltd v. Ewbank Preece Ltd* [1998] 1 Lloyd's Rep. 448, 455–456.

insurance cases in which the sub-contractors were suppliers of component parts to, respectively, a ship in course of construction and an off-shore oil production facility. In both cases it was held that the test for the existence of an insurable interest was whether the supplier might be adversely affected by the loss of or damage to the subject matter of the work by any of the perils insured against, and that this was satisfied if a defect in the component supplied by him might cause him to be liable for the loss or damage. That would in turn depend upon the size and function of the particular component. It is submitted that these decisions are also difficult to reconcile with established principles. First, the fact that a sub-contractor might suffer financial disadvantage if the contract works were to suffer loss or damage is not of itself a ground of insurable interest. It appears that the sub-contractors in question were unable to demonstrate that they possessed a legal or equitable interest in relation to the contract works. Nor could they show that the works were at their risk. The possibility of being held liable only for damage caused by their own employees would support an insurance against the risk of legal liability to the owners of the works but not an insurance of the works themselves. If the risk of becoming liable to the owner of property for negligently damaging it was a ground of insurable interest in property, cases in which the existence of an interest was denied should have been decided otherwise,[43] and it confuses the distinction between insurances on property, on the one hand, and product liability insurance on the other.[44]

1–157 Additional doubt is cast on the reasoning in the above decisions by the more recent decision of the Court of Appeal in *Deepak Fertilisers & Petrochemicals Corporation v. ICI Chemicals & Polymers Ltd.*[45] The litigation arose out of an explosion at a methanol production plant in India in October 1992. The plant had been built for Deepak between January 1988 and September 1991, and was commissioned in October 1991. Another party to the action, Davy McKee (London) Ltd ("Davy") provided technical and processing know-how to Deepak in connection with the construction and commissioning of the plant, the actual construction being performed by a third party. After the explosion Deepak claimed damages from Davy for

---

[43] *N. British & Mercantile Ins. Co. v. Moffat* (1871) L.R. 7 C.P. 25; *Macaura v. Northern Ass. Co.* [1925] A.C. 619.

[44] These decisions were concerned with denial of subrogated rights to insurers of parties engaged in building and engineering projects. Denying subrogated rights against such co-assureds would be better achieved either by the use of express waiver of subrogation clauses or by the implication into the construction contracts of terms that participants entitled to the benefit of the project insurance were not to be liable for damage to the project works caused by them and covered by the insurance. It is submitted that on close analysis the latter is the real ratio of the *Commonwealth Construction* case, see (1976) 69 D.L.R. (3d) 558, 561. It appears that the principle extends only to sub-contractors in the mainstream of the construction activity and not therefore either to a security company on the site—*Canadian Pacific Ltd v. Base Security Services (B.C.) Ltd* (1991) 77 D.L.R. (4th) 178 or to consultant engineers—*Hopewell v. Ewbank Preece* [1998] 1 Lloyd's Rep. 448. A test of insurable interest based on potential liability for property damage will lead to fine distinctions depending on the particular part of the contract works which are at risk from a particular sub-contractor's activities, and will not promote certainty and simplicity. The convenience in a supplier of goods to a project being able to claim for damage to contract works in which he has no direct involvement is not self-evident.

[45] [1999] 1 Lloyd's Rep. 387.

negligence. One of the defences raised by Davy was that the insurance arrangements in force disentitled Deepak from bringing its claim. The argument was that Davy was nominated as a co-insured sub-contractor under the all risks insurance policy taken out by Deepak to insure the plant, that the action was in reality a subrogated action brought for the benefit of Deepak's insurers, and that no claim could be brought against Davy as a co-assured entitled to be indemnified against loss or damage arising out of the explosion. The defence in turn raised the issue of whether Davy, as a sub-contractor providing services in connection with the construction of the plant, possessed an insurable interest in it at the time of the loss in October 1992.

1–158 In the Commercial Court Rix J. held that Davy possessed an insurable interest in the plant in October 1992 because it could potentially be held liable for causing damage thereto.[46] The Court of Appeal analysed the situation differently. While the plant was under construction and Davy were working on it, Davy did possess an insurable interest in it because, if it was damaged or destroyed by any of the perils insured against under the all risks policy, such as fire or flood, the opportunity to perform their retainer and earn their remuneration might be lost. In other words, they possessed a legal right to payment contingent upon the due completion of the project. But after it was completed they would suffer financial disadvantage from its damage or destruction only if that was caused by their own actionable breach of contractual or other legal duty. That was an appropriate subject-matter not of property insurance but rather of liability cover, and since the loss occurred after completion of the project and after Davy's work was finished, they were no longer a co-assured with a valid insurable interest in the plant. Accordingly the co-insurance provisions in their contract with Deepak afforded no defence to Deepak's claim.

1–159 It is submitted that the effect of the decision in *Deepak* is that the risk of being held liable for causing damage to the contract works does not of itself create a valid insurable interest for the purpose of an insurance of the project works. The sub-contractor named as a co-assured under the head contractor's or employer's insurance on the plant and construction needs to demonstrate a legal or equitable interest in the subject-matter or a legal right or obligation dependent upon its continued preservation. It is difficult to say whether the decisions in *Stone Vickers*, *National Oilwell* and *Hopewell Project Management* can still be supported on the basis of the judgment in *Deepak*. Most probably the decisions in the first two cases cannot be explained on that basis, whereas that in *Hopewell Project Management* and for that matter, *Petrofina (U.K.) v. Magnaload*[47] might possibly be, although the facts given in the reports of these cases do not permit a clear answer to be given.

(b) *Insurances Effected by the Assured on Behalf of Others*

1–160 Introductory. Complex and intricate problems have arisen concerning the extent to which a person who possesses either a limited interest

---

[46] [1998] 2 Lloyd's Rep. 139, 158–159.
[47] [1984] 1 Q.B. 127.

in property or no interest at all may effect a valid insurance on it for the benefit of someone else, and recover an indemnity to the full value of the property in the event of a loss. One reason for this has been the patchwork of statute law governing insurable interests in different types of insurance contracts. In addition, different rules govern insurances on goods effected on behalf of other persons by an assured having an insurable interest in them from those which apply when insurances on goods are effected by a nominal assured who has no insurable interest but acts as an agent. We consider insurances on real property first.

1–161 Real property. The question which has affected all discussion on this topic is whether the Life Assurance Act 1774 applies to insurances on buildings. Previous editions of this work have argued that it did, principally because of the wide wording of the Act, supported by a strong dictum in the Court of Appeal.[48] It was thought that buildings could not be within section 4 which excludes "ships, goods, or merchandises" from the ambit of the Act and that the references in section 1 to insurances on lives or "any other event or events whatsoever" and in section 2 to "any other event or events" were sufficiently wide to include an insurance against loss in the event of fire or other damage occurring to a building. The consequences were that section 2 prohibited the named insured with a limited interest in the property from recovering on behalf of any other person interested who was not named in the policy and it prevented the named insured with no interest from covering the interest of an undisclosed principal. Additionally section 3 appeared to prevent an insured with a limited interest from recovering an indemnity in excess of his interest for the benefit of another.

1–162 Doubts about this construction of the Act were, however, expressed in Commonwealth cases[49] and by commentators.[50] In *Davjoyda Estates Ltd v. National Insurance Co. of New Zealand*[51] an alternative construction was suggested whereby section 2 applied generally only where the named insured himself had no interest in the property and contracted solely for the benefit of another. If he had an interest, so that section 1 and the aim of the Act to strike down gambling policies were satisfied, there was no need to name the other parties interested in the property. In other cases the possibility of the Act applying to realty was discreetly circumvented[52] or simply ignored.[53] Now in *Siu (Yin Kwan) v. Eastern Insurance Co. Ltd*[54] the

---

[48] *Re King* [1963] Ch. 459, 485 *per* Lord Denning M.R. Earlier the point was left open in *Portavon Cinema v. Price* [1939] 4 All E.R. 601.

[49] e.g. *British Traders' Insurance Co. v. Monson* (1964) 111 C.L.R. 86, 103 *per* Menzies J. The question in that case whether the tenant had insured on behalf of the lessor as undisclosed principal was resolved against the lessor on the ground of the absence of intention on the part of the tenant to cover the lessor's interest, and not by reference to the 1774 Act.

[50] J. N. Quar 1971 S.L.T. (News) 141; Halsbury's *Laws*, (4th ed., 1978) Vol. 25, p. 328. *Ivamy, Fire and Motor Insurance* (4th ed.) p. 184.

[51] (1967) 65 S.R. (N.S.W.) 381, 428, *per* Manning J.

[52] *Petrofina (U.K.) Ltd v. Magnaload Ltd* [1984] Q.B. 127, 136.

[53] *Mumford Hotels Ltd v. Wheler* [1964] Ch. 117; *Lonsdale & Thompson Ltd v. Black Arrow Group plc* [1993] Ch. 361; *National Oilwell Ltd v. Davy Offshore Ltd* [1993] 2 Lloyd's Rep. 582. The Canadian courts ignored the possibility of the Act's application to policies on buildings in *Keefer v. Phoenix Insurance Co.* (1898) 29 Ont. R. 394 and *Caldwell v. Stadacona Fire & Life Ins. Co.* (1883) 11 S.C.R. 212. See also the unreported decision of the High Court of Ireland in *Church General Insurance Co. v. Connolly*, 7th May 1981, discussed (by Birds) in (1983) 5 Dublin University Law. Jo. at p. 291.

[54] [1994] 2 A.C. 199.

Privy Council has held, approving dicta of Kerr L.J. in *Mark Rowlands Ltd v. Berni Inns Ltd*,[55] that the 1774 Act was not intended to apply, and does not apply, to indemnity insurance of any kind, but only to insurances which provide for the payment of a specified sum upon the happening of an insured event. The earlier dicta of Lord Denning M.R. to the contrary were disapproved.[56] While technically it is still open to an English court to take a different view, it is realistic to conclude that all insurances on buildings and realty generally are outside the scope of the Act so long as they have the character of indemnity insurance.[57]

1–163 The insurable interest, however, of a person insuring property is, as we have seen, not necessarily limited to the actuarial value of his interest as a marketable asset.[58] Possession or legal title alone may give him an insurable interest to the full value of the property, and if any direct loss or legal liability may fall upon him as the result of the damage to, or destruction of, the property from any cause, he has an insurable interest to the amount of such possible loss or liability. In *Lonsdale & Thompson Ltd v. Black Arrow Group plc*[59] the lessor of demised property covenanted with the tenant to insure it for its full reinstatement value and in the event of damage or destruction by any insured risk to ensure that the insurance monies were laid out in reinstating it. The lessor concluded a contract for sale of the property. Before completion the property was destroyed by fire, but the sale proceeded and the lessor received the full price for it. The tenant, who was not a co-assured, served notice under section 83 of the Fire Prevention (Metropolis) Act 1774 requiring the insurers to discharge their full liability to the lessor by paying for reinstatement of the property, but the insurers refused on the ground that the lessor was completely indemnified for the loss to its personal interest. It was held that the lessor had insurable interest for the full reinstatement value of the property by virtue of its insurance obligation, and was entitled to recover the cost of reinstatement from the insurers. The fact that the lessor was obliged by the lease to apply the insurance proceeds for the benefit of the tenant meant that the lessor was not recovering an indemnity for itself in excess of its own loss.[60]

1–164 Even where the assured's interest in a house or other building would not otherwise be sufficient to entitle him to insure or recover the full value thereof, the Fires Prevention (Metropolis) Act 1774,[61] imposes upon

---

[55] [1986] 1 Q.B. 211, 227.

[56] In *Re King* [1963] Ch. 459, 485.

[57] In particular the judgments in *Hodson v. Observer Life Assurance Society* (1857) 8 E. & B. 40 and *Williams v. Baltic Insurance Association of London* [1924] 2 K.B. 282 were not cited to the Privy Council. The arguments to the contrary are rehearsed in *Birds' Modern Insurance Law* (5th ed., 2001), pp. 47–50.

[58] *Castellain v. Preston* (1883) 11 Q.B.D. 380–401; *Simpson v. Scottish Union Insurance Co.* (1863) 1 H. & M. 618, 623; *Kennedy v. Boolarra Butter Factory Pty Ltd* [1953] V.L.R. 548, 552; *Royal Insurance Co. v. Mylius* (1926) 38 C.L.R. 477.

[59] [1993] Ch. 361.

[60] It had already been held in other jurisdictions that an assured can recover the full value of real property destroyed by fire and hold the proceeds for other persons interested in as much as there remained a surplus to his own indemnity; see *e.g. Welsh v. London Assurance* 151 Pa. 607 (1892); *Keefer v. Phoenix Assurance Co.* (1898) 29 Ont. R. 394; *Howes v. Dominion Fire Ins. Co.* (1883) 8 Ont. A.R. 644. The suggestion in *British Traders Insurance Co. v. Monson* (1964) 111 C.L.R. 86, that this offended against the indemnity principle, does not represent English law—see note 76 on p. 66 of the 8th edition of this work.

[61] 14 Geo. 3, c. 78, s.83.

every person who insures house property a statutory liability which apparently justifies him in insuring it to its full value no matter how small his insurable interest apart from such liability would have been. The statute enacts that where houses or other buildings are insured and a loss arises, the company insuring shall, on the request of any person interested therein, cause the insurance money to be applied in reinstatement instead of paying it to the assured. The assured who has a limited interest is thus placed in this position: if he insures only to such amount as would if payment were made in cash give him an indemnity in respect of the value of his interest at stake, he will not in fact obtain an indemnity if other persons interested require the insurance money to be applied in partial reinstatement. He can only secure a certain indemnity to himself by insuring up to the full value of the property, and he has therefore an insurable interest up to that amount.[62] If reinstatement is claimed by the company or is insisted on by some third party interested, the company will then be liable to reinstate the property up to the full amount of the insurance. On the other hand, if the company elects to pay in cash and no demand is made by any third party for reinstatement, the company may probably refuse to pay more than the value of the assured's insurable interest calculated independently of the peculiar interest given by the statute.[63] The doubt which was at one time expressed whether section 83 of the Fires Prevention (Metropolis) Act 1774 applies to insurances on premises outside the area of the Bills of Mortality in London has been resolved in the affirmative.[64]

1–165 Mortgagee insuring for mortgagor. A mortgagee of land has, by reason of his interest in the property and the commercial sense of his position, the right to insure it for its full value for the benefit of the mortgagor. In the event of loss he holds the insurance proceeds in excess of his own interest on trust for the mortgagor.[65] Since the Life Assurance Act 1774 has been held to have no application to indemnity insurance,[66] it is not necessary in such case to name the mortgagor as a person for whose benefit the insurance is taken out. Whether the policy covers the interests of both parties is a question of construction,[67] and this is so whether or not they are both named. So where a mortgagee who had covenanted to insure insured in his own name "as mortgagee against all loss or damage not exceeding $6,000 as shall happen by fire to the property insured", it was held by the Supreme Court of New York that the terms of the contract whereby the assured was insured "as mortgagee" limited the insurance to an insurance of the mortgagee's security, and that he was not insured in respect of his liability on the covenant to insure.[68]

If both mortgagor and mortgagee are named in a policy, it is a question of

[62] *Andrews v. Patriotic Ins. Co. No. 2* (1886) 18 L.R.Ir. 355, 356. The right of the insurers to reduce their ultimate liability by subrogation is considered in Ch. 22, *post.*
[63] The explanation of the rights of an assured with a limited interest to demand reinstatement given in the corresponding paragraph of the 5th ed. of this work was approved by the High Court of Australia in *British Traders' Ins. Co. v. Monson* (1964) 111 C.L.R. 86.
[64] See para. 21–16, *post.*
[65] *Tomlinson (Hauliers) Ltd v. Hepburn* [1966] A.C. 451, 480; *Petrofina (U.K.) Ltd v. Magnaload Ltd* [1984] Q.B. 127, 136.
[66] See paras 1–161—1–162, *ante.*
[67] *Nichols v. Scottish Union & National Ins. Co.* (1885) 2 T.L.R. 190, reported in more detail in (1885) 14 R. (Ct. Sess.) 1094.
[68] *Xernochan v. New York Bowery Ins. Co.* 17 N.Y.App. 428 (1858).

construction whether the insurance is on behalf of one only or of both. The distinction may be important, not only because no more can be recovered than the amount of the interest of the person or persons on whose behalf the insurance is made, but because the insurers may have a defence against one which would not be available against the other. Thus, where a mortgagee has insured, if he insured on his own behalf only, he could not recover on the policy after repayment of the debt and reconveyance of the property, but if he insured on behalf of both he could still recover on behalf of the mortgagor. Where A, a mortgagee, effected an insurance on the mortgaged property "owned by B and now insured to cover a mortgage on the said property", it was held that the mortgagee insured on his own behalf alone and that the mortgagor could take no benefit.[69]

1–166 Mortgagor insuring for mortgagee. An insurance effected by a mortgagor may likewise enure for the benefit of a mortgagee even though he is not named either as a party or a person for whose benefit it is made. In *Garden v. Ingram*[70] the lessee of a property took out an insurance upon it in the joint names of lessor and lessee, as he had covenanted to do. It was further agreed between them that the insurance monies were to be used in reinstatement of the property. The lessee then mortgaged his interest in the property. Although the insurance policy was neither assigned to the mortgagee nor expressly mentioned in the mortgage deed, and the mortgagee was not referred to as a loss payee, the court was of the opinion that the mortgage had the effect of conferring the benefit of the insurance upon the mortgagee.

1–167 Where a mortgagor's policy is made payable to the mortgagee in case of loss, it is a question of construction whether the mortgagee is entitled to sue on it as an independent principal.[71] The American cases show a distinction between the "open" mortgagee clause—"loss payable to X (mortgagee) as interest may appear", and the "standard" clause—"not to be invalidated by any act or neglect of the mortgagor ... nor by any foreclosure or other proceedings or notice of sale of the property, nor by any change in the title of ownership of the property, nor by the occupation of the premises for purposes more hazardous than are permitted by the policy."[72] Where the "standard" clause has been used, the mortgagee has recovered notwithstanding lack of insurable interest and breach of warranty on the part of the mortgagor,[73] or misrepresentation by the mortgagor inducing the issue of the policy,[74] whereas under the "open" clause the mortgagee has been defeated by the arson of the mortgagor[75] and by the action of the mortgagor in recovering damages for the fire from the tortfeasor and thus depriving the insurers of their right of subrogation.[76]

[69] *Smith v. Columbia Ins. Co.* 17 Pa. 253 (1851).
[70] (1852) 23 L.J. Ch. 478.
[71] *Aetna Ins. Co. v. Kennedy* 301 U.S. 389 (1936).
[72] See generally, Appleman, *Insurance Law and Practice* (1981), Vol. 5A, para. 3401.
[73] *Goldstein v. National Liberty Ins. Co. of America*, 175 N.E. 359 (N.Y.C.A. 1931).
[74] *Fayetteville Building and Loan Association v. Mutual Fire Ins. Co. of W. Virginia*, 141 S.E. 634 (W.Va.Sup.Ct. 1928).
[75] *Whitney National Bank of New Orleans v. State Farm Fire and Casualty Co.* 518 F. Supp. 359 (U.S.D.C. 1981); compare *Rent-a-Car Co. v. Globe and Rutgers Fire* 148 A. 252 (Md. C.A. 1930).
[76] *Conard v. Moreland* 298 N.W. 628 (Iowa Sup.Ct. 1941). See the discussion in paras. 17–33 to 17–34 of the chapter on non-disclosure, *post.*

1–168 Goods: introductory. Insurance on personal chattels or goods rests on quite a different footing as regards the right of the limited owner to insure and recover on any interest other than his own. The Life Assurance Act 1774 does not apply,[77] and therefore the amount insurable is not limited by statute to the amount or value of the assured's personal interest. Further, as there is no obligation to insert in the policy the name or names of all persons on whose behalf the insurance is made, the nominal assured can insure not only on his own behalf but either wholly or partially on behalf of other persons interested in the goods. The Gaming Act 1845,[78] which prohibits all contracts made by way of gaming and wagering, is the only statute which applies to an insurance on goods against risks other than marine risks. Since the principles of insurable interest which are applicable are substantially the same as those which are applicable to marine insurance policies under the Marine Insurance Act 1745[79] which prohibited the making of policies of sea insurance by way of gaming or wagering, reference may be made to cases concerning marine insurances decided before the passing of the Marine Insurance Act 1906.[80]

1–169 Right to insure goods to full value. Any person with a limited interest in goods who is concerned in their safety and not merely in the preservation of his own personal interest in them, such as a bailee (who, although not an insurer of the goods entrusted to him, is ordinarily responsible to their owner for diligence in their custody) may insure such goods to their full value, irrespective of the amount of his own interest. In the event of a loss, he may then recover the full value of the goods from the insurers, and he will be a commercial trustee for the owners, or other parties interested, of all moneys remaining after he has been indemnified for his own personal loss, if any. Since he does not, in the final result, benefit beyond the extent of his own personal interest, the principle of indemnity is not contravened. Moreover, the policy is not rendered void by the Gaming Act 1845 because the assured has an interest in the subject-matter of the insurance, and he is not intending to gamble on the interest of others, but rather to effect an insurance on the goods in a commercially convenient and sensible manner.

1–170 The position is well illustrated by the leading case of *Waters v. Monarch Fire and Life Assurance Co.*,[81] which has been approved frequently in subsequent decisions. The plaintiffs were wharfingers and warehouse men, and they effected a policy of insurance against fire with the defendants, covering, *inter alia*, not only their own goods, but also "goods in trust or on commission" in their warehouse. The warehouse and everything in it was consumed by fire, and the defendants refused to pay to the plaintiffs more than the value of their own goods and the amount of their lien on their customers' goods for cartage and warehouse rent. The plaintiffs sued for the balance of the full value of all the goods, and it was held that they could recover. "Goods in trust" meant goods entrusted to them, and not goods held in trust in the strict technical sense of a trust enforceable by subpoena in

[77] 14 Geo. 3, c. 48, s.4; and see para. 1–27 *ante*.
[78] 8 & 9 Vict. c. 109.
[79] 19 Geo. 2, c. 37.
[80] Edw. 7, c. 41.
[81] (1856) 5 E. & B. 870.

Chancery. The customers' goods in the warehouse were accordingly covered by the policy, and it did not matter that the plaintiff's customers were ignorant of the insurance because ratification of the insurance by them was unnecessary. No statute or rule of law prevented the plaintiffs from recovering the full value of the insured goods, and they were entitled to apply the proceeds to cover their own personal interest, after which they would be trustees to the owners of the goods for the excess.[82]

1–171 It is obviously a matter of commercial importance to any person entrusted with the care of goods to be able in the event of loss to hand over their full value to the owner and so avoid any question of his own liability in respect of negligence or otherwise. Far from being a wager on the loss of the goods, such an insurance simply places the assured in an advantageous position *vis-à-vis* the owner of the goods in the event of a loss. If he were not able to insure for the full value, it would necessitate two or more insurances being effected on the same goods, so that insurers would receive several premiums in respect of what was to them the same risk.[83] For these reasons the courts have been prepared to uphold a doctrine which is, in substance, an exception to the principle of the English law of contract that the parties to a contract cannot confer enforceable rights under it on a third party.[84]

1–172 Cases in which the rule applies. The rule applies when the assured has taken out a policy on goods rather than on his personal liability to their owners.[85] Formerly it was essential that the insurance was on goods in order that the Life Assurance Act 1774 should not apply.[86] The distinction between a liability policy and one on goods has sometimes caused difficulties.[87] In *Tomlinson v. Hepburn*,[88] the plaintiffs were road hauliers and carriers who had effected a Lloyd's "goods in transit" policy to cover tobacco and cigarette consignments belonging to a customer. The policy was effected on their own behalf, naming themselves as the assured. A claim was brought in respect of the theft of a consignment of cigarettes during transit, and the insurers contended that it was not a policy on goods, but was rather one insuring the plaintiffs' own personal liability. This contention failed because, although the printed part of the Lloyd's "Form J Goods in Transit" policy did not appear to indicate that the insurance was on the property in the goods, there were typewritten insertions relating to such things as deterioration and loss of market which were apt for a policy on goods and inapt for a policy on the legal liability of the assured.[89] Where there is a policy on "goods" it seems that the courts will view it as one not confined to the personal liability of persons with a limited interest, such as carriers, unless precise words are employed to make the limitation clear.[90]

[82] (1856) 5 E. & B. 870, 881. It is more correct to say that the insurance proceeds are impressed with an equitable charge in favour of the bailor—see para. 20–26, *post.*

[83] *L.N.W.R. v. Glyn* (1859) 1 E. & E. 652, 661; *Ebsworth v. Alliance Marine Ins. Co.* (1873) L.R. 8 C.P. 596, 616–617; *Tomlinson v. Hepburn* [1966] A.C. 451, 481.

[84] *Tomlinson v. Hepburn* [1966] A.C. 451, 470–471.

[85] *Tomlinson (Hauliers) v. Hepburn* [1966] A.C. 451, 468, 474.

[86] Life Assurance Act 1774, s.4. and see para. 1–27, *ante.*

[87] See 17 Halsbury's *Statutes* (3rd ed.), pp. 828–829, and *Petrofina (U.K.) Ltd v. Magnaload Ltd* [1984] 1 Q.B. 127 at 134 and 136.

[88] [1966] A.C. 451.

[89] [1966] A.C. 451, 472, 474.

[90] [1966] A.C. 451, 475; *L.N.W.R. v. Glyn* (1859) 1 E. & E. 652, 663.

1–173 It is further essential that the assured should have an insurable interest (though limited) in the goods. Some of the classes of persons having a limited insurable interest in goods have already been considered above[91] but it is appropriate to summarise the different ways in which the assured may come to have an interest in the safety of the goods.

1–174 (i) *Possession with responsibility.* Possession by the assured of goods for which he is in some degree responsible in law grounds a personal interest to the extent of that liability.[92] This is the usual interest of all types of bailees, whether for reward or otherwise. The ordinary duty owed by a bailee at common law in the absence of special liabilities is, generally speaking, to exercise reasonable care to keep the bailed goods safe.[93] Though he has no strict or absolute responsibility for the safety of goods committed to his charge,[94] and in the absence of express terms to the contrary is liable only for loss or damage which may be caused by the negligence or wilful conduct of himself or his servants,[95] the risk of incurring such liability is real enough to give him an insurable interest. It would still be sufficient if the grounds of liability were restricted by special contractual terms or total liability were limited to a particular sum, although in the latter event he could not recover the full value of the goods in relation to his own personal interest.

1–175 (ii) *Responsibility of carrier.* The carrier's liability at law is some what complicated by the special liabilities attaching to those who are common carriers and by the operation of statutory provisions relating to different types of carriage.[96] As in the case of any person who is entrusted with goods on behalf of the owner, and is in possession of them, the carrier has an insurable interest to their full value in relation to his own personal liability to their owner, if there is any risk of his being liable to that extent.[97] If his liability is limited to a set figure under the contract of carriage, his liability cannot of itself ground a personal insurable interest in excess of that figure,[98] but it nevertheless suffices for the purpose now under discussion.

1–176 (iii) *Beneficial interest in the goods.* When a person is concerned with the safety of goods because the goods constitute a security for payment due to him, he has a limited interest in them to the extent of the sum owed. The most common example is that of a person entrusted with goods for any purpose, who has a lien or charge on them for advances made to the owner, or for work done or services rendered in relation to the goods.[99] This entitles him to insure the goods in his own name and for his own benefit under the description of goods which are his property, so that, in the event of loss by

---

[91] See, *e.g.* paras. 1–135 to 1–139; 1–154 to 1–159.
[92] *Boehm v. Bell* (1799) 8 T.R. 154; *Robertson v. Hamilton* (1811) 14 East 522, 527; *Petrofina (U.K.) Ltd v. Magnaload Ltd* [1984] 1 Q.B. 127, 135.
[93] See *Chitty on Contracts* (28th ed., 1999), Vol. 2, paras 33–042 to 33–046.
[94] *Garside v. Trent Nav. Co.* (1792) 4 T.R. 581; *Chapman v. G.W.R.* (1880) 5 Q.B.D. 278.
[95] *Thomas v. Day* (1803) 4 Esp. 262.
[96] As to who is a common carrier, and his liabilities of carriers in general, see *Chitty on Contracts* (28th ed., 1999) Vol. 2, paras 36–007 to 36–016.
[97] *Boehm v. Bell* (1799) 8 T.R. 154; *Robertson v. Hamilton* (1811) 14 East 522.
[98] *L.N.W.R. v. Glyn* (1859) 1 E. & E. 652 (where the assured carrier might have relied upon the Carriers Act 1830 to limit his liability to the owner) would have gone differently if his intention had been only to insure his own liability, rather than the goods themselves.
[99] *Crowley v. Cohen* (1832) 3 B. & Ad. 478; *Dixon v. Whitworth* (1879) 4 C.P.D. 371, 375.

perils insured against he can indemnify himself to the extent of his lien, but cannot recover beyond his own proprietary and beneficial interests.[1] Likewise a consignee of goods who has made an advance to the consignor by way of accepting a bill drawn on him and payable against shipping documents has an insurable interest in the goods consigned to him to the extent of his advance,[2] representing his own personal beneficial interest.

1–177 (iv) *Obligation to insure.* A person entrusted with goods who is obliged to insure them on behalf of and for the benefit of their owner has on that ground alone an insurable interest to the full value of the goods, because, if he failed to effect insurance, he would be liable in damages to the owner for breach of contract.[3] An obligation to insure which is not grounded on some proprietary or possessory interest in the goods is insufficient to constitute an insurable interest.[4]

1–178 (v) *Commercial convenience on construction sites.* In *Petrofina (U.K.) Ltd v. Magnaload Ltd*[5] the head contractor and sub-contractors on a refinery construction project were named co-assureds on a contractor's all risks policy which covered, *inter alia*, the contract works against loss or damage. It was held that a sub-contractor with a limited interest in part of the contract works possessed an insurable interest in all the contract works to their full value, and could recover a full indemnity for loss or damage, being accountable to the other co-assureds for the insurance proceeds received in excess of his own interest. The court relied upon the bailee cases by way of analogy, although it was accepted that a sub-contractor had no possessory interest in every part of the works and had not agreed to be responsible for them. The decision was based on commercial convenience. It is submitted elsewhere in this chapter[6] that there are considerable difficulties in reconciling this extension of insurable interest with earlier authorities. It is unclear now when the principle will be applied to property in other collaborative ventures.

1–179 Intention to cover other interests than that of the assured. It is essential, in order that a policy on goods effected by one with a limited interest in them should be held to cover the interests of other persons as well as his own, that it should have been the intention of the assured to cover their interests. This question has been discussed principally in connection with policies effected by a commercial trustee,[7] which afford an indemnity to the owner of the goods as well as to the warehouseman, consignee or wharfinger, as the case may be, only if it was intended to cover the proprietary interest of the owner as well as the limited interest of the nominal assured.

---

[1] *L.N.W.R. v. Glyn* (1859) 1 E. & E. 652.
[2] *Ebsworth v. Alliance Marine Ins. Co.* (1873) L.R. 8 C.P. 596. All the court were in agreement on this point, but were divided on the further question whether the consignee could insure the goods to their full value and recover in full from the insurers under the doctrine in *Waters v. Monarch Fire and Life Ass. Co.* (1856) 5 E. & B. 870.
[3] *Maurice v. Goldsbrough, Mort & Co.* [1939] A.C. 452, 462.
[4] *Prudential Staff Union v. Hall* [1947] K.B. 685, 689.
[5] [1984] 1 Q.B. 127.
[6] See para. 1–154, *ante.*
[7] This expression is a convenient description of any bailee to whom goods are entrusted for safe keeping, and derives from the references to trusteeship made by Lord Campbell C.J. in *Waters v. Monarch Fire and Life Assurance Co.* (1856) 5 E. & B. 870. The expression is also current elsewhere: *Johnson v. Union Fire Ins. Co. of New Zealand* (1884) 10 Vict.L.R. 154, 161.

1–180 In *Tomlinson v. Hepburn*,[8] the facts of which have been outlined above, the House of Lords held that the issue of what interests the assured intended to cover under the policy must be determined by construction of the policy itself. It was not necessary that evidence should be called to prove the subjective intention of the assured to cover interest other than his own[9] and the mistaken view that proof of such intention was necessary had resulted from confusing cases where policies on goods had been effected by persons having a limited interest with cases where policies were taken out by persons themselves having no interest at all.[10]

This is not to say, however, that other evidence of intention would in every case be irrelevant or inadmissible. If the insurers wish to disprove the prima facie conclusion to be drawn from the construction of the policy that the assured intended to cover the insurable interests of other persons, they may call evidence to prove that the assured was in fact intending to gamble on those interests, so that *quoad* those interests the insurance was a gaming transaction[11] and *pro tanto* void.[12]

1–181 "Goods his own in trust or on commission." The customary way of expressing the intention of a commercial trustee to insure beyond his own personal interest is to describe the subject-matter of the insurance as being "goods his own in trust or on commission". Where these words appear, although the policy appears in all other respects to be one effected by the commercial trustee on his own behalf and on his own insurable interest, and not as agent for the owner, nonetheless the rule in *Waters v. Monarch Fire and Life Assurance Co.*[13] will apply, and the assured will be entitled to recover the full value of the goods in case of loss.

1–182 "Goods held in trust for which they are responsible." In *North British and Mercantile Insurance Co. v. Moffat*[14] the assured were wholesale tea merchants who purchased and resold parcels of tea lying in bonded warehouses where they had been deposited by the importer. They took out two insurances to cover:

> "merchandise (jute, petroleum and its products excepted) the assured's own, in trust or on commission for which they are responsible, in or on all or any of the warehouses, vaults, cellars, sheds ... at"

certain wharves described in the policies. A fire occurred at one of these warehouses, so that certain chests of tea were consumed or damaged. On the assured claiming to be paid the full value of the teas in question, the insurers contended that they were not covered by the terms of the policy. The Court of Common Pleas held that the teas were not covered by the policy, because

---

[8] [1966] A.C. 451.

[9] [1966] A.C. 451, 470, 473–474, 480.

[10] [1966] A.C. 451, 469, 478–480. *Irving v. Richardson* (1831) 2 B. & Ad. 193 must be explained as a case in which the mortgagee of the insured ship had effected the insurance not as a person having a limited beneficial interest, but as an agent insuring on behalf of another. For this type of situation, see para. 1–189, *post.*

[11] [1966] A.C. 451, 482. Certain dicta of Bowen L.J. in *Castellain v. Preston* (1883) 11 Q.B.D. 380, 397–399, which might be considered authority for the proposition that evidence of intention is relevant, are, it seems, only making this point.

[12] *Rourke v. Short* (1856) 5 E. & B. 904, 912.

[13] (1856) 5 E. & B. 870. This was the wording construed in that case.

[14] (1871) L.R. 7 C.P. 25 followed in *Engel v. Lancashire and General Assurance* (1925) 41 T.L.R. 408.

effect had to be given to the words "for which they are responsible". On the facts it was found that the teas had been resold by the assured before the fire occurred, and that the purchase moneys had been paid. The property in the teas had passed to the purchasers, as had the risk. Consequently the assured no longer had any responsibility to the purchasers in respect of the teas in the case of fire, and the case was distinguishable from *Waters v. Monarch Fire and Life Assurance Co.*[15] where the assured's responsibility was not mentioned. By limiting the cover to goods for which the assured were responsible, the insurers had indicated that they did not intend to cover the proprietary interests of other persons in the goods insured.[16]

1–183 A modification of this formula is to be found in other words sometimes used, *viz.* "for which they may be liable in the event of loss or damage by fire" which words would seem to cover all goods in their possession (except in the rare cases where the terms of the contract relieve a person entrusted with the goods from liability for loss in any circumstances) and therefore to extend the cover to the owner's proprietary interest in any case where the assured might have been but in fact is not liable to the owner in respect of the loss or damage.[17]

1–184 Insurance simpliciter "on goods". Apart from the effect of any special condition in the policy affecting the matter, an insurance "on goods" would not without more cover interests beyond those of a commercial trustee named in the policy. It would be taken to cover his whole personal insurable interest in the goods, including both his beneficial interest in respect of his lien, if any, and his liability to the owner of the goods arising from his responsibility for their safety. It would operate to idemnify him from all personal loss or liability, but it would not cover the proprietary interest of the owner of the goods.[18] The fact that the policy names the commercial trustee as the assured and describes the property insured as the property of a named third party may be a neutral indication taken on its own, but the nature of the conditions set out in the policy may show that it was intended to insure the proprietary interest of the named third party, regardless of the absence of any mention of trusteeship.[19]

1–185 Other expressions of interest might suffice without any words of trust. Thus in *Ebsworth v. Alliance Marine Insurance Co.*[20] consignees of cotton shipped from India, who had made an advance to the consignors by

---

[15] (1856) 5 E. & B. 870.

[16] If however, the insurers chose to pay over the full value to the assured, it seems that cover expressed in this form would give the owner of the goods an equitable interest in the proceeds as *cestui que trust*, thus obtaining a preferential claim on the moneys in the event of the assured's bankruptcy: *Cochran v. Leckie's Trustee* (1906) 8 F. (Ct. of Sess.) 975.

[17] *Maurice v. Goldsbrough, Mort & Co.* [1939] A.C. 452.

[18] *L.N.W.R. v. Glyn* (1859) 1 E. & E. 652; *Globe and Rutgers Fire Ins. Co. v. U.S.*, 202 F. 2d 696 (1953).

[19] *Tomlinson v. Hepburn* [1966] A.C. 451, 468, 472, 474.

[20] (1873) L.R. 8 C.P. 596.

way of acceptance of a bill drawn on them and payable against shipping documents, insured the cotton in their own name and, in a form traditional in marine policies, "as well in their own names as for and in the name or names of all and every person to whom the same doth may or shall appertain in part or at all". The cotton being lost at sea, the consignees claimed in their own names and on a declaration of their own interest alone, the full value of the cotton. In the Court of Common Pleas Bovill C.J. and Denman J. agreed that the policy disclosed an intention on the part of the assured to cover the interest of the consignor as well, and that they could accordingly recover the full value of the goods lost, holding the residue of the proceeds on the policy in trust for the consignors. Brett and Keating JJ. did not dissent on this point, but held that, intention apart, it would offend the principle of indemnity if the assured were permitted to recover more than an indemnity for their own personal loss.[21]

1–186 Fire policies issued in respect of commercial risks or to cover goods employed in commerce usually contain a condition to the effect that "goods held in trust or on commission must be insured as such otherwise the policy will not extend to them". That condition has been construed as meaning that if the assured intends to insure beyond his own personal interest and to cover the proprietary interest of the owner in goods entrusted to him, they must be so described. If when a policy contains that condition a carrier or other person entrusted with the goods of others insures simply "on goods" or "on his own goods" his own proprietary interest in respect of any lien which he has on such goods will be covered notwithstanding the condition, but neither his liability to the owner in respect of such goods nor the owner's proprietary interest therein will be covered unless the goods are described as goods held in trust or on commission.[22]

1–187 Receipt of the proceeds of the policy. The last element of the rule in *Waters v. Monarch Fire Assurance Co.* concerns the receipt of the policy moneys by the assured after a loss has occurred. The assured may receive the full value of the goods lost, but only on the terms imposed by equity of holding in trust for the owners of the goods any surplus in the amount received over and above what is necessary to indemnify him in respect of his lien or personal liability.[23] The policy moneys thereupon represent the goods, and are apportionable according to the respective interests or property rights in the goods themselves.[24]

---

[21] (1873) L.R. 8 C.P. 596, 636–637. The objection taken by Brett J. on p. 637 is substantially the same one which was, *inter alia*, relied upon by counsel for the underwriters in *Tomlinson v. Hepburn* [1966] A.C. 451, 456, and there can be little doubt that the judgments of Bovill C.J. and Denman J. are to be preferred in the light of later authorities. It is significant that Brett J. did not attempt to distinguish the *Waters* case or the decisions following it. The decision in the Court of Common Pleas had a curious sequel. When the appeal came before the Exchequer Chamber, the parties agreed that the judgment of the trial judge, which still stood as the result of the equal division of opinion in the Common Pleas, be reversed by consent, and that judgment be entered for the plaintiffs in a sum representing only their admitted personal interest. This arrangement, which amounted to allowing an appeal by consent, would not be permitted today: *Slaney v. Kean* [1970] Ch. 243, 247, *per* Megarry J.; and, it is submitted, the settlement does not affect what is said above concerning the merits of the Common Pleas judgments. See the comments of Lord Wright in *Maurice v. Goldsbrough Mort* [1939] A.C. 452, 465.
[22] *L.N.W.R. v. Glyn* (1859) 1 E. & E. 652.
[23] *Waters v. Monarch Fire and Life Ass. Co.* (1856) 5 E. & B. 870, 881; *L. & N.W. R. v. Glyn* (1859) 1 E. & E. 652, 663.
[24] *Maurice v. Goldsbrough, Mort & Co.* [1939] A.C. 452, 464.

It has never been stated precisely how this "trust" is to be classified, or what is the exact nature of the remedy possessed by the beneficiary against the commercial trustee.[25] In the event of the commercial trustee retaining moneys paid out by the insurer, there is old authority suggesting that an action for moneys had and received to the plaintiff's use would be appropriate.[26] If the insurers refuse to pay out the full value, the commercial trustee should sue for the balance, and, if he does not, the beneficiary generally cannot bring a claim against the insurers.[27] If a bailee who has insured an owner's interest is bankrupt the owner, being beneficially entitled to any money paid by insurers, will be entitled to preferential ranking over the bailee's other creditors.[28]

1–188 Where an assured possessing a limited interest in goods has voluntarily included cover of the interests of other persons at no extra expense to them, he is entitled to apply the moneys received to cover his own loss or liability first, so that the others can only bring a claim for what is left over. If, however, he has been obliged to insure under contract, this rule might not apply.[29] The bailee may not retain a sum to recompense him for loss of profit and future charges not yet accrued, since an insurance on goods does not include profits unless so expressed.[30]

1–189 Insurances on goods by one possessing no interest. Quite apart from insurances effected on goods by persons possessing a limited insurable interest in them, it is also possible for a person with no insurable interest at all in the insured goods to effect a policy on behalf of others with proprietary interest in them. This is a consequence of the exclusion of goods insurances from the Life Assurance Act 1774.[31] The requirements for the validity of such a policy are different from those relating to policies taken out by an assured who possesses an insurable interest, and the policy may be taken out purely in the name of the assured as agent. If the Marine Insurance Act 1788 applies to such insurances on goods,[32] it seems that the lenient provisions of

---

[25] *Tomlinson v. Hepburn* [1966] A.C. 451, 467. It was partly on account of doubts concerning the beneficiary's ability to enforce the "trust" that Brett J. refused to countenance the recovery of the full value of the goods by the assured in *Ebsworth v. Alliance Marine Ass. Co.* (1873) L.R. 8 C.P. 596, 637. The bailee's duty is to account for the proceeds of the insurance to the bailor if he had undertaken to insure the goods—*Re Dibbens & Sons* [1990] B.C.L.C. 577. The modern analysis is that the insurance proceeds are impressed with an equitable charge in favour of the suitor—see para. 20–26, *post.*

[26] *Sidaways v. Todd* (1818) 2 Stark. 400; *Armitage v. Winterbottom* (1840) 1 M. & G. 130. The same action is available to an insurer in the exercise of his rights of subrogation against the assured. See chap. 22, s.1, *post* sub. title "Subrogation."

[27] An action by the bailor in his own name would fail at common law for want of privity of contract—*D.G. Finance v. Scott*, C.A. [1999] Lloyd's I.R. 387, 392 . The rights of the bailor to recover against (1) the bailee and (2) the insurer are considered in detail at paras 20–26 to 20–30, *post.*

[28] *Cochran v. Leckie's Trustees* (1906) 8 F. (Ct. of Sess.) 975.

[29] *Dalgleish v. Buchanan* (1854) 16 D. 322; *Ferguson v. Aberdeen Parish Council*, 1916 S.C. 715; *Martineau v. Kitching* (1872) L.R. 7 Q.B. 436. This may include a householder including cover in his home contents insurance for the property of members of his family residing with him—*Economides v. Comm. Union Ass. Co.* [1998] Q.B. 587. Wherever the assured with a limited interest is made liable for the whole value of the goods in the event of loss, and he does *not* insure for other interests, strangers to the contract have no control over the proceeds received by him; *Re Harrington Motor* [1928] Ch. 105.

[30] *Maurice v. Goldsbrough, Mort & Co.* [1939] A.C. 452.

[31] *Prudential Staff Union v. Hall* [1947] K.B. 685. See para. 1–16, *ante.*

[32] See para. 1–40, *ante.*

section 1 are satisfied by the insertion of the agent's name alone, so that the Act has no effect in practice.

1–190 The availability of a policy for persons not named in it depends upon rules formulated in cases concerned not only with assureds possessing no interest in the insured property, but also with assureds possessing an interest in it.

1. The policy itself must be construed as something more than a contract of mere personal indemnity on the interest of the nominal assured. It must appear to the insurer to have been effected by the named assured to insure the interests of other persons.[33]
2. The person for whose benefit the insurance is made must be in existence at the time the contract is concluded. There is authority to the effect that he must also have been capable of ascertainment at that time and not subsequently.[34] However, other authority suggests that subsequent ascertainment is no bar so long as that person belongs to a class of persons whose interests are expressly covered,[35] and it is submitted that commercial convenience favours this view.
3. The nominal insured must intend to insure on behalf of such a person.[36] The subjective intention of an agent who has no interest when effecting an insurance is important to the extent that, unless he intends to make it on behalf of a principal, he is simply wagering, and there is nothing which an undisclosed principal can ratify.[37] Rule (1) has the effect that a secret intention existing only in the mind of the person nominally insured is insufficient. Where a broker acts on instructions to effect an insurance the relevant intention will be that of his principal giving the instructions, and not that of the broker who carries them out.[38]

[33] Otherwise the contract would be deemed to be solely on the interest of the named assured. If the nominal insured had no authority to insure for others, they could not ratify unless the contract was expressed to be on behalf of a principal—*Keighley Maxstead & Co. v. Durant* [1901] A.C. 240; *Sharp v. Sphere Drake Ins. plc* [1992] 2 Lloyd's Rep. 501, 515; *National Oilwell Ltd v. Davy Offshore Ltd* [1993] 2 Lloyd's Rep. 582, 596.

[34] *Watson v. Swann* (1862) 11 C.B.(N.S.) 756, 771; *Ebsworth v. Alliance Marine Ins. Co.* (1873) L.R. 8 C.P. 596, 610. The statement by Willes J. in *Kelner v. Baxter* (1866) L.R. 2 C.P. 174 at p. 184 that the principal must actually be ascertained seems too restrictive.

[35] *Lyell v. Kennedy* (1889) 14 App.Cas. 437; *Williams v. Baltic Ins. Ass. Ltd* [1924] 2 K.B. 282; *Arnould, Law of Marine Insurance* (16th ed.), para. 243, which passage was approved in an earlier edition by Scrutton L.J. in *Graham Joint Stock Shipping Co. v. Merchants' Marine Ins. Co.* [1923] 1 K.B. 592, 634. The point was left open in *National Oilwell Ltd v. Davy Offshore Ltd* [1993] 2 Lloyd's Rep. 582, 597.

[36] *Boston Fruit Co. v. British & Foreign Marine Ins. Co.* [1906] A.C. 336; *Ferguson v. Aberdeen Parish Council* 1916 S.C. 715; *P. Samuel & Co. v. Dumas* [1923] 1 K.B. 592, 613, 627, 634; [1924] A.C. 431, 444; *Graham Joint Stock Shipping Co. v. Merchants Marine Ins. Co.* [1924] A.C. 294, 300; *Stone Vickers Ltd v. Appledore Ferguson Ltd* [1992] 2 Lloyd's Rep. 578; *National Oilwell Ltd. v. Davy Offshore Ltd* [1993] 2 Lloyd's Rep. 582, 596–597; *Colonia Versicherung A.G. v. Amoco Oil Co.* [1997] 1 Lloyd's Rep. 261, 271.

[37] *Tomlinson v. Hepburn* [1966] A.C. 451, 479–480 *per* Lord Pearce explaining *Irving v. Richardson* (1831) 2 B. & Ad. 193 as a case of agency. Intention may be deduced from the terms of the policy, from the terms of any other contract between the nominal assured and the unnamed party, and from extrinsic evidence of any kind so long as admissible—*Stone Vickers Ltd v. Appledore Ferguson Ltd* [1992] 2 Lloyd's Rep. 580, 584–585; *National Oilwell Ltd v. Davy Offshore Ltd* [1993] 2 Lloyd's Rep. 582, 597.

[38] *P. Samuel & Co. v. Dumas* [1923] 1 K.B. 592, 634.

4. The unnamed person claiming to be insured by the policy must either have authorised, or subsequently have ratified, the contract made on his behalf.[39]

1–191 Ratification after loss.[40] It is immaterial that the insurance was effected without the knowledge of the person subsequently ratifying it.[41] In marine insurance, ratification after knowledge of a loss is a good ratification of the contract made without the principal's authority. The received view in England and Scotland is that this rule is anomalous and peculiar to marine insurance, and that in fire insurance, and presumably therefore in all risks other than marine, the contract must be ratified before loss.[42] In a Canadian fire case the Saskatchewan Court of Appeal, after a full examination of the authorities, was equally divided on the point, with the result that the decision of the judge in the court below, allowing ratification after loss, was affirmed[43]; in America, ratification after loss has been allowed.[44] It is submitted that it is difficult to extract from the observations in *Williams v. The North China Insurance*[45] the inference that Hamilton J. drew from them in *Grover & Grover v. Mathews*,[46] and that the marine cases ought to be followed in cases of non-marine risks for reasons which are set out at greater length in the paragraphs of this book dealing generally with ratification.[47] This view was approved *obiter* by Colman J. in *National Oilwell Ltd v. Davy Offshore Ltd.*[48]

1–192 The result of the rules concerning ratification is that, if an agent takes out a policy on the chance that an interested principal will ratify it, it is purely optional whether the interested parties adopt it. The agent runs the risk of losing the premiums he has paid, which he cannot recover from the principal, as he has acted outside the scope of his authority. He cannot recover the premiums from the insurer before the risk ends, as the insurer may answer that it is still open to the principal to ratify.[49] Once the principal has adopted the policy, either he or the agent may sue on it.[50]

[39] *Routh v. Thompson* (1811) 13 East 274; *Williams v. The North China Ins. Co.* (1876) 1 C.P.D. 757.
[40] This paragraph in the 6th edition of this work was approved and followed by the High Court of Ontario in *Goldschlager v. Royal Insurance Co.* (1978) 84 D.L.R. (3d) 355, 376.
[41] *Routh v. Thompson* (1811) 13 East 274; *Hagedorn v. Oliverson* (1814) 2 M. & S. 485; *Williams v. The North China Insurance* (1876) 1 C.P.D. 757.
[42] Hamilton J. in *Grover & Grover v. Mathews* [1910] 2 K.B. 401, followed by Branson J. in *Portavon Cinema v. Price* [1939] 4 All E.R. 601; *Ferguson v. Aberdeen Parish Council*, 1916 S.C. 715.
[43] *Goulding v. Norwich Union* [1947] 4 D.L.R. 236; [1948] 1 D.L.R. 526.
[44] *Marqusee v. Hartford Fire Ins.*, 198 F. 475 (1912); *Automobile Ins. v. Barnes-Manley Wet Wash Laundry*, 168 F. 2d 381 (1948).
[45] (1876) 1 C.P.D. 757.
[46] [1910] 2 K.B. 401, 403.
[47] See Ch. 36, *post*.
[48] [1993] 2 Lloyd's Rep. 582, 607–608.
[49] *Hagedorn v. Oliverson* (1814) 2 M. & S. 485, 490, 492, 493; *Cory v. Patton* (1874) L.R. 9 Q.B. 577. There might well also be a breach of warranty of authority; see *Albion Fire & Life Ins. Co. v. Mills* (1828) 3 W. & S. 218.
[50] *Provincial Insurance Co. of Canada v. Leduc* (1874) L.R. 6 P.C. 224, 244; *Browning v. Provincial Insurance* (1873) L.R. 5 P.C. 263, 272–273; *Transcontinental Underwriting Agency v. Grand Union Ins. Co. Ltd* [1987] 2 Lloyd's Rep. 409, 414.

1–193 Third party claim on insurance money. Any concealment, misrepresentation or fraud by the nominal assured in connection with the effecting of the insurance would make the policy voidable, but after the insurance has been effected a breach of condition by the nominal assured would not necessarily avoid the contract with the principal who has complied with the conditions, and, conversely, a breach by the principal would not avoid the policy in so far as the nominal assured intended to insure his own interest. But where an agent insured in his own name and for all others interested, and intended the insurance to be for the benefit of his principal only, and the principal was unable to recover because his own act had caused the loss, it was held that the agent, who had in fact a limited interest, could not avail himself of the insurance to recover on that interest because he had not intended to insure it.[51] Where a policy on goods is effected by a nominal assured for the benefit of others interested, an action in respect of such interest may be brought either by the nominal assured or by the persons in fact interested.[52] The plaintiff must in his pleading name the person or persons for whose benefit the insurance was in fact made.[53]

When the insurers pay the policy moneys to the nominal assured, a third party on whose behalf and for whose benefit the policy was wholly effected is entitled to claim the moneys from the assured only if he was in a position to recover the money from the insurers as the person in fact interested in the policy to the extent of the amount claimed by him. The position is different from that relating to an assured who has a limited interest in the goods insured.[54]

1–194 Joint and composite insurance. It has become commonplace for reasons of commercial convenience to insure the interests of a number of assured persons under one policy of insurance, either because it concerns property in which they are all interested, as in *General Accident Fire & Life Assurance Corporation Ltd v. Midland Bank Ltd*[55] and *State of the Netherlands v. Youell*[56]; or because they are all companies within one corporate group which can obtain insurance more effectively and cheaply through a single policy than by individual negotiation of separate policies, as in *New Hampshire Insurance v. Mirror Group Newspapers*.[57] The fact that a number of assureds are insured by one policy does not by itself make the policy a joint insurance. There cannot be a joint insurance policy unless the interests of the several persons who are interested in the subject-matter are joint interests, so that they are exposed to the same risks and will suffer a joint loss by the occurrence of an insured peril. So if two persons are joint owners of property, an insurance to indemnify both against damage to it will afford an indemnity against their common loss which they will both necessarily have suffered.[58] The interests of such co-assureds are so inseparably connected that a loss or benefit must necessarily affect them

---

[51] *Conway v. Gray* (1809) 10 East 536.
[52] *Hagedorn v. Oliverson* (1814) 2 M. & S. 485; *Sutherland v. Pratt* (1843) 12 M. & W. 16, *Williams v. Baltic Ins. Ass. of London Ltd* [1924] 2 K.B. 282; *Fire Assurance v. Merchants*, 66 Md. 339 (1886).
[53] *Cohen v. Hannam* (1813) 5 Taunt. 101; *Bell v. Ansley* (1812) 16 East 141.
[54] For which see para. 1–187, *ante*.
[55] [1940] 2 K.B. 388.
[56] [1997] 2 Lloyd's Rep. 440; appealed on a different point [1998] 1 Lloyd's Rep. 236.
[57] [1997] L.R.L.R. 24.
[58] *General Accident Fire & Life Assurance v. Midland Bank* [1940] 2 K.B. 388, 404–405.

both.[59] One consequence is that a non-disclosure, mistrepresentation or wilful misconduct on the part of one assured will affect the rights of co-assureds to recover on the policy.[60]

1–195 Where the interests of different persons in the same insured subject-matter are diverse interests, a policy expressed to insure all interested persons must be construed as a composite policy which is intended to insure each co-assured separately in respect of his own interests. Not only does the policy wording show that it is intended to cover the different co-assureds separately for their respective interests, but perforce the elements of joint risk, joint interest and joint loss will be absent.[61] It is usual to describe the co-assureds in a composite policy as being insured "for their respective rights and interests",[62] but a policy lacking that wording may nonetheless be construed as composite.[63] By contrast, where an "over-redemption" insurance policy provided that co-assured A was insured against a particular loss but that on a certain contingency his rights of suit on the policy in respect of such loss were transferred to co-assured B, this was not a composite insurance, with the result that a misrepresentation, non-disclosure or breach of warranty by A would provide a defence to a claim brought by B.[64]

1–196 Another decision which shows that the naming of two or more co-assureds in a policy does not necessarily make it either a joint or composite policy is *Sumitomo Bank Ltd v. Banque Bruxelles Lambert S.A.*[65] ("BBL"), in which mortgage indemnity guarantee policies covering the interests of a number of banks making loans to finance the purchase of commercial properties in London were held to be single-assured policies and not composite policies. In this case BBL was described as "Agent" in the loan documentation, under which it was itself one of the lenders. BBL obtained two mortgage indemnity guarantee policies for the benefit of all the lending banks to protect them in the event that the borrowers defaulted on the loan agreements. When this occurred the insurers declined to pay on the ground of non-disclosure, and disputes arose between BBL and the other banks over responsibility for inadequate disclosure. On a trial of preliminary issues BBL contended that all the banks were co-assureds under the insurance policies, which were by nature composite policies, so that all the co-assureds owed separate duties of disclosure to the insurers and non-disclosure by BBL, if proved, would not affect the rights of the other banks to claim an indemnity. Langley J. held, however, that this was an impossible

[59] *Samuel & Co. Ltd v. Dumas* [1924] A.C. 431, 445.
[60] *Samuel & Co. Ltd v. Dumas, supra; Central Bank of India v. Guardian Assurance* (1936) 54 Ll.L.Rep. 247; *State of the Netherlands v. Youell* [1997] 2 Lloyd's Rep. 440, 445.
[61] *General Accident Fire & Life Assurance v. Midland Bank* [1940] 2 K.B. 388, 405–406; *New Hampshire Ins. Co. v. Mirror Group Newspapers* [1997] L.R.L.R. 24, 41, 57; *State of the Netherlands v. Youell* [1997] 2 Lloyd's Rep. 440, 447–448.
[62] *General Accident Fire & Life Assurance v. Midland Bank, supra.*
[63] *New Hampshire Ins. Co. v. Mirror Group Newspapers, supra.*
[64] *DSG v. QBE International Ins. Co. Ltd* [1999] Lloyd's Rep. I.R. 283.
[65] [1997] 1 Lloyd's Rep. 487.

construction of the policies. BBL was the sole "Insured", and was described not as having contracted "as agent for the Banks" but "as agent for the benefit of the Banks". In other words, BBL had been granted insurance as the sole assured, but additionally for the benefit of the other lending banks, so that in the event of a claim BBL was to recover sums in respect of its own and their interests and hold any recovery in excess of its own interest for their account.[66] It followed that BBL was the sole assured owing a duty of disclosure to the insurers. However, the court went on to hold that BBL owed to the other banks a duty to take care in performing its obligations under the loan agreement to arrange mortgage indemnity cover, and issues of breach of that duty and contributory negligence by the other banks arose for further determination.

7. SPECIFICATION OF INTEREST AND ALTERATION OF INTEREST

1–197 Specification not generally required. The general rule of law is that one who effects an insurance against the occurrence of an event need not, in the absence of specific inquiry, state the nature or extent of his interest in the subject-matter of the insurance unless the interest is such as to affect the risk being insured against.[67] It is sufficient to describe the subject-matter of the insurance itself in adequate terms, and this is so even where the assured has several differing interests in the same subject-matter.[68]

1–198 One who insures the life of another need not state whether he is interested in the life as a creditor or dependant.[69] Where property is insured, the assured need not state whether his title is legal or equitable,[70] so that a purchaser with a valid contract can insure as owner although the legal title or property has not passed to him.[71] A trustee need not disclose that he is a bare trustee without beneficial interest, and may insure to the full value.[72] A tenant who effects insurance in respect of his liability to repair need not disclose that his interest is not that of an owner.[73] A mortgagor insuring in the name of the mortgagee need not specify the amount of the mortgage,[74] and a mortgagee can insure the mortgaged property without stating that his interest is not that of the sole owner of it.[75] On the same principle, someone who insures goods need not specify his interest, although it may in fact be limited to that of a carrier or bailee in respect of his lien or liability to the

---

[66] *ibid.*, at p. 495.
[67] *Crowley v. Cohen* (1832) 3 B. & Ad. 478; *Dixon v. Whitworth* (1879) 4 C.P.D. 371, 375; *Mackenzie v. Whitworth* (1875) L.R. 10 Ex. 142, 148, explaining *Glover v. Black* (1763) 3 Burr. 1394; *Palmer v. Pratt* (1824) 2 Bing. 185; *Russell v. Union Ins. Co.*, 1 Wash. 409 (1806); *Bartlett v. Walter*, 13 Mass. 267 (1816); *Cross v. National Fire Ins. Co.*, 132 Sickel 133 (N.Y.C.A., 1892); *Tomlinson v. Hepburn* [1966] A.C. 451, 468; *Caldwell v. Stadacona Fire and Life Ins. Co.* (1883) 11 Can.S.C. 212, 226; *Insurance Co. v. Chase*, 72 U.S. (5 Wall.) 509, 515 (1866).
[68] *Carruthers v. Sheddon* (1815) 6 Taunt. 14.
[69] *McCormick v. Ferrier* (1832) Hayes & J. 12.
[70] *Inglis v. Stock* (1885) 10 App.Cas. 263, 270, 274; *Aetna Fire Ins. Co. v. Tyler*, 16 Wend. 385 (N.Y.Sup.Ct., 1836); *Dohn v. Farmers' Joint Stock Ins. Co.*, 5 Lans. 275 (N.Y.Sup.Ct., 1871).
[71] *Castellain v. Preston* (1883) 11 Q.B.D. 380.
[72] *Lucena v. Craufurd* (1806) 2 Bos. & Pul. (N.R.) 269, 324; *Ins. Co. v. Chase*, 72 U.S. (5 Wall.) 509 (1866).
[73] *Lawrence v. St Mark's Fire Ins. Co.*, 43 Barb. 479 (N.Y., 1865).
[74] *Ogden v. Montreal Ins. Co.* (1853) 3 U.C.C.P. 497.
[75] *King v. State Mutual Fire*, 61 Mass. (7 Cush.) 1 (1851).

owner in the case of loss.[76] An insurer of goods may effect a reinsurance of his risk by an insurance on the goods, not specifying his interest.[77]

1–199 Cases where interest must be stated. The terms of the proposal or policy may require the assured to have an interest of a particular kind or to specify his interest, and any such condition must be complied with as part of the contract between the parties. The ordinary form of fire policy provides that "the interest of the insured if other than that of absolute owner of the property must be stated". That clause has not been much discussed in the courts in this country. In North America it has been held that "absolute owner" does not necessarily imply that the assured must have the legal title vested in him. If he has an equitable title, or is sole beneficial owner of the property, it is sufficient.[78] If, on the other hand, he holds the legal title as trustee he is "absolute owner", notwithstanding that others may have an equitable or beneficial right to the property.[79] Unless the conditions expressly provide that the property must be unincumbered or that incumbrances must be disclosed, it is not necessary to disclose incumbrances on the property. The assured is "sole and unconditional owner", notwithstanding that he has mortgaged his property or that there is a lien upon it.[80] If a limited interest is expressly specified, the sole and unconditional ownership can apply only as a warranty of sole and unconditional ownership of that interest.[81]

Another condition found in fire policies is that the policy shall not extend to cover "goods held in trust or on commission" unless expressly insured as such. "Goods in trust" means goods with which the assured has been entrusted, and not goods held on trust in the technical, equitable sense of trusteeship.[82] A bailee, such as a wharfinger or carrier or mercantile agent,

---

[76] *L.N.W.R. v. Glyn* (1859) 1 E. & E. 652, 664; *Crowley v. Cohen* (1832) 3 B. & Ad. 478; *Walker v. Maitland* (1821) 5 B. & Ad. 171; *Western v. Home Ins. Co.*, 145 Pa. 346 (1891); *Pittsburgh Storage v. Scottish Union and National Ins. Co.*, 168 Pa. 522 (1895).

[77] *Mackenzie v. Whitworth* (1875) L.R. 10 Ex. 142; *Maurice v. Goldsbrough, Mort & Co.* [1939] A.C. 452, 461.

[78] *Hartford Fire v. Keating*, 86 Md. 130 (1898); *American Basket Co. v. Farmville Ins. Co.*, 3 Hughes 251 (C.C.A., 3 1878); *White v. Home Ins. Co.* (1870) 14 Low.Can.Jur. 301.

[79] *Gill v. Canada Fire and Marine Ins. Co.* (1882) 1 Ont.R. 341.

[80] *Hanover Fire Ins. Co. v. Bohn*, 48 Neb. 743 (1896); *Jones v. Protection Mutual Fire Ins. Co.* 93 F.Supp. 505 (1950), affirmed 192 F. 2d 1018 (1951).

[81] *Traders Ins. Co. v. Pacaud*, 150 Ill. 245 (1894); *Hanover Fire Ins. Co. v. Bohn*, 48 Neb. 743 (1898). In any event the company's knowledge, through its agent, of the assured's real interest may well preclude reliance on the "sole and unconditional owner" clause: see, *e.g. Cross v. National Fire Ins. Co.* 132 Sickel 133 (N.Y. 1892); *Welsh v. London Ass. Co.*, 151 Pa. 607 (1892); *Carpenter v. German American Ins. Co.*, 135 Sickel 298 (N.Y., 1892); *Hartford Fire Ins. Co. v. Keating*, 86 Md. 130 (1898); *Brooks v. Erie Fire Ins. Co.*, 76 N.Y. 275 (App.Div., 1902); *Dupuy v. Delaware Ins. Co.*, 63 Fed.Rep. 680 (1894). It might be otherwise if the clause was incorporated into the policy by legislation—see *North Empire Fire v. Vermette* [1943] S.C.R. 189.

[82] *Waters v. Monarch Fire and Life Ass. Co., supra; L.N.W.R. v. Glyn* (1859) 1 E. & E. 652; *Tomlinson v. Hepburn* [1966] A.C. 451, 467; *Lake v. Simmons* [1926] 1 K.B. 366, upheld in House of Lords [1927] A.C. 487. Goods entrusted to carriers through the handing over of a delivery order are held "in trust" by them: *Rigby Haulage Ltd v. Reliance Marine* [1956] 2 Q.B. 468.

holds goods "in trust" for their owner in this commercial sense.[83] If the assured thus situated omits to declare his interest and insures "on goods" *simpliciter*, he can recover on the policy in respect of his own personal loss, assuming there is no "absolute owner" clause, because the condition is only applicable to an insurance beyond the interest of the assured.[84]

1–200 In some cases the subject-matter of the insurance in respect of which the assured sought cover could not be known to the underwriter without the nature of the assured's interest being spelt out.[85] Thus, for example, while it is permissible to insure against loss of prospective profits,[86] an insurance on a building such as an inn or a shop would not of itself include profits earned on the business carried out there, and the policy would need to state in addition that profits were insured.[87] The insurer could not know from a mere description of the premises that this collateral interest existed, and a similar rule must apply wherever a description of property does not reveal a collateral interest in respect of which cover is sought.[88]

1–201 In some cases it is necessary to disclose the nature of the assured's interest in order that the insurance should not be avoided for concealment of a material fact which might have influenced the insurers in determining whether or not they should accept the risk and, if so, at what rate.[89] It was on that ground that Story J. expressed the view that a mortgagee's interest was of so special a nature that it ought to be disclosed.[90] In *Anderson v. Commercial Union*[91] it was said that the fact that the assured was a tenant at will ought to have been disclosed because it affected the exercise of the option to reinstate.

1–202 Misrepresentation as to insurable interest. If the assured has stated incorrectly the nature of his interest, the effect of such a mis-statement depends upon the policy and the proposal form. If the answer was warranted

---

[83] *Waters v. Monarch Fire and Life Ass. Co. supra*; *L.N.W.R. v. Glyn* (1859) 1 E. & E. 652; *Roberts v. Firemen's Ins. Co.*, 165 Pa. 55 (1894); *Pittsburgh Storage v. Scottish Union and National Ins. Co.*, 168 Pa. 522 (1895). In order for there to be a "commercial trusteeship" the owner of the goods must have a right to the return of the very same goods or the delivery of them to another on his order, so that the assured does not at any time acquire the property in them: *South Australian Ins. Co. v. Randell* (1869) L.R. 3 P.C. 101.

[84] *L.N.W.R. v. Glyn* (1859) 1 E. & E. 652.

[85] *Palmer v. Pratt* (1824) 2 Bing. 185; *Routh v. Thompson* (1809) 11 East 428.

[86] *Barclay v. Cousins* (1802) 2 East 544; *Lucena v. Craufurd* (1806) 2 Bos. & Pul. (N.R.) 269.

[87] *Re Wright and Pole* (1834) 1 Ad. & El. 621; *Menzies v. North British Ins. Co.* (1847) 9 D. 694; *Lucena v. Craufurd* (1806) 2 Bos. Pul. (N.R.) 269, 315; *Eyre v. Glover* (1812) 16 East 218; *Anderson v. Morice* (1875) L.R. 10 C.P. 609, 622, 624; *Maurice v. Goldsbrough Mort & Co.* [1939] A.C. 452, 463.

[88] *M'Swiney v. Royal Exchange Ass. Co.* (1849) 14 Q.B. 634; *Mackenzie v. Whitworth* (1875) L.R. 10 Ex. 142, affirmed (1875) 1 Ex.D. 36; *Dixon v. Whitworth* (1879) 4 C.P.D. 371, 375. Failure to define the assured's interest with precision may lead the court to infer that he possesses no insurable interest—*M'Swiney v. Royal Exchange* (1849) 14 Q.B. 634; *Anderson v. Morice* (1875) L.R. 10 C.P. 609, 622; *Macaura v. Northern Assurance* [1925] N.I. 141, 163.

[89] For non-disclosure, see Ch. 17 *post*.

[90] *Carpenter v. Providence Washington*, 41 U.S. (16 Pet.) 495, 505, (1842), in accord *Columbian Ins. Co. v. Lawrence*, 27 U.S. (2 Pet.) 25 (1829); *Kernochan v. N.Y. Bowery Ins. Co.*, 17 Barb. 428, 439 (N.Y., 1858); *sed contra King v. State Mutual Fire*, 61 Mass. (7 Cush.) 1 (1851); *Franklin Fire v. Coates*, 14 Md. 285 (1859).

[91] (1885) 34 W.R. 189; 55 L.J.Q.B. 146. See discussion on the materiality of a reinsurer's interest in *Mackenzie v. Whitworth* (1875) L.R. 10 Ex. 142; *Ins. Co. v. Chase*, 72 U.S. (5 Wall.) 509 (1866).

to be accurate, then naturally the insurers could repudiate liability on the policy. If it was not, and the insurers seek to avoid the policy on the misrepresentation alone, they will have to establish that it was material to the risk, and in many cases the degree of importance to be attached to one interest as opposed to another may well be insufficient.[92]

1–203 The problem arose in a case brought before the Industrial Assurance Commissioner where the society's agent had without the proposer's authority inserted in the proposal form the incorrect statement that the proposer was the wife of the life insured.[93] The statements in the proposal form were warranted to be true. The proposer was in fact unmarried and lived with the life insured as his salaried housekeeper. The Commissioner held that inasmuch as the incorrect statement was the statement of the society's agent and not the statement of the assured, the society could not set up its untruth as a defence to a claim on the policy and they were therefore estopped from alleging that the assured had not an insurable interest as the wife of the life insured. Alternatively the Commissioner held that the incorrect statement as to the nature of the interest did not prevent the assured from recovering in respect of her actual interest as housekeeper. That alternative finding appears to be sound inasmuch as the society could not avoid the policy for breach of warranty or misrepresentation, and if the assured in fact had an insurable interest she was entitled to recover on that interest. The decision that the society was estopped from denying that the assured was the wife of the life insured cannot, it is submitted, be supported. First, it is doubtful whether the statement of the agent could be used to estop the insurers, following the decision in *Newsholme v. Road Transport and General Ins. Co.*[94] Secondly, assuming that an assured has an insufficient interest to support an insurance, it cannot be the law that an insurer's agent can place the insurer in the position of being estopped from asserting the invalidity of the policy on the ground that it is illegal by statute. The doctrine of estoppel cannot be deployed so as to circumvent or nullify a statutory prohibition,[95] especially as the court is under a duty to take cognisance of such illegality.[96]

1–204 Change of interest. If the insurance is upon property and not upon any specified interest in it, and assuming that no condition in the policy prohibits an alteration in interest, the fact that the assured's interest changes during the risk does not affect the validity of the contract,[97] as where, for instance, a lessee becomes a mortgagor of the insured premises by charging his interest.[98] Even if an owner of premises insures them after mortgaging

---

[92] As to warranties and misrepresentation generally, see Chs 10 and 16, *post.*

[93] *Brunskill v. Pearl Assurance* [1926] I.A.C.Rep. 56.

[94] [1929] 2 K.B. 356.

[95] *Barrow Mutual Ship Ins. v. Ashburner* (1885) 54 L.J.Q.B. 377, 378; *Collins v. Nation Life and General* [1929] I.A.C.(N.I.)Rep. 57.

[96] *Gedge v. Royal Exchange Ass. Co.* [1900] 2 Q.B. 214; *Anctil v. Manufacturers Life Ins. Co.* [1899] A.C. 604; *Mercantile Credit Co. v. Hamblin* [1964] 1 All E.R. 680n. *Royal Exchange Ass. Co. v. Sjoforsokrings etc. Vega* [1902] 2 K.B. 384. *Bird v. British Celanese Ltd* [1945] K.B. 336, 339. See para. 1–17, *ante.*

[97] *Alston v. Campbell* (1779) 4 Bro.P.Cas. 476. *Ward v. Beck* (1863) 13 C.B.(N.S.) 668. *Collingridge v. Royal Exchange Ass. Corp.* (1877) 3 Q.B.D. 173, *Castellain v. Preston* (1883) 11 Q.B.D. 380, 385; *Martin v. Fishing Ins. Co.* 37 Mass. (21 Pick.) 389 (1838).

[98] *Garden v. Ingram* (1852) 23 L.J.Ch. 478.

them, and his equity of redemption is then sold under an execution, leaving him in possession as tenant to the mortgagee at the time of loss, he is entitled to the sums insured by the policy, notwithstanding the change in the nature of his interest.[99]

If, however, the contract is wholly one of personal indemnity, a diminution in the value of the interest of the assured diminishes proportionately the amount which he can recover. If the contract is one to indemnify him against loss to a specified interest, then he can recover only in respect of that interest.[1] If the policy requires the nature of the interest to be disclosed and specified, then the insurance is likely to be read as one on the interest disclosed and on that alone.[2]

1–205 Condition prohibiting sale or transfer. A usual condition in policies of insurance against fire and other property risks is to the effect that the insurance will cease to be in force "as to any property hereby insured which shall pass from the insured to any other person otherwise than by will or operation of law, unless notice thereof be given to and accepted by the company and the subsistence of the insurance in favour of such other person be declared by a memorandum endorsed hereon by or on behalf of the company". Where hay and straw was insured against destruction by fire on such terms, and the assured abandoned it when he left his farm on receipt of a notice to quit, he was divested of all his rights in the hay and straw by virtue of an Act of Parliament, and the property in it passed to his landlord. It was held that this transfer or property in the insured produce was one "by ... operation of law", so that the condition did not cause the insurance to terminate.[3]

1–206 Such a condition should be construed as referring not only to a transfer of the absolute property in the land or goods insured but also to a transfer of any interest which the assured may possess therein.[4] So where a mortgagor was insured as an owner, and later sold the equity of redemption, it was held that, although he retained an insurable interest in respect of his liability for the mortgage debt, the passing of the equity of redemption was a breach of the condition against transfer.[5] If, however, a person is insured expressly in respect of more than one interest in the insured property, the passing of one such interest does not normally avoid the policy *quoad* any remaining interest.[6]

1–207 Where a person is insured expressly in respect of a limited interest,

---

[99] *Strong v. Massachusetts Mutual Fire*, 27 Mass. (10 Pick.) 40 (1830).

[1] *Aetna Fire Ins. Co. v. Tyler*, 16 Wend 385 (N.Y.Sup.Ct. 1836).

[2] So where a car owner indemnifies himself as owner in respect of third party risks, the policy lapses when he sells the car: *Rogerson v. Scottish Auto and General Ins. Co.* (1931) 146 L.T. 26; *Tattersall v. Drysdale* [1935] 2 K.B. 174; *Peters v. General Accident Fire and Life Ins. Co.* [1937] 4 All E.R. 628. But see para. 29–16, *post.* Similarly when his interest ceases to be that of an owner: *Travellers' Indemnity Co. v. Leflèche* (1965) 47 D.L.R. (2d) 498, 501. If he was never really an owner at all the policy never attaches: *Zurich General Accident Co. v. Buck* (1939) 64 Ll.L.R. 115; *O'Leary v. Irish National Ins. Co.* [1958] Ir.Jur.Rep. 1; *Coen v. Employees Liability Ass. Corp* [1962] Ir.Rep. 314.

[3] *Thomas v. National Farmers' Union Mutual Ins. Soc.* [1961] 1 W.L.R. 386.

[4] *Pyman v. Marten* (1906) 13 Com.Cas. 64, 67; *Pinckney v. Mercantile Fire Ins. Co.* (1901) 2 O.L.R. 296.

[5] *Springfield Fire and Marine v. Allen*, 43 Hand 384 (N.Y.C.A., 1871).

[6] *Germania Fire Ins. Co. v. Thompson* 95 U.S. 547 (1877).

the passing of the property from one owner to another subject to that interest does not avoid the policy under the transfer clause. For instance, if an insurance were effected by a warehouseman expressly on goods in trust or on commission, the passing of the property in the goods would not affect the validity of his insurance. Where a person who was insured in respect of his interest as a purchaser of land under an executory contract sold half of his interest, it was held that the policy remained valid as to the other half of the interest which he retained.[7]

1–208 Where A, B and C insure property as co-partners, A retires and transfers his interest to B and C absolutely, and a loss occurs before the transfer is perfected, the insurance will not lapse under a "sale or transfer" clause.[8] Neither would it lapse if A were content to cede some of his interest without divesting himself of his share completely,[9] nor if A, B and C were to take D into the partnership.[10] Similarly, if A transfers his whole interest to B and C, the insurance does not cease.[11]

1–209 Where the condition was against "sale or conveyance", it was held that it applied to a voluntary sale only, and that a compulsory sale on execution did not terminate the insurance.[12] Where the assured insured as warehouseman, and the policy was declared to be void "if any change takes place in the possession of the subject-matter of the insurance", it was held that a constructive change of possession by the delivery of the warehouse receipt did not avoid the policy.[13] Where transfer without the company's consent by indorsement of the policy is prohibited, it is not sufficient to obtain an indorsement "payable in case of loss to B". Such an indorsement is not a consent to a transfer of the property to B but merely a substitution to B as payee.[14]

It may be asked, what happens if the subject-matter of the insurance is transferred to someone to whom the benefit of the policy is also assigned at the same time? At least one eminent judge thought that the condition against transfer could not apply,[15] and this serves to illustrate the difference between conditions prohibiting assignment and those prohibiting transfer of the *res*.

1–210 Assignment of life assurance policies and the Life Assurance Act 1774, s.2. Although the object of the statute is to prevent speculation, it applies only to the contract of insurance between the insurer and the assured, and it does not apply to contracts whereby the policy is subsequently assigned or otherwise dealt with between the assured and third parties. If the policy is valid in its inception, that is to say, if it was in fact effected for the use and benefit of the person named who had an insurable

---

[7] *Manley v. Ins. Co. of N. America*, 1 Lans. 20 (N.Y.Sup.Ct., 1869).
[8] *Forbes v. Border Counties Fire Ins. Co.* (1873) 11 M. 278.
[9] *ibid.*
[10] *Jenkins v. Deane* (1933) 47 Ll.L.R. 342, following New York authority.
[11] *Forbes v. Border Counties Fire Ins. Co., supra, obiter.* See too, Appleman, *Insurance Law and Practice* (1981), Vol. 4A, para. 2752, confirming that the weight of American authority is to the effect that the sale of one partner to the remaining partners does not relieve the insurer of liability.
[12] *Strong v. Massachusetts Mutual Fire Ins. Co.*, 27 Mass. (10 Pick.) 40 (1830).
[13] *California Ins. Co. v. Union Compress Co.*, 133 U.S. 387 (1889).
[14] *Bates v. Equitable Ins. Co.*, 77 U.S. (10 Wall.) 33 (1869).
[15] *Ward v. Beck* (1863) 13 C.B.(N.S.) 668, 673, *per* Willes J.

interest in the life assured, it cannot afterwards be invalidated by assignment to a person who has no interest, but who takes it merely as a speculation.[16]

1–211 In a case decided in the Supreme Court of Canada an assignment to a purchaser without interest was held to be valid even although the assignment was made before the assured had paid a single premium or even received delivery of his policy.[17] The assured had applied for a policy on his own life, and his proposal had been accepted and the policy forwarded to the company's local agent for delivery against payment of the first premium. The assured, however, found that he was unable to pay the premium and asked the agent to get the policy assigned for him, which he did, and the policy was assigned to a purchaser who had no interest in the life of the assured. The court held that as the contract was originally made bona fide by the assured without any intention to assign it, the subsequent dealing with it could not invalidate it, and that the assignment was not in itself unlawful. In an American case the assured had allowed a policy on his own life to lapse, and subsequently by arrangement with the company it was renewed and assigned to a purchaser.[18] The court held that the assignee could not recover, and although the ground of the decision, *viz.* that no assignment to a speculative purchaser is valid, cannot be approved,[19] the decision itself is probably right, because the renewal of the policy for the benefit of the assignee was in reality a fresh contract of insurance between the insurers and the assignee, and would in England have been void under 14 Geo. 3, c. 48.

1–212 Participation in payments made without interest. It has been held that if the insurers waive the illegality and pay the policy money on a policy effected without interest the absence of insurable interest cannot be raised by the person into whose hands the money has come as a defence against those claiming to participate in it as principals, assignees, beneficiaries or otherwise.[20]

---

[16] *Ashley v. Ashley* (1829) 3 Sim. 149; *M'Farlane v. Royal London F.S.* (1886) 2 T.L.R. 755. See para. 1–114, *ante.*

[17] *Vozina v. New York Life Ins. Co.* (1881) 6 Can.S.C. 30.

[18] *Carpenter v. U.S. Life.* 161 Pa. 9 (1894).

[19] Nor does it represent prevailing American law: see Appleman, *Insurance Law and Practice* (1981), Vol. 2, para. 854.

[20] *Worthington v. Curtis* (1875) 1 Ch.D. 419; *Att.-Gen. v. Murray* [1904] 1 K.B. 165; *Hadden v. Bryden* (1899) 1 F. 710; *Carmichael v. Carmichael's Executrix*, [1919] S.C. 636, 640, reversed on another point, [1920] S.C.(H.L.) 195; *Re Slattery* [1917] 2 Ir.R. 278. In previous editions of this work the propriety of these decisions was doubted. Following the analysis of the acquisition of property rights under illegal contracts in *Tinsley v. Milligan* [1994] 1 A.C. 340, the present editors think that these doubts are no longer appropriate.

CHAPTER 2

FORMATION OF THE CONTRACT

1. GENERAL PRINCIPLES

2–1 Introductory. In order that a binding contract of insurance shall be concluded there must be agreement between insurers and assured as to the terms of the insurance. In non-marine business it is usual for an offer to be made by the proposer, who completes a proposal form[1] and sends it to the insurers for their consideration and acceptance. If the insurers make a counter-proposal, negotiations may then end with the insurers making a final offer of cover to the applicant which is open for acceptance by signifying his assent either in words or by conduct such as tendering the premium demanded.[2]

2–2 An acceptance will be of no effect in law unless the parties have agreed upon every material term of the contract they wish to make.[3] The material terms of a contract of insurance are: the definition of the risk to be covered, the duration of the insurance cover, the amount and mode of payment of the premium and the amount of the insurance payable in the event of a loss. As to all these there must be a *consensus ad idem*, that is to say, there must either be an express agreement or the circumstances must be such as to admit of a reasonable inference that the parties were tacitly agreed. Without such agreement, it would be impossible for the courts to give effect to the parties' contract except by virtually writing the contract for them, which it is not the function of the courts to do.[4]

2–3 Agreement on these and other less essential terms of the proposed insurance may be achieved either at once, or only after a process of lengthy negotiations as is common in the case of large commercial risks. When negotiations become protracted, and there is subsequently a dispute concerning the existence of a binding contract or its terms, it is necessary to review the whole course of the negotiations in order to see if there was at any

[1] This may or may not be solicited by the insurers' agent. Proposal forms are rare in the commercial marine market.
[2] As for instance, in *Canning v. Farquhar* (1886) 16 Q.B.D. 727. The decision appealed from is at (1885) 1 T.L.R. 560, *sub nom. Canning v. Hoare.*
[3] *Allis-Chalmers Co. v. Maryland Fidelity and Deposit Co.* (1916) 114 L.T. 433. The corresponding paragraph to this in the 4th edition of this work was approved in *Davidson v. Global General Ins. Co.* (1965) 48 D.L.R. (2d) 503, 507.
[4] *Scammell Ltd v. Ouston* [1941] A.C. 251; *Charter Reins. Co. v. Fagan* [1997] A.C. 313, 388.

stage full agreement on the material terms of the insurance or, as the case may be, agreement that a particular term was agreed. In carrying out this exercise a tribunal should have regard to subsequent events which bear upon the question at issue.[5]

There is no rule of insurance law that there can be no binding contract of insurance until the premium has been actually paid or the policy has been issued.[6] Once the terms of the insurance have been agreed upon by the parties, there is prima facie a binding contract of insurance, and the assured is obliged to pay a premium as agreed, while the insurers for their part must deliver a policy containing the agreed terms.[7] If, therefore, insurers wish to guard against the eventuality of becoming bound to insure before they have secured payment of the premium, they must make it clear at the outset that there shall be no legally binding contract until some particular condition, such as payment of premium or issue of a policy, has been performed.[8] In practice such conditions are often stipulated, and the courts have shown themselves very ready to hold that, in life assurance, the insurers negotiate on the commercially sensible basis that they are not to be bound until the premium is paid and a policy issued.[9]

2–4 It is doubtful whether the courts would similarly lean in favour of insurers in cases involving any other kind of policy.[10] In fire, burglary and motor insurance the practice is to give temporary cover pending the insurers' consideration of the proposal, and, so far as temporary cover is concerned, there is no presumption whatsoever against an informal contract that is immediately binding—in fact rather the reverse. In motor insurance, indeed, the cover note must give the holder immediate protection in order to comply with sections 143(1) and 161(1) of the Road Traffic Act 1988. In the case of insurance with Lloyd's underwriters against fire and other risks, the slip once

---

[5] *Container Transport Int'l. v. Oceanus Mutual Underwriting Assoc.* [1984] 1 Lloyd's Rep. 476, 505.; *GNER Ltd v. Avon Ins. plc* [2001] 2 All E.R. (Comm) 526, 534.

[6] *Wooding v. Monmouthshire Indemnity Society Ltd* [1939] 4 All E.R. 570, 581; *Adie v. The Insurances Corporation Ltd* (1898) 14 T.L.R. 544; *Re Yager and Guardian Ass. Co. Ltd* (1912) 108 L.T. 38, 44; *Christie v. North British Insurance Co.* (1825) 3 S. & D. (Ct. of Sess.) 519, 522; *British Oak Ins. Co. Ltd v. Atmore* (1939) T.P.D. 9; *Lake v. Reins. Corporation Ltd* 1967 (3) S.A. 124, 127–128 (W).

[7] *Adie v. The Insurances Corporation Ltd* (1898) 14 T.L.R. 544; *Bhugwandass v. Netherlands India Sea and Fire Ins. Co. of Batavia* (1888) 14 App.Cas. 83; *Thompson v. Adams* (1889) 23 Q.B.D. 361; *General Accident Ins. Corp v. Cronk* (1901) 17 T.L.R. 233; *Queen Ins. Co. of America v. British Traders Ins. Co.* [1927] 1 W.W.R. 508. It is also settled by American decisions that equity has jurisdiction to decree specific performance of the insurers' obligation to issue a proper policy in accordance with the parties' agreement, whether the premium has been paid—*Franklin Ins. Co. v. Colt*, 87 U.S. (20 Wall.) 560 (1874); *Hebert v. Mutual Life Ins. Co.*, 12 Fed.Rep. 807 (1882); *Unions Central Life Ins. Co. v. Philips*, 102 Fed.Rep. 19 (1900)—or the assured is ready to pay— *Eames v. Home Ins. Co.*, 94 U.S. 621 (1876), in which case the sum due as premium ought to be deducted from any loss already payable by insurers by the time action is brought.

[8] For the effect of such conditions, see paras 2–38 to 2–50, *post.*

[9] *Canning v. Farquhar* (1886) 16 Q.B.D. 727; *Harrington v. Pearl Life Ass. Co. Ltd* (1914) 30 T.L.R. 613. In *Equitable Life Ass. Co. v. McElroy*, 83 Fed.Rep. 631 (1897), a U.S. federal court went so far as to say that there was actually a presumption in law to that effect regardless of express conditions, but, with respect, that does not appear ever to have been the general law in the United States, where, indeed, the widespread use of express conditions stipulating that no contract is in effect until the premium is paid and the policy delivered implies the contrary.

[10] See para. 6–10, *post.*

signed will constitute a binding contract for the whole term of the proposed insurance.[11]

(a) What Must be Agreed

2–5 Duration of the risk. The commencement and duration of the risk must be agreed. In a Canadian case it was held that, where an application for life insurance did not specify the date at which the risk was to commence, the issue of a policy antedated to the date of the application was a good acceptance.[12] If the *terminus a quo* is agreed upon, it will not as a rule be necessary that the *terminus ad quem* should be expressed. The universal practice in fire, burglary, and accident risks is to insure for a year, and, in the absence of anything to indicate the contrary, that may possibly be taken as an implied term of the contract, as has been suggested in two American decisions.[13] The duration of the risk might also be capable of being inferred from previous insurances between the same parties.[14]

2–6 Rate of premium. The rate of premium must be agreed,[15] but in the absence of an expressed figure it may be inferred to be the company's ordinary rate if it has a fixed tariff and there is no doubt as to how the risk should be classed,[16] or, again, it may be inferred to be the same rate as that at which the risk was previously insured.[17] All the parties have to do is to commit themselves to a certain arrangement for ascertaining the rate of premium.[18] Thus in insurances effected at Lloyd's, it is a common practice for underwriters to take certain risks at a rate to be agreed. The parties thereby agree to leave the rate open for future settlement, and if a loss occurs before settlement, the sum insured becomes payable subject to deduction of a reasonable premium.[19] In default of agreement between the parties, the

---

[11] *Thompson v. Adams* (1889) 23 Q.B.D. 361; *Jaglom v. Excess Ins. Co.* [1972] 2 Q.B. 250. See Ch. 35, *post.*

[12] *Armstrong v. Provident Savings Life* (1901) 2 Ont.L.R. 771. The court so held notwithstanding that the proposal and policy contained the express term that the insurance should not be binding, neither should the policy come into effect until payment of the first premium.

[13] *Eames v. Home Ins. Co.* (1876) 94 U.S. 621; *Kimball v. Lion Ins. Co.*, 17 Fed.Rep. 625 (1883).

[14] *Winne v. Niagara Fire Ins. Co.* (1883) 91 N.Y. 185.

[15] *Allis-Chalmers Co. v. Maryland Fidelity and Deposit Co.* (1916) 114 L.T. 433; *Canning v. Farquhar* (1886) 16 Q.B.D. 727, *Rose v. Medical Invalid Life Assurance Society* (1848) 11 D. 151; *Christie v. North British Ins. Co.* (1825) 3 S. & D. (Ct. of Sess.) 519.

[16] *Train v. Holland Purchase Ins. Co.* (1875) 62 N.Y. 598; *Boice v. Thames and Mersey Marine Ins. Co.*, 38 Hun. 246 (N.Y.Sup.Ct., 1885).

[17] *Winne v. Niagara Fire Ins. Co.*, 91 N.Y. 185 (1883); *Audubon v. Excelsior Ins. Co.*, 27 N.Y. 216 (1863); *Boice v. Thames and Mersey Marine Ins. Co.*, 38 Hun. 246 (N.Y.Sup.Ct., 1885).

[18] *Lake v. Reinsurance Corporation Ltd*, 1967 (3) S.A. 124 (W.); *Gliksten v. State Assurance Co.* (1922) 10 Ll.L.R. 604, where, however, it is hard to see how the parties were *ad idem* as to the risk.

[19] *Hyderabad (Deccan) Co. v. Willoughby* [1899] 2 Q.B. 530; *Banque Sabbag S.A.L. v. Hope* [1972] 1 Lloyd's Rep. 253, approving this paragraph in the 5th ed. of this work at pp. 260–261; affirmed [1973] 1 Lloyd's Rep. 233 in C.A. and [1974] 2 Lloyd's Rep. 301 in H.L., without reference to this point. The provision that a term is "to be agreed" may show that the conclusion of the contract depends upon that agreement, or that the contract is binding albeit the term is "t.b.a." according to the context—[1973] 1 Lloyd's Rep. 233, 240, 242, 250. For this case, see paras 35–19 *et seq.*, *post*. In marine insurance, where the position is governed by M.I.A. 1906 s.31(1) it has been held that such a term cannot apply if there is no reasonable commercial rate available: *Liberian Ins. Agency v. Mosse* [1977] 2 Lloyd's Rep. 560, 568.

amount of the premium will be settled by the court or an arbitrator. Insurance at a rate to be agreed is not usual in fire, life or accident insurance, but it is not unknown.

2–7 Amount and subject-matter of insurance. Another matter which must necessarily be defined is the amount of the insurance. If the amount of insurance requires to be apportioned upon different portions of the property to be insured, the contract is not complete until that has been done. Thus, where the parties contemplated apportionment between the real and personal property, and that had not been done when a loss occurred, it was held that there was no completed contract.[20] Again, where insurers offered to insure at a certain rate upon certain buildings, if in "specific form" (that is to say, if the various buildings and contents were specified with a separate amount on each) and the applicants accepted the rate and sent details of the amounts which they hoped would be sufficiently specific, it was held that there was no binding contract until the insurers had signified their approval of the apportionment.[21]

2–8 If there is any ambiguity as to the subject matter of the insurance, there is no contract.[22] In one case of life assurance the proposer intended to insure the life of her mother, Mary Ellen Ince, but the company's agent thought that she intended to insure the life of her grandmother and that Mary Ellen Ince was the grandmother's name, whereas the grandmother's name was Mary Ann Ince. The proposal was for a policy on the life of "Mary Ellen Ince", but the address and particulars of relationship and age which were filled in by the agent were inappropriate to the mother and appropriate to the grandmother. The policy contained the same inconsistencies, and the sum assured was calculated on the age of the grandmother. There was no evidence to show that the inconsistencies were due to the fault of either party. It was a clear case of a contract failing *ab initio* because the parties were never *ad idem* on an essential term. The Industrial Assurance Commissioner dismissed a claim for payment of the insurance moneys on the death of the mother, and the company agreed to return to the proposer a sum equal to the premiums she had paid.[23]

2–9 Two American fire insurance decisions illustrate the same principle. Where the proposal was to insure "my house" and the agent accepted the risk believing that the applicant referred to his previous residence, it was held that there was no contract.[24] Where, however, the property was defined, and the insurer agreed "to insure it", it was a reasonable inference that the intention was to insure it against fire and there was, therefore, a binding contract.[25]

2–10 Insurers' usual terms. A court will not require the parties to have

---

[20] *Kimball v. Lion Ins. Co.*, 17 Fed.Rep. 625 (1883).
[21] *Phoenix Ins. Co. v. Schultz*, 80 Fed.Rep. 337 (1897).
[22] e.g. whether a broker is placing a direct reinsurance on behalf of the primary insurer or a retrocession on behalf of a direct reinsurer of the primary insurer—*Commonwealth Ins. Co. v. Groupe Sprinks SA* [1983] 1 Lloyd's Rep. 67, 87–88.
[23] *Beach v. Pearl Assurance Co. Ltd* [1938] I.A.C.Rep. (1938–49) 3.
[24] *Mead v. Westchester Fire Ins. Co.*, 3 Hun. 608 (N.Y.Sup.Ct., 1875).
[25] *Bail v. St Joseph Ins. Co.* (1880) 73 Mo. 371.

reached separate agreement on all the terms of the insurance, apart from the essential terms described above, in order that a contract should be held to exist. It will readily be assumed that, when an applicant seeks insurance cover from particular insurers, he impliedly offers to take an insurance on the insurers' usual, or standard, terms of cover,[26] just as the insurers' interim cover note will be issued impliedly subject to the usual conditions contained in their policies.[27] When, therefore, the insurers come to issue their policy, their only obligation is to issue it with the terms and conditions usually attached to their policies, in so far as these are not inconsistent with the express terms of the parties' preliminary contract.[28]

This principle extends only to the implication of usual terms of cover and no more. Where a mutual company tendered to an applicant for fire insurance a policy which recited that he had agreed to become a member of the company, it was held that he was not bound to accept such a policy, as his proposal was for insurance only, and not also for membership in the company.[29] In the case of an application for a fidelity policy where the terms of the proposed contract had never been stated and there was no evidence of an intention to accept a policy in the usual terms contained in the company's policies, it was held that, until the applicant had seen and accepted the bond prepared by the company, there was no binding contract.[30]

2–11 The Statement of Insurance Practice issued by the insurers of the United Kingdom in 1977 and revised in 1986[31] includes the requirement in paragraph 1(f) that "unless the prospectus or the proposal form contains full details of the standard cover offered, and whether or not it contains an outline of that cover, the proposal form shall include a prominent statement that a specimen copy of the policy form is available on request".

2–12 The principle of incorporating the insurers' standard terms demonstrates that, once the essentials of the insurance are defined, the agreement to insure may be binding even though it does not express the whole terms and conditions of the insurance that will be contained in the policy when issued. To those unfamiliar with the business of insuring, or of insuring the particular risk in question, the agreement may on the face of it appear to be

---

[26] *Adie v. The Insurances Corporation* (1898) 14 T.L.R. 544; *General Accident Ins. Corp. v. Cronk* (1901) 17 T.L.R. 233; *Acme Wood Flooring Co. v. Marten* (1904) 9 Com.Cas. 157; *Sanderson v. Cunningham* [1919] 2 Ir.R. 234; *Rust v. Abbey Life Assurance Co. Ltd* [1979] 2 Lloyd's Rep. 334, 339 *per* Brandon L.J.; *S.E. Lancs. Inc. Co. v. Croisdale* (1931) 40 Ll.L.Rep. 22, 23.

[27] See Ch. 4 para. 4–15, *post*.

[28] *Palmer v. Commercial Travellers' Mutual Accident Association*, 53 Hun. 601 (N.Y.Sup.Ct., 1889).

[29] *Star Fire and Burglary Ins. Co. v. Davidson* (1903) 5 F. 83.

[30] *Allis-Chalmers Co. v. Maryland Fidelity and Deposit Co.* (1916) 114 L.T. 433. It is difficult to reconcile this reasoning with the authorities cited in note 26 above, but in any event clear agreement on the premium was wanting. *Cf. Rust v. Abbey Life Assurance Co. Ltd* [1979] 2 Lloyd's Rep. 334, where the company's agent explained the effect of their policy orally to the applicant, and a contract came into being before the applicant was able to study the prepared policy (p. 340).

[31] The revised version was announced on the House of Commons on February 21, 1986 (H.C.Deb., Vol. 92, No. 63, Cols 356–357). The text may be found in Part 7 of the *Encyclopedia of Insurance Law*. The statement applies only to consumer insurances. In other cases there is no need to bring the insurers' standard terms to the notice of the applicant unless any of them are for any reason unusual and not to be expected in that class of insurance—*Nsubuga v. Commercial Union Assce.* [1998] 2 Lloyd's Rep. 682, 686.

far from complete or precise, but to those familiar with the business the things left unexpressed may be a matter of necessary implication from the words or abbreviations used.[32] In one case where a commercial agreement was under scrutiny, Lord Wright said[33]: "Business men often record the most important agreements in crude and summary fashion; modes of expression sufficient and clear to them in the course of their business may appear to those unfamiliar with the business far from complete or precise. It is accordingly the duty of the court to construe such documents fairly and broadly without being too astute or subtle in finding defects." If, therefore, the overall contractual intention is clear, it is immaterial that the contract as expressed is silent as to some matters of detail which are either matters of necessary implication or may be inferred from a consideration of all the circumstances, having regard to the normal practice of insurers in the particular class of business in question.[34]

If, moreover, there is evidently agreement on the important terms, the presence of a meaningless term or phrase will not prevent a contract from being enforced. Such a term, if not essential to the performance of the contract, may be disregarded.[35]

(b) Offer and Acceptance

2–13 Withdrawal of offer. An offer when made remains open for acceptance for the time specified, if any, or for a reasonable time,[36] but the offeror can withdraw it at any time before acceptance.[37] In general a notice of withdrawal does not operate until it is actually communicated. It follows, therefore, that a withdrawal posted before acceptance will be ineffective unless communicated to the offeree before the latter has posted the letter of acceptance.[38]

A proposal for insurance may, therefore, be withdrawn by an applicant if notice of withdrawal is communicated to the company at any time before the company has posted its acceptance[39]; and thus, where an applicant, having made a proposal, afterwards made another proposal relating to the same risk but in different terms, it was held that the second proposal was a withdrawal of the first, and the subsequent acceptance of the first proposal by the company created no binding contract.[40]

2–14 Where a proposal for life insurance was made, the first premium was

---

[32] The truth in this statement should not, however, disguise the fact that on occasions even the experts are unable to agree on what the parties' hastily recorded agreement signifies, and the courts have sometimes been highly critical of loosely drafted contracts in litigation before them—*Marsden v. Reid* (1803) 3 East 572, 579, *per* Lawrence J.; *Trade Indemnity Co. v. Workington Harbour and Dock Board* [1937] A.C. 1, 17, *per* Lord Atkin.

[33] *Hillas & Co. Ltd v. Arcos Ltd* (1932) 38 Com.Cas. 23, 26.

[34] *Scammell v. Ouston* [1941] A.C. 251.

[35] *Nicolene Ltd v. Simmonds* [1953] 1 Q.B. 543.

[36] *Ramsgate v. Montefiore* (1866) L.R. 1 Ex. 109; *Dunlop v. Higgins* (1848) 1 H.L.Cas. 381.

[37] *Cooke v. Oxley* (1790) 3 T.R. 653; *Offord v. Davies* (1862) 12 C.B.(N.S.) 748; *Dickinson v. Dodds* (1876) 2 Ch.D. 463; *Cartwright v. Hoogstoel* (1911) 105 L.T. 628.

[38] *Byrne v. Van Tienhoven* (1880) 5 C.P.D. 344; *Henthorn v. Fraser* [1892] 2 Ch. 27. For the "postal acceptance rule," see para. 2–20; *post*.

[39] *Wolfe v. Equitable Life Assurance of U.S.A.*, *The Times*, January 26, 1906 (Mayor's Court); *Globe Mutual Life Ins. Co. v. Snell*, 19 Hun. 560 (N.Y.Sup.Ct., 1880).

[40] *Travis v. Nederland Life Ins. Co.*, 104 Fed.Rep. 486 (1900).

paid and an interim receipt was issued providing that the insurance should be effective from the date of the approval of the life-assured by the medical officer, it was held that the proposer could withdraw his proposal and recover back the premium at any time before the medical officer signified his approval.[41]

2–15 General rules as to acceptance. The general rule is that a contract of insurance will be concluded only when the party to whom an offer has been made accepts it unconditionally and communicates his acceptance to the person making the offer. Whether the final acceptance is that of the assured or insurers depends simply on the way in which the negotiations for an insurance have progressed. In many cases, both offer and acceptance are made and given respectively through the parties' authorised agents. It is particularly important that the person accepting for the insurers should be someone empowered to make contracts on their behalf. In life assurance especially it is traditional for the assured's proposal to be put before the directors for their appraisal and decision. A purported acceptance by someone without actual or ostensible authority to give it does not bind the insurers.[42]

Two qualifications must be borne in mind. First, certain market procedures employed to conclude insurance and, more especially, reinsurance contracts are difficult to explain by reference to the conventional analysis of offer and acceptance. Provided that there is a clear intention to create legal relations and the transaction is by nature commercial, the courts will be ready to recognise that a binding agreement has been created.[43] Secondly, insurers sometimes insert special stipulations into their contractual documentation which expressly delay the formation of a binding contract.[44] For the moment we consider the general rules in the absence of these complications.

2–16 Silence does not denote consent and therefore no binding contract arises until the person to whom an offer is made says or does something to signify his acceptance of it.[45] Mere delay in giving an answer cannot be construed as an acceptance,[46] as, prima facie, acceptance must be communicated to the offeror.[47] This is not always so; for instance, a motorist who is sent an insurance cover note by insurers may probably accept this offer of insurance cover by taking his car out on the road in reliance on it.[48] It seems

---

[41] *Henderson v. State Life Ins. Co.* (1905) 90 Ont.L.R. 540.

[42] For a discussion of agents' authority in such cases, see Ch. 36, *post*.

[43] *General Accident Fire & Life Ass. Corp. v. Tanter* [1984] 1 Lloyd's Rep. 58, 71; *Mander v. Commercial Union Ass. Co.* [1998] Lloyd's Rep.I.R. 93, 105.

[44] See paras 2–38 to 2–47, *post*.

[45] *Felthouse v. Bindley* (1862) 11 C.B.(N.S.) 869, affd. (1863) 1 New Rep. 401. The exact scope of this rule has never been established in English law. There is presumably nothing to prevent a person from agreeing in advance, either expressly or by implication from a course of dealing, that in a particular case his silence shall be taken to mean consent. See *Alexander Hamilton Institute v. Jones*, 234 Ill.App. 444 (1924).

[46] *Equitable Life Assurance Co. v. McElroy*, 83 Fed.Rep. 631 (1897); *Misselhorn v. Mutual Reserve Fund Life Association*, 30 Fed.Rep. 545 (1887); *Harp Lager v. Granger's Mutual Fire Ins. Co. of Frederick County*, 49 Md. 307 (1878); *More v. New York Bowery Fire Ins. Co.*, 130 N.Y. 537 (1892).

[47] *Powell v. Lee* (1908) 99 L.T. 284; *Rose v. Medical Invalid Life Ass. Soc.* (1848) 11 D. 151.

[48] *Taylor v. Allon* [1966] 1 Q.B. 304, 311. In that case there was no evidence offered to show that the assured sufficiently knew of the insurers' offer to accept it in this way.

that a person whose acceptance is expressed by conduct of this sort, and not by words, is not "silent" for the purposes of the rule that silence does not denote consent.[49] In *Rust v. Abbey Life Assurance Co. Ltd*[50] it was held that the applicant for a policy was under a duty to examine it when sent to her, and for that reason her failure to object to its terms within a reasonable time was an acceptance of the company's offer to issue it to her. On appeal the Court of Appeal affirmed the lower court, saying that it was an inevitable inference from the applicant's retention of the policy for seven months after receipt that she accepted it as a valid contract between herself and the company.[51]

2–17 Communication may be dispensed with through an acceptance being made in a manner expressly prescribed by the terms of the offer,[52] or by the general course of business.[53] For example, an offer to insure holders of newspaper coupons may be made in such a manner as to conclude a contract between the company and purchasers of the newspaper who sign the coupon, or are regular subscribers to the paper,[54] or their personal representatives.[55] Presumably, however, an offer to insure all purchasers of a particular newspaper issue could not be accepted by a person who bought the paper in ignorance of the offer.[56]

2–18 Where a coupon contained in Letts' Diaries was in the form of a promise by the company to pay £1,000 to the representatives of any person killed in a railway accident provided he was the owner of the diary and had caused his name to be registered at the head office of the company, and a claim was made within 12 months of registration, it was held that a contract was concluded at the latest when the letter of acceptance, applying for registration, was received by the company, but quite possibly at the date when it was posted.[57]

2–19 Where a newspaper offered to its registered subscribers a scheme of free insurance against fire, accident and sickness, and in response to applications for registration issued a registration certificate enumerating the benefits covered by the scheme, and containing an announcement that while the scheme did not involve any contractual liability, it had the financial backing and support of the proprietors of the newspapers whose issued

---

[49] *Roberts v. Hayward* (1828) 3 C. & P. 432.

[50] [1978] 2 Lloyd's Rep. 386, 393.

[51] [1979] 2 Lloyd's Rep. 334, 340, *per* Brandon L.J.; *Yona International v. L.R.F.* [1996] 2 Lloyd's Rep. 84, 110; *New Hampshire Ins. Co. v. M.G.N.* [1997] L.R.L.R. 24, 54.

[52] *Carlill v. Carbolic Smoke Ball Co.* [1893] 1 Q.B. 256; *Williams v. Carwardine* (1833) 4 B. & Ad. 621; *Adams v. Lindsell* (1818) 1 B. & Ad. 681.

[53] *Household Fire Ins. Co. v. Grant* (1879) 4 Ex.D. 216; *Dunlop v. Higgins* (1848) 1 H.L.Cas. 381; *Henthorn v. Fraser* [1892] 2 Ch. 27; *General Accident Fire and Life Ass. Corp. Ltd v. Tanter* [1984] 1 Lloyd's Rep. 58, 72 (fac. marine market usage), rev'd in part on a different ground [1985] 2 Lloyd's Rep. 529; *Mander v. Commercial Union Assce.* [1998] Lloyd's Rep.I.R. 93, 104–105.

[54] *Shanks v. Sun Life Ass. Co. of India* (1896) 4 S.L.T. 66; *Carlill v. Carbolic Smoke Ball Co.* [1893] 1 Q.B. 256.

[55] *Law v. George Newnes Ltd* (1894) 21 R. 1027.

[56] *R. v. Clarke* (1927) 40 C.L.R. 227, 233; *Gibson v. Proctor* (1891) 55 J.P. 616 (the report here is fuller than in 64 L.T. 594).

[57] *General Accident Fire and Life Ass. Corp. Ltd v. Robertson* [1909] A.C. 404, 411.

capital was over £1,250,000, it was held that there was no contract of insurance.[58]

2–20 In an analogous case before the Industrial Assurance Commissioner for Northern Ireland, it was held that the offer of increased benefits on current policies contained in a prospectus, circular or advertisement issued by the insurers may be accepted either by continuing to pay the premiums on the faith of such offer or by claiming the increased benefits on maturity.[59]

If the post is expressly or impliedly indicated as the manner of accepting an offer, a letter delivered to the Post Office concludes the contract at the time of the posting of the letter[60] and the subsequent delay or loss of the letter in course of transit is immaterial.[61] While the Post Office remains the customary medium of communication between persons at a distance, an invitation to use it will readily be inferred, but this is not by any means an irrebuttable presumption, and it is submitted that no such inference would be drawn if the service was likely to be disrupted or a more expeditious method of reply was reasonable in the circumstances.[62]

2–21 Correspondence of acceptance with offer. The mere communication of an acceptance will not conclude a contract of insurance unless it corresponds with an offer to which it relates. An acceptance emanating from insurers, whether it be by way of a letter or issue of a policy, must be in the terms of the assured's proposal. In other words, the insurers cannot effect a binding contract by purporting to accept an offer which has either never been made or was made on different terms.

This rule is of importance where upon analysis it is apparent that the proposer and the insurers are really at cross-purposes. In such a case no contract is formed and, if premiums have been paid in the mistaken belief that there was an effective contract of insurance, they are recoverable by the proposer in an action for money had and received to that person's use.

2–22 A good illustration of proposer and insurers being at cross-purposes may be found in a case referred to the Industrial Assurance Commissioner. Alice Grant, on being canvassed by the agent of an insurance company, agreed to effect a life endowment policy on the life of her son, Ralph Johnston, for her own benefit. The company did not issue life-of-another endowment policies and accordingly the agent procured the son's signature to a proposal for an own-life endowment policy, and on its acceptance delivered a policy in that form to Mrs Grant who paid all the premiums. On the death of Ralph Johnston, Mrs Grant and her son's widow were rival claimants for the policy moneys. The Industrial Assurance Commissioner held that inasmuch as Mrs Grant did not get the policy she asked for, there was no contract of assurance between her and the company. Neither was there a contract between the company and Ralph Johnston, inasmuch as he never intended to effect an own-life insurance but signed the proposal form

---

[58] *Woods v. Co-operative Ins. Society*, 1924 S.C. 692, where the very words of the advertisement expressly denied any intention of establishing legal liability.

[59] *McDermott v. The Refuge* [1930] I.A.C.(N.I.) Rep. 56.

[60] *Household Fire Ins. Co. v. Grant* (1879) 4 Ex.D. 216; *Henthorn v. Fraser* [1892] 2 Ch. 27.

[61] *ibid.*

[62] Is it reasonable to use the post in the case of parties linked by fax, or when the post is subject to disruption? See Treitel *Law of Contract* (10th ed. 1999) pp. 23–29.

so that his mother might effect an insurance of his life for her own benefit. The Commissioner accordingly dismissed both claims and held that Mrs Grant was entitled to be repaid the premiums paid by her.[63]

2–23 Another consequence of the rule that the acceptance must correspond with an offer is that the acceptance must be unconditional, for otherwise it is in point of law not a true acceptance at all, but a counterproposal.[64] Such a counter-proposal or counter-offer results when there is a material variation from the offer. The expression of the same terms in different words[65] or the expression of a term which if unexpressed would have been implied, does not constitute a departure from the terms of the offer. Therefore, the delivery of a policy containing some conditions not previously referred to between the parties may constitute a complete acceptance of the offer, if the policy contains nothing but the company's ordinary terms with reference to which the proposal must be deemed to have been made.[66]

2–24 Where there was a proposal for a pure endowment policy, but the insurance office in response thereto issued a whole-life policy with an option to convert it into an endowment policy if the life should attain a specified age, the Industrial Assurance Commissioner expressed some doubt whether the difference was sufficient to support a plea of no contract. In his view, if the annual premium had been thereby increased it would clearly have been a substantial variation, but if not, the difference would be in favour of the proposer and it would not be open to him to reject the policy on that ground.[67] It is submitted that the question of advantage or disadvantage to the proposer is beside the point; if there is a real variation the so-called acceptance is a counter-offer and does not create a binding contract until the proposer is seen to accept that counter-offer by words or by conduct evidencing an acceptance. The fact that the insurers' method of acceptance is to send a completed policy to the proposer makes no difference to this principle; if the policy delivered is not in accordance with the proposal, then it cannot constitute an acceptance in law or effect a binding contract, by the mere fact of delivery.[68] Where, therefore, a proposal for fire insurance was made to a mutual company, it was held that the issue of a policy wherein it was stated that the assured became a member of the company, did not effect a binding contract, since the assured had never proposed or agreed to become a member of the company.[69]

2–25 Difficulties arise where the policy sent to the assured appears on a

---

[63] *Johnston v. The Prudential Assurance Co.* [1946] I.A.C. (1938–49) Rep., 59.

[64] *Jordan v. Norton* (1838) 4 M. & W. 155; *Honeyman v. Marryat* (1857) 6 H.L.Cas. 112; *Tinn v. Hoffmann & Co.* (1873) 29 L.T. 271; *Canning v. Farquhar* (1886) 16 Q.B.D. 727; *Lark v. Outhwaite* [1991] 2 Lloyd's Rep. 132.

[65] *Clive v. Beaumont* (1847) 1 De G. & Sm. 397; *Colonial Ins. Co. of New Zealand v. Adelaide Marine Ins. Co.* (1886) 12 App.Cas. 128; *Lark v. Outhwaite* [1991] 2 Lloyd's Rep. 132, 139.

[66] *Sanderson v. Cunningham* [1919] 2 Ir.R. 234; *General Accident Ins. Corp. v. Cronk* (1901) 17 T.L.R. 233.

[67] *Harris v. Prudential Assurance Co.* [1928] I.A.C.Rep. 23.

[68] *National Benefit Trust v. Coulter*, 1911 1 S.L.T. 190. Once the assured has signed the policy or a note evidencing the acceptance of it, he cannot later be heard to say that he does not understand the terms and is not bound by it: *Laing v. Provincial Homes Investment Co. Ltd* 1909 S.C. 812.

[69] *Star Fire and Burglary Ins. Co. v. Davidson* (1903) 5 F. 83.

cursory reading to be an acceptance of the proposal sent by him, but is in fact a counter-offer, as would appear if the policy were scrutinised carefully. Is the assured's retention of the policy and payment of premiums to be seen as a conclusive acceptance by him of the counter-offer contained in the policy? In general it will bind him to the terms expressed in it, if the assured is able to read, has had ample opportunity to examine the policy, and could fairly have been expected to discover the alteration in terms if he had done so.[70] It would be different if the assured were led, by the insurers' agent or by a letter accompanying the policy, to believe that the policy did contain the terms of the insurance already agreed between them, so that he need not trouble to read it.[71] It is naturally a question of fact in each case whether the assured was careless or justified in not examining the policy sent to him. In reading the authorities on this point, care must be taken to distinguish cases such as *Wyld v. Liverpool and London and Globe Insurance Company*[72] where a binding contract has already been made before a policy purporting to evidence it is sent to the assured. That is quite a different situation, and in the event of any discrepancy, the policy may be rectified. Of course, if a policy is not received by the assured, there can be no basis for inferring his acceptance of a counter-offer contained in it.[73]

2–26 Refusal of policy tendered. The significance of the applicant's refusal to accept the policy tendered to him and insisting upon alterations being made in it depends upon the course of prior dealings between the parties. There are three distinct possibilities. First, if the policy sent to him represents an acceptance of his proposal in the same terms, the contract of insurance has already come into being upon the posting of the policy to him, and he is in effect requesting a variation of the terms of a concluded contract. The company is free to accept or refuse this request as it sees fit.

2–27 Secondly, there may already be a binding contract on the terms of a cover note or otherwise. If the policy as delivered does not embody the terms of the parties' contract, the assured is entitled to ask for rectification of it to make it comply with the terms already agreed. In the meantime, he remains insured under the prior agreement, which is not in these circumstances superseded by the policy.[74]

2–28 If, however, no contract already exists and the policy is different in material respects from the proposal sent to the insurers, the applicant, as we have already seen, is entitled to reject it. There is in that event no concluded contract until the parties are somehow agreed, expressly or impliedly, on the

---

[70] *Provident Savings Life Assurance Society of New York v. Mowat* (1902) 32 S.C.R. 147, where many authorities are cited; *Rust v. Abbey Life Assurance Co. Ltd* [1979] 2 Lloyd's Rep. 334, 340.
[71] *Provident Savings Life Assurance Society of New York v. Mowat* (1902) 32 S.C.R. 147 160 *per* Taschereau J., citing American authority.
[72] (1877) 1 S.C.R. 604.
[73] *Gardner v. Pearl Assurance Co.* [1932] I.A.C.(N.I.) Rep. 44.
[74] *Collett v. Morrison* (1851) 9 Hare 162, *Xenos v. Wickham* (1867) L.R. 2 H.L. 296, 324; *Armstrong v. Provident Savings Life Assurance Society* (1901) 2 Ont.L.R. 771, 778 *S.E. Lancs. Ins. Co. v. Croisdale* (1931) 40 Ll.L.R. 22, 24. As to rectification, see Ch. 12, *post.*

alterations to be made, and until that happens, the applicant cannot sue on the rejected policy. He is in fact uninsured pending further agreement.[75]

2–29 The reason for the discrepancy between the policy and the proposal is immaterial. Even if the discrepancy is the result not of a deliberate change of mind by the insurers but a purely clerical error, the legal position is still the same. The delivery of the policy out of conformity with the terms of the proposal represents a counter-offer which the applicant is free to accept by an appropriate act signifying his assent, or to reject.[76]

2–30 Agreement is objectively ascertained. We have seen that as a general rule a contract cannot be produced by cross-offers or by superficial agreement between two parties who are in reality in dispute over the terms supposedly agreed. A qualification needs to be expressed, however, before the topic of offer and acceptance is dismissed. It is a well established principle of law that, even where one party claims that he is not in agreement with another in his own mind, he may be estopped from pleading that he never meant to accept the terms put forward by the other party if his conduct, viewed objectively, is that of a man who in fact did accept the terms put to him.[77] This qualification of the doctrine that *consensus ad idem* is essential to the formation of a contract was well expressed by the Industrial Assurance Commissioner for Northern Ireland as follows:

> "Though the theoretical basis of contract lies in consensus of intention, the practical requirements of business and commerce have decreed, and the law has allowed, that in certain circumstances agreement must be presumed on the part of one of the contractors irrespective of his state of mind, and prima facie an alleged contracting party must be presumed to have read and understood a document which has been handed, sent or exhibited to him as a document purporting to contain the terms of a proposal or of a concluded contract, and *a fortiori* if he has signed such document or otherwise signified his acceptance of it."[78]

2–31 The clearest case of a party estopping himself from denying that full agreement has been reached is the case in which he has signed a contractual document. Thus, where three women of full age, in the presence of, and on the advice of, their father, signed without reading them proposals for own life policies which set out quite clearly the nature of the proposed contract as duly recorded in the policies afterwards issued to them, and there had been no misrepresentation by the agent who negotiated the insurances, they were estopped from alleging, by way of a plea of *non est factum*, that they intended to apply all the time for policies of a different character, and that they believed their applications to be to that end.[79]

---

[75] *Equitable Life Assurance v. McElroy*, 83 Fed.Rep. 631 (1897). There must be a clear rejection of the policy. Accepting it while grumbling to the insurers' agent will not do; *Smith v. Provident Savings Life Assurance Society of New York*, 65 Fed.Rep. 765 (1895).

[76] *Batty v. Pearl Assurance Co. Ltd* [1937] I.A.C.Rep. 12 (acceptance of non-conforming policy by payment of premiums for eight years).

[77] *Freeman v. Cooke* (1848) 2 Exch. 654, 663; *Smith v. Hughes* (1871) L.R. 6 Q.B. 597, 607; *Provident Savings Life Assurance Society of New York v. Mowat* (1902) 32 S.C.R. 147; *Inversiones Manria SA v. Sphere Drake Ins. Co.* [1989] 1 Lloyd's Rep. 69, 71–74 (declaration of primary yacht insurance against reinsurance open cover).

[78] *Ferguson v. Co-operative Ins. Society* [1930] I.A.C.(N.I.) Rep. 43.

[79] *Gardner v. Hearts of Oak Assurance* [1928] I.A.C.Rep. 21.

The principle of estoppel can, of course, benefit an assured as well, because insurers will not be allowed to deny the existence of a contract if, contrary to their own inner intentions, they have by their conduct induced the assured reasonably to think that his proposal was accepted.[80]

2–32 If a policy is delivered to the proposer which varies from the terms of his proposal, and he, being an educated person in full possession of his faculties, retains it and pays the premiums due under it over a substantial period of time, he cannot usually be heard to say later that he did not read it or did not understand its terms. His conduct in retaining it must prima facie be interpreted as an acceptance of its terms, which then bind both parties as a completed contract.[81] This prima facie rule might be displaced by the court finding that the insurers, by the manner in which they had delivered the policy to the proposer, with or without accompanying comment, had led him fairly to believe that a line-by-line scrutiny of the policy was unnecessary because his proposal was accepted *in toto*.[82] Again, the character and ability of the proposer must not be overlooked. If a policy issued to a blind or illiterate person is not in conformity with the proposal made by him or his amanuensis, he may repudiate it on discovering, even after a lapse of some years, that it is not in accordance with his proposal, and may recover the premiums paid.[83]

2. SPECIAL MARKET USAGE

2–33 Signature of a slip. In such insurance business as aviation, marine, reinsurance and insurance concluded at Lloyd's it is usual for the assured's broker to put down the terms of the proposed insurance on a document called a slip, which is put forward for the consideration of each underwriter.[84] The underwriter accepts the proposed risk by signing the slip and stating the proportion of risk to which he is prepared to subscribe. This creates a binding contract between the assured and each underwriter.[85] The insurers must then issue their policy in terms conforming to the slip. They are not at liberty to introduce inconsistent terms in the policy unless these are in some way authorised by the terms of the slip, so that it is agreed in certain respects not to record the final terms of the insurance.[86]

2–34 Types of slip. Not all slips are intended to create a binding contract when signed or initialled. A quotation slip, for instance, will not do so, and

---

[80] *Summers v. London and Manchester Assurance Co.* [1946] I.A.C.Rep. (1938–49) 56; *Provident Savings Life Assurance Society of New York v. Mowat* (1902) 32 S.C.R. 147, 160.
[81] *Laing v. Provincial Homes Investment Co.* 1909 S.C. 812.
[82] *Provident Savings Life Assurance Co. of New York v. Mowat* (1902) 32 S.C.R. 147, 160, *per* Taschereau J.; *MacMaster v. New York Life Ins. Co.*, 99 Fed.Rep. 856 (1899); 183 U.S. 25 (1901). Insurers often invite the assured to read his policy and inform them if it is not what he wants, and in that case the assured could have little excuse for omitting to do so in the belief that it was in accordance with his proposal, unless he had been expressly told that it was.
[83] *Irwin v. Liverpool Victoria F.S.* [1934] I.A.C.Rep. 19.
[84] The procedure for acceptance of risks in the Lloyd's market is considered in Ch. 35, *post*.
[85] *General Reinsurance Corp. v. Fennia Patria* [1983] Q.B. 856; *Napier v. Kershaw* [1997] L.R.L.R. 1, 7–8.
[86] *Symington & Co. v. Union Ins. Soc. of Canton Ltd (No. 2)* (1928) 34 Com.Cas. 233, 235.

nor will a slip expressed to be subject to conditions to be fulfilled.[87] A line slip is another type of slip which does not evidence a binding contract of insurance. It is a written facility granted by a number of insurers which empowers a leading underwriter to agree to proposals for insurance of risks within a prescribed defined classification on behalf of the insurers who subscribed to the line slip, so long as the proposed insurance falls within the scope of the authority conferred on him. Accordingly it is in the nature of a standing offer by subscribers to be bound to particular risks by their designated underwriter. Only when an off-slip is presented to the leading underwriter for acceptance, and unconditionally initialled by him, is a contract of insurance brought into being.[88] Another example of a slip which does not bring about a concluded contract of insurance immediately it is initialled is the reinsurance slip initialled in advance of the proposal for reinsurance by a reassured. A contract of reinsurance is brought about by the broker obtaining an order for reinsurance in terms of the slip from an intending reassured, even though there need be no communication of that order to the reinsurers who initialled the slip.[89] The same practice has been used in the case of facilities granted to brokers empowering them to declare to retrocessionaires proposals for reinsurance on the part of Lloyd's syndicates subscribing to designated marine insurance contracts. The brokers were thus authorised to make offers of reinsurance to these syndicates, which were to be accepted by placing orders for reinsurance in the form of declarations made against the retrocession facility by the same brokers.[90] Where a declaration was made in a bordereau stating "conditions as attached", when in fact none were attached, no contract of insurance could come into being when these could not be identified either from prior agreement or market usage.[91]

2–35 Leading underwriter clauses. When a leading underwriter clause is incorporated into a slip and policy, following underwriters thereby empower one or more leading underwriters to do such things as agree extensions of and variations to cover and to settle claims. The limits of such authority depend upon the express terms of the particular clause. There is no presumption that such clauses are to be construed restrictively and confined to amendments of minor importance.[92] There is no recognised market usage obliging a leading underwriter to consult followers when exercising his power pursuant to such a clause, and his decision binds them whether or not he has in their view used businesslike methods to settle a claim.[93]

2–36 When a leading underwriter is authorised to accept declarations under an open cover or line slip he is not the agent of following underwriters with power to bind them to declarations outside the ambit of the cover. It is

---

[87] *Eagle Star Ins. Co. v. Spratt* [1971] 2 Lloyd's Rep. 116, 124.

[88] *Denby v. English & Scottish Maritime Ins. Co. Ltd* [1998] Lloyd's Rep.I.R. 343, 354, *per* Hobhouse L.J. approving the analysis by Webster J. in *Balfour v. Beaumont* [1982] 2 Lloyd's Rep. 493, 494. The question of whether subscribers to a line slip are entitled to withdraw their authority from the leading underwriter to bind them to future risks was left open.

[89] *General Accident Fire & Life Ass. Corp. v. Tanter* [1984] 1 Lloyd's Rep. 58, 71–72; [1985] 2 Lloyd's Rep. 529, 532.

[90] *Mander v. Commercial Union Ass. Co.* [1998] Lloyd's Rep.I.R. 93, 104.

[91] *ibid* at p. 117.

[92] *Barlee Marine Corporation v. Mountain* [1987] 1 Lloyd's Rep. 471.

[93] *Roar Marine Ltd v. Bimeh Iran Ins. Co. Ltd* [1998] 1 Lloyd's Rep. 423.

said that his agreement "triggers" a binding contract, and is not an action which binds them as his principals.[94] The response that he possesses apparent authority to bind the following underwriters to the declaration which he accepts is met by the point that the assured are deemed to have knowledge of the terms of the open cover which is available for inspection.[95] Accordingly his acceptance of a risk does not preclude following underwriters from disputing that it comes within the cover, and the leading underwriter is not subject to a claim for damages for breach of an agent's implied warranty of authority if he initially accepts a declaration which is subsequently rejected by the following market as *ultra vires*.[96]

2–37 Certainty. Once a contract is concluded the fact that the parties have agreed that its terms may be varied by one of them at his discretion to take account of increased costs will not necessarily render the insurance too uncertain to be enforceable, at any rate where such terms were of minor importance.[97] Where an excess of loss reinsurance contract provided that an excess and a limit of liability were to be calculated on the basis of "each and every loss and/or series of losses arising out of one event", it was agreed that the reassured was to be the sole judge of what constituted "each and every loss" and "event", and that his decision was to be binding on reinsurers. This did not prevent the insurance from being binding and enforceable, although it would have done if fundamental questions of liability were left to the determination of one party to the insurance.[98]

3. SPECIAL CONDITIONS DELAYING COMMENCEMENT OF CONTRACT

2–38 "No insurance to be effective until premium paid." Insurers frequently stipulate that they will not come under a liability to indemnify the assured until the first premium is paid. Thus the applicant may find in the proposal which he signs a provision that no contract is to come into being, or no insurance is to be effective, until a premium is paid.[99] Alternatively, that provision may be found in a letter sent acknowledging receipt of the proposal and saying that the risk proposed is agreeable to the insurers.[1] The policy itself may also contain a condition providing that the risk shall not commence to run until a premium is received.[2]

2–39 When insurers purport to "accept" the applicant's proposal subject to such a stipulation, it is misleading to speak in general terms of their

---

[94] *The Tiburon* [1990] 2 Lloyd's Rep. 418, 422; *Mander v. Commercial Union Assurance* [1998] Lloyd's Rep.I.R. 93, 143, 144, not following *Roadworks (1952) Ltd v. Charman* [1994] 2 Lloyd's Rep. 99, 105–106.

[95] *Mander v. Commercial Union Assurance* [1998] Lloyd's Rep.I.R. 93, 144.

[96] *ibid.*

[97] *Baynham v. Philips Electronics (UK) Ltd, The Times*, July 19, 1995.

[98] *Brown v. GIO Insurance Ltd* [1998] Lloyd's Rep.I.R. 201, 208.

[99] *Paine v. Pacific Mutual Life Ins. Co.*, 51 Fed.Rep. 689 (1892); *Kohen v. Mutual Reserve Fund Life Association*, 28 Fed.Rep. 705 (1886); *MacMaster v. New York Life Ins. Co.*, 99 Fed.Rep. 856 (1899).

[1] *Canning v. Farquhar* (1886) 16 Q.B.D. 727. See also *Equitable Fire & Accident Office v. Ching Wo Hong* [1907] A.C. 96—insurance not to be in force until premium "actually paid".

[2] *Sickness and Accident Assurance Association v. General Accident Assurance Corporation* (1892) 19 R. 977.

"acceptance" of his offer, and to say that a "preliminary contract"[3] has come into being, since on legal analysis there is probably no binding contract at all at that time. The legal position of the parties will depend upon the negotiations which have taken place and the exact wording of the clause in question, from which the court will endeavour to deduce whether it was the parties' intention to enter into a legally binding agreement at that moment. There are certainly three alternative interpretations of such an "acceptance".

2–40 First, the insurers may have made a legal agreement to provide insurance, so that, on the one hand, the assured is bound to tender a premium within a reasonable time, and, on the other, they are bound to issue a policy, subject to the proviso that the assured will not be able to claim for any loss occurring before they receive the premium. Secondly, the insurers may be held to have made a counter-offer, which it is open to the applicant to ignore, or to accept by tendering a premium, whereupon the insurers will be bound. Lastly, the prior negotiations may indicate to the court that it was the insurers' intention to issue merely an invitation to treat, in response to which it was for the assured to make an offer by tendering a premium which they might or might not accept, as they pleased. It is accordingly impossible to state any universal rule concerning the effect of such stipulations, and the authorities mentioned in the next few paragraphs serve only to illustrate what the courts have held in particular instances where such clauses were used by insurers.

2–41 In *Canning v. Farquhar*[4] Mr Canning applied for life assurance upon one of the company's printed forms containing the usual questions and declarations. The risk was considered and approved by the directors, and the actuary wrote to Mr Canning's agent:

> "The proposal . . . on the life of Mr . . . Canning has been accepted at the annual premium of £47 18s. 4d. No assurance can take place until the first premium is paid."

No mention had been made of a premium until that moment. Before a premium was paid, or any policy issued, Mr Canning fell over a cliff and seriously injured himself. The premium was then tendered by his agent, who disclosed the occurrence of this unfortunate accident, whereupon the company refused the premium. Mr Canning then died. His administrator sued the company, claiming that a contract to insure had been made on the day the actuary wrote that the proposal was "accepted". The Court of Appeal held that the company was under no liability, but for differing reasons. Lord Esher M.R. believed that the insurers never intended to make an offer binding on themselves when their actuary wrote to Mr Canning's agent, so that they were not bound to accept the premium tendered whether or not there had been a material alteration in the terms of the risk.

2–42 It is, however, with respect, difficult to see why that letter was not a counter-offer in law, because it was unequivocal, and the insurers were at that stage clearly satisfied on all the essential terms of the insurance, so that

---

[3] See, *e.g.* Lord McLaren's speech in the *Sickness and Accident* case, *supra*, at p. 987, where he uses that phrase while at the same time stating that "matters are entire".
[4] (1886) 16 Q.B.D. 727.

the contract could be effected by the simple act of payment of the premium requested. It is submitted that the decision is best explained on the ground preferred by Lindley and Lopes L.JJ., namely that there had been a material change in the risk before a contract could be concluded by tender of a premium. The assured's agent, in disclosing it while at the same time tendering the premium, was in reality making a fresh (and obviously unwelcome) proposal, to obtain insurance on a sick man for the cost appropriate to a healthy person, so that his act of acceptance was not a true acceptance in law. Alternatively, it appears from the judgments of the Court of Appeal that the court may have thought that the actuary's counter-offer was made on the basis that the declaration of good health made by the assured should remain true up to the moment of acceptance, so that it lapsed when the declaration became invalid.

2–43 In *Harrington v. Pearl Life Assurance Company*,[5] one B applied to the Pearl office on October 1, 1912, for own-life assurance to £300, the policy to run from October 18. The applicant declared that there had been no material change in his health since he was examined on behalf of the office in the previous May in connection with another proposal. On October 18, the office wrote to B saying that his proposal was accepted, and the policy would be forwarded on receipt of the premium, provided it was received within 30 days. The policy applied for was the ordinary life policy issued by the Pearl, containing a condition that there was to be no insurance until the premium was paid. On November 4, B purported to assign all his interest in the policy to the plaintiff, Harrington, to whom he was indebted, and it was agreed between them that Harrington should pay the premiums on it. On November 6, B was taken seriously ill. On November 8 two things occurred; Harrington paid the premium due and, later on that day, B died. The Court of Appeal held that a bargain had been struck on October 18, between B and the insurers, that if he complied with certain stipulations (including that as to his health) he should have a policy, on which they should be at risk once a premium was paid. The warranty as to good health being broken, however, that discharged the insurers from performing their side of the bargain, and the *status quo ante* was restored. Although the case differed from the *Canning* case in that the insurers were ignorant of the increase of risk when the premium was tendered, the same rules applied, and the insurers could have refused to accept the premium when it was offered. When the increase in risk was later known to them, they could avoid the policy for breach of warranty and non-disclosure.

2–44 In *Looker v. Law Union and Rock Insurance Company Limited*[6] Dr Looker completed a proposal for own-life insurance, stating, *inter alia*, that he was free from disease or ailment, and that the particulars of his proposal were true. The company sent him a conditional acceptance, stating that the proposal was accepted, "and if the health of the life proposed remains meanwhile unaffected the policy will be issued on payment of the first premium. ... The risk of the company will not commence until receipt of the first premium, and the directors meanwhile reserve the power to alter or withdraw this acceptance." A few days later Dr Looker became indisposed;

[5] (1914) 30 T.L.R. 613.
[6] [1928] 1 K.B. 554.

a friend filled in the cheque for the first premium, and Dr Looker signed it, but it was not posted on that day. The next day (July 23) a doctor was called, who diagnosed pneumonia, and the friend posted the cheque on July 24. On the morning of July 26 the company received the cheque and posted a certificate of insurance. Dr Looker died on July 27. It is clear that in these circumstances the insurance company could not be liable. The communication of the directors could scarcely amount to more than a counter-offer which might be withdrawn at will, and was really no more than an invitation to Dr Looker to tender a premium by way of offer. The certificate was impliedly issued on the basis of the continued truth of the representations in the proposal form, and these had become untrue. Dr Looker had warranted the truth of them in the proposal form. The material change in the risk ought in any event to have been disclosed, so that the agreement concluded on July 26 was voidable both for breach of warranty and for non-disclosure.

2–45 Loss occurring before premium paid. In *Sickness and Accident Assurance Association v. General Accident Assurance Corporation*[7] a policy was issued, on November 16, 1888, to a tramway company against third party liability for accidents for a year from November 17, 1888, to November 17, 1889. The policy contained the clause: "No insurance shall be held to be effected until the premium due thereon shall have been paid." The secretary of the tramway company, on November 19, wrote to the insurers' agent:

> "I am duly in receipt of this policy, and will send you a cheque for the premium in the course of a few days. There are one or two points upon which I must confer with my directors. The date from which I desire to be covered is from the 24 inst. inclusive, and not the 17 inst., as stated herein."

He also requested that a particular firm of solicitors be given the conduct of all legal business bearing upon the policy. The agent replied on November 20, "I shall be pleased to make the alteration in policy required by your directors." On November 24 before the premium had been paid or a new policy issued, an accident occurred in respect of which the tramway company was liable. On November 26 a meeting took place between representatives of the two companies at which the accident was made known to the insurers' representative, who said they would not issue a policy "except from the twenty-fourth."[8] The same day the tramway company's secretary sent a cheque for the premium to the insurers' agent, who replied:

> "I am much obliged for your favour enclosing the cheque for the third party risk from the 24 inst. ... Please return policy for alterations."

The question accordingly was whether the insurers were liable in respect of the accident occurring on November 24 itself.

The Lord Ordinary, Lord Low, held that the insurers were bound to accept the premium when tendered and to issue a new policy, since a contract of insurance had been concluded prior to November 24, subject, however, to the suspensive condition present in the original policy, and in the altered one, to the effect that no cover was to be in effect until the premium was paid. The insurers had never waived that condition, their

[7] (1892) 19 R. 977.
[8] (1892) 19 R. 977, 982, 985.

receipt saying that the risk ran *"from* the 24 inst.," which meant, *not including* the twenty-fourth. The insurers had therefore not come on risk at the time of the accident, and were not liable.[9]

The Inner House of the Court of Session affirmed the judgment of the Lord Ordinary, but on other grounds and in speeches which are not, it is submitted, entirely free from difficulty. The Inner House cited and relied upon the English Court of Appeal's decision in *Canning v. Farquhar,*[10] and held that there was no binding contract prior to November 29 when the cheque sent on November 26 was accepted. The insurers were not bound to accept a premium after the loss occurred on November 24. It appears, particularly from Lord Adam's speech, that in the court's view the insurers had first simply made an offer to issue a policy and grant cover from November 24 inclusive, and, on the authority of *Canning v. Farquhar,*[11] that offer was incapable of acceptance by the tramway company once the loss occurred on November 24 because the offer was to indemnify against the risk of accidents happening, and not the actual consequences of one which had happened. It was impossible to overlook the meeting on November 26 which did not accord with the notion that a binding agreement was already in force. Lord Adam, indeed, went further, and, echoing Lord Esher M.R.'s judgment in *Canning v. Farquhar,*[12] doubted whether the insurers had even made a legally binding offer, in which case they could not be bound to accept the premium even if no accident had occurred in the meantime.[13]

2–46 The judgments in the Inner House are also susceptible of a different analysis, namely that there was a binding agreement prior to November 24 whereby the tramway company was to tender a premium and the insurers to deliver a policy under which cover would run from November 24 subject to the fulfilment of the special condition. No right to an indemnity could be acquired until such time as the premium was paid. This "preliminary contrast"[14] "fell"[15] when the accident occurred, because it was made on the basis that there would be no loss occurring before the policy was issued. The insurers were then free to contract on different terms, under which the risk ran from midnight on November 24 and did not cover an accident occurring earlier in the day.

2–47 If this interpretation of the *Sickness and Accident* case is correct, the judgments contain elements of three different analyses canvassed in paragraph 2–40, above. It is probably best explained on the basis that the insurers made an offer to issue a policy and to grant cover from November 24 inclusive and, on the authority of *Canning v. Farquhar,*[16] that offer was incapable of acceptance after the accident occurred on November 24.[17] It seems to follow that a special condition of the kind discussed is most likely

---

[9] (1892) 19 R. 977, 984.
[10] (1886) 16 Q.B.D. 727.
[11] *ibid.*
[12] *ibid.*
[13] (1892) 19 R 977, 986. See para. 4–37, *post.*
[14] (1892) 19 R 977, 987 *per* Lord McLaren.
[15] (1892) 19 R 977, 985 *per* Lord Adam.
[16] (1886) 16 Q.B.D. 727.
[17] In *McElroy v. The London Assurance Corporation* (1897) 24 R 287 which came before the same court, Lord McLaren described the former case as one where no insurance had been completed before the casualty occurred pp. 291–292.

not merely to suspend cover until the receipt of a premium but also to discharge the insurers from all liability in the event of a loss prior to payment. In the case where no preliminary agreement comes into being the assured is presumably under a duty to disclose all material circumstances occurring prior to a binding acceptance of the risk, and not merely an actual loss.

2–48 Delivery of policy a condition precedent. A proposal may be made and accepted on the terms that no contract shall be deemed to have been made unless and until the policy is delivered to the proposer.[18] It is a not uncommon condition of a proposal for life insurance, and, if the proposal is accepted, the condition may be repeated in the policy. Although there is a proposal and an acceptance and the parties are *ad idem* on the terms of the insurance, the effect of the condition is in fact to render the acceptance of no legal significance, because until the policy is delivered, there is no liability on either side and the position is as if no binding contract existed. The insurer is not on risk, and the proposer may recover any premium paid. The effect of the condition, thus, is to make clear that it was not the intention of the parties to make a binding contract of insurance when the insurers approved the proposal terms.

2–49 Delivery to a collector or other agent of the insurer is not a delivery within the meaning of the condition,[19] and the intention of the agent is immaterial.[20] Delivery by the agent to the proposer or his representative after the life proposed for insurance has dropped does not make the policy effective as a contract of insurance, and the insurer is not thereby brought on risk.[21] By an arrangement between the proposer and the company's agent, the latter may be constituted the agent of the proposer so far as the delivery of the policy is concerned, in which case delivery to the agent is delivery to the proposer within the meaning of the condition,[22] assuming that the agent has express or ostensible authority to make such arrangement.

2–50 The question what exactly constitutes delivery of a policy has been considered in several American cases and the balance of authority appears to support two propositions. First, there must be an intention to give legal effect to the policy, manifested by some word or act by the insurer putting the document outside his legal (but not necessarily his physical) control, and acquiesced in by the assured.[23] Secondly, delivery to an agent, if it satisfies the first proposition, is sufficient.[24]

---

[18] The American courts considered such clauses in *Kohen v. Mutual Reserve Fund Life Association*, 28 Fed.Rep. 705 (1886); *Misselhorn v. Same*, 30 Fed.Rep. 545 (1887); *Marks v. Hope Mutual Life Ins. Co.*, 117 Mass. 528 (1875); *MacMaster v. New York Life Ins. Co.*, 99 Fed.Rep. 856 (1900). For recent authority, see *Molton, Allen and Williams Inc. v. Harris*, 613 F. 2d 1176 (1980), and see generally, Appleman, *Insurance Law and Practice*, para. 133.

[19] *Clayton v. Liverpool Victoria F.S.* [1938] I.A.C.Rep. (1938–49) 1.

[20] *Shields v. Co-operative Ins. Soc.* [1949] I.A.C.Rep. (1938–49) 73.

[21] Note 19, *ante*.

[22] *Colquhoun v. London and Manchester Ass. Co.* [1949] I.A.C.Rep. (1938–49) 77.

[23] *Wood v. National Farmers' Union Automobile and Casualty Co.*, 114 F.Supp. 514 (U.S.D.C., Colo., 1953); *Life and Casualty Ins. Co. of Tennessee v. Gurley*, 229 F. 2d 326 (C.C.A., 4th Cir., 1956).

[24] *Progressive Life Ins. Co. v. Bohannon*, S.E. 2d 564 (Ga.Ct.App., 1946) 40; *Gilley v. Glen Falls Ins. Co.*, 58 S.E. 2d 218 (Ga.Ct.App., 1950); *Life and Casualty Ins. Co. of Tennessee v. Latham*, 50 So. 2d 727 (Sup.Ct.Ala., 1951).

If there is no express term postponing the operation of a policy until it has been delivered, no such term will be implied, for that would contravene the prima facie rule that a binding contract of insurance comes into being so soon as the parties are agreed upon the material terms of the insurance, and an offer from one of them has been unconditionally accepted in a lawful way by the other. Payment of a premium may in a proper case be itself construed as an act of acceptance by the assured, or a voluntary receipt of premiums may be construed as denoting acceptance on the part of insurers, in which event neither side will be free to resile from their contract.[25]

2–51 "Subject to approval of directors." An agent may be given authority to conclude a contract with an applicant on the terms that it shall not be effective until approved by the directors. It has been held that where negotiations between the applicant and the insurers' agent proceed on that basis, no notification of acceptance by the directors is necessary, and the contract becomes operative when, in fact, the directors do approve the risk even though that approval is not indicated by any outward act.[26] Thus in one American case the general agent of an English company, upon receiving a proposal, gave the following receipt:

> "Received the sum of £—premium on a proposal of assurance for £—on the life of A, which is to be forwarded immediately to the head office at Liverpool, England, for acceptance. If it be accepted, a policy will be issued in accordance therewith; if declined, the above-mentioned premium will be returned. But in case the said A die before the decision of the head office shall have been received the sum insured will be paid."

The proposal was transmitted and accepted and a policy issued and forwarded to the agent, who, in accordance with instructions, declined to deliver it to the assured on the grounds that his health was failing. A New York court held that, as the risk had been in fact accepted by the head office, there was a binding contract to issue a policy.[27] In another American case the agent accepted a fire risk "subject to acceptance by the directors of the premium agreed", and a loss occurred before the agent had communicated with the head office. It was held that the company was bound if the rate was a reasonable one.[28]

2–52 There is, however, no universal rule that the decision of the directors is sufficient, without more, to bring the contract into being. The course of negotiations may well have been such that the normal requirement of communication of acceptance applies at this stage.[29] It is also possible that there is still no contract even after the director's approval has been communicated, as this communication may be accompanied by the stipulation that some further step, such as the payment of a premium, is necessary.

---

[25] *Adie & Sons v. The Insurance Corporation* (1898) 14 T.L.R. 544; *McElhinney v. Northern Counties Life and General Assurance Co.* [1950] I.A.C.(N.I.) Rep. 21.
[26] *Welsh v. Continental Ins. Co.*, 47 Hun. 598 (N.Y.Sup.Ct., 1887).
[27] *Fried v. Royal Ins. Co.*, 50 N.Y. 243 (1872).
[28] *Perkins v. Washington Ins. Co.*, 4 Cow. 645 (N.Y.Sup.Ct., 1825).
[29] *Armstrong v. Provident Savings Life Assurance Soc.* (1901) 2 Ont.L.R. 771, and the decisions cited at note 47 to para. 2–16, *ante.*

2–53 An incidental question which arises in connection with acceptance by directors may be referred to here, and that is the effect, if any, of a delay on the part of the directors in giving their answer. The mere delay is of itself not an acceptance of the proposal, but a question much debated in America, on which there appears to be no English authority, is this; does unreasonable and inexcusable delay in dealing with the application for insurance give a right of action in tort to the applicant if he is damaged thereby? The prevailing opinion seems to be that it does.[30]

---

[30] See, *e.g. Barrera v. State Farm Mutual Automobile Ins. Co.*, 456 P. 2d 674 (1969); *Milbank Mutual Ins. Co. v. Schmidt*, 304 F. 2d 640 (1962). Compare *La Favour v. American National Ins. Co.* 155 N.W. 2d 286 (1967). See generally, Appleman, *Insurance Law and Practice*, paras. 7216–7223.

CHAPTER 3

FORM OF THE CONTRACT

1. GENERAL RULE

3–1 No particular form required. There is no rule of common law requiring contracts of insurance to be in any particular form, or, indeed in writing at all.[1] Statute law has, however, created certain important exceptions in relation to marine insurance, guarantee insurance, and industrial assurances on funeral expenses,[2] and these are examined below.

Requirements as to form may also be found in the memoranda of association, rules or internal instructions of insurance companies or the usages of certain insurance markets, and this will be considered later also.

3–2 As an illustration of the general rule a Lloyd's slip on, say, a fire risk on land, can be enforced as a binding contract[3] before it is embodied in a formal policy. There is nothing to prevent a valid contract of fire, accident or burglary insurance being constituted by informal writing or correspondence,[4] or even by mere oral communications.[5] In practice, however, it is very difficult to satisfy a court that there is an oral contract when one party disputes its existence,[6] and attempts to set up such an agreement are not to

---

[1] *London Life Assurance Co. v. Wright* (1880) 5 S.C.R. 466, 513; *Parsons v. Queen Ins. Co.* (1878) 43 U.C.Q.B. 271, 277; *Coulter v. Equity Fire Ins. Co.* (1904) 9 Ont.L.Rep. 35.

[2] This exception now applies only to Northern Ireland. It arises, according to the decision in *Gardner v. Pearl Assurance Co.* [1932] I.A.C.(N.I.) Rep. 44, upon the wording of the Assurance Companies Act 1909, s.36(1). That section has been repealed and has no equivalent in the extant legislation of England and Wales, but was re-enacted in the Industrial Assurance Act (Northern Ireland) 1924, s.3.

[3] *Thompson v. Adams* (1889) 23 Q.B.D. 361; *Jaglom v. Excess Ins. Co.* [1972] 2 Q.B. 250.

[4] *Salvin v. James* (1805) 6 East 571; *Bhugwandass v. Netherlands India Sea and Fire Ins. Co.* (1888) 14 App.Cas. 83; *General Accident Fire and Life Assurance Ltd. v. Robertson* [1909] A.C. 404; *Christie v. N. British Ins. Co.* (1825) 3 S. & D. (Ct. of Sess.) 519, 522; *Mills v. Albion Ins. Co.* (1826) 4 S. 575; *McElroy v. London Assurance Corp.* (1897) 24 R. 287; *Parker v. Western Assurance Co.* 1925 S.L.T. 131.

[5] *Murfitt v. Royal Ins. Co.* (1922) 38 T.L.R. 334; *Hochbaum v. Pioneer Ins. Co.* [1933] 1 W.W.R. 403; *Stockton v. Mason* [1978] 2 Lloyd's Rep. 430.

[6] *Allis-Chalmers Co. v. Maryland Fidelity and Deposit Co.* (1916) 114 L.T. 433; *Lines (A.S.) Sawmills v. N.A. Bronsten & Co.* [1954] 1 Lloyd's Rep. 384; *Sphere Drake Ins. PLC v. Denby* [1995] L.R.L.R. 1. In Scotland the doubt raised by conflicting decisions has been removed by the Requirements of Writing (Scotland) Act 1995 (c. 7). Pursuant to s.1 insurance contracts need not be in writing. Under s.11(3) privileged writings, including writs *in re mercatoria*, and *obligationes literis* are abolished. Although still to be tested the effect seems to be that Scots law recognises contracts, including insurance contracts, made, for example, on computers. In practice no doubt writing will continue to be used voluntarily and although not required the

be undertaken lightly. The small trouble involved in recording contracts in writing is amply justified to avoid later evidentiary difficulties. When an informal contract is recorded in writing, the written terms are not necessarily a conclusive statement of the contract in law, because oral evidence is admissible to prove other terms of the contract, if it is established that the document was not intended to be a complete record of it.[7]

3-3 The law in some countries requires all insurance contracts to be in writing, and it was argued in an American case that a custom to the same effect existed among insurers and businessmen and, because it was part of the law merchant, it ought to be recognised as part of the common law of the United States and England. The American Supreme Court rejected this contention, and held that where the president of an insurance company possessed ostensible authority to conclude oral contracts to grant insurances, and had done so several times, the company was bound by such a contract.[8]

3-4 **Statutory requirements not essential to validity.** Section 100 of the Stamp Act 1891 might appear on a cursory reading to jeopardise the general principle stated above, but, it is submitted, such is not the case. By that section any person who receives or takes the credit for any premium on any life insurance[9] and does not within one month make out and execute a duly stamped policy of insurance, incurs a penalty of £20. The Act does not, however, require any such contract of insurance to be expressed in a policy as a condition precedent to the validity of the contract itself. It is concerned with the stamping of policies in being.

It has been suggested that an oral contract of insurance must be void because it is evasive of the Stamp Act, but the absence of any provision in the Act to that effect and the contrast with the express provisions covering marine insurances point to the inference that the Act was never intended to prohibit informal contracts of insurance, other than marine insurance.

2. STATUTORY EXCEPTIONS

3-5 **Marine insurance.** The law requires every contract for marine insurance to be expressed in a policy.[10] Since the Finance Act 1970 repealed[11] section 30(2) of the Finance Act 1958, it has not been necessary for such a policy to be stamped, and the longstanding question whether a slip issued by

---

document will have formal validity if it is subscribed by the granter, from s.2. See s.3 for the provisions on self-proving documents replacing the previous law on the requirements of attestation. See s.11(3)(a) on the abolition of the common law rule that assignations of incorporeal moveables should be in writing although statutory provisions requiring writing remain unaffected.

[7] *Beckett v. Nurse* [1948] 1 K.B. 535. *Hutton v. Watling* [1948] Ch. 398.

[8] *Commercial Mutual Marine Ins. Co. v. Union Mutual Ins. Co. of New York* (1856) 60 U.S. (19 How.) 318.

[9] The section was originally of wider application but by the Finance Act 1970, s.32 and Sched. 7, para. 1(2)(b), stamp duty was abolished on insurance policies other than those of life insurance.

[10] Marine Insurance Act 1906, s.22.

[11] s.36(8), Sched. 8, Pt. IV.

Lloyd's underwriters was a policy within the meaning of the Stamp Act is no longer relevant.[12]

3–6 The Statute of Frauds. Section 4 of the Statute of Frauds[13] provided that no action should be brought upon an agreement which was not to be performed within the space of one year from the making thereof unless it was in writing or unless a memorandum or note thereof was in writing. This provision has been repealed as respects England and Wales,[14] save that it still applies to contracts of surety and guarantee,[15] namely, contracts whereby a person promises "to answer for the debt, default or miscarriage of another person". Translated into modern legal terminology the phrase "to answer for" means "to accept liability for", in the sense that the guarantor is to see to it that the debtor performs his obligation.[16] This is the crucial distinction between a contract of guarantee, which is within the section, and a contract of indemnity, which is not.[17] The surety promises a creditor that he will be paid, whereas an insurer promises to indemnify him if he is not.[18] We do not therefore propose to refer to the decisions on the section before its general repeal in England.[19]

3. OTHER EXCEPTIONS

3–7 Sources of other exceptions. Leaving aside those contracts of insurance subject to statutory requirements, any type of insurance may be subject to regulations on its form imposed by the memoranda of association, rules or internal instructions of insurance companies themselves. Another source of rules as to the form in which a contract of insurance ought to be expressed are the usages of insurance business, since these may authorise the insurers' agents to conclude contracts binding on the company only if these are in a particular form. These restrictions are considered at paragraphs 3–10 to 3–15 of the 9th edition of this book, but we have omitted them from the present edition as they have little relevance to the current law.

---

[12] The Finance Act 1959, s.30(2), (4) provided that cover notes, slips, etc., were not liable to stamp duty. See *Home Marine Ins. Co. v. Smith* [1898] 1 Q.B. 829.
[13] 29 Car.2, c. 3. The Act does not apply to Scotland or Northern Ireland.
[14] Law Reform (Enforcement of Contracts) Act 1954 (2 & 3 Eliz. 2, c. 34), s.1.
[15] *ibid.*, s.4.
[16] *Moschi v. Lep Air Services Ltd* [1973] A.C. 331, 347–348 *per* Lord Diplock.
[17] *Re Hoyle* [1893] 1 Ch. 84.
[18] The distinction between contracts of guarantee and contracts of credit or guarantee insurance is examined at paras. 31–40 to 31–42, *post.*
[19] See para. 269 of the 8th edition of this work.

CHAPTER 4

THE PERIOD PRIOR TO ISSUE OF THE POLICY

1. TEMPORARY COVER

(a) *Grant of Temporary Cover*

4–1 Introduction. It is usual for insurers to take some time to consider the applicant's proposal for insurance before giving a definite acceptance or refusal. Since the prospective assured often wishes to be covered from the time he applies for insurance, it is the practice of insurers to provide temporary cover, especially in the case of applications for fire, motor, burglary and accident insurance, during the interim period between the proposal and the final decision. This practice is common to Lloyd's underwriters as well as to insurance companies, for it represents a response to an undoubted customer demand, and in order to accommodate it elaborate arrangements have had to be made in Lloyd's insurance practice to permit the issue of interim cover notes.[1]

4–2 Life assurance formerly constituted an exception to this practice, but more recently it has become usual to issue interim protection pending the acceptance or rejection of a proposal by the directors or others. The interim cover is provided subject to appropriate monetary limits. In industrial assurance business, it is common practice for the collector or agent who secures a proposal to require payment of a first premium, to deliver a premium receipt book and to continue to collect premiums during such time as the proposal is under consideration by the head office. The premium receipt book usually contains a notice to the effect that it is issued subject to the acceptance or rejection of the proposal, and that the company does not accept liability in the event of a claim until a policy is issued. In the absence of such a notice being brought to the attention of the proposer, it might be contended that the receipt of premiums provided a temporary cover pending the consideration of the proposal but the general principles of life insurance

---

[1] The adaptation of Lloyd's practice to satisfy eager purchasers of new motor-cars who want instant insurance so that they can take to the road at once with their new possession is well described by Pearson J. in *Julien Praet et Cie SA v. H.G. Poland Ltd* [1960] 1 Lloyd's Rep. 416, 428. See para. 35–12, *post*.

are against any such inference being drawn from the mere receipt of premiums.[2]

4–3 The cover note. The general practice is for a cover note to be issued to the assured by the agent of the insurers who has undertaken to forward the proposal to them for consideration. This document may take a form similar to the cover note discussed in the leading case of *Mackie v. The European Assurance Society*,[3] which was as follows:

> "Memorandum of Deposit. A having this day proposed an insurance of £2,700 to the E Co. on property described in their fire order of this date, and having made a deposit of £2 in part payment of premium and duty, it is hereby declared that the property so described shall be held insured in virtue of such deposit for one month from this date or until notice be sooner given that the proposal is declined."

From this illustration it will be noted that the cover note records the receipt of a premium from the assured, in consideration of which the insurers agree to insure him for the period stated in the note. Because it is in part a receipt, the cover note has sometimes been described as an "interim receipt". That term is inappropriate as one of general description, because the typical cover note is, as has been observed before,[4] much more than a mere receipt. It is a document evidencing an actual agreement to insure for a maximum stated period, and, moreover, so far as its function as a receipt for the premium is concerned, it is a receipt valid for longer than just that interim period between application and the decision of the insurers.

4–4 The use of the term "interim receipt" is, besides being inapt, actually misleading in so far as it suggests that a mere acknowledgment of the receipt of a premium amounts in itself to an interim insurance. That is not so, as the decision in *Linford v. Provincial Horse and Cattle Insurance Co. Ltd*[5] illustrates. Upon an application for insurance on cattle, a local agent inspected the cattle, stated that they would be insured and accepted a year's premium, giving the company's printed receipt in the following form: "On account of the P Co. Received of A the sum of 35s. on insurance for cows." It was held by Sir J. Romilly M.R. that there was no contract of insurance on which the applicant could bring a claim. The receipt itself could not be construed as an agreement to insure, and the oral undertaking of the agent that the cows would be insured did not bind the company as it was not within the agent's authority to grant interim cover."[6]

4–5 Whether or not the cover note amounts to an agreement to insure depends upon the construction of its wording and not upon whether it is entitled "receipt" or "cover note". In *Patterson v. The Royal Insurance Co.*[7]

---

[2] *Trainor v. Refuge* [1930] I.A.C.(N.I.) Rep. 68; *Watson v. Northern Counties Life and General* [1931] I.A.C.(N.I.) Rep. 72; *Blain v. Royal Liver F.S.* [1938] I.A.C.(N.I.) Rep. 32.

[3] (1869) 21 L.T. 102.

[4] *McQueen v. Phoenix Mutual Insurance Co.* (1879) 29 U.C.C.P. 511, 520.

[5] (1864) 10 Jur.(N.S.) 1066. This report is much more full than that in 34 Beav. 291. As to the plight of those seeking support from cases reported in that period of Beavan's Reports, see the caution of Harman L.J. in *Beesly v. Hallwood Estates* [1961] Ch. 105, 118.

[6] On the question of agents' authority to grant temporary cover, see paras 4–22 to 4–27 *post*, and Ch. 36, *post*.

[7] (1867) 14 Grant 169.

the following receipt was issued by an agent on payment of the premium: "Agent's Provisional Receipt —— Received of A the sum of $—— being the premium of insurance upon property for twelve months and for which a policy will be issued by the R Co. within 60 days if approved by the manager in Toronto, otherwise this receipt will be cancelled and the amount of unearned premium refunded."

Although there was here no express undertaking to insure, the references to cancellation of the receipt and refunding of unearned premium upon refusal permitted the inference that there was a promise to insure the applicant pending the manager's decision.

4–6 Brokers' slip or cover note. Another term which may produce a misunderstanding is the phrase "Brokers' slip". It is necessary in each case to analyse the particular document issued by a broker in order to test its effect. A broker through whom insurance has been effected may issue a note certifying that an insurance has been effected on particular terms. This does not mean that he has undertaken to insure, or that the insurance company is necessarily bound by the document,[8] but the broker may be liable to the applicant, if there is in fact no insurance, for breach of warranty of authority,[9] or for making a fraudulent or negligent[10] statement upon which the applicant relied to his loss.

4–7 In complete contrast is the note issued by a Lloyd's "cover-holder" to perform the functions of a temporary cover note when insurance at Lloyd's has been applied for. This is a binding contract as between the underwriters and the applicant.[11]

Another analogous document is the traditional "slip" prepared by a broker for an application for insurance at Lloyd's.[12] Where insurances on fire, burglary and other non-marine risks are made at Lloyd's, the practice is for the broker there to prepare in the first instance a slip, as in marine insurance, indicating briefly the nature of the risk, the premium, the duration, the sum insured and any special limits or conditions imposed, which are usually denoted by abbreviations or initials familiar to those persons engaged in placing insurances at Lloyd's, though not necessarily to outsiders. The slip is then initialled by the various underwriters who are willing to underwrite that risk on behalf of the syndicates, and subsequently a policy is made out in conformity with the slip, and stamped and signed by Lloyd's Policy Signing Office on behalf of the underwriting syndicates involved. Until the policy is executed and signed, the slip operates as a binding contract of insurance, on which the underwriters are liable to be sued,[13] so that in this respect it is analogous to the usual temporary cover note.[14] The broker will normally retain this slip in his possession, while issuing to his client a note of the kind discussed in the previous paragraph.

---

[8] *Broit v. S. Cohen & Son (N.S.W.) Ltd* (1926) 27 S.R.N.S.W. 29.

[9] See para. 36–16, *post*. It would be material whether the broker was agent of the applicant or of the insurers.

[10] Under the rule from *Hedley Byrne v. Heller* [1964] A.C. 465.

[11] See *Praet v. Poland* [1960] 1 Lloyd's Rep. 416.

[12] The procedure outlined in this paragraph is analysed in greater detail in Chap. 35, *post*.

[13] *Thompson v. Adams* (1889) 23 Q.B.D. 361; *Jaglom v. Excess Insurance Co. Ltd* [1972] 2 Q.B. 250; *General Reinsurance Corporation v. Forsakringsaktiebolaget Fennia Patria* [1983] Q.B. 856.

[14] *The Queen Insurance Co. v. Parsons* (1881) 7 App.Cas. 96, 125.

4–8 Although the usual practice is for the agreement for interim insurance to be evidenced by a printed note. It is not necessary in point of law for such a contract to be in writing, and, if the insurers' agent is empowered by them to make oral contracts for temporary insurance, these will be effective to bind the insurers.[15] It has been held in a Canadian case[16] that it is for the insurers who allege that their agent lacked authority to conclude such a contract to prove the want of authority, it being otherwise presumed that he had power to do what he did.

4–9 Duration of temporary cover note. Once a cover note in the usual form has been issued, it creates a binding insurance for the period of time specified in it, but subject to determination by notice at any time within that period.[17] The temporary cover invariably takes effect at once, since its object is to give immediate protection pending the decision of the directors and the issue of a policy. A cover note will not readily be construed as affording merely conditional protection subject to the approval of the directors,[18] because such an interpretation would make it virtually useless. In motor insurance, the cover note must give immediate protection so as to comply with the provisions of section 147(1) of the Road Traffic Act 1988.[19]

4–10 Assuming that the insurers do not terminate the insurance before the period specified as a maximum limit of cover[20] has expired, it is sometimes difficult to define the moment of the termination of the insurance with precision, a point illustrated by three Canadian decisions. Each case depends upon the wording of the particular cover note, and it is quite possible that the receipt may be so worded as to insure beyond the specified days in the event of no notice to determine the risk being given by the company.

In *Patterson v. The Royal Insurance Co.*[21] the agent issued a receipt saying *inter alia*

> "Received ... the premium of insurance upon property for twelve months and for which a policy will be issued by the R Co. within 60 days if approved by the manager in Toronto, otherwise this receipt will be cancelled and the amount of unearned premium refunded."

It was held that this receipt constituted an agreement to provide temporary cover, made by an agent who had actual authority to conclude it.

---

[15] *Murfitt v. Royal Insurance Co.* (1922) 38 T.L.R. 334; *Hochbaum v. Pioneer Insurance Co.* [1933] 1 W.W.R. 403.

[16] *Hochbaum v. Pioneer Insurance Co.* [1933] 1 W.W.R. 403.

[17] *Mackie v. The European Assurance Co.* (1869) 21 L.T. 102, 104. In *Stockton v. Mason* [1978] 2 Lloyd's Rep. 430, 431, Lord Diplock said that the essential nature of a contract of interim insurance was that it was for a temporary period, usually up to a maximum of 30 days, but always terminable by notice from the insurers.

[18] *Goodfellow v. Times and Beacon Assurance Co.* (1859) 17 U.C.Q.B. 411. In *Mayne Nickless v. Pegler* [1974] 1 N.S.W.L.R. 228 the insertion of a condition in the cover that it was "subject to ... a satisfactory proposal for insurance" achieved precisely that result. See the note by Birds (1977) 40 M.L.R. 79, "What is a cover note worth?" The court also held that the duty of disclosure applied to interim cover.

[19] 1988, c.52.

[20] For a case illustrating the difficulty of computing the period itself, see *Cartwright v. MacCormack* [1963] 1 All E.R. 11.

[21] (1867) 14 Grant 169.

Consequently, even though the agent never informed the Toronto manager of the risk, the company was liable for a loss which occurred after 60 days had elapsed. The receipt bound the company until rejection, and, after the 60 days had expired, the applicant was entitled to a 12 months' policy subject to the company's usual conditions. The company, and not the applicant, must suffer for the fault of their agent in not giving them information upon which they might exercise the right of rejection.

4–11 A similar result was reached in *Hawke v. Niagara District Mutual Fire Insurance Co.*,[22] where the receipt ran:

> "The applicant will be considered insured until otherwise notified within one month from the date hereof, when, if declined, the receipt shall become void and be surrendered. N.B., should applicant not receive a policy in conformity with his application within 20 days from the date hereof, he must communicate with the secretary direct, as after one month from this date the receipt becomes void."

That was held to create an insurance which the insurers could terminate by notice within a month, but which after the expiration of a month without notice became binding and irrevocable for a year.

The wording of this receipt may be compared with that in *Barnes v. Dominion Grange Mutual Fire Insurance Association*,[23] where there was an application for a four years' fire policy. The receipt issued on payment of premium read:

> "Received from B $—— being a premium for an insurance to the extent of $—— on the property described in the application ... subject, however, to the approval of the board of directors, who shall have power to cancel this contract within fifty days from this date by causing a notice to that effect to be mailed to the applicant. And it is hereby mutually agreed that unless this receipt be followed by a policy within the said fifty days from this date the contract of insurance shall wholly cease and determine, and all liability on the part of the association shall be at an end."

The court was equally divided as to whether that was a four years' insurance determinable upon notice, or only a 50 days' insurance which would lapse by effluxion of time without notice.

4–12 Notice determining cover. Where the interim cover is determinable by notice, that notice will not be effective as a general rule until it has been received by the applicant himself or some person authorised by him to receive such notice on his behalf.[24] A broker instructed to place an insurance is not necessarily the applicant's agent to receive notice of the determination of the risk. As a rule the insurers would be safe in giving notice to a person authorised generally to manage the applicant's insurance business. If the

---

[22] (1876) 23 Grant 139. This was another case where the insurers' agent failed to forward the application, and the court followed *Patterson's* case, *supra*, on that point.

[23] (1895) 22 U.C.R. (C.A., Ont.) 68.

[24] *Goodfellow v. Times and Beacon Assurance Co.* (1859) 17 U.C.Q.B. 411; *Mackie v. European Assurance Co.* (1869) 21 L.T. 102, 104; *Queen Ins. Co. v. Parsons* (1881) 7 App.Cas. 96, 124.

applicant indicates a particular manner of communicating information, the insurers are not bound to do more than adopt the manner of communication indicated. Thus a Canadian court held, *obiter*, that, where the assured gave his address to an insurance company, and the company sent a notice to that address, but the applicant did not receive it because he had changed his place of abode without making proper provision for forwarding his correspondence, the notice was nonetheless effective.[25] This exception to the general rule was justified on the ground that the applicant knew that the company would be communicating with him, and must take the consequences of his own unbusinesslike attitude.

Similarly, if the normal manner of communication was to be through the Post Office, the act of posting a notice properly addressed would probably be sufficient to determine the risk at such time as in ordinary course of post the letter would have been received by the applicant, even if it be lost or delayed in the post through no fault of either party.[26]

4-13 Cover note superseded by policy. An interim receipt or cover note including any provisions in the company's usual form of policy which may be incorporated into it by reference, expresses the terms of the contract between the parties up to the date when a policy is issued. From that date, the contract expressed in the policy supersedes the contract evidenced by the cover note as to the future, but not as to the past. A claim arising out of an occurrence happening before the issue of the policy falls to be adjudicated by reference only to the contract as expressed in or evidenced by the cover note.[27] This distinction is important where the insurers have the right to introduce conditions into the policy which were not applicable to the cover note, and which might bar a claim under the policy that would succeed on the preliminary contract of insurance.[28] It must be remembered that, unless the parties have expressly bound themselves respectively to accept and to issue a policy, the contract of insurance may be terminated upon the expiration of the temporary cover.[29]

(b) *Terms of Temporary Cover*

4-14 Incorporation of policy conditions. The protection afforded by an interim receipt is not fully defined in the instrument itself, which is usually expressed to be on the company's usual terms, or subject to the conditions contained in the company's policies.[30] Where the conditions are thus referred to expressly, the insurer does not have to prove that they were brought to the notice of the assured, or even that he had an opportunity of making himself acquainted with them.[31] In such a case, the assured is bound

[25] *Henry v. Agricultural Mutual Assurance Association* (1865) 11 Grant 125.

[26] This would appear to follow from the statements made by the Court of Appeal in *James v. Institute of Chartered Accountants* (1908) 98 L.T. 225, 230, a case involving the posting of a notice of expulsion to a member by the Institute. It would be a very strict court which held that a mislaid notice would have been received in practice on the next morning after it was sent.

[27] *Neil v. South East Lancashire Ins. Co.*, 1932 S.C. 35.

[28] *Mackie v. European Assurance Society* (1869) 21 L.T. 102, 104.

[29] *ibid.*

[30] *Queen Ins. Co. v. Parsons* (1881) 7 App.Cas. 96; *General Accident, Fire and Life Assurance Corp. Ltd v. Shuttleworth* (1938) 60 Ll.L.Rep. 301.

[31] *McQueen v. Phoenix Mutual Ins. Co.* (1879) 29 U.C.C.P. 511.

by the conditions contained in the form of the company's policy currently in use and applicable to the case.[32]

4–15 If there is no express stipulation in a cover note that it is issued subject to the conditions contained in the insurers' policies, the insurance is subject to the conditions usually inserted in policies relating to the particular class of risk in question. In a Pennsylvanian decision,[33] where the only evidence of the preliminary contract of insurance was an entry in the insurers' books containing particulars such as would be given in a slip, it was held that the insurance was subject to the conditions contained in the insurers' policies. This decision was approved in *Hawke v. Niagara District Mutual Fire Insurance Co.* where Proudfoot V.-C. said[34]:

> "It would be unreasonable to hold that by giving an interim receipt the company meant to insure a larger liability than they were subject to on a policy; they must be understood as contracting for an insurance of the ordinary kind. The plaintiff asks for the completion of the insurance by the issuing of a policy, and he does not pretend that he is entitled to any other than the ordinary policy; he cannot, therefore, be in any better condition than if he had the policy in his possession."

These considerations were echoed by Sargant L.J. in *Wyndham Rather v. Eagle, Star and British Dominions Insurance Co.*,[35] without reference to these North American cases.

It is doubtful whether this principle of implied incorporation extends to a special addendum or marginal condition in the insurers' policy of which the assured has no actual knowledge, and which is not usual in policies covering the subject-matter in question issued by other insurers.[36]

4–16 Inapplicable policy conditions. Certain conditions contained in the company's policy may not be applicable to insurance provided by a temporary cover note. If a condition is wholly inapplicable, such as a condition with reference to renewal of cover at the end of a year, it is right to

---

[32] *McQueen v. Phoenix Mutual Ins. Co.* (1879) 29 U.C.C.P. 511, 522. The conditions of the policy may be expressly incorporated by a reference in the interim contract to the proposal form which itself makes any insurance subject to the policy conditions—*Wyndham Rather Ltd v. Eagle, Star and British Dominions Ins. Co. Ltd* (1925) 21 Ll.L.Rep. 214; *Houghton v. Trafalgar Insurance Co. Ltd* [1953] 2 Lloyd's Rep. 18; affd. on other grounds [1954] 1 Q.B. 247. It is not clear whether the assured must have signed the proposal form before being granted temporary cover in order for the reference to it to bind him. In the *Houghton* case he had; in the *Wyndham* case this is unclear, but the judgment of Sargant L.J. at p. 215 indicates that signature is immaterial. In modern practice, the proposal form is sometimes accompanied by a "prospectus" indicating the terms of the insurance offered and the applicant is expected to retain this in his possession after submitting the completed proposal form. It must be a question of fact whether the terms in such a "prospectus" form part of the agreement for interim cover.

[33] *Eureka Insurance Co. v. Robinson*, 56 Pa. 256, 264 (1867). Modern American authority is to the same effect: see Appleman, *Insurance Law and Practice*, para. 7232.

[34] (1876) 23 Grant 139, 148.

[35] (1925) 21 Ll.L.Rep. 214, 215.

[36] *Symington v. Union Ins. Soc. of Canton* (1929) 45 T.L.R. 181. This decision does not, however, appear to concern a typical interim cover situation, since it appears that the insurers had bound themselves to issue a policy in conformity with the slip, which did not have the marginal addition. Scrutton L.J.'s remarks about "obligations in honour" are, with respect, difficult to follow; if it was agreed that the f.p.a. clause in the slip was to be followed in the policy, it was not open to the insurers to introduce new clauses in the policy—45 T.L.R. 181, 182.

ignore it entirely. The same is true of any condition which negatives the main purpose of the temporary cover note or defeats its objects.[37]

4–17 Other conditions in the policy may be discarded as inapplicable on the ground that they impose obligations on the assured to do certain things which it would be unreasonable to expect him to do, unless he had actual notice of the condition in question. In *Re Coleman's Depositories*[38] a cover note was issued on December 28, 1904, pursuant to a proposal completed for insurance cover against employers' liability. The cover note contained no mention of any conditions. A policy was executed on January 3, 1905, but it was not received by the assured's brokers until January 9 or 10 whereupon it was delivered to the assured. In the meantime an employee of the assured was injured on January 2. The policy contained a condition that the assured should give immediate notice to the insurers of any accident occurring to an employee. Later the employee died, and a claim was made on the insurers, who repudiated liability on the ground that the condition that notice be given had never been performed. The Court of Appeal held, by a majority, that the condition was not applicable until the contents of the policy had been communicated to the assured. The assured had no opportunity of knowing of the condition until delivery of the policy, and it could not have been intended that he should be bound by it until either he was told of it or he received the policy.

4–18 The reasoning in that case was followed and approved, *obiter*, in *Parker & Co. v. Western Assurance Co.*,[39] where the pursuer sought to recover for a loss by fire and alleged an oral agreement by the company's agent to issue a cover note. The company's usual form of cover note purported to insure the proposer subject to the conditions printed in the company's policies. In the event the court held that the oral agreement was not proved, but expressed the opinion *obiter* that, if the alleged oral contract had been proved, it would have been free from the policy conditions relating to intimation of particulars of loss and to arbitration.

4–19 It is not entirely clear to what extent these cases create an exception to the general rule of implied incorporation of policy conditions into a cover note. In each case, the particular condition was of a usual kind and a standard term in the insurers policies, and it is difficult to justify the two decisions on the ground that it was not one which a reasonable assured could have expected to find. The exception probably therefore extends, on equitable grounds, to conditions requiring the assured to take positive steps of any kind, as opposed to conditions which merely restrict the insurers' liability or the scope of the risks run.

4–20 A condition contained in or incorporated into the policy may be excluded from application to the temporary cover if it is not appropriate to the situation at the inception of the temporary cover. In a Scottish case[40] where a claim arose under a cover note in respect of an accident which happened before a proposal was signed or policy issued, it was held that the

---

[37] *McQueen v. Phoenix Mutual Ins. Co.* (1879) 29 U.C.C.P. 511, 521.
[38] [1907] 2 K.B. 798.
[39] 1925 S.L.T. 131. See para. 3–2, *ante*, concerning oral agreements under Scots Law.
[40] *Neil v. South East Lancashire Ins. Co.*, 1932 S.C. 35.

insurance company could not rely upon a false answer to a question in the proposal form subsequently signed by the assured as constituting a breach of the warranty of accuracy therein contained, although the company's ordinary form of policy and the actual policy thereafter issued to the insured referred to the proposal as the basis of the contract, and despite the fact that the cover note provided expressly that it was "subject to the usual terms and conditions of the company's policy." One reason given was that that phrase referred only to such conditions as the assured would have been able to ascertain from the policy itself in isolation. A better reason was that the proposal form warranted the truth of answers contained in it and this warranty could not be a term of the contract for temporary insurance cover, which was completed nine days prior to the completion and signature of the proposal form.

4–21 Some conditions which are not altogether applicable to a temporary insurance cover may be applied "*mutatis mutandis*", as, for instance, where there is a condition that certain circumstances will vitiate the contract unless allowed by indorsement on the policy. In one Canadian case[41] a condition to that effect was held to be applicable, and the indorsement was required on the interim receipt, whereas in another case[42] it was held sufficient to give notice to the agent authorised to grant and indorse the receipt and obtain his express or implied consent to waive the requirement of indorsement.

(c) *General*

4–22 Authority of brokers to issue interim cover. Brokers transacting non-marine business will frequently have express authority to conclude an interim insurance contract on behalf of insurers. In the absence of an actual authority to do this, brokers may nonetheless have either apparent authority or implied authority to bind insurers to an interim cover.

4–23 Apparent authority. An agent in possession of cover notes will be held to have apparent authority to grant interim cover even if he lacks actual authority.[43] If the cover note is so framed as to give the applicant protection until the directors have approved or rejected the risk, the company is bound by the note to continue to provide cover, notwithstanding that the agent never communicates the proposal form to them and even appropriates the premiums to his own use.[44]

4–24 An applicant for insurance may not, however, plead the ostensible or apparent authority of the agent when the wording of the cover note or of the proposal form signed by him shows that the agent is in fact acting without authority, so that the applicant had notice of his want of authority, or would have had if he had read those documents.[45] Such notice, however received, is

---

[41] *Hawke v. Niagara District Mutual Fire Ins. Co.* (1876) 23 Grant 139, 148.
[42] *Parsons v. Queen Insurance Co.* (1878) 43 U.C.Q.B. 271, 279.
[43] *Mackie v. The European Assurance Co.* (1869) 21 L.T. 102.
[44] *Hawke v. Niagara District Mutual Fire Ins. Co.* (1876) 23 Grant 139; *Patterson v. The Royal Insurance Co.* (1867) 14 Grant 169.
[45] *Linford v. Provincial Horse and Cattle Ins. Co.* (1864) 10 Jur.(N.S.) 1066; *Levy v. Scottish Employers' Ins. Assoc.* (1901) 17 T.L.R. 229; *Henry v. Agricultural Mutual Assurance Association* (1865) 11 Grant 125.

fatal to a plea of ostensible or apparent authority. Thus, if the document handed over by the agent is in terms only a receipt for the premium, not purporting to grant cover, and the proposal form indicates that the agent cannot grant cover, the applicant will not be justified in relying upon oral promises by the agent that insurance cover is to be effected so soon as the premium is paid to him.[46]

Similarly, if the protection given by the interim cover note is for a specified number of days only, the agent has no apparent authority to grant cover for a longer period, or to grant a permanent insurance without submitting the proposal to the directors. In one Canadian case the agent granted a succession of interim receipts, each as the previous one expired, and it was held that he could not in that indirect manner grant an insurance for a longer period than 30 days without submitting a proposal to the company.[47]

4–25 Authority to conclude oral contracts of interim insurance. An applicant for insurance is sometimes told orally by a broker or agent speaking for insurers that he is temporarily held covered pending the insurers' decision on his proposal. Until the decision in *Stockton v. Mason*[48] it was thought that, if a broker made an oral interim contract without possessing actual authority to conclude it on behalf of the insurers, the applicant would need to adduce positive evidence of the agent's implied or ostensible authority if the insurers disputed the broker's authority. Thus in *Murfitt v. Royal Insurance Co. Ltd*[49] it was contended that a local agent had implied authority to grant oral cover against fire risks. Evidence was given, and apparently accepted, to the effect that the agent was a "full" agent, that it was a necessary incident of his work that he should be able to grant cover orally and that the company had knowledge of his habit of doing so previously. On what the learned judge McCardie J., termed "the special facts of the case", he held that the agent had implied authority to grant interim cover orally Ostensible authority to make oral interim contracts was not to be inferred from the mere fact of agency. In a South African case[50] where the English authorities were reviewed the court held that an applicant would not be justified in thinking that an agent was empowered to conclude such contracts unless he was in possession of cover notes.

4–26 A radically different approach to the broker's authority was revealed in *Stockton v. Mason*, a case concerning an application made on behalf of the assured to transfer an existing motor policy to a different car. The request was made to the assured's brokers, who replied, "Yes, that will be alright. We will see to that." In the circumstances which occurred the Court of Appeal[51] had to decide whether this response was an acknowledgment of the request and a promise to put it to the insurers, or a statement made on behalf of the insurers constituting a promise to insure the new car, while the request was considered further. In holding that a contract of interim insurance had been made, the court attached significance to an "implied authority" of the broker to enter into temporary insurance

---

[46] *Linford v. Provincial Horse and Cattle Ins. Co.* (1864) 10 Jur.(N.S.) 1066.
[47] *Hawke v. Niagara District Mutual Fire Ins. Co.* (1876) 23 Grant 139.
[48] [1978] 2 Lloyd's Rep. 430.
[49] (1922) 38 T.L.R. 334.
[50] *Dicks v. S.A. Mutual Fire and General Ins. Co.*, 1963 (4) S.A. 501 (N.).
[51] The court was composed, unusually, of three members of the House of Lords.

contracts on behalf of insurers. Lord Diplock said that it was "a principle of law" that "a broker in non-marine insurance has implied authority to issue on behalf of the insurer or enter into as agent for the insurer contracts of interim insurance".[52]

4–27 No actual or apparent authority was proved so far as one may judge from the report of the decision, and it appears that the court has implied this authority into the tripartite relationship of applicant, broker, and insurer as a matter of law without stating the precise grounds for the implication.[53] It may be that, since brokers invariably possess general binding authorities to grant interim cover, the court was taking judicial notice of it and implying the authority as a matter of market usage. It was recognised that the authority would not be present in "exceptional cases".

4–28 If an agent issues an interim receipt and makes an authorised oral agreement which is not inconsistent with the terms of the receipt, the assured will not be bound by the terms of the company's policy in so far as these are inconsistent with the oral agreement. Where any such agreement is alleged, however, the question must inevitably arise whether the agent had authority to make any contract other than in accordance with the terms of the company's interim receipts and policies.[54]

4–29 Admissibility of parol evidence. An interim cover note is not generally a contract in writing, but rather a memorandum evidencing a transaction, and so evidence is admissible to contradict the writing and prove that the agreement between the parties was different from that recorded in the document.[55] Although an interim cover note may be a "policy" for revenue purposes, it is not a policy of insurance in the ordinary sense of the word, and it does not purport to contain the whole, complete and final contract between the parties.[56]

Where the assured made an oral agreement with a duly authorised agent to insure him against fire for a year, and subsequently a sub-agent, as a matter of routine, issued on payment of premium an interim protection note purporting to insure for 30 days only, there was a binding contract for the year.[57]

2. Increase of Risk Before Policy is Issued

4–30 General principles. It may happen that after a proposal for insurance has been made by or to insurers but before it is accepted, a material change

---

[52] [1978] 2 Lloyd's Rep. 430, 431.

[53] The court complimented counsel on the brevity of their argument—[1978] 2 Lloyd's Rep. 430, 432.

[54] *Canadian Casualty and Boiler Ins. Co. v. Hawthorn* (1907) 39 S.C.R. 558, 565. The reasoning in the case on proximate cause is, with respect, very difficult to follow, and the decision is best supported on the grounds given by Davies J.

[55] *Beckett v. Nurse* [1948] 1 K.B. 535; *Hutton v. Watling* [1948] Ch. 398, 403.

[56] *Citizens' Insurance Co. v. Parsons* (1881) 7 App.Cas. 96; *Neil v. S.E. Lancashire Ins. Co.* 1932 S.C. 35. For the "parole evidence" rule, see Chap. 11, para. 11–37, *post*.

[57] *Coulter v. Equity Fire Ins. Co.* (1904) 9 Ont.L.R. 35. As to delegation to sub-agents, see *Rossiter v. Trafalgar Life Ass. Assoc.* (1859) 27 Beav. 377.

takes place in the nature of the risk it is proposed to insure. For instance, the life proposed for a life assurance policy may meet with a serious accident leaving him in a critical state of health. The general rule is that the insurers are not obliged to cover the altered risk but the practical operation of the rule depends on whether the assured tells them what has happened before the offer is accepted.

4–31 By reason of the principle of *uberrima fides* the putative assured is under a duty to disclose any material alteration in the risk which comes to his notice at any time up to the conclusion of a contract.[58] "Material" means, in this context, anything which would influence a prudent insurer in deciding whether to accept the risk and on what terms. The assured is also obliged to correct, in so far as it has ceased to be true, any material representation of fact made by him to the insurers in negotiations for the insurance, for instance, by way of statements in the proposal form. If he fails to do this, and the insurers accept his proposal for the risk to be covered in ignorance of material changes in the risk, they will be entitled to avoid the contract upon discovering the truth. If the assured, for his part, accepts their offer of insurance while concealing what has occurred, the same result follows.

4–32 The insurers are in no worse position if the assured does disclose a material change in the risk, and does so prior to or at the time when he or they communicate an acceptance of the other party's offer.[59] If the insurers are considering a proposal put by the assured when he tells them of a change in the circumstances of the risk, he is in substance making a new proposal to them while revoking the original offer. The insurers are then free to accept or reject the new offer. Suppose, however, that the insurers put a proposal to the assured, and he purports to accept it, while indicating at the same time that the risk has materially altered. The purported acceptance is of no effect, because, taken with the information accompanying it, it is in substance a counter-proposal to bind the insurers to a different contract. It no longer corresponds with their offer.

4–33 Apart from these general considerations of *uberrima fides* and offer and acceptance rules, a change in the risk may discharge a proposal by reason of an express provision in the proposal to that effect. If insurers were to put an offer to an assured on the express basis that it should lapse on the contingency of the risk altering in a material respect, any such alteration would discharge their offer of itself, regardless of any issue of a counter-offer being made by the assured.

4–34 The key to an understanding of the significance of alterations in the risk is to pin-point the moment at which the insurers become bound to grant insurance cover under a legally binding contract with the assured. Any change in the risk up to that moment is important for the reasons explained above; any such change subsequent to it is of no consequence,[60] whether or

---

[58] *Re Yager and The Guardian Assurance Co.* (1912) 108 L.T. 38, 44; *Whitwell v. Autocar Fire and Accident Ins. Co.* (1927) 27 Ll.L.Rep. 418. For the doctrine of "*uberrima fides*", see Ch. 17, *post.*
[59] *Canning v. Farquhar* (1886) 16 Q.B.D. 727.
[60] Except, of course, in the case of a continuing warranty regarding the facts which have changed; for that case, see Ch. 10, *post.*

not a policy has been issued or the premium actually paid. Bearing this in mind, we may proceed to consider certain situations in which the application of these principles is uncertain. The first is the case of an increase in the risk after the time at which the insurers say they have "accepted" the assured's proposal for insurance but before the time at which it is agreed they should come on risk.

4-35 Further steps required before contract binding. In accordance with the general principle stated above, a change of risk may still avoid the contract of insurance if it occurs after the insurers say that they have "accepted" the assured's proposal, because it does not necessarily follow that this is an "acceptance" in the legal sense, which concludes a binding contract. It may well be that, on closer analysis, such an acceptance is no more than an intimation by the insurers that the terms of the proposal are acceptable to them as the basis of a future contract of insurance between themselves and the assured, such contract to be concluded, if at all, upon the assured performing some fresh condition such as tendering the sum due as premium. This is especially true of life assurance contracts, as is illustrated by the Court of Appeal's decision in *Canning v. Farquhar*.[61]

4-36 In that case the court was confronted by the following facts. On December 8 a proposal by Mr Canning for assurance on his own life for a year was forwarded to the insurers. It contained a declaration that, "the whole of the statements made by me in the said proposal are true; and this declaration together with the certificate signed by me in the presence of the medical examiner, is to be the basis of the contract between me and the said society" (the insurers). The proposal stated, *inter alia*, that the applicant was in good health. On December 14 the insurers replied that, "The proposal ... on the life of Mr ... Canning has been accepted at the annual premium of £47 18s. 4d. No assurance can take place until the first premium is paid." On January 7 following, a letter was sent by the insurers saying that a new certificate of health would have to be prepared if the premium was not paid by January 14 but that on receipt of the premium a policy would be issued. In the meantime Canning had fallen over a cliff on January 5 and had seriously injured himself. On January 9 his agent went to the insurers and tendered the premium, disclosing the occurrence of this accident. The insurers thereupon declined to accept the premium. Canning then died and an action was brought against the insurers to recover the sum which would have been due under the policy if the insurers had issued it on January 9.

4-37 The chief point taken by the plaintiff, Canning's administrator, was that there was a binding contract to insure on December 14 when the proposal was accepted. This contention was rejected by all three judges in the Court of Appeal, who, however, expressed some uncertainty as to when a contract of insurance was concluded in those circumstances. On the view adopted by Lindley and Lopes L.JJ., and concurred in by Lord Esher M.R. with some hesitation,[62] the letter of December 14 amounted to a counter-

---

[61] (1886) 16 Q.B.D. 727.
[62] (1886) 16 Q.B.D. 727, 731, 734. Lord Esher's opinion that the insurers' letter of December 14 was merely a statement of intent and not a counter-offer is difficult to follow, as it was expressed in unqualified terms and was capable of creating a contract when the assured accepted it by tendering a premium. Counsel for the insurers did not argue this point; see p. 729.

offer, nothing having been said about the rate or payment of the premium in the proposal form. This counter-offer was to be accepted by the payment of the premium by the assured, whereupon the insurers ordinarily would be bound by a concluded contract of insurance, and must issue an executed policy forthwith. As events turned out, however, the accident to Mr Canning on January 5 had materially increased the risk, with the result that the insurers were not bound by the assured's purported acceptance on January 9. The serious injuries to Mr Canning rendered it impossible for him to accept the counter-offer put forward by the insurers on December 14 because that was an offer to cover a life in good health, and the assured's agent, in tendering the premium appropriate to that risk while at the same time asking the insurers to cover a seriously sick man, was in reality communicating an acceptance that did not correspond to the terms of the offer it was supposed to accept.

The judgments further suggest that the Court of Appeal may have thought that the insurers' counter-offer of December 14 was made on the condition that it was to lapse if the declaration of good health made by the assured should become untrue, this interpretation being suggested by the references to the declaration being "the basis" of their offer. If that is correct, it is an alternative ground for the decision in that case, and the agent for the assured was attempting to accept an offer which had already lapsed.

4–38 The decision in *Canning v. Farquhar*[63] has been approved in *Harrington v. Pearl Life Assurance Co.*[64] *and Looker v. Law Union and Rock Insurance Co.*,[65] where the change in the risk was not disclosed to the insurers.[66] These decisions show that, had the assured in *Canning's*[67] case concealed the increase in the risk, the insurers would still not have been bound by their receipt of the premium, since the resulting contract of insurance would have been liable to be avoided by them for non-disclosure on the part of the assured. By reason of the principle of *uberrima fides*, applicable to all contracts of insurance, the assured owed a duty to disclose to the insurers any material increase in the risk which occurred, to his knowledge, prior to the conclusion of a binding contract of insurance.[68] If he had failed to do so, the insurers could have avoided the contract upon discovery of the truth.

Even if there had not been a provision in the proposal form in *Canning's* case[69] by which the truth of the statements therein was to be the basis of the contract of insurance, it seems that on other general principles of contract law the insurers could have avoided liability on the policy. They had been induced to enter into the negotiations for a policy by the representation,

---

[63] (1886) 16 Q.B.D. 727.

[64] (1914) 30 T.L.R. 613.

[65] [1928] 1 K.B. 554.

[66] In addition the insurers' "acceptance" of the proposal in *Looker's* case stated expressly that no assurance was to become effective should the applicant's health worsen before the premium was received. For a doubtful application of the decision in *Canning's* case to a case of accident liability insurance, see *Sickness and Accident Assurance Association v. General Accident Assurance Corp.* (1892) 19 R. (Ct.Sess.) 977, and para. 2–45, *ante*.

[67] See note 63, *ante*.

[68] *Re Yager and The Guardian Assurance Co. Ltd* (1912) 108 L.T. 38, 44; *Looker v. Law Union and Rock Ins. Co. Ltd* [1928] 1 K.B. 554, 559; *Stiptich v. Metropolitan Life Ins. Co.*, 277 U.S. 311 (1928); *Watt v. Southern Cross Assurance Co.* [1927] N.Z.L.R. 106.

[69] (1886) 16 Q.B.D. 727.

inter alia, that the applicant was in good health. The applicant therefore owed them a duty to correct that statement if it became untrue before a contract was concluded.[70] If he failed to do so, any such contract would likewise be voidable for misrepresentation.

4–39 Contract binding, but risk not commenced. If the insurers have reached a binding agreement with the assured, the general rule is that any subsequent increase in the risk has no legal effect on the contract, and the assured need not disclose it. Thus, for example, where Lloyd's underwriters have reached agreement with the assured on the terms of a broker's slip, there is a binding contract of insurance concluded on those terms, and the insurers must issue a policy which records them faithfully.[71] Any subsequent increase in the risk insured is immaterial.

4–40 It is, however, possible that the contract of insurance is made subject to the condition that the risk will begin to run only from a specified date in the future. Is the assured bound to disclose to the insurers any increase in the risk prior to that date, and can the insurers refuse to be bound if they are told of such an event? The answer, it is thought, is plainly, "No". The insurers have bound themselves to grant cover from a specified date, and they must abide by their agreement regardless of any increase in the risk between the conclusion of the contract and that date, unless they have expressly stipulated that the contract may be terminated by themselves upon the risk increasing in specified ways during the interim period.[72]

4–41 A further difficulty arises where the parties conclude a contract of insurance before the premium is paid, and the contract is made subject to a condition that the risk is to commence upon payment or receipt of the first premium. Assuming for present purposes that a contract has actually been concluded,[73] what are the obligations of the assured in the event of an increase in the risk occurring before payment of the premium? It has been suggested,[74] on the authority of *Canning v. Farquhar*[75] and *Harrington v. Pearl Life Assurance Co. Ltd*,[76] that the effect of such a clause is to enlarge the period during which the duty of disclosure lies upon the assured up to the time when he pays the premium. With respect, it is submitted that this is

---

[70] Para. 16–56, *post*, and see Treitel, *Law of Contract* (10th ed., 1999), pp. 364–365.

[71] *Thompson v. Adams* (1889) 23 Q.B.D. 361; *Jaglom v. Excess Insurance Co.* [1972] 2 Q.B. 250; *General Reinsurance Corp. v. Forsakringsaktiebolaget Fennia Patria* [1983] Q.B. 856.

[72] The greater the freedom of withdrawal allowed to the insurers, the harder it is to sustain the conclusion that there was a binding contract of insurance. (See note 73 *infra*.) *British Equitable Ins. Co. v. Great Western Railway Co.* (1869) 20 L.T. 422 is, however, an example.

[73] The English cases suggest that a court would be more likely to find that there was no binding contract in such circumstances, unless a policy had been issued to the assured. The stipulations that "no assurance is to take place until the first premium is paid", and "no insurance shall be held to be effected until payment of premium" have been held to negative the existence of a contract, no policies having been executed and delivered—*Canning v. Farquhar* (1886) 16 Q.B.D. 727, 731; *Sickness and Accident Ass. Assoc. v. General Accident Ass. Corp.* (1892) 19 R. (Ct.Sess.) 977. These cases would be distinguishable if the stipulation were "no insurance cover to be in effect until payment of premium, which is to be made within 10 days from...," assuming that the communication containing it was otherwise capable of being an acceptance and not a counter-offer.

[74] Ivamy *General Principles* (6th ed.), p. 170.

[75] (1886) 16 Q.B.D. 727.

[76] (1914) 30 T.L.R. 613.

incorrect. In those cases, it was held that there was no binding contract of insurance in existence at the times when the assured knew of the increase in the risk and then endeavoured to pay a premium.[77] Once the insurers have agreed to be bound, the duty of disclosure has served its purpose, and they must abide by their obligations. If there is a loss prior to payment of the premium, however, they are not liable for it, not because the contract is in some way vitiated but because the risk has not begun to run in accordance with the contract.[78] It would certainly be wrong to imply, as a matter of law, any condition into the contract that the insurers were released from their contract if the risk increased prior to receipt of premium.[79]

4–42 It must, however, be emphasised that the problem discussed above is not very likely to arise in practice, since the most common interpretation of a clause postponing the commencement of risk until the premium has been paid is that no contract exists until then.[80]

If the insurers have executed and delivered a policy to the assured, it follows from what has been said above that no subsequent alteration in the circumstances, whether before or after commencement of the risk, entitles the insurers to withdraw from their obligations, and this is so regardless of whether the insurers have agreed to come on risk at some specified future date or on receipt of premium. In the first place, the policy would probably contain a recital to the effect that the premium had been paid, which would estop the insurers from denying receipt of the premium.[81]

Even in the absence of such a clause, the alteration in the risk could not of itself entitle the insurers to contend they were not bound. The issue of the policy would make it impossible for them to deny that a contract of insurance had been concluded.[82] The duty of disclosure would have lapsed accordingly, and the principle concerning the basis of the insurers' offer could not apply once the contract was complete.

4–43 Thus, if the policy in the case of *Canning v. Farquhar*[83] had been executed, and delivered subject to a condition that the insurance should not be in force until payment of premium by the assured, the fact that the premium was unpaid when the assured fell over the cliff would not have entitled the insurers to refuse a subsequent tender of the premium, and they would have been liable if the assured had died at any time after such tender. So in the case of fire insurance, if a policy is issued, say, on June 1, insuring premises for a year from June 24, and subject to the condition that the insurers are not to be liable for any loss occurring before payment of

[77] The same may be said of the authorities cited in Ivamy at pp. 171–172, including *Allis-Chalmers Co. v. Maryland Fidelity and Deposit Co.* (1916) 114 L.T. 433. *British Equitable Ins. Co. v. Great Western Ry.* (1869) 20 L.T. 422 seems to be a case where a contract was indeed concluded, but subject to a special condition defeasant. See note 72, *supra*.

[78] This point is illustrated by the judgment of the Lord Ordinary in *Sickness and Accident Ass. Assoc. v. General Accident Ass. Corp.* (1892) 19 R. 977, where he held, contrary to the Court of Session on appeal, that a contract of insurance had been concluded but the loss claimed was not covered by it since it occurred prior to payment of premium.

[79] This is not to deny the operation of other rules of insurance law concerning alterations in breach of express warranty or out of conformity with the description of the risk in the policy.

[80] See note 73, *supra*, and paras 2–45 to 2–47, *ante*.

[81] *Roberts v. Security Company Ltd* [1897] 1 Q.B. 111.

[82] [1897] 1 Q.B. 111, 115.

[83] (1886) 16 Q.B.D. 727.

premium, they could not refuse to accept the premium on the ground, for instance, that an extensive fire had broken out in adjoining premises on June 23, and was still burning when the premium was tendered. If events were to occur between June 1 and 24 which altered the premises to the extent that they ceased to correspond with the description of the insured premises in the policy, or involved a breach of other conditions therein, other considerations would apply. If such alterations were to have the effect of avoiding the policy in whole or in part, they would do so whether made or happening before or after the execution of the policy and whether before or after the commencement of the risk.

4–44 Retrospective insurance. It is competent to the insurers to agree that they shall be bound as from some prior date notwithstanding any loss or changes of risk which may have occurred at the time they accept the proposal and conclude a binding contract. That in effect is an agreement to insure "lost or not lost", to use the words familiar in marine policies. It has long been decided that this is a perfectly valid form of insurance and that the insurers are bound by their agreement, if both parties were equally cognisant or equally ignorant of the fact that a loss had occurred when the contract was made.[84] Marine policies almost invariably contain the "lost or not lost" clause, but it seems clear, and has actually been so held in America by the Supreme Court, that those exact words are not essential even in marine policies in order to create a good retrospective insurance, and that any form of words which expresses an intention to cover past losses is sufficient.[85] For example, a third-party liability policy expressed to cover "claims made" during the period of insurance is understood to cover such claims even though they arise out of events occurring prior to that period.

4–45 Where, therefore, insurers agree to insure from the date of a proposal or from some earlier specified date, they agree to bear losses which have in fact occurred at the time the contract was made, and, *a fortiori*, they undertake to bear the consequence of any increase in the risk. The general rule is illustrated by a case before the Industrial Assurance Commissioner,[86] in which a proposal for insurance on the life of another was signed on March 11, and the weekly premiums were paid on March 11, 18, and 25. The life assured died on March 24. This fact was communicated to the insurers' district office on March 25. On March 29 the society completed a policy, not under seal, antedated to March 11, and delivered it to the proposer. The Commissioner held that, as the policy was delivered with knowledge of the death, the insurers were bound to pay the amount insured.

An intention to make a contract of insurance retrospective must be clearly expressed, and prima facie an acceptance does not relate back to the date of the proposal.[87]

4–46 It is not doubted that an applicant for a retrospective insurance

[84] *Mead v. Davison* (1835) 3 Ad. & E. 303; *Stone v. Marine Ins. Co.* (1876) 1 Ex.D. 81; *Bradford v. Symondson* (1881) 7 Q.B.D. 456.
[85] *Mercantile Mutual Ins. Co. v. Folsom*, (1873) 85 U.S. (18 Wall) 237.
[86] *Pilling v. Scottish Legal Life* [1930] I.A.C.Rep. 24.
[87] *cf.* the duty imposed upon the assured's agent in *Proudfoot v. Montefiore* (1867) L.R. 2 Q.B. 511, 519.

cannot recover on a policy issued to him if he was aware at the time of the proposal that a loss had occurred and the insurers were then unaware of this fact. A slight doubt may arise, however, where knowledge of a loss or increase of risk comes to the applicant after he has made his proposal. There is no authority on a retrospective insurance which covers the point but it is submitted that, by the operation of the general principle of *uberrima fides* the applicant is obliged to disclose any such facts which he discovers prior to the insurers' acceptance of his proposal. The duty of disclosure binds him, as has been seen, up to the moment a contract is concluded. It might, however, be open to a court to conclude, on the facts of a particular case, that the insurers had waived their right to obtain further information from the assured as to developments occurring after the proposal was put to them.

All that the applicant is bound to do is to send notice to the insurers in the most expeditious manner available to him,[88] and, if they accept his proposal before the intimation of loss is received, they will be bound by the retrospective risk provision in their contract with him.

4–47 In a Canadian case,[89] company A had agreed to renew X's fire policy for 12 months from October 2. On October 15, desiring to be off the risk, company A went to company B and asked them to insure X. Company B agreed to take the risk and on October 17 issued a policy to X, insuring him for 12 months from October 2. Meanwhile, on October 13, a loss had occurred of which X was aware but both the companies were ignorant. It was held that X could recover from company B on their policy notwithstanding that it was effected after his knowledge of the loss. That, however, was not a case where *uberrima fides* was required on the part of the assured, inasmuch as the agreement was really one between the two insurance companies to the effect that company B should take over from company A their whole liability, whatever it might prove to be.

---

[88] *Rogers v. Equitable Mutual Life and Endowment Ass.*, (Sup.Ct. Iowa, 1897) 103 Iowa 337; 72 N.W. 538. In *Pritchard v. Merchants' & Tradesmen's Life* (1858) 3 C.B.(N.S.) 622, it was said that in a life assurance policy it was to be presumed that the insurers did not intend to insure "dead or alive" in the absence of strong contrary indications. See also Ch. 15, para. 15–6, *post*, for the application of the doctrine of common mistake.

[89] *Giffard v. Queen Ins. Co.* (1869) 1 Hannay (N.B.) 432.

CHAPTER 5

EXECUTION AND DELIVERY OF POLICY

1. INTRODUCTION

5–1 Completion of policy. From what has been said in Chapters 3 and 4 it will be seen that it may be of the utmost importance to determine the time at which a policy becomes effective as an operative insurance. For instance, the success of a claim brought by the assured may depend upon whether his rights are governed by the temporary cover agreement or by the policy which must supersede it.[1] Again, it may be a term of the parties' contract that the insurers are not to come on risk until the policy is "issued"[2] by them. The significance of the completion of a policy in these and other instances is best considered by treating policies which are under seal separately from those which are not.

5–2 Policy not under seal. If a policy is not under seal,[3] it is a simple contract representing the reduction into writing of the parties' agreement. The significance of the completion of a policy will depend upon the nature of the dealings between the parties prior to its being written. In many cases, the policy will do no more than evidence the terms of a binding contract of insurance already in force, as where cover has been obtained from Lloyd's underwriters on the terms of a slip.[4] It is possible, however, that no binding contract of insurance exists prior to the delivery of a policy to the assured, which act is to be the insurers' mode of acceptance of the assured's proposal for insurance. In that case the conclusion of the contract of insurance hangs upon the delivery of the policy to the assured, unless the "postal acceptance"[5] rule applies, in which case there will be a contract from the time that the insurers put the policy in the post for despatch to the assured or his agent.

The policy would not, of course, take effect in that manner if it varied from

---

[1] See paras 4–13, 4–16, *ante*. Whether the policy is intended to supersede the slip depends upon the circumstances of the particular transaction, see *HIH Casualty & General Ins. Co. v. New Hampshire Ins. Co.* [2001] 2 All E.R.(Comm.) 39, 59–66.

[2] For a discussion of what "issued" means, see *Pearl Life Assurance Co. v. Johnson* [1909] 2 K.B. 288.

[3] Though a seal appears on a Lloyd's policy, it does not purport to be the seal of the underwriters parties to the policy and the document is not "under seal" in the technical sense of those words.

[4] As, *e.g.* in *Thompson v. Adams* (1889) 23 Q.B.D. 361.

[5] *Henthorn v. Fraser* [1892] 2 Ch. 27, 38. See para. 2–20, *ante*.

the terms of the proposal.[6] It would then be a counter-offer by the insurers, and would not be operative until the assured accepted it by word or deed as the contract by which he intended to be bound.

2. POLICIES UNDER SEAL

5-3 Execution as deed. Where a policy is under seal, different consider-ations apply. In this case it is a specialty contract and becomes operative from the time when it is formally "signed, sealed, and delivered", although there may have been no physical delivery of it to the assured or his agent. The assured may acquire rights under a policy executed in this manner which he could not acquire if it were a simple contract. Before describing these, it is convenient to consider the way in which a policy may be executed as a deed binding on its maker through the process of signing, sealing and delivery.

5-4 The law regarding the creation of a deed has been altered by recent legislation.[7] A policy will take effect as a deed only if it shows on its face that it is intended to be a deed and has been validly executed as a deed.[8] In the case of an individual it need not be sealed, but it must be signed in the presence of a witness and must be delivered as a deed by him or his duly authorised agent.[9] In the case of a company, the deed must be executed by the affixing of its common seal, if it has one,[10] or signed by two directors or by one director and the company secretary, and it is then presumed to be delivered unless a contrary intention is proved.[11] so that actual delivery to the assured or to his agent is not necessary for it to bind the insurance company. We have accordingly not thought it necessary to retain the commentary on sealing of deeds in paragraphs 5-4 and 5-5 of the last edition of this book.

5-5 Delivery of deed. A deed, although signed and (where relevant) sealed, does not take effect until it is "delivered",[12] in the sense that that word is understood in the law as to deeds. As the oldest dictionary of English law says "After a deed is written and sealed, if it be not delivered, all the rest is to no purpose."[13] It follows, therefore, that a policy is capable of alteration between sealing and delivery without invalidating its effect when delivered.

5-6 If a deed has passed out of the possession of its grantor, that raises a presumption that it has been delivered,[14] but delivery does not in fact depend upon a transfer of possession. Delivery is simply any act or speech on the part of the maker of the instrument from which it can fairly be inferred that

---

[6] *Allis-Chalmers Co. v. Maryland Fidelity and Deposit Co.* (1916) 114 L.T. 433.
[7] Law of Property (Miscellaneous Provisions) Act 1989, s.1.
[8] *ibid.* s.1(2).
[9] *ibid.* s.1(3).
[10] Companies Act 1985, s.36A(2).
[11] *ibid.* s.36A(4) and s.36A(5).
[12] *Doe d. Cox and Kay v. Day* (1809) 10 East 427; *Styles v. Wardle* (1825) 4 B. & C. 908, 911; *Xenos v. Wickham* (1863) 14 C.B.(N.S.) 435, 473. For the change in the meaning of "delivery" over the years, see D. E. C. Yale, "The Delivery of a Deed" [1970] Camb.L.J. 52.
[13] *Termes de la Ley*, s.v. "Fait".
[14] *Hall v. Bainbridge* (1848) 12 Q.B. 699, 710.

he intends to execute it as his deed and be bound thereby.[15] Whether that intention was present is an issue of fact in each case.

Since there is nothing to prevent a deed being delivered in the legal sense although the grantor does not part with possession,[16] an insurance policy may become effective as a completed policy immediately after the last signature has been written.

5–7 In *Xenos v. Wickham*,[17] a marine policy had been executed by the insurance company, and purported on its face to be "signed, sealed and delivered" by two directors of the company. There was no other evidence of delivery, and the policy, on being executed, had been kept by the company until it should be sent for by the assured or his broker. A loss occurred while it was still in the company's possession. The House of Lords, after receiving advice from the judges, decided that the policy was complete and operative from the time it was executed. The statement on its face that all facts were done to render the execution complete was conclusive against the company that it was not only signed and sealed, but also delivered, there being no other evidence offered as to what took place at the time of execution. Although the policy was retained by the officers of the company after formal execution of it had taken place, they held it for the assured, whose property it became from that moment.

5–8 The principle was taken a stage further in *Roberts v. Security Co. Ltd.*[18] A burglary policy was signed and sealed in the prescribed manner by two directors and the secretary. The policy recited that the first premium had been paid, and it contained a condition that no insurance should be held to be effective until the premium due thereon had been paid. After it was signed and sealed, the policy remained at the company's office. The premium had not in fact been paid, but there was no other evidence tending to show that the execution of the policy was conditional. The Court of Appeal held that the policy was fully executed when signed, and no further act of delivery was required to make it a completely operative deed. Furthermore the company were estopped from denying the truth of the recital that the first premium was paid.

5–9 Whether or not a policy is delivered so as to complete the execution appears, therefore, to be a question of intention on the part of the company's officials who sign and seal the instrument. The requisite intention may be inferred from all the facts and circumstances of the case, and no direct evidence of any word or act indicating a formal delivery appears to be necessary, since in the *Roberts*[19] case there appears to have been no evidence at all beyond the fact that the policy was sealed and signed, and it did not, as in *Xenos v. Wickham*,[20] recite on its face that it had been "delivered". The principle there adopted seems to have been that, in the absence of evidence to the contrary, it may be inferred and presumed that a policy signed and

---

[15] *Xenos v. Wickham* (1876) L.R. 2 H.L. 296, 309, 312, 320, 323; *Vincent v. Premo Enterprises Ltd* [1969] 2 Q.B. 609, 619.
[16] *Doe d. Garnons v. Knight* (1826) 5 B. & C. 671; *Exton v. Scott* (1833) 6 Sim. 31.
[17] (1863) 14 C.B.(N.S.) 435; (1867) L.R. 2 H.L. 296.
[18] [1897] 1 Q.B. 111.
[19] [1897] 1 Q.B. 111.
[20] (1867) L.R. 2 H.L. 296.

sealed by a company in the prescribed form, and on the face of it complete, has thereby also been delivered as a complete deed.

5–10 The *Roberts*[21] case was for many years the only authority suggesting that the essential fact of delivery could be inferred, without additional proof of intention, from the other two essential facts of signing and sealing. The decision was, it could be argued, doubtful, in that it suggested that, in the case of a corporation, the requirement of delivery was virtually nugatory—a view criticised by the leading text book on the subject.[22] Recent authority suggests, however, that the principle of presuming delivery from signing and sealing is correct. In *Beesly v. Hallwood Estates Ltd* Buckley J. held without expressly mentioning *Roberts v. Security Co. Ltd*,[23] that the sealing of an instrument by a corporate body prima facie imported due delivery of it as a deed,[24] and the Court of Appeal, before whom that point was not contested, apparently approved that part of the learned judge's findings.[25]

If, therefore, the directors of an insurance company desire to execute a policy which shall not be immediately effective as a completed deed, they ought to indicate in some way or other that it has not been "delivered", or, preferably, that the policy is delivered as an escrow, and not as a completed deed.[26]

5–11 Delivery as an escrow. An escrow is an instrument which has been signed and executed, and is then delivered subject to a suspensive condition that it is not to take effect until the happening of some future event. Upon the happening of that event, whether it be performance of a specified condition by the grantee or some entirely extraneous occurrence, the grantor of the instrument is absolutely bound, whether he has parted with possession of it or not. When that happens, the escrow is transformed into a fully operative deed.[27]

Once delivered subject to its condition, the escrow is not as a general rule recallable by its maker. He must abide by the delivery of the instrument in escrow and cannot revoke it before it becomes an operative deed.[28] Equity

---

[21] [1897] 1 Q.B. 111.
[22] *Norton on Deeds* (1928 ed.) pp. 11–13.
[23] [1897] 1 Q.B. 111.
[24] [1960] 1 W.L.R. 549, 562.
[25] [1961] Ch. 105. It is not clear whether the Court of Appeal attached the same importance to s.74 of the Law of Property Act 1925 as Buckley J. did in reaching this conclusion.
[26] That might be done by a general standing resolution of the board of directors, or, better still, by introducing into each resolution which authorises the signing and sealing of policies words to the effect that if signed and sealed in advance of payment of premium, they are not to be treated as delivered and are not intended to operate as completed deeds until, in each case, the premium has actually been paid, and the policy sent to the assured or his agent. Another effective method would be to affix to the policy when executed a detachable slip to be removed by the agent on delivery of the policy against payment of the premium. It should be perfectly possible, as contemplated by Farwell L.J. in *Foundling Hospital (Governors and Guardians) v. Crane* [1911] 2 K.B. 367, 379, to arrange for a policy or other instrument to be handed to a broker for custody in a manner which negatives "delivery".
[27] *Xenos v. Wickham* (1867) L.R. 2 H.L. 296; *Beesly v. Hallwood Estates Ltd* [1961] Ch. 105; *Vincent v. Premo Enterprises Ltd* [1969] 2 Q.B. 609; *Windsor Refrigerator Co. Ltd v. Branch Nominees Ltd* [1961] Ch. 88, 99; *Alan Estates Ltd v. W.G. Stores Ltd* [1982] 1 Ch. 511.
[28] *Beesly v. Hallwood Estates Ltd* [1961] Ch. 105, 117–118, approving Sheppard's *Touchstone* at p. 58 of the 1820 edition— "No act of God or man can hinder or prevent its effect then". The condition specified can be virtually any future event, other than the death of the grantor, for in that case the document would become a testamentary disposition controlled by the Wills Act

provides one exception to this rule, however, in that, in a case where the grantee of the instrument delays an unreasonably long time in performing the condition upon which the maturity of the escrow into a deed depends, equity will relieve the grantor from his obligation.[29]

These characteristics distinguish the escrow from an ordinary instrument created subject to a condition. In the latter case, the maker is under no obligation at all pending the happening of the event specified in the condition, and the instrument is in no way an escrow or a deed because it is not "delivered" in the legal sense. It is not delivered, because it is not the intention of its maker that he shall be irrevocably bound, at once or at a future time.[30] So long, indeed, as an instrument, signed and sealed, remains in the possession of the grantor or of some third party for safe custody on his behalf, it may well be inferred that there is no delivery at all.[31]

5–12 It is now settled[32] that if the maker of an instrument retains it in his own hands, it may nonetheless be delivered as an escrow. On principle this appears to be entirely correct, since, if a grantor can unconditionally deliver a deed while it is in his own hands, there is no reason why he should not be able to deliver it conditionally as an escrow. If he can keep it in his hands as an escrow, *a fortiori* he can deliver it to his agent as an escrow. Delivery as an escrow is indeed commonly effected by conditional delivery to a stranger on behalf of the grantee. Delivery to the grantee himself probably cannot be conditional, but must be deemed to be an unconditional delivery of a completed deed,[33] although there are cases where an escrow has been delivered to one of several grantees[34] or to the grantee's solicitor.[35] All these instances are different from the case of the delivery of a policy not under seal to the assured, subject to a condition, in which case it will not be operative at all until the condition is fulfilled.[36]

5–13 The question whether an instrument is delivered as a deed or in escrow is seldom dependent on express words or a particular legal incantation,[37] but is usually to be inferred from the nature of the deed and from all the circumstances surrounding its execution.[38] The rule poses

1837—*Vincent v. Premo Enterprises Ltd* [1969] 2 Q.B. 609, 621; *Alan Estates Ltd v. W.G. Stores Ltd* [1982] 1 Ch. 511, 521, 527. It can even be a condition that the parties will reach agreement on a disputed point, as in *Vincent's* case. The effective date is that of delivery: *Alan Estates Ltd, supra.*

[29] *Beesly v. Hallwood Estates Ltd* [1961] Ch. 105; *Vincent v. Premo Enterprises Ltd* [1969] 2 Q.B. 609. The decisions in those two cases show, however, that equity is reluctant to do what Sheppard's *Touchstone* declared to be beyond the power of God or man.

[30] *Beesly v. Hallwood Estates Ltd* [1961] Ch. 105, 119, 120; *Windsor Refrigerator Co. Ltd v. Branch Nominees Ltd* [1961] Ch. 88, 103.

[31] *Doe d. Garnons v. Knight* (1826) 5 B. & C. 671; *Foundling Hospital (Governors and Guardians) v. Crane* [1911] 2 K.B. 367, 379.

[32] *Beesly v. Hallwood Estates Ltd* [1961] Ch. 105; *Vincent v. Premo Enterprises Ltd* [1969] 2 Q.B. 609, 620. Earlier in *Roberts v. Security Company Ltd* [1897] 1 Q.B. 111, Lord Esher M.R. had expressed some doubts as to whether this was possible.

[33] *Hall v. Bainbridge* (1848) 12 Q.B. 699, 710.

[34] *Johnson v. Baker* (1821) 4 B. & Ald. 440; *London Freehold v. Suffield* [1879] 2 Ch. 608.

[35] *Watkins v. Nash* (1875) L.R. 20 Eq. 262; *Millership v. Brookes* (1860) 5 H. & N. 797.

[36] As illustrated by the decision in the American case of *Hartford Fire Ins. Co. v. Wilson*, 187 U.S. 467 (1902).

[37] *Vincent v. Premo Enterprises Ltd* [1969] 2 Q.B. 609, 619.

[38] *Bowker v. Burdekin* (1843) 11 M. & W. 128; *Gudgen v. Besset* (1856) 6 E. & B. 986; *London Freehold v. Suffield* [1897] 2 Ch. 608.

considerable evidentiary problems, and it might well be better if the law were changed so as to require some clearly defined step to be taken by persons executing deeds and intending to deliver them unconditionally. One possibility would be to require transfer of possession to the grantee.[39] As the law stands at present, generalisation is not easy.

5–14 If a policy remains in the hands of the company or its agents after execution, and it is so held merely for the convenience of the assured until he demands it, authority both here and in America is clear to the effect that the policy is completely operative.[40] Where, however, the object of holding the policy is to obtain payment of the premium or to make inquiries before finally becoming committed to the risk, it is a natural inference that the directors did not intend to effect delivery of the policy.[41] So, where a policy is sent to an agent of the company who has standing instructions to hand over the policy only against payment of the premium by the assured, it is fair to infer that the directors, with those instructions in mind, did not intend to effect an unconditional delivery of the policy.[42]

5–15 Where a deed is produced from the custody of the grantee or his representatives, it is presumed prima facie to have been delivered unconditionally,[43] and, if shown to have been delivered conditionally it is presumed prima facie that the conditions have been fulfilled and that the deed has become fully operative.[44] The consequence of the performance of a condition precedent to the effective operation of a deed is to make the deed as effective as if it had been delivered unconditionally at the date it was delivered as an escrow.[45] If, therefore, the delivery of a policy by insurers to their own officials or agents is a delivery of the deed as an escrow, for instance if it is delivered conditionally and with the intention that it shall not be completely operative until the premium is paid, payment of the premium or the performance of any other suspensive condition would render the policy as effective for all purposes as if it had been delivered unconditionally at the time when it was delivered conditionally to the officials or agents of the company.[46] If a loss were to occur after the policy had been delivered in escrow upon condition that a premium be paid, and the premium were to be subsequently paid, it would appear that the loss would prima facie be

[39] See the interesting suggestions of Winn L.J. in *Vincent v. Premo Enterprises Ltd* [1969] 2 Q.B. 609, 623. It is, with respect, quite true that the authorities cited in *Norton on Deeds* could, prior to *Roberts v. Security Co. Ltd*, be interpreted as holding that a "constructive" change of possession was necessary before an instrument could be delivered as a deed or an escrow, but *Roberts v. Security Co. Ltd* [1897] 1 Q.B. 111, is not mentioned by Winn L.J. in that context. The Roberts case was itself not very cordially received by the Privy Council in *Equitable Fire and Accident Office v. The Ching Wo Hong* [1907] A.C. 96, but was not criticised when cited by Lord Maugham in *Wooding v. Monmouthshire Indemnity Soc.* [1939] 4 All E.R. 570, 581.
[40] *Xenos v. Wickham* (1867) L.R. 2 H.L. 296; *Franklin Insurance Co. of Philadelphia v. Colt* (1874) 87 U.S. (20 Wall) 560; *Bragdon v. Appleton Mutual Fire Ins. Col.* (1856) 42 Me. 259; *Union Central Life Ins. Co. v. Philips* (1900) 102 Fed.Rep 19.
[41] *Xenos v. Wickham* (1867) L.R. 2 H.L. 296.
[42] *Wainer v. Milford Mutual Fire Ins. Co.* (1891) 153 Mass. 335.
[43] *Mutual Life Assurance Co. of Canada v. Giguère* (1902) 32 S.C.R. 348.
[44] *Hare v. Horton* (1833) 5 B. & Ad. 715.
[45] *Graham v. Graham* (1791) 1 Ves. 272, 275; Sheppard's *Touchstone* (1820 ed.), p. 59, approved by Harman L.J. in *Beesly v. Hallwood Estates Ltd* [1961] Ch. 105, 117; *Alan Estates Ltd v. W.G. Stores Ltd* [1982] Ch. 511. But see Kenny [1982] Conv. 409.
[46] *Roberts v. Security Company Ltd* [1897] 1 Q.B. 111, 116.

covered by the policy. It is unlikely, moreover, that equity could release the insurers from their obligations in such a case. This example serves to illustrate the practical importance of inserting a term in policies to the effect that the insurers shall not be on risk until the first premium is paid.

5–16 Operative date of deed. Prima facie, if a deed is dated it is presumed to have been completely executed, that is, signed and delivered, on the date which it bears,[47] but the parties are not estopped from alleging that it was signed, sealed, or delivered on a date subsequent to the date shown.[48] A deed prima facie speaks from the date of delivery, unless it is clearly expressed to be retrospective in operation.[49] If a deed is dated, and time is computed from the date of the deed, the party executing it agrees that the date mentioned in the deed shall be the date for the purposes of such computation.[50]

5–17 Delivery subject to defeasance impossible. Although a policy may be delivered as an escrow not to take effect until a certain condition has been fulfilled, it cannot be delivered subject to a condition that it shall take effect at once but become void on the happening of some future event. Any such condition subsequent must be inserted in the policy, for once the policy is delivered as a fully completed deed no condition can be effective which is not part of the written instrument. Thus, if a policy were delivered subject to an oral condition that it should be surrendered and cease if and when cancelled by the company's head office, the condition must be inoperative, inasmuch as to give effect to it would be to introduce a term into the parties' contract inconsistent with their recorded written agreement.[51]

5–18 Effect of policy under seal. Assuming that a policy is issued as a deed and delivered, two principal benefits may accrue to the assured.

5–19 First, it is a peculiarity of a deed that it needs no acceptance on the part of the grantee to give it binding effect. Even in the case of a bilateral deed or indenture, where the covenants of the one party are expressed to be in consideration of the covenants by the other, the execution of the deed by the one party binds that party, even though the other party never executes his part.[52] As, in general, grants are for the benefit of the grantee, he may, so long as he has not rejected the deed, come in at any time and say, "By God and all His saints, I claim by the deed"; but he is entitled, so long as he has not assented to it, to say that he disclaims, and will have nothing to do with, the deed.[53] The grantee, therefore, so long as he has neither assented nor disclaimed, is free to elect whether he shall take the deed or not, and, although he can sue, he is not liable to be sued upon it.[54] If, however, he has assented to the deed by taking any benefit under it, or by otherwise

---

[47] *Steele v. Mart* (1825) 4 B. & C. 272.
[48] *Hall v. Cazenove* (1804) 4 East 477.
[49] *Jayne v. Hughes* (1854) 10 Ex. 430.
[50] *Styles v. Wardle* (1825) 4 B. & C. 908.
[51] This would approximate to the decision in *Hodge v. The Security Ins. Co. of New Haven*, 40 N.Y.S.C.R. (33 Hun.) 583 (1884), but it is unclear whether the policy in that case was under seal. The decision would, however, be the same.
[52] *Morgan v. Pike* (1854) 14 C.B. 473; *Rose v. Poulton* (1831) 2 B. & Ad. 822; *Naas v. Westminster Bank* [1940] A.C. 366.
[53] *Siggers v. Evans* (1855) 5 E. & B. 367, 381.
[54] *Petrie v. Bury* (1824) 3 B. & C. 353.

expressing an assent to it, he is bound to perform his part of the deed even though he has not in fact executed it.[55]

Upon those principles it follows that a policy made as a deed may be relied upon by the assured, notwithstanding that it varies from his proposal and that before the loss he neither acquiesced in nor even knew of its execution.[56] If he has seen it and disclaimed it, he can no longer rely on it but until he disclaims it, he has the right to elect whether to accept it or reject it. Disclaimer of a deed is a solemn, irrevocable, act; and where it is alleged the court must be satisfied that it is fully proved by the party alleging it, who must also establish that the disclaimer was made with full knowledge and full intention.[57]

5–20 Secondly, on general principles of estoppel, the assured may benefit from the insurers' inability to dispute certain statements made in a policy under seal.[58]

5–21 Reference may be made, in connection with both these benefits to the assured, to the interesting case of *Pearl Life Assurance Co. v. Johnson*.[59] There the company issued an industrial policy on the life of the assured's husband, which recited that it was granted in consideration of the assured having signed and caused to be delivered to the company a proposal dated July 26, 1907, such proposal being the agreed basis of the contract. A claim having been made on the policy, the company relied on a misrepresentation in the proposal sent to them. The proposal purported to be signed by the assured but in fact was completed and signed in her name (presumably by the company's agent) without her knowledge or authority. The policy was under seal. The assured accepted it and paid the premiums thereon. It was accordingly held that both parties were estopped from denying that the policy was granted on the basis of *a* proposal, and that it was not open to the company to contend that, as the assured had never signed any proposal form, there was no contract. On the other hand, the assured was not estopped from alleging that the proposal produced by the company was not her proposal, and that she was not responsible for the misstatements of fact contained in it.[60] As to the signature, the mere fact that the proposer had left it to the agent to do what was necessary to effect an insurance upon the lines indicated by her did not give the agent authority to sign the proposal form or bind the proposer by any warranty given without her knowledge.[61]

---

[55] *Webb v. Spicer* (1849) 13 Q.B. 894.

[56] *Yonge v. Equitable Life Ass. Soc.* (1887) 30 Fed. Rep. 902, where the assured died while an executed own-life policy was being mailed to him.

[57] *Naas v. Westminster Bank* [1940] A.C. 366.

[58] *Roberts v. Security Company Ltd* [1897] 1 Q.B. 111.

[59] [1909] 2 K.B. 288.

[60] See also *Maddock v. British Widows Assurance* [1926] I.A.C.Rep. 41; *Yates v. Liverpool Victoria F.S.* [1926] I.A.C.Rep. 50; *Wright v. Royal Liver F.S.* [1930] I.A.C.Rep. 89; *O'Kane v. City of Glasgow F.S.* [1931] I.A.C.(N.I.) Rep. 76.

[61] *O'Kane v. City of Glasgow F.S.*, *supra*. See also para. 18–2, *post*.

CHAPTER 6

COMMENCEMENT AND TERMINATION OF RISK

(A) COMMENCEMENT OF COVER

1. RISK COMMENCING WITH REFERENCE TO DATE OR EVENT

6–1 Commencement of risk. Where the risk is not described as running from any specified date, the presumption is that it runs from the date of the policy.[1] The risk may begin to run either before or after the policy is issued. It may run from the date of acceptance of the offer or from the payment of the first premium or from the execution or delivery of the policy. The date when a risk attaches is in each case a matter of construction of the terms of the preliminary agreement or of the policy when executed. There is no principle of law which compels a company to assume a risk as from the date of acceptance or from any other particular date. Unless so specified, an acceptance does not relate back to the date of the proposal or offer.[2] It is not uncommon, however, to antedate the policy to the date of the proposal, and if the assured accepts a policy in that form the period of risk will be computed as from the nominal date of the policy.[3]

6–2 Specified date. Where the risk is specified as running from or to a specified day or from the date of the policy, the question may arise whether the specified day is included or excluded. In an early life insurance case, Holt C.J. drew a distinction between the expressions "from the day of the date hereof" and "from the date hereof", holding that the former was exclusive of the day of the date, but the latter inclusive. Lord Mansfield, however, disapproved of any such rigid distinction, and said that the construction must vary according to the subject-matter, and that "from" a particular date may either include or exclude that day according to the context.[4]

6–3 It is now established, however, that in the absence of anything in the context to indicate a contrary intention of the parties, the word "from" will

---

[1] *McMaster v. New York Life* (1901) 183 U.S. 25; *Dunsheath v. Pearl* [1935] I.A.C.Rep. 18; *Barker v. Royal London Mutual* [1937] I.A.C.Rep. 10.
[2] *North American Life v. Elson* (1903) 33 S.C.R. 383; *Barker v. Royal London Mutual* [1937] I.A.C.Rep. 10; *McKillen v. Britannic* [1929] I.A.C.(N.I.) Rep. 59.
[3] *McConnell v. Provident Savings Life* (1899) 92 Fed.Rep. 769; *Johnson v. Mutual Benefit* (1906) 143 Fed.Rep. 950.
[4] *Pugh v. Duke of Leeds* (1777) 2 Cowp. 714.

be read in what the courts have said is its primary meaning, that is, exclusive of the specified day,[5] and where the duration of the risk is expressed as being until the corresponding day in the following month or year the whole of that day is included in the period of risk.[6] Thus, where a fire insurance policy was expressed to run "from the 14th day of February, 1868, until the 14th day of August, 1868", it was held that the period of risk excluded February 14 and included August 14.[7]

6–4 The importance of the prima facie rule of interpreting the word "from" a specified date as equivalent to "after" is illustrated by the decision in *Cartwright v. MacCormack*[8] concerning the duration of a cover note for motor-vehicle insurance. The commencement of the risk was expressed to be effective from 11.45 a.m. on December 2, 1959, and the cover note was stated to be valid "for 15 days from the commencement date of risk". It was held that the insurance company was still on risk in respect of an accident which took place at 5.45 p.m. on December 17, 1959, because the 15 days began to run at midnight on December 2 in accordance with this usual rule of construction. Had the 15 days been expressed in terms of the time of commencement of risk and not the date, the cover note would have time expired at 11.45 a.m. on December 17.[9] The same rule was applied also in two cases of insurance against risk of liability to third parties in respect of accident.[10]

6–5 Excluding the rule. The principle of computation may, however, vary with the nature of the case, and there are circumstances in which the court would compute the period of a month or a year from a specified date as including that date and excluding the corresponding date in the following month or year, as for example in a case where the sum assured was progressively increased in amount at the end of the first and second three months of insurance.[11] The usual rule may, of course, be varied by express words, as where the period of risk was said to be for two months "beginning with" the date of issue of the policy or cover note.[12] Another example would be where the insurance was expressed to be "from January 1st to July 1st, both days inclusive", in which case the period of risk would include both the commencement and terminating dates.[13] Wherever the period of the risk has to be computed in relation to an extension or renewal of cover, it is a relevant

---

[5] *Lester v. Garland* (1808) 15 Ves. 248; *Goldsmith's Co. v. West Metropolitan Ry* [1904] 1 K.B. 1; *Savory v. Bayley* (1922) 38 T.L.R. 619; *Stewart v. Chapman* [1951] 2 K.B. 792; *Re Figgis* [1969] 1 Ch. 123; *Carapanayoti v. Comptoir Commercial Andre* [1971] 1 Lloyd's Rep. 327; [1972] 1 Lloyd's Rep. 139.
[6] *Isaacs v. Royal Ins. Co.* (1870) L.R. 5 Ex. 296; *South Staffordshire Tramway Co. v. Sickness and Accident* [1891] 1 Q.B. 402; *Hirdes GmbH v. Edmund* [1991] 2 Lloyd's Rep. 546.
[7] *Isaacs v. Royal Ins. Co.* (1870) L.R. 5 Ex. 296.
[8] [1963] 1 W.L.R. 18.
[9] [1963] 1 W.L.R. 18, 21; *Dunn and Tarrant v. Campbell* (1920) 4 Ll.L.R. 36.
[10] *South Staffordshire Tramway Co. v. Sickness and Accident* [1891] 1 Q.B. 402; *Sickness and Accident Ass. Co. v. General Accident Ass.* (1892) 19 R. 977.
[11] *Butters v. Pearl* [1935] I.A.C.Rep. 16.
[12] *Hare v. Gocher* [1962] 1 Q.B. 641; *Trow v. Ind Coope* [1967] 2 Q.B. 899.
[13] *Hough & Co. v. Head* (1885) 55 L.J.Q.B. 43; *Scottish Metropolitan Ass. Co. v. Stewart* (1923) 39 T.L.R. 407; *Sickness and Accident Ass. v. General Accident Ass.* (1892) 19 R. 977.

consideration that the parties are likely to have intended to provide for an uninterrupted cover.[14]

6–6 Specified hour. If the period of risk runs from or to midnight or some specified hour of the day named, the hour will usually be determined by the local time of the place where the contract was made, that is to say, in the case of a policy issued by a British office, Greenwich mean time or summer time as the case may be.[15] A different intention may, of course, be expressed in the policy and may also be inferred from the circumstances of the case.

6–7 Specified event. The period of risk may equally well be expressed to run from the moment at which an event occurs. If, in such a case, the period of risk is expressed in days, these will be computed as periods of 24 hours starting at the relevant moment in time. So, where the risk was to run for 30 days from the arrival of the insured ship in port, and she arrived at 11.45 a.m., the period of insurance ran until 11.45 a.m. 30 days later.[16]

6–8 In certain types of insurance the risk must, by the very nature of the insurance cover requested, run from a named event, as where, for example, a marine insurance policy is taken out to cover risks on a particular voyage. In the field of non-marine insurance, it is common to obtain "transit" insurance covering persons or goods whilst in the course of a journey. In such cases the risk commences when the transit commences. In the present state of the authorities it is not certain whether the transit of goods can be said to start when they are handed over to the carrier[17] or when the actual carriage starts[18]—this question is discussed in more detail elsewhere in this work.[19]

6–9 Coupon insurance. Another instance of the risk commencing on the happening of an event is provided by accident or sickness insurances effected by means of coupons or advertisements inserted or printed in diaries, newspapers, or other periodicals. These become operative according to the terms in which the offer is made. The insurance may run from the time of signing, or from the date of posting the coupon with a remittance, or from the time of registration of the reader by the company. Usually the risk will run for 12 months from the date on which it attaches, but in the Scottish case of *General Accident Fire & Light Assurance v. Robertson,*[20] the wording of the coupon was unusual and it was held that the risk, although commencing at latest upon the date when the coupon and remittance were received by the office, ran until the expiration of a year from the date when the coupon was

---

[14] *Cornfoot v. Royal Exchange* [1904] 1 K.B. 40, explained in *Re Figgis* [1969] 1 Ch. 123, and *Carapanayoti v. Comptoir Commercial Andre* [1971] Lloyd's Rep. 327 (reversed by C.A. at [1972] 1 Lloyd's Rep. 139 but on other grounds not affecting these dicta). In a previous edition of this work it was suggested that there was a presumption that uninterrupted cover was intended; the existence of a presumption was questioned in *Hirdes GmbH v. Edmund* [1991] 2 Lloyd's Rep. 546.

[15] Pursuant to ss.9 and 23(3) of the Interpretation Act 1978, a reference to a time means, unless otherwise specified, Greenwich mean time.

[16] *Cornfoot v. Royal Exchange* [1904] 1 K.B. 40.

[17] *Crow's Transport v. Phoenix Assurance Co.* [1965] 1 W.L.R. 383, 388.

[18] *Sadler Bros & Co. v. Meredith* [1963] 2 Lloyd's Rep. 293, 307.

[19] See Ch. 27, paras 27–21 to 27–22, *post.*

[20] [1909] A.C. 404. For a case where cover attached to goods once entered in a register by the assured, see *Nigel Gold Mining v. Hoade* [1901] 2 K.B. 849.

"registered", and it was held to be "registered" when it was filed in alphabetical order along with other similar coupons.

2. RISK COMMENCING UPON PAYMENT OF PREMIUM

6–10 Prepayment of premium. There is no rule of law to the effect that there cannot be a complete contract of insurance concluded until the premium is paid, and it has been held in several jurisdictions that the courts will not imply a condition that the insurance is not to attach until payment.[21] It would seem to follow that, if credit has been given for the premium, the insurer is liable to pay in the event of a loss before payment, although, as has been held in a South African decision,[22] the insurer would be entitled to deduct the amount of the premium from the loss payable, at least where the period of credit had expired by that time, since the assured could not insist on payment when in breach of any obligation assumed on his part under the contract.

6–11 There can be no concluded contract, however, unless there is an express or implied agreement in respect of the amount of the premium and the mode of its payment. This is not to say that the parties must have agreed upon a particular figure for the premium. There can be an effective agreement to hold the assured covered under a policy at a rate of premium to be established later.[23]

It is, however, common practice in some classes of business, for the insurer to provide expressly in the policy[24] or in the proposal form[25] that the insurance is not to attach until the premium has been paid, and there is no doubt that the courts will give effect to such stipulations.[26] The effect of such stipulations depends on their true construction. They may prevent any contract from coming into force until premium is paid. Alternatively the coverage of risk may be affected in that coverage may only commence from the date of payment, or coverage may apply retrospectively from some earlier date once payment has been made.

6–12 Effect of express condition. Where there is a binding contract to insure or a policy has been issued, subject to a condition that there shall be no insurance until the first premium is paid, the condition saves the company from the unsatisfactory position of being on a risk for which they may never

---

[21] *Kelly v. London and Staffordshire Fire Ins. Co.* (1883) Cab. & Ell. 47, 48; *Wooding v. Monmouthshire Indemnity Soc.* [1939] 4 All E.R. 570, 581, 592; *Thompson v. Adams* (1889) 23 Q.B.D. 361; *Lake v. Reinsurance Corporation Ltd* [1967] 3 S.A. 124 (W), 128.

[22] *Lake v. Reinsurance Corporation Ltd* [1967] 3 S.A. 124 (W). See also *Long v. Pilot Life Ins. Co.*, 108 S.E. 2d 840 (N.C.Sup.Ct., 1959), where a condition provided for deduction of unpaid premium if assured died in Days of Grace with it unpaid.

[23] *Kirby v. Cosindit Societa per Azioni* [1969] 1 Lloyd's Rep. 75. S.31(1) of the Marine Insurance Act 1906 provides that where insurance is effected at a premium to be arranged, and no arrangement is made, a reasonable premium is payable.

[24] *Roberts v. Security Co.* [1897] 1 Q.B. 111; *Equitable Fire v. Ching Wo Hong* [1907] A.C. 96; *Re Yager and Guardian Ass. Co.* (1912) 108 L.T. 38.

[25] *Looker v. Law Union and Rock Ins. Co.* [1928] 1 K.B. 554.

[26] *Phoenix Life v. Sheridan* (1860) 8 H.L.Cas. 745.

receive the premium. The condition operates to suspend the risk where, but for the condition, it would have attached at the time the contract was made or at some specified date. Further than this, the condition does not affect the period of risk. It does not affect the date upon which the renewal premium is payable or the expiration of the risk upon non-payment.[27]

6–13 Specified commencement date. The expression that there shall be no insurance, or that the insurance shall not be in force, until the premium is paid is not altogether free from ambiguity. If it is coupled with an agreement to insure from a specified date it is open to argument that the condition has the effect of making the insurance subject to a suspensive condition, and that when the condition is satisfied by payment of the premium, the insurers are bound to indemnify the assured in respect of losses happening between the specified date and the payment of the premium.[28] Where no policy has been delivered or, in England, executed under seal the insurers may be able to escape liability by refusing to accept the premium on the ground that there has been a change of risk before a binding contract was concluded.[29] But if a policy has been delivered or, in England, executed under seal the insurers are more likely to be liable.[30]

6–14 Insurance from date of policy. Even where the insurance is not from a specified date, but is expressly or impliedly to run from the date of the policy or from the delivery of the policy, the condition that it shall not be in force until the premium is paid is probably not in itself sufficient to exclude all liability for loss happening after the execution or delivery of the policy and before payment of the premium. If insurers desire to avoid all risk of having to pay upon such a loss they must either delay execution, or in Scotland delivery, of the policy until the premium has been paid or else insert the less ambiguous proviso that they shall not be liable in respect of any loss happening before the premium is paid, and at the same time take care that they do not by declaration in the policy or otherwise admit payment of the premium before it has in fact been received. In own-life policies a proviso that "the policy shall not be in force until the premium is paid", might perhaps be sufficient, as payment means payment by the assured, and he cannot pay after his death; but a safer form of proviso, available also for

---

[27] *Armstrong v. Provident Savings Life* (1901) 2 Ont.L.R. 771; *North American Life v. Elson* (1903) 33 S.C.R. 383; *McConnell v. Provident Savings Life* (1899) 92 Fed.Rep. 769. This type of condition dates back to the early years of insurance law: see *Tarleton v. Staniforth* (1796) 1 Bos. & Pul. 471.

[28] See, *e.g.* observations of Avory J. in *Ocean Accident and Guarantee Corporation v. Cole* [1932] 2 K.B. 100, 105–106. This argument is strengthened where it is the practice of the office to accept the full premium for the specified period even though not paid until part of that period has elapsed. Many offices charge the premium only from the date of payment and acceptance thereof, and this is a much safer course. It is, of course, possible to stipulate that the insurance will not cover the period prior to payment of the premium or delivery of the policy to the assured: *Sharkey v. Yorkshire Ins. Co.* (1916) 54 S.C.R. 92.

[29] *Sickness and Accident Ass. v. General Accident Ass.* (1892) 19 R. 977; *Harrington v. Pearl Life Ass.* (1914) 30 T.L.R. 613.

[30] *Roberts v. Security Co.* [1897] 1 Q.B. 111, 116; For an argument to the contrary, see Lord Low, *obiter*, in *Sickness and Accident Ass. v. General Accident Ass.* (1892) 19 R. 977, but the learned Lord Ordinary's construction of the particular condition in that case was, with respect, questionable, and was not commented upon by the Court of Session on appeal. It is not possible to formulate a universal rule as to the effect of stipulations of this type—see the discussion in paras 2–41 to 2–43, *ante*.

insurances upon the lives of third parties, is that "the policy shall not be binding until the premium has been received during the lifetime of the party assured".[31]

6–15 Receipt of premium acknowledged in policy. A condition in a policy suspending the risk until payment of the first premium may be rendered inoperative if, in a policy under seal, the company formally acknowledge receipt of premium. This is said to follow from the doctrine of estoppel by deed. The company, having in a completely executed deed declared that it has received the first premium, is said to be estopped from thereafter denying such receipt. The Court of Appeal have carried that doctrine so far that they have held that even where the policy has not been handed to the assured or his agent, but is still in the custody of the company and its agents, yet if it is a completely executed deed, "sealed and delivered", the company is estopped from denying the receipt of premium therein acknowledged.[32] That decision was distinguished in a later case in the Privy Council, where it was held that the receipt clause in the particular policy then under consideration ought to be read as merely a matter of common form, and when taken in conjunction with an emphatic condition that the company should not be liable in respect of loss until the premium "is actually paid", could not reasonably be read as conclusive evidence of actual payment.[33]

In the US it has also been held that, even where the policy has been delivered to the assured, the acknowledgement of receipt of the premium is not conclusive when it is coupled with the condition that there shall be no insurance until the actual payment of the premium.[34] In Canada it has been held that where a policy which acknowledges receipt of the premium, and contains a condition suspending the risk until payment of the first premium, is executed and delivered to an agent of the company to exchange against the premium in cash, the company is not estopped from alleging non-payment of the premium.[35]

6–16 It will be noticed that the doctrine applies only to policies under seal, but it is thought that the recital in a Lloyd's policy that the premium has been paid must have the same effect as in a policy under seal, since the underwriter looks for payment to the broker, to whom he allows terms of credit. Failure of the assured to pay the broker is irrelevant, since the broker cannot cancel the contract without the authority of the assured.[36]

6–17 Estoppel by deed as against an assignee. Although acknowledgement of the receipt of premium contained in the policy may not be conclusive evidence of payment as against the assured, yet, if the policy is under seal, the insurers will be estopped, as against an assignee for value

---

[31] As in, *e.g. Armstrong v. Provident Savings Life Ass.* (1901) 2 Ont.L.R. 771.

[32] *Roberts v. Security Co.* [1897] 1 Q.B. 111. See para. 5–10, *ante* for a suggestion for avoiding this result by means of a resolution of the board of directors.

[33] *Equitable Fire and Life v. The Ching Wo Hong* [1907] A.C. 96.

[34] *Sheldon v. Atlantic Fire*, 26 N.Y. 460 (1863).

[35] *Western Ass. Co. v. Provincial Ass. Co.* (1880) 5 Ont.A.R. 190.

[36] *Xenos v. Wickham* (1867) L.R. 2 H.L. 296, 319. S.54 of the Marine Insurance Act 1906 provides that where a marine policy effected on behalf of an assured by a broker acknowledges receipt of the premium, such acknowledgment is, in the absence of fraud, conclusive as between insurer and insured, but not as between insurer and broker.

without notice of non-payment, from denying the payment of the premium so acknowledged to have been paid.[37]

6–18 Waiver of prepayment condition. Besides estoppel by deed, the insurers may be estopped by their conduct from relying upon the condition for prepayment of the premium—in other words they may expressly or impliedly waive it as a condition precedent to liability. Generally an unequivocal act leading the assured to believe that the contract will be effective without payment of premium amounts to a waiver of the condition.[38] Thus, for instance, the insurers will be held to have waived payment of the premium where credit is given,[39] or a negotiable instrument taken instead,[40] or where in any circumstances the assured is justified in believing, from what the insurers say or write, that payment of the premium is not necessary at that stage,[41] or that it has been paid even if this is not so.[42] If renewal premiums are habitually accepted by the insurers after the expiration of the days of grace, the assured may well be able to rely on their conduct as a waiver of the conditions for payment,[43] but it is always open to the insurers to notify the assured that in future they will insist on payment within the time laid down, and that will defeat a subsequent plea of waiver.[44] As a general rule, unless the insurers do or omit some act whereby the assured has just ground to believe and does believe that the contract will be made, continued or restored without payment of premium, there is no waiver or estoppel.[45]

6–19 The actual delivery of a policy to the assured without demanding payment of the premium may constitute a waiver notwithstanding that the condition is contained in the policy as delivered.[46] Where the usual practice is to insist upon payment of the premium against the delivery of the policy, a departure from that practice by delivering the policy without demanding payment may justify the assured in believing that the prepayment condition will not be insisted on. The question may be whether the delivery was made on such terms as to imply a giving of credit without prejudice to the immediate validity of the policy.[47] That is a question of inference from the

---

[37] Law of Property Act 1925, s.68.

[38] *Bragdon v. Appleton Mutual* (1856) 42 Me. 259; *Sheldon v. Atlantic Fire* (1863) 26 N.Y. 460; *O'Brien v. Union Insurance* (1884) 22 Fed.Rep. 586; *Supple v. Cann* (1858) 9 Ir.C.L.R. 1; *Bodine v. Exchange Fire* (1872) 51 N.Y. App. 117.

[39] *Prince of Wales Life Ass. v. Harding* (1858) E.B. & E. 183.

[40] *Masse v. Hochelaga Mutual Ins. Co.* (1878) 22 L.C.J. 124; *London and Lancashire Life Ass. Co. v. Fleming* [1897] A.C. 499, where, however, the assured failed to meet the terms on which the note was taken.

[41] *Benson v. Ottawa Agricultural Ins. Co.* (1877) 42 U.C.R. 282; *Farquharson v. Pearl Ass. Co. Ltd* [1937] 3 All E.R. 124.

[42] *Re Economic Fire Office Ltd* (1896) 12 T.L.R. 142.

[43] *Peppit v. North British and Mercantile Ins. Co.* (1878) 13 N.S.R.(I.R. & G.) 219.

[44] *Laing v. Commercial Union Ass. Co.* (1922) 11 Ll.L.R. 54; *Redmond v. Canadian Mutual Aid Association* (1891) 18 Ont.A.R. 335.

[45] *Equitable Life Assurance v. McElroy* (1897) 83 Fed.Rep. 631; *State Life v. Murray* (1908) 159 Fed.Rep. 408.

[46] *Roberts v. Security Co.* [1897] 1 Q.B. 111; *Boehen v. Williamsburgh Insurance* (1866) 35 N.Y. 131; *Trustees of First Baptist Church v. Brooklyn Fire* (1859) 19 N.Y. 305; *Washoe Tool Co. v. Hibernia Fire* (1876) 7 Hun. 74, affirmed 66 N.Y. 613; *Hodge v. Security Co. of New Haven* (1884) 33 Hun. 583; *Mutual Reserve Life v. Heidel* (1908) 161 Fed.Rep. 535.

[47] *Farnum v. Phoenix* (1890) 83 Cal. 246.

facts proved. Probably the bare fact that a policy was actually delivered to the assured would not be evidence upon which a finding could be made that a condition in the policy requiring prepayment of the premium was waived,[48] but very little more might be sufficient; as, for instance, the fact that the insurers usually did insist upon payment before delivery.[49]

A condition in a preliminary contract requiring prepayment of the premium would be waived by delivery of a policy which contained no such condition, and in a case in the US[50] where the company's policies contained the condition and there was an oral contract to insure, the court held that the fact that the company had previously issued policies to the same assured without demanding prepayment was evidence of the condition having been waived.

6–20 In considering the authorities on waiver summarised above, it is important to keep in mind the distinction now drawn between estoppel and election. Different principles apply to the two different types of waiver.[51]

(B) TERMINATION OF COVER

6–21 General rules. The period of risk ordinarily continues until the precise time fixed in the policy for its expiration arrives. If no hour is fixed for this, it expires at the last moment of the last day of the specified period.[52] In certain circumstances, however, the insurers may cease to be at risk at an earlier date for any one of various reasons which may be stated here briefly for the sake of completeness. The insurers may determine the policy on account of a breach of duty by the assured, or in exercise of a right given to them under it to determine it on notice to the assured.[53] The assured and insurers may together cancel the policy and substitute a new contract of insurance for it.[54]

If the policy provides that the insurers are to be liable only up to a particular sum, the payment of a loss or successive losses amounting to that sum discharges their liability so that in effect the risk has been terminated.[55]

6–22 Statutory rules as to cancellation. The assured under a long-term insurance contract, that is most forms of life and related insurance, may have the right to cancel the contract under rules made pursuant to statutory powers. The Financial Services and Markets Act 2000 provides generally for

---

[48] *Equitable Fire and Life Office v. The Ching Wo Hong* [1907] A.C. 96; *Wood v. Poughkeepsie* (1865) 32 N.Y. 619.

[49] *Miller v. Life Ins. Co.* (1870) 79 U.S. (12 Wall.) 285, where the policy also contained no condition requiring payment of premium as a condition precedent to operation of the policy.

[50] *Church v. La Fayette* (1876) 66 N.Y. 222.

[51] *Motor Oil Hellas v. Shipping Corp. of India* [1990] 1 Lloyd's Law Rep. 391, 397–400. See also paras 7–51 and 10–102 to 10–103, *post*.

[52] *Isaacs v. Royal Ins. Co.* (1870) L.R. 5 Ex. 296; *Hirdes GmbH v. Edmund* [1991] 2 Lloyd's Rep. 546.

[53] See *Bamberger v. Commercial Credit Mutual Ass. Co.* (1855) 15 C.B. 676; and para. 10–89, *post*.

[54] *Rowe v. Kenway* (1921) 8 Ll.L.R. 225.

[55] *Crowley v. Cohen* (1832) 3 B. & Ad. 478; *Gorsedd S.S. Co. v. Forbes* (1900) 5 Com.Cas. 413. The policy may contain a "buy-out" clause which allows insurers to pay a specified sum and to be relieved of any further liability: *John Wyeth & Brothers Ltd. v. Cigna Ins. Co.* [2001] Lloyd's Rep. I.R. 420.

the making of rules for the protection of consumers,[56] and specifically for the making of rules which confer rights to rescind agreements within specified time periods.[57]

6–23 The Financial Services Authority has promulgated rules[58] dealing with cancellation of, and withdrawal from, various types of contract.[59] The individual customer is given a right to cancel long-term insurance contracts, including life policies, appropriate pension policies and pure protection contracts.[60] Broadly, where there is a right of cancellation, it is to be exercised, in the case of a life policy within the shorter of 30 days or a period of 14 days or more specified by the insurer, and in other cases within 14 days. The time period runs from receipt of a post-sale notice by the customer. There are various exceptions to the right, and detailed provisions as to its exercise. Reference should be made to the rules for the full details of the cancellation regime which they implement.

6–24 Time of loss in relation to period of risk. Difficulties sometimes arise in relation to the time at which a loss, in respect of which a claim is made, occurs. The general rule is that, in the absence of express terms to the contrary, the assured must suffer a loss from a peril insured against during the currency of the risk. In this context it is helpful to remember that a contract of insurance is one whereby the insurer promises in return for a money consideration to pay money or convey some other benefit to the assured upon the occurrence of a named event.[61] The key to the legal significance of the time of loss depends upon the precise definition of that event.

6–25 In cases of indemnity insurance, the engagement of the insurer is to pay an indemnity for losses suffered by the assured, so that the event upon which payment depends is the actual occurrence of the loss.[62] The loss must accordingly be suffered inside the period of cover. Thus, in *Hough v. Head*,[63] shipowners insured against loss of charter freights due to them on a time charter, and the ship was damaged during the period of the insurance. The damage was not ascertained, however, until after the expiration of the policy, when the charterers withheld the charter freight under the off-hire clause in the charter until repairs were done. The Court of Appeal held that this loss of freight was not recoverable because, in the case of indemnity insurance, not only the accident but also the consequent loss must happen inside the period of the insurance. It follows that loss must be actually

---

[56] s.138.

[57] s.139(4)

[58] The rules are published on the FSA website, and are subject to change from time to time.

[59] FSA Conduct of Business Rules 6.7—Cancellation and Withdrawal.

[60] COB Rules: 6.7.7 and 6.7.15.

[61] *Prudential Ins. Co. v. I.R.C.* [1904] 2 K.B. 658, 663, *per* Channell J. See para. 1–1, *ante*.

[62] This proposition requires qualification in so far as the nature of the policy, or the particular terms, link payment to an event other than the occurrence of loss. In the case of liability insurance (other than claims-made cover), the event upon which coverage depends will commonly be the event giving rise to liability, while the event upon which payment depends will be the ascertainment of liability—see para. 28–86, *post*. In other types of insurance, the policy terms may provide for payment to depend upon something other than the actual occurrence of loss. For example, in political risk pecuniary loss insurance policies commonly stipulate that payment will not be made until a waiting period has elapsed after the event causing loss.

[63] (1885) 55 L.J.Q.B. 43.

suffered during the currency of the policy, and not merely threatened, however likely it is that the threat will materialise.[64]

6–26 A loss may be said to occur when the insured peril operates upon the subject-matter of the insurance, and the fact that the full extent of the loss is not discovered until after the expiration of the policy is immaterial.[65] Thus, if a ship be insured against seizure under a time policy, and she is seized during its currency, the underwriters will not escape liability on the ground that a Prize Court has not condemned her and assessed her value until after the expiration of the policy.[66]

6–27 Exceptions. The policy may, however, make it clear that the event upon which the insurer has engaged to pay the assured is not the occurrence of a loss caused by a peril insured against. Under a fidelity policy the insurer may undertake to pay in respect of all losses discovered during the running of the policy, no matter when the act of dishonesty was committed,[67] or, as is nowadays quite frequently stipulated in third-party liability insurances of various kinds, they may be bound to indemnify the assured against any claims made against him during the period covered regardless of the time at which the errors complained of had been made.[68]

6–28 Time of peril. Similar questions may arise concerning the time at which a peril insured against materialises. If a peril operates prior to and after the commencement of an insurance, and produces a loss while the risk is running, it would appear that the insurer is liable. In practice, however, the risk would probably never attach in such a case, because the assured would often be guilty of non-disclosure or breach of warranty in relation to the operation of the peril prior to the commencement of the cover.[69] Thus in *Demal v. British America Live Stock Association*,[70] an insurance on a horse named Jim took effect on July 18. Prior to that date Jim was inoculated against certain equine diseases, but the inoculation itself proved fatal, the symptoms appearing after July 18. The risk never attached, because the assured was in fact in breach of a warranty attesting to Jim's good health.

6–29 The facts in *Soole v. Royal Insurance Company Ltd*[71] raised the same problems in a more complex manner. The insurers undertook to indemnify the assured, a property speculator, against financial losses he might suffer in the event of neighbours proving able to enforce a restrictive covenant which

---

[64] *Moore v. Evans* [1918] A.C. 185; *Mitsui v. Mumford* [1915] 2 K.B. 27; *Campbell & Phillipps Ltd v. Denman* (1915) 21 Com.Cas. 357; *Fooks v. Smith* [1924] 2 K.B. 508.

[65] *Knight v. Faith* (1850) 15 Q.B. 649, 667, explaining *Meretony v. Dunlope* (cited in *Lockyer v. Offley* (1786) 1 T.R. 252, 260); *Daff v. Midland Colliery Owners Indemnity Co.* (1913) 109 L.T. 418, 427.

[66] *Andersen v. Marten* [1908] A.C. 334, 338–339.

[67] *Pennsylvania Co. for Insurances on Lives v. Mumford* [1920] 2 K.B. 537.

[68] *Maxwell v. Price* [1960] 2 Lloyd's Rep. 155; *Thorman v. New Hampshire Ins. Co.* [1988] 1 Lloyd's Rep. 7. For the usual position in an employers' liability policy—see *Victoria Ins. Co. v. Junction* [1925] A.C. 354; *Mayer v. Co-operative Ins.* [1939] 2 K.B. 627.

[69] This was the basis of the decision also in *Buchanan v. Faber* (1899) 4 Com.Cas. 223, a case of marine insurance where the warranty of seaworthiness was breached through the condition of the vessel at the commencement of the policy. *Buse v. Turner* (1815) 6 Taunt. 338 is an example of non-disclosure in such circumstances.

[70] (1910) 14 W.L.R. 250.

[71] [1971] 2 Lloyd's Rep. 332.

would drastically limit his building operations on a certain plot of land purchased for development. The cover clause in the policy provided, *inter alia*, that an indemnity was payable:

> "in the event of any person or persons at any time within a period of thirty years after the date shown above as commencing date claiming to be entitled to enforce such ... restrictive covenant."

The commencing date of the insurance was May 10, 1965. In September 1964 a claim to be entitled to the benefit of the covenant was intimated in correspondence by a neighbour, and eventually, in 1967, an injunction was granted against the assured, who made a claim on his policy. The insurers contended that the neighbour's claim had been initiated prior to May 10, 1965, and fell outside the scope of the policy. It was held that the words "claiming to be entitled" connoted more than the mere assertion of a claim in letters, and meant the enforcement of that claim in legal proceedings, so that the assured was not defeated on that ground.[72]

Most policies would not render the insurer liable for a loss suffered during the currency of the risk from a peril operating *wholly* before the commencement of the cover.[73] Neither would he ordinarily be liable for a loss suffered after expiry of the insurance whether due to a peril operating after the period of risk or during it.[74]

6–30 Contractual termination clauses. The insurance contract may contain a clause enabling the insurer or assured to terminate the contract in specified circumstances. Alternatively it may provide for automatic renewal unless notice of cancellation is given at a specified time prior to the renewal date.[75] A widely-drafted clause can give the insurer the option to terminate at will, without having to demonstrate that the exercise of the option is justifiable on objectively reasonable grounds.[76] The time at which cancellation becomes effective will depend upon the construction of the clause.[77] An

---

[72] The decision seems a little surprising on the wording of the policy, but less so when it appears from the facts that the neighbour first made his "claim" against the vendor of the land, not the assured—see [1971] 2 Lloyd's Rep. at 333. A defence of non-disclosure was abandoned for undisclosed reasons. The learned judge also held, *obiter*, that the insurers were not estopped from disputing liability on the policy by reason of the fact that they had taken over the defence of the neighbour's claim for an injunction against the assured, as, for one thing, any representation to be deduced from such conduct would have been one of law (at p. 340) and, secondly, such conduct was not inconsistent with a decision to deny liability under the policy. See para. 28–32, *post*.

[73] *Kelly v. Norwich Union Fire Ins. Soc.* [1990] 1 W.L.R. 139.

[74] *Lockyer v. Offley* (1786) 1 T.R. 252. In such circumstances issues as to causation may be linked with the question of the ambit of the insurance: *Fooks v. Smith* [1924] 2 K.B. 508.

[75] *Commercial Union Ass. Co. v. Sun Alliance Ins. Group* [1992] 1 Lloyd's Rep. 475 (120 days NCAD—Notice at Cancellation Date).

[76] *The Sun Fire Office v. Hart* (1889) 14 App.Cas. 98; *Carna Foods Ltd v. Eagle Star Ins. Co.* [1995] 2 I.L.R.M. 474 (H.C.); affirmed: [1997] 2 I.R. 193. The existence of a cancellation clause does not of itself impose a continuing duty of disclosure: *New Hampshire Ins. Co. v. MGN Ltd* [1997] L.R.L.R. 24.

[77] *e.g. Larizza v. Commercial Union Ass. Co.* (1990) 68 D.L.R. (4th) 460 (cancellation notice given by the assured was effective at the end of the day on which it was received: Ontario Court of Appeal).

insurer who exercises a contractual right of cancellation may, as a matter of contractual implication, be required to return all or some of the premium.[78]

Ambiguity in a termination clause would be likely to be construed against the insurer and so as to ensure that the insurer's contractual obligations were not effectively deprived of substance.[79] Furthermore, unfair terms not individually negotiated, and included in a contract with a consumer concluded after 31 December 1994 will not be binding on the consumer.[80] However, the assessment of the unfair nature of terms is not intended to apply to terms which clearly define or circumscribe the insured risk and which are taken into account in calculating the premium paid by the consumer.[81] A termination clause will be subject to the test of fairness unless it can be characterised as defining or circumscribing the ambit of the insured risk.

---

[78] *Re Drake Ins. Plc* [2001] Lloyd's Rep. I. R. 643. Return of premium is discussed further in Ch. 8, *post*. However, the contract may provide for the insurer to retain premium for cover which has been terminated, although it is to be expected that clear wording would be needed to achieve this result: *Kazakstan Wool Processors (Europe) Ltd v. NCM* [2000] Lloyd's Rep. I.R. 371.

[79] See, *e.g. Federation Ins. Ltd v. Wasson* (1987) 163 C.L.R. 303, where the High Court of Australia held that a composite policy of insurance did not permit termination to take place in relation to the interest of one co-assured who had purported to terminate without the consent of a co-assured. The exercise of a contractual termination clause would be most unlikely to relieve the insurer of liability for past, crystallised or settled losses, but a suitably-drafted clause can relieve the insurer of liability for contingent losses: *Kazakstan Wool Processors (Europe) Ltd v. NCM* [2000] Lloyd's Rep. I.R. 371.

[80] The Unfair Terms in Consumer Contracts Regulations, 1999 S.I. No. 2083. See also the discussion of the Regulations at paras 10–12 to 10–16, *post*.

[81] See preamble to Council Directive 93/13/EEC, O.J. L95/29.

CHAPTER 7

PAYMENT OF PREMIUM

7–1 This chapter deals with premium and rules regarding payment. The main topics considered are as as follows:

(1) general rules of payment;
(2) renewal premiums;
(3) the days of grace;
(4) non-payment: waiver, termination and related matters; and
(5) waiver by agents.

The relationship between premium and the formation of the contract of insurance is dealt with in Chapter 2. The effect of premium payment on the commencement of cover is dealt with in Chapter 6. Lloyd's practices with regard to premium are dealt with in Chapter 35.

7–2 Premium defined. The premium is the consideration required of the assured in return for which the insurer undertakes his obligations under the contract of insurance.[1] It will generally be a money payment but need not necessarily be so. Thus, in the case of a mutual insurance society it may consist of the liability of the member to contribute to a fund to indemnify other members of the society for their losses.[2] The amount or adequacy of the premium in relation to the risks run is a matter for the insurer rather than a court,[3] but it has been said that the amount of the premium charged might be of assistance in determining what risks the insurer intended to run if the premium was assessed on a fixed scale commensurate with the scope of the risk.[4]

---

[1] *Lewis Ltd v. Norwich Union Fire Ins. Co.* [1916] A.C. 509, 519.
[2] *Lion Mutual Marine Ins. Ass. v. Tucker* (1883) 12 Q.B.D. 176, 187; *Great Britain 100 A1 Steamship Ins. Ass. v. Wyllie* (1889) 22 Q.B.D. 710, 722; *Standard Steamship Owners P & I Assoc. v. Gann* [1992] 2 Lloyd's Rep. 528, 531–532. The provisions of the Marine Insurance Act 1906 relating to premium do not apply to mutual insurance: s.85 of the 1906 Act.
[3] The description of the premium as "a price paid adequate to the risk" in the old case of *Lucena v. Craufurd* (1806) 2 Bos. & Pul. (N.R.) 269, 301 was presumably a reference to insurance practice rather than to legal requirements. If insurance is effected at a premium to be arranged, and no sum is agreed, a reasonable premium is payable: s.31(1) of the Marine Insurance Act 1906.
[4] *Re George and Goldsmiths' Insurance* [1899] 1 Q.B. 595, 611.

1. GENERAL RULES OF PAYMENT

7–3 Theory and practice. Prima facie premiums are payable in cash to the insurers at their principal place of business, that is to say, in the case of a company, at the head office of the company.[5] In practice, the place and manner of payment are regulated by the terms of the policy or by the customary method of transacting the business of insurance.

The assured is presumed to have notice of any condition in his policy relating to the place of payment, and will be bound thereby.[6] But the conditions of the policy may be waived, and payment to an agent will be sufficient if the agent was expressly or impliedly authorised by the company to receive payment, or held out by the company as a person having such authority.[7] If the terms of a policy require payment to be made to one particular agent, payment to some other agent is not a valid payment, and the assured must use reasonable diligence to find the particular agent to whom payment must be made, and the fact that he has called once or twice and found the agent out is no excuse for non-payment of premium.[8] But, even where payment is directed to be made to a particular agent, the officials at the head office may probably be assumed, in the absence of express stipulation to the contrary, to have a concurrent authority to accept the premium.

7–4 Implied authority of agent. Payment to the company's examining physician, who undertook to transmit the money to the company, was held to be insufficient in the absence of evidence of authority or holding out of authority by the company.[9] An agent to whom a policy is transmitted for delivery to the assured has probably ostensible authority to collect the premium, and in one case in the US[10] a provision in the policy that payment should be made to the secretary or agent appointed in writing was held to be waived by the company transmitting the policy to an agent in such circumstances that authority to collect the premium would be implied. Where the assured has been in the habit of paying the premium to a particular local agent, payment to that agent is sufficient payment until the agent's authority has been revoked[11] and the assured has clear notice of the fact.[12]

7–5 Delegation of authority. An agent is not entitled to delegate his authority without the express or implied consent of his principal and, therefore, where an insurance company appoints a particular person to receive the premiums, that person cannot appoint anyone else to receive them on his behalf, unless authorised by the company to do so. But an agent

---

[5] *Montreal Assurance v. Macgillivray* (1859) 13 Moo.P.C. 87; *London and Lancashire life v. Fleming* [1897] A.C. 499.

[6] *Mulrey v. Shawmut Mutual*, 86 Mass. 116 (1862).

[7] *Palmer v. Phoenix Mutual Life Ins. Co.*, 39 Sickels 63 (84 N.Y.App.) (1881); *State Life v. Murray*, 159 Fed.Rep. 408 (1909); *Talbott v. Metropolitan Life*, 142 Fed.Rep. 694 (1906).

[8] *Cronkhite v. Accident*, 35 Fed.Rep. 26 (1888).

[9] *Teeter v. United Law*, 159 N.Y. 411 (1899).

[10] *Arthurholt v. Susquehanna*, 159 Pa. 1 (1893).

[11] *McNeilly v. Continental Life*, 66 N.Y.App. 23 (1876).

[12] *Insurance Co. v. McCain*, 96 U.S. 84 (1877). The decision indicates that the burden of proof of notice is on the insurer.

has implied authority to do his business in the ordinary way through a staff of clerks or other servants in his employment, and therefore payment to such persons would be deemed payment to the company. In one case in the US[13] the secretary's wife was in the habit of receiving premiums on behalf of the secretary. That practice was acquiesced in by the company, and payment to the wife was accordingly held to be sufficient payment. In another case in the US[14] an agent authorised his daughter to receive payment of premiums during his absence. The court held that the agent had acted within the scope of his authority in temporarily delegating that authority to his daughter, and that payment to the daughter was payment to the company.

7–6 Printed receipt. A condition may provide that no payment of premium will be recognised unless proved by the evidence of the company's printed receipt signed by the president and secretary. That condition may be waived. Thus, where the company terminated an agency, and did not send the agent the usual forms, but authorised him to remit to the head office the premiums then falling due, it was held that payment to the agent was sufficient, although no printed receipt had been given.[15] In an Australian case[16] a receipt for a renewal premium granted by an agent was expressed to be subject to the following terms:

> "This temporary receipt has the full force of the company's policy (and is subject to its conditions) for fourteen days only from the date of issue, but on the expiry of that time none other than the head office receipt will be acknowledged by the company."

A fire occurred after the 14 days, and before the agent had transmitted the premium to the head office, and it was held that there was an effective renewal for a year, although no receipt had been issued from the head office. The court was of opinion that the condition referred rather to the duty of the agent than to any obligation imposed on the assured.

7–7 Authority of broker. Prima facie, a broker employed by the assured to effect an insurance has no authority from the company to collect the premium for it, so that payment to him is not necessarily payment to the company. In any event the company can eliminate any doubt by inserting in the policy a condition that the broker or agent of the assured is deemed to be *his* agent in paying the premium.[17] But a broker may be held out by the company as having authority to collect the premium, and a clause in the policy providing that any person procuring the insurance shall be deemed the agent of the insured and not of the insurer has been construed as intended to prevent the insurer from being bound by the representations of a broker, and not to counteract the effect of his being held out as agent to receive the premium.[18]

7–8 Title to premiums paid. Where the insurers employ a broker or

---

[13] *Anderson v. Supreme Council of the Order of Chosen Friends*, 135 N.Y. 106 (1892).
[14] *McNeilly v. Continental Life*, 66 N.Y. 23 (1876).
[15] *McNeilly v. Continental Life*, 66 N.Y. 23 (1876).
[16] *Moore v. Halfay*, 9 Vict.L.R. 400 (1883).
[17] *Wilber v. Williamsburgh*, 122 N.Y. 439 (1890); *Becker v. Exchange Mutual*, 165 Fed.Rep. 816 (1908).
[18] *Kelly v. London and Staffordshire Fire* (1883) Cab. & El. 47.

insurance agency to collect premiums on their behalf, it is prudent to include in the agency agreement a clause providing that premiums are to be held in trust for them while in the agents' control, and are not to form part of the agents' personal estate. In *Vehicle and General Insurance Co. v. Elmbridge Insurances*,[19] the insurers went into liquidation while their dealings with their agents were governed by such a clause. It was held that the clause gave the liquidator title to premiums retained by the agents, and that the liquidation did not frustrate the parties' agreement.

7–9 Payment by cheque or bill. The insurers may accept a cheque, promissory note or bill of exchange as whole or part payment of the premium, and the question then arises whether they have accepted it as absolute payment or only as payment conditional on the document being honoured at maturity. Whether a negotiable instrument is accepted by a creditor as asbolute or conditional payment is a question of fact.[20] If a creditor were for his own convenience to take a bill drawn or accepted by a third party instead of payment in cash, the presumption would be that he accepted it as an absolute payment in satisfaction of the debt.[21]

7–10 The problem of conditional payment does not appear to have been considered in England so far as insurance premiums are concerned, except where the policy has contained special provisions,[22] but the decisions on conditional payments made under other types of agreement indicate that an English court would presume a payment by cheque or note to be a conditional payment unless the assured could prove an agreement to the contrary.[23] If the note of a third party were taken in satisfaction, the court would be more likely to find an intention to release the assured from the obligation to pay the premium and to leave the insurer to have recourse against the maker or acceptor of the note, particularly if the insurers might still have insisted upon payment by the assured himself.[24] The presumption does not necessarily apply to other methods of payment. A payment by credit card may fall to be treated as absolute in the light of the circumstances surrounding the payment.[25] The circumstances of each method of payment would have to be considered in order to decide whether it was absolute or conditional.

7–11 The US decisions are illuminating in that they concern insurance policies, but tend to a different conclusion, namely, that acceptance of a negotiable instrument in whole or part payment of premium is good

---

[19] [1973] 1 Lloyd's Rep. 325 (Mayor's and City of London Court). *cf. Re Attorney-General of Canada and Northumberland Ins. Co.* (1987) 36 D.L.R. (4th) 421; (1988) 52 D.L.R. (4th) 383, where, however, the trust arose pursuant to statute.

[20] *Goldshede v. Cottrell* (1836) 2 M. & W. 20; *Talbott v. Metropolitan Life*, 142 Fed.Rep. 694 (1906).

[21] *Anderson v. Hillies* (1852) 12 C.B. 499.

[22] As in *London and Lancashire Life Ass. Co. v. Fleming* [1897] A.C. 499. The point of payment by a cheque which is dishonoured was raised but not decided in *Looker v. Law Union and Rock Ass. Co.* [1928] 1 K.B. 554. See also *Barker v. N. British Ins. Co.* (1831) 9 S. 869; *Neill v. Union Mutual Life* (1881) 7 Ont.A.R. 171.

[23] *Marreco v. Richardson* [1908] 2 K.B. 584; Byles, *Bills of Exchange* (26th ed., 1988) p. 436 and cases cited at note 7, *ante*.

[24] Byles, *op. cit.* p. 439 and the cases cited at note 37, *post*.

[25] *Re Charge Card* [1989] Ch. 497 (payment for petrol).

payment and sufficient to waive all conditions in the contract concerning suspension or forfeiture in the event of non-payment in cash at the due date. It is not equivalent to an extension of time for payment.[26] If it were that, and if the cheque were to be dishonoured or the bill or note not met at maturity, the policy conditions relating to non-payment would revive and take effect. Thus, in *Thompson v. Knickerbocker Life Insurance Co.*,[27] the United States Supreme Court was of the view that, were there not in the policy in question a condition rendering it void if a note given for premium was not met at maturity, it would have held that such failure did not upset the policy. No presumption of law emerges from the 19th century US decisions to the effect that giving a note, whether drawn on or accepted by a third party or not, is without more conditional payment only.[28] If the insurer intended it to be a conditional payment, it should have been evidenced by a receipt describing it as such.[29]

7–12 Even where a clause provided that the policy should lapse if a note was not met at maturity, it was held in one case that forfeiture did not follow automatically, since on its true interpretation the clause gave the insurers the right to avoid the policy in that event, and unless they signified unmistakably their election to avoid it, the policy did not become void.[30]

7–13 Conditional payment. Conditional payment of a debt by bill or note suspends the debt until the bill or note has matured and become payable, and if at that time the instrument has passed into the hands of a third party, that is to say if the creditor has negotiated it, the debt remains suspended until the instrument gets back into the creditor's possession.[31] When the bill has matured and is in the creditor's own hands, the debt revives. If the debtor himself is primarily liable on the bill or note, there is no obligation on the creditor to give notice of the fact that it is overdue and unpaid, and it is for the debtor if charged with the debt to show that the bill or note is still current or has been met.[32] On the other hand, if a creditor accepts a bill drawn by the debtor on a third party, he must present the bill to the drawee and give notice of dishonour to the debtor before the original debt can be revived.[33] When the bill or note is met, conditional payment becomes actual payment, and relates back to the time when the bill or note was first given.[34] Applying the above general principles to the case of bills or notes accepted conditionally for payment of premium, it would seem that the effect of such acceptance is not to waive all conditions relating to the punctual payment of premium but merely to suspend their operation. If the bill or note is ultimately met, then

---

[26] *Thompson v. Knickerbocker Life Ins. Co.*, 104 U.S. 252 (1881); *Shaw v. Republic Life*, 69 N.Y. 286(1877); *McAllister v. New England Mutual Life*, 101 Mass. 558 (1869). The decision in *McGugan v. Manufacturers' & Merchants Mutual Fire Ins. Co.* (1879) 29 U.C.C.P. 494 turns on the wording of a Canadian statute and is not contrary to these authorities. *Brady v. Aid Association*,190 Pa. 595 (1899)is an unreasoned dissenter from the general doctrine.
[27] 104 U.S. 252 (1881).
[28] *MacMahon v. U.S. Life Ins. Co.*, 128 Fed.Rep. 389 (1904); *Mutual Life Ins. Co. v. French*, 30 Ohio StRep. 240, approved in the *Thompson* case, *supra*.
[29] *Thompson v. Knickerbocker Life Ins. Co. supra*.
[30] *Mutual Life Ins. Co. v. French* 30 Ohio StRep. 240; *Roehner v. Knickerbocker Life Ins. Co.*, 63 N.Y. 160 (1875).
[31] *Re A Debtor* [1908] 1 K.B. 344.
[32] *Price v. Price* (1847) 16 M. & W. 232.
[33] *Soward v. Palmer* (1818) 8 Taunt. 277.
[34] *Hadley v. Hadley* [1898] 2 Ch. 680.

the premium is deemed to have been paid on the date when the bill or note was first accepted[35]; but if the bill or note is not met, then the parties are in the same position as if no payment of any kind had ever been made. The result is practically the same as if there had been a condition for forfeiture on non-payment of the bill or note at maturity.

7–14 Notice of dishonour. Where there is a clause invoking forfeiture in the event of non-payment of a note or bill at maturity, and the assured is primarily liable on the note or bill, it is not necessary to give him notice when it is due,[36] nor to signify any election on the part of the insurers to avoid the policy.[37] Where a third party is primarily liable on a bill, it must be presented to him for payment on the due date; but, that having been done, the Supreme Court of the United States held that it was not necessary to give notice of dishonour to the assured in order to work a forfeiture under the express condition that "the policy shall become void if this draft is not paid at maturity".[38] Where there is an express condition of this kind, it would seem that non-payment of the note or bill at maturity will work an immediate forfeiture even although the instrument has been negotiated by the insurers and is in the hands of third persons.[39]

7–15 Forfeiture condition. Even although the policy acknowledges payment of the premium, it is competent to the insurers to show that it was paid not in cash, but by note, and that the policy has become void by reason of the dishonour of the note.[40] Where the policy contained no condition for forfeiture in the event of non-payment of a note, but the notes themselves given for the premium contained the proviso that the policy should be void if not paid on the day named, a Canadian court held that the assured could not rely upon the note as payment of the premium without being bound by the proviso.[41]

7–16 Payment by cheque. Prima facie, insurers are not bound to accept cheque in payment of premiums.[42] Posting a cheque is therefore not payment of premium, either conditionally or unconditionally, unless the company have authorised payment by cheque, either by express invitation or by a previous course of dealing.[43] Where payment by cheque is expressly or impliedly[44] sanctioned, it suffices for the assured to post the cheque in

---

[35] *American Credit Indemnity v. Champion*, 103 Fed.Rep. 609 (1900).

[36] *Roehner v. Knickerbocker Life Ins. Co.*, 63 N.Y. 160 (1875); *Thompson v. Same*, 104 U.S. 252 (1881).

[37] *McGeachie v. North American Life* (1894) 23 S.C.R. 148; *Frank v. Sun Life Ass. Co.* (1893) 20 Ont.A.R. 564.

[38] *Knickerbocker Life Ins. Co. v. Pendleton*, 112 U.S. 696 (1884).

[39] *London and Lancashire Life Ass. Co. v. Fleming* [1897] A.C. 499; *Hutchings v. National Life* (1905) 37 S.C.R. 124.

[40] *Baker v. Union Mutual Life Ins. Co.*, 43 N.Y. 283 (1871); *Pitt v. Berkshire Life*, 100 Mass. 500 (1868).

[41] *Frank v. Sun Life Ass. Co.* (1893) 20 Ont.A.R. 564 ; *Town Life v. Lewis*, 157 U.S. 335 (1902).

[42] *Bridges v. Garrett* (1870) L.R. 5 C.P. 451; *Pearson v. Scott* (1878) 9 Ch.D. 198 207; *Papé v. Westacott* [1894] 1 Q.B. 272; *Hine Brothers v. The Steamship Ins. Syndicate Ltd* (1895) 72 L.T. 79, 81.

[43] *Taylor v. Merchants' Fire*, 50 U.S. (9 How.) 390 (1850); *McNeilly v. Continental Life Ins. Co.*, 66 N.Y. App. 23 (1876); *Palmer v. Phoenix Mutual Life Ins.*, 84 N.Y. 63 (1881); *Kenyon v. Knights Templar*, 122 N.Y. 247 (1890).

[44] *Mitchell-Henry v. Norwich Union Life Ins. Society* [1918] 2 K.B. 67.

time to reach the company in ordinary course of post before the expiration of the time limited for payment, even if, owing to some accident outside the assured's control, the letter is delayed or lost in the post.[45] In that case, however, it would not usually be inferred that the insurance company agreed to bear the risk of loss or destruction in the post.[46] If a cheque is dishonoured on presentation at the bank there is no payment of premium, even though the company continues to hold the cheque, and there are subsequently sufficient funds of the assured in the bank to meet it,[47] but it is the duty of the company to represent the cheque within a reasonable time, and if it does not do so and the assured is prejudiced by the delay, the premium will be deemed to have been paid when the cheque was received, and the assured will be discharged from further liability on it.

7–17 Payment in bank notes. It has been held that a creditor who requests his debtor "to remit" a sum of money impliedly authorises him to send the money through the post in the ordinary way in which money is remitted by post, but that it is not usual to send a large sum in bank notes by registered post, and that if the money so sent is stolen in transit the debtor cannot plead payment of his debt.[48]

7–18 Allowance of credit. An insurance company may, by its course of business, in allowing credit to the assured for the amount of the premium on a periodical account to be settled at some unspecified future time, impliedly agree that the policy shall be treated as renewed on the renewal date, although the premium be not then paid.[49] The validity of the policy for the renewal period is not affected by the subsequent failure of the assured to pay the balance due by him on his account.[50]

7–19 Consumer Credit Act 1974.[51] If the insured is an individual or a partnership, an agreement to provide him with credit in an amount not exceeding £25,000 is a consumer credit agreement within the meaning of the Act.[52] It will further be a regulated agreement unless it falls under one or other of the exemptions made by or under section 16.[53] There are three exemptions of importance in the present context. The first covers agreements by which an insurer allows credit for the payment of a premium so long as the agreement provides for repayment in not more than four instalments.[54] The second covers the tripartite arrangements commonly made between insurers, building societies and mortgagors, by which the building society pays the premiums for insurance of the mortgaged property

---

[45] *Krebs v. Security Trust Life*, 156 Fed.Rep. 294 (1907); *Mutual Life Ins. Co. v. Tuchfeld*, 59 Fed.Rep. 833 (1908); *A/S Tankexpress v. Cie Financière Belge des Pétroles* [1949] A.C. 76.

[46] *Pennington v. Crossley & Son* (1897) 77 L.T. 43. Similarly, the insurer may bear the risk of a failure to implement a direct debit instruction: *Weldon v. GRE* [2000] 2 All E.R. (Comm.) 914.

[47] *Neill v. Union Mutual life* (1881) 7 Ont.A.R. 171.

[48] *Mitchell-Henry v. Norwich Union Life Ins. Society* [1918] 2 K.B. 67.

[49] *Holliday v. Western Australian Ins. Co.* (1936) 54 Ll.L.R. 373.

[50] *ibid.*

[51] 1974, c. 39.

[52] See ss.8(1), (2) and 189(1), and the Consumer Credit (Increase of Monetary Limits) Order 1983 S.I. No. 1878, as amended.

[53] See s.8(3).

[54] See the Consumer Credit (Exempt Agreements) Order 1989, S.I. 1989 No. 869, art. 3(1)(a), read with ss.10, 11(1) and 12 of the Act of 1974. Note that S.I. 1989 No. 869 has itself been amended.

and recovers the amount in instalments from the mortgagor. In this case there is no restriction as to the number of instalments.[55] The third covers transactions in connection with trade in goods or services between the United Kingdom and another country, or within or between countries outside the United Kingdom, if the debtor is provided with credit in the course of a business carried on by him.[56] Agreements falling within any of these exemptions are unaffected by the Act, save for its provisions[57] as to extortionate credit bargains.

7-20 An insurer who enters, otherwise than merely occasionally, into regulated agreements (for example one who allows annual premiums to be paid by monthly instalments otherwise than through a building society) is carrying on a consumer credit business and needs to be licensed under the Act.[58] There are requirements as to the form and content of regulated agreements and their execution.[59] If the agreement allows its provisions to be varied by the creditor, notice of such variation must be given in the prescribed manner.[60] There are requirements as to the notice of default to be given to the debtor before any remedies in the nature of forfeiture can be claimed against him.[61]

7-21 The payment of insurance premiums by means of credit cards occurs in the United Kingdom market. The Consumer Credit Act 1974 contans numerous provisions about credit cards, only one of which need be mentioned here. Section 75 gives the insured a concurrent remedy against the credit card company in any case where he has a claim for misrepresentation or breach of contract against the insurer. Subject to any agreement between them, the credit card company is entitled to be indemnified by the insurer in the event of its having to meet any such claim by the insured.[62]

7-22 Payment by agent. Although an agent may not be authorised to give credit on behalf of the company, or otherwise waive the conditions for punctual payment of the premium, he may himself pay the premium on behalf of the assured, and give the assured credit in respect of the personal debt then due by the assured to him.[63] But probably there must be an actual payment in cash made by the agent to the company within the time limited,

---

[55] See art. 3(1)(c) of the Order of 1989, read with ss.10, 11(1) and 12 of the Act of 1974.

[56] See art. 5 of the Order of 1989.

[57] See ss.137–139.

[58] Consumer Credit Act 1974, ss.21(1), 189(1), (2). As to licensing, see Pt. III (ss.21–42) of the Act and Orders made thereunder. Unlicensed trading is an offence under s.39. Agreements by unlicensed traders are largely unenforceable; see s.40. Section 40 does not apply to a regulated agreement (other than a non-commercial agreement) made by a consumer credit EEA firm, unless the firm was precluded from entering into the agreement by a consumer credit prohibition imposed under s.203 of the Financial Services and Markets Act 2000, or a restriction imposed under s.204 of that Act: s.40(6) of the Consumer Credit Act 1974, as amended. For the definition of "consumer credit EEA firm", see s.203(10) of, and para. 5 of Sched. 4, to the Financial Services and Markets Act 2000.

[59] See ss.60–65 and the Orders made thereunder.

[60] See s.82(1) and the Consumer Credit (Notice of Variation of Agreements) Regulations 1977, S.I. 1977 No. 328, as amended.

[61] See ss.87–89 and the Regulations made thereunder.

[62] Consumer Credit Act 1974, s.75(2). *Quaere* whether the financial limit in s.75(3)(b) has any application to insurance cases.

[63] *Newcastle Fire v. Macmorran* (1815) 3 Dow 255; *Yonge v. Equitable Life*, 30 Fed.Rep. 902 (1887); *Train v. Holland Purchase Ins.*, 62 N.Y. 598 (1875).

and the agent cannot by agreement with the assured to give him personal credit give the assured the benefit of his periodical account with the company, and, by merely debiting himself with the premium, claim that it was paid on behalf of the assured when he made the entry in his book.[64] *A fortiori*, in the absence of any agreement between the agent and the assured, the assured cannot avail himself of any arrangement between the company and the agent, whereby the agent is made personally liable for the premium if he does not immediately notify the company of the failure of the assured to pay the premium within the days of grace.[65]

7–23 Cheque cashed by agent. If an agent of an insurance company, whose authority is limited to receiving payment in cash, accepts a cheque payable to him personally and cashes the cheque, that is the equivalent of a cash payment of the premium, and the fact that the agent subsequently misappropriates the money is immaterial.[66]

7–24 Tender. A legal tender of money is equivalent to payment but, prima facie, a legal tender involves having the necessary cash ready and producing it unless production is expressly or impliedly dispensed with.[67] An offer to pay, which is something short of a legal tender, and a refusal to accept payment may be sufficient to estop the insurer (who but for such refusal would have been paid) from relying on non-payment of the premium as a defence to a claim on the policy.[68]

A tender of the premium may be made either by the holder of the policy, or by someone authorised by him to do so, such as a mortgagee of the policy, if the mortgage deed contains the necessary authority.[69] If a premium is tendered by some unauthorised person the insurers are not bound to accept it, and if it be refused, the holder of the policy cannot by subsequent ratification rely on it as a tender of the premium made on his behalf.[70] If, however, the premium tendered by an unauthorised person be accepted, it can probably be relied on as a payment enuring to the benefit of the holder of the policy[71] even though not ratified by him until after the expiration of the days of grace or even until after the policy has matured.[72]

7–25 Periodical accounts. Where there are frequent transactions between

---

[64] *Busteed v. West of England Fire and Life* (1857) 5 Ir.Ch.R. 553; *London and Lancashire Life v. Fleming* [1897] A.C. 499. As to the special accounting arrangements existing between Lloyd's underwriters and Lloyd's brokers, see Ch. 35, *post*. These arrangements provide considerable scope for the broker to allow credit to the assured. For the consequences of unauthorised payment by the broker, see *Pacific & General Ins. Co. Ltd (in liquidation) v. Hazell and Minet* [1997] L.R.L.R. 65.

[65] *Acey v. Fernie* (1840) 7 M. & W. 151.

[66] *Clay Hill Brick Co. v. Rawlings* (1938) 159 L.T. 482.

[67] *Finch v. Brook* (1834) 1 Bing. N.C. 253; *Re Farley* (1852) 2 De G.M. & G. 936; *Chitty on Contracts* (28th ed., 1999) vol. 1, pp. 1138, 1141.

[68] *Farquharson v. Pearl Ass. Co.* [1937] 3 All E.R. 124; *Weldon v. GRE* [2000] 2 All E.R. (Comm.) 914—where an insurer which failed to implement a direct debit could not rely on non-payment as a defence.

[69] *ibid.*

[70] *Walter v. James* (1871) L.R. 6 Ex. 124.

[71] On the principle of *Royal Exchange Ass. Corp. v. Hope* [1928] Ch. 179.

[72] It might, however, be argued that ratification comes too late after the expiration of the time within which payment must be made: *Dibbins v. Dibbins* [1896] 2 Ch. 348; or after the maturity of the policy: *Grover v. Mathews* [1910] 2 K.B. 401.

the same parties, actual payment of a cash premium upon each occasion might be extremely inconvenient, and therefore it is not unusual to arrange periodical settlements. Where that is the recognised course of business the premium may, for the purpose of the conditions in the policy, be deemed to be paid when an entry is made in the business books, or the transaction is in some other way recorded.[73] But, prima facie, agents of different companies have no authority to give one another credit, and unless the course of business is recognised by the companies themselves, their agents do not by debiting one another against periodical settlements effect payment of the premiums.[74] An agent authorised to collect premiums, who is himself insured with the company for which he is acting, cannot pay the premiums on his own policy by debiting his agency account therewith when the account is already in debit against him.[75]

In the US it has been held that where an insurance company deals with a broker on the terms of a monthly settlement, the broker being responsible to the company for the premiums, the premiums must be deemed as between company and assured to have been paid when the contract was concluded, and the fact that the assured has not paid the broker is immaterial.[76] This is in accordance with the law and practice in marine insurance in this country[77] and with the practice at Lloyd's,[78] and it would seem, even in the case of other risks, that if the insurers accept the credit of the broker and look to him alone for payment of the premium, the agreement with the broker for an account may be a waiver of all conditions in the policy requiring punctual payment by the assured.[79]

7–26 Consequences of failure to make punctual payment. The settlement of accounts may frequently involve delays, and it will be difficult to infer an intention to repudiate the contract by reason merely of non-payment of balances, without some specific demand for payment.[80] The principles relating to late payment were reviewed in *F.I.G. Re. Ltd v. Mander*.[81] In that case there were long delays in remitting premiums due under a retrocession (*i.e.* a reinsurance of reinsurance), attributable mainly to administrative errors and mistakes by the retrocedant's brokers. When the premium was eventually tendered, the retrocessionaires refused it on the ground that the failure to pay had constituted a repudiatory breach, and that the contract of

---

[73] *Prince of Wales Life v. Harding* (1858) El.B. & E. 183; *Comp. Tirrena di Ass. SpA v. Grand Union Ins. Co.* [1991] 2 Lloyd's Rep. 143.

[74] *Western Assurance v. Provincial Ass. Co.* (1880) 5 Ont.A.R. 190.

[75] *Hawkins v. Bristol and West of England F.S.* [1927] I.A.C.Rep. 52.

[76] *White v. Connecticut* (1876) 120 Mass. 330; *Potter v. Phoenix*, 63 Fed.Rep. 382 (1894).

[77] *Universo Insurance Co. of Milan v. Merchants' Marine* [1897] 2 Q.B. 93; s.54 of the Marine Insurance Act 1906.

[78] See Ch. 35, *post*. See also *Prentis Donegan & Partners Ltd v. Leeds Co. Inc.* [1998] 2 Lloyd's Rep. 326, 334–335, where Rix J. held that in such circumstances there could not be an automatic termination based upon late payment.

[79] Note, however, that it has been held in Australia that in non-marine business, a broker is not under any liability to pay to the insurer a sum in respect of a premium not received from the insured, even if running accounts are maintained between the insurer and the broker from which premiums due from the broker's clients are debited and to which commissions earned by the broker are credited: *Re Palmdale Insurance Ltd* [1982] V.R. 921.

[80] *Fenton v. Gothaer* [1991] 1 Lloyd's Rep. 172. For a case where the circumstances of non-payment did amount to repudiation, see *Pacific & General Ins. Co. Ltd (in liquidation) v. Hazell and Minet* [1997] L.R.L.R. 65.

[81] [1999] Lloyd's Rep.I.R. 193.

retrocession was terminated. Cresswell J. held that a failure to pay premium on a due date amounted to a repudiatory breach entitling an insurer to terminate the contract in three cases:

(a) where time was stipulated to be of the essence;
(b) where the circumstances of the contract or nature of the subject matter showed that time was impliedly of the essence, and
(c) where time was neither expressly nor impliedly of the essence, but the assured had been guilty of unreasonable delay, and the insurer then gave a notice requiring the premium to be paid within a reasonable time.

He further held that late payment would not, of itself, constitute renunciation of the contract. It was held that none of the three preconditions for repudiation were present, and that there had been no renunciation.

7–27 Liability for unpaid premium. In the marine insurance market and at Lloyd's, the placing broker is directly responsible as principal to the underwriter for the payment of premium, and he is entitled to be paid gross premium by the assured. In *Prentis Donegan & Partners Ltd. v. Leeds & Leeds Co. Inc.*[82] a Lloyd's placing broker who had given credit for net premium in his accounts with insurers sought to recover unpaid gross premium from New York producing brokers. The producing brokers denied that they were liable to reimburse the Lloyd's broker, and argued that the correct course was to claim directly from the assured. Rix J. gave summary judgment for the Lloyd's brokers. He held that there was no privity of contract between the assured and the Lloyd's placing brokers, so that it was impossible to establish a contractual liability of the former to the latter.

A marine broker is entitled to exercise a lien for unpaid premium and his charges over the policy, and on insurance monies received from the insurers, but he has no right to exercise a lien under a composite policy against assureds who are not indebted to him. The lien can only be exercised against an assured in default.[83] The marine usage with regard to the liability of the broker for payment can be displaced by clear contrary agreement, but a premium warranty stating "warranted each instalment of premium paid to underwriters within 60 days of due date" is not of itself an agreement to contract out of the usage.[84]

7–28 Appropriation of assured's credit. The insurers may, under certain circumstances, be bound to appropriate moneys in their hands, but belonging to the assured, to the payment of premiums falling due. For instance, where a firm of merchants who acted as agents for an insurance company, with whom they had also effected a number of policies on their own account, including a fire policy on their own stock-in-trade, paid a lump sum into a bank to the credit of the company's account and the company

---

[82] [1998] 2 Lloyd's Rep. 326. Rix J. also held that privity between the assured and a Lloyd's placing broker, to the exclusion of privity between brokers in the broking chain, would only arise in exceptional cases. He doubted that *Velos Group v. Harbour Insurance Services* [1997] 2 Lloyd's Rep. 461 was good authority to the contrary.

[83] *Eide v. Lowndes Lambert Group Ltd* [1999] Q.B. 199.

[84] *Chapman v. Kadirga Denizcilik ve Ticaret* [1999] Lloyd's Rep.I.R. 377. It followed that where premium was not apportionable, the broker was entitled to claim unpaid instalments of premium from the assured even though insurers might have been discharged from liability by breach of the premium payment warranty.

signed a receipt for that sum "on account of premiums", it was held that, as it was sufficient to cover all outstanding liability of the firm to the company in respect of the agency account and their own policies, part of it must be deemed to have been appropriated to the payment of the premium in arrears on their fire policy.[85]

7–29 Appropriation of dividends. It has been accepted in the US that insurers are bound to appropriate dividends due to the assured towards payment of premiums so as to save the policy from forfeiture:

> "an insurer is not justified in declaring a forfeiture of an insurance policy for the non-payment of a premium when, at the time such premium accrues, the insurer is indebted to the assured, either for dividends declared, or other funds which it may have in its hands belonging to the policy-holder."[86]

This rule does not apply where the assured has directed dividends to be paid or applied in a particular manner, for example where they must be left to accumulate,[87] nor where the moneys received are not yet accrued due to the assured at the moment when the premium is due.[88] Neither is an insurer bound to apply dividends due on one policy in payment of the premium due on another policy held by the same assured, in the absence of a request by the assured to do so.[89]

7–30 The situation is more complicated when the benefits due to the assured are not enough to cancel out the assured's indebtedness. It has been held that the insurers need not apply their debt in part settlement of the premium unless the assured offers to pay the balance,[90] and with respect this seems correct, since the foundation of the American principle of appropriation is equitable, and it would be vain for equity to insist upon appropriation when the debt for the premium would still not be discharged. The position would be different if the policy expressly or impliedly contemplated extension of cover for periods of less than a year upon receipt of pro rata payments, when the assured required it.[91]

7–31 Appropriation of surrender value. A life policy may contain a condition that the insurers shall apply any surrender value which the policy may have towards the payment of unpaid premiums until the surrender value is exhausted. (In some jurisdictions there may also be a statutory prohibition of the forfeiture of a policy so long as there is an uncharged surrender value of an amount sufficient to meet the premium.) The company

---

[85] *Kirkpatrick v. South Australian Ins. Co.* (1886) 11 App.Cas. 177.

[86] *American National Ins. Co. v. Yee Lion Shee*, 104 F. 2d 688, 694 (1939); *United States v. Morrell*, 204 F. 2d 490 (1953); *Federal Life Ins. Co. v. Jones*, 131 A. 2d. 879 (1957); *Winchester v. United Ins. Co.* (1957) 99 S.E. 2d; *Gaunt v. Prudential Ins. Co. of America*, 62 Cal.Rep. 624 (1967). This rule is followed where dividends have been assigned to the company in repayment of a loan: *State Mutual Life v. Fleischer*, 186 F. 2d 358 (1951).

[87] *United States v. Morrell*, 204 F. 2d 490, 493 (1953).

[88] *Mutual Life Ins. Co. v. Girard Life*, 100 Pa. 172 (1882).

[89] *Deposit Guaranty National Bank of Jackson v. Prudential Ins. Co. of America*, 195 So. 2d 506 (1967).

[90] *Dias v. Farm Bureau Mutual Fire of Columbus*, 155 F. 2d 660 (C.C.A. 1, 1946).

[91] *Price v. N.W. Mutual Life Ins. Co.*, 169 S.E. 613 (Va.Sup.Ct., 1933).

may be bound either to keep the policy on foot as a current policy for the amount assured thereby or to give the assured the option of taking a paid-up policy for a lesser amount, or of exercising one or other of the options provided for in the policy.[92] The conditions of the policy may, however, be such that it never acquires a surrender value, as, for instance, where the assured's only contractual right in the event of lapse owing to non-payment of premium is to a fully paid-up life or endowment policy of a reduced amount.[93] Some US policies contain complicated provisions with regard to the rights of the assured in the event of non-payment of premium which are not always easy to construe.[94]

7–32 Appropriation of claims. If the assured has a good claim against the insurers he can, while it is still unliquidated, set it off against premiums due under the same or other policies.[95] Thus, where the assured has a claim against a mutual company and tendered the balance of calls after setting off the amount of his claim, it was held that there was a sufficient tender in respect of the calls if the claim was well founded.[96] The insurers, however, are not bound to appropriate moneys due for claims towards payment of premiums unless directed to do so,[97] although in a case in the US where a member of a mutual society was in receipt of sick benefit it was held that the society could not cancel the policy for non-payment of dues when they could have deducted the amount thereof from the weekly allowances.[98]

7–33 Bankers' standing orders. The banker's standing order is an order signed by the assured and addressed by him to his bankers, instructing them to transfer money from his account to the account of the insurers. It may require an initial payment to be made on sight of the order or on a specified date and it usually requires further payments to be made at stated intervals. This method of payment is commonly adopted at the express suggestion of the insurers, who may supply a printed form for the purpose and invite the assured to send the completed form to them, for onward transmission to his bank. Such an order sufficiently resembles a cheque to enable many questions to be answered by way of analogy from the law governing cheques.

7–34 An assured who, at the insurers' invitation, sends them a duly completed order requiring funds to be transferred on sight must be taken to have made at least a conditional payment. If the order is not carried out owing to lack of funds in the account, the case is analogous to that of a dishonoured cheque. The case where the order is not carried out because of some negligence or default on the part of the banker may be more difficult.

It can certainly be argued that the assured's banker is acting as his agent and any failure to pay on the part of the banker is tantamount to a failure on the part of the assured. Yet if the insurer not only suggested the use of the standing order system but also took it upon himself to set the machinery in motion by sending the order to the bank, it might well be said that he assumed the risk of any miscarriage of the working of the system.

---

[92] *Equitable Life Assurance Society v. Reed* [1914] A.C. 587.
[93] *ibid.*
[94] See *Williams v. Union Central Ins. Co.* (1933) 291 U.S. 170.
[95] *Roberts v. Security Co.* [1897] 1 Q.B. 111, 117.
[96] *Williams v. British Mutual Marine* (1886) 57 L.T. 27.
[97] *Simpson v. Accidental Death* (1857) 2 C.B.(N.S.) 257.
[98] *Conley v. Washington Casualty*, 93 Me. 461 (1900).

7–35 Direct debit and bank giro. The last mentioned argument would apply *a fortiori* if the direct debit system were used.[99] This is a system by which the assured's bank accepts an order from the insurer to debit a specified sum to the account of the assured and transfer it to the account of the insurer. There is no written instruction from the assured relating to the specific payment; the bank apparently assumes that if a direct debit order is received from a payee of sufficient standing, it may safely be taken to have the assent of the payor.

7–36 The task of legal analysis of this system from the point of view of the relationship between banker and customer falls outside the scope of this work. As between insurer and assured, the analysis will depend upon the circumstances of each case. However, it may well be that if at the invitation of the insurer, the assured consents to the use of the direct debit system, the assured has no further obligations except to keep his account in funds. All further steps to obtain payment are to be taken by the insurer, who must take the consequences of anything which may go wrong.

7–37 The bank giro system permits any person to deposit money at any branch of a bank participating in the system, for transmission to any account at any other such branch. A question which may arise is whether the date of payment should be taken to be that on which the assured makes the deposit, or that on which the corresponding credit is passed to the insurer's account. The best answer probably is that if the assured uses the system on his own initiative, he must see to it that the money reaches the insurer's account by the due date of payment. If, however, the insurer holds the system out as an appropriate mode of payment (here again, printed forms may be supplied for the purpose by the insurer) it probably suffices for the assured to do what he has been invited to do, that is, deposit money with a bank, on or before the due date.

2. RENEWAL PREMIUMS

7–38 Right of renewal. A policy may be issued to cover a certain risk for a definite period at a definite premium without any provision for renewal; but often the policy is expressed to cover first a definite period, say a year, for which the premium is acknowledged to have been received, and secondly, an indefinite period thereafter, so long as an annual or other periodical payment shall be paid in accordance with the conditions of the policy. In the case of risks other than life, the assured is not given an absolute right of renewal, the continuance of the policy being conditional not only upon the payment of the premium by the assured but also upon the acceptance of it by the insurers.[1] In any such case the insurers may terminate the risk at each renewal period by refusing to accept the premium tendered.

7–39 Right to determine risk. In addition to the right to refuse acceptance

---

[99] Thus, in *Weldon v. GRE* [2000] 2 All E.R. (Comm.) 914, it was held that the presentation of a direct debit form constituted payment, or a tender of payment, and that the insurer was responsible for implementing the direct debit.

[1] *Law Accident Ins. Soc. v. Boyd* 1942 S.C. 384; *Simpson v. Accidental Death Ins. Co.* (1857) 2 C.B.(N.S.) 257.

of the renewal premium, the insurers may reserve the right to terminate the risk at any time upon giving notice and returning the unearned premium.[2]

The reservation of a right to terminate the risk may be qualified so as to be exercisable only in the event of some change or increase of risk occurring during the currency of the policy or it may give the insurers an absolute right to terminate the risk at their own discretion without assigning, or having, any reason for doing so other than their own desire, however capricious it may be.[3]

Notice to determine the risk must be given to the assured, or to some agent whose duty it is to receive and communicate the information to the assured. It has been held in the US that notice given to the assured's agent who procured the policy is not necessarily an effective notice to the assured, since his duty as an agent may have terminated when the policy was delivered by him to his principal.[4] If the condition is that the insurers may cancel the policy on repayment of a rateable proportion of the premium the insurers must, in addition to giving notice, have tendered a return of the unearned portion of the premium before the policy can be deemed to be cancelled.[5]

7–40 Life assurance. The contract of life assurance is essentially different from other classes of risk. In the normal contract of life assurance (as distinct from contracts intended to be for a term certain) the assured must have at least a right of renewal subject to reasonable conditions. There has, however, been a considerable difference of judicial opinon as to whether the contract of life assurance made in consideration of an annual premium is an insurance for a year with an irrevocable offer to renew upon payment of the agreed renewal premium, or an insurance for the entire life subject to defeasance or forfeiture upon non-payment of the renewal premium at the times stated. In *Pritchard v. The Merchants' and Tradesmen's Mutual Life Assurance Society,*[6] the annual premium was due on October 13 and a condition provided for forfeiture if premiums were not paid within 30 days after they should respectively have become due. The life assured died on November 12—the last day for payment. It was sought to keep the insurance on foot and the insurers were paid a cheque for the renewal premium on November 14; they were as yet ignorant of the life dropping. The plaintiffs were driven to contend that the receipt of the renewal premium evidenced an offer to insure for another year on the conditions of the old policy. They did not succeed, the court holding that it was never intended to insure in respect of a life actually not in being at the time. Willes J. said *obiter*[7] that the contract of life assurance was an annual one with the privilege of renewal. In *Stuart v. Freeman*[8] Collins M.R. referred to this dictum with apparent

---

[2] *Sun Fire Office v. Hart* (1889) 14 App.Cas. 98. The obligation to return premium may arise as a matter of contractual implication: *Re Drake Ins. Plc* [2001] Lloyd's Rep.I.R. 643. For a case where the policy permitted premium to be retained, and discussion of the effect of termination on claims, see *Kazakstan Wool Processors (Europe) Ltd v. NCM* [2000] Lloyd's Rep.I.R. 371.

[3] *ibid.*

[4] *Hodge v. Security Co. of New Haven*, 33 Hun. 583 (N.Y.Sup.Ct., 1884) ; *Grace v. American Central Ins. Co.*, 109 U.S. 278 (1883).

[5] *White v. Connecticut Fire Ins. Co.*, 120 Mass. 330 (1876).

[6] (1858) 3 C.B.(N.S.) 622.

[7] (1858) 3 C.B.(N.S.) 622, 643. In *Phoenix Life Ass. Co. v. Sheridan* (1860) 8 H.L.Cas. 745, 750, Lord Chelmsford said with reference to the confusingly worded policy construed in that case that it was an annual policy with renewal provisions, but on p. 749 Lord Cranford seems to have thought otherwise.

[8] [1903] 1 K.B. 47.

approval, but seems to have felt that it was justified by the scheme of the policy in the *Pritchard* case.[9] Mathew L.J. said he was unable to accept the opinion expressed in *Pritchard*,[10] and Romer L.J. hinted that he did not accept it as generally correct.[11]

7–41 In the US the subject has been considered, and the United States Supreme Court has held that a life insurance is not an insurance for a single year with a privilege of renewal from year to year by paying the annual premium, but is an entire contract of insurance for life, subject to discontinuance or forfeiture for non-payment of any of the stipulated premiums.[12] Bradley J. said:

> "Such is the form of the contract, and such its character ... It has been contended that the payment of each premium is the consideration for insurance during the next following year as in fire policies. But the position is untenable ... The value of insurance for one year of a man's life when he is young, strong and healthy, is manifestly not the same as when he is old and decrepit. There is no proper relation between the annual premium and the risk of insurance for the year in which it is made."[13]

In a Canadian case[14] the four judges of the Court of Appeal in Ontario were equally divided upon the question whether a life policy is an insurance continuing for life until forfeiture or an annual insurance from year to year. The distinction is one of considerable importance, particularly in relation to the legal effect of the days of grace, and the insurers' liability for losses occurring during the days of grace, but before payment of the renewal premium.[15]

7–42 Punctual payment. In some classes of insurance the punctual payment of the renewal premium according to the terms of the policy is a condition precedent to the continuance of the risk.[16] In the Canadian case of *Frank v. Sun Life*[17] the premium on a life policy was payable by quarterly instalments on specified days. It was held that default in the payment of any one quarterly instalment even for a day would release the company from further liability, notwithstanding the absence of any express forfeiture clause. Burton J. said[18]:

> "Promptness in payment is of the very essence of the business of life

[9] [1903] 1 K.B. 47, 52.
[10] [1903] 1 K.B. 47, 55.
[11] [1903] 1 K.B. 47, 53–54.
[12] *New York Life Ins. Co. v. Statham*, 93 U.S. 24 (1876); followed in *McMaster v. New York Life Ins. Co.*, 183 U.S. 25 (1901).
[13] 93 U.S. 24, 30 (1876).
[14] *Manufacturers' Life Ins. Co. v. Gordon* (1893) 20 Ont.A.R. 309.
[15] See para. 7–48, *post*.
[16] *Frank v. Sun Life Ass. Co.* (1893) 20 Ont.A.R. 564; *Nederland Life Ins. Co. v. Meinert*, 119 U.S. 171 (1905); *Thompson v. Knickerbocker Life Ins. Co.*, 104 U.S. 252, 258 (1881). In each case it is necessary to determine if time is of the essence for payment of the renewal premium—*Figre Ltd v. Mander* [1999] Lloyd's Rep.I.R. 193.
[17] (1893) 20 Ont.A.R. 564.
[18] (1893) 20 Ont.A.R. 564, 567; also see *New York Life Ins. Co. v. Statham*, 93 U.S. 24, 31 (1876).

insurance, and if, therefore, any one of the quarterly instalments remains unpaid the forfeiture is absolute, unless there is something in the contract itself to dispense with it. When no such stipulation exists it is the well-established understanding that time is material, or, as it is sometimes expressed, is of the essence of the contract."

7–43 Payable by instalments. A premium expressed to be an annual premium is sometimes, for the convenience of the assured, made payable in quarterly or other periodical instalments; but in order that the insurers may not lose thereby it is provided that if the assured die in any one year before the whole instalments for that year have been paid, the balance may be deducted from the sum insured. Such a proviso does not render the punctual payment of the instalments any less a condition precedent to the continuance of the risk.[19]

7–44 Wrongful refusal to accept. If the insurers wrongfully refuse to accept a renewal premium on a life policy, the assured may treat the refusal as a final breach of the contract and sue for the value of the policy at that time or tender the exact amount of each premium in cash until the policy money becomes payable.[20] The assured is not in all cases entitled, on account of the insurers' refusal to receive the premium, to a declaration of the court that his policy is valid.[21] If the insurers repudiate the contract the assured is relieved from the necessity of making any formal tender of further premiums,[22] but if he does not tender the premium he treats the repudiation as a final breach, and would therefore be bound to commence proceedings within the period allowed by the Limitation Act 1980,[23] that is, 12 years if the policy is under seal, and otherwise six years from the date when the insurers repudiated liability.

7–45 Ambiguity. A payment made to an agent for the insurers may be construed as a renewal premium on a current policy or as an initial premium on a newly accepted risk. In the absence of express words making this point clear, it is a question of inference from the facts and circumstances known to the parties.[24]

7–46 Friendly society. The rules of a friendly society may provide for the payment of a reduced benefit in the event of death within a year or six

---

[19] *Phoenix Life Ass. Co. v. Sheridan* (1860) 8 H.L.Cas. 745; followed in *McConnell v. Provident Savings Life*, 92 Fed.Rep. 769 (1899). Note that these are not cases where the premium was a true quarterly premium, when there could have been no question as to the effect of unpunctuality in payment. In the case of an annual premium payable by quarterly instalments the whole premium, that is all four instalments, is earned whenever the year begins to run. In the case of a true quarterly premium each quarterly premium is earned whenever the quarter in respect of which it is payable beings to run.

[20] *Day v. Connecticut General Life*, 45 Conn. 480 (1878).

[21] *Honour v. Equitable Life Ass. of U.S.A.* [1900] 1 Ch. 852. See, however, the further discussion of this point in paras 10–91 to 10–94, *post*.

[22] *Jones v. Barclay* (1781) 2 Doug. K.B. 684, 994, *per* Lord Mansfield; *Re Coleman's Depositories* [1907] 2 K.B. 798, 805; *McKenna v. City Life Ass. Co.* [1919] 2 K.B. 491, 496; *Mutual Ins. v. Home Benefit Society*, 181 Pa. 443 (1897); *Byram v. Sovereign Camp of the Woodmen of the World*, 108 Iowa 430 (1899).

[23] ss.5 and 8.

[24] *Protopapa v. Dominion Ins. Company* [1954] 1 Lloyd's Rep. 402.

months from the date of the policy. Thus, a quarter only of the full sum assured may be payable in the event of death within three months, and half benefit after the insurance has been in existence for three months, provided that 14 weeks' premium has been paid prior to the death, and full benefit after the insurance has been in existence for six months provided that 27 weeks' premium has been paid prior to the death. Where death occurs after the prescribed period, but the prescribed number of premiums has not been paid, the increased benefit is not payable and the society is entitled to deduct from the lower scale benefit the premiums in arrear at the date of death notwithstanding that if these had been paid when due the higher benefit would have been earned. Where a society has waived its right to deduct arrears in such cases, its action in so doing has been applauded by the Industrial Assurance Commissioner for Northern Ireland as being the proper course to take.[25]

3. The Days of Grace

7–47 Reason for days of grace. If the continuance of the risk under a policy were conditional on the payment of a premium on a certain specified date in each year or quarter, and no provision were made for the payment of overdue premiums, the policy would immediately lapse if a premium was even one day in arrear, and in consequence the assured would be placed in the position of having to apply for a new contract of insurance. In the case of life insurance, he could not obtain cover on the same terms, and the insurers, if they accepted the application, would in the past have had to prepare a new duly stamped policy in order to avoid the penalties of the Stamp Act.[26] To obviate this expense and inconvenience to the insurers and hardship to the assured, the practice has long been resorted to in many classes of insurance of making the future risk conditional on the payment of the renewal premium on a certain day, or within so many days thereafter, or else of declaring that the policy should not be considered void if the renewal premium was paid within so many days after it fell due. These days are called the days of grace, and the position of the assured during the days of grace, but before the renewal premium has been paid, depends upon the nature of the insurance, and the particular conditions as to renewal which are inserted in the policy.

The position of the assured when the last of the days of grace falls on a Sunday or other *dies non* is the subject of a divergence of trans-Atlantic opinion. It has been held in Canada that the period of grace expires at the end of the stipulated number of days from the due date for the payment of the renewal premium, even if the last of those days is a Sunday on which the receipt of the premium would have been unlawful.[27] In the US, it has been held that where the grace period expires on a Sunday the policy-holder is entitled to pay the premium on the following Monday provided that is a business day.[28]

---

[25] *Boyle v. Scottish Legal Life* [1927] I.A.C.(N.I.)Rep. 18.
[26] *Doe d. Pitt v. Sherwin* (1811) 3 Camp. 134.
[27] *Firth v. Western Life* (1956) 4 D.L.R. (2d) 284; affirmed (1957) 8 D.L.R. (2d) 129.
[28] *Friedmann v. Group Hospitalisation*, 220 F. 2d 827 (1955). See 53 A.L.R. 2d 877, 878.

7-48 Protection during days of grace. In fire, burglary and other risks where the insurers may refuse renewal, the days of grace do not primarily afford protection while the renewal premium is unpaid, that is, before it is tendered and accepted.[29] If the insurers expressly covenant that the assured shall be protected during the days of grace, notwithstanding the non-payment of the premium, then the assured is covered during those days for so long as the question of renewal is in abeyance[30]; but if the insurers decline to renew before the days of grace have begun to run, or perhaps even at any time before a loss has occurred, they thereby relieve themselves from liability during the days of grace.[31] In motor insurance there are no days of grace, although renewal notices normally include a cover note giving 15 days' protection against the statutory liability. In life insurance and in certain sickness policies written on a "permanent" basis the insurers cannot decline to renew the policy, and the question whether the assured is protected during the days of grace appears to depend upon the fundamental nature of the provisions for renewal. If the risk expires on the day when the renewal premium falls due and the days of grace are given merely as an opportunity for renewal, then death before payment of premium is not covered, because there is an implied condition that the subject-matter of the insurance is still in existence when renewal is claimed.[32] On the other hand, if there is a continuing risk carrying the insurance beyond the day on which the premium is payable, and subject only to defeasance upon non-payment of the premium upon that day or within the days of grace, then death before payment of premium is covered, because until the days of grace have expired there can be no forfeiture.[33]

7-49 Whether an insurance is of the one nature or the other is a matter of construction, although the better opinon probably is that as a general rule, a life policy creates a continuing risk subject to defeasance, and not merely an annual risk with a right of renewal.[34] Where the insurance is an own-life policy, and is expressed to be conditional upon the payment of the premiums by the assured, the proper inference may be that payment by his executors after death does not satisfy the condition.[35] That, however, would not be material if the risk were construed as a continuing risk subject to forfeiture, because, the insurers being liable until forfeiture, the rights of the parties become fixed at death, and the insurers are liable for the insurance moneys less the unpaid premium which has become due.[36] If a life policy provides expressly that the insurers will be liable in the event of death during the days of grace, but before payment of the premium, the matter is placed beyond

---

[29] *Tarleton v. Staniforth* (1794) 5 T.R. 695; *Simpson v. Accidental Death Ins. Co.* (1857) 2 C.B.(N.S.) 257.

[30] *Salvin v. James* (1805) 6 East 571, where the insurers' undertaking to extend the cover was contained in an advertisement on the faith of which the assured had effected insurance; *McDonnell v. Carr* (1833) Hayes & J. 256.

[31] *Salvin v. James* (1805) 6 East 571, 582.

[32] *Pritchard v. Merchants' and Tradesmen's Mutual Life* (1858) 3 C.B.(N.S.) 622, 643; *Stuart v. Freeman* [1903] 1 K.B. 47, 52.

[33] *Stuart v. Freeman* [1903] 1 K.B. 47; *New York Life Ins. Co. v. Statham*, 93 U.S. 24 (1876); *Manufacturers' Life Ins. Co. v. Gordon* (1893) 20 Ont.A.R. 309.

[34] See paras 7–40 to 7–41, *ante*.

[35] *Want v. Blunt* (1810) 12 East 183; *Simpson v. Accidental Death Ins. Co.* (1857) 2 C.B.(N.S.) 257. Contrast the wording and decision in *Provident Savings Life v. Taylor* (1906) 142 Fed.Rep. 709, and the remarks of Romer L.J. in *Stuart v. Freeman* [1903] 1 K.B. 47, 54.

[36] *Provident Savings Life v. Taylor*, 142 Fed.Rep. 709 (1906).

doubt.[37] If during the days of grace the assured intimates that he does not intend to pay the renewal premium on a life policy, that would probably relieve the insurers from further liability if the insurance fell to be construed as an annual insurance with an option to renew, but the insurers would not be relieved if the insurance fell to be construed as a continuing insurance subject to forfeiture, inasmuch as the assured might have changed his mind before forfeiture was actually incurred.[38]

7–50 Reinstatement after lapse. In fire, burglary and other similar policies there is usually no provision for revival of the policy after it has lapsed by non-payment of the premiums and expiration of the days of grace, but in life policies, where forfeiture is a much more serious thing, provision is usually made for revival of the policy within a specified time and upon the fulfilment of certain conditions, such as payment of a "fine" and satisfactory proof that the life is in good health.[39] There can be no doubt that during the period allowed for revival the policy is entirely ineffective, and no claim can be made for a death happening before the necessary conditions for revival have been fulfilled.

Proof of good health and payment of an extra premium as the conditions of revival of a lapsed policy may be waived by the company and prima facie would be waived by acceptance of the premium in arrear tendered after the expiration of the days of grace. If it is tendered only a day or two out of the time, the insurers will often make no demur to its acceptance on that footing, but any such acceptance is subject to an implied condition that the life assured has not already dropped. The intention in waiving the policy requirements is to revive the policy for the protection of the assured in the future without reference to the past.[40]

Where a policy contains the condition that it may be renewed within a certain time on proof of good health, it is a question of fact whether acceptance of the overdue premium within that time constitutes a waiver of the condition or whether it is accepted provisionally and subject to the condition that the assured shall prove to be in good health.[41]

7–51 Reinstatement *ex gratia*. Even after the expiration of the period allowed by the policy for renewal, the insurers may *ex gratia* renew the policy. On doing so they may either insist on examination of the life, or renew subject to the express condition that the life is in good health. If a lapsed policy is renewed without any express condition that the life is still in good health there may be an implied condition that the life has not

---

[37] This form of words is a common one.

[38] *McMaster v. New York Life Ins. Co.*, 90 Fed.Rep. 40 (1889); 99 Fed.Rep. 856 (1900); reversed on appeal in 183 U.S. 25 (1901) but not affecting the point of law for which cited here; *Provident Savings Life v. Taylor*, 142 Fed.Rep. 709 (1906).

[39] Some offices insert an even more liberal condition providing for revival of a lapsed policy without evidence of the health or the existence of the life or lives assured on payment of all arears and a "fine" within a period either absolutely fixed or depending on the surrender value of the policy at the time of lapsing. Provision is often made for the automatic non-forfeiture of the policy by the application of the surrender value towards payment of premium until the surrender value is exhausted: see para. 7–31, *ante*.

[40] *Pritchard v. Merchants' Life* (1858) 3 C.B.(N.S.) 622.

[41] *Barker v. North British Ins.* (1831) 9 S. 869; *Horton v. Provincial Provident Institution* (1888) 16 Ont.R. 382; *Wells v. Supreme Court* (1889) 17 Ont.R. 317; *Aetna Life v. Smith*, 88 Fed.Rep. 440 (1898); *Ronald v. Mutual Reserve Fund Life Ass.*, 132 N.Y. 378 (1892); *Rice v. New England*, 146 Mass. 248 (1888).

dropped,[42] but none as to good health. The burden of showing that there was an unconditional renewal rests upon the assured. If the receipt given to him for payment of premium after lapse contains a condition as to good health, it is not open to the assured or his representatives to say that he did not read the condition.[43]

In one case where a policy had lapsed, owing to non-payment of the premium before the expiration of the days of grace, there was a bonus due to the assured, and the company, although not required to do so by any condition in the policy, made an entry in their books by which they applied the cash value of the bonus towards the revival of the policy for such proportionate part of the year of insurance as the cash value bore to the amount of the premium with one year's interest thereon. That application of the bonus continued the policy in force for a period of 49 days. If the company had calculated the period for which they revived the policy on the premium without interest, the day on which the assured died would have been covered. In an action on the policy the court held that the assured had no legal right to have the bonus applied to a revival of the policy; that the revival was purely *ex gratia* on the part of the company; and that it did not therefore lie in the mouth of the assured's representative to complain of the method by which the period for which the policy was revived was calculated or to claim the benefit of thirty days of grace for payment of the premium after the expiration of such period.[44]

7–52 Conditional reinstatement. Where the assured had under a condition in the policy a right to be reinstated on proof of good health, and applied for such reinstatement, but the medical examiner refused to pass him unless he signed a new application which stated that there should be no contract until a policy was issued, and he signed such application and was examined and passed, but died before a new policy was issued, it was held that notwithstanding the new application the first policy was revived and the company was liable.[45]

Where it was a term of the company's prospectus that if after a policy had been in force for a specified time the policy-holder was unable to continue the payment of premiums he might surrender his policy for a free or paid-up policy for a reduced amount, it was held that a free policy could not be demanded on the bare statement by the assured that he was unable to pay. The right was conditional on his supplying the company with evidence which would enable it to judge whether or not he was able to pay, and it would then become the company's duty to consider the evidence impartially and decided whether the application was justified.[46]

---

[42] This would seem to follow from the decision in *Pritchard v. Merchants' & Tradesmen's Mutual Life* (1858) 3 C.B.(N.S.) 622, where an agreement to renew a life policy after the life had dropped without the parties knowing it was void for that common mistake; see also *Bennecke v. Connecticut Mutual*, 105 U.S. 355 (1881).

[43] *Handler v. Mutual Reserve Fund Life* (1904) 90 L.T. 192.

[44] *Bowan v. Atlas Assurance, The Times*, April 19, 1928.

[45] *Knights' Templars v. Masons' Life Ins. Co.*, 80 Fed.Rep. 202 (1897).

[46] *McClure v. Salvation Army Ass. Soc. Ltd* [1924] I.A.C.Rep. 98.

4. NON-PAYMENT: WAIVER, TERMINATION AND RELATED MATTERS

7–53 Waiver. A waiver of a term relating to the payment of premium may take the form of an election or an estoppel. An election involves the abandonment by an insurer of a contractual right (such as the right to treat the contract as at an end) on grounds of non-payment. An election must be communicated to the assured in clear and unequivocal terms, with knowledge by the insurer of the facts which give rise to the right. Once made an election is final and does not depend upon reliance by the assured. Promissory estoppel involves an unequivocal representation that the insurer does not intend to rely upon a right arising by reason of non-payment and action, or inaction, on the part of the assured in reliance on the representation, such that it would be inequitable for the insurer to enforce rights inconsistent with the representation. An estoppel is suspensory only, and does not involve particular knowledge on the part of the representor.[47] Apart from election and estoppel, the rights and obligations of the parties with regard to payment may have been modified over time by a course of dealing which has the effect of varying their original agreement.

7–54 Extension of time for payment. Notwithstanding the provisions in the policy, the insurers may extend the time for payment of the premium or waive any of the conditions precedent to the continuance of the risk, and even after the policy has lapsed the insurers may be held to have revived the insurance upon the same terms by any word or act which leads the assured to believe that the insurers have reassumed the risk.[48] In *Stuart v. Freeman*[49] an own-life policy allowed 30 days of grace for payment of the annual premium. The assured assigned the policy, and the insurers agreed orally with the assignee that if the original assured did not pay the premium within the 30 days it would be sufficient if the assignee paid it upon the following day. The court held that as between the insurers and the assignee, the policy must be read as if there were 31 days of grace instead of 30. A parol agreement to renew a fire policy and give credit for the premium may be binding notwithstanding the conditions in the policy,[50] but there must be a clear waiver of the conditions since an alleged oral agreement to renew may be merely a casual conversation of a preliminary nature or an intimation of willingness to renew in accordance with the conditions of the policy.[51] The issue of a renewal certificate or reciept for the premium without obtaining payment may be construed as a waiver of the conditions, even though it is expressly provided in the policy that the renewal insurance shall not be binding until the actual payment of the premium.[52]

7–55 Effect of waiver of forfeiture condition in life policy. The New York

[47] *Motor Oil Hellas v. Shipping Corp. of India* [1990] 1 Lloyd's Rep. 391; *Compagnia Tirrena di Ass. SpA v. Grand Union Ins. Co.* [1991] 2 Lloyd's Rep. 143. See also paras 10–96 to 10–97, *post.*
[48] *Kirkpatrick v. South Australian Ins. Co.* (1886) 11 App.Cas. 177.
[49] [1903] 1 K.B. 47.
[50] *Post v. Aetna Life Ins. Co.*, 43 Barb. 351 (N.Y.Sup.Ct., 1864).
[51] *O'Reilly v. Corporation*, 101 N.Y. 575 (1886).
[52] *Doherty v. Millers' Ins.* (1902) 4 Ont.L.R. 303. 6 Ont.L.R. 78. *Boehen v. Williamsburgh City Ins. Co.* (1866) 35 N.Y. 131; *Bordine v. Exchange Fire*, 51 N.Y. 117 (1872); *Tennant v. Travellers' Indemnity Ins. Co.*, 31 Fed.Rep. 332 (1887).

courts have held that an agreement with regard to a current life policy that it shall not be deemed void if the renewal premiums are paid within a reasonable time is a waiver of the conditions in the policy, so that a death occurring before a reasonable time has elapsed will be covered although the premium is unpaid.[53] This is because such an arrangement, whether express or implied, is not an agreement for renewal subject to the life being in existence at the time when payment is made, but is a definite waiver of suspension or forfeiture if payment is made in the extra time allowed.[54]

Sometimes a company intimates in its prospectus that it will grant more liberal terms for the revival of lapsed policies than it has hitherto done and that those terms will apply to all existing policies as well as to new policies. Such an announcement constitutes a standing offer to existing policy-holders which they may accept by continuing to pay their premiums on the faith of the announcement or by claiming the benefit of it.[55]

7–56 Evidence contradicting written terms of policy. In all cases where there is an extension of the time or other waiver of the conditions for punctual payment, evidence is properly admitted to prove an agreement or waiver made subsequent to the making of the original contract.[56] The parol evidence rule would (except in rectification cases) in theory prevent evidence being adduced of a prior oral agreement, if the parties intended that all terms should be reduced to writing. However, the practical scope of the rule is limited, since it is possible to admit evidence as to whether the parties did so intend.[57] Evidence would not be admitted to prove a custom to give credit contrary to the express terms of the written contract.[58] If the insurers subsequently acted in accordance with the alleged custom their conduct might amount to a waiver but the mere existence of the custom at the time the contract was made could not vary the express terms of the contract.

7–57 Acceptance of overdue premium. Forfeiture of a policy on the ground of non-payment of premium may be waived by subsequent demand for or acceptance of the premium in such circumstances as would naturally lead the assured to believe that the company intends to treat the policy as subsisting.[59] But the mere acceptance of a premium after forfeiture is not in itself conclusive. Thus, in a South African case, where the conditions of the policy provided for reinstatement of a lapse policy on payment of arrears and production of a health certificate, the acceptance of a premium after forfeiture was held insufficient to revive the policy.[60] Where a demand for an overdue premium is made, the assured will have a reasonable time to comply with it, but if he refuses to comply, or after a reasonable time fails to comply,

---

[53] *Howell v. Knickerbocker Life Ins. Co.*, 44 N.Y. 276 (1871); *Homer v. Guardian Mutual Ins. Co.*, 67 N.Y. 478 (1876); *Dilleber v. Knickerbocker Life Ins. Co.*, 76 N.Y. 567 (1879).

[54] *ibid.*

[55] *Salvin v. James* (1805) 6 East 571; explained felicitously by Cresswell J. in *Simpson v. Accidental Death* (1857) 2 C.B.(N.S.) 257.

[56] *De Freece v. National Life*, 136 N.Y. 144 (1892), an "instalment bond plan" case.

[57] For discussion of the parol evidence rule see *Chitty on Contracts* (28th ed., 1999) p. 624.

[58] *Re L, Sutro v. Heilbut, Symons & Co.* [1917] 2 K.B. 348.

[59] *Kirkpatrick v. South Australian Ins. Co.* (1886) 1 App.Cas. 177; *Morton v. Pearl Assurance Co.* [1926] I.A.C.Rep. 14; *Supple v. Cann* (1858) 8 Ir.C.L.R. 1; *Besant v. Northern Life* (1923) 2 D.L.R. 1086; *Comp. Tirrena di Ass. SpA v. Grand Union Ins. Co.* [1991] 2 Lloyd's Rep. 143.

[60] *Steyn's Estate v. S. African Mutual Life* (1948) 1 S.A.L.R. 359.

the policy will again lapse.[61] If a premium has been earned, in that the insurers have been actually on the risk during the whole or part of the period in respect of which it is payable, the acceptance of such premium does not necessarily waive a forfeiture incurred by reason of non-payment.[62] And on that principle where a premium note is taken for the whole or part of a premium on condition that if the note is not paid at maturity the policy shall be null and void, a demand for payment of an overdue note does not necessarily revive the policy,[63] but it may be made in such a way, or in such circumstances as to induce the assured to believe that the policy would be valid if he complied with the request, and if so, the insurers will be estopped from relying on non-payment as a forfeiture.[64] Similarly, an extension of the time for payment of an overdue note may be,[65] but is not necessarily, a waiver of the forfeiture.[66] In the case of mutual societies where the policy of the member is conditional on the punctual payment of assessments or death dues, a forfeiture for non-payment is not prima facie waived by demand for assessments which have fallen due before the forfeiture was incurred,[67] but a demand for assessments which have fallen due subsequently is prima facie a waiver of the forfeiture.[68]

7–58 Habitual acceptance of overdue premiums. There are numerous cases in the US courts where it has been held that the conduct of the insurers in continuing to accept without objection renewal premiums which are overdue may amount not only to a waiver of the forfeiture on each particular occasion, but to a general waiver for the future of the conditions in the policy requiring apyment on a particular date.[69] In one case it was said[70]:

> "There is no room for question about the rules of law applicable. A course of dealing which justifies the assured in believing that punctuality in paying premiums is not required or will be excused will relieve him from the consequences of delay. But it must be dealing which actually creates such belief, and justifies a jury in finding its existence",

and in a case in the Supreme Court the following direction to the jury was approved[71]:

> "If the company by its conduct led the assured, as a reasonable and prudent business man, to believe that he could make payments a few days after the due date, sick or well, it cannot turn around now and say,

---

[61] *Edge v. Duke* (1849) 18 L.J.Ch. 183. This is consistent with the general principle established in *Rickards v. Oppenheim* [1950] 1 K.B. 616.

[62] *McGeachie v. N. American Life Ins. Co.* (1894) 23 S.C.R. 148.

[63] *McGeachie*'s case, *supra*; *Manufacturers' Life Ins. Co. v. Gordon* (1893) 20 Ont.A.R. 309; *Duncan v. Missouri State Life*, 60 Fed.Rep. 646 (1908).

[64] *Hodson v. Guardian Life Ass*, 97 Mass. 144 (1867); *Palmer v. The Phoenix Mutual Life Ins. Co.*, 84 N.Y. 63 (1881).

[65] *Knickerbocker Life Ins. Co. v. Norton*, 96 U.S. 234 (1877).

[66] *Wall v. Home Ins. Co.*, 36 N.Y. 157 (1867).

[67] *Mandego v. Centennial Mutual*, 64 Iowa 134 (1884); *Crawford County v. Cochran*, (1878) 88 Pa. 230; *Rice v. Grand Lodge*, 92 Iowa 417 (1894); *Garbutt v. Citizens' Life* (1892) 84 Iowa 293; *Lycoming County v. Schollenberger*, 44 Pa. 259 (1863).

[68] *Knights of Pythias v. Kalinski*, 163 U.S. 289 (1895); *Beatty v. Mutual Reserve*, 75 Fed.Rep. 65 (1896).

[69] See, *e.g. Elkins v. Susquehanna Mutual Fire Ins. Co.*, 113 Pa. 386 (Sup.Ct.Pa., 1886).

[70] *Smith v. New England Mutual Life Ins. Co*, 63 Fed.Rep. 769, 772 (1894), *per* Butler J.

[71] *Hartford Life Ins. Co. v. Usell*, 144 U.S. 439 (1881).

'You did not pay at the time'. I cannot say to you as a matter of law that one receipt after the time specified would make a waiver or that fifty would. It is not in the numbers. The question is for you to consider and determine from all of them, and from the whole course of business whether, as a prudent business man, he had a right to believe that it was immaterial whether he paid on the day or a few days later. If the course of conduct was such that he had a right to believe that he could pay only in good health then there was no waiver applicable to the case."

7–59 It is, however, important to have exact regard to the precise conduct said to give rise to a waiver. The conduct must be unequivocal. Thus, habitual acceptance of overdue premiums under such circumstances that the insurers are satisfied each time that the insured life is in good health would not justify any inference of a general waiver of the condition for punctual payment in the future[72]; although it might be evidence of a waiver to this extent that the insurers would be bound to renew without penalty or increase of premium if the assured within a reasonable time tendered the premium, and satisfied the insurers that the life continued in good health.[73] On the other hand, where the insurers continue to accept overdue premiums without inquiry as to the health of the assured, an intention to waive strict punctuality would not be an unreasonable inference.[74] Thus, where the company had habitually received premiums on a life policy seven to 30 days after they were due without objection or inquiry, and the final premium was paid nine days after due, and accepted by the company in ignorance of the fact that the life had dropped on the previous day, it was held that the company was liable.[75]

7–60 An occasional indulgence to the assured by accepting an overdue premium, more especially if it is accompanied by a warning of the necessity of prompt payment and danger of delay, is no evidence of waiver of the right to exact punctual payment in the future.[76]

7–61 Annual contracts. Fire and other indemnity insurance contracts are commonly entered into for one year only and each renewal is a fresh contract. Different considerations apply to the question of late payment in such cases and even the habitual receipt of overdue premiums is probably no evidence of waiver. Where the policy contains the usual condition that the company shall not be liable for any loss occurring before the premium is paid, the acceptance of an overdue premium is clearly no waiver of that condition, and even if there is no such condition the acceptance of an

---

[72] *Thompson v. Knickerbocker Life Ins. Co.*, 104 U.S. 252 (1881); *Crossman v. Massachussetts Benefit Association*, 143 Mass. 435 (1887); *Ollie French v. Hartford Life and Annuity Ins. Co*, 169 Mass. 510 (1897); *Conway v. Phoenix Mutual Life Ins. Co.*, 140 N.Y. 79 (1893). Note that in the *Massachussets* decisions there were written conditions in the policies and association rules covering late payment.
[73] *Girard Life Ins. Co. v. Mutual Life Ins. Co.*, 86 Pa. 238 (1878).
[74] *Spoeri v. Massachussetts Mutual Life Ins. Co.*, 39 Fed.Rep. 752 (1889), distinguishing the *Crossman* decision.
[75] *ibid.*
[76] *Redmond v. Canadian Mutual Aid Association*, 19 Ont.A.R. 335 (1891); *Schmertz v. U.S. Life Ins. Co.*, 118 Fed.Rep. 250 (1902); *Smith v. New England Mutual Life Ins. Co.*, 63 Fed.Rep. 769 (1894). In the context of the obligation to pay charterparty hire, see *Scandinavian Trading Tanker Co. A.B. v. Flota Petrolera Ecuatoriana* [1983] 1 Q.B. 529; [1983] 2 A.C. 694.

overdue premium where no loss has occurred does not entitle the assured to assume that it will be accepted in the future after a loss has occurred.[77]

7–62 Incapacity to pay premium. The obligation to pay the premium according to the terms of the contract is prima facie absolute, and no sickness or infirmity will be accepted as an excuse for non-payment so as to avoid a forfeiture.[78] Even where the assured becomes insane, and is incapable of attending to any business, the incapacity is no excuse.[79] The conditions of the policy, however, may be such as to prevent the insurers insisting on a forfeiture, where non-payment was due to ill-health. Thus, where the condition in the policy of a mutual benefit society was that:

> "the policy shall lapse on failure to pay assessments, but for valid reasons given to officers of the association (such as failure to receive notice of assessment) a member may be reinstated on payment of arrears",

and the assured had, before the assessment was due or notified, become unconscious, and the assessment was not paid, it was held that the society were bound to reinstate after death.[80] Where a policy contained a provision that the policy should cease and determine if any premium was not paid on the date when due, "save as hereinafter provided", and that clause was followed by a provision that upon receipt of proof of total disability the company would pay for the assured all premiums becoming due after the receipt of such proof, the Supreme Court of the US held that a failure to pay after the disability but before proof forfeited the policy.[81]

7–63 No equitable relief. Equity will not, it seems, grant relief against forfeiture of a policy for non-payment of the premium within the time limited. Relief against a penalty or forfeiture will only be granted where the court can do so with proper regard for the interests of the other party. If the court cannot leave him in a position as good as if the agreement had been performed, it will not grant relief.[82] Applying that rule to contracts of life insurance, Woods J., in the Supreme Court of the United States, said[83]:

> "If the payment of the premiums and their payment on the day they fall due is of the essence of the contract, so is the stipulation for the release of the company from liability in default of punctual payment. No compensation can be made a life insurance company for the general want of punctuality on the part of its patrons."

Relief against forfeiture as a matter of English law appears to be limited to contracts involving a transfer of proprietary or possessory rights, and not to apply to contracts of insurance.[84]

---

[77] *Washington Mutual Fire Ins. Co. v. Rosenberger*, 84 Pa. 373 (1877).

[78] *Thompson v. Knickerbocker Life Ins. Co.*, 104 U.S. 252 (1881).

[79] *Klein v. New York Life Ins. Co.*, 104 U.S. 88 (1881); *Wheeler v. Connecticut Mutual Life Ins. Co.*, 82 N.Y. 543 (1880); *McCuaig v. Independent Order* (1909) 19 Ont.L.R. 613.

[80] *Dennis v. Massachussetts Benefit Association* (1890) 120 N.Y. 496.

[81] *Bergholm v. Peoria Life*, 284 U.S. 489 (1931).

[82] *Rose v. Rose* (1756) Amb. 331, 332, *per* Lord Hardwicke L.C.

[83] *Klein v. New York Life Ins. Co.*, 104 U.S. 88 at 91 (1881).

[84] *Socony Mobil Oil Co. Inc. v. West of England Shipowners Mutual Ins. Ass.* [1987] 2 Lloyd's Rep. 529, 539, applying *Scandinavian Trading Tanker Co. A.B. v. Flota Petrolera Ecuatoriana* [1983] 2 A.C. 694.

7–64 Unfair contract terms. A forfeiture term which is not individually negotiated and which is included in a contract with a consumer may have to satisfy a test of fairness arising from the Unfair Terms in Consumer Contracts Regulations 1999.[85] However, the test is not intended to apply to terms which are core terms, in other words terms that define the main subject matter of the contract or which concern the adequacy of the premium paid.[86] It is likely that a forfeiture clause would not be held to be a core term, so that the test of fairness would apply.

7–65 Default induced by conduct of insurers. The insurers cannot rely upon unpunctuality of payment induced by their own conduct. The general principle is thus stated in a case in the US[87]:

> "One, who by the terms of a contract is entitled to a forfeiture thereof to his own benefit on the occurrence of a certain act or omission which may be prevented by action taken in time by the other party, must not so act as to put the other party off his guard and induce him to refrain from preventive action. A forfeiture so induced will not prevail if the party in technical default with reasonable speed performs or offers to perform the omitted act ... Even if there be no primary hostile purpose in the action of one who may in a certain event become entitled to a forfeiture or other right arising from the non-performance of a condition, if by his act he has induced another to omit strict performance, he may not take the benefit or exact forfeiture."

7–66 Renewal notice. Prima facie insurers are not bound to give notice to the assured that the premium is due or that if unpaid a forfeiture will be incurred.[88] Thus, in *Simpson v. Accidental Death*,[89] where the assured met with a fatal accident during the days of grace while the premium was unpaid, it was held that, even if payment by the assured's executors would have revived the policy, there was no duty upon the insurers to intimate to them that the premium was unpaid, but that they might deliberately keep silence until the days of grace had expired, and then claim a forfeiture. Most insurance companies are in the habit of sending a notice to each assured before his renewal premium falls due, but the assured is not entitled to rely upon that act of courtesy being continued and, if for some reason or other a renewal notice is not sent or received, the assured cannot rely upon the omission as an excuse for unpunctuality in paying the premium.[90] If, however, the practice of giving notice of renewal can fairly be said to have become part of the usual course of dealing between the insurers and the assured, then it would not be open to the company to forfeit for

---

[85] 1999 S.I. No. 2083. Discussed further at paras 10–16 to 10–20, *post*.

[86] Preamble to Council Directive 93/13/EEC, O.J. L95/29.

[87] *Leslie v. Knickerbocker Life Ins. Co.*, 63 N.Y. 27 (1875); see also *Knight v. Rowe* (1826) 2 C. & P. 246; *West v. Blakeway* (1841) 2 M. & G. 729, 750; *Weldon v. GRE* [2000] 2 All E.R. (Comm.) 914.

[88] *Windus v. Tredegar* (1866) 15 L.T.(N.S.) 108; *Tredegar v. Windus* (1875) L.R. 19 Eq. 607; *Thompson v. Knickerbocker Life Ins. Co.*, 104 U.S. 252, 258 (1881). Many US state statutes provide for compulsory notice that renewal premiums are due: see, *e.g. Conway v. Phoenix Mutual Life Ins. Co.*, 140 N.Y. 79 (1893), where the early N.Y. Act is construed. The statues have nevertheless occasioned much litigation: see Richards, *Insurance*, para. 404.

[89] (1857) 2 C.B.(N.S.) 257. The decision would have been otherwise had the insurers actually represented that the policy was in force, rather than said nothing.

[90] *Thompson v. Knickerbocker Life Ins. Co.*, 104 U.S. 252 (1881).

non-payment on an occasion when it omitted to give such notice.[91] Where the assured was entitled to dividends as a shareholder, and the practice of the company was to apply the dividend for each year in part payment of the premium and send a note of the balance due, it was held that there was no default on the part of the assured until the usual note of the balance had been sent to him.[92]

7–67 If the insurers have expressly promised to give notice when the premium is due, the assured is entitled to rely upon their doing so.[93] Thus, where an assured inquired of an agent when the premium was due, and the agent said he would let him know, but no notice was ever sent, it was held that the insurers were estopped from claiming a forfeiture. There was evidence upon which it could be found that the agent had authority to promise that the general custom of the company would be kept up, and that notice would be given.[94] But where it was alleged that a promise to give notice of the due date of the renewal premiums was made by the agent at the time when the assured made his application, but the policy contained no such undertaking, it was held that the alleged promise was inconsistent with the terms of the written contract, and that the assured was attempting to vary that contract by parol evidence. Evidence of the promise was therefore inadmissible, and failure to give notice was no excuse for non-payment of the premium.[95] Where an assignee of a policy held it as security for a debt and the company promised to give him notice of the default of the assignor and an opportunity to pay the overdue premium, it was held that there could be no forfeiture, even of the assignor's interest, until the assignee had after due notice failed to pay within a reasonable time.[96] In one case where the insurers were in the habit of giving notice and of collecting the premiums by personal call, but suddenly, with the deliberate object of obtaining a forfeiture, omitted to give notice or call, it was held that they could not take advantage of their own trickery.[97] Where an insurance company had from time to time given the insured notice of the place where the premiums could be paid and the receipts obtained, but on one occasion, having changed its agency, omitted to send the usual notice, it was held that the company was estopped from refusing to receive a premium tendered within a reasonable time after the due date.[98] If a company discontinue the agency of an agent to whom the assured has been in the habit of paying his renewal premiums, the assured should, in the absence of notice, have a reasonable time after the due date to make inquiries and pay the premium to a person authorised to receive it.[99]

---

[91] *Minnick v. State Farm Mutual Automobile Ins. Co.* 174A. 2d 706 (Del.Sup.Ct., 1961); *Pester v. American Family Mutual Insurance Co.*, 186 N.W. 2d 711 (Neb.Sup.Ct., 1971); *New York Life Ins. Co. v. Eggleston*, 96 U.S. 572 (1877).

[92] *Phoenix Ins. Co. v. Doster*, 106 U.S. 30 (1882).

[93] *Selvage v. Hancock*, 12 Fed.Rep. 603 (1882).

[94] *Leslie v. Knickerbocker Life Ins. Co.*, 63 N.Y. 27 (1875).

[95] *Union Mutual Life Ins. Co. v. Mowry*, 96 U.S. (1877). However, as a matter of English law, the parol evidence rule is limited in its scope: see *Chitty on Contracts* (28th ed., 1999) vol. 1, p. 624.

[96] *Mutual Reserve Fund Life v. Cleveland Woollen Mills*, 82 Fed.Rep. 508 (1897).

[97] *Union Central v. Pottker*, 33 Ohio 459 (1878). The insurers could have insisted upon strict observance of the conditions only after giving reasonable notice of their intention to do so: *Edge v. Duke* (1849) 18 L.J.Ch. 183.

[98] *New York Life Ins. Co. v. Eggleston*, 96 U.S. 572 (1877); *Seaman's v. N.W. Mutual*, 3 Fed.Rep. 325 (1880).

[99] *Briggs v. National Life*, 11 Fed.Rep. 458 (1882).

Where a company notified the assured that the receipt for the annual premium was at a specified bank, and that payment might be made there, but before the time for payment arrived withdrew the receipt from the bank, it was held that it was estopped from claiming forfeiture for unpunctual payment of the premium.[1]

7–68 No waiver without knowledge. As a general rule a forfeiture for non-payment of premium is not waived by any word or deed on the part of the insurers unless they knew, or ought to have known, that a forefeiture had in fact been incurred.[2] Thus, in *Busteed v. West of England*[3] where an insurance company's agent had, without either actual or apparent authority given the assured credit for premiums due, but had, in his own monthly account with the company, included them as premiums paid, it was held that the acceptance of the premiums by the company could not be construed as a waiver of an irregularity on the part of the assured of which they had had no notice. But where the insurers are put upon inquiry by the fact that the agent has not forwarded the premiums to them in due course they cannot plead entire ignorance of the irregularity.[4] And if the company, having received a premium in ignorance of a forfeiture, does not, on becoming aware of the forfeiture, immediately return the premium, it may be bound.[5]

7–69 If a company has knowledge of a forfeiture, but accepts a premium through inadvertence, it may probably return it and insist on the forfeiture if it does so promptly and before the assured has, by reliance on the company's act, changed his position for the worse. Thus, in *Kelly v. Solari*[6] an insurance company paid a loss in forgetfulness of the fact that the policy had lapsed for non-payment of premium, and it was held that it could recover the money so paid by mistake; but in Canada where a mutual company, having cancelled a fire policy in its books for non-payment of assessments, subsequently in forgetfulness called for and received an assessment from the assured, it was held that there was a waiver of the forfeiture.[7] In a case in the US a man had insured his life for the benefit of his wife. After the premium was in arrear the wife called at the company's office and stated that she had come to attend to the premium. The secretary looked in his books and said the premium had been paid. Subsequently, the wife discovered that the premium had not been paid, and tendered it, but it was refused. It was held that the statement of the agent created no waiver or estoppel. There could be no waiver where there was no knowledge of the fact that the premium had not been paid, and, as the policy was already forfeited at the time, the assured was in no way prejudiced by the delay so as to create an estoppel against the company.[8]

7–70 Insolvency of insurers. In the US the question has been raised whether the insolvency of an insurance company affords a legal excuse to the

---

[1] *Provident Savings Life v. Duncan*, 115 Fed.Rep. 277 (1902).
[2] *Globe Mutual Life Ins. Co. v. Woolf* (1877) 95 U.S. 326; *Bennecke v. Connecticut Mutual*, 105 U.S. 355 (1881).
[3] (1857) 5 Ir.Ch.R. 553.
[4] *Hodson v. Guardian Life*, 97 Mass. 144 (1867).
[5] *Busteed v. West of England* (1857) 5 Ir.Ch.R. 553, 570.
[6] (1841) 11 L.J.Ex. 10.
[7] *Smith v. Mutual Ins. Co. of Clinton* (1877) 27 U.C.C.P. 441; *Lyons v Globe Mutual Life* (1877) 27 U.C.C.P. 567.
[8] *Robertson v. Metropolitan*, 88 N.Y. 541 (1882).

assured for non-payment of a premium which has fallen due on a life policy. It has been held that, while the mere suspicion of insolvency does not, of course, provide such excuse, the assured need not pay if the receiver declares that he will not accept further premiums,[9] or if the company has actually suspended business,[10] or if proceedings against it for a winding-up order have been irrevocably instituted.[11] The reason for these decisions is that there is an implied condition in the contract of insurance that the insurers will remain in a condition to perform their obligations under it towards policy-holders, and, once it is clear that they cannot do so, the assured is released from his obligations under the policy.[12]

7-71 In applying these principles in the United Kingdom, it is necessary to bear in mind the provisions of the Financial Services and Markets Act 2000, s.376(2), to the effect that the long term business of a company in liquidation is normally carried on with a view to its transfer as a going concern to another company.

5. WAIVER BY AGENTS

7-72 Authority to accept premiums otherwise than in cash. An agent is not ordinarily presumed in law to have actual authority to give credit for the premium or to take bills, notes or other consideration in lieu of cash payment,[13] although he probably has an implied authority to take a cheque in payment,[14] since this represents a usual method of payment.

7-73 On the other hand it may well be that an agent who is employed to settle the terms of cover and conclude the contract of insurance would be held to have an apparent authority to give credit or agree to special terms of payment, and the same might be true of an employee of the insurers who is authorised to take premiums and give receipts in return.[15] Wherever, in fact, it is reasonable for the assured dealing with the insurer's agent to assume that a power to relax the strict rules for payment of premiums is consistent with the latter's position, it should be held that, subject to general agency principles, the insurer who permitted him to act in that capacity is bound by the agent's decision to dispense with an immediate cash payment.[16] It makes no difference that the insurers have privately instructed their agent not to do

---

[9] *Att.-Gen. v. Guardian Mutual Life Ins. Co.*, 82 N.Y. 336 (1880).
[10] *Jones v. Life Assurance of America*, 83 Ky. 75 (1885).
[11] *People v Globe Mutual Life Ins. Co.*, 32 Hun. 147 (N.Y.Sup.Ct., 1884).
[12] *People v. Empire Mutual Life Ins. Co.*, 92 N.Y. 108 (1883).
[13] *Acey v. Fernie* (1840) 7 M. & W. 151; *Hine Bros. v. Steamship Syndicate* (1895) 72 L.T. 79, 81; *Legge v. Byas, Mosley & Co.* (1901) 7 Com.Cas. 16, 18; *Montreal Ass. Co. v. Macgillivray* (1859) 13 Moo.P.C.C. 87; *Busteed v. West of England* (1857) 5 Ir.Ch.R. 553; *Western Ass. v. Provincial Ins. Co.* (1880) 5 Ont.A.R. 190; *Hoffmann v. Hancock Mutual Life Ins. Co.*, 92 U.S. 161, 164 (1875).
[14] *Aetna Life v. Green* (1876) 38 U.C.Q.B. 459; *Taylor v. Merchants' Fire*, 50 U.S. (9 How.) 390 (1850).
[15] This is the view adopted in Gordon and Getz, *The South African Law of Insurance* (4th ed.) p. 149, and Vance, *Handbook on the Law of Insurance* (3rd ed.) pp. 438–439.
[16] *Edmunds v. Bushell & Jones* (1865) L.R. 1 Q.B. 97; *Manufacturers' Accident Ins. Co. v. Pudsey* (1897) 27 S.C.R. 374; *Scott v. Accident Assoc. of New Zealand* (1888) 6 N.Z.L.R. 263; *Kelly v. London and Staffs. Fire Ins.* (1883) Cab. & El. 47.

this, unless, of course, the assured knew of it. In this regard the assured will be held to have notice of any restrictions on the agent's powers explained in the policy, for he will be taken to have read them.[17] This rule does not, of course, apply to payment of the first premium before the policy is delivered.

7–74 The US authorities. It is submitted that great care should be taken in referring to the 19th century US state decisions on waiver of payment conditions by agents, since the principles enunciated differed widely from one state to another.[18] In *Mutual Reserve Fund Life Association v. Simmons*[19] Putnam C.J. gave the following warning[20]:

> "Nothing would be gained by undertaking to ... sift out the decisions of the state tribunals with reference to the questions here involved. How conflicting and, indeed, how absolutely irreconcilable they are, will be at once apparent on examining the citations made in *May on Insurance*."[21]

It is thought, however, that certain decisions of the state and federal courts may be consistent with English law. The US state and federal courts in different jurisdictions recognise a principle of apparent or ostensible authority similar to that discussed above.[22] Furthermore, there are cases where authority to relax conditions of payment has been implied in circumstances where it is believed an English court would do likewise.

7–75 Thus authority to give credit or accept bills for premiums may be implied from a local business custom or usage recognised by those carrying on the business of insurance in the particular county or district in question,[23] and if it is part of an agent's habitual mode of dealing to do this, and it is known to and recognised by the company, the latter will be held to have agreed to the practice and authorised it.[24] Where an agent is authorised to extend the time of payment on specified terms, and the assured knows this, and knows that the agent has no authority to extend the time on any other

---

[17] *Merserau v. Phoenix*, 66 N.Y. 274 (1876).

[18] These are cited in the footnotes to paras 790–793 of the 5th ed. of this work.

[19] 107 Fed. Rep. 418 (C.C.A. 1, 1901).

[20] 107 Fed. Rep. 418, 423.

[21] 4th ed., 1900, at paras 137, 137A, 345–345H, 360–360G.

[22] *Farnum v. Phoenix Ins. Co.*, 83 Cal. 246; 17 Am.St.Rep. 233 (Ca.Sup.Ct., 1890); *Baker v. Commercial Union Ass. Co.*, 162 Mass. 358 (1894); *Old Line Automobile Insurers v. Kuehl* 141 N.E. 2d 858 (Ind. App., 1957); *Buchanan v. Equitable Life Ass. Soc.*, 167 F.Supp. 832 (U.S.D.C.Cal., 1958); *Wyman v. Phoenix Mutual Life Ins. Co.*, 119 N.Y. 274 (1890); and see Richards, *Insurance*, paras 474, 478.

[23] *Boehen v. Williamsburgh City Ins. Co.*, 35 N.Y. 131 (1866); *Conway v. Phoenix Mutual Life Ins.* 140 N.Y. 79 (1893); *Franklin Ins. Co. of Phila. v. Colt*, 87 U.S. (20 Wall.) 560 (1874). See also *Manufacturers' Accident Ins. Co. v. Pudsey* (1897) 27 S.C.R. 374; *Moffatt v. Reliance Mutual Life Ass.* (1881) 45 U.C.Q.B. 561. The *Boehen* case indicates that the New York courts believed a general agent always had power to waive premium payment conditions. For definition of "general agent", see Richards, *Insurance*, paras 483, note 2.

[24] *O'Brien v. Union Ins. Co.*, 22 Fed. Rep. 586 (1884); *Tennant v. Travellers' Ins. Co.*, 31 Fed. Rep. 332 (1887); *Mutual Life Ins. Co. v. Logan*, 87 Fed. Rep. 637 (1898); *Payne v. Mutual Life Ins. Co.* 141 Fed. Rep. 339 (1905); *Dean v. Aetna Life*, 62 N.Y. 642 (1875); *Church v. La Fayette*, 66 N.Y. 222 (1876); *Marcus v. St Louis Mutual Life Ins.*, 68 N.Y. 625 (1876); *White v. Connecticut Fire Ins. Co.*, 120 Mass. 330 (1876).

terms, he cannot rely on an extension granted by the agent on substantially different terms.[25]

7–76 Authority to give credit for premiums may also be inferred from the terms of the instructions given to an agent by the company. Where the instructions were as follows:

> "Agents crediting premiums not actually received do so at their own risk, and must look to the policy-holder for reimbursement. The society does not ask or desire you to take this risk"

it was held that there was an implied authority to give credit and waive the condition requiring prepayment of the premium.[26] With this decision there should be contrasted that in *Acey v. Fernie*[27] where the instructions were that if the premiums on a life policy were not paid within 15 days the agent was:

> "to give immediate notice to the office of such fact, and in the event of your omitting to do so your account will be debited for the amount after the fifteen days are expired, and you will be held responsible to the directors for the same".

It was held that those instructions did not authorise the agent to give credit to the assured, but merely prescribed the penalty to be incurred by the agent if he did not comply with the company's instructions. Where the usual course of business was to transmit the renewal receipt to the agent and charge him with the premium, it was held that, if the agent delivered the receipt to the assured without receiving payment of the premium, the punctual payment of the premium was waived.[28]

7–77 Authority to revive lapsed policy. Prima facie, an agent has no authority to waive forfeitures and revive lapsed policies unless he is a general agent with authority to contract on behalf of the company[29]; but authority to waive forfeitures may be implied from a course of previous dealing recognised by the company.[30]

7–78 Conditions restricting authority of agent. In order to protect the company from liability arising out of the unauthorised acts of its agents, a

[25] *Slocum v. New York Life Ins. Co.*, 228 U.S. 364 (1912). Some American decisions hold that, wherever an agent gives credit on terms involving any advantage to himself, the resulting conflict of interest prevents the company being bound: *Union Central Life Ins. Co. v. Robinson*, 148 Fed. Rep. 358 (1906); *Union Central Life Ins. Co. v. Berlin*, 90 Fed. Rep. 779 (1899). Moreover, if chattels were taken in lieu of cash, or some highly unusual payment accepted, this could be a payment which it was outside the company's power to accept, or one which put the assured on notice that the agent was exceeding his authority: *Hoffmann v. Hancock Mutual Life Ins. Co.*, 92 U.S. 161 (1875); *Manufacturers' Accidents Ins. Co. v. Pudsey*, (1897) 27 S.C.R. 374, 379.
[26] *Smith v. Provident Savings Life*, 65 Fed. Rep. 765 (1895).
[27] *Acey v. Fernie*, (1840) 7 M. & W. 151; see also *Miller v. Brooklyn Life Ins. Co.*, 79 U.S. (12 Wall.) 285 (1870).
[28] *Fidelity and Casualty v. Willey*, 80 Fed. Rep. 497 (1897).
[29] *Post v. Aetna Ins. Co.*, 43 Barb. 351 (1864); *Foxwell v. Policy Holders' Mutual Life*, (1918) 42 Ont.L.R. 347 (Canada).
[30] *Campbell v. National Life*, (1874) 24 U.C.C.P. 133; *Globe Mutual Ins. Co. v. Wolff*, 95 U.S 326 (1877); *Knickerbocker Life Ins. Co. v. Norton*, 96 U.S. 234, 240 (1887); *Aetna Life Ins. Co. v. Smith*, 88 Fed. Rep. 440; *Wyman v. Phoenix Manual Life Ins. Co.*, 19 N.Y. 274 (1890).

condition is frequently inserted in the policy to the effect that agents are "not authorised to make, alter or discharge contracts or waive forfeitures", or that "nothing less than a distinct agreement indorsed on the policy shall be construed as a waiver". Such conditions are valuable in that they give notice to the assured of a definite restriction on the agent's authority, and may prevent the company being bound by acts which would otherwise be within the agent's apparent authority[31] but, like all other conditions in the policy, they may be waived by the subsequent conduct of the company or of the company's agent recognised and permitted by the company.[32] Conditions, therefore, may be waived by an agent, notwithstanding the provisions of the policy, if, subsequent to the granting of the policy, the words or conduct of the agent known to and acquiesced in by the company have been such as to induce the assured to believe that a forfeiture will not be insisted on or that other conditions in the policy will be waived.[33]

---

[31] *Morton v. Pearl Ass. Co.*, [1926] I.A.C. Rep.14; *Marvin v. Universal Life Ins. Co.*, 85 N.Y. 278 (1881).

[32] *Knickerbocker Life Ins. Co. v. Norton*, 96 U.S. 234, 240 (1877).

[33] *Tennant v. Travellers' Ins. Co.*, 31 Fed. Rep. 322 (1887); *Marcus v. St Louis Mutual Life Ins.*, 68 N.Y. 625 (1876); *Mutual Reserve Fund v. Cleveland Woollen Mills*, 82 Fed. Rep. 508 (1897); *Campbell v. National Life*, (1874) 24 U.C.C.P. 133. It has also been held that, if the restrictions upon the agent's authority to waive are contained in the policy, they do not affect the agent's actions *vis-à-vis*, the assured prior to the delivery of it: *Wood v. American Fire Ins. Co.*, 149 N.Y. 382 (1896) and see generally Richards, *Insurance*, (5th ed.), para. 485.

CHAPTER 8

RETURN OF PREMIUM

1. GENERAL PRINCIPLES

8–1 Principle of recovery: "no risk no premium". Premiums, like any moneys paid in return for a promise of a service or benefit, are recoverable when paid for a consideration which has wholly failed.[1] The principle was expounded in typically clear language by the progenitor of modern insurance law, Lord Mansfield, in the early marine insurance case of *Tyrie v. Fletcher*:[2]

> "I take it, there are two general rules established, applicable to this question: The first is, That where the risk has not been run, whether its not having been run was due to the fault pleasure or will of the insured, or to any other cause, the premium shall be returned: Because a policy of insurance is a contract of indemnity. The underwriter receives a premium for running the risk of indemnifying the insured, and whatever cause it be owing to, if he does not run the risk, the consideration for which the premium or money is put into his hands, fails and therefore he ought to return it.
>
> Another rule is, that if the risk of that contract of indemnity has once commenced, there shall be no apportionment or return of premium afterwards. For though the premium is estimated, and the risk depends upon the nature and length of the voyage, yet, if it has commenced, though it be only for twenty-four hours or less, the risk is run; the contract is for the whole entire risk, and no part of the consideration shall be returned."[3]

Thus, if the day after a risk has attached there is a breach of warranty or the assured's interest ceases, the whole premium is earned, and there can be no

---

[1] *Henkle v. Royal Exchange Assurance Co.* (1749) 1 Ven.Sen. 317, 319, *per* Lord Hardwicke L.C.; *Loraine v. Thomlinson* (1781) 2 Doug. K.B. 585, 587; *Goldsmith v. Martin* (1842) 4 M. & G. 5, 6; *Anderson v. Thornton* (1853) 8 Exch. 425, 427–428; *Thomson v. Weems* (1884) 9 App.Cas. 671, 682; *Wolenberg v. Royal Co-op etc. Society* (1915) 112 L.T. 1036; Marine Insurance Act 1906, s.84(1)(3)(a), (b). Thus there can never be a return of premium under P. & I. cover in a Mutual Insurance Association—*N. Eastern 100A S.S. etc. Association v. Red "S" S.S. Co.* (1906) 12 Com.Cas. 26.

[2] (1777) 2 Cowp. 666, 668.

[3] See also *Anderson v. Fitzgerald* (1853) 4 H.L.Cas. 484, 508; *Bermon v. Woodbridge* (1781) 2 Doug. K.B. 781; *Stone v. Marine Ins. Co.* (1876) 1 Ex.D. 81; *Provident Savings Life Association v. Bellew* (1904) 35 Can.S.C.R. 35.

return.[4] These principles may be reflected in, or modified by, the express or implied terms of the contract.[5]

8–2 Divisibility of risk. Where for some reason the risk does not attach as to part of the insurance, but does as to the remainder, the assured cannot recover any part of the premium,[6] but, as was decided in eighteenth century marine insurance cases, if the contract is on its true construction severable, so that separately identifiable risks are being run, the assured is entitled to a partial return of premium, commensurate with those risks which had not yet attached at the time of loss.[7] There is a lack of authority on the application of this principle to non-marine insurances. In respect of time, the insurance is often divisible into the periods for which the premiums are payable. Thus an insurance upon condition that a premium is paid every week is prima facie divisible into separate weekly insurances; but on the other hand, the policy may be framed as an annual insurance with an annual premium payable in instalments,[8] in which case the risk for the year would be indivisible,[9] and the whole premium would be earned immediately the year began to run.

8–3 Mistake. Where the contract is void for mistake, it is obvious that the consideration has wholly failed, and premiums paid are returnable. The fact that the cause of action in most cases is in quasi-contract for money paid in return for a consideration which has wholly failed,[10] and is in no sense an action on the policy, is well illustrated here, for, owing to the mistake, no contract ever came into being.

8–4 Non-disclosure and misrepresentation. Where the contract is avoided at the election of the insurers for an innocent (*i.e.* non-fraudulent) concealment or misstatement of material facts, the contract is retroactively avoided, *ab initio* when the election to avoid is effectively and validly

---

[4] Thus if the assured never possessed an insurable interest in property before it was lost during the period of cover, premium is returnable (subject to the rules relating to gaming and illegality, where relevant): *Routh v. Thompson* (1809) 11 East 428; Marine Insurance Act 1906, s.84(3)(c). But if the assured possessed an insurable interest which was, though unknown to him, defeasible, and he was divested of it after the period of cover had terminated without loss, premium is not returnable for want of interest. This is the real ground of Lord Ellenborough's decision in *M'Culloch v. Royal Exchange Ass. Co.* (1813) 3 Camp. 406. He did not mean to state a rule that a claim for premium had to be made during the currency of the risk—see Arnould's *Law of Marine Insurance* Vol. 2 para. 1335.

[5] Marine Insurance Act 1906, s.83; *C.T. Bowring Reinsurance v. Baxter* [1987] 2 Lloyd's Rep. 416; *Re Drake Ins. plc* [2001] Lloyd's Rep. I.R. 643 (return of premium after exercise of right of cancellation).

[6] *Canadian Pacific Ry v. Ottawa Fire Ins. Co.* (1907) 39 S.C.R. 405.

[7] *Stevenson v. Snow* (1971) 3 Burr. 1237; *Rothwell v. Cooke* (1797) 1 B. & P. 172; Marine Insurance Act 1906, s.84(2)(3)(b).

[8] If the terms of an instalment contract are such as to bring the Consumer Credit Act 1974 into operation, the provisions of that Act may affect the question of a return of premium.

[9] See *Loraine v. Thomlinson* (1781) 2 Doug. K.B. 585.

[10] *Stevenson v. Snow* (1761) 3 Burr. 1237, 1240; *Anderson v. Thornton* (1853) 8 Exch. 425, 427; *Feise v. Parkinson* (1812) 4 Taunt. 640, 641. A court can also decree a return of premiums paid under a mistake of fact; see paras 8–21, 8–35 and 8–37, *infra*, and when granting cancellation and delivery-up of a policy: *Da Costa v. Scandret* (1723) 2 P.Wms. 170; *Barker v. Walters* (1844) 8 Beav. 92; *Joel v. Law Union and Crown Ins. Co.* [1908] 2 K.B. 431, not reversed on this point in the C.A. [1908] 2 K.B. 863. Money paid under a mistake of law is also recoverable: *Kleinwort Benson v. Lincoln City Council* [1999] 2 A.C. 349.

exercised.[11] There is consequently a failure of consideration *ex post facto* and premiums are recoverable by the assured.

8-5 Breach of warranty. Where the insurers do not waive a breach of warranty by the assured, they are discharged from liability as from the time of breach.[12] If the term broken by the assured was a condition precedent to the inception of the risk, as where a warranted answer in the proposal form was false at the time when it was made,[13] the risk never attached,[14] and in the absence of fraud on his part the assured may recover the premium paid. If, however, the term was by nature a condition subsequent, as, for example, a continuing promissory warranty, and the breach occurred after the commencement of the risk, then the insurers were on risk for a time and no premiums are recoverable.[15] The breach of a condition precedent to recovery or a term suspending the risk while the assured contravenes it must logically have the same effect. But where the risk is divisible into periods corresponding to the dates when the premium is payable, premiums paid after the breach of warranty may be recovered because no part of the risk for the future periods was ever run by the insurers.[16]

Where a policy contains an express provision that in the event of a breach of warranty or misrepresentation the premiums paid shall be forfeited, the assured cannot recover his premiums even although the policy was void *ab initio* and there was no fraud on his part.[17] Where a policy provided that if the assured should reside or travel beyond the prescribed limits the policy would be void and that "the premiums paid shall be forfeited", it was held that "premiums" meant all premiums, and included not only the premiums paid before forfeiture but the premiums paid over a period of 12 years after the breach but before it became known to the company.[18]

8-6 Contract never validly concluded. If premiums have been paid to the insurer with an application for insurance, but no binding contract of insurance is in fact concluded, the money is recoverable as paid for a consideration which has wholly failed. There is no concluded contract, for example, where there was never in fact mutual consent,[19] where the insured

---

[11] *Carter v. Boehm* (1766) 3 Burr. 1905, 1909; *Anderson v. Thornton* (1853) 8 Exch. 425; *Fowkes v. Manchester and London Life Assurance and Loan Association* (1863) 3 B. & S.917, 927; *Hemmings v. Sceptre Life Assurance Ltd* [1905] 1 Ch. 365 (these two last cases illustrating that insurers may make their own conditions for forfeiture of premiums); *Towle v. National Guardian Assurance Co.* (1861) 30 L.J.Ch. 900, 911; *London Assurance Co. v. Mansel* (1879) 11 Ch.D. 363, 372. For the effect of non-disclosure, see Ch. 17, *post*. For fraudulent misrepresentation, see paras 16–4 and 16–5, *post*. See also Marine Insurance Act 1906, s.84(3)(*a*).

[12] *Bank of Nova Scotia v. Hellenic Mutual War Risks Ass'n* [1992] 1 A.C. 233, 262–264. See paras 10–89 *et seq.*, *post*.

[13] *e.g. Thomson v. Weems* (1884) 9 App.Cas. 671.

[14] *Macdonald v. Law Union Ins. Co.* (1874) L.R. 9 Q.B. 328; *Feise v. Parkinson* (1812) 4 Taunt. 640; *Colly v. Hunter* (1827) 3 C. & P. 7; *Henkle v. Royal Exchange Co.* (1749) 1 Ves.Sen. 317; *Allen v. Long* Marshall, *Insurance* (1785), p. 529.

[15] *Annen v. Woodman* (1810) 3 Taunt. 299; *Langhorn v. Cologan* (1812) 4 Taunt. 330; *Hawke v. Niagara District Fire Ins. Co.* (1876) 23 Grant 139.

[16] *Bunyon on Life Insurance* (5th ed.) p. 113; *Imperial Bank v. Royal Ins. Co.* (1906) 12 Ont.L.R. 519.

[17] *Duckett v. Williams* (1834) 2 Cr. & M. 348; *Thomson v. Weems* (1884) 9 App.Cas. 671; *Howarth v. Pioneer Life Assurance Co.* (1912) 107 L.T. 155; *Broad & Montague v. S.E. Lancashire Ins. Co.* (1931) 40 Ll.L.R. 328.

[18] *Sparenborg v. Edinburgh Life Assurance Co.* [1912] 1 K.B. 185.

[19] *Johnstone v. Prudential Assurance Co.* [1927] I.A.C.Rep. 31.

withdrew his proposal before final acceptance,[20] where the agent who had no power to contract submitted to the directors terms different from those in fact proposed, and the risk was accepted, and the policy issued upon a proposal which was never in fact made;[21] where the policy was issued to a person on a proposal which was not his proposal and which he had not signed although he had accepted the policy and paid the premiums;[22] where an agent induced a woman to sign another person's name but without that other's knowledge or consent on a proposal for an own-life policy and the woman paid the premiums on a policy written in terms of the proposal in the belief that it was an insurance effected on the life assured for her own benefit;[23] or where an industrial policy on the life of a child was issued on a form the table on which did not specify any benefit appropriate to the payment of the weekly premium of twopence.[24] The cases of cancellation of long-term policies under statutory provisions are governed by the same rule.[25]

8–7 The contract of insurance may be unenforceable because it is *ultra vires* the insurance company, as where, for example, the policy issued was of a type of insurance which the insurance company was not empowered to grant.[26] In such a case, so long as the policy is not illegal on other grounds as well,[27] the assured is entitled to recover back premiums paid.[28]

8–8 Loss from excepted peril. Where a loss arises from an excepted peril no premium can be recovered if the risk has attached; for example, where the assured on a life policy paid the premium for a year and committed suicide the next day.[29]

8–9 Unauthorised insurance effected by agent. Where a policy is effected by an agent without the authority of the person for whose benefit it is made, and the agent pays the premium, he cannot afterwards recover it back on the

---

[20] *Henderson v. State Life Ins. Co.* (1905) 9 Ont.L.R. 540.

[21] *Fowler v. Scottish Equitable Life Ins. Society* (1858) 4 Jur.(N.S.) 1169; *Harnickell v. New York Mutual Life Ins. Co.*, 111 N.Y. 390 (1888); *Key v. National Life*, 107 Iowa 446 (1899).

[22] *McKenna v. Catholic Life and General Ass. Co.* [1927] I.A.C.(N.I.)Rep. 23; *Hall v. Refuge Ass. Co.* [1928] I.A.C.(N.I.)Rep. 28.

[23] *Hewitt v. City of Glasgow F.S.* [1933] I.A.C.Rep. 39; *Scaley v. London and Manchester Ass. Co.* [1936] I.A.C.Rep. 25.

[24] *Cook v. British Widows' Ass. Co.* [1930] I.A.C.Rep. 34.

[25] See para. 6–22, *ante.*

[26] *Re Argonaut Marine Ins. Co.* [1932] 2 Ch. 34; *Re Arthur Average Association, ex parte Hargrave & Co.* (1875) L.R. 10 Ch.App. 542, where the assured were not claiming a return of premiums and the point was left open; *Hooper Grain Co. v. Colonial Assurance Co.* [1917] 1 W.W.R. 1226. As to the restricted ambit of the doctrine of *ultra vires* since the passing of what is now the Companies Act 1985, s.35, see para. 36–50, *post.*

[27] *Re London County Commercial Re-insurance Office Ltd* [1922] 2 Ch. 67.

[28] *Re Phoenix Life Assurance Co., Burges & Stock's Case* (1862) 2 J. & H. 441; *Flood v. Irish Provident Ass. Co. Ltd* [1912] 2 Ch. 597n. These cases were doubted in their application to contracts of loan by Lord Haldane and Lord Sumner in *Sinclair v. Brougham* [1914] A.C. 398, 417, 452–453, where to return the money would have been tantamount to performance of the *ultra vires* contract; distinguished as to insurance contracts in *Hooper v. Colonial Assurance Co.* [1917] 1 W.W.R. 1226, 1228. In each case it must be clear that the assured received no valuable consideration—see *per* Lord Sumner in *Sinclair v. Brougham, supra.*

[29] *Bermon v. Woodbridge* (1781) 2 Doug. K.B. 781, 789; *Tyrie v. Fletcher* (1777) 2 Cowp. 666, 669.

ground that his principal has refused to ratify the contract.[30] But where a wife effected a policy in her husband's name without his authority but with his money, it was held that the husband was entitled to recover the premiums.[31]

2. PRINCIPLES RELATING TO ILLEGAL INSURANCE

8–10 Illegal insurance. In the case of insurances which are illegal whether by statute,[32] such as insurances without interest, or by common law,[33] such as insurances on property unlawfully employed, the general rule is that the insured can recover neither the policy moneys nor the premiums which he has paid.[34] It will not avail the insured to plead that he was ignorant of the law and thought that there was an insurable interest where in fact there was none,[35] or even that the mistake as to the law was induced by the innocent misrepresentation of the insurer or his agent.[36] Where application was made for a policy which, if issued, would have been illegal, and the company issued a policy in a form which did not conform to the application but was equally illegal, it was held that the assured could not recover the premiums on a plea of *non est factum*, inasmuch as he had asked for an illegal policy, and the particular form of illegality which he got was not material.[37] Equally where a policy is illegal, the assured cannot recover the premiums paid on the ground that it was *ultra vires* the company to issue such a policy.[38]

8–11 There is a distinction, however, between policies that are illegal in the sense that they are prohibited or penalised and those that are merely declared to be void. P.p.i. policies of marine insurance which are declared to be void by section 4 of the Marine Insurance Act 1906[39] are in the latter category, and the premiums paid on these may be recovered. Policies to which the Life Assurance Act 1774[40] applies are, on the other hand, prohibited if made without interest or if they are otherwise in contravention

---

[30] *Routh v. Thompson* (1811) 13 East 274, 290; *Hagedorn v. Oliverson* (1814) 2 M. & S. 485, 490–491.

[31] *Fenwick v. London and Manchester Ass. Co.* [1925] I.A.C.Rep. 8.

[32] See para. 14–2, *post.*

[33] See para. 14–12, *post.*

[34] *Howard v. Refuge Friendly Society* (1886) 54 L.T. 644; *Harse v. Pearl Life Ass. Co.* [1904] 1 K.B. 558; *Forgan v. Pearl Life Ass. Co.* (1907) 51 S.J. 230; *Evanson v. Crooks* (1911) 106 L.T. 264; *Elson v. Crookes* (1911) 106 L.T. 462; *Lowry v. Bourdieu* (1780) 2 Doug. K.B. 468; *Andree v. Fletcher* (1789) 3 T.R. 266; *Morck v. Abel* (1802) 3 B. & P. 35; *Oom v. Bruce* (1810) 12 East 225; *Hentig v. Staniforth* (1816) 5 M. & S.122; *Paterson v. Powell* (1832) 9 Bing. 320, 333; *Allkins v. Jupe* (1877) 2 C.P.D. 375, 388, 390; *Brophy v. N. American Life Ass. Co.* (1902) 32 S.C.R. 261, where the familiar maxim was quoted as *"in pari delicto, melio est causa possidentis".*

[35] *Lubbock v. Potts* (1806) 7 East 449; *Lowry v. Bourdieu* (1780) 2 Doug. K.B. 468.

[36] *Harse v. Pearl Life Assurance Co.* [1904] 1 K.B. 558; *Phillips v. Royal London Mutual Ins. Co.* (1911) 105 L.T. 136; *Evanson v. Crooks* (1911) 106 L.T. 264; *Hughes v. Liverpool Victoria Legal Friendly Society* [1916] 2 K.B. 482; *Wolenberg v. Royal Co-op. Collecting Society* (1915) 112 L.T. 1036; *Dickinson v. Prudential Ass. Co.* [1926] I.A.C.Rep. 26.

[37] *Elson v. Crookes* (1911) 106 L.T. 462.

[38] *Evanson v. Crooks* (1911) 106 L.T. 264.

[39] 6 Edw. 7, c. 41.

[40] 14 Geo. 3, c. 48.

of that Act, and are therefore illegal as well as void, and the premiums paid are prima facie non-returnable.[41]

In certain circumstances, however, the assured may recover premiums notwithstanding the illegality of the insurance. These may be summarised as follows:

1. Where the assured has been induced to contract by the fraud of the insurer or his agent.
2. Where the illegality arises from the form of the policy as issued by the insurers.
3. Where the assured was ignorant of the facts which made the insurance illegal.
4. Where the assured claims rescission of the contract before the risk has attached.
5. Where, in the case of statutory illegality, the statute is intended to protect assureds as a class so that they are not to be regarded as *in pari delicto*.
6. Where the assured has a right of recovery conferred by statute.[42]

8–12 Illegal policy solicited by agent of insurers. Where an agent persuades a person whom he canvasses to take an illegal policy on the life of another in whose life that person has no interest, the agent may be innocent in the matter either because he erroneously thinks that the relationship or other facts are such as to give the assured an insurable interest, or because he erroneously thinks that in law the assured has an insurable interest in the life assured. In such cases the premiums cannot be recovered, whether the agent has said nothing about the policy's legality or has in good faith stated that it is valid in law. Thus in *Harse v. Pearl Life Assurance Company*,[43] a case decided in the Court of Appeal, the plaintiff was induced by the agent of an assurance company to effect a policy on the life of his mother to cover funeral expenses. At the date when the policy was effected such a policy was illegal for want of insurable interest, but it was the practice of companies to issue such policies, and the agent, in the belief that there was an insurable interest, told the plaintiff that the policy would be valid and the plaintiff relied on that statement in effecting the policy. In an action to recover the premiums, the Court of Appeal held that as there was no fraud, duress or oppression on the part of the insurers the parties were *in pari delicto*, and the assured was not entitled to recover the premiums which he had paid on an illegal policy. Agents of insurance companies, they said, were not to be treated as being under any greater obligation to know the law than ordinary persons whom they approach to make insurances.[44]

8–13 This may seem a harsh decision. A layman who accepts the

---

[41] *Harse v. Pearl Life Ass. Co.* [1904] 1 K.B. 558, 563; *Hughes v. Liverpool Victoria Legal Friendly Society* [1916] 2 K.B. 482, 489, 493; *Re London County Commercial Re-insurance* [1922] 2 Ch. 67; *Re National Benefit Assurance Co.* [1931] 1 Ch. 46. Note also the reference to "void" contracts in the Marine Insurance Act 1906, s.84(3)(a).

[42] These exceptions to the general rule of irrecoverability reflect the limits of the application of the general maxims of "*in pari delicto potior est conditio defendentis*" and "*ex turpi causa non oritur actio*", for which see Ch. 14, *post*.

[43] [1904] 1 K.B. 558, approved in *Hughes v. Liverpool Victoria Legal Friendly Society* [1916] 2 K.B. 482, 492.

[44] [1904] 1 K.B. 558, 564. See also *Evanson v. Crooks* (1911) 106 L.T. 264, 268; *Goldstein v. Salvation Army* [1917] 2 K.B. 291.

assurance of a professional that a transaction is legal does not, in the eyes of most people, bear an equal share of blameworthiness for what proves to be an illegality. The decision is to be explained, however, as an illustration of the general rule that ignorance of the law is no excuse. Just as an innocent misrepresentation of law is not a ground for rescission of a contract,[45] and a mistake of law is no defence to a criminal charge, so an innocent misrepresentation of law is to be left out of account in the application of the *par delictum* rule. The reported English cases on this point are all cases of misrepresentations of law in so far as misrepresentations were material to these decisions.[46] The position would be different, it is submitted, if the insurer or his agent had represented facts which, if true, would render the transaction legal. A person who enters into an illegal transaction reasonably believing in a state of facts which, if true, would justify his action, is not *in delicto* at all.[47] There is, in any event, no doubt that the assured can recover premiums paid if he was misled by the fraudulent representations of the insurer or his agent, and we proceed to consider that case in more detail.

8–14 Fraud of agent. Regardless of the legal distinction between "innocent" misrepresentation and fraudulent misrepresentation, an agent touting for policies may know very well when a policy is legal and when it is not, and those whom he solicits may be ignorant and easily imposed upon by a fraudulent agent. If the premiums are obtained by fraud on the part of an agent, they may be recovered by the assured on his discovering the fraud.[48] The onus is on the assured to prove that he was ignorant of the fraud being practised by the agent upon the company and believed the policy to be legal, and that it was the agent's fraudulent representation and not merely his own cupidity or a desire to gamble on a human life that induced him to take the policy and pay the premiums.[49] It is not sufficient for the assured to say that, being ignorant of the law, he relied on the agent as a man of skill and assumed that everything was in order,[50] or that, knowing the proposed insurance was illegal, he relied on the agent's statement that the company would nevertheless pay.[51]

8–15 A variety of fraudulent devices have been resorted to historically by agents, in particular in life business, who hope to sell illegal policies. The simplest of them is to ask A to take a policy on the life of B, in whose life he

---

[45] See para. 16–14, *post*.

[46] *Harse v. Pearl Life Ass. Co.* [1904] 1 K.B. 558, 563; *Phillips v. Royal London Mut. Ins. Co.* (1911) 105 L.T. 136; *Hughes v. Liverpool Victoria Legal Friendly Society* [1916] 2 K.B. 482, 492–493. In *Evanson v. Crooks* (*supra*) there was no clear misrepresentation at all: 106 L.T. 264, 267. In *Elson v. Crookes* (*supra*) and *Howard v. Refuge Friendly Soc.* (1886) 54 L.T. 644 and *Wolenberg v. Royal Co-op. Collecting Society* (1915) 112. L.T. 1036 no misrepresentations were relied upon.

[47] *cf.* para. 8–25, *post*. There might be also a misrepresentation, *e.g.* as to what benefit would accrue under the policy. To misdescribe the functioning of a policy can be a statement of fact: see *Hyams v. The Paragon Ins. Co.* (1927) 27 Ll.L.R. 448. Equity is adept on occasions at construing statements of the law as representations of fact: *Solle v. Butcher* [1950] 1 K.B. 671.

[48] *Tofts v. Pearl Life Ass. Co.* [1915] 1 K.B. 189.

[49] *Howarth v. Pioneer Life Ass. Co.* (1912) 107 L.T. 155; *Whitaker v. Royal Co-op. Collecting Soc.* [1937] I.A.C.Rep. 7; *McCartan v. Nation Life and General* [1929] I.A.C.(N.I.)Rep. 50; *McGeown v. Pearl Life Ass. Co.* [1928] I.A.C.(N.I.)Rep. 33; *Simpson v. Catholic Life & General* [1928] I.A.C.(N.I.)Rep. 34.

[50] *Harse v. Pearl Life Ass. Co.* [1904] 1 K.B. 558.

[51] *Howarth v. Pioneer Life Ass. Co.* (1912) 107 L.T. 155.

has no interest, and then procure B to sign a proposal for a policy on his own life with the intention that the policy when issued will be handed to A for his sole benefit and that A will pay the premiums. A policy so procured is illegal and if A can satisfy the court that he believed that the policy would be legal and that he was induced to take it by the fraudulent representation of the agent to that effect, he can recover the premiums.[52] Unless, however, the person concerned is illiterate, uneducated or very young, the court will not readily accept the plea that he did not know that the policy was illegal or that he was actuated by the fraudulent statement that the transaction was legal, and not by a desire to participate in the fraud by indulging in a gamble on the life assured.[53]

A similar but slightly different form of the fraud is for an agent to procure C, who has an insurable interest in the life to be insured, to make a proposal in his own name for a policy on the life of B with the intention that when the policy is issued it will be handed to A for his sole benefit and that A will pay the premiums. It will not be easy in such cases for A to satisfy the court that he acted innocently. In a case where a policy for funeral expenses taken out by the daughter of the life assured was intended for the benefit of a boy aged 11 who had no insurable interest in the life and who paid the premiums, the Industrial Assurance Commissioner for Northern Ireland was of opinion that the boy was too young to understand the transaction and exculpated him from any participation in the fraud and made an award in his favour for a return of the premiums which he had paid.[54]

8–16 It is not always, however, that the life to be insured, or some person having an insurable interest in that life, is so complacent and unsuspicious or so fraudulent as to put his signature to a proposal for a policy which is intended to enure for the benefit of another who is to pay the premiums, and when the fraud cannot be worked in that way the agent may have to go a little more underground. The crudest method is for the agent to forge the name of the life assured to an own-life proposal and then hand the policy when issued to A. If A was ignorant of the intended forgery, the same considerations arise on a claim for return of premiums as in a case where the life assured gave his name to the proposal. If A, being an illiterate or uneducated person, is induced by an agent to believe that, apart from the forgery of which he is ignorant, the proposed transaction is lawful, he can recover the premium.[55] A cannot recover the premiums on the ground of fraud if, although ignorant of the forgery, he must have known that the proposed transaction was an illegal one[56] or that he was indulging in an obvious gamble on human life.[57]

8–17 Another variation of the fraud is for the agent to get A to sign a proposal for an own-life policy in the name of B, the life to be assured, on the promise that he, the agent, will see B and "get him to put everything right", but B is told nothing about it and a policy is issued on the proposal bearing B's signature written by A. If in such a case A was induced by the agent to

---

[52] *Hughes v. Prudential Ass. Soc.* [1931] I.A.C.(N.I.)Rep. 38.
[53] *Gamble v. City of Glasgow F.S.* [1930] I.A.C.(N.I.)Rep. 35.
[54] *Heagney v. Refuge Friendly Soc.* [1931] I.A.C.(N.I.)Rep. 47.
[55] *McMullan v. City of Glasgow F.S.* [1931] I.A.C.(N.I.)Rep. 36; *McCooe v. Scottish Legal Life* [1935] I.A.C.(N.I.)Rep. 22; *Heagney v. National Life and General* [1932] I.A.C.(N.I.)Rep. 30.
[56] *Nevin v. Scottish Legal Life* [1935] I.A.C.(N.I.)Rep. 27; *McNeeley v. Pearl* [1936] I.A.C.(N.I.)Rep. 40.
[57] *Quinn v. Refuge* [1932] I.A.C.(N.I.)Rep. 30.

believe that what was proposed was a lawful transaction he can recover the premiums.[58]

8-18 Another device is for an agent to put forward to his company a proposal signed by the person on whose behalf the insurance is to be effected but with an inaccurate description of the relationship between the proposer and the life to be assured, thus falsely representing that the proposer has an insurable interest in the life. Thus, when CM, on the suggestion of an agent and in the belief that it was legal, agreed with the agent to take out a funeral expenses policy on the life of her aunt, HB, but CM signed no proposal, and a policy was issued on a proposal purporting to be, but not in fact, signed by her, in which HB was described as her sister, it was held that as CM was innocent of any fraud or illegality she was entitled to recover the premiums which she had paid.[59]

8-19 In order to recover the premiums paid on an illegal policy effected without interest in the life assured, it is not always necessary to prove that the agent told the assured in so many words that the policy would be legal or that it would be all right. A false representation may be made by conduct and action without any spoken word. It is fraud on the part of an agent in taking a proposal to conceal from the intending assured the fact that he, the agent, is intending to deceive his own company as well as the assured by a falsified proposal. In another case where the statement in the proposal as to the proposer's relationship to the life assured was untrue and made it appear that there was an insurable interest, whereas there was none, the agent who knew the true relationship told the assured that the policy would be legal whereas he knew that it would be illegal. The assured signed the proposal form not knowing that it contained the false statement in question and relying on the agent's statement that the policy would be legal. The Industrial Assurance Commissioner held that the assured was entitled to recover the premiums which she had paid.[60]

8-20 Form of policy illegal. In a Canadian case it was held that where a life policy was void by reason of the name of the person for whose benefit it was made not being inserted in the policy, the assured was entitled to recover the premiums paid. The parties, said the court, were not *in pari delicto* since there was no improper conduct on the part of the assured, who had fully disclosed the facts, and the sole fault was on the part of the company in issuing an irregular policy.[61]

8-21 Insured ignorant of relevant facts. If the assured contracted in ignorance of the facts which made the insurance illegal, he is entitled to a return of premium if the insurers repudiate the policy on the ground of the illegality.[62] In these cases a state of facts is reasonably believed to exist which, if it does, makes the insurance legal.

Where a company carrying on business in Northern Ireland had made the

[58] *White v. Pearl Ass. Co.* [1933] I.A.C.Rep. 31.
[59] *McGeown v. Refuge Friendly Soc.* [1931] I.A.C.(N.I.)Rep. 44.
[60] *Whitworth v. Pearl Life Ass. Co.* [1927] I.A.C.Rep. 26.
[61] *Dowker v. Canada Life Ass. Co.* (1865) 24 U.C.Q.B. 591.
[62] *Oom v. Bruce* (1810) 12 East 225; *Cousins v. Nantes* (1811) 3 Taunt. 513, 515; *Hentig v. Staniforth* (1816) 5 M. & S. 122. The rule was referred to in *Re Cavalier Ins. Co. Ltd* [1989] 2 Lloyd's Rep. 430, but was not the basis of the decision in that case.

necessary deposit of £20,000 to entitle it to carry on industrial assurance business there, but had not made an additional deposit of £20,000 in respect of ordinary life assurance business and it issued a policy on a form applicable to industrial assurance business, but the terms of which constituted an ordinary branch policy, the Industrial Assurance Commissioner held that the policy was illegal. As the assured was not aware of the illegality, he was entitled to a return of the premiums. The decision would appear to be correct on general principles, but as the policy was not an industrial policy it may be questioned whether the Commissioner had jurisdiction in the matter or whether he was right in dealing with the case as one covered by section 5 of the Industrial Assurance Act (Northern Ireland) 1924.[63]

8–22 Contract wholly executory. The general rule applicable to illegal contracts is that if either party desires to cancel the contract while it is still executory, that is, when nothing has been done to carry out the illegal purpose, he may do so and claim a return of any consideration paid by him, provided that the non-performance is due to the plaintiff's abandonment of his illegal purpose and not to the operation of external circumstances.[64] The soundness of the rule has been doubted,[65] and it is, perhaps, not very logical, but it offers an inducement to the wrongdoer to repent before it is too late, and a long series of decisions have placed the recognition of the rule beyond dispute.[66] In the majority of insurances which are illegal for want of insurable interest, the rule has no application, since those insurances are not only illegal under the insurance statutes, but are void under the Gaming Acts as wagers, and any claim for the return of money paid in respect of a wager is expressly disallowed by these Acts.[67] But in other classes of illegal insurance the rule applies, and it therefore becomes necessary to consider when the contract of insurance ceases to be executory, and becomes partly performed so as to bar the assured's claim to recovery of the premium. In one sense it may be said that the contract to insure is executed when the policy is issued,[68] and in another sense it may be said that the contract of insurance is not executed until either an event insured against happens or the risk has expired.[69] There is no very direct decision upon this point, but it is submitted that the contract is executory so long as the risk has not begun to run. As soon as the risk attaches, or would have attached but for the illegality, the contract is at least partly performed, and if the parties are *in pari delicto* the assured cannot recover the premium on the ground of illegality.[70]

---

[63] *McWilliams v. Northern Counties Life and General* [1930] I.A.C.(N.I.)Rep. 40. As to the position now in respect of unauthorised contracts, see para. 8–24, *post*.

[64] For the importance of the proviso, see *Bigos v. Bousted* [1951] 1 All E.R. 92.

[65] *Palyart v. Leckie* (1817) 6 M. & S. 290; *Kearly v. Thomson* (1890) 24 Q.B.D. 742. See Trietel, *The Law of Contract* (10th ed., 1999) p. 455.

[66] *Lowry v. Bourdieu* (1780) 2 Doug. K.B. 468, 471; *Tappenden v. Randall* (1801) 2 B. & P. 467; *Aubert v. Walsh* (1810) 3 Taunt. 277; *Taylor v. Bowers* (1876) 1 Q.B.D. 291; *Kearly v. Thomson* (*supra*); *Re National Benefit Ass. Co.* [1931] 1 Ch. 46.

[67] 8 & 9 Vict. c. 109. 55 & 56 Vict. c. 9. The provisions in the statutes against contracts "by way of gaming or wagering" will not touch insurances made by the assured in the belief, although a mistaken belief, that he has in fact an interest in the subject-matter. The position of such contracts was not affected by the Betting and Gaming Act 1960 (8 & 9 Eliz. 2, c. 60) or the Betting Gaming and Lotteries Acts 1963 to 1985.

[68] *Palyart v. Leckie* (1817) 6 M. & S. 290, 294.

[69] *Lowry v. Bourdieu* (1780) 2 Doug. K.B. 468, 471.

[70] *Herman v. Jeuchner* (1885) 15 Q.B.D. 561; *Alexander v. Rayson* [1936] 1 K.B. 169; and *Kettlewell v. Refuge* [1907] 2 K.B. 242; [1908] 1 K.B. 545.

8–23 Class-protecting statutes. In cases of statutory illegality the assured will be able to recover premium if it is clear that the statute was intended to protect assureds as a class from insurers so that the parties cannot be regarded as being *in pari delicto*. This principle was applied in *Re Cavalier Insurance Co.*[71] so as to enable consumer assureds to recover premium paid for extended warranty cover which was held to be illegal as a result of lack of authorisation of the insurer.

8–24 Statutory right of recovery. An insured who entered into a contract with an insurer who was not authorised under section 2 of the Insurance Companies Act 1982 was entitled, subject to certain qualifications, to recover premium pursuant to section 132(1) of the Financial Services Act 1986.[72] The insured has a similar right of recovery under section 26 of the Financial Services and Markets Act 2000, in relation to contracts made after that section came into force.

8–25 Illegal policy issued to infant. In certain circumstances an infant or minor may recover the premiums paid on a policy made without interest, or otherwise illegal, although an adult could not do so in the same circumstances. An illegal contract of insurance cannot be one for the infant's benefit even although he may have thought that he was entering into a profitable speculative transaction. For that reason, apart from any other, the contract is void and there is a total failure of consideration.[73] Further, the principle of *in pari delicto* cannot be applied as between an adult and an infant who has had no proper advice. An improvident contract entered into by an infant without independent advice will be set aside at any time, and delay in making the claim after attaining majority will not necessarily be a bar to the claim, because the contract is void and not merely voidable.[74] The Industrial Assurance Commissioner held that a policy without interest effected by an infant, aged 18, on the life of his uncle could be repudiated by him at the age of 37 and all the premiums paid by him recovered.[75] The company had never been on the risk and the infant had received no benefit from it.[76]

8–26 Supervening illegality of risk. Where the insurance is legal in its inception, but subsequently becomes illegal, as when war breaks out between the states of which the insurer and insured are respectively subjects, the insurer is not liable to return any part of the premium because he has been on the risk, and according to the general rule has thereby earned the whole premium.[77]

---

[71] [1989] 2 Lloyd's Rep. 430.
[72] Insurance contracts which fall within the definition of investment business under the 1986 Act, *i.e.* most forms of life insurance, are governed by s.5 of the 1986 Act which is to the same effect.
[73] *R. v. Lord* (1848) 12 Q.B. 757; *De Francesco v. Barnum* (1890) 45 Ch.D. 430; *Bromley v. Smith* [1909] 2 K.B. 235; *Flower v. London and North Western Ry* [1894] 2 Q.B. 65; *Clements v. London and North Western Ry* [1894] 2 Q.B. 482
[74] *Kempson v. Ashbee* (1874) L.R. 10 Ch.App. 15.
[75] *Gardner v. Hearts of Oak* (1928) I.A.C.Rep. 21.
[76] *Corpe v. Overton* (1833) 10 Bing. 252. *Hamilton v. Vaughan Sherrin Electrical Engineering Co.* [1894] 3 Ch. 589; *Steinberg v. Scala (Leeds) Ltd* [1923] 2 Ch. 452.
[77] *Furtado v. Rogers* (1802) 3 B. & P. 191; *Oom v. Bruce* (1810) 12 East 225, 227.

3. OTHER MATTERS AFFECTING RETURN OF PREMIUM

8–27 Application by insurers to cancel illegal policy. It has been held in Canada that where a company had insured in the belief that the assured had an insurable interest, and subsequently during the currency of the risk discovered that he had no such interest, it might apply to the court for cancellation of the contract, and was not bound to return the premium where the policy amounted to an illegal wagering contract.[78]

8–28 Policy obtained by fraud. There is some conflict of authority as to whether premiums are returnable where the insurers prove fraud on the part of the assured. In an early case of life insurance,[79] where at the suit of the insurers the Court of Chancery ordered the policy to be delivered up on the ground of fraud with full costs to the plaintiffs, the reporter states that the moneys received by way of premium were ordered to be applied in part payment of the costs. The actual decree, however, in this case is silent as to the premium. In a marine insurance case[80] Lord Macclesfield set aside the policy on the ground that the assured had not disclosed the fact that he had, at the time he proposed the insurance, information which induced him to have grave doubts as to the safety of his vessel. The decree was that the policy be delivered up with costs, and that the premium be paid back and allowed out of the costs. Those two Chancery cases, neither of which as reported is satisfactory, were apparently accepted in the Court of Chancery as binding authority for the proposition that where the insurers came to a court of equity for cancellation the premium should be returned even if the policy were cancelled on the ground of the fraud of the assured.

8–29 In an early case at common law,[81] where a marine policy was found by a jury to have been obtained by fraud, the underwriters having been induced to subscribe the policy by the signature of a "decoy duck" heading the subscriptions, Lord Mansfield ordered a return of premiums, but in a later case,[82] where when he effected the insurance the assured knew that his ship was lost, the same judge held that "the fraud was so gross that the premium should not be recovered from the underwriter." This was followed by a decision of the whole Court of King's Bench,[83] to the effect that in all cases where there was actual fraud on the part either of the assured or of his agent, the assured cannot recover the premiums which he has paid. That decision appears to have been generally followed at common law,[84] though

---

[78] *Brophy v. N. American Life Ass. Co.* (1902) 32 S.C.R. 261.
[79] *Whittingham v. Thornburgh* (1690) 2 Vern. 206.
[80] *Da Costa v. Scandret* (1723) 2 P.Wms. 170.
[81] *Wilson v. Ducket* (1762) 3 Burr. 1361. But the case was decided on the basis that the insurer was bound by a tender of premium.
[82] *Tyler v. Horne* (1785) Park (8th ed.) p. 456.
[83] *Chapman v. Fraser* (1793) Park (8th ed.) p. 456.
[84] *Feise v. Parkinson* (1812) 4 Taunt. 640, 641; *Anderson v. Thornton* (1853) 8 Exch. 425, 427; *Anderson v. Fitzgerald* (1853) H.L.Cas. 484, 508; *Fowkes v. Manchester etc. Association* (1863) 3 B. & S.917, 927; *Rivaz v. Gerussi* (1880) 6 Q.B.D. 222, 230; *British Equitable Ins. Co. v. Musgrave* (1887) 3 T.L.R. 630; Marine Insurance Act 1906, s.84(1). See also *Prince of Wales etc. Association v. Palmer* (1858) 25 Beav. 605, where a forfeited premium was applied to meet costs in a case of what appeared to be fraudulent mis-statement.

not without dissent in the 19th century.[85] It may be supported on the grounds that the assured may not be heard to rely upon his own fraud or wrongdoing in order to claim a benefit of relief,[86] just as we have seen he cannot plead the illegality of his contract in order to claim back premiums,[87] unless the insurers or their agent fraudulently stated that the policy was valid and legal.[88]

8–30 Whether fraud is always a bar to return of premiums has not been discussed in modern case-law. In marine insurance there is no return of premium in the case of fraud on the part of the assured where there has been either a total failure of consideration or an avoidance of the policy by the insurer.[89] In non-marine insurance there have been tentative expressions of opinion in favour of,[90] and against,[91] return of premium in the case of avoidance for fraud. While a claim by the assured for a return of premium might be defeated on the ground that he was driven to rely upon his own fraud, it is arguable that the insurer cannot seek the equitable remedy of rescission without offering to make restitution by tendering a return to premium.[92] It seems unsatisfactory, however, that the insurers' liability to return the premium in the case of fraud by the assured should turn on the nature of the action in which the issue arises. The courts are more likely to apply the marine insurance principle in a non-marine context, on the ground that insurance is a contract of utmost good faith and this justifies an exception from the general equitable requirement of restitution as a precondition of rescission.

8–31 Misrepresentation by insurers' agent. The effect of an illegal policy has already been discussed. If the insured has been induced to effect an insurance by reason of a fraudulent misrepresentation of fact or law made by the insurers or their agent to him he can claim rescission and return of premiums.[93]

8–32 An unscrupulous agent may make a false and fraudulent representation to a person whom he canvasses for a policy as to the benefits which the policy will secure and even although the incorrectness of the statement would have been apparent on an examination of the policy, yet if the insured

---

[85] *Anderson v. Fitzgerald* (1853) 4 H.L.Cas. 508, 510; *Fowkes v. Manchester etc. Association* (1863) 3 B. & S. 917, 929; *Desborough v. Curlewis* (1838) 3 Y. & C. 175, 178. The pre-1873 equity cases are examined in *Brophy v. N. American Life Ins. Co.* (1902) 32 S.C.R. 261.

[86] See note 91, *infra*.

[87] *Langhorn v. Cologan* (1812) 4 Taunt. 330; *Harse v. Pearl Life Ass. Co.* [1904] 1 K.B. 558; *Phillips v. Royal London Mut. Ins. Co.* (1911) 105 L.T. 136; *Elson v. Crookes* (1911) 106 L.T. 462; Marine Insurance Act, 1906, s.84(1).

[88] *British Workman's and General Assurance Co. v. Cunliffe* (1902) 18 T.L.R. 425, 502; *Hughes v. Liverpool Victoria Legal Friendly Society* [1916] 2 K.B. 482.

[89] Marine Insurance Act 1906, s.84(1) and s.84(3)(a).

[90] *Biggar v. Rock Life Ass. Co.* [1902] 1 K.B. 516, 526.

[91] *Joel v. Law Union and Crown Ins. Co.* [1908] 2 K.B. 431, 440.

[92] In the older case of *Barker v. Walters* (1844) 8 Beav. 92, 96 the court was not sure whether the tender of premium was a necessary precondition to the exercise of the equitable jurisdiction, but the Canadian Supreme Court thought it was in *Brophy v. N. American Life Ass. Co.* (1902) 32 S.C.R. 261, 270, 276. See *Spence v. Crawford* [1939] 3 All E.R. 271, in which the presence of fraud is said to be material to the defendant's plea for restitution of benefit.

[93] *Hughes v. Liverpool Victoria Legal Friendly Society* [1916] 2 K.B. 482 and the earlier decisions concerning illegal policies cited at notes 41–44 in this chapter, *supra*. For fraudulent and innocent misrepresentation generally, see Ch. 16, *post*.

is an illiterate or uneducated person and was in fact induced by the statement to take the policy, he may recover the premiums which he has paid on it notwithstanding that the incorrectness of the statement was not discovered by him nor action taken until a considerable time later.[94] In an Irish case an agent of an assurance society procured the assured to effect a policy on his own life by the false and fraudulent representation that on payment of the first premium he could obtain from the society a loan of £100 on the security of the policy. It was held that although the representation made by the agent was *ultra vires* and outside the scope of the agent's authority, that did not affect the right of the assured to rescind the contract and recover from the society the money which it had received under it. The society could not repudiate the agent's authority and at the same time keep the money obtained by his fraud.[95]

8–33 In the case of *Kettlewell v. Refuge Assurance Company*[96] the assured was induced to continue paying her premiums on a life policy on the false representation of the agent that in five years she would become entitled to a paid-up policy. After paying the premiums for four years she discovered the fraud, and sued the insurers for a return of the premiums paid. The Court of Appeal held that she was entitled to have the premiums returned. Two of the judges based their decision on the ground that she was entitled to have the contract rescinded. Buckley L.J., on the other hand, thought that it was too late to rescind after the insurers had been on the risk, but he agreed with the decision on the ground that money obtained by the fraud of the company's agent could not be retained by the company against the person defrauded. The House of Lords affirmed the decision of the Court of Appeal without comment upon the difference of opinion in that court.[97]

If the opinion expressed by Buckley L.J. in the above case is right, that is to say, that there can be no rescission after the company has been on the risk, then it would seem to follow that an assured cannot recover premiums paid upon a policy induced by the innocent misrepresentation of the insurer or its agent.[98] It is submitted that the view taken by the majority of the Court of Appeal is to be preferred, and, if so, a claim for return of premiums can be made on the ground of the insurers' misrepresentation, whether innocent or fraudulent, and this view is supported by other decisions, and particularly by the decision of the House of Lords in *Mutual Reserve Life v. Foster.*[99]

---

[94] *Mutual Reserve Life Ins. Co. v. Foster* (1904) 20 T.L.R. 715 (principle applicable to misrepresentations generally. For a slightly barbed tribute to the argument of losing counsel, see *per* Lord Lindley at p. 717); *Brown v. Pearl Life Ass. Co.* [1930] I.A.C.Rep. 36; *McCabe v. Northern Counties Life and General Ins. Co.* [1930] I.A.C.(N.I.)Rep.

[95] *Byrne v. Rudd* [1920] 2 Ir.R. 12.

[96] [1908] 1 K.B. 545, affirming the Divisional Court at [1907] 2 K.B. 242. The lower court's decision seems to be grounded on reasoning similar to that of the majority in the C.A., although Phillimore J. at one point puts the plaintiff's claim in quasi-contrast: p. 245.

[97] [1909] A.C. 243.

[98] Buckley L.J.'s view does not, with respect, represent the law; see *Spence v. Crawford* [1939] 3 All E.R. 271 (H.L.); *Duffell v. Wilson* (1808) 1 Camp. 401; *Cross v. Mutual Reserve Life Ins. Co.* (1904) 21 T.L.R. 15 (a decision of Buckley J. himself); *Merino v. Mutual Reserve Life Ins. Co.* (1904) 21 T.L.R. 167; *Molloy v. Mutual Reserve Life Ins. Co.* (1905) 22 T.L.R. 59. In the *Mutual Reserve* cases, which instance a dogged persistence on the defendants' part, contracts of insurance were rescinded at equity for misrepresentation after the company had been on the risk for some years, and the sole issue of real contention was *laches*.

[99] (1904) 20 T.L.R. 715. The decisions in *Angers v. Mutual Reserve Fund Life Ass. Co.* (1904) 35 S.C.R. 330 and *Tomlinson v. Britannic Ass. Co.* [1927] I.A.C.Rep. 24 do not represent the English law correctly.

8–34 Complicity or fault of assured. The maintenance of the assured's claim for a return of premiums is rendered much more complicated when his own conduct is not beyond reproach, and the consequences of such conduct have been examined in some North American decisions which afford guidance on the point. If the assured is a willing party to a fraud practised on the insurers by their own agent, as where a man crippled with rheumatism warrants in a declaration that he is free from any such disease, he cannot later set up the fraud of the agent as a cause for rescission of the policy and recovery of premiums.[1] It has been suggested in a Canadian decision,[2] moreover, that if the assured is ignorant of a fraud perpetrated by the agent to secure a policy, but, upon discovery of it later, acquiesces in the fraud by paying premiums on the policy so obtained, he loses his right to demand rescission of the policy for the agent's fraud. In such cases the assured is bound to perform his part of the contract if the company elects to affirm it with knowledge of the fraud.[3]

8–35 An assured whose claim for the policy moneys is defeated by a breach of warranty due to the agent's fraud, but which he could have prevented if he had perused the application form completed by the agent before signing it, may, it seems, maintain an action in quasi-contract for the recovery of premiums upon discovering what had been done by the agent,[4] but he could not maintain such an action if his conduct was also fraudulent and not merely negligent.[5] US decisions also hold that an assured who is entirely innocent in respect of a fraud perpetrated by the agent on the insurers to secure acceptance of the proposal may demand a return of premiums if the company cancels the policy for breach of warranty,[6] and that the assured, if induced to enter into the insurance by fraudulent statements by the agent, may rescind the contract and claim back premiums paid.[7]

8–36 Rescission by insured. As misrepresentation or non-disclosure does not make a contract void, but merely voidable at the option of the other party, the insured cannot claim rescission and return of premiums where he himself was at fault but the insurer elects to treat the insurance as valid and

---

[1] *Palmer v. Metropolitan Life Ins. Co.*, 21 Hun. 287 (N.Y.App.Div., 1897); *Fisher v. Same*, 160 Mass. 386 (1894); *Malhoit v. Same*, 87 Me. 374 (1895); *Lewis v. Phoenix Mutual Life Ins. Co.*, 3 9 Conn. 100 (1872).

[2] *Wakeman v. Metropolitan Life Ins. Co.* (1899) 30 Ont.R. 705, following, on acquiescence, *Robinson v. Gleadow* (1835) 2 Bing.N.C. 156; *French v. Backhouse* (1771) 5 Burr. 2727.

[3] For a valiant attempt by the assured to set up a fraudulent misrepresentation of law by the insurers *subsequent* to the conclusion of the contract, see *Palmer v. Metropolitan Life Ins. Co.*, *supra*.

[4] *New York Mutual Life Ins. Co. v. Fletcher*, 117 U.S. 579 (1885), very much *obiter dicta*; followed in *Biggar v. Rock Life Ass. Co.* [1902] 1 K.B. 516, 526 (*obiter*).

[5] *Lewis v. Phoenix Mutual Life Ins. Co.*, 39 Conn. 100 (1872). The reason given, however, that there was no failure of consideration, is insupportable, and the case must be upheld on the other ground given, that the assured was a party to the agent's fraud and could not counter-claim for a return of premiums alleging his own fraud.

[6] *Miller v. Union Central Life Ins. Co.*, 86 Hun. 6 (N.Y.S.C., 1895). The court did not advert to the fact that the assured had signed the proposal form wrongly filled in by the company's medical adviser, but the decision seems to follow the *obiter dicta* expressed in *Fletcher*'s case, *supra*.

[7] *Fisher v. Metropolitan Life Ins. Co.*, 160 Mass. 3867 (1894); *Rohrschneider v. Knickerbocker Life Ins. Co.*, N.Y. Rpts (Appeals) 216 (1879).

subsisting.[8] By the same token the assured cannot of his own motion claim a rescission of the policy and return of premium on the ground that he has broken his own warranty and that accordingly the risk has never attached. Even although the policy is declared to be null and void in the event of a breach the insurer may waive the breach, and if he does so he earns the premium. In the US, however, it was held that where the assured had an interest in property as mortgagee, but was not sole and unconditional owner as warranted, he could, after the period of risk had expired without loss, claim a return of premium on the ground that the insurance was void *ab initio*.[9]

8–37 Premiums paid by mistake. Premiums paid by a stranger to the contract under a mistake of fact[10] may be recovered by the party who has so paid them, as where the holder of a policy on the life of her grandfather for funeral expenses had married and gone to Canada and her sister thereafter paid the premiums in the mistaken belief that the holder had abandoned all claims to the policy in her favour, and, when a claim came to be made, would be ready and willing to facilitate payment to her of the sum assured. The Commissioner for Northern Ireland held that the premiums paid by the sister were payments made under a mistake of fact which she was entitled to recover.[11] Similarly, payments made under a fundamental mutual mistake as to the rights of the parties may be recovered. In a case before the Industrial Assurance Commissioner in 1958 the claimant recovered premiums paid by her since 1947. Down to 1955, the payments had been made under the erroneous supposition, common to both parties, that they were due under policies then current and effective, which the Commissioner held were not effective until that date because of non-delivery; after that date, they were made by the claimant under a mistake as to her rights innocently induced by the society.[12]

Where at the request of the society's agent and on his assurance that it would be all right, a third party paid the premiums on the own-life policy of another and afterwards continued to pay the premiums in the belief that she was the nominee under a valid nomination which was in fact invalid, but was represented to her to be valid by the society's district manager, she was held entitled to a return of the premiums paid by her as money paid on a consideration which had failed, *i.e.* the supposed contractual obligation of the society to pay her as nominee.[13]

8–38 Wrongful repudiation by insurers. If while the risk is still current the insurers wrongfully repudiate the validity of the contract, the assured may

---

[8] *Bunyon on Life Insurance* (5th ed., 1914), p. 113; *Fisher v. Metropolitan Life Ins. Co.*, 160 Mass. 386 (1894); *Palmer v. Metropolitan Life Ins. Co.*, 21 Hun. 287 (N.Y.App.Div., 1897); *Malhoit v. Metropolitan Life Ins. Co.*, 87 Me. 374 (1895); *Wakeman v. Metropolitan Life Ins. Co.* (1899) 30 Ont.R. 705. This rule is perhaps an illustration of the general principle that no man may rely upon his own unlawful act to claim relief or a benefit: *New Zealand Shipping Co. v. Société des Ateliers et Chantiers de France* [1919] A.C. 1.

[9] *Waller v. Northern Ins. Co.*, 64 Iowa 101 (1884).

[10] Sums paid under a mistake of law are now also potentially recoverable: *Kleinwort Benson v. Lincoln City Council* [1999] 2 A.C. 349.

[11] *Montgomery v. Refuge Ass. Co.* [1929] I.A.C.(N.I.)Rep. 53.

[12] *Hands v. Wesleyan and General* [1958] I.A.C.Rep. 2.

[13] *Baines v. National Friendly Collecting Society* [1938] I.A.C. Rep. 20.

either enforce the contract in due course or treat the repudiation as a final breach and sue for a return of premiums as damages for breach of contract.[14]

If the assured intends to treat the repudiation as a final breach he must give notice within a reasonable time after the act of repudiation and where the assured did nothing for 11 months after the insurers had refused to accept a renewal premium, it was held that it was too late for the assured to sue for a return of premiums.[15]

The repudiation by the company of collateral agreements may be sufficient to entitle the assured to cancel the policy. Where the contract of insurance and the collateral contract form part of one entire transaction, the company cannot repudiate the one and insist on the validity of the other. Thus, where the agent of an insurance company promised to lend money to an intending borrower and he insured his life with the company as part security for the loan, it was held that if the company afterwards refused to advance the money, the assured might cancel the policy and recover the premiums paid.[16] Where an agent promised that the company would pay the surrender value of old policies if the assured took out a new one which the assured did, it was held that if the company repudiated the agent's promise the assured might rescind the policy.[17] But where a collateral agreement is wholly independent of the insurance, as where the assured was appointed medical officer of the company, the cancellation of his appointment as such did not entitle him to rescind the insurance and recover the premiums.[18]

8–39 Return of rateable proportion in marine insurance. In marine insurance the underwriter is bound to return a rateable proportion of the premium when, by reason of accidental over-valuation, short interest, or double insurance, the underwriter has never been on the risk to the full amount insured.[19] No such rule, however, seems to have been established in the case of fire and similar risks. In most cases the express conditions of the policy would preclude any claim for return of premium on such grounds, but even where there are no such conditions the rule in marine insurance would not be extended to other classes of risk in the absence of any custom or practice to return a proportion of the premium in cases of over-insurance. The nearest approach to the application of such a principle in life cases is the practice of returning an additional premium paid in respect of a licence to go beyond the limits of the risk where in fact the life assured has not availed himself of the licence.[20] It is common in motor insurance for the insurer to return a part of the premium if, during the currency of the policy, the insured intimates that he no longer requires insurance, has substituted a cheaper

---

[14] *Brewster v. National Life Ins. Soc.* (1892) 8 T.L.R. 648; *McCall v. Phoenix Mutual Life Ins. Co.*, 9 W.Va. 237 (1876) (this decision does not represent the English law as to imputed knowledge, the other point in the case); *American Life Ins. Co. v. McAden*, 109 Pa. 399 (1885); *Fischer v. Hope Mutual Life Ins. Co.* (1877) 69 N.Y. 161; *Van Werden v. Assurance Co.*, 99 Iowa 621 (1896).

[15] *Howland v. Continental Life Ins. Co.*, 121 Mass. 499 (1877).

[16] *Key v. National Life*, 107 Iowa 446 (1899).

[17] *Harnickell v. New York Life Ins. Co.* (1888) 111 N.Y. 390. No contract was thus concluded, but the principle is the same.

[18] *Labergé v. Equitable Life Ass. Co.* (1895) 24 S.C.R. 595.

[19] *Fisk v. Masterman* (1841) 8 M. & W. 165; Marine Insurance Act 1906, s.84(3)(e)(f).

[20] *Bunyon on Life Insurance* (5th ed., 1914), p. 113. Premiums continued in ignorance of the death of the life assured should be returned by the office without any deduction for expenses: *Cash v. Liverpool Victoria F.S.* [1925] I.A.C.Rep. 26.

vehicle for the one originally insured, or has moved to an area where a lower premium rate is applicable. It may be that such repayments are made *ex gratia*. There is at all events no authority for the existence of an enforceable practice or custom.

8–40 Claim barred by Statute of Limitation. Claims for the return of premium may be barred by the Limitation Act 1980 if no action is brought within six years after the cause of action arose.[21] Where the contract is illegal, or where there is no contract at all, for want of agreement or because there was a mutual mistake, or where the assured may set aside the contract on the ground of misrepresentation by the insurers, the cause of action arises when each premium is paid, and, therefore, premiums which were paid more than six years before the action is brought cannot be recovered, except where the assured can rely upon a postponement of the limitation period in cases of fraud, concealment or mistake.[22] Where the insurance is voidable by the insurer on the ground of misrepresentation or breach of warranty by the assured, the cause of action does not arise until the insurer has elected to avoid the contract.[23] If therefore the assured has, in the circumstances, any right at all to recover his premiums such right is not barred in whole or in part until six years after the insurer has elected to avoid.

8–41 Receipt of premium. Where an action is brought for return of premium the acknowledgement of the receipt of the premium in a policy properly executed under the seal of the insurers is said to be conclusive evidence of payment of the premium.[24]

8–42 Restoration of policy. Where a return of premium has been made, the policy is cancelled and the assured cannot afterwards have the benefit of it. Error in law does not entitle the assured to have the policy restored;[25] but, on the other hand, if the premium was returned on a mutual mistake of the facts upon which the validity of the policy depended the assured might, even after loss, claim to have the policy restored.[26]

8–43 Cancellation by statutory notice. An assured under a long-term policy who avails himself of a statutory right to serve a cancellation notice may be able to recover any sum which he has paid by way of premium or otherwise to the insurer or his agent, subject to the provisions of the relevant cancellation rules.

8–44 Amount of premium returned to assured. One question which does not appear to have been considered in the English authorities is whether the premium refunded to the assured should be a gross sum or a sum net of commission deducted by the assured's broker. On one view, the appropriate refund would be the net amount since that would be the sum which had been received by underwriters as consideration for undertaking the insured risk.

---

[21] s.5.
[22] s.32.
[23] *Bunyon on Life Insurance* (5th ed., 1914), p. 113.
[24] *Dalzell v. Mair* (1808) 1 Camp. 532; *Anderson v. Thornton* (1853) 8 Exch. 425, 428; see, however, *Roberts v. Security Co.* [1897] 1 Q.B. 111, 115, where it was said that such an acknowledgment would not bar an action for the premium by the insurers.
[25] *May v. Christie* (1815) Holt N.P. 67.
[26] *Reyner v. Hall* (1813) 4 Taunt. 725.

Whether the assured would also be able to recover the commission from the broker would depend in the particular circumstances upon whether the broker could be said to have earned commission in placing a contract which later transpired to be voidable or void. An alternative view is that the assured is entitled to a refund of the gross amount of premium from the underwriter, but the underwriter could then face difficulties in formulating a claim over against the broker for the sum representing the commission which had been allowed to the broker. The former approach is perhaps preferable since it reflects the distinction between a claim for repayment of premium and a claim for repayment of commission. However, the correct approach in any particular case may depend on the accounting arrangements adopted by the parties.

8–45 The matter may be resolved by reference to the terms of the particular policy. In the case of marine insurances incorporating the Institute Time Clauses (Hulls) and (Freight) 1995, it is provided that, if the cover is cancelled by agreement, premium will be returned pro rata monthly net of commission for each uncommenced month of cover. In *Velos Group Ltd v. Harbour Insurance Services Ltd*[27] premium was payable in instalments. The insurance was cancelled in mid term. The insurers returned premium to the assured via placing brokers. The broker retained a sum equivalent to their commission on outstanding instalments. The assured sought recovery of the amount deducted. It was held that the claim failed. The brokers earned the total commission when the risk was placed. They were entitled to deduct outstanding commission from monies received from insurers before accounting for the balance to the assured. Under the ITC (Hulls) the entitlement was to a return of premium net of commission, whatever the overall entitlement to commission might be.

---

[27] [1997] 2 Lloyd's Rep. 461.

CHAPTER 9

SALVAGE PREMIUMS

9–1 Premium paid by third person. Frequently, where a person beneficially entitled to a life policy is unable or unwilling to continue the
payment of the premiums, some other person steps in and, either for his own
benefit or for the benefit of the person who has failed to pay, pays the
premiums and so keeps the policy on foot. Where the person beneficially
entitled or his representative finally reaps the benefit of a policy which has
been kept alive in this way, the question arises whether he is not under a legal
as well as a moral obligation to repay out of the policy moneys the amount of
the premiums to the person who paid them to the insurers, and so saved the
policy.

9–2 Voluntary payment by stranger. Apart from any contractual relationship between the parties, it has been contended that a mere stranger who has
saved the policy by paying the premiums is entitled to claim at least
repayment out of the policy moneys on the grounds: (a) that as a salvor he is
entitled to a lien for salvage remuneration[1]; (b) that the assured having
adopted his acts and taken the fruits of his payments, he is entitled to a lien
for his disbursements.[2]

It has been held, however, that the doctrine of salvage is peculiar to
maritime law and cannot be extended to cases of this kind,[3] and that the
doctrine of adoption is not applicable to the case of a man enforcing his own
contract or using his own property even although incidentally he thereby
reaps the benefit of the uninvited expenditure or labours of another in
respect thereof.[4] A stranger, therefore, who steps in uninvited and by paying
the premiums keeps on foot a policy which but for his intervention would
have lapsed, not only has no direct claim on the policy moneys but has no
right to recover the premiums either personally against the assured or by
way of lien on the policy.[5] The mere fact that he thought he had a beneficial
interest in the policy does not place him in any better position.[6]

---

[1] See *Shearman v. British Empire Mutual Life* (1872) L.R. 14 Eq. 4; *Re Tharp* (1852) 2 Sm. &
Giff. 578n.
[2] See *Busteed v. West of England* (1857) 5 Ir.Ch.R. 553.
[3] *Falcke v. Scottish Imperial* (1886) 34 Ch.D. 234; *Re Leslie* (1883) 23 Ch.D. 552.
[4] *Falcke v. Scottish Imperial* (1886) 34 Ch.D. 234.
[5] *Falcke v. Scottish Imperial* (1886) 34 Ch.D. 234; *Re Leslie* (1883) 23 Ch.D. 552; *Clack v.
Holland* (1854) 19 Beav. 262; *Burridge v. Row* (1842) 1 Y. & C.Ch. 183; *Re Jones Settlement*
[1915] 1 Ch. 373; *Fidelity Trust Co. v. Fenwick* (1921) 51 Ont.L.R. 23 (Can.).
[6] *Re Winn* (1887) 57 L.T. 382; *Urquhart v. Butterfield* (1887) 37 Ch.D. 357; *Montgomery v.
Scottish Legal Life* [1936] I.A.C.(N.I.) Rep. 19; *Diamond v. Refuge Ass. Co.* [1928] I.A.C.(N.I.)
Rep. 35.

9–3 Officer of the court. Although the voluntary payment of premiums creates no legal claim against the person who takes the benefit of the policy, he may be under a moral obligation, and accordingly when the person taking such benefit is an officer of the court, such as a trustee in bankruptcy, the court will not permit him to retain money which morally belongs to someone else.[7] Thus, where a trustee in bankruptcy claims a policy of the bankrupt, the court has in certain cases ordered the repayment of premiums which have even after the date of the bankruptcy been paid by a third person to keep the policy on foot.[8] But where, in the case of a policy on joint lives payable to the survivor of husband and wife on the death of the predeceasing spouse, the husband became bankrupt and the wife paid the premiums to protect her own contingent interest, it was held on her death in the lifetime of her husband that the trustee in bankruptcy was entitled to the policy money and that the wife's estate was not entitled to be reimbursed the amount of the premiums paid by her.[9]

9–4 Payment at request of insured. If a person beneficially entitled to the policy moneys requests another to pay the premiums on his behalf, he, by implication, promises to repay the amount so advanced.[10] The transaction is presumed to be a loan and not a gift, and the insured is under a personal obligation to repay the loan.

9–5 Implied promise to refund. A promise to repay may sometimes be implied from slight circumstances,[11] and this inference may the more easily be drawn where small industrial policies are concerned.[12] Knowledge and acquiescence in the fact that the premiums are being paid by another for the assured's benefit is generally sufficient to raise the inference that the assured accepts the payments as being made on his behalf and impliedly promises to repay them.[13] In *Falcke v. Scottish Imperial* Bowen L.J. said:

> "wherever you find that the owner of the property saved knew of the service being performed you will have to ask yourself, and the question will become one of fact, whether, under all circumstances, there was what the law calls an implied contract for repayment or a contract which would give rise to a lien."[14]

9–6 Presumption of advancement. Where the premiums are paid by the husband or parent of the assured, there is a presumption of advancement and that the premiums were intended as a gift to the assured and not as a loan. Where a father effected a policy on the life of his son payable on the son's death to the father, his executors, administrators, or assigns as trustees for the life assured, and the premiums were paid by the father until his death and thereafter by the trustees of his will until the death of the life assured, it was held that the premiums paid by the father were paid by way of

---

[7] *Re Tyler* [1907] 1 K.B. 865; *Schondler v. Wace* (1808) 1 Camp. 487.
[8] *ibid.*
[9] *Rogerson v. Refuge Life Ass.* [1937] I.A.C.Rep. 6.
[10] *Falcke v. Scottish Imperial* (1886) 34 Ch.D. 234, *per* Cotton L.J. at 241, *per* Fry L.J. at 252.
[11] *Falcke v. Scottish Imperial* (1886) 34 Ch.D. 234, *per* Cotton L.J. at 241.
[12] *Davidson v. Refuge* [1955] I.A.C.Rep. 5; *Thomas v. Royal London Mutual* [1958] I.A.C.Rep. 7.
[13] *Re Power's Policies* [1899] 1 Ir.R. 6; *Re Walker* (1893) 68 L.T. 517; *Drew v. Pearl* [1940] I.A.C. (1938–49) Rep. 31.
[14] 34 Ch.D. 234, 248.

advancement and that there was no lien on the policy for the repayment of these to his estate. The premiums paid by the trustees after his death, however, were not paid by way of advancement and the trustees were entitled to be recouped out of the policy money the premiums which they had paid to preserve the property of the trust.[15]

9–7 Lien on policy. It has been suggested[16] that a request to pay the premiums not only gives rise to a personal obligation on the part of the assured, but also creates a charge upon the policy moneys, so that the person who pays the premiums can follow the policy into the hands of assignees, and when the policy moneys become due can insist on the payment of his debt in priority to other creditors or to any claimants on the fund. It is submitted, however, that a bare request and express or implied promise to repay the premiums advanced do not in themselves create a charge on the policy,[17] but that there may be circumstances from which it can be implied that the parties intended to create not merely a personal obligation but a charge.[18] In an industrial assurance case the Industrial Assurance Commissioner thought that the retention by the assured's wife of the premium receipt book, without production of which the company would not pay a claim, was sufficient to create a lien on the policy in her favour for the premiums which she paid at her husband's request when he became financially embarrassed.[19] On the other hand, the Industrial Assurance Commissioner for Northern Ireland has held that delivery of the policy to a stranger, coupled with the request that he pay the premiums, does not by itself justify the inference of an intention to create a charge on the policy moneys in his favour.[20] If, however, the beneficial owner of a policy stands by and allows another to pay the premiums in the belief that he is the owner, and the beneficial owner knows that he pays in that belief and knows that he is wrong, equity will not allow the beneficial owner to profit by the other's mistake which he could have prevented, and therefore gives that other a charge upon the policy for the repayment of his outlay.[21] Payment in belief of ownership without full knowledge of the circumstances on the part of the true owner does not give rise to any right to have the premiums repaid.[22] But where all parties concerned have acted at all times under the mistaken belief that the policy belonged to the person paying the premiums and they were paid by him in accordance with an implied arrangement between them, he is entitled to a charge on the policy moneys for the premiums so paid.[23]

9–8 Payment of premium by party interested. It has sometimes been contended that one who has an interest in a policy as a part owner or

[15] *Re Roberts* [1946] Ch. 1.
[16] *Falcke v. Scottish Imperial* (1886) 34 Ch.D. 234, *per* Cotton L.J. at 241; *Diamond v. Refuge* [1928] I.A.C.(N.I.) Rep. 35; *Smith v. Pearl* [1924] I.A.C.Rep. 105.
[17] *Falcke v. Scottish Imperial* (1886) 34 Ch.D. 234, *per* Fry L.J. at 252. See as to Scots law *Wylie's Executrix v. McJannet* (1901) 4 F. 195.
[18] See *Cranston v. Prudential* [1927] I.A.C.Rep. 21.
[19] *Walker v. Prudential Ass. Co.* [1927] I.A.C.Rep. 21.
[20] *Johnson v. Prudential Ass. Co.* [1930] I.A.C.Rep. 58.
[21] *Falcke v. Scottish Imperial* (1886) 34 Ch.D. 234, *per* Cotton L.J. at 243; *Re Leslie* (1883) 23 Ch.D. 552, *per* Fry L.J. at 565.
[22] *Falcke v. Scottish Imperial* (1886) 34 Ch.D. 234.
[23] *Re Foster (No. 2)* (1938) 54 T.L.R. 1059; *Gibbs v. Pioneer Life* [1954] I.A.C.Rep. 8.

reversioner, and who pays the premiums in order to preserve his interest, acquires thereby a right of contribution against all others who are beneficially interested and a lien on the policy for their proportions of the premiums.[24]

The right of contribution, however, in respect of a voluntary payment is limited to tenants in common, joint tenants, and coparceners, and does not extend so as to be applicable as between those entitled to successive interests such as life-tenants and remaindermen.[25] One, therefore, who has an interest in the nature of a reversion or spes successionis in a policy of insurance has no right to indemnity on paying the premiums even although he never receives any benefit from the policy.[26] So where property which included a policy on the husband's life was settled upon trusts under which the wife had the first life interest, the husband covenanting to pay the premiums, and on the husband's death it appeared that the wife had expended a large sum in premiums to keep the policy on foot, it was held on the authority of *Re Leslie*[27] that she was not entitled to recoupment from the trustees.[28] A joint tenant or tenant in common who pays the premium has a right of action for a contribution against his co-owners, but except by contract he has no charge on the policy.[29] Such a contract, however, may be inferred where the payment has been made at the request of the other co-owner, and in such a case the co-owner who pays the premiums has a lien on the policy.[30]

In one case cited in the *Journal of the Institute of Actuaries* A mortgaged certain leaseholds and a policy on his own life to an insurance company. He assigned the equity of redemption of the leaseholds to B, but retained the equity to redeem the policy, and afterwards became bankrupt. The office informed B that if the premiums on the policy were not paid they would call in the loan. B accordingly paid the premiums and, on the policy being assigned to A's trustee in bankruptcy, claimed repayment of the premiums by the trustee. It was held by the Court of Appeal that as B had paid the premiums voluntarily as a stranger he had no claim.[31]

9–9 Payment by mortgagee. A mortgagee, however, is in a different position from other part owners. He holds the policy as security for a debt, and unless he had the power of paying the premiums and adding them to the charge, the security might be of little value. The mortgagee therefore is entitled to preserve his security by paying the premiums to keep the policy on foot, and if he does so he can add them to the charge.[32] It is doubtful whether the premiums can be recovered as a personal debt from the

---

[24] *Money v. Gibbs* (1837) 1 Dr. & Wal. 394.

[25] *Re Waugh's Trustees* (1877) 46 L.J.Ch. 629; but see as to Scots law *Morgan v. Morgan's Judicial Factor* [1922] S.L.T. 247.

[26] *Re Leslie* (1883) 23 Ch.D. 552; *Rogerson v. Refuge Ass. Co.* [1937] I.A.C.Rep. 6.

[27] *ibid.*

[28] *Re Jones's Settlement* [1915] 1 Ch. 373.

[29] *Re Leslie* (1883) 23 Ch.D. 552; *Teasdale v. Sanderson* (1864) 33 Beav. 534; *Kay v. Johnston* (1856) 21 Beav. 536; *Ex p. Young* (1813) 2 V. & B. 242; *Ex p. Harrison* (1814) 2 Rose 76; *Wood v. Birch*, Sug.V. & P. 700. Two cases contra (*Swan v. Swan* (1819) 8 Price 516 and *Hamilton v. Denny* (1809) 1 Ball & B. 199) were disapproved by Fry L.J. in the case of *Re Leslie, supra*, at 563.

[30] *Re McKerrell* [1912] 2 Ch. 648; *Rogerson v. Refuge* [1937] I.A.C.Rep. 6.

[31] *Journal of the Institute of Actuaries*, vol. 33, p. 392.

[32] *Gill v. Downing* (1874) L.R. 17 Eq. 316; *Aylwin v. Witty* (1861) 30 L.J.Ch. 860; *Drysdale v. Piggott* (1856) 8 De G.M. & G. 546; *Re City of Glasgow Life* (1914) 84 L.J.Ch. 684; *Shaw v. Scottish Widows' Fund* (1917) 87 L.J.Ch. 76.

mortgagor; but if the mortgagor has undertaken to pay the premiums, they can be recovered from him as damages for breach of contract. In one case where the mortgage of a policy and other property was set aside, it was held that the mortgagee who had for some years paid the premiums was entitled to a charge on the policy for the sums actually advanced by and owing to him, and for the premiums; but that he was not entitled to any personal remedy against the mortgagor in respect of the premiums. Therefore, if the mortgagor elected to abandon all claim to the policy, the mortgagee could not recover the amount of premiums paid, although considerably in excess of the value of the policy.[33]

9–10 Payment by mortgagor. A mortgagor who has not covenanted to keep up a mortgaged policy does not by voluntarily paying premiums to preserve his equity of redemption acquire thereby any right as against the mortgagee to repayment of such premiums out of the policy moneys.[34] Nor, prima facie, can any assignee of the equity of redemption claim repayment of premiums against the mortgagee, and consequently a second mortgagee having paid the premiums on a policy in order to preserve the security was not entitled to any charge in respect thereof in priority to the claim of the first mortgagee.[35] An assignee of the equity of redemption may have a right to be reimbursed in respect of premiums or other costs of preserving the security such as the costs of an action against the company, but whether he has or has not such right depends not on the bare fact that the mortgagee gets the benefit of his expenditure, but on special circumstances from which the inference may be drawn that there was an undertaking to repay.[36]

9–11 Payment by trustees. Trustees and other persons who hold a policy in a fiduciary capacity are entitled to preserve the policy for their beneficiaries, and to pay the premiums if the person who primarily ought to pay them fails to do so. Where a man effected a policy of assurance under section 11 of the Married Women's Property Act 1882 on his own life for the benefit of his wife absolutely and was the trustee of the policy under the Act, the premiums paid by him after the death of his wife were presumed to have been paid by him as trustee for the preservation of the trust property and his personal representative was held to be entitled to an indemnity in respect thereof out of the policy moneys payable on maturity.[37] And where a man effected a policy on the life of his son payable on the son's death to the assured, his executors, administrators or assigns as trustees for the life assured, and after the father's death the trustees of the father's will paid the premiums until the death of the son, it was held that they were entitled to recoup themselves out of the policy moneys received by them on the son's death.[38]

9–12 Trustees ought to pay the premiums from trust funds if any are available for that purpose, but if there are none and they pay them out of

---

[33] *Pennell v. Millar* (1856) 23 Beav. 172.
[34] *Norris v. Caledonian Ins. Co.* (1869) L.R. 8 Eq. 127; *Saunders v. Dunman* (1878) 7 Ch.D. 825; *Falcke v. Scottish Imperial* (1886) 34 Ch.D. 234; see contra *Shearman v. British Empire* (1872) L.R. 14 Eq. 4.
[35] *Re Power's Policies* [1899] 1 Ir.R. 6.
[36] *Strutt v. Tippett* (1890) 62 L.T. 475; *Myers v. United Guarantee* (1855) 7 De G.M. & G. 112.
[37] *Re Smith's Estate* [1937] Ch. 636.
[38] *Re Roberts* [1946] Ch. 1.

their own pockets, they are entitled to a first charge on the policy to indemnify themselves.[39] Where the trustees had the means of procuring trust funds properly available for the purpose of paying premiums, it was held that they did not acquire a charge on the policy by paying out of their own pockets.[40]

Not only are trustees entitled to a charge in respect of disbursements for premiums paid out of their own pockets, but they may give a like charge to others who advance the premiums at their request.[41] It has been said that if the trustees have trust funds available for the premiums, they cannot charge the policy by borrowing from strangers any more than they can by paying out of their own pockets[42]; but, on the other hand, if a trustee requests a beneficiary of the trust to pay the premiums, the beneficiary has a charge on the policy even although there are available funds in the possession of the trustee.[43]

9–13 Payment by beneficiary of trust. There is some authority for saying that if a beneficiary of a trust pays the premiums in default of the person who ought to pay them, he is entitled to a charge even although he did not act on the request of the trustees[44]; but there seems to be no reason why a beneficial part owner under a trust should have any greater right to an indemnity than a part owner at law, and therefore the better opinion seems to be that only in the case of joint tenancy or tenancy in common has a beneficiary a right to contribution against the other beneficiaries, and even then he has no lien on the policy unless he has acted by request of the trustees.[45]

Where a person has an interest in a policy under an assignment which is voidable, as in the case of a voluntary assignment which is voidable by the assignor's trustee in bankruptcy, the premiums which he has paid before the date when the assignment is avoided constitute a first charge on the policy moneys.[46] Equity makes such a charge a condition of the right to have the assignment set aside against an innocent holder.[47]

9–14 Lien on policy. Any person can by contract with the beneficial owner of a policy acquire a right to recover the premiums which he has paid to keep it on foot, and his contract may give him a charge on the policy for that purpose.[48] Once a lien has been acquired he can keep the policy on foot for his own benefit, and add the further premiums to the charge,[49] and he may, by requesting others to advance the premiums, give them a charge upon the policy, since that is the same as if he had borrowed the money and assigned his security.[50]

---

[39] *Clack v. Holland* (1854) 19 Beav. 262, *per* Romily M.R. at 273; *Re Walker* (1893) 68 L.T. 517; *Re Earl of Winchelsea* (1888) 39 Ch.D. 168; *Norris v. Caledonian Ins. Co.* (1869) L.R. 8 Eq. 127; *McElroy v. Hancock Mutual Life*, 88 Md. 137 (1898).

[40] *Clack v. Holland* (1854) 19 Beav. 262.

[41] *ibid.*

[42] *ibid.*

[43] *Todd v. Moorhouse* (1874) L.R. 19 Eq. 69.

[44] *Burridge v. Row* (1842) 1 Y. & C.Ch. 183; *Re Tharp* (1852) 2 Sm. & G. 578n.

[45] See para. 9–08, *ante.*

[46] *West v. Reid* (1843) 2 Hare 249; *Edwards v. Martin* (1865) L.R. 1 Eq. 121.

[47] *ibid.*

[48] *Aylwin v. Witty* (1861) 30 L.J.Ch. 860.

[49] *ibid.*

[50] *ibid.*

9–15 Scots law. The law of Scotland with regard to salvage premiums has developed in some respects differently from the law of England. It is now beginning to acquire a conceptual and linguistic coherence which was hitherto lacking. The trend of more recent judicial authority has been to consider, as a general question, whether one party has been unjustifiably enriched at the expense of another party without there being a legal ground which would justify him in retaining that benefit.[51] The appropriate remedy to recover a sum paid to keep in force the policy of another is recompense, as is illustrated by earlier case-law, and the awarding of this remedy does not depend upon an express or implied request by the policyholder.[52] Stair speaks of recompense as "a most natural obligation" giving rise to "the action in law *de in rem verso* whereby whatsoever turneth to the behoof of any makes him liable for recompense, though without any engagement of his own".[53] All that is necessary to lay a foundation for a claim for the recovery of the premiums paid is either that the premiums have been paid with the direct intention of benefiting the owner of the policy, but without any intention of making a gift of the premiums, or that the premiums have been paid in the bona fide belief that the policy belonged to the claimant, or that the claimant, having a partial interest in the policy, has found it necessary to pay the premiums both for his own benefit and that of the owner.[54] Where a husband and wife had joined in an assignation, in security for the husband's debts, of a policy effected by the husband under the Married Women's Policies of Assurance (Scotland) Act 1880,[55] for the benefit of his wife, the assurance company raised a multiplepoinding in which the claimants were the widow and the assignees in security. Lord Mackenzie held that the assignation was invalid in that it was inconsistent with, and amounted to an attempt to revoke, the irrevocable statutory trust contained in the policy.[56] Since the assignees had paid the whole premiums on the policy since the date of the assignation in the belief that the assignation was valid, they were nevertheless entitled to be recouped the money expended by them. Accordingly, he held that they were entitled to be paid out of the policy moneys a sum equal to the total amount of the premiums paid by them with interest at five per cent on each premium paid from the date of payment thereof and that the widow was entitled to the balance of the policy money.[57]

9–16 Where a policy effected by a husband on his own life was assigned by him to trustees in trust to hold the policy money and pay his widow the interest thereon during her life and thereafter for the benefit of the children of the marriage and the husband covenanted to pay the premiums, he, after paying a number of premiums, became bankrupt, and thereafter until his death his wife's father and later his wife herself paid the premiums for

---

[51] *Dollar Land (Cumbernauld) Ltd v. CIN Properties Ltd* 1996 S.C. 331, 348–349 *per* Lord Cullen, and applied in the seminal case of *Shilliday v. Smith* 1998 S.C. 725.

[52] *Edinburgh and District Tramways Co. Ltd v. Courtenay* 1909 S.C. 99; *Varney (Scotland) Ltd v. Lanark Town Council* 1974 S.C. 245; *Lawrence Building Co. Ltd v. Lanark County Council*, [1978] S.C. 60; *Christie's Executor v. Armstrong*, 1996 S.L.T. 948.

[53] Inst. 1.8.6 and 7 (5th edition); Erskine, Inst. 3.1.11; Bell's *Principles*, s.538.

[54] *Morgan v. Morgan's Judicial Factor*, 1922 S.L.T. 247.

[55] 43 & 44 Vict. c. 26.

[56] Following *Beith's Trs. v. Beith* 1950 S.C. 66, this aspect of the decision can no longer be regarded as correct.

[57] *The Edinburgh Life Ass. Co. v. Balderston* [1909] 2 S.L.T. 323.

behoof of the trust and in order to prevent the policy lapsing. It was admitted that the widow paid the premiums in the expectation of recovering them on maturity. After the husband's death the widow brought an action against the judicial factor appointed by the court as trustee to administer the trust and Lord Hunter held on the facts admitted that she was entitled to recover from him the actual amount of her outlay with interest thereon, provided the amount so recoverable did not exceed the difference between the amount recovered under the policy and what would have been its value on the assumption that no premiums had been paid by her.[58] The reason for the proviso was that the practical application of the doctrine of recompense is subject to two limitations, *viz.*:

(1) that the person making the expenditure is not entitled to any profit, and
(2) that he cannot claim from the person benefited a sum in excess of the increased value of the subject-matter arising from his expenditure.

The precise scope of this Outer House decision is not easy to determine. Where a person who has an interest in a subject spends money on it, there is a presumption against him recovering his expenditure from another person who also benefited from it.[59] Lord Hunter considered that on the facts of the case the widow could overcome that presumption, but he does not explain which facts he considered relevant in this connection. It may, however, be that he had in mind the provisions for payment of capital and income to the children in the event of the widow's death or remarriage, since these meant that the widow's payments were not ultimately entirely for her own benefit. If so, the decision might be different where the only possible beneficiary of the policy was the person paying the premiums.

9–17 No lien on policy. Except in the case of premiums paid by a trustee for the preservation of the trust subjects it would seem that the doctrine of recompense gives rise only to a personal obligation by the owner of the policy to the person who has paid the premiums, and creates no right *in rem* against the proceeds of the policy so as to give the claimant a preference against other creditors. This was the clear decision of the Inner House in a case where a solicitor had induced a client to insure his life in order to provide security for advances which he, the solicitor, had made to him. The solicitor took possession of the policy and paid all the premiums, but there was no assignation of it to him or intimation to the association. In a multiple-poinding raised to decide the conflicting claims to the policy money of the executrix on the deceased's estate and the solicitor, the court held that no valid security had been created over the policy and that, although the premiums paid together with the other advances constituted a debt owing by the assured, it gave the creditor no preferential right over any other creditor of the estate to the fund produced by the policy.[60] The decision of Lord Mackenzie in the *Balderston* Case would seem to support the view that the right of the claimant in respect of salvage premiums is a right of lien, because in that case also there was a multiplepoinding and the policy money constituted the fund *in medio* and the claimants were ranked and preferred

[58] *Morgan v. Morgan's Judicial Factor*, 1922 S.L.T. 247, 250.
[59] This is illustrated particularly by the cases on expenditure by liferenters. See, *e.g. Morrisons v. Allan* (1886) 13 R. 1156. *cf.* Gloag, *The Law of Contract* (2nd ed., 1929), 322.
[60] *Wylie's Executrix v. McJannet* (1901) 4 F. 195.

against the fund for the amount of the premiums paid by them and interest.[61] It does not appear, however, that any distinction was sought to be made between lien and unsecured personal obligation, and if the deceased's estate was solvent it was a matter of indifference to the parties and the decision can carry no weight on this point as against the decision of the Inner House in the *Wylie* Case. In two cases heard by the Industrial Commissioner in Scotland he considered the authorities and held that payment of the premiums at the request of the owner of the policy created a lien on the policy moneys, but it is submitted that these decisions are not in accordance with the Scottish authorities which he cited.[62]

9–18 Payment by trustees. In the event of trustees, in the absence of available trust funds, paying out of their own pockets premiums to preserve a policy included in the trust estate which is in danger of lapse, they are entitled to be recouped out of the policy money in preference to beneficiaries and other creditors. They have in effect a possessory lien and may retain out of the policy money when it comes into their hands sufficient to meet their claims for premiums paid by them. One of the several trustees who has paid the premiums on a policy which is subject to the trust cannot during the currency of the policy call his co-trustees to contribute to such payments or reimburse him out of their own pockets an appropriate proportion of their expenditure.[63] Neither can a trustee while the policy is current require his co-trustees to realise the policy by surrender or otherwise so that he may be immediately reimbursed. He must wait until the policy matures, when he can exercise his right of lien by retaining out of the policy money the amount of premiums and interest not exceeding in all the amount by which the estate is *lucratus* by the payment of the premiums which he has advanced.[64]

---

[61] *The Edinburgh Life Ass. Co. v. Balderston*, 1909 2 S.L.T. 323.
[62] *Walker v. Prudential* [1927] I.A.C.Rep. 21; *British Legal Life v. Lighton* [1926] I.A.C.Rep. 21.
[63] *Brown v. Brown* (1896) 4 S.L.T. 46.
[64] *ibid.*

CHAPTER 10

WARRANTIES AND OTHER POLICY TERMS*

1. CLASSIFICATION OF TERMS

10–1 All insurance policies contain provisions inserted for the benefit of the insurer, which are intended to restrict his liability under the policy in one manner or another, or to impose requirements upon the assured in order to assist the insurer in dealing with claims. These have been the subject of judicial interpretation for over two hundred years. In particular, warranties which, when not fulfilled, discharge the insurer from liability, have been the subject of criticism by the courts. So far as terms in consumer insurance contracts are concerned, new requirements of intelligibility and fairness to the assured were imposed by the Unfair Terms in Consumer Contracts Regulations 1994[1] (now revoked and replaced by the Unfair Terms in Consumer Contracts Regulations 1999[2]) which are going to have a major impact upon the drafting and enforceability of these sorts of clauses. In the present chapter we consider the position both at common law and under the Regulations.

10–2 Nature of warranty. Any attempt at a comprehensive definition of "warranty" in insurance law is complicated by the sometimes indiscriminate use of the word to refer to clauses in policies which do not possess the traditional attributes of a warranty, and by changes in legal terminology over the years. It has a different meaning from a warranty in the general law of contract. An insurance law warranty is a term of the contract of insurance in the nature of a condition precedent to the liability of the insurer.[3] Typically it is a promissory term whereby the assured promises either that a given state of affairs existed prior to the inception of the insurance or that it will continue to exist during the currency of the risk, and breach of the warranty discharges the insurer's liability on the policy from the time of the breach.[4]

---

* We are grateful to Mr Christopher Hancock Q.C. for undertaking the revision of this chapter.

[1] S.I. 1994 No. 3159.

[2] S.I. 1999 No. 2083.

[3] *Newcastle Fire Ins. Co. v. Macmorran* (1815) 3 Dow. 255, 259; *Thomson v. Weems* (1884) 9 App.Cas. 671, 684; *Barnard v. Faber* [1893] 1 Q.B. 340; *Hambrough v. Mut. Life Ins. Co. of New York* (1895) 72 L.T. 140; *Bank of Nova Scotia v. Hellenic Mut. War Risks Assoc.* [1992] 1 A.C. 233, 263.

[4] See paras 10–88 to 10–90, *post.*

Thus the liability of the insurer is made to depend upon the existence of the thing warranted by the assured. If, for instance, in a motor policy there is a warranty that the assured had never been convicted of a motoring offence, the insurer's liability will not attach if the warranted statement was untrue,[5] and if there is a warranty in a buildings policy that a security alarm shall be maintained on the insured premises, the insurer's liability will cease if the alarm ceases to be operative.[6]

10–3 The essential characteristics of a warranty are briefly these:
  (i) it must be a term of the contract;
 (ii) the matter warranted need not be material to the risk;
(iii) it must be exactly complied with;
(iv) a breach discharges the insurer from liability on the contract notwithstanding that the loss has no connection with the breach or that the breach has been remedied before the time of loss.

10–4 Warranty distinguished from representation. The differences between warranty and a representation were first established two centuries ago in a series of decisions of Lord Mansfield who, in the words of his biographer, did much to rescue insurance law from the incoherence in which previous judges had left it.[7] The case commonly cited on the elementary distinction between a warranty and representation is *Pawson v. Watson*,[8] where Lord Mansfield emphasised that a warranty or condition "makes part of a written policy" whereas a representation is made outside the written contract, and added that, where there was a warranty, "Nothing tantamount will do or answer the purpose; It must be strictly performed, as being part of the agreement".[9] If, therefore, the insured vessel was there warranted to carry 12 carriage guns and 20 men the warranty would not be fulfilled if there were 10 carriage guns, nine swivel guns and 16 men and 11 boys, although the latter might be the stronger force. In *De Hahn v. Hartley*[10] he returned to this theme and said:

> "There is a material distinction between a warranty and a representation. A representation may be equitably and substantially answered; but a warranty must be strictly complied with. Supposing a warranty to sail on the 1st of August, and the ship did not sail till the 2nd, the warranty would not be complied with. A warranty in a contract of insurance is a condition or a contingency, and unless that be performed, there is no contract. It is perfectly immaterial for what purpose a warranty is introduced; but, being inserted, the contract does not exist unless it be literally complied with."[11]

10–5 A breach of warranty discharges the insurer from all liability as from the date of the breach, but without prejudice to any liability already incurred

[5] *Mackay v. London General Ins. Co.* (1935) 51 Ll.L.Rep. 201, applying *Dawsons v. Bonnin* [1922] 2 A.C. 413.
[6] *Hussain v. Brown* [1996] 1 Lloyd's Rep. 627, 628.
[7] Fifoot, *Lord Mansfield*, Chap. 4, p. 83, and see the preface to the 1st edition of Park's *System of the Law on Marine Insurances*, dedicated to that "venerable magistrate" in 1787. For a definition of representations, see Ch. 16, para. 16–10, *post*.
[8] (1778) 2 Cowp. 785.
[9] *ibid.*, 787–788.
[10] (1786) 1 T.R. 343.
[11] *ibid.*, 345.

by that date.[12] Warranties are therefore to be contrasted with certain other terms which are equally terms of the insurance contract but do not attract the same consequences on breach.

10–6 Collateral promise. A stipulation in a policy may be merely a collateral promise by the assured to do some act without making his right to recover dependent on his fulfilment of the promise.[13] Here the only remedy of the insurer in the event of breach is a counterclaim for damages. If insurers desire to create a condition precedent then sufficiently clear wording should be used to demonstrate that intention, and a clause which is not clearly expressed as a condition is likely to be read as a collateral stipulation unless a cross action for damages would be an inadequate redress in the event of breach.[14] In *Re Bradley & Essex and Suffolk Accident*[15] a stipulation in an employer's liability policy that the assured should keep a proper wages book was held to be merely a collateral promise relating to the adjustment of premiums, and a breach did not discharge the insurers from liability. Although described on its face as a "condition precedent", the clause in question formed part of a larger provision which could not take effect as a condition precedent and created an ambiguity which had to be resolved against the insurers.[16]

In *Stoneham v. Ocean Railway and General Accident*[17] it was held that the condition that, "in case of fatal accident notice must be given to the company within seven days", was not a condition precedent to recovery, but was merely a contractual term the breach of which imposed an obligation upon the assured's representatives to reimburse the company for any extra expense which they might incur from having to investigate the circumstances of an accident at a long interval after its occurrence. Since the "condition" was not expressed to be a condition precedent to recovery on the policy, whereas others were, and since the result of holding it to be one would in that case have produced an unreasonable result, the decision is not surprising.

10–7 Suspensive condition. A warranty must also be distinguished from a term which delimits the risks covered under the policy with the effect that, while the promise made by the assured is being broken, the insurer is not on risk and the cover is temporarily suspended until the breach is remedied. *Farr v. Motor Traders Mutual Society*[18] affords a useful illustration. The applicant for insurance on two taxi-cabs was asked in the proposal form whether the cabs were "driven in one or more shifts per twenty-four hours" and answered "Just one". The policy was issued in February 1918. In August one cab was driven for a brief period in two shifts per 24 hours, after which

---

[12] See paras 10–88 to 10–90, *post.*
[13] *London Guarantie Co. v. Fearnley* (1880) 5 App.Cas. 911, 916; *Cowell v. Yorkshire Provident Life Ass. Co.* (1901) 17 T.L.R. 452; *Ballantine v. Employers' Ins. Co.* (1893) 21 R. 305.
[14] *London Guarantie Co. v. Fearnley* (1880) 5 App.Cas. 911; *Barnard v. Faber* [1893] 1 Q.B. 340; *Ellinger v. Mutual Life Ins. Co. of New York* [1905] 1 K.B. 31; *Jones v. Provincial Ins. Co.* (1929) 35 Ll.L.Rep. 135.
[15] [1912] 1 K.B. 415.
[16] *ibid.*, 432–433.
[17] (1887) 19 Q.B.D. 237.
[18] [1920] 3 K.B. 669.

ordinary working was resumed, and in November the cab was damaged in an accident. The insurers resisted payment on the ground that the statement relating to the user of the cabs was a warranty, so that the breach in August entitled them to repudiate liability. It was held, however, that the statement amounted on its true construction to no more than a term delimiting the scope of the risk. Therefore the cover provided by the policy had re-attached when the assured resumed single shift working, and the insurers were accordingly liable to satisfy the claim in respect of the accident in November, though they would not, of course, have been liable for any loss or damage occurring during the period of double shift working. Had the term suspending the risk been a warranty, the breach in August would have discharged the insurers' liability.[19]

Clauses of this nature are sometimes referred to as "warranties descriptive of the risk" or "delimiting the risk".[20] This usage is not an accurate one,[21] but it serves as a reminder that a court may be prepared to construe a clause as one descriptive of the risk even though the word "warranty" or "warranted" appears in it, as where a car was "warranted used only for the following purposes".[22] That case illustrates the point that there is no magic in the word "warranted"[23] which is frequently used with considerable ambiguity in policies.[24]

10–8 Conditions precedent. Apart from suspensory conditions, there are also other terms which are termed conditions precedent. These may be conditions precedent to the contract itself[25] or they may be conditions precedent to liability.[26] In addition, such clauses may, as a matter of construction, be found to be conditions precedent to any liability, or simply conditions precedent to liability in relation to particular claims.[27] Such clauses may serve to postpone the running of limitation periods.[28]

10–9 Exceptions clauses. Other clauses take the form of exceptions from the general risk described in the policy as, for instance, "not to cover loss arising from explosion of gun-powder". Here there is no question of the insurers' liability being either avoided or suspended, but the general risk described in the policy is limited by certain classes of loss being excluded. Nonetheless it is not unusual to find a clause of this type introduced by the word "warranted" as, for example, in marine policies where it is provided

---

[19] See the cases cited in paras 10–77 to 10–78, *post.*

[20] *De Maurier v. Bastion Inc. Co.* [1967] 2 Lloyd's Rep. 550, 558–559.

[21] As noted by Scrutton L.J. in *Re Morgan and Provincial Ins. Co.* [1932] 2 K.B. 70, 80—"so-called warranty".

[22] *Roberts v. Anglo-Saxon Ins. Co.* (1927) 27 Ll.L.Rep. 313 (C.A.); *De Maurier v. Bastion Ins. Co.* [1967] 2 Lloyd's Rep. 550; *Cohen v. Plaistow Transport* [1968] 2 Lloyd's Rep. 587, 592; *CTN Cash & Carry v. General Accident Fire & Life Ass. Corp.* [1989] 1 Lloyd's Rep. 299, 302–303; *Kler Knitwear v Lombard General Insurance Co.* [2000] Lloyd's Rep. I.R. 47.

[23] *Barnard v. Faber* [1893] 1 Q.B. 340, 342, 345. The verb "to warrant" is not a term of art corresponding to the noun "warranty"—*Lindsay v. European Grain & Shipping Agency* [1963] 1 Lloyd's Rep. 437, 443, *per* Diplock L.J. "Warranty" has more than one meaning depending on the context—*Wickman Machine Tools v. Schuler AG* [1974] A.C. 235, 256 *per* Lord Morris.

[24] *Roberts v. Anglo Saxon Ins. Co.* (1926) 26 Ll.L.Rep. 154, 157 (Div.Ct.) where MacKinnon J. said "Now, nothing turns upon the use of the word 'warranted' ... always used with the greatest ambiguity in a policy ...".

[25] See, *e.g. The Zeus V* [2000] 2 Lloyd's Rep. 587.

[26] See the discussion in paras 10–11 and 10–36, *post.*

[27] See, *e.g. Kazakstan v. NCM* [2000] Lloyd's Rep. I.R. 371.

[28] As in the case of *Virk v. Gan Life* [2000] Lloyd's Rep. I.R. 159.

"warranted free from particular average". That does not mean that if there is a partial loss the insurer's liability is discharged, but it is simply excluding partial loss from the subject-matter of the insurance.[29] Another example is "warranted free of capture and seizure".[30]

10–10 Duties to be performed by the assured. There are terms in every policy which impose certain obligations on the assured. For example there are clauses which require the assured to do certain things in the event of a loss, such as give notice of loss within a specified time,[31] notify the insurer of claims brought against the assured,[32] deliver particulars of loss in a limited time,[33] initiate a reference to arbitration,[34] or prosecute a dishonest employee.[35] Other clauses impose duties on the assured during the currency of the risk, such as the common condition in a motor policy requiring the assured to take all reasonable steps to safeguard the insured vehicle from loss or damage and to maintain it in efficient condition.[36]

10–11 The effect of the assured's breach of such a term depends upon an interpretation of the clause in question in the context of the whole policy. Clauses requiring delivery of particulars of loss within a specified time have been construed as conditions precedent to recovery even where not expressed to be either a warranty or condition precedent,[37] but it is unlikely that a court would take the same view today. The modern drafting technique is to include a general clause which declares that the due observance and fulfilment by the assured of all the obligations cast upon him by the policy terms shall be conditions precedent to any liability of the insurers to make any payment under the policy.[38] Breach by the assured of a term of the kind described above then provides the insurer with a defence to payment, regardless of whether it was either remedied before or causally connected with the loss.[39] A literal interpretation of the general condition precedent

---

[29] In *Re Morgan and Provincial Ins. Co.* [1932] 2 K.B. 70, 80, *per* Scrutton L.J. He gave as another example the clause "warranted no St Lawrence between October 1 and April 1", citing *Birrell v. Dryer* (1884) 9 App.Cas. 345, although in that case the House of Lords appears to have treated it as a promissory warranty.

[30] *De Maurier v. Bastion Ins. Co.* [1967] 2 Lloyd's Rep. 550, 558–559; *The "Good Luck"* [1992] A.C. 233, 261; *The "Vasso"* [1993] 2 Lloyd's Rep. 309, 313.

[31] E.g. Cawley v. National Employers (1885) 1 T.L.R. 255.

[32] E.g. Allen v. Robles [1969] 1 W.L.R. 1193; *Farrell v. Federated Employers Ins. Assoc.* [1970] 1 W.L.R. 498, 1400.

[33] *Roper v. Lendon* (1859) 1 E. & E. 825; *Elliott v. Royal Exchange Ass. Co.* (1867) L.R. 2 Ex. 237, 244.

[34] *Elliott v. Royal Exchange Ass. Co.* (1867) L.R. 2 Ex. 237.

[35] *London Guarantie Co. v. Fearnley* (1880) 5 App.Cas. 911.

[36] E.g. *Jones v. Provincial Ins. Co.* (1929) 35 Ll.L.Rep. 135; *Brown v. Zürich General Accident & Liability Ins. Co.* [1954] 2 Lloyd's Rep. 243; *Conn v. Westminster Motor Ins. Assoc.* [1966] 1 Lloyd's Rep. 407; *Devco Holder Ltd v. Legal & General Ass. Soc. Ltd* [1993] 2 Lloyd's Rep. 567.

[37] *Roper v. Lendon* (1859) 1 E. & E. 825; *Elliott v. Royal Exchange Ass. Co.* (1867) L.R. 2 Ex. 237; *Mason v. Harvey* (1853) 8 Exch. 819.

[38] See the cases in note 36 *ante*; *Farrell v. Federated Employers' Ins. Co.* [1970] 1 W.L.R. 498, 500; 1400; *Cox v. Orion Ins. Co.* [1982] R.T.R. 1.

[39] *Conn v. Westminster Motor Ins. Assoc.* [1966] 1 Lloyd's Rep. 407, 414; *Provincial Ins. Co. v. Morgan* [1933] A.C. 240. Such clauses may well be unenforceable against consumer assureds under the Unfair Terms etc. Regulations—see para. 10–20, *post*. Contrast *Lane v. Spratt* [1970] 2 Q.B. 480, in which a "Due Diligence" clause was not reinforced by a general condition precedent clause and was held to provide a defence only if there was a causal connection between breach and loss. Roskill J. described it as a "warranty", but this is inconsistent with the usual definition of warranties.

clause suggests that the insurer is altogether discharged from liability under the policy for the future, and not merely from liability to meet the particular claim, but it is submitted that the courts would endeavour to interpret it as not barring recovery for future claims if at all possible as, for example in a case where the assured's breach consisted of a failure to intimate a claim within a time limit. Where the assured's compliance with a policy term is expressed to be a "condition precedent to recovery", the insurer may have a defence to payment only so long as the breach remains un-remedied.[40]

10–12 Innominate or intermediate terms. An innominate or intermediate term is, in the general law of contract, a term which is neither a condition nor a warranty (using the word warranty in its non-insurance sense, as a term which does not give the other party to the contract a right to terminate the contract).[41] A party will have the right to terminate the contract for breach of an innominate term only if that breach is "repudiatory", in the sense that it goes to the root of the contract.[42] If the breach is not repudiatory, or if the right to terminate is not exercised or lost, then the remedy for such breach is limited to damages. In the insurance field, such damages are often likely to be difficult to establish.

10–13 However, the Courts have recently begun to construe terms as innominate terms of a slightly different type. In the case of *McAlpine (Alfred) Plc v. BAI (Run-Off) Ltd*,[43] The Court was prepared to hold that a notice provision was to be construed as an innominate term, a repudiatory breach of which would give rise, not to a right to terminate the contract, but instead simply to a right to reject the particular claim in question. That case was followed by the Court of Appeal in *K/S Merc-Skandia v. Certain Lloyd's Underwriters*,[44] though in each case the relevant breach was held not to be repudiatory on the facts. The increased flexibility in remedy which the introduction of such a term gives to the Courts is welcome, though the legal basis for the term is, perhaps, open to question.[45]

10–14 The type of terms which have in the past been found to be innominate are varied. In the cases referred to in the previous paragraph, the obligations involved the giving of notice of claim and keeping underwriters informed. Other examples of such terms may be found in *Phoenix General Insurance Co. of Greece S.A. v. Halvanon Insurance Co. Ltd*,[46] where there

---

[40] *Mint Security Ltd v. Blair* [1982] 1 Lloyd's Rep. 188, 198–199. The court referred to this condition as a "warranty", but it did not possess equivalent force to the traditional warranty. In *Welch v. Royal Exchange Ass.* [1939] 1 K.B. 294 a general clause provided that certain conditions in the policy were deemed to be "conditions precedent to the right of the insured to recover hereunder", and Mackinnon L.J. seems to have thought that a breach in relation to one claim was irremediable and would bar later claims—p. 312. See para. 10–91, *post*.

[41] See, *e.g. Hongkong Fir Shipping Co. v. Kawasaki Kisen Kaisha* [1962] 2 Q.B. 26; *Chitty on Contracts* (28th ed., 1999) para. 12–034.

[42] See *Federal Commerce & Navigation Co. Ltd v. Molena Alpha Inc.* [1979] A.C. 757, 779; *Chitty on Contracts* (28th ed., 1999) para. 25–039.

[43] [2000] 1 Lloyd's Rep. 437.

[44] [2001] 2 Lloyd's Rep. 563.

[45] In the *MacAlpine* case, reliance was placed on the New Zealand decision of *Trans Pacific Insurance Co. (Australia) Ltd v. Grand Union Insurance Co. Ltd* (1989) 18 NSWLR 675. However, that case involved the possibility of termination of a contract of reinsurance entered into pursuant to a surplus treaty and, it is submitted, is not good authority for the proposition derived by the Court of Appeal.

[46] [1988] Q.B. 216.

were found to be implied terms of a reinsurance contract that the reassured would conduct business in a proper and businesslike manner; and *The Beursgracht (No. 2)*,[47] where the term was as to the making of declarations under an open cover. The extent to which this analysis will be adopted in the future remains to be seen.

10–15 Rights of cancellation. The policy may contain a clause entitling the insurer to cancel it at will.[48] If procedural conditions are attached to the decision to cancel, such as the service of a notice at a particular time,[49] the insurer must comply with them in order to exercise his right to terminate.[50] The policy may also confer a right to terminate upon the assured, as where a life policy may be surrendered against payment of its surrender value.[51] A clause in a composite policy conferring a right to cancel on the assureds would be construed as a right to be exercised by all the assureds jointly unless it was very clearly worded to provide for cancellation by any one of them singly.[52]

10–16 The Unfair Terms in Consumer Contracts Regulations 1999.[53] As from 1 October 1999, these Regulations have replaced the Unfair Terms in Consumer Contracts Regulations 1994. The Regulations implement the European Community Directive[54] on unfair terms in consumer contracts. By paragraph 1 of Regulation 4 they are expressed to apply to unfair terms[55] in contracts cncluded between a seller or a supplier and a consumer. In turn, by Regulation 5, a term which is not individually negotiated will be unfair if, contrary to the requirements of good faith, it causes a significant imbalance in the parties' rights and obligations arising under the contract, to the detriment of the consumer. This affects an insurance granted by an insurer to an assured who is (1) a natural person and (2) who, in obtaining the insurance is "acting for purposes which are outside his trade, business or profession."[56] The meaning of "business" in this context was considered in *Standard Bank Ltd v. Apostolakis*[57] where it was held that substantial foreign exchange transactions entered into by a lawyer and a civil engineer were not made as part of those individuals' businesses, despite the scale of the transactions. The definition of "consumer" is accordingly narrower than that of "private policy holder" in section 6(7) of the Policyholders' Protection Act 1975.[58] It excludes business partnerships but seems to include recreational clubs in the form of unincorporated associations. It is unclear whether the Regulations apply to an insurance obtained partly for business

---

[47] [2002] Lloyd's Rep. I.R. 335.

[48] *Sun Fire Office v. Hart* (1889) 14 App.Cas. 98.

[49] *Commercial Union Ass. Co. v. Sun Alliance Ins. Group* [1992] 1 Lloyd's Rep. 475, 480.

[50] This is the general rule relating to the exercise of options—see, e.g. *The "Foresight Driller 2"* [1995] 1 Lloyd's Rep. 251, 264–266.

[51] *Ingram-Johnson v. Century Ins. Co.* 1909 S.C. 1032.

[52] *Federation Ins. Co. v. Wasson* (1987) 163 C.L.R. 303.

[53] For a fuller discussion of these regulations, see *e.g. Chitty on Contracts* (28th ed., 1999) paras 15–004 to 15–076.

[54] Council Directive 93/13/EEC, 5 April 1993 (O.J. 1993 L95/29); S.I. 1994 No. 1359 (now S.I. 1999 No. 2083).

[55] Other than terms which reflect mandatory statutory or regulatory provisions of English law or the provisions of international conventions.

[56] Reg. 3(1).

[57] 2000 I.L.Pr. 766.

[58] See *Ackman v. Policyholders Protection Board* [1994] 2 A.C. 57, 75, 115.

purposes, as, for instance, where a professional person insures a car which is to be used only partly for purposes of his profession, or whether the insurance must be wholly unconnected with any business.[59] It is also unclear whether the Regulations apply to an insurance granted to a consumer and to a business concern, such as the composite buildings policy covering the interests of the householder and his building society.

10–17 Few terms in consumer insurance policies are "individually negotiated". No definition of these words is given but regulation 5(3) states:

"... a term shall always be regarded as not having been individually negotiated where it has been drafted in advance and the consumer has not been able to influence the substance of the term."

The standard terms and conditions of insurance policies fall easily within that description.

10–18 Fairness and plain wording. The Regulations divide terms into two basic categories. The first consists of terms which define the main subject matter of the contract or concern the adequacy of the remuneration.[60] We may call these "core terms". The Court of Appeal considered the question of what constituted a "core term" in the case of *Director General of Fair Trading v. First National Bank Plc.*[61] The Court held that a provision for default interest in a consumer credit agreement was not a core term since it did not define the main subject matter of the contract or concern the adequacy of the remuneration. This indicates that a strict approach will be taken to this question by the Courts. So long as it is in plain intelligible language, a core term will not be scrutinised for unfairness,[62] although it will form part of the context in which other terms are assessed for unfairness. The second category consists of all non-core terms, and these will not be enforceable against a consumer if they are unfair.[63] An unfair term is one which "contrary to the requirement of good faith causes a significant imbalance in the parties' rights and obligations under the contract to the detriment of the consumer."[64] Unfairness is to be assessed by reference to certain prescribed factors including the nature of the contracted performance provided and the circumstances in which it was concluded.[65] Good faith is not defined under the 1999 Regulations, and the Schedule to the 1994 regulations which gave guidance as to the meaning of the phrase is not reproduced in the new regulations. However, since the matters referred to in that schedule form part of the preamble to the Directive, it would be surprising if those matters were not still relevant. The meaning of the phrase was considered (in the context of the old regulations) by the Court of Appeal in *Director General of Fair Trading v. First National Bank Plc*[66] in which the Court approved a test proposed by Professor Beale, to the effect that the

---

[59] The construction placed on ss.5(2)(a), 6(2) and 12(1) of the Unfair Contract Terms Act 1977 suggests that the contract will be made for a purpose outside the business unless it is made exclusively for business purposes—*R. & B. Brokers Ltd v. U.D.T. Ltd* [1988] 1 W.L.R. 321, 334.
[60] Reg. 6(2).
[61] [2000] Q.B. 672.
[62] *ibid.*
[63] Reg. 8(1).
[64] Reg. 5(1).
[65] Reg. 6(1).
[66] [2000] Q.B. 672.

concept has both a procedural aspect (to prevent unfair surprise) and a substantive aspect (looking to the content of the term itself). Illustrations of terms which may be regarded as unfair are given in Schedule 2.[67] All written terms should be in plain intelligible language, and if there is any doubt about their meaning the interpretation most favourable to the consumer shall prevail.[68]

10–19 Core terms in insurance contracts. It seems that clauses in policies which define the scope of the cover and the measure of indemnity will be read as core terms,[69] including exceptions clauses, suspensive conditions, and limitations on liability. A warranty will therefore not be a core term unless it serves to define the risk run by the insurer.

10–20 Non-core terms in insurance policies. These will encompass procedural clauses stipulating time limits and procedures for making claims and resolving disputes arising under the policy, and clauses requiring notification of specified events during the currency of the policy. They would appear to include forfeiture clauses, and basis of contract clauses whereby the accuracy of pre-contractual statements is warranted. It would be strange if the latter could not be scrutinised for fairness, against the background of judicial[70] and other[71] criticisms of them. At present one can only speculate which types of clauses might be declared unfair but they could include terms in life assurance contracts providing substantial early surrender penalties,[72] terms permitting the insurer to terminate cover at discretion on short notice,[73] terms making the assured's compliance with procedural requirements a condition precedent to indemnity,[74] and terms reversing the usual burden of proof to the disadvantage of the assured.[75] The Director General of Fair Trading (and certain other authorised bodies) are given the power to seek injunctions against insurers to restrain the use of unfair standard terms and conditions in consumer insurance contracts.[76] In addition, the Director General and the authorised bodies are given power to obtain documents and information[77] and may take and publicise undertakings not to continue with the use of unfair terms.[78]

---

[67] Reg. 5(5).

[68] Reg. 7, and see *Re Drake Insurance plc* [2001] Lloyd's Rep. I.R. 643.

[69] See Recital 20 to the Directive.

[70] *Joel v. Law Union & Crown Ins. Co.* [1908] 2 K.B. 863, 885; *Zurich General Accident & Liability Ins. Co. v. Morrison* [1942] 2 K.B. 53, 58; *Provincial Ins. Co. v. Morgan* [1933] A.C. 240, 251–252.

[71] Law Commission Report No. 104, paras 7.5, 9.1; Statement of General Insurance Practice 1986, para. 1(b).

[72] Sched. 2, paras 1(d), (e).

[73] Sched. 2, para. 1(f). See, *e.g. Sun Fire Office v. Hart* (1889) 14 App.Cas. 98.

[74] Sched. 2, para. 1(n). See the cases mentioned in Ch. 19, *post*, at paras 19–35, 19–39 and 19–47.

[75] Sched. 2, para. 1(q). See, *e.g. Levy v. Assicurazioni Generali* [1940] A.C. 791.

[76] Reg 12. The case of *Director General of Fair Trading v. First National Bank Plc*, at [2000] Q.B. 672, involved such an application.

[77] Reg. 13.

[78] Regs 14 and 15.

2. WARRANTIES—DETAILED SURVEY

(a) *Definition and How Created*

10–21 General definition. A warranty may be defined briefly as a written term of the contract of insurance in which the assured warrants, owing to the force of express words or through the operation of law, either that certain statements of fact are accurate, or that certain statements of fact are and will remain accurate, or that he will undertake the due performance of an obligation specified therein. The result of a breach of the warranty is to release the insurer from liability from the date of breach, notwithstanding that the content of the warranty may not have been material to the risk and that the breach of warranty may not have caused a loss in respect of which a claim is brought. What is said in this section is prima facie applicable to terms which are expressly or impliedly conditions precedent to the liability of the insurer, except that it must be remembered that, despite the tendency of lawyers to use the words "warranty" and "condition" indifferently, a condition may not on closer analysis possess all the attributes of a full warranty.[79]

10–22 A warranty is contractual. Since a warranty is necessarily a term of the contract, as opposed to a representation, which is not,[80] it must be found in the contractual documents evidencing the parties' agreements. Therefore it will generally be found in the policy or in some other document which is incorporated by reference into the policy and made part of it.[81] Usually that document is the proposal form, and the policy itself contains a recital incorporating the proposal and the applicant's declaration therein.[82] In marine insurance it is a statutory rule that an express warranty must be stated in the policy or incorporated into it by words of reference appearing in the policy itself,[83] and this is only fair to the assured who would perhaps otherwise forget, if not possessing a copy of the proposal form, what he had warranted in it. This does not now appear, however, to be the general rule in non-marine insurance, where it is sufficient for an insurer to obtain the signature of the applicant to a declaration saying that, "This proposal is to serve as the basis of the contract", whereupon the warranty is an effective term of the contract of insurance even if not expressly mentioned in the policy when that is issued.[84] The juristic basis for this practice is unclear. One explanation is that the policy evidences the main contract between the parties but the promises in the proposal form are collateral warranties given

---

[79] See paras 10–7 to 10–14, *supra*.

[80] *Pawson v. Watson* (1778) 2 Cowp. 785, 787, *per* Lord Mansfield C.J.

[81] *Routledge v. Burrell* (1789) 1 Hy.Bl. 254; *Worsley v. Wood* (1796) 6 T.R. 710; *Lothian v. Henderson* (1803) 3 Bos. & P.N.R. 499, 509; *Sceales v. Scanlan* (1843) 6 Ir.L.R. 367; *Sillem v. Thornton* (1854) 3 E. & B. 868, 880.

[82] *Provincial Insurance v. Morgan* [1933] A.C. 240, 251, *per* Lord Wright: *Yorkshire Insurance v. Campbell* [1917] A.C. 218.

[83] Marine Insurance Act 1906, s.35(2). For earlier law, see *Bean v. Stupart* (1778) 1 Doug. K.B. 11, 12n.

[84] *Duckett v. Williams* (1834) 2 Cr. & M. 348; *Joel v. Law Union* [1908] 2 K.B. 431, 437; *Condogianis v. Guardian* [1921] 2 A.C. 125; *Rozanes v. Bowen* (1928) 32 Ll.L.R. 98, overruling 31 Ll.L.R. 231, despite the opening sentence of Scrutton L.J. at p. 100; *Unipac (Scotland) Ltd v. Aegon Ins. Co.* 1996 S.L.T. 1197.

prior to the conclusion of the contract.[85] Another explanation might be that, since the insurer would presumably be able to rectify the policy to include words incorporating the assured's warranties therein in accordance with their prior agreement, the court is prepared to see as done what ought to be done and to treat the policy as if it already included words of incorporation. Whatever is the reasoning behind this practice, it is in our submission an objectionable one in so far as it makes the extent of the assured's obligations extremely unclear to him, particularly where continuing warranties have been made.[86]

10–23 Even the less dubious practice of incorporating the proposal form into the policy by reference has been criticised as making it difficult for the assured to see the extent of his obligations and rights until he has co-ordinated separate types of clauses appearing in different parts of the policy,[87] and the omission of words of reference altogether is still worse and quite contrary to the insistence of the Legislature in other areas of the law of contract that onerous or vital terms in a complex agreement must be delineated with especial clarity.[88]

10–24 Unsigned declarations. In life assurance, a warranty of good health is usually contained in a signed declaration attached to the proposal and incorporated into the policy by reference. There have been cases, however, where the assured did not in fact sign the declaration and it has been held that in the absence of such signature, he is not bound by the warranty contained therein.[89] This does not mean, however, that the warranty in the declaration would have no effect. Where a condition in the policy was that, if it were discovered that at the date of the policy the assured was afflicted with any mental or bodily disease or infirmity, the policy should be void and all premiums paid be forfeited, there was also a similar declaration in the proposal form, which was unsigned. The court held that it must give regard to the latter term and read the warranty in the policy not as superseding or repeating the warranty in the declaration, but as covering only a possible alteration in the health of the assured between the date of the proposal and the date of the issue of the policy. Therefore, where the assured's health had not changed between these two dates, there was no breach of warranty, however bad it had been at the date of the proposal.[90]

10–25 Warranty in any part of policy. A warranty may be written in any part of the policy, either at the top or bottom[91] or transversely on the

---

[85] For the creation of a collateral warranty or contract, see Treitel, *Law of Contract* (10th ed., 1999), p. 182, and see *per* Walton J. in *Anglo-Californian Bank v. London, etc., Marine* (1904) 10 Com.Cas. 1. It could also be said that the policy does not evidence the entire contract between the parties.

[86] For continuing warranties, see paras 10–70 to 10–79.

[87] *Provincial Insurances v. Morgan* [1933] A.C. 240, 252.

[88] See *e.g.* the Consumer Credit Act 1974. For general criticism of the "basis of the contract" clause, see R.A. Hasson (1971) 34 M.L.R. 29, and the Law Commission report of 1980, Cmnd. 8064. Insurers have volunteered not to use a "basis of the contract" clause in insurances of private individuals: para. 1(b) of the Statement of General Insurance Practice and of the Statement of Long-Term Insurance Practice 1986. They are open to challenge under the Unfair Terms in Consumer Contracts Regulations, 1999; see para. 10–20, *ante.*

[89] *Royal v. Royal Co-operative Society* [1933] I.A.C.Rep. 45.

[90] *Street v. Pearl* [1934] I.A.C.Rep. 27.

[91] *Blackhurst v. Cockell* (1789) 3 T.R. 360.

margin[92] or on the back. If written on the back, it should be referred to on the face of the policy, since if the policy is apparently complete on the face of it, the assured's attention might never have been directed to the back, and he would be entitled to accept what appeared on the face as constituting the whole contract between the parties.

10–26 There are some decisions of Lord Mansfield where it was held that a separate document, even if delivered with the policy, could not form part of it,[93] and he so held even where the document was wafered on to the policy.[94] Accordingly the ordinary gummed slip would not be a part of the policy and a warranty contained therein would be only a representation. These decisions cannot, however, have any force today. There are modern authorities in which appellate courts have accepted that a warranty can be effective even if not embodied in the policy itself,[95] whether expressly or by incorporation, and this strikes at the root of Lord Mansfield's objections, though that is not to agree that the modern tendency is to be applauded. In a case[96] involving a marine policy, the House of Lords gave effect to an exclusion clause in a slip pasted on to the policy, and Lord Halsbury dismissed as far-fetched the notion that the pasted slip could not form part of the policy[97] owing to the nature of its relationship to it.

The place in which a warranty is found may, however, indicate the extent of its scope where this is at all in doubt. Thus if a continuing warranty be annexed by indorsement to the burglary section of a policy covering jewellers' premises for various risks, it must be taken to apply only to that section of the policy and not to the whole policy.[98]

10–27 Creation of warranties. In order to give a statement or promise the force of a warranty, the insurers must be able to demonstrate that it was the intention of the parties that this should be so. When a court has to decide the status of a term in a contract of insurance, it is endeavouring to ascertain the intention of the parties with regard to it.[99] Consequently, warranties are created in two ways. First, a term or stipulation, although possibly not conclusively expressed as a warranty, is given the force of a warranty because the court is satisfied that, having regard to the business sense of the clause, the parties to the contract cannot have intended it to be anything else. This category of warranties also includes those implied warranties imported into the contract as a necessary part of the agreement. Secondly a term is made a warranty by reference to a declaration in the proposal form or policy, which decrees quite clearly that it shall have that status, and therefore leaves the parties' intention in no doubt.

[92] *Bean v. Stupart* (1778) 1 Doug. K.B. 11; *Kenyon v. Berthon* (1778) 1 Doug. K.B. 12n.
[93] *Pawson v. Barnevelt* (1779) 1 Doug. K.B. 12n.
[94] *Bize v. Fletcher* (1779) 1 Doug. K.B. 12n.
[95] *Condogianis v. Guardian* [1921] 2 A.C. 125; *Rozanes v. Bowen* (1928) 32 Ll.L.R. 98.
[96] *Bensaude v. Thames and Mersey Ins. Co.* [1897] A.C. 609.
[97] [1897] A.C. 609, 612.
[98] *Allan Peters v. Brocks Alarms* [1968] 1 Lloyd's Rep. 387, 391. See also *Printpak v. AGF Insurance Ltd* [1999] Lloyd's Rep I.R. 542, where, as a matter of construction, a warranty was found to relate only to one section of a policy and not the whole policy.
[99] *Wheelton v. Hardisty* (1857) 8 E. & B. 232, 300, 302; *Barnard v. Faber* [1893] 1 Q.B. 340.

10–28 No technical words necessary. No formal or technical wording is requisite for the creation of a warranty,[1] and the court will consider the substance of the statement or promise made to see if it is fundamental to the contract, bearing in mind its relation to the risk, its business purpose, and whether it would be unfair to leave the insurers without a defence to a claim in the event of a breach of it.[2] This is a question of construction of the whole instrument containing it, and in appropriate circumstances words affirming facts on the faith of which the parties contract are as competent to make a warranty as any strictly technical declaration in the policy.[3]

10–29 On the other hand, it must not be thought that the words "warranty" or "warranted" are of no importance. They are good evidence of the parties' intention to create a warranty, and even though a promise which is "warranted" may in some cases be construed as an exclusion clause or term delimiting the risk,[4] it will usually be elevated at least from the level of a statement of intention or collateral stipulation.[5] Prima facie, the use of the word "warranted" shows that the parties understood that a breach of it should be a permanent or temporary bar to the insurers' liability.[6]

10–30 Presumption of warranty. In marine policies there is a presumption that any statement of fact bearing upon the risks underwritten is, if introduced into the written policy, to be construed as a warranty.[7] In *Sceales v. Scanlan*,[8] Lefroy B. was inclined to follow these early marine cases in a case of life assurance, so that the mere affirmation of a matter of fact which forms part of the contract by actual insertion or by reference to another instrument does make it a matter of warranty. In another Irish case, *Quin v. National Assurance Company*[9] which concerned the description of premises in a fire policy, Jay C.B. thought that a description of premises written in the policy must *ipso facto* be a warranty. The general tendency in English law, however, is to consider the relevance of the disputed term to the policy as a whole in order to determine the parties' intention in regard to it.[10] Thus, in *HIH Casualty and General Insurance Ltd v. New Hampshire Co*,[11] Rix L.J. noted three tests which might be used in determining whether, as a matter of construction, a term was to be construed as a warranty. One was whether the term went to the root of the transaction; a second was whether the term was descriptive of, or bore materially, on the risk of loss; and a third was whether

---

[1] *Union Insurance Society of Canton Ltd v. Wills* [1916] 1 A.C. 281; *Dawsons v. Bonnin* [1922] 2 A.C. 413, 429.

[2] *Barnard v. Faber* [1893] 1 Q.B. 340; *Ellinger v. Mutual Life of N.Y.* [1905] 1 K.B. 31; *Yorkshire Ins. v. Campbell* [1917] A.C. 218; *Union Insurance v. Wills* [1916] 1 A.C. 281, 287.

[3] *Sceales v. Scanlan* (1843) 6 Ir.L.R. 367, 371, *per* Lefroy B; *Thomson v. Weems* (1884) 9 App.Cas. 671, 684; *Yorkshire Ins. Co. v. Campbell* [1917] A.C. 218, 224; *HIH Casualty and General Insurance Ltd v. New Hampshire Co.* [2001] 2 Lloyd's Rep. 161.

[4] See paras 10–7 to 10–9, *ante*.

[5] *Roberts v. Anglo-Saxon* (1926) 26 Ll.L.R. 154, 157; *Palatine Ins. v. Gregory* [1926] A.C. 90, 92.

[6] *Newcastle Fire v. Macmorran* (1815) 3 Dow. 255; *Ellinger v. Mutual Life* [1905] 1 K.B. 31, 38.

[7] *Thomson v. Weems* (1884) 9 App.Cas. 671, 684; *Yorkshire Ins. Co. v. Campbell* [1917] A.C. 218, 224.

[8] (1843) 6 Ir.L.R. 367.

[9] (1839) Jo. & Car. 316, 340.

[10] *Thomson v. Weems* (1884) 9 App.Cas. 671, 684; *Barnard v. Faber* [1893] 1 Q.B. 340.

[11] [2001] 2 Lloyd's Rep. 161.

damages would be an unsatisfactory or inadequate remedy for breach of the term. He noted also, with approval, the views expressed in the previous edition of this work that a description of the subject matter of the insurance written into the policy and obviously material would be likely to be construed as a warranty.[12]

10–31 Implied warranties. Marine insurance has long been familiar with the implied warranty of seaworthiness, whereby the shipowner is held to warrant that the ship is in a seaworthy state at the commencement of a voyage. In other insurances, however, warranties of fitness are not usually implied. There is no implied warranty in life assurance that the "life" is in good health or free from disease and there is no implied warranty in fire insurance that the premises are well-built and incorporate fire precautions, as opposed to any warranty attaching to the description of them. The implied warranty of seaworthiness has, however, a limited relevance in motor insurance in so far as it has assisted judges in the construction of exclusion clauses in motor policies whereby the car in question is not covered while being driven in an "unsafe" or "unroadworthy" condition. In *Barrett v. London General Insurance Co.*[13] Goddard J. applied the marine doctrine in holding that such a clause meant only that the car must be roadworthy at the commencement of a journey; and in *Clarke v. National Insurance*,[14] the Court of Appeal followed the marine decisions in saying that a car could be made unroadworthy because of overloading. The analogy has been criticised, however,[15] and there is nothing in the above cases to suggest that a court would imply a warranty of roadworthiness into a motor policy.

10–32 Creation of warranties by declarations in proposal form. It has already been remarked that the modern practice is for insurers to enquire the assured to warrant the accuracy of statements made in his proposal form by inserting an appropriate declaration at the foot of his answers which applies to all of them. This practice seems to have begun with life assurance policies in the third decade of the nineteenth century. The declarations which the proposer had to sign contained two elements, namely, first that the answers to the insurers' questions were made the basis of the contract between the assured and insurer, and secondly, that any untrue statement should render the insurance policy null and void.[16] The courts accepted that the requirement that facts should be "truly stated" meant that they must be accurate irrespective of the assured's knowledge, and that the immateriality of the matters warranted did not matter so long as the parties' intention was to create a warranty.[17] In more recent cases it has been held that the all-important element in such a declaration is the phrase which makes the declaration the "basis of the contract". These words alone show that the proposer is warranting the truth of his statements, so that in the event of a

---

[12] See, for instance, the cases where the description of premises in a fire policy is interpreted as a warranty, para. 10–76, *infra*.

[13] [1935] 1 K.B. 238.

[14] [1964] 1 Q.B. 199.

[15] *Trickett v. Queensland Insurance Co.* [1936] A.C. 159, 165.

[16] *Everett v. Desborough* (1829) 5 Bing. 503; *Duckett v. Williams* (1834) 2 Cr. & M. 348; *Southcombe v. Merriman* (1842) Car. & Mar. 286; *Maynard v. Rhode* (1824) 5 Dow. & Ry. 266; *Anderson v. Fitzgerald* (1853) 4 H.L.Cas. 484.

[17] *Thomson v. Weems* (1884) 9 App.Cas. 671.

breach of this warranty, the insurer can repudiate liability on the policy irrespective of issues of materiality.[18]

10–33 Whether affected by other conditions. It is sometimes a nice question whether or not the effect of a "basis of the contract" clause is restricted by other conditions in the policy. It has been held that the effect of the recital was not cut down by a condition to the effect that "material misstatement or concealment of any circumstance by the insured material to assessing the premium herein or in connection with any claim shall render the policy void", since the latter condition was not rendered nugatory by the "basis of the contract" clause.[19] In *Holmes v. Scottish Legal Life Assurance Society*[20] this clause was held not to be affected by a provision that the policy would be rendered void by "any fraudulent or untrue statement" and a rule of the Society incorporated in the contract that fraudulent misstatements as to age or health would avoid the contract. In *Condogianis v. Guardian Assurance*[21] a condition providing that any material misdescription of the property insured or its whereabouts or material misrepresentation of facts affecting the risk would release the insurers from liability did not have the effect of restricting the "basis of the contract" clause in the proposal form. In *Fowkes v. Manchester and London Assurance*[22] the "basis of contract" clause was immediately followed by a provision that any fraudulent concealment or designedly untrue statement would avoid the policy, which, in the way it was inserted, appeared to state the consequences of the other clause. The court held accordingly that the declaration that the proposer's statements were "true" must mean "true so far as he knew" in order to harmonise with the words "designedly untrue", although prima facie, "true" would mean "true in fact".

10–34 Where the answers to questions in the proposal form were declared to be the basis of the policy and to be true and certain items were selected from the proposal and made matters of specific warranty in the policy, it was held that the other items not so specifically warranted were nevertheless warranted under the general declaration in the proposal form.[23] As has been said earlier,[24] a warranty can be created by an appropriate declaration in the proposal form alone, and without any express recital in the policy incorporating the declaration into it. In this respect our law is less favourable to the assured than the law of the United States, where appropriate words of reference or incorporation must be found in the policy.[25] There is no reason, of course, why the policy alone should not contain a "basis of contract"

---

[18] *Condogianis v. Guardian Assurance* [1921] 2 A.C. 125; *Dawsons Ltd v. Bonnin* [1922] 2 A.C. 413; *Provincial Insurance v. Morgan* [1933] A.C. 240. Note that this type of clause should not now be used in consumer insurance policies. See note 88, *supra*.

[19] *Dawsons v. Bonnin* [1922] 2 A.C. 413.

[20] (1932) 48 T.L.R. 306.

[21] [1921] 2 A.C. 125.

[22] (1863) 3 B. & S. 917, distinguished in *Unipac (Scotland) Ltd v. Aegon Ins. Co.* 1996 S.L.T. 1197.

[23] *Anderson v. Fitzgerald* (1853) 4 H.L.Cas. 484; *Sceales v. Scanlan* (1843) 6 Ir.L.R. 367.

[24] See paras 10–22 and 10–32, *ante*.

[25] *Campbell v. New England Mutual*, 98 Mass. 381 (1867); *Missouri Trust v. German Bank*, 77 Fed.Rep. 117 (1896); *Daniels v. Hudson River*, 66 Mass. 416 (1853); *Vilas v. N.Y.*, 72 N.Y. 590 (1878); *Cumberland Valley Mutual v. Mitchell*, 48 Pa. 374 (1864); *Hubbard v. Mutual*, 100 Fed.Rep. 719 (1900).

clause rather than the proposal form, so long as this is brought to the assured's notice before the contract is concluded.[26]

10–35 Creation of warranties—ambiguity. Whether a warranty be created by force of its own content and wording or by reference to a general declaration in the proposal form, it has been said by the courts that if insurers intend to extract a warranty from the assured, they ought to express the obligation to warrant in clear terms without ambiguity.[27] The policy is prepared by them and any ambiguity in the creation of warranties ought, as in their interpretation, to be construed against the insurers.[28] This is particularly the case in life assurance, where the applicant is obliged to warrant the accuracy of statements concerning his health of which he cannot be certain.[29]

10–36 Creation of conditions precedent. In modern policies those terms the due observance of which is intended to be a condition precedent to the insurer's liability or a pre-condition of recovery are usually described expressly as conditions precedent. Where the policy wording demonstrates a clear intention to give a clause the status of a condition precedent, the clause will be recognised as such. Either the policy describes an individual clause in such a way as to show that it is a condition precedent,[30] such as "No claim . . . shall be payable unless the terms of this condition shall have been complied with",[31] or a general condition precedent clause states that compliance by the assured with obligations cast on him by the policy is a condition precedent to the insurer's liability to pay claims. A variety of different formulations have been used to that end,[32] but any ambiguity in the wording will be construed against the insurers.[33] In one case[34] a clause stating that observance of all policy conditions was a condition precedent to liability was not conclusive as to a particular condition the nature of which made it inappropriate to possess that status. This decision is open to question in as much as the majority of the Court of Appeal treated the clause in question as if it said that observance of all conditions precedent in the policy was a condition precedent to liability, and the dissenting judgment of Fletcher Moulton L.J. is persuasive.

---

[26] *Macdonald v. Law Union* (1874) L.R. 9 Q.B. 328.

[27] *Braunstein v. Accidental Death* (1861) 1 B. & S. 782, 799.

[28] *De Maurier v. Bastion* [1967] 2 Lloyd's Rep. 550.

[29] *Joel v. Law Union* [1908] 2 K.B. 863, 886.

[30] *Vaughan Motors v. Scottish General Ins. Co.* [1960] 1 Lloyd's Rep. 479, 481; *Shoot v. Hill* (1936) 55 Ll.L.Rep. 29, 34.

[31] *Welch v. Royal Exchange Ass.* [1939] 1 K.B. 294. See also, more recently, *Gan Insurance Co. Ltd v. Tai Ping Insurance Co. Ltd (Nos 2 and 3)* [2001] Lloyd's Rep. I.R. 667.

[32] *e.g. Welch v. Royal Exchange Ass., supra; Bennett v. Yorkshire Ins. Co.* [1962] 2 Lloyd's Rep. 270; *Conn v. Westminster Motor Ins. Assoc.* [1966] 1 Lloyd's Rep. 407; *Pioneer Concrete (UK) Ltd v. Nat. Employers' Mutual Gen. Ins. Assoc.* [1985] 1 Lloyd's Rep. 274; *M/S Aswan Engineering Establishment Co. v. Iron Trades Mut. Ins. Co.* [1989] 1 Lloyd's Rep. 289; *Devco Holder v. Legal & General Ass. Soc.* [1993] 2 Lloyd's Rep. 567.

[33] *London Guarantie Co. v. Fearnley* (1880) 5 App.Cas. 911.

[34] *Re Bradley and Essex & Suffolk Accident Indemnity Soc.* [1912] 1 K.B. 415.

(b) *Special Rules about Warranties*

(i) *Materiality not required*

10–37 Materiality: general rule. With small exceptions, a warranty is independent of all questions of materiality. If a warranty is not fulfilled, the insurer is discharged from liability, whether or not the fact warranted affected the risk or in any way influenced the insurer when he took it. One object of having a warranty is to avoid the difficulty faced by an insurer who has to satisfy the court that a misrepresentation or concealment concerned a fact material to the risk and induced him to take the risk. Thus in *Anderson v. Fitzgerald*, Lord Cranworth said[35]:

> "Nothing, therefore, can be more reasonable than that the parties entering into the contract should determine for themselves what they think to be material, and, if they choose to do so, to stipulate that unless the assured shall answer a certain question accurately the policy or contract which they are entering into shall be void, it is perfectly open to them to do so, and his [the assured's] false answer will then avoid the policy."

In *Thomson v. Weems*, Lord Watson said[36]:

> "Where the truth of a particular statement has been made the subject of warranty no question can arise as to its materiality or immateriality to the risk, it being the very purpose of the warranty to exclude all controversy upon that point."

This general principle manifests itself in two particular respects:

> (i) the fact warranted may be of no relevance to the risk; (ii) a loss need not be occasioned by the breach of warranty in order that the breach may protect the insurer.[37]

10–38 Immateriality of facts warranted or of the breach of warranty. The parties to the contract of insurance may make a bargain about anything, even if it be absurd or fanciful,[38] so long as they make clear what they wish to do. Thus the facts warranted may be of a sort which could not affect the risk in any manner. Thus, if a proposer for motor insurance uses her maiden name when she is in fact married, albeit secretly, that is a breach of the warranty that all her answers are in all respects accurate, even if a spinster could hardly be said to be a worse risk than a married woman.[39] More

---

[35] (1853) 4 H.L.Cas. 484, 503. See also *Glicksman v. Lancs. and General* [1927] A.C. 139, 143, *per* Lord Dunedin.

[36] (1884) 9 App.Cas. 671 689; approved and followed in *Yorkshire Insurance v. Campbell* [1917] A.C. 218; *Condogianis v. Guardian Assurance* [1921] 2 A.C. 125; *Dawsons Ltd v. Bonnin* [1922] 2 A.C. 413; *Paxman v. Union Assurance* (1923) 39 T.L.R. 424.

[37] The Law Commission has reviewed the law of warranties in insurance contracts and has made proposals for reform which would substantially alter the principle stated in this paragraph. See Law Com. No. 104, paras 10.32–10.38. Their proposals have not been implemented, but warranties in insurance policies are now open to challenge on the ground of unfairness—see paras 10–19 to 10–20, *ante*.

[38] *Farr v. Motor Traders Mutual Ins.* [1920] 3 K.B. 669, 673, *per* Bankes L.J.

[39] *Dunn v. Ocean Accident and Guarantee Corporation* (1933) 45 Ll.L.R. 276.

usually, however, the matter warranted concerns things which could well be material in a general way, although the particular breach by the assured is not important at all.[40] Thus if an assured warrants that he has not been attended by a medical man since a certain date, the insurance will be void if he has been so attended, even if a jury might think the attendance immaterial for purposes of the assurance.[41] Where the insurance was on a horse against marine perils and risks of mortality during a sea voyage, and it was described in the proposal form as—"Bay gelding by Soult x St. Paul (mare) 5 years", the pedigree as stated was incorrect and the Privy Council held that, since on its construction the description of the horse was a warranty, the inaccuracy provided insurers with a defence to the owner's claim when the horse died on the voyage.[42]

As a last illustration, it will suffice to consider *Mackay v. London General Insurance Co.*,[43] where the assured had omitted to state when applying for motor insurance that he had been fined 10 shillings many months previously for driving without efficient brakes when a nut had become loose on his motorcycle. Swift J. held that this conviction was not material for the purposes of non-disclosure, but, since the assured had stated that he had never been convicted, and had signed a "basis of the contract" declaration, the insurers could rely on the breach of warranty as a defence to a claim brought on the policy.[44]

10–39 Loss unconnected with breach. Where there is a claim brought in respect of a loss under the policy and the insurer wishes to plead breach of warranty as a defence to it, it is no answer that the loss was not caused by or contributed to by the breach of warranty.[45] Thus, if a man warrants that he is of sober and temperate habits, and the insurers on a policy on his life dispute the accuracy of his statement, then the only issue will be whether he was so or not, and, if not, it is no good his representatives saying that he was a man of exceptionally strong constitution so that his occasional bouts of intemperance had no effect upon his system and did not hasten his death.[46] It is the same with continuing warranties. In *Glen v. Lewis*,[47] there was a warranty that "no steam engine shall be introduced". One was introduced experimentally into the premises for a few days. The court held that the insurance was thereby terminated, and Parke B. said[48]:

[40] *Newcastle Fire v. Macmorran* (1815) 3 Dow 255.
[41] *Cazenove v. British Equitable* (1859) 6 C.B.(N.S.) 437.
[42] *Yorkshire Insurance v. Campbell* [1917] A.C. 218. There is a suggestion on p. 225 that the Privy Council might have been prepared to label the pedigree material.
[43] (1935) 51 Ll.L.R. 201. See also *Grogan v. London and Manchester Industrial Life* (1885) 53 L.T. 761; *Allen v. Universal Auto. Ins. Co.* (1933) 45 Ll.L.R. 55; *Dawsons v. Bonnin* [1922] 2 A.C. 413.
[44] Under the Statements of Insurance Practice, insurers are supposed not to extract immaterial warranties save in insurances on the life of another: para. 1(b) of the Statement of General Insurance Practice and of the Statement of Long-Term Insurance Practice 1986.
[45] *Woolmer v. Muilman* (1763) 3 Burr. 1419; *Weir v. Aberdeen* (1819) 2 B. & Ald. 320; *Maynard v. Rhode* (1824) 3 L.J.(O.S.) K.B. 64 (the warranty appears to this report only); *Southcombe v. Merriman* (1842) Car. & Mar. 286; *Glen v. Lewis* (1853) 8 Ex. 607; *Beacon Life and Fire Ass. v. Gibb* (1862) 1 Moo.P.C.(N.S.) 73; *Foley v. Tabor* (1861) 2 F. & F. 663; *Conn v. Westminster Insurance* [1966] 1 Lloyd's Rep. 407; *Yorkshire Insurance v. Campbell* [1917] A.C. 218. The Commercial Court has deplored reliance on such defences—*De Maurier v. Bastion Insurance* [1967] 2 Lloyd's Rep. 550, 560, *per* Donaldson J.
[46] *Southcombe v. Merriman* (1842) Car. & Mar. 286; *Thomson v. Weems* (1884) 9 App.Cas. 671.
[47] (1853) 8 Ex. 607.
[48] *ibid.*, 617.

"It appears to have been on the premises insured for several days, and then the fire happened, whether in consequence of the steam engine being worked or not is quite immaterial."

If the assured under a motor policy warrants that, as a condition of the insurers' liability, he will maintain the insured vehicle in an "efficient" or "roadworthy" condition, and the insurers can show that the vehicle was not in such a state, they will have a defence to his claim arising out of an accident involving the insured vehicle without going so far as to prove that the poor condition of the vehicle caused or contributed to the accident.[49] It makes no difference, moreover, that the breach of warranty is remedied before a loss occurs, as where an unseaworthy ship sets forth on her voyage, puts into port to repair the cause of unseaworthiness, departs again on her voyage, and is lost thereafter.[50] Since the breach of warranty discharges the insurer from liability irrespective of how loss occurs, it must be the logical consequence that the insurer can at once disclaim liability under the policy for a breach of warranty before any claim is brought. This point is considered later.[51]

10–40 Exceptions to principles of immateriality. It is convenient to bear in mind certain exceptions to the general rule that materiality is of no account in warranty law. First, when the intention of the parties to give a particular term the status of a warranty is in doubt, the fact that it is material to the risk is, as we have seen, a good indication that a warranty was intended.[52] Secondly, the effect of breach of warranty may be cut down by a proviso, as long as the wording of the proviso is apt to cover breaches of warranty,[53] which states that the policy can only be avoided for untrue statements or concealment of material facts. In that case, the materiality of the false answer is made a relevant issue.[54] There is also a possible third exception, inasmuch as a court may be more ready to construe a warranty in the assured's favour, in order to find that he had complied with it, if the matter warranted was trivial and not fundamental to the risk.[55]

10–41 Statements of Insurance Practice. Paragraph 2(b) of the Statement of General Insurance Practice 1986 provides that insurers will not repudiate liability towards an assured on the grounds of a breach of warranty or

---

[49] *Jones v. Provincial Insurance* (1929) 35 Ll.L.R. 135; *Brown v. Zurich General Accident* [1954] 2 Lloyd's Rep. 243; *Conn v. Westminster Ins. Co.* [1966] 1 Lloyd's Rep. 407.

[50] *Foley v. Tabor* (1861) 2 F. & F. 663; *Farr v. Motor Traders Mutual* [1920] 3 K.B. 669; *Newcastle Fire v. Macmorran* (1815) 3 Dow. 255.

[51] See para. 10–97, *infra*.

[52] *Barnard v. Faber* [1893] 1 Q.B. 340; *Yorkshire Ins. Co. v. Campbell* [1917] A.C. 218; *HIH Casualty and General Insurance Ltd v. New Hampshire Co.* [2001] Lloyd's Rep. 161.

[53] See, *e.g. Kumar v. AGF Insurance* [1999] 1 W.L.R. in which the wording was held to be apposite; contrast *HIH Casualty and General Insurance Ltd v. New Hampshire Co.* [2001] Lloyd's Rep. 161 where the wording was held not to be apposite.

[54] *Fowkes v. Manchester and London Life Ass. Assoc.* (1863) 3 B. & S. 917; *Mutual Life of N.Y. v. Ontario Metal Products* [1925] A.C. 344; *Gauvrement v. Prudential Ins. Co. of America* [1941] S.C.R. 139. For the American state legislation abrogating the rule that breach of warranty need not be material to the risk, see Richards, *Law of Insurance* (1952), paras 320–321.

[55] *Provincial Ins. Co. v. Morgan* [1933] A.C. 240.

condition where the circumstances of the loss are unconnected with the breach unless fraud is involved. This paragraph does not apply to marine and aviation policies. The Statement of Long-Term Insurance Practice 1986, which covers life assurance, provides in paragraph 3(b) that, fraud apart, an insurer will not rely on breach of warranty unless the circumstances of the claim are connected with the breach and unless (1) either the warranty relates to a statement of fact concerning the life on a life of another policy which the life assured could reasonably have been expected to disclose had he proposed for an own life policy, or (2) the warranty was material to the particular risk and was drawn to the attention of the proposer at or prior to the conclusion of the contract.[56]

(ii) *Strict compliance*

10–42 General rule. It has always been the law since Lord Mansfield's day that there must be strict and exact compliance with the obligation or statement which is warranted, so that, as he himself said in *Pawson v. Watson*, "Nothing tantamount will do or answer the purpose".[57] It is, therefore, not open to the assured to say that the obligation has been substantially complied with, or that the answer he made to a question was more or less accurate. This rule is presumably related to the general doctrine that a warranty is independent of any question of materiality, since an assured who gave an answer which was false only in a trifling detail, and contended that it was accurate, would in a sense be contending that the difference was not material or important to the insurers' calculations.

10–43 Where, therefore, a proposer for motor insurance was asked, "What was actual price paid by owner?", and answered, "£285", it was held that there had been a breach of warranty because he had paid only £271.[58] A stove pipe which is three feet long does not answer a warranty that it is two feet long.[59] Where the age of an applicant for life assurance was warranted to be 30, the warranty was broken when it was shown to be 35, and the issue of materiality had to be withheld from the jury.[60] Where the answers in a fire policy were warranted true, and in answer to a question concerning incumbrances the assured stated the property was mortgaged for £6,600, whereas it was in fact mortgaged for £6,684, it was held that the insurer was discharged from liability.[61]

10–44 Exact compliance sufficient. The rule of strict compliance demands only an exact performance of the warranty or condition, and the insurer is not permitted to say that it was in the power of the assured to do more to comply with the warranty than he did, if what he did was an exact

---

[56] For the text of the Statements see Part 7 of the *Encyclopaedia of Insurance Law*.

[57] (1778) 2 Cowp. 785, 787; *De Hahn v. Hartley* (1786) 1 T.R. 343; *Yorkshire Insurance v. Campbell* [1917] A.C. 218, 224; Marine Insurance Act 1906, s.33; *Union Insurance v. Wills* [1916] 1 A.C. 281; *Overseas Commodities v. Style* [1958] 1 Lloyd's Rep. 546, 558.

[58] *Allen v. Universal Automobile Ins. Co.* (1933) 45 Ll.L.R. 55. See also *Santer v. Poland* (1924) 19 Ll.L.R. 29.

[59] *Newcastle Fire v. Macmorran* (1815) 3 Dow. 255.

[60] *Aetna Life v. France*, 91 U.S. 510 (1875).

[61] *Abbott v. Shawmut Mutual*, 85 Mass. 213 (1861).

compliance.[62] This principle dates back to Lord Mansfield's day also, and he held in *Hide v. Bruce*[63] that a warranty that a ship had 20 guns was not one which additionally required her to have sufficient men to work them.

10–45 Exact compliance and alteration of user. One application of the rule that exact compliance is sufficient is where the assured wishes to alter a user of premises described in a policy. Where, in a fire or burglary policy, for instance, there is an alteration in the user of the insured premises which may increase the risk or liability of the insurer, and the assured has warranted that the user will correspond to a particular description, the issue is whether the new user is outside the description or not. If it is not, it does not invalidate the policy even if it increases the risk or liability of the insurers,[64] for the assured need not conduct his business or occupation in the way least prejudicial to the insurers' interests.

10–46 In *Pim v. Reid*,[65] the insurance was on machinery in a mill. When the policy was effected the mill was being used for the manufacture of paper, but during the currency of the policy the assured started the business of a cleaner and dyer of cotton waste, which involved a user of a more hazardous sort, and a loss occurred. It was held that in the absence of any express condition prohibiting alterations in user, and in the absence of the alteration contravening any description of the subject-matter of the insurance, the change of trade did not invalidate the policy. In *Baxendale v. Harvey*[66] the insurance was on a warehouse containing a steam engine ordinarily used for hoisting goods. After the insurance was effected the assured began to use it to grind provender for their horses, and it was held that, even though the danger of fire might thereby be increased, the policy was not invalidated. Pollock C.B. said[67]:

> "This is a mere increase of danger. It is like the case of a person who has an oven on his premises using it for some other purpose. ... A person who insures may light as many candles as he pleases in his house though each additional candle increases the danger."

In one US fire case[68] it was held that, in the absence of express conditions, the erection of contiguous buildings, although increasing the risk, did not affect the validity of the policy, and in another it was held that, express conditions apart, change of tenancy from a careful to a careless tenant does not affect the validity of the policy.[69]

10–47 The above cases must be contrasted with cases where the description of the trade carried on by the assured is warranted, and the

---

[62] *Whitehead v. Price* (1835) 2 Cr. M. & R. 447; *Mayall v. Mitford* (1837) 6 Ad. & El. 670.
[63] (1783) 3 Doug. K.B. 213.
[64] *Shaw v. Robberds* (1837) 6 Ad. & El. 75. See paras 26–49 to 26–58, *post.*
[65] (1843) 6 Scott N.R. 982, 1004; 6 M. & G. 1.
[66] (1859) 4 H. & N. 445.
[67] (1859) 4 H. & N. 445, 452.
[68] *Young v. Washington Mutual*, 14 Barb. 545 (N.Y.S.C. 1853).
[69] *Gates v. Madison Mutual*, 5 N.Y. 469 (1851).

alteration of user or trade makes the description cease to be correct. Where in a proposal for insurance on the contents of a factory the applicants were described as paper board manufacturers but were in fact waste paper merchants, and stocked between four and five hundred tons of that commodity in the premises, it was held that owing to the misdescription of the trade, the risk was not covered.[70] These principles are not confined to fire and burglary policies[71] and they also show that there is no implied warranty in a policy that the risk will not be increased during the policy.

10–48 Express conditions relating to alterations. In practice there may be express conditions which determine the questions discussed above. Thus, if there is an express condition in the policy that any alteration increasing the risk will render the policy void, the description of the premises or user can amount at most to an absolute warranty of the same at the commencement of the insurance, but the express condition precludes any interpretation of the description as a continuing warranty preventing any alterations whatsoever during the risk.[72] Conversely, if there is a warranty that the subject-matter of the insurance comes within a particular classification defined in the policy, and it does not. the policy will be invalidated regardless of the risk being increased or not. So in *Newcastle Fire Insurance v. Macmorran*,[73] an often cited decision of Lord Eldon, the premises insured were warranted to be within Class 1 of the risks defined in the policy. Class 1 was defined as including buildings which had, *inter alia*, "not more than two feet of stove pipe". The building contained a stove which had more than two feet of metal pipe and the House of Lords, reversing the Court of Session, held that the breach of warranty avoided the policy regardless of its materiality to the risk.

10–49 Interpretation of warranty. The rule of strict compliance is, however, mitigated in practice by rules of construction which sometimes have the effect of reducing the scope of a warranty to the extent that, when it is read in a more limited sense than that contended for by the insurer, it is seen that there has been no breach of the warranty thus interpreted. These rules of construction are considered in more detail in the chapter on principles of construction, but it may be useful to mention their effect in the context of warranties.

10–50 The first relevant rule of construction is that the apparently literal meaning of the words of the warranty must be restricted if they produce a result inconsistent with a reasonable and businesslike interpretation of such a warranty.[74] A warranty in a contract must, like a clause in any other commercial contract, receive a reasonable interpretation and must, if necessary, be read with such limitations and qualifications as will render it reasonable.[75] The words used ought to be given the interpretation which,

---

[70] *A. F. Watkinson & Co. v. Hallett* (1938) 61 Ll.L.R. 145.

[71] *Thompson v. Hopper* (1858) E.B. & E. 1038, 1049; *Trinder Anderson v. Thames and Mersey Ins. Co.* [1898] 2 Q.B. 114, 128 (marine); *Mitchell Conveyor and Transporter Co. v. Pulbrook* (1933) 45 Ll.L.R. 239, 245 (construction risks policy).

[72] *Stokes v. Cox* (1856) 1 H. & N. 320, 553.

[73] (1815) 3 Dow. 255.

[74] *Barnard v. Faber* [1893] 1 Q.B. 340, 344; *Equitable Fire and Accident v. Ching Wo Hong* [1907] A.C. 96.

[75] *National Protector Fire Ins. Co. v. Nivert* [1913] A.C. 507, 513; *Mammone v. RACV Ins. Pty Ltd* [1976] V.R. 617.

having regard to the context and circumstances, would be placed upon them by ordinary men of normal intelligence conversant with the subject-matter of the insurance. The courts' interpretation of a warranty is a question of law.[76]

10–51 The courts' tendency to place a limited interpretation on a phrase with potentially wide scope is well illustrated by the cases on continuing warranties.[77] Thus there are cases where the assured under a fire policy has undertaken and warranted that the user of the insured premises shall correspond to a particular description in the proposal form during the continuation of the risk, but the courts have interpreted the warranty as referring to habitual user only, so that a temporary departure from the described user was not a breach of warranty at all.[78] Where the assured under a burglary policy warranted that the insured premises would be "always occupied", the insurer contended that this meant, quite literally, that the premises should never be left unattended, but the court held that the words meant that the premises should be continuously occupied as a residence.[79] To hold otherwise would be quite unreasonable on the assured, especially during an air-raid on that locality.[80]

10–52 Interpretation in favour of feasible answer. The same principle applies where it would be very hard or virtually impossible for the assured to provide an entirely accurate answer to the question put to him, and the court interprets the question in a more limited sense which makes it feasible for the assured to answer it, and also shows that his answer was correct. Where the applicant for life assurance is asked, "Have you had any other illness, local disease or personal injury?" and answers "No", the warranty will not be held to cover slight indispositions or trivial injuries occurring possibly many years before.[81] The company could not reasonably expect a man of mature age to recollect and disclose every illness, however slight, or every personal injury, consisting of a contusion or cut or blow, which he might have suffered in the course of his life. "Personal injury" must therefore be interpreted as "serious personal injury". Similarly, where the assured was warranted to be in "good health", Lord Mansfield was of opinion that the warranty might be complied with even if the assured had some particular infirmity not endangering life,[82] such as, for example, gout.[83]

10–53 The second principle of construction which assists the assured who

---

[76] *Dunn v. Ocean Accident* (1933) 45 Ll.L.R. 276, 280; *Simmonds v. Cockell* [1920] 1 K.B. 843; *Yorkshire Ins. Co. v. Campbell* [1917] A.C. 218, 221.

[77] See paras 10–80 to 10–85, *infra*.

[78] *Dobson v. Sotheby* (1827) Moo. & M. 90; *Shaw v. Robberds* (1837) 6 Ad. & El. 75; *Provincial Insurance v. Morgan* [1933] A.C. 240.

[79] *Simmonds v. Cockell* [1920] 1 K.B. 843.

[80] *Winicofsky v. Army and Navy* (1919) 35 T.L.R. 283.

[81] *Connecticut Mutual Life v. Moore* (1881) 6 App.Cas. 644, 648; and see *Broad & Montague v. S.E. Lancs. Ins. Co.* (1931) 40 Ll.L.R. 328, 331 for analogous treatment of question concerning prior insurance in a motor policy.

[82] *Ross v. Bradshaw* (1761) 1 Wm.Bl. 312; 2 Park 934.

[83] *Willis v. Poole* (1780) 2 Park 935; Park, *Insurance* (1817), p. 650. See *Yorke v. Yorkshire Ins. Co.* [1918] 1 K.B. 662 for definitions of "good health"; also *Burrow v. Nation Life and General* [1925] I.A.C.(N.I.)Rep. 53.

contends he has complied with a warranty is that any ambiguity in the terms of a policy must be construed against the insurer, so that if the assured has taken a statement or question in a particular sense which is not an unreasonable interpretation of the words, the insurer cannot contend for the reading more favourable to him. This principle is frequently applied to ambiguous questions in a proposal form in which the truth of the assured's answer is warranted and several examples are given in another chapter.[84] Where, also, an applicant for life insurance was asked to state his "residence", and thought that this meant the place where he was residing for some months when making his application rather than his permanent home in Ireland, a Divisional Court held that, if the insurers wanted to know the place where the applicant would be residing in the future, they should put the question in appropriate words, and the assured was justified in answering the question as he did, so that the warranty of its accuracy was complied with.[85]

In a case of an insurance upon the machinery in certain cotton mills, there was a warranty that the mills would be worked by day only. The insurers pleaded a breach of warranty inasmuch as a certain steam engine, being contained in the mill, was worked by night and not by day only. The court held that the plea was bad in that the working of a single engine in the mill was not necessarily a working of the mill.[86] And where the applicant for a life policy was asked "Are you now, and have you always been, of sober and temperate habits?" and answered "Yes", it was held that he was right to think that the insurers were concerned only with the excessive consumption of alcohol and not with drug taking. Consequently his addiction to veronal did not make his answer incorrect.[87] The words "sober and temperate", said McCardie J., must receive such an interpretation as would ordinarily be put on them by ordinary men of normal intelligence and average knowledge of the world.

10–54 Basis of rules of interpretation. This principle rests in part upon the general *contra proferentem* rule, but also upon the courts' sympathy for ordinary people unaccustomed to legal documents who find it difficult to relate the different parts of a complex policy and understand what is being asked of them, especially when insurers could with more care remove the ambiguities present in it.[88] It has been remarked justly that "the result of using ambiguous expressions is generally a decision against those who deal in such ambiguities",[89] and the following words of Lord St Leonards in *Anderson v. Fitzgerald* have been cited and approved on many occasions: "A policy ought to be so framed that he who runs can read. It ought to be framed with such deliberate care, that no form of expression by which, on the one hand, the party assured can be caught, or by which, on the other hand the company can be cheated, shall be found upon the face of it."[90] Nonetheless, it is not open to the assured to exploit a possible ambiguity where a normal

[84] Ch. 16, paras 16–25 to 16–28, *post*.
[85] *Grogan v. London and Manchester* (1885) 53 L.T. 761.
[86] *Mayall v. Mitford* (1837) 6 Ad. & El. 670.
[87] *Yorke v. Yorkshire Insurance Co.* [1918] 1 K.B. 662.
[88] *Woolfall & Rimmer v. Moyle* [1942] 1 K.B. 66, 73; *Provincial Ins. Co. v. Morgan* [1933] A.C. 240, 250; *Glicksman v. Lancashire and General* [1927] A.C. 139, 144; *Sweeney v. Kennedy* (1949) 82 Ll.L.R. 294, 301.
[89] *Sweeney v. Kennedy* (1948) 82 Ll.L.R. 294, 302.
[90] (1853) 4 H.L.Cas. 484, 510.

intelligent person would, on reflection, know what was really meant.[91] In this respect the *contra proferentem* rule is subordinate to the first principle here mentioned—that of reasonable interpretation. Thus in *Yorke v. Yorkshire Insurance*[92] the proposer for life assurance was also asked "What illnesses have you suffered?" and answered "None of any consequence". The answer was warranted true. In fact he had taken an overdose of veronal and had lain in a critical condition while relatives were sent for. However, it was argued that, since the question was obscurely framed and ambiguous, the meaning of "illness" was to be taken in a way favourable to the assured and his answer must be at most an expression of opinion. McCardie J. held that the word "illness" must be construed in a "fair business manner", and that the assured's answer was one of fact even if it involved him in expressing a "mixture of fact and opinion".[93] Consequently the word "illness" was unambiguous, and the assured's answer was wrong.[94]

10–55 In *Kumar v. Life Assurance Corporation of India*[95] the applicant was asked in the proposal form "Have you consulted a medical practitioner within the last five years, if so give details", "Did you ever have any operation, accident or injury, if so give details", and "Have you ever been in any hospital ... for a check-up, observation, treatment or an operation, if so give details". She answered all three questions, "No". It was held by Kerr J. that her answers were wrong. She had previously had a Caesarean delivery in hospital, which was relevant to the second question. She had consulted a doctor thereafter concerning the advisability of her "going on the pill", which was within the ambit of the first question. The Caesarean delivery was also material to the third question.

10–56 A similar decision was reached in *Thomson v. Weems*[96] with regard to the question "(1) Are you temperate in your habits and (2) have you always been strictly so?" to which the assured had replied "(1) Temperate (2) Yes". It was argued that the answer must be necessarily a matter of opinion, which meant that it need only be honest, but the House of Lords held that a man's sobriety was a matter of fact and the answer's accuracy did not depend upon the assured's own opinion of his habits. And in *Roberts v. Avon Insurance Co.*[97] the question "Have you ever sustained a loss?" was held to include any loss in respect of which the insurer had indemnified the proposer, for that was the intended meaning of the question.

(c) *Types of Warranty and Related Clauses*

10–57 Warranty irrespective of knowledge. The rule of strict compliance makes it very important for the assured to know exactly what he is

---

[91] *Condogianis v. Guardian* [1912] 2 A.C. 125, 130; *Hart v. Standard Marine* (1889) 22 Q.B.D. 499; *Jacobson v. Yorkshire Ins. Co.* (1933) 49 T.L.R. 389.
[92] [1918] 1 K.B. 662.
[93] *ibid.*, 668–669.
[94] Neither pregnancy, child-birth nor a miscarriage is an "illness" or "infirmity" within the meaning of such a question: *Anstey v. British Natural* (1908) 99 L.T. 16, 765; *Dunk v. Bristol etc., F.S.* [1924] I.A.C.Rep. 115; *Capiter v. Bristol Widows Ass. Co.* [1926] I.A.C.Rep. 71. See also *Gardner v. London General Ins. Co.* [1926] I.A.C.Rep. 46 (mental defective).
[95] [1974] 1 Lloyd's Rep. 147.
[96] (1884) 9 App.Cas. 671.
[97] [1956] 2 Lloyd's Rep. 240.

warranting when he signs the proposal form, and this is especially true of life assurance policies, where the declaration may mean that the assured is warranting that his answers are not only truthfully given but entirely accurate.

10–58 It has been recognised by the courts in England that an insurer may require the assured to warrant the accuracy of all statements made by him in the proposal form irrespective of his own personal knowledge. Where an assured warrants that his statements are "true", not only is subjective truthfulness warranted but also their absolute accuracy.[98] In *Duckett v. Williams*, an early case on this type of warranty, Lord Lyndhurst remarked that "a statement is not the less untrue because the party making it is not apprised of the untruth".[99] Thus if the applicant states that he has no disease or symptoms of disease, and in fact he had some latent disease or some symptom of disease of which he was unconscious or which he did not recognise as such, the policy will be invalidated, however fully and honestly he may have stated the facts within his knowledge, and even though the accuracy of his statements could sometimes only be tested by a post-mortem examination.[1] In *Thomson v. Weems*, Lord Blackburn said[2]:

> "It seems to me a very reasonable stipulation on the part of the insurer, and that it is not at all absurd or improper on the part of the assured to assent to such being a term in the contract. It is seldom that a derangement of one important function can have gone so far as to amount to disease without some symptoms having developed themselves, but the insurers have a right, if they please, to take a warranty against such disease, whether latent or not; and it has very long been the course of business to insert a warranty to that effect."

10–59 Warranty of opinion or belief. In contrast to the above warranty is the warranty by which the assured has warranted only the truth of his statements so far as he knew it. In many cases this is quite clear, as where he declares that he is "not aware of any disorder tending to shorten life"[3] or that "he believes the statements to be true"[4] or that "the answers are true to the best of his knowledge and belief"[5] or where the condition in the policy states that "the policy will be void in case of any false and fraudulent averments".[6] In some cases, the words used in the declaration may be inaptly chosen and create an ambiguity, in which case the courts will readily assume that the

---

[98] *Duckett v. Williams* (1834) 2 Cr. & M. 348; *Anderson v. Fitzgerald* (1853) 4 H.L.Cas. 484; *Cazenove v. British Equitable* (1859) 6 C.B.(N.S.) 437; (1860) 29 L.J.C.P. 160; *Macdonald v. Law Union* (1874) L.R. 9 Q.B. 328; *Hamborough v. Mutual Life* (1895) 72 L.T. 140; *Fowkes v. Manchester and London Life* (1863) 3 B. & S. 917, 929; *Grogan v. London and Manchester Industrial Life* (1885) 53 L.T. 761; *Holmes v. Scottish Legal Life* (1932) 48 T.L.R. 306.

[99] (1834) 2 Cr. & M. 348, 351.

[1] This point was made in *Hutchison v. National Loan* (1845) 7 D. 467, where the Court of Session said the court ought not to give effect to such a warranty. The Scottish courts refused to follow *Duckett v. Williams (supra)*—see *McLaws v. U.K. Temperance, etc., Ass. Co.* (1861) 23 D. 559—and in *Thomson v. Weems* the House of Lords expressly overruled the Scottish authorities opposed to it.

[2] (1884) 9 App.Cas. 671, 682.

[3] *Jones v. Provincial Life* (1857) 3 C.B.(N.S.) 65.

[4] *Wheelton v. Hardisty* (1857) 8 E. & B. 232.

[5] *Confederation Life Ass. v. Millar* (1887) 14 S.C.R. 330; *McLoughlin v. Hearts of Oak Ass. Co.* [1931] I.A.C.(N.I.) Rep. 74.

[6] *Scottish Provident v. Boddam* (1893) 9 T.L.R. 385.

assured is only required to warrant his belief that the answers are correct. The context may justify the court in construing the words "false" and "untrue" in the narrower sense of dishonest.[7] Thus, where the declaration signed by the assured was to the effect that the policy should be void in case "any designedly untrue statement" had been made, but there was also a condition in the policy providing that it should be void if "any false averment" was made, the condition was construed in the light of the declaration, so that "false averment" was held to mean "wilfully false averment".[8]

10–60 The sort of question which elicits only an opinion is one such as "Do you consider yourself of sound constitution"—a question relating clearly to the applicant's opinion of himself, so that the answer can only be untrue if dishonest.[9] The question "Have you had" certain diseases relates only to matters of which the assured must have been previously conscious and not to antecedent latent diseases of which he or she was unconscious.[10] However, if the assured had suffered from one of the stated diseases, but had forgotten about it, a denial would be untrue, notwithstanding the honesty of the answer, since the question would seem to elicit more than just an honest answer. The correctness of the denial would raise a nice point if the disease was attended by characteristic symptoms of which the assured was conscious, although he did not know what disease they signified. If the question was "do you enjoy good health?" the inclusion of the word "enjoy" might well mean that the applicant was being asked merely whether he was conscious of ordinary vitality and freedom from distressing symptoms. The question "Are you in good health?" is more ambiguous. Some authority suggests that it elicits only the assured's opinion of his health,[11] but these cases were decided prior to *Thomson v. Weems*, and it is submitted that it poses a question of fact.[12] No doubt a court would be prepared to say that "good health" does not mean "perfect health", and a man might still be in good health even if he were an insomniac[13] or was short-sighted or possessed some other slight ailment which did not endanger life or seriously reduce his enjoyment of it. As Lord Mansfield said in *Willes v. Poole* "such a warranty could never mean, that a man has not in him the seeds of some disorder. We are all born with the seeds of mortality in us."[14]

However, it must be said that the courts have criticised the severity of warranties of accuracy of statements regarding health, and will be very ready to construe any ambiguous declaration signed by the assured either as no

---

[7] *Moulor v. American Life*, 111 U.S. 335 (1884); *Phoenix Life v. Raddin*, 120 U.S. 183 (1887).

[8] *Fowkes v. Manchester and London Life* (1863) 3 B. & S. 917. Cf. *Hemmings v. Sceptre Life* [1905] 1 Ch. 365. *Contra: Unipac (Scotland) Ltd. v. Aegon Ins. Co. (UK) Ltd.* 1996 S.L.T. 1197.

[9] *Thomson v. Weems* (1884) 9 App.Cas. 671, 690.

[10] *Life Association of Scotland v. Forster* (1873) 11 M. 351; *Thompson v. Weems* (1884) 9 App.Cas. 671, 693.

[11] *Swete v. Fairlie* (1833) 6 C. & P. 1; *Hutchison v. National Loan* (1845) 7 D. 467.

[12] *Yorke v. Yorkshire Insurance* [1918] 1 K.B. 662, 669.

[13] *Yorke v. Yorkshire Insurance* [1918] 1 K.B. 662.

[14] (1780) Marsh, Ins. 771; Park, *Insurance*, p. 649 (ed. 1817); reported also in note to *Ross v. Bradshaw* (1761) 1 Wm.Bl. 312, 313.

warranty[15] or else as a warranty limited in scope.[16] A declaration that the applicant has made true answers to a medical referee has been interpreted as meaning they were truthfully made.[17]

10–61 Health of third party. A distinction has also been drawn between questions put to the assured concerning his own health and habits, and questions put concerning the health and habits of another when the insurance is on the life of a third party. The former are readily susceptible of the construction that they are only put to elicit facts within the knowledge of the applicant, whereas the latter are directed to facts not necessarily within his knowledge at all, and may be more readily construed to require an absolute warranty of the facts stated.[18]

10–62 Promissory or continuing warranties. A warranty of a promissory character is a warranty that a given state of affairs will exist during the continuation of the risk and not merely at its inception, a breach of which will discharge the insurer's liability.[19] The word "promissory" is, however, an ambiguous one despite its frequent use in this context,[20] since any warranty is in a sense "promissory" in so far as the assured is giving an undertaking in respect of any facts warranted, present or future,[21] and it might accordingly be preferable to style these warranties as "continuing".[22]

10–63 The continuing warranty must be distinguished from other types of statement. If, for example, the applicant for motor insurance were to state in his proposal form that the vehicle, was "driven only by proposer", those words might after issue of a policy constitute any one of five different types of statement—(i) a statement of intention as to the driving of the car; (ii) a warranty as to the present situation regarding it; (iii) a term delimiting the risk; (iv) a collateral stipulation; (v) a continuing warranty that no one else would drive the car. In the following paragraphs we consider, first, examples of these different statements; secondly, the considerations which influence

---

[15] *Joel v. Law Union* [1908] 2 K.B 863 *per* Fletcher Moulton L.J.; *Wheelton v. Hardisty* (1857) 8 E. & B. 232, 300.

[16] *Yorke v. Yorkshire Insurance* [1918] 1 K.B. 662; *Burrow v. Nation Life and General* [1925] I.A.C.(N.I.) Rep. 53 (latent tuberculosis did not invalidate declaration of good health); *Willis v. Poole* (1780) 2 Park 935; Park, *Insurance* (1817), p. 650.

[17] *Joel v. Law Union* [1908] 2 K.B. 863. Paragraph 1(e) of the Statement of Long Term Insurance Practice 1989 provides that "Insurers should avoid asking questions which would require knowledge beyond that which the signatory could reasonably be expected to possess". Para. 1(e) of the Statement of General Insurance Practice 1986 provides that, so far as is practicable, insurers will avoid asking questions which would require expert knowledge beyond that which the proposer would reasonably be expected to possess or to obtain, or which would require a value judgment on his part.

[18] *Life Association of Scotland v. Forster* (1873) 11 M. 351.

[19] *Bank of Nova Scotia v. Hellenic Mut. War. Risks Assoc.* [1992] 1 A.C. 233, 263. See paras 10–88 to 10–90, *post.*

[20] *Provincial Insurance v. Morgan* [1933] A.C. 240, 254 *per* Lord Wright; *Hearts of Oak v. Law Union* [1936] 2 All E.R. 619, 623; *Beauchamp v. National Mutual* [1937] 3 All E.R. 19, 21 *per* Finlay J.; *De Maurier v. Bastion* [1967] 2 Lloyd's Rep. 550, 558 *per* Donaldson J.; *Kirkbride v. Donner* [1974] 1 Lloyd's Rep. 549, 553, *per* His Honour Deputy Judge Tibber; *"The Milasan"* [2000] 2 Lloyd's Rep. 458, 466, per Aikens J.

[21] See definition of "promissory warranty" in Marine Insurance Act 1906, s.33(1).

[22] *Hales v. Reliance Fire and Accident* [1960] 2 Lloyd's Rep. 391, 395 *per* McNair J.

the courts when they classify a statement which is not clearly expressed to be a continuing warranty; lastly, the interpretation of continuing warranties by the courts when it is not obvious that there has been a breach by the assured.

10–64 Statement of intention. Since the future cannot be definitely ascertained statements with regard to it are more readily susceptible of the construction that they are only representations of expectation or intention, whereas with statements relating to the present the presumption is that there is a warranty of present fact,[23] unless the things represented are necessarily matters of opinion,[24] such as statements concerning value or health. If a statement of intention does not correspond with what eventually happened or was done, there is no prejudice to the assured unless he never entertained the intention as claimed.

10–65 In a fidelity policy the assured stated that a finance committee would examine the accounts of the employee in question every fortnight, and signed a declaration that the statements in the proposal form were true. The Court of Exchequer decided that this was a declaration of the course intended to be pursued with regard to the committee, so that if it was made honestly there was no breach of what was at most a warranty of intention entertained if the committee failed to meet fortnightly.[25]

This case[26] has been followed in similar cases in Australia,[27] and it is only where a policy has contained an express condition that the course of business and supervision to be pursued would be in accordance with the statements in the proposal form that the latter have been held to constitute absolute warranties as to the future.[28]

10–66 Two policies of fire insurance on a steamship which was burned while lying in Tate's Dock, Montreal, are of interest in that in the claim on one policy the description of the vessel's intended user and locality was construed as a mere expression of intention, whereas in the claim on the other policy a description in slightly different terms was construed as an express warranty as to her future use. In the one case the vessel was described as "The Steamer *Malakoff* now lying in Tate's Dock, Montreal, and intended to navigate the St Lawrence and lakes from Hamilton to Quebec principally as a freight boat to be laid up for the winter in a place approved by the Company", and it was here held that there was no warranty that the ship would so navigate but merely an expression of intention and a licence to do so.[29] But in the other case where the description was "the Steamer *Malakoff* (now in Tate's Dock, Montreal) navigating the river St

---

[23] *Herrick v. Union Mutual Fire.* 48 Me. 558 (1860).

[24] See paras 10–59 to 10–60, *supra.*

[25] *Benham v. United Guarantee* (1852) 7 Ex. 744. *Towle v. National Guardian Assurance* (1861) 10 W.R. 49; 30 L.J.Ch. 900 is another decision on a fidelity policy, but the court's classification of the assured's statements is uncertain.

[26] *ibid.*

[27] *R. v. National Insurance* (1887) 13 Vict.L.R. 914; *Att.-Gen. v. Adelaide Life* (1888) 22 S.Aus.L.R. 5.

[28] *Haworth & Co. v. Sickness and Accident* (1891) 18 R. 563; *Dougherty v. London Guarantee* (1880) 6 Vict.L.R. 376; also *Harbour Commissioners of Montreal v. Guarantee Co. of North America* (1893) 22 S.C.R. 542.

[29] *Grant v. Aetna Fire* (1862) 15 Moo.P.C. 516.

Lawrence between Quebec and Hamilton stopping at intermediate ports", it was held to be an express warranty that the steamer would navigate, and that inasmuch as she remained in dock from the time of the issue of the policy until she was burned there was a breach of warranty and the policy was void.[30]

10–67 Warranty as to present fact only. Where it is consistent with business sense to read an ambiguous term as either a present or continuing warranty the courts are prepared to interpret it as a warranty relating to the situation up to the inception of the policy.[31] Thus in an employers' liability policy the assured was asked "Are your machinery, plant and ways properly fenced and guarded and otherwise in good order and condition?" and answered "Yes".[32] The case posed the issue[33] whether the answer amounted to a promise that this state of affairs would continue to be true throughout the currency of the risk, and the Court of Appeal held that it did not, but related only to the situation when it was made. Lord Greene M.R. remarked that there was "not a particle of justification for reading into that perfectly simple question any element of futurity whatsoever".[34] This case was followed in *Sweeney v. Kennedy*,[35] where the assured had answered "No" to the question "Are any of your drivers under twenty-one years of age or with less than twelve months' driving experience?" and had further agreed that the declaration should "be held to be promissory and so form the basis of the contract". This answer was true at the commencement of the risk but was invalidated subsequently. The Divisional Court of the High Court of Eire held that the effect of the word "promissory" was to give the answers the status of warranties, but that this answer was confined to the facts as they existed at the time of the proposal being made. In *Kirkbride v. Donner*[36] the proposal form put out by a Lloyd's motor syndicate asked "Will the car to your knowledge be driven by any person under 25 years of age?" The applicant answered, "Yes, self". The declaration at the foot of the form included the words, "I further agree that this declaration signed by me is promissory and forms the basis of the contract". The underwriters contended that in signing the form the applicant warranted that the car would not be driven by anyone under 25 besides herself throughout the currency of the policy. It was held that this was not so, and that the applicant merely warranted her existing state of knowledge, and her intentions, at the time she signed the proposal form.

10–68 Terms delimiting the risk. Where the user of the thing insured is potentially flexible and changeable from day to day, such as the user of a motorvehicle, the courts have on several occasions interpreted the statement of that user as a term descriptive of, or delimiting, the risk.[37] In *Roberts*

---

[30] *Grant v. Equitable* (1864) 14 Law.Can.R. 493.

[31] *Hussain v. Brown* [1996] 1 Lloyd's Rep. 627.

[32] *Woolfall & Rimmer v. Moyle* [1942] 1 K.B. 66.

[33] The other issue concerned the interpretation of the clause requiring the assured to take "all reasonable precautions". See para. 28–51, *infra*.

[34] [1942] 1 K.B. 66, 71.

[35] [1950] Ir.R. 85; (1948) 82 Ll.L.R. 294.

[36] [1974] 1 Lloyd's Rep. 549.

[37] *Farr v. Motor Traders* [1920] 3 K.B. 669; *De Maurier v. Bastion* [1967] 2 Lloyd's Rep. 550; *A. Cohen & Co. v. Plaistow Transport* [1968] 2 Lloyd's Rep. 587; *Kler Knitwear v. Lombard General Insurance Co.* [2000] Lloyd's Rep. I.R. 47.

v. Anglo-Saxon Insurance Co.[38] the proposal form for motor insurance included a statement that the insured car was "warranted used only for the following purposes—commercial travelling". It was destroyed by fire while carrying four passengers on a Sunday drive through the Black Mountains in Wales, and the Court of Appeal held that such descriptions of user in motor policies were to be construed as delimiting the risk, so that the insurers were not liable if there was a loss by a peril insured against while the vehicle was being used in a manner at variance with the words of the clause, as here, but their liability re-attached to the vehicle when the agreed user was resumed. They could not avoid the policy as for breach of warranty when they learned what the insured had been doing. In the later case of *Provincial Insurance v. Morgan*,[39] the assured owned a lorry and was asked in the proposal form to "State (a) purposes in full for which the vehicle will be used; (b) nature of the goods." He answered, "(a) Delivery of coal; (b) Coal." The lorry was involved in an accident shortly after it had been carrying timber, as it had done on isolated occasions, and the insurers contended that they were entitled to repudiate all liability on the policy, since the declaration was made the "basis of the contract"[40] so that the statement, which referred to future user, was a continuing warranty. The House of Lords held that the policy was valid. One of their Lordships' *rationes decidendi* was that the statement concerning user of the lorry was a term descriptive of the risk, and accordingly, since the lorry was carrying coal at the time of the accident, the insurers were liable.[41]

10–69 Collateral stipulation.[42] A clause which quite clearly refers to the future may, of course, be only a collateral undertaking, a breach of which gives the insurer only a claim for damages. The best known instance is *Re Bradley and Essex & Suffolk Accident Indemnity Society*.[43] Here a claim was brought on a workman's compensation policy and the case turned upon the interpretation of a provision in the policy the relevant part of which read, "and the amount of wages, salary and other earnings paid to him shall be duly recorded in a proper wages book". The Court of Appeal by a majority, Fletcher Moulton L.J. dissenting, held that the provision was neither a warranty nor condition precedent to liability, but merely a term providing a mechanism for the purpose of premium adjustment in accordance with the wages actually paid, which accordingly provided no defence to the claim.

10–70 Continuing warranty. In contrast to all the foregoing provisions in

---

[38] (1927) 27 Ll.L.R. 313.

[39] [1933] A.C. 240.

[40] See paras 10–32 to 10–34, *ante*, for the effect of this form of declaration.

[41] This was the *ratio* of the Court of Appeal [1932] 2 K.B. 70 and was the *ratio* of Lord Russell's opinion [1933] A.C. 240, 249. Lord Wright agreed with the opinions expressed in the Court of Appeal (p. 256), but also described the clause in issue as a continuing condition or warranty (p. 254) and cited *Shaw v. Robberds* (1837) 6 Ad. & El. 75, a case concerning temporary deviation in user—para. 10–79, *infra*. Lord Buckmaster, with whom the other Law Lords concurred, construed the clause as a term which, on its true meaning was never breached (p. 247).

[42] See paras 10–6 and 10–36, *ante*. See also the discussion of conditions precedent and innominate terms at 10–8 and 10–12 to 10–14, *ante*.

[43] [1912] 1 K.B. 415. Contrast later decisions in which the keeping of proper accounts was held to be a condition precedent to insurers' liability under the policy—*Shoot v. Hill* (1936) 55 Ll.L.Rep. 29; *Jacobson v. Yorkshire Ins. Co.* (1933) 45 Ll.L.Rep. 281; *Bennett v. Yorkshire Ins. Co.* [1962] 2 Lloyd's Rep. 270.

policies is the continuing or "future" warranty, which provides much greater protection to the insurer against any increase in the risk and in his liability on the policy. These warranties are sometimes found in fire policies, where the description of the premises insured may well be held to import a warranty that the structure and user will not be altered so as to increase the risk during the continuation of the policy.[44] Thus in an application for insurance on a general shop, the question: "Are any inflammable oils or goods used or kept on the premises?" received the answer: "Lighter fuel", and the applicant declared that his answers were true and complete and that his declaration and answers were the basis of the contract. The fire out of which the claim arose occurred while the insured had between 30 and 50 lbs. of fireworks on his premises, as he normally did at that time of year. McNair J. held that the answer amounted to a warranty concerning inflammable oils or goods during the duration of the policy, which was broken by the presence of the fireworks on the premises, and this entitled the insurers to repudiate liability.[45]

10–71 Principles of construction. The interpretation of a clause which is not expressed clearly as a future or continuing warranty, and its subsequent classification in one of the categories of terms outlined in the preceding paragraphs, is not a process which invites easy generalisations, but it may be helpful to mention some of the factors emphasised by the courts in the past. The courts have in general tended to construe an ambiguously worded term as something other than a continuing warranty, and this is because they disapprove of insurers whom they suspect of misleading their assured by exacting promises for the future through the medium of words appearing sometimes to relate to the present. It has been stated that insurers are fully entitled to stipulate for the future performance of obligations by the assured,[46] and wherever these duties are stipulated in clear words, whether expressed as warranties or as conditions precedent to liability, the courts will readily enforce them.[47] The sometimes divergent decisions reached in this area of insurance law are best understood in terms of the courts' readiness to construe ambiguous terms against insurers who could, with more forethought, have used unexceptionable wording.[48]

10–72 In determining whether a clause shall be construed as a continuing warranty the courts have emphasised the following criteria[49]:

(i) does the clause have the appearance of a warranty;
(ii) is it clearly referable to a future situation;

---

[44] *Sillem v. Thornton* (1854) 3 E. & B. 868; *Farnham v. Royal Insurance Co. Ltd* [1976] 2 Lloyd's Rep. 437.
[45] *Hales v. Reliance Fire and Accident* [1960] 2 Lloyd's Rep. 391.
[46] *Weber & Berger v. Employers Liability Ass. Co.* (1926) 24 Ll.L.R. 321 *per* MacKinnon J.; *Woolfall & Rimmer v. Moyle* [1942] 1 K.B. 66, 71 *per* Lord Green M.R.; *Sweeney v. Kennedy* (1948) 82 Ll.L.R. 294, 299.
[47] *e.g. Vaughan v. Scottish General Ins. Co.* [1960] 1 Lloyd's Rep. 479; *Welch v. Royal Exchange Ass. Co.* [1939] 1 K.B. 294, *Brown v. Zurich General Accident* [1954] 2 Lloyd's Rep. 243 and other cases concerning the maintenance of vehicles in an efficient condition— see Ch. 29, *post.*
[48] *Provincial Ins. Co. v. Morgan* [1933] A.C. 240, 247, 250, 256; *Sweeney v. Kennedy* (1948) 82 Ll.L.R. 295, 301.
[49] These criteria set out in what was then paragraph 754 in the 7th edition of this work were applied in *Hair v. Prudential Ass. Co. Ltd* [1983] 2 Lloyd's Rep. 667, 672.

(iii) is it a provision which would be of little or no value to the insurers if it related only to present facts;

(iv) does a breach of the clause permanently prejudice the insurers even if it is subsequently remedied?

10–73 Appearance of warranty. If it is clear that the statement is being warranted accurate, usually by a "basis of the contract" clause involving all the answers given by the applicant, it is most unlikely to be interpreted as a mere statement of intention.[50] In the absence of such a clause the statement in question would very probably be construed as a warranty nonetheless, if it had a real bearing upon the risk run by the insurer.[51] If it related to matters unconnected with the risk a court might well interpret it as a collateral stipulation.

10–74 Reference to the future. Where a statement or description is obviously intended to refer to a future situation, as indicated by the tense employed or the particular subject-matter of the description,[52] no doubts can arise on this point. However, a provision which appears on its face to refer to the future may well be found to be restricted to the present, either expressly or impliedly, by its relationship with other provisions in the policy.[53] So, if the insurers have inserted an express provision in the policy providing that any alteration in the premises insured which increased the risk would render the policy void unless the insurers are notified of it and the policy is indorsed accordingly, this will have the effect of restricting the description of the premises in the policy to a warranty of the situation at the commencement of the insurance.[54] It is clear that in such a case the presence of the express condition envisaging alterations during the running of the policy shows that the parties could not intend the assured to warrant that the premises would correspond to the description in all respects during the risk.

10–75 In *Sweeney v. Kennedy*,[55] the assured under a motor policy had answered "No" to the question, "Are any of your drivers under 21 years of age …?" and his declaration of facts in the proposal form was expressed "to be promissory and so form the basis of the contract". On the face of it the answer therefore appeared to refer to the future, but since the whole declaration was covered by the word "promissory", and most of the answers related clearly to the past, the word could not extend this answer to the future and was interpreted as "declaratory", in which sense it was consistent with all the assured's answers. If there is any suggestion that the insurers are trying to extract a future warranty under the camouflage of surrounding terms which are not expressed in a future tense, the courts will uphold the assured's reading of the clause as relating to the present.[56]

---

[50] *Roberts v. Anglo-Saxon Ins. Co.* (1927) 27 Ll.L.R. 313.

[51] *Barnard v. Faber* [1893] 1 Q.B. 340; *Re Bradley and Essex and Suffolk Indemnity* [1912] 1 K.B. 415.

[52] *Beauchamp v. National Mutual Indemnity* [1973] 3 All E.R. 19.

[53] *Pim v. Reid* (1843) 6 M. & G. 1; *Weber & Berger v. Employers' Liability* (1926) 24 Ll.L.R. 321; *Woolfall & Rimmer v. Moyle* [1942] 1 K.B. 66; *Farnham v. Royal Insurance Co. Ltd* [1976] 2 Lloyd's Rep. 437.

[54] *ibid.*

[55] [1950] Ir.R. 85; (1948) 82 Ll.L.R. 294.

[56] (1948) 82 Ll.L.R. 294, 300.

10–76 Protection of insurer. An argument in favour of a provision being a future warranty is that it would serve little or no purpose if compliance was confined to the situation when it was made. Accordingly statements in burglary policies that buildings are "always occupied" have been held to be continuing warranties.[57] Where, however, the insurers clearly obtain a useful degree of protection even when the clause's operation is confined to present facts and it is not worded so as to apply to the future as well, that is a good reason for limiting its scope accordingly.[58] There is no presumption that warranties as to the nature or use of insured premises will be construed as continuing warranties,[59] and earlier dicta to that effect[60] are incorrect.

10–77 Undue restriction on assured. If the statement of user or description is contained in the policy and the accuracy of it is expressed to be warranted, the court will be inclined to construe it as a suspensive condition where the user of the insured object is potentially highly varied and it would be harsh on the assured to lose his entire policy through one departure from the situation so described. Thus in motor policies, a statement concerning the user of the vehicle is likely to be a condition suspending the risk while being disregarded.[61] It would be unduly harsh on the owner of a commercial vehicle who had stated the user as "goods carrying" that he should find his policy avoided because he stopped to take the victim of a road accident to hospital.[62] The insurer, who is not on risk when the term is not complied with, is not prejudiced by the breach; he undertook to insure against risks incidental to a goods vehicle and these are not increased by the temporary alteration of user.[63] If the temporary alteration were, however, to increase the risk resumed by the insurer the decision should go the other way, it is submitted.[64] Thus if a car were to be described as "warranted no competition work or racing", that description of user might fairly be classified as a warranty, since the vehicle would quite probably be in a mechanically weaker state after a spell of rallying or racing and the likelihood of an accident subsequently would be increased. The doctrine of suspensive conditions is not confined to motor policies but has been applied to all-risks cover on jewellery and a goods in transit policy where the assured undertook to equip[65] or garage[66] a vehicle in a particular fashion. Where, however, the construction or user of premises is described, the tendency is to construe the description as a warranty,[67] and not a mere limitation of the risk, so that the risk does not re-attach by the property being again brought into conformity with the description of it.[68]

[57] *Winicofsky v. Army and Navy General Ins. Co.* (1919) 35 T.L.R. 283; *Simmonds v. Cockell* [1920] 1 K.B. 843.
[58] *Woolfall & Rimmer v. Moyle* [1942] 1 K.B. 66; *Sweeney v. Kennedy* (1948) 82 Ll.L.R. 294.
[59] *Hussain v. Brown* [1996] 1 Lloyd's Rep. 627, 629.
[60] *Hales v. Reliance Fire & Accident Ins. Co.* [1960] 2 Lloyd's Rep. 391, 395.
[61] *Farr v. Motor Traders* [1920] 3 K.B. 669; *Roberts v. Anglo-Saxon Ins.* (1927) 27 Ll.L.R. 313; *Provincial Insurance v. Morgan* [1933] A.C. 240.
[62] Per MacKinnon J. in *Roberts v. Anglo-Saxon* (1926) 26 Ll.L.R. 154, 157.
[63] *De Maurier v. Bastion* [1967] 2 Lloyd's Rep. 550, 559 per Donaldson J.
[64] This is supported by *Powell Valley Elect Co-op v. U.S. Aviation Underwriters*, 179 F.Supp. 616 (D.C.W.D.Va.).
[65] *De Maurier v. Bastion* [1967] 2 Lloyd's Rep. 550.
[66] *Cohen v. Plaistow Transport* [1968] 2 Lloyd's Rep. 587.
[67] e.g. *Newcastle Fire v. Macmorran* (1815) 3 Dow 255.
[68] *Fidelity Phoenix Fire Ins. Co. of N.Y. v. Raper*, 6 So. 2d 513 (Ala. 1942) is an exception although the court did not resolve the question of the clause's nature.

10–78 It is not certain whether movable property insured against fire or burglary is warranted to remain in the place or location where it is described to be at the commencement of the insurance. It is submitted that the description of their locality ought to be interpreted as a definition of the risk so that the policy ceases to attach when the goods are removed from the locality stated, but re-attaches when they are returned to it. It would be very hard on the assured if the policy could be avoided for a breach of warranty in the event of their removal, when, for example the building in which they are housed became temporarily unsafe. Thus in *Gorman v. Hand-in-Hand*,[69] certain agricultural implements were described as being "in coach-house, stable, and cow-house". It was held that they were not covered by the policy when lying in the adjoining yard, but it was the opinion of the court that the policy would re-attach on their return to the coach-house, stable or cow-house.

10–79 The American decisions on future warranties do not correspond closely with the English decisions. Thus the description of an insured vehicle as "ordinarily kept in X" had been construed as a continuing warranty and not as a mere limitation of the risk.[70] In states in which, like New York, a statutory rule entitles the assured to recover despite breach of warranty unless the breach increased the risk, there is naturally a tendency for the insurers to frame their clauses as limiting the risk rather than as warranties, and for the assured to contend for the contrary interpretation.[71] In other states there are statutes providing that the breach of warranty justifies avoidance only if the breach contributed to the loss.[72]

10–80 Construction of continuing warranties. Once it is established that a warranty is a continuing warranty, and the assured's breach of it would therefore discharge the insurer from liability, it is necessary to determine what is the scope of the obligation there laid down, in order to ascertain whether in fact there has been a breach. Here again the courts have been willing to construe ambiguous or uncertain wording against the interpretation contended for by the company whose drafting it is, particularly where the wider interpretation would impose hardship on the assured in efforts to comply with it.

10–81 Where the assured under a burglary policy warranted that the premises covered were "always occupied", it was held that the warranty did not mean that the premises should be at no time left unattended which would be unreasonable for the assured, but that they should be continuously occupied as a residence.[73] This still gave useful protection to the insurer, since it prevented the building being left empty and unused, which would constitute greater encouragement to thieves. Where the applicant for a fidelity policy was asked concerning the employees in question, "How often do you require them to pay over to you and are they then allowed to retain a

---

[69] *Gorman v. Hand-in-Hand* (1877) Ir.R. 11 C.L. 224.

[70] *Marone v. Hartford Fire Ins. Co.*, 176 A. 320 (N.J., 1935).

[71] *Erie County v. Continental Casualty Co.*, 68 N.E. 2d 48 (N.Y.Ct.App., 1946), "whilst such safe is located in X", decided under New York Insurance Law, s.150.

[72] See Richards, *The Law of Insurance* (5th ed.), vol. II, paras 320–321.

[73] *Winicofsky v. Army and Navy, etc., Ins. Co.* (1919) 35 T.L.R. 283; *Simmonds v. Cockell* [1920] 1 K.B. 843.

balance in hand?" and answered, "M should not retain and should pay over as received", it was held (1) that by reference to a clause in the policy this was a continuing warranty concerning M's course of employment; but (2) that it was a warranty of what the employee's duties were to be, and not a warranty that at no time would any money be retained by M. It would be impossible to guarantee an employee's strict conformity to the system enjoined upon him, and that would be tantamount to warranting that no claim would ever be made upon the policy.[74] There are several American decisions where continuing warranties of this sort in fidelity policies have been interpreted as relating only to the course of business enjoined upon employees, and not to their complete adherence to it.[75]

10–82 The courts have on several occasions interpreted a statement of user or description of a building in such a manner as to license occasional deviations from the description there given. In *Dobson v. Sotheby*[76] the policy covered a barn against fire risks, and there was a condition providing that if the insured buildings "shall at any time after this insurance be made use of to stow or warehouse any hazardous goods ..." the policy would be forfeited. A fire occurred after a tar barrel had been introduced into the barn and a fire lit for tarring. The insurers contended that the insurance was invalidated, but it was held that the condition was intended to exclude only the habitual use of fire and ordinary deposit of hazardous goods, so that an "occasional introduction" was not a breach of the obligation undertaken in the condition.

10–83 In *Shaw v. Robberds*,[77] the policy concerned fire risks on a building described as "a kiln for drying corn in use". On one occasion during the currency of the policy the kiln was used to dry bark from a vessel which had sunk near it, this being an isolated act of kindness unconnected with the habitual business user of the kiln. In the process a fire occurred and the premises were destroyed. Although the jury found as facts that the drying of bark was a different business, more hazardous, and only covered at a higher premium, the plaintiff succeeded in his claim, since the words related only to the habitual user of the kiln, and were not contravened by a single act of kindness outside the usual business user altogether. In *Provincial Insurance v. Morgan*,[78] the facts of which case are related above, the *ratio* of the majority of the House of Lords' opinions was that where the applicant was asked to state "(a) the purposes (in full) for which the vehicle will be used", that did not mean that he must state in full the purposes for which the vehicle would be exclusively used, so that this term was not broken by the occasional carriage of timber when the applicant had answered "Delivery of coal". Lord Wright cited[79] *Shaw v. Robberds* with approval and it would seem that

---

[74] *Hearts of Oak v. Law Union* [1936] 2 All E.R. 619. The same reasoning is applicable to the courts' treatment of the clause obliging the assured to take "reasonable precautions" to prevent an accident, etc.: see *Woolfall and Rimmer v. Moyle* [1942] 1 K.B. 66; *Fraser v. Furman* [1967] 1 W.L.R. 898.

[75] *Rice v. Fidelity and Deposit Co.*, 103 Fed.Rep. 427 (1900); *Hunt v. Fidelity and Casualty*, 99 Fed.Rep. 242 (1900); *Phoenix Ins. v. Guarantee Co.*, 115 Fed.Rep. 964 (1902).

[76] (1827) Moo. & M. 90.

[77] (1837) 6 Ad. & El. 75.

[78] [1933] A.C. 240.

[79] [1933] A.C. 240, 255. It is unclear whether Lord Buckmaster considered the term a warranty or a term within the general condition precedent clause in the policy.

the principle that occasional divergences are permitted now extends in such a case to where the change of use is nonetheless a business use.

In American cases concerning fire policies it has been held that where the assured warrants to observe certain rules relating to management of the premises, the warranty is not broken by a temporary breach,[80] as where a "constant watch" was warranted to be kept, and premises were burned down in the temporary absence of the watchman.[81]

10–84 Compliance with continuing warranty in fire policies. As we have already seen, the description of premises or of their user in a fire policy or burglary policy is usually interpreted not as a suspensive condition defining and limiting the risk but as a warranty that the premises or user will continue to correspond to the description during the currency of the risk. The question then arises, in order that the assured shall comply with the warranty, must he refrain from altering the premises or user at all, thus fulfilling the warranty literally, or is it sufficient if he refrains from altering the premises or user in a way which increases the liability of, or risk on the insurers?

10–85 In *Sillem v. Thornton*,[82] the property insured was situated in California and described as a two-storied house. The description was accurate when the proposal was sent off from California, but, before the insurance was effected in London, the assured had added another storey. The court held that there was a breach of warranty, since it could be said that the description was inaccurate on the date when the policy was effected. But Lord Campbell C.J. said,[83] *obiter*: "But we are further of opinion that the description in the policy amounts to a warranty that the assured would not during the time specified in the policy, voluntarily do anything to make the condition of the building vary from this description, so as thereby to increase the risk or liability of the underwriter." The last part of Lord Campbell's statement would appear to show that the assured warrants only that the building will not vary from the description in such a manner as to increase the risk.

10–86 In Ireland, however, it was held in *Quin v. National Assurance*[84] that the warranty contained in the description of premises is absolute and must be literally complied with, regardless of any increase of risk. The premises were described as "a dwelling-house occupied by a caretaker", and the court held that if they were not so occupied, the policy would be void, and no question could be raised as to whether the change was material to the risk or not. The distinction is perhaps an academic one, since most alterations to premises might be expected to affect the risk or liability of underwriters. Inasmuch as a warranty requires exact compliance, it would seem that the Irish decision, following early English marine cases, is to be preferred to the dicta in *Sillem v. Thornton*.[85] It is noteworthy that in *Benham v. United*

---

[80] *Hosford v. Germania Fire*, (1888) 127 U.S. 399; *Daniels v. Hudson River Fire*, 66 Mass. 416 (1853).
[81] *King v. Phoenix*, 164 Mass. 291 (1895).
[82] (1854) 3 E. & B. 868.
[83] *ibid.*, 881–882.
[84] (1839) Jo. & Car. 316.
[85] (1854) 3 E. & B. 868.

Guarantee,[86] a case involving a fidelity policy and mentioned *supra*, one of the reasons which induced Pollock C.B. to hold that in that case there was no continuing warranty was the consideration that the assured would be unable to depart from the practice warranted even though they could decrease the risk by so doing.[87]

(d) *Breach of Warranty*

10–87 Onus of proof of breach. It is for the insurer who alleges that the assured's breach of warranty or condition provides him with a defence to a claim to prove that there has actually been a breach.[88] This has been accepted at least since Parke B.'s judgment in *Barrett v. Jermy*.[89] It is open to the parties to insert express words to shift the burden of proof, but clear words would be needed to alter what has been an established principle of insurance law for over a century.[90] If insurers dispute liability in a life policy because they allege that the assured had a disease which he warranted himself to be free from, they will need to give particulars of the symptoms of the disease which they rely upon.[91]

10–88 Effect of breach of warranty. A breach of warranty by the assured provides the insurer with a defence to any claim brought in respect of a time subsequent to the breach. The legal analysis of breach of warranty given in earlier editions of this book,[92] and shared by other writers on the subject,[93] was that the breach gave the insurers the right to avoid the contract of insurance and that, if the right was exercised, the contract was avoided with effect from the time of the breach. However, the decision of the House of Lords in *Bank of Nova Scotia v. Hellenic Mutual War Risks Association (Bermuda) Ltd (The "Good Luck")*[94] disapproved this analysis.

10–89 In the *"Good Luck"* case Lord Goff interpreted section 33(3) of the Marine Insurance Act 1906 to provide that, subject to any express provision in the policy, a breach of warranty discharges the insurer from liability as from the date of the breach, automatically and without the need for any election on his part. This is because a promissory warranty is in the nature of a condition precedent to the liability of the insurer. Lord Goff said[95]:

---

[86] (1852) 7 Ex. 744.
[87] *ibid.*, 752.
[88] *Stebbing v. Liverpool and London and Globe* [1917] 2 K.B. 433, 438; *Bonney v. Cornhill Ins. Co.* (1931) 40 Ll.L.R. 39, 41; *Bond Air Services v. Hill* [1955] 2 Q.B. 417; *Lane v. Spratt* [1970] 2 Q.B. 480; *Sofi v. Prudential Ass. Co.* [1993] 2 Lloyd's Rep. 559, 564.
[89] (1849) 3 Ex. 535, 542.
[90] *Bond Air Services v. Hill* [1955] 2 Q.B. 417, 427.
[91] *Marshall v. Emperor Life* (1865) L.R. 1 Q.B. 35; *Girdlestone v. N. British Mercantile Ins.* (1870) L.R. 11 Eq. 197.
[92] 8th ed., paras 790–792.
[93] Clarke, *The Law of Insurance Contracts* (1st ed.), para. 20–6C; Colinvaux's *Law of Insurance* (6th ed.), para. 6–27; *Halsbury's Laws* (4th ed.), vol. 25, para. 420.
[94] [1992] 1 A.C. 233.
[95] [1992] 1 A.C. 233, 263. The other members of the House of Lords agreed with Lord Goff's speech.

"This moreover reflects the fact that the rationale of warranties in insurance law is that the insurer only accepts the risk so long as the warranty is fulfilled. This is entirely understandable; and it follows that the immediate effect of a breach of a promissory warranty is to discharge the insurer from liability as from the date of the breach ... Even if in the result no further obligations rest on either party, it is not correct to speak of the contract being avoided."

The House of Lords did not expressly state whether this analysis applied to non-marine insurance.

10–90 In the preceding edition of this book,[96] the view was expressed that, despite some doubts,[97] a breach of warranty would have the effect of discharging the insurer from liability in all classes of insurance. It would now appear that this is the case, and certainly a number of cases at first instance and in the Court of Appeal have proceeded on this basis (though without the point being expressly argued). Thus Thomas J. in *Kumar v. AGF Insurance Ltd*[98] accepted that this was the case in a non-marine context, as did the Court of Appeal in the later cases of *Printpak v. AGF Insurance Co. Ltd*[99] and *HIH Casualty and General Insurance v. New Hampshire Co.*[1]

10–91 Effect of breach of condition. The first question is whether the clause is a condition in the nature of a collateral stipulation or a condition precedent. If it be the former, the insurer's remedy is a cross claim in damages.[2] The second question is whether the wording of the condition precedent is such that a breach is remediable and does not for ever bar recovery.[3] If the assured's breach of a condition precedent to recovery provides the insurer with a permanent defence to the instant claim, the next question will be whether the breach serves not only to relieve the insurer of liability to pay that claim but also discharges him from all liability on the policy thereafter. The answer depends upon the clarity of the wording employed and the nature of the particular breach of condition.[4] If the effect of the breach is to discharge the insurer from all liability for the future even where the assured's default was only a failure to comply once with a procedural requirement for giving notice of claim or particulars of loss, the prospects of challenge for unfairness under the Unfair Terms in Consumer Contracts Regulations 1999[5] must be good.

10–92 Effect of express provisions. The consequences which the law

---

[96] 9th ed. at para. 10–87.

[97] The reasons for the doubts are set out in para. 10–87 of the previous edition, to which the reader is referred for a full account.

[98] [1999] 1 W.L.R. 1747.

[99] [1999] Lloyd's Rep. I.R. 542.

[1] [2001] 2 Lloyd's Rep. 161. This approach was reiterated by the Court of Appeal in a later decision in the same case, as yet unreported.

[2] See para. 10–6, *ante*.

[3] As in *Weir v. Northern Counties of England Ins. Co.* (1879) 4 Ir.L.R. 689, commented upon in *Welch v. Royal Exchange Ass.* [1939] 1 K.B. 294, 308 by Slesser L.J.

[4] See *e.g. Welch v. Royal Exchange Ass.*, *supra, per* MacKinnon L.J. at p. 312. It is unlikely that a court would read a condition precedent as discharging the insurer from all liability for the future unless the wording was clearly to that effect—see *Kazakstan Wool Processors v. N.C.M.* [2000] Lloyd's Rep. I.R. 371, where it was argued also (unsuccessfully) that the clause had retroactive effect.

[5] See paras 10–18 to 10–20, *ante*, and *Cox v. Orion Ins. Co.* [1982] R.T.R. 1.

prescribes shall ordinarily attend the breach of a warranty or condition may be altered by the presence of an express provision as to what shall happen in the event of breach. In life assurance policies it was common[6] to provide that the effect of a mis-statement in a proposal form, the accuracy of which was warranted in a basis of contract clause, was to avoid the policy, and accordingly it was stated by courts construing such insurances that the effect of a breach of such warranties was to avoid the contract of insurance.[7] These authorities are not affected by the decision in the *Good Luck* case,[8] and it is submitted that a provision that, in the event of a breach of warranty, the policy is to be "void" is to be interpreted as meaning that the insurer possesses the right to avoid it, so that the assured cannot bring about the termination of the cover by is own breach of contract.[9]

10–93 If a policy is expressed to be "indisputable" after it has been in force for a specified time, it cannot be challenged for breach of warranty after that time has elapsed.[10] Again a condition in the policy, or in the case of industrial assurance a statutory provision,[11] may prohibit the insurers from challenging the validity of a life policy on the ground of breach of warranty or misrepresentation as to the state of health of the life assured unless fraud be proved. In such a case the court will not readily infer fraud but will require it to be proved conclusively. In a case of industrial assurance where there was a warranty of good health, the Industrial Assurance Commissioner for Northern Ireland refused to draw the inference of fraud although the medical evidence was to the effect that the assured knew her heart was not in good condition and that for several years she had been suffering from and under treatment for a form of heart disease known as myocarditis.[12]

10–94 Where the insurers have provided that a particular penalty has to be paid in the event of a breach of stipulation, such as an increased premium, they are limited to that penalty and cannot avoid the policy.[13] In *Sun Fire Office v. Hart*,[14] there was a condition in a fire policy that the insurers should have the right to terminate the insurance by notice to the assured if it so desired for any reason whatever, in which case the policy would not be avoided *ab initio*, and a rateable proportion of premiums would be due to be returned to the assured. The Privy Council gave effect to the clause, but it was not suggested that the insurers had, by including it in the policy, excluded their right to avoid the contract for breach of warranty.

10–95 The insurers may also have excluded their right to rely on a breach

---

[6] *Dawsons v. Bonnin* [1922] 2 A.C. 413, 430 *per* Viscount Finlay.
[7] *Duckett v. Williams* (1834) 2 Cr. & M. 348; *Anderson v. Fitzgerald* (1853) 4 H.L.Cas. 484; *Thomson v. Weems* (1884) 9 App.Cas. 671.
[8] [1992] 1 A.C. 233
[9] *New Zealand Shipping Co. v. Soc. des Atelier.* [1919] A.C. 1; *Quesnel Forks Gold Mining Co. v. Ward* [1920] A.C. 222, 227; *Torquay Hotel Co. v. Cousins* [1969] 2 Ch. 106, 137; *Cheall v. APEX* [1983] 2 A.C. 180, 188; *Alghussein Establishment v. Eton College* [1988] 1 W.L.R. 587. See, however, *Dawsons v. Bonnin* [1922] 2 A.C. 413, 437 *per* Lord Wrenbury.
[10] *Anstey v. British Natural* (1908) 24 T.L.R. 871 and see para. 16–60, *post.*
[11] Indust. Ass. Act 1923, s.20(4); Indust. Ass. and Friendly Societies Act 1948, s.9(2).
[12] *McLister v. Refuge Ass. Co.* [1948] I.A.C.(N.I.)Rep. 46.
[13] *London Loan and Savings v. Union Ins. Co. of Canton* (1925) 56 Ont.L.R. 590; *Hussain v. Brown* [1996] 1 Lloyd's Rep. 627, 631.
[14] (1889) 14 App.Cas. 98.

of warranty as discharging them from liability. Whether a clause is apt to achieve this end is a matter of construction of the clause. Thus, for example, in *Kumar v. AGF Insurance Co. Ltd*,[15] a clause was held effective to exclude the insurers' rights to rely on a breach of warranty; whereas in the later case of *HIH Casualty and General Insurance Co. Ltd v. New Hampshire Insurance Co.*[16] the particular clause, though far reaching, was held not to be apt to exclude such rights.

10–96 In addition, where a clause is relied on in this regard, it is necessary to determine whether insurers have only agreed to forego their right to rely on the breach as discharging them from liability, or whether they have, in addition, agreed to forego any right to damages that they would otherwise have. In *Kumar v. AGF Insurance Co. Ltd*,[17] the judge held that insurers had also agreed to forego any right to damages in relation to breaches of the sort alleged in the case.

10–97 Cancellation of policy and declaration of non-liability. We have seen that a breach of warranty discharges the insurer from liability from the date of the breach,[18] but we have so far considered the position in the context when a claim is brought. What happens, by contrast, in the situation where, say, a life policy is forfeited early on by breach of warranty, but a long time will elapse before a claim can be brought on it? There used to be authority[19] to the effect that in such a case the insurers could not safeguard their position by applying either for an order that the policy be cancelled and delivered up or for a declaration that they were discharged from liability on the policy, but subsequent changes to rules of court[20] have conferred jurisdiction on the courts to award a declaration of non-liability regardless of whether consequential relief could then be obtained by the plaintiff, and the practice has changed.

10–98 Recent authority has established the right of an insurer to seek a declaration of non-liability where he contends that a policy is voidable for non-disclosure by the assured.[21] In principle he should be entitled to seek the same relief where the contention is that his liability has been discharged by a breach of warranty or, for that matter, a breach of a condition precedent to liability. The remedy is, of course, discretionary, and will not be granted if productive of substantial inconvenience or injustice.[22] There is in particular a reluctance to permit an insurer to seek a declaration of non liability concerning a policy granted by others, as where a reinsurer seeks a declaration that his reassured is not under a liability towards an original assured. Although it was formerly held that a declaration could be sought by any party with an interest in the subject matter of a transaction and whether

---

[15] [1999] 1 W.L.R. 1747.
[16] [2001] 2 Lloyd's Rep. 161.
[17] [1999] 1 W.L.R. 1747.
[18] Paras 10–88 to 10–90, *ante*.
[19] *Thornton v. Knight* (1849) 16 Sim. 509; *Brooking v. Maudslay* (1888) 38 Ch.D. 636.
[20] The current rule is C.P.R. Part 40.20.
[21] *Ins. Corp. of Ireland v. Strombus International Ins. Co.* [1985] 2 Lloyd's Rep. 139; *Meadows Indemnity Co. v. Ins. Corp. of Ireland* [1989] 2 Lloyd's Rep. 298; *St Paul Fire & Marine Ins. Co. (UK) Ltd v. McDonnell Dowell Constructors Ltd* [1995] 2 Lloyd's Rep 116; *Booker v. Bell* [1989] 1 Lloyd's Rep. 516.
[22] *Ins. Corp. of Ireland v. Strombus International Ins. Co.* [1985] 2 Lloyd's Rep. 139, 144.

there be a cause of action or not,[23] the current position is that a reinsurer cannot seek a declaration of his reassured's non-liability because there could not be under English law any disputed rights of claim between the original assured and the reinsurer, and declarations should be restricted to the existence or non-existence of legally enforceable liabilities between parties before the court.[24] When statements made by the assured prior to contract are later made the subject of warranty it has been said that the policy could be cancelled for misrepresentation notwithstanding that there would also be a breach of warranty,[25] but it may be said in answer that the insurers should be held to the parties agreement that the assured's statements must be treated as terms of the contract.

10–99 It is also possible that the insurers may repudiate the contract of insurance wrongfully, before any claim has arisen upon it, by refusing to accept further premiums or by asserting, without any good cause, that it is invalid for breach of warranty or, for that matter, illegality or non-disclosure. The rights of the assured are then determined by the ordinary principles of the law of contract. The assured may accept the repudiation as an anticipatory breach of contract and sue for damages. The measure of damages would depend on the nature of the policy. In the case of a life policy the measure would probably include the present value of the disputed policy having regard to the contingency upon which the sum is to be payable and the amount of the future premiums. On the other hand, the assured is not bound to accept a repudiation by the insurers and may, in appropriate circumstances, continue to tender the renewal premiums until the maturity of the policy. If this course is followed the assured will in all probability desire to obtain a declaration that the policy is valid and still subsisting. The award of this remedy is discretionary and depends upon the circumstances of the particular case, but two factors may be mentioned. First, there must be a dispute concerning the validity of the policy before the court can entertain an action for a declaration. Thus, in one case the insurers denied the validity of a life policy after being told that a condition in the policy had been broken. The assured demanded the return of premiums paid after the date of the breach. He did not assert the validity of the policy until after a considerable interval when he amended his statement of claim a few weeks before the trial to include an alternative claim for a declaration that the policy was valid. It was held that the assured could not claim the declaration.[26]

10–100 Secondly, the court may be of the opinion that the action for a declaration is premature and that injustice might be done to the insurers if

---

[23] *Guaranty Trust Co. of N.Y. v. Hannay* [1915] 2 K.B. 536, 562.

[24] *Meadows Indemnity Co. v. Ins. Corp. of Ireland* [1989] 2 Lloyd's Rep. 298, applying statements of principle in *Gouriet v. Union of Post Office Workers* [1978] A.C. 435. Thus, too, an application by a plaintiff injured by the assured's motor car for a declaration that the assured's motor insurers were liable to satisfy any judgment obtained by the plaintiff against the assured was premature and vexatious and liable to be struck out—*Carpenter v. Ebblewhite* [1939] 1 K.B. 347, 358 *per* Greer L.J. See most recently *Burns v. Shuttlehurst* [1999] 1 W.L.R. 1449, 1459. However, the Law Commission has put forward a draft bill to enable disclosure and suit against insurers in cases where the assured is insolvent—see Law Commission Report 272 (2001), the recommendations in which have recently been accepted by the Government, and it is possible that, with the advent of the CPR, the Court may look at this point afresh, in an appropriate case.

[25] *Smith v. Grand Orange Lodge* (1903) 6 Ont.L.R. 588.

[26] *Sparenborg v. Edinburgh Life Assurance* [1912] 1 K.B. 185.

the declaration were granted. In *Honour v. Equitable Life Assurance*,[27] the office had refused a renewal premium on a life policy on the ground that the policy was effected without interest in the life assured and had been obtained by fraudulent misrepresentation. The court was of opinion that the assured's action for a declaration that the policy was valid and subsisting was premature inasmuch as the office might, when the life dropped, be in possession of information which they had not then and could not for the moment entertain. In that case the court was prepared to dismiss the action for a declaration of the validity of the policy on the defendants' undertaking that in case any action should be brought on the policy they would not rely on the non-payment of the subsequent premiums on the due dates as a defence to the claim.

(e) *Waiver*

10–101 We have seen that the breach of a term of the policy by the assured gives the insurer a remedy which varies according to the status of the term which is broken.[28] Circumstances may arise in which the insurer is held to have waived the right to exercise that remedy as a result of his conduct either before or (more frequently) after the breach by the assured. In order to appreciate how the doctrine of waiver applies to breaches of policy terms it is first necessary to consider its juristic basis.

10–102 "Waiver" is not a term of art[29] and has been criticised as vague.[30] In the present context it means the abandonment or relinquishment of a right or a defence which may occur as the result either of an election by the insurer or of the creation of an estoppel precluding him from relying upon his contractual rights against the assured.[31] Election arises where the insurer becomes entitled to exercise a right on the commission of the assured's breach of contract, and he must decide whether to do so. An example would be the right to avoid the policy in reliance on a forfeiture clause.[32] If the insurer is aware of the facts which create the right in question and (though this is not completely clear) is also aware of his legal right, and he acts in such a way as clearly to evince a decision to relinquish it, he will be held to have elected not to exercise it against the assured, and that election is irrevocable.[33] The time may come when the law will deem him to have elected to

---

[27] [1900] 1 Ch. 852.
[28] See paras 10–6 (collateral stipulation), 10–11 and 10–91 (condition) and 10–88 to 10–90, *ante* (warranty).
[29] *Banning v. Wright* [1972] 1 W.L.R. 972, 981, *per* Lord Reid.
[30] *Ross T. Smyth & Co. v. Bailey* [1940] 3 All E.R. 60, 70, *per* Lord Wright, approved in *Banning v. Wright, supra.*
[31] *P. Samuel & Co. v. Dumas* [1924] A.C. 431, 442; *Kammins Ballrooms Co. v. Zenith Investments (Torquay) Ltd* [1971] A.C. 850, 882–883; *Telfair Shipping Corp. v. Athos Shipping Co. SA* [1981] 2 Lloyd's Rep. 74, 87–88; *Motor Oil Hellas SA v. Shipping Corp. of India* [1990] 1 Lloyd's Rep. 391, 397–399.
[32] *Croft v. Lumley* (1858) 6 H.L.Cas. 672, 705; *Matthews v. Smallwood* [1910] 1 Ch. 777; *Kammins Ballrooms Co. v. Zenith Investments (Torquay) Ltd* [1971] A.C. 850, 883.
[33] *Motor Oil Hellas SA v. Shipping Corp. of India* [1990] 1 Lloyd's Rep. 391, 399. It is not necessary that the insurer should subjectively intend to excuse the breach of contract—*Cia Tirrena Assicurazioni v. Grand Union Ins. Co.* [1991] 2 Lloyd's Rep. 143, 153, 154. Nor is it necessary for the assured to prove reliance upon the insurer's decision: *ibid.* As to whether the insurer needs to have knowledge of its legal rights, see *Peyman v. Lanjani* [1985] Ch. 457 and, more recently, *Bhopal v. Sphere Drake Insurance Plc* [2002] Lloyd's Rep. I.R. 413.

exercise or to forgo his right, as the case may be, when he takes no action to communicate a decision.[34]

10–103 Election is to be contrasted with equitable, or "promissory", estoppel. Where a person who possesses a legal right or defence against another unequivocally represents by words or conduct that he does not intend to rely upon it, and the other party acts, or desists from acting, in reliance on that representation, the representor will be estopped from enforcing his legal rights inconsistently with his representation to the extent that it would be inequitable for him to do so.[35] Whereas election requires a party to have knowledge of the facts which create a right exercisable by him (and, at least possibly, knowledge of the legal right) before he can be held to have made an election in respect of it, the principle of equitable estoppel does not require any particular state of knowledge on his part, although it is submitted that in practice it will be difficult for an assured to make out the elements of an equitable estoppel against an insurer unless the latter is known to be aware of the assured's breach of contract. Another point of distinction is that an election, once communicated or deemed to be made, is irrevocable, whereas an equitable estoppel may in certain cases only suspend the exercise of a right temporarily. As applied to breaches of contract the concept of equitable estoppel means that when one party represents to the other that the latter's breach of contract will be overlooked, he will not be allowed later to rely upon it where to do so would be unjust to that other party.

10–104 Waiver of breach of warranty. The effect of the assured's breach of warranty is automatically to discharge the insurer from liability as from the date of the breach.[36] Consequently the insurer possesses an immediate defence to a claim by the assured and is not required to elect to exercise a remedy, such as rescission of the contract, in order to acquire a defence. In the last edition of this work,[37] it was submitted that waiver by election is therefore inapplicable to breach of warranty, not because the contract of insurance has terminated,[38] which is not the case,[39] but because the insurer is not put to any election by the occurrence of the breach, and cases decided before *Bank of Nova Scotia v. Hellenic Mutual War Risks Association*[40] in which an insurer was said to have elected not to avoid liability for breach of warranty must be regarded as wrongly applying the law.[41] The view that the election is inapplicable to a case of breach of warranty has now been

---

[34] *The "Laconia"* [1977] A.C. 850, 872; *Motor Oil Hellas SA v. Shipping Corp. of India* [1990] 1 Lloyd's Rep. 391, 398.
[35] *Kammins Ballrooms Co. v. Zenith Investments (Torquay) Ltd* [1971] A.C. 850, 883–884; *Motor Oil Hellas SA v. Shipping Corp. of India* [1990] 1 Lloyd's Rep. 391, 399. This type of estoppel can be traced back to *Hughes v. Metropolitan Railway Co.* (1877) 2 App.Cas. 439 *via Central London Property Trust v. High Trees House* [1947] K.B. 130.
[36] See paras 10–88 to 10–90, *ante.*
[37] At para. 10–98.
[38] This was the suggestion in Clarke, *Law of Insurance Contracts* (2nd ed.), para. 20–7A.
[39] *Bank of Nova Scotia v. Hellenic Mutual War Risks Assoc.* [1992] 1 A.C. 233, 263.
[40] [1992] 1 A.C. 233.
[41] *e.g. Cia. Tirrena Assicurazioni v. Grayd Union Ins. Co.* [1991] 2 Lloyd's Rep. 143, although there could well have been a waiver by estoppel on the facts of that case.

accepted by a number of first instance judges and, more recently, the Court of Appeal.[42] An assured who wishes to contend that an insurer has waived a breach of warranty must therefore establish waiver by estoppel, which invariably means equitable estoppel. The same analysis must be true of waiver of a breach of a condition precedent to liability which affords a defence to all claims originating after the breach.[43]

10–105 It follows that the onus upon an assured pleading waiver of breach of warranty is to establish his reliance upon the unequivocal representation of the insurer, by words or conduct, that he intends not to rely upon it as a defence to further liability under the policy. An example of a successful plea of waiver by equitable estoppel to a breach of a condition precedent is *Barrett Bros (Taxis) Ltd v. Davies*.[44] The assured was obliged by a condition in his motor policy to forward immediately to the insurers any letter, notice of intended prosecution, writ, summons, or process relating to an accident in which he was involved. He failed to send them the notice of prosecution and summons which he received after an accident, and pleaded guilty to charges brought against him. The insurers sought to rely on this breach of condition precedent as a defence to payment of his loss, although they had in fact received clear and reliable information of the pending proceedings from the police, and had written to the assured before the trial of his liability towards the claimant asking him why he had not forwarded the relevant documents, but without requesting that they be sent on to them. The Court of Appeal agreed unanimously that the insurers' failure to request the documents in their letter to the assured was a waiver of the requirement to forward them.[45]

10–106 Acts constituting waiver by estoppel. Apart from replying to the assured in terms that amount to an express promise to overlook a breach of warranty or condition precedents, the insurers' conduct may found a waiver because it is inconsistent with an intention to rely upon it as a defence to liability on the policy, and thus possesses the character of an implied representation that they will not take advantage of it. As Scrutton J. said in *Toronto Railway Co. v. National British & Irish Millers Insurance Co. Ltd*,[46] citing an American decision[47]:

---

[42] See *J. Kirkaldy & Sons Ltd v. Walker* [1999] Lloyds' Rep. I.R. 410; *"The Milasan"* [2000] 2 Lloyd's Rep. 458; *HIH Casualty and General Insurance Ltd v. Axa Corporate Solutions* [2002] Lloyd's Rep. I.R. 325 (at first instance). The decision in this last case was upheld by the Court of Appeal in a decision which is, as yet, unreported. For a contrary view, see Soyer, *Warranties in Marine Insurance* (2001). In *Bhopal v. Sphere Drake Insurance Plc* [2002] Lloyd's Rep. I.R. 413, Timothy Walker J. and the Court of Appeal were prepared to treat the matter as one of election, without deciding whether this was the appropriate doctrine. It is submitted that this case should not be treated as authority running counter to the proposition in the text.

[43] See *Banning v. Wright* [1972] 1 W.L.R. 972, 990 *per* Lord Simon as to waiver of future performance of a condition precedent.

[44] [1966] 1 W.L.R. 1334.

[45] The alternative dictum of Lord Denning M.R. and Danckwerts L.J. that insurers could not rely on a breach of a condition precedent when the breach caused no prejudice to them is not now accepted as correct—*Pioneer Concrete (U.K.) Ltd v. National Employers' Mut. Gen. Ins. Assoc.* [1985] 1 Lloyd's Rep. 274, 281, approved in *Motor & General Ins. Co. v. Pavey* [1994] 1 W.L.R. 462, 469 (P.C.); *Cox v. Orion Ins. Co.* [1982] R.T.R. 1. See also; *Farrell v. Federated Employers' Ins. Assoc.* [1970] 1 W.L.R. 498, 502; [1970] 1 W.L.R. 1400, 1409, and *The "Mozart"* [1985] 1 Lloyd's Rep. 239, 245.

[46] (1914) 111 L.T. 555, 563.

[47] *Hanscom v. Home Ins. Co.* 90 Me. 339 (1897), referred to at p. 342 of the first edition of this work.

"It may happen that a waiver of a breach of the condition in the policy was not actually intended; but if the conduct and declaration of the insurer are of such a character as to justify the belief that waiver was intended and, acting upon this belief, the insured is induced to incur trouble and expense and is subjected to delay to his injury and prejudice, the insurer may be prohibited from claiming a forfeiture for such a breach upon the principle of equitable estoppel."

10–107 However, the representation must be to the effect that the insurer is content not to rely on his rights. This in turn means that his conduct, or statements, must give the assured to understand that he, the insurer, knows that he has a defence to liability and yet is content not to rely on that defence.[48] As Phillips J. put it in *The Superhulls Cover Case*:

"A party can represent that he will not enforce a specific legal right by words or conduct. He can say so expressly—this of course he can only do if he is aware of the right. Alternatively he can adopt a course of conduct which is inconsistent with the exercise of that right. Such a course of conduct will only constitute a representation that he will not exercise the right if the circumstances are such as to suggest either that he was aware of the right when he embarked on the course of conduct inconsistent with it or that he was content to abandon any rights that he might enjoy which were inconsistent with that course of conduct."[49]

10–108 The decisions cited below[50] provide instances in which the insurers' conduct may found waiver in this way. They are principally useful in demonstrating conduct which expressly or impliedly constitutes a representation that a waiver is intended. In some cases the need for the assured to prove his reliance[51] on the representation and the injustice of permitting the insurer to rely upon the breach was not spelt out. Either it was tacitly accepted that these elements of equitable estoppel were present, or the court was not applying the current principles of equitable estoppel and did not require them to be proved.[52] It should however be noted that it would be dangerous to place too much reliance on cases decided before the decision in *The Good Luck*.[53]

10–109 Waiver by acceptance of premium. The acceptance of premium after receipt of knowledge of a breach of warranty or condition is an act so inconsistent with an intention to repudiate liability that it is frequently a ground of waiver.[54] If insurers accept a renewal premium which falls due after the occurrence of the breach, this is inconsistent with a wish to treat the

---

[48] *Youell v. Bland Welch & Co. Ltd (The "Superhulls Cover" Case)* [1990] 2 Lloyd's Rep. 431; *J Kirkaldy & Sons Ltd v. Walker* [1999] 1 Lloyd's Rep. 410; *HIH Casualty v. AXA Corporate Solutions* [2002] Lloyd's Rep. I.R. 325. This last decision has been upheld by the Court of Appeal in a decision which is, as yet, unreported.
[49] [1990] 2 Lloyd's Rep. 431, 450.
[50] See paras 10–109 to 10–113, *post*.
[51] The assured need not prove that he has acted to his detriment or prejudice, but merely that he conducted himself in reliance on the insurers' words or conduct differently than he would otherwise have done—*The "Athos"* [1981] 2 Lloyd's Rep. 74, 88.
[52] *e.g. Ayrey v. British Legal & United Provident Ass. Co.* [1918] 1 K.B. 136; *De Maurier v. Bastion Ins. Co.* [1967] 2 Lloyd's Rep. 550.
[53] [1992] 1 A.C. 233.
[54] *Wing v. Harvey* (1854) 5 De G.M. & G. 265; *Armstrong v. Turquand* (1858) 9 Ir.R.C.L. 32; *Jones v. Bangor Mut. Shipping Ins. Soc.* (1889) 61 L.T. 727; *Hemmings v. Sceptre Life Ass.* [1905] 1 Ch. 365; *Ayrey v. British Legal etc. Ass. Co.* [1918] 1 K.B. 136; *Besant v. Northern Life Ass. Co.* [1923] 1 W.W.R. 362; *Yorkshire Ins. Co. v. Craine* [1922] 2 A.C. 541, 547; *Cia. Tirrena Assicurazioni. v. Grand Union Ins. Co.* [1991] 2 Lloyd's Rep. 143.

breach as discharging their liability, and will be regarded as an implied representation that they will not exercise their right to do so.[55] If, however, it fell due or was earned before the breach then their acceptance of the premium is not an unequivocal representation that the insurers are accepting their liability for claims arising thereafter, and there is no waiver. If the insurers accept a premium while reserving their position or on condition that special terms are imposed, the assured cannot say that they are waiving their rights to disclaim liability, and in the latter case he must comply with the new terms if cover is to be continued.[56]

10–110 Waiver in handling the claim. When a claim is made, and the insurers discover, or have discovered, a breach by the assured in its presentation or earlier, their treatment of the claim may well amount to waiver. Thus where the assured under a fire insurance made a claim which was insufficiently detailed to comply with a condition precedent in the policy, but the insurers took possession of his premiums and property under a salvage condition, they were held to have waived the breach of condition, especially as the words of the salvage term envisaged that only adjustment remained to be settled.[57] Where a fire policy contained a condition precedent which provided for the tender of a magistrate's certificate testifying to a loss and for the joint appointment of appraisers to assess it in the event of disagreement, the conduct of the insurers in concurring in the appointment of an adjuster by the assured alone was held to debar them from complaining of the assured's non-compliance with the terms of the policy.[58] In another case a condition precedent in an equestrian driving accident policy provided that, in the event of an accident resulting in the death of a horse, a qualified veterinary surgeon should duly certify that death was caused by a peril insured against under the policy. The insurers first misled the assured by saying that this meant their own surgeon, who had already dissected the horse, and then said that they would accept evidence of the cause of death otherwise than as prescribed in the policy. It was held that the insurers had represented their willingness to dispense with the assured's performance of the condition and had waived their right to insist upon its fulfilment.[59]

10–111 If insurers take steps to discover information which the assured failed to give them, that may found a waiver.[60] A mere request that a claim form be completed may be equivocal in regard to past breaches by the assured[61] but the demand by life insurers for a post mortem has been treated as an implied representation that they regard the policy as in force.[62] If the insurers dispute the claim on a ground unconnected with the breach of warranty or condition, they may be held to be displaying an intention to overlook it.[63]

---

[55] *Holdsworth v. Lancs & Yorks Ins. Co.* (1907) 23 T.L.R. 521.

[56] *Handler v. Mut. Reserve Fund* (1904) 90 L.T. 192.

[57] *Yorkshire Ins. Co. v. Craine* [1922] 2 A.C. 541.

[58] *Toronto Railway Co. v. National British etc. Ins. Co.* (1914) 111 L.T. 555.

[59] *Burridge & Son v. Haines & Sons* (1918) 114 L.T. 681.

[60] *Globe Savings etc. Co. v. Employer's Liability Ass. Co.* (1901) 13 Man.R. 531.

[61] *James v. Royal Ins. Co.* (1907) 10 N.Z.Gaz.L.R. 244; contrast *McNally v. Phoenix Ass. Co.*, 137 N.Y. 389 (1893); *Canada Landed Credit v. Canadian Agricultural Ins. Co.* (1870) 17 Grant 418.

[62] *Donnison v. Employers' Acc. & Life Stock Ins. Co.* (1897) 24 R. 681.

[63] *Ocean Accident & Guarantee Corp. v. Fowlie* (1902) 33 S.C.R. 253; *McCormick v. The Royal Ins. Co.* (1894) 163 Pa. 184; *Accident Ins. Co. of North America v. Young* (1891) 20 S.C.R. 280.

10–112 There is no waiver when the insurers, in answer to a claim, merely deny liability in general terms, without giving specific reasons, for it is not clear that they intended to waive a breach of condition of which they have knowledge.[64] If, however, the proper inference to be drawn was that another particular reason for refusing payment was specified, then that may well raise waiver of the unspecified grounds.[65] In an American case where the action was tried a second time, the company was held to be estopped from setting up technical breaches of warranty as to which they had knowledge at the time but did not set up the defence at the first trial,[66] but it was held in *London and Manchester Plate Glass v. Heath*[67] that an insurer is not estopped from setting up an exception in answer to one claim when he did not see fit to avail himself of the same exception on other policies containing it.

10–113 Waiver in issuing policy with knowledge of breach. If the insurers renew or issue a policy with knowledge of a breach of warranty or condition, that should normally be construed as a waiver of that breach,[68] as where a policy warranted "no fireworks kept" and the agent issued the policy with knowledge that fireworks were kept,[69] or where a policy was issued by the insurers who knew all along that a condition forbidding double insurance was being broken.[70] Where the proposer for life assurance completed the proposal form in such a manner that the answers concerning the date of birth and age next birthday of the life assured were inconsistent, so that it was obvious that one of the answers was wrong, if not both, the insurers could not take this breach of warranty as a defence to a claim after they had issued the policy despite the inconsistency.[71]

10–114 Other acts of waiver. Any conduct of the insurers which is consistent only with an intention to keep the policy in force can ground waiver. In *De Maurier v. Bastion*,[72] the assured brought a claim on a jewellers' all risks policy in respect of the theft of jewellery from his car, and the insurers rejected the claim while not repudiating their liability on the policy. Subsequently they specified certain safes as suitable for keeping jewellery insured under the policy. A second loss then occurred, and it was held that the insurers' action in approving the type of safe was a waiver of the right to repudiate liability for breach of warranty.

10–115 Waiver of future compliance with term. The representations or conduct of the insurers may as well found a waiver of their right to insist upon the assured's future compliance with a continuing warranty or condition precedent as a waiver of their right to disclaim liability for a past

---

[64] *Whyte v. Western Ass. Co.* (1875) 22 L.C.J. 215, PC. The return of proofs of loss together with a repudiation of liability has been held to be a waiver of any defect in the proofs—*Rumsey v. Phoenix Ins. Co.* (U.S.D.C. 1880) 17 Blatchf. 527.

[65] *McCormick v. Royal Insurance Co.*, 163 Pa. 184 (1894).

[66] *Cleaver v. Traders Ins. Co.* (1889) 40 Fed.Rep. 711.

[67] [1913] 3 K.B. 411.

[68] *Sulphate Pulp Co. v. Faber* (1895) 1 Com.Cas. 146, 153–154.

[69] *Phoenix v. Flemming* 65 (1898) Ark. 54; 67 Am.S.R. 900.

[70] *Jones v. Bangor Mut. Shipping Ins. Soc.* (1889) 61 L.T. 727.

[71] *Keeling v. Pearl Ass. Co.* (1923) 129 L.T. 573.

[72] [1967] 2 Lloyd's Rep. 550. The waiver was based on election not to avoid the policy for breach of warranty, but could have been put on estoppel.

breach.[73] Where an express dispensation is relied upon it must be construed carefully to see if it was an unrestricted waiver or subject to limitations.[74] In short, any act or communication by the insurers may have the effect of dispensing the assured from future performance of a condition or warranty in the policy or proposal form so long as the assured is fairly misled into receiving that impression, whether this be connected with the issue[75] or renewal[76] of cover or the bringing of a claim upon the policy.[77]

10–116 Waiver of right to avoid policy. The policy may provide that in the event of a breach of warranty or other term it is to become void,[78] in a similar way to the provisions of a forfeiture clause in a lease.[79] This means, it is submitted, that the policy becomes voidable at the election of the insurer.[80] The right of avoidance may be lost not only by a waiver founded upon the principles of equitable estoppel but also by waiver founded upon the doctrine of election. The insurer has a choice whether to avoid the policy in order to repudiate his liability to the assured. If, with knowledge of the assured's breach, he manifests an unequivocal intention to keep the policy on foot, he will be taken to have waived his right to avoid it, regardless of his subjective intentions,[81] and his deemed election is irrevocable.[82]

10–117 Knowledge. A waiver by election involves an express or implied choice by the insurer. An informed choice presupposes that the insurer has knowledge of his rights and that the contingency upon which they are exercisable has come about. The assured should prove that the insurer had full knowledge of the facts which constitute a breach, or at least sufficient to put them on enquiry as to the extent of a breach known to have occurred.[83] Being put on inquiry as to the possible commission of a breach is insufficient to found waiver by election.[84] The manner in which the insurers acquire

[73] *Toronto Railway Co. v. National British etc. Ins. Co.* (1914) 111 L.T. 555; *Burridge v. Haines* (1918) 118 L.T. 681; *Ayrey v. British Legal etc. Ass. Co.* [1918] 1 K.B. 136; *Barrett Bros. v. Davies* [1966] 1 W.L.R. 1334.

[74] *Re Carr and Sun Fire Ins. Co.* (1897) 13 T.L.R. 186.

[75] *Roberts v. Security Co.* [1897] 1 Q.B. 111, 116; *Lawrence v. Pennsylvania Mut. Life Ins. Co.*, 36 So. 898 (La.Sup.Ct. 1904); *Pottsville Mut. v. Fromm*, 100 Pa. 347 (1882).

[76] *Ayrey v. British Legal etc. Ass. Co.* [1918] 1 K.B. 136; *Allen v. Home Ins. Co.*, 65 P 138 (Cal.Sup.Ct. 1901).

[77] *Strong v. Harvey* (1825) 3 Bing. 304; *Harrison v. Douglas* (1835) 3 Ad. & El. 396; *Provident Life v. Bellew* (1904) 35 S.C.R. 35.

[78] *Wing v. Harvey* (1854) 5 De G.M. & G. 265; *Thomson v. Weems* (1884) 9 App.Cas. 671; *Hemmings v. Sceptre Life Ass. Co.* [1905] 1 Ch. 365.

[79] *Matthews v. Smallwood* [1910] 1 Ch. 777; *Kammins Ballrooms Co. v. Zenith Investments (Torquay) Ltd* [1971] A.C. 850, 883.

[80] See note 9 to para. 10–92, *ante*.

[81] *Cia. di Tirrena Assicurazioni v. Grand Union Ins. Co.* [1991] 2 Lloyd's Rep. 143; *Central Estates v. Woolgar* [1972] 1 W.L.R. 1048, 1052. Another way of putting it is that his intention is conclusively presumed—*The "Brimnes"* [1973] 1 W.L.R. 386, 413.

[82] *Scarf v. Jardine* (1882) 7 App.Cas. 345, 360; *Central Estates v. Woolgar* [1972] 1 W.L.R. 1048, 1054.

[83] *McCormick v. National Motor & Accident Ins. Union* (1934) 49 Ll.L.R. 361, 365; *Locker & Woolf v. W. Australian Ins. Co.* [1936] 1 K.B. 408; *Busteed v. West of England Fire & Life Ins. Co.* (1857) 5 Ir.Ch.R. 553; *Phillips v. Gd. River Farmers' Mut. Fire Ins. Co.* (1881) 46 U.C.R. 334; *Pritchard v. Merchants' & Tradesmen's Life Ass.* (1858) 3 C.B.(N.S.) 622; *Melik v. Norwich Union Fire Ins. Soc.* [1980] 1 Lloyd's Rep. 523, 533–534.

[84] *McCormick v. National Motor etc. Union* (1934) 49 Ll.L.R. 362, 365; *Allan Peters v. Brocks Alarms* [1968] 1 Lloyd's Rep. 387, 395 (failure by insurers' surveyor to notice improperly fixed security grille); *McEwan v. Guthridge* (1860) 13 Moo.P.C. 304.

knowledge of the breach does not matter in English law,[85] although it has been held in an American case[86] that the informal receipt of information which was required by the policy to be given by formal written notice did not found a waiver of the breach of the relevant provision.

10–118 Knowledge possessed by agent of insurers. In order that the insurance company should be held to have knowledge of the assured's breach, it is not necessary that the relevant information should have been received directly by the same employee or official of the company whose act is relied upon as constituting a waiver. It suffices that the agent who received the information was authorised to do so and to transmit it to other employees of the company. Where the information received reveals a breach by the assured only when it is placed in the context of earlier statements by the assured in, for instance, proposal forms or declarations of health, the company will be held to have acquired knowledge of the breach only when the relevant agent is actually aware of the entire picture or when he ought to have been in the ordinary course of his duties.

These propositions are illustrated in two decisions of the Court of Appeal. In *Evans v. Employers' Mutual Insurance Association Ltd*[87] the assured had stated in his proposal form that he had held a driving licence for five years and had five years driving experience. His answers were warranted true. About four months later he completed a claim form after an accident in which he stated that he had been driving motors for six weeks. He also told a company claims inspector orally that he had held a licence for only six weeks prior to the accident, so that he must have obtained it almost three months after completing the proposal form. The inspector handed over the claim form and his own report to a clerk whose duty it was to check the claim form and report and to note any discrepancy with the proposal form. He noticed the discrepancy but did not consider it sufficiently important to bring it to the attention of his superior. Consequently the company paid the part of the claim relating to damage to the assured's car and took over the conduct of third party proceedings. Over one month later the claims superintendent noticed the discrepancy between the various documents and repudiated liability. It was held that the company had waived the assured's breach of warranty by payment of part of the claim and by conducting the proceedings. The clerk's knowledge of the breach was imputed to the company because he was the duly authorised employee of the company to discover this kind of misstatement and to notify others in the company of his discovery, and he had received knowledge of it in the ordinary course of his work.[88] It would make no difference if his conduct was properly described as negligent, but his knowledge would not have been imputed to the company if he had acquired it while acting fraudulently or in breach of duty towards his employers.[89]

By contrast, in *Malhi v. Abbey Life Assurance Co. Ltd*[90] a proposal form

---

[85] *Barrett Bros (Taxis) v. Davies* [1966] 1 W.L.R. 1334.
[86] *Fitchpatrick v. Hawkeye Ins. Co.*, 53 Iowa 335 (1880).
[87] [1936] 1 K.B. 505.
[88] *Wing v. Harvey* (1854) 5 De G.M. & G. 265; *Ayrey v. British Legal etc. Ass. Co.* [1918] 1 K.B. 136; *Houghton & Co. v. Nothard, Lowe & Wills* [1928] A.C. 1, 14–15.
[89] *Newsholme Bros. v. Road Transport and General Ins. Co.* [1929] 2 K.B. 356, 374.
[90] [1996] L.R.L.R. 237.

for life assurance would have revealed earlier non-disclosures by the assured in negotiations for an existing policy if its contents had been compared with earlier proposals and declarations made for the purposes of the latter. The underwriter who read (and rejected) the proposal did not have before him the earlier documents completed by the assured and so did not appreciate the assured's breaches of duty. The actions of the insurers in continuing to accept premiums for the existing cover was held by a majority of the Court of Appeal not to constitute a waiver of the non-disclosures, because the underwriter was unaware of the discrepancy between the documents and it was not company practice that he should have called for copies of the earlier records. The mere fact that the company had in its possession the documents which, if perused, would have revealed the non-disclosure was not enough to fix it with knowledge of their contents and hence the assured's default.

10–119 Delay. It has been held that insurers are entitled to delay a decision whether to affirm or avoid a policy after they acquire knowledge of the assured's breach, so that inaction on their part does not itself ground waiver of the right of avoidance. In *Allen v. Robles, Compagnie Parisienne de Garantie (Third Party)*,[91] the assured was obliged by a condition in his motor policy to advise the insurers "immediately he has knowledge of a claim and at the latest within five days ...". On April 9, 1967, he negligently drove into a house and injured the plaintiff occupier. In July 1967 he informed the insurers that a claim had been made against him by the plaintiff. On November 29, 1967, the insurers told the occupier that they would indemnify the assured only in respect of the plaintiff's damages covered by statutory third-party insurance and not in respect of the damage to the plaintiff's house, which was much greater in quantum. The plaintiff obtained a judgment against the assured for all his loss and the assured joined the insurers as third parties. They contended that the assured's breach of the procedural condition entitled them to elect not to indemnify him. Mocatta J. held that the insurers had to make their election within a reasonable time, and that they had lost their right by delaying a decision for an unreasonably long time. The Court of Appeal allowed the insurers' appeal, holding that the insurers were entitled to delay as long as they wished, subject to the loss of their right to repudiate liability if—

(i) delay occasioned prejudice to the assured, or
(ii) in some way the rights of third parties intervened, or
(iii) the lapse of time were itself evidence of an intention to affirm their liability.

This is not an easy decision. First, it is unclear what legal right accrued to the insurers as a result of the breach of condition, and it may be that it provided an automatic defence to payment. If so, it was not a true case of election. Secondly, assuming that it was a case where insurers possessed a right of avoidance, it is hard to see why their right to elect to avoid the policy was not subject to the general principle that, where a party possesses a right in the nature of an option, and no express time limit for its exercise is stipulated, it should be exercised within a reasonable time,[92] regardless of prejudice to the

---

[91] [1969] 1 W.L.R 1198.
[92] *The "Laconia"* [1977] A.C. 850, 872; *Reardon Smith Line v. Ministry of Agriculture* [1963] A.C. 691, 731–732, applied in *The "Foresight Driller 2"* [1995] 1 Lloyd's Rep. 251, 266.

assured. Even if this is incorrect as a general proposition the courts are free to achieve the same result in particular cases. If the delay is so unreasonable as to be excessive, it can properly be treated as evidence of a decision to affirm the contract,[93] and it can ground waiver by equitable estoppel if the assured, believing that insurers had evidently decided not to avoid the policy, decides in an appropriate case not to insure elsewhere.[94]

10–120 Waiver by agent. It has been seen that the insurers may be affected by the knowledge of an agent duly authorised to be informed of the facts concerning a breach by the assured. It is equally clear that in certain circumstances the express representation or conduct of an agent may be described as the act of waiver by the insurers themselves. In order to claim that an express representation or act on the part of an agent amounts to a waiver and is binding on the insurers, the assured must show that the representation or act itself constitutes a waiver in the relevant circumstances[95] and that it fell within the category of insurance work which that agent had actual or ostensible authority to conduct.[96] "Ostensible authority" may be defined for these purposes as the authority which the agent appears to possess ostensibly by reference to the position which the insurers have permitted him to occupy, so that, even if he does not in fact have actual authority to do the act in question, the insurers are estopped from denying that he has it.[97] Some illustrations may be helpful.

10–121 If an agent has authority to receive and give receipts for premiums on behalf of the insurance company, his acceptance of a premium with knowledge of a prior breach of a provision in the policy is an act waiving that breach which binds the insurers.[98] An agent who has authority to settle claims has ostensible authority to waive any breach of warranty. In one American case an agent had "power to issue policies, receive premiums, consent to assignments and attend to all other duties and business of the agency". There was a condition that the policy should become void if, without the written consent of the company first obtained, the house should become vacant. It was held that the agent had apparent authority to indorse the policy with permission to leave the premises unoccupied, and that, if the premises had been left unoccupied without previous indorsement, he had authority to waive the breach, and that he did so by subsequent indorsement.[99] In a Canadian case the insurers' policies contained a condition against double insurance unless noted and indorsed on the policy. The agent, being informed that the applicant held another insurance, told him that he would obtain particulars and insert them in the proposal. He then issued an interim protection note and forwarded the proposal to the head office without entering the particulars of other insurance. The proposal was accepted, and a policy issued. It was held that the protection note was valid,

---

[93] *Clough v. L.N.W.R.* (1871) L.R. 7 Ex. 26, 35.

[94] *Morrison v. Universal Marine Ins. Co.* (1873) L.R. 8 Ex. 197, 205–206.

[95] *Wing v. Harvey* (1854) 5 De G.M. & G. 265, 269; *Davies v. National Fire and Marine Ins. Co.* [1891] A.C. 485, 496.

[96] *Houghton & Co. v. Northard, Lowe & Wills* [1928] A.C. 1, 14.

[97] The reader should be warned that some of the older decisions before 1900 were reached before the doctrine of ostensible authority was developed and cannot be relied upon today.

[98] *Ayrey v. British Legal and Provident* [1918] 1 K.B. 136; *Wing v. Harvey* (1854) 5 De G.M. & G. 265.

[99] *Wheeler v. Waterton Fire*, 131 Mass. 1 (1881).

as the agent knew of the double insurance and had authority to issue the note, but the policy was void because the head office which accepted the contract had no knowledge of the double insurance.[1]

10–122 An agent whose authority is limited to receiving premiums in the days of grace cannot waive the non-payment by taking a premium later and revive the lapsed policy.[2] A loss adjuster employed by the insurers cannot waive a term requiring proof of loss.[3] A local agent has no authority to waive a condition requiring the giving of notice of loss to the head office in a particular time.[4] It can happen that the agent's authority is restricted by provisions in the policy, such as "no condition can be waived except in writing signed by the secretary". In such a case the assured is put on notice as to the lack of authority of the company's agents to waive breaches of condition or warranty, and he cannot plead ostensible authority when his policy tells him the true state of affairs.[5] Other conditions lay down a formal mode in which the waiver must be exercised, and then, on analogous principles, the assured cannot rely on informal acts of waiver by an agent.[6]

10–123 Plea of waiver. The plea of waiver has been described as a "serious step"[7] and its proper place is in the assured's reply to the insurers' defence of a breach of condition or warranty. The onus of proof is on the assured to establish the elements of waiver,[8] and he must specifically plead that the insurers' words or actions led him to believe that they intended to treat the policy as subsisting or to waive future performance of a term in the policy, as the case may be.[9]

10–124 Waiver in Scots law. Waiver is the abandonment of a right. It may be express or inferred from facts and circumstances.[10] In *Donnison v. Employers' Accident and Live Stock Ins. Co. Ltd*[11] an accident policy provided for notification of any accident within 14 days, and the assured, prior to his death, gave notice outside that period. The insurers requested a post-mortem examination under a term of the policy and the assured's widow consented. The insurers were held to have waived their right to rely on the notice provision. A party pleading waiver as opposed to personal bar

---

[1] *Billington v. Provincial Insurance* (1877) 2 Ont.A.R. 158; (1879) 3 S.C.R. 182.

[2] *Acey v. Fernie* (1840) 7 M. & W. 151.

[3] *Atlas Ass. Co. v. Brownell* (1899) 29 S.C.R. 537; *Commercial Union Ass. Co. v. Margeson* (1899) 29 S.C.R. 601.

[4] *Brook v. Trafalgar Ins. Co. Ltd* (1947) 19 Ll.L.R. 365.

[5] *O'Brien v. Prescott Ins. Co.*, 134 N.Y. 28 (1892); *Levy v. Scottish Employers Ins.* (1901) 17 T.L.R. 229.

[6] *Atlas Ass. Co. v. Brownell* (1899) 29 S.C.R. 537; *M'Millan v. Accident Ins. Co.* [1907] S.C. 484.

[7] *Brook v. Trafalgar Ins. Co. Ltd* (1947) 79 Ll.L.R. 365, 367.

[8] *De Maurier v. Bastion Ins. Co.* [1967] 2 Lloyd's Rep. 550. The assured has to satisfy the court that his interpretation of the insurers' behaviour was reasonable. *Marcovitch v. Liverpool Victoria Soc.* (1912) 28 T.L.R. 188 is not good authority to the contrary; the insurers' evidence of breach was very unsatisfactory.

[9] *Morrison v. Universal Marine Ins. Co.* (1873) L.R. 8 Ex. 197, 206. (This was a non-disclosure case, but the principle seems to be equally applicable to waiver of breach of condition or warranty.) *Ocean Trawling Co. v. Fire and All Risks Ins. Co. Ltd* [1965] W.A.R. 65, 71.

[10] *Arma Ltd v. Daejan Developments Ltd* [1979] S.C.H.L. 56, 71, *per* Lord Keith of Kinkel, followed in *Gordon v. E. Kilbride Development Corporation* [1995] S.L.T. 62, 64, where it was stated that waiver generally involves the irrevocable abandonment of the right.

[11] (1897) 24 R. 681, cited by Lord Keith in *Armia, supra*.

need not show that he acted to his prejudice on the basis of the waiver,[12] but it has been held that he must at least prove that he acted in reliance on the waiver,[13] which means there must be averments of some overt acceptance of the waiver.[14]

[12] *Arma*, pp. 68–69, *per* Lord Fraser of Tullybelton; *Banks v. Mecca Bookmakers (Scotland) Ltd* [1982] S.C. 7, 10–13.
[13] *Morrison's Exrs v. Rendall* [1986] S.L.T. 227; *D. & J. McDougall Ltd v. Argyll & Bute District Council* [1987] S.L.T. 7.
[14] *Barrett Scotland Ltd v. Keith* [1993] S.C. 142.

CHAPTER 11

CONSTRUCTION OF POLICIES

1. ORDINARY MEANING OF WORDS

11–1 General rules. Insurance policies are to be construed according to the principles of construction applicable to commercial contracts generally, and there are no peculiar rules of construction applicable to the terms and conditions in a policy which are not equally applicable to the terms of other mercantile contracts.[1] The task of a tribunal endeavouring to interpret the contract of insurance is to ascertain the intention of the parties in relation to the facts in dispute.[2] Such intention is, however, to be gathered from the wording of the policy itself[3] and from the wording of any other documents which may be incorporated with it,[4] so that

> "the true construction of a document means no more than that the court puts on it the true meaning, and the true meaning is the meaning which the party to whom the document was handed or who is relying on it would put on it as an ordinarily intelligent person construing the words in the proper way in the light of the relevant circumstances".[5]

The courts have developed various canons or maxims of construction to assist in the process of interpretation. The drafting and construction of policies are also affected by certain provisions of the Unfair Terms in

---

[1] *Drinkwater v. Corp. of the London Assurance* (1767) 2 Wils. 363, 364; *Robertson v. French* (1803) 4 East 130, 135, *per* Lord Ellenborough; *Reid v. Marsden* (1803) 3 East 572, 579; *Abbott v. Howard* (1832) Hayes 381, 401; *Glen v. Lewis* (1853) 8 Ex. 607, 617; *Smith v. Accident Ins. Co.* (1870) L.R. 5 Ex. 302, 307; *Hart v. Standard Marine* (1889) 22 Q.B.D. 499, 501; *Jason v. British Traders' Ins. Co. Ltd* [1969] 1 Lloyd's Rep. 281, 290; *Cementation Piling & Foundations Ltd v. Aegon Ins. Co. Ltd* [1995] 1 Lloyd's Rep. 97, 101.

[2] *Drinkwater v. Corp. of the London Assurance* (1767) 2 Wils. 363, 364; *Tarleton v. Staniforth* (1794) 5 T.R. 695, 699; *Braunstein v. Accidental Death* (1861) 1 B. & S. 782, 799.

[3] *Want v. Blunt* (1810) 12 East 183, 187; *Borradaile v. Hunter* (1843) 5 M. & G. 639, 653, 657, 664; *M'Swiney v. Royal Exchange Assurance* (1849) 14 Q.B. 634, 661; *Beacon Life, etc. v. Gibb* (1862) 1 Moo.P.C.(N.S.) 73, 97; *Re George and Goldsmiths' and General Burglary Ins. Ass.* [1899] 1 Q.B. 595; *Wickman Machine Tool Sales v. L. Schuler AG* [1972] 1 W.L.R. 840, 857 affirmed in H.L. [1974] A.C. 235; *M. W. Wilson (Lace) Ltd v. Eagle Star Ins. Co. Ltd* 1993 S.L.T. 938, 944.

[4] *e.g.* the proposal form or a slip pasted on to the policy. See paras 10–21 to 10–22, *ante*.

[5] *Hutton v. Watling* [1948] Ch. 398, 403, *per* Greene M.R.; approved and followed in *Randazzo v. Goulding* [1968] Qd.R. 433. The same principle is to be found in the first of Lord Hoffmann's five principles of interpretation stated in *Investors Compensation Scheme Ltd v. West Bromwich Bldg. Soc.* [1998] 1 W.L.R. 896, 912.

Consumer Contracts Regulations 1999.[6] These are considered in the course of this chapter.

11–2 Previous interpretation. The first and overriding consideration in construing any phrase or form of words in a policy is to inquire whether these have been the subject of any prior decision by a court. The proper construction to be placed on words is a matter of law for the court.[7] Consequently, as with all questions of law, the ordinary rules of the doctrine of precedent apply, and the tribunal interpreting the words in question will either be bound to follow the previous court's interpretation or strongly persuaded to do so, depending on the tribunal's relationship to the court which decided the earlier case. When a higher court has placed an interpretation upon the phrase to be construed by the later and inferior tribunal, the latter has no option but to follow that interpretation.[8] As Parke B. said in *Glen v. Lewis*[9]: "If a construction had already been put upon a clause precisely similar in any decided case we should defer to that authority."

11–3 Even where the tribunal is not bound to follow an earlier interpretation, it frequently happens that it will nevertheless do so in order not to create confusion in the insurance industry, which may have been accustomed to understand a particular form of words in a particular sense for very many years since the court first gave their view of its meaning.[10]

"It is a salutary rule that the courts should be chary in interfering with the interpretation given to a well-known document and acted on for any considerable period of time."[11]

Parties to commercial contracts are taken to be cognisant of prior decisions upon the construction of similar contracts.[12]

11–4 In order that either principle be invoked, however, it is necessary that the words to be construed are identical to those construed in an earlier case,[13] or else differ only in immaterial details,[14] since:

---

[6] S.I. 1999 No. 2083.

[7] *Simond v. Boydell* (1779) 1 Doug. K.B. 268; *Clift v. Schwabe* (1846) 3 C.B. 437, 469; *Simmonds v. Cockell* [1920] 1 K.B. 843; *Starfire Diamond Rings Ltd v. Angel* [1962] 2 Lloyd's Rep. 217, 219.

[8] See, *per* Roskill J. in *W. J. Lane v. Spratt* [1970] 2 Q.B. 480, 491–492, following *Fraser v. B. N. Furman* [1967] 1 W.L.R. 898 and *Woolfall & Rimmer v. Moyle* [1942] 1 K.B. 66.

[9] (1846) 3 C.B. 437, 470.

[10] *Andersen v. Marten* [1908] A.C. 334, 340, following *Goss v. Withers* (1758) 2 Burr. 683; *Becker, Gray & Co. v. London Assurance Corp.* [1918] A.C. 101, 108; *Louden v. British Merchants Ins. Co. Ltd* [1961] 1 Lloyd's Rep. 155, following *Mair v. Railway Passengers Ass. Co.* (1877) 37 L.T. 356.

[11] *Re Hooley Hill Rubber and Royal Insurance Co.* [1920] 1 K.B. 257, 269 *per* Bankes L.J. See also *Louden v. British Merchants Ins. Co. Ltd* [1961] 1 W.L.R. 798 *per* Lawton J.: *The Annefield* [1970] 2 Lloyd's Rep. 252, 262; *Bourne v. Keane* [1919] A.C. 815, 858, 871, 922; *Atlantic Shipping Co. v. Dreyfus* [1922] 2 A.C. 250, 257; *Spinney's (1948) Ltd v. Royal Insurance Co. Ltd* [1980] 1 Lloyd's Rep. 406, 435.

[12] *Toomey v. Eagle Star Ins. Co. Ltd* [1994] 1 Lloyd's Rep 516, 520.

[13] *Clift v. Schwabe* (1846) 3 C.B. 437, 470; *Re Calf and Sun Insurance Office* [1920] 2 K.B. 366, 382.

[14] *Lawrence v. Accidental Ins. Co.* (1881) 7 Q.B.D. 216, 220; *Dodson v. Dodson Insurance Services* [2001] 1 All E.R. (Comm.) 300, 310.

"Authorities may determine principles of construction, but a decision upon one form of words is no authority upon the construction of another form of words."[15]

It must, indeed, be borne in mind that a clause cannot be said to be "precisely similar" to another unless its context is the same. Words are always to be construed in their context,[16] and a difference in context will often afford valid grounds for distinguishing an earlier decision, though it dealt with words which also occur in the policy under consideration.

11–5 Reliance upon decisions in other jurisdictions. Decisions reached on points of interpretation in other common-law jurisdictions are not of binding force on English tribunals, but they are frequently entitled to respect. The degree of authority a case possesses depends upon the quality of the judgment's reasoning and the status of the court in question. It is rare, however, for a court to follow a decision in a foreign jurisdiction rather than an English authority at variance with it, and in one case Scrutton L.J. was moved to say:

"I am not impressed by the fact that a different view has been taken by American courts on American policies. Those courts frequently differ from ours on the construction of mercantile documents. English courts construe documents by the light of English decisions."[17]

English law does not follow the principle adopted in some American jurisdictions whereby policies are construed to produce a result which satisfies the reasonable expectations of the assured.[18]

11–6 Ordinary meaning. There is a presumption that the words to be construed should be construed in their ordinary and popular sense,[19] since the parties to the contract must be taken to have intended, as reasonable men, to use words and phrases in their commonly understood and accepted sense. This presumption can be rebutted in certain circumstances which are examined later in this chapter,[20] but it is frequently the case that there is no reason to depart from the ordinary meaning of the words in question. Thus

---

[15] *Re Coleman's Depositories Ltd and Life and Health Assurance Ass.* [1907] 2 K.B. 798.

[16] See para. 11–17, *infra*.

[17] *Re Hooley Hill Rubber and Royal Ins. Co.* [1920] 1 K.B. 257, 272. Another instance is *American Surety Co. of New York v. Wrighton* (1911) 103 L.T. 633, 666, *per* Hamilton J. citing James L.J. in *North British and Mercantile Ins. Co. v. London, Liverpool and Globe Ins. Co.* (1877) L.R. 5 Ch.D. 569; 36 L.T. 629 concerning the authority of decisions of U.S. state and federal courts.

[18] *Smit Tak Offshore Services v. Youell* [1992] 1 Lloyd's Rep. 154, 159, *per* Mustill L.J.; *Yorkshire Water Services v. Sun Alliance & London Ins. plc* [1997] 2 Lloyd's Rep. 21, 28, *per* Stuart-Smith L.J.

[19] *Robertson v. French* (1803) 4 East 130, 135; *Stanley v. Western Insurance* (1868) L.R. 3 Ex. 71; *Thomson v. Weems* (1884) 9 App.Cas. 671, 687; *Hart v. Standard Marine Ins. Co.* (1889) 22 Q.B.D. 499, 500; *Re George and Goldsmiths' and General Burglary Ins. Assoc. Ltd* [1899] 1 Q.B. 595, 610; *Yangtze Ins. Assoc. v. Indemnity Mutual Marine Ass. Co.* [1908] 2 K.B. 504, 509; *Leo Rapp v. McClure* [1955] 1 Lloyd's Rep. 292, 293; *S. & M. Hotels Ltd v. Legal and General Ass. Soc. Ltd* [1972] 1 Lloyd's Rep. 157, 162–163; *Young v. Sun Alliance & London Ins. Co.* [1977] 1 W.L.R. 104 ("flood")—*cf. Anderson v. Norwich Union Soc. Ltd* [1977] 1 Lloyd's Rep. 253. "[W]e do not easily accept that people have made linguistic mistakes, particularly in formal documents"—*Investors Compensation Scheme v. West Bromwich Bldg. Soc.* [1998] 1 W.L.R. 896, 913.

[20] See paras 11–12 to 11–13, *post*.

in *Starfire Diamond Rings Ltd v. Angel*[21] the court had to determine the scope of an exclusions clause in a jewellers' Block Policy excepting liability for theft when the assured's car was "left unattended". The driver had gone thirty-seven yards from the car in order to relieve himself, and a suitcase containing jewellery was stolen by a thief in that short period of time. It was held that in the circumstances the car had been "left unattended", and Upjohn L.J. commented:

> "I deprecate any attempt to expound the meaning or further to define words such as these which are common words in everyday use, having a perfectly ordinary and clear meaning."[22]

It follows that, if a word or phrase has an accepted popular meaning, that meaning should prevail rather than a more limited scientific or technical meaning unless the context demands the latter. Thus "gas" in a fire policy has been held to mean ordinary coal gas and not to include a vapour given off in the course of an oil extraction process,[23] and "subsidence" has been held to include "settlement" in accordance with its popular meaning, although its more accurate scientific meaning denoted only vertical movement.[24] There are many examples of the application of this presumption in the reports. Similarly, the words in the policy will be construed on the footing that the parties intended the ordinary rules of grammar to apply to them.[25]

11–7 Businesslike interpretation. It is an accepted canon of construction that a commercial document, such as an insurance policy, should be construed in accordance with sound commercial principles and good business sense, so that its provisions receive a fair and sensible application.[26] Several consequences flow from this principle. The literal meaning of words must not be permitted to prevail where it would produce an unrealistic and generally unanticipated result,[27] as, for example, where it would unwarrantably reduce the cover which it was the purpose of the policy to afford.[28] Thus, in a policy of which the main purpose was to insure against damages arising from negligent acts by the insured, it was held that a condition that "the insured shall take reasonable precautions" could not be so construed

---

[21] [1962] 2 Lloyd's Rep. 217; followed in *Ingleton of Ilford v. General Accident, etc., Ass. Corp.* [1967] 2 Lloyd's Rep. 179; *cf. Langford v. Legal and General Ass. Soc. Ltd* [1986] 2 Lloyd's Rep. 103.

[22] [1962] 2 Lloyd's Rep. 217, 219.

[23] *Stanley v. Western Ins. Co.* (1868) L.R. 3 Ex. 71.

[24] *D. Allen & Sons (Billposting) Ltd v. Drysdale* [1939] 4 All E.R. 113.

[25] *Weir v. Northern Counties of England Ins. Co.* (1879) L.R. 4 Ir. 689, 693; *L. Emanuel & Son Ltd v. Hepburn* [1960] 1 Lloyd's Rep. 304, 308. But "insurance documents in the London market are rarely drawn with the precision of language needed for grammatical contrasts to be a reliable guide to intention"—*Touche Ross & Co. v. Baker* [1992] 2 Lloyd's Rep. 207, 213, *per* Lord Mustill.

[26] *Clift v. Schwabe* (1846) 3 C.B. 437, 469; *Glen v. Lewis* (1853) 8 Ex. 607, 610; *Hydarnes v. Indemnity Mutual* [1895] 1 Q.B. 500, 504; *J. Martin of London Ltd v. Russell* [1960] 1 Lloyd's Rep. 554, 565; *Lowenstein v. Poplar Motor Transport Ltd* [1968] 2 Lloyd's Rep. 233, 238; *Suncorp Ins. v. Milano Assic. SpA* [1993] 2 Lloyd's Rep. 225, 231; *Turner v. Manx Line* [1990] 1 Lloyd's Rep. 137, 142.

[27] *M'Cowan v. Baine & Johnston* [1891] A.C. 401, 403; *Re Etherington and the Lancashire and Yorkshire Accident Ins. Co.* [1909] 1 K.B. 591, 597; *North British, etc., Ins. Co. v. London, Liverpool, etc., Ins. Co.* (1877) 5 Ch.D. 569, 576–577; *Borradaile v. Hunter* (1843) 5 M. & G. 639; *Connecticut Mutual Life Ins. Co. v. Moore* (1881) 6 App.Cas. 644, 648; *Westminster Fire Office v. Reliance Marine Ins. Co.* (1903) 19 T.L.R. 668.

[28] *Morely v. United Friendly Ins. PLC* [1993] 1 Lloyd's Rep. 490.

that every negligent act was a breach of it.[29] It is probably by virtue of this maxim also that the court should be prepared to overlook obvious grammatical errors, such as an inadvertent negative obviously out of context,[30] and will interpret for the purposes of the particular cover inappropriate phrases in a standard printed policy primarily intended for other sorts of insurance,[31] or else disregard them as matters of surplusage to the cover in question.[32] A further result of this maxim is that a court may imply into the express words granting cover an extended scope beyond their strictly literal meaning in order to give effect to the only sound interpretation of the contract. In *Pearson v. Commercial Union Assurance Co.*[33] a ship was insured while "lying in the Victoria Docks, London, with liberty to go into dry dock, and light boiler fires once or twice during the currency of this policy". The ship was expressly covered when either in the Victoria Docks or in a London dry dock, but it was agreed that the insurance must by implication cover the transit from the Victoria Docks to the dry dock and back again, together with any necessary deviations or delay on the way.

11–8 Commercial object. It follows that in interpreting any clause of a policy, it is correct to bear in mind the commercial object or function of the clause and its apparent relation to the contract as a whole.[34] It may then become apparent that the literal meaning of the clause must yield to business sense or that an ambiguity in the wording can be resolved, or that the ordinary meaning of the words used may need to be modified.

11–9 Construction to avoid unreasonable results. If the wording of a clause is ambiguous, and one reading produces a fairer result than the

---

[29] *Fraser v. Furman* [1967] 1 W.L.R. 989; *Sofi v. Prudential Ass. Co.* [1993] 2 Lloyd's Rep. 559; *Devco Holder v. Legal & General Ass. Soc.* [1993] 2 Lloyd's Rep. 567. See also *Cornish v. Accident Ins. Co.* (1889) 23 Q.B.D. 453; *Trew v. Railway Passengers Assurance Co.* (1861) 6 H. & N. 839, 844. It has also been said, in wider terms, that it is for the benefit of trade that policies be construed in favour of trade and against forfeiture; *Pelly v. Royal Exchange Ins.* (1757) 1 Burr. 341, 349; *Phoenix Life v. Sheridan* (1858) E.B. & E. 156, 166; *Newbury v. Armstrong* (1829) 6 Bing. 201, 202.

[30] *Glen's Trustees v. Lancashire and Yorkshire Accident Ins.* (1906) 8 F. 915. Recent examples are in *American Airlines v. Hope* [1974] 2 Lloyd's Rep. 301, 305—deletion of the first two letters of "unprovoked"; *Farnham v. Royal Insurance* [1976] 2 Lloyd's Rep. 437, 443—erroneous description of insured property; and *Nittan U.K. v. Solent Steel* [1981] 1 Lloyd's Rep. 633, 637, misnomer.

[31] *North British, etc., Ins. Co. v. London, Liverpool, etc. Ins. Co.* (1877) 5 Ch.D. 569.

[32] *Western Assurance Co. of Toronto v. Poole* [1903] 1 K.B. 376, 389; *South British Fire, etc., Co. v. Da Costa* [1906] 1 K.B. 456, 460. Surplussage is by no means unknown in insurance contracts—*Flying Colours Film Co. v. Assic. Generali SpA* [1993] 2 Lloyd's Rep. 184, 192; *Arbuthnott v. Fagan* [1996] L.R.L.R. 135, 142.

[33] (1876) 1 App.Cas. 498. Contrast *Ewing & Co. v. Sicklemore* (1918) 34 T.L.R. 501. The extent of cover may be implied from the wording of a clause setting out what is excluded from cover—*Cementation Piling & Foundation v. Aegon Ins. Co.* [1995] 1 Lloyd's Rep. 97, 103.

[34] *Clift v. Schwabe* (1846) 3 C.B. 437, 477; *Borradaile v. Hunter* (1843) 5 M. & G. 639, 659, 664; *Smith v. Accident Ins. Co.* (1870) L.R. 5 Ex. 302, 305; *Hart v. Standard Marine Insurance Co.* (1889) 22 Q.B.D. 499; *Lake v. Simmons* [1927] A.C. 487, 508; *Leo Rapp v. McClure* [1955] 1 Lloyd's Rep. 292, 293; *Starfire Diamond Rings v. Angel* [1962] 2 Lloyd's Rep. 217, 219; *Barnard v. Faber* [1893] 1 Q.B. 340, 341, 343–345; *Kearney v. General Accident Fire and Life Assurance Corp. Ltd* [1968] 2 Lloyd's Rep. 240; *L. Schuler A.G. v. Wickman Machine Tool Sales Ltd* [1974] A.C. 235, 251, 265; *Wilson (Lace) Ltd v. Eagle Star Ins. Co. Ltd* 1993 S.L.T. 938, 944; *Morely v. United Friendly Ins. PLC* [1993] 1 Lloyd's Rep. 490, 495; *Australian Agricultural Co. v. Saunders* (1875) L.R. 10 C.P. 668; *Sargent v. GRE (UK) Ltd* [2000] Lloyd's Rep.I.R. 77.

alternative, the reasonable interpretation should be adopted.[35] It is to be presumed that the parties, as reasonable men, would have intended to include reasonable stipulations in their contract, and this presumption may assist either party depending on the circumstances. Thus in *Hooper v. Accidental Death Insurance Co.*,[36] a solicitor was insured under an accident policy which bound the insurers to pay him a weekly sum if an injury was so serious "*as wholly* to disable him from following his usual business, occupation or pursuits". Having sprained his ankle very badly, he was confined to a sofa in his bedroom for a time, being unable to get downstairs. The insurers disputed liability on the grounds that he was not "wholly" disabled, taking the words "as wholly to disable" at their face value. The court held, however, that the meaning of the clause looked at in its entirety was that the assured should be disabled from conducting his usual business in the normal manner, and this more reasonable construction of the clause should be followed.

11–10 Secondly, even though the wording of a condition in a policy is apparently plain, the court will sometimes narrow its scope or place a gloss on its words in order to make it reasonable in application.[37] So, where a policy contains a condition requiring that "Every claim, notice, letter, writ or process ... served on the employer shall be notified or forwarded to the Association *immediately on receipt*", the words "immediately on receipt" have been construed to mean "with all reasonable speed".[38] In this case, the element of ambiguity arises from the fact that an absolutely literal interpretation produces results which are not merely unfair but quite impracticable. Therefore some gloss on the words becomes essential and their superficially plain meaning is seen to be illusory. In less strong cases, it must always be remembered the courts have said expressly that it is not their function to make for the parties a reasonable contract in place of what is there already.[39] If the policy is expressed in such clear and precise words that only one interpretation of them is possible, the court generally ought to adopt that construction even though it appears harsh to the assured.[40]

11–11 Implied terms. Where a policy does not by its express terms cover a situation which has arisen, it is permissible to imply a term which does cover those facts if either the proper inference from the reading of the policy as a

[35] *Gamble v. Accident Assurance Co. Ltd* (1869) I.R. 4 C.L. 204, 214; *Lion Ins. Association v. Tucker* (1883) 12 Q.B.D. 176, 190; *Century Bank of City of New York v. Mountain* (1914) 112 L.T. 484, 486; *London Guarantee Co. v. Fearnley* (1880) 5 App.Cas. 911, 916; *Daff v. Midland Colliery Owners Mutual Indemnity Co.* [1913] 6 B.W.C.C. 799. See also the cases on promissory warranties and suspensive conditions—para. 10–7, *ante.*
[36] (1860) 5 H. & N. 546.
[37] *Australian Agricultural Co. v. Saunders* (1875) L.R. 10 C.P. 668; *E. Hulton v. Mountain* (1921) 8 Ll.L.R. 249; *Braunstein v. Accidental Death* (1861) 1 B. & S. 782; *Smellie v. British General Ins. Co.* [1918] W.C. & Ins.Rep. 233; *Stadhard v. Lee* (1863) 3 B. & S. 364; and see comment in *Diggle v. Ogston Motor Co.* (1915) 112 L.T. 1029.
[38] *Re Coleman's Depositories Ltd and Life and Health Assurance Ass.* [1907] 2 K.B. 798, 807; *Farrell v. Federated Employers Ins. Ltd* [1970] 1 W.L.R. 1400 (C.A.).
[39] *Re George and Goldsmiths' and General Burglary Ins. Ass. Ltd* [1899] 1 Q.B. 595, 609; *Union of India v. E. B. Aaby's Rederi* [1975] A.C. 797, 818; *Abrahams v. Mediterranean Ins.* [1991] 1 Lloyd's Rep. 216, 237; *Jason v. British Traders' Ins. Co.* [1969] 1 Lloyd's Rep. 281, 290.
[40] *Gamble v. Accident Assurance Co.* (1869) I.R. 4 C.L. 204, 214; *Cole v. Accident Ins. Co.* (1889) 5 T.L.R. 736, 737; *Re United London and Scottish Ins. Co. Ltd, Brown's Claim* [1915] 2 Ch. 167, 170.

whole is that the parties would have so expressed themselves if they had addressed their minds to the possibility of those particular facts arising, or on the grounds that it was necessary for the business efficacy of the contract.[41] A court will not imply a term into a contract merely because the contract might be considered more reasonable as a result,[42] but no term will be implied unless it is reasonable.[43]

However, terms may be implied in order to give effect to the principle of utmost good faith underlying every contract of insurance, such as those obliging insurers to exercise rights conferred on them for their benefit with proper regard for the interests of their assured.[44]

2. SPECIAL MEANINGS OF WORDS

11–12 Departure from ordinary meaning of words. The presumption that words in a policy should receive their ordinary, natural and unrestricted meaning is displaced if it be shown that:

(a) they are legal terms of art, or
(b) they have acquired a special meaning by force of long usage in a particular trade or business, or
(c) the context in which they appear compels a restricted or modified meaning to be given to them.

11–13 Technical legal meaning. A word or phrase which has a recognised technical meaning in law will usually be taken to bear that meaning, and not a wider or narrower popular meaning.[45] When, therefore, a word which is established as a term of legal art in the criminal law appears in a policy, the criminal law definition of that word should govern its interpretation,[46] for, as Viscount Sumner said in *Lake v. Simmons*:

> "I dissent from the view that criminal law should be regarded as irrelevant merely because a document is commercial. After all, criminal law is still law, and so are its rules and definitions."[47]

Thus, for example, the word "theft" will now[48] receive the current criminal

---

[41] *The Moorcock* (1889) 14 P.D. 64; *Shirlaw v. Southern Foundries* [1939] 2 K.B. 206; *Yorkshire Ins. Co. v. Nisbet* [1962] 2 Q.B. 330, 340; *Ashmore v. Corporation of Lloyd's* [1992] 2 Lloyd's Rep. 620, 626–627; *Euro-Diam Ltd v. Bathurst* [1990] 1 Q.B. 1, 41.

[42] *City Tailors Ltd v. Evans* (1921) 126 L.T. 439.

[43] *Liverpool City Council v. Irwin* [1977] A.C. 239, 262.

[44] *The Mercandian Continent* [2001] 2 Lloyd's Rep. 563, 571–572, citing *Phoenix General Ins. Co. v. Halvanon Ins. Co.* [1988] Q.B. 216, 240–241; *Cox v. Bankside Agency Ltd* [1995] 2 Lloyd's Rep. 437, 462.

[45] *London and Lancashire Fire Ins. Co. v. Bolands* [1924] A.C. 836; *Saqui v. Stearns* [1911] 1 K.B. 426, 436; *Sturge v. Hackett* [1962] 1 Lloyd's Rep. 626. A word capable of bearing one meaning as a term of legal art, such as "condition", may be interpreted in a popular sense if the context requires it: *Wickman Tool Sales Ltd v. L. Schuler AG* [1974] A.C. 235; *Turner v. Manx Line* [1990] 1 Lloyd's Rep. 137 ("interest").

[46] *London and Lancashire Fire Ins. Co. v. Bolands* [1924] A.C. 836; *Debenhams v. Excess Ins. Co. Ltd* (1912) 28 T.L.R. 505; *Re Calf and The Sun Insurance Office* [1920] 2 K.B. 366.

[47] [1927] A.C. 487, 509.

[48] Compare the position before the passing of the Theft Act 1968 when the relevant term was "larceny": *Algemeene Bankvereenigigng v. Langton* (1935) 40 Com. Cas. 247; *Lake v. Simmons* [1927] A.C. 487, 498; *Nishina Trading Co. v. Chiyoda Fire & Marine Ins. Co.* [1969] 2 Q.B. 449.

law definition according to the Theft Act 1968.[49] It is important, however, to distinguish words which are not terms of legal art, but rather popular descriptions of criminal acts having a different technical definition in law, such as "suicide".[50]

11–14 If the parties have provided express definitions in their policy for particular words which are also technical legal words, their own definition must, of course, prevail.[51] The context may also show by implication that a word capable of being understood as a technical legal term is not to be so understood. Thus, in *Algemeene Bankvereeniging v. Langton,*[52] the fact that a policy was issued to a Belgian bank to cover risks arising entirely in Belgium was held to suggest that words describing crimes were not used in their technical sense in English law. Conversely, the context may import a technical definition. Thus it has been held that words in a motor policy are to be construed "in the context of motor insurance", with the result that "motor car" should prima facie have the meaning which it has in the Road Traffic Act 1972.[53]

11–15 When it is sought to show that there has been a loss under the policy occasioned by conduct constituting a crime under the definitions of the criminal law, the court need not be satisfied beyond reasonable doubt of what is alleged, but only on the preponderance of probabilities.[54]

11–16 Trade usage. If words have acquired an artificial or technical meaning in the usage of a particular trade or business, it must be presumed that parties contracting in that context intended their words to receive their customary meaning.[55] Thus "average" in the context of marine insurance means a partial loss of ship or cargo,[56] and in the clothing trade unused Government surplus goods may be described as "new" even though they are not of recent manufacture.[57]

11–17 Meaning affected by context. The natural and ordinary meaning of the words to be construed may have to be modified or restricted if the context in which they appear indicates that the parties to the contract cannot

---

[49] *Grundy (Teddington) Ltd v. Fulton* [1981] 2 Lloyd's Rep. 666, 670, approving a comment in the 6th edition of this book; affirmed without discussing the point [1983] 1 Lloyd's Rep. 16; *Dobson v. General Accident PLC* [1990] 1 Q.B. 274.

[50] *Clift v. Schwabe* (1846) 3 C.B. 437, 458, 462, 464, 470.

[51] *Re George and Goldsmiths' and General Burglary Insurance Association Ltd* [1899] 1 Q.B. 595.

[52] (1935) 40 Com.Cas. 247.

[53] *Laurence v. Davies* [1972] 2 Lloyd's Rep. 231.

[54] *Nishina Trading Co. v. Chiyoda Fire and Marine Ins. Co.* [1969] 2 Q.B. 449.

[55] *Robertson v. French* (1803) 4 East 130, 135; *Clift v. Schwabe* (1846) 3 C.B. 437, 469; *Hart v. Standard Marine* (1889) 22 Q.B.D. 499, 502; *M'Cowan v. Baine & Johnston* [1891] A.C. 401. The same principle applies to words which acquire a usage in a particular sport—*Scragg v. U.K. Temperance, etc., Institution* [1976] 2 Lloyd's Rep. 227—"motor racing" does not include a Silverstone sprint event.

[56] *Price & Co. v. Al Ships' etc. Association* (1889) 22 Q.B.D. 580, 584.

[57] *Anglo-African Merchants v. Bayley* [1970] 1 Q.B. 311.

have intended them to be read in their usual sense.[58] In *Kearney v. General Accident Fire and Life Assurance Corporation Ltd*,[59] an employer's liability insurance policy contained an exception which provided, *inter alia*, that any work in connection with gasometers, towers, steeples, bridges, viaducts, blast furnaces, colliery overhead winding gear, hangars and roofs was not covered by the policy. An employee of the assured company died from injuries received when he fell from the roof girders of a building which had originally been a hangar but was at the time being converted for use as a factory. The insurers disclaimed liability on the ground that the injuries resulted from work in connection with a hangar. It was held that, although the ordinary meaning of "hangar" was a building used to house aeroplanes, and that user did not apply to the building in question, yet it was still a hangar for the purposes of the insurance. The other buildings enumerated were all of a sort which involved some special kind of hazard, mainly the risk of falling from a great height, and a building which had the physical characteristics of a hangar was covered by the exceptions clause even though it was not used as such. It was also held that the roof girders were part of the roof. In *Curtis & Sons v. Mathews*,[60] a claim was brought on a "war and bombardment" policy in respect of a building destroyed by fire. The fire had spread from a nearby building which was being shelled by Crown forces. The policy contained a clause excluding any claim "for confiscation or destruction by the Government of the country in which the property is situated." It was held that the destruction of the building was not covered by the exclusion clause since the act of destruction therein referred to was confined to an act of deliberate destruction in the same sense that confiscation would be deliberate, so that cases of accidental destruction resulting from the operations of Government forces were not inside the clause's scope.

11–18 Ejusdem generis rule. One particular application of the general principle that the primary meaning of words may be affected by their context is the well-known canon of construction that where a particular enumeration is followed by general words such as "or other", the general words ought to be limited to matters *ejusdem generis* with those specifically enumerated.[61] The rule has sometimes been said to be confined to cases where the general words used are added to a context containing specific words which can be grouped under a genus, and the general words can be readily interpreted as extending only to specific things within that genus. It would follow that when a genus cannot be found or when everything which could come within the

---

[58] See, *e.g.* decisions concerning the assured's "total disablement"; *Williams v. Lloyd's Underwriters* [1957] 1 Lloyd's Rep. 118; *Cathay Pacific Airways v. Nation Life and General Ins. Co.* [1966] 2 Lloyd's Rep. 179; *Pocock v. Century Insurance* [1960] 2 Lloyd's Rep. 150. A recent example is *Charter Re. v. Fagan* [1997] A.C. 313, in which "actually paid" was interpreted to mean "ultimately liable to pay", see Lord Mustill at p. 386, remarking at p. 384 that "paid" was "a slippery word" which could have more than one ordinary meaning depending on its context. *Cf. Equitable Fire & Accident Office Ltd v. The Ching Wo Hong* [1907] A.C. 96, in which a condition that an insurance was not to be in force until the premium was "actually paid" was held to refer to the act of payment.

[59] [1968] 2 Lloyd's Rep 240.

[60] [1919] 1 K.B. 425.

[61] *Sun Fire Office v. Hart* (1889) 14 App.Cas. 98, 103; *Mair v. Railway Passengers Assurance Co.* (1877) 37 L.T. 356; *Palmer v. Naylor* (1854) 10 Ex. 382; *King v. Traveller's Ins. Ass.* (1931) 48 T.L.R. 53; *Knutsford S.S. Ltd v. Tillmanns & Co.* [1908] A.C. 406; *Thames and Mersey Ins. Co. v. Hamilton* (1887) 12 App.Cas. 484; *Lee v. Alexander* (1883) 8 App.Cas. 853; *Thorman v. Dowgate S.S. Co.* [1910] 1 K.B. 410; *Lambourn v. McLlellan* [1903] 2 Ch. 268; *Herman v. Morris* (1919) 35 T.L.R. 574; *The Lapwing* [1940] P. 112.

genus has been specifically enumerated, the *ejusdem generis* rule is inapplicable.[62] No doubt these are factors which may indicate that the parties did not intend to restrict the literal meaning of the general words, but it cannot be taken as universally true that in all other cases the general words must have been intended to have their literal meaning whatever other indications there may be to the contrary. There is no reason why, if it accords with the apparent intention of the parties, the general words should not be treated as inserted in order to prevent disputes founded on nice distinctions and to cover all such other things as may be within the spirit of the matters previously enumerated. Like any other rule of construction, it is no more than a guide to enable the court to arrive at the true meaning of the parties. It is not a rule of automatic application. The so-called rule is, in short, only a recognition of the fact that parties with their minds concerned with the particular objects about which they are contracting are apt to use words, phrases and clauses which taken literally are wider than they intend. Words, even though general, must be limited to circumstances within the contemplation of the parties unless they have used other words which clearly indicate an intention to exclude the *ejusdem generis* rule.[63] Thus, where a charterparty contained an exemption from liability arising from "frosts floods strikes ... and any other unavoidable accidents or hindrances of what kind soever beyond their control", it was held that the rule did not apply because the use of the words "of what kind soever" was intended to exclude the application of the rule.[64]

Similarly, where a list of specified causes was ended by the phrase "or from any other cause whatsoever" those words would not be governed by the rule.[65]

11–19 Noscitur a sociis. This maxim affords another illustration of the importance of context; in a list of words a word of uncertain scope may take its character from those surrounding it if they have a recognisable characteristic. Thus in *Watchorn v. Langford*[66] the assured, who was not a linen draper, insured his "stock in trade, household furniture, linen, wearing apparel and plate". He claimed the value of some linen-drapery goods destroyed in a fire. It was held by Lord Ellenborough that, having regard to the articles preceding and succeeding it in the list, the "linen" there mentioned must be "household linen or apparel", and there was no cover under the policy.

3. What Documents to be Considered

11–20 General context. The meaning of a word or phrase is not affected only by the immediate context in which it appears, but also by its general context in the sense of the policy as a whole and the circumstances prevailing

---

[62] *Sun Fire Office v. Hart* (1889) 14 App.Cas. 98, 104.

[63] *Thorman v. Dowgate S.S. Co.* [1910] 1 K.B. 410; *Herman v. Morris* (1919) 35 T.L.R. 574; *S. Magnhild v. McIntyre Bros & Co.* [1921] 2 K.B. 97; *Ambatielos v. Jurgens* [1923] A.C. 175.

[64] *Larsen v. Sylvester* [1908] A.C. 295.

[65] *Beaumont-Thomas v. Blue Star Line Ltd* (1939) 55 T.L.R. 852. All the important cases on this principle of construction are cited and commented upon by Devlin J. in *Chandris v. Isbrandtsen-Moller Co. Inc.* [1951] 1 K.B. 256.

[66] (1813) 3 Camp. 422; *Emanuel v. Hepburn* [1960] 1 Lloyd's Rep. 304, 308. *Diana Maritime Corp. v. Southern's Ltd* [1967] 1 Lloyd's Rep. 114 turned on a similar principle.

at the time that the policy was entered into. It is therefore necessary to inquire what other clauses, documents and extrinsic circumstances the court is permitted to consider in determining the meaning of the words in dispute.

11–21 The entire policy to be considered. Where there is doubt as to the meaning of a clause or phrase, the whole of the policy should be examined in order to see what intention the parties appear to have had concerning the matters governed by the words in question,[67] and in order to discover also whether the same phrase or words appear elsewhere in it.[68] Words should not be given an interpretation which nullifies other provisions in the contract of insurance,[69] or which involves different meanings being attributed to the same words in different parts of the policy, since the same words should prima facie receive the same meaning throughout.[70] The context may indicate, however, that the parties cannot have intended this to happen, especially where the word is one often having widely differing legal significance such as "property".[71] The recital is to be considered as a part of the policy to assist in the interpretation of ambiguous words in the body of the policy.[72]

11–22 Other documents incorporated into policy. Other documents may be incorporated into, and considered as part of, the policy if they are physically stuck on to it,[73] like a slip, or incorporated therein by words of reference, usually contained in the policy itself.[74] The mere delivery of a document with the policy does not without more make it a part of the contract of insurance.[75]

11–23 Incorporation of proposal. The proposal and the statements and declarations therein contained may be and usually are incorporated into the contract by reference, and being so incorporated must be read with the policy as part of the written contract so that every part of the contract may receive effect. Even where the policy is under seal, it may by reference incorporate as part of the deed a proposal under hand only.[76] A mere reference to the proposal as having been made is not an incorporation of it into the contract, because there must be something to show that it is referred to not by way of recital but as part of the contract.[77] It is sufficient to say that

[67] *Cornish v. Accident Ins. Co.* (1889) 23 Q.B.D. 453, 456; *Re George and Goldsmiths' and General Burglary Ins. Ass. Ltd* [1899] 1 Q.B. 595, 605; *Hamlyn v. Crown Accidental Ins. Co.* [1893] 1 Q.B. 750, 754; *City Tailors v. Evans* (1921) 126 L.T. 439, 444; *J. Martin v. Russell* [1960] 1 Lloyd's Rep. 554, 560.

[68] *South Staffordshire Tramways Co. v. Sickness and Accident Assurance* [1891] 1 Q.B. 402.

[69] *Gale v. Motor Union Ins. Co.* [1928] 1 K.B. 359; *Cornish v. Accident Ins. Co.* (1889) 23 Q.B.D. 453.

[70] *South Staffordshire Tramways Co. v. Sickness and Accident Assurance* [1891] 1 Q.B. 402; *Lake v. Simmons* [1927] A.C. 487, 507.

[71] *Andrews v. Patriotic Assurance Co. (No. 2)* (1886) 18 L.R.Ir. 355, 362; *Shera v. Ocean Accident and Guarantee Corp.* (1900) 32 O.R. 411.

[72] *Notman v. Anchor Life Assurance Co.* (1858) 4 C.B.(N.S.) 476, 480; *Blascheck v. Bussell* (1916) 33 T.L.R. 74.

[73] *Heath v. Durant* (1844) 12 M. & W. 438; *Cheshire v. Vaughan* [1920] 3 K.B. 240.

[74] *Worsley v. Wood* (1796) 6 T.R. 710; *Newcastle Fire v. Macmorran* (1815) 3 Dow 255; *Re George and Goldsmiths' and General Burglary Insurance Assoc.* [1899] 1 Q.B. 595, 601.

[75] *Pawson v. Barnevelt* (1779) 1 Doug. K.B. 12n.; *Bize v. Fletcher* (1779) 1 Doug. K.B. 12n.

[76] *Routledge v. Burrell* (1789) 1 H.Bl. 254.

[77] *Wheelton v. Hardisty* (1857) 8 E. & B. 232.

the proposal or the declaration therein is the basis of the contract of insurance,[78] and it has been held that the proposal can become part of the contract of insurance by force of express words of incorporation in the proposal form itself and not in the policy at all.[79]

11–24 Articles or byelaws. It is quite usual to import into a policy by reference the company's articles of association, deed of settlement or byelaws. Inasmuch as a company may during the currency of its policy alter its articles or byelaws, the question arises whether the contract is one made on the basis that any alteration will not affect the contractual rights of the assured, or whether it is one made subject to the right of the company to affect the contractual rights of the assured by such alteration. The answer depends on the intention of the parties as expressed in the policy, but prima facie the assured must be taken as contracting subject to the power of the company to alter its rules.[80]

11–25 In one case the question was whether a company could so alter its byelaws as to the division of profits and maintenance of a reserve fund as to diminish the share of profits of a participating policy-holder who had effected his insurance at a time when the byelaws provided that all profits should be divided without any deduction for a reserve fund. The company's deed of settlement provided that any byelaw of the company might be altered, repealed or suspended by a byelaw or byelaws. It was held that although the company advertised the provision of the byelaws with regard to the distribution of profits as an inducement to the public to insure with the company, it did not thereby bind itself to perpetuate the system, and policy-holders must be deemed to have contracted on the basis that the byelaws could be altered.[81] But where a friendly society had taken over and agreed to fulfil the obligations under the policies of another society it was held that although it had power by its rules to vary the benefits payable to its own members it could not by any alteration of its rules or otherwise vary the contracts under the policies which it had taken over unless it obtained the consent of the policy-holders.[82]

Where a policy provided that "the provisions contained in the articles of association shall be deemed and considered part of this policy", and the company had five years previously resolved to alter the articles and had registered a copy of the altered articles, and the altered articles were printed on the policy, the court held that the assured was bound by the articles as altered, notwithstanding that the alteration was invalid under the Companies Act by reason of the fact that it had not been confirmed by a resolution.[83]

Even when the company's articles are not expressly incorporated into its policy, they can nonetheless affect the rights of an assured. Where a retirement annuity policy entitled the policyholder to an annuity increased by such bonuses as might be declared by the directors in the exercise of the

[78] *Thomson v. Weems* (1884) 9 App.Cas. 671; *Provincial Insurance v. Morgan* [1933] A.C. 240.
[79] *Rozanes v. Bowen* (1928) 32 Ll.L.R. 98.
[80] *Yelland v. Yelland* (1898) 25 Ont.A.R. 91; *Knights Templars v. Jarman.* 104 Fed.Rep. 638 (1900); *Lloyd v. Supreme Lodge*, 98 Fed.Rep. 66 (1899); *Sieverts v. National Benevolent*, 95 Iowa 710 (1895).
[81] *British Equitable v. Baily* [1906] A.C. 35; *Johnstone v. British Empire Collecting Soc.* [1925] I.A.C.Rep. 9.
[82] *Adamsbaum v. Bristol West of England Ins. F.S.* [1926] I.A.C.Rep. 73.
[83] *Muirhead v. Forth, etc., Ins.* [1894] A.C. 72.

discretionary powers conferred on them by its articles of association, the rights of the policyholder to receipt of bonus had to be read subject to the discretion granted by the articles, but it was held that the discretion itself was not unrestricted, and could not be exercised in such a way as to defeat the expectation of the policyholder based upon a reasonable interpretation of his policy.[84]

11–26 Statements in company's prospectus. Statements made by a company in its prospectus or other advertisement are frequently urged by the assured as matter which should be taken into consideration as part of the contract between the parties. It will seldom happen that any such advertisement is referred to in a policy in such a way as to be imported into it as part of the written contract. It must therefore, if at all, be given effect to in some other way. If the statements are to be regarded only as representations inducing the contract they may afford ground for rescission or return of premiums, but cannot be read as part of the bargain between the parties, unless a court exercises its discretion to award damages under section 2 of the Misrepresentation Act 1967. Statements made in an advertisement may, however, operate as terms of the contract in one or other of the following ways: (1) they may form part of the preliminary contract, and, if the policy does not correspond with the advertisement, it may be rectified in order to represent the true contract between the parties[85]; (2) they may constitute a collateral agreement not varying the terms of the policy, but representing a supplementary part of the bargain.[86] In *Sun Life Assurance Co. of Canada v. Jervis*[87] it was held that the terms of an "Illustration" or prospectus sent to the assured with an application form for life assurance were intended on their true construction to become part of the contract of insurance together with the policy, and that in so far as the "Illustration" was made the basis of the contract, the policy would have to be rectified to avoid inconsistency with it.

Even where a document other than the policy cannot be said to be incorporated therein, it may sometimes be resorted to as a guide in case of ambiguity in the policy—a question referred to later in this chapter.[88]

11–27 Evidence of extrinsic facts. In gathering the intention of the parties from the words in the policy and incorporated documents, the wording is not to be construed in isolation. Evidence may be adduced of the background to the contract, so that the court can appreciate its genesis and purpose, and the facts of which the parties were both aware when making it.[89] There are limits

---

[84] *Equitable Life Assurance Society v. Hyman* [2000] 3 W.L.R. 529.
[85] *Anstey v. British Natural Premium Life* (1908) 24 T.L.R. 871.
[86] *Bowtle v. Salvation Army Ass. Soc.* [1927] I.A.C.Rep. 47.
[87] [1943] 2 All E.R. 425. Rectification is considered in Chap. 12, *post.* Reference should be made also to the incorporation of another company's policy provisions: *Walker & Sons v. Uzielli* (1896) 1 Com.Cas. 452, 455.
[88] See paras 11–33 to 11–35, *infra.*
[89] *Youell v. Bland Welch & Co.* [1992] 2 Lloyd's Rep. 127, 133; *Toomey v. Eagle Star Ins. Co.* [1994] 1 Lloyd's Rep. 516, 519–520; *Arbuthnot v. Fagan* [1996] L.R.L.R. 135, 139, 140; *NLA Group Ltd v. Bowers'* [1999] 1 Lloyd's Rep. 109, applying *Prenn v. Simmonds* [1971] 1 W.L.R. 1381, 1385; *Reardon-Smith Line v. Hansen-Tangen* [1976] 1 W.L.R. 989, 995–997. The modern approach was anticipated in such cases as *Birrell v. Dryer* (1884) 9 App.Cas. 345, 353; *Union Ins. Soc. of Canton v. Wills* [1916] 1 A.C. 281, 288; *Yorkshire Ins. Co. v. Campbell* [1917] A.C. 218,

to the admissibility of such evidence. Evidence of negotiations is inadmissible as an aid to interpretation unless they are alleged to demonstrate an agreed meaning for the language used, and the slip is likewise inadmissible as an aid to construction of the policy where it was intended to be superseded by a complete policy recording the parties' entire agreement.[90] The admissibility of extrinsic evidence is a technical and complicated subject and is further considered in the last section of this chapter.

4. INCONSISTENCY AND AMBIGUITY

11–28 Inconsistencies. Where different words or provisions in the contract of insurance appear to bear conflicting meanings, the court will try wherever possible to reconcile the inconsistencies in order to be able to give effect to the whole contract.[91] Where this is impossible, certain principles have been established to settle the problem of contradiction. The problem can, of course, arise only with reference to express terms, as it is well established that no term may be implied in a policy which is inconsistent with an express term therein.[92]

11–29 Earlier and later provisions. Where two clauses in one deed or instrument are repugnant, the general rule is that the first shall stand and the later be rejected.[93] This rule has to be applied with caution in the sphere of insurance policies, however, since many policies are drafted according to a scheme by which clauses appearing early on in the policy are drastically qualified by later clauses apparently in conflict with them, and the true sense is apparent only when words such as "provided always that" are imagined to precede the later clauses. Clauses of specific application may contradict clauses of general application which, if they stood alone, would control the specific subject-matter, and the clause of specific application then controls.[94]

Where terms in the proposal form conflict with provisions in the policy, the usual rule is that the policy, being the later document and representing the formal reduction of the contract into writing should prevail.[95] It is, however, open to either of the parties to demonstrate through extrinsic

---

225 and *Simon Brooks Ltd v. Hepburn* [1961] 2 Lloyd's Rep. 43. The relevant background may include the history and commercial development of a standard market working, such as the "ultimate net loss" clause—*Charter Re. v. Fagan* [1997] A.C. 313, 392–394, and the comments of Staughton L.J. at p. 340.

[90] *Prenn v. Simmonds* [1971] 1 W.L.R. 1381, 1383–1384; *HIH Casualty & General Ins. Ltd v. New Hampshire Ins. Co.* [2001] 2 All E.R. (Comm.) 39, 59–66.

[91] *Crane v. City Ins. Co*, 3 Fed.Rep. 558 (S.D. Ohio, 1880) is an excellent example of adroit interpretation.

[92] *Anglo-Californian Bank v. London and Provincial Marine, etc., Ins. Co.* (1904) 10 Com.Cas. 1, 12; *Sterling Engineering v. Patchett* [1955] A.C. 534, 547.

[93] *Forbes v. Git* [1922] A.C. 256, 259.

[94] *Williamson v. Commercial Union* (1876) 26 U.C.C.P. 591, 595. In marine policies it is common to find cover granted by a clause which is by nature an exception upon an exception: *Izzard v. Universal Ins. Co.* [1937] A.C. 773, 779; *Panamanian Oriental S.S. Co. v. Wright* [1970] 2 Lloyd's Rep. 365, 372; [1971] 1 W.L.R. 882, 886 (C.A.). Lord Atkin himself was once moved to say that the traditional form of marine policy was "past praying for": *Trade Indemnity Co. v. Workington Harbour and Dock Board* [1937] A.C. 1, 17; and for a recent criticism of obscure wording in an aviation policy, see *American Airline Inc. v. Hope* [1972] 1 Lloyd's Rep. 253, 256.

[95] *Kaufmann v. British Surety Ins. Co.* (1929) 33 Ll.L.R. 315, 318; *Izzard v. Universal Ins. Co.* [1937] A.C. 773, 780.

evidence that the proposal form represented the real intention of the parties and that the policy is incorrect in some material particular giving grounds for a claim for rectification.[96]

11–30 Written and printed clauses. Where a policy contains clauses in print and type the court will endeavour to give effect to both equally,[97] but, if it is plain that a written clause manifestly cannot be reconciled with one or more printed conditions, the former overrides the latter, inasmuch as the written words are the immediate language and terms selected by the parties themselves for the expression of their meaning with relation to the particular risk and the printed words are a general formula applied equally to all insurances in the same class of risk.[98]

11–31 Printed clauses inapplicable. It sometimes happens that certain of the standard printed clauses contained in the contract cannot be reconciled with the expressed objects and subject-matter of the insurance. It is frequently the case with commercial contracts such as contracts of insurance and charterparties that there are to be found in them all sorts of provisions and clauses which may or may not be applicable to the particular contract,[99] so that a court will not be afraid to ignore them in so far as they are inapplicable.[1] The printed form of policy used, moreover, may be inapplicable to the particular risk, as where a policy adapted for marine risk is used to cover risks on land[2] or vice versa,[3] or where a policy adapted for original insurance is used to express a contract of reinsurance,[4] or where the conditions in some other company's policy are incorporated by reference.[5] In such cases the conditions will be enforced in so far as they are not inconsistent with the contract to which they are applied.[6] A condition not in terms applicable to the risk may be applied *mutatis mutandis*.[7] Thus, where a

---

[96] See Ch. 12, *post*.
[97] *Foster v. Mentor Life Assurance Co.* (1854) 3 E. & B. 48, 82; *Yorkshire Ins. Co. v. Campbell* [1917] A.C. 218, 224; *Farmers' Co-operative Ltd v. National Benefit Assurance Co.* (1922) 13 Ll.L.R. 417, 530, 533.
[98] *Robertson v. French* (1830) 4 East 130, 136; *Joyce v. Realm Marine Ins. Co.* (1872) L.R. 7 Q.B. 580, 583; *St Paul Fire and Marine v. Morice* (1906) 22 T.L.R. 449; *Farmers Co-operative Ltd v. National Benefit Ass. Co.* (1922) 13 Ll.L.R. 417, 530, 533; *Glynn v. Margetson* [1893] A.C. 351; *Kaufmann v. British Surety Ins. Co.* (1929) 33 Ll.L.R. 315, 318.
[99] *South British Fire and Marine Ins. Co. of New Zealand v. Da Costa* [1906] 1 K.B. 456, 460; *Dudgeon v. Pembroke* (1877) 2 App.Cas. 284, 293; *Western Assurance Co. v. Poole* [1903] 1 K.B. 376, 389; *Compagnie Tunisienne de Navigation SA v. Compagnie d'Armement Maritime SA* [1971] A.C. 572, 585, 591.
[1] *Hydarnes S.S. Co. v. Indemnity Mutual Marine Ass. Co.* [1895] 1 Q.B. 500. The small size of the print is no ground for ignoring it unless it is positively illegible; *Koskas v. Standard Marine Ins. Co.* (1927) 17 Ll.L.R. 59; neither may one discriminate against particular founts of type; *Yorkshire Ins. Co. v. Campbell* [1918] A.C. 218, 222.
[2] *Baring Bros. v. Marine Ins. Co.* (1894) 10 T.L.R. 276; *Robinson Gold Mining Co. v. Alliance Ins. Co.* [1902] 2 K.B. 489, 500; *Hoff Trading Co. v. Union Ins. Soc. of Canton* (1929) 34 Ll.L.R. 81.
[3] *Beacon Life and Fire v. Gibb* (1862) 1 Moo.P.C.(N.S.) 73.
[4] *Foster v. Mentor Life Assurance Co.* (1854) 3 E. & B. 48; *South British, etc., Ins. of New Zealand v. Da Costa* [1906] 1 K.B. 456.
[5] *ibid.*
[6] *Sulphite Pulp Co. v. Faber* (1895) 11 T.L.R. 547; *New India Ass. Co. v. Yeo Beng Chow* [1972] 1 W.L.R. 786; [1972] 3 All E.R. 293; *Armadora Occidental SA v. Horace Mann Insurance* [1977] 1 W.L.R. 1098.
[7] *Robinson Gold Mining Co. v. Alliance Ins. Co.* [1902] 2 K.B. 489, 500.

vessel was insured against fire and the contract of insurance was embodied in a policy ordinarily used for insuring buildings, it was held that the clause which prohibited the storing of gunpowder "on the premises" was applicable, and that for "premises" must be read "ship".[8] On the other hand, the conditions or some of them may be totally inapplicable and may be disregarded.[9] In one case of a reinsurance contract, expressed in the form of a printed slip pasted on to the form of a policy applicable to an original insurance, the whole of the conditions were totally inapplicable to a reinsurance contract except the condition providing that the right to bring an action on the policy should be limited to 12 months after the date of the loss. That condition, apart from its context, would have been applicable, but on the other hand it was an unreasonable condition inasmuch as the ceding insurer could not sue until the original loss was settled, and the settlement of that loss might be delayed without any fault on his part. The court, therefore, declined to read the condition into the contract and held that the conditions as a whole were inapplicable.[10] In a Canadian case, a rider to a bank's policy provided cover against

"any loss sustained by the insured through having in good faith and the course of business ... purchased or otherwise acquired, accepted or received or sold or delivered, or guaranteed in writing or witnessed any signature upon, or given any value, extended any credit or assumed any liability on the faith of, or otherwise acted upon any securities, documents or other written instruments which prove to have been counterfeited or forged ... or raised or altered or lost or stolen".

It was held that, although not framed as a third party risk policy, the rider was apt to cover liability of the bank in conversion to the true owner of a stolen stock certificate, and consequently that a clause in the main body of the policy, limiting the value of securities to that on the day of the discovery of the loss, was inappropriate and could be disregarded.[11]

11–32 Printed clauses deleted by the parties. It is uncertain at present whether the court may look at printed words which the parties have deleted as being inapplicable to their transaction for the purpose of ascertaining the intention of the parties concerning other clauses left in the policy. The court's right to do this has been asserted firmly,[12] and equally categorically denied,[13] it has been exercised with trepidation[14] and also without concern.[15] It is submitted that the parties' action in striking out particular provisions ought to be a factor in enabling a tribunal to determine what liabilities they intended to create by their contract.[16] It has been said that a court may draw

---

[8] *Beacon Life and Fire v. Gibb* (1862) 1 Moo.P.C.(N.S.) 73.

[9] *Australian Widows' Fund Life Assurance Society v. National Mutual Life Association of Australasia* [1914] A.C. 615, 630; *Hydarnes S.S. Co. v. Indemnity Mutual Marine Ass. Co.* [1895] 1 Q.B. 500; *City Tailors Ltd v. Evans* (1921) 126 L.T. 439.

[10] *Home Ins. Co. of New York v. Victoria Montreal Fire Ins. Co.* [1907] A.C. 59.

[11] *Aitken v. Gardiner* (1956) 4 D.L.R. (2d) 119.

[12] *Baumwoll v. Gilchrist & Co.* [1892] 1 Q.B. 253, 256.

[13] *Sassoon v. International Banking Corporation* [1927] A.C. 711, 721.

[14] *Wyllie v. Povah* (1907) 12 Com.Cas. 317, 323.

[15] *Thomasson Shipping Co. v. Henry Peabody & Co.* [1959] 2 Lloyd's Rep. 296, 304; *London Transport Co. v. Trechmann Bros* [1904] 1 K.B. 635, 645; *Louis Dreyfus v. Parnaso Cia Naviera SA* [1959] 1 Q.B. 498, 515.

[16] *Punjab National Bank v. de Boinville* [1992] 1 W.L.R. 1138, 1148, *per* Staughton L.J. citing earlier appellate authority.

conclusions from spaces left blank.[17] There seems little difference in principle between the two cases.

11–33 Ambiguity and the contract proferentem rule. The established common law rule applying to all contracts of insurance must be distinguished from the rule of interpretation of terms in favour of consumers introduced by The Unfair Terms in Consumer Contracts Regulations 1999.[18] The common law rule of construction, that *verba chartarum fortius accipiuntur contra proferentem*, means that ambiguity in the wording in a policy, or slip, is to be resolved against the party who prepared it.[19] In the majority of cases this means the insurer. It has been said that a party who proffers an instrument cannot be permitted to use ambiguous words in the hope that the other party will understand them in a particular sense and that the court which has to construe them will give them a different meaning,[20] but the ambiguity usually arises inadvertently from including conflicting standard printed clauses in the same policy.

11–34 The language used in a policy, more particularly in the written part of it, may be the language of the assured, as, for instance, where the description of the property or limits of the risk are taken verbatim from the proposal. Sometimes clauses may be drafted by a broker to express the particular needs of the assured. In such cases the rule that the instrument is to be construed against the party who prepared it is likely to operate in favour of the insurer.[21]

11–35 Ambiguity must be real. The *contra proferentem* rule of construction arises only where there is a wording employed by those drafting the clause which leaves the court unable to decide by ordinary principles of

---

[17] *Compagnie Tunisienne de Navigation SA v. Compagnie d'Armement Maritime* [1971] A.C. 572, 592, 595. There is a list of authorities bearing on the issue in Scrutton on *Charterparties* (20th ed.) p. 22.

[18] S.I. 1999 No 2083, reg. 6.

[19] *Tarleton v. Staniforth* (1794) 5 T.R. 695, 699; *Anderson v. Fitzgerald* (1853) 4 H.L.Cas. 484, 507; *Braunstein v. Accidental Death Ins. Co.* (1861) 1 B. & S. 782, 799; *Notman v. Anchor Ass. Co.* (1858) 4 C.B.(N.S.) 476, 481; *Smith v. Accident Ins. Co.* (1870) L.R. 5 Ex. 302, 309; *Cornish v. Accident Ins. Co.* (1889) 23 Q.B.D. 453, 456; *Re Etherington and Lancashire and Yorkshire Accident Insurance Co.* [1909] 1 K.B. 591, 596; *Simmonds v. Cockell* [1920] 1 K.B. 843, 845; *Lake v. Simmons* [1927] A.C. 487, 508; *Kaufmann v. British Surety Ins. Co. Ltd* (1929) 33 Ll.L.R. 315, 318; *Provincial Ins. Co. v. Morgan* [1933] A.C. 240, 255; *English v. Western* [1940] 2 K.B. 156, 165; *Metal Scrap and By-products Ltd v. Federated Conveyors Ltd* [1953] 1 Lloyd's Rep. 221, 227; *Re Sweeney and Kennedy's Arbitration* [1950] Ir.R. 85, 99; *McLean Enterprises v. Ecclesiastical Ins. Office PLC* [1986] 2 Lloyd's Rep. 416, 426; *Youell v. Bland Welch* [1992] 2 Lloyd's Rep. 127, 134; *Hitchens v. Prudential Ass. Co.* [1991] 2 Lloyd's Rep. 580, 586; *London Tobacco Co. v. DFDS Transport* [1993] 2 Lloyd's Rep. 306; *De Maurier v. Bastion Ins. Co.* [1967] 2 Lloyd's Rep. 550, 559 (slip); *Zeus Tradition Marine Ltd v. Bell* [2000] 2 Lloyd's Rep. 587, 597.

[20] *Fowkes v. Manchester and London Life Assurance* (1863) 3 B. & S. 917, 929; *Wawanesa Mutual v. Bell* (1957) 8 D.L.R. 577, where the Supreme Court of Canada approved the text in the corresponding paragraph of an earlier edition of this work.

[21] *Birrell v. Dryer* (1884) 9 App.Cas. 345, 352; *Bartlett & Partners v. Meller* [1961] 1 Lloyd's Rep. 487; *A/S Ocean v. Black Sea and Baltic General Ins. Co.* (1935) 51 Ll.L.R. 305, 307; *Balfour v. Beaumont* [1982] 2 Lloyd's Rep. 493, 503. For the situation where the insurer prepares an exemption relied on by the reinsurer, see *Youell v. Bland Welch* [1992] 2 Lloyd's Rep. 127, 134.

interpretation which of two meanings is the right one.[22] "One must not use the rule to create the ambiguity—one must find the ambiguity first."[23] The words should receive their ordinary and natural meaning unless that is displaced by a real ambiguity either appearing on the face of the policy[24] or, possibly, by extrinsic evidence of surrounding circumstances.[25] If the meaning of the words used is reasonably clear it should be followed even if it is unreasonable or operates harshly against the assured,[26] although the more unreasonable the result the clearer the words must be in order to lead to it.[27] The courts may be less ready to reach an interpretation of the terms of a consumer insurance contract[28] which is unfavourable to the assured.

11–36 Terms in consumer insurance contracts. Special rules govern terms to which the Unfair Terms in Consumer Contracts Regulations 1999[29] apply, being any term in a contract of insurance concluded with an assured who is a natural person and who has not obtained the insurance for purposes of his business, so long as that term has not been individually negotiated with him.[30] The insurer will not be able to establish individual negotiation when the term is drafted in advance and the assured is not able to influence its substance.[31] All written terms to which the Regulations apply must be expressed in plain intelligible language.[32] If there is doubt about the meaning of a written term the interpretation most favourable to the assured will prevail, regardless of its provenance.[33] Failure to word a core term of the insurance clearly will result in it losing its exemption from assessment for fairness.[34] Core terms in insurance contracts will include terms which stipulate premium, describe the perils insured against, and specify the measure of indemnity afforded by the cover.

5. ADMISSIBILITY OF EXTRINSIC EVIDENCE

11–37 Two separate rules of law restrict the admissibility of extrinsic evidence to affect or explain the contents of a contract of insurance. First, once the terms of the insurance have been recorded in a policy there is a presumption that the policy contains all the terms of the cover, with the

---

[22] *London & Lancs. Fire Ins. Co. v. Bolands* [1924] A.C. 836, 848, and see to the same effect *Cornish v. Accident Ins. Co.* (1889) 23 Q.B.D. 453, 456 and *M. W. Wilson (Lace) Ltd v. Eagle Star Ins. Co.* 1993 S.L.T. 938.

[23] *Cole v. Accident Ins. Co.* (1889) 5 T.L.R. 736, 737.

[24] *Birrell v. Dryer* (1884) 9 App.Cas. 345, 350; *Thomson v. Weems* (1884) 9 App.Cas. 671; *Yorke v. Yorkshire Ins. Co.* [1918] 1 K.B. 662, 668; *Condogianis v. Guardian Ass. Co.* [1912] 2 A.C. 125, 130–131; *Fitton v. Accidental Death Ins. Co.* (1864) 17 C.B.(N.S.) 122, 135; *Passmore v. Vulcan Boiler & General Ins. Co.* (1936) 54 Ll.L.Rep. 92, 94.

[25] *Hordern v. Commercial Union Ins. Co.* (1887) 56 L.J.P.C. 78.

[26] *Smith v. Accident Ins. Co.* (1870) L.R. 5 Ex. 302, 307; *Sulphite Pulp v. Faber* (1895) 11 T.L.R. 547; *Jason v. British Traders Ins. Co.* [1969] 1 Lloyd's Rep. 281, 290.

[27] *Charter Re. v. Fagan* [1997] A.C. 313, 355, *per* Staughton L.J., 388, *per* Lord Mustill.

[28] See para. 11–36, *post.*

[29] S.I. 1999 No. 2083.

[30] Regs 2(1), 3(1).

[31] Reg. 3(3).

[32] Reg. 6.

[33] *ibid.*

[34] Reg. 3(2). "Core term" is our shorthand for the class of term to which this Regulation applies—see para. 10–14, *ante.*

consequences that extrinsic evidence, whether oral or in writing, cannot be introduced to contradict, vary, add to or cut down the terms set out in the policy.[35] This is the "parol evidence" rule. Evidence is admissible in a variety of instances to rebut the presumption that the policy records the entire agreement of the parties, such as:

(1) to show that the policy does not express the true agreement of the parties, and to support a plea for rectification[36];

(2) to establish a collateral contract containing a separate undertaking which may vary the terms of the policy[37];

(3) to evidence the whole contract where it can be shown that the policy was not intended to be a memorandum of the complete agreement, and to complete blanks or other omissions[38];

(4) to prove and annex to the contract a custom or usage in a particular trade, business or market, in contemplation of which the parties must be deemed to have contracted,[39] so long as it is not inconsistent with express terms of the contract[40];

(5) to prove a subsequent agreement, written or oral, by which the parties have varied[41] or discharged[42] the original contract contained in the policy, or to prove an act of waiver on the part of one of them.[43]

11–38 There is a second rule, one of construction of contracts, to the effect that where the words of a policy or other document recording the terms of the insurance contract possess a clear meaning, extrinsic evidence is inadmissible to show that the parties intended them to bear a different

---

[35] *Gillespie Bros. v. Cheney, Eggar & Co.* [1896] 2 Q.B. 59, 62; *Davies v. National Fire & Marine Ins. Co.* [1891] A.C. 485, 496–497; *Burges v. Wickham* (1863) 3 B. & S. 669, 696; *Horncastle v. Equitable Life Ass. Soc.* (1906) 22 T.L.R. 735 (where the policy stated that it set forth all the terms of the parties' contract).

[36] *British Equitable Ass. v. Bailey* [1906] A.C. 35, 41; *Griffiths v. Fleming* [1909] 1 K.B. 805, 817; *American Airlines Inc. v. Hope* [1974] 2 Lloyd's Rep. 301, 307; *Investors Compensation Scheme v. West Bromwich Bldg. Soc.* [1998] 1 W.L.R. 869, 913.

[37] *De Lassalle v. Guildford* [1901] 2 K.B. 215; *City and Westminster Properties (1934) Ltd v. Mudd* [1959] Ch.129; *Hurst-Bannister v. New Cap Reinsurance Co.* [2000] Lloyd's Rep.I.R. 166, 172.

[38] *Mercantile Bank of Sydney v. Taylor* [1893] A.C. 317, 321; *Anglo-Californian Bank v. London Provincial Marine Ins. Co.* (1904) 10 Com.Cas. 1, 11–12. Extrinsic evidence of additional terms would most probably be inadmissible where the written contract was expressed to contain all the terms of the transaction—*Horncastle v. Equitable Life Ass. Soc.* (1906) 22 T.L.R. 735.

[39] *Syers v. Bridge* (1780) 2 Doug. K.B. 526, 530; *Blackett v. Royal Exchange Ass. Co.* (1832) 2 Cr. & J. 244, 250; *Gibson v. Small* (1853) 4 H.L. Cas. 353, 397; *Anglo-Californian Bank v. London & Provincial Ins. Co.* (1904) 10 Com.Cas. 1.

[40] *Re L. Sutro and Heilbut Symons & Co.* [1917] 2 K.B. 348; *Les Affréteurs Réunis v. Walford* [1919] A.C. 801, 809, 813; *Palgrave Brown & Son v. S.S. Turid* [1922] 1 A.C. 397. The custom or usage must be notorious, uniform, certain and reasonable. Evidence of a voluntary practice, even if frequent, will not suffice—*Anderson v. Commercial Union Ass. Plc.* 1998 S.L.T. 826; *NLA Group Ltd v. Bower's* [1999] 1 Lloyd's Rep. 109; *Roar Marine v. Bimeh Iran Ins. Co.* [1998] 1 Lloyd's Rep. 423.

[41] *Stuart v. Freeman* [1903] 1 K.B. 47.

[42] *Morris v. Baron* [1918] A.C. 1.

[43] *Davies v. National Fire and Marine Ins. Co. of New Zealand* [1891] A.C. 485, 497; *Brook v. Trafalgar Ins. Co.* (1947) 79 Ll.L.R. 365, 367.

meaning.[44] However, there are several instances in which extrinsic evidence is admissible, consistent with the above rule, to explain and interpret the wording of a written contract of insurance, such as:

(1) to explain words which are susceptible of explanation such as words in a foreign language,[45] technical terms,[46] or market abbreviations and shorthand[47];

(2) to show the circumstances in which the insurance was concluded in order to appreciate its genesis and purpose[48];

(3) to identify references in the contract which are of themselves incomplete or uncertain[49];

(4) to show the intention of the parties where there is a patent ambiguity in the wording[50] or where there is a latent ambiguity,[51] that is to say, one which does not appear on the face of the document but which is disclosed only by evidence of the circumstances prevailing when the contract was made;

(5) to prove conduct which estops a party from asserting a particular meaning of the words used,[52] or which establishes an agreement between the parties to attach a given meaning to words in the contract[53];

(6) to prove that certain words or phrases have a technical trade or market meaning which is different from their meaning in ordinary speech,[54] but such interpretation will not prevail over other plainly worded terms with a contrary meaning.[55]

(7) to establish the background facts to the contract of insurance in order to show that the parties have mistakenly used the wrong words or syntax to carry out their intention,[56] since "if detailed semantic and

[44] *Shore v. Wilson* (1842) 9 Cl. & F. 355; *Bank of New Zealand v. Simpson* [1900] A.C. 182, 189; *Inglis v. Buttery* (1878) 3 App.Cas. 552, 577; *Reliance Marine Ins. Co. v. Duder* [1913] 1 K.B. 265, 273; *Wickman Tools v. Schuler AG* [1974] A.C. 235, 261; *Marine Ins. Co. v. Grimmer* (1944) 77 Ll.L.R. 224, 234–235.

[45] *Shore v. Wilson* (1842) 9 Cl. & F. 355, 555–556, approved in *Wickman Tools v. Schuler AG* [1974] A.C. 235, 269.

[46] *Wickman Tools v. Schuler AG* [1974] A.C. 235, 269.

[47] *American Airlines Inc. v. Hope* [1973] 1 Lloyd's Rep. 233, 245–246; [1974] 2 Lloyd's Rep. 301, 305.

[48] *Youell v. Bland Welch* [1992] 2 Lloyd's Rep. 127, 133, *Charter Reinsurance Co. v. Fagan* [1997] A.C. 313, 395; *Touche Ross & Co. v. Baker* [1992] 2 Lloyd's Rep. 207, 208; *Arbuthnott v. Fagan* [1996] L.R.L.R. 135, 139, 140; *Kumar v. AGF Ins. Ltd* [1998] 4 All E.R. 788; *Arab Bank v. Zurich Ins. Ltd* [1999] 1 Lloyd's Rep. 262. See para. 11–27, *ante.*

[49] *Moss v. Norwich & London Accident Ins. Assoc.* (1922) 10 Ll.L.R. 395; *Burges v. Wickham* (1863) 3 B. & S. 669, 698.

[50] *Shore v. Wilson* (1842) 9 Cl. & F. 355, 565.

[51] *Wickman Tools v. Schuler AG* [1974] A.C. 235, 261; *Hordern v. Commercial Union Ins. Co.* (1887) 56 L.J.P.C. 78; *Simon Brooks v. Hepburn* [1961] 2 Lloyd's Rep. 43.

[52] *Salvin v. James* (1805) 6 East 571; *Smith & Son v. Eagle Star & British Dominions Ins. Co.* (1934) 50 T.L.R. 208.

[53] *Lamb v. Goring Brick Co.* [1932] 1 K.B. 710, 722; *Cie Tunisienne de Navigation SA v. Cie d'Armement Maritime SA* [1971] A.C. 572, 603; *M.S. Karen Oltmann v. Scarsdale Shipping Co.* [1976] 2 Lloyd's Rep. 708, 712.

[54] *Bowes v. Shand* (1877) 2 App.Cas. 455, 468; *Birrell v. Dryer* (1884) 9 App.Cas. 345, 353; *Crofts v. Marshall* (1836) 7 C & P. 597; *Scragg v. U.K. Temperance etc. Inst.* [1976] 2 Lloyd's Rep. 227 (motor sport technical term); *London & Lancs. Fire Ins. Co. v. Bolands* [1924] A.C. 836, 847 ("riot").

[55] *Mowbray, Robinson & Co. v. Rosser* (1922) 91 L.J.K.B. 524.

[56] *Investors Compensation Scheme v. West Bromwich Bldg. Soc.* [1998] 1 W.L.R. 896, 913; *Mannai Investment Co. v. Eagle Star Life Ass. Co.* [1997] A.C. 749, 779.

syntactical analysis of words in a commercial contract is going to lead to a conclusion that flouts business common sense, it must be made to yield to business common sense".[57] Unless, however, this use of extrinsic evidence is restricted to cases where there have been errors in drafting, there is a risk that time and costs will be wasted by parties trying to cast doubt on terms which are clearly expressed and which make sense in their commercial context.[58]

---

[57] *Antaios Cia. Naviera S.A. v. Salen Rederierna A.B.* [1985] A.C. 191, 201.

[58] *NLA Group Ltd v. Bowers* [1999] 1 Lloyd's Rep. 109, where the costs of the hearing were awarded on an indemnity basis against a party who had adduced evidence to such ends. See Clarke, "Interpreting Contracts—the price of perspective" [2000] Camb. L.J. 18 and Sir Christopher Staughton, "How do the Courts Interpret Commercial Contracts" [1999] Camb. L.J. 303.

CHAPTER 12

RECTIFICATION

12–1 Introductory. Where either party to a contract of insurance establishes that the policy formally embodying the terms of the parties' contract does not record the real agreement of the parties, he is entitled to have the policy rectified so that it properly expresses their true agreement[1]:

> "If there be an agreement for a policy in a particular form, and the policy be drawn up by the office in a different form, varying the right of the party assured, a Court of Equity will interfere and deal with the case upon the footing of the agreement, and not of the policy."[2]

If the clerical staff in the insurance office had made a mistake to the prejudice of the company and not the assured, the company would be entitled to rectification of the policy to conform to the real agreement reached by the parties before issue of the policy.[3]

12–2 There is a presumption that a policy which is issued by the insurer and accepted by the assured contains the complete and final contract between the parties.[4] Consequently, the courts' equitable jurisdiction to rectify insurance policies is exercised with restraint inside certain well established limitations, or else it would tend to destroy certainty in insurance business.[5] When a plaintiff seeks rectification, he must establish as a fact that the parties were agreed upon the point in question, and that the policy accidentally fails to record their agreement. The Court is not rectifying the

[1] *Motteux v. London Assurance Co.* (1739) 1 Atk. 545, 547; *Henkle v. Royal Exchange Assurance Co.* (1749) 1 Ves.Sen. 317; *Collett v. Morrison* (1851) 9 Hare 162; *Xenos v. Wickham* (1867) L.R. 2 H.L. 296, 324; *Mackenzie v. Coulson* (1869) L.R. 8 Eq. 368; *Letts v. Excess Ins. Co.* (1916) 32 T.L.R. 361; *Eagle Star and British Dominions Ins. Co. v. A. V. Reiner* (1927) 27 Ll.L.R. 173. Lord Hardwicke L.C. explained rectification as an illustration of the equity maxim that equity considered as done what ought to have been done; *Henkle's* case, *supra*, at 318.
[2] *Collett v. Morrison* (1851) 9 Hare 162, 173, *per* Turner V.-C., approved in *Griffiths v. Fleming* [1909] 1 K.B. 805, 817, *per* Kennedy and Farwell L.JJ.
[3] *Ball v. Storie* (1823) 1 Sim. & St. 210; *Alliance Aeroplane Co. v. Union Ins. Co. of Canton Ltd* (1920) 5 Ll.L.R. 341, 406.
[4] *Wheelton v. Hardisty* (1858) 8 E. & B. 232, 263, *per* Erle J.; reversed on other grounds (1858) 8 E. & B. 285; *Alliance Aeroplane Co. v. Union Ins. Co. of Canton* (1920) 5 Ll.L.R. 406; *Provident Savings Life Assurance Society v. Mowatt* (1902) 32 S.C.R. 147, 155, 165.
[5] *Pasquali v. Traders' and General Ins. Association* (1921) 9 Ll.L.R. 514, 515, *per* Rowlatt J. The Chancery courts always exercised the discretionary remedy of rectification with caution: see *Whiteside v. Whiteside* [1950] Ch. 65, 71.

contract, but rectifying the document purporting to contain its terms, so that the rectified document contains the terms of the original agreement.[6]

12–3 Requirements for rectification. The conditions to be satisfied to support rectification have been summarised as follows.[7]

1. There must be a common intention in regard to the particular provisions of the agreement in question, together with some outward expression of accord.
2. This common intention must continue up to the time of execution of the instrument.
3. There must be clear evidence that the instrument as executed does not accurately represent the true agreement of the parties at the time of its execution.
4. The instrument, if rectified as claimed, must then accurately record the true agreement of the parties at that time.

As to the third requirement, the onus of proof is dischargeable on a balance of probabilities, but clear and convincing evidence is required on the parties' true bargain.[8]

12–4 Prior agreement. It is not necessary for the party claiming rectification to prove that there was a legally binding agreement concluded prior to the issue of the policy,[9] although in many cases he might well be able to do so. He need only establish the fact of common intention manifested in some form or other as to the form and terms of the contract which would be set out in the policy when issued. In other words, he must prove that a bargain was struck, even if it was unenforceable at the outset. Thus when it is claimed that the true terms of an insurance are contained in a slip used by the brokers to submit to the insurers, it does not matter in principle whether the slip constituted a legally enforceable agreement, as in the case of a Lloyd's slip,[10] or was only a memorandum of the agreement to be concluded later.[11] It follows also that the slip, even if legally binding, can be called in question as being inaccurate.[12]

12–5 Evidence of common intention. A strong burden of proof lies upon the party seeking rectification. He must adduce convincing proof of the

[6] *Lovell & Christmas v. Wall* (1911) 104 L.T. 84, 93, *per* Buckley L.J.; *Youell v. Bland Welch & Co.* [1992] 2 Lloyd's Rep. 127, 140, *per* Beldam L.J.
[7] *AGIP SpA v. Navigazione Alta Italia SpA* [1984] 1 Lloyd's Rep. 353, 359, *per* Slade L.J., applied by Steyn J. in *Commercial Union Ass. Co. v. Sun Alliance Group PLC* [1992] 1 Lloyd's Rep. 475, 482.
[8] *ibid.* In *Crane v. Hegeman Harris Co.* [1939] 1 All E.R. 662, 664 Simonds J. had used the phrase "beyond reasonable doubt".
[9] *Earl v. Hector Whaling* [1961] 1 Lloyd's Rep. 459, 470, *per* Harman L.J.; *Joscelyne v. Nissen* [1970] 2 Q.B. 86, where the Court of Appeal disapproved of earlier authorities to the contrary. The heresy probably arose from the ambiguous nature of the word "agreement": see [1970] 2 Q.B. 86 at p. 97. The earliest cases of rectification of policies such as *Motteux* and *Henkle, supra,* do not appear to have required a prior legal agreement.
[10] *Thompson v. Adams* (1889) 23 Q.B.D. 361; *Jaglom v. Excess Ins. Co* [1972] 2 Q.B. 250.
[11] *Motteux v. London Assurance Co.* (1739) 1 Atk. 545, 547; *Alliance Aeroplane Co. v. Union Ins. Co. of Canton* (1920) 5 Ll.L.R. 341, 406.
[12] *Spalding v. Crocker* (1897) 2 Com.Cas. 189; *Eagle Star and British Dominions Ins. Co. v. Reiner* (1927) 27 Ll.L.R. 173, 175.

parties' outward expression of accord or common intention,[13] so that the court is in no doubt that his contention is to be preferred to that of the opposite party alleging that the policy contains their agreement.[14] Thus in *Parsons v. Bignold*,[15] A applied to an insurance office for a policy on the life of B, his son. The insurers' agent gave him a form to complete. It included a question as to his interest in the life assured. A did not complete the answer to the question in writing, but explained orally to the agent that he possessed an interest in certain lands, held of the Dean and Chapter of Wells, for so long as his son, B, lived. The agent then filled up the form incorrectly, including certain other lands in the declaration of interest. On B's death, the insurers declined to pay on the ground that the declaration of interest was untrue and avoided the policy, into which it had been incorporated as the basis of the contract. A claimed rectification of the policy to accord with his answer given to the agent, who, it was assumed for the sake of argument, had acted as the insurers' agent in writing down the answer. No adequate evidence of their conversation was, however, given by A and, although the agent had freely admitted in a letter that he might well have made a mistake, he did not give evidence to support that admission. Rectification was refused, the Lord Chancellor saying that "nothing short of the most clear and distinct evidence would be sufficient".[16]

12–6 The burden of discrediting a policy on oral evidence alone is an exceptionally difficult one to discharge, and rectification is achieved usually only in cases where there has been some written expression of the parties' intention, such as a slip,[17] or a proposal form accepted by the insurers,[18] or a printed table or schedule to be incorporated in the policy.[19] A policy cannot be rectified on the ground that a prior agreement would have been concluded differently in the light of events known to the parties subsequently to that agreement but prior to issue of the policy.[20]

12–7 "Mutual mistake." It is sometimes said that there must be a "mutual

---

[13] *Joscelyne v. Nissen* [1970] 2 Q.B. 86, 98. The phrase "irrefragable evidence" was used by Thurlow L.C. in the old case of *Shelburne v. Inchiquin* (1748) 1 Bro.C.C. 338, 341, not Lord Eldon as Simonds J. thought in *Crane v. Hegeman-Harris & Co.* [1939] 1 All E.R. 662, 664.

[14] *Gagnière & Co. Ltd v. Eastern Co. of Warehouses Insurance & Transport of Goods with Advances* (1921) 8 Ll.L.R. 365, 366–367, *per* Bankes L.J. Cases where rectification was refused because the burden of proof was not discharged by the party seeking rectification include *Maignen & Co. v. National Benefit Assurance Co. Ltd* (1922) 38 T.L.R. 257; *Pasquali v. Traders' and General Ins. Association* (1921) 9 Ll.L.R. 514; *Rogers v. Whitaker* [1917] 1 K.B. 942; *American Airlines v. Hope* [1974] 2 Lloyd's Rep. 301; see at p. 307, *per* Lord Diplock; *Mint Security Ltd v. Blair* [1982] 1 Lloyd's Rep. 188.

[15] (1846) 15 L.J.Ch.379.

[16] Lord Lyndhurst, at p. 382.

[17] *Wilson, Holgate & Co. Ltd v. The Lancashire and Cheshire Ins. Corp. Ltd* (1922) 13 Ll.L.R. 486; *Eagle Star and British Dominions Ins. Co. v. Reiner* (1927) 27 Ll.L.R. 173; *Alliance Aeroplane Co. v. Union Ins. Co. of Canton* (1920) 5 Ll.L.R. 341, 406; *Letts v. Excess Ins. Co.* (1916) 32 T.L.R. 361; *Collett v. Morrison* (1851) 9 Hare 162; *Commercial Union Ass. Co. v. Sun Alliance Group PLC* [1992] 1 Lloyd's Rep. 475, 483.

[18] *Griffiths v. Fleming* [1909] 1 K.B. 805, 817; *Re Bradley and Essex and Suffolk Accident Indemnity Society* [1912] 1 K.B. 415, 430; *Solvency Mutual Guarantee Co. v. Freeman* (1861) 7 H. & N. 17; *Braund v. Mutual Life and Citizens Assurance Co.* [1926] N.Z.L.R. 529 (Sup.Ct.N.Z.); *Brodigan v. Imperial Livestock and General Ins. Co.* [1928] W.C. & Ins.Rep. 160.

[19] *Watson v. Abundance and Northern F.S.* [1930] I.A.C.Rep. 44.

[20] *Pasquali v. Traders' and General Ins. Co.* (1921) 9 Ll.L.R. 514, 515; *Townshend v. Stangroom* (1801) 6 Ves. 328, 332.

mistake" in order to ground a claim for rectification.[21] This expression is inapt and, in so far as it suggests that the parties must mutually make the mistake in drawing up the policy, it is also inaccurate.[22] The importance of mutuality is in the context of the prior agreement or outward expression of intention upon which the claimant relies, because he must establish the assent of the other party to that which he intended should be recorded in the policy. If the other party never assented to the claimant's terms, the unilateral error of the claimant in not presenting the right terms to the other party affords no ground for rectification.[23]

12–8 Thus in *Fowler v. Scottish Equitable Life Insurance Society*,[24] the assured negotiated with Captain Cook, the agent of the Society in London, for a life policy on the life of H. They told Cook that H must have leave to travel to ports outside Europe. Cook, however, left it to them to draft a suitable condition for insertion in the policy, which they did. Cook sent it off to the Society with a covering letter saying that cover was requested incorporating the draft condition, and giving a muddled interpretation of its purpose.[25] As drafted by the assured, the condition did not fulfil their intention, because it did not permit H to travel outside the Mediterranean, which was what they had wished to achieve by it. H travelled to the Atlantic coast of Morocco and died there. The insurance society refused to pay on the policy, which contained the draft condition restricting travel to the Mediterranean ports of Africa. The assured claimed rectification of the policy to make it conform to the intention of themselves and Cook as regards travel by the life assured. Stuart V.-C. refused it because Cook had no power to bind the Society to agree to any condition, and the Society had never intended to license travel beyond the Mediterranean since the draft clause sent to them did not convey to them that this was the wish of the assured. No doubt if Cook had possessed authority to contract on behalf of the company, it would have been possible to point to an agreement between him and the assured, with which the policy could have been made to conform.

12–9 Difficulties arise where an agent with power to contract manifests a different intention from that of his principal. In *Stanton & Stanton v. Starr*,[26] the assured employed a broker called Lee to effect a comprehensive insurance policy at Lloyd's which would cover, *inter alia*, the risk of theft of furs and skins from their premises. Lee went to Lloyd's brokers, who told him it would be difficult to get cover on goods on the assured's premises. Lee

---

[21] *Slack v. Hancock* (1912) 107 L.T. 14, 17; *Shipley U.D.C. v. Bradford Corporation* [1936] Ch. 375, 395; *Stanton & Stanton Ltd v. Starr* (1920) 3 Ll.L.R. 259; *Eagle Star, etc. v. Reiner* (1927) 27 Ll.L.R. 173, 175.

[22] *Gagnière & Co. v. Eastern Co. of Warehouses Insurance & Transport of Goods with Advances Ltd* (1921) 8 Ll.L.R. 365, 366. See para. 12–10, *post*.

[23] *Fowler v. Scottish Equitable Life Ins. Soc.* (1858) 28 L.J.Ch. 225; *Billington v. Provincial Ins. Co.* (1879) 3 S.C.R. 182; *Royal Liver F.S. v. Shearer* [1930] I.A.C.(N.I.)Rep. 73; *Batty v. Pearl Ass. Co.* [1937] I.A.C.Rep. 12.

[24] (1858) 28 L.J.Ch. 225.

[25] On p. 229 Stuart V.-C. seems to say at one point that the fault for the mistake lay with Captain Cook, but it is clear from the full report of the facts that it was the fault of the assured, although the covering letter contributed to the misunderstanding. *Snell on Equity* (28th ed.), p. 614 seems to blame Cook, but this is incorrect, it is submitted with respect.

[26] (1920) 3 Ll.L.R. 259.

agreed, without consulting the assured, to delete that part of the cover. The Lloyd's brokers accordingly submitted a slip to underwriters which excluded that risk and it was initialled. A draft policy was then drawn up by the brokers, which by mistake included the risk of theft from the assured's own premises. The assured inspected the draft policy and confirmed that it was what they wanted. The underwriter's deputy then signed the policy. A burglary occurred on the assured's premises. The underwriter denied liability and claimed rectification of the policy to comply with the terms of the slip, and so excluding that risk. Bailhache J. refused to order rectification on the ground that there had been no "mutual mistake", and held that the underwriters were bound by the signed policy. It is submitted with respect that it is difficult to support that ground for the decision in the case. The broker, Lee, had power to bind the assured, and presumably possessed ostensible authority to assent to the exclusion of the risk of theft from the assured's premises. He agreed to exclude it. The slip therefore evidenced a common intention to exclude that risk, even if the assured themselves were ignorant of it, and their remedy should have been against the broker, Lee, for breach of his instructions. The authority of the agent to conclude a contract distinguishes the case from *Fowler v. Scottish Equitable Life Insurance Society*,[27] where the agent could not enter into a preliminary agreement evidencing an intention at variance with the policy. It would be possible to explain the case on the ground that, because the underwriter was originally shown the assured's proposal form at the same time as the slip, and in terms inconsistent with the slip, he was put on notice as to the brokers' lack of authority to exclude the risk in question, with the result that the assured were not bound by the slip at any time, and the draft policy was in effect their offer which was accepted by the insurer. The court, however, did not say as much expressly.

12–10 Continuing common intention. The second condition set out in paragraph 12–3 above is that the applicant for rectification of the contract document must show a common intention continuing up to the time of its execution. Cases have occurred in which one party mistakenly accepts a draft prepared for signature without realising that it either omits a provision previously agreed or contains an additional provision not hitherto accepted, and the other party executes the draft after realising that the former has failed to spot the alteration and believes the draft to be in the form previously agreed. Can the second party resist a decree of rectification on the ground that his intention altered just before he executed the contract? It has been held that, if the applicant was mistaken as to the contents of the document, and the defendant knew this but refrained from drawing it to his attention because the alteration was to the defendant's advantage, the defendant may be precluded from resisting rectification on the ground that his intention had changed prior to execution.[28]

---

[27] (1858) 28 L.J.Ch. 225.

[28] *AGIP SpA v. Navigazione Alta Italia SpA* [1984] 1 Lloyd's Rep. 353, 361, applying *A. Roberts & Co. v. Leics. C.C.* [1961] Ch. 555, *Riverlate Properties v. Paul* [1975] Ch. 133, and *T. Bates & Son v. Wyndham's (Lingerie) Ltd* [1981] 1 W.L.R. 505. The principle presumably rests upon an estoppel created by the defendant's deliberate failure to disclose the mistake in circumstances in which a responsible person would have regarded it as his duty to do so—see *Tradax Export v. Dorada Cia Nav.* [1982] 2 Lloyd's Rep. 140, 157, *per* Bingham J.

12–11 Time of pleading rectification. Rectification can be pleaded after a loss has occurred,[29] although the evidentiary difficulties obviously increase with the passage of time. An insurer can raise it as a defence in answer to a claim on the policy.[30] The assured, however, must be careful not to sue on the uncorrected policy before claiming rectification, for if he does so with knowledge of the error, he will be held to have adopted it as his contract.[31] A company which seals and delivers a policy not in conformity with the slip will be bound by it if it is adopted.[32]

12–12 Where rectification unnecessary or impossible. If a binding agreement to insure was concluded prior to issue of a policy, the purpose of which was merely to record the terms of that agreement, the assured has the option of suing upon the earlier contract in lieu of seeking rectification of the policy.[33]

12–13 If in answer to the assured's application the insurers deliver a policy inconsistent with the application, then, generally speaking, rectification is irrelevant. The issue of the policy is a counter-offer by the insurers.[34] The assured is entitled to reject it and request a different policy, in which case he can recover any premiums already paid in advance.[35] If he keeps the policy, prima facie he knowingly accepts the insurers' counter-offer, and there is no room for rectification.[36] There may, however, be circumstances where an assured who keeps his policy without noticing that it is inconsistent with his application, can claim that the insurers are estopped from saying that they sought to alter the application for insurance, since their conduct led him to suppose reasonably that his proposal was accepted without qualification.[37]

---

[29] *Henkle v. Royal Exchange Assurance Co.* (1749) 1 Ves.Sen. 317; *Eagle Star and British Dominions Ins. Co. v. Reiner* (1927) 27 Ll.L.R. 173; *Braund v. Mutual Life and Citizens Assurance Co.* [1926] N.Z.L.R. 529; *Wyld v. Liverpool and London and Globe Ins. Co.* (1877) 1 S.C.R. 604; *Allom v. Property Ins. Co., The Times,* February 10, 1911.

[30] *Eagle Star and British Dominions Ins. Co. v. Reiner, supra; Harley v. Canada Life Ins. Co.* (1911) 20 Ont.W.R. 54; *Alliance Aeroplane Co. v. Union Ins. Co. of Canton* (1920) 5 Ll.L.R. 341, 406.

[31] *Baker v. Yorkshire Fire Assurance Co.* [1892] 1 Q.B. 144; *Foster v. Mentor Life Assurance Co.* (1854) 3 E. & B. 48, 65; *Macdonald v. Law Union Ins. Co.* (1874) L.R. 9 Q.B. 328; *Dawsons Ltd v. Bonnin* [1922] 2 A.C. 413, 431–432.

[32] *Xenos v. Wickham* (1866) L.R. 2 H.L. 296, 324.

[33] *Pattison v. Mills* (1828) 1 Dow. & Cl. 342 (where the policy was in fact void by statute in England); *Wyld v. Liverpool and London and Globe Ins. Co.* (1877) 1 S.C.R. 604; *Canadian Casualty and Boiler Ins. Co. v. Hawthorn & Co.* (1907) 39 S.C.R. 558; *American Airlines Inc. v. Hope* [1972] 1 Lloyd's Rep. 253; affirmed on slightly different grounds [1974] 2 Lloyd's Rep. 301. *Sed contra* as to Scotland: *McKinlay v. Life and Health Assurance Association* (1905) 13 S.L.T. 102.

[34] *Canning v. Farquhar* (1886) 16 Q.B.D. 727; *Star Fire and Burglary Ins. Co. v. Davidson* (1903) 5 F. 83; *National Benefit Trust v. Coulter* 1911 1 S.L.T. 190; *Pattison v. Mills* (1828) 1 Dow. & Cl. 342, 361.

[35] *Fowler v. Scottish Equitable Life Ins. Soc.* (1858) 28 L.J.Ch. 225.

[36] *Smith v. Provident Savings Life Assurance Society of New York,* 65 Fed. Rep. 765 (1895); *Laing v. Provincial Homes Investment Society Ltd,* 1909 S.C. 812; *Batty v. Pearl Ass. Co. Ltd* [1937] I.A.C.Rep. 12; *Rust v. Abbey Life Ass. Co.* [1979] 2 Lloyd's Rep. 334; *Yona v. La Reunion Francaise* [1996] 2 Lloyd's Rep. 84, 110.

[37] *Freeman v. Cooke* (1848) 2 Exch. 654, 663; *Smith v. Hughes* (1871) L.R. 6 Q.B. 597; 607. The different views which a court might take in such a situation are well illustrated by the decision of the Ontario Court of Appeals in *Mowat v. Provident Life Savings Ass. Soc* (1900) 27 U.C.R. (CA Ont.) 675, and its reversal on appeal by the Supreme Court of Canada at (1902) 32 S.C.R. 147. The Ontario court held that it was incumbent on the insurer to point out that the policy sent in answer to the application was a counter-offer, and the assured was justified in not reading it,

In practice this is unlikely to happen unless an accompanying letter or other message gives that impression to the assured.[38] If it does happen, there must be a contract on the basis of the proposal form conditions, and the assured must in principle be entitled to rectification of the policy sent to him as a purported counter-offer.

12–14 The argument likely to be used by insurers in that situation would be that a party to a contract may not rely upon his mistake concerning a matter which it was his duty to know correctly or concerning which, having the means of knowledge, it was in the circumstances wilful or negligent of him not to know the truth. Knowledge of the true facts is then imputed to him.[39] Whether the applicant, who receives a policy apparently in answer to his application, falls within that principle when he fails to perceive that a counter-offer has been made, would depend upon the test of any accompanying letter or prior notification.

12–15 Misrepresentation of policy terms by agent. Misrepresentation by an officer or agent of the legal effect of the company's policy may be a good ground for rescission or return of premiums.[40] It is not good ground for rectification unless the officer or agent had authority to bind the company.[41] As a rule an officer or agent of the company who has no authority to contract on its behalf, has no authority to bind the company by construing the policy for the applicant and stating its legal effect,[42] or by assuring the applicant on his own responsibility that the contract of insurance would have an effect other than that to be deduced from reading the policy.[43]

---

so that the insurers were estopped from denying an agreement on the terms of the application. The Supreme Court said that this was not a case where agreement already existed, as was the case in *Wyld v. Liverpool and London and Globe Ins. Co.* (1877) 1 S.C.R. 604, and the applicant was therefore guilty of negligence in not perusing the policy sent to him, from which it would have been at once apparent that it was a counter-offer.

[38] *Braund v. Mutual Life and Citizens' Ass. Co.* [1926] N.Z.L.R. 529; *MacMaster v. New York Life Ins. Co.*, 99 Fed.Rep. 856; 183 U.S. 25 (1901) (oral assurance by agent).

[39] *Leake on Contracts* (8th ed.), p. 215; *Mowat v. Provident Life Savings Ass. Soc.* (1902) 32 S.C.R. 147; following *MacMaster v. New York Life Ins. Co.*, 99 Fed.Rep. 856, not reversed on the statement of the principle in Supreme Court but on its application.

[40] See Ch. 16, paras 16–4 and 16–9, *post*. Ch. 8, para. 8–31, *ante*.

[41] *Newsholme Bros. Ltd v. Road Transport and General Ass. Co.* [1929] 2 K.B. 356.

[42] *Re Hooley Hill Rubber Co. and the Royal Ins. Co.* [1920] 1 K.B. 257; *Chatt v. Prudential Ass. Co.* [1926] 1 A.C. 24.

[43] *Comerford v. The Britannic Assurance Co.* (1908) 24 T.L.R. 593; *Horncastle v. Equitable Life Ass. Co. of the U.S.A.* (1906) 22 T.L.R. 735.

CHAPTER 13

CONFLICT OF LAWS

13–1 Introduction. An insurance transaction may have links with more than one country. It may be that the parties come from different countries, as where a policy is issued by an English office to a Scotsman; or different aspects of a complex transaction may be located in different countries, as where a policy issued in Rome is the subject of re-insurance in Geneva, both policies providing for the settlement of any dispute by arbitration in London. In any such case it is necessary to turn to the principles of private international law, or the conflict of laws, in order to determine by reference to which system of law disputes are to be resolved; that is, which system of law governs the contract of insurance. If a dispute must be resolved by litigation those same principles will be relevant in defining the limits of the jurisdiction of the courts of a particular country, and in regulating the enforceability of a judgment in any third country.[1] This chapter deals first with jurisdiction and then with proper law. It concludes with a section on other related matters—the plurality of proper law; the rights of third parties; the law of the place of performance and the proof of foreign law.

1. JURISDICTION

13–2 Brussels and Lugano Conventions. These Conventions are no longer relevant in most cases involving EC Member States, but form an important part of the background to the current jurisdictional regime. The Civil Jurisdiction and Judgments Act 1982[2] gave effect in the law of the United Kingdom to the 1968 Convention on Jurisdiction and the Enforcement of Judgments in Civil and Commercial Matters as amended,[3] which contained

---

[1] For general reference and for detailed discussion of particular issues the reader is referred to *Dicey & Morris on the Conflict of Laws* (13th ed., 2000); O'Malley and Layton, *European Civil Practice* (1989 (new ed. announced 2002/2003); Plender, *The European Contracts Convention* (2001); Briggs and Rees, *Civil Jurisdiction and Judgments* (2002); Kaye, *Civil Jurisdiction and Enforcement of Foreign Judgments* (1987).

[2] 1982 c. 27.

[3] The Convention, often referred to as the Brussels Convention, was signed in 1968. The original parties were Belgium, France, Germany, Italy, Luxembourg, and The Netherlands. The Accession Convention of 1978, by which Denmark, Ireland and the United Kingdom became parties, led to amendment of the text of the 1968 Convention. The 1982 Act came into force on January 1, 1987. The 1968 Convention was further amended as a result of further accessions. Greece acceded to the Convention by an Accession Convention of 1982. In 1989, Spain and Portugal did likewise by an Accession Convention, often referred to as the San Sebastian

special provisions dealing with the jurisdiction of courts in insurance cases.[4] Schedule 1 to the 1982 Act contained the text of the 1968 Convention. The 1982 Act also implemented a parallel convention, the Lugano Convention, which extended the scheme of the 1968 Convention to EFTA States and potentially to other states.[5] Schedule 3C to the 1982 Act contained the text of the Lugano Convention, being inserted by the provisions of the Civil Jurisdiction and Judgments Act 1991.[6]

13–3 Regulation 44/2001. The Brussels Convention has been superseded, with effect from 1 March 2002, by EC Council Regulation No. 44/2001.[7] The Regulation takes effect, for the purpose of providing a uniform set of rules relating the allocation of jurisdiction and the enforcement of judgments, as between all EC Member States except Denmark. Its text is largely identical to the text of the Brussels Convention in relation to the allocation of jurisdiction (notwithstanding a confusingly different scheme for the numbering of some of its provisions). However, some changes were made to the Convention text, and it is now important to check the Regulation for the latest formulation of the relevant jurisdictional rules for the allocation of jurisdiction between Member States.

As a result of the current fragmentation of jurisdictional rules, there are now five sets of rules relevant to determining jurisdiction in the United Kingdom. Broadly, they operate as follows. First, Regulation 44/2001 allocates jurisdiction as between the courts of the United Kingdom and the courts of European Community states, with the solitary exception of Denmark. Secondly, jurisdiction as between the courts of the United Kingdom and Denmark is governed by the Brussels Convention, as amended, and the 1982 Act. Thirdly, the Lugano Convention deals with jurisdiction as between the courts of the United Kingdom and courts of certain other states. Fourthly, common law principles, supplemented by the Civil Procedure Rules and specific statutory provisions, deal with jurisdiction as between the courts of the United Kingdom and courts of other states, and with matters outside the ambit of the Conventions. Fifthly, rules contained in Part II of Schedule 2 of the Civil Jurisdiction and Judgments Order 2001[8] allocate jurisdiction between courts in the United Kingdom.

The commentary below concentrates on Regulation 44/2001. In relation

Convention, which involved amendment of the original 1968 Convention. The amendments resulting from the San Sebastian Convention came into force in the United Kingdom on December 1, 1991, being implemented by S.I. 1990 No. 2591. By an Accession Convention in 1996 Austria, Finland and Sweden became parties.

[4] Section 3 of the Convention.

[5] Currently the parties to the Lugano Convention are Iceland, Norway, Switzerland, and Poland. The Czech Republic has applied to become a party.

[6] 1991 c. 12. The amendments made to the 1982 Act in order to implement the Lugano Convention came into force on May 1, 1992—S.I. 1992 No. 745.

[7] O.J. [2001] L12/1, 16.1.2001. As a Regulation, its provisions become law without the need for implementation by Parliament. Legislative changes required as a result of the Regulation are made by the Civil Jurisdiction and Judgments Order 2001, S.I. 2001 No. 3929. Schedule 1 of the Order applies various provisions of the 1982 Act with modifications. Schedule 2 amends the 1982 Act, and Schedule 3 contains consequential amendments. The Regulation provides that it only applies to legal proceedings instituted after it comes into force—Art. 66(1). Amendments to the Civil Procedure Rules are effected by the Civil Procedure (Amendment No. 5) Rules 2001 (S.I. 2001 No. 4015).

[8] S.I. 2001 No. 3929. Jurisdiction in Scotland is dealt with by Pt III of Sched. 2 of the Order.

to proceedings involving parties domiciled in Denmark, it will be necessary to refer to the identical or substantially similar provisions of the Brussels Convention. Similarly in relation to proceedings involving parties domiciled in a state which is a party to the Lugano Convention, it will be necessary to refer to the parallel provisions of that Convention. This chapter also does not deal with jurisdictional rules arising as a matter of common law or pursuant to the Civil Procedure Rules[9] or specific enactments, nor with the enforcement of judgments.

13–4 Regulation 44/2001 and the Conventions: general points. As already noted, the provisions of the Regulation, the Brussels Convention and the Lugano Convention are complex and very similar.[10] Authorities on the meaning of provisions in the Brussels Convention are cited below in relation

[9] For guidance on the approach adopted under old RSC Ord. 11 r.1—the precursor to Civil Procedure Rule 6.20, see *Seaconsar Far East Ltd v. Bank Markazi* [1994] 1 A.C. 438. For the manner in which jurisdictional issues have been dealt with in authorities dealing with insurance disputes, see the following: *Amin Rasheed Shipping Corp. v. Kuwait Ins. Co.* [1984] A.C. 50 (English law as proper law; principles as to jurisdiction); *Britannia Steamship Ins. Assoc. v. Ausonia Ass. SA* [1984] 2 Lloyd's Rep. 98 (English putative proper law); *Ins. Corp. of Ireland v. Strombus International Ins. Co.* [1985] 2 Lloyd's Rep. 139 (negative declaratory relief); *Islamic Arab Ins. Co. v. Saudi Egyptian American Reins. Co.* [1987] 1 Lloyd's Rep. 315 (English proper law; lack of expertise in alternative forum); *The Irish Rowan* [1989] 2 Lloyd's Rep. 144 (representative proceedings); *Meadows Ins. Co. v. Ins. Corp. of Ireland* [1989] 2 Lloyd's Rep. 298 (declaratory relief); *The Golden Mariner* [1989] 2 Lloyd's Rep. 390 (joinder of co-insurers as proper or necessary parties); *Finnish Marine Ins. Co. v. Protective National Ins. Co.* [1990] 1 Q.B. 1078 (declaration that contract was void); *Overseas Union Ins. Ltd v. Incorporated General Ins.* [1992] 1 Lloyd's Rep. 439 (English proper law; defence of illegality); *Bank of America National Trust and Savings Assoc. v. Taylor* [1992] 1 Lloyd's Rep. 484 (representative procedure); *SCOR v. ERAS International Ltd* [1992] 2 All E.R. 82 (dependent claims); *Standard Steamship Owners P. & I. Assoc. v. Gann* [1992] 2 Lloyd's Rep. 528 (construction of English documents; illegality); *Trade Indemnity plc v. Forsakrings. A.B. Njord* [1995] 1 All E.R. 796 (overseas court to rule on foreign business practices); *SCOR v. ERAS (No. 2)* [1995] 2 All E.R. 278 (anti-suit injunction); *DR Ins. Co. v. Central National Ins. Co.* [1996] 1 Lloyd's Rep. 74 (declaration that contract void; allegations of illegality); *D.R. Ins. Co. v. Central National Ins. Co.* [1996] Lloyd's Rep. I.R. 74 (claims by assignees and insurers bringing subrogated claims depend for purpose of jurisdictional categorisation upon nature of the underlying assigned or subrogated claim); *Von Appen GmbH v. Voest Alpine Intertrading GmbH* [1997] 2 Lloyd's Rep. 279; *HIB Ltd v. Guardian Ins. Co. Ltd* [1997] 1 Lloyd's Rep. 412 (claim for a declaration that broker not in breach of a contract admitted to exist was one "affecting" a contract, although a claim that a contract of insurance is non-existent because void is not—see *Finnish Marine Ins. Co. v. Protective National Ins. Co. Ltd* [1990] 1 Q.B. 1078); *New Hampshire Ins. Co. v. Aerospace Finance Ltd* [1998] 2 Lloyd's Rep. 539 (followed *HIB*, although the claim was struck out for other reasons); *New Hampshire Ins. Co. v. Philips Electronics N. Am. Corp.* [1999] Lloyd's Rep. I.R. 58 (application for declaration of non liability: approach to be adopted); *Gan Ins. Co. Ltd v. Tai Ping Ins. Co. Ltd* [1999] Lloyd's Rep. I.R. 229, upheld [1999] Lloyd's Rep. I.R. 472 (negative declaration); *Youell v. Kara Mara Shipping Co Ltd* [2001] Lloyd's Rep. I.R. 553 (negative declaratory relief; necessary and proper parties; claim affecting a contract); *Messier-Dowty Ltd v. Sabena SA* [2001] 1 Lloyd's Rep. 428 (negative declarations); *Raiffeisen Zentralbank Osterreich AG v. Five Star General Trading* [2001] Lloyd's Rep. I.R. 460 (declaratory relief); *Excess Ins. Co Ltd v. Allendale Mutual Ins. Co* [2001] Lloyd's Rep. I.R. 524 (English proceedings not in breach of U.S. Service of Suit clause). For the common law regime generally, see *Dicey & Morris on the Conflict of Laws* (13th ed., 2000) vol. 1. The Civil Procedure Rules now provide, by CPR 6.20(8), for jurisdiction where a claim is made for a declaration that no contract exists when, if the contract existed, the Court would have jurisdiction. This over-rules *Finnish Marine, supra.*

[10] This chapter deals with the provisions as they appear in the Regulation. For the 1968 Convention, see Sched. 1 to the 1982 Act. For the Lugano Convention it is necessary to refer to Sched. 3C to the 1982 Act.

to the identical, or substantially similar, provisions of the Regulation. Whilst such authorities are potentially open to review in the context of the Regulation, they presumably still offer relevant guidance, bearing in mind first that the underlying aims of the Regulation coincide with those of the previous Conventions, and secondly that the language of relevant provisions is identical or substantially similar. It has been established that a purposive interpretation should be applied to the provisions of the Conventions;[11] no doubt a similar approach should be adopted to the Regulation. It is necessary to observe carefully the distinctions between an insured, a policyholder (a term which is intended to refer to the original party to the contract of insurance, he who "took out" the policy),[12] and a beneficiary; and to note the importance of determining where the defendant is domiciled. In view of the significance of arbitration to insurance disputes, it is important to note that the Regulation does not apply to arbitration.[13]

13–5 A primary aim of Regulation 44/2001 is to allocate jurisdiction between courts of EC Member States. As between those courts, the English discretionary principles as to *forum non conveniens* do not apply. However, the Court of Appeal has held,[14] reversing previous first instance decisions,[15] in relation to the Brussels Convention, that in the case of a jurisdictional contest between an English court and the courts of a non-Contracting State where the defendant was domiciled in England, the English courts retain a discretion to stay English proceedings on grounds of *forum non conveniens*.[16]

13–6 Domicile. Under Article 2 of Regulation 44/2001 a person domiciled

---

[11] For examples relating to insurance provisions, see *New Hampshire Ins. Co. v. Strabag Bau AG* [1992] 2 Lloyd's Rep. 361, 365; and *Charman v. WOC Offshore BV* [1993] 2 Lloyd's Rep. 551. In interpreting the 1968 Convention, the English Courts are to have regard to the reports prepared by M. Jenard and Professor Schlosser: Civil Jurisdiction and Judgments Act 1982, s.3(3). The reports are at O.J. [1979] C59/1, 66, 71. In interpreting the Lugano Convention, regard is to be had to the report prepared by M. Jenard and Mr Moller: Civil Jurisdiction and Judgments Act 1982, s.3B(2). The report is at O.J. [1990] C189/57. These reports will presumably continue to provide guidance to the identical, or similar, provisions now contained in the Regulation.

[12] The French term is *preneur d'assurance*. For discussion of "policyholder" in s.96(1) of the Insurance Companies Act 1982 and the Policyholders' Protection Act 1975, see *Scher v. Policyholders Protection Board* [1994] 2 A.C. 57, 73–74 (Lord Donaldson M.R.), 110, 118–122, 128 (Lord Mustill).

[13] Art. 1(2)(d); *The Atlantic Emperor* [1989] 1 Lloyd's Rep. 548; [1992] 1 Lloyd's Rep 342 (English Court proceedings relating to appointment of arbitrator fell within Convention exclusion); *The Atlantic Emperor (No. 2)* [1992] 1 Lloyd's Rep. 624 (submission to jurisdiction); *Partenreederei M/S Heidberg v. Grovesnor Grain & Feed Co. Ltd* [1994] 2 Lloyd's Rep. 287; *Toepfer International GmbH v. Molino Boschi SRL* [1996] 1 Lloyd's Rep. 510; *Toepfer International GmbH v. Societe Cargill France* [1997] 2 Lloyd's Rep. 98; *Vale do Rio Doce Navegacao SA v. Shanghai Bao Steel Ocean Shipping Co. Ltd* [2000] C.L.C. 1200.

[14] *Re Harrods (Buenos Aires) Ltd* [1992] Ch. 72.

[15] *Berisford v. New Hampshire Ins. Co.* [1990] 2 Q.B. 631; *Arkwright Mutual Ins. Co. v. Bryanston Ins. Co.* [1990] 2 Q.B. 649.

[16] The discretion to stay, where it was not inconsistent with the 1968 Convention, was preserved by s.49 of the 1982 Act. An appeal to the House of Lords in *Re Harrods* was instituted, and the matter was referred to the European Court of Justice. The parties thereafter settled their dispute. *Re Harrods* was applied in *Ace Ins. SA-NV v. Zurich Ins. Co* [2001] Lloyd's Rep. I.R. 504, where the defendant insurer was domiciled in Switzerland, a Lugano state. It is understood that an appeal to the House of Lords in *Ace*, which would have involved further consideration of the *Re Harrods* decision, was compromised. See also *SCOR v. ERAS (No. 2)* [1995] 1 Lloyd's Rep. 64, 75–77: effect of *Re Harrods* on application for injunction to restrain

in a Member State is to be sued in that state.[17] A corporate entity is domiciled where it has its statutory seat, or central administration, or principal place of business.[18] If a defendant is not domiciled in any Member State, the jurisdiction of the courts of each Member State shall be determined by the law of each state.[19]

13–7 Special jurisdiction. Alternatives to domicile as a basis of jurisdiction are provided by Articles 5 to 6 of the Regulation. Two provisions in Article 5 are of particular relevance.[20] Article 5(1) provides for the defendant to be sued in the courts for the place of performance of the obligation in question, *i.e.* the obligation which forms the basis of the action.[21] The obligation must be contractual. The obligation to exercise good faith prior to the conclusion of an insurance contract comes within the scope of Article 5(1).[22] The court must be satisfied that there is a good arguable case to establish jurisdiction.[23] Article 5(1) does not apply to matters relating to insurance, which are governed by special rules discussed below. It does apply to reinsurance contracts, because reinsurance falls outside the special rules for insurance. Where, as commonly occurs in reinsurance disputes, the claimant seeks a declaration of non-liability, the obligation in question is the obligation which the claimant contends has been breached.[24] If a number of such obligations are in issue, the Court must identify the principal obligation on which the claim is founded.[25] Under Article 5(5), as regards a dispute arising out of the operations of a branch, agency or other establishment, the defendant may be sued in the courts of the country where the branch, agency or establishment

proceedings in a non-Contracting State. With regard to the scope of the European jurisdictional regime, note that the European Court has held that the 1968 Convention does not apply to proceedings in Contracting States to enforce judgments given in non-Contracting States: Case C-129/92, *Owens Bank v. Bracco (No. 2)* [1994] Q.B. 509.

[17] Courts are to apply their internal law to decide if a party is domiciled in the state seised—Art. 59(1). In order to decide if a party is domiciled in a Member State other than the state seised, the court must apply the law of that other state—Art. 59(2).

[18] Art. 60(1).

[19] Art. 4(1) subject to Art. 22 (exclusive jurisdiction) and Art. 23 (prorogation of jurisdiction).

[20] Reference should be made to specialist works for detailed commentary on these Articles.

[21] See, for example, *Union Transport plc v. Continental Lines SA* [1992] 1 W.L.R. 15 (failure to nominate vessel for charter). Note that the Regulation has introduced special sub-rules for sales of goods and provision of services; these do not appear to be relevant to a contract of insurance.

[22] In *Trade Indemnity plc v. Forsakrings. A.B. Njord* [1995] 1 All E.R. 796 (a reinsurance case where it was accepted that the special rules as to insurance in section 3 of the Convention did not apply) it was held by Rix J. that the obligation did not come within Art. 5(1). However, the opposite conclusion was reached by Mance J. in *Agnew v. Lansforsakringsbolagens AB* [1996] L.R.L.R. 392. The decision in *Agnew* was affirmed by the Court of Appeal, [1997] L.R.L.R. 671, and by the House of Lords: [2001] 1 A.C. 223. A claim to recover monies pursuant to a contract subsequently admitted to be void is not a matter relating to a contract within Art. 5(1), *Kleinwort Benson Ltd v. Glasgow City Council* [1997] 1 A.C. 153, HL. Presumably a claim by the insurer to avoid a contract, coupled with a claim for repayment of monies previously paid to the insured, would fall within Art. 5(1), although the point is not free from difficulty. In *Fisher v. Unione Italiana de Riassicurazione SpA* [1999] Lloyd's Rep. I.R. 215, a claim for rescission based on an alleged breach of the duty of disclosure was held to be within Art. 5(1). Where a reinsurer claimed a declaration of non-liability to its Greek reinsured based upon a failure to comply with an obligation to notify loss under a claims co-operation clause, it was held that Art.5(1) applied to give the English Court jurisdiction, notwithstanding an alternative claim by the reinsurer for damages: *AIG Europe (UK) Ltd v. The Ethniki* [2000] Lloyd's Rep. I.R. 343.

[23] *Canada Trust Co. v. Stolzenberg* [1998] 1 W.L.R. 547, 553–559, CA; [2000] 4 All E.R. 481, HL; *Deutsche Ruck. A.G. v. La Fondiara* [2001] 2 Lloyd's Rep. 621.

[24] *Fisher v. Unione Italiana de Riassicurazione SpA* [1999] Lloyd's Rep. I.R. 215.

[25] *AIG Europe (UK) Ltd v. The Ethniki* [2000] Lloyd's Rep. I.R. 343.

is situated.[26] Article 6 provides special grounds for jurisdiction relating to co-defendants, third party proceedings and counterclaims.[27]

13–8 Jurisdiction in matters relating to insurance. Section 3 of Regulation 44/2001, comprising Articles 8 to 14, contains special jurisdictional rules for "matters relating to insurance".[28] The rules in section 3 are not applicable to reinsurance.[29] They do not, it is submitted, apply to subrogated claims brought on behalf of insurers against third parties. The rules are not restricted to consumer contracts of insurance, nor to contracts where there is inequality of bargaining power.[30] They apply without prejudice to Articles 4 and 5(5) of Regulation 44/2001.[31] They do not apply to the jurisdictional regime for different parts of the United Kingdom which is contained in Schedule 2 of the Civil and Jurisdiction and Judgments Order 2001.[32] Article 9 of the Regulation contains a special rule as to domicile under which an insurer who would not otherwise be domiciled in a Member State but has a branch, agency or other establishment in that Member State is, in disputes arising out of the branch, agency or establishment, deemed to be domiciled in that State.[33] If a judgment conflicts with rules in Section 3, that will be a ground for the judgment not to be recognised or enforced in other Member States.[34]

13–9 Actions against insurers. If an action is brought against an insurer who is domiciled in Scotland or Northern Ireland, the jurisdiction of the English courts is limited to the cases specified in Part II of Schedule 2 of the Civil and Jurisdiction and Judgments Order 2001.[35] In essence a modified version of the Regulation regime is applied, so that English courts will have jurisdiction under provisions very similar to those pursuant to which they

---

[26] *New Hampshire Ins. Co. v. Strabag Bau AG* [1990] 2 Lloyd's Rep. 61; affirmed [1992] 1 Lloyd's Rep. 361, CA, where it was pointed out that the relevant branch is that of the defendant not the plaintiff, and that a broker who acts as an independent entity for particular transactions does not come within Art. 5(5). It appears that Art. 5(5) is not limited to contracts which are to be performed in the State where the branch is situated: see *Dicey & Morris on the Conflict of Laws* (13th ed., 2000) vol. 1, p. 358.

[27] For the use of Art. 6 to found jurisdiction for an anti-suit injunction, see *SCOR v. ERAS (No. 2)* [1995] 1 Lloyd's Rep. 64.

[28] The rules have been described as a "self contained and exclusive code governing insurance": *Baltic Ins. Group v. Jordan Grand Prix* [1999] Lloyd's Rep. I.R. 93, at 95.

[29] Case C-412/98 *Group Josi Reins. Co. SA v. Universal General Ins. Co.* [2001] Lloyd's Rep. I.R. 483, anticipated by the House of Lords in *Agnew v. Lansforsakringsbolagens AB* [2001] 1 A.C. 223. For prior consideration of the point, see Schlosser report O.J. [1979] C59, para. 151; *Citadel Ins. Co. v. Atlantic Union Ins. Co.* [1982] 2 Lloyd's Rep. 543; *Arkwright Mutual Ins. Co. v. Bryanston Ins. Co. Ltd* [1990] 2 Q.B. 649; Case C–351/89, *Overseas Union Ins. Ltd v. New Hampshire Ins. Co.* [1992] Q.B. 434; *New Hampshire Ins. Co. v. Strabag Bau AG* [1992] 1 Lloyd's Rep 361; *Trade Indemnity v. Forsakrings. A.B. Njord* [1995] 1 All E.R. 796.

[30] *New Hampshire Ins. Co. v. Strabag Bau AG* [1990] 2 Lloyd's Rep. 61; affirmed [1992] 1 Lloyd's Rep. 361.

[31] Art. 8.

[32] S.I. 2001 No. 3929.

[33] Art. 9(2), applied in *Berisford v. New Hampshire Ins. Co.* [1990] 2 Q.B. 631. If the State is the United Kingdom, the insurer will be deemed to be domiciled in the part of the United Kingdom in which the branch, agency or establishment is situated: s.44 of the 1982 Act and s.11 of Sch. 1 of S.I. 2001 No. 3929. "Part of the United Kingdom" means England and Wales, Scotland or Northern Ireland: s.50 of the 1982 Act.

[34] Art. 35(1).

[35] S.I. 2001 No. 3929, which by s.4 of Sch. 2 of the Order implements a new version of Sch. 4 of the 1982 Act.

have jurisdiction in cases involving other Member States.[36] If an action is brought against an insurer not domiciled in any of the Member States (nor domiciled in any state which is a party to the Lugano Convention), the jurisdiction of the English courts is governed by the traditional principles as to service of process within the jurisdiction or, in accordance with the Civil Procedure Rules, outside the jurisdiction.[37] The court has power under section 51 of the Supreme Court Act 1981 to order a third party to pay the costs of proceedings to which it was not a party, but which were contested and financed by it to protect its own interests.[38] This power could presumably be exercised against a liability insurer which had financed the defence of a third party claim against the assured for such reasons.

13–10 Jurisdiction in actions against insurers domiciled in Member States[39] is subject to the special rules in section 3 of Regulation 44/2001, the effect of which may be stated as follows: the English courts will have jurisdiction

(a) if the insurer is domiciled in England (or deemed to be domiciled in England, as discussed above)[40];

(b) if the policy-holder, insured, or beneficiary under the insurance is domiciled in England[41];

(c) if the insurer is a co-insurer, and proceedings against the leading insurer are brought in England[42];

(d) in the case of liability insurance, if the harmful event occurred in England[43];

(e) in the case of insurance of immovable property (or where movable and immovable property are covered by the same policy and both are adversely affected by the same contingency), if the harmful event occurred in England[44];

(f) in the case of liability insurance, in third-party claims by the insured, where the injured party has brought proceedings against the insured in England[45]; and

---

[36] See Sch. 4 of the 1982 Act, as modified by S.I. 2001 No. 3929, arts. 1, 3(a) (where England is the place of performance of the relevant contractual obligation), 3(e) (disputes arising out of the operations of a branch, agency or other establishment in England), 5 (co-defendants, third-party proceedings and counterclaims), 12 (jurisdiction clauses) and 13 (submission). In *Davenport v. Corinthian Motor Policies at Lloyd's* [1991] S.L.T. 774 the Scottish court had no jurisdiction over an English insurer under Sch. 4, art. 5 (now art. 3) in respect of a claim under s.151 of the Road Traffic Act 1958.

[37] Regulation 44/2001 Art. 4 (saved by art. 8).

[38] The power under s.51 is discussed at para. 28–41 *post*. The procedure for service out was discussed by the Court of Appeal in *National Justice Compania Naviera SA v. Prudential Ass. Co. Ltd (The Ikarian Reefer (No. 2))* [2000] Lloyd's Rep.I.R. 230. The situation is now covered by CPR 6.20(17).

[39] In the case of an insurer domiciled in Denmark, section 3 of the Brussels Convention applies. In the case of insurers domiciled in states which are parties to the Lugano Convention, the similar provisions of the Lugano Convention apply.

[40] Arts 9(1)(a), (2).

[41] Art. 9(1)(b).

[42] Art. 9(1)(c). This facilitates but does not require the consolidation of proceedings in one jurisdiction.

[43] Art.10. For the location of the harmful event see Case 21/76, *Handelskwekerij G.J. Bier NV v. Mines de Potasse d'Alsace SA* [1978] Q.B. 708; *Minster v. Hyundai* [1988] 2 Lloyd's Rep. 621; *Domicrest v. Swiss Bank Corp.* [1999] Q.B. 548 (where *Minster* was not followed).

[44] Art. 10.

[45] Art. 11.

(g) in the case of a counter-claim, if the insurer has commenced proceedings in England based on the same contract or facts.[46]

The above rules apply to actions brought by the injured party directly against the insurer where such direct actions are permitted, *e.g.* under the Third Parties (Rights against Insurers) Act 1930.[47] The effect of jurisdiction clauses on these rules is considered below. The English court will always have jurisdiction where the defendant insurer submits to the jurisdiction.[48] As discussed above, the English court will also have jurisdiction under Article 5(5) in respect of disputes arising out of the operations of a branch, agency or other establishment situated in England.

13–11 Actions by insurers. If an action is brought by an insurer against a defendant (whether policy-holder, insured or beneficiary) domiciled in Scotland or Northern Ireland, the jurisdiction of the English courts is limited to the cases specified in Part II of Schedule 2 of the Civil and Jurisdiction and Judgments Order 2001.[49] If the defendant is not domiciled in any of the Member States (nor in a state which is a party to the Lugano Convention), the jurisdiction of the English courts rests upon the traditional principles as to service of process within the jurisdiction or, in accordance with the Civil Procedure Rules, outside the jurisdiction.

13–12 Jurisdiction in all other actions by an insurer against a policy-holder, insured or beneficiary domiciled in a Member State[50] is subject to the special rules in section 3 of Regulation 44/2001. The primary rule is that an insurer may bring such proceedings in the English courts only if the defendant is domiciled in England.[51] To this there are a number of exceptions. If the dispute arises out of the operations of a branch, agency or other establishment, the action may be brought in England if the branch, agency of other establishment is situated in England, even if the defendant is domiciled in another Contracting State.[52] The English courts will also have jurisdiction in the case of a counter-claim if proceedings against the insurer based on the same contract or facts have been commenced in England.[53] But an insurer, whether or not domiciled in a contracting state, is not permitted to bring a counterclaim against parties other than the original claimant. So in *Baltic Insurance Group v. Jordan Grand Prix Ltd*[54] an insurer against whom

---

[46] Arts 6(3), 12(2).

[47] Art. 11(2). It seems unlikely that an action under the 1930 Act would be excluded from the scope of the Regulations on grounds that it related to winding up. This accords with the views of the Law Commission: Law Com. No. 272, July 2001, para. 8.22.

[48] See art. 24 and (for the position at common law) *Dicey & Morris on the Conflict of Laws* (13th ed., 2000) vol. 1, pp. 310–314.

[49] S.I. 2001 No. 3929. s.4 of Pt II of Sch. 2 of the Order implements a modified version of Sch. 4 of the 1982 Act.

[50] If the defendant is domiciled in Denmark, section 3 of the Brussels Convention applies. If domiciled in a state which is a party to the Lugano Convention, section 3 of that Convention applies.

[51] Regulation 44/2001, Art. 12(1).

[52] *ibid*. art. 5(5) as expressly saved by art. 8.

[53] *ibid*. arts 6(3), 12(2).

[54] [1999] 2 A.C.127.

a claim was brought in England by a corporate assured, and which had responded by avoiding the policy for alleged fraud and by instituting a counterclaim for damages, was unable to join parties situated in Ireland as additional defendants to the counterclaim. Where an injured party has brought an action in England directly against the insurer, *e.g.* under the Third Parties (Rights Against Insurers) Act 1930, the English courts will also have jurisdiction over a policy-holder or insured who is joined as a party to the action.[55] The effect of jurisdiction clauses on these rules is considered below. The English court will always have jurisdiction where the defendant submits to the jurisdiction.[56]

13–13 Jurisdiction clauses. A clause by which the parties agree that disputes are to be resolved in the English courts will generally be effective in conferring jurisdiction upon those courts.[57] The clause must on its true construction oblige the parties to resort to the English jurisdiction.[58] General words of incorporation will normally not demonstrate that the parties to a reinsurance contract intend to incorporate a jurisdiction clause from the underlying insurance.[59] Rather different considerations apply in insurance cases which attract the special rules in section 3 of Regulation 44/2001 which have been examined in the preceding paragraphs. Those rules may be departed from only by an agreement on jurisdiction which satisfies a number of specified requirements. The agreement must be either in writing or evidenced in writing or in a form which accords with practices which the parties have established between themselves, or, in international trade or commerce, in a form which accords with a usage of which the parties are or ought to have been aware and which in such trade or commerce is widely known to, and regularly observed by, parties to contracts of the type involved in the particular trade or commerce concerned.[60]

13–14 The agreement must also comply with the special rules for insurance cases in Articles 13 and 14 of Regulation 44/2001.[61] Under those rules an agreement allowing the policy-holder, the insured or a beneficiary to bring proceedings in courts other than those indicated in section 3 of the

---

[55] *ibid*. art. 11(3); such joinder would be most unusual under English procedures.

[56] *ibid*. art. 24 and (for the position at common law) *Dicey & Morris on the Conflict of Laws* (13th ed., 2000) vol. 1, pp. 301–305.

[57] See *Dicey & Morris on the Conflict of Laws* (13th ed., 2000) vol. 1 p. 424; CPR 6.20(5)(d); Civil Jurisdiction and Judgments Act 1982, Sch. 4, art. 12, as enacted by S.I. 2001 No. 3929 Sch. 2 Pt II s.4 (where the defendant is domiciled in Scotland or Northern Ireland). The choice must be express: *New Hampshire Ins. Co. v. Strabag Bau AG* [1992] 1 Lloyd's Rep. 361, 371.

[58] *Berisford v. New Hampshire Ins. Co.* [1990] 2 Q.B. 631. But it does not have to refer exclusively to the English jurisdiction: *Kurz v. Stella Musical Veranstaltungs GmbH* [1992] Ch. 196.

[59] *AIG Europe (UK) Ltd v. The Ethniki* [2000] Lloyd's Rep. I.R. 343; *AIG Europe SA v. QBE International Ins. Ltd* [2001] 2 Lloyd's Rep. 268.

[60] Regulation 44/2001 art. 23(1). In the Brussels and Lugano Conventions the relevant provision is art. 17(1). The wording in the text reflects changes to art. 17 agreed in negotiations concerning the Lugano Convention and the 1989 Accession Convention. Although the relevant article (i.e. 23(1) in the Regulation) is in effect subject to the special insurance rules in arts. 13 and 14, its formal requirements apply in all cases. See Case 201/82, *Gerling v. Treasury Administration* [1983] E.C.R. 2503, and *Berisford v. New Hampshire Ins. Co.* [1990] 2 Q.B. 631, 643. For the interpretation of those requirements, see *Dicey & Morris on the Conflict of Laws* (13th ed., 2000) p. 435, and *Denby v. Hellenic Mediterranean Lines* [1994] 1 Lloyd's Rep. 320.

[61] In so far as the Lugano or Brussels Convention applies, art. 12 is the relevant provision.

Regulation will be effective. An agreement allowing an insurer to bring proceedings in such courts will only be effective if:

(a) it is entered into after the dispute has arisen; or

(b) it is concluded between a policy-holder and an insurer, both of whom are at the time of the conclusion of the contract domiciled or habitually resident in the same Member State and which has the effect of conferring jurisdiction on the courts of that State even if the harmful event were to occur abroad, provided the agreement is not contrary to the law of that State; or

(c) it is concluded with a policy-holder who is not domiciled in a Member State, except in so far as the insurance is compulsory or relates to immovable property in a Member State; or

(d) it relates to a contract of insurance in so far as it covers certain risks to ships, aircraft and goods in transit.[62]

Those risks are as follows[63]:

(i) any loss of or damage to sea-going ships, installations situated offshore or on the high seas, or aircraft arising from perils which relate to their use for commercial purposes, or to goods in transit other than passengers' baggage where the transit consists of or includes carriage by such ships or aircraft;

(ii) any liability, other than for bodily injury to passengers or loss of or damage to their baggage, arising out of the use or operation of such ships, installations or aircraft (in so far as the law of the Member State in which such aircraft are registered does not prohibit agreements on jurisdiction regarding insurance of such risks), or for loss or damage caused by goods in such transit;

(iii)any financial loss connected with the use or operation of such ships, installations or aircraft, in particular loss of freight or charter-hire;

(iv)any risk or interest connected with any of those listed above, and

(v) all "large risks".[64]

With regard to such risks, the jurisdiction clause must relate to a contract of insurance which covers only risks of the specified kinds.[65]

13–15 Concurrent jurisdiction. Under Article 27 of Regulation 44/2001, where proceedings involving the same cause of action and between the same parties[66] are brought in courts of different Contracting States, any court

---

[62] Regulation 44/2001, art. 13.

[63] *ibid.* art. 14.

[64] As defined by Council Directive 73/239/EEC, as amended by Directives 88/357/EEC, and 90/618/EEC. "Large risks" are defined to include a wide range of risks where the policy holder satisfies specified tests for minimum balance sheet figures, turnover or numbers of employees. The inclusion of "large risks" in the category of contracts in which the insurer is permitted to rely on a jurisdiction clause was achieved by Regulation 44/2001. The result is that insurers of substantial commercial risks will be increasingly likely to be able to rely on jurisdiction clauses.

[65] *Charman v. WOC Offshore BV* [1993] 2 Lloyd's Rep. 551 (decided in relation to similar provisions in the Brussels Convention—held there was sufficient connection between coverage of land-based equipment and of vessels for the jurisdiction agreement to apply).

[66] Case 144/86, *Gubisch Maschinenfabrik KG v. Palumbo* [1987] E.C.R. 4861; *Ass. Generales de France I.A.R.T. v. Chiyoda Fire and Marine Co. (U.K.) Ltd* [1992] 1 Lloyd's Rep. 325; Case C–406/92, *The Maciej Ratal* [1995] 1 Lloyd's Rep. 302. Where an insurer is involved in one set of proceedings, and an assured is involved in another, they will not be treated as a single party unless their interests in both disputes are identical and indissociable: *Drouot Ass. SA v. Consolidated Metallurgical Industries*; Case C–351/96, [1999] Q.B. 497.

other than the court first seised must decline jurisdiction.[67] The court which is second seised should not normally investigate the jurisdiction of the court first seised.[68] If the jurisdiction of the first seised court is challenged, the second court can stay its proceedings pending the outcome of the challenge in the first court. Article 21 is not restricted to cases where the defendant is domiciled in a Contracting State or where jurisdiction is founded on Regulation 44/2001.[69] Under Article 22, where related actions are brought in courts of different Contracting States any court other than the court first seised may stay its proceedings.[70]

13–16 The court becomes seised for the purposes of the Regulation:

(a) at the time when the document instituting the proceedings, or equivalent document, is lodged with the court, provided that the defendant has not subsequently failed to take steps required to effect service, or

(b) if the document has to be served before being lodged, at the time when it is received by the authority responsible for service, provided that the claimant has not subsequently failed to take steps required to lodge the document with the court.[71]

2. The Proper Law of the Contract

13–17 The ascertainment of the proper law of a contract of insurance now largely depends on rules contained in the Contracts (Applicable Law) Act 1990 and regulations made pursuant to the Financial Services and Markets Act 2000. However, common law principles cannot be entirely ignored. They remain relevant for some purposes (for example, the determination of the proper law of an arbitration agreement in a contract otherwise governed by the Rome Convention). They may also affect the interpretation of the

---

[67] Case 351/89, *Overseas Union Ins. v. New Hampshire Ins. Co.* [1992] Q.B. 434; *Ass. Generales de France I.A.R.T. v. Chiyoda Fire and Marine Co. (U.K.) Ltd* [1992] 1 Lloyd's Rep. 325.

[68] The position is different if the court second seised has, or is alleged to have, exclusive jurisdiction under 23 of the Regulation (equivalent to art. 17 of the Brussels Convention): *Kloeckner v. Gatoil* [1990] 1 Lloyd's Rep. 177; *Denby v. Hellenic Mediterranean Lines* [1994] 1 Lloyd's Rep. 320; *Continental Bank N.A. v. Aeakos Cia Naviera* [1994] 1 W.L.R. 588.

[69] Case 351/89, *Overseas Union Ins. v. New Hampshire Ins. Co.* [1992] Q.B. 434.

[70] Case 406/92, *The Maciej Rataj* [1995] 1 Lloyd's Rep. 302.

[71] Regulation 44/2001, art. 30. There is no equivalent provision in the Brussels and Lugano Conventions. Under the Brussels Convention, it was held that in England the court became seised upon service of a writ—see *Dresser UK Ltd v. Falcongate Freight Management Ltd* [1991] 2 Lloyd's Rep 557; *Neste Chemicals SA v. D.K. Line Ltd* [1994] 2 Lloyd's Rep. 6; *Grupo Torras SA v. Sheikh Fahd Mohammed Al-Sabah* [1996] 1 Lloyd's Rep. 7. For examples of the English court, under the Brussels regime, investigating an issue as to the date of seisin by reference to foreign procedural law, see *Ass. Generales de France I.A.R.T. v. Chiyoda Fire and Marine Co. (U.K.) Ltd* [1992] 1 Lloyd's Rep. 325, 334–337; *Grupo Torras SA v. Al-Sabah* [1996] 1 Lloyd's Rep. Under the rule for all Member States (excluding Denmark) which now applies pursuant to art. 30 of Regulation 44/2001, it seems that the court will be seised at the time of issue of proceedings provided that there is subsequent compliance with CPR requirements for service.

statutory rules. This section therefore summarises common law principles before turning to the statutory regime.

(a) *Proper Law: Common Law Principles*

13–18 The proper law. Contracts of insurance, like other types of contract, are governed by a system of law identified as "the proper law of the contract". As a matter of common law the proper law of an insurance contract governs almost all issues relating to the essential validity of the contract and so determines the major question whether the insurer is liable to make a payment to the insured. Thus the discharge of a contract is governed by its proper law.[72] It applies also to such matters as the interpretation of the terms of the policy[73] and whether the insurer has a defence to a claim made by the insured. It is also relevant to resolving any dispute concerning the intrinsic validity of the insurance contract, as where it is contended that its payment provisions contravene the statute law of a particular country.[74]

13–19 Express choice of the proper law. The first step in the determination of the proper law, as a matter of common law, is to examine the policy in order to see whether the parties have by its express terms evinced a common intention as to the system of law by reference to which their mutual rights and obligations under it are to be ascertained.[75] The selection of the proper law made by the parties will be recognised provided it is a bona fide choice[76] and does not contravene imperative rules of public policy, including those incorporated in statutes intended to override the usual conflict of laws rules.[77] Generally, the parties' choice is conclusive, and a selection of English law as the proper law will be recognised even if the circumstances of the case reveal few, if any, other links with England.[78] It is possible in some circumstances for the parties validly to select a system of legal rules which correspond with the law of no particular country.[79] But they cannot employ a floating choice of law clause which leaves the applicable law undetermined at the time of the contract.[80]

[72] *e.g. Anderson v. Equitable Ass. Soc. of the United States* (1926) 134 L.T. 557, CA. Discharge also includes the question where policy monies are to be paid: *Pick v. Manufacturers Life Ins. Co.* [1958] 2 Lloyd's Rep. 93, 97.
[73] *e.g. Rowett, Leakey & Co. v. Scottish Provident Institution* [1927] 1 Ch. 55, CA.
[74] *Rossano v. Manufacturers' Life Insurance Co.* [1963] 2 Q.B. 352.
[75] *Amin Rasheed Shipping Corp. v. Kuwait Ins. Co.* [1984] A.C. 50, 61.
[76] *cf. Golden Acres Ltd v. Queensland Estates Pty Ltd* [1969] Qd.R. 378, affirmed on other grounds *sub. nom. Freehold Land Investments Ltd v. Queensland Estates Pty Ltd* (1970) 123 C.L.R. 418.
[77] In *DR Ins. Co. v. Central National Ins. Co.* [1996] 1 Lloyd's Rep. 74 the provisions of the Insurance Companies Acts relating to authorisation of insurers were regarded as overriding. *Cf.* also the Unfair Contract Terms Act 1977, s.27(2) and *The Hollandia* [1983] 1 A.C. 565.
[78] *Greer v. Poole* (1880) 5 Q.B.D. 272, 274; *R. v. International Trustee for the Protection of International Bondholders Aktiengesellschaft* [1937] A.C. 500, 529; *Vita Food Products Inc. v. Unus Shipping Co. Ltd* [1939] A.C. 277, 290; *Mount Albert Borough Council v. Australasian Temperance and General Mutual Life Ass. Soc. Ltd* [1938] A.C. 224, 240; *Whitworth Street Estates Ltd v. Miller* [1970] A.C. 583, 603.
[79] *Deutsche Schachtbau-und Tiefbohrgesellschaft mbH v. R'AS Al-Khaimah National Oil Co.* [1990] 1 A.C. 295.
[80] *Armar Shipping Co. Ltd v. Caisse Algerienne d'Assurance et de Reassurance* [1981] 1 W.L.R. 207, 215; *Amin Rasheed Shipping Corp. v. Kuwait Ins. Co.* [1984] A.C. 50, 65; *E.I. Du Pont de Nemours & Co. v. Agnew* [1987] 2 Lloyd's Rep. 585, 592; *CGU International Ins. Plc v.*

13–20 Incorporation by reference. It may be that a reference in a contract to a system of law does not represent the selection of a proper law but rather an intention to incorporate certain provisions of that law as terms of the contract. This does not amount to the selection of the proper law. The courts will ascertain the proper law by reference to ordinary principles and will then construe the entire contract, including the incorporated terms, according to the proper law so ascertained.[81] A foreign statute incorporated in this way may be interpreted not as an Act but simply as a contractual term;[82] but an English statute so incorporated will bear the same meaning in an English contract as it does when standing alone.[83] A reference to a foreign statute may be intended as an aid to the interpretation of the contract and not as a choice of proper law.[84] The incorporation of contractual terms devised for use in the insurance practice of a particular country, while a factor which may be weighed in the determination of the proper law, does not itself amount to a selection of the law of that country as the proper law.[85] The use of general words of incorporation in a reinsurance contract (*e.g.* "as original") will not demonstrate unequivocally that a choice of law in the underlying contract is to be incorporated, and may be outweighed by circumstances surrounding the placing which point to a different applicable law.[86]

13–21 Where no express choice of law. In a case where the contract does not expressly provide which law is to govern it, the court must ascertain the proper law for itself. It is commonly said that this inquiry proceeds in two stages. The court first endeavours to deduce the presumed intention of the parties as to the proper law from an examination of the terms of the contract construed in the light of the circumstances of its formation. The presence of certain types of material in the contract will provide a basis for this "inferred intention" or "implied choice of law" as a matter of common law. In the absence of such material the court must determine the system of law with which the transaction has its closest and most real connection. In practice these two stages are not always kept distinct but merge into each other.[87]

13–22 Arbitration and jurisdiction clauses. The parties to a contract

Szabo [2002] Lloyd's Rep. I.R. 196. The rule has been criticised. See *e.g. Howard* [1995] L.M.C.L.Q. 1. A common clause in insurance contracts with a connection with the United States is the "New York suable" clause. It provides that at the option of the assured the place of issue and delivery of the policy shall be New York, and that all matters thereunder shall be determined in accordance with American law and practice. It does not leave proper law indeterminate from the outset, but the option to change the proper law suggests that it may be objectionable as a variant of a floating choice of law clause: *Cantieri Navali Riuniti SpA. v. NV Omne Justitia (The Stolt Marmaro)* [1985] 2 Lloyd's Rep. 428, 435. *Cf. The Iran Vojdan* [1984] 2 Lloyd's Rep. 380. It is not merely a clause which offers a choice of jurisdiction, which would not be objectionable: *Star Shipping A.S. v. China National Foreign Trade Transportation Corporation* [1993] 2 Lloyd's Rep. 445.

[81] *e.g. Nea Agrex SA v. Baltic Shipping Co. Ltd* [1976] Q.B. 933.

[82] *Dobell & Co. v. Steamship Rossmore Co. Ltd* [1895] 2 Q.B. 408, 413.

[83] *Compania Colombiana de Seguras v. Pacific Steam Navigation Co.* [1965] 1 Q.B. 101, 127.

[84] *Ex parte Dever* (1887) 18 Q.B.D. 660.

[85] *Amin Rasheed Shipping Corp. v. Kuwait Ins. Co.* [1984] A.C. 50, 71; *The Stolt Marmaro* [1985] 2 Lloyd's Rep. 428, CA.

[86] *Gan Ins. Co. v. Tai Ping Ins. Co. Ltd* [1999] Lloyd's Rep. I.R. 472. A similar approach has been followed in relation to jurisdiction clauses: *AIG Europe (UK) Ltd v. The Ethniki* [2000] Lloyd's Rep. I.R. 343; *AIG Europe SA v. QBE International Ins. Ltd* [2001] 2 Lloyd's Rep. 268; *Ass. Gen. SpA v. Ege Sigorta AS* [2002] Lloyd's Rep. I.R. 480.

[87] See *Amin Rasheed Shipping Corp. v. Kuwait Ins. Co.* [1984] A.C. 50, 69.

frequently provide that any disputes arising under it shall be referred either to arbitration in a named country (an arbitration clause) or to the courts of such a country (a jurisdiction clause). The presence of an arbitration or jurisdiction clause in a contract is taken to be a strong indication of the parties' intention to choose as the proper law the law of the jurisdiction named.[88] It was thought at one time that the presence of such a clause necessarily and conclusively determined the proper law, but it is now clear that there is no absolute rule.[89]

13–23 Choice of a validating law. Where rival systems of law are contended for as the proper law, and one or more terms of the contract are invalid by one of these and valid by the other, it is sometimes argued that the parties must have intended the latter system of law to govern their contract for otherwise they cannot give effect to their whole bargain.[90] However, more recent cases have played down the importance of this consideration as one the significance of which should not be exaggerated,[91] and the factor is one which has an especial artificiality in the case of standard form policies and contracts. However, it can still be of relevance, in that it is difficult to infer that the parties intended their contract to be governed by a system of law which would put its validity in doubt.[92]

13–24 Closest and most real connection. In the absence of clear indications of an express or implied choice of law by the parties, the court will determine the proper law by deciding with which system of law the contract has its closest and most real connection. This involves the examination of a variety of factors related to the parties, the making of the contract, its terms, the expected place of performance, and also the considerations as to jurisdiction clauses and a validating law examined above. In the process of weighing these factors the mode of performance of the contract matters more than the residence or nationality of the insured and the place where the contract was negotiated. The place of contracting was formerly given considerable weight, although it was always recognised that the circumstances in which the contract came to be made in a particular place had to be examined.[93] In modern cases, the place of contracting may depend upon purely technical factors such as the business procedures adopted within a large international corporation or the precise sequence of telex messages

---

[88] *Royal Exchange Assurance Corp. v. Sjokorsakrings Aktiebolaget Vega* [1902] 2 K.B. 384 CA; *Spurrier v. La Cloche* [1902] A.C. 466; *Norske Atlas Ins. Co. Ltd v. London General Insurance Co. Ltd* (1927) 28 Ll.L.Rep. 104; *Compagnie Tunisienne de Navigation SA v. Compagnie d'Armement Maritime SA* [1971] A.C. 572; *Atlantic Underwriting Agencies Ltd v. Compagnia di Ass. di Milano* [1979] 2 Lloyd's Rep. 240; *The Mariannina* [1983] 1 Lloyd's Rep. 12 CA; *Afia Worldwide Ins. Co. v. Deutsche Ruck* (1983) 133 N.L.J. 621; *The Komninos S* [1991] 1 Lloyd's Rep. 371, 375. Contrast *The Stolt Marmaro* [1985] 2 Lloyd's Rep. 428, 434, which concerned a non-mandatory, New York suable clause.

[89] *Compagnie Tunisienne de Navigation SA v. Compagnie d'Armement Maritime SA* [1971] A.C. 572, 600. For examples relating to insurance, see *Spurrier v. La Cloche* [1902] A.C. 446; *Atlantic Underwriting Agencies Ltd v. Comp. di Ass. di Milano* [1979] 2 Lloyd's Rep. 240.

[90] *Peninsular and Oriental Steam Co. v. Shand* (1865) 3 Moo.P.C.(N.S.) 272; *N.V. Handel Maatschappij J. Smits v. English Exporters (London) Ltd* [1955] 2 Lloyd's Rep. 317; *Coast Lines Ltd v. Hudig and Veder Chartering N.V.* [1972] 2 Q.B. 34, CA.

[91] *Sayers v. International Drilling Co.* [1971] 1 W.LR. 1176, CA; *Monterosso Shipping Co. Ltd v. International Transport Workers Federation* [1982] I.C.R. 675, CA.

[92] *Islamic Arab Ins. Co. v. Saudi Egyptian American Reins. Co.* [1987] 1 Lloyd's Rep. 315, 320.

[93] *Maritime Ins. Co. Ltd v. Assekuranz-Union von.* 1865 (1935) 52 Ll.L.R. 16, 19; *Sayers v. International Drilling Co.* [1971] 1 W.L.R. 1176, 1187, CA.

exchanged by the parties.[94] In some types of contract, the place of performance is of great significance, but this is not necessarily the case where, as in a contract of insurance, performance consists in the payment of money by one party or the other, sometimes using an international rather than a national currency.[95] The courts have given considerable weight, particularly in the case of life insurance, to the system of law governing the conduct of the insurer's business, which is often identified with the insurer's principal place of business.[96] As explained below, the law of the country of the insured's residence will assume greater significance in the case of risks situated within Member States of the European Economic Community, as a result of the application of statutory rules.

13–25 Centre of gravity. The general trend, particularly in cases of complex international insurance or reinsurance transactions, has been for the courts to identify the "centre of gravity" of the contract, in order to ascertain the system of law with which the contract has its closest connection.[97] This has involved consideration of matters such as the market in which the contract was negotiated and made; the identity of other participants; the existence of clauses such as the "follow London" clause[98] and the method of processing premiums and claims.

13–26 The application of common law principles is illustrated by *Amin Rasheed Shipping Corp. v. Kuwait Insurance Co.*,[99] which concerned a contract of marine insurance issued by the respondents, an insurance company incorporated in and carrying on business in Kuwait. The insured was a Liberian shipping company, which had its head office in Dubai. The policy was issued in Kuwait and claims were payable there, but the form used, the insurer's standard form of hull policy, was wholly in English and followed the Lloyd's S.G. policy scheduled to the Marine Insurance Act 1906, but with a few added clauses which also reflected the then current English practice. The House of Lords held that English law was the proper law of the contract. Lord Diplock (with whom three other Law Lords agreed) identified as the crucial circumstance the absence at the relevant time of any indigenous Kuwaiti law of marine insurance. The general

---

[94] *Pick v. Manufacturers Life Ins. Co.* [1958] 2 Lloyd's Rep. 93, 98; *Amin Rasheed Shipping Corp. v. Kuwait Ins. Co.* [1984] A.C. 50, 62.

[95] *Amin Rasheed Shipping Corp. v. Kuwait Ins. Co.* [1984] A.C. 50, 62.

[96] *Pick v. Manufacturers Life Ins. Co.* [1958] 2 Lloyd's Rep. 93; *Rossano v. Manufacturers Life Ins. Co.* [1963] 2 Q.B. 352. *Cf. Buerger v. N.Y. Life Ins. Co.* (1927) 43 T.L.R. 601.

[97] *Citadel Ins. Co. v. Atlantic Union Ins. Co. SA* [1982] 2 Lloyd's Rep. 543; *Britannia Steamship Ins. Ass. v. Ausonia Ass. SpA* [1984] 2 Lloyd's Rep. 98; *The Stolt Marmaro* [1985] 2 Lloyd's Rep. 428; *E.I. Du Pont de Nemours & Co. v. Agnew* [1987] 2 Lloyd's Rep. 585; *Islamic Arab Ins. Co. v. Saudi Egyptian American Reins. Co.* [1987] 1 Lloyd's Rep. 315; *Overseas Union Ins. Ltd v. Incorporated Gen. Ins. Ltd* [1992] 1 Lloyd's Rep. 439; *DR Ins. Co. v. Central National Ins. Co.* [1996] 1 Lloyd's Rep. 74, 81; *Ass. Gen. SpA v. Ege Sigorta AS* [2002] Lloyd's Rep. I.R. 480.

[98] The inference is that the following contract is governed by the same law as the contract which it follows: *Armadora Occidental SA v. Horace Mann Ins. Co.* [1977] 1 W.L.R. 520, 524 (*per* Kerr J.); 1098, 1102 (*per* Lord Denning M.R.); *Islamic Arab Ins. Co. v. Saudi Egyptian American Reins. Co.* [1987] 1 Lloyd's Rep. 315, 320; *E.I. Du Pont De Nemours & Co. v. Agnew* [1987] 2 Lloyd's Rep. 585, 591.

[99] [1984] A.C. 50.

commercial law of Kuwait could answer few of the issues arising in the "idiosyncratic" field of marine insurance; the only way in which a Kuwaiti court could interpret the policy (which makes much use of expressions whose meaning can only be discovered from the 1906 Act) was by applying English law. Lord Wilberforce reached the same conclusion by a slightly different route, giving weight not only to the use of a form of policy expressed in the English language and requiring interpretation according to English rules and practice but also to the (differing) nationality of the parties and the use of English sterling as the money of account.

(b) *Proper Law: The Statutory Rules*

13–27 Common law principles have been largely superseded by statutory rules for the ascertainment of the proper law of an insurance contract. Different sets of rules apply to different types of contract. The Rome Convention, as implemented by the Contracts (Applicable Law) Act 1990,[1] applies to insurance contracts covering risks situated outside the territories of EEA States; it does not apply to contracts covering risks situated within such States.[2] The latter contracts are governed by rules, arising from European Directives, which are largely set out in the Financial Services and Markets Act 2000 (Law Applicable to Contracts of Insurance) Regulations.[3] The scheme of the rules is explained below; reference should be made to specialist works for further discussion.[4]

13–28 The proper law of a contract of original insurance now depends upon where the risk covered by the contract is situated. Different regulations apply to:

(a) risks situated outside the territory of an EEA State[5];

(b) general (non-life) risks situated within the territory of an EEA State, and

(c) long term (life) risks situated within the territory of an EEA State.

The rules relating to reinsurance require separate consideration. The statutory rules apply, with modifications, to insurance provided by friendly societies.[6]

13–29 Common law principles. The common law principles discussed above remain applicable to contracts entered into prior to the implementation of the statutory rules. They also still apply to arbitration agreements and choice of court agreements, which are excluded from the ambit of the Rome Convention. They are likely to continue to provide guidance on whether a choice of law has been made by the parties, and the identification of the law of the country with which a contract is most closely connected.

---

[1] 1990 c. 36.

[2] Rome Convention, Art. 1(3).

[3] S.I. 2001 No. 2635. The regulations were amended in relation to friendly societies by S.I. 2001 No. 3542.

[4] *e.g.*, *Dicey & Morris on the Conflict of Laws* (13th ed., 2000); Plender, *The European Contracts Convention* (2001).

[5] An EEA State is defined by the Financial Services and Markets Act 2000 as a state which is a contracting party to the agreement on the European Economic Area signed at Oporto on 2 May 1992: Financial Services and Markets Act 2000, Sch. 3, s.8.

[6] S.I. 2001 No. 2635 reg. 3(2), as amended, deals with the application of the regulations to contracts with friendly societies.

13–30 The situation of the risk. The situation of the risk determines which set of statutory rules applies. The Rome Convention stipulates that in order to determine whether a risk is situated in the territory of a Member State the court shall apply its internal law.[7]

13–31 The following rules establish where a risk is situated:

(a) where the insurance relates to buildings, or to buildings and contents in so far as contents are covered by the same policy, the risk is situated in the EEA State in which the property is situated;

(b) where the insurance relates to vehicles of any type, the risk is situated in the EEA State of registration;

(c) where policies with a duration of four months or less cover travel or holiday risks, the risk is situated in the EEA State where the policy holder took out the policy;

(d) in other cases, (i) where the policy holder is an individual, the risk is situated where the policy holder had his habitual residence at the date when the contract was entered into; otherwise, (ii) the risk is situated where the establishment of the policy holder to which the policy relates is situated at that date.[8]

In the majority of cases, comprised within category (d) above, it will be necessary to identify the habitual residence of the policy holder, or the establishment to which the policy relates.[9] The statutory rules offer no guidance on the approach to be adopted if a single risk is situated both within and outside EEA States, or a contract covers multiple risks situated within and outside EEA States.[10]

(i) Risks situated outside Member States

13–32 The Contracts (Applicable Law) Act 1990. The Rome Convention as implemented by the Contracts (Applicable Law) Act 1990[11] applies to risks situated outside EEA States. It deals with contractual obligations in any situation involving a choice between the laws of different countries.[12]

---

[7] Rome Convention, Art. 1(3).

[8] S.I. 2001 No. 2635 reg. 2(2). Although the rules appear to be formulated in terms of identifying in which EEA State a risk is situated, they presumably also determine whether a risk is situated in an EEA State at all.

[9] Neither the Rome Convention nor the regulations in S.I. 2001 No. 2635 define "habitual residence". S.I. 2001 No. 2635 reg. 2(1) defines "establishment" by reference to: a head office; agency; branch or permanent presence. The concept of the establishment to which a policy relates might cause difficulties, for example in the case of a policy covering branches in a number of different countries, or a policy covering international risks, *e.g.* on a vessel engaged in international trade with a registered owner and a manager in different countries.

[10] The point is discussed in *Dicey & Morris on the Conflict of Laws* (13th ed., 2000) vol. 2 at p. 1342. The tentative suggestion is made that the contract is regarded as severable, with the potential for different legal regimes to be applied to different risks. This solution was rejected in *American Motorists Ins. Co. v. Cellstar Corp.* [2002] 2 Lloyd's Rep. I.R. 216, where it was held, *obiter*, that risks should only be treated as situated within a Member State if they are predominantly so situated. (*Cf. CGU International Ins. Co. v. Szabo* [2002] Lloyd's Rep. I.R. 196 at 202 for a similar rejection of severance by reference to different systems of law.) We suggest that Art. 1.3 of the Rome Convention should be construed so as to exclude from the Convention only those risks which are within the scope of the Statutory Instrument, being exclusively in one or more EEA Member States.

[11] 1990 c. 36. References to Articles below are references to Articles of the Rome Convention, as set out in Sch. 1 of the 1990 Act.

[12] Art. 1(1).

Arbitration agreements and agreements on the choice of court are amongst the matters excluded from the Convention.[13] The Convention regime permits wide-ranging freedom of choice of law, and in the absence of choice provides for the application of the law with which the contract is most closely connected. Separate rules apply to consumer contracts. Guidance on the interpretation of the Convention is to be obtained from a report prepared by Professors Giuliano and Lagarde.[14] The Convention came into force on April 1, 1991.[15] Common law principles would apply to contracts made prior to that date.

13–33 Choice of law by the parties. Article 3 of the Convention enshrines the principle of freedom of choice of law. A contract is governed by the law chosen by the parties.[16] The choice must be express or demonstrated with reasonable certainty by the terms of the contract or the circumstances of the case.[17] The use of a standard Lloyd's policy of marine insurance is likely to lead to the inference that English law has been chosen. A similar inference may arise from the use of a clause providing for arbitration in England.[18] The parties are free to amend the proper law at any time.[19] The existence and validity of consent as to the choice of law is governed by Articles 8, 9 and 11 of the Convention.[20] An issue as to the existence of the contract, and as to its material validity, is to be determined by the putative proper law of the contract.[21]

13–34 Mandatory rules. The effect of a choice of proper law is limited in respect of mandatory rules. Article 3(3) of the Convention provides as follows:

> "The fact that the parties have chosen a foreign law, whether or not accompanied by the choice of a foreign tribunal, shall not, where all the other elements relevant to the situation at the time of the choice are connected with one country only, prejudice the application of rules of the law of that country which cannot be derogated from by contract, hereinafter called mandatory rules."

[13] Art. 1(2)(d). Common law conflicts principles apply to such agreements. For the ambit and implications of the exclusion see Plender, *The European Contracts Convention* (2001) pp. 67–74. The exclusion does not prevent arbitration agreements being taken into consideration under Art. 3(1) of the Convention: Giuliano-Lagarde Report, Art. 1 para. 5.

[14] O.J. 1980 C 282/1, reprinted in Plender, *The European Contracts Convention* (2001). Provision is made in s.3(3)(a) of the Contracts (Applicable Law) Act 1990 for courts to have regard to the report.

[15] Contracts (Applicable Law) Act 1990 (Commencement No. 1) Order 1991, S.I. 1991 No. 707.

[16] Art. 3(1).

[17] Art. 3(1).

[18] Giuliano-Lagarde Report, Art. 3, para. 3 which suggests that a choice of law will be recognised where there is a choice of a place for arbitration in circumstances indicating that the arbitrator should apply the law of that place.

[19] Art. 3(2). Whilst the parties may be able to choose different laws to apply to different parts of the contract, they will not be able to conclude a contract with no fixed system of applicable law at the time of contracting: *CGU International Plc v. Szabo* [2002] Lloyd's Rep. I.R. 196.

[20] Art. 3(4).

[21] Art. 8(1). However, an alleged party can rely on the law of his habitual residence to establish that he did not consent to the contract, if it would be unreasonable to decide on the effect of his conduct by resort to the putative proper law: Art. 8(2). It seems that this rule was intended to deal with the inference to be drawn from silence on the part of a party alleged to be bound: Giuliano-Lagarde Report, Art. 8, para. 2.

This provision would be applicable where all elements of the situation at the time of choice linked an insurance contract with country A, but the contract contained a choice of law of country B. It is only applicable where the situation has no international element other than the choice of law. It would therefore not appear to be relevant where the insurer and insured are based in different countries. The intention is that a choice of law should not, in the case of a domestic insurance contract, be used to circumvent the application of the mandatory rules of country A. Uncertainty exists as to whether Article 3(3) means that the mandatory rules must be applied even if (absent the Convention) the law of country A would permit such application to be avoided by the choice of law of country B.[22]

13–35 The effect of a choice of law may also be restricted by the law of the forum.[23] Article 7(2) provides that nothing in the Convention shall restrict the application of the rules of the law of the forum in a situation where they are mandatory irrespective of the law otherwise applicable to the contract. This article will apply to the limited class of English statutes which are regarded as overriding in effect, *i.e.* which apply regardless of the proper law of the contract. It is likely that provisions of the Insurance Companies Acts and of the Financial Services and Markets Act 2000 relating to the need for authorisation, which are intended for the protection of insureds, are of this character.[24] Article 16 provides for a court to refuse to apply a rule of law which is manifestly incompatible with the public policy (*"ordre public"*) of the forum.

13–36 Closest connection. Article 4(1) of the Rome Convention provides that, to the extent that the proper law has not been chosen in accordance with Article 3, the contract shall be governed by the law of the country with which it is most closely connected.[25] A severable part of the contract which has a closer connection with another country may by way of exception be governed by the law of that other country.[26] The concept of closest

---

[22] It is submitted that the preferable approach is that the avoidance of the application of mandatory rules of country A ought to be permitted by a choice of law where such avoidance is otherwise permitted by the law of country A—see Plender, *The European Contracts Convention* (2001) pp. 106–107, and *Dicey & Morris on the Conflict of Laws* (13th ed., 2000) vol. 2 at p. 1242. If the Convention made mandatory rules applicable even where they could otherwise legitimately be circumvented by a choice of law, the result would arguably go beyond the compromise intended by Art. 3(3)—see Giuliano-Lagarde Report, Art. 3, para. 8.

[23] Recourse to mandatory rules of a law with which "the situation has a close connection" is also envisaged by art. 7(1), but this does not have the force of law in the United Kingdom: Contracts (Applicable Law) Act 1990, s.2(2).

[24] *DR Ins. Co. v. Central National Ins. Co.* [1996] 1 Lloyd's Rep. 74, 82—a case which did not concern the Rome Convention.

[25] The Convention refers to the country, rather than the legal system, most closely connected with the contract. The distinction might arise where an insurance contract is sold to an insured by a branch office in the insured's country of residence, establishing close connections with that country, but the most closely connected legal system is arguably that of the country of the insurer's head office (*cf. Rossano v. Manufacturer's Life Ins. Co.* [1963] 2 Q.B. 352). Art. 4(5) of the Convention would in any event enable the Court to take all relevant circumstances into account.

[26] Art. 4(1). However, this does not mean that the system of law could remain unascertained until some event after conclusion of the contract; nor would it be easy to see how a policy providing global coverage could be subject to different systems of law in relation to matters such as the identification of the insured: *CGU International Ins. Plc v. Szabo* [2002] Lloyd's Rep. I.R. 196.

connection is familiar as a matter of English common law. However, the concept is to be applied in a different manner under the Convention, by reference to a rebuttable presumption as to performance.

13–37 Article 4(2) provides for a presumption as to closest connection based on the performance which is characteristic of the contract. It will be presumed that the contract is most closely connected with the country where the party who is to effect the performance which is characteristic of the contract has, at the time of the conclusion of the contract, his habitual residence or, in the case of a body corporate or unincorporate, its central administration. If the contract is one entered into in the course of that party's trade or profession, the relevant country is that in which the principal place of business is situated, or if under the terms of the contract the performance is to be effected through a place of business other than the principal place of business, the relevant country is that in which the other place of business is situated.[27] Thus in *HIB Ltd v. Guardian Insurance Co.*[28] London reinsurance brokers sought a declaration that they were not liable to a client insurance company domiciled in the U.S. Virgin Islands. The jurisdiction of the English courts depended upon whether the law of the broking contract was English law. The brokers' central administration was in London, where they were to perform agency services. London was their principal place of business. It was held that the law of the broking contract was English law, applying Article 4(2) of the Convention.

13–38 Some doubt has been expressed as to whether the concept of characteristic performance is applicable to a contract of insurance.[29] It is submitted that the concept is applicable to insurance, and that the characteristic performance is the provision of cover by the insurer.[30] An insurance contract will inevitably be entered into in the course of the insurer's trade. On this basis, the proper law of an insurance contract will rebuttably be presumed, for the purpose of Article 4(2), to be the law of the country in which the insurer's principal place of business is situated. Alternatively, where the insurer's performance is to be effected through another place of business, the proper law will be presumed to be the law of the country in which the other place of business is situated. Three points should be noted about these presumptions. First the concept of the place through which the insurer's performance is to be effected may give rise to difficulty when contracts are concluded or performed through a branch office or an agent. If authority to underwrite is delegated to the branch or agent, the characteristic performance would appear to be effected through the branch or agent. The same result would not necessarily follow if the branch or agent was no more than a conduit for communication, because it would be questionable whether the characteristic performance (provision of insurance cover) was "effected through" the branch or agent. Secondly, notwithstanding the importance of the broker in international insurance

---

[27] Art. 4(2).

[28] [1997] 1 Lloyd's Rep. 412.

[29] See Merkin, *Insurance Contract Law*, Ch. D.4.2 and *Dicey & Morris on the Conflict of Laws* (13th ed., 2000) vol. 2 at p. 1345.

[30] The Giuliano-Lagarde Report, art. 4, para. 3 refers specifically to provision of insurance. The concept of characteristic performance is derived from Swiss law, which appears to recognise that, in the case of a contract of insurance, the characteristic performance is that of the insurer: Plender, *The European Contracts Convention* (2001) p. 116.

transactions, the location of the place of business of the insured's broker appears to be irrelevant for the purpose of Article 4(2). The insurer's performance in providing cover is probably not effected through a broker acting as an agent of the insured.[31] Thirdly, complex composite insurance contracts involve numerous insurers and agents with places of business in different countries; this could produce the unattractive result of a presumption that a number of different proper laws applied to single risk.

13–39 These difficulties are likely to be more apparent than real. There is a recognition in Article 4 that the presumption as to the place of performance may not be applicable and is rebuttable.[32] If the characteristic performance of a contract cannot be determined, the presumption will not apply. Nor will it apply if it appears from the circumstances as a whole that the contract is more closely connected with another country.[33] The strength of any presumption that the applicable law is the law of the country of the insurer's principal place of business (or that of a branch or an agent) will therefore vary in the circumstances of each case. This enables a flexible approach to be adopted, consistent with common law principles and the trend in complex cases to ascertain the proper law of an insurance contract by reference to its centre of gravity.[34]

13–40 Consumer contracts. A contract the object of which is the supply of services to a consumer for a purpose outside his trade or profession is governed by Article 5 of the Rome Convention. It is intended that this Article should apply to insurance.[35] Two particular rules apply to such contracts. First, the parties are free to make a choice of proper law, in accordance with Article 3, but any such choice does not, in circumstances specified in Article 5(2), deprive the consumer insured of the protection afforded by the mandatory rules of the country in which he has his habitual residence.[36] Secondly, in the absence of an express or implied choice of law, and in the circumstances specified in Article 5(2), the contract is governed by the law of the country of the habitual residence of the consumer insured.[37]

13–41 The circumstances specified in Article 5(2) which are relevant to insurance are:

[31] However, the broker's role would be relevant for the purpose of the inquiry into circumstances as a whole envisaged by art. 4(5). The country where the broker is situated will also be relevant to determining the proper law of the broking contract: *HIB Ltd v. Guardian Ins. Co.* [1997] 1 Lloyd's Rep. 412.
[32] Art. 4(5).
[33] Art. 4(5).
[34] See para. 13–25, *ante*. For an example, in the context of banking, of the use of art. 4(5) to displace a presumption under Art. 4(2), see *Bank of Baroda v. Vysya Bank* [1994] 2 Lloyd's Rep. 87. The distinction between the potential flexibility of the Rome Convention and the more restrictive rules applicable to risks situated in Member States is emphasised in *Credit Lyonnais v. New Hampshire Ins. Co.* [1997] 2 Lloyd's Rep. 1.
[35] Giuliano-Lagarde Report, Art. 5 para. 2. But the rules relating to consumer contracts do not apply if the insurance services are to be supplied exclusively in a country other than that in which the consumer insured has his habitual residence: art. 5(4)(b).
[36] Art. 5(2). The term "habitual residence" is not defined by the Convention.
[37] Art. 5(3).

(a) that in the country of the consumer insured's habitual residence the conclusion of the contract was preceded by a specific invitation addressed to him or by advertising, and that the insured had taken in that country all the steps necessary on his part for the conclusion of the contract, or

(b) that the insurer or the insurer's agent received the insured's order in the country of the insured's habitual residence.[38]

13–42 Scope of applicable law. Article 10 deals with the scope of applicable law. In summary the applicable law identified in accordance with the Convention governs the following matters: (a) interpretation; (b) performance; (c) consequences of breach (within the limits of procedural law); (d) extinguishment of obligations, prescription and limitation, and (e) consequences of nullity of the contract.

13–43 Different parts of United Kingdom. The Rome Convention applies to conflicts between the laws of different parts of the United Kingdom in relation to risks situated outside EEA States.[39]

(ii) *General (Non-life) risks[40] situated within EEA States*

13–44 Source and application of rules. The relevant rules are contained in the Financial Services and Markets Act 2000 (Law Applicable to Contracts of Insurance) Regulations.[41]

13–45 Relationship with Rome Convention. The regulations apply independently of the Rome Convention. However, it may be necessary to refer to the Convention, as implemented by the Contracts (Applicable Law) Act 1990, for the purpose of establishing, in particular, what freedom of choice the parties have under English law; whether mandatory rules are to be applied, and generally for guidance on matters not dealt with in the regulations.[42]

13–46 The regulations apply where risks are situated in the United Kingdom or another EEA State.[43] Different regulations apply to different types of non-life contract. The result is a labyrinthine set of choice of law rules.

13–47 Choice of law. The rules permit freedom to choose proper law, but the extent of that freedom varies between different types of contract. The effect of a choice of law is restricted in circumstances where all elements relevant to the situation at the time of choice are connected with one EEA State only. In this situation, a choice of law does not prejudice the application of mandatory rules of law of that State.[44] Nothing in the rules

---

[38] Art. 5(2).

[39] Contracts (Applicable Law) Act 1990, s.2(3).

[40] These are non-life risks of the types identified in Part 1 of Schedule 1 of the Financial Services and Markets Act 2000 (Regulated Activities) Order 2001, S.I. 2001 No. 544.

[41] S.I. 2001 No. 2635, Part II. The regulations came into force on 1 December 2001, pursuant to S.I. No. 3538, reg. 2 (1).

[42] Reg. 7.

[43] Reg. 4 (1).

[44] Reg. 5(2). Mandatory rules, as defined by reg. 1(1), are rules from which the law of the State allows no derogation by means of contract.

restricts the application of rules of a part of the United Kingdom in a situation where they are mandatory irrespective of the law otherwise applicable to the contract.[45]

13–48 A choice of law must be expressed or demonstrated with reasonable certainty by the terms of the contract or the circumstances of the case.[46] Where a choice is not so expressed or demonstrated, the contract is governed by the law of the country with which it is most closely connected.[47] A severable part of the contract which has a closer connection with another country may by way of exception be governed by the law of that other country.[48]

13–49 Choice of law: large risks. Parties to contracts relating to certain large risks situated in an EEA State are permitted to choose any law as the applicable law.[49]

13–50 Choice of law: risks other than large risks. The rules are more restrictive for contracts in respect of other types of risk. It is necessary to take account of the location of the policy holder's habitual residence or central administration, and the situation of the risk. Three main rules apply, as discussed below.

13–51 (i) *Coincidence of habitual residence and situation of risk.* Where the policy holder has his or her habitual residence (in the case of an individual), or its central administration (in other cases), within the territory of the EEA State where the risk is situated, the law applicable to the contract is the law of that State. However, where the law of that State so allows, the parties may choose the law of another country.[50] Thus, if a policy holder has its central administration in England and the risk is situated in England, the law applicable to the contract will be either English law, or any other law chosen by the parties which is permitted by English conflict of law rules. For the purpose of determining what choice is permitted as a matter of English law, reference is to be made to the Contracts (Applicable Law) Act 1990.[51] The requirement that a choice of law must be validated by reference to the law of the place where the risk is situated marks a significant departure from common law principles. It is to be contrasted with the wide freedom of choice permitted under the Rome Convention.

13–52 (ii) *Habitual residence not in the EEA State where the risk is situated.* If the policy holder does not have his habitual residence, or its

[45] Reg. 5(1).
[46] Reg. 6 (1). It is submitted that this wording covers an implied choice of law.
[47] Reg. 4(8).
[48] *ibid.*
[49] Reg. 4(7). "Large risks" are defined in Art. 5(d) of the first non-life insurance directive, *i.e.* Council Directive 73/239/EEC, as amended by Art. 5 of Directive 88/357/EEC, and Art. 2 of Directive 90/618/EEC. In summary, large risks are risks of the following types: (a) aircraft; (b) ships; (c) goods in transit; (d) aircraft liability and liability for ships; (e) credit and suretyship risks which relate to business carried on by the policy holder, and (f) vehicle, fire, property, motor vehicle liability, general liability or miscellaneous financial loss risks where the policy holder carries on a business which satisfies certain conditions as to balance sheet total, net turnover and number of employees
[50] Reg. 4(2).
[51] Reg. 7(3).

central administration, in the EEA State where the risk is situated, the parties may choose to apply either (a) the law of the EEA State where the risk is situated, or (b) the law of the country in which the policy holder has his habitual residence, or its central administration.[52] However, the parties may choose some other proper law if the law of the State where the risk is situated grants them greater freedom of choice.[53] Thus if a policy holder has its central administration in France and the risk is situated in England, the chosen law can be French law, English law or any other law the choice of which is permitted under English conflict of law rules. If a policy holder carries on a business and the contract covers two or more risks relating to the business which are situated in different EEA States, the freedom of choice as to the law applicable to the contract extends to the laws of those States and of the country in which the policy holder has his habitual residence or its central administration.[54] Where the relevant States grant greater freedom of choice as to proper law, the parties may take advantage of that freedom.[55] It is unclear if the greater freedom of choice must be permitted by the law of all relevant EEA States, or if it is sufficient that such freedom is granted only by the law of one relevant State. In that the intention appears to be to increase flexibility, the parties ought to be permitted to take advantage of a greater freedom of choice of law permitted by the law of any one of the relevant States.[56]

13–53 (iii) *Risks limited to events in an EEA State other than the State where the risk is situated.* Where the risks covered by a contract are limited to events occurring in an EEA State other than the EEA State where the risk is situated, the parties may choose the law of the former State.[57] This rule provides a further option as to proper law in a case where the contract of insurance relates solely to non-domestic activities of the policy-holder, and where the risk would be regarded as situated in the EEA State of the policy holder's habitual residence or central administration. However, it may not be clear from the contract whether risks are limited to events occurring in a particular EEA State.

13–54 Absence of choice of law: country most closely connected. If a choice of law is not expressed or demonstrated with reasonable certainty, the guiding principle is that the contract is governed by the law of the country with which it is most closely connected. It appears that the relevant countries are restricted to those considered above, namely:

(a) EEA States where the risk is situated;
(b) the EEA State or country where the policy holder has his habitual residence or its central administration;
(c) EEA States where the risks covered by the contract are limited to events occurring in that State and which are not the State where the risk is situated.[58]

---

[52] Reg. 4(3).
[53] Reg. 4(5).
[54] Reg. 4(4).
[55] Reg. 4(5).
[56] See *Dicey & Morris on the Conflict of Laws* (13th ed., 2000) Vol. 2 at p. 1359.
[57] S.I. 2001 No. 2635, reg. 4(6).
[58] Reg. 4(8).The drafting is not particularly satisfactory, but the restriction is imposed by the requirement that the contract is to be governed by the law of the country "from amongst those considered in the relevant paragraph" of regulation 4.

This restriction is to be contrasted with the flexibility as to proper law permitted by the Rome Convention and as a matter of common law. The contract is rebuttably presumed to be most closely connected with the EEA State where the risk is situated.[59] The presumption was applied in *Credit Lyonnais v. New Hampshire Insurance Co.*[60] where the establishment of the policyholder was the London branch of the claimant bank. The risk was situated in England. The insurers sought to rebut the presumption in favour of English law, in order to apply French law, under which the claim would have been time-barred. They relied on matters such as the currency of the policy (French francs), and the negotiation and agreement of the contract in France. It was held that these considerations did not rebut the presumption. Factors which might have rebutted the presumption would have been those which linked the subject-matter and performance of the contract with another country.

13–55 Different territorial units. Where an EEA State, including the United Kingdom, includes different territorial units, subject to different laws concerning contractual obligations, each unit is treated as a separate state for the purpose of identifying the proper law.[61]

(iii) *Long-term (Life) risks*[62] *situated within EEA States*

13–56 Source and application of rules. The relevant rules are set out in the Financial Services and Markets Act 2000 (Law Applicable to Contracts of Insurance) Regulations.[63]

13–57 The rules operate independently of the Rome Convention. However, it may be necessary to refer to the Rome Convention, as implemented by the Contracts (Applicable Law) Act 1990, for the purpose of ascertaining what freedom of choice of law the parties have under English law, and for guidance on matters not dealt with in the rules.[64]

13–58 The rules apply (in the case of an individual) if the policy holder is habitually resident in an EEA State, or (in other cases) if the establishment of the policy holder to which the contract relates is situated in an EEA State.[65]

13–59 The law of the EEA State of commitment. The law applicable to the contract is the law of the EEA State of commitment.[66] This means (if the policy holder is an individual) the EEA State where the policy holder has his

---

[59] Reg. 4(9).
[60] [1997] 2 Lloyd's Rep. 1, CA.
[61] S.I. 2001 No. 2635, reg. 2(4).
[62] These are life and similar risks (*e.g.* permanent health) of the types identified in Pt II of Sch. 1 to the Financial Services and Markets Act 2000 (Regulated Activities) Order 2001, S.I. 2001 No. 544.
[63] S.I. 2001 No. 2635, Pt III. The regulations came into force on 1 December 2001, pursuant to S.I. No. 3538, reg. 2 (1).
[64] Reg. 10.
[65] Reg. 8(1).
[66] Reg. 8(2).

habitual residence at the date of entry into the contract, or (if the policy holder is not an individual) the EEA State where the establishment of the policy holder to which the commitment relates is situated at the date of entry into the contract.[67] Nothing in the rules restricts the application of the rules of a part of the United Kingdom in a situation where they are mandatory irrespective of the law otherwise applicable to the contract.[68]

13–60 Choice of another proper law if permitted by the law of the EEA State of commitment. Where the law of the EEA State of commitment allows, the parties may choose the law of another country as the proper law of the contract.[69] Thus if the law of the EEA State of commitment is English, the parties may choose a proper law other than English law where such choice is permitted by English conflict of law rules. Reference is to be made to the Contracts (Applicable Law) Act 1990 for the purpose of ascertaining the relevant English rules.[70]

13–61 Choice of national law of individual policy-holder. Where the policy holder is an individual and has his habitual residence in an EEA State other than that of which he is a national or citizen, the parties may choose the law of the State of which he is a national or citizen.[71]

13–62 Different territorial units. Where an EEA State, including the United Kingdom, includes different territorial units, subject to different laws concerning contractual obligations, each unit is treated as a separate state for the purpose of identifying the proper law.[72]

(iv) *Reinsurance*

13–63 Reinsurance. By contrast with original insurance, there is a single scheme of proper law rules for reinsurance, regardless of the situation of the risk and the nature of the contract. Reinsurance contracts are governed by the Rome Convention, as implemented by the Contracts (Applicable Law) Act 1990.[73] The Convention applies to all reinsurance contracts entered into after April 1, 1991.[74] Common law principles apply to reinsurance contracts entered into on or prior to that date.

[67] Reg. 2(1).
[68] Reg. 9.
[69] Reg. 8(2).
[70] Reg. 10(2).
[71] Reg. 8(3). The concept of linking proper law to nationality may give rise to difficulties, for example in cases of dual nationality. See *Dicey & Morris on the Conflict of Laws* (13th ed., 2000) vol. 2 at p. 1373.
[72] Reg. 2(4).
[73] Rome Convention, art. 1(4). Contracts of reinsurance are expressly excluded from the regulations governing the applicable law of contracts of original insurance covering risks situated in EEA States: S.I. 2001 No. 2635, reg. 3 (1).
[74] Contracts (Applicable Law) Act 1990 (Commencement No. 1) Order, S.I. 1991 No. 707.

13–64 Where the risk covered by the original insurance is situated in an EEA State, the Rome Convention will not apply to the contract of original insurance but will apply to a contract for the reinsurance of the risk. This could give rise to a difference between the proper laws of the contracts of original insurance and reinsurance, and to inconsistency between the two contracts. One solution to such inconsistency would be to construe terms in the two contracts so as to have the same legal effect; an alternative solution would be to treat particular terms as governed by the same proper law.[75]

13–65 The effect of the Rome Convention has been described above.[76] In summary, the parties to a reinsurance contract have considerable freedom as to choice of proper law, in accordance with the provisions of Article 3 of the Convention. If no choice of law has been made, Article 4 provides that the reinsurance contract will be governed by the law of the country with which it is most closely connected. It is probable that, for the purposes of Article 4(2), the performance which is characteristic of a contract of reinsurance is the provision of reinsurance cover by the reinsurer. This gives rise to a rebuttable presumption that the proper law is the law of country in which the reinsurer's principal place of business is situated. Alternatively, where the reinsurer's performance is to be effected through another place of business, the proper law would rebuttably be presumed to be that of the country in which the other place of business is situated. However, it is clear from Article 4(5) of the Convention that the presumption is to be disregarded if it appears from the circumstances as a whole that the contract is more closely connected with another country. It is therefore likely that it will continue to be relevant to identify the centre of gravity of a reinsurance contract, as part of the process of identifying its proper law.[77]

3. OTHER RELATED MATTERS

13–66 Plurality of proper laws. In the usual case, a contract is governed by a single proper law. It is possible for there to be two or even more proper laws, different issues or aspects of the contract being governed by different laws. This possibility is recognised in Article 3(1) of the Rome Convention, which provides that parties can select the law applicable to the whole or a part only of the contract.[78] A clearly expressed decision by the parties to this effect will be recognised, but in other circumstances English authorities

---

[75] cf. *Forsikrings. Vesta v. Butcher* [1989] A.C. 852 a case which did not involve the Rome Convention, and in which the House of Lords adopted the first solution. The second solution could derive support from art. 3(1) of the Rome Convention, which envisages that different proper laws may apply to different parts of the contract.

[76] See para. 13–32.

[77] See para. 13–25. In *Gan Ins. Co. Ltd v. Tai Ping Ins. Co. Ltd* [1999] Lloyd's Rep I.R. 472, it was necessary to determine the proper law of reinsurance contracts placed in London on the London market. In one case all reinsurers had their principal place of business in London; in another the majority were so established. It was held that there was an implied choice of English law under art. 3(1) of the Rome Convention, or that the presumption of English law under art. 4(2) could be applied. A reference to terms "as original" did not import into the reinsurance a choice of law clause from the underlying insurance.

[78] The Giuliano-Lagarde Report, art. 3, para. 4 explains that there was a difference of expert view on the point, and suggests that severability has to be shown to be logically consistent, *i.e.* it must relate to distinct elements of the contract.

suggest that the courts will only treat the contract as having been split in this way if there are compelling reasons to do so.[79] If the parties' selection of a particular law is expressed to be for a particular, limited purpose (such as the resolution of disputes arising out of a specified clause in the policy), this may suggest that the same law governs the contract as a whole,[80] but there is no necessary presumption to this effect.[81] In the absence of any choice of law by the parties the courts are likely to treat closely related contracts as prima facie governed by the same proper law, subject to any constraints imposed by the statutory rules discussed above. If an insurance contract is governed by the law of one country, a reinsurance contract based on the same terms and conditions may be construed to give the same coverage, notwithstanding the difference between the proper laws of the contracts.[82] Where a reinsurance contract relates to a whole series of underlying policies, themselves governed by a variety of laws, this approach will not be appropriate, and more weight will be given to the centre of gravity of the transaction.[83]

13–67 Rights of third parties. Where the obligation of the insurer to meet the claim is not in doubt but the problem concerns the right of a third party to receive payment in place of the insured, the proper law of the insurance contract is not necessarily relevant. If the third party claims by virtue of a transaction or principle of succession extrinsic to the contract, it is necessary to ascertain the law governing that transaction or principle. Thus there are distinct rules of the conflict of laws governing bankruptcy, and testate and intestate succession. In the case of assignment, the assignment agreement will have its own proper law.[84] Article 12 of the Rome Convention[85] contains two rules relating to assignments. First, the mutual obligations of assignor and assignee under a voluntary assignment of a right against another person are governed by the law which, under the Convention, applies to the contract between the assignor and the assignee.[86] Therefore, where an insured enters into a contract of assignment of rights under a contract of insurance, questions as to the validity of the assignment and the obligations of assignor and assignee are governed by the proper law of the assignment.[87] Secondly, the law governing the right to which the assignment relates determines its assignability, the relationship between the assignee and the debtor, the conditions under which the assignment can be invoked against the debtor and any question whether the debtor's obligations have been discharged.[88] Thus, if a contract of insurance is governed by English law and a contract of

---

[79] *Kahler v. Midland Bank* [1950] A.C. 24, 42.

[80] See, *e.g. Jones v. Oceanic Steam Navigation Co. Ltd* [1924] 2 K.B. 730.

[81] For contracts to which the Rome Convention applies, the Giuliano-Lagarde Report, art. 3, para. 4 points out that the Convention does not adopt the idea that a partial choice of law gives rise to a presumption that the law so chosen will govern a contract in its entirety. Recourse should be had to art. 4 of the Convention in the case of a partial choice of law.

[82] *Forsikrings. Vesta v. Butcher* [1989] A.C. 852.

[83] *Citadel Ins. Co. v. Atlantic Union Ins. Co. SA* [1982] 2 Lloyd's Rep. 543, CA.

[84] See *Dicey and Morris on the Conflict of Laws* (13th ed., 2000) Vol. 2 at p. 981.

[85] As implemented by the Contracts (Applicable Law) Act 1990, Sch. 1.

[86] Art. 12(1).

[87] The same result would be reached as a matter of common law: *Lee v. Abdy* (1886) 17 Q.B.D. 309. See also *Republica de Guatemala v. Nunez* (1926) 95 L.J.K.B. 955; [1927] 1 K.B. 669.

[88] Art. 12(2); *Raiffeisen Zentralbank Osterreich AB v. Five Star General Trading* [2001] Lloyd's Rep.I.R. 460.

assignment is governed by Panamanian law, questions as to whether rights under the contract of insurance are capable of being assigned and as to the effect of the assignment on the insurer's obligations will be determined by English law, since it governs the rights arising from the insurance contract.[89] Where the Rome Convention is not applicable, the same principles apply as a matter of common law. The question of the priority of successive assignees of rights created under a contract of insurance is to be determined by reference to the proper law of the insurance contract.[90]

13–68 Article 13 of the Rome Convention,[91] under the heading subrogation, provides that where a person ("the creditor") has a contractual claim upon another ("the debtor"), and a third person has a duty to satisfy the creditor, or has in fact satisfied the creditor in discharge of that duty, the law which governs the third person's duty to satisfy the creditor shall determine whether the third person is entitled to exercise against the debtor the rights which the creditor had against the debtor under the law governing their relationship and, if so, whether he may do so in full or only to a limited extent. It has been emphasised[92] that this rule only applies to the transfer of rights which are contractual in nature. It does not to apply to subrogation by operation of law when the debt to be paid has its origin in tort.[93] Therefore Article 13 is not applicable where an insurer succeeds by operation of law to the rights of the insured against a tortfeasor.[94]

13–69 Difficulty is presented by situations in which a third party obtains a right to claim directly against an insurer under some special statutory provision, such as the Third Parties (Rights against Insurers) Act 1930. There is no conclusive English authority on the proper choice of law rules applicable in such cases, although the complex issues have received some examination in Australia and the United States and by the Law Commission. The balance of Australian authority appears to treat the proper law of the insurance contract as governing the availability of direct action by the third party.[95]

13–70 Law of the place of performance. While the material validity of a

---

[89] The same result would be reached as a matter of common law. See *Re Fry* [1946] Ch. 312; *N.W. Mutual Life v. Adams*, 155 Wis. 335, 144 N.W. 1108 (1914); *Campbell Connelly & Co. v. Noble* [1963] 1 W.L.R. 252; *Baytur v. Finagro* [1992] 1 Lloyd's Rep. 134, 141–142, not contested on appeal [1992] 1 Q.B. 610.

[90] *Le Feuvre v. Sullivan* (1885) 10 Moore P.C. 1; *Kelly v. Selwyn* [1905] 2 Ch. 117, 122; *Republica de Guatemala v. Nunez* (1926) 95 L.J.K.B. 955; [1927] 1 K.B. 669.

[91] Implemented by the Contracts (Applicable Law) Act 1990, Sch. 1.

[92] Giuliano-Lagarde Report, art. 13, para. 1.

[93] See para. 13–72 on tort-related conflict rules.

[94] Giuliano-Lagarde Report, art. 13, para. 1. It is not clear from the commentary if article 13 is applicable to subrogation by operation of law to the contractual rights of an insured.

[95] See *Dicey & Morris on the Conflict of Laws* (13th ed., 2000) vol. 2 at pp. 1525–1527, and Kaye, *Civil Jurisdiction and Enforcement of Foreign Judgments* (1987) p. 809. The point is touched on inconclusively in *Irish Shipping Ltd v. Commercial Union Ass. Co.* [1991] 2 Q.B. 206. In cases relating to the Third Parties (Rights Against Insurers) Act 1930 the application of the proper law of the insurance contract is consistent with the suggestion that the Act achieves a form of statutory assignment of rights under the contract: *Post Office v. Norwich Union Fire Ins. Soc. Ltd* [1967] 2 Q.B. 363, 367 (*per* Harman L.J.). But it might be more satisfactory to treat the Act as applicable in any English bankruptcy or winding up regardless of the proper law of the insurance policy—see "Insolvency at Sea" by Sir Jonathan Mance in [1995] L.M.C.L.Q. 34. This broadly reflects the view favoured by the Law Commission: Law Com. 272, July 2001, Part 8.

contract is governed by its proper law, the law of the place of performance has been regarded as relevant to the question whether an English court will enforce a contract, irrespective of its proper law. Where a contract requires an act to be done in a foreign country, it has been held, in the absence of very special circumstances, to be an implied term of the continuing validity of such a provision that the act to be done in the foreign country shall not be illegal by the law of that country.[96] On this basis, where the payment of a particular sum of money, for example premiums or insurance proceeds, would necessarily be illegal by the place of payment, the English courts would not compel payment even if the proper law of the contract were English. It is not clear whether this rule has survived the enactment of the Contracts (Applicable Law) Act 1990.[97] The law of the place of performance is also relevant in that it may affect the incidents or mode of performance, that is, performance as contrasted with obligation. So, where the proper law of a contract was that of New Zealand, an obligation to pay in the State of Victoria a sum of money expressed in pounds was interpreted as meaning pounds in Victorian currency.[98]

13–71 Proof of foreign law. Where the proper law of the contract is that of a foreign country, an English court must have evidence as to the content and effect of the foreign law from experts in that law.[99] So far as construction of the policy is concerned, evidence is admissible to prove rules of construction or other legal principles of the foreign law in question, but it is inadmissible as to the actual meaning of the policy after those rules and principles have been applied[1]: the experts on the foreign law are not to tell the court what it means. So far as the meaning of a foreign statute or regulation is concerned, the court will in the main be guided by experts in the foreign law in question, but, when experts differ as to the meaning, by reading it.[2] Where the correctness of a foreign court's decision is genuinely in doubt, an English court should be prepared to form its own view of the foreign authority cited

---

[96] *Ralli Brothers v. Compania Naviera Sota y Aznar* [1920] 2 K.B. 287, 304, *per* Scrutton L.J.; *Foster v. Driscoll* [1929] 1 K.B. 470 (no enforcement if contract has as its purpose the breaching of laws of another country); *Regazzoni v. K.C. Sethia (1944) Ltd* [1958] A.C. 301 (no enforcement of contract with purpose of breaching laws even if capable of being performed otherwise); *Euro Diam v. Bathurst* [1990] 1 Q.B. 1 (enforcement of insurance did not breach *Ralli* principle). Conversely, the fact that an English law contract would be tainted by illegality under some other law (*e.g.* foreign regulatory provisions) does not prevent it being enforced in England pursuant to its proper law, if that does not involve performance of acts in the foreign country of acts in breach of that country's law, and does not offend against comity: *Soc. of Lloyd's v. Fraser* [1999] Lloyd's Rep. I.R. 156, 172.

[97] See *Dicey & Morris on the Conflict of Laws* (13th ed., 2000) vol. 2, p. 1248, and Reynolds (1992) 109 L.Q.R. 553.

[98] *Mount Albert Borough Council v. Australasian, etc., Society* [1938] A.C. 224, 241.

[99] To a limited extent the court may take judicial notice of a foreign law: Civil Evidence Act 1972, s.4(2). On the approach of an appellate court to disputed issues of foreign law, see *Grupo Torras SA v. Sheikh Fahad Mohammed Al-Sabah* [1996] 1 Lloyd's Rep. 7, 18.

[1] *Rouyer Guillet et Cie v. Rouyer Guillet & Co. Ltd* [1949] 1 All E.R. 244 CA. Foreign law is a matter of fact which must be proved by expert evidence: *Nelson v. Bridport* (1845) 8 Beav. 527, 542; *Castique v. Imrie* (1870) L.R. 4 H.L. 414; *Buerger v. New York Life Ass. Co.* (1927) 96 L.J.K.B. 930 CA. A finding as to foreign law does not give rise to an appealable point of English law under s.69 of the Arbitration Act 1996: *Egmatra v. Marco* [1999] 1 Lloyd's Rep. 862.

[2] *Concha v. Murietta* (1889) 40 Ch.D. 543, CA (Civil Code of Peru); *Buerger v. New York Life Ass. Co.* (1927) 96 L.J.K.B. 930 CA (Tsarist Russian law as modified by Soviet decrees; doubts expressed by Scrutton L.J.); *Rouyer Guillet et Cie v. Rouyer Guillet & Co. Ltd* [1949] 1 All E.R. 244 (French civil law); *Bankers and Shippers Ins. Co. of New York v. Liverpool Marine and General Ins. Co. Ltd* (1926) 24 Ll.L.R. 85, especially at 93 HL (New York Arbitration Act).

to it, again relying for assistance on foreign law experts.[3] In the absence of satisfactory evidence of foreign law, it will be presumed to be the same as English law.[4] This is a rule of evidence and procedure which appears to be unaffected by the Rome Convention.[5] Therefore if the parties do not rely upon and prove any foreign law, the court will apply English law to the issues before it.

13–72 Tort claims. Different conflict rules apply to tort claims such as a claim for damages for deceit brought against a broker or intermediary. Detailed discussion of them is beyond the scope of this work.[6] Briefly, at common law the rule was that an act performed in a foreign country would be actionable as a tort in England only if it was both actionable as a matter of English law and actionable as a matter of the law of the country where the act was performed.[7] The rule became subject to exceptions.[8] Statute has intervened, in the form of Part III of the Private International Law (Miscellaneous Provisions) Act 1995.[9] It abolishes the rule of double actionability,[10] and introduces a concept of the applicable law of the tort.[11] The general rule is that the applicable law is the law of the country in which the events constituting the tort or delict in question occur.[12] Provision is made for situations where elements of the tort occur in different countries.[13] The general rule is displaced where it appears from all the circumstances that it is substantially more appropriate for the law of another country to apply.[14]

---

[3] *Guaranty Trust Co. of New York v. Hannay & Co.* [1918] 2 K.B. 623, 638–639, CA; *Rouyer et Cie v. Royer Guillet & Co. Ltd* [1949] 1 All E.R. 244, CA; *Glencore International A.G. v. Metro Trading International Inc.* [2001] 1 Lloyd's Rep. 284.

[4] *Gold v. Life Ass. Co. of Pennsylvania* [1971] 2 Lloyd's Rep. 164, 167 ("perhaps the most presumptious presumption of English law" *per* Donaldson J.); *Bumper Development Corp. v. Commissioner of Police of the Metropolis* [1991] 1 W.L.R. 1362; *El Ajou v. Dollar Land Holdings* [1993] 3 All E.R. 717, 736, reversed on a different point: [1994] 2 All E.R. 687.

[5] Rome Convention, Art. 2(h).

[6] See *Dicey & Morris on the Conflict of Laws* (13th ed., 2000) Ch. 35.

[7] *ibid.*, pp. 1488ff.

[8] *Red Sea Ins. Co. Ltd v. Bouygues SA* [1995] 1 A.C. 190, PC.

[9] 1995 c. 42. Part III came into force on May 1, 1996, pursuant to S.I. 1996 No. 995.

[10] s.10.

[11] s.9.

[12] s.11(1).

[13] s.11(2).

[14] s.12.

CHAPTER 14

ILLEGALITY

14–1 Introduction. This chapter is concerned with four inter-related aspects of illegality:

(1) the rules by which parties to insurance contracts may be precluded from enforcing rights conferred by them;
(2) the position of the assured when loss is caused by his own unlawful act;
(3) the ability of third parties to recover when a loss is caused by the unlawful conduct of the assured, and
(4) the effect of war and dealings with enemy aliens.

1. CLAIMS TAINTED BY ILLEGALITY

14–2 General principles. The courts will not permit a person to enforce his rights under a contract of any kind if it is tainted by illegality.[1] This principle of public policy is expressed in the familiar Latin maxim *ex turpi causa non oritur actio*. Although this maxim is lacking in precise legal definition,[2] it is reflected in two rules affecting the enforceability of rights under contracts of insurance. First, a claim is unenforceable when the grant of relief to the plaintiff would enable him to benefit from his criminal conduct.[3] Secondly, a claim is unenforceable when the plaintiff either has to found his claim on an illegal contract or to plead its illegality in order to support his claim.[4] Once a court has determined that one or other rule applies to the facts of a given case, it has no discretion whether or not to apply the rule depending upon the degree to which the plaintiff has affronted the public conscience.[5]

---

[1] *Tinsley v. Milligan* [1994] 1 A.C. 340, 354 and 363, *per* Lord Goff, citing *Holman v. Johnson* (1775) 1 Cowp. 341, 343.
[2] *Beresford v. Royal Ins. Co.* [1937] 2 K.B. 197, 219–220.
[3] *Cleaver v. Mutual Reserve Fund Life Assoc.* [1892] 1 Q.B. 147; *Beresford v. Royal Ins. Co.* [1938] A.C. 586; *Hardy v. Motor Insurers' Bureau* [1964] 2 Q.B. 745, 760, 762, 769; *Geismar v. Sun Alliance & London Ins. Ltd* [1978] 1 Q.B. 383; *Euro-Diam Ltd v. Bathurst* [1990] 1 Q.B. 1 at p. 19, *per* Staughton J. and 35, *per* Kerr L.J. It is submitted that this established category of *ex turpis causa* has survived the decision in *Tinsley v. Milligan* [1994] 1 A.C. 340. The "public conscience" test, to which Staughton L.J. referred in *Group Josi Re. v. Wallbrook Ins. Co.* [1996] 1 W.L.R. 1152, 1164, related to the court's supposed discretion whether or not to give effect to a defence of illegality depending upon whether the public conscience was affronted.
[4] *Bowmakers Ltd v. Barnet Instruments Ltd* [1945] K.B. 65; *Euro-Diam Ltd v. Bathurst* [1990] 1 Q.B. 1, at pp. 18 and 35; *Tinsley v. Milligan* [1994] 1 A.C. 340, at pp. 366 and 369.
[5] *Tinsley v. Milligan* [1994] 1 A.C. 340.

14–3 Illegal contracts. The contract sued upon may be illegal in its inception or in its performance. It is illegal in inception when it is made to achieve or further an objective which is unlawful[6] or contrary to public policy,[7] or when the contract is one prohibited by law. Examples of prohibited contracts are a contract of insurance granted by an insurer lacking statutory authorisation,[8] and a contract of life insurance made without the insurable interest in the life assured which is required by the Life Assurance Act 1774.[9] The contract is illegal as performed if:

(a) the purpose of the contract is lawful but it has been performed in an unlawful manner by the plaintiff, or by the defendant with the knowledge and consent of the plaintiff,[10] or

(b) the action is brought by a plaintiff who intended from the outset to perform the contract in an unlawful manner, or knew that the other party to it intended to do so.[11]

14–4 Transfers of property. Property transferred pursuant to an illegal contract vests in the transferee and is not in general recoverable by the transferor, but there are special exceptions to this rule apart from when the transferor does not need to plead the illegality of the contract.[12] As regards insurance, this is relevant principally to claims for return of premium paid under an illegal contract, a topic dealt with separately in Chapter 8.

14–5 Contract illegal from its inception. A contract of insurance is illegal if it constitutes a contract to commit an illegal act or to reward someone for doing so, as if, for instance, the insurers undertook to indemnify the assured against the consequences of crimes which they knew he intended to commit,[13] or to indemnify him against liability for fraud or deceit or any other tort which the assured chose intentionally to commit.[14] A policy of insurance upon such terms would be no more than a contract to indemnify someone for knowingly committing a crime or civil wrong. Similarly, an insurance upon the property of an enemy national in time of war would be illegal from the outset,[15] since as a matter of public policy a contract

---

[6] *St John Shipping Corporation v. Joseph Rank Ltd* [1957] 1 Q.B. 267, 283. Examples are collected in Treitel, *Law of Contract* (10th ed., 1999), p. 395.

[7] *Fender v. St John Mildmay* [1938] A.C. 1

[8] Under the Insurance Companies Act 1982, s.2 see paras. 14–07 to 14–10, *post*, or under the Financial Services and Markets Act 2000, s.19—see para.14–10A, *post*.

[9] s.1—see paras 1–22 to 1–31, *ante*. By contrast, a reinsurance contract which permits the insured to determine the meaning and application of the phrases "each and every loss" and "one event" in an excess of loss cover is neither illegal nor against public policy as an ouster of jurisdiction of the court. The situation might well be different if one of the parties was empowered to decide a fundamental question of law, such as the contractual liability of the insurer: *Brown v. GIO Ins. Ltd* [1998] Lloyd's Rep. I.R. 201, 208.

[10] *St John Shipping Corporation v. Joseph Rank Ltd* [1957] 1 Q.B. 267, 283; *Archbold v. Spanglett* [1961] 1 Q.B. 374; *Shaw v. Groom* [1970] 2 Q.B. 504; *Smith v. Mawhood* (1845) 14 M. & W. 452, 463; *Ashmore, Benson, Pease & Co. Ltd v. A. v. Dawson Ltd* [1973] 1 W.L.R. 828.

[11] *Archbold v. Spanglett* [1961] 1 Q.B. 374, 384; *Pearce v. Brooks* (1866) L.R. 1 Ex. 213.

[12] See para. 14–02, *ante*.

[13] *Hardy v. Motor Insurers' Bureau* [1964] 2 Q.B. 745, 760; *Burrows v. Rhodes* [1899] 1 Q.B. 816, 828.

[14] *Brown Jenkinson & Co. v. Percy Dalton* [1957] 2 Q.B. 621; *Shackell v. Rosier* (1836) 2 Bing.N.C. 634.

[15] *Kellner v. Le Mesurier* (1803) 4 East 396; *Gamba v. Le Mesurier* (1803) 4 East 407; *Brandon v. Curling* (1803) 4 East 410.

involving commercial intercourse with an enemy is illegal as tending to assist the enemy.[16]

14–6 Contracts have been declared illegal at common law because their tendency is to lead to the commission of crimes or other conduct of which the law disapproves on grounds of public policy.[17] A strict application of this rule to insurance contracts would result in certain types of policies being held illegal, and, for example, it was at one time held that seamen could not validly insure their wages, because this might make them less diligent in bringing their ship home to port.[18] It is clear, however, that insurances are not illegal or void simply because they may lead to the commission of crimes or immoral acts in the sense of providing a motive for such conduct.[19] Thus if A insures his life in B's favour, B in theory has a motive for plotting A's death, but the contract of life insurance will not be vitiated unless B in fact succumbs to such temptation.[20] The explanation of this policy in regard to insurance is probably not so much that insurance is an exception to any general rule, but that a class of contracts will not be held to have a harmful tendency unless it can fairly be said that such contracts generally conduce towards the commission of acts which are either unlawful or contrary to public policy, in some more direct way than the mere creation of a possible motive.[21]

14–7 Insurer acting without authorisation. An insurer carrying on insurance business in the United Kingdom required authorisation pursuant to section 2 of the Insurance Companies Act 1982.[22] Authorisation is now required under the Financial Services and Markets Act 2000.[23] The question whether business is being carried on in the United Kingdom is determined by reference to the insurer's business as a whole; the insurer may be carrying on business within the jurisdiction by virtue of the activities of a broker conducting tasks such as claims handling on behalf of the insurer.[24] One important question is as to the effect on its contracts of an insurer acting without authorisation. The position under the 1982 Act was the subject of

---

[16] *Ertel Bieber v. Rio Tinto Co.* [1918] A.C. 260, 273. See the fourth section of this chapter.

[17] *e.g.* a promise made by a married man to marry another woman after his wife dies is unenforceable on this ground, *Spiers v. Hunt* [1908] 1 K.B. 720; *Wilson v. Carnley* [1908] 1 K.B. 720.

[18] *Fender v. St John Mildmay* [1938] A.C. 1, 13.

[19] *Beresford v. Royal Ins. Co.* [1938] A.C. 586; *Re Michelham's Will Trusts* [1964] 1 Ch. 550.

[20] *Wainwright v. Bland* (1835) 1 Moo. & R. 481, 486. In *Re Chantiam and Packall Packaging Inc.* (1998) 38 O.R. (3d) 401, an employer insured the life of its manager under a "keyman" policy. He later resigned from his post and set up a competitor company. He applied to court for cancellation of the policy, contending that it was against public policy to permit speculation on the life of a competitor. The Ontario Court of Appeal declined the application, noting that the Insurance Act 1990 of Ontario impliedly supported the continuation of the policy after the relationship of employer-employee had ceased.

[21] *Fender v. St John Mildmay* [1938] A.C. 1, 13. Any temptation on the part of the assured to destroy insured property in order to collect the property moneys is effectively removed by the rule that the assured cannot recover for a loss deliberately caused by his own act—see para. 30, *post.*

[22] As to this, see also Ch. 34 on Insurance Companies and Ch. 33 on Reinsurance, *post.*

[23] See para. 14–10A, *post.*

[24] *Secretary of State for Trade and Industry v. Great Western Ins. Co. SA* [1997] 2 B.C.L.C. 685. Failure to obtain authorisation can lead to winding up of the insurer, or criminal sanctions. Criminal liability can arise even if no contract of insurance is in fact concluded: *R. v. Wilson* [1997] 1 All E.R. 119.

conflicting decisions at first instance,[25] although the conflict was subsequently resolved so far as the common law was concerned by the Court of Appeal.[26] The matter was then put on a statutory footing by section 132 of the Financial Services Act 1986.[27] Section 132(1) of the 1986 Act renders an insurance contract entered into by an unauthorised insurer, which does not fall within the definition of insurance contracts which are investment agreements,[28] unenforceable by the insurer. However, the assured can elect to enforce the contract since section 132(6) provides that a contravention of section 2 of the 1982 Act "shall not make a contract of insurance illegal or invalid to any greater extent than is provided in this section".[29] Alternatively, the assured may in effect, by virtue of section 132(1), elect to treat the contract as invalid and may recover any money or other property[30] paid or transferred by him under the contract.[31]

14-8 However, the court can give relief from the consequences of section 132(1)[32] if it is satisfied (a) that the insurer reasonably believed that his entering into the contract did not constitute a contravention of section 2 of the 1982 Act, and (b) that it is just and equitable for the contract to be enforced or, as the case may be, for the money or property paid or transferred under it to be retained.

14-9 By section 132(4), where an assured elects not to perform[33] a contract unenforceable against him under the section or recovers money paid or property transferred under a contract, he is not entitled to any

[25] *Bedford Ins. Co. Ltd v. Instituto de Resseguros do Brasil* [1984] 1 Lloyd's Rep. 210; *Stewart v. Oriental Fire and Marine Ins. Co. Ltd* [1984] 2 Lloyd's Rep. 109; *Phoenix General Ins. Co. Greece SA v. Halvanon Ins. Ltd* [1985] 2 Lloyd's Rep. 599.

[26] *Phoenix General Ins. Co. of Greece SA v. Administratia Asiguraliror de Stat* [1986] 2 Lloyd's Rep. 552. Followed in *Re Cavalier Ins. Co. Ltd* [1989] 2 Lloyd's Rep. 430.

[27] The view expressed in previous editions of this book, relying on *Joseph v. Law Integrity Ins. Co. Ltd* [1912] 2 Ch. 581 (a decision on s.2 of the Assurance Companies Act 1909, a forerunner of the present statute), was that all policies issued by an unauthorised insurer were illegal and void. This view was supported by the *Bedford* case, *supra*, and by the Court of Appeal in the *Phoenix* case, *supra*. In contrast, in both the *Stewart* case and the *Phoenix* case at first instance, it was held that an innocent assured (or reassured) could enforce his contract against his unauthorised insurer (or reinsurer). However, a contract of reinsurance entered into by an insurer to reinsure risks which it was not authorised to insure was unenforceable: see the *Bedford* and *Phoenix* cases, *supra* (contra, the *Stewart* case). *Joseph v. Law Integrity*, *supra* concerned a successful action brought by a shareholder to restrain the company from acting *ultra vires* and is clearly still good authority on this point. In any given case, the effect of a statutory or similar prohibition is a matter of construction. Thus in *P & B Ltd v. Wooley* [2002] Lloyd's Rep. I.R. 344, it was held that a failure to comply with a Lloyd's Bye-law regulating agreements between members and managing agents did not render void the contract conferring authority on the agent.

[28] These are most "long-term insurance contracts", *i.e.* life insurance contracts, excluding principally pure life and accident and sickness insurance where benefits are payable only on death or disability and term policies of 10 years or less; see Sch 1 to the 1986 Act. "Investment insurance" is subject to the general provisions of the Act and unauthorised contracts of this sort are governed by s.5, the terms of which are similar to those of s.132.

[29] It seems to follow from this provision that an insurer can rely on any defences to a claim by the assured, *e.g.* non-disclosure or breach of warranty or condition, and can pursue subrogation rights following payment of a claim, since these are hardly matters of "enforcement" which are what s.132(1) strikes down; *cf. McCall v. Brooks* [1984] R.T.R. 99.

[30] Where property has passed to a third party, a reference to property in the section is a reference to its value at the time of its transfer under the contract of insurance: s.132(5).

[31] Together with compensation for any loss sustained by him as a result of having parted with it: s.132(2).

[32] s.132(3).

[33] *Quaere* whether "performance" can refer to anything other than payment of a premium.

benefits under the contract and must repay any money and return any other property received by him under the contract. A contravention of section 2 of the 1982 Act in respect of a contract of insurance does not affect the validity of any reinsurance contract entered into in respect of that contract.[34]

14–10 Section 132 entered into force on 12 January 1987. There were conflicting first instance decisions as to whether it applied retrospectively to contracts entered into before that date.[35] The Court of Appeal has held that section 132 enables contracts to be enforced which were made before the section came into force, including contracts which are illegal under the Insurance Companies Act 1974.[36]

14–10A The Financial Services and Markets Act 2000. The relevant provisions of the Act apply to agreements made after section 26 came into force.[37] If such agreements are made in the course of carrying out a regulated activity without any authorisation, contrary to the general prohibition in section 19 of the Act, they are unenforceable (absent court order) by the unauthorised insurer against the insured.[38] It appears that the insured can enforce the contract; alternatively, the insured can recover premium paid or compensation for any relevant loss suffered as a result of such payment.[39] The court has power to permit the insurer to enforce the contract, or to retain premium, if satisfied that it is just and equitable to do so.[40] The court must have regard to whether the insurer reasonably believed that he was not contravening the general prohibition.[41] If the insured elects not to perform, or recovers premium paid, any sums received by the insured under the insurance must be returned.[42] The foregoing applies where the insurer lacks any authorisation under the Act. If an authorised insurer carries on a class of business otherwise than in accordance with authorisation granted under the Act, transactions entered into as a result of the unauthorised activity are enforceable.[43] If an agreement is made by an authorised insurer through a third party carrying out a regulated activity without authorisation, the agreement will be unenforceable by the insurer against the insured.[44]

14–11 Other statutory provisions. A contract of insurance is not vitiated by reason of the fact that in relation to a policy there has been a contravention of the Trade Descriptions Act 1968,[45] or of the provisions of the Insurance Companies Act 1982 or of the rules made under the Financial

---

[34] s.132(6).

[35] In *D.R. Ins. Co. v. Seguros America Banamex* [1993] 1 Lloyd's Rep. 120 it was held that the section did not apply retrospectively. The opposite conclusion was reached in *Bates v. Barrow* [1995] 1 Lloyd's Rep. 680, applying the reasoning of the House of Lords in *The Boucraa* [1994] 1 A.C. 486 as to the presumption against retrospectivity.

[36] *Group Josi Re v. Walbrook Ins. Co. Ltd.* [1996] 1 W.L.R. 1152.

[37] s.26 came into force on 1 December 2001, together with (*inter alia*) s.19 which contains a general prohibition of unauthorised regulated activity, as a result of the Financial Services and Markets Act 2000 (Commencement No. 7) Order (S.I. 2001/3538). The regulatory regime is discussed in further detail at para. 34–16 *post*.

[38] FSMA 2000, s.26(1).

[39] *ibid.* s.26(2).

[40] *ibid.* s.28(3).

[41] *ibid.* s.28(5).

[42] *ibid.* s.28(7).

[43] *ibid.* s.20(2)(b).

[44] *ibid.* s.27(1).

[45] s.35 of that Act makes express provision only for the case of contracts for the supply of goods, but it is submitted that the position is the same in respect of other contracts.

Services Act 1986 relating to statutory notices.[46] The Acts of 1982 and 1986 contained no provision concerning the validity or otherwise of policies in connection with which there has been a contravention of their provisions about advertising non-investment insurance contracts,[47] misleading state-ments[48] or disclosure of information concerning agents.[49] These provisions, however, dealt with matters prior to the contract and not with its actual conclusion. It seems arguable that unless a contravention involves a misrepresentation capable of vitiating the contract at common law, it is not relevant to the validity of the contract. In contrast, in respect of one matter prior to the contract, detailed provision was made[50] in respect of contracts entered into following a breach of the section. This was in respect of the promotion of insurance contracts which amount to investment agreements under the 1986 Act[51] other than by, *inter alia*, authorised insurers.[52] Under section 30 of the Financial Services and Markets Act 2000, an agreement is unenforceable if made in consequence of a contravention of restrictions on financial promotion in section 21 of that Act. The foregoing provisions deal with breaches of statutory provisions prior to entry into a contract of insurance. An insurer subject to the regulatory regime of the Financial Services and Markets Act 2000 is also prohibited from carrying on commercial business other than insurance business and activities directly arising from that business, but contravention of this prohibition does not make any transaction void or unenforceable.[53]

14–12 Property unlawfully employed. If the property which is covered by a policy of insurance is being used by the assured, or with his knowledge or assent, in an illegal manner or in the furtherance of an unlawful object, the policy may be invalidated by the illegal user. The source of this rule is a line of marine insurance cases decided in the time of the Napoleonic Wars in which it was held that an insurance on ship or cargo or freight was vitiated if the vessel was bound upon an adventure which was prohibited by statute.[54] In the mid-nineteenth century it was held that an insurance on a ship was invalid if with the owner's knowledge she sailed in a condition prohibited by the Merchant Shipping Acts; for instance with a deck cargo of timber in cases where that was prohibited,[55] or carrying passengers where that was forbidden.[56] Whether the statute in question prohibited the voyage thus

---

[46] s.75(4) of the 1982 Act and s.62(4) of the 1986 Act.

[47] s.72 of the 1982 Act.

[48] s.133 of the 1986 Act.

[49] s.74 of the 1982 Act.

[50] s.131 of the 1986 Act.

[51] As to investment agreements, see note 27, *supra*.

[52] s.130 of the 1986 Act.

[53] The prohibition of other business arises from the Interim Prudential Sourcebook for Insurers, promulgated pursuant to s.141(1) of the FSMA 2000. It is discussed further at para. 34–24, *post*. Previously, s.16 of the Insurance Companies Act 1982 prohibited the carrying out of activities other than insurance business. In *Fuji Finance v. Aetna Ins. Co.* [1997] Ch. 173 the Court of Appeal expressed differing views, *obiter*, as to the consequences of a breach of s.16.

[54] *Johnston v. Sutton* (1779) 1 Doug. K.B. 254; *Camden v. Anderson* (1798) 1 B. & P. 272; *Chalmers v. Bell* (1804) 3 B. & P. 604; *Lubbock v. Potts* (1806) 7 East 449; *Toulmin v. Anderson* (1808) 1 Taunt. 227; *Parkin v. Dick* (1809) 11 East 502; *Gray v. Lloyd* (1811) 4 Taunt. 136; *Wainhouse v. Cowie* (1811) 4 Taunt. 178; *Ingham v. Agnew* (1812) 15 East 517; *Gibson v. Service* (1814) 5 Taunt. 433; *Cowie v. Barber* (1814) 4 Camp. 100; *Darby v. Newton* (1816) 6 Taunt. 544.

[55] *Wilson v. Rankin* (1865) L.R. 1 Q.B. 162; *Cunard v. Hyde* (1858) E. B. & E. 670; (1859) 2 E. & E. 1.

[56] *Dudgeon v. Pembroke* (1874) L.R. 9 Q.B. 581.

begun besides merely exacting a penalty for its contravention depended on its interpretation.[57]

14–13 The extent to which such a rule should be applied to insurances on property and goods on land depends upon the precise basis for the rule. This cannot be said to emerge very clearly from the reported decisions, although certain explanations have been offered. In *Redmond v. Smith*[58] Tindal C.J. suggested that,

> "A policy on an illegal voyage cannot be enforced; for it would be singular if, the original contract being invalid and therefore incapable to be enforced, a collateral contract founded on it could be enforced."[59]

This reasoning is very apt in the case of an insurance upon freight[60] to be earned on an illegal voyage, since, if the assured has no legal right to claim the freight, he has no insurable interest in it which the law will recognise.[61]

14–14 Another explanation of these marine insurance decisions is that policies on vessels used in defiance of the navigation and wartime statutes were impliedly prohibited by the statutes themselves, or, possibly, rendered void by the policy of the common law in order to make the legislation effective in the public interest.[62] In *Parkin v. Dick*, Lord Ellenborough C.J. held that a policy on cargo was avoided when the cargo consisted in part of naval stores the export of which was prohibited, and said:

> "The statute having made the exportation of and trade in naval stores, contrary to the king's proclamation, illegal, impliedly avoids all contracts made for protecting the stores so exported."[63]

The idea that the navigation statutes contained such an implied prohibition, or that public policy compelled such insurances to be avoided, may well have been reinforced by a consideration of section 4 of the Convoy Act[64] section 4 of which expressly avoided the insurance on a vessel which, contrary to the Act, sailed alone without convoy.[65]

14–15 This explanation is not, however, entirely satisfactory. In the later cases of *Cunard v. Hyde*,[66] *Wilson v. Rankin*[67] and *Dudgeon v. Pembroke*[68] it was made quite clear that the insurance was avoided only if the assured was privy to the infringement of the relevant Act of Parliament, and that it was valid if he did not know of this. This emphasis on the assured's intention to

---

[57] *Redmond v. Smith* (1844) 7 Man. & G. 457.

[58] *ibid.*

[59] (1844) 7 Man. & G. 457, 474, adopted in Arnould, *Marine Insurance* (16th. ed.) vol. II, para. 744. The older decisions did not turn upon any such reasoning.

[60] *e.g. Wilson v. Rankin* (1865) L.R. 1 Q.B. 162; *Cunard v. Hyde* (1859) 2 E. & E. 1 (policy on cargo and freight).

[61] See Chap. 1 on insurable interest, *ante.*

[62] *Camden v. Anderson* (1798) 1 B. & P. 272, 278–279; *Parkin v. Dick* (1809) 11 East 502; *Dudgeon v. Pembroke* (1874) L.R. 9 Q.B. 581, 585.

[63] *Parkin v. Dick* (1809) 11 East 502, 503.

[64] Geo. 3, c. 57.

[65] See *Camden v. Anderson* (1798) 1 B. & P. 272, 274.

[66] (1858) E. & E. 70; (1859) 2 E. & E. 1.

[67] (1865) L.R. 1 Q.B. 162.

[68] (1874) L.R. 9 Q.B. 581. The privity of the assured was made the decisive factor in two cases decided at the end of the Napoleonic Wars on breaches of the Convoy Act (*Carstairs v. Allnutt* (1813) 3 Camp. 497; *Metcalfe v. Parry* (1814) 4 Camp. 123).

break the law as the vital factor in vitiating the policy cannot now be supported in the light of modern authorities which hold that, once it is shown that a statute actually prohibits a particular type of contract from being performed as opposed to merely exacting a penalty for something done in the course of the transaction, it is irrelevant whether the plaintiff intended to break the law or not.[69] It is enough that the contract as performed was one which was prohibited by the statute, and, presumably, this reasoning would apply to a contract prohibited on grounds of public policy by the common law. It follows that the nineteenth-century marine insurance cases were not decided upon rules of public policy and illegality as these are understood today.

14–16 The best explanation of these decisions, it is submitted, is that suggested by the Marine Insurance Act 1906, which provides in section 41 that the assured under a marine policy impliedly warrants that, so far as he can control the matter, the adventure upon which insured property is bound shall be carried out in a lawful manner. Such a warranty explains the importance attached to the assured's knowledge of the illegality in the later cases where, in some instances, the courts were not at all certain whether the statute in question was intended to affect the insurance directly, or even to prohibit the voyage.[70]

14–17 If we are right in suggesting that the maritime insurance cases concerning illegal user depend upon the implication of a warranty of legal user, it would be quite wrong to apply the same rule by simple analogy to non-marine policies, where no such warranty will be implied, as has been decided in a non-marine case.[71] In *Leggate v. Brown*[72] a motor tractor was held covered under a policy expressed to be operative while it was being used with not more than two trailers attached to it. The assured took it on the highway with two laden trailers attached, contrary to section 18(1)(b) of the Road Traffic Act 1930, and he was prosecuted for using it when it was not covered by an effective insurance policy. It was held that the insurance policy was effective and not void as contrary to public policy, and that the insurers would be bound to indemnify the assured for liability incurred to a third party. This decision at least suggests that the assured under a policy of motor insurance does not impliedly warrant lawful user of the insured vehicle in terms similar to those in section 41 of the Marine Insurance Act, and shows clearly that something more than merely a temporary illegal user of property has to be shown before an insurance on it is without more rendered unenforceable.

14–18 In *Euro-Diam Ltd v. Bathurst*[73] the plaintiff claimed under an all-risks policy in respect of goods stolen whilst in Germany on a "sale or

---

[69] *St John Shipping v. Rank* [1957] 1 Q.B. 267, 283 *et seq.*; *Archbold v. Spanglett* [1961] 1 Q.B. 374; *Shaw v. Groom* [1970] 2 Q.B. 504; *Chitty on Contracts* (28th ed., 1999) p. 841.
[70] *Cunard v. Hyde* (1859) 2 E. & E. 1.
[71] *Euro-Diam Ltd v. Bathurst* [1990] 1 Q.B. 1.
[72] (1950) 66(2) T.L.R. 281.
[73] [1990] 1 Q.B. 1.

return" basis. At the request of its customer the plaintiff had issued a false invoice showing a value lower than the true value of the goods. This gave rise to an offence under German law. It was held that the policy was not subject to an implied warranty as to the legality of the venture. Furthermore there were no other grounds to refuse to enforce the claim. The plaintiff did not need to rely on its reprehensible conduct in order to prove its claim, nor had it derived any tangible benefit from the false invoice. The receipt of the insurance proceeds would not enable the plaintiff to derive a benefit from crime. In these circumstances the defence of illegality failed.

14–19 It is submitted that the application of the ordinary rules of illegality and public policy affecting contracts will not result in a contract of insurance being rendered unenforceable by an unlawful user of the insured property in more than a few instances; some examples are suggested below.

(i) *Unlawful interest.* If the assured's insurable interest is founded on illegality, clearly the policy is unenforceable by him. Thus if an assured first leases a house to a prostitute knowing that she will use it as a brothel, an insurance against loss of rent will be unenforceable because the rent could not be claimed in an action on the illegal lease.[74]

14–20 (ii) *Express warranty.* If the assured has warranted that the property will be used for lawful purposes in so far as he knows of its user, it is again obvious that the unlawful use of it with his consent or acquiescence will avoid the policy.[75]

14–21 (iii) *Contract tending to assist or further a crime.* If the assured took out a policy of insurance on property he intended to use to further a criminal purpose, the policy might be unenforceable by him for that reason.

14–22 (iv) *Public policy to deter certain types of user invalidating insurances.* In a case where the assured used the insured property to carry on a trade forbidden by statute or to further an objective contrary to public policy, it would be open to a court to hold that the public interest was best served by making it impossible for him to protect himself by insurance against loss or damage occurring to it.[76] The tendency of the courts in recent years has been, however, to interpret statutes as imposing penalties for their contravention rather than in fact prohibiting contracts which involve such an offence being committed, and it is doubtful whether the public interest is necessarily best served by the latter approach. If, for example, a building is erected contrary to statutory building regulations, and falls down, injuring people in the highway, it may well be doubted whether public policy demands that the building owner be denied recourse against his insurers when he lacks the money with which to pay damages to injured persons.[77]

---

[74] *Upfill v. Wright* [1911] 1 K.B. 506.

[75] The illegal user might, of course, incidentally increase the risk of loss or damage occurring to the insured property contrary to a condition in the policy.

[76] This is very much the approach taken by Lord Ellenborough in *Parkin v. Dick* (1809) 11 East 502, 503. A good instance would be where the assured tried to enforce an insurance upon a ship under construction without Admiralty licence under legislation such as the Naval Treaties Acts 1922–37, or where he insured an aeroplane which was to be used to carry supplies to a belligerent in a war in which Britain was neutral contrary to legislation such as the Foreign Enlistment Act 1870.

[77] See the further discussion in para. 14–50, *post.*

14-23 It is helpful to remember that the contract of insurance is performed by the assured tendering a premium and the insurer paying money to the assured on the happening of a specified event. In this sense the policy money is the subject matter of the contract of insurance, and not the insured property itself.[78] Consequently, it is not correct to speak of the contract of insurance as being performed illegally when the insured property is used illegally by the assured; if this were the case the consequence of unlawful user would be invariably an illegality in performance of the contract of insurance and the results would be much more far-reaching.

14-24 (v) *Illegal user of property prior to inception of risk*. The principle that the courts will not assist a plaintiff endeavouring to secure to himself a benefit accruing from a crime committed by him may result in a property insurance being invalidated by the assured's prior dealings with the insured property, provided that there is sufficient proximity between the prior crime and the claim under the insurance.[79] In *Geismar v. Sun Alliance and London Insurance Ltd*[80] the plaintiff insured the contents of his house under three policies issued by the defendants. The contents included some jewels which the plaintiff had previously imported into this country without declaring them to the customs and excise authorities and without paying duty on them, contrary to the Customs and Excise Act 1952. The defendants took the point that public policy debarred the plaintiff from suing them on the insurance in respect of the theft of the jewels. It was held that public policy required the court to assist the enforcement of the 1952 Act by denying to the plaintiff the benefit of an insurance upon goods deliberately imported in contravention of the statute.[81] Were this not so the court would be assisting him to secure a benefit accruing, albeit indirectly, from his criminal importation of the jewels.

14-25 By contrast, in *Euro-Diam Ltd v. Bathurst*[82] the illegality defence failed. There was an insufficiently close link between the insurance claim and the plaintiff's prior conduct in supplying a false invoice. The supply of the invoice at the request of the customer provided no tangible benefit. Nor did it affect the plaintiff's entitlement to the stolen goods. Payment of the insurance claim would not secure for the plaintiff any benefit accruing from crime. Similarly, it has been held that the fact that the subject-matter of the insurance has been purchased with proceeds attributable to some prior, wholly separate, illegal transaction does not prevent a claim being upheld in respect of loss or damage to the insured subject-matter.[83]

---

[78] *Rayner v. Preston* (1881) 18 Ch.D. 1, 9; *Castellain v. Preston* (1883) 11, Q.B.D. 380, 397.

[79] *Euro-Diam Ltd v. Bathurst* [1990] 1 Q.B. 1, 19—"the more remote the crime, the less reason to apply the principle", *per* Staughton J., citing *Bird v. Appleton* (1800) 8 T.R. 562; 101 E.R. 1547.

[80] [1978] 1 Q.B. 383.

[81] The court confined its decision to cases of deliberate infringements of the law: [1978] 1 Q.B. 383, 395.

[82] [1990] 1 Q.B. 1, discussed in para. 14–18, *ante*.

[83] *Bird v. Appleton* (1800) 8 T.R. 562, 101 E.R. 1547. A court might, however, today be unwilling to enforce a claim relating to goods bought with the proceeds of crime if presented with evidence of systematic "laundering" of the proceeds.

14–26 Performance contrary to foreign law. The contract of insurance might be rendered unenforceable by reason of the fact that it was performed in a manner infringing foreign laws. For example, an English assured might take out a policy with foreign insurers, governed by English law, and providing that premiums were to be paid at the insurers' place of business in a manner contravening the currency regulations of the insurers' country. It has been held that a contract is unenforceable in an English court if its performance involved the commission of acts in a friendly and foreign country in violation of that country's law,[84] and this principle would extend to currency regulations.[85] The same principle could apply to the payment of claims in contravention of the law of the country in which they were to be paid.[86] In *Society of Lloyd's v. Fraser*[87] a Canadian citizen applied to become a member of Lloyd's, with his application being accepted in London and recorded in a contract subject to English law and jurisdiction. Under Ontario law the application procedure was arguably illegal. However, that did not make the contract unenforceable in England as a matter of public policy, even if Lloyd's could not have enforced it in Canada. The validity of the contract depended upon its proper law, which was English. It did not involve the performance of acts in Ontario contrary to Ontario law, and was not intended to breach Canadian law, so that the principles derived from *Foster v. Driscoll* and *Regazzoni v. Sethia* had no application.

14–27 Whether a contract would be unenforceable if the payment of premium contravened a revenue law of a foreign country is questionable. In former times Lord Mansfield once said that "no country ever takes notice of the revenue laws of another",[88] and he was prepared to countenance an insurance on a marine adventure expressly intended to defraud the revenue laws of another state.[89] It is true that the courts of this country will not enforce the revenue laws of another country directly or indirectly,[90] but, although the point has been left open in recent decisions, it is probable that a court would not now enforce a contract that necessarily involved a breach of a friendly state's revenue laws. The Court of Appeal has indicated that it is prepared to have regard to a foreign revenue law in order to see if a foreign government has acquired title to a taxpayer's movables under its provisions.[91]

14–28 Insurer's knowledge of illegality. An action by the assured for

---

[84] *Foster v. Driscoll* [1929] 1 K.B. 470; *Reggazoni v. K. C. Sethia (1944)* [1958] A.C. 301. There is an exception if the law in question has never been enforced, *Francis v. Sea Ins. Co.* (1898) 3 Com.Cas. 229. For a discussion of the principle, see *Dicey & Morris on the Conflict of Laws* (13th ed., 2000) vol. 2 p. 1246.

[85] *Kahler v. Midland Bank Ltd* [1950] A.C. 24; *Zivnostenska Banka National Corp. v. Frankman* [1950] A.C. 57.

[86] *Rossano v. Manufacturers' Life Ins. Co.* [1963] 2 Q.B. 352, 372. Contrast *Euro-Diam Ltd v. Bathurst* [1990] 1 Q.B. 1 where the claim under an English policy to be performed in England was enforced, although the insured had participated in actions that contravened German law.

[87] [1999] Lloyd's Rep. I.R. 156.

[88] *Holman v. Johnson* (1775) 1 Cowp. 341, 343.

[89] *Planché v. Fletcher* (1779) 1 Doug. 251; *Lever v. Fletcher* (1780) 1 Park, *Law of Marine Insurance*, 507.

[90] *Government of India v. Taylor* [1955] A.C. 491; *Brokaw v. Seatrain U.K. Ltd* [1971] 2 Q.B. 476, 482; *Rossano v. Manufacturers' Life Ins. Co.* [1963] 2 Q.B. 352, 377.

[91] *Brokaw v. Seatrain U.K. Ltd* [1971] 2 Q.B. 476. In *Euro-Diam Ltd v. Bathurst* [1990] 1 Q.B. 1 it was not necessary to decide the point, but the Court of Appeal was unimpressed by the distinction between revenue laws and other laws.

recovery of the policy moneys may be countered with a plea of illegality whether or not the insurers knew of it beforehand. In *Toulmin v. Anderson*[92] the insurers resisted payment upon a marine policy on account of the illegality of the adventure, of which they were aware when the policy was taken out, and Lord Mansfield said[93]:

> "It appears a monstrous thing that persons standing in the situation of these defendants, and having known the objection to exist at the time they made the contract, should avail themselves of it, but they are certainly legally entitled to do so if they think fit."

In many instances the illegality would vitiate the insurance regardless of the insurers' knowledge. But where the insurers are aware of the illegality they can still resist payment, as was recognised in another decision of Lord Mansfield,[94] on account of the maxim *in pari delicto, potior est conditio defendentis*.

14–29 Proof of illegality. The general rule is that where illegality is alleged by the insurers it lies upon them to prove it, and the presumption is always against illegality.[95] Thus, in the case of a death from unascertained causes, suicide would not readily be inferred, but if the insurers proved that the assured destroyed himself, the burden of proof shifted to the plaintiff, who had then to prove insanity in order to rebut the plea of illegality.[96] Similarly, where it was proved that a husband shot his wife and afterwards committed suicide, and there was nothing to show whether he was sane or not at the time, the presumption was that he murdered his wife.[97] Where an accused person has been convicted in a criminal court the conviction is only prima facie evidence of guilt in a civil court,[98] but the verdict of a coroner's jury is not even prima facie proof, against anyone, of the facts found.[99] An important qualification to these rules is that, even if the insurers do not allege illegality, the court must take due note of it if it is clearly disclosed in evidence even if inadvertently.[1] In such a case, it is submitted, the evidence of illegality would need to be strong before the presumption against it could be displaced.

---

[92] (1808) 1 Taunt. 227.

[93] (1808) 1 Taunt. 227, 232.

[94] *Johnston v. Sutton* (1779) 1 Doug. K.B. 254. As to a claim for the return of premiums, see Ch. 8.

[95] *Thurtell v. Beaumont* (1823) 1 Bing. 339; *Fender v. St John Mildmay* [1938] A.C. 1, 36–37; *Overseas Union Ins. Ltd v. Incorporated General Ins. Ltd* [1992] 1 Lloyd's Rep. 439.

[96] *Stormont v. Waterloo Life* (1858) 1 F. & F. 22. It is not now a crime to commit suicide and a policy may now provide for payment of policy moneys in that event. See paras 14–66 to 14–71, *post*.

[97] *Re Pollock* [1941] Ch. 219.

[98] Civil Evidence Act 1968, s.11 (the exception in s.13 being irrelevant for present purposes). See also *In the Estate of Crippen* [1911] P. 108. The civil court is at liberty to doubt the verdict of the criminal court: *Gray v. Barr* [1971] 2 Q.B. 554, 565, 577.

[99] *Bird v. Keep* [1918] 2 K.B. 692; *Barnett v. Cohen* [1921] 2 K.B. 461, but see *Prince of Wales Assurance v. Palmer* (1858) 25 Beav. 605.

[1] *Gedge v. Royal Exchange Ass.* [1900] 2 Q.B. 214; *MacDonald v. Green* (1950) 66 T.L.R. (Part 2) 649, reversed on other grounds in C.A. [1951] 1 K.B. 594. The relevant principles are discussed in *Bank of India v. Trans Continental Commodity Merchants* [1982] 1 Lloyd's Rep. 427. See para. 1–17, *ante*.

2. L<small>OSS</small> C<small>AUSED BY</small> A<small>SSURED'S</small> U<small>NLAWFUL</small> A<small>CT</small>

14–30 Loss caused by deliberate act. Another instance where illegality will defeat a claim on a policy is where the assured has intentionally brought about a loss under the policy by an act which is itself unlawful. In such a case his claim is barred by two rules of law which need to be carefully distinguished. First, as a matter of public policy, no man will be given assistance by the courts to recover a profit from or an indemnity for his own deliberate crime. Secondly, it is a rule of insurance law that an assured cannot normally recover the policy moneys when he has intentionally brought about the event upon which the policy specifies the moneys to be payable. We shall consider this latter principle first in order to distinguish it from the former.

14–31 There is a presumption in the case of every insurance contract that the assured cannot by his own intentional act bring about the event upon which the insurance money is payable and then recover under the policy.[2] That is not the result of any rule of public policy, but of a prima facie rule of construction of the contract, by which it is presumed that the insurers have not agreed to pay on that happening.[3] Thus a life policy does not prima facie cover the contingency of the assured committing suicide while sane, or, put another way, the event of the assured's death does not mean or include the event of his self-caused death while sane.[4] This presumption can, however, be displaced if the policy provides either expressly or by clear implication that the policy money is payable to his representatives in the event of sane suicide, in which case a claim will be maintainable by the assured's representatives, or by an innocent assignee of the policy before the suicide,[5] especially where the policy contains an express term to this effect limited in its scope to benefit assignees only.[6]

14–32 The assured's own wilful act (not being illegal) is, however, no bar to recovery on the policy if such act, even though it may have indirectly contributed to the result, was not the immediate cause of the loss. Thus, where the owners of a vessel, having insured her, wilfully permitted her to go to sea in an unseaworthy condition, which under the circumstances was not illegal, it was held they could recover, even although the loss was indirectly attributable to her unseaworthy condition.[7] The case was distinguished from those where through the absence of proper documents a neutral vessel was

---

[2] *Bell v. Carstairs* (1811) 14 East 374; *Thompson v. Hopper*, 6 E. & B. 172, 191; *Britton v. Royal Ins. Co.* (1866) 4 F. & F. 905, 908. This rule does not extend to losses caused by the wilful act of the Government of the country to which the assured belongs, *Aubert v. Gray* (1861) 3 B. & S. 169.

[3] *Beresford v. Royal Ins. Co.* [1938] A.C. 586, 595; *Gray v. Barr* [1971] 2 Q.B. 554, 587. The presumption would appear to be irrebuttable in the case of an indemnity policy where money is payable in the event of an accidental loss: *Dhak v. Ins. Co. of North America (U.K.) Ltd* [1996] 1 W.L.R. 936. Cf. *Fire and All Risks Ins. Co. v. Powell* [1966] V.R. 513.

[4] *Beresford v. Royal Ins. Co.* [1938] A.C. 586, 602.

[5] *ibid.* at 600. The policy provided for payment on such an event by implication, but the assured's personal representative was barred from recovery by the first rule mentioned in the paragraph above; see paras 14–66 to 14–71, *post.*

[6] *Moore v. Woolsey* (1854) 4 E. & B. 243.

[7] *Thompson v. Hopper* (1858) E.B. & E. 1038. This decision may, however, be doubted after the authoritative statements of the doctrine of *causa proxima* in *Leyland Shipping Co. v. Norwich Fire Ins. Soc. Ltd* [1918] A.C. 350, applied in *Gray v. Barr* [1971] 2 Q.B. 554.

captured by belligerents, and it was held that the assured could not recover because the loss was the direct and immediate consequence of his own deliberate act in not providing proper papers.[8] So in insurance other than marine, the wilful act of the assured in directly causing the loss, as, for instance, if he deliberately set his house on fire, would prevent him from recovering, even although the policy contained no express condition to that effect;[9] but if the assured got drunk and set his house on fire while intoxicated he could recover because the loss would not have been the immediate consequence of his wilful act of getting drunk but would have only been indirectly attributable to that act.[10]

14–33 The assured will be held to have caused a loss through his own deliberate act in a case where, even if the loss was not directly intended by him, he embarked upon a course of conduct in which there was a clear risk of the loss occurring. So, if a man insured against liability for accidents permits himself to grapple with another man while he is carrying a loaded gun, he cannot enforce a claim against insurers on a policy indemnifying him for liability arising out of bodily injury caused to any third party by accident. The proximate cause of such injury is the risk taken by the assured, and that sort of accident is not one which the insurers intend to cover.[11] A similar result would follow if the assured takes a calculated risk of injury or death as a result of drinking to excess.[12]

14–34 Loss caused by criminal or tortious act. The assured may not recover under a policy of insurance in respect of a loss intentionally caused by his own criminal or tortious act.[13] This rule is founded on a principle of public policy applicable to all contracts, that a court will not assist a criminal who seeks to recover any kind of benefit or indemnity for his crime, for to do so would be to remove a restraint upon the commission of crimes.[14] The rule may be instanced as an application of the maxim *ex turpi causa, non oritur actio.*

Thus, in life assurance, a man who has insured the life of another cannot recover if he murders the person whose life he has insured[15]; just as a

---

[8] *Bell v. Carstairs* (1811) 14 East 374; *Horneyer v. Lushington* (1812) 15 East 46; *Oswell v. Vigne* (1812) 15 East 70. *Cf.* the discussion of wilful default in the context of marine insurance in *National Oilwell (U.K) Ltd v. Davy Offshore Ltd* [1993] 2 Lloyd's Rep. 582. The decision was appealed, but the case settled before the Court of Appeal gave judgment.

[9] *Britton v. Royal Ins. Co.* (1866) 4 F. & F. 905, 908.

[10] *Aubert v. Gray* (1861) 3 B. & S.169, 171. The same consideration would presumably apply if the assured committed arson while insane, for his mind could not then accompany the act to make it "intentional" in law. See *Beresford v. Royal Ins. Co.* [1938] A.C. 586, 595. *Cf. Stats v. Mutual of Omaha Ins. Co.* (1977) 73 D.L.R. (3d) 324 (Ont. Ct. App.), where the severely intoxicated driver did not intend the death of the victim. By contrast, in *Dhak v. Ins. Co. of North America (U.K.) Ltd* [1996] 1 W.L.R. 936 the assured's death from inhalation of vomit was directly caused by drinking a bottle of gin in a short period of time and was a foreseeable consequence of her conduct.

[11] *Gray v. Barr* [1971] 2 Q.B. 554, 567, 580, 587; *Charlton v. Fisher and Churchill Ins. Co.* [2001] Lloyd's Rep. I.R. 387. Contrast *Trynor v. Canadian Surety* (1970) 10 D.L.R. (3d) 482, where the damage was quite unexpected.

[12] *Dhak v. Ins. Co. of North America (U.K.) Ltd* [1996] 1 W.L.R. 936.

[13] *Beresford v. Royal Ins. Co.* [1938] A.C. 586; *Hardy v. Motor Insurers' Bureau* [1964] 2 Q.B. 745, 760, 762, 769; *Cleaver v. Mutual Reserve Fund Life Assoc.* [1892] 1 Q.B. 147: *In the Estate of Crippen* [1911] P. 108.

[14] *Gray v. Barr* [1971] 2 Q.B. 554, 580–581.

[15] *Prince of Wales Assurance v. Palmer* (1858) 25 Beav. 605. See also para. 14–57, *post.*

murderer may not take any benefit under the will of his victim.[16] But a verdict of "guilty but insane" is not, properly speaking, a conviction, and the public policy that prevents a sane murderer from recovering was held by the Industrial Assurance Commissioner to have no application in such a case.[17] If a man insures his own life, his representatives cannot normally recover if he takes his own life while sane, but that is now due only to the rule against recovery for loss deliberately caused, since it is no longer in England a crime to commit suicide.[18] If, on the other hand, a man committed a capital offence and thence suffered the death penalty, the rule of public policy would doubtless apply.[19] In this connection, the Supreme Court of the Cape of Good Hope once refused to extend the doctrine of illegality so far as to prevent recovery on an own-life insurance policy by the representatives of the assured on the ground that he was a rebel and was killed while fighting against His Majesty's troops engaging in suppressing the rebellion[20]; but it is difficult to see how this decision could be supported without disregarding the principles of public policy endorsed by the House of Lords in the *Beresford* case.[21]

14–35 The *ex turpi causa* rule has been applied to a claim for social security benefits by a widow found guilty of the manslaughter of her husband,[22] though in the United States of America the rule, in its application to life policies, does not extend to the case of manslaughter where there was not intent to inflict injury of a kind likely to cause death.[23] In this country account must now be taken of the provisions of the Forfeiture Act 1982.

14–36 The Forfeiture Act 1982. Under this Act, the court is empowered to allow the claim of someone who has "unlawfully killed"[24] another to the benefits of, *inter alia*, a life assurance policy. The court has a very wide discretion.[25] The Act has been applied to a claim on life insurance by a surviving party to a suicide pact.[26] It is submitted that it would be apt to cover

---

[16] *In the Estate of Crippen* [1911] P. 108; *In the Estate of Hall* [1914] P. 1.

[17] *Chaplin v. Royal London Mutual* [1958] I.A.C.Rep. 2.

[18] Suicide Act 1961, s.l. Suicide while insane never was, in the absence of special conditions, a bar to recovery, *Horn v. Anglo-American Life* (1861) 30 L.J.Ch. 511. See the discussion of suicide in paras 14–31, 14–37 and 14–66 to 14–75, *post*.

[19] *Amicable Ins. Co. v. Bolland* (1830) 4 Bligh (N.S.) 194.

[20] *Burger v. South African Mutual Life* (1903) 20 S.C. (Cape of Good Hope) 538.

[21] [1938] A.C. 586. *Cf. Molloy v. John Hancock Mutual Life* (1951) 97 N.E. 2d 423, where the assured was shot in the course of committing an armed robbery and it was held that a beneficiary under his life policy could not recover. See also *Hewitson v. Prudential Ass. Co.* (1985) 12 N.I.J.B. 65 (Northern Ireland Court of Appeal), where the assured's claim under a life policy was disallowed because she had participated with the life assured, her husband, in a criminal act, an attempted armed robbery, as a consequence of which her husband was shot by someone who reasonably believed him to be a terrorist.

[22] *R. v. National Ins. Commissioner, ex parte Connor* [1981] 1 Q.B. 758, applying *Gray v. Barr* [1971] 2 Q.B. 554, but note the possible effects of the Forfeiture Act 1982 discussed below.

[23] See, *e.g. Minasian v. Aetna Life* (1936) 3 N.E. 2d 17; *Shoemaker v. Shoemaker* (1959) 263 F. 2d 931.

[24] Not including murder: s.5.

[25] s.2.

[26] *Dunbar v. Plant* [1998] Ch. 412. The test under s.2(2) of the Act is whether, having regard to the conduct of the offender-applicant and deceased, the justice of the case requires the forfeiture rule to be modified. In *Dunbar* the survivor of a suicide pact aided and abetted

a case of manslaughter where there was no intention or recklessness. The Act applies only when one person has unlawfully killed "another"[27] and thus has no effect on the *Beresford* case.[28] Further, by reason of the definition of "interest in property" in section 2(4), it cannot apply to any third party insurance.[29]

14–37 Suicide—express policy term. It is usual in policies of life insurance to insert a clause to the effect that if the assured dies by his own hand, whether sane or insane, within the period of one or two years from the issue of the policy the policy will be void, and it has been argued that the effect of that is to include in the risk death by suicide, whether sane or insane, committed at any time after the expiration of the excepted period. That argument appears to have found favour in America,[30] but in this country it was rejected by the House of Lords in *Beresford v. The Royal Insurance Co.*,[31] decided at a time when suicide was still a crime, where it was held that no term in the policy expressed or implied can escape the general prohibition of illegality and so enable the representatives of the assured to recover in the event of the assured's death by suicide while sane at any time in the currency of the policy. In that case it was held that the policy was intended to cover the risk of suicide after a year from its inception; the decision would have been different after the passing of the Suicide Act 1961.[32]

14–38 Intentional crime and unintended loss. In the case of the murder of a life assured there can be no doubt that the assured who committed the crime directly intended the loss. The position is more difficult when the assured intentionally commits a crime which leads indirectly to a loss being sustained under the policy, the loss itself not being actually intended. In such cases, the loss will be said to have been caused by the criminal act of the assured if it was the natural or probable result of that act, and so was clearly risked by the assured.

14–39 In *Hardy v. Motor Insurers' Bureau*[33] the plaintiff, a chief security officer, stopped to talk to the driver of a van displaying a stolen road fund licence. The driver drove off while the plaintiff was holding on to the open van door with his head inside the window, with the result that the plaintiff was severely injured. In proceedings against the Bureau, necessitated by the fact that the driver was uninsured, the Bureau raised in defence the contention that the plaintiff's injury was caused by an intentional criminal act on the part of the van driver, who had subsequently been convicted of maliciously causing grievous bodily harm with intent. The Court of Appeal agreed that the plaintiff's bodily injuries were intentionally caused by a

---

suicide. A majority of the Court of Appeal held that the public interest did not require the imposition of a penal sanction, and that in such a case the normal approach should be to give relief against forfeiture. Other cases where the Act has been applied are *Re Royse* [1985] 1 Ch. 22; *Re K.* [1985] Ch. 85, affirmed [1985] Fam. 180; *Re H. (dec'd)* [1990] Fam. Law 175.

[27] s.1.

[28] [1938] A.C. 586.

[29] As, *e.g.* in *Gray v. Barr* [1971] 2 Q.B. 554, discussed in para. 14–40, *post.*

[30] *North Western Life v. Johnson* (1920) 254 U.S. 96. For a full discussion of the voluminous American case law in this area, see Appleman, *Insurance Law and Practice*, Ch. 26.

[31] [1938] A.C. 586.

[32] In *Gray v. Barr*, Salmon L.J. suggested that, apart from the Suicide Act, public policy might not compel the courts now to decide the case in the same way [1971] 2 Q.B. 554, 582.

[33] [1964] 2 Q.B. 745.

criminal act in the sense that, although the driver did not intend to injure him as an end in itself, he nevertheless intended to make good his escape even if that necessarily entailed inflicting considerable injuries on the plaintiff.[34] The driver would have been precluded from making a claim on insurance, but this did not prevent the plaintiff from recovering from the Bureau.[35]

14–40 The case of *Gray v. Barr*[36] illustrates the same principle in circumstances of greater complexity. The defendant, Barr, suspected he would find his wife in the house of Gray, a neighbour with whom she had been having an affair. Being in a state of extreme emotion and distress, he took a gun and went to Gray's house, where, on entering, he encountered Gray at the top of the stairs. When Gray denied (correctly) that Mrs Barr was there, the defendant disbelieved him and started up the stairs to look for her himself. As he came up to Gray he fired a shot into the ceiling to frighten him. Fearing no doubt for his life, Gray grappled with the defendant, who fell downstairs. During this struggle the gun went off and the shot killed Gray. It was accepted that the defendant never intended to fire the shot or to kill Gray, and he was acquitted of manslaughter at his trial. The administrators of Gray's estate then sued the defendant in negligence, and the defendant joined as third party his insurance company who had undertaken in a "hearth and home" policy, to indemnify him in respect of all sums which he should "become legally liable to pay as damages in respect of (a) bodily injury to any person caused by accident".

14–41 The Court of Appeal held that the defendant's claim failed because (1) Gray's injuries were not caused by an accident, and (2) public policy made the claim unenforceable. The effective and dominant cause of Gray's death, said Lord Denning M.R. and Phillimore L.J.[37] was the defendant's deliberate act of threatening Gray with a loaded gun and firing a shot into the ceiling, since the whole tragic sequence of events which followed was the foreseeable and probable result of that conduct. Moreover, the defendant's conduct undoubtedly amounted to an unlawful assault with violence, so that in truth the defendant was seeking an indemnity in respect of the consequences of his deliberate crime.[38]

14–42 Ignorance of the law is immaterial. If the assured causes a loss under his policy by the deliberate commission of an act which, through ignorance of the law alone, he wrongly believes to be lawful, that loss is nonetheless caused by an intentional criminal act. A man is presumed to know the law.[39] In *Haseldine v. Hosken*[40] the plaintiff, who was a solicitor, claimed against the defendant, an underwriting member of Lloyd's, a

---

[34] *ibid.*, 759, 764.
[35] See para. 14–77, *post.*
[36] [1971] 2 Q.B. 554.
[37] [1971] 2 Q.B. 554, 567, 587.
[38] *ibid.*, 581. *Cf. S.Y. Investments (No. 2) Pty Ltd v. Commercial Union Ass. Co. of Australia Ltd* (1986) 82 F.L.R. 130; reversed in part (1986) 44 N.T.R. 14; *Co-Op. Fire and Casualty Co. v. Saindon* (1975) 56 D.L.R. 556. Contrast *Fire & All Risks Ins. Co. v. Powell* [1966] V.R. 513, where deliberate breach of road traffic regulations was not treated as the cause of subsequent damage to goods.
[39] *Lubbock v. Potts* (1806) 7 East 449, 456; *Burrows v. Rhodes* [1899] 1 Q.B. 816, 829; *Haseldine v. Hosken* [1933] 1 K.B. 822, 836; *Allan (J.M.) (Merchandising) v. Cloke* [1963] 2 Q.B. 340, 348.
[40] [1933] 1 K.B. 822.

declaration that the defendant was liable to indemnify him, under a solicitor's indemnity policy, in respect of a loss sustained by him, and an order for payment of the amount due. The policy covered:

> "loss arising from any claim or claims which may be made against them by reason of any neglect, omission or error whenever or wherever the same was or may have been committed on the part of the firm during the subsistence of this policy in or about the conduct of any business conducted by or on behalf of the firm in their professional capacity as solicitors".

The plaintiff entered into agreements with a client for whom he conducted an action which was held to be champertous. The other parties to the action, who were unable to recover from the nominal plaintiff all the costs awarded in their favour, sued the plaintiff for damages arising from his tort. He paid £950 to settle that claim, and then claimed for this as a loss under his policy. Swift J. held that he was covered: he said that the plaintiff had acted innocently, though ignorantly, and that the loss was a consequence of an error of judgement in entering into a contract which turned out to be illegal. The Court of Appeal, however (Scrutton, Greer and Slesser L.JJ.), allowed the appeal of the underwriter and dismissed the action.

14-43 Two reasons were given for allowing the appeal. First it was said that the solicitor's indemnity policy was intended to cover only losses sustained by the assured in the conduct of business carried on in his professional capacity as a solicitor acting on behalf of a client, and in this case the plaintiff had sustained a loss as the result of a speculation for his own benefit alone.[41] Secondly, the claim against the plaintiff had not been occasioned by "any neglect, omission or error" on his part, because the plaintiff had at all times intended to make the champertous agreements while knowing all the facts and circumstances which made them illegal. His action was entirely deliberate, and it was no answer to say that he did not realise it was criminal. "If a person does not know the law so much the worse for him".[42]

14-44 The decision in *Haseldine v. Hosken*[43] is in line with the authorities determining when it is permissible for a plaintiff to claim an indemnity otherwise than by way of an insurance, for a liability or loss resulting to him from his commission of a tortious or criminal act. The plaintiff may not bring an action by way of indemnity, however it is framed, if

(1) he knew he was committing a crime, or
(2) the act in question was manifestly unlawful in the eyes of any reasonable person, or
(3) the plaintiff knew all the facts and circumstances which made the act unlawful even though he did not know the law which stated it to be such.[44]

On the other hand, if he is ignorant of the circumstances which make an

---

[41] This emerges most clearly from the judgments of Greer and Slesser L.JJ. [1933] 1 K.B. 822, 837–839.
[42] [1933] 1 K.B. 822, 836.
[43] *ibid.*
[44] *Burrows v. Rhodes* [1899] 1 Q.B. 816, 829–830. *Leslie v. Reliable Advertising Agency* [1915] 1 K.B. 652, 660.

otherwise lawful act a crime, he may seek to be indemnified for his loss, whether by express contract or otherwise. A famous decision to that effect is *Burrows v. Rhodes*[45] where it was held that the plaintiff could maintain an action in deceit against defendants who had induced him to ride in the Jameson Raid of 1895, in contravention of the Foreign Enlistment Act 1870, by representing to him that the expedition had the sanction of the British Government.

14–45 No indemnity in respect of punishment for a crime. One qualification to these principles must be added. In no circumstances may a plaintiff maintain an action to be indemnified for a fine or other punishment imposed for the commission of a crime.[46] It is against public policy that a punishment imposed on an offender partly or wholly as a deterrent against further offences should be shifted onto the shoulders of another. It follows that an insurance against such loss would be unenforceable or void.[47] However, this does not mean that it is contrary to public policy to provide an indemnity against an award of exemplary damages, at least if the assured's liability arises vicariously.[48]

14–46 Loss caused by negligence of assured. There is no rule of public policy which prevents a man from insuring against the consequences of his own negligence, and, for instance, this is done in the ordinary motor-car accident policy covering third party risks.[49] So a man may insure against liability for other wrongful acts committed by him which are committed innocently or through carelessness and without any deliberate intention to do wrong, such as infringement of copyright or publication of a libel.[50] Although a man cannot recover an indemnity in respect of the consequences of his own criminal act intentionally committed, he may nevertheless be entitled to recover in respect of liability accidentally and unintentionally incurred while committing a statutory offence as, for instance, in respect of an accident happening whilst the assured was driving his car in excess of the statutory speed limit,[51] or even whilst the assured was driving his car recklessly because he was drunk.[52] Even the fact that the assured has been convicted of manslaughter is not a bar to recovery on the policy.[53]

---

[45] [1899] 1 Q.B. 816.

[46] *Colburn v. Patmore* (1834) 1 C.M. & R. 73; *Leslie v. Reliable Advertising Agency* [1915] 1 K.B. 652, 659; *Askey v. Golden Wine Co.* (1948) 64 T.L.R. 379.

[47] *Haseldine v. Hosken* [1933] 1 K.B. 822, 837.

[48] *Lancashire County Council v. Municipal Mutual Ins. Ltd* [1996] 3 W.L.R. 493.

[49] *Shaw v. Robberds* (1837) 6 Ad. & E. 75; *Tinline v. White Cross Ins. Ass. Ltd* [1921] 3 K.B. 327; *Weld-Blundell v. Stephens* [1919] 1 K.B. 520, 529, 544; [1920] A.C. 956; *Robertson v. London Guarantee and Accident* [1915] 1 S.L.T. 195. While a policy can therefore provide cover against negligent use of the vehicle, it is necessary to consider the effect on cover of other conditions. For example, an assured who is in breach of an obligation to maintain a vehicle may be unable to recover for loss caused by his own negligent maintenance: *Amey Properties Ltd v. Cornhill Ins. plc* [1996] L.R.L.R. 259.

[50] The policy may, however, contain a term requiring the assured not deliberately to court the danger of loss: *Fraser v. B.N. Furman (Productions) Ltd* [1967] 1 W.L.R. 898; *Sofi v. Prudential* [1993] 2 Lloyd's Rep. 559; *Devco Holder v. Legal and General Ins. Soc.* [1993] 2 Lloyd's Rep. 567; *Hayward v. Norwich Union Ins. Co.* [2001] Lloyd's Rep.I.R.410.

[51] *Tinline v. White Cross Ins. Ass. Ltd* [1921] 3 K.B. 327.

[52] *Robertson v. London Guarantee and Accident*, 1915, 1 S.L.T. 195; *James v. British General Ins. Co.* [1927] 2 K.B. 311.

[53] *Tinline v. White Cross Ins. Ass., Ltd* [1921] 3 K.B. 327; *James v. British General Ins. Co.* [1927] 2 K.B. 311.

The correctness of these decisions was at one time doubted,[54] but is now established beyond doubt, at least in the sphere of motor insurance.[55] What is not clear, however, is the correctness of the wider principle which may be deduced from them, namely that an assured may recover an indemnity in respect of liability for any damage or injury he has caused otherwise than on purpose, a principle which has been cast in doubt by the decision in *Gray v. Barr*.[56] An example will illustrate the difficulty.

14–47 Suppose that a motorist in a great hurry decides to overtake a slow-moving car in a place where it is unlawful to do so. The motorist can see that it is unlawful by reason of the double white lines marked on the road, but he decides nonetheless to take the risk despite the danger and the illegality involved in his manoeuvre. He collides with an oncoming car, the occupants of which are killed, and his own car is damaged as well. According to the motor insurance cases cited above, the motorist has a valid claim against his insurers even if convicted of causing death by dangerous driving or of manslaughter, because he did not intend to cause that loss. Certainly the current practice would be for the insurers not to take his act of negligence as a defence to payment.

14–48 In *Gray v. Barr*[57] (the facts of which case have been stated above) it was held, however, that an assured who deliberately embarks on a course of conduct which is (i) criminal and (ii) likely to occasion a loss under the policy as a foreseeable and probable result of that conduct, may not on grounds of public policy be indemnified for that loss even though it was unintended.[58] This is a fair description of the conduct of the reckless motorist instanced above, in which case he should be debarred from claiming by the same rule of public policy, although the Court of Appeal in *Gray v. Barr*[59] in no way sought to impugn the established interpretation of the motor insurance cases.

14–49 In the light of the foregoing discussion, we do not believe that it is now possible to state a simple distinction between a loss intentionally caused by a criminal act, in respect of which no indemnity is permitted, and a loss caused by a negligent act of the assured, also criminal, in respect of which a claim is maintainable. The distinction should be sought in terms of the requirements of public policy, a solution which is suggested by some remarks made by the Court of Appeal in *Gray v. Barr*.[60]

The motor insurance cases must be seen as an instance where the overwhelming requirement of public policy is that insurances against casualties inflicted by the wrongdoer must be fully effective (short of the point where the assured actually inflicts damage on purpose) especially when the position of the innocent victims of dangerous drivers is considered. Driving cars is not in itself a particularly anti-social activity and it is

---

[54] *Haseldine v. Hosken* [1933] 1 K.B. 822; *Beresford v. Royal Ins. Co.* [1937] 2 K.B. 197, 220.
[55] *Gray v. Barr* [1971] 2 Q.B. 554, 568, 581; *Marles v. Trant* [1954] 1 Q.B. 29, 39.
[56] [1971] 2 Q.B. 554.
[57] [1971] 2 Q.B. 554.
[58] *ibid.*, 569, 581.
[59] *ibid.*
[60] *ibid.*

recognised that the best-intentioned of road users can commit errors of judgment or be careless behind the wheel. Carrying a loaded fire-arm with the intent of persuading another person to comply with your wishes is quite another matter, and at a time when "crimes of violence, particularly when committed with loaded guns, are among the worst curses of this age"[61] public policy demands that any assured who permits himself to commit a crime with a loaded gun be debarred from recovering an indemnity in respect of any unintended injury which may foreseeably result from his actions.[62] Future cases involving a loss caused by a negligent and criminal act of the assured will have to be considered primarily in relation to the type of crime committed, and the question whether it is so anti-social that public policy requires the rule in *Gray v. Barr*[63] to be applied to it.[64]

14–50 It is submitted, however, that certain categories of case can confidently be placed on the same side of the dividing line as the motor cases. These are cases involving negligence in the conduct of industrial, mining, building and engineering operations. Such activities are basically innocent, but also dangerous. It is both common and desirable for those engaged in such activities to insure against the consequences of negligence and in one case insurance is compulsory.[65] In many cases, an act of negligence will involve a contravention of the Factories Act 1961, the building regulations or some similar enactment and will therefore be punishable by the criminal courts. There is no consideration of public policy which demands that insurers be excused from liability in those cases.

14–51 The North American motor insurance cases. In Canada the reasoning in the *Tinline* case[66] has been dissented from, and the opposite view was taken in Ontario in a case of reckless driving, where it was held that public policy prevented the assured from recovering.[67] This view was upheld by the Supreme Court of Canada. Legislation followed in order to protect victims of traffic accidents, and generally to limit the application of the *ex turpi* principle to cases where the assured intends to cause the loss.[68]

14–52 In the United States, the tendency has been to follow the *Tinline* case.[69] In *Henell v. Hicock*[70] the court cited that case with approval, and

[61] *ibid.*, 581, *per* Salmon L.J.

[62] *ibid.*, 581, 587.

[63] *ibid.*

[64] See the remarks of Diplock L.J. on public policy in *Hardy v. Motor Insurers' Bureau* [1964] 2 Q.B. 745, 767–770, approved in *Gardner v. Moore* [1984] A.C. 548. See too *Meah v. McCreamer (No. 2)* [1986] 1 All E.R. 943, 950–951. Policy as to road accidents is also discussed in *Pitts v. Hunt* [1991] 1 Q.B. 24, 39–46 and *Fire & All Risks Ins. Co. Ltd v. Powell* [1966] V.R. 513. In *Charlton v. Fisher and Churchill Ins. Co.* [2001] Lloyd's Rep. I.R. 387, the Court of Appeal held that a claim on motor insurance was precluded by the assured's deliberate infliction of damage.

[65] Under the Employer's Liability (Compulsory Insurance) Act 1969, which is discussed in Ch. 28.

[66] [1921] 3 K.B. 327.

[67] *O'Hearn v. Yorkshire Ins. Co.* (1921) 50 Ont.L.R. 377; 51 Ont.L.R. 130; discussed in *James v. British General* [1927] 2 K.B. 311.

[68] See *Home Ins. Co. of New York v. Lindal* [1934] S.C.R. 33; *Stats v. Mutual of Omaha Ins. Co.* (1977) 73 D.L.R. (3d) 324, and the discussion in Brown and Menezes, *Insurance Law in Canada* (2nd ed. 1991).

[69] As to the American cases in general, see Holmes's Appleman, *Insurance Law and Practice* (2nd ed. 1996).

[70] 13 N.E. 2d 358 (1937).

quoted from the judgment of Cardozo J. in *Messersmith v. American Fidelity*.[71] where he said:

"To restrict insurance to cases where liability is incurred without fault of the insured would reduce indemnity to a shadow. Liability of the owner (of an automobile) who is also the operator, can never be incurred without fault that is personal. Indeed the statute has so covered the field that it can seldom, if ever, be incurred without fault that is also a crime."

In *New Amsterdam Casualty v. Jones*,[72] J was insured against liability for bodily injury suffered by any person as the result of an accident on his premises. J shot M under a misapprehension and served a sentence for wilful and felonious assault. M sued J for damages, and on obtaining judgment which was unsatisfied garnished the insurers. It was held:

(i) that the contract was valid, as not specifically directed to unlawful acts, nor offering any temptation towards their commission;
(ii) that M. could recover under the terms of the Michigan statute because the defence of public policy, even if it would have prevailed against J, was not a defence "under the terms of the policy" but outside it.

14–53 Special provision in policy. The occurrence of a loss caused by a criminal act of the assured may be covered by an exemption clause in the policy. In *Marcel Beller Ltd v. Hayden*[73] the plaintiff company insured an employee, M, under a Lloyd's personal accident policy covering death resulting from accidental bodily injury. Liability was excluded in the case of death resulting from "deliberate exposure to exceptional danger or the insured person's own criminal act". M consumed a considerable quantity of alcohol, and then drove his car in excess of the speed limit, entered a bend at too high a speed, lost control of the car and was killed in the resulting crash. His employers claimed under the policy. It was held that there had been no "deliberate exposure to exceptional danger", but that death had resulted from a "criminal act" within the meaning of the clause. The court left open the question of what precise limitation be put upon the words "criminal act" but held that, if moral culpability was required, it was present in that case.

14–54 Unlawful acts of assured's servant. A man may insure against loss caused by the illegal acts of his employees or defendants. Thus it would be no objection to his recovery on a fire policy to show that his servant or probably even his wife[74] had wilfully burned the premises, provided that the assured himself was not privy to the act. Similarly, a chief constable can recover under a liability policy in respect of his vicarious liability for the criminal or unconstitutional conduct of his police officers.[75] In America objection was taken to an employee's fidelity insurance on the ground that it was contrary to public policy to permit an employer to insure against the dishonesty of his servants, as it would tend to make him less careful in his choice, but the objection was overruled.[76] In Australia it has been held that the unlawful

---

[71] 133 N.E. 432 (1921).
[72] 135 F. 2d 191 (1943).
[73] [1978] Q.B. 694.
[74] *Midland Ins. Co. v. Smith* (1881) 6 Q.B.D. 561. Or his partner: *Higgins v. Orion Ins. Co.* [1985] C.C.L.I. 139 (Ontario C.A.).
[75] *Lancashire County Council v. Municipal Mutual Ins. Ltd* [1996] 3 W.L.R. 493.
[76] *Fidelity and Casualty v. Eickhoff*, 63 Minn. 170 (1895).

conduct of an employee in killing a supposed intruder was not to be attributed to the corporate assured for the purpose of a claim on insurance in respect of damages payable as a result of the incident.[77]

3. THIRD PARTIES' RIGHTS AFTER LOSS CAUSED BY ASSURED'S UNLAWFUL ACT

(a) *General Principle*

14–55 Third party not barred. What is the position if a third party wishes to enforce rights he has acquired under a policy by way of assignment or otherwise, although the assured himself would find his claim barred by the maxim *ex turpi causa non oritur actio*? It must be remembered that, unless the contract of insurance is void because it is illegal from the outset or absolutely prohibited by statute, the *ex turpi causa* rule is not concerned with the lawfulness of the contract itself.[78] In a case where the assured has caused a loss by his illegal act, the rule operates to make his claim unenforceable because, on public policy grounds, the courts will not give their assistance to someone who has behaved in a criminal or anti-social way. It follows, therefore, that persons who are regarded in law as the successors of the assured will find their claims tainted by his illegality, but other third parties in whom his rights may vest by assignment or operation of statute will not be barred by an impediment attaching to him personally.[79] The precise extent of the rights of such a person against the insurers must be determined by a construction of the contract of insurance. We now consider these principles in relation to (i) life assurance policies and (ii) indemnity policies generally.

14–56 It should first be noted in relation to the common law principles described below that their operation may be affected by the jurisdiction given to the court under the Forfeiture Act 1982 to allow someone who has unlawfully killed another, other than by murdering them,[80] to benefit from, *inter alia*, a policy of life assurance on the deceased's life.[81]

(b) *Life Assurance Policies*

14–57 No recovery by or through wrongdoer. Where a policy of life assurance is on the life of another and the life assured dies by the unlawful act of the assured and no other person has any interest in the policy, the money cannot be recovered at all.[82] In the case of an own-life policy where

---

[77] *S.Y. Investments (No. 2) Pty Ltd v. Commercial Union Ass. Co. of Australia* (1986) 44 N.T.R. 14.

[78] *Hardy v. M.I.B.* [1964] 2 Q.B. 745, 767–769, *per* Diplock L.J. If the insurance in general terms covers risks which are legal and risks which are illegal, it will be valid as to the former and the latter will be excepted: *Glaser v. Cowie* (1813) 1 M. & S.52; *Janson v. Driefontein Consolidated* [1902] A.C. 484, 506; *Beresford v. Royal Ins. Co.* [1938] A.C. 586.

[79] One reason to uphold the rights of such parties is the need to ensure that the *ex turpi* principle should not destroy the value of life policies held by third parties as security: *Beresford v. Royal Ins. Co.* [1938] A.C. 586, 599–600.

[80] s.5.

[81] See para. 14–36, *ante*.

[82] *Keef v. Pearl Ass. Co.* [1926] I.A.C.Rep. 35.

the death of the assured is the result of the unlawful[83] act of some other person who has an interest in the policy, no one claiming by or through that interest can take the insurance money, and the benefit of the policy reverts to the assured's personal representatives and assigns other than the guilty party.[84] The validity of a policy on the life of another is not affected by the fact that the life assured dies as the result of his own criminal wrongdoing, and so where a woman effected an industrial policy for funeral expenses on the life of her son, the fact that he suffered the death penalty for murder did not bar her from recovering the sum assured.[85]

14–58 Where the assured is debarred from recovering by reason that the loss is caused by his own wrongdoing, all who claim through him as representing his estate or claiming a share of his estate as a beneficiary under his will or on intestacy or as a creditor are equally barred.[86] If losses caused by the assured's illegal act were deemed to be excepted in all circumstances from the risks covered, it would follow that no person claiming under any derivative title whatsoever from the assured could recover, and that the claim of assignees for value and mortgagees would be barred even although the claimant was unaware of the illegal act. However, the better view is that the rule against illegality does not necessarily create an absolute exception from the risk, but is an application of the wider rule that no man can be allowed to profit by his own wrongdoing.[87] In *Cleaver v. Mutual Reserve Fund Life*[88] Fry L.J. said:

> "No system of jurisprudence can with reason include amongst the rights which it enforces rights directly resulting to the person asserting them from the crime of such person."

In *Crippen*'s case,[89] Sir Samuel Evans P. said:

> "No person can obtain or enforce any rights resulting from his own crime."

In *Beresford v. The Royal Insurance Co.*,[90] Lord Atkin said:

> "I think that the principle is that a man is not to be allowed to have recourse to a court of justice to claim a benefit from his crime whether under a contract or a gift."

So explained, the rule would hit the assured's estate and all those claiming in respect of any interest held by the assured at the date of loss, but would not necessarily hit irrevocable interests previously acquired such as those of an assignee or mortgagee.[91]

---

[83] *ibid.*

[84] *Cleaver v. Mutual Reserve Fund Life* [1892] 1 Q.B. 147; *In the Estate of Crippen* [1911] P. 108; *In the Estate of Hall* [1914] P. 1; *Re Pollock* [1941] Ch. 219.

[85] *Podmore v. Tunstall and District Assurance Collecting Society* [1930] I.A.C.Rep. 38.

[86] *Cleaver v. Mutual Reserve Fund Life* [1892] 1 Q.B. 147, 152; *Beresford v. Royal Ins. Co.* [1937] 2 K.B. 197 (C.A.); [1938] A.C. 586 (H.L.); *Re Pitts* [1931] 1 Ch. 546; *Re Sigsworth* [1935] Ch. 89; *In the Estate of Crippen* [1911] P. 108; *Re Pollock* [1941] Ch. 219.

[87] See Lord Sumner in *P. Samuel & Co. v. Dumas* [1924] A.C. 431, 474.

[88] [1892] 1 Q.B. 147.

[89] *In the Estate of Crippen* [1911] P. 108.

[90] [1938] A.C. 586, 598; *Hardy v. M.I.B.* [1964 2 Q.B. 745, 769.

[91] *Cleaver v. Mutual Reserve Fund Life* [1892] 1 Q.B. 147, 159; but see *Burt v. Union Central* 187 U.S. 362 (1902).

14–59 In *Moore v. Woolsey*[92] a life policy was granted to the assured on his own life, with a suicide clause providing that if the assured should die by his own hands, the policy should become void so far as regards his executors or administrators and should remain in force only to the extent of any bona fide interest which might have been acquired by any other person for valuable consideration. The policy was handed by the assured to a trustee to hold on behalf of his wife to satisfy in part an obligation contained in his marriage settlement, and the assured having subsequently committed suicide, it was held that the executors of the assured could recover on behalf of his widow. In that case Lord Campbell C.J. said:

> "Where we are called upon to nullify a contract on the grounds of public policy we must take care that we do not lay down a rule which may interfere with the innocent and useful transactions of mankind. That the condition [in favour of a bona fide assignee for valuable consideration] may promote evil by leading to suicide is a very remote and improbable contingency, and it may frequently be very beneficial by rendering a life policy a safe security in the hands of an assignee."

This case is authority for the proposition that there is nothing illegal in the insurers agreeing with the assured that if he assigns the policy bona fide for valuable consideration and thereafter causes his own death by a criminal act they will pay the policy moneys to his assignee. If that be so, public policy does not demand that a loss caused by the illegal act of the assured should be an absolute exception from the risk, at any rate in the case of life policies and other policies which are not contracts of indemnity.[93]

14–60 Assignment by way of security. Where the assignment is by way of security only, different considerations may arise. If the mortgage is a legal mortgage in the sense that there was an assignment of the policy which was "an absolute assignment not purporting to be by way of charge only" within the meaning of section 136 of the Law of Property Act 1925, and which would therefore entitle the mortgagee to sue in his own name, it is clear that but for the illegal act of the mortgagor the mortgagee could have recovered at least the amount of his debt from the office without reference to the mortgagor. Thus, if we regard the illegality on the part of the mortgagor not as bringing the event within an absolute exception to the risk but merely as a personal bar to any claim made by the assured or those representing him or his estate, the only ground on which the plea of public policy would justify the office in withholding from the mortgagee a sum of money otherwise payable to him would be that the assured or his estate might indirectly obtain a benefit from such payment. The assured or his estate, it is submitted, can claim no direct benefit by requiring the mortgagee to credit the insurance money as payment in whole or in part of the secured debt. The personal bar would operate to prevent the result although it did not operate to prevent the mortgagee from recovering.[94]

---

[92] (1854) 4 El. & Bl. 243.
[93] See also *Dufaur v. Professional Life* (1858) 25 Beav. 599; *Rowett, Leaky & Co. v. Scottish Provident* [1927] 1 Ch. 55.
[94] The decisions on suicide clauses such a *White v. British Empire Mutual* (1868) L.R. 7 Eq. 394, and *The Solicitors and General Life v. Lamb* (1864) 1 H. & M. 716, to the effect that the exception in favour of assignees for value may, where the suicide is not felonious, operate in favour of the assured's estate by discharging his debt are no authority against the proposition that where the act causing death is illegal, payment of the insurance money to the mortgagee does not operate to discharge the debt due by the assured to him.

14–61 In *Davitt v. Titcumb*[95] a house was purchased in joint names and a joint names policy was effected to secure a mortgage loan. The policy was assigned to a building society. One of the joint assured murdered the other. The insurance proceeds were paid out to the building society which applied them in discharge of the mortgage debt. It was held that the victim's estate was entitled to the proceeds of the sale of the house, so as to ensure that no benefit accrued to the murderer, and to reflect the fact that the benefit of the entire insurance proceeds had vested in the estate of the victim.

14–62 The rights of an innocent mortgagee of a life policy in a case where the illegal act of the assured has brought about his own death were much discussed during the European War of 1914–18, in relation to policies on the lives of alien enemies killed fighting against the armed forces of Great Britain or her allies. It was pointed out that if a British subject had taken as security for a debt due to him an assignment of a life policy effected in a British office by a German subject, and the assured was killed in action, the office could not pay without in effect conferring benefit on the alien enemy's estate by paying his debt to the extent of the insurance money. The answer seems to be that in law the alien enemy's estate is not discharged inasmuch as no British court would permit his representatives to claim the benefit of the policy money, and although as a practical result the alien enemy's estate would probably be relieved of the debt, such indirect benefit is no good reason for depriving a British subject of his security.

14–63 In this connection the decision of the House of Lords in *Rodriguez v. Speyer Brothers*[96] seems to be in point. That was an action by a British firm for an acknowledged debt of £30,000. The defence was that one of the partners holding an interest of 2 per cent of the profits of the firm was an alien enemy and that on that account the firm could not sue. The majority of the Court of Appeal and of the Law Lords held that the plaintiffs could nevertheless recover. The Lord Chancellor (Lord Finlay) said:

> "The rule [which prohibited an alien enemy from being a plaintiff in an action] was founded on public policy, but if there might be a state of circumstances in which to prevent an alien enemy being a party to an action as plaintiff would do much more harm to British subjects or friendly neutrals than to the enemy, that was a consideration most material to be taken into account in determining whether such a case fell within the true intent and scope of the rule."

It may be said that if a mortgagee could recover where the mortgagor's claim is barred by reason of his illegal act one would get the startling result that the mortgagee might obtain payment of his debt twice over. That result, however, does not seem any more repugnant to justice or commonsense than the opposite conclusion that the mortgagee should run the risk of never being paid at all while the insurer who has received the premiums retains the insurance money.

14–64 When the assignment of the policy falls short of an assignment of the legal chose in action and the title of the assignee is equitable only, as in

[95] [1990] 1 Ch. 110.
[96] [1919] A.C. 59. See also Lord Parker's speech in *Daimler Co. v. Continental Tyre & Rubber Co.* [1916] 2 A.C. 307, and *Tingley v. Müller* [1917] 2 Ch. 144.

the case of a mortgage by deposit, there seems to be no reason why a different rule of public policy should apply, and it is submitted that an equitable assignee for value, including an equitable mortgagee, is equally entitled to recover on a life or other policy which is not a contract of indemnity, notwithstanding that the illegal act of the assured has occasioned the event upon which the money becomes payable.[97]

14–65 Criminal act of assignee. If a policy of life assurance has been assigned absolutely, and the assured's death is caused by the criminal act of the assignee, such assignee cannot recover, with the result that the insurers escape all liability; but if the death is caused by a beneficiary under a settlement policy, although the beneficiary is thereby excluded from benefit, there is a resulting trust in favour of the assured's representatives and they are entitled to claim the money for the benefit of the assured's estate.[98]

14–66 The effect of suicide. In considering whether in any particular case suicide while sane will bar recovery at the suit of one who does not claim as a personal representative of the assured, or as one entitled to share in the distribution of his estate, but claims independently as an assignee of the policy from the assured, it is important to distinguish between that which is a matter of construction of the policy and that which brings into play the principle of public policy. As a matter of construction, suicide while sane is prima facie excepted from the risk, not because it is contrary to public policy, but because there is a presumption that the promise of the insurers to pay on the happening of a specified event does not include a promise to pay when that event is directly caused by the wilful act of the assured. If a policy contains no express term rebutting the presumption that suicide while sane is an exception from the risk, an assignee, whether voluntary or for valuable consideration, cannot recover in the event of suicide of the assured while sane for the simple reason that the risk is not covered by the policy. But if as a matter of construction the risk of suicide while sane is covered by the policy, then the secondary issue arises, does any principle of public policy intervene to prevent recovery by anyone representing the assured or claiming to participate in the distribution of his estate?

14–67 The question of construction is often determined by an express clause in the policy. The clause may expressly exclude suicide sane or insane from the risk, and then except from that exclusion the bona fide interests of third parties by way of assignment for valuable consideration, and in such a case there may be two questions for the court:

(a) whether on the true construction of the clause the claimant is within the exception;
(b) whether, if he is, there is any principle of public policy which bars his claim.

The suicide clause may by inference contain a promise that the insurers will pay the assured's representatives or assigns whomsoever in the event of

---

[97] The fact that he would have to sue in the name of the assured or his representatives is not a good ground for rejecting his claim. The name of an alien enemy may be used as a nominal plaintiff without offending against any rule of public policy: *Rodriguez v. Speyer Brothers* [1919] A.C. 59; *Continho, Cargo & Co. v. Vermont & Co.* [1917] 2 K.B. 587.

[98] *Cleaver v. Mutual Reserve Fund Life* [1892] 1 Q.B. 147. Note, however, the possible effects of the Forfeiture Act 1982—see para. 14–36, *ante*.

suicide sane or insane, and this is so where the clause provides that if the assured shall die by his own hand, whether sane or insane, within a specified time from the commencement of the assurance, the policy shall be void except to the extent of any bona fide interest acquired for pecuniary consideration or as a security for money. On the true construction of that clause there is a promise to pay the assured's representatives or assigns if the assured dies by his own hand, whether sane or insane, after the expiration of the specified period, and then the only question for the court is whether there is any principle of public policy which bars the particular claimant from enforcing the contract in his favour.[99]

14–68 A life policy without any reservation in favour of assignees or incumbrancers in the event of suicide is not a proper security for a debt. It is the usual practice in this country to insert in the suicide clause a reservation in favour of assignees and incumbrancers duly intimated during the lifetime of the assured, and the policy is thereby rendered effective as a marketable asset. There is nothing illegal in the reservation, even although it may indirectly operate to the benefit of the assured's estate. Thus where the insurers held a policy as security for a loan made by them to the assured, it was held that, as they were incumbrancers, the policy was valid in their hands to the amount of the debt, and that they were bound to discharge the debt from the policy proceeds[1]; and similarly where policies were mortgaged by deposit to third parties, creditors of the assured, it was held that they were entitled to recover from the insurers, and that the insurers had no claim to the other securities in their hands, nor could they require the incumbrancers to have recourse to such other securities first or even *pari passu*,[2] the result being that the assured's representatives had the debt discharged from the policy moneys, and were entitled to a conveyance of the other securities unencumbered.[3] Whether a reservation in favour of assignees and incumbrancers includes the insurers themselves is a question of construction. Where the reservation was in favour of "the pecuniary interest of third parties bona fide acquired for valuable consideration", Tomlin J. (as he then was) distinguished *Solicitors and General Life v. Lamb*[4] and *White v. British Empire Mutual Life*,[5] and held that "third parties" meant "other than insurers or assured" and so did not include the insurers.[6] The assured's trustee in bankruptcy is in the same position as his personal representatives, and therefore, if the assured commits suicide while sane, the trustee cannot under any circumstances recover,[7] and the ordinary reservation in favour of assignees does not include the trustee in bankruptcy.[8]

14–69 In the policies of some Scottish insurance companies the exception

[99] *Beresford v. Royal Ins. Co.* [1937] 2 K.B. 197, CA; [1938] A.C. 586, HL.

[1] *White v. British Empire Mutual Life* (1868) L.R. 7 Eq. 394.

[2] *The Solicitors and General Life v. Lamb* (1864) 1 H. & M. 716; *City Bank v. Sovereign Life* (1884) 50 L.T. 565.

[3] But the reservation in favour of assignees may be limited so as to operate by way of indemnity only, and if so the company will, on paying an indemnity to the assignee, be subrogated to his claims against the assured's estate.

[4] (1864) 1 H. & M. 716.

[5] (1868) L.R. 7 Eq. 394.

[6] *Royal London Mutual v. Barrett* [1928] Ch. 411.

[7] *Amicable Society v. Bolland* (1830) 4 Bligh (N.S.) 194.

[8] *Jackson v. Forster* (1860) 1 E. & E. 463.

from the suicide clause is expressed to be in favour of the interests of "bona fide onerous holders", which phrase has been held to be equivalent to "assigns for valuable consideration".[9] It has been held to cover the interest of the assured's wife under a provision in a separation agreement, but not to cover the interest of the assured in a policy effected by him on the life of his debtor.[10]

14–70 On the other hand, if it is a term of the policy that it shall be void if the assured commit suicide, whether sane or insane, within a specified period from the date of issue and there is no exception in favour of an assignee of the policy, the condition must be given effect to, and if suicide takes place within the specified period there can be no recovery of the policy money even by an assignee for value for whose benefit the policy was effected.[11]

14–71 Public policy and suicide. So far as the law of England and Wales is concerned, the Suicide Act 1961 provides that suicide is no longer a crime, with the result that no rule of public policy prevents recovery of the policy money by the assured's personal representatives or by his assigns. The act of the assured in taking his own life is no longer illegal, so that the reasoning of the decision in the *Beresford*[12] case no longer applies to invalidate a payment to the assured's estate or to his successors in title, or to assignees, whether for value or not. The sophisticated distinctions made in the case law prior to the passing of the Suicide Act 1961 between claims brought by assignees for value and claims brought on behalf of the assured's estate are no longer important in English law, but their reasoning is still of interest in jurisdictions where suicide is still a crime and may perhaps also throw light upon principles applicable in other cases of illegality.[13]

14–72 The right of an assignee for value to recover on a life policy, prior to the passing of the Suicide Act 1961, when the assured had committed suicide while sane was considered in *Beresford v. The Royal Insurance Co.*[14] Although no decision on the point was actually called for Lord Wright M.R., who delivered the judgment of the Court of Appeal, having stated that in a case of sane suicide the personal representative of the assured had no better title than the assured, added, "the same is true of assigns", and then further on in the judgment he says that in the event of a claim brought by a murderer neither the murderer nor his estate nor his assigns can take any benefit under the policy. But, notwithstanding these dicta, we find towards the close of the judgment that after discussing some of the suicide clauses in the usual policy conditions he said:

> "Where the condition was that the policy though void in the event of suicide should operate to entitle the holder to recover to the extent of an

---

[9] *Rowett, Leaky & Co. v. Scottish Provident* [1927] 1 Ch. 55; *Ballantyne's Trustees v. Scottish Amicable* [1921] 2 S.L.T. 75; 1921 W.C. & Ins. Rep. 262.

[10] *ibid.*

[11] *Ellinger v. Mutual Life* [1905] 1 K.B. 31.

[12] [1938] A.C. 586.

[13] English policy as to suicide is considered in *Kirkham v. Chief Constable of Manchester* [1990] 2 Q.B. 283. In Australia legislation has intervened which provides that recovery on insurance in cases of suicide depends on the construction of the policy: Life Assurance Act 1945, s.120.

[14] [1937] 2 K.B. 197; [1938] A.C. 586.

assignment or bona fide interest, the interest of onerous holders was protected."[15]

In support of that statement he cites *Dufaur v. Professional Life*[16] and *Rowett, Leaky & Co. v. Scottish Provident.*[17]

In the House of Lords, Lord Atkin was clearly of opinion that the exception in the suicide clause in favour of assignees for value is effective. He said:

> "Anxiety is naturally aroused by the thought that this principle [of public policy] may be invoked so as to destroy the security given to lenders and others by policies of life assurance which are in daily use for that purpose. I consider myself free to say that I cannot see that there is any objection to an assignee for value before the suicide enforcing a policy which contains an express promise to pay upon sane suicide at any rate so far as the payment is to extend to the actual interest of the assignee. It is plain that a lender may himself insure the life of the borrower against sane suicide."

Lord Macmillan, on the other hand, said that he desired to reserve his opinion as to the position of third parties who have bona fide acquired rights for value under such policies.

14-73 It is submitted that in life and other policies which are not policies of indemnity, a voluntary assignee under an assignment which is absolute and irrevocable would be entitled to recover on a policy containing a suicide clause such as that in the *Beresford* case, which, as a matter of construction, included the risk of suicide while sane. There seems to be no sound reason why his claim should be rejected on the ground of public policy if there was no intent to commit suicide at the time the policy was assigned, and even if suicide was a criminal act.

14-74 The principles of public policy which the court applied in cases where the death of the life assured was caused by the felonious act of the assured were discussed at length by the Industrial Assurance Commissioner in the case of a claim on a life policy issued by a friendly society.[18] The insured member killed himself and the coroner's verdict was *felo de se*. The rules of the society provided that:

> "on the death of a member the sum assured shall be paid to the person nominated by him or in default of nomination to his widow, personal representative or next-of-kin".

The Commissioner was of opinion that the widow was entitled to the money in her own right and not through the deceased, and that she was therefore entitled to recover it notwithstanding the unlawful act of the deceased. The Commissioner, after referring to the reported cases, said[19]:

> "The result of all these cases, in my opinion, is that, where the event is brought about by a felonious act, the person guilty of the felony, and

---

[15] [1937] 2 K.B. 197, 210, 211, 215.
[16] (1858) 25 Beav. 599.
[17] [1927] 1 Ch. 55.
[18] *Bird v. L.C.C. Tramway Employees etc. Soc.* [1925] I.A.C.Rep. 44.
[19] [1925] I.A.C.Rep. 44.

those who claim through him, are debarred from claiming on grounds of public policy and on the grounds of public policy alone, and not because the event was unduly accelerated by the felonious act, or because the felonious act was a risk which was not within the contemplation of the assurers. If these latter were the reasons, no one could recover at all. But it is perfectly clear to me that the sum assured can be recovered so long as it is claimed by someone who can claim independently of the felon, and not under or through the felon."

14–75 These decisions collectively support the sensible opinion that, in appraising a defence based on public policy, the court ought not to be astute to discover how many persons it is possible to exclude by rules of public policy, but that rather it should limit the effect of rules of policy which invalidate contracts freely entered into, so that only those are excluded who in the actual public interest should be denied payment.[20]

(c) *Indemnity Policies*

14–76 General principles. In contracts of indemnity such as policies covering fire, burglary and accident risks, different issues arise. A contract of indemnity obliges the insurers to indemnify the assured and no other, and is at common law accordingly incapable of assignment because the assignee would have no valid interest in the subject-matter insured. That is not to say, however, that third parties may not acquire rights under the policy if they also possess rights in the subject-matter of the insurance. Thus in *P. Samuel & Co. v. Dumas*[21] where there was a marine insurance on a ship against perils of the sea and the ship was deliberately scuttled with the connivance of the owners, it was assumed that an innocent mortgagee of ship and policy could not recover if his interest in the policy was a derivative one by assignment from the guilty owner.

14–77 A similar question arose in the complex case of *Hardy v. Motor Insurers' Bureau*,[22] where a security officer was injured by the driver of a van bearing a stolen road fund licence when he sought to apprehend him. The act of the driver in driving away when the security officer was holding onto the open door of the van amounted to an intentional criminal act (causing grievous bodily harm with intent). The van driver was uninsured. The plaintiff obtained a judgment against him for £300 and then sued the Motor Insurers' Bureau for that amount. To succeed in his claim he had to establish that the driver's liability towards him was one which had to be "covered by a policy of insurance" under section 203 of the Road Traffic Act 1960.[23] The

---

[20] *Macdonald v. Prudential Ass. Co.* (1972) 24 D.L.R. (3d) 185, 192. This is consistent with the approach adopted by the Court of Appeal in *Dunbar v. Plant* [1998] Ch. 412 to a claim made by the survivor of a suicide pact.
[21] [1924] A.C. 431. *Cf. Bank of Scotland v. Guardian Royal Exchange* 1995 S.L.T. 763, where the bank had a separate interest as a heritable creditor, unaffected by any misconduct of the assured.
[22] [1964] 2 Q.B. 745.
[23] Now the Road Traffic Act 1988, s.145.

SECT. 3] THIRD PARTIES' RIGHTS **14–79**

Court of Appeal held that it was. Although an assured who deliberately injured a pedestrian could not himself recover an indemnity in respect of that liability from his insurers, the disability attaching to him by reason of the maxim *ex turpi causa non oritur actio* did not extend to a plaintiff exercising his statutory right to sue them under section 207[24] of that Act. What the Act did was

"not to effect a statutory assignment of the assured's rights under the contract of insurance, but to confer on a third party who suffers bodily injury as a result of the tortious act of the assured, and obtains a judgment against him, a direct right of action against the insurers."[25]

14–78 The decision in *Hardy v. Motor Insurers' Bureau*[26] was approved and followed by the House of Lords in the case of *Gardner v. Moore*,[27] where the injured plaintiff was also a pedestrian deliberately run down by an uninsured motorist who was convicted of the same offence as the van driver in the earlier case. The proper construction of the Road Traffic Act 1972 and the Motor Insurers' Bureau agreements, and the policy underlying them, required the Motor Insurers' Bureau to satisfy the motorist's liability to the innocent plaintiff:

"To invoke, as (the Motor Insurers' Bureau) now do, the well-known doctrine of public policy that a man may not profit by the consequences of his own wrongdoing seems to me to stand the principle of public policy on its head."[28]

14–79 Independent interests. Where an independent interest is separately insured there can be no question of avoiding the policy *quoad* that interest unless the person so separately insured was privy to the illegality. Thus, a creditor insuring his debtor's life on his own behalf can recover notwithstanding that the debtor has feloniously taken his own life or otherwise by his criminal act or wilful wrongdoing compassed his own death. Inasmuch as in life and other policies to which the Life Assurance Act 1774 applies, the name of the person interested must be inserted as such in the policy, no person can claim under any such policy in respect of an independent interest unless he is named in the policy as a person insured in respect of that interest.[29] As regards insurance on goods, however, and other insurances to which that Act does not apply, an independent interest may be separately insured although the name of the person so insured in respect of that interest is not named in the policy, and it may then be a nice question of fact whether a claimant, such as a mortgagee of the property insured, has been insured

---

[24] Now the Road Traffic Act 1988, s.151.

[25] [1964] 2 Q.B. 745, 768–769, *per* Diplock L.J. *cf. Lombard Australia Ltd v. NRMA Ins. Ltd* [1969] 1 Lloyd's Rep. 575 (co-assureds with separate interests); *Stats v. Mutual of Omaha Ins. Co.* (1977) 73 D.L.R. (3d) 324 (separate statutory right of beneficiary).

[26] [1964] 2 Q.B. 745.

[27] [1984] A.C. 548.

[28] *ibid.*, 561–562, *per* Lord Hailsham L.C. In *Total Graphics v. AGF Ins. Ltd* [1997] 1 Lloyd's Rep. 599 at 606 Mance J. held that public policy did not prevent a claim under the Third Party (Rights against Insurers) Act 1930 by a client insured against a broker's professional indemnity insurers in circumstances in which the broker had been fraudulent. The claimant was an innocent victim of the fraud. Public policy was regarded as creating a personal disability, so that the claimant was not affected by any public policy which precluded a claim by the fraudulent broker.

[29] Life Assurance Act 1774, s.2.

independently in respect of his own interest or can claim, if at all, only on a derivative title in respect of the insurance by the owner on the owner's own interest.[30] In the latter case, the contract being one of indemnity of the owner against loss sustained by him, the claimant cannot recover on a derivative title if the loss was caused by the criminal or wilfully wrongful act of the owner.[31] In the former case the claimant can recover if he was not privy to the illegality. There may, however, be cases where two persons are insured jointly or where the several interests insured are so inseparably connected that the misconduct of one person interested would be sufficient to invalidate the whole insurance.[32] The mortgagee may protect its interest by insurance enabling it to claim where the mortgagor's misconduct would preclude a claim by the mortgagor.[33]

4. ALIEN ENEMIES[34]

14–80 Effect of war on contracts. The effect of war[35] upon contracts made between British subjects or residents in the British Dominions,[36] on the one part, and aliens and others who, on the outbreak of war, became enemies on

[30] See para. 1–183, *ante*.

[31] *P. Samuel & Co. v. Dumas* [1924] A.C. 431, 445.

[32] *ibid*. at 445 *per* Viscount Cave. In *New Hampshire Ins. Co. v. MGN Ltd* [1997] L.R.L.R. 24 the Maxwell group of companies had fidelity coverage under a group policy. It was held that each company had a separate interest to insure and the insurance was composite. Therefore breaches of duty by one company did not affect the claims of other companies. But see paras 17–33 to 17–34 *post*.

[33] *Continental Illinois National Bank v. Bathurst* [1985] 1 Lloyd's Rep. 625; *The Alexion Hope* [1988] 1 Lloyd's Rep. 311.

[34] This section has been shortened, by the removal of passages on the general effects of war and matters of historical interest. For the previous full text, see the eighth edition pp. 202–215.

[35] In recent times declarations of war seem to have gone out of fashion, and the question whether a war exists or not may be further complicated by the fact that the other side is not recognised as a state. It was decided in *Re Al-Fin Corporation's Patent* [1970] Ch. 160, that the Korean war constituted "hostilities between His Majesty and any foreign state" for the purposes of the Patents Act 1949, s.24. Whether it was a war and the citizens of the "Democratic People's Republic of Korea" were enemy aliens for the purposes of the statement in the text may nevertheless be doubted. The practical answer is that in the future case in which residents are required to desist from dealing with the inhabitants of some other country, the legislature can be expected to make express provision accordingly.

[36] The persons whose freedom of action is fettered by a declaration of war are those who owe allegiance to the Crown and could therefore be charged with treason if they adhered to the enemies of the Crown. It is well established that these include not only the subjects of the Crown but also resident aliens (see, *e.g. Joyce v. Director of Public Prosecutions* [1946] A.C. 347). The phrase "British dominions" has traditionally been used to describe the territories whose residents are thus affected, but it is a phrase which causes some difficulty. It was established in 1939, both by the neutrality of Eire and by the separate declaration of war of the Union of South Africa, that a declaration of war by His Majesty's Government in the United Kingdom did not bind the self-governing dominions. In recent times, a large number of territories have become republics within the Commonwealth, but in most cases the legislation by which that status was conferred does not have the effect of taking the territory concerned outside the meaning of the words "Her Majesty's dominions". It is clear, not only as a matter of legal theory but also as a matter of practical politics, that many of these territories may in future be involved in wars in which the United Kingdom is not involved and vice versa. That being so, "British Dominions" in the text must be given some narrower meaning than that which "Her Majesty's dominions" still possesses in constitutional law. It is submitted that the term should here be understood to mean the United Kingdom and colonies, the Channel Islands and the Isle of Man and, possibly, any Commonwealth country which is in fact a cobelligerent with the United Kingdom.

the other part, consequent upon the disabilities and prohibitions imposed by the common law and upon the prohibitions contained in the Trading with the Enemy Act 1939, and orders made thereunder, is summarised below.

14–81 In so far as rights and obligations have become enforceable, or payments have become due before the outbreak of war:
  (a) such rights and obligations continue to be enforceable;
  (b) any such rights which have accrued to a party who is a British subject or is resident in the British Dominions may, during war, be enforced by action against a party who is an enemy,
  (c) but any right of action which has accrued to an enemy in respect thereof is suspended until the termination of the war, or until he has otherwise ceased to be an enemy.[37]

14–82 A contract between a British subject or a resident in the British Dominions and an enemy is not necessarily dissolved by the outbreak of war; if it has such natural life as may outlive the war and may be adequately performed during war without intercourse between the parties, and if the suspension of intercourse during war does not alter the essentials of the contract[38] the rights and obligations under such a contract may mature and become enforceable during war,[39] subject to the qualifications that any right accruing to either party, the exercise of which would involve intercourse between them,[40] and any right of action accruing to the enemy is suspended until the termination of the war or until the enemy otherwise ceases to be such.[41]

14–83 However, a contract between a British subject or a resident in the British Dominions and an enemy is dissolved by the outbreak of war if it cannot be adequately performed during war without intercourse between the parties, or if the adequate performance of it may involve such intercourse, or if the suspension of intercourse during the indefinite period of war would alter the essentials of the contract.[42]

14–84 Enemy policy on life of enemy. Where the title to a policy is vested in an enemy, whether it be on his own life or on the life of another, and the death of the life assured is the proximate result of service in the armed forces of the enemy against Great Britain or her allies, the risk is illegal and the policy-holder cannot recover. It would seem to be immaterial whether in any such case the life assured was killed in action, or died of wounds received in action, or died in consequence of disease directly attributable to military or naval service, or whether death so caused occurred during the war or after the conclusion of peace. It is also illegal during war to insure for the benefit

---

[37] *Janson v. Driefontein Consolidated Mines Ltd* [1902] A.C. 484; *Porter v. Freudenberg* [1915] 1 K.B. 857; *Robinson & Co. v. Continental Ins. of Mannheim* [1915] 1 K.B. 155.
[38] *Schering Ltd v. Stockholms Enskilda Bank* [1944] Ch. 13; [1946] 1 All E.R. 36, HL.
[39] *Porter v. Freudenberg* [1915] 1 K.B. 857; *Halsey v. Lowenfeld* [1916] 2 K.B. 707.
[40] *Robson v. Premier Oil & Pipe Line Co.* [1915] 2 Ch. 124.
[41] *Porter v. Freudenberg* [1915] 1 K.B. 857; *Sovfracht (V/O) v. Van Udens Scheepvaart* [1943] A.C. 203; *Arnhold Karberg & Co. v. Blythe, Green, Jourdain & Co.* [1916] 1 K.B. 495.
[42] *Janson v. Driefontein Consolidated Mines Ltd* [1902] A.C. 484; *Ertel Bieber & Co. v. Rio Tinto Co.* [1918] A.C. 260; *Hugh Stevenson & Sons. Ltd v. Aktiengesellschaft für Cartonnagen Industrie* [1917] 1 K.B. 842; *Re Badische Co.* [1921] 2 Ch. 331; *Distington Hematite Iron Co. Ltd v. Possehl & Co.* [1916] 1 K.B. 811; *Edward H. Lewis & Son v. Morelli* [1948] 2 All E.R. 1021.

of an enemy the lives of persons serving in the armed forces of the enemy. Where, however, an alien enemy takes no part in hostile operations either by service in the armed forces of the enemy or otherwise, an insurance on his life for the benefit of an enemy is not illegal except in so far as it extends to death which is the direct consequence of naval or military action by Great Britain or her allies. Thus, on the conclusion of peace, if the treaty or legislation consequent on peace contains no provision to the contrary, the insurance money may be recovered by or on behalf of an ex-enemy where the insurance was on the life of an enemy civilian who died a natural death, even although such death may have been accelerated by privations suffered during war; but the insurance money cannot be recovered if the enemy civilian was killed in a British or allied bombardment or air raid or died of wounds then inflicted.

14–85 Life of British rebel. The Supreme Court of the Cape of Good Hope refused to extend the doctrine of illegality so as to bar the right of the assured's representatives to recover on his life insurance policy on the ground that the assured, who was a British subject, was killed while fighting as a rebel against His Majesty's troops.[43] The court appeared to have laid some stress on the fact that rebellion and its consequences were not contemplated when the policy was effected. The *Burger* case was cited in the Court of Appeal in England in the case of *Beresford v. The Royal Insurance Co.*,[44] and the Master of the Rolls said that they could not agree with the view that inability to recover depended on proof that the illegal act was contemplated at the time the policy was effected. The court expressed no opinion as to whether or not the case was otherwise rightly decided.

14–86 British policy on life of enemy. Where a policy on the life of a person who has become an enemy is vested solely in a British subject or alien, its legality is not affected by the fact that the life assured becomes an enemy and dies during or as a result of hostilities. Thus, a British creditor who has insured the life of his debtor, who becomes an enemy, may recover the policy money if he has insured his own interest only, inasmuch as the enemy debtor takes no direct benefit from the insurance.[45] A creditor may, however, have insured for the benefit of both himself and his debtor, that is to say, on terms which would entitle his debtor in equity to have the policy money brought into account and applied to discharge his debt, and the balance paid to him.[46] In such cases, where the risk is illegal in respect of the enemy debtor, his representatives could not in a British court claim any benefit from the insurance money. The result seems to be that the British creditor could claim payment in full from the office, but would be relieved of any liability to account to his enemy's debtor's representatives, and the debt would remain undischarged.[47] It may be that if the creditor had to take

---

[43] *Burger v. South African Mutual Life* (1903) 20 S.C. (Cape of Good Hope) 538.
[44] [1937] 2 K.B. 197.
[45] *Dalby v. India and London Life* (1854) 15 C.B. 365; *Humphrey v. Arabin* (1836) L. & G. 318; *Bell v. Ahearne* (1849) 12 Ir.Eq.R. 576.
[46] *Salt v. Marquess of Northampton* [1892] A.C. 1; *Holland v. Smith* (1806) 6 Esp. 11; *Courtenay v. Wright* (1860) 2 Giff. 337; *Drysdale v. Piggott* (1856) 8 De G.M. & G. 546.
[47] *Cleaver v. Mutual Reserve* [1892] 1 Q.B. 147.

proceedings after the conclusion of peace in the foreign court of his debtor's domicile he would there be compelled to bring the policy money into account, but that possible advantage accruing to the alien enemy after the war does not seem to be a sound answer to the British creditor's right to recover the whole insurance money from a British office.[48]

14–87 Enemy policy on life of British subject. A life policy on the life of a British subject or alien, the title to which is vested in an enemy, is only illegal to the extent to which it protects the assured against the direct consequence of the war. After the conclusion of peace, the ex-enemy assured can recover in respect of the death of the life assured during war unless such death was the proximate consequence of hostilities.

14–88 Insurance on enemy property. Applying the same principles to insurance on property, it would seem to be illegal for a British office to insure a person who has become an enemy against any war risk, *e.g.* against consequences of invasion or bombardment from ships at sea or from aircraft. A fire or burglary policy on a dwelling-house or its contents, even although situated in enemy territory, against risks other than war risk, would not be contrary to public policy; but a policy on commercial property such as factories, warehouses and merchandise, or on munitions of war, would probably be illegal. In *Nigel v. Hoade*[49] an insurance upon the production of a gold mine in the Transvaal was held not to be immediately dissolved by the outbreak of the Boer War, and the assured was not barred by public policy from recovering for a loss of gold through capture by the Transvaal government, since it was not their intention to continue their mining business after the war started. This authority suggests that an assured might be afforded a reasonable time to reorganise his business after the outbreak of war.

14–89 Hostilities imminent. The law recognises no intermediate state between peace and war, and therefore, however imminent war may be, an alien who subsequently becomes an enemy can after the conclusion of war recover in respect of any loss which occurred before a state of war actually existed, even although that loss was occasioned by an act of the state which subsequently became an enemy state done in contemplation of and for the purpose of the war which subsequently broke out.[50]

14–90 Non-enemy assignee of enemy policy. Whether or not an innocent assignee can recover where, as against the original assured, the risk is illegal has already been discussed, and the same principles must apply where the illegality alleged is that of insuring an enemy against the consequences of war. The conclusion is that as regards life policies the non-enemy assignee is prima facie entitled to recover, but as regards policies of fire insurance and other policies-of indemnity the non-enemy assignee can have no better title than the original assured.

14–91 Payment of sum assured during war. The payment of any insurance

---

[48] *Daimler v. Continental Tyre & Rubber Co.* [1916] 2 A.C. 307; *Tingley v. Müller* [1917] 2 Ch. 144.
[49] [1901] 2 K.B. 849.
[50] *Janson v. Driefontein Consolidated* [1902] A.C. 484.

money to an alien enemy during war is clearly illegal at common law, and constituted a trading with the enemy under the relevant statutes and proclamations at the time of the First and Second World Wars.[51]

14–92 Payment of premiums during war. In an early edition of this work the opinion was expressed that there was nothing either in the principles of the common law or in the Trading with the Enemy Acts and Proclamations enacted during the war of 1914–18 which prohibited a British office from accepting payment by or on behalf of an enemy assured of the premium accruing due on his policy during war. It was considered that the acceptance of money due from an alien enemy was not "intercourse" with the enemy either at common law or within the meaning of the Proclamations and did not infringe the prohibition in the Proclamation of September 9, 1914, not "to accept or give effect to any insurance made or entered into with or for the benefit of an enemy before the outbreak of war". In *Seligman v. The Eagle Insurance Co.*,[52] Neville J. held that a life policy which was effected with a British office by an alien on his own life and was assigned by him to the insurance company by way of mortgage to secure a loan made to him by the company was not avoided when the assured became an enemy, and that a surety who had since the outbreak of war paid the premiums and subsequently paid off the assured's debt to the company was entitled to demand of the company an assignment of the policy to him without any reservation indorsed on it to the effect that the company did not warrant the validity of the policy. In the course of his judgment Neville J. said:

> "I also think that it cannot possibly be said that the mere receipt of a premium by the company is an unlawful intercourse with the enemy. The payment itself cannot be illegal. Then, having regard to the result of the payment, can it be illegal? I say 'no' because as regards the enemy alien he gains nothing by the transaction while he is an enemy."

14–93 Trading with the Enemy Act 1939 and licence to receive premiums. The provisions of the Trading with the Enemy Act 1939,[53] with regard to the receipt of money from an enemy were, however, much more stringent than those of the 1914 Proclamation and would seem to have prohibited an insurance company, except by licence, from accepting payment from or on behalf of an enemy of the premiums becoming due during the war on a policy of life assurance held by him. The serious effect of prohibiting the life offices from receiving premiums to keep on foot enemy policies was soon recognised by the Board of Trade, and by a letter dated November 16, 1939, addressed to the Life Offices Association, a general licence to receive premiums from or on behalf of an enemy assured was granted to all life offices, and by the same letter the offices were authorised to apply the surrender value of a policy or any other money in their hands to the payment of premiums whether or not such application was authorised by the terms of the policy.

14–94 Notwithstanding the licence given to the life offices to receive

---

[51] Trading with the Enemy Proclamation (No. 2) September 9, 1914; Trading with the Enemy Act 1939, s.1(2); Trading with the Enemy (Custodian Order) 1939 (S.R. & O. 1939 No. 520) art. 1.

[52] [1917] 1 Ch. 519.

[53] 2 & 3 Geo. 6, c. 89. Amended by the Emergency Laws (Miscellaneous Provisions) Act 1953.

payment of premiums from or on behalf of an enemy assured, it must have been in comparatively few cases during the years of hostilities that such payments were possible. During and after the cessation of hostilities, the life offices differentiated between those enemy policy-holders who were enemy nationals and those who were technical enemies only by reason of their residence in enemy or enemy-occupied territory. With regard to the former the policy conditions were adhered to and no concessions were made, but with regard to the latter every effort was made to keep the policy in force whenever that was possible by means of special war loans, the voluntary application of non-forfeiture provisions and otherwise. When technical enemies ceased to be so and resumption of intercourse became possible, the reinstatement of lapsed policies was allowed on the most lenient terms with regard to payment of arrears, loan bonds, interest and requirements regarding evidence of health.

14–95 Premiums on fire policies. Fire policies and others which are renewable only upon acceptance of the renewal premium stood on a different footing from a life policy. The tender of the payment was not sufficient to renew the policy. If the office refused the renewal premium the risk was terminated. Offer and acceptance of a renewal premium in any such case involved intercourse with the enemy, and was an acceptance of and a giving effect to an insurance of the risk under the policy and was prohibited by common law principles and by the Proclamation of September 9, 1914, and *a fortiori* by the Trading with the Enemy Act 1939.

14–96 Dissolution, suspension or lapse of policies. It is submitted that a contract of insurance is never dissolved by war. Where the assured or other person entitled to payment of the policy money becomes an enemy and the policy money becomes payable during the war, payment is suspended until after the conclusion of peace, but such suspension of payment does not make the contract one essentially different from what it originally was.[54] In life assurance and other contracts of insurance which are not annual or short term contracts, the payment of the annual premium may become impossible and the effect of consequent non-payment will be lapse in accordance with the terms of the policy. If the policy is subject to reinstatement within a specified time, that, too, may be rendered impossible as the result of war, and there will be an absolute lapse. An insurance policy is not in suspense during war because the assured has become an enemy.[55] Certain risks may have become illegal, with the result that nothing can be claimed in respect of a loss or event which but for the war would have given rise to a claim, but in so far as the risk has not become illegal the policy matures in favour of an enemy assured in the same manner as if war had not intervened. Payment only is suspended. But although the benefit of a policy is not suspended and rights under it may accrue in favour of the enemy assured, the latter is not excused from performance of his part according to the tenor of the contract.[56] Impossibility of performance caused by war is no excuse for non-performance on the part of the enemy assured, and if the premiums are not paid the

---

[54] *Seligman v. Eagle Ins. Co.* [1917] 1 Ch. 519. See, however, *New York Life Ins. Co. v. Statham* (1876) 93 U.S. 24.

[55] *Tingley v. Müller* [1917] 2 Ch. 144; but see Neville J. in *Seligman v. Eagle Ins. Co.* [1917] 1 Ch. 519.

[56] *Halsey v. Lowenfeld* [1916] 2 K.B. 707.

policy lapses in the same manner as if war had not intervened.[57] War does not alter the terms of the contract in favour of the enemy assured.[58] If a policy gives the assured a right to claim the surrender value of the policy by giving notice to the office at any time before or within a specified time after lapse, that is not a right which an enemy assured can exercise during war, and on non-payment of the premium the policy lapses without any right to relief on the conclusion of peace other than such as may be decided by special enactment following on the terms of the treaty of peace.[59]

14–97 Policies issued by agent in enemy country. Where a life policy of a British office is issued to a person resident in a foreign country by or through its agent resident in that country and the country in question afterwards becomes an enemy country or allied or neutral territory in hostile occupation, the effect of war is to revoke the direction to the assured to pay the premiums to the agent and the authority of the agent to receive them.[60] During the war of 1914–18 special licences were granted by the Board of Trade to agents of British offices in enemy countries to receive payment of premiums on behalf of the British offices, and thus the policies were kept alive. If no such licence were granted, the premiums would in law remain unpaid, even if actually paid to the foreign agent, and the policy would lapse. Such a policy might, however, remain valid against the foreign agent who issued it, to the extent of the funds of the office in his hands, and payment or tender of the premium to the agent might and probably would keep the policy in force as against such funds. The issue could well depend on the law of the enemy or enemy-occupied country, which in this respect would be likely to favour the assured.

14–98 Policies subject to foreign law. The contract contained in a policy issued by a British office through an agent in a foreign country may be a contract of which the proper law is that of the enemy country, and the question may then arise as to what law is applicable to the solution of questions arising out of the state of war. If action on the policy were brought in this country after the determination of the war, any question whether the risk was illegal, as being a contract to make good to an enemy losses suffered in consequence of the war, being a question of public policy, would be decided by English law.[61] Similarly, English law would be applied to the question whether the benefit of the contract was suspended in whole or in part during war. Where, however, the question turns on the construction of the policy, the law of the ex-enemy country would be applied and would decide whether or not the policy had lapsed during the war by reason of non-payment of premiums. Whether or not the contract was wholly dissolved by war would also depend on the law of the ex-enemy country. Where the law applicable is that of an enemy country, the question may arise as to how far the war emergency legislation of that country is to be applied as part of that law.[62] If the emergency legislation be one-sided and penal in its

[57] *ibid.*
[58] *Zinc Corporation Ltd v. Hirsh* [1916] 1 K.B. 541.
[59] Notice exercising an option under a contract cannot be given by an enemy: *Zinc Corporation Ltd v. Hirsh* [1916] 1 K.B. 541
[60] *New York Life Ins. Co. v. Davis* (1877) 95 U.S. 425.
[61] *Rousillon v. Rousillon* (1880) 14 Ch.D. 351.
[62] *Re Fried. Krupp* [1917] 2 Ch. 188. *Re Francke & Basch* [1918] 1 Ch. 470.

nature, or directed against particular classes of persons (particularly if it be directed against British subjects), the courts of this country would not give effect to it[63]; but if it be of a general nature, altering the law which governs the contract between the parties (*e.g.* postponing the due date of all bills held outside the country), then on the principle of *Rouquette v. Overmann*[64] an English court would give effect to the alteration in the law.[65] These issues would now have to be reconsidered in the light of the Contracts (Applicable Law) Act 1990.[66]

14–99 The Insurance Contracts (War Settlements) Act 1952.[67] This Act illustrates the type of legislation which may be necessary to clarify the rights of parties to insurance contracts after war. The 1952 Act empowered Her Majesty by Order in Council to give effect:

(a) to an agreement with the Government of Finland effected in 1949, and
(b) to any future agreement with a foreign government regarding all contracts of insurance and reinsurance made by persons who subsequently became enemies.

In summary the Finland agreement[68] divided contracts of insurance into different classes, and made specific provision for the effect of war upon them. Effect was given to this agreement, and to a similar agreement with the Government of Italy, in 1954, and to an agreement with the Federal Republic of Germany in 1961.[69]

14–100 Economic sanctions. It is a trite proposition of constitutional law that international treaties produce no effects in municipal law, save in so far as their provisions are incorporated in United Kingdom legislation.[70] The same must be true of the decisions of a body such as the United Nations Security Council, which exercises powers derived from a treaty. Whatever obligations may flow in international law from a decision of the Security Council, the private individual remains unaffected and no contract becomes unenforceable merely by reason of a prohibition issued by the Security Council. If legislation is adopted to implement such a prohibition it is to the legislation alone that the individual must look to see what he is prohibited from doing. The acts in international law which lie behind the legislation are relevant, at most, as a possible source of clarification in case of ambiguity in the legislation.[71]

14–101 When sanctions are imposed, there may be a specific prohibition of provision of insurance, or of the payment of claims. Alternatively, the

---

[63] *Re Fried. Krupp* [1917] 2 Ch. 188 at 193.
[64] (1875) L.R. 10 Q.B. 525.
[65] *Re Francke & Rasch* [1918] 1 Ch. 470 at 484, 486.
[66] 1990 c. 36. In particular, see Sch. 1, arts 7 and 16 which deal with mandatory rules of the forum and public policy, and art. 10 which deals with the scope of applicable law.
[67] 15 & 16 Geo. 6 and Eliz. 2, c. 56.
[68] Exchange of Notes between the Government of the United Kingdom and the Government of Finland. Treaty Series No. 9 of 1950, Cmd. 6886.
[69] Insurance Contracts (War Settlement) (Finland) Order 1954, S.I. 1954 No. 1464; Insurance Contracts (War Settlement) (Italy) Order 1954, S.I. 1954 No. 1463. Insurance Contracts (War Settlement) (Germany) Order 1961, S.I. 1961 No. 1497.
[70] See *Oppenheim's International Law* (9th ed., 1992), at pp. 59–61, and *e.g. Cheney v. Conn* [1968] 1 All E.R. 779.
[71] On the principles of construction adopted, see *e.g. Post Office v. Estuary Radio Ltd* [1968] 2 Q.B. 740, and *The Andrea Ursula* [1971] 1 Lloyd's Rep. 145.

sanctions legislation may contain a more generalised prohibition on conduct such as the promotion of trade or the provision of services; in such cases it is necessary to determine whether the legislation extends on its true construction to the provision of insurance or to the payment of claims under existing contracts.[72]

---

[72] For examples of earlier sanctions regimes (now repealed), see the Southern Rhodesia Act 1965 s.2; the Southern Rhodesia (United Nations Sanctions) (No. 2) Order 1968, S.I. 1968 No. 1020; the Iran (Temporary Powers) Act 1980, and the Iran (Trading Sanctions) Order 1980, S.I. 1980 No. 737. For a summary of measures adopted against Iraq after the invasion of Kuwait, see Bethlehem (ed.) *The Kuwait Crisis*, Grotius Publications 1991. Sanctions against the Federal Republic of Yugoslavia were adopted pursuant to Resolution 757 (1992) of the UN Security Council. It specifically required states to prohibit insurance and payment of claims in respect of aircraft registered in Serbia or Montenegro, or operated for Serbian or Montenegran entities. The prohibition was effected in the United Kingdom by means of the Serbia and Montenegro (United Nations Sanctions) Order 1992, S.I. 1992 No. 1302.

CHAPTER 15

MISTAKE

15–1 General principles. There are several different categories of case in which a contract may be affected by mistake. Those cases in which no agreement is ever reached because the parties are not *ad idem*, and those in which an error in the written expression of the parties' intention may be rectified, are considered elsewhere.[1] The cases now under consideration are those in which the parties agree, but are both mistaken about a relevant fact. Such cases have been a fruitful source of judicial and academic controversy, for a full account of which the reader is referred to the standard textbooks on the law of contract.[2]

15–2 Certain propositions command general assent. First, a contract may be vitiated because of the common mistake of the parties. Secondly, the mistakes which have that effect are not mistakes concerning any relevant fact, but only those concerning "something which both must necessarily have accepted in their minds as an essential and integral element of the subject matter."[3] Thirdly, even a mistake of such a fundamental kind will not vitiate a contract if one party has undertaken to guarantee the existence of the facts in question, or to take upon himself the risk that the facts may prove to be otherwise.[4]

15–3 The main difficulty lies in giving to the definition of the category of mistakes which are so "fundamental" as to vitiate a contract, sufficient precision to afford practical guidance. It has been said that the mistake must go to the substance, or to the identity, of the subject-matter, and not merely to its qualities or its value.[5] That is clear enough in cases of sale of goods, but leaves a great deal of room for disagreement when it comes to a contract of which the subject-matter is an incorporeal right. Another point of doubt is

---

[1] See paras 2–02 and 12–3, *ante*.

[2] See *Chitty on Contracts* (27th ed., 1994); Treitel, *Law of Contract* (9th ed., 1995).

[3] *Per* Lord Thankerton in *Bell v. Lever Bros.* [1932] A.C. 161, 235. Put another way, the mistake must render the subject-matter of the contract essentially and radically different from that which the parties believed it to be—*per* Lord Atkin [1932] A.C. 161, 218; *Assoc. Japanese Bank v. Crédit du Nord SA* [1989] 1 W.L.R. 255, 268. The party relying upon a common mistake should have reasonable grounds for his mistaken belief—*ibid.* at pp. 268–269.

[4] *McRae v. Commonwealth Disposals Commission* (1951) 84 C.L.R. 377; *Assoc. Japanese Bank v. Credit du Nord SA* [1989] 1 W.L.R. 255, 268; *Sindall v. Cambridgeshire C.C.* [1994] 1 W.L.R. 1016, 1035.

[5] See *Bell v. Lever Bros.* [1932] A.C. 161, *per* Lord Atkin at p. 226 and, *per* Lord Thankerton at p. 235, and *Kennedy v. Panama, New Zealand and Australian Royal Mail Co.* (1867) L.R. 2 Q.B. 580, *per* Blackburn J. at p. 586.

[377]

the effect of a common mistake upon a contract. It seems that at law the contract is void, but in equity only voidable.[6] It is part of the equitable doctrine that the voidable contract should be avoided only if the party claiming avoidance is not at fault and no injustice will be caused to third parties.[7] Therefore the choice between the two doctrines will be crucial in a case where either of these factors is present.[8]

15–4 There would seem to be three main classes of case in which the doctrine of common mistake is likely to be applicable in insurance law. They are cases in which insured property does not exist, cases in which a life assured is already dead and cases of compromise of claims under policies, or assignments or other dealings with policies, which are voidable, inoperative or for some other reason different from the policies which the parties thought them to be.

15–5 Non-existent property. It seems clear in principle that the non-existence of the property insured is a sufficiently fundamental mistake to avoid a contract of insurance.[9] In the majority of cases, however, a description of the property will appear in the proposal form and the assured will have warranted the correctness of the statements in that form.[10] If that is so, the insurer is discharged from liability as from the date of breach,[11] and there is no room for the application of the doctrine of mistake.

Even in the absence of an express warranty, the same result might follow if it were to be held that the fact to which the mistake related lay within the ambit of the assured's duty to disclose, with the result that the policy would be voidable on grounds of non-disclosure.[12]

It is also possible to have a policy in which the insurer expressly contracts to assume the risk that the property has already perished at the time when the policy is entered into. The well-known "lost or not lost" clause in a marine insurance policy has the effect that both parties agree to contract regardless of the present existence or non-existence of the thing insured, with the result that the insurer must pay for a loss occurring through a peril, insured against, even though the loss occurred prior to the contract, while the assured must still pay the premium if the thing has perished through a

---

[6] See *Bell v. Lever Bros.* [1932] A.C. 161, *per* Lord Warrington at p. 206 and, *per* Lord Atkin at p. 218; *Solle v. Butcher* [1950] 1 K.B. 671; *Magee v. Pennine Insurance Co.* [1969] 2 Q.B. 507; *Assoc. Japanese Bank v. Credit du Nord SA* [1989] 1 W.L.R. 255, 266.

[7] See *Solle v. Butcher* [1950] 1 K.B. 671, 692, 693. In avoiding the contract, a court of equity may also impose such terms as are required to deal justly with the whole relationship between the parties: see *Cooper v. Phibbs* (1867) L.R. 2 H.L. 149.

[8] Compare *Solle v. Butcher* [1950] 1 K.B. 671 with *Leaf v. International Galleries* [1950] 2 K.B. 86, and see the explanation of the distinction between these cases given by Denning L.J. in *Oscar Chess Ltd v. Williams* [1957] 1 W.L.R. 370, 373. In *Assoc. Japanese Bank, supra,* Steyn J. suggests that the first step is to see if the contract is void for common mistake at law. If it is valid, then one may see if equity would nonetheless hold it voidable on terms—p. 268; *Sindall v. Cambridgeshire C.C.* [1994] 1 W.L.R. 1016, 1042.

[9] *cf.* the case of purchase and sale of an article which has perished, mentioned in the Sale of Goods Act 1979, s.6, and in the speech of Lord Atkin *Bell v. Lever Bros* [1932] A.C. 161, 217.

[10] para. 10–22, *ante.*

[11] See para. 10–89, *ante.*

[12] See para. 17–8, *post,* and *cf.* the remarks of Lord Atkin in *Bell v. Lever Bros* [1932] A.C. 161, 227.

cause not insured against.[13] Though unusual in practice, such clauses could appear outside the field of marine insurance.

15–6 Life assured already dead. In *Pritchard v. Merchants' Life*,[14] an insurance company obtained a policy by way of reinsurance upon a life which they had insured. Having allowed a premium due to remain unpaid for more than 30 days, they were entitled to reinstatement only upon payment of a fine and on satisfactory proof of good health. The reinsurer in fact waived proof and accepted the premium unconditionally, but, unknown to either party, the life had dropped two days prior to payment. It was held, distinguishing the old case of *Earl of March v. Pigot*,[15] that on a true construction of the policy the parties had intended to contract only on the mutual and fundamental assumption that the life was still in being, so that the basis of the contract was gone and it was void for the mistake. Byles J. remarked that it was impossible to ascertain an intention to renew "dead or alive" analogous to the "lost or not lost" clause in marine policies.[16] In practice, original contracts of life assurance on such a basis are unknown, and it is probably only in contracts of reinsurance or in reinstatement agreements that a company would be prepared to insure "dead or alive." Neither has it been said that a proposer for life assurance warrants the existence of the life assured except by express warranties contained in the proposal form where these are present. A similar case is *Strickland v. Turner*,[17] where it was held that the purchase of an annuity was void for mistake if the annuitant was in fact dead at the time of the purchase, for there was accordingly no annuity in existence.

15–7 A mistake going merely to some attribute of a life assured or annuitant seems on principle to be insufficient to avoid a contract.

15–8 In *Att.-Gen. v. Ray*[18] the grant of an annuity made by the Commissioners for the Reduction of the National Debt to a life assurance company was held void because the annuitant's age had been erroneously certified by the company. It has been said that the true ground of that decision was common mistake,[19] but it is clear that the company was obliged by the relevant Act of Parliament to certify the age of the annuitant, and it seems that the Act made the correctness of that representation the basis of the contract, so that if it was wrong the contract must be voidable. Mellish L.J. remarked that,[20]

> "It is the same thing as in an ordinary case of a policy of life assurance where certain representations as to the age of the person insured, and as regards his state of health are made the basis of the contract, and if they are not true, the insurance office is not bound by the contract."

---

[13] Marine Insurance Act 1906, Sched. 1, r. 1; *Sutherland v. Pratt* (1843) 11 M. & W. 296; *Reinhart v. Hoyle* [1961] 1 Lloyd's Rep. 346.

[14] (1858) 3 C.B.(N.S.) 622.

[15] (1771) 5 Burr. 2802.

[16] At pp. 644–645.

[17] (1852) 7 Exch. 208, cited with apparent approval by Lord Thankerton in *Bell v. Lever Bros* [1932] A.C. 161, 236.

[18] (1874) L.R. 9 Ch. 397.

[19] See the fifth edition of this work, para. 798.

[20] At p. 407. Viscount Haldane explained the decision on this ground in *Dawsons Ltd v. Bonnin* [1922] 2 A.C. 413, 423.

15–9 Dealing with policies. It is a matter of daily occurrence that insurers compromise claims without making any exhaustive inquiry into, for example, the truth of all the warranties contained in the proposal form. If such an insurer subsequently discovers that a warranty has been breached, can he set the compromise aside on the ground of mistake? The answer must obviously be negative if an intention to compromise "liable or not liable" can be inferred from the conduct of the insurer. It is by no means unknown for insurers to pay out, as a matter of business practice, on claims which they know or suspect to be unenforceable.

15–10 If in pursuance of that practice a claim on a suspect policy is deliberately compromised, the doubts about its validity being taken into account in arriving at the compromise, the insurer cannot later resile if a new fact emerges to reinforce his suspicions.

If in pursuance of a similar practice, an insurer deliberately refrains from exploring certain aspects of the claim and then compromises it, he cannot later be allowed the benefit of a defence upon which he happens to stumble in the unexplored territory.

15–11 In the leading case on this point, *Magee v. Pennine Insurance Co.*,[21] it was not contended, neither does it seem that the facts could have supported a contention, that the insurer deliberately elected to compromise regardless of the validity of the policy. The offer to compromise a motor accident claim was contained in a letter written by an agent of the insurer after the damaged vehicle had been inspected. Other servants of the insurer, a few days later, investigated other aspects of the matter, and they discovered a breach of warranty. It seems to have been a case of the company's left hand not knowing what its right hand was doing. A majority of the Court of Appeal held that the compromise agreement was voidable in equity.

15–12 In principle the decision appears easy to support. It is difficult to think of anything more fundamental to an agreement of compromise than the validity of the claim which is compromised. The question is, however, whether *Magee*'s case is reconcilable with the decision of the House of Lords in *Bell v. Lever Bros*[22] Lord Denning M.R. boldly disposed of *Bell*'s case by saying that it showed that a common mistake never made a contract void in law, but did not affect the equitable jurisdiction to set aside a contract for common mistake.[23] It would be better to say that a contract can be void for a fundamental common mistake of fact, but that the House of Lords did not consider whether the termination agreement before them was voidable in equity and concentrated upon the common law doctrine.[24] Even that view, with respect, poses difficulties.[25]

15–13 There are, however, fine but real distinctions of fact to be drawn

---

[21] [1969] 2 Q.B. 507.
[22] [1932] A.C. 161. Winn L.J. dissented on this ground—[1969] 2 Q.B. 507, 515.
[23] [1969] 2 Q.B. 507, 514.
[24] *Assoc. Japanese Bank v. Credit du Nord SA* [1989] 1 W.L.R. 255, 266. This was what Lord Denning M.R. had said in *Solle v. Butcher* [1951] 1 K.B. 671, 694, and Goff J. in *Grist v. Bailey* [1967] Ch. 532, 538.
[25] It cannot be suggested that the House of Lords in *Bell*'s case was unaware of the existence of an equitable doctrine: see the remarks of Lord Warrington at p. 210 and note the citation of the leading case on the equitable doctrine (*Cooper v. Phibbs* (1867) L.R. 2 H.L. 149) in

between *Bell*'s case and *Magee*'s case. The contract impugned in *Bell*'s case was not one of compromise pure and simple. The directors in that case were "bought out" of their offices by payments far in excess of anything which they could have recovered by way of damages for wrongful dismissal. The payments contained a substantial element of reward for distinguished past services which they had in fact rendered, and which were quite unaffected by the misconduct which had made their contracts of employment terminable.[26] Additionally the company was keen to terminate their contracts to pursue a corporate merger, and it was doubtful whether the indefeasibility of their service contracts would have been seen as essential at the time of concluding the agreement.[27]

15–14 It is submitted that *Magee v. Pennine Insurance Co.* can be accepted as authority for the following rule: If a claim on an insurance policy is compromised and for reasons not present to the mind of either party at the time of compromise, the policy was voidable, the compromise may be set aside unless it appears either that the insurer intended to compromise regardless of legal liability, or that the existence of a possible defence against the claim was taken into account in arriving at the compromise.

15–15 Other dealings with voidable policies, *e.g.* the assignment of such a policy, should presumably follow the same rule. The rule can also be extended without difficulty to cover policies which are inoperative for some other reason, such as the effluxion of time. A more doubtful case is *Scott v. Coulson*,[28] where a policy on the life on one A. T. Death was assigned for a consideration of £460 on the assumption that Death was alive and well. The price paid was fixed in relation to the surrender value. In fact Death was dead, so that the policy had matured and was worth £777. The vendor asked for the transaction to be set aside, invoking, so it seems, the court's equitable jurisdiction, but Vaughan-Williams L.J. stated[29] that the contract to assign was in any event void at law because the parties had entered into it upon the basis of a common mistake. Since the subject-matter of the contract to assign was the insurance policy itself, the mistake was not as to the existence of the *res* but rather as to its value and a quality of it, *i.e.* whether it had matured or not, so that the buyer believed he was purchasing a contingent right to payment whereas it had in fact accrued.

15–16 It is submitted that a mistake of this kind has some difficulty in passing the tests laid down in *Bell v. Lever Bros.*[30] However, Lord Thankerton in that case approved *Scott v. Coulson*[31] on the grounds that

---

argument, by Lord Atkin at p. 218 and by Lord Thankerton at p. 236. It is also interesting to observe that the form of relief claimed by the plaintiff in *Bell*'s case was rescission. If the plaintiff was entitled to relief in equity, the failure of the House of Lords to grant him that relief is inexplicable.

[26] See particularly the speech of Lord Blanesburgh at p. 181, where this aspect of the case is strongly emphasised.

[27] *Assoc. Japanese Bank v. Credit du Nord SA* [1989] 1 W.L.R. 255, 267.

[28] [1903] 2 Ch. 249.

[29] At p. 252. The other judgments seem to approve his reasoning.

[30] [1932] A.C. 161. See Treitel, *Law of Contract* (10th ed., 1999) pp. 267–268.

[31] [1903] 2 Ch. 249.

"the subject-matter of the contract was a policy still current with a surrender value and that accordingly the subject matter did not exist at the date of the contract".

The practical view of the matter therefore seems to be that *Scott v. Coulson*[32] is still good law, and that a mistake as to whether the assured is alive or dead suffices to avoid, not only a life assurance policy itself, but also a contract of which such a policy is the subject-matter.

---

[32] [1932] A.C. 161, 236.

CHAPTER 16

MISREPRESENTATION

(a) *Fraudulent Misrepresentation*

16–1 In order to constitute an actionable fraudulent misrepresentation the statement of which complaint is made must be:

(1) false
(2) made dishonestly, and
(3) acted upon by the recipient in the sense that it induced him to make the proposed contract.

Requirements (1) and (3) are discussed below[1] Requirement (2) is the hall-mark of fraudulent mis-statements. It means that the false statement is made without an honest belief on the part of its maker that it is true but with the intention nonetheless that the recipient shall act on it. Either the maker knows that what he says is false or he makes the statement recklessly without caring whether it be true or false.[2]

16–2 It is therefore fraud if a man takes it upon himself to make a statement of fact as to the accuracy of which he knows he is entirely ignorant,[3] but there will be no fraud if a false statement is made merely through want of care in investigating or stating the facts. Although the Court of Chancery would, before the Judicature Act, set aside a contract on the wider basis of what was called "constructive fraud",[4] it is clear that "fraud" must now always be interpreted according to the strict limitations laid down in *Derry v. Peek*.[5] Fraud is a serious allegation which must be clearly substantiated, and must not be confused with carelessness, however gross that may be.

16–3 Effect of fraudulent statement. Fraud renders a contract voidable at the option of the injured party. He may thus rescind the contract and recover back what he gave.[6] It has been said that the right to rescind cannot be

---

[1] Paras 16–16 *et seq.* and 16–46 *et seq.*
[2] *Derry v. Peek* (1889) 14 App.Cas. 337; *Akerhielm v. De Mare* [1959] A.C. 789, 805–806.
[3] *Bree v. Holbech* (1781) 2 Doug. K.B. 654, 655; *Pawson v. Watson* (1778) 2 Cowp. 785, 788; *Evans v. Edmonds* (1853) 13 C.B. 777, 786. Other authorities are cited by Lord Herschell in *Derry v. Peek* (1889) 14 App.Cas. 337, 359.
[4] *Pulsford v. Richards* (1853) 17 Beav. 87, 94; *Rawlins v. Wickham* (1858) 3 De G. & J. 304. *Slim v. Croucher* (1860) 1 De G., F. & J. 518; *Reese River Co. v. Smith* (1869) L.R. 6 H.L. 64.
[5] (1889) 14 App.Cas. 337.
[6] *Clough v. L.N.W.R.* (1871) L.R. 7 Ex. 26, 34.

exercised if the other party cannot be restored to his status quo,[7] but that does not mean that he must be placed literally in as good a position as he was in at the time of entering into the contract, and it is sufficient if the aggrieved party can return the actual consideration he received under it. Thus, while the purchaser of a business enterprise cannot rescind after he has disposed of some or all, of its assets,[8] the right to rescind is not lost merely because the subject-matter of the contract has deteriorated without the fault of the defrauded party. A merchant who has been induced by fraud to purchase goods may rescind the contract if he can restore the goods, and the fact that the market value has fallen does not entitle the vendor to resist rescission on the ground that he cannot be restored to his status quo.[9] It appears also that someone guilty of fraud cannot rely on his own dealings with the thing obtained by him through the fraud as a bar to the exercise of the innocent party's right to rescind,[10] and this principle extends to cases where the innocent party has dealt with the subject-matter at the defrauding party's request.[11]

16-4 In the context of insurance in particular, it has been suggested that restitution is impossible where an insurance company has been on risk, for the assured has then had a benefit which he cannot restore. In *Kettlewell v. Refuge*,[12] the assured was induced to continue the payment of the weekly premiums on her policy by the fraudulent statement of the company's agent that if she continued to pay them for five years, she would get a free policy. On discovery that the company would not grant a free policy, the assured claimed rescission of her policy and return of the premiums paid. The Court of Appeal were unanimous in granting her the return of her premiums, but Buckley L.J. so held on the ground that a principal could not retain profits made through the fraud of his agent, and he thought that the contract could not be rescinded because the assured had enjoyed the benefit of the company being on risk. Lord Alverstone C.J. and Sir Gorell Barnes P. held that the contract could be rescinded, there being no such performance by the company as would prevent rescission. It is submitted that this latter opinion is right, and can be supported on two separate grounds. First, it may be said that the assured never received any actual benefit from the contract, and the chance of benefit which she had from the company being on risk is similar to the chance which a purchaser of goods or shares would have of the contract turning out for his benefit if the market rose. Alternatively, if it is thought that she received a benefit through enjoying the security of the company being on risk, this should not have been fatal to her claim, since it appears to be the law that the receipt of a benefit by the misrepresentee is no bar to rescission so long as the misrepresentor did not suffer actual loss in conferring it.[13] It seems arguable that an insurer who has paid reinsurance

---

[7] *First National Reinsurance Co. v. Greenfield* [1921] 2 K.B. 260, 267; *Sheffield Nickel Co. v. Unwin* (1877) 2 Q.B.D. 214, 223; *Clarke v. Dickson* (1858) E.B. & E. 148.

[8] *Sheffield Nickel Co. v. Unwin* (1877) 2 Q.B.D. 214.

[9] *Armstrong v. Jackson* [1917] 2 K.B. 822.

[10] *Spence v. Crawford* [1939] 3 All E.R. 271.

[11] *Hulton v. Hulton* [1917] 1 K.B. 813.

[12] [1908] 1 K.B. 545. Affirmed in H.L. without opinion *sub nom. Refuge v. Kettlewell* [1909] A.C. 243; see also in Div.Ct. [1907] 2 K.B. 242.

[13] *Spence v. Crawford* [1939] 3 All E.R. 271, where the misrepresentor relieved the innocent party of liability to a bank by entering into a personal guarantee with the bank himself, but was not called upon to pay any sum under it.

premiums while on risk can resist rescission. But it seems reasonable to ignore normal administrative overheads incurred by insurers in conducting their business.

16–5 Where the insurer seeks to rescind the policy on the ground of fraud, there is some authority for the proposition that, contrary to the general rule, he is not even bound to restore the consideration he has received, and may cancel the policy without offering to return the premiums.[14] In any event fraud by the assured is always a defence to a claim brought on the policy, in which case the insurer is not bound to return the premiums. If the insurer discovers that a claim was fraudulent only after paying the loss, he can recover the amount paid out as damages for fraud.[15]

16–6 Election of innocent party. Where there is fraud the defrauded party may elect to affirm the contract if it is beneficial to his interest to do so, in which case it remains valid. He is not bound to make his election until in possession of all the facts material to the fraud, and so he does not lose his right to rescind because he has treated the policy as valid and enforceable up to the discovery of the fraudulent misrepresentation.[16]

16–7 What statements actionable. Certain features must be present in order that any fraudulent misrepresentation should give grounds for a remedy. These are that the misrepresentation must be of present fact, not of law, of opinion or *de futuro* and that it must have induced the injured party to enter into the contract. These points are considered below in the context of innocent misrepresentation.[17]

(b) *Innocent Misrepresentation*

16–8 Definition. In a general sense an "innocent" misrepresentation is one which falls short of being fraudulent, but it is necessary to distinguish between a misrepresentation made owing to carelessness on the part of the maker and a misrepresentation made in error under a pardonable misapprehension in the absence of negligence and with reasonable grounds for thinking it was correct. In the first instance the recipient of a negligent misrepresentation who has acted on it to his loss and damage may have a cause of action in tort against the maker for damages where:

(a) the latter had voluntarily assumed a responsibility to take reasonable care in what was said, and

---

[14] *Feise v. Parkinson* (1812) 4 Taunt. 640, 641; *Anderson v. Fitzgerald* (1853) 4 H.L.C. 484, 508; *Fowkes v. Manchester and London Assurance* (1863) 3 B. & S. 917, 927, 931 (*sed contra at* 929); *Prince of Wales Association v. Palmer* (1858) 25 Beav. 605; *Rivaz v. Gerussi* (1880) 6 Q.B.D. 222, 229–230; Marine Insurance Act 1906, s.84(1), (2). As to return of premiums in the converse case of fraud by the insurer or his agent, see *British Workman's Ass. Co. v. Cunliffe* (1902) 18 T.L.R. 425, 502; *Harse v. Pearl Life Ass. Co.* [1904] 1 K.B. 558, 563, explained in *Hughes v. Liverpool Victoria Legal Friendly Soc.* [1916] 2 K.B. 482 CA. See Ch. 8, para. 8–30, *ante*.
[15] *London Assurance v. Clare* (1937) 57 Ll.L.R. 254.
[16] *Mutual Reserve Life v. Foster* (1904) 20 T.L.R. 715. This was a case of innocent misrepresentation, but seems to be applicable here.
[17] See paras 16–10 *et seq., post.*

(b) it was reasonably foreseeable that he would suffer loss if the statement were incorrect.[18]

The existence of a duty of good faith on the part of the assured and insurer does not of itself create or promote a "special relationship" within which such responsibility is presumed to arise.[19] Moreover, a person who is induced to enter into a contract on the strength of erroneous statements made to him by the other party to the contract may have a statute-based claim for either damages or for rescission of the contract when the latter cannot show that he had reasonable grounds for believing that what he stated was true.[20] It is established that the Misrepresentation Act 1967 applies to insurance contracts,[21] although it has been said that avoidance is the sole appropriate remedy in the context of commercial contracts of insurance and reinsurance.[22] We do not propose to discuss these two remedies for negligent misrepresentation because section 20 of the Marine Insurance Act 1906 requires every material representation made by the assured and his agent to the insurer during negotiations for an insurance, and before conclusion of the contract, to be true. If it be untrue, the insurer may avoid the contract regardless of whether or not a misrepresentation was made negligently or even fraudulently. This strict requirement is a creation of the duty of utmost good faith set out in section 17 of the Act.[23] It is an exception to the general rule at common law that an innocent misrepresentation did not affect the validity of a contract or provide a defence to an action upon it.[24] It was recognised in marine insurance in the time of Lord Mansfield that an innocent misrepresentation by the assured gave the insurer a defence to an action on a policy of marine insurance.[25] At first this exception was explained on somewhat unsatisfactory grounds such as "legal fraud", but it was later held that in every such policy there was an implied condition that no material misrepresentation had been made in the procuring of the insurance.[26] This principle was not extended to non-marine insurance so far as the common law was concerned,[27] although the Court of Chancery exercised a jurisdiction in equity to set aside a contract for a wholly innocent misrepresentation when:

---

[18] *Hedley Byrne v. Heller* [1964] A.C. 465; *Spring v. Guardian Ass. Plc* [1995] 2 A.C. 296, 317–320.

[19] *Banque Keyser Ullmann SA v. Skandia (UK) Ins. Co.* [1990] 1 Q.B. 665, 801; *HIH Casualty & General Ins. Ltd v. Chase Manhattan Bank* [2001] 2 Lloyd's Rep. 483, 496–498.

[20] Misrepresentation Act 1967, s.2. The statutory remedy, unlike the tortious remedy, is not available to an insurer wishing to claim against a broker, since the broker is not a party to the insurance contract.

[21] *HIH Cas. & Gen. Ins. Ltd. v. Chase Manhattan, supra* at p. 496.

[22] *Highland Ins. Co. v. Continental Ins. Co.* [1987] 1 Lloyd's Rep. 109, 118.

[23] *HIH Cas. & Gen. Ins. Ltd. v. Chase Manhattan Bank* [2001] 1 All E.R. (Comm) 719, 735, not dissented from on appeal at [2001] 2 Lloyd's Rep. 483, *supra*.

[24] Unless there was a total failure of consideration—*Kennedy v. Panama, New Zealand and Australian Royal Mail Co.* (1867) L.R. 2 Q.B. 580, 587; *Pan Atlantic Ins. Co. v. Pine Top Ins. Co.* [1995] 1 A.C. 503, 543.

[25] *Macdowell v. Fraser* (1779) 1 Dougl. K.B. 260; *Fitzherbert v. Mather* (1785) 1 T.R. 12; *Dennistoun v. Lillie* (1821) 3 Bligh 202; *Anderson v. Thornton* (1853) 8 Exch. 425; *Ionides v. Pacific Fire & Marine Ins. Co.* (1871) L.R. 6 Q.B. 674, 683; *Anderson v. Pacific Fire & Marine Ins. Co.* (1872) L.R.7 C.P. 65.

[26] *Blackburn v. Vigors* (1887) 17 Q.B.D. 553, 578, 583; approved (1887) 12 App. Cas. 531, HL.

[27] *Anderson v. Fitzgerald* (1853) 4 H.L.Cas. 484, 504 (although *cf.* p. 508); *Wheelton v. Hardisty* (1858) 8 E. & B. 232; *Byrne v. Muzio* (1881) 8 L.R.Ir. 396; *Fowkes v. London & Manchester Assurance* (1863) 3 B. & S. 917, 929; *Behn v. Burness* (1863) 3 B. & S. 751, 753.

(a) the applicant for rescission could restore the consideration received under the contract or, if that were impossible, the benefit bestowed on him did not cause the misrepresentor to suffer loss, and

(b) the exercise of the remedy of rescission was not inequitable in the circumstances.[28]

Since the Judicature Acts this jurisdiction has been exercisable in courts of law determining insurance disputes.

16–9 Marine Insurance Act 1906. It is accepted in recent authority that the principles set out in section 20 of the 1906 Act apply to all classes of insurance contracts.[29] The Act, however, deals only with the remedy of the insurer. Presumably the equitable jurisdiction, which applies to all types of contracts,[30] will provide a remedy to an assured who is induced to contract by an innocent misstatement of the insurer or his agent. Moreover, section 20 does not apply to negotiations for a contract *for* insurance as opposed to one *of* insurance,[31] so that an insurer wishing to avoid a binding facility or a lineslip on the ground of innocent (non-negligent) misrepresentation would also need to seek relief in equity, although such contracts are of course also within the ambit of the remedies for negligent misrepresentation provided in tort and under statute law.[32] For these reasons, it is proposed to devote less space to the equitable jurisdiction than in the previous edition of this work, while drawing attention to differences between the two regimes.

(c) *Characteristics of Actionable Misrepresentation*

16–10 Requirements of actionable misrepresentation. In order for an innocent misrepresentation to entitle a party to avoid the contract of insurance it must satisfy the following conditions:

(1) it must be a statement of fact or, in relation to the insurer's remedy under section 20 of the 1906 Act only, a statement of opinion or belief;

(2) it must be untrue;

(3) if made to the insurer, it must be material to his appraisal of the risk, and in other cases material in the wider sense;

(4) it must be a statement as to present or past fact and not *de futuro*;

(5) it must have induced the aggrieved party to enter into the contract of insurance.

16–11 Fact distinguished from opinion. It is necessary to distinguish between a statement of fact and a statement of opinion of belief or opinion, because they are treated differently under both section 20 of the 1906 Act

---

[28] The authorities on the origins and development of the equitable jurisdiction are collected at the notes to paragraphs 16–10 to 16–12 of the 9th edition of this work. The grant of a decree of rescission in equity is subject to the usual bars to rescission—Treitel, *Law of Contract* (10th edition, 1999) pp. 350–357.

[29] *Pan Atlantic Ins. Co. v. Pine Top Ins. Co.* [1995] 1 A.C. 503, 518, 541; *Economides v. Commercial Union Assurance Co.* [1998] Q.B. 587; *HIH Casualty & General Ins. Ltd. v. Chase Manhattan Bank* [2001] 2 Lloyd's Rep. 483; *Avon Ins. plc v. Swire Fraser Ltd.* [2000] 1 All E.R.(Comm) 573, 579.

[30] See Treitel, *The Law of Contract* (10th ed., 1999) p. 342.

[31] *Avon Ins. plc v. Swire Fraser Ltd.* [2000] 1 All E.R. (Comm) 573, 579; *HIH Casualty & General Ins. Ltd. v. Chase Manhattan Bank* [2001] 2 Lloyd's Rep. 483, 495.

[32] 32 *Avon Ins. Plc v. Swire Fraser Ltd., supra.*

and in equity. If the representee knows or ought to know that the representor has no first-hand knowledge of the matters stated, that together with the words used may lead his statement to be construed as an expression of opinion rather than a statement of fact.[33] A statement that an anchorage was "good and safe", made by a party who professed not to have first-hand experience of it, was construed as a mere expression of opinion.[34] Again, certain matters are by their nature such that statements about them can only be expressions of opinion, such as questions of valuation,[35] predictions of future events, or certain statements as to good health.[36] Under the Act a statement of opinion is required to be true, but it is deemed to be true if it be made in good faith, meaning that the opinion is honestly held, so that no liability attaches merely because the opinion turns out to be wrong.[37] Under the general law an expression of opinion is in itself not actionable, although the speaker will be held to have represented impliedly that the opinion is genuinely held, so creating a representation of fact which is actionable as a fraudulent misstatement if he does not truly believe it,[38] and reaching the same result as the Act.

16–12 The representee's position is stronger than the above summary might suggest. First, what at first blush may seem to be an expression of belief may turn out on closer examination to be a statement of fact where the maker is in a good position to know the facts in question.[39] Where the assured said that "he thought" that the ship on which insured cargo was shipped was the new Norwegian vessel *Socrates* and not the old French vessel *Socrate*, this was treated as a statement of fact.[40] A plain "No" to a question in a proposal form will generally be construed to relate to the facts and not merely the proposer's belief in them,[41] although it would be otherwise if he was required to declare that his answers were true to the best of his knowledge and belief.

16–13 Secondly, it has been held in a number of cases that an opinion given by a proposer for insurance may well give rise to an implied representation of fact accompanying it that the speaker possesses reasonable grounds for his opinion.[42] However, in *Economides v. Commercial Union Assurance Company Plc*[43] a majority of the Court of Appeal (Simon

---

[33] *Bissett v. Wilkinson* [1927] A.C. 177; *Hubbard v. Glover* (1812) 3 Camp. 313; *Brine v. Featherstone* (1813) 4 Taunt. 869.

[34] *Anderson v. Pacific Fire & Marine Ins. Co.* (1872) L.R.7 C.P.65.

[35] *Economides v. Commercial Union Ass. Co. Plc* [1998] Q.B. 587.

[36] *Joel v. Law Union & Crown Ins. Co.*[1908] 2 K.B. 863; *Life Association of Scotland v. Forster* (1873) 11 M. 351; *Delahaye v. British Empire Mutual Life* (1897) 13 T.L.R. 245. *Cf. Thomson v. Weems* (1884) 9 App.Cas. 671, where the statement that assured was of temperate habits was held to be one of fact.

[37] S.20(5). Based upon *Anderson v. Pacific Fire & Marine Ins. Co.* (1872) L.R. 7 C.P. 65.

[38] *Brown v. Raphael* [1958] Ch. 636, 641; Treitel, *Law of Contract* (10th ed., 1999) pp. 305–306; *Hercules Ins. Co. v. Hunter* (1837) 15 S. 800.

[39] *Yorke v. Yorkshire Ins. Co.* [1918] K.B. 662, 669.

[40] *Ionides v. Pacific Fire & Marine Ins. Co.* (1871) L.R. 6 Q.B. 674.

[41] *Zurich General Accident & Liability Ins. Co. v. Leven* 1940 S.C. 407.

[42] *Ionides v. Pacific Fire & Marine Ins. Co.* (1871) L.R. 6 Q.B. 674, 683; *Irish National Ins. Co. v. Oman Ins. Co.* [1983] 2 Lloyd's Rep. 453, 461; *Highland Ins. Co. v. Continental Ins. (Note)* [1987] 1 Lloyd's Rep. 109, 112; *Bank Leumi Le Israel v. British National Ins. Co.* [1988] 1 Lloyd's Rep. 71, 75; *Credit Lyonnais Bank Nederland v. E.C.G.D.* [1996] 1 Lloyd's Rep. 200, 216; *Sirius Int. Ins. Corp. v. Oriental Ass. Gp.* [1999] Lloyd's Rep.I.R. 343, 351.

[43] [1998] Q.B. 587.

Brown and Peter Gibson L.JJ.) held that no such representation could be implied because it contradicted the words of section 20(5) of the Act, which provide that a statement of expectation or belief is true if honestly held. The assured had applied for renewal of his household contents insurance, and stated that the total value of the contents was £16,000 and that valuables did not account for more than one third of the total value. In truth, the total value was about £40,000 and the valuables accounted for much more than one third of it. The reason was that the assured's parents had come to reside with him, bringing with them a quantity of jewellery. The assured did not obtain a professional valuation of the jewellery but relied upon his father's opinion that it was worth between £3,000 to £4,000, whereas it was worth about £27,000. The Court of Appeal rejected the insurers' argument that the assured had impliedly misrepresented that he had reasonable grounds for his belief as to the value of the contents, when in fact he did not. He had relied on his father's opinion and honestly believed what he declared was true. The result of the decision is to give an insurer less protection against ill – founded statements of belief than other persons relying on the general equitable jurisdiction to give relief for misrepresentation, despite the good faith nature of the contract. It is submitted that a better ground for the decision is that the assured had declared his statements to be true to the best of his knowledge and belief, so that the insurers had to be content with his honest opinion of value, and could not expect him to engage a professional valuer. This was the primary ground for the decision of Sir Iain Glidewell and an additional ground for that of Peter Gibson L.J. If this is right, the earlier decisions, which did not concern similar declarations, should still be treated as good law.[44]

16–14 Fact distinguished from law. A misrepresentation as to a matter of law is generally not actionable.[45] One ground for this rule is that all are presumed to know the law of the land and so it must be presumed that a party to whom misrepresentations of law were made cannot have been misled by an erroneous statement on matters concerning which he must be taken to be as well informed as the person who made the representation.[46] It has been doubted, however, whether this presumption is not an unfounded exaggeration of the much more limited maxim that ignorance of the law does not excuse,[47] and a better ground for the rule may be that, since statements as to the law involve complex and difficult questions of judgment on which legal experts can and do frequently differ, statements of law must be regarded as statements of opinion or belief rather than dogmatic assertions of something not infallibly ascertainable. As such they are not actionable as misrepresentations of fact.

16–15 There are important exceptions, however. It has been held that wilful misstatements of law are actionable,[48] and this is explicable on the basis that the maker has expressed an opinion which he never actually held.

---

[44] *Economides* was distinguished on this ground in the commercial reinsurance case of *Sirius v. Oriental, supra.*

[45] *Rashdall v. Ford* (1866) L.R. 2 Eq. 750, 754; *Beattie v. Lord Edbury* (1872) L.R. 7 Ch.App. 777, 802; *Eaglesfield v. Marquis of Londonderry* (1876) 4 Ch.D. 693, 709.

[46] *West London Commercial Bank v. Kitson* (1884) 13 Q.B.D. 360, 362, *per* Bowen L.J.

[47] *Evans v. Bartlam* [1937] A.C. 473, 479, *per* Lord Atkin.

[48] *West London Commercial Bank v. Kitson* (1884) 13 Q.B.D. 360, 362; *Harse v. Pearl Life Assurance* [1904] 1 K.B. 558, 563; *British Workman's etc., Co. v. Cunliffe* (1902) 18 T.L.R. 502.

Secondly, although the distinction is a narrow one, it has been held that to misrepresent the effect of a legal deed, document or enactment is to misstate a fact, and gives rise to liability.[49] Thus if an applicant for insurance misrepresented the effect of any relevant legal document, the policy would be voidable accordingly. If the insurer or his authorised agent were to misrepresent the benefits[50] or obligations[51] attaching to a policy, the assured would be able to have it set aside and claim a return of premiums paid, but, if on its proper construction the insurer's statement was a representation of the meaning of a clause of the policy rather than of the assured's consequent position, such a statement would be an ineffectual statement of law.[52] To represent that an applicant for a policy would have a valid insurable interest under the policy contemplated is, it seems, to state the law relating to such a policy, because it is tantamount to asserting the legal validity of the policy.[53] On the other hand, it has been held that to say that a man owns, or has an interest in, certain property is a statement of fact although such a statement strictly speaking involves conclusions of law which may be debatable.[54]

16–16 Statement must be false. Section 20(4) of the Act of 1906 states the following test of truth and falsity:

"(4) A representation as to a matter of fact is true if it be substantially correct, that is to say, if the difference between what is represented and what is actually correct would not be considered material by a prudent insurer."

This test can have the effect of merging the separate questions of falsity and materiality into a single question. Thus in a case where buildings were described for fire insurance as roofed with slate, whereas in fact a part of the roof was of tarred felt which was inflammable, Malins V.-C. decided the point in favour of the assured and said: "If the description of the property be substantially correct and a more accurate answer would not have varied the premium, the error is not material."[55]

16–17 The above test is applicable to representations which are governed by the rules set out in the section.[56] The truth of representations made by assureds or by parties to contracts *for* insurance should be determined in the exercise of the equitable jurisdiction by a test adopted from the above. A test adopted for statements made by parties to contracts *for* insurance is—

---

[49] *Hirschfield v. London, Brighton and South Coast Ry* (1876) 2 Q.B.D. 1, 5; *West London, etc., v. Kitson* (1884) 13 Q.B.D. 360; *British Workman's and General v. Cunliffe* (1902) 18 T.L.R. 425; *Gibbon v. Mitchell* [1990] 1 W.L.R. 1304, 1310. (deed set aside for mistake as to its legal effect).

[50] *British Workman's, etc. v. Cunliffe* (1902) 18 T.L.R. 425, affirmed in the Court of Appeal on another ground at p. 502.

[51] *Cross v. Mutual Reserve Life Co.* (1904) 21 T.L.R. 15; *Merino v. Mutual Reserve Co.* (1904) 21 T.L.R. 167.

[52] *Re Hooley Hill Rubber Co. & Royal Ins. Co.* [1920] 1 K.B. 257, 263.

[53] *Harse v. Pearl Life* [1904] 1 K.B. 558, explained in *Hughes v. Liverpool Victoria Legal Friendly Soc.* [1916] 2 K.B. 482.

[54] *Cooper v. Phibbs* (1867) L.R. 2 H.L. 149, 170.

[55] *Re Universal Non-Tariff Fire Ins Co.* (1875) L.R. 19 Eq. 485, 496.

[56] See para. 16–9, *supra*.

"A representation may be true without being entirely correct, provided that it is substantially correct and the difference between what is represented and what is actually correct would not induce a reasonable person in the position of the (representee) to enter into the contract(s)."[57]

A test for statements made by insurers which does not merge the separate concepts of materiality and inducement might be: A representation is true if it is substantially correct and the difference between what was represented and what is actually correct would not influence the judgment of a reasonable assured in deciding whether to contract on the terms offered by the insurer. In considering the decisions referred to in the following paragraphs, it should be recalled that in some instances the assured may have warranted the truth of his answers to questions in a proposal form, so that materiality was not in question.

16–18 Where a statement is false in the sense that it is completely untrue,[58] whether intentionally or not, no difficulty arises. Thus, if it is said that no other insurances exist upon the same subject matter, whereas in fact they do,[59] or if it is said that no company has ever declined a proposal for motor insurance whereas two underwriters have in fact done so on different occasions,[60] then the statement's falsity is clear. Other sorts of statements, however, give rise to difficulties concerning their accuracy.

16–19 Suggestio falsi. There may be a false representation without any false statement having been made in plain terms. It is enough if the language taken as a whole and reasonably interpreted conveyed a false impression of the relevant facts. In reference to representations of that kind Lord Halsbury said:

"It is said there is no specific allegation of fact which is proved to be false. Again I protest, as I have said, against that being the true test. I should say, taking the whole thing together, was there a false representation? I do not care by what means it is conveyed, by what trick or device or ambiguous language, all those are expedients by which fraudulent people seem to think they can escape from the real substance of the transaction. If, by a number of statements, you intentionally give a false impression, and induce a person to act upon it, it is not the less false, although, if one takes each statement by itself, there may be a difficulty in showing that any specific statement is untrue."[61]

16–20 Suppressio veri. A statement may also be false because it is incomplete. Although true so far as it goes, it may suppress a part of the truth to give a misleading impression. This omission to state material facts will

---

[57] *Avon Ins. Plc. v. Swire Fraser Ltd* [2000] 1 All E.R. (Comm) 573, 579, *per* Rix J.

[58] *Re Marshall and Scottish Employers Liability, etc., Co.* (1901) 85 L.T. 757.

[59] *Wainwright v. Bland* (1836) 1 M. & W. 32.

[60] *Trustee of G. H. Mundy v. Blackmore* (1928) 32 Ll.L.Rep. 150.

[61] *Aarons Reefs v. Twiss* [1896] A.C. 273, 281; and see *per* Lord Colonsay in *Peek v. Gurney* (1873) L.R. 6 H.L. 377, 400; *Galle Gowns v. Licenses and General Ins. Co.* (1933) 47 Ll.L.Rep. 186, 191; *Pulsford v. Richards* (1853) 17 Beav. 87, 96. So in *Sirius Ins. Corp. v. Oriental Ass. Gp.* [1999] Lloyd's Rep. I.R. 343 a statement that the insured premises were equipped with five hydrants (true) was construed to mean that they were operational (false).

amount not only to non-disclosure but to actual misrepresentation, since the whole truth has not been told although the impression given is that it has been.[62]

Where among the questions put to an applicant for life assurance was the question, "How often has medical attendance been required?" and the answer was "Two years ago for a disordered stomach", and in fact the assured had had a serious illness with two doctors in attendance within a year of the proposal, there was in substance a false statement, although it may have been literally true that two years before the assured was attended for a disordered stomach.[63] Where, also, an applicant for life insurance was asked whether he had made any previous proposals to any other office or offices and whether they were accepted or refused, and answered that he had been accepted by two offices whereas he had also been refused by five others, the answer was adjudged false. Although literally a true answer in so far as it went, it carried with it the inference that he had never been declined, which was false.[64] Where the question put was simply, had any proposals been made to other offices on the life assured, and the assured answered, "Yes, in the Edinburgh Life, in April", and other proposals had been made to four other insurance companies, of which three had fallen through in connection with the necessary medical examinations, the answer was held to be untrue in material particulars.[65]

16–21 It is also established in motor insurance that, if an applicant is asked whether any underwriter or company has declined to insure or required an increase of premium, an answer to the effect that one company declined the risk is an untrue statement if in fact more than one did.[66] In a burglary insurance the question "Have you ever sustained a loss? If so, give short particulars" means on its true construction "what losses have you sustained?" and an answer giving one out of three previous losses is incomplete and so untrue.[67] Where, on a fire insurance proposal, the question was whether the proposer "had ever been a claimant on a fire insurance company in respect of the property now proposed, or any other property? If so, state when and name of company", and he answered, "Yes, 1917, Ocean", this was held to be true so far as it went but incomplete inasmuch as in 1912 another claim had been made. The answer was accordingly false.[68] When a proposer is asked for the names of any previous insurer, he should give all the previous insurers,[69] and where a proposer is asked whether the risk is insured elsewhere, he should state all the offices insuring it.[70] Similarly, a statement that the tenants of a building are A, B and C is untrue if D is also a tenant.[71]

16–22 Context in which statement made. Sometimes a statement may appear to be false, but only because it was intended to apply to quite

[62] *HIH Casualty & General Ins. Co. v. Chase Manhattan Bank* [2001] 2 Lloyd's App. 483, 494.
[63] *Cazenove v. British Equitable* (1859) 6 C.B.(N.S.) 437.
[64] *London Assurance v. Mansel* (1879) 11 Ch.D. 363; *Re General Provincial Life* (1870) 18 W.R. 396.
[65] *Scottish Provident Institution v. Boddam* (1893) 9 T.L.R. 385.
[66] *Broad v. S.E. Lancashire Ins. Co.* (1931) 40 Ll.L.R. 328.
[67] *Krantz v. Allan* (1921) 9 Ll.L.Rep. 410; *Rozanes v. Bowen* (1928) 32 Ll.L.R. 98.
[68] *Condogianis v. Guardian Ass. Co.* [1921] 2 A.C. 125.
[69] *Dent v. Blackmore* (1927) 29 Ll.L.R. 9.
[70] *Pennsylvania Mutual v. Mechanics*, 72 Fed. 413 (1896).
[71] *Abbott v. Shawmut Mutual*, 85 Mass. 213 (1861).

different circumstances, and so it is always important to check the accuracy of a disputed statement by reference to the purposes for which the insurer required it at the time the proposal was made.[72] Once an apparently false statement as to, for example, the value of the insured property is placed in its proper context, it may be seen to be accurate.[73] In *Anderson v. Pacific Fire and Marine Assurance Co.*[74] underwriters represented to reinsurers that a ship was, "insured only for £4,000". This might be taken to have meant that there was no other original insurance on the ship but for £4,000 with these insurers, and this was untrue. However, it was held by the Privy Council that, since this was a reinsurance contract and it was always open to the owner to insure in any sum he liked, the reinsurers could not reasonably take the statement in this unlimited sense, but must understand it as meaning that the original insurance made with the insurers was for £4,000 only.

16–23 The true meaning of a statement by the assured must be considered in the light of all facts concerning the subject-matter of the insurance known to the insurers, and this may have the effect of restricting the apparently literal meaning of the assured's words.[75]

16–24 Statement must be considered in its entirety. A statement which is basically accurate will not be vitiated on account of a trivial misstatement or omission,[76] and, as Burrough J. said in *Morrison v. Muspratt*, "Advantage ought not to be taken of trifling circumstances."[77] Thus in *O'Neill v. Ottawa Agricultural Insurance Co.*[78] it was held that it was correct for the assured to say he owned the relevant property in fee simple though he had not yet paid for it.

16–25 Questions and answers: ambiguous questions. Another difficulty frequently arises in connection with the accuracy of the proposer's statements where an ambiguous question has been put by the insurer, with the result that, taken in one sense the proposer's answer is correct, but, if read in another sense, the answer would be incorrect. The cardinal principle in such a case is that a fair and reasonable construction must be placed upon the question. If, therefore, there is ambiguity in a question put to an applicant by insurers in a proposal form or elsewhere, the latter cannot rely upon the answer as a misrepresentation of fact if that answer is true having regard to the construction which a reasonable man might put upon the question and which the applicant did in fact put upon it.[79] This principle is

---

[72] *Carter v. Boehm* (1766) 3 Burr. 1905, 1911; *Revell v. London General Ins. Co.* (1934) 50 Ll.L.R. 114, 117; *Golding v. Royal London Auxiliary Insurance* (1914) 30 T.L.R. 350.

[73] *Price Bros Ltd v. Heath* (1928) 32 Ll.L.R. 166.

[74] (1869) 21 L.T. 408.

[75] *St Margarets Trust Ltd v. Navigators and General Ins. Co. Ltd* (1949) 82 Ll.L.R. 752, 762.

[76] *De Hahn v. Hartley* (1786) 1 T.R. 343, 345, *per* Lord Mansfield; *Quin v. National Assurance* (1839) Jo. & Car. 316, 328; *Fowkes v. Manchester and London Life Assurance* (1863) 3 B. & S. 917, 924; *Dawsons v. Bonnin* [1922] 2 A.C. 413, 425.

[77] (1827) 4 Bing. 60, 63.

[78] (1879) 30 U.C.C.P. 151.

[79] *Condogianis v. Guardian Assurance* [1921] 2 A.C. 125, 130; *Revell v. London General Ins. Co.* (1934) 50 Ll.L.R. 114, 116; *Corcos v. De Rougemont* (1925) 23 Ll.L.R. 164, 166; *Yorke v. Yorkshire Ins. Co.* [1918] 1 K.B. 662, 666; *Sweeney v. Kennedy* (1948) 82 Ll.L.R. 294, 300; *Whyte's Estate v. Dominion Ins. Co.* [1945] A.D. 382 (S.A.)

well illustrated by certain decisions in motor insurance. Where the question was: "Have you or any of your drivers ever been convicted of any offence in connection with the driving of any motor vehicle?" and the answer was "No", it was shown that a driver of the assured had in fact been convicted of using a vehicle without a suitable reflecting mirror and of unlawfully using a vehicle without having in force an insurance policy in respect of third party risks. The insurance company contended that the answer was therefore untrue, but it was held that the question was ambiguous. It might quite reasonably be construed as referring only to offences concerning the actual careless or reckless driving of the vehicle, rather than offences which could be committed while it was stationary. This was what the assured had thought, and her answer was adjudged to be true.[80]

16–26 In another case where a similar question was asked and a similar answer given, a previous conviction for using a car without a current road fund licence did not render the answer untrue.[81] Where the question was "Do you ... suffer from ... defective vision ...?," the assured answered, "No", although he wore glasses with "thick" lenses. It was held that the answer was correct because the question, when construed in relation to the circumstances in which it was put, referred to defects in vision which affected the proposer's competence as a driver, and the vision of the assured with his glasses was more than adequate.[82]

16–27 The same principle has been applied in life insurance cases.[83] Thus where the question was "Are you now and have you always been of sober and temperate habits?", and the answer was "Yes", it was not an untrue reply despite the assured's addiction to veronal.[84] The question must be construed according to the understanding of "ordinary men of normal intelligence and average knowledge of the world",[85] and, so interpreted, they applied only to the use or abuse of alcohol.

16–28 In *Golding v. Royal London Auxiliary Ins. Co.*[86] this rule of "fair construction" was applied to questions concerning previous insurances, the first being, "Are you or have you been insured in this or any other office?" The insured replied "No". In fact he had an insurance on his dwellinghouse and once had cover on another workshop. The answer was held correct on the ground that, since other questions in the proposal form referred to "these premises", the question must be given a similar interpretation, and applied only to the premises in respect of which cover was sought. In the same case the proponent was asked "Has any other office declined to accept or renew your insurance?" He answered "No", although he had at one time been refused the transfer of another person's policy. The answer was said to

---

[80] *Revell v. London General Ins. Co.* (1935) 50 Ll.L.R. 114. See also *Cleland v. London General* (1935) 51 Ll.L.R. 156, where the question "Have you ... ever been convicted or had your motor licence endorsed?" was held to refer only to motoring convictions.

[81] *Taylor v. Eagle Star Ins. Co.* (1940) 67 Ll.L.R. 136.

[82] *Austin v. Zurich General Accident and Liability Ins. Co.* (1944) 77 Ll.L.R. 409 (affirmed in (1945) 78 Ll.L.R. 185 on other grounds, this point not being contested on the appeal).

[83] *Connecticut Mutual Life Assurance v. Moore* (1881) 6 App.Cas. 644; *Joel v. Law Union & Crown Ins. Co.* [1908] 2 K.B. 863.

[84] *Yorke v. Yorkshire Ins. Co.* [1918] 1 K.B. 662.

[85] [1918] 1 K.B. 662, 666.

[86] (1914) 30 T.L.R. 350.

be correct, since "accept" and "renew" had commonly understood meanings distinct from "transfer".

16–29 No presumption in favour of assured. There is no presumption that the interpretation of an ambiguous question most favourable to the assured will be that which is necessarily fair and reasonable.[87] Thus in *Holt's Motors v. S.E. Lancashire Ins. Co.*[88] it was held by Scrutton L.J.[89] that it was not accurate to answer "No" to the question, "Has any company or underwriter declined to insure?" when a company had stated that it did not "invite renewal", although the question could possibly have been thought to refer only to the express refusal of a proposal.

16–30 Assured must be consistent in his answers. If a question is ambiguous and the assured places a particular interpretation on the words occasioning the difficulty, he must hold to that view when answering other ambiguous questions in the proposal form, and cannot say later that the insurer should have understood the answers to the latter in another sense favourable to himself. Thus where one member of a partnership answered questions in a proposal for burglary insurance which were addressed to "you" there was obviously an ambiguity in so far as the pronoun might mean "you, the partnership as such" or "you, or either of you, the partners". The assured placed the latter interpretation on the word "you" in answering two questions, but argued that he had understood it differently in answering another question which was, accordingly, true. It was held, however, that the insurance company was right in contending that his answer to the last question was false.[90] The situation described above is that the proposer's answers are on their face consistent, although their accuracy is found to be dependent upon his varying interpretation of ambiguities contained in the questions. It must be distinguished from the situation where the proposer's answers are obviously inconsistent on their face, as where in an application for life assurance the date of birth and the figure given for the applicant's age at his next birthday are contradictory.[91] If the inconsistency is such as to be self-evident to anyone reading the completed proposal form, and yet the insurers issue a policy and receive a premium without making further inquiry, they must be held to have waived their right to repudiate liability on the policy on account of incorrect answers or non-disclosure.[92]

16–31 The unanswered question. Where a question in the proposal form is left entirely unanswered, the issue of the policy without further inquiry has been held to be a waiver of information[93]; the omission to answer a question cannot be regarded as a misstatement of fact[94] unless the obvious inference is

---

[87] *Yorke v. Yorkshire Ins. Co.* [1918] 1 K.B. 662, 668–669.

[88] (1930) 37 Ll.L.R. 1.

[89] (1930) Ll.L.R. at 4. Greer L.J. chose not to reach a decision on the point, p. 5.

[90] *Glicksman v. Lancashire and General Assurance* [1925] 2 K.B. 593. For ambiguity in cases concerning proposals by partnerships, see *Becker v. Marshall* (1922) 12 Ll.L.R. 413; *Locker & Woolf v. W. Australian Ins. Co.* [1936] 1 K.B. 408. The Court of Appeal's reasoning was approved in the House of Lords [1927] A.C. 127.

[91] *Keeling v. Pearl Ass. Co. Ltd* (1923) 129 L.T. 573.

[92] (1923) 129 L.T. 573, 574; *Thomson v. Weems* (1884) 9 App.Cas. 671, 694.

[93] *Armenia Fire v. Paul*, 91 Pa. 520 (1879).

[94] *Connecticut Mutual Life v. Luchs*, 108 U.S. 498 (1882); *Markovitch v. Liverpool Victoria Friendly Society* (1912) 28 T.L.R. 188, 189.

that the applicant intended the blank to represent a negative answer. The foregoing passage in the third edition of this work was approved by Barry J. in *Roberts v. Avon Insurance*.[95] In *London Assurance v. Mansel*, Jessel M.R. said[96] *obiter* that, if a proposer purposely avoids answering a question and does not state a fact which it is his duty to communicate, that is non-disclosure. That, with respect, is undoubtedly so,[97] but the question considered in that case was in fact a partially answered question, and it is submitted that Sir George Jessel's dicta do not affect the principle of law whereby an insurer who issues a policy despite a wholly unanswered question in the proposal form waives his rights to repudiate liability unless the blank answer must read as "No".

16–32 The incomplete answer. In *Roberts v. Avon Insurance*,[98] Barry J. remarked that similar principles applied to questions which were only partially answered, so that,

> "If the omission to deal with some part of an answer carries with it the irresistible inference that the proposer intends that part of the answer to be negative, then the answer cannot be said to be incomplete and the insurers are not, in my judgment, put upon their inquiry, nor are they precluded at a later stage from saying that the answer was inaccurate."[99]

As Sir George Jessel said in *London Assurance v. Mansel*,[1] if the fair meaning of an incomplete answer to a question is a comprehensible negative answer to the question, then the assured is not to be allowed to say afterwards "I did not answer the question", and this is an example of *suppressio veri* discussed above.[2]

16–33 If, on the other hand, the answer is obviously incomplete and unsatisfactory on its face, the acceptance of the form without making further inquiry may operate as a waiver of the insurer's right to obtain correct answers and full disclosure of material facts.[3] The test must be, ought the form of the incomplete answer put the insurer on his guard? This must be, it is submitted, the explanation of the decision in *Perrins v. Marine and General Travellers*,[4] where the applicant for insurance on his own life was required to state the "name, residence, profession or occupation of the person whose life is proposed to be insured", and he wrote as follows: "I.T.P. Esquire, Saltley Hall, Warwickshire". He was in fact an ironmonger by occupation. The materiality of the concealment was irrelevant[5]; because he had warranted the truth of his answers, and the central issue in the case was therefore whether the answer on its face conveyed the impression that the applicant was not in trade. Cockburn C.J. thought the word "Esquire"

---

[95] [1956] 2 Lloyd's Rep. 240, 249.
[96] (1879) 11 Ch.D. 363, 369.
[97] See *Thornton-Smith v. Motor Union Ins. Co.* (1913) 30 T.L.R. 139; *Taylor v. Yorkshire Ins. Co.* [1913] 2 Ir.R. 1.
[98] [1956] 2 Lloyd's Rep. 240.
[99] [1956] 2 Lloyd's Rep. 240, 249
[1] (1879) 11 Ch.D. 363, 369.
[2] See para. 16–20, *ante*.
[3] *Roberts v. Avon Ins. Co.* [1956] 2 Lloyd's Rep. 240.
[4] (1859) 2 E. & E. 317.
[5] A second ground for the decision of Wightman J. was that the omission was not material.

conveyed the impression that the applicant was not in trade,[6] but the majority of the court thought that the answer did not amount to a statement that he had no occupation, but was on the face of it incomplete.[7] The company had issued a policy despite receiving this imperfect answer, so it could not avoid the policy.[8]

16–34 Materiality. The requirement that a representation must be material in order to ground avoidance is of limited effect in practice. If it has already been found to be false by the application of the tests set out at paragraphs 16–16 to 16–17 above, the statement will already have been found to be material. If the assured has warranted the truth of his answers to questions put by the insurer, any inaccurate answer will release the insurer from liability regardless of materiality, and the matter will be governed by the law concerning warranties and conditions precedent.[9] If, however, the policy contains a term entitling the insurer to avoid it only in cases of material omissions and misstatements by the assured, the reference to materiality will serve to prevent reliance on trivial misstatements. A material fact is one which would be taken into account by a prudent insurer in deciding whether to accept the proposed risk and, if so, on what terms.[10] Examples of material facts are given in the chapter on non-disclosure below.[11]

16–35 Trivial errors. If a misstatement is trivial, the court may well form the opinion that it could not have affected the mind of a reasonable underwriter at all, or induced him to enter into the contract,[12] as where premises were described as roofed with slate whereas a small part of them was roofed with felt, but the misdescription was immaterial.[13]

Similarly, a discrepancy of four days between the real and the stated age of a life assured has been held to be immaterial.[14] It is noteworthy that in both the examples just mentioned, the misrepresentation was immaterial because of the limited extent to which it departed from the truth, although it undoubtedly related to a material subject-matter (the construction of the insured premises in the one case and the age of the life assured in the other).

16–36 *Dawsons v. Bonnin*[15] is also an authority for the proposition that, if a misrepresentation does not vary the premium, the facts misstated are immaterial. A firm of contractors in Glasgow insured a motor lorry at Lloyd's against damage by fire and third-party risks, and misstated in the proposal form the address at which the vehicle would be garaged. The lorry

---

[6] (1859) 2 E. & E. 317, pp. 321–322.

[7] *ibid.*, pp. 322–323.

[8] Under s.21(3) of the Insurance Contracts Act 1984 (Australia) an insurer who accepts an incompletely answered proposal form without further enquiry is deemed to have waived compliance by the assured with the duty of disclosure in relation to the matter which should have been stated.

[9] *Re Marshall and Scottish Employers' Liability & Gen. Ins. Co.* (1901) 85 L.T. 757; *Thomson v. Weems* (1884) 9 App.Cas. 671; *Dawsons v. Bonnin* [1922] 2 A.C. 413. Further authority is given at para. 10–28, *ante*.

[10] *Pan Atlantic Ins. Co. v. Pine Top Ins. Co.* [1995] 1 A.C. 503.

[11] See paras 17–46, *et seq.*, *post*.

[12] *Smith v. Chadwick* (1882) 20 Ch.D. 27, pp. 45–46.

[13] *Re Universal Non-Tariff Fire Co.* (1875) L.R. 19 Eq. 485.

[14] *Mutual Relief Society of Nova Scotia v. Webster* (1889) 16 S.C.R. 718.

[15] [1922] 2 A.C. 413.

was destroyed by fire in the garage and a claim was brought. The decision in the House of Lords turned on a different point,[16] but a majority of their Lordships agreed that the inaccuracy was immaterial since the evidence showed that the misstatement was not material to the assessment of the premium.

16–37 Nowadays, insurers take the view that risks of collision and theft vary from one locality to another, with the result that most companies charge appreciably different premiums according to the place where a motor vehicle is kept. Evidence of this modern practice would justify a court in reaching a different conclusion about the materiality of a similar misrepresentation in a case heard today. Furthermore, in this particular proposal form there was a separate question asking in what area the vehicle would be used. That was clearly the important factor in determining the third-party risks covered, and if, as is usual, the only indication of the locality where the vehicle would be used had come from the answer concerning the garage, then it would surely, it is submitted, have been material.[17] Proof that the facts misrepresented would not have varied the premium is not, however, conclusive proof of their immateriality. There may be circumstances where the insurers might have declined the risk, although, if they had taken it, they would have taken it at the same premium; or there may be circumstances where the insurers might have accepted the risk at the same premium but upon other terms.[18]

16–38 Evidence of materiality. The question whether a fact misrepresented is or is not material is one of fact, to be determined, if necessary, with the assistance of expert evidence.[19] Materiality can, however, be determined without evidence being called, and the ultimate decision depends upon a critical assessment of the evidence by the trier of fact.[20] If the same or similar questions of fact are asked by practically every insurer, that is strong evidence of that fact's materiality.[21]

16–39 Materiality of fraudulent statement. A fraudulent statement, unlike an innocent misrepresentation, is actionable without proof that it concerned

---

[16] See para. 10–33, *ante.*

[17] The case might have been decided on the ground that the insurers' own agent had been responsible for the inadvertent error, but this was not pleaded [1922] 2 A.C. 413, 427.

[18] In any event, following *Container Transport International Inc. v. Oceanus Mutual Underwriting Association (Bermuda) Ltd* [1984] 1 Lloyd's Rep. 476, it does not have to be shown that the insurers' decision would have been different; see paras. 16–34, *ante* and 17–35, *post.*

[19] There are useful discussions of the courts' practice in admitting expert evidence by McCardie J. in *Yorke v. Yorkshire Ins. Co.* [1918] 1 K.B. 662, 670; by Pape J. in *Babatsikos v. Car Owners' Mutual Ins. Co.* [1970] 2 Lloyd's Rep. 314; and by Forbes J. in *Reynolds and Anderson v. Phoenix Assurance Co. Ltd* [1978] 2 Lloyd's Rep. 440, 457, 459. See also judgment of McNair J. in *Roselodge v. Castle* [1966] 2 Lloyd's Rep. 113.

[20] *Glicksman v. Lancashire and General* [1925] 2 K.B. 593, 609; *Mitchell v. Scottish Eagle Ins. Co. Ltd* 1997 S.L.T. 793. To the extent that an appeal court must decide whether the evidence received by a trial court could substantiate a finding of materiality, it is also a question of law—*Dawson's Bank v. Vulcan Ins. Co.* (1934) 50 Ll.L.R. 129, 130.

[21] See note 18, *ante.*

a fact material to a prudent underwriter.[22] The principle of *uberrima fides*, in particular, does not permit an assured who has deliberately misled an insurer by a false representation to defend himself on the ground that it was not material in that sense. On the other hand the materiality or otherwise of the false statement is relevant to the separate issue of whether it induced the insurer to contract. Proof that a fraudulent representation was made concerning a fact material to the risk will often raise a presumption of fact that the insurer was influenced by it, thereby putting on the assured the onus of rebutting that presumption.[23] If the fact in question is not material, it will be more difficult for the insurer to prove that the misrepresentation did influence him. A mere attempt to deceive is not actionable.[24]

16–40 Statements as to the future. Strictly speaking, there can be no representation as to facts *in futuro*, and therefore a statement relating to such facts must be either a promise, a statement of intention or a statement of opinion or belief.

16–41 Promissory representation. If a representation relating to the future amounts to a statement that something will be done, and is therefore a promissory representation, it has, generally speaking, no legal significance unless it is binding either as a term of the contract or as a collateral promissory warranty.[25] Mellish L.J. said:

> "There is a clear difference between a misrepresentation in point of fact, a representation that something exists at that moment which does not exist, and a representation that something will be done in the future. Of course, a representation that something will be done in the future cannot either be true or false at the moment it is made, and although you may call it a representation, if it is anything, it is a contract or promise."[26]

This promise must, therefore, either be incorporated in the written instrument of contract, the policy, as an express term in the nature of a promissory warranty, or it must stand alongside the main contract of insurance as a collateral promise or contract in which the promise was the consideration for the insurer agreeing to run the risk.[27]

This general principle of law notwithstanding, a promissory representation may have a limited legal effect although it is not a contractual term or promise but merely operated as an inducement to the contract. First, in the

---

[22] *Smith v. Kay* (1859) 7 H.L.Cas. 750, 759, 770; *The "Bedouin"* [1894] P. 1, 12; *Gordon v. Street* [1899] 2 Q.B. 641, 645–646; *Pan Atlantic Ins. Co. v. Pine Top Ins. Co.* [1995] 1 A.C. 501, 533. For the elements of actionable fraudulent misstatements, see para. 16–1, *ante*. See also Treitel, *Law of Contract* (10th ed., 1999) p. 317.

[23] *Smith v. Chadwick* (1884) 9 App.Cas. 187, 196; *Pan Atlantic Ins. Co. v. Pine Top Ins. Co.* [1995] 1 A.C. 501; *St Paul Fire & Marine Ins. Co. v. McConnell Dowell* [1995] 2 Lloyd's Rep. 116, 127.

[24] *Macleay v. Tait* [1906] A.C. 24; *Horwood v. Statesman Publishing Co.* (1929) 141 L.T. 54, 58; *Smith v. Chadwick* (1884) 9 App.Cas. 187.

[25] *Yorkshire Insurance v. Craine* [1922] 2 A.C. 541, 553; for the nature of promissory warranties see paras 10–62 and 10–70, *et seq.*, *ante*.

[26] *Beattie v. Lord Edbury* (1872) L.R. 7 Ch.App. 777, 804. See also *Maddison v. Alderson* (1883) 8 App.Cas. 467, 473 *per* Lord Selborne L.C. In *Dawsons v. Bonnin* [1922] 2 A.C. 413, 423, Viscount Haldane described Mellish L.J. as a great master of accuracy in legal phraseology.

[27] The elements of collateral contracts are outlined in Treitel, *Laws of Contract* (10th ed., 1999) pp. 540–542.

law of marine insurance it may still be the law, following the House of Lords decision in *Dennistoun v. Lillie*,[28] that a promissory representation of a material fact will render the contract voidable if unfulfilled, whether made fraudulently or not. The decision has not been followed in non-marine insurance cases and may well not have survived the Marine Insurance Act 1906, in which the wording of section 20 seems to exclude this type of representation.[29]

16–42 Secondly, non-performance of a promissory representation has been held to be a bar to the granting of the equitable relief of a decree for specific performance, because "the conduct of the party applying for relief is always an important element for consideration",[30] although the promise had no other legal significance at all. Lord Cairns remarked

"I quite agree that this representation was not a guarantee. It was not introduced into the agreement on the face of it, and the result is that in all probability the plaintiff could not sue in a court of law for a breach of any such guarantee or undertaking, and very probably he could not maintain a suit in a court of equity to cancel the agreement on the ground of misrepresentation. At the same time . . . it is a perfectly good defence in a suit for specific performance, if it is proved in point of fact that the representation made has not been fulfilled."[31]

Therefore, if for instance, an applicant for a fire insurance policy promised to have some alterations made on the premises so as to minimise the risk of fire, and the company thereupon accepted the proposal and issued a cover note, they would not be bound to issue a policy until the promised alterations had been made, but if they issued a policy without insisting on the alterations and without any promise or warranty in the policy, they could not afterwards resist a claim on the ground that the representation was not fulfilled, even though the loss arose directly by reason of its non-fulfilment. It is possible that a similar rule applies to expressions of intention made prior to contract.

16–43 Statement of intention. If the applicant makes a representation *de futuro* relating to something which is or may be within his control, it may very well be upon its true construction an expression of his then existing intention to see that something shall be done without amounting to a promise that it will be realised. It is then not a representation as to the future at all but a representation of present intention, and it will be a misrepresentation in law only when it is shown that the applicant never entertained the intention which he represented himself as having. The only statement of fact involved in a statement of intention is that the stated intention is currently present in the mind of the applicant.[32] It follows that a subsequent change of intention or acts done contrary to the expressed intention will not invalidate

[28] (1821) 3 Bligh 202.
[29] The marine cases on promissory representations are discussed very usefully in Arnould (16th ed.), Vol. II at paras 600–603.
[30] *Lamare v. Dixon* (1873) L.R. 6 H.L. 414, 423.
[31] (1873) L.R. 6 H.L. 414, 428; see too *Myers v. Watson* (1851) 1 Sim.(N.S.) 523, 529; *Chappell v. Gregory* (1863) 34 Beav. 250.
[32] *Benham v. United Guarantee and Life Assurance* (1852) 7 Ex. 744; *Grant v. Aetna Ins. Co.* (1862) 15 Moo.P.C.C. 516; *British Airways Board v. Taylor* [1976] 1 W.L.R. 17, 23–24; *Avon Ins. Plc v. Swire Fraser Ltd* [2001] 1 All E.R. (Comm) 573, 598–599; *Seismik Securitie A.G. v. Sphere Drake Ins. Plc.* [1997] 2 C.L.Y. 3157.

the policy. Thus, in *Benham v. United Guarantee and Life Assurance*[33] the applicant had, as treasurer of a literary institution, sought to obtain a fidelity policy for his institution, declaring, *inter alia*, that there would be a fortnightly check made by a finance committee on the secretary's accounts. The committee did not sit regularly, and a claim was made on account of the secretary's dishonesty. It was held that the assured could recover inasmuch as the statement about the committee was only a declaration of the course intended to be pursued at the time, despite the fact that the answers of the applicant were made the basis of the contract. Since this decision was reached before the important House of Lords decisions on the effect of "basis of contract" clauses,[34] it is probable that the statement would today be interpreted as a promissory warranty, and it would therefore be a condition of the policy that the stated intention would be carried out. Even in the case of a mere representation, any change of intention prior to the issue of the policy must be communicated, because the declaration of intent continues up to the execution of the policy.[35]

16–44 It will be clear from the foregoing paragraph that the rules concerning statements of intention to some extent mitigate the effect of the law on promissory representations as to future conduct. A statement that a man will do a thing can be construed either as a statement as to his future conduct or a statement as to his present intention concerning the future. The courts are prepared to lean in favour of the latter construction, especially where there is deceit. The result is the fulfilment of the requirement that there must be a misstatement of an existing fact, because the present state of a man's mind is as much a fact as anything else.[36]

16–45 Implied representation of reasonable grounds. A statement as to a future state of affairs is one of expectation or belief about future events, but it often carries with it an implied representation of fact, that the maker possesses reasonable grounds for his opinion or forecast. The latter statement is one of fact, so that it can be tested by reference to the present or past facts which are said to justify his views.[37] Thus it is usual in the presentation of a risk for reinsurance to give estimates of future claims and premium income. While these are in themselves merely predictions and not representations of fact, they can be interpreted as entailing implied representations that there exist reasonable grounds for them, and the loss and income statistics available at the time of placement can be scrutinised in order to see if they provide a reasonable justification for what is being said.[38]

16–46 Inducement of contract. A misrepresentation by one party to a contract of insurance does not entitle the other to avoid the policy unless it "induced" the making of the contract in the sense that "induced" has in the general law of contract.[39] The plaintiff must show that the misrepresentation

---

[33] (1852) 7 Ex. 744. Contrast, *Towle v. National Guardian* (1861) 30 L.J.Ch. 900.

[34] *Anderson v. Fitzgerald* (1853) 4 H.L.Cas. 484; *Thomson v. Weems* (1884) 9 App.Cas. 671.

[35] *Re Marshall and Scottish Employers' Liability, Co.* (1901) 85 L.T. 757; *Traill v. Baring* (1864) 4 De G., J. & S. 318; *Notman v. Anchor Assurance* (1858) 4 C.B.(N.S.) 476.

[36] *Edgington v. Fitzmaurice* (1884) 29 Ch.D. 459, 483 *per* Bowen L.J.

[37] See the discussion of the authorities at para. 16–13, *supra*.

[38] *Hill v. Citadel Ins. Co. Ltd* [1995] L.R.L.R. 218, 227; *Simner v. New India Ass. Co. Ltd* [1995] L.R.L.R. 240, 259.

[39] *Pan Atlantic Ins. Co. v. Pine Top Ins. Co.* [1995] 1 A.C. 501, 549.

was a real and substantial cause of his entering into the contract on terms that he would not have accepted if he had been appraised of the truth.[40] It may well be reasonable to infer, in the absence of evidence from the plaintiff, that he would not have contracted, either on the same terms or at all, if the misrepresentation had not been made.[41] When the assured has made a misrepresentation about a fact material to the risk and which, by definition, would influence the mind of a prudent insurer in deciding whether to take the risk and on what terms, it should not be difficult for a court to presume that it induced the making of the contract. The assured can rebut this presumption only by showing that, even if the misrepresentation had not been made, the particular insurer would still have granted cover on the same terms.[42] Or that while the misrepresentation encouraged him to contract as he did, it was not a substantial cause which induced the contract.[43]

16–47 Rebuttal of presumption. The assured who wishes to prove that his misrepresentation did not influence the particular insurer may do so in a variety of ways. For instance, he may prove either that the misstatement was never communicated to the insurers, that they were aware of the truth, that they acted on their own investigation without any real reliance on the misrepresentation, or that some statement was made by the insurers to the effect that little or no importance was attached to that particular aspect of the matter.

16–48 It is obviously impossible for insurers who accepted a proposal in ignorance of the assured's misrepresentation to claim that they were misled by it. Thus a misrepresentation made to an agent of the insurance company cannot vitiate the policy unless it was communicated by the agent to the directors, or unless they acted on the agent's report which would, but for the misstatement, have been unfavourable. Neither can the insurers be misled if they know the truth. If the true facts are made known to, or discovered by, the agent of the insurers, in circumstances where the knowledge of the agent can properly be deemed to be the knowledge of his principals, the company must be taken to know the true facts.[44] Where, however, the insurers merely have the opportunity or means of discovering the truth *aliunde* and fail to do so, they are not precluded from relying upon the misrepresentation[45] even though their conduct in not pursuing the chance offered them may have amounted to negligence.[46] Thus if the assured shows to the insurers papers or plans relating to the risk and states what is contained in them, he cannot be

---

[40] *St Paul Fire & Marine Ins. Co. v. McConnell Dowell* [1995] 2 Lloyd's Rep. 116, 124–125 (innocent misrepresentation/non disclosure); *JEB Fasteners v. Marks Bloom & Co.* [1983] 1 All E.R. 583 (action for damages for negligent misrepresentation); *Edgington v. Fitzmaurice* (1884) 29 Ch.D. 459; *Pulsford v. Richards* (1853) 17 Beav. 87, 96 (fraudulent misrepresentations); *Avon Ins. Plc. v. Swire Fraser Ltd* [2000] 1 All E.R. (Comm) 573, 580, 633 (action for damages under Misrepresentation Act 1967).
[41] *Smith v. Chadwick* (1884) L.R. 9 App.Cas. 187, 196.
[42] *Zurich General Accident & Liability Co. v. Morrison* [1942] 2 K.B. 53, 58, 65. This was a case in which s.10(3) of the R.T.A. 1934 (now s.151 of the R.T.A. 1988) required the insurer to show that the policy was obtained by a material misrepresentation.
[43] *Avon Ins. Plc. v. Swire Fraser Ltd* [2000] 1 All E.R. (Comm) 573, 633–637.
[44] *Bawden v. London, Edinburgh and Glasgow Life Ass. Co.* [1892] 2 Q.B. 534; *Holdsworth v. Lancs. and Yorks Ins. Co.* (1907) 23 T.L.R. 521.
[45] *Mackintosh v. Marshall* (1843) 11 M. & W. 116; *Scottish Equitable v. Buist* (1876) 3 R. 1078; (1878) 5 R. (H.L.) 64.
[46] *Redgrave v. Hurd* (1882) 20 Ch.D. 1, 13, 23, 24.

heard to say afterwards that the insurers ought to have verified his statements by checking the documents.

16–49 There is authority to show that this rule applies to the careless recipients of both fraudulent and innocent misrepresentations,[47] but it is arguable that it should be confined to cases where the "innocent" (*i.e.* non-fraudulent) misrepresentor has been careless as well as the misrepresentee who has failed to check the accuracy of his statement.[48] The law now distinguishes between careless misstatements and wholly excusable ones, and it is perhaps just that the negligent recipient of inaccurate statements of fact ought not to make a wholly innocent misrepresentor bear the loss occasioned by his mistake, at least where it is normal business practice to check information that is easy to verify without any extra expense being incurred.

16–50 Insurers' own investigations. If the assured can prove that the insurers, instead of relying on the false statement which was made to them, investigated the facts for themselves and acted on the results of their investigations, the false statement cannot be said to have induced them to issue a policy, whether they have actually discovered the truth or not, for they disregarded it and acted on their own inquiry. It must be shown clearly that the insurers not only investigated the facts[49] but also relied eventually on the result of their own investigation, since it might be the case that the investigation was perfunctory precisely because the insurers relied upon the assured's definite statements concerning the subject-matter of the risk. The test, therefore, is not whether the insurers simply investigated the facts for themselves, but whether it is a reasonable inference from their conduct that they relied mainly upon their own investigation.[50] Where, for instance, an agent of the insurers has examined the premises proposed for a fire risk, it would probably be assumed that the insurers acted upon the result of their agent's examination rather than the representations of the applicant concerning matters which ought to have been obvious to the agent in the course of a reasonably diligent examination.[51]

16–51 Finally, there is the possibility that the assured may be able to prove, by the insurer's own admission or otherwise, that certain facts are of no account to him, even if material to other insurers generally. In such a case the facts in dispute do not cease to be material facts, but the insurer cannot afterwards say that he relied upon them in issuing a policy.[52]

16–52 The decoy policy. Where an insurance obtained by fraud or concealment is put forward as a decoy to induce other insurers to accept the risk, the policy obtained by such representation is voidable. In *Hanley v. Pacific Fire & Marine Insurance Co.*[53] an applicant, in answer to the usual

---

[47] *ibid.*
[48] See Treitel, *Law of Contract* (10th ed., 1999), pp. 314–315.
[49] *Sweeney v. Promoter Life* (1863) 14 Ir.C.L.R. 476.
[50] *Attwood v. Small* (1838) 6 Cl. & F. 232, 344, 497; *Redgrave v. Hurd* (1882) 20 Ch.D. 1; *Edgington v. Fitzmaurice* (1884) 29 Ch.D. 459.
[51] *Re Universal Non-Tariff Fire Co.* (1875) L.R. 19 Eq. 485.
[52] *Berger v. Pollock* [1973] 2 Lloyd's Rep. 442; *Pan Atlantic Ins. Co. v. Pine Top Ins. Co.* [1995] 1 A.C. 501, 550, 567.
[53] (1893)14 N.S.W.R. (Law) 224.

question, stated that he was insured elsewhere, but the insurances mentioned had been obtained by fraud and the policy obtained on the faith of them was set aside. A statement that a previous insurer covered the same risk at a particular rate carries with it an implied representation that full disclosure was made to the prior insurer.[54]

16–53 Leaders and followers. A related problem arises when an applicant induces one insurer by misrepresentation or fraud to subscribe to a policy and thereby following insurers are drawn in to underwrite it. In a very early life insurance case[55] where this occurred the whole policy was cancelled on the ground of fraud. In the Lloyd's marine insurance market it was established in the late eighteenth and early nineteenth centuries that a material misrepresentation of fact made to the first-named underwriter on a slip or policy was a ground of avoidance not only by him but by following underwriters even though the misrepresentation was not repeated to them.[56] As Lord Mansfield said in *Barber v. Fletcher*,[57] "a representation to the first underwriter extends to the others." It appears that this rule rested upon a presumption that the following underwriters were induced to subscribe by their confidence in the skill and judgment of the first-named where he was a "good man"[58] The rule was described by Lord Ellenborough C.J. as a "proposition ... to be received with great qualification"[59] and one which was difficult to support on principle.[60] In more recent times it has been doubted,[61] and said to be inconsistent with the provisions of section 20 of the Marine Insurance Act 1906.[62] It is difficult to envisage an insurer successfully relying on it today.

16–54 Correction of facts represented. Representations and warranties as to present facts must be read as continuing to apply to the facts stated up to the time when a binding contract is concluded between the parties. In marine insurance, where the material time is the issue of the slip,[63] no change occurring after that time need be notified to the insurers, since the insurer who has issued a slip is in honour bound to issue a policy. In other classes of insurance there is no such rule of practice, and the material time is the time when the contract becomes legally complete. If, therefore, after a representation has been made the circumstances alter before the contract is complete, and that fact is not disclosed, the original representation becomes untrue, rendering the applicant guilty not only of non-disclosure but of

---

[54] *Container Transport International v. Oceanus Mut. Underwriting Assoc.* [1984] 1 Lloyd's Rep. 476, 522.

[55] *Whittingham v. Thornburgh* (1690) 2 Vern. 206.

[56] Arnould, *Law of Marine Insurance* (16th ed., 1981), Vol. 2, paras 623–624, and see the citations from the 19th century marine insurance text books in *Grant v. Aetna Ins. Co.* (1860) 11 Low.Can.R. 128, 136–139.

[57] (1779) 1 Dougl. 305, 306.

[58] *Pawson v. Watson* (1778) 2 Cowp. 785, 786, 789.

[59] *Forrester v. Pigou* (1813) 1 M. & S. 9, 13.

[60] *Bell v. Carstairs* (1810) 2 Camp. 543, 544.

[61] *The "Zephyr"* [1985] 2 Lloyd's Rep. 529, 539, *per* Mustill L.J.

[62] *Bank Leumi le Israel v. British National Ins. Co.* [1988] 1 Lloyd's Rep. 71, 77–78, *per* Saville J. A market usage cannot be accorded judicial recognition if contrary to statute.

[63] Marine Insurance Act 1906, ss.20(1), 21; and *Lishman v. Northern Maritime Ins. Co.* (1873) L.R. 8 C.P. 216; (1875) L.R. 10 C.P. 179.

misrepresentation also.[64] Thus, where on an application for life assurance the insurers intimated to the applicant that his life had been accepted for insurance, but the applicant was severely injured before the first premium was paid or the policy issued, it was held that statements made in the proposal as to the good health of the applicant had become untrue.[65] A declaration in a proposal form to the effect that the applicant was not insured elsewhere was rendered untrue when before the issue of the policy the applicant did insure elsewhere,[66] and where an applicant for a life policy who had been medically examined and passed for acceptance, suddenly became alarmed about his health and consulted a specialist, the statement in the proposal that he ordinarily enjoyed good health became untrue.[67] And where in an application for reinsurance on a life policy the applicant company stated that it intended to retain a certain proportion of the risk, but the directors then changed their minds and reinsured the balance of the risk before the contract of reinsurance was concluded, it was held that there was a misrepresentation of their intention.[68]

A representation made in the course of previous negotiations unconnected with the particular insurance in question cannot be relied upon by the insurer as a continuing representation so as to affect the contract.[69]

16–55 Reinsurance. In reinsurance situations, the relevance of representations made by the assured for the original insurance depends upon the wording of the terms of the reinsurance policy. If the assured's statements are warranted true in the original policy and these are in turn made the basis of the reinsurance policy, the reinsurer will be entitled to repudiate liability in the event of any statement made by the assured turning out to have been untrue at the date of the issue of the original policy.[70] If the proper interpretation of the reinsurance terms is that the insurers applying for reinsurance have themselves adopted the statements of the original insured, they may be held to have warranted their accuracy at the time of the issue of the reinsurance policy, although the object of the recital of the original declaration may, alternatively, be simply to inform the reinsurers of the declaration which formed the basis of the original policy.[71]

16–56 Substituted policy. Where a policy is issued to supersede another which is thereupon surrendered, the practice has been to insert a specific recital in the substituted policy to the effect that, if there is neither any increase in the sum assured nor other new benefit, nor any reduction of premium unaccompanied by a reduction in the sum assured (*i.e.* if the

---

[64] This is true of the law outside insurance contracts—*Davies v. London and Provincial Marine* (1878) 8 Ch. D. 469, 475; *With v. O'Flanagan* [1936] Ch. 575—as well as in insurance law itself, *Re Yager and Guardian Ass. Co. Ltd* (1912) 108 L.T. 38; *Piedmont and Arlington Life v. Ewing*, 92 U.S. 377 (1875).

[65] *Canning v. Farquhar* (1886) 16 Q.B.D. 727.

[66] *Re Marshall and Scottish Employers' Liability Co.* (1901) 85 L.T. 757, really a case where an intention was warranted to be held.

[67] *British Equitable v. Great Western Ry* (1869) 20 L.T. 422.

[68] *Traill v. Baring* (1864) 4 De G., J. & S. 318.

[69] *Dawson v. Atty* (1806) 7 East 367.

[70] *Australian Widows Fund Life v. National Mutual Life* [1914] A.C. 615.

[71] *Foster v. Mentor Life* (1854) 3 E. & B. 48, where the Court of Queen's Bench was equally divided upon the construction of the reinsurance declaration.

insurers' risk is no greater than before), then the substituted policy is expressly stated to be based on the original proposal and declaration. If the insurers' risk is increased in any way, a new declaration is required.[72] When one insurer transfers a policy in force to another, and the latter issues a substitute policy, it may well be a question of construction whether a declaration in the new policy is to be correct at that date or at the time the first policy was issued.[73]

16–57 Substitution of vehicle. Where a policy of motor insurance is worded to cover a vehicle which is the subject of the policy, and that car is sold and another substituted for it, the owner's rights under the policy cease,[74] and the policy is at an end, so that when he negotiates for cover in respect of a new vehicle, a new policy must be issued, necessitating disclosure of material facts and accurate answers to any questions asked. If none were asked, the understanding being that the earlier answers should stand, then the assured must correct them if no longer accurate. Even where a policy is altered to cover a second vehicle, but continues in force, the insurers can avoid the policy if their agreement to cover a new risk was procured by an incorrect declaration or concealment of a material fact.[75]

16–58 Onus of proof. If the insurers rely upon fraudulent or innocent misrepresentation by the assured as a defence to liability, the onus is on them to prove clearly that the contract was induced by the misrepresentation made to them by or on behalf of the assured.[76] Similarly, the onus is on the assured if he seeks to avoid the contract by reason of misrepresentations made by or on behalf of the insurers.

16–59 Exclusion of insurers' remedies for misrepresentation. The law will give effect to a term in an insurance policy whereby the insurers restrict or exclude the duty of their assured to make true statements, or absolve him from liability for misrepresentation, or alternatively agree to waive their right to avoid the policy for misrepresentation, in so far as it excuses non-fraudulent misrepresentation.[77] For reasons of public policy the law will not enforce a term which purports to protect the assured from the consequences of his own fraudulent statements, because no-one should be allowed to benefit from his own wilful wrongdoing, There are two qualifications to that general rule. First, the courts will enforce a clearly expressed term whereby the assured excludes his responsibility for the fraud of his agent, or the insurers agree not to exercise a right of avoidance in consequence of it, so long as the assured is not implicated in the agent's fraud.[78]

[72] *Martin v. Home Insurance* (1870) 20 U.C.C.P. 447.
[73] *Cahan v. Continental Life*, 41 N.Y. 296 (1877).
[74] *Rogerson v. Scottish Automobile, etc., Ins. Co.* (1931) 146 L.T. 26, 27.
[75] *General Accident v. Shuttleworth* (1938) 60 Ll.L.R. 301.
[76] *Davies v. National Fire and Marine* [1891] A.C. 485, 489; *Joel v. Law Union and Crown* [1908] 2 K.B. 863; *Goldstein v. Salvation Army Assurance Society* [1917] 2 K.B. 291; *Elkin v. Janson* (1845) 13 M. & W. 655, 666.
[77] *Svenska Handelsbanken v. Sun Alliance & London Ins. Plc* [1996] 1 Lloyd's Rep. 519, 551; *Sumitomo Bank Ltd v. Banque Bruxelles Lambert SA* [1997] 1 Lloyd's Rep. 487, 495; *HIH Casualty & General Ins. Ltd v. Chase Manhattan Bank* [2001] 2 Lloyd's Rep. 483 (under appeal to the House of Lords at the time of writing); *HIH Casualty & General Ins. Ltd v. New Hampshire Ins. Co.* [2001] 2 All E.R. (Comm) 39, 94–95.
[78] *HIH Casualty & General Ins. Co. v. Chase Manhattan Bank, supra,* at p. 503.

Secondly, where a number of assureds are insured under a composite policy in respect of their several and distinct interests, a clause whereby the insurers agree to waive their right to avoid the policy for innocent misrepresentation or non-disclosure by their assured may be construed as preventing the insurers from avoiding their contracts of insurance with those assureds not complicit in a fraudulent misstatement made by one or more of their co-assureds, and therefore limiting the exercise of the right to their contracts of insurance with the dishonest assureds who made the fraudulent misstatement.[79] In *Kumar v. AGF Insurance Ltd*[80] a solicitors' professional indemnity policy contained a "Non-avoidance" clause in which the insurers promised not to seek to avoid repudiate or rescind the insurance on any ground whatsoever, but which expressly entitled them to seek reimbursement of any claim against any member of the insured firm who had procured the policy by fraudulent misrepresentation concerning the likelihood of future claims, thereby indirectly making the dishonest assured responsible for the consequences of his fraud. It was held that the clause prevented the insurers from avoiding the policy in the event of a prior fraudulent misrepresentation by the partner who had signed the proposal form for the firm's insurance. The need to protect clients against loss from incompetence on the part of professional advisers is paramount to the undesirability of binding insurers to insurance cover obtained by fraud.

16–60 Indisputable policy. Where a policy was expressed to be "indisputable" after being in force for a particular time, except on the ground of fraud, it could not be challenged on the grounds of non-fraudulent misrepresentation, concealment or breach of warranty. If a policy is expressed to be "indisputable" *simpliciter*, it is nonetheless avoidable for fraudulent misstatement by the assured.[81] So if an assured had procured an "indisputable" policy by fraud, neither he nor his representatives could enforce it, and even an innocent assignee for value would be barred by the fraud of his assignor. Where, however, the assured has made an insurance on the life of another and it is declared in general terms to be indisputable, a fraudulent misstatement by the life will not vitiate the insurance.[82]

16–61 Incontestable policy. In many American states, the insertion of a clause rendering the policy indisputable or "incontestable" after a stated period of years is required by statute. The effect of such a clause was summarised by Cardozo C.J. in *Mutual Life v. Conway*[83] as follows: "the provision that a policy shall be incontestable after it has been in force during the lifetime of the insured for two years is not a mandate as to coverage or a definition of the risks to be run by the insurer. It means only this, that within the limits of the coverage the policy shall stand unaffected by any defence that it was invalid in its inception, or thereafter became invalid by reason of a condition broken." Consistently with the principle so stated, insurers have been held entitled to rely, in spite of the fact that the policy had become incontestable, on clauses excluding the right of double indemnity for

---

[79] *Arab Bank v. Zurich Ins. Co.* [1999] 1 Lloyd's Rep. 262.
[80] [1998] 4 All E.R.788.
[81] *Anstey v. British Natural Premium Life* (1908) 24 T.L.R. 871; *Re General Provincial Life Ass. Co.* (1870) 18 W.R. 396.
[82] See para. 18–17, *post.*
[83] 169 N.E. 642 (1930).

accidental death, if death results by bodily injury by another person,[84] excluding risks arising from aviation[85]; limiting disability benefit to the consequences of disease arising after the date of the policy[86]; and providing for adjustment of benefit in the event of misstatement of age[87]; but not on fraudulent concealment inducing the issue of the policy,[88] though there have been differing views on the issue of fraud in some American jurisdictions, where it has been held to constitute an exception to the incontestability clause. While this may be a debatable point in jurisdictions where the clause has statutory recognition, it is submitted that in England the view stated above would be preferred.

16–62 In *Anctil v. Manufacturers' Life Insurance Company* [89] a life policy contained an incontestability clause providing that after it had been in force for one year it should be incontestable on any ground whatsoever, provided that premiums were punctually paid. On the death of the life assured after the year had run, the insurers accepted that premiums had been punctually paid but raised a defence of lack of insurable interest. The assured relied on the clause. The Privy Council held that the assured did not possess an insurable interest as required by the Civil Code of Lower Canada, and that:

> "The rule of the Code appears to them to be one which rests upon general principles of public policy of expediency, and which cannot be defeated by the private convention of the parties. Any other view would lead to the sanction of wager policies".

The English authorities cited in paragraphs 16–59 to 16–60 above indicate that an incontestable clause would not be permitted for reasons of public policy to defeat an insurer's defence that the policy had been obtained by fraudulent misrepresentation.

16–63 Criminal liability for fraudulent statements. By section 379 of the Financial Services and Markets Act 2000, which re-enacts the substance of what was section 133 of the Financial Services Act 1986, it is provided that a person who makes a statement, promise or forecast which he knows to be misleading, false or deceptive in a material particular, or recklessly[90] makes a statement, promise or forecast of a similar nature, is guilty of an offence if it is made to induce someone to enter or offer to enter a "relevant agreement". By sub-section 397(9) and regulations made under the Act[91] this classification includes a contract of insurance to which the direct or indirect recipient of the statement becomes a party. Unlike its predecessor this section appears to apply to false statements made by either party to the insurance contract and to their respective agents, but it appears to follow it in applying to statements *de futuro* as well as to *de praesenti*.

---

[84] *ibid.*

[85] *McBride v. Prudential*, 72 N.E. 2d 98 (1947); *Waller v. Life and Casualty of Tennessee*, 191 F. 2d 768 (1951).

[86] *Apter v. Home Life of N.Y.*, 194 N.E. 846 (1935).

[87] *New York Life v. Hollenden*, 225 P. 2d 581 (1951).

[88] *Apter v. Home Life of N.Y.*, 194 N.E. 846 (1935).

[89] [1899] A.C. 604.

[90] *i.e.* made not caring whether it be true or false—see para. 16–1, *supra.*

[91] Financial Services and Markets Act 2000 (Regulated Activities) Order 2001, S.I. 2001 No. 3645.

CHAPTER 17

GOOD FAITH AND THE DUTY OF DISCLOSURE

(a) *Duty of Utmost Good Faith*

17–1 Insurance is one of a small number of contracts based upon the principle of utmost good faith[1]—*uberrimae fidei*. Section 17 of the Marine Insurance Act 1906 states this principle and goes on to provide that if the utmost good faith be not observed by either party, the contract may be avoided by the other party. It thus appears indirectly to impose on the parties a duty to act in good faith in their mutual dealings. The principle governs all contracts of insurance and reinsurance, and it applies both before a contract is concluded (the pre-formation period) and during the performance of the contract (the post-formation period).[2]

17–2 In the pre-formation period the principle of utmost good faith creates well-established duties owed by the assured and by his agent effecting the insurance to disclose material facts and to refrain from making untrue statements when negotiating the contract. The law is summarised in sections 18 to 20 of the 1906 Act, which again apply to all classes of insurance.[3] These sections are not, however, exhaustive of the concept of utmost good faith.[4] During the post-formation period it continues to affect the insurance, but the content and effect of the duty is flexible and varies depending upon the circumstances. If the assured seeks a variation to, or renewal of, the insurance contract, then he again becomes subject to duties similar to those set out in sections 18 to 20 of the Act. Here a new agreement is being negotiated, and the insurer's sole remedy for breach is avoidance of

[1] *Bell v. Lever Bros. Ltd* [1932] A.C. 161, 227; *Banque Keyser S.A. v. Skandia (UK) Ins. Co. Ltd* [1990] 1 Q.B. 665, 769. The expression "*uberrimae fidei*" was in use in the late 18th century—*Wolff v. Horncastle* (1789) 1 Bos. & Pul. 316, 322, *per* Buller J. The categories of such contracts are closed—*Bell v. Lever Bros., supra* at pp. 227, 231–232. Neither a line slip facility nor a binding authority nor an agreement to indemnify contained in a novating transaction are contracts of utmost good faith, as they are contracts *to insure* and not *of insurance*—*HIH Casualty & General Ins. Ltd v. Chase Manhattan Bank* [2001] 1 All E.R. (Comm) 719, 744, *per* Aikens J. citing earlier authority.
[2] *London Assurance Co. v. Mansel* (1897) 11 Ch. D. 363, 367; *Cantieri Meccanico Brindisino v. Janson* [1912] 3 K.B. 452; *Manifest Shipping Co. Ltd v. Uni-Polaris Co. Ltd The Star Sea* [2001] 1 All E.R. (Comm) 193, 198, 209–210.
[3] *Joel v. Law Union* [1908] 2 K.B. 863, 878; *Economides v. Commercial Union Ass. Co. Plc.* [1998] Q.B. 587, 598.
[4] *Manifest Shipping Co. Ltd v. Uni-Polaris Co. Ltd The Star Sea* [2001] 1 All E.R. (Comm) 193, 198, 209, 221.

the particular agreement in respect of which the breach is committed.[5] In contrast both parties are required to act in good faith towards each other in the performance of the contract, although there are few instances in which the courts have held that the duty applies. One is when a term of the insurance requires the assured to provide the insurer with information in particular circumstances.[6] Another is when a liability insurer exercises his right to conduct his assured's defence to a claim made by a third party.[7] It is said that the party in question must in such cases act in good faith and with regard to the interests of the other party, although with respect it is difficult to see how the duty of good faith relates to the performance of duties and exercise of rights which have their source in the terms of the contract itself, and for which the contract provides remedies in the event of breach.[8] The irrelevance of the statutory duty is emphasised by the very limited circumstances in which the draconian and often disproportionately severe right of avoidance can be exercised. It is available only in cases when the breach of duty occasions such serious prejudice to the innocent party that it permits him to terminate the insurance contract prospectively under the law of contract.[9] Such cases will be extremely rare. It would, with respect, have been simpler to curb the exercise of the remedy of avoidance by interpreting the post-formation duty of good faith as resting on an implied condition of the contract rather than on the separate rule enshrined in section 17 of the Act, but in *The Star Sea* the House of Lords preferred to describe it as a principle independent from contract law and with its own statutory sanction for breach.[10]

17–3 Fraudulent claims. It is appropriate to refer in this context to the content of the duty of good faith owed by an assured making a claim. The assured acts in good faith by refraining from dishonesty in the presentation of a claim, and fraud in the making of a claim entitles the insurer to avoid the insurance under section 17.[11] Matters are complicated by the separate existence of a common law rule of public policy, ante-dating the Marine Insurance Act 1906, that an assured who makes a fraudulent claim forfeits

---

[5] *K/S Merc-Scandia XXXXII v. Certain Lloyd's Underwriters The Mercandian Continent* [2001] 2 Lloyd's Rep. 563, 573–574; *HIH Casualty & General Ins. Ltd v. Chase Manhattan Bank* [2001] 2 Lloyd's Rep. 483, 494; *Manifest Shipping Co. Ltd v. Uni-Polaris Shipping Co. Ltd The Star Sea* [1997] 1 Lloyd's Rep. 360, 370, not commented upon in the H.L.

[6] *K/S Merc-Scandia XXXXII v. Certain Lloyd's Underwriters The Mercandian Continent* [2001] 2 Lloyd's Rep. 563, 571–572, citing *Phoenix General Co. v. Halvanon Ins. Co.* [1988] Q.B. 216.

[7] *ibid.* citing *Cox v. Bankside Agency Ltd* [1995] 2 Lloyd's Rep. 437, 462. Another instance may be the duty of the assured to have regard to the interests of the insurer when taking proceedings against a third party who has caused an insured loss—see paras. 22–41 to 22–42, *post.*

[8] It may be more accurate to describe the concept of good faith as the basis of terms implied to restrict the unfettered exercise of rights possessed by one party when this could harm the interests of the other. See the previous note.

[9] *K/S Merc-Scandia XXXXII v. Certain Lloyd's Underwriters The Mercandian Continent* [2001] 2 Lloyd's Rep. 563, 575; *Agapitos v. Agnew* [2002] 1 All E.R.(Comm) 714, 729.

[10] It is true that Lord Hobhouse said that a coherent scheme could be achieved by placing the post-formation duty on a contractual implied condition basis—[2001] 1 All E.R. (Comm) 193,211, and that Lord Steyn and Lord Hoffmann agreed with his speech. But they also agreed with Lord Scott, who treated the duty as imposed by s. 17, and it appears that Lord Hobhouse ultimately abided by the concession of counsel that the continuing duty of good faith was based upon an independent rule of law stated by the Act of 1906—p. 210. Lord Clyde did not advert to this point.

[11] *Agapitos v. Agnew* [2002] 1 All E.R.(Comm) 714, 717, 730.

the benefit of his policy.[12] Both the common law rule and the section 17 duty cease to apply to the assured's conduct of a claim once litigation is commenced.[13] The law relating to fraudulent claims is considered in detail in Chapter 19, below.[14]

(b) *The Duty of Disclosure*

17–4 The general principles upon which the duty of disclosure is based were stated by Lord Mansfield in the well-known leading case of *Carter* v. *Boehm*.[15] This case concerned an action on a policy for the benefit of George Carter, the Governor of Fort Marlborough in the island of Sumatra in the East Indies, against the fort being attacked by a foreign enemy. It was alleged by the underwriters that the weakness of the fort and the likelihood of its being attacked by the French were material facts known to the assured which ought to have been disclosed to the underwriters. This defence failed, but Lord Mansfield took the occasion to explain the principles necessitating a duty of disclosure in these words:

> "Insurance is a contract of speculation. The special facts upon which the contingent chance is to be computed lie most commonly in the knowledge of the assured only; the underwriter trusts to his representation, and proceeds upon confidence that he does not keep back any circumstance in his knowledge to mislead the underwriter into a belief that the circumstance does not exist. The keeping back such circumstance is a fraud, and therefore the policy is void. Although the suppression should happen through mistake, without any fraudulent intention, yet still the underwriter is deceived and the policy is void; because the *risque* run is really different from the *risque* understood and intended to be run at the time of the agreement ... The policy would be equally void against the underwriter if he concealed ... Good faith forbids either party, by concealing what he privately knows, to draw the other into a bargain from his ignorance of the fact, and his believing the contrary."[16]

17–5 Probably no better justification for the doctrine of non-disclosure has been stated since Lord Mansfield delivered his classic judgment over 200 years ago. More recent judicial pronouncements have reiterated the ideal of fair dealing and emphasised the assured's possession of superior knowledge of, or means of discovering, matters material to the proposed risk.[17] So far as

---

[12] *ibid.* at pp. 719–720.

[13] *ibid.* at pp. 733–734.

[14] See paras. 19–54, *et seq., post.*

[15] (1766) 3 Burr. 1905. The policy was written "interest or no interest", and "without benefit of salvage", but no point could be taken on this prior to the Life Assurance Act 1774.

[16] (1766) 3 Burr. 1905, 1909–1910.

[17] *Seaton* v. *Burnand* [1899] 1 Q.B. 782, 792; *London General Omnibus Co. Ltd* v. *Holloway* [1912] 2 K.B. 72, 86; *Rozanes* v. *Bowen* (1928) 32 Ll.L.R. 98, 102; *Greenhill* v. *Federal Ins.* [1927] 1 K.B. 65, 76; *Banque Keyser SA* v. *Skandia (U.K.) Ins. Co.* [1990] 1 Q.B. 665, 769; [1991] 2 A.C. 249, 281; *Pan Atlantic Ins. Co. Ltd* v. *Pine Top Ins. Co.* [1995] 1 A.C. 501, 542; *Soc. Anon d'Intermediaires Luxembourgeois* v. *Farex Gie.* [1995] L.R.L.R. 116, 149.

marine insurance is concerned, the rules of disclosure developed from *Carter* v. *Boehm* have been codified and given statutory authority in sections 17, 18 and 19 of the Marine Insurance Act 1906.

17–6 Applicable to all classes of insurance. It is by now established beyond doubt that the duty of disclosure applies to all species of insurance,[18] and this must be right in principle when the reasons for the existence of the duty are considered, although this does not necessarily mean that the scope and application of the duty are identical in every type of insurance. As Jessell M.R. said in *London Assurance* v. *Mansel*[19]:

> "As regards the general principle I am not prepared to lay down the law as making any difference in substance between one contract of insurance and another. Whether it is life, or fire, or marine insurance, I take it good faith is required in all cases, and though there may be certain circumstances from the peculiar nature of marine insurance, which require to be disclosed, and which do not apply to other contracts of insurance, that is rather, in my opinion, an illustration of the application of the principle than a distinction in principle."

17–7 Basis of duty of disclosure. Although it has been stated that the duty is imposed by an implied condition of the contract of insurance,[20] the preponderant view is that it arises outside, and independently of, the contract.[21] Section 18 of the Marine Insurance Act 1906 imposes a statutory duty upon a proposer for marine insurance. The reciprocal duty of the marine insurer arises by implication from section 17 of the Act.[22]

(c) *Duty of the Assured*

17–8 The general rule stated. Subject to certain qualifications considered below, the assured must disclose to the insurer all facts material to an insurer's appraisal of the risk which are known or deemed to be known by the assured but neither known nor deemed to be known by the insurer. Breach of this duty by the assured entitles the insurer to avoid the contract of insurance so long as he can show that the non-disclosure induced the making of the contract on the relevant terms.[23] The question of materiality is treated separately after a consideration of the other elements of the doctrine.

---

[18] *Lindenau v. Desborough* (1828) 8 B & C. 586; *Brownlie v. Campbell* (1880) 5 App. Cas. 925, 954; *Seaton v. Heath* [1899] 1 Q.B. 782; *Krantz v. Allan* (1921) 9 Ll.L.R. 410, 412; *Godfrey v. Britannic Ass.* [1963] 2 Lloyds Rep. 515, 528.

[19] (1879) 11 Ch. D. 363, 367 followed in *Joel v. Law Union* [1908] 2 K.B. 863, 878.

[20] *Blackburn v. Vigors* (1886) 17 QBD 553; (1887) 12 App. Cas. 531; *William Pickersgill & Sons Ltd v. London & Provincial Marine & General Ins. Co. Ltd* [1912] 3 K.B. 614; *Jester-Barnes v. Licenses & General Ins. Co. Ltd* (1934) 49 Ll.L.R. 231, 234–235.

[21] *Bell v. Lever Brothers Ltd* [1932] A.C. 161, 227; *Merchants & Manufacturers Ins. Co. Ltd v. Hunt* [1941] 1 K.B. 295, 313; *March Cabaret Club & Casino Ltd v. London Ass.* [1975] 1 Lloyd's Rep. 169, 175; *Banque Keyser SA v. Skandia (U.K.) Ins.* [1990] 1 Q.B. 665, 778–780; *Bank of Nova Scotia v. Hellenic Mutual Ltd* [1990] 1 Q.B. 818, 888; *Manifest Shipping Co. Ltd v. Uni-Polaris Co. Ltd The Star Sea* [2001] 1 All E.R. (Comm) 193, 209–211.

[22] *Banque Keyser SA v. Skandia (U.K.) Ins.* [1990] 1 Q.B. 665, 770. See para. 17–88, *post*.

[23] *Pan Atlantic Ins. Co. Ltd v. Pine Top Ins. Co.* [1995] A.C. 501; *St Paul Fire & Marine Ins. Co. v. McConnell Dowell* [1995] 2 Lloyd's Rep. 116. The corresponding paragraph in the 8th edition of this work was approved in *Unipac (Scotland) v. Aegon Ins. Co.* 1996 S.L.T. 1197.

17–9 Facts known to the assured. The duty of disclosure extends only to facts which are known (or deemed in law to be known) to one party and not to the other.[24] "The duty is a duty to disclose," said Fletcher Moulton L.J. in *Joel v. Law Union and Crown Insurance*,[25] "and you cannot disclose what you do not know. The obligation to disclose, therefore, necessarily depends upon the knowledge you possess."

17–10 Actual knowledge of natural and corporate assureds. Whether a material circumstance is known by a natural assured is simply a question of fact—"he knows what he knows".[26] Thus a proposer for life or sickness insurance need not disclose the existence of a medical condition of which his doctors have not told him, so long as he is genuinely ignorant of it and is not shutting his eyes to the truth.[27] The knowledge of a corporate assured is more complex. It depends upon the identification of those persons whose actual knowledge is to count as the knowledge of a company for the purpose of the disclosure rule imposed upon all proposers for insurance in order to enable insurers to make an informed assessment of the risks presented to them.[28] There is little authority on this question, which in practice arises when the director or manager responsible for arranging the company's insurances is ignorant of a fact known to another director or employee.[29]

17–11 It is submitted that the knowledge of those who represent the directing mind and will of the company, and who control what it does, is to be identified as the company's knowledge, whether or not they are responsible for arranging the insurance cover in question.[30] This class of persons usually consists of directors and officers of the company. It can include non-directors to whom the exercise of the company's powers has been delegated by the board of directors, whether generally or in relation to a particular business activity. It has been said *obiter*[31] that the knowledge of a person responsible for arranging the insurance cover should count as the company's knowledge even if not identifiable as part of its directing mind and will, but it is

---

[24] *Hearts of Oak Building Society v. Law Union Ins. Co.* [1936] 2 All E.R. 619, 620; *Whitwell v. Autocar Ins.* (1927) 27 Ll.L.R. 418; *Wheelton v. Hardisty* (1858) 8 E. & B. 232, 269; *Swete v. Fairlie* (1833) 6 C. & P. 1; *Fowkes v. Manchester & London Life Ins. Co.* (1862) 3 F. & F. 440; *Jones v. Provincial Ins. Co.* (1857) 3 C.B.(N.S.) 65; *Haydenfayre v. British National Ins. Soc.* [1984] 2 Lloyd's Rep. 393, 403.

[25] [1908] 2 K.B. 863, 884; *Economides v. Commercial Union Assce. Co.* [1998] Q.B. 587, 601, 607.

[26] *PCW Syndicates v. PCW Reinsurers* [1996] 1 Lloyd's Rep. 241, 253 *per* Staughton L.J.

[27] *Lee v. British Law Ins. Co.* [1972] 2 Lloyd's Rep. 49; *Keating v. New Ireland Ass. Co.* [1990] 2 I.R. 383; *Economides v. Commercial Union Assce. Co.* [1998] Q.B. 587, 602. He would have to disclose the fact that he had undergone tests for an unknown medical condition if he appreciated their importance.

[28] *El Ajou v. Dollar Holdings* [1994] 2 All E.R. 685, 706; *Meridian Global Funds Management Asia v. Securities Commission* [1995] 2 A.C. 500, 507; *PCW Syndicates v. PCW Reinsurers* [1996] 1 Lloyd's Rep. 241, 253.

[29] *e.g.* a director is aware of his own previous conviction involving dishonesty but his fellow directors have not been told of it, as in *Regina Fur Co. v. Bossom* [1957] 2 Lloyd's Rep. 466, aff'd. [1958] 2 Lloyd's Rep. 425.

[30] *PCW Syndicates v. PCW Reinsurers* [1996] 1 Lloyd's Rep. 241, 253; *Johns v. Kelly* [1986] 1 Lloyd's Rep. 468, 474, applying *Tesco Stores v. Nattrass* [1972] A.C. 153; *Ins. Corp. of the Channel Islands v. Royal Hotel* [1998] Lloyd's Rep. I.R. 151, 156. *Regina Fur Co. v. Bossom*, *supra*, could have been put on this ground alone without the unconvincing attribution to the director in question of a role in arranging the insurance—see [1957] 2 Lloyd's Rep. 466, 484. See further note 42 to para. 28–81, *post*.

[31] *PCW Syndicates v. PCW Reinsurers, supra*, at p. 253.

submitted that corporate knowledge is restricted to the knowledge possessed by the company's directing minds, and that the knowledge of employees and agents is not the actual knowledge of the company, although it may be deemed to know what they know on other grounds. Section 18(1) of the Marine Insurance Act 1906 provides that in certain circumstances a corporate assured is deemed to know what its agents and employees know, and this appears to be based on the imputation of such knowledge to the persons who embody the directing mind of the company. The courts have interpreted the deemed knowledge provision in section 18(1) restrictively,[32] and, if the actual knowledge of employees below the status of director is too readily identified as the actual knowledge of the company, there is a risk that the limitations placed on the imputation of their knowledge, *qua* agents, to the directing minds of the company will be circumvented. The nature and terms of the particular insurance policy may also make it inappropriate to attribute the knowledge of one or more directors to a corporate assured.[33]

17–12 Constructive knowledge. It is necessary to distinguish between the proposer seeking insurance cover in the course of a business from a proposer seeking it for purposes unconnected with a business,[34] such as an individual purchasing life or property cover, because the rule of deemed knowledge expressed in section 18(1) of the Marine Insurance Act 1906 applies to the former but not to the latter.

17–13 Business insurance. Section 18(1) of the Marine Insurance Act 1906 provides that an assured is "deemed to know every circumstance which, in the ordinary course of business, ought to be known by him". It expresses a rule applicable to both natural and corporate assureds and to both marine and non-marine insurances. Although on a first reading of the section it might appear that an assured is deemed to know matters which a person should reasonably be expected to know in the ordinary course of his line of business, the courts have in fact interpreted it more restrictively.[35] The assured is deemed to know only what he would be expected to know in the ordinary course of his own business, making allowance for its imperfect organisation, prior to the conclusion of the insurance. Therefore he is not deemed to be aware of matters which should be known to him in the course of a well run business which he would have found out if he had re-organised his schedule or business system at the time in question. He need not undertake any special enquiry for the benefit of the insurer, although, if he does, the findings, if material, should not be kept back. The principle is that if he should have been informed of certain facts in the ordinary course of his actual business, he will be deemed to know them even if, due to a failure in communication, he is not actually made aware of them.[36] He cannot rely on the incompetence or ignorance of an employee or agent whose duty in the ordinary course of the business was to keep him informed,[37] and he cannot

---

[32] See para. 17–13 and paras 18–12 to 18–16, *post.*

[33] *Arab Bank Plc v. Zurich Ins. Co.* [1999] 1 Lloyd's Rep. 262.

[34] A similar distinction between business and consumer insurance appears in Reg. 2(1) of the Unfair Terms in Consumer Contracts Regulations 1999—see para. 10–12 *ante.*

[35] *Australia & New Zealand Bank v. Colonial & Eagle Wharves* [1960] 2 Lloyd's Rep. 241, 252; *Simner v. New India Ass. Co.* [1995] L.R.L.R. 240, 253–255.

[36] *London General Ins. Co. v. General Marine Underwriters Assoc.* [1921] 1 K.B. 104.

[37] *Inversiones Manria SA v. Sphere Drake Ins. Co.* [1989] 1 Lloyd's Rep. 69, 95, applying *Proudfoot v. Montefiore* (1867) L.R. 2 Q.B. 511, 521.

turn a blind eye to material circumstances which he has good reason to suspect exist.[38]

17–14 The category of employees and agents whose actual knowledge is imputed to the assured pursuant to the above rule is limited, and it is not the knowledge of every agent or employee which is so attributed.[39] It includes agents employed (i) to manage a property or activity which is the subject matter of the insurance[40] and (ii) to prepare the proposal for insurance or to transmit it to the broker engaged to negotiate it with the insurers,[41] but it does not include a former agent who acquired the relevant knowledge after completion of the work he was engaged to perform or in circumstances where he was not under a duty to report it to the assured. If the agent is acting in fraud of the assured or is guilty of misconduct in his duties, and disclosure of material facts to the assured would involve the agent in revealing his own fraud or misconduct, as the case may be, the agent's knowledge will not be imputed to the assured as it is fanciful to suppose that the assured would receive knowledge of the facts in question.[42]

17–15 Consumer insurance. The deemed knowledge provisions of section 18 of the Marine Insurance Act 1906 do not apply to disclosure by private individuals who are not obtaining insurance in the course of a business. In *Economides v. Commercial Union Assurance Co*[43] all three members of the Court of Appeal stated that such an assured was not to have ascribed to him any form of deemed or constructive knowledge, and that in this context "knowledge" means actual knowledge, subject only to the qualification that an assured may not say that he has no knowledge of something if he has deliberately shut his eyes to evidence of it. It appears therefore that an individual assured will not be deemed to know matters known to his agent even if the latter is legally obliged to communicate them to him.[44]

17–16 Innocent omissions. If a fact is material and within the knowledge of the assured or his agent, the assured is under an absolute duty to disclose it. There is a long line of decisions from Lord Mansfield's judgment in *Carter v. Boehm*[45] itself where it has been said that an insurer can avoid the insurance in the absence of fraudulent intent on the part of the assured.[46] Mistake or forgetfulness affords no defence. "It is well-established law," said Cockburn C.J. in *Bates v. Hewitt,*[47] "that it is immaterial whether the

---

[38] *Blackburn, Low & Co. v. Vigors* (1887) 12 App.Cas. 531, 537.

[39] *Regina Fur Co. v. Bossom* [1957] 2 Lloyd's Rep. 466, 484.

[40] See paras 18–12 to 18–14, *post.*

[41] *Blackburn Low & Co. v. Haslam* (1888) 21 Q.B.D. 144.

[42] See para. 18–16, *post.* Misconduct may include irregularities—*Kingscroft v. Nissan Fire etc. Ins. Co.* [1999] Lloyd's Rep. I.R. 371, 375.

[43] [1998] Q.B. 587.

[44] *Sed contra*, Clarke, *Law of Insurance Contracts* (looseleaf ed., 1999) para. 23–8A.

[45] (1766) 3 Burr. 1905, 1909. For a different view see R. A. Hasson in (1969) 32 M.L.R. 615, 616–617.

[46] *Macdowall v. Fraser* (1779) 1 Doug. K.B. 260; *Buse v. Turner* (1815) 6 Taunt. 338; *Lindenau v. Desborough* (1828) 8 B. & C. 586; *Wheelton v. Hardisty* (1857) 8 E. & B. 232, 255; *Traill v. Baring* (1864) 4 De G.J. & S. 318, 328; *Joel v. Law Union & Crown Ins. Co.* [1908] 2 K.B. 863; *Godfrey v. Britannic Ass. Co.* [1963] 2 Lloyd's Rep. 515; *Anglo-African Merchants v. Bayley* [1969] 1 Lloyd's Rep. 268, 2275; *Murphy v. Sun Life Ass. Co. of Canada* (1964) 44 D.L.R. (2d) 369.

[47] (1867) L.R. 2 Q.B. 595, 607.

omission to communicate a material fact arises from indifference or a mistake or from it not being present to the mind of the assured that the fact was one which it was material to make known."

17–17 Effect of questions in proposal form. The questions put by insurers in their proposal forms may either enlarge or limit the applicant's duty of disclosure.[48] As a general rule the fact that particular questions relating to the risk are put to the proposer does not *per se* relieve him of his independent obligation to disclose all material facts.[49] Thus, if a burglary insurance proposal form asks questions chiefly concerned with the nature of the proposer's premises and the business carried on there, this will not of itself relieve him of his duty to disclose material facts relating to his personal experience, such as the possession of a criminal record.[50]

17–18 It is possible that the form of the questions asked may make the applicant's duty more strict. The applicant may well be reminded by a particular question that the general duty of disclosure enjoins him to state material facts in his possession relating to the subject-matter of the question but outside its ambit.[51]

17–19 It is more likely, however, that the questions asked will limit the duty of disclosure, in that, if questions are asked on particular subjects and the answers to them are warranted, it may be inferred that the insurer has waived his right to information, either on the same matters but outside the scope of the questions, or on matters kindred to the subject matter of the questions.[52] Thus, if an insurer asks, "How many accidents have you had in the last three years?" it may well be implied that he does not want to know of accidents before that time, though these would still be material. If it were asked whether any of the proposer's parents, brothers or sisters had died of consumption or been afflicted with insanity, it might well be inferred that the insurer had waived similar information concerning more remote relatives, so that he could not avoid the policy for non-disclosure of an aunt's death of consumption or an uncle's insanity. Whether or not such waiver is present depends on a true construction of the proposal form, the test being, would a reasonable man reading the proposal form be justified in thinking that the

---

[48] *Roselodge Ltd v. Castle* [1966] 2 Lloyd's Rep. 113, 131. This paragraph and the two following in the 8th edition of this work were approved in *Vrbanic v. London Life Ins. Co.* (1996) 25 O.R. (3d) 710, 727 (C.A. Ont.).

[49] *Joel v. Law Union* [1908] 2 K.B. 863, 878, 892; *Becker v. Marshall* (1922) 11 Ll.L.R. 113; *Glicksman v. Lancashire & General* [1927] A.C. 139; *Bond v. Commercial Union* (1930) 35 Com.Cas. 171; *Holt's Motors v. S.E.Lancs Ins. Co.* (1930) 35 Com.Cas. 281; *McCormick v. National Motor* (1934) 40 Com.Cas. 76, 78; *Taylor v. Eagle Star Ins. Co.* (1940) 67 Ll.L.R. 136; *Schoolman v. Hall* [1951] 1 Lloyd's Rep. 139; *Godfrey v. Britannic Ass.* [1963] 2 Lloyd's Rep. 515; *Roselodge v. Castle* [1966] 2 Lloyd's Rep. 113; *Lee v. British Law Ins. Co.* [1972] 2 Lloyd's Rep. 49, 58.

[50] *Schoolman v. Hall* [1951] 1 Lloyd's Rep. 139.

[51] *Becker v. Marshall* (1922) 11 Ll.L.R. 113, 117, affirmed in C.A. at 12 Ll.L.R. 413; *Glicksman v. Lancashire & General* [1925] 2 K.B. 593, 609; [1927] A.C. 139, 143; *Ins. Corp. of the Channel Islands v. Royal Hotel* [1998] Lloyd's Rep. I.R. 151, 158.

[52] *Laing v. Union Marine Ins. Co.* (1895) 1 Com.Cas. 11, 15; *Schoolman v. Hall* [1951] 1 Lloyd's Rep. 139; *Taylor v. Eagle Star Ins.* (1940) 67 Ll.L.R. 136; *Joel v. Law Union* [1908] 2 K.B. 863, 878; *Roberts v. Plaisted* [1989] 2 Lloyd's Rep. 341.

insurer had restricted his right to receive all material information, and consented to the omission of the particular information in issue?[53]

17–20 The authorities do not give any clear indication as to when such an implication will be made, but it is probable that when certain information is sought in respect of a particular period of time, this necessarily implies a waiver concerning the same sort of facts occurring outside it.[54] Where, however, insurers ask whether a business partnership has had any burglary losses, this has been held not to be a waiver of their right to know of each partner's *individual* losses.[55] It is possible, also, that when questions are put on certain matters but not on other related material points, the insurers may be held to have waived information on the latter through omitting to ask any question on them at all,[56] and Scrutton L.J. twice said[57] that, if insurance companies fail to put questions on material matters, they run the risk of the contention that failure to ask the question prevents them from relying upon non-disclosure afterwards. Thus in *Golding v. London Auxiliary Insurance Co. Ltd*[58] the assured was asked, "Has any other office declined to accept or renew your insurance?" and answered "No". It was not said that another office's refusal to *transfer* an existing policy to him ought to have been disclosed by him as a material fact.[59] Generally, however, the risk referred to by Scrutton L.J. is a slight one, as is illustrated by *Taylor v. Eagle Star Ins. Co. Ltd*[60] where the assured had been asked the following question in a proposal form for motor insurance, "Have you or has your driver been convicted of any offence in connection with the driving of any motor vehicle?" He answered "No". This was correct, but even so, it was held, he ought to have disclosed not only previous drinking convictions unconnected with the driving of a car, but also a conviction for permitting a car to be used without proper insurance. The insurers had not waived their right to know of offences concerning the ownership of a car as opposed to the actual driving of it.

17–21 Declarations in the policy. Quite apart from the subject matter of the questions asked, the proposal form may limit the duty of disclosure in other ways. Where a proposer for life assurance signed a declaration that he was not aware of any disorder or circumstances tending to shorten his life or make the insurance more hazardous, the court held that the company had limited their right to disclosure to matters which in the assured's own

---

[53] The corresponding paragraph in the previous edition of this work was cited with approval by Woolf J. in *Hair v. Prudential Ass. Co. Ltd* [1983] 2 Lloyd's Rep. 667, 673 (see para. 17–21, *post*) and by the Supreme Court of Ireland in *Kelleher v. Irish Life Ass. Co.* [1993] I.L.R.M. 643 (S.C.).

[54] *Jester-Barnes v. Licenses & General* (1934) 49 Ll.L.R. 231, 237; *Parker v. Salvation Army Ass. Soc.* [1928] I.A.C.Rep. 25.

[55] *Becker v. Marshall* (1922) 11 Ll.L.R. 113; 12 Ll.L.R. 413.

[56] *Zurich Accident v. Morrison* [1942] 2 K.B. 53, 64. *Sweeney v. Kennedy* (1949) 82 Ll.L.R. 294, 300.

[57] *Newsholme Bros v. Road Transport & General* [1929] 2 K.B. 356, 363; *McCormick v. National Motor* (1934) 40 Com.Cas. 76. 78.

[58] (1914) 30 T.L.R. 350.

[59] Contrast *Holt's Motors v. S.E. Lancashire Ins. Co.* (1930) 35 Com.Cas. 281, 286, where Scrutton L.J. seems to have thought that the question "Has any company ... declined to insure ...?" did not excuse non-disclosure of an insurer's warning that he did not invite renewal, even if the failure to mention the warning did not amount to a false answer.

[60] (1940) 67 Ll.L.R. 136.

opinion were injurious to health.[61] Where a proposer for household contents insurance completed a proposal form in which he supplied values for certain chattels and declared that his answers were true and complete to the best of his knowledge and belief, honestly believing that the values given were correct, he was not under a duty to disclose that they were substantial undervaluations. By requiring him only to give his own honest opinion of the matter, the insurers had impliedly waived disclosure of the true values.[62] It is possible also that the policy may contain a condition that it shall be disputed or avoided only on the ground of fraud, in which case the insurer cannot rely on any non-disclosure which is less than fraudulent concealment.[63] If a policy provides that in the event of an incorrect definition of the subject-matter insured, the insurers agree to hold the assured covered at a premium to be negotiated, that will protect the assured from avoidance of the policy by reason of an inadequate description, provided that the assured acted in good faith.[64] In *Hair v. Prudential Assurance Co. Ltd*[65] it was held that where the proposal form contained a declaration that "I warrant that all the information entered above is true and complete and that nothing materially affecting the risk has been concealed", the assured was not bound to disclose any material fact outside the scope of the specific questions asked, on the ground that, if it was intended that the assured should answer matters even though he was not questioned about them, the insurers should have stated clearly the need for such disclosure and left space on the proposal form for the assured to put in details.[66]

17–22 Duration of duty of disclosure. The time up to which full disclosure of facts material to the risk proposed must be made is the moment when a binding contract is concluded.[67] The practical effect of this rule is that the applicant for assurance is bound to disclose any material facts concerning the insurance proposed which come to his notice while negotiations are proceeding and before the proposal is accepted. This is especially important in life assurance, where the applicant's health may alter in some respect while the insurers are perusing the proposal and medical reports sent to

---

[61] *Jones v. Provincial Life* (1857) 3 C.B.(N.S.) 65, 86.

[62] *Economides v. Commercial Union Assurance Co* [1998] Q.B. 587.

[63] *Fowkes v. Manchester and London Life* (1863) 3 B. & S. 917; *Scottish Provident v. Boddam* (1893) 9 T.L.R. 385; *Naughter v. Ottawa Agricultural* (1878) 43 U.C.Q.B. 121.

[64] *Hewitt Bros. v. Wilson* [1915] 2 K.B. 739.

[65] [1983] 2 Lloyd's Rep. 667.

[66] *ibid.* at 673, applying the test in para. 17–19, *ante*. A prominent warning of the need for disclosure should be inserted in proposal forms for non-commercial insurances according to the Statement of General Insurance Practice. para. 1(c) and the Statement of Long-Term Insurance Practice para. 1(a). These may be found in s.7 of the *Encyclopaedia of Insurance Law*.

[67] *Ionides v. Pacific Ins. Co.* (1871) L.R. 6 Q.B. 674, 684; (1872) L.R. 7 Q.B. 517; *Cory v. Patton* (1872) L.R. 7 Q.B. 304, 309; affirmed (1874) L.R. 9 Q.B. 577; *Lishman v. Northern Maritime Ins. Co.* (1875) L.R. 10 CP 179, 181–182; *Canning v. Farquhar* (1886) 16 Q.B.D. 727; *Re Yager and the Guardian Ass. Co.* (1912) 108 L.T. 38; *Commercial Union Ass. Co. v. Niger Co. Ltd* (1922) 13 Ll.L.R. 75; *Haydenfayre v. British National Ins. Soc. Ltd* [1984] 2 Lloyd's Rep. 393, 398; *Newbury Int. Ltd v. Reliance National Ins. Co. (U.K.) Ltd* [1994] 1 Lloyd's Rep. 83, 85. For application to open covers, see *The La Pointe* [1986] 2 Lloyd's Rep. 513, 520; not considered on appeal at [1989] 2 Lloyd's Rep. 536. For negotiation of binding authorities, see *Pryke v. Gibbs Hartley Cooper Ltd* [1991] 1 Lloyd's Rep. 602, 615–616. For re-insurance, *Traill v. Baring* (1864) 4 De G., J. & S. 318 and para. 33–33, *post*.

them.[68] Thus in *Looker v. Law Union and Rock Insurance Co. Ltd*[69] the applicant represented in his proposal form that he was free from disease and ailments. The insurers informed him that the insurance would become effective when the first premium due was received. Five days after this information came he became seriously ill with what was diagnosed as pneumonia. Four days later he died, a cheque for the premium being received one day prior to his death.[70] Acton J. held that the insurers were not liable. One reason for the decision was the effect of an express condition in the insurers' acceptance of the risk, but he also held, that:

> "there was here a failure to discharge a duty incumbent upon all proposers of contracts of insurance such as these ... namely a duty to inform the insurers of any material change in the nature of the risk to be undertaken by them".[71]

17–23 It is very usual in life assurance policies for a clause to be inserted into the contract providing that the insurance company shall not become bound until receipt of the first premium. Such a clause creates an express extension of the period wherein disclosure is required, so that any new or altered material circumstance affecting the insurers' calculations must be communicated to them right up to the time of the receipt by them of the premium.[72] Another version of this clause provides that the insurance company will not become bound until the policy is delivered to the assured, and the effect of this is to prolong the period of disclosure still further.[73]

17–24 Renewals. When, as is usual in risks other than life, an insurance contract is for a fixed period which expires, it is renewable only upon the consent of the insurer unless it contains provision for its extension at the option of the assured. When renewal is dependent on the insurer's consent, the full duty of disclosure attaches.[74] The assured must disclose not only circumstances which have occurred during the expiring period of cover, but also any matters which he omitted to disclose when the old insurance was concluded and are still relevant to the new one, assuming them to be material and unknown to the insurer. It has been mooted that the assured might have to disclose on renewal his own prior failure to disclose a fact once material to the expiring risk but no longer material.[75] It is submitted that this would only be so in an exceptional case in which the assured had acted so dishonestly as to raise a real question of moral hazard with regard to the new insurance.[76]

---

[68] There are many American decisions upholding this principle—compare *Stipcich v. Metropolitan Life Ins. Co.*, 277 U.S. 311 (1928) with *Wilkins v. Travelers Co.*, 117 F. 2d 646 (1941).

[69] [1928] 1 K.B. 554.

[70] The cheque was dishonoured but nothing seems to turn on this.

[71] [1928] 1 K.B. 554, 558.

[72] *British Equitable Ins. Co. v. G.W.Ry* (1869) 20 L.T. 422; *Canning v. Farquhar* (1886) 16 Q.B.D. 727; *Harrington v. Pearl Life Ass. Co.* (1913) 30 T.L.R. 24; (1914) 30 T.L.R. 613; *Looker v. Law Union & Rock Ins. Co.* [1928] 1 K.B. 554; followed in *Mander v. Commercial Union Ass. Co.* [1998] Lloyd's Rep. I.R. 93, 136–137.

[73] *Allis-Chalmers Co. v. Maryland Fidelity & Deposit Co.* (1916) 114 L.T. 433. On "delivery" see *Jackson v. New York Life Ins. Co.*, 7 F. 2d 31 (1925).

[74] *Re Wilson & Scottish Ins. Corp.* [1920] 2 Ch. 28; *Lambert v. Co-operative Ins. Soc.* [1975] 2 Lloyd's Rep. 485, 487; *K/S Merc-Scandia XXXXII v. Certain Lloyd's Underwriters The Mercandian Continent* [2001] 2 Lloyd's Rep. 563, 571.

[75] Clarke, *Law of Insurance Contracts* (looseleaf ed., 1999) para. 23–4C.

[76] *CTI Inc. v. Oceanus Mutual Underwriting Assoc.* [1982] 1 Lloyd's Rep. 178, 199.

17–25 Disclosure after inception of risk. The general principle is that the duty of disclosure comes to an end when the insurance contract is made. There is no duty on the assured to keep the insurer informed of matters affecting the risk even in cases where the insurer has an option to terminate cover on giving a stipulated notice and might like to be appraised of events inclining him to exercise it.[77] By contrast, if the assured negotiates a variation to the terms of cover for his benefit, a limited duty of disclosure applies. It is to disclose matters material to the insurer's decision to agree the variation in cover, including the amount of premium, but does not extend to matters relating to the original un-amended risk to which the insurer is already bound.[78] The insurer's remedy for breach of this limited duty is to avoid the agreement by which the policy was amended, not the entire contract of insurance.[79] This makes the timing of any casualty critical. If it is covered under the un-amended contract terms, the assured should be able to recover. Note, however, that if the alteration to the insurance amounts in law to the discharge of the original insurance and its replacement by a new contract, then there will be a duty to disclose all material facts without this limitation. Whether the alteration is a variation of the old contract or creates a new one will depend upon the intention of the parties deduced from the new terms agreed.[80] The assured owes no duty of disclosure of material facts when making a claim. His duty is to act with complete honesty towards the insurer.[81]

17–26 Burden of proof. The onus of proving non-disclosure is on the insurer.[82] In *Joel v. Law Union and Crown*, the company alleged that the assured had not disclosed the fact that she had suffered from nervous depression after influenza, and had been attended by a brain specialist. In support of that allegation it put in evidence the printed form containing the questions put by the medical examiner. The medical examiner had been instructed to put the questions with "any necessary explanation", to write down the answers, and to obtain the applicant's signature to a declaration that the answers were true. The answers were filled in and the declaration signed by the assured. In answer to the question, "What medical men have you consulted?" the names of two doctors were filled in but no mention was

---

[77] *Lishman v. Northern Maritime Ins. Co.* (1875) L.R. 10 C.P. 179, 181; *Commercial Union Ass. Co. v. Niger Co.* (1922) 13 Ll.L.Rep. 75, 82; *MGN v. New Hampshire Ins. Co.* [1997] L.R.L.R. 24, 58–61; *Manifest Shipping Co. Ltd v. Uni-Polaris Co. Ltd The Star Sea* [2001] 1 All E.R.(Comm) 193, 212.

[78] *Lishman v. Northern Maritime Ins. Co., supra; Manifest Shipping Co. Ltd v. Uni-Polaris Co. Ltd The Star Sea, supra,* at pp. 211–212. The same principle applies to an application for extended cover pursuant to a "held covered" clause in a marine policy, so that the insurer can assess the additional premium to be charged—see *Overseas Commodities v. Style* [1958] 1 Lloyd's Rep. 546, 559; *Liberian Ins. Agency v. Mosse* [1977] 2 Lloyd's Rep. 560, 568; *K/S Merc-Scandia XXXXII v. Certain Lloyd's Underwriters The Mercandian Continent* [2001] 2 Lloyd's Rep. 563, 571.

[79] *Manifest Shipping Co. Ltd v. Uni-Polaris Co. Ltd The Star Sea* [1997] 1 Lloyd's Rep. 360, 370 CA; *K/S Merc-Scandia XXXXII v. Certain Lloyd's Underwriters The Mercandian Continent* [2001] 2 Lloyd's Rep. 563, 571. The point seems not to have been contested in *Fraser v. Colton* [1997] 1 Lloyd's Rep. 586.

[80] *Kensington v. Inglis* (1807) 8 East 273; *Royal Exch. Ass. Co. v. Hope* [1928] 1 Ch. 179; *Cornhill Ins. Co. v. Assenheim* (1937) 58 Ll.L.Rep. 27, 29.

[81] *Manifest Shipping Co. Ltd v. Uni-Polaris Co. Ltd The Star Sea* [2001] 1 All E.R. (Comm) 193, disapproving the decision of Hirst J. in *The Litsion Pride* [1985] 1 Lloyd's Rep. 437.

[82] *Joel v. Law Union Ins. Co.* [1908] 2 K.B. 863; *Roselodge Ltd v. Castle* [1966] 2 Lloyd's Rep. 113, 127; *Murphy v. Sun Life Ass. Co. of Canada* (1964) 44 D.L.R. (2d) 369; *Butcher v. Dowlen* [1981] 1 Lloyd's Rep. 310, 313.

made of the brain specialist. The medical examiner who put the questions and filled in the answers was not called as a witness, although he was in court at the trial. The court held there was no evidence of non-disclosure. The printed form and answers proved nothing, because the court did not know what questions and explanations were put to the assured by the medical examiner, and the whole facts might have been disclosed to him.

17–27 On the other hand, it has been held that a negative answer to the question, "Has any company declined to accept or refuse to renew your burglary insurance?" was prima facie evidence of non-disclosure of a previous refusal to insure by another company, so that it was not necessary to call the insurers' agent to testify that he was never told of the refusal.[83] Only if the assured were to plead that he had disclosed it to that agent would it be necessary to call the agent to rebut that reply by the assured. The case differs from *Joel v. Law Union and Crown* in that there was nothing to suggest that it was the agent's function to interpret or explain the question to the assured.

17–28 Inducement. To succeed in a defence of non-disclosure the insurer must prove not only that the assured failed to disclose a material fact but also that the non-disclosure induced the making of the contract in the sense that he would not have made the same contract if he had known the matters in question.[84] Where the materiality of the undisclosed matter is obvious it may justify the court in presuming that the underwriter was induced, but this an evidential presumption which may be rebutted by contradictory evidence adduced by the assured.[85] It is most useful where for good reason an underwriter cannot be called to give evidence and other underwriters on the risk have given satisfactory evidence that they were induced by the non-disclosure.[86] The court is reluctant to allow the assured to refer back to risks previously written by the underwriter for other assureds because of the potentially oppressive discovery of documents involved and the difficulty of assessing the relevance of decisions taken in considering proposals made by other assureds in which the overall complexion of the risk was different. It does not necessarily follow from the fact that the underwriter was acting carelessly and imprudently that he would have agreed the same terms if his mind had been directed to an obviously material fact, but where the underwriter found the business attractive for commercial reasons, then he might well have written it on the same terms even with full disclosure.[87] The defence will fail even if the reason why the underwriter would have attached little importance to the facts in issue was that he was relying on an incorrect interpretation of an exclusion term in the policy.[88]

[83] *Glicksman v. Lancashire & General Ass. Co.* [1925] 2 K.B. 593, affirmed [1927] A.C. 139, HL.

[84] *Pan Atlantic Ins. Co. v. Pine Top Ins. Co.* [1995] A.C. 501, 549–550; *St. Paul Fire & Marine Ins. Co. v. McConnell Dowell Constructors* [1995] 2 Lloyd's Rep. 116, 124–125; *Marc Rich v. Portman* [1997] 1 Lloyd's Rep. 225, 234–235, affirming [1996] 1 Lloyd's Rep. 430, 442; *Ins. Co. of the Channel Islands* [1998] Lloyd's Rep. I.R. 154, 158.

[85] *St Paul Fire & Marine Ins. Co., supra* at p. 117; *Gaelic Assignments Ltd v. Sharp* 2001 SLT 914, 918.

[86] *Rich v. Portman* [1996] 1 Lloyd's Rep. 430, 440–442; *Sirius Ins. Corp. v. Oriental Ass. Corp.* [1999] Lloyd's Rep. I.R. 343, 351; *Aneco Re. v. Johnson v. Higgins* [1998] 1 Lloyd's Rep. 565, 597.

[87] *Rich v. Portman* [1996] 1 Lloyd's Rep. 430, 440–442; *Kingscroft Ins. Co. v. Nissan Fire & Marine Ins. Co.* [1999] Lloyd's Rep. I.R. 603, 631.

[88] *Kausar v. Eagle Star Ins. Co.* [2000] Lloyd's Rep. I.R. 154.

17–29 The effect of non-disclosure. If the assured has failed in his duty of making full disclosure, the insurer may, on discovering the full facts, elect to avoid the contract of insurance,[89] and he may do so either before or after a loss has occurred. The contract cannot therefore be said to be automatically avoided by non-disclosure; it remains in force until avoided by the insurer.[90] The exercise of the insurer's right does not depend upon his ability to make restitution.[91] Unless there has been wilful or fraudulent concealment on the part of the assured, the premiums paid are returnable, but the basis for such recovery is not equitable restitution but quasi-contractual. Non-disclosure does not confer a remedy in damages, and there is high appellate authority that avoidance is the insurer's sole remedy.[92] Dicta that the insurer may simply raise non-disclosure as a defence to a claim without avoiding the contract of insurance[93] cannot, it is submitted, stand with these statements of principle.

17–30 Avoidance is retroactive. The rule for the return of premiums illustrates the point that the contract of insurance is avoided *ab initio*, and not merely for the future, from the moment of avoidance by the insurer.[94] This point is usually irrelevant, but circumstances may arise in which it is important. If, for example, the assured is paid for a loss under a fire policy, and then, on the occasion of a second loss shortly afterwards, the insurers discover that there has been a non-disclosure by the assured, it is very material to know the moment in time from which the policy is deemed to be avoided. If the contract is avoided only from the moment of avoidance, the assured would keep the money paid to him in settlement of his earlier claim, and, it may be presumed, he would not be able to recover past premiums paid, for it would mean that the insurers had been irrevocably at risk up to the moment of avoidance. But the law is otherwise. "Avoidance of the policy, of course, results in it being set aside *ab initio*, the repayment of any losses and the return of any premiums paid under it."[95] The premiums are recoverable only on the footing that the insurers have never been at risk under the void contract of insurance; the assured has a quasi-contractual action for money paid against a total failure of consideration.[96] The losses are repaid as money paid under a mistake of fact; had the insurers known of the non-disclosure at the time they need not have paid them.

---

[89] *Locker & Woolf v. W. Australian Ins. Co.* [1936] 1 K.B. 408, 415; *Joel v. Law Union & Crown Ins. Co.* [1908] 2 K.B. 863, 884; *Krantz v. Allan* (1921) 9 Ll.L.R. 410, 412; *Godfrey v. Britannic Ass.* [1963] 2 Lloyd's Rep. 515, 532. For the effect of recent insurance company codes of practice upon this right, see paras 17–98 to 17–100, *post*.

[90] *Mackender v. Feldia AG* [1966] 2 Lloyd's Rep. 449, 455; *Holland v. Russell* (1863) 4 B.&S. 14.

[91] *Joel v. Law Union & Crown* [1908] 2 K.B. 863.

[92] *Banque Keyser Ullmann SA v. Skandia (U.K.) Ins. Co. Ltd* [1990] 1 Q.B. 665, 778–781; [1991] 2 A.C. 249, 280, 281, *Bank of Nova Scotia v. Hellenic Mutual War Risks Ass.* [1990] 1 Q.B. 818, 888, not considered by the H.L. [1992] 1 A.C. 233. *HIH Casualty & General Ins. Ltd. v. Chase Manhattan Bank* [2001] 2 Lloyd's Rep. 483, 494. In *Pan Atlantic Ins. Co. Ltd v. Pine Top Ins. Co. Ltd* [1995] 1 A.C. 501, the sole remedy mentioned was avoidance—see at pp. 680, 682 and 717—although the nature of the remedy was not directly in point.

[93] *The Litsion Pride* [1985] 1 Lloyd's Rep. 437, 515; *Roadworks (1952) Ltd v. Charman* [1994] 2 Lloyd's Rep. 99, 107–108. See para. 17–2, *ante*.

[94] *Wheelton v. Hardisty* (1857) 8 E. & B. 232, 275 *per* Lord Campbell C.J.

[95] *Cornhill Insurance Co. v. Assenheim* (1937) 58 Ll.L.R. 27, 31, *per* Mackinnon J.; *Marks v. First Federal Ins. Co.* (1963) 6 W.I.R. 185; *Manifest Shipping Co. Ltd v. Uni-Polaris Co. Ltd The Star Sea* [2001] 1 All E.R. (Comm) 193, 210.

[96] *Feise v. Parkinson* (1812) 4 Taunt. 640; *Anderson v. Thornton* (1853) 8 Ex. 425, 427–428; Marine Ins. Act 1906, s.84(3)(a).

17–31 There are statements in the judgments of the Court of Appeal in *Mackender v. Feldia A.-G.*[97] which appear to suggest that avoidance for non-disclosure is not retroactive but discharges the insurer for the future, albeit with consequential adjustments of premiums and losses already paid. This is a difficult decision. But the issue was whether a dispute, as to whether insurers were entitled to avoid a policy for non-disclosure, was a dispute "arising under the contract" and so referable to the Belgian courts under a Belgian law and exclusive jurisdiction clause. The decision can perhaps best be explained on the basis of the autonomy of the Belgian exclusive jurisdiction clause.[98]

17–32 Effect of non-disclosure upon assignee of policy. It seems correct to say that an assignee of the policy is affected by any right which the insurers may have against the first assured (the assignor) to avoid the policy for non-disclosure.[99] This right is a remedy granted to them in equity[1] and the assignee presumably takes subject to prior equities.[2] Section 50(2) of the Marine Insurance Act 1906 provides that an insurer is entitled to raise against an assignee "any defence arising out of the contract" which would have been available against the first assured. This has been held to cover a defence based on non-disclosure,[3] despite the difficulty that the non-disclosure, being prior to the contract's conclusion, might be said not to arise out of it.

17–33 Effect of non-disclosure on composite policy. Supposing that two or more persons are insured under one policy in respect of their separate interests, such as mortgagor and mortgagee, and one co-assured is guilty of non-disclosure but the other is innocent, the question has arisen whether the insurer is entitled to avoid the policy as against both assureds or is restricted to avoiding it against the assured in breach of duty while remaining liable to the innocent assured.[4] In principle, avoidance against the one assured is possible only where the policy contains separate contracts of insurance with each assured, because where the policy is construed as containing one contract, as in *Federation Insurance v. Wasson*,[5] it is impossible to conceive of the contract being partly avoided and partly affirmed.[6] Even in the case of separate contracts, there may well be problems concerning return of premium and the employment of one broker as agent to conclude the

---

[97] [1967] 2 Q.B. 590, 598, 603.
[98] Mustill & Boyd, *Commercial Arbitration.* (2nd ed.), pp. 110–111; *FAI General Ins. Co. v. Ocean Marine Mutual P. & I. Assoc.* [1998] Lloyd's Rep. I.R. 24 (N.S.W. Comm. Div).
[99] *Scottish Equitable Ass. Co. v. Buist* (1876) 3 R. 1078; (1877) 4 R. 1076; (1878) 5 R.(H.L.) 64; *Locker & Woolf Ltd v. W. Australian Ins. Co.* [1936] 1 K.B. 408.
[1] *Merchants & Manufacturers Ins. Co. v. Hunt* [1941] 1 K.B. 295, 313, 318.
[2] *Roxburghe v. Cox* (1881) 17 Ch.D. 520.
[3] *Pickersgill & Son Ltd v. London etc., Ins. Co.* [1912] 3 K.B. 614; *The Litsion Pride* [1985] 1 Lloyd's Rep. 437, 517–519.
[4] *Woolcott v. Sun Alliance & London Ins. Co.* [1978] 1 W.L.R. 493; *The Litsion Pride* [1985] 1 Lloyd's Rep. 437, 516.
[5] (1987) 163 C.L.R. 303.
[6] *United Shoe Machinery v. Brunet* [1909] A.C. 330, 340, and see *New Hampshire Ins. Co. v. Mirror Group Newspapers* [1997] L.R.L.R. 24, 57–58.

insurance for both assureds, and these have not been addressed in the reported decisions. In Canada it has become customary for a mortgagee to protect himself against the consequences of non-disclosure, misrepresentation, and breach of conditions by the mortgagor by incorporating a special mortgagee clause in the policy, which has been held to create a separate contract between the mortgagee and insurer independent of that between the insurer and mortgagor.[7] By agreeing to enter into separate contracts with borrower and lender in this way, the insurer signifies its consent to forgo the right to complain that the borrower's non-disclosure induced the making of both contracts.

17-34 Such clauses have been employed in this jurisdiction in non-marine property insurances.[8] Recent decisions suggest that the courts will readily construe composite policies as containing separate contracts between the insurer and each co-assured in order to ensure that each interest is adequately protected and to avoid injustice to those assureds who would otherwise be deprived of cover through no fault of their own. If cover is granted under one composite policy to a number of companies within one corporate group for their respective separate interests, it would be unjust if insurers could avoid the entire insurance for the failure of one co-assured to give full disclosure of facts relevant only to its own cover.[9] Where a liability policy granted to an incorporated firm of estate agents and valuers and to its individual directors for their several interests was construed to provide that the dishonesty of one co-assured would not result in the denial of coverage to others not complicit in his dishonesty, the court had no difficulty in interpreting it as a bundle of separate contracts of insurance between each co-assured and the insurers, so that deliberate concealment by the managing director did not entitle the insurers to avoid the insurances of the other directors and the company itself.[10] It was held that this should be the prima facie construction of a composite policy.

(d) Materiality

17-35 Criterion of materiality in English law. The common law test for materiality is stated in section 18(2) of the Marine Insurance Act 1906[11] which provides that: "Every circumstance is material which would influence the judgment of a prudent insurer in fixing the premium or determining whether he will take the risk." The word "judgment" does not mean "final

---

[7] *London & Midland Gen. Ins. Co. v. Bonser* [1973] S.C.R. 10; *Canadian Imperial Bank of Commerce v. Dominion of Canada Gen. Ins. Co.* (1988) 46 D.L.R. (4th) 77 (Sup. Ct. B.C.); *Nat. Bank of Greece v. Katsikonouris* [1990] 2 S.C.R. 1029; *Royal Bank of Canada v. N. Waterloo Farmers Mut. Ins. Co.* (1992) 7 O.R. (3d) 723, following the analysis of mortgagee interest clauses by the courts in the U.S.A., summarised in Couch, *Cyclopedia of Insurance Law* (2nd ed., 1982) vol. 10, p. 761.

[8] Evidence to this effect was accepted in *F.N.C.B. v. Barnet Devanney (Harrow) Ltd* [1999] Lloyd's Rep. I.R. 43; [1999] Lloyd's Rep. I.R. 459 C.A., where the assured recovered damages from its broker for failure to advise that a mortgage clause should be included in the insurance on the mortgaged property.

[9] *New Hampshire Ins. Co. v. Mirror Group Newspapers* [1997] L.R.L.R. 24, 57.

[10] *Arab Bank Plc. v. Zurich Ins. Co.* [1999] 1 Lloyd's Rep. 262.

[11] *Lambert v. Co-operative Ins. Soc. Ltd* [1975] 2 Lloyd's Rep. 485; *Pan Atlantic Ins. Co. Ltd v. Pine Top Ins. Co. Ltd* [1995] 1 A.C. 501. The Irish High Court has adopted the same test—*Chariot Ins. Ltd v. Assicurazioni Generali SpA* [1981] I.R. 199.

decision" but simply "formation of an opinion". Accordingly a fact may be material although, if disclosed, it would not have led the prudent insurer to decline the risk or stipulate an increased premium.[12] It is enough that he would rightly take it into account as a factor in coming to his decision. It has been suggested by Scrutton L.J. that the statutory definition should be glossed by adding the words "in that type of insurance" after "prudent insurer".[13]

17–36 Life assurance and Scots law. It was held by Lord President Inglis in *Life Association of Scotland v. Foster*[14] that the test of materiality in life assurance under Scots law was whether a reasonable man in the position of the assured and with knowledge of the facts in dispute should have realised that they were material to the risk. In *Hooper v. Royal London General Insurance Co. Ltd*[15] the court considered *Foster*, and held that the "reasonable assured" test applies, exceptionally, only to life assurance, but that in all other types of insurance the English law test of materiality would be followed in Scots law.

17–37 Opinion of the assured is irrelevant. The opinion of the particular assured as to the materiality of a fact will not as a rule be considered, because it follows from the accepted test of materiality that the question is whether a prudent insurer would have considered that any particular circumstance was a material fact and not whether the assured believed it to be so.[16] The maxim *uberrima fides* is therefore to an extent misleading, since an assured might believe in all honesty that he was complying with the duty of good faith, and yet fail to discharge the duty of disclosure. In Scots law, which follows the "reasonable assured" test in life assurance, it is recognised that the opinion of the individual assured is irrelevant in law, although the opinion of the particular assured may well be held to have been that tenable by a reasonable assured in the same circumstances. In *Life Association of Scotland v. Foster*[17] the assured had at the date of her proposal a slight swelling in her groin. It gave her no pain or uneasiness of any kind and, since she attached no importance to it, she did not mention it to the company's doctor. To a medical man this swelling would have indicated the presence of a rupture which might become dangerous to life, and it was therefore argued that there had been non-disclosure of a material fact. The court did not agree, and Lord President Inglis, after stating the nature of the duty of disclosure, said[18]:

---

[12] *Pan Atlantic Ins. Co. Ltd v. Pine Top Ins. Co. Ltd, supra,* approving the earlier decision of the Court of Appeal in *Container Transport International Inc. v. Oceanus Mutual Underwriting Ass.* [1984] 1 Lloyd's Rep. 476.
[13] *Becker v. Marshall* (1922) 12 Ll.L.R. 413, 414, followed by Scott L.J. in *Locker & Woolf v. W. Australian Ins. Co.* [1936] 1 K.B. 408, 415.
[14] (1873) 11 M. 351.
[15] 1993 S.C. 242, followed in *Unipac Scotland Ltd v. Aegon Ins. Co.* 1996 S.L.T. 1197, 1199.
[16] *Dalglish v. Jarvie* (1850) 2 M. & G. 231, 243; *Brownlie v. Campbell* (1880) 5 App.Cas. 925, 954; *Bates v. Hewitt* (1867) L.R. 2 Q.B. 595, 607–608; *Re Yager & Guardian Ass. Co.* (1912) 108 L.T, 38, 44; *Joel v. Law Union & Crown Ins. Co.* [1908] 2 K.B. 863, 884; *Zurich General Accident & Liability Co. v. Morrison* [1942] 2 K.B. 53, 64; *Regina Fur Co. v. Bossom* [1957] 2 Lloyd's Rep. 466, 483; *Godfrey v. Britannic Ass. Co.* [1963] 2 Lloyd's Rep. 515, 529; *Roselodge Ltd v. Castle* [1966] 2 Lloyd's Rep. 113, 131; *Murphy v. Sun Life Ass. of Canada,* approving the corresponding passage in the 5th ed. of this work at pp. 894–896, (1964) 44 D.L.R. (2d) 369.
[17] (1873) 11 M. 351.
[18] (1873) 11 M. 351, 359.

"My opinion is, upon a consideration of the whole circumstances as disclosed in the evidence, that the swelling which is proved to have existed at the date of the contract of insurance has not been shown to be such a fact as a reasonable and cautious person unskilled in medical science, and with no special knowledge of the law and practice of insurance, would believe to be of any materiality or in any way calculated to influence the insurers in considering and deciding on the risk."

17–38 The reasons for disregarding the assured's opinion of materiality were stated succinctly by Bayley J. in *Lindenau v. Desborough*, a well-known decision in life assurance, where he said[19]:

"The contrary doctrine would lead to frequent suppression of information, and it would often be extremely difficult to show that the party neglecting to give the information thought it material. But if it be held that all material facts must be disclosed, it will be the interest of the assured to make a full and fair disclosure of all the information within their reach."

It must be emphasised, however, that this rule does not affect the operation of the rule already mentioned, that the assured need disclose only those material facts which are within his knowledge or which he is deemed to know.[20]

17–39 Opinion of particular insurer. A fact does not become material merely because the particular insurer personally regards it as such,[21] but his subjective opinion is relevant as evidence that he would not have contracted, either on the same terms or at all, if the fact had been disclosed by the assured, so that the non-disclosure can be shown to have induced the conclusion of the contract.[22] The view has been expressed, however, that a fact is material if to the knowledge of the assured, the insurer regards it as material,[23] but this seems to contradict the established criterion for materiality. It is submitted that, if the assured does owe a duty of disclosure in these circumstances, it rests on a different basis. The principle of *uberrimae fidei* and the rule of disclosure are not synonymous. The latter is the best known consequence of the former. There remains a residual duty to act in the utmost good faith with regard to matters which may not technically be the subject of the duty of disclosure, and it is submitted that an assured who is aware that his insurers regard particular facts as important does not discharge his residual duty to demonstrate good faith if he conceals them, regardless of their materiality. Thus in *Cantiere Meccanico Brindisino v. Janson*[24] Vaughan-Williams L.J. remarked that in marine insurance a party

---

[19] (1828) 8 B. & C. 586, 592, approved in *Marks v. First Federal Ins. Co.* (1963) 6 W.I.R. 185.

[20] See paras 17–9 to 17–10, *ante*.

[21] *Glasgow Assurance Corp. v. Symondson* (1911) 16 Com.Cas 109, 119.

[22] *Pan Atlantic Ins. Co. Ltd v. Pine Top Ins. Co. Ltd* [1995] A.C. 501, approving Kerr J. in *Berger v. Pollock* [1973] 2 Lloyd's Rep. 442, 463. See para. 17–28, *ante*.

[23] Ivamy, *General Principles*, (6th ed.), p. 153, citing *Tate v. Hyslop* (1885) 15 Q.B.D. 368, *Glicksman v. Lancashire and General Ass. Co.* [1927] A.C. 139, and *Holmes v. Cornhill Ins. Co. Ltd* (1949) 82 Ll.L.R. 575. In *Tate*, however, the court regarded the undisclosed fact as satisfying the objective test of materiality, and in *Holmes* the court was interpreting the word "material facts" in a warranty contained in a proposal form.

[24] [1912] 3 K.B. 452, 463. See also *CTI v. Oceanus Mutual Underwriting Ass.* [1984] 1 Lloyd's Rep. 476, 512, 525.

might well be obliged to disclose facts under section 17 of the Marine Insurance Act 1906 which enjoins a general duty to act in good faith, although he might not be obliged to do so under section 18 of that Act, which contains the detailed rules relating to communication of material facts. It is submitted that this is the true explanation of certain remarks made by Scrutton L.J. and Viscount Dunedin in *Glicksman v. Lancashire and General Assurance*,[25] where it was said that the assured should disclose facts known by him to be treated as material by the insurers. It was not there meant that the underwriters' belief determined whether they were truly material or not. In practice the insurers will usually ask specific questions about facts regarded as important by themselves, so this issue is not likely to arise often.

17–40 Evidence of materiality. Although it is proper for the court to formulate legal tests governing the materiality of facts, the question whether a given fact is or is not material is one of fact to be determined by a jury or a judge as the trier of fact.[26] The decision rests on the judge's own appraisal of the relevance of the disputed fact to the subject-matter of the insurance; it is not something which is settled automatically by the current practice or opinion of insurers.

17–41 Thus the materiality of an uncommunicated fact may be so obvious that it is unnecessary to call any expert evidence to establish this point.[27] Scrutton L.J. put the matter forcibly in *Glicksman v. Lancashire and General Assurance Co.*[28] in the following way:

"[It was argued] that before a court can find that a fact is material, somebody must give evidence of the materiality. That is entirely contrary to the whole course of insurance litigation; it is so far contrary that it is frequently objected that a party is not entitled to call other people to say what they think is material; that is a matter for the court on the nature of the facts. I entirely agree with Roche J. that the nature of the facts may be such that you do not need anybody to come and say, 'This is material'. If a shipowner desiring to insure his ship for the month of January knew that in that month she was heavily damaged in a storm, it would, with deference to counsel who has suggested the opposite, be ridiculous to call evidence of the materiality of that fact; the fact speaks for itself."

17–42 Where, however, the court is unsure of the materiality of a given fact, it is usual to call expert evidence from persons engaged in the insurance business in order to assist the court in making its decision. This appears to have been permissible at least in connection with marine risks since an early

[25] [1925] 2 K.B. 593, 609; [1927] A.C. 139, 143–144.

[26] *Morrison v. Muspratt* (1827) 4 Bing. 60; *Lindenau v. Desborough* (1828) 8 B. & C. 586; *Huguenin v. Bayley* (1815) 6 Taunt. 186; *Swete v. Fairlie* (1833) 6 C. & P. 1; *Rawlins v. Desborough* (1840) 2 Moo. & Ry. 328, 333; *Seaton v. Heath* [1899] 1 Q.B. 782, 791.

[27] *Mitchell v. Scottish Eagle Ins. Co. Ltd* 1997 SLT 793, following *Marene Knitting Mills Pty. Ltd v. Greater Pacific Ins. Ltd* [1976] 2 Lloyd's Rep. 631, 642.

[28] [1925] 2 K.B. 593, 609. See also [1927] A.C. 139, 143 *per* Viscount Dunedin.

date,[29] and Lord Mansfield's remarks in *Carter v. Boehm* about the irrelevance of such evidence seem to have been prompted by the actual opinion tendered by the broker called in that case; it appears to have been a personal view based on hindsight and "without the least Foundation from any previous Precedent or Usage".[30] Hence it has been said that expert evidence ought to be directed to the practice of the insurance profession as a whole, and not to the particular opinion of the witness in question as to what he would do, which might be inadmissible.[31]

17–43 Expert evidence. The categories of expert evidence admissible to prove materiality are not restricted to witnesses engaged in insurance. Thus, in the case of life assurance, where the insurers would naturally be guided by their medical advisers in gauging the health and prospects of the life proposed for assurance, it is permissible to adduce expert medical testimony concerning the relevance of undisclosed facts relating to medical matters.[32] It is only right that opinions on such matters should come from the medical profession, by whose opinions life assurance offices are guided, and not from the insurers themselves, who must be ignorant of the significance of such facts. It is submitted that expert evidence on the materiality of undisclosed facts ought to be admitted whenever it is the usual practice of insurers to be guided by the opinions of that class of experts whose evidence is offered in the case in question.

17–44 Even when evidence is restricted to general insurance usage and criteria there remains the possibility that the witness, in representing current practice, may too easily be made the embodiment of the "prudent insurer". The notional prudent insurer should not, it is submitted, follow the usages of his profession without question any more than the notional "reasonable man" of tort law is permitted to follow the usages of a given profession or employment or trade without reflecting upon them,[33] and a review of the decisions on materiality may prompt the feeling that accepted practice has sometimes carried too much weight.[34] Be that as it may, even greater care should be given to the evaluation of expert evidence when the test of materiality followed by the court is what the reasonable man would conceive to be of relevance to the insurers.[35] In a sense the view of the insurers

---

[29] *Chaurand v. Angerstain* (1791) Peake 43; *Littledale v. Dixon* (1805) 1 Bos. & P.N.R. 151; *Berthon v. Loughman* (1817) 2 St. 258; *Herring v. Janson* (1895) 1 Com.Cas. 177, 179; *Trading Co. Hoff v. de Rougemont* (1929) 34 Com.Cas. 291. See Smith's *Leading Cases* Vol. I, pp. 560–561 (1929 ed.), for a survey of older decisions on admissibility of evidence to prove materiality.

[30] (1766) 3 Burr. 1905, 1918.

[31] *Horne v. Poland* [1922] 2 K.B. 364, 365. Evidence from the actual underwriter or his in-house experts, as received in *Henwood v. Prudential Ass. Co.* (1967) 64 D.L.R. (2d) 715 and *Babatsikos v. Car Owners Mutual Ins. Co. Ltd* [1970] 2 Lloyd's Rep. 314, 323, would be admissible to establish inducement of contract.

[32] *Yorke v. Yorkshire Ins. Co.* [1918] 1 K.B. 662; *Godfrey v. Britannic Ass. Co.* [1963] 2 Lloyd's Rep. 515; see also *Murphy v. Sun Life Ass. Co. of Canada* (1964) 44 D.L.R. (2d) 369 where an actuary's evidence was admitted.

[33] *Atkinson v. Tyne-Tees Steam Shipping Co.* [1956] 1 Lloyd's Rep. 244. This paragraph in the 7th edition of this work was approved by Forbes J. in *Reynolds v. Phoenix Ass. Co.* [1978] 2 Lloyd's Rep. 440, 459.

[34] See the cases discussed by R. A. Hasson in (1969) 32 M.L.R. 615.

[35] This is the correct test in life assurance in Scots Law: see para. 17–36, *ante*.

themselves on what they would like to be told is irrelevant. The courts undoubtedly have the power to make their own evaluation of the practice put in evidence, however,[36] and the decision in *Roselodge Ltd v. Castle*[37] is a good illustration. In that case a Lloyd's underwriter gave evidence to the effect that it was material to know that an employee of a firm of jewellers insured against loss or damage to its property had been convicted of bribing a police officer 12 years previously, but McNair J. decided that a prudent underwriter would not regard it as such.

17–45 Information and opinions. A proposer for insurance is required to disclose not only material facts known to him but also information and opinions concerning the risk which have come to his notice. Mere unsubstantiated rumours do not count,[38] but reports and opinions from credible sources should be disclosed so that the underwriter can exercise his judgment upon them, even though the proposer himself believes them to be wrong. This rule was established in a line of marine insurance cases concerning reports that a ship was in trouble, and even if the report ultimately turned out to have been unfounded it was held that the failure to disclose it entitled the insurer to avoid the insurance.[39] More recently it has been applied to a report made by an expert with whom another expert disagrees.[40] In *British Equitable Insurance Co. v. Great Western Ry.*[41] the assured had consulted a specialist concerning the swelling of his feet, and was told that he was in a dangerous state of health. His own doctor said that the specialist was wrong, and the assured did not mention it to the insurance when applying for an own-life policy. He died of a heart attack shortly after the policy was issued. It was avoided. The specialist's opinion, even if wrong, should have been disclosed to the insurers. Conversely, the failure to disclose a fact which prior to issue of a policy was not material does not entitle the insurer to avoid the insurance when with hindsight it is later realised that it was material after all.[42]

17–46 Examples of material facts. The definitions of material facts discussed above may usefully be illustrated by taking certain categories of facts decided by the courts to be material in different types of insurances.

---

[36] *Carter v. Boehm* (1766) 3 Burr. 1905; *Rickards v. Murdock* (1830) 10 B. & C. 527, 541; *Fracis Times & Co. v. Sea Insurance Co.* (1898) 3 Com.Cas. 229; *Thames and Mersey Marine v. Gunford Ship Co.* [1911] A.C. 529; *Yorke v. Yorkshire Ins. Co.* [1918] 1 K.B. 662, 670; *Johnson & Perrott Ltd v. Holmes* (1925) 21 Ll.L.R. 330, 332.

[37] [1966] 2 Lloyd's Rep. 113.

[38] *Decorum Investments Ltd v. Atkin* [2001] 2 Lloyd's Rep. 378, 382.

[39] *Da Costa v. Scandret* (1723) 2 P. Wms. 170; *Seaman v. Fonnereau* (1743) 2 Str. 1813; *Shirley v. Wilkinson* (1781) 3 Dougl. K.B. 41; *Lynch v. Hamilton* (1810) 3 Taunt. 37, affirmed *sub nom. Lynch v. Dunsford* (1811) 14 East 494; *Durrell v. Bederley* (1816) Holt N.P. 283, 285; *Morrison v. Universal Marine* (1873) L.R. 8 Exch. 40, 53, not challenged on appeal at p.197; *Stribley v. Imperial Mar. Ins. Co.* (1876) 1 Q.B.D. 507. *Sed contra Gate v. Sun Alliance Ins. Ltd* [1995] L.R.L.R. 385, 399.

[40] *Cantiere Meccanico Brindisino v. Janson* [1912] 3 K.B. 452, 471; *St. Paul Fire & Marine Ins. Co.* [1995] 2 Lloyd's Rep. 116, 120.

[41] (1869) 20 L.T. 422.

[42] *Watson v. Mainwaring* (1813) 4 Taunt. 763; *Assoc. Oil Carriers v. Union Ins. Co.* [1917] 2 K.B. 184; *Sharp v. Sphere Drake Ins. Plc, The Moonacre* [1992] 2 Lloyd's Rep. 501, 521.

17–47 Exposure to unusual risk of loss. If the assured knows facts which indicate that the subject-matter of the insurance is exposed to abnormal physical danger from perils insured against, he should disclose them to the insurer. Any fact suggesting that the life assured will be shorter than expected by the insurer on a reading of the proposal form ought to be disclosed, quite apart from the specific questions put in the proposal form.[43] Thus, notwithstanding that all the questions put to an applicant for life assurance have been answered correctly it has been held to be a question of fact whether the following additional matters were material to be disclosed, *viz.*: that the applicant for insurance on her own life was then in a debtor's prison[44]; that after the applicant had been medically examined he had become troubled with a cough, emaciated, and had consulted a doctor[45]; that the life proposed for insurance had lost the use of his speech and mental faculties[46]; that some years previously the applicant had been operated on for a tumour[47]; that about four years previously the applicant had exhibited symptoms of consumption[48]; that the life assured was a mental defective as the result of a traumatic lesion of the brain inflicted during the process of childbirth.[49] It is material that the life assured had been told that he had a minor kidney condition and suffered from attacks of pharyngitis,[50] and an applicant for life insurance ought to disclose that he had been to consult a specialist about loss of weight and suspected dropsy,[51] or a psychiatrist about suspected nervous disorders,[52] or had to have an electrocardiographic test after a syncope episode,[53] or that he had had hepatitis shortly before obtaining insurance.[54]

17–48 Living conditions and habits. Symptoms of illness are not the only material facts indicating that a life assured may drop sooner than anticipated. Intemperate habits[55] or the taking of possibly harmful drugs[56] may well be material facts, and the occupation of the assured ought to be disclosed if especially hazardous. In one case[57] the assured was killed while driving in the celebrated Paris to Bordeaux motor race of 1903. His proposal form stated that his occupation was "driving motor cars", occasionally in races. In an application for reinsurance the insurers produced their policy where he was described as a "gentleman" and did not disclose the assured's occasional motor racing. It was held that the reinsurers were entitled to

---

[43] *Joel v. Law Union & Crown Ins. Co.* [1908] 2 K.B. 863; *Piedmont, etc., Life v. Ewing*, 92 U.S. 377 (1875); *Stiptich v. Insurance Co.*, 277 U.S. 311 (1928).
[44] *Huguenin v. Bayley* (1815) 6 Taunt. 186.
[45] *Morrison v. Muspratt* (1827) 4 Bing 60.
[46] *Lindenau v. Desborough* (1828) 8 B. & C. 586.
[47] *Abbott v. Howard* (1832) Hayes 381.
[48] *Geach v. Ingall* (1845) 14 M. & W. 95.
[49] *Gardner v. London General Ins. Co.* [1926] I.A.C.Rep. 46.
[50] *Godfrey v. Britannic Assurance* [1963] 2 Lloyd's Rep. 515.
[51] *British Equitable v. G.W.R.* (1869) 20 L.T. 422; and see *Joel v. Law Union & Crown Ins. Co.* [1908] 2 K.B. 863.
[52] *Henwood v. Prudential Ass. Co.* (1967) 64 D.L.R. 2d. 715.
[53] *Murphy v. Sun Life Ass. of Canada* (1964) 44 D.L.R. (2d) 369.
[54] *Marks v. First Federal Ins. Co.* (1963) 6 W.I.R. 185.
[55] *Rawlins v. Desborough* (1840) 2 Moo. & Ry. 328, 333.
[56] *Yorke v. Yorkshire Insurance* [1918] 1 K.B. 662.
[57] *Equitable Life Ass. Soc. v. General Accident Ass. Corp.* (1904) 12 S.L.T. 348.

repudiate liability on the reinsurance contract. In an accident insurance case where the insured described himself as a tea-traveller, omitting to state he was also a publican, Wright J. seemed to agree with the arbitrator's decision that this was material.[58] Not every change of occupation is, of course, material. If the assured resigned from his post after completing a proposal but before the policy was issued, he would not need to disclose this unless he knew that he was going to take up another particular calling which involved greater risks.[59] It has been held that where the proposer described himself as a "bricklayer", but had for some time been unable to lay bricks owing to poor eyesight, there was no misdescription or concealment of a material fact.[60] The shortness of vision would be material in itself only if it was produced by a disease, as was the case in *Lee v. British Law Insurance Co.* where the applicant for personal accident insurance ought to have disclosed a condition of myopia.[61]

17–49 Threats of murder. In an American decision it was left to the jury to say whether the fact that the assured's life had been threatened was material and ought to have been disclosed.[62] Provided that the threat is not believed to be baseless, this seems to be entirely correct, since it has been held several times that threats to burn down property ought to be disclosed to fire insurers.[63]

17–50 Insurances on property and chattels: fire. The situation or user of a building may well be material if these suggest that the subject-matter of the insurance is particularly vulnerable to the risk of damage by fire. Thus in the old case of *Buse v. Turner,*[64] where the insured on applying for an insurance on his warehouse had failed to disclose that there had been a fire the same evening in a house nearby adjoining the warehouse proposed to be insured, it was held he could not recover in respect of the subsequent destruction of his warehouse consequent on a fresh outbreak of the fire in the adjoining house. If there are present in the insured building goods the presence of which the insurer would not know from the proposal alone, and which increase the fire hazard, this fact should be disclosed,[65] as should any abnormal user of any part of the building which could increase the danger of fire.[66] Where a car is insured against fire, the nature and situation of its garage will normally be material facts if these could affect the chances of fire breaking out or being difficult to extinguish,[67] although if the risk of fire in the garage is insignificant in relation to other risks insured against they are too trivial to be material.[68] If there have been attempts to set fire to the building insured (or in which insured goods are stored) whether successful or

---

[58] *Biggar v. Rock Life Ass. Co.* [1902] 1 K.B. 516.
[59] *Turnbull v. Scottish Provident* (1896) 34 S.L.R. 146.
[60] *Jarvis v. Liverpool Victoria Friendly Society* [1927] I.A.C.Rep. 34.
[61] [1972] 2 Lloyd's Rep. 49.
[62] *Connecticut Mutual Life v. McWhirter,* 73 Fed.Rep. 444 (1896); *N.Y. Life Ins. Co. v. Bacalis,* 94 F. 2d 200 (1938).
[63] See note 69, *infra* and *Leen v. Hall* (1923) 16 Ll.L.R. 100.
[64] (1815) 6 Taunt. 338.
[65] *Watkinson v. Hullett* (1938) 61 Ll.L.R. 145.
[66] *Barsalou v. Royal Insurance Co.* (1864) 15 L.C.R. 3; *James v. CGU Ins. Plc.* [2002] Lloyd's Rep. I.R. 206, 220; *Hales v. Reliance Fire and Accident Ins. Corp.* [1960] 2 Lloyd's Rep. 391 (*obiter*), such as the presence of squatters—*Aldridge Estates v. MacCarthy* [1996] E.G.C.S. 167.
[67] *Dawsons Ltd v. Bonnin* [1922] 2 A.C. 413, 429.
[68] [1922] 2 A.C. 413.

not, or if there have been threats of incendiarism, these should as a rule be disclosed,[69] unless the threats in question are not such that a reasonable man would take them seriously.[70]

17–51 As is the case with burglary insurance applications, previous losses by the peril insured against are material and ought to be disclosed. In one case a company applied for fire cover on premises where it carried on the business of manufacturing caravans. This business was essentially that of its sole director and major shareholder, who was described as the *alter ego* of the company. He failed to disclose that, some three years earlier, there had been a loss by fire on premises of another company which he had used as a vehicle for the same business. It was held that this loss was material, and that the insurers were entitled to avoid the contract of insurance.[71]

17–52 Burglary insurance. If goods are insured against theft, any fact suggesting that they are exposed to an unusual risk of loss by theft is material. Any characteristic of the building where the goods were kept which made it impossible, for instance, to take the usual precautions against unauthorised entry would presumably be material. Previous losses are also relevant to the risk of future losses,[72] even if the assured has been indemnified by his insurers,[73] because a prudent insurer would wish to investigate such losses in order to see to what extent the assured's carelessness might have contributed to them.[74] A householder is not as a rule bound to investigate and disclose the past insurance history of all persons residing under his roof to his insurers on a burglary insurance policy.[75] Theft of a radio worth £350 from a yacht laid up in Spain is not a material fact when it is to be regarded as an ordinary incident in that locality.[76]

17–53 Motor insurance. An applicant for motor insurance ought to make full disclosure of any accidents in which he has been involved,[77] whether he was driving on his own account or on behalf of some other person.[78] This disclosure should extend to the accident record of any driver who to his knowledge is going to drive the car.[79] It seems that an accident occurring to

---

[69] *Leen v. Hall* (1923) 16 Ll.L.R. 100; *Mitchell v. Scottish Eagle Ins. Co. Ltd* 1997 S.L.T. 793; *Herbert v. Mercantile Fire Ins. Co.* (1878) 43 U.C.R. 384; *Campbell v. Victoria Mutual Fire Ins. Co.* (1880) 45 U.C.R. 412.

[70] *Watt v. Union Insurance* (1884) 5 N.S.W.L.R. 48.

[71] *Arterial Caravans Ltd v. Yorkshire Insurance Co. Ltd* [1973] 1 Lloyd's Rep. 169, followed in *Marene Knitting Mills Pty Ltd v. Greater Pacific General Insurance Ltd* [1976] 2 Lloyd's Rep. 631 (P.C.).

[72] *Krantz v. Allan* (1921) 9 Ll.L.R. 410; *Rozanes v. Bowen* (1928) Ll.L.R. 98; *Morser v. Eagle Star, etc., Co.* (1931) 40 Ll.L.R. 254; *Becker v. Marshall* (1922) 12 Ll.L.R. 413; *Lyons v. Bentley* (1944) 77 Ll.L.R. 355.

[73] *Roberts v. Avon Ins. Co.* [1956] 2 Lloyd's Rep. 240. A previous loss by theft is also relevant even if the property is restored by the police, *Morser v. Eagle Star, etc., Ins. Co.* (1931) 40 Ll.L.R. 254.

[74] *Becker v. Marshall* (1922) 11 Ll.L.R. 113, 114, 117.

[75] *Lyons v. Bentley* (1944) 77 Ll.L.R. 335, 338.

[76] *The Moonacre* [1992] 2 Lloyd's Rep. 501, 517–518, also holding that the forgery of the assured's signature on the proposal form by the broker is material and disclosable—pp. 518–522. The decision would have been different if the insurer had had to prove inducement because the insurer would have simply demanded that the assured sign the proposal.

[77] *Dent v. Blackmore* (1927) 29 Ll.L.R. 9.

[78] *Furey v. Eagle Star* (1922) W.C. & Ins. Rep. 149.

[79] *Dunn v. Ocean, Accident and Guarantee Corp. Ltd* (1933) 47 Ll.L.R. 129.

the proposer's car when he was not driving it is nonetheless material,[80] so long as no reasonably minded man could dismiss it as a "minor accident" or trivial knock.[81] The fact that other sorts of damage have occurred to the applicant's cars may well be material. It has been held to be a material fact that the applicant's previous car was taken and driven away on three occasions, although it was recovered undamaged each time, because this might indicate carelessness on the part of the applicant.[82] It would normally also be material that the car was garaged in a building where there had been fires previously or which was subject to unusual fire risks or theft risks of which the insurer could not be aware.[83]

17-54 In motor insurance, as is well known, the insurer estimates the risk according to certain characteristics of the car and the assured on which there is statistical evidence permitting him to grade the risk. These matters are usually covered by questions in the proposal form. If by chance the proposal form omitted them, or if a change in circumstances occurred prior to a renewal of the policy (to which, it will be recalled, the duty of disclosure attaches),[84] they would no doubt be considered material facts. Thus the age of the car would be material, because this would affect its value under a comprehensive policy, and so would any modifications to the manufacturers' standard specification affecting the vehicle's performance. The age of the proposer is material,[85] as this is always relevant to the premium charged, particularly under certain new types of policy issued recently, and so is his physical condition in so far as it affects his capabilities as a driver.[86] The proposer's occupation is material,[87] since there are some professions and callings with significantly higher accident rates than others. It seems that it would be concealment of a material fact for the proposer to omit to state he did not own the insured vehicle if the proposal form gave the impression that he did.[88]

It has been held immaterial that the proposer for motor insurance failed his driving test,[89] at least where the policy was intended to cover inexperienced drivers.

17-55 Character and motive of assured. All facts are material which suggest that the business integrity of the proposer for insurance is open to doubt, or that his motive in seeking cover is not merely the prudent one of covering himself against losses which might occur in the ordinary course of events. The types of facts which have been held to relate to this "moral hazard" are very varied and call for separate discussion.

[80] *Trustee of G. H. Mundy (a Bankrupt) v. Blackmore* (1928) 32 Ll.L.R. 150.
[81] 32 Ll.L.R. 150, 152.
[82] *Farra v. Hetherington* (1931) 40 Ll.L.R. 132. The court did not consider that the obligation to disclose these "borrowings" was excluded by asking a question specifically concerning "accidents" and "losses" only, though this does not seem to have been argued.
[83] *Johnson & Perrot v. Holmes* (1925) 21 Ll.L.R. 330 does not contradict this proposition. In that case the fact that the insured car was kept in a garage used by the IRA was found to *decrease* the risk for insurer, since a seizure by the IRA would fall inside an exception in the policy.
[84] *Re Wilson and Scottish Insurance* [1920] 2 Ch. 28, and para. 17-24, *supra*.
[85] *Broad v. Waland* (1942) 73 Ll.L.R. 263.
[86] *James v. British General Ins. Co. Ltd* (1927) 27 Ll.L.R. 328.
[87] *Holmes v. Cornhill Ins. Co.* (1949) 82 Ll.L.R. 575; *McNealy v. Pennine Insce Co.* [1978] 2 Lloyd's Rep. 18.
[88] *Guardian Assurance v. Sutherland* (1939) 63 Ll.L.R. 220.
[89] *Zurich General Accident and Liability v. Morrison* [1942] 2 K.B. 53.

17–56 Previous convictions. The most obvious type of fact which falls under the rubric "moral hazard" is where the proposer has been convicted in the past of a criminal offence. Indeed, before the Rehabilitation of Offenders Act 1974 the non-disclosure of such facts often came before the courts as a basis for avoidance. In motor insurance not only previous convictions for driving offences of the assured[90] or of intended drivers of the insured car are material,[91] but also convictions for quite different offences. Thus convictions of the assured for garage-breaking, forgery, breach of recognisances and theft are material,[92] and in another case convictions of the assured for drinking offences in no way connected with the driving of motor vehicles were held material, and also a conviction for permitting a car to be used without proper insurance.[93] In other types of insurance a similar rule has prevailed. A jeweller who effected a policy against loss by burglary had as a young man been convicted of larceny on six occasions over a period of seven years ending 14 years before the date of the policy, and a jury found that these were material facts.[94] The Court of Appeal refused to disturb this finding, despite the fact that the assured's record related, as Asquith L.J. said, to a "dim and remote past".[95]

A wife who renews a policy on jewellery belonging partly to herself and partly to her husband is under a duty to disclose the fact that her husband, though not the assured, had been convicted of two crimes involving dishonesty during the previous year in which the policy was in force, at least when it was not the first time he had been convicted of such a crime.[96] A director of a company should disclose when applying for renewal of its traders' combined policy that he had been convicted of handling stolen property in the year prior to renewal.[97] The non-disclosure of a conviction in 1960 for a robbery on the part of a mortgagor was held to entitle the insurance company to avoid liability to him under a building society block policy to which he was added in 1972, although not to the building society in respect of its separate interest.[98] A conviction for attempting to extort money from an insurance company is by its very nature material to a fire policy[99] and no doubt to any other type of policy. A conviction for vandalism some 18 months prior to proposal is material to an insurance of home contents against fire, theft and vandalism.[1] It is material to a proposal for yacht insurance that the skipper has been convicted seven times under a foreign law of drawing cheques against insufficient funds within a period of five years before proposal.[2] The question therefore arises, disregarding the

---

[90] *Jester-Barnes v. Licenses and General Ins. Co. Ltd* (1934) 49 Ll.L.R. 231. *Aliter* if the offence was trivial, *Mackay v. London General Ins.* (1935) 51 Ll.L.R. 201.

[91] *Bond v. Commercial Union Ass. Co.* (1930) 35 Com.Cas. 171; *Jester-Barnes v. Licenses and General* (1934) 49 Ll.L.R. 231.

[92] *Cleland v. London General Ins. Co.* (1935) 51 Ll.L.R. 156.

[93] *Taylor v. Eagle Star Ins. Co. Ltd* (1940) 67 Ll.L.R. 136.

[94] *Schoolman v. Hall* [1951] 1 Lloyd's Rep. 139.

[95] [1951] 1 Lloyd's Rep. 139, 143.

[96] *Lambert v. Co-operative Ins. Soc. Ltd* [1975] 1 Lloyd's Rep. 485.

[97] *March Cabaret Club v. London Assurance* [1975] 1 Lloyd's Rep. 169.

[98] *Woolcott v. Sun Alliance and London Ins. Ltd* [1978] 1 W.L.R. 493. But see para. 17–33 *ante* on this aspect.

[99] *Arif v. Excess Ins. Group Ltd* 1987 S.L.T. 183, 186.

[1] *Hooper v. Royal London General Ins. Co. Ltd* 1993 S.C. 242.

[2] *Inversiones Manna v. Sphere Drake Ins. Co., The Dora* [1989] 1 Lloyd's Rep. 69. A conviction for corruption of a public official involves dishonesty and is a material fact—*Stewart v. Commercial Union Ass. Co.* 1993 S.C. 1.

provisions of the Rehabilitation of Offenders Act 1974, as to what previous convictions should be disclosed.

It is submitted that the assured must disclose his previous convictions at least in cases where (i) these involved a degree of dishonesty or irresponsibility repugnant to ordinary social or business standards of integrity, and (ii) they were *either* directly related to the risks insured against under the policy in question *or*, if not so related, would by their nature and proximity in time indicate to a reasonably prudent insurer that there was a likelihood of continuing dishonesty on the part of the assured. The refusal of an insurer to accept a risk offered to him has important consequences for the applicant, who is bound to disclose the fact of the refusal to other insurers, and insurers ought not to regard a conviction as material unless it can fairly be said to have a bearing on the risk proposed.[3]

17–57 Rehabilitation of Offenders Act 1974. The Rehabilitation of Offenders Act 1974 provides that an applicant is entitled to withhold from the insurers information about certain of his or her previous convictions. The purpose of the Act is, *inter alia*, "to rehabilitate offenders who have not been reconvicted of any serious offence for periods of years".[4] This object is achieved by providing that after the expiry of the "rehabilitation period" a conviction becomes "spent".[5] There are different rehabilitation periods according to the seriousness of the sentence. Under section 4 a spent conviction is to be treated "for all purposes in law" as though it had never happened, and the person who has a spent conviction is to be treated as though he had not committed or been charged with the offence in question. As a result of section 3(2) the insurer will have no remedy if the assured has failed to acknowledge a spent conviction in an answer in a proposal form. Even if the assured has warranted the truth of all his answers, which thus become terms of the contract, the insurer is not entitled to treat the assured's failure to acknowledge a spent conviction as a breach of warranty entitling him to repudiate the policy or reject a claim made under it. As a result of section 4(3)(a) the proposer for insurance is relieved of any duty to disclose not only a spent conviction but also the events (for example a motor accident) out of which it arose.[6]

17–58 Allegation of criminal offences. Is a proposer for insurance obliged

---

[3] *Reynolds v. Phoenix Ass. Co.* [1978] 2 Lloyd's Rep. 440, 459. In interlocutory proceedings Lord Denning M.R. had thought it debatable whether a conviction of 10 years' standing for receiving resulting in a fine, ought to be disclosed: [1978] 2 Lloyd's Rep. 22, 25, and Forbes J. held at the trial of the action that it was not material: [1978] 2 Lloyd's Rep. 440, 461. In *Deutsche Rückversicherung Akt. v. Wallbrook Ins. Co. Ltd* [1995] 1 Lloyd's Rep. 153, Phillips J. stated that dishonest conduct should have an impact on the risk if it was to be material.

[4] See the long title to the Act, which applies to convictions in foreign jurisdictions as well as in the U.K.

[5] The most important exception to the Act is that a conviction in respect of an offence punished by "a sentence of imprisonment for a term exceeding 30 months" cannot become spent: s.5(1).

[6] s.7(3) of the Act provides for the admission of evidence as to spent convictions before a court if that court is satisfied that justice cannot be done except by admitting it. This provision, and the extent to which it affects the insured's duty of disclosure, was left uncertain by the Court of Appeal in *Reynolds v. Phoenix Ass. Co. Ltd* [1978] 2 Lloyd's Rep. 22. In *The Dora* the subsection was used to permit evidence of convictions which, though spent at the time of the trial, were not spent at the date of the proposal [1989] 1 Lloyd's Rep. 69, 80–81.

to disclose that he has been charged with a criminal offence which itself would be material to the risk if he had in truth committed it? If guilt is established by admission or conviction subsequent to the conclusion of the contract, the charge will be held to have been disclosable.[7] If, prior to contract, the charge is dropped or the assured is acquitted, then nothing need be disclosed.[8] The position is less clear where, at the time of making the contract, the assured is denying the charge and is subsequently acquitted or has the charge against him dropped. In *Reynolds v. Phoenix Assurance Co. Ltd*[9] Forbes J. held that the allegation did not have to be disclosed, but that only if the assured knew it to be well founded, the commission of a criminal act would itself have to be disclosed. But in *March Cabaret Club & Casino Ltd v. The London Assurance*[10] and in *The "Dora"*,[11] it was held *obiter* by May J. and by Phillips J. respectively that the allegation itself must be disclosed regardless of the subsequent events. It is submitted, with great respect, that the assured should not have to disclose an unfounded allegation. It seems strange that he should be excused by the 1974 Act from disclosing a conviction for dishonesty of comparatively recent date and yet be obliged to disclose the existence of a charge which he knew to be baseless at a time while presumed in law to be innocent.

17–59 Dishonest conduct. The moral hazard principle extends beyond criminal charges and convictions. Dishonest conduct of the assured which demonstrates a real risk that the insurers will be asked to pay for fictitious or inflated losses is a material fact. Although in practice intending assureds are unlikely to reveal their misdeeds when these have not become the subject of criminal convictions, the test of materiality is not what a prudent insurer expects to be told, but rather on his reaction if he were told. Where a director of the assured company had caused false invoices to be prepared with a view to showing them to its bankers if it became desirable to give them a rosier impression of its trading position and profitability than was warranted by its actual receipts, insurers on a fire policy were entitled to treat this dishonesty as material, although no use had been made of them before the policy incepted.[12] The false invoices came to light when they were used to bolster a claim on a business interruption insurance granted by the same insurers. In another case the assured under a motor traders combined policy failed to disclose to the insurers that he was in dispute with the Inland Revenue and Customs & Excise over allegations that he had withheld in each case sums of about £40,000, and that he had deliberately misappropriated premiums paid to him by customers for warranty cover.[13] It was held that the former matter was material because it showed that the business was in financial trouble and that adequate business records were not kept, while the latter demonstrated dishonesty in the running of the insured business. The dishonest use of

[7] *March Cabaret Club & Casino Ltd v. The London Assurance* [1975] 1 Lloyd's Rep. 169.
[8] *Reynolds v. Phoenix Ass. Co. Ltd* [1978] 2 Lloyd's Rep. 440; *March Cabaret Club & Casino v. The London Assurance* [1975] 1 Lloyd's Rep. 169, 177.
[9] [1978] 2 Lloyd's Rep. 440, 460; *Gate v. Sun Alliance Ins. Ltd* [1995] L.R.L.R. 385, 408 (N.Z. High Court), following a test based on whether the assured was in due course acquitted, which is not the approach followed in the English cases.
[10] [1975] 1 Lloyd's Rep. 169, 177.
[11] [1989] 1 Lloyd's Rep. 69, 93–94. The point was left open by Mance J. in *I.C.C.I. v. Royal Hotel* [1998] Lloyd's Rep. I.R. 151, 157.
[12] *Ins. Co. of the Channel Islands v. Royal Hotel* [1998] Lloyd's Rep. I.R. 151.
[13] *James v. CGU Ins. Co. Plc.* [2002] Lloyd's Rep. I.R. 206, 224–228.

customers' money no doubt coloured the court's approach to the allegations made by the tax authorities in this case. A readiness to infer a risk of dishonesty from untested allegations could be unjust to honest assureds lacking in business acumen.

17–60 Race or nationality. Before the Race Relations Act 1976 problems arose as to whether the national origins or nationality of the proposer did constitute a material fact, and there was a line of cases on this question.[14] The Race Relations Act 1976 renders unlawful discrimination on "racial grounds" and "racial grounds" are defined as meaning colour, race, nationality or ethnic or national origins.[15]

Section 20 of the Act provides that it is unlawful for any person concerned with the provision of goods, facilities or services to the public to discriminate on racial grounds against a person by refusing or deliberately omitting to provide that person with any of them or by refusing or deliberately omitting to provide that person with them on the same terms as are normal in relation to other members of the public. The result of the 1976 Act is that the assured's duty of disclosure does not extend to his colour, race, nationality or ethnic or national origins. Thus not only is the assured entitled to refuse to volunteer this information to the insurer, but he is also entitled to refuse to answer any question in a proposal form which relates to it. In any event, an insurer is not entitled to avoid a policy on the ground of its concealment.

17–61 Sex and Disability. Section 29 of the Sex Discrimination Act 1975 contains provisions to the like effect, *mutatis mutandis*, as section 20 of the Race Relations Act 1976. However, section 45 of the 1975 Act allows insurers to discriminate against women as regards acceptance of the risk and assessment of the premium on the basis of actuarial or other data where it is reasonable to rely on such data and where, having regard to the data and any other relevant factors, such discrimination is reasonable. The proviso is limited to annuities, life insurance policies, accident insurance policies and other similar matters involving the assessment of the risk. In view of this provision it appears that the 1975 Act will have little or no effect on the assured's duty of disclosure.[16]

In similar fashion section 20 of the Disability Discrimination Act 1995 and the provisions of the Disability Discrimination (Services and Premises) Regulations 1996[17] permit an insurer to discriminate against a disabled person by showing that he reasonably relies upon relevant information such as medical reports or actuarial or statistical data, and that his treatment of the disabled person is reasonable in the particular circumstances. This permits an insurer to refuse a risk or impose special terms for reasons based upon accepted actuarial and rating criteria, so that an applicant's disability remains a material fact in the field of life, accident and health insurance despite the general prohibition against discrimination in the Act.

17–62 Previous refusals. In marine insurance the fact that the same risk has been refused by other underwriters is not regarded as a material fact

---

[14] See *Horne v. Poland* [1922] 2 K.B. 364, 365; *Lyons v. Bentley* (J.W.) (1944) 77 Ll.L.R. 335, 337; *Becker v. Marshall* (1922) 12 Ll.L.R. 413, 414.
[15] See Race Relations Act 1976, ss. 1 and 3.
[16] Khan, Sexual Discrimination in Insurance (1986) 139 N.L.J. 839.
[17] S.I. 1996 No. 1836.

which ought to be disclosed. In non-marine insurance the position is uncertain. Refusal of the risk was said to be material by Greer J. in *Arthrude Press Ltd v. Eagle Star & British Dominions Insurance Co. Ltd*[18] and by Sir George Jessel M.R., *obiter*, in *London Assurance v. Mansel*,[19] but the *Arthrude* case was decided on a different ground on appeal and Scrutton L.J. expressed doubts concerning what was said by Greer J.[20] Doubt was also expressed by Malins V.-C. in *Re General Provincial Life*.[21] From cases in which materiality of prior refusals has been conceded[22] or barely argued[23] it would appear that the bare fact of refusal is not in itself material but rather the reason given for it, such as claims experience, where that is known to the assured.[24] A refusal to renew except upon the imposition of special terms could likewise be material for the same reason.[25] Where the assured has made proposals to other companies and then withdrawn them, there is no obligation to disclose the incomplete negotiations.[26]

17–63 Refusals on other risks. There is no general duty to disclose either refusals or claims in respect of insurances on other risks, but the reasons for the refusal of a proposal,[27] or the circumstances in which a previous claim was made, may make the refusal or claim a fact which would influence the judgment of a prudent underwriter considering the assured's proposal. Thus in *Locker and Woolf Ltd v. Western Australian Insurance Co. Ltd*[28] it was held that insurers were entitled to avoid a fire insurance on account of the assured's failure to disclose that an application for motor insurance had been declined on the ground that untrue answers had been given in the proposal in order to conceal previous claims and losses. In another case[29] it was conceded that a refusal to renew a motor policy on the grounds of poor claims experience should be disclosed to insurers to whom the assured was proposing for motor insurance on a different vehicle three weeks later.

17–64 Over-valuation. Excessive over-valuation of the subject-matter of the insurance for the purpose of a valued policy is a material fact which ought to be disclosed.[30] A valuation will be declared excessive for this purpose if it changes the character of the risk from a business risk to a speculative risk.[31] It was explained by Blackburn J. in the leading case of *Ionides v. Pender*,[32] that

---

[18] (1924) 18 Ll.L.R. 383, 385.

[19] (1879) 11 Ch.D. 363, 370.

[20] (1924) 19 Ll.L.R. 373, 374. See also *Rozanes v. Bowen* (1928) 32 Ll.L.R. 98, 102.

[21] (1870) 18 W.R. 396.

[22] *Cornhill Insurance Co. Ltd v. Assenheim* (1937) 58 Ll.L.R. 27.

[23] *Re Yager and Guardian Ass. Co.* (1912) 108 L.T. 38.

[24] *Holt's Motors Ltd v. South East Lancashire Ins. Co. Ltd* (1930) 35 Com.Cas. 281, 285–286 (refusal to renew); *Container Transport International Inc. v. Oceanus Mutual Underwriting Ass. (Bermuda) Ltd* [1984] 1 Lloyd's Rep. 476, 522, 530.

[25] *Rozanes v. Bowen* (1928) 31 Ll.L.R. 231, 235; (1928) 32 Ll.L.R. 98, 102, 104.

[26] *Watt v. Union Insurance* (1884) 5 N.S.W.L.R. 48.

[27] *Ewer v. National Employers' Mutual General Ins. Ass. Ltd* [1937] 2 All E.R. 193.

[28] [1936] 1 K.B. 408.

[29] *Cornhill Ins. Ltd v. Assenheim* (1937) 58 Ll.L.R. 27, 30.

[30] *Ionides v. Pender* (1874) L.R. 9 Q.B. 531; *Gooding v. White* (1912) 29 T.L.R. 312; *Visscherrig Maatschappij Nieuwe Onderening v. Scottish Metropolitan Ass. Co.* (1921) 9 Ll.L.R. 420.

[31] *Ionides v. Pender* (1874) L.R. 9 Q.B. 531–539; *Mathie v. Argonaut Marine Ins. Co. Ltd* (1925) 21 Ll.L.R. 145.

[32] (1874) L.R. 9 Q.B. 531.

excessive valuation did not lead only to suspicions of foul play but, in a case of marine insurance, might tend to make the assured less careful in selecting a competent crew and making other efforts to avert a loss, although the court did not base its judgment on that ground.[33]

17–65 The burden of proving that the discrepancy between the insured value and the actual insurable value is so great as to make the risk speculative is on the insurer who wishes to avoid the policy.[34] While it is legitimate to include in the value placed upon a cargo in a marine policy a reasonable sum in respect of the anticipated profits on its sale at its destination, that value was excessive when based upon the chance of a foreign government imposing a duty on that commodity at a time convenient to the assured,[35] and where bearer shares in a Russian railway company were valued at a figure greatly above their actual current value by reference to optimistic expectations of their future value, this was held to be an excessive valuation,[36] since what was valued for the underwriters was "not a bird in the hand but a bird in a very far away and possibly unobtainable bush".[37] If, however, the over-valuation can be explained as part of an ordinary business transaction, it will not be found to be excessive.[38] When an assured took out a valued policy on a yacht, valuing her at the price paid for her, the fact that this was appreciably more than the open market value was held not to be material.[39]

17–66 Underinsurance. In *Economides v. Commercial Union Assurance Co. Plc.*[40] the assured did not disclose that the full replacement value of his household contents substantially exceeded their declared value and that the contents included valuables worth much more than one third of their total value as stated. The assured conceded that these were material facts. Simon Brown L.J. doubted the correctness of the concession, stating obiter that underinsurance was not material where the policy contained an average clause, because the assured would then be required to bear a share of any loss and the insurer would not be disadvantaged. The argument to the contrary, it is submitted, is that the value of the property is important in calculating the applicable premium, and the presence of a number of articles of disproportionately high value might have a bearing on the risk of theft.

17–67 Other insurance. It has been held that as a general rule the assured is not bound to disclose the fact that he is insured elsewhere unless the question is asked or the non-existence of other insurance is made a condition of the policy.[41] If, however, the other insurance is for such an amount that on

---

[33] (1874) L.R. 9 Q.B. 531, 539. This reasoning was approved by Lord Robson in *Thames and Mersey Marine v. Gunford Ship Co.* [1911] A.C. 529, 550.

[34] *Mathie v. Argonaut Marine* (1925) 21 Ll.L.R. 145, 146; *Berger v. Pollock* [1973] 2 Lloyd's Rep. 442, 465.

[35] *Ionides v. Pender* (1874) L.R. 9 Q.B. 531.

[36] *Hoff v. Union Ins. Soc. of Canton* (1929) 34 Ll.L.R. 81.

[37] (1929) 34 Ll.L.R. 81, 92, *per* Greer L.J.

[38] *Mathie v. Argonaut Marine* (1925) 21 Ll.L.R. 145.

[39] *The Dora* [1989] 1 Lloyd's Rep. 69, 92 (misrepresentation case).

[40] [1998] Q.B. 587, 603.

[41] *McDonnell v. Beacon* (1858) 7 U.C.C.P. 308; *Parsons v. Citizens Insurance* (1878) 43 U.C.Q.B. 261.

the acceptance of the proposal put forward, the assured would become over-insured to an extent out of all proportion to any possible fluctuation in the value of his insurable interest, that would be a material fact.[42] In *Thames and Mersey Marine v. Gunford Ship Co.*[43] the assured effected extra insurance against marine risks by means of honour or "p.p.i." policies, and it was held that this was "over-insurance by double insurance"[44] and ought to have been disclosed.

17–68 Facts relevant to subrogation. Matters affecting the insurers' right to subrogation may well be material, since, if the assured has fettered, or deprived himself of, his right to recover against third parties, the ultimate risk of loss borne by the underwriter is thereby increased. In *Tate v. Hyslop*[45] the insurers advertised two rates of premium on marine cargo insurances which included risks of loading and unloading goods from lighters. The lower rate was to be charged where the lightermen owed the strict liability of a common carrier, and the higher rate when there was no recourse but for negligence on the part of the lightermen. The assured knew that the insurers charged these different rates, but they accepted a policy at the lower rate without disclosing that they had an exclusive arrangement with a particular lighterman on the basis that he should be liable only for losses caused by his own negligence. The court held that there was concealment of a material fact which vitiated the policy. Although Brett M.R. laid emphasis upon the assured's knowledge of the significance of their non-disclosure,[46] it is submitted that the arrangement made with the lighterman was a material fact regardless of that knowledge, judged by the current test of materiality.[47]

17–69 In America the courts have generally followed the opinion of Brett M.R. in *Tate v. Hyslop* and it has been held that there is no obligation on the assured to disclose arrangements whereby other parties may be relieved from liability and so receive the benefit of the insurance, unless either the assured knows that it would affect the premium if known to the insurers or there is a condition written into the policy specifically subrogating the insurers to all rights of the assured against third parties responsible for the loss.[48] It must be remembered, however, that in the bulk of American jurisdictions the doctrine of concealment requires the assured to disclose only those facts *known* to him to be material, so that the American courts were bound to stress the element of knowledge in *Tate v. Hyslop.*[49] If in any class of risk the insurers are known not to consider subrogation rights as an element in risk computation then there is clearly no duty to disclose the fact that third persons were protected from liability.[50] Where it is in the usual

[42] *Tate v. Hyslop* (1885) 15 Q.B.D. 368; *Pickersgill v. London and Provincial Marine* [1912] 3 K.B. 614, 619.
[43] [1911] A.C. 529.
[44] [1911] A.C. 529, 549.
[45] (1885) 15 Q.B.D. 368.
[46] (1885) 15 Q.B.D. 368, 375–376.
[47] See para. 17–35, *ante.*
[48] *British and Foreign Marine v. Gulf,* 63 Tex. 475 (1885); *Phoenix v. Erie Transportation,* 117 U.S. 312 (1886); *Lett v. Guardian Fire,* 52 Hun. 570 (N.Y.S.C., 1889); *Jackson v. Boston Mutual,* 139 Mass. 508 (1885); *Fayerweather v. Phoenix,* 118 N.Y. 324 (1890).
[49] (1885) 15 Q.B.D. 368.
[50] *Pelzer Manufacturing Co. v. St Paul,* 41 Fed. Rep. 271 (1890).

course of the assured's business that the parties contract on terms that one of the parties shall be relieved entirely or in part from his common-law liability the insurers are deemed to be acquainted with such course of business and therefore to have knowledge of the usual terms of contract. In a New South Wales case certain concurrent insurances were specified in the policy, and it was held that there was no duty to communicate the fact that during the currency of the policy these had been allowed to lapse.[51]

17–70 Interest in subject-matter of insurance. Apart from specific questions or special conditions, the assured is not bound to disclose either the nature or extent of his interest in the subject-matter of the insurance.[52] Thus where property is insured, the assured need not state that his interest is that of a mortgagee[53] or bailee.[54] Only where the concealment of the assured's interest also conceals other material facts which would necessarily have come to light if it were disclosed is the assured liable to disclose it.[55] In an early American decision Storey J. took the view that the assured's interest was important, since the smaller it was the less likely he was to use the necessary precautions to avoid the calamity assured against.[56] The protection afforded by full insurance is, however, equally likely to encourage the carelessness of any assured, so it does not seem right to single out the assured with a limited interest for special consideration. This is the view supported by the authorities. The assured is not required to disclose his title to real property.[57] He need not disclose that he has merely an equitable title, such as that of a purchaser before completion.[58] If he holds the legal title, as in the case of a mortgagor or trustee, and insures for the full value, he need not disclose the fact that he is not beneficially interested to the full amount.[59] An owner of real property need not as a rule disclose the existence of incumbrances upon it, unless the terms of the particular policy make the existence of other interests in or over it a matter of concern to the insurers, or if questions are asked as to title, interest, or incumbrances.[60]

---

[51] *Hordern v. Commercial Union* (1887) 5 N.S.W.L.R. (Law) 309.

[52] *Crowley v. Cohen* (1832) 3 B & Ad. 478; *Mackenzie v. Whitworth* (1875) 1 Ex.D. 36. In *James v. British General Ins. Co.* [1927] 2 K.B. 311 Roche J. preferred to dismiss a defence, based on concealment of interest by a consideration of the evidence rather than on a point of law.

[53] *Ogden v. Montreal Ins. Co.* (1853) 3 C.P. 497; *Reesor v. Provincial Ins. Co.* (1873) 33 U.C.R. 357.

[54] *London & North Western Ry v. Glyn* (1859) 1 E. & E. 652, 664.

[55] *The Spathari* 1925 S.C.(HL) 6; *Mackenzie v. Whitworth* (1875) 1 Ex.D. 36, 43; *Anderson v. Commercial Union* (1886) 1 T.L.R. 511, *obiter*, not commented upon in the CA (1886) 55 L.J.Q.B.(N.S.) 146; *Mitchell v. Scottish Eagle Ins. Co.* 1997 S.L.T. 793.

[56] *Columbian Insurance v. Lawrence*, 10 Pet. 507 (1836).

[57] *Klein v. Union Fire* (1883) 3 Ont. R. 234; *Reddick v. Saugeen Mutual* (1888) 15 Ont. A.R. 363; *Clement v. British American Ass. Co.* 141 Mass. 298 (1886); *Kernochan v. New York Bowery Ins. Co.*, 17 N.Y. 428 (1858); *Cumberland Valley Mutual v. Mitchell*, 48 Pa. 374 (1864).

[58] *Rumsey v. Phoenix Ins. Co.*, 17 Blatchf. 527 (U.S.D.C. 1880).

[59] *Provincial Ins. v. Reesor* (1874) 21 Grant 296. The mortgagor may insure on behalf of the mortgagee and vice versa, *Kernochan v. New York Bowery Ins. Co.*, 17 N.Y. 428 (1858).

[60] *Ocean Accident and Guarantee Corp. v. Williams* (1915) 34 N.Z.L.R. 924; *Fritzley v. Germania Farmers Mutual Fire Ins.* (1909) 19 O.L.R. 49; *Parsons v. Bignold* (1846) 15 L.J.Ch. 379; *Bleakley v. Niagara District Mutual* (1869) 16 Grant 198, 201–202 (statutory lien on insured property).

(e) *What Need not be Disclosed by the Assured*

17–71 General principles. The situations in which facts need not be disclosed were anticipated by Lord Mansfield C.J. in *Carter v. Boehm*, where he said:

> "There are many matters as to which the insured may be innocently silent. He need not mention what the underwriter knows: what way soever he came to the knowledge. The insured need not mention what the underwriter ought to know: what he takes upon himself the knowledge of: or what he waives being informed of. The underwriter need not be told what lessens the *risque* agreed and understood to be run by the express terms of the policy. He needs not to be told general topics of speculation, and either party may be innocently silent as to grounds open to both to exercise their judgment upon."[61]

These rules and modern additions to them are discussed in the following sections of this chapter.

17–72 Facts known to insurers. It is obvious that the insurers cannot complain of having been misled by the assured's concealment when from some other source they had received knowledge of the facts which they say were not communicated.[62] This would seem to apply even to fraudulent concealment by the assured, since the concealment could not have induced the insurers to contract. This principle applies where knowledge is received by an agent of the company, but is subject to the general limitation that the agent must have received it in the ordinary course of his duty and employment.[63] Thus where a water corn-mill was insured against fire risks, the assured used rice chaff in place of pollard in the mill, but did not disclose this to the insurers, although it was more inflammable. Since the insurers' agent had, however, inspected the mill and seen what was done there, the insurers were deemed to have knowledge of the use of rice chaff and could not rely upon the assured's non-disclosure.[64]

17–73 Constructive knowledge of insurers. Section 18(3)(b) of the Marine Insurance Act 1906 provides that, in the absence of inquiry, the assured need not disclose any circumstance presumed to be known to the insurer, and it may be taken to state the law applicable to non-marine insurances.[65] Apart from the particular examples of presumed knowledge given in the subsection,[66] the insurers may be presumed to know facts which are reasonably clear to them from information in their possession, even if not expressly mentioned by the assured.[67] They may also be presumed to know matters

---

[61] (1766) 3 Burr. 1905, 1911.

[62] *Bates v. Hewitt* (1867) L.R. 2 Q.B. 595; *Carter v. Boehm* (1766) 3 Burr. 1905, 1911; *Anglo-California Bank Ltd v. London & Provincial, etc., Ins. Co. Ltd* (1904) 10 Com.Cas. 1; Marine Insurance Act 1906, s.18(3)(b).

[63] *Pimm v. Lewis* (1862) 2 F. & F. 778; *Ayrey v. British Legal etc.*, [1918] 1 K.B. 136; *Woolcott v. Excess Ins. Co. Ltd* [1979] 1 Lloyd's Rep. 231; [1979] 2 Lloyd's Rep. 210; *Latham v. Hibernian Ins. Co. Ltd* (1992) 10 I.L.T.R. 266; *Haydenfayre v. British National Ins. Soc. Ltd* [1984] 2 Lloyd's Rep. 393, 401.

[64] *Pimm v. Lewis* (1862) 2 F. & F. 778.

[65] *Pan Atlantic Ins. Co. Ltd v. Pine Top Ins. Co. Ltd* [1995] 1 A.C. 501, 518, 554.

[66] See paras 17–74 to 17–77, *infra*.

[67] *St Margaret's Trust Ltd v. Navigators & General Ins. Co. Ltd* (1949) 82 Ll.L.R. 752, 762; *Kingscroft Ins. Co. v. Nissan Fire & Marine Ins. Co.* [1999] Lloyd's Rep. I.R. 603.

which they have the means of learning from sources available to them. Thus in *Foley v. Tabor*[68] it was said that an insurer who knew that a vessel proposed for insurance on a voyage from England to India was likely to be carrying iron rails, but neglected to ascertain the precise quantity from a source available at Lloyd's, should be treated as knowing the quantity as a fact "within his knowledge".

17-74 Common knowledge. The insurers are credited with knowledge of matters of public knowledge or notoriety which a generally well-informed person might fairly be expected to know. As Cockburn C.J. said in *Bates v. Hewitt*: "It is also true that when a fact is one of public notoriety, as of war ... the party proposing the insurance is not bound to communicate what he is fully warranted in assuming the underwriter already knows."[69] So, where a castle in Ireland was insured against damage by riot, civil commotion, war, rebellion and fire, and was destroyed by the I.R.A. in 1921, the insurers failed in their defence based upon the assured's non-disclosure of the previous use of the castle by Crown forces as a dungeon for Sinn Fein prisoners.[70] It appears that the jury considered the previous strife in that part of Ireland to be a matter of public knowledge. It has also been held that insurers must be taken to know that fireworks are likely to be stocked for sale by retail shopkeepers in the period prior to November 5 each year.[71] However, the decision in *Bates v. Hewitt*[72] is a caution against crediting the insurers with a good memory of even recent events, since the court did not disturb a jury finding that the vessel *Georgia*, on which cover was obtained in that case, could not be realised by the insurers to be the ex-Confederate warship dismantled and rebuilt some months previously, although the exploits of the vessel and her arrival in England were widely publicised and agreed to be matters of general report at that time.

17-75 That decision illustrates the point that a plea of knowledge, on whatever it is based, must establish that the facts not disclosed were present to the minds of the insurers at the time that the risk was accepted. The assured cannot be heard to say "You, the insurers, once had the knowledge of these facts in the past, and you ought still to remember them," because they are not bound to rack their brains for information they once possessed. To hold that they were would derogate greatly from the assured's duty to display good faith as it would enable him to calculate the minimum facts necessary for disclosure rather than discharge his duty frankly and honestly.[73] This consideration is relevant whenever constructive knowledge is pleaded by the assured.

17-76 Business practice and custom. The insurer is presumed to know not only the ordinary incidents of ordinary risks but the ordinary incidents of

---

[68] (1862) 2 F. & F. 663.
[69] (1867) L.R. 2 Q.B. 595, 605. See also *Carter v. Boehm* (1766) 3 Burr. 1905, 1911 *per* Lord Mansfield.
[70] *Leen v. Hall* (1923) 16 Ll.L.R. 100.
[71] *Hales v. Reliance Fire and Accident Ins. Corp. Ltd* [1960] 2 Lloyd's Rep. 391.
[72] (1867) L.R. 2 Q.B. 595.
[73] (1867) L.R. 2 Q.B. 595, 606–607; *Morrison v. Universal Marine Ins. Co.* (1872) L.R. 8 Exch. 40; 197.

peculiar risks if he undertakes them.[74] "Every underwriter," said Lord Mansfield, "is presumed to be acquainted with the practice of the trade he insures. If he does not know, he ought to inform himself."[75] So, if insurers cover a building where celluloid is stored, and they are informed of it, they cannot afterwards complain that they did not know celluloid was inflammable. If, however, the assured carried on his manufacture or trade by an unusually hazardous or novel process, he ought to disclose this fact.

17–77 In the insurance of risks depending on contractual rights and obligations, the insurers are presumed to know the ordinary terms and conditions under which the contracts in question are usually made.[76] In fidelity cover the assured need not, therefore, state the terms of employment unless there is something unusual in them, and in contracts of reinsurance the original risk will be presumed to be subject to all the clauses and conditions usually inserted in policies covering that particular class of risk. The reinsured should disclose such omissions or additions as one would not normally expect to find in such policies.[77]

17–78 Ordinary attributes of the risk. It follows that, so far as business or industrial risks are concerned, the insurers are taken to know the ordinary attributes of the risk, so that they will know what goods a tradesman of the specified class would normally have in his stores, and if dangerous goods are ordinarily included in such stock, it is unnecessary to disclose the presence of such goods.[78] In domestic risks, the assured need not disclose matters which could be inferred from the general description of the risk. If a man insures a house, he need not disclose how it is heated. The insurer is taken to know that houses have some form of heating, and must ask specific questions about it if he wants further details. He cannot expect the assured to disclose how many people occupy the house.[79] Only unusual elements affecting the risk ought to be disclosed.[80] Thus in motor insurance an assured who owns a very fast motorcar of a particular make need do no more than declare the usual description of the vehicle, but if he has altered the specification in any way so as to increase the speed that, it is submitted, should be disclosed.

17–79 Insurer's information incomplete. If the information of the insurer is a matter of rumour and report only, that will not entitle the assured to say that the insurer knew the fact of which the assured had definite knowledge.[81] This must have been one of the situations envisaged by the United States Supreme Court in *Sun Mutual Insurance Co. v. Ocean Insurance Co*,[82] where

---

[74] *Salvador v. Hopkins* (1765) 3 Burr. 1707; *Carter v. Boehm* (1766) 3 Burr. 1906, 1911; *Freeland v. Glover* (1806) 7 East 457; *Stewart v. Bell* (1821) 5 B. & Ad. 238; *Glasgow Assurance v. Symondson* (1911) 16 Com.Cas. 109; *Bates v. Hewitt* (1867) L.R. 2 Q.B. 595, 611.

[75] *Noble v. Kennoway* (1780) 2 Doug. K.B. 510, 512; *Planche v. Fletcher* (1779) 1 Doug. K.B. 251; *Western v. Home Insurance*, 145 Pa. 346 (1891); *Laing v. Union Marine Co.* (1895) 1 Com.Cas. 11, 15. This presumption is most probably confined to a known and established trade—*Harrower v. Hutchinson* (1870) L.R. 5 Q.B. 584, 591; *Tate v. Hyslop* (1885) 15 Q.B.D. 368, 377; *British & Foreign Mar. Ins. Co. v. Gaunt* [1921] 2 A.C. 41, 63–64.

[76] *The Bedouin* [1894] P. 1.

[77] *Charlesworth v. Faber* (1900) 5 Com.Cas. 408; *Vallance v. Dewar* (1808) 1 Camp. 503.

[78] *Nicholson v. Phoenix* (1880) 45 U.C.Q.B. 359.

[79] *Browning v. Home Insurance*, 71 N.Y. 508 (1877).

[80] *Baxendale v. Harvey* (1859) 4 H. & N. 445.

[81] *Lindenau v. Desborough* (1828) 8 B. & C. 586.

[82] 107 U.S. 485 (1882); see also *Davey v. Royal Liver F.S.* [1929] I.A.C. (N.I.) Rep. 70.

it was said that if the assured has more complete knowledge of certain material facts, he is bound to give the insurers the benefit of his knowledge, even though they may have a general, but less complete, knowledge. If undisclosed, the question will be whether the additional information possessed by the assured was in fact material.

17–80 Assured's opinion. The assured is not bound to disclose what is merely a matter of inference or judgment from the facts known to the insurers. He is bound to supply the insurers with the facts, but he is not bound to estimate the risk for them.[83] If the insurers are unfamiliar with the natural inferences to be drawn from what they are told, they should ask, only counting upon the assured to disclose unusual attributes of the risk which could not ordinarily be appreciated from the facts given.[84] Neither is the assured bound to give the insurers advice on the legal consequences of the facts disclosed or on other matters.[85]

Thus when loss experience on marine business is recorded in triangulated form, the data itself is material and ought to be disclosed, but the assured's own estimates of future losses calculated from the loss statistics need not be disclosed since the insurer is in as good a position to calculate them as is the assured.[86] In such cases the concept of utmost good faith has to be accommodated within the framework of a commercial negotiation. " As I see it", said Waller J. in *Pan Atlantic Ins. Co. v. Pine Top Ins. Co.*,[87] "the negotiation is a commercial one, the broker does not have an obligation to tell the underwriter how to do his job".[88] The same point was made by Davitt P. in *Kreglinger & Fernau Ltd. v. Irish National Ins. Co. Ltd*[89] when he said that "the insured does not have to conduct the insurer's business for him".

17–81 Facts tending to diminish the risk. Lord Mansfield said in *Carter v. Boehm*: "the underwriter needs not be told what lessens the *risque* agreed and understood to be run by the express terms of the policy ... if he insures for three years he need not be told any circumstance to show it may be over in two; or if he insures a voyage, with liberty of deviation, he needs not be told what tends to show there will be no deviation".[90] This may seem obvious, but such a fact does literally fall within the definition of a material fact, since it would influence the underwriter in deciding whether to take the risk or not, or in fixing the premium.

17–82 Facts covered by or dispensed with by a warranty or condition. Where a matter is covered by a warranty or condition, it is not necessary for the assured to disclose facts relevant only to the matter so warranted or

---

[83] *Carter v. Boehm* (1766) 3 Burr. 1905, 1911; *Bates v. Hewitt* (1867) L.R. 2 Q.B. 595; *Gandy v. Adelaide Marine Ins. Co.* (1871) L.R. 6 Q.B. 746; *Cantiere Meccanico Brindisino v. Janson* [1912] 3 K.B. 452.

[84] *Greenhill v. Federal Ins. Co.* [1927] 1 K.B. 65, 84.

[85] *The Bedouin* [1894] P. 1, 12. This paragraph was approved by David Steel J. in *Decorum Investments v. Atkin* [2001] 2 Lloyd's Rep. 378, 382.

[86] *Aiken v. Stewart-Wrightson* [1995] 2 Lloyd's Rep. 618, 648, reinsurance, (this point does not appear from the other reports of the case).

[87] 1992 1 Lloyd's Rep. 101, 105.

[88] Followed by Longmore J. in *Marc Rich v. Portman* [1996] 1 Lloyd's Rep. 430, 445.

[89] [1956] I.R. 116, 151.

[90] (1766) 3 Burr. 1905, 1911. See now Marine Insurance Act 1906, s.18(3)(b).

stipulated.[91] The reason for that is that the insurers have full protection in the warranty. So, in a case of life insurance if the life is warranted good, or there is a warranty of good health, it is unnecessary for the protection of the insurer that he should be informed of symptoms tending to show that the life is not in good health.[92]

This principle extends to matters of implied warranty,[93] for the same reasoning applies, and also presumably to matters covered by an exceptions clause,[94] and a suspensive condition.[95]

17–83 Facts as to which the insurer waives information. If the insurers have waived disclosure by the assured of a particular matter prior to the commencement of the risk, it is obvious that they cannot later raise the non-disclosure of that fact in answer to a claim or otherwise.[96] Waiver of information as to facts material to the risk is not to be inferred too readily, or else it might subvert the assured's duty to disclose them in good faith.[97] The test appears to be as follows: The assured must perform his duty of disclosure properly by making a fair presentation of the risk proposed for insurance.[98] If the insurers thereby receive information from the assured or his agent which, taken on its own or in conjunction with other facts known to them or which they are presumed to know, would naturally prompt a reasonably careful insurer to make further inquiries, then, if they omit to make the appropriate check or inquiry, assuming it can be made simply,[99] they will be held to have waived disclosure of the material fact which that inquiry would necessarily have revealed.[1] Waiver is not established by showing merely that

---

[91] *Grant v. Aetna Fire* (1860) 11 Low.Can.R. 128; *De Maurier v. Bastion Ins. Co.* [1967] 2 Lloyd's Rep. 550; Marine Ins. Act 1906, s.18(3)(d); *The Dora* [1989] 1 Lloyd's Rep. 69, 92; *Kircaldy v. Walker* [1999] Lloyd's Rep. I. 410, 423.

[92] *Ross v. Bradshaw* (1761) 1 Wm. Bl. 312, 313.

[93] *Hayward v. Rodgers* (1804) 4 East 590.

[94] *Johnson & Perrott v. Holmes* (1925) 21 Ll.L.R. 330; *Thames and Mersey v. Gunford S.S. Co.* [1911] A.C. 529; *International Lottery Management v. Dumas* [2002] Lloyd's Rep. I.R. 237; *Kausar v. Eagle Star Ins. Co.* [2000] Lloyd's Rep. I.R. 154, 158. The contrary view apparently expressed by Willes J. in *Seymour v. London and Provincial Marine* (1872) 41 L.J.C.P. 193 is difficult to understand; it is hard to see how "matters falling within a warranty" ought to be disclosed consistently with the authorities just cited.

[95] See para. 10–7, *ante*.

[96] *Carter v. Boehm* (1766) 3 Burr. 1905, 1911; *Court v. Martineau* (1782) 3 Doug. K.B. 161; *Laing v. Union Marine Ins. Co.* (1895) 1 Com.Cas. 11, 15; Marine Insurance Act 1906, s.18(3)(c).

[97] *Mann, Macneal & Steeves v. Capital and Counties Ins. Co.* [1921] 2 K.B. 300, 317; *Greenhill v. Federal Ins. Co.* [1927] 1 K.B. 65, 89; *Container Transport International Inc. v. Oceanus Mutual Underwriting Assoc. (Bermuda) Ltd* [1984] 1 Lloyd's Rep. 476, 511.

[98] *Container Transport International Inc. v. Oceanus Mutual Underwriting Assoc. (Bermuda) Ltd* [1984] 1 Lloyd's Rep. 476, 496–497, 511; *Hadenfayre v. British National Ins. Soc. Ltd* [1984] 2 Lloyd's Rep. 393, 403; *The Dora* [1989] 1 Lloyd's Rep. 69, 88; *St Paul Fire & Marine Ins. Co. (UK) Ltd v. McConnell Dowell Constructors Ltd* [1993] 2 Lloyd's Rep. 503, 512; *Newbury International Ltd v. Reliance National Ins. Co. (U.K.) Ltd* [1994] 1 Lloyd's Rep. 83, 90; *Marc Rich v. Portman* [1996] 1 Lloyd's Rep. 430, 442; affirmed [1997] 1 Lloyd's Rep. 225, 234; *Hill v. Citadel Ins. Co.* [1997] L.R.L.R. 167, 171.

[99] *Container Transport International Inc. v. Oceanus Mutual Underwriting Assoc. (Bermuda) Ltd* [1984] 1 Lloyd's Rep. 476, 529, *per* Stephenson L.J. ("an underwriter is not a detective").

[1] *Freeland v. Glover* (1806) 7 East 457; *Bates v. Hewitt* (1867) L.R. 2 Q.B. 595; *Harrower v. Hutchinson* (1870) L.R. 5 Q.B. 584, 590; *Asfar v. Blundell* [1896] 1 Q.B. 123, 129; *Mann, Macneal & Steeves v. Capital and Counties Ins. Co.* [1921] 2 K.B. 300; *Cantiere Meccanico Brindisino v. Janson* [1912] 3 K.B. 452; *Greenhill v. Federal Insurance Co.* [1927] 1 K.B. 65, 89; *Anglo-African Merchants v. Bayley* [1969] 1 Lloyd's Rep. 268, 278; *Arterial Caravans Ltd v. Yorkshire Insurance Co.* [1973] 1 Lloyd's Rep. 169, 181; *Container Transport International Inc. v. Oceanus Mutual Underwriting Assoc. (Bermuda) Ltd* [1984] 1 Lloyd's Rep. 476, 497, 511, 529.

the insurers were aware of the possibility of the existence of other material facts; they must be put fairly on inquiry about them.[2] A presentation which makes no reference to an existing loss experience is not fair unless the losses are modest or insignificant, so that the underwriter does not waive disclosure of a history of substantial losses by failing to ask for the claims experience.[3]

17–84 Information which prompts inquiry. The assured's description of the risk may itself suffice to raise doubts in the insurer's mind.[4] So in *Cohen v. Standard Marine Insurance Co.*,[5] the insurance was upon an obsolete battleship which was to be towed across the North Sea and then, broken up. During the voyage she was abandoned by her tugs and stranded on the Dutch coast, where she became a constructive total loss. The insurers denied liability on the ground, *inter alia*, of failure to disclose the fact that the vessel had no steam power of her own. Roche J. held that they must be presumed to know that a dismantled warship which needed a tow was not likely to have her own usual sources of power available, and that as, with this knowledge, they had abstained from asking any questions about the precise position on board, they had waived any further disclosure by the assured on how she was going to be steered. By way of comparison, the decision in *Anglo-African Merchants v. Bayley*[6] may be mentioned. Here insurers were asked to cover "New Men's Clothes in Bales for Export" while in storage. The insured goods were stolen and it turned out that they were in fact unused war surplus clothing some 20 years old. The insurers repudiated liability for non-disclosure of this fact, since war-surplus clothing was much more susceptible to theft, and the assured contended in reply that this disclosure was waived by the insurers in failing to make further inquiries. Megaw J. held that a reasonable underwriter would not be put on inquiry by the description given him, and the plea failed.

17–85 Incomplete answers. The insurers may also be put on inquiry concerning uncommunicated information when the proposal form received by them is seen to contain one or more answers which are wholly or partially incomplete.[7] The question in each case is whether the natural and proper inference to be drawn from the absence of a complete answer is that there remains further material information to be communicated. If the need for further facts is clear, then the issue of a policy without further inquiry will support the assured's contention that disclosure was waived.[8] So, if in a motor policy proposal the applicant is asked "How many accidents have you

---

[2] *Harrower v. Hutchinson* (1870) L.R. 5 Q.B. 584; *Greenhill v. Federal Insurance Co.* [1927] 1 K.B. 65; *Container Transport International Inc. v. Oceanus Mutual Underwriting Assoc. (Bermuda) Ltd* [1984] 1 Lloyd's Rep. 476, 511; *Aiken v. Stewart Wrightson Agency* [1995] 1 W.L.R. 1281, 1316.

[3] *Marc Rich v. Portman* [1996] 1 Lloyd's Rep. 430, 433, aff'd [1997] 1 Lloyd's Rep. 225, 234.

[4] *Mann, Macneal & Steeves v. Capital and Counties Ins. Co.* [1921] 2 K.B. 300; *Cantiere Meccanico Brindisino v. Janson* [1912] 3 K.B. 452

[5] (1925) 21 Ll.L.R. 30.

[6] [1970] 1 Q.B. 311.

[7] *Connecticut Mutual Life Ins. Co. v. Luchs* 108 U.S. 498 (1883); *Phoenix Mutual Life Ins. Co. v. Raddin* 120 U.S. 183 (1887); *Williams v. Metropolitan Life Ins. Co.*, 139 Va. 341 (1924); *Bowles v. Mutual Benefits Accident etc. Ass.*, 99 F. 2d 44 (C.C.A. 4, 1938); *Roberts v. Avon Ins. Co.* [1956] 2 Lloyd's Rep. 240. The remarks of Sir George Jessel M.R. in *London Assurance v. Mansel* (1879) 11 Ch.D. 363 are explained under *Misrepresentation*, para. 16–31, *ante*.

[8] *Forbes & Co. v. Edinburgh Life* (1832) 10 S. 451 can be explained on its facts, but some dicta concerning the limits of waiver are unsupported by later authority: (1832) 10 S. 451, 461.

had in the last ten years?" and replies "Cannot say yet" or "Details unavailable at present", the insurers would waive disclosure of all the accidents, it is submitted, if they made no more inquiries. On the other hand, if the form of the applicant's answer seems in substance to amount to a meaningful negative or affirmative reply to the question, the insurers would not be held to waive the non-disclosure if no more was said.[9] In this connection evidence of the practice commonly followed as to the disclosure of the particular matters in dispute is admissible, and evidence to the effect that information of a particular kind is not ordinarily disclosed may not only allow but require the court to hold that the insurers waived that class of information.[10]

17–86 Indifference of insurers. Quite apart from any statements made by the assured which ground waiver, the assured can assume that the insurers are waiving disclosure of matters concerning which they appear to be indifferent or disinterested.[11] The mere fact that a prima facie material matter is not made the subject of a question in the proposal form is not, however, a ground for inferring such a lack of concern.[12]

17–87 High rate of premium. The payment of a high rate of premium may be *ipso facto* evidence of the insurers' knowledge or waiver of an undisclosed fact.[13] Conversely, the receipt of the standard rate of premium is some evidence of the insurers' ignorance of the circumstances in dispute where the assured is alleging knowledge on their part.[14]

(f) *The Insurer's Duty of Disclosure*

17–88 The duty of disclosure is mutual. Concealment of material facts by the insurer prior to conclusion of the insurance entitles the assured to avoid the contract,[15] although instances are likely to be rare. In *Banque Keyser Ullmann SA v. Skandia (U.K.) Insurance Co. Ltd* the Court of Appeal held that:

> "... the duty falling upon the insurer must at least extend to disclosing all facts known to him which are material either to the nature of the risk sought to be covered or the recoverability of a claim under the policy which a prudent insured would take into account in deciding whether or not to place the risk for which he seeks cover with that insurer."[16]

---

[9] See the related topic of misrepresentation in a partially complete answer: *Roberts v. Avon Ins. Co.* [1956] 2 Lloyd's Rep. 240, 249. For inconsistent answers and waiver, see *Keeling v. Pearl Life* (1923) 129 L.T. 573. The answer given by the applicant in the proposal form must be interpreted in the light of any oral or written statements made by him earlier in negotiations: *Claude R. Ogden & Co. Pty. Ltd v. Reliance Fire Sprinkler Co. Pty Ltd* [1975] 1 Lloyd's Rep. 52, 65 (Aus. High Ct.).

[10] *Mann, Macneal & Steeves v. Capital and Counties Ins. Co.* [1921] 2 K.B. 300, 306.

[11] *Laing v. Union Marine Ins. Co.* (1895) 1 Com.Cas. 11, 15; *Everett v. Desborough* (1829) 5 Bing. 503, 520; *Paling v. Refuge* [1945] I.A.C.Rep. (1938–49) 53; *Sweeney v. Co-operative Ins. Soc.* [1949] I.A.C.Rep. (1938–49) 78.

[12] *Roselodge v. Castle* [1966] 2 Lloyd's Rep. 113.

[13] *Court v. Martineau* (1782) 3 Doug. K.B. 161.

[14] *Greenhill v. Federal Ins. Co.* [1927] 1 K.B. 65, 79.

[15] *Carter v. Boehm* (1766) 3 Burr. 1905, 1909; *Banque Keyser Ullmann SA v. Skandia (U.K.) Ins. Co. Ltd* [1990] 1 Q.B. 665, 770; [1991] 2 A.C. 249, 268, 280, 281–282; *Pan Atlantic Ins. Co. Ltd v. Pine Top Insurance Co. Ltd* [1995] 1 A.C. 501, 555.

[16] [1990] 1 Q.B. 665, 772.

On appeal to the House of Lords Lord Bridge was disposed to accept this statement of the insurer's duty.[17] Presumably the assured must also show that the relevant non-disclosure induced him to contract on the terms agreed.[18] The duty does not extend to giving the assured the benefit of the insurer's market experience, such as, for instance, that the same risk could be covered for a lower premium by another insurer,[19] or presumably, by the same insurer under a different type of insurance contract. The insurer is not required to perform the role of the assured's broker in this regard. In any event, the sole remedy for breach by the insurer is avoidance, which is of little use to the assured.[20]

(g) *Miscellaneous*

17–89 Waiver of non-disclosure. We have seen that the insurers may waive disclosure of a particular, material fact, prior to the commencement of the insurance. This might happen either because the contents of the proposal form had the effect of dispensing with the need to disclose it, or because the insurers acted in such a manner during negotiations for insurance cover as to give the assured the impression that a particular material matter need not in this case be disclosed in full or at all. Waiver may, however, arise at a much later stage and after the inception of the policy. The insurers may expressly waive a non-disclosure by the assured when they learn of it, in which case they cannot later change their minds and attempt to use it as a pretext for avoiding the policy. Even if the insurers do not themselves have the actual intention to affirm the contract of insurance by waiving the assured's breach of the duty of disclosure, they will be deemed in law to have done so if their representations or conduct upon discovery of the undisclosed facts fairly convey to the assured the impression that it is not their intention to exercise their right to avoid the contract, since they will then be estopped from so doing later.

17–90 Affirmation. An insurer is said to waive the right to avoid a contract of insurance when, with knowledge of the facts entitling him to avoid it, he elects to continue it and so affirms it. The principles governing affirmation were recently reviewed by Mance J. in *Insurance Corporation of the Channel Islands v. Royal Hotel Ltd.*[21] They may be summarised as follows:

1. The insurer must have actual knowledge of the facts not disclosed prior to contract. Constructive knowledge is insufficient.[22]
2. He must also know that non-disclosure creates a right to avoid.[23]
3. He has a reasonable time in which to decide what to do.[24]

---

[17] [1991] 2 A.C. 249, 268.
[18] See para 17–26, *ante*.
[19] [1990] 1 Q.B. 665, 772.
[20] *HIH Casualty & General Ins. Co. Ltd v. Chase Manhattan Bank* [2001] 2 Lloyd's Rep. 483, 497.
[21] [1998] Lloyd's Rep. I.R. 151, 161.
[22] *Evans v. Bartlam* [1937] A.C. 473, 479; *C.T.I. v. Oceaus Mut. Underwriting Assoc.* [1984] 1 Lloyd's Rep. 476, 498, 530; *Malhi v. Abbey Life Ass. Co.* [1996] L.R.L.R. 237.
[23] *Peyman v. Lanjani* [1985] 1 Ch. 457.
[24] *McCormick v. National Motor & Accident Ins. Union* (1934) 49 Ll.L.R. 361.

4. There must be an unequivocal communication to the assured by words or conduct that the insurer has made an informed choice to affirm the contract.[25]

5. Whether such a communication is found depends upon how a reasonable person in the position of the assured would interpret the insurer's words or conduct. In particular, mere delay or inactivity does not demonstrate an intention to waive the assured's breach of duty but it will affect the insurer's position if the assured is prejudiced by it or is led to believe that the delay is explicable only on the basis that the insurer is affirming the policy.[26]

6. Failure to return the premium is not *per se* a waiver of the right to avoid for non-disclosure.[27] But refusal to pay a claim while not declaring avoidance and making a return of premium is evidence of an intent to affirm the contract.[28] Payment of an interim loss with knowledge of an undisclosed previous conviction has constituted waiver.[29] Acceptance of a premium after receiving knowledge of a non-disclosure is good evidence of waiver,[30] and giving instructions to the assured concerning the subject-matter of the insurance would usually be so too.[31] In short, any kind of conduct by the insurer that leads the assured reasonably to believe that the insurers intend to continue to insure him can ground waiver. When the assured acts in reliance on that belief and refrains from seeking cover elsewhere, the doctrine of promissory estoppel may well additionally debar the insurer from avoiding the insurance.[32]

17–91 Exclusion of duty and remedy for breach. The law will enforce a clause in a contract of insurance which unequivocally either releases the assured from his duty of disclosure[33] or which restricts[34] or excludes[35] the exercise by the insurer of his right to avoid the contract in the event of the assured's breach of the duty of disclosure. Neither the duty of utmost good

[25] *Peyman v. Lanjani* [1985] 1 Ch. 457, 502–503; *Ins. Corp. of the Channel Islands v. Royal Hotel Ltd* [1997] L.R.L.R. 94, 132–133.

[26] *Morrison v. Universal Mar. Ins. Co.* (1873) L.R. 8 Ex. 43; 197; *Allen v. Robles* [1969] 1 W.L.R. 1193; *Simon, Haynes & Barlas v. Beer* (1946) 78 Ll.L.R. 337.

[27] *March Cabaret Club v. London Assurance Co.* [1975] 1 Lloyd's Rep. 169, 178.

[28] *Simon Haynes & Barlas v. Beer* (1946) 78 Ll.L.R. 337; *West v. National Motor Accident & Ins. Union* [1955] 1 All E.R. 800.

[29] *Callaghan v. Thompson* [1998] C.L.Y. 3360 (C.A.).

[30] *Hemmings v. Sceptre Life* [1905] 1 Ch. 365; *Holdsworth v. L. & Y. Ins.* (1907) 23 T.L.R. 521; *Ayrey v. British Legal & Provident* [1918] 1 K.B. 136; *Simon Hayes & Barlas v. Beer* (1946) 78 Ll.L.R. 337.

[31] *De Maurier v. Bastion* [1967] 2 Lloyd's Rep. 550, 559.

[32] If relying on estoppel the assured must expressly plead a representation and how he came to rely on it—*Morrison v. Universal Mar. Ins. Co.*, *supra*.

[33] *Svenska Handelsbank v. Sun Alliance & London Ins. Plc.* [1996] 1 Lloyd's Rep. 519, 551; *Sumitomo Bank Ltd v. Banque Bruxelles Lambert S.A.* [1997] 1 Lloyd's Rep. 487, 495; *HIH Casualty & General Ins. Ltd v. Chase Manhattan Bank* [2001] 1 All E.R. (Comm) 719; [2001] 2 Lloyd's Rep. 438.

[34] *Arab Bank Ltd v. Zurich Ins. Co.* [1999] Lloyd's Rep. 262; *Kumar v. AGF Ins. Ltd* [1998] 4 All E.R. 788.

[35] *Pan Atlantic Ins. Co. v. Pine Top Ins. Co.* [1993] 1 Lloyd's Rep. 496, 502, where however the clause was not sufficiently clear to achieve this end; *HIH Casualty & General Ins. Ltd v. Chase Manhattan Bank* [2001] 2 Lloyd's Rep. 483, where it was, despite being "ungrammatical, poor in its syntax, and obscure" [2001] 1 All E.R.(Comm) 719, 745.

faith nor any other rule of public policy invalidates such provisions.[36] In the former case the contractual waiver extends to the duty of disclosure owed by the assured's agent to insure under section 19 of the Marine Insurance Act 1906, because, if the assured has no duty to disclose, his agent to insure can have none either.[37] In the latter case, an exclusion of the right to avoid will cover all non-disclosure regardless of whether it is innocent, negligent, intentional, or fraudulent, because the duty to disclose is unitary and absolute, and the remedy of avoidance applies regardless of the assured's motive and culpability.[38]

17–92 Problems in guarantee insurance. The duty of disclosure applies to guarantee insurance as to other classes of business. In this type of insurance, the insurer in effect guarantees to pay a sum to the assured in the event of a debt not being paid to the assured on a named date or on the occurrence of some other form of breach of contract. It is thus an insurance against the non-performance of a contract and must be distinguished from contracts of surety or guarantee where the duty of disclosure is limited to disclosure of anything unusual and unexpected in the transaction between the debtor and creditor, because they are not contracts *uberrimae fidei*.[39]

17–93 This distinction is not an easy one to apply in practice, since both types of contract involve an undertaking to pay upon the event of a default by another, and it turns on the construction of the agreement in issue. Where the guarantor (whether described as "surety" or "insurer") is engaged by the debtor and is also a party to a transaction with the creditor whereby he guarantees its performance by the debtor or agrees to answer in some other manner for the debt, default or miscarriage of another, then the agreement is a contract of surety, because it creates the tripartite contractual relationship of creditor, debtor and surety.[40] If, however, the guarantor is engaged by the creditor and charges a realistic premium in consideration for paying a set sum in the contingency of the creditor suffering a default by the debtor, but his obligation is not mentioned in or required by the original contract between the creditor and debtor, then the guarantee given is in substance made in the form of an insurance.[41] It is quite logical that there should be a

---

[36] *HIH Casualty & General Ins. Co. v. Chase Manhattan Bank* [2001] 1 All E.R. (Comm) 719, 737, *per* Aikens J.; [2001] 2 Lloyd's Rep. 438, 509, C.A.

[37] *HIH Casualty & General Ins. Ltd v. Chase Manhattan Bank* [2001] 2 Lloyd's Rep. 438, 507–509.

[38] *ibid.*, at pp. 513–515 impliedly disapproving *Toomey v. Eagle Star Ins. Co. (No. 2)* [1995] 1 Lloyd's Rep. 88, 92–93. For clauses excluding remedies for misrepresentation and breach of warranty, see paras 16–59 and 10–95, *ante*.

[39] *Credit Lyonnais Bank v. E.C.G.D.* [1996] 1 Lloyd's Rep. 200, 226–227; *Davies v. London and Provincial Marine* (1878) 8 Ch.D. 469; *North British Ins. Co. v. Lloyd* (1854) 10 Exch. 523; *London General Omnibus Co. Ltd v. Holloway* [1912] 2 K.B. 72. The issue may not be completely resolved—see *Mackenzie v. Royal Bank of Canada* [1934] A.C. 468, 475; *Trade Indemnity v. Workington etc. Board* [1937] A.C. 1, 18. See the discussion in paras 31–40 to 31–44, *post*.

[40] *Trade Indemnity Co. v. Workington Harbour and Dock Board* [1937] A.C. 1.

[41] *Seaton v. Burnand* [1899] 1 Q.B. 782, C.A. The H.L. disagreed on appeal only with the materiality of the particular fact at issue—[1900] A.C. 135.

duty of disclosure owed to the insurer by the creditor, since there is no reason why the insurer should be conversant with the situation of the debtor. In a contract of surety, however, the surety is engaged by the debtor, and has as good a chance of knowing or discovering facts relevant to the debtor's capacity to perform as the creditor.

17–94 It has been held that under a policy guaranteeing the solvency of a third party, it is a material fact that the third party is in considerable financial difficulties.[42] But details of the original creditor-debtor contract may well be immaterial. In *Seaton v. Burnand*,[43] X had made a loan to Y, and Z guaranteed it. The insurers then issued a policy of guarantee insurance to X covering the risk of Z becoming insolvent. The fact that the loan by X to Y was made at a very high rate of interest was held to be immaterial to the insurers.

17–95 Criminal liability. By section 133(1) of the Financial Services Act 1986[44]:

"any person who ... dishonestly conceals any material facts ... is guilty of an offence if he ... conceals the facts for the purpose of inducing, or is reckless as to whether it may induce, another person (whether or not the person ... from whom the facts are concealed) to enter into or offer to enter into, or to refrain from entering or offering to enter into, a contract of insurance with an insurance company (not being an investment agreement)[45] or to exercise or refrain from exercising, any rights conferred by such a contract".

Commission of the offence can lead to seven years' imprisonment or a fine or both on conviction on indictment, or to six months' imprisonment or a fine not exceeding the statutory maximum or both on summary conviction.[46]

The wording of the section seems designed to deter dishonest concealment on the part of insurers or their agents only, and does not apparently apply to the assured or his agent, since they could not induce an insurer to contract with an insurance company, but it seems to apply to a re-assured and reinsurer where both are insurance companies.

17–96 Criticism of the duty of disclosure. This chapter would be incomplete without mention of calls for reform of disclosure law, questioning the need to retain in its present form a doctrine developed to meet eighteenth century requirements which is today unduly harsh on the assured and disproportionately favourable to the insurer. Three issues arise:

(1) Whether the duty of disclosure should be retained at all;
(2) if so, whether the current law should be amended;
(3) if so, in which respects it should be amended.

17–97 Retention or abolition. The duty of disclosure is so well established

[42] *Anglo-Californian Bank v. London and Provincial Marine* (1904) 10 Com.Cas. 1.
[43] *Seaton v. Burnand* [1900] A.C. 135.
[44] Replacing and extending s.73 of the Insurance Companies Act 1982, but note the territorial limits in subs. (2).
[45] Contracts of insurance which amount to investment agreements under the Act are most forms of life insurance contracts (see para 3–06, *ante* at footnote 15). They are governed in this respect by the substantially similar section 47.
[46] s.133(3).

in English law that it is necessary to go back many years in the authorities to discover a rationale for it which is not simply a recital of precedents or an incantation of the mantra of *uberrima fides*: The generally accepted justification for the doctrine is that the assured expects the insurer to run the risk of becoming liable to pay substantial sums in the event of loss in return for a premium which is small in comparison. The viability of the insurer's business depends on an accurate assessment of a proposed risk, and it is inequitable to expect the insurer to keep his side of the bargain if he is deprived of the information needed to appraise and rate the risk, of which he is ignorant and the assured is cognisant. What was emphasised is the insurer's lack of knowledge and the means to obtain it, while the assured has the relevant information to hand.[47]

17–98 Lord Mansfield's rationale for the duty of disclosure was a response to conditions prevailing in the nascent marine insurance market of his day. The assured would be likely to know more than the insurer did about the condition of a vessel or the state of an intended cargo, and the means of communication to enable the insurer to make enquiries and maintain up to date records were inadequate. The national polity depended on the availability of affordable insurance against marine and war risks in those turbulent times, and a rule of law which lightened the burdens of the emerging London market accorded with sound commercial policy. Today, it is argued, the insurer's position has altered. He requires the assured to answer a list of questions which experience has taught are important in rating the risk, and he has the assistance of expert staff such as surveyors to inspect property risks and medical advisers to assess lives proposed for life and accident cover. Scientific data and actuarial statistics are available to assist insurers evaluate the risk. In short the insurer has the means of knowledge and the previous imbalance in the relationship of insurer and proposer is no more.

17–99 There is force in these arguments,[48] but it is wrong to assume that the insurer's knowledge is always either adequate or easily obtainable. Interim cover is often granted without the benefit of a proposal form, and the assured may obtain variation or renewal of cover without completing one. There is always the possibility that the risk is affected by circumstances outside the scope of a proposal form—the house next door has been burgled twice in the last year, there have been credible threats of arson, or the condition of the proposed life assured worsens between signature and acceptance. In some markets, such as marine and reinsurance, business is done without the use of proposal forms, and premiums are kept competitive by imposing a duty on the assured to volunteer information, allowing the insurer to process acceptance of risks more cheaply and expeditiously than if he had find out everything about the risk.[49] A unitary duty of disclosure

---

[47] *Carter v. Boehm* (1766) 3 Burr. 1905; *Friere v. Woodhouse* (1817) 1 Holt N.P. 572; *Seaton v. Burnand* (1899) 1 Q.B. 782; *Hoff v. de Rougemont* (1929) 34 Ll. L. Rep. 81, 87.

[48] *Richards on Insurance* (5th ed., 1952) Vol. 2, Ch. 10, "The Anachronistic Doctrine of Concealment"; Hartnett, " A Remnant in the Law of Insurance" (1950) 15 Law & Contemp. Prob. 391; Hasson, "The Doctrine of Uberrima Fides—A Critical Evaluation" (1969) 32 M.L.R. 615.

[49] *Manifest Shipping Co. Ltd v. Uni-Polaris Co. Ltd, The Star Sea* [2001] 1 All E.R. (Comm) 193, 208.

which does not require proof of fraud to establish a breach provides a simple remedy for an insurer who has been misled. We would not go so far as to say that the duty of disclosure is otiose.

17–100 Defects in the current law. Critics of the present law have dwelt on four main defects in the law. First, in many cases assureds are unaware of their duty to disclose material facts. This is a less cogent criticism now that insurers following the Statements of Insurance Practice have agreed to insert clear warnings of its existence in proposal forms, and both the law and regulatory authority have obliged brokers to advise assureds what is expected of them.[50] Secondly, a layman is unlikely to know what an insurer regards as a material fact. To some extent the problem is answered by a broker's advice, but when business is done directly between the parties without the intervention of a broker this will not be so. Thirdly, it is said that the law favours incompetent underwriters by permitting them to escape liability for a loss by reference to the standard of underwriting diligence and prudence of the notional prudent insurer, although the undisclosed circumstances would not have affected their readiness to write the risk if disclosed.[51] The inclusion of the requirement of inducement as an element of the defence of non-disclosure was intended to address the complaint.[52] In practice it is not difficult for even the most incompetent underwriter to show (with the benefit of hindsight) that disclosure of important facts, such as a poor loss record, would have persuaded him not to write the risk on the same terms.[53] The courts' reluctance to order discovery of the insurer's files for other comparable risks further limits the assured's chances of challenging the insurer's assertion of inducement, although it must be said that seeking to demonstrate an underwriting practice to overlook a particular fact from the insurer's reactions to a succession of proposals each possessing different attractive and negative factors would probably be unproductive. In our experience the need to prove inducement tends to be significant in cases of insurance and reinsurance of large commercial risks, where interpretations of loss statistics may reasonably differ, the insurer/reinsurer may be keen to have the business for commercial reasons,[54] and when he may be prepared to overlook unattractive aspects of the risk in order to encourage future business from the broker concerned.

17–101 Finally, the only remedy for non-disclosure is avoidance of the contract, an inflexible and draconian remedy in cases of inadvertent and borderline breaches of the duty, especially where the insurer would have written the contract for an increase in premium if disclosure had been made. There have been calls for a more sophisticated and flexible choice of remedies.[55] Taken together these criticisms do in our view justify reform of

---

[50] See Ch. 36, *post.*

[51] *Haydenfayre v. British National Ins. Soc.Ltd.* [1984] 2 Lloyd's Rep. 393, 400, *per* Lloyd J.; *Pan Atlantic Ins. Co. v. Pine Top Ins. Co.* [1993] 1 Lloyd's Rep. 496, 508, *per* Sir Donald Nicholls V.-C.

[52] *Pan Atlantic Ins. Co. v. Pine Top Ins. Co.* [1995] A.C. 501, in which Lord Mustill discussed criticisms of the current law at pp. 528–509.

[53] *Marc Rich v. Portman* [1996] 1 Lloyd's Rep. 430; affirmed at [1997] 1 Lloyd's Rep. 225.

[54] See *e.g. Kingscroft Ins. Co. v. Nissan Fire & Marine Ins. Co.* [1999] Lloyd's Rep. I.R. 603.

[55] *Pan Atlantic Ins. Co. v. Pine Top Ins. Co.* [1993] 1 Lloyd's Rep. 496, 508; [1995] 1 A.C. 501, 528; *Kausar v. Eagle Star Ins. Co.* [2000] Lloyd's Rep. 154, 157, *per* Staughton L.J.; Sir Andrew Longmore, "An Insurance Contracts Act for a new Century?", [2001] L.M.C.L.Q. 356.

the present law, although it is not easy to say exactly what form this should take. There is support in the insurance industry for further self-regulation on the lines of the Statements of Insurance Practice and the Insurance Ombudsman's service to claimants under private consumer insurance policies, and we consider this first.

17–102 Statements of Insurance Practice. In 1977 the insurance industry in the United Kingdom made voluntary proposals to mitigate some of the severity in the present law of non-disclosure. The British Insurance Association (now the Association of British Insurers) and Lloyd's issued Statements of Insurance Practice which their members were recommended to accept. In 1986, these statements were revised to take account of criticisms of their terms and recommendations for law reform made by the Law Commission.[56] One statement refers to general (*i.e.* non-life) insurances of United Kingdom resident private policyholders. The second statement covers "long-term insurances", which means principally life assurances held by the same category of assureds.[57]

The General Insurance Practice Statement contains provisions concerning proposal forms. By paragraph 1(b) a prominent warning of the existence of the duty of disclosure must be put into the proposal form, together with a statement of the consequences of breach of it. By paragraph 3 the insurer is to remind the assured of the relevance of the duty upon renewal by a warning in the renewal notice. By paragraph 2(b) the effect of a non-disclosure or misrepresentation is restricted by a provision that the insurer will not repudiate liability to a policyholder on grounds of non-disclosure of a material fact which a policyholder could not reasonably be expected to have disclosed or on grounds of misrepresentation unless it is a deliberate or negligent misrepresentation of a material fact. Paragraph 2(b) does not apply to marine or aviation policies.

17–103 The Long-Term Insurance Practice Statement contains similar provisions on proposal forms. By paragraph 3(a) it states that a claim will not be "unreasonably" rejected, and that a claim will not be rejected for non-disclosure or misrepresentation of facts unknown to the assured, but a proviso states that fraud will, and negligence or non-disclosure or misrepresentation of a material fact may, result in adjustment or constitute grounds for rejection.

17–104 We do not regard these statements of self-regulatory practice as a substitute for reform of the law. Although as revised in 1986 they are clearer than the earlier versions and, in particular, in respect of general insurance, the insurers have not retained their right to judge whether it is reasonable to reject a claim, that general discretion is retained in paragraph 3(a) of the Long-Term Statement. Further, and most importantly, the statements lack the force of law.[58] A liquidator of an insurance company would be bound to reject legally invalid claims, irrespective of the statements, and insurers who

---

[56] Law Reform Committee Report, "Conditions & Exceptions in Insurance Policies", Cmnd. 62 (1957); Law Commission Report, "Non-Disclosure and Breach of Warranty", Cmnd. 8064 (1980).

[57] The full texts can be found in Part 7 of the *Encyclopedia of Insurance Law*.

[58] For more detailed commentary on the statements, see Birds, "Self-regulation and insurance contracts", Ch. 1 in *New Foundations for Insurance Law* (ed. Rose, 1987) and Forte (1986) 49 M.L.R. 754.

are not members of the Association of British Insurers or of Lloyd's can in no way be said to be bound by them.

17–105 Insurance Ombudsman. Another measure of self-regulation was the creation in 1981 of the Insurance Ombudsman's Bureau, which enabled assureds whose claims were rejected for any reason, including alleged non-disclosure, to complain to the Ombudsman, who had power to reverse the insurance company's decision in an appropriate case. The Ombudsman's jurisdiction was restricted to complaints by private individuals and over the years the IOB created "a body of consumer insurance law",[59] which included remedies for non-disclosure other than avoidance.[60] At the time of writing the IOB is being reconstituted as a statutory body under the Financial Services & Markets Act 2000, and will continue to determine complaints by reference to what is "fair and reasonable in all the circumstances of the case".[61] The valuable work of the IOB lessens the impact of the duty of disclosure on consumer insurance, but in our view does not remove the need for reform. What is unfair to individuals is also unfair to small businesses and difficult to justify in commercial insurance law.[62]

17–106 Reform of the law. In its Report on "Non-disclosure and Breach of Warranty"[63] in 1980 the Law Commission recommended that the test of materiality should be the opinion of the reasonable assured as to whether a fact known to him would influence the judgment of a prudent insurer. The Insurance Contracts Act 1984 (Australia) has adopted a similar test, whereby the assured must disclose matters known to him which either he knows are relevant to the insurer's decision whether to accept the risk and on what terms, or which a reasonable assured in the circumstances could be expected to know was relevant in that context.[64] Avoidance is permitted only in cases of fraudulent non-disclosure, and in other cases the liability of the insurer is to be reduced to reflect what he would have agreed if disclosure had been made.[65] Reported cases show that this solution is not free from difficulty,[66] but it would provide a good basis for reform of the English law. It would, we submit, be better than continuing to rely on the existence of a separate regime for consumer insurance.

---

[59] *Birds' Modern Insurance Law* (5th ed., 2001) p. 6.
[60] Including on occasions the proportionate reduction of the claim.
[61] Financial Services and Markets Act 2000, s.228(2).
[62] Sir Peter North *Law Reform: Processes and Problems* (1985) 101 L.Q.R. 338; Sir Andrew Longmore [2001] L.M.C.L.Q. 356, 368.
[63] Cmnd. 8064.
[64] s.22. In certain instances the duty is deemed to be waived—s.21. The Australian Law Reform Commission has now recommended that these provisions be applied to marine insurance, which was excluded from the 1984 Act—Report 91, April 2001.
[65] s.28.
[66] There is a useful account by A.A. and J-A. Tarr in "The Insured's Non-Disclosure in the Formation of Insurance Contracts: A Comparative Perspective", 50 I.C.L.Q. 577 (2001).

CHAPTER 18

FRAUD, MISREPRESENTATION AND NON-DISCLOSURE BY THIRD PARTIES

(a) *General Principles*

18-1 General rule. It is a general rule in the law of contract that fraud, misrepresentation, or non-disclosure by persons who are not parties to a contract or agents for those parties does not affect the validity of the contract[1] though it may be a ground for proceeding against those persons for damages in deceit[2] or negligence,[3] or for breach of collateral warranty.[4] This rule applies to contracts of insurance as to other contracts, and prima facie it is no defence for the insurers to allege that some person other than the assured or his agent made false or inaccurate statements to them or did not disclose some material fact within his knowledge. Thus, where a proposal form was completed and signed in the name of the assured but was in fact signed by some other person without the assured's authority or knowledge, it was held that the company could not rely on misstatements contained therein as a defence to the assured's claim on the policy.[5]

18-2 Proposal not signed by assured. In *Pearl Life v. Johnson,*[6] the company on a proposal purporting to be signed by S.A.J. issued a policy under seal covenanting to pay S.A.J. a named sum upon the death of W.J. The policy recited that S.A.J. had signed a proposal, and that such proposal was to be the basis of the contract, and that if there was any false averment contained therein, the policy should be null and void. The proposal contained untrue statements, but it was not in fact signed by S.A.J., nor had she any knowledge of its contents, nor had she given any authority to make the statements on her behalf. It was held that S.A.J. could recover on the policy because no proposal was made which could be said to be the basis of the contract, and the company, having issued the policy and received the premiums, was estopped from repudiating it unless it could show that the untrue statements were made by or with the authority of the assured.

18-3 These principles were followed by the Industrial Assurance

[1] *Connecticut Mutual Life v. Luchs*, 108 U.S. 498 (1883).
[2] *Pasley v. Freeman* (1789) 3 T.R. 51; *Wells v. Smith* [1914] 3 K.B. 722.
[3] *Hedley Byrne v. Heller* [1964] A.C. 465.
[4] *Shanklin Pier v. Detel Products* [1951] 2 K.B. 854.
[5] *Pearl Life v. Johnson* [1909] 2 K.B. 288; *Yates v. Liverpool Victoria F.S.* [1926] I.A.C. Rep. 50; *Wright v. Royal Liver* [1930] I.A.C.(N.I.) Rep. 89.
[6] [1909] 2 K.B. 288.

Commissioner in *Jones v. Pearl Assurance Co.*[7] The assured signed a proposal for an insurance on the life of her son. The agent, having reason to believe that the proposal contained a misstatement of the son's age, obtained from the son a correct proposal signed by him, and destroyed the original proposal. The company issued a policy to the assured on the proposal signed by the son. The assured had no knowledge of this and supposed that the policy was issued on the proposal which she had signed. The company sought to avoid the policy on the ground of misrepresentation as to the health of the life assured. The Commissioner held that for that purpose they could not rely on the statement made in either proposal. In *Ashworth v. Scottish Legal Life*,[8] the society produced a proposal containing inaccuracies which purported to be signed by the assured, but the signature had in the first instance been written in pencil and then been inked over by an agent of the society so that the pencil writing was obliterated. The Commissioner held that inasmuch as the original writing could not be produced expert evidence was inadmissible to prove that the signature on the policy was the signature of the assured. In the absence of any other reliable evidence to prove that, contrary to her assertions, the assured did sign the proposal form, the Commissioner held that her claim was not affected by the inaccurate statements contained therein.

18–4 Warranty by assured. The only true exception to the general rule considered above is where the assured has warranted that the statements made by a third party to the insurance contract are accurate, or that he has not concealed any material fact. In such a case it is obvious that a misstatement or non-disclosure by that third person will invalidate the policy. Examples of such warranties occur sometimes in life insurance, and are considered below.

18–5 Agency. All other cases in which a contract is vitiated by the misrepresentation or non-disclosure of a third party will be found to be cases in which the misrepresentation or omission complained of is made by an agent for one of the parties who is directly concerned with the placing of the insurance cover. On general principles the principal whose agent he was cannot escape responsibility for the default of the agent, and will usually suffer just as if he himself had made the misrepresentation or concealed the undisclosed fact. The underlying reason for this rule is the principle of imputed knowledge, whereby, in short, knowledge acquired by the agent in relation to the insurance is treated as knowledge possessed by the principal employing him to deal with it.

The significance of misstatements or omissions by an agent depends upon whose agent he is—assured's or insurer's—and we shall therefore consider these matters first in relation to the assured's agent and, secondly, in relation to the insurers' agent. It may be that in a given case the same person acts as agent for both parties, but on a legal analysis of his position he will probably be agent for the assured to perform certain functions, and an agent for the

[7] [1927] I.A.C. Rep. 42.
[8] [1927] I.A.C. Rep. 40.

insurer in performing others, so that it must be asked at the outset, whose agent he was concerning the matters in question.[9]

18–6 Insurance broker. An independent broker who places an insurance between the assured and underwriters at Lloyd's or an insurance company is prima facie the agent of the assured and not of the insurers.[10] The fact that he places most of the business entrusted to him with the same underwriters or companies and is remunerated by way of commission on premiums received by him and deducted in account with the insurers does not make him the insurers' agent. Even if he solicits business from prospective applicants for insurance, that does not make him the insurers' agent in the placement of the insurance unless the solicitation is done on the instructions of the insurers with whom the risk is placed.[11] The kind of case where the broker is found to be the insurers' agent is where he is employed by them or is tied to them and, in that capacity, initiates the relationship between the insurers and assured.[12]

(b) *Agents of the Assured*

18–7 It is convenient to refer at the outset to sections 18 and 19 of the Marine Insurance Act 1906,[13] which are now accepted as stating the law applicable both to marine and non-marine insurance.[14] Section 18(1) provides that the assured is deemed to know every circumstance which, in the ordinary course of business, ought to be known by him, and so involves the imputation to the assured of the knowledge of agents employed to conduct his business. Section 19 stipulates what the agent effecting the insurance must disclose to the insurers. For purposes of disclosure of material facts this class of agent means the agent who actually deals with the insurer and concludes the insurance with them on behalf of the assured.[15] In the following paragraphs we observe the distinction between these types of agent derived from the statute.

---

[9] *Equitable Life Ass. Soc. v. General Accident Ass. Corp.* (1904) 12 S.L.T. 348; *St. Margarets Trust Ltd v. Navigators & General Ins. Co.* (1949) 82 Ll.L.R. 752; *Callaghan & Hedges v. Thompson* [2000] Lloyd's Rep.I.R. 125, 131–132.

[10] *Rozanes v. Bowen* (1928) 32 Ll.L.R. 98, 101; *Newsholme Bros. v. Road Transport & General Ins. Co.* [1929] 2 K.B. 356, 362; *Anglo-African Merchants Ltd v. Bayley* [1970] 1 Q.B. 311, 322; *Arif v. Excess Ins. Group Ltd* 1987 S.L.T. 473; *Searle v. Hales & Co.* [1996] L.R.L.R. 68.

[11] *Arif v. Excess Ins. Group Ltd* 1987 S.L.T. 473, 474, following para. 817 in the 7th edition of this book.

[12] *Winter v. Irish Life Ass. PLC* [1995] 2 Lloyd's Rep. 274, 282.

[13] 6 Edw. 7, c.41.

[14] *Simner v. New India Ass. Co.* [1995] L.R.L.R. 240, 252; *Soc. Anon. d'Intermédiaires Luxembourgeois v. Farex Gie.* [1995] L.R.L.R. 116, 141; *Pan Atlantic Ins. Co. v. Pine Top Ins. Co.* [1995] A.C. 501, 518. In *PCW Syndicates v. PCW Reinsurers* [1996] 1 Lloyd's Rep. 241 the C.A. was content to proceed upon the parties' agreement to this effect.

[15] *PCW Syndicates v. PCW Reinsurers* [1996] 1 Lloyd's Rep. 241, 257, *per* Rose L.J. and 258, *per* Saville L.J., approving Waller J. at 248. Staughton L.J. left the point open—p. 257; *Group Jose Re v. Walbrook Ins. Co.* [1996] 1 Lloyd's Rep. 345, 361.

18–8 Agent to effect insurance. If the assured employs an agent to effect the insurance for him, any fraud,[16] misrepresentation[17] or non-disclosure[18] by the agent in effecting the insurance will give the insurers the same entitlement to avoid the policy as if it had been that of the principal. It makes no difference that the assured was not privy to the fraud or that incorrect statements were made either without his knowledge or even against express instructions.[19]

18–9 Disclosure by agent to effect insurance. As a general rule the assured will be held responsible for any failure by his agent to effect the insurance to disclose a material fact actually known to, or deemed to be known to, either of them. This is the result of three separate rules derived from section 19 of the Marine Insurance Act 1906[20]:

(1) The agent is bound to disclose what the assured knows, unless it comes to the assured's notice too late for communication to the agent.
(2) The agent must disclose material facts known to him, whether or not also known to the assured.
(3) The agent must also disclose facts which in the ordinary course of business he should have known or been told, whether or not the assured should have known of them or told him about them.

It follows that the insurers may be entitled to avoid a policy for non-disclosure of a material fact actually known to neither the assured nor his agent to effect the insurance.

18–10 Reasons for agent's default immaterial. It makes no difference whether the agent concerned intentionally concealed the facts omitted[21] or merely forgot to mention them or thought bona fide that it did not matter or said what he believed, albeit wrongly, to be correct.[22] Nor is the insurers' position affected by whether the agent was given wrong information or failed to perform his proper instructions correctly.[23] The courts will not allow the insurers to be prejudiced by the assured's employment of an agent to deal with them, and are entitled to the same accuracy of statement and unstinted disclosure of material facts as they would be justified in demanding from the assured in person.

18–11 Restriction on disclosure of facts known to agent to insure. Despite *dicta* to the contrary[24] it has been held that material circumstances known to

---

[16] *Hambrough v. Mutual Life Ins. Co. of N.Y.* (1895) 72 L.T. 140; *Dunn v. Ocean, Accident & Guarantee Corp.* (1933) 45 Ll.L.R. 276, approved in (1933) 47 Ll.L.R. 129; *Allen v. Universal Automobile Ins. Co.* (1933) 45 Ll.L.R. 55, 58.

[17] *Wheelton v. Hardisty* (1858) 8 E & B 232, 270; *Anderson v. Pacific Fire and Marine Ins. Co.* (1872) L.R. 7 C.P. 65; *Bancroft v. Heath* (1901) 6 Com.Cas. 137; *Hambrough v. Mutual Life Ins. Co. of N.Y.* (1895) 72 L.T. 140; *Krantz v. Allan* (1921) 9 Ll.L.R. 410.

[18] *Blackburn, Low & Co. v. Haslam* (1888) 21 Q.B.D. 144; *Winter v. Irish Life Ass. plc* [1995] 2 Lloyd's Rep. 274.

[19] *Hambrough v. Mutual Life Ins. Co. of N.Y.* (1895) 72 L.T. 140; *Holland v. Russell* (1863) 4 B. & S. 14; *Russell v. Thornton* (1860) 6 H. & N. 140.

[20] *PCW Syndicates v. PCW Reinsurers* [1996] 1 Lloyd's Rep. 241, 258.

[21] *Biggar v. Rock Life Ass. Co.* [1902] 1 K.B. 516.

[22] *Krantz v. Allan* (1921) 9 Ll.L.R. 410.

[23] *Dawsons v. Bonnin* [1922] 2 A.C. 413, 427, 439; *Winter v. Irish Life Ass. plc* [1995] 2 Lloyd's Rep. 274.

[24] *El Ajou v. Dollar Land Holdings* [1994] 2 All E.R. 685, 702; *Soc. Anonyme d'Intermédiaires v. Farex* [1995] L.R.L.R. 116, 149.

the agent effecting the insurance are not disclosable unless knowledge of them was acquired in his capacity as agent for the assured, and would be disclosable by the assured if known to him.[25] It follows that the agent's awareness that he is defrauding the assured, for example with regard to premiums, is not disclosable to the insurer (assuming that it be a material fact) because that is not knowledge gained in the regular performance of his agency. Furthermore it will not be imputed to the assured because of it is not information which will be communicated to him in the ordinary course of business, so that the agent's fraud is not something which the assured is deemed to know and accordingly bound to disclose.[26]

18–12 Knowledge of agents employed in the assured's business. We are here concerned with the question of when an individual assured (or the directing mind of a corporate assured) is deemed to know a material fact of which he has no actual knowledge, but which is known by an agent employed in his business. The principle upon which knowledge possessed by such an agent is imputed to the assured is expressed in section 18(1) of the Marine Insurance Act, which has been interpreted restrictively by reference to marine insurance cases decided before the Act was passed. It is not all agents whose knowledge is imputed in that way for purposes of non-disclosure but only those agents who are "agents to know", that is to say, are responsible for keeping the assured informed about the subject matter of the insurance, either because they are responsible for placing the insurance or because they have the management of it for the assured.[27] If such an agent owes a duty to communicate information which is relevant to the insurance, but fails to do so, the assured is deemed to know what in the ordinary routine of his business he should have been told if the agent had performed his duty, but he will not be deemed to know facts which, whether or not owing to the deficient organisation of the business, no agent was responsible for communicating to him.[28]

18–13 Thus in *Australia & New Zealand Bank v. Colonial & Eagle Wharves*[29] insurers sought to avoid for non-disclosure of the fact that the assured wharfingers' business possessed a deficient system for ensuring that imported wool was not misdelivered, and that wool held to the order of particular persons was habitually released without their assent. The board of directors were unaware of this fact, but it was known to the company's chief entry clerk who liaised with the warehouse delivery clerks when delivery orders were presented. His knowledge was not imputed to the assured.

[25] *PCW Syndicates v. PCW Reinsurers* [1996] 1 Lloyd's Rep. 241, 256–257 *per* Staughton and Rose L.JJ., approving Waller J. at 250; *Soc. Anonyme d'Intermédiaires Luxembourgeois v. Farex Gie.* [1995] L.R.L.R. 116, 143, 156–157; *International Commercial Bank v. Ins. Corp. of Ireland* [1991] I.R.L.M. 726, HC approving para. 811 in the 7th edition of this work.
[26] *PCW Syndicates v. PCW Reinsurers, supra.*
[27] *Proudfoot v. Montefiore* (1867) L.R. 2 Q.B. 511; *Blackburn, Low & Co. v. Vigors* (1887) 12 App. Cas. 531; *Blackburn Low & Co. v. Haslam* (1888) 21 Q.B.D. 144; *PCW Syndicates v. PCW Reinsurers* [1996] 1 Lloyd's Rep. 241, 253–254; *Group Josi Re v. Walbrook Ins. Co.* [1996] 1 W.L.R. 1152, 1169.
[28] *Australia & New Zealand Bank v. Colonial & Eagle Wharves* [1960] 2 Lloyd's Rep. 241; *Simner v. New India Ass. Co.* [1995] L.R.L.R. 240.
[29] [1960] 2 Lloyd's Rep. 241.

Although he was crucial to the efficiency of the system, he was neither an agent under a duty to monitor it and report on its operation nor an agent with executive authority placed in charge of the goods in the assured's warehouses.

18–14 In *Simner v. New India Assurance Company*[30] the reassured syndicate had a participating line in business written under a binding authority by an underwriting agency. The reinsurers sought to avoid for non-disclosure of the claims record under the binder, which was known to the agency but not to the reassured. The agency's knowledge was not imputed to the reassured because the agency owed no reporting duty to the reassured, but only to the leading underwriter who, in turn, owed no duty to report to the reassured. By contrast in *London General Insurance Company v. General Marine Underwriters' Association*[31] there was in place a system whereby casualty lists received from Lloyd's were to be disseminated to the reinsurance department of the reinsured company via its underwriting and claims departments. On the day in question the underwriting departmental manager put the casualty lists in a drawer without looking at them, and omitted to pass them on to the other departments due either to oversight or pressure of work, with the result that a material fact was not disclosed to reinsurers. It was held that the reassured company was deemed to know the fact in question because in the ordinary course of business it should have been known to those concerned in the reinsurance.[32]

18–15 Non-disclosure of partial loss. It has been held in two marine cases that where an agent in charge of property, acting without fraud, failed to disclose a partial loss, in ignorance of which the policy was effected, the result of the non-disclosure was not to make the contract voidable but to create an implied exception from the risk in respect of the loss which had occurred.[33] The soundness of these decisions has, however, been doubted,[34] and their authority is suspect.

18–16 Agent acting to defraud principal. While an assured cannot avoid responsibility for false statements made on his behalf to the insurers by his agent acting within his authority on the ground that the agent was defrauding him,[35] an agent's fraud is important in the context of imputation of knowledge. An agent's knowledge of his own fraud or misconduct and matters relevant to it will not be imputed to the assured in accordance with the principles set out in paragraph 18–13 above, because it cannot be supposed that in the ordinary course of business an agent will disclose his

---

[30] [1995] L.R.L.R. 240.

[31] [1921] 1 K.B. 104.

[32] There seems to have been a difference of opinion in the Court of Appeal as to whether the failure was attributable to human failing or to an inherently defective system, *cf.* Lord Sterndale M.R. at p. 110 with Younger L.J. at p. 112. If the failure in communication was the result of poor organisation, then the case is authority for the proposition that the assured is deemed to know what he ought to have known if the business was well run.

[33] *Gladstone v. King* (1813) 1 M. & S. 35; *Stribley v. Imperial Marine Ins. Co.* (1876) 1 Q.B.D. 507.

[34] *Blackburn, Low & Co. v. Vigors* (1887) 12 App.Cas. 531, 540, per Lord Watson; *Arnould, Marine Insurance*, (16th ed.) Vol. 2, paras 635–636.

[35] *Wheelton v. Hardisty* (1858) 8 E. & B. 232, 270; *Hambrough v. Mut. Life Ins. Co. of N.Y.* (1895) 72 L.T. 140.

own fraud, misconduct or serious breach of duty to his principal.[36] Thus another reason for the decision in *Australia & New Zealand Bank v. Colonial & Eagle Wharves*[37] that the knowledge of the assured's chief entry clerk concerning the company's delivery systems was not to be imputed to the assured was that it would have revealed his own misconduct and he had no duty to report that to his superiors.

18–17 Life of another policy. In life assurance the misrepresentation, fraud, or non-disclosure of the "life" (not being the assured) or referee does not of itself affect the validity of the policy. It may do so, but on one of two prima facie grounds only; either:

(i) because the "life" or referee is acting as agent of the assured; or
(ii) because there is some condition in the contract, express or implied, by which the truth of the statements made by the "life" or referee is warranted or made the basis of the contract.

Some of the earlier cases seem at first sight to support the theory that in the case of an insurance upon the life of another the "life" is necessarily the agent of the assured for the purpose of answering such questions as the insurers may think proper to ask, and that the policy is therefore voidable if the "life" answers any of such questions inaccurately. In some of the cases there is an expression of judicial opinion that the "life" is the agent of the assured for that purpose. In *Everett v. Desborough*[38] the "life" made a false statement as to his "usual medical attendant," and the court in setting aside the policy proceeded partly on the ground that the "life" must be considered to be the agent of the assured, but partly also on the ground that there was a condition in the policy that the usual medical attendant of the life insured must be truly declared. Also in *Maynard v. Rhodes*,[39] *Morrison v. Muspratt*,[40] *Huckman v. Fernie*, [41] *Swete v. Fairlie*,[42] and *Rawlins v. Desborough*[43] the opinion of some of the judges was that the assured must be held responsible for any false statements made by the "life" although not for the non-disclosure by him of material facts. In a Scottish case, *Forbes v. Edinburgh Life*,[44] Lord President Hope said that even non-disclosure by the "life" would invalidate the policy, and in *Rawlins v. Desborough*,[45] Denman C.J. said that wilful concealment by the "life" would invalidate. But if all those cases are carefully examined it will be found that either:

---

[36] *PCW Syndicates v. PCW Reinsurers* [1996] 1 Lloyd's Rep. 241, 255, 2587, applying *Re Hampshire Land Co.* [1896] 2 Ch. 743, *Houghton v. Nothard, Lowe & Wills* [1928] A.C. 1, *Newsholme Bros. v. Road Transport & General Ins. Co.*. [1929] 2 K.B. 356, 374; *Soc. Anonyme d'Intermédiaires v. Farex* [1995] L.R.L.R. 116, 143; *Arab Bank Plc v. Zurich Ins. Co.* [1999] 1 Lloyd's Rep. 262, 282–283; *Australia & New Zealand Bank v. Colonial & Eagle Wharves* [1960] 2 Lloyd's Rep. 241; *Kingscroft Ins. Co v. Nissan Fire & Marine Ins. Co.* [1999] Lloyd's Rep.I.R. 371, 375.
[37] [1960] 2 Lloyd's Rep. 241, 254–255, para. 18–13, *ante*. In this case there was no fraud but merely incompetence.
[38] (1829) 5 Bing. 503.
[39] (1824) 5 Dow. & R. 266.
[40] (1827) 4 Bing. 60.
[41] (1838) 3 M. & W. 505.
[42] (1833) 6 C. & P. 1.
[43] (1840) 2 Moo. & Ry. 328.
[44] (1832) 10 S. 451.
[45] (1840) 2 Moo. & Ry. 328.

   (i) there was an express condition in the policy that the statement made by the "life" must be accurate[46]; or

   (ii) the facts were probably known to the assured as well as to the "life", and therefore there was non-disclosure by the assured himself[47]; or

   (iii) the questions were put to the assured and by him handed on to the "life" to answer on his behalf.[48]

There is, therefore, no authority for holding that the "life" is necessarily the agent of the assured for any purpose.

18–18 Two later cases may be referred to in this connection. Where an agent obtained the assured's signature to a proposal for a policy on her husband's life, on which proposal certain questions were left unanswered, and the agent with the assured's knowledge and consent took the signed proposal to the assured's husband for the purpose of obtaining the necessary information for completing it, it was held that the assured was bound by her husband's answers as if they were her own.[49] On the other hand, where an agent without the knowledge or authority of the assured went to the "life" and procured him to fill up and sign the proposal it was held that the assured was not responsible for the inaccuracy of the statements made therein.[50] In the case of statements made by a referee, that is by a medical man or friend, whom the assured has named as a person to whom the insurers may refer for information relating to the health or habits of the "life", there has been a tendency to consider the referee as the agent of the assured in respect of the information given.[51] In *Lindenau v. Desborough*[52] it would appear that the policy was set aside on the ground that the former medical attendants of the "life" had made false statements or failed to disclose material facts in answer to questions put to them. The report, however, of that case does not show whether or not there was any express condition in the policy, or whether the assured himself was aware of the facts alleged to have been misrepresented or concealed, and from the fact that Brougham, in moving for a new trial on behalf of the assured, does not appear to have taken the objection that the misrepresentation or non-disclosure, if any, was not that of the assured, but of the referee, and from the fact that the judgments lay stress on the duty of the assured to make full disclosure, it may be inferred that the court thought that the assured himself knew or ought to have known of the facts which were not disclosed. In *Rawlins v. Desborough*[53] the plea of the defendants, and the direction of Denman C.J. to the jury, proceed on the assumption that a wilfully false statement by the referee would vitiate the policy, but there is no discussion or actual decision upon the point.

18–19 Neither as to "life" or referee is there any conclusive authority to the effect that a policy is voidable on the ground of his false statement or

---

[46] *Maynard v. Rhodes* (1824) 5 Dow. & R. 266; *Everett v. Desborough* (1829) 5 Bing. 503; *Forbes v. Edinburgh Life* (1832) 10 S. 451. In practice, statements by the "life" are usually warranted.

[47] *Morrison v. Muspratt* (1827) 4 Bing. 60; *Huckman v. Fernie* (1838) 3 M. & W. 505.

[48] *Huckman v. Fernie* (1838) 3 M. & W. 505, where the insurance was effected by the husband on the life of his wife.

[49] *Kelling v. Pearl Ass. Co.* (1923) 129 L.T. 573.

[50] *Jones v. Pearl Ass. Co.* [1927] I.A.C. Rep. 42.

[51] *Rawls v. American Mutual Life*, 27 N.Y. 282 (1863).

[52] (1828) 8 B. & C. 586; 3 Man. & Ry. 45.

[53] (1840) 2 Moo. & Ry. 328.

non-disclosure. On general principle there is no foundation for such a rule, and what is submitted to be an accurate statement of the law is contained in the judgment of Lord Campbell C.J. in *Wheelton v. Hardisty*.[54] In that case the insurance was upon the life of another, and the insurers alleged that the "life" and medical and other referees had been guilty of fraudulent misrepresentations. In the proposal the assured declared his belief that the answers given by the "life" and medical referees were true. It was argued that the "life" and referees were the agents of the assured at least for the purpose of answering the questions put to them. The court held that the "life" and referees were not necessarily the agents of the assured, and in particular that they could not be held to be so when the assured was only asked to state his belief as to the truth of their answers. Lord Campbell C.J. said,[55] in reference to the previous authorities:

> "On behalf of the defendants it has been very powerfully argued, before us, that the person whose life is to be insured (as he is usually called, the 'life') and the referees are always to be considered, if not the agents of the assured to effect the policy, at least the agents of the assured in giving answers to all material questions which may be put to them respecting the matters as to which they may be properly interrogated. Although this doctrine has some sanction from language which has been used by judges, it seems to me to be contrary to principle; and the decisions cited in support of it admit of an explanation which leaves me at liberty to condemn it. A policy may, no doubt, be framed which shall make the assured liable for any material misrepresentation or concealment by the 'life' or the referees; but what we have to consider is whether when the policy contains no express condition for this purpose, and is made on a declaration by the assured that they believe the statements of the 'life' and the referees to be true, the 'life' and referees are still the agents of the assured in the manner contended for. In the first place, it seems rather strange if they are employed, not in any respect to negotiate or effect the insurance, but only to give information as to facts exclusively known to themselves, they should be denominated agents. It often happens that the assured have never seen the 'life' and are wholly unacquainted with the state of his health, and with his habits. But an agent is supposed to do what could be done by the principal were the principal present. A more serious objection arises from the consideration that this doctrine would entirely prevent a life policy from being a security upon which a man could safely rely as a provision for his family, however honestly and however prudently he may have acted when the policy was effected. But the assurer and assured being equally ignorant of material facts to influence their contract, if the assurer asks for information and the assured does his best to put the assurer in a situation to obtain the information and to form his own opinion as to whether the information is sincere, can it be permitted where the assurer, without any blame being imputable to the assured, has allowed himself to be deceived, that he shall be able to say to the assured: 'You warranted all the information I received to be true; and having received your premiums for many years now the "life" drops and I tell you I was incautious, and the policy I gave you is a nullity'?

---

[54] (1858) 8 E. & B. 232.
[55] (1858) 8 E. & B. 232, 268.

The *uberrima fides* is to be observed with respect to life insurances as well as marine insurances. The assured is always bound not only to make a true answer to the questions put to him, but spontaneously to disclose any fact exclusively within his knowledge which it is material for the assurer to know; and any fraud by an agent employed to effect the insurance is the fraud of the principal; but there is no analogy between the statements of the 'life' or the referees in the negotiation of a life insurance and the statements of an insurance broker to underwriters, by which he induces them to subscribe the policy."

The question in each case is whether the terms of the contract or the circumstances are such that the assured has made himself responsible for the information supplied by, or for the integrity of, the person to whom he has referred the company for information.[56]

18–20 Guarantee or fidelity policy. Where an insurance company issues a guarantee or fidelity policy it may be approached, not by the creditor or employer whom it insures but by the debtor or employee. The latter has to procure a policy in favour of the former as a condition of the credit or employment. In such cases the debtor or employee is not necessarily the agent of the creditor or employer for the purpose of effecting the insurance, and prima facie his fraud does not avoid the policy as against the creditor or employer.

18–21 In the unreported case of *Comptoire Nationale v. Law Car and General*[57] the plaintiffs, as bankers, had made advances to certain merchants, O Brothers, to enable them to fulfil a contract for the delivery of coal to the Danish Government. As a condition precedent to further advances the bank required security, and O, a member of the merchants' firm, said he would procure a policy. He procured a policy from the defendants, indemnifying the bank against loss consequent upon O Brothers failing to fulfil their contract with the Danish Government, and in the course of the negotiations made a false statement to the defendants' manager as to his financial position. Mr. Justice Bray held that the fraud of O did not affect the bank as O was not their agent for the purpose of making representations. He said:

"It was O's affair to get this policy. He wanted it in order that the advances might be continued. He could go to what insurance company he liked, provided the policy eventually turned out satisfactorily; it was quite immaterial to the plaintiffs what premium he gave or agreed to give, quite immaterial what the conditions were, provided the policy, when it was produced, was a satisfactory one, and therefore it seems to me that it would be entirely wrong to conclude from this that the

[56] *cf.* company prospectus cases where promoters put before the public the report of an expert which they believe to be true but which in fact is false and fraudulent: *Mair v. Rio Grande Rubber Estates Ltd* [1913] A.C. 853 and cases therein cited.
[57] Bray J. October 21, 1908; Court of Appeal, June 10, 1909. The editors have not been able to sight a transcript of the judgments in this case, but the present text first appeared in the 1st edition of this work, at p. 353, and is presumed to be accurate.

plaintiffs constituted O their agent. No authority was cited for that proposition except the case of *Wheelton v. Hardisty*, which really did not decide anything of the kind, but hinted that, under certain circumstances, a person who negotiated might be the agent of the person in whose favour the policy was eventually given, but it did not say under what circumstances, and no opinion was expressed at all and no authority, except that one was cited, and I know of none for that proposition. But there is a very familiar case that arises every day: A man is asked to lend money, and the proposed lender says: 'I must have a guarantee or security.' 'Very well,' says the intending borrower, 'I will try and get one,' and thereupon he may bring either the surety himself, or he may bring a document signed by the surety. Is the debtor or intending borrower the agent of the lender to make representations? Surely not."

This judgment was affirmed in the Court of Appeal. Vaughan Williams L.J. said:

"It is said that O was acting as agent for the bank. In my opinion there is nothing to justify such a finding of fact. The proper conclusion is that O, wanting to persuade the bank to render him financial assistance, and finding that he could not get it without security, he went on his own account to get such security as would be acceptable to the bank."

Fletcher Moulton L.J. said:

"It all turns on one point: was O agent or principal in negotiating the contract? If he had been agent he would have had authority to make the bank liable to pay the consideration, but it is clear that he had no such authority; he, as debtor, was bound to pay the premiums on the policy which he obtained."

And Buckley L.J. said: "I do not think he was agent any more than a lessee is who covenants to obtain an insurance in the name of the lessor."

This decision is authority for the proposition that when a borrower, lessee or employee procures an insurance company to issue a policy insuring his lender, lessor or employer, the company cannot avoid the policy on the ground of false statements made by him unless:

(1) on the facts of the particular case he was authorised to conclude the insurance on their behalf or
(2) the policy contains an express provision which entitled the company to do so.

(c) *Agent of Insurers*

18–22 Introduction. A misrepresentation or a concealment by the insurers' agent may take, broadly speaking, one of two forms. First the agent may, mistakenly or deliberately, misrepresent to the intending assured the benefits obtainable under the policy or the liabilities imposed by its terms, with the result that the assured is induced to enter into the contract of insurance by false or misleading information. In that case he may be entitled to avoid the contract[58] and recover his premium.[59] We are here concerned

---

[58] Ch. 16, paras. 16–3 to 16–9, *ante*; Ch. 36, paras 36–68 to 36–69, *post*.
[59] Para. 8–14, *ante*.

with the other situation in which the insurers' agent is wholly or partly responsible for the intending assured making a misstatement to, or concealing a fact from, the insurers themselves.

18–23 For instance, it may happen that the assured gives full and accurate information to the person acting as the insurers' agent to solicit and receive proposals for insurance, but the agent forgets to pass on something disclosed to him, so that the insurers later complain of non-disclosure by the assured. The agent may even deliberately misrepresent matters to the insurers in order to make the assured's proposal seem more attractive to them, in order to secure his commission on the completed contract. He may inadvertently misrepresent to the assured the meaning of a question in the proposal form, so that the assured gives an incorrect answer to it. It is in fact possible to envisage many ways in which an agent could cause an assured to be guilty of a non-disclosure or misrepresentation.

18–24 If the person acting on behalf of the insurers were to be seen, in law, as their agent in everything he did in dealing with the assured's application, no doubt the company would always have to bear responsibility for the kind of defaults which were given as examples above. The legal position is unfortunately more complex than that, because the rights of the assured and the insurers depend upon the actual or apparent authority of the agent and the particular circumstances in which knowledge of the true facts was acquired by him.

18–25 If the assured wishes to rescind the contract, the important question is whether the agent was acting inside his authority at the time. Thus, if the agent has actual or apparent or implied authority to explain questions in the proposal form, and misleads the applicant in so doing, then the applicant may claim rescission of the contract despite the fact that he may have warranted the accuracy of his own answers.[60] If, however, the insurers wish to avoid the contract on discovering the truth, and the assured wants to hold them to it, then the use of imputed knowledge comes into the picture. As a general rule the knowledge acquired by an agent in the course of his duties is imputed to his principal, so that the latter is estopped from denying that he knows the matters in question.[61] The assured, therefore, may claim that he gave accurate and complete information about the risk to the agent dealing with him on the part of the insurers, and, as the agent was in possession of the true facts, the insurers are in law estopped from alleging non-disclosure or saying that they were misled, and may be held to have waived the right to invoke a breach of warranty of which their agent was aware.

The law on this topic is undoubtedly complex, but we shall set out some guide lines before examining the effect of these rules in individual cases.

18–26 Conditions necessary to found estoppel. In order that the assured may claim the benefit of this rule the court must be satisfied that:

---

[60] *Newsholme Bros. v. Road Transport, etc., Ins. Co.* [1929] 2 K.B. 356, 364; *New York Life Ins. Co. v. Fletcher*, 117 U.S. 579 (1885); *McNally v. Phoenix Assurance Co.*, 137 N.Y. 389 (1893).
[61] In general see Bowstead & Reynolds, *Agency* (17th ed., 2001) Art. 97(1).

(i) The person acting as agent was in fact an agent of the insurers;
(ii) He acquired knowledge of the matters in dispute in the ordinary performance of his duties as an agent;
(iii) The agent was not acting for his own private ends in fraud of his principals.

18–27 An agent of the insurers. It is for the assured to prove that the person with whom he dealt in obtaining insurance was the agent of the insurers.[62] Thus, where insurance is obtained through a Lloyd's broker his knowledge is irrelevant, since he is not the agent of Lloyd's underwriters,[63] and where one agent acts for assured and insurers it will be for the assured to prove that at the material time he was the insurers' agent.[64]

18–28 Acquisition of knowledge in ordinary course of duty. This principle involves two quite separate issues. The first is an issue of the time at which the agent discovered the truth; the insurers are not to have imputed to them knowledge acquired by the agent otherwise than in his employment as their insurance agent.[65] Thus, if the assured is refused a renewal by Company A, and subsequently he denies to Company B that anyone has ever refused to renew his cover, he cannot rely upon the knowledge of B's agent to the contrary where that agent learned of the truth while acting as agent for Company A when the assured had a policy with them.[66] Secondly, the agent must have had authority to acquire the knowledge at the time he discovered the true facts and in the manner in which he learns of them. This requirement raises some problems when the assured has had the agent's assistance in filling up a proposal form wherein his answers are warranted true, and these are considered separately. So far as non-disclosure is concerned, quite apart from any untruth contained in the proposal form, there should be no difficulty in establishing authority—express or ostensible. Ostensible authority will be shown if, although the insurers have not given the particular agent authority to act as the medium for communicating to them facts disclosed by the assured, the impression reasonably received by the assured is that the person sent to him to obtain a proposal for insurance is the proper person to whom to disclose them.[67] The insurers are then estopped from denying his want of actual authority. The assured will therefore have discharged his duty of disclosure regardless of any forgetfulness or inadvertent mistake on the part of the agent subsequently, and that will ground a plea of knowledge on the part of the insurers,[68] or waiver if that is appropriate in the circumstances.[69]

[62] *Bancroft v. Heath* (1901) 6 Com.Cas. 137; *Tate v. Hyslop* (1885) 15 Q.B.D. 368. See para. 18–6, *ante.*
[63] *Rozanes v. Bowen* (1928) 32 Ll.L.R. 98.
[64] *Equitable Life Assurance Society v. General Accident Assurance Corp.* (1904) 12 S.L.T. 348; *Bancroft v. Heath* (1900) 5 Com.Cas. 110; affirmed 6 Com.Cas. 137.
[65] *Tate v. Hyslop* (1885) 15 Q.B.D. 368; *Wilkinson v. General Accident, etc.* [1967] 2 Lloyd's Rep. 182; *Holt v. S.E. Lancashire Ins. Co.* (1930) 35 Com.Cas. 281, 284; *Wells v. Smith* [1914] 3 K.B. 722.
[66] *Taylor v. Yorkshire Ins. Co.* [1913] 2 Ir.R. 1; *O'Keefe v. London and Edinburgh Ins. Co. Ltd* [1928] N.I. 85.
[67] Bowstead & Reynolds, *Agency* (17th ed., 2001), Art. 74.
[68] *Parsons v. Bignold* (1846) 15 L.J. Ch. 379; *Re Universal Non-Tariff Fire Insurance Co.* (1875) L.R. 19 Eq. 485, 495; *Chopra v. New Zealand Ins. Co.* (1967) 4 A.I.R. (Cal.) 35.
[69] *Ayrey v. British Legal and United Provident Ass. Co.* [1918] 1 K.B. 136; *Holdsworth v. L. & Y. Ins. Co.* (1907) 23 T.L.R. 521.

18–29 Agent defrauding his principals. If the agent deliberately fails to pass on a material fact disclosed to him by the assured, or deliberately inserts an erroneous answer in the application form, probably to obtain his commission on an accepted proposal, and his fraud on the insurers is established, then his knowledge of the true facts is not to be imputed to them.[70] If the assured defrauds the insurers, and the insurers' agent knows of this but fails to tell them, it is no answer for the assured to say that the insurers cannot complain because their agent ought to have warned them.[71]

18–30 The agent who completes the proposal form. The application of the principles concerning imputation of knowledge to the insurers becomes more complicated, however, when the agent fills up the proposal form for the applicant and either inadvertently writes erroneous answers in it contrary to what he is told, or discovers that the truth is otherwise than what he is told to write. The main difficulty concerns the authority of the agent to assist the proposer in this way, and the leading modern authority is the Court of Appeal decision in *Newsholme Bros v. Road Transport and General Insurance Co.*[72]

18–31 The *Newsholme* case came before the court on a case stated by an arbitrator. The assured (appellants) made a proposal to the (respondent) insurance company for a motorcar insurance on their motor bus. The proposal form was signed by a partner in the appellant firm but in fact the answers were filled in by an agent of the company. The answers were declared to be true and to be the basis of the contract. A policy was issued and the premium paid. An accident having occurred whereby the motor bus was damaged and some passengers were injured, the assured brought a claim on the policy. The insurance company, however, discovered that some of the answers in the proposal form were untrue, and they repudiated liability under the policy. The assured said that the agent had been told the true facts when filling up the form, and that the company accordingly had no defence.

18–32 The arbitrator found that the agent had been told the correct answers to put down on the form, and that it did not appear why he had not done so correctly. He also found that the duties of the agent were to canvass for insurances, to obtain duly completed and signed proposals, and to receive premiums, but that he had no authority to complete a proposal form himself. Rowlatt J. held that on these facts the breach of warranty nonetheless discharged the company's liability, and the Court of Appeal affirmed this decision. Scrutton L.J. said that, in writing down the answers given to him orally by the applicant for insurance, the agent could only have been acting as the agent or amanuensis of the applicant. He could not be the agent of the company because a man cannot contract with himself and, therefore, the person who fills up the proposal cannot be the agent, at that time, of the person to whom the proposal is made. Consequently any mistake or error in writing down the answers was not perpetrated by the agent in performance of any duty to the company, and, if the mistake was committed wilfully in order to earn his commission, there was an additional reason for

---

[70] *Newsholme Bros v. Road Transport and General Ins. Co.* [1929] 2 K.B. 356, 375; *Dunn v. Ocean Accident and Guarantee Corp.* (1933) 45 Ll.L.R. 276, 279; 47 Ll.L.R. 129; *Biggar v. Rock Life Ass. Co.* [1902] 1 K.B. 516, 525.
[71] *Wells v. Smith* [1914] 3 K.B. 722.
[72] [1929] 2 K.B. 356.

refusing to impute his knowledge to the insurance company since he would have been defrauding his principals. Greer L.J. agreed with this analysis[73] in a concurring judgment and Russell L.J. concurred briefly with both of the judgments delivered.

18–33 It will be observed, therefore, that the assured's attempt to impute the agent's knowledge to the company failed on at least two of the requirements stated above and possibly also on the third one. It must, however, be noted that the Court of Appeal was concerned with a case where the agent had a limited actual authority, there was no reason in the circumstances to imply a greater authority in law, and there were no printed terms in the proposal form making provision for the event of the agent committing an error in this manner. Had these facts been otherwise, the decision could have been different, and this must be borne in mind in the ensuing discussion of particular cases and authorities.

18–34 Misunderstanding the applicant. Assuming that, as was held by the Court of Appeal in the *Newsholme* case,[74] the agent completing the proposal form for the applicant is acting usually as the agent of the latter in so doing, it follows that, if the agent mishears the applicant or misunderstands a colloquial reply given to a question, the only relevant fact is the falsity of the written answer, and the applicant must take the responsibility for the agent's error.[75] It is submitted that the American authorities suggesting that the court ought to inquire what was the verbal reply given to the agent are inconsistent with English authority.[76]

18–35 Obvious mistakes. Similarly, if an agent makes an obvious error such as putting down "No" when the applicant said "Yes", or "fifty" when he said "sixty", then the applicant cannot be excused because although the company's agent made the mistake, he was acting on behalf of the applicant when he committed it.

18–36 Proposal form signed in blank or completed by agent from own knowledge. Another class of case is where an applicant gives an agent the necessary information and at the agent's request signs the proposal form in blank and leaves it to the agent to complete it. In so doing the agent is exceeding his authority in the usual case, and is acting as the applicant's agent,[77] as to render the applicant responsible for the proposal as completed.

---

[73] [1929] 2 K.B. 356, 382. This analysis has been approved or followed in *Dunn v. Ocean Accident and Guarantee Corp.* (1933) 45 Ll.L.R. 276, 279, *per* Avory J., and at (1933) 47 Ll.L.R. 129 by the CA; *Facer v. Vehicle and General Ins. Co.* [1965] 1 Lloyd's Rep. 113, 119 (sub-agent of insurers); *Le Blanc v. Co-operative Fire and Casualty Co.* (1964) 46 D.L.R. (2d) 79; *Stone v. Reliance Mutual Ins. Soc.* [1972] 1 Lloyd's Rep. 469, 474–475; *Winter v. Irish Life Ass.* [1955] 2 Lloyd's Rep. 274, 282.

[74] [1929] 2 K.B. 356.

[75] [1929] 2 K.B. 356, 364; *Parsons v. Bignold* (1846) 15 L.J.Ch. 379; *Paxman v. Union Assurance Soc.* (1923) 15 Ll.L.R. 206.

[76] They will be found in note 14 to para. 991 in the 5th ed. of this book.

[77] *Parsons v. Bignold* (1846) 15 L.J. Ch. 379 as interpreted in *Re. Universal Non-Tariff Fire Co.* (1875) L.R. 19 Eq. 485, 494–495; *Billington v. Provincial Ins. Co.* (1879) 3 S.C.R. 182. The Canadian courts have held that even where the agent of the insurers has authority to complete a proposal form for signature by the assured, the insurers may still rely upon incorrect answers inserted by the agent in a form signed in blank by the assured unless the agent told the assured that it was not necessary to check the form after completion—*Blanchette v. C.I.S.* [1973] S.C.R. 833; *Vrbanic v. London Life Ins. Co.* (1996) 25 O.R. (3rd) 710, 718–724 (C.A. Ont.)

If, however, the applicant on reading over the completed form afterwards, finds an error in it and tells the agent, it is the agent's duty to transmit the correction to the company, and the company will then be treated as having constructive knowledge of the true facts.[78]

18–37 Similarly, where an agent fills in the proposal form from his own knowledge, or from his own inquiries and investigations, and then procures the applicant's signature, he is not acting in the regular manner permitted by his authority. In *Biggar v. Rock Life Assurance Co.*,[79] a local agent solicited the assured to take out an accident policy. The assured, who appears unusually to have been at the same time a publican and also teetotal, was reluctant to do so, but was ultimately persuaded during a game of billiards with the agent and the company's inspector of agents. The agent filled up the proposal form himself, and the assured signed it without reading it or knowing its contents. Several of the answers written down by the agent were untrue and he acted either with gross negligence or fraudulently in order to secure his commission. The proposal contained the usual declaration that the statements therein were to be the basis of the contract, and the policy was expressed to be granted "on the express condition of the truthfulness of the statements contained in the proposal". A further condition read:

> "Any of the circumstances in relation to these conditions coming to the knowledge of any local agent shall not be notice to or . . . prejudicially affect the company."

18–38 Wright J. held that the policy was avoided and the assured could not recover on it. He did not rest his decision on the clause as to the knowledge of a local agent, but expressly found for the company on other grounds. The agent, he said, was not the company's agent to invent answers for the proposal, and must be taken as having been allowed to act in so doing as the agent of the applicant. Moreoever, the applicant was under a duty to the insurers to check the answers inserted by someone else in his name, and in signing the form he adopted them as they were stated on it. No knowledge was to be imputed to the company. This decision might have been explained on the ground of fraud or the presence of the condition as to the agent's knowledge, but the Court of Appeal in the *Newsholme*[80] case approved it on the broader ground that the agent was acting for the applicant in completing the proposal. It is also possible that, in this type of case, the agent will be unaware of the untruth of what he has written, and in that case, as Scrutton L.J. said in the *Newsholme* case, there is no knowledge on his part to be imputed to the company.[81]

18–39 Agent possessing wider authority. So far we have considered the situations in which the company's agent might commit errors in connection with the proposal form on the footing that his authority is restricted, as it was in the *Newsholme* case,[82] to obtaining completed forms from applicants and forwarding them to the company. The significance of his errors would be

---

[78] *Golding v. Royal London Auxiliary Inst. Co.* (1914) 30 T.L.R. 350.
[79] [1902] 1 K.B. 516.
[80] [1929] 2 K.B. 356.
[81] *ibid.*, at p. 364. *Paxman v. Union Ass. Soc.* (1923) 15 Ll.L.R. 206. *Marks v. First Federal Ins. Co.* (1963) 6 W.I.R. 185.
[82] [1929] 2 K.B. 356.

different if his authority were wider in fact,[83] or deemed to be wider by operation of law, and this possibility will now be considered.

18–40 Authority of general agent. If the agent has actual authority to give a receipt for premiums and issue a policy or temporary cover note which binds the insurance company, then he has authority to make a contract after considering all the facts material thereto, and in such a case any knowledge he may have of facts inconsistent with or contrary to those stated in the proposal form should be imputed to the insurers.[84] This is the distinction taken in the Canadian authorities concerning imputation of knowledge[85] and in some American state jurisdictions.[86]

18–41 Authority increased by law. In certain situations an agent whose authority is limited to obtaining completed proposal forms from an applicant may be held in law to have a wider authority, which will in turn be relevent to the imputation of his knowledge to the insurance company where this is in issue. Thus a court would probably be prepared to hold that such an agent had either implied or ostensible authority to explain the meaning of questions in the proposal form in order that an applicant would know how to answer them and possibly to put the answers when received into proper shape. Consequently if an agent, in explaining the meaning of a question, puts a wrong interpretation on it, the issue is whether the answer is true in relation to the question as explained. This applies more particularly to the case of questions put by a medical examiner who is directed to explain them,[87] but it would seem to apply equally to agents. If the agent has authority to negotiate and settle the terms of a proposal, he must, by necessary implication have some authority to explain the matter to the applicant.[88]

18–42 Proposer blind or illiterate. If the proposer for insurance is blind or illiterate, it is very probably the case that the agent has an implied authority to write in the answers and thereby become the company's medium of receiving knowledge of all facts relevant to the insurance, even if he cannot bind the company to accept the written proposal. Alternatively it could be said that the agent has ostensible authority to complete the form, since this would be a reasonable conclusion for the applicant to draw when the agent comes to him on behalf of the company. Thus the agent has been constituted an "agent to know"[89] and the insurers should then be bound by his knowledge of the true facts despite any warranty of the accuracy of the answers in the proposal form.

[83] *Stone v. Reliance Mutual Ins. Soc.* [1972] 1 Lloyd's Rep. 469.

[84] Suggested by Scrutton L.J. [1929] 2 K.B. 356, 373–374. In such a case the agent would possess ostensible authority to explain the questions: *Cie Equitable d'Assurances v. Gagne* (1965) 58 D.L.R. (2d) 56.

[85] *Westside Construction Co. v. Saskatchewan Government Insurance Office* (1959) 18 D.L.R. (2d) 285 and cases therein cited.

[86] *Rogers v. Atlantic Life*, 133 S.E. 215, 220 (S.C., 1926); *Arant v. Mutual Benefit Health and Accident*, 150 F.Supp. 82 (1957).

[87] *Joel v. Law Union and Crown Ins. Co.* [1908] 2 K.B. 863.

[88] *Newscastle Fire v. Macmorran* (1815) 3 Dow 255, 262; *Wheelton v. Hardisty* (1858) 8 E. & B. 232, 276; *Carollton Manufacturing Co. v. American Indemnity Co.*, 124 Fed.Rep. 25 (1904); *Compagnie Equitable d'Assurances v. Gagne* (1965) 58 D.L.R. (2d) 56, approving this passage in the 5th ed. of this work at para. 990.

[89] See *per* Lord Halsbury L.C. in (1887) 12 App.Cas. 531, 537.

18–43 The decision in *Bawden v. London, Edinburgh and Glasgow Life Insurance Co.*[90] ought, it is submitted, to be explained on one of these grounds. In that case the assured, who was illiterate and almost unable to read or write beyond signing his own name, had lost the sight of one eye by the time he applied for an accident policy. The proposal form was completed by the insurance company's agent in accordance with the answers dictated to him by the assured, and was signed by the assured. It contained a declaration that the assured was in good health and had no physical infirmity, and that the statements therein would be the basis of the contract. In the margin opposite this declaration there was a note: "If not strictly applicable any deviation must be given at back." The proposal contained no reference to the fact that the assured had only one good eye. During the currency of the policy the assured met with an accident through which he lost the sight of the good eye. The Court of Appeal held that he was entitled to receive the sum insured in the event of loss of sight of both eyes. It was agreed that the agent knew of the assured's infirmity and had forgotten to note it on the back of the proposal; there was no fraud.[91] No evidence was offered by the insurance company of any restrictions on the agent's authority, so it was "to be gathered from what he did.[92] Even if he could not contract on the company's behalf, he had authority to negotiate and settle the terms of the proposal, and, if he knew that he was making a contract with a one-eyed man, that knowledge must be imputed to the company. The breach of warranty was therefore waived by the issue of the policy.

18–44 For some years after it was decided the *Bawden* case[93] was interpreted as authority for the wide proposition that any knowledge on the part of the insurers' agent concerning inaccuracies in the proposal must be imputed to them.[94] This interpretation created serious difficulties with regard to the agent's authority to complete a proposal form, which were not discussed in the judgments, and the case was accordingly criticised by the Court of Apeal in *Newsholme Brothers v. Road Transport and General Insurance Co.*[95] Certain decisions reported before the *Newsholme* case cannot now be regarded as right,[96] but it is submitted that the actual decision in *Bawden's*[97] case was correct. Quite apart from general principles of implied or ostensible authority applicable to proposal forms submitted in the

[90] [1892] 2 Q.B. 534.
[91] As Scrutton L.J. said in *Wells v. Smith* [1914] 3 K.B. 722, 725, if the agent had written down that the assured had two good eyes, the decision would have been otherwise.
[92] [1892] 2 Q.B. 534, 539.
[93] [1892] 2 Q.B. 534.
[94] *e.g. Brewster v. National Life* (1892) 8 T.L.R. 648. See the comments of McCardie J. in *Paxman v. Union Ass. Co.* (1923) 15 Ll.L.R. 206, 207.
[95] [1929] 2 K.B. 356.
[96] The decisions in *Brewster v. National life* (1892) 8 T.L.R. 648 and *Thornton-Smith v. Motor Union Ins. Co.* (1913) 30 T.L.R. 139 cannot be supported in the light of the later authorities. In *Kaufmann v. British Surety Ins. Co.* (1929) 33 Ll.L.R. 315 and *Holdsworth v. L. & Y. Ins. Co.* (1907) 23 T.L.R. 521 there were express representations by the superior agents of the insurers themselves, which are sufficient to justify the decision reached. *Hough v. Guardian Fire and Life Ass. Co.* (1902) 18 T.L.R. 273 seems to be explicable on the ground of rectification or an undisclosed agency, though not in the way the court reached its decision. The Scottish courts took a narrow view of *Bawden's* case—*Yule v. Life and Health Assurance Association* (1904) 6 F. 437; *M'Millan v. Accident Ins. Co.* 1907 S.C. 484, and in the Irish case of *Taylor v. Yorkshire Ins. Co.* [1913] 2 Ir.R. 1. Palles C.B. confined the decision to the facts before the Court of Appeal.
[97] [1892] 2 Q.B. 534.

names of illiterate persons.[98] it appears, at least from the judgments of Kay and Lindley L.JJ.[99] that the company intended the agent to complete the particulars of infirmities on the back of the proposal form, so that he was authorised by them to obtain that information and pass it on to them. In so doing he would not be acting, therefore, as agent of the assured. This ground of distinction was first suggested by Palles C.B. in *Taylor v. Yorkshire Insurance Co.*[1] and has now been followed in *Stone v. Reliance Mutual Insurance Society*[2] by the Court of Appeal in England, though without express reference to the *Taylor* case.[3]

18–45 In a case before the High Court of Ontario,[4] the applicant for motor insurance, who was illiterate, had a wooden leg; he informed the agent of this, but in answer to the question, "will the automobile be operated by any person suffering from the loss of a foot or limb?" the agent wrote, "No". This error was inadvertent and not fraudulent, and the court held that the agent's knowledge could be imputed to the company. Where, also, an applicant was to the agent's knowledge illiterate and the agent wrote down an answer which was not justified by the statements made to him by the applicant, who then put his mark to the form without having it read over to him, the Industrial Assurance Commissioner for Northern Ireland held that the false answer could not be set up as a ground for repudiating liability for breach of warranty.[5] It is likely that the plea of *non est factum* is open to an illiterate applicant whose answers are filled up incorrectly, but if he does not request the agent to read them over to him, he will very probably be estopped by negligence on his own part.[6]

18–46 Policy conditions. The company can strengthen its position by inserting in the proposal form a notification that the agent filling up the proposal form is the agent of the applicant and not of the company.[7] This does not necessarily mean that he is the agent of the applicant for all purposes connected with the application for insurance, and, for example, it might still be the case that he was the company's agent to explain the questions in the form, so that, if he misled the applicant by an erroneous explanation, the company would bear responsibility for the mistake.[8] The company might further protect itself by inserting a condition that neither the knowledge of, nor statements made to, the agent shall bind the company

---

[98] See para. 18–42, *supra.*
[99] [1892] 2 Q.B. 534, 540–541.
[1] [1913] 2 Ir.R.1.
[2] [1972] 1 Lloyd's Rep. 469. Lord Denning M.R. relied additionally upon an implied representation by the agent who completed the proposal form that the answers were correct, so that it need not be checked (p. 475). The Canadian courts have treated this as essential to the decision—see note 77 to para. 18–36, *supra.*
[3] [1913] 2 Ir.R.1.
[4] *Lewis v. Northern* (1956) 4 D.L.R. (2d) 496.
[5] *Gibson v. Liverpool F.S.* [1933] 1 A.C.(N.I.) Rep. 44.
[6] *Gallie v. Lee* [1971] A.C. 1004. See also *Murphy v. Sun Life Assurance of Canada*, where it was suggested that the insurers must bear responsibility for incorrect answers in a claims form when obtained by an agent from an assured in a state of distress and shock—(1964) 44 D.L.R. (2d) 369, 371.
[7] *Facer v. Vehicle and General Ins. Co.* [1965] 1 Lloyd's Rep. 113.
[8] *Graham v. Ontario Mutual* (1887) 14 Ont.R. 358; *Naughter v. Ottawa Agricultural* (1878) 43 U.C.Q.B. 121.

unless embodied in writing in the proposal form.[9] Certain states in America, however, have statutory rules banning such clauses and providing that persons soliciting or procuring insurances are always to be deemed the agents of the company.[10]

18–47 Policy conditions. Recent authority has confirmed that the courts will recognise a clause whereby the parties to an insurance contract exclude the right of each party to avoid it on the ground of pre-contractual misrepresentation or non-disclosure by the other, so long as it is sufficiently clearly drafted to evince that intention.[11] The exclusion can in principle be for the benefit of one party alone, as in *HIH Casualty & General Ins. Co. v. Chase Manhattan Bank* [12] in which the Court of Appeal held that insurers could agree by a term in a specially negotiated film finance pecuniary loss insurance policy to exclude their remedies for misrepresentation and non-disclosure by their assured, fraudulent misstatement and non-disclosure apart. The court held, however, that it was competent for the parties to exclude the insurers' remedies for fraudulent mis-statements and non-disclosure by the agent of the assured, provided that the relevant clause made express reference to fraud and did not seek to cloak its true purpose in general terms, because "Fraud is a thing apart".[13] The clause in question was construed as failing to exclude remedies for fraud by the agent which would give the insurers a cause of action for the tort of deceit.

18–48 In theory, therefore, an insurer is entitled at common law to include a term in a policy which excludes the exercise by the assured of his remedies for all kinds of pre-contractual misrepresentation by the agent of the insurer. It may be doubted whether this would be realistic in practice. The clause would have to satisfy the requirement in section 3 of the Misrepresentation Act 1967 that any contractual term which restricts or excludes a remedy available to a contracting party by reason of a pre-contractual misrepresentation is of no effect unless it is shown by the party relying thereon to satisfy the requirement of reasonableness stated in section 11(1) of the Unfair Contract Terms Act 1977.[14] It is also likely that if the clause appeared in a consumer insurance policy it would fail the test of fairness imposed by the Unfair Terms in Consumer Contracts Regulations 1999 for causing a significant imbalance in the parties' rights and obligations, contrary to the requirement of good faith in consumer contracts.[15] At the extreme it is hard to conceive that a clause excluding the assured's remedy for fraud by the insurer's agent could be effective in the type of consumer insurance cases discussed earlier in this chapter. An earlier defender of consumer rights, the

---

[9] *Biggar v. Rock Life* [1902] 1 K.B. 516; *M'Millan v. Accident Ins. Co.* 1907 S.C. 484; *Bleakley v. Niagara District* (1869) 16 Grant 198; *Peck v. Agricultural Insurance* (1890) 19 Ont.R. 494; *New York Life v. Fletcher*, 117 U.S. 579 (1885); *Aetna Life v. Moore*, 231 U.S. 543 (1912); *Broad & Montague v. S.E. Lancashire Insurance Co.* (1931) 40 Ll.L.R. 328.

[10] For examples, see *National Union Fire v. Wanberg*, 260 U.S. 71 (1922); *Stipcich v. Metropolitan Life Insurance Co.*, 277 U.S. 311 (1928); *World Ins. Co. v. Bethea*, 93 So. 2d 624 (1957); also Alberta Insurance Act, R.S.A. 1955, c. 159, s.236.

[11] *Pan Atlantic Ins. Co. v. Pine Top Ins. Co.* [1993] 1 Lloyd's Rep. 496, 502; *Toomey v. Eagle Star Ins. Co.* [1995] 2 Lloyd's Rep. 88, 91. These were reinsurance cases.

[12] [2001] 2 Lloyd's Rep. 483. At the time of writing the decision is under appeal to the House of Lords.

[13] *ibid*. at pp. 503–504.

[14] *ibid*. at p. 503.

[15] Reg. 5(1).

Industrial Insurance Commissioner, came to the same conclusion on the simple ground that such a clause was "illegal". [16]

18–49 Onus of proof is on assured. Where the assured has signed a proposal or warranted the accuracy of a declaration the onus of proof is on him to establish that, despite formal appearances, he did not in fact give the answers written down and attributed to him. The proposal is itself prima facie evidence against him as to what he said to the agent.[17] This rule would not apply where an agent or medical referee is instructed by the insurers to explain the printed questions, because then the printed form cannot of itself constitute evidence that an untrue answer was given to a question contained in it.[18]

[16] *Yates v. Liverpool Victoria F.S.* [1926] I.A.C. Rep. 50.
[17] *Parsons v. Bignold* (1846) 15 L.J.Ch. 379.
[18] *Joel v. Law Union and Crown* [1908] 2 K.B. 863; *Murphy v. Sun Life Assurance Co. of Canada* (1964) 44 D.L.R. (2d) 369, 375.

CHAPTER 19

THE LOSS

1. CAUSATION

19–1   General rule. It is a fundamental rule of insurance law that the insurer is only liable for losses proximately caused by the peril covered by the policy. This rule is easily stated in general terms, but its application in particular cases has been hotly disputed. In so far as problems arise in connection with specific clauses they are considered in the appropriate chapter but it may also be helpful to attempt to formulate certain general principles.

A proximate cause is not the first, or the last[1] or the sole cause[2] of the loss; it is the dominant[3] or effective or operative cause.[4] The insurer is liable if such a cause is within the risks covered by the policy and is not liable if it is within the perils excepted.

19–2   Chain of events. The peril insured against need not be the actual instrument of destruction. For instance where fire causes an explosion[5] or causes a building to fall,[6] the damage caused by the explosion or fall is damage by fire. Similarly if a fire has begun and property is thrown into the sea or otherwise destroyed, that loss is proximately caused by the fire.[7]

If the loss or damage is the necessary consequence of the peril insured against under the existing physical conditions, there is, prima facie, damage

---

[1] *Yorkshire Dale S.S. Co. v. Minister of War Transport* [1942] A.C. 691; *Monarch Steamship Co. Ltd v. Karlshamns* [1949] A.C. 196, 227; *Boiler Inspection and Ins. Co. of Canada v. Sherwin-Williams Co. of Canada* [1951] A.C. 319.

[2] *Reischer v. Borwick* [1894] 2 Q.B. 548.

[3] *Leyland Shipping Co. v. Norwich Union Fire Ins. Society* [1918] A.C. 350; *Yorkshire Dale S.S. Co. v. Minister of War Transport* [1942] A.C. 691.

[4] *P. Samuel & Co. v. Dumas* [1924] A.C. 431; *Bovis Construction Co. v. Commercial Union Assce. Co.* [2001] 1 Lloyd's Rep. 416, 420. The test should be a commonplace one which would be adopted by the ordinary businessman, see *per* Lord Macmillan in *Yorkshire Dale S.S. Co. v. Minister of War Transport* [1942] A.C. 691, 702, *per* Roskill J. in *W. J. Lane v. Spratt* [1970] 2 Q.B. 480 and *per* Aikens J. in *Brownsville Holdings v. Adamjee Ins. Co.* [2000] 2 Lloyd's Rep. 458, 466.

[5] *Waters v. Merchants* (1837) 11 Peters 213; *Re Hooley Hill Rubber and Chemical Co. and the Royal Ins. Co. Ltd* [1920] 1 K.B. 257; *Shea and Foubert v. Halifax* (1957) 10 D.L.R. (2d) 664; (1958) 5 D.L.R. (2d) 667.

[6] *Johnston v. West of Scotland* (1828) 7 S. 52.

[7] *Symington & Co. v. Union Ins. Society of Canton Ltd* (1928) 34 Com.Cas. 23; 97 L.J.K.B. 646; *Stanley v. Western Ins. Co.* (1868) L.R. 3 Ex. 71, 74.

by that particular peril.[8] Similarly, if the peril is one of the causes in a chain of events leading naturally and in the ordinary course to loss or damage to the insured object, such loss or damage will be proximately caused by the peril.[9] Where, however, the loss or damage is very far removed from the particular peril, the assured cannot recover even if his loss could be said to be a necessary consequence of that peril.[10]

It is not, however, sufficient for the peril insured against to have facilitated the loss; it must have caused the loss. Thus if goods are stolen from a building during an air-raid, it is the theft and not the air-raid which is the proximate cause of their loss.[11]

19-3 New cause. Where a new cause independent of and subsequent to the peril insured against contributes to the loss, it is often difficult to say which cause is the proximate cause. If the peril insured against has merely given occasion for the operation of the independent cause, the insurer will not be liable for the loss.[12] Thus, if a gable left standing by a fire were afterwards blown down by a violent gale, the damage caused by the falling gable would not be damage by fire.[13] But if the subsequent peril operates concurrently with the peril insured against, both perils may be proximate causes of the loss[14] and the assured may thus be entitled to recover.[15] All that can be said is that it is difficult to extract from the cases any clear definition of what will amount to an independent cause.

Loss resulting from action taken in fear of a peril insured against before it begins to operate cannot be said to be proximately caused by that peril.[16] The voluntary act of the master of a ship putting into port to avoid risk of capture is not a loss by capture and seizure[17]; similarly a collision occurring between

---

[8] *Lawrence v. Aberdein* (1821) 5 B. & Ad. 107; *Montoya v. London Ass. Co.* (1851) 6 Exch. 451.

[9] *cf.* Welford and Otter-Barry, *Fire Insurance* (4th ed.) p. 258. *Reischer v. Borwick* [1894] 2 Q.B. 548.

[10] *Everett v. London Assurance* (1865) 19 C.B.(N.S.) 126; *Taylor v. Dunbar* (1869) L.R. 4 C.P. 206; *Bird v. St. Paul Fire & Marine* 120 N.E. 86, 88, *per* Cardozo J.

[11] *Winicofsky v. Army and Navy General Ins. Co.* (1919) 35 T.L.R. 283; *cf. Yorkshire Dale SS. Co. v. Minister of War Transport* [1942] A.C. 691.

[12] *De Vaux v. Salvador* (1836) 4 Ad. & E. 420; *Pink v. Fleming* (1890) 25 Q.B.D. 396; *Field SS. Co. v. Burr* [1899] 1 Q.B. 579; *Williams & Co. v. Canton Ins. Office Ltd* [1901] A.C. 462; *Mordy v. Jones* (1825) 4 B. & C. 394; *Scottish Marine v. Turner* (1853) 1 Macq. 334; *Philpott v. Swann* (1861) 11 C.B.(N.S.) 270; *Fooks v. Smith* [1924] 2 K.B. 508; *Adelaide SS. Co. v. R.* (1924) 93 L.J.K.B. 871.

[13] *Gaskarth v. Law Union Ins. Co.* (1876) Bunyon, Fire Insurance (7th ed., 1923) p. 163.

[14] *Reischer v. Borwick* [1894] 2 Q.B. 548, 550–551, *per* Lindley L.J.; *Board of Trade v. Hain SS. Co.* [1929] A.C. 534, 539, *per* Lord Buckmaster; *Ocean SS. Co. v. Liverpool and London War Risks Ass. Ltd* [1946] 1 K.B. 561, 575, *per* Scott L.J. The view that there can be two proximate causes has been criticised by Devlin J. in *Heskell v. Continental Express* [1950] 1 All E.R. 1033, 1048 and *West Wake Price & Co. v. Ching* [1957] 1 W.L.R. 45, 49 and (inferentially) by Lord Dunedin in *Leyland Shipping Co. v. Norwich Union Fire Ins. Society* [1918] A.C. 350, 363. In *Liverpool and London War Risks Ass. Ltd v. Ocean SS. Co.* [1948] A.C. 243 the point was argued (pp. 252, 253) but not decided. The Court of Appeal has, however, now accepted that there can be two proximate causes of loss, *Miss Jay Jay* [1987] 1 Lloyd's Rep. 32.

[15] See para. 19–5, *post.*

[16] *The Knight of St. Michael* [1898] P. 30; *Moore v. Evans* [1918] A.C. 185. But see para. 26–17, *post*, and the principle in marine insurance that the cost of salvage services incurred to save the ship from a peril insured against is treated as a loss caused by that peril—*Pyman S.S. Co. v. Admiralty Commrs.* [1919] 1 K.B. 49.

[17] *Becker, Gray & Co. v. London Ass. Cpn* [1918] A.C. 101.

ships in convoy due to lights being extinguished from fear of submarines, or a stranding due to zigzagging on an unaccustomed course under orders from a naval officer in charge of a convoy (there being no evidence that any enemy warship was in fact nearby) is not a consequence of warlike operations.[18]

19–4 Special provisions in policy. The rule can be displaced by clear words, thus insurers might be liable for loss "directly or indirectly",[19] caused, or loss caused "directly or jointly"[20] with some other cause. But the words "in consequence of"[21] or "originating from"[22] or "arising from"[23] will not prevent the operation of the rule.

The requirement of proximate cause can also be qualified, *e.g.* by providing that the cause must be accidental or external[24] or extraneous.[25] In *The Miss Jay Jay*[24] a yacht was insured against damage "directly caused by external accidental means" and was damaged in the course of a difficult Channel crossing. The Court of Appeal held that, on the judge's findings that the weather conditions were markedly worse than average and that such conditions had contributed to the damage, the damage had been caused by means which were both external and accidental.

19–5 Two effective causes. It often happens that the insured's loss is attributable to at least two causes each of which is a proximate cause in the sense that the loss would not have happened if only one of the causes had been operative. In *The Miss Jay Jay*,[24] for example, it was held that the damage was caused by the frequent and violent impacts of an adverse sea on a badly designed hull. The adverse sea was a peril insured against but the bad design of the hull was not. The Court of Appeal held there were two proximate causes and the assured could recover on the basis that it was sufficient if one of the causes was a peril insured. It is different, however, if there are two proximate causes of the loss, one of which is insured and the other of which is excluded. In *Wayne Tank and Pump Co. v. Employers' Liability Assurance Corporation*[26] a factory was destroyed by fire partly due to the negligence of the assured's servant (which was insured) and partly due to the unsuitable nature of plastic material used in the installation (which was expressly excepted under the policy). In this situation it was held that, since the insured had promised that the insurers would not be liable for loss caused by the excepted peril, the insured could not recover.

---

[18] *Britain S.S. Co. v. R.* [1921] 1 A.C. 99.

[19] *Coxe v. Employers' Liability Ins.* [1916] 2 K.B. 629; *American Tobacco v. Guardian Ass. Co.* (1925) 22 Ll.L.R. 37 *Oei v. Foster* [1982] 2 Lloyd's Rep. 170; *Grell-Taurel v. Caribbean Home Ins. Co.* [2000] Lloyd's Rep.I.R. 614.

[20] *Smith v. Accident Ins. Co.* (1870) L.R. 5 Ex. 302. A "direct" cause is a proximate cause *Martini Investments v. McGuin* [2000] 2 Lloyd's Rep. 313.

[21] *Ionides v. Universal Marine Ins. Co.* (1863) 14 C.B.(n.s.) 259; *Liverpool and London War Risks Ass. Ltd v. Ocean SS. Co.* [1948] A.C. 243.

[22] *Marsden v. City and County Ass. Co.* (1865) L.R. 1 C.P. 232.

[23] *Bell v. Lothiansure Ltd* 1993 S.L.T. 421. *Sed contra, G.I.O. v. Green & Lloyd* (1965) 114 C.L.R. 93; *Dunthorne v. Bentley* [1999] Lloyd's Rep.I.R. 560, in which it was said that "arising out of" was a wider phrase than "caused by", while retaining the requirement of some causal element.

[24] *Miss Jay Jay* [1987] 1 Lloyd's Rep. 32.

[25] *Linden Alimak v. British Engine Ins.* [1984] 1 Lloyd's Rep. 416, 423–425 where the absence of a retaining bolt in the structure of a crane was held not to be an extraneous cause.

[26] [1974] Q.B. 57. *Cory v. Burr* (1883) 8 App.Cas. 393, 400–401.

2. BURDEN OF PROOF

19–6 Generally on the assured. The burden of proving that the loss was caused by a peril insured against is on the assured.[27] It is not necessary for him to prove precisely how the casualty occurred, but he must show that the proximate cause falls within the perils insured against. For example, the assured will discharge his burden under an all risks policy if he can show that the loss occurred accidentally.[28]

19–7 Exceptions. Once the assured has proved that the loss was caused by the general peril insured against, it is for the insurer to bring himself within any exception in the policy on which he relies.[29] But it may be a difficult matter of construction to decide whether the contract of insurance affords a limited cover or a general cover subject to exceptions. If the policy gives only a limited cover it is still for the assured to bring himself within the terms of the policy. In *Hurst v. Evans*[30] jewellery was insured against "loss or damage arising from any cause whatever on land or water save and except . . . loss by theft or dishonesty committed by any servant . . . of the assured". The facts proved established a loss by theft and threw suspicion on a servant of the assured either as a wrongdoer or an accomplice. Lush J. held that the onus was on the assured to prove that the theft was not committed by any of his servants. This case has been severely criticised and some of the language used by the learned judge was undoubtedly too wide; it can be defended, if at all, only on the ground that it affords an extreme illustration of the principle stated above. Bailhache J. refused to follow the decision in *Munro Brice & Co. v. War Risks Association*,[31] in which he laid down certain general rules as to the onus of proof in insurance cases. Although the decision concerned a dispute as to whether a ship was lost from perils of the seas or in consequence of hostilities and war-like operations, the principles accepted by the judge are applicable to all classes of insurance:

1. The assured must prove that the loss or damage was caused by the operation of the general risk insured against;
2. If the general risk is qualified by the exception of specific risks, which but for the exception would fall within the general risk, and some part of the general risks is left unqualified, the burden is on the insurer to prove facts which bring the case within the exception relied on;
3. If there is a qualification of the general risk which covers its whole scope so that there is no unqualified risk left, the burden is on the

[27] *Austin v. Drewe* (1815) 4 Camp. 360; (1816) 6 Taunt. 436; *Everett v. London Ass. Co.* (1865) 19 C.B. (N.S.) 126; *Marsden v. City and County Ass. Co.* (1865) L.R. 1 C.P. 232.

[28] *British and Foreign Marine Ins. Co. v. Gaunt* [1921] 2 A.C. 41. But if the insured makes specific allegations in order to prove that the loss was accidental, he must make good those allegations, *Regina Fur Co. Ltd v. Bossom* [1958] 2 Lloyd's Rep. 425.

[29] *Hercules Ins. Co. v. Hunter* (1836) 14 S. 1137; *Gorman v. Hand-in-Hand Ins. Co.* (1877) Ir.R. 11 C.L. 224; *American Tobacco Co. Inc. v. Guardian Ass. Co.* (1925) 22 Ll.L.R. 37; *Greaves v. Drysdale* (1935) 53 Ll.L.Rep. 16; *Bond Air Services v. Hill* [1955] 2 Q.B. 417, 426.

[30] [1917] 1 K.B. 352.

[31] [1918] 2 K.B. 78; reversed on a different point [1920] 3 K.B. 94. The view of Bailhache J. was followed in *Greaves v. Drysdale* (1935) 53 Ll.L.R. 16; *cf.* also *Firestone Tyre and Rubber Co. v. Vokins & Co. Ltd* [1951] 1 Lloyd's Rep. 32 and *Eagle Star Ins. Co. v. Willey* [1956] 1 S.A.L.R. 330.

insured to prove facts which bring the case within the general risk as qualified[32];

4. Whether a qualification of the general risk is in the nature of an exception or a qualification of the whole risk is in every case a question of construction of the policy as a whole;

5. In construing a policy it must be borne in mind that a general risk with exceptions can generally be turned by an alteration of phraseology into a general risk with a qualification covering its whole scope.

One of the factors which clearly influenced Lush J. in *Hurst v. Evans*[33] was that in an all risks policy, unless the onus was on the assured, he would only have to prove a loss of the thing insured and it would then be for the insurer to show that it was occasioned by a peril which was not insured against. It is submitted, however, that the same rules apply to all risks policies as to ordinary contracts of insurance and that the onus will be on the assured to prove that the loss was accidental in the sense that it was occasioned by the intervention of something fortuitous which could be regarded as a casualty within the meaning of an insurance contract. It will then be for the insurer to prove that it was caused by an excepted peril.[34] It cannot, however, be too strongly emphasised that the prime duty of a court is to make up its mind how the loss occurred; the rules about burden of proof need only be resorted to when the evidence is insufficient for the court to make a decision.[35]

19–8 Wilful act of the assured. Since the burden of proving that the loss was caused by a peril insured against is always on the assured, it may sometimes be the case that, if the insurers raise the possibililty that the insured himself wilfully caused the loss, the assured will have to prove that he did not so cause the loss. Thus in an all risks policy the assured must prove that the loss was fortuitous and under an ordinary marine policy the assured must prove that the loss was caused by a peril of the sea.[36] If the insurer chooses to plead positively that the assured deliberately destroyed the property insured he will assume the burden of proving that assertion; but even if he fails to discharge that burden, the assured may nevertheless be unable to recover if he in his turn cannot prove that the property was lost by a peril insured against.[37]

If, however, there is no doubt that the peril insured against has operated to cause the loss, the burden of proof will be different. Thus if the assured sets fire to his own property insured under a fire policy, the assured can easily establish that there has been a loss by fire and the onus will then shift to the

---

[32] See, *e.g. Sohier v. Norwich Fire Ins. Co.*, 93 Mass. 336 (1865).

[33] [1917] 1 K.B. 352.

[34] *British and Foreign Marine Ins. Co. v. Gaunt* [1921] 2 A.C. 41. For consideration of the words "accident or casualty" see *London and Provincial Leather Processes Ltd v. Hudson* [1939] 2 K.B. 724 and *Webster v. General Accident Fire and Life Ass. Cpn* [1953] 1 Q.B. 520, and para. 27–11 below.

[35] *Cooper v. General Accident Fire and Life Ass. Cpn* [1922] 2 Ir.R. 38 and 214 (H.L.), where the rules laid down by Bailhache J. were accepted by the Court of Appeal for Ireland.

[36] *Rhesa Shipping Co. v. Edmunds* [1985] 1 W.L.R. 948.

[37] *Astrovlanis Compania Naviera SA. v. Linard* [1972] 2 Q.B. 611 and [1972] 2 Lloyd's Rep. 187; *Palamisto General Enterprises S.A. v. Ocean Marine Ins. Ltd* [1972] 2 Q.B. 625; *Lambhead Shipping Co. v. Jennings* [1994] 1 Lloyd's Rep. 624.

insurer to plead and prove that the fire was caused by the wilful act of the assured.[38]

19–9 Special provisions in policy. The burden of proof may, of course, be displaced by the express words of the policy itself[39] and the burden of proving any particular fact may by agreement be put on either party to the contract.[40]

3. AMOUNT OF LOSS PAYABLE[41]

(a) *General Rules*

19–10 Valued policy. If the insurance policy is a valued policy the amount recoverable by the assured is the agreed value[42]; this will benefit the insurer in cases where the loss is greater than the sum stated in the policy, but will benefit the assured if his actual loss is less than the agreed valuation.[43] The same principle applies to a partial loss, in which case it is necessary to calculate the amount of actual depreciation and express it as a fraction of the actual value. The insurer will then be liable to pay that fraction of the agreed value,[44] although it is arguable that he can limit his liability to the cost of re-instatement.[45] It is a question of construction whether a policy is a valued policy but the valuation need not be a precise figure if it is capable of being calculated.[46]

---

[38] *Slattery v. Mance* [1962] 1 Q.B. 676, 681; *The Alexion Hope* [1987] 1 Lloyd's Rep. 60, 67; [1988] 1 Lloyd's Rep. 311, 317. The standard of proof is not proof beyond a reasonable doubt. It is proof on the balance of probabilities that the assured wilfully caused the loss. There is a line of authority to the effect that the degree of probability varies with the degree of fraud or criminality alleged, amounting to "a standard falling not far short of the rigorous criminal standard"—*The Zinovia* [1984] 2 Lloyd's Rep. 264, 272. Those cases include *Grunther v. Federated Employers' Ins. Ass.* [1976] 2 Lloyd's Rep. 259; *S. & M. Carpets (London) Ltd v. Cornhill Ins. Co.* [1982] 1 Lloyd's Rep. 423; *Continental Illinois v. Alliance Ass. Co.* [1989] 1 Lloyd's Rep. 33; *Polivette v. Commercial Union Ass. Co.* [1987] 1 Lloyd's Rep. 379. This is an imprecise formulation, difficult to apply in practice. A better formulation is that the standard of proof required is the mere balance of probabilities but the gravity of the plea and implausibility of respectable persons (where appropriate) committing frauds are taken into account as weighting the balance in favour of the assured—*The Filiatra Legacy* [1991] 2 Lloyd's Rep. 337, 365–366; *The Ikarian Reefer* [1995] 1 Lloyd's Rep. 455, 459. See [1995] L.M.C.L.Q. 305.
[39] *Levy v. Assicurazioni Generali* [1940] A.C. 791; *Spinney's (1948) Ltd v. Royal Ins.* [1980] Lloyd's Rep. 406, 426; *Grell-Taurel v. Caribbean Home Ins. Co.* [2000] Lloyd's Rep.I.R. 614.
[40] *America Tobacco Cpn Inc. v. Guardian Ass. Co.* (1925) 22 Ll.L.R. 37; *Scottish Union and National Fire Ins. Co. v. Alfred Pawsey & Co., The Times,* October 17, 1908, P.C.
[41] See "Valuation and Measure of Recovery under Fire Insurance Policies," 49 Col.L.Rev. 818 (1949).
[42] *Feise v. Aguilar* (1811) 3 Taunt, 506; *Irving v. Manning* (1847) 6 C.B. 391; 1 H.L.Cas. 287; *Burnand v. Rodocanachi* (1882) 7 App.Cas. 333; *British Traders' Ins. Ltd v. Monson* (1964) 111 C.L.R. 86.
[43] *Maurice v. Goldsbrough, Mort & Co. Ltd* [1939] A.C. 452.
[44] *Elcock v. Thomson* [1949] 2 K.B. 755; *Compania Maritima Astra SA v. Archdale* [1954] 2 Lloyd's Rep. 95.
[45] *Elcock v. Thomson* [1949] 2 K.B. 755, 764, *per* Morris J., at any rate if the premises actually have been re-instated by the insured.
[46] *City Tailors Ltd v. Evans* (1921) 126 L.T. 439. It is unusual for a court to construe a non-marine policy as a valued policy—*Leppard v. Excess Ins. Co. Ltd* [1979] 1 W.L.R. 512.

19–11 Unvalued policy. If the policy contains no agreed valuation, the measure of indemnity is calculated with reference to the value at the date and place of the loss.[47] The value of the object insured may have increased during the currency of the policy and thus the assured may be able to recover more than he paid for it.[48] The policy may state the amount for which the object is insured but if it is not an agreed value policy this cannot bind the insurer, the only effect of such a statement is to fix the maximum amount for which the insurer can be held liable, and the assured will still have to prove the extent of his loss.[49]

19–12 Consequential loss. An insurance policy will prima facie cover only loss of or damage to the property insured and not consequential damage. Thus a simple insurance on property does not cover loss of rent, occupancy, business profits, wages of servants or workmen rendered idle or other consequential damages.[50] Any such loss can, however, be expressly insured and loss of rent and non-occupancy during repairs are very common subjects of insurance. Business profits may also be specially insured,[51] and owners of monopolies, such as patent rights, may insure against diminution of royalties consequent upon the premises of a licensee being destroyed by fire.[52] Similarly, no policy will be held to cover either a merely sentimental loss or a claim for personal hardship, stress, or inconvenience. It is usually said that such losses are too remote to be recoverable since they are not proximately caused by the peril insured against, but a better view is probably that on a true construction of the policies concerned, such losses are not provided for.[53]

19–13 Assessment of loss. If there is a total loss, the amount payable to the assured will be the value of the thing insured at the time of the loss, but if there has only been a partial loss, the correct measure of indemnity is the

---

[47] *Vance v. Forster* (1841) Ir.Circ.Rep. 47; *Chapman v. Pole* (1870) 22 L.T. 306; *Hercules Ins. Co. v. Hunter* (1836) 14 S. 1137 (Ct. of Sess.); *Rice v. Baxendale* (1861) 7 H. & N. 96 at p. 101, *per* Bramwell B. *arguendo*; *Richard Aubrey Film Productions Ltd v. Graham* [1960] 2 Lloyd's Rep. 101; *Leppard v. Excess Ins. Co. Ltd* [1979] 1 W.L.R. 512; *Quorum A/S v. Schramm* [2002] 1 Lloyd's Rep. 249.

[48] *Re Wilson and Scottish Ins. Cpn Ltd* [1920] 2 Ch. 28. Conversely it may well have depreciated—*Edney v. De Rougemont* (1927) 28 Ll.L.R. 215.

[49] *Vance v. Forster* (1841) Ir.Circ.Rep. 47, 50; *Curtis & Sons v. Mathews* (1918) 24 Com.Cas. 57, 67 (varied on appeal but only on the figures [1919] 1 K.B. 425); *Re Wilson and Scottish Insce. Corp. Ltd* [1920] 2 Ch. 28; *Glasgow Provident Investment Society v. Westminster Fire Office* (1887) 14 R. 947, 988, *per* Lord Young; *British Traders' Ins. Ltd v. Monson* (1964) 111 C.L.R. 86; *Quorum A/S v. Schramm* [2002] 1 Lloyd's Rep. 249.

[50] *Re Wright and Pole* (1834) 1 Ad. & El. 621; *sub. nom. Sun Fire Office v. Wright* 3 Nev. & M.K.B. 819; *Theobald v. Railway Passengers' Ass. Co.* (1854) 10 Exch. 45, 58, *per* Pollock C.B.; *Shelbourne & Co. v. Law Investment and Ins. Corp. Ltd* [1898] 2 Q.B. 626; *Maurice v. Goldsbrough, Mort & Co. Ltd* [1939] A.C. 452; *cf. Molinos de Arroz v. Mumford* (1900) 16 T.L.R. 469, where rice had deteriorated because the owner had been compelled to store it in wartime; *Menzies v. North British Insce. Co.* (1847) 9 D. 694; *Farmers' Mutual Ins. Co. v. New Holland Turnpike Co.*, 122 Pa. 37 (1888) (turnpike company held unable to recover for loss of tolls when bridge was destroyed by fire); *Leger v. Royal Ins. Co.* (1968) 70 D.L.R. (2d) 344; *Sprung v. Royal Ins. Co.* [1999] Lloyd's Rep.I.R. 111 (no claim for consequential loss when payment for loss under policy delayed.) See paras 19–70 to 19–71, *post*.

[51] *City Tailors Ltd v. Evans* (1921) 38 T.L.R. 230.

[52] *National Filtering Oil Co. v. Citizens Ins. Co.*, 106 N.Y. 535 (1887).

[53] *Re Egmont's Trusts* [1908] 1 Ch. 821, 826 *per* Warrington J.; *Richard Aubrey Film Productions Ltd v. Graham* [1960] 2 Lloyd's Rep. 101, 103 *per* Winn J.; *Ventouris v. Mountain (No. 3)* [1992] 2 Lloyd's Rep. 281, 293, followed in *Sprung v. Royal Ins. Co.* [1999] Lloyd's Rep.I.R. 111; *England v. Guardian Ins. Ltd.* [2000] Lloyd's Rep.I.R. 404, 422.

difference between the value of the damaged property before and after the loss.[54] The policy may make specific provision for the calculation of the loss and if, for example, the assured is expressly entitled to the cost of reinstatement, he is entitled to recover on that basis.[55]

19–14 Value of property before the loss. The undamaged value before the loss is to be taken at the market value immediately before the loss occurred.[56] Although the value taken in cases of marine insurance is the value at the commencement of the risk, this principle has not been extended to fire risks. The assured is not entitled to take the cost price or the cost of construction or manufacture as conclusive evidence of the value of the property at the time of the fire.[57] It may be prima facie evidence but it must be remembered that:

(1) the assured may have paid more than its value;
(2) the market value may have fallen since the time of purchase;
(3) wear and tear or damage different from that insured against may have depreciated the value of the particular property.

Conversely, the property may have risen in value and the assured is entitled to the benefit of the rise[58] subject, however, to any express or implied condition that the property is insured only for the value as declared by the assured either in the proposal or elsewhere.

In *Carreras Ltd v. Cunard Steamship Co.*[59] the plaintiffs, who imported paper goods for the manufacture of cigarettes, made an agreement with the defendants whereby the defendants undertook to warehouse the goods arriving on their ships at a rental of 4d. per cubic ton per week, to include insurance against loss or damage by fire. When the goods arrived, the plaintiffs used to hand to the defendants the customs entries on which was stated the cost price of the goods in London at the date of their arrival. Some of the plaintiffs goods were damaged by fire; the value of these goods was £1,125 according to the customs entries but the plaintiffs alleged that at the time of the fire they were in fact worth £1,968. It was held by Bailhache J. that the defendants were liable solely for the value as shown in the customs entries. Whether the defendants insured the contents of their warehouse by means of a floating policy on goods (as in fact they had done) or were their own insurers, they were entitled to know the maximum sum for which they were liable. As the figures in the customs entries were the only available

---

[54] *Westminster Fire Office v. Glasgow Provident Investment Society* (1888) 13 App.Cas. 699; *Grant v. Aetna Fire Ins. Co.* (1860) 11 Low.Can.R. 128. In many cases the measure of indemnity will be equivalent to the cost of re-instatement but by no means necessarily so; *cf. Pitman v. Universal Marine Ins. Co.* (1882) 9 Q.B.D. 192; *Jackson v. Canada Accident and Fire Ins. Co.* (1924) 52 N.B.R. 33, and para. 19–16 below.

[55] *McLean Enterprises v. Ecclesiastical Ins. Office* [1986] 2 Lloyd's Rep. 416.

[56] *Leppard v. Excess Ins. Co. Ltd* [1979] 1 W.L.R. 512 and cases cited in note 47, *supra*; *Equitable Fire Ins. Co. v. Quinn* (1861) 11 Low.Can.R. 170. In some cases the market value of the assured's interest may not afford a true indemnity, especially where the assured has a limited interest in real property, *Castellain v. Preston* (1883) 11 Q.B.D. 380, 400, 401, *per* Bowen L.J. In such cases the assured is still entitled to a full indemnity, *cf. Westminster Fire Office v. Glasgow Provident Investment Society* (1888) 13 App.Cas. 699, 713, *per* Lord Selborne.

[57] *Richard Aubrey Film Productions Ltd v. Graham* [1960] 2 Lloyd's Rep. 101; *Equitable Fire Ins. Co. v. Quinn* (1861) 11 Low.Can.R. 170.

[58] *Re Wilson and Scottish Ins. Cpn* [1920] 2 Ch. 28.

[59] [1918] 1 K.B. 118.

information as to the value of the goods, they must be deemed to be the
declared value for insurance purposes.

19–15 The market value of a parcel of whisky in bonded store has been
held to include an amount of unpaid government tax for which the assured
remained liable[60]; but a merchant or shopkeeper who insures his stock
cannot recover the retail value of the stock because he would thereby be
recovering the loss of profits on his retail business and more than the actual
damage to the property.[61] For the same reason, where wool brokers had
insured wool entrusted to them for sale and had recovered the value under
the policy, the Privy Council prevented them from deducting from sums due
to their principals anything for commission which they would have earned
on the sale of the wool.[62]

A problem which has been much discussed is that of a fire in which a large
quantity of a scarce commodity is consumed and the market price thereby
greatly enhanced.[63] If the assured only receives the value of the goods
immediately before the fire, he cannot restock his premises without great
additional expense. But this expense is only incurred so that he may not lose
his profits, and if there was no specific insurance on profits it seems clear that
he can only recover the value of the goods according to the market price
immediately before the fire. In *Saunders (P.H.) & Co. v. Phoenix Assce Co.
Ltd*[64] goods were insured which were imported into New Zealand from
Great Britain and Germany; the sale price was limited by statutory order to
the landed cost plus a percentage profit. At the time of the loss there had
been a substantial rise in the price of similar goods in Great Britain and
Germany and the landed cost and sale price had increased in proportion but
it was held that the assured could recover only the original cost and not the
cost of replacement at the date of the fire.

If there is no market for the property before the loss, the value will have to
be measured in some other way. If the insurer relies on a market, he must
prove its existence and, if he fails, a court will probably award the insured the
cost of repair or replacement up to the amount of the sum insured.[65]

19–16 Value of property after loss. It is often difficult to decide the
appropriate value of the property after loss. The rival views are usually:

(a) the market value of the property in its damaged condition or
(b) the value of the property before the loss minus the cost of repair (with
or without an allowance for betterment).

The insured will often wish to contend for the second alternative because the
sum payable will usually be greater and he will thus have a greater possibility
of restoring his property to its original use. For this reason courts tend to lean
in favour of calculating the value of property after loss by reference to the
cost of repair rather than the market value as damaged.[66] This tendency is,

---

[60] *Hedger v. Union Ins. Co.*, 17 Fed.Rep. 498 (1883); *cf. Wolfe v. Howard Ins. Co.*, 7 N.Y. 583
(1853).
[61] *Fisher v. Crescent Ins. Co.*, 33 Fed.Rep. 544 (1887).
[62] *Maurice v. Goldsbrough, Mort & Co.* [1939] A.C. 452.
[63] Bunyon, *Fire Insurance* (3rd ed.), p. 156.
[64] [1953] N.Z.L.R. 598.
[65] *Carrick Furniture House Ltd v. General Accident Fire and Life Ass.* 1977 S.C. 308.
[66] *Pleasurama v. Sun Alliance* [1979] 1 Lloyd's Rep. 389, 393, *per* Parker J.

however, by no means invariable and if the insured does not have a sufficient interest in the property to be able to demand that the owner should repair it or if the insured does not, in fact, intend to repair the property or if he never intended to use the property himself but was at the time of the loss prepared to sell it for an ascertainable price,[67] the cost of repair may not be representative of his actual loss. In such cases it would be appropriate to take the actual saleable value of the damaged property.[68]

19–17 Difficulties will arise if the cost of repair is greater than the value of the property before loss or greater than the cost of replacement. In such cases courts will usually only allow the cost of repair if (a) the insured genuinely intends to repair and (b) such a course is not eccentric or absurd. In *Reynolds v. Phoenix Assurance Co.*[69] the plaintiff acquired some old maltings in Suffolk for the storage and milling of grain and insured them for £550,000. There was a serious fire in November 1973 which destroyed about seven-tenths of the buildings. The cost of reinstatement was held to be £246,583 but the money required to buy and erect a suitable building of modern steel and asbestos construction together with the land on which to erect it was no more than £50,000. Forbes J. held that the plaintiff genuinely intended to repair if he got sufficient money for the purpose and that, although a sensible commercial concern might well not choose to reinstate if using its own money, the plaintiff's intention was not a mere eccentricity but arose from the fact that he would not be properly indemnified unless he was given the means to reinstate the buildings substantially as they were before the fire.

19–18 Betterment. If an old house or an old article is destroyed or damaged and the assured replaces or repairs, he may end up with a house or article which is considerably better than the old and the question arises whether he should make any allowance to the insurers to the extent that he is better off after the loss than before. The conventional view is that such allowance should be made and in marine insurance custom has fixed an allowance of one-third "new for old" which is said to be deductible.[70] No such fixed allowance exists in non-marine insurance but an allowance is generally made to ensure that the assured does not make a profit out of his contract of insurance.[71]

This can work hardship on the assured and it is submitted that in cases where the assured has no practicable alternative to repairing real property that has been damaged (as opposed to replacing property that has been lost), it may in some circumstances be appropriate to allow the full cost of reinstatement subject always to the limit of the total sum insured in the policy. It is now clear that a tortfeasor who destroys real property is

---

[67] *Leppard v. Excess Ins. Co. Ltd* [1979] 1 W.L.R. 512.

[68] As in *Glad Tidings v. Wellington Fire Ins. Co.* (1964) 46 D.L.R. (2d) 475 where repair was prohibited by local bye-laws.

[69] [1978] 2 Lloyd's Rep. 440. If no claim is made for the cost of repair as such, it will usually be appropriate to award the cost of replacement *Exchange Theatre v. Iron Trades Mutual* [1983] 1 Lloyd's Rep. 674, reversed on other points [1984] 2 Lloyd's Rep. 169.

[70] *Pitman v. Universal Marine Ins. Co.* (1882) 9 Q.B.D. 192 and s.69(1) of Marine Insurance Act 1906.

[71] *Vance v. Forster* (1841) Ir.Circ.Rep. 47; *Hercules Ins. v. Hunter* (1836) 14S. (Ct. Sess.) 1137, 1141; *Brinley v. National Ins. Co.*, 52 Mass. 195 (1864); *Reynolds and Anderson v. Phoenix Ins. Co.* [1978] 2 Lloyd's Rep. 440.

ordinarily liable for the full replacement value,[72] and it could, therefore, be argued that the insurer of real property should afford a similar indemnity. It has to be recognised, however, that there is as yet no authority for such a proposition and Forbes J. has said that the principle of betterment is too well established in the law of insurance to be departed from even though it may sometimes work hardship on the assured who has not insured on a replacement cost basis.[73]

19–19 Sum recoverable. Where it is appropriate to calculate the damaged value by reference to the cost of repair or reinstatement, the appropriate figure may be reached by deducting the cost of repair from the repaired value. The sum payable by the insurers is then calculated by taking the difference between the undamaged value and the damaged value, and this calculation automatically gives allowance for betterment.

	£	£
Undamaged value..........................		100
Repaired value	110	
Cost of repair................................	70	
Damaged value		40
Amount recoverable		60

or in a case where the repaired value is less than the undamaged value:

	£	£
Undamaged value..........................		100
Repaired value	90	
Cost of repair................................	70	
Damaged value		20
Amount recoverable		80

The same result is achieved by taking the cost of repair or reinstatement and deducting from or adding to that the difference between the repaired value and the undamaged value.[74]

19–20 Reinstatement clauses. Sometimes the insurers will expressly promise to pay the cost of reinstatement of property destroyed or damaged and clauses to this effect are now comparatively common in real property insurance.[75] They can, however, give rise to difficulty because it is commonly

---

[72] *Harbutt's Plasticine v. Wayne Tank and Pump Co. Ltd* [1970] 1 Q.B. 447; *Dominion Mosaics Co. v. Trafalgar Trucking Co.* [1990] 2 All E.R. 246.

[73] [1978] 2 Lloyd's Rep. 440, 453. The principle of betterment was upheld in *Fire & All Risks Ins. Co. v. Rousianos* (1989) 19 N.S.W.L.R. 57 by the New South Wales Court of Appeal, followed in *Vintix v. Lumley General Ins. LH* (1991) 24 N.S.W.L.R. 627, 636–637, refusing to follow the English decisions in tort law.

[74] *Vance v. Forster* (1841) Ir.Circ.R. 47; *cf. Canada National Fire Ins. Co. v. Colonsay Hotel* [1923] 3 D.L.R. 1001; *Walker v. Co-operative Co.* (1966) 58 D.L.R. (2d) 10 where the above approach was adopted. If the repaired value is less than the undamaged value, then the difference must, of course, be added to, not deducted from, the cost of repair.

[75] *McLean Enterprises v. Ecclesiastical Ins. Office* [1986] 2 Lloyds Rep. 416, where the policy was, after some hesitation, construed to mean that the cost of reinstatement was to be the measure of indemnity; *Lonsdale Thompson v. Black Arrow Group* [1993] Ch. 361, 365.

provided that the work of reinstatement must be commenced and carried out with reasonable despatch and that no payment (or no payment beyond what would otherwise be payable) is to be made until the cost of reinstatement has been actually incurred. It has been held in the United States of America that these clauses must be interpreted according to their terms.[76] but it is rather hard that an insured, who needs the money with which to repair his property, should be expected to incur the cost of reinstatement from his own funds. This is particularly so, if the insurers, in breach of contract, deny liability under the policy or assert that the insured should be compensated on a basis other than that of reinstatement. It is, therefore, submitted that the requirement that the insured should commence and carry out the work of reinstatement with reasonable despatch should only operate if the insurers in accordance with their contractual obligations, accept that reinstatement is the appropriate measure of indemnity.[77] In *McLean Enterprises v. Ecclesiastical Insurance Co.*[78] Staughton J. declined to decide this point. In that case the assured had agreed before the fire to sell the property insured, subject to contract and, although the sale went off, he did in fact sell after the fire to another purchaser for a much lesser amount. The judge held that, because the assured had a settled intention to sell, he would not have reinstated the premises even if he had had the necessary resources or the insurers had paid the claim promptly. The absence of any intention to reinstate was fatal to the argument that it was only the insurers' breach of contract which rendered the assured unable to reinstate.

19–21 Loss of value due to severance may be taken into account in estimating the damaged value of the property. Thus a site and a building may together be worth more than the cost of the bare site plus the cost of constructing the building. Where the building is burned, the loss is the difference in the market value of the site and premises before the fire and the site and premises after the fire; if part of that loss is the depreciation in the value of the site, that may be recovered on a policy which purports to insure the building.[79] Similarly where an assortment of goods is insured, and certain of the goods are lost, the assured should, it is submitted, be entitled to recover for any consequent loss of value of the remaining goods.[80]

(b) *Particular Cases*

19–22 Salvage. Where the insured property is totally destroyed and cannot be repaired and the debris is of no value whatever, the assured is entitled to a cash payment of the full value of the property.[81] In cases of

---

[76] *Bourazak v. North River Ins. Co.*, 379 Fed. 2d. 530 (1967); *Higgins v. Ins. Co. of North America*, 469 Pac. 2d. 766 (1970).

[77] *Carlyle v. Elite Ins. Co.* (1984) 56 B.C.L.R. 331.

[78] [1986] 2 Lloyd's Rep. 416.

[79] *Westminster Fire Office v. Glasgow Provident Investment Society* (1888) 13 App.Cas. 699, 711–712, *per* Earl of Selborne; in the same case Lord Watson expressed the view (p. 704, *arguendo*) that if two houses, side by side, were insured in one policy by the owner of both and one was burned down, part of the insured recoverable loss was the depreciation in the value of the adjoining house. This could hardly be the case if only the destroyed building was insured.

[80] This should follow from the statement of Lord Watson referred to in the above note, but it is contrary to the opinion of Lord Young in the same case in the Court of Session; *Glasgow Provident Investment Society v. Westminster Fire Office* (1887) 14 R. 947, 989.

[81] *Monteleone v. Royal Ins. Co.*, 47 La.Ann. 1563 (1895).

marine insurance where the cost of repairs will exceed the repaired value, the doctrine of constructive total loss comes into play whereby the assured is entitled to give notice of abandonment and underwriters are bound to pay the full value as for a total loss, but are entitled to the damaged property as salvage.[82] There is no such doctrine in non-marine insurance law and the assured is, strictly speaking, only entitled to the difference between the value of the undamaged property and the value of what remains.[83] In practice, however, insurers often pay as for a total loss on goods which are seriously damaged and when they do so they are entitled to the damaged goods as salvage, or their value.[84] Similarly if they pay a total loss on real property, they are entitled to anything which may be realised or realisable from the ruins. Sometimes a policy contains a specific clause to the effect that before a claim is adjusted, the insurers may take possession and have power to sell the property insured; if in such a case the insurers do take possession, they will probably be estopped from thereafter saying that they are not liable to the insured.[85]

19–23 Insurers' right to inspect. After a fire the insurers should be afforded all reasonable opportunity of entering and inspecting the premises in order to ascertain the extent of the damage or the value of the salvage. The right to enter the assured's premises is sometimes made a condition of the policy but in the absence of any express condition, such a right will probably be implied as flowing from the nature of the contract and the custom of the insurance business.[86] If the insurers remain longer than reasonably necessary for the purpose of investigating the damage, they run the risk of an action for trespass and in *Cumberland v. The Albert Insurance Co.*[87] the judge in the Mayor's Court awarded damages on the grounds that the insurers had kept possession for two months and entirely stopped the plaintiff's business. Moreover, it has been held by the Privy Council that the extent of the damage flowing from the peril insured against must, subject to the principles of remoteness, be assessed as at the time when the insurance company gives back possession and not at the time of the cessation of the peril.[88] When the property damaged is inspected by the insurers, the assured should be given an opportunity of being present.[89]

When the property is not in the control or possession of the assured, there can presumably be no implied condition that the insurers shall have access to the premises and probably any express condition in the policy would be held inapplicable.

19–24 Statutory rights of salvage corps. Under the Metropolitan Fire

[82] See Arnould, *Marine Insurance*, (16th ed., 1981), Ch. 29.
[83] *Hough v. People's Fire Ins. Co.*, 36 Md. 398 (1872).
[84] *Skipper v. Grant* (1861) 10 C.B.(N.S.) 237; *Rankin v. Potter* (1873) L.R. 6 H.L. 83, 118; *Roux v. Salvador* (1836) 3 Bing.N.C. 266, 288; *Oldfield v. Price* (1860) 2 F. & F. 80; *Kaltenbach v. Mackenzie* (1878) 3 C.P.D. 467, 470–471, per Brett J.; *Dane v. Mortgage Ins. Cpn* [1894] 1 Q.B. 54, 61, per Lord Esher M.R.; *Holmes v. Payne* [1930] 2 K.B. 301. The insurer cannot both claim salvage and disclaim liability for any excess, *Mueller v. Western Union Ass. Co.* [1974] 5 W.W.R. 530, decided on the wording of the relevant Alberta statute.
[85] *Yorkshire Ins. Co. v. Craine* [1922] 2 A.C. 541.
[86] *Oldfield v. Price* (1860) 2 F. & F. 80.
[87] Ins. Rec., May 11, 1866, cited in Bunyon, *Fire Insurance* (7th ed., 1923), p. 184.
[88] *Ahmedbhoy Habbibhoy v. Bombay Fire and Marine Ins. Co.* (1912) L.R. 40 Ind.App. 10; 29 T.L.R. 96.
[89] *Masters v. Le fevre*, Bunyon, *op. cit.*, p.184.

Brigade Act 1865[90] the insurers may, through the salvage corps, have a greater right of entry and possession than they would have under the contract of insurance. The fire brigade has statutory power to enter and take possession of any property within the metropolis for the purpose of extinguishing fires, and by section 29 it is provided that if the insurance companies or a sufficient number of them establish a salvage corps, the fire brigade shall, without charge, render such salvage corps all necessary assistance, and hand over to its custody the property salved. The salvage corps has therefore a statutory right to the custody of the salvage, not only against the assured but against all others. No doubt this right must be deemed to be restricted so as to give it custody for such time only as is reasonably necessary for the purpose of ascertaining the damage done, and realising the salvage, if the insurers have become entitled to it, but, during the time the salvage corps has the custody, the right of the assured or other owner or occupier to the possession or control of the property must be in abeyance.

19–25 Claims against third parties. The amount recoverable by the assured must be assessed without any deduction in respect of claims which the assured may have against others in respect of the loss. Thus, even if the assured has entered into a binding contract of sale when the property insured is destroyed, he can recover the full amount of the loss irrespective of the claim which he has against the purchaser.[91] When the insurer has paid the loss, he is subrogated to the benefit of all rights which have accrued or may in future accrue to the assured in diminution or extinction of the loss so that, if the assured has realised claims or received benefits in diminution of his loss before he brings any action against the insurer, such sums must be brought into account when calculating any sum due from insurers.[92]

19–26 Reinstatement by third party. The question has been raised whether the assured is entitled to recover the insurance money if, before action brought, some third person has reinstated the premises, for example, where a mortgagee has insured on his own interest and the mortgagor or his insurers have reinstated the premises. In *Westminster Life and Fire Office v. Glasgow Provident Investment Society*[93] it was said that if the first incumbrancer had reinstated the premises the second incumbrancer would have suffered no loss, but it is doubtful whether this is strictly accurate. It is submitted that the right of action by the second incumbrancer against his insurers accrued when the premises were burned, that the insurers were bound to pay the damage to the extent of their assured's debt, and that the benefit arising from the reinstatement of the premises, whether reinstated before or after action brought, would be a matter for subrogation, the insurers being entitled, if the insurance was for the benefit of the incumbrancer alone, to an assignment of the debt and transfer of the security, including therein the benefit of the reinstatement.[94] It has been decided in America[95] that a mortgagee is entitled to recover from his insurer,

---

[90] s.29. This section is not repealed by the Fire Services Act 1947.
[91] *Collingridge v. Royal Exchange Ass. Cpn* (1877) 3 Q.B.D. 173.
[92] *British Traders' Ins. Co. v. Monson* (1964) 111 C.L.R. 86. See Ch. 22, *post*, for subrogation generally.
[93] (1888) 13 App.Cas. 699 at p. 712, *per* Earl of Selborne.
[94] *cf. Naumann v. Ford* (1985) 275 E.G. 542, a case between tenant and landlord.
[95] *Foster v. Equitable, Mutual Fire, Ins. Co.*, 68 Mass. 216 (1854).

notwithstanding that the owner of the equity of redemption has reinstated the premises, whereas in Canada[96] there is an opinion to the opposite effect. It is submitted that the American decision is correct.

19–27 Indemnity limited by insurable interest. Problems may arise where the assured has a limited interest in the property insured. It is well established that a person with a limited interest may insure the full value of the property on behalf of himself and other persons interested; in such a case he can recover the full value from the insurer and will be accountable for all sums over and above the value of his interest to those on whose behalf he took out the insurance. Likewise it is settled that some classes of insured persons, such as bailees, have an insurable interest in the full value of goods even though they are not the owners of them. If a bailee intends to insure the full value of goods, he can recover the full value from the insurer and is then accountable to the owner.[97] For this purpose it is not necessary for a bailee or other assured with a limited interest to contract on behalf of those with other interests in the subject-matter of the insurance. It is sufficient that the law will require the assured to account to such persons or requires that the insurance proceeds be expended for their benefit. In *Lonsdale v. Black Arrow Group plc*[98] the defendant landlords leased warehouse premises to the plaintiff and undertook to insure the premises at the plaintiff tenant's cost. They further undertook to apply any insurance proceeds to reinstating the premises. They then contracted to sell the premises, subject to the plaintiffs' lease. Between contract and conveyance, the warehouse was destroyed by fire but the defendants received the agreed price on the due date for completion. The insurers claimed that they were not liable to the landlords since the landlords had only a limited interest and had been paid in full for that limited interest when they received the purchase price. The landlords, who were the only contracting party, had thus received a full indemnity. Deputy Judge Sumption Q.C. held, however, that the landlords had an insurable interest up to the full reinstatement value of the premises and that they could recover that value from the insurers, even though the landlords had no general obligation to reinstate under the lease but only an obligation to lay out in reinstatement any proceeds of insurance which they actually received from insurers. But if a person with a limited interest expressly insures his own interest only, he cannot recover from the insurer any more than the value of his interest at the time of the loss.[99] If the principles set out in the earlier part of this chapter apply, it would be said that the assured is entitled to recover the depreciation in the market value of his interest, calculated by reference to the market value before and after the loss. This is straightforward if the insured is, for example, a mortgagee since his interest has an obvious correlation with the amount of the debt which he is owed. But in the case of a tenant who has insured his limited interest, it is doubtful whether the depreciation in the market value of his interest is the

---

[96] *Mathewson v. Western Ass. Co.* (1859) 10 Low Can.R. 8.
[97] *Waters v. Monarch Fire Ass. Co.* (1856) 5 E. & B. 870; *A. Tomlinson (Hauliers) v. Hepburn* [1966] A.C. 451.
[98] [1993] Ch. 361 (See note in [1993] C.L.J. 387).
[99] *Anderson v. Commercial Union Assurance Co.* (1885) 55 L J.Q.B 146. 149, *per* Bowen L.J.; *Castellain v. Preston* (1883) 11 Q.B.D 380, 397, *per* Bowen L.J.; *British Traders' Ins. Co. v. Monson* (1964) 111 C.L.R. 86.

proper test of the amount recoverable. A partial loss might for the time being entirely destroy the market value of a tenant's interest and the immediate depreciation of the market value of the tenant's interest might be greater than the total damage to the property. Conversely, a tenant loses more than the mere marketable value of his interest in the property; he loses the house in which he is living and the enjoyment of doing so and this is something for which he should be compensated.[1] It is therefore submitted that the proper rule for estimating the primary liability of the insurers on a limited proprietary interest is not to calculate the depreciation in value of the interest but to calculate the loss or damage to the property and to allow the insured to recover that amount up to the extent of his interest in the property.

19–28 Insurance of separate interests. Where several persons having separate interests have insured each on his own interest, it is no answer to A's claim for indemnity against his own insurer for the insurer to say that B has already been paid by his insurer the total fire damage. Recovery by B can only satisfy A's claim if B recovered with the authority of A in respect of A's interest as well as his own.[2] Several persons interested in a single property may cover their interests by a single policy. If they are joint owners the contract may well be to afford a joint indemnity for a joint loss; but where, as is more usual, parties with diverse interests (*e.g.* landlord, tenant and mortgagee) combine to insure, there is neither a joint interest nor a joint risk, and the policy is a composite one insuring the different parties severally to the extent of their respective interests.[3] Thus a hire-purchase contract for a car often stipulates that the hirer shall take out a policy to cover the car and, in the absence of any contrary intention, this will be held to cover the interest of both the hirer and the owner.[4]

19–29 In *Westminster Life and Fire Office v. Glasgow Provident Investment Society*[5] the owners of certain mills in Scotland had borrowed money on the security of their mills, and granted bonds and dispositions in security (mortgages) to their creditors A, B and C, the security of the later bondholders being postponed to the security of the earlier. Each of the

---

[1] *Castellain v. Preston* (1883) 11 Q.B.D. 380, 400, *per* Bowen L.J.; similarly if the lease contains a covenant whereby the tenant agrees to make good damage covered by fire. *British Traders' Ins. Co. v. Monson* (1964) 111 C.L.R. 86.

[2] *Scottish Amicable Heritable Securities Ass. Ltd v. Northern Ass. Co.* (1883) 11 R. 287; *Swan and Cleland's Graving Dock and Slipway Co. v. Maritime Ins. Co.* [1907] 1 K.B. 116.

[3] *General Accident, Fire and Life Ass. Cpn Ltd v. Midland Bank Ltd* [1940] 2 K.B. 388. *Cf. Woolcott v. Sun Alliance* [1978] 1 Lloyd's Rep. 629; *Black King Shipping v. Massie* [1985] 1 Lloyd's Rep. 437, 516–517; *Rowlands v. Berni Inns* [1986] Q.B. 211; *New Hampshire Ins. Co. v. M.G.N. Ltd* [1997] L.R.L.R. 24.

[4] *Lombard Australia v. N.R.M.A. Ins. Ltd* [1969] 1 Lloyd's Rep. 575. A problem might arise if the insurer paid the hirer in full who became insolvent and the owner then sued the insurer in respect of his (the owner's) interest. The insurer would have to argue that the hirer was the authorised agent of the owner to receive the insurance money but this might be difficult if there was the standard question about ownership of the vehicle in the propsal form and the answer had revealed the existence of an owner, see para. 20–30 below.

[5] (1888) 13 App.Cas. 699, *sub. nom. Glasgow Provident v. Westminster Fire Office* (1887) 14 R. 947. This report of the case in the Court of Session should be consulted as well as the report in the House of Lords.

bondholders caused insurance to be effected each to protect his own interest, and each with a different office. These were all in practically the same form, and were in the names of the respective bondholders *primo loco*, and in the name of the owners in reversion, but there was no privity of agreement between the bondholders. The premiums were paid by the bondholders, but were debited in account against the owners. C's original bond had been for £1,000 and they had subsequently been granted a bond of corroboration for £917 11s. 6d. At the time when the action was raised the amount remaining due to C was £800 2s. Their insurance was for £900. The policy recited that the assured were "C and X, Y (the owners) jointly and severally, in reversion". Then followed the condition for payment:

> "The Society hereby agrees with the insured . . . that if the said property, or any part thereof, shall be destroyed or damaged by fire . . . the Society will . . . pay or make good all such loss or damage, to an amount not exceeding, in respect of the several matters described in the margin hereof, the sum set opposite thereto respectively, and not exceeding in the whole the sum of £900."

In the margin this sum was apportioned over different parts of the premises insured. The premises were damaged by fire. Immediately before the fire the value of the site and premises was sufficient to satisfy all the bondholders. The value of the site and salvage after the fire was valued by C's valuators at £3,500, and by the insurers' valuators at £6,900, that is to say, in either case it was insufficient to satisfy the prior bonds, which amounted to £8,600. The value of the insurable subjects, *i.e.* the premises apart from the site was never sufficient to satisfy the prior bonds. The prior bondholders recovered from their insurers the total fire damage, amounting to £5,668 16s. 8d., and applied it in reduction of their debt against the owners. This sum would have been sufficient for the complete reinstatement of the premises. C, with the consent and concurrence of the owners, then raised an action in the Court of Session against their insurers, claiming in respect of each item in their policy, the total amount of fire damage to the extent of the sums apportioned thereon. The insurers contended that where there were several policies upon different interests in the same premises no more could be recovered in the aggregate upon all the policies than the total damage done by the fire. This argument was rejected by a majority of the whole court of the Court of Session, and by a unanimous decision of the House of Lords. It was held that each insurance was a separate insurance on the interest of each incumbrancer, and each was entitled to an indemnity from his own insurer. If the premises were so damaged by fire that what was left was insufficient to satisfy the prior incumbrancer, a postponed incumbrancer was entitled to recover the amount of his debt from his insurers. The judgment in the House of Lords was upon this basis, that whereas the value of the premises before the fire was sufficient to cover all the incumbrancers, the fire had so reduced the value that even after the first incumbrancer had applied the insurance money received by them in part extinction of their debt, the value of the land and salvage was insufficient to meet the balance of the first incumbrancer's debt. The security of the postponed incumbrancer was in this view practically extinguished and each was clearly entitled to the total fire damage not exceeding the amount insured by him on each item or the amount of his debt.

19–30 Interest of postponed incumbrancer. The judgment of the House of

Lords in the above case leaves open the question whether a postponed incumbrancer would be entitled to recover in all or any of these four cases:

(1) if the premises before the fire had been insufficient to satisfy the prior incumbrancer;
(2) if after the fire the premises had been sufficient to satisfy the balance of the prior incumbrancer's debt (after payment by their insurers) and leave sufficient to satisfy the postponed incumbrancer's debt, but with a smaller margin of security;
(3) if the value of the premises had not been reduced by more than the amount paid to the prior incumbrancer so that after the fire the premises had been sufficient to satisfy the balance of the prior incumbrancer's debt and leave the same margin of security as before;
(4) if the owner or prior incumbrancer reinstated the premises so that after reinstatement the postponed incumbrancer were left with the same margin of security as before the fire.

It is submitted that in each of these four cases the postponed incumbrancer would primarily be entitled to recover from his insurers the amount of the fire damage done to the premises not exceeding the amount of his debt.

19–31 In the first case, the fact that a prior incumbrancer could not, even before the fire, have been satisfied out of the premises, does not divest a postponed incumbrancer of all interest in them. The prior incumbrancer might be paid off without having recourse to the security, and then the security would be available to the postponed incumbrancer.

In the second case the fact that the margin of security is reduced should entitle an incumbrancer to an indemnity, even although a bare security is left. His interest is to have the security maintained with the same ample margin. This appears to be the view that was taken in the Court of Session.[6]

In the third and fourth cases the question is whether the amount payable is the amount of damage at the time of the fire or whether subsequent benefits which reduce the damage are to be set off against this amount. It has already been submitted in another part of this work[7] that the benefit accruing to the assured from reinstatement is properly matter of subrogation and the same rule appears to be applicable to the case where the amount paid to the prior incumbrancer is equivalent to the damage done, so that when he has reduced his debt by that amount the security of the assured is undiminished. Primarily the assured is entitled to the whole amount of damage, but the insurer may counterclaim in respect of the benefit which the assured has received from the fact that prior charges on the property have been paid off.

19–32 Assessor's clause. Where it is necessary to make complex mathematical calculations in order to decide the amount of the indemnity due to the insured, policies sometimes provide for an assessor to be appointed whose conclusions are to be binding on both parties. It is sometimes difficult to know on what grounds the assessor's decision can be challenged[8]; he is different from an arbitrator although he occupies an

---

[6] (1887) 14 R. 947, 963.
[7] Para. 19–26, *supra*.
[8] See the remarks of Donaldson J. in *Frewin v. Poland* [1968] 1 Lloyd's Rep. 100.

analogous position. An assessor's certificate can be challenged if he made a mistake in law or in the construction of the insurance policy and applied an erroneous method of assessment; if he omitted to take into account a material fact or took into account a fact which was not material, his decision could probably be set aside; but a mere error of fact or mistake in calculation will not be sufficient, provided he has applied the correct method of assessment. The assessor can be called as a witness and cross-examined in order to determine whether he made his assessment in accordance with the provisions of the policy.[9]

19–33 Cost of repair. If the assured intends to repair he should try to obtain the insurer's agreement to the cost of repair; if he fails to do so, the insurer may afterwards argue that repairs could have been done more economically or that unnecessary work was carried out.[10] Many policies give insurers rights with regard to the cost of repairs and the obligation to submit estimates but, in the absence of an express clause, insurers cannot insist on repairs being done at any particular place by any particular person.[11]

Problems can arise if the assured obtains estimates but then leaves everything else to be arranged by the insurer. If this happens and the insurer accepts an estimate and orders the repairs to be done by the repairer whose estimate he accepts, it will usually be held that the contract of repair is made between the repairer and the insurer with the result that the assured will not himself be liable for the cost of the repair.[12] If, however, the assured is to bear a part of the loss himself it seems that there may be a contract made by the insurer as agent of the assured to the extent of the excess and there will, in any event, be a contract whereby the repairer agrees with the assured to do the repair work within a reasonable time and with all reasonable skill.[13]

It has been held by the Court of Session that in the absence of express agreement insurers are not obliged either to reimburse their assured for the cost of borrowing money in order to finance the performance of repairs to insured property, or to meet demands for interim payments demanded by contractors during the course of the repairs.[14] Although insurers customarily do meet interim payments, the evidence fell short of establishing a legally binding custom to that effect. It is understandable that the cost of borrowing might be said to arise from the impecuniosity of the assured and so not be covered by the policy, but it is less clear why the insurers should not indemnify the assured against interim payments where that is a usual term in a construction contract, at least up to the point that the total of such payments reaches what insurers consider to be the reasonable overall repair cost when that has not been agreed.

---

[9] *Recher & Co. v. North British and Mercantile Ins. Co.* [1915] 3 K.B. 277.

[10] *Adcock v. Co-Operative Ins. Soc. Ltd* [2000] Lloyd's Rep.I.R. 657.

[11] *cf.* the detailed arrangements contained in clause 13 of the Institute Time Clauses (Hulls) 1995 in the context of marine insurance.

[12] *Cooter and Green v. Tyrell* [1962] 2 Lloyd's Rep. 377; *Godfrey Davis v. Culling* [1962] 2 Lloyd's Rep. 349.

[13] *Charnock v. Liverpool Cpn* [1968] 1 W.L.R. 1498; *Brown and Davis v. Galbraith* [1972] 1 W.L.R. 997.

[14] *Anderson v. Commercial Union Assce. Co.* 1998 S.L.T. 826.

4. NOTICE OF LOSS

19–34 Necessity for notice. Insurance policies used almost always to require notice of the loss sustained by the assured to be given to the insurer within a specified time, though this is nowadays less common. The statement of General Insurance Practice adopted in January 1986 by the Association of British Insurers' (applicable only to the contracts of private individuals) provides that:

"Under the conditions regarding notification of a claim, the policyholder shall not be asked to do more than report a claim and subsequent developments as soon as reasonably possible except in the case of legal processes and claims which a third party requires the policyholder to notify within a fixed time, where immediate advice may be required."[15]

The purpose of a notice clause is to enable the insurer to test the genuineness of the claim within a reasonably short time of the occurrence of the loss and to ensure that immediate steps are taken to mitigate the consequences of the loss. Some policies, however, do not contain any express stipulation about notice and the question arises whether there is an implied obligation on the assured to give notice. There is a curious absence of authority on the point, but it is submitted that the assured should give notice of his loss within a reasonable time as part of his general obligation to act with good faith towards his insurer.[16]

19–35 Condition precedent. It is not always easy to decide whether clauses requiring notice of a claim are conditions precedent to the liability of the insurer under the policy, or merely terms of the policy for breach of which the insurer's only remedy is to claim damages for the extra expense flowing from the assured's failure to give notice within the proper time.[17] Little more can be said than that it is a matter of construing the policy as a whole.[18] Such clauses should not be treated as a mere formality which is to be evaded at the cost of a forced and unnatural construction of the words used in the policy but should be construed fairly to give effect to the object for which they were inserted, but at the same time so as to protect the assured from being trapped by obscure or ambiguous phraseology.[19] No express words are necessary to create a condition precedent[20] but, conversely, the

---

[15] The statement is an updated version of the statement announced in the House of Commons on May 4, 1977 (H.C.Deb., Vol. 931, No. 98, cols 217–220) and published on the same day in a Press Release by the Department of Trade (ref. 117).

[16] Welford, *Accident Insurance*, (2nd ed., 1932) p.194; *Haydenfayre v. British National Ins. Soc. Ltd* [1984] 2 Lloyd's Rep. 393, 402, *per* Lloyd J. *Contra*, Colinvaux's *Law of Insurance* (7th ed., 1997) para. 9–2.

[17] There is no requirement for the insurer to show prejudice if a notice clause is a condition precedent, *Pioneer Concrete (U.K.) Ltd v. National Employers Ass. Ltd* [1985] 1 Lloyd's Rep. 274; *Motor and General Ins. v. Pavy* [1994] 1 W.L.R. 462, 469. If, however, the court were to construe the notice clause as an "innominate" term, and the assured's breach had very serious consequences for the insurers, this could entitle the insurers to reject the claim in question— *Alfred MacAlpine v. BAI (Run-Off) Ltd* [2000] 1 All E.R. (Comm) 545; *K/S Merc-Scandia XXXXII v. Certain Lloyd's Underwriters, The "Mercandian Continent"* [2001] 2 Lloyd's Rep. 563. See para. 10–13, *ante*.

[18] *Stoneham v. Ocean, Railway and General Accident Co.* (1887) 19 Q.B.D. 237, 239; *Cox v. Bankside Members Agency Ltd* [1995] 2 Lloyd's Rep. 437, 453, *per* Phillips J. approving this paragraph in the 8th edition of this work.

[19] *George Hunt Cranes Ltd v. Scottish Boiler & General Ins. Co. Ltd* [2002] 1 All E.R. (Comm) 366, 370, approving this passage in the 9th edition of this work.

[20] *Hollister v. Accident Ass. of New Zealand* (1886) 5 N.Z.L.R. (S.C.) 49.

fact that the policy states that certain clauses (of which the notice clause is one) are conditions precedent is not necessarily conclusive.[21] Where some conditions are expressed to be precedent to liability and other conditions have no such sanction attached, it is difficult to avoid giving effect to the differences in expression.[22] In *Re Coleman's Depositories Ltd and Life and Health Assurance Association*[23] the policy (which indemnified employers for liability to their employees) provided

> "the observance and performance by the employer of the times and terms above set out so far as they contain anything to be done by the employer are of the essence of the contract".

Bray J. held that this did not make the clause requiring notice a condition precedent and that breach by the insured only entitled the insurer to counterclaim for damages. The Court of Appeal decided that the clause was not incorporated in the contract of insurance but Vaughan Williams and Buckley L.JJ. were not disposed to differ from Bray J.'s conclusion although Vaughan Williams L.J. expressed "great doubt". Fletcher Moulton L.J. took the opposite view and held that any clause which was expressed to be of the essence of the contract was a condition precedent.[24]

19–36 Impossibility of performance. The fact that it may have been impossible for the claimant to give notice within the prescribed time (*e.g.* because he did not know of the facts giving rise to his right to claim[25] or because an injury only became apparent after the time for notice had expired[26]) will not prevent a court from denying the right to recover under the policy. An accident may result in instantaneous death and those having the right to claim may not know of the death of the assured or even that he was insured.[27] There are, however, cases in which the courts have mitigated the harshness of this doctrine. In *Re Coleman's Depositories and Life and*

---

[21] *Re Bradley and Essex and Suffolk Accident Indemnity Society* [1912] 1 K.B. 415.
[22] *Stoneham v. Ocean, Railway and General Accident Ins. Co.* (1887) 19 Q.B.D. 237.
[23] [1907] 2 K.B. 798.
[24] The following are examples of cases in which a clause requiring notice was held to be a condition precedent: *Roper v. Lendon* (1859) 1 E. & E. 825; *Gamble v. Accident Ins. Co. Ltd* (1870) I.R. 4 C.L. 204; *Cawley v. National Employers' Accident and General Ass. Ltd* (1885) Cab. & El. 597; 1 T.L.R. 255; *Cassel v. Lancashire and Yorkshire Accident Ins. Co. Ltd* (1885) 1 T.L.R. 495; *Hollister v. Accident Ass. of New Zealand* (1886) 5 N.Z.L.R.(S.C.) 49; *Patton v. Employers' Liability Ass. Cpn* (1887) 20 L.R. Ir. 93; *Accident Ins. Co. of North America v. Young* (1892) 20 S.C.R. 280; *Montreal Harbour Commissioners v. Guarantee Co. of North America* (1893) 22 S.C.R. 542; *Employers' Liability Ass. Cpn v. Taylor* (1898) 29 S.C.R. 104; *Re Williams and Lancashire and Yorkshire Accident Ins. Co.'s Arbitration* (1902) 51 W.R. 222; 19 T L.R. 82; *Evans v. Railway Passengers Ass. Co.* (1912) 3 D.L.R. 61; *General Motors Ltd v. Crowder* (1931) 40 Ll.L.R. 87; *Allen v. Robles* [1969] 1 W.L.R. 1193. *Pioneer Concrete U.K. v. National Employers Ass. Ltd* [1985] 1 Lloyd's Rep. 274; *Geo. Hunt Cranes Ltd. v. Scottish Boiler & General Ins. Co. Ltd* [2002] 1 All E.R. 366. Examples of cases where such clauses were not construed as conditions precedent are *Stoneham v. Ocean, Railway and General Accident Ins. Co.* (1887) 19 Q.B.D. 237; *Re Coleman's Depositories Ltd and Life and Health Ass.* [1907] 2 K.B. 798; *Shera v. Ocean Accident and Guarantee Cpn* (1900) 32 O.R. 411; *Haydenfayre v. British National Ins. Soc. Ltd* [1984] 2 Lloyd's Rep. 393; *Cox v. Bankside Members Agency Ltd* [1995] 2 Lloyd's Rep. 437, 453–454; *Adamson & Sons v. Liverpool and London and Globe Ins. Co.* [1953] 2 Lloyd's Rep. 355; *Re Williams and Lancashire and Yorkshire Accident Ins. Co.'s Arbitration* (1902) 51 W.R. 222; 19 T.L.R. 82.
[25] *Verelst's Administratrix v. Motor Union Ins. Co.* [1925] 2 K.B. 137.
[26] *Cassel v. Lancashire and Yorkshire Accident Ins. Co.* (1885) 1 T.L.R. 495.
[27] *Gamble v. Accident Ins. Co. Ltd* (1869) I.R. 4 C.L. 204, followed in *Patton v. Employers' Liability Ass. Cpn* (1887) 20 L.R.Ir. 93 and *Evans v. Railway Passengers' Ass. Co.* (1912) 3 D.L.R. 61. See also *Accident Ins. Co. of North America v. Young* (1892) 20 S.C.R. 280.

Health Assurance Association[28] the accident occurred before the policy containing a notice clause was delivered to the assured; meanwhile he had been covered by a cover note which neither contained a condition as to notice nor referred to the conditions in the policy. It was held by the Court of Appeal that the insurers could not rely on the clause requiring notice in the policy. It has also been suggested that in cases of liability insurance, time for giving notice will only run when it is clear that insurers will be concerned in the case[29] but this must be regarded as doubtful.[30] Sometimes the notice clause can be construed so as to excuse the delay which has occurred, as in *Ward v. Law Property Assurance and Trust Society*[31] where, in a guarantee policy, the assured was obliged to give notice "within six days of any liability being incurred". It was held that this meant notice of any criminal misconduct whereby it was clear that a liability had been incurred and that the assured was not therefore bound to give notice until he had ascertained that a liability had actually been incurred.

19–37 Canadian and American cases have been more favourable to the assured and it has been held that where the insured had an accident in July but did not discover that he had suffered any injury until the following March, he could still give notice to the insurer.[32] Similarly it was held that where the assured was drowned but the claimant did not discover his fate until six months later, notice could be given immediately after discovery[33]; and again where the insured died, but the accidental cause of death was not apparent until after a post-mortem examination, it was held sufficient to give notice immediately after discovery of the facts on which the claim was based.[34]

19–38 Apparently trivial injuries. Difficulties may arise where the assured has an accident but no injury or only a very trivial injury is apparent at the time and no notice is given because the assured never contemplated that it would give rise to any liability under the policy. Much will depend on the precise wording of the relevant clause. If there is a clear obligation to give notice within a specified number of days after the accident, a court will probably give literal effect to the condition[35] but in a case where the clause provided for "written notice of any occurrence and of all claims relating thereto" to be given "as soon as practicable", Hawke J. expressly declined to decide the point.[36] Where the clause provided that notice must be given within a certain number of days of "an accident causing disability or death" it has been held in America that until disability or death has supervened the

---

[28] [1907] 2 K.B. 798.
[29] *Smellie v. British General Ins. Co.*, 1918 2 S.L.T. 58; W.C. & Ins.Rep. 233.
[30] See *Re Williams and Lancashire and Yorkshire Accident Ins. Co.'s Arbitration* (1902) 19 T.L.R. 82; 51 W.R. 222 and *General Motors Ltd v. Crowder* (1931) 40 Ll.L.R. 87.
[31] (1856) 27 L.T.(o.s.) 155; 4 W.R. 605.
[32] *Gill v. Yorkshire Ins. Co.* (1913) 24 W.L.R. 389; *cf. Warne v. London Guarantee Accident Co.* (1900) 20 C.L.T. 227 and *Parent v. Merchant's Ins. Co.* (1918) 54 Q.R.S.C. 106.
[33] *Kentzler v. American Mutual Accident Ass.*, 88 Wis. 589; 43 Am.S.R. 934 (1894); *cf. Globe Accident Ins. Co. v. Gerisch*, 163 Ill. 625; 54 Am.S.R. 486 (1896) where it was held that no claim could exist until the representatives of the insured had completed their title by probate.
[34] *Trippe v. Provident Fund Society*, 37 Am.S.R. 529 (1893). See also *Woodmen's Accidental Ins. Co. v. Pratt*, 62 Neb. 673; 89 Am.S.R. 777 (1901).
[35] *Cassel v. Lancashire and Yorkshire Accident Ins. Co. Ltd* (1885) 1 T.L.R. 495.
[36] *General Motors Ltd v. Crowder* (1931) 40 Ll.L.R. 87.

event of which notice has to be given has not occurred; although there is an accident there is no accident causing disability or death.[37]

19–39 Immediate notice. There is very little English authority on the meaning of the words "immediately" or "forthwith" when used in insurance policies.[38] But in a licensing case where the statute provided that an appellant should enter into recognisances immediately after giving notice of appeal, the Court of Queen's Bench held that an unexplained delay of four days was not a compliance with the statute.[39] Cockburn C.J. said:

> "It is impossible to lay down any hard and fast rule as to what is the meaning of the word 'immediately' in all cases. The words 'forthwith' and 'immediately' have the same meaning. They are stronger than the expression 'within a reasonable time,' and imply prompt, vigorous action, without any delay, and whether there has been such action is a question of fact, having regard to the circumstances of the particular case."

In South Africa, where the policy required immediate notice to be given, a delay of nine days was held to be too long[40]; in Canada it has been held that notice within five days was given promptly,[41] whereas one week was too long.[42] American courts have construed the word rather more liberally as "within a reasonable time"[43] but it is doubtful whether their decisions would be followed in this country.

19–40 As soon as possible. The words "as soon as possible" are not so stringent. In *Verelst's Administratrix v. Motor Union Insurance Co.*[44] the policy provided:

> "in case of any accident ... the insured's representative ... shall give notice ... in writing of such accident ... as soon as possible after it has come to the knowledge of the assured's representative".

[37] *Rorick v. Railway Officials' and Employers' Accidental Ass.*, 119 Fed.Rep. 63 (1902); *Western Commercial Travellers' Ass. v. Smith*, 85 Fed.Rep. 400 (1898). See also *Odd Fellows' Fraternal Accident Ass. v. Earl*, 70 Fed.Rep. 16 (1895) where it was held that, if the disability supervened after the prescribed number of days from the date of the accident the clause had no application and it was sufficient if notice was given within a reasonable time.

[38] But see *Re Williams and the Lancashire and Yorkshire Accident Ins. Co.'s Arbitration* (1902) 19 T.L.R. 82 where a delay of nearly two months was held to preclude the assured from recovering: *Farrell v. Federated Employers Ins. Ass. Ltd* [1970] 1 W.L.R. 1400 (six months); *Berliner Motor Cpn v. Sun Alliance Ltd* [1983] 1 Lloyd's Rep. 320 (10 months).

[39] *R. v. Berkshire Justices* (1878) 4 Q.B.D. 469; considered in *Prairie City Oil Co. v. Standard Mutual Fire Ins. Co.* (1910) 14 W.L.R. 41, 380, reversed 44 S.C.R. 40. An employee, dismissed on a Friday and employed by a different employer to whom the business had been transferred on a Monday, was held to have been employed "immediately before" the transfer, see *Alphafield v. Barratt* [1984] 1 W.L.R. 1062.

[40] *Hean v. General Accident Fire and Life Ass. Co.* [1931] N.L.R. 215.

[41] *North Lethbridge Garage Ltd v. Continental Casualty Co.* [1930] 2 D.L.R. 835.

[42] *Montreal Harbour Commissioners v. Guarantee Co. of North America* (1893) 22 S.C.R. 542; *Johnston v. Dominion of Canada Guarantee and Accident Ins. Co.* (1908) 17 Ont.L.R. 462 ("immediate notice means reasonably expeditious notice").

[43] *Rokes v. Amazon Ins. Co.* 34 Am.Rep. 323 (1879); *Kentzler v. American Mutual Accident Ass.*, 88 Wis. 589, 43 Am.S.R. 934 (1894); *Shera v. Ocean Accident and Guarantee Cpn* (1900) 32 O.R. 411; *Griffey v. New York Central Ins. Co.*, 53 Am.Rep. 202 (1885). Other American authorities are collected in Appleman, *Insurance Law and Practice*, paras 3502–3.

[44] [1925] 2 K.B. 137. Cf. *R. v. Board of Visitors of Dartmoor Prison* [1987] Q.B. 106. For the words "as soon as practicable" see *General Motors Ltd v Crowder* (1931) 40 Ll.L.R. 87 and *Black King Shipping Corp. v. Massie* [1985] 1 Lloyd's Rep. 437.

The assured was killed in an accident in India in January 1923 and her administratrix, though she knew of the death within a month, did not know of the existence of the policy until the following January. She then gave notice and it was held that the arbitrator was entitled to find that she had given notice as soon as possible. Roche J. held that all existing circumstances must be taken into account such as the available means of knowledge of the policy and of the identity of the insurance company on the part of the claimant. Absence of any threat of proceedings against the assured does not affect the obligation to give notice of the accident "as soon as possible".[45]

19–41 Notice need not be in writing. Oral notice is sufficient[46] unless the policy expressly requires notice to be given in writing.[47] Such a requirement can, of course, be waived,[48] but the fact that the insurer may have received notice from another source will probably not absolve the asssured from his obligation to give written notice.[49]

19–42 To whom notice must be given. Although notice need not be given to the insurer personally, and can be given to his agent, the agent must be one who has authority to receive it. It is only necessary that the agent should have ostensible authority[50] and an assured who is ignorant that an agent has ceased to represent the insurer may still be able to recover.[51] If the policy requires notice to be given to the head office, notice to a local agent is insufficient[52] unless the insured can show that the information was in fact communicated to the head office.[53]

19–43 By whom notice can be given. Notice need not be given by the assured personally but can be given by his agent or anyone acting on his behalf.[54] It is not clear whether notice received from any source or knowledge on the part of the insurer, however acquired, will be sufficient for

---

[45] *Glenburn Dairy Ltd v. Canadian General Ins. Co.* [1953] 4 D.L.R. 33.

[46] *Re The Solvency Mutual Guarantee Society; Hawthorn's Case* (1862) 31 L.J.Ch. 625.

[47] *Cawley v. National Employers' Accident and General Ass. Ass. Ltd* (1885) Cab. & El. 597; 1 T.L.R. 255; *Brook v. Trafalgar Ins. Co. Ltd* (1946) 79 Ll.L.R. 365.

[48] *Webster v. General Accident Fire and Life Ass. Cpn Ltd* [1953] 1 Q.B. 520.

[49] See para. 19–43 and *Prairie City Oil Co. v. Standard Mutual Fire Ins. Co.* (1910) 14 W.L.R. 41 (on appeal 380), reversed on other grounds 44 S.C.R. 40.

[50] *Gale v. Lewis* (1846) 9 Q.B. 730; *Roche v. Roberts* (1921) 9 Ll.L.R. 59 (notice to broker who negotiated policy on behalf of the insured insufficient); *Re Solvency Mutual Guarantee Society; Hawthorn's Case* (1862) 31 L.J.Ch. 625.

[51] *Marsden v. City and County Ins. Co.* (1865) L.R. 1 C.P. 232.

[52] *Brook v. Trafalgar Ins. Co. Ltd* (1946) 79 Ll.L.R. 365 (local agent probably does not have authority to waive such a condition).

[53] *Shiells v. Scottish Ass. Cpn Ltd* (1889) 16 R. 1014; *Gill v. Yorkshire Ins. Co.* (1913) 24 W.L.R. 389; *American Accident v. Carol*, 13 Ohio C.C. 154 (1896). But see *Young v. Travellers' Ins. Co.*, 80 Me. 244 (1888) where an agent incorrectly filled in the notice form and the insurer was not allowed to rely on the error. See also *Rendal v. Arcos* (1937) 43 Com.Cas. 1 where the House of Lords held that if notice had been given to an agent acting for a principal in a transaction, there is a rebuttable presumption that the agent will have passed the notice on to his principal.

[54] *Patton v. Employers' Liability Ass. Corp.* (1887) 20 L.R.Ir. 93, 100; *C.V.G. Siderurgicia Del Orinoco S.A. v. London Steamship Ows. Mut. Ins. Assoc. Ltd* [1979] 1 Lloyd's Rep. 557, 565.

the purposes of a notice clause.[55] But a majority of the Court of Appeal held in *Barrett Bros (Taxis) Ltd v. Davies*[56] that, since the insurers had received all the necessary information from the police, it was unnecessary for the assured to give the insurers the same information and that the insurers could not rely on the notice clause in the policy. If, however, the insurers had received only ambiguous or doubtful information they would presumably not be under any obligation to discover the truth for themselves but would be entitled to await a communication from the insured.

19–44 Meaning of notice. It is difficult to say what will amount to a sufficient notice of loss within the terms of an insurance policy. In *A/S Rendal v. Arcos Ltd*[57] a charterparty required that notice of any claim must be given within 12 months of arrival at the port of discharge. The House of Lords held that the notice need not be a precisely formulated claim but "such a notice as will enable the party to whom it is given to take steps to meet the claim by preparing and obtaining appropriate evidence for that purpose".[58] It is suggested that a similar approach should be adopted for the meaning of "notice" in insurance policies, *i.e.* the notice must be sufficient for the insurer to decide whether he is liable under the policy and, if not, to collect evidence in order to prove that he is not.

The condition as to notice must be complied with according to its terms; if it requires "notice of an accident" it is not enough to give notice of an injury but notice of the accidental cause must be given.[59] A claimant need not prove notice as part of his case; absence of proper notice must be pleaded and proved in defence.[60] A requirement that the insured is to give notice of any claim or occurrence of which he becomes aware looks to claims or

---

[55] In *Shiells v. Scottish Ass. Corp. Ltd* (1889) 16 R. 1014 notice received by the insurers from their own agent was held sufficient; *cf. Abel v. Potts* (1860) 3 Esp. 242 and *Mildred Goyeneche v. Maspons* (1883) 8 App.Cas. 874, 885 *per* Lord Blackburn, 888, *per* Lord Selborne L.C. and *Prairie City Oil Co. v. Standard Mutual Fire Ins. Co.* (1910) 14 W.L.R. 41, 380 and 44, S.C.R. 40. In *The Vainqueur Jose* [1979] 1 Lloyd's Rep. 557 it was held, under a liability policy, that notice of claim had to be given by or on behalf of the insured, if it was to be effective.

[56] [1966] 1 W.L.R. 1334. This ground for the decision was followed in *M.V. Mozart (Owner) v. Ferrum G.m.b.H.* [1985] 1 Lloyd's Rep. 239 and *Valla Giovanni & C. S.p.A. v. Gebr. Van Weelde, The Chanda* [1985] 1 Lloyd's Rep. 563. In *Bass Brewers v. Independent Ins. Co. Ltd* 2002 S.L.T. 512 it was held that failure by one assured under a composite policy to notify an occurrence likely to rise to a claim was a breach of a notice clause in the form of a condition precedent even when the other co-assured had given the relevant notice. The English authorities were not cited. The wider observation by Lord Denning M.R. in *Barrett Bros* that insurers can never rely on a breach of a notice clause in the form of a condition precedent unless they can show that it has caused them prejudice has been doubted and cannot now be regarded as good law—*Pioneer Concrete (UK) Ltd v. National Employers Mutual Ins. Assoc. Ltd* [1985] 2 All E.R. 395, approved by the Privy Council in *Motor & General Ins. Co. v. Pavy* [1994] 1 W.L.R. 462, 469.

[57] (1937) 43 Com.Cas. 1; *Mozart* and *Chanda, ante.*

[58] At p. 4. See also the word "notice" construed in statutory contexts, *Herbert v. Railway Passenger Ass. Co.* [1938] 1 All E.R. 650 (a casual conversation with insurer's agent not sufficient for "notice of the bringing of proceedings" against the insured); *Weldrick v. Essex and Suffolk Equitable Ins. Society Ltd* (1949) 83 Ll.L.R. 91; *Ceylon Motor Ins. Ass. Ltd v. Thambugala* [1953] A.C. 584; *McGoona v. Motor Insurers' Bureau* [1969] 2 Lloyd's Rep. 34, 46; *Harrington v. Pinkney* [1989] 2 Lloyd's Rep. 310.

[59] *Simons v. Iowa State Travelling Men's Ins. Co.*, 102 Iowa 267 (1897); but if the policy requires the insured to forward every written notice as to any verbal notice of claim arising through any accident (to his employee) there is no obligation on him to forward a notice of arbitration; *Wilkinson v. Car and General Ins. Cpn Ltd* (1913) 110 L.T. 468.

[60] *Coburn v. Travellers' Ins. Co.*, 145 Mass. 227 (1887); *Baker v. Provident Accident and White Cross Ins. Co. Ltd.* [1939] 2 All E.R. 690.

occurrences which arise during the policy year, rather than claims or occurrences which exist at the inception of the policy.[61]

19–45 Waiver. The condition as to notice may be waived by the conduct of the company. This may be done before or after there has been a breach of the condition: before, by conduct inducing the claimant to rely on an informal notice or to delay giving formal notice; after, by conduct inducing the claimant to incur further trouble or expense in the prosecution of his claim in the belief that no point would be taken on the defective notice.[62] If the insurer receives an insufficient notice before the time for giving it has expired and the defect is apparent on the face of the notice, it is his duty to inform the claimant and give him an opportunity to put the defect right while there is yet time; if he does not do so his silence will be taken as a waiver of the defect[63]; if he acts upon a defective notice which can still be put right, *e.g.* by sending a medical officer to investigate the case or requiring a post-mortem examination, the defect will likewise be held to have been waived.[64]

If no notice has been received before the time has expired, mere silence on the part of the insurer cannot operate as a waiver and even an investigation of the claim, without repudiation on the ground that no notice has been given, cannot be a waiver unless the claimant has been put to trouble and expense.[65] Where, for example, the insurers received the proofs, investigated the claim and denied liability on the merits, it was held that the insurers had not waived any of their rights, in relation to the notice clause.[66] No party is required to name all his reasons at once or any reason at all and the assignment of one reason for a refusal to pay cannot be a waiver of any other existing reason unless the silence of the insurer has misled the plaintiff in such a way that the insurer should be estopped from relying on the clause.

19–46 In *Allen v. Robles*[67] where the assured had failed to give notice of his claim within the required five days but gave notice about two months later, the insurers did not deny liability for a further five months. The Court of Appeal held that they could not lose their rights by lapse of time unless

---

[61] *Tilley and Noad v. Dominion Ins. Co.* (1987) 254 E.G. 1056.

[62] *Toronto Railway Co. v. National British and Irish Millers Ins. Co. Ltd* (1914) 111 L.T. 555; 20 Com.Cas. 1; *Burridge & Son v. Haines* (1918) 87 L.J.K.B. 641; *Webster v. General Accident Fire and Life Ass. Corp. Ltd* [1953] 1 Q.B. 520; *Barrett Bros (Taxis) Ltd v. Davies* [1966] 1 W.L.R. 1334; *The Vainqueur Jose* [1979] 1 Lloyd's Rep. 557 and *Italmare Co. v. Ocean Tanker Inc. (No. 2)* [1982] 3 All E.R. 273.

[63] *Welsh v. London Ass. Co. Ltd*, 151 Pa. 607; 31 Am.S.R. 786, 789 (1892). *Cf. Panchaud Frères v. Et. General Grain* [1970] 1 Lloyd's Rep. 53.

[64] *Martin v. Equitable Accident Ins. Co.*, 61 Hun. 467 (1891).

[65] *Heywood v. Marine Mutual Accident Ass.*, 85 Me. 789 (1893); *cf. Whyte v. Western Assurance Co.* (1875) 22 L.C.J. 215, P.C.

[66] *Accident Ins. Co. of North America v. Young* (1892) 20 Can.S.C. 280. There are cases where insurers have been held to waive defective notices by proceeding to investigate; *e.g. Donnison v. Employers' Accident and Live Stock Ins. Co. Ltd* (1897) 24 R. 681; *Carbray v. Strathcona Fire Ins. Co.* (1915) 47 Q.R.S.C. 212; *Sproul v. National Fire Ins. Co.* [1925] 1 D.L.R. 1152; but they seem contrary to principle. *Webster v. General Accident Fire and Life Ass. Corp. Ltd* [1953] 1 Q.B. 520, where the claimant's solicitor gave oral instead of written notice, was a case in which the judge merely held that there was evidence to support the arbitrator's conclusion that the insurers had waived their right to rely on the defective notice.

[67] [1969] 1 W.L.R. 1193; followed in *Forsikringsaktieselskapter Vesta v. Butcher* [1986] 2 All E.R. 488.

there was prejudice to the assured or third party rights had intervened, or the delay was so long as to be evidence that the insurers had accepted liability.

In practice insurers who intend to take advantage of the lateness of the notice should immediately repudiate liability on that ground. They may then ask for proofs and evidence "without prejudice" and the claimant is obliged to supply them according to the conditions in the policy because the insurers are entitled to a full opportunity of investigating the claim on its merits as well as relying on the ground that notice has not been given. In the absence of any such request, the claimant is not bound to comply with the conditions of the policy as to proofs or anything else once the defence of no notice has been taken.[68]

At no time can any act of the insurers amount to a waiver unless they were at the time aware of the insufficiency of the notice.

5. PARTICULARS AND PROOF OF LOSS

19–47 Construction of conditions. It is the practice of insurers to incorporate into their policies provisions to the effect that particulars or proof of loss are to be delivered in a certain way or within a certain time. These clauses are often expressed to be conditions precedent to recovery and what has been said in relation to clauses requiring notice of loss applies with equal force to clauses requiring particulars or proof of loss.[69] In *Welch v. Royal Exchange Assurance*,[70] for example, the policy provided that no claim was to be payable unless the required particulars were given within a reasonable time. It was held by the Court of Appeal that production of the particulars within a reasonable time was a condition precedent to recovery and that, even if the assured ultimately did produce them, he could not succeed in his claim.

If the stipulation as to time is a condition precedent, a failure to furnish particulars puts an end to the insurer's liability and the assured cannot revive his rights by delivering particulars at a later time.[71]

The benefit of any such clause can be waived by the insurer and the same principle will apply as in the case of waiver of notice clauses[72]; a mere failure to mention the clause as a defence to a claim at an early stage will not amount to a waiver.[73]

---

[68] *Re Coleman's Depositories Ltd and Life and Health Assurance Ass.* [1907] 2 K.B. 798, 805–806.

[69] *Worsley v. Wood* (1796) 6 T.R. 710. *Routledge v. Burrell* (1789) 1 Hy.Bl. 254; *Oldham v. Bewicke* (1786) 2 Hy.Bl. 577n.; *Mason v. Harvey* (1853) 8 Exch. 819; *Roper v. Lendon* (1859) 1 E. & E. 825; *Elliott v. Royal Exchange Ass. Co.* (1867) L.R. 2 Ex. 237; *Hiddle v. National Fire and Marine Ins. Co. of New Zealand* [1896] A.C. 372, *Hollister v. Accident Ass. of New Zealand* (1886) 5 N.Z.L.R.(S.C.) 49; *Johnston v. Dominion of Canada Guarantee and Accident Ins. Co.* (1908) 17 Ont.L.R. 462. In *Cowell v. Yorkshire Provident Life Ass. Co.* (1901) 17 T.L.R. 452 it was held that proof of insurable interest, though required by the policy, was not a condition precedent.

[70] [1939] 1 K.B. 294. But see *Weir v. Northern Counties Ins. Co.* (1879) 4 L.R.Ir 689 (no claim was payable "until" an account of the loss had been given; held that claim could be made provided that account was given at some time) and *Western Australian Bank v. Royal Ins. Co.* (1908) 5 C.L.R. 533.

[71] *Whyte v. Western Ass. Co.* (1875) 22 L.C.J. 215, P.C.

[72] *Toronto Railway Co. v. National British and Irish Millers Ins. Co. Ltd* (1914) 111 L.T. 555; 20 Com.Cas. 1; *Yorkshire Ins. Co. Ltd v. Craine* [1922] 2 A.C. 541.

[73] *Whyte v. Western Ass. Co.* (1875) 22 L.C.J. 215, P.C.

The insurer may grant an extension of time but any conditions attached to such extension must be strictly followed.[74]

19–48 Particulars required. Sufficient particulars must be given by the assured. It is a question of fact whether particulars are sufficient, which must depend on all the circumstances of the case, such as the means of information open to the assured and, no doubt, the time within which particulars must be delivered.[75] The phrase "full particulars" has been said to mean "the best particulars the assured can reasonably give",[76] and if the assured has failed to give a detailed account of his loss when he could have done so, he will be unable to recover.[77]

The assured will not be prevented or estopped from recovering for his loss by the fact that his particulars are inaccurate since, unless the policy otherwise provides, he is entitled to deliver further particulars or to amend the original ones.[78]

19–49 Proof required. When the assured is under an obligation to produce proofs of his loss, *e.g.* by verifying the particulars by documentary evidence as required by the insurer, the same principles will apply as for the furnishing of particulars. Inaccuracies in the proofs will not prelude recovery since they can be amended even during the trial.[79] A condition as to proof may be waived by the insurer's accepting other evidence[80]; as with conditions of notice and particulars, if the insurer repudiates liability the claimant is under no liability to furnish proofs[81] unless asked to do so without prejudice to the defence.

It is usually stipulated that proof is to be satisfactory to the insurer, which means that reasonably satisfactory proof will be sufficient.[82] What is reasonable must depend on the circumstances and, in life insurance cases, the insurer will not be compelled to be satisfied by a legal presumption against suicide or even necessarily an order presuming death made by the court.[83] On the other hand, it has been held in Canada that the insurer is

---

[74] *Re Carr and Sun Fire Ins. Co.* (1897) 13 T.L.R. 186.

[75] *National Bank of Australasia v. Brock* (1864) 1 W.W. & A.B. 208; *Hiddle v. National Fire and Marine Ins. Co. of New Zealand* [1896] A.C. 372; *National Trust Co. v. Sterling Accident and Guarantee Ins. Co. of Canada* (1917) Q.R. 51 S.C. 481.

[76] *Per* Pollock C.B. in *Mason v. Harvey* (1853) 8 Exch. 819, 820 *arguendo.*

[77] *Hiddle v. National Fire and Marine Ins. Co. of New Zealand* [1896] A.C. 372; *Banting v. Niagara District Mutual Fire Ins. Co.* (1866) 25 U.C.Q.B. 431.

[78] *Vance v. Forster* (1841) Ir.Circ.Rep. 47; *Mason v. Harvey* (1853) 8 Exch. 819, 820 *per* Pollock C.B. *arguendo*; *Northern Suburban Property Ltd v. British Law Fire Ins. Co. Ltd* (1919) 1 Ll.L.R. 403.

[79] *McMaster v. Ins. Co. of North America*, 55 N.Y. 222 (1873) at p. 228; *North American Life and Accident Ins. Co. v. Burroughs*, 69 Pa. 43 (1871).

[80] *Toronto Railway Co. v. National British and Irish Millers Ins. Co. Ltd* (1914) 111 L.T. 555; 20 Com.Cas. 1; *Burridge & Son v. Haines* (1918) 87 L.J.K.B. 641; *Ocean Guarantee and Accident Cpn v. Fowlie* (1902) 33 S.C.R. 253; *Pim v. Reid* (1843) 6 Man. & G. 1; *Glagovsky v. National Fire Ins. Co. of Hartford* [1931] 1 W.W.R 573.

[81] *Re Coleman's Depositories and Life and Health Ass.* [1907] 2 K.B. 798; *Shiells v. Scottish Assurance Cpn Ltd* (1889) 16 R. 1014; *cf. Passaportis v. Guardian Ass. Co. Ltd* [1916] S.R. 14.

[82] *Braunstein v. Accidental Death Ins. Co.* (1861) 1 B. & S. 782; *Trew v. Railway Passengers' Assc. Co.* (1861) 6 H. & N. 839; *London Guarantee Co. v. Fearnley* (1880) 5 App.Cas. 911, 916; *Macdonald v. Refuge Ass. Co.* (1890) 17 R. 955; *Moore v. Wolsey* (1854) 4 E. & B. 243.

[83] *Harvey v. Ocean Accident Guarantee Cpn* [1905] 2 Ir.R. 1; *Doyle v. City of Glasgow Life Ass. Co.* (1884) 53 L.J.Ch. 527. See Ch. 24, *post.*

entitled to call for vouchers, accounts, invoices,[84] and a builder's certificate of the value of a house.[85] The proof must be reasonably detailed. A mere notice that an accident has happened and that an injury has resulted is not proof,[86] nor is a mere affidavit sworn by the assured of the value of goods which he claims to have lost.[87]

The policy may provide that the assured should make a statutory declaration verifying his claims and the particulars[88]; the clause may go on to provide that such a declaration shall be prima facie evidence that the loss is not of a kind excluded by the policy. Such a provision will not, however, prevent the onus for proving his loss at the trial from remaining on the assured.[89] Where a permanent health policy entitled the assured to benefits "on production of proof satisfactory to [the insurers] of the insured's entitlement", it was held that the insurers could insist on proofs which vouched the claim to benefit but that the clause did not bar the assured from disputing their rejection of his claim by taking legal proceedings.[90]

19–50 There is no obligation on the insurers to furnish forms of proof to the assured, but if they lead him to believe that they will furnish him with forms and do not do so, they cannot complain of the assured's neglect in failing to send the proofs.[91]

If no time is fixed for delivery of proofs, they can be delivered at any time before the limitation period expires.[92]

19–51 Evidence required for proof. The ordinary rules of evidence apply to insurance claims. The assured must prove his loss but the parties may agree to reverse the burden of proof or to dispense with proof of any particular fact or requirement for recovery.[93] Inferences can, of course, be drawn from circumstantial evidence.[94] Where the assured has died, the claimant may find difficulty in proving that an accident took place, but since

---

[84] See *Cinqmars v. Equitable Ins. Co.* (1875) 15 U.C.Q.B. 143; *Greaves v. Niagara District Mutual Fire Ins. Co.* (1865) 25 U.C.Q.B. 127; *Mulvey v. Gore District Mutual Fire Ass. Co.* (1866) 25 U.C.Q.B. 424; *Carter v. Niagara District Mutual Ins. Co.* (1868) 19 U.C.C.P. 143; *cf. Gordon v. Transatlantic Fire Ins. Co.* [1905] T.H. 146.

[85] *Fawcett v. London, Liverpool and Globe Ins. Co.* (1868) 27 U.C.Q.B. 255. In cases of personal accident insurance, the policy may entitle the insurers' medical officer to examine the insured, but this will not entitle the insurers to call for an exhumation, *Wehle v. U.S. Mutual Accident Ass.*, 153 N.Y. 116 (1897); *Ewing v. Commercial Travellers' Ins. Soc.*, 55 App. Div. 241 (1900).

[86] *Johnston v. Dominion of Canada Guarantee and Accident Ins. Co.* (1908) 17 Ont.L.R. 462.

[87] *Greaves v. Niagara District Mutual Ins. Co.* (1865) 25 U.C.Q.B. 127; *Mulvey v. Gore District Mutual Fire Ins. Co.* (1866) 25 U.C.Q.B. 424; *cf. Atlantic Metal Co. Ltd v. Hepburn* [1960] 2 Lloyd's Rep. 42 where it appeared that stock cards recording stocks of metal were unreliable in supporting the plaintiffs' claim; *Forsikringsaktieselskapter Vesta v. Butcher* [1986] 2 All E.R. 488.

[88] See Statutory Declarations Act 1835 and *Beeck v. Yorkshire Ins. Co.* (1909) 11 W.A.L.R. 88; *Glagovsky v. National Fire Ins. Co. of Hartford* [1931] 1 W.W.R. 573. It is an offence knowingly and wilfully to make a false statement in a statutory declaration, Perjury Act 1911, s.5; *R. v. Baynes* (1843) 1 Car. & Kir. 65.

[89] *Watts v. Simmons* (1924) 18 Ll.L.R. 177.

[90] *Napier v. UNUM Ltd* [1996] 2 Lloyd's Rep. 550.

[91] *Standard Life and Accident v. Schmaltz*, 66 Ark. 508; 74 Am.S.R. 112 (1899).

[92] See *Harvey v. Ocean Accident and Guarantee Cpn* [1905] 2 Ir.R. 1 and *Welch v. Royal Exchange Ass. Co.* [1939] 1 K.B. 294.

[93] Apart, presumably, from proof of insurable interest where required by statute—see para. 1–13, *ante.*

[94] *Wright v. Sun Mutual Life Ins. Co.* (1878) 29 C.P. 221, 233, *per* Hagarty C.J.

the Civil Evidence Act 1968, hearsay evidence of what the deceased said before the trial as to the nature of the accident will be admissible subject to the qualifications laid down in the statute and rules of court made thereunder.

Certain injuries are themselves prima facie evidence of accidental death[95] and, in the absence of other evidence, a court will presume that violence was accidental and not intentionally self-inflicted.[96] But if the facts point to suicide as the only reasonable conclusion or even as a justifiable conclusion, a court should not be influenced by presumptions in favour of accidental death but should decide the cause of death on the balance of probabilities.[97] Where the issue is between death by accident and death from natural causes, there is no presumption in favour of accidental death; once again, the court or jury must decide the question on the balance of probabilities.[98]

19–52 Obligation to furnish evidence. The policy may provide that the claimant shall furnish all such information and evidence as the insurers may from time to time require. Under this clause the insurers can ask for evidence and information which may not be absolutely necessary to prove the claimant's case.[99] Any such evidence or information must not, however, be asked for unreasonably.[1] In a case where death was alleged to have resulted from an accident, the insurers requested a post-mortem examination and the judges of the Inner House of the Court of Session could not agree whether this was a reasonable requirement.[2] The demand for evidence must be made directly on the claimant or on those acting for him. If the claimant is obliged merely to "furnish" evidence or information, it is submitted that he can only be asked for evidence or information within his own possession and cannot be required to procure evidence or information from others in the absence of a clear indication to the contrary in the policy.

19–53 Whether notice a prerequisite to accrual of cause of action. In the absence of express provision that the insurers are not to be under a liability to the assured until notice is given or a demand is made, the accrual of a cause of action to the assured does not depend upon either of these things. In *Callaghan v. Dominion Insurance Company Ltd*[3] insurers contended that a claim on a fire insurance was time-barred because proceedings were commenced after the lapse of six years from the date of the loss. The assured argued that certain conditions in the policy delayed the accrual of a cause of action to a time within six years prior to issue of writ. The court followed earlier authorities holding that a cause of action for unliquidated damages

---

[95] *Macdonald v. Refuge Ass. Co.* (1890) 17 R. 955, 957; *Ballantine v. Employers Ins. Co. of Great Britain* (1893) 21 R. 305; *McAlea v. Scottish Legal Life* [1927] I.A.C.(N.I.) Rep. 16.

[96] *Macdonald v. Refuge Ass. Co.* (1890) 17 R. 955, 957, *per* Macdonald L.J.-C.; *Bender v. Owners of SS. Zent* [1909] 2 K.B. 41; *Harvey v Ocean Accident and Guarantee Cpn* [1905] 2 Ir.R. 1; *Goodwillie v. Scottish Legal Life* [1933] I.A.C.Rep. 10; *Boyle v. Royal Co-operative Collecting Society* I.A.C.(N.I.) Rep. 1947, p. 19; *Barnard v. Prudential Ins. Co. of America* [1949] 4 D.L.R. 235.

[97] *Williams v. U.S. Mutual Accident*, 133 N.Y. 366 (1892); *New York Life Ins. Co. v. Ganer*, 303 U.S. 161 (1937).

[98] *Trew v. Railway Passenger Ass. Co.* (1861) 6 H. & N. 839; *Bender v. Owners of SS. Zent* [1909] 2 K.B. 41; *Marshall v. Owners of SS. Wild Rose* [1909] 2 K.B. 46.

[99] *Wilkinson v. Car and General Ins. Cpn Ltd* (1913) 110 L.T. 468.

[1] *A.B. v. Northern Accident* (1896) 24 R. 758.

[2] *Ballantine v. Employers' Ins. Co. of Great Britain* (1893) 21 R. 305.

[3] [1997] 2 Lloyd's Rep. 541.

on an indemnity insurance arose when the loss occurred, because at that moment the insurers were in breach of a promise to hold their assured harmless against loss.[4] The conditions relied on by the assured were construed either to relate to the quantification of the indemnity as opposed to the accrual of the right to be indemnified, or to provide a defence to payment of a claim made pursuant to it. In *Universities Superannuation Scheme Ltd v. Royal Insurance (UK) Ltd*[5] it was recognised that the policy wording could postpone the accrual of a cause of action, but the clause in question was intended to exclude liability for losses under a fidelity insurance if not discovered within a fixed time after loss, and not to delay the accrual of a right to indemnity until discovery of the loss which was the subject of a claim. It seems illogical to deem that the insurer is in breach of a promise to indemnify before he has had an opportunity to perform it, but the proposition is established by appellate authority.[6]

6. FRAUDULENT CLAIMS

19–54 Introductory. Most non-marine policies contain a clause providing that in the event of a fraudulent claim being made the assured forfeits all benefit under the policy, so that his claim entirely fails and the policy may possibly be prospectively terminated.[7] Even when the policy does not contain such a clause, there is a rule that the assured is penalised for fraud in the making of a claim. The rule is based upon two separate principles of insurance law, each of which can be invoked in defence by the insurer. The first is a rule of the common law established in the nineteenth century, and mirrored in the fraud clauses of the day, to the effect that when the assured makes a fraudulent claim it is wholly defeated and he forfeits all benefit under the policy. The second is the continuing duty of utmost good faith expressed in section 17 of the Marine Insurance Act 1906 which provides that either party may avoid the policy in the event that the other fails to comply with it. Since an attempt to obtain a benefit by deception is as clear an example of bad faith as can be imagined, insurers have in more recent times relied specifically upon the section to rebut a dishonest claim. In consequence the law concerning fraudulent claims has become more

---

[4] *Ventouris v. Mountain* [1992] 2 Lloyd's Rep. 281; *Bank of America National Trust & Savings Assoc. v. Christmas* [1993] 1 Lloyd's Rep. 137, and authorities there cited. In liability insurance the relevant loss arises only when the assured's liability is ascertained by admission, agreement or judgment, and a cause of action arises in equity before the assured discharges it—*Firma C-Trade S.A. v. Newcastle P. & I. Assoc.* [1991] 2 A.C. 1.

[5] [2000] 1 All E.R. (Comm) 266.

[6] It is unclear how the principle became established. Under the old rules of pleading it was sufficient to plead that the insurer had promised to indemnify the assured against a loss and that a loss had been caused by an insured peril—Park, *A System of the Law of Marine Insurance* (4th ed., 1842) at pp. 838–841. "Damages" did not mean compensation for breach of contract but simply an unliquidated sum requiring proof and quantification—*Jabbour v. Custodian of Israeli Absentee Property* [1954] 1 W.L.R. 139, 143–144. See the discussion at para. 19–71 *infra*. In Scots law a claim on a policy is one for payment of a debt—*Scott Lithgow v. Secretary of State for Defence* 1989 S.C. 9, 20 *per* Lord Keith; *Gaelic Assignments v. Sharp* 2001 S.L.T. 914, 924. An Irish court has held that an insurer's liability to indemnify his assured does not arise while the latter has failed to comply with a condition that particulars of loss be lodged with the insurer—*Superwood Holdings Plc. v. Sun Alliance & London Ins. Plc.* [1995] 3 I.R. 303.

[7] See para. 19–59, *infra*.

complicated than previously, and we therefore consider these different defences separately.

(a) *Policy Conditions*

19–55 Conditions relating to fraudulent claims. Insurers, in the nature of their profession, are particularly exposed to fraudulent claims which are difficult to refute since the evidence in support will almost always be in the sole hands of the assured or his witnesses. They have therefore sought the protection of express conditions in their policies against fraudulent claims in terms that sometimes caused harshness to the assured. In the eighteenth century it was common to find a clause requiring the insured to procure a:

> "certificate under the hand of the minister and churchwardens, together with some other reputable inhabitants of the parish ... importing that they were well acquainted with the character and the circumstances of the person ... insured and do know or verily believe that he she or they really and by misfortune without any fraud or evil practice have sustained the claimed loss or damage by fire".[8]

This could work hardship if the assured could not produce a certificate and the requirement for such a certificate was expressed to be a condition precedent to liability.[9] By the early nineteenth century it was more usual to find a clause in these terms: "If there appear fraud in the claim made, or false swearing or affirming in support thereof, the claimant shall forfeit all benefit under the policy"[10] and the common Lloyd's form in use in the twentieth century has been: "If the assured shall make any claim knowing the same to be false or fraudulent, as regards amount or otherwise, this policy shall become void and all claim thereunder shall be forfeited."[11]

19–56 If the assured makes a claim where he has suffered no loss or claims for a loss which he has himself caused, insurers do not need to rely on any condition relating to fraudulent claims; but in practice, where the circumstances are suspicious, it may be much easier to show that the assured has made a fradulent statement in the advancement of his claim than it is to show that he wilfully destroyed his own property. The clause thus enables the insurers to assume a lesser burden and still defeat the claim. This approach had the full support of, at any rate, Willes J. in his summing-up to the jury in *Britton v. Royal Insurance Co.*[12]:

> "Of course, if the assured set fire to his house, he could not recover. That is clear. But it is not less clear that, even supposing it were not

---

[8] *Oldman v. Bewicke* (1786) 2 Hy.Bl. 577 note (a).

[9] *Routledge v. Burrell* (1793) 1 Hy.Bl. 254; *Worsley v. Wood* (1796) 6 T.R. 710.

[10] *Levy v. Baillie* (1831) 7 Bing. 349.

[11] *Albion Mills Co. v. Hill* (1922) 12 Ll.L.R. 96; *Harris v. Evans* (1924) 19 Ll.L.R. 346; *Dome Mining Cpn Ltd v. Drysdale* (1931) 41 Ll.L.R. 109. Sometimes the clause says "all claims hereunder" shall be forfeited—*K/S Merc-Scandia XXXXII v. Certain Lloyd's Underwriters, The "Mercandian Continent"* [2001] 2 Lloyd's Rep. 563, 568. A modern variant is—"If the claim be in any respect fraudulent or if any fraudulent means or devices be used by the insured ... to obtain any benefit under this Policy ... all benefit under this Policy shall be forfeited"—*Insurance Corp. of the Channel Islands v. McHugh* [1997] L.R.L.R. 94, 98; *Baghbadrani v. Commercial Union Ass. Co.* [2000] Lloyd's Rep.I.R. 94, 102; *Nsubuga v. Commercial Union Ass. Co.* [1998] 2 Lloyd's Rep.682, 684.

[12] (1866) 4 F. & F. 905. In effect, the judge withdrew the issue of arson from the jury leaving them to decide merely whether the claim had been presented fraudulently.

wilful, yet as it is a contract of indemnity only, that is, a contract to recoup the insured the value of the property insured by fire, if the claim is fraudulent, it is defeated altogether. That is, suppose the insured made a claim for twice the amount insured and lost, thus seeking to put the office off its guard, and in the result to recover more than he is entitled to, that would be a wilful fraud, and the consequence is that he could not recover anything. This is a defence quite different from that of wilful arson. It gives the go-by to the origin of the fire, and it amounts to this—that the assured took advantage of the fire to make a fraudulent claim. The law upon such a case is in accordance with justice, and also with sound policy. The law is, that a person who has made such a fraudulent claim could not be permitted to recover at all. The contract of insurance is one of perfect good faith on both sides, and it is most important that such good faith should be maintained. It is common practice to insert in fire-policies conditions that they shall be void in the event of a fraudulent claim; and there was such a condition in the present case. Such a condition is only in accordance with legal principle and sound policy. It would be dangerous to permit parties to practise such frauds, and then, notwithstanding their falsehood and fraud, to recover the real value of the goods consumed. And if there is wilful falsehood and fraud in claim, the insured forfeits all claim whatever upon the policy."

The clause is most commonly invoked where the assured includes a claim for goods which he either never had or which were disposed of before the fire or burglary in question,[13] or where the claim is inflated deliberately.[14] Being a clause of a kind frequently found in policies, it is un-necessary to bring it specifically to the notice of an assured in order for him to be bound by it.[15] Since it is an agreed term of the contract, questions concerning its meaning and effect are to be resolved according to its proper interpretation. In this regard assistance is to be gained from decisions on the common law rule referred to above, since the clause has been said to produce the same results as the latter.[16] What is clear is that the assured who is detected in dishonestly making a false statement only as to part of his claim automatically forfeits the entire claim. In *Lek v. Mathews* Lord Phillimore thought that this was harsh on the assured—*Dura lex sed ita scripta est.*[17] Today, however, this principle is regarded as a sound rule of public policy intended to deter fraud because, "The logic is simple. The fraudulent assured must not be allowed to think: if the fraud is successful, then I will gain; if it is unsuccessful, I will lose nothing"[18]

---

[13] *Britton v. Royal Ins. Co.* (1866) 4 F. & F. 905, 907, 913; *Albion Mills Co. v. Hill* (1922) 12 Ll.L.R. 96; *Cuppitman v. Marshall* (1924) 18 Ll.L.R. 277; *Herman v. Phoenix* (1924) 18 Ll.L.R. 371; *Lek v. Mathews* (1927) 29 Ll.L.R. 141; *Nsubuga v. Royal Ins. Co.*[1998] 2 Lloyd's Rep. 682.
[14] *Goulstone v. Royal Ins. Co.*(1858) 1 F. & F. 276; *London Ass. Co. v. Clare* (1937) 57 Ll.L.R. 254; *Central Bank of India v. Guardian Ass. Co.*(1934) 54 Ll.L.R. 247; *Insurance Co. of the Channel Islands v. McHugh* [1997] L.R.L.R. 94
[15] *Nsubuga v. Royal Ins.Co.* [1998] 2 Lloyd's Rep. 682, 685
[16] *Galloway v. Guardian Royal Exchange (U.K.) Ltd.* [1999] Lloyd's Rep.I.R. 209, 211; *Nsubuga v. Royal Ins. Co.*[1998] 2 Lloyd's Rep. 682, 686.
[17] (1927) 29 Ll.L.R. 141, 164.
[18] *Manifest Shipping Co. Ltd v. Uni-Polaris Co. Ltd, The Star Sea* [2001] 1 All E.R. (Comm) 193, 214–215, *per* Lord Hobhouse. See also *per* Millett L.J.—"It is in my opinion a necessary and salutary rule which deserves to be better known by the public", *Galloway v. Guardian Royal Exchange (UK) Ltd.* [1999] Lloyd's Rep.I.R. 209, 214.

19–57 Exaggeration and fraudulent devices. It has been said that some exaggeration in a claim is permissible and does not amount to fraud, as where the assured seeks to bargain with the insurers.[19] The true position, it is submitted, is that exaggeration in itself is not automatically fraud, but that in many cases a fraudulent intent can properly be inferred from the presentation of a deliberately inflated claim.[20] Another problem concerns the case of the assured who possesses a valid claim but embellishes it by deliberately giving false information in support of it. Under the modern clause "fraudulent devices" are expressly included, and under the traditional Lloyd's clause it seems that this would amount to falsehood and fraud in the claim. [21] An assured who ante-dates a cheque for the premium to a date before the loss has been held to have used a "fraudulent device" to obtain a benefit under a policy.[22]

19–58 It must presumably follow that if the assured asserts a loss by a peril insured against when he knows such assertion to be false, he cannot recover even if the policy applies to the loss that has, in fact, happened. Thus an assured who makes a claim for a total loss knowing it to be a false claim cannot later recover for a partial loss.[23] Similarly if the assured claims a loss by perils of the seas under a marine policy when he knows the vessel has been scuttled deliberately by one of the crew, he probably cannot recover for barratry.[24] Both these instances would fall within Lord Sumner's exposition of the clause in *Lek v. Mathews*.[25]

"... I think it refers to anything falsely claimed, that is, anything not so unsubstantial as to make the maxim *de minimis* applicable,[26] and is not limited to a claim which as to the whole is false. It means claims as to particular subject-matters in respect of which a right to indemnity is asserted, not the mere amount of money claimed without regard to the particulars or contents of the claim; and a claim is false not only if it is deliberately invented but also if it is made recklessly,[27] not caring whether it is true or false but only seeking to succeed in the claim.

Finally ... I incline to think that as this is a clause of defeasance of the cause of action as existing at the date of the writ, it will extend to false

---

[19] *London Ass. Co. v. Clare* (1937) 58 Ll.L.R. 254, 268; *Ewer v. National Employers' Mutual* [1937] 2 All E.R. 193; *Orakpo v. Barclays Ins. Services* [1995] L.R.L.R. 443, 450; *Nsubuga v. Royal Ins. Co.* [1998] 2 Lloyd's Rep. 682, 686.

[20] *Royal Boskalis Westminster v. Mountain* [1997] L.R.L.R. 523, 593; *Pole v. Chapman* (1870) 22 L.T. 306, 307; *Transthene v. Royal Ins. Co.* [1996] L.R.L.R. 32, 44; *Superwood Holdings Plc. v. Sun Alliance & London Ins. Plc.* [1995] 3 I.R. 303.

[21] *Lek v. Mathews* (1927) 29 Ll.L.R. 141, 164. The clause was in the common Lloyd's form, as appears from the Court of Appeal report at (1925) 25 Ll.L.R. 525, 526.

[22] *Newis v. General Accident Fire & Life Ass. Corp.* (1910) 11 C.L.R. 620.

[23] *Dome Mining Cpn Ltd v. Drysdale* (1931) 41 Ll.L.R. 109.

[24] This point was left undecided in *Piermay Shipping v. Chester* [1979] 2 Lloyd's Rep. 55, 88–89, because Kerr J. held that the owners did not believe their original claim for a loss by perils of the sea to be false. The assured put their pleaded case solely on barratry. There was no need to decide the point in the Court of Appeal [1979] 2 Lloyd's Rep. 1.

[25] (1927) 29 Ll.L.R. 141, 145.

[26] Presumably the false statement must be material, see *Steeves v. Sovereign Fire Ins. Co.* (1880) 20 N.B.R. (4 Pugsley) 394.

[27] Followed in *Bucks Printing Press v. Prudential Ass. Co.* [1994] 3 Re L.R. 196, 199, *per* Saville J.

statements made during the trial[28] as to the items claimed in the action, for otherwise judgment in full might go to the Plaintiff if no stamps had been recovered and no particulars had been given before action, though his evidence as to his several possessions was perjured. Equally little can it avail, if a false claim has once been made, that in face of difficulties arising at the trial it is abandoned when the case is in the hands of Counsel."[29]

If insurers have innocently paid a claim which was made fraudulently they will be able in an appropriate case to recover the sums paid.[30] There is no implied term in the policy, however, that will entitle them to the cost of investigating a false claim by way of damages (as opposed to costs) although it is arguable that such damages might be recovered as damages for the tort of deceit.

19–59 The insurer's remedy. The question of what is meant by forfeiture of claims or the policy becoming void is to be determined by construction of the clause.[31] In *Insurance Company of the Channel Islands v. McHugh*[32] Mance J. construed a condition which provided that all benefit under the policy was to be forfeited as automatically releasing the insurers from liability to pay the claim in question and at the least prospectively to deprive the assured of cover under all sections of the policy. He left open the question of retrospective avoidance. Bearing in mind recent criticisms of the draconian and disproportionate severity of this remedy in insurance law[33] it is reasonable to suppose that a court would construe the forfeiture provision as equating to prospective termination of the insurance contract, and it is noteworthy that Mance L.J. has recently held, albeit "tentatively", that the common law rule on fraudulent claims does not result in retrospective avoidance of the policy.[34] There seems no reason why a court should not construe a clause which provided that the policy should become void as having the same effect, as the meaning of "void" depends on its context and could well be read as meaning "unenforceable".

(b) *The Common Law Rule*

19–60 Ambit of the rule. It is well established that an assured who has made a fraudulent claim is not permitted to recover at all and forfeits any part of the claim which could have been made in all honesty. This is the consequence of a rule of public policy that the courts will not allow such an

---

[28] Including an arbitration hearing, *Singh v. Yorkshire Ins. Co.* (1917) 17 N.S.W.L.R. 312. It has been held, however, that the common law rule has no application to fraudulent conduct after issue of proceedings—*Agapitos v. Agnew* [2002] 1 All E.R. (Comm) 714, 733, *per* Mance L.J.

[29] Or, probably, if it is abandoned before proceedings are instituted or a Statement of Claim served as happened in *Piermay Shipping Co. v. Chester* [1979] 1 Lloyd's Rep. 55, 88–89.

[30] *London Assurance Co. v. Clare* (1937) 57 Ll.L.R. 254; *Direct Line Insurance v. Khan* [2002] Lloyd's Rep. I.R. 364.

[31] *Insurance Corp. of the Channel Islands v. McHugh* [1997] L.R.L.R. 94, 133; *Fargnoli v. Bonus Plc* [1997] C.L.C. 653.

[32] [1997] L.R.L.R. 94, 133–134.

[33] *Manifest Shipping Co. Ltd v. Uni-Polaris Co. Ltd, The Star Sea* [2001] 1 All E.R. (Comm) 193, 210, *per* Lord Hobhouse.

[34] *Agapitos v. Agnew* [2002] 1 All E.R. (Comm) 714, 730. Decisions in other jurisdictions to the same effect are *Lehmbackers Earthmoving v. Incorporated General Ins. Co.* [1983] 3 S.A. 513 (App. Div.); *Fargnoli v. GA Bonus Plc* [1997] CLC 653.

assured to recover.[35] Quite apart from cases in which the claim is baseless or dishonestly inflated from the start, the rule also applies to a claim which was honestly believed in at the outset but is subsequently maintained after the assured realises that it is exaggerated, as where missing property thought to have been stolen is found in a hiding place.[36] To come within the rule, the assured's fraud must be substantial,[37], meaning not trivial, it must be relevant to the claim made, and the assured must either know that he is providing incorrect information in order to obtain a benefit, or be reckless as to whether what he says is true.[38] A "sub-species" of the rule has been held to apply to dishonest devices used to promote a claim for which the assured has a good cause of action, such as the concealment of facts which provide the insurer with a defence to payment, such as a breach of warranty.[39] Here the fraud is not in the formulation of the claim itself, but in masking the breach of a condition precedent to the insurers' liability, so that it is material to the insurers' ultimate liability. The position is less clear when the fraud relates to something which, contrary to what the assured believes, turns out to be irrelevant to the insurers' liability, such as the concoction and back-dating of the letter of advice considered in *The Litsion Pride*.[40] In *Agapitos v. Agnew*[41] Mance L.J. suggested tentatively that, in order to be relevant to the claim, a lie had to be intended by the assured to improve his chances of recovery and also (if believed) one which would tend (objectively) to yield a not insignificant improvement in the assured's prospects prior to trial, even if with hindsight it was seen to serve no useful purpose. With respect, this is an elaborate test which will be not be easy to apply, and one may question the necessity to extend the ambit of the fraudulent claim rule to conduct which is immaterial to the liability of the insurer.[42] He is already protected by powerful defences against fraud which are not enjoyed by parties to other types of contract.

19–61 Forfeiture of benefit. It is clear from the discussion of authorities upon conditions providing forfeiture of all benefits in the event of a fraudulent claim that the assured automatically forfeits his whole claim under the common law rule also.[43] In Scotland the view has been taken that only the claim itself is forfeit, and the assured retains the right to bring valid claims on the policy for the remainder of the cover.[44] In *Orakpo v. Barclays Insurance Services*[45] the Court of Appeal analysed the common law rule as an implied term of the contract of insurance, incorporated by operation of law to give effect to the over-riding principle of utmost good faith. Fraud in making a claim therefore struck at the root of the contract and entitled the

---

[35] *Manifest Shipping Co. Ltd v. Uni-Polaris Co. Ltd*, *The Star Sea* [2001] 1 All E.R. (Comm) 193, 214–215.

[36] *Agapitos v. Agnew* [2002] 1 All E.R. (Comm) 714, 720.

[37] *Galloway v. Guardian Royal Exchange (UK) Ltd* [1999] Lloyd's Rep.I.R. 209, 212, 214; *Lek v. Mathews* (1927) 29 Ll. L. Rep. 141, 145.

[38] *Lek v. Mathews, supra, Bucks Printing Press v. Prudential Ass.Co.* [1994] 3 Re L.R. 196, 199.

[39] *Agapitos v. Agnew* [2002] 1 All E.R. (Comm) 714, 730.

[40] [1985] 1 Lloyd's Rep. 437, on which see comment by Mance L.J. in [2002] 1 All E.R. (Comm) 714, 728–729.

[41] [2002] 1 All E.R. (Comm) 714, 728, 730.

[42] *Wisental v. World Auxiliary Ins. Corp.* (1930) 38 Ll.L.R. 54 was cited, but this appears to have been a case of lies told to conceal earlier non-disclosure of material facts.

[43] See para. 19–56, *supra*

[44] *Reid & Co. v. Employers' Accident & Livestock Ins. Co.* (1899) 1 F. 1031, 1036, *per* Lord Trayner.

[45] [1995] L.R.L.R. 443.

insurer to be discharged from prospective liability, but without disturbing valid claims previously paid. However, in *The Star Sea* Lord Hobhouse stopped short of endorsing the contractual analysis of the rule [46] and the House of Lords appear to have treated the insurers' defence as one arising under section 17 of the Marine Insurance Act 1906. *Dicta* of Millett L.J. in *Galloway v.Guardian Royal Exchange (UK) Ltd*[47] suggest that the policy is "avoided", but the nature of the insurer's remedy was not in issue and the point was not being addressed. In *Agapitos v. Agnew*[48] Mance L.J. took the "tentative view" that the common law rule fell outside the scope of section 17 and that accordingly no question of avoidance *ab initio* arose. *Tot judices quot sententiae.* In our view the desirability of fashioning defences to insurance claims which are not disproportionately severe to the assured militates against interpreting forfeiture of benefits as encompassing retro-spective avoidance of the policy.

19–62 In litigation. In contrast to authority upon fraud conditions in policies[49] it has been held that neither the common law rule nor its "sub-species" apply to fraud by the assured after the commencement of proceedings.[50]

(c) *Utmost Good Faith Disclosure*

19–63 Duty and sanction for breach. The parties to the insurance contract remain subject to a continuing duty of utmost good faith after the formation of the contract, as stated in section 17 of the Marine Insurance Act 1906. The duty does not arise from an implied condition of the contract but as an independent rule of law enshrined in the statute.[51] While it is no longer the law that an insurer may avoid the contract for breach of the duty of good faith when the assured either is guilty of "culpable" non-disclosure or misrepresentation in the making of a claim, or acts unconscionably in failing to be completely open with the insurer, this does not mean that actual fraud in making a claim is tolerated by section 17.[52] Making a fraudulent claim is a breach of the duty of utmost good faith, and the section states that the insurer may therefore avoid the contract. The Court of Appeal in *The Mercandian Continent* has placed a restriction upon the right to avoid. It is restricted to a case where (a) the fraud would have an effect upon underwriters' ultimate liability and (b) the gravity of the fraud or its consequences would entitle the underwriters, if they wished to do so, to terminate the policy for breach of contract.[53] It follows that the right to avoid the insurance retrospectively arises only where the insurer could accept the

---

[46] [2001] 1 All E.R. (Comm) 193, 215–216; *Agapitos v. Agnew* [2002] 1 All E.R. (Comm) 714, 722.
[47] [1999] Lloyd's Rep.I.R. 209, 214.
[48] [2002] 1 All E.R. (Comm) 714, 730.
[49] *Lek v. Mathews* (1927) 29 Ll.L.R. 141, 145.
[50] *Agapitos v. Agnew* [2002] 1 All E.R. (Comm) 714.
[51] Although Lord Hobhouse in *The Star Sea* said that a "coherent scheme" could be achieved on such an analysis, his speech was in fact founded on the parties' consensus that the relevant principle was not a contractual term but a principle of law supporting a right of retrospective avoidance—[2001] 1 All E.R. (Comm) 193, 210. Were this not so, it is difficult to see how Lord Steyn and Lord Hoffmann could have agreed with both his speech and that of Lord Scott, who founded his speech upon the duty of good faith expressed in s.17.
[52] *The Star Sea* [2001] 1 All E.R. (Comm) 193, over-ruling *The Litsion Pride* [1985] 1 Lloyd's Rep. 437 on this issue.
[53] [2001] 2 Lloyd's Rep. 563, 575.

assured's conduct as repudiatory and terminate the contract. Applying the contractual yardstick, the paradigm cases of the baseless claim, the inflated claim, and the suppression of a defence would most probably pass not only test "a" but also test "b", as both Hoffmann L.J.[54] and Lord Hobhouse [55] thought when viewing the common law rule as one based on a contract term. However, the insurer could not rely on section 17 when the assured was guilty of knowingly putting forward false evidence in support of a valid claim, since this would not pass test "a".[56]

19–64 In litigation. Although the point has not been decided as such, there are strong *obiter dicta* at the highest level to the effect that the duty of good faith under section 17 is superseded by the rules of civil procedure once litigation has begun with regard to the subject-matter of that litigation.[57]

19–65 Assignees. An assignee claiming in right of the assured as his assignor will be defeated by the asssured's fraud in making the claim.[58] Similarly the fraud of one out of two joint assureds will defeat a joint claim by both of them.[59] The fraud of one co-assured in making a claim will not defeat a separate claim by another co-assured where the latter is not party to the fraud and has a right of claim not derived from that of the fraudulent assured.[60]

7. INTEREST & COSTS

19–66 Power of tribunal to award interest. Section 35A of the Supreme Court Act 1981 empowers the High Court[61] in proceedings for recovery of a debt or damages to award simple interest on the sum for which interim or final judgment is given, or which is paid before judgment, for all or any part of the period between the date when the cause of action[62] arose, and the date of the judgment or prior payment.[63] The rate of interest and the period for which it is to run are in the discretion of the court, although the parameters within which the discretion is exercisable are indicated by authority. An award of interest is appealable only if the judge has misdirected himself or his conclusion is outside the generous ambit within which a reasonable disagreement is possible.[64]

19–67 Interest runs from date of default. As a general rule the court will

---

[54] *Orakpo v. Barclays Ins. Services* [1995] L.R.L.R. 443, 451.
[55] *Manifest Shipping Co. Ltd v. Uni-Polaris Co. Ltd, The Star Sea* [2001] 1 All E.R. (Comm) 193, 216.
[56] *Agapitos v. Agnew* [2002] 1 All E.R. (Comm) 714, 730.
[57] *ibid.* at p. 733.
[58] *In re Carr and the Sun Fire Ins. Co.* (1897) 13 T.L.R. 186; *The Litsion Pride* [1985] 1 Lloyd's Rep. 437, 518–519.
[59] *General Accident Fire & Life Ass. Corp. v. Midland Bank* [1940] 2 K.B. 388.
[60] *Samuel v. Dumas* [1924] A.C. 431; *New Hampshire Ins. Co. v. MGN* [1997] L.R.L.R. 24, 57; *Bass Breweries Ltd v. Independent Ins. Co. Ltd* 2002 S.L.T. 512; but if the fraudulent assured acts as agent for the other, neither can recover, *Direct Line Insurance v. Khan* [2002] Lloyd's Rep. I.R. 364.
[61] Arbitrators possess a similar power under the Arbitration Act 1996, s.49, but in addition have the power to award compound interest.
[62] *The Khian Captain No. 2* [1986] 1 Lloyd's Rep. 429, 434.
[63] *Edmunds v. Lloyd's Italico & L'Ancora Cia.* [1986] 1 Lloyd's Rep. 326.
[64] *Adcock v. Co-Operative Ins. Soc. Ltd* [2000] Lloyd's Rep.I.R. 657, 663.

award interest from the date at which the insurer is in default for not paying the claim, because the basic function of an award of interest is to compensate the claimant for being kept out of his money. In indemnity insurance this is, strictly speaking, the date on which the assured's cause of action arose, and in property insurance this will be the date of the casualty, at which according to the established but unrealistic analysis of a claim for an indemnity as one for damages for breach of contract, the insurer is deemed to be in breach of an obligation to hold his assured harmless against loss caused by an insured peril.[65] In practice, the courts are sometimes prepared to postpone the running of interest not only to the date at which a claim is notified to the insurers, because it cannot be said that he is being kept out of his money until the insurer is aware that a payment is demanded, but to that at which a reasonable investigation of the claim ought to have been completed.[66] In cases where the claim is inadequately formulated or documented the time for a reasonable investigation may well be extended in consequence.[67] Regard will be had to the terms of the policy stipulating provision of particulars and evidence of loss and allowing the insurer a time for investigation of the claim.[68] In life insurance the company will usually be entitled to refuse payment until proper proof of death and a good title to receipt of the policy monies is tendered so that a valid legal discharge can be given.[69]

The court may abridge the period for the running of interest to mark its disapproval of the claimant's delay in bringing or pursuing his claim, although this has the effect of providing a windfall to the insurer who should not have had the use of the money.[70] It can be explained on the basis that the assured's unreasonable delay becomes a cause of the money remaining unpaid.[71]

19–68 Rate of interest. The modern practice is to award a rate of interest sufficient to compensate the assured on the assumption that he has borrowed the judgment sum for the period for the period during which he was kept out of his money.[72] There is no enquiry into what he would have done with it,[73] and the only enquiry is as to the rate which would have been charged to an assured in his position for borrowing an equivalent sum, whether he actually did or did not borrow it, which may require evidence of rates in force in the

---

[65] *Callaghan v. Dominion Ins. Co.* [1997] 2 Lloyd's Rep. 541; *Rhesa Shipping Co. S.A. v.Edmunds* [1984] 2 Lloyd's Rep. 555, 559; *Firma C-Trade S.A. v. Newcastle Protection & Indemnity Association* [1991] 2 A.C. 1; *Kuwait Airways Corp. v. Kuwait Ins. Co.* [2000] Lloyd's Rep. 678, 684, 689. In Scots law the action is in debt, and interest runs from the time of a "judicial demand", including an action for a declaratory conclusion when insurers have agreed to honour a declarator if made against them—*Gaelic Assignments v. Sharp* 2001 S.L.T. 914.

[66] *Rhesa Shipping Co. S.A. v. Edmunds* [1984] 2 Lloyd's Rep. 555; *McLean v. Ecclesiastical Ins. Office Plc.* [1986] 2 Lloyd's Rep. 416, 427–428; *Kuwait Airways Corp. v. Kuwait Ins. Co.* [2000] Lloyd's Rep.I.R. 678, 689; *Quorm A/S v. Schramm (No. 2)* [2002] 2 Lloyd's Rep. 72, 75.

[67] *Rhesa Shipping Co. S.A. v. Edmunds* [1984] 2 Lloyd's Rep. 555, 559; *Adcock v. Co-Operative Ins. Soc. Ltd* [2000] Lloyd's Rep.I.R. 657,663–664.

[68] *Suncorp Ins. v. Milano Assicurazioni SpA.* [1993] 2 Lloyd's Rep. 225, 242.

[69] *Webster v.British Empire Mut. Life* (1880) 15 Ch.D. 169.

[70] *Whiting v. New Zealand Ins. Co.*(1932) 44 Ll.L.R. 179, 181; *Adcock v. Co-Operative Ins. Soc.Ltd* [2000] Lloyd's Rep.I.R. 657, 663–664; *Kuwait Airways Corp. v.Kuwait Ins. Co.* [2000] Lloyd's Rep.I.R. 678, 689; *Metal Box Ltd v. Currys* [1988] 1 All E.R. 341, 346.

[71] *Kuwait Airways Corp. v. Kuwait Ins. Co.* [2000] Lloyd's Rep.I.R. 678, 689; *Quorm A/S v. Schramm (No. 2)* [2002] 2 Lloyd's Rep. 72, 76.

[72] *Cremer v. General Carriers* [1974] 1 W.L.R. 341, 355–358; *Kuwait Airways Corp. v. Kuwait Ins. Co.* [2000] Lloyd's Rep.I.R. 678, 691.

[73] *La Pintada Cia. Nav. v. President of India* [1983] 1 Lloyd's Rep. 37, 43.

foreign jurisdiction in which he does business. A secondary function of interest is to compensate a claimant for diminution of the purchasing power of the sum awarded in a time of substantial inflation, and in such cases higher rates have been said to be available.[74] The usual practice in the English Commercial Court is to award 1 per cent over base rate(s) or Libor for the period in question.[75]

19–69 Indemnity costs. An insurer who delays unreasonably long in paying a claim may be ordered to pay the assured's costs on an indemnity basis,[76] and conversely an assured who persists in an unjustified claim may have to pay the insurers' costs on a similar basis.[77]

1970 Compensation for unreasonable delay in payment. English law does not allow an action by an assured against an insurer to recover damages for consequential loss caused by the insurer's unjustified refusal to pay a valid claim.[78] This is based on a combination of two separate rules. First, the cause of action for payment of an indemnity is analysed as one for payment of unliquidated damages.[79] The insurer is said to be in breach of a promise to hold the assured harmless against loss caused by an insured peril as from the time of its occurrence, regardless of when a claim is made or rejected. The second rule is one of the law of damages, namely that there can be no cause of action for damages for late payment of damages.[80] The assured's sole remedy is an award of interest, which in serious cases is inadequate compensation.

19–71 It is unclear when the first rule became established. Under the old rules of pleading it seems to have been sufficient either in covenant or assumpsit to plead the underwriter's promise to indemnify the assured for loss caused by a peril insured against, the occurrence of the peril, and the resultant loss. While the assured claimed to have suffered "damage" or "damages" this was simply unquantified loss caused by the peril and not by any breach of contract by the underwriter.[81] It did not involve the illogicality

---

[74] *Cookson v. Knowles* [1979] A.C. 556, 570.

[75] *Shearson Lehman Hutton Inc. v. Maclaine Watson & Co. Ltd (No. 2)* [1990] 3 All E.R. 723; *Kuwait Airways Corp. v. Kuwait Ins. Co.* [2000] Lloyd's Rep.I.R. 678, 691 and authorities there cited.

[76] *Wailes v. Stapleton Construction & Commercial Services* [1997] 2 Lloyd's Rep. 112; *Martini Investments v. McGuin* [2000] 2 Lloyd's Rep. 313, 317.

[77] *Cepheus Shipping Corp. v. Guardian Royal Exchange Ass. Plc.* [1995] 1 Lloyd's Rep. 622, 647; *NLA Group v. Bowers* [1999] 1 Lloyd's Rep. 109 (unsuccessful claimant ordered to pay half of defendant's costs on indemnity basis).

[78] This rule bars a claim for damages for hardship, inconvenience and mental distress caused by insurers' unreasonable behaviour—*Ventouris v. Mountain* [1992] 2 Lloyd's Rep. 281; *England v. Guardian Ins. Ltd.* [2000] Lloyd's Rep.I.R. 404, 422. It also bars a claim for financial loss consequent upon insurers' refusal to accept liability or to pay a valid claim—*Sprung v. Royal Ins. (UK) Ltd* [1999] Lloyd's Rep.I.R. 111.

[79] *Ventouris v. Mountain* [1992] 2 Lloyd's Rep. 281; *Bank of America National Trust & Savings Assoc. v. Christmas* [1993] 1 Lloyd's Rep. 137; *Edmunds v. Lloyd Italico & L'Ancora Cia. Di Assicurazioni* [1986] 1 Lloyd's Rep. 326, 327; *Callaghan v. Dominion Ins. Co. Ltd* [1997] 2 Lloyd's Rep. 541; *Firma C-Trade S.A. v. Newcastle Protection & Indemnity Assoc.* [1991] 2 A.C. 1. The description of the assured's claim as one for a "debt" in *England v. Guardian Ins. Ltd.* [2000] Lloyd's Rep.I.R. 404, 422, is with respect incorrect.

[80] *President of India v. La Pintada Cia. Nav.* [1985] A.C. 104; *President of India v. Lips Maritime Corp.* [1988] A.C. 395; *Ventouris v. Mountain* [1992] 2 Lloyd's Rep. 281.

[81] Park, *A System of the Law of Marine Insurances* (4th ed. 1842) Ch. 21, pp. 838–841.

of the present law of deeming the insurer to be in breach of an obligation to indemnify before he had an opportunity to perform it. At some stage the reference to "damages", necessarily unliquidated because requiring proof and quantification, became associated with damages awarded for breach of contract.[82] Be that as it may, the breach analysis is now established at the highest level.[83] What is needed to circumvent the two rules is the recognition of a separate obligation upon the insurer when handling a claim over and above the liability to indemnify. One possible obligation was the insurer's post-contractual duty to observe the utmost good faith towards the assured, but the opportunity to give it the status of an implied condition affording damages for its breach was missed in *The Star Sea*[84] and the only remedy for a breach of the duty in itself is avoidance.[85] It is on the basis of damages for breach of a contractual duty of good faith that the Supreme Court of Canada has recently allowed a claim by an assured for punitive damages when an unjustifiable defence of arson was persisted in for several years.[86] Another possibility is to say that the insurer has to exercise its express rights to investigate claims and to require proof of loss with due regard to the interests of the assured, in the same way that a liability insurer is obliged to exercise its right to conduct the defence of a claim against the assured in good faith and with regard to the assured's interests.[87] This, however, fails to meet persistence in an unjustified defence after all details of the claim have been supplied, and complete redress would require the implication of a term, based on the over-riding principle of good faith, that insurers would not dispute their obligation to indemnify in the absence of reasonable grounds. We know of no precedent for such a term in English law, and in *Insurance Corporation of the Channel Islands v. McHugh*[88] Mance J. refused to imply a term in a fire policy to the effect that insurers would assess, negotiate and settle claims with reasonable expedition.

---

[82] *Jabbour v. Custodian of Israeli Absentee Property* [1954] 1 W.L.R. 139, 143–144, *per* Pearson J.

[83] See note 79 *supra*. Academic criticism has not been lacking—Campbell [2000] LMCLQ 42; Hemsworth [2001] LMCLQ 296; Clarke, *Law of Insurance Contracts* (Looseleaf ed., 1999) para. 30–6B.

[84] [2001] 1 All E.R. (Comm) 193.

[85] The duty gives rise to no contractual or tortious duties—*HIH Casualty & General Ins. Ltd. v. Chase Manhattan Bank* [2001] 2 Lloyd's Rep. 483, 494.

[86] *Whiten v. Pilot Ins. Co.* [2002] 209 D.L.R. (4th) 257. Another case is *Clarfield v. Crown Life Ins. Co.* (2001) 50 O.R. (3d) 696 (unfair delay in dealing with claim on disability policy; Can$75,000 aggravated damages and Can$200,000 punitive damages).

[87] *Cox v. Bankside Agency Ltd* [1995] 2 Lloyd's Rep. 437, 462; *The Mercandian Continent* [2001] 2 Lloyd's Rep. 563, 572.

[88] *Ins. Corp. of the Channel Islands v. McHugh* [1997] L.R.L.R. 94, 136–137.

CHAPTER 20

THE CLAIMANT

1. ASSIGNMENT

(a) *Voluntary Assignment*

20–1 Rights under insurance policies are choses in action and as such are capable of assignment, but their assignability is complicated by the existence of different rules depending on the type of policy in question and the precise nature of the rights which are to be assigned. Life policies and marine policies are assignable under the Policies of Assurance Act 1867 and the Marine Insurance Act 1906 respectively. The former Act is considered in detail in chapter 24. The latter lies outside the scope of this work, although reference will be made to marine insurance cases for illustrative purposes. Rights under all contracts of insurance including life and marine are assignable under section 136 of the Law of Property Act 1925 if they satisfy the requirements of that section, chiefly that they are existing legal choses in action and are assigned absolutely, while those which do not are assignable in equity, assuming in both cases that assignment is not prohibited either by statute or by the terms of the insurance. Another distinction must be made between assignment (transfer) of the subject-matter insured under the policy and the assignment of the policy itself because they have entirely different effects.

20–2 Assignment of the subject-matter insured. If the assured voluntarily parts with all his interest in the subject-matter of the insurance policy, the policy lapses since the assured no longer has any insurable interest and can have suffered no loss.[1] The assignment must, however, be complete[2] and if the assured retains any insurable interest he will be able to recover under the policy.[3] Thus, if he enters into a contract to convey the subject-matter and the subject-matter is lost or damaged, the assured can still recover even

---

[1] *Rayner v. Preston* (1881) 18 Ch.D. 1, 7, *per* Cotton L.J., *Ecclesiastical Commissioners v. Royal Exchange Assurance Corporation* (1895) 11 T.L.R. 476; *Robson v. Liverpool, London and Globe Ins. Co.* (1900) *The Times*, June 23; *Rogerson v. Scottish Automobile and General Ins. Co. Ltd* (1931) 48 T.L.R. 17; *Tattersall v. Drysdale* [1935] 2 K.B. 174; *Boss and Hansford v. Kingston* [1962] 2 Lloyd's Rep. 431; *Dodson v. P. H. Dodson Ins. Services* [2001] 1 All E.R. (Comm) 300.
[2] *Forbes & Co. v. Border Counties Fire Office* (1873) 11 M. 278.
[3] See Ch. 1, *ante*.

though the risk has passed to the purchaser.[4] Until the vendor is paid he cannot be certain of receiving the purchase price and it is in effect this risk which, in such a case, is the subject of insurance.[5] The policy will probably remain in force even after conveyance if the purchase price has not been paid, provided that the vendor has not parted with his lien. The lien will ensure that the assured still has an insurable interest.[6] An assured who enters into a contract of sale will often agree to transfer the insurance policy and, if he effectively does so, the transferee will be able to recover under it.[7]

20–3 Change of interest. A change of interest is something different from an assignment of the subject-matter insured. It is not only the unpaid seller of goods who retains a sufficient insurable interest to recover under the policy; the creation of a mortgage or a charge does not affect the validity of the policy since the assured retains the equity of redemption.[8] If, however, the mortgagor disposes of his equity of redemption[9] or if the mortgagee lawfully exercises his power of sale,[10] there will be an assignment and the insured will be unable to recover. The position might be different if the mortgagor's equity of redemption was compulsorily sold by way of execution, but the mortgagor continued in possession as a tenant of the mortgagee.[11]

20–4 A sale of land will constitute an assignment even where only the buildings and chattels are insured,[12] but a conveyance of the legal estate will not prevent the insured from recovering if he retains the beneficial interest.[13] A hire-purchaser who enters into a sub-hire-purchase agreement will be held to have assigned the subject-matter.[14]

A change in the constitution of a partnership can give rise to difficulties. If a partner retires, he remains liable for debts and liabilities arising before his retirement and the interest of the other partners continues. It is therefore submitted that, as far as liability insurance is concerned, the insurance policy continues to be effective and can be enforced by the partner liable or in the name of the firm.[15] Insurance on property is more difficult; if it can be said

---

[4] *Collingridge v. Royal Exchange Assurance Corporation* (1877) 3 Q.B.D. 173. Conversely if goods are sold and paid for but the risk remains with the seller, the seller's insurance will continue, *Martineau v. Kitching* (1872) L.R. 7 Q.B. 436. Similarly, where the seller retains a bare legal title, *Caledonian Ins. Co. v. Montreal Trust Co.* [1932] 3 D.L.R. 657.

[5] *Castellain v. Preston* (1883) 11 Q.B.D. 380, 385 *per* Brett L.J.; *A. R. Williams Machinery Co. v. British Crown Assurance Corporation Ltd* (1921) 29 B.C.R. 481. It is, of course, possible that the insurance will also continue to protect concurrent limited interests as in *Lonsdale v. Black Arrow* [1993] Ch. 361.

[6] *Castellain v. Preston* (1883) 11 Q.B.D. at 401 and 405 *per* Bowen L.J. Once the vendor is fully paid, however, his interest will cease and he will be unable to recover; *Bank of New South Wales v. North British and Mercantile Ins. Co.* (1881) 2 N.S.W.L.R. 239.

[7] See para. 20–23, *post.* This is the invariable procedure under a c.i.f. contract for the sale of goods.

[8] *Alston v. Campbell* (1779) 4 Bro.P.C. 476; *Ward v. Beck* (1863) 13 C.B.(N.S.) 668; *Garden v. Ingram* (1852) 23 L.J.Ch. 478. *Cf. Smith v. Royal Ins. Co.* (1867) 27 U.C.Q.B. 54 (conveyance to guarantor security), *Sovereign Fire Ins. Co. v Peters* (1885) 12 S.C.R. 33.

[9] *Springfield Fire and Marine Ins. Co. v. Allen*, 43 N.Y. 389 (1871); *Pinhey v. Mercantile Fire Ins. Co.* (1901) 2 O.L.R. 296.

[10] *Pyman v. Marten* (1907) 13 Com.Cas. 64, 67, *per* Lord Alverstone C.J.

[11] *Strong v. Manufacturers' Insurance*, 27 Mass. 40 (1830).

[12] *Dunlop v. Usborne and Hibbert Fire Ins. Co.* (1895) 22 O.A.R. 364.

[13] *Ward v. Beck* (1863) 13 C.B.(N.S.) 668.

[14] *Reilly Bros. v. Mercantile Mutual Ins. Co.* (1928) 30 W.A.L.R. 72.

[15] *Jenkins v. Deane* (1933) 150 L.T. 314, 318.

that the property lost or damaged was always owned by the surviving partner, that partner can enforce the policy,[16] but if the property was owned by the retiring partner and was transferred to the remaining partners, the insurance might well be held to have lapsed.[17] This would certainly be the case if a new partner was admitted and became a co-owner of the property.[18] A liability insurance policy will not cover a new partner, unless the insurers have given their consent, but there is no reason why the original partners should not continue to be covered for their personal liability, unless the risk of their liability has been altered by the advent of a new partner.[19]

20-5 Assignment of policy contrasted with assignment of right of recovery. It is vital to distinguish between an assignment of the contract of insurance and an assignment of any claim that arises under that contract. The assured may wish to transfer the subject-matter of the insurance and at the same time transfer the benefit of the insurance policy so that the transferee can sue under the policy for the damage sustained by what is now his interest. This can only be done in accordance with settled rules of law and, since there is to be a substitution of the original assured by a new assured, there is, in effect, a novation and the consent of the insurers will be required. On the other hand the assured may wish merely to transfer the right to recover under the policy. This is a chose in action and can be effectively assigned at common law provided that the requirements of section 136 of the Law of Property Act 1925 are fulfilled. Even if they are not, the transfer will operate as an equitable assignment.[20] The consent of the insurer is not required because there is no change in the scope or the terms of the policy.[21] The insurer must, however, receive notice of the assignment before it will be complete and he will then be entitled and bound to pay any proceeds over to the assignee.[22] It is important to realise that whereas an assignee of a contract of insurance is able to recover for the damage sustained by him to his interest, an assignee of the debt arising under the contract can only recover in respect of the loss sustained by his assignor.[23] It

[16] *Forbes & Co. v. Border Counties Fire Office* (1873) 11 M. 278.
[17] *cf. Ferguson v. National Fire and Marine Ins. Co. of New Zealand* (1886) N.S.W. Law R. 392.
[18] *Jenkins v. Deane* (1933) 150 L.T. at p. 317.
[19] This seems to be the effect of the decision in *Jenkins v. Deane, supra.*
[20] *Raiffeisen Zentralbank v. Five Star Trading* [2001] 1 All E.R. (Comm) 961, 987; *Williams v. Atlantic Assurance Co.* [1933] 1 K.B. 81, 106.
[21] *McPhillips v. London Mutual Fire Ins. Co.* (1896) 23 O.A.R. 524. The parties can presumably agree that the insurers' consent is necessary for this type of assignment but only in the clearest possible words, *Re Birkbeck Permanent Benefit Building Society* [1913] 2 Ch. 34.
[22] *Scheidermann v. Barnet* [1951] N.Z.L.R. 301. If no notice is given to the insurers, they will not be bound to pay the asignee, *London Investment Co. v. Montefiore* (1864) 9 L.T. 688. For the formalities required by the law of Quebec for an effective assignment of the rights arising under the Contract of Insurance, see *Bank of Toronto v. St. Lawrence Fire Ins. Co.* [1903] A.C. 59 and *Boiler Inspection and Insurance Co. of Canada v. Sherwin-Williams Company of Canada* [1951] A.C. 319. Assignment of life assurance policies are in the nature of assignments of the right to recover thereon.
[23] See *Hazzard v. Canada Agricultural Ins. Co.* (1886) 39 U.C.Q.B. 419 where a mortgagor assigned the benefit of insurance contract to his mortgagee who later, after loss, assigned the right of recovery to the mortgagor; *Landauer v. Asser* [1905] 2 K.B. 184 where, by contrast, the seller of goods no longer possessed any interest in the insured cargo and in the insurance, and *Jan de Nul v. Assoc. British Ports* [2001] Lloyd's Rep. I.R. 324, 355–356, where the assignee was unable to prove that the assignor had suffered loss, affirmed [2002] 1 Lloyd's Rep. 583.

is proposed to distinguish between the two types of assignment by referring to them as assignment of the contract and assignment of the right of recovery respectively. Assignment of the right of recovery depends solely on the ordinary principles of the law of contract[24] and this section will be chiefly concerned with the rules relating to the valid assignment of the contract.

20–6 Assignment of the contract of insurance. A contract of insurance is a personal contract and does not run with the property which is the subject matter of the insurance[25]; thus, if the subject-matter is sold or otherwise alienated by the assured, the policy does not pass to the assignee unless the policy is also assigned in accordance with the rules set out in this paragraph.[26] In fact, as we have seen, once the subject-matter of the insurance policy is completely transferred by the assured, the policy itself immediately lapses.[27] There are two rules for the assignment of contracts of insurance: (1) the consent of the insurers must be obtained to the assignment in the form (if any) required by the policy, and (2) the assignment of the policy must accompany the assignment of the subject-matter of the insurance.

20–7 Consent of the insurer. In the case of a fire policy it is always necessary to obtain the consent of the insurer to the assignment.[28] An indemnity insurance is a contract of personal indemnity between the insurer and the assured and, if a new assured is to be substituted for an original assured, there must, in effect, be a novation of the contract.[29] Moreover, the assignee must know and consent to the assignment before it can be effective.[30]

The policy may contain a clause expressly prohibiting assignment but this adds nothing to the position at common law.[31] On the other hand, assignment may be permitted, provided that the assured gives notice within a specified time of the assignment.[32] If no such notice is given, any assignment can be avoided by the insurer.[33]

---

[24] This assignment can take place either before or after loss; compare *Bank of Toronto v. St. Lawrence Fire Ass. Co.* [1903] A.C. 59 and *English and Scottish Mercantile Investment Co. v. Brunton* [1892] 2 Q.B. 700.

[25] *Rayner v. Preston* (1881) 18 Ch.D. 1, 6, *per* Cotton L.J., 11 *per* Brett L.J.; *Phoenix Ass. Co. v. Spooner* [1905] 2 K.B. 753 overruled (on different grounds) in *West Midland Baptist Association v. Birmingham Corporation* [1970] A.C. 874. *Ocean Accident and Guarantee Corporation v. Williams* (1915) 34 N.Z.L.R. 924. This characteristic does not preclude intervention by an undisclosed principal for whom the insurance was made—*Siu Yin Kwan v. Eastern Ins. Co. Ltd* [1994] 2 A.C. 199, 210.

[26] *Mildmay v. Folgham* (1799) 3 Ves. 471; *Poole v. Adams* (1864) 33 L.J.Ch. 639; *Rayner v. Preston* (1881) 18 Ch.D. 1, 12.

[27] See para. 20–2, *ante*.

[28] *Sadlers' Co. v. Badcock* (1743) 2 Atk. 554, 556–557 *per* Lord Hardwicke L.C.; *Hendrickson v. Queen Ins. Co.* (1870) 30 U.C.Q.B. 547. The insurers' consent might be given at the outset through the grant of a policy to the assured and his assigns—*Noack v. Lanark County Mut. Fire Ins. Co.* [1932] 4 D.L.R. 64.

[29] *Peters v. General Accident Fire and Life Assurance Corporation Ltd* [1938] 2 All E.R. 267. See also the judgment of Goddard J. at first instance [1937] 4 All E.R. 628 and *Murchie v. Victoria Insurance Co.* (1885) 4 N.Z.L.R.(S.C.) 14.

[30] *Crozier v. Phoenix Ins. Co.* (1871) 13 N.B.R. 200.

[31] See para. 20–15, *post*.

[32] *cf. Re Birkbeck Permanent Benefit Building Society* [1913] 2 Ch. 34.

[33] *Doe d. Pitt v. Laming* (1814) 4 Camp. 73.

The above principles apply to all contracts of insurance except and marine insurance which is subject to special rules.[34]

20–8 Assignment of subject-matter must accompany assignment of the contract. An assignment of the contract of insurance must be accompanied by a contemporaneous transfer of interest in the subject-matter insured, if the assignment is to be valid.[35] Thus if a contract of insurance is assigned before the subject-matter is transferred, the assignee will have no insurable interest and the policy will become void, whereas if it is assigned after transfer the policy will have already ceased to be in force as the assured will have lost all interest in the subject-matter. In *Lynch v. Dalzell*,[36] a house was sold and subsequently caught fire; the vendor purported to assign the policy to the purchaser after the fire, and the purchaser made a claim. The House of Lords held that the policy lapsed when the vendor sold the property, and the assignee could not recover. The insurers had not consented to the assignment but, even if they had, there would have been no valid assignment to which consent could be given and any such consent would be ineffective unless a completely new contract to indemnify the assignee could be inferred.[37]

It may well be that the assignment of the subject-matter for the purposes of this rule need not be absolute. If, for example, a mortgagor at the same time as mortgaging the property assigns the benefit of a policy to the mortgagee with the consent of the insurers, the mortgage would presumably be a sufficient assignment.[38] Moreover, an assignee would probably not be precluded from recovering to the extent of his interest by the fact that the policy originally insured additional property over and above the property transferred to him.[39]

20–9 Assignment of the right of recovery. If the insured validly assigns his right to recover under the policy, the assignee becomes the payee of the proceeds, and the insurer will pay the assignor at his peril.[40] The assignee will, however, be bound to perform any conditions precedent to recovery, such as giving notice of loss, and, since he takes subject to equities, the

---

[34] *Peters v. General Accident Fire and Life Assurance Corporation* [1937] 4 All E.R. 628, 633, *per* Goddard J. See further s.50 of the Marine Insurance Act 1906 and, as an illustration of the substitution of assignee for assignor as the assured, *Landauer v. Asser* [1905] 2 K.B. 184.

[35] There is remarkably little authority for this principle except in cases of marine insurance, see *Lloyd v. Fleming* (1872) L.R. 7 Q.B. 299 and *North of England Pure Oil Cake Co. v. Archangel Ins. Co.* (1875) L.R. 10 Q.B. 249. An agreement to transfer the subject-matter would probably suffice, *cf.* the converse case of a transfer of the subject-matter and a contemporaneous agreement to assign, *Powles v. Innes* (1834) 11 M. & W. 10. After loss the assignment of the benefit of the claim will satisfy this requirement where the loss has exhausted the policy or the policy is then time expired—*Raiffeisen Zentralbank v. Five Star Trading* [2001] 1 All E.R. (Comm) 961, 983.

[36] (1729) 4 Bro.P.C. 431.

[37] *cf.* cases cited in note 46, *infra.*

[38] *cf. Burton v. Gore District Mutual Fire Ins. Co.* (1857) 14 U.C.Q.B. 342; (1865) 12 Gr. 156 where, however, the mortgage took the form of an absolute assignment. But see *Stevens v. Queen Ins. Co.* (1894) 32 N.B.R. 387.

[39] *cf.* the facts of *Hazzard v. Canada Agricultural Ins. Co.* (1876) 39 U.C.Q.B. where the assignee had succeeded in persuading the insurers to pay him the amount insured on the buildings which had been mortgaged to him.

[40] *Watt v. Gore District Mutual Ins. Co.* (1861) 8 Gr. 523; *Greet v. Citizens' Ins. Co.* (1879) 27 Gr. 121, reversed on different grounds (1880) 5 O.A.R. 596.

insurers can rely on any breach of condition by the assured.[41] Moreover, since the assignor remains the insured, any cancellation of the policy by the assignee will be ineffective.[42]

20–10 Assignment of the contract of insurance. Where the policy is effectively assigned together with the subject-matter insured, the assignee still takes subject to equities and the insurer will, for example, be able to rely on any non-disclosure which takes place before the assignment is made.[43] It is not entirely clear whether the insurers can rely on any breach of condition or duty on the part of the original assured after he has assigned the policy but if he retains an interest they probably can.[44] But, they cannot rely on any such misconduct where the new assured has an original interest in the subject-matter of the policy which is not derived by way of assignment,[45] or where they have, in effect, entered into a completely new contract with the assured.[46]

After an assignment of this kind has taken place, the assignor drops out of the picture and the assignee becomes the insured.[47] If, therefore, the insurers wish to cancel the policy for non-payment of premiums and notice to the insured is required, that notice must be given to the assignee.[48] The assignor can no longer sue even if he becomes interested in the subject-matter again; thus a mortgagor, who executes a transfer of the property and an assignment of the insurance policy and later repays the debt and obtains the property again, cannot recover under the policy[49] unless the policy is re-assigned at the time of the reconveyance.[50]

20–11 Other Rights. Rights other than those arising from the contract of insurance will not be assigned with the contract. If, for example, the assignor has acquired rights against his insurance brokers, those rights will not pass to

---

[41] *Re Carr and Sun Fire Ins. Co.* (1897) 13 T.L.R. 186; *Samuel & Co. v. Dumas* [1924] A.C. 431; *Williams v. Atlantic Ass. Co. Ltd* [1933] 1 K.B. 81; *McEntire v. Sun Fire Office* (1895) 29 I.L.T. 103. When the right of recovery is assigned, the insurer owes a duty to act in good faith to the assignor before and after the assignment. When the insurance policy is assigned, the duty is then owed to the assignee—*The "Good Luck"* [1988] 1 Lloyd's Rep. 514, 546; [1989] 2 Lloyd's Rep. 238, 264.

[42] *Morrow v. Lancashire Ins. Co.* (1898) 26 O.A.R. 173; *Raiffeisen Zentralbank v. Five Star Trading* [2001] 1 All E.R. (Comm) 961, 982–983.

[43] *William Pickersgill & Sons Ltd v. London and Provincial Marine and General Ins. Co. Ltd* [1912] 3 K.B. 614.

[44] *Black King Shipping v. Massie* [1985] 1 Lloyd's Rep. 437, 517–519 (mortgagees were defeated by insured's absence of good faith in pursuing a fraudulent claim). Contrast *Burton v. Gore District Mutual Ins. Co.* (1865) 12 Gr. 156 (previous proceedings 14 U.C.Q.B. 342) with *Kanady v. Gore District Mutual Fire Ins. Co.* (1879) 44 U.C.Q.B. 261.

[45] *Samuel & Co. v. Dumas* [1924] A.C. 431. Cf. *Omnium Securities Co. v. Canada Fire and Mutual Ins. Co.* (1882) 1 O.R. 494 and *Liverpool and London Globe Ins. Co. v. Agricultural Savings and Loan Co.* (1903) 33 S.C.R. 94.

[46] *Chapman v. Gore District Mutual Ins. Co.* (1876) 26 U.C.C.P. 89; *Weyman v. Imperial Ins. Co.* (1888) 16 S.C.R. 715; *Western Australian Bank v. Royal Ins. Co.* (1908) 5 C.L.R. 533; *Springfield Fire and Marine Ins. Co. v. Maxim* [1946] S.C.R. 604.

[47] *Landauer v. Asser* [1905] 2 K.B. 184.

[48] *Guggisberg v. Waterloo Mutual Fire Ins. Co.* (1876) 24 Gr. 350.

[49] *Fitzgerald v. Gore District Mutual Fire Ins. Co.* (1870) 30 U.C.Q.B. 97. The position would be different if the original assignment was invalid: *Crozier v. Phoenix Ins. Co.* (1870) 13 N.B.R. 200.

[50] *De Launay v. Northern Ass. Co.* (1883) 2 N.Z.L.R.(S.C.) 1.

the assignee, but if the broker knows of an impending assignment, he may well assume a tortious duty of care to the assignee.[51]

(b) *Involuntary Assignment*

20–12 Introduction. On the death or bankruptcy of the assured, both the subject-matter insured and the policy itself pass to the personal representatives,[52] or the trustee in bankruptcy,[53] as the case may be. Similarly if any company is compulsorily wound up, its property may, by order of the court, vest in the liquidator.[54] But the loss may arise either before or after the event which gives rise to the involuntary assignment and different principles will apply.

20–13 Loss before the event. If the loss occurs before the insured dies or goes bankrupt, his personal representatives or his trustee in bankruptcy will be entitled to make a claim on behalf of the insured's estate. The right of action against the insurance company is a chose in action which can be enforced in the ordinary way by the personal representative or the trustee.[55] The same principle applies to a company in liquidation when the liquidator will be able to enforce the claim that accrued to the company before liquidation took place.[56] Since the assignee is enforcing the claim of the insured, he is bound by the terms of the policy and must perform all conditions precedent to recovery. He will, moreover, be liable to be defeated by any misconduct or breach of condition on the part of the assured before the assignment takes effect.[57] If the insurer pays or settles with a bankrupt insured after the trustee has become entitled to enforce the policy, the trustee's rights are unaffected and the insurer may have to pay twice.[58]

20–14 Loss after the event. If the insured dies and the executors or administrators distribute the property to those entitled and the property is then lost or damaged, it is very doubtful whether the new owners can recover in the absence of consent on the part of the insurers. Thus in *Mildmay v. Folgham*[59] it was held that the heirs at law to whom the property had passed after the death of the insured could not recover for a fire which occurred after the death. But most policies at the present time undertake to indemnify

---

[51] *Punjab Bank Ltd v. De Boinville* [1992] 1 W.L.R. 1138.

[52] Administration of Estates Act 1925, s.1(1) which brought the law of real property into line with that for personal property; *Doe* d. *Pitt v. Laming* (1814) 4 Camp. 73.

[53] Insolvency Act 1986, s.306. As to the right of the injured third party to be subrogated to the rights of the bankrupt insured in liability insurance, see Chap. 28, *post.*

[54] Insolvency Act 1986, s.145.

[55] *Marriage v. Royal Exchange Ass. Co.* (1849) 18 L.J.Ch. 216; *Durrant v. Friend* (1851) 5 De G. & Sm. 343; *Manchester Fire Ass. Co. v. Wykes* (1875) 33 L.T. 142; *Re Carr and Sun Fire Ins. Co.* (1897) 13 T.L.R. 186; *Hood's Trustees v. Southern Union General Ins. Co.* [1928] Ch. 793. The trustee may sue either in his official name or in his own name, *Leeming v. Lady Murray* (1879) 13 Ch.D. 123.

[56] *Re Harrington Motor Co. Ltd* [1928] Ch. 105.

[57] *Re Carr and Sun Fire Ins. Co.* (1897) 13 T.L.R. 186; *McEntire v. Sun Fire Office* (1895) 29 I.L.T. 103.

[58] *McEntire v. Potter & Co.* (1889) 22 Q.B.D. 438; *Hood's Trustees v. Southern Union General Ins. Co.* [1928] Ch. 793.

[59] (1797) 3 Ves. 471. Although real property now passes to the personal representatives just like the insurance policy, the principle of this decision is presumably still valid, at any rate if the fire occurs after distribution of the assets.

the insured and all persons to whom his interest in the property may pass by will or by operation of law and the insurer's consent to the assignment of the interest and the policy is then signified in advance.[60]

A trustee in bankruptcy or a liquidator cannot, without the consent of the insurers, assign the insurance policy at the same time as he disposes of the property of the bankrupt or the company in liquidation; and, in the absence of a term in the policy providing for loss or damage to the property while in their own hands, they probably cannot recover for damage which occurs after the bankruptcy or the liquidation as the case may be.

(c) Conditions Prohibiting Assignment

20–15 Effect of various clauses. The policy may contain a clause prohibiting the assignment of the subject matter; this adds nothing to the common law position.[61] Alternatively it may contain a clause prohibiting assignment otherwise than by will or operation of law. This will have the effect of actually permitting an assignment which takes place in one of those ways.[62] The words "operation of law" are not always easy to construe but they have been held to include the statutory transfer of property from one person to another[63] and even the transfer of property by someone who is under a statutory obligation to assign, such as the liquidator of an unregistered company.[64]

Sometimes the policy may be framed so as to prevent even a mortgage or lease of the property insured,[65] which would not normally constitute an assignment of the subject-matter.[66]

20–16 A policy which provides that it is not assignable in one sense states no more than the common law position, since it is impossible to assign the burden (as opposed to the benefit) of the contract. The effect of such a clause is, however, always a matter of construction of the contract. Such a clause would be likely to be construed to mean that the assured was not permitted to assign either the benefit of the contract or, even, the right to recover in the event of a loss.[67]

---

[60] cf. Doe d. Pitt v. Laming (1815) 4 Camp. 73. A clause that the policy is to cease to have effect if the subject-matter is assigned otherwise than by will or operation of law would presumably have a similiar effect, Thomas v. National Farmers' Union Mutual Ins. Society Ltd [1961] 1 W.L.R. 386 and Re Birkbeck Permanent Benefit Building Society [1913] 2 Ch. 34.

[61] cf. the clause in Pyman v. Marten (1907) 13 Com.Cas. 64. There will be no breach of such a clause until the assignment is complete, Forbes & Co. v. Border Counties Fire Office (1873) 11 M. 278.

[62] See para. 20–12, ante.

[63] Thomas v. National Farmers' Union Mutual Ins. Society Ltd [1961] 1 W.L.R. 386.

[64] Re Birkbeck Permanent Benefit Building Society [1913] 2 Ch. 34. Quaere whether an assignee from a trustee in bankruptcy or a trustee for sale might be able to argue that a transfer to him was likewise an assignment by operation of law.

[65] cf. National Protector Fire Ins. Co. Ltd v. Nivert [1913] A.C. 507; and Citizens' Ins. Co. of Canada v. Salterio (1894) 23 S.C.R. 155.

[66] See para. 20–3, ante.

[67] Linden Gardens Trust Ltd v. Lenesta Sludge Disposals Ltd [1994] 1 A.C. 85. This was a building contract case and it could be argued that somewhat different considerations apply to contracts of insurance. In Kerr v. Hastings Mutual Fire Insurance Co. (1877) 41 U.C.Q.B. 217 it was held that a purported assignment of the policy was to be construed merely as an assignment of the right to recover under the policy with the result that there was no breach of a clause prohibiting assignment.

2. Limited Interests in Property

(a) *Vendors and Purchasers*[68]

20–17 Insurance by vendor of land. Apart from statute, the purchaser of real property is not entitled to the benefit of any insurance effected by the vendor on the property, unless the benefit of the policy has been assigned to the purchaser by the contract and the insurers have consented to the assignment.[69] After contract and before conveyance the vendor still has an insurable interest and can recover for any loss under the policy[70]; the purchaser, however, despite any loss or damage to the property, must still pay the agreed purchase price and has no right to the insurance money at common law in the absence of any express assignment of the benefit of the policy. Thus in *Rayner v. Preston*[71] R purchased a workshop from P who had insured against fire. Between the date of the contract and the date of completion a fire took place and the property was damaged. The loss was paid to P and R claimed that he was entitled to the benefit of the sums paid by the insurance company. The Court of Appeal by a majority held that R was not entitled to any such benefit because the contract of sale made no reference to the contract of insurance; the contract of sale passed the benefit of contracts necessarily connected with the use and enjoyment of the property but not the benefit of contracts which were merely collateral. A contract to reinstate the buildings might be closely enough connected, but a contract to pay an indemnity was not; in this case the only liability of the company was to pay the money and there was no liability to rebuild although the company might elect to do so. The plaintiff had relied on the doctrine that a vendor is a trustee for the purchaser but it was pointed out that a vendor is only a trustee of the actual subject-matter of the contract, not even of the rents accruing before the time for completion and still less of money paid under a contract of insurance.

R also argued that under the Fires Prevention (Metropolis) Act 1774,[72] he was entitled to insist that the insurers should reinstate the property and that therefore he should also be entitled to use the money in the hands of P for that purpose. The court held, however, that the right of reinstatement gave no right to claim the insurance money from P after it had been paid over.

20–18 American jurisdictions are much divided on the question whether a purchaser can claim the benefit of the insurance money if a fire occurs

---

[68] For the respective insurable interests of vendor and purchaser, see paras 1–124 to 1–130, *ante*.

[69] *Paine v. Meller* (1801) 6 Ves. 349; *Poole v. Adams* (1864) 33 L.J.Ch. 639; *Rayner v. Preston* (1881) 18 Ch.D. 1.

[70] *Collingridge v. Royal Exchange Assurance Corporation* (1877) 3 Q.B.D. 173; *Lonsdale v. Black Arrow Group* [1993] Ch. 361.

[71] (1881) 18 Ch.D. 1; *cf. Royal Insurance Co. v. Mylius* (1926) 38 C.L.R. 477.

[72] It is submitted (see para. 21–18 below) that the purchaser has a right to call for reinstatement unless (1) there is an express term in the contract to the contrary, or (2) the vendor covenants to give the purchaser the benefit of his insurance in certain specified circumstances only, see *e.g. Edwards v. West* (1878) 7 Ch.D. 858.

between contract and completion.[73] In England, however, an attempt has now been made to mitigate the injustice of the result by statute.[74]

After completion, neither party can recover on a policy taken out by the vendor since the vendor no longer has an interest in the subject-matter of the insurance.[75]

A policy taken out in the name of the vendor after the contract of sale was made might be construed as intended to benefit both parties and the purchaser would accordingly be able to share in the recovery.[76]

20–19 Law of Property Act 1925,[77] s.47. The section provides that where, after the date of a contract for the sale or exchange of property, money becomes payable under any contract of insurance maintained by the vendor in respect of damage to or destruction of property included in the contract, the money shall upon completion be held or receivable by the vendor on behalf of the purchaser and paid by the vendor to the purchaser on completion, or so soon thereafter as the same shall be received by the vendor. It is expressed to have effect subject to:

(a) any contrary stipulation in the contract,
(b) any requisite consents of the insurers and
(c) payment by the purchaser of a proportionate part of the premium.

It overrules *Rayner v. Preston* by imposing a duty on the vendor to account to the purchaser for such monies as are received by him, and accordingly appears not to work an assignment of either the insurance policy itself or the right of recovery thereunder, but rather to follow the grounds of the dissenting judgment of James L.J. by impressing the monies in the vendor's hands with a statutory trust or charge in favour of the purchaser.

Because the section operates only upon the insurance proceeds payable to the vendor it is not in practice a satisfactory alternative for the purchaser to taking out his own policy. It relies upon the vendor having maintained an insurance on the property for its full value and the insurers having no defence to payment. In the case where the insurance proceeds become payable after the receipt of the purchase monies, the insurers would have a defence to payment on the ground that the vendor had suffered no loss in consequence of the damage to the insured property.[78] Since the Standard Conditions of Sale (1990) provide that the vendor retains the risk until completion and that section 47 does not apply to the transaction, these problems have ceased to be important.[79]

---

[73] Contrast *Bronwell v. Board of Education*, 146 N.E. 630 (1925) in which the dissenting reasoning of James L.J. was criticised as "general and manifestly unsound" and *Edlin v. Security Ins. Co.* 269 F.2d. 159 (1959) with *Brady v. Welsh*, 204 N.W. 235 (1925), *Millville Aerie No. 1836, Fraternal Order of Eagles v Weatherby*, 88 A.847 (1913) and *Dublin Paper Co. v. Ins. Co. of North America*, 63 A.2d 85, 94–96; 8 A.L.R. 2d 1393 (1949).

[74] Law of Property Act 1925, s.47.

[75] *Ecclesiastical Commissioners v. Royal Exchange Ass. Corporation* (1895) 11 T.L.R. 476.

[76] *Brady v. Irish Land Commission* [1921] 1 I.R. 56, where the transaction was an unusual one and the form of policy was described as unique.

[77] 15 Geo. 5, c. 20. See the Review by the Law Commission of the law relating to the transfer of risk under sales of land in their Working Paper No. 109 (1988) and published Report No. 191 (1990).

[78] *Ziel Nominees Pty Ltd v. VACC Insurance Co.* (1975) 7 ALR 667, where there was an assignment of the vendor's insurance to the purchaser.

[79] In practice this section of the Conditions is normally deleted, and the purchaser takes out his own insurance cover—*Birds' Modern Insurance Law* (5th ed., 2001) p. 171.

20–20 Obligation of vendor to insure. The vendor of property is not bound to insure pending completion unless he has contracted to do so.[80] But since the vendor contracts to give the purchaser a good title, he must keep up the insurance if the title depends on it. Thus, where the property is leasehold subject to forfeiture for breach of convenant to insure, the vendor must insure up to the day fixed for completion.[81] A single day's non-insurance will incur forfeiture and although the lessor has not taken advantage of it, the breach is a continuing one and he may do so at any time if he does not waive the forfeiture.[82] If the purchase is not completed on or before the day fixed, the vendor is not bound to insure up to the actual date of completion[83] unless the delay was solely due to his default[84]; but he ought to inform the purchaser when the insurance expires so as to give him an opportunity of insuring on his own account.[85]

The vendor of a leasehold having insured in pursuance of his covenant to do so is no doubt bound to do all that he can to give the purchaser the benefit of the insurance money, since it is paid under a contract necessarily connected with the use and enjoyment of the property sold. Thus, if the insurance were in the joint names of the vendor and his lessor, it would be the vendor's duty not to sign the receipt for the insurance money without obtaining from the lessor reasonable security that it would be expended in reinstatement for the benefit of his purchaser.[86]

20–21 Lessee with option to purchase. Where a lessee has an option to purchase the premises and the buildings are insured under the lease in the joint names of both parties, the lessee on exercising the option is entitled to the full benefit of the insurance, but not where the buildings are insured by the lessor alone.

Thus in *Reynard v. Arnold*[87] A let premises to R with an option to purchase at £800. R covenanted to insure in joint names for £800, and that the policy money was to be applied towards reinstatement. In fact, R insured in joint names for £1,080. Without R's knowledge, A insured in another company in his own name for £515. Damage by fire occurred to the amount of £600, and the two offices apportioned the loss, A's insurer paying £220 4s. and the other insurers being ready to pay £379 16s. R then gave notice to

---

[80] *Paine v. Meller* (1801) 6 Ves. 349.

[81] *Palmer v. Goren* (1856) 25 L.J.Ch. 841; *Dowson v. Solomon* (1859) 1 Dr. & Sm. 1. See also *Newman v. Maxwell* (1899) 80 L.T. 681.

[82] *Wilson v. Wilson* (1854) 14 C.B. 616. S.146 of the Law of Property Act 1925 has greatly mitigated the effect of a breach of covenant involving forfeiture, but the vendor of leasehold is still bound to give a title which cannot be defeated and therefore if there has been a breach of covenant to insure which at the date fixed for completion has not been waived or compensated, the purchaser may refuse to accept the title.

[83] *Dowson v. Solomon* (1859) 1 Dr. & Sm. 1.

[84] *Palmer v. Goren* (1856) 25 L.J.Ch. 841.

[85] See *Rayner v. Preston* (1881) 18 Ch.D. 1, 6 *per* Cotton L.J.

[86] Similarly the vendor of the reversion, who has covenanted to insure and expend on reinstatement, will be bound to spend his recovery on such reinstatement, *Lonsdale v. Black Arrow Group* [1993] Ch. 361.

[87] (1875) L.R. 10 Ch.App. 386. Distinguished in *Edwards v. West* (1878) 7 Ch.D. 858 where a lessor had insured and contracted to spend money on reinstatement if the damage was less than £4,000. In fact the damage was greater and it was held that a lessee who subsequently exercised an option to purchase had no claim to the benefit of the insurance money. *Cf. London Holeproof Hosiery Co. Ltd v. Padmore* (1928) 44 T.L.R. 499.

exercise his option and suggested that all the policy moneys should be applied in part payment of the price. A insisted that all the moneys should be applied in reinstatement and notified the insurers accordingly. It was held that R was entitled to a declaration that all the policy moneys belonged to him absolutely without any obligation to spend them in rebuilding. On exercising the option he was entitled to the full benefit of the joint policy but that had become to a great extent unproductive in consequence of the existence of the other policy of which he had no notice:

> "The money in the lessor's pocket was the measure of the injury which the lessor had done to the lessee by diminishing his right to receive under his (sc. the joint) policy."[88]

If a lessee insures in his own name and does not exercise his option to purchase, he can only recover enough to compensate him for the loss or damage to his limited interest, unless he intended to insure the lessor's interest as well.[89]

20–22 Insurance by purchaser. When a purchaser insures he insures prima facie entirely for his own benefit, and at his own cost, and if completion does not take place or the sale is afterwards set aside, the vendor cannot claim the benefit of the insurance,[90] nor can the purchaser charge the vendor with the premiums. Thus, in *Fry v. Lane*[91] the purchaser of a contingent reversionary interest insured the vendor's life to provide against the failure of the contingency. The sale was set aside on grounds of unfair dealing, and it was held that the purchaser was not entitled to charge the premiums on accounting with the vendor. In *Foster v. Roberts*[92] A was entitled to a vested reversionary interest in a trust fund of £1,000. He obtained a loan of £300 from an insurance company and to secure the repayment he took out life policies for £600 in the same office and mortgaged the policies and the reversionary interest to the company. B bought the reversionary interest for £370 by paying £70 to A and taking an assignment of the policies and the reversionary interest subject to the company's mortgage. B paid the premiums on the policies during A's life and after A's death the reversion fell into possession. A's widow was held able to set aside the sale of the reversion to B but B was entitled to retain the policies as he had voluntarily paid the premiums and taken the risk.

20–23 Buyers and sellers of goods. [93] There is little difference between the principles applicable to the sale of insured goods and those applicable to the sale of real property which is the subject of insurance.[94] At common law the purchaser could not take the benefit of a contract of insurance unless the seller had agreed to transfer the insurance and the insurer had consented. These requirements are satisfied under c.i.f. contracts of sale where the obligation of the seller is to procure an insurance policy which will entitle the

---

[88] (1878) 7 Ch.D. 858, 864, *per* Fry J.
[89] *British Traders' Ins. Co. Ltd v. Monson* [1964] 111 C.L.R. 86.
[90] *Bartlett v. Looney* (1877) 3 V.L.R. 14.
[91] (1888) 40 Ch.D. 312.
[92] (1861) 29 Beav. 467.
[93] For the respective insurable interests of buyer and seller, see Ch. 1, para. 1–128, *ante*.
[94] See para. 20–17, *ante*.

buyer to recover for loss of or damage to the goods in transit.[95] In such cases, therefore, the buyer is able to recover from the insurers and is even entitled to the whole of the policy moneys, although such recovery may exceed the price he has paid or the actual value of the goods.[96]

If, however, the contract of sale does not purport to transfer to the buyer any insurance taken out by the seller, the buyer will be unable to recover[97] unless he can bring himself within section 47 of the Law of Property Act 1925, which applies to goods as well as to land.[98]

Conversely, an insurance effected by the purchaser will not enure to the benefit of a seller who regains the goods by exercising his right of stopping the goods *in transitu*[99]; similarly, no doubt, the seller would not be able to recover under a policy taken out by a purchaser who subsequently rejected the goods.

(b) *Bailor and Bailee*

20–24 Insurance by bailee. A goods-owner may sometimes be able to take advantage of the fact that a bailee has effected an insurance policy. It is well settled that a bailee has an insurable interest in the full value of goods entrusted to him.[1] He may, of course, insure only his own liability in respect of goods entrusted to him but he often insures for the full value either because he has agreed with the goods-owner to do so or merely because he knows that such insurance will operate as an inducement to goods-owners to put their goods in his hands.[2] In such a case the bailee will be entitled, if the goods are lost, to recover their full value from the insurers and retain so much as covers his own interest in the goods. He will be acountable to the goods owner for the remainder.[3]

Thus in *Maurice v. Goldsbrough Mort & Co. Ltd*,[4] the respondent wool brokers insured "merchandise the assureds' own property or held by them in

---

[95] See, *e.g. Biddell Bros v. E. Clemens Horst Co.* [1911] 1 K.B. 214, 220, *per* Hamilton J.; *Johnson v. Taylor Bros* [1920] A.C. 144, 156, *per* Lord Atkinson. Since the buyer is an assignee of the cargo insurance under s.50 of the M.I.A. 1906, he takes the benefit of any waiver of subrogation clause in the policy, and can enforce it against the insurer when the latter seeks to recover his outlay, after payment of a loss, from a third party covered by the clause—*The Surf City* [1995] 2 Lloyd's Rep. 242—and see para. 20–64, *post*.

[96] *Ralli v. Universal Marine Ins. Co.* (1862) 31 L.J.Ch. 313; *Landauer v. Asser* [1905] 2 K.B. 184. But where the seller takes out an honour policy on increased value as a private speculation of his own, the buyer is not entitled to the proceeds, *Strass v. Spillers and Bakers Ltd* [1911] 2 K.B. 759. See Arnould, *Marine Insurance* (16th ed), vol. 1, para. 260.

[97] *Martineau v. Kitching* (1872) L.R. 7 Q.B. 436.

[98] See para. 20–19 above and s.205(1)(xx) of the Act.

[99] *Berndston v. Strang* (1868) L.R. 3 Ch.App. 588.

[1] See para. 1–162, *ante*.

[2] *cf. Coupar Transport (London) Ltd v. Smith's (Acton) Ltd* [1959] 1 Lloyd's Rep. 369, in which the goods-owner's agents procured their own (inadequate) cover for the transit.

[3] *Tomlinson (Hauliers) Ltd v. Hepburn* [1966] A.C. 451; *Dalgleish v. Buchanan* (1854) 16 D. 332. It should follow that if the insured becomes bankrupt, after payment under the policy, the goods-owner will be entitled to claim the policy moneys in preference to other creditors. *Cf. Cochran & Son v. Leckie's Trustee* (1906) 8 F. 975.

[4] [1939] A.C. 452.

trust or on commission" against the risk of fire, but not against loss of profit. Mr. Maurice sent a consignment of wool to the respondents for sale but while in their store it was destroyed by fire. It was held that the respondents had not insured on Mr. Maurice's behalf but on their own behalf and were therefore entitled to recover the value of the wool from the insurers and retain enough to cover their own interest. The respondents argued that they were entitled to deduct from the proceeds the commission which they would have earned on the sale of the wool and the charges they would have been entitled to make for receiving, weighing and valuing the wool, inasmuch as this was part of their interest. The High Court of Australia upheld this contention but their judgment was reversed by the Judicial Committee of the Privy Council, who held that such commission and charges amounted to a claim for loss of profit which was excluded from the policy. The respondents' interest was therefore confined to their charge for services actually rendered and expenses paid in connection with the wool before the fire. They were entitled to retain that amount from the insurance proceeds but were accountable to Mr. Maurice for the remainder.

20–25 Bailee's right to recover full indemnity. The bailee's right to recover the full value of goods entrusted to him by maintaining a policy covering the goods themselves and not his own potential liability to their owners, is not dependent upon proof of his unilateral intention to cover the goods-owners' interests. In *Tomlinson (Hauliers) Ltd v. Hepburn*,[5] carriers had insured goods in transit not merely their own interest in the consignment, but the insurer argued that they were not entitled to recover the full amount recoverable under the policy, unless they could prove that they intended to insure the interest of the goods-owners as well as their own interest; in the absence of any such intention, they could only recover such sum as would indemnify them for their own loss. The Court of Appeal accepted this argument but held that the carriers did have the requisite intention and could therefore recover in full. The House of Lords, however, held that it was unnecessary for the carriers to show any such intention. Since the carriers, as bailees, had an insurable interest in the full value of the goods, they were entitled to recover in full the amount of the insurance but, if there was any surplus remaining after they had indemnified themselves in respect of their loss, that surplus was held on trust for the goods-owners. As Lord Hodson pointed out,[6] the intention of the person effecting the insurance is only relevant where there is an issue of insurable interest. Thus if someone acting merely as an agent or broker effects an insurance, he cannot recover unless he shows that he intended to act for someone who did have an insurable interest at the relevant time. But a bailee has an insurable interest by virtue of his position as bailee and can therefore recover in full without proving an intention to insure on the goods-owners' behalf.[7]

20–26 Bailor's rights of recovery (1) against the bailee. It is well

---

[5] [1966] A.C. 451.
[6] [1966] A.C. at p. 472.
[7] On pp. 467–468 *per* Lord Reid, pp. 480 and 481–482 *per* Lord Pearce. The dictum of Lord Pearce at p. 482 that it is open to the insurer to prove positively that the bailee intended not to insure the goods-owner's interest but only his own may be too wide. If the bailee undertakes to hold any surplus on trust for the goods-owner, it should be no concern of the insurer to try to ascertain the bailee's intentions, see *per* Lord Hodson at p. 473.

established that the bailor is entitled to have his loss satisfied by the bailee out of the insurance proceeds received by the latter, after satisfaction of the bailee's own legitimate interest.[8] The basis of the bailee's liability to account is not a trust in the strict sense of a trust enforceable in Chancery,[9] but an obligation arising on receipt of the monies to account for money had and received to the bailor's use.[10] When the bailee has insured the goods for their full value pursuant to a term in the contract of bailment, he comes under a fiduciary duty to account to the bailor out of the insurance proceeds received from the insurers, and most probably they are subject in his hands to an equitable charge in favour of the bailor, but they do not constitute a trust fund.[11]

20–27 Bailor's rights of recovery (2) against the insurer. The decision in *Tomlinson v. Hepburn*[12] left open the question whether the goods-owner himself has a right of action under the insurance policy. This can be important because the bailee may be insolvent or may, for some other reason, decline to claim the full amount from the insurer; moreover, the insurer may, on payment to the bailee and on the bailee's accounting to the goods-owner, wish to be subrogated not only to the bailee's rights but also to the goods-owner's rights against any wrongdoer who caused loss or damage to the goods. The insurer can only be subrogated to the rights of persons who have a claim against him under the policy and can, therefore, only sue in the name of a goods-owner who could have recovered directly from him. The mere fact that the bailee intended to cover the bailor's interest in the goods and so insured them for their full value did not until recently entitle the bailor to recover on the bailee's insurance, even where the bailment expressly stipulated that they would be so insured.[13] The bailor had to go further and show either that the bailee acted as his agent when concluding the contract of insurance or constituted himself trustee of his rights of suit thereon for the benefit of the bailor. It is submitted that the action of the bailee in insuring the bailor's interest in the goods, and so obliging himself to account to the bailor for the proceeds of the insurance, would now entitle the bailor to bring a claim directly against the bailee's insurers under the Contracts (Rights of Third Parties) Act 1999.[14]

20–28 Undisclosed agency. A bailee may insure both his own interest and the interest of the goods-owner, disclosing that he is making the policy on the goods-owner's behalf as well as his own. In such a case there can be no doubt that the goods-owner will be entitled to sue the insurers. If, however, he does

---

[8] *Maurice v. Goldsbrough Mort & Co.* [1939] A.C. 452; *Tomlinson v. Hepburn* [1966] A.C. 451. Whether the bailee is entitled to deduct monies when the balance is insufficient to satisfy the bailor's loss must depend upon the terms of the contract of bailment and the nature of the bailee's undertaking, if any, to insure the goods—*Re Dibbens* [1990] B.C.L.C. 577.

[9] *Tomlinson v. Hepburn* [1996] A.C. 451, 467, and [1996] 1 Q.B. 21, 57; *Re Dibbens* [1990] B.C.L.C. 577, 583; *DG Finance v. Scott* [1999] Lloyd's Rep. I.R. 387.

[10] *DG Finance v. Scott, supra*, relying on the analysis by Lord Diplock in *The "Albazero"* [1977] A.C. 774, 845–846.

[11] *Re Dibbens* [1990] B.C.L.C. 577.

[12] [1966] A.C. 451.

[13] *Re Dibbens* [1990] B.C.L.C. 577; *DG Finance v. Scott* [1999] Lloyd's Rep I.R. 387.

[14] See para. 20–63, *post.*

not disclose that he is acting as an agent, the goods-owner can only sue subject to the rules relating to undisclosed principals. While it may be easy to demonstrate the bailee's intention to cover the bailor's interest, particularly where their contract provides that he shall do it, that does not without more amount to an intention to contract on behalf of the bailor as an intended contracting party.[15] In the normal case the bailee has an open cover against which goods are directly or indirectly declared in the course of his business. At the time at which the insurance is taken out the bailor may not be known to the bailee at all, and this will be an additional bar to his claim to be the bailee's undisclosed principal unless it suffices that he is a member of a limited class of persons whose interests were intended to be covered by a suitably worded policy giving them the right of suit.[16] The bailor will also be ignorant of the policy until after loss, and the authorities do not yet conclusively establish that he is entitled to adopt the contract of insurance after a loss has occurred.[17]

20–29　When trust inferred. Whether a bailee has constituted himself a trustee of rights of suit under an insurance policy (as opposed to a commercial trustee of the policy monies when received by him) for a bailor must depend upon a close examination of the facts of the individual case. The mere fact that a bailee insures goods to their full value, even if by agreement with their bailor, is insufficient to achieve it.[18] The courts have always been reluctant to decide that one party to a contract holds his rights as trustee for another if they suspect that the invocation of a trust is an attempt to evade the doctrine of privity of contract,[19] but there may still be cases in which dealings with the goods create a presumption of a trust, as where a husband gives his car to his wife but retains the policy in his own name.[20] Although in *Tomlinson v. Hepburn*[21] the House of Lords did not find it necessary to decide whether the bailee was trustee of his rights under the policy for the benefit of the bailor, both Roskill J.[22] and Pearson L.J.[23] in the courts below were prepared to hold that he held the policy in trust for the bailor. In such a case, if a bailee were then to refuse or be unable to sue on the policy, the bailor could do so and join the bailee as a defendant,[24] but the invocation of a trust is now somewhat academic after the passing of the contracts (Rights of Third Parties) Act 1999.

20–30　Discharge of insurers' liability. Difficulties can arise if the insurers pay the full amount of the indemnity to the bailee who does not account to

---

[15] Dicta of Diplock L.J. in *Re King* [1963] Ch. 459, 499 to the contrary have been disapproved in the *DG Finance* case, partly on the ground that they were difficult to reconcile with Lord Diplock's subsequent *dicta* in The *"Albazero"* [1977] A.C. 774, 845, as well as with *Tomlinson v. Hepburn* [1966] A.C. 451.

[16] See para. 1–190, *ante* and para. 36–11, *post*.

[17] See para. 1–191, *ante* and para. 36–14, *post*.

[18] *DG Finance v. Scott* [1999] Lloyd's Rep. I.R. 387.

[19] *Vandepitte v. Preferred Accident Ins. Corp. of New York* [1933] A.C. 70; *Green v. Russell* [1959] 2 Q.B. 266; *Tomlinson v. Hepburn* in the C.A. [1966] 1 Q.B. 21.

[20] *Payne v. Payne, The Times*, November 5, 1908.

[21] [1966] A.C. 451.

[22] [1966] 1 Q.B. 21, 28.

[23] [1966] 1 Q.B. 21, 47.

[24] *Harmer v. Armstrong* [1934] Ch. 65, 82–84, *per* Lord Hanworth M.R.

the bailor. Although they might speculate that the bailee will be accountable to a number of third parties, the insurers must normally be discharged by payment to the bailee policy holder. There is a possible exception in the case of hire purchase agreements. Since 1956 arrangements have existed for the noting of hire purchase interests on motor policies. It has been agreed between a number of finance houses and a number of insurers that the interest of financial companies will be noted through the adoption of a standard question in proposal forms.[25] If the answer reveals the existence of a finance house or other owner of the vehicle, the insurers might have difficulty in claiming that they were discharged merely by payment to the hirer, because it could well be argued that the noting of the interest of the finance house or owner operated by way of a partial equitable assignment.[26]

(c) *Mortgagor and Mortgagee*[27]

20–31 Common Law. Formerly a mortgagee was not entitled to insure the mortgaged premises and charge the premiums in account against the mortgagor in the absence of a covenant to that effect.[28] Any insurance which he effected was therefore at his own cost and for his own benefit. If the mortgagor covenanted to insure and failed to do so, the mortgagee had probably the right to insure at the mortgagor's expense, in which case he could charge the cost in account with the mortgagor and subject to the mortgage debt would hold the proceeds for the mortgagor's benefit. But unless the mortgage deed gave the mortgagee express power to insure and add the cost of insurance to the mortgage debt he could not tack it so as to obtain priority over subsequent mortgagees.[29] Where there was express power to insure and add the cost of insurance to the mortgage debt, the mortgagee was not entitled to charge premiums for insurance unless he did in fact insure.[30] Where an insurance company is itself a mortgagee and has power to insure and charge the premiums on its security, it may be able to insure even in its own office and still be entitled to charge the premiums to the mortgagor's account.[31]

---

[25] Noting of Hire Purchase Interest on Motor Vehicle Insurance Policies, published by the Finance Houses Association Ltd, revised 1 July 1966.

[26] *Colonial Mutual General Ins. Co. v. ANZ Banking Group (New Zealand) Ltd* [1995] 1 W.L.R. 1140 (bank's request to insurer to note its interest in mortgaged property constituted notice of assignment). See para. 20–41, *post.*

[27] For insurable interest, subrogation and rights of separate mortgagees where there is insurance of separate interests see paras 1–147 *et seq.*, 22–86 *et seq.* and 19–28 *et seq.* respectively, *post.*

[28] *Dobson v. Land* (1850) 8 Hare 216; *Bellamy v. Brickenden* (1861) 2 J. & H. 137; *Brooke v. Stone* (1865) 34 L.J.Ch. 251. But see *Scholefield v. Lockwood* (1863) 33 L.J.Ch. 106, 111 *per* Romilly M.R. The same principle applies to ship mortgages, *The Basildon* [1967] 2 Lloyd's Rep. 134, but if the mortgagor fails to insure, the mortgagee may well be justified in taking possession since his security will have been impaired; once he has done so, he can then charge the mortgagor with the premiums, *The Manor* [1907] P. 339. An agreement by the mortgagor of a chattel that, if he fails to insure, the mortgagee may do so and that the premiums will be a charge on the property does not offend the Bills of Sale Acts, *Ex p. Stanford* (1886) 17 Q.B.D. 259; *Briggs v. Pike* (1892) 61 L.J.Q.B. 418.

[29] *Brook v. Stone* (1865) 34 L.J.Ch. 251.

[30] *Lawley v. Hooper* (1745) 3 Atk. 278; *Hutchinson v. Wilson* (1794) 4 Bro.C.C. 488.

[31] See *Fitzwilliam v. Price* (1858) 4 Jur.(N.S) 889 where the insurance company had suffered a loss as a result of the mortgagor's failure to pay the premiums, *contra. Grey v. Ellison* (1856) 1 Giff. 438 where the insurers had power to charge an additional premium to the mortgage debt in a certain event.

20–32 Statutory power of mortgagee. Section 101(1) of the Law of Property Act 1925[32] provides:

"A mortgagee, where the mortgage is made by deed, shall, by virtue of this Act, have the following powers, to the like extent as if they had been in terms conferred by the mortgage deed, but not further (namely);

...

(ii) A power, at any time after the date of the mortgage deed, to insure and keep insured against loss or damage by fire[33] any building, or any effects, or property of an insurable nature, whether affixed to the freehold or not, being or forming part of the property which or an estate or interest wherein is mortgaged, and the premiums paid for any such insurance shall be a charge on the mortgaged property or estate or interest, in addition to the mortgage money, and with the same priority, and with interest at the same rate, as the mortgage money."

Thus a mortgagee now has by statute full powers of insurance against fire which he could previously only secure by express covenant. It is further laid down[34] that the amount of an insurance effected by a mortgagee under the power conferred by the Law of Property Act must not exceed the amount specified in the mortgage deed, or if no amount is specified then must not exceed two-thirds of the amount that would be required in case of total destruction to restore the property insured.

20–33 The mortgagee has no power under the Act to effect an insurance

(i) Where the mortgage deed expressly provides to the contrary[35];
(ii) Where there is a declaration in the mortgage deed that no insurance is required[36];
(iii) Where an insurance is kept up by or on behalf of the mortgagor in accordance with the mortgage deed[37];
(iv) Where the mortgage deed contains no stipulation respecting insurance and an insurance is kept up by or on behalf of the mortgagor, with the consent of the mortgagee, to the amount in which the mortgagee is by the Act authorised to insure.[38]

20–34 Benefit of mortgagor's insurance. Apart from the statute the mortagee is not prima facie entitled to the benefit of an insurance effected on the property by the mortgagor.[39] Even where a mortgagor of chattels covenanted to insure and did so in his own name, it was held that the mortgagee had no claim to the insurance moneys as against the mortgagor's

---

[32] Reproducing s.19(1)(ii) of the Conveyancing Act 1881.
[33] The section gives no power to insure against risks other than fire, *The Basildon* [1967] 2 Lloyd's Rep. 134.
[34] s. 108(1).
[35] s. 101(4).
[36] s. 108(2)(i).
[37] s. 108(2)(ii).
[38] s. 108(2)(iii).
[39] *Lees v. Whiteley* (1866) L.R. 2 Eq. 143; *Harryman v. Collins* (1835) 18 Beav. 11; *Sinnott v. Bowden* [1912] 2 Ch. 414; *Graham Joint Stock Shipping Co. v. Merchants' Marine Ins. Co.* [1924] A.C. 294; *Halifax Building Society v. Keighley* [1931] 2 K.B. 248. The mortgagee is therefore entitled to interest on the amount outstanding until the date for repayment, *Austin v. Story* (1863) 10 Gr. 306.

trustee in bankruptcy.[40] In order to entitle the mortgagee to any claim on the policy there must have been an intention to insure on the mortgagee's behalf,[41] which might well be evidenced by a covenant to insure for the benefit of the mortgagee, or to apply the policy moneys in reinstatement or otherwise for the benefit of the mortgagee. Thus in *Garden v. Ingram*[42] a mortgagor of leaseholds had insured in pursuance of his covenant in the lease, which provided that the lessee was to insure in joint names of himself and the lessor and apply the policy moneys in reinstatement. It was held that the mortgagee was entitled to the benefit of such insurance because the effect of the provision as to reinstatement was to benefit the mortgagee. The situation is now governed to all intents and purposes by section 108 or the Law of Property Act 1925.

20–35 Benefit of mortagee's insurance. Similarly the mortgagor cannot claim the benefit of a policy effected by the mortgagee unless it has been effected on behalf of both mortgagor and mortgagee[43] or the mortgagee has covenanted to apply the policy moneys in reinstatement or extinction of the debt or otherwise for the benefit of the mortgagor. If the security is in the form of a conveyance to the creditor in trust to pay himself and hold the balance in trust for the debtor, the creditor is then in the position of any other trustee and bound not to take advantage of the trust for his own benefit except in so far as he may be a beneficiary under the trust; and therefore if he insures he must apply the insurance money in accordance with the trust.[44]

20–36 Application of insurance money under statute. Section 108 of the Law of Property Act provides:

"(3) All money received on an insurance of mortgaged property against loss or damage by fire or otherwise effected under this Act, or any enactment replaced by this Act, or an insurance for the maintenance of which the mortgagor is liable under the mortgage deed, shall, if the mortgagee so requires, be applied by the mortgagor in making good the loss or damage in respect of which the money is received

(4) Without prejudice to any obligation to the contrary imposed by law, or by special contract, a mortgagee may require that all money received on an insurance of mortgaged property against loss or damage by fire or otherwise effected under this Act, or any enactment replaced by this Act, or on an insurance for the maintenance of which the

---

[40] *Lees v. Whiteley* (1866) L.R. 2 Eq. 143, distinguished in *Mumford Hotels Ltd v. Wheler* [1964] Ch. 117 where a covenant to insure was held to enure for the benefit of both landlord and tenant.

[41] *Samuel & Co. v. Dumas* [1924] A.C. 431.

[42] (1825) 23 L.J.Ch. 478 followed in *Greet v. Citizens' Ins. Co.* (1879) 27 Gr. 121, criticised in *Rayner v. Preston* (1881) 18 Ch.D. 1., and distinguished in *Lees v. Whiteley* (1866) L.R. 2 Eq. 143, 149 on the point of the covenant to apply the insurance proceeds in reinstatement.

[43] *Irving v. Richardson* (1831) 2 B. & Ad. 193, but see the explanation of this case in *Tomlinson (Hauliers) Ltd v. Hepburn* [1966] A.C. 451, 478–479, *per* Lord Pearce. See also *Kenney v. Employers' Liability Assurance Corporation* [1901] 1 Ir.R. 301 and *Horden v. Federal Mutual Ins. Co. of Australia Ltd* (1924) 24 S.R. (N.S.W.) 267.

[44] *Ex p. Andrews* (1816) 2 Rose 410, followed in *Henson v. Blackwell* (1845) 14 L.J.Ch. 329.

mortgagor is liable under the mortgage deed, be applied in or towards the discharge of the mortgage money."[45]

20–37 An insurance effected by the mortgagors before the mortgage and renewed by them thereafter, the mortgage deed containing a covenant to insure, is within section 108 and the mortgagee can demand that the money be spent on reinstatement, notwithstanding the existence of an order garnisheeing the money due under the policy.[46] In *Halifax Building Society v. Keighley*[47] the mortgagors not only paid the premiums on policies kept up by the mortgagees, but also insured for their own account. A fire occurred and both insurance companies paid up on their respective policies. The mortgagees claimed the benefit of the money paid to the mortgagors but it was held that they were not entitled to it since the mortgagors had not insured "under the Act" or in pursuance of a covenant in the mortgage deed and the mortgagees could not therefore bring themselves within section 108(4). Apart from statute, the mortgagees could not claim the benefit of the mortgagors' insurance even by claiming that the mortgagors were constructive trustees of the insurance money.

20–38 This decision has created a difficulty for building societies, because if there is more than one insurance, the insurers will be able to take advantage of the usual clause limiting their liability to the rateable proportion of the damage. If the mortgagor's own insurance is not available to the building society, the society will not be able to recover the full amount of the insurance, and might well not be able to reinstate. This difficulty could, no doubt, be avoided if the mortgagor were prohibited from insuring; in fact, building societies often include a provision in the mortgage deed that any money received under an independent insurance effected by the borrower is to be held in trust for the society.

Mortgages of leaseholds can create a problem because the lessee will, no doubt, have entered into a covenant to insure in joint names and apply the insurance money in reinstatement, while the consequence of a mortgage by the lessee may be such that he is obliged to hold the proceeds of his independent insurance on trust for the building society who can then apply the proceeds to the reduction of the debt instead of reinstatement. The answer to this problem may be that the mortgagees would have to take the money subject to the terms of the lease, which would constitute a "special contract" within section 108(4) and thus permit it to be used for reinstatement, if the lessor so wished. If, indeed, the policy were in the joint names of lessor and lessee, no use could be made of the proceeds without the lessor's consent.[48]

20–39 The right of the mortgagee to demand that the insurance money

---

[45] *cf.* for marine insurance, *Swan and Cleland's Graving Dock and Slipway Co. v. Maritime Ins. Co. and Croshaw* [1907] 1 K.B. 116, where in the absence of a covenant in the mortgage deed that the policy monies be applied towards the cost of repairs to the ship, they were applied to the reduction of the mortgage debt.

[46] *Sinnott v. Bowden* [1912] 2 Ch. 414.

[47] [1931] 2 K.B. 248. The Supreme Court of the Irish Free State was able to come to a different conclusion in *Re Doherty* [1925] 2 Ir.R. 246 on the rather different wording of the Conveyancing Act 1881, discussed in (1910) 54 S.J. 358.

[48] See the argument of Sir Andrew Clark K.C. in *Earl of Radnor v. Folkestone Pier and Lift Co.* [1950] 2 All E.R. 690 accepted by Vaisey J. and, in general the article signed by "X" in (1953) 103 L.Jo. 230.

shall be applied towards discharge of the mortgage debt is subject to any statutory or contractual rights which the mortgagor or any other person may have in respect of the insurance money. The right of the mortgagee is in effect an implied term in the contract between mortgagor and mortgagee and as such must yield to any statutory or contractual obligation towards third parties or to any express term in the contract between mortgagor and mortgagee. Where the insurance company exercises its option under a reinstatement clause in the policy, there is a contractual obligation towards the company which prevents the subsection coming into operation, and it seems reasonably clear that the mortgagee would have no right as against the company to make it pay in cash when it had elected to reinstate. Where the provisions of section 83 of the Fires Prevention (Metropolis) Act 1774 are applicable,[49] it is submitted that the mortgagor could not demand reinstatement under that section because the Law of Property Act 1925 imports an implied term into his contract with his mortgagee that the insurance money shall be applied in discharge of the mortgage debt, and the statutory right to call upon the insurers to expend the insurance money in reinstatement cannot be exercised to the prejudice of contractual obligations.[50] It seems to follow that any third parties taking their title from the mortgagor after the date of the mortgage are equally bound by the implied term imported by the Law of Property Act, and cannot rely on section 83 of the Fires Prevention Act. This category would include subsequent mortgagees and others becoming entitled to or interested in the equity of redemption. On the other hand, third parties whose interests are independent of the mortgagor, or who have acquired title from him before the date of the mortgage, would be entitled to demand reinstatement notwithstanding the provisions of the Law of Property Act. This category would include ground landlords, in the case of leaseholds and prior mortgagees.

20–40 Policy effected by receiver. Where a mortgagee has appointed a receiver under the Law of Property Act to receive the income of the property the receiver must, if so directed in writing by the mortgagee, insure to the extent, if any, to which the mortgagee might have insured, and keep insured against loss or damage by fire, out of the money received by him, any building, effects or property comprised in the mortgage, whether affixed to the freehold or not, being of an insurable nature, and may apply the money received by him *inter alia* in payment of the premiums on insurances authorised by the mortgage or under section 109 of the Act.[51] A policy thus effected is the property of the mortgagor subject to the right of the mortgagee to have the policy moneys applied in reinstatement or in discharge of his debt.

20–41 Loss payable clause. Policies on mortgaged property commonly contain a "loss payable" clause. The degree of protection which it provides depends on the wording of the clause. In its simple form it constitutes the mortgagee as no more than a mere appointee to whom payment is to be made. It does not make him either an assured with a right of suit on the policy or an assignee of the right to recover claims paid under it,[52] and it

[49] See paras 21–14 *et seq, post.*
[50] *cf. Reynard v. Arnold* (1875) L.R. 10 Ch.App. 386.
[51] Law of Property Act 1925, s. 109(7), (8).
[52] *Iraqi Ministry of Defence v. Avcepey Shipping Co. S.A.* [1979] 2 Lloyd's Rep. 491, 497, *per* Donaldson J.

leaves the mortgagee vulnerable to the claims of other claimants to the insurance monies. In *Amalgamated General Finance v.Golding*[53] the policy incorporated the U.S.M.A.Payee Hull Clause, providing that "Loss, if any, including claims under the Collision Clause and not withstanding any provision therein to the contrary, payable to the ... Bank ...". Insurers had followed a practice, evidently without objection by the Loss Payee, of paying all claims to the mortgagor shipowner's broker for onward transmission. The shipowner made an equitable assignment of certain claims to a second lender and instructed the collecting broker to pay the assignee, while deliberately not notifying either the insurers or the Loss Payee of the assignment. The assignee would have obtained the monies had they not been retained by the broker and set off against a larger sum of unpaid premiums owed to it by the mortgagor, and the court upheld the broker's right to intercept them. If, however, the mortgage contains a covenant obliging the mortgagor to insure the mortgaged property, and the mortgagee requests the insurers to note its interest on the policy, as is standard practice, such request will suffice to notify the insurer of the existence of a partial equitable assignment of the insurance proceeds in its favour, thereby giving it an interest by way of charge over them.[54] Loss payee clauses which contain a notice of this kind will make the mortgagee an equitable assignee of the proceeds. The insurer cannot then pay the mortgagor or agree to apply the policy monies towards rebuilding without the mortgagee's consent, and if he does so he may be liable to pay twice over.[55] An assignee, however, takes subject to defences to payment available to the insurers against the assignor, and his claim is liable to be defeated by any default on the part of the mortgagor which entitles the insurer to deny liability, such as misrepresentation or non-disclosure, wilful causation of loss, or release of the insurers' rights of subrogation.[56]

20–42 In order to avoid this situation it is customary to incorporate a "mortgage clause"[57] in addition to a loss payee clause. This might typically provide:

> "This insurance shall not be invalidated by any act or neglect of the mortgagor or owner of the property ... nor by any changein the title or ownership of the property, nor by the occupation of the property for purposes more hazardous than are permitted by this policy."

In the United States this clause (known as the "standard clause" to distinguish it from the "open clause" which provides only that the loss is payable to the mortgagee) has been held to protect the mortgagee when the acts or neglects of the mortgagor occur after the inception of a valid policy and also from the consequences of non-disclosure and misrepresentation by

---

[53] [1964] 2 Lloyd's Rep. 163.

[54] *Colonial Mutual General Ins. Co. v. ANZ Banking Group Ltd* [1995] 1 W.L.R. 1140

[55] *Swan and Cleland's Graving Dock and Slipway Co. v. Maritime Ins. Co.* [1907] 1 K.B. 116; *London & Lancs. Guarantee and Accident Co. of Canada v. M & P Enterprises Ltd* (1968) 69 D.L.R. 2d 461, affirmed (1969) 1 D.L.R. 3d 731.

[56] *Wm. Pickersgill & Sons v. London & Provincial Marine & General Ins. Co.* [1912] 3 K.B. 614; *Graham Joint Stock Shipping Co. v. Merchants' Marine Ins. Co.* [1924] A.C. 294 (no loss payable clause but the mortgagor had covenanted to procure an indorsement of the mortgagee's interest on the policy); *P. Samuel & Co. v. Dumas* [1924] A.C. 431, 450 *(obiter).*

[57] Expert evidence of the use of mortgage clauses in non-marine insurances on mortgaged property was considered in *First National Commercial Bank v. Barnet Devanney* [1999] Lloyd's Rep. I.R. 43; reversed on appeal [2000] 2 All E.R. (Comm.) 233.

the mortgagor.[58] It has also been held to create a separate contract of insurance with the insurers covering the mortgagee's several interest[59]. The English courts have recently shown a readiness to interpret composite policies as containing separate contracts between each assured and the insurers whenever this is needed to achieve the implicit purpose of all composite policies to provide cover to each co-assured which is unaffected by the defaults of other co-assureds, and this approach would most probably now be followed even in the absence of a mortgage clause.[60]

20–43 The mortgagee's interests can best be protected either by taking out the insurance in the names of mortgagor and mortgagee for their several and respective interests. The insurer cannot then obtain a good discharge from the mortgagor alone,[61] and the interest of the mortgagee will not be prejudiced by the acts of the mortgagor,[62] unless the mortgagor can be held to have been the agent of the mortgagee in taking out the policy, a problem not yet fully considered in the English authorities. Alternatively, the mortgagee could obtain a special mortgagee interest insurance of the kind familiar in marine insurance, whereby the insurers promise to indemnify him in the contingency that the ship-owner's hull insurers are discharged from liability owing to the default of the owner.[63] Such contingency policies are not unknown in non-marine insurances of mortgaged property.[64]

(d) Landlord and Tenant[65]

20–44 Insurance by landlord. Unless a landlord has agreed to insure for the benefit of his tenant or to apply the insurance money in reinstating the premises, the tenant has no claim to the proceeds of an insurance policy

---

[58] *Fayetteville Building and Loan Association v. Mutual Fire Ins. Co.,* 141 S.E. 634 (1928), and see para. 1–194, *ante*.

[59] *Aetna Ins. Co. v. Kennedy,* 301 U.S.389 (1936); *Mutual Creamery Ins. Co. v. Iowa National Ins. Co.,* 294 F. Supp. 337 (1968). Recent Canadian authority has followed this approach—*Panzera v. Simcoe & Erie Ins. Co.* (1990) 74 D.L.R. (4th) 197; *Canadian Imperial Bank v. Ins. Co. of Ireland* (1991) 75 D.L.R. (4th) 482, following *London & Midland General Ins. Co. v. Bonser* [1973] S.C.R. 10 and *Caisse Populaire v. Soc. Mut.d'Assurances* (1991) 74 D.L.R. (4th) 161.

[60] *Arab Bank v. Zurich Ins. Co.* [1999] 1 Lloyd's Rep. 262, interpreting and applying *P Samuel v. Dumas* [1924] A.C. 431, *General Accident Fire & Life Ass. Corp. Ltd v. Midland Bank* [1940] 2 K.B. 388, and *New Hampshire Ins. Co. v. Mirror Group Newspapers* [1997] L.R.L.R. 24.

[61] *Re King* [1963] Ch. 459, 492–493, *per* Upjohn L.J., *sed contra Penniall v. Harborne* (1848) 11 Q.B. 368, 376, *per* Lord Denman C.J. The mortgagee may insist that the money be brought into court for the respective interests in it to be determined—*Rogers v. Grazebrooke* (1842) 12 Sim. 557.

[62] Including wilful destruction of the subject-matter—*P. Samuel & Co. v. Dumas* [1924] A.C. 431, where the mortgagee's claim failed because a ship wilfully cast away is not lost by perils of the seas; *Bank of Scotland v. Guardian Royal Exchange Ins. Plc.* 1995 S.L.T. 763.

[63] See the study of the Institute Mortgagees Interest Clauses Hulls (1986) by Dr Susan Hodges in *The Modern Law of Marine Insurance* (Rhidian Thomas ed., 1996) Ch. 8.

[64] *First National Commercial Bank v. Barnet Devanney* [2000] 2 All E.R. (Comm.) 233 where the question arose whether the lender had to give credit for monies received under such a policy when assessing damages recoverable from the brokers who had failed to include a mortgage clause in the insurance taken out on the mortgaged property in the names of the borrower and lender.

[65] For the respective insurable interests of landlord and tenant, see paras 1–140 *et seq, ante*.

effected by the landlord for his own benefit.[66] Apart from express contract and his rights, if any, under section 83 of the Fires Prevention (Metropolis) Act 1774, he cannot compel the landlord to apply the policy moneys in reinstatement or in discharge of rent payable during the time the premises are unfit for occupation or otherwise to apply them for his benefit.[67] If, however, on a true construction of the lease, the landlord can be treated as having insured for the joint benefit of himself and his lessee, the lessee may well be able to share in the recovery or require that the insurance money be spent in reinstating the premises. Difficult questions of construction of the lease may arise, but if the tenant has paid or contributed to the insurance premiums, a court will usually hold that the landlord has insured the premises for the benefit of himself and his tenant either jointly or for their respective rights and interests.[68] This was the conclusion reached in *Mark Rowlands Ltd v. Berni Inns*[69] where the lease provided, in addition, that the tenant was to be relieved from his obligation to repair in the event of fire.

20-45 Insurance by tenant. A landlord is in a similar position as regards insurance by the tenant. If the insurance is effected by the tenant for his own benefit, the landlord has no right to the proceeds. He can only claim the benefit of the insurance by reason of the covenants in the lease or under section 83 of the 1774 Act. Even if a lessee has convenanted to insure in the joint names of lessor and lessee, or otherwise for the benefit of the landlord but, instead of doing so, insures in his own name for his own benefit, the landlord will have no right to the insurance moneys and, apart from any right under the 1774 Act, his only remedy is an action for breach of covenant.[70]

20-46 A joint insurance in the names of both lessor and lessee is very commonly arranged. In such cases a court may hold that each party has insured for his respective interests and is entitled to the money in proportion to his interest.

Thus in *Beacon Carpets v. Kirby*,[71] the landlords were required by the lease to keep the premises insured in the joint names of themselves and the tenants, but the tenants were required to provide the money by way of additional rent and to keep the premises in repair. The landlords effected a policy in joint names "for their respective rights and interests" for a sum which proved insufficient to pay for the cost of rebuilding after destruction by fire. The parties agreed that the premises should not be rebuilt but could not agree as to the destination of the insurance proceeds. The Court of Appeal held that both parties were intended to have an interest in the insurance and their interests in the property would have to be valued so that

---

[66] This does not mean that an insurer can refuse to pay a landlord who has sold his reversion and been paid the price, if the landlord is under an obligation to his tenant to apply any proceeds of insurance to reinstating the premises, *Lonsdale v. Black Arrow Group* [1993] Ch. 361.

[67] *Leeds v. Cheetham* (1829) 1 Sim. 146; *Lofft v. Dennis* (1859) 1 E. & E. 474; *Re King* [1963] Ch. 459, 484-485, *per* Lord Denning M.R.

[68] *Mumford Hotels Ltd v. Wheler* [1964] Ch. 117. See (1964) 28 Conv.(N.S.) 307.

[69] [1986] Q.B. 211, 225-228. See comment in [1986] C.L.J. 23.

[70] The statutory provision to the contrary in s.7 of Law of Property Amendment Act 1859 was repealed by s.14(7) of the Conveyancing Act 1881 and has not been re-enacted. S.83 of the 1774 Act will usually, however, provide the landlord with an adequate remedy, see paras 21-17 *et seq., post*.

[71] [1985] Q.B. 755.

the insurance proceeds could be divided accordingly. A different result had been previously reached in *Re King*[72] where the lessee covenanted:

(1) to keep the premises insured in the joint names of himself and the lessor;
(2) to lay out all insurance moneys in rebuilding;
(3) to keep the premises in good repair; and
(4) to reinstate in the event of fire.

A fire occurred in 1944 and, before a building licence could be obtained, the premises became the subject of a compulsory purchase order so that it was impossible to use the insurance money for the purpose of reinstatement. It therefore had to be decided to whom the money belonged and the majority of the Court of Appeal held that the only reason why the policy was taken out in joint names was to enable the lessor to ensure that the money would be spent on reinstatement; the insurers would not obtain a good discharge without the signature of both parties and there would thus be no danger of the lessee obtaining the proceeds without the lessor's knowledge. Since there was no possibility of reinstatement, the proceeds were the property of the lessee who had paid the premiums—"he who pays the piper calls the tune".[73] Diplock L.J. pointed out that there was no business reason why the lessor should insure his interest in the premises because he was fully secured by the policy being in joint names.[74] Lord Denning M.R. dissented and held that the moneys were payable to both parties for their respective interests; but it would be difficult to calculate with any precision the interests of the parties without resort to expert valuers and it is unlikely that the parties intended that this should be done.

20–47 Covenant to insure.[75] Where a lease contains a covenant on the part of the tenant to insure, the tenant usually covenants to insure and keep insured in the name of the lessor or in joint names of the lessor and the lessee for a specified sum either in a named office or generally in some substantial fire office. The fact that the covenant may become impossible to perform because no office will accept the risk will not prevent the tenant from being in breach of covenant.[76] A covenant to insure with a named office, "or some other responsible insurance office to be approved by the lessor", imports a primary obligation to insure in the named office, and the landlord may withhold his approval of an alternative without giving reasons.[77] The tenant must insure within a reasonable time after the execution of the lease.[78] If afterwards the policy is allowed to lapse for however a short a time there is a

---

[72] [1963] Ch. 459.

[73] At p. 473, *per* R. W. Goff Q.C. *arguendo*.

[74] At p. 498, *per* Diplock L.J. This derives some support from the shortly reported case of *Hamer v. Drummond* (1939) 187 L.T.Jo. 156 where it was held that the lessee could not require insurance money, held in a joint account, to be paid out to him, without giving some security for rebuilding.

[75] See Woodfall, *Landlord and Tenant* (28th ed., 1994), paras 11.090, *et seq.*

[76] *Moorgate Estates Ltd v. Trower* [1940] Ch. 206; reversed pursuant to Landlord & Tenant (War Damage) (Amendment) Act 1941, s.11.

[77] *Tredgar v. Harwood* [1929] A.C. 72. If no office is named, it is the tenant's right and duty to select an office if he is the covenantor, *Hare v. Garland* 1955 (3) S.A. 306. If it is the landlord who gives the covenant, then his right to nominate is unqualified, provided the company chosen is reputable *Berrycroft Management v. Sinclair Gardens* [1996] E.G.C.S. 143.

[78] *Doe d. Darlington v. Ulph* (1849) 13 Q.B. 204. *Hare v. Garland*, 1955 (3) S.A. 306.

breach of the covenant.[79] But the tenant is not bound to keep up the original policy. If some effective policy is always in force that is sufficient.[80] If the tenant is obliged to insure but does not do so and the landlord then insures the property, the landlord is under no duty to inform the tenant of any decision not to renew the insurance.[81] A covenant to insure in the joint names of the lessor and lessee is satisfied by an insurance in the name of the lessor alone[82]; but a covenant to insure in the name of the lessor is not satisfied by an insurance in the joint names of the lessor and lessee.[83] Where a tenant covenanted to insure in joint names but insured in his own name and showed the policy to the landlord, who approved of it and afterwards received rent, it was held that there was a breach of the covenant, and that although the breach was waived up to the time when the last rent was received, there was a continuing breach after that date, for which the tenant was liable.[84] If a policy is effected and kept in force, the fact that for some reason it is voidable at the option of the company does not constitute a breach of the covenant to insure if in fact the company does not avoid it.[85] A covenant to "insure and keep insured . . . the sum of £800 at the least in some sufficient insurance office" is not void for uncertainty but was held to refer to insurance against fire, to be made where policies against fire are usually effected.[86] A covenant to insure all buildings "which at any time during the said term may be erected or placed upon or fixed upon the demised premises" was held to apply to buildings erected at the time of the demise as well as to those erected during the term.[87] If the tenant covenants to pay a premium to cover "the full cost of reinstatement", the lessor will be entitled to charge for a premium calculated by reference to the cost of reinstatement beginning at the end of the policy period and ending up to 18 months later.[88]

20–48 A covenant to insure has been held to run with the land and therefore to be enforceable by and against assignees, because under section 83 of the Fires Prevention (Metropolis) Act[89] the landlord is empowered to require the insurance money to be applied in reinstatement.[90] This must be

[79] *Doe d. Pitt v. Shewin* (1811) 3 Camp. 134; *Wilson v. Wilson* (1854) 14 C.B. 616; *Job v. Banister* (1856) 26 L.J.Ch. 125; *Heckman v. Isaac* (1862) 6 L.T. 383. The breach is not remedied by the insurers' receiving the premium after the lapse of the policy and dating back the receipt, *Wilson v. Wilson* (1854) 14 C.B. 616, *Howell v. Kightley* (1856) 21 Beav. 331.

[80] *Doe d. Flower v. Peck* (1830) 1 B. & Ad. 428.

[81] *Argy Trading v. Lapid Developments Ltd* [1977] 1 Lloyd's Rep. 67.

[82] *Havens v. Middleton* (1853) 10 Hare 641.

[83] *Penniall v. Harborne* (1848) 11 Q.B. 368. But if the lessee is willing to declare himself a trustee for the lessor, the damages will be nominal, *cf. Matthey v. Curling* [1922] 2 A.C. 180, 141 *per* Lord Atkinson.

[84] *Doe d. Muston v. Gladwin* (1845) 6 Q.B. 953; *Doe d. Flower v. Peck* (1830) 1 B. & Ad. 428; *Hyde v. Watts* (1843) 12 M. & W. 254. But a breach of a covenant to use insurance money to reinstate the premises is a single breach committed when the tenant has declined to reinstate within a reasonable time of receipt of the money. A subsequent acceptance of rent will, therefore, constitute a waiver of such breach, *Farimani v. Gates* (1984) 271 E.G. 887.

[85] *Doe d. Pitt v. Laming* (1814) 4 Camp. 73.

[86] *Doe d. Pitt v. Shewin* (1811) 3 Camp. 134.

[87] *Sims v. Castiglione* [1905] W.N. 112.

[88] *Gleniffer Finance v. Bamar Wood and Products* [1978] 2 Lloyd's Rep. 49. *Quaere* whether the lessor can charge more than the cost of a reasonable premium. Compare *Bandar Property Holdings v. Darwen* [1968] 2 All E.R. 305 with *Finchbourne v. Rodrigues* [1976] 3 All E.R. 581 and *Taygetos* [1982] 2 Lloyd's Rep. 272.

[89] See paras 21–14 *et seq, post.*

[90] *Vernon v. Smith* (1821) 5 B. & Ald 1. See s.141 of the Law of Property Act 1925.

true of all such covenants if, as is submitted below, the Act applies throughout the country.[91]

A covenant to insure against loss or damage by fire without qualification is not fully satisfied by a policy containing the usual war risk exceptions; and if the premises are damaged by fire caused by the act of an enemy the covenantor will be liable in damages for breach of his covenant[92]; but a covenant to insure against loss or damage by fire in a designated office is fully satisfied by a policy in the form ordinarily issued by that office, and if it contains the usual war risk exception the landlord cannot require the tenant to insure the premises against damage by enemy aircraft.[93]

20–49 It has been held that a landlord does not commit a breach of a covenant to keep premises adequately insured if the sum insured is insufficent to replace the buildings destroyed or damaged, but not only was the tenant informed of the amount insured, to which he raised no objection, but the landlord had received proper advice from the insurers as to the amount to be insured.[94] Nor is it a breach of covenant, if a landlord agrees to insure but refuses to enforce the tenant's rights under the policy at his own cost. If the tenant wishes an action to be brought against the insurers his correct course is to offer the landlord an indemnity against the cost of proceedings and, if the landlord still declines to enforce the policy, he can then sue the insurers in his own name and join the landlord as defendant.[95]

Where a covenant to insure is broken and the premises are burned the landlord is entitled to recover from the tenant, as damages for breach of the covenant, the amount of the loss which but for the breach would have been recovered from the insurers.[96] In the event of the tenant failing to insure, the landlord cannot charge him with the premium of an insurance effected by himself unless the lease gives him authority to do so; but, on the other hand, he is entitled to recover from the tenant damages for breach of the contract to insure even although there has been no fire, and more than nominal damages may be awarded for the risk to which he has been exposed.[97]

A covenant to use insurance money in reinstatement is not broken until the money has been received[98] and reinstatement has not been made or, at any rate, begun within a reasonable time after such receipt.[99] Moreover, the party obliged to reinstate is not discharged by any reinstatement carried out by the other party who can still sue for breach of covenant.[1]

20–50 Increase in risk. If the landlord has covenanted to insure and pay the premiums and if the premium is increased by reason of any improvement executed by the tenant, the landlord can recover any increase in premium

---

[91] See para. 21–16.
[92] *Enlayde Ltd v. Roberts* [1917] 1 Ch. 109.
[93] *Upjohn v. Hitchens* [1918] 2 K.B. 48.
[94] *Mumford Hotels Ltd. v. Wheler* [1963] 3 All E.R. 250; not reported at [1964] Ch. 117.
[95] *Williams Torrey v. Knight* [1894] P. 342.
[96] *Newman v. Maxwell* (1899) 80 L.T. 681; *cf. Williams v. Lassell and Sharman* (1906) 22 T.L.R. 443.
[97] *Hey v. Wyche* (1842) 2 G. & D. 569; *Schlesinger and Joseph v. Mostyn* [1932] 1 K.B. 349.
[98] *Beacon Carpets v. Kirby* [1985] Q.B. 755, 763.
[99] *Farimani v. Gates* (1984) 271 E.G. 887.
[1] *Naumann v. Ford* (1985) 275 E.G. 542.

from the tenant.[2] If the landlord insures but there is no covenant on the part of either party to insure, or if the landlord is bound to insure and the premium increases for some reason other than that the tenant has improved the property, the landlord cannot call on the tenant to bear the additional premiums.[3] Conversely, if the tenant is bound to insure, any increase in premium resulting from the activities of the landlord, *e.g.* in his use of adjacent land, must be borne by the tenant.[4]

(e) Tenant for Life and Remainderman; Trustee and Beneficiary[5]

20–51 General rules. A tenant for life is not liable to the remainderman for permissive waste and, therefore, unless the terms of the settlement expressly lay such an obligation on him, he is not bound to execute any repairs to the premises during his life tenancy.[6] A tenant for life who is not bound to repair is not bound to insure the premises unless that obligation is laid upon him by the terms of the settlement.[7] Section 88 of the Settled Land Act 1925[8] does, however, lay upon a tenant for life the obligation at his own expense to maintain and insure improvements made under the provisions of the Act in such manner and in such amount as the Minister of Agriculture by certificate in any case prescribes.

20–52 If a tenant for life does insure without any obligation to do so he is prima facie entitled to the proceeds of the policy for his own benefit.[9] But if he treats the insurance of the policy moneys as part of the settled estate, it will on his death follow the settlement instead of passing as part of his estate.[10] The mere fact, however, that a tenant for life invested the proceeds in the name of the trustees and allowed them to remain so invested for 14 years pending a decision whether or not to rebuild, was held not to imply an abandonment of the money for the benefit of the settlement.[11]

But the remainderman, although not otherwise entitled to the benefit of the insurance of a tenant for life, may obtain the benefit by exercising his right under section 83 of the Fires Prevention (Metropolis) Act 1774 and

---

[2] See s.16 of Landlord and Tenant Act 1927, as amended by the Finance Act 1963, s.73(7), and the Housing Act 1980, s.152(3), Sch. 26

[3] *cf. Hickman v. Isaacs* (1861) 4 L.T. 285.

[4] *O'Cedar Ltd v. Slough Trading Co. Ltd* [1927] 2 K.B. 123.

[5] For the respective insurable interests of tenants for life and remaindermen, see paras 1–136 *et seq. ante*; for trustees and beneficiaries, see paras 1–119 *et seq., ante*.

[6] *Re Cartwright* (1889) 41 Ch.D 532 (freehold estate); *Re Parry and Hopkin* [1900] 1 Ch. 160 (leasehold estate).

[7] *Re Bennett* [1896] 1 Ch. 778, 787; *Re Kingham* [1897] 1 Ir.R. 170; *Re Betty* [1899] 1 Ch. 821, 829.

[8] 15 & 16 Geo. 5, c. 18.

[9] *Seymour v. Vernon* (1852) 21 L.J.Ch. 433; *Warwicker v. Bretnall* (1882) 23 Ch.D. 188; *Gaussen v. Whatman* (1905) 93 L.T. 101; *Re Quicke's Trusts* [1908] 1 Ch. 887. It is arguable that since the tenant for life is, after 1925, a trustee of the settlement in whom the settled land is vested he must, like ordinary trustees, hold any insurance money for the beneficiary, see Colinvaux, *The Law of Insurance* (7th ed.), para. 14–26. But it is submitted that in relation to settled land the tenant for life has an independent interest by virtue of his equitable interest under the settlement, and that, therefore, the old cases are still good law.

[10] *Norris v. Harrison* (1817) 2 Madd. 268; *cf. Welsh v. London Assurance Corporation*, 151 Pa. 607 (1892).

[11] *Gaussen v. Whatman* (1905) 93 L.T. 101.

calling on the insurers to apply the policy moneys in rebuilding the premises destroyed.[12]

If the terms of the settlement lay upon the tenant for life an obligation to repair he will be liable to reinstate the premises if they are burned down,[13] but the remainderman will not necessarily have any lien on the policy moneys. If, however, the tenant for life is bound to insure and does insure, the moneys from any policy will belong to the settled estate.[14]

20–53 Section 95 of the Settled Land Act 1925 empowers the trustees of a settlement to give the insurance company a complete discharge for moneys paid to them in respect of insurances on property comprised in the settlement.

20–54 Settlement of leasehold property. Where an onerous property such as a leasehold is settled, the prima facie intention is that the tenant for life shall take the benefit with the burden and that the income he is to derive from it is to be the net income and not the gross income. All payments which are necessarily incidental to the production of the income must be deducted from it. Thus, where leaseholds are settled and there is a covenant to insure the trustees must, at the expense of the tenant for life, perform the covenant and pay the premiums out of the income.[15] The tenant for life is not, however, bound to make good breaches of covenant committed before his title vested in possession.[16]

20–55 Obligation of trustees to insure. Trustees and executors are not bound to insure trust property unless they are directed to do so and are supplied with funds for the purpose, and they are not even bound to inform their beneficiaries when existing insurances expire unless they have acted so as to induce beneficiaries to rely on them to keep up such insurances.[17] The power to insure conferred on trustees by the Trustee Act 1925[18] does not impose a duty to insure, nor is any such duty imposed by a direction in the trust deed to pay "necessary expenses" out of rents and profits.[19]

But trustees are bound to see that obligations upon which the existence of the trust property depends are duly performed; in the case of leaseholds with a covenant to insure and repair they are bound to see that these covenants

---

[12] *Re Quicke's Trusts* [1908] 1 Ch. 887; see paras 21–14 *et seq., post.*
[13] *Gregg v. Coates* (1856) 23 Beav. 33.
[14] *Re Quicke's Trusts* [1908] 1 Ch. 887; *Re Bladon* [1911] 2 Ch. 350; [1912] 1 Ch. 45.
[15] *Re Fowler* (1881) 16 Ch.D. 723; *Debney v. Eckett* (1894) 71 L.T. 659; *Re Waldron* [1904] 1 Ir.R. 240. The contrary decisions of Kekewich J. in *Re Baring* [1893] 1 Ch. 61 and *Re Tomlinson* [1898] 1 Ch. 232 were based on a misapprehension of the decision in *Re Courtier* (1886) 34 Ch.D. 136 and after his brother judges had refused to follow it (see *Re Redding* [1897] 1 Ch. 876; *Re Betty* [1899] 1 Ch. 821, and *Re Kingham* [1897] 1 Ir.R. 170) he bowed in *Re Gjers* to the superior weight of authority [1899] 2 Ch. 54.
[16] *Re Courtier* (1886) 34 Ch.D. 136; *cf. Brereton v. Day* [1895] 1 Ir.R. 518.
[17] *Bailey v. Gould* (1840) 4 Y. & C. Ex. 221; *Garner v. Moore* (1855) 3 Drew. 277; *Fry v. Fry* (1859) 27 Beav. 144, 146; *Dowson v. Solomon* (1859) 1 Dr. & Sm. 1
[18] See para. 20–57, *post.*
[19] *Re McEacharn* (1911) 103 L.T. 900.

are performed and, if necessary, to perform them themselves in so far as the funds at their disposal will permit.[20]

If persons in fiduciary position do insure trust property, they must hold the insurance for the benefit of the trust, and will not be allowed to allege that they made the insurance on their own interest or for their own benefit.[21] Even if the trustees have paid premiums out of their own private funds, they can be compelled to give the benefit of the insurance to the trust.[22]

20–56 Application of trust funds to effect insurance. Trustees have authority to insure trust property out of trust funds (1) if authorised by the trust; (2) by statute.

The trustees may be authorised expressly, or impliedly from the other terms of the trust (as in the case of a bequest of leaseholds with a covenant to insure), to insure the trust property out of the income of the trust estate. The power is presumably to insure for the benefit of the estate and not solely for the benefit of the persons entitled to the income for the time being, and therefore the policy moneys, if not applied in reinstatement, must be applied as capital subject to the same trusts as affected the property destroyed or damaged.

Section 102 of the Settled Land Act 1925[23] provides that if and so long as any person who is entitled to a beneficial interest in possession affecting land is an infant, the trustees may insure against fire and pay the premiums out of the income of the land.

20–57 Section 19 of the Trustee Act 1925,[24] re-enacting earlier provisions to similar effect, provides that any trustee may insure against loss or damage by fire any building or other insurable property to any amount (including the amount of any insurance already on foot), not exceeding three-quarters of the full value of such building or property, and pay the premiums for such insurance out of the income thereof, or out of the income of any other property subject to the same trusts without obtaining the consent of any person who may be entitled wholly or partly to such income. Chattels such as jewels and family portraits, settled along with the land, are within the section.[25]

20–58 Application of insurance money on trust property. Section 20 of the Trustee Act 1925,[26] which is new, contains elaborate provision as to the

---

[20] *Re Fowler* (1881) 16 Ch.D. 723. This was a decision as to the duties of trustees under a settlement; since 1925 the tenant for life is himself a trustee of the settlement and the remaining trustees have much less active duties in relation to the trust property than under the previous law. But although *Re Fowler* may now be a doubtful guide to the obligations of trustees of settled land, it is submitted that it is authoritative in relation to other trustees such as trustees for sale, personal representatives and even trustees of a settlement who are in the position of a statutory owner where there is no adult tenant for life.

[21] *Parry v. Ashley* (1829) 3 Sim. 97. As submitted in note 9 above this probably does not apply to a tenant for life under a settlement.

[22] *Ex p. Andrews* (1816) 2 Rose 410; *cf. Re McGaw* [1919] W.N. 288 where trustees were authorised by the court to proceed against insurers at the risk (for costs) of the trust estate.

[23] 15 & 16 Geo. 5, c. 18.

[24] 15 & 16 Geo. 5, c. 19.

[25] *Re Earl of Egmont's Trust* [1908] 1 Ch. 821.

[26] This section reverses the effect of the decision in *Re Quicke's Trusts* [1908] 1 Ch. 887 and applies only to insurance payments, not to other payments such as indemnities from the State for war damage; *Re Scholfield* [1949] Ch. 341.

application of insurance moneys receivable under a policy on property subject to a trust or settlement, kept up under a trust power or obligation, or by a tenant for life impeachable for waste. The effect of the section is to make the insurance money capital moneys under the Settled Land Act 1925, or under the trust, and there are subsidiary provisions empowering the trustees to apply the money in reinstatement and saving the existing rights (if any) to require the insurance money to be applied in reinstating the property lost or damaged.

20–59 Inherent power of trustees to insure. In view of the statutory powers, it is no longer necessary to decide whether a trustee has power on general equitable principles to insure out of capital.[27]

20–60 Personal representatives. There may well be no obligation on a personal representative to insure property which was not insured by the deceased,[28] but, if he does insure he will be entitled to recover the premiums from the part of the property which is protected.[29]

3. CLAIMS BROUGHT BY THIRD PARTIES PURSUANT TO THE CONTRACTS (RIGHTS OF THIRD PARTIES) ACT 1999

20–61 At common law persons who are strangers to a contract are not entitled to enforce it even when it purports to confer benefits upon them.[30] Individual exceptions have been created by statute in relation to particular classes of insurance, such as motor,[31] life and accident policies made for the benefit of spouses and children,[32] fire insurances on buildings,[33] and liability policies.[34] By contrast, the Contracts (Rights of Third Parties) Act 1999[35] applies potentially to all types of contract and therefore to all classes of insurance. It provides that a third party may in his own right enforce a term of a contract:

(a) if the contract expressly provides that he may, or

(b) if it purports to confer a benefit upon him, subject to it appearing from the contract that the parties did not intend the term to be enforceable by him.[36] The Act does not affect rights and remedies already afforded to third parties by common law, equity or statute.[37]

20–62 The reader should consult other works for a detailed treatment of

---

[27] See *Re Bennett* [1896] 1 Ch. 778, 786 *per* Kay L.J.; *Re Sherry* [1913] 2 Ch. 508; *Re Seibel Estate* [1931] 2 W.W.R. 581 (power in trustee to effect hail insurance where it would be prudent and proper to do so).

[28] *cf. Re McEacharn* (1911) 103 L.T. 900.

[29] *Re Smith* [1937] 1 Ch. 636.

[30] *Vandepitte v. Preferred Accident Insurance Corporation* [1933] A.C. 70, 79.

[31] Road Traffic Act 1988, s.148(7), s.151.

[32] Married Women's Property Act 1882, s.11.

[33] Fire Prevention (Metropolis) Act 1774, s.83.

[34] Third Parties (Rights against Insurers) Act 1930

[35] The Act applies to contracts concluded on or after November 11, 1999 if expressly made subject to it, and otherwise to contracts concluded six months thereafter.

[36] s.1(1) and 1(2).

[37] s.7(1)

the Act.[38] In this section we aim to give a brief account as to how it may affect third party beneficiaries of insurance policies. First, there are cases in which the Act may permit third parties to enforce rights under policies for the first time. Secondly, there are instances in which it provides a more satisfactory juristic basis for certain third party claims for which exceptions to the privity rule have already been allowed. Thirdly, there are cases in which claimants might appear to possess a right of enforcement under section 1 of the Act, but in which their claims are likely to be defeated either under other sections of the Act or by separate rules of insurance law.

20–63 The first category consists of potential third party claimants whose claims were previously defeated by the privity doctrine. A bailee who insures goods "his own in trust or on commission" is entitled to insure them to their full value and so cover the interests of their owners. While a bailor is entitled at common law to require the bailee-assured to account to him for the proceeds of the insurance once received from the insurers, he cannot directly enforce the bailee's insurance himself.[39] Since the insurance is worded to cover the interests of the class of persons to which he belongs, namely the present and future customers of the assured, it should be possible to describe him as a person on whom the coverage clause purports to confer a benefit, so that he would be able to bring a claim directly against the insurers if the bailee was unwilling to enforce a claim for the benefit of his customers. Another example is that of the personal accident group insurance policy effected by an employer under which the insurers undertake to pay certain sums in the event of accidental injury to his employees.[40] While the employees are described as "insured persons" who are to benefit indirectly from the payments made to their employer, he alone is the assured, and the decision in *Green v. Russell*[41] shows that they are unable to enforce the policy at law or in equity in the absence of clear wording to show that he intended to constitute himself trustee of his rights of suit on the policy for their benefit. In that case the employees had no right under their employment contracts to require the employer to account to them for the proceeds of the insurance, but it would not have made a difference if they did. In principle a direct claim would now lie against the insurers under the Act, although if a policy were to contain a clause similar to that in *Green v. Russell*[42] providing that the insurers were not bound " to recognise any equitable or other claim to or interest in the policy and the receipt of the insured…alone shall be an effectual discharge", it might well show that the parties did not intend the policy to be directly enforceable by an employee.

20–64 Another area in which the Act will have an effect is that of waiver of subrogation clauses contained in insurance policies. It is not unusual for contractors' risks policies to contain a clause whereby the insurer promises not to exercise his rights of subrogation against a defined group of persons,

---

[38] *Chitty on Contracts* (28th ed., 1999) Vol. 1 paras 19–075 to 19–102; *Privity of Contract* (Merkin ed., 2000); Burrows, The Contracts (Rights of Third Parties) Act 1999 and its implications for commercial contracts, [2000] L.M.C.L.Q. 540.
[39] *DG Finance v. Scott* [1999] Lloyd's Rep. I.R. 387 and see paras 20–27 to 20–29, *ante*.
[40] Group sickness policies often employ similar wording.
[41] [1959] 2 Q.B. 226
[42] *ibid.*

such as sub-contractors, in the event that one them causes a loss for which the insurer has to indemnify the assured. Unless the beneficiary of the waiver clause is a co-assured on the policy, he will be unable to enforce it against the insurer who brings suit. Two cases in marine insurance illustrate the problem. In the Canadian case of *Fraser River Pile and Dredge v. Can-Dive Services*[43] the charterer of the assured ship-owner's barge was protected by a waiver of subrogation clause in the owner's hull policy on the barge. It sank, and the insurers paid their assured, the owner. They also agreed with their assured that they would bring a subrogated claim against the charterer despite the clause. Having brought proceedings the insurers invoked the privity of contract doctrine to stop the charterer enforcing the clause. The Supreme Court of Canada allowed him to do so under its doctrine of "principled exceptions" to the privity rule, which is not part of English law. The charterer would in principle possess the right to enforce the clause under the Act. In *The Surf City*[44] the owner of a vessel carrying goods sold under a c.i.f. sale sought to avail himself of the benefit of a waiver of subrogation clause contained in the cargo insurance on the goods when cargo insurers brought a subrogated claim in the name of the c.i.f. buyer. He successfully established that he was in the class of persons protected by the clause, but was not able to enforce it against the insurers. Luckily for him the insurers conceded that it would be inequitable to pursue their claim in these circumstances. The 1999 Act would not now leave him dependent on their magnanimity.

20–65 The second category of case can be illustrated by reference to a loss-payee clause. In its most simple form this is no more than a term of a policy constituting a direction by the assured to the insurers to make payments of claims to that person. In the absence of an intention by the assured to assign his right to payment it is merely a mandate to the insurer to pay the third party.[45] Unless the loss payee is a co-assured, or the loss-payee term constitutes or evidences an assignment of the assured's rights of recovery to the third party, he has no right at common law to enforce the clause in his favour.[46] In practice this can lead to attempts to find an assignment in the absence of satisfactory evidence of an intention to assign and to further argument as to whether the assignment takes effect in law or equity. Under the Act the loss-payee would seem to have the right to enforce the clause directly against the insurer. Another example is the case of a property insurance taken out by a trades union or other similar association for the benefit of its members. The members have insurable interest but are not assureds, while the union has a right of suit but no interest. In *Prudential Staff Union v. Hall*[47] the court held that the union was entitled to recover on such a policy in reliance on its member's interest because "no doubt the union would regard themselves as trustees for the particular members of any amounts recovered", although there were no words of trust in the policy.[48]

---

[43] [2000] 1 Lloyd's Rep. 199 and see Green, "Privity a la Canadienne" [2000] L.M.C.L.Q. 322.

[44] [1995] 2 Lloyd's Rep. 242.

[45] *Timpson's Executors v. Yerbury* [1936] 1 K.B. 645, 658–659. See paras 20–41 *et seq.*, *ante*.

[46] *Iraqi Ministry of Defence v. Avcepey Shipping Co. S.A. The Angel Bell* [1979] 1 Lloyd's Rep. 491, 497, *per* Donaldson J.

[47] [1947] K.B. 685.

[48] The authorities requiring clear evidence of an intention to create a trust, such as *Vandepitte v. Preferred Accident Insurance Corporation* [1933] A.C. 70 and *Re Schebsman* [1944] Ch. 83, were not discussed in the judgment.

Today the union members would be able to claim directly on the policy covering their interests in reliance on the Act.

20–66 There are a variety of ways in which claims brought by a third party are liable to be defeated. First they are made subject to all defences which arise in connection with the contract and which would have been available to the insurer as a defence to a claim by the named assured, such as rescission for non-disclosure or misrepresentation, a defence of breach of warranty, or avoidance for breach of utmost good faith.[49] In this respect a mortgagee would still remain in a worse position as a loss-payee than if he were a named co-assured on the policy.[50] The third party's claim may also fail for lack of insurable interest, for the Act is not expressed to relieve third party claimants from demonstrating interest in circumstances in which the named assured[51] must do so. In paragraph 7.34 of the Law Commission's Report[51] it is said that an own-life policy taken out by B and expressed to be for the benefit of his co-habitee C could be enforced by C against the insurers on B's death under section 1(1) (a) of the Act. C, however, would be required by section 1 of the Life Assurance Act 1774 to show that she possessed an insurable interest in B's life in order to prevent the insurance from being illegal and void under that Act, and under the existing law she cannot do so because she is not his wife.[52] Another difficulty may be caused by notice clauses in policies which require notice of claim to be given by the named assured and are not adapted to permit notice to be given by a third party claimant.[53] It has also been remarked that attempts by persons to whom an assured is liable to claim directly on his liability cover (when he is not yet insolvent) would fail because the wording of the policy would not be expressed to confer a benefit on the third party but rather to give an indemnity to the assured, and because a potential victim of a negligent act committed by the assured cannot be said to belong to a class of persons capable of being defined as less than the public at large.[54] Another difficulty is created by section 2 of the 1999 Act, which permits the parties to the contract to extinguish or alter the rights of the third party unless they are aware that he has relied on the term confers a benefit on him or can reasonably foresee that he would and in fact he has done so. If the right of the charterer in the *Fraser River Pile & Dredge* case[55] to enforce the waiver of subrogation clause in his favour was to be adjudicated under the Act, it is hard to see how his claim would survive section 2(1). The agreement of the parties to amend the waiver clause to exclude charterers was made after the casualty but before a claim was brought against the charterer. At that time reliance was indeed foreseeable, but it does not appear that the charterer was in fact relying on it before he realised that a subrogated action was being taken against him.

---

[49] Contracts (Rights of Third Parties) Act 1999, s.3(2).
[50] See paras 17–33 *et seq., ante.*
[51] Law Commission Report No. 242.
[52] See Hemsworth, (1998) 57 Camb.L.J. 55.
[53] *Senate Electrical Wholesalers v. Alcatel Submarine Networks* [1999] 2 Lloyd's Rep. 423, and see the discussion by C. Henley in *Privity of Contract* (2000) at pp. 239–240.
[54] *Privity of Contract* (2000) pp. 105–106.
[55] [2000] 1 Lloyd's Rep. 199

CHAPTER 21

REINSTATEMENT

1. GENERALLY

21–1 Introduction. A fire policy will almost invariably provide that the insurer shall have the right of replacing or repairing the property instead of paying a money indemnity to the assured. This right can be particularly valuable to the insurer where, for example, there are several insurers on several interests and their total liability may be far greater than the total amount of fire damage. If, in *Westminster Fire Office v. Glagow Provident Investment Society*,[1] the insurance companies had taken advantage of their right to reinstate and had joined in giving notice to their several insured that they elected to reinstate, they would have discharged their liability by one payment of the fire damage divided between them instead of each having to pay to their assured the total fire damage up to the amount insured without any right of contribution from the other companies.

The insurer may insist on the right to reinstate:

(1) if by his contract he has expressly reserved the power to do so;
(2) if he has any suspicion of fraud or arson;
(3) if he is requested to do so by any person other than the assured, who is interested in or entitled to the premises damaged by fire.

The right under the last two heads is conferred by the Fires Prevention (Metropolis) Act 1774, which will be discussed later. Where the insurer has neither a statutory nor an express contractual right to reinstate he cannot, as against his assured, insist on doing so, but must pay a money indemnity.[2]

21–2 Reinstatement clause. The usual form of reinstatement clause gives the insurers an option to pay a money indemnity or to restore to the assured *in specie* the property damaged or destroyed. The alternative is not merely to lay out the insurance money in reinstatement as far as it will go but to reinstate completely. If the insurers elect to reinstate, their liability is not limited either by the amount insured,[3] the amount of the damage,[4] or the assured's insurable interest.

[1] (1888) 13 App.Cas. 699. The facts are set out in para. 19–29, *ante*.
[2] *Rayner v. Preston* (1881) 18 Ch.D. 1, 9–10, *per* Brett L.J.
[3] *cf. Brown v. Royal Ins. Co.* (1859) 1 E. & E. 853, 860, *per* Crompton J.; *Morrell v. Irving Fire Ins. Co.*, 33 N. Y. 429 (1865); *Argy Trading v. Lapid Developments Ltd* [1977] 1 Lloyd's Rep. 67, 74; *contra*, if the policy gives the insurer the right to limit his liability, *Home Mutual Fire Ins. Co. v. Garfield*, 14 Am.Rep. 27 (1871).
[4] *Swift v. New Zealand Ins. Co.* [1927] V.L.R. 249.

The clause is for the benefit of the insurer[5] and, if he elects to pay, the assured cannot either insist on reinstatement or upon a sum being paid equivalent to the cost of reinstatement.[6] On the other hand once the insurer has paid, he cannot insist that the assured must spend the money on reinstating the premises, unless he has made an express agreement to that effect before payment for the loss.[7] If, however, the insurer does elect to reinstate, the assured is bound to allow the insurer to enter his land and neither the assured nor an assignee of the proceeds of the policy will be granted an injunction to restrain the insurer from carrying out the work of reinstatement.[8]

21–3 Notice of election. If the insurer wishes to reinstate the must give the assured unequivocal notice that he intends to exercise his option.[9] If the policy does not stipulate a period within which the notice must be given,[10] it must be given within a reasonable time[11] to the assured or his agent having authority to receive such notice on his behalf.[12] Where the policy was indorsed "loss, if any, payable to mortgagee" it was held that notice of election to reinstate was properly given to the owner, and notice to the mortgagee was unnecessary.[13] It is sometimes provided in the policy that the option to reinstate is conditional on giving notice within a certain time of completion of proofs; it has been held that such a clause refers to the formal preliminary proof for loss and not proof of loss before a court or arbitrator.[14]

21–4 Election to pay or reinstate. Once the insurer has made his election he is bound by it and cannot thereafter change his mind.[15] But it may often be difficult to say whether conduct of any kind by the insurer constitutes an election. In *Sutherland v. Sun Fire Office*[16] a stationer's stock and furniture

---

[5] *Anderson v. Commercial Union Ass. Co.* (1885) 55 L.J.Q.B. 146, 149, *per* Bowen L.J.

[6] *Rayner v. Preston* (1881) 18 Ch.D. 1, 6; *Leppard v. Excess Ins. Co. Ltd* [1979] 1 W.L.R. 512.

[7] *Queen Ins. Co. v. Vey* (1867) 16 L.T. 239, *re Law Guarantee Trust and Accident Society Ltd, Liverpool Mortgage Ins. Co. Ltd's Case* [1914] 2 Ch. 617, 632–633, *per* Buckley L.J., 639, *per* Kennedy L.J.; *Lees v. Whiteley* (1866) L.R. 2 Eq. 143, 149.

[8] *Bissett v. Royal Exchange Ass. Co.* (1822) 1 S. 174, where the assured claimed a money sum but the insurer insisted on reinstating before the court decided whether the assured was entitled to claim the sum in cash.

[9] Compare generally the law on options, see, *e.g.* Halsbury, *Laws of England* (4th ed.), vol. 9, para. 235; *Daul v. Fireman's Ins. Co.*, 35 La.Ann. 98 (1888).

[10] See, *e.g. Maryland Home Fire Ins. Co. v. Kimmel*, 89 Md. 437 (1899).

[11] *Sutherland v. Sun Fire Office* (1852) 14 D. 775; *cf.* the statement of facts in *Anderson v. Commercial Union Ass. Co.* (1885) 55 L.J.Q.B. 146, where it is stated that notice was given within a reasonable time.

[12] See Ch. 36, *post.*

[13] *Heilman v. Westchester Fire Ins. Co.*, 75 N.Y. 7 (1878).

[14] *Clover v. Greenwich Ins. Co.*, 101 N.Y. 277(1866); see also *Kelly v. Sun Fire Office*, 141 Pa. 10 (1891) where time was held to run from the delivery of corrected preliminary proofs.

[15] *Sutherland v. Sun Fire Office* 14 D. 775 (1852); *Scottish Amicable Heritable Securities Association Ltd v. Northern Ass. Co.* (1883) 11 R. 287; *Brown v. Royal Ins. Co.* (1859) 1 E. & E. 853, 860, *per* Crompton J.; *Bowes v. National Fire & Marine Ins. Co. of New Zealand* (1889) 7 N.Z.L.R. 27. (partial reinstatement invalid unless contract is divisible). If the insurer makes a money payment on the faith of a promise by the insured to use the money for reinstatement and the insured does not do so, the insurer may be able to recover his payment, see *Queen's Ins. Co. v. Vey* (1867) 16 L.T. 239.

[16] (1852) 14 D. 775.

were insured and damaged by fire. Before any formal claim was made the defendant insurance company sent an expert to examine the stock and fittings and to report on the damage. After a formal claim was made the company made an offer of a cash payment which was refused and subsequently an offer to refer the amount of damage to arbitration which was also declined by the assured. The company then siad it would exercise its option to reinstate but the assured brought an action for a money indemnity. It was held by the Court of Session that it was still open to the office to elect to reinstate.[17] The Court of Session arrived at a different conclusion, however, in *Scottish Amicable Heritable Securities Association v. Northern Assurance Co.,*[18] where the different incumbrancers (mortgagees) were insured with different insurance companies. After a fire had occurred on August 1, 1882, there were prolonged negotiations for a settlement. The prior incumbrancers claimed a certain sum or reinstatement. The insurers took no notice of the alternative claim for reinstatement, but disputed the amount claimed, and they prepared a minute of reference to arbitration on the question of damage; this minute was not, however, signed as the insurers insisted upon all the other insurers being made parties to the reference. On February 5, 1883, the assured raised their action for payment and for the first time the insurers offered to reinstate in their defence. It was held that the offer was too late since it was clear from the terms of the correspondence that the insurers had elected to settle in money for the loss covered by the policy and that the only difference between the parties was the amount payable which would be fixed by arbitration. In an American case the assured, after loss, signed an indorsement on the policy, "Pay the loss under the written policy to B," and the company added their indorsement, "Assented to". It was held that the company had not waived their right to reinstate, but had merely assented to an assignment of the benefit of the policy as it stood to B.[19]

21-5 In the light of these authorities it is not easy to lay down any general principles as to what conduct constitutes an election, since in each case it is a question of fact. But a court would be reluctant to hold that an insurer had exercised an election by conduct unless it was satisfied that the insurer had all the available information before him on which to decide which of the two courses was more advantageous to him.[20] In particular, a mere offer to settle by payment of a certain sum of money will probably not of itself be an election to pay if that offer is refused; insurers would however be wise to state that any such offer was made without prejudice to their right to reinstate.

---

[17] The only judge to express any doubt was Lord Ivory who thought that the offer of a cash payment might be an election to pay rather than to reinstate; but he held that the refusal to go to arbitration threw the whole question open again, and entitled the company once more to make its election.

[18] (1883) 11 R. 287. This case arose out of the same fire as gave rise to *Westminster Fire Office v. Glasgow Provident Investment Society* (1888) 13 App.Cas. 699. See also *Lalands v. Phoenix Ins. Co. of Hartford* (1918) 54 Q.R.S.C. 461.

[19] *Tolman v. Manufacturer's Ins. Co.* 55 Mass. 73 (1848). For a case where the consent of a third party was allegedly necessary before reinstatement could be made, see *Bank of New South Wales v. Royal Ins. Co.* (1880) 2 N.Z.L.R.(S.C.) 337.

[20] *Sutherland v. Sun Fire Office* (1852) 14 D. 775, 778, *per* the Lord President.

21–6 Effect of election. If the insurer elects to reinstate property damaged by fire, the contract ceases to be a contract of indemnity and becomes a contract to reinstate, as if the insurer had originally agreed to reinstate.[21] In short, the insurance policy becomes a building contract[22] or a repair contract[23] and is enforceable as such. Thus if the insurer fails to perform the contract adequately or at all, he will be liable for damages,[24] although he will not be compelled to perform the contract specifically.[25] Moreover he cannot excuse himself on the grounds that reinstatement has turned out to be more expensive than he anticipated or than the amount for which the property was originally insured[26] or than the assured's actual loss.[27]

21–7 Impossibility of reinstatement. It seems necessary to distinguish between impossibility existing at the time when the insurer has to make his election, and impossibility supervening after the insurer has elected to reinstate. The former case presents little difficulty. In *Anderson v. Commercial Union Assurance Co.*,[28] Bowen L.J. said:

> "It is clear law that if one of two things which had been contracted for subsequently becomes impossible, it becomes a question of construction whether, according to the true intention of the parties, the obligor is bound to perform the alternative or is discharged altogether."[29]

He went on to say that on the policy before the court in that case, it was "hopeless" to contend that total discharge was the intention. The same conclusion would in all probability be reached on any policy. The effect of impossibility of reinstatement, exising at the time of election, is therefore to exclude the option to reinstate and to leave the insurer with the single obligation to make a money payment.

The question what amounts to impossibility must be considered in the light of the precise tenor of the obligation to reinstate. It has been said that the obligation is, where the property has been totally destroyed, to "replace it by other things which are equivalent to the property destroyed".[30] There is no implication that chattels must be restored in the same place where they were before. Thus the fact that the premises in which the insured chattels were housed have themselves been destroyed, or are no longer at the disposal of the insured, raises no impossibility in the way of reinstatement. The insured in such a case should nominate another place at which the

---

[21] *Brown v. Royal Ins. Co.* (1859) 1 E. & E. 853, 858–859, *per* Lord Campbell C.J.; *Bank of New South Wales v. Royal Ins. Co.* (1880) 2 N.Z.L.R.(S.C.) 337; *Robson v. New Zealand Ins. Co. Ltd* [1931] N.Z.L.R. 35; *Maher v. Lumbermens' Mut. Casualty Co.* [1932] 2 D.L.R. 593, 600–601; *Carlyle v. Elite Ins. Co.* (1984) 56 B.C.L.R. 331, 335. It is a matter of construction whether clauses of the policy such as the arbitration clause will be applicable to the contract to reinstate; contrast *Wynkoop v. Niagara Fire Ins. Co.*, 43 Am.Rep. 686 (1883) with *Jordan v. Scottish Ass. Corporation* (1922) O.P.D. 129.
[22] *Morrell v. Irving Fire Ins. Co.*, 33 N.Y. 429 (1865); *cf. Times Fire Ass. Co. v. Hawke* (1859) 28 L.J.(Ex.) 317, at Nisi Prius (1858) 1 F. & F. 406.
[23] *Maher v. Lumberman's Mutual Ins. Co.* [1932] D.L.R. 593; *Robson v. New Zealand Ins. Co.* [1931] N.Z.L.R. 35.
[24] *Brown v. Royal Ins. Co.* (1859) 1 E. & E. 853, *Davidson v. Guardian Royal Exchange Ass.* [1979] 1 Lloyd's Rep. 406 and cases cited in note 41, *infra*.
[25] *Home District Mutual Ins. Co. v. Thompson* (1847) 1 U.C.Err. & App. 247.
[26] *Brown v. Royal Ins. Co.* (1859) 1 E. & E. 853.
[27] *Swift v. New Zealand Ins. Co. Ltd* [1927] V.L.R. 249.
[28] (1885) 55 L.J.Q.B. 146.
[29] At p. 150.
[30] *Anderson v. Commercial Union Ass. Co.*, *per* Lord Esher M.R. *Supra* at p. 148.

reinstatement can take place; he has no right to insist on a money payment[31] Again, the fact that building regulations do not permit a building to be restored exactly as it was before does not necessarily amount to impossibility.[32] If, on the other hand, the effect of reinstating the original building would be the erection of a building which would be condemned as unsafe, a court would probably say that reinstatement was impossible and require the insurer to pay the value of the loss of damage.[33]

21–8 Though the dictum of Bowen L.J., quoted above, is on the face of it applicable both before and after the insurer's election, it can well be argued that different considerations arise after the contract has been transformed, by the election to reinstate, into a contract to build or repair. Such a contract is, normally, capable of being discharged by frustration.[34] There seems to be no good reason why the ordinary rules of frustration should not operate in this case.[35]

21–9 The only relevant decision is *Brown v. Royal Insurance Co.*,[36] which was decided before the principles of frustration were established and must now be considered a doubtful authority. The insurers elected to reinstate but, after they had begun, the house was condemned under the Metropolis Management Act 1855 by the Commissioners of Sewers, who ordered it to be demolished. To the assured's claims for damages for failure to reinstate, the insurers pleaded that the contract had become impossible and that they were therefore discharged. This argument was not accepted by the Court of Queeen's Bench, who held that the assured's action could proceed, on the ground that impossibility arising after the conclusion of the contract was no defence. Today a court could hardly fail to discuss whether the contract was frustrated or not.

21–10 In principle the position of the insurer is probably no different from that of a builder under a building contract and it would clearly be impossible for an insurer to plead frustration on the ground that the project had become more expensive that he expected. It may be, however, that an insurer will have greater difficulty in maintaining a successful plea of frustration than a builder. If, for example, in the course of an ordinary building contract, the site is compulsorily purchased by the local authority, a builder would no doubt be able to maintain that the contract had been frustrated, because, even if the compulsory acquisition should have been foreseen, it would be the owners' responsibility to make the necessary investigations. If the same event occurred while an insurer was rebuilding, it would at least be arguable

---

[31] *Anderson v. Commercial Union Ass. Co. supra.*

[32] See *Fire Association v. Rosenthal*, 108 Pa. 474 (1885), where insurers were held liable to reinstate using different building materials from those originally used, and *Alchorne v. Favill* (1825) 4 L.J.(o.s) Ch. 47, where insurers rebuilt to a new building line required by legislation. They were, however, held bound to indemnify the insured by a money payment for the short-fall in value of the new premises as compared with the old.

[33] *Monteleone v. Royal Ins. Co. of America and London*, 47 La.Ann, 1563 (1895).

[34] See Chitty, *Contracts* (27th ed.), Ch. 23; Hudson, *Building Contracts* (11th ed.), pp. 633–655.

[35] In *Bank of New South Wales v. Royal Ins. Co.* (1880) 2 N.Z.L.R.(S.C.) 337, Richmond J. said (at p. 344) that the insurers would not be bound to reinstate if, after election, it was discovered to be impossible. *Wright, Stephenson & Co. v. Holmes* [1932] N.Z.L.R. 815 is to like effect (insured car destroyed by fire in earthquake while insurer liable to repair it.).

[36] (1859) 1 E & E. 853.

that the insurer, before reinstating, should have taken steps to find out whether there was any risk of compulsory purchase.

The most equitable step after holding the contract of reinstatement frustrated would be to restore the insurers's obligation to pay the amount of the loss or damage, but there is a strong argument to the effect that frustration has dischargd the insurer altogether from further liability to the assured.[37] If the insurer had already incurred considerable expenditure in restoring or repairing, it might be thought unjust that he should pay the whole amount of the loss, but the assured is entitled to payment according to the insurance policy.[38] In similar circumstances it has been held that where an insurer has elected to reinstate and after partial completion the premises are again burned down, he must make good the fresh damage as part of his obligation to reinstate.[39]

21–11 Measure of insurer's obligation. An insurer who has elected to reinstate is bound to put the premises in substantially the same condition as before the fire. He is not bound to give the assured a new house for an old one; when, therefore, premises are only partially destroyed, he is not bound to pull down the old walls and rebuild them even if there is a defect in their foundation. If the old material is combined with the new so that the repaired building is as good as the old one, the insurer has done all that can be required of him.[40] If, however, the work of reconstruction is done badly and the result is less valuable than the old building, the insurer will be liable in damages for the deficiency.[41] Such damages will include all consequential damages which flow from the defective reinstatement and can reasonably be foreseen by the defendant such as loss of business or loss of rent. Although the insurer is liable to make good the difference, if he produces an inferior article, he gets no credit if he produces a superior article unless there is an

---

[37] In *Bank of New South Wales v. Royal Ins. Co.* (1880) 2 N.Z.L.R.(S.C.) 337 Richmond J. said (at p. 344) that the insurers would not be bound to reinstate if, after election, it was discovered to be impossible: "The clause relating to reinstatement is inapplicable." This stops short, however, of an answer to the problem. Clarke, *Law of Insurance Contracts*, (looseleaf, ed., 1999) paras 29–2c, suggests on the basis of the speech of Lord Wilberforce in *Johnson v. Agnew* [1980] A.C. 367, 398–399, that the insurer's election to reinstate is not irrevocable because departure from it is not impossible, and that he is bound to perform in the alternative manner of payment for the loss. But Lord Wilberforce was considering the exercise of the equitable remedy of election and not the exercise of a contracted option to perform a contract in an alternative manner. Nor was it a case where the other party to the contract sought to enforce a return to the primary mode of performance. It is submitted that the answer must lie in the implication of a term obliging the insurer to pay money when the contract to reinstate is frustrated, based upon the fundamental principle of providing an indemnity.

[38] s.2(5)(b) of the Law Reform (Frustrated Contracts) Act 1943 provides that the Act does not apply to any contract for insurance, but it is submitted that in the circumstances envisaged above the contract has become a building contract and is no longer a contract of insurance within the section.

[39] *Smith v. Colonial Mutual Life Ins. Co.* (1880) 5 V.L.R. 200.

[40] *Times Fire Ass. Co. v. Hawke* (1859) 28 L.J.Ex. 317; 1 F. & F., 406; *Anderson v. Commercial Union Ass. Co.* (1885) 55 L.J.Q.B. 146, 148, *per* Lord Esher M.R..

[41] *Brown v. Royal Ins. Co.* (1859) 1 E. & E. 853; *Kaffrarian Colonial Bank v. Grahamstown Fire Ins. Co.* (1885) 5 Buch. (East Dist. Ct.) 61; *Robson v. New Zealand Ins. Co.* [1931] N.Z.L.R. 35; *Ryder v. Commonwealth Fire Ins. Co.*, 52 Barb. 447 (1868); *Alchorne v. Savill* (1825) 4 L.J.(o.s.) Ch. 47. If the insurer elects to replace a chattel, the insured will be entitled to reject it (if it is not as good as the original) and claim for a money payment, *Braithwaite v. Employer's Liability Ass. Corporation* [1964] 1 Lloyd's Rep. 94.

express agreement to such effect. That is a matter which he must take into consideration before he offers to reinstate.

21–12 The reinstatement must be completed within a reasonable time or the insurer will be liable to pay damages for delay.[42] If he fails to complete after beginning to reinstate the assured may himself complete and sue the insurer for the cost.[43] In some cases policies have been framed so that, if the insurer does not complete within a reasonable time, the assured can sue on the policy for the total amount of fire damage, but this is the exception rather than the rule.[44]

Where the right of reinstatement is exercised in respect of buildings, the insurer must reinstate them on the same site. The fact that the site has passed out of the possession or control of the assured into the hands of, for example, a mortgagee does not deprive him of his right to reinstate if he can obtain permission to do so.[45] But when the right of reinstatement is exercised in respect of goods or other movable property, the locality of the thing is not an essential element of the reinstatement. Thus, if premises have been destroyed or possession has passed into the hands of another so that the goods cannot be restored to the same place as before, the assured can request that similar goods be given to him in another place while the insurer will be discharged by offering to supply goods of a similar nature in such reaonable place as the assured may be willing to receive them.[46]

21–13 In *Robson v. New Zealand Insurance Co.*,[47] a motor-vehicle policy contained a reinstatement clause giving the insurer the option of repairing the car or allowing the owner to effect repairs and paying him the cost and a clause which provided "the insured shall not without the consent of the company repair or alter the damaged motor-car." The car was damaged and the insurance company elected to have repairs done at a garage of their choice. These repairs were, however, faulty and unsatisfactory. The owner had the defective repairs remedied at his own garage but the insurance company refused to pay the necessary amount. It was held that the insurer had elected to repair and that the clause quoted above was only applicable where the insurance company exercised the alternative option of allowing the insured to do his own repairs; since the contract for reinstatement had not been properly performed, the plaintiff was entitled to damages.

If the assured denies the right of the insurer to reinstate, the insurer has two courses open to him. He can wait to be sued for the policy money and then plead his election by way of defence[48] or he can proceed immediately to

---

[42] *Davidson v. Guardian Royal Exchange Assurance* [1979] 1 Lloyd's Rep. 406; *Maher v. Lumbermens' Mutual Casualty Co.* [1932] 2 D.L.R. 593, 601. But see *Mylius v. Royal Ins. Co.* [1928] V.L.R. 126 where damages were not recoverable for delay where reinstatement was not required under the 1774 Act, *infra*.

[43] *Fire Association v. Rosenthal*, 108 Pa. 474 (1885); *Morrell v. Irving Fire Insurance Co.*, 33 N.Y. 429 (1865).

[44] *Haskins v. Hamilton Mutual Ins. Co.*, 71 Mass. 432 (1855); *Langan v. Aetna Ins. Co.*, 99 Fed.Rep. 374 (1900).

[45] *Morrell v. Irving Fire Insurance Co.*, 33 N.Y. 429 (1865); *Wynkoop v. Niagara Fire Ins. Co.*, 91 N.Y. 478 (1883).

[46] *Anderson v. Commercial Union Ass. Co.* (1885) 55 L.J.Q.B. 146.

[47] [1931] N.Z.L.R. 35.

[48] *Kelly v. Sun Fire Office*, 141 Pa. 10 (1891).

reinstate. If he adopts the second course, he runs the risk that the court will eventually decide that he is bound to pay the policy money, but, if this is a risk he wishes to take, there is no reasons why a court should exercise its discretion to restrain him from reinstating the property pending the trial of the action.[49] If the assured prevents the insurer from reinstating and reinstates himself, and it is ultimately decided that the insurers had correctly exercised their option, the assured may well be unable to recover anything, not even the sum which the insurer must necessarily have spent on reinstatement.[50]

If several companies agree to reinstate, they will be jointly and severally liable for the fulfillment of the obligation.[51]

2. UNDER STATUTE

21–14 Statutory obligation. Under section 83 of the Fires Prevention (Metropolis) Act 1774[52] companies which insure houses or other buildings against loss by fire are required to spend the insurance money in reinstating so far as it will go, if requested to do so by anyone interested in the premises. A second limb of the section provises that if an insurance company has any ground of suspicion that the owner, occupier or other person who has insured the premises is guilty of fraud or arson, it is authorised[53] to spend the money so far as it will go in reinstatement. Both these provisions are subject to the proviso that if, within 60 days of the claim being adjusted, the party claiming the insurance money gives a sufficient security to the company that the insurance money will be laid out in reinstatement or that if, by that time, the money has been settled and disposed of to and among the contending parties to the satisfaction of the company's directors, the company ceases to be under any obligation or to be able to insist on its right to reinstate.

21–15 The Act applies only to the respective governors or directors of the several insurance offices and does not therefore extend to Lloyd's under-writers.[54] Moreover, only insurances on "houses or other buildings" are within the Act which is therefore inapplicable to policies on goods or other movable property such as trade fixtures or tenant's fixtures, which would not pass under a conveyance of "all that house and buildings".[55] The right or duty of the insurer under the Act must be distinguished from his right or election under a contract. When the insurer exercises his contractual right to reinstate he must restore the premises to their original condition, no matter what the ultimate cost may be. The obligation under the statute is merely to

---

[49] See, *e.g. Bisset v. Royal Exchange Assurance Co.* (1822) 1 S. 174.

[50] See *Beals v. Home Insurance Co.*, 36 N.Y. 522 (1867).

[51] *Hartford Fire Insurance Co. v. Peebles Hotel*, 82 Fed.Rep. 546 (1897).

[52] 14 Geo. 3, c. 78. The act was given its short title by the Short Titles Act 1896 (59 & 60 Vict. c. 14).

[53] The Act itself coalesces the two provisions which are preceded by the words "they [*i.e.* the directors of the insurance offices] are hereby authorised and required". It is reasonably clear, however, that the word "required" applies only to the first provision and that if the company suspects fraud or arson it is not required to reinstate but merely has the right to do so.

[54] *Portavon Cinema Co. Ltd v. Price & Century Ins. Co.* [1939] 4 All E.R. 601, 607–608. The learned judge's remarks are *obiter* but it is submitted that they are correct.

[55] *Ex. p. Goreley* (1864) 4 De G.J. & S. 477; *Re Quicke's Trusts* [1908] 1 Ch. 887; *Randolph v. Randolph* (1907) 3 N.B.Eq.Rep. 576.

expend the money in rebuilding or repairing "as far as the same will go". There is no obligation to make complete reinstatement if the insurance money is insufficient.

21–16 Application outside the Bills of Mortality. The statute was originally entitled "An Act for the further and better Regulation of Buildings and Party Walls, and for the more effectually preventing mischiefs by fire within the Cities of London and Westminster and the Liberties thereof, and other the Parishes, Precincts and Places within the weekly Bills of Mortality,[56] the Parishes of St Mary-le-Bow, Paddington, St Pancras and St Luke at Chelsea, in the county of Middlesex". It has, however, been held that section 83 of the Act is of general application to the whole of England[57] but probably not to Scotland[58] and not to Ireland.[59]

Other places where the Act has been held to be in force are Ontario[60] and British Columbia[61] (but not Saskatchewan),[62] Western Australia,[63] New Zealand[64] and Hong Kong.[65]

21–17 Persons interested. The statute requires the insurance company to cause the insurance money to be laid out in rebuilding "upon the request of any person or persons interested in or entitled unto any house or houses or other buildings which may hereafter be burnt down, demolished or damaged by fire".[66] The concluding words of the section, however, provide that the insurers may pay out the appropriate sum if the insurance money shall be settled and disposed of among all the contending parties to the satisfaction of the insurers and it has been argued that in the light of these words the section is only available to persons who are interested in the sense that they have a claim upon the insurance money.[67] In *Westminster Fire Office v. Glasgow Provident Investment Society*, this argument met with some sympathy from the Earl of Selborne, who doubted whether the section applied so as to

---

[56] This is the area within which prior to the Births and Deaths Registration Act 1836 (6 & 7 Will. 4, c. 86) provision had been made by the London Company of Parish Clerks for the recording of deaths in 109 parishes in and around London. It corresponds substantially to the metropolitan area as defined in the Metropolis Management Act 1855 (18 & 19 Vict. c. 120), s.250, now repealed by S.I. 1965 No. 540.

[57] *Ex p. Goreley* (1864) 4 De G.J. & S. 477 (reversing the decision of the Commissioner in Bankruptcy *sub nom. ex p. Leney and Evenden* (1864) 10 L.T. 697); *Re Quicke's Trusts* [1908] 1 Ch. 887; *Sinnott v. Bowden* [1912] 2 Ch. 414. In *Westminster Fire Office v. Glasgow Provident Investment Society* (1888) 13 App.Cas. 699 Lord Watson said, with regard to the application of the statute outside the Bills of Mortality in England, that the decision in *ex p. Goreley* would have to be carefully considered. In spite of this dictum, the law must be accepted as settled.

[58] *Westminster Fire Office v. Glasgow Provident Investment Society* (1888) 13 App.Cas. 699, *per* Lord Watson.

[59] *Andrews v. Patriotic Ass. Co. of Ireland* (1886) 18 L.R.Ir. 355, 366, *per* Palles C.B.

[60] *Canada South Railway Co. v. Phelps* (1884) 14 S.C.R. 132.

[61] *Re Alliance Ass. Co.* (1960) 25 D.L.R. (2d) 316.

[62] *Royal Bank of Canada v. Pischke* [1933] 1 W.W.R. 145.

[63] *Goldman v. Hargrave* [1967] 1 A.C. 645, 648, 664.

[64] *Searl v. South British Assurance Co.* [1916] N.Z.L.R. 137. The New Zealand Law Commission has recommended that section 83 be removed from the New Zealand statute book—Report No. 46, 1998, para. 55.

[65] Application of English Law Ordinance, Laws of Hong Kong, c. 88.

[66] The section cannot be relied on by the assured but only by persons, other than the assured, who have an interest in the property, *Reynolds v. Phoenix Ass. Co.* [1978] 2 Lloyd's Rep. 440, 462, *per* Forbes J.

[67] *per* Rigby Q.C. in *Westminster Fire Office v. Glasgow Provident Investment Society* (1888) 13 App.Cas. 699, 707.

entitle a postponed bondholder to call upon the insurer of a prior bondholder to lay out the insurance money payable to the latter in reinstatement when each bondholder had insured his own interest and clearly had no claim on the other's insurance. He said[68]:

> "It has not, as far as I know, ever been decided that it applies as between mortgagor and mortgagee, or (which is the same thing in effect) as between prior and puisne incumbrancer. The concluding words of the section are sufficient, at least, to suggest grave doubts whether it ought to be so applied."

But in *Sinnott v. Bowden,*[69] it was held that the section did apply as between mortgagor and mortgagee. B had by indenture charged his house with payment to C of a sum of £30, and he covenanted to insure the premises against fire. At the date of the deed, B had already insured the premises and he subsequently renewed the insurance. The premises were destroyed by fire and the sum payable by the insurance company to B exceeded the amount of the charge. S, a judgment creditor of B, obtained a garnishee order nisi attaching the insurance money. After the date of the order C served the company with a notice requiring the money to be applied in rebuilding the premises. S applied to make the garnishee order absolute and C opposed the application. Parker J. discharged the order and held that section 83 of the statute applied outside the bills of mortality and could be invoked by a mortgagee. He further held that the mortgagee's right to have the insurance money spent in rebuildintg was an equitable right which could not be displaced even by a garnishee order absolute provided that relief was sought before payment had in fact been made. The judge was not sure that he could follow the Earl of Selborne's suggestion that the concluding words of the section prevented the statute from applying as between mortgagor and mortgagee:

> "The words in question exempt the insurance company from having to lay out or take security for the laying out of the policy moneys in rebuilding the insured premises if, within 60 days, those moneys shall have been settled and disposed of to and amongst all 'the contending parties' to the satisfaction and approval of the insurance company. If 'the contending parties' means the parties claiming to be interested in the policy moneys the clause may possibly appear to suggest that no one except the persons so interested has any right to require the policy moneys to be laid out in rebuilding; but, as a matter of fact, this right is expressly given not to the persons interested in the policy moneys, but to the persons interested in the premises destroyed by fire, and I can see no reason why 'the contending parties' should not include the persons who, though not interested in the policy moneys, are interested in the subject-matter of the insurance and are insisting on the insurance money being laid out in rebuilding. This construction seems to me in full accordance with the general object of the enactment, which is to deter fraudulent people from arson, and not to provide a solution of difficulties arising out of rival claims to policy moneys."

---

[68] (1888) 13 App.Cas. 699, 714.
[69] [1912] 2 Ch. 414; *cf. Stinson v. Pennock* (1868) Gr. 604; *Royal Ins. Co. v. Mylius* (1926) 38 C.L.R. 477; [1927] V.L.R. 1 where a purchaser from a mortgagor was held entitled to invoke the section as against the mortgagees; *Re Alliance Ass. Co.* (1960) 25 D.L.R. (2d) 316.

21–18　Similarly, it has been held that a lessor can take advantage of the section where the lessee has insured the premises and the lessor would therefore have no claim as such to the policy moneys[70] and conversely where the lessor has insured the premises the statute will endure to the benefit of the lessee.[71] It may also be the case that a purchaser of land who has not yet completed can avail himself of the statute since equity regards him as the owner[72] and in *Re Quicke's Trusts*[73] where trustees of settled land had insured under their statutory powers and had paid premiums out of income, it was held that the remaindermen were entitled to the benefit of the statute as against the tenant for life. In the light of these authorities it is submitted that the person claiming the right to enforce the statute need not show that he has otherwise any claim to the benefit of the insurance money.

The assured must, however, have a valid and subsisting claim under the policy before an interested party can require the company to rebuild; if the assured has no insurable interest[74] or has a claim which has been satisfied,[75] or has suffered no loss,[76] or the company is entitled to avoid the policy[77] no right under the statute can be exercised.

21–19　Procedure to enforce statutory right. In *Simpson v. Scottish Union Insurance Co.*[78] where the lessor of certain buildings brought an action to recover from the insurance company moneys which he had himself expending on rebuilding, it was held by Sir W. Page Wood V.-C. that the proper way in which to enforce a statutory remedy was by mandatory injunction and not by proceeding in equity for a declaration and an order for payment. In *Wimbledon Park Golf Club v. Imperial Insurance Co.,*[79]

---

[70] *Vernon v. Smith* (1821) 5 B. & Ald. 1; *Matthey v. Curling* [1922] A.C. 180, 198, *per* Atkin L.J.; *Ex p. Goreley* (1864) 4 De G.J. & S. 477, where, however, the precise point was not argued. Another applicant for reinstatement was the lessee's mortgagee and it is perhaps significant that no suggestion is made in the report that the section was not enforceable by a mortgagee desiring to obtain the benefit of the mortgagor's insurance. See also *Auckland City Corporation v. Mercantile and General Insurance Co.* [1930] N.Z.L.R. 809 where it was assumed that a lessor could invoke the statute.

[71] *Wimbledon Park Golf Club v. Imperial Ins. Co.* (1902) 18 T.L.R. 815; but if the lessee is obliged by his lease to repair at his own cost, he cannot avail himself of the statute to evade his obligations. Thus a lessee was refused a remedy against the insurers of the lessor in such a case since the insurers would have been subrogated to the lessor's rights; see *Searl v. South British Assurance Co.* [1916] N.Z.L.R. 137. A sale by the lessor of his interest and receipt by him of the purchase price will not affect the rights of the lessee, *Lonsdale v. Black Arrow Group* [1993] Ch. 361.

[72] *Rayner v. Preston* (1881) 18 Ch.D. 1, 15, *per* James L.J. dissenting; *Royal Ins. Co. v. Mylius* (1926) 38 C.L.R. 477. A purchaser will probably have no right against the insurer under the Act if the sale contract expressly provides to the contrary or if there is an express covenant by the vendor to give the benefit of the insurance to the purchaser in specified circumstances only. See also the note on *Lonsdale v. Black Arrow* by A.J. Oakley in [1993] C.L.J. 387.

[73] [1908] 1 Ch. 887.

[74] *Matthey v. Curling* [1922] 2 A.C. 180, 219, *per* Younger L.J.

[75] As would have been the position if insurers' arguments had been upheld in *Lonsdale v. Black Arrow Group plc.* [1993] Ch. 361.

[76] *Kern Corp. v. Walter Reid Trading Pty* (1987) 61 A.L.J.R. 319.

[77] *Auckland City Corporation v. Mercantile and General Ins. Co. Ltd* [1930] N.Z.L.R. 809; *Logan v. Hall* (1847) 4 C.B. 622–623, *per* Maule J. *arguendo*, presupposing arson by the assured.

[78] (1863) 1 H. & M. 618.

[79] (1902) 18 T.L.R. 815, doubted by Kennedy L.J. in *Sun Ins. Office v. Galinsky* [1914] 2 K.B. 545. See further *Stinson v. Pennock* (1868) 14 Gr. 604; *Searl v. South British Assurance Co.* [1916] N.Z.L.R. 137 land in particular the judgment of the High Court of Australia in *Royal Ins. Co. v. Mylius* (1926) 38 C.L.R. 477. It appears that an injunction in the terms envisaged by Wright J. was sought in *Marriage v. Royal Exchange Ass. Co.* (1849) 18 L.J.Ch. 216.

however, Wright J. expressed the view that an interested party had no right to compel the insurers to undertake reinstatement but that his proper remedy was an injunction to restrain the insurers from paying over the insurance money until they should have obtained a sufficient security from the assured that the money would be spent in reinstatement. If the assured does tender a sufficient security[80] the insurers are bound to hand the money over to him and the fact that such security has been given is a complete answer to any claim made by an interested party against the insurers. But if the assured is unable or unwilling to offer sufficient security the party claiming reinstatement will obtain no benefit from an order against the insurers restraining them from parting with the money. Wright J. objected that in the case before him the parties interested were not agreed as to what should be rebuilt and that the insurers had no power to enter on the premises. It can, however, be argued that the statute gives the insurers implied power to enter and reinstate any premises which they have insured, and if the parties cannot agree as to the form of reinstatement they must be content to have the insurance money expended so far as it will go in a replica of the old building. It is therefore submitted that the statutory right does entitle an interested party to compel the insurers to cause the insurance money to be spent in rebuilding and that Page Wood V.-C. was right when he suggested that a mandatory injunction was the proper remedy.[81] The assured probably cannot claim damages if the insurer refuses to comply or delays in complying with his statutory obligation.[82]

21–20 Interpleader. Before the Judicature Act 1873 it was held that an insurer, who was subjected to a demand for payment of the insurance money by the insured, on the one hand, and a request by a party interested to expend the money in reinstating the insured premises, on the other hand, was entitled to seek relief by filing an interpleader bill in accordance with the old practice of the Court of Chancery[83] This form of relief is no longer available. In *Sun Insurance Office v. Galinsky*[84] a house was insured against fire in the joint names of lessor and lessee. A fire occurred and the lessee proceeded to rebuild and requested the insurance company to pay him the insurance money for this purpose; but the lessor disapproved of the builder employed by the lessee and served a notice on the insurance company requiring them to spend the insurance money on rebuilding. The insurance company sought relief by way of interpleader summons under what became Order 17, r. 1 of the Rules of the Supreme Court. This order is only available to an applicant who is under liability for some debt, money, goods or chattels in respect of which he is or expects to be sued by two or more parties making adverse claims thereto and the Court of Appeal held that the parties were not making adverse claims to the insurance money although they were making inconsistent claims as to the manner in which the company should

---

[80] It seems from the above case that a performance bond without sureties will be sufficient at any rate if the assured is financially sound.

[81] This is the conclusion reached by the majority of the High Court in *Royal Ins. Co. v. Mylius* (1926) 38 C.L.R. 477.

[82] *Mylius v. Royal Ins. Co.* [1928] V.L.R. 126.

[83] *Paris v. Gilham* (1813) Coop.G. 56.

[84] [1914] 2 K.B. 545. *Cf.* the very similar process of multiple-poinding, *Commercial Union Ass. Co. v. Globe* (1916) 1 S.L.T. 343.

apply that money. Under the old Chancery procedure the rival claimants were cited as defendants and the issue between them was determined in the presence of the plaintiff; the present practice is that the applicant pays the money into court and is discharged from any further liability in respect of it, the issue between the rival claimants being decided in his absence. It could hardly be right to discharge an insurer of his obligations under the statute when it is his right to be so discharged that is the very issue between the parties. The proper course is presumably for the insurer to defend both actions, apply for them to be consolidated or to be heard one after the other by the same judge, and serve notice on both claimants that the court will be asked to order the unsuccessful claimant to pay the costs of both proceedings.

21–21 Insurance money. The words "insurance money" in the statute are ambiguous. Prima facie they refer to money which, but for the statute, would be payable to the assured in cash, *viz.* the sum necessary to indemnify the assured. Difficulty, however, arises where the assured's interest in the buildings is less than their total value as in the case of a lessee or a tenant for life. A cash payment to him of, say, £100 might represent the full value of his interest in the buildings, and would therefore completely indemnify him; but if the landlord or reversioner demands reinstatement, the expenditure of £100 in rebuilding might mean only a partial reinstatement, which would be a strange and unsatisfactory result if the amount insured were sufficient to cover a complete reinstatement. On the other hand, if the company is bound to make complete reinstatement the statute which is primarily designed for the protection of the community operates to increase the contractual liability of the company. In *Simpson v. Scottish Union Insurance Co.*[85] a tenant from year to year had insured and the landlord claimed that he had given notice to the insurance company to reinstate. One of the arguments advanced by the company was that they were only bound to reinstate, if at all, to the extent of the tenant's interest in his tenancy from year to year. This argument was rejected by Page Wood V.-C. although the company succeeded on other grounds. He said:

> "... a tenant from year to year, having insured, would have a right to say that the premises should be rebuilt for him to occupy, and ... his insurable interest is not limited to the value of his tenancy from year to year. Then the statute gives the landlord the right to require the money insured by his tenant's policy to be laid out in rebuilding."[86]

It is submitted that this approach is correct. The "insurance money" is the sum which the company contracts to pay. Although it contracts to pay an indemnity, the proportion of the amount insured required to indemnify the assured may vary according to circumstances. If the statute is invoked, a larger sum is required to indemnify an assured with a limited interest than would be required if the statute were not invoked, and the company must pay accordingly.[87] An alternative way of putting the assured's case, which perhaps accords more closely to the analysis of Page Wood V.-C., is that

---

[85] (1863) 1 H. & M. 618.

[86] At p. 628; *cf. Andrews v. Patriotic Ass. Co.* (No. 2) (1886) 18 L.R. Ir. 355, 366, *per* Palles C.B., the dissenting judgment of James L.J. in *Rayner v. Preston* (1881) 18 Ch.D. 1, 15 and the observations thereon by Bowen L.J. in *Castellain v. Preston* (1883) 11 Q.B.D. 380, 399–401.

[87] *cf. British Traders Ins. Co. v. Monson* (1964) 111 C.L.R. 86.

where the statute may be invoked he has an insurable interest to the full value of the property and is thus prima facie entitled to recover the full value.

21–22 Contracting out. If there is a contract between the assured and the party claiming reinstatement to the effect that the assured is entitled to payment of the insurance money in cash, the assured will be able to obtain an injunction restraining the party so claiming from giving notice to the insurers or otherwise enforcing the statute.[88]

As between mortgagor and mortgagee, the mortgagee may be entitled, either by the express terms of the morgage deed or under the terms of section 108 of the Law of Property Act 1925[89] to have any insurance money applied towards discharge of the mortgage debt, and, if the mortgagee so elects, he can restrain the mortgagor from demanding that the insurers should apply the money in reinstatement.[90]

21–23 Request necessary before company settles with assured. A person who requires an insurance company to spend the insurance money in reinstatement must make an unequivocal demand to this effect specifying that he is requiring the company to act upon the statute. It is not sufficient merely to make a claim to the benefit of the insurance money. Moreover, the demand must be made before the company pays or otherwise settles with the assured[91]; the statute does not give any right in the insurance money,[92] nor can an assured who has received the insurance money be compelled to reinstate or otherwise apply the money for the benefit of those interested under the statute. In *Simpson v. Scottish Union Insurance Co.*[93] the plaintiff was the landlord of premises insured by his tenants in the office of the defendant company. After a fire he wrote to the defendants claiming that he was entitled to the benefit of the insurance policy and requiring them not to pay the money to his tenants. In spite of this, they agreed with the tenants that in consideration for the payments to the tenants of a sum insured on their stock-in-trade under a separate policy, the policy on the premises would be delivered up for cancellation and all claims under it would be abandoned. On hearing that this settlement had been reached between the company and his tenants the plaintiff proceeded to rebuild and then to claim from the company the sum insured, by invoking the provisions of the statute. Page Wood V.-C. held that there had been no sufficient request for reinstatement under the statute and that the time to make such a request must be before and not after any settlement with the assured. He also pointed out that the statute did not authorise the plaintiff to rebuild and then claim the money:

"the company themselves are the persons to rebuild, in order that they

---

[88] *Reynard v. Arnold* (1875) L.R. 10 Ch.App. 386.

[89] 15 Geo. 5 c. 20.

[90] This would not however affect the right of the insurance company to exercise its option under a reinstatement clause in the policy, or to rely upon the statute if they suspected fraud.

[91] *Re Quicke's Trusts* [1908] 1 Ch. 887 is no authority to the contrary, although application to the court was made after payment, since all parties desired the money to be spent on reinstatement.

[92] It follows that a right under the statute is not an insurance for the purpose of conditions relating to double insurance, *Portavon Cinema Co Ltd v. Price* [1939] 4 All E.R. 601.

[93] (1863) 1 H. & M. 618 followed in *Randolph v. Randolph* (1907) 3 N.B.Eq.Rep. 576.

may see that the money is really laid out in reinstating the property, and that it is judiciously expended."[94]

In *Rayner v. Preston*[95] property which was the subject of a contract of sale was destroyed by a fire between the time of the contract and the time fixed for completion. The vendor had insured the property and received the insurance money but the purchaser claimed that it had been received for his benefit. Cotton L.J. said that, even if the purchaser could have availed himself of the statute before the money had been paid to the vendor, it was too late for him to seek to recover the sum insured from the vendor once he had received it.[96]

21–24 If a purchaser of property cannot recover insurance money from his vendor even though he might have been able to require an insurance company to apply it in reinstating the property, it seems to follow that there is no equity entitling him to compel the vendor to spend the insurance money which he has received in reinstatement, in the absence of any agreement to that effect,[97] and the result must be the same as between a lessor and lessee.[98]

21–25 Critique. It is difficult to believe that section 83 works satisfactorily in its present form. There is no doubt good reason for a statutory provision enabling any person interested in property to require insurers to reinstate the premises as far as the insurance money will go but, if the reported cases are any guide, it is not a provision which is often invoked. There is, however, no good reason why it should apply only to insurance companies and not to Lloyd's; nor does the provision authorising the insurer to reinstate if he suspects arson or fraud seem to have any practical effect. In the first place, unless it be given a very liberal interpretation,[99] the section both authorises and requires the insurer to reinstate in these circumstances, which is nonsense. Secondly, if the insurer suspects fraud or arson he is more likely to refuse payment than to insist on reinstatement. Since the policy usually contains a reinstatement clause in any event, the insurer scarcely needs any additional statutory protection. It is submitted that Section 83 should now be repealed and replaced by a short statute requiring any insurer to use the insurance money for reinstatement if he is requested to do so by any person interested in the property. The New Zealand Law Commission has recommended total repeal of the section.[1]

---

[94] pp. 628–629, cited with approval by Younger L.J. in *Matthey v. Curling* [1922] 2 A.C. 180, 219.

[95] (1881) 18 Ch.D. 1.

[96] (1881) 18 Ch.D. at p. 7. Brett L.J. expressed no opinion on this point and James L.J. dissented.

[97] For a case where there was such agreement see *Garden v. Ingram* (1852) 23 L.J.Ch. 478.

[98] *cf. Leeds v. Cheetham* (1829) 1 Sim. 146 where, however, the statute was not referred to in the judgment or the argument; *Randolph v. Randolph* (1907) 3 N.B.Eq.Rep. 576.

[99] See n. 35 to para. 21–14, *ante*.

[1] See n. 64 to para. 21–16 *ante*.

CHAPTER 22

SUBROGATION

1. INTRODUCTION

22–1 General principle. "Subrogation" means literally the substitution of one person for another.[1] The concept was known to the Roman law, where it appears to have enabled a third party who discharged a debt for which another was liable to succeed to the rights of the creditor against the debtor.[2] Such a third party was entitled to be "subrogated to" the rights of the creditor. By the close of the eighteenth century the English courts of law and equity had come to recognise rights of subrogation in a number of separate legal relationships, one of which was the contract of indemnity. This is how rights of subrogation attached to insurance contracts. In insurance law "subrogation" is the name given to the right of the insurer who has paid a loss to be put in the place of the assured so that he can take advantage of any means available to the assured to extinguish or diminish the loss for which the insurer has indemnified the assured. It is an instance of the fundamental principle of indemnity insurance that the assured shall receive no more than a full indemnity for his real loss, and must not be permitted to make a profit out of being insured.[3]

22–2 Nature of the doctrine. The doctrine confers two distinct rights on the insurer after payment of a loss. The first is to receive the benefit of all rights and remedies of the assured against third parties which, if satisfied, will extinguish or diminish the ultimate loss sustained.[4] The insurer is thus entitled to exercise, in the name of the assured, whatever rights the assured possesses to seek compensation for the loss from third parties. This right is the corollary of two fundamental principles of the common law. (1) If a person suffers a loss for which he can recover against a third party, and is also insured against such a loss, his insurer cannot avoid liability on the ground

---

[1] Compact Edition of the *Oxford English Dictionary, sub.tit. "subrogation"*. Generally see Goff and Jones, *The Law of Restitution* (5th ed, 1998) Ch. 3; Halsbury, *Laws of England* (4th ed.), Vol. 16 (Reissue) (Equity), paras 888–893, Derham, *Subrogation in Insurance Law* (1985); Mitchell, *The Law of Subrogation* (Oxford, 1994).

[2] Bouvier's, *Law Dictionary* (1926) p. 1143; *J. Edwards & Co. v. Motor Union Ins. Co.* [1922] 2 K.B. 249, 252, *per* McCardie J.; Goff and Jones, *op. cit.*, p. 121.

[3] *Castellain v. Preston* (1883) 11 Q.B.D. 380; *H. Cousins & Co. Ltd v. D. & C. Carriers Ltd* [1971] 2 Q.B. 230, 242, *per* Widgery L.J.

[4] *Castellain v. Preston* (1883) 11 Q.B.D. 380; *H. Cousins & Co. Ltd v. D. & C. Carriers Ltd* [1971] 2 Q.B. 230.

that the assured has the right to claim against the third party.[5] (2) Conversely, the third party, if sued by the assured, cannot avoid liability on the ground that the assured has been or will be fully indemnified for his loss.[6]

22-3 The insurer's right to sue third parties has been recognised in the case of non-marine insurance at least since the decision in *Mason v. Sainsbury*,[7] in which the plaintiff's house had been demolished in the riots of 1780. He had insured his house and collected the money from his insurers who proceeded to exercise the plaintiff's remedy against the Hundred under the Riot Act of 1714. The action was brought in the name of the householder and it was contended on behalf of the Hundred that there could be no recovery because the insurers had received their premium and had not suffered "by any act of the defendant". The Court of King's Bench unanimously rejected this argument, Lord Mansfield saying:

> "The office paid without suit not in ease of the Hundred, and not as co-obligators, but without prejudice. It is, to all intents, as if it had not been paid. ... Every day the insurer is put in the place of the insured. In every abandonment it is so. The insurer used the name of the insured. ... I am satisfied that it is to be considered as if the insurers had not paid a farthing."[8]

22-4 The width of the doctrine was described by Brett L.J. in the leading case of *Castellain v. Preston*[9]:

> "... as between the underwriter and the assured, the underwriter is entitled to the advantage of every right of the assured, whether such a right consists of contract, fulfilled or unfulfilled, or in remedy for tort capable of being insisted on or already insisted on, or in any other right whether by way of condition or otherwise, legal or equitable, which can be, or has been exercised or has accrued, and whether such a right could or could not be enforced by the insurer in the name of the assured, by the exercise or acquiring of which right or condition the loss against which the assured is insured, can be, or has been diminished."

Accordingly the insurer may require the assured to enforce a right to be indemnified against the loss under an indemnity clause contained in a contract between the assured and the indemnifier, so long as the indemnifier

---

[5] *Colingridge v. Royal Exchange Ass.* (1877) 3 Q.B.D. 173, 176–177; *Dickenson v. Jardine* (1868) L.R. 3 C.P. 639; *Cullen v. Butler* (1816) 5 M. & S. 461, 466; *Darrell v. Tibbitts* (1880) 5 Q.B.D. 560, 562; *Bristol & West Building Society v. May, May and Merrimans (No. 2)* [1998] 1 W.L.R. 338, 345–346.

[6] *Bradburn v. Great Western Ry.* (1874) L.R. 10 Ex. 1; *Mason v. Sainsbury* (1782) 3 Doug. K.B. 61, 63; *Yates v. Whyte* (1838) 4 Bing.N.C. 272; *H. Cousins & Co. Ltd v. D. & C. Carriers Ltd* [1971] 2 Q.B. 230, 240, 243; *Driscoll v. Driscoll* [1918] 1 I.R. 152, 156, *per* O'Connor M.R.; *Parry v. Cleaver* [1970] A.C.1. *Dominion Mosaics Co. v. Trafalgar Trucking Co.* [1990] 2 All E.R. 246, 251. It makes no difference that the defendant was required by contract to effect the insurance and to pay the premium—*The "Yasin"* [1979] 2 Lloyd's Rep. 45, 56.

[7] (1782) 3 Doug. 61. This was a case at law. Earlier cases in equity had already established the second right referred to below.

[8] *ibid.* at p. 63.

[9] (1883) 11 Q.B.D. 380, 388, described by Diplock J. in *Yorkshire Ins. Co. v. Nisbet Shipping Co.* [1962] 2 Q.B. 330, 339 as the *locus classicus* of the doctrine of subrogation in insurance law.

is the party with primary liability for the loss in question.[10] Where the insurer and indemnifier have co-ordinate obligations to indemnify the assured, as where both are insurers, the insurer who has paid the assured should claim contribution from the other indemnifier in his own name, since the assured no longer has a claim for indemnity.[11]

22–5 The second right vested in the insurer by the doctrine of subrogation is to claim from the assured any benefit conferred on the assured by third parties with the aim of compensating the assured for the loss in respect of which the insurer has indemnified him.[12] The right is usually exercised by an insurer claiming from the assured a sum equivalent to any sum of damages paid to the assured by a third party legally liable for the loss. The right is wider in scope than that, however, and the insurer is entitled to moneys paid to the assured *ex gratia* to diminish his loss unless intended by the donor to benefit the assured to the exclusion of the insurers.[13]

22–6 Difference between subrogation and abandonment. Both these doctrines are applications of the basic rule of indemnity insurance that the assured should not receive more than a complete indemnity against his loss,[14] but they are distinct.

22–7 "Abandonment" denotes, principally, the voluntary cession by the assured to the insurer of his rights over the subject-matter of the insurance in the case of a total loss. Abandonment in this sense originated in the field of marine insurance, in which sphere it is governed by sections 61 to 63 of the Marine Insurance Act 1906. Abandonment is achieved when the assured tenders notice of abandonment to the insurer and the insurer accepts it. Ownership of the *res* is then vested in the insurer, who thereby acquires all proprietary rights to the *res*, including, for example, the right to earn and keep freight in the process of being earned by an abandoned ship at the time of the abandonment to her insurers.[15] The insurer, as her new owner, is entitled to all the profits he can make on the ship, even if they far exceed the amount of the loss.[16]

22–8 The word "abandonment" has been given a secondary meaning applicable to all indemnity insurance, namely, a rule that, on being paid for an actual total loss of the *res*, the assured is required to abandon his interest

---

[10] *Caledonia North Sea Ltd. v. Norton (No. 2)* [2002] 1 All E.R. (Comm) 321, 330, 340, 348–349; *Speno Rail Maintenance Australia Pty Ltd. v. Hammersley Iron Pty Ltd* [2000] 23 W.A.R. 291.

[11] *Sickness & Accident Ass .v. General Accident Ass. Corp.* (1892) 19 R. 977; *Austin v. Zurich General Accident & Liability Ins. Co. Ltd.* [1945] K.B. 250, 258; *Bovis Construction Co. v. Commercial Union Ass. Co. Plc.* [2001] 1 Lloyd's Rep. 416, 418.

[12] See *Randal v. Cockran* (1748) 1 Ves. sen 98 and paras 22–67 to 22–68, *post*. This paragraph in the 8th edition of this work was cited with approval in *Colonia Versicherung AG v. Amoco Oil Co.* [1997] 1 Lloyd's Rep. 261, 270.

[13] See para. 22–71, *post*.

[14] *Rankin v. Potter* (1873) L.R. 6. H.L. 83, 101–102, *per* Brett J.

[15] Marine Insurance Act 1906, s.63; *Glen Line v. Att.-Gen.* (1930) 36 Com.Cas. 1, 13, *per* Lord Atkin, *Rankin v. Potter* (1873) L.R. 6 H.L. 83, 144, *per* Martin B., 156, *per* Lord Chelmsford.

[16] *Lucas v. Export Credit Guarantee Dept.* [1973] 1 W.L.R. 914, 924, *per* Megaw L.J.; *Page v. Scottish Ins. Corp.* (1929) 140 L.T. 571, 575, *per* Scrutton L.J.

in the *res* to the insurer.[17] Thus, if a chattel is lost and then is found after the assured has been paid for a total loss, the insurer is said to be entitled to have it. In the case of an antique article which has increased in value during the period of its disappearance the insurer might well thus realise a profit through exercising his rights of ownership over it.

22–9 Subrogation operates very differently from the doctrine of abandonment in its primary sense.[18] It occurs in all contracts of indemnity insurance. The rights of the insurer arise automatically upon payment of a loss, whether the loss be total or partial. No notice of election is required to perfect the process. The insurer is not permitted to keep sums acquired by the exercise of his rights of subrogation in an amount exceeding the amount of the payment made to the assured.[19] He acquires no proprietary rights over the subject-matter of the insurance as a result of subrogation, but rather is subrogated to the assured's personal rights of suit against third parties in respect of the event causing the loss.

22–10 In its secondary sense abandonmnent is more closely related to subrogation in that the insurers' rights arise upon payment and not on a voluntary cession of interest prior to payment. There remain significant differences between the two doctrines with regard to the type of loss which brings each into operation, and the value of the exercise of the rights conferred by them.

22–11 Difference between subrogation and assignment. Both subrogation and assignment permit one party to enjoy the rights of another, but it is well-established that subrogation is not a species of assignment.[20] Rights of subrogation vest by operation of law rather than as the product of express agreement. Whereas rights of subrogation can be enjoyed by the insurer as soon as payment is made,[21] an assignment requires an agreement that the rights of the assured be assigned to the insurer. The insurer cannot require the assured to assign to him his rights against third parties as a condition of

---

[17] *Rankin v. Potter* (1873) L.R. 6 H.L. 83, 118, *per* Blackburn J. approved by Brett L.J. in *Kaltenbach v. Mackenzie* (1878) 3 C.P.D. 467, 471; Chitty, *Contracts* (28th ed., 1999) Vol. II, para. 41–078 *sub.tit.* "Salvage". *Sed quaere.* The example given by Blackburn J. of the cession of rights is *Mason v. Sainsbury* (1782) 3 Doug. K.B. 61, a case of ordinary subrogation, and it may be that he was referring only to the exercise by the insurer of the assured's rights of action in order to try to salve something of value from the aftermath of the loss. His language is strikingly similar to s.79 of the Marine Insurance Act 1906. The same comment applies to his citation from *Randal v. Cockran* (1748) 1 Ves. 98, unless that case is interpreted as one of abandonment of the insured vessel to underwriters after her loss by capture to the Spaniards. In *Dane v. Mortgage Ins. Corp.* [1894] 1 Q.B. 54, 61 Lord Esher M.R. appears to use the expression "salvage" to describe the exercise by insurers of subrogation rights. *Holmes v. Payne* [1930] 2 K.B. 301 turned upon a replacement agreement concluded after the claim was lodged. The assured voluntarily tendered the brooch when it was found, and the issue of ownership did not arise for decision.

[18] *Glen Line v. Att.-Gen.* (1930) 36 Com.Cas. 1, 13–14, *per* Lord Atkin; *Simpson v. Thomson* (1877) 3 App.Cas. 279, 292, *per* Lord Blackburn.

[19] *Yorkshire Ins. Co. v. Nisbet Shipping Co.* [1962] 2 Q.B. 330.

[20] *Morris v. Ford Motor Co.* [1973] Q.B. 792, 800, 809; *Orakpo v. Manson Investments Ltd* [1978] A.C. 95, 104; *King v. Victoria Ins. Co.* [1896] A.C. 250; *James Nelson & Sons Ltd v. Nelson Line Liverpool Ltd* [1906] 2 K.B. 217, 222, 225.

[21] *Castellain v. Preston* (1883) 11 Q.B.D. 380; *West of England Fire Ins. Co. v. Isaacs* [1897] 1 Q.B. 226; *Re Miller, Gibb & Co.* [1957] 1 W.L.R. 703.

payment[22] unless there is a special clause in the policy obliging the assured to do so.[23] This distinction is of some importance, since in certain circumstances an insurer might prefer to take an assignment of an assured's rights[24] rather than rely upon his rights of subrogation. If, for example, there was any prospect of the insured being able to recover more than his actual loss from a third party, an insurer, who had taken an assignment of the assured's rights, would be able to recover the extra money for himself whereas an insurer who was confined to rights of subrogation would have to allow the assured to retain the excess.

22–12 Another distinction lies in the prodecure of enforcing the rights acquired by virtue of the two doctrines. An insurer exercising rights of subrogation against third parties must do so in the name of the assured.[25] An insurer who has taken a legal assignment of his assured's rights under statute should proceed in his own name, while, if he is an equitable assignee of the assured's legal rights he will generally be required to join the assured, his assignor, as a necessary and proper party to proceedings taken on the assignment.[26] Before the Judicature Acts and the fusion of law and equity this distinction was less marked, in as much as an equitable assignee of a legal chose in action was abliged to sue in the name of his assignor and equity would if necessary compel the assignor to lend his name for the purpose. Similarly an insurer, who has to sue in the name of his assured, must seek the aid of equity to compel a recalcitrant assured to lend his name to the insurer's proceedings.[27] These similarities may have been responsible for Lord Blackburn's remark in *Simpson v. Thomson*[28] that the insurer exercising rights of subrogation was an "assignee" of the rights of the assured who, one day, might be permitted to sue in his own name.[29] That day has not

---

[22] *Ins. Co. of North America v. Fidelity Co.* 123 Pa. 523 (1889); *King v. State Mutual Fire Ins. Co.* 6 Mass. 1 (1851).

[23] *Lucas v. Export Credits Dept.* [1974] 1 W.L.R. 909; *Niagara Fire Ins. Co. v. Fidelity Co.* 123 Pa. 516 (1889).

[24] Such an assignment is not invalid as the assignment of a bare right of suit because it is supported by the insurer's legitimate interest in recovering the amount he has paid in respect of a loss—*Cia Colombiana de Seguros v. Pacific Steam Navigation* [1965] 1 Q.B. 101. The terms of a subrogation receipt may, on analysis, constitute an assignment, *Central Ins. Co. v. Seacalf Shipping Corporation* [1983] 2 Lloyd's Rep. 25.

[25] *Mason v. Sainsbury* (1782) 3 Doug. K.B. 61; *London Ass. Co. v. Sainsbury* (1783) 3 Doug. K.B. 245; *Clark v. Inhabitants of Blything* (1823) 2 B. & C. 254; *Yates v. Whyte* (1838) 4 Bing. N.C. 272; *King v. Victoria Ins. Co.* [1896] A.C. 250; *Edwards (J.) v. Motor Union Ins. Co.* [1922] 2 K.B. 249, 254; *Yorkshire Ins. Co. v. Nisbet Shipping Co.* [1962] 2 Q.B. 330, 340; *Morris v. Ford Motor Co.* [1973] Q.B. 792, 800, 812; *Simpson v. Thomson* (1877) 3 App.Cas. 279, 284; *Dane v. Mortgage Ins. Corp.* [1894] 1 Q.B. 54, 61; *Central Ins. Co. v. Seacalf Shipping Corporation* [1983] 2 Lloyd's Rep. 25, 33; *Smith (M.H.) (Plant Hire) v. Mainwaring* [1986] 2 Lloyd's Rep. 244; *Esso Petroleum Ltd v. Hall Russell & Co.* [1989] A.C. 643.

[26] Chitty, *Contracts* (28th ed., 1999) Vol. 1, para. 20–037; *Central Ins. Co. v. Seacalf Shipping Corporation* [1983] 2 Lloyd's Rep. 25, 33–34.

[27] *John Edwards & Co. v. Motor Union Ins. Co* [1922] 2 K.B. 249; *Yorkshire Ins. Co. v. Nisbet Shipping Co.* [1962] 2 Q.B. 330, 339, 341; *Morris v. Ford Motor Co.* [1973] Q.B. 792.

[28] (1877) 3 App.Cas. 279.

[29] (1877) 3 App.Cas. 279, 293. See also *per* Lord Cairns at p. 286 and Lord Gordon at p. 295. In *Jenner v. Morris* (1861) 3 De G.F. & J. 45, 52 Lord Campbell sought to analyse the equitable right of subrogation possessed by the lender of money to a deserted wife for the purchase of necessaries as a species of equitable assignment. *Sed quaere* when the lender does not always acquire the right to sue for the full value of the goods. See also *Hobbs v. Marlow* [1978] A.C. 16, 39, *per* Lord Diplock.

yet dawned, and there is strong authority against the view that subrogation is a species of assignment.[30]

22-13　Disputed basis of the doctrine of subrogation It has been accepted for over 100 years that subrogation in insurance law is grounded in the nature of a contract of indemnity and is not a doctrine peculiar to contracts of insurance.[31] Judicial opinion has differed, however, concerning the origins and juristic basis of the doctrine as it is found in insurance law.

22-14　Subrogation an equitable doctrine? One school of thought holds that subrogation is a principle of equity[32] and that insurers' rights of subrogation were acquired from Chancery. Judicial statements of this proposition have relied in support of it on a remark by Lord Hardwicke in an early case in Chancery[33] that an insurer possessed "the plainest equity", on the recognition by courts of equity in the eighteenth century of the notion of subrogation.[34] and on the assistance given by equity to an insurer wishing to compel an unco-operative assured to lend his name to proceedings to be taken against a third party.[35] Indirect support is lent to this view by those decisions in which subrogation has been described as achieving an assignment by operation of law,[36] since the closest analogy would be equitable assignment.

22-15 The theory is not free from difficulty. The brief report of Lord Hardwicke's judgment in *Randal v. Cockran*[37] is a frail foundation for it. Lord Hardwicke probably intended to say no more than that the insurers possessed a plainly meritorious claim,[38] and was not attempting an analysis of their right of suit. Secondly, the principle of subrogation was applied to contracts of insurance by the courts of law long before the fusion of law and equity,[39] and without any acknowledgment to equitable inspiration. In the

---

[30] See note 18, *supra.*

[31] *Simpson v. Thomson* (1877) 3 App.Cas. 279, 284; *Castellain v. Preston* (1883) 11 Q.B.D. 380, 394, 401–403; *Burnand v. Rodocanachi* (1882) 7 App.Cas. 333, 339; *Morris v. Ford Motor Co.* [1973] Q.B. 792, which was not an insurance case.

[32] *Burnand v. Rodocanachi* (1882) 7 App.Cas. 333, 339, *per* Lord Blackburn; *J. Edwards & Co. v. Motor Union Ins. Co.* [1922] 2 K.B. 249, 254–255, *per* McCardie J.; *Morris v. Ford Motor Co.* [1973] Q.B. 792, 801, *per* Lord Denning M.R. and p. 807, *per* Stamp L.J.; *Re Miller, Gibb & Co.* [1957] 1 W.L.R. 703, 707, *per* Wynn Parry J. Derham, *Subrogation in Insurance Law*, Ch. 1; *Smith (M.H.) (Plant Hire) v. Mainwaring* [1986] 2 Lloyd's Rep. 244, 246, *per* Kerr L.J.; *Linsley v. Petrie* [1998] 1 V.R. 427.

[33] *Randal v. Cockran* (1748) 1 Ves.Sen.97, cited in *Yates v. Whyte* (1838) 4 Bing. N.C. 272, *J. Edwards & Co. v. Motor Union Ins. Co.* [1922] 2 K.B. 249, 252, *Morris v. Ford Motor Co.* [1973] Q.B. 792, 800, and *Re Miller, Gibb & Co.* [1957] W.L.R. 703, 707.

[34] *Morris v. Ford Motor Co.* [1973] Q.B. 792, 809.

[35] *Morris v. Ford Motor Co.* [1973] Q.B. 792, 800.

[36] *Burnand v. Rodocanachi* (1882) 7 App.Cas. 333.

[37] (1748) 1 Ves.Sen. 97.

[38] Judges have often described causes of action as "equitable" in that sense—see *Sadler v. Evans* (1766) 4 Burr. 1986, *per* Lord Mansfield, explained by Farwell L.J. in *Baylis v. London (Bishop)* [1913] 1 Ch. 127, 136–137; *Collins v. Brook* (1860) 5 H. & N. 700, 708, *per* Byles J. In *Strang, Steel & Co. v. Scott & Co.* (1899) 14 App.Cas. 601, 608 Lord Watson described the right of contribution in general average as having its foundation in "the plainest equity", and this dictum was approved by Lord Atkinson in *Kish v. Taylor* [1912] A.C. 604, 619. The origin of the right to contribution is the Rhodian maritime law, as Lord Watson himself acknowledged, *ubi cit.*

[39] *Yorkshire Insurance Co. v. Nisbet Shipping Co.* [1962] 2 Q.B. 330, 339, *per* Diplock J.

celebrated leading case of *Mason v. Sainsbury*,[40] the defendants objected to the attempted exercise of the assured's rights by his insurers after they had indemnified him. Dismissing the argument that, once indemnified, the assured could not be said to have suffered a loss,[41] the Court of King's Bench upheld the insurers' right to sue in his name on the grounds that the practice was already well established, that it was irrelevant whether the insurers had made payment, and that an analogous right was recognised in the doctrine of abandonment[42] and in the enforcement of debts.[43] No reference was made to the courts of equity. The judges appear to have been familiar with the concept of subrogation in insurance law, and experienced no need to draw on equitable doctrine to support it.[44] When subrogation was again challenged in *Clark v. Inhabitants of Blything*[45] the challenge foundered on the hitherto undisturbed precedent of *Mason v. Sainsbury*,[46] and no chancery precedents were referred to.

22–16 It is very doubtful whether the eighteenth-century common law judges could have deduced a general principle from the two isolated cases in which equity then permitted one person to stand in the shoes of another,[47] particularly as the doctrine operated differently in each case.[48] Even today it is very difficult to find a satisfactory classification for all the categories of case where rights of subrogation exist.[49] The same problem existed in 1782, as can be illustrated by reference to the rights of subrogation possessed by lenders of money to infants and deserted wives for the purchase of necessaries. It had been established by *Harris v. Lee*[50] and *Marlow v. Pittfield*[51] that a person

[40] (1782) 3 Doug. K.B. 61.

[41] Accordingly *Derham, Subrogation in Insurance Law*, p. 11, interprets the case as merely determining a question of damages rather than enforcing rights of subrogation. But the Court did enforce the insurers' rights, which the damages argument was intended to subvert. The view expressed in the text is supported by Blackburn J. in *Stringer v. English & Scottish Marine Ins. Co. Ltd* (1869) L.R. 4 Q.B. 676, 692 and *Rankin v. Potter* (1873) L.R. 6 H.L. 83, 118, and by Park on *Marine Insurances* (8th ed), Vol. 2, p. 969.

[42] (1782) 3 Doug. K.B. 61, 64, *per* Lord Mansfield and Ashurst J., the former saying: "We every day see the insurer put in the place of the insured."

[43] *ibid.* at p. 64, *per* Willes J. The sheriff who permitted a gaoled debtor to escape was in certain cases liable to the creditors in the amount of their losses. After paying them he was subrogated to the right of the creditors to sue the debtor. See: Anderson, *Execution* (1889) pp. 121–124; Addison, *Wrongs*, p. 500; *Bastard v. Trutch* (1835) 1 N. & M. 109; *R. v. Sheriff of Surrey* (1808) 9 East 467.

[44] Buller J. said, at (1782) 3 Doug. 61, 64: "whether this case be considered upon strict legal principles or upon the more liberal principles of insurance law, the plaintiff is entitled to recover".

[45] (1823) 2 B. & C. 254.

[46] (1782) 3 Doug. K.B. 61.

[47] These were (1) the right of the surety who had discharged a debt to sue in the place of the creditor, (2) the right of the lender of money to deserted wives and to infants for the purchase of necessaries to sue the husband or infant respectively in the place of the tradesman who supplied the necessaries.

[48] The surety clearly succeeded to the creditor's rights to sue the debtor and have security for the debt, where stipulated for. Early cases concerned sureties suing debtors whose debts due to the Crown had been discharged by them—see *R. v. Doughty*, (1702) and other cases cited in *R. v. Bennett* (1810) 1 Wight. 1. Later the surety's right became almost statutory by section 5 of the Mercantile Law Amendment Act 1856. See: *Re Lord Churchill* (1888) 39 Ch.D. 174. By contrast the lender's right to sue in the name of a tradesman was different in nature—see note 53, *infra*.

[49] *Orakpo v. Manson Investments Ltd* [1978] A.C. 95, 104, *per* Lord Diplock.

[50] (1718) 1 P. Wms. 482.

[51] (1719) 1 P. Wms. 558.

who lent money to an infant or to a deserted wife for the purchase of necessaries was put into the place of the tradesman to enable him to sue the infant or the husband, respectively, for the repayment of so much of the money as had been applied in the purchase of the necessaries. This is said to have been a good example of equitable subrogation,[52] but it is clear that the creditor was not exercising the rights of the tradesman in the way that subrogation is understood in insurance law. The creditor was not permitted to sue for the full value of the goods, unless his loan had been applied to that extent,[53] and in any event the price of the goods had *ex hypothesi* been paid to the tradesman, who accordingly possessed no right of action against the infant or husband. The creditor in truth did not stand in the shoes of the tradesman but rather donned the tradesman's cloak in order covertly to bring his own action.

22–17 Finally, the need of an insurer to invoke the assistance of equity (whether to enforce his right of subrogation against an unwilling assured or in other respects), does not of itself mean that the very right itself was conferred on him by equity in the first instance.[54] It was a case of equity performing its traditional function of providing a remedy to permit the enforcement of a right bestowed by law. It is established too that, however close subrogation may approach to equitable assignment, the doctrines are distinct.[55] The proceedings against the third party are treated as proceedings taken by the assured for the benefit of the insurer, and not as proceedings taken by the insurer in his own right. Thus, the assured is entitled to the fruits of a judgment if successful,[56] and the burden of costs falls upon him in the first instance if the action does not succeed.[57] The position of the equitable assignee of a legal chose is different from the position of the insurer. He sues in his own name, joining his assignor as a second party where this is necessary in order to avoid future disputes concerning the validity of the assignment.[58]

22–18 Subrogation a principle of law? According to a second school of thought, the insurer's rights of subrogation rest upon terms implied into the contract of insurance by operation of law, whereby the assured owes a duty to take proceedings against third parties to reduce his loss and to account to the insurer for any benefits received by him which do reduce it.[59] This analysis was developed by Diplock J. in *Yorkshire Insurance Co Ltd v. Nisbet*

---

[52] *Morris v. Ford Motor Co.* [1973] Q.B. 792, 809 *per* James L.J.; *Orakpo v. Manson Investments Ltd* [1978] A.C. 95, 112, *per* Lord Edmund-Davies.

[53] *Jenner v. Morris* (1861) 3 De G.F. & J. 45.

[54] *Yorkshire Insurance Co. v. Nisbet Shipping Co.* [1962] 2 Q.B. 330, 339, *per* Diplock J.

[55] *Morris v. Ford Motor Co.* [1973] Q.B. 792, 800, 809.

[56] *Yorkshire Insurance Co. v. Nisbet Shipping Co.* [1962] 2 Q.B. 330, 341.

[57] *Morris v. Ford Motor Co.* [1973] Q.B. 792, 800, *per* Lord Denning M.R. See also paras. 22–43 to 22–45, *infra*.

[58] Chitty, *Contracts* (28th ed., 1999) Vol. I, para. 20–037; *Central Ins. Co. v. Seacalf Shipping Corporation* [1983] 2 Lloyd's Rep. 25, 33–34.

[59] *Yorkshire Insurance Co. v. Nisbet Shipping Co.* [1962] 2 Q.B. 330, 339, 340–341, applied in *H. Cousins & Co. v. D. & C. Carriers Ltd* [1971] 2 Q.B. 230, 242–243, *per* Widgery L.J.; *Orakpo v. Manson Investments Ltd* [1978] A.C. 95, 104, *per* Lord Diplock; *Hobbs v. Marlowe* [1978] A.C. 16, 39, *per* Lord Diplock, with whose speech Lord Elwyn-Jones L.C. and Lord Salmon agreed, p. 32 and p. 42. In *Boag v. Standard Marine Insurance Co.* [1937] 2 K.B. 113, 128 Scott L.J. seems to have taken this view—"contractual right". Two other cases where judges appear to have thought subrogation rights were creatures of the contract of indemnity are *Darrell v. Tibbitts* (1880) 5 Q.B.D. 560, 562, *per* Brett L.J. and *Morris v. Ford Motor Co.* [1973] Q.B. 792, 812, *per* James L.J.

Shipping Co. Ltd,[60] where he referred to the fundamental principle that an assured was never to receive more than a full indemnity and said:

> "The expression 'subrogation' in relation to a contract of marine insurance is thus no more than a convenient way of referring to those terms which are to be implied in the contract between the assured and the insurer to give business efficacy to an agreement whereby the assured in the case of a loss against which the policy has been made shall be fully indemnified and never more than fully indemnified"[61]

22–19 The term governing the exercise of rights against third parties was defined by him in the following way:

> "It is … an implied term of the contract that if it is within the power of the assured to reduce the amount of the loss for which he has received payment from the insurer, by exercising remedies against third parties, he must do so upon being indemnified by the insurer against the costs involved."[62]

The term governing the restitution to the insurer of benefits received in diminution or extinction of the assured's loss was not precisely defined. It is suggested that it is one which imposes on the assured a duty to account to the insurer for, and pay to him a sum equivalent to, the pecuniary value of all benefits received by him from third parties which diminish or extinguish his loss. Whatever be the precise definition of the assured's duty, it has been recognised, taking the other side of the coin, that the insurer has not merely a right of action in quasi-contract to recover the money so received and held by the assured as money had and received to his use,[63] but also an equitable lien while the money constitutes a defined and traceable fund.[64]

22–20 The conflicting theories—a suggested reconciliation. It is submitted on the basis of House of Lords authority[65] and as a matter of legal history that subrogation in insurance law is a legal doctrine by origin. Equity later came to play a useful supporting role in the development of the doctrine. Equity's effective performance in that role may have created the impression that subrogation was an entirely equitable doctrine, but equity should not be permitted to upstage the common law in that way. The court's "task nowadays is to see the two strands of authority, at law and in equity, moulded into a coherent whole".[66]

22–21 Origins of subrogation. It has already been said that there are considerable difficulties attendant on the theory that subrogation in insurance law is a creature of the equitable jurisdiction.[67] Although its

---

[60] [1962] 2 Q.B. 330. Faint doubts concerning this case were voiced by Megaw L.J. in *Lucas v. E.C.G.D.* [1973] 1 W.L.R. 914, 924.
[61] *ibid.* at pp. 339–340.
[62] *ibid.* at p. 341.
[63] [1962] 2 Q.B. 330, 341; *Burnand v. Rochocanachi* (1882) 7 App.Cas. 333, 344, *per* Lord Fitzgerald; *Darrell v. Tibbitts* (1880) 5 Q.B.D. 560, 568, *per* Thesiger L.J; *Horse Carriage & General Insurance Co. v. Petch* (1916) 33 T.L.R. 131; *Phoenix Assurance Co. v. Spooner* [1905] 2 K.B. 753, 756; *The "Albazero"* [1977] A.C. 774, 846.
[64] *Napier and Ettrick v. Hunter* [1993] A.C. 713.
[65] *Hobbs v. Marlowe* [1978] A.C. 16; *Napier and Ettrick v. Hunter* [1993] A.C. 713.
[66] *ibid.*, p. 743.
[67] See paras 22–15 to 22–17, *supra.*

historical origins are obscure, it is more probable that subrogation emerged as a development of the principle of abandonment, which itself was a doctrine of the old marine insurance law preserved in the Continental codes of insurance, and that it was received into the common law from that source.[68] The word "subrogation" itself seems to have been unknown to the early insurance law treatises,[69] and the confusion which persisted for some time between subrogation and abandonment may testify to their common origin in a doctrine designed to preserve the cardinal principle of marine insurance that the assured should recover no more than an indemnity.[70]

22–22   For its part the common law in Lord Mansfield's day did not need to borrow from Chancery to give effect to the basic rights of subrogation. So far as the insurer's right to sue in the name of the assured was concerned, there were common law precedents already to hand.[71] These were not rooted in assignment, and this may explain how the proceedings against the third party were always treated as the assured's proceedings, and not as the insurer's,[72] in a way inconsistent with the effect of an assignment. The other right of the insurer—to recover moneys obtained by the assured in diminution of his loss—was exercised by the quasi-contractual action for money had and received to the use of the plaintiff.[73] Although Lord Mansfield once described this action as a "liberal action in the nature of a bill in equity",[74] the action *ex quasi contractu* was not a creature of Chancery but of the common law.[75]

22–23 The role of equity. Equity has reinforced the insurer's rights of subrogation in two ways. First, equity would compel an unco-operative assured to consent to proceedings being take in his name for the benefit of

[68] Lord Mansfield, the father of English insurance law, was undeniably influenced by the writers of the Continental Codes on marine insurance law such as Roccus, Emerigon, Valin and Le Guidon—see Marshall, *Law of Marine Insurance* (4th ed.), Ch. 1, p. 20.

[69] Thus, *Park, Marine Insurance* places *Randal v. Cockran* (1748) 1 Ves. Sen. 98 in a chapter entitled "Salvage" (7th ed., 1817) p. 229 (8th ed., 1842) p. 330. *Mason v. Sainsbury* (1782) 3 Doug. K.B. 61 is in the same chapter, while in *Marshall, op. cit.*, it appears under "Risks". There is no entry of "subrogation" in the indexes to these works, nor in that of *Arnould, Marine Insurance* (2nd ed., 1857).

[70] The confusion between abandonment and subrogation has been remarked upon by Lord Atkin in *Glen Line Ltd v. A.-G.* (1930) 36 Com.Cas. 1, 13–14 and Diplock J. in *Yorkshire Ins. Co. v. Nisbet Shipping Co. Ltd* [1962] 2 Q.B. 330, 343. The recognition of a doctrine of subrogation distinct from abandonment may perhaps be traced to the 1870's. In the case of *North of England Iron S.S. Ins. Assoc. v. Armstrong* (1870) L.R. 5 Q.B. 244 counsel referred to the insurers being "subrogated" for the assured upon abandonment and upon an actual total loss, but the court did not use the word. In *Stringer v. English & Scottish Mar. Ins. Co.* Blackburn J. also said that the insurers paying for a total loss were "subrogated" for their assured, (1869) L.R. 4 Q.B. 676, 692. In *Rankin v. Potter* he criticised "abandonment" as an ambiguous word referring to two separate things, namely (1) the transfer of rights upon notice of abandonment and (2) the transfer of salvage upon a loss in fire insurance, exemplified by *Mason v. Sainsbury*. Finally in *Simpson v. Thomson* (1877) L.R. 3 App.Cas. 279, 292–293 Lord Blackburn identified a right of insurers to be "subrogated" to the rights of their assured upon payment of either a total or a partial loss, not dependent upon any such transfer of rights over the thing insured as occurred on abandonment in its primary sense. *Mason v. Sainsbury* and *Yates v. Whyte* (1838) 4 Bing. N.C. 272 were interpreted as cases of subrogation upon payment of partial losses.

[71] See para. 22–15, *ante.*

[72] See para. 22–12, *ante.*

[73] See note 63, *ante.*

[74] *Clarke v. Shee & Johnson* (1744) Cowp. 197, 199.

[75] *Miller v. Atlee* (1849) 13 Jur. 431, *per* Pollock C.B. See also Winfield, *The Province of the Law of Tort* (1931), pp. 129–130.

the insurer.[76] Secondly, equity has in more recent years imposed an equitable lien in favour of the insurer on moneys received by the assured in diminution of his loss after he has been paid by the insurer.[77] This was a welcome development from the standpoint of the insurer. It has served to clarify the status of these moneys once in the hands of the assured in a way not possible in reliance on quasi-contract alone. Thus it has been held that in the event of the liquidation of a corporate assured, the insurers are entitled to such moneys in priority to other creditors.[78] The imposition of a lien may yet create further developments, such as the right of an insurer to sue in tort a party, such as a receiver, who has caused the assured to pay to a third party the moneys destined to the insurer, thereby arguably committing the tort of inducing a breach of trust by the assured. In these respects equity is building on the foundations laid by the common law.[79]

2. CONDITIONS PRECEDENT TO THE EXERCISE OF RIGHTS OF SUBROGATION

22–24 The insurer is entitled to exercise rights of subrogation if:
(a) the insurance is an indemnity insurance,
(b) he has made payment under it and
(c) his rights of subrogation are not excluded by a term of the parties' contract.

These prerequisites to his enjoyment of the rights of subrogation are considered separately.

(a) *Contract of Indemnity*

22–25 Subrogation applies only in cases of indemnity insurance, but it applies to all types of insurances within that classification.[80] It has been held to apply to contracts of marine insurance,[81] fire insurance,[82] motor insurance,[83] burglary[84] and solvency insurance,[85] insurance of securities[86] and export credit guarantees.[87] In the days when life insurance was still believed to be indemnity insurance prior to the decision in *Dalby v. India & London*

---

[76] *Morris v. Ford Motor Co.* [1973] Q.B. 792, 800; *Yorkshire Insurance Co. v. Nisbet Shipping Co.* [1962] 2 Q.B. 330, 339.

[77] *Napier and Ettrick v. Hunter* [1993] A.C. 713; *Re Miller, Gibb & Co.* [1957] 1 W.L.R. 703, 707; *King v. Victoria Insurance Co.* [1896] A.C. 250, 255. in *Randal v. Cockran* (1748) 1 Ves.Sen. 98 Lord Hardwicke L.C. referred to the assured as "trustee for the insurer". This prophetic utterance by a Chancery court could not be echoed in the common law courts until after 1873. An analogous case is the "charge" impressed upon insurance moneys in the hands of a bailee of goods in favour of the bailor, para. 20–26, *supra*.

[78] *Re Miller, Gibb & Co.* [1957] 1 W.L.R. 703.

[79] *Banque Financière de la Cité v. Parc (Battersea) Ltd* [1998] 1 All E.R. 737, 744–745.

[80] *Burnand v. Rodocanachi* (1882) 7 App.Cas. 333, 339; *Simpson v. Thomson* (1877) 3 App.Cas. 279, 2284. The doctrine of subrogation is not, of course, confined to contracts of insurance. If a broker compensates an insured he may acquire subrogation rights, see *Nahhas v. Pierhouse* (1984) 270 E.G. 328.

[81] Marine Insurance Act 1906, s.79.

[82] *Castellain v. Preston* (1883) 11 Q.B.D. 380.

[83] *Page v. Scottish Insurance Corporation Ltd* (1929) 140 L.T. 571.

[84] *Symons v. Mulhern* (1882) 46 L.T. 763, 764.

[85] *Parr's Bank Ltd v. Albert Mines Syndicate* (1900) 5 Com.Cas. 116.

[86] *Finlay v. Mexican Investment Corporation* [1897] 1 Q.B. 517.

[87] *Re Miller, Gibb & Co. Ltd* [1957] 1 W.L.R. 703.

Life Assurance Co.,[88] the principle of subrogation was applied, logically,[89] to a contract of life insurance.[90]

22-26 If, on a proper construction of the contract of insurance, the insurer has promised to pay a certain sum of money on the happening of a certain event (*e.g.* on accident or death) regardless of the actual loss suffered by the assured, there is no room for the doctrine of subrogation.[91] Insurance policies other than life or accident policies are usually held to be indemnity policies,[92] but difficult cases can sometimes arise. In *Meacock v. Bryant & Co.*,[93] defendants wanted to insure against the possibility that sums of money which had been deposited on their behalf in Spain would fail to arrive in England within 15 months of the deposit being made. They accordingly took out policies, described as contingency policies, which provided that the insurer was to pay a "loss" in the event of sums deposited in banks in Spain not being received within the period of 15 months. The plaintiff paid the defendants for a loss but at a later date the defendants received £2,747 out of the deposited money. The plaintiff claimed this sum by virtue of the doctrine of subrogation and argued that the policy was a contract of indemnity, while the defendants contended that it was a contract against a contingency, *viz.* that the money would not be in England by the due date. Atkinson J. held that the policy was a contract of indemnity and pointed out that some meaning must be given to the word "loss" in the policy. It could mean either the loss of the capital sums referred to in the policy or the loss suffered by the defendants in not having their money at the time when they expected it. If it meant the former, the defendants should not be entitled to keep both the insurance money and the money eventually received from Spain; if it meant the latter, it could not be quantified until the length of the period during which the money was not paid was known. The policy provided that payment was to be made "within seven days after such loss is proved" and both parties had considered this to mean that payment was to be made within seven days after the defendants had proved that the due date was past but the money had not arrived in England. The judge held that this was correct and that the word "loss" must accordingly refer to the capital sums and not the loss sustained by the defendants while out of their money. The defendants were therefore liable to pay to the plaintiff the amount of the sums received by them eventually from Spain.

(b) *Payment to Assured*

22-27 The insurer's right of subrogation cannot be exercised until he has made payment under the policy.[94] Thus in *Page v. Scottish Insurance*

---

[88] (1854) 15 C.B. 365.

[89] *Burnand v. Rodocanachi* (1882) 7 App.Cas. 333, 340–341 *per* Lord Blackburn.

[90] *Godsall v. Boldero* (1807) 9 East 72.

[91] *The Solicitors' & General Life Assurance Society v. Lamb* (1864) 2 De G.J. & S. 251; *Crab Orchard Improvement Co. v. Chesapeake & Ohio R.R. Co.* 118 F.2d. 277 (1940). See further Chap. 25, *post*—personal accident policies.

[92] *e.g. Blascheck v. Bussell* (1916) 33 T.L.R. 74.

[93] [1942] 2 All E.R. 661.

[94] *Simpson v. Thomson* (1877) 3 App.Cas. 279, 284; *Castellain v. Preston* (1883) 11 Q.B.D. 380, 389; *Driscoll v. Driscoll* [1918] 1 I.R. 152, 159; *Burnand v. Rodocanachi Sons & Co.* (1882) 7 App.Cas. 333, 339; *Dickenson v. Jardine* (1868) L.R. 3 C.P. 639, 644. Motor insurers do not

Corporation,[95] the defendant insurers of a car claimed to be subrogated to the rights of their assured against the plaintiff who had damaged the car by careless driving. A third party involved in the accident had a claim against the assured for damages for injury to her car and the defendants at first denied that they were liable to their assured to pay this claim under the policy. Meanwhile they asked the plaintiff to repair the car and, when he sued for the cost of the repair, the defendants instituted an action against him in the name of the assured for the loss arising from the accident. The actions were consolidated and the insurers claimed to set off the damages, to which their assured was entitled, against the plaintiff's claim. Since the insurers were still denying liability under their policy with the assured when they issued their writ against the plaintiff, the Court of Appeal held that no rights of subrogation had arisen and the writ had therefore been issued without the authority of the assured. Thus, the second action was improperly constituted and could not be the foundation of a set-off.[96]

22–28 Although the right of subrogation cannot be exercised until payment is made by the insurer, it is a contingent right, vesting at the time when the policy is entered into[97] and it cannot be diminished by the assured effecting another policy with a different insurer.[98] There may, however, be a right of contribution if there is a case of double insurance.[99]

22–29 If an insurer is liable under the policy for different types of loss to the assured, he must pay for all types of damage before he can be subrogated to any particular right of the insured. Thus a motorist may take out a policy covering third-party liability, personal injury to himself and injury to his car. The insurer may be liable in all three respects but will not be subrogated to the rights of the assured in respect of damage to the car unless he has made payment in full in respect of each head of liablity under the policy.[1]

22–30 Restraint on exercise of rights of subrogation. It has been asserted by certain textbook writers that until the assured has received a full indemnity against his loss, no rights of subrogation can be exercised by an insurer even when he has paid his maximum liability under the policy.[2] Irish

---

acquire rights of subrogation by paying for repairs to the insured vehicle which have not in fact been properly performed to the reasonable satisfaction of the assured, since he has not been indemnified against his loss—*Scottish Union and National Insurance Co. v. Davis* [1970] 1 Lloyd's Rep. 1.

[95] (1929) 140 L.T. 571.

[96] It was therefore unnecessary to decide whether an insurer, when sued in his own name, can use a claim in the name of the assured as a set-off.

[97] *John Edwards & Co. v. Motor Union Insurance Co.* [1922] 2 K.B. 249, 254–255, *per* McCardie J.

[98] *Boag v. Standard Marine Insurance Co.* [1937] 2 K.B. 113; *City General Insurance Co. Ltd v. St. Paul Fire & Marine Insurance Co. Ltd* [1964] 1 Lloyd's Rep. 225 (S.D.N.Y.).

[99] See Ch. 23, *post.*

[1] *Page v. Scottish Ins. Corporation* (1929) 140 L.T. 571. it has been held by the New York courts that rights of subrogation do not arise in the case of an insurer making a loan to the assured in the sum of the loss pending an action against the wrong-doer in the name of the assured—*City General Ins. Co. Ltd v. St Paul Fire & Marine Ins. Co. Ltd* [1964] 1 Lloyd's Rep. 225, 229, and the authorities there cited. For a discussion of loan receipts see *Derham, op. cit.*, Ch. 9.

[2] Bunyon, *Fire Insurance* (7th ed.) p. 274; Halsbury, *Laws of England* (4th ed.) Vol. 25, reissue, p. 191 para. 317(3).

and Canadian decisions support this view,[3] but the proposition was reserved for future consideration by Scrutton L.J. in *Page v. Scottish Insurance Corporation*,[4] and it is too wide as a general proposition. It is inconsistent with the result, if not the reasoning, of a decision of the Privy Council.[5] The decision which is usually cited in support of the proposition is in fact only authority for the much narrower principle that untl the assured has been fully indemnified he is entitled to remain *dominus litis*. This is the case of *Commercial Union Assurance Co. v. Lister*[6] in which the plaintiff insurance company sought to restrain the defendant assured (whose loss was not fully covered by insurance) from proceedings against third parties unless he proceeded for the whole loss and not merely the loss which was not recoverable from the insurers. The company also sought a declaration that they were entitled to the benefit of any right of action vested in the defendant. The court refused to grant the declaration and made no order on the defendant's undertaking to sue for the full amount. The Court of Appeal held that, since the assured had not recovered his loss in full from the insurance company, he was still *dominus litis* and entitled to conduct proceedings himself, if he chose. The court did not say that no rights of subrogation had arisen by virtue of the company's making only a partial indemnity.

22–31 The case is therefore no authority for the view that the assured can refuse to take proceedings and prevent the insurers from doing so on the ground that no rights of subrogation have arisen. Indeed, by making the defendant undertake to sue for the whole amount of his loss, the court indicated that the insurers had an interest which was worthy of protection. Confusion may have arisen because counsel equated the insurers' rights of subrogation with the particular right to conduct the third party proceedings.[7] It is therefore submitted that rights of subrogation may arise after payment even if the assured is not fully indemnified, allthough the manner in which those rights are exercisable will depend on whether the insurer or the assured is *dominus litis*.[8]

22–32 Voluntary payment by insurers. Difficulty may arise where the insurer pays for a loss under the policy for which he was not strictly under any liability to pay. It was decided by the Judicial Committee of the Privy Council in *King v. Victoria Insurance Co.*[9] that, where a payment has been made honestly purporting to be in satisfaction of a potential liability under a policy, a defendant cannot be allowed to allege that the payment was not strictly within the terms of the policy. But if the contract of insurance is void or illegal or a nullity, it is unlikely that a court will hold that an insurer is subrogated to the rights of an assured whom he has purported to indemnify and it has been held that an insurer is not entitled to be subrogated to any

---

[3] *Driscoll v. Driscoll* [1918] 1 Ir.Rep. 152; *Sheridan v. Tynes* (1971) 19 D.L.R. (3d) 277; *Lawton v. Dartmouth Moving & Storage Ltd* (1976) 64 D.L.R. (3d) 326.
[4] (1929) 140 L.T. 571, 576.
[5] *Quebec Fire Ins. Co. v.. St. Louis* (1851) 7 Moo.P.C. 286. This case was in any event decided under the civil law in Quebec. See also *Morley v. Moore* [1936] 2 K.B. 359, 365.
[6] (1874) L.R. 9 Ch.App. 483; see the comment by Scrutton L.J. in (1929) 140 L.T. 571, 576.
[7] (1874) L.R. 9 Ch.App. 483, 485.
[8] See further para. 22–72, *post.*.
[9] [1896] A.C. 250; see also *Austin v. Zurich General Accident & Liability Ins. Co. Ltd* [1944] 2 All E.R. 243, not disapproved in the Court of Appeal [1945] K.B. 250.

rights arising out of a P.P.I. policy, even though he has made a payment under it, since such a policy is avoided *in toto* by section 4 of the Marine Insurance Act.[10] Decisions in the United States are possibly rather more strict, and give little encouragement to the ininsurer who claims "to be subrogated to a recovery for a loss against which it did not insure".[11] Where insurers paid the victims of careless driving by an un-insured driver, an attempt to obtain recompense from him on principles of unjust enrichment failed in the absence of an assignment.[12]

(c) *Exclusion of Rights of Subrogation*[13]

22–33 It is possible to exclude all or some of the insurers rights of subrogation by means of a term in the policy.[14] More frequently it happens that rights of subrogation do vest in the insurer, but cannot be exercised by the insurer in proceedings against a particular third party because the assured is himself not entitled to sue the third party owing to a prior agreement between them[15] or by reason of a trade usage incorporated into a contract between the assured and the third party.[16] The existence of such a usage is a material fact, and should be disclosed to the insurer at the time of proposal for the cover.[17] Other instances are where the wrongdoer is also a co-assured,[18] and where there is a contract between them providing for insurance to be effected in terms which exclude the wrongdoer's liability to the assured for the kind of loss which has occurred.[19]

22–34 An insurer may also be affected by an agreement between himself and another insurer. The "knock-for-knock" agreement common among motor insurers is one example.[20] An assured is in no way debarred by the agreement from suing another insured motorist who is liable to him in tort for causing damage to his person or property.[21] He is not a party to the agreement between the two insurers. But the insurer of the innocent motorist cannot cause his assured to exercise his right of suit for his own

---

[10] *John Edwards & Co. v. Motor Union Ins. Co.* [1922] 2 K.B. 249. In the United States a P.P.I. policy is valid if the insured has an interest and the doctrine of subrogation will therefore apply in such cases, *Frank B. Hall & Co. v. Jefferson Ins. Co.*, 279 F. 892 (1921).

[11] *Standard Marine Ins. Co. v. Scottish Metropolitan Ass. Co.*, 283 U.S. 289, 290 (1931), *per* Stone J.; *Bonnie v. Maryland Casualty Co.*, 133 S.W. 2d 904 (1939); *Old Colony Ins. Co. v. Kansas Public Service Co.*, 121 P.2d 193 (1942). But *cf. Maryland Casualty Ins. Co. of North America*, 110 F. 420 (1901).

[12] *Norwich Union Fire Ins. Soc. v. Ross* [1995] S.L.T. (Sh.Ct.) 103.

[13] See "Defences to an Insurer's Subrogated Action" by Dr. C. Mitchell, [1996] L.M.C.L.Q 343–367.

[14] *Morris v. Ford Motor Co.* [1973] Q.B. 792, 812; *Thomas & Co. v. Brown* (1899) 4 Com.Cas. 186; *The "Surf City"* [1995] 2 Lloyd's Rep. 242; *National Oilwell Ltd v. Davy Offshore Ltd* [1993] 2 Lloyd's Rep. 582, 591. The insurers' rights of subrogation may also be waived, expressly or by necessary implication, as a term of an agreement compromising the assured's claim for payment—*Brooks v. MacDonnell* (1835) 1 Y. & C. Ex. 500.

[15] *Coupar Transport (London) Ltd v. Smith's (Acton) Ltd* [1959] 1 Lloyd's Rep. 369.

[16] *Tate v. Hyslop* (1885) 15 Q.B.D. 368.

[17] *ibid.*

[18] *Petrofina (U.K.) Ltd v. Magnaload Ltd* [1984] Q.B. 127. See paras. 22–98 to 22–100, *infra.*

[19] *Rowlands (Mark) Ltd v. Berni Inns Ltd* [1986] Q.B. 211. See para. 22–94, *infra.*

[20] *Morley v. Moore* [1936] 2 K.B. 359; *Bourne v. Stanbridge* [1965] 1 W.L.R. 189, over-ruled on an issue of the award of costs in *Hobbs v. Marlowe* [1978] A.C. 16; *Bell Assurance Assoc. v. Licenses & General Insurance Corp. & Guarantee Fund* (1923) 17 Ll.L.Rep. 100.

[21] *Morley v. Moore* [1936] 2 K.B. 359, approved in *Hobbs v. Marlowe* [1978] A.C. 16.

benefit, for that would put him in breach of the "knock-for-knock" agreement with the other insurer. Other examples of agreements made by insurers which restrict their enjoyment of rights of subrogation are the agreement of employers' liability insurers not to procure the institution of claims against an employee of their assured,[22] and the so-called "Gold Clause Agreement" of August 1, 1950.[23]

3. EXERCISE OF RIGHTS OF SUBROGATION

22-35 It has already been remarked that the doctrine of subrogation confers two distinct rights on the insurer.[24] These are the right to oblige the assured to pursue remedies against third parties for the insurer's ultimate benefit,[25] and the right to recover from the assured any benefits received by the assured in extinction or diminution of the loss for which he has been indemnified.

(a) *Claims against Third Parties*

22-36 Claims to which the insurer is subrogated. The insurer is subrogated to any claim of any character which the assured is entitled to bring in proceedings agains a third party to diminish his loss.[26] It matters not whether the right of suit is legal, equitable or statutory. It is submitted, for instance, that a motor insurer, who had indemnified his assured against the cost of repair to the insured vehicle necessitated after a third party took it without consent and crashed it, would be entitled to request the assured to seek a compensation order against the convicted wrongdoer in criminal proceedings.[27]

22-37 The right is exercisable by reinsurers. Thus in *Assicurazioni Generali di Trieste v. Empress Assurance Corporation Ltd*[28] the defendants had insured certain vessels and then reinsured them with the plaintiffs. The defendants paid for a loss, for which they supposed themselves to be liable, only as a result of a fraudulent misrepresentation on the part of the insured. After they had recovered from the plaintiffs under the policy of reinsurance, they discovered the truth and obtained damages for fraud from the insured. The plaintiffs claimed that they were subrogated to the rights of the defendants against the insured and were entitled to be reimbursed the sums they had paid out. The defendants argued that the damages recovered by

---

[22] *Morris v. Ford Motor Co.* [1973] Q.B. 792, 799
[23] Scrutton, *Charterparties & Bills of Lading* (18th ed.) p. 528.
[24] See para. 22–2, *supra*.
[25] Subject to a tender of costs: *Morris v. Ford Motor Co.* [1973] Q.B. 792, 796; *Yorkshire Insurance Co. v. Nisbet Shipping Co.* [1962] 2 Q.B. 330, 341. Adherents to the "equitable" theory of the origins of subrogation might prefer to describe the right of suit as being exercised by the insurer in the assured's name, but this is, strictly, incorrect.
[26] *Castellain v. Preston* (1883) 11 Q.B.D. 380, 388; *Morley v. Moore* [1936] 2 K.B. 359
[27] Power of Criminal Courts Act 1973, s.35(1). The example is based on *R. v. Vivian* [1979] 1 W.L.R. 291. Whether the deputy circuit judge in that case should have enquired whether the car owner had been indemnified by his insurers is, with respect, open to question—see para. 22–2, *supra*.
[28] [1907] 2 K.B. 814.

them were personal damages for a personal wrong not connected with the subject matter of the insurace but it was held that the damages were received by them in diminution of their loss and that the reinsurers were entitled to succeed in their claim.

It has, furthermore, been held that the insurer is subrogated not merely to the rights of the assured but also to any benefits which a court may in its discretion award to the insured. Thus, awards of interest to a successful plaintiff pursuant to statute are not matters of right but a matter for the court's discretion; it was nevertheless held in *Cousins H. Ltd v. D. & C. Carriers Ltd*[29] after some initial doubts[30] that an insurer is subrogated to an award of interest in respect of any period after the assured has been indemnified by the insurer for his loss. Similarly, if costs are awarded in favour of a plaintiff who is insured, it is thought that they can be claimed by an insurer who has, in fact but not in name, fought the action.[31]

22–38 An insurer cannot, however, be subrogated to rights which have no connection with the subject-matter of the insurance. Thus a hull underwriter is not subrogated to the rights of the assured to freight under a charter party,[32] nor will, an underwriter usually be subrogated to damages awarded to the assured for libel.[33] Similarly, if a man insures his property against fire and both he and his property are injured, the insurer is subrogated only to his rights in respect of the property and not to any personal rights arising out of the injury sustained.[34]

22–39 Subrogation only to assured's rights. An insurer is not entitled to make any claim which the assured himself could not have made. The best known example of the principle is the case of *Simpson v. Thomson*,[35] in which two ships owned by the same person collided through the fault of one. It was held that the insurers of the ship not at fault could not recover from the owner for the negligence of the other ship because, the owner could not bring an action against himself. Similarly if the assured has, before a loss is incurred, agreed to limit his rights against the wrong-doer, the insurer will only be subrogated to the rights so limited.[36] For example, a contract

---

[29] [1971] 2 Q.B. 230; followed in *Metal Box Ltd v. Currys Ltd* [1988] 1 All E.R. 341.

[30] See *Harbutt's "Plasticine" Ltd v. Wayne Tank and Pump Co. Ltd* [1970] 1 Q.B. 447.

[31] See [1971] 2 Q.B. 230, 242, *per* Widgery L.J. and *Gough v. Toronto and York Radial R.W. Co.* (1918) 42 Ont.L.R. 415.

[32] See *Ins. Co. v. Hadden* (1884) 13 Q.B.D. 706. *Cf. South British Ins. Co. Ltd v. Broun's Wharf Pty. Ltd* (1960) 1 N.S.W.R. 80, 84.

[33] *Assicurazioni Generali di Trieste v. Empress Ass. Corporation Ltd* [1907] 2 K.B. 814, 820.

[34] *Law Fire Ass. Co. v. Oakley* (1888) 4 T.L.R. 309. See also *Young v. Merchants' Marine Ins. Co. Ltd* [1932] 2 K.B. 705. Derham suggests the test is whether the exercise of the assured's right in question by the insurer will diminish the loss insured against, *Subrogation in Insurance Law*, Ch. 4, p. 35

[35] (1877) 3 App.Cas 279; *cf. Midland Ins. Co. v. Smith* (1881) 6 Q.B.D. 561 where it was held that there was no right of subrogation where the only right of the insured was against his wife.

[36] *Thomas & Co. v. Brown* (1899) 4 Com.Cas 186; *Germania Fire Ins. Co. v. Memphis R.R. Co.*, 72 N.Y. 90 (1878); *Savannah Fire and Marine Ins. Co. v. Pelzer Manufacturing Co.*, 60 Fed.Rep. 39 (1894); *cf. Lister v. Romford Ice and Cold Storage Co. Ltd* [1957] A.C. 555, 579, *per* Viscount Simonds, 600, *per* Lord Somervell, and *Coupar Transport (London) Ltd v. Smith's (Acton) Ltd* [1959] 1 Lloyd's Rep. 369. In the U.S., clauses preventing the exercise of rights against defendants (often known as waiver of subrogation clauses) are not always enforceable, *Tenneco Oil Co. v. Tug "Tony"* [1972] 1 Lloyd's Rep. 514.

between a goods-owner and a carrier may provide that, if the carrier is liable for the loss, he shall have the benefit of any insurance effected on the goods. In such a case the insurer has no rights enforceable by subrogation since if the carrier is not liable, the assured has no right to which underwriters can be subrogated. If he is liable, the assured has no right to which underwriters can be subrogated, because the assured has contracted that he can have the benefit of any insurance money and the insurer is bound by this stipulation.

22–40 This will probably be so even where the contract between the insurer and the assured is to indemnify the insured only. Thus if a vendor of property has taken out an insurance policy and agreed with the purchaser that he should have the benefit of the insurance, there would be no subrogation to the vendor's claim for the purchase money.[37] In *Canadian Transport Co. Ltd v. Court Line Ltd*[38] however, shipowners by a time charterparty agreed to give charterers the benefit of their insurance so far as the rules of the insurer's club allowed, and those rules provided that the insurers could recover from third parties any damages due to their neglect and that no assignment of the insurance cover was to bind the insurers. The House of Lords held that the rules of the insurers' club rendered inoperative the clause in the charterparty giving the benefit of the insurance to the charterers.

4. COMMENCEMENT AND CONDUCT OF PROCEEDINGS

22–41 Institution of proceedings. The assured is entitled to take proceedings against third parties to recover his loss, and cannot be restrained from doing so by the insurer before[39] or after[40] payment of what is due under the policy.[41] The insurer is safeguarded by the possibility of the assured becoming liable to him in damages if he conducts proceedings without regard to the insurer's interests before or after he is indemnified,[42] and by the duty of the assured to hold as chargee for him moneys received in the proceedings in excess of his actual loss.[43]

22–42 Control of the proceedings. Until he is paid by the insurer, the assured is entitled to control any proceedings brought in his name. Even if he has been paid out under the policy, but continues proceedings to gain

---

[37] See para. 22–84, *infra*. If the contract of insurance contained an express term to the effect that the insured would not prejudice the insurer's rights of subrogation, the insurer would presumably be able to sue the insured for breach of the express term. In the absence of such a term, it is very doubtful whether one would be implied.

[38] [1940] A.C. 934; *cf.* the judgment of Scott L.J. in the Court of Appeal [1939] 2 All E.R. 761, and *Inman v. South Carolina Railway Co.*, 129 U.S. 128 (1889).

[39] *Commercial Union Ass. Co. v. Lister* (1874) L.R. 9 Ch.App. 483; *Page v. Scottish Ins. Corp.* (1929) 140 L.T. 571, 576

[40] *Morley v. Moore* [1936] 2 K.B. 359. In *Hobbs v. Marlowe* [1978] A.C. 16, the House of Lords declined to decide the point. It is usually covered by express provision in the policy.

[41] *Commercial Union Ass. Co. v. Lister* (1874) L.R. 9 Ch.App. 483; *Page v. Scottish Ins. Corp.* (1929) 140 L.T. 571, 576.

[42] *West of England Fire Insurance Co. v. Isaacs* [1897] 1 Q.B. 226; *Commercial Union Ass. Co. v. Lister* (1874) L.R. 9 Ch.App. 483; *Horse Carriage & General Ins. Co. v. Petch* (1916) 33 T.L.R. 131; *Sheridan v. Tynes* (1971) 19 D.L.R. (3d) 277, 285

[43] Para. 22–23, *supra*; *A. Barnett Ltd v. National Ins. Co. of New Zealand* [1965] N.Z.L.R. 874, 885.

compensation for his uninsured loss, the insurers cannot interfere if he is willing to prosecute a claim for the whole loss.[44] The insured must conduct the litigation with proper regard for the insurers' interest, and may be liable in damages for misconducting the litigation, in particular abandoning rights to the prejudice of the insurers.[45] It has been said in a New Zealand decision[46] that the assured has a discretion as to what *quantum* of loss is claimed in the action, and he may be able to justify his failure to sue for all or some of his insured loss.

22–43 Insurer has no right to sue in own name. The cause of action for damages remains in the assured, and the insurer subrogated to the assured's rights brings the action in the name of his assured,[47] whose action it is.[48] By contrast, if the assured has made an express assignment of his rights to the insurer, the cause of action has vested in the insurer who can exercise in his own name the rights originally belonging to the assured.[49]

22–44 Consistently with this rule the law ignores the fact that, when proceedings are instituted at the behest of the insurer, he is the real plaintiff.[50] Thus a Canadian court has held that an order for security for costs may be made against a foreign assured in whose name a domestic insurance company is bringing an action.[51] Similarly the assured, as the plaintiff on the record, is liable to comply with the court's rules of procedure and must, for instance, make proper discovery in the action,[52] The insurer is under no obligation, under the English Rules of Court, to give discovery of documents in his possession, custody or power to a defendant but only to procure the discovery of documents in the possession, custody or power of the assured.[53] An insurer, who is the defendant in proceedings brought by a person against whom the assured has a cause of action, cannot counterclaim in those proceedings even though he is subrogated to the rights of the assured.[54] Judgment must be entered in the name of the nominal plaintiff, the assured,

---

[44] *Commercial Union Ass. Co. v. Lister* (1874) L.R. 9 Ch.App. 483; *A. Barnett Ltd v. National Ins. Co. of New Zealand* [1965] N.Z.L.R. 874, 883, 885, 889.

[45] See note 37, *supra*.

[46] *Barnett A. Ltd v. National Insurance Co. of New Zealand* [1965] N.Z.L.R. 874.

[47] *Mason v. Sainsbury* (1782) 3 Doug. K.B. 61; *London Assurance v. Sainsbury* (1782) 3 Doug. K.B. 245 and the cases cited in note 25 to para. 22–12, *supra*.

[48] *Wilson v. Raffalovich* (1881) 7 Q.B.D. 553, 558; *Smith (M.H.) (Plant Hire) v. Mainwaring* [1986] 2 Lloyd's Rep. 244.

[49] *King v. Victoria Ins. Co.* [1896] A.C. 250; *Cia Colombiana de Seguros v. Pacific Steam Navigation Co.* [1965] 1 Q.B. 101.

[50] *Russell v. Wilson, The Times*, May 26, 1989, where the insurer was compelled to submit to the small claims procedure in the County Court.

[51] *Gough v. Toronto & York Radial R. W. Co.* (1918) 42 Ont.L.R. 415. For the English procedure see R.S.C. Ord. 23, r. 1(1)(b). The insurers' undertaking to indemnify the assured against his costs would make it unlikely that the assured would fail to meet an order for costs, but problems could be created by the assured becoming bankrupt or being put into liquidation.

[52] *Wilson v. Raffalovich* (1881) 7 Q.B.D. 553.

[53] *Nelson J. & Sons Ltd v. Nelson Line (Liverpool) Ltd* [1906] 2 K.B. 217. Admittedly in that case the insurer had paid only part of the loss and the assured-plaintiff retained an actual interest in the proceedings, which led Cozens-Hardy L.J. at p. 225 to leave open what might happen if the assured had been paid in full. However, the obligation to give discovery attaches only to the party on the record, under R.S.C., Ord. 24, and it is difficult to see how an order could be made against an underwriter. The Court could not employ the sanction of staying the proceedings under R.S.C., Ord. 24, r. 16, since the nominal plaintiff would not have had an order made against him to produce these documents.

[54] *Page v. Scottish Ins. Corporation* (1929) 140 L.T. 571, 576.

and the defendant will obtain a good discharge only if he pays the assured, not if he pays the insurer.[55]

22–45 A rigid application of these principles would lead to absurd results in a case where the assured was awarded costs against an unsuccessful defendant. In a Canadian case the defendant argued that he could resist an order to pay solicitors' costs if (as usually happens) the action was conducted by the insurers' solicitors, on the ground that the assured was under no liability to pay such costs himself.[56] The court did not accept this contention and ordered the defendant to pay the costs because, it was held, the insurer was the real litigant and the judgment and costs awarded to the nominal plaintiff were in reality the "property" of the insurer. This analysis is, strictly speaking, incorrect. It would prompt the conclusion, for instance, that an order for discovery could be had against the insurer as the real party in suit, as the court averred,[57] but this is not the English law.[58] It is submitted, however, that the decision ought to be followed on grounds of good sense even if the court's reasoning is difficult to accept. Presumably the solicitors appointed by the insurer appear on the record as solicitors conducting the proceedings for the assured. It might be preferable to uphold the decision on the basis that the defendant, like the court, cannot look beyond the record and so cannot dispute the presumption from the record alone that the solicitors are retained by the assured. Otherwise the wrongdoer would be permitted to profit from the fact that his victim was insured.[59]

22–46 If the assured refuses to allow the insurer to use his name as a plaintiff, the insurer may institute an action against the defendant in his own name, join the assured as a second defendant and ask the court to order him to lend his name to the action as a plaintiff or, perhaps, ask for an order that the first defendant pay damages to the second defendant and for a declaration that the second defendant holds such damages on behalf of the insurer.[60]

22–47 English law is remarkably strict in its rigid separation between assured and insurer. In most of the cases mentioned no injustice will result to the insurer, but it is not difficult to imagine cases where an insurer might suffer from the inflexibility of the law. Thus, an assured might lend his name to the action as a plaintiff but, when the trial takes place, refuse to give evidence. In such a case the insurer should be able to ask for the court to issue a *subpoena*, but it is unlikely that a court would feel free to do so, since a plaintiff can hardly requst an order for a *subpoena* to be served on himself. At present the insurer would be obliged to ask the court to adjourn the

---

[55] *Yorkshire Ins. Co. v. Nisbet Shipping Co.* [1962] 2 Q.B. 330, 341, *per* Diplock J.
[56] *Gough v. Toronto & York Radial R.W. Co.* (1918) 42 Ont.L.R. 415.
[57] *ibid.* at p. 417.
[58] *Wilson v. Raffalovich* (1881) 7 Q.B.D. 553; *Nelson J. & Sons Ltd v. Nelson Line (Liverpool) Ltd* [1906] 2 K.B. 217. See note 51, *supra*.
[59] See note to para. 22–2, *supra*.
[60] *King v. Victoria Ins. Co.* [1896] A.C. 250, 255–256; *John Edwards & Co. v. Motor Union Assurance Co.* [1922] 2 K.B. 249, 254; *Re Miller, Gibb & Co.* [1957] 1 W.L.R. 703, 707.

proceedings, and then, shedding the mantle of the assured and donning his own, to commence proceedings in his own name against the assured to obtain enforcement of the terms of the contract of insurance obliging the assured to give all assistance necessary to permit the insurer to enjoy his rights to subrogation.

22–48 Insurer's right to control proceedings. When the insurer has fully indemnified the assured, he can take over the control of proceedings on undertaking to indemnify the assured against his costs. This does not, however, prevent the assured from proceeding in his own name and on his own behalf. Even if the insurer requests the assured not to sue the wrongdoer, and disclaims any desire to receive anything which the assured may recover, the assured may proceed against the wrongdoer and hold what he receives as chargee to repay the insurer what he has paid out under the policy.[61]

22–49 Duty to commence proceedings. Insurance policies frequently contain a clause expressly requiring the assured to take all necessary steps to protect the insurer's rights. If an assured under such a policy allowed a time-bar to elapse, thereby precluding the insurer from enjoying the exercise of remedies against a third party, the insurers could, it is submitted, recover damages for the breach of that stipulation in the amount which would have been recoverable from the third party. If it was clear that the clause possessed the status of a condition, or "warranty" in insurance parlance, the insurers could decline liability altogther.[62]

22–50 It has never been decided in English law whether, in the absence of an express clause, there is an obligation on the assured to take active steps to prosecute a claim against a third party, so as to stop it becoming time barred to the detriment of the insurer. This is a very real problem in cases where there is a contract between the assured and the third party stating that claims must be brought within a short period of time, as is common in contracts for the carriage of goods by land or sea. in *Andrews v. The Patriotic Assurance Company*[63] Palles C.B. held that an insurer on a buildings policy was not entitled to repudiate liability by reason of the failure of the assured to sue the wrongdoer before the latter became bankrupt, in the absence of any request by the insurer to do so. The English authorities hold that the assured may not actively deal with rights against third parties to the prejudice of the insurer. Consequently he will be liable to the insurer in damages for the value of any right wrongfully renounced or any claim wrongfully settled.[64] These cases

---

[61] *Morley v. Moore* [1936] 2 K.B. 359, applied in *Bourne v. Stanbridge* [1965] 1 W.L.R. 189. In *Hobbs v. Marlowe* [1978] A.C. 16 the House of Lords refrained from examining this part of the decision in *Morley v. Moore,* while upholding it on the point concerning knock-for-knock agreements between motor insurers. See para. 22–68, *infra.*

[62] The "Duty of Assured" clause, no. 16, in the Institute Cargo Clauses is not a warranty, and a breach sounds in damages—*Noble Resources v. Greenwood (The Vasso)* [1993] 2 Lloyd's Rep. 309, where the assured committed no breach by omitting to apply for a *Mareva* injunction. See comment by C. Henley in (1993) 3 Ins. Law & Practice 86.

[63] (1886) 18 L.R.Ir. 355. *Cf. Carter v. White* (1883) 25 Ch.D. 666 where a surety was held not to be discharged merely because the creditor had allowed his action against the principal debtor to become time-barred.

[64] *Defourcet & Co. v. Bishop* (1886) 18 Q.B.D. 373; *West of England Fire Ins. Co. v. Isaacs* [1897] 1 Q.B. 226; *Phoenix Ass. Co. v. Spooner* [1905] 2 K.B. 753; *Horse Carriage & General Ins. Co. v. Petch* (1916) 33 T.L.R. 131; *Boag v. Standard Marine Ins. Co.* [1937] 2 K.B. 113.

concerned actual transactions by the assured which caused the insurer to lose the enjoyment of a right or remedy against a wrongdoer. They do not deal with the issue of whether the duty extends to a mere omission to act in the insurer's interests.

22–51 In most cases the insurers do not suffer from the absence of a general duty on the assured to preserve their rights of subrogation, even when there is no express term in the policy enjoining him to do so. Once they know of a claim and there is any danger of it being lost by lapse of time, loss of evidence, bankruptcy, or any other cause, the insurers have the remedy in their own hands, namely, to pay the loss and commence proceedings in the assured's name. Where the insurer knows the position there is no injustice in fixing him with the conduct of the assured who can be compelled to lend his name to any proceedings which the insurer may bring.[65] The insurer could, however, be prejudiced if the claims were notified after a relevant time-bar had expired. This is not necessarily an argument for the imposition of a general duty not to allow the insurer's position to become prejudiced in any way, because the insurer is invariably protected by an express term of the policy in cases of late notification of a claim, but there is certainly something to be said for it. According to the theory which bases rights of subrogation on terms implied into the contract of insurance by operation of law, it would be relatively simple for the courts to imply into indemnity insurance contracts a duty upon the assured to take all reasonable steps to preserve the insurer's rights of subrogation. "Reasonable steps" would mean, we submit, no more than protecting the claim against any relevant legal or arbitration time bar, and then inviting the insurer to make payment and take over the conduct of the action.

5. Release and Settlement

22–52 Release or settlement of claims. So far as third parties are concerned the insurer and the assured are a single entity, and an unconditional settlement or abandonment of a claim by the assured will prima facie bind the insurer. But, as between the insurer and the assured, that is not the end of the matter. The assured is under an obligation not to deal with any claim he possesses, or will possess, against a third party in such a manner as to prejudice the insurer's rights of subrogation in relation to it.[66] The insurer's remedy will be to repudiate liability on the policy, or to counterclaim for damages for the loss of, or diminution of, their rights, depending on the circumstances. The position varies slightly depending on whether the insurer has paid for the loss.

22–53 Release before payment. After a loss has occurred but before the insurer has made payment, any release or settlement made by the assured with third parties to the prejudice of the insurer will entitle the insurer to set up, in answer to the assured's claim, a counterclaim for damages in the amount of the loss thereby suffered by the insurer. The insurer might be

---

[65] *Yorkshire Ins. Co. v. Nisbet Shipping Co. Ltd* [1962] 2 Q.B. 330, *Morris v. Ford Motor Co.* [1973] Q.B. 792, 796.
[66] See note 64, *supra.*

entitled to repudiate liability if express provision were made for such a contingency in the policy. The assured is not precluded, however, from settling a doubtful claim in good faith for the benefit of himself and his insurers, and such a settlement is not a defence to his claim on the policy in the absence of an express term forbidding such conduct. The insurers can have the question of settlement in their own hands, either by means of such a clause, or by paying a full indemnity to the assured so as to be entitled to take over control of the proceedings.

22–54 The insurers will, of course, be prejudiced by the assured's unconditional release of a third party, since it binds them indirectly just as it binds the assured. It is possible to conceive of a release being held to be, in its context, an incomplete release, so that there could still be a claim, made on behalf of the insurers, in respect of that portion of the loss which was covered by insurance.[67] Care needs to be exercised by an assured suing to recover the amount of an uninsured excess in a motor policy. If the defendant pays the sum claimed into court, and the assured accepts it, his action will be stayed. That does not bar the insurer from suing the defendant to recover the amount of the insured loss which he has paid, as he can apply for the stay on the assured's action to be lifted.[68] But if judgment had been entered on the assured's claim, the cause of action would have been barred, to the prejudice of the insurer.[69]

22–55 Release after payment. If the assured makes a release or settlement with the third party after he has been paid by the insurers, and to their prejudice, he will be liable to compensate them for the amount by which he has diminished the value of their rights of subrogation.[70] Prejudice depends upon the nature of the transaction with the third party, and upon whether the insurers are effectively bound by it. It has been held that insurers who have paid out under their policy are never bound by a release or compromise made by their assured if the third party has notice of the payment before concluding the transaction,[71] but it is submitted that this is too wide. This part of the decision was *obiter* and proceeded on the assumption that, upon payment of the insurance moneys, the insurers had received an equitable assignment of the assured's right of action with the knowledge of the third party. Subrogation does not operate, however, as an assignment of the assured's rights to the insurers[72] The decision should rest on the court's interpretation of the receipt alleged to constitute a total release, namely, that in the context in which it was signed by the assured it was not capable of being read as relating to his insured loss.[73]

---

[67] *Taylor v. O. Wray & Co. Ltd* [1971] 1 Lloyd's Rep. 497, *Smidmore v. Australian Gas Light Co.* (1881) 2 N.S.W.L.R. 219.

[68] *Buckland v. Palmer* [1984] 1 W.L.R. 1109.

[69] *ibid.* at p. 1115. A judgment after a contested action could only be set aside if procured inequitably, *Hayler v. Chapman* [1989] 1 Lloyds Rep. 490.

[70] *Defourcet & Co. v. Bishop* (1886) 18 Q.B.D. 373; *West of England Fire Ins. Co. v. Isaacs* [1897] 1 Q.B. 226; *Phoenix Ass. Co. v. Spooner* [1905] 2 K.B. 753; *Boag v. Standard Marine Ins. Co.* [1937] 2 K.B. 113, 127–129.

[71] *Haigh v. Lawford* (1964) 114 N.L.J. 208 (Salisbury County Court, Judge Bulger Q.C.).

[72] Paras 22–11 to 22–12, *supra*.

[73] This is the ground of the decision in the *Smidmore* case—note 67, *supra*—on which the learned judge relied. American authorities are not reliable guides to the English law on this topic as the American law tends to see the insurer as the real party in suit in a subrogation action.

22–56 In *Horse, Carriage and General Insce. Co. v. Petch*[74] the assured had a claim against a third party for personal injury and for damage to his car. The insurer was subrogated only to the action for damage to the car but the assured compromised both claims for one unapportioned sum of £1,250. The insurer had paid £81 15s. to the assured in respect of the damaged car. It was held that the insurer was entitled to recover the full amount which had been paid in respect of the damaged car, either as damages for being deprived of the right to have the conduct of the claim[75] or because the assured must be assumed, in favour of the insurer, to have settled the action for the full amount.[76]

22–57 If the assured has been paid the insurance money but has not received a full indemnity, he is still entitled to make a bona fide settlement in the joint interest of himself and his insurer.[77]

22–58 Settlement by the insurer. Any settlement by the insurer will probably bind the assured but this question will be answered by applying the rules of agency rather than insurance.[78]

22–59 If an insurer does settle an assured's claim so that the assured is in some way prejudiced, the assured may be able to claim damages from the insurer by relying on an implied term of the contract to the effect that the insurer shall not exercise rights of subrogation to his prejudice.[79] This is unlikely to be of much practical importance save where the assured has lost the prospect of recovering more than his actual loss on facts similar to *Yorkshire Insurance Co. v. Nisbet Shipping Co.*[80] or where the insurer has settled a claim for a loss which was not insured.

22–60 Cost of proceedings. Difficulties can often arise in connection with costs of proceedings brought in the name of the assured, especially if both insurer and assured have an interest in the proceedings. Various situations must be considered.

22–61 If the assured has been fully indemnified, the insurer becomes *dominus litis*, and is entitled to start proceedings in the name of the assured provided that he undertakes to indemnify the assured in respect of all costs incurred.[81] It follows from this that the insurer must bear all the costs of the

---

[74] (1916) 33 T.L.R. 131. There is some American authority holding that the insurer must prove that the settlement was by way of payment for the same loss as that for which the assured had been indemnified—*Hamilton Fire v. Greger*, 158 N.E. 60 (1972); *Illinois Automobile Exchange v. Brown*, 124 A. 691 (1924).

[75] *cf. per curiam arguendo* in *Law Fire Ass. Co. v. Oakley* (1888) 4 T.L.R. 309.

[76] See para. 22–29, *supra*.

[77] *Globe & Rutgers Fire Ins. Co. v. Truedell* [1927] 2 D.L.R. 659.

[78] *Kitchen Design Ltd v. Lea Valley Water Co.* [1989] 2 Lloyds Rep. 221.

[79] *England v. Guardian Ins. Ltd* [2000] Lloyd's Rep. I.R. 404, 418.

[80] [1962] 2 Q.B. 330.

[81] *Netherlands Ins. Co. v. Karl Lijungberg & Co.* [1986] 3 All E.R. 767, 770, *per* Lord Goff of Chieveley.

proceedings and, if a greater sum is recovered than the insurer has paid to the assured, the insurer, although he can claim back what he has paid, cannot claim any extra on account of his costs.

22–62 The assured is, of course, free to sue the wrongdoer even though he has received a full indemnity and the insurer is unwilling for the proceedings to be instituted.[82] He may well, however, exercise this right of suit at some risk to himself so far as costs are concerned. It was held in one American case that if the assured insists on starting proceedings himself in spite of being fully indemnified, he cannot deduct costs before accounting to the insurer for the proceeds.[83] He may also find that the fact that he has been indemnified adversely affects the award of costs in the third party proceedings. In *Hobbs v. Marlowe*[84] the plaintiff's car was damaged in a collision caused by the negligence of the defendant. The cost of repairs to it was £237.59. He hired another car for the duration of the repairs. This cost £63.53. His insurers paid him £227.59 under his policy for the repair costs, there being a £10 excess. The hiring costs were not covered by the policy. To recover his out-of-pocket expenses totalling £73.53 he sued in the county court. His insurers had no interest in the proceedings, since they had concluded a "knock-for-knock" agreement with the defendant's insurers. The County Court Rules then in force provided that no solicitors' charges were to be awarded to a successful plaintiff claiming £75 or less. The plaintiff therefore increased his claim to the full amount of his initial loss— £301.12—in order to obtain an award of costs on scale 3. The county court judge held, following *Morley v. Moore*[85] that he was entitled to have judgment for the £301.12 despite the "knock-for-knock" agreement, since the fact that the plaintiff was insured was not to benefit the defendant. But he exercised his discretion on costs to deprive him of all his costs save £7.50, the sum appropriate to a claim not exceeding £75. His decision was upheld in the Court of Appeal and the House of Lords.

22–63 The House of Lords approved *Morley v. Moore*,[86] but overruled *Bourne v. Stanbridge*[87] on the issue of costs. The policy underlying the rules governing small claims was to remove the threat of a heavy award of costs in the event of failure, and accordingly to encourage litigants to assert small claims without legal representation. The inflation of the claim beyond the plaintiff's real loss was a technical misuse of the county court procedure, and the judge was entitled to exercise his discretion against the plaintiff, although in a sense this ran counter to the principle that the plaintiff's insurance was not to benefit the defendant.

22–64 No full indemnity. If the assured is not fully indemnified, he is entitled to start proceedigns himself and remain *dominus litis*, provided that he protects the insurer's interest as well as his own.

The assured may begin proceedings and carry them through to a successful conclusion. In such a case, costs will usually be awarded against

---

[82] *Morley v. Moore* [1936] 2 K.B. 359.
[83] *Hardman v. Brett*, 37 Fed.Rep. 803 (1899).
[84] [1978] A.C. 16.
[85] [1936] 2 K.B. 359
[86] *ibid.*
[87] [1965] 1 W.L.R. 189. See further *Smith v. Springer* [1987] 1 W.L.R. 1720 which held that the facts had to be determined before issues of costs could be decided.

the defendant, but there may well be irrecoverable costs incurred by the assured. It seems to be well settled that reasonable costs can be deducted from the sum recovered before accounting to the insurer.[88] The assured may carry on proceedings but lose them. In such a case liability for costs may be very large and the insurer can only be expected to bear the costs if he authorised the proceedings. If he did give such authority, liability for costs will be borne according to the respective interests of the assured and the insurer in the proceedings.[89] If no authority is given, the assured will probably be held to have taken the burden of litigation on himself and he therefore cannot recover costs. There is, however, often a clause in the policy to the effect that the assured is bound to take all necessary proceedings in the interests of the insurer. Where such a clause is present a term may be implied that expenses incurred by the assured in compliance therewith shall be recoverable by him from the insurers in so far as they relate to the preservation or exercise of rights in respect of loss or damage for which the insurers are liable under the policy.[90]

22–65 A New Zealand decision should be contrasted with the preceding one. In *A. Barnett Ltd v. National Insurance Company of New Zealand*,[91] the assured has suffered a loss not fully covered by the insurance and instituted proceedings to claim his uninsured loss. He later amended his statement of claim to claim the insured loss as well, consistent with the decision in *Commercial Union Assurance Co. v. Lister*,[92] but contended that the insurers should bear a proportionate part of the cost because their policy required him to maintain the proceedings. The policy provided:

> "The insured shall, at the expense of the company, do and concur in doing, and permit to be done, all such acts and things as may be necessary or reasonably required by the company for the purpose of enforcing any rights and remedies. ...."

The New Zealand Court of Appeal held that this clause did not entitle the assured to conduct litigation at the expense of his insurers and that unless the insurers authorised the action to proceed he could not look to them for costs.

22–66 Proceedings by insurer. If the assured decides against taking proceedings but the insurer takes proceedings in his name in respect of the part of the loss for which he has paid, and the insurer loses those proceedings, the costs must be paid by the insurer.

If the insurer wins such proceedings, he may in fact recover more than he has paid to the assured. The assured will receive the recovery, since it is only by payment to him that a defendant can satisfy a judgment.[93] The question will then arise whether the insurer can claim from the assured not only the

---

[88] *Assicurazioni Generali di Triesto v. Empress Ass. Corporation Ltd* [1907] 2 K.B. 814; *National Fire Ins. Co. v. McLaren* (1886) 12 O.R. 682; *Baloise Fire Ins. Co. v. Martin* (1937) 2 D.L.R. 24.
[89] *Duus Brown v. Binning* (1906) 11 Com.Cas. 190.
[90] *Netherlands Ins. Co. v. Karl Lijunbgerg & Co.* [1986] 3 All E.R. 767, approving the view expressed in para. 1184 of the 7th edition of this work, while applying a different rationale.
[91] [1965] N.Z.L.R. 874. This case can be distinguished from the *Netherlands Ins. Co.* case on the ground that the court construed the policy as not requiring proceedings to be taken in the absence of an express request. See Birds, [1979] J.B.L. 124, 127–128.
[92] (1874) L.R. 9 Ch.App. 483.
[93] *Yorkshire Ins. Co. Ltd v. Nisbet Shipping Co. Ltd* [1962] 2 Q.B. 330, 341

sum which he originally paid but also the costs of making the recovery. There seems to be little authority on this point and it can clearly be argued that the insurer, by assuming the burden of litigation, assumes liability for all the costs. It is submitted, however, that the costs should be shared by the insurer and insured in accordance with their respective interests.[94] The assured is, in effect, obtaining a windfall and justice requires that he should participate in the costs of obtaining it.

If the insurer recovers any sum beyond the value of his payment to the assured and the costs of the recovery, by exercising the rights of the assured, he is bound to account to the assured for the excess.[95] Except when the subject-matter of the insurance is abandoned to the insurer the problem should not arise in English law. In our law the action and the judgment against the wrongdoer in a case of subrogation are the assured's, and judgment is given in his favour, not the insurer's.

6. Claims against Assured

22–67 Insurer's right of recovery against the assured. This is the second species of right vested in the insurer by the doctrine of subrogation, namely to recover from the assured any benefit received by the assured in extinction or diminution of the loss for which he has been indemnified.[96]

22–68 If the assured recovers any sums from a third party by way of diminution of his loss before the insurer has made any payment, all such sums should be deducted from the sums payable by the insurer.[97] If the insurer makes a payment to the assured not knowing that the assured has made a recovery, he is entitled to any sum in the hands of the assured up to but not beyond the value of his own payment.[98]

If the insured makes a recovery from a third party, after the insurer has made a payment under the policy, the assured can retain what he has recovered until he is fully indemnified,[99] but holds the rest subject to any equitable lien in favour of the insurer[1] up to the value of the insurer's

---

[94] *England v. Guardian Ins. Ltd* [2000] Lloyd's Rep. I.R. 404, 426.

[95] *Lonrho v. E.C.G.D.* [1996] 2 Lloyd's Rep. 649 which decided that the excess is held on trust for the assured.

[96] See para. 22–5, *supra*.

[97] *West of England Fire Ins. Co. v. Isaacs* [1897] 1 Q.B. 226; *Connecticut Fire Ins. Co. v. Erie*, 73 N.Y.App. 399 (1878); if the insurer is sued he can claim a set-off in respect of any such sums received by the assured, see para. 22–19, *supra* and *British Traders Ins. Co. Ltd v. Monson* (1964) A.L.R. 845.

[98] *Castellain v. Preston* (1883) 11 Q.B.D. 380; *Stearns v. Village Main Reef Gold Mining Co. Ltd* (1905) 10 Com.Cas. 89; *Yorkshire Ins. Co. v. Nisbet Shipping Co. Ltd* [1962] 2 Q.B. 330, 341, *per* Diplock J.

[99] But see paras 22–72 *et seq.*, *infra*.

[1] *Napier and Ettrick v. Hunter* [1993] A.C. 713; *White v. Dobinson* (1844) 14 Sim. 273; *Commercial Union Ass. Co. v. Lister* (1874) L.R. 9 Ch.App. 483, 484, *per* Jessel M.R.; *King v. Victoria Ins. Co.* [1896] A.C. 250; *Morley v. Moore* [1936] 2 K.B. 359; *Re Miller, Gibb & Co. Ltd* [1957] 1 W.L.R. 703. There is some conflict whether *ex gratia* payments to the insured of which the insurer is entitled to avail himself (see para. 22–71, *infra*) are also held subject to an equitable lien. An analogous rule applies to recoveries made by the insurer—*Lonrho Exports' Ltd v. Export Credit Guarantee Department* [1996] 2 Lloyd's Rep. 649, 661, where however the monies were recovered pursuant to a treaty and were available for distribution at the Crown's

payment.[2] The assured is, however, entitled to deduct the costs of recovery from the third party before he is obliged to account to the insurer.[3] The insurer cannot recover more than he has himself paid and if the insurer has paid for a total loss but the assured recovers more than the value of the subject-matter insured, he can only be made to reimburse the insurer for his payment and may retain any excess.[4]

22–69 One requirement for the exercise of an equitable lien is that a fund should exist over which the lien can take effect. In *Lord Napier and Ettrick v. Hunter,*[5] the facts of which are summarised below in paragraph 22–74 the monies recovered by the Names at Lloyd's in proceedings against the negligent party had been paid to the names' solicitors. There was thus a fund in existence. In the courts below the House of Lords, the Names had argued that their stop loss insurers could only recover sums to which they were subrogated by an action for money had and received, after the Names had received the money (many of them being outside the jurisdiction) while the stop loss insurers contended that the money recovered and held by the Names' solicitors was held on trust to the extent of their entitlement. Saville J. and the Court of Appeal did not wish to impose the duties of a trustee on the solicitors and held that there was no trust. The House of Lords decided, however, that previous authority supported the intervention of equity but did not require the imposition of a trust since it was sufficient to hold that the damages paid by the third party were subject to an equitable lien or charge in favour of the stop loss insurers. They decided, therefore, to grant an injunction to restrain the solicitors from distributing the proceeds of the third party action to the Names without first paying whatever was due to stop loss insurers by way of subrogation.

22–70 One matter expressly left undecided by *Napier and Ettrick* was whether the equitable lien or charge attaches to any right of action which the insured has against a third party as opposed to attaching only to the proceeds realised by the exercise of such right of action. It is submitted that there should be no lien or charge attaching to the cause of action since that would make it difficult for the third party to know whether he is safe to compromise the claim brought by the insured or even whether he is safe to pay the insured

---

discretion. In *Randal v. Cockran* (1748) 1 Ves. Sen. 98 Lord Hardwicke L.C. said that they were held on trust but in *Stearns v. Village Main Reef Gold Mining Co.* (1905) 10 Com.Cas. 89 Stirling L.J. expressed a contrary view, but that may well have been because there was no defined fund over which the lien could be exercised.

[2] *Darrel v. Tibbits* (1880) 5 Q.B.D. 560; *Horse, Carriage and General Ins. Co. v. Petch* (1916) 33 T.L.R. 131. In *Re Halifax Ins. Co.* (1964) 44 D.L.R. (2d) 339 the same insurer insured both the plaintiff and the wrong-doing third party; the plaintiff recovered a sum from the third party but the insurer was held unable to participate in the recovery because he had represented to the plaintiff, by his conduct in assisting in the settlement of the claim, that he would not seek to recover anything from the plaintiff.

[3] *Assicurazioni Generali di Trieste v. Empress Ass. Co. Ltd* [1907] 2 K.B. 814; *Hatch Mansfield & Co. Ltd v. Weingott* (1906) 22 T.L.R. 366.

[4] *Yorkshire Insurance Co. v. Nisbet Shipping Co.* (1962) 2 Q.B. 330. However, see *Lucas Ltd v. Export Credit Guarantee Department* [1973] 1 W.L.R. 914 where it was held that the parties had agreed for the insurer to have the excess (reversed without discussing the point [1974] 1 W.L.R. 909).

[5] [1993] A.C. 713. Where monies paid into court by third parties became subject to insurers' equitable lien, it was held that the lien took precedence over the statutory charge of the Legal Aid Board attaching to recoveries made by the legally aided claimant assureds, since they did not possess title to the money—*England v. Guardian Ins. Ltd* [2000] Lloyd's Rep. I.R. 404, 415.

in full without also obtaining a discharge from the insurers. Since the insurer has the remedy of suing the third party in his own name if the insured refuses to do so, subject to the requirement of joining the insured as a second defendant to the proceedings,[6] he has sufficient protection from the common law without the need for equitable intervention.

22–71 Gifts to the insured. It is not always easy to decide whether an insurer who has paid under the policy is entitled to any *ex gratia* payments made to the assured. The principle is that if such a payment was made with the intention of reducing or extinguishing the loss against which the insurer was obliged to indemnify the assured, the insurer is entitled to recover what he has paid,[7] but if the payment was made with the intention of benefiting the assured rather than diminishing or extinguishing the loss, the latter can keep the full value of the benefit.[8]

22–72 No recovery pending full indemnity. The general principle is that an assured, who is paid out on his policy and then proceeds to recover from a third partry, is entitled to retain the recovery until he is fully indemnified against his loss. Thus, if a policy provides cover up to, say, £10, 000 and the assured suffers a loss of £25,000 for which he recovers £20,000 from a third party, he can claim £10,000 under the policy, retain £15,000 out of his recovery, and hand over only £5,000 to the insurer.[9]

This principle is no doubt correct in so far as it is applied to cases where the assured's interest was fully covered. It does not take account, however, of cases of partial insurance where problems can be created by the presumption that the parties intend that the assured is to be his own insurer for the amount which is uninsured. In marine insurance contracts the assured is always deemed to be his own insurer in respect of any uninsured part of the risk[10] and, to take the example given above, if the subject-matter of the insurance is worth £50,000 and the amount recoverable under the policy is £10,000, the assured will be presumed to have borne four-fifths of the risk himself. For a total loss he can only recover £10,000. For a partial loss of £30,000 he can only recover £6,000. However, in cases of non-marine insurance there is no such presumption. The assured is not his own insurer for the under-insured property unless there is an average clause in the policy. So if he suffers a partial loss exceeding £10,000 he will always be able to recover £10,000. Most property insurances do contain such a clause,[11] which brings the marine insurance principle into play.

22–73 If these principles are borne in mind, it can be seen that it is not

[6] See para. 22–46, *supra*.
[7] *Randal v. Cockran* (1748) 1 Ves.Sen. 98; *Stearns v. Village Main Reef Gold Mining Co.* (1904) 10 Com.Cas 89. But see *Castellain v. Preston* (1883) 1 1 Q.B.D. 380, 395, *per* Cotton L.J. This principle applies even when the source of payment was a person not strictly liable to the assured, *e.g.* a broker funding a claim by the assured, *Merrett v. Capital Indemnity Corporation* [1991] 1 Lloyds Rep. 169, or a non-adjacent party in a string of contracts, *Colonia Versicherung AG v. Amoco Oil Co.* [1995] 1 Lloyd's Rep. 570, *affirmed.* [1997] 1 Lloyd's Rep. 261.
[8] *Burnand v. Rodocanachi Sons & Co.* (1882) 7 App.Cas. 333.
[9] *Driscoll v. Driscoll* (1918) 1 Ir.R. 152; *National Fire Ins. Co. v. MacLaren* (1886) 12 O.R. 682; *Globe and Rutgers Fire Ins. Co. v. Truedell* [1927] 2 D.L.R. 659; *Scottish Union and National Ins. Co. v. Davis* [1970] 1 Lloyd's Rep. 1; *Commercial Union Ass. Co. v. Lister* (1874) L.R. 9 Ch.App. 483 *arguendo*; Goff and Jones, *Law of Restitution* (5th ed., 1998) pp. 141–142.
[10] See Marine Insurance Act 1906, s.81; Arnould, *Marine Insurance*, 16th ed. (1982) para. 447.
[11] See Ch. 23, s.2, *infra*.

wholly accurate to say that the assured is entitled to keep whatever he recovers from third parties until he has received a full indemnity. If the example given were a case of marine insurance, one would expect that the sum of £20,000 recovered by the assured should be divided between him and the insurer in accordance with their respective interests; the insurer would therefore receive £4,000 and the assured £16,000 out of the proceeds of £20,000. This procedure was in fact adopted in *The Commonwealth*.[12] The fact that the assured has not been fully indemnified in the sense that he has not received full compensation for his loss does not prevent the insurer from claiming his share of the proceeds. It is submitted that the same principle must apply to those cases of non-marine insurance in which there is an average clause in the policy.[13] Where there is no such clause, the assured is entitled to claim the full amount insured and, if this is insufficient to compensate him, he can no doubt retain whatever he recovers from third parties until he has received a full indemnity and need only hand over any excess to the insurer.

22–74 Another case of partial insurance occurs when insurance is given for different layers of risk. In the case of *Lord Napier and Ettrick v. Hunter*[14] stop loss insurers had insured Names at Lloyd's for the amount by which the Names' overall net underwriting loss exceeded a defined "excess" in the policy, and this stop loss insurance was itself subject to a limit. The illustration used for the purpose of argument was a Name who suffered a net underwriting loss of £160,000 and had stop loss for £100,000 excess of £25,000. The stop loss insurer paid the Name £100,000. Subsequently, the Name recovered £130,000, and argued that he need only pay the stop loss insurer £70,000 (being the sum he had received over and above what would be for him a full indemnity) or, in mathematical terms, £230,000 − £160,000. Stop loss insurers argued he had agreed to bear the first £25,000 in any event and he should therefore pay £95,000. The House of Lords held that stop loss insurers' contention was correct because the principle that the insurer cannot recover until the insured is fully indemnified contemplates only an indemnification against the loss actually insured. As Lord Templeman put it "an insured is not entitled to be indemnified against a loss which he has agreed to bear".[15]

22–75 Further difficult problems may arise in connection with valued policies, if the agreed value is less than the true value of the thing insured. In such cases it has been held that the insurers are subrogated to any benefit

---

[12] [1907] P. 216; *Napier and Ettrick v. Kershaw*, [1993] 1 Lloyd's Rep. 10, 23, *per* Staughton L.J. It seems that this result will not apply in cases of aviation insurance, *Kuwait Airways Cpn v. Kuwait Ins. Co.* [1996] 1 Lloyd's Rep. 664, 694–5 [1997] 2 Lloyd's Rep. 687, 697.

[13] There was no indication in the cases cited at note 7 above that the policies contained an average clause. Most property insurance policies nowadays do contain one.

[14] [1993] A.C. 713.

[15] At page 731E. The result in layer insurance can be summarised by the phrase that the layer insurers "pay up and recover down", see, *per* Staughton L.J. at [1993] 1 Lloyd's Rep. 10, 24. It seems to follow that in the simple case of a policy containing a deductible, the assured cannot apply a recovery to the amount of the deductible until the insurer is fully indemnified for the amount of the insured loss. This is an important exception to the general rule in para. 22–72, *supra*.

received by the assured which diminishes the loss up to the amount of their payment, although the assured has not in fact received a full indemnity.[16]

7. APPLICATION TO PARTICULAR CASES

22-76 Carriers and bailees. When goods which have been insured by their owner are lost or damaged, the insurers on payment are subrogated to the owner's remedy against any carrier, warehouseman or other bailee responsible for the safety of the goods,[17] and they are entitled to recover the whole loss from the carrier or bailee who is liable to the owner irrespective of the extent of their liability to the insured.[18] A common carrier is absolutely responsible for goods in his possession and is commonly called an insurer of the goods; but he is not an insurer in the strict sense of the word and cannot claim contribution from the insurers.[19] The owner's insurers are only deprived of their right of subrogation when they have in fact insured both owner and bailee[20] or where the owner has contracted that the bailee shall not be liable for loss.[21] A bailee can exempt himself from liability for negligence provided he does so in express terms but general words of exclusion will be presumed not to exclude negligence on the part of the bailee if there is any other liability on his part to which the excluding words can apply.[22] If there are two recognised rates of carriage, it may be held that carriage at the cheaper rate will entail no liability for negligence on the part of the carrier and in a case where the goods-owner insured his goods under a policy expressed to be "without recourse to lightermen" it was held that underwriters were precluded from recovering in the name of their assured against the lightermen.[23] Where a bailee has contracted to insure for the benefit of the bailor but has omitted to do so, he is liable in the case of loss by fire to pay damages for breach of contract amounting to the sum which the bailor would have recovered on the policy if it had been effected.[24]

22-77 Rights of the carrier's or bailee's insurers. Since insurers are subrogated to the rights of those whom they have contracted to indemnify, they cannot, in the absence of express provision in the policy, be subrogated to the rights of a mere payee who is entitled to receive the money but whose

---

[16] An example is *Goole & Hull Steam Towing Co. v. Ocean Marine Ins. Co.* [1928] 1 K.B. 589. Valued policies are almost entirely confined to the field of marine insurance. For discussion of the much criticised cases in which this principle was laid down, see Arnould, *Marine Insurance*, Vol. 10, British Shipping Laws, Ch. 30, paras 1217–1221.

[17] *North British and Mercantial Ins. Co. v. London Liverpool and Globe Ins. Co.* (1877) 5 Ch.D. 569; *Hall and Long v. Railroad Companies*, 13 Wall. 367 (1871).

[18] *Mobile and Montgomery Ry. Co. v. Jurey*, 111 U.S. 584 (1883).

[19] *Hall and Long v. Railroad Companies*, 13 Wall. 367 (1871).

[20] *Wager v. Providence Insce. Co*, 150 U.S. 99 (1893). In the "*Surf City*" [1995] 2 Lloyds Rep. 242 a waiver of subrogation clause in the contract between insurer and c.i.f. seller was held to enure to the benefit of the carrier. Problems of privity were circumvented by a concession made by the subrogated cargo insurers. See para. 20–64 *ante*.

[21] See para. 22–33, *supra*; *Thomas & Co. v. Brown* (1899) 4 Com.Cas. 186; *Phoenix Ins. Co. v. Erie and Western Transportation Co.*, 117 U.S. 312 (1886).

[21] *Rutter v. Palmer* [1922] 2 K.B. 87; *Alderslade v. Hendon Laundry* [1945] K.B. 189.

[23] *Thomas & Co. v. Brown* (1899) 4 Com.Cas. 186.

[24] *Ex p. Bateman* (1856) 8 De G.M. & G. 263.

interest is not separately insured.[25] Such a payee may, however, effectively possess cover under the policy, and one case is where a carrier takes out a "goods in transit" policy which covers the full value of the goods. It is settled law that a bailee, such as a carrier, has an insurable interest in the full value of the goods and that any sum which he recovers from the insurer in excess of his own loss (if any) is held by him for the owner of the goods.[26] But it has never been considered whether the insurer, on payment of a loss to the carrier, is subrogated to the rights of the goods-owner after he has received the insurance money from the carrier. This may be a problem which will not often arise in practice, because the carrier will usually possess a right of suit against a wrong-doing third party and these rights can then be exercised by the insurers in the carrier's name; but such rights may be defeated by an exclusion clause in a contract or for some other reason, and it will then be important to know if the insurer can exercise the rights of the goods-owner.[27]

22–78 If it is correct that an insurer is subrogated only to the rights of parties to the contract of insurance who have a right to payment under the policy, it follows that the insurer will be subrogated to the rights of a goods-owner only where that owner was himself an assured because the carrier specifically effected the cover on behalf of the goods-owner as his agent. In the usual case, however, the carrier will have effected the policy before the goods are entrusted to him and cannot be said to have acted as the goods-owners' agent. In practice the bailor will not be aware of the policy until after the loss. Quite apart from the difficulties attendant on ratification after loss,[28] he will not normally be entitled to sue on the policy as the bailee's undisclosed principal.[29]

22–79 In such a case, the orthodox view is that because the goods-owner cannot directly enforce the contract of insurance against the insurer, there being no privity of contract, the insurer likewise cannot exercise rights of subrogation in his name. It might be argued, however, that the law, by allowing the carrier to claim an indemnity for the benefit of the goods-owner and by obliging the carrier to account to the goods-owner for his successful recovery, is sanctioning an exception to the doctrine of privity of contract, so that the insurer is, however indirectly, obliged to indemnify the goods owner. If that is correct, it could be said that on equitable grounds an insurer should be permitted to sue in the name of the goods-owner who can in this manner claim an indemnity from him, especially as the insurers' rights of subrogation, to some extent, derive from equitable principles.[30] However, the so-called obligation of the insurer towards the goods-owner has never been upheld in a situation where the carrier refuses to claim the insurance money for the latter's benefit or where the goods-owner wishes to make a direct recovery under the policy. Although it has been said *obiter* that the

---

[25] *Wager v. Providence Ins. Co.* 150 U.S. 99 (1893). The contract may expressly provide for insurers to be subrogated to the rights of a third party to whom payment is to be made—see, *e.g. Anderson v. Saugeen Mutual Fire Ins. Co.* (1889) 18 Ont.R. 355, 359, 367–368.

[26] *Tomlinson (Hauliers) Ltd v. Hepburn* [1966] A.C. 451.

[27] See *Morris v. C. W. Marten & Sons* [1966] 1 Q.B. 716.

[28] See para. 1–184, *ante* and para. 36–14, *post.*

[29] See the discussion at paras. 20–26 to 20–28, *supra.*

[30] See para. 22–23, *supra.*

goods-owner is entitled to claim the value of his goods from the insurer,[31] it has never been spelled out what form his action should take and such statements have been doubted in the Court of Appeal.[32] It would be wrong to assume that, because the policy moneys are impressed with a charge in favour of the goods-owner once they are received by the carrier, the goods-owner possesses any direct action against the insurer.[33]

22–80 Negligence of assured or his servants. If the assured would be disentitled to claim from a third party by reason of his own negligence or that of his servants, the insurer is in no better position and will fail in any claim brought against that third party in the name of the assured.[34]

If the assured is rendered liable as a result of his servant's negligence, the servant may be in breach of his contractual duty to perform his service with reasonable care and skill; although an employer might well not wish to sue his employee for breach of contract in such a situation, there is no doubt that he has the right to do so and to this right the insurer can, in theory, be subrogated. Thus in *Lister v. Romford Ice and Cold Storage Co.*[35] a father and son were both employed by the respondent company. The son negligently injured the father while driving a vehicle on company business and the father recovered damages from the company as vicariously liable for the son's negligence. The company then sued the son as a joint tortfeasor and for breach of his contract of service and the House of Lords held that the company was entitled to recover. In the absence of special circumstances, it was said that there was no implied term in a contract of service that the master would indemnify the servant against claims arising out of acts done in the course of his employment or that the servant would receive the benefit of any contract of insurance taken out by the master.

22–81 This decision created problems because liability insurers were, in effect, held entitled to require the use of an employer's name (by virtue of their rights or subrogation) to sue the employer's own servants. If employers, or insurers in the employers' name, were to sue their own servants in such circumstances, good industrial relations would be in constant peril. Accordingly, members of the British Insurance Association entered as a "gentleman's agreement" in the following terms:

> "Employers' Liability Insurers agree that they will not institute a claim against the employee of an insured employer in respect of the death of or injury to a fellow-employee unless the weight of evidence clearly

---

[31] *Re King* [1963] Ch. 459, 491, *per* Upjohn L.J., and at p. 499, *per* Diplock L.J. who referred to agency in more guarded words.

[32] *D.G. Finance Ltd v. Scott* [1999] Lloyd's Rep. I.R. 387.

[33] *D.G. Finance Ltd v. Scott, supra,* applying *Tomlinson (Hauliers) Ltd v. Hepburn* [1966] A.C. 451, *Re Dibbens* [1990] B.C.L.C. 577, and *The "Albazero"* [1977] A.C. 774, 845. The better view today, it is submitted, is that the goods-owner possesses a statutory right to enforce the bailee's insurance under section 1 of the Contracts (Rights of Third Parties) Act 1999—see para. 20–63, *ante.*

[34] See *Simpson v. Thomson* (1877) 3 App.Cas. 279; but in *Williams v. Hays* (1892) 64 Hun. 202 where one insurer insured two part-owners of a vessel and a loss occurred through the negligence of one, the insurer was held to be subrogated to the claim of the other part-owner and could recover what he had paid to him from the negligent part owner. *Cf. Eagle Star Ins. Co. v. Bean* 134 F. 2d 755 (1934).

[35] [1957] A.C. 555.

indicates (i) collusion, or (ii) wilful misconduct on the part of the employee against whom a claim is made."[36]

This agreement has effectively negatived *Lister's* case as far as insurance claims are concerned.

It has also had a surprising influence in a situation where insurers were not concerned. In *Morris v. Ford Motor Co.*[37] the plaintiff was employed by a firm of cleaners at Fords' car factory. The cleaners' contract with Fords contained a clause indemnifying Fords in respect of any liability for the negligence of their (Fords') servants or agents. The plaintiff was injured as a result of the negligence of one of Fords' servants and brought an action against Fords who claimed against the cleaners under their indemnity clause. The cleaners, on general principles of subrogation, sought to use Fords' name to sue the servant who had injured the plaintiff. This was a situation where rights of subrogation could arise once the cleaners indemnified Fords and one would have expected that, on the authority of *Lister's* case, the cleaners would have been held entitled to use Fords' name to sue the negligent servant. The Court of Appeal, however, decided that the cleaners were not so entitled. Lord Denning M.R. stated that it was not just or equitable for Fords to be compelled against their will to sue their own servant and that, since the doctrine of subrogation was a creature of equity, it could not be used for inequitable purposes. James L.J. preferred to rest his decision on the view that there was an implied term in the contract of indemnity that the cleaners should not have any rights of subrogation. Both judges relied on the fact that liability insurers had agreed not to exercise their rights under *Lister's* case and clearly thought that it would be anomalous if other persons could avail themselves of rights which insurers had expressly disavowed.

22–82 It is difficult to avoid the conclusion that the result of this case is directly contrary to the decision in *Lister's* case and the dissenting judgment of Stamp L.J. is particularly persuasive. There is no doubt that *Lister's* case can, in theory, give rise to awkward situations but, once the doctrine of subrogation is applied at all, the conclusion reached by the House of Lords is inescapable. Any mitigation of the potential hardships should be a matter for legislation in the context of industrial relations as a whole, rather than a matter dealt with piecemeal by the courts.

22–83 Rights of vendor against purchaser. The right of an insurer to be subrogated is not confined to claims which the insured may make in respect of the loss, but extends to all claims which, if satisfied, will diminish the loss.[38] In *Castellain v. Preston,*[39] the owner of a house contracted to sell his house which he had already insured. Before completion of the purchase, the house was destroyed by fire. The insurance company paid the vendor the amount of the loss and the purchase was subsequently completed with the result that the vendor received the full contract price from the purchaser. It was held that the insurers were entitled to recover the sum paid to their insured, the

---

[36] *Morris v. Ford Motor Co.* [1973] Q.B. 792, 799, 814, 847 and 861.
[37] [1973] 1 Q.B. 792.
[38] See para. 22–5, *supra.*
[39] (1883) 11 Q.B.D. 380; *cf. Hoffman v. Calgary Fire Ins. Co.* (1909) 2 Alta.L.R. 1 and *Phoenix Ass. Co. v. Spooner* [1905] 2 K.B. 753 which applied the same principle to a case of compulsory purchase.

vendor; the insurers were even entitled to exercise the vendor's lien as against the purchaser to enforce payment. Brett L.J. expressed himself in the widest possible way:

"It seems to me that to carry out the fundamental rule of insurance law this doctrine of subrogation must be carried to the extent which I am now about to endeavour to express, namely, that as between the underwriter and the assured the underwriter is entitled to the advantage of every right of the assured, whether such right consists in contract fulfilled or unfulfilled, or in a remedy for tort capable of being insisted on or already insisted on, or in any other right, whether by way of condition or otherwise, legal or equitable, which can be or has been exercised or has accrued, and whether such right could or could not be enforced by the insurer in the name of the assured, by the exercising or acquiring of which right or condition the loss against which the assured is insured can be or has been diminished. That seems to me to put this doctrine of subrogation in the largest possible form and if in that form, large as it is, it is short of fulfilling that which is the fundamental condition, I must have omitted to state something which ought to have been stated."[40]

The fundamental condition referred to by Brett L.J. in the above passage is that the contract of insurance is one of indemnity and indemnity only, and it is upon that alone that he bases the right of subrogation.

22–84 The Court of Appeal doubted whether the vendor's insurers could bring a suit for specific performance in the name of the vendor, but on general principles there seems to be no reason why they should not be entitled to exercise that right, which might be their only chance of obtaining repayment. There is, however, no subrogation to the vendor's claim for the purchase money where the vendor has contracted with the purchaser that he shall have the benefit of his insurance,[41] or where the policy does in fact insure both vendor and purchaser.[42] Moreover, a question arises as to the effect of section 47 of the Law of Property Act 1925 which enacts that in certain circumstances insurance money becoming payable to the vendor after the contract is held by the vendor to the purchaser's use. It would probably be held that, if the section applies, there are no rights of subrogation, but in so far as the qualifications to section 47 apply and the right so given to the purchaser is taken away by the terms of his contract or by the absence of the necessary consent, it is submitted that the principles stated remain valid.

22–85 Separate insurance on conflicting interests. Where each of two parties interested in property has insured separately in respect of his own

---

[40] (1883) 11 Q.B.D 380, 388.

[41] *Washington Fire Ins. Co. v. Kelly*, 32 Md. 421, 455–458 (1870). (This may be the explanation of *Hoffman v. Calgary Fire Ins. Co.* (1909) 2 Alta.L.R. 1.)

[42] *Benjamin v. Saratoga County Mutual Fire Ins. Co.*, 17 N.Y. 415 (1858). American cases are not necessarily reliable in connection with rights of subrogation arising from contracts of sale of property since it has been held in some jurisdictions that no such right exists. A distinction is taken between insuring the receipt of the purchase money and insuring the property; in the latter case it is said there is no subrogation because there is no claim arising out of the loss. Compare *Ins. Co. v. Updegraff*, 21 Pa. 513 (1853); *Washington Fire Ins. Co. v. Kelly*, 32 Md. 421, 443, 458 (1870) and *Aetna Fire Ins. Co. v. Tyler*, 16 Wend. 385, 399 (1836).

interest, the effect of the doctrine of subrogation may be to throw the whole of the loss on one insurer. Thus in *North British and Mercantile Insurance Co. v. London, Liverpool and Globe Insurance Co.*[43] B & Co., who were wharfingers, held grain belonging to R and Co. and by the custom of the trade the wharfingers were liable for loss, however it occurred. Each firm insured the grain for its own benefit and when a loss occurred it was held that the insurers of R and Co., upon paying the loss, were entitled to be subrogated to the claim of their insured against B & Co. The result was that, in spite of the *pro rata* conditions in the insurance policies, B & Co.'s insurers bore the whole loss. Similarly in *Andrews v. Patriotic Assce Co.*[44] where a landlord and his tenant had insured independently, the court was of opinion that the landlord's insurers could, by subrogation to the landlord's claim under the covenant to repair, recover the loss against the tenant, so that the tenant's insurers would ultimately bear the whole loss.

22–86 Subrogation to debt and security of mortgagee. When property is lost which is subject to a mortgage and is insured by the mortgagee and the insurer pays the amount of the loss to the mortgagee, the question arises whether he is subrogated to the rights of the mortgagee to the security and the payment of his debt. There is no English authority directly in point and American cases are in conflict,[45] but the decisions which deny the right of subrogation to the insurer seem to be based on the theory that the insurer is only subrogated to the rights of the insured to recover satisfaction for the loss.[46] The current of modern American authority does not accept this theory[47] and for English law *Castellain v. Preston*[48] has decided that the right of subrogation is not limited to the right of the insured to recover satisfaction, but includes all rights of the insured which will diminish the loss. The right of a mortgagee to payment of the secured debt is such a right and, on principle, the mortgagee's insurer is prima facie entitled to be subrogated to the mortgagee's right against the mortgagor.[49]

22–87 In *North British and Mercantile Insurance Co. v. London, Liverpool and Globe Insurance Co.*[50] Mellish L.J. stated that, where two persons are interested in the same property to the full value, each is entitled to insure and recover the full value from their respective insurers and he cites the case of mortgagor and mortgagee as an illustration of that principle; but in order that the insurers may not ultimately pay more than the total value of the property between them, one of them must be subrogated to the right of their insured against the other party interested in the property. In *Glasgow*

---

[43] (1877) 5 Ch. D. 569.
[44] (1886) 18 L.R. Ir. 355.
[45] *King v. State Mutual Fire Ins. Co.*, 61 Mass. 1 (1851); *Suffolk Fire Ins. Co. v. Boyden*, 91 Mass. 123 (1864) (denying the right of subrogation); *Carpenter v. Providence Washington Ins. Co.*, 41 U.S. 16 Pet. 495, 501 (1842); *Excelsior Fire Ins. Co. v. The Royal Ins. Co. of Liverpool*, 55 N.Y. 343, 359 (1873) (accepting the right).
[46] *Provincial Ins. Co. v. Reesor* (1874) 21 Grant Ch. U.C. 296 (the mortgagee insures "not the debt but the buildings" *per* Blake V.-C.).
[47] See, *e.g. Gainsville National Bank v. Martin*, 1 S.E. 2d 636 (1939); *Noble v. Equity fire Ins. Co.*, 297 N.W. 349 (1941).
[48] (1883) 11 Q.B.D. 380.
[49] See *Samuel & Co. v. Dumas* [1924] A.C. 431, 445, *per* Lord Cave; *Woolwich Building Society v. Brown*, [1996] C.L.C. 625 (mortgage indemnity insurance).
[50] (1877) 5 Ch.D. 569; *cf. Holmes and Bell v. National Fire Ins. Co.* (1887) 5 N.Z.L.R.(S.C.) 360.

Provident Investment Society v. Westminster Fire Office,[51] the majority of the consulted judges in the Court of Session expressed the opinion that, when a bondholder's insurers paid for a loss the bondholder was bound to assign to them his rights against the debtor.

22–88 The right of subrogation in the case of a mortgagee's insurance depends partly on the terms of the mortgage and partly on the terms of the insurance policy. There can be no subrogation in the following circumstances:

(1) where the mortgagee is merely payee of the insurance money payable upon the interest of the mortgagor, and is not separately insured in respect of his own interest[52];

(2) where the mortgagee is insured in respect of his own interest but the insurers have also agreed to indemnify the mortgagor as well as the mortgagee and such agreement is enforceable by the mortgagor;

(3) where the mortgagee has contracted to insure the mortgagor or to give him the benefit of his insurance by applying the insurance money in reduction of the mortgage debt.

22–89 Policy insuring mortgagor's interest. If a mortgagor takes out a policy of insurance or if a mortgagee takes out a policy on the mortgagor's behalf, the insurer is prima facie under an obligation to make payment in case of loss to the mortgagor. Many such policies expressly provide that payment is to be made to "the mortgagee in case of loss" but such a provision will not convert the policy to an insurance of the mortgagee's interest[53] and accordingly the insurer will not be subrogated to the rights of the mortgagee[54] The mortgagee is merely in the position of having a charge on the mortgagor's policy.[55] Payment to the mortgagee prima facie extinguishes the debt *pro tanto*, and if the payment exceeds the debt the mortgagee will hold the balance in trust for the mortgagor.[56]

A policy "payable to mortgagee in case of loss" often contains a condition that the mortgagee's right shall not be affected by acts or deeds of the mortgagor; this probably does not make the policy a separate insurance of the mortgagee on his own interest, but is only an agreement to pay upon the mortgagor's interest without reference to any conduct of the mortgagor which, as between him and the insurer, might invalidate the policy[57] If this is

---

[51] (1887) 14 R. 947, 966; affirmed without reference to this point (1883) 13 App.Cas. 699.

[52] See para. 22–89, *infra*.

[53] *Livingstone v. Western Ins. Co.* (1869) 16 Gr.Ch.U.C. 9; *Anderson v. Saugeen Mutual Fire Ins. Co.* (1889) 18 Ont.R. 355, 366–367, *per* Ferguson J. But see *Hastings v. Westchester Fire Ins. Co.*, 73 N.Y. 141 (1878). For a discussion of the question of whose interest is insured compare *Graham Joint Stock Stock Shipping Co. v. Merchants Marine Ins. Co.* [1924] A.C. 294 and *P. Samuel & Co. Ltd v. Dumas* [1924] A.C. 431.

[54] *Imperial Fire Ins. Co. v. Bull* (1889) 18 Can.S.C. 697; *Klein v. Union Fire Ins. Co.* (1883) 3 Ont.R. 234. Both those cases show that there is no subrogation even if the insurer stipulates for it from the mortgagee.

[55] See para. 20–41, *ante*.

[56] *Graves v. Hampden Fire Ins. Co.* 92 Mass. 281 (1865). But when the mortgagor wilfully burned the premises and the insurers voluntarily paid the loss to the mortgagee and took an assignment of the mortgage, it has been held that they could enforce the whole debt against the mortgagor without giving credit for the sum paid to the mortgagee, *Westmacott v. Hanley* (1875) 22 Gr.Ch.U.C.

[57] *Anderson v. Saugeen Mutual Fire Ins. Co.* (1889) 18 Ont.R. 355, 367; but see *Hastings v. Westchester Fire Ins. Co.*, 73 N.Y. 141 (1878).

the case, there will be no subrogation on payment to the mortgagee unless it is expressly provided for in the policy.[58] The ordinary form of mortgage clause does so provide and runs somewhat on the following lines:

> "It is agreed that whenever this company shall pay the mortgagee any sum for loss under this policy, and shall claim that, as to the mortgagor or owner no liability therefor exists, it shall at once and to the extent of such payment, be legally subrogated to all the rights of the party to whom such payments shall be made, . . . and if required to do so by this company, the mortgagee shall execute an assignment to the extent of such payment."

In *Anderson v. Saugeen Mutual Fire Insce. Co.*[59] the policy contained the mortgage clause in the above terms and also a clause making proofs of loss by the owner a condition of recovery. Since proofs of loss had not been delivered, the company claimed that they were under no liability to the mortgagor and were therefore subrogated to the rights of the mortgagee on payment of the loss to him. It was held, however, that the proofs of loss were a condition precedent to action but not a condition precedent to liability and that, although the mortgagor could not sue on the policy, there was a subsisting liability to him and therefore the company was not entitled to be subrogated to the rights of the mortgagee.

22–90   Assignment of policy to mortgagee. If the mortgagor assigns absolutely his policy to the mortgagee with the consent of the insurer, the policy becomes prima facie an insurance of the mortgagee on his own interest. The mortgagor ceases to be the insured and consequently the insurers on payment to the mortgagee are subrogated to his rights against the mortgagor.[60]

22–91   Policy insuring mortgagee's interest. If a policy is granted to a mortgagee in his own name it may be intended to cover both his own and the mortgagor's interests or only his own interest. If the policy is intended to insure the mortgagee only, or if the mortgagor is not named and not an assured, the right of subrogation will arise on payment to the mortgagee,[61] unless the mortgagee has agreed to insure for the benefit of the mortgagor or to apply the insurance money in discharge of the debt. If such an agreement has been made, there is no claim open to the mortgagee against the mortgagor to which the insurer can be subrogated. Where, however, a mortgagee insures his own interest on his own behalf without any obligation

---

[58] *Allen v. Watertown Fire Ins. Co.*, 132, Mass. 480 (1882).

[59] (1889) 18 Ont.R. 355. For other cases on the clause, see *Phoenix Ins. Co. of Brooklyn*, 19 Hun. 287 (1879) (if mortgagor has insured elsewhere and, as against him, the insurer is only liable to pay a rateable proportion of the loss, on payment of the whole loss to the mortgagee he is entitled to be subrogated to recover the difference between the sum which would have been payable to him to the mortgagor and the sum in fact paid to the mortgagee); *Eddy v. London Ins. Corporation*, 64 Hun. 307 (1892) (where the amount paid by the insurer to the mortgagee was insufficient to extinguish the mortgage debt, the insurer was not entitled to rank *pari passu* with the mortgagee, but the mortgagee was entitled to repayment of his debt in full before the insurer could proceed for any benefit from the debt or the securities); *Attleborough Savings Bank v. Security Ins. Co.*, 168 Mass. 147 (1897) (if the mortgagee releases any of the securities for the debt before payment and thus cannot comply with the mortgage clause, the insurer is discharged from liability).

[60] *Burton v. Gore District Mutual Fire Ins. Co.* (1865) 12 Gr.Ch.U.C. 156.

[61] *Woolwich Building Society v. Brown* [1996] C.L.C. 625.

to the mortgagor, he may not, at common law, include the premiums in the mortgage debt[62] and therefore he is not bound to account to the mortgagor for any insurance money received by him; not only can he retain the insurance money but he may also recover the whole debt from the mortgagor.[63]

If a mortgage contains a covenant by the mortgagor to insure and, failing such insurance, empowers the mortgagee to insure and add the premium to the debt and the mortgagee accordingly insures in his own name and charges the premiums to the mortgagor, such insurance may be held to have been made for the benefit of both mortgagor and mortgagee and the mortgagee would be bound to apply the insurance money in discharge of the debt.[64] But the mortgagee is not bound to insure for the benefit of both and he can expressly insure his own interest only and provide that on payment the insurer shall be subrogated to his rights under the mortgage.[65]

22–92 Separate insurances. If mortgagor and mortgagee insure independently in different offices, each on his own interest, each is entitled to a full indemnity up to the value of his interest which may be in each case the total value of the property.

If the mortgagee has agreed to apply his insurance money towards the extinction of the debt, this is a benefit accruing to the mortgagor and is therefore available to the mortgagor's insurers. In a case where the mortgagee insures for the amount of his debt and the mortgagor for the full value of the property, the ultimate result will be that the mortgagee's insurers pay the amount of the debt and the mortgagor's insurers the difference between that amount and the total loss, if the latter exceeds the former. But if the mortgagee is not bound to apply his insurance money towards the extinction of the debt, he or his insurers in his name can enforce payment and the ultimate result will be that the mortgagor's insurers will pay the total loss. In these cases the policies are effected on different interests and there is, therefore, no double insurance and no place for the application of the *pro rata* clause.

A more difficult case arises when the mortgagee has insured for the full value of the property and for the benefit of both mortgagor and mortgagee, and at the same time the mortgagor has insured in another office for the full value and solely for his own benefit. Here, as far as the mortgagor is concerned, there is a double insurance and each office is prima facie liable to him for half the loss. But the mortgagor is entitled to demand that the mortgagee shall apply the whole of the insurance money in reduction of the debt. The mortgagor's insurers are entitled to this benefit and therefore the ultimate result should be that, notwithstanding any *pro rata* clause, the mortgagee's insurers bear the total loss. The facts in *Nichols & Co. v. Scottish Union*[66] presented in substance the above problem but the question of

---

[62] *Dobson v. Land* (1850) 8 Hare 216. See a note on this case in (1851) 61 Mass. at p. 14. For the current position under the Law of Property Act 1925, see para. 20–31, *ante*.

[63] In such a case, the insurer would be able to recover the amount he has paid, *cf. Excelsior Fire Ins. Co. v. The Royal Ins. Co. of Liverpool*, 55 N.Y. 343, 359 (1873).

[64] *Howes v. Dominion Fire and Marine Ins. Co.* (1883) 8 Ont.A.R. 644; *Provincial Ins. Co. v. Reesor* (1874) 21 Gr.Ch.U.C. 296

[65] *Foster v. Van Reed*, 70 N.Y. 19 (1877). The mortgagee's insurers will usually be subrogated to other claims of the mortgagee, *e.g.* against negligent valuers *Europe Mortgage Co. v. Halifax Estate Agencies, The Times*, May 23, 1996.

[66] (1885) 2 T.L.R. 190; 14 R. 1094; *cf.* para. 23–12, *post*.

subrogation was not discussed or decided. The mortgagor claimed against his insurers and it was held that there was double insurance since his interest was also insured by the mortgagee's policy and that under the *pro rata* clause he could only recover half the loss from his insurers. Although it is not clear that the mortgagee's policy did in fact insure the mortgagor, the mortgagee was bound to apply the insurance money in reduction of the debt and it is therefore submitted that the ultimate result ought to have been that the mortgagee's insurers bore the whole loss.

22–93 Landlord and tenant. The insurers of a landlord and a tenant are entitled to subrogation and the ultimate loss falls upon the insurer of the party who would have borne it if there had been no insurance. Thus the insurer of a landlord is entitled after payment to the benefit of the tenant's covenant to repair or reinstate,[67] or if the tenant has reinstated the premises the landlord must account to his insurer for the value of the reinstatement.[68] Accordingly, when a tenant settled a claim for breach of repairing covenants brought by his lessor on terms that he would not make any claim in respect of the lessor's covenant to lay out insurance monies on rebuilding, the tenant's insurers, having paid him in respect of fire damage to the demised premises, were entitled to recover from the tenant the value of the claim against the lessor of which they has been deprived by his settlement.[69] Rights of subrogation may, however, be excluded by the terms of the particular lease. In *Mark Rowlands Ltd v. Berni Inns Ltd*[70] the lease provided that the lessor would insure the building against fire and lay out the insurance monies to rebuild it, while the tenant was to contribute to the cost of the premium by an "insurance rent" and was relieved from its repairing obligations in the event of damage by fire. There was a fire caused by the tenant's negligence. The lessor reinstated the building with monies received from its insurers. These insurers then sought to exercise their right of subrogation to sue the tenant for negligence in the name of the lessor. It was held that they could not do so, because the lessor did not possess the right to bring such a claim. The insurance had been effected for the benefit of the tenant as well as of the lessor[71] and, following Canadian authority,[72] the terms of the lease signified an intention to exclude the tenant's liability in the event of fire and to leave the lessor to recoup its loss out of the proceeds of the insurance for which the tenant had in part paid the premium.

That a bare covenant by the landlord to insure the building does not raise a presumption that the insurance is intended to be for the benefit and relief of both parties is illustrated by *Lambert v. Keymood Ltd.*[73] Here the lease contained merely a bare covenant by the landlord to insure the demised premises and lacked the additional terms which persuaded the Court in *Mark Rowlands* that the insurance was intended to provide an indemnity to

---

[67] *Re King* [1963] Ch. 459, 499–500, *per* Diplock L.J.; *Andrews v. Patriotic Assurance Co. of Ireland* (1886) 18 L.R. Ir. 355.

[68] *Darrell v. Tibbits* (1880) 5 Q.B.D. 560.

[69] *West of England Fire Ins. Co. v. Isaacs* [1897] 1 Q.B. 226.

[70] [1986] Q.B. 211; followed in *Barras v. Hamilton* 1994 S.L.T. 949.

[71] The tenant was not a co-insured.

[72] In particular *T. Easton Co. Ltd v. Smith* (1977) 92 D.L.R. 3d 425; *Greenwood Shopping Plaza Ltd v. Neil J. Buchanan Ltd* (1979) 99 D.L.R. (3d) 289. Although the Court of Appeal did not think it essential that the insurance was effected for the tenant's benefit—[1986] Q.B. 211, 225—it seems that this was a material part of the reasoning of the Canadian courts.

[73] [1999] Lloyd's Rep. I.R. 80.

satisfy both parties' loss, notably a requirement that the tenant should contribute to the cost of insurance, a provision relieving the tenant from his repairing obligations in the event of damage to the building by fire and an express obligation on the landlord's part to apply the insurance monies in reinstatement after a fire. The earlier decision was accordingly distinguished. Presumably where the tenant has his own insurance, his insurers will be subrogated to the benefit of the landlord's covenant to insure and apply the proceeds to reinstatement.

22–94 Reinsurers. Reinsurers are entitled to be subrogated to all the rights of the original insurers, including the rights of the assured to which the original insurers are subrogated.[74]

22–95 Guarantee policy. In the case of a guarantee policy which is a contract of insurance and not of suretyship, the insurers on paying the debt to the insured creditor, are entitled to be subrogated to his claims against the debtor and sureties and the insurers and sureties are not co-sureties of one another.[75] The insurers may thus recover the whole debt from the sureties in the name of the creditor.

22–96 Mortgage indemnity insurance or guarantee. It is common for lenders against the security of real property to insure against loss which they will suffer if the borrower defaults and the value of the property falls short of the outstanding mortgage debt. The borrower pays the premium, although the cover is for the relief of the lender. In *Bristol Building Society v. May May & Merrimans*[76] these arrangements had been made in circumstances where the lender had a claim for breach of fiduciary duty against the solicitors who had acted for it and who had been held liable in damages for the whole amount of its loss on certain transactions. The issue before the court was one of measure of damages. The solicitors argued that they should be given credit for money received by the lender under its mortgage indemnity insurance, because otherwise the lender would benefit from a double recovery and because they would be exposed to the risk of double jeopardy, namely having to pay both the lender and the insurers, the latter possibly having a direct action for damages in their own right and not by way of subrogation. The first argument was based on the fact that the lender had compromised its claim against the insurers on terms which excluded any liability to account to them for recoveries, and which was said to take the case outside the rule that a defendant cannot benefit from the fact that the claimant is insured.[77] This argument failed on the ground that the compromise was a commercial deal whereby the lender accepted less than its claim and gave up its demand to retain certain types of recovery in return for being allowed to retain others. The second argument succeeded to the extent that the court stayed enforcement of the judgment against the solicitors to enable them to join the insurers to the proceedings in order to decide whether they were liable to pay damages to the insurers.

---

[74] *Assicurazioni Generali de Trieste v. Empress Ass. Co. Ltd* [1907] 2 K.B. 814; *The Ocean Wave*, 5 Biss. 378 (1873).

[75] *Parr's Bank Ltd v. Albert Mines Syndicate Ltd* (1900) 5 Com.Cas. 116.

[76] [1998] 1 W.L.R. 336, approved in *Arab Bank Plc v. John D Wood Commercial Ltd* [2000] Lloyd's Rep. I.R. 471, 498–499.

[77] For this rule see para. 22–2, *supra*.

22–97 Insurance in joint names. If an insurance is taken out in joint names by two or more parties for their respective rights and interests and the subject-matter of the insurance is damaged or lost by the actionable fault of one or other party, the insurer may wish to pay the "innocent" party and then claim to be subrogated to his right of action against the "guilty" party. For example, a landlord and tenant may insure and the house be burnt down, so that the insurers wish to enforce the landlord's covenant to repair. A mortgagor and mortgagee may insure as co-assureds and the insurer may wish to be subrogated to the mortgagee's claim to repayment of the advance. Again, an employer, a head contractor and sub-contractors all engaged upon a single construction project may be co-assureds on a policy insuring their respective interests in the contract works, and the insurer who pays for damage to the works caused by a sub-contractor may wish then to claim damages from that party through a subrogated action in the name of the employer or head contractor. The insurer's attempt to claim against one co-assured in the name of another will usually fail for one of two reasons. Either the insurance policy itself may well contain a bar to the claim or the underlying agreement between the parties, pursuant to which the insurance is effected, may expressly or impliedly deprive the "innocent" party from taking action against the potential defendant for the loss or damage in question.

22–98 The insurance policy—express waiver. The first possibility is that the policy contains an express waiver of subrogation clause by which the insurers relinquish their rights to seek reimbursement from named parties or a category of co-assureds. The waiver may be in unqualified terms or it may be limited to particular types of losses.[78] The insurer may even waive the exercise of rights of subrogation against a third party not a co-assured, and that party may be able to enforce the waiver in his favour by invoking the Contract (Rights of Third Parties) Act 1999.[79]

22–99 Circuity of action. In the absence of a waiver clause rights of subrogation existing between co-assureds are likely to be defeated by what has been called circuity of action, so long as the defendant co-assured is himself insured under the policy against the loss in question and has a valid insurable interest in the property which is damaged.[80] The analysis can be illustrated by reference to an insurance of leasehold property insured in the joint names of landlord and tenant. Suppose that the building is damaged and that the insurers pay the landlord for the costs of repair. An attempt by the insurers to enforce the covenant to repair against the tenant will be met by a cross-claim by the tenant seeking an indemnity against the very claim being asserted by the insurers.[81] If, however, one of the co-assureds has

---

[78] *Thomas & Co. v. Brown* (1899) 4 Com. Cas. 186; "*The Surf City*" [1995] 2 Loyd's Rep. 242; *National Oilwell Ltd v. Davy Offshore Ltd* [1993] 2 Lloyd's Rep. 582, 591, 603; *State of the Netherlands v. Youell* [1997] 2 Lloyd's Rep. 440, 443, 449.

[79] See para. 20–64, *ante*.

[80] "*The Yasin*" [1979] 2 Lloyd's Rep. 45, 54–55; *Petrofina (UK) Ltd v. Magnaload Ltd* [1984] Q.B. 127, 139–140; Derham *op. cit.*, Ch. 7, note 4.

[81] *Mark Rowlands v. Berni Inns Ltd* [1986] Q.B. 211, 229 *obiter*, approving the decision in the *Petrofina* Case. In the *Mark Rowlands* Case the defendant was not a co-assured—see para. 22–94, *supra*.

wilfully destroyed the insured property, the position may be different. Thus, if a house be insured in the joint names of mortgagor and mortgagee and the mortgagor deliberately burns it down, the mortgagor's claim is barred by his wilful misconduct but the mortgagee may claim on their composite policy so long as his right of claim is original and not derived from that of the mortgagor.[82] The insurers must then pay the mortgagee and are subrogated to his rights against the "guilty" co-assured. If there are no rights of subrogation, payment of the proceeds of insurance to the mortgagee merely reduces the outstanding mortgage debt, permitting the mortgagor to benefit from his own wrong. That cannot be right, and there is high authority for the view that in these circumstances the insurer may exercise rights of subrogation.[83]

22–100 The implied term analysis. There are difficulties with the circuity of action analysis. It rests on the notion that the co-assured who is made defendant to the subrogated proceedings can bring his own claim on the policy in respect of the loss in answer to the insurers' claim. In practice this is debatable because:

(1) the party in suit is the "innocent" co-assured and not the insurer, and
(2) the insurer could not be liable to pay the claim having already indemnified the "innocent" co-assured.

It has recently been stated by the House of Lords[84] that it is preferable to follow a different analysis, namely, that where two or more parties are co-assureds in respect of the loss or damage which has occurred, there is an implied term of the contract of insurance that an insurer will not seek by the exercise of rights of subrogation to recoup from a co-assured the indemnity which he has paid to the assured. This obviates the need to issue third party proceedings against the insurer, which he would have to do if he were to plead circuity of action, and the difficulties attendant thereon.[85] The recent authorities indicate that there should be little difficulty in implying such a term where the contract which is the source of the obligation to insure requires the policy to be taken out in joint names. The courts will view this as a compelling indication that both parties are intended to have the benefit of the insurance, because the law will not allow an action between two or more persons who are insured under the same policy against the same risk.[86]

---

[82] *Samuel v. Dumas* [1924] A.C. 431. We have changed the factual example given in the text from the ship mortgage example in the last edition because the mortgagee could not recover for a loss by perils of the sea if the ship was scuttled, as was decided in the *Dumas* Case.

[83] [1924] A.C. 431, 445–446, *per* Lord Cave. Had the co-assureds been joint owners with identical interests, the fraud of one assured would have tainted the claim of the other—*General Accident Fire & Life Ass. Co. v. Midland Bank Ltd* [1940] 2 K.B. 388, 405.

[84] *Co-operative Retail Services Ltd v. Taylor Young Partnership Ltd* [2002] 1 W.L.R. 1419, 1423, 1438 approving similar comments by the Court of Appeal at [2000] 2 All E.R. (Comm) 865, 879–885. See Birds [2001] L.M.C.L.Q. 193.

[85] *Stone Vickers Ltd v. Appledore Ferguson* [1991] 2 Lloyd's Rep. 288, 301–302 (reversed for another reason at [1992] 2 Lloyd's Rep. 578); *National Oilwell Ltd v. Davy Offshore Ltd* [1993] 2 Lloyd's Rep. 582, 612–614.

[86] See *Co-operative Retail Services Ltd v. Taylor Young Partnership Ltd* [2002] 1 W.L.R. 1419, 1423, *per* Lord Bingham and 1437, *per* Lord Hope. In *Re King* [1963] Ch. 459 the Court of Appeal held, however, that the purpose of insurance in the joint names of landlord and tenant was merely to ensure that the insurance monies were laid out in rebuilding. It does not matter if the insurance does not cover the liability of the co-assured so long as it covers his interest in the insured property—*Petrofina v. Magnaload* [1984] Q.B. 127; *National Oilwell v. Davy* [1993] 2 Lloyd's Rep. 582, 613.

Whether the co-assured is insured in respect of the loss in question may be more difficult to establish when his interest is not co-extensive with that of the assured who took out the policy.[87]

22–101 Subrogation barred by the underlying contract. It is trite law that an insurer is only subrogated to such rights of action as his assured is able to exercise.[88] Consequently an attempt to claim reimbursement will fail where the commercial contract between the co-assureds, which is the source of the obligation to insure, contains terms which expressly or impliedly debar the party in whose name the subrogated claim is made from claiming against the intended defendant, a situation commonly found in large construction projects.[89] Even when the intended defendant is not a co-assured, it will be impossible to bring proceedings against him if the contract between the assured and the defendant is construed to provide that the insurance in question is intended for their joint benefit so that the assured will look only to his insurers for compensation for loss, whether or not it has been caused by the defendant's negligence. Such intention is of course essential and must be derived from the construction of the contract which is the source of the obligation to insure, such as a lease[90] or building contract.[91]

22–102 North American decisions. While the decisions of courts in Canada and North America have provided inspiration to English courts in defining limits to the insurer's exercise of subrogated rights against a co-assured, they must be treated with care because they proceed upon principles which do not form part of English law.[92] The Canadian courts have applied a different test to determine whether rights of subrogation are excluded which is stated in the leading case of *Commonwealth Construction Co. Ltd v. Imperial Oil Ltd and Wellman-Lord (Alberta) Ltd.*[93] The question is whether the different co-assureds must be regarded in law as one assured. If there is joint insurance with an identical interest, this is the case. Where the co-assureds have different interests, then "... if the different interests are pervasive and if each relates to the entire property, albeit from different angles, again there is no question that the several assureds must be regarded as one and that no subrogation is possible".[94] The difficulty with this approach is that it is based on a fiction of unpredictable application. It is not clear what is to happen where one insurance covers a building of which only a part is demised to a tenant. It appears also that there cannot be subrogation where one co-assured wilfully caused the loss.[95] The American courts apply a

---

[87] *National Oilwell v. Davy, ubi cit.* at pp. 597–604.

[88] *Co-operative Retail Services Ltd v. Taylor Young Partnership Ltd* [2000] 2 All E.R. (Comm) 865, 878.

[89] *Co-operative Retail Services Ltd v. Taylor Young Partnership Ltd, supra* at note 77. Cases in which by contrast the contract has not barred subrogation rights include *Caledonia North Sea Ltd v. Norton (No. 2) Ltd* [2002] 1 All E.R.(Comm) 321.

[90] *Mark Rowlands Ltd v. Berni Inns Ltd* [1986] Q.B. 211, followed in *Barras v. Hamilton* 1994 S.L.T. 949. See para. 22–93 *supra*.

[91] *Co-operative Retail Services Ltd v. Taylor Young Partnership Ltd* [2002] 1 W.L.R. 1419.

[92] There is a useful summary of the several doctrines in Derham, *op. cit.* at Ch. 7.

[93] (1976) 69 D.L.R. (3d) 558.

[94] (1976) 69 D.L.R. (3d) 558, 561, *per* De Grandpre J.

[95] In the *Petrofina* Case Lloyd J. followed the *Commonwealth* case as being "high persuasive authority", [1984] Q.B. 127, 138, but he nonetheless subscribed to the circuity of action analysis which formed no part of the reasoning of the Canadian court—[1984] 1 Q.B. 127, 139–140. It is unclear to what extent, if at all, he relied upon the Canadian law fiction of the one assured. Another difficulty is to know when the interest of a party engaged in the project is "pervasive".

different criterion. Starting from the premise that subrogation is an equitable right, the theory is that the insurer seeking equity must do equity, and that an insurer who sues its own assured is acting inequitably, and against public policy.[96] There appears now to be an inflexible rule that an insurer is never permitted to sue a named assured,[97] although it is possible that there is an exception if that assured has wilfully caused a loss.[98] This analysis runs counter to the analysis in English law that subrogation is not exclusively an equitable right or remedy.[99]

That of a security company is not—*Canadian Pacific Ltd v. Base Security Services (B.C.) Ltd* (1991) 77 D.L.R. (4th) 178. See para. 1–156, note 44 *ante*. It is submitted that the real *ratio* of *Commonwealth* is that, on a true interpretation of the building contract in that case, a term was implied into it to the effect that participants in the construction project were not to be liable to each other *inter se*—see para. 1–156, *ante*.

[96] *Home Ins. Co. v. Pinski Bros Inc.* (1972) 500 P. 2d 945, and see comment in *Caledonia North Sea Ltd v. Norton (No. 2) Ltd* [2002] 1 All E.R. (Comm) 321, 330, 342.

[97] *Great American Ins. Co. v. Curl* (1961) 181 N.E. 2d 916, *Federal Ins. Co. v. Tamiami Trail Tours*, 117 F. 2d (1941); *General Ins. Co. of America v. Stoddard Wendle*, 410 P. 2d 904 (1966) *New Amsterdam Casualty Co. v. Homans-Kohler Inc.*, 305 F. Supp. 1017 (1969).

[98] *Louisiana Fire Ins. Co. v. Royal Indemnity Co.* (1949) 38 So. 2d 807, 810. Derham, *op. cit.*, Chap. 7, pp. 78–81 contains detailed references to the American case law. The insurer is permitted to preserve rights of subrogation by an express clause—*Fields v. Western Millers Mut. Fire Ins. Co.*, 48 N.E. 2d 489 (1943).

[99] See para. 22–23 *ante*.

CHAPTER 23

RIGHTS OF TWO OR MORE INSURERS

1. Double Insurance

23–1 Several liability of insurers. Double insurance occurs when the assured insures the same risk on the same interest in the same property with two or more independent insurers. Over-insurance occurs when the aggregate of all the insurances is more than the total value of the assured's interest. Apart from express condition, both double insurance and over-insurance are perfectly lawful; one may insure with as many insurers as one pleases and up to the full amount of one's interest with each one.[1] If a loss occurs, the assured may, in the absence of a *pro rata* contribution clause, select any one or more insurers and recover from him or them the total amount of the loss.[2] If he fails to recover his whole loss from those against whom he has proceeded in the first instance, he may recover the balance from any one or more of the others. But in no event is he entitled to recover more than his loss because each contract is a contract of indemnity only, and, therefore, when he has recovered his total loss from some one or more of his insurers his claims against the others abate.[3] The right to sue his insurers in any order is a valuable right for the assured, for it protects him against loss in the event of one or more of his insurers becoming insolvent; but as it would have been a considerable hardship on the insurers that one alone of several co-insurers should bear the whole loss, the doctrine of contribution was evolved, apparently by Lord Mansfield, who held that in marine insurance an insurer who paid more than his rateable proportion of the loss should have a right to recover the excess from his co-insurers, who had paid less than their rateable proportion.[4] The same general principles of liability and

---

[1] *Millandon v. Western Marine and Fire Ins. Co.*, 9 La. 27. 32 (1836).
[2] *Godin v. London Ass. Co.* (1758) 1 Burr. 489; 1 W.Bl. 105; *Bank of British North America v. Western Ass. Co.* (1884) 7 Ont.R. 166.
[3] *Bovis Construction Ltd v. Commercial Union Ass. Co. Plc.* [2001] 1 Lloyd's Rep. 416, 418. A similar result is reached in life assurance, although it is not indemnity insurance, by reason of the interpretation of the Life Assurance Act 1774, s.3. See *Hebdon v. West* (1863) 3 B. & S. 579; *Simcock v. Scottish Imperial Ins. Co.* (1902) 10 S.L.T. 286 (where an employer insured the life of his foreman in two separate offices; the first office paid and it was held that, since the first payment fully compensated the assured, he could make no claim against the second office). See also para. 1–33, *ante*.
[4] *Godin v. London Ass. Co.* (1758) 1 Burr. 489, 492; *Newby v. Reed* (1763) 1 W.Bl. 416; *Rogers v. Davis* (1777) 2 Park 601; *Davis v. Gildard* (1777) 2 Park 601.

contribution have been held to apply to fire insurance[5] and, liability insurance.[6] As a rule, however, insurers are not content to leave their liability on this basis, and have accordingly inserted conditions in their policies to protect themselves as far as possible against fraudulent over-insurances, and at the same time to obtain the maximum benefit from the contributory liability of co-insurers.

23–2 Policy conditions. Most fire and other indemnity policies contain one or other or both of the following conditions:

(1) requiring the assured to disclose other insurances upon the same property subsisting at the time the policy is issued or coming into existence thereafter;
(2) providing that in the event of other insurances subsisting at the time of the loss the insurer shall only be bound to pay to the assured their proper proportion of the loss.

The clauses designed to effect these objects appear in many different forms and with many variations in detail, but in construing them it is always important to remember that they are aimed primarily at double insurance, that is, at cases where the assured has made contracts with other insurers upon the same property and the same interest and against the same risk, and, unless a condition contains words which compel a different construction, it ought only to be applied to cases which are strictly cases of double insurance.[7]

23–3 Separate insurances on same property. The first essential element of double insurance is that the insurances must be on the same property.[8] It is not entirely clear whether it is necessary that the insurances should be on the identical property or whether it is sufficient if another policy does in effect cover a substantial part of the property already insured.[9] It is submitted that there is double insurance where item A is insured by one insurer and items A

---

[5] *North British and Mercantile Ins. Co. v. London, Liverpool and Globe Ins. Co.* (1877) 5 Ch.D. 569, 583 *per* Mellish L.J.; 587, *per* Baggallay J.A.

[6] *Commercial Union Ass. Co. v. Hayden* [1977] 1 Lloyd's Rep. 1; *Sickness and Accident Ass. Assoc. Ltd v. General Accident Ass. Corpn Ltd* (1892) 19 R. 972, 977, *per* Lord Low, Lord Ordinary. The rules as to double insurance and contribution might also apply to guarantee and fidelity insurances; *cf. Seaton v. Heath* [1899] 1 Q.B. 782, but see the cautionary remarks of Hamilton J. in *American Surety Co. of New York v. Wrightson* (1910) 16 Com.Cas. 37, 51.

[7] The statement in the text was adopted by Branson J. in *Portavon Cinema v. Price* [1939] 4 All E.R. 601, 604. See also *American Surety Co. of New York v. Wrightson* (1910) 16 Com.Cas. 37, 56 and *Blue Anchor Overall Co. v. Pennsylvania Lumbermen's Mutual Ins. Co.*, 123 A. 2d 413 (1956) for a discussion of the words "whether concurrent or not" as applied to other insurance policies.

[8] *Godin v. London Ass. Co.* (1758) 1 Burr. 489, 492, *per* Lord Mansfield C.J.; *American Surety Co. of New York v. Wrightson* (1910) 16 Com.Cas. 37, 56, *per* Hamilton J.

[9] There does not seem to be any English authority directly in point. The courts of Pennsylvania do require the policies to cover identically the same property no more no less, *Sloat v. Royal Insurance Co.*; 49 Pa. 14 (1865), *Lumbermen's Exchange v. American Central Ins. Co.*, 183 Pa. 366 (1898); *Liberty Mutual Ins. Co. v. Home Ins. Co.*, 583 F.Supp. 849 (1984). But the courts of Ontario and New York have not insisted on so strict a test—see *Ramsay Woollen Cloth Manufacturing Co. v. Mutual Fire Ins. Co. of Johnstown* (1854) 11 U.C.Q.B. 517; *Ogden v. East River Ins. Co.*, 50 N.Y. 388 (1872); *cf. Trustees of the First Unitarian Congregation of Toronto v. Western Ass. Co.* (1866) 26 U.C.Q.B. 175; *Page v. Sun Ins. Office*, 74 Fed.Rep. 203 (1896).

and B are insured for a single undivided premium by another insurer and also where goods are covered by a floating policy and part of the goods so covered is also insured specifically. In *American Surety Co. of New York v. Wrightson*[10] a bank was insured through loss by dishonesty of its employees up to $2,500 in the case of a particular employee and was also, insured in a sum of £40,000 covering loss caused not only by the bad faith of their employees but also loss by their negligence or by dishonesty of persons not their employees or by burglary or by fire or while documents were in transit in New York. Although it was conceded that there was double insurance and the issue was as to the method of assessing contribution, Hamilton J. doubted whether (apart from the concession) the doctrine would have applied. But it is submitted that this doubt related to the nature of the risk rather than the identity of the subject-matter insured and therefore that the statement in the text is not in any way affected by the *obiter dicta* of the judge.

23–4 The same risk. There is no double insurance unless at least a substantial part of the same risk is covered by both insurances, and the fact that two insurances may under certain circumstances overlap so as to insure the same property against the same risk for a brief period does not constitute a double insurance within the meaning of a clause requiring notice of double insurance to be given. In *Australian Agricultural Co. v. Saunders*,[11] an insurance against fire was effected on wool "in all or any shed or store, on station, or in transit to Sydney by land only, or in any shed or store, or any wharf in Sydney until placed in ship". The policy contained a clause:

> "No claim shall be recoverable if the property insured be previously or subsequently insured elsewhere, unless the particulars of such insurance be notified to the company in writing."

Subsequently the assured effected a marine insurance,

> "at and from the River Hunter to Sydney per ships and steamers, and thence per ship or ships to London, including the risk of craft from the time that the wools are first waterborne, and of trans-shipment or landing, and reshipment at Sydney".

The wool was shipped to Sydney, where it was landed and deposited in the stevedore's warehouse to await reshipment. While in the warehouse the wool was burned; the insurers pleaded double insurance without notice. The Court of Exchequer Chamber held the loss was not covered by the marine policy so that there was no double insurance in fact. The court also thought there was no possibility of the policies overlapping, but even if there was such a possibility during a short period, that was not "insurance elsewhere" within the meaning of the clause. Pollock B. said[12]:

> "These conditions have been of late inserted—into fire policies with the object of enabling the insurers to know the character of the risk and that

[10] (1910) 16 Com.Cas. 37, 103 L.T. 663.
[11] (1875) L.R. 10 C.P. 668; 33 L.T. 447.
[12] 33 L.T. at p. 450.

the parties had the real value of the goods insured. But it would manifestly be quite immaterial to the underwriters of a fire policy, whether they knew or not that the assured had a wide marine policy also, even if the two policies might possibly in some event overlap."

Blackburn J. said[13]:

"I think the meaning of an insurance elsewhere in the fire policy is an assurance specifically covering the same risk and not a mere possibility that at some point another policy should attach";

Lush J. said[14]: "That clause refers to subsequent insurances obviously intended to cover the same risk."

23-5 It could well be argued that if, in such a case, a loss does in fact happen when the property is covered by both insurances, there would be double insurance, but it has been held in New York that an incidental double insurance by operation of law will not affect the assured, if he had no intention to create a double insurance.[15]

The locality of the insured property may be an essential element of the risk. In *Boag v. Economic Insurance Company Ltd*[16] the assured owned two factories at Luton and insured a parcel of cigarettes loaded at factory A under an "all risks" transit policy. The cigarettes were moved to factory B for the night, where they were destroyed by fire. The insurers paid the loss and it was held that they were not entitled to contribution from other insurers who had insured factory B against fire under a policy which covered the stock-in-trade at factory B but not stock temporarily at factory B, not A while in transit.

23-6 Difficult problems of double insurance can occur in liability policies especially if the insured is covered in a "claims occurring" basis for one year and a "claims made" basis for another year. This happened when some solicitors renewed their professional indemnity policies with Lloyd's under a master policy sponsored by the Law Society. In *National Employers Mutual General Insurance Ltd v. Haydon*[17] the plaintiff insurers had paid a solicitors' negligence claim of which the solicitors became aware before the expiry of their policy which covered them until March 24, 1976. They had notified the insurers before the claim on them was made and in accordance with the policy the claim was then deemed to have been made during the currency of the policy. The Law Society scheme underwritten by Lloyd's insured the solicitors against all loss arising from claims made against the firm during the insurance which began on March 25, 1976. When the claim was made on the solicitors, they passed it on to Lloyd's at the request of the plaintiff insurers who claimed that there was double insurance so that Lloyd's should contribute 50 per cent. of the claim. The Lloyd's policy provided:

---

[13] L.R. 10 C.P. 668, 676.

[14] L.R. 10 C.P. 668, 677. The right to contribution between two insurers exists where both policies cover the same risk that has given rise to the claim—*Bovis Construction Ltd v. Commercial Union Ass. Co. Plc.* [2001] 1 Lloyd's Rep. 416, 418.

[15] *Mead v. American Fire Ins. Co.* 13 Hun.App. 476 (1897).

[16] [1954] 2 Lloyd's Rep. 581.

[17] [1980] 2 Lloyd's Rep. 149.

"This insurance shall not indemnify the Assured in respect of any loss
... in respect of any circumstances or occurrence which has been
notified under any other insurance attaching prior to the inception of
this Certificate."

The Court of Appeal held that the Lloyd's policy excluded absolutely all
claims notified under prior insurance and that there was, therefore, no
double insurance at all. They also held (but with more hesitation) that since
under the first policy the claim was deemed to have been made on March 24,
and since, at that time there was no Lloyd's policy in existence, there would
not be double insurance for that reason also. As Stephenson L.J. said: "The
two policies are not concurrent, but consecutive." They did not cover the
same risk.

23–7 Complex building operations can sometimes give rise to problems of
double insurance which require the true nature of different insurances to be
determined. Thus a contractor may take out all risks insurance on works,
temporary works, plant and equipment at a building site and this insurance
may be not only for his own benefit but also for the benefit of sub-contractors
and sub-sub-contractors. These sub-contractors may have their own
insurance against third-party liability. If an accident occurs causing loss of
life or damage to property at the building site for which a sub-contractor is
responsible, the question may arise whether he is doubly insured. In
Petrofina (U.K.) Ltd v. Magnaload Ltd[18] there was insurance under section 1
of which the assured and his sub-contractors were indemnified "against loss
or damage to the insured property whilst at the contract site" and the policy
included the following exception:

"The insurer shall not be liable in respect of loss, damage or liability
which ... is insured by or would but for the existence of this policy be
insured by any other policy or policies except in respect of any excess.
..."

Lloyd J. held that each sub-contractor and sub-sub-contractor was insured in
respect of the whole contract works (including property belonging to any
other insured or for which such other insured was responsible) and that such
insurance was insurance on property not liability insurance. The insurers
were thus liable to the particular sub-sub-contractor insured under section 1
of the policy. The sub-sub-contractor, however, had liability policies with
other insurers and one of the arguments was that such other insurances were
"other policies" within the words of the exception. Lloyd J. held that they
were not, because the exception was only intended to apply to true cases of
double insurance where "the same insured is covered in respect of the same
property against the same risks". In this case there were two separate risks in
that section 1 of the policy which was the subject-matter of the action was a
policy on property while the "other policies" were liability policies. There
was thus no double insurance and the exception clause did not apply.

---

[18] [1984] Q.B. 127. This decision was followed in *Wimpey Construction U.K. Ltd v. Poole*
[1984] 2 Lloyd's Rep. 499 where it was held that a claim under a financial loss extension to a
professional indemnity policy was not defeated by the existence of either a public liability or a
contractors' all risks policy.

23–8 The same interest. It is not, however, sufficient for the policies to relate to the same risk and the same property; they must also cover the same interest since it is not the subject-matter of the insurance as such which is covered by the policy but the assured's interest in that subject-matter.[19] Where two people have different interests in the same property, and each insures his own interest on his own behalf, there is no double insurance, even though the aggregate of the two insurances is more than the total value of the property. Thus, there may be independent insurance by the owner and bailee of goods,[19] by the owner and mortgagee of house property[20] or successive mortgagees,[21] by a vendor and purchaser,[22] or by a landlord and his tenant.[23] If each insures his own interest only there is no double insurance, and each as between his insurer and himself is entitled to a full indemnity in respect of his interest, but if the one has, apart from the insurance, a right of recourse against the other in respect of the damage, his insurer is subrogated to that right, and thus in the result one insurer may have to bear the whole loss.[24] Similarly, if one party with a limited interest in the premises in fact receives the benefit of the insurance effected by the owner to the full amount of his insurable interest he can recover nothing from his own insurer.[25] On the other hand, a bailee, mortgagee or lessee may insure the owner's interest as well as his own, and if the insurance is with the owner's consent, and he also has insured, there is a double insurance of the owner's interest.[26]

23–9 In *North British and Mercantile Insurance Co. v. London, Liverpool and Globe Insurance Co.*,[27] wharfingers held grain belonging to Rodoca-nachi & Co. who were merchants and by the custom of the trade the wharfingers were liable for any loss, however occurring. The wharfingers insured, with the defendant company, grain in their warehouse at Rother-hithe, "the assured's own, in trust, or on commission, for which they are responsible". The merchants also insured their grain with the plaintiff company. Both policies contained a clause that if at the time of the loss there

---

[19] *North British and Mercantile Ins. Co. v. London, Liverpool and Globe Ins. Co.* (1877) 5 Ch.D. 569 esp. at p. 577, *per* Jessel M.R.; *cf. California Ins. Co. v. Union Compress Co.*, 133 U.S. 387, 419–421 (1889).

[20] *Burton v. Gore District Mutual Fire Ins. Co.* (1865) 12 Grant Ch.U.C. 156 (where a policy on premises was assigned to a mortgagee and the mortgagor subsequently took out another policy and it was held that there was no double insurance); *Marrow v. Lancashire Ins. Co.*, (1898) 26 O.A.R. 173; *Foster v. Equitable Mutual Fire Ins. Co.*, 68 Mass. 216 (1854); *Tuck v. Hartford Fire Ins. Co.* 56 N.H. 326 (1876); *De Witt v. Agricultural Ins. Co.*, 157 N.Y. 353 (1898).

[21] *Scottish Amicable Heritable Securities Association v. Northern Ass. Co.* (1883) 11 R. 287; *Glasgow Provident Investment Society v. Westminster Fire Office* (1887) 14 R. 947; (1888) 13 App.Cas. 699.

[22] *Acer v. Merchant's Ins. Co.*, 57 Barb. 68 (1870); *Economical Mutual Ins. Co. v. Federation Ins. Co. of Canada* (1961) 27 D.L.R. (2d) 539.

[23] *Andrews v. Patriotic Ass. Co.* (1886) 18 L.R.Ir 355; *Portavon Cinema v. Price* [1939] 4 All E.R. 601; *cf. Reynard v. Arnold* (1875) L.R. 10 Ch.App. 386.

[24] *North British and Mercantile Ins. Co. v. London, Liverpool and Globe Ins. Co.* (1877) 5 Ch.D. 569.

[25] *Brown v. London Mutual Fire Ins. Co.* (1914) 29 W.L.R. 711.

[26] *Home Ins. Co. v. Baltimore Warehouse Co.*, 93 U.S. 527, 545–546 (1876); *Robbins v. Firemen's Fund Ins. Co.*, 16 Blatchf. 122 (1879). But a mere right to the policy moneys in the hands of assured will probably not constitute a double insurance in these circumstances: see *Portavon Cinema v. Price* [1939] 4 All E.R. 601, 604–606, and paras 23–12, *et seq.*, *infra*.

[27] (1877) 5 Ch.D. 569.

should be any other subsisting insurances, whether effected by the insured or by any other person, covering the same property the company should not be liable for more than a rateable contribution. A fire occurred in the warehouse and the merchant's grain was destroyed. The wharfingers were paid in full and the companies took proceedings in order to have it decided which should bear the ultimate liability. It was held that there was no double insurance as each party had insured his own interest. The wharfingers were insured in respect of their own interest and liability, and the merchants could make no claim on that insurance. Apart from the condition, the merchants' insurers would, after payment, be subrogated to the merchant's claim against the wharfingers who would be entitled to an indemnity from the defendant company who would thus have to bear the whole loss. Since there was no double insurance there was no right of contribution either on general principle or by reason of the *pro rata* clause which had no application.

23–10 Similarly in *Scottish Amicable Heritable Securities Association v. Northern Assurance Co.*,[28] certain property in Scotland was disponed in security to successive incumbrancers. The proprietors took out insurance policies in the name of the loan company in each case and in their own name in reversion, and each policy contained the *pro rata* liability clause. After a loss the first incumbrancer sued their insurers who contended that they were only liable to pay a rateable proportion with the insurers of the other incumbrancer. It was held that the clause did not apply, since no individual interest was doubly insured except that of the proprietors, and as there was not sufficient to satisfy the various incumbrancer there could be no claim in respect of their interest.

23–11 In *Andrews v. Patriotic Assurance Co.*[29] a landlord and tenant insured certain house property independently. The lease contained a covenant to repair but no covenant to insure and each party insured without specifying his interest. After a fire had occurred, the tenant recovered the full loss from his insurers, and subsequently became bankrupt without having reinstated the premises. The landlord then sued his insurers who contended that they were only liable for a *pro rata* contribution under the clause in their policy. It was held that the landlord and tenant had each insured only his own interest in the premises and that as the landlord could obtain no direct benefit from the tenant's insurance there was, therefore, no double insurance, and the landlord was entitled to recover the whole loss from his insurers, whose only recourse would be against the tenant in respect of his covenant to repair.

23–12 Indirect interest in other insurance. Difficult questions may arise where, although the assured has not himself doubly insured, he may have taken out an insurance policy and also have an indirect interest in policy moneys received under another policy by another assured. For example, under section 83 of the Fires Prevention (Metropolis) Act 1774[30] a person interested in or entitled to any building damaged by fire can require the insurers to cause the money to be laid out in rebuilding. Suppose that a lessor

---

[28] (1883) 11 R. 287; approved by the Court of Session in *Glasgow Provident Investment Society v. Westminster Fire Office* (1887) 14 R. 947.
[29] (1886) 18 L.R.Ir. 355.
[30] See paras 21–14, *et seq.*, *supra*.

who has himself insured invokes the statute and compels reinstatement by the lessee's insurer, can the lessee's insurer call upon the lessor's insurer to contribute rateably to the reinstatement? Similarly if a mortgagor takes out an insurance policy on his own interest and also an insurance policy on the mortgagee's interest which provides that any insurance money shall be applied towards reducing the mortgage debt, is there a double insurance?

23–13 In *Port Avon Cinema v. Price*,[31] a lessor and a lessee of a theatre had separately insured their respective interests. The theatre was destroyed by fire and the lessee claimed from its insurers who contended, *inter alia*, that the lessee had an equitable interest in the policy taken out by the lessor thus giving rise to a double insurance or alternatively that the lessor's right to call upon them to reinstate under section 83 of the 1774 Act gave rise to a double insurance. Both these contentions were rejected by Branson J. who held first that no equity could be created in the lessee since the lessor had never intended to give any interest in the policy moneys to the lessee and secondly that section 83 does not make anyone an assured; it merely gives him a right to direct those who have to pay insurance moneys to expend them in a particular way. There is nothing in the report to show that a demand for reinstatement had, in fact, been made. The decision is authority for the proposition that, so long as each party relies on his own insurers to pay the loss, there is no double insurance; it may still be open to argument that if the lessor does invoke the statute and compels reinstatement by the lessee's insurer, then there is double insurance and the lessee's insurer can, if his policy contains the appropriate condition, call upon the lessor's insurer to contribute to the cost of reinstatement. The whole tenor of the judgment is adverse to such a construction of the section, but it may be that, if the assured is so placed that he must necessarily derive benefit from another party's insurance, there is *pro tanto* a double insurance, even though the insurances are on different interests.

23–14 In *Nichols & Co. v. Scottish Union and National Insurance Co.*[32] the rules of a building society provided that any property mortgaged to the society should be insured in the name of trustees, and that the premiums should be charged to the member; that in the case of loss the insurance moneys should be applied in paying off the debt or, at the option of the board, in repairing the damage. The society sold certain paper mills to A & Co. who mortgaged the property to the society in order to secure part of the purchase price remaining unpaid. An insurance with X & Co. was effected in accordance with the society's rules, and subsequently A & Co. insured the property for their own benefit with Y & Co. Both policies contained the usual *pro rata* clause. After a loss had occurred, A & Co. sued their insurers, who contended that they were only liable to a *pro rata* contribution. A Divisional Court sustained this contention on the ground that the society's policy insured the interest of both parties, since the debt was to be paid off with the insurance money. There was therefore a double insurance and the *pro rata* clause applied.

23–15 If, as seems from the report, the mortgagees insured their own

[31] [1939] 4 All E.R. 601.
[32] (1885) 2 T.L.R. 190; 14 R. 1094.

interest, the decision must be open to question. It is true that they charged the mortgagor with the insurance premiums and contracted to give him the benefit of the insurance by paying off the debt, but that was not an insurance of the mortgagor upon his own interest, and the decision can only be supported on the ground that there is a double insurance where the assured has a contractual right to the benefit of another party's insurance on his own interest. This is, at least, a doubtful proposition and the better view is perhaps that in circumstances similar to *Nichols & Co. v. Scottish Union and National Insurance Co.* each party insures his own interest and can recover in full against his insurer; since, however, the mortgagor has a contractual right to have the debt paid off by the mortgagee, the mortgagor's insurers will be subrogated to that right after payment by them to the mortgagor. Although neither the mortgagor, nor his insurer, can compel the mortgagee to make any recovery, the overall result would probably be that the loss fell on the insurers of the mortgagee.

23–16 The same assured. Whether or not the insurances must in every case be strictly on the same interests, there can be no double insurance unless at or before the time of the loss the same person has become entitled to the benefit of the whole or part of both insurances, either directly as the assured or indirectly by being in a position to claim the benefit of the insurance money.[33]

23–17 Conditions relating to double insurance. Some policies contain clauses stating that if the subject-matter of the insurance is subsequently insured, then the insurance shall cease to have effect or that if a second insurance is taken out the policy shall be void.[34] It is more usual to provide that in such circumstances the policy will be void, unless the insurers have previously signified their assent to the second insurance in writing.[35] In such cases the clause prohibiting double insurance is in effect a condition of the policy which can, however, be waived.[36] If the clause merely provides that any other insurance should be notified to the insurers and their consent obtained, it is an open question whether such notification is a condition of the policy. It has been held in Ontario that it is a condition and that if the insurers have not been notified and have not consented, they are entitled to avoid liability altogether.[37]

The wording of the clauses may vary considerably in detail and sometimes it is merely provided that notice should be given[38]; in these cases there is no

---

[33] *North British Mercantile Ins. Co. v. London, Liverpool & Globe Ins. Co.* (1877) 5 Ch.D. 569. See *Godin v. London Ass. Co.* (1758) 1 Burr. 489 where goods were insured both by the shipowner at the request of the shipper and by the receiver. Held that although the receiver might be entitled to the benefit of the shipowner's policy by virtue of the indorsement of the bills of lading, he could not obtain it without first paying off a debt owed to the shipowner by the shipper and there was therefore a double insurance, see also *De Witt v. Agricultural Ins. Co.,* 157 N.Y. 353 (1898).

[34] *Re Marshall and Scottish Employers' Liability Ins. Co. Ltd* (1901) 85 L.T. 757.

[35] *Australian Agricultural Co. v. Saunders* (1875) L.R. 10 C.P. 668; *Noad v. Provincial Ins. Co.* (1859) 18 U.C.Q.B. 584; *Osser v. Provincial Ins. Co.* (1862) 12 U.C.C.P. 133; *Weinaugh v. Provincial Ins. Co.* (1870) 20 U.C.C.P. 405.

[36] *Lancashire Ins. Co. v. Chapman* (1875) 7 Rev. Leg. 47, P.C.; *Emmett v. Canada Accident and Fire Ins. Co.* [1924] 3 D.L.R. 125.

[37] *McBride v. Gore District Mutual Fire Ins. Co.* (1870) 30 U.C.Q.B. 451, relying on *Mason v. Harvey* (1853) 8 Ex. 819.

[38] *Hendrickson v. Queen Ins. Co.* (1871) 31 U.C.Q.B. 3473.

breach of the clause until a reasonable time has expired without notice being given.[39] A mistake in the particulars contained in the notice will not necessarily be fatal to the assured's claims.[40]

23–18 There is no implied warranty that a second insurance once notified to the first insurer and accepted by him will be maintained[41] and, in the absence of any express condition,[42] there is probably no warranty that an existing insurance, of which the insurers know at the time the policy is made, will be renewed.

The words "warranted highest rate" means that if there is any other insurance the premium is no higher than that received by the insurer under the policy which contains the clause.[43]

23–19 Waiver. The condition relating to double insurance, or any breach thereof, may be waived by the company or its agents having proper authority.[44] An indorsement on the policy may expressly or impliedly sanction concurrent insurance up to a specified amount.[45] A company's officer or agent with authority to make the contract of insurance would probably have ostensible authority to waive the condition.[46] The making or acknowledgment of the contract with knowledge of other insurance would be a waiver of the breach. Thus, if a policy is issued or a renewal premium accepted with full knowledge of other subsisting insurance, notice and consent in the prescribed form is waived and in certain circumstances the knowledge of an agent may be the knowledge of the company.[47] Where an agent was authorised to bind the company by interim receipt, but not otherwise, his issuing of the receipt with knowledge of other insurance was a waiver of the condition as far as the interim protection was concerned, but it was held that the company was not liable on the permanent insurance, because the directors, when they issued the policy, had no knowledge of the other insurance.[48] Insurers do not waive the breach of a condition against double insurance by merely investigating a claim and asking for further proof of loss after obtaining knowledge of double insurance and without taking an objection to it.[49] Neither the local agent nor an inspector of the company with authority to adjust claims can be presumed to have authority to waive a breach of the condition.[50]

---

[39] *Commercial Union Ass. Co. v. Temple* (1898) 29 Can.S.C. 206.

[40] *Osser v. Provincial Ins. Co.* (1862) 12 U.C.C.P. 133; *cf. Parsons v. Standard Fire Ins. Co.* (1879) 4 O.A.R. 326 where the mistake was made on the proposal form; on appeal (1880) 5 Can.S.C. 233.

[41] *Hordern v. Commercial Union Ass. Co.* (1884) 5 N.S.W.R. (Law) 309, affirmed on another ground (1887) 56 L.J.P.C. 78; *cf. Hoffman v. Manufacturers' Mutual Fire Ins. Co.*, 38 Fed.Rep. 487 (1889).

[42] *Sulphite Pulp Co. Ltd v. Faber* (1895) 1 Com.Cas. 146.

[43] *Walker & Sons v. Uzielli* (1896) 1 Com.Cas. 452.

[44] See *Marcovitch v. Liverpool Victoria Friendly Society* (1912) 28 T.L.R. 188.

[45] *General Ins. Co. of Trieste v. Cory* [1897] 1 Q.B. 335; *Parsons v. Standard Fire Ins. Co.* (1880) 5 Can.S.C. 233; *Palatine Ins. Co. v. Ewing*, 92 Fed.Rep. 111 (1899).

[46] See *Jacobs v. Equitable Ins. Co.* (1858) 17 U.C.Q.B. 35 and (for the role of agents generally), Ch. 36.

[47] *McIntyre v. East Williams Mutual Fire Ins. Co.* (1889) 18 Ont.R. 79; *Carroll v. Charter Oak Ins. Co.*, 40 Barb. 292 (1863), *Northern Assurance v. Grand View, Building Co.*, 183 U.S. 308 (1901).

[48] *Billington v. Provincial Ins. Co.* (1879) 3 Can.S.C. 182.

[49] *Fair v. Niagara District Mutual Fire Ins. Co.* (1876) 26 U.C.C.P. 398.

[50] *Western Assurance Co. v. Doull* (1886) 12 Can.S.C. 446.

23–20 Rateable proportion of the loss. A common form of rateable proportion clause provides:

> "If at the time of any claim ... there shall be any other insurance covering the same risk or any part thereof the Company shall not be liable for more than its rateable proportion thereof."

The meaning of this clause is that, if there is double insurance, the assured cannot recover from any one insurer more than the appropriate amount for which the insurer would be liable as between himself and his co-insurers.[51] Although such a clause may not be intended to prevent the assured from recovering the full sum insured, it does require him to recover the appropriate proportion from each of his insurers,[52] and it may work injustice if one of the insurers is insolvent.[53]

23–21 Both policies prohibiting double insurance. Difficult questions may arise where two or more policies contain conditions exempting the insurers from all liability if the assured is entitled to be indemnified under another policy. In *Gale v. Motor Union Insurance Co.*[54] L became liable in damages to a motor-cyclist while he was driving G's car. Both G and L had policies covering this event which contained a condition that if the risk was covered by another policy the insurers should not be liable and a further condition that where two policies existed which covered the same risk the insurers should pay rateably. Roche J. held that the words "provided that there is no other insurance in respect of such car whereby the insured may be indemnified" in the second contract of insurance referred to a full indemnity and not such a partial indemnity as would be obtained under the first policy. He further held that the conditions purporting to exclude liability must be qualified by the rateable proportion clause and that therefore neither policy operated so as to deprive its assured of a right to indemnity under the other and each insurance company was obliged to pay half the claim. In *Weddell v. Road Transport and General Insurance Co. Ltd,*[55] the facts were very similar but no rateable proportion clause existed in either policy. It was accordingly argued that, since the driver was insured under a second policy, he came within the proviso in the first policy exempting the insurer if such a driver was "entitled to indemnity under any other policy." Rowlatt J. considered

---

[51] The manner in which such calculation should be made is discussed in the following section "Contribution". Should the insurer pay the assured in full, he is a volunteer as regards payment of the sum in excess of his rateable proportion, and consequently is limited to seeking contribution from a second insurer to the amount which he was liable to pay pursuant to the clause—*Bovis Construction Ltd. v. Commercial Union Ass. Co. Plc.* [2001] 1 Lloyd's Rep. 416, 419.

[52] *North British and Mercantile Ins. Co. v. London, Liverpool and Globe Ins. Co.* (1877) 5 Ch.D. 569, 588, *per* Baggallay J.A.

[53] Donaldson J. has said that this is a "surprising" result of the rateable proportion clause in *Commercial Union v. Hayden* [1977] 1 Lloyd's Rep. 1, 3 but it appears to follow from the wording of the clause.

[54] [1928] 1 K.B. 359. The clause cited was considered in *Commercial Union v. Hayden* [1977] 1 Lloyd's Rep. 1. Slightly different wording was used for the clause in *Legal & General Ass. Co. v. Drake Ins. Co.* [1992] Q.B. 887.

[55] [1932] 2 K.B. 563 approved, *obiter* in *National Employers Mutual General Ins. v. Haydon* [1980] 2 Lloyd's Rep. 149, and followed in *Structural Polymer Systems Ltd. v. Brown* [2000] Lloyd's Rep. I.R. 64, 75.

that the reasonable construction of such a clause was to exclude from the category of co-existing cover any cover which was expressed to be itself cancelled by such co-existence, and held that the insurers should each pay half the claim. A similar result might have followed in *Austin v. Zurich General Accident and Liability Insurance Co. Ltd*[56] but for the failure of the driver to give notice to the owner's insurers of a prosecution against him arising out of the accident, so that they were relieved from liability by a term in the policy. In this case one policy contained a "rateable contribution" clause, while the other provided that in the event of the existence of collateral cover the insurers should be liable only in excess of the sum or sums actually recovered or recoverable under such insurance.

23–22 A slightly different form of clause was considered in *Steelclad Ltd v. Iron Trades Mutual Insurance Co. Ltd*[57] which concerned the roofing of a generating station at Peterhead. The North of Scotland Hydro-Electric Board had taken out a "project policy" insuring themselves, their contractors and sub-contractors which provided:

> "This insurance does not cover any loss, damage or accident which ... is insured by or would but for the existence of this Policy be insured by any other policy or policies except in respect of any excess beyond the amount which would have been payable under such other policy or policies had this insurance not been effected."

The roofing sub-contractors suffered a loss of £168,915 of which they recovered £80,000 under the project policy. They then endeavoured to recover the remainder under a policy which they had themselves taken out with the defenders and which had a clause in almost identical terms to the clause quoted above, except that it was an express requirement that the "other policy" had to be "effected by the insured jointly or severally on his behalf." It was held by the Court of Session that the defenders could not successfully argue that the project policy had been effected by the pursuers on their behalf since it had been effected by the Hydro-Electric Board on behalf of others besides the pursuers. The Court also followed the reasoning of Rowlatt J. in *Weddell's* case and adopted his reasoning that co-existing cover could not include any cover which was expressed to be cancelled by such co-existence. They accepted that the words "or would but for the existence of this policy be insured" created a difficulty if literally applied but, even so, were able to apply the construction favoured by Rowlatt J. so as to arrive at the conclusion that the pursuers' own insurers were liable for the balance of the loss.

23–23 A somewhat similar problem arose before the New Zealand Court of Appeal in *State Fire Insurance General Manager v. Liverpool and London and Globe Insurance Co.*[58] A "State" policy indemnified a hospital board

---

[56] [1944] 2 All E.R. 243 and [1945] K.B. 250. Another difficulty was that the action was wrongly taken in the assured's name as one of subrogation, but it should have been a contribution claim in the name of the insurer which had paid in full—[1945] K.B. 250, 258.

[57] 1984 S.L.T. 304.

[58] [1952] N.Z.L.R. 5; see also *Gauthier v. Waterloo Mutual Ins. Co.* (1881) Ont.A.R. 231; *Nicols v. London and Provincial Fire Ins. Co.* (1884) 5 N.S.W.R. (Law) 333; *Home Insurance of New York v. Gavel* [1927] 3 D.L.R. 929; [1927] S.C.R. 481; *Hayes v. Milford Mutual Fire Ins. Co.* 170 Mass.492 (1898).

and its officers against legal liability for negligence; a "Globe" policy similarly indemnified one of the officers. The "State" policy provided that:

> "if the assured's officers are otherwise indemnified … the indemnity under this policy … shall not apply until the full amount of the indemnity otherwise provided has been applied as far as it will go in satisfaction of the liability",

It also contained a rateable proportion clause as did the "Globe" policy. It was held that since the "State" policy afforded an indemnity only against the balance of liability remaining after payment in full under another policy, no question of contribution arose; the loss payable was less than the maximum insured by the "Globe" policy and the "State" policy therefore paid nothing. The English authorities were distinguished on the grounds that they were concerned with reconciling two clauses in separate policies which might be construed so as to produce absurdity, whereas in the New Zealand case the problem was to resolve a conflict between the indemnity clause and the "rateable" proportion clause in the "State" policy. *Gale*'s case helped to resolve the conflict because it indicated that a rateable proportion clause should be subordinated to the provision for indemnity.

23–24 Meaning of "other insurance". It may be important to know whether there is "other insurance" in effect for the purposes of a double insurance clause. If, at the time of a loss, the assured is negotiating for a second insurance but has not concluded a contract or if a second insurance has been concluded through an agent acting without authority, one may safely conclude that no "other insurance" is in existence. In *Equitable Fire and Accident Office Ltd v. Ching Wo Hong*[59] the second policy entered into by the respondent, provided that it was not to come into force until the premium had been paid and a receipt for it had been given. No premium had been paid and the Privy Council held that the second insurance had never attached and did not fall within a clause in the first policy requiring notice of any insurance effected during the currency of the policy. The same result should follow where a contract has been purportedly made but through an agent acting without authority.[60] If, however, there is a dispute and the insured asserts that the second insurance company is bound to him, he will be precluded from denying the validity of the second insurance in proceedings against the first insurer.[61]

23–25 Greater difficulties arise if the second insurer can deny liability because, for example, the insured has committed a breach of warranty or has not complied with a condition precedent to the liability of the insurer or the insurer has the right to avoid the policy for non-disclosure or misrepresentation. No doubt if the insured has repudiated the contract and that

---

[59] [1907] A.C. 96. Compare *Western Ass. Co. v. Temple* (1901) 31 Can.S.C. 373 with *Manitoba Ass. Co. v. Whitla* (1903) 34 Can.S.C. 191.

[60] *Morrow v. Lancashire Ins. Co.* (1898) 26 O.A.R. 173; *Lumbermen's Exchange Co. v. American Central Ins. Co.* 183 Pa. 366 (1898); *Taylor v. State Ins. Co.* 107 Iowa 275 (1899). The position will be different if there is an adoption of the unauthorised insurance or receipt of payment thereunder, *Dafoe v. Johnston District Mutual Ins. Co.* (1858) 7 U.C.C.P. 55; *Park v. Phoenix Ins. Co.* (1859) 19 U.C.Q.B. 110.

[61] *Mason v. Andes Ins. Co.* (1873) 23 U.C.C.P. 37.

repudiation has been accepted by the insurer or if the insurer has correctly avoided the insurance before the loss occurred, it could not be said that there was relevant "other insurance". But if it is only after the loss that the second insurer seeks to say that a condition (*e.g.* as to notice) has not been complied with or seeks to avoid for non-disclosure, what then is the position?

23–26 In *Legal and General Assurance v. Drake Insurance*[62] there was a claim by a motorist's first insurer, who had indemnified a third party claimant (as by statute he was bound to do), for a contribution from a second insurer of the motorist. Both policies contained terms providing that it was a condition precedent to insurers' liability that immediate notice of the claim must have been to the insurers. The motorist gave such notice to the first insurer who settled the claim in full; he did not give notice or make any claim against the second insurer. The first insurer then sued for a 50 per cent contribution from the second insurer who said it could not be liable because no notice had been given and it had had no opportunity of investigating the claim. The Court of Appeal held by a majority that the right of a co-insurer to contribution from another co-insurer was not based on contract but, like the right of a co-surety, "on what has been said to be the plainest equity, that burdens should be shared equally". Lloyd L.J. then said:

"Since the existence of the equity depends on the ability of the assured to claim against either A or B at his choice, the obvious date to determine whether the conditions are satisfied is the date when the assured is assumed to exercise his choice, namely the date of the loss."

At the date of the loss there was double insurance even though the liability of the second insurer (indeed both insurers) depended on the insured subsequently giving immediate notice of the third party's claim. The first insurer's action for contribution, therefore, succeeded. Ralph Gibson L.J. dissented on the ground that the right of contribution could always be excluded by contract and it must, therefore, be permissible for the second insured to rely on a clause excusing him from liability if immediate notice of a claim is not given, just as much as if the insured were in breach of warranty at the date of the loss.

23–27 In the similar case of *Eagle Star Insurance v. Provincial Insurance*[63] the Privy Council in a Bahamian case preferred the dissenting judgment of Ralph Gibson L.J. The facts were almost identical save that the first insurer, while being liable in the full to the third party claimant under the relevant motor vehicle insurance statute, was not liable to its insured at all because it had cancelled its insurance contract with him before the accident. The claim against the second insurer was thus that it was only the second insurer who was liable and the second insurer therefore should pay the full amount of the claim. The second insurer argued that it was not liable to the insured at all since it had never been notified of the claim and this argument was upheld by the Judicial Committee, Lord Woolf stating there was no justification for creating a special cut off point at the date of the loss and continuing:

[62] [1992] Q.B. 887.
[63] [1994] 1 A.C. 130.

"Looking at the issue from the insurer's and insured's standpoint, it makes no difference if an insurer defeats a claim by relying on action taken before or after the loss has occurred."

It is submitted that, if precedent permits,[64] the advice of the Privy Council should be preferred to the decision of the Court of Appeal. If, which is uncontroversial, the right of contribution can be excluded or limited by agreement, it is artificial (as well as contrary to the parties' agreement) to treat exclusions or limitations operating after loss differently from exclusions or limitations operating before loss.

23–28 The same principles must apply when the second insurer alleges breach of warranty or asserts that he is entitled to avoid for misrepresentation or non-disclosure.[65] If a policy provides that "other insurance" includes all other insurances "whether valid or invalid", this will put the matter beyond doubt.[66]

The form of the other insurance is immaterial if there is a contract to insure; an interim protection note will be sufficient to constitute a double insurance.[67]

23–29 If a condition requires all other insurances to be notified and the assured substitutes a new policy for one already notified, he does not have to notify the substituted insurance to the first insurer, even though the new policy is for a larger amount than the old.[68]

If the second policy is avoided by statute or is an "honour" policy, it will probably not be "other insurance" within the meaning of a double insurance clause, because a policy which is unenforceable on its face can hardly be "insurance" in the eyes of the law.[69]

23–30 A clause which prohibits other insurance beyond a certain amount will not be infringed by the assured's taking out policies to cover the possibility of insolvency on the part of the underwriters insuring him for the permitted amount.[70]

---

[64] And surely precedent does so permit to judge by the way in which lower courts have followed *Wagon Mound (No. 1)* [1961] A.C. 388.

[65] This seems to have been accepted by both Lloyd L.J. and Lord Woolf. *Cf. Jenkins v. Deane* (1934) 47 Ll.L Rep. 342, 346. No doubt a court will be cautious before holding in a case between two co-insurers and, in the absence of the insured, that there has in fact, been a breach of warranty, misrepresentation or non-disclosure. Conversely, a court will also be cautious if it is the insured who asserts a second contract is voidable for non-disclosure in response to the first insurer's reliance on a rateable proportion clause.

[66] *Hammond v. Citizens Ins. Co. of Canada* (1886) 26 N.B.R. 371.

[67] *Hatton v. Beacon Ins. Co.* (1858) 16 U.C.Q.B. 316; *cf. Greet v. Citizens Ins. Co.* (1880) 5 Ont.A.R. 596 and *Mason v. Andes Ins. Co.* (1873) 23 U.C.C.P. 37.

[68] *National Protector Fire Ins. Co. v. Nivert* [1913] A.C. 507; the result of this case might have been different if the names of the other companies had been required to be endorsed on the policy. See further *Parsons v. Standard Fire Insurance Co.* (1880) 5 Can.S.C. 233; *Lowson v. Canada Farmers' Fire Ins. Co.* (1881) 6 O.A.R. 512; *Klein v. Union Fire Ins. Co.* (1883) 3 Ont.R. 234, 261, *et seq.; Moore v. Citizens Fire Ins. Co.* (1888) 14 O.A.R. 582.

[69] In *Roddick v. Mutual Marine Ins. Co.* [1895] 1 Q.B. 836 Kennedy J. decided that a p.p.i. policy infringed a warranty that a vessel was uninsured but it is submitted that the case would now be decided differently in the light of s.4(2) of the Marine Insurance Act 1906 and the judgments in *Cheshire v. Vaughan* [1920] 3 K.B. 240. The Court of Appeal in *Roddick's Case* [1895] 2 Q.B. 380 expressly reserved their opinion. See also *Thames and Mersey v. Gunford Ship Co.* [1911] A.C. 529, 538.

[70] *General Ins. Co. of Trieste v. Cory* [1897] 1 Q.B. 335.

23–31 Onus of proof. The burden of proving another subsisting contract of insurance on the same property and on the same interest lies upon the insurers,[71] and it has been said that in considering the effect of another insurance the assured is not prevented by the rule against parol evidence from showing that another insurance, although apparently covering the same property, was not intended by the parties to cover the particular property in question.[72] If one assured has two policies on different terms, it may be necessary for the court to determine whether the second insurance applies, in the absence of any argument from the second insurers. Thus a bailee may have a general policy on goods and a second policy covering him for loss resulting from negligence of his employees. The court will have to decide whether the bailee's employees were, in fact, negligent in order to decide whether there is double insurance.[73]

A statement by the assured in his proofs of loss that he is insured elsewhere is not conclusive evidence against him as to the existence or as to the actual terms of such other insurance.[74]

2. CONTRIBUTION[75]

(a) *Introduction*

23–32 Principle of contribution. Where there are two or more insurances covering the same rights and interests in any risk, the principle of contribution applies as between the different insurers.[76] Apart from any condition in the policies, any one insurer is bound to pay to the assured the full amount for which he would be liable if his policy stood alone; but, having paid, he is entitled to an equitable contribution from the other insurers on the same principle as co-sureties are bound to contribute *inter se* when any one is called upon by the creditor to pay.[77] In fact, however, most fire and many other policies contain a condition which provides that, if more than

---

[71] *Jenkins v. Deane* (1933) 47 Ll.L.R. 342, 346 where Goddard J. said that it was insufficient to put in evidence an insurance policy which purported to cover the same interest as the policy sued on.

[72] *McMaster v. Ins. Co. of North America*, 55 N.Y. 222 (1873); *Lowell Manufacturing Co. v. Safeguard Fire Ins. Co.* 88 N.Y. 591 (1882).

[73] *Mint Security v. Blair* [1982] 1 Lloyd's Rep. 188.

[74] *Manitoba Ass. Co. v. Whitla* (1903) 34 Can.S.C. 191; *McMaster v. Ins. Co. of North America*, 55 N.Y. 222 (1873); *Mead v. American Fire Ins. Co.*, 13 Hun.App. 476 (1897).

[75] We are most grateful to officials of the Fire Loss Association for providing much of the material upon which this chapter is based. They are not, of course, in any way responsible for its contents.

[76] E. H. Minnion, *Average Clauses and Fire Loss Apportionments* (1947); and for further reference T. J. Milnes, *Fire Loss Apportionments* (1906); John and James Laird, *Fire Loss Apportionments* (1909); W. H. Hore, *Remarks on the Apportionment of Fire Losses* (1869), reissued (1909) with preface by T. J. Milnes; F. H. Kitchen, *The Principles and Finance of Fire Insurance* (1904) Ch. 6; H. S. Bell, *Contribution in Fire Insurance* (1935); S. J. Pipkin, "The Average Conditions of a Fire Insurance Policy" (1896); J.F.I.I., Vol. 1, p. 243; H. C. Evans, "Contribution in Respect of Fire Losses" (1909), J.F.I.I., Vol. 12, p. 143; W. T. Watson, "Law of Contribution as it Affects Insurance Companies" (1909) J.F.I.I., Vol. 13, p. 321; T. C. Howes, "Problem of Full Value in Relation to Average" (1969) J.C.I.I., Vol. 66, p. 43; A. R. Doublet, *Fire Insurance Claims* (1963) especially Chs 7 and 8.

[77] See paras 23–01 *et seq.*, *supra* where the necessary conditions for the right of contribution are examined in the context of double insurance.

one policy covers the loss, each insurer is only responsible to the insured for his own proportion of the loss.[78] The rateable proportion for which the insurers are liable under such a condition is calculated in accordance with the principles set out in this chapter.

The manner in which contributions between different insurers were calculated used sometimes to be complex. During recent years, however, average clauses have been incorporated into most policies of insurance and this makes the calculation somewhat more simple since claims are, in such cases, shared in proportion to the independent liability of each insurer. Where there is no average clause, contribution is based on the respective sums insured by each insurer.

(b) *Contribution Under the Average Clause*

23–33 Under-insurance. Under a non-marine policy of insurance[79] the insured can recover the whole amount of his loss up to the limit of the sum insured. He may, therefore, obtain insurance at a small premium by understating the value of the subject-matter insured, but nevertheless make recovery in a sum up to the amount insured[80]; where there is a partial loss he may even be able to recover the full amount of his loss and suffer no penalty for being under-insured.

23–34 It has therefore become the almost invariable practice for insurers to declare that the policy is "subject to average"[81] or "subject to the undermentioned condition of average" which means that, if the sum insured does not represent the value of the property insured at the time of the loss or damage, the insured is to be his own insurer for the requisite proportion of the insurance and must therefore bear a part of the loss accordingly. In *Carreras Ltd v. Cunard Steamship Co.*[82] where the plaintiff company warehoused goods with the defendant company at a fixed rental to include insurance against loss or damage by fire, Bailhache J. held that the so-called pro-rata condition of average was so common in fire insurances on merchandise that it must be implied as a term of the warehouse agreement. The average clause now occurs in almost all policies, except those relating to private dwelling-houses and household goods, and to buildings (and their contents) used wholly or mainly for religious worship.[83]

The first record of the average principle in relation to fire insurance

---

[78] See para. 23–20, *supra*.

[79] For marine insurance, s.81 of the Marine Insurance Act 1906 provides that where the insurance is for an amount less than the insurable value, the assured is deemed to be his own insurer in respect of the uninsured balance. Compare *Joyce v. Kennard* (1871) L.R. 7 Q.B. 78 with *Holmes & Sons Ltd v. Merchants' Marine Ins. Co. Ltd* [1919] 1 K.B. 383.

[80] *Sillem v. Thornton* (1854) 3 E. & B. 868, 888, *per* Lord Campbell C.J.; *Anglo-Californian Bank Ltd v. London and Provincial Marine and General Ins. Co.* (1904) 10 Com.Cas. 1, 9, *per* Walton J. See also *Fifth Liverpool Starr-Bowkett Building Society v. Travellers' Accident Ins. Co.* (1893) 9 T.L.R. 221; *Newman v. Maxwell* (1899) 80 L.T. 681.

[81] *Acme Wood Flooring Co. Ltd v. Marten* (1904) 9 Com.Cas. 157; 20 T.L.R. 229; *Aetna Wood Paving v. Ross* (1910) 15 Com.Cas. 24. It may sometimes be difficult to ascertain whether the parties to the insurance contract intended the policy to be subject to average, see *Niger Co. Ltd v. Yorkshire Ins. Co. Ltd* (1920) 2 Ll.L.R. 509.

[82] [1918] 1 K.B. 118.

[83] These exceptions were agreed by the Fire Offices' Committee in 1967. The non-tariff companies and Lloyd's underwriters follow the same practice.

appears to be a minute of the Fire Committee of the Royal Exchange Assurance Corporation in January 1722 when it was ordered that the following note should be added to all policies of £500 and upwards:

> "If in case of loss or damage it appears that there was a greater value than the sum insured hereby and part thereof is saved, then this loss or damage shall be taken and born (*sic*) in an average."[84]

Average clauses have taken different forms over the years and there are now three conditions of average in common use, but the words "average clause" or "condition of average" or "subject to average", without more, will always refer to what is known as the *pro rata* condition of average.

23–35 Pro rata condition of average. The first condition of average is the *pro rata* condition of average and is usually in some such form as the following:

> "Wherever a sum insured is declared to be subject to Average, if the property covered thereby shall, at the breaking out of any fire or at the commencement of any destruction of or damage to such property by any other peril hereby insured against, be collectively of greater value than such sum insured, then the Insured shall be considered as being his own insurer for the difference and shall bear a rateable share of the loss accordingly."

The opening words of the clause render it necessary for the policy to declare, first, the sum for which each item is insured and, secondly, that the sum insured is subject to the Condition of Average set out in the policy.

23–36 Concurrent average policies. Where insurances are concurrent, that is to say, where the contributing policies are of the same range and cover precisely the same property, the proper basis of contribution is according to the liabilities of the several policies for the actual loss.

Value of property insured	Insured in Office A	Insured in Office B	Loss
300	100	150	150

The property is under-insured in respect of 50 and, if the policy is subject to average, the insured must bear his proportion of the loss.

Thus

$$\text{A pays } \frac{100}{300} \times \frac{150}{1} = 50$$

$$\text{B pays } \frac{150}{300} \times \frac{150}{1} = 75$$

$$\text{Assured bears } \frac{50}{300} \times 150 = 25$$

---

[84] For this and other interesting historical information see the paper read to the Insurance Institute of London by Mr. G. F. Lambert F.C.I.I. on 26 February, 1969. We are grateful to the Institute for allowing us to consult this paper, which is their property; a copy of the paper is held in the Institute, and copies may be obtained from them.

23–37 Non-concurrent average policies.[85] When non-concurrent policies are subject to *pro rata* average condition, policies covering more than one property are liable in respect of each property for the proportion which the total sum assured bears to the total value of all the properties covered.

When upon any one property the total of the liabilities calculated as above is less than the loss upon that property then the assured bears the balance of such loss, and the policies will contribute in proportion to their resulting liabilities.

23–38 When upon any one property the total of the liabilities is more than the loss upon that item, then the contributing policies bear the whole of such loss in proportion to such liabilities.

The following case will illustrate the present practice in apportioning losses:

Value of property insured	*Insured in Office A*	*Insured in Office B*	*Insured in Office C*	*Loss*
X 10000	5000 ⎤	4000(I) ⎤		6000
Y 5000	⎬	⎬	3000	4000
Z 3000	⎦	2000(II) ⎦		3000

$\dfrac{\text{Loss X}}{6000}$

$$\text{Liability of A} \quad \frac{5000}{10000} \times \frac{6000}{1} = 3000$$

$$\text{Liability of B} \quad \frac{4000}{15000} \times \frac{6000}{1} = 1600$$

Assured bears the balance of 1400

$\dfrac{\text{Loss Y}}{4000}$

$$\text{Liability of B} \quad \frac{4000}{15000} \times \frac{4000}{1} = 1066\frac{10}{15}$$

$$\text{Liability of C} \quad \frac{3000}{8000} \times \frac{4000}{1} = 1500$$

Assured bears the balance of $1433\frac{5}{15}$

$\dfrac{\text{Loss Z}}{3000}$

$$\text{Liability of B} \quad \frac{2000}{3000} \times \frac{3000}{1} = 2000 \quad \Big\rbrace$$

$$\text{Liability of C} \quad \frac{3000}{8000} \times \frac{3000}{1} = 1125 \quad 3125$$

$$\text{B pays} \quad \frac{2000}{3125} \times \frac{3000}{1} = 1920$$

$$\text{C pays} \quad \frac{1125}{3125} \times \frac{3000}{1} = 1080$$

Result: A pays 3000; B pays $4586\frac{10}{15}$; C pays 2580; Assured bears $2833\frac{5}{15}$

---

[85] For a full discussion of average policies and calculations of contributions thereunder, see Minnion, *op. cit.* Chs 6–9.

23–39 The special (75 per cent) condition. Sometimes the subject-matter of the insurance has a fluctuating value and in such cases it is considered unjust to expect the insured to pay a full year's premium on a maximum value which arises only once a year. Thus the value of property on a farm will vary from time to time throughout the year and a farmer cannot reasonably be expected to pay a premium for a full year based on the value of his crops at harvest time. A condition is, therefore, introduced which provides that if the sum insured is not less than 75 per cent of the value of all agricultural produce and growing crops at the time of the fire the *pro rata* condition of average will not take effect. If, however, the sum insured is less than 75 per cent of such full value, then the condition will operate. The normal wording is as follows:

"Whenever a sum insured is declared to be subject to the special condition of average, then, if such sum shall at the breaking out of any fire at the commencement of any destruction of or damage to the property by any other peril hereby insured against, be less than three-fourths of the value of the property insured in that amount, the Insured shall be considered as being his own insurer for the difference between the sum insured and the full value of the property insured at the time of such fire or at the commencement of such destruction or damage and shall bear a rateable share of the loss accordingly."

Examples

(a) Sum insured   800
     Value   1000
     Loss   500
     Average does not operate. Insurer pays 500

(b) Sum insured   600
     Value   1000
     Loss   500
     Sum insured is less than 75 per cent.
     Therefore average does operate
     Insurer pays $\dfrac{600}{1000} \times 500 = 300.$

23–40 Second condition of average. The second condition of average is designed to regulate contribution among non-concurrent policies which are subject to average.

It provides that where part of the property insured by a policy of wider range is also covered by a policy of lesser range, which covers that part of the property only, the policy of wider range shall insure that part of the property only in respect of the excess of value not covered by the policy of lesser range.

23–41 The following is an example of the modern second condition of average:

"But if any of the property included in such average shall at the breaking out of any fire, or at the commencement of any destruction of or damage to such property by any other peril hereby insured against, be also covered by any other more specific insurance, *i.e.* by an insurance which at the time of such fire or at the commencement of such destruction or damage applies to part only of the property actually at risk and protected by this insurance and to no other property whatsoever, then this Policy shall not insure the same except only as regards any excess of value beyond the amount of such more specific insurance or insurances, which said excess is declared to be under the protection of this Policy, and subject to average as aforesaid."

23–42 In applying the second condition of average the range of a policy is not to be deemed restricted by reason of the fact that part of the property covered is fully insured by another policy of lesser range. Thus, in the following case:

Value of property insured		Insured in Office A	Insured in Office B	Insured in Office C	Loss
X	100	100			100
				50	
Y	200		100		50

the value of X is fully covered by the policy A, and if X were eliminated altogether from policy C, policies B and C would be concurrent insurances, and the second condition of average would not apply to their contribution *inter se*. In accordance, however, with the above rule, X cannot be altogether eliminated from policy C, and that policy is still deemed to be a policy of wider range than policy B, and the second condition of average applies, so that C insures Y only in respect of the excess of value not covered by policy B.

23–43 Application of both conditions of average. Now, if one takes again the example in paragraph 23–38 and considers it on the assumption that the policies contain both the conditions of average, the following result is obtained:

Applying the second condition of average:

Policy B(I) applies to X only in so far as there is an excess of value over the amount covered by policy A, that is to say, it covers 5000 only of X, and the total value covered by policy B(I) is 10000.

Policy C applies to Z only in so far as there is an excess of value over the amount covered by policy B(II), that is to say, it covers 1000 only of Z, and the total value covered by policy C is 6000.

23–44 Applying the *pro rata* average condition:

$\dfrac{\text{Loss X}}{6000}$ Liability of A $\dfrac{5000}{10000} \times \dfrac{6000}{1} = 3000$ (leaving a loss of 3000)

Liability of B $\dfrac{4000}{10000} \times \dfrac{3000}{1} = 1200$

Assured bears the balance, 1800

$\dfrac{\text{Loss Y}}{4000}$ Liability of B $\dfrac{4000}{1} \times \dfrac{4000}{1} = 1600$

Liability of C $\dfrac{3000}{6000} \times \dfrac{4000}{1} = 2000$

Assured bears the balance, 400

$\dfrac{\text{Loss } Z}{3000}$ Liability of B $\quad \dfrac{2000}{3000} \times \dfrac{3000}{1} = 2000$ (leaving a loss of 1000)

Liability of C $\quad \dfrac{3000}{6000} \times \dfrac{1000}{1} = 500$

Assured bears the balance, 500

Result: A pays 3000; B pays 4800; C pays 2500; Assured bears 2700.

(c) Contribution Without Average

23-45 Concurrenct non-average policies. Where insurances are concurrent, the proper basis of contribution is according to the amounts insured upon the property, and not according to the liabilities of the several policies for the actual loss.
Thus:

Value of property insured	Insured in Office A	Insured in Office B	Loss
300	100	150	100

A pays $\dfrac{100}{250} \times \dfrac{100}{1} = 40$

B pays $\dfrac{150}{250} \times \dfrac{100}{1} = 60$

23-46 Non-concurrent non-average policies. The practice among the British offices is to adhere to the same basis as in concurrent policies—that is to say, to make each policy contribute in proportion to the amount insured by it and applicable to the common subject of insurance. Where a policy has contributed in respect of any one item it is *pro tanto* diminished as to the amount of its insurance, and is only available to contribute in respect of other items as to the balance of the sum insured, and consequently the result of the apportionment may vary according to the order in which the items of insurance are apportioned. When this is the case the ususal practice is to apportion them in the first instance from the item upon which there is the greatest loss down to the item upon which there is the least loss, and then to apportion them in the reverse order and take the mean of the two apportionments.
Sometimes, instead of taking only two apportionments as above, a separate apportionment is taken in each possible order of rotation of the several items. Thus, where there are three items of insurance upon which loss has occurred there would be six apportionments, and contribution would be upon the mean of the six. It is more usual, however, to rely upon the mean of the two apportionments only.
The result of taking the mean of the apportionments as indicated above may be that the loss is not fully met. Where the sums insured, when added together, are insufficient to meet the whole loss, the insured will be given the benefit of the apportionment which allocates to him the smaller or smallest proportion of the total loss. Where, however, the sums insured are together

sufficient to meet the whole loss, then an alternative method of apportionment must be found since the insured is entitled to be fully indemnified if the overall sums insured are adequate. In such a case the proportion might have to be calculated on the basis of liability of the insurer rather than on the basis of the sums insured.[86]

23-47 The following simple case will illustrate the practice in relation to mean apportionment:[87]

Value of property insured	Insured in Office A	Insured in Office B	Loss
Stock 2000	1000 ⎫	1500	1500
Fittings 1000	⎬	500	

Larger Loss First

		A	B

1. Stock

$$A \ \frac{1000}{2500} \times \frac{1500}{1} = 600$$

$$B \ \frac{1500}{2500} \times \frac{1500}{1} = 900 \qquad\qquad 600 \qquad\qquad 900$$

2. Fittings
   B 1500 − 900 = 600
   Therefore B pays 500

   $$\qquad\qquad\qquad\qquad\qquad\qquad 500$$

Smaller Loss First

		A	B

2. Fittings
   B pays 500 of his total
   sum insured of 1500

   $$\qquad\qquad\qquad\qquad\qquad\qquad 500$$

1. Stock

$$A \ 1000$$

Total Insurance

$$B$$

$$(1500 - 500) = \frac{1000}{2000}$$

$$A \ \frac{1000}{2000} \times \frac{1500}{1} = 750$$

$$B \ \frac{1000}{2000} \times \frac{1500}{1} = 750$$

		750	750
	Aggregate	1350	2650
	Mean	675	1325

[86] An alternative method would be to apportion the balance remaining to the account of the insured in the same proportion as the rest of the loss is borne by the insurers.

[87] For a more complex example setting out an instance of failure to indemnify the insured by the method of mean apportionment, see para. 1865 of the fifth edition of this work.

Therefore A pays on Stock   675 (Half of 1350)
          B pays on Stock   825 (Half of 1650)
          B pays on Fittings 500 (Half of 1000)
                             ————
                             2000

23–48 Contribution in proportion to liability. Messrs Laird[88] suggested that in dealing with non-concurrent insurances the basis of contribution in proportion to the sums assured should be abandoned, and that contribution ought to be in proportion to the liability of each insurer for the loss on each item. This method was strenuously advocated by Mr Hore[89] many years ago, but the method of contribution in proportion to sums assured was so firmly established in practice that it successfully resisted and still resists the logic of Mr Hore's arguments. Contribution in proportion to liability has, however, received judicial support in the context of liability insurance where the Court of Appeal has held that contribution, where there is no condition of average, should be assessed on an independent liability and not a maximum liability basis.

23–49 In *Commercial Union Assurance Co. v. Hayden*[90] the insured had effected a public liability policy with the Commercial Union with a limit of £100,000 on any one accident and a similar policy with Lloyd's with a limit of £10,000 on any one accident. A Mr Parsons was injured on the insured's premises and the Commercial Union met his claim by paying £4,425.45. They then sought to claim contribution from Lloyd's underwriters on an "independent liability basis" saying that since both policies would have been liable in full, they should share the claim equally. Lloyd's underwriters resisted the claim and argued that contribution should be made in proportion to the total limits of the respective policies *viz*. 10:1 and that they were liable for only one-eleventh of the total claim. This was referred to as the "maximum liability basis". Donaldson J. found in favour of Lloyd's largely because the maximum liability basis had always been applied to concurrent non-average policies insuring property. The Court of Appeal, however, took the opposite view and preferred the independent liability basis, mainly on the ground that it was that approach which was more likely to be intended by reasonable businessmen. Cairns L.J. said:

> "It is difficult to suppose that when a limit of £10,000 was fixed by Lloyd's it could be intended that if there happened to be another policy with a limit of £100,000. Lloyd's underwriters should be liable for only one-eleventh of any claim, however small. ... The obvious purpose of having a limit under an insurance policy is to protect the insurer from the effect of exceptionally large claims: it seems to me artificial to use the limits under two policies to adjust liability in respect of claims which are within the limits of either policy."

The result of this decision is that for a claim which falls within the limits of both policies, insurers bear the loss equally; while for a claim which falls only

[88] *Fire Loss Apportionments* (1909), see note 76, *supra*.
[89] *Remarks on the Apportionments of Fire Losses* (1869), see note 76, *supra*.
[90] [1977] Q.B. 804; [1977] 1 Lloyd's Rep. 1.

within the policy with the higher limit, the smaller policy will contribute half the loss up to its own limit and the larger policy will contribute the balance.

It is respectfully submitted that this decision is correct. It is in accordance with the earlier decision of *American Surety Co. v. Wrightson*[91] where Hamilton J. adopted the independent liability basis to a similar question because the maximum liability basis proved to be unworkable. Moreover, the maximum liability basis would be very difficult to operate in cases where the sum recoverable under one of the policies is unlimited, as, for example, a motor insurance policy complying with the requirements of the Road Traffic Act 1972.

23–50 Policies on property. The Court of Appeal were careful to confine their decision to the method of contribution between liability policies but the question remains whether the independent liability method is not also the correct basis in law for ascertaining contribution between insurances on property. It is clear that the present practice where there is no average clause is to assess contribution by reference to the maximum liability method but it may well be only a matter of time before the courts hold that, in law, the independent liability method leads to a fairer result and is, therefore, to be preferred.[92]

23–51 Voluntary payment in excess of liability. Where a policy contains a rateable proportion clause the insurer is not entitled to contribution from the other insurers, if he pays out more than he is required to do by his policy, since contribution only arises out of a legal obligation to pay.[93]

23–52 Conditional average clause. In order to avoid the difficulty which arises when a policy subject to average has to contribute with a policy not subject to average, it is usual[94] to provide in a policy not primarily subject to average that where any of the property covered thereby is covered by any other policy which is subject to average, then the first policy shall be subject to average in like manner. An example of a clause in general use until 1922 and still sometimes found is:

> "In all cases where any other subsisting Insurance or Insurances, whether effected by the Insured or by any other person or persons on his behalf, covering any of the property hereby insured either alone or together with any other property in and subject to the same risk only, shall be subject to average, the Insurance on such property under this Policy shall be subject to average in like manner."

Since 1922 it has been more usual to add two clauses after the standard contribution clause as set out in paragraph 23–20 above.[95] "If any such other insurance shall be subject to any Condition of Average this policy, if not

---

[91] (1910) 16 Com.Cas. 37, 103 L.T. 663.

[92] See [1977] C.L.J. 231.

[93] *Legal and General Ass. Co. v. Drake Ins. Co.* [1992] Q.B. 887. The decision is difficult to understand on the facts, since, under the relevant provisions of the Road Traffic Acts the plaintiffs were obliged to pay the whole amount to the third party claimant. Lloyd L.J. seems to have thought it relevant that they could recover 50 per cent of that amount from their insured, but it is difficult to see why they should have been obliged to sue their own insured in order to relieve their co-insurer, see *The Yasin* [1979] 2 Lloyd's Rep. 45, 52, *per* Lloyd J., as he then was.

[94] Except in policies on dwelling-houses.

[95] See in general Minnion, *op. cit.* Ch. 9.

already subject to any Condition of Average, shall be subject to Average in like manner."

"If any other insurance effected by or on behalf of the insured is expressed to cover any of the property hereby insured, but is subject to any provision whereby it is excluded from ranking concurrently with this policy either in whole or in part or from contributing rateably to the destruction or damage, the liability of the Company hereunder shall be limited to such proportion of the destruction or damage as the sum hereby insured bears to the value of the property."

The second of these two clauses is designed to prevent an insured from recovering in full for a partial loss if he has insured for only a part of the value of the property with one insurer and the balance (at a lower rate of premium) under a policy designed only to operate over and above the sum insured under the first policy. In such cases the insured may be obtaining full cover for a total loss at less premium than he would otherwise pay.

23–53 Contribution by agreement between insurers. In the apportionment of losses on certain types of property including private house property, most insurers apportion the loss *inter se* without regard to the different interests which may be insured in the property. Almost all non-tariff offices, but not Lloyd's, subscribe to an Agreement made by members of the Fire Offices Committee whereby contribution is accepted even where the policies cover different interests. In other words the decision in *North British and Mercantile v. London Liverpool and Globe*[96] is disregarded and the insurances are treated as double insurance subject to contribution, instead of as several insurances upon separate interests giving rise to possible rights of subrogation but not contribution.

The Agreement does not affect mercantile insurances and applies to the contents of buildings only in certain cases; thus there is no apportionment in the case of losses on commercial risks or the contents of buildings not covered by the Agreement, unless there is double insurance in the strict legal sense.[97]

[96] (1877) 5 Ch.D. 569.
[97] For further information, see Mr Lambert's paper referred to in note 84, *supra*, which, however, deals with the form of Agreement which existed in 1969. The Agreement has now been re-drafted and revised.

SECTION 2

PARTICULAR CLASSES OF BUSINESS

CHAPTER 24

LIFE INSURANCE

1. PROOF OF DEATH AND AGE

24–1 Proof satisfactory to the directors. The insurance money on a whole-life policy is usually made payable when proof satisfactory to the directors shall have been made of the death of the assured, and of the title of the party or parties claiming under the policy. Sometimes the policy money is made payable after the lapse of a specified period, such as three months, after such proof shall have been made: but the tendency of modern practice is to make claims payable immediately on proof of death and title. Proof satisfactory to the directors means proof which ought to be satisfactory to them.[1] Death must be proved by such evidence as the directors may reasonably require, but the directors are not justified in refusing payment merely because their unreasonable or capricious demands have not been satisfied.[2] There may be "reasonable proof" although the evidence is such as would be excluded by the technical rules applied in a court of justice.[3] Reasonable persons may reasonably take different views, and therefore it does not follow that, because a judge or jury subsequently find the death proved, it was therefore the duty of the company to have paid when the claim was first made, even although practically the same evidence was placed before them at that time as was afterwards placed before the court. Where the evidence is not clear the company under such a clause is entitled to the protection of an order of the court, and if they act reasonably in declining to pay in a doubtful case, they will be entitled to deduct from the sum insured the costs incurred by them in defending an action.[4] The question, however, of reasonableness is a question of fact, and a judge or jury having found the death proved on the evidence before them may also find as a fact that an insurance company was unreasonable in not accepting that evidence as sufficient, and upon such a finding the company will have to pay the costs of the action.[5]

24–2 Certified evidence of death and of age. The most common way in

---

[1] *London Guarantee v. Fearnley* (1880) 5 App.Cas. 911, 916. The obligation to vouch the claim by satisfactory proof does not mean that the directors' evaluation of the proof as evidence cannot be challenged in a court or arbitration proceedings—*Napier v. UNUM Ltd* [1996] 2 Lloyd's Rep. 550, 553.

[2] *Braunstein v. Accidental Death* (1861) 1 B. & S. 782.

[3] *Wilson v. Esquimalt Ry* [1922] 1 A.C. 202

[4] *Doyle v. City of Glasgow Life* (1884) 53 L.J.Ch. 527.

[5] *Ballantine v. Employers' Insurance* (1893) 21 R. 305.

which death and, if not already admitted, the age of the deceased are proved is by the production of the death certificate and birth certificate, in other words by production of an appropriate certified copy entry in the Register of births, deaths and marriages.[6]

The Births and Deaths Registration Act 1953 contains the English provisions regarding the registration of births and deaths[7] and provides, *inter alia*,[8] that a certified copy of any entry is admissible as evidence of the facts properly recorded therein.[9] This includes the date of birth or death as well as the fact thereof.[10] No evidence need be given of the authenticity of the certificate nor of the official capacity of the person by whom it purports to be signed.

24–3 Other public records. Any other public records regularly kept and produced from proper custody are admissible as evidence of death and of age. A copy or extract is admissible if proved to have been examined or certified as a true copy by the officer to whose custody the book or document is entrusted.[11] Such records have been held to include a muster book of a vessel of the Royal Navy recording the death of a seaman,[12] a parochial register of baptisms or burials,[13] and an entry in a family Bible recording the date of birth of a member of the family.[14]

There are provisions confirming the admissibility in evidence of army and air force records,[15] parish registers,[16] non-parochial registers,[17] and foreign registers and other public records.[18]

[6] The certificate should be accompanied by evidence of identity if there is any room for doubt as to whether the person named in the certificate and the person whose life is insured are one and the same: *Parkinson v. Francis* (1846) 15 Sim. 160.
[7] Substantially the same provisions are made for Northern Ireland and Scotland by the Births and Deaths Registration (Northern Ireland) Acts 1863 to 1947 and the Registration of Births, Deaths and Marriages (Scotland) Act 1965, respectively.
[8] For detail, see *Halsbury's Laws of England*, (4th ed.) Vol. 39, paras 1001, *et seq.*
[9] In respect of births and deaths occurring at sea see the Merchant Shipping Act 1995, s.108; the Merchant Shipping (Returns of Births and Deaths) Regulations 1979 (S.I. 1979 No. 1577); and the Registration of Births, Deaths and Marriages (Special Provisions) Act 1957, s.2. In respect of the registration of births and deaths in aircraft registered in the U.K. see the Civil Aviation Act 1982, s.83 and the Civil Aviation (Births, Deaths and Missing Persons) Regulations 1948 (S.I. 1984 No. 1411).
[10] *In the Estate of Goodrich* [1904] P. 138; *Brierley v. Brierley* [1918] P. 257.
[11] Evidence Act 1851, s.14.
[12] *R. v. Rhodes* (1742) Leach 24.
[13] However, this is not in itself evidence of the date of birth (*Robinson v. Buccleugh* (1886) 3 T.L.R. 472) but merely of the fact and date of baptism and that the person baptised was born before that date (*Re Bulley's Settlement* [1866] W.N. 80). However, combined with parol evidence that the person was very young when baptised, it could be evidence of the approximate date of birth.
[14] *Hubbard v. Lees* (1866) L.R. 1 Ex. 255.
[15] Army Act 1955, s.198(5) and the Air Force Act 1955, s.198(5), as amended by the Army and Air Force Act 1961, s.38(1) and Sch. 11.
[16] The Baptismal and Burial Registers Act 1812. Parish registers in Scotland are now in the hands of the Registrar-General for Scotland: the Registration of Births, Deaths and Marriages (Scotland) Act 1965, ss.45–47.
[17] The Non-Parochial Registers Act 1840, under which these records were deposited with the Registrar-General of Births, Deaths and Marriages.
[18] These, and certified extracts therefrom, are admissible in evidence as to matters properly and regularly recorded therein, where it appears that they have been kept under the sanction of public authority, and are recognised by the tribunals of the country where they are kept as authentic records: *Lyell v. Kennedy* (1889) 14 App.Cas. 437; see also Oaths and Evidence (Overseas Authorities and Countries) Act 1963, s.5(1).

24–4 Direct evidence. Death or age may be proved by direct evidence, that is by the oath of some person present at the death or birth, as the case may be.

24–5 Presumption of death. If a person has disappeared and no direct evidence of his life or death can be obtained, his death may be proved either by

(1) circumstantial evidence, that is, by proof of facts from which a jury might reasonably infer the fact of death; or

(2) a presumption of law which arises after the expiry of seven years from the time a person was last seen or heard of.[19]

For the prima facie presumption of death to arise, there must in general be evidence that those who would be likely to hear of the missing person, if alive, have not heard of him[20] and evidence that reasonable enquiries have been made by advertisement and otherwise in or about the place or places where he was last seen or heard of, or where he was likely to have gone.[21] The presumption does not arise if a person disappears in circumstances which lead to the inference that even if he were alive, it would be unlikely that his friends or relatives would hear of him.[22]

24–6 Date of death. In general there is no presumption as to the date of death within the seven-year period,[23] and the onus of proving life or death at any particular time rests on the person alleging it.[24] However, as a rule the date of disappearance is a more probable date of death than any other time during the seven years. In one situation, namely the death of two or more persons in circumstances rendering it uncertain which of them survived the other or others, there is a statutory presumption that the younger survived the elder.[25]

24–7 Presumption of earlier death. When a person has disappeared, it is possible to prove death without waiting for the expiry of the seven-year period, if the circumstances are such that a court or jury may reasonably find, as a matter of fact, that the missing person is dead.[26] Such circumstances could include a missing or shipwrecked vessel[27] and a sailor, soldier or airman reported missing and afterwards officially presumed killed.[28]

24–8 Leave to swear death. If a missing person holds a policy of insurance

[19] This is a common law presumption in England, based on the analogy of statutes relating to the presumption of death in special cases. A more detailed account may be found in Phipson, *Evidence* (14th ed., 1990) para. 5–10. As to Scotland, see paras 24–14, *et seq.*

[20] *Doe v. Andrews* (1850) 15 Q.B.D. 756.

[21] See, especially, *Prudential Assurance v. Edmonds* (1877) 2 App.Cas. 487; *Chard v. Chard* [1956] P. 259.

[22] See, *e.g. Watson v. England* (1844) 14 Sim. 28; *Bowden v. Henderson* (1854) 2 Sm. & G. 360.

[23] *Re Phené's Trusts* (1870) L.R. 5 Ch. 139.

[24] *Re Rhodes* (1887) 36 Ch.D. 586, and see generally, Phipson, *Evidence* (14th ed., 1990).

[25] Law of Property Act 1925, s.184; see *Hickman v. Peacey* [1945] A.C. 304 as to the construction of s.184. As to Scotland, see the Succession (Scotland) Act 1964, s.31 which provides to the same effect, subject to the exceptions therein. See para. 24–15, *post.*

[26] *R. v. Tolson* (1889) 23 Q.B.D. 168.

[27] See, *e.g. In the Goods of Norris* (1858) 1 Sw. & Tr. 6; *In the Goods of Main* (1858) 1 Sw. & Tr. 11; *In the Goods of Hurlston* [1898] P. 27.

[28] *Re Butler's Settlement Trusts* [1942] Ch. 403.

on his own life, no action can be brought upon it until his personal representatives have completed their title by probate or letters of administration, and they cannot do this until they have obtained leave to swear the death.[29]

24–9 Notice of application. Notice of an application for leave to swear death must be given to any insurance company which has insured the missing person's life,[30] and if the company successfully resists the application, it may be allowed its costs against the applicant.[31]

24–10 Liability of insurer. The company is not bound by the order of the court giving leave to swear the death. Leave is usually granted to swear the death on or after the date upon which the missing person was last seen or heard of, but it is still open to the company to defend proceedings against it either on the ground that there is no evidence of death or that there is no evidence of death before the date when the policy expired. If, however, the company disputes the death after a judge has upon full investigation and inquiry presumed death, it will do so at the risk of having to pay the costs of all subsequent proceedings.

A life office is under no obligation to pay a claim on a certificate of presumption of death issued by the competent authority in respect of a man or woman who has been serving with one of the fighting services in wartime and is presumed to have died on active service. Not being under any obligation to pay the claim on such evidence the office may, without prejudice to a subsequent denial of liability, offer to pay the sum assured in exchange for an undertaking on the part of the payee to refund it if the life assured should afterwards be proved to be alive or for such further or other security for repayment as it may think fit to demand.

24–11 Proceedings by personal representative. In the case of the presumed death of the insured on an own-life policy, it is only when death has been presumed and the will proved or an administrator appointed that the office becomes liable to an action to enforce payment. If it does not pay, it runs the risk of judgment being given against it for the sum assured and the costs of the action. The office is in a better position if it pays before judgment, because if the life assured is in fact alive, the money can then be more readily recovered in an action for money had and received on the ground that it was paid on a mistake of fact than if full judgment had been given against the office. A judgment against the office would be res judicata between the office and the legal representative so long as it stood, and it could only be got rid of by the office applying to the Court of Appeal to extend the time for appealing, and then, on an appeal against the judgment, obtaining leave of the court to adduce the new evidence proving that the assured is alive.

---

[29] See, generally, Tristram & Coote, *Probate Practice* (28th ed., 1995) pp. 562–565.

[30] An application for leave to swear to the death must include an affidavit, one of the terms of which is whether the life of the deceased was insured, and if so giving particulars of all relevant policies. This includes the name of the insurance company and whether notice of the application has been given to the insurance office: see *In the Goods of Barber* (1886) 11 P.D. 78; *In the Goods of Kirkbride* (1891) 55 J.P. 503 and Non-Contentious Probate Rules 1987, (S.I. 1987 No. 2024) (L.10) r. 53. Furthermore the applicant must produce a reply from the office or file an affidavit of service of the notice of application for leave to swear: see *In the Goods of Saul* [1896] P. 151.

[31] *Re Lidderdale, The Times*, March 24, 1910; see further (1912) 57 S.J. 3.

24–12 Rights of assured if living. So far as the assured is concerned, the presumption of his death, the grant of representation and the judgment against the office are wholly ineffectual to deprive him, if alive, of any right against the office, and he may exercise all such rights by way of reinstatement of the policy or otherwise as the terms of his policy may entitle him to. In such cases it has been sought to pray in aid of the office the protection given by section 27 of the Administration of Estates Act 1925, to persons who make any payment in good faith under a grant of representation. There has been no legal decision on the point, but the wording of the section read as a whole and the definitions of the words "representation" and "administration" in section 55 of the Act seem to show that section 27 applies only to a grant of representation to the estate of a deceased person which may afterwards be revoked on the ground that the executor or administrator was not entitled to a grant and that the section has no application to a grant of representation erroneously made to the estate of a person who is still alive.

24–13 Right of insurers to be refunded. As against the executor or administrator to whom the policy money has been paid the onus is on the office to prove that the payment was made under a mistake of fact, that is to say, that it was made in the belief that the assured was dead whereas in fact he was alive. The right of the office to recover is independent of any revocation of the grant because, even while the grant stands, proof that the assured was alive is sufficient to establish the fact that the sum assured was not payable. The liability to refund the money is that of the executor or administrator to whom it was paid, but it is not trust money and the office cannot follow it into the hands of the supposed beneficiaries to whom it may have been paid over by the personal representative. He no doubt could in his turn recover it from them as money paid under a mistake of fact.

24–14 Presumption of death in Scots Law. The Presumption of Death (Scotland) Act 1977[32] replaced the common law and previous statutory rules and introduced a single action of declarator.[33] The action may be brought by "any person having an interest" whether patrimonial or personal.[34] Apparently therefore an insurer can raise such proceedings.[35] The action may be raised either where someone is thought to have died (for example, where an aircraft has gone missing but has not been found), or where he has not been known to be alive for a period of at least seven years. The Scottish courts have jurisdiction where, on the date when the missing person was last known to be alive, he either was domiciled in Scotland or had been resident there for the year prior to that date.[36] In addition they have jurisdiction where the pursuer is the spouse of the missing person and is domiciled or habitually resident in Scotland.[37] It follows that the Scottish courts will have jurisdiction

---

[32] c. 27. This Act was passed following the Scottish Law Commission Report on Presumption of Death (Scot. Law Com. Report No. 34, 1974).
[33] s.1(2).
[34] s.1(1).
[35] s.1(1) read with s.5 and Sch. 1 of the Interpretation Act 1978 (c. 30).
[36] s.1(3)(a). For the sheriff court, see s.1(4)(a).
[37] s.1(3)(b). In such cases the Scottish court will accept as sufficient proof a decree or judgment of the court of the missing person's domicile or habitual residence: s.10. For the sheriff court, see s.1(4)(b).

even though the death may have occurred abroad or the missing person was abroad when last known to be alive.[38]

24–15 Types of decree. If death is actually established on a balance of probabilities, then the court will grant a decree specifying the date and time of death so far as ascertainable.[39] In reaching its decision the court will generally proceed on evidence rather than on presumptions. Where, however, two persons are found to have died in a common calamity and the court is unable to determine on a balance of probabilities[40] that one survived the other, then, as a rule, the younger is presumed to have survived the older.[41] The rule admits of two exceptions, one of which is directly relevant to insurance, *viz.* that where the deceased were spouses it is presumed that neither survived the other.[42] In some cases, of course, the court will not be able to find that death has been established but merely, again on a balance of probabilities, that the missing person has not been known to be alive for a period of at least seven years. In such cases the court will grant decree that the missing person died at the end of the day[43] occurring seven years after he was last known to be alive.[44]

24–16 Effect of decree. The decree of declarator is of general effect.[45] It is conclusive of the matters contained in it and is effective against any person and for all purposes—including the dissolution of the missing person's marriage[46] and the acquisition of rights to or in any person's property. So any decree is binding on insurers even though they were not parties to the action, but where insurers have an interest in the outcome of an action they may lodge a minute seeking a determination not sought by the pursuer.[47]

24–17 Recall or variation of decree. While the declarator has the widespread effects indicated, provision is made for recall or variation of the decree provided that application is made within five years.[48] Again any person having an interest, apparently including an insurer, may apply for such variation or recall[49] by lodging a minute in the original process.[50] Such an application would be appropriate, for instance, where the missing person turned up alive or where information became available indicating that the death occurred at a time other than that specified in the decree. Even where the court recalls or varies its original decree, however, the recall or variation does not affect property rights acquired by virtue of the original decree[51] unless the court makes a further order.[52] In making any further order the

---

[38] The missing person shall be called as a defender: Rules of the Court of Session (1994 S.I. No. 1443), r. 50.2.

[39] s.2(1)(a).

[40] *Lamb v. Lord Advocate* [1976] S.C. 110.

[41] Succession (Scotland) Act 1964 (c. 41), s.31(1)(b).

[42] Succession (Scotland) Act 1964, s.31(1)(a).

[43] Interpretation Act 1978, s.9.

[44] 1977 Act, s.2(1)(b).

[45] s.3(1).

[46] Even if the missing person is subsequently found to be alive, the marriage remains dissolved: s.3(3) and 4(5). For bigamy see s.13.

[47] s.1(5) read with Interpretation Act 1978, s.5 and Sch. 1.

[48] s.5(4).

[49] s.4(1) read with s.5 and Sch. 1 of the Interpretation Act 1978.

[50] s.4(3).

[51] s.5(1).

[52] s.5(2).

court must have regard to what is fair and reasonable in the circumstances, but, so far as practicable, the court must have regard to the consideration that insurers should be repaid any capital sum paid out on the strength of the original decree.[53] This safeguard for insurers is backed up by the provisions of section 6(3) by which, before paying out any capital sum on the basis of the original decree of declarator, insurers[54] are entitled to insist on the payee insuring against this kind of contingency.

2. Statutes of Limitation

24–18 Limitation Act 1980. By section 5 of this Act, all actions of debt grounded upon any simple contract must be commenced within six years next after the cause of action has arisen. Where, therefore, a policy of life assurance is not under seal any action to recover the sum assured or any other money payable thereunder must be commenced within six years after the cause of action in respect of the money claimed has arisen. Prima facie the cause of action in respect of the sum assured arises upon the maturity of the policy, i.e. upon the happening of the death of the life assured or such other event on the happening of which it is expressed to be payable. Where a policy provides that the office shall pay the sum assured on proof satisfactory to the directors of the death of the life assured and the title of the claimant, or at some specified period of time after such proof has been furnished, the operation of the statute is not suspended until after the furnishing of such proof or the lapse of such time as may be specified, because these are matters which lie within the power of the claimant to proceed with or not as he pleases, and if he does not proceed to perfect his right to sue by furnishing the necessary proof the fault lies with him alone. The condition requiring proof is a condition precedent to the right to demand payment and the right to sue: but it does not touch the cause of action, only the proof of it and the remedy.[55]

If a policy of life assurance is issued under seal the promise or covenant to pay is a specialty debt, and the right of action in respect of a claim thereunder is not barred until 12 years after the cause of action has arisen.[56]

24–19 Application to arbitrations. The Limitation Act applies to all arbitrations whether the reference is by agreement under an arbitration clause in the policy or under an Act of Parliament. In the application of the Limitation Act to arbitrations time begins to run from the date when the cause of action is complete, and not on the date when the claimant refers the dispute to arbitration.[57]

24–20 Prescription of obligation in Scots Law. The obligation of an insurer to pay a sum due under a policy is an obligation arising from a contract of insurance. The insurer's obligation to pay will prescribe five years

---

[53] s.5(3)(b).
[54] As defined in s.17.
[55] *Coburn v. Colledge* [1897] 1 Q.B. 702; *Monckton v. Page* [1899] 2 Q.B. 603; *Cheshire C.C. v. Hopley* (1923) 21 L.G.R. 524.
[56] Limitation Act 1980, s.8.
[57] Arbitration Act 1996, s.13(1); *Pegler v. Railway Executive* [1948] A.C. 332; *Central Electricity Board v. Halifax Corp'n* [1963] A.C. 785.

after it becomes enforceable,[58] unless a relevant claim is made[59] or the subsistence of the obligation has been relevantly acknowledged.[60] It was formerly the law in Scotland that the long negative presumption[61] applied to obligations constituted by probative (self proving) documents.[62] The disapplication of the long negative prescription to probative deeds,[63] consequent upon the abolition of probativity,[64] has removed the anomaly whereby obligations embodied in a probative contract of insurance subsisted for a longer period than obligations embodied in non-probative contracts of insurance. In calculating the five year period, as opposed to the twenty year period, certain periods of time are excluded.[65]

3. INTEREST AND RATE OF EXCHANGE

24-21 Power of court to award interest. Tribunals are given a statutory power to award interest upon sums awarded by them to a claimant.[66] The reader is referred to the coverage of this topic in the chapter on payment of losses.[67]

24-22 Interest runs from date of default. The court will not award interest against an insurance company unless the company was in default in making payment, and then interest will run only from the time of such default. A claimant is not entitled to interest until he has tendered to the company proper proof of death, and a good title to the policy moneys.[68] He must be able to give the company a legal discharge before interest will begin to run.[69]

24-23 Conflicting claims. Conflicting claims do not justify an insurance company in keeping the money after the time for payment has passed. Its duty is to pay into court or interplead, and, if it has improperly delayed doing so, it may be ordered to pay interest from the date when the money was payable, until the date of payment in. Where an insurance company makes a payment into court in the honest although mistaken belief that it cannot otherwise obtain a good discharge, it will not be ordered to pay interest after the date of payment in.[70] In the case of an interpleader, even though the company may be entitled to its costs of the interpleader summons, it may

---

[58] s.6(1). *Flynn v. Unum Ltd* 1996 S.L.T. 1067, following *Scott Lithgow Ltd v. Secretary of State for Defence* 1989 S.C. (H.L.) 9. For the position in relation to a contract of guarantee see *Royal Bank of Scotland v. Brown* 1982 S.C. 89. See also Lord Kincraig's discussion in *McPhail v. Cunninghame District Council* 1983 S.C. 246.

[59] See n. 40, *ante*.

[60] See n. 41, *ante*.

[61] Prescription and Limitation (Scotland) Act 1973, s.7(1).

[62] Prescription and Limitation (Scotland) Act 1973, Sch. 1 paras 2(c) and 4.

[63] Requirements of Writing (Scotland) Act 1975, Sch. 5 repealing paras. 2(c), 3 and 4(b) of Sch. 1 of the Act of 1973.

[64] Probativity has been replaced by certain presumptions: see ss.3 and 4 of the Act of 1995.

[65] s.6(4).

[66] Supreme Court of Judicature Act 1981, s.35A (High Court); County Court Act 1984, s.69 (County Court); Arbitration Act 1996 s.49 (arbitration).

[67] See paras 19–66 to 19–69, *ante*.

[68] The time of payment is frequently the end of a fixed period, such as three or six months, after proof satisfactory to the directors.

[69] *Webster v. British Empire Mutual Life* (1880) 15 Ch.D. 169; *Wells v. Prudential Assurance Co. Ltd*, I.A.C.Rep. (1930) p. 40.

[70] *Re Waterhouse's Policy* [1937] Ch. 415.

nevertheless be ordered to pay interest on the sum paid.[71] Where an insurance company was requested by the claimants not to pay the money into court pending the settlement of the dispute between them the company was not ordered to pay interest.[72]

24–24 Industrial assurance. Where, from the policy money payable on an industrial policy, the insuring society was entitled to deduct arrears of premiums, the Industrial Assurance Commissioner doubted whether he had a discretion to allow it to deduct interest on such premiums under the provisions of section 29 of the Civil Procedure Act 1833, but in the case before him he said that even if he had the jurisdiction he would not be disposed to exercise such a discretion in favour of the society inasmuch as it had benefited by avoiding the expense of collection.[73]

24–25 Rate of interest. The rate of interest payable by an insurance company on policy moneys which are overdue will vary according to the prevailing rates of interest at the relevant time and the conduct of the claimant.[74] It is usual to award interest at a small percentage over base rate.[75]

24–26 Repayment of policy money. In an Irish case it was held that the Act applied to an action by an insurance company to recover back from the assured policy moneys paid to him in ignorance of the fact subsequently discovered that the policy had been obtained by fraudulent misrepresentation. The policy-holder was ordered to repay the money with interest at four per cent.[76]

24–27 Deduction of income tax. Interest awarded by the court under section 35A of the Supreme Court Act 1981, is "interest" on which income tax is chargeable under Schedule D and the defendant in satisfying a judgment for a debt and the interest awarded thereon is entitled and bound under section 349 of the Income and Corporation Taxes Act 1988 to deduct from that part of the judgment debt which represents interest income tax at the then standard rate and to account for the same to the Crown.[77]

24–28 Policy payable in foreign currency. Where the policy money is payable in a foreign country otherwise than in sterling, it is a question of construction of the contract as to what foreign currency it is payable in. In order to ascertain this, it is necessary to discover what at the date of payment would constitute legal tender in the foreign country for the amount due under the policy.[78]

24–29 It is, however, no longer necessary to convert policy money payable in a foreign currency into sterling.[79] Judgment in an English court may be

---

[71] *French v. Royal Exchange* (1857) 7 Ir.Ch.R. 523; *Re Rosier's Trusts* (1877) 37 L.T. 426.
[72] *French v. Royal Exchange* (1857) 7 Ir.Ch.R. 523.
[73] *Bone v. Royal Liver Friendly Society* (1932) I.A.C.Rep. p. 11.
[74] See para. 19–66, *ante*.
[75] The award of simple interest over a lengthy period does not in practice compensate the claimant. Power is now given to arbitrators by s.49 of the Arbitration Act 1996 to award compound interest where the justice of the case requires it.
[76] *Edinburgh Life v. Byrne* (1911) J.I.A., Vol. xlvii, p. 306.
[77] *Westminster Bank Ltd v. Riches* [1947] A.C. 390.
[78] *Anderson v. Equitable Life Assurance Society of the United States* (1926) 42 T.L.R. 302.
[79] For a fuller discussion, see McGregor, *Damages* (16th ed., 1997) paras 704–737.

expressed in the currency of the debt,[80] even where the proper law of the contract is English.[81] For procedural reasons, however, before execution is levied, the amount of the judgment must be converted into sterling. The proper date for conversion is the date of payment, i.e. the date when the court authorises enforcement of the judgment.[82]

4. CLAIMANT'S TITLE TO POLICY

24–30 An insurance company may only safely pay out the policy moneys to the person or persons entitled to them at the date when they become due. In this part of the chapter the principal means will be considered whereby title to the policy moneys is established and whereby the company may obtain a good discharge for the policy moneys.

(a) *Discharge for Policy Moneys*

24–31 (a) The general rule. As a general rule, but subject to the exceptions set out below, the company should in all cases obtain a discharge from both the person entitled to sue at law for the policy moneys[83] and from the person entitled to the policy moneys in equity[84] at the time when the policy falls due for payment. If the office accepts anything less it stands the risk of having to pay out twice over on the policy. Thus if the office omits to obtain a legal discharge and instead pays out directly to, for example, an equitable assignee, it may find itself with no defence to an action brought by another equitable assignee, in the name of the person entitled at law to the policy moneys, who gave notice to the legal proprietor before the persons whom the office had already paid.[85] Thus the company ought always to obtain a legal discharge. However it is a defence to a company which has not obtained a legal discharge to show that it has paid out the moneys to the person beneficially entitled in equity.[86]

24–32 (b) Formal discharge. A legal discharge means that the person to whom the money is paid has a legal and not just an equitable title to it. The company is obliged to pay out to the claimant upon the production to it of such evidence as does or ought reasonably to satisfy it that he is entitled at law to the policy moneys. In this respect the obligations of an insurance company do not differ from that of any other debtor. It is not entitled to insist on any formal discharge from the claimant as a precondition to payment[87]; and, whilst it may ask for a receipt, the refusal to give a receipt does not justify the company in withholding payment.[88]

---

[80] *Miliangos v. George Frank (Textiles) Ltd (No. 1)* [1976] A.C. 443; as to Scotland see *Commerzbank AG v. Large* 1977 S.C. 375 and Rules of the Court of Session 1994 (S.I. 1994 No. 1443) r. 7.5.

[81] *Federal Commerce & Navigation Co. Ltd v. Tradax Export SA* [1977] Q.B. 324.

[82] *Miliangos v. George Frank (Textiles) Ltd, supra.*

[83] *i.e.* The person entitled to the legal chose in action.

[84] *i.e.* The person entitled to the equitable chose in action.

[85] See paras 24–69, *et seq., post.*

[86] *Da Costa v. Prudential* (1918) 88 L.J.K.B. 884.

[87] *Cole v. Blake* (1793) Peake 238; *Finch v. Miller* (1848) 5 C.B. 428.

[88] *ibid.*

(b) *Proof of Title*

24–33 The company is always entitled to insist upon strict proof of the claimant's title, and every step in the title ought to be established by the proper documentary evidence.

24–34 (a) Production of policy. The fact that a claimant is unable to produce the policy does not in itself afford the company a good reason for withholding payment, provided that the non-production of it is satisfactorily explained.[89]

24–35 (i) Policy in hands of third person. Where the policy is in the hands of a third person, that person may well have a right to retain the document, although he has no claim at all to the policy moneys. The most frequent example of this is where a solicitor has a lien on the policy for his charges. Another example is where the policy has been subject to an imperfect gift, which is sufficient to pass property in the document but not sufficient to transfer the chose in action. In such circumstances the company is not entitled to insist on the production of the policy but must pay out to the claimant notwithstanding. The claimant is in a position to prove his claim to the full, and if the matter were litigated, he could serve a *subpoena duces tecum* upon the person in possession of the policy. The company is probably entitled to insist upon a statutory declaration by the claimant that he has asked for production of the policy but that such production has been refused.[90] In a case where the person in possession of the policy has no right to retain it as against the claimant, the company may probably insist that the claimant take all the appropriate steps to recover it.[91]

24–36 (ii) Non-production of policy in Scotland. In Scotland the company is entitled to refuse payment except on the production and the delivery up to it of the policy if it is admittedly in existence. Thus, where a company refused payment of the policy money to an executrix who said that the policy had been deposited by the assured with a bank as security for a cash credit, it was held, dismissing the executrix's claim, that the policy was a document of debt and that the company was not legally bound to pay its creditor without delivery of such document.[92]

24–37 (iii) Lost policy. If the policy is alleged to be lost the company is probably entitled to insist that the claimant give a statutory declaration stating the circumstances under which it was lost, that all diligent searches and inquiries as to its whereabouts have been made and that the claimant has not himself made any assignment, deposit or charge of the policy and knows of no claim to the policy moneys conflicting with his own. It is usual for the company to ask for an indemnity, but strictly it cannot insist upon one.[93] If

---

[89] *e.g.* that it has been lost or is in the hands of some other person who refuses to give it up.

[90] In this connection it should be noted that a mortgagee exercising the statutory power of sale ought under Law of Property Act 1925, s.106(4) to recover the policy and all other documents of title from any person other than one having a prior charge.

[91] N.B. If the company itself by its own default, allowed the policy to fall in the hands of the third person it can make no such demand—see *Worsfauld v. Pearl*, [1934] I.A.C.Rep. p. 32.

[92] *Scott v. Edinburgh Life* (1907) J.I.A. Vol. xlvi, p. 396.

[93] *Crockett v. Ford* (1855) 25 L.J.Ch. 552; *England v. Tredegar* (1866) L.R. 1 Eq. 344.

the matter were litigated the company would be ordered to pay out, and the decree of the court would be sufficient indemnity.[94]

24–38 (b) Surrender of policy. A surrender of the policy is tantamount to a sale. Thus, where a policy is offered for surrender the company ought to satisfy itself not only that the claimant has a good title but also that he has power to sell the policy. Where the claimant is a trustee or mortgagee, his power of sale must be carefully considered.[95]

24–39 (c) Assignee's documents of title. The company is not entitled to delivery up of an assignee's documents of title showing his title from the original assured. The assignee will, of course, have to produce them to the company to satisfy them as to his claim, but, once having done so, he is entitled to retain them to protect himself against any claims which may subsequently be made against him.[96] In practice, where the deeds of assignment relate only to the policy, they are handed over to the company together with the policy, and, where they relate to other property, the claimant gives the company an acknowledgment of the right to production of the deeds and an undertaking to produce them when required.[97] Notwithstanding, however, that this is the long-established practice, the company is not strictly entitled to insist upon such an acknowledgment, and is liable to be sued by the claimant if it withholds payments pending his giving the required acknowledgment.[98]

24–40 Claimant's agent. If payment is to be made to an agent for the claimant the company should satisfy itself that the agent has sufficient authority to receive the money. Normally this will take the form of a written authority signed by the claimant appointing the person to whom payment is to be made an agent to receive the policy moneys on his behalf. Such authority could take the form of a clause in the policy appointing that person as payee of the policy.[99] Trustees[1] have wide powers to appoint an agent for this purpose under section 11 of the Trustee Act 2000.[2] It has been suggested that the company may safely pay to a solicitor acting for any claimant upon production of the policy with the receipt of the claimant indorsed thereon pursuant to the provisions of section 69 of the Law of Property Act 1925. It is submitted, however, that this section is inapplicable even where the policy is under seal, since the receipt for policy moneys can scarcely be considered "a receipt for consideration money" within the meaning of the section.[3]

---

[94] Thus, if the company pays the policy moneys into court because an indemnity is refused, and the title of the claimant is reasonably clear, the company may be ordered to pay the claimant's costs of applying to the court for payment out—see *Harrison v. Alliance Assurance* [1903] 1 K.B. 184.

[95] See paras 24–134 and 24–214, *post.*

[96] *Re Palmer* [1907] 1 Ch. 486.

[97] For the effect of such an acknowledgment and undertaking see Law of Property Act 1925, s.64.

[98] *Dockray v. Refuge Assurance* (1912) J.I.A. Vol. xlvii, p. 422.

[99] See as to receipt clauses, paras 24–75 to 24–76, *post.*

[1] Which expression includes a personal representative but not a mortgagee (Trustee Act 1925, s.68).

[2] This section and the other provisions of Pt. IV of the 2000 Act replaced s.23 of the Trustee Act 1925, which contained a specific provision authorising a trustee to appoint a solicitor or banker as his agent for these purposes.

[3] But, *quaere* whether this section would apply to a surrender of the policy for cash, which is tantamount to a sale of the policy.

24-41 Agent in Scotland. In Scotland there is no statutory authority similar to that provided in England by the Trustee Act and the Law of Property Act, but, as regards the consideration money on a sale of property, or the repayment of money invested upon heritable security, the possession by a law agent of a disposition and discharge signed by his client is a sufficient mandate authorising him to receive the consideration money.[4] There would appear to be no sound reason for refusing to extend this reasoning to the payment of the policy money to an agent of the claimant on production of the policy with the receipt of the claimant indorsed thereon. The better opinion would seem to be that such an agent has an implied mandate to receive the money, and that an insurance company would get a good discharge on payment to him.

(c) *Legal Discharge*

24-42 (a) The assured. The person prima facie entitled to the legal chose in action is the assured, and his legal personal representatives after his death. The assured is the person with whom the contract of insurance is made,[5] and it is to him that the promise or covenant to pay is made. The simplest form of insurance is a covenant to pay the assured, his executors, administrators or assigns. The promise may, however, be to pay some third person; and, in these circumstances, further considerations will apply.

24-43 (b) Payee. If the policy moneys are made payable to some person other than the assured, that person, being a stranger to the contract and not privy to the consideration, is prima facie precluded from suing upon it; and the legal title remains vested in the assured, who alone can afford the company a good legal discharge.[6]

24-44 However, if it is an essential term of the contract contained in the policy that payment shall be made to a named person and no other, the company is entitled to pay the money to that person notwithstanding any attempt to intercept it or any objection raised by the assured or his representatives,[7] and from this it would seem to follow that the receipt of that person is a sufficient legal discharge to the company. Whether that person is to receive the money beneficially or merely as agent for the assured depends upon the intention of the parties.[8] It has been suggested that, where the payee is to receive the moneys merely as agent for the assured, like any other form of agency his mandate can be withdrawn at any time. Moreover, it could also be argued that, like any other form of agency, the mandate is automatically withdrawn upon the death of the assured. It is submitted that there is no automatic withdrawal on death and that, until the mandate is expressly revoked by the assured, payment may safely be made to the payee.

---

[4] *Wyman v. Paterson* (1899) 2 F. 37, 41, HL: Wood, *Lectures on Conveyancing*, 1903, p. 21.

[5] N.B. The expression "the assured" must therefore be distinguished from "the life assured."

[6] *Scher v. Policyholders' Protection Board (No. 2)* [1994] 2 A.C. 57, 119. But as to equitable discharge, see paras 24–50 *et seq., post.* In Scots law a person intended to benefit although not a party to the contract of insurance may have title to claim on the policy under the doctrine of *jus quaesitum tertio*—*Peddie v. Brown* (1857) 3 Macq. 65 and para. 24–164, *post.* A beneficiary under a contract in England effected after the Contract (Rights of Third Parties) Act, 1999 came into force may be entitled to sue on it.

[7] See *Re Schebsman* [1943] Ch. 366; [1944] Ch. 83; and see further paras 24–160 *et seq., post.*

[8] *ibid.*

However, since the matter is not entirely free from doubt, it is suggested that in all cases the company ought, if possible, to obtain a discharge from the assured or his personal representatives in addition to the receipt of the payee.

24–45 (c) Receipt clause. It is not uncommon, particularly in industrial assurance business, for a clause to be inserted in the policy providing that the production by the company of a receipt for the policy moneys signed by any person being the personal representative, or husband or wife, or relative by blood or connection by marriage shall be a good discharge to the company. Such a clause does not entirely relieve the company from the obligation to obtain a discharge from the person entitled to the legal chose in action. It has, however, been held by the Court of Appeal and the Industrial Assurance Commissioner, that such a clause is effective to protect the company where it makes a bona fide payment to any such person in a case where either such person may be presumed to have the authority of the legal owner or there is no legal owner, owing to no legal representation to the deceased's estate having been constituted.[9] It has also been held that the company is protected by such a clause when it bona fide makes payment to a blood relative of the assured, all parties being in ignorance at the time of payment that the assured had left a will, and may be relied upon by the company in an action by the executors after the will is discovered.[10] It would seem that this rule also applies where the company pays out bona fide and without negligence to the assured's widow, on her false representation that the assured left no will.[11]

24–46 This type of clause will not, however, protect the company if it pays out the policy moneys to a person whom the company knows is not entitled to receive it,[12] particularly when it has received notice from the legal or beneficial owner of the policy not to pay the money except to him. Thus, it has been held that the company was not protected by such a clause in a case where the assured was entitled to the policy moneys on the death of her husband[13] but, at the time of the death, was, to the knowledge of the company, in a mental home, and the company paid out to the step-daughter of the assured.[14] In a case where the company paid out to the assured's wife in exchange for a document purporting to be signed by the wife as agent for the assured, when in fact the wife had no authority from the assured to receive the policy moneys, it was held that there was no "receipt" at all, and therefore no "receipt signed by the wife" within the meaning of the receipt clause.[15]

24–47 (d) Transfer of legal title. The legal chose in action may pass from the assured either by express assignment or by operation of law.

An assignment of the legal chose in action is established by production of a properly stamped instrument of assignment, notice in writing of the

---

[9] *Da Costa v. Prudential* (1918) 88 L.J.K.B. 884; *Worrall v. Prudential* [1924] I.A.C.Rep. 109; *Mullan v. Hearts of Oak* [1928] I.A.C.(N.I.) Rep. 43.

[10] *O'Reilly v. Prudential* [1934] 1 Ch. 519.

[11] *Fearing v. Royal Liverpool Friendly Society* [1943] I.A.C.Rep. (1938–1949), 42.

[12] *Yardley v. Pearl* [1926] I.A.C.Rep. 36; *Hearts of Oak v. Pearl* [1933] I.A.C.(N.I.) Rep. 39. See also *O'Reilly v. Prudential, supra,* at 534, 535.

[13] *i.e.* Under a "life-of-another" policy.

[14] *Almey v. Co-operative Ins. Soc. Ltd* [1940] I.A.C.Rep. (1938–49) 24.

[15] *Welsh v. Royal London Mutual Ins. Soc.* [1925] I.A.C.Rep. 23.

assignment having been given to the company before it received notice of any other assignment.[16]

24–48 The legal chose in action passes by operation of law—(1) on death to the deceased's personal representative and (2) on bankruptcy to the bankrupt's trustee in bankruptcy.

The passing of the legal chose in action to the personal representative is established by the production of probate or letters of administration granted by the Family Division of the High Court of Justice in England, or of a Scottish, Northern Ireland or Colonial grant sealed by the Family Division.[17] A trustee in bankruptcy establishes his title by production of a sealed copy of the order of appointment (where he has been appointed by the Court under section 297 of the Insolvency Act 1986) or a copy of the certificate of his appointment (where he has been appointed by a creditors' meeting under section 293 or 294 or by the Secretary of State under section 295, 296 or 300).[18]

24–49 (e) Compromise with legal owner. Until the company has notice of any equitable claim to the policy moneys it is entitled to deal with the legal owner as though he were solely entitled and a receipt from the legal owner is a sufficient discharge.[19] Persons with equitable claims of which the company did not have notice at the date of payment must look to the recipient for satisfaction.[20] Precisely the same rule applies to any bona fide compromise of the claim.[21] The company is in the position of a person dealing with his creditor, and until it has notice that another person has an equitable interest in the debt, it is perfectly entitled to come to any kind of arrangement with the legal owner for the purposes of extinguishing or modifying the debt.[22]

(d) Equitable Discharge

24–50 Once the company has notice of any outstanding equitable interest it cannot by payment or otherwise do anything to take away or diminish the rights of the person entitled to such interest as they stood at the time the company received such notice, and, if the company disregards the notice and pays or settles only with the person entitled to the legal chose in action,[23] on proof it may well be called to account by the person entitled to the equitable chose in action, and have to pay out the policy moneys over to him again.[24]

24–51 The above rule does not, however, apply to any payments to or settlements with trustees (under express trusts),[25] personal representatives[26] or mortgagees.[27] These persons, if entitled to the legal chose in action, may

---

[16] See further paras 24–69, *et seq., post.*
[17] See Supreme Court Act 1981, Pt V.
[18] See the Insolvency Rules 1986 (S.I. 1986 No. 1925) rr 6.120 to 6.122.
[19] *London Investment Co. v. Montefiore* (1864) 9 L.T. 688.
[20] *Williams v. Sorrell* (1799) 4 Ves. 389.
[21] *Stocks v. Dobson* (1853) 4 De G.M. & G. 11, 16.
[22] *Phipps v. Lovegrove* (1873) L.R. 16 Eq. 80; *Newman v. Newman* (1885) 28 Ch.D. 674.
[23] *Roxburghe v. Cox* (1881) 17 Ch.D. 520; *Brice v. Bannister* (1873) 3 Q.B.D. 569.
[24] *Brice v. Bannister, supra.*
[25] Trustee Act 1925, s.14. See para. 24–203, *post.*
[26] Administration of Estates Act 1925, ss.27 and 39.
[27] Law of Property Act 1925, s.107, see para. 24–143, *post.*

so deal with the policy as to overreach the equitable interest of the beneficiaries or the mortgagor, and so may give a complete discharge for the policy moneys when due notwithstanding the claim of the beneficiaries or the person entitled to the mortgagor's equity of redemption.

24–52 (a) Payment to person entitled to the equitable chose in action. Subject to the discharge of the legal chose in action the company may safely pay an equitable assignee or other person entitled in equity to the policy moneys provided that it has no notice of any competing equitable claim.[28] The same applies to any settlement, surrender or other arrangement made with the equitable assignee or other person entitled in equity.

24–53 (b) Purchaser of the policy. There is a presumption that the person who purchases the policy, that is to say the person on whom the ultimate burden of paying the premiums has in fact fallen or will fall, is entitled to the beneficial interest in the policy money.[29] This presumption, frequently referred to as the presumption of a resulting trust, can be rebutted by evidence tending to show that the purchaser intended the policy to be a gift to the person in whose name the policy was taken (that is to say the nominal assured).[30] The presumption may also be ousted by the presumption, often referred to as the presumption of advancement, arising out of the particular relationship between the purchaser and the nominal assured, that the nominal assured was intended to take beneficially.[31] The presumption, of course, has no application at all where there is an express (or implied) declaration of trust in favour of the nominal assured, or where the policy was taken out under the Married Women's Property Act 1870 or 1882, or the Married Women's Policies of Assurance (Scotland) Act 1880, for the benefit of the nominal assured.[32]

24–54 The purchaser of the policy may, however, have no insurable interest in the life assured and the policy may, therefore, be illegal either on this ground or because the purchaser, being a person for whose use and benefit or on whose account the policy was made, is not named therein. Such a policy is illegal and void as between the office and the assured, and in the case of an industrial policy the purchaser, as "owner of the policy", would be entitled to recover the premiums.[33] Thus, where a woman who had taken out an industrial policy in the name of and upon the life of her daughter maintained a claim against the company on her daughter's death; it was held that there was a resulting trust in favour of the mother, but that on that footing the policy was illegal for want of any insurable interest, and hence neither the mother nor the daughter's personal representatives could

---

[28] *Stocks v. Dobson* (1853) 4 De G.M. & G. 11, 16; *Ottley v. Grey* (1847) 16 L.J.Ch. 512; *Desborough v. Harris* (1855) 5 De G.M. & G. 439.
[29] *Re A Policy, No. 6402 of the Scottish Equitable* [1902] 1 Ch. 282; *Ex parte Dever* (1887) 18 Q.B.D. 660; *Cleaver v. Mutual Reserve* [1892] 1 Q.B. 147; *Hadden v. Bryden* (1899) 1 F. 710; *Forrester v. Robson's Trustees* (1875) 2 R. 755.
[30] See, *e.g.*, *Fowkes v. Pascoe* (1875) L.R. 10 Ch.App. 343.
[31] *Thomley v. Thomley* [1893] 2 Ch. 229 (husband and wife); *Shephard v. Cartwright* [1955] A.C. 431 (father and child). It would now seem that neither of the above two presumptions have much application in disputes between husband and wife: see *Pettitt v. Pettitt* [1970] A.C. 777. The position may be obiter in connection with life insurance policies.
[32] See paras 24–146, *et seq., post.*
[33] Industrial Assurance Act 1923, ss.5, 45(1).

recover from the insurers.[34] It has been stated that if the company waives the illegality and pays the policy moneys no one else can plead the illegality on any question of title to the money[35]; but the better view would seem to be that this proposition applies only when the company has made payment to the purchaser and the policy moneys are in his hands. If the policy moneys have in fact been paid to the nominal assured or his personal representatives (not being the purchasers) the purchaser cannot establish any claim of his own to those moneys without pleading his own illegal act in taking out an illegal policy, and therefore in principle he should not be able to recover.[36]

24–55 (c) Nominal assured. Prima facie the legal title and hence the ability to give the company a good discharge rests in the person in whose name the policy was taken out. As stated above where that person does not provide the premiums there is a presumption of a resulting trust to the purchaser which can either be rebutted by evidence of intention to advance or ousted in favour of the presumption of advancement, which arises where the assured is the wife or child of the purchaser or is a near relative to whom the purchaser stands *in loco parentis*.[37] The presumption of advancement can also be rebutted by circumstances tending to show that the nominal assured was not intended to take beneficially.[38]

24–56 The general rule, therefore, is that where the nominal assured is a stranger to the proposer (i.e. not a wife, child of or person to whom the purchaser stands *in loco parentis*) there is no presumption of advancement and, prima facie, unless he can show as a matter of fact that the purchaser intended him to have the beneficial interest, he holds the policy and its proceeds in trust for the purchaser and must account to him for it.[39]

24–57 (d) Payee. The position of the payee in relation to the legal discharge for the policy moneys has already been examined.[40] Basically

[34] *Jones v. Pearl Ass. Co.* [1937] I.A.C.Rep. 1937, at 18—N.B. the presumption of advancement does not strictly apply as between mother and children—*Bennet v. Bennet* (1879) 10 Ch.D. 474.

[35] *Worthington v. Curtis* (1875) 1 Ch.D. 419; *Carmichael v. Carmichael's Executrix* [1919] S.C. 636.

[36] This view is lent support by the Industrial Assurance Commissioner for Great Britain (Sir George Robertson)—see *Fitzsimmons v. City of Glasgow Friendly Society* [1933] I.A.C.Rep. at 24; *McMeeken v. Prudential Ass. Co.* [1936] I.A.C.Rep. p. 21. See, for the operation of the Life Assurance Act 1774, paras 1–22 to 1–31, *ante*.

[37] See further *Re Richardson* (1882) 47 L.T. 514; *Re McKerrell* [1912] 2 Ch. 648; *Re Hicks* (1917) 117 L.T. 360; *Re Engelbach's Estate* [1924] 2 Ch. 348, *per* Romer J. at 354; *Re A Policy, No. 6402, of the Scottish Equitable* [1902] 1 Ch. 282 and the cases cited in the judgment of Joyce J.; *Smith v. Ker* (1869) 6 M. 863; *Grainger v. Pearl Ass. Co.* [1937] I.A.C.Rep. at 4; *Neill v. Refuge Ass. Co.*, [1928] I.A.C.(N.I.) Rep. at 46. The presumption applies even where it is shown that the sole object of putting the property in the wife's name was to protect it from creditors: *Gascoigne v. Gascoigne* [1918] 1 K.B. 223.

[38] *Worthington v. Curtis* (1875) 1 Ch.D. 419 (where the agreement under which policy effected made it clear that a policy taken out by a father in the name of his son was intended for the benefit of the father); *Hatley v. Liverpool Victoria Legal Friendly Society* (1919) 88 L.J.K.B. 237 (where the circumstances disclosed that a policy taken out by a father in the name of his two-year-old son was designed for the benefit of the father to cover any possible expenses of his child's funeral); see also *Hadden v. Bryden* (1899) 1 F. 710.

[39] See cases at n. 29, *supra* and see also *Da Costa v. Prudential Ass. Co.* (1918) 88 L.J.K.B. 884; *Re Slattery* [1917] 2 Ir.R. 278.

[40] See paras 24–43 to 24–44, *ante*.

there are three capacities in which the payee may be named. He may be either:

(1) a beneficiary under an express or implied declaration of trust contained in the policy[41];

(2) a donee of the policy moneys under a gift from the assured; or

(3) a nominee or agent to receive the policy moneys on behalf of and to the use of the assured.[42]

24–58 (1) A beneficiary under a trust created by the terms of the policy cannot sue the insurers at law, but he may enforce his beneficial interest in equity against the assured or his representatives, if they have received the policy moneys, or by proceedings against the insurers joining the assured or his representatives as a party.[43] (2) A mere donee of the policy not being a beneficiary under a trust and not being a party to the contract has no claim to the policy moneys either at law or in equity,[44] but if he actually receives the policy moneys he is entitled to retain them for his own use, and is not accountable further to the assured or his representatives.[45] It may be an essential term of the contract that the insurers make payment to the payee and no other. In these circumstances the insurers must obtain a discharge from the payee and the assured cannot unilaterally intercept or counter-mand the payment. Since, however, the payee has no enforceable interest in the policy moneys, it is open at any time for the insurers and the assured to agree between themselves that payment be made to the assured or some other person, and thereby to defeat the expectations of the payee. (3) In the absence of a trust or of evidence to show that the payee was intended to take for his own benefit, the presumption is that the payee is to take as agent or nominee for the assured and that the term for payment constitutes merely a mandate by the insured to the payee which, like any other mandate, can be revoked by the assured at any time, and, on one argument, is *ipso facto* revoked by the death of the assured.[46]

In which of these three capacities a payee is named in the policy is a question which falls to be decided on the construction of the policy in the light of the relevant facts.[47]

(e) *Remedies of the Insurers in the Event of Rival Claims*

24–59 (a) Payment into court under the Payments into Court Act 1896. An insurance company which cannot otherwise obtain a satisfactory discharge for the policy moneys may do so by paying the moneys into court under the provisions of the Life Assurance Companies (Payment into Court) Act 1896. Subject to the Rules of Court any life assurance company may pay into the Supreme Court any moneys payable by it under a life policy

---

[41] For the circumstances in which this is the case see paras 24–144, *et seq., post.*

[42] See paras 24–43 to 24–44, *ante.*

[43] *Re Webb* [1941] Ch. 225; *Re Gordon* [1940] Ch. 769.

[44] See paras 24–144, *et seq., post.*

[45] *Re Schebsman* [1944] Ch. 83—until the policy moneys are paid there is a mere incompletely constituted gift, which becomes completely constituted on payment to the assured.

[46] See paras 24–43 to 24–44, *ante.*

[47] See paras 24–147, *et seq., post.*

in respect of which, in the opinion of its board of directors, no sufficient discharge can otherwise be obtained.[48]

The receipt or certificate of the proper officer of the court is a sufficient discharge to the company for the moneys so paid into court, and such moneys are, subject to the Rules of Court, to be dealt with according to the orders of the High Court.[49] The Act does not extend to Scotland.[50]

24–60 (i) Rules of Court. Under the Civil Procedure Rules 1998,[51] R.S.C. Order 92, r. 1, an insurance company wishing to make a payment into court under the Life Assurance Companies (Payment into Court) Act 1896[52] must, by its secretary or other authorised officer, file a witness statement or affidavit setting out the following:

(a) a short description of the policy in question and a statement of the persons entitled thereunder with their names and addresses so far as known to the company;

(b) a short statement of the notices received by the company claiming an interest in or title to the money assured, or withdrawing any such claim, with the dates of receipt thereof and the names and addresses of the persons by whom they were given;

(c) a statement that, in the opinion of the board of directors of the company, no sufficient discharge can be obtained otherwise than by payment into court under the Act of 1896;

(d) the submission by the company to pay into court such further sum, if any, as the Court may direct and to pay any costs ordered by the Court to be paid by the company;

(e) an undertaking by the company forthwith to send to the Accountant General any notice of claim received by the company after the making of the witness statement or affidavit with a letter referring to the title of the witness statement or affidavit, and

(f) an address where the company may be served with any application, claim form, court order, or notice of any proceedings, relating to the money paid into court.

The company is not permitted to deduct any costs of and incidental to the payment into court.[53] No payment may be made into court under the Act where any proceedings to which the company is a party are pending in relation to the policy or the moneys thereby assured except with the leave of the court to be obtained by an application made in accordance with C.P.R. Part 23.[54] The company is required to give immediate notice of any such payment into court to every person appearing from the witness statement or affidavit to be entitled to or to have an interest in the moneys lodged.[55] Any person claiming to be entitled to or interested in the moneys paid into court may apply in the Chancery Division by the issue of a claim form for payment

[48] s.3.
[49] s.4, as amended by the Courts Act 1971.
[50] s.5. See para. 24–68, *post.*
[51] S.I. 1998 No. 3132.
[52] As to this Act see *supra.*
[53] r. 1(2).
[54] r. 1(3).
[55] Ord. 92, r. 4.

out,[56] unless the amount does not exceed £15,000, in which case application may be made by witness statement or affidavit and need not be served on any other person.[57] Unless the Court otherwise directs, a C.P.R. Part 23 application by which a claim with respect to money paid into court under the Act is made shall not, except where the application includes an application for payment of a further sum of costs by the company who made the payment, be served on that company, but it must be served on every person who appears by the witness statement or affidavit on which the payment into court was made to be entitled to, or interested in, the money in court or to have a claim upon it or who has given a notice of claim which has been sent to the Accountant General in accordance with the undertaking in para. (e), above.[58]

24–61 (ii) Advantages of payment in. The advantage of proceeding under the Act of 1896 is that the company is thereby afforded an absolute discharge against all claims present and future and not only, as in the case of interpleader, in respect of an existing contest between rival claimants. Thus payment into court under the Act provides a simple remedy for the company when faced with the fact that the person who can sue at law or the person or persons of whose equitable claims the company has actual or constructive notice either cannot be ascertained or cannot be traced, or where, owing to amateur or bad conveyancing, the title is not satisfactory.

24–62 (iii) Disadvantage of payment in. The disadvantage of proceedings under the Act of 1896 is that the company has in any event to bear its own costs of payment in,[59] and is at risk, if the court should determine that the company was acting over-cautiously and that it was unnecessary for there to have been any payment in, of being ordered to pay the costs of the claimant's application for payment out. In one case, however, where the court had held that the company ought to have paid the money to the claimant when it became due, the claimant, although he was awarded interest on the money from the date it became due, was not awarded the costs of his application for payment out on the grounds that, by his summons, he had claimed a sum larger than that to which he was entitled.[60] The company will only be relieved from liability to pay the costs of the application for payment out if the court comes to the conclusion that the opinion of the director of the company that no sufficient discharge could be obtained otherwise than by payment into court was an opinion which was not only honestly given but was reached on reasonable grounds.[61]

24–63 (iv) Conflict of jurisdiction. Where the company is liable to be sued in more than one jurisdiction,[62] payment into court in one action is not an

---

[56] Ord. 92, r. 5(2). Unless the application is made in a pending cause or matter or an application for the same purpose has previously been made by petition or originating summons, the summons must be an originating summons.

[57] Ord. 92, r. 5(3).

[58] Ord. 92, r. 1(4).

[59] In Ireland this was so held even in the absence of the express rules of court to cover the point: *Re Power's Policies* [1899] 1 Ir.R. 6.

[60] *Re Waterhouse's Policy* [1937] Ch. 415.

[61] *Harrison v. Alliance* [1903] 1 K.B. 184; *Re Waterhouse's Policy* [1937] Ch. 415; *Re Carroll's Policy* (1892) 29 L.R.Ir. 86.

[62] *e.g.* in Scotland and in England.

absolute bar to proceedings in the other country,[63] although, as a general rule, if payment into court is made in the country in which the claim is made payable, the court in any other country would be likely to stay any proceedings until the claim against the fund paid in has been adjudicated upon. Similarly there is no legal or procedural bar to payment into court in England after proceedings have been commenced abroad; and this would seem to be an appropriate course where the money is payable in England and the company is liable to be sued in England.

24–64 (b) Payment into court under the Trustee Act 1925. An insurance company is not a trustee of the policy moneys.[64] It is in the position of an ordinary debtor and accordingly cannot avail itself of section 63 of the Trustee Act 1925 relating to payments into court except in so far as any debtor may do so under the provision of section 136 of the Law of Property Act 1925.[65] The proviso to that section provides that in the case of assignment of choses in action to which the Act applies, if the debtor, trustee or other person liable in respect of the debt shall have had notice that such assignment is disputed by the assignor or anyone claiming under him, or by any other opposing or conflicting claims, he is to be entitled to call upon the various claimants to interplead,[66] or he may, if he thinks fit, pay the money into court under and in conformity with the provisions of the Trustee Act 1925.

24–65 In view of the provisions of the Act of 1896 specifically relating to insurance companies, it is doubtful whether an insurance company can ever be advised to make payment into court under the Trustee Act since it would probably be said that it ought to have proceeded under the former Act. In any event it is unlikely that the company will derive any benefit from proceeding under the Trustee Act in preference to the Act of 1896. Under the Trustee Act the costs of payment in are in the discretion of the court,[67] and, although it was formerly the practice to give the company paying in under the Trustee Relief Act 1847 the costs of payment in any case where there was a reasonable doubt, it is now unlikely, it is submitted, that the court will give to a company paying into court under the Trustee Act 1925 any better order as to costs than would have been given had the company paid in under the Act of 1896.[68]

24–66 (c) Interpleader. An alternative remedy to payment into court is by interpleader. The condition for and the procedure to be followed in the case of an interpleader are governed by the Civil Procedure Rules 1998, Order 17.[69] Order 17, r. 1 permits the application to the court for relief by way of interpleader where, inter alia, a person is under a liability in respect of a debt and is, or expects to be, sued for or in respect of that debt by two or more persons making adverse claims to it. The wording of Order 17, r. 1 is clearly wide enough to cover an insurance company's liability in respect of policy

---

[63] *Cook v. Scottish Equitable* (1872) 26 L.T. 571.

[64] *Re Haycock's Policy* (1876) 1 Ch.D. 611. Even if the policy takes the form of a charge upon the company's funds with no direct promise to pay.

[65] Re-enacting Judicature Act 1873, s.25(6).

[66] See para. 24–66, *post.*

[67] *Re Carroll's Policy* (1892) 29 L.R.Ir. 86.

[68] The company would, at least, have to bear its own costs of the payment in.

[69] S.I. 1998 No. 3132.

moneys.[70] The advantage of proceeding by way of interpleader rather than by way of payment into court is that if there is a bona fide dispute between two or more claimants the company will in the ordinary course receive out of the policy moneys the whole of its solicitors' and own client costs, such costs being ultimately borne by the unsuccessful claimant or claimants.[71] The disadvantage of interpleader is that it affords the company a discharge only as regards the actual claimants that the company has joined to the summons. Interpleader should, therefore, only be resorted to in a case where the company is satisfied that one or other of the claimants is the person entitled to the money, and that there can be no other person other than the claimant who might at a later stage come forward with a superior claim.

24–67 The company is not entitled in interpleader proceedings to raise any question between itself and a claimant.[72] Thus, where the company claims a charge or other interest in the policy moneys, it should deduct the amount claimed by it and interplead for the balance. A similar rule applies in connection with payment into court. Payment into court by the company of the whole of the policy moneys without deducting amounts claimed by the company, has been held to be equivalent to an admission by the company that it has no claim upon the fund in court, thereby debarring it from later putting forward any claim of its own to the moneys paid in.[73]

24–68 (d) Action of multiplepoinding. The Life Assurance Companies (Payment into Court) Act 1896, does not apply to Scotland, where the remedy of a company faced with conflicting claims on its policy is to raise an action of multiplepoinding in the Court of Session.[74] This process is in many respects similar to an interpleader summons in England. It is only available when the policy money has become payable and the office, as holder, admits its liability to pay to the person or persons entitled thereto the whole or the balance of the money after deduction of any advance and interest thereon or premium arrears. The sole interest of the holder must be that of obtaining a discharge and there must be conflicting claims to the money or what in Scotland is called a double distress. The procedure is not competent where the inability to obtain a discharge satisfactory to the directors arises from inability to find a claimant, or from some doubt as to the validity of the title produced by a sole claimant. The holder is the pursuer and real raiser of the action and it cites as defenders to the summons all parties who have intimated a claim or who are believed by the holder to be entitled or likely to make a claim. The jurisdiction of the court over all possible claimants arises from the fact that the fund in respect of which the dispute arises is locally situated in Scotland.[75] The procedure is laid down in the Rules of the Court

[70] cf. *Chapman v. Besnard & Keays* (1869) 17 W.R. 358, where the court refused a bill of interpleader on the grounds that the company's proper remedy was to pay into court. This case was decided before the Rules of Court in their present form had come into effect.
[71] This fact alone will often induce the claimants to offer an absolute indemnity to the company as to its costs of payment into court to persuade it not to interplead—and see *Re Weniger's Policy (No. 2)* [1910] W.N. 278 (where such an indemnity is given the costs are not mortgagee's costs payable out of the policy moneys).
[72] *Bignold v. Audland* (1840) 11 Sim. 23.
[73] *Re Jeffrey's Policy* (1872) 20 W.R. 857.
[74] Stair, *Institutes*, IV.16.3; *Mackay's Manual of Practice*, Ch. 56; *Encyclopaedia of the Laws of Scotland*, Vol. 10, pp. 117–134; Rules of the Court of Session 1994, Ch. 51.
[75] Civil Jurisdiction and Judgments Act 1982, Sch. 4, art. 5(8)(b); Sch. 8, art. 2(9).

of Session 1994.[76] After the fund *in medio*, which is the property in dispute, is lodged in a bank to abide the order of the court, the holder is exonerated and discharged from all actings and intromissions with the fund and the court adjudicates on the competing claims. The effect of the decree of exoneration is to relieve the office of all further responsibility or liability in respect of the policy even though the money may be awarded to the wrong claimant in the absence of one who has a better title. The responsibility of the office is at an end when it has cited all who are known to it as possible claimants and lodged the money to abide the order of the court.[77]

5. ASSIGNMENT

(1) *Legal Assignment*

24–69 Before the coming into effect of the Policies of Assurance Act 1867 a policy of life insurance, in common with other legal choses in action, could not be assigned at law[78] although it could always be assigned in equity. The right to sue at law before 1867 always remained vested in the assignor, and the equitable assignee could only sue by joining the assignor as a party[79] to the action. Equally the insurance company could not obtain a legal discharge from the assignee. The Policies of Assurance Act 1867 which applies only to policies of life insurance, and section 136 of the Law of Property Act 1925 (re-enacting s.25(6) of the Judicature Act 1873), which applies to all choses in action including life policies, now enable the benefit of a policy of life insurance to be assigned at law so that the assignee may sue in his own name without joining the assignor. These statutory provisions were primarily aimed at affording a simpler remedy for the assignee and do not make assignable any chose in action which before these Acts were passed was not assignable in equity, nor do they affect the rules that governed equitable assignments. It follows that if an assignment fails as a legal assignment, because, for instance, the requisite notice to the debtor has not been given, it may still be operative as a valid equitable assignment.[80]

(a) *Legal assignment under the Policies of Assurance Act 1867*

24–70 (i) *Requirements.* In order for the right to sue at law without joining the assignor to pass to the assignee, and hence his ability to give a legal discharge to the life office, three conditions have to be satisfied:

(1) At the time when the action is brought the assignee must be entitled in equity to receive the policy.[81]
(2) The assignee must have a properly stamped assignment in writing in the words or to the effect set out in the Schedule to the Act.[82]

---

[76] Ch. 51.
[77] *Farquhar v. Farquhar* (1886) 13 R. 596.
[78] Except to the Crown—*Dufaur v. Professional Life* (1858) 25 Beav. 599.
[79] As a plaintiff if the assignor consented, otherwise as a defendant.
[80] *Brandt Sons & Co. v. Dunlop* [1905] A.C. 454; *Holt v. Heatherfield Trust Ltd* [1942] 2 K.B. 1.
[81] Policies of Assurance Act 1867, s.1.
[82] *ibid.* s.5 and see para. 24–72, *post.*

(3) Written notice must have been given to the company at its principal place of business.[83]

24–71 The first condition requires some explanation. It was a qualification introduced to ensure that the assignee obtaining the legal title under the Act did not obtain a better right to the insurance money than he would have had as an equitable assignee before the passing of the Act.[84] The claimant must show that he would, before the Act, have been entitled either beneficially or as a trustee to receive the insurance money. Although the Act[85] provides that the date on which the requisite notice is received shall regulate the priority of claims under the Act, since the entitlement in equity at the time when the action is brought is a condition precedent to the validity in law of the assignment it follows that the company, before being able to pay out to the claimant, must consider all equities of which they have notice, whether formal or informal, in order to determine whether or not the claimant has the equitable right to receive the insurance money. This can lead to a certain degree of difficulty, since if, after considering all the other equities of which they have notice, the only conclusion is that the person who gave first formal notice under the Act is not, under the equitable rules governing the priority of assignments, entitled to the policy, the company will not be able to have a valid legal discharge from him or any other assignee. The Act, therefore, only operates when the assignee under the Act is also the person entitled in equity to priority over all other equitable assignments. This provision therefore goes further than the corresponding provision in section 136 of the Law of Property Act 1925 making all legal assignments thereunder "subject to equities." Both Acts make the legal assignee subject to prior equitable interest, but the 1867 Act alone makes the equitable entitlement a condition precedent to the legal validity of the assignment. For this reason most assignments of life insurance policies are now made not under the Policies of Assurance Act 1867 but under the Law of Property Act 1925.

24–72 (ii) *Form of assignment.* The form prescribed in the Schedule to the Act is as follows:

"I AB of etc. in consideration of etc. do hereby assign unto CD of etc. his Executors Administrators and Assigns, the [within] Policy of Assurance granted etc. [Here describe the Policy.] In witness etc."

This form must either be indorsed on the actual policy or be contained in a separate instrument. The exact words need not, of course, be used, so long as the parties and the policy are sufficiently identified and there is a clear intention shown to effect an immediate and unqualified assignment of the policy. Although the assignor must clearly testify that the instrument is his own by signing it, there is nothing in the words "In witness etc." that can imply any requirement that the assignor's signature must itself be attested by a witness.

24–73 (iii) *Essentials of validity of an assignment.* To come within the provisions of the Act there must be an immediate and outright assignment of

---

[83] *ibid.* s.3.
[84] *Scottish Amicable Life v. Fuller* (1867) Ir.R. 2 Eq. 53. For the rules governing the right in equity to receive the insurance money see paras 24–80, *et seq., post.*
[85] *ibid.* s.3.

the policy. An agreement to effect a transfer at a certain future date, even though supported by valuable consideration, would not be an assignment for purposes of the Act. Thus in *Spencer v. Clarke*[86] the assured deposited the policy of life insurance with A by way of equitable mortgage to secure certain advances. A retained the policy but gave no notice at all to the company. B later, in ignorance of the prior equitable mortgage, agreed to lend money to the insured upon the security of the same policy. The assured told B that he had left the policy at home by mistake and promised to deliver it forthwith to B. He also signed a memorandum that he had deposited the policy and undertook on B's request to execute a transfer of the policy in B's favour. B gave the company formal notice of an assignment. The court held that the policy had not been assigned to B within the meaning of the Act, and that since B had constructive notice, by reason of the absence of the policy, of A's interest, A had priority.[87]

24–74 The Act applies to an assignment by way of security as well as to one by sale or gift. In *Re Haycock's Policy*[88] the assured in 1852 assigned his policy to B absolutely who in turn in 1869 assigned it to C. C gave formal notice to the company. After A's death in 1875 the company admitted C's title subject only to requiring C to show that a mortgage made by the assured in 1851 of which the company had notice had been satisfied. The court held that the requisition by the company was a proper one since if the mortgage had not been satisfied the mortgagee might, by virtue of the Policies of Assurance Act 1867, have sued the company in his own name on the assignment. It is probable, however, that only mortgages by way of absolute assignment[89] come within the Act, and that an assignment which is contingent or subject to defeasance would not be covered by the statute.

(b) *Legal assignment under the Law of Property Act 1925*

24–75 (i) *Requirements.* The right to sue at law under section 136 of this Act is not dependent on the assignee, as under the Policies of Assurance Act, having the right in equity to receive the insurance money.[90] Two require-ments only must be satisfied in order to give the assignee the right to sue at law and the ability to give a valid legal discharge to the company:

(1) The assignment must be absolute and in writing under the hand of the assignor, not purporting to be by way of charge only.
(2) Express notice in writing must be given to the company.[91]

24–76 The first assignee to satisfy these two requirements receives the

---

[86] (1878) 9 Ch.D. 137.
[87] Though the decision by itself might suggest that had the assignment been within the Act it would have had priority, this would not be correct in the context of a contest by claimants *inter se*. The point probably is that had B's assignment been within the Act the company could have obtained a good legal discharge from him without needing the discharge of the assured.
[88] (1876) 1 Ch.D. 611.
[89] See para. 24–78, *post.*
[90] *West of England Bank v. Batchelor* (1882) 51 L.J.Ch. 199 "The one (i.e. the 1867 Act) makes the right to receive the money a condition precedent to the right to sue at law, and the other (*i.e.* s.25(6) of the Judicature Act 1873) makes the assignment of a chose in action subject to existing equities"—*per* Fry J., at 200.
[91] The effective date of the notice is its reception by the debtor: *Holt v. Heatherfield Trust* [1942] 2 K.B. 1.

right to sue at law, even though there may have been a previous assignment which does not satisfy these requirements but which in equity has priority. Under section 136 the company can safely obtain a legal discharge from the subsequent assignee that satisfies the requirements of the section, even though it has notice of an equitable assignee having priority. Had the assignment in these circumstances been under the Policies of Assurance Act 1867 only the assignor could have given a valid legal discharge. Section 136 expressly provides that it does not affect the Policies of Assurance Act and, although, prima facie it should be possible for a life insurance policy to be assigned under section 136 like any other legal chose in action, it is just arguable that the effect of this provision is to exclude life insurance policies from the ambit of section 136. To guard against this, albeit remote, possibility the safest course for the company when faced with an assignment is to assume that only the Policies of Assurance Act 1867 applies, and hence, when circumstances demand, to obtain a legal discharge from the assignor as well as the assignee.

24–77 (ii) *Essentials.* Although an assignment "by way of charge only" does not come within the section, an assignment of the whole debt by way of mortgage with a proviso for redemption is an "absolute" assignment for the purposes of the section.[92] It is otherwise where there is an assignment of so much to the chose in action as is required to meet the indebtedness to the assignee to the assignor.[93]

Consideration is not essential to the validity of an assignment within either Act.[94]

An assignment to a person upon trust for someone else is an absolute assignment within the meaning of section 136.[95]

24–78 To constitute an absolute assignment the instrument must express a final and settled intention to make an immediate and outright transfer of the whole chose in action.[96] It follows that any assignment subject to a condition for defeasance and revesting of the chose in the assignor upon the happening of a future event[97] and an assignment subject to a condition precedent do not constitute valid legal assignments within the Act. The governing principle is that the debtor must not be placed in any position of uncertainty as to the person to whom he should pay the money.[98] It follows that the assignment of a life insurance policy contingently upon the assignee surviving the assignor is not a valid legal assignment of the policy within the Act, and would not operate as a valid testamentary disposition unless the formalities of the Wills Act 1837 have been complied with,[99] although, if

---

[92] *Tancred v. Delagoa Bay Ry Co.* (1889) 23 Q.B.D. 239. "A document given 'by way of charge' is not one which transfers the property with a condition for reconveyance, but is a document which only gives a right of payment out of a particular fund or particular property without transferring the fund or property" *per* Denman J. at 242.

[93] *Durham Bros v. Robertson* [1898] 1 Q.B. 765; *Mercantile Bank of London v. Evans* [1899] 2 Q.B. 613.

[94] *Re Westerton* [1919] 2 Ch. 104.

[95] *Comfort v. Betts* [1891] 1 Q.B. 737.

[96] *Re Williams* [1917] Ch. 1, 8.

[97] *Durham Bros v. Robertson* [1898] 1 Q.B. 765.

[98] [1898] 1 Q.B. 765; *per* Chitty L.J. at 773.

[99] See n. 96, *ante.*

there is valuable consideration given, it may be a valid equitable assignment. For similar reasons it would seem that the assignment of part only of a chose in action is not an "absolute" assignment within the meaning of the Act.[1] Hence a policy of life insurance can only be assigned in law as a whole, and this would seem to include the total sums assured by the policy, including any bonuses, unless (semble) the bonuses were payable upon a contingency different from that attached to the other sums assured.

(c) *Effect of Legal Assignment*

24–79 A legal assignment gives the assignee the right to sue for the debt at law, and hence the ability to give the company a good legal discharge, without the necessity of joining the assignor. Neither under the Policies of Assurance Act nor under the Law of Property Act 1925 does a legal assignment affect the equitable right of any assignee to receive the policy moneys. Under the Policies of Assurance Act the equitable right to receive the policy moneys is an essential condition for the validity of the assignment,[2] and a legal assignment under the Law of Property Act is expressly made subject to all prior equities.[3] The ultimate right to receive the policy moneys must therefore be determined as between competing assignees by the ordinary rules governing the priority of equitable assignments[4] irrespective of whether there has been a valid legal assignment or not.

(2) *Equitable Assignment*

24–80 The whole or any part of the proceeds of an insurance policy have always been assignable in equity, whether by way of gift, sale, mortgage or other charge. The equitable right could either be enforced by suing both the assured (or his legal representatives) and the company as joint defendants, or by compelling the assured to allow the assignee to sue the company at law in the name of the assured. The modern procedure is for the equitable assignee either with consent of the assured to sue the company in the name of the assured or, without such consent, to join the assured (or his legal representatives) as a joint defendant in an action against the company.

A policy of life insurance is assignable in equity notwithstanding that the assignee has no insurable interest in the life of the assured,[5] and an equitable assignment may be enforced against the assured or his legal representatives, but not against the company, in any case where the policy is expressed to be "not assignable."[6]

---

[1] *Re Steel Wing Co.* [1921] 1 Ch. 349. Cf. *Skipper & Tucker v. Holloway* [1910] 2 K.B. 636. See also Greer L.J. in *Williams v. Atlantic Assurance Co. Ltd* [1933] 1 K.B. 81, 100.

[2] See paras 24–70 to 24–71, *ante*.

[3] See para. 24–76, *ante*.

[4] Discussed at para. 24–87, *post*.

[5] *Ashley v. Ashley* (1829) 3 Sim. 149.

[6] *Re Turcan* (1888) 40 Ch.D. 5—*quaere* whether the company can safely disregard notices of equitable assignments.

(a) *Essentials of an Equitable Assignment*

24-81 Where the assignment is for valuable consideration no special form of assignment is required and, except where the assignment must be in writing,[7] a purely oral assignment will suffice. Anything which shows an intention to effect an assignment between the assignor and the assignee will suffice,[8] notwithstanding the absence of notice to the company,[9] deposit of the policy[10] or any other act other than an expression of intention inter se.[11] "Whether or not what has been done in any particular transaction amounts to an equitable assignment is a matter of inference from the facts and documents concerned."[12]

24-82 In the case of a voluntary assignment also no particular form of assignment is required, but a voluntary assignee may only enforce the assignment where the assignment is complete between the assignor and the assignee. Mere words showing an intention to make an assignment will not suffice.[13] To constitute a complete assignment the assignor must either have done everything required to be done by him in order to transfer the chose in action[14] or have in some manner constituted himself a trustee for the assignee. The former can only be fulfilled by satisfying the requirements necessary for a legal assignment,[15] but the latter condition is satisfied wherever the assignor says or does something showing a present intention to make an immediate and outright assignment of the policy. Thus a letter written by the assignor stating that "the enclosed is the formal letter of assignment"[16] and a verbal declaration accompanied by the delivery of the policy[17] have both been held to constitute valid equitable assignments although unsupported by consideration. It has also been held in *Holt v. Heatherfield Trust Ltd*[18] that a voluntary assignment which failed as a valid legal assignment because formal notice had not been given to the debtor nevertheless constituted a valid equitable assignment.[19] Because, however, of the special nature of the transaction an assignment by way of charge only must always be supported by consideration.[20]

24-83 Whether or not the transaction is for value it is clear that a direction by a creditor to his debtor to pay the debt to a third party is merely a revocable mandate to the debtor and does not constitute in itself a valid

---

[7] As in the case of marriage settlements.
[8] *Brandt Sons & Co. v. Dunlop* [1905] A.C. 454, 462; *Re Warren* [1938] 1 Ch. 725.
[9] *Gorringe v. Irwell* (1886) 34 Ch.D. 128—but see para. 24–89, *post.*
[10] *Claune v. Baylis* (1862) 31 Beav. 351.
[11] *Myers v. United Guarantee* (1855) 1 De G.M. & G. 112.
[12] *I.R.C. v. Electric and Musical Industries* [1949] 1 All E.R. 120, 126, *per* Cohen L.J.; see also *Claune v. Baylis*, 31 Beav. 351.
[13] *Re Williams* [1917] 1 Ch. 1.
[14] *Re Williams, supra,* at 8.
[15] See *Re Westerton* [1919] 2 Ch. 104.
[16] *Re King, Sewell v. King* (1880) 14 Ch.D. 179.
[17] *Thomas v. Harris* [1947] 1 All E.R. 444.
[18] [1942] 2 K.B. 1—see also *Re McArdle* [1951] Ch. 669.
[19] But it may be that this decision is not reconcilable with the decision in *Milroy v. Lord* (1862) 4 De G.F. & J. 264 since, *quaere,* the donor has not done everything he could have done to complete the gift. The answer, probably, is that he has shown a clear intention to constitute himself trustee for the donee.
[20] *Re Lucan (Earl)* (1890) 45 Ch.D. 470.

equitable assignment in favour of the third party unless and until it is communicated to the third party.[21]

(b) *Particular Transactions*

24–84 (i) *Garnishee.* A garnishee order does not constitute an equitable assignment,[22] and a judgment creditor cannot garnishee a debt which the judgment debtor has already assigned at the date of the order, even where the assignment is valid only in equity, since the judgment creditor cannot be put in any better a position than that of his debtor.[23]

24–85 (ii) *Deposit of policy.* In England the delivery of the policy of assurance for valuable consideration is sufficient in itself to constitute a valid equitable assignment, even though the delivery is unaccompanied by any written memorandum.[24] The exact nature of the transaction will be determined by the surrounding circumstances and parol evidence.

Similarly, where a life policy was deposited with a creditor of the assured accompanied by a memorandum stating "I will leave in your hands a policy for collaterally securing to you the payment of £260 due and I will assign the same to you whenever requested so to do", this was held to be a valid equitable assignment of the policy.[25]

In Scotland a deposit of a policy without any written assignment or memorandum is insufficient to pass any title or give any security to the depositee, but if the policy is accompanied by a letter stating that it is deposited in security, that, when duly intimated, constitutes a valid security.[26]

24–86 (iii) *Charge in favour of office.* The deposit of the policy with the issuing office as security for the assured's indebtedness to the office cannot strictly be an equitable assignment in favour of the office, since the office cannot be both creditor and debtor simultaneously in respect of the same debt.[27] If such a charge is intended the proper course is for the policy to be assigned to trustees on behalf of the office.[28]

However, the private Act of Parliament incorporating the insurance

---

[21] *Morrell v. Wootten* (1852) 16 Beav. 197; *Field v. Lonsdale* (1850) 13 Beav. 78; see also *Re Foster* (1873) Ir.R. 7 Eq. 294.

[22] *Re Combined Weighing & Advertising Machine Co.* (1890) 43 Ch.D. 99.

[23] *Holt v. Heatherfield Trust Ltd* [1942] 2 K.B. 1.

[24] *Maughan v. Ridley* (1863) 8 L.T.(N.S.) 309; *Le Feuvre v. Sullivan* (1855) 10 Moore P.C. 1; see also *Shaw v. Foster* (1872) L.R. 5 H.L. 321, 340.

[25] *Cook v. Black* (1842) 1 Hare 390.

[26] *Scottish Provident v. Cohen* (1886) 16 R. 117; Gloag and Henderson, *Introduction to the Law of Scotland* (10th ed.) para. 19.16.

[27] *Grey v. Ellison* (1856) 1 Giff. 438—but the transaction has sometimes been treated as such in regard to the exception of bona fide assignments in "suicide clauses"—on this see *White v. Brit. Empire Mutual Life* (1868) L.R. 7 Eq. 394.

[28] As in *Fitzwilliam v. Price* (1858) 4 Jur.(N.S.) 889.

company may provide for an assignment of its own policies to itself by way of security having the same effect as though the assignment was to a third party.

(3) *Priority of Assignments*

24–87 As stated supra[29] in all questions concerning the priority amongst assignees and encumbrancers of a policy, so long as the money still remains in the hands of the company or is deposited in court, all priorities *inter se* must be determined as though all were equitable assignees, even though there may have been a valid legal assignment under the Policies of Assurance Act or the Law of Property Act 1925. In *Newman v. Newman*[30] a question of priority arose in connection with certain claims on a life policy and it was contended that an assignee who had given formal notice to the company under the Policies of Assurance Act had priority over a prior assignee who had only given informal notice. North J. rejected this contention, holding that it was not the intention of the statute to enact that a person who had advanced money upon a second charge with notice of the first should, by giving statutory notice to the office, exclude the person who had the prior incumbrance.

24–88 The general rule is that equitable assignees rank in priority in order of date regardless of whether or not they had notice of prior equities.

However, an equitable assignee for value can acquire priority over a prior encumbrancer of whom he had no notice, actual or constructive if:

(a) he has given formal notice to the company before the company had acquired knowledge of the prior equity[31] or

(b) the holder of the prior equity by his words or conduct misled the later assignee or induced him to take an assignment which he would otherwise not have taken[32] or

(c) the holder of the prior equity has contributed by his negligence to the creation of the subsequent assignment.

24–89 (i) *Formal notice.* In order to gain priority, formal notice to the company or its authorised agent must be given. The notice should be in writing, specifying the policy that is being assigned and must be given with the intention of perfecting an assignment. Notice given in general terms that a policy has been assigned by a particular deed is notice of the content of the deed and the content of the charge,[33] but if the notice specifies a particular charge it is not notice of another charge not specified in the notice but which is contained in the deed.[34]

Policies of insurance frequently contain a condition that the agents of the company are not authorised to accept any notice of intimation of an assignment, which can only be given at the company's head office. It is submitted that the effect of such condition is that notice given merely to an agent of the company is not formal notice and priority cannot thereby be

---

[29] See paras 24–59, *et seq. ante.*
[30] (1885) 28 Ch.D. 674.
[31] *Dearle v. Hall* (1828) 3 Russ. 1; *Wood v. Duncombe* [1893] A.C. 369.
[32] *Shropshire Union v. Queen* (1875) L.R. 7 H.L. 496; *Justice v. Wynne* (1860) 12 Ir.Ch.R. 289.
[33] *Re Bright's Trusts* (1856) 21 Beav. 430.
[34] *Re Bright's Trusts, supra; Crawford v. Canada Life* (1897) 24 Ont. A.R. 643.

acquired, although, if the agent communicates the notice to the head office, this would probably rank as informal notice to the company.

24–90 (ii) *Informal notice.* An informal notice to the company of an equitable claim is not sufficient to give that claim priority over prior equities, but it is sufficient to prevent subsequent equities gaining priority over it by giving formal notice.[35] Knowledge by the company's directors, principal officers or any agent whose duty it is to communicate the matter to the directors would constitute sufficient informal notice to the company.

24–91 (iii) *Notice by voluntary assignee.* A voluntary assignee can never gain priority over a prior assignment, whether or not the prior assignment is for value.[36] Nevertheless, by giving either formal or informal notice to the company, the voluntary assignee will prevent subsequent assignments for value gaining priority by giving formal notice.

24–92 (iv) *Notice by sub-assignee.* A sub-assignee (i.e. a person who takes an assignment from an assignee) must give notice of his sub-assignment to the company in order to acquire or preserve priority among other sub-assignees. For this purpose notice to the original assignor is not necessary. Provided the assignee has already given notice, the sub-assignee need not give any further notice to acquire or preserve priority amongst other assignees.[37] A sub-assignee steps into the shoes of the assignee, with the result that he gains whatever priority over prior equities the assignee may have gained by giving notice and conversely loses any priority which the assignee may have lost by failing to give notice, and in both cases it is quite irrelevant whether or not the sub-assignee had himself notice of any prior equities.[38]

24–93 (v) *Notice to trustees and personal representatives.* As a general rule notice ought to be given to all the trustees, and if possible a note or memorandum of the assignment ought to be endorsed on the trust deed.[39] If notice is given to all the trustees a person who has a subsequent assignment after the death of all the trustees who were given the prior notice will not be entitled to any priority over the prior assignment, even if the subsequent assignee has given notice to all the new trustees and they have no knowledge of the prior assignment.[40] Notice to one of several trustees, not being the assignor himself,[41] is sufficient to protect the assignment against subsequent assignments (but not to acquire priority over any previous assignments without notice) so long as the trustee who is given the notice remains a trustee, and the priority of the first assignee is retained notwithstanding that the trustee dies after without having communicated the notice to his co-trustees and after the trustees have received notice of a second

---

[35] *Lloyd v. Banks* (1868) L.R. 3 Ch. 488; *Ipswich Permanent Money Club v. Arthy* [1920] 2 Ch. 257. Informal notice is also sufficient to bind the policy moneys in the hands of the company and prevent it from paying out to the assignor or his representatives.
[36] *Justice v. Wynne* (1860) 12 Ir.Ch.R. 289.
[37] *Ex p. Barnett* (1845) De G. 194; *Jones v. Gibbons* (1804) 9 Ves. 407.
[38] *Lowther v. Carlton* (1741) 2 Atk. 242; *Ford v. White* (1852) 16 Beav. 120.
[39] *Re Hall* (1880) 7 L.R. Ir. 180.
[40] *Re Warsdale* [1899] 1 Ch. 163; see also *Ward v. Duncombe* [1893] A.C. 369.
[41] *Brown v. Savage* (1859) 4 Dow. 635; *Lloyds Bank v. Pearson* [1901] 1 Ch. 865; *Re Dallas* [1904] 2 Ch. 385, 401, 402.

assignment.[42] If, however, the second assignment is made and notice of it given after the death of the only trustee who had notice of the first assignment, it will be postponed in priority to the second assignment.[43]

24–94 The same principles apply in the case of notice to be given to personal representatives. Notice given to an executor named in the will but who subsequently renounces probate is ineffective.[44] This could lead to some harsh results since until an administrator cum testamento annexo is appointed there is no one having dominion over the fund to whom notice can be given. Thus if a person entitled under a will were to assign his interest to a large number of people before an administrator *cum testamento* was appointed, their order of priority *inter se* would be determined exclusively by the order in which they each managed, on hearing of the grant of administration, to serve notice on the administrator, irrespective of the order of their creation.

24–95 (vi) *Knowledge of prior equity.* An equitable assignee for value can never gain priority by giving formal notice to the company over any prior equity of which he had notice, actual or constructive, at the time that he took his assignment.[45] It is the time that the assignment was made that is important, the knowledge of the assignee at the time of his giving notice being immaterial.[46]

By constructive notice is meant knowledge of such facts as would have put a prudent man on inquiry. In these circumstances an assignee is deemed to have notice of any prior equitable assignment which a reasonable inquiry would have revealed. In *Re Weniger's Policy*[47] a policy was deposited with the company to secure certain advances. Subsequently the policy was assigned to various people in succession and one of these paid off the advance by the company. It was held that all the assignees took subject to the charge in favour of the company (and transferred to the other assignees) since the absence of the policy was constructive notice to each of them of this charge. An assignee should therefore always insist on the production of the policy itself or a satisfactory[48] explanation of its non-production, since otherwise he will be unable to gain priority over any prior equity of which he had no actual notice.

24–96 (vii) *Effect of leaving policy in the hands of the assignor.* It is doubtful to what extent the leaving of the policy in the hands of the assignor will postpone the assignee to a subsequent assignee who takes without notice of the earlier assignment. In the case of realty it has been held that even the purchaser of a legal estate will be postponed to a subsequent purchaser if he negligently allows the vendor to retain custody of the title deeds,[49] but it is

---

[42] *Ward v. Duncombe* [1893] A.C. 369.

[43] *Re Hall* (1880) 7 L.R.Ir. 180; *Timson v. Ramsbottom* (1837) 2 Keen 35, 50; *Re Phillips' Trusts* [1903] 1 Ch. 183; *Ward v. Duncombe* [1893] A.C. 369.

[44] *Re Dallas* [1904] 2 Ch. 385.

[45] *Spencer v. Clarke* (1878) 9 Ch.D. 137; *Newman v. Newman* (1885) 28 Ch.D. 674; *Re Weniger's Policy* [1910] 2 Ch. 291.

[46] *Mutual Life v. Langley* (1886) 32 Ch.D. 460.

[47] [1910] 2 Ch. 291; see also *Spencer v. Clarke* (1878) 9 Ch.D. 137; *Hiern v. Mole* (1806) 13 Ves. 114.

[48] It is not a satisfactory explanation that the policy was "left at home by mistake" (*Spencer v. Clarke*) or was "at his bank for safe custody" (*Maxfield v. Burton* (1873) L.R. 17 Eq. 15).

[49] *Walker v. Linom* [1907] 2 Ch. 104.

doubtful whether this applies by analogy to the assignment of a chose in action. In *Neal v. Molineux*[50] it was held that the assignee of a policy of insurance was not postponed to a subsequent assignee even though he had left the policy in the hands of the assignor. It should be noted, however, that this was a decision before the doctrine of estoppel by negligence had been developed, and it may well be that the same rule as has been applied in the case of realty will be held to apply in the case of assignment of choses in action.

If the assignee not only leaves the policy in the hands of the assignor but gives no notice to the company he may be postponed to a subsequent assignee who takes without notice.[51]

24–97 (viii) *Stop order.* If the policy moneys have been paid into court an assignee should not give notice to the company, but instead should obtain a "stop order", the effect of which is precisely the same as formal notice to the company would have produced if the money had been in the company's hands.[52] Equally the company, if it has a charge on the policy and has not deducted it before paying the moneys into court, ought to obtain a stop order to preserve its priority.[53]

24–98 (ix) *Position of trustee in bankruptcy.* A trustee in bankruptcy is a statutory assignee of all the bankrupt's property which he takes subject to existing equities. He is not considered to be an assignee for value and cannot therefore gain priority over existing equities by giving notice,[54] although he ought to give notice of his appointment to the company to prevent subsequent assignees who took their assignment without notice of the bankruptcy from gaining priority over him by giving prior notice.[55]

(4) *Miscellaneous Topics*

24–99 (a) Unenforceable or illegal policy. Although, if the policy itself is unenforceable, the assignee will be unable to enforce his claim against the company, the assignment is valid and enforceable as between the assignor and the assignee, and thus the assignee can claim the policy moneys from the person to whom the company has paid out on the policy.[56] But, semble, an assignee will have no claim where the company makes a purely *ex gratia* payment in respect of a policy on which it has denied all liability.

24–100 (b) Substituted policy. If a policy-holder surrenders the policy and takes a new policy in its place, the new policy will be subject to the same equities as the old, and fresh notice to the company is not required.[57]

24–101 (c) Possessory lien. A possessory lien on the document itself, such

[50] (1847) 2 Cor. & K. 722.
[51] *Shropshire Union v. The Queen* (1875) L.R. 7 H.L. 496, 506.
[52] *Stephens v. Green* [1895] 2 Ch. 148; *Montifiore v. Guadella* [1903] 2 Ch. 26; *Re Holmes* (1885) 29 Ch.D. 786; see also *Pinnock v. Bailey* (1883) 23 Ch.D. 497.
[53] *Swayne v. Swayne* (1848) 11 Beav. 463.
[54] *Re Wallis* [1902] 1 K.B. 719; *Re Anderson* [1911] 1 K.B. 896.
[55] *Re Russell's Policy Trusts* (1872) L.R. 15 Eq. 26.
[56] *Worthington v. Curtis* (1875) 1 Ch.D. 419; *A.G. v. Murray* [1903] 2 K.B. 64.
[57] *Nesbitt v. Berridge* (1864) 10 Jur.(N.S.) 53.

as a solicitor's lien for unpaid fees, may be enforced against the person entitled to the policy moneys,[58] and this right does not depend upon notice being given to the company.[59]

24–102 (d) Policy as chattel. Unless the policy is given in contemplation of death so as to constitute a valid *donatio mortis causa*,[60] the mere delivery of the policy with the intention of making a gift of it is probably not a valid equitable assignment.[61] Nevertheless the gift of the document itself may be valid, so that the donee can hold it against the person entitled to the policy moneys.[62]

24–103 (e) Accretions to policy. In the absence of any contrary indication in the assignment, an assignment of a policy of life insurance gives the assignee the benefit of all past and future bonus additions and other accretions to the rights of the policy-holder.[63] It would seem, too, that where the assured assigns by way of gift a policy on his life for a one-year term, and later extends the policy and dies within the period of extension, it is presumed that the extension was effected for the benefit of the assignee, who is thereby entitled to claim the policy moneys.[64]

(5) *Conflict of Laws*

24–104 Where the assignment of a policy of life insurance involves a foreign element a question may arise as to which system of law should apply, and this must be determined by the rules of private international law. A foreign element will be involved wherever either the policy was taken out abroad or the assignment of the policy was made abroad or both. It is not intended in this chapter to set out the rules of conflict of laws concerned in this matter, which are discussed in chapter 13 to which reference may be made.[65]

(6) *Voidable and Void Assignments*

24–105 An assignment of a life policy may be void or voidable for one of several grounds, particularly for misrepresentation, mistake, duress, and undue influence or under the doctrine of non est factum or for reasons of public policy.[66]

---

[58] *Head v. Egerton* (1734) 3 P.W. 280.

[59] *West of England v. Batchelor* (1882) 51 L.J.Ch. 199; *Gibson v. Overbury* (1841) 7 M. & W. 535.

[60] *Re Dillon* (1890) 44 Ch.D. 76; *Re Weston* [1902] 1 Ch. 680; see also *Amis v. Witt* (1863) 33 Beav. 619; *Savage v. Prudential Ass. Co.*, [1925] I.A.C.Rep. 16.

[61] See paras 24–85, *et seq., ante*.

[62] *Rummens v. Hare* (1876) 1 Ex.D. 169; *Diamond v. Refuge Ass. Co.* (1928) I.A.C.(N.I.) Rep. 35.

[63] *Gilly v. Burley* (1856) 22 Beav. 619; *Courtney v. Ferrers* (1827) 1 Sim. 137; *Parkes v. Bott* (1838) 9 Sim. 388.

[64] *Royal Exchange Ass. v. Hope* [1928] Ch. 179; see also *Sparks v. Burnett* (1890) 17 R. 997.

[65] See para. 13–67, *ante*, concerning rules governing the assignment of a policy.

[66] As to mistake and misrepresentation, see Chs 15 & 16, *ante*. Details of the other principles may be found in any standard work on the law of contract.

(7) *Voluntary Assignment*

(a) *The general rule*

24–106 Subject to the exceptions mentioned below the general rule is that a voluntary assignment[67] of a policy of insurance is not enforceable against the assignor or his personal representative unless:

(1) the assignment is complete as between assignor and assignee; or
(2) the assignor has constituted himself a trustee of the policy for the assignee.

24–107 The above rule is based upon the doctrine developed in the Court of Chancery that equity will not complete an incompletely constituted gift.[68] If the assignor has declared himself a trustee of the policy for the assignee, the court of equity would always enforce the trust, although purely voluntary.[69] A mere promise to assign in the future was never deemed sufficient to constitute a trust and, although there were a number of decisions, particularly as regards assignments between husband and wife to the contrary effect,[70] it was held by the Court of Appeal in *Milroy v. Lord*[71] in the case of a gift between strangers, that words purporting to assign the property de praesenti were insufficient, since an imperfect gift could not be construed as a declaration of trust unless there was something besides the mere intention to give to show that that donor intended to constitute himself a trustee.

(b) *Application to Policies of Assurance*

24–108 The general rule mentioned above was applied by the court of equity to property assignable at law. Policies of assurance, being choses in action, were, before 1867, not assignable at law and could, like any other purely equitable right, only be assigned in equity. It was therefore arguable on the one hand that, since the assignee had to come to equity to enforce his rights, the equitable rules should apply, and on the other hand that those rules did not apply where there were words of present gift since either:

(1) these words were themselves sufficient in equity to complete the gift,[72] or
(2) that at least these words in the context of a purely equitable right should be construed as amounting to a declaration of trust.[73]

24–109 The result of the decisions appears to be as follows:

---

[67] *i.e.* one that is not supported by consideration moving from the assignee.
[68] *Duffield v. Elwes* (1827) 1 Bligh (N.S.) 497.
[69] *Ex p. Pye* (1811) 18 Ves. 140, 149.
[70] *Grant v. Grant* (1865) 34 Beav. 623; *Richardson v. Richardson* (1867) L.R. 3 Eq. 686; *Morgan v. Malleson* (1870) L.R. 10 Eq. 425; *Baddeley v. Baddeley* (1878) 9 Ch.D. 113; *Bridge v. Bridge* (1852) 16 Beav. 315.
[71] (1862) 4 De G.F. & J. 264; followed in *Richards v. Delbridge* (1874) L.R. 18 Eq. 11; *Heartley v. Nicholson* (1875) L.R. 19 Eq. 233.
[72] *Ellison v. Ellison* (1802) 6 Ves. 656.
[73] *Re Magawley's Trust* (1851) 5 De G. & Sm. 1.

(1) A mere voluntary promise to assign in the future a chose in action, such as a policy of assurance, is not enforceable against the promisor or his personal representatives[74];

(2) Where there are written words purporting to assign the policy *de praesenti*, there is a complete assignment which is enforceable, although voluntary.[75] If notice of the assignment is given to the company the assignment will be complete at law and the voluntary assignee will be capable of calling upon the policy in his own name. Even if no notice has been given to the company it appears on the authorities that the assignment, being complete as between assignor and assignee, takes effect as an equitable assignment[76];

(3) Oral words purporting to assign the policy de praesenti even if accompanied by delivery of the policy itself,[77] do not amount to a complete assignment conferring any equitable right upon the intended donee unless it can be clearly shown from the words used that the donor intended to constitute himself a trustee of the policy for the donee.[78] It follows that a bare oral statement by a policyholder that he gives it to another confers upon that other no interest which can be enforced either at law or in equity.[79]

(c) *Exceptions to the Rule*

24–110 Donee becomes personal representative. Where there is otherwise an imperfect gift and the donor appoints the donee an executor of his will, or the donee takes out letters of administration to the donor's estate, the passing of the legal title by operation of law completes the gift, and gives the donee, as against creditors or beneficiaries under the will as good a title as if the gift had been complete *inter vivos*.[80] It is immaterial for this purpose that the donee is only one of two or more executors or administrators. The rule is however, subject to the qualification that the donee must show a settled intention on the part of the donor to make a present gift of the chose to the

---

[74] *Re McArdle* [1951] Ch. 669; *Re D'Angibau* (1880) 15 Ch.D. 228, 235; *Re King* (1880) 14 Ch.D. 179; *Vavasseur v. Vavasseur* (1909) 25 T.L.R. 250. A promise under deed creates no legal or equitable interest in the policy but only entitles the promisee to sue at law for damages on the covenant: *Ward v. Audland* (1846) 16 M. & W. 862; *Cox v. Barnard* (1850) 8 Hare 310. Sed quaere in the light of *Beswick v. Beswick* [1968] A.C. 58.

[75] *Re King* (1880) 14 Ch.D. 179; *Pearson v. Amicable* (1859) 27 Beav. 229; *Re Griffin* [1899] 1 Ch. 408; *Brownlee v. Robb* (1907) 9 F. 1302; *cf. Re Westerton* [1919] 2 Ch. 104; *cf. Re Williams* [1917] 1 Ch. 1 (where the words endorsed on the policy were held not to amount to words of present assignment); and see also *Crisp v. Pearl* [1931] I.A.C.Rep. 75.

[76] *Holt v. Heatherfield Trust* [1942] 2 K.B. 1; *Fortescue v. Barnett* (1834) 3 My. & K. 36; *Re King* (1880) 14 Ch.D. 179; *Justice v. Wynne* (1860) 12 Ir.Ch.R. 289; *Re Patrick* [1891] 1 Ch. 82. *Cf.* the contrary opinion of the Industrial Assurance Commissioner for Great Britain (Sir George Robertson) in *Blackburn v. Prudential Ass. Co.*, [1930] I.A.C.Rep. 16 which it is submitted failed to distinguish between that which is necessary to give the assignee the right to sue in his own name and that which is necessary to perfect a proprietary right in equity.

[77] *James v. Bydder* (1841) 4 Beav. 600; *Maggison v. Foster* (1843) 2 Y. & C. 336; delivery of the policy may, however, confer upon the donee a good title to the policy as a document: *Rummens v. Hare* (1876) 1 Ex.D. 169; *Diamond v. Refuge*, [1928] I.A.C.(N.I.) Rep. 35.

[78] *Vavasseur v. Vavasseur* (1909) 25 T.L.R. 250; *McFadden v. Jenkins* (1842) 1 Ph. 153, 157; *cf. Kekewich v. Manning* (1851) 1 De G.M. & G. 176.

[79] *Howes v. Prudential* (1883) 49 L.T. 133; *Frost v. Prudential*, [1957] I.A.C.Rep. 2 (where the Industrial Assurance Commissioner accepted the correctness of this statement).

[80] *Strong v. Bird* (1874) L.R. 18 Eq. 315; *Re Stewart* [1908] 2 Ch. 251; *Re Pink* [1912] 2 Ch. 528; *Re James* [1935] Ch. 449.

donee and that this intention continued unaltered right up to the date of his death.[81]

24-111 *Donatio mortis causa.* Where a document which represents or is the evidence of a chose in action is delivered by a person in contemplation of death on condition that it shall be the property of the donee in the event but only in the event of the death of the donor in the circumstances then threatening him, there is a *donatio mortis causa* of the chose in action which the court will enforce against the donor's representatives.[82] It is a question of fact whether the delivery of a document was made as a gift inter vivos or mortis causa. To establish a *donatio mortis causa* there must be evidence that the donor made the gift in contemplation of death.[83] In order to be the subject-matter of a valid *donatio mortis causa* the document itself must be "the essential indicia or evidence of title, possession or production of which entitles the possessor to the money or property purported to be given".[84] Following this authority, the Industrial Assurance Commissioner for Northern Ireland held that the delivery of a free policy certificate, showing on its face that it would be accepted by the company "in place of the original policy in support of any claim in respect of such free paid-up policy", was a valid *donatio mortis causa* of the policy moneys.[85] Savings or deposit bank books are sufficient indiciae of title to the money in the bank and their delivery to a donee may constitute a valid *donatio mortis causa* of the chose in action.[86] A policy of insurance has been held to be a subject of *donatio mortis causa.*[87] If the policy is delivered by a person in the extremity of sickness and in contemplation of death in circumstances which indicate an intention to give, the court will presume that it was given to be retained only in the event of death and to be returned if the donor should recover.[88] In an Irish case it was said that the nature of a policy of insurance on the life of the donor is such that an intention to make a gift to take effect only on death is readily presumed.[89] *Sed quaere*: does not this beg the question, "was this the death contemplated?" Readers of the case cited may wonder whether the gift was made in contemplation of death at all.

24-112 An essential part of the validity of a *donatio mortis causa* is that the donor should part with the dominion over the policy so as to prevent its being dealt with by him in the interval between the *donatio* and his death.[90]

---

[81] *Re Greene* [1949] Ch. 333; *Re Freeland* [1952] Ch. 110; *Re Wale* [1956] 1 W.L.R. 1346.

[82] *Ward v. Turner* (1751) 2 Ves.Sen. 431; *Duffield v. Elwes* (1827) 1 Bligh (N.S.) 497; *Re Dillon* (1890) 44 Ch.D. 76; *Re Weston* [1902] 1 Ch. 680. In Scots law immediate apprehension of death is not an essential element of a *donatio mortis causa*. It is sufficient if there is an actual or constructive delivery of a document of title to the donee with the intention of making a gift to take effect as between donor and donee on the death of the donor: *Aiken's Executors v. Aiken*, 1937 S.C. 678.

[83] *Lord Advocate v. King* [1953] T.R. 119.

[84] *Per* Lord Evershed M.R., in *Birch v. Treasury Solicitor* [1951] Ch. 298, 311.

[85] *Brown v. Britannic.* [1951] I.A.C.(N.I.) Rep. 17.

[86] *Birch v. Treasury Solicitor* [1951] Ch. 298.

[87] *Amis v. Witt* (1863) 33 Beav. 619; *Witt v. Amis* (1861) 1 B. & S. 109; *Savage v. Prudential Ass. Co.*, [1925] I.A.C.Rep. 16.

[88] *Gardner v. Parker* (1818) 3 Madd. 184; *Macgowan v. Pearl Ass. Co.* [1928] I.A.C.(N.I.) Rep. 39.

[89] *Nelson v. Prudential* [1929] N.Ir.R. 113.

[90] *Re Craven's Estate* [1937] 3 All E.R. 33; *Sen v. Headley* [1991] Ch. 425, 431–432.

Delivery of the policy directly to the donee is the normal way of parting with such dominion, but when the donee is already in possession of the policy for some other purpose the delivery need not be repeated.[91] Delivery to a third party on behalf of the donee may be sufficient,[92] but delivery to an agent of the donor is not,[93] nor if such agent is already in possession of the policy is a request to him to hand it over to the donee.[94] The delivery of the key of a box in which the policy is kept by the donor may be a sufficient constructive delivery of the policy.[95] A direction to the intended donee by the deceased who was in hospital to go to her house and get a bag which contained the documents of title was held to be a sufficient delivery of the documents.[96] The delivery of a deposit receipt for a policy deposited in a bank for safe custody may constitute an effective delivery of the policy.[97] A *donatio mortis causa* of a policy of life assurance may be made subject to payment by the donee of the donor's funeral expenses or of his debts or both and where the gift is thus qualified the obligation to discharge these claims is a valid charge on the policy money.[98] The uncorroborated evidence of the donee may be sufficient to establish the gift, but it is the duty of the court to sift such evidence very carefully.[99]

A *donatio mortis causa* is invalid if made when the donor was contemplating suicide: but if made in contemplation of death as the result of sickness or an operation it is not invalidated by the suicide of the donor not contemplated by him at the date of the gift.[1]

6. MORTGAGES[2]

(1) *Creation and Definition of Mortgages*

24–113 (a) Definition. A mortgage of a policy of insurance is an assignment of the assured's right to recover the policy moneys but only "as a security for the payment of a debt or the discharge of some other obligation for which it is given".[3]

Being merely an assignment of the policy no particular formality is required[4] and, subject only to the difficulties of proof and the questions of

---

[91] *Cain v. Moon* [1896] 2 Q.B. 283; *Andrews v. Pearl Ass. Co.* [1940], I.A.C.Rep. (1938–49) 28.
[92] *Drury v. Small* (1717) 1 P.Wms. 404.
[93] *Farquharson v. Cave* (1846) 2 Coll. 356, 368.
[94] *Bunn v. Markham* (1816) 7 Taunt. 224; *Re Hawkins* [1924] 2 Ch. 47; *Kelsall v. Pearl Ass. Co.* [1928] I.A.C.Rep. 13.
[95] *McGreevy v. Britannic Ass. Co.* [1930] I.A.C.(N.I.) Rep. 54; *Re Ward* [1946] 2 All E.R. 206. Cf. *Sen v. Headley* [1991] Ch. 425 (delivery of key to steel box containing title deeds). This decision contains a comprehensive review of the authorities.
[96] *Birch v. Treasury Solicitor* [1951] Ch. 298.
[97] *British Linen Bank v. Gammie* (1948) 64 Sh.Ct.Rep. 23, and see *Aiken's Executors v. Aiken*, n. 82 to para. 24–111, *ante*.
[98] See n. 69 to para. 24–22, *ante*.
[99] *Re Dillon* (1890) 44 Ch.D. 76.
[1] *Mills v. Shields and Kelly* [1948] Ir.R. 367.
[2] This section is confined to those aspects of the law of mortgages thought to be of relevance to mortgages of life assurance policies. The question of the priority of competing mortgages is resolved by applying the rules already discussed in paras 24–87, *et seq., ante*.
[3] *Santley v. Wilde* [1899] 2 Ch. 474, *per* Lindley M.R.
[4] See paras 24–79, *et seq., ante*.

priority between successive encumbrancers a mortgage may be created merely by an oral agreement between the parties without writing, deposit of the policy or notice to the company.

24–114 (b) Methods of creating a mortgage. The most formal way of creating a mortgage is by a deed of mortgage whereby the policy is assigned in security with the usual conditions for redemption and powers of sale. A method, however, which is frequently used to create a mortgage is to deposit the policy with the lender together with a memorandum of deposit or some similar document specifying the extent and conditions of the charge which it is intended to create.

24–115 (i) *Deposit with memorandum.* Where the policy is deposited with a memorandum of deposit there is generally no difficulty; the terms set out in the memorandum will determine the nature and extent of the charge and these cannot be contradicted by oral evidence.[5] Thus if the memorandum states that the deposit was made to serve a specific advance, parol evidence is not admissible to prove that it was the intention of the parties that further advances should be included in the charge.[6] However, if the memorandum is ambiguous, parol evidence may be introduced to show what the intention of the parties really was.[7]

24–116 (ii) *Deposit without memorandum.* It has been held[8] that a policy may be mortgaged merely by a deposit of the policy without notice, without writing, and without even word of mouth passing between the depositor and the depositee, as long as the circumstances under which the deposit was made show sufficiently that it was the intention of the parties that a charge on the policy moneys should be created. Mere possession of the policy is not sufficient itself to support a claim to a charge on the policy moneys[9] since the policy may have been delivered with some other intention.[10] Prima facie, however, wherever a debtor deposits a policy with his creditor as security for a debt, it will be presumed in the absence of a contrary intention that he intended thereby to charge the policy moneys and not merely to pledge the piece of paper.[11]

Where there is no memorandum the extent of the charge must be ascertained from parol evidence and from the circumstances surrounding the deposit. If, for example, there are continuous transactions between the parties and a constantly varying balance of account, a court will readily construe the deposit as having been made to serve not only the balance at the date of deposit, but also any further balance of account.

In Scotland a deposit of a policy unaccompanied by any note or memorandum in writing able to constitute an assignation can give the depositee no charge on the policy moneys.[12] The usual practice in Scotland is

---

[5] *Shaw v. Foster* (1872) L.R. 5 H.L. 321, 340.

[6] *Vandezee v. Willis* (1789) 3 Bro.C.C. 21.

[7] See, *e.g. Jones v. Consolidated Investment* (1858) 26 Beav. 256, where it was ambiguous whether the charge was to cover only debts due at the date of the deposit or future debts as well.

[8] See *Shaw v. Foster* (1872) L.R. 5 H.L. 321, 340.

[9] *Chapman v. Chapman* (1851) 13 Beav. 308.

[10] *e.g.* for safe custody; as a pledge of the paper—see *Carter v. Wake* (1877) 4 Ch.D. 605; to enable a final charge to be drawn up—see *Norris v. Wilkinson* (1806) 12 Ves. 192.

[11] *Norris v. Wilkinson* (1806) 12 Ves. 192.

[12] *Wylie's Executor. v. McJannet* (1901) 4 F. 195, and see para. 24–85, *ante.*

to take an assignment in security with a proviso for redemption and not a memorandum of deposit.

24-117 (c) Subsequent additions to charge. If a policy has been initially charged to secure a specified debt, nothing can prevent the charge being subsequently enlarged to secure other debts. No particular formality, such as a surrender and redeposit of the policy,[13] is required and the enlargement of the charge may be created by oral agreement even where the initial charge has been defined by a written memorandum.[14] It is submitted that the rule[15] whereby subsequent advances cannot be added to a legal mortgage of land has no application to a charge of a chose in action, such as an insurance policy, and that even where the charge has been created by deed subsequent advances may be added by oral agreement. The reverse, however, is not so. Thus, if there is an initial deposit on terms orally agreed between the parties and subsequently a formal deed is drawn up to secure a specific debt, the original oral agreement is deemed to have merged in the subsequent agreement under seal and the charge will be limited to the debt mentioned in the deed.[16]

24-118 (d) Assignment *ex facie* absolute. In determining whether a transaction is a mortgage the court looks at the substance of the transaction and not merely at the form.[17] Thus, whether a particular transaction is merely a sale with an option to repurchase or in reality a mortgage depends on the surrounding circumstances.[18] Parol evidence is admissible to show that an assignment *ex facie* absolute is neither a sale nor a gift but a mortgage, and this is so even where the assignment is by a deed which expressly states that it is by way of an unconditional sale; although it would need cogent evidence to overcome the natural presumption that the deed sets out the true nature of the transaction.[19] An example, however, is afforded by the case of *Murphy v. Taylor*.[20] There A, having taken out a policy on the life of X for £999, executed a deed whereby he purported to assign it to B for a consideration expressed of £144, a receipt for which was indorsed on the deed. Evidence was admitted to show (1) that A had executed a bond for £144 in favour of B at the same time and (2) that A was already indebted to B for £119 at the time of the transaction and had received only £25 in cash. Later B received £600 on the policy after a compromise with the life office and A sued B for the balance after deducting the £144. The court held that the transaction constituted a mortgage and not a sale and that A was therefore entitled to redeem.

24-119 (e) Mortgages of Life Policies under the Consumer Credit Act 1974. The use of a life policy as security for a loan may be affected by the

---

[13] *Ex p. Whitbread* (1812) 19 Ves. 209.
[14] *Ex p. Kensington* (1813) 2 V. & B. 79; *Ede v. Knowles* (1843) 2 Y. & C.Ch.Cas. 172.
[15] For which see *Ex p. Hooper* (1815) 19 Ves. 177; and see (1815) 1 Mer. 7, 9.
[16] See *Vaughan v. Vandersteyen* (1854) 2 Drew. 289, where the original deposit was to secure the bill of costs owed to a solicitor on terms orally agreed, but the subsequent deed covered other debts only.
[17] *Re Watson* (1890) 25 Q.B.D. 27; *Re Lovegrove* [1935] Ch. 464.
[18] *Re Watson, supra*; *Mears v. Pepper* [1905] A.C. 102.
[19] *Boston v. Bank of N.S. Wales* (1890) 15 App.Cas. 379.
[20] (1850) 1 Ir.Ch.R. 92. See also *Salt v. Marquess of Northampton* [1892] A.C. 1.

provisions of the Consumer Credit Act 1974.[21] Section 105 of that Act requires securities provided in relation to regulated agreements[22] to be in writing and to comply with regulations as to form and content and with provisions as to proper execution. Non-compliance renders the security enforceable only by order of the court, and if such order is refused, under section 106 the security is void, any document lodged with the creditor must be returned to the debtor, and any money received by the creditor on realisation of the security must be repaid. Section 106 also applies, by virtue of section 113, to securities given in connection with credit agreements which are in various ways defective under other terms of the Act. The court has wide powers under section 129 to give debtors time for payment and under section 136 to amend agreements and securities.

Sections 137 to 139 contain provisions empowering the court to reopen extortionate credit bargains, whether or not they are regulated agreements under the Act. These sections replace the more rigid and less comprehensive provisions of the Moneylenders Acts 1900 and 1927, which are repealed. The powers of the court include the setting aside of the transaction in whole or in part, the amendment of the credit agreement or any security instrument and ordering the return of money paid or documents handed over.

24–120 (f) Competing claims to a joint mortgaged policy. It is common practice for two people jointly purchasing a house for occupation to use a joint endowment insurance policy, with life cover in the event of death earlier than the specified date of maturity, as a means of financing the purchase.[23] A loan is secured on a mortgage of the property and the benefit of the policy is assigned to the mortgagee. The normal intention in the event of death, or when the policy matures, is that the proceeds are used to repay the mortgagee and the mortgage on the house is discharged. However, if in fact, on the death of one of the assureds, the claim of the mortgagee is satisfied by other means, the surviving assured, and not the estate of the deceased assured, is entitled to the policy proceeds.[24]

(2) *Redemption*

24–121 The right to redeem. Quite apart from the contractual right of the mortgagor to redeem the mortgage on the day, if any, fixed by its terms, customarily six months from the date of the mortgage,[25] he always has the equitable right to redeem at any date thereafter, although he must, in the normal case, give six months' notice (or interest in lieu of notice) of his

---

[21] The relevant provisions were brought into force from May 19, 1985 by the Consumer Credit Act (Commencement No. 8) Order 1983 (S.I. 1983 No. 1551). For more detail, see *The Encyclopedia of Consumer Credit Law*.

[22] "Regulated Agreement" includes a consumer credit agreement (s.189), defined by s.8 (as amended by S.I. 1983 No. 1878) as an agreement providing credit not exceeding £25,000 to an individual (including a partnership), which is not exempt under s.16.

[23] The same practice is used, of course, when there is a single purchaser, but that case cannot give rise to a situation of competing claims.

[24] *Smith v. Clerical Medical and General Life Assurance Society* [1993] 1 F.L.R. 47.

[25] This can be extended, provided there is no oppression or undue influence and the right to redeem is not rendered illusory: see Megarry and Wade, *The Law of Real Property* (5th ed., 1984) pp. 965–968.

intention[26] and pay the proper price.[27] Apart from the mortgagor, any person interested in the equity of redemption, including any subsequent mortgagee,[28] has the right to redeem.

24–122 The equity of redemption. The mortgagor's equity of redemption comprises his equitable right to redeem together with all his other rights over the property charged. There must be no clogs or fetters on this equity and, in particular, after redemption, the mortgagor must be free from all conditions in the mortgage.[29] So, too, an option to purchase the mortgaged property granted to the mortgagee at the time of the loan is generally void.[30] An example in relation to insurance policies is an unreported decision of the Appellate Court of Madras,[31] where it was held that a proviso in a charge of a life policy to the company to the effect that if the mortgagor fell behind in his payments, the company was to be entitled to cancel the policies at their surrender value was void as a clog on the equity of redemption.[32]

(3) *The Price of Redemption*

24–123 Besides payment of the principal sum advanced with interest thereon a mortgagor, in order to redeem, must also in certain circumstances pay additional amounts to the mortgagee.

(a) *Premiums on the Mortgaged Policy*

24–124 (i) *Implied power to add premiums to charge.* Wherever a policy of life insurance is mortgaged it is prima facie an implied term of the agreement that the mortgagor will pay the premiums on the policy as they become due, and that if he fails to do so the mortgagee may pay them and may add the amount so expended by him with interest from the date of payment to the security.[33] It would seem, however, that in the absence of express agreement by the mortgagor to repay the amount of the premiums, a mortgagee who has paid the premium cannot recover the amount of the premium as damages for breach of the mortgagor's express or implied covenant, since the only damages he could claim is for loss of the security if the policy was allowed to drop. Clearly if the mortgagee has not in fact paid any premiums the damages he can obtain will not bear any necessary relation with the amount of the premiums not paid by the mortgagor.[34]

---

[26] See, *e.g. Smith v. Smith* [1891] 3 Ch. 550. Less notice than this, or even no notice, may be justified if the mortgage was only temporary or the mortgagee shows that he wishes to call in the loan straightaway.

[27] See paras 24–123, *et seq., post.*

[28] See Megarry and Wade, *op. cit.*, pp. 971–972.

[29] See Megarry and Wade, *op. cit.*, pp. 968–971.

[30] *Samuel v. Jarrah Timber & Wood Paving Corp.* [1904] A.C. 323.

[31] *Darbha v. Nat. Ins. Co.*, noted J.I.A. (1946), vol. lxxiii, Pt. II Legal Notes, p. 17.

[32] *i.e.*, the proviso was treated in the same way as an option to purchase the policy.

[33] *Hodgson v. Hodgson* (1837) 2 Keen 704.

[34] See *National Assurance v. Best* (1857) 2 H. & N. 605—where the mortgagee was in fact held entitled only to nominal damages.

24–125 (ii) *Express power to add premiums to charge.* If there is an express term in the mortgage deed entitling the mortgagee to pay the premiums on the policy and to add these to the security it would seem that the express remedy excludes an action for damages for breach of the mortgagor's covenant. In *Browne v. Price*[35] A assigned to trustees for an insurance company, *inter alia*, a policy on his life taken out at that office as security for a loan. A covenanted to pay the premiums and, in default, the trustees had power to pay them and charge the payments on all the property mortgaged. After a time A ceased to pay the premiums and the life office credited the premiums as paid and debited the amount against A's mortgage account. The trustees sued to recover the amount of the premiums. The Court of Common Pleas held that as there was no express covenant to repay the premiums the trustees could only in any event sue for damages,[36] and, treating the back entries by the company as equivalent to a payment of the premiums by the trustees, as the trustees had exercised their express remedy of adding the premiums to the charge, this excluded by implication their remedy by way of an action for damages.

24–126 (iii) *Loan on policy by insurers.* Where an insurance company makes a loan on the security of a policy in its own office, the transaction is frequently carried out in the name of trustees for the company who contract with the assured as if they were third persons taking the policy in security for a loan made by them.[37] On the whole the court tends to have regard to the substance of the matter and to determine the right of the parties on the basis that the trustees and the company are the same person. In *Fitzwilliam v. Price*,[38] for example, the same transaction as was the subject of proceedings in *Browne v. Price*,[39] was the subject of a redemption action in Chancery. The court held that, looking at the substance of the transaction, it constituted an agreement between A and the company that the company could add the premiums to the charge if A failed to pay them.

If a debtor agrees with a life insurance company to pay all premiums on any policy of life insurance on the debtor's life taken out by the company, the debtor will not be obliged to pay the premiums on a policy effected by the company in its own office, unless such a policy was contemplated at the time the agreement was made.[40]

24–127 (iv) *Premiums paid by mortgagee by deposit.* Where a life policy is deposited to secure payment of a debt there is, in the absence of anything to the contrary in the memorandum or the oral agreement, an implied agreement by the debtor to pay interest and premiums, and the creditor is impliedly entitled to add to the security any premiums paid by him to keep the policy alive, together with interest on such premiums from the date of payment.[41] It has been held that the mortgagee is entitled to add to the

---

[35] (1858) 4 C.B.(N.S.) 598; *cf. Schlesinger & Joseph v. Mostyn* [1932] 1 K.B. 349, 354.

[36] *i.e.* following *National Assurance v. Best, supra.*

[37] This practice is particularly common where the insurers are an unincorporated association.

[38] (1858) 4 Jur.(N.S.) 889.

[39] See para. 24–125, *ante.*

[40] *Grey v. Ellison* (1856) 1 Giff. 438—The point of this case is that the policy was to be in favour of the company, and such a "policy" taken out by the company in favour of itself was held not to be a policy at all. If the company wished it could have stipulated for the debtor simply to pay extra charges, equivalent to a premium, to the company at regular intervals.

[41] *Re Kerr's Policy* (1869) L.R. 8 Eq. 331; *Bellamy v. Brickenden* (1861) 2 John. & H. 137.

security the full amount of the premiums paid by him notwithstanding that he (or his solicitor on his behalf) has deducted a commission therefrom.[42]

(b) *Capitalisation of Arrears of Interest*

24–128 Where it is desired to capitalise arrears of interest so as to enable the mortgagee to obtain compound interest on such arrears, this should be done by express provision in the instrument creating the charge. The provision should be an outright one and not one in the form of an option to the mortgagee to capitalise arrears of interest, since this may be held to constitute a clog upon the equity of redemption.[43]

(c) *Costs and Expenses of Mortgagee*

24–129 A mortgagee is entitled to all proper costs, charges and expenses incurred by him in relation to the mortgage debt or the security. In particular he is entitled as of right (and without the order of the court) to his legal costs as between solicitor and own client incurred by him and properly incidental to an action for foreclosure or redemption. Although his entitlement to these costs rests on contract, the court may disallow all or part of such costs where the mortgagee has acted unreasonably or vexatiously in bringing or defending such proceedings.[44]

In the Irish case of *Murphy v. Taylor*[45] the mortgagee was held to be entitled to all his costs of a redemption action, even though the bulk of these costs were incurred through his defence, which the court rejected, that the assignment was absolute and not by way of mortgage. In England, however, the practice would appear to be to allow the mortgagee in a redemption action only such costs as are attributable to the taking of an account between the parties, and not the costs fairly attributable to a defence of the mortgagee which has failed.[46]

(4) *Remedies of the Mortgagee*

24–130 The mortgagee of a life policy has available to him a number of remedies when the mortgagor is in default.[47]

24–131 Foreclosure or judicial sale. The mortgagee can apply to the court for an order for sale or, possibly, for foreclosure.[48] Such orders have the

---

[42] *Leete v. Wallace* (1888) 58 L.T. 577.
[43] See para. 24–119, *ante*.
[44] *Cotterell v. Stratton* (1872) L.R. 8 Ch. 295; *Bank of N.S.W. v. O'Connor* (1889) 14 App.Cas. 273, 278; *Rourke v. Robinson* [1911] 1 Ch. 480.
[45] (1850) 1 Ir.Ch. 92, the full facts of which are set out in para. 24–118, *ante*.
[46] *Kinnaird v. Trollope* (1889) 42 Ch.D. 610.
[47] More detailed description of remedies can be found in Megarry and Wade, *op. cit.*
[48] Strictly speaking, foreclosure should not be available to the mortgagee of a chose in action such as an insurance policy, since the remedy is confined to legal mortgagees or equitable mortgagees who have the right to have a legal mortgage executed: see *Dyson v. Morris* (1842) 1 Hare 413, where Wigram V.C. said that the proper remedy of a mortgagee of a policy of insurance was sale. However, there are cases where foreclosure orders have been made over property including choses in action: see e.g. *Beaton v. Boulton* [1891] W.N. 30.

effect of extinguishing the mortgagor's equity of redemption, but are little used in practice nowadays.

24–132 Statutory right to require sale. In addition to the common law remedy just described, section 91 of the Law of Property Act 1925[49] gives the mortgagee, and the mortgagor or any other person interested in the equity of redemption, the right, at any time before foreclosure absolute, to apply to the court for an order for sale. The remedy applies as much to an equitable mortgagee by deposit as to any other mortgagee,[50] and can be used in exceptional cases to ensure that the sale is unimpeachable.[51]

24–133 The mortgagee's power of sale. In addition to the right to ask for the court to order sale, the mortgagee may have the right to sell the mortgaged property without resorting to the court under section 101 of the Law of Property Act 1925[52] or under the power commonly reserved in the mortgage.

The statutory power of sale arises, subject to a contrary provision in the instrument creating the mortgage, whenever a mortgage is made by deed after 1881 and the legal date for redemption has passed, and provided that either:

(1) notice requiring repayment of the capital has been served on the mortgagor and he is in default of repayment for more than three months; or

(2) some interest is in arrear for more than two months after having become due; or

(3) the mortgagor has committed a breach of some condition contained in the deed or implied by statute other than the covenant to repay the capital and interest.[53]

The power of sale may be exercised under a properly framed power of attorney,[54] and the mortgagee whose power of sale has become exercisable is entitled to call for all deeds and documents relating to the mortgaged property which a purchaser would be entitled to demand; this would presumably cover a policy of insurance.

24–134 Title of purchaser from mortgagee. So long as the power of sale has arisen, the title of a bona fide purchaser is not generally impeachable on the grounds that the power was not exercisable,[55] and accordingly a purchaser is not concerned to enquire whether the conditions laid down in section 103 have been fulfilled. It is doubtful whether this provision protects

---

[49] Replacing, with amendments, Conveyancing Act 1881, s.25.
[50] *Oldham v. Stringer* (1884) 51 L.T. 895.
[51] *cf.* the power under s.184, described below. See *Arab Bank p.l.c. v. Merchantile Holdings Ltd* [1994] Ch. 71.
[52] Replacing Conveyancing Act 1881, s.19.
[53] Law of Property Act 1925, s.103.
[54] Law of Property Act 1925, s.106(1).
[55] Law of Property Act 1925, s.104(2).

a purchaser of a life policy which has merely been charged to the extent of the debt, although this is otherwise a "mortgage" for the purpose of the statutory power of sale. Section 104 is only effective to transfer to the purchaser "the subject of the mortgage", which in this case is not the policy itself but only a charge thereon. Hence the chargee cannot give a complete legal title to the purchaser or a legal discharge to the office on surrender.

24–135 Right to appoint a receiver. Where the statutory power of sale has become exercisable, the mortgagee may, without prejudice to his other remedies, realise his security either in whole or in part by appointing a receiver of the income of the mortgaged property or any part of it.[56] It is therefore to the advantage of the mortgagee, and quite usual in practice, for the lender of money on the security of a life policy to insist that the borrower offers him some collateral security in respect of which, on default of payment of the premiums on the policy or interest on the money advanced, a receiver may be appointed and the money received by him applied in payment of premiums and interest.

24–136 Conditions in mortgage deed. It is usual for the mortgage deed to provide for a power of sale and other remedies in wider terms than under the statutory provisions just described. Where the mortgage gives the mortgagee an express and unfettered right of sale, the mortgagee may sell at any time, after the legal date for redemption has passed,[57] upon giving the mortgagor notice and a reasonable time to find and pay the money due.[58]

24–137 Duties of mortgagee exercising power to sell. The mortgagee is in no sense a trustee of the power of sale, either for the mortgagor or for any other person interested in the equity of redemption. So, in general, he is not under a duty to obtain the best price obtainable for the property,[59] but he does owe a duty to the mortgagor[60] to take reasonable care to obtain a proper price or the true market value.[61] A great disparity between the purchase price and the best price obtainable may be evidence of unreasonable or reckless conduct. Neither the mortgagee nor his solicitor or agent acting for him in the sale is entitled to purchase the property in his own account.[62]

24–138 Sale of policy by surrender. The surrender of a policy to the company is usually the most convenient mode of exercising the power of sale, but it is not certain whether it is a permissible mode of exercising the power under the statute, and hence whether the mortgagee can give the company a sufficient discharge from further liability on the policy. Technically a surrender is not a sale, since it is merely a release of the insured's

---

[56] Law of Property Act 1925, ss.101(1) and 109(1).

[57] *Brougham v. Squire* (1852) 1 Drew 151.

[58] *Ex p. Official Receiver* (1886) 18 Q.B.D. 222.

[59] But note Building Societies Act 1962, s.36(1) which does impose such a duty on a building society exercising a power of sale. See *Reliance Permanent Building Society v. Harwood-Stamper* [1944] Ch. 362.

[60] And to a guarantor: *Standard Chartered Bank v. Walker* [1982] 1 W.L.R. 1410.

[61] *Cuckmere Brick Co. v. Mutual Finance Ltd* [1971] Ch. 949 and the authorities discussed therein explained in *Downsview Nominees Ltd v. First City Corporation Ltd* [1993] A.C. 295, 315.

[62] *Hodson v. Deans* [1903] 2 Ch. 647; *Henderson v. Astwood* [1894] A.C. 150.

rights, but in substance its effect upon the mortgagor is precisely the same as a sale. The surrender value may not be the best price obtainable but the mortgagor cannot object on that account. Moreover, if the mortgagee sold the policy at its surrender value to trustees for the company, this could not be impeached as an improper exercise of the power, although the effect would be precisely the same as a surrender.[63] It is submitted that a court would hold that, so long as the surrender value is equal to the sort of price which the mortgagor might reasonably have obtained, it is a proper exercise of the power of sale to surrender the policy directly to the company.

24–139 Payment of policy money into court. If there is any reasonable doubt as to the entitlement in equity to the policy moneys as between the mortgagor and the mortgagee or other persons interested in the equity of redemption, the company may pay the money into court under the Life Assurance (Payment into Court) Act 1896,[64] and the company will not have to pay the costs of subsequent proceedings even where the mortgagee could have given an effective receipt under the Law of Property Act 1925,[65] unless, semble, the mortgagor or other person interested in the equity of redemption had made a claim which was quite untenable on the face of it.[66]

Where the mortgagee does not have the right to sue at law,[67] and it is therefore necessary or at least advisable for the company to obtain a legal discharge from the mortgagor but for some particular reason[68] this cannot be done, the company may either take the risk and pay out the moneys to the mortgagee or retain the moneys. If it takes the latter course, upon the mortgagee's bringing an action against it, the court may, if the mortgage debt exceeds the amount of the policy moneys, order that the receipt of the mortgagor or his representatives be dispensed with and give judgment to the mortgagee against the company for the policy moneys without interest and subject to the deduction by the company of its taxed costs in the action.[69]

24–140 Receipt for bonus declared on policy. Where a bonus declared on a mortgaged policy is payable immediately in cash the mortgagee's right to receive it and ability to give a complete discharge is the same as his right to receive and give a discharge for the principal policy moneys. Where, however, a bonus is declared as an addition to the principal policy moneys, payment can only be obtained before the policy falls in by surrendering the bonus to the company at its surrender value, and since this amounts to a sale of part of the policy, the mortgagee can only surrender the policy if he is entitled to exercise the power of sale.[70] For this reason and in view of the

---

[63] It would seem advisable, therefore, until the matter is finally resolved, for an insurance company to use this method rather than accept a direct surrender by the mortgagee, but in practice it is usual for life offices to follow the latter course.

[64] See para. 24–59, *ante.*

[65] *Hockey v. Western* [1898] 1 Ch. 350.

[66] See *Desborough v. Harris* (1855) 5 De G.M. & G. 439.

[67] See paras 24–69, *et seq., ante.*

[68] *e.g.* because he has died and no personal representatives have been appointed.

[69] *Curtius v. Caledonian Fire & Life* (1881) 19 Ch.D. 534; *Crossley v. City of Glasgow Life* (1876) 4 Ch.D. 421; *Webster v. British Empire Mutual* (1880) 15 Ch.D. 169.

[70] See the article by Mr A. R. Barrand in *Journal of Institute of Actuaries*, Vol. xxxiii, at p. 214.

difficulties that may arise it is usual in these circumstances for the company to insist on the mortgagor's consent being obtained.

24–141 Assignment of policy to creditor on trust. Where the security takes the form of an assignment to the creditor of the policy upon trust to hold the policy moneys to discharge his debt out of them and then to remit the surplus to the debtor, subject only to any question as to the validity of the instrument purporting to create the trust, the company may pay the creditor without regard to any question between him and the debtor. The latter comes in only as a beneficiary under the trust, with whom the company is not concerned,[71] and the company would not be entitled, and would consequently be at risk as to costs, to pay the policy moneys into court.

24–142 Receipt when mortgage redeemed. A receipt indorsed on or annexed to a mortgage stating the name of the person who pays the money and executed by the mortgagee or other person entitled to give a receipt for the mortgage money operates without any express reconveyance, surrender or release as a reconveyance of the mortgaged property to the person immediately entitled before the execution of the receipt to the equity of redemption and as a discharge of that property from all moneys secured by the mortgage.[72] Thus a company can safely rely on this receipt in paying the mortgagor or a person claiming through him.

(5) *Receipt for Policy Money*

24–143 Mortgagee's receipt. Insurance companies, once satisfied that a mortgage of a life policy is valid, may safely pay the policy moneys on the sole receipt of the mortgagee, without enquiring as to the state of account between him and the mortgagor and disregarding any dispute between them on this matter.[73] However, they are not bound to do so, and can distribute the moneys amongst those beneficially entitled thereto according to their respective rights.[74] Further, they may do so if the mortgagee is a trustee or merely an equitable mortgagee by deposit.[75]

7. TRUSTS AND SETTLED POLICIES

(1) *Creation of Trusts*

24–144 There are a number of ways in which a policy of insurance or the insurance moneys can become the subject of a trust in favour of persons other than the assured. Thus a trust may be created by an express declaration of trust on the part of the assured, or he may assign the policy to trustees to hold it on trusts declared by him.[76] Alternatively the policy may be

---

[71] See paras 24–144, *et seq.*, *post.*
[72] Law of Property Act 1925, s.115.
[73] Law of Property Act 1925, s.107; see Barrand, J.I.A., Vol. xxxiii, p. 211.
[74] *Re Bell* [1896] 1 Ch. 1.
[75] Law of Property Act 1925, s.113. As to the position regarding the survivor(s) of joint mortgagees, see section 111.
[76] See paras 24–69, *et seq.*, *ante.*

purchased by someone not an assured, with the consequence that a resulting trust arises in favour of the person who paid premiums,[77] or a policy may be effected for the benefit of someone other than the assured by reason of the Married Women's Property Acts 1870 and 1882.

In this part we consider certain problems attaching to the creation of trusts of life policies before treating of the incidents which attach to a policy once it has been settled on trusts.

24–145 Unambiguous declaration of trust. Leaving aside the statutory trusts arising under the 19th century Married Women's Property Acts,[78] it is a fundamental principle that a trust of a policy is not to be inferred from a general intention, expressed orally or in writing, to benefit a third party in circumstances where it would be meritorious to do so, but only from language clearly revealing an intention to create a trust. This general principle rests on two separate rules of English law, one of equity and one of common law. Equity would not hold that a person had declared himself a trustee of property unless he had used words clearly evincing an intention to constitute himself trustee of it.[79] At common law the doctrine of privity of contract necessitated a clear distinction between a contract between two parties for the benefit of a third (who could not enforce it), and the creation of a trust by two or more persons for a beneficiary (who could obtain execution of the trust).[80] To the extent that the law was prepared to find trusts and grant remedies to third party beneficiaries, it was undermining the doctrine of privity.

24–146 The courts' consciousness of these two rules is illustrated by the judgments of the Court of Appeal in *Re Schebsman*,[81] case concerning a company's promise to an employee to pay a pension to his widow. Lord Greene M.R. remarked:

> "To interpret this contract as creating a trust would, in my judgment, be to disregard the dividing line between the case of a trust and the simple case of a contract made between two persons for the benefit of a third. That dividing line exists, although it may not always be easy to determine where it is to be drawn."[82]

Du Parcq L.J. said:

> "It is true that by the use of possibly unguarded language a person may create a trust, as Monsieur Jourdain talked prose, without knowing it; but unless an intention to create a trust is clearly to be collected from the language used and the circumstances of the case, I think that the court ought not to be astute to discover any indication of such an intention."[83]

---

[77] See paras 24–53, *et seq.*, *ante*.
[78] See paras 24–168, *et seq.*, *post*. These Acts are the 1870 and 1882 Acts in England and Wales, and the Married Women's Policies of Assurance (Scotland) Act 1880 as amended by the Married Women's Policies of Assurance (Scotland) (Amendment) Act 1980 in Scotland.
[79] See, *e.g. Jones v. Lock* [1865] L.R. 1 Ch.App. 25; *Richards v. Delbridge* (1874) L.R. 18 Eq. 11.
[80] This distinction, and the few common law exceptions to the privity rule, were clarified in *Beswick v. Beswick* [1968] A.C. 58. *Green v. Russell* [1959] 2 Q.B. 226 is an illustration in a life insurance context of the application of the distinction.
[81] [1944] Ch. 83. This case is discussed at para. 24–158, *post*.
[82] [1944] Ch. 83, 89.
[83] [1944] Ch. 83, 104. The case was approved by the House of Lords in *Beswick v. Beswick* [1968] A.C. 58.

The application of this principle can only be determined by an examination of the decided cases, but it must be noted that the doctrine of privity of contract has been substantially modified by the Contracts (Rights of Third Parties) Act 1999, in respect of contracts entered into on or after May 11, 2000. A more detailed consideration of the effect of this Act can be found elsewhere in this work,[84] but the fact that a third party will now be able to enforce a life policy effected for his benefit after that date means that one of the principal reasons for trying to establish a trust of a policy no longer exists. The authorities discussed in the following paragraphs must therefore now be read in this light.

24–147 In *Cleaver v. Mutual Reserve Fund Life Ass.,*[85] a policy effected by a man on his own life was expressed to be payable to F.M., his wife, if living at his death and otherwise to his personal representatives. It was held that there was an effective statutory trust in favour of his wife under section 11 of the Married Women's Property Act 1882 but that, apart from section 11, the words of the policy would not have been sufficient to create a trust.

24–148 In *Re A Policy No. 6402 of the Scottish Equitable*[86] a policy was effected in a Scottish office by A on his own life "for behoof of B" (his wife's sister) and the policy money was made payable to B. It was held that the words "for behoof of" were not apt to create a trust, that as A had paid all the premiums there was a resulting trust of the proceeds of the policy to A and that consequently B was a mere agent to receive the money on behalf of A.

24–149 In *Re Burgess's Policy*[87] a married woman effected a policy on her own life "in terms of the Married Women's Property Act 1870 for the benefit of her children". The Act of 1870 did not apply to such a policy effected by a married woman. It was held that no trust in favour of the children was created by the words "for the benefit of" and that the policy and its proceeds therefore belonged to the assured and her personal representatives.

24–150 In *Re Engelbach's Estate*[88] there was a proposal for an endowment policy in which the proposer described himself as the proposer "for his daughter M.M., aged one month", and the policy issued on that proposal was expressed to be payable at the end of the endowment period to the daughter (called "the nominee") her executors, administrators or assigns, if she should survive to the specified age but otherwise all premiums were to be repaid without interest to the proposer or his executors, administrators or assigns. On maturity of the policy after the death of the proposer the office paid the policy money upon the daughter's receipt to a firm of solicitors to hold for whoever might be entitled thereto. Romer J. held that the proposer had not constituted himself a trustee of the policy for his daughter and that accordingly the policy moneys formed part of the proposer's estate.[89]

24–151 In *Re Sinclair's Policy*[90] A signed a proposal form for a "special

---

[84] See paras. 20–61 to 20–66, *ante*.
[85] [1892] 1 Q.B. 147.
[86] [1902] 1 Ch. 282.
[87] (1915) 113 L.T. 443.
[88] [1924] 2 Ch. 348.
[89] The decision in this case has been doubted by the majority of the House of Lords in *Beswick v. Beswick* [1968] A.C. 58 but see para. 24–159, *post*.
[90] [1938] Ch. 799; see also *Re Clay's Policy* [1937] 2 All E.R. 548.

child's endowment" in which he described himself as the godfather of B, then six months old, to be referred to in the policy as "the nominee" and the policy moneys were expressed to be payable to the child on maturity, but in the event of the child's dying before the date that the policy matured all premiums were to be repaid to A or his personal representatives. A handed the policy to B's father and told him to retain it and in due course to collect payment for his son. On maturity after A's death the insurance company paid the policy moneys into court. Farwell J. held that the evidence was insufficient to establish a trust in favour of his godson. There was no doubt that A's intention was to make provision for his godson, but he did not constitute himself a trustee of the moneys payable.[91]

24–152 In *Re Foster*,[92] A took out what is usually termed a "Child Deferred Policy" on the life of his son B, then aged 13 years. The terms of the policy were that £5,000 plus bonuses was to be paid to the personal representatives or assigns of B in the event of his death after the age of 21 years, but if he should die before then 90 per cent of the premiums with interest at 21 per cent was to be repaid to A. A paid all the premiums until he died, and then premiums were paid by or on behalf of B who by this time had attained the age of 21. On B's death it was held[93] that the proceeds of the policy belonged to the personal representatives of A and not of B since the policy created no trust in B's favour. All that B's representatives were entitled to was a lien on the policy moneys to the extent of the premiums paid by or on behalf of B.

24–153 In all the above cases it was held that the words used in the policy were not sufficient to create a trust. The principle of these cases has recently been stated to be as follows:

> "First, that the mere fact that A takes out a policy which is expressed to be for the benefit of B does not constitute a trust for B; and the second is this, that the mere fact that the policy provides that the policy moneys are to be payable to B does not create a trust in favour of B."[94]

In the following three cases it was held that the words used in the policy were sufficient to create a trust in favour of the payee.

24–154 In *Re Gordon*[95] the question before the court was whether under the rules of a certain friendly society the widow of a member was entitled to retain for her own benefit the gratuity and pension payable on the death of her husband, or whether they formed part of her husband's estate. The rules of the society, after providing that the widow was to be entitled to these payments on the death of her husband, went on to provide that all the property of the society, though legally vested in trustees, was to be dealt with in accordance with the rules. Simonds J. held that whether a trust in favour of the widow was created depended upon the true construction of the rules, and

---

[91] It should be noted that Lord Upjohn in *Beswick v. Beswick* [1968] A.C. 58, 96 held that the distinguishing feature of this case was that the policy moneys were paid into court—and he disagreed with so much of Farwell J.'s judgment as was to the effect that had the moneys been paid to the child he would have held them as a constructive trustee for the proposer.

[92] (1938) 54 T.L.R. 903; [1938] 3 All E.R. 357, 610.

[93] *Per* Crossman J.

[94] *Re Foster's Policy* [1966] 1 W.L.R. 222, 227, *per* Plowman J.

[95] [1940] Ch. 851.

on their true construction the rules imposed a trust in favour of anyone who under the rules was entitled to a benefit.

24–155 In *Re Webb*[96] Farwell J. found sufficient indication in the terms of the particular child's deferred assurance before him to distinguish it from the policies considered in the *Engelbach, Sinclair* and *Foster* cases above cited and to enable him to hold that a trust in favour of the child had been created. The policy was generally in standard form, i.e. it was expressed to have been taken out by the proposer on the life of and for the benefit of the child, the policy moneys were expressed to be payable to the child's representatives if he died after his twenty-first birthday, and if he died before then the premiums were to be returned to the proposer. The policy also conferred certain options of, for example, converting the policy into an endowment policy and other powers to be exercised by the proposer (therein called "the grantee") "on behalf of the life assured". The policy then went on to state—and this was the provision upon which Farwell J. relied—that upon the life assured attaining the age of 21 the proposer's rights and powers would cease and the life assured would become solely interested in and entitled to deal with the policy. The proposer died before his children had attained the age of 21 years and his executors took out a summons to determine whether they held the policy for the benefit of the estate or upon trust for his child. Farwell J. held that, having regard to the other cases cited above, the policy would belong to the father's estate unless there was in the policy something establishing reasonably clearly that the assured was in fact constituting himself a trustee for his children. He proceeded to hold that there was sufficient in the policy to establish a trust. In the first place throughout the policy the grantee (i.e. the proposer) was said to be acting and to be exercising his various powers on behalf of the infant, and if he had, for example, surrendered the policy, the money so acquired would have to belong to the infant and not to the grantee since this would be a term of the bargain between him and the insurance company. The most striking feature of the policy, however, was the express provision that on the child's attaining the age of 21 the grantee's powers would cease and all his interest in the policy would completely disappear. This was sufficient, in Farwell J.'s judgment, to distinguish this policy from the policies under consideration in the other cases and to establish a trust in favour of the infant.

24–156 The above decision has been considered and applied by Plowman J. in *Re Foster's Policy*,[97] who interpreted the ratio in *Re Webb* as being that if, according to the terms of the policy, a time comes when the proposer (or grantee) ceases to have any beneficial interest in it, the court will imply a trust in favour of the person for whose benefit the policy is expressed to have been taken out and to whose personal representatives payment is to be made.[98] In this case the policy was expressed in similar terms to the one considered in *Re Webb*, except that there was no express provision that the grantee's interest in the policy would cease when the life assured attained the age of 21 years. There was, however, a provision to the effect that until the life assured attained the age of 21 years the grantee or his personal representatives was to have the right (without the consent of the insured) to

[96] [1941] Ch. 225.
[97] [1966] 1 W.L.R. 222.
[98] *ibid.* at 229.

surrender, to reduce or to borrow upon the policy, but that after the assured attained the age of 21 years all these rights were to be vested in and for the benefit of the assured or his personal representatives. Plowman J. held that the fact that these rights became vested in and for the benefit of the assured after he attained the age of 21 years was inconsistent with the grantee's retaining any beneficial interest after that date and consistent only with the beneficial interest being in the assured. Since the policy moneys only became payable after that date the policy accordingly established a trust in favour of the infant.

24–157 The payee's right to the proceeds. If there is no trust of the policy or proceeds in favour of the payee, but he receives the proceeds for some other reason, he will ordinarily be entitled to retain the money. However, if a reading of the policy compels the conclusion that he was not intended to take as a donee from the assured, but as a nominee or agent for the assured, he will be compelled to account to the proposer or his personal representatives for the moneys received by him. This was established by the Court of Appeal in *Re Schebsman*,[99] a decision approved by a majority of the House of Lords in *Beswick v. Beswick*.[1]

24–158 In *Re Schebsman*[2] a company covenanted with its employee S by his contract of employment to make certain payments to S's widow in the event of his death occurring within six years of the termination of his employment. S died within the six-year period and his estate was bankrupt. The trustee in bankruptcy sought to divert the payments to S's widow to the estate of S, and claimed a declaration that all the sums payable by the company under the agreement formed part of the estate. His claim failed. At common law the company was not only entitled but bound to make the stipulated payments to the widow,[3] and there was no reason to describe her as an agent to receive the moneys for the account of S's estate, so that she could spend them as she chose. The trustee could claim no right to intercept the payments which S himself did not possess, and S could not have done this. Only S and the company together could vary the company's obligation and it was not open to S or his trustee to seek to alter it unilaterally. Neither did equity oblige the widow to cede priority to the trustee. As the court rejected the idea that S had constituted himself trustee of the benefit of the contract for his wife, the trustee sought to persuade the court to find a resulting trust of the benefit of the payments in favour of S. The court held, however, that there was no pretext for equity to intervene to enable the company to break the terms of its agreement with S.[4]

24–159 The result of the decision in *Re Schebsman*[5] is that it is now difficult to envisage a situation in which a payee, in a similar position to S's widow, could be described as an agent to receive policy moneys for the assured. Such an obligation would arise, if at all, at common law. It was found

[99] [1943] Ch. 366; [1944] Ch. 83.
[1] [1968] A.C. 58, *per* Lord Reid at 71, Lord Pearce at 94 and Lord Upjohn at 96. Lord Hodson and Lord Guest did not comment on the decision.
[2] [1943] Ch. 366; [1944] Ch. 83.
[3] See *per* du Parcq L.J. at [1944] Ch. 83, 103–104.
[4] Another way of expressing it is that there was no necessity for equity to intervene, S having perfected a gift to his wife by entering into the contract with the company.
[5] [1943] Ch. 366; [1944] Ch. 83.

to exist in the *Engelbach*[6] case where the child was held not entitled to keep the policy moneys, and there are sympathetic dicta in the *Sinclair*[7] and *Foster*[8] cases, but in those cases the payee had never received the money, which had been paid into court. Moreover in *Beswick v. Beswick*[9] Lord Upjohn disapproved the *Engelbach* case on this point, and criticised the *Sinclair* case in so far as it suggested that the policy moneys, once received by the payee, would have had to be paid to the proposer's estate. His remarks were concurred in by Lord Reid and Lord Wilberforce. It can therefore be said that, although the doctrine propounded in the *Engelbach* case remains, it is now hard to see a court holding that, if the same or similar facts arose for decision today, the recipient of the moneys was accountable to the proposer for them.

(2) *Particular Types of Trust Policy*

24–160 (a) Child Endowment Policies. This type of policy has already been considered in relation to a number of the cases cited above.[10] It is, perhaps, worth noting that if the policy is held to enure for the benefit of the proposer it is prima facie an illegal policy, since a man ordinarily has no insurable interest in his child,[11] and on the principle "ut res magis valeat quam pereat," this in itself might persuade a court to hold that a trust in favour of the child has been created.

24–161 The actual legal relationship created by a policy such as that considered in *Re Webb* and *Re Foster's Policy* is a complex one. The proposer, as a party to the contract with the insurance company, is a trustee of the benefit of that contract until the child reaches the specified age. After that date the child alone is interested beneficially in the policy and entitled to deal with it. The insurance company can only fulfil their obligations under the contract by paying the child or his representatives, and so in a sense the child can be said to be in the position of a mere payee who is the donee of the policy as was the widow in *Re Schebsman*.[12] His position differs only in this respect that, whereas in *Re Schebsman* the wife could not sue upon the contract if the company refused to pay, since she was not a party to the contract, the child, as a beneficiary under a trust, may enforce his rights by compelling the proposer to sue the company. Thus indirectly he may enforce the contract in circumstances in which the mere payee and donee of the policy cannot. Of course, once the child commences to pay the premiums to the life office and the office accepts such payments from the child, there can

---

[6] [1924] 2 Ch. 348.
[7] [1938] Ch. 799.
[8] (1938) 54 T.L.R. 903.
[9] [1968] A.C. 58.
[10] See *Re Engelbach*; *Re Foster*; *Re Sinclair*; *Re Webb*; *Re Foster's Policy*, cited in paras 24–150, 24–152, 24–151, 24–155, 24–156, *ante*.
[11] *Halford v. Kymer* (1830) 10 B. & C. 724. And see paras 1–90 to 1–100, *ante*.
[12] [1943] Ch. 366; [1944] Ch. 83.

be said to be a novation of the agreement such that from then onwards the child ceases to be entitled merely as a beneficiary under a trust but becomes entitled to sue upon the policy in his own right as a contracting party.

24–162 (b) Group Insurance Policy. A group insurance is one where a person, generally an employer, takes out a policy on the lives of a group of people, generally his employees, for the benefit of the lives insured.

Two forms of such policy have been considered by the courts. In *Bowskill v. Dawson (No. 2)*[13] a group life policy was effected by a trustee company under the terms of a trust deed made between it and the employing company. Under the policy the trustee company was designated the "person assured"; and the employees of the employing company were "the lives assured." The premiums on the policy were calculated so as to secure for each employee on death while in the employment of the company, or on total disablement, a sum calculated by reference to his age and salary. All sums payable under the policy and received by the trustee company were expressed in the trust deed to be held by it upon trust for the employee or his representatives. In these circumstances the court[14] had no difficulty at all in holding that such employee, upon whose death a sum became payable, was a beneficiary under the trusts of the deed.

24–163 In *Green v. Russell*[15] on the other hand, a group accident policy was taken out by an employer, called "the insured", in the policy, expressed to be for the benefit of the employees named in a schedule, with sums payable on death or disablement in each case. In this case, however, the policy provided that:

> "the company shall be entitled to treat the insured as the absolute owner and shall not be bound to recognise any equitable or other claim or interest in the policy and the receipt of the insured alone shall be an effectual discharge".

The Court of Appeal held that an employee, upon whose death by accident a sum became payable under the policy was not entitled to it either at common law, because he was not a party to the contract, or in equity, because on a true construction of the policy the employer had not constituted himself a trustee for his employees.

In both the above cases the issue before the court was whether the benefits under the policies, which had in each case been paid to the deceased's representatives, were deductible from the amount of damages recoverable against the employer under the Fatal Accidents Acts, or were excluded by section 1 of the Fatal Accidents (Damages) Act 1908,[16] and in both cases it was held that they were so excluded.

---

[13] [1955] 1 Q.B. 13.

[14] See particularly Romer L.J., *ibid.* at 27. *cf. Buxton v. Stamp Duties Commrs.* [1953] N.Z.L.R. 92.

[15] [1959] 2 Q.B. 226. See also *McCamley v. Cammell Laird Shipbuilders Ltd* [1990] 1 W.L.R. 963, where the policy was a group personal accident policy in very similar form.

[16] N.B. This section has now been repealed and has been replaced with modifications by s.2 of the Fatal Accidents Act 1959—*cf. Malyon v. Plummer* [1964] 1 Q.B. 330.

(3) *Rights of Third Parties in Scots Law*

24-164 (i) *In general.* In Scotland different principles of law arise in relation to a child's endowment or deferred assurance policy, or any other policy expressed to be payable to an intended donee of the policy and its proceeds.[17] In Scotland, law and equity were never separate, and any person who acquires a right in relation to the performance of a contract can enforce his right by action in his own name against the obligor. Where a person other than the assured or his personal representative is named as payee in a policy, two questions arise: (1) may the payee enforce the promise to pay by action in his own name against the insurer? (2) is he entitled to receive and retain the proceeds of the policy for his own use as against the assured? As regards the first question, the form of the obligation is sufficient to give the payee a right of action against the insurer. As regards the second question, the form of the obligation is not enough and his right depends on whether the obligation in his favour has as between the assured and him become irrevocable. Until then the assured may recall the provision and revoke the mandate to the insurer to make payment to the payee. Irrevocability may be established in different ways and is essentially a question of evidence. The most obvious evidence is the delivery of the policy to the child or other donee. Registration in the Books of Council and Session for publication would be conclusive evidence of irrevocability, because a deed or contract, once it is registered, cannot be recalled. Intimation to the child or other donee is also sufficient, because it implies a declaration by the assured that the child or other donee may look to the policy as a provision made for his benefit. Where the tertius has undertaken an onerous obligation in reliance upon his right under the contract, then the provision in his favour will be irrevocable, even though it has not been intimated to him. But these do not exhaust the ways in which the intention to make an irrevocable donation may be proved, and in particular it should be noted that, according to the most distinguished authority, the possibility has not been excluded that the terms of the deed themselves may be sufficient to show the necessary intention to make the provision irrevocable.[18]

24-165 The present state of the law on this subject is summed up in the speech of Lord Dunedin in the case of *Carmichael v. Carmichael's Executrix*.[19] The policy under consideration in that case was one issued by the English and Scottish Law Life Assurance Association. The policy recited the proposal of H. F. Carmichael therein referred to as "the grantee" to effect an assurance for the sum of £1,000 on the life of his son I. N. Carmichael (then eight years of age), and witnessed that if the life assured should die before attaining the age of 21 years the premiums would be repaid by the office to the grantee, but if the life assured should attain the age of 21

---

[17] In Scotland children have contractual capacity on attaining 16 years—Age of Legal Capacity (Scotland) Act 1991 (c. 50), as amended by the Children (Scotland) Act 1995 (c. 36) s.105 (4) and Sch. 4, para. 53, which provides that in civil matters a person of 12 years or more is presumed to be of sufficient age and maturity to have a general understanding of what it means to instruct a solicitor—Sch. 4, para. 53(3), inserting s.2 (4A) and 2 (4B) in the 1991 Act. Prejudicial transactions entered into by persons aged between 16 and 18 may be set aside.

[18] Lord Reid in *Allan's Trs. v. Lord Advocate* [1971] S.C. 45, 54, HL holding that the intimation of the trust to only one of three prospective beneficiaries was equivalent to delivery of the trust deed and sufficed to bring the whole trust into effect.

[19] 1919 S.C. 636; 1920 S.C. 195, HL.

years and pay the annual premiums thereafter, the funds of the association would be liable to pay to the executors, administrators or assigns of the life assured immediately on his death the sum of £1,000. Up to the time of the son's majority the father was entitled to discontinue the payment of premiums and surrender the policy to the office for the cash surrender value. Upon attaining majority the life assured was given several options: to pay the premiums and keep up the policy; to convert it into a paid-up policy, or to take the cash surrender value. The father kept the policy in his possession and paid the premiums until the son attained majority. The son knew of the existence of the policy but there was no evidence of any direct intimation of it to him. When the son attained majority the father wrote a letter to the insurance company based on the assumption that the son would now exercise his rights under the policy. The son died about nine months after attaining majority before any action was taken by him and before any further premium became payable. The policy money was claimed by the son's executrix and by the father. The latter, in the statement annexed to his claim, averred that at the age of 21 the son had certain options, including that of taking up the policy and paying the premiums. The House of Lords, reversing the decision of a majority of a court of seven judges in the Court of Session, held that taking all the circumstances together there was sufficient evidence when taken along with the terms of the document to show that an irrevocable jus quaesitum was constituted in favour of the son, and that the claim of his executrix must prevail against the claim of the father. Lord Dunedin, in whose speech Viscount Haldane, Viscount Finlay, and Viscount Cave concurred, and with which Lord Shaw of Dunfermline agreed except on one small point, summarised the position in this way[20]:

> "I have gone through these various ways in which the intention that a vested jus tertio should be created can be shown, but, after all they are only examples and not an exhaustive list, for in the end it is a question of evidence, and the only real rule to be deduced is that the mere expression of the obligation as giving a jus tertio is not sufficient. In short, I entirely agree with the one sentence in which Lord Mackenzie states the case, where he says: 'The question always must be—can the article in favour of the third party be recalled or not?'"

24–166 Even though the unanimous decision of the House of Lords in *Carmichael* laid down the law in such plain terms, the reasoning which led to the formulation cannot unfortunately be regarded as convincing[21] since it proceeds in part upon a misinterpretation of a passage in Stair's *Institutions*.[22] Despite what Lord Dunedin said in *Carmichael*, Stair certainly thought that the *jus quaesitum* could be irrevocable without the necessity for intimation or the like. In *Allan's Trustees v. Lord Advocate*,[23] Lord Reid described *Carmichael* "as in some respects a difficult case to interpret".[24] Notwithstanding these criticisms, *Carmichael* must be taken as representing the state of the law, unless and until it is re-examined by the House of Lords. In that regard it is at least possible that the law in *Carmichael* is too firmly

---

[20] 1920 S.C. 203, HL.
[21] Rodger [1969] *Juridical Review* 34 and 128; MacCormick [1970] *Juridical Review* 228. For a full discussion see W.W. McBryde, *The Law of Contract in Scotland*, (2nd ed.) Ch. 10.
[22] 1.10.5.
[23] 1971 S.C. 45, HL.
[24] 1971 S.C. 54, HL His Lordship's observation was strictly *obiter*.

established to be reformed by anything other than statute, especially since the advantages of altering the law are by no means immediately apparent.[25]

24–167 (ii) *Testamentary effect of policy.* There are many writings other than formal wills and testaments which the law of Scotland allows to have testamentary effect. Among these are the rights conferred by marriage contracts on parties other than the spouses and their issue, and the directions in favour of third parties contained in personal bonds and stock certificates. In conformity with this principle, a policy of life assurance on the life of the assured made payable to a third party may operate as a testamentary bequest if, during the life of the assured, the payee has not acquired an irrevocable jus quaesitum. The destination being testamentary is revocable by the assured either by inter vivos deed or by a will or other testamentary writing executed after the date of the policy. Whether a clause or general revocation of all former testamentary writings will operate to revoke a special destination of a testamentary character contained in a deed was discussed by Lord Skerrington in *Drysdale's Trustees v. Drysdale,*[26] and he expressed it as his opinion that it would so operate. The Lord President (Clyde) and Lord Mackenzie reserved their opinion, and so the law on that point is left, as they found it, in what Lord Skerrington described as a state of painful uncertainty.

(4) *Settlement Policies under the Provisions of the Married Women's Property Act 1870, s.10 and Married Women's Property Act 1882, s.11*

24–168 Section 10 of the 1870 Act enabled a married man, by effecting a policy of assurance on his life, expressed on the face of it to be for the benefit of his wife and children, or both or any of them, to create a trust in their favour which removed their beneficial interest in the policy and its proceeds out of his reach and that of his creditors.

On the repeal of the 1870 Act by the 1882 Act section 10 of the 1870 Act was reproduced with slight modification by section 11 of the 1882 Act. The major alterations brought about by the later Act were (i) it enabled an unmarried man to effect a policy under the Act[27] and (ii) it extended the right to effect a Settlement Policy to women.

24–169 It will rarely be necessary today to consider any longer the wording of the original enactment, and one need only concentrate on the wording of section 11 of the Married Women's Property Act 1882. This enacts that a policy of assurance effected by any man on his own life and

[25] The Scottish Law Commission Memorandum No. 38: "Constitution and Proof of Voluntary Obligations: Stipulations in Favour of Third Parties" (1977) recommends reform of this aspect of the law: paras 32 and 33.
[26] 1922 S.C. 741.
[27] By substituting the words "by any man" for the words "by any married man". It was uncertain before this whether a man could take out the policy before he was actually married.

expressed to be for the benefit of his wife, or of his children, or of his wife and children, or any of them, or by any woman on her own life and expressed to be for the benefit of her husband, or of her children, or of her husband and children, or any of them, shall create a trust in favour of the objects therein named; and that the moneys payable under such a policy shall not, so long as any object of the trust remains unperformed, form part of the estate of the assured or be subject to his or her debts: provided that if it shall be proved that the policy effected and the premiums paid with intent to defraud the creditors of the insured, they shall be entitled to receive out of the moneys payable under the policy a sum equal to the premiums so paid. For the purposes of this section references to a person's children include and are deemed always to have included reference to children adopted by that person under an adoption order[28] and the expression "children" includes illegitimate children.[29]

24–170 The insured may by the policy or by any memorandum under his or her hand appoint a trustee or trustees of the money payable under the policy, and from time to time appoint a new trustee or trustees thereof, and may make provision for the appointment of a new trustee or new trustees thereof, and for the investment of the moneys payable under any such policy.[30] In default of any such appointment of a trustee such policy immediately on its being effected shall vest in the insured and his or her legal personal representative in trust for the purposes aforesaid. If at the time of the death of the insured or at any time afterwards, there should be no trustee, or it shall be expedient to appoint a new trustee or new trustees, a trustee or trustees, or a new trustee or new trustees may be appointed by the court.

The receipt of a trustee or trustees duly appointed, or in default of any such appointment, or in default of notice to the insurance office, the receipt of the legal personal representative of the insured shall be a discharge to the office for the sum secured by the policy, or for the value thereof in whole or in part.

24–171 Protection afforded by settlement policy. The Act not only affords a simple method of creating a trust of the policy, but it also gives the

---

[28] Adoption Act 1958, s.14(3).

[29] Family Law Reform Act 1969, s.19(1). The effect of this provision is to enable the policy to be taken for the benefit of illegitimate (as well as legitimate) children under the Act. The expression "children" used in a policy effected before January 1, 1970, will still, however, be restricted to legitimate children since a reference to "children" is only deemed to include a reference to illegitimate children in a disposition made after the coming into effect of the Act—see s.15 of the Family Law Reform Act 1969.

[30] It is undecided whether the words "new trustee" include an additional trustee as well as a replacement trustee. It was held in *Re Gregson's Trusts* (1887) 34 Ch.D. 209 that the same words in section 31(2) of the Conveyancing Act 1881 referred only to a replacement trustee, but note that the court had jurisdiction to appoint an additional trustee under section 32 of the Trustee Act 1850, which expressly referred to substitutional and additional trustees: *ibid.*; *Re Brackenbury Trust* (1870) L.R. 10 Eq. 45. In previous editions of this work, this decision was cited as authority for a similar construction of these words in section 11, on which there is no authority. However, it may be argued that in section 11 these words bear their ordinary meaning (and the sense expressly provided for in section 32 of the 1850 Act) and that the assured has power to appoint an additional trustee as well as one in substitution, quite apart from the power to that effect in section 36(6) of the Trustee Act 1925.

beneficiaries a degree of protection that they would not get under a voluntary settlement outside the Act.

24–172 As stated above, so long as anyone is entitled to a beneficial interest under the trust, the policy moneys cannot be made available, with one exception, for the benefit of the creditors of the assured. The one exception is where the policy was taken out with intent to defraud creditors, but even in this case the creditors are only entitled to claim a sum equal to the amount of the premiums.[31] The trust under a settlement policy cannot, like any other trust, be set aside on the ground that it is a transaction at an undervalue within section 243 of the Insolvency Act 1986.[32]

It is submitted that, notwithstanding the general rule that the Crown is not bound by any provisions of any statute unless specifically named therein or bound by necessary implication,[33] the Act also provides protection against claims by the Crown. This is because the Act does not in terms protect the proceeds of the policy against claims by creditors, but in terms provides that the policy or its proceeds should not form part of the assured's estate. The Crown cannot, any more than any other creditor, except where there is an express enactment to the contrary, take in satisfaction of its debt property that does not form part of the debtor's estate. It follows that the Act affords protection also against debts of the assured owed to the Crown.

24–173 Policies within the Act. To come within the provisions of the Act a policy must satisfy the following conditions:
  (i) It must be a policy effected by a man on his life or a woman on her life. The policy is effected by the person who signs the proposal form; and generally the fact that one or more of the premiums have been paid by someone else does not matter.[34]
  (ii) The policy must be one of life insurance. So long, however, as one of the contingencies upon which the policy moneys are payable is the death, from whatever cause, of the insured, it is for this purpose deemed to be a policy of life assurance even though the policy moneys are payable as well in other events. Thus in one case an accident policy taken out for the benefit of the assured's wife, the policy moneys being payable either on the death of the assured or on his disablement as a result of an accident, was held to be a policy within the provisions of the Act.[35] It may be taken, therefore, that any form of life combined with endowment assurance policy is within the provisions of the Act.
  (iii) The policy must be expressed to be for the benefit of a husband, wife or children. It is no impediment, however, to the creation of the statutory trust that the policy moneys are payable to the beneficiaries only upon the occurrence of a contingency that may in fact never occur. The statutory trusts will attach to the policy (or the proceeds thereof) for so long as the contingency or contingencies upon which the wife, husband or children are to take is or are still capable of

---

[31] *Holt v. Everall* (1876) 2 Ch.D. 266. "Premiums," however, include the proceeds by surrender of an earlier M.W.P.A. policy utilised to defray the premiums on a later policy.

[32] *Holt v. Everall, supra.* Section 243 replaces and extends section 42 of the Bankruptcy Act 1914 and section 172 of the Law of Property Act 1925.

[33] See *Att.-Gen. for N.S.W. v. Curator of Intestate Estates* [1907] A.C. 319.

[34] *Re Oakes' Settlement* [1951] Ch. 156.

[35] *Re Gladitz* [1937] Ch. 588.

occurring, as well as upon the happening of the contingency or contingencies.[36]

24–174 Words apt to create the trust. In order to create the statutory trust the policy must be expressed to be "for the benefit of wife or children or husband or children" of the assured, as the case may be.

In many cases the policy is expressed to be issued in terms of section 11 of the Act, but it is not necessary that the statute should be mentioned in order to create a valid trust under its protection.[37] Express words of trust are not required and it is sufficient if the policy is merely expressed in terms showing that it is taken out for the benefit of the beneficiaries. However, even a joint life policy effected by husband and wife, but with no reference to the Act nor any other words indicating that each assured effected the policy for the benefit of the other, is not within the Act.[38]

24–175 In *Cleaver v. Mutual Reserve Fund Life Association*[39] the policy was expressed to be for the benefit of the assured's wife, and she was named as the payee of the policy money in the event of her surviving the assured. It was held that the policy was one to which the Act applied and that it created a trust in favour of the assured's wife.

24–176 In *Re Fleetwood's Policy*[40] the company agreed to pay the policy moneys to the wife of the assured, or, in the event of her prior death, to the assured's personal representatives. There was also a reference in the printed conditions of the policy to "the beneficiary designated herein". It was held that the policy was one expressed to be for the benefit of the wife and that the statutory trust accordingly arose in her favour.

24–177 In *Re Gladitz*[41] the proceeds of an accident policy were expressed to be payable to the wife of the assured if she was living at the date on which the policy moneys became payable, otherwise it was payable to the insured's personal representatives. It was held that the fact that policy moneys were payable to the wife was itself sufficient to show that the policy was "expressed to be for the benefit" of the wife.

It would seem to follow from these cases:

(a) that no particular form of words is needed to create the statutory trust and any indication that the wife, husband or children are intended to take the benefit of the policy will bring the statutory trust into effect;

---

[36] *Re Ioakimidis' Policy Trusts* [1925] Ch. 403 (payable to wife if husband died within 20 years leaving wife surviving)—see also *Chrystal's Trustees v. Chrystal*, 1912 S.C. 1003; *Re Fleetwood's Policy* [1926] Ch. 48 (payable to wife if alive at assured's death); *Re Equitable Life Ass. Society of U.S. and Mitchell* (1911) 27 T.L.R. 213 (payable to wife if alive at end of tontine period, otherwise to children if alive, assured to have right to withdraw policy moneys at end of tontine period).

[37] *Per contra* see Wallington J. in *Bown v. Bown and Weston* [1949] P. 91 whose view is not borne out by other authorities.

[38] *Rooney v. Cardona* [1999] 1 W.L.R. 1388.

[39] [1892] 1 Q.B. 147.

[40] [1926] Ch. 48.

[41] [1937] Ch. 588; and see *Chrystal's Trustees v. Chrystal*, 1912 S.C. 1003.

(b) that whether or not the insured intended the provisions of the section to apply is irrelevant.

24–178 Persons within the statutory trust. The benefits of the section are available only to the spouse or children of the assured. Grandchildren or remoter issue are not within the protected class.[42] A policy may be effected, however, by an unmarried man for the benefit of any wife he may thereafter marry. It may also be effected by a married man for the benefit of his wife then living or of any future wife.[43] As regards children the policy may be effected for the benefit either of existing children of the assured or of all children of the assured both then existing and future, either of his present marriage or of any future marriage.[44]

24–179 If a policy is expressed to be for the benefit of persons outside of this class it will not be protected by the section—even though the spouse or children of the assured are also named as beneficiaries. In such a case no statutory trust in favour of any of the beneficiaries will arise.[45] If the wording of the policy is such it may well create a trust in favour of the person named, enforceable as a voluntary settlement[46]; but words sufficient to create a trust under the Act are not necessarily a sufficient declaration of trust in themselves. If the policy is not within the section owing to the introduction of persons outside the protected class and there are no words sufficient to constitute a declaration of trust, the policy will remain the absolute property of the assured and his estate; and if the policy moneys are made payable to some other person or persons they may be accountable to the assured or his estate if they receive the money.[47]

Interests of beneficiaries under statutory trust

24–180 (i) *Creation of immediate vested interest.* It is now reasonably clear, despite earlier decisions to the contrary, that a policy effected under section 11 of the 1882 Act is perfectly capable of creating an immediate absolute vested interest in the policy and its proceeds in favour of the assured's spouse or any child or children of the assured.[48]

24–181 In *Re Collier*[49] Clauson J. expressed an opinion to the effect that the Act of 1870 was aimed at enabling a husband to make provision for his widow and was so framed as not to give a husband power to confer the

---

[42] *Bowen v. Lewis* (1884) 9 App.Cas. 890, 915.

[43] *Re Browne's Policy* [1903] 1 Ch. 188; *Re Parker's Policy* [1906] 1 Ch. 526—in this regard there is no difference between Married Women's Property Act 1870, s.10 and Married Women's Property Act 1882, s.11.

[44] It should be noted in this regard that in a policy taken out after 1 January 1970, the expression "children" will also include all the assured's illegitimate children: see Family Law Reform Act 1969, ss.15 and 19.

[45] *Re Parker's Policy*: see n. 43.

[46] See as to voluntary assignments paras 24–106 *et seq.*, *ante*.

[47] *Re Clay's Policy* [1937] 2 All E.R. 548. *Cleaver v. Mutual Reserve Fund Life* [1892] 1 Q.B. 147. *Cf. Re Schebsman* [1944] Ch. 83—whether they are to be accountable depends upon whether the proper inference from the policy is that the person is named as payee purely for convenience so that the words "or as the assured may direct" can properly be inferred: see Simonds J. in *Re Stapleton-Brotherton* [1941] Ch. 482.

[48] *Cousins v. Sun Life Ass. Co.* [1933] Ch. 126.

[49] [1930] 2 Ch. 37.

benefit of the Act upon any wife of his unless she, by surviving her husband, became his widow.[50] Clauson J. was thus following the earlier Irish decision of *Robb v. Watson*[51] in preference to the earlier Irish decision of *Prescott v. Prescott*.[52] In *Robb v. Watson* a policy purporting to be effected under the Act of 1870 was expressed to be for the benefit of E.W., the wife of the deceased and it was held that on the death of E.W. during the lifetime of the assured her interest in the policy ceased and reverted to the assured. In *Prescott v. Prescott* a policy effected by a married woman under the Act of 1882 was expressed to be for the benefit of and payable to W.P., the husband of the assured. It was held that on the death of the assured after her husband's death the policy moneys fell into W.P.'s estate notwithstanding the fact that he had predeceased his wife, since he was entitled to an absolute vested interest immediately the policy was taken out.

24–182 These cases were all considered by the Court of Appeal in *Cousins v. Sun Life Ass. Co.*[53] In this case a policy taken out under the Act of 1882 was expressed to be "for the benefit of L.C. the wife of the assured under the Married Women's Property Act 1882". The wife predeceased the assured and in these circumstances the assured claimed to be entitled to the sole beneficial interest in the policy. The Court of Appeal held, following *Prescott v. Prescott*, that there was nothing in the wording of the Act of 1882 which prevented a spouse conferring an immediate absolute vested interest on the other spouse, and that since there was nothing in the policy in question to suggest that the interest of the assured's wife was contingent, she took an absolute vested interest in the policy which passed on her death to her personal representatives to the exclusion of her husband.[54] Although the Court of Appeal expressed doubt as to the correctness of the decision in *Robb v. Watson*[55] and so much of Clauson J.'s decision in *Re Collier*[56] as followed *Robb v. Watson*, it was not prepared directly to overrule them but preferred to distinguish them upon the grounds that they were both decisions upon the slightly different wording of the Act of 1870.

24–183 (ii) *Construction of policy.* The Act itself authorises the creation of a trust in favour of a spouse or children, but in order to determine the nature of the beneficial interest created one must look at the words used in the policy itself, bearing always in mind that, upon the principle "*ut res magis valeat quam pereat*," if the words used are capable of bearing two meanings, one which would bring the policy within the section and one which would not, the court leans in favour of the construction which brings the policy within the section.[57]

---

[50] Note, however, that the principal reason given by Clauson J. for his decision was that the policy did not name the wife and was therefore to be construed as being in favour of whatever wife the assured might leave upon his death. This ground of decision can still be supported.

[51] [1910] 1 Ir.R. 243.

[52] [1906] 1 Ir.R. 155.

[53] [1933] Ch. 126; see also the Australian case of *Perpetual Trustee v. Tindal* (1940) 63 C.L.R. 232.

[54] In *Re Kilpatrick's Policies Trusts* [1966] 1 Ch. 730, where it was held that the particular policy in question created a vested but defeasible interest in favour of the assured's spouse, no question at all was raised as to the capability of creating such an interest by means of a settlement policy.

[55] See n. 51.

[56] See n. 49.

[57] *Re Seyton* (1887) 34 Ch.D. 511.

24–184 There may be a certain ambiguity in the use of such words as "wife", "husband" or "children" particularly in cases where the assured dies having been married more than once and having had children by more than one marriage. The following, therefore, is a summary of the decisions on the meaning of words commonly used to express the assured's intention as to the persons to be benefited:

"for the benefit of his wife A.B."—immediately on the issue of the policy the named wife takes an absolute vested interest in the policy and its proceeds[58];

"for the benefit of his wife"—means the person who at his death shall become his widow, whether it be his wife living at the date of the policy or some future wife who shall survive him[59];

"for the benefit of his wife and children"—means his widow and such of his children by any marriage and whenever born who shall survive him;[60];

"his widow or widow and children"—means the same as the expression last mentioned[61];

"for the benefit of his wife A.B. and the children of their marriage"— means the named wife if she survives the assured and such of the children of their marriage as survive him[62];

"for the benefit of his wife or, if she be dead, between his children in equal proportions"—means the wife at the time that the policy was effected (and no other) if she survives the assured, or if she shall predecease him, his children by any marriage and whenever born who shall survive him[63];

"for the benefit of his wife in the event of her surviving him, and failing her for the benefit of his children born or to be born or any of them"—means the wife at the time the policy was effected (and no other) if she shall survive him, or if she shall predecease him, his children[64];

"for the absolute benefit of the wife of the assured should the amount of insurance become payable during her lifetime failing which for the absolute benefit of such of the children of the assured as shall survive the assured"—means the wife at the time the policy was effected (and no other) if she is living at the maturity of the policy, and if not the children of the assured surviving him.[65]

24–185 (iii) *Interests of beneficiaries* inter se The policy may be expressed in general terms for the benefit of wife and children or children without specifying the respective interests of the beneficiaries *inter se*, or the policy

---

[58] *Cousins v. Sun Life Ass. Co.* [1933] Ch. 126.
[59] *Re Collier* [1930] 2 Ch. 37.
[60] *Re Browne's Policy* [1903] 1 Ch. 188; *Re Davies' Policy Trusts* [1892] 1 Ch. 90.
[61] *Re Parker's Policies* [1906] 1 Ch. 526.
[62] *Re Seyton* (1887) 34 Ch.D. 511.
[63] *Re Griffiths' Policy* [1903] 1 Ch. 739.
[64] *Watson, Petitioners* Patrick (Ld. Ordinary), July 18, 1944 unreported. See para. 24–198, *post.*
[65] *Wood v. James* (1954) 92 C.L.R. 142, a decision on the corresponding position in the Married Women's Property Act 1892 (Western Australia).

may be expressed to be for the benefit of the persons designated in such shares and proportions and interest and generally in such manner as the assured shall by will or deed appoint.[66] In the absence of any appointment or apportionment of interests either in the policy or by will or deed of the assured the persons designated as beneficiaries will take in equal shares as joint tenants.[67] When the beneficiaries are the widow and children of the assured the widow shares equally as a joint tenant with the children unless the wording or some special circumstance indicates an intention that the widow is to have a life interest in the whole with remainder to the children.[68] A joint tenancy means that until there is a division of the policy moneys among the beneficiaries they take with benefit of survivorship and the share of any beneficiary who dies before division accrues to the survivor or survivors.[69]

24–186 Exercise of options. If a policy contains options exercisable by the assured and the policy is effected for the benefit of a spouse or children so as to create a trust under the Act then, so long as any of the trust purposes remain unperformed, the trust may not be defeated by the exercise of any of the options, and the assured is a trustee of the powers granted to him by the policy and may also exercise the options for the benefit of the beneficiaries, whether their interests be vested or contingent.[70]

The fact that some of the options are capable of being exercised against the interest of the beneficiaries does not entitle the court to construe the policy as one conferring interest on the beneficiaries defeasible to the extent to which the assured can exercise the options. The assured's duty is still to exercise the options for the best benefit of the beneficiaries and if, for example, the assured is unable or unwilling to continue to pay the premiums, his duty in those circumstances may be to elect to have the policy converted into a paid-up insurance payable on his death.[71]

24–187 In *Re Fleetwood's Policy*[72] the wife of the assured was the sole beneficiary of a settlement policy contingent upon her surviving the assured. The assured exercised an option contained in the policy of receiving the entire cash value and of discontinuing the policy. The company paid the proceeds into court. It was held that by exercising the option the assured could not defeat the beneficial interest of his wife, and that the proceeds must accordingly remain in court and be accumulated to await the event determining who was to be ultimately entitled to it.

24–188 Resulting trust in favour of assured. If the whole trust purposes fail there is a resulting trust for the assured and his estate.[73] In *Cleaver v. Mutual Reserve Fund Life*[74] a policy effected by a married man was expressed to be

[66] *Re Parker's Policies* [1906] 1 Ch. 526.
[67] *Re Seyton* (1887) 34 Ch.D. 511. *Re Davies' Policy Trusts* [1892] Ch. 90; *Re Griffiths' Policy* [1903] 1 Ch. 739; *Re Browne's Policy* [1903] 1 Ch. 188.
[68] *Re Seyton* (1887) 34 Ch.D. 511.
[69] *ibid.*
[70] *Re Fleetwood's Policy* [1926] Ch. 48; *Re Equitable Life Ass. Society of U.S. and Mitchell* (1911) 27 T.L.R. 213.
[71] *ibid. Re Fleetwood's Policy.*
[72] [1926] Ch. 48.
[73] Regardless of whether this is specifically stated in the policy.
[74] [1892] 1 Q.B. 147.

for the benefit of his named wife, and the policy moneys were made payable to her if living at the death of the assured, otherwise to the assured's personal representatives. The assured died and his wife was convicted of murdering him. A joint action was thereupon brought against the company by a representative of the wife and her estate on the one hand and the personal representatives of the husband on the other hand. The company argued that the wife could not claim since the death of the assured was the consequence of her own felony,[75] and that the personal representatives of the assured could not claim as the assured was only entitled if he survived his wife. It was held that, as the wife's claim was barred on the grounds of public policy, the sole object of the statutory trust had failed. There was, therefore, no object of the trust remaining unperformed and accordingly there was a resulting trust of the policy moneys in favour of the assured. The policy moneys were therefore recoverable by the assured's personal representatives.

24–189 Discharge for policy money. As stated below in this chapter,[76] in relation to any dealing with a settled policy the company ought to obtain a discharge from the trustees of the settlement under which the policy is held. In paying the policy moneys or advancing money to pay premiums or accepting a surrender of a policy effected under the Married Women's Property Acts, the company ought therefore to be satisfied that it is dealing with the properly constituted trustee of the policy, and that such trustee has power to bind all the persons with beneficial interests in the policy.

24–190 The Act of 1870 contained no provision for determining the trustee of the policy, and consequently, when a policy was effected under that Act, it was necessary, before the company could obtain a valid discharge for the proceeds of the policy and before there could be any dealing with the policy, to apply to the court for the appointment of a trustee.[77]

24–191 This deficiency was remedied by section 11 of the Act of 1882. This section provides that the assured may, by the policy or by any memorandum under his or her hand, appoint a trustee or trustees of the policy and from time to time appoint a new trustee or trustees thereof, and may make provision for the appointment of a new trustee or new trustees thereof and for the investment of the moneys payable under the policy; and that, in default of appointment, the policy shall vest in the assured or his or her personal representatives as trustee of the policy. The assured is specifically given no power to remove a trustee or to appoint another in his place, but it is reasonably clear that the statutory power conferred by section 36 of the Trustee Act 1925 would apply. Although it is open to some doubt, it is submitted that the assured is the person who, within the meaning of section 36(1)(a) of the Trustee Act 1925, is the "person nominated for the purpose of appointing new trustees by the instrument, if any, creating the trust", and hence the person given power under section 36 to discharge trustees for the reasons there given and appoint new trustees in their place. This would stem from the fact that, although the "instrument creating the

---

[75] *i.e.* applying the legal maxim "*ex turpi causa non oritur actio.*"

[76] See paras 24–203, *et seq.*, *post.*

[77] *Re Turnbull* [1897] 2 Ch. 415; *Re Kuyper's Policy Trusts* [1899] 1 Ch. 38. The application was either to the High Court or to the County Court for the district in which the insurance office was situated.

trust" is the policy, the policy may be said to incorporate by reference the provisions of section 11 of the Act of 1882.

24–192 It follows from the above that when the policy moneys become payable on the death of the assured and no trustees have been appointed, the company may safely pay the assured's personal representatives. Similarly, in relation to any surrendering or charge of the policy, the company may safely deal with the assured as trustee, in default of an express appointment of trustees, though it is usual, in order to guard against a possible breach of trust, to take a joint receipt of husband and wife. If the assured goes bankrupt before the appointment of trustees the policy does not pass to the trustee in bankruptcy,[78] even if it was effected whilst the assured was insolvent, since the creditors are only entitled to claim the repayment of the premiums when the policy moneys fall in.[79]

Where, however, the personal representative is also the sole beneficiary under the statutory trust and he becomes bankrupt before the death of the assured, the policy vests in the trustee in bankruptcy and only he can give a good receipt for the proceeds. The specific provisions of the Insolvency Act 1986 take priority over the general provisions of the 1882 Act. It is irrelevant whether or not the insurers have actual notice of the bankruptcy.[80]

If there is any difficulty in the way of having a trustee appointed under the statutory power, application may be made in the usual way to the court.[81]

Where the beneficiaries are infants and the policy moneys are to be held for their benefit, two trustees ought to be appointed[82]; and the court has power in such circumstances under its inherent jurisdiction to appoint two trustees even where the policy was effected under the Act of 1870.[83]

24–193 Effect of divorce. If the terms of the policy are such that the named spouse of the assured takes an immediately vested interest not subject to defeasance, a divorce will not in itself affect that spouse's beneficial interest. The assured may, however, apply to the court for an order varying the settlement made by the policy, under the court's power to vary any ante-or post-nuptial settlement,[84] and the court has on a number of occasions made orders varying the terms of a policy effected under the Act.[85]

24–194 Proof of marriage and legitimacy. The company is not generally concerned to inquire whether those claiming to be beneficiaries are persons protected under a settlement policy and therefore whether the marriage is in fact valid and the children legitimate.[86] This is a question as between the trustee and the beneficiaries, and the trust may still be a valid one although not protected by the Acts. If, however, the validity of the appointment of the

---

[78] See paras 24–211, *et seq.*, *post.*
[79] See the Scottish case of *Stewart v. Hodge* 1901 8 S.L.T. 436.
[80] *Rooney v. Cardona* [1999] 1 W.L.R. 1388.
[81] *Re Kuyper's Policy Trusts* [1899] 1 Ch. 38. *Re Smith's Policy Trusts* (1898) 33 L.J.N.C. 187; *Schultze v. Schultze* (1887) 56 L.J.Ch. 356; and see para. 24–212, *post.*
[82] *Re Hewson's Policy Trusts* [1885] W.N. 213; *Re Smith's Policy Trusts, supra.*
[83] *Schultze v. Schultze, supra.*
[84] See Matrimonial Causes Act 1973, s.24(1)(c)(d).
[85] See *Lort-Williams v. Lort-Williams* [1951] P. 395; *Gulbenkian v. Gulbenkian* [1927] P. 237; *Gunner v. Gunner and Stirling* [1949] P. 77.
[86] N.B. If a policy is effected after January 1, 1970, any reference to "children" will, in the absence of any contrary expressed intention, be taken to include illegitimate as well as legitimate children: see Family Law Reform Act 1969, ss.15 and 19.

trustee or trustees depends upon the terms of the Act, or if the company has notice that the assured's estate is insolvent,[87] strict proof of marriage and legitimacy ought to be required in the form of proper marriage and birth certificates.[88]

(5) *Scots Law Relating to Settlement Policies*

24–195 Married Women's Policies of Assurance (Scotland) Act 1880. The Married Women's Property Acts 1870 and 1882 do not apply in Scotland, but similar provisions operate under the Married Women's Policies of Assurance (Scotland) Act 1880[89] as amended by the Married Women's Policies of Assurance (Scotland) (Amendment) Act 1980.[90]

By section 1 of the 1880 Act:

> "A married woman may effect a policy of assurance, on her own life or on the life of her husband, for her separate use; and the same and all benefit thereof, if expressed to be for her separate use, shall, immediately on being so effected, vest in her and shall be payable to her, and her heirs, executors and assignees, excluding the jus mariti and right of administration of her husband, and shall be assignable by her either *inter vivos* or *mortis causa* without consent of her husband; and the contract in such policy shall be as valid and effectual as if made with an unmarried woman."

By section 2

> "A policy of assurance effected by a man or woman on his or her own life, and expressed upon the face of it to be for the benefit of his or her spouse or children, or any of them, shall together with all benefit thereof, be deemed a trust for their benefit, and such policy, immediately on its being so effected, shall vest in him or her and his or her legal representatives in trust for the purpose or purposes so expressed, or in any trustee nominated in the policy; or appointed by separate writing duly intimated to the assurance office,[91] but in trust always as aforesaid, and shall not otherwise be subject to his or her control or form part of his or her estate or be liable to the diligence of his or her creditors, or be revocable as a donation, or reducible on any ground of excess or

---

[87] Thereby rendering the validity of trusts of the policy vulnerable at the instance of creditors unless it is protected by the Act.

[88] The Family Law Reform Act 1969, s.15, has introduced certain complications into this branch of the law. If, for example, A, a male, after January 1, 1970, takes out a policy for the benefit of his children B and C, and B and C are not his legitimate children, the validity of the trust in favour of B and C and hence the validity of the appointment of the trustees may depend upon whether it can be shown that B and C are A's illegitimate children. Unless there has been an affiliation order, it may be very difficult for satisfactory proof of B and C's paternity to be furnished. In these circumstances the company would be justified, it is submitted, in paying the policy moneys into court.

[89] 43 & 44 Vict. c. 26. For the background, see *Barclay's Tr. v. Inland Revenue* 1975 S.C. 1, 23, H.L. *per* Lord Kilbrandon.

[90] 1980 c. 56 The Act was the result of a Report of the Scottish Law Commission (Scot. Law Com. No. 52, July 1978).

[91] By section 3(b) of the Trusts (Scotland) Act 1921 (11 & 12 Geo. 5, c. 58), all trusts, unless the contrary be expressed, are held to include power to the trustee if there be only one, or to the trustees if there be more than one, or to a quorum of the trustees, if there be more than two, to assume new trustees.

insolvency: and the receipt of such trustee for the sums secured by the policy, or for the value thereof, in whole or in part shall be a sufficient and effectual discharge to the insurance office: provided always, that if it shall be proved that the policy was effected and premiums thereon paid with intent to defraud creditors, or if the person on whose life the policy is effected shall be made bankrupt within two years from the date of such policy, it shall be competent to the creditors to claim repayment of the premiums so paid from the trustee of the policy out of the proceeds thereof."

It should be noted that as a result of the amending legislation, unmarried persons may now effect such a policy in favour of their prospective spouse or children.[92] Moreover, references to a person's children include references to that person's illegitimate or adopted children.[93]

24-196 Delivery or intimation of policy. In Scotland at common law a deed of trust, although executed by the truster, is ineffective by itself to constitute a trust. There must be "delivery of the trust deed or subject of the trust or a sufficient and satisfactory equivalent to delivery, so as to achieve irrevocable divestiture of the truster and investiture to the trustee in the trust estate."[94] So in *Jarvie's Trustee v. Jarvie's Trustees*,[95] a life policy was effected by a married man in 1870. By its terms, certain trustees were entitled, on his death, to receive the policy moneys as directed by writing under his hand for behoof of his wife and the children of their marriage, whom failing his heirs and assignees. The man kept the policy in his custody. The trustees were unaware of its existence until 1885 when along with the man's wife and children, they assigned their interest to him. The man died in 1886, having executed a trust deed in favour of his creditors. In a multiplepoinding it was held that the policy proceeds formed part of the estate available to the man's creditors, since, there having been no equivalent of delivery of the trust deed, no valid trust had been constituted. Where, however, a policy effected for the benefit of the assured's spouse and children comes within the Married Women's Policies of Assurance (Scotland) Act 1880 as amended, no delivery or intimation of the policy is necessary to constitute an effective trust since the Act expressly provides that immediately on such a policy being effected it shall vest in the assured and his or her personal representatives for the purpose or purposes expressed, or in any trustee nominated in the policy or appointed by separate writing duly intimated to the assurance office.[96] Furthermore on the policy so vesting in trust, the trust constitutes a trust within the meaning of the Trusts (Scotland) Act 1921 and any person in whom the policy vests is a trustee within the meaning of that Act.[97]

24-197 Policies covered by the legislation. The amendments introduced by the 1980 Act considerably extended the range of policies covered by the

---

[92] 1980 Act, s.1(c).
[93] *ibid.*
[94] *Clark Taylor & Co. Ltd v. Quality Site Development (Edinburgh) Ltd* 1981 S.C. 111, 118, *per* Lord President Emslie; *Tay Valley Joinery Ltd v. C.F. Financial Services Ltd* 1987 S.L.T. 207; *Allan's Trustees v. Lord Advocate*, 1971 S.C. 45, HL.
[95] (1887) 14 R. 411.
[96] s.2 (as amended).
[97] 1980 Act, s.2(1).

legislation. So, policies effected by wives in favour of their husbands as well as policies executed by husbands in favour of their wives are covered.[98] So also are policies effected by unmarried persons in favour of their prospective spouse or children. Moreover, references in any policy to a person's children include that person's illegitimate or adopted children.[99] The protection of the 1880 Act is afforded to a policy expressed upon the face of it to be for the benefit of the settlor's spouse or children, or any of them.[1] It appears that, if any person other than the spouse or children would be entitled to benefit from the policy, the policy is not covered by the Act.[2] "It will not do, therefore, if the matter is so left that the 'benefit' of the policy may pass for the 'benefit' of persons other than those within the statutory words."[3] At any rate:

> "if the expressed purposes do not extend to the whole policy, or to the whole beneficial interest in the policy, the statutory trust would only operate over such part or such interest as would be included in the purposes expressed."[4]

But a policy may be covered by the Act even though the settlor is no longer married at the time when he executes it. So where a widower executed a policy in favour of his children by his deceased wife, the policy was held to fall within the Act.[5]

24–198 Meaning of "for the benefit of his wife". In an unreported case decided by Lord Patrick (Lord Ordinary), one George Macdonald effected in 1894 an assurance on his own life with the Scottish Union and National Insurance Company. The policy was expressed to be issued under the provisions of the Married Women's Policies of Assurance (Scotland) Act 1880, "for the benefit of his Wife, in the event of her surviving him, and failing her, then for the benefit of his children, born or to be born or any of them". The assured was married when the policy was effected, and a son of the marriage had been born in 1892. In 1927 the assured's wife died, and in 1942 he married a second wife who had herself been born, after the execution of the policy, in 1902. There was no issue of the second marriage. The assured died in 1943 and was survived by his son and his second wife. The widow and son each claimed to be entitled to the policy money. Lord Patrick dealt with the case as one which depended solely on the true construction of the beneficial interest expressed in the policy. He said that there was a presumption that a married man speaking of his wife referred only to his wife at that time, and the presumption was still stronger when there was a destination over to his children if his wife did not survive him. The learned judge said that he read the words "for the benefit of his wife", as

---

[98] s.2 of the 1880 Act as amended by s.1(a) of the 1980 Act.
[99] s.2 of the 1880 Act as amended by s.1(c) of the 1980 Act.
[1] s.2 of the 1880 Act as amended by s.1 of the 1980 Act.
[2] cf. *Barclay's Tr. v. Inland Revenue* 1975 S.C., 1 HL. So far as suggesting otherwise, Lord Kincairney's obiter remarks in *Dickie's Trs. v. Dickie* (1892) 29 S.L.R. 908 must be held to be wrong. They were followed in *Stewart v. Hodge* 1901 8 S.L.T. 436.
[3] 1975 S.C. 17, HL, *per* Lord Morris of Borth-y-Gest.
[4] 1975 S.C. 21, HL, *per* Lord Wilberforce.
[5] *Kennedy's Trs. v. Sharpe* (1895) 23 R. 146.

meaning "for the benefit of his then wife" and not as meaning "for the benefit of his widow". The latter words he never used, and might so easily and naturally have used if it had occurred to him that his then wife might predecease him and that he might marry again. He thought that the assured never thought of such an event and never intended to provide for it. He held, accordingly, that the son and not the widow was entitled to the policy money. Construing the policy as he did, it was not necessary for him to consider, nor did he consider, whether a second wife or children by his second marriage would have come within the protection of the Act under a policy effected by him during the continuance of his first marriage.[6]

24–199 Power of trustees. Since any person in whom the policy vests is a trustee within the meaning of the Trusts (Scotland) Act 1921, he accordingly enjoys all the relevant powers available under that Act and in particular sections 4 and 5.[7] In addition, where such acts are not at variance with the terms or purposes of the trust, a trustee has power:

(a) to exercise any option under the policy or under any deed of trust or other document constituting a trust in relation to the policy,
(b) to convert the policy to a partially or fully paid-up assurance,
(c) to convert it into any other form of assurance on the life of the person effecting the policy,
(d) to increase or reduce the amount of the annual premiums payable under the policy,
(e) to alter the period during which the premiums under the policy are payable and
(f) to surrender the policy.[8]

24–200 Beneficiary's rights to deal with his interest. A beneficiary, who is of full age and not suffering from any legal disability, may, subject to the terms of the policy (a) assign his or her interest[9] under the policy whether in security or otherwise or (b) renounce the interest.[10] The beneficiary can do this even though the result may be to make the policy or any benefits under it subject to the control of the person effecting the policy, or part of that person's estate or liable to the diligence of his creditors. Applications may also be made to vary the trust under section 1 of the Trusts (Scotland) Act 1961.

24–201 Right to possession of policy. If the assured is the trustee of a policy which comes under the protection of the Act he is entitled as trustee to the possession of it, and in the event of his becoming insolvent he may recover it from the trustee in the sequestration if it has come into the latter's possession, and the assured's wife as beneficiary under the trust can in her own name obtain an order against the trustee in the sequestration directing him to deliver it to her husband to be held in trust according to its terms. If

---

[6] *Watson Petitioners* 18 July 1944 (unreported).
[7] See W. A. Wilson & A. G. M. Duncan, *Trusts, Trustees and Executors* (1975), Ch. 21. The trustee may charge for his professional services: 1980 Act. s.2(3). For power of trustees to effect insurance, see *Governors of Dollar Academy Trust v. Lord Advocate* 1995 S.L.T. 596.
[8] 1980 Act, s.2(2). Surrender may be for cash: *Schumann v. Scottish Widows' Fund Society* (1886) 13 R. 678; *Stevenson's Exrs. v. Inland Revenue* 1981 S.C. 44, HL.
[9] The definition of "interest" is wide: 1980 Act. s.3(3).
[10] 1980 Act, s.3(1). The beneficiary has this power whether the policy was dated before or after October 29, 1980.

the policy was effected with intent to defraud creditors the only remedy open to the trustee in the sequestration on behalf of the creditors is to claim repayment of the premiums out of the proceeds of the policy on maturity.[11] That remedy affords no basis on which the trustee in the sequestration can claim possession of the policy.[12]

24–202 Effect of divorce. As in England, a decree of divorce does not by itself deprive the spouse of any rights under the policy which have already vested.[13] But by sections 8(2) and 14(2)(h) and (6) of the Family Law (Scotland) Act 1985 (c. 37),[14] in a divorce process a party may apply for an order setting aside or varying any term of the settlement of the policy. The order may be made before, on, or after, the granting or refusing of decree of divorce.[15] The principles to be applied are found in sections 9, 10 and 11.[16]

(6) *Role of Trustees*

Discharge for policy moneys in relation to settled policies

24–203 (i) *Discharge from trustees.* Formerly a person liable to pay money to a trustee was under an obligation to the beneficiaries to see that the trust was performed.[17] The only exceptions were:

(1) where the trustee was given an express power to give receipts in full discharge; and

(2) where such a power might be implied from the fact that the trust was for the benefit of infants unborn or unascertained persons, or for general purposes such as the payment of debts.

Trustees now have a statutory power to give a complete discharge conferred by section 14 of the Trustee Act 1925,[18] which provides that the receipt in writing of a trustee[19] for any money, securities, investments or other personal property or effects payable, transferable or deliverable to him under any trust or power shall be a sufficient discharge to the person paying, transferring, or delivering the same and shall effectually exonerate him from seeing to the application or being answerable for any loss or misapplication thereof. The section applies notwithstanding anything to the contrary in the instrument, if any, creating the trust.[20]

24–204 Despite the express wording of the section it may be taken that a person will not obtain an effectual discharge from a trustee if he pays the

[11] Section 2 of the 1880 Act, preserved by s.34(7) of the Bankruptcy (Scotland) Act 1985 (c. 66).

[12] *Stewart v. Hodge* (1901) 8 S.L.T. 436.

[13] Before the Succession (Scotland) Act 1964, the position was different. *cf. Wallace v. Wallace* 1916 1 S.L.T. 163.

[14] As amended by the Pensions Act 1995 (c. 26).

[15] s.14(1) of the 1985 Act.

[16] See J. M. Thomson, *Family Law in Scotland*, (3rd ed.) Ch. 7.

[17] *i.e.* he had to obtain a discharge from them.

[18] As amended by the Trustee Act 2000, Sch. 2.

[19] If there is more than one trustee all must join in the receipt; N.B. The term "trustee" as used in the Trustee Act 1925 includes, where context so admits, a personal representative—*ibid.* s.68(17).

[20] Trustee Act 1925, s.14(3).

money to him with the knowledge that the trustee is going to apply it in breach of trust. It follows that if trustees of a policy apply to the company for the surrender of the policy or for the application of a bonus in a particular way, the company, before complying with the request, ought to satisfy itself that the trustees have power under the trust to deal with the policy in the manner proposed or are authorised so to do by an order of the court.[21]

24-205 (ii) *Trustees power of compromise.* Section 15 of the Trustee Act 1925 gives wide powers to compromise and value claims to a personal representative, or two or more trustees acting together, or to a sole trustee authorised to act alone.[22]

24-206 (iii) *Discharge from person invested with legal chose in action.* Where the trustees have acquired the legal chose in action, that is, the right to sue at law for the policy moneys in their own names,[23] the only obligation upon the company is to inquire into the validity of the settlement and the title of the trustees; and, once satisfied that the settlement is unimpeachable and that the claimants are the properly appointed trustees and invested with the legal title, the company may safely pay the policy moneys to them, notwithstanding objections made by beneficiaries or by purchasers or incumbrancers taking from the settlor after the creation of the trust.

The company would not be justified in paying the policy moneys into court merely on account of conflicting claims of beneficiaries who do not dispute the validity of the settlement or the title of the beneficiaries; and, if it did so, it may be held liable to pay the costs thereby occasioned. Where, however, there is a trust, but without a completed assignment of the legal chose in action to the trustees, the company ought to obtain a discharge not only from the trustees but also from the person or persons entitled to the legal chose in action; and, if this cannot be obtained, it ought to pay the policy moneys into court.

24-207 (iv) *Discharge from agent for trustees.* An insurance company may safely pay the policy moneys to an agent for the trustees merely upon the agent producing the appropriate authority under section 11 of the Trustee Act 2000. Such an agent can be one of the trustees other than a beneficiary.[24]

24-208 (v) *Payment to beneficiaries.* In principle if all the beneficiaries are ascertained and are sui juris they can direct the company to make payment to anyone they wish, including one of their number and the company would be safe in paying in accordance with their direction. It is submitted, however, that nevertheless the company is fully justified in insisting upon and ought always to have a full discharge from the trustees who have the legal title. This is because one or more of the beneficiaries may have charged or assigned their beneficial interest, and the company would have no way of knowing about this. If it paid the beneficiary and subsequently that beneficiary's chargee or assignee made a claim against the company, the company in the absence of a legal discharge from the trustees, would have no defence.

---

[21] See article by A. R. Barrand in *Journal of Institute of Actuaries*, Vol. xxxiii, p. 220; and for the powers of trustees see paras 24–214, *et seq., post.*
[22] For more detail, see Snell, *Principles of Equity* (29th ed.) p. 270.
[23] See further paras 24–69, *et seq., ante.*
[24] Trustee Act 2000, s.12.

24–209 Appointment of new trustees. Before making any payment to trustees the office ought to be satisfied that the trustees making the claim and giving the receipt have been regularly appointed and that the legal chose in action has duly vested in them.[25] The following are the means whereby new trustees are appointed.[26]

24–210 (1) By means of an express provision contained in the trust instrument. The office should ensure that the appointment has been properly made by the donee of the power.

24–211 (2) By means of the statutory power. Section 36 of the Trustee Act 1925 confers wide powers to appoint new trustees in a number of circumstances. The power is vested first in the person nominated for the purpose of appointing new trustees, but if there is no such person, then in the continuing trustee or trustees or the personal representatives of the last surviving trustee.

24–212 (3) By the court. The court has a wide power to appoint new trustees either under the terms of section 41 of the Trustee Act or under its inherent jurisdiction.

24–213 It should be noted that the mere appointment of a new trustee under these powers does not itself vest the trust property in him. The office should ensure that this has been properly done. Vesting can take place either, if the appointment is by deed, by means of an express declaration as to vesting in the deed[27]; or, if the appointment is made by the court or special application for that purpose made, by means of a vesting order of the court[28]; or, if none of these methods has been utilised, by means of an express assignment or conveyance of the trust property from the existing body of trustees to themselves and the new trustee.

24–214 Powers of trustees to surrender or borrow on policy. Difficult questions may arise when an insurance company is asked by the trustee or trustees of a settled policy to pay the surrender value of the policy, or to grant a paid-up policy for a reduced amount or make an advance on the security of the policy. In this section will be considered the powers of the trustees in this regard and the circumstances and the manner in which such powers arise and may be exercised.

24–215 (i) *Powers given by trust deed or statute.* The necessary power must be sought either in the instrument creating the trust or in the statutory powers given to trustees. For this purpose it is submitted that a surrender of the policy either for cash or for a paid-up policy may be regarded as the sale of the trust property or, where it is intended to invest the proceeds in some other security, as a change of investment; while an advance by the office

---

[25] N.B. The original trustees are those designated as such in the instrument (if any) creating the trust: if none is designated the property will remain vested in the settlor upon trust: see *Mallott v. Wilson* [1903] 2 Ch. 494.

[26] For more detail, see Snell, *Principles of Equity* (29th ed.) pp. 200–207.

[27] Trustee Act 1925, s.40. A deed made after the commencement of the Act without an express declaration will operate as if it had contained such a declaration in the absence of an express provision to the contrary ibid. s.40(1)(b).

[28] *ibid.* ss.44–53.

against the surrender value of the policy may be regarded as a borrowing by the trustees upon the security of the trust property.

24-216 (ii) *Statutory powers.* In England, except under section 16 of the Trustee Act 1925, there is no statutory power for trustees to sell or borrow on the security of trust property without the consent of the court. Section 16 confers such a power upon trustees but only as regards any part of the trust property "for the time being in possession". Inasmuch as a policy of life insurance is a chose in action of a reversionary nature which cannot be reduced into possession until it becomes payable,[29] it is submitted that it is not property that can be sold or mortgaged under the power contained in this section. It follows accordingly that, for an English trust at any rate, the power to sell or to borrow on the security of a life assurance policy must be contained in the policy or in the instrument creating the trust.

24-217 In Scotland trustees have general power under section 4(1) of the Trusts (Scotland) Act 1921 to sell all the trust estate or any part thereof and to borrow money on the security of the trust estate or any part thereof provided only that the exercise of such power is not at variance with the terms or purposes of the trust.

24-218 (iii) *Power conferred by terms of policy.* If by the terms of the policy the assured has a contractual right to demand payment of the surrender value or a paid-up policy, or a loan, as the case may be, that is a power which might be exercised by the assured or other trustee of an M.W.P. policy, or by the trustees of a trust deed as the holders of the policy by virtue of the assignment of the policy to them. If the policy gives the assured no contractual right to surrender or borrow, the necessary power of sale or borrowing, or power to alter investments, must be found if at all in the trust deed. If it cannot be found there the office would not be safe in accepting the surrender of a policy for cash, or granting a paid-up policy or making an advance on the security of the policy when not contractually bound to do so.

24-219 (iv) *Powers of the court.* Where the transaction which it is desired to be carried out is not within the powers of the trustees, whether statutory or conferred upon them by the policy or the trust instrument, it may be possible to carry it out under an order of the court pursuant to section 53 or 57 of the Trustee Act 1925. Section 53 enables the court, where an infant is beneficially entitled to any trust property, to appoint a person to convey or transfer the property with a view to the application of the capital or income for the maintenance, education or benefit of the infant. Under this section the court has authorised the mortgage of an infant's entailed interest in remainder[30] and there seems no reason why it should not apply to authorise the surrender or mortgage of a life assurance policy. A power of somewhat wider application is contained in section 57. By this section, where in the management or administration of any property vested in trustees, any sale, lease, mortgage, surrender, release or other disposition, or any purchase, investment, requisition, expenditure, or other transaction, is in the opinion of the court expedient, but the same cannot be effected by reason of the

---

[29] See *Purdew v. Jackson* (1824) 1 Russ. 1, 43; *Aitcheson v. Dixon* (1870) L.R. 10 Eq. 589; *Re Watson* (1890) 7 Mor. 155.
[30] *Re Gower's Settmt.* [1934] 1 Ch. 365.

absence of any power for this purpose vested in the trustees by the trust instrument or by law, the court[31] may by order confer upon the trustees either generally or in any particular instance, the necessary powers for the purpose, on such terms, and subject to such provisions and conditions, if any, as the court may think fit. The power contained in this section is wider than the older power of the court under its inherent jurisdiction in cases of "salvage operations,"[32] and is unaffected by the Variation of Trusts Act 1958, application under which should only be made when a variation of beneficial interests is being asked.

24–220 The court has a complete discretion under these sections whether to make the order being sought, and will be bound to have regard to the best interests of the beneficiaries. The circumstances in which the court is most likely to exercise its power in favour of sale or surrender is where the settlor has ceased paying the premiums on the policy and there is no fund available out of which the premiums can be paid.[33]

24–221 (v) *Exercise of the power to sell or borrow.* Whether or not the power is contained in the policy or trust deed or, in the case of a Scottish trust, is implied by statute, the proposed exercise of the power must not be at variance with the purposes of the trust. Accordingly whether it is an English or a Scottish trust the office cannot safely accede to the application if either:

(1) the granting of the application would be inconsistent with the purposes of the trust; or
(2) the office is aware that the intended purpose is not one within the purposes of the trust.

The duty of the office in this connection is not a particularly high one. In particular, so long as the exercise of the power could serve some legitimate purpose of the trust, it is not incumbent upon the office to enter upon an inquiry to determine whether the proposal is for that legitimate purpose; and, indeed, it is better not to make any inquiry unless the facts already known are so suspicious as to make it a moral duty to inquire. In the absence of known facts tending to show that a breach of trust is intended the office may safely accede to the application to pay the surrender value, issue a paid-up policy or make a loan on the security of the policy.

24–222 Two types of cases must be distinguished in this regard. In the first place there are the cases in which no legitimate purpose of the trust could possibly be served by the proposed exercise of the power. This might be the case where, for example, an advance is sought by the trustees on a fully paid-up policy the sole purpose of which is expressed to be that of making provision for the assured's widow and children after his death. Secondly, on the other hand, there are those cases where the purposes of the trust are such that the proposed exercise of the power might fall within them. For example, if a policy under the Married Women's Property Act 1870 or 1882 is expressed in general terms to be for the benefit of the assured's then wife and

---

[31] "The court" means the High Court or the county court in respect of an estate or fund worth less than £30,000: see The Trustee Act 1925, s.63A; County Courts Act 1984, s.148(1) and Sch. 2, Pt I.

[32] See *Chapman v. Chapman* [1954] A.C. 429.

[33] See para. 24–240, *post,* and the cases there cited.

the children of their marriage, a loan made to the trustee on the security of the policy might well be used for the legitimate purpose of providing maintenance for the wife or children during the subsistence of the marriage, without incurring any breach of trust. The obligation of the office is only carefully to scrutinise the trust purposes to see whether, if the loan were granted the money could possibly be applied for one legitimate trust purpose. As another example, a surrender of the policy in return either for cash or for a fully paid-up policy of a reduced amount may often be the only way of preserving the trust property where the assured is unable or unwilling to continue payment of the premiums. An application in such circumstances would be for a legitimate purpose of the trust and, unless the office has reason to suspect that, in the case of an application for the surrender value in cash, the money would be misapplied by the trustee, the office is safe in acceding to the application.

24–223 There is very little authority on this aspect. In the Scottish case of *Schumann v. Scottish Widows' Fund and Life Ass. Soc.*[34] during the currency of a policy effected by a married man and expressed to be for the benefit of his existing wife if she survived him or otherwise for his personal representatives, the assured and his wife made a joint application for the payment of the surrender value. The office was unwilling to accede to the application without the sanction of the court. The Court of Session was unanimously of the opinion that the office could so accede, at least on the joint receipt of the husband and wife, and Lords Shand and Adam thought that, in accordance with the terms of the office's prospectus which provided for the surrender of the policy, it could even have acceded to the application on the sole receipt of the assured as the trustee of the policy. In *Schultze v. Schultze*[35] a policy effected by a married man under the Act of 1870 was expressed to be for the benefit of the assured's wife for life with remainder for the children of the marriage. The company's rules permitted the policy to be surrendered for a fully paid-up policy of lower value but, when the assured went bankrupt and subsequently insane resulting in a danger that the policy would lapse for want of payment of premiums, and an application was made to have the policy surrendered, the company refused to accede to the application in the absence of the authority of the court. The wife, as beneficiary, therefore brought an action against her husband as trustee asking for the appointment of a new trustee and for power in him to surrender the policy for a fully paid-up policy. As there were infant beneficiaries the court appointed two trustees in place of the husband and directed them to exchange the policy for a paid-up policy.[36]

24–224 (vi) *Concurrence of all the beneficiaries.* Whether the trustees have the power to do so and whether or not the exercise of the power is for a legitimate trust purpose, if all the present beneficiaries are sui juris and there is no possibility of any other beneficiaries the company is quite safe in acceding to the application upon the joint receipt of all the beneficiaries. The company ought first to satisfy itself that there is no prospect of any other

[34] (1886) 13 R. 678.
[35] (1887) 56 L.J.Ch. 356.
[36] N.B. This case is not a direct authority on the power of the trustees out of court, but it is illustrative of the sort of circumstances in which the exercise of the power would be for a legitimate trust purpose.

beneficiaries[37] and that all the present beneficiaries are of full legal capacity and able to give a valid receipt. Moreover, in the light of *Re Pauling's Settlement Trusts (No. 1)*,[38] it is submitted that the office would not be altogether safe in acceding to the application where some of the consenting beneficiaries are just over the age of 18 years and there is a suspicion that they are acting under the undue influence of their parents. This would be particularly so where it is clear that the application is not to further any legitimate trust purpose at all.

(7) *Rights and Obligations of the Settlor*

Covenants by the settlor

24–225 (i) *Covenant to insure.* A settlor who has covenanted with trustees to insure his own life is liable for breach of the covenant if the insurance companies refuse to insure him.[39] The covenant is prima facie absolute and is not conditional on the office's accepting him as a good life.

24–226 (ii) *Covenant to settle after-acquired property.* A life policy effected by a settlor may fall within the covenant to bring all "acquirenda" into the settlement. Thus, where a husband by an ante-nuptial settlement covenanted to assign to the trustees any property whatsoever which he thereafter acquired and subsequently and during the marriage he took out a life insurance policy, it was held that he was bound to bring the policy into the settlement as property purchased by him, and notwithstanding that the policy contained a condition against assignment.[40]

24–227 (iii) *Covenant to pay premiums.* Where a settlor covenants to pay the premiums and then fails to do so, the trustees may pay the premiums themselves and recover the amount they have paid from the settlor by way of damages for breach of the covenant, even though the settlement contains no clause expressly entitling the trustees to recoup the premiums from him.[41]

If the settlor becomes bankrupt the trustees are entitled to prove in the bankruptcy for an amount equal to the value of the settlor's covenant, which is equivalent to the amount necessary to purchase a paid-up policy. If, however, although the trustees have proved for this amount and their proof has been accepted, the settlor dies before the trustees have received a dividend in the bankruptcy, resulting in the whole policy moneys becoming payable, the proof must be expunged except as to premiums actually paid by the trustees.[42]

If the insurance company goes into liquidation, before the settlor's death, this in itself releases[43] the settlor from any further obligations under his

---

[37] *e.g.* if the beneficiaries are "all the children of A", so long as A is alive the class of possible beneficiaries is not generally closed.

[38] [1964] Ch. 303.

[39] *Re Arthur* (1880) 14 Ch.D. 603: the measure of damages would presumably be such sum as when invested in current high yielding securities and the dividends reinvested and added thereto by way of accumulation for the remainder of the life of the settlor (as actuarially determined) would produce the sum for which his life was to be insured.

[40] *Re Turcan* (1889) 40 Ch.D. 5; *Re Holland* [1902] 2 Ch. 360.

[41] *Schlesinger & Joseph v. Mostyn* [1932] 1 K.B. 349.

[42] *Re Miller* (1877) 6 Ch.D. 790.

[43] *i.e.* it is an event causing a frustration of the original covenant.

covenant to pay the premiums, and the only recourse of the trustees is to prove in the winding up for the value of a paid-up policy.[44]

24-228 (iv) *Specific performance of the settlor's covenants.* A covenant made by the settlor is made with the trustees and, on the principle that only parties to an agreement may sue upon it, at common law only the trustees could claim damages for breach of the covenant.[45] Based upon the principle that equity will not assist a volunteer, only those beneficiaries under a settlement who have given valuable consideration, or in the case of a marriage settlement, are within the marriage consideration,[46] may obtain specific performance of the covenant.

The covenant, being under seal, is, of course, enforceable by the trustees, but the court will not direct the trustees to seek specific performance of it at the instance of beneficiaries who are mere volunteers,[47] and, indeed, in one case[48] even directed the trustees not to sue.[49]

24-229 (v) *Security for settlor's covenants.* The settlor's covenant may be secured by the settlor's assigning the policy to the trustees and at the same time entering into a covenant, bond or warrant of attorney whereby the settlor consents to have judgment entered against him for a specified sum, but subject to the condition that the trustees shall not sue or enter judgment so long as the settlor punctually pays the premiums and does nothing to invalidate the policy.[50]

24-230 (vi) *Covenant not to invalidate the policy.* In addition to a covenant to pay the premiums a properly drawn settlement of a life policy should contain a covenant by the settlor not to do any act which may invalidate the policy. The damages for breach of this covenant as for example where the settlor went beyond the territorial limits of the policy and thereby rendered the policy void, is not the total amount insured but the actuarial value of the forfeited policy plus the value of the settlor's covenant to pay the future premiums.[51] The settlor will not, however, be liable for breaking a term of the policy of which he was totally unaware, as where all that the settlor has done is to present himself for a medical examination and the policy effected by the trustees contained a clause against foreign travel which had not been brought to his notice.[52] The positive covenant to pay the premiums and to do all acts necessary to keep the policy on foot does not, it seems, incorporate by implication the negative covenant not to do anything to invalidate the policy.[53]

24-231 Bonus additions to policy. Difficult questions can arise as to whether a bonus addition to the settled policy enures for the benefit of the

---

[44] *Garniss v. Heinke* (1871) 41 L.J.Ch. 306.

[45] *cf. Fletcher v. Fletcher* (1844) 4 Hare 67.

[46] See *Pullan v. Koe* [1913] 1 Ch. 9. Cf. *Re Plumptre's Marriage Settlement* [1910] 1 Ch. 609.

[47] *Re D'Angibau* (1880) 15 Ch.D. 228; *Re Pryce* [1917] 1 Ch. 234. Cf. *Re Cook's S.T.* [1965] 1 Ch. 902.

[48] *Re Kay's Settmt.* [1939] Ch. 329; see also *Re Ralli's W.T.* [1964] Ch. 288, 301.

[49] This extension of the equitable doctrine is, however, somewhat doubtful.

[50] See *Winthorp v. Murray* (1850) 14 Jur. 302.

[51] *Hawkins v. Coulthurst* (1864) 5 B. & S. 343.

[52] *Vyse v. Wakefield* (1840) 6 M. & W. 442.

[53] *Dormay v. Borrodaile* (1847) 10 Beav. 335 (where the settlor committed suicide and the policy was invalidated by a suicide clause).

settlor or comes within the settlement. Prima facie the settlement of a policy will include all bonus additions to the amount insured by the policy, and if the settlor wishes to retain the bonuses for his own benefit he should do so by inserting an express clause to this effect in the trust instrument. However, difficult questions of construction can arise where the settlor settles, in terms, not the policy itself but the sum assured by the policy. It will be a matter of construction as to whether the settlor intended only that amount, expressed as a sum of money and charged on the policy, to be included in the settlement, or whether he intended to settle the policy as a whole including all bonus additions to it.

24–232 In *Gilly v. Burley*,[54] an ante-nuptial settlement recited that the settlor had agreed to effect and had effected a policy on his life for £2,500 in the name of the trustees, and then proceeded to set out the trusts of "the sum of £2,500" when the same became due. In fact, contrary to the recital, the policy was not effected until after the marriage and was effected in the name of the settlor. The rules of the company provided that bonuses could be applied either (1) by payment to the holder, or (2) by reduction of premiums, or (3) by addition to the insured amount. The settlor allowed the bonus additions to be added to the assured amount. Upon the settlor's death it was held that the bonus additions fell to the trustees of the settlement and not to the settlor's personal representatives. The court held that the intention of the settlor was to settle the whole policy, including bonus additions, and not merely the sum of £2,500 charged on the policy. The settlor could have elected to have the bonuses applied in reduction of the premiums, but he had not done so, and they therefore became part of the settled property.[55]

24–233 In *Courtney v. Ferrers*[56] a settlor assigned, inter alia, a policy of life assurance on his life to the trustees of his marriage settlement under which, in the events that happened, his daughter was absolutely entitled subject to the settlor's life interest. On her marriage the daughter assigned to her trustees "all that the sum of £3,000 assured by" the policy to be held, in the events that happened, for the daughter's testamentary appointees. By her will the daughter appointed "£1,000 part of the sum of £3,000 which my father covenants to keep insured on his life " to A and the "remaining £2,000" to B. On the father's death £6,000 bonus additions were due upon the policy. The court held that the daughter's intention was to settle her whole interest in the policy, including bonus additions, and by her will to divide the whole proceeds thereof between A and B in the proportions one-third to two-thirds. A and B were therefore, between them entitled to the whole £9,000 that became due on the policy.

24–234 In *Parkes v. Bott*[57] an ante-nuptial settlement provided that, after the marriage, the trustees should stand possessed of "the said sum of £3,000," being the amount of a life policy to be effected by the settlor, upon certain trusts for the benefit of the intended wife and children of the marriage. The husband died a bankrupt at a time when £885 by way of

---

[54] (1856) 22 Beav. 619.
[55] *i.e.* by adding the bonuses to the policy moneys and continuing to pay the full premiums the settlor had, in effect, elected to bring further moneys into the settlement.
[56] (1827) 1 Sim. 137.
[57] (1838) 9 Sim. 388.

bonuses had accrued on the policy. The court held that the settlor's intention was to settle the whole policy, and not merely the £3,000 secured upon it, and that accordingly the £885 belonged to the trustees of the settlement and not to the settlor's trustee in bankruptcy.

24–235 Finally in *Roberts v. Edwards*[58] a testator, who at the date of his will had two life policies of £1,000 each, bequeathed "the £2,000 insured on my life." Subsequently he surrendered one of his policies and a bonus of £112 10s. was declared on the other. It was held that the legatee took the policy money plus the bonus.

It is a moot point whether a term of the settlement allowing the bonus additions to be applied "in the reduction of future premiums" permits the bonus additions to be applied in the payment of the current premiums in full, until the bonus is exhausted, or only permits the bonus to be applied in reduction of all future premiums *pro rata*. This case is mentioned by Mr Barrand[59] as having arisen in practice, on which occasion the company, adopting the latter interpretation, refused to comply with the request of the settlor and the trustees that the bonus be applied in the discharge of current premiums. Although "reduction of future premiums" could, on a liberal construction, be held to include the discharge either wholly or in part of current premiums, it is submitted that the expression as used in a settlement is more likely to be taken as a reference to one of the usual options given by insurance offices, that is to say the method of permanent reduction of premiums.[60]

Settlor's right of revocation

24–236 (i) *Express power.* A settlor is perfectly at liberty to reserve for himself the right to withdraw the policy from the settlement, and if he has the right to withdraw it "in toto", also has the right to withdraw it in part, as by allowing it to remain in the settlement but encumbered with debts that he has charged upon it.[61]

Whether or not, in the absence of a clear and unambiguous provision, the settlor has reserved for himself this power is a matter of construction. If, on a true construction of the settlement, there is a present gift of an appropriated fund to be kept apart for distribution after death, a trust is thereby created in favour of the beneficiaries which is irrevocable by the settlor.[62]

It is not, however, open to a settlor to make a power of revocation subject to the consent of a judge of the Chancery Division. This would be an attempt to make the judge an arbitrator without his consent and is not permissible.[63]

24–237 (ii) *Scots Law.* By Scots law, before the Married Women's

---

[58] (1863) 9 Jur.(N.S.) 1219.

[59] *Journal of Institute of Actuaries*, Vol. xxxiii, p. 20.

[60] If the trustees had express power to borrow to pay the premiums, or could be said to be exercising their implied power (see para. 24–238), the difficulty could probably have been overcome by the trustees each year borrowing the annual premium on the security of the bonus.

[61] See *Pedder v. Mosely* (1862) 31 Beav. 159, where settlor reserved right to sell policy; and later charged policy to a bank.

[62] *Torrance v. Torrance's Trustees* 1950 S.C. 78, 90, *per* Lord Justice-Clerk Thomson. See also W. A. Wilson & A. G. M. Duncan, *Trusts, Trustees and Executors*, Ch. 10.

[63] *Re Hooker's Settmt.* [1955] Ch. 55.

Property (Scotland) Act 1920, a gift from a husband to a wife was revocable during the subsistence of the marriage[64] except that a post-nuptial provision for the wife of a reasonable amount was irrevocable.[65] Now, however, all gifts and provisions between husband and wife are irrevocable[66] except in the event of the sequestration of the estate of the donor within five years after the completion of the gift.[67]

24–238 (iii) *Revocation by will.* If the settlor reserves for himself an express right of revocation in general terms this right can prima facie be exercised by a properly executed will, and a bequest of the policy in the will to a person other than the beneficiary will be taken as an exercise of the power of revocation. If the settlor purports to exercise the power of revocation by an instrument that is intended to take effect on his death, that instrument, to be valid, must conform with the formalities required by the Wills Act 1837, since it is an appointment by a "writing in the nature of a will in the exercise of a power" within the meaning of section 1 of that Act and therefore void under section 10 if the formalities requisite for the execution of wills are not complied with.[68] If the instrument is testamentary in character it is not sufficient that it complies with the formalities specified in the settlement; it must also comply with the Wills Act.[68]

Rights and Obligations of the Trustees

24–239 (i) *Obligation to keep policy on foot.* Trustees are never bound to pay the premiums on a policy unless they have trust funds available out of which to pay them. If they do have such funds then they are obliged generally to pay the premiums from such funds, since not to do so will probably amount to a breach of the obligation to act in the conduct of the trust as ordinary prudent men of business. In the absence of funds available trustees are quite entitled to pay the premiums from their own pocket or to borrow, and if they do so they will be entitled to a charge on the policy moneys for the amount they have expended.[69] It follows that the company may safely advance sufficient money to trustees of the policy to pay the premiums by way of a charge on the policy provided only that they are satisfied, by means of a statutory declaration or other evidence, that the trustees have no funds available for this purpose, and there is a consequent danger of the policy otherwise lapsing. Trustees cannot in these circumstances renew the policy for their own benefit, and if they purport to do so, the policy will remain trust property.[70]

24–240 (ii) *Obligation to enforce settlor's covenants.* The trustees of a

---

[64] *Dunlop v. Johnston* (1867) 5M. 22, HL.

[65] *Hay's Trustees v. Hay* (1904) 6 F. 978.

[66] Bankruptcy (Scotland) Act 1985 (c. 66), ss.34 and 74(2). Reasonable gifts of a conventional kind are protected: s.34(4).

[67] Married Women's Property (Scotland) Act 1920, s.5, repealed by s.28(2) and Sch. 2 of the Family Law (Scotland) Act 1985 (c. 37).

[68] *Re Barnett* [1908] 1 Ch. 402; *Re Schintz's W. T.* [1951] 1 All E.R. 1095.

[69] *Clark v. Holland* (1854) 19 Beav. 262, 273, 277; *Todd v. Moorhouse* (1874) L.R. 19 Eq. 69; *Re Leslie* (1883) 23 Ch.D. 552; *Re Jones' Settlement* [1915] 1 Ch. 373.

[70] *Fitzgibbon v. Scanlon* (1813) 1 Dow. 261; merely an illustration of the doctrine that trustees may not purchase trust property: compare *Keech v. Sandford* (1726) Sel.Cas.t.King 61.

settlement are prima facie bound to enforce the settlor's covenant to insure his life and to pay the premiums, but the beneficiaries cannot hold them liable for failure to do so unless they can show that proceedings against the settlor would have been productive.[71] Moreover beneficiaries who are volunteers cannot compel the trustees to sue since to do so they will be enabled to invoke the assistance of equity (indirectly) to complete their gift in a way that directly they cannot do.[72]

24–241 (iii) *Leave to sell policy.* Where the settlor is unable (or unwilling) to pay the premiums and there are no funds available, the proper course for trustees is to apply to the court for leave to sell or surrender the policy and to apply the proceeds to the trust purposes.[73] In a proper case the court will sanction the surrender of the policy for a paid-up policy of lower amount.

24–242 (iv) *Failure by trustees to keep policy on foot.* Where trustees are neglectful in their duty to keep up a settled policy out of the income of other trust property, the court may, on the application of a beneficiary, appoint some other person to receive the income and to apply a sufficient portion of it for that purpose on his giving security for the amount of the principal sum insured.[74]

24–243 (v) *Apportionment of policy money.* Where a policy is part of residuary personalty settled by will upon trust for a person for life with remainders over, and the policy moneys do not become payable until some time after the trust has become operative, they must be apportioned as between capital and income by ascertaining the sum which, put out at interest at 4 per cent per annum on the day when the trust became operative and accumulating at compound interest calculated at that rate with yearly rests and deducting income tax, would, with the accumulations of interest, have produced at the day of receipt of the policy moneys the amount actually received, and the sum so ascertained should be treated as capital and the residue as income.[75] Where the premiums on such a policy have been paid by the trustees out of income the premiums ought to be recouped to the tenant for life with interest at 4 per cent out of the policy moneys, and the balance should then be divided between capital and income in the manner already indicated.[76] If the policy was subject to a mortgage and the trustees kept down the interest thereon out of income, such payments must also be recouped to the tenant for life with interest at 4 per cent before division of the balance.[77]

24–244 Assignment by trustees in breach of trust. If trustees assign a

---

[71] *Hobday v. Peters (No. 3)* (1860) 28 Beav. 603; *Ball v. Ball* (1847) 11 Ir.Eq.R. 370.

[72] See para. 24–227, *ante.*

[73] *Hill v. Trenery* (1857) 23 Beav. 16; *Beresford v. Beresford* (1857) 23 Beav. 292; *Vicars v. Scott* (1837) 1 Jur. 402; *Steen v. Peebles* (1890) 25 L.R.Ir. 544; and see *Ex p. Hays* (1849) 3 De G. & Sm. 485.

[74] *Vicars v. Scott* (1837) 1 Jur. 402; *Re Wells* [1903] 1 Ch. 848, 853.

[75] *Re Earl of Chesterfield's Trusts* (1883) 24 Ch.D. 643. Having regard to the present rate of interest which may be obtained by trustees, 4 per cent is now the current rate for calculation of interest in all questions relating to trust funds where no statute or rule of court interferes to prevent it: *Re Beech* [1920] 1 Ch. 40; *Re Baker* [1924] 2 Ch. 271. The rate was at one time reduced to 3 per cent: *Re Woods* [1904] 2 Ch. 4.

[76] *Re Morley* [1895] 2 Ch. 738.

[77] *Capell v. Winter* [1907] 2 Ch. 376.

policy in breach of trust the assignee acquires no title if he knew of the breach. If he did not, the question of priority between a purchaser and the beneficiaries depends on the usual rules of priority of notice to the company. That is to say, if the company had knowledge of the trust the title of the beneficiary must prevail against a subsequent assignment in breach of trust even though made to a bona fide purchaser for value.[78]

Where trustees assigned a policy in alleged breach of trust and then assigned the rest of the trust funds to new trustees, it was held that the new trustees had no right to recover the proceeds from the purchaser. If there was any breach of trust the old trustees, and the purchaser unless he took for value and without notice, were liable to account to the beneficiaries but not to the new trustees who had acquired no interest in the policy.[79]

8. Bankruptcy of the Insured[80]

24-245 Proceedings in bankruptcy. When a petition in bankruptcy is presented, the court may appoint an interim receiver of the debtor's property[81] otherwise the official receiver acts as receiver and manager of the bankrupt's estate.[82] Bankruptcy commences on the day a bankruptcy order is made by the court.[83] A trustee in bankruptcy is appointed either by a creditors' meeting,[84] by the Secretary of State[85] or by the court.[86]

24-246 Passing of property to trustee. The bankrupt's estate vests in the trustee immediately on his appointment taking effect or, if the official receiver is appointed trustee, on his becoming trustee.[87] The estate comprises all property belonging to or vested in the bankrupt[88] which includes every beneficial right or interest which the bankrupt may have in or in relation to a policy of insurance.

Where during the bankruptcy a policy lapsed through non-payment of premiums and the office voluntarily indorsed it as a paid-up policy for a reduced amount it was held that the trustee was entitled to the benefit of the policy so indorsed.[89]

24-247 Insurance policy. The trustee in bankruptcy on becoming entitled to the bankrupt's policy of insurance may realise it by sale or surrender for the benefit of the creditors, or he may keep it up for the benefit of the estate in the event of the bankrupt's death. But where the trustee refused to pay the

---

[78] *Johnson v. Swire* (1861) 3 Giff. 194.

[79] *ibid.*

[80] This section gives only the broadest outline of bankruptcy law, much of which was recast by the Insolvency Act 1986 and the Insolvency Rules 1986, and retains detailed consideration only of those points of bankruptcy law of particular reference to life insurance.

[81] Insolvency Act 1986, s.286.

[82] *ibid.*, s.287.

[83] *ibid.*, s.278.

[84] *ibid.*, ss.293 or 294.

[85] *ibid.*, ss.295, 296 or 300.

[86] *ibid.*, s.297. The detailed procedure is prescribed in the Insolvency Rules 1986 (S.I. 1986 No. 1925), Ch. 10.

[87] *ibid.*, s.306.

[88] *ibid.*, s.283.

[89] *Re Shrager* (1913) 108 L.T. 346.

premiums on the bankrupt's policies and disclaimed all interest in them, and the bankrupt died, his representatives were held entitled to the policy moneys as against the trustee.[90] The trustee in bankruptcy is neither bound to pay the premiums nor disclaim the policy; but if not having disclaimed, a third person has kept the policy on foot during the bankrupt's insolvency, and the trustee afterwards claims the benefit of the policy moneys, the court will require the trustee to repay to such third person out of the policy moneys the sums expended by him in so keeping the policy on foot.[91]

24–248 Lien for premiums. Where a third person has kept the policy on foot by payment of premiums before the bankruptcy, and at the request of the bankrupt, such person will have a lien on the policy as against the bankrupt, and the trustee will take subject to that equity. Where the payment of premiums has been made by a third person after the bankruptcy without any request by the trustee, the trustee is not bound at law or in equity to repay the premium so paid[92] but may be directed as an officer of the court to do so, on the principle of *Ex p. James*.[93]

If a bankrupt does not disclose the fact that he has a policy on his life, and continues to pay the premiums thereon after he has obtained his discharge, the trustee in bankruptcy may claim the policy or its proceeds whenever he becomes aware of its existence, and is not bound to allow the bankrupt or his representatives anything in respect of premiums paid.[94]

It seems, as the law now stands, that the distinction between the cases cited in support of the last paragraph and *Re Tyler*[95] lies in the fact that in the former the trustee was not aware of the existence of the policy. It is by no means clear, however, that the knowledge of the officer was an indispensable factor to the decision in *Re Tyler*.[96] The value of *Re Stokes*[97] has been somewhat discounted by the unfavourable observations of Younger L.J. in *Re Wigzell*[98] but again it is by no means clear why the principle *Ex p. James*[99] was invoked.[1]

9. POLICY ON LIFE OF DEBTOR

24–249 Insurance by creditor. Where a policy is effected upon the life of a debtor in order to give security to the creditor, the question frequently arises as to whether, in the absence of any express agreement, the creditor is entitled to the policy absolutely or whether he is only entitled as mortgagee and bound to account to the debtor after satisfaction of the debt. Whether

---

[90] *Re Learmouth* (1866) 14 W.R. 628.
[91] *Re Tyler* [1907] 1 K.B. 865; *Re Hall* [1907] 1 K.B. 875.
[92] *Re Leslie* (1883) 23 Ch.D. 552.
[93] (1874) L.R. 9 Ch.App. 609.
[94] *Tapster v. Ward* (1909) 101 L.T. 503; *Re Stokes* [1919] 2 K.B. 256; *Re Phillips* [1914] 2 K.B. 689, *Nicholas v. Prudential Ass. Co.* [1940] I.A.C.Rep. (1938–1949) 26.
[95] [1907] 1 K.B. 865.
[96] *ibid.*
[97] [1919] 2 K.B. 256. See also *Re Phillips* [1914] 2 K.B. 689.
[98] [1921] 2 K.B. 835, 869–870.
[99] (1874) L.R. 9 Ch.App. 609.
[1] The policy of insurance in fact represented in part the debtor's savings out of an allowance paid to him by the trustee, and in part moneys acquired by him after his discharge. See further Williams, *Bankruptcy* (18th ed., 1968) pp. 275–278.

the policy is in the name of the debtor or creditor is not material, except as prima facie evidence of ownership, and as a general rule the policy must be deemed to belong to that one of them who, as between themselves, is ultimately liable to pay for it.[2]

24–250 Title of debtor to policy. If the debtor expressly or impliedly agrees to pay the premiums for an insurance on his life, the policy belongs to him in whatever form it may be effected.[3] An agreement to pay the premiums may be implied if the creditor, in his account with the debtor, debits the premiums to the debtor, and the debtor either pays them,[4] or admits that they are properly charged.[5] But where the creditor has merely charged the premiums against the debtor in his own books that is only evidence of his intention to charge the debtor if he could, and is not sufficient to show that the debtor agreed to pay the premiums or that the policy was his.[6]

24–251 Transfer of policy on repayment. Where there was no obligation on the debtor to pay premiums during the non-payment of the debt, but he agreed on the debt being paid off to pay a proportion of the premium for the unexpired portion of the current year, it was held that that obligation implied an obligation on the creditor to transfer the policy.[7] But in such a case the policy belongs to the creditor absolutely until the debt is paid off, and where the creditor merely undertakes that on repayment he will transfer a policy which the debtor is under no obligation to pay for, the creditor is not bound to account for the proceeds if the debtor dies before repayment.[8] And similarly, if the debtor has a mere option to purchase the policy on repayment that is not an option which can be exercised by his representatives after his death.[9] A creditor who has covenanted to assign a policy on repayment of the debt does not thereby undertake to keep the policy on foot; but, on the other hand, he could not sell it or surrender it so as to defeat the debtor's right to it.[10]

24–252 Interest calculated to cover cost of insurance. The fact that a debtor has agreed to pay interest which is obviously calculated so as to include the cost of insurance is not enough to entitle him to claim as his a policy effected by the creditor on his life.[11] In such a case the creditor is entitled to the additional interest, whether he effects a policy or not. He is not bound to insure, and if he does insure he insures entirely at his own

---

[2] *Brown v. Freeman* (1851) 4 De G. & Sm. 444; *Pennell v. Millar* (1857) 23 Beav. 172; *Drysdale v. Piggott* (1856) 8 De G.M. & G. 546; *Gottlieb v. Cranch* (1853) 4 De G.M. & G. 440; *Courtenay v. Wright* (1860) 2 Giff. 337; *Salt v. Marquess of Northampton* [1892] A.C. 1.

[3] *Re Storie's Will Trusts* (1859) 1 Giff. 94; *Simpson v. Walker* (1833) 1 L.J.Ch. 55; *Martin v. West of England Life and Fire* (1858) 4 Jur.(N.S.) 158.

[4] *Holland v. Smith* (1806) 6 Esp. 11.

[5] *Morland v. Isaac* (1855) 20 Beav. 389.

[6] *Bruce v. Garden* (1869) L.R. 5 Ch.App. 32.

[7] *Williams v. Atkyns* (1845) 2 Jo. & La. T. 603.

[8] *Bashford v. Cann* (1863) 11 W.R. 1037.

[9] *Lewis v. King* (1875) 44 L.J.Ch. 259.

[10] *Hawkins v. Woodgate* (1844) 7 Beav. 565.

[11] *Gottlieb v. Cranch* (1853) 4 De G.M. & G. 440; *Freme v. Brade* (1858) 2 De G. & J. 582; *Preston v. Neele* (1879) 12 Ch.D. 760; *Knox v. Turner* (1870) L.R. 5 Ch.App. 515; *Kavanagh v. Waldron* (1846) 9 Ir.Eq.R. 279; *Ex p. Lancaster* (1851) 4 De G. & Sm. 524; but see *Courtenay v. Wright* (1860) 2 Giff. 337.

expense with money which but for the insurance would go into his own pocket.

24–253 Debtor's equity of redemption. Where the policy is effected at the debtor's expense he is entitled to the equity of redemption even though the policy is in the name of the creditor as assured, or has been assigned to him.[12] Any condition that the creditor may not redeem is void if made at the time the security was created.[13] On repayment of the debt the debtor is entitled to have the policy assigned to him if not already in his name, and if he dies while the debt is unpaid, his representatives are entitled to have the policy moneys applied in discharge of the debt, and to have the balance paid over to them. Failure on the part of the debtor to pay the premiums in accordance with his promise to do so does not entitle the creditor, who has paid the premiums on the debtor's default, to treat the policy as his absolute property.[14] He may add the premiums to the debt, but otherwise the policy still belongs to the debtor.[15]

24–254 Insurance at sole expense of creditor. If the policy is effected entirely at the creditor's expense, the debtor's representatives have no concern with the application of the policy moneys, and apart from agreement the debtor has no right to a transfer on paying the debt.[16]

24–255 Application of policy money to extinguish debt. Before the case of *Godsall v. Boldero*[17] was overruled[18] it was held that a policy of life insurance was a policy of indemnity, and that therefore a creditor insuring the life of his debtor could not recover from the insurance company after he had received payment of his debt from the debtor, and as a sort of corollary to that rule it was held that if the creditor received the insurance money on the death of the debtor it ought primarily to be applied in extinguishing the debt.[19] Both these theories have long been exploded, and now if a creditor insures on his own account without being bound to do so, and without any agreement express or implied to give the debtor the benefit, he may recover both the debt and the insurance money for his own sole benefit. At first sight it seems perhaps unfair that he should be paid twice over, but neither the debtor nor the insurance company have any reason to complain. Each pays in strict accordance with the contract he has made. And there is no reason why either should claim as a windfall the benefit of another contract with which he has no concern.

24–256 Insurance by creditor as trustee. Where a creditor has assumed the position of a trustee towards his debtor he may, as trustee, be bound to

---

[12] *Martin v. West of England Life and Fire* (1858) 4 Jur.(N.S.) 158; *Simpson v. Walker* (1833) 2 L.J.Ch. 55; *Re Storie's Will Trusts* (1859) 1 Giff. 94; *Holland v. Smith* (1806) 6 Esp. 11; *Morland v. Isaac* (1855) 20 Beav. 389.

[13] *Salt v. Marquess of Northampton* [1892] A.C. 1.

[14] *Drysdale v. Piggott* (1856) 8 De G.M. & G. 546.

[15] *ibid.*

[16] *Brown v. Freeman* (1851) 4 De G. & Sm. 444; *Humphrey v. Arabin* (1836) Ll. & G. (Plunket) 318; *Bell v. Ahearne* (1849) 12 Ir.Eq.R. 576; *Law v. Warren* (1843) Drury 31; *Foster v. Roberts* (1861) 7 Jur.(N.S.) 400; *Lea v. Hinton* (1854) 5 De G.M. & G. 823; *Barron v. Fitzgerald* (1840) 6 Bing.N.C. 201; *Milliken v. Kidd* (1843) 4 Drury & Warren 274.

[17] (1807) 9 East 72.

[18] *Dalby v. India and London Life* (1854) 15 C.B. 365.

[19] *Henson v. Blackwell* (1845) 4 Hare 434.

account for a policy on the debtor's life; as where the debtor assigned to his creditor a contingent reversionary interest in trust to pay the debt and hold the balance to the use of the debtor, and the creditor insured the debtor's life to provide against the contingency.[20]

24-257 Loan transaction set aside. Where a transaction between creditor and debtor is set aside, the right to a policy effected on the debtor's life does not depend on whether the debtor would or would not have been ultimately liable to pay for it under the agreement between them because *ex hypothesi* the agreement has ceased to exist.[21] It is submitted that the policy must be considered as the policy of the party who has actually paid the premiums, and if the creditor has paid the premiums he will not, as a rule, be allowed to charge them in account against the debtor,[22] but where the debtor in applying to have the transaction set aside offered to refund the money and interest and to comply with "any other fair and reasonable demand", the court set aside the transaction on condition that he paid the premiums in exchange for a transfer of the policy.[23]

24-258 Illegal policy. If the insurance company has paid the policy moneys without questioning the validity of the policy, the plea that the policy was illegal or void cannot be set up by a creditor as against the debtor or vice versa.[24]

24-259 Own-life policy effected by debtor. A debtor effecting a policy on his own life in order to give security to his creditor is a trustee of the policy to the extent of the debt from the time it is effected.[25]

---

[20] *Ex p. Andrews* (1816) 2 Rose 410.
[21] *Pennell v. Millar* (1857) 23 Beav. 172.
[22] *Pennell v. Millar* (1857) 23 Beav. 172; *Ex p. Shaw* (1800) 5 Ves. 620; *Bromley v. Smith* (1859) 26 Beav. 644.
[23] *Hoffman v. Cooke* (1801) 5 Ves. 622.
[24] *Freme v. Brade* (1858) 2 De G. & J. 582; but see *Henson v. Blackwell* (1854) 4 Hare 434.
[25] *Winter v. Easum* (1864) 2 De G.J. & S. 272.

CHAPTER 25

PERSONAL ACCIDENT POLICIES

1. MEANING OF "ACCIDENT"

25–1 Introduction. The word "accident" is not susceptible of any very precise definition; in the context of an accident insurance policy the word is usually contained in phrases such as "injury by accident", "accidental injury", "injury caused by or resulting from an accident" or "injury caused by accidental means" and in each of these phrases it has the connotation of an unexpected occurrence outside the normal course of events. It is difficult to improve the definition of Lord Macnaughten who said that the popular and ordinary sense of the word was "an unlooked-for mishap or an untoward event which is not expected or designed".[1] One aspect of the word is its contrast with the concept of intention or design; no intended event can be described as accidental from the point of view of the person who is responsible for it.[2] Another element in the word is its contrast with an event that happens naturally; thus death or injury as a result of disease is not death or injury from accident, unless some accidental event has given rise to the disease.[3]

25–2 Although there is a certain amount of authority on the meaning of the word "accident" in accident insurance policies, it is also instructive to see how the word has been interpreted by the courts when dealing with the question whether an injury was "caused by an accident" within the Workmen's Compensation Acts since it has been observed that the fundamental conception of those Acts is that of insurance.[4] But cases

---

[1] *Fenton v. Thorley & Co. Ltd* [1903] A.C. 443, 448; *cf. per* Lord Lindley at p. 453 who spoke of any unintended or unexpected occurrence and *per* Lord Shand at p. 451. The House of Lords was considering the meaning of the phrase "injury by accident" in the Workmen's Compensation Act 1897—see para. 25–2, *supra.* Lord Lindley's definition was cited to the Court of Appeal in *R. v. Morris* [1972] 1 W.L.R. 228 but the court preferred to define the word accident as an "unintended occurrence which has an adverse physical result". Lord Macnaughten's definition was followed by the Court of Appeal of Nova Scotia in *Pickford & Black v. Canadian General Ins. Co.* [1975] 1 Lloyd's Rep. 267, 271, affirmed [1976] 2 Lloyd's Rep. 108.

[2] See para. 25–7, *infra.*

[3] See *Sinclair v. Maritime Passengers' Ass. Co.* (1861) 3 E. & E. 478; *De Souza v. Home & Overseas Ins. Co.* [1995] L.R.L.R. 453, 460; and para. 25–14, *post.*

[4] *Trim Joint District School Board of Management v. Kelly* [1914] A.C. 667, 675–676, *per* Lord Haldane L.C.

decided under those Acts must be treated with some caution before being accepted as authoritative in the various situations that can arise in connection with policies of accident insurance. Thus one essential element in workmen's compensation cases was that the accident had to have happened in the course of the workman's employment before he could recover, a consideration which is completely immaterial to contracts of accident insurance. It is, moreover, well-established that the test of causation is much less strict in the context of workmen's compensation than in that of accident insurance[5]; in fact it is true, as a general proposition, that the Workmen's Compensation Acts were construed more liberally than contracts of insurance[6] and it would therefore not be safe to say that any event or course of events that has been held to be accidental for the purposes of the Acts must necessarily be accidental for the purpose of an accident policy. For example the principle that death or injury must not be caused by any natural phenomenon[7] or any existing disease[8] if it is to be death or injury by accident plays a much stronger part in accident insurance than in workmen's compensation. While cases decided under the Acts may deserve attention when the policy uses the statutory words "injury or damage caused by accident",[9] it has recently been said in the Court of Appeal that:

"although it would be absurd to ignore the existence of [such cases] it would equally be unwise to put much weight upon them, and in my judgment one can put it no higher than to say ... that they 'afford some clue' as to the meaning of the word accident".[10]

25-3 Result of assured's voluntary act. If the assured intends a certain event to happen, and achieves its occurrence, no one would say that it happened by accident. So if the assured conceives the desire to do away with himself, and succeeds in so doing, his death is not accidental.[11]

---

[5] *Fenton v. Thorley & Co.* [1903] A.C. 443, 455, *per* Lord Lindley. See also *Re Etherington and Lancashire and Yorkshire Accident Insurance Co.* [1909] 1 K.B. 591, 602, *per* Kennedy L.J; *Fidelity and Casualty Co. of New York v. Mitchell* [1917] A.C. 592, 596, *per* Lord Dunedin.

[6] *Trim Joint District School Board of Management v. Kelly* [1914] A.C. 667, 677, *per* Lord Haldane L.C.; *Wicks v. Dowell & Co. Ltd* [1905] 2 K.B. 225, 229, *per* Collins M.R.

[7] Thus death or injury caused by sunstroke has been held to be accidental for the purpose of the Workmen's Compensation Acts—see *Morgan v. Owners of the "Zenaida"* (1909) 25 T.L.R. 446 and *Davies v. Gillespie* (1911) 105 L.T. 494—but not to be death by accident for the purpose of an insurance policy—see *Sinclair v. Maritime Passengers' Assurance Co.* (1861) 3 E. & E. 478. The learned editors of Halsbury, *Laws of England* (4th ed. Reissue) Vol. 25, p. 323, para. 571, note 3 consider that the latter case is probably wrong; but it is submitted that the distinction drawn in that case between the sailor who suffer sunstroke in the ordinary course of working on a ship in the tropics and the sailor who is shipwrecked and then suffers sunstroke as a result of exposure is correct for claims under insurance policies and was rightly applied in that case. One would not expect such a distinction to be decisive in a scheme of workmen's compensation. *Sinclair* was approved in *De Souza v. Home & Overseas Ins. Co.* [1995] L.R.L.R. 453.

[8] Compare *Re Scarr and General Accident Ass. Corporation* [1905] 1 K.B. 387 (accident insurance), with *Clover, Clayton & Co. Ltd v. Hughes* [1910] A.C. 242 (workmen's compensation).

[9] *Smith v. Cornhill Ins. Co. Ltd* [1938] 3 All E.R. 145; *Mills v. Smith* [1964] 1 Q.B. 30.

[10] *De Souza v. Home & Overseas Ins. Co.* [1995] L.R.L.R. 453, 458, *per* Mustill L.J., citing from Colinvaux, *Law of Insurance* (5th ed., 1984) para. 17–10.

[11] *Griessel v. SA Myn en Algemene Assuransie* (1952) (4) S.A. 473; *Beresford v. Royal Ins. Co.* [1938] A.C. 586, 595, *per* Lord Atkin. *Secus* if the assured is insane and cannot form an intention: *Horn v. Anglo-Australian Life Ins. Co.* (1861) 30 L.J. Ch. 511.

The same principle extends to situations where the assured deliberately courts the risk of injury by embarking on a course of action which is obviously hazardous, such as taking great risks on the road to avoid capture by a police patrol car.[12] So where a young man, given to feats of daring, drank a quantity of vodka and lime and then fell to his death while balancing on a thirteenth storey patio wall, his death was risked in undertaking this dangerous feat as a test of nerve, and was not caused "solely by accident".[13]

For injury or loss to be other than accidental it is not necessary that the assured made a subjective decision to run the risk of harm. It suffices that he embarked upon a deliberate course of conduct where the occurrence of injury or loss was, objectively viewed, a natural and probable consequence of his actions. Even if his conduct does not lead to the inference that he was courting the risk of injury and was taking a calculated risk, it means that the resulting injury was caused by the assured's own voluntary conduct without the intervention of a fortuitous event, and was not therefore accidental.[14] This can be illustrated by decisions in three jurisdictions.

25–4 In *Gray v. Barr*[15] the assured believed that his wife was visiting a neighbour with whom she had been having an affair. Determined to see into his neighbour's bedroom, where he suspected she was, he took a loaded shot-gun and tried to force his way in there past his neighbour, who denied that she was there. During the struggle the gun went off, killing the neighbour. A majority of the English Court of Appeal held that his death was not an accident, since it was a foreseeable, although unintended, consequence of his decision to force his way into the bedroom with the loaded gun.

In *Dhak v. Insurance Company of North America (U.K.) Ltd*,[16] the assured, a ward sister with many years of experience as a nurse, who consumed at least the contents of a bottle of gin over a relatively short period, died from asphyxiation having inhaled her own vomit. The Court of Appeal held that her death was not "caused by accidental means" because it was the direct consequence of drinking to excess, and, moreover, there must have been a point when she realised that any further drinking would be dangerous and thus took a calculated risk of sustaining some injury.

The Canadian courts have followed the same principle.[17] In *Jones v. Prudential Insurance Co. of America*[18] the assured lay down on his hotel bed, opened a couple of "girlie" magazines, put a plastic bag over his head and inhaled the fumes of a bottle of "Cutex" nail polish remover. It was found as a fact by the court, that his death was not caused by suicide or homicide, but by the consequences of this eccentric "thrill-seeking", to quote the coroner's

---

[12] *Greenway v. Saskatchewan Governmental Ins. Office* (1967) 59 W.W.R. 673.

[13] *Candler v. London and Lancashire Guarantee and Accident Co. of Canada* (1963) 40 D.L R. (2d) 408, in which there is a full citation of relevant common law authorities in Canada, England and the U.S.A.

[14] *Dhak v. Insurance Co. of North America (U.K.) Ltd* [1996] 1 Lloyd's Rep. 632 at 640; *National & General Ins. Co. v. Chick* [1984] 2 N.S.W.L.R. 86, 104–105, *per* Samuels J.A.

[15] [1971] 2 Q.B. 554.

[16] [1996] 1 Lloyd's Rep. 632.

[17] *Candler's case, supra; Turner v. Northern Life Ass. Corp.* (1953) 1 D.L.R. 427, 431–432. *Trynor v. Canadian Surety Co.* (1970) 10 D.L.R. (3d) 482.

[18] (1972) 24 D.L.R. (3d) 683.

verdict. Was this "death by accidental bodily injury"? The court held it was not, because, whether the assured realised it or not, his death was a foreseeable, probable consequence of his deliberate and foolhardy conduct.

In America it has been held that death from playing "Russian Roulette" was not accidental,[19] and that a man with a severe heart condition does not die by accident when he tries to push an automobile up a hill.[20]

25-5 The principles laid down in these cases give rise to difficulty in cases of driving under the influence of drink. If a person consumes an excessive amount of alcoholic drink and then proceeds to drive home in his car, it could well be said that any collision or other event resulting in death or injury was a foreseeable though unintended consequence of his driving after imbibing an excessive quantity of alcohol and therefore not caused by accident. In *Beller v. Hayden* [21] the driver of a car died in a collision with railings at the side of the road. He had a blood alcohol level three times the permitted maximum and was exceeding the speed limit. The court held that he had failed to appreciate that he had to slow down to negotiate a bend in the road, and that this was caused by his excessive drinking. The learned judge declined to follow *Jones v. Prudential* and held that the driver had sustained accidental bodily injury resulting in death, since the man in the street would say that he died in an accident, although the claim on the accident policy was defeated by an exception of death resulting from the assured's own criminal act. It is difficult to reconcile the finding of accidental bodily injury with the decision in *Dhak v. Insurance Company of North America (UK) Ltd* . The crash was the natural and direct consequence of the assured's voluntary conduct in drinking to excess and then taking the wheel. Since the court also stated that the assured had committed crimes involving moral turpitude, it is hard to see why the assured was not found to have decided at some stage in the evening to run the risks inherent in driving under the influence of alcohol.

25-6 The same question arose in an acute form in *Glenlight Shipping Ltd v. Excess Insurance Co. Ltd*[22] in which the pursuers employed a Mr Grierson as a shore engineer in connection with the construction of a concrete oil platform at Loch Kishorn. He lived about a mile from Kyleakin in Skye and, to return home, took the Skye ferry at around 9.30 p.m. on May 12, 1977, (*viz.* just after lighting-up time). He drove his car and parked on the ferry and, before the ferry had completed the journey, suddenly started up the engine of his car, drove past the vehicles which had boarded before him, up the ramp (which was in a raised position) at the end of the vessel, over the

---

[19] *Thompson v. Prudential Ins. Co.*, 66 S.E. 2d 119 (1951); *Linder v. Prudential Ins. Co.* 250 S.E. 2d 662 (1979). Contrast *National & General Ins. Co. v. Chick* [1984] 2 N.S.W.L.R. 86, where the assured checked the position of the round before firing a revolver, but miscalculated, his ensuing death was caused by accidental means.

[20] *Evans v. Metropolitan Life Ins. Co.*, 174 P. 2d 961 (1946); *Kasper v. Provident Life Ins. Co.* 285 N.W. 2d 548 (1979). There is, however, also American authority for the proposition that death from the activation of a heart condition while playing basketball or performing other operations instinctively is accidental, *Gottfried v. Prudential Ins. Co.* 414 A.2d. 544 (1980); *Commercial Travellers' Co. v. Walsh* 228 F.2d. 200 (1955). It has also been held that death of a fugitive from the police whose car crashed at high speed was accidental, *Schwartz v. John Hancock Mutual Life Ins. Co.* 233 A.2d. 416 (1967). See in general, Appleman, *Insurance Law and Practice*, (1981), Vol. 1A, para. 360.

[21] [1978] Q.B. 694.

[22] 1983 S.L.T. 241 affirming. 1981 S.C. 267.

top and into the sea. He drowned and the post-mortem revealed 307 milligrammes of alcohol per 100 millilitres of blood. Suicide was rejected and the question for the purpose of the pursuers' employers' liability policy was whether Grierson had sustained "bodily injury caused by violent accidental, external and visible means" resulting in his death. Both Lord Ross and the Inner House of the Court of Session held that the death was caused by accidental means, Lord Hunter saying:

> "If suicide is discounted, an onlooker of ordinary intelligence would in my opinion rightly describe such an event as an accident and the means directly causing the death as accidental."

In *MacLeod v. New Hampshire Ins. Co.*[23] the decision in Glenlight was interpreted as turning on the assured's mistaken belief that the ferry had berthed when in fact she had not, so that driving into the sea was not the intended result of his action.

25–7 Unforeseeable result of assured's deliberate act. The kind of case under consideration is where the assured deliberately makes some physical movement, or engages in a particular activity, and as a result unexpectedly injures himself either because unknown to him his organs were weakened by disease or because they were healthy but he miscalculated the extent of the stress to which he was subjecting them. Where the assured is covered against "accidental injury" there should be no difficulty in holding that claims for such injuries are valid. But there has been a divergence of judicial opinion as to whether such injuries are within an accident policy covering "bodily injury caused by violent, accidental, external and visible means", the phrase commonly used to define the ambit of the cover. This wording is considered in detail below in section 2, but in the present context we will consider the question of whether such injuries can be said to be caused by accident or by accidental means.

25–8 The English law on this topic has been clarified by two recent decisions of the Court of Appeal. In *De Souza v. Home & Overseas Insurance Company*[24] the assured was covered against "accidental bodily injury caused solely and directly by outward violence and visible means". He died of heat stroke after excessive exposure to the sun while on holiday in Spain. The Court held that the mere fact that the result of exposure to the sun was unexpected and unwanted was insufficient to satisfy the policy wording. In his illuminating analysis of the authorities Mustill L.J. adopted the summary of the law by Mr Baker Welford in his book on accident insurance.[25] Accordingly an injury is caused by accident either where the injury is the natural result of a fortuitous and unexpected cause, or where the injury is the fortuitous and unexpected result of a natural cause. An injury is not caused by accident when it is the natural result of a natural cause, such as sunstroke following voluntary exposure to the heat of a tropical sun.[26] On these principles the claim could not succeed.

25–9 This analysis was later approved and applied by the Court of Appeal

---

[23] 1998 S.L.T. 1191.
[24] [1995] L.R.L.R. 453.
[25] 1st ed., (1923) pp 295–296 and 299.
[26] The authority for this example was *Sinclair v. Maritime Passengers Assurance Co* (1861) 2 E & E 478, approved by the Court of Appeal.

in *Dhak v. Insurance Company of North America (UK) Ltd*,[27] the facts of which case are briefly summarised in paragraph 25–4, above. The policy there covered the assured against bodily injury resulting in death and caused by accidental means. Applying a further passage from Mr Welford's work[28] the Court held[29] that an injury which is the natural and direct consequence of an act deliberately done by the assured is caused neither by accident nor by accidental means. In this context the fact that the assured is not aware that he has a medical condition which threatens to produce an injury in consequence of his actions does not make the injury accidental when it occurs. Furthermore, if the assured sustains injury as the result of a voluntary action, such as the excessive consumption of alchohol in *Dhak*, the injury will not be caused by accident or accidental means when a reasonable person in the position of the assured must have taken a calculated risk that injury might result from what he was doing.

25–10 Exertion beyond natural strength. It has been held for the purpose of the Workmen's Compensation Acts that any injury caused by exertion beyond one's natural strength is an accident.[30] In *Fenton v. Thorley & Co.*[31] for example, a workman operated a machine for pressing cattlecakes. The machine jammed and in his effort to move it the workman ruptured himself. There was no previous weakness and no evidence of any slip or unintentional movement on the part of the workman, but there was held to be an injury caused by accident within the meaning of the Workmen's Compensation Act 1897. This class of case is similar to those considered in the above paragraph since the insured intended to do everything that he did but did not foresee the result. One approach would be to say that in this respect accident insurance differs from workmen's compensation and that although the injury may have been caused by accident for the latter purpose, the element of intention precludes it from being accidental for the purpose of insurance.[32] This is unsatisfactory since the element of intention should prevent any injury from being an accident regardless of the context in which the word "accident" is used. Another approach would distinguish between the words "injury caused by accident" and the words "injury caused by

---

[27] [1996] 1 Lloyd's Rep. 632

[28] (2nd ed., 1932), pp. 268–269; 272–273.

[29] [1996] 1 Lloyd's Rep. 632, 639–640.

[30] *Stewart v. Wilsons and Clyde Coal Co. Ltd* (1902) 5 F. 120; *Fenton v. Thorley* [1903] A.C. 443; *Aitken v. Finlayson, Bousfield & Co. Ltd*, 1914 S.C. 770; *Boardman v. Scott and Whitworth* [1902] 1 K.B. 43; *McInnes v. Dunsmuir and Jackson*, 1908 S.C. 1021 (where there was a latent defect but the over-exertion was held to be the primary and proximate cause of the injury); *Horsfall v. Pacific Mutual Life Ins. Co.*, 98 Am.St.R. 846 (1903).

[31] [1903] A.C. 443. To the same effect is *R. v. Deputy Industrial Injuries Commissioner, ex p. A.E.U., Re Dowling* [1967] 1 A.C. 725 (hernia caused by lifting heavy flagstone was a "personal injury caused by accident" within s.7(1) of the National Insurance (Industrial Injuries) Act 1946).

[32] Halsbury, *Laws of England*, (4th ed. reissue) vol. 25 p. 324, para. 572 takes the opposite view, suggesting that an injury resulting from exertion beyond one's natural strength should be regarded as "accidental", "caused by accident" or "caused by an accident" for insurance policy purposes, following the Workmens' Compensation Act cases. It is submitted in para. 25–13, *post*, that this view is incorrect. In certain cases, it may be relevant to inquire what the cause of the over-exertion was. For example it seems clear that a person who injures himself in an attempt to escape when he is trapped in a vehicle after a collision may be regarded as injured by accident. *Commercial Traveller's Co. v. Walsh*, 228 F. 2d. 200 (1955) can also be regarded in this light. It would seem, however, to be taking this concept too far to regard the stopping of the machine in *Fenton v. Thorley & Co.* as an accident and the act of the assured as caused by it.

accidental means" which are the words found in most insurance policies. On this view injury from over-exertion might be injury caused by accident but not injury caused by accidental means, because the assured did not act involuntarily in adopting the course of conduct leading to the injury. There is support for both distinctions in the judgments of the Court of Appeal in *De Souza v. Home & Overseas Insurance Company*[33] and *Dhak v. Insurance Company of North America (U.K.) Ltd.*[34]

25-11 In *Martin v. Travellers' Insurance Co.*[35] the insured recovered where the disability was caused by lifting a heavy weight, but the policy in that case covered accident "provided that the injury should be occasioned by any external or material cause" and it is therefore not safe to treat the case as authority for the construction of policies which require the injury to have been caused by accidental means.

25-12 Events happening naturally. Events that happen in the course of nature and all ordinary and foreseeable consequences of such events are not accidents. Such events fall into two main categories, pre-existing latent weakness or disease and exposure to the elements.

25-13 Pre-existing latent weakness or disease. Many insurance policies have an express exception for disease existing at the time of the accident but it is well settled that accident policies do not cover death or injury as a result of a pre-existing weakness or disease,[36] whether its existence or extent was known to the insured or not.[37] Thus in *Re Scarr and General Accident Assurance Corporation*,[38] the insured had been suffering from a condition known as fatty degeneration of the heart; he attempted to eject a drunken man from his office and the effort and excitement operating upon the defective condition of the heart caused dilatation and subsequently death. It was held that there had been no accident. Similarly where the insured took a long bicycle ride and the natural action of the psoas muscle rubbing against abnormal concretions in the appendix set up inflammation and caused death, the death was due to natural and not accidental means.[39] In all such cases the only accidental element is that the assured is not aware of his own condition or of the natural consequence which is likely to ensue from the voluntary effort which he makes.

[33] [1995] L.R.L.R. 453.

[34] [1996] 1 Lloyd's Rep. 632, 640. This was the view taken in earlier editions of this book (see 5th ed. at paras. 1639 and 1642) but not in more recent editions (see 8th ed. at para. 1770). The distinction is supported by the reasoning in *Mills v. Smith* [1964] 1 Q.B. 30, 36, concerning the words "damage to property caused by accident", and has found favour with the Supreme Court of Canada in *Smith v. British Pacific Life Ins. Co.* (1964) 45 D.L.R. 2d 91; (1965) 51 D.L.R. 2d 1. See paras 25–8 and 25–9, *ante*, and paras 25–32 and 25–34, *post*.

[35] (1859) 1 F. & F. 505, *cf. Youlden v. London Guarantee and Accident Co.* (1912) 26 O.L.R. 75; affirmed (1913) 28 O.L.R. 161.

[36] It may of course, be difficult to say in any given case that the disease rather than the accident caused the injury, see para. 25–46, *post*.

[37] *Sinclair v. Maritime Passengers' Ass. Co.* (1861) 3 E. & E. 478; *Drylie v. Alloa Coal Co. Ltd* 1913 S.C. 549, 553, *per*, Lord Dundas; *Weyerhauser v. Evans* (1932) 43 Ll.L.R. 62; *Mills v. Smith* [1964] 1 Q.B. 30, 36; *Smith v. British Pacific Life Ins. Co.* (1964) 45 D.L.R. 2d 1; and (1965) 51 D.L.R. 2d 1; *Milashenko v. Co-operative Fire and Casualty Co.* (1968) 1 D.L.R. 3d 89.

[38] [1905] 1 K B. 387. *Shanberg v. Fidelity and Casualty Company of New York*, 158 Fed. Rep. 1 (1907).

[39] *Appel v. Aetna Life Ins. Co.*, 83 N.Y.S. 238 (1903).

25–14 If, however, disease which gives rise to injury or death is caused by an accident, the insured may well be able to recover, and there is a group of workmen's compensation cases in which it has been held that a workman who dies or suffers injury as a result of a disease which he catches accidentally suffers injury caused by accident within the meaning of the Acts. In *Brintons Ltd v. Turvey*,[40] for example, a workman was engaged in sorting wool when a bacillus from the wool came into contact with the tender membrane of the eye and he became infected by anthrax. There was no evidence of any abrasion or wound and the only accidental element was the contact made by the bacillus with a susceptible part of the body, but the House of Lords held that there had been an injury caused by accident within the Workmen's Compensation Act 1897. It is not clear whether injury caused by disease coming into existence in this manner would be an accident within the meaning of an accident policy, but it is submitted that if a disease is proximately caused by an accident and injury or death is the ordinary or foreseeable result of that chain of events, and if the consequences of disease are not expressly excepted by the contract of insurance, an assured should be entitled to recover under an accident policy.[41]

25–15 Express exception for disease. An accident insurance policy will often have an express exception for the consequence of disease in general or certain diseases in particular. The policy in *Weyerhauser v. Evans*[42] had such a clause, but it was doubted if a pimple giving rise to septicaemia could be said to be a disease. On the other hand gallstones,[43] kidney disease[44] and anthrax[45] are clearly diseases which fall within such an exception and it has also been held that an arterial disease comes within a clause excepting liability for "injury directly or indirectly caused by or arising or resulting from or traceable to any physical defect or infirmity which existed prior to the accident".[46] If disease is defined in the policy so as to restrict the cases in which compensation for disability will be given, the same definition will be applied to the word "disease" in an exception in the policy.[47]

---

[40] [1905] A.C. 230. Contrast *Steel v. Cammel Laird & Co.* [1905] 2 K.B. 232 where the Court of Appeal held that lead poisoning resulting from the gradual absorption of lead into the workman's system was not an injury caused by accident since it was the result of a gradual process and not of any accidental event. For other cases in which the accidental infliction of disease was "injury caused by accident" see *Ismay, Imrie & Co. v. Williams* [1908] A.C. 437 (heatstroke); *Innes v. Kynoch* [1919] A.C. 765; *Warner v. Couchman* [1912] A.C. 35 (frostbite), *Drylie v. Alloa Coal Co.*, [1913] S.C. 549 (chill); *Coyle or Brown v. John Watson Ltd* [1915] A.C. 1 (chill); *Pyrah v. Doncaster Corporation* [1949] 1 All E.R. 883 (tuberculosis).

[41] cf. *Fitton v. Accidental Death Ins. Co.* (1864) 17 C.B.(N.S.) 122 and *Western Commercial Travelers' Ass v. Smith*, 85 Fed. Rep. 400 (1898). The problem in such cases is likely to be that of causation, see paras 25–36, *et seq.*

[42] (1932) 43 Ll.L.R. 62; it is similarly doubtful whether a condition which can give rise to ulcers could be said to be a disease rather than a "predisposing tendency," see the judgment of Cardozo C.J. in *Silverstein v. Metropolitan Life Ins. Co.*, 171 N.E. 914 (1930).

[43] *Cawley v. National Employers' Accident and General Ass. Assn. Ltd* (1885) Cab. & El. 597.

[44] *McKechnie's Trustees v. Scottish Accident Ins. Co.* (1889) 17 R. 6.

[45] *Bacon v. United States Mutual Accident Assn.* 123 N.Y. 304 (1890); *Brintons Ltd v. Turvey* [1905] A.C. 230.

[46] *Jason v. Batten (1930) Ltd* [1969] 1 Lloyd's Rep. 281. But a fainting spell produced by indigestion or lack of proper food is not to be considered a disease, *Manufacturers' Accident Indemnity Co. v. Jargan*, 58 Fed. Rep. 945, 955–956 (1893).

[47] *Mardorf v. Accident Ins. Co.* [1903] 1 K.B. 584.

25–16 Express exception for condition the subject of prior medical consultation. A variant of the above exception is a clause found in sickness policies which excludes liability for disease in respect of which the assured has received medical advice, treatment or counselling within a period preceding the commencement of cover. In *Cook v. Financial Insurance Co. Ltd*[48] the appellant was insured under a "group disability insurance policy" and was issued with a certificate of insurance containing the following exclusion:

> "No benefit will be payable for disability resulting from (a) Any sickness, disease, condition or injury for which an insured person received advice,treatment or counselling from any registered medical practitioner during the 12 months preceding the commencement date. ....".

He claimed under the insurance when he had to give up work because he was diagnosed as suffering from angina. Some three months before the commencement of the policy he had consulted his general practitioner complaining of pain and breathlessness while out running. She thought that he was probably suffering from a viral infection and prescribed a mild anti-biotic. She also referred him to a consultant cardiologist because she wanted "to exclude angina". Shortly after the cover had incepted, he was diagnosed as having angina. The insurers declined liability in reliance on the exclusion. The House of Lords held by a majority that the claim succeeded. The assured had not received advice, treatment or counselling for angina because at that stage he was not recognised to be suffering from it. It was not enough for the insurers to say that he received advice for symptoms which subsequently turned out to be those of angina. "Condition" meant a recognised medical condition, and a doctor does not give advice about, or treatment for, a sickness, disease or condition when unaware what illness the patient has.

25–17 Where a disease which comes within the exception clause causes an accident which gives rise to injury or death, the injury or death will usually be held to have been caused by the accident rather than the disease, since it is the immediate and not the remote cause of the injury that must be considered. Thus, where the insured was seized by an epileptic fit while crossing a stream and consequently fell in and was drowned, the injury and death were held to be due to accidental means.[49] More difficult questions arise where an accident gives rise to a disease which is excepted by the policy. In this situation the court must decide whether it is the accident or the disease that is the proximate cause of the injury. If the disease arose contemporaneously with the accident and was, so to speak, all part and parcel of it, it may well be held that the injury was proximately caused by the accident with the result that the insured can recover,[50] but if the disease comes into existence some time after the accident, death or injury is more

---

[48] [1999] Lloyd's Rep. I.R. 1.
[49] *Winspear v. Accident Ins. Co. Ltd* (1880) 6 Q.B.D. 42; *Lawrence v. Accidental Ins. Co.* (1881) 7 Q.B.D. 216; *cf. Reynolds v. Accidental Ins. Co.* (1870) 22 L.T. 820 and *Wicks v. Dowell & Co. Ltd* [1905] 2 K.B. 225. See further paras 25–37, *et seq.*
[50] *Fitton v. Accidental Death Ins. Co.* (1864) 17 C.B.(N.S.) 122 (hernia); *Accident Ins. Company of North America v. Young* (1892) 20 S.C.R. 280 (erysipelas); *Bailey v. Interstate Casualty Company of New York*, 8 App.Div. 127 (1896).

likely to be held to have been proximately caused by the disease and therefore excluded by the terms of the policy.[51]

25–18 Surgical operations and medical treatment. If an insured dies while under an operation, the operation itself will be disregarded and death will be attributed to the circumstances which made it necessary to have the operation; thus if the insured was suffering from disease, his death will be considered to have been caused by the disease and he will not be able to recover,[52] but if the operation is performed in order to alleviate the consequences of an accidental injury, his death is caused by the accident and he can recover under the policy.[53] Similarly in America death resulting from proper medical treatment of an accidental injury will be death caused by accident.[54] But there can also be death by accident when death occurs during treatment of or an operation for disease, if it happens in a manner independent of the operation although perhaps connected with it.[55]

25–19 Many policies have an express exception for injury or death occurring as a result of medical or surgical treatment and difficulties may arise in connection with treatment given not by a doctor or surgeon but by a nurse, osteopath or even a layman.[56] If there is an express exception for death occurring as a result of surgical treatment and the insured meets with an accidental injury necessitating an operation, the exception will not apply if the insured dies while the operation is being skillfully performed, even though the death is directly due to the operation and not to the original injury.[57] In one case the insured's doctor prescribed opium as a remedy for nervous excitement and the insured died from taking more than the prescribed dose; it was held that the death was caused by medical treatment and was, therefore, within the exception.[58] The exception excludes the consequences of acts done by way of diagnosis, as well as of actual attempts to relieve or cure the patient's condition.[59]

25–20 Exposure to natural elements. The cases on this topic are somewhat conflicting, but it seems clear that if the assured suffers injury through being

[51] *Smith v. Accident Insurance Co.* (1870) L.R. 5 Exch. 302 (erysipelas), where *Fitton's* case was distinguished partly on the grounds mentioned in the text and partly on the grounds that the hernia had there arisen from external violence outside the system of the human body, while the erysipelas in *Smith's* case had arisen within the system. *Cf. Bacon v. United States Mutual Accident Association*, 123 N.Y. 304 (1890).
[52] *Charles v. Walker Ltd* (1909) 25 T.L.R. 609. If death were due not to the effects of the operation but to the negligence of the surgeon, a fresh accidental cause has intervened and the assured can, presumably, recover.
[53] *Fitton v. Accidental Death Ins. Co.* (1864) 16 C.B.(N.S.) 122; *Shirt v. Calico Printers' Association* [1909] 2 K.B. 51; *Thompson v. Mutter, Howey & Co.* 1913 S.C. 619.
[54] *Insce. Co. of North America v. Thompson* 381 F.2d 677 (1967) and, generally, 25 A.L.R. 3d. 1386.
[55] Contrast *McMahon v. Mutual Benefit Health and Accident Association*, 206 P. 2d. 292 (1949) (dislodging of embolus and death from pulmonary thrombosis) and *Johnson v. National Life and Accident Ins. Co.*, 905 F. 2d 36 (1955) (death from a normal dose of penicillin) with *Linn v. Equitable Life Ins. Co. of Iowa*, 107 P. 2d 921 (1940) (germs entering through incision made by surgeon) and *Life and Casualty Ins. Co. of Tennessee v. Brown*, 98 S.E. 2d 68 (1957) (food particles becoming lodged in windpipe) reversed on different ground 99 S.E. 2d 98. See further Appleman, *Insurance Law and Practice* (1981), Vol. 1B, para. 414.
[56] See *Weyerhauser v. Evans* (1932) 43 Ll.L.R. 62.
[57] *Travelers' Ins. Co. v. Murray*, 25 Am.S.R. 267, 273 (1891); *Westmoreland v. Preferred Accident Ins. Co.*, 75 Fed. Rep. 244 (1896).
[58] *Bayless v. Travelers' Ins. Co.*, 14 Blatchf. 143 (1877).
[59] *Provident Life and Accident Ins. Co. v. Hutson*, 305 S.W. 2d 837 (1959).

in contact with the ordinary forces of nature in the ordinary course of his work or his leisure, that injury is not accidental. In *Sinclair v. Maritime Passengers Co.*[60] it was held that death from sunstroke resulting from exposure to heat on board ship was not covered by a policy insuring against "injury caused by accident." If the exposure had itself been accidentally caused, *e.g.* by shipwreck, then the resulting sunstroke might well have been held to be injury by accident, but since the injury was sustained in the ordinary course of the insured's work, it could not be said to be accidental. The decision in *Sinclair* was followed in *De Souza v. Home & Overseas Insurance Co. Ltd*,[61] where death from heat stroke on holiday following exposure to a normal Mediterranean summer climate was held not to be accidental. Similarly it is submitted that a mountaineer who suffers injury from exposure to cold or the rarefied atmosphere does not suffer injury by accident, nor does a seaman who contracts a cold from exposure to a gale at sea. Different considerations might well apply to a motorist who breaks down and then gets caught in a blizzard,[62] or to a mountaineer who slips or becomes cut off from his base by an avalanche; in each of these cases an accidental event has intervened and any resulting injury is probably caused by accident.[63]

In a previous edition of this work,[64] it was suggested that the decision in *Sinclair's* case conflicted with the recent decision in *The Miss Jay Jay*[65] and that the line of the Workmen's Compensation cases,[66] which incline to the view that exposure to natural elements can be accidental in the sense that it is not incurred intentionally, was to be preferred. In *The Miss Jay Jay*, a yacht was insured against loss or damage caused by external accidental means. The yacht was badly built and sustained damage during a cross-channel voyage where the sea was adverse but by no means exceptional. The Court of Appeal held that the damage had been caused by external accidental means because it was not inevitable and the owner of the yacht did not intend it to happen, Slade L.J. commenting:

> "Even if the occurrence of a particular unwanted event, which may or may not occur, is a readily foreseeable risk, the event may still be properly regarded as accidental when it does in fact occur."[67]

In *De Souza's* case, the Court of Appeal held that the suggestion of a conflict was misconceived and regarded the decision in *The Miss Jay Jay* as turning on the fact that the policy there was a marine one construed in the context of

---

[60] (1861) 3 E. & E. 478; *cf. Landress v. Phoenix Ins. Co.*, 291 U.S. 491 (1933) where a majority of the Supreme Court of the United States held sunstroke was not covered by an insurance against death "through external violent and accidental means."

[61] [1995] L.R.L.R. 453.

[62] *North-West Commercial Travellers' Association v. London Guarantee and Accident Co.* (1895) 10 Man. R. 537; *Sklar v. Saskatchewan Government Ins. Office* (1965) 54 D.L.R. (2d) 455.

[63] Injury by being struck by lightning is probably accidental, although it is a natural force, which may or may not occur; see *Andrew v. Failsworth Industrial Society* [1904] 2 K.B. 32.

[64] 8th edition at para. 1779.

[65] [1987] 1 Lloyd's Rep. 32.

[66] See *Morgan v. Owners of "Zenaida"* (1909) 25 T.L.R. 446 and *Davies v. Gillespie* (1911) 105 L.T. 494 (sunstroke); *Ismay, Imrie & Co. v. Williamson* [1908] A.C. 437 (heat stroke); *Brooker v. Thomas Borthwick & Sons (Australasia) Ltd* [1933] A.C. 669 (earthquake); *Alloa Coal Co. Ltd v. Drylie* 1913 S.C. 549 (pneumonia as a result of standing in cold water); *Coyle or Brown v. John Watson Ltd* [1915] A.C. 1 (pneumonia through exposure to draught); *Glasgow Coal Co. v. Welsh* [1916] 2 A.C. 1 (rheumatism incurred while baling out flooded mine).

[67] At p. 39.

an accident at sea. While it seems illogical that the construction of the words "accidental means" in a marine policy should differ from their construction in a non-marine policy, it has to be accepted that that is the current legal position. The Court of Appeal also cautioned against treating decisions under the Workmens Compensation Acts as authoritative for the construction of accident policies.[68]

25–21 Drowning. Death caused by drowning will usually be held to be accidental, or a death caused by violent accidental external and visible means. This is obvious where the assured accidentally falls into the water.[69] If nothing is known save that the body of the assured has been washed up, there is a presumption of accident and if the insurers wish to assert that the assured committed suicide[70] or was affected by some disease while in the water such as apoplexy or cramp,[71] the burden is upon them to show how the assured died. The fact that the personal representatives do not permit a post-mortem to be made will not necessarily be sufficient to discharge that burden,[72] but if the insurers can show that the assured suffered some such attack, it will probably be held that his death was not accidental within the meaning of the policy.

25–22 Concussion. If the assured is accidentally concussed and while in a concussed state incurs further injury, he may recover for such injury under an accident insurance policy.[73]

25–23 Death from poison or inhaling gas. Many policies contain express exceptions excluding death or injury resulting from taking poison or inhaling gas,[74] but where there is no such express exception the question arises whether such occurrences are within the general risk. If the assured takes poison by mistake for medicine, he should be able to recover[75] but if he takes an overdose, two situations must be distinguished. If the assured believed that the dose he took was the proper amount but he miscalculated the effect of the quantity taken, there is no accident, but if he mistakenly pours out and takes a larger dose than he intended, death is caused accidentally.[76] Death resulting from the inhalation of gas may well be death from accident,[77] but in

---

[68] [1995] L.R.L.R. 453, 456–458.

[69] Even if the accident is caused by some disease such as an epileptic fit, *Winspear v. Accident Insurance Co.* (1880) 6 Q.B.D. 42; *Reynolds v. Accidental Ins. Co.* (1870) 22 L.T. 820.

[70] *Macdonald v. Refuge Ass. Co.* (1890) 17 R. 955; *Harvey v. Ocean Accident and Guarantee Corporation* [1905] 2 Ir.R. 1, *cf. Young v. Maryland Casualty Co.* (1909) 14 B.C.R. 146 and *Dominion, etc., Guarantee Co. v. Mckercher* (1911) 18 Rev.Jr. 136.

[71] *Trew v. Railway Passengers' Ass. Co.* (1861) 6 H. & N. 839.

[72] *Ballantine v. Employers' Ins. Co. of Great Britain Ltd* (1893) 21 R. 305.

[73] *Smith v. Cornhill Ins. Co.* [1938] 3 All E.R. 145.

[74] *Cole v. Accident Ins. Co. Ltd.* (1889) 5 T.L.R. 736; *Re United London and Scottish Ins. Co., Brown's Claim* [1915] 2 Ch. 167.

[75] *Cole v. Accident Ins. Co. Ltd* (1889) 5 T.L.R. 736.

[76] *Carnes v. Iowa Traveling Men's Association* 76 N.W. 683 (1898) and *Prudential Ins. Co. of America v. Gutowski,* 113 A. 2d 579 (1955). In both these cases the evidence was consistent with either hypothesis and the claimant had therefore failed to prove his case. *Cf. Price v. Dominion of Canada General Ins. Co.* [1941] S.C.R. 509 where the claimant would not have been able to recover had it not been for the statutory addition to the policy of the words "bodily injury ... happening ... as the indirect result of his intentional act" by virtue of s.5 of the New Brunswick Accident Insurance Act.

[77] *Hunter v. Royal London Mutual Ins. Co.,* I.A.C. Rep. (1933), p. 14; *Paul v. Travelers' Ins. Co.* 112 N.Y. 472 (1889).

Re United London and Scottish Insurance Co., Brown's Claim[78] there was an exceptions clause excluding "death or disablement by accident directly or indirectly caused by ... anything swallowed or administered or inhaled" and it was therefore held that the assured who had been accidentally asphyxiated could not recover. Moreover, if there is a requirement of bodily injury in the policy, the mere inhalation of poisonous fumes will not entitle the assured to recover.[79]

25–24 An express exception in the policy may exclude the insurer's liability if death or disability results from taking poison or inhaling gas or it may exclude simply "death resulting from poison". In the first case it has been said that, if the exception is to apply, there must be a conscious and voluntary act done with knowledge of the nature of the substance taken or inhaled.[80] This view has been disapproved by the Court of Appeal and the federal courts of the United States[81] and if the exception takes the second form any conscious or voluntary element which may be implied from the word "taking" is eliminated.[82] An exception against death from poison will probably not prevent recovery where there is an accidental wound and blood poisoning supervenes as a direct result of the original injury.[83]

25–25 Obstruction of windpipe. Death caused by choking due to some particle of food blocking the windpipe has been held to be death caused by external, violent and accidental means.[84]

25–26 Intended injuries by another. Intended injuries inflicted by another are accidental from the point of view of assured and are therefore covered unless they were invited or provoked by the assured.[85] Fist fighting is not calculated to result in death, and the death of an assured who fell and hit his head on the pavement while so fighting was held to have been caused by accidental means.[86]

25–27 Shock without physical contact. In *Pugh v. London, Brighton and South Coast Ry,*[87] the assured was a signalman who noticed a defect in a carriage of a passing train which might have caused an immediate accident. He leaned out of his box and waved violently to the driver to stop. The

[78] [1915] 2 Ch. 167.

[79] *Milashenko v. Co-operative Fire and Casualty Company* [1968] 1 D.L.R. 3d 89.

[80] *Travelers' Ins. Co. v. Dunlop*, 160 Ill. 642 (1896); *Menneiley v. Employers' Liability Ass. Corporation*, 148 N.Y. 596 (1896).

[81] *Re United London and Scottish Ins. Co., Brown's Claim* [1915] 2 Ch. 167; *McGlother v. Provident Mutual Accident Co. of Philadelphia* 89 Fed. Rep. 685 (1898); *cf. Hill v. Hartford Accident Ins. Co.*, 22 Hun. 187 (1880).

[82] *Cole v. Accident Ins. Co. Ltd* (1889) 5 T.L.R. 736; *McGlother v. Provident Mutual Accident Co. of Philadelphia*, 89 Fed. Rep. 685 (1898).

[83] *Hill v. Hartford Accident Ins. Co.*, 22 Hun. 187, 193 (1880); *Omberg v. U.S. Mutual Accident Association*, 72 Am.S.R. 413 (1897).

[84] *American Accident Co. of Louisville v. Reigart*, 23 S.W. 191 (1893), followed in *Ponsford v. Royal Co-operative Coll. Soc.*, I.A.C. Rep. [1928], p. 9; *cf. Burridge & Son v. Haines* (1918) 87 L.J.K.B. 641 (suffocation of a horse).

[85] *Trim Joint District School Board of Management v. Kelly* [1914] A.C. 667; *cf. Letts v. Excess Ins. Co.* (1916) 32 T.L.R. 361; *Morran v. Railway Passenger's Ass. Co.* (1919) 43 O.L.R. 561; *Mills v. Smith* [1964] 1 Q.B. 30 and *Anderson v. Balfour* [1910] 2 Ir.R. 497; *Robinson v. United States Mutual Accident Association of City of New York*, 68 Fed. Rep. 825 (1895).

[86] *Rooney v. Mutual Benefit Health and Accident Association*, 170 P. 2d 72 (1947).

[87] [1896] 2 Q.B. 248.

excitement caused severe nervous shock and, although there was no physical contact with the cause of the injury, it was held that the assured fell within the provision of the policy, "in case of his being incapacitated by reason of accident"; he would probably have also recovered under a policy insuring against "injury caused by violent, accidental, external and visible means". It is important to note, however, that some form of bodily injury must have been sustained by the assured if that is a requirement of the policy.[88]

25–28 Negligence not a bar. The fact that an accident arises from the negligence of the assured does not prevent him from recovering under the policy,[89] although there will often be a clause excepting accidents happening as a result of voluntary exposure to obvious risk.[90] But if the intentional act of the assured gives rise to death or injury, he will be unable to recover unless, perhaps, the act is proximately caused by an accident.[91]

25–29 Originating incident or result? It may sometimes be important to know if the word "accident" is applicable to the event that causes the ultimate loss or damage or to the loss or damage itself. The question will usually arise under a liability policy by which the assured is entitled to indemnity against, e.g. "liability for damage to the property of others caused by accident" or "liability for damages because of injury to or destruction of property resulting from an accident due to the operations of the assured". Under a policy where the first of these phrases was used, it was necessary to decide whether damage caused by defectively manufactured glue fell within the contract of insurance. The Supreme Court of Canada held that, although it was impossible to say where the manufacturing process had gone wrong there was nevertheless an accident causing damage to the property of another and the insured could accordingly recover under his liability policy.[92]

A more difficult problem arose under a stevedores' liability policy containing the second phrase which also contained an exemption for "Risk at sea outside Halifax Harbour limits." The stevedores were held to have

---

[88] *Milashenko v. Co-operative Fire and Casualty Co.* (1968) 1 D.L.R. 3d 89.

[89] *Cornish v. Accident Ins. Co.* (1889) 23 Q.B.D. 453, 457, *per* Lindley L.J.; *Cole v. Accident Ins. Co. Ltd* (1889) 5 T.L.R. 736; *Life and Casualty Co. of Tennessee v. Benion*, 61 S.E. 2d 579 (1950) *Marcel Beller v. Hayden* [1978] Q.B. 694. Similarly negligent conduct after the injury has been incurred will probably not prevent recovery in the absence of an express clause to that effect, unless it amounts to an intervening cause, see *Maryland Casualty Co. v. Gehrmann*, 96 Md. 634 (1903).

[90] See paras 25–74, *et seq.*, *infra*.

[91] Thus it has been held in cases of workmen's compensation that an accident which causes insanity or physical derangement which gives rise to suicide is an accident within the statutes, see *Marriott v. Maltby Main Colliery Co.* (1920) 90 L.J.K.B. 349 and *Dixon v. Sutton Heath and Lea Green Colliery Ltd (No. 2)* (1930) 23 B.W.C.C. 135. It is doubtful whether injury due to an act, intentionally done in order to prevent an accident from happening or to minimise its consequences, would fall within an accident policy. In *Trew v. Railway Passengers Ass. Co.* (1861) 6 H. & N. 839, Cockburn C.J. asked (p. 842) whether death incurred when running into a burning house to save the life of a child would be covered by an accident policy. The court gave no answer to the question but it is difficult to see how it could be covered, unless the death arising from the rescue was proximately caused by the accidental occurrence of a fire. Usually a rescuer's decision to rescue is a new intervening cause.

[92] *Canadian Indemnity Co. v. Andrews & George Ltd* [1953] 1 S.C.R. 19.

negligently stowed a cargo of hydroelectric components on board the vessel *Lake Bosomtwe* at Halifax and as a result the cargo shifted after two days in normal weather at sea with considerable consequent damage. The Supreme Court of Canada held first that the "accident" for the purpose of the operative words of the policy was the shifting of the cargo not the negligence at the dockside in the stowing of the cargo and secondly that it followed that the event fell within the exception and insurers were therefore not liable.[93]

2. BODILY INJURY CAUSED BY VIOLENT, ACCIDENTAL, EXTERNAL AND VISIBLE MEANS

25–30 A common definition. Insurance companies have always experienced difficulty in defining the risk which they are prepared to undertake in an accident policy. In a sense every death or injury, unless intentionally inflicted by the assured himself, is accidental in that its time, manner and cause are unforeseen and unexpected, and insurers have sought to define the risk much more narrowly. For some time a common definition of the risk has been "bodily injury caused by violent, accidental, external and visible means" and in spite of or, perhaps, as a result of the unfavourable comments of Cozens-Hardy M.R. who said "it is open to doubt whether this does not exempt the company upon every occasion that is likely to occur",[94] the clause retains its popularity.[95]

25–31 Bodily injury. Bodily injury will usually be of an obvious kind, but it is not necessary that there should be any outward and visible sign of the injury.[96] Thus Bray J. was prepared to assume that dilatation of the heart amounted to bodily injury[97] and the fact that injury and death occur at the same moment will not prevent the clause from coming into operation.[98] If a knee is accidentally wrenched, that will be bodily injury within the clause.[99]

---

[93] *Pickford & Black Ltd v. Canadian General Ins. Co.* [1976] 2 Lloyd's Rep. 108. In the Court of Appeal of Nova Scotia it was pointed out that the policy in the earlier case would have given no effective cover at all unless the word "accident" applied to the original defect in the manufacture of the glue, see [1975] 1 Lloyd's Rep. 267, 272.

[94] *Re United London and Scottish Ins. Co., Brown's Claim* [1915] 2 Ch. 167, 170. In *Australian Casualty Co. v. Federico* (1986) 66 A.L.R. 99, 110, the court described the phrase as "notoriously obscure". Such a cover clause probably contravenes Reg. 6 of the Unfair Terms in Consumer Contracts Regulations 1999 (S.I. 1999 No. 2083) and might form the basis of a complaint to the Director General of Fair Trading under Reg. 8.

[95] A variant is "accidental bodily injury caused solely and directly by outward violence and visible means". Here the words after "directly by" serve to expound the accidental bodily injury—*De Souza v. Home & Overseas Ins. Co.* [1995] L.R.L.R. 453, 462.

[96] If two objects collide, they can both suffer an accident even though one or other of them is completely uninjured, *Captain Boyton's World's Water Show Syndicate Ltd v. Employers' Liability Ass. Corporation Ltd* (1895) 11 T.L.R. 384.

[97] *Re Scarr and General Accident Ass. Cpn.* [1905] 1 K.B. 387. Likewise Fisher J. was prepared to assume that a coronary thrombosis was bodily injury in *Jason v. Batten (1930) Ltd.* [1969] 1 Lloyd's Rep. 281.

[98] *Trew v. Railway Passengers Assurance Co.* (1861) 5 H. & N. 839, 844, *per* Cockburn C.J. Internal injuries caused by excessive consumption of alcohol leading to asphyxiation were held to constitute "bodily injury" in *Dhak v. Ins. Co. of N. America (U.K.) Ltd.* [1996] 1 Lloyd's Rep. 632, 637, and in *Connolly v. New Hampshire Ins. Co.* 1997 SLT (0) 1341, post traumatic stress disorder was held to constitute "bodily injury".

[99] *Hamlyn v. Crown Accidental Ins. Co.* [1893] 1 Q.B. 750; *cf. Burridge & Son v. Haines* (1918) 87 L.J.K.B. 641 (pressure on windpipe but no external injury).

Accidentally inhaling poisonous fumes is not bodily injury as such,[1] but may in due course give rise to bodily injury.[2] Disease may itself amount to bodily injury if it has been caused by accident.[3]

25–32 Violent means. Often the element of violence in an accident will be as evident as the bodily injury; the insured may, for example, be bitten by a dog[4] or knocked down by a train[5] or merely slip and fall.[6] In other cases it will not be so obvious and it has been held that the phrase violent means is the antithesis of without any violence at all.[7] Thus injury from any extra exertion such as stooping to pick up a marble may be injury by violent means[8] and the phrase seems to include almost any external cause of injury such as drowning[9] or the inhalation of gas.[10]

25–33 Accidental means. The phrase "injury by accidental means" has given rise to difficulties in jurisdictions outside England. If interpreted strictly it is to be contrasted with a phrase such as "accidental injury" because it focuses upon the means by which the resultant injury is achieved and not upon the resultant injury itself. Whereas many injuries are accidental in the sense that the assured neither expected nor intended them to occur, many such injuries would not be caused by accidental means. The cases start with the Scottish decision of *Clidero v. Scottish Accident Insurance Company.*[11] The assured, a stout man, got out of bed in the usual way one morning and bent over to put on his stockings. While doing so his colon slipped and became distended, putting such pressure on his heart that he died within a few days. The Court of Session held unanimously that the bodily injury was not caused by accidental means because his conduct was entirely intentional. Although the result of his activities may have been accidental, the means by which it was achieved was not accidental.[12] This decision was followed by the Court of Appeal of New Zealand in *Long v. Colonial Mutual Life Assurance Society.*[13] The assured threw a tennis ball and sprained his shoulder. He was a

[1] *Milashenko v. Co-operative Fire and Casualty Co.* (1968) 1 D.L.R. 3d 89.
[2] See *Re United London and Scottish Ins. Co., Brown's Claim* [1915] 2 Ch. 167, where it seems to have been assumed that the insurance company would have been liable in the absence of the relevant exceptions clause.
[3] *Fitton v. Accidental Death Ins. Co.* (1864) 17 C.B.(N.S.) 122 (hernia); *Mardorf v. Accident Ins. Co.* [1903] 1 K.B. 584 and *Accident Ins. Co. of North America v. Young* (1891) 20 S.C.R. 280 (erysipelas); *Re Etherington and Lancashire and Yorkshire Accident Ins. Co.* [1909] 1 K.B. 591.
[4] *Mardorf v. Accident Ins. Co.* [1903] 1 K.B. 584, 588, *per* Wright J.
[5] *Lawrence v. Accidental Ins. Co.* (1881) 7 Q.B.D. 216.
[6] *Hooper v. Accidental Death Ins. Co.* (1860) 5 H. & N. 546.
[7] *Hamlyn v. Crown Accidental Ins. Co.* [1893] 1 Q.B. 750, 753, *per* Lord Esher M.R.
[8] ibid. *Re Scarr and General Accident Ass. Corporation* [1905] 1 K.B. 387, 393, *per* Bray J.; *De Souza v. Home & Overseas Ins. Co.* [1995] L.R.L.R. 453, 462.
[9] *Trew v. Railway Passengers' Assurance Co.* (1861) 6 H. & N. 839; *Reynolds v. Accidental Insurance Co.* (1870) 22 L.T. 820.
[10] *Re United London and Scottish Ins. Co., Brown's Claim* [1915] 2 Ch. 167 (where the actual decision turned on the meaning of the exception clause). See also *Henley v. Mutual Accident Association,* 133 Ill. 556 (1890) and *Mutual Accident Association of the Northwest v. Tuggle,* 39 Ill.App. 509 (1891) where it was held that death by poison acting on the intestines was death by violent means; *Paul v. Travelers' Ins. Co.,* 112 N.Y. 472 (1889) (arresting of the action of the lungs so that suffocation resulted held to be "violent means").
[11] (1892) 19R. 355.
[12] See at p. 362, *per* Lord Adam.
[13] [1931] N.Z.L.R. 528. Contrast *Claxton v. Travelers' Ins. Co.* (1917) 52 Que. R. (S.C.) 239, where the assured recovered for a rupture done while playing golf.

man "in his prime", in perfect health and accustomed to playing games. In the absence of any involuntary or unintended movement by the assured the injury, however unexpected, was not caused by accidental means. In *Landress v. Phoenix Insurance Company*[14] the United States Supreme Court held that death by sunstroke was not death by accidental means because the means by which death resulted were not accidental in that the assured intended to do everything which he did, namely, to play golf in the August sun. The distinction between accidental results and accidental means was followed in other jurisdictions.[15]

25-34 In *Landress* Cardozo J. delivered a powerful dissent in which he said that there was no distinction between "accidental injury" and "injury by accidental means", and predicted that, "The attempted distinction between accidental results and accidental means will plunge this branch of the law into a Serbonian bog."[16]

Whether English law has avoided this misfortune depends upon the correct interpretation to be placed on the "puzzling"[17] and "delphic"[18] decision in *Hamlyn v. Crown Accidental Insurance Company*.[19] The assured was a grocer. A child dropped a marble on the floor of his shop. The floor sloped and the marble began to roll away. The assured stooped and made a grab for the marble. In so doing he wrenched his knee, dislocating a cartilage in the knee joint. The Court of Appeal held that this constituted "bodily injury caused by accidental external and visible means", rejecting the argument that it was merely the result of his deliberate movement. One interpretation[20] of the decision was that, in grabbing at the marble, the assured involuntarily got into an awkward position in which he wrenched his knee, so that the injury was the result of an un-natural movement, and therefore came within the definition of accidental means laid down in *Clidero v. Scottish Accident Insurance Company*.[21] An alternative interpretation favoured by a number of English textbook writers[22] was that the Court of Appeal had given a liberal interpretation to the policy, deciding that an

---

[14] 219 U.S. 491 (1933), reaffirming the earlier Supreme Court decision in *U.S. Mutual Accident Association v. Barry* 131 U.S. 100 (1889). English law has reached the same conclusion by deciding that sunstroke is an illness resulting from natural causes and so not the result of accident unless the exposure to the sun was involuntary—*Sinclair v. Maritime Passengers' Ass. Co.* (1861) 3 E. & E. 478 ("injury by accident") and *De Souza v. Home & Overseas Ins. Co.* [1995] L.R.L.R. 453, 460, 463 ("bodily accidental injury").

[15] Canada: *Candler v. London etc. Accident Co. of Canada* (1963) 40 D.L.R. 2d 408; *Smith v. British Pacific Life Ins. Co.* (1964) 45 D.L.R. 2d 91; (1965) 51 D.L.R. 2d 1; *Leontowicz v. Seaboard Life Ins. Co.* (1985) 16 D.L.R. 4th 95; *Aguilar v. London Life Ins. Co.* (1990) 70 D.L.R. 4th 510. Australia: *Steinke v. Australia Provident Ass. Association* [1944] Q.S.R. 7; *Dennis v. City Mutual Life Ass. Society* [1979] V.R. 75; *National & General Ins. Co. v. Chick* [1984] 2 N.S.W.L.R. 86.

[16] 219 U.S. 491, 499–500.

[17] *De Souza v. Home & Overseas Ins. Co.* [1995] L.R.L.R. 453, 461, *per* Mustill L.J.

[18] *Australian Casualty Co. v. Federico* (1986) 66 A.L.R. 99, 102, *per* Gibbs C.J.

[19] [1893] 1 Q.B. 750.

[20] *In re Scarr and General Accident Ass. Corp.* [1905] 1 K.B. 387, 393–394, *per* Bray J; *Long v. Colonial Mutual Life Ass. Society* [1931] N.Z.L.R. 528, 541, *per* Kennedy J., *National & General Ins. Co. v. Chick* [1984] 2 N.S.W.L.R. 86, 102 *per*, Samuels J.A. The judgment of A.L. Smith L.J. affords most support to this interpretation [1893] 1 Q.B. 750, 755.

[21] (1892) I.G.R. 355.

[22] MacGillivray, 8th ed. paras 1792–1794; Halsbury's Laws (4th ed. Reissue) Vol. 25, para. 576; Colinvaux's *Law of Insurance* (4th ed.) para. 17–16; Clarke, *Law of Insurance Contracts* (2nd ed., 1994), para. 17–5FI. The judgment of Lopes L.J. gives most support to this interpretation—see [1893] 1 Q.B. 750, 754.

injury which was the fortuitous and unexpected consequence of a deliberate movement was nonetheless caused by accidental means.

It was submitted in three previous editions of this book[23] that this was the better interpretation of the decision, because injuries which were the fortuitous and unexpected result of a natural cause should not be excluded from the ambit of a personal accident policy, and because the distinction between accidental means and accidental results was very difficult to apply in individual cases such as death by drowning or injury by unprovoked assault. In recent years the tide of judicial opinion in the United States has been turning in favour of the dissenting view of Cardozo J. to equate "injury by accidental means" with "accidental injury".[24] Courts in Scotland,[25] New Zealand,[26] Australia,[27] and Canada[28] also expressed dissatisfaction with the distinction between "accidental results" and "accidental means".

25–35 Two recent decision of the Court of Appeal in England, however, have established the distinction in English law. In *De Souza v. Home & Overseas Insurance Company*[29] the Court had to construe the words "accidental bodily injury", and Mustill L.J. cited with approval the decisions in *Re Scarr and The General Accident Assurance Corporation*[30] and *Long v. Colonial Mutual Life Assurance Society*[31] in which *Hamlyn v. Crown Accident Insurance Company*[32] had been interpreted as one of involuntary conduct on the part of the assured, consistent with the distinction between accidental results and accidental means. In the subsequent case of *Dhak v. Insurance Company of North America (U.K.) Ltd*[33] the Court of Appeal followed this analysis of the authorities in a case where the policy covered "bodily injury caused by accidental means". The assured had died from asphyxiation from inhaling her own vomit due to drinking alcohol to excess.

---

[23] See 8th ed., para. 1794.

[24] The trend was charted recently by the federal court of appeals for the 1st Circuit in *Wickman v. Northwestern Ins. Co.* 908 F. 2d 1077 (1990) at p. 1086. The court rejected the distinction between "accidental death" and "death by accidental means". In *Beckham v. Travelers' Ins. Co.* 225 A. 2d. 529 (Sup. Ct. Pa. 1967) the Supreme Court of Pennsylvania regretted that the prediction of Cardozo J. had come to pass, as did the Supreme Court of Texas in *Republic National Life Ins. Co. v. Heymans* 536 S.W. 2d 549 (Sup. Ct. Tex. 1976). The division of opinion in state courts was earlier summarised in para. 1640 of the 5th edition of this book. An Australian court has wittily observed that "there are American decisions which, seeking to skirt the bog, mire themselves nonetheless, but in the quicksands of judicial legislation"— *National & General Ins. Co. v. Chick* [1984] 2 N.S.W.L.R. 86, 102, *per* Samuels J.A.

[25] *Glenlight Shipping Ltd v. Excess Ins. Co.* 1983 S.L.T. 241, in which Lord Stott said at p. 245 that there was no substance in the distinction between "accidental injury" and "injury occasioned by accidental means", followed in *MacLeod v. New Hampshire Ins. Co.* 1998 S.L.T. 1191; *Connolly v. New Hampshire Ins. Co.* 1997 S.L.T. (O) 1341.

[26] *Groves v. A.M.P. Fire & General Ins. Co. (N.Z.) Ltd* [1990] 1 N.Z.L.R. 122, refusing to follow the *Clidero Case*.

[27] *Australian Casualty Co. v. Federico* (1986) 66 A.L.R. 99, 112, *per* Wilson, Deane and Dawson J.J., expressing disagreement with the reasoning in *Clidero*.

[28] *C.N.A. Ass. Co. v. MacIsaac* (1979) 102 D.L.R. 3d 160; *Voison v. Royal Ins. Co. of Canada* (1989) 53 D.L.R. 4th 299, 304, approving the view that "injury by accidental means" included the unexpected result of voluntary actions; *Tracy-Gould v. Maritime Life Ins. Co.* (1992) 89 D.L.R. 4th 726.

[29] [1995] L.R.L.R. 453, 461–462.

[30] [1905] 1 K.B. 387.

[31] [1931] N.Z.L.R. 528.

[32] [1893] 1 Q.B. 750. The conclusion drawn from the authorities was that an unexpected injury which naturally resulted from an ordinary, voluntary movement could not be described as an injury either caused by accident or by accidental means.

[33] [1996] 1 Lloyd's Rep. 632. See para. 25–4, *ante*.

One reason for denying recovery was that she must have realised the danger inherent in what she was doing.[34] The Court also expressly stated that English law recognises the distinction between accidental means and accidental results, and that it was accordingly necessary to show bodily injury was proximately caused by an accident. Since the assured had intended to drink as she did, she failed on that ground also.[35] The decision of the Court of Appeal to apply a stricter definition of "injury caused by accidental means" could be supported on the ground that personal accident insurance has hitherto been a "cheap and useful product"[36], but would not remain so for very long if it was allowed to become a form of personal health insurance, a traditionally higher risk and more expensive cover. It is now open only to the House of Lords to place a more liberal interpretation upon *Hamlyn v. Crown Accident Insurance Company.*[37]

25–36 External and Visible Means. The word "external" is meant to express anything which is not internal[38] and refers to the cause of the injury not the injury itself. Thus, an insured who stoops to pick up a marble and wrenches his knee is injured by external means.[39] And so is someone who suffers death by drowning.[40] The contrast is with disorders that arise within the body such as senility or certain types of disease. Some diseases can, of course, be brought into existence by external causes [41] and injury caused by such diseases will be injury caused by external means. Many accidents are only fatal because they result in a failure of the heart; this will seldom be due to a cause which only operates internally and even injury as a result of taking poison would be injury caused by external means. Policies on property may likewise require that damage be caused by external accidental means if it is to be recoverable. In this context it has been held that a vessel damaged in adverse seas is damaged by external accidental means,[42] whereas damage to a crane, which collapses due the absence of a particular kind of retaining bolt, is not damage from any accidental extraneous cause.[43]

"Visible means" does not add anything to the phrase "external means" since it has been held that any cause which is external must be visible.[44]

---

[34] [1996] 1 Lloyd's Rep. 632, 641.

[35] At pp. 640–641.

[36] Clarke, *Law of Insurance Contracts* (2nd ed, 1994) para. 17–5F2.

[37] [1893] 1 Q.B. 750.

[38] *Hamlyn v. Crown Accidental Ins. Co.* [1893] 1 Q.B. 750, 753, *per* Lord Esher M.R., 754, *per* Lopes L.J. and 755, *per* A. L. Smith L.J., followed in *North-West Commercial Travellers' Association v. London Guarantee and Accident Co.* (1895) 10 Man.R. 537; *De Souza v. Home & Overseas Ins. Co.* [1995] L.R.L.R. 453, 462; *cf. Burridge & Son v. Haines & Sons Ltd* (1918) 87 L.J.K.B. 641.

[39] *Hamlyn v. Crown Accidental Ins. Co.* [1893] 1 Q.B. 750. See also *MacLeod v. New Hampshire Ins. Co.* 1998 S.L.T. 1191 (backstrain caused by lifting truck wheel).

[40] *Trew v. Railway Passengers' Ass. Co.* (1861) 6 H. & N. 839; *Winspear v. Accident Ins. Co.* (1880) 6 Q.B.D. 42.

[41] See para. 25–14, *ante.*

[42] *Miss Jay Jay* [1987] 1 Lloyd's Rep. 32. "External" was said to be merely the antithesis of "internal", *per* Dillon L.J. at p. 39.

[43] *Linden Alimak v. British Engine Ins. Ltd* [1984] 1 Lloyd's Rep. 416, 423–5.

[44] *Hamlyn v. Crown Accidental Ins. Co.* [1893] 1 Q.B. 750, 753, *per* Lord Esher M.R., 754, *per* Lopes L.J.; *Burridge & Son v. Haines & Sons Ltd* (1918) 87 L.J.K.B. 641.

3. Causation

25–37 General principles. As in other branches of insurance law the assured must show that his injury was proximately caused by the operation of a peril insured against. The reader is referred to the general discussion of proximate cause[45] but policies of accident insurance give rise to peculiar problems which must be discussed in greater detail. For example, it has already been pointed out that policies with an express exception for disease are liable to give rise to difficulty either because the accident relied on was caused or contributed to by a disease or because a disease was caused or contributed to by an accident.[46] Where a disease of the assured actually causes the accident, it is held that the injury or death is proximately caused by the accident, not the disease so that the exceptions clause does not operate and the insurer is liable. Thus an assured who has an epileptic fit and is drowned by falling into a stream[47] or hit by a train as a result of falling onto the railway line[48] can recover in spite of an express exception for disease. The converse case has given rise to greater difficulty. In *Fitton v. Accidental Death Insurance Co.*[49] the accident gave rise to hernia in the assured; there was an exception for "hernia ... or any other disease or cause arising within the system of the insured" but it was held that the hernia was caused by (and arose at the same time as) the accident and did not therefore come within the exception since the accident not the hernia was the proximate cause of death. This case was distinguished in *Smith v. Accident Insurance Co.*[50] where erysipelas caused by an accident was held to fall within the exception:

> "erysipelas or any other disease or secondary cause or causes arising within the system of the assured before or at the time of or following such accidental injury (whether causing such death directly or jointly with such accidental injury)".

The first ground of distinction was that erysipelas caused by the accident came within the phrase "secondary cause",[51] while a second distinction was that the erysipelas was a later development, and, unlike the hernia in *Fitton's* case, did not arise instantaneously with the accident. The second ground of distinction seems to indicate that while death by hernia was proximately caused by the accident in *Fitton's* case, the death by erysipelas was not proximately caused by the accident in *Smith's* case; no doubt cases can arise

---

[45] See paras 19–01, *et seq.*, *supra.*

[46] See para. 25–17, *supra.*

[47] *Winspear v. Accident Ins. Co.* (1880) 6 Q.B.D. 42; the position would be different if there were an intervening cause between the accident and death, see *Wadsworth v. Canadian Railway Accident Ins. Co.* (1912) 26 O.L.R. 55.

[48] *Lawrence v. Accidental Ins. Co.* (1881) 7 Q.B.D. 216.

[49] (1864) 17 C.B.(N.S.) 122.

[50] (1870) L.R. 5 Ex 302. This case has been adversely criticised by Welford, *Accident Insurance* (2nd ed.), p. 289, note (i) and the second ground of decision is certainly open to criticism in that it is out of line with the thinking behind the doctrine of proximate cause, see in particular *Re Etherington and the Lancashire and Yorkshire Accident Ins. Co.* [1909] 1 K.B. 591 (see para. 25–40, *infra*). The case can, however, be supported on the ground that the right meaning was attached to the words "secondary cause", which have the same effect as an exception for disability or death "caused directly or indirectly by disease", see *Manufacturers' Accident Indemnity Co. v. Dorgan,* 58 Fed.Rep. 945, 955 (1893).

[51] The meaning of this term is not altogether clear, but it would seem to have the result that although the accident be the proximate cause, disease being a contributory cause will bring the exception into operation. See, further, para. 25–46, *post.*

in which death by erysipelas would be proximately caused by accident and such a case would fall outside an ordinary exception for disease.[52]

25–38 Where there are two proximate causes of the injury and one (*e.g.* disease) is an excepted peril, the insurer will be under no liability since the exceptions clause will apply.[53] But in ascertaining the proximate cause of injury or death in such cases, a distinction should probably be drawn between cases where injury or death was caused by the disease and cases where the disease merely aggravates the consequences of an injury caused by some other agency. In the first case the insurer will not be liable if disease is an excepted cause, while in the second case he will be liable.[54] Moreover, disease will not be a proximate cause of disability or death if it merely weakens the system of the insured so that he becomes more vulnerable to accident,[55] but if the accident aggravates an already existing disease the resulting disability or death has been held to have been caused by disease.[56]

25–39 Death from the effects of injury caused by accident. In *Isitt v. Railway Passengers Assurance Co.*[57] the policy insured against death from the effects of injury caused by accident. The insured fell and dislocated his shoulder and was put to bed. The accident had rendered him susceptible to colds and, having caught a cold, he died from pneumonia a month after the accident. It was held that the insured had suffered death from the effects of the injury. It was not necessary that the death itself should be immediately caused by the injury but only that the injury should be immediately caused by the accident and that the death should be the natural consequence of the injury. Thus the doctrine of proximate cause does not apply in its strictest sense to a phrase such as "death from the effects of injury caused by accident".

25–40 Direct or proximate cause. It is often specifically stated that the accident must be a direct or proximate cause of death or injury in order to give rise to liability. Even if these words are not used, this is the normal construction of the word "cause" unless there are express terms to a different effect. There is no difference in meaning between the word "direct" and the word "proximate"[58]; the word "indirect" will, however,

---

[52] See *Accident Ins. Co. of North America v. Young*, 20 S.C.R. 280 (1892); and compare *Bacon v. United States Mutual Accident Association*, 123 N.Y. 304 (1890) with *Bailey v. Interstate Casualty Co. of New York*, 8 App.Div. 127 (1896). In *Martin v. Manufacturers' Accident Indemnity Co.*, 151 N.Y. 94 (1896) it was held that death by blood poisoning where the poison is communicated at the same time as the injury is inflicted is death proximately caused by accident not by disease.

[53] *Cawley v. National Employers' Accident and General Ass. Association* (1885) 1 Cab. & El. 597; *Jason v. Batten (1930) Ltd* [1969] 1 Lloyd's Rep. 281; *National Masonic Accident Association v. Shryock*, 73 Fed.Rep. 774 (1896).

[54] *cf. Prudential Ins. Co. of America v. Kellar*, 98 S.E. 2d 90 (1957).

[55] *Thornton v. Travelers' Ins. Co.*, 94 Am.S.R. 99, 106–107 (1902).

[56] *Freeman v. Mercantile Mutual Accident Association*, 156 Mass. 351 (1892); *cf. McKechnie's Trustees v. Scottish Accident Ins. Co.* (1893) 17 R. 6, 9, *per* the Lord Ordinary and *Travelers' Ins. Co. v. Selden*, 78 Fed.Rep. 285 (1897).

[57] (1889) 22 Q.B.D. 504.

[58] *Fitton v. Accidental Death Ins. Co.* (1864) 17 C.B.(N.S.) 122; *Lawrence v. Accidental Ins. Co.* (1881) 7 Q.B.D. 216; *Mardorf v. Accident Ins. Co.* [1903] 1 K.B. 584; *Re Etherington and the Lancashire and Yorkshire Accident Ins. Co.* [1909] 1 K.B. 591, especially at p. 602, *per* Kennedy L.J.

indicate that the doctrine of proximate cause is not to apply.[59] In *Re Etherington and Lancashire and Yorkshire Accident Insurance Co.*[60] the policy insured against bodily injury caused by violent, accidental, external and visible means and provided that the policy would operate "where the accident is the direct or proximate cause of death, not where the direct or proximate cause is disease or other intervening cause". The insured fell from his horse and became wet to the skin with a subsequent lowering of vitality. He had to ride home in his wet clothes and as a result of the lowering of his vitality caught pneumonia and died. It was held that the death was directly caused by the accident and that if an accident is followed by natural results, the whole train of events is a proximate cause of the death.[61]

25–41 Sole cause. It is sometimes provided that the accident must be the sole cause of the injury or death; this probably adds nothing to the implied requirement that the accident must be the proximate cause, except in a case where there are two proximate causes.[62] The first inquiry is to discover the proximate cause of the injury or death; once it is found, it will also be the sole cause, regardless of subsequent events that may have hastened the death or aggravated the injury, unless there is another proximate cause. Thus in *Mardorf v. Accident Insurance Co.*[63] the policy provided that accidental injury had to be the "direct and sole" cause of death.[64] The insured accidentally wounded his leg with his thumb nail. This caused inflammation which in turn gave rise to erysipelas, septicaemia, septic pneumonia and finally death. It was held that none of the medical conditions so identified was an intervening cause but they were merely different stages in the development of the septic condition brought about by the wound. Similarly in *Smith v. Cornhill Insurance Co. Ltd*[65] the policy provided that the policy moneys would be payable "on death occurring as a result solely of bodily injury caused by violent, accidental, external and visible means, sustained by the insured whilst riding in … the insured car". The insured had an accident while in the car, became concussed, wandered for some distance and made her way into a river where she died not by drowning but as a result of shock sustained by coming into contact with the water. Atkinson J. held that each event which occurred after the crash was due to brain injury resulting from the accident and that the true proximate cause of the death was the accident

---

[59] *Jason v. Batten (1930) Ltd.* [1969] 1 Lloyd's Rep. 281; *cf. Coxe v. Employers' Liability Ass. Corporation* [1916] 2 K.B. 629 and para. 19–4, *ante*.

[60] [1909] 1 K.B. 591. In so far as *Smith v. Accident Ins. Co.* (1870) L.R. 5 Ex. 302 (which was not cited to the Court of Appeal in this case) is inconsistent with this decision (see para. 25–36, *ante*) the reasoning of the earlier case about proximate cause should be treated with considerable caution.

[61] *cf. McCarthy v. Travelers' Ins. Co.*, 8 Biss. 362, 366–367 (1878).

[62] See para. 19–5, *ante* as to the controversy whether a peril can have more than one proximate cause.

[63] [1903] 1 K.B. 584; *cf. Fitton v. Accidental Death Ins. Co.* (1864) 17 C.B.(N.S.) 122; *Lawrence v. Accidental Ins. Co.* (1881) 7 Q.B.D. 216.

[64] See the similar provision in *Lawrence v. Accidental Ins. Co.* (1881) 7 Q.B.D. 216, and in *Marks v. Commercial Travelers' Mutual Accident Association* [1956] 4 D.L.R. 2d 113 where the insured fractured his femur by falling on ice, contracted peritonitis and then pneumonia. His death was held to be within the policy.

[65] [1938] 3 All E.R. 145. In an exceptions clause the word "solely" has been held to mean "without the intervention of any peril", see *Miss Jay Jay* [1985] 1 Lloyd's Rep. 264, 273, *per* Mustill J., affirmed [1987] 1 Lloyd's Rep. 32.

not the contact of the insured with the cold water. The chain of causation is operative until there is an intervening cause.

25–42 Immediate cause. Sometimes a policy provides that the accident is to be the "immediate cause" of the injury; this is usually construed as equivalent to proximate and not as an adjective of time, and it has been held that a gap of three months between accident and death will not prevent an insured from recovering under a policy with such a provision.[66] On this construction of the word "immediate" an accidental injury might be the immediate cause of disability occurring years afterwards, and the policy may therefore provide that there shall be no recovery unless disability supervenes within a specified time after the accidental injury.[67] For the same reason the right to compensation may be limited to cases where the disability is continuous.[68]

25–43 Intervening cause. Whether the accident has to be the direct, proximate, or sole cause of the injury or death, it is clear that only an intervening cause will suffice to break the chain of causation and exempt the insurer from liability. Thus if the insured has received an accidental injury to his leg and is later run over by a bus and killed because he had difficulty in getting out of the way, the death is the result of an intervening cause and is not due to the accidental injury to his leg.[69] The policy in *Re Etherington*[70] provided that the insurance was only operative "where the accident is the direct or proximate cause of death, not where the direct or proximate cause is disease or other intervening cause, even although the disease or other intervening cause may itself have been aggravated by such accident or have been due to weakness or exhaustion consequent thereon, or the death accelerated thereby". It was argued that the pneumonia caught by the assured was a "disease or other intervening cause" but the Court of Appeal said that those words referred to something new and independent of the accident not a new cause which was dependent on the accident; anything which was a mere "sequela" of the accident could not be an intervening cause.[71] It was further argued that since the vitality of the assured had been lessened, the pneumonia was due to a weakness consequent on the accident, and that therefore the exception applied; but it was held that the exception only applied where there was a completely new and independent cause and that it was intended to cover cases where the assured was weakened by the accident and, by reason of that weakness, was attacked by a disease or other intervening cause wholly unconnected with the accident.[72] If the clause were to mean that whenever death resulted from a cold which was due to weakness caused by the accident, the insurers would be liable only in cases of sudden death, this cannot have been contemplated by the policy.

[66] *Shera v. Ocean Accident and Guarantee Corpn Ltd* (1900) 32 Ont.R. 411; *Claxton v. Travelers' Ins. Co. of Hartford* (1917) 52 Que.R. (S.C.) 239; *cf. Jason v. Batten (1930) Ltd* [1969] 1 Lloyd's Rep. 281 (6 days), *Hagadorn v. Masonic Equitable Accident Association*, 69 N.Y.S. 831 (1901) and *Brendon v. Traders' and Travelers' Accident Co. of New York*, 69 N.Y. 831 (1903).
[67] *Trew v. Railway Passengers Ass. Co.* (1861) 6 H. & N. 839.
[68] *Shera v. Ocean Accident* (1900) 32 Ont.R. 411.
[69] *Isitt v. Railway Passengers' Ass. Co.* (1889) 22 Q.B.D. 504, 512.
[70] [1909] 1 K.B. 591, see para. 25–40, *ante*.
[71] At p. 598, *per* Vaughan Williams L.J. and pp. 602–603, *per* Kennedy L.J.; *cf. Smith v. Cornhill Ins. Co.* [1938] 3 All E.R. 145, 153, *per* Atkinson J.
[72] At p. 600, *per* Vaughan Williams L.J. and at p. 603, *per* Kennedy L.J.

25–44 Independently and exclusively of all other causes. Insurers who have been disturbed to find that the courts have given a wide meaning to the words "sole cause" and a narrow meaning to the words "intervening cause" have sought other words with which to limit the risk which they are prepared to undertake. One such phrase which is narrower than the words "sole cause" is that which requires the death or injury to result from an accident "independently and exclusively of all other causes". Thus the policy in *Fidelity and Casualty Company of New York v. Mitchell*[73] covered bodily injury sustained through accidental means and resulting "directly independently and exclusively of all other causes" in total disablement from performing the duties of the assured's occupation. The assured had once had a tubercular infection of the left lung and there was therefore a form of latent tuberculosis in his system. He accidentally sprained his wrist and in the normal course of events would have recovered fairly quickly, but the injury caused the tuberculosis to revive and the insured became disabled. The Judicial Committee of the Privy Council held that the disablement resulted directly, independently and exclusively of all other causes so that the assured could recover. They pointed out that the accident had two distinct effects in that it sprained the wrist and at the same time induced the tubercular condition. It is important to note that the tuberculosis would never have come into existence again but for the accident and that the case is therefore dissimilar to a case where a condition exists at the time of the accident and co-operates with the accident to bring about injury or death.

25–45 *Jason v. Batten (1930) Ltd*[74] was just such a case. The policy provided that the insurers would make payments in respect of any bodily injury sustained in any accident "resulting in and being—independently of all other causes—the exclusive direct and immediate cause of the injury". It further provided that no benefit was payable for injury "directly or indirectly caused by or arising or resulting from or traceable to any physical defect or infirmity which existed prior to the accident". The assured, who suffered from arterial disease, had a car accident and six days later suffered a coronary thrombosis which incapacitated him for several weeks. The judge found that the stress associated with the accident precipitated the attack but the assured would in any event have had a coronary thrombosis within three years as a result of his diseased condition. He went on to hold that the accident was not the cause of the coronary thrombosis independently of all other causes because the arterial disease was a concurrent and co-operative cause. The distinction envisaged by the policy was between conditions in which the effect of the accident operated and co-operative causes. The arterial disease and the accident were examples of co-operative causes and the case thus differed from *Mitchell's* case[75] where the accident gave rise to the tubercular condition, which would not have come into existence at all if there had been no accident to induce it. A further ground of decision was that the events that had occurred were within the exception for injury caused

---

[73] [1917] A.C. 592; followed in *Morran v. Railway Passengers' Ass. Co.* (1918) 43 O.L.R. 561. *Cf. Candler v. London and Lancashire Guarantee and Accident Co. of Canada* (1963) 40 D.L.R. 2d 408 and *Wayne Tank and Pump Co. v. Employers Liability Ass. Corporation* [1974] Q.B. 57, 68.
[74] [1969] 1 Lloyd's Rep. 281.
[75] See note 73, *ante.*

directly or indirectly by physical defect or infirmity; just as the body of the policy defined the risk more narrowly than by the common law doctrine of proximate cause, so the exception was phrased in terminology wider than the doctrine of proximate cause and it was, therefore, unnecessary to decide whether the arterial disease or the accident was the proximate cause of the assured's incapacity.

25–46 Existing disease or infirmity contributing to injury or death. Cases in which a disease has caused an accident or an accident has caused a disease have already been discussed. There is, however, a third category of case which is particularly difficult and that is those cases in which an assured who is already suffering from a disease meets with an accident and both the disease and the accident contribute to the injury or death. Where the terms of the policy require the injury or death to be proximately caused by the accident, a court will have to decide whether the disease or the accident is the proximate cause. Thus in *Re Scarr and General Accident Assurance Corporation*[76] it was held that the cause of death was, at any rate in part, the defective condition of the assured's heart and the insurers were not liable under the policy, while in *Casey v. Continental Casualty Co.*[77] an assured with defective kidneys broke his leg and died of uraemia and it was held that the insurers were liable since the accident was the proximate cause of death. It may be impossible for a court to say more than that both the disease and the accident were the proximate cause of the death or injury; in such a case the assured should be able to recover[78] unless the policy specifies that the accident is to be the sole cause of the death or injury. If the policy states that the accident is to be the exclusive clause, independently of all other causes, then the mere fact that there is another contributing cause will preclude recovery.[79] There is so little English authority on this topic that it may be helpful to draw attention to some American cases.[80] Thus, the assured was entitled to recover where he had an accident handling a milk-can, causing fatal perforation of the duodenum which had been weakened by a dormant ulcer[81] and where glaucoma was exacerbated by accidental exposure to an electric arc, causing blindness[82] but he has not recovered where a pre-existing heart condition was exacerbated by a fall[83] or by over-exertion[84] resulting in death. It is difficult to find a rational basis on which to rest a

---

[76] [1905] 1 K.B. 387.

[77] [1933] 2 D.L.R. 46; revsd. on other grounds [1934] S.C.R. 54. *Cf. Claxton v. Travellers' Ins. Co. of Hartford* (1917) 52 Que.R. (S.C.) 239 where an assured with a predisposition to hernia ruptured himself while playing golf.

[78] See paras 25–37 and 25–41, *supra*. The principle stated in the text must be subject to any express exception in the policy, see *Cawley v. National Employers' Accident and General Ass. Association* (1885) 1 Cab. & El. 597.

[79] *Jason v. Batten (1930) Ltd* [1969] 1 Lloyd's Rep. 281, distinguished in *Robbins v. Travellers' Ins. Co.* (1978) 84 D.L.R. (3d.) 727 where the insured died from cardiac arrest induced by a car accident and his representatives were held entitled to recover even though his heart was previously diseased.

[80] See, generally, Appleman, *Insurance Law and Practice*, (1981), Vol. 2, para. 793.

[81] *Silverstein v. Metropolitan Life Ins. Co.*, 171 N.E. 914 (1930).

[82] *Emergency Aid Ins. Co. v. Dobbs*, 83 So. 2d 335 (1955). *Stokes v. Police and Firemen's Ins. Association*, 243 P. 2d 144 (1951) where a fireman, who was exposed to heat and smoke when he had a pre-existing cardiac sclerosis both of which caused death, was held able to recover was not followed by Fisher J. in *Jason v. Batten (1930) Ltd* [1969] 1 Lloyd's Rep. 281.

[83] *National Masonic Accident Ins. Co. v. Shryock*, 73 Fed.Rep. 774 (1896).

[84] *Scharmer v. Accidental Life Ins. Co.*, 84 N.W. 2d 866 (1957) followed in *Jason v. Batten (1930) Ltd* [1969] 1 Lloyd's Rep. 281.

decision in this type of case but one that has found some favour is that suggested in *Penn v. Standard Life Insurance Co.*[85]:

(1) If at the time of the accident the assured is suffering from disease, but the disease has no causal connection with the injury or death, the accident is the sole cause;
(2) If at the time of the accident there is an existing disease which co-operating with the accident resulted in injury or death, the accident is not the sole or independent cause.[86]

4. PARTICULAR CLAUSES

(a) *Clauses Defining Total or Partial Disability*

25–47 Total incapacity for business. These clauses must receive a reasonable construction in relation to their object. If the insurance is limited to accidents wholly disabling the insured from following his usual business or occupation, full effect must be given to the word "usual". Thus a solicitor who sprains his ankle and is confined to his bedroom for a period of time is incapable of following his usual occupation, business or pursuits even if he can and does conduct some business from his bed.[87] If a man cannot follow his usual business and pursuits he is, as Pollock C.B. points out, wholly disabled from following them. His usual pursuit is not to do a little, but embraces the whole scope and compass of his mode of obtaining a livelihood.[88] Similarly, if an ear, nose and throat specialist sprains his wrist he is totally disabled from performing the duties of his occupation.[89] In *Williams v. Lloyd's Underwriters*[90] a steel worker was insured against permanent total disability which was defined as

> "the inability to resume his normal calling or occupation of any kind within 12 months from the date of receiving the injury, and at the end of the 12 months being so permanently or incurably incapacitated as to render it impossible for him to resume any such calling or occupation."

After an accidental injury he was no longer capable of being employed as a steel worker and could only do the duties of a night watchman. It was held that he could not resume his normal calling, nor could he "resume …

---

[85] 76 S.E. 262 (1912). This statement, as far as it goes, was accepted by the Supreme Court of Canada as correctly stating the law of New York in *Marks v. Commercial Travelers' Mutual Accident Association* [1956] 4 D.L.R. 2d 113 and was also accepted by Fisher J. in *Jason v. Batten (1930) Ltd* [1969] 1 Lloyd's Rep. 281.

[86] The word "sole" must be treated with some caution as English cases have given a wide meaning to the word, see para. 25–41, *ante*.

[87] *Hooper v. Accidental Death Ins. Co.* (1860) 5 H. & N. 546.

[88] At p. 556; thus a dancing master who sprains his ankle would be wholly disabled within the meaning of the policy (at p. 556 *per* Pollock C.B.) while in similar circumstances a teacher of mathematics might not be (at p. 558 *per* Wightman J.). *cf. Tucker v. South British Ins. Co.* [1916] N.Z.L.R. 1142 where the policy covered inability to pursue the insured's ordinary occupation or to attend any business affairs and it was held that compensation was payable for the whole period of his inability to pursue his ordinary occupation, although he was only unable to attend to business completely for part of that period.

[89] *Fidelity and Casualty Co. of New York v. Mitchell* [1917] A.C. 592.

[90] [1957] 1 Lloyd's Rep. 118.

occupation of any kind" because the use of the word "resume" implied a taking up of his former employment or one that was substantially similar to it. He was therefore able to recover under the policy.

25–48 The policy may provide that payment is to be made if the insured is wholly disabled from engaging in or giving attention to his business or occupation.[91] It has been suggested, *obiter*, that in such a case no compensation can be given if the insured is able to do any part of his business[92] but it is not clear that this view is now consistent with the reasonable construction of such clauses supported by the later authorities cited in the preceding and succeeding paragraphs.

25–49 Incapacity for any kind of business. Clauses which make the payment of benefit dependent upon the assured being unfit for any kind of work are apt to be construed in favour of the assured. In *Pocock v. Century Insurance Co. Ltd.*[93] the policy required the assured to be totally disabled "from attending to business of each and every kind". He was a wholesale grocer, and the test applied by the court was whether he was fit to attend to business and play a worthwhile role in the conduct of his own or some substitute business to which he might turn. The fact that he could perform some unimportant part of the business rather badly, or do some utterly insignificant job which was unworthy of him, did not mean that he was fit to attend to business or was not totally disabled.[94] In *Sargent v. GRE(UK) Ltd.*[95] the policy paid a benefit of £10,000 in the event of "permanent total disablement from attending to any occupation". The insurers contended that this meant disablement from attending to any occupation at all, while the assured understood it to mean an inability to follow the occupation he was in at the time of the accident which disabled him. The court held for the assured on two grounds. First, separate benefits were payable under the policy in different circumstances when the assured could not follow his own or any alternative occupation, and the insurers could have used that formulation if they wanted to make the clause mean what they said it did. Secondly, the wording in question was ambiguous and the *contra proferentem* rule of construction required it to be interpreted in favour of the assured.[96]

Where the payment of benefits is dependent on the inability of the assured as the result of an accident or sickness either to perform the occupation in which he was engaged at the time or, as the case may be, to carry on any gainful occupation whatsoever, the test of entitlement to be applied is objective. In *Haghiran v. Allied Dunbar Insurance*[97] the assured suffered serious spinal injury which in turn produced a pain syndrome aggravating his physical state. In addition he genuinely believed himself to be far more disabled than in fact he was, so that he could not in his view be expected to work. The Court of Appeal held that the pain syndrome was rightly to be

---

[91] *Fidelity and Casualty Co. of New York v. Mitchell* [1917] A.C. 592.

[92] *Hooper v. Accidental Death Ins. Co.* (1860) 5 H. & N. 546, 554, *per* Wilde B., 555, *per* Pollock C.B.

[93] [1960] 2 Lloyd's Rep. 150.

[94] *Aliter* if he could make a substantial contribution to it, or carry on some other substantial business—*Neill v. Order of United Friends* 149 N.E. 430 (1896).

[95] [2000] Lloyd's Rep. I.R. 77.

[96] *Per* Leggatt L.J. at p. 79.

[97] [2001] 1 All E.R. (Comm.) 97.

taken into account in determining his disability but that the assured's own belief that he was disabled from working must be excluded from the assessment, although it was in a sense a consequence of the illness, and his claim failed.

25–50 Any gainful occupation. Total disability is commonly defined in America as any impairment of mind or body which renders it impossible for the assured to follow "a" or "any" gainful occupation; this phrase has been held to refer to the ordinary employment of the particular assured, or another similar employment which the assured might fairly be expected to follow in view of his station, circumstances and physical and mental capabilities. Thus a physician who suffered a complete breakdown recovered on the ground of total disability though holding occasional small municipal employment[98]; so did a newspaper circulation manager, reduced to part-time work only,[99] a cotton merchant who became totally deaf,[1] and a tailor who contracted phlebitis,[2] while a miner who obtained employment as a motor salesman did not.[3] It therefore seems that no American court would interpret "any gainful occupation" so strictly as to ignore the previous employment, training and capabilities of the actual insured.[4]

25–51 Clauses defining disability. Total disability may be expressly defined in the policy as the period of time during which the assured is confined to bed or to his house[5] or is attended by a physician. In *Froelich v. Continental Casualty Co.*,[6] for example, the policy provided that the assured must be "under the regular care and attendance of a legally qualified physician". The assured had been seriously disabled by a motor accident, but had discontinued medical treatment because he could get no benefit from it and could not afford it. The Saskatchewan Court of Appeal decided that the condition, being clear and unambiguous, prevented the assured from recovering even though there would have been little, if any, point in the assured complying with it.

25–52 Sometimes total and partial disability are defined so as to limit them to specific injuries such as the loss of sight, hands or feet. Such limitations must be expressed in clear language, and where the proviso was that partial disablement "implied" the loss of one hand, one foot or complete loss of sight the Court of Session held that the definition was not exhaustive but merely explanatory, and that there might be partial disablement within the meaning of the policy although the assured had suffered none of the

---

[98] *Mutual Life Ins. Co. of New York v. Barron*, 30 S.E. 2d 879 (1944).
[99] *Metropolitan Life Ins. Co. v. Hawley*, 198 S.W. 2d 171 (1947).
[1] *Norney v. Pacific Mutual Life Ins. Co.*, 33 So. 2d 531 (1947).
[2] *Stahlberg v. Metropolitan Life Ins. Co.*, 55 N.E. 2d 640 (1944).
[3] Appleman, *Insurance Law and Practice*, (1981), Vol. 1C, para. 632.
[4] *Huffman v. Equitable Life Ass. Society of the United States*, 241 S.W. 2d 536 (1951). So where payment was dependent upon the inability of the assured to carry on a "similar gainful occupation", this was construed to mean a similar occupation for which he was qualified and which generated a living wage—*Johnson v. IGI Ins. Co. Ltd* [1997] 2 C.L.Y. 3142 (taxi driver).
[5] *Guay v. Provident Accident and Guarantee Co.* (1917) 51 Que.R. (S.C.) 328 (outings on doctor's advice do not prevent recovery).
[6] (1956) 4 D.L.R. 2d 62. In New York it has been held that such a clause presupposes that some advantageous treatment is possible. If no such treatment can be obtained, the clause need not be complied with, *Liston v. New York Casualty Co.*, 58 N.Y.S. 1090 (1897); *Hunter v. Federal Casualty Co. of Detroit*, 191 N.Y.S. 474 (1921).

specified injuries.[7] In *Bawden v. London, Edinburgh and Glasgow Assurance Co.*[8] it was held that a man who had only one eye when he obtained an insurance and lost his other eye during the currency of the policy was entitled to recover for "complete and irrecoverable loss of sight in both eyes". This case has been criticised by Scrutton L.J. on the ground that it is difficult to see how the accident caused loss of sight in both eyes when the loss of sight in one eye had been caused long before[9] but it is submitted that the case should still be followed since what the policy covered was a total loss of sight.

There is some conflict as to what constitutes total loss of sight. Thus the Court of Appeal of British Columbia has held that an assured had irrevocably lost the entire sight of one eye, when he had lost all useful sight in that eye, although he was still able to distinguish light from darkness and to see a shadow if an object was placed close to his injured eye.[10] But it has been held in New Zealand[11] and Ontario[12] that there is no total loss of sight if the eye can distinguish daylight from darkness even though the eye is useless for the purpose of the assured's occupation.

25–53 Loss of hands, feet or limbs means loss as a matter of practical utility[13] and is not confined to loss by severance, unless so expressed.[14] Where a loss is expressly limited to loss by severance it is not necessary that the whole member should be severed provided that there is a partial severance and a total loss of practical utility.[15]

The word "disability" may include disability arising from old age.[16]

(b) *Clauses Defining the Compensation Payable*

25–54 Fixed sum or indemnity. It is often said that an accident policy, like a life policy, is not an indemnity policy[17] and it is certainly true that in modern accident policies the compensation payable is almost invariably a fixed sum, usually a lump sum in the case of death, a smaller lump sum in the case of permanent disability and a weekly payment in case of temporary disability; sometimes a 5 or 10 per cent. addition to the sum insured is made annually over a specified period.[18]

25–55 But accident policies can, of course, provide for an indemnity

---

[7] *Scott v. Scottish Accident Ins. Co.* (1889) 16 R. 630.

[8] [1892] 2 Q.B. 534 where knowledge that the assured only had one eye could be imputed to the insurers at the time they accepted the proposal.

[9] *Newsholme Bros v. Road Transport and General Ins. Co.* [1929] 2 K.B. 356, 369; *cf. per* Greer L.J. at p. 381.

[10] *Shaw v. Globe Indemnity Co.* [1921] 1 W.W.R. 674.

[11] *Macdonald v. Mutual Life and Citizens' Ass. Co.* (1910) 29 N.Z.L.R. 478, 1073.

[12] *Copeland v. Locomotive Engineers' Ins. Association* (1910) 16 O.W.R. 739.

[13] *Supreme Court of Honor v. Turner*, 99 Ill. App. 310 (1901). *Stevers v. People's Mutual Accident Ins. Association*, 150 Pa. 131 (1892).

[14] *Sheanon v. Pacific Mutual Life Ins. Co.*, 77 Wis. 618 (1890); 20 Am.St.Rep. 151; *Lord v. American Mutual Accident Association*, 61 N.W. 293 (1894).

[15] *Sneck v. Travelers' Ins. Co.*, 88 Hun. 94 (1895). But a policy covering "loss by physical separation of one hand" may not cover the loss of only two fingers, *Cook v. Southern Life Association* (1894) 15 Natal L.R.(N.S.) 127.

[16] *Dodds v. Canadian Mutual Aid Association* (1890) 19 O.R. 70.

[17] *Theobald v. Railway Passengers' Ass. Co.* (1854) 10 Exch. 45, 53, *per* Alderson B. *arguendo*; *Hooper v. Accidental Death Ins. Co.* (1860) 5 H. & N. 546, 555, *per* counsel *arguendo*.

[18] *Depue v. Travelers' Ins. Co.*, 166 Fed.Rep. 183 (1909).

instead of a fixed sum; in *Theobald v. Railway Passengers' Assurance Co.*,[19] for example, the insurers promised to pay £1,000 in the event of death and a proportionate part of £1,000 in the event of personal injury, expressed to be payable for "expense, pain and loss immediately connected with the accident". The assured was injured and claimed £34.95 as medical expenses and £1,000 for loss of time and profit from his business. The court held that he was entitled to an indemnity up to £1,000 within the ordinary rule as to remoteness and that he was therefore entitled to the amount claimed for medical expenses but the claim for loss of time and profit was too remote.

(c) *Exceptions for Intentional Injuries, Unlawful Activities, Fighting, etc.*

25–56 Self-inflicted injuries. In so far as this exception relates to injuries intentionally inflicted by the assured upon himself, it is not really an exception, because such an injury is not accidental and therefore would not fall within the general risk.[20] Where, however, the injury is inflicted under the influence of insanity or drink, the injury probably is within the general risk and it is a matter of construction whether suicide while insane or drunk falls within such an exception. In cases of life insurance it has been held that an exception of suicide applies to all acts of self-destruction, even if the assured was incapable of judging between right and wrong.[21] Those cases turned on the distinction between felonious and non-felonious suicide but will presumably be followed although no such distinction exists today. The act must, however, be the intentional act of a person capable of realising the probable consequences of what he is doing[22]; an accidental act of self-destruction will not come within the exception.[23] Suicide while insane may be expressly excluded from the risk by the addition to the exception of the words "sane or insane" or words to that effect.

Even where suicide, sane or insane, is excepted from the risk, the exception does not apply where insanity supervenes as the direct result of an accidental injury as in a case where tetanus produced delirium and the assured destroyed himself while under the influence of the delirium.[24] The exception must be read as excluding suicide only when it is an independent cause of death and not when it is merely a link in the natural consequences of an accidental injury.

25–57 Intentional injuries inflicted by another. Such injuries fall within the general risk[25] and it is therefore necessary for the insurer to stipulate expressly if he wishes to exclude liability for them. It has been argued that

---

[19] (1854) 10 Exch. 45; *cf. Blascheck v. Bussell* (1916) 33 T.L.R. 74 where the insurer had undertaken to insure the plaintiff against cancellation of lectures scheduled to be delivered by Ellen Terry, by promising to make good "all such loss not exceeding the sum of £100 for each performance". It was held that the insured was only entitled to be paid the actual loss suffered by him.

[20] See para. 25–3, *ante.*

[21] *Clift v. Schwabe* (1846) 3 C.B. 437; *Borradaile v. Hunter* (1843) 5 M. & G. 639.

[22] *Clift v. Schwabe* (1846) 3 C.B. 437, 464, *per* Rolfe B.; *Borradaile v. Hunter* (1843) 5 M. & G. 639, 648 *per* Erskine J.; *Re Davis* [1968] 1 Q.B. 72, 82, *per* Sellers L.J. *cf. Accident Ins. Co. v. Crandal*, 120 U.S. 527 (1886).

[23] *Borradaile v. Hunter* (1843) 5 M. & G. 639, 654, *per* Maule J.; *Clift v. Schwabe* (1846) 3 C.B. 437, 465 *per* Patteson J.; *Stormont v. Waterloo Life & Casualty Ass. Co.* (1858) 1 F. & F. 22.

[24] *Travelers' Ins. Co. of Hartford v. Mellick*, 65 Fed.Rep. 178 (1894).

[25] See para. 25–26, *ante.*

the exception should be confined to injuries inflicted with the consent of the assured, such as surgical operations or injuries naturally resulting from a fight voluntarily engaged in by the assured. This argument has, however, failed[26] and cases of wilful wounding or murder have been held to fall within the exception.[27]

25–58 The injury must be intentional in the sense that it must be directed against the assured[28] and that the person inflicting the injury intended to inflict the actual injury which he did inflict[29] or at any rate that such injury was the natural and probable cause of his wilful act. Thus, where the assured was murdered for the purpose of highway robbery it was held that there was no intentional injury within the meaning of the exception because no act was directed against the assured as an individual but merely as a member of the public whom it was the intention of the assailant to rob without respect of persons.[30] Where the assailant intended to kill some other person and killed the assured by mistake, it was likewise held that the assured had not been killed intentionally.[31] But the idea that an injury is not intentional because it is not the precise injury which the assailant intended must not be carried too far. If a man aims a blow at another's head and the latter wards it off with his arm and gets his arm broken the injury is clearly intentional as the assailant intended to inflict some serious injury.[32] But if a man merely intends to inflict some minor injury, such as a light blow not intended to cause death or a tripping to cause a fall, but death in fact results, the fatal injury is not intentional within the meaning of the exception.[33] An injury inflicted by a person who is so insane or drunk that he does not know the nature or quality of his act is not within the exception.[34]

25–59 In old policies there was often an exception for being killed or wounded in a duel; in such cases death or injury was within the exception even if the opponent of the assured did not intend to wound or kill him[35] and, apparently, even if his opponent was insane.[36]

25–60 Violation of law.[37] Where the insurers rely upon this exception, they must prove a wilful violation of the law by the assured,[38] but in the case of a

[26] *De Graw v. National Accident Society*, 51 Hun. 142 (1889).
[27] *Travelers' Ins. Co. v. McConkey*, 127 U.S. 661 (1887); *Jarnagin v. Travelers' Protective Association*, 133 Fed.Rep. 892 (1904).
[28] *Hutchcraft v. Travelers' Ins. Co.*, 12 Am.S.R. 484, 487 (1888).
[29] *Utter v. Travelers' Ins. Co.*, 8 Am.S.R. 913, 919 (1887).
[30] *Hutchcraft v. Travelers' Ins. Co.*, 12 Am.S.R. 484 (1888); 87 Ky. 300.
[31] *Utter v. Travelers' Ins. Co.*, 8 Am.S.R. 913 (1887); 65 Mich. 545.
[32] See *Matson v. Travelers' Ins. Co.*, 93 Me. 469 (1900).
[33] *Richards v. Travelers Ins. Co.*, 23 Am.S.R. 455 (1891); 89 Cal. 170 (1891).
[34] *Berger v. Pacific Mutual Life Ins. Co. of California*, 88 Fed.Rep. 241 (1898); *Corley v. Travelers' Protective Association*, 105 Fed.Rep. 854 (1900).
[35] *Clift v. Schwabe* (1846) 3 C.B. 437, 466, *per* Patteson J.
[36] *Borradaile v. Hunter* (1843) 5 M. & G. 639, 662, *per* Erskine J.; *Clift v. Schwabe* (1846) 3 C.B. 437, 468, *per* Alderson B. But *quaere* whether these decisions would be treated as truly analogous today, if a court had to construe an exception of intentional injury in an accident policy and it were proved that the insured's assailant was not aware of the nature and quality of his act. It is submitted that the American authorities, cited in note 34, *supra*, should be followed.
[37] See Ch. 14 on illegality for the position where there is no express provision for violation of the law in the policy.
[38] *Givens v. Baloise Marine Ins. Co. Ltd* (1958) 13 D.L.R. 2d 416, reversed on a different ground (1959) 17 D.L.R. 2d 7. *cf Wells v. New England Mutual Life Ins. Co. Ltd*, 191 Pa. 207 (1889) (death in course of illegal abortion).

public law (as opposed to, *e.g.* the internal regulations of a company) they are not required to show that the assured knew that his act was a violation of the law, because every person is presumed to know the law of the land. Violation of the law means violation of the criminal law and not merely the infringement of some private right giving rise only to a civil action.[39] Difficulty has arisen in applying the clause to driving offences. The words "death or disablement resulting from the assured's own criminal act" have been held sufficient to exclude liability where the deceased had driven with an excess of alcohol in his blood[40] contrary to the provisions of the Road Traffic Act 1972. In one Canadian case the assured had been convicted of exceeding the speed limit and was, therefore, held unable to recover under the exception.[41] In a later case, however, it was said that such an exception is capable of two meanings in that it could exclude all injuries caused by a breach of the law whether inadvertently or otherwise, or only such injuries as were not caused by inadvertence.[42] It was then said that if the policy was to exclude liability even for negligent acts of the assured it must do so clearly and that, in the absence of such clear words, the exception applied only to acts done intentionally or "so recklessly as to denote that the assured did not care what the consequences of his act might be". In Australia a violation of the traffic laws has been held to be a violation of law within the meaning of the exception.[43]

25–61 Where the exception extends to violation of the rules of a corporation such as a railway company, the insurers must prove that the assured wilfully violated the rule in the sense that he knew of the existence of the rule. There is no presumption that the assured knows of such rules. Moreover, if the rule has fallen into disuse and is systematically ignored by the servants of the company and the public, there is no wilful violation of the rule.[44]

25–62 Causal connection between illegality and injury. The exception against violation of law or the internal regulations of a company is sometimes so worded as to exclude, if read literally, not only injuries happening in consequence of the violation but all injuries happening while violating the law or the regulation. In Australia it has been held, in accordance with the English decisions on the words "while under the

---

[39] *Chamberlain v. Mutual Benefit Health and Accident Association*, 260 S.W. 2d 790 (1953).

[40] *Marcel Beller v. Hayden* [1978] Q.B. 694, where the judge held that the wording of the policy probably applied to all criminal acts other than those of inadvertence, but that, if they only applied to offences of moral turpitude, driving with an excess of alcohol in the blood stream was such an offence.

[41] *Ingles v. Sun Life Ass. Co. Ltd* [1937] 1 D.L.R. 706; affirmed [1938] 3 D.L.R. 80. At least one judge (Henderson J.A.) seems to have thought it relevant that the assured must have known that what he was doing was wrong.

[42] *Robinson v. L'Union St Joseph* [1950] 4 D.L.R. 541. The observations set out in the text were *obiter* since the court held that no driving offence had in fact been committed. The judge relied on *Burrows v. Rhodes* [1899] 1 Q.B. 816 in support of his construction of the clause but it is submitted that, while it is a relevant authority in determining the extent to which it is permissible to insure against the consequences of one's own unlawful act, it is of no relevance to the construction of an express clause in the policy.

[43] *Re United Insurance Co. and Absalom* [1932] V.L.R. 494. For conflicting American views, see *Provident Life and Accident Ins. Co. v. Eaton*, 84 F. 2d 528 (1936) and *Thomas v. First National Life Ins. Co.* 250 So.2d. 42 (1971); Appleman, *Insurance Law and Practice*, (1981), Vol. 1B, para. 513.

[44] *Travelers' Ins. Co. of Hartford v. Randolph*, 78 Fed.Rep. 754 (1897).

influence of intoxicating liquor",[45] that the word "while" has a temporal and not a causal connotation.[46] But American courts have refused to read such clauses literally and have held that a causal connection must be shown between the unlawful act and the injury,[47] and they have also held, at least where the exception is confined to the consequences of an illegal act, that the consequences must be such as might naturally be expected to follow from the act done by the assured and not the remote and wholly unexpected consequences.[48]

25–63 Clauses excepting injuries resulting from fighting, quarrelling or drinking. Any such provision must receive a reasonable construction and will not be held to include every frivolous controversy which could not reasonably have been expected to provoke anger or lead to injury.[49] The exception applies only to fighting and quarrelling for which the assured is in some way to blame[50] and to such injuries as might naturally result from the fight or quarrel in which the assured voluntarily engaged; thus, if the assured consented to fight with fists and his opponent afterwards shot him the injury would presumably not be within the exception. It cannot be construed as depriving the assured of the right of self-defence,[51] nor can it apply if the assured is obliged to use force in the performance of his duty or in the lawful vindication of his rights.[52]

25–64 Where the exception excludes liability for injuries sustained "whilst under the influence of intoxicating liquor", the word "influence" means such influence as disturbs the balance of a man's mind[53] or the quiet and equable exercise of the intellectual faculties.[54] The word "whilst" has a temporal meaning, and no causal relation between the injury and being under the influence of liquor is required,[55] but if the insurers can only prove

---

[45] See para. 25–64, *post.*
[46] *Re United Ins. Co. and Absalom* [1932] V.L.R. 494. *cf Western Finance Cpn Ltd v. London and Lancashire, etc., Co. of Canada* [1928] 2 W.W.R. 454.
[47] *Ins. Co. v. Bennett,* 25 Am.S.R. 685 (1891) (where the illegal act was living with a mistress); *Utter v. Travelers' Ins. Co.,* 8 Am.S.R. 913, 919; 65 Mich. 545 (1887).
[48] *Ins. Co. v. Seaver,* 19 Wall. 531, 542 (1873); *Turner v. Northern Life Ass. Co.* [1953] 1 D.L.R. 427 where the exception was for death resulting directly or indirectly from any violation of the law by the insured and it was held that the insured's own act in firing at a lorry was a cause of his death.
[49] *Ins. Co. v. Bennett,* 25 Am.S.R. 685, 690 (1891).
[50] *Ins. Co. v. Bennett,* 25 Am.S.R. 685 (1891); *Gresham v. Equitable Accident Ins. Co.,* 27 Am.S.R. 263 (1891).
[51] *Gresham v. Equitable Accident Ins. Co.,* 27 Am.S.R. 263, 265 (1891); *Coles v. New York Casualty Co.,* 87 App.Div. 41 (1903).
[52] *Coles v. New York Casualty Co.,* 87 App.Div. 41 (1903).
[53] *Mair v. Railway Passengers' Ass. Co.* (1877) 37 L.T. 356, 358, *per* Coleridge C.J.
[54] *Mair v. Railway Passengers' Ass. Co.* (1877) 37 L.T. 356, 359, *per* Denman J.; *Louden v. British Merchants' Ins. Co.* [1961] 1 W.L.R. 798; *Kennedy v. Smith* 1976 S.L.T. 110.
[55] *Mair v. Railway Passengers' Ass. Co.* (1877) 37 L.T. 356 (where it was held that, where death or injury while under the influence of intoxicating liquor was excepted and death resulted from an injury, it was the injury that must occur during the specified time, if liability was to be excluded); *MacRobbie v. Accident Insurance Co.* (1886) 23 S.C.L.R. 391; *Louden v. British Merchants Ins. Co.* [1961] 1 W.L.R. 798; *Re United Ins. Co. and Absalom* [1932] V.L.R. 494; *Givens v. Baloise Marine Ins. Co. Ltd* (1959) 17 D.L.R. 2d 7; *Ludlow v. Life and Casualty Ins. Co. of Tennessee,* 217 S.W. 2d 361 (1948); affirmed 218 S.W. 2d 65 (1949) and 63 *Harvard Law Review* 359 (1949).

that the assured was drunk when last seen and that some time elapsed before his injury or his death, they may not discharge the onus of proof.[56]

(d) *Clauses Limiting the Risk to Accidents Happening in a Particular Place or Manner*

25–65 Risk of transit. Insurance against the risk of transit on a railway or other public conveyance may be limited to accidents happening in a particular way. In *Theobald v. Railway Passengers' Assurance Co.*[57] the insurance was against injury by reason of a railway accident and the assured, who was on his way to Shrewsbury, injured himself when alighting from his train at Wolverhampton where it was necessary to change. The insurers contended that the risk was confined to accidents happening to the train in which the assured was travelling while the assured argued that the insurance extended to any accident happening to a person while travelling by railway. The judges did not completely accept the assured's argument[58] but held that he was entitled to recover on the ground that the risk at any rate included all accidents happening while the assured was doing something necessarily connected with his journey and attributable to the fact that he was travelling as a passenger on a railway. Thus, it is doubtful whether an accident wholly unconnected with the journey would be covered, for instance if the assured while sitting in the carriage cut his finger with a penknife, or got up from his seat and struck his head against the top of the carriage.[59] Most railway accident policies now insure only against "injury by reason of an accident to the passenger train in which the insured is travelling", thereby eliminating a large percentage of the risks of railway travelling.

25–66 Travelling as a passenger. The risk is frequently confined to accidents happening "while the insured is travelling as a passenger."[60] This will include an accident happening to a passenger in a vehicle hired for a pleasure drive[61] and the risks of boarding[62] and alighting from[63] the vehicle in a proper manner will be covered. The fact that a passenger may be unable to recover in negligence from the person or company operating the vehicle if he boards or dismounts from the vehicle while it is moving will not necessarily

---

[56] *Haines v. Canadian Railway Accident Co.* (1910) 13 W.L.R. 709.

[57] (1854) 10 Ex. 45. See also *Fire and All Risks v. Turner* (1976) 50 A.L.J.R. 767.

[58] But Alderson B. was clearly attracted by it.

[59] *Per* Pollock C.B. at p. 52, *arguendo*. But see *per* Alderson B. *arguendo* in 23 L.J. Ex. 249, 251.

[60] See *Fidelity and Casualty Co. of New York v. Mitchell* [1917] A.C. 592 where double benefit was payable for bodily injury sustained "while in or on a public conveyance (including the platform, steps and running board thereof) provided by a common carrier for passenger service."

[61] *Shanks v. Sun Life Assurance Co. of India* 1896 4 S.L.T. 65. It is not clear from the report whether the assured was the driver or a passenger but it is submitted that a driver could not recover under a policy covering the assured while travelling as a passenger.

[62] *Powis v. Ontario Accident Insurance Co.* (1901) 1 O.L.R. 54; *Champlin v. Railway Passengers Assurance Co.*, 6 Lans. 71 (1872). *Cf. Wallace v. Employers' Liability Assurance Co.* (1912) 26 O.L.R. 10 where the assured, having alighted from a streetcar, tried to mount it again to avoid an on-coming car. He accidentally fell and was held unable to recover because he was no longer "travelling" nor was he then a passenger.

[63] *King v. Travelers' Ins. Co. of Hartford*, 28 S.E. 661 (1897). *cf Theobald v. Railway Passengers' Ass. Co.* (1854) 10 Ex. 45.

prevent him from "travelling as a passenger" within the words of the policy.[64] The words "while the insured is travelling as a passenger" will, however, exclude:

(1) cases where the assured is travelling on duty as a servant of the railway company or other carrier,[65] although an employee of a steamship company may be a passenger on his employer's ship if during that voyage his time is his own and not his employer's[66];

(2) cases where the assured, although a passenger, is travelling on a part of the vehicle not intended for the conveyance of passengers.[67]

25–67 Where the risk insured was "whilst travelling by public or private conveyances", a passenger walking from a wharf to a railway station in prosecution of a continuous journey by steamer and rail was held to be covered.[68] But if the assured deviates from the journey he is not covered, as where a passenger crossed the platform after arrival at his destination in order to speak to an acquaintance in another train.[69] A deviation rendered necessary by temporary illness is covered, as where the assured went on to the platform of the train to vomit.[70]

If the risk is not limited to travelling by public conveyances, it may include all forms of private conveyance.[71] It has been held however, that a person riding a bicycle is not travelling in a vehicle as an ordinary passenger.[72]

25–68 "In or upon." There is much American authority on the construction of policies covering risks of accident to the assured arising out of the use by him of a specified vehicle "while in or upon, entering or alighting from it".[73] Thus the assured has recovered where the accident happened while he was changing a wheel,[74] standing with his hand on the door ready to open it,[75] locking the door,[76] placing a tyre in the boot[77] and pushing the vehicle to stop

---

[64] *Aschenbrenner v. U.S. Fidelity and Guarantee Co.*, 292 U.S. 80 (1933).

[65] *Travelers' Ins. Co. v. Austin*, 42 S.E. 522 (1902); *Wood v. General Accident Ins. Co. of Philadelphia*, 160 Fed.Rep. 926 (1908).

[66] *Interstate Life and Accident Ins. Co. v. Hulsey*, 94 S.E. 2d 34 (1957); *Prudential Ins. Co. v. Barnes*, 285 F. 2d 299 (1960). But see *Braley v. Commercial Casualty Ins. Co.*, 227 P. 2d 571 (1951).

[67] Compare *Van Bokkelen v. Travelers' Ins. Co.*, 34 App.Div. 399 (1898); affirmed 167 N.Y. 590 (1901) and *Aetna Life Ins. Co. v. Vandecar*, 86 Fed.Rep. 282 (1898) with *Berliner Travelers' Ins. Co.*, 53 P. 918 (1898).

[68] *Northrup v. Railway Passenger Ass. Co.*, 43 N.Y. 516 (1871); *cf. Rock v. Fidelity and Casualty Co.*, 219 N.Y.S. 2d 550 (1961) (woman assaulted in subway held not to be boarding or riding in a conveyance as a fare paying passenger).

[69] *Hendrick v. Employers' Liability Ass. Corporation*, 62 Fed.Rep. 893 (1894).

[70] *Preferred Accident Ins. Co. v. Muir*, 126 Fed.Rep. 926 (1904).

[71] *e.g.* a car hired for a pleasure drive, *Shanks v. Sun Life Ass. Co. of India Ltd* [1896] 4 S.L.T. 65 or a privately owned river steamer used for exploration in Alaska; *Aetna Life Ins. Co. v. Frierson*, 114 Fed.Rep. 56 (1902).

[72] *McMillan v. Sun Life Ass. Co. of India Ltd* [1896] 4 S.L.T. 66; *cf. Harsford v. London Express Newspapers Ltd* (1928) 44 T.L.R. 349 where the word "vehicle" was held to include a bicycle.

[73] Appleman, *Insurance Law and Practice*, (1981), Vol. 1C, para. 571.

[74] *Christoffer v. Hartford Accident and Indemnity Co.* 267 P. 2d 887 (1954).

[75] *Goodwin v. Lumbermen's Mutual Casualty Co.*, 85 A. 2d 759 (1952).

[76] *Katz v. Ocean Accident and Guarantee Corporation*, 112 N.Y.S. 2d. 737 (1952).

[77] *Madden v. Farm Bureau Mutual Automobile Ins.Co.*, 79 N.E. 2d 586 (1948).

it rolling.[78] He has failed to recover where the accident happened six feet away from his vehicle while he was returning to it,[79] and where, in the course changing a wheel, the jack slipped and the car fell onto him.[80]

25-69 Contravention of regulations. If the risk is limited to travelling in a public conveyance in compliance with the rules and regulations of the carrier, any accident happening when the assured is contravening such rules, as where he is riding on an open platform or leaving the train while in motion, will be excluded.[81] In one case an aviation policy excluded night flying unless carried out according to regulations and it was held that the onus was on the assured to show that he had complied with the regulations.[82]

25-70 Risk limited to United Kingdom. It has been held that, if the risk is limited to accidents happening in the United Kingdom, an accident is covered if it happened in Jersey,[83] but the question has been left open in the Court of Appeal where conflicting views have been expressed.[84]

25-71 Age limit of risk. In *Lloyds Bank Limited v. Eagle Star Insurance Co.*[85] a motor insurance policy provided that the insurers would pay to the assured's executors:

> "If the insured shall sustain any personal injury ... whilst riding in ... any private motor-car ... and if such injury shall be the sole direct and immediate cause ... of: (a) death of the insured, the sum of £1,000 ... provided always that ... the company shall not be liable to pay compensation in respect of personal injuries sustained by or happening to the insured if ... over the age of sixty-five years."

The assured died as a result of injuries received the previous day while riding in a private motorcar. At the time of his death he was aged 65 years and seven months. It was held first, that the words "personal injuries" included death resulting from such injuries and, secondly, that the words "over the age of sixty-five years" included a person aged 65 years and seven months, and that the proviso applied to anyone who had lived beyond the attainment of his 65th birthday, with the result that the company was not liable under the policy.

25-72 Newspaper coupon insurance. Difficulties have arisen on the construction of insurances against railway accidents contained in newspapers.[86] In *Hunter v. Hunter*,[87] the proprietors of *Answers* undertook, in a free insurance coupon printed in the paper, to pay, in the event of a person's possession of the current number being killed in a railway accident, the sum

---

[78] *Sherman v. New York Casualty Co.* 82 A. 2d 839 (1951).

[79] *New Amsterdam Casualty Co. v. Fromer*, 75 A. 2d 645 (1950).

[80] *Green v. Farm Bureau Mutual Automobile Insurance Co.*, 80 S.E. 2d 424 (1954).

[81] *Bon v. Railway Passengers' Assurance Co.*, 56 Iowa 664 (1881).

[82] *Bjorkman and Toronto Flying Club Ltd v. British Aviation Insurance Co. Ltd* [1953] 2 D.L.R. 249, following *Munro v. Brice*, see para. 19–07, *ante*.

[83] *Stoneham v. Ocean Railway and General Accident Insurance Co.* (1887) 19 Q.B.D. 237.

[84] *Navigators and General Insurance Co. Ltd v. Ringrose* [1962] 1 W.L.R. 173.

[85] [1951] 1 All E.R. 914.

[86] For problems relating to the formation of the contract see Ch. [2] *ante* and, in particular, *Law v. George Newnes Ltd* (1894) 21 R. 1027.

[87] (1904) 7 F. 136 following *Law v. George Newnes Ltd* (1894) 21 R. 1027; *cf Ashby v. Costin* (1888) 21 Q.B.D. 401.

of £1,000 to "the person adjudged by the Editor to be the next-of-kin of the deceased". It was held that, even if there was an obligation to pay, which was doubtful, it was an obligation to pay the person whom the Editor should select as most in need of the money, for his or her own benefit, and not as trustee for the whole next-of-kin. In another case,[88] the *Daily Mail* printed an insurance coupon stating that the Norwich Union would pay, *inter alia*, £1,000 to the personal representatives of the bona fide holder of the coupon if he should be killed as the result of a railway accident. One of the conditions of the coupon stated that the husband or wife of a subscriber or regular reader should be entitled to certain of the benefits covered by the coupon including the one mentioned above. A regular reader was so killed and the *Daily Mail* gave the widow a cheque for £1,000 made out to the "executors and/or administrators of" the deceased. The Public Trustee, claiming as sole executor, argued that the money belonged to the deceased's estate, while the widow contended that by reason of the above condition she was herself entitled to the money. Eve J. upholding the claim of the Public Trustee, held that the condition, on its true construction, secured an independent benefit to the husband or wife of a subscriber in the event of such a husband or wife being killed in an accident and did not entitle the wife of a subscriber to claim the money payable on his death. If both husband and wife were killed the liability of the insurer would be limited to one single sum of £1,000.[89] A condition providing for compensation if "the insured or his wife" were injured was held not to include the assured's husband where the assured was a married woman.[90]

25–73 External Mark. Accident policies sometimes used to require that there was an external mark on the body. Such clauses were always commoner in America than English policies and are now uncommon.[91]

(e) *Exception for Exposure to Unnecessary Danger*

25–74 Construction. These exceptions are framed by different companies in a great variety of phrases which, if literally construed, would defeat altogether the main object of the policy. No man travels by land or sea without wilfully exposing himself to danger, and if he travels for pleasure, and not because he must, the danger may be said to be unnecessary.[92] A man who crosses an ordinary crowded street is exposed to obvious risk of injury and it is clear that some qualification must be put on the words used.[93]

25–75 Unnecessary danger. The exception does not exclude recovery where the conduct of the assured is that of a reasonably prudent man[94] and even an occasional lapse from extreme prudence will not bring the case within the exception. The ordinary prudent man is occasionally careless or

---

[88] *Re Lambert* (1916) 114 L.T. 453
[89] *Re Caire* [1927] S.A.S.R. 220.
[90] *Automobile Fire and General Insurance Co. of Australia v. Davey* (1936) 54 C.L.R. 534.
[91] See the discussion in the 7th edition of this work at paras 1832–4 and in Appleman, *Insurance Law and Practice*, (1981), Vol. 1A, para. 364.
[92] *Sanger's Trustees v. General Accident Ins. Corporation Ltd* (1896) 24 R. 56, 57, *per* Lord Stormonth-Darling, Lord Ordinary.
[93] *Cornish v. Accident Ins. Co.* (1889) 23 Q.B.D. 453, 456.
[94] *Cornwall v. Fraternal Accident Association*, 66 Am.S.R 601, 603 (1896).

thoughtless, and mere negligence, such as might give rise to an action against the assured if his act caused injury to others or might prevent him recovering from the person from whom he received the injury, will not necessarily prevent him from recovering under the policy.[95]

The act must be one of gross or wanton negligence with regard to his own security[96] and the danger must be a substantial danger,[97] not merely one of those risks which are incidental to the everyday conduct of life. This is expressed by the words "unnecessary danger" and will be implied even though the word "unnecessary" is not used. Crossing[98] or walking along[99] a railway track without looking to see if trains are coming,[1] going too near the edge of a cliff in search of wild flowers,[2] travelling in an unlighted vehicle at dusk or in the dark,[3] boarding a moving train,[4] climbing a fence with a loaded gun[5] have all been held to be unnecessary exposure to danger within the meaning of the exception.

25–76 The ordinary pleasures of a healthy man, however, such as swimming, riding, bicycling or motoring are not unnecessary dangers if done in a ordinarily prudent manner.[6] It has even been held that accosting a woman walking with another man is not to expose oneself wilfully to unnecessary danger.[7] The dangers and risks incidental to a man's ordinary occupation or means of livelihood are not unnecessary.[8] A farmer must tend his cattle, although one of them is a dangerous bull,[9] and a railway employee may uncouple wagons or board moving trains or do other more or less

---

[95] *Cornish v. Accident Ins. Co.* (1889) 23 Q.B.D. 453, 457; *Schneider v. Provident Life Ins. Co.*, 1 Am.R. 157, 161 (1869); *Thomas v. Masons' Fraternal Accident Association* 64 App.Div. 22 (1901); *Keene v. New England Mutual Accident Association*, 161 Mass. 149 (1894).

[96] *Sangster's Trustees v. General Accident Ins. Corporation Ltd* (1896) 24 R. 56, 57, *per* Lord Stormonth-Darling, Lord Ordinary; *Traders' and Travelers' Accident Co. v. Wagley*, 74 Fed.Rep. 457 (1896).

[97] *Travelers' Ins. Co. of Hartford v. Randolph*, 78 Fed.Rep. 754, 762 (1897), *per* Harlan J.

[98] *Cornish v. Accident Insurance Co.* (1889) 23 Q.B.D. 453.

[99] *Lovell v. Accident Ins. Co.* reported in *Post Magazine* for the years 1874, 1875 and 1876 at pp. 255, 419 and 59 respectively and referred to in *Wright v. Sun Mutual Life Ins. Co.* (1878) 29 C.P. 221 where it was held that it could not be assumed from the presence of the insured's body on a railway line that he had exposed himself to unnecessary danger.

[1] Contrast *Keene v. New England Mutual Accident Association*, 161 Mass. 149 (1894) where the railway had expressly prohibited members of the public from using the railway line but it was held that the question whether the insured had exposed himself to unnecessary danger should be left to the jury.

[2] *Walker v. Railway Passengers' Ass. Co.* (1910) 129 L.T. Jo. 64.

[3] *Re United Ins. Co. v. Absalom* [1932] V.L.R. 494.

[4] *Small v. Travelers' Protective Association of America*, 45 S.E. 706 (1903); contrast the case of a railway superintendent whose job requires him to board moving trains, *Accident Ins. Co. of North America v. McFee* (1891) 7 M.L.R. (Q.B.) 255. *cf.* the express exception in *Mair v. Railway Passengers Ass. Co.* (1877) 37 L.T. 356.

[5] Contrast *Sargent v. Central Accident Ins. Co.* 88 Am.S.R. 946 (1901) with *Cornwall v. Fraternal Accident Association*, 66 Am.S.R. 601 (1896).

[6] *Sangster's Trustees v. General Accident Ins. Corporation Ltd* (1896) 24 R. 56; *Keiffe v. National Accident Ins. Co.*, 4 App.Div. 392 (1896). But if an activity is illegal, it will not be an ordinary pleasure even if done frequently in a certain locality and may therefore be held to be an unnecessary danger: *Ins. Co. v. Seaver*, 19 Wall. 531 (1873).

[7] *Mair v. Railway Passengers Ass. Co.* (1877) 37 L.T. 356.

[8] *Pacific Mutual Life Ins. Co. v. Snowden*, 58 Fed.Rep. 342, 346 (1893).

[9] *Johnson v. London Guarantee Ins. Co.*, 15 Mich. 86 (1897).

dangerous things.[10] The only question is whether he performed his duty in a reasonably prudent manner or whether he went beyond it and did something reckless and foolish.[11]

Similarly a danger which is inevitable will not be held to be an unnecessary one.[12]

25–77 Moral obligation. The ordinary duties of humanity cannot be said to be unnecessary and a man may incur danger in voluntarily helping another[13]; he may run the most extreme risks in order to save life,[14] and yet it will not be unnecessary danger. The test is, was the risk run reasonably appropriate to the end to be attained?

25–78 Obvious risk of injury. If a danger is a hidden danger or an unavoidable one, there can be no "voluntary" exposure to it because the word "voluntary" implies that the assured recognised the dangerous character of the situation but nevertheless intentionally and consciously assumed the risk.[15]

25–79 In this connection a distinction has been drawn between two differently worded forms of the exception:

(1) in respect of injuries happening "by exposure of the insured to obvious risk of injury", and
(2) in respect of injuries caused by "voluntary exposure to unnecessary danger".

The first form of the exception was considered in *Cornish v. Accident Insurance Co.*,[16] where it was held that such a clause would exclude two classes of accidents,

(a) those which arose from an exposure by the assured to a risk of injury which was obvious to him at the time he exposed himself to it, and
(b) those which arose from an exposure by the assured to a risk of injury which would have been obvious to him if he had been paying reasonable attention to what he was doing.

---

[10] *Canadian Railway Accident Ins. Co. v. McNevin* (1902) 32 Can.S.C. 194; *Accident Ins. Co. of North America v. McFee* (1891) 7 M.L.R. (Q.B.) 255; *cf. De Loy v. Travelers' Ins. Co.*, 50 Am.S.R. 787 (1894).

[11] *Ashenfelter v. Employers' Liability Ass. Corporation Ltd*, 87 Fed.Rep. 682 (1898).

[12] *North West Commercial Travelers' Association v. London Guarantee and Accident Co.* (1895) 10 Man.R. 537

[13] *Canadian Railway Accident Ins. Co. v. McNevin* (1902) 32 Can.S.C. 194, 204, *per* Sedgwick J.

[14] *Tucker v. Mutual Benefit Life Co.*, 50 Hun. 50 (1888); *cf. Williams v. U.S. Mutual Accident Association*, 82 Hun. 268 (1894).

[15] See for hidden dangers, *Ashenfelter v. Employers' Liability Ass. Corporation Ltd*, 87 Fed.Rep. 682 (1898) and *Buckhard v. Travelers' Ins. Co.*, 102 Pa. 262 (1883); and for inevitable dangers, *N.W. Commercial Travelers' Association v. London Guarantee and Accident Co.* (1895) 10 Man.R. 537.

[16] (1889) 23 Q.B.D. 453.

The assured had crossed a railway line where there was nothing to intercept his view of passing trains and he was knocked down; the court decided that the accident was excluded from the risk under one or other of the above categories; under (a) if he saw the train coming and attempted to pass in front of it, and under (b) if he crossed the line without looking to see if the line was clear.

25–80 In *Lehman v. Great Eastern Casualty and Indemnity Co. of New York*,[17] the Appellate Division of the Supreme Court of New York considered the second form of the exception and held that it only excluded the accidents contained in category (a). The assured was crossing a railway track and saw a train coming one way; while his attention was directed to observing and avoiding that train, a train coming the other way which he did not see knocked him down. The court held that the insurers had to prove that actual danger, which caused the injury, was present to the mind of the assured when he exposed himself to it and that there was no voluntary exposure in this case because the assured was not aware of the particular danger. If the wording of the policy had been the same as in the *Cornish* case,[18] the accident would have been excepted, because there was a risk which would have been obvious to the assured if he had exercised ordinary prudence and looked both up and down the line.

A third form of the exception, "deliberate exposure to exceptional danger" or "wilful exposure to needless peril" is even more restrictive and the insurer will not be excused unless the assured chooses deliberately to run the risk of an accident.[19] An impulsive response to a practical joke when the risk of injury is not appreciated does not bring the exception into play.[20]

25–81 Contributory negligence of another. If the assured exposes himself to obvious danger and meets with an accident of the kind which might have been anticipated from the risks taken, the accident is nonetheless within the exception because it is immediately due to the contributory negligence of another. Thus, in the case of an assured walking along a railway track in the dark, the fact that the driver of the locomotive might have avoided the accident by blowing the whistle or applying his brakes or keeping a proper look-out does not take the case out of the exception.[21]

25–82 Burden of proof. Difficulties may arise in connection with the burden of proving that the facts of any particular case fall within this exception. The usual rule is that once the assured has proved that the case comes within the general risk, it is for the insurers to prove that it comes within an exception. It has therefore been suggested in some American decisions that, where the insurers prove only that the assured exposed himself to danger and there is no evidence to show why he did so, they cannot succeed, because they have not proved that his behaviour was

---

[17] 7 App.Div. 424 (1896); *cf. Canadian Railway Accident Ins. Co. v. McNevin* (1902) 32 Can.S.C. 194.

[18] (1889) 23 Q.B.D. 453.

[19] *Marcel Beller Ltd v. Hayden* [1978] Q.B. 694. *Glenlight Shipping Ltd v. Excess Ins. Co. Ltd* 1983 S.L.T. 241, esp. 243, *per* Lord Hunter and 245–6, *per* Lord Stott. In both these cases (the facts of which are set out at paras 25–5 to 25–6, *ante*) the assured was under the influence of drink and was, therefore, unable to form the necessary intent.

[20] *Morley v. United Friendly Ins. plc* [1993] 1 Lloyd's Rep. 490.

[21] *Tuttle v. Travelers' Ins. Co.*, 45 Am.R. 316 (1883).

voluntary or that the danger was unnecessary.[22] Since an extremely heavy burden is imposed on the insurers if they have to prove the state of mind of the assured, it has been suggested in Canadian decisions that the court should presume that the assured acted voluntarily and that, where he does an apparently dangerous and foolish act, such danger was unnecessary, until the contrary is shown.[23] In practical terms, therefore, the onus does in fact lie on the claimant to explain the conduct of the assured where there is no apparent reason for exposing himself to an obvious danger.[24]

(f) *Exceptions for Specified Hazards, or for Hazardous Occupations*

25–83 Construction. These exceptions will prima facie be construed as limited to conscious and voluntary acts[25] and as excluding only such injuries as might naturally be expected to result from the particular nature of the excepted hazard.[26] An exception may, however, be so worded as to cover engaging in a hazardous risk under compulsion. Thus where a condition in a life policy provided that the life assured should not become engaged in any active naval or military occupation, it was held that the words covered compulsory military service, but that they did not cover the death of the life assured in an air raid in London when on leave from a Royal Artillery training unit in which he was serving as a conscript.[27]

25–84 If the occupation of the assured is specifically described in the policy, any exception from or separate provision for liability for injury while the assured is employed in a hazardous occupation will not be construed as extending to such acts as are ordinarily incidental to the specified occupation.[28] Moreover even if there is a general exception for hazardous occupations, the exception will not apply if the injury occurs while the assured is performing an isolated act, because he is not performing his occupation.[29] Injury received while returning from his occupation is not excluded by an exception for hazards of the assured's occupation.[30]

25–85 If words of causation are used in the policy, the ordinary rules of proximate cause will apply[31] but the words "directly or indirectly arising from or traceable to" will exclude the doctrine of proximate cause. Thus where a policy exempted liability for injury "directly or indirectly caused by

---

[22] *Williams v. U.S. Mutual Accident Association*, 92 Hun. 268 (1894); *Meadows v. Pacific Mutual Life Ins. Co.*, 50 Am.S.R. 427 (1895).

[23] *Neill v. Travelers' Ins. Co.* (1885) 12 Can. S.C. 55, 63, *per* Strong J.; *Fowlie v. Ocean Accident and Guarantee Corporation Ltd* (1901) 4 O.L.R. 146. *Contra, North-West Commercial Travelers' Association v. London Guarantee and Accident Corporation* (1895) 10 Man.R. 537, 563, *per* Killan J.

[24] *Walker v. Railway Passengers' Ass. Co.* (1910) 129 L.T.Jo. 64.

[25] *Scheiderer v. Travelers' Ins. Co.*, 46 Am.R. 618; 58 Wis. 13 (1883).

[26] *Buckhard v. Travelers' Ins. Co.*, 102 Pa. 262 (1883).

[27] *Aslett v. National Life and General* (1941) I.A.C. Rep. 1938–1949, p. 40.

[28] *De Loy v. Travelers' Ins. Co.* 50 Am.S.R. 787 (1894); *Standard Life and Accident Ins. Co. v. Schmaltz*, 74 Am.S.R. 112, 119–120; 66 Ark 588 (1899).

[29] *Canadian Railway Accident Ins. Co. v. McNevin* (1902) 32 Can.S.C. 194. But liability will be excluded where the policy excluded injuries received while the assured is "temporarily or permanently" engaged in a hazardous occupation, *Stanford v. Imperial Guarantee and Accident Ins. Co.* (1909) 18 O.L.R. 562.

[30] *Graham v. London Guarantee and Accident Co.* (1925) 56 O.L.R. 494.

[31] See paras 19–1, *et seq.*

arising from or traceable to war" and the assured was accidentally killed on a railway line which he was guarding in the performance of his military duties, the court upheld the arbitrator's award that the exception applied.[32] If no words of causation are used but the exception is merely for accidents received while the assured is engaged in, *e.g.* military service, a court would presumably hold that no causal connection between military service and the injury need be shown, any more than when a policy excludes injuries received while the assured is under the influence of intoxicating liquor.[33]

25–86 Hazardous occupation. The word "occupation" in exception clauses has reference to the vocation, profession, trade or calling in which the assured is engaged for hire or profit, and does not preclude him from the performance of acts and duties which are simply incidents connected with the daily life of men in any or all occupations.[34] Occasional acts do not amount to an occupation[35] and, even though they are acts which are ordinarily incidental to some other occupation, they are not acts pertaining to that occupation unless the assured has temporarily or permanently engaged in such occupation as a means of livelihood.[36] When the acts are done merely by way of recreation or to give temporary assistance to another, they are acts pertaining to the daily life of anyone whatever his occupation may be and not acts pertaining to any particular occupation.[37]

25–87 Policy covering travel undertaken for specific purpose. In *Killick v. Rendall*[38] a corporate assured maintained a personal accident cover for the benefit of its directors which covered them *inter alia* on journeys in the United Kingdom made "on behalf of the assured". Two directors were killed in a helicopter crash while returning to London from Bolton where they had been attending a football match. Before arriving in Bolton they had met business contacts on a social basis and had visited a factory making a balloon which was sponsored by the assured. It was held that it was necessary to identify the primary purpose of the entire journey in order to say whether it was for business purposes. One director had been travelling primarily for social purposes. The journey of the second director had two purposes of equal weight, one business and the other social. In his case it was sufficient that one was within the cover while the other was not excluded, and the claim made in respect of his death succeeded.

---

[32] *Coxe v. Employers' Liability Ass. Corporation Ltd* [1916] 2 K.B. 629; *cf. Oei v. Foster* [1982] 2 Lloyd's Rep. 170 and *Turner v. Northern Life Ass. Co.* [1953] 1 D.L.R. 427. For other cases where clauses exempting death arising from war or hostilities or whilst on active service were considered, see *Howarth v. Britannic* (1942) I.A.C. Rep. 1938–49, p. 46 and *Frew v. Scottish Legal Life Ass. Society* (1951) I.A.C. Rep. 1953, p. 5 (death during operations against Communist terrorists in Malaya when no state of war had been declared).

[33] See para. 25–63 above. In America the authorities are divided; compare *Life and Casualty Ins. Co. v. McLeod*, 27 S.E. 2d 89 (1943) and *Beeding v. Metropolitan Life and Casualty Ins. Co.* N.E. 2d 71 (1944) (which support the proposition in the text) with *Smith v. Sovereign Camp of the Woodmen of the World*, 28 S.E. 2d 808 (1944) and *Young v. Life and Casualty Ins. Co. of Tennessee* 29 S.E. 2d, 482 (1944).

[34] *Union Mutual Accident Association v. Frohard*, 23 Am.S.R. 664, 668 (1890); 134 Ill. 288; *Holiday v. American Mutual Accident Association*, 103 Iowa 178 (1897). *Cf.* the strange judgment of Lennox J. in *Graham v. London Guarantee and Accident Co.* (1925) 56 O.L.R. 494.

[35] *Berliner v. Travelers' Ins. Co.*, 66 Am.S.R. 49, 55; 121 Cal. 458 (1898).

[36] *Canadian Railway Accident Ins. Co. v. McNevin* (1902) 32 Can.S.C. 194; *Johnson v. London Guarantee and Accident Co.*, 69 Am.S.R. 549; 15 Mich. 86 (1897).

[37] *Hobday v. American Mutual Accident Association*, 103 Iowa 178 (1897).

[38] [2000] Lloyd's Rep. I.R. 581.

5. Proof of Claim

25–88 Circumstantial evidence. Claims requiring direct and positive proof of an accident or of the nature, cause or manner of the injury have been considered in American cases. It is not necessary to establish the facts by evidence from persons who were present and can give testimony as eye-witnesses; the facts may be proved by circumstantial evidence, inferences may be drawn according to the ordinary laws[39] and the American courts have in effect refused to permit the parties to restrict by their contract the usual methods of proof in a court of law.[40]

25–89 Statements by deceased. If the assured died from the effects of an injury, the claimant was frequently in difficulty at common law in proving an accident, where there were no independent witnesses. Hearsay evidence was admissible under the doctrine of *res gestae* to prove what the deceased said to his doctor or his friends about his state of health, but not what he said about the cause of his injury.[41] Since the Civil Evidence Act 1968, however, first-hand hearsay has been admissible provided that the conditions laid down in the Act and the rules of court made thereunder have been fulfilled.[42]

25–90 Nature of injury. Certain injuries afford by themselves prima facie proof of accidental means. If a man is found with a pistol shot in his heart,[43] or if his body is found in the water bearing symptoms of death by drowning,[44] or if he is found with marks of violence on his back[45] or with a fractured arm[46] or cut to pieces on a railway,[47] or if he fell out of a railway train,[48] there is direct evidence of injury by violence. In such cases the law presumes that the violence was accidental rather than that it was intentionally self-inflicted[49] and, in the absence of other evidence, there is proof of injury by violent and accidental means. The reason for this presumption has been said to be that the law will not assume that the assured committed a crime, but it is submitted that the presumption should still apply even though suicide is no longer a crime,[50] since there is inevitably a certain moral or social stigma that

---

[39] *Wright v. Sun Mutual Ins. Co.* (1878) 29 C.P. 221, 233, *per* Hagarty C.J.; *Perk v. Equitable Accident Association*, 52 Hun. 255 (1889). English courts will readily draw inferences concerning the assured's state of mind—see, *e.g. Morley v. United Friendly Ins. plc* [1993] 1 Lloyd's Rep. 490.

[40] *Utter v. Travelers' Ins. Co.*, 65 Mich. 545, 553–554 (1887), *per* Morse J.; *Travelers' Ins. Co. v. McConkey*, 127 U.S. 661 (1887), *per* Harlan J.

[41] *Amys v. Barton* [1912] 1 K.B. 40. *cf. Insurance Co. v. Mosley*, 8 Wall. 397 (1869).

[42] Civil Evidence Act 1968 (c. 64) and R.S.C., Ord. 38.

[43] *Travelers' Ins. Co. v. McConkey*, 127 U.S. 61 (1887); *Accident Ins. Co. v. Bennett*, 16 S.W. 723 (1891).

[44] *Macdonald v. Refuge Ass. Co. Ltd* (1890) 17 R. 955; *Ballantine v. Employers' Ins. Co. of Great Britain Ltd* (1893) 21 R. 305.

[45] *Cronkhite v. Travelers' Ins. Co.*, 43 N.W. 731 (1889).

[46] *Peek v. Equitable Accident Association*, 52 Hun. 255 (1889).

[47] *Meadows v. Pacific Mutual Life Ins. Co.*, 50 Am.S.R. 427 (1895).

[48] *Standard Life and Accident Ins. Co. v. Thornton*, 100 Fed. Rep. 582 (1900).

[49] *Macdonald v. Refuge Ass. Co. Ltd* (1890) 17 R. 955, 957, *per* Macdonald L.J.-C.; *Bender v. Owners of SS Zent* [1909] 2 K.B. 41, 45, *per* Farwell L.J.; *Harvey v. Ocean Accident and Guarantee Corporation* [1905] 2 Ir.R. 1; *Barnard v. Prudential Ins. Co. of America* [1949] 4 D.L.R. 235. But see *Fowlie v. Ocean Accident Corporation* (1901) 4 O.L.R. 146, affirmed 33 Can.S.C. 253 where a new trial was ordered because the jury's verdict was incomprehensible.

[50] Suicide Act 1961.

attaches to a person who commits suicide. If, however, the facts proved point to suicide as the only reasonable conclusion, the fact that there is some possible explanation consistent with accidental death will not justify a finding of accident.[51]

25–91 Where the evidence is equally consistent with an accidental and a non-accidental cause of death, not involving suicide or breach of the law, there is no presumption in favour of accidental death, as, for instance, where the question is between death by accident and death from natural causes.[52] The usual principle applies that the plaintiff must prove his case. Thus where the assured died from an overdose of opium and the facts proved were equally consistent with his having accidentally taken more than he intended and with his having taken exactly what he intended, erroneously believing it to be a proper dose, it was held that the claimant was not entitled to recover.[53] But if there is a distinct probability that the cause of death was accidental, a finding of accident will be supported even though the evidence may be consistent with a non-accidental cause. Thus where the body of the assured was found in the water, but was so decomposed as to afford no direct proof of actual death by drowning and the facts proved were entirely consistent with the assured having died from natural causes such as heart failure while bathing, it was held that there was evidence upon which the jury might properly return a verdict of death by accidental drowning.[54] Similarly, where a man fell from a buggy whilst driving it and was picked up dead, it was left to the jury to say on the medical evidence whether the immediate cause of death was apoplexy or the fall from the buggy.[55]

25–92 Proof satisfactory to the directors. A policy may stipulate that there shall be no claim unless the injury is caused by outward and visible means of which proof satisfactory to the directors is to be furnished. This is an attempt to make the directors judge in their own cause and a court would almost certainly hold that a claim must be allowed if the directors ought to have been satisfied by the proof that has been provided.[56]

25–93 Obligation to furnish evidence. A claimant may be required to furnish such evidence as the directors may require. This empowers the directors to call for evidence over and above such evidence as would satisfy a judge or jury in order to test or corroborate the evidence before them.[57] But

---

[51] *Williams v. U.S. Mutual Accident Association*, 133 N.Y. 366 (1892); *New York Life Ins. Co. v. Ganer* 303 U.S. 161 (1937). This paragraph is commented upon by Thomas J. in *Clark v. N.Z.I. Life Ltd* [1991] 2 Qd.R. 11, 16–17.

[52] *Bender v. Owners of SS Zent* [1909] 2 K.B. 41; *Marshall v. Owners of SS. Wild Rose* [1909] 2 K.B, 46. See also *A.B. v. Northern Accident Ins. Co.* (1896) 24 R. 758, where a doctor who refused to disclose the name of a patient from whom he caught a disease was held not to be entitled to recover.

[53] *Carnes v. Iowa Traveling Men's Association*, 76 N.W. 683 (1898); *cf.* the test of negligence, in *Wakelin v. London and South Western Ry* (1886) 12 App.Cas. 41.

[54] *Trew v. Railway Passengers Ass. Co.* (1861) 6 H. & N. 839. *Cf. Sangster's Trustees v. General Accident Co. Ltd* (1896) 24 R. 56.

[55] *McCormack v. Illinois Commercial Men's Association*, 159 Fed.Rep. 114 (1907).

[56] *Trew v. Railway Passengers Ass. Co.* (1861) 6 Jur.(N.S.) 759, *per* Martin B. and Pollock C.B. *arguendo*; rvsd 6 H. & N. 839; *Napier v. UNUM Ltd* [1996] 2 Lloyd's Rep. 550. See the policies in *Winspear v. Accident Ins. Co.* (1880) 6 Q.B.D. 42 and *Macdonald v. Refuge Ass. Co.* (1890) 17 R. 955.

[57] *Ballantine v. Employers' Ins. Co. of Great Britain Ltd* (1893) 21 R. 305; *A.B. v. Northern Accident Ins. Co. Ltd* (1896) 24 R. 758.

the evidence or information must not be required unreasonably[58] and the fact that even a reasonable request is refused will not necessarily prevent the claimant from recovering.[59] The demand for evidence must be made directly on the claimant or on some person or persons who have been acting for him in respect of the claim.[60] It is submitted that if the claimant is merely required to "furnish" evidence or information, the evidence or information asked for must be such as is in the possession or power of the claimant, and that he cannot be required to procure evidence or information from other persons unless the clause expressly requires him to do so.

25–94 Demand for examination of body. If there is a clause in the policy to the effect that the company's medical adviser shall be permitted to examine the person of the insured in respect of any alleged injury or cause of death, the company is not entitled to call for exhumation after burial, at any rate if they have had an opportunity of examining the body before burial but did not do so.[61] The position is not clear if, after burial, facts come to the knowledge of the insurer which indicate that the accident was due to an excepted cause[62] but it has been held in New York that, even though notice of the accident was not given to the insurance company until after burial, it was not entitled to call for exhumation.[63]

---

[58] In *Ballantine v. Employers' Ins. Co. of Great Britain Ltd* (1893) 21 R. 305, differing views were expressed on the question whether it was reasonable to require a post-mortem examination.

[59] See the judgment of Lord Young in *Ballantine's* case.

[60] *Ballantine v. Employers Ins. Co. of Great Britain Ltd* (1893) 21 R. 305.

[61] *American Employers' Liability Ins. Co. v. Barr*, 68 Fed.Rep. 873 (1895); *Wehle v. U.S. Mutual Accident Association*, 153 N.Y. 116 (1897); *Root v. London Guarantee and Accident Co.* 92 App.Div. 578 (1904).

[62] *Wehle v. U.S. Mutual Accident Association*, 153 N.Y. 116 (1897).

[63] *Ewing v. Commercial Travelers' Mutual Accident Association*, 55 App.Div. 241 (1900).

CHAPTER 26

FIRE POLICIES

1. NATURE OF THE RISK

26–1 Definition of "fire". The word "fire" is used in its ordinary popular meaning in a fire policy. It follows that there must be ignition of some kind[1] and it has been said that there is loss or damage by fire:

> "when there has been ignition of insured property which was not intended to be ignited, or when insured property has been damaged otherwise than by ignition, as a direct consequence of the ignition of other property not intended to be ignited".[2]

There is no distinction in English law between an ordinary fire and a fire "where no fire ought to be". If there is actual ignition of property not intended to be ignited and property insured is damaged as a proximate consequence of that ignition, it is no defence for the insurer to prove that the fire was in a place where fires usually are. In *Harris v. Poland*[3] the assured concealed valuables such as jewellery and banknotes in her grate as a precaution against theft and inadvertently lit a fire forgetting what she had done. Atkinson J. held that she could recover and refused to draw a distinction between a fortuitous fire and an intended fire (or, to adopt the American phraseology, between a hostile and a friendly fire[4]); he expressed the view that the ordinary assured would never suspect that, if something is blown by the wind or accidentally dropped into the fire, he was not covered.

26–2 Excessive heat. Damage to property caused by excessive heat will not, as such, be covered by an ordinary fire policy unless there is also ignition

---

[1] *Everett v. London Ass. Co.* (1865) 19 C.B.(N.S.) 126, 133, *per* Byles J. A fire in a chimney entails the ignition of soot and will therefore be within the usual fire policy. *Austin v. Drewe* (1816) 6 Taunt. 436. 438, *per* Shepherd S.G. *arguendo. Way v. Abington Mutual Fire Ins. Co.*, 166 Mass. 67 (1896). *Wasserman v. Caledonian-American Insurance*, 95 N.E. 2d 547 (1950).

[2] *Harris v. Poland* [1941] 1 K.B. 462.

[3] [1941] 1 K.B. 462.

[4] American courts have traditionally regarded as a "friendly fire" any fire burning in a place where it is intended to burn, although damage may result where none is intended: see 46 Col.L.R. 362 (1946); *Yonge v. Employers Fire Ins. Co.*, 238 P. 2d 472 (1951). However, some modern cases reveal a tendency to confine friendly fires to fires under control and to allow recovery for damage done by any fire beyond control, whether in or out of its proper place: see, *e.g. Barcalo Manufacturing Co. v. Firemen's Mutual Ins. Co.*, 263 N.Y.S. 2d 807 (1965); *Engel v. Redwood County Farmers Mutual Ins. Co.*, 281 N.W. 2d 331 (1979); *Shulze & Burch Biscuit Co. v. American Protection Ins. Co.*, 421 N.E. 2d (1981).

of property not intended to be ignited. In *Austin v. Drewe*[5] there was insurance "against all damage which the assured should suffer by fire on stock and utensils in their regular built sugar house". The buildings consisted of eight storeys and from a stove on the ground floor a flue passed up through the other floors for the purpose of heating them. At the top of the flue was a register which was closed at night in order to retain as much heat as possible. When the fire was lit in the morning the assured's servant forgot to open the register and the intense heat which resulted damaged the sugar which was being refined on the top floors. The building was filled with smoke and sparks but the flames never got beyond the flue and nothing took fire. It was held that the damage to the sugar was not damage by fire. Gibbs C.J. said:

> "There was no more fire than always exists when the manufacture is going on. Nothing was consumed by fire. The plaintiff's loss arose from the negligent mismanagement of their machinery.[6] The sugar was chiefly damaged by the heat; and what produced that heat? Not any fire against which the company insures, but the fire for heating the pans which continued all the time to burn without any excess ... Had the fire been brought out of the flue and anything had been burnt the company would have been liable. .... This is not a fire within the warranty of the policy, nor a loss for which the company undertake. They might as well be sued for damage done to drawing-room furniture by a smokey chimney."

26-3 Other examples of damage caused by excessive heat which would probably be beyond the protection of an ordinary fire policy are damage done by the bursting of a boiler caused by excess of ordinary fire-heat and absence of water in the boiler[7] or damage done by reason of a boiler's corrosion by contact with bilge water so as to become too thin to resist the pressure of steam.[8]

26-4 It may happen that damage through excessive fire-heat is expressly included in the policy. It can even be impliedly included. For example, in *Jameson v. Royal Insurance Co.*[9] the insurance policy on premises and stock-in-trade contained an express condition that the insurers should not be liable "for any loss or damage to still, coppers, or such like, occasioned by the ordinary fire-heat under same, nor for loss to spirits or such like, therein at the time of such loss or damage". The assured made a claim for damage to spirits and the insurers pleaded that the property destroyed consisted of

---

[5] (1815) 4 Camp. 360; Holt N.P. 126; in banc (1816) 6 Taunt. 436.
[6] The negligence of a servant of the assured is now regarded as affording no defence to the insurer; see para. 26–27, post.
[7] *American Touring Co. v. German Fire Ins. Co.*, 74 Md. 25 (1891); *Wasserman v. Caledonian-American Ins. Co.*, 95 N.E. 2d 547 (1950). Compare, however, *Barcalo Manufacturing Co. v. Firemen's Mutual Ins. Co.*, 421 N.E. 2d 331 (1981), where damage caused by, respectively, a gas furnace and an oven being left on inadvertently was held to fall within an ordinary fire policy.
[8] *West India Telegraph Co. v. Home and Colonial Ins. Co.* (1880) 6 Q.B.D. 51, 60, *per* Brett L.J. who, however, held this case to be sufficiently analogous to one of fire to be covered by the general words at the end of a marine policy.
[9] (1873) Ir.R. 7 C.L. 126.

"spirits and such like in a still, and that the loss complained of was occasioned by the ordinary fire-heat under the said still". This plea was held to be bad since there was no allegation that the still was damaged by ordinary fire-heat and that the loss happened to the spirits at the time of such loss or damage. Since damage arising from only a particular kind of fire-heat had been excluded, it could be assumed that the parties intended the policy to cover other forms of fire-heat and it was the duty of the insurer to bring himself within the exception by pleading and proving that the damage to the spirits happened at the time the still itself was damaged by ordinary fire heat.

26–5 Damage by smoke. If property has been ignited which was not intended to be ignited, and property insured is damaged by smoke, the insurer will be liable to compensate the assured for such damage, provided it is a proximate consequence of the fire.[10] No recovery can be had when the damage is done by smoke from an intended fire. In *Harris v. Poland* Atkinson J. thought that smoke was a source of damage from fire along with heat, sparks and the flames themselves,[11] but would presumably have concluded that damage by smoke without any unintended ignition of property could not of itself render an insurer liable under a fire policy.

26–6 Damage by fire in an adjoining property. The improper ignition which is prima facie an essential element of "fire" within the meaning of a fire policy need not, however, be an ignition of the property insured. If other property in the vicinity is alight and damage is caused to the insured property by falling walls,[12] water[13] or otherwise, there is "fire" and "damage by fire" within the meaning of the policy subject to the principles of causation discussed below.[14]

26–7 Lightning. If lighting results in ignition, any loss occasioned by such ignition is a loss by fire[15]; but damage caused by lightning without ignition is not damage by fire.[16] Frequently, however, a fire policy will expressly include any loss by lightning.[17]

2. CAUSATION OF LOSS

26–8 Proximate cause. If there is a "fire" within the meaning of the policy, it must still be decided whether the fire was the proximate cause of the

---

[10] See *"The Diamond"* [1906] P. 282.

[11] [1941] K.B. 462, 469. In America, damage by smoke from a friendly fire has repeatedly been held not to be loss or damage by fire—see *Cannon v. Phoenix Ins. Co.*, 35 S.D. 775 (1900); *Lavitt v. Hartford County Fire Mutual Ins. Co.*, 136 A. 572 (1927).

[12] *Johnston v. West of Scotland Ins. Co.* (1828) 7 S. 52; *Ermentrout v. Girard Fire and Marine Ins. Co.*, 63 Minn. 305; 56 Am.S.R. 481 (1895).

[13] See paras 26–13, *et seq.*, *post*.

[14] See *Everett v. London Ass. Co.* (1865) 19 C.B.(N.S.) 126. This paragraph was cited with approval in *Edwards v. Wawanesa Mutual Ins. Co.* (1959) 17 D.L.R. 2d 229, 232.

[15] *Gordon v. Rimmington* (1807) 1 Camp. 123, *per* Lord Ellenborough C.J. at pp. 123–124.

[16] *Kenniston v. Merchants' County Mutual Ins. Co.*, 14 N.H. 341 (1843); *Babcock v. Montgomery County Mutual Ins. Co.*, 6 Barb.N.Y. 637 (1849); *Emerigon* (1827 ed.) Vol. 1, c. 12, s.17, p. 428; Bunyon, *Fire Insurance* (7th ed.) p. 175 (citing two cases reported in the Insurance Record); Arnould, *Marine Insurance* (16th ed.) para. 806, note 92.

[17] As in *Roth v. South Easthope Farmers' Mutual Ins. Co.* (1918) 41 O.L.R. 52 and *Edwards v. Wawanesa Mutual Ins. Co.* (1959) 17 D.L.R. 2d 229.

damage. The general rules for determining whether damage has been proximately caused by the peril insured against have already been stated[18] but it is still necessary to discuss their application to particular cases.

In *Everett v. London Assurance Co.*[19] a house was insured against "such loss or damage as should or might be occasioned by fire". There was an explosion of gunpowder half a mile away from the assured's premises which damaged the premises by concussion of the atmosphere. The Court of Common Plea held that this particular loss was not covered by the policy. Willes J. said:

> "We are bound to look to the immediate cause of the loss or damage and not to some remote or speculative cause. Speaking of this injury no person would say that it was occasioned by fire. It was occasioned by a concussion or disturbance of the air caused by fire elsewhere. It would be going into the causes of causes to say that this was an injury caused by fire to the property insured. The rule 'in jure non remota causa sed proxima spectatur' determines this case."

26–9 This case may be usefully contrasted with *Johnston v. West of Scotland Insurance Co.*[20] in which a house in Glasgow was insured against "loss or damage which the insured shall suffer by fire on the property". A house adjacent to the assured's premises was burned down and a gable wall was left standing in a dangerous condition. The Dean of Guild, who had authority in such matters, ordered the gable to be pulled down, and as it was being demolished in accordance with his instructions it fell and damaged the premises of the assured. It was held that the damage was damage by fire within the meaning of the policy. On any analysis this must be a borderline case since if it could have been proved that the gable would not have fallen but for the action of the Dean of Guild, the fire could hardly be said to have been the proximate cause of the damage.

26–10 In *Shea and Foubert v. Halifax Insurance Co.*[21] the insurance was against "direct and accidental loss or damage caused solely by fire". The insured vehicle, a fuel oil tanker-trailer, was destroyed during the delivery of fuel oil in very cold weather. In order to heat the oil so as to make it flow, a heating device was employed which was not turned off at the required time. Damage to the vehicle was caused by the combustion of vapour, with consequent explosion, when the level of oil in the tank fell. There was no express exception for explosions in the policy and it was held that the fire was the proximate cause of the loss.

26–11 Excepted perils. The doctrine of proximate cause applies just as

---

[18] See paras 19–1, *et seq.*, *ante*.

[19] (1865) 19 C.B.(N.S.) 126. The statement of Byles J. that there must be ignition either of the property insured or of the premises in which it is contained must be regarded as too wide in the light of *Harris v. Poland* [1941] 1 K.B. 462, 473; see para. 26–1, *ante*. For an interesting contrast see *Lynn Gas and Electric Co. v. Meriden Fire Ass. Co.*, 158 Mass. 570 (1893) where a fire produced great heat which caused a short circuit and an increase in electric current with resulting damage to insured property.

[20] (1828) 7 S. 52. Cf. *Rutherford v. Royal Ins. Co.*, 12 F.2d 880 (1926) where it was held that there can be a total loss of a building when, after partial destruction by fire, it has been demolished by order of the municipal authority. See also *A. H. Jacobson & Co. v. Commercial Union Ass. Co.*, 83 F. Supp. 674 (1949).

[21] (1957) 10 D.L.R. 2d 664; (1958) 15 D.L.R. 2d 667.

much to excepted perils[22] as to those insured against. Thus an insurer cannot escape liability unless he can show that the loss or damage was proximately caused by an excepted peril and, conversely, once it is shown that an excepted peril was in operation, the assured will be unable to recover for any loss or damage which is the proximate result of that peril.[23] Thus, if explosion is excepted from a fire policy, the exception will exclude not only damage caused by an explosion consequent upon a fire but also damage caused by a fire consequent upon an explosion.[24] Similarly where a fire policy excepted loss or damage by fire occasioned by any earthquake and an earthquake caused a lighted stove in one house to be upset and in consequence the house caught fire and the fire spread to other houses, in so far as it spread without the intervention of other than natural causes it was a fire caused by or through an earthquake.[25]

26–12 Partial loss. In marine insurance if a partial loss from perils insured against is followed by a total loss from an excepted peril, so that the assured is not ultimately prejudiced by the partial loss, no recovery can be had in respect of such partial loss.[26] It is doubtful whether this principle has any application to an ordinary fire risk. But an insurer might be discharged from liability where, for instance, property was damaged by fire but immediately thereafter destroyed by an earthquake which was an excepted peril, because he would be unable to exercise the usual option to reinstate the premises and would have to pay on very doubtful evidence as to the extent of the loss.

26–13 Damage caused by effort to avert or extinguish fire. Although loss or damage may have occurred to the property of the assured by reason of efforts made to avert or extinguish a fire and not by reason of the fire itself, it by no means follows that the loss is not proximately caused by the fire.[27] In *Stanley v. Western Insurance Co.*[28] Kelly C.B. said:

> "I agree that any loss resulting from an apparently necessary and bona fide effort to put out a fire, whether it be by spoiling the goods by water or throwing the article of furniture out of a window or even the destroying of a neighbouring house by an explosion for the purpose of checking the progress of the flames, in a word, every loss that clearly and proximately results whether directly or indirectly from the fire is within the policy."

---

[22] Particular excepted perils are considered in paras 26–28, *et seq., post.*

[23] *Marsden v. City and County Ass. Co.* (1866) L.R. 1 C.P. 232; *Stanley v. Western Ins. Co.* (1868) L.R. 3 Ex. 71; *Ford Motor Co. v. Prudential Ass. Co.* (1958) 14 D.L.R. 2d 7.

[24] *Re Hooley Hill Rubber and Chemical Co. and the Royal Ins. Co.* [1920] 1 K.B. 257 and para. 26–47, *post.*

[25] *Tootal Broadhurst, Lee & Co. Ltd v. London and Lancashire Fire Ins. Co.* (1908) *The Times*, May 21.

[26] *Wilson Shipping Co. v. British & Foreigh Mar. Ins. Co.* [1921] 1 A.C. 188; *Livie v. Janson* (1810) 12 East 648; *Knight v. Faith* (1850) 15 Q.B. 649; Arnould, *Marine Insurance* (16th ed.) 1126–1128.

[27] s.12(2) of the Metropolitan Fire Brigade Act 1865 provided that, as regards fire within the Metropolitan area, any damage done by the brigade in the due execution of its duty should be deemed to be damage by fire within any policy of insurance against fire. Although this provision has been repealed by Sched. VI to the Fire Services Act 1947, it is submitted that it was in this respect merely declaratory of the common law, and that such damage is recoverable.

[28] (1868) L.R. 3 Ex. 71.

26–14 The dictum has been followed by the Court of Appeal[29] and the Privy Council.[30] It is, however, often difficult to draw a distinction between loss caused in such a way and loss caused by a voluntary act merely done in apprehension that loss will result. The principle seems to be that once the peril insured against begins to operate, loss and harm in efforts to check or avert the casualty will be proximately caused by that peril, but where the peril has not come into existence at all, loss or damage due to the fear that it will occur cannot be said to be the proximate result of that peril (unless perhaps there is a very real and pressing danger). In *Symington v. Union Insurance Society of Canton Ltd*[31] a shipment of cork was insured against fire, while waiting at a jetty to be shipped. A fire broke out some distance away and local authorities threw some of the cork into the sea and poured water on the rest to avoid consumption by the fire. It was held by the Court of Appeal that the consequent loss could be reasonably attributed to the fire and was proximately caused by it, Scrutton L.J. putting the test in these words: "Is it a fear of something that will happen in the future or has the peril already happened and is it so imminent it is immediately necessary to avert the danger by action?"[32]

26–15 Thus, if there was reasonable justification for the measures taken to avert damage by fire, damage to property caused by water[33] or demolition[34] is covered as damage by fire. It has been held in Canada that even if such avoiding action results in a peril which is expressly excepted by the policy, the insurer may still be liable. In *Glen Falls Insurance Co. v. Spencer*,[35] a motorcar was insured against fire but not against collision, a fire broke out in the dashboard and while the assured was trying to put it out the car collided with a tree and was totally destroyed by fire. The Supreme Court of New Brunswick held by a majority that the fire was the proximate cause of the entire loss.

26–16 Another consequence of fire may be that property is removed from a building in order to preserve it or to deprive the fire of inflammable

---

[29] *Symington v. Union Ins. Society of Canton Ltd* (1928) 97 L.J.K.B. 646; 34 Com.Cas. 23.
[30] *Canada Rice Mills Ltd v. Union Marine and General Ins. Co. Ltd* [1941] A.C. 55, 71. See also *Johnston v. West of Scotland Ins. Co.* (1828) 7 S. 52, 54; *Re Etherington and the Lancashire and Yorkshire Accident Ins. Co.* [1909] 1 K.B. 591, 599, *per* Vaughan Williams L.J. In *The Knight of St. Michael* [1898] P. 30 where part of a cargo became overheated and had to be discharged in order to avoid a loss by fire, Gorell Barnes J. held that the consequent loss of freight was sufficiently analogous to a loss by fire to fall within the general (not the particular) words of a marine policy. Contrast *Kacianoff v. China Traders Ins. Co.* [1914] 3 K.B. 1121 and *Becker Gray & Co. v. London Ass. Corporation* [1918] A.C. 102.
[31] (1928) 97 L.J.K.B. 646; 34 Com. Cas. 23.
[32] (1928) 97 L.J.K.B. 650. See also *MacMillan Bloedel Ltd v. Youell (The "Warschau")* (1993) 79 B.C.L.R. (2d) 326; (1994) 95 B.C.L.R. (2d) 130 in which the Court of Appeal of British Columbia held that the cost of discharging a cargo of coal in imminent danger of overheating was irrecoverable under a charterers' liability policy, either as sue and labour or as loss proximately caused by a peril insured against.
[33] *Ahmedbhoy Habbibhoy v. Bombay Fire and Marine Ins. Co.* (1912) L.R. 40 Ind.App. 10; 107 L.T. 668; *Symington v. Union Ins. Society of Canton Ltd* (1928) 97 L.J.K.B. 646; *McPherson v. Guardian Ins. Co.* (1893) 7 Nfld.L.R. 768; *Geisek v. Crescent Mutual Ins. Co.*, 19 La.Ann. 297 (1867); *Lewis v. Springfield Fire and Marine Ins. Co.*, 76 Mass. 159 (1857).
[34] *Stanley v. Western Ins. Co.* (1868) L.R. 3 Ex. 71, 74, *per* Kelly C.B.; *City Fire Ins. Co. v. Corlies*, 21 Wend. 367 (1839).
[35] (1956) 3 D.L.R. 2d 745.

material. If such property is damaged by being left out in bad weather[36] or by being thrown down from a window,[37] such damage may be recoverable under a fire policy.

It does not seem to have been decided in England whether it is a defence for the insurer to prove that, if no measures had been taken to avert or extinguish the fire, the property would not have been damaged. It is submitted that, if the measures were reasonably taken, any resulting damage should be recoverable by the insured, irrespective of the fact that no damage would have occurred if no such measures had been taken.[38]

26–17 Averting or minimising damage in general. Marine insurance policies often contain a "sue and labour" clause which (in its old form) permitted the insured to "sue, labour and travel" for the purpose of defending the ship or her cargo and required underwriters to pay the cost of such steps and (in the new forms) imposes a duty on the assured to take reasonable measures for averting or minimising a loss and likewise requires insurers to pay the reasonable cost thereof.[39] Aviation policies may also contain such a clause.[40] Property damage policies have no uniform terminology but it is not uncommon to find a clause in both marine and non-marine policies in some such terms as the following: "It is the duty of the assured to take such measures as may be reasonable for the purpose of averting or minimising a loss." It is relevant to ask:

(1) whether such a term, if not expressed, would be implied into a property damage policy and
(2) whether the cost of complying with the clause or of taking reasonable measures to prevent loss (or further loss) will be recoverable from insurers.

26–18 (1) It is doubtful whether a court would imply any general term that an insured should take reasonable steps to avert or minimise a loss. This is partly because it is easy to make express provision for such an obligation and business efficacy will not usually require the implication of a term which is commonly incorporated as an express term. Another reason is that the doctrine of proximate causation can often do the work of such an implied term. If the insured suffers loss because he has decided not to take a step which it would be reasonable for him to have taken, his loss will be held to have been proximately caused by that decision rather than the operation of any peril insured against.[41]

26–19 (2) The cost of taking measures to avert or minimise a loss will not

---

[36] *Cf. McLaren v. Commercial Union Ins. Co.* (1885) 12 Ont. App. 279; *Thompson v. Montreal Ins. Co.* (1850) 6 U.C.Q.B. 319; *Balestracci v. Firemen's Ins. Co.*, 34 La.Ann. 844 (1882).

[37] *Stanley v. Western Ins. Co.* (1868) L.R. 3 Ex. 71, 74, *per* Kelly C.B.

[38] The great majority of U.S. decisions support this view—see, *e.g. Balestracci v. Firemen's Ins. Co.*, 34 La.Ann. 844 (1882); *Queen's Ins. Co. v. Patterson*, 74 So. 807 (1917); *Harper v. Pelican Trucking Co.*, 176 So. 2d. 767 (1965).

[39] Compare the various terms set out in *Integrated Container Services v. British Traders Ins. Co.* [1981] 2 Lloyd's Rep. 460.

[40] See, *e.g. Kuwait Airways Corp. v. Kuwait Ins. Co. S.A.K.* [1999] 1 Lloyd's Rep. 803—see para. 30–10, *post*.

[41] The authorities do not speak unambiguously, see the *dicta* of Scrutton L.J. in *City Tailors Ltd v. Evans* (1921) 38 T.L.R. 230, 233–4, criticised in para. 26–28, *post* and not referred to in *Yorkshire Water Services v. Sun Alliance* [1997] 2 Lloyd's Rep. 21.

often be recoverable from insurers. If no provision for such costs are included in the policy, any recoverability will have to be implied and it may be difficult to formulate an implied term with any great precision. In *Netherlands Insurance v. Karl Ljungberg & Co.*[42] the marine insurance policy in that case contained the clause quoted above and the insurers conceded that they should reimburse the assured the costs of complying with the clause. This concession was, perhaps, made because the policy also contained the old form of sue and labour clause and because it was necessary for both provisions to be read together. It is unlikely that the case will be treated as any general authority for the implication of a term that insurers will pay the costs of measures taken to avert a loss, particularly as Lord Goff of Chieveley said in the course of delivering the advice of the Judicial Committee:

> "Their Lordships do not feel able to accept that, as a general proposition, the mere fact that an obligation is imposed on one party to a contract for the benefit of the other carries with it an implied term that the latter shall reimburse the former for his costs incurred in the performance of that obligation."

In *Yorkshire Water Services Ltd v. Sun Alliance*[43] the insured had incurred considerable expense in doing flood alleviation works in order to avoid additional damage to the property of third parties; if that work had not been done, the insured would have been liable in damages for nuisance or negligence to those third parties and they contended that their liability insurers would have been liable for such damages. They argued that insurers should, therefore, be liable for the cost of averting that liability. The Court of Appeal held that on the true construction of the relevant liability policies, the obligation was on the insured to pay for the expense of averting further damage to the third parties. But they also considered whether, if that were wrong, a term could be implied indemnifying the insured for costs reasonably incurred to prevent or minimise further loss which might otherwise fall on the insurer. The court concluded that such a term could not be implied into a liability policy. A liability policy normally affords an indemnity against sums which the insured becomes legally liable to pay as damages or compensation in respect of loss or damage to property. Sums paid to avert or lessen his liability are not sums of that description.

The position under a property damage policy is, perhaps more debatable. Suppose, for example, a householder insures his house but not his garden against subsidence and the garden subsides to such an extent that the house is itself in imminent danger of collapse. If the householder then erects a retaining wall to avert the risk of further subsidence as well as to reduce the risk of insurers becoming liable under the policy, can he recover the cost of erecting the retaining wall? We submit that he should be so entitled[44] and that any other result would be manifestly unjust.

---

[42] [1986] 3 All E.R. 767.

[43] [1997] 2 Lloyd's Rep. 21.

[44] This is the position in some jurisdictions in the U.S.: see *Leebov v. United States Fidelity & Guaranty Co.*, 401 Pa. 477 (1960); 71 Col.L.R. 1309 (1971), but the Supreme Court of Canada has held that there must be an operating peril of the type or category described in the policy and damage must be reasonably anticipated from the peril—see *Liverpool & London & Globe Ins. Ltd v. Canadian General Electric Co. Ltd* (1981) 123 D.L.R. 3d 513.

26–20 Wilful act of the assured. The assured cannot recover for a loss where his own deliberate act is the proximate cause of it.[45] This rule is the result of the application of one or both of two separate principles of law. First, on ordinary principles of insurance law an assured cannot by his own deliberate act bring about the event upon which the insurance money is payable, because it is presumed that the insurance was never intended to cover that kind of loss, but only a loss occasioned by a fortuitous peril.[46] This presumption must be virtually irrebuttable in relation to indemnity policies, but it also applies to life insurance policies which will not, prima facie, cover the self-inflicted death of the assured while sane.[47] Secondly, on a principle of public policy applicable to all sorts of legal claims, the assured is not entitled to recover a benefit or indemnity in respect of his own criminal or civil wrong, because the courts desire to impose that restraint upon the commission of crimes and illegal acts.[48] This principle is perhaps itself a special application of the general doctrine that no man may take advantage of his own wrong.[49]

26–21 The second of these two principles may sometimes be of greater importance than the first. Thus if a policy covers two assured (not being joint owners) for their respective, right, and interest, the wilful act of one will not debar the other's claim.[50] Sometimes a person with a limited interest, such as a mortgagee, may take out his own policy so as to avoid any difficulty with the insurance should the mortgagor be tempted to destroy the property. In *Schiffshypothekenbank zu Luebeck v. Compton ("The Alexion Hope")*[51] a mortgagee had a policy which was to pay "if an occurrence causes loss or damage and the Assured is unable to recover from the vessel's underwriters and the cause of the non-payment is not the bankruptcy of the Hull underwriters". Hull underwriters alleged that the owners set fire to the vessel deliberately and the question was whether that was an occurrence within the mortgagee's policy. The mortgagee's insurers argued that an occurrence had to be something which hull insurers had insured and wilful destruction by fire was not an insured peril. Staughton J. held that, since fire was a named peril in the hull insurance, even a deliberate fire was covered although, of course, hull insurers were not bound to indemnify the owners if

---

[45] *Horneyer v. Lushington* (1812) 15 East 46; *Oswell v. Vigne* (1812) 15 East 70; *Thurtell v. Beaumont* (1824) 1 Bing. 339; *Upjohn v. Hitchens* [1918] 2 K.B. 48, 58, *per* Scrutton L.J.; *City Tailors v. Evans* (1921) 38 T.L.R. 230, 233–234, *per* Scrutton L.J.; *Beresford v. Royal Ins. Co.* [1938] A.C. 586, 595, *per* Lord Atkin.
[46] *Beresford v. Royal Ins. Co.* [1938] A.C. 586, 595; *Gray v. Barr* [1971] 2 Q.B. 554, 580, 587; *Trinder Anderson v. Thames and Mersey Ins. Co.* [1898] 2 Q.B. 1 14, 127–128; *Smit Tak Offshore Services v. Youell* [1992] 1 Lloyd's Rep. 154, 158.
[47] *Beresford v. Royal Ins. Co.* [1938] A.C. 586, 602.
[48] *Gray v. Barr* [1971] 2 Q.B. 554 (where the modern authorities are reviewed by the Court of Appeal); *Geismar v. Sun Alliance Ltd* [1978] Q.B. 383. For a full examination of these principles see paras 14–22, *et seq.*, *ante*.
[49] *Société des Ateliers & Chantiers de France v. New Zealand Shipping Co.* [1919] A.C. 1; *Torquay Hotel Co. v. Cousins* [1969] 2 Ch. 106, 137; *Thompson v. Hopper* (1858) E.B. & E. 1038. 1045; *Slattery v. Mance* [1962] 1 Q.B. 676.
[50] *Lombard Australia Ltd v. N.R.M.A. Insurance Ltd* [1969] 1 Lloyd's Rep. 575; *Higgins v. Orion Ins. Co.* [1985] C.C.L.I. 139 (Ontario); *Samuel v. Dumas* [1924] A.C. 431, 445, 469; *New Hampshire Ins. Co. v. Mirror Group Newspapers* [1997] L.R.L.R. 24; *Scott v. Wawanesa Mutual Ins. Co.* (1898) 59 D.L.R. (4th) 660, 676. See para. 1–194, *ante*.
[51] [1987] 1 Lloyd's Rep. 60, affirmed by the Court of Appeal [1988] 1 Lloyd's Rep. 311.

they had deliberately set fire to the vessel, because the owners could not be allowed to take advantage of their own wrong. The Court of Appeal agreed but took the view that a deliberate fire was, in any event, an "occurrence" within the meaning of the mortgagee's policy.

26–22 Fraudulent intent. For the sake of completeness it may be added that if the assured were shown to have effected the insurance with the intention of causing a loss and pocketing the insurance moneys, it would be unenforceable ab initio at the suit of the assured if his chosen method of bringing about a loss involved a criminal or unlawful act.[52] Over-valuation of the property insured may well constitute important evidence in support of the plea of arson or insurance with fraudulent intent.[53] Clauses dealing with the making of fraudulent claims are discussed elsewhere in this work.[54]

26–23 Burden of proof. Once the assured establishes that a loss by fire has occurred, the onus of proof shifts to the insurer to plead and prove by cogent evidence that the fire was caused by the wilful act of the assured.[55]

26–24 Proximate cause of the loss. At the outset it was said that the prohibition of recovery applied only if the assured's action was the proximate cause of the loss. Thus, if the assured introduces highly inflammable goods or naked flames into dangerous positions, that does not ipso facto affect the insurers' position, because a wilful act of the assured which merely increases the risk does not, apart from a warranty prohibiting it, affect the policy. It is not the effective cause of the loss.[56] If, however, the necessary consequence of the act was to bring about a loss, or if, on the analogy of recent decisions of the courts, the assured deliberately took a serious risk that it would do so,[57] then his act would be regarded as the proximate cause of the loss.

26–25 Circumstances justifying assured's act. If the wilful act of the assured was done for the purpose of avoiding a peril insured against, the loss may be recoverable, since it may be said to result from the operation of the peril rather than from the free volition of the assured, as where certain property is destroyed in order to check a wider conflagration.[58] It has been suggested in ancient treatises on insurance by foreign writers[59] that if a wilful burning is not done solely to obtain insurance money, but is otherwise

---

[52] *Archbolds v. Spanglett* [1961] 1 Q.B. 374, 387, 388. In *Hercules Ins. Co. v. Hunter* (1835) 14 S. 147; (1836) 14 S. 1137 it was said that the insurer could avoid the policy for concealment of the assured's intention. In the improbable event that the insurer was also party to the fraudulent intention of the assured, the policy would presumably be void *ab initio*.

[53] *Hercules Ins. v. Hunter* (1836) 14 S. 1137; *Britton v. Royal Ins. Co.* (1866) 4 F. & F. 905.

[54] See para. 19–54, *ante*.

[55] The authorities are considered in note 38 to para. 19–8, *ante*. See also *McGregor v. Prudential Insurance Co. Ltd* [1998] 1 Lloyd's Rep. 112, where the equivalent paragraph in the 8th edition of this work (para. 1881) was cited by the learned judge. It is the same in marine insurance where fire is a specified peril—see *National Justice Cia v. Prudential Ass. Co.* [1995] 1 Lloyd's Rep. 455. The same approach was followed in *Shakur v. Pilot Ins. Co.* (1991) 73 D.L.R. (4th) 337, 344, Ont.C.A.

[56] *Thompson v. Hopper* (1858) E.B. & E. 1038.

[57] *Gray v. Barr* [1971] 2 Q.B. 554, 567, 587; *Hardy v. Motor Insurers' Bureau* [1964] 2 Q.B. 745, 759, 764.

[58] *Stanley v. Western Ins. Co.* (1868) L.R. 3 Ex. 71, and para. 26–13, *ante*.

[59] Pothier; Valin; Emerigon, cited in *Gordon v. Rimmington* (1807) 1 Camp. 123, 124 by the reporter.

justifiable, it is a loss by fire for which recovery may be had under the policy, and Emerigon, for instance, said that an insurer on a marine policy was liable where the ship was deliberately burned to prevent plague spreading.[60] The English law, however, is not so wide as that, and in *Gordon v. Rimmington*,[61] where a vessel was set alight to avoid her capture by enemy forces, and recovery was permitted for a loss by fire, it is clear that Lord Ellenborough regarded the action of the crew as being one which they were bound to take out of duty to the State. Although the court described it as a loss by fire, the case is better explained as concerning a loss by enemy action. It could not be said, for instance, that, if bedding or furniture were set alight after an infectious illness, such loss would be recoverable from the insurers as a loss by fire, but, if it were done by order of competent medical authorities the loss could well be recoverable under some other head of a comprehensive policy.

26–26 Wilful act of servant of assured. A claim will not be defeated by the wilful act of the assured's servants or agents, provided it was not done with the privity or consent of the assured.[62] If the assured's wife[63] or some other member of his household[64] without his connivance burns his property, the assured will be able to recover. But where a corporation is insured it cannot recover if the fire was wilfully caused by one of its principal officers.[65]

26–27 Negligence of assured. If the proximate cause of the loss is fire, it is immaterial in the absence of relevant warranties that the fire has been caused by the negligence of the assured[66] or his servants.[67] Thus, where the assured hid her jewellery in a grate and later forgot that she had done so and lit a fire there, it was held that she was entitled to recover under a fire policy for the resulting damage.[68] Even gross negligence will not debar the assured from recovering under the policy unless his conduct was so reckless and careless of consequences that it amounts in law to a wilful act.[69]

26–28 If the assured refuses to take obvious precautions to prevent or stop a fire, for instance if he leaves a coal which has fallen out of the grate or a candle shade which has caught alight to set fire to the house, it might be argued that he is not entitled to recover.[70] But the better view is probably

---

[60] See Book 1 at p. 434.
[61] (1807) 1 Camp. 123.
[62] *General Accident Fire and Life Ass. Corporation v. Midland Bank Ltd* [1940] 2 K.B. 388.
[63] *Midland Ins. Co. v. Smith* (1881) 6 Q.B.D. 561.
[64] *Shaw v. Robberds* (1837) 6 Ad. & El. 75, 84, *per* Lord Denman C.J.; *Perry v. Mechanics' Mutual Ins. Co.*, 11 Fed.Rep. 485 (1882); see also *Brewster v. Blackmore* (1925) 21 Ll.L.R. 258.
[65] *S. & M. Carpets (London) Ltd v. Cornhill Ins. Co. Ltd* [1982] 1 Lloyd's Rep. 423. It has been held in California that a corporation can recover if it can show that the officer of the company who caused the fire will not benefit directly or indirectly—see *Erwin-Lawler Enterprises Inc. v. Fire Ins. Exchange*, 73 Cal.Rep. 182 (1968). It is doubtful if this decision would be followed in this country.
[66] *Shaw v. Robberds* (1837) 6 Ad. & El. 75; *Jameson v. Royal Ins. Co.* (1873) Ir.R. 7 C.L. 126; *Davidson v. Burnand* (1868) L.R. 4 C.P. 117; *"The Diane"* [1977] 1 Lloyd's Rep. 61.
[67] *Austin v. Drewe* (1815) 4 Camp. 360, 362; *Dobson v. Sotheby* (1827) 1 M. & M. 90; *Busk v. Royal Exchange Ass. Co.* (1818) 2 B. & Ald. 73; *Att.-Gen. v. Adelaide S.S. Co.* [1923] A.C. 292, 308, *per* Lord Wrenbury.
[68] *Harris v. Poland* [1941] 1 K.B. 462.
[69] *Pipon v. Cope* (1808) 1 Camp. 434 as explained in *Trinder Anderson v. Thames and Mersey Marine Insurance* [1898] 2 Q.B. 114, 129, *per* Collins L.J.
[70] *Cf. Chandler v. Worcester Mutual Fire Ins. Co.*, 57 Mass. 328 (1849); Appleman, *Insurance Law and Practice*, (1981), para. 3115.

that the insurer cannot rely on any negligent act of the assured (even after the fire has started[71]) except as evidence of a wilful act. Sometimes a policy contains a specific clause requiring the assured to use due diligence and to do and concur in doing all things reasonably practicable to minimise the loss. In *City Tailors Ltd v. Evans*[72] Scrutton L.J. expressed the view (in an unreserved judgment) that such a clause added nothing to the ordinary obligation of the assured since if the assured failed to exercise due diligence any loss would have been caused by his own act. The difficulty with this approach is that, if the assured's act was negligent and not wilful it should be covered by the policy. It is therefore submitted that Scrutton L.J.'s remarks are too wide.

26–29 Insanity and drunkenness of the assured. If the assured is so insane as not to be legally responsible for his acts, an act of incendiarism will not prevent him from recovering under the policy.[73] The question of the assured's insanity will probably have to be decided with reference to the McNaghten rules.[74]

The criminal law acquits on the ground of drunkenness when the assured is so drunk as to be incapable of forming the specific intent which must be proved by the Crown and, where no specific intent need be proved, drunkenness is no defence. It could be argued by analogy that, since a specific intent must be proved to establish the defence of wilful incendiarism in an insurance case, the drunkenness of the assured may be a relevant factor. Just as a man who kills another in a manner which would normally justify the inference that he did so intentionally may escape that inference and be convicted only of manslaughter if he was severely intoxicated, so acts which appear on the face of them to amount to wilful burning of property may for the same reason be held not to be wilful.

3. PERILS COMMONLY EXCEPTED

26–30 Loss or damage by theft or riot. As a matter of general principle theft or riot might well be considered a nova causa interveniens but as a matter of practice many insurance companies pay for loss or damage by thieves or rioters during the confusion caused by fire.[75] It is desirable that, at any rate, theft during the removal of goods from the scene of the fire should be covered since otherwise the assured might be tempted to leave them to burn, and in Canada a claim has been allowed on this ground.[76]

26–31 It is doubtful whether English law would follow the Canadian cases

---

[71] *Dixon v. Sadler* (1839) 5 M. & W. 405, 414, *per* Parke B.
[72] (1921) 38 T.L.R. 230, 233–234.
[73] *D'Autremont v. Fire Association of Philadelphia*, 65 Hun. 475 (1892).
[74] (1843) 10 Cl. & Fin. 200.
[75] *Levy v. Baillie* (1831) 7 Bing. 349 where a claim was made both for goods injured during removal and for goods abstracted by the crowd. No objection was made that loss by theft was not covered by the policy.
[76] *Thompson v. Montreal Ins. Co.* (1850) 6 U.C.Q.B. 319. See also *McGibbon v. Queen's Ins. Co.* (1866) 10 L.C.J. 227; *Harris v. London and Lancashire Fire Ins. Co.* (1866) 10 L.C.J. 268 (both these last cases were cited by Gorell Barnes J. in the *Knight of St. Michael* [1898] P. 30.); *McPherson v. Guardian Ins. Co.* (1893) 7 Nfld.L.R. 768; *Belastracci v. Firemen's Ins. Co.*, 34 La.Ann. 844 (1882).

on this point since it can usually be said only that the fire provides the opportunity for the intervention of an entirely independent cause of damage. In *Marsden v. City and County Assurance Co.*[77] there was a policy on plate glass "against loss or damage originating from any cause whatsoever except fire, breakage during removal, alteration or repair of premises". A fire broke out in some premises adjoining those of the assured, who began to remove his furniture and stock-in-trade; while he was so engaged a mob broke in the windows for the purpose of plunder. The insurers sought to argue that the loss was caused by the fire and was therefore within the exception clause but it was held that the fire was not the proximate cause of the breakage. Erle C.J. said:

> "No doubt the remote cause of the damage was fire, but the proximate cause was the lawless violence of the mob ... the breakage was not caused by the fire; it was the result of the plaintiff's attempt to save his stock and furniture coupled with the desire of the mob to seize what they could lay their hands on."

It seems to follow from this decision that even if riot or theft are not expressly excepted from the risk in a fire policy, loss or damage caused by thieves or rioters can seldom be recovered as loss or damage by fire.[78]

26–32 Riot and civil commotion. Insurance policies frequently provide that the insurer is not to be liable for loss arising from various forms of disturbance. Such a clause, in one form or another, has been inserted in fire policies since the "Gordon Riots"[79] and will now usually exclude the consequences of invasion, insurrection, riot, civil commotion, military and usurped power. Sankey J. has thus described the clause[80]:

> "The clause has two limbs—(1) insurrection, riots, civil commotions (2) military or usurped power. The first refers to domestic disturbances of different degrees of intensity, down to civil commotion. ... The words 'military or usurped power' seem to open a new and another category of events, to import more than mere internal incidents ... military and usurped power suggest something more in the nature of war or civil war than riot and tumult. This is a riot clause and a war clause combined."

26–33 Riot is a technical term of the criminal law and will be interpreted accordingly.[81] The fact that the authorities on the topic concerned the old common law offence of riot which has now been abolished and replaced by a new statutory definition contained in section 1 of the Public Order Act 1986[82] makes no difference to the general principle that technical terms of the

---

[77] (1865) L.R. 1 C.P. 232.
[78] But see *Bondrett v. Hentigg* (1816) Holt N.P. 149 where goods were landed after a vessel had run ashore owing to a fire and pilferage of the goods by landsmen was held to be a peril of the sea. See also *Queen's Insurance Co. v. Patterson Drug Co.*, 74 So. 807 (1917) where the assured had a duty to use all reasonable means to save his property in the event of a fire and was held able to recover for theft while he removed them.
[79] See the historical analysis by Hamilton L.J. in *London and Manchester Plate Glass Co. v. Heath* [1914] 3 K.B. 411.
[80] *Rogers v. Whittaker* [1917] 1 K.B. 942.
[81] *London and Lancashire Fire Ins. Co. v. Bolands* [1924] A.C. 836; *Athens Maritime Enterprises Cpn v. Hellenic Mutual War Risk Assn (Andreas Lemos)* [1983] Q.B. 647—see para. 11–13, *ante*.
[82] Smith and Hogan, *Criminal Law* (10th ed.) pp. 761–764.

criminal law will be given their technical meaning when they are used in insurance policies. The old authorities are, accordingly, not now of assistance in interpreting the term "riot". Canadian and American authorities have adopted a more flexible approach[83] but that is not likely to commend itself to an English court. Now that a riot can only occur "where 12 or more persons present together use or threaten unlawful violence for a common purpose", the statutory meaning is much closer to the ordinary sense of the word and there is likely to be less difference of interpretation than formerly between English courts and those of other common law jurisdictions. If an assured has suffered loss from riot he can still claim damages under the Riot (Damages) Act 1886.[84]

26–34 "Civil Commotion" has been defined by Lord Mansfield "as an insurrection of the people for general purposes, not necessarily amounting to a rebellion."[85] The acts constituting the commotion must be done by the rioters together, not merely in concert and simultaneously; thus, where a plate glass policy covered damage caused directly by or arising from civil commotion, it was held that the breaking of a window by a single suffragist demonstrator was not within the policy, although a number of women had separately broken windows in pursuance of a preconceived plan.[86] The element of turbulence or tumult or popular rising is essential, and the fact that some disorder exists, and that emergency regulations have been promulgated, is not in itself sufficient.[87] In *Cooper v. General Accident Fire and Life Assurance Corporation*[88] a car was insured by the appellant who heard a noise in the yard near the garage where his car was parked. He opened the back door and a voice said "shut that door". All that the appellant could see was an arm, holding what might have been a revolver or a stick, and the car being driven off. The House of Lords accepted the contention of the insurers that the loss was caused by civil commotion. It was common knowledge that a state of guerrilla warfare existed in certain parts of Ireland and the acts of the participants could not be said to be those of ordinary thieves. The insurers did not have to prove that there was a commotion at the time and place where the loss occurred provided that the loss did occur as a consequence of civil commotion.

26–35 Insurrections, rebellion, civil war. These expressions describe various ascending stages of civil conflict. The first two may well be included in the phrase civil commotion but, because civil commotion is intended to indicate a stage between a riot and a civil war,[89] civil war will not itself come within an exception for civil commotion.[90] In order to decide whether a state

---

[83] *Ford Motor Co. of Canada Ltd v. Prudential Ass. Co.* (1958) 14 D.L.R. 2d 7; *Pan American World Airways Inc. v. Aetna Casualty and Surety Co.* [1975] 1 Lloyd's Rep. 77.

[84] For compensation payable in cases of terrorism in Northern Ireland see para. 26–37, note 2, post.

[85] *Langdale v. Mason* (1780) Park, *Insurance*, Vol. 2, p. 965.

[86] *London and Manchester Plate Glass Co. v. Heath* [1914] 3 K.B. 411.

[87] *Levy v. Assicurazioni Generali* [1940] A.C. 791. *Spinney's v. Royal Ins. Co.* [1980] 1 Lloyd's Rep. 406, 437.

[88] (1923) 128 L.T. 481; 13 Ll.L.R. 219; followed in *Boggan v. Motor Union Ins. Co.* (1923) 130 L.T. 588; 16 Ll.L.R. 64. The words "civil commotion" do not apply to hijacking—*Pan American World Airways Inc. v. Aetna Casualty and Surety Co.* [1975] 1 Lloyd's Rep. 77.

[89] *Bolivia Republic v. Indemnity Mutual Insurance* [1909] 1 K.B. 785, 801; *Crozier v. Thompson* (1922) 12 Ll.L.R. 291; *Johnson and Perrott v. Holmes* (1925) 21 Ll.L.R. 330.

[90] *Curtis & Sons v. Mathews* [1919] 1 K.B. 425.

of civil war exists, it will be necessary to consider whether there are persons inside a particular state fighting against one another, what their objectives are, and what the scale of the conflict is. Activities of militarised bands of men were, accordingly, not held to amount to civil war in *Spinney's v. Royal Insurance*.[91] The activities of Renamo in Mozambique in the early 1980's were held to amount at least to insurrection, if not rebellion, in *National Oil Co. of Zimbabwe v. Sturge*.[92] In the latter case Saville J. said:

> " 'Rebellion' and 'insurrection' have somewhat similar meanings to each other. To my mind, each means an organised and violent internal uprising in a country with, as a main purpose, the object of trying to overthrow or supplant the government of that country, though 'insurrection' denotes a lesser degree of organisation and size than 'rebellion'."

26–36 Military or usurped power. This exclusion describes two different state of affairs and does not mean "usurped military power".[93] It seems to date from the early 18th century and first came before the courts in *Drinkwater v. London Assurance*[94] where a distinction was drawn between a common mob (which might be committing riot) and a rebellious mob (which would be committing treason). Since damage had been inflicted by a common mob incensed by increased prices, there could be no question of the loss being caused by "invasion, foreign enemy, or any military or usurped power whatsoever". It is less clear whether damage caused by a rebellious mob will always fall within an exception for "usurped power" especially if there is a further exception for "insurrection or rebellion". The perpetrators of a rebellion must have the intention to force a change of government by acts of violence, but it is possible to contemplate a situation:

(a) where a mob has no wish to force a change of government but wishes to do acts within the sphere of aiding government activity and

(b) where a mob which does wish to force a change of government (and is thus a rebellious mob) nevertheless fails effectively to achieve any of its objects.

The first situation is not a rebellion but it seems that it can constitute usurped power. In *Spinney's v. Royal Insurance*,[95] Mustill J. held that, although there was no rebellion or insurrection in the sense that there was an intention to supplant the existing rulers or to deprive them of authority over part of their territory, the relevant Lebanese militia took action to relieve public grievances by, *e.g.* promoting or weakening Palestinian influence in Lebanon, making efforts to displace sections of the population and preventing freedom of movement. Since these acts were within the proper sphere of government, the militia were arrogating to themselves functions of the state and exercised or constituted a usurped power. It is submitted that in the second situation, where the rebellion or insurrection fails to achieve its objects but causes loss or damage to property, a court would be unlikely to hold that such loss or damage was caused by military or usurped power.

---

[91] *Spinney's v. Royal Ins. Co.* [1980] 1 Lloyd's Rep. 406.

[92] [1991] 2 Lloyd's Rep. 281.

[93] *Rogers v. Whittaker* [1917] 1 K.B. 942. *Cf. Pan American World Airways v. Aetna Casualty and Surety Co.* [1975] 1 Lloyd's Rep. 77.

[94] (1767) 2 Wils. 363.

[95] [1980] 1 Lloyd's Rep. 406.

Examples of "military power" are fire caused by an enemy air-raid[96] and acts done by military force in repelling an enemy or suppressing a rebellion.[97] "Usurped power" does not include the act of a magistrate exceeding his jurisdiction[98] or an act of a government de facto recognised by the British Government.[99]

26–37 Terrorism. In recent years, exceptions aimed at acts of terrorism have begun to appear in fire policies. One such clause excepts "any activity of any organisation the objects of which are or include the overthrowing or influencing of any *de jure* or *de facto* government by terrorism or by any violent means".[1] In Northern Ireland since 1978 it has been usual to include in commercial and industrial fire policies an exception designed to exclude all those cases in which compensation can be claimed from the Government.[2] The definition of "terrorism" used for this purpose "includes any use of violence for the purpose of putting the public or any section of the public in fear". In insurances on residential property, this exclusion is not generally used but there may be a warranty requiring the insured to take all necessary steps to claim government compensation.

26–38 War risk. Where there is an exception for war risks, the word "war" does not have a technical meaning[3]; the civil strife in Dublin in 1916, *e.g.* was held to amount to war within the terms of an insurance policy[4] and the revolutionaries were held to be "king's enemies".[5] Unless a contrary intention appears, the word "war" will include "civil war".[6] In *Curtis & Sons v. Mathews,*[7] the plaintiffs insured their business premises in Dublin under a policy containing a "war and bombardment" clause:

> "This policy is to cover the risk of loss and/or damage to the property hereby insured directly caused by war, bombardment, military or usurped power, or by aerial craft (hostile or otherwise), including bombs, shells, and/or missiles dropped or thrown therefrom, or discharged thereat, and fire and/or explosion directly caused by any of the foregoing, whether originating on the premises insured or elsewhere ... No claim to attach hereto for confiscation or destruction by the Government of the country in which the property is situated."

---

[96] *Rogers v. Whittaker* [1917] 1 K.B. 942.
[97] *Curtis & Sons v. Mathews* [1919] 1 K.B. 425; *cf. Johnson and Perrott Ltd v. Holmes* (1925) 21 Ll.L.R. 330 (damage caused by the military and/or police unless acting under military or police authority).
[98] *City Fire Ins. Co. v. Corlies*, 21 Wend. 367 (1839).
[99] *White, Child and Beney v. Simmons and Eagle Star Ins. Co.* (1922) 127 L.J. 571; 11 Ll.L.R. 7, *per* Bankes L.J.
[1] *Cf. Spinney's v. Royal Ins. Co.* [1980] 1 Lloyd's Rep. 406, 438.
[2] Under the Criminal Damage (Compensation) (Northern Ireland) Order 1977 (S.I. 1977 No. 1247) and the regulations (S.R.N.I. 1978 No. 72) made thereunder.
[3] *Cf. Kawasaki Kisen Kaisha v. Bantham SS. Co.* [1939] 2 K.B. 544 (construction of the word in a charterparty); *Kuwait Airways Cpn v. Kuwait Ins. Co.* [1996] 1 Lloyd's Rep. 664, 691.
[4] *Curtis & Sons v. Mathews* [1919] 1 K.B. 425.
[5] *Secretary of State for War v. Midland Great Western Ry of Ireland* [1923] 2 Ir.R. 102.
[6] *Curtis & Sons v. Mathews* [1919] 1 K.B. 425; *Pesquerías y Secaderos de Bacalao de España v. Beer* [1949] 1 All E.R. 845; 82 Ll.L.R. 501, 514, *per* Lord Morton.
[7] [1918] 2 K.B. 825; [1919] 1 K.B. 425.

The premises were set on fire during the Easter rising of 1916; the fire originated in the General Post Office, as the result of a bombardment by the forces of the Crown, and spread until it consumed the insured premises. Roche J. held first that Easter week in Dublin was a week not of mere riot but of civil strife amounting to warfare and involving bombardment, and secondly, that, in view of the close collocation of the words "destruction" and "confiscation", the proviso related only to intentional and direct destruction, *e.g.* of buildings, as a hindrance to military operations. His decision that the assured was entitled to succeed was affirmed in the Court of Appeal and later approved in the House of Lords.[8]

26–39 A useful comparison may be made with the *American Tobacco Co. Inc. v. Guardian Assurance Co.*[9] arising out of a conflagration at Smyrna which occurred between September 13 and 16 in 1922 and destroyed the greater part of the city. The insurance on the plaintiffs' warehouses in Smyrna contained a war risks clause excepting:

> "Loss or damage directly or indirectly proximately or remotely occasioned or contributed to by or in connection with or in consequence of invasion, the act of foreign enemy, hostilities or war-like operations the administration of any place or area under martial law or in a state of siege or any of the events or causes which determined the proclamation or maintenance or martial law or state of siege or any consequence of any of the said occurrences or incendiarism directly connected therewith."

The Greek army had occupied Smyrna in 1919 and the Turks had withdrawn into the interior. In 1922 the Angora Turks, under Mustapha Kemal, defeated the Greeks, who retreated through Smyrna and ultimately evacuated it on September 9, 1922; the Turkish army entered Smyrna without any fighting and proclaimed martial law, but from that day the policing of the city, at any rate in the Armenian quarter, failed entirely with the result that disorderly groups of individuals—Turkish civilians and soldiers—began committing outrages, including murder and arson, with impunity, and this state of anarchy continued from September 9 to 13 when a number of fires broke out in the Armenian quarter in quick succession and Rowlatt J. drew the inference that they were due to incendiarism committed by disorderly people. He held that the fire was sufficiently connected with the military occupation to prevent the plaintiff from recovering and the Court of Appeal agreed with him. Bankes L.J. said he desired to base his judgment on the ground that the loss or damage of which the plaintiffs complained was proximately or remotely contributed to by or in connection with or in consequence of events or causes which determined the proclamation or maintenance of martial law or state of siege. Scrutton L.J. said that the fire was at any rate contributed to by incendiarism directly caused by the state of war.

26–40 There is little modern authority on the meaning of "war risks" but sometimes policies are very particular as to the precise terms of cover afforded. The latent (and often patent) hostilities in the Middle East have caused underwriters and their assured much difficulty. In *American Airlines*

---

[8] *Pesquerías y Secaderos de Bacalao de España v. Beer* [1949] 1 All E.R. 845; 82 Ll.L.R. 501
[9] (1925) 22 Ll.L.R. 37.

v. Hope[10] three aircraft had been destroyed by the Israeli Government while grounded at Beirut airport, in retaliation for a previous attack by Arab terrorists on Israeli aircraft at Athens two days before. No policy had been issued but the slip excluded war risks. There was, however, much argument whether the contract of insurance included two clauses which had been in previous insurances:

(1) "This policy is extended to cover loss or damage arising out of any unprovoked or accidentally provoked incidents which arise during the normal course of the Assured's operations between Israel/Arab countries";

(2) "Including liability for loss or damage arising out of any unprovoked or accidentally provoked incident or incidents which occur during normal course of the Assured's operations over Arab/Israel territory."

The House of Lords eventually held that neither of these clauses was incorporated in the contract of insurance, but it was also held (obiter) that a deliberate act of retaliation was not an unprovoked or accidentally provoked incident and that an attack on grounded aircraft did not occur during the normal course of operations "over" the relevant territories.

26–41 Acts of State. Certain old cases in law of marine insurance lay down a principle to the effect that an assured cannot recover in respect of damage wilfully done by an alien government of which the assured was a subject[11]: The rationale of the rule appears to be that in such a case an alien assured must be identified with the acts of his own government for otherwise it would be impossible to prevent fraudulent collusion between the assured and his government for the purpose of obtaining the insurance money. The rule has been criticised[12] and has been doubted in the U.S.[13] and it is doubtful whether it would be extended to cases of fire insurance.

It is perhaps unlikely that the question will be decided since most policies have an exception for loss by military power, but cases not within the exception might arise. In *Curtis & Sons v. Mathews*[14] there was an express term in the policy excepting confiscation or destruction by the government of the country in which the property was situated and the Court of Appeal held that this referred only to intentional and direct destruction such as destruction of buildings which were a hindrance to military operations.

26–42 Spontaneous combustion. Many policies contain an exception of "loss or damage to property occasioned by or happening through its own spontaneous fermentation or heating". It is submitted that if a stackyard was

---

[10] [1974] 2 Lloyd's Rep. 301; see also the judgments of the Court of Appeal and Mocatta J. at [1973] 1 Lloyd's Rep. 233 and [1972] 1 Lloyd's Rep. 253, respectively, and *Pan American World Airways Inc. v. Aetna Casualty and Surety Co.* [1975] 1 Lloyd's Rep. 77.

[11] *Conway v. Gray* (1809) 10 East 536; *Campbell v. Innes* (1821) 4 B. & Ald. 423; Arnould, *Marine Insurance* (16th ed.) para. 787.

[12] *Aubert v. Gray* (1862) 3 B. & S. 169.

[13] *Ocean Ins. Co. v. Francis*, 2 Wend. 64 (1828).

[14] [1919] 1 K.B. 425.

insured, and one stack were to ignite through spontaneous combustion, the loss of that stack would fall within the exception; but if the fire were to spread to the rest of the stacks their loss would be recoverable. The exception only excludes the loss of the particular thing which has been lost through its own spontaneous combustion.

26–43 It is not clear whether a fire policy without such an exception will extend to loss through spontaneous combustion; it is submitted that it should, since there has been an ignition of something which is not intended to be ignited. There is, however, authority in the law of marine insurance that where loss or damage is caused solely by the defective condition of the thing insured, there can be no recovery, *e.g.* when a vessel on a time policy goes to sea in an unseaworthy condition and has to put into a port of refuge for repairs[15] or when cargo shipped is liable to catch fire.[16] These cases can be distinguished on the ground that loss due to inherent vice is not a loss covered by a marine policy but is a loss due solely to an independent cause. In the case of a fire policy, however, the intention of the parties is to insure against the happening of any unintended fire and it has been held in Quebec that a fire policy on a quantity of coal stored on land covered the risk of spontaneous combustion due to the negligent stacking of the coal in a damp condition.[17] It is submitted that, in any event, if the inherent defect is brought into activity by a peril insured against or if it gives rise to a peril insured against, the loss or damage so caused should be within a fire policy.

26–44 Earthquake. Earthquakes are often the subject of an exception in fire policies, and two cases arose out of the earthquake in Jamaica in 1907. In each case, it is for the insurer to prove that the loss or damage occurred as a proximate result of the earthquake, unless the policy provides to the contrary.[18]

26–45 Incendiarism. A policy may contain a provision excepting liability for incendiarism. In *Walker v. London and Provincial Insurance Co.*[19] a neighbour of the assured wilfully set fire to his own house and the wind carried the flames to the house of the assured. It was held that if the fire spread in consequence of the ordinary elements the destruction of the assured's house was the proximate result of the incendiary act and he could not recover; but if the fire had been communicated by a fireman removing goods from the burning house and accidentally throwing some portion of the burning material upon or near the assured's premises, there would have been the intervention of an independent cause and the loss would have been not the proximate but the remote result of the incendiary act so that the assured could recover notwithstanding the exception. In the absence of evidence indicating some independent cause the court presumed that the fire spread by natural causes and held that the loss was not covered.

---

[15] *Fawcus v. Sarsfield* (1856) 6 E. & B. 192.

[16] *Boyd v. Dubois* (1811) 3 Camp. 133; *Providence Washington Insurance Co. v. Adler*, 65 Md. 162 (1885); *Sassoon v. Yorkshire Ins. Co.* (1923) 14 Ll.L.R. 167; affirmed 16 Ll.L.R. 129.

[17] *British American Ins. Co. v. Joseph* (1857) 9 Low.Can.R. 448.

[18] *Tootal Broadhurst, Lee and Co. Ltd v. London and Lancashire Fire Co.* (1908) *The Times*, May 21; *Scottish Union and National Fire Ins. Co. v. Alfred Pawsey and Co.* (1908) *The Times*, October 17, P.C.

[19] (1888) 22 L.R.Ir. 572; *cf. American Tobacco Co. Inc. v. Guardian Ass. Co.* (1925) 22 Ll.L.R. 37, para. 26–39, *ante.*

26–46 Explosion. The ordinary form of fire policy, apart from any exceptions, will cover loss or damage caused by an explosion which was itself caused by a fire.[20] Explosion may also be separately insured and, in the absence of an appropriate exclusion, will cover a volcanic explosion.[21]

If, however, cover is afforded or there is an exception for "explosion", the court will have to consider whether an explosion did, in fact, occur. In *Commonwealth Smelting Ltd v. Guardian Royal Exchange Assurance Ltd*[22] the question arose at a blower house in a smelting complex at Avonmouth. The blower house was designed to provide air to a furnace and consisted of a steel impeller attached to a shaft. The impeller failed, shattering its casing pieces of which flew outwards expelled by the air pressure. It was held that this was not an explosion which must be given its ordinary English meaning and the Court of Appeal upheld the trial judge who had held that an explosion denoted:

> "an event that is violent noisy and caused by a very rapid chemical or nuclear reaction, or the bursting out of gas or vapour under pressure."[23]

26–47 Where there is an exception for loss or damage caused by explosion, it becomes important to distinguish the respective consequences of fire and explosion. Thus it has been held that such an exception applies not merely to loss suffered as a result of a fire following an explosion but also to loss suffered by an explosion occurring in the course of and caused by a fire.[24] Two cases may usefully be contrasted. In *Re Hooley Hill Rubber and Chemical Company and the Royal Insurance Co. Ltd*[25] manufacturers of explosives took out a fire policy, condition 3 of which excepted loss or damage by explosion. A memorandum was also endorsed on the policy stating that loss or damage by fire following an explosion was not covered unless the fire "was not caused directly or indirectly thereby or was not the result thereof". A fire occurred in the assured's premises followed by an explosion which shattered the premises and blew out the fire. The Court of Appeal held that the assured could not recover for the damage done by the explosion. In *Boiler Inspection and Insurance Company of Canada v. Sherwin-Williams Company of Canada Ltd*[26] the insurer undertook to pay for loss on property directly damaged by accident, excluding loss from fire The assured used a bleaching tank to bleach turpentine and internal pressure blew off the tank door; a large quantity of gas escaped which when mixed with air became highly explosive and almost immediately after the tank door

---

[20] *Hobbs v. Guardian Ass. Co.* (1886) 12 S.C.R. 631; *Re Hooley Hill Rubber and Chemical Co. and The Royal Ins. Co. Ltd* [1920] 1 K.B. 257, 271–272, *per* Scrutton L.J.; *Curtis's and Harvey (Canada) Ltd v. North British and Mercantile Ins. Co.* [1921] 1 A.C. 303, 310, *per* Lord Dunedin; *Shea and Foubert v. Halifax Ins. Co.* (1958) 15 D.L.R. 2d 667; *Waters v. Merchants' Louisville Ins. Co.*, 11 Peters 213 (1837); *Scripture v. Lowell Mutual Fire Ins. Co.*, 64 Mass. 356 (1852). Explosion is not a fire as such—see *Everett v. London Ass. Co.* (1865) 19 C.B.(N.S.) 126.

[21] *Martini Investments Ltd v. McGinn* [2001] Lloyd's Rep. I.R. 374.

[22] [1986] 1 Lloyd's Rep. 121.

[23] [1984] 2 Lloyd's Rep. 608, 612.

[24] *Stanley v. Western Ins. Co.* (1868) L.R. 3 Ex. 71; see also *Curtis's and Harvey (Canada) Ltd v. North British and Mercantile Ins. Co.* [1921] 1 A.C. 303.

[25] [1920] 1 K.B. 257. *Contra, Vareno v. Home Mutual Fire Ins. Co.*, 63 A. 2d 97 (1949). See also cases where there is an exception for "blow-out", *e.g. Feeney and Meyers v. Empire State Ins. Co.*, 228 F. 2d 770 (1955) and *Central Manufacturers' Mutual Ins. Co. v. Elliott*, 177 F. 2d 1011 (1949).

[26] [1951] A.C. 319. See also *Abasand Oils Ltd v. Boiler Inspection and Ins. Co. of Canada* (1949) 65 T.L.R. 713.

had been blown off, it became ignited in an unexplained way and exploded, shattering most of the building where the accident happened. The insurers argued that since there was an ignition the damage was caused by fire and not by explosion. The Judicial Committee of the Privy Council however, held that the fire in the explosive mixture was merely an incident in the explosion and that the subsequent loss was thus effectively caused not by the fire but by the explosion:

> "when it has to be determined whether the tearing asunder of the tank or the ignition of the gases thereby released is the cause of the explosion and of the loss which it occasions, their lordships have no hesitation in choosing the former."

26–48 Other risks and exceptions. The following phrases have also been construed in the context of a fire insurance policy: "Explosion of boilers used for domestic purposes[27]; subsidence and collapse."[28]

4. Miscellaneous Clauses in Fire Policies

26–49 Conditions against alterations increasing the risk. Many fire policies contain conditions prohibiting any alterations increasing the risk or requiring any such alteration to be notified to the insurer and his consent obtained. It is a question of fact whether an alteration has increased the risk, and no alteration which does not increase the risk will affect the validity of the policy, even though it may cause the property to differ from the description in the proposal or the policy, provided that there is no warranty that the description is accurate. A condition of this kind adds little or nothing to the common law which would ask whether circumstances have so changed that the new situation is something which insurers have not agreed to cover.[29]

26–50 Temporary alterations. A condition of this kind does not preclude temporary variations, but only alterations of a substantially permanent character. In *Shaw v. Robberds*[30] the premises were described as "a kiln for drying corn in use"; the policy was declared to be forfeited if the buildings were not accurately described or if the trades carried on were not specified and further provided "if any alteration or addition be made in or to the

---

[27] *Willesden Corporation v. Municipal Mutual Insurance Ltd* [1945] 1 All E.R. 444; 78 Ll.L.R. 256.

[28] *David Allen & Sons (Billposting) v. Drysdale* [1939] 4 All E.R. 113.

[29] *Kausar v. Eagle Star Ins. Co.* [1997] C.L.C. 129, [2000] Lloyd's Rep. I.R. 154.

[30] (1837) 6 Ad. & E. 75; see also *Barrett v. Jermy* (1849) 3 Exch. 535, 545. But reconstruction work may constitute an alteration of the risk—see *Marzouca v. Atlantic and British Commercial Ins. Co. Ltd* [1971] 1 Lloyd's Rep. 449.

building or the risk of fire to which such building is exposed be by any means increased", such alteration or addition must be immediately notified or the policy would be void. On one occasion the assured permitted the owner of some bark which had been shipwrecked near the kiln to dry it in the kiln. He made no charge for this service; the bark caught fire and the kiln was destroyed. It was found as a fact by the jury that the process of drying bark was more hazardous than that of drying corn, and that the fire was occasioned by the drying of the bark. The Court of King's Bench held that there had been no breach of the condition against alterations increasing the risk. Lord Denman C.J. said:

> "The condition points at an alteration of business, at something permanent and habitual; and if the plaintiff had either dropped his business of corn drying, and taken up that of bark drying, or added the latter to the former, no doubt the case would have been within that condition. Perhaps if he had made any charge for drying this bark, it might have been a question for the jury whether he had done so as a matter of business, and whether he had not thereby made an alteration in his business within the meaning of that condition. ... No clause in this policy amounts to an express warranty that nothing but corn should ever be dried in the kiln, and there are no facts, or rule of legal construction, from which an implied warranty can be raised."[31]

26–51 Ten years earlier Lord Tenterden C.J. had reached a similar conclusion in *Dobson v. Sotheby*[32] in which the premises were described as a barn "wherein no fire is kept and no hazardous goods are deposited". Since the premises required to be tarred, a fire was lit in the building and a tar barrel was brought inside for the purpose of performing the necessary operations. The tar boiled over and set fire to the premises as a result of the negligence of the assured's servants. Lord Tenterden said, in directing the jury, that he thought there was no breach of warranty:

> "If the company intended to stipulate not merely that no fire should habitually be kept on the premises, but that none should ever be introduced upon them, they might have expressed themselves to that effect; and the same remark applies to the case of hazardous goods also. In the absence of any such stipulation, I think that the condition must be understood as forbidding only the habitual use of fire or the ordinary deposit of hazardous goods, not their occasional introduction, as in this case, for a temporary purpose connected with the occupation of the premises. The common repairs of a building necessarily require the introduction of fire upon the premises, and one of the great objects of insuring is security against the negligence of servants and workmen."

26–52 Ordinary use. When the condition prohibits "alterations by which, risk of fire may be increased" the question to be considered in the case of an alteration in construction is whether the alteration is such as to increase the risk during the normal and ordinary use and occupation of the premises. An

---

[31] The last sentence of the quotation was cited with apparent approval by Lord Wright in *Provincial Ins. Co. v. Morgan* [1933] A.C. 240. See also *Johnston v. Grange Mutual Fire Ins. Co.* (1893) 23 O.A.R. 729.
[32] (1827) Moo. & M. 90.

increase in the size of a building must almost necessarily increase the risk, whether the building is occupied or not, since the area throughout which it is possible for a fire to arise is increased. But some alterations are such that they cannot possibly increase the risk unless there is user. Thus the mere insertion into the premises of an additional furnace or steam engine does not in itself increase the risk. In such cases the question is not whether the alteration increases the risk, but whether the use of the additional object in the ordinary way increases the risk; if it is not used at all or on an extraordinary occasion only for some temporary purposes, there is no breach of warranty.[33]

26–53 Alteration contemplated or consented to. If the alteration comes within the terms of the risk as described in the policy, it cannot be an alteration within the meaning of the condition.[34] Thus in *Exchange Theatre Ltd v. Iron Trades Mutual Insurance Co. Ltd*[35] the policy identified items insured, one of which was a bingo hall described in detail in the policy, which also provided:

> "This policy shall be avoided with respect to any item thereof in regard to which there be any alteration whereby the risk of destruction or damage is increased. ..."

Insurers alleged that a petrol generator and a petrol container had been brought into the hall and that there had been an alteration with regard to the building. The Court of Appeal held that, for the exception to apply, there had to be an alteration in the description of the building and that since there had been no such alteration, the assured were entitled to recover.[36] Moreover, there can be no alteration in the risk if the alteration in fact made was within the contemplation of the parties at the time when the policy was taken out.[37] In one case the insurers had allowed the assured to use a room (which was the subject of insurance) in order to boil varnish. It was held the introduction of boilers for this purpose was no breach of a condition requiring immediate notification or any alteration or addition to the risk.[38]

26–54 The burden is always upon the insurer to prove that an alteration has taken place which has increased the risk[39] and, where relevant, that no notice or consent has been given.[40] Where, however, the assured wishes to extend his policy beyond a specified period, he cannot rely on a clause requiring notification of alteration to show that an extension was contemplated by the policy.[41]

---

[33] *Barrett v. Jermy* (1849) 3 Exch. 535; *cf. Stokes v. Cox* (1856) 1 H. & N. 533, 538–539, *per* Willes J. *arguendo* and *Naughter v. Ottawa Agricultural Ins. Co.* (1878) 43 U.C.Q.B. 121.
[34] *Whitehead v. Price* (1835) 2 Cr.M. & R. 447; *Baxendale v. Harvey* (1859) 4 H. & N. 445; *Kausar v. Eagle Star Ins. Co.* [1997] C.L.C. 129; [2000] Lloyd's Rep. I.R. 154.
[35] [1984] 1 Lloyd's Rep. 149.
[36] In fact the Court of Appeal later ordered a new trial on other grounds [1984] 2 Lloyd's Rep. 169.
[37] *Law, Guarantee, Trust and Accident Society v. Munich Reins. Co.* [1912] 1 Ch. 138, 154, *per* Warrington J.; followed in *Exchange Theatre v. Iron Trades Mutual Ins. Co. Ltd* [1984] 1 Lloyd's Rep. 149, 152. *A fortiori*, if the alteration took place before the policy was taken out, *Fourdrinier v. Hartford Fire Ins. Co.* (1865) 15 U.C.C.P. 403.
[38] *Barrett v. Jermy* (1849) 3 Exch. 535.
[39] *Whitehead v. Price* (1835) 2 Cr.M. & R. 447; *Baxendale v. Harvey* (1859) 4 H. & N. 445.
[40] *Barrett v. Jermy* (1849) 3 Exch. 535, 542, *per* Parke B.
[41] *Jones Construction Company v. Alliance Ass. Co. Ltd* [1961] 1 Lloyd's Rep. 121.

It has been held that there is no alteration, which increases the risk, if an elevator is brought into a warehouse,[42] but that there is such an alteration if there is a change of user from that of a store to a printing-office.[43]

26–55 Sometimes the clause refers merely to an "increase of risk" or to an "increase or change of risk".[44] Under such a clause it had been held that the following are all increases of risk—bringing a steam engine into premises,[45] hat bleaching in premises described as a dry goods store or an architect's office,[46] repairing metal containers with welding equipment in buildings of a business classified as carriers and transit warehousing,[47] putting a crane into commercial use when it was insured while in the process of erection and commissioning[48] and a change of user from a dwelling to a hotel.[49] If there is a series of alterations any one of which increases the risk, the insurers will be discharged[50] but if all the alterations are inextricably connected the question will be whether there is an overall increase of the risk.[51] If the insured leaves houses unoccupied for some months there may well be an increase of risk,[52] but since occupation may cease without the knowledge of the insured,[53] the policy may provide a defence only where the increase of risk occurs "by any means within the control of the insured".[54] A threat of damage to premises

[42] *Todd v. Liverpool and London and Globe Ins. Co.* (1868) 18 U.C.C.P. 192.

[43] *Hervey v. Mutual Fire Ins. Co.* (1865) 15 U.C.C.P. 175; *cf. Wilshire v. Guardian Ass. Co. Ltd* (1912) 15 C.L.R. 516 (change from storage to wool-scouring) and *Lount v. London Mutual Fire Ins. Co.* (1905) 9 O.L.R. 549 (change from water power to steam power).

[44] The words "increase or change of risk" have been held to mean "change increasing the risk,"—see *Gill v. Canada Fire and Marine Ins. Co.* (1882) 1 O.R. 341. For accident insurance, see *General Insurance v. Fulton* (1991) 75 D.L.R. 4th 382.

[45] *Reid v. Gore District Mutual Fire Ins. Co.* (1853) 11 U.C.Q.B. 345.

[46] *Merrick v. Provincial Ins. Co.* (1856) 14 U.C.Q.B. 439. In this case the policy also provided that no cover was given, except at an additional premium, for hazardous activities—*cf. Sovereign Fire Ins. Co. v. Moir* (1887) 14 Can.S.C. 613.

[47] *Farnham v. Royal Ins. Co. Ltd* [1976] 2 Lloyd's Rep. 437 distinguished in *Exchange Theatre Ltd v. Iron Trades Mutual Ins. Co. Ltd* [1984] 1 Lloyd's Rep. 149

[48] *Linden Alimak Ltd v. British Engine Ins. Ltd* [1984] 1 Lloyd's Rep. 416.

[49] *Guerin v. Manchester Fire Ass. Co.* (1898) 29 Can.S.C. 139. On the other hand, building an oven or a change in tenancy do not constitute *per se* an increase of risk—see *Naughter v. Ottawa Agricultural Ins. Co.* (1878) 43 U.C.Q.B. 121 and *Irving v. Sun Ins. Office* [1906] O.R.C. 24.

[50] *Heneker v. British American Ass. Co.* (1863) 13 U.C.C.P. 99. An alteration to a building near the premises insured will prevent recovery if there is an increase in risk to the premises insured—see *Wydrick v. Saltfleet and Binbrook Mutual Fire Ins. Co.* [1930] 1 D.L.R. 241.

[51] *Date v. Gore District Mutual Fire Ins. Co.* (1865) 15 U.C.C.P. 175. If alterations are made by a neighbouring landowner to his property and such alterations increase the risk to the property insured, the insurers probably cannot deny liability—*Copp v. Glasgow and London Ins. Co.* (1890) 30 N.B.R. 197. But see previous note.

[52] Compare *Foy v. Aetna Ins. Co.* (1854) 3 Allen (N.Br.) 29 and *Boardman v. North Waterloo Ins. Co.* (1899) 31 O.R. 525 with *McKay v. Norwich Union Ins. Co.* (1895) 27 O.R. 251 and *Payson v. Equitable Fire Ins. Co.* (1908) 38 N.B.R. 436. A condition against change in the nature of occupation of premises does not apply when the premises have merely become vacant—*Littlejohn v. Norwich Union Ins. Co.* [1905] T.H. 374.

[53] *Cf. Abrahams v. Agricultural Mutual Ass. Assoc.* (1876) 40 U.C.Q.B. 175. Policies often contain an express warranty as to occupation—*Peck v. Agricultural Ins. Co.* (1890) 19 O.R. 494; *Bishop v. Norwich Union Ass. Co.* (1893) 25 N.S.R. 492. An express clause relating to occupation will override an express clause relating to increases of risk on the principle *generalia specialibus non derogant*—see *Laurentian Ins. Co. v. Davison* [1931] 4 D.L.R. 720; affirmed [1932] 2 D.L.R. 750.

[54] *Heneker v. British American Ass. Co.* (1864) 14 U.C.C.P. 57; *London and Western Trust Co. v. Canada Fire Ins. Co.* (1906) 13 O.L.R. 540. For a condition relating to things done "within the knowledge of the assured," see *Hillerman v. National Ins. Co.* (1870) 1 V.R.(L) 155. *Cf. Goldman v. Piedmont Fire Ins. Co.*, 198 F.2d 712 (1952).

by a person to whom a tenant has unlawfully sub-let is not an increase of risk under the freeholder's policy because it did not amount to a new situation which the insurers had not agreed to cover.[55]

26–56 Notification required. Some policies provide that any addition or alteration to the premises must be notified to the insurers and that, if this is not done, the insurers will not be liable.[56] Other policies provide that notification must be given of any increase of risk,[57] or of a particular change—*e.g.* loss of licence (in the case of a hotel)[58] or any change in the nature of the adjoining premises.[59] The policy will usually provide for notice to be given to the company secretary,[60] in the absence of such provision, notice to the local agent will be sufficient. It can be oral and need not be detailed[61] but must be given within a reasonable time.[62]

26–57 Conditions preventing introduction of specified objects. As a result of the decisions referred to in the previous paragraphs, clauses have been introduced into fire policies which forbid not merely alterations in the risk but also the introduction of certain specified objects. A condition of this kind will prevent even a temporary introduction of the prohibited object and a breach of it will prevent the assured from recovering, although the object may not have caused the loss.

In *Glen v. Lewis*[63] the policy provided that no steam engine should be introduced into the premises. These words were held to amount to a warranty that no steam engine would ever be used even temporarily on the premises, and the policy was held to have been avoided by the introduction and use of a steam engine experimentally for a few days only. By way of contrast, in *Stokes v. Cox*[64] the policy provided "no steam engine employed on the premises". This more elliptical form of words was held to mean that no steam engine was employed on the premises at the time when the policy was effected. There was a separate condition avoiding the policy if there was increase on the risk, in the light of which the court was reluctant to hold that the clause relating to the steam engine could operate after the contract had been made.

26–58 No express term about alteration in the risk. It is not clear whether in the event of an alteration in the risk, the insurer can decline liability in the absence of any term to that effect in the policy. No problem arises if the risk is described in the policy and the claim of the assured does not fall within the original description by reason of the alteration.[65] There can be little doubt,

[55] *Kausar v. Eagle Star Ins. Co.* [1997] C.L.C. 129, [2000] Lloyd's Rep. I.R. 154.

[56] It will not matter that there is no increase in risk—*Lyndsay v. Niagara District Mutual Fire Ins. Co.* (1869) 28 U.C.Q.B. 326.

[57] Cover will not cease on this form of clause merely because notification has not been given—*Hussain v. Brown* [1996] 1 Lloyd's Rep. 627.

[58] *Rhodes v. Union Ins. Co.* (1883) 2 N.Z.L.R. (S.C.) 106.

[59] *Littlejohn v. Norwich Union Ins. Co.* [1905] T.H. 374. *Cf. Canada Landed Credit Co. v. Canada Agricultural Ins. Co.* (1870) 17 Gr. 418.

[60] *Cf. Lount v. London Mutual Fire Ins. Co.* (1905) 9 O.L.R. 549.

[61] *Peck v. Phoenix Mutual Ins. Co.* (1881) 45 U.C.Q.B. 620.

[62] *Canada Landed Credit Co. v. Canada Agricultural Ins. Co.* (1870) 17 Gr. 418; *Rhodes v. Union Ins. Co.* (1883) 2 N.Z.L.R.(S.C.) 106.

[63] (1853) 8 Exch. 607 followed in *Payson v. Equitable Fire Ins. Co.* (1908) 38 N.B.R. 436. *Cf. McEwan v. Guthridge* (1860) 13 Moo.P.C. 304.

[64] (1856) 1 H. & N. 533.

[65] *Kausar v. Eagle Star Ins. Co.* [1997] C.L.C. 129, [2000] Lloyd's Rep. I.R. 154.

however, that some alterations of the risk will discharge the insurer; even though it may be difficult to say that the description of the risk in the policy is no longer accurate. If for example, an insurer covers the risk that a debtor of the assured will not pay his debt, any material alteration of the underlying contract between the assured and his debtor may have a serious effect on the insurer's obligation. In these circumstances it seems only right that the insurer should be entitled to deny liability in the same way that a guarantor can claim he is discharged from his guarantee.[66] Whether this principle will be extended to other types of insurance remains to be seen.[67]

26–59 Locality of movable property. If movable property insured against fire or burglary is described as being in a particular place, the locality of the property is of the essence of the contract. If the insurer insures property in a house A, the insurance does not cover the same property when removed to house B, unless the policy expressly so provides. Property insured "whilst in warehouse" is not covered while it is in a lorry parked in the compound[68] and property stolen in the assured's yard is not lost in the assured's premises but "between vehicles and premises".[69]

26–60 In *Pearson v. Commercial Union Assurance Co*[70] the policy insured against loss by fire on a ship "lying in the Victoria Docks, London, with liberty to go into dry dock and light the boiler fires once or twice during the currency of the policy". The vessel went into dry dock two miles up the river, and when the repairs were completed, instead of returning directly to the Victoria Docks, she was moored in the river so that her paddle wheels might be more conveniently replaced. The paddle wheels could have been replaced in dock, but it would have been a more expensive operation. While lying in the river the vessel was destroyed by fire, and the House of Lords held that the loss was not covered by the policy. The vessel, by remaining in the river longer than was necessary for the purpose of transit from dock to dock, had gone outside the defined limits of the risk.

A description of the locality of goods insured does not amount to a warranty that they will never be moved outside the defined locality. Prima facie it is a definition of the risk so that the policy ceases to attach if the goods are removed, but reattaches when they are returned to the specified locality.[71]

26–61 Description of interest of assured. The interest of the assured need not be stated in the policy unless there is a condition to that effect and it need not usually be disclosed.[72] If it is stated, however, the assured must state it correctly,[73] and it is quite common to find a clause in these or similar terms:

---

[66] *Hadenfayre Ltd v. British National Ins. Society Ltd* [1984] 2 Lloyd's Rep. 393 where, however, the essential terms of the underlying contract of sale were set out in the slip and insurers were able to argue that a variation in that contract constituted a breach of a term in the insurance contract for which the insurers could repudiate liability.

[67] There is no general duty of disclosure during the currency of the policy: *New Hampshire Ins. Co. v. Mirror Group Newspapers* [1997] L.R.L.R. 24, 61.

[68] *Leo Rapp Ltd v. McClure* [1955] 1 Lloyd's Rep. 292. *Cf. Arnold v. British Colonial Fire Ins. Co.* (1917) 45 N.B.R. 285 and *Laidlow v. Monteath*, 1979 S.L.T. 78.

[69] *Mint Security Ltd v. Blair* [1982] 1 Lloyd's Rep. 188.

[70] (1876) 1 App.Cas. 498; "*The Delfini*" [1976] 2 Lloyd's Rep. 741.

[71] *Gorman v. Hand-in-Hand Ins. Co.* (1877) Ir.R. 11 C.L. 224.

[72] See para. 17–65, *ante.*

[73] *Parsons v. Bignold* (1846) 15 L.J.Ch. 379.

"If the interest of the assured be any other than the entire and sole ownership, it must be so represented otherwise the policy shall be void."[74]

A condition in a policy on goods that the house or other place where the goods are deposited shall be accurately described relates to the physical attributes of the house and not to any description of the interest. Thus a statement that the goods were in the dwelling-house of the insured when the insured was only a lodger in the house, was held not to be a breach of condition.[75]

26–62 A statement by an assured who is acquiring a car under a hire-purchase agreement, that the car belongs to him, is sufficiently accurate[76] and the possessor of a car under a conditional sale agreement is probably a sole and unconditional owner for the purposes of an insurance policy[77]; the same applies to a mortgagor[78] who, provided he has the equity of redemption, is even entitled to warrant that the property is free from all liens.[79] Moreover, the fact that the assured describes property as "his" does not mean that he warrants that he is the owner.[80]

26–63 If there is no warranty that the interest as described is correct, any misdescription will only enable the insurers to escape liability if it was material to the risk.[81]

A bailee's mercantile policy usually excludes goods held on trust or commission unless expressly described as such and a bailee who intends to cover a goods-owner's interest, as well as his own, must so specify.[82]

26–64 Use or occupancy. Any description of premises which specifies, expressly or by implication, a particular user will prevent the insured from recovering if the premises are used habitually for some other purpose; he will not, however, be prejudiced by a mere temporary user.[83] A description of a house as two-storied will mean that no cover will be provided if a third storey is added,[84] but the mere description of premises as a dwelling-house

---

[74] It has been held that a clause in a form similar to this cannot be relied on by the insurers unless there is a question in the proposal form directed to the interest of the assured: *Dohn v. Farmers' Joint Stock Ins. Co.*, 5 Lans. 275 (1871). *Cf. Rohrback v. Germania Fire Ins. Co.*, 62 N.Y. 47 (1875).

[75] *Friedlander v. London Ass. Co.* (1832) 1 Moo. & Rob. 171.

[76] The decision of Bailhache J. in *Banton v. Home and Colonial Ass. Co.*, *The Times*, April 27, 1921, was reversed on July 6, 1921—see Welford, *Accident Insurance* (2nd ed.), p. 314, note (u).

[77] *Forsyth v. Imperial Guarantee and Accident Ins. Co.* [1925] 4 D.L.R. 479; 3 W.W.R. 669.

[78] *Western Ass. Co. v. Temple* (1901) 33 Can.S.C. 373; *Foster v. Standard Ins. Co. of New Zealand* [1924] N.Z.L.R. 1093.

[79] *Bidwell v. Northwestern Ins. Co.*, 24 N.Y. 302 (1862).

[80] *Rohrbach v. Germania Fire Ins. Co.*, 62 N.Y. 47 (1875); *cf. James v. British General Ins. Co.* [1927] 2 K.B. 311 where a car was paid for by and registered in the name of a father, but was held to belong to the son, and *Gill v. Canada Fire and Marine Ins. Co.* (1882) 1 O.R. 341 where a vendor under a contract of sale was held entitled to call the property "his".

[81] *Kerr v. Hastings Mutual Fire Ins. Co.* (1877) 41 U.C.Q.B. 217; *cf. North British and Mercantile Ins. Co. v. McLellan* (1892) 21 Can.S.C. 288 and *James v. British General Ins. Co.* [1927] 2 K.B. 311.

[82] See *Waters v. Monarch Fire etc. Assurance Co.* (1856) 5 E. & B. 870; *London and Northwestern Ry v. Glyn* (1859) 1 E. & E. 652; *North British and Mercantile Ins. Co. v. Moffatt* (1871) L.R. 7 C.P. 25.

[83] *Shaw v. Robberds* (1837) 6 A. & E. 75; *Sillem v. Thornton* (1854) 3 E. & B. 868; *Wall v. East River Mutual Ins. Co.*, 7 N.Y. 370 (1852).

[84] *Sillem v. Thornton* (1854) 3 E. & B. 868.

does not import a warranty of occupation throughout the risk.[85] The most that words such as "occupied as a dwelling" or "occupied by the assured" are likely to mean is that the building is so occupied at the commencement of the risk,[86] although if buildings remain unoccupied for a long time there may be an alteration of the risk within the terms of a condition in the policy.[87]

26–65 It is often difficult to decide whether a description of premises in a policy is intended to refer to the commencement of the risk or to apply throughout the duration of the insurance.[88]

When questions are asked in the proposal form as to use or occupation of the premises, or as to precautions taken against fire, and it is clear that they relate to the time of asking, there will probably be no warranty as to future use or occupation or observance of precautions.[89] In *Hair v. Prudential Assurance Co. Ltd*,[90] it was held that an answer in a proposal form that property was in a good state of repair related to the time of the answer, although there might have been a material alteration if the property had subsequently fallen into disrepair. Likewise an answer as to the identity of the occupiers related to the time of the answer and did not amount to a warranty that no change would occur. In many cases, however, there will be no point in asking the questions unless the insurer can rely on them as being truthful for the duration of the risk. Thus in *Whitlaw v. Phoenix Insurance Co.*,[91] there was a question on the application form "Is there a watchman kept on the premises at night?" and the answer was "Yes", and the declaration was that the statements in the proposal should form the basis of the liability of the company and should form a part and be a condition of the insurance contract. The court held that there was a warranty that a night-watchman would be kept throughout the risk. A different construction, however, was permitted where the assured making the statement had not the control of the premises as in another Canadian case where a mortgagee insured his interest in a mill, and, in answer to a question on the application form, stated that there was always a watchman on the premises. The application was referred to in the policy as the assured's warranty, and a part of the contract, but the court held there was no continuing warranty, although a similar statement made by the owner or occupier might have been so construed.[92]

The English Court of Appeal was more robust in *Hussain v. Brown*[93]

---

[85] *Quin v. National Ins. Co.* (1839) Jones & Carey 316; *Browning v. Home Ins. Co.*, 71 N.Y. 508 (1877).

[86] *O'Niel v. Buffalo Fire Ins. Co.*, 3 N.Y. 122 (1849); *Parmelee v. Hoffman Fire Ins. Co.*, 54 N.Y. 193 (1873); *Woodruff v. Imperial Fire Ins. Co.*, 83 N.Y. 133 (1880). For the meaning of "occupation" in an exceptions clause, see *Oei v. Foster* [1982] 2 Lloyd's Rep. 170.

[87] See para. 26–55, *ante*.

[88] See paras 26–57 and 26–64, *ante*.

[89] *Daniels v. Hudson River Fire Ins. Co.*, 66 Mass. 416 (1853).

[90] [1983] 2 Lloyd's Rep. 667.

[91] (1877) 28 U.C.C.P. 53.

[92] *Worswick v. Canada Fire and Marine Insurance Co.* (1879) 3 Ont.A.R. 487. See further para. 10–66, *ante*.

[93] [1996] 1 Lloyd's Rep. 627. The draconian consequences of a breach of warranty was an important influence on the decision of the court. While English law continues to hold that an insurer is discharged from liability by any breach of warranty even if the breach has no relation to the loss, the rather strict approach of the Court of Appeal to the language of the proposal form can only be applauded. See paras 10–39 to 10–40, *ante*.

where the proposal form had asked whether the premises were fitted with any sort of intruder alarm and the assured had replied "Yes". Five months later there was a fire and the assured admitted that the alarm system was inoperative before and at the time of the fire. The insurers claimed that the warranty was a continuing warranty and that they were, therefore, discharged. The Court of Appeal held that the question in the proposal form had been posed in the present tense and that, since no information had been sought as to the proposer's practice in connection with the alarm, the affirmative answer could not constitute a continuing warranty.

26–66 Clerical errors of description. If the assured makes a mistake describing the risk on the application form or to the agent of the insurers, he must as a rule suffer for the mistake, since he cannot hold the company to a risk other than that which they have accepted.[94] In certain cases, however, where there is no doubt as to the identity of the premises insured a misnomer will not affect the validity of the policy.[95] If the description is not sufficiently specific, and there is consequently doubt as to the identity of the premises, the assured may prove by, evidence outside the terms of the policy which property he intended to insure, and unless it appears that the insurers thought they were insuring other property, the property which the assured intended to insure will be taken to be the property insured.[96] Where the premises were described as Nos. 754 and 756 George Street, Sydney, it appeared that the numbers had been changed, and parol evidence was admitted to show what premises were in fact covered.[97] Where there is no doubt as to the general identity of the premises, parol evidence is not admissible to explain patent ambiguities as to the scope of the insurance. Thus, where on the construction of the policy it was doubtful whether it was intended to cover the machinery in all the insured buildings, or only in some of them, it was held to be inadmissible to prove by other evidence that the intention was to insure all the machinery.[98]

26–67 Divisibility of the risk. Apart from special circumstances or conditions, misrepresentation or non-disclosure as to any part of the property insured will avoid the whole policy, for prima facie the contract is one and indivisible.[99] But if the property covered by the policy is severable into and described in distinct parts, to each of which the premium is separately apportioned, a misrepresentation or non-disclosure affecting one part only will not, apart from an express condition to that effect, avoid the contract as to those risks which are not affected.[1] Even if the premium is a single unapportioned sum, yet if the risks are clearly severable, the policy will be voidable in respect only of those risks which are affected by the misrepresentation or concealment.[2]

---

[94] *Ionides v. Pacific Fire and Marine Insurance Co.* (1871) L.R. 6 Q.B. 674, 686; *Youell v. Bland Welch* [1992] 2 Lloyd's Rep. 127, 141.

[95] See n. 94 *supra.*

[96] See n. 94 *supra.*

[97] *Hordern v. Commercial Union Insurance Co.* (1887) 56 L.J.P.C. 78; 56 L.T. 240.

[98] *Hare v. Barstow* (1844) 8 Jur. 928.

[99] *Gore District Mutual v. Samo* (1878) 2 Can.S.C. 411; *Hopkins v. Prescott* (1847) 4 C.B. 578; *United Shoe Machinery Co. of Canada v. Brunet* [1909] A.C. 330, 340.

[1] *Pickering v. Ilfracombe Ry* (1868) L.R. 3 C.P. 235, 250; *Kearney v. Whitehaven* [1893] 1 Q.B. 700.

[2] *Greenwood v. Bishop of London* (1814) 5 Taunt. 727; *New Hampshire Ins. Co. v. Mirror Group Newspapers* [1997] L.R.L.R. 24 and see para. 17–33, *ante.*

Similarly, as regards a breach of warranty, if the risks are clearly severable so that the breach does not relate to the risk that has materialised, it is unlikely that the breach would now be regarded as discharging the insurers from liability in respect of the risk in question.[3]

26–68 Conditions relating to divisibility. A usual condition in a fire policy is that misdescription, misstatement or omission, makes the policy void as to the property affected by such misdescription, misstatement, or omission. Whether any circumstance directly affecting part of the property does or does not indirectly affect the whole property is a question of fact, and in a Canadian case where three out of seven tenement dwellings insured as one risk were left vacant it was held that the whole property was affected.[4] If, however, the condition is that the policy will be void in case of any misdescription, change of risk, or any other like matter, the policy will be void as to the whole insurance, even though the contravention of the condition has been in respect of and affects only a small portion of the risk.[5]

26–69 Conditions reserving liberty to terminate the risk. A fire policy may provide that either party shall have the right to terminate the risk at any time during the currency thereof subject to the return of a proportionate part of the premium for the unexpired term. In some policies the return of the unearned portion of the premium is made a condition precedent to the insurers' right to terminate the risk,[6] but in others the risk is determined either immediately upon or within a specified number of days after notice by the insurers and the obligation to return the premium is merely collateral.[7] The right of the insurers to terminate the risk may be limited to cases where there is an increase of hazard, but as a rule the policy reserves to them an absolute discretion to terminate in any circumstances.[8] If the insurers are already discharged from liability by reason of some breach of warranty on the part of the assured, the assured cannot elect to cancel the policy and claim a return of unearned premium.[9] The notice to terminate the risk must, of course, be given to the contracting party or to some person who has authority to receive such notice on his behalf.

---

[3] *Printpak v. AGF Insurance Ltd* [1999] Lloyd's Rep. I.R. 542; see note 98 to para. 10–27, *ante*.
[4] *McKay v. Norwich Union* (1895) 27 Ont.R. 251.
[5] *Gore District Mutual v. Samo* (1878) 2 Can.S.C. 411; *Russ v. Mutual Fire of Clinton* (1869) 29 U.C.Q.B. 73; *Cashman v. London & Liverpool Insurance Co.* (1862) 5 Allen (10 N.Br.) 246.
[6] *Caldwell v. Stadacon Fire* (1883) 11 Can.S.C. 212.
[7] *Swarzchild v. Phoenix*, 124 Fed.Rep. 52 (1903).
[8] *Sun Fire v. Hart* (1889) 14 App.Cas. 98; *New Hampshire Ins. Co. v. Mirror Group Newspapers* [1997] L.R.L.R. 24, 59.
[9] *Colby v. Cedar Rapids*, 66 Iowa 577 (1885).

CHAPTER 27

OTHER INSURANCES ON PROPERTY[1]

1. BURGLARY AND THEFT

27–1 Technical terms. There is some conflict in the authorities on the question whether criminal offences that are the subject of insurance should, in the absence of any definition in the policy, be defined in accordance with the definitions settled by the criminal law. Thus it has been doubted whether the words "larceny" or "forgery" in a policy of insurance should be given their technical meaning[2]; but the better view is that where terms to which the criminal law has given a technical meaning are used in a policy which offers no further definition or elaboration, such terms should be given the same meaning as that assigned to them by the criminal law.[3] Before 1969, for example, the word "burglary" could be expected to be given the same meaning as in the Larceny Act 1916,[4] while the word "theft" would have been given a broad meaning untrammelled by the intricacies of the criminal law,[5] since theft was not a concept to which the criminal law attached any very precise significance. This has changed since the passing of the Theft Act 1968, which provides a precise definition of theft for the purposes of the criminal law.[6] "Theft" in an insurance policy must now be construed in accordance with that technical meaning.[7] The same must apply to policies that cover burglary or robbery.

[1] "Property" is not a word readily capable of definition but it does not include human beings: *H.T.V. v. Lintner* [1984] 2 Lloyd's Rep. 125.

[2] *Algemeene Bankvereeniging v. Langton* (1935) 40 Com.Cas. 247, 259, *per* Maugham L.J.; *Equitable Trust Co. of New York v. Henderson* (1930) 47 T.L.R. 90.

[3] *Re Calf and Sun Insurance Office* [1920] 2 K.B. 366, 380, *per* Atkin L.J.; *Lake v. Simmons* [1927] A.C. 487, 509, *per* Viscount Sumner. *cf. London and Lancashire Fire Ins. Co. v. Bolands Ltd* [1924] A.C. 836 (riot). See also paras 11–13 and 26–33, *ante*.

[4] *Re Calf and Sun Insurance Office* [1920] 2 K.B. 366, 380.

[5] *Lake v. Simmons* [1927] A.C. 487, 507, *per* Viscount Sumner; *Pawle & Co. v. Bussell* (1916) 114 L.T. 805, "the word theft ... means only what the ordinary commercial man would consider to be theft." *Nishina Trading Co. Ltd v. Chiyoda Fire and Marine Ins. Co. Ltd* [1969] 2 Q.B. 449, 462, *per* Lord Denning M.R. Larceny by a trick would, for example, be included and larceny by a bailee (see *Lake v. Simmons* [1927] A.C. 487) and embezzlement (see *Algemeene Bank-vereeniging v. Langton* (1935) 40 Comm.Cas. 247). But *cf. Lim Trading Co. v. Haydon* [1968] 1 Lloyd's Rep. 159 (where the High Court of Singapore held that obtaining by false pretences did not amount to theft within a Lloyd's in and out stockbrokers' policy since "theft" was contrasted with the words "fraud" and "other dishonesty").

[6] ss.1–6.

[7] *Dobson v. General Accident Ass. Co.* [1990] 1 Q.B. 274; *Hayward v. Norwich Union Ins. Ltd* [2001] Lloyd's Rep. I.R. 410, 418.

27-2 If the policy provides for cover in respect of theft at a particular place, *e.g.* in the assured's yard, a problem can arise since theft requires an intention as well as an act. If a thief intends to steal while in the assured's yard but does not commit an act inconsistent with the owner's rights until later, there is no theft in the yard.[8]

27-3 Some insurance companies have thought it necessary to add their own definitions of the crimes covered by their policies and it is not uncommon to see memoranda attached to policies stating that the word "burglary" shall be defined as "theft" involving entry to or exit from a building by forcible and violent means.

27-4 Forcible and violent entry. The parties to an insurance policy are always free to "make their own dictionary" and to agree a definition of a risk different from that adopted by the criminal law. Thus in *Re George and Goldsmiths and General Burglary Insurance Association Ltd*,[9] a policy was taken out against burglary and housebreaking "as hereafter defined" and the risk insured was loss "by theft following upon actual forcible and violent entry upon the premises." Before business hours, a criminal entered the premises merely by turning the door handle and stole goods for which a claim was made against the insurance company. The Court of Appeal held that there had been no forcible and violent entry and therefore no loss within the terms of the policy. In another case, a subsequent Court of Appeal held that the sliding back of a latch of a lock by means of an instrument was sufficient to constitute a forcible and violent entry.[10] In *Dino Services v. Prudential Assurance*[11] the keys of premises had been stolen and used by the thief to gain access and steal. The Court of Appeal decided that there had been forcible but not violent entry. The word "violent" meant that the use of force (which might be minimal) must be accentuated or accompanied by some act that could properly be regarded as violent. It is not sufficient that the act is unlawful.

27-5 If the policy is expressed to cover business premises it will be no defence for the insurer to prove that peaceful entry was effected to part of a house, which was used for residential purposes, if there had later been a forcible and violent entry into the business premises. Moreover, it may be the case that although entry to the business premises as a whole was effected without force and violence, forcible entry into a particular room on the premises will be within the terms of the policy[12] although the subsequent use of the violence while in a room which had been peaceably entered will not be covered by the policy.[13] In a policy insuring property on premises which consisted of a building and a yard, the qualification of the meaning of the "premises" to exclude the yard for the purposes of the location of the property insured was held not to apply to the insuring clause "theft (or any attempt thereat) involving entry to or exit from the Premises by forcible and

[8] *Grundy (Teddington) Ltd v. Fulton* [1983] 1 Lloyd's Rep. 16: *cf. Shell International Petroleum Co. v. Gibbs* [1983] 2 A.C. 375.
[9] [1899] 1 Q.B. 595. Collins L.J. (p. 610) expressed the view that to effect entry by using a skeleton key would not be a forcible and violent entry.
[10] *Re Calf and Sun Ins. Office* [1920] 2 K.B. 366.
[11] [1989] 1 All E.R. 422.
[12] *Re Calf and Sun Ins. Office* [1920] 2 K.B. 366.
[13] *Re George and Goldsmiths and General Burglary Ins. Ass. Ltd* [1899] 1 Q.B. 595.

violent means." Thus, when thieves forced open gates to the yard to gain entry and exit, and then proceeded to gain access to the building possibly without using forcible and violent means, the loss was within the terms of the policy.[14]

27–6 Theft by servant or customer of assured. Policies against burglary or theft may expressly except from the risk any loss by theft or dishonesty of the assured's servants or any members of his household, and policies issued to merchants insuring their stock frequently contain a clause excepting loss occasioned by the theft or dishonesty of any customer or broker in respect of goods entrusted to him. In accordance with general principle, it will be for the insurer to prove that the loss was caused in the manner specified in the exception.[15] If a servant aids, abets, counsels or procures the commission of a theft in concert with others, the insurer will be able to take advantage of the exception just as much as if the servant committed theft himself and neither loss nor liability can be apportioned.[16] In *Lake v. Simmons*[17] the assured was induced to let a woman have possession of two pearl necklets by her fraudulent representation that she wanted to show them to her husband and to another (purely fictitious) person. The assured entered the name of the husband and the fictitious person in his books and, after the woman had disposed of the necklets, claimed on his theft policy, which excepted "loss by theft or dishonesty committed by ... any customer ... in respect of goods entrusted to [him] by the assured". The House of Lords held that since the handing over of the jewellery had been fraudulently induced there had been no entrusting within the exception clause and that the insurer was therefore liable and they further held that, as a matter of fact, possession had not been given to a "customer", since it was the husband and the fictitious person who were the customers of the assured.

27–7 Other exceptions. It is common to find an exception in burglary and theft policies excluding losses capable of being covered by some other kind of insurance, *e.g.* the usual fire or plate-glass policies. There is often an exception for war risks but it has been held that an isolated case of burglary committed during the opportunity afforded by a hostile air raid in time of war was not a loss "occasioned by hostilities or loot, sack or pillage in connection therewith".[18]

27–8 Common conditions. It is often provided in burglary and theft policies in relation to residential premises that they shall be occupied during the night or shall not be left unoccupied for longer than a specified number of days. Temporary absence for a short time is not a breach of a condition in general terms that the house shall be occupied.[19] Occupation means occupation by someone sleeping on the premises and a caretaker living on

---

[14] *John A. Pike (Butchers) Ltd v. Independent Insurance Co. Ltd* [1998] Lloyd's Rep. I.R. 410.
[15] In so far as *Hurst v. Evans* [1917] 1 K.B. 352 decided otherwise, it will probably not be followed—see para. 19–7, *ante* and *Greaves v. Drysdale* (1935) 53 Ll.L.R. 16.
[16] *Saqui and Lawrence v. Stearns* [1911] 1 K.B. 426.
[17] [1927] A.C. 487.
[18] *Winicofsky v. Army and Navy General Ass. Co.* (1919) 35 T.L.R. 283.
[19] *Simmonds v. Cockell* [1920] 3 K.B. 843; *Winicofsky v. Army and Navy General Ass. Co.* (1919) 35 T.L.R. 283. The phrase "to be attended at all times" is stricter—*CTN Cash and Carry Co. v. General Accident Fire and Life Ass. Corp.* [1989] 1 Lloyd's Rep. 299 (cash kiosk unattended when operator on floor above).

the premises by day only does not constitute occupation.[20] An alternative condition is that if the premises are left unattended a burglar alarm should be put into operation.[21] A clause requiring a burglar alarm to be kept in efficient working order will not be contravened unless the insured is (or ought to be) aware that the alarm was not working and had done nothing about it.[22] Another clause frequently found in policies is that the assured shall take all due and reasonable precautions to safeguard the property concerned.[23] As with liability policies, there will only be a breach of this clause if the insured has a reckless disregard of the safety of the property insured. It has been held in this context that it was reckless to leave a Ferrari car unlocked in the street with the keys in the ignition,[24] but it was not reckless to leave jewellery in the locked glove compartment of a locked car,[25] nor to leave a lorry containing a cargo of vodka in a secure warehouse with the ignition keys inside the vehicle, this being the assured's practice in order to permit quick removal in case of fire.[26] A positive answer to the question whether the premises are fitted with any form of intruder alarm will be held to relate to the date of the policy.[27]

27–9 Defences. There can be no recovery under a theft policy in respect of goods liable to confiscation because the assured has failed to pay the requisite import duty.[28] The same principle may well apply to stolen property or property unlawfully employed.[29]

27–10 Loss of chattels from any cause. Jewellery and other valuables are frequently insured against "all risks" or all loss from any cause whatsoever with certain specified exceptions.[30] In such a case it is enough for the assured to prove that an insured article has disappeared and after diligent search and a lapse of reasonable time cannot be found or (as Roche J. has said) "recovery is uncertain".[31] The assured must prove that the loss was due to an accident or a fortuitous cause or was otherwise within the policy[32] but in an ordinary case it may well be a matter of inference, once a loss has been proved, that it has happened accidentally. The phrase "all risks" will not, however, apply to loss or damage due to fair wear and tear, unlawful risks, inherent vice or the act of the assured himself.[33]

---

[20] *Clements v. National General Ins. Co., The Times,* June 11, 1910; *cf. Starfire Diamond Rings Ltd v. Angel* [1962] 2 Lloyd's Rep. 217.

[21] *Roberts v. Eagle Star Ins. Co.* [1960] 1 Lloyd's Rep. 615.

[22] *Victor Melik & Co. v. Norwich Union Fire Ins. Soc.* [1980] 1 Lloyd's Rep. 523; *O'Donoghue v. Harding* [1988] 2 Lloyd's Rep. 281, 289.

[23] *Carlton v. Park* (1922) 10 Ll.L.R. 818; *H.T.V. v. Lintner* [1984] 2 Lloyd's Rep. 125.

[24] *Devco v. Legal & General Ass. Co.* [1993] 2 Lloyd's Rep. 567. See also *Gunns v. Par Insurance Brokers* [1997] 1 Lloyd's Rep. 173 (failure to turn on alarm).

[25] *Sofi v. Prudential Ass. Co.* [1993] 2 Lloyd's Rep. 559.

[26] *Gordon Leslie Ltd v. General Accident Fire & Life Assurance Corp. plc* 1998 S.L.T. 391.

[27] *Hussain v. Brown* [1996] 1 Lloyd's Rep. 627.

[28] *Geismar v. Sun Alliance Ltd* [1978] Q.B. 383, unaffected by *Euro-Diam v. Bathurst* [1990] 1 Q.B. 1.

[29] See paras 14–24 to 14–25, *ante*.

[30] See, *e.g. Lazard Bros Ltd v. Brooks* (1932) 38 Com.Cas. 46 where it was held that the wide terms of the policy were not cut down by the recital.

[31] *Holmes v. Payne* [1930] 2 K.B. 301; *Webster v. General Accident etc. Corpn Ltd* [1953] 1 Q.B. 520, 532.

[32] *London and Provincial Leather Processes Ltd v. Hudson* [1939] 2 K.B. 724; *Regina Fur Company Ltd v. Bossom* [1958] 2 Lloyd's Rep. 425.

[33] *British and Foreign Marine Ins. Co. v. Gaunt* [1921] 2 A.C. 41.

27–11 In *Holmes v. Payne*[34] a pearl necklace was held to have been lost when the owner had searched but could not find it and it was nonetheless a loss because, some time after the insurers had agreed to settle the claim, the necklace fell out of the owner's evening cloak in which it had been concealed. In *Moore v. Evans*,[35] however, dealers in jewellery and precious stones had insured their merchandise against "loss of and/or damage or misfortune to the before mentioned property or any part thereof arising from any cause whatsoever", subject to certain specified exceptions. The assured had sent pearls to Germany on sale or return and on the outbreak of war they were detained in Germany but were placed in safe custody in a bank there, and there was no reason to suppose that they would be irrecoverable once peace was restored. The House of Lords refused to hold there had been any loss or damage or misfortune to the pearls and refused to extend the doctrine of constructive total loss to policies of non-marine insurance. A different situation arose in *London and Provincial Leather Processes Ltd v. Hudson*[36] where skins insured against "all and every risk" had likewise been sent to Germany where they were wrongfully detained under circumstances that in English law amounted to conversion and to a wrong in German law. It was held that there had been a loss within the meaning of the policy in that there had been a "fortuitous occurrence" or an "accidental loss". In another case the owner of a car had insured it against loss or damage. He was induced to part with possession by a fraudulent representation on the part of a stranger who said he had a buyer for it, but in fact sold the car by auction in his own name and misappropriated the proceeds. Although the assured knew where the car was, he had been advised that it was irrecoverable and it was held that there had been a loss of the car.[37] This case can be contrasted with that of parting with a car for a worthless cheque, which has been held to be a loss not of the car but of the proceeds of sale.[38] Since the Theft Act 1968, however, it would be held that the car was stolen and that there was, therefore, a loss of the car.[39]

27–12 Insurance against loss of money or securities. There are a number of cases concerning policies taken out by banks or other depositories against loss of securities or valuables. One policy indemnified a banking company against all losses discovered during the currency of the policy of "securities ... which now are or are by them supposed to or believed to be ... in or upon their premises", and also for loss of securities "whilst in transit between any houses or places within 100 miles" of the assured's premises. One of the bank's officers obtained securities from the vault clerk by the fraudulent

---

[34] [1930] 2 K.B. 301. The underwriters were entitled to the necklace. In *Federation Ins. Co. of Canada v. Coret Accessories Inc.* [1968] 2 Lloyd's Rep. 109, a judge of the Quebec Superior Court held that there was not a loss within a marine open cargo policy when, after payment, the goods were found, but only a loss arising from delay in delivery, which was excepted by the policy. Accordingly the insured was compelled to return the sums paid to him by the insurer. The fact that he had agreed to do so seems to have been only a secondary ground of decision.

[35] [1918] A.C. 185.

[36] [1939] 2 K.B. 724. Similarly there can be a "loss" of aircraft at a captured airfield, *Kuwait Airways v. Kuwait Ins. Co.* [1996] 1 Lloyd's Rep. 664, 686–689.

[37] *Webster v. General Accident Fire and Life Assurance Cpn Ltd* [1953] 1 Q.B. 520. It must be emphasised that in this case there was no actual sale to the rogue but only a parting with possession with a view to a sale.

[38] *Eisinger v. General Accident Fire and Life Assurance Cpn Ltd* [1953] 1 W.L.R. 869.

[39] *Dobson v. General Accident Fire and Life Assce Cpn* [1990] 1 Q.B. 274; *D.P.P. v. Gomez* [1993] A.C. 442.

pretence that he was going to hand them back to their owners. It was held that it was not sufficient that the customer to whom the securities belonged believed them to be on the premises at the date of the policy. The bank did not believe they were still on the premises since the vault clerk had delivered them to the fraudulent officer who produced a forged receipt to the customer. It was also held that an intramural transit between the vault and the customer's reception rooms was not within the terms of the policy.[40] Cover for loss by theft or false pretences committed by persons present on the premises of the bank does not apply to a case of theft by an innocent agent on behalf of a principal or company not itself present on the premises.[41]

27–13 Different consequences may result from the fraud of a customer on the one hand and that of an officer of the bank itself on the other. Thus in *Century Bank of the City of New York v. Mountain*,[42] the policy indemnified the bank from all losses by reason of cheques, banknotes, currency or cash being taken out of its possession by fraudulent means. The bank was fraudulently induced to discount promissory notes, which were forgeries, by a customer who thus obtained a substantial credit that was later withdrawn in the normal way. It was held that money had not been taken out of the possession of the bank by fraudulent means since they had merely been induced to create the relationship of creditor and debtor between their customer and themselves. In *Algemeene Bankvereeniging v. Langton*,[43] however, a bank was insured against losses incurred:

> "by reason of any money and/or securities in which they are interested or the custody of which they have undertaken ... being lost or destroyed or otherwise made away with by ... theft, robbery or hold up. ..."

One of the branch managers of the bank appropriated sums of money received by him from customers for and on behalf of the bank. It was held that this loss was covered by the policy since the sums had been made away with by the theft of the bank manager.

27–14 Provisions for notice are often inserted in policies of this nature. In one case money was insured against loss in transit and it was provided that the insurers would not be liable in respect of any loss that was not notified within 14 days of its occurrence. Money was given to an employee of the assured for the purpose of purchasing insurance stamps but was systematically stolen over a period of three years. The assured gave notice as soon as the loss was discovered but it was held that each sum stolen was a separate loss[44] and that the assured could recover only for the two losses which occurred within 14 days before notification.[45]

---

[40] *Pennsylvannia Co. for Insurance on Lives v. Mumford* [1920] 2 K.B. 537.

[41] *Deutsche Genossenschaftsbank v. Burnhope* [1995] 1 W.L.R. 1580.

[42] (1913) 19 Com.Cas. 178; (1914) 20 Com.Cas. 90; 112 L.T. 484 distinguished in *Liberty National Bank of New York v. Bolton* (1925) 21 Ll.L.R. 3. In *Wasserman v. Blackburn* (1926) 43 T.L.R. 95, 26 Ll.L.R. 127 an assured recovered for loss arising from discounting bills of exchange which were subsequently dishonoured. See also *Lazard Bros v. Brooks* (1932) 38 Com.Cas. 46.

[43] (1935) 40 Com.Cas. 247; 51 Ll.L.R. 275.

[44] *Pennsylvania Co. for Insurance on Lives v. Mumford* [1920] 2 K.B. 537.

[45] *T. H. Adamson & Sons v. Liverpool and London and Globe Ins. Co. Ltd* [1953] 2 Lloyd's Rep. 355.

27–15 Insurance against forgery. A policy issued in London indemnifying a businessman in New York against loss caused by acting in the ordinary course of business on documents proved to have been forged or invalid was held not to cover loss occasioned by the assured acting on a document containing a knowingly false statement as to the assets and liabilities of a certain firm although according to the law of New York such a document would have been a forgery.[46] A policy in respect of forgery will not usually afford compensation for loss of use of the money that was lost by reason of the forgery.[47]

27–16 Advances against forged documents. Banks frequently take out insurance policies against the possibility of loss arising through advancing money against forged documents; in these circumstances each advance is a separate loss. In one case the policy provided that the insurer should only pay the excess over 2,500 dollars ultimate net loss in respect of each and every loss. The bank operated a credit up to a specified amount in favour of a customer on the terms that the advances were secured by the deposit of securities; seven advances were made at different times before it was discovered that the securities were forged and it was held that there were seven separate losses and that, as each advance was less than the franchise limit, nothing could be recovered.[48] In a similar case, a bank made daily advances to a merchant of sums not exceeding the franchise limit in any one day against invoices for goods sold by him; many of the invoices were forgeries so that when the merchant became bankrupt the bank lost a sum in excess of the franchise limit. The Court of Appeal held that there was a series of losses or occurrences resulting in a net loss of less than the franchise limit on each, and that the bank could recover nothing.[49]

27–17 Detailed statements of loss. Delivery of a detailed statement of loss may be a condition precedent to recovery, although the detail required may vary with circumstances. It has been held that the details must be sufficient to enable the insurer to ascertain the character and amount of the loss, and to check exaggeration or falsity.[50] If the assured fails to comply with this requirement in respect of the loss as a whole, he cannot recover even in respect of the items that were supplied.

27–18 Books of account. Similarly it may sometimes be a condition of the policy that books of account or records of purchases and sales should be kept so that the insurer can determine the amount of the loss.[51]

2. GOODS IN TRANSIT

27–19 Position of carrier or bailee. Insurance on goods in transit may take the form of insurance of the carrier's or bailee's liability to the goods-owner

---

[46] *Equitable Trust Co. of New York v. Henderson* (1930) 47 T.L.R. 90.
[47] *Courtaulds plc v. Lissenden* [1986] 1 Lloyd's Rep. 368.
[48] *Equitable Trust Co. of New York v. Whittaker* (1923) 17 Ll.L.R. 153.
[49] *Philadelphia National Bank v. Price* [1938] 2 All E.R. 199; *cf.* para. 28–40, *post.*
[50] *L'Union Fire Accident and General Ins. Co. v. Klinker Knitting Mills* (1938) 59 C.L.R. 709.
[51] *Jacobson v. Yorkshire Ins. Co. Ltd* (1933) 45 Ll.L.R. 281; *Shoot v. Hill* (1936) 55 Ll.L.R. 29; *Dattner v. Guardian Ins. Co.* (1957) 11 D.L.R. 2d 44; *Bennett v. Yorkshire Ins. Co.* [1962] 2 Lloyd's Rep. 270.

or insurance of the goods themselves. In the former case the bailee may only recover to the extent of his own liability but in the latter case he uses his insurable interest in the goods to insure them for their full value; in such a case he is able to recover the value of the goods but, once he has been indemnified for his own loss, if any, he holds the remainder of the sum received as trustee for the goods-owner.[52] The phrase "goods in transit" insurance is normally used to mean this second type of insurance.[53] It is sometimes difficult to decide whether a policy covers only the bailee's own interest in the goods or the full value of the goods but it has now been determined that this is purely a matter of construing the policy and the parties' intentions are irrelevant unless they are communicated to each other.[54] When a bailee insures his own goods and "goods in trust or on commission", he will usually be held to have covered both his own interest and the interest of the goods-owner, even if the owner has not expressly assented to the insurance.[55] In this context the phrase "in trust" does not have any technical meaning but merely means that the goods have been entrusted to the bailee in the ordinary commercial sense of the word.[56] Thus in a case where the insured sub-contracted the carriage of the goods and the sub-contractor's driver fraudulently induced the goods-owner to hand over the goods, which he promptly stole, the insured was able to recover on the grounds that once the goods had been handed over to the driver of the sub-contractor they had been entrusted to him as the main contractor pursuant to his contract with the goods-owner.[57] The main contractor remains responsible to the goods-owner for the performance of the contract whether or not he sub-contracts the actual carriage and even the fact that the sub-contract may be voidable for fraud will not mean that he has not received the goods "on trust" within the wording of the insurance policy.[58]

27–20 Goods in transit policies are now so common that it can be assumed that both parties to a bailment contract have such policies in mind when they are negotiating about the obligation to insure. It has even been held that when the goods-owner undertakes to insure, it is to be implied that the carrier's liability for negligence is excluded and that the owner's insurers will have no rights of subrogation against him.[59]

27–21 "In transit." The concept of "in transit" sometimes gives rise to difficulty and has been worked out in cases concerning marine policies in much more detail than in cases where land policies have had to be construed.[60] There is nevertheless a sharp distinction to be drawn between the two types of policy and it has even been held that a policy covering transit by land does not include conveyance in barges on inland waterways.[61]

---

[52] See para. 20–24, *ante* and *Tomlinson v. Hepburn* [1966] A.C. 451.
[53] *Coupar v. Smith's* [1959] 1 Lloyd's Rep. 369, 374, *per* Winn J.
[54] *Tomlinson v. Hepburn* [1966] A.C. 451.
[55] *Waters v. Monarch Fire and Life Ass. Co.* (1856) 5 E. & B. 870.
[56] *ibid., per* Lord Campbell C.J. at 880.
[57] *Rigby (Haulage) Ltd v. Reliance Marine Ins. Co.* [1956] 2 Q.B. 468. Contrast *Lake v. Simmons* [1927] A.C. 487 where it was held that goods obtained by larceny by a trick had not been entrusted to the recipient.
[58] *Metal Scrap and By-Products Ltd v. Federated Conveyers Ltd* [1953] 1 Lloyd's Rep. 221.
[59] *Coupar Transport (London) Ltd v. Smith's (Acton) Ltd* [1959] 1 Lloyd's Rep. 369.
[60] See Arnould, *Marine Insurance* (16th ed.), chap. 16.
[61] *Ewing & Co. v. Sicklemore* (1918) 35 T.L.R. 55.

27-22 It is usually considered that transit begins when the goods are individually received by the carrier,[62] which may be well before he begins to transport them. It has been suggested that transit begins when the goods are placed upon the vehicle[63] but this is unnecessarily late in time. In *Crow's Transport Ltd v. Phoenix Assurance Co. Ltd*[64] goods were covered against all risks in transit and "while temporarily housed during the course of transit". Goods were delivered to the insured and left in their yard but were stolen before being loaded. The Court of Appeal held that the transit had already begun at the moment when the goods were received at the haulier's premises and that the goods were, therefore, temporarily housed during transit within the meaning of the policy.

If, during the transit, the lorry is temporarily parked and the goods are stolen, the loss will be covered since the goods are still in transit, even if it can be argued that the lorry is not.[65]

27-23 The moment when transit ends has never been authoritatively determined. Sometimes the policy will itself give some guidance; in *Tomlinson v. Hepburn*,[66] for example, the policy covered goods "whilst being carried and/or in transit ... including loading or unloading". All the judges who considered the case agreed that the policy covered a loss after the goods had arrived at their destination but before they were unloaded. It has been said that the transit does not cease at the moment of arrival but only when the goods are individually removed from the vehicle[67] or are delivered into the hands of the consignees' staff[68]; on this analysis a loss that occurred before unloading would probably be covered but it would probably not be necessary for the goods, once unloaded, to cross the threshold of the consignees' warehouse before the insurer can deny liability. On the other hand it has also been held in a case concerning a contract of carriage of goods in barges that transit ended when the barge arrived at the consignees' wharf.[69] If the point were to arise for decision on a policy which merely provided that cover was afforded while the goods were in transit, a court would probably draw an analogy with the commencement of transit and hold that, just as transit begins once the goods are delivered to the carrier, even before they are loaded on the vehicle, so transit does not end until the goods have been "redelivered" to the goods-owner or consignee and this cannot take place (in the ordinary sense of the word "redelivery") until the goods have been unloaded and given into the custody of the recipient. Sometimes insurers will insist on a limit in the policy for loss that happens at the dangerous time between the unloading of goods and their arrival in the hands of the consignee. It has been held, pursuant to such a provision, that cash lost in a post office yard after it left the vehicle but before it arrived in

[62] *Kilroy Thompson Ltd v. Perkins and Homer Ltd* [1956] 2 Lloyd's Rep. 49, 53.
[63] *Sadler Bros v. Meredith* [1963] 2 Lloyd's Rep. 293, 307, *per* Roskill J.
[64] [1965] 1 W.L.R. 383.
[65] *Sadler Bros. v. Meredith* [1963] 2 Lloyd's Rep. 293, following *dicta* in *Kilroy Thompson Ltd v. Perkins & Homer Ltd* [1956] 2 Lloyd's Rep. 49, 53. But not if the driver deviates from the normal course of transit as in *S.C.A. (Freight) Ltd v. Gibson, per* Ackner J. [1974] 2 Lloyd's Rep. 533.
[66] [1964] 1 Lloyd's Rep. 416; [1966] 1 Q.B. 21; [1966] A.C. 451.
[67] *Kilroy Thompson Ltd v. Perkins and Homer Ltd* [1956] 2 Lloyd's Rep. 49, 53.
[68] *Bartlett and Partners Ltd v. Meller* [1961] 1 Lloyd's Rep. 487; *cf. Heinekey v. Earle* (1857) 8 E. & B. 410, 423.
[69] *William Soanes Ltd v. F. E. Walker Ltd* (1946) 79 Ll.L.R. 646.

the building was lost "between the vehicle and the premises" rather than on the premises.[70]

27–24 Warranties and exceptions relating to security. A very common exclusion of liability in a goods in transit policy is for loss "if the vehicle is left unattended" or "if the vehicle is left unattended in a public place" or "if the vehicle is not individually attended".[71] It has been held that, if a driver leaves a vehicle but keeps it in view during his absence, the vehicle is unattended unless he can give effective chase to any one who attempts to make off with the vehicle or its goods.[72] In *Ingleton Ltd v. General Accident Fire and Life Assurance Corporation,*[73] the driver stopped for 15 minutes to deliver goods to a customer; he made sure that he could observe his vehicle while he was on the customer's premises but he had no reasonable prospect of preventing any unauthorised interference with the vehicle and Phillimore J. therefore held that the vehicle had been left unattended. Similarly, in *Sanger v. Beazley,*[74] a vehicle was unattended when the owner, feeling unwell, stopped at a motorway service station and went to the lavatory. He was not in a position to observe any attempt at interference nor to have any reasonable prospect of preventing interference. Conversely a vehicle will not be held to be unattended if the driver unloads goods into his house with a view to returning to the vehicle immediately.[75] A vehicle is not unattended if the driver is asleep inside,[76] or if he is merely paying for petrol while his vehicle is locked,[77] provided that he keeps reasonable observation of the vehicle.[78]

Insurers may very well now insert even more specific exclusions. In *Hayward v. Norwich Union Ins. Ltd,*[79] a motor policy excluded loss or damage arising from theft whilst the ignition keys of the car had been left in or on the car. The car was stolen from a garage forecourt while the owner paid for petrol at the kiosk. He had left the car unlocked with the keys in the ignition, although he had set the immobiliser, believing that this was sufficient to prevent theft, and kept the car under observation. The Court of Appeal held that the keys had been left in the car in breach of the clearly worded exclusion and the insurers were not liable for the loss.

27–25 It is frequently provided that the vehicle must be garaged in a locked garage by night, unless employed on night journeys when it is not to be left unattended. In such cases it is insufficient to leave the vehicle in a yard behind locked gates, and it has been tentatively suggested that "night" means during lighting up time.[80] In another case the policy excluded liability for thefts from a vehicle left unattended between 6 p.m. and 6 a.m. unless the vehicle was (a) locked and garaged in a building securely closed and locked, or (b) locked and parked in a yard fully enclosed and securely closed and locked. It was further provided that if this clause could not be complied with,

---

[70] *Mint Security v. Blair* [1982] 1 Lloyd's Rep. 188.
[71] As in *Harvest Trucking v. Davis* [1991] 2 Lloyd's Rep. 638.
[72] *Starfire Diamond Rings Ltd v. Angel* [1962] 2 Lloyd's Rep. 217.
[73] [1967] 2 Lloyd's Rep. 179.
[74] [1999] Lloyd's Rep. I.R. 424.
[75] *Langford v. Legal and General Ass. Co.* [1986] 2 Lloyd's Rep. 103.
[76] *Plaistow Transport Ltd v. Graham* [1966] 1 Lloyd's Rep. 639.
[77] *O'Donoghue v. Harding* [1988] 2 Lloyd's Rep. 281.
[78] See the *dictum* of Longmore J. in *Sanger v. Beazley, supra* at 429.
[79] [2001] Lloyd's Rep. I.R. 410.
[80] *A. Cohen & Co. Ltd v. Plaistow Transport Ltd* [1968] 2 Lloyd's Rep. 587.

there was to be 20 per cent coinsurance. It was held that the clause could not be complied with if, at the relevant time, a driver had to have a rest period in accordance with the requirements of section 73 of the Road Traffic Act 1960; but it was further held that it was the driver's duty not to start a journey at all if he would have insufficient driving time to reach a proper parking place before he was obliged to have a rest period.[81]

Where a policy, which differentiated between carrying, handling and storing goods in transit, provided that the insurers were not liable for loss or damage resulting from theft from an unattended vehicle unless it was securely locked and the keys removed, it was held that the exception only applied when a driver was attending on a vehicle and had no application when the goods were being properly stored.[82]

27–26 In *Princette Models Ltd v. Reliance Fire and Accident Insurance Corporation*[83] the policy provided that there was to be no liability unless the vehicle was left securely locked or unless the door, window or windscreen had been smashed by violent forcible means wherever entry, access or theft had been effected. It was held that this clause referred to the place at which entry to the vehicle was first effected and there had to be a forcible entry at that point if the insurer was to be held liable. The insured could, therefore, not recover if entry to the cab of the van had been achieved through an unlocked door and there was later a smashing to get into the part of the van in which the goods were placed.

27–27 A policy, covering money in transit during business hours and in the safe after business hours, provided that a record was to be kept of money in transit and money on the premises and that it was to be deposited in some place other than a place where money was kept. Diplock J. held that the requirement for a record was a condition of the policy and that such record must be deposited all the time not just in business hours.[84]

27–28 Sometimes warranties relating to security concentrate on the reliability of employees. In *Mint Security v. Blair*[85] the assured stated on its proposal form that he had certain procedures for checking on staff employed to carry cash, which included that they had been employed for at least a year and that their references had been checked. There was then a warranty in the policy that the procedures specified in the proposal form should not be varied to the detriment of underwriters. Staughton J. held that a casual non-compliance did not constitute a variation but that non-compliance as a result of a decision at some level of management would be a breach of warranty with the result that the insured could not recover.

27–29 Other provisions. Goods may be covered "whilst in warehouse" or "whilst in store". Where insurance was provided "whilst in a public warehouse" it was held that the question to be decided was whether the owner of the warehouse carried on a business of warehousing and it was accordingly held that a friendly arrangement whereby goods were stored

[81] *Lowenstein & Co. Ltd v. Poplar Motor Transport Ltd* [1968] 2 Lloyd's Rep. 233.
[82] *Gordon Leslie Ltd v. General Accident Fire & Life Assurance Corp. plc* [1998] S.L.T. 391
[83] [1960] 1 Lloyd's Rep. 49.
[84] *Vaughan Motors Ltd v. Scottish General Ins. Co.* [1960] 1 Lloyd's Rep. 479.
[85] [1982] 1 Lloyd's Rep. 188.

under an archway of a nearby railway was not sufficient to bring the goods within the cover.[86]

It has been held that it is not necessary for goods covered "whilst in store" to be kept in a covered building, but the question whether such a phrase implies that the goods must be properly stored has been left open.[87] Sometimes a policy will contain a limited liability for specified goods and a general indemnity for legal liability (e.g. under the C.M.R. Convention); in such cases the limit will prevail over the more general indemnity.[88] If cover is afforded for loss or damage to goods on vehicles operated by sub-contractors, but not by bogus sub-contractors, it will apply to a loss caused or contributed to by a genuine but criminal sub-contractor.[89]

3. POLICIES COVERING RISK OF STORM AND TEMPEST

27–30 Nature of the risk. Losses caused by storm and other types of water damage are often excluded from fire policies but are usually included in a householder's ordinary comprehensive policy. Separate cover is not particularly common in the United Kingdom but is more frequent in the United States and Canada where policies may cover loss by lightning, hurricanes, cyclones, tornadoes, windstorm or hail.

In *Oddy v. Phoenix Assurance Co. Ltd*[90] Veale J. defined storm in the following terms:

> "'storm' means storm, and to me it connotes some sort of violent wind usually accompanied by rain or hail or snow. Storm does not mean persistent bad weather, nor does it mean heavy rain or persistent rain by itself."

He further said that the word "tempest" meant no more than a severe storm and that the word "storm" is therefore the operative word in such a policy.

It follows from this that a storm is more prolonged and widespread than a gust of wind[91] and it is doubtful whether wind or rain on their own would constitute a storm.[92] Heavy snowfall together with the existence of some significant wind has been held to be a storm in Scotland.[93]

27–31 U.S. policies often provide cover for loss caused by "windstorm". This word, while indicating something different from mere wind,[94] may contemplate an absence of rain, hail or snow. It has been said that there must be an outburst of tumultuous force[95] or a wind of unusual violence but that it

---

[86] *Firmin and Collins Ltd v. Allied Shippers Ltd* [1961] 1 Lloyd's Rep. 633. For the meaning of the words "final warehouse" see *John Martin of London Ltd v. Russell* [1960] 1 Lloyd's Rep. 554, followed in *Bayview Motors v. Mitsui Marine Ins. Co.* [2002] 1 Lloyd's Rep. 652, 656.

[87] *Wulfson v. Switzerland General Ins. Co. Ltd* (1940) 163 L.T. 136.

[88] *Avandero v. National Transit Insce.* [1984] 2 Lloyd's Rep. 613.

[89] *London Tobacco v. DFDS Transport* [1994] 1 Lloyd's Rep. 394.

[90] [1966] 1 Lloyd's Rep. 134, 138.

[91] *S. & M. Hotels Ltd v. Legal and General Ass. Soc. Ltd* [1972] 1 Lloyd's Rep. 157; *Metropolitan Ice Cream Co. v. Union Mutual Fire Ins. Co.*, 210 S.W. 2d 700 (1948).

[92] This point was expressly left open for future decision in *Anderson v. Norwich Union Fire Insurance Society Ltd* [1977] 1 Lloyd's Rep. 253.

[93] *Glasgow Training v. Lombard Continental* 1989 S.C. 30.

[94] *Kaufman v. New York Underwriters Ins. Co.* [1955] 2 D.L.R. 555.

[95] *Lunn v. Indiana Lumbermen's Mutual Ins. Co.* 201 S.W. 2d 978 (1948).

need not be sufficiently ferocious to amount to a cyclone or tornado.[96] It has been said that a windstorm must be a wind of such extraordinary force and violence as "to injuriously disturb the ordinary condition of the property insured",[97] or "to be capable of damaging the insured property, assuming the property to be in a reasonable state of repair".[98] Sometimes the insurer will stipulate that the insured should maintain the building at all times in a proper state of repair, but if cover is afforded while the building is actually in the course of repair, the insurer will probably be unable to rely on the condition.[99]

27–32 Causation. The insured must, of course, prove that the damage was proximately caused by the peril insured against. Thus, the destruction of a bungalow by the collapse of a retaining wall was held not to fall within a policy covering loss from "storm or tempest" when it was shown that the collapse of the wall was due to the pressure of water building up behind it over a long period of time rather than to the combination of rain and wind at a particular moment.[1] Similarly, a building that collapsed because the supports were over-stressed was held not to have been damaged as a result of wind or storm.[2]

On the other hand, if, during a storm, the wind makes openings in the roof of a building and rain then enters and damages property inside the building, such damage will be covered by a windstorm policy.[3] If a structure has been previously weakened by rain but the wind is the effective cause of the damage the loss will likewise be covered.[4]

Loss or damage from burst water mains[5] may be covered if the bursting occurs during the policy year, but it will not be enough if it is only the damage that occurs during the year.[6]

27–33 Exceptions. Policies may expressly exclude certain events. Storms or cyclones may themselves be excluded from ordinary accident policies,[7] while damage by lightning or minor damage by wind may be excluded from

---

[96] *Schaeffer v. Northern Ass. Co.* 177 S.W. 2d 688 (1944); *Metropolitan Ice Cream Co. v. Union Mutual Fire Ins. Co.*, 210 S.W. 2d 700 (1948).

[97] *Fidelity-Phoenix Fire Ins. Co. of New York v. Board of Education of Town of Rosedale*, 204 P. 2d 982 (1948); *cf. Adam's Apple Products Corporation v. National Fire Ins. Co. of Pittsburgh*, 85 A. 2d 702 (1952); *Kemp v. American Universal Ins. Co.*, 391 F. 2d 533 (1968).

[98] *Druggist Mutual Ins. Co. v. Baker*, 254 S.W. 2d 691 (1952); *Old Colony Ins. Co. v. Reynolds*, 256 S.W. 2d 362 (1953); *Pearson v. Aroostook County Patrons Mutual Fire Ins. Co.*, 101 A. 2d 183 (1953); *Beattie Bonded Warehouse Co. v. General Accident Fire and Life Assurance Corporation*, 315 F. Supp. 996 (1970). *Cf.* 93 A.L.R. 2d 135 (1964).

[99] *S. & M. Hotels Ltd v. Legal and General Ass. Society Ltd* [1972] 1 Lloyd's Rep. 157, 165, *per* Thesiger J.

[1] *Oddy v. Phoenix Ass. Co. Ltd* [1966] 1 Lloyd's Rep. 134.

[2] *S. & M. Hotels Ltd v. Legal and General Ass. Society Ltd* [1972] 1 Lloyd's Rep. 157.

[3] *Loyola University v. Sun Underwriters of New York*, 196 F. 2d 169 (1952); *Magnolia-Broadway Corporation v. Fire Association of Philadelphia*, 137 N.Y.S. 2d 918 (1955); *cf.* the express provision in *Stephanie v. Consumers Mutual Ins. Co.*, 74 N.W. 2d 116 (1955).

[4] *Wood v. Michigan Millers Mutual Fire Ins. Co.*, 96 S.E. 2d 28 (1957). For a policy covering "direct loss" only, see *Kintzel v. Wheatland Mutual Ins. Assn.* 203 N.W. 2d 799 (1973) and 65 A.L.R. 3d 1128 *et seq.* 1975).

[5] Such bursting will usually be held to require a rupture from within—see *Computer Engineering v. Lelliott* (1989) 54 B.L.R. 1.

[6] *Kelly v. Norwich Union Fire Ins.* [1990] 1 W.L.R. 139.

[7] *Maryland Casualty Ins. Co. v. Finch*, 147 Fed.Rep. 388 (1906), where a cyclone was held to mean a violent windstorm specially destructive to buildings in its path rather than a technical meteorological phenomenon.

an ordinary storm policy.[8] Damage from flood will be covered by a policy insuring against loss or damage by water[9] but is sometimes expressly excluded from a storm and tempest policy.[10] In *Oakleaf v. Home Insurance Co.*,[11] a householder's policy covered loss and damage caused by windstorm or by rain entering an aperture made by windstorm. Loss or damage caused by flood or overflow was excluded. The insured left a stepladder leaning against a wall; it was dislodged by high winds accompanied by heavy rainfall and broke the basement window. A gutter outside the window had become obstructed and then filled with rainwater, which overflowed and poured through the broken window and into the basement. The insured was able to recover under the policy for the broken window but the majority of the Court of Appeal of Ontario held that he could not recover for the damage to the basement because there had been an overflow.[12] It was argued that the loss was caused by rain entering the aperture made by the windstorm but it was held that, even if this were so, the water was in the form of an overflow and was therefore excluded by the express terms of the policy and it was further held that the fact that the overflow had itself been caused by the windstorm could not avail the insured because the overflow, not the windstorm, was the proximate cause of the damage. The dissenting judge, Lebel J.A., said that the exception for overflow and flood referred to the behaviour of a pre-existing body of water and that, if water came into existence as a result of a windstorm and then overflowed, the exception did not apply; it is submitted, however, that this opinion unjustifiably reads words into the exception that were not present in the policy and that the majority view is to be preferred.

27–34 Where loss has been caused both by a peril insured against and an excepted peril it is always difficult to say which peril a court will regard as the proximate cause.[13] In some cases it may be possible to attribute parts of the damage to separate causes, *e.g.* a policy covering damage by lightning and excluding damage caused by the wind.[14] In one case in the U.S. a bridge was insured against damage from windstorms, cyclones and tornadoes but damage from high water or floods was excluded. A violent wind caused vessels to be blown against the bridge and there was also a high tide. Because

---

[8] *Holmes v. Phenix Ins. Co.*, 98 Fed. Rep. 240 (1899) where the exclusion for damage by lightning or minor damage by wind was qualified by the words "unless other damage occur". These words were held to apply only to the damage by wind and damage by lightning was thus completely excluded.

[9] *Kündig v. Hepburn* [1959] 1 Lloyd's Rep. 183. A flood has been said to be a natural phenomenon that has some element of violence, suddenness or largeness about it and does not include a seepage of water from an underground watercourse that covers the floor to a depth of three inches. *Young v. Sun Alliance* [1976] 2 Lloyd's Rep. 189. Nor is it apposite to describe as a "flood" an accidental discharge of water from a building's existing fire protection system—see *Computer Engineering v. Lelliott* (1989) 54 B.L.R. 1. On the other hand, an ingress of water some three to four inches deep which had entered a house over the flashings following a period of heavy rainfall was held to constitute a "flood" in *Rohan Investments Ltd. v. Cunningham* [1999] Lloyd's Rep. I.R. 190.

[10] *Howard Farrow Ltd v. Ocean Accident and Guarantee Corporation Ltd* (1940) 67 Ll.L.R. 27; *Oddy v. Phoenix Ass. Co. Ltd* [1966] 1 Lloyd's Rep. 134; *Pennsylvania Fire Ins. Co. v. Sikes*, 168 P. 2d 1016 (1946), where damage to goods blown by wind into a flooded street was nevertheless held to be recoverable.

[11] (1959) 14 D.L.R. 2d 535.

[12] On this point the trial judge was upheld, see (1957) 10 D.L.R. 2d 765.

[13] See para. 19–05, *ante*.

[14] *Beakes v. Phoenix Ins. Co.*, 143 N.Y. 402 (1894).

there was no evidence that the action of the water caused any damage apart from the wind, the court held that it was open to the jury to decide that all the damage was caused by the wind.[15] If, however, there is such evidence, it is clear that the insured cannot recover for damage caused by the action of both wind and water.[16] Where a windstorm policy excludes damage by water and damage is caused by water driven by the wind, the damage will probably be covered by the policy, at any rate if the windstorm can be said to be the proximate cause of the damage,[17] but if the water is the predominant cause or even substantial contributing factor, the damage will not be covered.[18]

An exception for flood will preclude recovery by the insured where the flood is caused by the negligence of his servants or agents even though the purpose of the policy as a whole may be to afford cover for such negligence.[19]

4. PLATE-GLASS POLICIES

27–35 Usual scope of cover. These policies are usually issued in respect of shop premises. The policy contains a detailed description of the glass which is insured, and insures it against damage from specified causes, such as civil commotion,[20] or against damage from any cause with specified exceptions such as fire, breakage during removal, alteration or repair of the premises. The policy in *Marsden v. City and County Assurance Co.*[21] was in this latter form. A fire broke out in the house next door to the plaintiff's shop, and, although it slightly damaged the rear of the shop, it did not approach the shop-front. While the plaintiff was removing his stock and his furniture to a safe place, a mob tore down the shop's shutters and broke the glass in order to steal what was inside. The defendants argued that the plaintiff's loss was proximately caused by the fire or by breakage during removal, but the Court of Common Pleas held that the fire on the neighbour's premises was only a remote cause of the damage, the proximate cause of which was the lawless violence of the mob.

27–36 Although the judges all agreed that the cause of the damage was not "breakage during removal", there was some difference of opinion about the meaning of this exception. The policy did not afford cover while the glass was "horizontally placed or moveable" and Byles J. thought these words should be read with the exception so that the insured was not covered if the glass was removed from one part of the premises to another or from one set of premises to another.[22] Erle C.J. originally inclined to this view but recognised that the true meaning might well be that breakage of the glass was not covered while the insured's goods were being removed from the

---

[15] *Phenix Ins. Co. v. Charleston Bridge Co.*, 65 Fed.Rep. 628 (1895).
[16] *Niagara Fire Ins. Co. v. Muhle*, 208 F. 2d 191 (1953).
[17] *Kaufman v. New York Underwriters Incorporated [1955] 2 D.L.R. 555, followed in Oakleaf v. Home Ins. Co.* (1957) 14 D.L.R. 2d 535. *Cf. Anderson v. Connecticut Fire Ins. Co.*, 43 N.W. 2d 807 (1950) where a building was weakened by the wind but finally collapsed as a result of an excepted peril.
[18] *Protzmann v. Eagle Fire Co. of New York*, 71 N.Y.S. 2d 43 (1947); *Niagara Fire Ins. Co. v. Muhle*, 208 F. 2d 191 (1953).
[19] *Howard Farrow Ltd v. Ocean Accident and Guarantee Corpn Ltd* (1940) 67 Ll.L.R. 27.
[20] *London and Manchester Plate Glass Co. v. Heath* [1913] 3 K.B. 411.
[21] (1865) L.R. 1 C.P. 232.
[22] *ibid.* at pp. 240–241.

premises in ordinary circumstances such as moving shop. Even if this was so, the exception did not apply to the removal of the insured's goods as a result of a sudden emergency.[23] Willes J. considered that the exception applied to a breakage due to some accident resulting from or incidental to the removal of the insured's business or plant and taking place during such removal.[24] This construction, which was accepted by Keating J.,[25] seems to accord most readily with the parties' likely intentions.[26]

27–37 Risk of breakage during (or as a result of) alterations or repairs on the premises may be excepted if the insured does not give notice of the proposed alterations and pay any such additional premium as may be required to cover any increase of risk. The liability of the insurer is usually limited to the cost value of the glass insured, and the insurer usually reserves the right to reinstate instead of making a money payment.

5. LIVESTOCK POLICIES

27–38 Scope of policies. There are many different forms of livestock policy in use covering all kinds of risks to horses, cattle and other animals. An annual insurance covering farm stock is usually an insurance against loss by death arising from any accident[27] or disease[28] with certain specified exceptions such as poisoning, docking, surgical operation, improper use, overloading, unskilful treatment, wilful neglect, malicious injuries, slaughtering, war, tumult or riot. Certain other specified causes of death are not insured unless an extra premium is paid, such as death occurring during transport by rail or sea, or arising from foaling, castration, fire, lightning, glanders or farcy. The insurance is conditional upon every animal insured being in perfect health and free from any injury at the time of proposal[29] and at the time the first premium is paid; upon each renewal of the policy the insured is required to furnish a satisfactory written declaration of health and soundness. The animals insured by the policy are specified in a schedule showing the numbers of each class and distinguishing marks[30] and stating the price paid for the animal by the insured or its value.[31] The policy is not usually a valued policy and the liability of the insurer will not exceed either the sum insured or the actual market value at the date of death. Special policies are sometimes issued for foaling and castration. It is commonly required that the assured be the owner of the animal.[32]

---

[23] *ibid.* at p. 239.

[24] *ibid.* at p. 240.

[25] *ibid.* at p. 242

[26] But see para. 25–63, *ante.*

[27] *cf. Burridge v. Haines* (1918) 87 L.J.K.B. 641; 118 L.T. 681 where insurance was given for death caused by accidental, external and visible injury, see para. 25–29, *ante.*

[28] Insurance against "mortality" will cover death from natural causes only—see *St Paul Fire and Marine Ins. Co. v. Morice* (1906) 11 Com.Cas. 153.

[29] See *Demal v. British American Live Stock Association* (1910) 14 W.L.R. 250.

[30] See *Yorkshire Ins. Co. v. Campbell* [1917] A.C. 218 where the pedigree of a horse had been wrongly stated in the proposal form.

[31] Compare *Great Northern Ins. Co. v. Whitney* (1918) 57 Can. S.C.R. 543 with *Clarke v. British Empire Ins. Co.* (1912) 22 W.L.R. 89.

[32] *O'Connell v. Pearl Assurance PLC* [1995] 2 Lloyd's Rep. 479.

27–39 Where a policy makes different provisions for injury to and death of an animal and the animal is so seriously injured that the proper course is to slaughter it at once, the loss will fall within the provisions for death.[33] Any provision in the policy requiring the written consent of the insurer before the animal is slaughtered does not apply where death is accelerated so as to save the animal from unnecessary suffering.[34]

27–40 Livestock policies frequently require that a certificate or report from a qualified veterinary surgeon should be forwarded with or shortly after the claim. Any such requirements can, of course, be waived if, for example, the insurer repudiates the claim as soon as he is notified of it and before the insured has an opportunity of obtaining a report.[35]

The insurer may be entitled to ask the insured to make a statutory declaration as to the loss but, if so, the insured is probably entitled to make the declaration in a form of his own choice.[36]

27–41 Safe arrival. In one case a fox terrier dog was insured for £150 against risk of transport from England to India "against all risks, including mortality from any cause, jettison, and washing overboard, but walking at Lahore, Punjab, to be deemed a safe arrival". On arrival at Lahore the dog was suffering from periostitis of the right hind leg, and was unable by reason of such injury to walk upon four legs, and therefore only used three legs. It was held that the "deeming" clause applied to all the risks and not that of mortality only, but that there had not, in fact, been a safe arrival. The clause meant that the dog must be capable of locomotion in the usual way upon four legs. In this case it was incapable of using one leg at all and the insurers had to pay a total loss.[37]

27–42 Alteration of circumstances. There will usually be a provision entitling the insured to substitute other animals for those specified in the policy with the consent of the insurer; if the insured sells his stock, however, the benefit of the policy does not pass to the buyer unless it is expressly assigned.[38] If the policy specifies the use that is to be made of the stock and an animal suffers an accident while being used in a different manner, the loss will not be covered.[39] Sometimes the policy will require the animals to remain in a specified locality. If they leave the place, they will not be covered, but the policy will re-attach when they return.[40]

---

[33] *Shiells v. Scottish Assurance Corporation Ltd* (1889) 16 R. 1014. The policy may provide that the cause of death must arise within a specified period as in *Demal v. British American Live Stock Association* (1910) 14 W.L.R. 250; *Sharkey v. Yorkshire Ins. Co.* (1916) 54 Can. S.C.R. 92.

[34] *Shiells v. Scottish Assurance Corporation Ltd* (1889) 16 R. 1014.

[35] *Shiells v. Scottish Assurance Corporation Ltd* (1889) 16 R. 1014; *Burridge v. Haines* (1918) 87 L.J.K.B. 641; 118 L.T. 681.

[36] *Beeck v. Yorkshire Ins. Co.* (1909) 11 W.A.L.R. 88.

[37] *Jacob v. Gaviller* (1902) 7 Com.Cas. 116.

[38] *Gill v. Yorkshire Ins. Co.* (1913) 24 W.L.R. 389.

[39] *Stuart v. Horse Ins. Co.* (1893) 1 S.L.T. 91.

[40] *Gorman v. Hand-in-Hand Ins. Co.* (1877) I.R. 11 C.L. 224.

CHAPTER 28

THIRD PARTY RISKS

1. Liability Insurance Generally

28–1 Introduction. There has been a considerable extension of the practice of insurance against various forms of legal liability which the assured may incur to third parties. The subsequent sections of this chapter will deal in detail with the principal types of liability insurance, while in this section some questions of general importance are considered.

(a) Accrual of Cause of Action

28–2 Right to indemnity. It will often be necessary to determine when the right to an indemnity arises. An insurance against liability, like an insurance on property, is a contract of indemnity,[1] and no obligation arises on the part of the insurer to pay a claim until the assured has suffered a loss.[2] The common law doctrine was that nothing less than payment would suffice as proof of loss.[3] Equity, however, accepted that a loss was suffered once the fact and extent of the liability of the party seeking to enforce the indemnity had been ascertained in proceedings or otherwise.[4] Since the passing of the Judicature Acts the equitable rule has prevailed.[5] Consistent with these principles a majority[6] of the Court of Appeal has held in *Post Office v.*

---

[1] *Lancashire Insurance Co. v. Inland Revenue Commissioners* [1899] 1 Q.B. 353, 359, *per* Bruce J.; *British Cash and Parcel Conveyors Ltd v. Lamson Store Service Co. Ltd* [1908] 1 K.B. 1006, 1014–1015, *per* Fletcher Moulton L.J.

[2] *West Wake Price & Co. v. Ching* [1957] 1 W.L.R. 45, 49, *per* Devlin J., approved in *Post Office v. Norwich Union Fire Insurance Society Ltd*, *per* Lord Denning M.R. and Salmon L.J. [1967] 2 Q.B. 363, 374, 378.

[3] *Collinge v. Heywood* (1839) 9 A. & E. 633; *Re Richardson ex parte Governors of St Thomas's Hospital* [1911] 2 K.B. 705, 709–710, 712–713; *M'Gillivray v. Hope* [1935] A.C. 1, 10.

[4] *Re Richardson ex parte Governors of St Thomas's Hospital* [1911] 2 K.B. 705. A "pay to be paid" clause in marine policies has the effect of restoring the common law rule—see *Firma C-Trade SA v. Newcastle P. & I. Association* [1991] A.C. 1. The courts will, however, lean against this result if an alternative construction is possible: compare *Hong Kong Borneo Services v. Pilcher* [1992] 2 Lloyd's Rep. 593 with *Charter Reins. Co. Ltd v. Fagan* [1997] A.C. 313.

[5] *County and District Properties Ltd v. C. Jenner & Son Ltd* [1976] 2 Lloyd's Rep. 728; *R. & H. Green & Silley Weir Ltd v. British Railways Board* [1985] 1 W.L.R. 570; *Telfair Shipping Corp. v. Inersea SA* [1985] 1 W.L.R. 553, 568; *Firma C-Trade SA v. Newcastle P & I Association* [1991] 2 A.C. 1, 28, *per* Lord Brandon.

[6] Lord Denning M.R. and Salmon L.J.

[821]

Norwich Union Fire Insurance Society Ltd[7] that the insured's right to be indemnified under a liability insurance policy arises only once the insured's liability to the third party claimant is ascertained and determined by agreement, award or judgment,[8] and not upon the occurrence of the event which gives rise to a liability on the part of the insured to the third party.

28–3 Previous editions of this work recorded some reservations about the correctness of this case, but it has been approved in *Bradley v. Eagle Star Insurance Co. Ltd*[9] and must now be regarded as authoritative. This probably means that *Chandris v. Argo Insurance Co. Ltd*[10] can no longer be supported. In that case Megaw J. held that the cause of action for an indemnity under a marine policy against liability to contribute in general average arose at the time of the general average loss. It was not cited to the Court of Appeal in *Post Office v. Norwich Union* and can be justified, if at all, only by reference to specific provisions of the Marine Insurance Act 1906.

28–4 Limitation. It follows from the above principles that, for the purposes of limitation, time will start to run against the assured, in respect of any cause of action he has against the insurer, from the date of the agreement, award or judgment which establishes the extent of the insurer's liability to indemnify him.[11]

28–5 Third-party proceedings. The time at which a right to indemnity arises is relevant to the practice of joining liability insurers as third parties in proceedings brought by a claimant against the assured.[12] Since juries ceased to try issues of fact in civil cases it has been commonplace for this to be done in order to avoid multiplicity of proceedings and the risk of inconsistent decisions.[13] It might be thought that it was premature to proceed against the insurer in this way before the assured's liability was ascertained, but the Court of Appeal has disagreed with this contention.[14] It is submitted that so

---

[7] [1967] 2 Q.B. 363. Harman L.J. dissented from this statement of principle but concurred in the result of the appeal for a different reason also relied on by the majority, namely, that the insured could not claim against the insurers before he had been found liable without being in breach of a condition in the policy in question which stipulated that no admission of liability was to be made without insurers' consent. This is a clause commonly found in all liability policies. The majority decision is supported by the judgment of Scrutton L.J. in *Versicherungs und Transport AG Daugava v. Henderson* (1934) 39 Com.Cas. 312, 316–317.

[8] To which there have to be added, interim payment order and taxation of costs if appropriate; *Cox v. Bankside Members Agency Ltd* [1995] 2 Lloyd's Rep. 437, 453, *per* Phillips J.

[9] [1989] A.C. 957.

[10] [1963] 2 Lloyd's Rep. 65. See the discussion of this case in [1995] L.C.M.L.Q. 34, 37–40, *per* Sir Jonathan Mance. Cases and *dicta* relying on this authority must also be suspect, *e.g. Bosma v. Larsen* [1966] 1 Lloyd's Rep. 22 and the first instance decision in *Phoenix v. Halvanon* [1988] Q.B. 216. It must, however, be remembered that the principle set out in the text applies only to liability insurance and reinsurance. It does not necessarily apply to every contract of indemnity—see *Callaghan v. Dominion Ins. Co.* [1997] 2 Lloyd's Rep. 541.

[11] *Lefevre v. White* [1990] 1 Lloyd's Rep. 569; *Versicherungs Daugava v. Henderson* (1934) 39 Com.Cas. 312, 316.

[12] This can be achieved under the Civil Procedure Rules Part 20.

[13] *Harman v. Crilly* [1943] 1 K.B. 168; *Brice v. Wackerbarth* [1974] 2 Lloyd's Rep. 274.

[14] *Brice v. Wackerbarth* [1974] 2 Lloyd's Rep. 274. It must be said that in the decisions upon the permissibility of joinder prior to *Harman v. Crilly*, *supra*, no point was made that the third-party claim against the insurer was in any event premature—*Lothian v. Epworth Press* [1928] 1 K.B. 199; *Gowar v. Hales* [1928] 1 K.B. 191; *Jones v. Birch Bros Ltd* [1933] 2 K.B. 597. *Carpenter v. Ebblewhite* [1939] 1 K.B. 347 is different in that there the third party claimant was

long as the insured is seeking a declaration of liability rather than actual payment there is no objection in principle to such proceedings.[15] No doubt in practice the insurers are not concerned with niceties of this kind when they cannot be altogether rid of third-party proceedings against them.[16]

28–6 Legal liability. In order to recover under a conventional liability policy, the assured must show that it was under a legal liability to the third party claimant; that the liability is covered by the insurance, and (in the case of a settlement) that any amount paid by way of settlement was reasonable.[17] The general principle is that liability insurance provides an indemnity against actual established liability, as opposed to mere allegations.[18] Where liability has been established by a judgment or similar determination, it is not normally permissible to look beyond the determination in order to establish the basis of the liability.[19] A liability which is actionable only because the assured has waived his right to diplomatic immunity is a legally enforceable liability against which insurers must indemnify their assured.[20] A liability that arises by estoppel will be covered by the ordinary form of liability policy, at any rate where the estoppel arises from the negligent, as opposed to wilful, conduct of the assured or those for whom he is responsible.[21] By contrast, a payment made by the assured by reason of commercial pressure rather than on account of any liability will not be covered.[22]

28–7 Legality. Since the assured under a liability policy is always seeking to be indemnified against the consequences of his own wrongdoing, this is a

---

seeking a declaration against the insurer before obtaining judgment against the insured. See also *Wright v. Donne Mileham, The Times,* 9 November 1976; *Du Pont v. Agnew* [1987] 2 Lloyd's Rep. 585, 595. The Commercial Court has entertained actions for such declarations before the insured's liability was determined—*Thorman v. New Hampshire Ins. Co.* [1988] 1 Lloyd's Rep. 7.

[15] *Brice v. Wackerbarth* [1974] 2 Lloyd's Rep. 274, 276, *per* Lord Denning M.R. It is unclear from the report precisely what relief was claimed in the third-party proceedings. Although apparently equity may not previously have granted a declaration of liability to indemnify before the liability was ascertained, *Re Richardson* [1911] 2 K.B. 705, 709–710, presumably the width of the modern equitable jurisdiction to grant declarations has overcome that difficulty. See also *Post Office v. Norwich Union Fire Ins. Society Ltd* [1967] 2 Q.B. 363, 374C; *Rigby v. Sun Alliance & London Ins. Ltd* [1980] 1 Lloyd's Rep. 359, 362–363.

[16] See, *e.g. Dunbar v. A. & B. Painters Ltd, Economic Ins. Co. Ltd and Whitehouse & Co., Third Parties* [1986] 2 Lloyd's Rep. 38, 40; *Gray v. Barr* [1970] 2 Q.B. 626 (declaration claimed); *Barrett Bros v. Davies* [1966] 2 Lloyd's Rep. 1. The insurers may in fact be permitted to be joined as defendants, to ensure that the defence is conducted properly and that all relevant issues can be resolved: *Wood v. Perfection Travel* [1996] L.R.L.R. 233.

[17] *Structural Polymer Systems v. Brown* [2000] Lloyd's Rep. I.R. 64, 67.

[18] *MDIS v. Swinbank* [1999] Lloyd's Rep. I.R. 516; *Thornton Springer v. NEM Ins. Co. Ltd* [2000] Lloyd's Rep. I.R. 590. In *Skandia International Corp. v. N.R.G. Victory Reinsurance Ltd* [1998] Lloyd's Rep. I.R. 446, which involved a claim under reinsurance, a legal opinion that a Texan jury instructed by a judge without experience in insurance law would be likely to find against the reassured did not suffice to establish liability.

[19] *London Borough of Redbridge v. Municipal Mutual Ins. Ltd* [2001] Lloyd's Rep. I.R. 545.

[20] *Dickinson v. Del Solar* [1930] 1 K.B. 376.

[21] *"The Diane"* [1977] 1 Lloyd's Rep. 61, 66–67.

[22] *Smit Tak v. Youell* [1992] 1 Lloyd's Rep. 154. But amounts paid pursuant to *ex gratia* settlements will be covered, if there was in fact a liability: *Peninsular & Oriental Steam Co. v. Youell* [1997] 2 Lloyd's Rep. 136. Similarly, if the assured can demonstrate it was liable for at least the settlement sum, it is no bar to recovery that commercial considerations may in part

field in which questions of illegality are particularly likely to arise. The general principles governing these questions are discussed elsewhere.[23]

A particular case in which this question has arisen is that of insurance for libel.

28–8 Libel. Policies are commonly issued insuring authors and publishers against liability for libel. It has never been conclusively decided whether such policies are enforceable at common law[24] but section 11 of the Defamation Act 1952[25] provides that an agreement for indemnifying any person against civil liability for libel in respect of the publication of any matter shall not be unlawful unless at the time of publication that person knows that the matter is defamatory, and does not reasonably believe there is a good defence to any action brought upon it.[26]

(b) Rights of Third Party Against Insurer

28–9 Rights of third party against insurer. Among the most important questions arising in this field is whether, and to what extent, the injured party can recover directly against the insurer the damages awarded to him against the assured. At common law there is in general no possibility of his doing so.

28–10 Common law. There have been several cases in which a third party who has recovered damages against an assured has sought a remedy against the insurers by way of garnishee proceedings. These attempts have always failed and, in any event, have now become unimportant as far as motor-vehicle insurance is concerned since section 151 of the Road Traffic Act 1988 (re-enacting previous legislation) gives a third party a direct remedy against

---

have affected the amount paid to particular claimants: *Structural Polymer Systems Ltd v. Brown* [2000] Lloyd's Rep. I.R. 64. It is common for liability policies to exclude cover if the assured assumes by agreement a liability to which it would not otherwise have been subject—see *A.S. Screenprint Ltd v. British Reserve Ins. Co. Ltd* [1999] Lloyd's Rep. I.R. 430, 435.

[23] Ch. 14, *supra*. Punitive damages present problems, but are a legitimate subject of liability insurance. See *Lancashire County Council v. Municipal Mutual Ins. Co.* [1997] Q.B. 897. Many policies, however, expressly exclude any liability for punitive damages. A policy covering the liability of the assured for amounts awarded as "compensation" will not necessarily exclude liability for punitive damages, nor will it exclude statutory liability if such liability can be regarded as compensatory, see *Charterhouse Development v. Sharpe* [1998] Lloyd's Rep. I.R. 266.

[24] Since libel can be a crime if it tends to provoke a breach of the peace, it has been argued that any insurance against the consequences of committing libel should be void. There is authority for the view that a contract purporting to indemnify a person against the consequences of libel is void—see *Colbourn v. Patmore* (1834) 1 C.M. & R. 73; *Shackell v. Rosier* (1836) 2 Bing N.C. 634; *Burrows v. Rhodes* [1899] 1 Q.B. 816, 828; *W. H. Smith & Son v. Clinton* (1908) 25 T.L.R. 34; *Weld-Blundell v. Stephens* [1920] A.C. 956, 998; *Broadstreets British Ltd v. Harold Mitchell* [1933] Ch. 190. On the other hand, libel policies have come before the courts without any suggestion that they are unenforceable—see *"Daily Express" (1908) Ltd v. Mountain* (1916) 32 T.L.R. 592; *E. Hulton & Co. v. Mountain* (1921) 37 T.L.R. 869 and the note of Sir Frederick Pollock in [1908] 1 K.B. at p. 1015.

[25] 15 & 16 Geo. 6 & 1 Eliz. 2, c. 66; see also s.14 of New Zealand Defamation Act 1954.

[26] In earlier editions of this work, the editor retained a full discussion of the extent to which libel policies are enforceable at common law since it would be useful in jurisdiction to which the Defamation Act 1952 did not apply. The conclusion reached was that policies could be enforced in so far as they afforded indemnity for unintentional defamation but that defamatory statements intentionally made by a person who reasonably believed that he had a good defence could not be the subject of insurance. The reader is referred to the discussion at pp. 989–991 of the 5th ed. but it should be read in the light of the additional cases cited in note 24, *ante*.

the insurer.[27] In *Israelson v. Dawson*[28] it was held that no debt was due from an insurer to his assured, but there was only a promise to indemnify the assured against such payment as the assured was legally liable to make. If the promise is not honoured, the assured has a claim for breach of contract but since no debt is due, there is nothing which can be garnished in the hands of the insurers. Moreover, the obligation of the insurer can be discharged by satisfying any judgment obtained against the assured by the third party and it is therefore impossible to say that the insurer in any way owes a debt to the assured.[29]

28–11 Statutory assignment. Before 1930 the right of a person to be indemnified under a contract of insurance against claims made against him by persons whom he might have injured was one personal to himself, and there was no privity of any sort between the injured person and the insurers. The injured person had no interest at law or in equity in the insurance money, either before or after it was paid by the insurers to their assured. If the assured became bankrupt or, being a company, went into liquidation the insurance money became part of the general assets distributable among creditors, and if the injured person had not already obtained judgment and levied execution in respect of his claim for damages his only right was to prove in the bankruptcy or winding-up.[30] To correct this injustice the Third Parties (Rights against Insurers) Act 1930[31] was passed, which effects a statutory assignment of the rights of the assured to the injured person. Section 1 provides that where, under any contract of insurance,[32] a person is

[27] See para. 29–23, *infra*.
[28] [1933] 1 K.B. 301. A claim upon an insurance policy is classified as a claim for unliquidated damages: *Jabbour v. Custodian of Israeli Absentee Property* [1954] 1 W.L.R. 139, 143; *Chandris v. Argo Ins. Co.* [1963] 2 Lloyd's Rep. 65, 73–74; *Edmunds v. ADAS* [1986] 1 Lloyd's Rep. 326, 327; *Phoenix General Ins. Co. v. Halvanon Ins. Co.* [1985] 2 Lloyd's Rep. 599, 609. This does not, however, mean that an assured can get damages at large for an insurer's failure to pay—*"Italia Express"* [1992] 2 Lloyd's Rep. 281, 293, in which damages for inconvenience, hardship and mental distress as well as other consequential pecuniary loss were refused to an insured shipowner: *Sprung v. Royal Ins. (UK) Ltd* [1999] Lloyd's Rep. I.R. 111. (Permission was granted by the Court of Appeal to argue to the contrary in *Pride Valley Foods Ltd v. Independent Ins. Co. Ltd* [1999] 1 Lloyd's Rep. I.R. 120.) In Scots law the action is not classified as one for damages—*Scott Lithgow v. Secretary of State for Defence* 1989 S.C., H.L. 9, 20 (a case on prescription).
[29] *Israelson v. Dawson* [1933] 1 K.B. 301 at p. 306, *per* Greer L.J.; *France v. Piddington* (1932) 43 Ll.L.R. 491; *Loftus v. Port of Manchester Ins. Co.* (1933) 45 Ll.L.R. 452. The policies in all these cases contained an arbitration clause in the *Scott v. Avery* form and it could be argued that it was for this reason that it was held that no debt was owed by the insurer to the assured. But this ground is not relied on in the judgments and the law as stated in the text was accepted by Pearson J. in *Jabbour v. Custodian of Israeli Absentee Property* [1954] 1 W.L.R. 139, 144. The assumption by Swift J. in *Adams v. London General Ins. Co.* (1932) 42 Ll.L.R. 56 to the opposite effect must now be regarded as wrong.
[30] *Re Harrington Motor Co. Ltd* [1928] Ch. 105; *Hood's Trustees v. Southern Union General of Australia* [1928] Ch. 793.
[31] 20 & 21 Geo. 5, c. 25. A similar principle is embodied in the Marine and Aviation (Insurance) War Risks Act 1952 (15 & 16 Geo. 6 & 1 Eliz. 2, c. 57). For a penetrating critique of the Act, see the lecture of Sir Jonathan Mance, "Insolvency at Sea", published in [1995] L.M.C.L.Q. 34.
[32] Difficulty has sometimes arisen in deciding whether a particular agreement is a contract of insurance. An agreement between an employer and a mutual indemnity association whereby the association in reality advances payment to meet claims and is reimbursed by calls on the employer is not a contract of insurance: *Pailin v. Northern Employers' Mut. Indemnity Co.* [1925] 2 K.B. 73. But the mechanism whereby a mutual insurance association is funded by calls on its members is not enough, *per se*, to prevent the establishment of a contract of insurance:

insured[33] against liability which he may incur to third parties, then, if he becomes bankrupt or makes a composition with his creditors, or if (the insured being a company) a winding-up order is made, or a resolution for voluntary winding-up is passed,[34] or a receiver or manager is appointed or possession taken by or on behalf of debenture-holders, the rights of the assured against the insurer in respect of any such liability incurred before or after such event shall be transferred to the third party to whom the liability was incurred.[35] The Act applies to liability insurance, *i.e.* insurance which provides an indemnity against a liability to a third party. It does not apply to insurance relating to sums voluntarily incurred, such as legal expenses insurance and health insurance.[36]

In *Sea Voyager Maritime Inc. v. Bielecki*[37] the inter-relationship between the 1930 Act and individual voluntary arrangements was considered. It was held that where a third party had a potential claim against an assured who was the subject of a proposed individual voluntary arrangement under the Insolvency Act 1986, and that arrangement would prejudice the third party's right to proceed to judgment for the full amount of his claim against the assured, and thus his rights under the 1930 Act, the third party was entitled to relief under section 262 of the 1986 Act on grounds of unfair prejudice. To allow the arrangement to proceed without qualification would have been a derogation from the statutory scheme in insolvency, of which the 1930 Act forms a part.

28–12 Liability to be established first. This provision does not give the third party any right to sue the insurer before the liability of the assured has been established. In *Post Office v. Norwich Union Fire Insurance Society Ltd*[38] the Post Office had a claim against certain contractors who had damaged one of their cables. The contractors (who denied liability) were insured under a public liability policy with the defendant company which undertook to indemnify them against all sums which they "shall become

---

Wooding v. Monmouthshire and S. Wales Indemnity Soc. [1939] 4 All E.R. 570; *Compania Maritima San Basilio SA v. The Oceanus Mut. Underwriting Association* [1977] 1 Q.B. 49; *Re Allobrogia S.S. Corporation* [1978] 3 All E.R. 423. Reinsurance is excluded: s.1(5). So is compulsory insurance against oil pollution liability: Merchant Shipping (Oil Pollution) Act 1971, s.12(5).

[33] If a term of a contract of insurance states that there is no cover for a particular head of liability unless the insurers shall otherwise determine in their discretion, the insured is not a person who "is insured" in respect of that liability for purposes of the 1930 Act: *"The Vainqueur Jose"* [1979] 1 Lloyd's Rep. 557, 580, *per* Mocatta J.

[34] The Act does not apply to a voluntary winding up merely for reconstruction or amalgamation (s.1(6)) nor where a company has been dissolved as a result of being struck off the register under s.353 of the Companies Act 1948—*Re Harvest Lane Motor Bodies Ltd* [1969] 1 Ch. 457. The provisions of the Act apply where there is an order for the administration in bankruptcy of the estate of a deceased debtor (s.1(3)). There seems to be no right to recover the costs incurred in petitioning from the insurers, unless they opposed the petition unsuccessfully. It seems that the Act does not apply to an insolvency order made against a partnership. It does, however, apply to a winding-up under the Limited Liability Partnerships Act 2000.

[35] It may be doubted whether the term "statutory subrogation" is strictly accurate. Actions under the 1930 Act are brought by claimants in their own names, and the better term is "statutory assignment": *Post Office v. Norwich Union Fire Ins. Society Ltd* [1967] 2 Q.B. 363, 376, *per* Harman L.J.

[36] *Tarbuck v. Avon Ins. Co* [2001] 1 All E.R. (Comm) 422.

[37] [1999] 1 B.C.L.C. 133; [1999] Lloyd's Rep. I.R. 356.

[38] [1967] 2 Q.B. 363. See paras 28–2 to 28–3, *supra.* and *Socony Mobil Oil Inc. v. West of England Ship Owners' Mutual Ins. Association; The Padre Island (No. 2)* [1987] 2 Lloyd's Rep. 529.

legally liable to pay as compensation in respect of ... loss of or damage to property". Before the claim against the contractors was heard, they went into liquidation and the Post Office sued the insurance company, invoking the provisions of the Act of 1930. The Court of Appeal held that their action was premature, since the Post Office could not be in any better position than the assured who would have been unable to sue the insurers until the amount of their liability had been ascertained. The correct procedure therefore is for the third party to sue the insured person. In the case of a company in liquidation the leave of the court will be necessary but the Court of Appeal made it clear that, in such a case, leave should automatically be given.[39] However, the insurers may be permitted to join in proceedings against the insured person.[40]

The *Post Office* decision was approved by the House of Lords in *Bradley v. Eagle Star Insurance Co. Ltd*[41] in which it was held that, if the insured was a company which had been dissolved, no right could vest in the third party at all, because there was not in existence any insured whose liability could ever be ascertained. This decision worked an obvious injustice on third parties such as employees whose diseases were acquired in the course of employment but did not manifest themselves for several years after their initial impact. The actual decision was, therefore, changed by the Companies Act 1989[42] which provided that existing provisions, enabling the court to declare a dissolution void and allow the company to be restored to the register, could be invoked at any time up to 20 years from its dissolution in an application to bring proceedings for personal injury or wrongful death against a dissolved company. There is no equivalent provision for physical or financial loss to a third party.

28–13 Procedure. If the assured, at the time of bankruptcy or liquidation, has taken no steps against the insurer, the third party is entitled to sue the insurer in his own name once the assured's liability has been ascertained. The position is more complicated if the assured has begun proceedings by, for example, issuing a claim form and progressing an action before bankruptcy or liquidation occurs. The Act appears to contemplate an automatic assignment and it must presumably follow that it would be a defence for the insurer to say that he is no longer liable in an action continued in the name of the assured. The third party would, however, be entitled to ask the court that he be substituted for the original plaintiff pursuant to Part 19 of the Civil Procedure Rules. The action could then continue. He could also institute a fresh action in his own name provided he was not time-barred.[43] If the assured has instituted arbitration proceedings

---

[39] [1967] 2 Q.B. 367, 375, 377, 378.

[40] *Wood v. Perfection Travel* [1996] L.R.L.R. 233. Contrast *Myers v. Dortex International Ltd* [2000] Lloyd's Rep. I.R. 529, where the insurer did not have conduct of the matter, had been unable to agree with the insured or other insurers as to the conduct of the defence, and was effectively threatening to confront the claimant with a defence different from that of the insured defendant.

[41] [1989] A.C. 957.

[42] s.141, amending s.651 of the Companies Act 1985. No order can be made by the court if the action would, in any event, be time-barred—s.651(5) of the 1985 Act. But if it is arguable that such action would not be time-barred or that any primary time-limit might be disapplied, an order should be made: *Re Workvale Ltd* [1992] 1 W.L.R. 416.

[43] In *Lefevre v. White* [1990] 1 Lloyd's Rep. 569 the third party sought to bring his own action in his own name more than six years after the liability of the assured had been ascertained. The action was held to be time-barred. The assured had issued a writ, which was in time, the day

rather than began an action, the Civil Procedure Rules will not apply. By analogy with such rules, however, it would probably be held that the third party could take advantage of the pending arbitration by notifying the insurer of his intention to carry on the arbitration and submitting to the jurisdiction of the arbitrators.[44] Where the third party has obtained a judgment, there is no special rule under the 1930 Act which prevents the insurer from disputing its liability, or the amount recoverable under the policy, by reference to matters relevant to proceedings in which it has not participated.[45]

A claim under the 1930 Act, even where the third party's claim against the assured is for damages in respect of personal injuries, is not itself a claim for such damages. It is a claim for indemnity under a contract of insurance of which the third party is the statutory assignee. Thus there is no basis for an application for pre-action disclosure on the basis that the claim is one in respect of personal injury.[46]

28–14 Foreign corporations. If a foreign corporation incurs liability to a third party in respect of which the foreign corporation is insured but it makes no attempt to discharge that liability because it is insolvent, the third party may wish to invoke the Act of 1930. He can only do so, however, if a winding-up order is made and the question thus arises whether an English court can make a winding-up order of a foreign corporation on the petition of a creditor who has obtained an unsatisfied judgment against the foreign corporation. *Re Compania Merabello*,[47] Megarry V.-C. held that the court had jurisdiction to make such a winding-up order provided that there were "assets" within the jurisdiction and that the concept of "assets" included a chose in action such as a claim against an insurer.[48] He, therefore, made a winding-up order on the petition of owners of cargo carried by a one-ship Panamanian company who had obtained an unsatisfied judgment, despite the objections of the company's P. & I. Club who would, or might, thus become liable to indemnify the cargo-owners pursuant to the 1930 Act.

The jurisdiction will not be exercised if there is no reasonable possibility of benefit accruing to the creditors of the foreign corporation from the making of the winding-up order. If, therefore, the only alleged asset of the foreign corporation is a right of action against its insurers, the court will to some extent be concerned whether any action against its insurers has a reasonable prospect of success. *Re Allobrogia Steamship Corporation*,[49] unsatisfied judgment creditors sought an order winding up a Liberian corporation on the grounds that there was an asset within the jurisdiction in the form of a

---

before he went bankrupt. Popplewell J. held that that writ did not preserve the plaintiff's position. This was, no doubt, correct in that the existence of the assured's writ could not prevent the third party's writ from being time-barred. The learned judge does not seem to have been asked to permit the third party to be substituted for the assured on the assured's writ.

[44] *Montedipe SpA v. JTP-Ro Jugotanker (The Jordan Nicolov)* [1990] 2 Lloyd's Rep. 11, approved in *Baytur SA v. Finagro Holding SA* [1992] Q.B. 610, 618.

[45] *Cheltenham & Gloucester v. Royal* [2001] S.L.T. 1151. The insurer who participates in the defence of the claim may be estopped from denying cover: see para. 28–29, *infra*.

[46] *Burns v. Shuttlehurst Ltd* [1999] 1 W.L.R. 1449.

[47] [1973] Ch. 75.

[48] The jurisdiction does not depend upon the presence of assets. An order may be made if there is a reasonable possibility of benefit to the petitioners from a source other than the company if the order is made: *Re Eloc Electro-Optieck* [1982] 1 Ch. 43 (provision of redundancy money by Department of Employment where employer is insolvent).

[49] [1978] 3 All E.R. 423.

claim against the corporation's P. & I. Club. The Club was also a creditor of the corporation in respect of unpaid premiums (or calls) and, therefore, was entitled to oppose the petition. The Club did oppose the petition and argued that the asset had no value since the corporation's claim against the Club would not succeed. Slade J. held that the Club was guilty of no abuse of process in opposing the petition on this ground but that it was for the opposing creditor to satisfy the court that the claim had no real prospect of success. It was sufficient for the petitioning creditors to show merely that the action had a reasonable prospect of success. It thus appears that on the winding-up petition, the court will not conduct a trial of the issues arising between the foreign corporation and the insurer, but will make an order if the claim is reasonably likely to succeed.[50] If the claim is made against a party domiciled in an EC Member State, jurisdiction will probably be determined in accordance with the insurance provisions of EC Council Regulation 44/2001.[51]

28–15 No contracting out. Section 1(3) of the Act of 1930 provides that in so far as a contract of insurance purports to avoid the contract, whether directly or indirectly, or to alter the rights of the parties thereunder upon the happening to the insured of any of the events set out in section 1, the contract shall be of no effect. It has been debated whether a clause requiring the assured to have paid the claimant before recovering from his insurer is avoided by section 1(3). Many different views had been expressed[52] but the House of Lords has now decided that such a requirement is not avoided by the section. In *Firma C-Trade SA v. Newcastle P. & I. Association ("The Fanti")*[53] the insurance contracts provided that the assured was to be indemnified against claims which "he shall have become liable to pay and shall in fact have paid". In other words the assured had to pay the claim in order to be paid by the insurers.[54] The House of Lords held that this was a condition precedent to the liability of the insurers; the question then arose whether the fact that an insolvent assured (usually a company) could not first pay the claim before recovering from his insurer meant that the contract of insurance purported directly or indirectly to avoid the contract or alter the rights of the parties upon the happening of the insolvency or the company's winding-up, with the result that the "pay to be paid" provision should be regarded as of no effect. The House of Lords held that the contract did not provide that the rights of the assured should alter on insolvency or winding-up nor did the rights, in fact, alter. The right remained the same *viz.* a right to be paid if the claimant had first been paid. As Lord Goff of Chieveley put it:

"Following the insolvency of the member [the assured], or a winding-up

---

[50] It is interesting to compare the doctrine evolved in these cases with that of the New York Court of Appeal in *Seider v. Roth*, 17 N.Y. 2d 111 (1966) (not followed in, *inter alios, Shaffer v. Heitner*, 433 U.S. 186 (1977)). The New York practice allows a defendant in tort, not otherwise subject to the jurisdiction of the New York courts, to be brought within that jurisdiction by attachment of his (albeit only contingent) rights under an insurance policy issued by an insurer carrying on business in the State.

[51] [2001] O.J. L12/1. The Regulation almost entirely replaces the Brussels Convention, and is discussed in Chap. 13.

[52] See, *e.g. Re Allobrogia* [1978] 3 A.E.R. 423, 433 and the judgment of Staughton J. at first instance in *"The Fanti"* [1987] 2 Lloyd's Rep. 299.

[53] [1991] 2 A.C. 1.

[54] That is the meaning of the expression "pay to be paid".

order, his contractual rights remain the same; there is a contingent right of reimbursement as before, though it is one which the member is, in the new circumstances, less able to exercise."[55]

28–16 The statutory subrogation does not affect either:

(a) any rights of the assured against the insurer where the liability of the insurer is greater than the liability of the assured to the third party, or
(b) any rights of the third party against the assured where the insurer's liability is less than the liability of the assured to the third party, in respect of the excess, or the balance of liability, as the case may be.[56]

The Act does not apply to contracts of reinsurance.[57]

28–17 Third party in no better position than the assured.[58] The third party can be in no better position than the assured. The Act transfers to him the rights of the assured under the contract of insurance. The determination of those rights necessarily involves the application of all the terms of the contract and the consideration of any defence which would have been available to the insurers against the assured.[59] As Harman L.J. has said, the assured cannot "pick out the plums and leave the duff behind".[60] Thus he will be bound to arbitrate if there is an arbitration clause in the policy.[61] If the insurer has the right to avoid the policy or accepts a repudiation of the policy by the assured, the third party cannot recover under the Act.[62] Where the

---

[55] [1991] 2 A.C. 1 at page 37E.

[56] s.1(4). The implication of this section and indeed of the statute as a whole seems to be that the rights of the assured are completely transferred to the third party on the happening of any of the events specified in s.1(1), with the saving in s.1(4) for any balance over and above the amount for which the insurer is liable under his contract, which can still be recovered from the assured. If, therefore, the third party cannot recover against the insurer, *e.g.* because the insurer is himself insolvent, it must logically follow that he cannot prove for the full amount in the assured's bankruptcy or liquidation; he can only seek to obtain the amount which he could not have recovered in any event from the insurer. This was actually decided under s.5 of the Workmen's Compensation Act of 1906 which enacted a similar scheme to the Act of 1930 in the limited field of workmen's compensation—see *Re Pethick, Dix* [1915] 1 Ch. 26 and *Re Renishaw* [1917] 1 Ch. 199.

[57] s.1(5); in this respect the Act differs from the Marine and Aviation (Insurance) War Risks Act 1952.

[58] *Firma C-Trade v. Newcastle P. & I. Association* [1991] 2 A.C. 1.

[59] *Freshwater v. Western Australia Ass. Co. Ltd* [1933] 1 K.B. 515; *Jones v. Birch Bros Ltd* [1933] 2 K.B. 597, 608, *per* Scrutton L.J.; *McCormick v. National Motor & Accident Ins. Union Ltd* (1934) 40 Com.Cas. 76, 82, *per* Scrutton L.J., p. 91, *per* Slesser L.J.; *Farrell v. Federated Employers' Ins. Association Ltd* [1970] 2 Lloyd's Rep. 170, 173, *per* Lord Denning M.R.; *Post Office v. Norwich Union Fire Ins. Society Ltd* [1967] 2 Q.B. 363, 374, *per* Lord Denning M.R. and at p. 376, *per* Harman L.J.; *Re Allobrogia S.S. Corp.* [1978] 3 All E.R. 423, 431, *per* Slade J.; *"The Padre Island"* [1984] 2 Lloyd's Rep. 408, 414, *per* Leggatt J.

[60] *Post Office v. Norwich Union Fire Ins. Society Ltd* [1967] 2 Q.B. 367, 376.

[61] *Freshwater v. Western Australia Ass. Co. Ltd* [1933] 1 K.B. 515; *Smith v. Pearl Ass. Co.* [1939] 1 All E.R. 95. *Cunningham v. Anglian Ins. Co.* [1934] S.L.T. 273; *Dennehy v. Bellamy* [1938] 2 All E.R. 262; *The "Padre Island"* [1984] 2 Lloyd's Rep. 408; *Baytur SA v. Finagro Holding SA* [1992] Q.B. 610.

[62] *McCormick v. National Motor and Accident Ins. Union Ltd* (1934) 40 Com.Cas. 76; *Greenlee's v. Port of Manchester Ins. Co.*, 1933 S.C. 383; *Cleland v. London General Ins. Co.* (1935) 51 Ll.L.R. 156. See also *Total Graphics Ltd v. AGF Ins. Ltd* [1997] 1 Lloyd's Rep. 599, where the third party was bound by the insurers' avoidance of the policy for a fraudulent claim. However, Mance J. held, *obiter*, that the third party would not have been prevented from recovery under the 1930 Act by reason of public policy if the assured's liability had fallen within the scope of the insurance. Public policy created a personal disability to recovery which would not affect an innocent party.

insurer has the right to require the assured not to admit liability, the third party is equally bound by a term to that effect.[63] A clause making it a condition precedent to liability that any claim form or notice of proceedings should be sent to the insurer affects the third party as much as the assured,[64] and so does a provision limiting the insurer's liability.[65] It has however been held that a third party is not affected by a counterclaim which the insurer has against the assured for premiums, at any rate where the right to set off such sums as are due is not a condition of the policy.[66] In *Horne v. Prudential Assurance Co. Ltd*[67] it was held that a condition requiring claims to be reported "as soon as reasonably possible" could not be complied with as the assured was a company which had gone into liquidation before the claim was made. Compliance would have been impossible.[68] If a condition in the policy as to the giving of notice of a claim is not, on its proper construction, a condition precedent to the liability of the insurers, the term is likely to be an innominate term. A breach is unlikely to be repudiatory, but if it has sufficiently serious consequences it could bar the claim.[69]

The policy may, in certain events, render the claim of the assured subject to the discretion of the insurer. Thus in many covers afforded by P. & I. Clubs there is an obligation on the assured to notify the Club of any claim within a certain period and, if it is not done, the claim is disallowed subject to the discretionary power of the Committee to admit it wholly or in part. Another type of clause provides that the insured is, at the Committee's discretion, liable to have a deduction made from any claim where the Committee is of the view that he has not taken such steps to protect his interests as he would have done if uninsured. These clauses apply equally to claims pursued under the Act.[70] It is the duty of the insurers to exercise their discretion in such a case honestly, fairly and reasonably, and in accordance with law.[71] If they do so, the Court will not interfere with their decision, and in any event it will not expect a lay body to give "the same expert,

---

[63] *Post Office v. Norwich Union Fire Ins. Society Ltd* [1967] 2 Q.B. 363. If the assured compromises his claim against the insurer or releases him from liability the insurer can probably (in the absence of fraud and subject to s.3 of the Act) resist a claim under the Act—see *Barlow v. Merchants' Casualty Ins. Co.* [1929] 4 D.L.R. 701 and *Rowe v. Kenway* (1921) 8 Ll.L.R. 225. See para. 28–21, *infra*.

[64] *Hassett v. Legal and General Ass. Society Ltd* (1939) 63 Ll.L.R. 278; *Farrell v. Federated Employers' Ins. Association Ltd* [1970] 1 W.L.R. 1400; *"The Vainqueur Jose"* [1979] 1 Lloyd's Rep. 557; *Pioneer Concrete (U.K.) Ltd v. National Employers Mutual General Ins. Association* [1985] 1 Lloyd's Rep. 274.

[65] *Avandero v. National Transit Ins. Co. Ltd* [1984] 2 Lloyd's Rep. 613.

[66] *Murray v. Legal and General Ass. Soc. Ltd* [1970] 2 Q.B. 495. The reasoning was that the Act transfers only the particular rights and liabilities "in respect of the liability" incurred to third parties. Rights in connection with premiums are not referable to such liability unless there is an express clause making payment of outstanding premium a condition precedent to payment. *Sed quaere.* The Act does not speak of a transfer of liabilities, as opposed to rights. The third party is assigned rights subject to any defences which the insurers possess against the assured, and these include, it is submitted, general equitable rights of set-off. *Murray* was not followed in *Cox v. Bankside Members Agency* at first instance, [1995] 2 Lloyd's Rep. 437, 451.

[67] 1997 S.L.T. (Sh. Ct) 75.

[68] Similarly, in *Saunders v. Royal Ins. Inc.* 1999 S.L.T. 358, the third party obtained decree in absence against the assured, no writ or equivalent document being served. Insurers were unable to resist the third party's claim under the Act by relying on a condition requiring the assured to send any such document to them immediately upon receipt.

[69] *Alfred McAlpine Plc v. BAI (Run-off) Ltd* [2000] Lloyd's Rep. I.R. 352, discussed in para. 28–26, *infra*.

[70] *The "Vainqueur Jose"* [1979] 1 Lloyd's Rep. 557.

[71] *ibid.* at p. 573.

professional and almost microscopic investigation of the problems, both factual and legal, that is demanded of a suit in a court of law".[72]

28–18 Duty to give information. When the provisions of section 1 of the 1930 Act come into effect, it becomes the duty of the bankrupt debtor, personal representative of the deceased debtor or company, and of the trustee in bankruptcy, liquidator, administrator, receiver or manager, or person in possession, as the case may be, to give such information as may reasonably be required to any person claiming that a liability exists to which the Act applies, to enable him to ascertain whether any right has been vested in him by the Act, or to enable him to enforce such right, and any contract of insurance purporting to avoid the contract or to alter the rights of the parties on the giving of such information, or to prohibit or prevent such information being given, is to that extent ineffective.[73] The duty to give information includes a duty to allow policies and other relevant documents to be inspected and copies to be taken.[74] If the information so given discloses reasonable ground for supposing that rights against a particular insurer have been transferred by the Act, that insurer becomes liable to the same duty.[75]

Once the provisions of the Act as to transference of rights have come into play, no subsequent agreement, waiver, assignment or disposition by, or payment to, the assured affects the rights transferred to the third party.[76]

28–19 Retrospective operation. The Third Parties (Rights Against Insurers) Act 1930, was retrospective to the extent that it operated to transfer to the third party the benefit of the bankrupt's policy notwithstanding that the liability to indemnify him had arisen before the passing of the Act,[77] provided that before that date the bankruptcy had not supervened and so given the assured's creditors an accrued right.[78]

28–20 Competing claimants. An assured will sometimes be liable to more than one person. A building contractor could, for example, be liable both to his employer and to someone injured on the site. If the insurance is only enough to satisfy one claim, to which claim will the insurance money be applied? The answer is that the first party to obtain judgment against the insurer will be entitled to the fruits of that judgment and will not be restrained from entering on the process of execution, unless there is good reason for departing from that basic rule. In *Cox v. Bankside Members Agency*,[79] a number of members' agents and managing agents had many claims made against them by Names at Lloyd's in respect of allegedly negligent underwriting. Many such agents were in liquidation and more were likely to go into liquidation if the claims were held good. The agents

---

[72] *ibid.* at p. 577.

[73] 20 & 21 Geo. 5, c. 25, s.2(1) and (1A), as amended by Sch. 8, para. 7 of the Insolvency Act 1985.

[74] *ibid.* s.2(3).

[75] *ibid.* s.2(2). The duty to provide the information does not arise until the assured's liability has been established by judgment, award or agreement—*Nigel Upchurch Assocs. v. Aldridge Estates Tnv. Co.* [1993] 1 Lloyd's Rep. 535; *Woolwich Building Soc. v. Taylor* [1994] C.L.C. 516 (Ch.). See the critique of these cases by Sir Jonathan Mance in [1995] L.M.C.L.Q. 34, 40.

[76] *Ibid.* s.3. See *Total Graphics v. AGF Ins. Co. Ltd* [1997] 1 Lloyd's Rep. 599.

[77] *Re Nautilus SS. Co. Ltd* [1936] 1 Ch. 17.

[78] *Ward v. British Oak Ins. Co. Ltd* [1932] 1 K.B. 392.

[79] [1995] 2 Lloyd's Rep. 437. The reader is referred to the analysis of the problem by Sir Jonathan Mance in [1995] L.C.M.L.Q. 34, 53–55.

had errors and omissions cover which was likely to be inadequate to meet all claims. It was, therefore, important for Names to know whether the court would allow the first claims in respect of which judgment was given to scoop the limited amount of insurance cover or whether the court would apply some form of rateable allocation so that both claimants who already had a judgment and those who would obtain one in future would be able to share in the amount of insurance available. The Court of Appeal rejected the submission that the insurance money was, or would (when available) become, subject to a trust since there was no certainty of terms, no certainty of beneficiaries and no clear intention that the insurance proceeds would be held for the benefit of others. There was thus no alternative to the approach of chronological priority whereby the first Names to obtain judgment were entitled to be satisfied from the insurance proceeds. The Court countenanced the idea that, in a case where there might, perhaps, be just two claimants to an identifiable fund and there was a competition between claimants, both of whom were ready for trial, as to whose case should be tried first, the court could arrange its affairs so that a final judgment was pronounced at the same time in each case. The Lloyd's litigation was quite different from that, so chronological priority prevailed.

28–21 Settlements. The Act does not apply to settlements which take place before the assured is insolvent. The third party will be bound by a settlement so reached, even if he does not regard it as a satisfactory settlement. Nor will a third party normally be able to obtain an injunction to prevent such a settlement.[80] The position might be different, however, if the assured were under a statutory, professional, or contractual duty to effect insurance but was, nevertheless, proposing to surrender or repudiate cover to which he was apparently entitled.[81] If there was no bona fide reason for that proposed conduct, the court might infer collusion and grant an injunction to prevent any such settlement being implemented.

28–22 Proposals for reform. The Law Commission has reviewed the operation of the 1930 Act. It has put forward proposals for reform,[82] which maintain the overall scheme of Act but seek to deal with particular shortcomings.[83] In summary the Law Commission has proposed the following changes to the law: (a) The third party claimant should acquire rights against the insurer upon the insolvency event, and should be able to claim against the insured and insurer in a single set of proceedings. It should not be obliged to sue the insured, and should not have to revive a defunct company for this purpose. (b) The claimant should have improved rights to information about insurance. (c) The Act should apply in a wider range of insolvency-type events, and its application to cases with a foreign element should be clarified. (d) Claims covered by legal expenses insurance and health insurance should come within the ambit of the Act. (e) Insurers' ability to rely on lack of notice defences should be modified (so that the third

---

[80] *Normid Housing Assoc. v. Ralphs* [1989] 1 Lloyd's Rep. 265; *Jackson v. Greenfield* [1998] B.P.I.R. 699 (rights against insurers were assets in an individual voluntary arrangement of the assured, and prior to ascertainment of liability to the claimant third party could be compromised).

[81] *Cox v. Bankside Members Agency* [1995] 2 Lloyd's Rep. 437, 458.

[82] Law Com No. 272, Cm. 5217, July 2001.

[83] For criticism of the Law Commission's overall approach, see Jess, "Reform of direct rights of action by third parties against non-motor liability insurers" [2000] L.M.C.L.Q. 192.

party can give requisite notice), and "pay to be paid" clauses should not operate to the prejudice of claimants or insureds (except in the case of maritime claims not involving personal injury or death).

28–23 Contract (Rights of Third Parties) Act 1999.[84] This Act allows a third party to bring an action on a contract if the contract so provides or if the contract confers benefits on the third party and does not restrict a direct action. However, this is unlikely to be a route by which a claimant can generally recover from liability insurers. The claimant will not normally be specifically identifiable as an intended beneficiary of the insurance, nor be intended to benefit from the liability insurance in the manner contemplated by the Act.

(c) Terms in Liability Policies

28–24 Notice to insurers. Liability policies often contain a term, expressed to be a condition precedent to insurers' liability to make payment, which requires the assured to give written notice within a particular time of any accident likely[85] to give rise to a claim, and of all claims and legal proceedings brought against him.[86] If the clause is a condition precedent, non-compliance gives the insurer a defence to payment of the claim in respect of which a requisite notice ought to have been given. Thus where a clause in a public liability policy required written notice of "any accident or claim or proceedings", and the insured gave notice only of proceedings and not of the occurrence and claim preceding them, there was a breach of the clause and the insurers were relieved from liability to meet the claim.[87]

28–25 Whether prejudice to insurers required. In *Barrett Bros Taxis (Ltd) v. Davies*[88] an assured was required to forward to his motor insurers any legal process received with regard to an accident, but failed to do so. The Court of Appeal held that the insurers waived that non-compliance in subsequent correspondence, and that the insurers had received the requisite information from the police. Lord Denning M.R. went on to say[89] that in any

---

[84] 1999 c.31.

[85] "Likely" means that there must be at least a 50 per cent chance of a claim being made—*Layher v. Lowe* (1997) 58 Con.L.R. 42; [2000] Lloyd's Rep. I.R. 510. This construction of "likely" was followed in *Jacobs v. Coster* [2000] Lloyd's Rep. I.R. 506, where the third party slipped on the assured's garage forecourt and was taken to hospital. The assured failed to notify insurers until the third party indicated that she would make a claim, which was well after the 30 day period required by the policy. The Court of Appeal, reversing the judgment below, held that the assured could not conclude merely from the fact that an injury had occurred that a claim was likely to occur. In *Bass Brewers v. Independent Ins. Co.* 2002 S.L.T. 512, a different approach was adopted. "Likely to give rise to a claim" was treated as meaning "liable to give rise to a claim", but the English authorities were not cited.

[86] For a commentary on "notice" clauses, see Ch. 19, *supra*, at paras 19–34 to 19–46.

[87] *Pioneer Concrete (U.K.) Ltd v. National Employers' Mutual General Ins. Association* [1985] 1 Lloyd's Rep. 274. See also *George Hunt Cranes Ltd. v. Scottish Boiler and General Ins. Co. Ltd.* [2002] Lloyd's Rep. I.R. 178, where the Court of Appeal adopted the approach to construction of notice clauses formulated in Ch. 19 of this work. Difficulty can arise with phrases such as "circumstances of which the assured shall become aware and which may give rise to a claim": see *Hamptons Residential v. Field* [1998] 2 Lloyd's Rep. 248, reversing [1997] 1 Lloyd's Rep. 502. See para. 28–82, *infra*.

[88] [1966] 1 W.L.R. 1334.

[89] [1966] 1 W.L.R., at 1340. Danckwerts L.J. agreed generally with Lord Denning's judgment. Salmon L.J. agreed only on the ground of waiver.

event the insurers could not rely on breach of the policy condition to defeat his claim unless they were prejudiced by it. Since they had been told of the intended prosecution by the police, there was no prejudice. These remarks have been interpreted subsequently as *obiter dicta* which ought not to be followed.[90]

28–26 However, if the clause is not a condition precedent to liability, failure to give notice would only preclude a claim in the case of a serious breach. If – as is likely – the breach is not repudiatory of the contract as a whole, insurers would probably need to demonstrate that they had suffered very serious consequences as a result of the lack of timely notice, in order to have a defence to the claim based on late notice.[91]

28–27 Defence and settlement of claims. Apart from requiring that all claims made or legal process served upon the assured shall be forwarded immediately to the insurers,[92] liability policies also usually provide that the insurers shall be entitled to defend claims brought against him, and to settle them if need be.[93] If insurers receive notice of a claim on their assured and decline to take over the defence, they will be precluded from contesting the quantum of any bona fide settlement, although the assured must still

---

[90] *Farrell v. Federated Employers' Ins. Association Ltd* [1970] 1 W.L.R. 498; [1970] 2 Lloyd's Rep. 170 (the report at [1970] 1 W.L.R. 1400 reports the constitution of the court inaccurately); *"The Vainqueur Jose"* [1979] 1 Lloyd's Rep. 557 (where Mocatta J. did not reject the *obiter dicta*, but strained to find prejudice); *Pioneer Concrete (U.K.) Ltd v. National Employers' Mutual General Ins. Association* [1985] 1 Lloyd's Rep. 274, 281; *Motor and General Ins. Co. v. Pavy* [1994] 1 W.L.R. 462, 469, in which the insurers were told by a third party what the assured should have told them; *Total Graphics Ltd v. AGF Ins. Co. Ltd* [1997] 1 Lloyd's Rep. 599. *Cf. CNA Int. Reins. Co. Ltd. v. Companhia de Seguros Tranquilidade SA* [1999] Lloyd's Rep. I.R. 289, where it was not necessary for the Court to decide the point. See also para. 19–43, *ante*. In *Bass Brewers v. Independent Ins. Co.* 2002 S.L.T. 512 it was held that where one co-assured told the insurers of damage to insured property, but the other did not, the latter was in breach of a condition precedent, and lost his claim. This result is difficult to reconcile with proposition, derived from *Barrett*, that the insurers cannot rely on a failure to notify where they have received the requisite information from a source other than the insured.

[91] This was the approach suggested by the Court of Appeal in *Alfred McAlpine Plc v. BAI (Run-off) Ltd* [2000] Lloyd's Rep. I.R. 352, although it did not find that the requisite degree of prejudice had been suffered in that case. It is respectfully suggested that the difficulty with this approach is that it leads to uncertainty as to when insurers can rely on late notice as a defence. It might be thought that, if timely notice was important, they could provide expressly for it in terms of a condition precedent, or could be compensated in damages if late notice caused demonstrable loss (including a loss of a chance). It may be that circumstances justifying the defence, adopting the approach in *McAlpine*, will be relatively rare. For examples of similar defences failing see: *K/S Merc-Scandia XXXXII v. Lloyd's Underwriters* [2001] 2 Lloyd's Rep. 563, and *"The Beursgracht"* [2002] 1 Lloyd's Rep. 574.

[92] *Wilkinson v. Car and General Ins. Corp. Ltd* (1914) 110 L.T. 468 (request for arbitration was not of itself a notice of claim but only a step in procedure): *Hassett v. Legal and General Ass. Society Ltd* (1939) 63 Ll.L.Rep. 278; *Barrett Bros (Taxis) Ltd v. Davies* [1966] 1 W.L.R. 1334; *Farrell v. Federated Employers' Ins. Association Ltd* [1970] 1 W.L.R. 1400; *Pioneer Concrete (U.K.) Ltd v. National Employers' Mutual General Ins. Association Ltd* [1985] 1 Lloyd's Rep. 274; *Smellie v. British General Ins. Co.* 1918, 2 S.L.T. 58 ("notice of accident" held to mean "notice of claim"); *Canadian Bank of Commerce v. London and Lancashire Guarantee and Accident Co. of Canada* (1958) 14 D.L.R. 2d 623.

[93] See, *e.g. British General Ins. Co. Ltd v. Mountain* (1919) 36 T.L.R. 171; 1 Ll.L.Rep. 605; *Post Office v. Norwich Union Fire Ins. Society Ltd* [1967] 2 Q.B. 363. Such a clause does not compel the assured to accept the services of the insurers' solicitor: *Barrett Bros (Taxis) Ltd v. Davies* [1966] 1 W.L.R. 1334. Where an insurer exercised his rights under such a clause and made an offer which was accepted by the third party, he was not himself liable to pay the third party the agreed sum: *Nairn v. South East Lancashire Ins. Co.* 1930 S.C. 606.

establish that there was a liability.[94] If the assured fails to take relevant points in the defence, it may not be possible to establish that there was a liability.[95] On the other hand care is needed in undertaking the defence of the claim on behalf of the assured, or else the insurers may become precluded from denying liability under the policy. How this trap may be avoided we shall see later.[96]

28–28 If the assured has settled the claim, it will have to establish that the amount of the settlement was reasonable. If the insured was liable for claims covered by the insurance for at least the amount paid by way of settlement, the settlement is not rendered unreasonable merely because commercial considerations affected the amount paid to a particular claimant, nor because claims not covered by the insurance were included in the settlement.[97]

28–29 Estoppel by conduct of defence. Where insurers discover a breach of condition or warranty, or a concealment on the part of the assured, which would permit them to avoid liability on that account, their undertaking or continuing the defence of the claim, whether to a judgment or settlement, is likely to be construed as a waiver of their right to refuse payment because of the assured's breach of duty.[98] The situation becomes more complicated when there is doubt as to whether the claim brought by a third party against the assured is covered by the policy at all, regardless of any breach on the part of the assured which would provide the insurers with a defence on the policy if the claim were covered. In such a case there is no breach of duty by the assured to be waived by insurers, and the significance of the insurers' conduct in defending the third party's claim pursuant to their rights under the policy depends upon the strictness of the doctrine of estoppel in whatever jurisdiction is concerned.

28–30 In U.S. insurance law it is very easy for the assured to allege an

---

[94] *Captain Boyton's World's Water Show Syndicate Ltd v. Employers' Liability Ass. Corporation Ltd* (1895) 11 T.L.R. 384. In *Cheltenham & Gloucester v. Royal* [2001] S.L.T. 1151, the insurer had withdrawn from conducting the defence, and was not precluded by the judgment against the assured from disputing liability and the amount recoverable under the policy. If a third party asserts a claim against the assured on the basis of a liability in respect of which there is no cover, and the assured settles the claim because he knows he is liable on the basis of a different liability in respect of which he is covered and because underwriters have refused to take over his defence, he may well be able to recover from liability underwriters: see *Kuhne & Nagel Inc. v. Baiden* [1977] 1 Lloyd's Rep. 90. In *Structural Polymer Systems v. Brown* [2000] Lloyd's Rep. I.R. 64 the insurers decided at an early stage that the claim was not covered, and declined to investigate. They were not subsequently granted leave to defend when they contended that they were entitled to look into the background to the claim.

[95] See *Liberian Ins. Agency Inc. v. Mosse* [1977] 2 Lloyd's Rep. 560 where the assured entered no defence on the merits. He claimed that this was with underwriters' knowledge but the judge declined to hold that underwriters were thereby rendered liable.

[96] See para. 28–30, *post*. Another course open to insurers is to apply to be joined in the action brought by the third party against their assured—*Wood v. Perfection Travel Ltd* [1996] L.R.L.R. 233. However, an insurer potentially liable, but without conduct of the matter, will not be permitted to participate as an additional defendant on the basis that it has been unable to agree with the assured (or other insurers) as to how the defence should be conducted: *Myers v. Dortex International Ltd* [2000] Lloyd's Rep. I.R. 529.

[97] *Structural Polymer Systems v. Brown* [2000] Lloyd's Rep. I.R. 64.

[98] *Evans v. Employers' Mutual Ins. Assoc.* [1936] 1 K.B. 505; *Fraser v. B. N. Furman (Productions) Ltd* [1967] 1 W.L.R. 898, 909; *Barrett Bros. (Taxis) Ltd v. Davies* [1966] 1 W.L.R. 1334.

estoppel, and it is almost invariably the case that an insurer who defends a claim against his assured without expressly reserving a right to dispute liability under the policy will become estopped by his conduct from contending that the claim is not covered by the policy as a matter of its legal interpretation. So far as the requirement of prejudice to the assured is concerned, it suffices that, by acquiescing in the control of the matter by the insurers, he is deprived of the chance to do better.[99] This mechanical view of the doctrine of estoppel was applied by an Australian court in *Hansen v. Marco Engineering (Pty)*,[1] following the U.S. decisions. In that case a company was insured under two motor policies. One was a comprehensive policy but specifically excluded liability to passengers. The other was a third-party liability policy with a limit of A£2,000 for any one claim. A passenger was hurt riding in a company vehicle and brought suit to recover damages. The insurers, as they were entitled to do, took charge of the defence of this action, and it actually proceeded to a jury trial. After six days a settlement was arrived at between counsel, involving a payment of A£3,750 by the defendant-assured, and the insurers approved it because they mistakenly believed that they were liable for that amount under the comprehensive policy. Later they refused to pay more than A£2,000, and the assured, now defendant in an action to enforce the settlement, joined them as a third party, claiming the balance of the settlement figure. It was held that the insurers were estopped from disputing their liability to pay a full indemnity by their conduct in defending the claim.

28–31 The decision was not free from difficulty. In the first place it is hard to see how there could be any prejudice to the assured in his acquiescence in their conduct of his defence, because the court admitted that in all probability the plaintiff would have been awarded judgment for over A£4,000. More seriously, the judgment does not disclose any statement or conduct on the insurers' part which unequivocally indicated their intention to pay a loss under the comprehensive policy. When the insurers took over the conduct of the defence of the company, their action was consistent with the intention to defeat the plaintiff's claim and so extinguish or minimise their own liability on the third-party liability policy, the limitation on which the company must have been aware of. The court seems to have interpreted their conduct in settling for A£3,750 as founding a fresh estoppel, depriving them of their right to deny liability at all on the comprehensive policy,[2] although one cannot see how the comprehensive policy should have been in anyone's mind at that stage. To the extent that *Hansen* was regarded as authority that an estoppel could arise without any real detriment to the assured, it no longer appears to be good law.[3]

28–32 English law. The decision in and reasoning of the *Hansen* Case were dissented from in *Soole v. Royal Insurance Co.*[4] where the issue of estoppel by conduct of a defence was raised in relation to English law. The assured

---

[99] *Gerka v. Fidelity and Casualty Co. of New York*, 251 N.Y. 51 (1929); *Malley v. American Indemnity Co.*, 297 Pa. 216 (1929), and other authorities cited at A.L.R. 81, pp. 1326, *et seq.* Later American decisions are cited at 38 A.L.R. 2d, pp. 1148, *et seq.*

[1] [1948] V.L.R. 198, 209, *et seq.*

[2] [1948] V.L.R. 198, 212.

[3] *Territory Ins. Office v. Adlington* No. AP 16/1999; (1992) 84 N.T.R. 7, where the above analysis of *Hansen* was adopted.

[4] [1971] 2 Lloyd's Rep. 332.

purchased a plot of land in Richmond on which one house stood. He decided to increase its value while diminishing the value of the surrounding properties by demolishing the one house and erecting six. The neighbours fought an application for planning permission but in vain. However, there was another more formidable weapon in their armoury. One of them checked his title deeds and claimed that the assured's land was subject to a covenant restricting the number of houses on it to one. There was, however, some doubt as to the enforceability of the restrictive covenant by the neighbour, and cautiously optimistic opinions to that effect were obtained by the assured from counsel. Armed with these, the assured obtained cover against damage resulting to him from successful enforcement of the covenant "in the event of any person … claiming to be entitled to enforce" it. The neighbour, together with two other neighbours, duly brought proceedings to enforce the covenant. The insurers conducted the defence. The neighbours succeeded. The insurers then disputed liability on the ground that a claim had first been brought before the inception of the policy, and so was not covered by it. The court found against them on construction of the policy, but also held that the insurers were not estopped from denying that the claim was covered.[5] Their conduct of the defence could not be construed unequivocally as a representation that they were liable to indemnify the assured if the claim succeeded, and, in any event, such a representation would have been one of law, which could not found an estoppel.[6]

28–33 It is submitted with respect that the decision in *Soole* correctly represents the English law. There is good authority for the proposition that an estoppel requires:

(i) a clear representation by word or conduct of a present fact,
(ii) made to someone who is expected to act on it, and
(iii) who does so, to his "detriment".[7] The insurers' conduct did not constitute a clear representation that they would meet the claim, and it could not be so construed as a matter of law. The assured was in no way prejudiced, as his freedom to develop despite the covenant was asserted by as eminent a counsel as he could ever have secured for himself if the insurers had abandoned him. The decision in *Hansen v. Marco Engineering Co. (Pty)*[8] was rightly disregarded, as there was no case in English law for applying an automatic estoppel as in U.S. law, and it might also be distinguished as turning upon an estoppel by conclusion of a settlement, a feature absent from the *Soole* case in which insurers conducted the defence of their assured up to the point at which judgment was given against him.

---

[5] [1971] 2 Lloyd's Rep. 332, 338–342.
[6] It would not, however, have been difficult to interpret a representation of liability to indemnify as a representation of a present intention to meet the claim.
[7] *Greenwood v. Martins Bank Ltd* [1933] A.C. 51, 57, applied in *Canadian Bank of Commerce v. London and Lancashire Guarantee and Accident Co. of Canada* (1958) 14 D.L.R. (2d) 623 where estoppel was not established by the assured. The very similar requirements set out by Humphreys J. in *Algar v. Middlesex County Council* [1945] 2 All E.R. 243 were applied to defeat the plea of estoppel in *Pentagon Contruction (1969) Co. Ltd v. U.S. Fidelity & Guaranty Co.* [1978] 1 Lloyd's Rep. 93, where the Court of Appeal of British Columbia pointed out that in order to bring a risk not originally accepted by underwriters within the cover there would need to be a new agreement supported by fresh consideration, whatever might be the position where underwriters merely had a right to avoid or repudiate which could be waived.
[8] [1948] V.L.R. 198.

28-34 "Non-waiver" agreement. Insurers have a reasonable time in which to make up their minds concerning a claim[9] and they have the opportunity to record their decision to reserve their rights under the policy while conducting the assured's defence.[10] In North America it is common form for insurers to conclude "non-waiver" agreements for that purpose before embarking on the defence of a third party's claim.[11]

28-35 Conduct of proceedings. If the insurers assume the conduct of the defence of an action brought against the assured and appoint solicitors to act therein, the solicitors so appointed are the solicitors of the assured, and the assured is entitled to have all the documents in the action produced to him for his inspection.[12] Both the insurers and the solicitors appointed by them owe a duty to the assured to conduct the proceedings with due regard to his interests, and an action for damages will lie for breach of that duty.[13] Where the solicitors at the instance of the insurers, and with a view to the latter's protection admitted, contrary to the facts, that the assured had been negligent in the driving of his car, and in consequence of that admission damages had been awarded against him, it was held by the Court of Appeal that there had been a breach of duty, but that, in the circumstances, the damages were nominal, since the judgment against the assured had immediately been satisfied by the insurers, and there was no evidence of any other pecuniary loss.[14] In cases of this kind the insurers have the right to decide upon the proper tactics to pursue in the conduct of the action, provided that they do so in what they bona fide consider to be the interests of themselves and the assured.[15] Insurers, whether they have paid a claim or

---

[9] *McCormick v. National Motor etc.* (1934) 40 Com. Cas. 76; *Liberian Ins. Agency Inc. v. Mosse* [1977] 2 Lloyd's Rep. 560, 565.

[10] *Chicago Coulterville Coal v. Fidelity and Casualty Co. of New York*, 130 Fed.Rep. 957 (1904).

[11] But any "non-waiver agreement" will be strictly construed against the insurer. See *Federal Ins. Co. v. Matthews* (1956) 3 D.L.R. (2d) 322 where it was held that such an agreement merely postponed the right of the insurer to elect whether he would defend the proceedings and admit liability or whether he would deny liability and refuse to have anything to do with the proceedings; and that if the insurer defended proceedings after he had issued a writ claiming a declaration that he was not liable under the policy that would preclude him from continuing his action.

[12] *Re Crocker* [1936] Ch. 696. If the policy so provides, solicitors' reports must be furnished in full to the insurers: *Brown v. Guardian Royal Exchange* [1994] 2 Lloyd's Rep. 325. Questions of common interest privilege may arise. The waiver of privilege that arises from the common interest of insurer and assured comes to an end when any conflict of interest surfaces: *TSB v. Irving and Burns* [1999] Lloyd's Rep. I.R. 528.

[13] *Groom v. Crocker* [1939] 1 K.B. 194; *K/S Merc-Scandia XXXXII v. Lloyd's Underwriters* [2001] 2 Lloyd's Rep. 563, 566. *Cf. Patterson v. Northern Accident Ass. Co.* [1901] 2 Ir.R. 262 where, owing to the negligence of the insurer, excessive damages were awarded to the third party.

[14] *Groom v. Crocker* [1939] 1 K.B. 194.

[15] At p. 203, *per* Lord Greene M.R.; a bona fide settlement by the insurer, where he has a right to conduct the defence and settle claims, will bind the assured even if he has to pay part of the damages awarded himself (*e.g.* the first £5): *Beacon Ins. Co. v. Langdale* [1934] 4 All E.R. 204. It appears that, when the insurer takes over conduct of the assured's defence, each party comes under an obligation, as a matter of contractual implication, to act in good faith with due regard to the interests of the other: *K/S Merc-Scandia XXXXII v. Lloyd's Underwriters* [2001] 2 Lloyd's Rep. 563, 572, 574. Generally the interest of insurer and insured will coincide. However, there is potential for conflict (e.g. if the limit of cover is likely to be exceeded). In this event, the insurer should pay regard to the separate interest of the insured, as well the insurer's own

not, have no right to direct the assured not to pursue a claim against a third party.[16]

28–36 Costs. The policy will usually make express provisions for the costs of defending a claim. Thus a common clause provides:

"In respect of a claim for damages to which the indemnity expressed in this policy applies the Company will also indemnify the insured against:
(a) all costs and expenses of litigation recovered by any claimant from the insured,
(b) all costs and expenses of litigation incurred with the written consent of the company."

Such a clause would certainly cover the third party's costs of a successful claim and the assured's costs if incurred with written consent. It would probably not apply to the assured's own costs of meeting an unsuccessful claim since such a claim would not be "a claim to which the indemnity expressed in this policy applies".[17] However, other forms of clause are expressed more broadly, so as to permit recovery of costs where the third party claim is unsuccessful,[18] or does not fall within the scope of the liability insurance.[19]

28–37 A provision that "the Company will indemnify the Insured against all sums for which the Insured shall become legally liable to pay as compensation" refers only to damages and not to costs.[20] A promise by insurers to pay "all costs and expenses incurred with its written consent" covers only the costs and expenses of the insured himself.[21] A clause to the effect that the insurers will not pay costs unless incurred with their consent does not give them the right to decide whether the action should be fought, and a term will probably be implied that such consent is not to be unreasonably withheld.[22] Consent at the outset of proceedings will not

---

interest: *Cormack v. Washbourne* [2000] Lloyd's Rep. P.N. 459, 466 (C.A). *Cf. Distillers Co. Biochemical (Australia) v. Ajax Ins.* (1974) 48 A.L.J.R. 136 (High Ct. of Australia). Similar considerations arise under claims co-operation clauses in re-insurance: *Gan v. Tai Ping* [2001] Lloyd's Rep. I.R. 667 (C.A.).

[16] *Morley v. Moore* [1936] 2 K.B. 359; followed in *Bourne v. Stanbridge* [1965] 1 W.L.R. 189; *Hobbs v. Marlowe* [1978] A.C. 16. These cases concerned "knock for knock" agreements between insurers. For a case construing such an agreement, see *Bell Assurance Association v. Licenses and General Ins. Corporation* (1923) 17 Ll.L.R. 100.

[17] *Cross v. British Oak Ins. Co.* [1938] 2 K.B. 167, 174. *Cf. Xenos v. Fox* (1869) L.R. 4 C.P. 665, 668. The fact that the insurer has agreed to indemnify the assured in respect of his costs will not preclude the assured from recovering his costs from an unsuccessful third party; see *Cornish v. Lynch* (1910) 3 B.W.C.C. 343.

[18] *Thornton Springer v. NEM Ins. Co. Ltd* [2000] Lloyd's Rep. I.R. 590.

[19] *Poole Harbour Yacht Club Marina Ltd v. Excess Ins. Co. Ltd* [2001] Lloyd's Rep. I.R. 580.

[20] *Aluminium Wire & Cable v. Allstate Ins. Co. Ltd* [1985] 2 Lloyd's Rep. 280, 288.

[21] *ibid.*

[22] See *Hulton & Co. Ltd v. Mountain* (1921) 8 Ll.L.R. 249; 37 T.L.R. 869 where there was an express term that such consent should not be unreasonably withheld. The Court of Appeal did not, however, seem to rely on the express term in their judgments. Moreover, they seemed prepared to infer from the inactivity of the insurer that he had in fact consented by conduct to such costs being incurred. In *Poole Harbour Yacht Club Marina Ltd v. Excess Ins. Co. Ltd* [2001] Lloyd's Rep. I.R. 580, it was stated that consent could not be unreasonably withheld (although this was not essential to the decision). The implied term was held to exist in *"The Beursgracht (No. 2)"* [2001] 2 Lloyd's Rep. 608, at 619; not challenged on appeal: [2002] 1 Lloyd's Rep. 574. In *Thornton Springer v. NEM Ins. Co. Ltd* [2000] Lloyd's Rep. I.R. 590 it was suggested, *obiter*, that, in the particular policy, there was no implied term. However this was in

necessarily cover all stages of the ensuing litigation; therefore, consent should be confirmed or obtained in respect of each major stage of the proceedings.[23]

28–38 A limit of liability that referred to "all ... costs and expenses payable by the insured" meant only the costs of the claimant, not the costs of defending the claim. The key word was "payable". In practice, the costs of defending a claim are borne by the insurers and are not "payable" by the assured.[24] Unless the policy stipulates otherwise, it will be construed as covering all costs incurred in the defence of the claim which were reasonably related to the assured's liability, even if that might benefit co-defendants of the assured who may be uninsured or insured by other insurers.[25] Where the policy provides for the payment of costs incurred in the settlement of any claim which falls to be dealt with under the policy, this covers the costs of settling the claim incurred before, as well as after, the claim has actually been made.[26]

28–39 "Liability under the policy": costs. The question of costs in relation to reinsurance was considered in *British General Insurance Co. Ltd v. Mountain*[27] in which the plaintiff insurance company, which was under an obligation to indemnify insured persons against third-party liability and litigation expenses, reinsured their "liability under the policy" with the defendant. The insurance company had the right to defend any action brought against their assured. The House of Lords considered two distinct situations. First, the assured might defend any action themselves. In such a case they would be entitled to recover the amount of their legal expenses from the insurance company who could in turn claim that amount from the defendant under their reinsurance policy. The second situation was that the insurance company would themselves take over the defence of their assured under the express term of the policy empowering them to do so. In this case

---

the context of a claim for which the assured was not liable to the claimant, where the underlying question will be whether the policy covers the costs of dealing with unsuccessful claims. In *Gan Ins. Co. Ltd v. Tai Ping Ins. Co. Ltd* (2 & 3) [2001] Lloyd's Rep I.R.667, the Court of Appeal held that there was no implied term in a reinsurance that reinsurers could not decline to approve settlements unless there were reasonable grounds for doing so. This arguably involves different considerations. It is one thing to say that reinsurers are not (by way of implied term) required to justify an insistence that proceedings should be determined by a judgment rather than settled. It is another to say that liability insurers are not required to justify a refusal to sanction the incurring of costs which may be essential to the assured's defence of the third party claim.

[23] *Poole Harbour Yacht Club Marina Ltd v. Excess Ins. Co. Ltd* [2001] Lloyd's Rep. I.R. 580, where it was, however, held that underwriters had, whilst debating coverage, never withdrawn their consent.

[24] *Citibank NA v. Excess Ins. Co. Ltd* [1999] Lloyd's Rep. I.R. 122.

[25] *New Zealand Forest Products Ltd v. New Zealand Ins. Co Ltd* [1997] 1 W.L.R. 1237, PC. If some distinct costs relate to claims outside the scope of the insurance, it will presumably be necessary to apportion costs; this was assumed to be correct in *Structural Polymer Systems v. Brown* [2000] Lloyd's Rep. I.R. 64 at 75. However, costs relating to matters which are covered should be recoverable even if the costs are "dual-purpose" in the sense that they overlap with matters which are not covered: *Thornton Springer v. NEM Ins. Co. Ltd* [2000] Lloyd's Rep. I.R. 590, 612–613.

[26] *J Rothschild Ass. Plc v. Collyear* [1999] Lloyd's Rep. I.R. 6.

[27] (1919) 1 Ll.L.R. 605; 36 T.L.R. 171. See also, in relation to reinsurance, para. 33–79.

they might become liable to pay the costs of the successful plaintiff and the costs of their own solicitors. Since this would be a liability incurred under an arrangement which was expressly sanctioned by the policy of insurance, it was a "liability under the policy" for the purposes of the contract of reinsurance and could be recovered from the defendant.

28–40 Where the policy contains an undertaking by the insurers to pay all costs if they require a claim to be contested, there is no consideration for an agreement by the assured to contribute to the costs of proceedings taken at the direction of the insurers.[28] If a third party obtains judgment against the assured for damages and costs, neither the judge nor the registrar in the county court, nor the taxing officer in the High Court has any jurisdiction to determine what portion of the costs should be borne by the insurers who are not parties to the action.[29]

28–41 Section 51(1) Supreme Court Act 1981. In certain exceptional circumstances, the liability insurers of an unsuccessful defendant may be ordered to pay the claimant's costs, irrespective of the terms of the policy, including any limits, pursuant to section 51(1) of the Supreme Court Act 1981. The insurers do not have to be joined as a party to the application for costs, they may be ordered to pay costs for a part only of the proceedings,[30] and defendants to the third party's claim other than the assured can make an application. The application should only be made in clear cases. It should not be used as a springboard for costly satellite litigation.[31] The Court can consider an application after it has ordered the defendant to pay costs.[32] The Court has jurisdiction over a non-domiciled party to decide if it should pay costs under section 51.[33]

28–42 The general principles enabling the court under this section to order a non-party to pay costs were established by the House of Lords in *Aiden Shipping Co Ltd v. Interbulk Ltd.*[34] The features which should normally be present for costs to be awarded against a liability insurer have been established by the Court of Appeal[35] as follows:

(1) the insurers determined that the claim would be defended;
(2) the insurers funded the defence;

[28] *Knight v. Hosken* (1943) 75 Ll.L.R. 74.
[29] *Re Taxation of Costs* [1937] 3 All E.R. 113.
[30] See, e.g. *Citibank NA v. Excess Ins. Co. Ltd* [1999] Lloyd's Rep. I.R. 122.
[31] *Bristol & West Plc v. Bhadresa* [1999] Lloyd's Rep. I.R. 138.
[32] *Gloucestershire Health Authority v. MA Torpy and Partners Ltd* [1999] Lloyd's Rep. I.R. 203.
[33] *National Justice Comp. Nav. SA v. Prudential Ass. Co. Ltd ("The Ikarian Reefer")* [2001] 1 All E.R. (Comm) 37, where it was held that an application under s.51 either did not involve a party being "sued" for the purpose of the Brussels Convention, or could be accommodated within the Convention provision for third-party proceedings. The rules are now enshrined in Council Regulation (EC) No.44/2001, [2001] O.J. L12/1. CPR r.6.20(7) provides for an application to be made for permission to serve the relevant proceedings on an insurer out of the jurisdiction.
[34] [1986] A.C. 965.
[35] *Murphy v. Young & Co's Brewery Plc* [1997] 1 W.L.R. 1591; *TGA Chapman Ltd v. Christopher* [1998] 1 W.L.R. 12. In *Cormack v. Washbourne* [2000] Lloyd's Rep. P.N. 459 the Court of Appeal treated an insurer's overriding self-interest as being a key constituent of the relevant exceptional circumstances.

(3) the insurers had the conduct or control of the litigation;
(4) the insurers fought the claim exclusively to defend their own interests; and
(5) the defence failed in its entirety.

The second and fifth features will almost always be present in practice.[36] The other features are primary material factors which will generally be determinative. The discretion should only be exercised where the circumstances are sufficiently exceptional.[37] Whether a case is exceptional enough for costs to be awarded is to be judged, not in the context of the insurance industry, but in the context of litigation as a whole. In *Chapman*[38] Phillips L.J. commented: "It must be rare for litigation to be funded, controlled and directed by a third party motivated entirely by its own interests." He explained that the basis for rejecting the argument that a limit in the policy should be respected was not that the policy was being re-written, but that a liability was being imposed on underwriters independent of the policy. The requirement that insurers have conduct of the proceedings is likely to involve an analysis of the nature of the instructions given to the solicitors retained to defend the claim. The insurers may have overall control and conduct of the matter notwithstanding the fact that the assured provides information and assistance to solicitors.[39] Applications under section 51 have been made in a number of cases in recent years.[40] In *Bristol and West plc v. Bhadresa*[41] an application was made against the Solicitors' Indemnity Fund. It has a duty to defend solicitors against claims for professional negligence, but is prohibited from indemnifying those found to have acted dishonestly. It was held that in principle section 51 conferred jurisdiction to award costs against the Fund, but the circumstances were not so exceptional for costs to be awarded. The fact that the Fund had defended the solicitors in question for a lengthy period before finally concluding that there had been dishonesty was justifiable, given the effect of such a finding on the Fund and on the solicitors.

28–43 Liability for costs. If no express provision is made as to costs in the policy, they may be recoverable under the general indemnity clause.[42] But if

---

[36] See the analysis in *Citibank NA v. Excess Ins. Co. Ltd* [1999] Lloyd's Rep. I.R. 122 esp. at 129–131.

[37] *Cormack v. Washbourne* [2000] Lloyd's Rep. P.N. 459, where the Court of Appeal rejected a test based merely upon considerations of broad fairness.

[38] [1998] 1 W.L.R. 12 at 20.

[39] *Citibank NA v. Excess Ins. Co. Ltd* [1999] Lloyd's Rep. I.R. 122; *Monkton Court Ltd v. Perry Prowse (Insurance Services) Ltd* [2001] 1 All E.R. (Comm) 566. In *Citibank* at 136 Thomas J. suggested that the terms of any joint retainer of solicitors should be clearly spelt out, and that insurers and insured should set out their involvement in decision-making in written form.

[40] See for example, apart from authorities mentioned above, *Tharros Shipping Co. Ltd v. Bias Shipping A.G.* [1997] 1 Lloyd's Rep. 246; *Pendennis Shipyard v. Magrathea* [1998] 1 Lloyd's Rep. 315; *Citibank NA v. Excess Ins. Co. Ltd* [1999] Lloyd's Rep. I.R. 122 (application allowed in part—order made for period after judgment on liability, as the circumstances then became exceptional); *Gloucestershire Health Authority v. MA Torpy and Partners Ltd* [1999] Lloyd's Rep. I.R. 203 (application refused—no exceptional features); *Monkton Court Ltd v. Perry Prowse (Insurance Services) Ltd* [2001] 1 All E.R. (Comm) 566 (application granted—claim was fought almost exclusively to defend the insurer's interests). *Worsley v. Tambrands* [2002] Lloyd's Rep. I.R. 382 (application refused).

[41] [1999] Lloyd's Rep. I.R. 138.

[42] In *Forney v. Dominion Ins. Co. Ltd* [1969] 1 W.L.R. 928 Donaldson J. held that a limit of liability of £3,000 included liability for a principal sum and the third parties' costs. Since the principal sum exceeded £3,000 nothing was recoverable in respect of costs, but if the principal

there is a clause entitling the insurer to defend a claim and the insurer insists on defending without consulting the assured, the insurer may be liable for the costs in any event, in the absence of any specific provision.[43] Where, however, the amount insured includes liability for costs, the assured must meet the costs, once the limit of liability is exceeded.[44] If the insurer wrongfully repudiates liability under the policy so that the assured has to defend a claim himself, the assured will be entitled to the costs of doing so as part of his damages for the wrongful repudiation.[45]

28–44 Limitation on insurer's total liability under the policy. The policy usually provides that the total liability thereunder, either in respect of damages recovered or costs, shall in no event exceed a particular sum.[46] Such a provision will be construed strictly since it could operate harshly against the assured if, for example, the insurer has the right to defend and does defend a doubtful case with the result that damages and costs are recovered far in excess of the sum insured, although in the first instance the claim might have been settled for a sum which would have been covered by the policy. If the parties have not expressly agreed an aggregation clause which limits the right to make claims arising from the same act or series of acts, it will not ordinarily be possible to imply any such clause.[47] Another limit often found in liability policies is that a certain maximum sum will be paid in respect of "any one accident" or "any one occurrence". The former wording is less restrictive since there may be many accidents arising out of one occurrence, *e.g.* a train crash where each injury has been held to be an accident.[48] In *Forney v. Dominion Insurance Co. Ltd*[49] the insurance was limited to £3,000 "in respect of any one claim or number of claims arising out of the same occurrence". An accident had occurred while a family was being driven in a car by the father. Both the father and his father-in-law were killed and three other members of the family were injured. The father was insured and the injured members of the family were advised by the assistant of the plaintiff

---

sum had been less the judge would presumably have permitted the plaintiff to recover in respect of the costs for which he was liable to the third parties. He was also prepared to hold that the plaintiff's own costs of contesting the claims were covered by the words "loss arising from any claim": see also *Xenos v. Fox* (1869) L.R. 4 C.P. 665, 668. See para. 33–67, *post.*

[43] *Allen v. London Guarantee and Accident Co. Ltd* (1912) 28 T.L.R. 254.

[44] *Cox v. Bankside Members Agency* [1995] 2 Lloyd's Rep. 437, 460–463. But see *Chapman v. Christopher, supra.*

[45] *Pictorial Machinery Ltd v. Nicolls* (1940) 67 Ll.L.R. 524; *Forney v. Dominion Ins. Co.* [1969] 1 W.L.R. 928 where it was held that the insurers acting reasonably, would have authorised costs to be incurred if they had not wrongfully repudiated the policy.

[46] As in *British General Ins. Co. v. Mountain* (1919) 1 Ll.L.R. 605.

[47] *Mabey & Johnson v. Ecclesiastical Ins. Office Plc* [2001] Lloyd's Rep. I.R. 369, where it was pointed out that the variety of clauses which could potentially be used would prevent implication.

[48] *South Staffordshire Tramways Co. v. Sickness and Accident Assurance Association Ltd* [1891] 1 Q.B. 402; *Allen v. London Guarantee and Accident Co. Ltd* (1912) 28 T.L.R. 254; *Distillers Co. Biochemicals (Australia) v. Ajax Ins. Co.* (1974) 48 A.L.J.R. 136. *Cf. Equitable Trust Co. of New York v. Whittaker* (1923) 17 Ll.L.R. 153 (series of frauds on bank). In *Kuwait Airways Cpn. v. Kuwait Ins. Co.* [1996] 1 Lloyd's Rep. 664 it was held that the invasion of Kuwait and the capture of the airport was the relevant "occurrence" for the purpose of a limit on the sum insured, even though the aircraft covered were flown to Iraq on separate subsequent occasions. The subsequent appeal proceedings concerned other issues: [1997] 2 Lloyd's Rep. 687 (CA); [1999] 1 Lloyd's Rep. 803 (HL).

[49] [1969] 1 W.L.R. 928.

solicitor to pursue a remedy against the father's insurers. On the assistant's advice letters of administration were taken out by the mother; this was negligent advice since if litigation ensured the mother would be the nominal defendant to the action as having the administration of her husband's estate and would therefore be unable to sue in respect of her own injuries. The assistant committed a further act of negligence in failing to issue writs against the husband's estate within the six months required by the Law Reform (Miscellaneous Provisions) Act 1934. As a result the husband's insurers repudiated all the claims on the ground that they were time-barred. The solicitor notified his professional negligence insurers who claimed they could limit their liability to £3,000. Donaldson J. held, however, that there were, in effect, two occurrences. The assistant's negligence had occurred twice, first in arranging for the mother to be the administratrix or in failing to obtain revocation of the grant of administration and secondly in failing to issue writs within the limitation period. The mother's claim did not arise because of the assistant's failure to issue a writ on her behalf (which would not have been a useless proceeding) but arose because the assistant allowed her to become administratrix of her husband's estate or failed to revoke the letters of administration before her claim became statute-barred. The judge further held that the limit of £3,000 included any liability in costs to the third parties and that the plaintiff therefore could not recover any sum in respect of the costs incurred but only two sums of £3,000.

28–45 Other words of limitation. Other phrases construed by the courts have been variants of "any one event", "each and every loss arising out of one event", "each and every loss and/or occurrence and/or series of losses and/or occurrences arising out of one event", and "claim or claims arising from one originating cause". It is difficult to say much more than that each such phrase must be construed in its context with particular attention to the actual words used.[50] In *Caudle v. Sharp*[51] it was held at first instance that a continuing state of affairs amounted, or could amount, to an event. On that view it was held that the negligent underwriting of 32 run-off contracts of reinsurance without the necessary investigation into the problems of asbestosis was one event. The Court of Appeal reversed this decision on the basis that the underwriting of each contract was an occurrence and so there were 32 occurrences. It was held not to be apposite to call a failure to conduct the necessary investigation an "event".[52]

28–46 Before *Caudle v. Sharp* went to the Court of Appeal it was held that the negligence of three separate underwriters did not amount to one "originating cause" but three "originating causes".[53] Subsequently, it has been held by the House of Lords that "event" and "originating cause" are different concepts in that an "event" is "something which happens at a particular time, at a particular place, in a particular way",[54] whereas a "cause" can be a continuing state of affairs or the absence of something

---

[50] *Lloyds TSB v. Lloyds Bank Group Ins. Co. Ltd* [2001] Lloyd's Rep. I.R. 237, 241; affirmed by the Court or Appeal, with different reasoning: [2002] 1 All E.R. (Comm.) 42.

[51] [1995] L.R. L.R. 433.

[52] [1995] L.R. L.R. 433.

[53] *Cox v. Bankside Members Agency Ltd* [1995] 2 Lloyd's Rep. 437, 454–455.

[54] If cover is given against named "events" occurring during the period of insurance, it requires the peril to occur at that time, and not merely loss resulting from its earlier occurrence—*Kelly v. Norwich Union Fire Ins. Ltd* [1990] 1 W.L.R. 139.

happening and, especially in the form "originating cause", has a much wider connotation than the word "event".[55] Furthermore it may be possible to aggregate by reference to an underlying cause of losses if the contract provides for the aggregation in terms such as "a related series of acts or omissions".[56]

28–47 Liability policies sometimes provide that, when judgment is given against the insured for more than the limit of indemnity in the policy, the insurer will indemnify the assured additionally against a proportion of the costs he is ordered to pay determined by the relationship of the indemnity limit to the sum for which judgment is given exclusive of costs.[57]

28–48 Meaning of "claims". It is often provided that the insurer is liable for a limited amount in respect of each claim or that the assured is to bear a certain proportion of each claim and it may, therefore, become important to know precisely what is meant by a "claim" in the context of liability insurance.[58] The word was defined by McNair J. in *Australia and New Zealand Bank v. Colonial and Eagle Wharves*[59] as "the occurrence of a state of affairs which justifies a claim on underwriters" and it is clear from this definition that the learned judge regarded the word "claim" as referring to the claim on underwriters rather than to the claim on the insured. A difficult question of construction arose under a building contractor's liability insurance in *Trollope & Colls Ltd v. Hayden*[60] where the builders erected

---

[55] *Axa Reinsurance v. Field* [1996] 1 W.L.R. 1026 especially at page 1035 *per* Lord Mustill; *Municipal Mutual Ins. Ltd v. Sea Ins. Co. Ltd* [1998] Lloyd's Rep. I.R. 421, 434. See also para. 33–66, *post*.

[56] *Lloyds TSB v. Lloyds Bank Group Ins. Co. Ltd* [2001] Lloyd's Rep. I.R. 237, affirmed, with different reasoning by the Court of Appeal [2002] 1 All E.R. (Comm.) 42, where a large number of claims for pension mis-selling were made against the assured. It was held that a single deductible could be applied to the claims on the basis that they arose from a related series of negligent acts or omissions, which stemmed from a failure to train the sales force properly.

[57] *Aluminium Wire & Cable v. Allstate Ins. Co. Ltd* [1985] 2 Lloyd's Rep. 280, 288, in which a third party claimant suing under the 1930 Act was entitled to the benefit of such a condition.

[58] For difficulties that arose in connection with insurances against theft and forgery, see *Philadelphia National Bank v. Price* [1938] 2 All E.R. 199 and para. 27–16, *ante*. Where indemnity was promised against the consequences of persons "claiming to be entitled to enforce" a covenant within a specified period, it was held that "claiming" included not only the assertion of a right to enforce but also the sequential process of enforcement of the right: *Soole v. Royal Ins. Co. Ltd* [1971] 2 Lloyd's Rep. 332, 337–338.

[59] [1960] 2 Lloyd's Rep. 241.

[60] [1977] 1 Lloyd's Rep. 244. It is clear that the context is very important. In *Thorman v. New Hampshire Ins. Co.* Q.B.D. (Com. Ct.) 23 December 1986, unrep., Steyn J. defined "claim" in a professional indemnity policy as "the assertion by a third party against the insured of a right to some relief because of the breach of the insured of the duty referred to in the ... cover." The C.A. affirmed this definition, although not the final decision, [1988] 1 Lloyd's Rep. 7. Several causes of action may support a single claim, *West Wake Price v. Ching* [1957] 1 W.L.R. 45, 57; approved in *Haydon v. Lo & Lo* [1997] 1 W.L.R. 198. The primary meaning of "claim" is a demand made on the assured—*Thorman v. New Hampshire Ins. Co.* [1988] 1 Lloyd's Rep. 7, 15, and whether one or more claims are made is an issue of fact depending on the underlying facts although the manner in which the claimant makes its demand is a starting-point—*Municipal Mutual Ins. Ltd v. Sea Ins. Co.* [1996] L.R.I.R. 265 (but on appeal the analysis focussed on the nature of the aggregation clause: [1998] Lloyd's Rep. I.R. 421); *Haydon v. Lo & Lo* [1997] 1 W.L.R. 198, 204–205; *Citibank NA v. Excess Ins. Co. Ltd* [1999] Lloyd's Rep. I.R. 122. There must be notification of the claim to the assured: *Robert Irving & Burns v. Stone* [1998] Lloyd's Rep. I.R. 258 (no claim made when writ issued but not served, and assured not aware of relevant circumstances). Claims may be made by participating in a review process into the conduct of the assured: *J.Rothschild Assurance Plc v. Collyear* [1999] Lloyd's Rep. I.R. 6.—see para. 28–86, *ante*.

houses and garages for Harlow Development Corporation and warranted that they were and would remain weathertight for a period of five years. Numerous failures and defects appeared and the builders carried out extensive remedial works, the cost of which they then tried to recover from the underwriters. The policy provided that the builders were to bear the first £25 of each and every claim and underwriters contended that each separate defect which required remedy constituted a separate claim while the builders contended that the only claim was based on the failure to make the buildings weathertight. Neither argument was accepted by the judge or the Court of Appeal. The judge held that there were a number of separate defects which appeared several times in the various buildings constructed by the assured and that each such separate defect constituted one claim within the meaning of the policy, regardless of the number of the houses or garages in which it was to be found. The Court of Appeal held first that the word "claim" meant a claim on underwriters in the sense defined by McNair J. and then proceeded to hold that there was a claim in respect of each house or garage to which repair work had been done, regardless of the number of separate defects there may have been in each house or garage. As there were 481 houses and a similar number of garages, most of which had to have remedial work done to them, there was a substantial excess which had to be borne by the assured.

28–49 Admission of liability. There is usually a condition avoiding the policy in the event of any admission of liability or other conduct by the insured to the prejudice of the insurers' interests.[61] It has been held that the driver of a traction engine in the employment of the assured was not his agent to make admission of liability, and that an admission so made was not the admission of the assured within the meaning of the condition.[62] Where a secretary of a foreign legation against whom a writ had been issued by a person injured in a motor accident, waived his diplomatic immunity on the instructions of his government and submitted to the jurisdiction of the court, it was held that the insurers could not object since the privilege was that of the government, not the individual defendant.[63] Breach of such a condition is waived if the solicitor conducting the defence for the insurers, with knowledge of the breach, elects to continue to defend the action.[64] Liability insurance will often be expressed not to apply if the assured assumes by agreement a liability to which it was not otherwise exposed.[65]

28–50 Judgment by default. Where judgment has been obtained against the assured by default, the insurers have the right to apply to set aside the

[61] *e.g. Post Office v. Norwich Union Fire Ins. Society Ltd* [1967] 2 Q.B. 363; *Total Graphics v. AGF Ins. Co. Ltd* [1997] 1 Lloyd's Rep. 599. Such a condition in a motor policy was held not to be contrary to public policy: *Terry v. Trafalgar Ins. Co.* [1970] 1 Lloyd's Rep. 524. It has been held by a majority of the High Court of Australia to apply even if the insurers do not themselves deal with the claim: *Distillers Co. Biochemical (Australia) v. Ajax Ins.* (1974) 48 A.L.J.R. 136, although the decision turned on the construction of the particular term. In *Distillers* it was pointed out that such a condition will almost certainly not prevent an insured from answering forensic questions, or making a payment in satisfaction of a judgment.

[62] *Tustin v. Arnold* (1915) 31 T.L.R. 368. *Cf.. Burr v. Ware R.D.C.* [1939] 2 All E.R. 688.

[63] *Dickinson v. Del Solar* [1930] 1 K.B. 376.

[64] *Cadeddu v. Mount Royal Ins. Co.* [1929] 2 D.L.R. 867.

[65] *A.S. Screenprint Ltd v. British Reserve Ins. Co. Ltd* [1999] Lloyd's Rep. I.R. 430, 435—where it is pointed out that such provision is not an exclusion of all liability founded on contract.

judgment under the rules of court, a right which arises either from their contractual right to conduct the litigation or, where section 151 of the Road Traffic Act 1972 applies, from their statutory obligation to satisfy the judgment,[66] but they are not, by virtue of having entered an appearance on behalf of their assured, parties to the action, and no application or appeal should be made in their own name.[67]

28–51 Obligation of assured to take precautions. Many indemnity policies contain a clause requiring the assured to take reasonable precautions. Employers' liability policies, for example, frequently provide that the assured shall take reasonable precautions to prevent accidents and disease, while goods in transit policies may contain some such clause as "the assured shall take all reasonable precautions for the protection and safe-guarding of the goods". Such clauses will not be construed as warranties, breach of which will entitle the insurer to repudiate liability irrespective of whether there is a causal connection between the breach and the loss.[68]

28–52 It has frequently been pointed out that unless some restriction is placed upon the clause, the insurers would be entitled to avoid liability wherever they establish negligence on the part of the assured, which will usually be the very conduct which the policy is chiefly desired to cover.[69] In *Woolfall and Rimmer v. Moyle*[70] the insurer contended that a clause requiring the assured to take reasonable precautions to prevent accidents imposed a duty of care coterminous with an employer's duty to his workmen. The Court of Appeal rejected this contention on the ground that such a construction would altogether exclude a large and important class of case from the area of liability expressed to be covered by the policy. The court held that the effect of the clause was to impose a personal obligation on the assured to conduct his business in an ordinarily prudent manner and not in a way that invites accidents. Thus if a servant or employee fails to take reasonable precautions so that the assured is vicariously liable for such failure, that is not a breach of the clause. Moreover there will be no breach if the assured provides all the normal safety equipment for his employees and the employee is made aware of such provision.[71]

28–53 Recklessness required to avoid liability. An obligation to take reasonable precautions to prevent accidents is an obligation to take

---

[66] *Windsor v. Chalcraft* [1939] 1 K.B. 279.

[67] *Murfin v. Ashbridge* [1941] 1 All E.R. 231.

[68] *W. & J. Lane v. Spratt* [1970] 2 Q.B. 480, followed by Neill J. in *H.T.V. Ltd v. Lintner* [1984] 2 Lloyd's Rep. 125, 128. In *Pictorial Machinery Ltd v. Nicholls* (1940) 45 Com.Cas. 334, 344 Humphreys J. refused to hold that a similar clause was a condition precedent to liability even though it was expressly described as such. It must depend upon the wording of the particular clause. A clause requiring the assured to take reasonable precautions to maintain his vehicle was construed to relieve insurers of liability regardless of causal connection with an accident—*Lefevre v. White* [1990] 1 Lloyd's Rep. 569, 571; *Amey Properties v. Cornhill Ins. plc* [1995] L.R.L.R. 259, 264. It is likely that, if not construed as conditions precedent, many such clauses will now be regarded as innominate terms, releasing insurers from liability for a claim only if the breach is sufficiently serious: *Alfred McAlpine Plc v. BAI (Run-off) Ltd* [2000] Lloyd's Rep. I.R. 352.

[69] See, *e.g. Beauchamp v. National Mutual Indemnity Ins. Co.* [1937] 3 All E.R. 19, 27, *per* Finlay J.; *Woolfall and Rimmer v. Moyle* [1942] 1 K.B. 66.

[70] [1942] 1 K.B. 66. *Cf. T. F. Maltby Ltd v. Pelton S.S. Co. Ltd* [1951] 2 Lloyd's Rep. 332.

[71] *London Crystal Window Cleaning Co. Ltd v. National Mutual Indemnity Ins. Co. Ltd* [1952] 2 Lloyd's Rep. 360.

reasonable measures to avert dangers which are likely to cause bodily injury to employees. The precautions taken need only be reasonable ones and that does not mean reasonable as between the employer and the employees but as between the assured and the insurer. The clause cannot mean that the assured must take measures to avert dangers which he does not himself foresee or that, if he does foresee dangers, he must take all the measures which a reasonable employer would take in order to avert them. If it did have this meaning it would be repugnant to the commercial purpose of the policy which is to indemnify the assured for the consequences of his negligence.[72] Diplock L.J. has said:[73]

> "What, in my judgment, is reasonable as between the insured and the insurer, without being repugnant to the commercial purpose of the contract is that the insured where he does recognise a danger should not deliberately court it by taking measures which he himself knows are inadequate to avert it. In other words, it is not enough that the employer's omission to take any particular precautions to avoid accidents should be negligent; it must be at least reckless, that is to say, made with actual recognition by the insured himself that a danger exists, and not caring whether or not it is averted. The purpose of the condition is to ensure that the insured will not, because he is covered against loss by the policy, refrain from taking precautions which he knows ought to be taken."

These remarks were followed, obiter, in *W. & J. Lane v. Spratt*[74] in which it was contended that the assured, under a goods in transit policy, had failed to take reasonable precautions in selecting their drivers in that they had taken no steps to check the references of a new driver beyond making an abortive telephone call to which there was no reply. Roskill J. had little doubt that the assured had been negligent but no doubt at all that they were not reckless in the sense of refraining from taking precautions which they realised ought to be taken because they knew they were covered against loss by the policy. Similarly, a failure to fence machinery in which an employee has caught her hand will not of itself constitute recklessness within the meaning of the clause.[75]

28–54 Provision of safeguards. Another form of the condition under discussion is that the assured will at all times exercise reasonable care in seeing that all reasonable safeguards against accident are provided and used. It has been held that the word "provided" indicates that the safeguards and

---

[72] *Fraser v. B. N. Furman (Productions) Ltd* [1967] 1 W.L.R. 898.

[73] *ibid.* at p. 906, applied in *Aluminium Wire & Cable v. Allstate Ins. Co. Ltd* [1985] 2 Lloyd's Rep. 280 and *Aswan Engineering v. Iron Trades Mutual Ins. Co.* [1989] 1 Lloyd's Rep. 289 where Hobhouse J. held that it was reckless to decide to send forward goods known to be damaged. The principle also applies to property insurance—*Sofi v. Prudential Ass. Co.* [1993] 2 Lloyd's Rep. 559; *Devco Holder v. Legal & General Ass. Soc. Ltd* [1993] 2 Lloyd's Rep. 567; *Gunns v. Par Insurance Brokers* [1997] 1 Lloyd's Rep. 173 (failure to switch on a burglar alarm).

[74] [1970] 2 Q.B. 480.

[75] *Fraser v. B. N. Furman (Productions) Ltd* [1967] 1 W.L.R. 898 where the judge at the trial of the action between the employee and the employer had held that the employers probably did not ever appreciate the sort of risk to which they were subjecting their employees.

precautions envisaged are material things.[76] A clause in a carrier's goods in transit policy provided: "The insured shall take all reasonable precautions for the protection and safeguarding of the goods and/or merchandise and use such protective appliances as may be specified in the policy and all vehicles and protective devices shall be maintained in good order." It was held that the clause was limited to the need to protect the safety of the goods and was not intended to require precautions to be taken in the selection of staff by the assured.[77]

28–55 Description of assured's business. The nature and scope of the assured's business will usually be defined in the policy and read as part of it. Thus a builder who had not previously carried out demolition work took out a policy to indemnify him in respect of the work involved in the demolition of a mill. He was asked in the proposal form whether he used explosives in his business; he did not use explosives in his business of a builder and he answered the questions in the negative, but he did intend to use explosives in the course of the demolition and it was held that the question related not to his general business as a builder but to the specific business of demolition covered by the policy.[78]

28–56 Liability in course of business. Similarly, professional indemnity policies may undertake to indemnify the assured for negligence while acting in the course of his profession, e.g. as a solicitor. A solicitor who commits champerty has been held not to be acting in the course of his profession and is therefore unable to recover.[79] Conversely, some household policies provide cover against liability for accidents excluding liability arising from a trade, occupation or business. This exclusion relates to liability incurred whilst acting in the course of an occupation, but not to liability arising outside the occupation from the use of skills derived from the assured's work.[80]

28–57 If the assured's business is inaccurately described in the policy but the insurer's agent knows the real nature of his business, the insurer may be deemed to have had the agent's knowledge and to have insured the

---

[76] *Concrete Ltd v. Attenborough* (1939) 65 Ll.L.R. 174. (In *Woolfall and Rimmer v. Moyle* [1942] 1 K.B. 66 Goddard L.J. stated that he did not agree with all the reasoning in this case; but he did not specify the points to which he took exception and seems to have approved the actual decision.) See also *Pictorial Machinery Ltd v. Nicholls* (1940) 45 Com.Cas. 334.

[77] *W. & J. Lane v. Spratt* [1970] 2 Q.B. 480. See *Liverpool Corporation v. Roberts* [1965] 1 W.L.R. 938 (no system of vehicle maintenance) and *Lefevre v. White* [1990] 1 Lloyd's Rep. 569 (driving with a bald tyre).

[78] *Beauchamp v. National Mutual Indemnity Ins. Co.* [1937] 3 All E.R. 19.

[79] *Haseldine v. Hosken* [1933] 1 K.B. 822, 839. The policy may also require that liability should arise "out of the ordinary course" of provision of services by the assured. Where a development capital company acted as a director of another company, it was held to be acting in the ordinary course of provision of financial and associated services: *Charterhouse Development (France) v. Sharp* [1998] Lloyd's Rep. I.R. 266.

[80] *Dignan v. Irving* 2001 S.L.T. 32, where the assured was liable for building work which he had carried out as a favour, using skills he also used in his employment. The exclusion did not apply. The contrary construction would have involved "a bleak view of society in which the Good Samaritan finds no place".

employer in respect of his actual business as known to the agent, not merely in respect of the business described in the policy.[81]

28–58 Deemed abandonment of proceedings. It is not unknown for policies to contain a clause providing that if insurers disclaim liability for a claim and, if within 12 calendar months of such disclaimer, legal proceedings have not been instituted, the claim shall be deemed to be abandoned and shall not thereafter be recoverable. Such a clause may be reasonable enough in an ordinary policy but in a liability policy it is a trap for the unwary since the assured may notify his insurers of a claim against him in such terms as to constitute a claim made by him against his insurers. The party making the claim on the assured may well delay for more than a year before issuing proceedings and it will often not occur to the insured that he should himself issue proceedings against the insurers at an earlier stage. In *Walker v. Pennine Insurance Co.*[82] the plaintiff, after receiving notice of a claim to be made by his passenger arising from a collision, wrote to his insurers stating that he expected to be indemnified under the policy. This was held to be a "claim" within the clause by Sheen J. and the claim was deemed to be abandoned within the 12 months after insurers' rejection on March 22, 1971, even though the passenger did not issue a writ until October 25, 1972. On the face of it this is a hard decision, especially as, if the passenger had obtained a judgment against the plaintiff, the clause would no doubt have been invalidated by section 148(1) of the Road Traffic Act 1972.

28–59 The Unfair Contract Terms Act 1977. It was common practice for enterprises of various kinds to deal with the public on contractual terms which limited or excluded the liability otherwise arising in tort towards members of the public suffering personal injury or property damage through the negligence of the enterprise. The use of such terms was sometimes a condition of the public liability insurance policies of such enterprises. The Unfair Contract Terms Act 1977[83] renders such terms wholly ineffectual in so far as they relate to personal injury[84] and subjects them to a test of reasonableness in so far as they relate to property damage.[85] The Act does not, however, apply to insurance policies[86] and on the face of it does not affect a policy condition of the kind mentioned above. It might perhaps be argued that such a condition is now against public policy, at least if it requires the assured to employ terms relating to personal injury, of a kind which the Act totally prohibits. The situation would be very complicated in a case where the test of reasonableness applied as between the assured and the injured party, since the outcome of that test might depend on factors which were not known or ascertained, as between insurer and assured, at the time when the policy was entered into. The conditions of public liability insurances ought to be carefully scrutinised, with the provisions of the Act of 1977 in mind. It is likely, in any event, that these kind of provisions are now

---

[81] *Holdsworth v. Lancashire and Yorkshire Insurance Co.* (1907) 23 T.L.R. 521. For a case where the court corrected a misnomer, see *Nittan v. Solent Steel Fabrication Ltd* [1981] 1 Lloyd's Rep. 633.

[82] [1979] 2 Lloyd's Rep. 139.

[83] 1977, c. 50.

[84] s.2(1).

[85] s.2(2). For the test of what is reasonable, see s.11.

[86] See s.1(2) and Sch. 1 for exceptions to the provisions of ss.2–4.

unenforceable by reason of the Unfair Terms in Consumer Contracts Regulations, 1999, as regards consumer insurance contracts.[87]

(d) *Types of Liability Insurance*

28–60 There are many types of liability insurance policy. The more usual are considered in subsequent sections of this chapter and in chapters 29 and 32. But there are many other types. Many companies take out public liability cover to indemnify them "against all sums which they shall become legally liable to pay as compensation in respect of loss of or damage to property."[88] Manufacturers commonly effect product liability insurance to indemnify them against liability at law for damages awarded in actions bought by purchasers of defective products.[89] Householders commonly purchase a composite insurance cover under which they are covered not only against damage to their house but also liability towards third parties.[90] Besides the policies available for every category of contractor,[91] builder[92] or repairer[93] who wishes to cover his liability towards third parties, mention should be made of the specialised covers for particular trades which incorporate liability cover, such as an "entertainment package policy" for companies producing films.[94] Many working in professions are required to carry liability

---

[87] See para. 10–16, *ante*.

[88] *Post Office v. Norwich Fire Ins. Society Ltd* [1967] 2 Q.B. 363.

[89] *Nittan (U.K.) Ltd v. Solent Steel Fabrication Ltd* [1981] 1 Lloyd's Rep. 633; *Berliner Motor Corporation v. Sun Alliance and London Ins. Ltd* [1983] 1 Lloyd's Rep. 320. In general product liability cover relates to loss in respect of some physical event involving the product during the period of cover. It will not, therefore, (absent clear wording) provide cover for a loss of goodwill arising from a lack of repeat orders after an incident involving a product. The loss of goodwill is a separate form of pecuniary loss, not related (in the relevant sense) to a physical occurrence involving the product; rather, it arises from a separate decision not to order, or to supply, further quantities of goods. See *Rodan Int. Ltd v. Commercial Union Ass. Co. Plc* [1999] Lloyd's Rep. I.R. 495; *A.S. Screenprint Ltd v. British Reserve Ins. Co. Ltd [1999] Lloyd's Rep. I.R. 430.*

[90] *Gray v. Barr* [1971] 2 Q.B. 554 ("hearth and home" policy); *Hair v. Prudential Ass. Co. Ltd* [1983] 2 Lloyd's Rep. 667 (same); *Oei v. Foster* [1982] 2 Lloyd's Rep. 170 ("house-holder's and house-owner's all-in policy"). See also *Sturge v. Hackett* [1962] 1 W.L.R. 1257 where it was held that a policy which was expressed to cover "all sums for which the assured (as occupier of the said private dwelling-house) may be held legally liable" applied to liability in any action which could be framed in a form in which it would be a necessary averment that the assured was an occupier; it applied therefore to indemnify the assured in respect of any liability for allowing fire to escape from his premises. The word "occupier" is, however, a term of art and relates to "a well-defined group of liabilities imposed upon occupiers of premises"; it is not merely descriptive of the identity or status of the person to whom liability attaches, *per* McNair J. [1962] 1 Lloyd's Rep. 117, 124 and approved by the Court of Appeal [1962] 1 W.L.R. 1257, 1267, followed in *Rigby v. Sun Alliance & London Ins. Co.* [1980] 1 Lloyd's Rep. 359, 364, where the cover was against the liability attaching to the insured "solely as owner (not occupier) of the house." A phrase such as "liability arising by reason of the assured's interest" may be construed more widely—*Turner v. Manx Line* [1990] 1 Lloyd's Rep. 137. See also *Christmas v. Taylor Woodrow Civil Engineering Ltd* [1997] 1 Lloyd's Rep. 407 ("legally liable as owners").

[91] *Rowlinson Construction Ltd v. Insurance Co. of N. America* [1981] 1 Lloyd's Rep. 332. See the discussion on contractors' "all-risks" policies in Ch. 32, *infra*. For a "contractors' public liability policy" effected for a firm of stevedores, see *Pickford & Black Ltd v. Canadian General Ins. Co.* [1976] 2 Lloyd's Rep. 108.

[92] See, *e.g. Gold v. Patman* [1958] 1 W.L.R. 697—requirement for insurance in R.I.B.A. contract satisfied if contractor alone was insured against liability for subsidence of neighbouring property, and not the owner as well.

[93] *American Shipbuilding Co. v. Orion Ins. Co.* [1969] 2 Lloyd's Rep. 251 (ship-repairer); *Pillgrem v. Richardson* [1977] 1 Lloyd's Rep. 297 (marine operator and ship repairer).

[94] *H.T.V. Ltd v. Lintner* [1984] 2 Lloyd's Rep. 125.

insurance, either by rules of their professional associations (which may also provide insurance schemes),[95] or by statute or subordinate legislation. The categories of liability against which indemnity is offered may be restricted. An insurance against "liability imposed by the law" has been held to refer to statutory and tortious liability, and not to liability arising out of breach of contract or to liability in tort co-extensive with contractual liability.[96]

2. Professional Indemnity Policies

28–61 Introduction. One of the most important forms of insurance is that required to cover professional people for negligence in the course of their professions. The number of such insurances increased rapidly in the aftermath of the decision in the House of Lords in *Hedley Byrne & Co. v. Heller and Partners.*[97] Before this decision it was generally considered that professional people owed a duty of care only to their clients or to those with whom they had a fiduciary relationship, but the House of Lords decided in 1963 that in some circumstances a duty of care could be owed by those who made statements which were intended to be relied upon to those who in fact relied upon such statements and suffered loss thereby. Members of the professions are now faced with the prospects of a much wider and more far-reaching liability than they had previously contemplated.

28–62 Scope of the policy. It is essential to appreciate that the purpose of the usual professional indemnity policy, subject to special wordings in particular cases, is to afford cover in respect of the liability of the insured for negligence on the part of himself or his employees. Accordingly, it does not cover either clients of the assured[98] or the assured himself against loss suffered in his business due to his negligence or that of his employees where that negligence does not give rise to a liability towards a third party.[99] It is not the purpose of such a policy to afford cover for liability incurred by the insured as the result of any dishonest or fraudulent act on the part of his employees.[1] This form of liability is the province of the fidelity policy not of an indemnity policy in the traditional form. However it is now common for a

[95] See para. 28–71, *post*.

[96] *Canadian Indemnity Co. v. Andrews & George Co. Ltd* [1952] 4 D.L.R. 690 and *Dominion Bridge Co. Ltd v. Toronto General Ins. Co.* [1964] 1 Lloyd's Rep. 194 where, however, there was an express exclusion for liability assumed by contract. In *Aswan Engineering v. Iron Trades Ins. Co.* [1989] 1 Lloyd's Rep. 289, it was held that cover against liability "at law" included liability under a contract. See also para. 32–16, *post*.

[97] [1964] A.C. 465.

[98] *Macmillan v. Knott Becker Scott* [1990] 1 Lloyd's Rep. 98, in which there is a useful summary of the development of E. & O. insurance

[99] *Goddard & Smith v. Frew* [1939] 4 All E.R. 358; *Walton v. National Employers Mutual General Ass. Ass'n Ltd* [1974] 2 Lloyd's Rep. 385 (N.S.W. Sup. Ct.). There is one exception to this rule in the case of policies which indemnify large concerns which possess different departments acting in different capacities on a common project, and it may suffice to show that one department of the insured possesses a notional claim for negligence against another, as in *Wimpey Construction U.K. Ltd v. Poole* [1984] 2 Lloyd's Rep. 499, 513.

[1] *Davies v. Hosken* [1937] 3 All E.R. 192; *Whitworth v. Hosken* [1939] 65 Ll.L.R. 48; *Goddard and Smith v. Frew* [1939] 4 All E.R. 358; *West Wake Price & Co. v. Ching* [1957] 1 W.L.R. 45; *Johns v. Kelly* [1986] 1 Lloyd's Rep. 468. The Court must look at the substance of the complaint against the assured in order to say whether liability rests on negligence or fraud—see para. 28–59, *infra*.

professional indemnity policy to include cover against such liability, excluding liability where the assured could reasonably have discovered or suspected the dishonesty.[2] Still less is it the purpose of such a policy to afford cover for liability incurred by the insured as a result of his own dishonesty or fraud.[3] It is, indeed, doubtful whether cover of that kind could ever be effective, because an insured cannot recover for a loss caused by his own wilful act or omission[4] and, if and in so far as that act amounts to a crime, a contract to indemnify the criminal for the consequences of his crime will be in most cases void.[5]

28–63 Whether cover for non-negligent act. Confusion has arisen as a result of the wording of the indemnity clauses in some professional negligence policies as to whether liability for a non-negligent breach of contract would be covered. In *Wimpey Construction U.K. Ltd v. Poole*[6] the insurers granted indemnity against loss arising from any claim or claims arising out of "any omission, error or negligent act". Webster J. held that in the context of the particular policy cover was granted against omissions and errors occurring without negligence.[7] In practice this is often of little importance since generally liability towards the third party rests upon breach of a contractual or tortious duty of care by the insured and no liability arises in the absence of negligence.[8]

28–64 Act of employee. In *Goddard and Smith v. Frew*[9] a firm of auctioneers and estate agents insured themselves against "all losses cost, charges and demands whatsoever by reason of any act, neglect, omission, misstatement or error ... on the part of the firm or any person employed by the firm ..." An agent of the plaintiffs collected rents from property belonging to Covent Garden Properties Co. Ltd and embezzled them. The plaintiffs paid over the amounts which had been embezzled and claimed to recover the sum so paid from the insurers under the policy. It was held that they could not do so since the policy only covered liability for negligent conduct on the part of the assured or his employees. Scott L.J. said:[10]

---

[2] See the wording of the insurance in *MDIS v. Swinbank* [1999] Lloyd's Rep. I.R. 516—discussed in para. 28–59, *infra*.

[3] *Haseldine v. Hosken* [1933] 1 K.B. 822.

[4] *Wimpey Construction U.K. Ltd v. Poole* [1984] 2 Lloyd's Rep. 499, 514, *per* Webster J. See paras 14–30–14–33, *ante*.

[5] See para. 14–34, *ante*.

[6] [1984] 2 Lloyd's Rep. 499. The slip had provided cover for "negligent act, error or omission" which could not have been intended to have any different meaning—see p. 513.

[7] In *West Wake Price & Co. v. Ching* [1957] 1 W.L.R. 45, 47, Devlin J. was of the view that innocent acts of conversion attracting legal liability without negligence might be covered by professional indemnity policies. See also *MDIS v. Swinbank* [1999] Lloyd's Rep. I.R. 516, affirming [1999] Lloyd's Rep. I.R. 98 (discussed in para. 28–69, *post*) where it was common ground that the phrase "any neglect error or omission including breach of contract occasioned by the same" extended beyond negligence alone.

[8] This was indeed the case in *Wimpey Construction U.K. Ltd v. Poole* [1984] 2 Lloyd's Rep. 499, 514. The test for whether a professional man has been negligent is "the standard of the ordinary skilled man exercising and professing to have that special skill": *Bolam v. Friern Hospital Management Committee* [1957] 1 W.L.R. 582, 586, approved in *Whitehouse v. Jordan* [1981] 1 W.L.R. 246. *Sed quaere* whether a client retaining a practitioner of international renown may expect a higher standard than that of the average humble practitioner: *Duchess of Argyll v. Beuselinck* [1972] 2 Lloyd's Rep. 172, discussed in *Wimpey Construction U.K. Ltd v. Poole* [1984] 2 Lloyd's Rep. 499, 505–506.

[9] [1939] 4 All E.R. 358.

[10] *ibid.* at p. 361.

"The real cause of the loss of the firm was embezzlement by their servant. That was the true proximate cause of the loss and, in my view, as this is not a fidelity policy, but only an indemnity policy against certain carefully described liabilities, the loss cannot be brought within this policy."

He went on to point out that any statement of claim drafted on behalf of the Covent Garden Properties Co. Ltd against the plaintiffs would have made a claim for money had and received and would not have had to allege any negligent conduct or indeed any specific conduct on the part of the employee at all. In these circumstances it could not be said that the plaintiffs' loss was due to any act, neglect or error on the part of their employee.

28–65 It may be difficult to determine whether in a given case liability has arisen through the act of a person capable of being described as an "employee" of the assured. In *Johns v. Kelly*[11] a firm of Lloyd's brokers permitted another firm of non-Lloyd's brokers to use its printed slips and to transact business in its name under an "umbrella" or "piggy-back" arrangement sanctioned by the Committee of Lloyd's. It was held by Bingham J. that, applying the usual criteria for the existence of a contract of employment, a director of the second firm whose acts were called in question was not an employee of the Lloyd's brokers. Nor could he be an "assured" under the Lloyd's brokers' indemnity policy.[12]

28–66 Act of "assured". Policies usually distinguish between the acts of the insured person and acts of employees and other persons working for the insured. In the case of a sole trader or partnership the distinction is easy to apply. In the case of a limited company being the assured named in the policy it is the senior management, its *"alter ego"*, who are the assured as opposed to employees of the assured.[13]

28–67 Deliberate act of employee. In *West Wake Price & Co. v. Ching*[14] the plaintiff firm of accountants were insured against loss from:

"any claim or claims which may be made against them ... in respect of any act of neglect, default or error on the part of the assured ... or their partners or their servants in the conduct of their business as accountants".

The insurers also agreed to pay:

"any such claim or claims which may arise without requiring the assured to dispute any claim, unless a King's Counsel ... advise that the same could be successfully contested by the assured, and the assured consents to such a claim being contested, but such consent not to be unreasonably withheld".

This latter clause (which is now usually referred to as the Q.C. clause) appears in virtually all professional indemnity policies in order to prevent underwriters from insisting that an assured should dispute liability to the third party and thus face the publicity of legal proceedings which, whether

---

[11] [1986] 1 Lloyd's Rep. 468.
[12] [1986] 1 Lloyd's Rep. 468, 474–476.
[13] *Johns v. Kelly* [1986] 1 Lloyd's Rep. 468, 474.
[14] [1957] 1 W.L.R. 45.

successful or not, might be damaging to his reputation. The plaintiffs were in the habit of receiving money from a particular client and using it for certain purposes and it came to light that one of their clerks had received about £20,000 but had not accounted for it. The client brought proceedings against the firm of accountants claiming:

(1) damages for negligence or breach of duty as accountants in failing to keep proper books or to supervise the activities of their clerk;
(2) money had and received to the plaintiff's use; and
(3) damages for converting the money to their own use.

The plaintiffs claimed that their loss fell within the policy and also within the Q.C. clause so that the underwriters were obliged to pay out without requiring the accountants to dispute the claim. It was held by Devlin J. in accordance with previous authority, that the policy covered only professional negligence and not loss incurred as a result of the dishonesty of an employee and that, in essence, the plaintiff's claim was a claim in fraud or at any rate a claim based partly on fraud and partly in negligence, whereas only an unmixed claim in negligence was intended to fall within the terms of the policy and the Q.C. clause. In determining this question, the court was not restricted by the way in which the third party had framed his claim against the plaintiffs but was entitled (and indeed bound) to ascertain the true nature of the claim and if, as in this case, the claim was really in respect of an employee's dishonesty it would not be covered by the policy.[15]

28–68 In *Simon Warrender Proprietary Ltd v. Swain*[16] it was assumed for purposes of a preliminary point of law that an employee in a company of insurance brokers deliberately failed to effect insurance on a client's fishing boat, and falsely represented that it had been effected. The company settled the client's claim for damages and claimed on its Brokers' Errors and Omissions Policy whereby it was insured against "all losses . . . resulting from errors or omissions by themselves or their employees in the conduct of their business". The underwriters argued that the employee's deliberate conduct was not covered by "errors and omissions". It might be thought that this was correct, inasmuch as the root cause of the client's claim was deliberate misconduct by an employee as in the *Ching*[17] Case. However, while the policy did not define indemnity by reference to claims, the Court considered that the company's liability to the client had been based on "some form of

---

[15] If, however, one event gives rise to a cause of action in negligence and, at the same time, to other causes of action not covered by the policy, the insurance should respond—*Capel-Cure Myers v. McCarthy* [1995] L.R. L.R. 498, 503, *per* Potter J., distinguishing the facts in the *Ching* Case. The facts in *Ching* were also distinguished in *Charterhouse (Development) Ltd v. Sharp* [1998] Lloyd's Rep. I.R. 266. A policy issued to a development capitalist provided indemnity against "compensatory damages" for "financial loss caused by a negligent act, negligent error or negligent omission on the part of an officer or Employee of the Assured" which arose "out of the ordinary course of the provision by the Assured of the financial and associated services described in the Proposal Form." The assured had provided capital to a French business and assumed a directorship in the business. When the business went into insolvent liquidation, it was held liable in France for what was described as the equivalent of liability for wrongful trading under s.214 of the Insolvency Act 1986, with the French court using language of negligence. It was held that the assured's liability arose out of the provision of a service and was based on negligence. Further the liability under French law was essentially "compensatory".
[16] [1960] 2 Lloyd's Rep. 111.
[17] [1957] 1 W.L.R. 45.

neglect" by the company rather than on the company's vicarious liability for a deliberate and wilful default by its employee. The underwriter had not contended that the company itself had acted deliberately and wilfully, and accordingly its failure to effect a policy fell within the words "errors or omissions".

28–69 Modern policies may now provide cover against the assured's liability arising out of the fraud or dishonesty of his employees, except where the fraud could have been discovered or suspected by the assured. This is likely to be construed as a separate head of cover, distinct from the basic cover against negligence. In *MDIS Ltd v. Swinbank & Others*[18] insurance covering a computer consultancy company provided indemnity against:

> "any claim for which the Assured may become legally liable, first made against the Assured and notified to the Underwriters during the period of this Certificate arising out of the professional conduct of the assured's business ... alleging:"
>
> (a) "any neglect error or omission including breach of contract occasioned by the same,"
> (b) "any dishonest, fraudulent, criminal or malicious act(s) or omission(s) of any person employed at any time by the Assured", and "any claim arising from"
> (c) infringement of intellectual property rights or
> (d) defamation.

Cover under paragraph (b) was qualified by the following proviso:

> "The Assured will not be indemnified against any claim or loss, resulting from the dishonest, fraudulent, criminal or malicious act(s) or omission(s) perpetrated after the Assured could reasonably have discovered or suspected the improper conduct of the employee(s)."

The assured had compromised a claim made against them by a client which the insurers maintained was based on the dishonesty of the employees of the assured and which fell within the proviso to paragraph (b). The assured argued that the word "alleging" meant that the policy responded to allegations rather than proven causes of liability, and that any allegation falling within paragraph (a) was covered if there was a judgment or compromise based on the allegation, whether or not liability could have been established under paragraph (b). That contention was rejected at first instance and in the Court of Appeal. By a majority[19] the Court of Appeal held that "alleging" could not be read literally in the sense suggested by the assured. The clause was construed as providing an indemnity where the proximate cause of the assured's loss was one of the insured perils. Cover under the insurance was not determined by the manner in which the claim against the assured was put by the claimant. This conclusion is consistent with the general principle that liability insurance is concerned with actual, established liability.[20]

---

[18] [1999] Lloyd's Rep. I.R. 516, affirming [1999] Lloyd's Rep. I.R. 98.

[19] Peter Gibson L.J. disagreed with the majority reasoning, on the basis that "alleging" could not be treated as meaning "resulting from". However, he concluded that the proviso to paragraph (b) related to all claims, and would preclude recovery even if the claim against the assured only alleged negligence.

[20] *Thornton Springer v. NEM Ins. Co. Ltd* [2000] Lloyd's Rep. I.R. 590; *London Borough of Redbridge v. Municipal Mutual Ins. Ltd* [2001] Lloyd's Rep. I.R. 545.

28–70 Intentional act of assured. *Haseldine v. Hosken*[21] provides an example of a case in which an assured was not entitled to recover under a professional indemnity policy as a result of his own conduct. Mr Haseldine was a solicitor who acted for a client named Mr Broad in an action brought by him for commission against Messrs Stern & Co. Mr Haseldine agreed to pay all the disbursements incurred in connection with the action and not to charge his client anything if the action failed; but if it succeeded he was to be rewarded by the sum of £500 or 40 per cent of the damages recovered whichever was the greater. The action was tried and dismissed but Messrs Stern & Co. could not recover their costs and therefore sued Mr Haseldine for damages for maintenance or champerty. Mr Haseldine settled the claim and then claimed an indemnity from his insurers. The Court of Appeal rejected his claim and two connected but distinct lines of reasoning underlie their judgment. First, a contract to indemnify a person from the consequences of committing a crime was illegal and could not be enforced. Since 1967[22] champerty has no longer been a crime and the case could probably no longer be supported on that ground; moreover the court itself recognised that not every contract to indemnify a person from the consequences of his crime would necessarily be void since otherwise many motor insurance contracts would be entirely useless. But the second line of reasoning was that the insured had acted intentionally and that since the policy was intended to cover negligent acts, the plaintiff's conduct precluded him from recovery. At first instance Swift J. had held that the plaintiff had no idea he was committing a crime but the Court of Appeal held that this was irrelevant; his actions were intended although their legal consequences may not have been and his deliberate conduct was not a "neglect, omission or error" within the terms of the policy.[23] In *Total Graphics Ltd v. AGF Insurance Ltd*[24] a broker's "flagrant misconduct" in failing to place insurance for their client was held not to be covered by their professional indemnity policy.

28–71 Insurance through professional association. The difficulty of devising a professional indemnity policy which will cover all the cases likely to arise has led certain professional associations to adopt an ingenious solution. The Royal Institution of Chartered Surveyors undertakes to reimburse any client of a member against loss resulting from the misconduct of the member himself and the Institution has taken out an insurance policy covering the resulting loss to itself.[25] In this way, cover is obtained for those cases of deliberate misfeasance of the principal in a firm of chartered surveyors which would otherwise be uninsurable. It is expected that similar schemes will be entered into by other organisations of estate agents in order to comply with the requirements of the Estate Agents Act 1979.[26] The Law

[21] [1933] 1 K.B. 822.
[22] Criminal Law Act 1967, s.15.
[23] A third ground for the decision was that the insured was not acting "as a solicitor" within the terms of the policy when he made the champertous agreement, [1933] 1 K.B. 822, 839.
[24] [1997] 1 Lloyd's Rep. 599.
[25] The RICS standard policy was referred to in *Arab Bank plc v. Zurich Ins. Co* [1999] 1 Lloyd's Rep. 262, discussed in para. 28–72, although the policy in that case did not follow exactly that model.
[26] 1979 c. 38. See s.16 of that Act (still not in force) for the requirements of insurance where estate agents accept deposits from their clients.

Society insures practising solicitors under the Solicitors' Indemnity Fund.[27] It is common for solicitors to insure liability in excess of the limit covered by the Fund under a separate policy.[28]

28–72 Fraud of one assured not to affect co-assureds. The sort of provisions referred to in the previous paragraph were considered in *Arab Bank Plc v. Zurich Insurance Co.*[29] The defendant insurers provided professional indemnity insurance to JDW, a company which carried out estate agency and valuation business. The plaintiff obtained judgment against JDW and, JDW having gone into insolvent liquidation, sought to enforce the judgment against insurers under the Third Parties (Rights against Insurers) Act 1930. The insurers repudiated liability on the basis of non-disclosure and breach of warranty, based upon the assumed fraud of JDW's managing director (B), who was also a substantial shareholder in JDW, in making valuations for the plaintiff. Under the terms of the policy, various persons were included within the definition of "the insured". The primary insured was the "firm", but also included were partners, directors and others, subject to a proviso that the definition of insured was not to be construed as meaning that insurers would indemnify any person knowingly committing, making or condoning any dishonest, fraudulent or malicious act or omission. The policy contained a term waiving the right to avoid for non-disclosure or misrepresentation, provided that the insured could establish to the insurers' satisfaction that any such non-disclosure or misrepresentation was innocent and free from any fraudulent conduct or intent. It provided that rights of subrogation would not be exercised against partners, directors or employees unless the claim was brought about by, *inter alia*, fraudulent acts or omission of any such person. Rix J. construed the policy as providing separate insurances for all the co-assureds.[30] He held that as JDW was vicariously liable for the fraud of B, and there was no question of B claiming directly under the policy, the insurers were liable to indemnify JDW.[31]

28–73 Negligence of predecessors in business. Many people who seek professional indemnity insurance practise in partnership and problems can arise in deciding the scope of the insurance cover with reference to retiring and incoming partners. Most policies will make it clear that the firm itself, the individual partners and any new partner who may be appointed during the currency of the policy are all indemnified. But even if only the firm is expressly indemnified, there can be no doubt that the indemnity would extend to each of the individual partners if they were sued in their individual names and, conversely, if the partners are expressly insured in their

[27] The scheme is discussed briefly in *Bristol and West Plc v. Bhadresa* [1999] Lloyd's Rep. I.R. 138.
[28] The terms of such cover were considered in *Kumar v. AGF Insurance Ltd* [1998] 2 All E.R. 788. *Cf.* para. 28–76, *post.*
[29] [1999] 1 Lloyd's Rep. 262. See also para. 17–34, *ante.*
[30] Applying *New Hampshire Ins. Co. v. MGN Ltd* [1997] L.R.L.R. 24, see para. 17–34, *ante.*
[31] Note that it was held that there was no basis for attributing B's knowledge to JDW, applying principles derived from *Re Hampshire Land Co.* [1896] 2 Ch. 743, and *Meridian Global Funds Management Asia v. Securities Commission* [1995] A.C. 500.

individual names, an action brought against the firm in the firm's name would presumably be covered by the policy.

28–74 When old partners retire and new partners come into the business or the profession, the constitution of the partnership changes but the remaining partners will be liable for any negligence which occurred while the partnership was in its previous form. Thus any partnership will require cover for the partners against liability arising from such negligence and it is common for professional indemnity policies to afford cover for the negligent acts or omissions of "the insured or their predecessors in business or any employee of the insured or their predecessors in business". This form of wording will ensure that both the partnership and the individual partners will be indemnified in respect of negligence which occurred before one of the partners retired[32] but the retiring partner himself will not, of course, be covered by such a policy although he will remain liable to the third party; his own liability must be the subject of separate cover.

28–75 In *Maxwell v. Price*[33] two solicitors practised in partnership, under the name of Ellis and Price. During the currency of the policy, a claim was made against Mr Price for negligence committed while he was practising on his own and before he entered into the partnership with Mr Ellis. The policy contained a "predecessors in business clause" but the underwriters argued that the purpose of the clause was to give the insured partners an indemnity for liability for the negligence of a partnership of which they had previously been partners not an indemnity for liability incurred by a present partner when he was practising on his own before the partnership came into existence. It was held, however, by the High Court of Australia that the clause had a wider meaning and was intended to cover all liability for the past negligence of the individual partners so as to avoid the necessity for a number of policies. Thus it seems that the policy covered the negligence of a partner committed while practising on his own account and perhaps even negligence committed while the partner was in partnership with another firm of solicitors. It is difficult, however, to see how either a solicitor practising on his own or a completely different partnership can be said to be the "predecessor in business" of the partnership insured and an English court might well prefer to accept the reasoning of the dissenting judgment of Taylor J.

28–76 Waiver of right to avoid. A professional indemnity policy may restrict the insurer's ability to avoid for non-disclosure, misrepresentation or breach of warranty.[34] In *Kumar v. AGF Insurance Ltd*[35] a policy effected by

---

[32] It was held in *Jenkins v. Deane* (1933) 47 Ll.L.R. 342 that the admission of a new partner could not excuse the insurer from indemnifying the original partners under a liability policy since the admission of a new partner could make no difference to the insurers. Similarly, it could be argued that the retirement of a partner makes no difference to the insurers in that the remaining partners might be called upon to pay the whole loss and therefore that the insurers would in any event be obliged to indemnify the remaining partners even if the policy did not contain wording similar to that given in the text.

[33] [1960] 2 Lloyd's Rep. 155 (High Ct. of Aust.).

[34] See, for example, provisions in *Arab Bank Plc v. Zurich Ins. Co.* [1999] 1 Lloyd's Rep. 262 (discussed in para. 28–72) and *J. Rothschild Assurance Plc v. Collyear* [1999] Lloyd's Rep. I.R. 6.

[35] [1999] 2 All E.R. 788.

a firm of solicitors to cover excess liability above that covered by Solicitors' Indemnity Fund provided as follows:

> "Non-Avoidance: the Insurers will not seek to avoid repudiate or rescind this Insurance upon any ground whatsoever including in particular non-disclosure or misrepresentation. However, in circumstances where before the inception or renewal of this Insurance a principal has fraudulently failed to disclose and/or fraudulently misrepresented circumstances which might give rise to a claim or claims, the Insurers shall be entitled to seek reimbursement from that principal in respect of any loss arising from such claim or claims."

In completing the proposal form, the plaintiff's former partner failed to disclose certain circumstances for which the firm was later held liable. It was held that insurers were not relieved from liability to the plaintiff on the basis of a breach of warranty when his partner completed the proposal form. The waiver clause, construed against the background to the policy and the rules of the Solicitors' Indemnity scheme, was to be read as preventing the insurers from escaping from liability in any way, even though the clause did not literally cover a discharge from liability by reason of a breach of warranty.[36]

28–77 Exceptions. It is not common for there to be many exceptions in professional indemnity policies but liability for libel and slander is frequently excluded and there is sometimes an exclusion for "claims brought about or contributed to by the dishonest, fraudulent, criminal or malicious act or omission of the insured, their predecessors in business or employees of the insured or their predecessors in business". It is doubtful whether these words add anything to the position at common law[37] and they may have been inserted merely for the avoidance of doubt. Of course, such conduct may be the subject of an extension to the policy (usually known as the "fidelity extension") and likewise liability for libel and slander may be the subject of a separate extension. It is increasingly common for professional indemnity policies to exclude liability for circumstances notified under any prior policy, because the policies are effected on a "claims made" basis.

28–78 Gratuitous advice. Some professional indemnity policies exclude liability where advice given by the insured is gratuitous. This exclusion will apply where the advice in genuinely gratuitous, in the sense of not being given under some arrangement under which remuneration is charged. Advice given in the context of an overall contract, with no separate fee, but included as part of the services offered for the original contract price, is covered.[38]

28–79 Conditions. Most of the conditions of a professional indemnity policy are common to all liability policies and have been discussed in that context. Thus, there are often conditions against repudiating or admitting liability without the written consent of the insurers, requiring the assured to notify the insurers in writing as soon as any claim is made against him and

---

[36] See para. 10–95 *ante*. In relation to the construction of a waiver clause generally, see *HIH Casualty and General Ins. Co. Ltd v. Chase Manhattan Bank* [2001] Lloyd's Rep. I.R. 703.

[37] See para. 28–54, *ante*.

[38] *Structural Polymer Systems v. Brown* [2000] Lloyd's Rep. I.R. 64.

requiring the assured to give such information and assistance to the insurers as they may require. One clause that is found only in professional indemnity policies is the Queen's Counsel clause, which has already been mentioned in the context of *West Wake Price & Co. v. Ching*.[39]

28–80 Q.C. clause. In its present form the Q.C. clause in a Lloyd's policy reads:

"... the Assured shall not be required to contest any legal proceedings unless a Queen's Counsel (to be mutually agreed upon by the Assured and the underwriter) shall advise that such proceedings should be contested."

In *West Wake Price & Co. v. Ching* Devlin J. analysed the K.C. clause in the policy before him as a supplementary contract outside the main contract of insurance.[40] It is submitted, with respect, that the clause was not inconsistent with the principles of indemnity insurance, and merely restricted the circumstances in which insurers could deny that liability was established by the terms of the assured's settlement with the third party. Be that as it may with regard to the K.C. clause in that case, it is submitted that there is no need to define the abbreviated Q.C. clause as a supplementary contract. It was held in *Simon, Haynes Barlas & Ireland v. Beer*[41] that, where the insurers do not put the clause into operation, they cannot complain if the assured settles a third party's claim.

28–81 Duty to disclose negligence. In accordance with ordinary principles of insurance law, it is the duty of the assured to disclose all facts which would influence a prudent insurer in determining whether to accept the risk. In the case of professional indemnity insurance, an assured must therefore disclose any negligent acts or omissions of which he knows and which might give rise to liability under the policy.[42] This casts a heavy burden on the assured at the beginning of the policy but when the policy is about to come to an end and the assured seeks renewal he may well feel that, if there are circumstances which might give rise to a claim, it will be in his interest to ensure that they do give rise to a claim before the policy expires rather than to be under an obligation to disclose such facts at the time for renewal. This is hardly a satisfactory situation and in order to avoid it a condition is frequently inserted in the policy in some such words as[43]:

---

[39] [1957] 1 W.L.R. 45; para. 28–59, *ante*.

[40] [1957] 1 W.L.R. 45.

[41] (1945) 78 Ll.L.Rep. 337, 377. The Q.C. clause appears to follow the maxim, "Always remember a bad settlement is better than a good case", a principle which has not always commended itself to insurers.

[42] See *Simon, Haynes, Barlas & Ireland v. Beer* (1945) 78 Ll.L.R. 337. The assured ought also to disclose any feature of the practice which may make him responsible for the negligence of others, such as the Lloyd's brokers' "piggy-back" facility: *Johns v. Kelly* [1986] 1 Lloyd's Rep. 468, 479–483. Any fraud of the assured must be disclosed even if it is the fraud of a partner or co-director of which the signer of the proposed form may be ignorant: *Yorkville v. Lissenden* (1986) 63 A.L.R. 611; *Advance v. Matthews* (1989) 85 A.L.R. 161. A clause excluding liability for loss resulting from an occurrence known to the assured and likely to give rise to a claim applies to cases where a partner knows or suspects that a consultant has made a negligent survey—*Tilley v. Dominion Ins. Co.* (1987) 254 E.G. 1056.

[43] See the more restrictive clause set out in the report of *Forney v. Dominion Insurance Co. Ltd* [1969] 1 W.L.R. 928. If a number of insurers subscribe the policy under separate contracts and one declines to renew, he can be required to give the extension cover on his own, while other underwriters renew in the ordinary way, *Touche Ross v. Baker* [1992] 2 Lloyd's Rep. 209.

"If during the subsistence of this policy the assured shall become aware of any occurrence which may subsequently give rise to a claim against him for breach of professional duty by reason of any negligent act, event or omission he shall give written notice to the Company of such occurrence immediately. Such notice having been given any such claim which may subsequently be made against the assured arising out of that occurrence shall for the purposes of this policy be deemed to have been made during the subsistence hereof."

28–82 The duty of the assured under such a clause has been considered in recent cases. They have adopted a liberal view of the obligation regarding notification of possible claims. In *Hamptons Residential Ltd v. Field*[44] the assured was bound, under condition 2 of their policy, to give notice as soon as possible:

"(a) any circumstances of which the assured shall first become aware which may give rise to a claim or loss against them or any of them ... (c) of the discovery (or reasonable cause for suspicion) of dishonesty or fraud on the part of a past or present ... employee. Such notice having been given to Underwriters the Assured shall give to the Underwriters as soon as possible full details in writing of the circumstance which may give rise to a claim or loss."

The assured estate agents employed a land buyer who, unknown to them, participated in mortgage frauds on lending institutions. Having been alerted to this by one institution, the assured notified the insurers of the fraud on that institution, and subsequently passed on details of their employee's other activities. It was held that notification of the one fraud was sufficient compliance with condition 2(c) to alert the insurers to the possibility of frauds committed by that employee, so that the subsequent giving of full details of other frauds was compliance with condition 2. Conditions 2(a) and (c) were treated as overlapping alternatives, and separate compliance with condition 2(a) was unnecessary.

28–83 In *J Rothschild Assurance Plc v. Collyear*[45] the claimant claimed under its professional indemnity policy in respect of losses it had suffered or might yet suffer arising from their obligation to compensate investors to whom it had sold private pensions. The requirement to compensate was imposed by the regulatory authorities, following a general review of pensions mis-selling. The notification clause was virtually identical to that in the policy in the *Hamptons* Case. It was held that a letter written to insurers identifying some 2,500 pensions issued by the claimant, describing the review and stating that these circumstances might "give rise to a claim by each client against the Assured" was sufficient compliance with the condition.

28–84 The duty to disclose negligence is in practice linked with other common exclusions and conditions, so as to reinforce the "claims made" nature of professional indemnity insurance.[46] Thus, a policy may expressly exclude liability arising out of any circumstances or occurrences notified

---

[44] [1998] 2 Lloyd's Rep. 248 (reversing [1997] 1 Lloyd's Rep. 302).
[45] [1999] Lloyd's Rep. I.R. 6.
[46] Discussed further in para. 28–85, *post*.

under any other policy attaching prior to the commencement of the policy, or which were known to the assured prior to the commencement of the policy. It is also common to find "special conditions" which allow the insurers to avoid the policy for non-disclosure or mis-representation only if there was fraudulent intent. They often further provide that where there are circumstances which could give rise to a claim which should have been notified under a preceding insurance, the insurers will remain liable but only to the extent and amount of the preceding insurance. The apparent conflict between such provisions was reconciled in *J Rothschild Assurance Plc v. Collyear*.[47] Rix J. held that the exclusion was to be given limited scope, and would apply where the assured had been unable to establish that its presentation of the risk was free from fraudulent intent, but where the insurers did not wish to avoid the whole policy and wished to be free to indemnify in respect of claims arising out of circumstances known prior to inception. If there was no fraudulent intent, the special conditions prevailed, removing the right of avoidance and guaranteeing cover limited to that under a preceding insurance.

28–85 Basis of cover. It is usual for professional indemnity policies to cover claims made during their currency whenever the act giving rise to liability takes place and difficulties can arise if the insurer declines to renew or offer run-off cover. It is unlikely that an insurer would do this wholly capriciously. If he learns of the existence of potential claims of which the assured has failed to notify him, the assured can hardly complain. If the assured has notified such claims the insurer will, in any event, be on risk if, as is usual, the policy contains some such clause as that mentioned in the previous paragraph. In the improbable event of the assured being unable to obtain cover elsewhere, his only remedy would be to argue that it is a breach of an implied duty of good faith for the insurer to decline to give cover for any future claims arising from business done in the policy year, but there would be formidable difficulties in the way of such an argument.[48]

28–86 Nature of a claim. The nature of what is a claim for the purposes of "claims made" cover has been considered in recent decisions. In *Robert Irving & Burns v. Stone*[49] the Court of Appeal held that a claim is made against the assured only when there is notification by the third party to the assured. So, when a writ was issued within the relevant policy period against the assured, but was not served in that period, and the assured knew nothing about the claim within that period, insurers were not liable. In *J Rothschild Assurance Plc v. Collyear*[50] it was held that "claims made" included a situation in which the assured had volunteered investigation and recompense to investors who had bought its pensions. Investors made claims by participating in a review process, or in accepting redress offered. This approach to construction was justified by the fact that the insurers had provided insurance against the background of a regulatory regime with

---

[47] [1999] Lloyd's Rep. I.R. 6. See also *Kumar v. AGF Ins. Ltd* [1998] 4 All E.R. 799 and para. 28–76, *ante*.

[48] *Cf.* Professor Goode's review of the sixth edition of this work: (1977) 93 L.Q.R. 458.

[49] [1998] Lloyd's Rep. I.R. 258. Reliance was placed upon the decision of the Ontario Court of Appeal in *St Paul Fire & Marine Ins. Co. v. Guardian Ins. Co. of Canada* [1983] 1 D.L.R. (4th) 342.

[50] [1999] Lloyd's Rep. I.R. 6.

which they were familiar, and which allowed for this method of claiming by investors.

3. EMPLOYERS' LIABILITY POLICIES

28–87 Compulsion to insure. An employer[51] carrying on any business in Great Britain[52] must insure and maintain insurance under one or more approved policies with an authorised insurer or insurers against liability for bodily injury or disease sustained by his employees arising out of and in the course of their employment in Great Britain in that business.[53] An approved policy must not contain provisions rendering the insurer's liability conditional upon the exercise of reasonable care, the compliance with safety legislation or the keeping of specified records by the employer or provisions defeating a claim by reason of acts or omissions by the employer subsequent to the event giving rise to the claims.[54] Neither must a policy contain any condition requiring a relevant employee to pay or an insured employer to pay the relevant employee the first amount of any claim or any aggregation of claims.[55] Cover must extend to an amount of five million pounds in respect of claims relating to any one or more of his employees arising out of any one occurrence.[56] A certificate of insurance must be displayed at every place of business where persons are employed.[57] It has been remarked that such a certificate can be misleading, inasmuch as there are clauses suspending cover under certain circumstances which are not proscribed by statute and of which the employee will be ignorant.[58]

[51] This applies to all employers with certain exceptions, for which, see the Employer's Liability (Compulsory Insurance) Act 1969, s.3; Local Government Act 1972, ss.1(10), 179(3); Employers' Liability (Compulsory Insurance) Exemption Regulations 1998 (S.I. 1998 No. 2573), reg. 9 and Sch. 2. The exemptions relate principally to bodies with exemption certificates from government departments; foreign and Commonwealth governments, and certain public bodies. Certain members of shipowners mutual assurance associations are exempted, as are employers required to insure under a compulsory motor insurance scheme by virtue of the fact that employees are carried in or use vehicles.

[52] Similar legislation is in force in Northern Ireland, the Channel Islands and the Isle of Man. The legislation extends to offshore installations, see the Offshore Installations (Application of the Employers' Liability (Compulsory Insurance) Act 1969) Regulations 1975) (S.I. 1975 No. 1289), and the Employers' Liability (Compulsory Insurance) Regulations 1998 (S.I. 1998 No. 2573).

[53] Employers' Liability (Compulsory Insurance) Act 1969, s.1(1).

[54] Employers' Liability (Compulsory Insurance) Regulations 1998 (S.I. 1998 No. 2573), reg. 2(1).

[55] *ibid.,* reg. 2(2). A relevant employee is an employee who is ordinarily resident in the United Kingdom, or who, though not ordinarily resident in the United Kingdom, has been employed on or from an offshore installation or associated structure for a continuous period of not less than seven days, or who, though not ordinarily resident in Great Britain, is present in Great Britain in the course of employment for a continuous period of not less than 14 days (*ibid.,* reg. 1(2)). The purpose of the regulations is to prevent a policy excess from affecting the employee's right to receive full compensation. It is permissible to provide that, if the employee is so compensated, the insurer will seek reimbursement for part of the claim from the employer: *Aitken v. Independent Ins. Co.* [2001] S.L.T. 376.

[56] *ibid.* reg. 3.

[57] Employers' Liability (Compulsory Insurance) Act 1969, s.4(1). For further provisions as to certificates, see the Employers' Liability (Compulsory Insurance) Exemption Regulations 1998 (S.I. 1998 No. 2573), regs 4–6 and Sch. 1.

[58] *Dunbar v. A. & B. Painters Ltd* [1986] 2 Lloyd's Rep. 38, 43, *per* Balcombe L.J. (clause excluding cover arising in connection with work carried out at over 40 feet from the ground).

28–88 Transfer of undertaking. Where there is a transfer of an undertaking pursuant to the Transfer of Undertakings (Protection of Employment) Regulations 1981,[59] the transferor employer's contingent or vested rights to claim under its employers' liability insurance are part of the rights in connection with the employee's contract of employment which are transferred.[60]

28–89 Extent of liability. Before 1946 an employer's liability policy would have protected the assured against all claims whether at common law or under the Employers' Liability Act 1880 or under the Workmen's Compensation Acts 1925 to 1945.[61] The Workmen's Compensation Acts have now been repealed and replaced by a compulsory scheme of national insurance[62] and the Employers' Liability Act 1880 has been repealed by the Law Reform (Personal Injuries) Act 1948,[63] which abolished the doctrine of common employment[64] and further provided that in assessing damages for personal injuries there should be taken into account, against loss of earnings or profits, one-half of the value of any rights which have accrued or probably will accrue to an employee in respect of industrial insurance benefit, industrial disablement benefit or sickness benefit for five years from the accrual of the cause of action.[65] Now, therefore, employers need only insure against their common law liability for negligence as modified by the Act of 1948.

It is to be noted that failure to take out employer's liability insurance on the part of a responsible director or company secretary, or connivance with that failure on the part of other directors, in the present state of the law, will not give rise to an action against such persons for breach of statutory duty.[66]

28–90 Scope of insurance. Employers' liability policies are contracts of indemnity[67] and are governed by the general principles of insurance applicable to fire and other indemnity policies. The question whether a particular workman is the employee of the assured for the purposes of an employers' liability policy may give rise to difficulty especially if a workman, employed and paid by one employer, is temporarily working for another. The general test for the purposes of liability, is not who employs and pays the

---

[59] S.I. 1981 No. 1794.

[60] *Martin v. Lancs. County Council* [2000] Lloyd's Rep. I.R. 665.

[61] A policy which insured an employer's liability "under or by virtue of the Employers Liability Act 1880" was held not to cover a case in which the employee had been awarded damages in a common law action of negligence, even though the same damages could have been recovered under the Act, *Morrison and Mason v. Scottish Employers' Liability Ins. Co.* (1888) 16 R. 212.

[62] See National Insurance (Industrial Injuries) Act 1946, replaced by National Insurance (Industrial Injuries) Act 1965, c. 52, which was in turn replaced by the Social Security Act 1975, c. 14.

[63] 11 & 12 Geo. 6, c. 41. *Cf.* Law Reform (Miscellaneous Provisions) Act (Northern Ireland) 1948, 11 & 12 Geo. 6, c. 23 (N.I.).

[64] *ibid.* s.1.

[65] *ibid.* s.2.

[66] *Richardson v. Pitt-Stanley* [1995] Q.B. 123; *contra, Cameron v. Fraser* 1990 S.L.T. 652, where, however, the claimant was unable to prove his loss.

[67] *British Cash and Parcel Conveyors Ltd v. Lamson Store Service Co. Ltd* [1908] 1 K.B. 1006, 1014–1015, *per* Fletcher Moulton L.J.; *Lancashire Ins. Co. v. Inland Revenue Commissioners* [1899] 1 Q.B. 353; *Dunbar v. A. & B. Painters Ltd* [1986] 2 Lloyd's Rep. 38, 42 citing *Fraser v. B.N. Furman Productions* [1967] 1 W.L.R. 898, 904.

workman, but "who has at the moment the right to control the manner of execution of the acts of the servant".[68]

But the policy may be limited to those who are under a contract of service with the assured; thus where an employee is paid by a firm of builders and not by the assured, the assured may find that he is liable to the employee but cannot recover under his policy.[69] Conversely, an employee does not cease to be under a contract of service to his regular employer merely because his services are temporarily lent to another, who neither pays his wages nor has the power to dismiss him.[70]

28–91 The usual form of employers' liability policy covers the employer against liability to any person under a contract of service with the employer for any injuries "arising out of and in the course of his employment". It was held in *Vandyke v. Fender*[71] that these words should receive the same interpretation as was given to them in the cases arising under the old Workmen's Compensation Acts[72] and that the specific interpretation adopted by the National Insurance (Industrial Injuries) Act 1946 should not be followed in construing the words in an insurance policy. It was accordingly held that a workman who suffered injury while a passenger in a car provided by his employer to take him to work was not injured in the course of his employment because he was not obliged by the terms of his contract of employment to travel to work in the vehicle provided.[73] The position is, of course, different if it is the duty of the employer to transport his employees to work.[74]

28–92 Ascertainment of premium. The premium in respect of employer's liability policies is often based upon the amount of wages paid by the insured to his employees during the year of insurance. At the commencement of the risk a premium is paid upon the estimated amount of wages, and the policy provides that the assured shall keep a proper wages book and render an account of the actual wages paid so that at the end of the year the premium may be adjusted and any balance due by or to the assured paid accordingly. Since the keeping of a proper wages book is a matter which affects only the amount of premium, it has been held that the condition requiring such a book to be kept is not a condition precedent to the insurer's liability on the policy unless it is clearly and unequivocally stated to be so.[75]

---

[68] *Mersey Docks and Harbour Board v. Coggins and Griffiths (Liverpool) Ltd* [1947] A.C. 1; Atiyah, *Vicarious Liability*, Ch. 18.

[69] *Etchells, Congdon and Muir Ltd v. Eagle Star and British Dominions Ins. Co.* (1928) 72 S.J. 242.

[70] *Denham v. Midland Employers' Mutual Ins. Co.* [1955] 2 Q.B. 437. The authorities are considered in *Johns v. Kelly* [1986] 1 Lloyd's Rep. 468, 474–476 by Bingham J. in determining when a person was "employed by" the insured firm of brokers.

[71] [1970] 2 Q.B. 292.

[72] *cf.* Halsbury, *Laws* (3rd ed.) vol. 27, paras 1403, *et seq.*

[73] [1970] 2 Q.B. 292, 304–306, *per* Lord Denning M.R., 309–311, *per* Sachs L.J.; following *St Helens Colliery Co. Ltd v. Hewitson* [1924] A.C. 59 and *Weaver v. Tredegar Iron and Coal Co. Ltd* [1940] A.C. 955; approved in *Smith v. Stages* [1989] A.C. 928, and applied by the Hong Kong Court of Appeal in *Low Kwai-chun v. Hong Kong Oxygen Co.* [1980] H.K.L.R. 420.

[74] *Paterson v. Costain & Press (Overseas) Ltd* [1979] 2 Lloyd's Rep. 204.

[75] *Re Bradley and Essex and Suffolk Accident Indemnity Society* [1912] 1 K.B. 415; distinguished as a "very special . . . case" in *Southern Union Ins. Co. v. Altimer* [1969] 2 N.S.W.R. 333.

28–93 Action for an account. If the employer declines to render a proper account of wages at the expiration of the risk the insurer may bring an action for an account and for payment of such balance of premium as may be found due. The insurer is not bound to show that there will be any balance in his favour nor is he bound to supply the assured with a form upon which to make his return. At the hearing of such an action for an account, the court will order an account to be delivered and the insurer will have the costs of the action down to the date of the order, subsequent costs being reserved.[76] It is no defence to an action for an account to allege that an account was rendered to the brokers, since the brokers are not the agents of the insurer.[77]

28–94 Claims. It is beyond the scope of this work to discuss in detail the types of claims which may be made against employers, and to which liability insurance may respond. As with other forms of insurance, the employer must comply with any relevant conditions precedent to liability.[78] Employers, and their insurers, are not infrequently confronted with claims which are dishonest or exaggerated. It is quite common for private investigators to be employed to investigate suspicious claims. Such investigations may involve an element of illegality or deception; the evidence so obtained will generally be admissible if relevant, subject to the overriding criterion that it does not cause injustice or unfairness.[79]

28–95 Directors and Officers Liability. Section 310(1) of the Companies Act 1985 declares void any contractual provision indemnifying any officer of the company in respect of any negligence, default, breach of duty or breach of trust of which he may be guilty in relation to the company. This made it doubtful, to say the least, whether company directors or other officers could obtain insurance for any personal liability. The position was ameliorated by section 137(1) of the Companies Act 1989 which provides that nothing in section 310 prevents a company from purchasing or maintaining for an officer (or auditor) of the company insurance against such personal liability. It is thus probably still ineffective for a company officer to take out his own insurance but, if the company takes it out, that will be effective.

---

[76] *General Accident Ass. Corporation v. Day* (1904) 21 T.L.R. 88.
[77] *Garthwaite v. Rowland* (1948) 81 Ll.L.R. 417.
[78] *LEC v. Glover* [2001] Lloyd's Rep. I.R. 315 (failure to comply with fire watch provision when hot work carried out).
[79] *McNally v. RG Manufacturing* [2001] Lloyd's Rep. I.R. 379.

CHAPTER 29

MOTOR VEHICLE INSURANCE

29–1 The modern motor-vehicle policy covers the assured against a variety of different risks. In addition to providing cover against third-party risks and, in many instances, the costs of litigation associated therewith, it provides cover against the risk of personal injury or death to the assured while travelling in the insured vehicle, the risks of loss of or damage to the vehicle itself, and, frequently, a variety of ancillary risks such as loss or damage to the contents of the car, destruction of or damage to the garage in which the car is kept and the cost of legal representation in the criminal courts.[1] Accordingly a motor insurance policy can be at the same time a liability cover, a personal accident insurance and a property insurance. These characteristics have been responsible for the wide range of terms and conditions usually found in motor policies, and they also create a far-reaching catalogue of facts material to the several risks embraced by the policy which have to be considered at inception or renewal.[2] In this chapter we consider aspects of these risks peculiar to motor-vehicle insurance,[3] the classes of persons entitled to bring, and liable to meet, claims for indemnity in respect of motor-vehicle accidents,[4] and certain terms and conditions generally found in motor policies.[5] It must be emphasised that motor insurance has been the subject of much legislation, originally enacted in the Road Traffic Acts 1930[6] and 1934,[7] and now consolidated in Part VI of the Road Traffic Act 1988,[8] to which subsequent references to statutory provisions relate except where the contrary is stated.

---

[1] The leading monograph was Shawcross, *Motor Insurance* (2nd ed., 1949), inevitably out of date. See also Ivamy, *Fire & Motor Insurance* (1996).

[2] See paras 17–50 to 17–51, *ante.*

[3] See paras 29–2 to 29–15, *ante.*

[4] See paras 29–16 to 29–54, *ante.*

[5] See paras 29–59 to 29–87, *ante.*

[6] 20 & 21 Geo, 5, c. 43.

[7] 24 & 25 Geo, 5, c. 50.

[8] 1988, c. 52. Many of the changes recently introduced are the result of E.C. Directives. For a useful description of the history, see *Norman v. Aziz* [2000] Lloyd's Rep. I.R. 52 at 54–56. The latest Directive (Directive 2000/26/E.C.), which must be implemented by January 20, 2003, is designed to ensure equivalent protection for the victims of road accidents injured in a member State that is not their State of residence. In some member States, the liability that compulsory insurance backs up is in some circumstances strict rather than fault-based. For the requirements of E.C. law in this respect, see *Ferreira v. Companhia de Seguros Mundial Confiança SA* [2000] All E.R. (D.) 1197.

(a) *Risks Covered*

29–2 Compulsory cover against third party risks. The general effect of section 143 of the Road Traffic Act 1988 is to make compulsory insurance against liability in respect of death or bodily injury to third parties, including passengers, and in respect of liability for damage to a third party's property. The section makes it an offence for any person[9] to use,[10] or to cause or permit any other person to use,[11] a motor vehicle[12] on a road or other public place[13] unless there is in force in relation to such use a policy of insurance or such a security in respect of third-party risks as complies with the requirements of the Act.[14]

29–3 Using and causing or permitting use. The meaning of these words, which are the core words in section 143, has been the subject of a fair amount of case law.[15] "Use" includes the leaving of a car on a road, even though it is incapable at present of being mechanically propelled.[16] However, the word implies an element of controlling, managing or operating the vehicle at the relevant time and does not include "use" as a passenger,[17] unless the latter

[9] "Person" includes a limited company (*Briggs v. Gibson's Bakery Ltd* [1948] N.I. 165) and is not confined to the owner of a vehicle (*Williamson v. O'Keefe* [1947] 1 All E.R. 307).

[10] See para. 29–3, below.

[11] See *ibid.*

[12] "Motor vehicle" is defined by s.185(1) as "a mechanically propelled vehicle intended or adapted for use on roads." A vehicle without its propulsive unit may be within the section if there is reasonable prospect of it being made mobile again (*Newberry v. Simmonds* [1961] 2 Q.B. 345; *Law v. Thomas* (1964) 108 Sol. Jo. 158) but not otherwise: *Lawrence v. Howlett* [1952] 2 All E.R. 74; *Smart v. Allan* [1963] 1 Q.B. 291. *A fortiori*, a vehicle with its propulsive unit but otherwise propelled is inside the section: *Floyd v. Bush* [1953] 1 W.L.R. 242. A vehicle is "intended" for use on the road if that was reasonably to be contemplated as one of its uses. It is "adapted" to that end if fit and apt for road use: *Burns v. Currell* [1963] 2 Q.B. 433, 441. A farm tractor has come within the section (*Woodward v. James Young* 1958 S.C. (J) 28), while dumper trucks, a go-kart and a Ford Anglia prepared for racing were not (*Daley v. Hargreaves* [1961] 1 W.L.R. 487; *Burns v. Currell, supra*; *Brown v. Abbott* (1965) 109 Sol. Jo. 437), nor was a motor cycle adapted for "scrambling": *Chief Constable of Avon and Somerset v. Fleming* [1987] 1 All E.R. 318. A pedestrian-controlled motor mower is not a motor vehicle: see s.189.

[13] Section 192(1) defines a road as "any highway and any other road to which the public has access and including bridges over which a road passes." The extension of s.143 to a "public place" was made by the Motor Vehicles (Compulsory Insurance) Regulations 2000 (S.I. 2002 No. 726), following the decision of the House of Lords in *Cutter v. Eagle Star Ins. Co. Ltd* [1998] 1 W.L.R. 1647 to the effect that a car park would not normally be regarded as a road. See also *Griffin v. Squires* [1958] 1 W.L.R. 1106; *Randall v. M.I.B.* [1968] 1 W.L.R. 1900 (school driveway); *Oxford v. Austin* [1981] R.T.R. 416. See also on this section *Price v. D.P.P.* [1990] R.T.R. 413; *D.P.P. v. Coulman* [1993] R.T.R. 230; *McGurk v. Coster* [1995] C.L.Y. 2912; *Severn Trent Water v. Williams* [1995] C.L.Y. 3724; *O'Connor v. Royal Ins. Co.* [1996] C.L.Y. 463. See especially now, [1997] 1 W.L.R. 1082.

[14] Set out in s.145; see para. 29–5, *post.* As to securities, see para. 29–10, *post.*

[15] See also para. 29–55, *post,* where the matter is also discussed in the context of the common law remedy for breach of statutory duty.

[16] *Elliott v. Grey* [1960] 1 Q.B. 367; *Dunthorne v. Bentley, The Times,* March 11, 1996. It is otherwise if the vehicle is totally immovable: *Thomas v. Hooper* [1986] R.T.R. 1., unless it can be made to run after performing mechanical repairs—*Pumbien v. Vines* [1996] R.T.R. 37.

[17] *Brown v. Roberts* [1965] 1 Q.B. 1 at 15, *per* Megaw J. Here, the passenger in a car was negligent in opening her door and thereby injured a pedestrian. It was held that she was not using the car in the statutory sense, because she had no control over the vehicle, so the driver was not therefore causing or permitting her to use it and thus not liable in damages for breach of statutory duty in not insuring her against her potential liability; see also *A. v. Bundy* (1960) 58 L.G.R. 344; *Hatton v. Hall* [1999] Lloyd's Rep. I.R. 313 (pillion passenger not a "user" of a motor cycle).

owns the vehicle,[18] or is the driver's employer or is controlling and enjoying the use of the vehicle for his own purposes.[19]

The word "cause" involves an express or positive mandate to use a car in a particular way, whereas "permit" is looser, and merely denotes express implied licence to use a vehicle.[20] In *McLeod v. Buchanan*,[21] a man appointed his brother as manager of his farm and bought him a car that was insured for business and private use. The car having proved unsatisfactory, the man authorised his brother to buy a van instead; this was insured for business use only, but was in fact used for private purposes. It was held that the man had permitted his brother to use the van while uninsured. The van was given to him for the same purposes as the car, and the brother was not told not to use it for private purposes. In *Lyons v. May*,[22] a garage owner was driving a car back from the garage after repair, at the request of the car's owner. It was held that the latter had caused or permitted the use of the car. In contrast, in *Watkins v. O'Shaughnessy*,[23] an auctioneer sold a car which the purchaser drove away immediately without, to the auctioneer's knowledge, being insured. It was held that the auctioneer had not caused or permitted the use of the car because, having sold it, he not longer had any control over it. In *Thompson v. Lodwick*,[24] a driving instructor was held not to have caused or permitted his pupil to use the vehicle when the latter owned it.

29–4 Exempted classes of vehicles. The following classes of vehicles are totally exempt from Part VI of the 1988 Act:

    (a) invalid carriages[25];
    (b) tramcars or trolley vehicles operated under statutory powers[26];
    (c) vehicles in the public service of the Crown.[27]

The obligation under section 143 to insure against third party risks does not apply to the following classes of vehicles:

    (a) vehicles owned by a person who has deposited and keeps deposited with the Accountant-General of the Supreme Court the sum of

[18] *Cobb v. Williams* [1973] R.T.R. 113.

[19] *B. (A Minor) v. Knight* [1981] R.T.R. 136; *Leathley v. Tatton* [1980] R.T.R. 21; *Stinton v. M.I.B.* [1995] R.T.R. 167; *O'Mahony v. Joliffe* [1999] Lloyd's Rep. I.R. 321. It is submitted, with respect, that *Bennett v. Richardson* [1980] R.T.R. 358 (passenger driven by business partner in firm's van not using the van) is difficult to reconcile with the other decisions on the meaning of "use".

[20] Lord Wright in *McLeod v. Buchanan* [1940] 2 All E.R. 179 at 187. Permission for these purposes may be granted by one who is not the owner, but who is responsible for the care, management or control of the vehicle: *Lloyd v. Singleton* [1953] 1 Q.B. 357.

[21] *ibid.*

[22] [1948] 2 All E.R. 1062.

[23] [1939] 1 All E.R. 385.

[24] [1983] R.T.R. 76.

[25] s.143(4). An invalid carriage is defined as a mechanically propelled vehicle with a weight of not more than 5 cwt which is specially designed and constructed and not merely adapted for the use of a person suffering from some physical defect or disability and is used solely by such person.

[26] s.193.

[27] Pt. VI of the Act is not included among the sections made applicable to such vehicles by s.183, and it is submitted that accordingly they are exempted.

£500,000 at a time when the vehicle is being driven under the owner's control[28];

(b) vehicles owned by certain local and other public authorities, while being driven under their control[29];

(c) vehicles owned by a police authority while being driven under the owner's control, or to a vehicle at a time when it is being driven for police purposes by or under the direction of a constable, or a police employee[30];

(d) vehicles owned by the Service Authorities for the National Criminal Intelligence Service or National Crime Squad when being driven under their control, or a vehicle at a time when it is being driven for the purposes of the body maintained by either of the Authorities by or under the direction of a constable, or by a person employed by either Authority[31];

(e) vehicles being driven on a journey for salvage purposes under the Merchant Shipping Act 1995,[32] or used for certain purposes under the Army or Air Force Acts 1955[33];

(f) vehicles owned by a national health service body,[34] by a Primary Care Trust[35] or by the Commission for Health Improvement at a time when the vehicle is being driven under the owner's control[36];

(g) ambulances owned by an NHS Trust[37] at a time when the vehicle is being driven under the owner's control[38];

(h) vehicles made available by the Secretary of State to any person, body or local authority for certain purposes under the National Health Service Act 1977, while being used on the terms on which it is made available.[39]

29–5 Essentials of valid policy. To comply with the Act, policies must be

---

[28] s.144(1), as amended by s.20 Road Traffic Act 1991. The Secretary of State may by order, subject to the affirmative resolution procedure, increase the sum required. "Being driven under the owner's control" means being driven by the owner or by a servant of the owner in the course of his employment or otherwise subject to the control of the owner: s.161(1). A sum deposited under s.144(1) cannot be used to discharge any other liabilities of the depositor so long as there are undischarged liabilities that would require to be insured against under s.145. Section 144(1) is supplemented by the Motor Vehicles (Third Party Risks Deposits) Regulations 1992 (S.I. 1992 No. 1284), which provide the detail as to the making of deposits and allow for withdrawal of them in appropriate cases, e.g. when the depositor satisfies the court that he intends to comply with s.143 in some other way or ceases to own a motor vehicle.

[29] s.144(2)(a), which sets out the types of local authorities exempted. These do not include parish councils or community councils.

[30] s.144(2)(b). See *Jones v. Chief Constable of Bedfordshire* [1987] R.T.R. 332 (police officer on duty using his own vehicle for police purposes is covered by the exemption).

[31] s.144(2)(ba), inserted by the Police Act 1997, s.134(1).

[32] s.144(2)(c).

[33] s.144(2)(d).

[34] As defined in s.60(7) of the National Health Service and Community Care Act 1990.

[35] Established under s. 16A of the National Health Service Act 1997.

[36] s.144(2)(da), as inserted by the National Health Service and Community Care Act 1990, Sch. 8 and the Health Act 1999 (Supplementary, Consequential etc Provisions) Order 2000 (S.I. 2000 No. 90).

[37] Established under Pt I of the National Health Service and Community Care Act 1990 or the National Health Service (Scotland) Act 1978.

[38] s.144(2)(db), as inserted by the National Health Service and Community Care Act 1990, Sch. 8.

[39] s.144(2)(e); similar provision is made in s.144(2)(f) regarding the National Health (Scotland) Act 1978.

issued by an authorised insurer, *i.e.* a person or body of persons carrying on motor vehicle insurance business in Great Britain, who is a member of the Motor Insurers' Bureau.[40] A policy must insure the persons specified in it:

(i) against liability[41] in respect of death or bodily injury to any person or damage to property caused by or arising out of, the use of the vehicle[42] on a road or other public place[43] in Great Britain[44]; "person" includes any passenger,[45] but not the driver[46];

(ii) in the case of a vehicle normally based in the territory of another E.C. Member State, against any civil liability occurring as a result of an event related to the use of the vehicle in Great Britain if:

    (a) the law of that member State would require such insurance in respect of an event occurring in that country and

    (b) the cover required by that law would be higher than that required by (i) above[47];

(iii) in the case of a vehicle normally based in Great Britain, against any liability in respect of the use of the vehicle[48] in the territory other than Great Britain of each of the Member States of the E.C. according to

    (a) the law on compulsory motor vehicle insurance of the State where the event occurred or

    (b) if it would give higher cover, the law which would apply if the place where the event occurred was in Great Britain[49];

(iv) against the statutory liabilities for payment for emergency treatment.[50]

Insurance is not required in respect of the following:

(a) the liability of an employer to an employee in respect of death or bodily injury out of and in the course of his employment, where there is effective cover under the Employers' Liability (Compulsory Insurance) Act 1969[51]; however, a policy under the 1969 Act is not now required to cover motor liability risks;[52]

---

[40] s.145(2) and (5). As to authorised insurers, see Ch. 34, *post*. Cessation of M.I.B. membership does not affect policies issued or obligations arising before such cessation: s.145(6).

[41] Including liability to a husband for the loss of the society and services of his wife: *Ladd v. Jones* [1975] R.T.R. 67.

[42] "Vehicle" is defined by s.185(1); see note 12, *ante*. This may include death or injury arising from the vehicle's cargo: *Fire and All Risks Insurance v. Turner* (1976) 50 A.L.J.R. 767 (accidental discharge of gas being carried in the vehicle).

[43] See note 13, *ante*.

[44] s.145(3)(a).

[45] Unless they are covered by an effective employer's liability policy as described below.

[46] *R. v. Secretary of State for Transport, ex parte National Insurance Guarantee Corporation plc, The Times*, June 3, 1996.

[47] s.145(3)(aa), inserted by the Motor Vehicles (Compulsory Insurance) Regulations 1992 (S.I. 1992 No. 3036).

[48] And of any trailer, whether or not coupled.

[49] s.145(3)(b), as amended by the Motor Vehicles (Compulsory Insurance) Regulations 1992 (S.I. No. 1992 3036).

[50] See para. 29–11, *post*.

[51] s.149(4) and s.149(4A) as inserted by the Motor Vehicles (Compulsory Insurance) Regulations 1992 (S.I. 1992 No. 3036). As to the 1969 Act, see Ch. 28, *ante*.

[52] Employers' Liability (Compulsory Insurance) Regulations 1998 (S.I. 1998 No. 2573), Sch. 2, para. 14.

(b) cover in respect of property damage of more than £250,000 "caused by, or arising out of, any one accident involving the vehicle"[53];

(c) liability in respect of damage to the vehicle;

(d) liability in respect of damage to goods carried for hire or reward in or on the vehicle or in or on any trailer drawn by the vehicle[54];

(e) liability of a person in respect of damage to property in his custody or under his control[55]; and

(f) any contractual liability.[56]

The policy must cover liability for death or injury irrespective of whether it was caused accidentally or intentionally.[57] The liability of an insured owner of a vehicle towards someone permitted to drive or ride it is not required to be covered,[58] nor does the Act require a policy to be in force covering the personal liability of the driver of the vehicle.[59] As Humphreys J. said in *John T. Ellis Ltd v. Hinds*[60]:

> "It is not any particular person who uses the vehicle who is required by section 35 to be insured. What is required is that the user on the road by the person or persons, in fact, using the road should be covered by insurance in respect of third party risks."

(b) *Policy "In Force"*

Section 143(1) requires there to be "in force" at the material time a policy of insurance covering the then user of the vehicle against third-party risks.

29–6 Problems can arise where policies contain clauses restricting the liability of the insurers in various ways, *e.g.* by reference to the qualifications of the driver of the vehicle or the purposes for which it is used.[61] Whether or not the policy is in force when the restrictions are breached depends upon the precise language in which they are expressed. Thus in *John T. Ellis Ltd v.*

---

[53] s.161(3) provides that any reference to an accident includes a reference to two or more causally related accidents. Note that there is a broad construction of "accident" in this context: see *South Staffordshire Tramways Co. v. Sickness and Accident Assurance Association* [1891] 1 Q.B. 402, where a liability policy effected by a tramway company had a limit of "£250 in respect of any one accident." It was held that when a tram overturned injuring 40 passengers, each passenger suffered an accident and therefore the insurer's maximum liability was 40 times £250.

[54] This does not exclude liability in respect of goods carried gratuitously, although the next exception may do so.

[55] *e.g.* the belongings of passengers. It is unclear how far this exception goes. It would probably apply to luggage in the boot of a car, although it can hardly apply to items of clothing or other things on the person of a passenger.

[56] s.145(4).

[57] *Hardy v. M.I.B.* [1964] 2 Q.B. 745; *Gardner v. Moore* [1984] A.C. 548. If death or injury is caused intentionally, the assured himself will not be entitled to recover on the policy (see para. 14–30, *ante*), but the injured third party will have a claim under s.151 (see para. 29–23, *post*).

[58] *Cooper v. M.I.B.* [1985] 1 Q.B. 575.

[59] *John T. Ellis v. Hinds* [1947] K.B. 475; *March v. Moores* [1949] 2 K.B. 208; *Lees v. Motor Insurers' Bureau* [1952] 2 All E.R. 511, 513; *Lister v. Romford Ice & Cold Storage Co. Ltd* [1957] A.C. 555, 582, 593. In *Lees*, Lord Goddard C.J. said that in *Ellis* the Divisional Court had overruled the contrary view of Atkinson J. in *Sutch v. Burns* [1943] 2 All E.R. 441 (not considered in the Court of Appeal in [1944] 1 K.B. 406). Whether this be correct or not, clearly *Sutch v. Burns* cannot now stand with the views expressed in *Lister*.

[60] [1947] K.B. 475, 487.

[61] Certain types of restrictions are invalid against third parties by reason of s.148, see para. 29–30, *post*.

Hinds,[62] the appellants held a policy of insurance covering their liability to third parties, subject to an exception excluding liability whilst the insured vehicle was being driven with the general consent of the assured by any person who to the knowledge of the assured did not hold a licence to drive it. An accident happened when the insured vehicle was being driven by a boy of 17 who neither held nor was qualified to hold a driving licence. The appellants neither knew the age of the boy, nor that he did not hold a licence. Accordingly the exception clause did not operate, the policy was in force when the boy was driving the vehicle, and the appellants' conviction was quashed. Had the policy excluded cover while the vehicle was driven by a driver without a licence regardless of the consent and knowledge of the assured, the policy would not have been in force and an offence would have been committed.[63] Where a car owner permits another to drive his car in such circumstances in the honest but erroneous belief that the driver holds a valid licence, he is guilty of permitting the use of the car without the required insurance being in force, but if he makes permission conditional upon the driver being covered by insurance then no offence is committed by him even if the condition is broken.[64]

29–7 When a policy is voidable, for instance on account of misrepresentation, it remains "in force" for purposes of section 143 unless and until the insurer takes steps to avoid the policy as provided in section 152.[65] No offence is committed under section 143 where a policy, which covers third-party risks, allows the vehicle to be driven in a manner constituting an offence under the Road Traffic Act, even if a separate offence is committed by the user of the vehicle.[66]

29–8 Evidence that policy "in force". Where there is a doubt as to whether a particular use is covered by the policy owing to an ambiguous exceptions clause or other term, it appears that the court may accept evidence from the insurers, that they regard themselves as on risk, as establishing that cover was in force.[67] But such evidence will be of no account if the construction of the relevant clause is clear,[68] or if the question is whether or not an enforceable contract of insurance has been concluded,[69] or if the relevant user is forbidden by law.[70] It seems that the facility of consultation with

---

[62] [1947] K.B. 475.

[63] *Baugh v. Crago* [1976] 1 Lloyd's Rep. 563. As to restrictions imposed on the user of the vehicle compare *Leggate v. Brown* [1950] 2 All E.R. 564 (no offence) with *Kerridge v. Rush* [1952] 2 Lloyd's Rep. 305 (conviction). See also *Goodwin v. Leckey* [1946] N.I. 40 (named driver policy); *Williamson v. Wilson* [1947] 1 All E.R. 306 (named driver); *Sands v. O'Connell* [1981] R.T.R. 42 (under-age driver).

[64] *Newbury v. Davis* [1974] R.T.R. 367; *Baugh v. Crago* [1976] 1 Lloyd's Rep. 563.

[65] See para. 29–26, *post*; *Durrant v. McClaren* [1956] 2 Lloyd's Rep. 170. *Sed aliter* if a policy never comes into existence at all, because it cannot then be said that insurers remain liable to injured persons under s.152 and that there is a policy in force to satisfy s.143: *Evans v. Lewis* [1964] 1 Lloyd's Rep. 258 (policy expressed to cover class of persons other than driver of hired car).

[66] *Leggate v. Brown* [1950] 2 All E.R. 564; contrast *Robb v. M'Knechie* 1936 S.C. (J) 25; *Kerridge v. Rush* [1952] 2 Lloyd's Rep. 305.

[67] *Carnhill v. Rowland* [1953] 1 W.L.R. 380.

[68] *Carnhill v. Rowland, ante*; *Boss v. Kingston* [1963] 1 W.L.R. 99, 105.

[69] *Taylor v. Allon* [1966] 1 Q.B. 304.

[70] *Mumford v. Hardy* [1956] 1 W.L.R. 163.

underwriters was intended for the assistance of prosecuting authorities rather than for a court deciding an issue of law.[71]

29–9 Insurance certificate. A policy[72] is of no effect for the purposes of these provisions of the Act until the insurer has delivered to the person by whom the policy is effected a certificate of insurance in a prescribed form.[73] "For the purposes ... of the Act" means for the purpose of insuring the driver against the liabilities against which he is required to be insured. If a certificate has not been delivered, the insurers are not at risk in respect of such liabilities,[74] but the policy can be effective at common law and a certificate subsequently issued can operate retrospectively.[75] "Person by whom the policy is effected" means the insured or his agent.[76] Where a finance company supplying a car on hire purchase took delivery of the certificate, which was hypothecated to them as security, the Act was not complied with,[77] and the driver was placed in breach of the section[78] requiring him to produce his certificate on request by a police constable. A certificate of insurance is not itself the contract of insurance and cannot be the policy of insurance required by section 143 of the Act.[79] Detailed regulations have been made under the Act prescribing the form, time of issue, replacement, and record of issue of such certificates.[80] The issue of a certificate does not estop the insurer from pleading subsequently that the policy was obtained by fraud.[81]

29–10 Requirements in respect of securities. A security, in order to comply with the requirements of the Act, must:

(a) be given by an authorised insurer, or by some body of persons which carries on in the United Kingdom the business of giving such securities, and has deposited and keeps deposited with the Account-ant-General of the Supreme Court the sum of £500,000 in respect of that business, and,

(b) consist of an undertaking to make good, in the case of public service vehicles up to £25,000, and in other cases up to £5,000, any failure by the owner of the vehicle, or such other persons as may be specified, duly to discharge such liabilities as are by section 145 of the Act required to be covered by a policy of insurance.[82]

---

[71] *Edwards v. Griffiths* [1953] 1 W.L.R. 1199, 1202.
[72] "Policy" includes a cover note: s.161(1).
[73] s.147(1).
[74] *General Accident Fire and Life Assurance Corp. v. Shuttleworth* (1938) 60 Ll.L.R. 301, 306, *per* Humphreys J.
[75] *Motor and General Ins. Co. v. Cox* [1990] 1 W.L.R. 1443.
[76] *Starkey v. Hall* [1936] 2 All E.R. 18, 20–21.
[77] *Starkey v. Hall, ante.*
[78] s.40 of the 1930 Act, now s.165(1).
[79] *Biddle v. Johnston* [1965] 2 Lloyd's Rep. 121.
[80] Motor Vehicle (Third Party Risks) Regulations 1972, (S.I. 1972 No. 1217) as amended by S.I. 1974 No. 792. These also provide for the recognition of equivalent documents issued by insurers in other European countries. The Motor Vehicles (International Motor Insurance Card) Regulations 1971, (S.I. 1971 No. 792) as amended, prescribe the forms of cards to be carried by temporary visitors to this country who wish to be insured by foreign insurers.
[81] *McCormick v. National Motor Insurance Co.* (1934) 40 Com.Cas. 76.
[82] s.146, as amended by s.20 Road Traffic Act 1991. The Secretary of State may by order, subject to the affirmative resolution procedure, increase the sum required.

29–11 Hospital treatment and emergency medical attention. Sections 157 and 158[83] provide that where any payment is made (whether or not with an admission of liability) by an authorised insurer under or in consequence of a policy issued under Part VI of the Act in respect of the death of or bodily injury to any person arising out of the use of a motor-vehicle on a road or in a place to which the public have a right of access, and the person who has so died or been bodily injured has to the knowledge of the authorised insurer received treatment at a hospital in respect of the injury so arising, there shall also be paid by the authorised insurer to such hospital the expenses reasonably incurred in affording such treatment, and provision is also made for payment to a doctor who has given emergency treatment.[84] A policy is one issued under Part VI if it gives the cover required by the Act and complies with the statutory requirements, notwithstanding that it includes cover beyond the statutory minimum; and "any person" means "any person" and not "any person of the class required to be covered by the Act".[85] For the sections to apply, the insurers must have knowledge of the treatment before payment to the third party; it is not sufficient that they should have acquired this knowledge before the issue of a writ by the hospital authority claiming payment of the expenses of treatment.[86]

A broader scheme for the recovery of National Health Service charges was introduced by the Road Traffic (NHS Charges) Act 1999.[87] This applies if a person (described as the "traffic casualty") has suffered injury, or has suffered injury and died, as a result of the use of a motor vehicle on a road, a compensation payment has been made in respect of the injury or death and the traffic casualty received NHS treatment[88] at a health service hospital in respect of his injury.[89] A compensation payment includes a payment made by an authorised insurer under, or in consequence of, a policy issued under section 145 of the 1988 Act and one made by the owner of a vehicle where a security has been issued or a deposit made under the 1988 Act; it also includes a payment made in pursuance of a compensation scheme for motor accidents,[90] which effectively means the Motor Insurers' Bureau under one of the agreements described later in this chapter, but it does not include a payment made under section 158 of the 1988 Act.[91] Payments made outside the United Kingdom and payments made voluntarily, as well as in pursuance of a court order or agreement, are covered,[92] and it is irrelevant whether a payment is made with or without an admission of liability.[93] The person

---

[83] As amended by the Road Traffic Accidents (Payment for Treatment) Order 1995, (S.I. 1995 No. 889) in respect of the levels of payment.

[84] Similar provisions apply where there is a security in force, or the owner has made a deposit according to s.144(1) and the Motor Vehicles (Third Party Risks Deposits) Regulations 1992 (S.I. 1992 No. 1284).

[85] *Barnet Group Hospital Management Committee v. Eagle Star Insurance Co.* [1960] 1 Q.B. 107. *Cf. Royal Victoria Hospital v. London Guarantee and Accident Corp.* [1937] N.I. 64.

[86] *Barnet Group Hospital Management Committee v. Eagle Star Ins. Co., ante.*

[87] See also the Road Traffic (NHS Charges) Regulations 1999 (S.I. 1999 No. 785).

[88] Defined in s.1(6).

[89] s.1(1).

[90] Defined in s.17.

[91] s.1(3).

[92] s.1(4).

[93] s.1(9)

making the compensation payment is liable to pay the appropriate NHS charges[94] to the Secretary of State in respect of the treatment.[95] The Secretary of State must account to the appropriate hospital.[96]

29–12 Passengers. Before 1972 it was not compulsory to insure in respect of liability for death or bodily injury sustained by passengers carried in the insured vehicle unless they were carried for hire or reward or by reason or in pursuance of a contract of employment.[97] There were therefore decisions on the meaning of the phrase "by reason of or in pursuance of a contract of employment".[98] Since this phrase does not appear in the current legislation[99] and will not appear in current motor policies as opposed to employers' liability policies, little purpose would be served by examining the relevant decisions in this chapter. Under the present legislation policies must cover passengers on the same footing as any other injured third parties.

29–13 Under the former law, the advice often offered to drivers whose policies did not cover liability to passengers was to obtain from the passengers an agreement that they were carried "at their own risk" or something to the same effect. Despite having removed the incentive to such agreements, the legislature proceeded in 1971 to pass legislation avoiding them.[1] Section 149(2) provides that when a person uses a motor vehicle under circumstances requiring third-party insurance,[2] any antecedent agreement (whether intended to be legally binding or not) between the user and a passenger is of no effect in so far as it purports to negative or restrict any such liability of the user in respect of persons carried[3] in or upon the vehicle as is required by section 145[4] to be covered by a policy of insurance, or to impose any conditions with respect to the enforcement of any such liability of the user. Furthermore, the fact that a person so carried has willingly accepted as his the risk of negligence on the part of the user is not to be treated as negativing such liability of the user. The effect of these provisions is to

---

[94] This is the amount or amounts specified in a certificate (s.1(7)). The detailed provisions on certificates are contained in ss.2–5, and ss.6–10, supplemented by the Road Traffic (NHS Charges) (Reviews and Appeals) Regulations 1999 (S.I. 1999 No. 786) and the Road Traffic (NHS Charges) (Reviews and Appeals) (Scotland) Regulations 1999 (S.I. 1999 No. 1843), make provision for reviews and appeals. Sections 11 and 12, supplemented by the Road Traffic (NHS Charges) Regulations 1999 (S.I. 1999 No. 785), deal with the provision of information to, and the use of information by, the Secretary of State.

[95] s.1(2).

[96] s.13.

[97] Road Traffic Act 1960, s.203(4)(b), repealed by the Motor Vehicles (Passenger Insurance) Act 1971, s.1(1).

[98] See the seventh edition of this work at note 68 to para. 2063. The decisions on the phrase "for hire or reward" are referred to in para. 29–14, *infra*. See also *Tan Keng Hong v. New India Ass. Co.* [1978] 1 W.L.R. 297 (P.C.)"by reason of or in pursuance of a contract of employment".

[99] Nor can it because of the provisions of EC Directive 90/232, which requires insurance against liability for injuries to passengers throughout the EC; as already indicated, the United Kingdom has required such insurance since 1972.

[1] Motor Vehicles (Passenger Insurance) Act 1971, s.1(2), now s.149(2).

[2] i.e., circumstances in which s.143(1) requires either a policy of insurance or a security to be in force.

[3] s.149(4) provides that persons entering, getting on to, or alighting from a vehicle are included within the meaning of "persons carried".

[4] See para. 29–5, *ante*.

eliminate the doctrine of volenti non fit injuria from the field of motor accident cases involving passengers.

29–14 Car sharing. Section 150 aims to ensure that a policy or security is not invalidated by the assured's participation in a non-profit-making car sharing arrangement. Subject to conditions described below, the use of a vehicle on a journey in the course of which one or more passengers are carried at separate fares is to be treated as either:

(1) falling within a restriction limiting the use of the vehicle to specified purposes (for example, social, domestic and pleasure purposes)[5] of a non-commercial character, or

(2) not falling within an exclusion relating to use of the vehicle for hire or reward,[6] business or commercial use of the vehicle or use of the vehicle for specified purposes of a business or commercial character.[7]

The conditions are:

(a) the vehicle is not adapted to carry more than eight passengers and is not a motor cycle;

(b) the fare(s) paid in respect of the journey do not exceed the amount of the running costs of the vehicle for the journey[8]; and

(c) the arrangements for the payment of fares were made before the journey began.[9]

29–15 Risks against which cover is not compulsory. A motor policy may well provide cover against damage to, or loss of, the vehicle and its accessories by a variety of perils. In the case of a policy on a taxicab and "accessories belonging thereto", the taximeter was covered as an accessory.[10] An essential part of the vehicle, such as its engine, is not an accessory.[11] A policy on a motor vehicle covers all parts of that vehicle, and accordingly damage to, or loss of, a part of the vehicle occurring while it has been removed from the vehicle for repair or refurbishment will be covered by the policy subject to any exclusion of liability arising under the particular circumstances of its removal.[12] It is not uncommon for policies to cover the contents of the vehicle and the garage in which it is housed. The personal accident element of a motor policy may cover the assured and other persons against accidental personal injury sustained in connection with travel in the assured's own vehicle and other vehicles.[13] A proviso excluding liability to

---

[5] As to the meaning of this phrase, see paras 29–65 to 29–69, *post.*

[6] The following cases consider the meaning of the phrase "for hire or reward", being decisions either on those words appearing in proposal forms or policies or on the provision of the former legislation referred to in para. 29–12: *Wyatt v. Guildhall Ins. Co.* [1937] 1 K.B. 653; *Bonham v. Zurich General Accident and Liability Ins. Co. Ltd* [1945] 1 K.B. 292; *Coward v. M.I.B.* [1963] 1 Q.B. 259; *McGoona v. M.I.B.* [1969] 2 Lloyd's Rep. 34; *Connell v. M.I.B.* [1969] 2 Q.B. 494; *Albert v. M.I.B.* [1972] A.C. 301.

[7] s.150(1). The section applies however the restrictions or exclusions are framed or worded, for example they may be warranties, conditions, terms delimiting the risk or exceptions: s.150(3).

[8] For these purposes to include an appropriate amount in respect of depreciation and general wear.

[9] s.150(2).

[10] *Rowan v. Universal Ins. Co. Ltd* (1939) 64 Ll.L.R. 288.

[11] *Seaton v. London General Ins. Co. Ltd* (1932) 43 Ll.L.R. 398, 400.

[12] *Seaton v. London General Ins. Co. Ltd, ante.*

[13] As to this, see Ch. 25, *ante.*

pay compensation in respect of personal injuries to the assured after the attainment of a certain age has been held to apply to personal injuries resulting in the death of the assured.[14] The subjects of further cover ancillary to the foregoing vary from one insurer to another and a detailed description is beyond the scope of this chapter.

(c) Persons Entitled to Indemnity or Compensation from Motor Insurers

29–16 The assured—extension of cover when driving other vehicles. Motor vehicle policies frequently contain clauses extending to the assured when driving another vehicle[15] that does not belong to him and is not hired to him under a hire-purchase agreement. A car being driven by the assured pursuant to a sale on approval does not "belong to" the assured prior to approval being signified.[16] Sometimes a proviso is added to the effect that such vehicle must have been being used at the relevant time instead of the insured car.[17] This restricts the facility to the temporary use of another car while the car named in the schedule to the policy cannot be driven, so that, once the scheduled vehicle is sold, cover lapses and the extension is inoperative.[18] Even in the absence of such a proviso the same result would follow if, upon a true interpretation of the insurance, the insurers were granting cover on the basis of the continuing user or ownership of the scheduled vehicle, and that vehicle were then sold.[19] However, the matter depends on the true interpretation of the policy as a whole and the section covering third party risks may be read as quite independent of the insurance of a named vehicle. In *Dodson v. Peter H. Dodson Insurance Services*,[20] where the policy separately covered the driving by the assured (with the owner's permission) of any vehicle neither owned by nor on hire purchase to the assured and had no provision indicating that this cover was to end on the disposal of the insured vehicle, the Court of Appeal held that the insurers must be taken to have accepted that this cover could continue after disposal of the insured car, whether or not the assured had obtained a replacement vehicle of his own.[21] The ownership of a vehicle insured by a partnership does not completely change so as to terminate a policy merely because a new partner joins the partnership.[22]

---

[14] *Lloyd's Bank Ltd v. Eagle Star Ins. Co. Ltd* [1951] 1 Lloyd's Rep. 385.

[15] The clause may define the type of vehicle covered by the extension. In *Laurence v. Davies* [1972] 2 Lloyd's Rep. 231, a Ford Transit van was held to be a "motor car" for the purpose of an extension clause, applying the definition in s.190(2) of the Road Traffic Act 1972.

[16] *Bullock v. Bellamy* (1940) 67 Ll.L.R. 392.

[17] As in *Rogerson v. Scottish Automobile and General Ins. Co. Ltd* (1932) 48 T.L.R. 17.

[18] *Rogerson v. Scottish Automobile and General Ins. Co. Ltd, ante.*

[19] *Tattersall v. Drysdale* [1935] 2 K.B. 174; *Wilkinson v. General Accident Fire and Life Ass. Corp. Ltd* [1967] 2 Lloyd's Rep. 182; *Boss v. Kingston* [1963] 1 W.L.R. 99. The reasoning in the last case was disapproved of by the Court of Appeal in *Dodson v. Peter H. Dodson Insurance Services* [2001] Lloyd's Rep. I.R. 278; see *ante.*

[20] [2001] Lloyd's Rep. I.R. 278, distinguishing *Rogerson v. Scottish Automobile and General Ins. Co. Ltd* and *Tattersall v. Drysdale* [1935] 2 K.B. 174, *ante.*

[21] The reasoning in *Boss v. Kingston, ante,* that the terms of the policy that required, as a condition precedent to liability of the insurers, the insured to maintain the insured vehicle implied the retention of the vehicle was disapproved. So also was the view that, because the premium was fixed partly by reference to the insured vehicle, this implied that insurance cover ceased on disposal of that vehicle.

[22] *Jenkins v. Deane* (1933) 47 Ll.L.R. 342.

29–17 Extension clauses of this kind sometimes exclude liability where the assured is driving a car "owned by a person of the household of which the assured is a member". A Canadian court has held that the assured was not a member of the same household as his brother, with whom he was living as a boarder,[23] and in *English v. Western Insurance Co.*,[24] where the clause referred to "members of the insured's household" it was construed as meaning "members of the household of which the insured was head".

29–18 Extension of cover to driver of vehicles. A motor insurance policy frequently contains a clause extending the cover to persons driving the vehicle with the permission of the assured.[25] In *Williams v. Baltic Insurance Association of London Ltd*[26] the insurers agreed to indemnify the assured against, inter alia, "all sums for which the insured (or any licensed personal friend or relative of the insured while driving the car with the insured's general knowledge and consent) shall become legally liable". The assured's sister drove the car with the assured's consent and accidentally caused injury to third parties who recovered a judgment for damages against her. The assured made a claim for an indemnity against the amount of the judgment, to be paid to her or to himself as her trustee. It was held by Roche J. that the purpose and effect of the extension clause was to bind insurers to indemnify the persons referred to in it rather than to indemnify the assured for a liability falling on him as a result of their driving the car, so that the insurance became one for the named assured and for those persons' benefit. Applying the rule from *Waters v. Monarch Fire and Life Assurance Co. Ltd*[27] the assured was entitled to recover an indemnity and hold the proceeds on trust for his sister. It was further held that the policy was one "on goods" within section 4 of the Life Assurance Act 1774, so that the requirement of section 2 thereof for the beneficiaries' names to be inserted in the policy did not apply.[28] A further difficulty might have arisen in later cases if, for some reason, the assured had been unwilling to claim against his insurers for the benefit of another driver, since the latter is not a party to the contract of insurance.[29] However, this difficulty was overcome by the enactment of section 36(4) of the Road Traffic Act 1930, now reproduced in section 148(7) of the 1988 Act.

29–19 Section 148(7). This section provides that:

> "notwithstanding anything in any enactment, a person issuing a policy of insurance under section 145 of this Act shall be liable to indemnify the persons or classes of persons specified in the policy in respect of any liability which the policy purports to cover in the case of those persons or classes of persons".

[23] *Bell v. Wawanesa Mutual Ins. Co.* (1956) 5 D.L.R. 2d 759; (1957) 8 D.L.R. 2d 577.
[24] [1940] 2 K.B. 156. For the meaning of "ordinarily residing with the insured", see *Clarke v. Insurance Office of Australia Ltd* [1965] 1 Lloyd's Rep. 308.
[25] For a more detailed survey of such clauses, see paras 29–60 to 29–64, *post.*
[26] [1924] 2 K.B. 282.
[27] (1856) 5 E. & B. 870. See paras 1–172 to 1–180, *ante.*
[28] See para. 1–107, *ante.* Recent authority has held the 1774 Act to be inapplicable to ordinary indemnity policies such as a motor policy; see para. 1–23, *ante.*
[29] The insured could not have been compelled to take action unless it were held that he was trustee of his right of action on the policy for the benefit of a permitted driver—see *Vandepitte v. Preferred Accident Ins. Corp.* [1933] A.C. 70. See para. 20–29, *ante.*

The effect of this subsection is that if the policy purports to cover not only the owner but also the driver of the motor-vehicle, the driver can recover on the insurance policy although his name is not inserted under the policy and although he is not a party to the contract of insurance.[30] As Goddard J. said in *Tattersall v. Drysdale*,[31] the subsection "has given a cause of action which hitherto did not exist to a person indicated in the policy but not a party to it." The enactments referred to in section 148(7) are presumably sections 1 and 2 of the Life Assurance Act 1774 and possibly section 18 of the Gaming Act 1845.[32] There is no enactment providing that a contract is enforceable only between the parties to it and their privies but it is clear that the subsection was intended to overcome this difficulty also.[33] Any person taking the benefit of this provision is bound by any condition in the policy, for example as to the giving notice of claims or an arbitration clause,[34] and the insurer can avoid the policy for misrepresentation by the assured.[35]

29–20 The question arises whether the liability to specified third parties is restricted to the compulsory cover required by section 145 or extends to an indemnity against wider liabilities incurred by them if covered by the policy wording, e.g. liability in a situation within the exceptions in section 145(4).[36] This depends on the meaning of the words "issuing a policy ... under section 145". These words do not expressly define such a policy by reference to the liabilities required by statute to be covered by insurance.[37] Moreover Salmon J. gave wide construction to the words "issued under Part II of this Act" when considering what are now sections 157 and 158 of the Road Traffic Act[38] and, by parity of reasoning, a policy providing more extensive cover than the statutory minimum should be held to have been "issued under section 145" for the purposes of section 148(7). If this is correct, then a policy purporting to indemnify the assured and any friend or relative driving the insured car with his permission, against all liabilities arising from the use of the insured car, would be within the subsection, and such a friend might claim indemnity against liability for damage caused by him to the car, although section 145(4)(c) does not require such liability to be covered by insurance.

---

[30] *McCormick v. National Motor etc. Ltd* (1934) 40 Com.Cas. 76; *Tattersall v. Drysdale* [1935] 2 K.B. 174.

[31] [1935] 2 K.B. 174, 181–182.

[32] Although given the modern views about the 1774 Act referred to in note 28, *ante*, this piece of drafting now appears superfluous.

[33] *McCormick v. National Motor etc. Ltd* (1934) 40 Com.Cas. 76, 90; *Guardian Ass. Co. v. Sutherland* [1939] 2 All E.R. 246, 250. This difficulty, arising from the common law doctrine of privity of contract, has been substantially lessened by the Contracts (Rights of Third Parties) Act 1999—see paras 20–61—20–66 *ante*.

[34] *Austin v. Zurich General Accident etc. Ltd* [1945] 1 K.B. 250; *Freshwater v. Western Australian Ass. Co.* [1933] 1 K.B. 515.

[35] *Guardian Ass. Co. v. Sutherland* [1939] 2 All E.R. 246 applying *McCormick v. National Motor etc. Ltd*, *supra*. The guiding principle is that the claimant is given a statutory right to enforce the policy against the insurer, and is subject to all its terms, including those which afford defences to the insurer: *Freshwater v. Western Australian Ass. Co.* [1933] 1 K.B. 515, 521, 524, 526; *Austin v. Zurich General Accident and Liability Ins. Co. Ltd* [1945] 1 K.B. 250, 256—but subject to s.148(2) of the Act, *ante*. An analogous principle applies in the case of claims under the Third Parties (Rights Against Insurers) Act 1930—see para. 28–17, *ante*.

[36] See para. 29–5, *ante*.

[37] *Austin v. Zurich General Accident etc. Ltd* [1944] 2 All E.R. 243, 248, *per* Tucker J.

[38] *Barnet Group Hospital Management Committee v. Eagle Star Ins. Co. Ltd* [1960] 1 Q.B. 107. See para. 29–11, *ante*.

29–21 Contract (Rights of Third Parties) Act 1999. In any event, the Contract (Rights of Third Parties) Act 1999, which is discussed more fully elsewhere in this book,[39] now gives a right to sue on the policy to a third party who is covered thereby. Note, however, that this right, unlike that conferred by section 148(7), can be excluded by the terms of the policy.

29–22 Claims by third parties not specified in the policy. Parliament has passed legislation assisting third parties to whom an assured has incurred a liability covered by a motor policy. Depending on the circumstances, such persons may be entitled by statute to sue the relevant insurers, either under the Third Parties (Rights Against Insurers) Act 1930 or the Road Traffic Act 1988. Alternatively they may be able to make a claim on the Motor Insurers' Bureau where a claim against motor insurers is not feasible for particular reasons. Each has to be considered separately.

29–23 Claim under the 1930 Act. This Act is considered in detail in Chapter 28. It was passed to assist third party claimants entitled to judgment against a bankrupt or insolvent assured, who were left by the general law before the statute to prove for the claim in the bankruptcy or liquidation together with the general body of creditors.[40] Section 1 of the Act transfers to a third party the rights of the assured against the insurers in respect of the liability incurred to the third party where that is covered by the policy.[41] The general principle is that, subject to section 1(3) of this Act,[42] and sections 148(1) and (2) of the 1988 Act,[43] the third party's claim is subject to all the terms and conditions of the policy and to all defences, such as non-disclosure, which the insurer could have raised against the assured himself.[44]

29–24 Liability of insurer to third party under the 1988 Act. A more extensive remedy is conferred by section 151 upon those who have obtained judgment against the user of a vehicle.[45] After delivery of a certificate of insurance under section 147,[46] and after a third party has obtained[47] a

---

[39] See paras 20–61—20–66, *ante*.

[40] *Re Harrington Motor Co. Ltd ex p. Chaplin* [1928] Ch. 105; *Hood's Trustees v. Southern Union General Ins. Co. of Australasia* [1928] Ch. 793; *Jones v. Birch Brothers Ltd* [1933] 2 K.B. 597, 608, 611–612; *McCormick v. National Motor and Accident Insurance Union Ltd* (1934) 40 Com.Cas. 76; *Croxford v. Universal Ins. Co. Ltd* [1936] 2 K.B. 253; *Post Office v. Norwich Union Fire Ins. Society Ltd* [1967] 2 Q.B. 363, 373.

[41] *McCormick v. National Motor and Accident Ins. Union Ltd* (1934) 40 Com.Cas. 76: *Post Office v. Norwich Union Fire Ins. Society Ltd* [1967] 2 Q.B. 363, 373, 376, 379; *Firma C-Trade SA v. Newcastle Protection and Indemnity Association* ("The Fanti"), *Socony Mobil Oil Inc. v. West of England Shipowners Mutual Insurance Association*, ("The Padre Island") [1991] 2 A.C. 1.

[42] See para. 28–17, *ante*.

[43] See paras 29–30 to 29–36, *post*.

[44] *Freshwater v. Western Australian Ins. Co. Ltd* [1933] 1 K.B. 515; *McCormick v. National Motor and Accident Ltd* (1934) 40 Com.Cas. 76; *Post Office v. Norwich Union Fire Ins. Society Ltd* [1967] 2 Q.B. 363.

[45] The section (and its predecessors) is not retrospective: *Croxford v. Universal Ins. Co. Ltd* [1936] 2 K.B. 253; *Dolan v. Dominion of Canada General Ins. Co.* [1936] 2 All E.R. 1354.

[46] But all that this requires is that a certificate is issued and a policy effected prior to judgment which covers the liability in question, even retrospectively: *Motor and General Ins. Co. v. Cox* [1990] 1 W.L.R. 1443.

[47] The court will not grant a declaration in favour of the claimant pending judgment to the effect that, if a judgment be got, the insurer will be liable to meet it: *Carpenter v. Ebblewhite* [1939] 1 K.B. 347.

judgment against any person insured by the policy in respect of a liability required to be covered by section 145, the whole of the judgment in respect of liability for bodily injury,[48] and up to £250,000 of it in respect of liability for damage to property,[49] must be satisfied by the insurer, notwithstanding that the insurer may be entitled to avoid or to cancel the policy or may in fact have done so.[50] Further, the same obligation applies in respect of a judgment against a person not insured by the policy in respect of such a liability, but who would have been covered if the policy had covered the liability of all persons, except that in respect of liability for death or bodily injury, it does not apply if the third party was allowing himself to be carried in or upon the vehicle knowing or having reason to believe that the vehicle had been stolen or unlawfully taken.[51] In determining whether a liability is, or would be, covered, as the case may be, a provision restricting cover to drivers in possession of a valid licence is to be disregarded.[52]

29–25 For section 151 to operate, it appears that there must be an apparently valid policy which in terms covered the use to which the insured vehicle was being put at the time, but assuming, for the purposes of the section, that the policy covers driving by any person regardless of whether or not that person holds a valid driving licence.[53] On the other hand, the insurers are disentitled from reliance on a non-disclosure or misrepresentation or breach of warranty which would entitle them to avoid or cancel the policy as against their insured, subject to their due compliance with the procedure laid down by section 152.[54] The third party is further assisted by section 148(1) and (2) which avoid certain terms of policies otherwise providing a defence to insurers against claims made on the policy.[55]

29–26 Insurer's rights of recovery. In situations where, under section 151, the insurer is liable to meet a judgment notwithstanding that his liability to the assured is nil or is for a lesser sum, he will have a remedy under section 151(7) or (8). By section 151(7), he has a remedy against a person insured for the whole of the amount he has paid out where he is liable by virtue of section 151(3), i.e. the person was driving without a valid licence; he also has a remedy for the excess where the amount of the judgment exceeds the amount for which he would otherwise have been liable. Where an insurer

---

[48] In other jurisdictions the insurer's liability under such a provision is sometimes limited to a particular sum by the wording of the statute: *Sri Lanka Ins. Co. v. Ranasinghe* [1964] A.C. 541; *Harker v. Caledonian Ins. Co.* [1980] 1 Lloyd's Rep. 556; *Suttle v. Simmons* [1989] 2 Lloyd's Rep. 227.

[49] And interest thereon where awarded.

[50] s.151(1), (2), (5) and (6). The award that must be satisfied include costs and interest awarded. Where a property damage judgment exceeds £250,000, s.151(6)(b) provides as to how the insurer's exact liability is to be assessed.

[51] s.151(4).

[52] s.151(3).

[53] The section assumes that the insurer was on risk under a validly concluded contract: *Norman v. Gresham Fire & Accident Ins. Society* [1936] 2 K.B. 253, 277–278; *Spraggon v. Dominion Insurance* (1941) 69 Ll.L.R. 1. It seems that it will still not apply to a user outside the policy terms, e.g. other than for social domestic and pleasure purposes: *Jones v. Welsh Ins. Corp.* [1937] 4 All E.R. 149. If the act giving rise to liability was intentional the insurer has a defence to a claim by the insured for reasons of public policy but would remain liable to an injured third party under the principles stated in *Hardy v. M.I.B.* [1964] 2 Q.B. 745 and *Gardner v. Moore* [1984] A.C. 548. See Ch. 14, *ante*.

[54] See para. 29–26, *ante*. and *Motor & General Ins. Co. v. Pavy* [1994] 1 W.L.R. 462, 473–474.

[55] See paras 29–31 to 29–36, *ante*.

meets a judgment against someone not insured by the policy, he can recover the amount from that person or from any person who was insured by the policy and who caused or permitted the use of the vehicle which gave rise to the liability.[56]

29–27 Qualifications upon insurer's liability to satisfy a judgment. The insurer is not liable:

(a) unless he had notice of the bringing of the proceedings in which the judgment was given, before or within seven days after their commencement[57];

(b) while execution is stayed pending an appeal[58];

(c) if the policy was cancelled before the accident, and within the period of 14 days from the cancellation either the certificate was surrendered, or the holder made a statutory declaration that it was lost or destroyed, or the insurer commenced proceedings in respect of failure to surrender it[59];

(d) if in an action commenced not later than three months from the commencement of the proceedings in which the judgment was given, he has obtained a declaration[60] that he is entitled to avoid the policy for non-disclosure of a material fact or material misrepresentation,[61] but in order to get the benefit of such a declaration he must give notice of the proceedings within seven days of commencing the action to the plaintiff in those proceedings, specifying the non-disclosure or misrepresentation on which he proposes to rely.[62]

29–28 Notice of bringing of proceedings. The notice ought to be a formal notification, particularly when given to an agent on behalf of the insurer.[63] However, there is no requirement of notice in writing,[64] so that a clear oral notice of the commencement of legal proceedings should suffice. What is essential is notice that is unambiguous as to the commencement of formal legal proceedings, not notice that is conditional or simply notice that a claim might be made.[65] It is a matter of fact and degree in every case.[66] A letter seeking clarification as to whether or not liability is declined is not a good notice even if it might well be inferred that proceedings would be brought if liability were declined,[67] nor is a solicitor's letter stating that the victim of the road accident is being advised to issue proceedings.[68] On the other hand, it is not necessary to specify the court where the action will be or has been

[56] s.151(8).

[57] s.152(1)(a). "Proceedings" means "legal proceedings": *McGoona v. M.I.B.* [1969] 2 Lloyd's Rep. 34, 46–47.

[58] s.152(1)(b).

[59] s.152(1)(c).

[60] s.152(2).

[61] Defined in s.152(2), as amended by the Road Traffic Act 1991, Sch. 4.

[62] s.152(3).

[63] *Herbert v. Railway Passengers Ass. Co.* (1938) 60 Ll.L.Rep. 143.

[64] *Harrington v. Pinkey* [1989] 2 Lloyd's Rep. 310, *per* Sir Denis Buckley at 316.

[65] *Desouza v. Waterlow* [1999] R.T.R. 71; *Wake v. Wylie* [2001] R.T.R. 20.

[66] *Desouza v. Waterlow, ante.*

[67] *Weldrick v. Essex & Suffolk Equitable Ins. Society* (1950) 83 Ll.L.R. 91, 102. However, it has been doubted whether this decision can stand other than as confined to its own peculiar facts: *Wake v. Wylie, ante.*

[68] *Harrington v. Pinkey* [1989] 2 Lloyd's Rep. 310. However, this was only "just on the wrong side of the line": *per* Woolf L.J. at 315.

commenced, nor the date.[69] It is for the plaintiff to show that notice was given or waived,[70] but insurers who wish to rely upon the absence of notice should plead the point.[71]

29–29 Notice of proceedings to plaintiff. The word "plaintiff" in section 151(2) must include a counterclaiming defendant since it will sometimes be the case that the person who recovers judgment against the assured is not technically a plaintiff, but a defendant who has brought a successful counterclaim. It follows also that "the commencement of the proceedings in which judgment was given" must be construed in subsection (2) and (3) of section 152 to mean, where necessary, the delivery of a defendant's counterclaim, or else if the counterclaim was delivered more than seven days after the insurers had begun their actions for a declaration, they would then be unable to comply with the requirements of the proviso to section 152(2).[72] Thus where the assured, on being sued for negligence as the result of an accident, serves a third-party notice against another person involved in the accident, and that person counterclaims and recovers judgment on his counterclaim against the assured, it is not sufficient, to make the insurers liable to satisfy that judgment where they have avoided the policy, that they should receive notice of the third-party proceedings. They must also have received notice of the delivery of the counterclaim.[73]

29–30 Action for declaration. The object of the proviso to section 152(3) is to forewarn the third party claimant of the insurers' intention to avoid the policy for material non-disclosure or misrepresentation and to give him the right to oppose the declaration sought.[74] Accordingly the insurers are not free to adduce further allegations of non-disclosure or misrepresentation beyond those specified in their statutory notice.[75] The court will grant a declaration in the absence of the assured.[76] Under section 152(2) the insurers have to establish not only that there was a non-disclosure or misrepresentation of a material fact as defined in the subsection, but also that the policy was "obtained" by it in the sense that it influenced them in granting cover.[77] Admissions of the assured are not evidence against the third party who has been joined as co-defendant and is opposing the grant of a declaration.[78] In *Trafalgar Insurance Co. v. McGregor*[79] the insurers sought a declaration of

---

[69] *Ceylon Motor Ins. Association Ltd v. Thambugula* [1953] A.C. 584; *Harrington v. Pinkey, ante*, at 315. This is clearly correct as the section allows the notice to be given before proceedings are commenced. See also *McBlain v. Dolan* [1998] S.L.T. 512.

[70] *Herbert v. Railway Passengers Ass. Co., ante*, at 146.

[71] *Baker v. Provident Accident and White Cross Ins. Co.* [1939] 2 All E.R. 690, 697.

[72] *Cross v. British Oak Ins. Co.* [1938] 2 K.B. 167.

[73] *ibid.*

[74] *Merchants' & Manufacturers' Ins. Co. v. Hunt* [1941] 1 K.B. 295, 308. By s.154(4) the third party is entitled to be joined in the proceedings.

[75] *Zurich General Accident & Liability Ins. Co. Ltd v. Morrison* [1942] 2 K.B. 53.

[76] *Guardian Ass. Co. v. Sutherland* (1939) 55 T.L.R. 576.

[77] *Merchants & Manufacturers' Ins. Co. v. Hunt* [1941] 1 K.B. 295; *Zurich General Accident & Liability Ins. Co. v. Morrison* [1942] 2 K.B. 53, 58, 60, 65; *General Accident etc. Corp. v. Shuttleworth* (1938) 60 Ll.L.R. 301, 304. However, now the general law on non-disclosure and misrepresentation is to similar effect; see para. 17–26, ante.

[78] *Merchants' & Manufacturers' Ins. Co. v. Hunt* [1941] 1 K.B. 295.

[79] [1942] 1 K.B. 275.

entitlement to avoid the policy for non-disclosure and misrepresentation. The third party, who had been made a co-defendant, sought particulars of the convictions for motor-offences alleged by the insurers, while the assured did not defend the action. On failing to provide particulars within a reasonable time, the insurers were precluded from giving evidence of the convictions at the trial.[80]

29–31 Avoidance of certain terms in policies. Section 148 assists third parties by avoiding certain conditions and terms in policies that could otherwise defeat claims. Section 148(1) provides that, where a certificate of insurance has been delivered under section 147 to an insured, restrictions on the insurers' liability by reference to any of the matters listed in subsection (2) are of no effect "as respect such liabilities as are required to be covered by a policy under section 145 of this Act":

the age or physical or mental condition of persons driving the insured vehicle;
the condition of the vehicle;
the number of persons that the vehicle carries;
the weight or physical characteristics of the goods that the vehicle carries;
the time at which or the area within which the vehicle is used;
the horsepower or cylinder capacity or value of the vehicle;
the carrying on the vehicle of any particular apparatus;
the carrying on the vehicle of any particular means of identification other than those required by the Vehicle Excise and Registration Act 1994.[81]

29–32 Physical or mental condition of drivers. A condition that the assured shall keep every motor car insured by the policy in an efficient state of repair, and shall use all care and diligence to avoid accidents and to employ only steady and sober drivers, is not a condition restricting the insurance by reference to the physical or mental condition of persons driving the vehicle.[82]

29–33 Weight or physical characteristics of the goods. A condition negativing liability if the insured vehicle is used otherwise than for "social, domestic and pleasure purposes" or in connection with a specified business, is not invalidated by section 148(2)(d) as being a condition relating to the physical characteristics of the goods carried.[83]

29–34 Subsection (3) of section 148 provides that nothing in subsection

---

[80] See *Butcher v. Dowlen* [1981] 1 Lloyd's Rep. 310 concerning particulars of convictions.
[81] 1994, c. 22.
[82] *National Farmers' Union Mutual Ins. Society v. Dawson* [1941] 2 K.B. 424. Lord Caldecote L.C.J. upheld the arbitrator's award on the alternative ground that the sum that the insurers had paid to the third party was recoverable from the assured as damages for breach of the condition. But if, as the Lord Chief Justice had held, the condition was not invalidated by the section, the insurers could have refused to pay the third party and should have been unable to show that they had suffered any damages as a result of the breach.
[83] *Jones v. Welsh Ins. Corp. Ltd* [1937] 4 All E.R. 149.

(1) requires the insurer to pay any sum other than in discharge of the insured liability, and subsection (4) provides that any sum paid in or towards the discharge of that liability which is covered only by virtue of subsection (1) is recoverable by the insurer from the person whose liability has been discharged. It is submitted that the effect of these provisions is to enable insurers who have settled a claim, or satisfied a judgment, against their assured or against another driver covered by the policy,[84] to recover the amount paid from the latter if, but for subsection (1), there would have been no liability on their part to indemnify. Presumably the subsections apply equally where insurers are sued by a third party under section 152 of the Act,[85] so long as they would not have been liable to indemnify but for section 148(1). The ultimate effect of them is to make the relevant terms of motor policies ineffective as against third parties.

29–35 Conditions precedent invalid against third parties. By section 148(5), conditions in a policy issued under Part VI of the Act, relieving the insurers from liability by reason of some act or omission by the assured after the happening of the event giving rise to a claim under the policy, are of no effect against third parties in respect of such liabilities as are required to be covered by section 145. By subsection (6), which, significantly, is worded in a different form from subsection (4),[86] a policy term requiring the assured to repay to the insurers sums which they have become liable to pay and have paid in satisfaction of such claims is valid.[87] A provision negativing liability, if notice is not given within a specified time, or if an action in respect of a repudiated claim is not brought within three months after repudiation, is invalidated by the Act.[88] The effect of this part of section 148 is that if all was in order between the assured and the insurers when the accident occurred, the position cannot be altered by subsequent breaches or by acts or omissions on the part of the assured.[89] But if the insurers were not on risk at the time of the accident, they cannot, of course, be liable to third parties and therefore a provision negativing liability if the vehicle is used in connection with the motor trade[90] or if a passenger is carried on a motor-cycle otherwise than in a sidecar,[91] cannot be affected by the section because the use of the vehicle in the manner specified prevents the risk from ever attaching.

---

[84] See paras 29–18 to 29–20, *ante*.

[85] See paras 29–24 to 29–30, *ante*.

[86] See para. 29–34, *ante*.

[87] This first appeared as a proviso in section 38 of the Road Traffic Act 1930, upon which Scrutton L.J. commented in *Jones v. Birch Bros. Ltd* [1933] 2 K.B. 597 at 610 that he had the "impression that the draftsman did not quite understand what he meant to do and has not unnaturally left it doubtful what he has done." Greer L.J. described it as "a very odd provision", (at 613) but said that it entitled the insurers to recover from the insured under the relevant policy provision any sums they had paid to discharge a compulsory insurance liability, which they would not have had to pay in the absence of s.38. It is submitted that this is correct, with respect. *Jester-Barnes v. Licenses & General Ins. Co.* (1934) 49 Ll.L.R. 231, a case arising out of the same events as the case of *Jones, supra*, illustrates the kind of provision referred to in s.38. In that case Mackinnon J. apparently agreed with a legal arbitrator's view that s.38 disentitled the insurers from relying on breach of a condition precedent requiring the assured to give information and assistance after an accident in answer to a claim for indemnity brought by the assured himself, p. 236. *Sed quaere*. The point was not argued.

[88] *Revell v. London General Ins. Co.* (1934) 50 Ll.L.R. 114; *McCormick v. National Motor Ltd* (1934) 40 Com.Cas. 76, 89–90.

[89] *Gray v. Blackmore* [1934] 1 K.B. 95; *Croxford v. Universal Ins. Co.* [1936] 2 K.B. 253, 268.

[90] *ibid*.

[91] *Bright v. Ashfold* [1932] 2 K.B. 153.

29–36 Arbitration clause. It has been held that an arbitration clause is effective, despite the provisions of section 148(5).[92] It was argued in *Jones v. Birch Bros. Ltd*[93] that a clause in the *Scott v. Avery* form[94] was caught by the section since it required the assured to do some act after the happening of the event giving rise to the claim. Greer L.J. favoured this argument while Scrutton L.J. seemed to take the opposite view. All three judges in the Court of Appeal, however, held that the provision making the obtaining of an award a condition precedent to the right of action was severable from the remainder of the arbitration clause, which remained effective, although the court could refuse in its discretion to order a stay of the action. The court did order a stay since otherwise there would have had to be separate arbitration proceedings between the insurers and the assured to establish whether the assured was bound to make repayment of sums paid by the insurers to the third party, pursuant to what is now section 148(6).

29–37 Condition saving rights of third parties. Motor-vehicle policies may contain a clause to the effect that nothing in the policy is to affect the right of any person indemnified by the policy or of any other person to recover an amount under section 148 or 151 of the Road Traffic Act, but that the assured shall repay to the company all sums which the company would not have been liable to pay but for the said provisions of the Act. Stable J. has said that the meaning of such a clause is that the insurers contract out of their right to sue for a declaration of avoidance under section 152(2)[95] but the Court of Appeal, while deciding the case on another ground, were inclined to disagree with Stable J.'s view[96] and in a later case Atkinson J., while admitting that the words appeared to be meaningless, followed the views of the Court of Appeal and said that the clause had no effect except to remind the assured of what the law is.[97]

29–38 Other statutory provisions assisting third-party claims. Section 153(1) provides that where a certificate of insurance has been delivered, the happening of any of the events specified in subsection (2) shall, notwithstanding anything in the Third Parties (Rights against Insurers) Act 1930,[98] not effect any such liability of the person insured as is required to be covered by insurance, but, by subsection (3) nothing in section 153(1) affects any rights conferred by the 1930 Act on the third party against the insurer. The events specified in section 153(2) are where the assured is made bankrupt,[99] dies insolvent[1] or, if a company, becomes subject to any of a number of

---

[92] *Jones v. Birch Bros. Ltd* [1933] 2 K.B. 597.

[93] *ibid.* This point was not argued in *Freshwater v. Western Australian Ass. Co.* [1933] 1 K.B. 515 in which it was held that a claimant under section 1(1) of the Third Parties (Rights Against Insurers) Act 1930 was bound by an arbitration clause in the policy, containing a *Scott v. Avery* provision.

[94] See Ambrose & Maxwell, *London Maritime Arbitration* (1996) P. 30.

[95] *Merchants' and Manufacturers' Ins. Co. v. Hunt* [1940] 4 All E.R. 205.

[96] [1941] 1 K.B. 295.

[97] *Zurich General Accident & Liability Ins. Co. v. Morrison* [1942] 1 All E.R. 529, 535. The point was not considered in the Court of Appeal, [1942] 2 K.B. 53.

[98] See Ch. 28, *ante.*

[99] Or he makes a composition or arrangement with his creditors, or his estate is sequestrated, or he grants a trust deed for his creditors.

[1] i.e. his estate falls to be administered under s.421 of the Insolvency Act 1986, an award of sequestration of his estate is made, or a judicial factor is appointed under s.11A of the Judicial Factors (Scotland) Act 1889.

insolvency proceedings.[2] The section appears to do no more than make it clear that, if there is any significant difference between the rights of the third party under section 151 and the 1930 Act, he can avail himself of either.

By section 154(1) a person against whom a claim is made in respect of third-party motor liability is bound to give certain information concerning the existence of any insurance policy insuring him against it. Failure to comply in the absence of reasonable excuse, and the making of a wilfully false statement in response to a demand for such information, constitute criminal offences punishable on summary conviction.[3]

29–39 The Motor Insurers' Bureau: The two agreements. Since July 1, 1946, much of the law about the rights of a third party to sue an insurer has become less important as the result of an agreement of June 17, 1946 between the Ministry of Transport and a corporation called the Motor Insurers' Bureau ("M.I.B.") whereby the M.I.B. undertook to compensate the accident victims of uninsured drivers. By a separate agreement of April 21, 1969, between M.I.B. and the Ministry of Transport, M.I.B. undertook to compensate the victims of untraced drivers. These agreements were replaced by those of November 22, 1972, between the Secretary of State for the Environment and M.I.B. covering the same subject matter. A revised version of the agreement concerning uninsured drivers was agreed on December 21, 1988 and a further version was agreed on August 13, 1999. The agreement regarding untraced drivers was replaced by one dated June 14, 1996. Although first agreed long before the E.C. Second Motor Insurance Directive,[4] they have subsequently been recognised as implementing the requirements thereof, although the question of whether they do so sufficiently has been referred to the European Court of Justice.[5] In the following account, the two agreements are considered separately.

29–40 The 1999 Agreement—Uninsured Drivers.[6] Clause 5 of this agreement, read with the definitions in clause 1, provides that, if a claimant has obtained against any person in a court in Great Britain a judgment, which is unsatisfied, in respect of any relevant liability,[7] whether or not the defendant is in fact covered by insurance, and that judgment is not satisfied in full within seven days of the date upon which the person in whose favour it was given became entitled to enforce it, then M.I.B. will pay or cause to be paid to the person in whose favour it was given the amount remaining payable thereunder, including interest and costs awarded by the court in respect of the liability. By clause 6(1)(b), M.I.B.'s liability extends to claims

---

[2] (i) a winding up order, (ii) an administration order, (iii) a voluntary winding up, (iv) the due appointment of a receiver or manager of the company's business or undertaking, (v) the taking of possession of property subject to a floating charge by the chargee.

[3] s.154(2). The penalty is prescribed by the Road Traffic Offenders Act 1988, c.53.

[4] 84/5/EEC.

[5] *Evans v. Secretary of State for the Environment, Transport and the Regions* [2001] E.W.C.A. Civ 32, [2001] 2 C.M.L.R. 10, [2002] Lloyd's Rep. I.R. 1. See further at paras. 29–46 and 29–48, *ante*. The M.I.B. is not an emanation of the State for the purposes of E.C. law: *Mighell v. Reading, White v. White* [1999] Lloyd's Rep. I.R. 30, *Norman v. Aziz* [2000] Lloyd's Rep. I.R. 52.

[6] This Agreement, which operates in respect of accidents occurring on or after October 1, 1999, replaced that of 1946 and the subsequent ones of February 1, 1971, November 22, 1972 and December 21, 1988. The text of the agreement is published by HMSO and is reproduced in the *Encyclopedia of Insurance Law*, Part 9. All authorised motor insurers must be members of M.I.B.: s.145(5). The 1946 text is appended to the report of *Hardy v. M.I.B.* [1964] 2 Q.B. 745.

[7] Defined as a liability to be covered under the Act—see para. 29–5, *ante*.

arising out of the use of a vehicle which is not required to be covered by compulsory insurance by virtue of section 144 if the use is in fact covered by a contract of insurance, as where, for instance, vehicles are owned by a local or police authority or are used for police purposes.[8]

The agreement is determinable by the Secretary of State or by M.I.B. on 12 months' notice.[9]

Contracts of insurance can provide that any sums paid by the insurers or by M.I.B. by virtue of the agreement shall be recoverable from the assured or any other person.[10]

Nothing in the agreement prevents M.I.B. from acting through agents,[11] and where a policy has been issued to the tortfeasor, but the insurer is entitled to avoid it despite the provisions of section 151 of the Act,[12] the usual practice is for the M.I.B. to nominate that insurer to deal with the claim.

29–41 Conditions precedent. There are a number of conditions precedent to M.I.B.'s liability[13]:

(1) Application must be made in the form reasonably required by M.I.B. giving such information about the relevant proceedings and other matters relevant to the agreement and accompanied by such documents as it may reasonably require.[14]

(2) By clause 9, proper notice of the bringing of the proceedings[15] must be given not later than 14 days after the commencement of the proceedings[16] (i) to the insurer where the liability is covered by a contract of insurance with an ascertainable insurer or (ii) in any other case to M.I.B. Proper notice means the following, except in so far as any of them has already been supplied with the application:

(a) notice in writing that proceedings have been commenced by claim form, writ or other means;

(b) a copy of the sealed claim form, writ or other document providing evidence of the commencement of the proceedings[17];

(c) a copy or details of any insurance policy providing benefits in the case of the death, bodily injury or damage to property to which the proceedings relate where the claimant is the insured party and the benefits are available to him;

---

[8] ss.144(2)(a) and (b); see para. 29–4, *ante*. See also para. 29–44, *post*.

[9] cl. 4(2).

[10] cl. 20.

[11] cl. 22.

[12] See para. 29–23, *ante*.

[13] Note that these are more onerous than those applying under the earlier agreements. Any notice required or documents to be supplied to M.I.B. must be sent by fax or by registered or recorded delivery post: cl. 8.

[14] cl. 7. MIB may not ultimately refuse to accept an application signed by a person other than the claimant or his solicitor, but it may do so until it is reasonably satisfied that, having regard to the status of the signatory and his relationship to the claimant, the claimant is fully aware of the contents and effect of the application.

[15] The "bringing of the proceedings" is when the court prepares, issues and seals the summons for service: *Silverton v. Goodall* [1997] P.I.Q.R. 451.

[16] The phrase "commencement of the proceedings" bears its ordinary meaning, namely the point in time at which the proceedings commenced: *Silverton v. Goodall*, *ante*. The time limit is strictly enforced: *Stinton v. M.I.B.* [1995] R.T.R. 167.

[17] And in Scotland a statement of the means of service. See *Cambridge v. Callaghan* [1998] R.T.R. 365.

(d) copies of all correspondence in the possession of the claimant or his solicitor or agent to or from the defendant (or defender) or his solicitor, insurers or agent which is relevant to (i) the death, bodily injury or damage for which the defendant is alleged to be responsible or (ii) any contract of insurance which covers, or which may or has been alleged to cover, liability for such death, injury or damage the benefit of which is, or is claimed to be, available to the defendant;

(e) a copy of the particulars of claim[18];

(f) a copy of all other documents required under the appropriate rules of procedure to be served on a defendant with the claim form, writ or other originating process or with the particulars of claim;

(g) such other information about the relevant proceedings as M.I.B. may reasonably specify

(3) In England and Wales, the claimant must give notice in writing of the date of service of the claim form or other originating process not later than the day falling (a) seven days after the date when the claimant receives notification from the court that the service of the claim form or other originating process has occurred, the date when the claimant receives notification from the defendant that service has occurred or the date of personal service or (b) 14 days after the date when service is deemed to have occurred in accordance with the Civil Procedure Rules, whichever of those days occurs first.[19]

(4) The claimant must, within seven days of the occurrence of (a) the filing of a defence in the relevant proceedings (b) any amendment to the particulars of claim or amendment or addition to any schedule or other document required to be reserved therewith and (c) either the setting down of the case for trial or the date of receipt of notice of the trial date, give notice in writing and supply a copy of any of the documents referred to.[20]

(5) The claimant must give notice in writing of his intention to apply for or sign judgment in the relevant proceedings after commencement of the proceedings and not less than 35 days before the date when the application for judgment is made or the signing of judgment occurs.[21]

(6) As soon as reasonably practicable, the claimant must demand the information and particulars specified in section 154 of the 1988 Act[22] and, if the respondent fails to comply, must make a formal complaint to a police officer and use all reasonable endeavours to obtain the name and address of the registered keeper of the vehicle.[23]

(7) If M.I.B. so requires and subject to an indemnity as to costs, the person bringing the proceedings must have taken all reasonable steps to obtain judgment against all the responsible tortfeasors, including any person who may be vicariously liable;

---

[18] Whether or not indorsed on the claim form or writ and whether or not served on the defendant, except that in England and Wales, if the particulars have not been served with the claim form, it is sufficient if a copy is served on M.I.B. not later than seven days after it is served on the defendant.

[19] cl. 10.

[20] cl. 11.

[21] cl. 12.

[22] See para. 29–38, *ante*.

[23] cl. 13. Alternatively the claimant must authorise M.I.B. to act on his behalf is so requested.

(8) Any judgment obtained must be assigned to M.I.B. or its nominee and the claimant must undertake to repay to M.I.B. (a) any sum paid to him by M.I.B. if a relevant judgment is subsequently set aside and (b) any sum paid by any other person by way of compensation or benefit for the death, bodily injury or other damage to which the relevant proceedings relate.[24]

If there is any dispute as to whether any step required by M.I.B. is reasonable, it is to be referred to the Secretary of State whose decision is to be final.[25]

It is possible for the requirements of notice, etc., within a specified time limit to be waived.[26]

29–42 Property damage. The agreement covers liability in respect of property damage, since it is now compulsory to insure against such liability, but M.I.B.'s liability is limited to a maximum of £250,000, and there is an excess of £300, *i.e.* the M.I.B. will not pay a claim of that amount or less and will deduct the first £300 from a claim of greater amount.[27]

29–43 Compensation received from other sources. By clause 17, where a claimant has received compensation from (a) the Policyholders Protection Board,[28] (b) an insurer under an insurance agreement or arrangement, or (c) any other source, in respect of the death, bodily injury or other damage to which the relevant proceedings relate, and the compensation has not been taken into account in the calculation of the amount of the unsatisfied judgment, M.I.B. may deduct from its liability an amount equal to that compensation.[29] The exact scope of this clause is unclear. The equivalent clause in the 1988 agreement[30] referred only to property damage; this covered, for example, indemnity received from the claimant's own first party insurer in respect of damage to his vehicle.[31] In respect of death or bodily injury, it could be argued that it is not apt to permit the deduction of money received under a personal accident or life insurance policy, as such proceeds are not "compensation" in the normal sense.[32] On the other hand, payments received under a medical expenses insurance policy, for example, which are calculated on an indemnity basis, are probably certainly deductible.

29–44 Liability in respect of intentional criminal act. In *Hardy v. M.I.B.*[33] a

---

[24] cl. 15. The latter includes a sum that would have been deductible under cl. 17 (see *post*) if it had been received before M.I.B. was obliged to satisfy a judgment.

[25] cl.19. There is no other right to challenge a decision by the M.I.B. on the grounds that it failed to act reasonably: *Norman v. Ali* [2000] Lloyd's Rep. I.R. 395

[26] *Cooper v. M.I.B.* [1983] 1 W.L.R. 592; [1985] 1 Q.B. 575, where on the facts there was no waiver.

[27] cl. 16. Unreasonable involvement of the M.I.B. where a claim is unlikely to exceed the £300 excess is likely to result in costs being awarded against the claimant's solicitors personally: *Martin v. Blanchard* [1995] C.L.Y. 3727.

[28] As to this, see paras 34–41 to 34–52, *post*, and note that the Policyholders Protection scheme is replaced by the Financial Services Compensation Scheme.

[29] In addition to the excess for property damage.

[30] cl. 2(3).

[31] The insurer's potential subrogated claim in this respect is also excluded—see para. 29–45, *ante*.

[32] The notes to the agreement state that "claims for loss and damage for which the claimant has been compensated or indemnified may be deducted." Payments under a personal accident or life policy are certainly not indemnities.

[33] [1964] 2 Q.B. 745.

security officer stopped a van driven by a factory employee because a stolen Road Fund licence was on the windscreen. The driver was uninsured and suddenly drove off while the officer had his head and shoulders inside the van, thus intentionally causing him serious injury. If the driver had been insured as the law required, he would not have been able to recover on grounds of public policy, but the Court of Appeal held that nevertheless M.I.B. was liable to the plaintiff, who was not affected by the disability attaching to the motorist. This decision has been followed and approved in the House of Lords.[34]

29–45 Exemptions. Liability under clause 5 is excluded in the following cases[35]:

(a) a claim arising out of the use of a vehicle owned by or in the possession of the Crown except where any other person has undertaken responsibility for the existence of a contract of insurance under Part VI of the Act or the liability is in fact covered by a contract of insurance.[36] A vehicle that has been unlawfully taken from the possession of the Crown is deemed to continue in that possession while it is so removed.[37]

(b) a claim arising out of the use of a vehicle not required to be covered by insurance by virtue of section 144 of the Act unless the use was in fact covered by a contract of insurance.[38]

(c) a claim by, or for the benefit of, someone (the beneficiary) other than the person suffering death, injury or other damage, which is made either in respect of a cause of action or judgment assigned to the beneficiary or pursuant to a right of subrogation or contractual or other right belonging to the beneficiary.

(d) a claim in respect of damage to a motor vehicle or losses arising therefrom where, at the time the damage was sustained, there was no insurance in force as required by Part VI of the Act and the claimant either knew or ought to have known of the lack of insurance.

(e) a claim by a person being carried in the vehicle[39] who, at the time of the use giving rise to the liability, was voluntarily allowing himself to be carried and either before the commencement of this journey in the vehicle or after such commencement if he could reasonably be expected to have alighted from the vehicle he knew or ought to have known[40] that:

(1) the vehicle had been stolen or unlawfully taken;

(2) the vehicle was being used without an insurance in force to comply with Part VI of the Act,

---

[34] *Gardner v. Moore* [1984] A.C. 548. See also para. 14–39, *ante*.
[35] cl. 6.
[36] cl. 6(1)(a).
[37] cl. 6(5)(a). This provision seems curious since vehicles owned by or in the possession of the Crown are not made subject to Part VI of the Act—see note 27 to para. 29–4, *ante*. But since 1947 the Crown has been vicariously liable for the torts of its servants under Crown Proceedings Act 1947, s.2. It may be that the purpose of cl. 6(1)(a) is to ensure that M.I.B. will not be liable to pay damages awarded against the Crown except in the two specified instances.
[38] See para. 29–39, *ante*.
[39] "Being carried in a vehicle" includes being carried upon or entering or getting on to or alighting from a vehicle—cl. 6(5)(b).
[40] This includes knowledge of matters of which he could reasonably be expected to have been aware had he not been under the self-induced influence of drink or drugs—cl. 6(4).

(3) the vehicle was being used in the course or furtherance of a crime, or

(4) the vehicle was being used as a means of escape from, or avoidance of, lawful apprehension.

The burden of proving knowledge is on M.I.B., but, in the absence of evidence to the contrary, proof of any of the following is to be taken as proof of knowledge:

(i) that the claimant was the owner[41] or registered keeper of the vehicle or had caused or permitted its use;

(ii) that the claimant knew the vehicle was being used by a person who was below the legal minimum age for driving such a vehicle;

(iii) that the claimant knew that the person driving was disqualified from holding or obtaining a driving licence;

(iv) that the claimant knew that the user of the vehicle was neither its owner or registered keeper nor the owner or registered keeper of any other vehicle.[42]

29–46 "Ought to have known". The meaning of this phrase in the equivalent exemption in the 1988 agreement was the subject of the House of Lords' decision in *White v. White*.[43] Article 1(4) of the second Motor Insurance E.C. Directive,[44] which the relevant part of both the 1988 and 1999 agreements implements, only permits exemption "in respect of persons who voluntarily entered the vehicle which caused the damage or injury when the [M.I.B.] can prove that they knew it was uninsured." Construing the agreement in the light of this, it was held that this meant primarily that the claimant passenger possessed information leading to the conclusion that the driver was uninsured. While this included the situation where the passenger had information leading to the conclusion that the driver might well not be insured but deliberately refrained from asking, it did not cover the situation where the passenger did not think about insurance even if this was negligent in the sense that an ordinary prudent passenger in this position would have inquired about it. The same construction must be placed on all the exemptions in clause 5 described in para. 29–45 (e).

[41] "Owner" includes the person in possession of a vehicle subject to a hire purchase agreement—cl. 6(5)(c).

[42] Note that the presumptions and the exemption relating to intoxification were new in the 1999 agreement. For authorities on the much less expansively worded equivalent clause in the earlier agreements see *Porter v. Addo*; *Porter v. M.I.B.* [1978] 2 Lloyd's Rep. 463. See also *Stinton v. M.I.B.* [1995] R.T.R. 167.

[43] [2001] U.K.H.L.9; [2001] 1 W.L.R. 481. The Court of Appeal (*Mighell v. Reading*; *White v. White* [1999] Lloyd's Rep. I.R. 30) had been prepared to assume that the wording of the agreement was incompatible with the Directive, but held that the latter did not have direct effect and that the phrase could not be struck out of the agreement. They held that a claimant without actual knowledge might have a claim for damages against the Secretary of State for failing properly to implement the Directive, under the principle established in *Francovich v. Italy* [1991] E.C.R. I–5337, although following the House of Lords' decision, this became academic. However, a similar question has arisen under the untraced drivers agreement; see para. 29–48, *ante*. In the light of the Court of Appeal decision, which was issued before the date of the 1999 agreement, it is perhaps surprising that the wording of this agreement does not better reflect the wording of the Directive.

[44] 84/5/E.E.C.

29–47 Untraced drivers. Before 1969, there was no liability on M.I.B. to make any payment where damage resulted from the use of a vehicle, the owner or driver of which could not be traced, because it was impossible to obtain a judgment. Sometimes ex gratia payments were made[45] but on April 21 1969 a further agreement was made between the Minister of Transport and M.I.B. to deal with this problem. This agreement was replaced by an Agreement of November 22 1972 entitled "Compensation of Victims of Untraced Drivers", and this in turned was replaced by one with the same title of June 14, 1996.

These agreements put on a formal basis that practice that was followed in making ex gratia payments under the 1946 Agreement. The 1996 agreement applies in respect of events giving rise to death or injury on or after July 12, 1996.[46] The provisions of the agreement are rather complex and only the most salient features of the scheme can be set out here. It is determinable by either party giving to the other not less than 12 months' notice in writing.[47]

29–48 Coverage of the agreement. M.I.B. will accept applications for payment in respect of death or bodily injury resulting from the use of a motor-vehicle on a road in Great Britain where[48]:

(1) the applicant cannot trace any person responsible or, where more than one person was responsible, cannot trace one of those persons[49]; and

(2) the death or injury was caused in such circumstances that the untraced person would be liable in damages on the balance of probabilities; and

(3) the untraced person's liability is one that is required to be covered by insurance under the Road Traffic Act.

M.I.B. will not accept cases of deliberate "running down."[50] Also excluded[51] are cases where the injured party was allowing himself to be carried in a vehicle and either before or after the commencement of his journey in the vehicle, if he could reasonably be expected to have alighted from the vehicle, he knew or had reason to believe that the vehicle:

(i) had been stolen or unlawfully taken, or

(ii) was being used without there being in force in relation to its use a contract of insurance complying with the 1988 Act, or

(iii) was being used in the course or furtherance of crime, or

(iv) was being used as a means of escape from or avoidance of lawful apprehension.[52]

As this Agreement also implements the second E.C. Motor Insurance

---

[45] Note 6 to the Agreement of 1946. In *Adams v. Andrews* [1964] 2 Lloyd's Rep. 347, no *ex gratia* payment was made.

[46] cl. 1(1)(a). The 1972 agreement will still apply to events occurring up to that date.

[47] cl. 27.

[48] cl. 1(1).

[49] Difficulty may arise as to the meaning of the word "trace". Clearly a driver who disappears immediately after an accident is an "untraced driver", but suppose the driver is taken into custody and subsequently escapes, or disappears after a writ has been served, is he untraced? It is submitted that a driver is "untraced" if he cannot be served. If he can be or is served, a judgment can be obtained and, if he is uninsured, the Agreement relating to uninsured drivers will apply.

[50] cl. 1(1)(e).

[51] cl. 1(2)(b)(i).

[52] The 1972 agreement was more narrowly worded in the equivalent clause, applying to cases where the injured party was being carried in a vehicle taken without the consent of its owner when he knew or had reason to believe that there was no consent.

Directive, the phrase "had reason to believe" must be construed in accordance with the decision of the House of Lords on the Uninsured Drivers' Agreement in *White v. White*.[53] The Agreement excludes cases where the vehicle was owned by or in the possession of the Crown unless someone else has undertaken responsibility for the existence of a contract of insurance.[54] Applications must be made in writing to M.I.B. within three years of the date of the accident,[55] and the incident must be reported to the police within 14 days or as soon as the applicant reasonably can, and the applicant must co-operate with the police.[56]

Clause 5 of the agreement provides for cases where an untraced person and an identified person are each partly responsible for a death or injury and defines the conditions under which M.I.B. will make a contribution in respect of the responsibility of the untraced person.

29–49 Amount payable. The amount which M.I.B. will award to the applicant will be assessed in the same way as a court would have assessed the amount of damages payable by the untraced person if the applicant had been able to bring a successful claim, but M.I.B. is not required to include any sum representing loss of earnings if the applicant has received his wages or salary in full or in part from his employer.[57] Interest is not payable on an award under the Agreement,[58] but the question of whether or not this is compatible with the second Motor Insurance Directive has been referred to the European Court of Justice.[59]

29–50 Conditions precedent. There are three conditions precedent to M.I.B.'s liability[60]:

(1) The applicant must give all such assistance as may be reasonably required by M.I.B., to enable any necessary investigation to be carried out;

(2) The applicant must, if so required, take all reasonable steps to obtain judgment against any person or persons in respect of their liability to the applicant subject to an indemnity as to costs;

(3) The applicant must, if so required, assign to M.I.B. or their nominee any judgment obtained by him, but M.I.B. or their nominee shall be accountable for any excess over what M.I.B. shall have paid to the applicant, after deducting the reasonable expenses of recovering the sum for which judgment was given.

29–51 M.I.B. procedure. Once the application is made, M.I.B. must cause it to be investigated. They can then, if they wish, make an offer of immediate settlement stating to the claimant the evidence relating to the circumstances of the death or injury and the circumstances and evidence relevant to the

---

[53] [2001] U.K.H.L. 9, [2001] 1 W.L.R. 481. See para. 29–46, *ante*.

[54] cl. 1(2)(a).

[55] cl. 1(1)(f).

[56] cl. 1(1)(g).

[57] cll 3 and 4. The 1972 agreement also excluded liability for any amount in respect of loss of expectation of life.

[58] *Evans v. M.I.B.* [1999] Lloyd's Rep. I.R. 30.

[59] *Evans v. Secretary of State for the Environment, Transport and the Regions and the Motor Insurers' Bureau* [2001] EWCA Civ 32, [2001] 2 C.M.L.R. 10, [2002] Lloyd's Rep. I.R. 1. See also para. 29–39, *ante*.

[60] cl. 6.

quantum of the offer. If the claimant accepts this offer, M.I.B. are then discharged.[61] If the offer is not accepted or if M.I.B. decide not to make an offer, M.I.B. must cause a report to be made on the application and then decide whether to make an award and, if so, in what amount.[62] Clause 9 of the agreement provides that when M.I.B. have decided whether to make a payment, they are to notify the applicant of their decision, setting out the circumstances and the evidence on which they base their decision and, if they refuse to make a payment, their reasons for that refusal. The applicant has a right to appeal within six weeks to an arbitrator selected by the Minister from a panel of Queen's Counsel appointed by the Lord Chancellor and the Lord Advocate.[63] As a result of receiving the applicant's comments, M.I.B. may investigate the application further and communicate with the applicant again; if they do this, the applicant has six weeks from the date of the further communication to decide whether to go on with this appeal.[64] Where the applicant appeals on the ground only that the amount awarded is too low, M.I.B. will ask the arbitrator to decide the issue of M.I.B.'s liability to make any payment.[65] M.I.B. will send the relevant documents to the arbitrator on which he will base his decision; if he requests M.I.B. to make a further investigation, the applicant will have an opportunity to comment on the result of that investigation.[66] If he considers the appeal to be unreasonable, the arbitrator may award that the applicant pays his fees; otherwise each party to the appeal will bear his own costs, the arbitrator's fee being paid by M.I.B.[67]

29–52 M.I.B. as party to litigation. As a matter of strict law, an injured claimant has no cause of action against M.I.B. because he is not a party to its agreements with the Secretary of State.[68] It has been said that the Secretary of State could seek an order for specific performance of its agreements by the Bureau, following which the injured claimant could enforce it for his own benefit.[69] If the Secretary of State refused to sue, it might be possible to join him as a defendant to the action brought by the claimant against M.I.B.[70]

29–53 In practice claimants sue M.I.B. directly. The point that they have no cause of action is not taken by M.I.B., and the court does not of its own volition raise either that objection or the absence of the Secretary of State as a party to the proceedings.[71] The court is entitled to proceed upon the

[61] cll. 24–26..
[62] cl. 7.
[63] cll 11, 12 and 18. There is no right to go to the courts: *Persson v. London Country Buses* [1974] 1 W.L.R. 569. But an arbitrator's award will be set aside or remitted if it is wrong in law, *Elizabeth v. M.I.B.* [1981] R.T.R. 405.
[64] cl. 13.
[65] cl. 14.
[66] cll. 15 and 17.
[67] cll. 21 and 22.
[68] *Gurtner v. Circuit* [1968] 2 Q.B. 587, 596, 598–599, 606; *Hardy v. M.I.B.* [1964] 2 Q.B. 745, 757, 766; *Albert v. M.I.B.* [1971] 2 All E.R. 1345, 1354. As was pointed out in *Evans v. Secretary of State for the Environment, Transport and the Regions* [2001] E.W.C.A. Civ 32, para. 4, [2002] Lloyd's Rep. I.R. 1, 4 the Contracts (Rights of Third Parties) Act 1999 might produce a different result if either of the agreements is renewed or replaced after its date of commencement (May 11, 2000).
[69] *Gurtner v. Circuit* [1968] 2 Q.B. 587, 596, 598–599, 606.
[70] *Gurtner v. Circuit* [1968] 2 Q.B. 587, 596, *per* Lord Denning M.R. No opinion was expressed on this point by the other members of the court.
[71] *Coward v. M.I.B.* [1963] 1 Q.B. 259, 265.

assumption that the bureau has for good consideration contracted with the claimant to perform its agreement with the Secretary of State, or that for some reason it is estopped from denying privity of contract.[72] The House of Lords has been prepared to turn a blind eye to the legal position of the claimant,[73] while deprecating the practice.[74] Lord Denning M.R. has said that he hopes this point will never be taken.[75] The bureau has said that it never will be.[76] Lord Hailsham L.C. has commented that the foundations of the 1972 agreements in jurisprudence are better not questioned any more than were the demises of John Doe and the behaviour of Richard Roe in the old ejectment actions.[77] However, it is not clear that M.I.B.'s status as a "private law contractor"[78] is compatible with the second EC Motor Insurance Directive, a question that has been referred to the European Court of Justice.[79]

29–54 Adding as a new party. Much more difficulty used to be caused by the question whether M.I.B. can be joined in an action that has been commenced against some other defendant.[80] The wording of the Civil Procedure Rules[81] now permits the court to order a person to be joined as a new party

> "if (a) it is desirable to add the new party so that the court can resolve all the matters in dispute in the proceedings; or (b) there is an issue involving the new party and an existing party which is connected to the matters in dispute in the proceedings, and it is desirable to add the new party so that the court can resolve that issue."

This is clearly wide enough to allow the M.I.B. to be added as a party in any case whose outcome might impose a liability on it,[82] except perhaps a case that might impose liability under the untraced drivers agreement, under which it has wide powers to direct the action.[83]

---

[72] *Gurtner v. Circuit* [1968] 2 Q.B. 587, 599, *per* Diplock L.J., who in *Hardy v. M.I.B.* [1964] 2 Q.B. 745, 766 suggested that M.I.B. could not take the point without being in breach of their agreement with the minister.

[73] *Albert v. M.I.B.* [1971] 2 All E.R. 1345, 1347–1348, *per* Lord Donovan; *M.I.B. v. Meanen* [1971] 2 All E.R. 1372; *Gardner v. Moore* [1984] A.C. 548.

[74] *Albert v. M.I.B.* [1971] 2 All E.R. 1345, 1354, *per* Viscount Dilhorne.

[75] *Hardy v. M.I.B.* [1964] 2 Q.B. 745, 757. But there may be occasions in litigation between a claimant and an insured person in which the court is obliged to consider it: *Gurtner v. Circuit* [1968] 2 Q.B. 587, 599, *per* Diplock L.J.

[76] *Albert v. M.I.B.* [1971] 2 All E.R. 1345, 1354; *Persson v. London Country Buses* [1974] 1 W.L.R. 569, 572.

[77] *Gardner v. Moore* [1984] A.C. 548, 556.

[78] *Per* Hobhouse L.J. in *Mighell v. Reading* [1999] Lloyd's Rep. I.R. 30 at 42. Compare, though, the views of Lord Cooke of Thornton in *White v. White* [2001] U.K.H.L. 9, [2001] 1 W.L.R. 381 at 490, para. 35.

[79] *Evans v. Secretary of State for the Environment, Transport and the Regions* [2001] E.W.C.A. Civ 32, [2002] Lloyd's Rep. I.R. 1.

[80] For a more detailed consideration of this question under the former Rules of the Supreme Court, see the 9th edition of this book at paras. 29–51 to 29–54.

[81] S.I. 1998 No. 3132.

[82] For example, an action brought by an insurer for a declaration that it was entitled to avoid the policy for non-disclosure and misrepresentation (compare *Fire Auto and Marine Ins. Co. v. Greene* [1964] 2 Q.B. 687) and as to the liability of an uninsured driver (*Gurtner v. Circuit* [1968] 2 Q.B. 587).

[83] Compare *White v. London Transport* [1971] 2 Q.B. 721.

(d) *Breach of Duty to Insure*

29–55 Common law remedy. It has been seen that it is an offence for any person to use, or cause or permit any other person to sue, a motor vehicle on a road or other public place without there being in force a valid policy or security complying with the requirements of the Act.[84] Several years before the establishment of M.I.B., the courts had provided a remedy at common law to the victims of uninsured and impecunious drivers in the form of an action for damages for breach of the statutory duty to insure. It has been held that the commission of an offence under section 143 is a breach of statutory duty, which will support an action for damages at the suit of any person who suffers loss as a result.[85] Difficulties have arisen in construing the words of the section "causing or permitting" a vehicle to be used.[86] Where the owner had lent his car to a friend who was not insured, who in turn had allowed it to be driven by another person who was not insured, and neither the borrower nor the driver had the means to pay damages, a person injured by the negligent driving of the car was held in *Monk v. Warbey*[87] entitled to recover against the owner the damages awarded against the driver. Where an owner, who was covered against third-party risks only while the car was being used for business purposes, gave general permission to another person to use it, and an accident happened while that person was using it for private purposes, it was held by the House of Lords that the owner was guilty of causing or permitting it to be used uninsured, and that the injured plaintiff could recover against him.[88] But where a person who was not the owner of the vehicle had participated in a fraudulent scheme, allowing it to be registered in his name and conniving at the forgery of his name by his brother in the application for insurance, it was held that he had neither caused nor permitted the use of the vehicle.[89] Nor has a trader or auctioneer who sells a car to a person who drives it away uninsured, since he has parted with control of the car and had no control over the driver and cannot be said either to cause or permit what is done.[90] In another case an insurer issued a policy to a motor trader who hired out cars to be driven by the hirers; the trader was empowered to issue sub-policies in respect of each hiring, subject to a proviso excluding Jews from cover. The trader hired the car to a Jew who injured a third party and it was held that the insurer had not caused or permitted the use of the car.[91]

The principle of *Monk v. Warbey* has been applied in Australia under the Tasmania Traffic Act 1925, which contains provisions similar to those of section 143. Accordingly a finance company from whom a car had been obtained on the usual hire-purchase terms was held guilty of causing or permitting its use in breach of the Act where the hirer was uninsured, and to

---

[84] s.143; see para. 29–2, *ante*.
[85] *Monk v. Warbey* [1935] 1 K.B. 75. The action is "in respect of personal injuries" and therefore the limitation period is three years under the Limitation Act 1980, s.11: *Norman v. Ali* [2000] Lloyd's Rep. I.R. 395.
[86] See also para. 29–3, *ante*.
[87] [1935] 1 K.B. 75.
[88] *McLeod v. Buchanan* [1940] 2 All E.R. 179.
[89] *Goodbarne v. Buck* [1940] 1 K.B. 771.
[90] *Watkins v. O'Shaugnessy* [1939] 1 All E.R. 385; *Peters v. General Accident Corporation Ltd* [1938] 2 All E.R. 267.
[91] *Richards v. Brain and Port of Manchester* [1934] 4 All E.R. 458 (Goddard J.); 152 L.T. 413.

have incurred liability to satisfy a judgment in favour of an injured third party for damages which the hirer was unable to pay.[92]

29–56 An employer has no statutory duty towards his employee to keep insured a vehicle driven by his employee[93] but there is an implied term of the contract of employment that the employer will comply with the provisions of the statute and thus he will be liable to an employee who suffers any loss or damage as a result of the vehicle being uninsured.[94] In *British School of Motoring Ltd v. Simms*[95] it was held that the contract between a driving school and its pupil contained an implied term that the car used for the lessons would be so insured as to cover it while being driven by the pupil in the course of the lessons.

29–57 Damage caused by breach. For an action to lie for breach of the duty imposed by section 143, it is necessary for the plaintiff to show, not only that the defendant used, or caused or permitted to be used, the vehicle in breach of the Act, but also that the damage he suffered flowed from the breach.[96] Thus, where a person whose negligence caused an accident died after the lapse of six months and before the issue of a writ against him, an attempt to sue the owner of the car failed, because the damage suffered by the plaintiff resulted not from the defendant's breach of duty, but from the plaintiff's failure to comply with the provisions of the Law Reform (Miscellaneous Provisions) Act 1934.[97]

　Though it is not essential for the injured person to sue the uninsured driver first, before proceeding against the owner on the grounds of his breach of the duty to insure,[98] it is necessary to prove that the driver is unable to pay the damages which have been incurred. Ability to pay the damages in full within a short time after judgment is the relevant criterion. The owner cannot escape liability on the grounds that the driver can satisfy the judgment in instalments over a period of years.[99]

29–58 It will now often be the case that, where the driver has no means, an unsatisfied judgment will be satisfied by the M.I.B.[1] Where a plaintiff succeeded against both an impecunious driver and against the owner for breach of statutory duty, judgment was entered subject to the proviso that if the M.I.B. satisfied the judgment against the driver, the plaintiff could not enforce judgment against the owner.[2] However, the fact that the Bureau might be liable does not affect the right to sue for breach of statutory duty.[3]

---

[92] *Broad v. Parish* (1941) 64 C.L.R. 588.
[93] *Gregory v. Ford* [1951] 1 All E.R. 121.
[94] *Semtex v. Gladstone* [1954] 1 W.L.R. 945.
[95] [1971] 1 All E.R. 317.
[96] *Richards v. Brain and Port of Manchester* [1934] 4 All E.R. 458, 464.
[97] *Daniels v. Vaux* [1938] 2 K.B. 203. The provision in question was repealed in this respect by s.4 of the Law Reform (Limitation of Actions) Act 1954, 2 & 3 Eliz. 2, c. 36. The decision might have been different if the deceased had been impecunious and at all times unable to meet a judgement, p. 209.
[98] *Monk v. Warbey* [1935] 1 K.B. 75.
[99] *Martin v. Dean* [1971] 2 Q.B. 208.
[1] See para. 29–40, *ante*.
[2] *Corfield v. Groves* [1950] 1 All E.R. 488.
[3] *Norman v. Aziz* [2000] Lloyd's Rep. I.R. 52.

(e) *Terms and Conditions of Motor Policies*

29–59 Categories of clauses. Motor insurance policies commonly contain provisions extending cover to other drivers besides the assured[4] and the assured when driving cars other than those in the policy schedule.[5] They also contain clauses limiting the insurers' liability by reference to such matters as the purpose and manner of the user of the insured vehicle, its condition and upkeep, the qualifications and fitness of persons permitted to drive, and the obligations placed on the assured in the event of an accident and subsequent claim on the policy. In every case it is necessary to consider the juristic status of the particular clause under review, because the consequences of non-compliance will vary depending upon whether it is construed as a warranty, an exclusion clause, a suspensive condition, or a condition precedent to liability.[6]

29–60 Extension of cover to other drivers. A motor vehicle policy frequently contains a clause extending the cover to relatives and friends of the assured driving the insured vehicle with his permission. It has long been settled that the purpose of such a clause is to indemnify such persons for sums which they become liable to pay and not merely to indemnify the assured for sums which he becomes liable to pay by reason of such a person being the driver,[7] and it has been pointed out that the Road Traffic Act 1988 contains provisions designed to overcome any objections based on the statutory requirement that the name of the assured must be inserted in the policy or on the common law rule that a third party cannot sue on a contract to which he is not a party.[8]

In each case it is a matter of fact whether permission has been granted[9] and whether, if it has been granted subject to terms, those terms have been complied with. If the assured permits a friend to drive his car for a particular purpose, the insurers will not be at risk if the car is used for any other purpose.[10] The insurers will be liable if the relevant permission has been granted by the agent of the assured.[11]

29–61 Where the extension clause agreed to treat "any person in the insured's employ" as though he were the assured, it was held that the clause covered a person employed under a contract of agency with the assured as well as one employed under a contract of service.[12] In one case an extension clause applied to "any person who holds a licence to drive and is driving the vehicle with the insured's consent". It was held in the county court that this included the holder of a provisional licence even when he was not

---

[4] See paras 29–60 to 29–64, *ante.*
[5] See para. 29–16, *ante.*
[6] See Ch. 10, especially at paras 10–1 to 10–10, *ante.*
[7] *Williams v. Baltic Insurance Association of London Ltd* [1924] 2 K.B. 282.
[8] See paras 29–16 to 29–20, *ante.*
[9] *Paget v. Poland* (1947) 80 Ll.L.R. 283; *Tattersall v. Drysdale* [1935] 2 K.B. 174. A person employed to drive on his master's business will not usually be driving "with the general consent of the insured": *Lester Bros. (Coal Merchants) Ltd v. Avon Ins. Co. Ltd* (1942) 72 Ll.L.R. 109.
[10] *Browning v. Phoenix Ass. Co. Ltd* [1960] 2 Lloyd's Rep. 360; *Singh v. Rathour* [1988] 1 W.L.R. 422
[11] *Pailor v. Co-operative Ins. Society Ltd* (1930) 38 Ll.L.R. 237, 239 per Scrutton L.J.
[12] *Burton v. Road Transport & General Ins. Co. Ltd* (1939) 63 Ll.L.R. 253. *Quaere* whether this case would be extended to an independent contractor employed by the assured.

accompanied by a qualified driver as required by the Road Traffic Act.[13] If a policy covers a person driving with the permission of the assured, provided that he is not disqualified from holding a licence, the word "disqualified" means disqualified either by an order of the court or by reason of the driver's age. It does not mean prohibited from holding a licence by reason of mental or physical disability.[14]

29–62 A clause extending cover to persons driving the insured car with the permission of the assured has no effect once the insured car has been sold, and purchaser from the assured cannot claim an indemnity either as a purchaser or as an assignee of the policy unless the assignment was made with the consent of the insurers. This is because only the owner of the car can give permission within the terms of the clause, and one who sells a car ceases to be the owner.[15] On the other hand in *Kelly v. Cornhill Insurance Co.*[16] a father, who had permitted his son to drive his car, died and eight months after his death, while the car was still insured, the son had an accident. The House of Lords held that the permission continued until it was shown to have terminated and that the insurance company were therefore liable. It is not easy to reconcile the reasoning in the cases, since on the father's death the ownership of the car became vested in the father's executor who could not be said to have permitted the son to drive, but any other conclusion would lead to anomalous consequences, for example that the son might have started a journey in an insured vehicle but, by the time he arrived at his destination, be committing a criminal offence, by driving an uninsured vehicle.

29–63 The clause extending the insurers' liability is usually made expressly subject to the other terms and conditions of the policy in so far as they are applicable, and sometimes there is an express provision that one who drives with the permission of the assured is to be treated as if he were the insured person. Thus a clause requiring the assured to give notice of any claim or prosecution arising out of an accident is binding on a person seeking to rely on the extension clause.[17] When read in conjunction with the other provisions in the policy, such a clause may have unexpected consequences. For instance, when Miss Merle Oberon was injured while being driven by her chauffeur and recovered damages against him, it was held by the House of Lords that the insurers were liable to indemnify the chauffeur under the extension clause.[18] In such a case the assured, while being driven by someone else, becomes in effect a third party within the meaning of his own insurance policy. In *Richards v. Cox*[19] liability to the employees of the assured was excluded and the insurers undertook to treat an authorised driver of the insured vehicle if he were the assured. It was held that, for the purposes of a

---

[13] *Rendlesham v. Dunne* [1964] 1 Lloyd's Rep. 192 (Westminster County Court).
[14] *Edwards v. Griffiths* [1953] 1 W.L.R. 1199; *Mumford v. Hardy* [1956] 1 W.L.R. 163.
[15] *Peters v. General Accident Fire and Life Assurance Corporation Ltd* [1938] 2 All E.R. 267; *Smith v. Ralph* [1963] 2 Lloyd's Rep. 439.
[16] [1964] 1 W.L.R. 158.
[17] *Austin v. Zurich General Accident and Liability Insurance Co. Ltd* [1945] 1 K.B. 250.
[18] *Digby v. General Accident Fire and Life Assurance Corporation Ltd* [1943] A.C. 121.
[19] [1943] 1 K.B. 139.

claim by a driver other than the assured, the exception of liability to employees must be read as referring to employees of that driver, and the driver could recover the damages for which he was liable to an employee of the assured. On the other hand, in *Pailor v. Co-operative Insurance Society Ltd*[20] in the absence of words in the policy to the effect that an authorised driver was to be treated as if he were the assured, it was held that a clause permitting the car to be used about the business of the assured could not be construed so as to include the business of another authorised driver.

29–64 Where a policy specified the persons who might drive the insured vehicle as "the above-named proposer and his paid driver", it was held that these words included a driver who was driving for the assured but was paid by a customer of his.[21]

29–65 User of the vehicle—private, social domestic and pleasure purposes. Of the various conditions restricting the liability of the insurers by reference to the purposes for which the insured vehicle is used, the commonest are those which negative liability when the vehicle is being used for other than private or social, domestic or pleasure purposes, with or without an express exclusion of use for hire. Use for "private pleasure" includes carrying tools or timber for use in a garden.[22] A trip to see the Southend illuminations is clearly a use for "social domestic or pleasure purposes".[23] But using one's own car to visit a firm with which one intends to negotiate a contract is not a use for such purposes, although it may be more comfortable, pleasurable and restful than travelling in a hire car.[24] "Social purposes" are not necessarily confined to the private social life of the assured, but have been held to include social activities of a local authority of which the assured was a member.[25]

29–66 If a vehicle is used for giving lifts it can be difficult to decide whether it falls within the clause. Du Parcq J. has said that if an assured driving for social purposes gave a lift out of kindness courtesy or charity to someone who happened to be on business of his own, that would not cause the vehicle to be used other than for a social purpose.[26] But the question is what was the essential character or primary purpose of the journey, and it is submitted that the answer would be different if the journey was made from the outset only to accommodate the assured's acquaintance. Thus where the assured was asked to take an employee of his son to the dentist in the son's car, it was held that he was not using the car for a social domestic or pleasure purpose even though he would in any event have used the car to go home for lunch and return in the afternoon to help his son.[27]

29–67 Dual purposes. If the car is on a journey that has two purposes, neither being predominant, and one is a permitted user while the other is excluded, it is not being used only for the permitted user and is not covered

[20] (1930) 38 Ll.L.R. 237.
[21] *Bryan v. Forrow* [1950] 1 All E.R. 294.
[22] *Piddington v. Co-operative Ins. Co.* [1934] 2 K.B. 236.
[23] *McCarthy v. British Oak Ins. Co.* (1938) 61 Ll.L.R. 194.
[24] *Wood v. General Accident Fire and Life Assurance Corporation Ltd* (1948) 82 Ll.L.R. 77.
[25] *D.H.R. Moody (Chemists) Ltd v. Iron Trades Mutual Ins. Co.* [1971] 1 Lloyd's Rep. 386.
[26] *Passmore v. Vulcan Boiler & General Ins. Co.* (1936) 54 Ll.L.R. 92, 94.
[27] *Seddon v. Binions* [1978] 1 Lloyd's Rep. 381.

by the policy.[28] If the car is used for purposes other than those specified in the clause, the policy ceases to cover the car,[29] but the insurers are not entitled to avoid the insurance for breach of contract, or be discharged from all liability thereunder, unless the assured had warranted that it would be used only for the specified purposes.[30]

29–68 Use for hiring. This is often specifically excluded and has been held to refer to a journey on which a person pays the assured or driver of the car for its use, provided that (i) there is a genuine business arrangement for a stipulated sum[31] and (ii) there is an express or implied legal obligation to make that payment.[32] Where there is an exclusion of use "for hire or reward", more informal arrangements are caught by the wording, and liability was excluded where the assured carried fellow-employees to their place of work in return for a sum equivalent to the rail fare, there being no binding contract but merely an expectation, justified by a longstanding practice, that he would be paid.[33]

29–69 Statement by insurers. In 1975 motor insurers issued a statement[34] that the receipt of contributions as part of a car-sharing arrangement for social or similar purposes in respect of passenger carriage in a private car would not be regarded as carriage for hire or reward, or the use of the vehicle for hiring, provided that:

(i) the vehicle is not constructed or adapted to carry more than seven passengers;
(ii) the passengers are not being carried in the business of carrying passengers;
(iii) the total contributions received for the journey concerned do not involve an element of profit.

29–70 User of car for business of assured. A policy covering use for private purposes only or for social, domestic or pleasure purposes may well be expressed also to include "business or professional" use by the assured. Such clauses have been strictly construed and do not extend to business use by others driving the car with the consent of the assured.[35] In one case the permitted user was defined as "use for social, domestic and pleasure

---

[28] *Seddon v. Binions* [1978] 1 Lloyd's Rep. 381; *Browning v. Phoenix Ass. Co.* [1960] 2 Lloyd's Rep. 360, 367; *Passmore v. Vulcan Boiler & General Ins. Co.* (1936) 54 Ll.L.R. 92; *McGoona v. M.I.B.* [1969] 2 Lloyd's Rep. 34. The same principle was applied to a similar provision in a personal accident policy in *Killick v. Rendall* [2000] Lloyd's Rep. I.R. 581

[29] *Farr v. Motor Traders' Mutual Ins. Soc.* [1920] 3 K.B. 669.

[30] *Provincial Ins. Co. v. Morgan* [1933] A.C. 240—see Ch. 10, *ante*.

[31] *McCarthy v. British Oak Ins. Co.* (1938) 61 Ll.L.R. 194 (especially at 196).

[32] *Wyatt v. Guildhall Ins. Co.* [1937] 1 K.B. 653; *Bonham v. Zurich General Accident and Liability Ins. Co.* [1945] 1 K.B. 292, where the decision turned on the added words "or reward"; *Orr v. Trafalgar Insurance Co.* (1948) 82 Ll.L.R. 1.

[33] *Bonham v. Zurich General Accident and Liability Ins. Co.* [1945] K.B. 292, Mackinnon L.J. dissenting. In *Albert v. M.I.B.* [1971] 2 All E.R. 1345, the House of Lords was asked to define the words "vehicle in which passengers are carried for hire and reward" in s.203(4) of the 1960 Act. It was recognised that the wording was not identical with the policy exclusion wordings, but the decision in *Bonham* was cited with apparent approval by Lord Donovan at 1350 and Viscount Dilhorne at 1356. The receipt of contributions from passengers should not per se make the use one for hire or reward. There must be a business arrangement, *per* Lord Pearson at 1364.

[34] D.o.T. Circular 9/78, Annex 4. Compare the similar, although different, wording of s.150 of the Road Traffic Act 1988; see para. 29–14, *ante*.

[35] *Pailor v. Co-operative Ins. Society* (1930) 38 Ll.L.R. 237.

purposes and use for the business of the insured", and it was held that a journey by the assured and another person on the business of the firm by which they were both employed was not covered.[36] In a similar case the assured was described in the schedule as "carrying on or engaged in the business or profession of millinery"; in fact she had owned the business herself, but it had subsequently been converted into a limited company. It was held that a journey on the business of the company was not covered, since the plaintiff's business ceased to exist when the company was formed.[37] It has been held that there is no inconsistency between a clause giving cover for "use by assured in connection with this business" and an exclusion "for any purpose in connection with the motor trade" even where the assured is a garage proprietor, because the second clause is narrower than the first and excludes a liability which would otherwise be covered by the wide words of the first clause.[38]

29–71 In *D.H.R. Moody Ltd v. Iron Trades Mutual Insurance Company Ltd*[39] the "description of use" clause confined cover to use "for social domestic and pleasure purposes and use for the business of the Insured including carriage of goods [namely the business of pharmacists and no other]". An employee of the assured was a member of Clacton U.D.C., and procured the loan of the assured's car to be used to drive council visitors from abroad back to the airport, being driven by the clerk to the council. It was held that on that journey the car was being used for social purposes and not for the purpose of the clerk's employment. When "use for the carriage of goods in connection with any trade or business" is excluded from cover, it is a question of fact whether goods are carried on a given occasion as part of a business of the assured or only as a hobby.[40] Use for "agricultural purposes" may include taking a show pony to show.[41]

29–72 Use for hire or reward other than private hire. Where such a use was excluded, and private hire was defined to mean "letting of the vehicle supplied from the policyholder's garage", it was held that "private hire" so defined meant hire for a definite journey as distinct from plying for hire, and included the picking up of passengers for that journey away from the policyholder's garage.[42]

29–73 Other exclusions as to use. In *A.P. Salmon Contractors Ltd v. Monksfield*[43] liability was excluded for death or injury caused by the

---

[36] *Passmore v. Vulcan Boiler and General Ins. Co. Ltd* (1936) 54 Ll.L.R. 92; followed in *Browning v. Phoenix Ass. Co.* [1960] 2 Lloyd's Rep. 360 and *McGoona v. M.I.B.* [1969] 2 Lloyd's Rep. 34.

[37] *Levinger v. Licenses and General Ins. Co. Ltd* (1936) 54 Ll.L.R. 68.

[38] *Gray v. Blackmore* [1934] 1 K.B. 95.

[39] [1971] 1 Lloyd's Rep. 386, 388–389.

[40] *Jones v. Welsh Insurance Corporation Ltd* [1937] 4 All E.R. 149 (keeping sheep as a side-line held not to be a hobby—in Wales).

[41] *Henderson v. Robson* (1949) 113 J.P. 313.

[42] *Lyons v. Denscombe* [1949] 1 All E.R. 977 (disapproved in *Wurzal v. Addison* [1965] 2 Q.B. 131 on another point).

[43] [1970] 1 Lloyd's Rep. 387.

spreading of material or substance from the insured vehicle or load carried by it. Part of a load of plywood fell off the insured lorry, being inadequately secured. It was held that "spreading" was ambiguous, since it might refer either to a deliberate dissemination or to an accidental spillage, and the exception was construed contra proferentem to refer only to deliberate spreading, as of grit on to a road. In *Palmer v. Cornhill Insurance Co.*[44] a term was orally agreed that the cover was limited to use of the vehicle in a particular locality, and the assured was unable to claim an indemnity when an accident occurred outside it.[45] Policies usually exclude liability while the vehicle is used for racing, pace-making or speed trials or is taking part in motor rallies. In a case on a life policy it was held, applying evidence of motor sport usage, that motor racing did not include a motor club sprint event.[46] Where liability is excluded "while the insured vehicle has a trailer attached thereto", the exception is not apt to cover the towing of another vehicle.[47]

29–74 Vehicle in the charge of a person not authorised to drive. In *Samuelson v. National Insurance and Guarantee Corporation*[48] the policy excluded liability while the insured vehicle was "being driven by, or for the purpose of being driven, is in charge of any person other than an authorised driver described in the Schedule". The assured was the only scheduled driver. The car was stolen while outside a spare parts agency and in the custody of a repairer who had driven it there to select some spare parts for it. The insurers relied upon the exception. It was held that the exception required a determination of whether the repairer was in charge of the car for the purpose of driving it at the precise moment of the loss, and that, because he was at that moment inside the spare parts agency selecting parts for the purpose of seeing if they fitted the car and, if so, purchasing them, the car was in his charge for that purpose and not for the purpose of driving it, albeit that he would then have driven it away. It was further held that a proviso that the exclusion of use for any purpose in connection with the motor trade was not to apply to a time when the car was in the custody of a motor trader for its upkeep did not create an exception to the clause dealing with unauthorised drivers so as to provide cover while the car was in the charge of the repairer for any purpose whatsoever.[49]

29–75 Condition of the vehicle. Many motor vehicles policies contain an exception stating that the company will not be liable "while the vehicle is being driven in an unsafe or unroadworthy condition". In *Barrett v. London General Insurance Co.*[50] Goddard J. held, applying marine insurance

---

[44] (1935) 52 Ll.L.R. 78.
[45] s.148(2)(e) (see para. 29–32, *ante.*) would prevent insurers from reliance on such a term as against a third party unless it were held that an oral term is not within the written policy, as in that case.
[46] *Scragg v. United Kingdom Temperance & General Provident Institution* [1976] 2 Lloyd's Rep. 227.
[47] *Jenkins v. Deane* (1933) 47 Ll.L.R. 342. The definition of trailer applied by the court would not cover a caravan.
[48] [1985] 2 Lloyd's Rep. 541.
[49] [1985] 2 Lloyd's Rep. 541, 543–544, *per* Robert Goff L.J.
[50] [1935] 1 K.B. 238.

decisions on unseaworthiness, that the insurer, in order to rely on the exclusion, must prove that the vehicle was unroadworthy when it set out on its journey, and not merely that it was unroadworthy at the time of the accident. He evidently thought that, were this not so, the insurers could avoid liability in a case where, for instance, a braking system became unserviceable in use and precipitated an almost simultaneous accident. In *Trickett v. Queensland Insurance Co.*[51] a vehicle was driven at night without lights for some time before an accident occurred. It was not shown whether the lights had been defective at the start of the journey, but the Privy Council held that liability was excluded by an exemption applying "while any motor-vehicle ... under this policy is: (e) being driven in a damaged or unsafe condition", disapproving the reasoning of Goddard J. It was further held that insurers did not have to prove the assured's knowledge of the defect.[52] In *Clarke v. National Insurance and Guarantee Corporation Ltd*[53] the exceptions clause in a policy on a Ford Anglia with four seats provided that the insurers should not be liable while the car was being driven in an unsafe or unroadworthy condition. The owner of the car drove the car with eight adult passengers in addition to himself and thus seriously impaired the steering, braking and control of the car, although there would have been nothing wrong with the car if it had been driven with a normal load. It was held by the Court of Appeal that when the car was being driven it was unroadworthy and that therefore it was being driven in an unroadworthy condition within the meaning of the clause. As Pearson L.J. said[54]

"There was nothing wrong with the intrinsic character of the vehicle, it is true: it was properly designed and manufactured and (so far as we know) maintained. But there was on this journey something wrong with its condition: it was in an overloaded condition."

29-76 In reaching this decision, the Court of Appeal relied upon marine cases in which it had been held that bad stowage and an excess of cargo could render a ship unseaworthy. It was held that such cases could be of assistance in construing roadworthiness conditions in motor policies, but that Goddard J. was wrong in *Barrett v. London General Insurance Co.*[55] to apply the warranty of seaworthiness cases to a policy term plainly dealing with the course of a journey and not merely its commencement.[56]

29-77 In *A.P. Salmon Contractors v. Monksfield*[57] liability was excluded while a lorry was "driven or used in an unsafe condition". Part of its load of plywood fell off and injured a pedestrian, because it was inadequately secured contrary to the Motor Vehicles (Construction & Use) Regulations 1960. It was held that the exclusion did not apply because the faulty loading did not make the lorry itself unsafe.[58]

It has also been held in a case where the insured vehicle was towing

---

[51] [1936] A.C. 159.
[52] *ibid.* at 165.
[53] [1964] 1 Q.B. 199.
[54] *ibid.* at 210.
[55] [1935] 1 K.B. 238.
[56] [1964] 1 Q.B. 199, 206, *per* Harman L.J.
[57] [1970] 1 Lloyd's Rep. 387 (Mayor's and City of London Court.)
[58] This is consistent with marine cases holding that bad stowage that affects only the cargo and not the safety of the ship does not make her unseaworthy; see *Scrutton on Charterparties* (20th ed., 1996), p. 98.

another vehicle, which had broken down, and the tow rope broke, that it did not follow that the vehicle was being driven in an unsafe condition since the tow rope was no part of the vehicle.[59]

29–78 Conveyance of excess load. An exception applying while the insured vehicle is conveying a load in excess of that for which it was constructed does not refer to the weight of a vehicle towed by it, but only to the weight carried upon the insured vehicle.[60] In *Houghton v. Trafalgar Insurance Co.*[61] the insurers argued that such an exemption excluded their liability while a car constructed to carry four persons was in fact carrying five. The defence failed. It was held that the clause only applied in cases where a weight load was specified for the particular vehicle, be it lorry or van, and did not apply to carrying an extra passenger in a private car.

29–79 Sometimes the exception as to the vehicle's being unsafe is added to a clause requiring the assured to keep the car in good repair as follows:

> "The insured shall take all due and reasonable precautions to safeguard the property insured and to keep it in a good state of repair. The insurers shall not be liable for damage or injury caused through driving the motor-vehicle in an unsafe condition either before or after the accident."

In such a case there is only one obligation, *viz.* to safeguard the vehicle and keep in it a good state of repair and the second sentence expresses the consequences of a failure on the part of the assured to exercise the duty imposed by the first sentence.[62]

29–80 Maintaining the vehicle in an efficient condition. Motor vehicle policies often provide that the assured shall take all reasonable steps to maintain the vehicle in an efficient condition. Thus, where a vehicle had no footbrake, the assured was not entitled to recover since he was in breach of this condition,[63] and a similar result was reached where the tyres of a vehicle had worn smooth and the vehicle skidded on icy ground.[64] In the latter case, Sellers J. said that the words "efficient condition" involved the taking of reasonable steps to make the vehicle or keep the vehicle roadworthy.[65] In a later case,[66] the learned judge repeated this opinion, which was approved in the Court of Appeal,[67] but it has been criticised in Scotland on the grounds that if that was what the condition meant, one would have expected it to say so.[68] The sheriff-substitute considered that the words "efficient condition" meant capable of doing what is normally and reasonably required of a

---

[59] *Jenkins v. Deane* (1933) 47 Ll.L.R. 342.

[60] *ibid.* at 345.

[61] [1954] 1 Q.B. 247.

[62] *Liverpool Corporation v. T. & H.R. Roberts* [1965] 1 W.L.R. 938. *Cf.* the policy in *Jenkins v. Deane* (1933) 47 Ll.L.R. 342 where, however, this point does not seem to have been taken. The first sentence in the clause was held to impose an obligation to implement a system for the maintenance of the vehicle, but not impose vicarious liability on the assured if a competent person instructed to follow that system negligently failed to do so, following Woolfall & *Rimmer v. Moyle* [1942] 1 K.B. 66. See para. 28–44, *ante.*

[63] *Jones v. Provincial Ins. Co. Ltd* (1929) 35 Ll.L.R. 135.

[64] *Brown v. Zurich General Accident and Liability Ins. Co. Ltd* [1954] 2 Lloyd's Rep. 243.

[65] At 246, followed in *Amey Properties v. Cornhill Ins. plc* [1996] L.R.L.R. 259.

[66] *Conn v. Westminster Motor Ins. Association Ltd* [1966] 1 Lloyd's Rep. 123.

[67] [1966] 1 Lloyd's Rep. 407, 409, *per* Willmer L.J.

[68] *McInnes v. National Motor and Accident Ins. Union Ltd* [1963] 2 Lloyd's Rep. 415.

vehicle, but it will not be often that these two approaches to the clause will produce any difference in the result of a particular case.

29–81 It will sometimes be necessary to consider this clause in connection with a clause providing that the observance and fulfilment of the conditions in the policy shall be a condition precedent to the liability of the insurers to make any payment under the policy. Where this is the case, the insurers will be able to escape liability if the vehicle has in fact not been maintained in an efficient condition, regardless of the question whether such inefficiency caused or contributed to an accident.[69] Thus in *Conn v. Westminster Motor Insurance Association Ltd*[70] the assured had allowed the tyres of a vehicle to become defective and, on proof of this, the court entered judgment for the insurance company without considering whether the defective tyres had contributed in any way to the accident out of which the claim arose.

29–82 Another clause in motor-vehicle policies that has a similar effect is a clause requiring the assured to "take all due and reasonable precautions to safeguard the property insured, and to keep it in a good state of repair". It has been held that this clause imposes a personal obligation on the assured to operate an adequate system of maintenance and repair, and where a motor-coach caused a collision, because the braking system failed as a result of an inadequate system on the part of the insured for the procuring of proper maintenance and repair, it was held that the assured could not recover.[71]

29–83 Conditions relating to the driver. Section 192(1) of the Road Traffic Act 1988 provides:

> " 'Driver', where a separate person acts as steersman of a motor vehicle, includes that person as well as any other person engaged in the driving of the vehicle, and the expression 'drive' shall be construed accordingly."

There may, therefore, be more than one driver of a vehicle. If one such driver holds a licence to drive, the fact that the other driver does not is immaterial and the vehicle remains insured notwithstanding an exceptions clause in the policy providing that the insurers shall not be liable if the insured vehicle is driven by a person not holding a driving licence.[72]

It is common to find exceptions to the effect that the insurers are not to be liable unless the person driving holds a licence to drive or has held and is not disqualified for holding or obtaining such a licence. In such a case if the driver has no licence the insurance will afford no cover.[73] The meaning of the world "disqualified" has already been considered.[74]

---

[69] The term is in effect a warranty—see para. 10–10, *ante*. However, a person insuring in an individual capacity should be protected against this consequence by virtue of the Statement of General Insurance Practice—see para. 2(b)(iii) of the Statement in Pt 7 of the *Encyclopedia of Insurance Law*, and para. 10–41, *ante*.

[70] [1966] 1 Lloyd's Rep. 407.

[71] *Liverpool Corporation v. T. & H.R. Roberts* [1965] 1 W.L.R. 938. Such a clause refers to the condition of the vehicle not to the quality of the driver: *Rendlesham v. Dunne* [1964] 1 Lloyd's Rep. 192.

[72] *R. v. Wilkins* (1951) 115 J.P. 443.

[73] *Lester (Coal Merchants) Ltd v. Avon Ins. Co. Ltd* (1942) 72 Ll.L.R. 109; *Haworth v. Dawson* (1946) 80 Ll.L.R. 19; *Spraggon v. Dominion Ins. Co. Ltd* (1941) 69 Ll.L.R. 1.

[74] See para. 29–6, *ante*, and *Edwards v. Griffiths* [1953] 1 W.L.R. 1199.

29–84 A clause referring to a vehicle "being driven by the insured" means being driven by or on behalf of the assured.[75] In *G.F.P. Units Ltd v. Monksfield*[76] the policy contained a "named driver" clause to the effect that the insurer would not be liable for any loss caused while the car was being driven by any person other than B or Mrs B. The court refused to read into this exception an implied term that would have restricted it to driving by another person with the knowledge and consent of the assured. Therefore, damage sustained while the car was in the hands of an unauthorised borrower was not covered.

29–85 Motor vehicle policies may contain clauses exempting liability for injury sustained by the assured while under the influence of drugs or intoxicating liquor. The question is whether the drugs or liquor disturb the quiet, calm, intelligent exercise of the faculties.[77] In Scotland one pint of lager is sufficient to have this effect.[78] The drug or liquor does not have to cause the injury.[79]

29–86 Sometimes a further clause is added to the obligation to maintain the vehicle in efficient condition to the effect that the assured shall use all care and diligence to avoid accidents and to employ only steady and sober drivers. Drunkenness on the part of the assured in such a case has been held to be a breach of the clause entitling the insurers to recover from the assured any sum payable by them to a third party.[80]

29–87 After the accident. Motor policies may contain a clause stating that the assured is not to act to the detriment or prejudice of the insurers' interests. It was held in *Dickinson v. Del Solar*[81] that an insured diplomat was not in breach of this clause when, at the instruction of the minister in charge of his legation, he waived his diplomatic immunity when served with process by the third party whom he had injured.

Another clause provides that the assured is not to make any admission of liability or offer or promise or payment to third parties without the insurers' consent. Such clauses, which are found in other liability insurance policies,[82] are not contrary to public policy, since they do not require the assured to lie about what has happened, but merely to refrain from making admissions of liability.[83]

A provision requiring the assured to obtain the approval of insurers in writing before authorising repairs to the insured vehicle may be waived by insurers' oral indication that the plaintiff could proceed with the repairs in

---

[75] *Lester Bros. (Coal Merchants) Ltd v. Avon Ins. Co Ltd* (1942) 72 Ll.L.R. 109.

[76] [1972] 2 Lloyd's Rep. 79. See also *Herbert v. Railway Passengers Ass. Co.* (1938) 60 Ll.L.R. 143; *Goodwin v. Lecky* [1946] N.I. 40.

[77] *Louden v. British Merchants Ins. Co.* [1961] 1 Lloyd's Rep. 155; applying *Mair v. Railway Passengers Ass. Co.* (1877) 37 L.T. 356.

[78] *Kennedy v. Smith* [1976] S.L.T. 110.

[79] *Louden v. British Merchants Ins. Co.* [1961] 1 Lloyd's Rep. 154, 158; *Givens v. Baloise Marine Insurance Co.* (1959) 17 D.L.R. 2d 7.

[80] *National Farmers Union Mutual Ins. Society v. Dawson* [1941] 2 K.B. 424—but see para. 29–31, *ante*; *Robertson v. London Guarantee & Accident Co.* [1915] 1 S.L.T. 195.

[81] [1930] 1 K.B. 376. The decision is not entirely free from difficulty but it seems that the insured's actions must be voluntary in order to attract the clause.

[82] See further para. 28–41, *ante*.

[83] *Terry v. Trafalgar Ins. Co. Ltd* [1970] 1 Lloyd's Rep. 524 (Mayor's & City of London Court).

question.[84] The manner in which repairs are authorised is important in determining the creation of rights and duties between the assured, the insurers and the repairers.[85]

Finally, motor policies invariably require the assured to give notice of the accident, and particulars in writing, within specified periods of time.[86] When fanciful particulars were given in support of a claim it was held that the "particulars" required were particulars of the accident, and that the condition was broken because the assured had not given detailed particulars of the accident which occurred but rather of an entirely different one.[87]

---

[84] *McConnell v. Poland* (1925) 23 Ll.L.R. 77.
[85] The several reported decisions on this question are discussed at para. 19–33, *ante.*
[86] See generally, paras 19–34 to 19–46, *ante.*
[87] *Cox v. Orion Ins. Ltd* [1982] R.T.R. 1. *Sed quaere.* This seems a little contrived, with respect, but it might have been described as a dishonest claim, leading to avoidance of the policy.

CHAPTER 30

AVIATION INSURANCE[1]

30–1 Compulsory insurance. The United Kingdom has signed both the Rome Convention of 1933 and the Rome Convention of 1952[2] but neither of these conventions has been implemented by legislation so as to form part of the municipal law. The conventions made provisions in respect of liability to persons or property on the surface of the ground or water, and included provisions for compulsory insurance against such liability. Pursuant to the 1933 Convention, Parliament passed Part IV of the Civil Aviation Act 1949, sections 43 to 46 of which contained provisions for such compulsory insurance. They never came into effect, however, and have now been repealed by section 128 of the Companies Act 1967. A further section conferring power to give effect to the Rome Convention of 1933 has likewise been repealed by section 26 of the Civil Aviation Act 1968.[3]

30–2 At the present time, therefore, there is no compulsory insurance against surface damage. Moreover, there is no compulsory insurance in respect of liability to passengers or cargo-owners. Any applicant for an air service licence, however, will be refused a licence if the Civil Aviation Authority is not satisfied that the resources of the applicant and financial arrangements made by him are adequate for discharging any obligations in respect of the business activities in which he will engage if he is granted a licence.[4] For all practical purposes, this has the effect of compulsory insurance for any aircraft operator under the Civil Aviation (Licensing) Act 1960.

30–3 Standard policies. Insurance of aviation risks has developed from the marine market. Much of the terminology and practice in the aviation market derives from the marine market, although there are differences between the practices in the two markets.[5] It is normal to insure aviation risks in comprehensive terms under a form of "all risks" cover, which is cut down by

---

[1] See, in general, McNair, *Law of the Air* (3rd ed., 1964), Ch. 11 and Shawcross and Beaumont, *Air Law*, (2002) Ch. 34.

[2] For the terms of the Conventions, see Shawcross and Beaumont, *op. cit.*, vol. 2, App. A.

[3] For a discussion of the provisions of the Civil Aviation Act 1949, see the fifth edition of this work at paras 1840–1844.

[4] Civil Aviation Act 1982 s.65(2)(b) together with the regulations made thereunder. See also for E.C. air transport operations, Reg. 2407/92, [1992] O.J. L240/1.

[5] *Kuwait Airways Corporation v. Kuwait Ins. Co. S.A.K* [1999] 1 Lloyd's Rep. 803, 809.

exclusions. Certain of the perils so excluded will be covered by separate extension clauses or agreements.[6]

Standard aviation policies will usually afford cover in respect of loss, or damage to the aircraft, third-party liability and passenger liability. Accidental loss or damage to the aircraft will be covered but liability will usually be excluded for wear and tear, structural defect and electrical or mechanical damage or breakdown. Consequential loss or damage may also be covered and the policy usually provides cover while the aircraft is in flight, taxi-ing on the ground or moored.[7] The policy may only give cover "during the normal course of the assured's operations", which will probably preclude cover for aeroplanes whose airworthiness certificates have expired, or which are about to be sold.[8] Any cover for aircraft spares will have to be separately granted.[9]

30–4 The standard aviation hull policy will also exclude war risks, but separate war risks cover may be available. Some points of construction of such cover arose in *Kuwait Airways Corporation v. Kuwait Insurance Company S.A.K.*[10] In giving judgment, the House of Lords was critical of the lack of care in the preparation and drafting of the insurance contract, and held that inter-underwriter agreements relating to war risks cover were of no help in construing a contract which did not incorporate them. The assured's aircraft were insured against loss or damage caused by:

    (a) war, invasion, acts of foreign enemies, hostilities etc;
    (b) strikes, riots, civil commotions or labour disturbances;
    (c) political or terrorist acts;
    (d) any malicious act or act of sabotage;
    (e) confiscation, nationalisation, seizure, restraint, detention, appropriation, requisition by Government, and
    (f) hijacking.

An extension provided that "it is noted and agreed that the indemnity provided by the Policy other than [(a)] is extended to include loss of or damage to Aircraft Spares."

The principal question for the House of Lords concerned the loss of spares which had been taken from Kuwait airport by the Iraqi military when Iraq invaded Kuwait in 1990. The insurers argued that the risk fell within (a), and so was excluded from the spares cover, and that head (e) was only intended to apply to peaceful acts of an internal government. The majority of the House of Lords rejected this argument, finding no reason to disapply the

---

[6] *ibid.*
[7] Cover afforded during the course of operation "over" certain territories will only be effective while the aircraft is in the air, not when on the ground: *Banque Sabbag v. Hope* [1972] 1 Lloyd's Rep. 253; [1973] 1 Lloyd's Rep. 233; [1974] 2 Lloyd's Rep. 301 H.L. The expression "ground risks" describes all relevant risks which occur on the ground: *Kuwait Airways Cpn. v. Kuwait Ins. Co.* [1996] 1 Lloyd's Rep. 664 at 681.
[8] *Banque Sabbag v. Hope* [1973] 1 Lloyd's Rep. 233 where the Court of Appeal differed from the views of Mocatta J. at first instance [1972] 1 Lloyd's Rep. 253. The point was not considered by the House of Lords.
[9] *Kuwait Airways Cpn. v. Kuwait Ins. Co.* [1996] 1 Lloyd's Rep. 664, 692.
[10] [1999] 1 Lloyd's Rep.803, reversing in part the Court of Appeal decision at [1997] 2 Lloyd's Rep. 687. The points from the first instance decision referred to at notes 5 and 7, *ante*, were not the subject of appeal.

ordinary meaning of the word "seizure". In this respect, they agreed with the unanimous view of the Court of Appeal. However, the majority of the Court of Appeal had then construed paragraph (a) as in effect an exclusion from cover in relation to spares, and denied recovery on the ground that the assured is not entitled to recover where an exclusion is a proximate cause of loss. The House of Lords, by contrast, construed the spares cover as a qualified extension and not an exclusion clause, as a matter of plain language. They rejected the further argument by insurers that to construe the contract as providing cover for spares not in transit where a cause of the loss was the occurrence or existence of a war would produce exorbitant risks which could not have been intended to be covered.

30–5 Premium adjustment clauses. Aviation hull policies employ different techniques for rewarding the insured for a good claims record. One method is to charge a high premium and then to give a refund at expiry, called "profit commission" or "good experience return", in the nature of a retrospective no claims bonus. Another is to charge a low initial premium, but to charge additional premiums in the event of claims, these being called "burning differentials", "burning costs", or "penalty premiums". Yet another method is where instalments of premium are deferred, but become payable in the event of a total loss. The risks of loss of profit commission or, alternatively, of becoming liable to pay the additional premiums, are insured separately under aviation contingency risk policies, usually by a different insurer from the insurers on the hull cover. In order to write hull cover, liability cover and contingency business in the United Kingdom, aviation insurers should be authorised to write aviation, aviation liability and miscellaneous financial loss business.[11]

30–6 Third-party liability. The policy will provide indemnity against liability to third parties for death or personal injury or damage to property. This will include the statutory liability under section 40(2) of the Civil Aviation Act 1949 for damage caused "by, or by a person in, or an article or person falling from, an aircraft while in flight, taking off or landing". It has been held that an aircraft does not begin to take off until the pilot has brought the aeroplane to the position where he begins his take-off run, so that any preliminary taxi-ing is not part of the taking off.[12]

30–7 The meaning of "in flight" has also given rise to difficulties, and its interpretation must depend on the context. In connection with the wording of the statutory liability mentioned above, it is to be distinguished from take off or landing; but a pilot may take out a life or personal accident policy which is to attach as soon as the aircraft is "in flight". In *Dunn v. Campbell*,[13]

---

[11] *Phoenix General Ins. Co. v. Halvanon Ins. Co.* [1988] 1 Q.B. 216—although, as that case illustrated, the classification of such risks, and the result of non-compliance, will depend upon the precise form of the regulatory regime at the relevant time. In *Phoenix*, certain transitional provisions prevented a finding that insurers had acted illegally. For the regulatory regime under the Financial Services and Markets Act 2000—see Ch. 34.

[12] *Blankley v. Godley* [1952] 1 All E.R. 436; *cf. Ilford Airways Ltd v. Stevenson*, U.S. C.Av.R. 55 (1957).

[13] (1920) 2 Ll.L.R. 98, 101; affirmed on other grounds (1920) 4 Ll.L.R. 36; *Bresse v. Automobile Ins. Co.*, U.S.Av.R. 53 (1932).

the policy provided that flight was to be "deemed to commence from the time the aircraft moves forward in taking off for the actual air transit and shall be deemed to end on the aircraft coming to rest after contact with ground or water". It seems that such a policy would not attach during a taxi-ing made with no immediate intention of flight but would attach once the pilot began to taxi preparatory to getting into the air.

Liability to passengers, who are the family, servants or sub-contractors of the insured is usually excluded.

Insurance will usually be provided for liability to passengers for accidental injury while in the aircraft, entering or leaving it. Some policies may also insure liability for loss of or damage to the baggage of the passengers.

30–8 Terms and conditions. Warranties relating to the airworthiness of the aircraft are invariably found in aviation policies in some such terms as:

> "The insured will comply with all air navigation and airworthiness orders and requirements issued by any competent authority and will take all reasonable steps to ensure that such orders and requirements are complied with by his agents and employees and that the aircraft shall be airworthy at the commencement of each flight."[14]

Although the burden of proving a breach of warranty lies upon the insurer,[15] the orders and requirements are so complex and numerous that this warranty can impose a heavy obligation on the assured. If the assured fails to comply with the warranty, the insurer is entitled to repudiate liability for any claim, however immaterial to the cause of the loss the breach of warranty may be.[16] If, however, the policy is so framed that flights in breach of regulations are excluded from the cover, the loss or damage must occur during such a flight, before the insurer can deny liability.[17]

It is usual to find a clause providing:

> "The due observance and fulfilment of the terms, provisions, conditions, and endorsements of this policy shall be conditions precedent to any liability of the insurers to make any payment under this policy."

It has been held that it is for the insurer to prove that there has been a breach of condition before he can rely on this clause; although the observance and fulfilment of the terms of the policy are expressed to be a condition precedent to liability, the onus is not on the assured to prove such compliance with all the terms before he can recover.[18]

There may be other conditions requiring the keeping of proper log books by the insured and the giving of notice of any change in the nature of the risk.[19] "Usual trial flights" did not, in 1920, cover a flight to Australia.[20]

---

[14] *Obalski Chibougamou Mining Co. v. Aero Ins. Co.* [1932] S.C.R. 540; *R. v. Burgess* (1936) 55 C.L.R. 618.

[15] *Bond Air Services Ltd v. Hill* [1955] 2 Q.B. 417.

[16] *Bruce v. Lumbermen's Mutual Casualty Co.*, U.S.C.Av.R. 108 (1955); *Marais v. Thomas*, U.S.C.Av.R. 647 (1955).

[17] *Lloyd's Underwriters v. Cordova Airlines Inc.*, U.S.C.Av.R. 474 (1960); *Visco Flying Co. Inc. v. Hansen and Rowland Inc.*, U.S.C.Av.R. 579 (1960). A policy specifying that the aircraft should fly under visual flight rules was held not to exclude night flying: *Orion Insurance Co. v. Crone* (1966) 60 D.L.R. 2d 630; [1968] 1 Lloyd's Rep. 443.

[18] *Bond Air Services Ltd v. Hill* [1955] 2 Q.B. 417.

[19] *Lineas Aereas v. Travellers' Fire Ins. Co.* U.S.C.Av.R. 298 (1958).

[20] *Alliance Aeroplane Co. Ltd v. Union Ins. Soc. of Canton Ltd* (1920) 5 Ll.L.R. 406.

30–9 Exceptions. The first flight of an aircraft may be excluded by the terms of the policy.[21] So may war-risks,[22] racing,[23] aerobatics,[24] crop-spraying, flights when more than the declared number of passengers are carried, or when the aircraft is piloted by a person not named in the schedule, and flights for purposes other than those authorised by the policy itself or by any licence issued by the relevant licensing board.[25]

30–10 Ordinary life or accident insurance policies may exclude liability in respect of death or injury caused by or resulting from "aeronautic activity" or "participating in aeronautics".[26] It was held in *Tierney v. Occidental Life Insurance Co. of California*[27] that an alighting passenger who walked into a propeller did not suffer an accident "in consequence of having participated in aeronautics"; but an assured who was injured in swinging the propeller of a machine he was about to fly himself was held to be "engaging or participating as a passenger or otherwise in aviation or aeronautics".[28] It is not unusual for accident policies to exclude flying other than as a "fare-paying passenger".[29]

30–11 Sue and labour. An aviation hull policy, being closely based on a marine insurance policy, will often contain a sue and labour clause.[30] In *Kuwait Airways Corporation v. Kuwait Insurance Company S.A.K.*[31] the policy covered "sue, labour and costs and expenses and salvage charges and expenses incurred by or on behalf of the assured in or about the defence, safety, preservation and recovery of the insured property. ...". However, a proviso stated that such costs and expenses should "be included in computing the losses hereinbefore provided for, notwithstanding that the [insurers] may have paid for a total loss." Reversing the lower courts, the House of Lords held that the clear meaning of the proviso was that, where there was a limit on the indemnity, that limit must be applied to the aggregate of the primary loss and the sue and labour expenses.

---

[21] *Dunn v. Campbell* (1920) 4 Ll.L.R. 36 where the proposal form stated that the first flight was excluded "unless specially arranged for" and it was held that special arrangements had been made. It was also held that the words "from the date and time of the first flight" meant from the beginning, not the end, of the first flight.
[22] *Banque Sabbag v. Hope* [1973] 1 Lloyd's Rep. 233; [1974] 2 Lloyd's Rep. 301; *Pan American World Airways v. Aetna Casualty Co.* [1975] 1 Lloyd's Rep. 77.
[23] *Alliance Aeroplane Co. Ltd v. Union Ins. Soc. of Canton Ltd* (1920) 5 Ll.L.R. 406 where it was held that taking part in a race amounted to "racing" even though the aeroplane was not travelling fast.
[24] See the proposal form in *Dunn v. Campbell* (1920) 4 Ll.L.R. 36, 38.
[25] *Orion Ins. Co. v. Crone* [1968] 1 Lloyd's Rep. 443.
[26] See *Aetna Life Ins. Co. v. Reed*, U.S.Av.R. 528 (1952); *Downs v. National Casualty Co.*, U.S.Av.R. 645 (1960).
[27] U.S.Av.R., 191 (1928); *cf. Kinarch v. Mutual Benefit Health and Accident Ass. of Omaha*, U.S.C.Av.R. 253 (1953).
[28] *Blonski v. Bankers' Life Ins. Co.*, U.S.Av.R. 57 (1932).
[29] *Metropolitan Life Ins. Co. v. Halcombe*, U.S.Av.R. 154 (1936); *Good v. Metropolitan Life Ins. Co.*, U.S.Av.R. 286 (1950); *Burns v. Mutual Benefit Life Ins. Co.*, U.S.Av.R. 281 (1950).
[30] See paragraph 26–17, *ante.*
[31] [1999] 1 Lloyd's Rep. 803.

CHAPTER 31

INSURANCE AGAINST PECUNIARY LOSS

1. Consequential Loss Insurance[1]

31–1 Loss of profits. Many businesses wish to insure against the possibility of a fire or other catastrophe giving rise to a loss of profits or additional expense during the period after the occurrence of the peril insured against. It is accepted law that an ordinary insurance policy on property against, for example, fire does not cover loss of profits[2] and it has even been held that a loss of market caused by delay arising from a peril insured against is not covered by a standard form policy.[3] Any type of consequential loss can be insured[4] but loss of profits or additional expenditure are the most usual subjects of insurance and for this reason the insurance discussed in this chapter is often referred to as loss of profits insurance. This is, however, an unsatisfactory term since it directs attention to one form only of consequential loss; moreover it may be required even when a business is experiencing a period of trading loss and to talk of loss of profits in this context is somewhat inappropriate.[5]

It follows that loss of profits and other forms of consequential loss must be described in the policy and insured as such.[6] The purpose of the insurance is to put the insured into the position he would be in if the profits had been earned (subject to the conditions of the policy) and he will therefore be liable to tax on the indemnity received.[7] It may well be material to disclose that a business, for which a loss of profits insurance is sought, is running at a loss.[8]

---

[1] See Riley, *Consequential Loss Insurances and Claims* (7th ed., 1991), hereafter referred to as "*Riley*".

[2] *Re Wright and Pole* (1834) 1 Ad. & E. 621 (insurance on property); *Cator v. Great Western Ins. Co. of New York* (1873) L.R. 8 C.P. 552 and *Maurice v. Goldsborough, Mort & Co.* [1939] A.C. 452 (insurances on goods).

[3] *Lewis Emanuel & Son Ltd v. Hepburn* [1960] 1 Lloyd's Rep. 304.

[4] *e.g.* loss of a market or even loss of a particular contract: see *Farmers Co-operative Ltd v. National Benefit Ass. Co. Ltd* (1922) 13 Ll.L.R. 530, where the insurer was to pay for a loss if a vessel was unable to load and a contract was cancelled thereby. It was held that the vessel must be prevented from loading by an ordinary marine peril, *cf. The Megara* [1974] 1 Lloyd's Rep. 590. For a case concerning loss arising from the breakdown of a machine, see *Burts and Harvey Ltd v. Vulcan Boiler and General Ins. Co.* [1966] 1 Lloyd's Rep. 161. *Cf. De Meza v. Apple* [1975] 1 Lloyd's Rep. 498 (insuring solicitors' fees).

[5] *Riley* at para. 7.

[6] *Maurice v. Goldsborough, Mort & Co.* [1939] A.C. 452; *Mackenzie v. Whitworth* (1875) 1 Ex.D. 36, 43.

[7] *R. v. Fir and Cedar Lumber Co. Ltd* [1932] A.C. 441; *London and Thames Haven Oil Wharves Ltd v. Attwood* [1967] Ch. 772.

[8] *Stavers v. Mountain, The Times*, July 27, 1912.

31–2 Measure of indemnity. The indemnity afforded by consequential loss insurance is intended to be as complete as possible and is usually based on the turnover of the business, which is made up from three items.[9] These may be called:

(a) the prime costs (which will vary according to the amount of turnover) such as purchases for resale or manufacture, fuel, electricity or consumable stores,

(b) overhead expenses (which are constant) such as rent, insurance premiums, salaries to permanent staff and wages to skilled employees, usually referred to as "standing charges" and

(c) the net profit.

If a fire occurs, prime costs will not be incurred but the standing charges will be incurred and will form a much larger proportion of the turnover than before. At the same time there will be a loss of net profit since the turnover on which it can be earned is reduced. The usual form of consequential loss policy must compensate for these two factors and therefore agrees to pay, on the amount of turnover lost, the percentage which net profit plus standing charges bore[10] to the turnover in the financial year preceding the loss (this percentage is known as the Rate of Gross Profit).[11] Thus if, in the relevant year preceding the fire, the standing charges and net profit constitute 40 per cent of a turnover of £80,000 and the turnover in the relevant year after the fire is £30,000, the consequential loss claim will be £20,000. This sum will afford an indemnity in respect of reduction in the turnover of the business; but the insured will also require compensation for the additional expenditure incurred in order to reduce the prospective loss of turnover, and the standard form of consequential loss policy therefore includes a further agreement to pay such compensation which may frequently exceed the loss suffered by a reduction of turnover.[12]

31–3 Specification. The standard policy usually provides that the insured is to be indemnified according to the terms of the specification which is attached to the policy and the specification lays down that the insurance is limited to loss of Gross Profit due to (a) Reduction in Turnover and (b) Increase in cost of working. It continues:

"… and the amount payable as indemnity thereunder shall be:

(a) In respect of reduction in Turnover: the sum produced by applying the Rate of Gross Profit to the amount by which the turnover during the Indemnity Period shall, in consequence of the damage, fall short of the Standard Turnover,

(b) In respect of Increase in Cost of Working, the additional expenditure … necessarily and reasonably incurred for the sole purpose of avoiding or diminishing the reduction in Turnover which but for that expenditure would have taken place during the Indemnity Period, in consequence of the damage, but not exceeding the sum

---

[9] *Riley* at para. 3.

[10] These standing charges are invariably set out in the policy.

[11] *Riley* at paras 4 and 40. If it is impossible to assess the loss by reference to the preceding year, *e.g.* because the business had not been running for a full year before the peril occurred, the court must do its best to assess the amount which would have been earned during the period of interruption: *Burts and Harvey v. Vulcan Boiler and General Ins. Co.* [1966] 1 Lloyd's Rep. 161.

[12] *Riley* at paras 8 and 50.

produced by applying the Rate of Gross Profit to the amount of the reduction thereby avoided,

less any sum saved during the Indemnity Period in respect of such of the Insured Standing Charges as may cease or be reduced in consequence of the damage ..."

There is a definition section which defines the terms used. Gross Profit is defined as "the sum produced by adding to the Net Profit the amount of the Insured Standing Charges"[13] and the Rate of Gross Profit as "the rate of Gross Profit earned on the Turnover during the financial year immediately before the date of the damage".[14]

31–4 The modern method. The standard form of policy calculates the insurable gross profit by adding the standing charges to the net profit. During the last 30 years, however, another method has been used to calculate the gross profit, *viz.*, the deduction of the prime costs from the turnover. This method arrives at exactly the same result as the older calculation but is considered simpler by loss adjusters and accountants. The prime costs are the converse of "standing charges" and are usually described as "uninsured working expenses" or "specified working expenses".[15]

31–5 The only difference between the wording of the old standard form and the new form is in the definition of gross profit in the specification. Instead of being defined as the sum produced by adding the standing charges to the net profit, it is defined as follows.[16]

"the amount by which
   (1) the sum of the Turnover and the amount of the Closing Stock shall exceed
   (2) the sum of the amount of the Opening Stock and the amount of the Uninsured Working Expenses
Note. The amount of the Opening and Closing Stocks shall be arrived at in accordance with the Insured's normal accountancy methods, due provision being made for depreciation."

31–6 Increase in cost of working. It is in the interest of both the insured and the insurer to restore the business to normal trading conditions as quickly as possible and, under the policy, it may well be the duty of the insured to do so. In these circumstances it is right and proper for the policy to provide cover for the additional expenditure incurred by the insured. It must be noted that an increase in the ratio of the cost of working to the turnover is not covered by this provision in the policy. Not every item in the costs of working will be taken into account under the heading of standing charges and in *Polikoff v. North British and Mercantile Insurance Co. Ltd,*[17] the uninsured wages and expenses formed a much higher percentage of turnover after a fire than before. Branson J. nevertheless disallowed the claim for these on the grounds that an increased ratio of wages to turnover was not covered by the words "additional expenditure".

---

[13] See note 10, *ante.*
[14] *Riley* at para. 40
[15] *Riley* at paras 83–84.
[16] *Riley* at para. 81.
[17] (1936) 55 Ll.L.R. 279.

In *Henry Booth v. Commercial Union Assurance Co.*[18] cover was provided in respect of "such sums as the insured shall necessarily pay for increase in the cost of working to continue the business for twelve months from the day of the fire". It was held that the insured was entitled to both the extra cost of continuing in business and the cost of having to buy partly manufactured goods to replace those destroyed. Other items which might fall within this clause are payment of additional overtime in trying to make good the loss of production, temporary repairs which have subsequently to be discarded, extra advertising and even the occupation of temporary premises.

31–7 Duty of Insured to minimise loss. It is probably the duty of the insured at common law to take all reasonable steps to minimise his loss[19] and, in any event, the policy will often contain a condition to this effect.[20] In so far as the insured incurs expenditure in so doing he will be entitled to recover this expenditure under the terms of the policy just discussed. It may also be that, in mitigating loss, the assured sustains some further loss which is covered by the policy.[21] But it is doubtful how far this duty extends. Is the insured obliged, for example, to take on fresh premises to conduct his business and, if he does so, can the insurers claim to have any profits made at the new premises taken into account in adjusting the claim? It is submitted that the answer to both these questions is "no". In *City Tailors Ltd v. Evans*[22] the plaintiffs suffered a fire which destroyed their premises at Old Street in the City of London and in order to preserve their goodwill they took temporary premises at Craven Street, where they managed to make a profit. The policy provided:

> "The assured shall use due diligence and do and concur in doing all things reasonably practicable to minimise any interruption of or interference with the business and to avoid or diminish the loss."

The insurer contended[23] that this clause obliged the insured to obtain temporary premises and to take the profits made there into account when presenting his claim. It seems that all three members of the Court of Appeal must have rejected both contentions. Both Scrutton and Atkin L.JJ. made it

---

[18] (1923) 14 Ll.L.R. 114.

[19] *City Tailors Ltd v. Evans* (1921) 126 L.T. 439, 443, *per* Scrutton L.J. In marine insurance, the duty is reflected in s.78(4) of the Marine Insurance Act 1906. The effect of that statutory duty has caused difficulties where insurance is intended to provide cover against negligence. It has been held that, in such circumstances, the duty under s.78(4) only applies in rare cases in which negligence is not covered, and the breach is so significant as to displace the prior insured peril as the proximate cause of loss: *State of Netherlands v. Youell* [1998] 1 Lloyd's Rep. 236, 245.

[20] *Brunton v. Marshall* (1922) 10 Ll.L.R. 689; *City Tailors Ltd v. Evans* (1921) 126 L.T. 439.

[21] Thus, in *Quinta Communications SA v. Warrington* [2000] Lloyd's Rep. I.R. 81, the insured was covered against defined loss in the event of the non-appearance of Michael Jackson at pop concerts as a result of any cause beyond the insured's control. As a result of the death of Princess Diana, Michael Jackson was too unwell to attend a concert at Ostende. It was rescheduled, pursuant to the obligation to mitigate. The rescheduling necessitated cancellation of another concert, at Barcelona. The insured was able to recover the loss arising from the second cancellation, effectively as part of the loss flowing from the non-appearance at the original Ostende concert. (The recovery was in fact not under the primary policy, but under a secondary "deductible buy-back" policy.)

[22] (1921) 126 L.T. 439.

[23] See insurer's defence summarised at p. 440.

clear that the subject-matter of the policy was loss of profits at Old Street and that the quoted condition only referred to efforts at Old Street to minimise or avoid the loss at those premises. It was quite immaterial that other profits had been made elsewhere, although it was possible that, once payment had been made, the insurer might be entitled to some share of the profits so made by virtue of his rights of subrogation.[24] Atkin L.J. said[25]:

> "The clause merely compels the plaintiffs to do what they can to diminish the loss at Old Street by reducing so far as possible the effect of the fire there and producing as much output there after the fire as is reasonably necessary. ... I do not think that it involves them in the obligation to take any steps to carry on the business elsewhere; nor do I think that if they did carry on the business elsewhere it would import an obligation to account to the defendant for the profits. I can find no such obligation in the words. Whether if the plaintiffs in fact use the same staff and skilled employees to make profits the defendant would on payment of the loss be entitled by subrogation to such profits is a question that does not arise, inasmuch as the defendant has not yet made any payment."

31–8 As a result of this case, it must now be taken to be settled law that, if the insured conducts business elsewhere, any profit made by him need not be brought into account when he claims from his insurers. It is therefore common to find an express term in consequential loss policies in the following words:

> "If during the indemnity period goods shall be sold or services shall be rendered elsewhere than at the premises for the benefit of the business either by the insured or by others on the insured's behalf the money paid or payable in respect of such sales or services shall be brought into account in arriving at the turnover during the indemnity period."

31–9 Valued policies. In order to avoid complex calculations of loss of profit and additional expenditure, the parties sometimes agree that the loss of profit shall be a certain definite amount. Thus there are examples of policies which provided for the indemnity to be a certain percentage of the amount by which the turnover in each month after the fire should be less than the turnover for the corresponding month of the year preceding the fire, with provision for the insured's auditors to assess the amount of the loss[26]; alternatively the policy might provide for payment of a percentage of the "ultimate net loss" as paid on some other policy.[27] On the other hand, an

---

[24] It is doubtful whether the insurer could have recovered anything out of the Craven Street profits by way of subrogation, since such profits were entirely collateral to the contract of insurance and did not arise by virtue of the insured exercising any legal right in existence at the time of the loss but rather by his exercising an independent choice to acquire by purchase new premises and the hope of a profit to be made there. It would be difficult to fit the suggested right of the insurer into the wide words of Brett L.J. in *Castellain v. Preston* (1883) 11 Q.B.D. 380.

[25] At p. 445; *cf.* Scrutton L.J. at p. 443 and Bankes L.J. at p. 441.

[26] *Recher & Co. v. North British and Mercantile Ins.* [1915] 3 K.B. 277 where it was held that the auditor's assessment was conclusive unless it could be shown he went wrong in law or omitted to take into account some material fact, *e.g.* the possibility that some of the damage might have been caused by something other than the peril insured against.

[27] *Bailliere, Tindal and Cox v. Drysdale* (1948) 82 Ll.L.R. 736.

agreement to pay the "same percentage of the sum insured as the total sum paid on fire policies bears to total sum insured thereunder" does not make the policy a valued policy as such but merely obliges the insurer to pay an amount so calculated, subject to other conditions of the policy.[28]

31–10 Sometimes the use of terms intended for non-valued policies can give rise to difficulty, if the policy is in fact a valued policy.[29] Thus, in *City Tailors Ltd v. Evans*[30] it was agreed that the loss of profits should be valued at £100 per working day for each working day that work might be wholly stopped owing to fire and a proportionate amount of £100 if work were partially stopped. There was thus no reference to standing charges and it was impossible to say whether they had been taken into account in arriving at the agreed figure of £100 per day. Nevertheless a standard printed clause (Condition 1) provided:

> "In the event of the amount insured by this policy exceeding the total of the probable annual profits of the business to be determined by an assessor (to be mutually agreed upon) after taking into consideration any extraordinary or unusual circumstances or if the standing charges [these were defined and set out in another printed clause] shall be reduced or ceased to be paid, the amount of loss hereunder shall be reduced accordingly."

All the members of the Court of Appeal agreed that the first part of the clause was inapplicable to a valued policy[31]; if the parties agreed to value the loss of profits at £100 per day, it would not be consistent for an assessor to be appointed with a view to determining whether the figure of £100 exceeded the probable annual daily profit. But the court was divided on the question whether the second part of the clause applied so as to reduce the amount of £100 per day if any of the standing charges were reduced or ceased to be paid. Scrutton L.J. thought that the fact that the policy was a valued policy precluded any account being taken of a reduction in standing charges and that, once the first part of the condition was excluded, it was impossible to retain the second part.[32] The majority of the Court of Appeal concluded, however, that any reduction of the standing charges should be taken into account on the ground that such charges must have been an element in the calculation of the sum of £100 per day and that it was therefore reasonable that any reduction in them should go to diminish the agreed sum *pro tanto*.[33] Atkin L.J. went so far as to say that if the provision had not been there the contract would have been a mere wager[34] but, since the plaintiffs clearly had an interest in the subject-matter insured, this remark is rather difficult to understand.

31–11 Terms and conditions. The policy will always be for a definite duration and it has been held that the loss of profit must be incurred during

---

[28] *Brunton v. Marshall* (1922) 10 Ll.L.R. 689.
[29] For discussion of the distinction between valued and unvalued policies generally, see *Kyzuna Investments Ltd. v. Ocean Marine Mutual Ins. Assoc. (Europe)* [2000] 1 Lloyd's Rep. 505; *Quorum v. Schramm* [2002] Lloyd's Rep. I.R. 292.
[30] (1921) 126 L.T. 439.
[31] *per* Bankes L.J. at 441; *per* Scrutton L.J. at 442; *per* Atkin L.J. at 444.
[32] *ibid.* at 442–443.
[33] *ibid.* at 441, *per* Bankes L.J.; *per* Atkin L.J. at 444–445
[34] *ibid.* at 444, *per* Atkin L.J.

the duration of the policy if it is to be covered[35]; it is not sufficient for the peril (*e.g.* a fire) to occur during the existence of the policy if the loss of profits occurs afterwards, no doubt because the true peril insured against is the loss of profit, not the fire or even loss directly caused by the fire.

The clause providing for a reduction in the amount payable if the standing charges are reduced or cease to be paid has already been discussed in the context of a valued policy.[36] It has been suggested that this clause will apply even though the reduction is not caused by and is completely collateral to the fire, but that no extra compensation can be given for any increase in loss as a result of the standing charges themselves increasing or being a greater proportion of the reduced turnover than before the fire.[37] The standing charges are always set out in the policy and the Polikoff Case[38] discusses the meaning of "salaries and commissions to directors and permanent staff",[39] "wages to skilled employees",[40] insurance premiums,[41] general expenses,[42] rent, rates and taxes,[43] depreciation,[44] extra cost of machinery.[45]

31–12 Material Damage Proviso. It is a common proviso of consequential loss or business interruption insurance that, at the time of any interruption to the relevant business of the insured consequent on damage to property used by the insured for the purposes of the business:

> "there shall be in force an insurance covering the interest of the insured in the property at the premises against such damage and that payment shall have been made or liability admitted".

It has been held that this clause requires the assured to insure only that property in which he possesses a personal proprietary interest or which is at his risk.[46] So, where architects' drawings were destroyed by fire in the course of a redevelopment, and the insured developer lost revenue for a period of 22 weeks during which progress was delayed largely as a result of the plans having to be redrawn, it did not matter that the assured had not insured them. The assured had no personal contractual or proprietary right in them.

31–13 Another common clause in consequential loss policies is the clause loosely known as the "Special Circumstances Clause". An early form of the clause can be found in *City Tailors Ltd v. Evans*[47] where the assessor who was to calculate the probable annual profits of the business had to take "into

---

[35] *Sexton v. Mountain* (1919) 1 Ll.L.R. 507.

[36] *cf.* the different wording used in *Mount Royal Assurance Co. Ltd v. Cameron Lumber Co.* [1937] A.C. 313, 319–320.

[37] *Polikoff Ltd v. North British and Mercantile Ins. Co. Ltd* (1936) 55 Ll.L.R. 279. See especially at 286.

[38] *ibid.*

[39] Held not to include wages paid to packers. *ibid.* at 285.

[40] *ibid.* at 287–288.

[41] Held not to include national insurance contributions. *ibid.* at 288.

[42] *ibid.* at 288.

[43] *ibid.* at 288–289.

[44] *ibid.* at 289.

[45] *ibid.* at 289–290.

[46] *Glengate-KG Properties Ltd v. Norwich Union Fire Insurance Society Ltd* [1996] 2 All E.R. 487. The majority construed the word "interest" restrictively to mean a personal right or title in the property. Auld L.J. appears, however, to have considered that it would suffice if the property was at the assured's risk, and if so, it is hard to see why the assured's obligation to pay the architects for preparing replacement drawings did not create the requisite interest.

[47] (1921) 126 L.T. 439.

consideration any extraordinary or unusual circumstances"—a phrase which provoked a parenthetical "whatever that may mean" from Scrutton L.J.[48] Branson J. has suggested that a heavy advertising campaign at a particular time might distort the profits made in a particular month and have to be taken into account in comparing the profits of one month or year with that of the preceding month or year.[49] In its present form, the clause is bracketed jointly against the policy definitions of Rate of Gross Profit, Annual Turnover and Standard Turnover and reads:

> "to which such adjustments shall be made as may be necessary to provide for the trend of the business and for variations in or special circumstances affecting the business either before or after the damage or which would have affected the business had the damage not occurred, so that the figures thus adjusted shall represent as nearly as may be reasonably practicable the results which but for the damage would have been obtained during the relative period after the damage".

For other clauses, which have not yet come before the courts, the reader is referred to Mr Riley's book, Consequential Loss Insurances and Claims which fully discusses other usual terms and conditions in consequential loss policies.

31–14 Loss of rent. Another form of consequential loss insurance is insurance on the rent payable in respect of property. If the insured is a tenant, he may wish to insure his liability to pay rent after destruction of or damage to the buildings[50] and, conversely, if the insured is a landlord, he may insure against loss of rent by reason of its being suspended during reinstatement in accordance with the terms of the lease. The usual form of policy provides that the insurers are not to become liable unless the premises become untenantable and their liability will only continue while the premises remain in that state.[51] If a policy covers loss of rent for a building in the course of redevelopment and fire occurs before the redevelopment is complete, the policy may require that for the purposes of an average clause the rent lost is to be calculated on the assumption that the building has in fact been completed and is fully tenanted as in *Glengate-KG Properties Ltd v. Norwich Union Fire Insurance Society Ltd.*[52]

31–15 Other forms of policy. A similar type of policy to one covering loss of rent is a policy covering loss on hire-purchase transactions. It has been held by the House of Lords that under such a policy the owner is only entitled to recover from the insurers sum due from the hirer on determination of the hire purchase contract and that they cannot recover instalments falling due after termination.[53] Another form of loss sometimes

---

[48] *ibid.* at 442.
[49] *Polikoff Ltd v. North British and Mercantile Ins. Co. Ltd* (1936) 55 Ll.L.R. 279, 285–286.
[50] *cf. Matthey v. Curling* [1922] 2 A.C. 180.
[51] *Buchanan v. Liverpool and London and Globe Ins. Co.* (1884) 11 R. 1032.
[52] [1996] 1 Lloyd's Rep. 614.
[53] *Constructive Finance Co. Ltd v. English Ins. Co.* (1924) 19 Ll.L.R. 144.

insured is loss sustained by reason of postponement or cancellation of some projected event, such as the making of a film.[54]

2. CREDIT INSURANCE[55]

31–16 Nature of the risk. A creditor will often wish to insure himself against the possibility of a debtor failing to pay his debts and credit insurance has become a common form of insurance.[56] Such insurance may cover debts in general[57] or a particular debt[58] or debts which will be incurred after the policy is effected.[59] The debtor will not necessarily be the principal debtor, since it may be a surety[60] or even an insurer[61] whose liability is the subject-matter of the insurance.

The event on the happening of which the insurer is to become liable differs from policy to policy. Usually, it is non-payment of a debt on the due date[62]

---

[54] *Flying Colours v. Assicurazioni General* [1991] 1 Lloyd's Rep. 536. For an example of insurance covering investment in film production, see *HIH Casualty & General Ins. Ltd v. Chase Manhattan* [2001] Lloyd's Rep.I.R. 703. For examples of cover against non-appearance at public events, see *CNA International Reins. Co. v. Companhia de Seguros Tranquilidade SA* [1999] Lloyd's Rep. I.R. 289 (Placido Domingo); *Quinta Communications SA v. Warrington* [2000] Lloyd's Rep. I.R. 81 (Michael Jackson).

[55] Also known as guarantee insurance or financial guarantee. For the distinction between contracts of credit (or guarantee) insurance and contracts of guarantee (or suretyship), see paras 31–40 *et seq., post.*

[56] One particularly important form of credit insurance used to be that conducted by the Export Credits Guarantee Department of the Department of Trade which issued policies to exporters in this country covering them for loss incurred if the buyer fails to pay for or to accept goods supplied or if difficulty arises in connection with transfers of currency. See *Re Miller, Gibb & Co. Ltd* [1957] 1 W.L.R. 703. These policies may also underlie guarantees given by E.C.G.D. to banks who purchase bills of exchange drawn by the exporter and accepted by the foreign importer, *Credit Lyonnais v. E.C.G.D.* [1996] 1 Lloyd's Rep. 200. E.C.G.D. has now been privatised. See also *Simon Container Machinery Ltd. v. EMBA Machinery A.B.* [1998] 2 Lloyd's Rep. 429, where the E.C.G.D. had insured the plaintiff against risks of loss arising out of its sub-contract with the defendant for the supply of machinery to the defendant's purchaser in the former USSR. The purchaser defaulted. The defendant recovered from its credit insurers. The amount recovered sums owed to the plaintiff. In order to satisfy the E.C.G.D., the agreement between the plaintiff and defendant required the latter on the occurrence of a loss to take all necessary steps to recover from the purchaser or from any other person from whom recoveries may be made. It was held that the defendant was liable to account to the plaintiff, "loss" in the agreement meaning a loss for the purposes of the plaintiff's credit insurance. Under its policy with E.C.G.D., the plaintiff would have to account for 90% of what it recovered by way of subrogation.

[57] *Solvency Mutual Guarantee Co. v. York* (1858) 3 H. & N. 588; *Solvency Mutual Guarantee Co. v. Froane* (1861) 7 H. & N. 5; *Solvency Mutual Guarantee Co. v. Freeman* (1861) 7 H. & N. 17.

[58] *e.g.* a loan—*Parr's Bank v. Albert Mines Syndicate Ltd* (1900) 5 Com.Cas. 116; a bank deposit—*Dane v. Mortgage Ins. Corporation* [1894] 1 Q.B. 54; a mortgage—*Re Law Guarantee Trust and Accident Society* (1913) 108 L.T. 830; a debenture—*Shaw v. Royce Ltd* [1911] 1 Ch. 318; *Re Law Guarantee Trust and Accident Society Ltd (Liverpool Mortgage Insurance Co. Ltd's Case)* [1914] 2 Ch. 617; or the sum outstanding on a hire-purchase agreement—*Constructive Finance Co. v. English Ins. Co.* (1924) 19 Ll.L.R. 144.

[59] *Seaton v. Burnand* [1900] A.C. 135, 141, *per* Lord Halsbury; *Anglo-Californian Bank Ltd v. London and Provincial Marine and General Ins. Co. Ltd* (1904) 10 Com.Cas. 1.

[60] *Seaton v. Burnand* [1900] A.C. 135.

[61] *MacVicar v. Poland* (1894) 10 T.L.R. 566.

[62] *Shaw v. Royce Ltd* [1911] 1 Ch. 138.

or within a specified time thereafter[63]; if this is the case is it irrelevant to consider the reason why payment is not made.[64] In other cases the policy specifically provides for payment in the event of insolvency of the debtor,[65] but any allegation that a debt has not been paid for some other reason will be scrutinised closely if the debtor is, in fact, insolvent.[66]

31–17 In *Waterkeyn v. Eagle Star & British Dominions Insurance Co. Ltd*[67] the policy covered:

> "the risk of ... loss arising from the bankruptcy or insolvency of all or any of the said banks ... directly due to damage or destruction of the premises and contents of the said banks through riots, civil commotions, war, civil war, revolutions, rebellions, military or usurped power ..."

The subject-matter was money deposited in Russian banks and the plaintiff had taken out the policy with the defendants while the Kerensky government was in power. The Bolshevists subsequently abolished private banks and confiscated their assets and the plaintiff then claimed to recover under the policy. Greer J. held that three things had to be proved, *viz.* (1) insolvency; (2) damage or destruction of the premises and contents; and (3) that the damage or destruction was due to one of the specified perils. There was no evidence that the premises of the banks had been destroyed or damaged in any way and he therefore gave judgment for the defendants, saying it was impossible to read the words "damage or destruction" as if they were equivalent to damage or destruction of the banks' business.

31–18 Alteration of the risk. There is usually an express condition in the policy preventing the creditor from assenting to any arrangements which modify his rights or remedies against the debtor[68] and, if this condition is not fulfilled, the insurer will be able to decline liability. In the absence of any such condition, the question will be whether such alteration or modification gives rise to a material alteration in the risk.[69] The policy may, however, give the insured an express power to alter the risk; thus an insurance of debentures may expressly reserve a power to the debenture-holders to sanction any modification or compromise of their rights against the debtor company, *e.g.* a postponement of payment, and in such a case the insurer will

---

[63] *Finlay v. Mexican Investment Corporation* [1897] 1 Q.B. 517; *Kazakstan Wool Process (Europe) Ltd v. NCM* [2000] Lloyd's Rep. I.R. 371.

[64] *Mortgage Ins. Corporation v. Inland Revenue Commissioners* (1887) 57 L.J.Q.B. 174, 181, *per* Hawkins J.; *Laird v. Securities Ins. Co.* (1895) 22 R. 452, 459, *per* Lord McLaren.

[65] *Hambro v. Burnand* [1904] 2 K.B. 10, 19 *per* Collins M.R.; *Waterkeyn v. Eagle Star & British Dominions Ins. Co.* (1920) 5 Ll.L.R. 42. *cf. Murdock v. Heath* (1899) 80 L.T. 50.

[66] *MacVicar v. Poland* (1894) 10 T.L.R. 566.

[67] (1920) 5 Ll.L.R. 42.

[68] See *e.g. Finlay v. Mexican Investment Corporation* [1897] 1 Q.B. 517. In *HIH Casualty & General Ins. Co. v. New Hampshire Ins. Co* [2001] Lloyd's Rep. I.R. 596, it was held (at 623) that a term in reinsurance of film finance cover that the reinsured would obtain the reinsurers' approval to all amendments was a warranty, and that this result reflected the position at common law.

[69] See paras 26–49, *et seq., ante.* If it appears that any alteration was within the contemplation of the parties when the contract was made, any such alteration will not be held sufficient to discharge the insurer—see *Law Guarantee Trust and Accident Society v. Munich Reinsurance Co.* [1912] 1 Ch. 138, 154, *per* Warrington J. Where, however, the amount of the instalments payable by a debtor was significantly reduced, that was held sufficiently material to discharge the insurer: *Hadenfayre v. British National Ins. Soc.* [1984] 2 Lloyd's Rep. 393.

be bound despite any such modifications.[70] A creditor, who does not consent to any such modification, is nevertheless entitled to payment from the insurer once the event insured against has happened, and the insurer will be subrogated to the creditor's rights against the company, as modified.[71] Where, however, a creditor's rights are not modified but extinguished, the insurer can no longer be liable (unless there is an express clause covering that additional risk). Thus a creditor may find that he is bound, pursuant to the terms of his contract with the debtor, by a majority decision of other creditors extinguishing old rights, creating new ones and releasing the insurer from his obligations. In such a case he will have no remedy against his insurer even if he does not consent to the new arrangement and he will only be able to pursue his new and, perhaps, less satisfactory rights against his debtor.[72]

31–19 Irrelevance of alterations after the event. Once the event insured against has happened, the insurer is liable to pay and any subsequent alteration in the relationship between the debtor and the creditor will not discharge him,[73] unless the creditor agrees to surrender some right to which the insurer ought to be subrogated.[74] The mere fact that a debtor such as a company goes into liquidation and the court sanctions a scheme of arrangement discharging the liabilities of the company and, in effect, preventing the insurer from deriving any benefit from his rights of subrogation, will not affect the liability of the insurer.[75]

31–20 Non-disclosure of material facts. There is surprisingly little authority in relation to non-disclosure in contracts of credit insurance.[76] It must, on any view, be material for the insurer to know whether the debtor is insolvent or in serious financial difficulties. If the insurer has such knowledge, it will not be necessary for the creditor to inform him, but if he does not, and information in the creditor's possession is not disclosed to him, he will probably be entitled to avoid the contract.[77] It has been held that a surety is entitled to know whether anything in the transaction between the debtor and the creditor is different from the surety's reasonable expectations[78] and it must follow from this that an assured is bound to disclose anything unusual about the contract with his debtor, since the doctrine of non-disclosure applies to contracts of insurance much more stringently than

[70] *Laird v. Securities Ins. Co. Ltd* (1895) 22 R. 452.
[71] *Finlay v. Medican Investment Corporation* [1897] 1 Q.B. 517. If the modification does not bind the creditor, the insurers can presumably exercise the creditor's original unmodified rights.
[72] *Shaw v. Royce Ltd* [1911] 1 Ch. 138, 147–148, *per* Warrington J. where the insurers were themselves parties to the agreement whereby the original rights were extinguished and new ones created. There is no indication, however, that the decision would have been any different if the insurers had been strangers to the agreement.
[73] *Dane v. Mortgage Insurance Corporation* [1894] 1 Q.B. 54.
[74] See para. 22–25, *ante.*
[75] cf. *Laird v. Securities Insurance Co.* (1893) 22 R. 452 and *Young v. Trustees Assets Co.* (1893) 21 R. 222.
[76] A defence of non-disclosure in *Bank Leumi v. British National Ins. Co.* [1988] 1 Lloyd's Rep. 71 failed on the facts.
[77] *Anglo-Californian Bank Ltd v. London and Provincial Marine and General Insurance Co. Ltd* (1904) 20 T.L.R. 665.
[78] *Pidcock v. Bishop* (1825) 3 B. & C. 605; *Hamilton v. Watson* (1845) 12 Cl. & F. 109; *Lee v. Jones* (1864) 17 C.B.(N.S.) 482 especially, *per* Blackburn J. at 503–504; *Credit Lyonnais v. E.C.G.D.* [1996] 1 Lloyd's Rep. 200, 225–227; *Royal Bank of Scotland v. Etridge* [2002] 1 Lloyd's Rep. 343, 387.

to contracts of guarantee.[79] If the solvency of a surety is insured, it is much less material for the insurer to know the circumstances of the original loan made by the creditor to the debtor and it has been further held that the terms of the original loan, *e.g.* the rate of interest, are not material to the risk undertaken by the insurer.[80] All questions of materiality are, however, questions partly of fact and different courts may come to different conclusions depending on the evidence before them. In any event, it must be relevant for the insurer to know the financial standing of the surety whose solvency he is insuring.[81]

31–21 Measure of liability. The insurer is often liable to pay the full sum insured, once a debtor is in default[82]; but the policy sometimes provides that the insured must first recover what he can from the debtor[83] or that the insurer is only to be liable for the balance which remains due after a final dividend is declared. In *Murdock v. Heath*[84] the plaintiff deposited certain sums in a bank and the policy undertook to pay interest on the deposit if the bank made default and they also undertook to pay the principal sum "less any portion of the principal previously received from the bank when the final dividend in bankruptcy or liquidation is declared". The bank went into liquidation and was reconstructed; it went into liquidation again and, after paying a dividend of 5s. 7d. in the pound, transferred the remaining assets, which were practically exhausted, to a new company for realisation. This dividend was not called a final dividend and the new company offered shares to the plaintiff, but he rejected this offer and sued his insurers; they argued that the last dividend was not a final dividend in the liquidation, which had not yet been completed. Bigham J. held that there had been a final dividend and that the liquidation of the bank had come to an end; there could be no further declarations of dividend and the last dividend was therefore a final dividend. The insurers, on paying the balance of the deposit, would be entitled to the shares in the new company as salvage.

31–22 Gold clause. Where policies were issued covering bonds issued by Provinces of the Dominion of Canada, containing a gold clause, and payments of interest and principal under the bonds had been made in paper dollars, it was held that the gold clause could not be imported into the policies, which merely obliged the insurers to pay certain stated sums of United States dollars, if the issuers of the bonds did not fulfil their obligations. There had therefore been no loss within the terms of the policies.[85]

---

[79] It may even be material to know if the bargain insured is a bad bargain: *Kreglinger & Fernau v. Irish National Ins. Co.* [1956] I.R. 116, noted (1975) 38 M.L.R. 212.

[80] *Seaton v. Burnand* [1900] A.C. 135.

[81] *ibid.* In *Banque Keyser v. Skandia Ins. Co.* [1991] 2 A.C. 249, credit insurers, who discovered that their insured's broker was defrauding him and did not inform the insured of that fact, would have been in breach of their duty of disclosure to the insured, if the broker's fraud had been such as to entitle insurers to repudiate liability: *per* Lord Bridge at 268.

[82] *Dane v. Mortgage Ins. Corporation* [1894] 1 Q.B. 54.

[83] *cf. Re Law Guarantee Trust and Accident Society Ltd, Liverpool Mortgage Ins. Co. Ltd's Case* [1914] 2 Ch. 617. *Mercantile Credit Guarantee Co. v. Wood*, 68 Fed.Rep. 529 (1895).

[84] (1899) 80 L.T. 50.

[85] *Sturge & Co. v. Excess Ins. Co. Ltd* [1938] 4 All E.R. 424; 159 L.T. 606.

31–23 Reinsurance of the risk. Where the insurers reinsure a proportion of the risk, and subsequently become bankrupt or go into liquidation, the liability of the reinsurers is to pay the specified proportion of the amount which the original insurers become liable to pay, not of the amount they actually pay as a dividend.[86] Money paid by reinsurers to the insurers is divisible among the general creditors of the insurers and, in the absence of a fiduciary relationship between the insurers and the creditor, the creditor cannot claim that the reinsurance money belongs to him. The fact that an insurance company, as well as guaranteeing a debenture, acts as trustee of the trust deed for the debenture-holders does not create a fiduciary relationship in respect of the guarantee, which is a separate transaction, so that the debenture-holders have no specific claim on the money paid by the reinsurers.[87] Neither will they be able to avail themselves of the provisions contained in the Third Parties (Rights against Insurers) Act 1930.[88] The insurers may, however, impose a charge on any money received under a policy of reinsurance and this will protect the insured.[89]

31–24 Subrogation and contribution. Primarily the obligation of the insurers upon a guarantee of a specified debt is to pay the whole debt upon the failure of the debtor to pay the debt when due or upon the insolvency of the debtor, as the case may be, and any sum which may be ultimately recovered from the debtor, and all securities for the debt belong to the insurers.[90] The policy may even expressly provide that, if the insurers pay a claim, the creditor shall be bound to transfer to them his rights in respect of the debt and the securities;[91] in such a case the insured need only transfer such rights as he has.[92]

Where a creditor obtains a double security, the question may arise whether the second guarantor is a co-surety with the first or whether his obligation only arises upon the failure both of the debtor and the first guarantor. The distinction is of importance not only with regard to the primary liability of the second guarantor but also upon the question whether he is entitled to be subrogated to the debt and the creditor's securities or whether he is merely entitled to a contribution from the first guarantor as a co-surety.[93] *Re Denton's Estate*[94] a debt was secured by a mortgage deed in which D joined as surety for repayment of the debt and the mortgagee

[86] *Re Law Guarantee Trust and Accident Society Ltd, Liverpool Mortgage Ins Co. Ltd's Case* [1914] 2 Ch. 617. The reinsurers may, however, expressly exclude liability for anything more than the insurers actually pay—see *Neplan v. Marten* (1895) 11 T.L.R. 256, 480. In *Charter Reins. Co. v. Fagan* [1997] A.C. 313 it was held, taking account of the nature of the reinsurance, that actual payment by the reinsured was not a precondition to recovery from the reinsurer.

[87] *Re Law Guarantee Trust and Accident Society Ltd Godson's Claim* [1915] 1 Ch. 340; *Re Harrington Motor Co.* [1928] Ch. 105.

[88] s.1(5) of that Act expressly excludes reinsurance liabilities from the meaning of the words "liabilities to third parties". The Law Commission has proposed changes to the 1930 Act, but has advocated maintaining the exclusion of reinsurance liabilities: Law Com No. 272, Cm 5217, July 2001.

[89] *General Ins. Co. Ltd of Trieste v. Miller* (1896) 1 Com.Cas. 379.

[90] *Dane v. Mortgage Ins. Corporation* [1894] 1 Q.B. 54; *Finlay v. Mexican Investment Corporation* [1897] 1 Q.B. 517; *Parr's Bank v. Albert Mines Syndicate* (1900) 5 Com.Cas. 116.

[91] *Re Denton's Estate* [1904] 2 Ch. 178; *Re Law Guarantee Trust and Accident Society* (1913) 108 L.T. 830, 831.

[92] *Laird v. Securities Ins. Co. Ltd* (1895) 22 R. 452.

[93] The insurers may, of course, have rights under an independent agreement with third parties, as in *Mortgage Ins. Co. v. Pound* (1895) 65 L.J.Q.B. 129.

[94] [1904] 2 Ch. 178.

obtained what was called a "mortgage insurance policy" from a guarantee company guaranteeing payment of the mortgage debt. It was held that the contract between the mortgagee and the company was not a contract of insurance but a contract of guarantee of the mortgage debt in the event of default of the mortgagor and the surety. The company's obligation was, however, held to be supplemental and not collateral so that the company was not a co-surety who could only recover a contribution but, upon payment of the debt, it was entitled to the mortgagee's securities and therefore entitled to sue D for his proportion of the debt according to his covenant in the mortgage deed.

31–25 Duration of insurance. If a policy is issued covering the default of a debtor, and premiums are payable at stated intervals, the policy will not lapse automatically if the premium is not paid, at any rate in cases where the premium is payable by the debtor.[95] It may, however, be expressly provided that the premium must be paid within a certain period of grace if the insurer is to be liable.[96]

In one case a general guarantee policy provided that it should be treated as renewed on the same conditions at the end of the two-year term of the policy, unless two months' notice of an intention not to renew was given. It was held that the automatic renewal operated once only and that the risk ceased after four years had elapsed, unless the policy was expressly renewed.[97] Another policy provided that cover should cease upon the insured trader retiring from business; it was held that the whole risk determined upon the retirement from the insured firm of one of the two partners.[98] Where the insurer is given a contractual right to terminate (e.g. upon any breach by the insured), the effect of termination will depend upon the contract terms. One would generally expect that termination would prevent liability arising for losses occurring after the date of termination, and that it would not affect liabilities which had already been settled. The position with regard to contingent losses (e.g. where a waiting period after non-payment of a debt has not expired as at the date of termination) is more difficult. Appropriately-drafted terms can relieve the insurer of liability for such losses upon termination.[99]

31–26 Bonds of guarantee societies accepted by court. The bonds[1] of guarantee societies or insurance companies are accepted by the court in cases where security is required to be given by a litigant, liquidator, receiver or any other person.[2] The fact that the liability on the bond is confined to

---

[95] *Shaw v. Royce Ltd* [1911] 1 Ch. 138, 148 *per* Warrington J.

[96] *Re Law Guarantee Trust and Accident Society Ltd, Liverpool Mortgage Ins. Co. Ltd's Case* [1914] 2 Ch. 617. The fact that the risk of non-payment has turned into a certainty will not absolve the insured from complying with the condition: *Employers' Ins. Co. of Great Britain v. Benton* (1897) 24 R. 908; *Simpson v. Mortgage Ins. Corporation* (1893) 38 S.J. 99.

[97] *Solvency Mutual Guarantee Co. v. Froane* (1861) 7 H. & N. 5.

[98] *Solvency Mutual Guarantee Co. v. Freeman* (1861) 7 H. & N. 17.

[99] *Kazakstan Wool Producers (Europe) Ltd v. NCM* [2000] Lloyd's Rep.I.R. 371.

[1] It should be noted that the bonds in question are different from insurance policies. They contain an acknowledgment of indebtedness to the public officer to whom the insured owes his duties. They are invariably given under seal, in view of the absence of consideration following from the promisee.

[2] *Colemore v. North* (1872) 27 L.T. 405.

payment out of the capital stock and funds of the society, and that the personal liability of the directors is expressly excluded, is not a valid objection to the bond as a sufficient security.[3] The court will consider in each case the sufficiency of the company offered as surety, in the same way as it would consider the sufficiency of an individual. The bond of a foreign company may be accepted if, under the special circumstances of the case, the court deems it to be sufficient security.[4]

31–27 Premiums paid by receiver. A receiver appointed without salary or remuneration is entitled to charge as part of his expenditure premiums paid by him to a guarantee society on the bond which constitutes his security.[5] A receiver who is remunerated must pay the premiums out of his salary.[6]

3. Fidelity Policies

31–28 Scope of fidelity policies. Fidelity insurance is a branch of contingency insurance designed to cover the insured for loss incurred by a breach of fidelity on the part of an employee or other person in whom the insured has placed confidence.[7] The policy will usually specify in fairly precise terms the conduct on the part of the employee which will give rise to liability on the part of the insurer; thus cover may be given for theft or embezzlement in which case the words will be construed in accordance with their meaning in criminal law.[8] Cover may also be afforded against loss from fraud or dishonesty of the servant[9] or want of integrity, honesty or fidelity on his part. In *European Assurance Society v. Bank of Toronto*,[10] a policy was issued to the bank against loss occasioned by want of integrity, honesty or fidelity or negligence, defaults or irregularities on the part of their agent at Montreal.

---

[3] *Carpenter v. Treasury Solicitor* (1882) 7 P.D. 235.

[4] *Aldrich v. British Griffin Chilled Iron and Steel Co.* [1904] 2 K.B. 850.

[5] *Aldrich v. British Griffin Chilled Iron & Steel Co.*, *supra*.

[6] *Harris v. Sleep* [1897] 2 Ch. 80.

[7] Normally a fidelity policy covers employees rather than any larger category of persons: *Excess Life Ass. Co. v. Firemen's Ins. Co. of Newark* [1982] 2 Lloyd's Rep. 599. In *Proudfoot Plc v. Federal Ins. Co.* [1997] L.R.L.R. 659, the policy defined "employee" as including "any director or trustee of an insured while performing acts coming within the scope of the usual duties of an employee." It was argued that an independent company which administered the assured's payroll was within the definition, on the basis that it was a trustee of the assured. It was held that although the company received money in trust, it was as trustee for the assured, not of the assured.

[8] *Debenhams Ltd v. Excess Ins. Co. Ltd* (1912) 28 T.L.R. 505; *London Guarantee and Accident Co. v. City of Halifax* [1927] Can.S.C. 165. See further the discussion of terms of the criminal law in theft policies, paras 27–01 *et seq.*, *ante*. The fact that the servant may have been acquitted of the criminal charge will not prevent the employer from recovering: *Protestant Board of School Commissioners v. Guarantee Co. of North America* (1887) 31 L.C.J. 254.

[9] *Ravenscroft v. Provident Clerks' and General and Guarantee Association* (1888) 5 T.L.R. 3. The words "fraud or dishonesty amounting to embezzlement" may cover loss by embezzlement only (*cf. London Guarantee Co. v. Fearnley* (1880) 5 App.Cas. 911, 916, *per* Lord Blackburn) or may be used in a wider, less technical sense—see *London Guarantee and Accident Co. v. Hochelaga Bank* (1893) 3 Q.R.Q.B. 25. If the policy covers against acts of dishonesty undertaken "with manifest intent", it is likely that the employee must act with clear, obvious and apparent intent to cause loss, and that such intent would be established if the employee believed that the loss was substantially certain: *New Hampshire Ins. Co. v. Philips Electronics (No. 2)* [1999] Lloyd's Rep. I.R. 66, 79 (where the point was not seriously disputed between the parties).

[10] (1875) 7 Rev. Leg. 57.

The agent allowed one of the bank's customers to overdraw his account by a large sum, although he knew that the customer would be unable to repay the overdraft. The Judicial Committee of the Privy Council held that the agent's conduct constituted a "want of fidelity" within the policy; there could be no liability for loss caused by an honest exercise of discretion to allow overdrafts to customers of the bank, but, if the discretion was not exercised bona fide in the interests of the bank, the insurers would be liable.[11] The policy may cover conduct of a non-criminal nature such as the wilful default[12] or negligence of the servant.[13] In a Canadian case[14] the policy covered "loss directly occasioned by ... dishonesty or negligence"; money was abstracted by some unknown person but by reason of the employee's failure to check the accounts the abstraction was not discovered until it was too late to arrest the defaulter and recover the money. It was held that the loss was occasioned by the negligence of the employee and was, therefore, within the policy. The policy will not, however, cover losses due to a crime which is not the fault of the employee, as, for instance where the servant is robbed of his master's money;[15] nor will a liability policy, protecting the insured from the consequences of his servant's negligence, afford cover in respect of his criminal activities.[16]

31–29 In modern practice, fidelity cover may be part of what are often described as "comprehensive crime policies". Issues arising under such a policy were the subject of *New Hampshire Insurance Co. v. Philips Electronics North America Corporation (No. 2)*.[17] The section of the policy conferring fidelity cover provided:

> "This section indemnifies the Insured following loss of Money, Securities and other property which the Insured sustains ... resulting directly from one or more fraudulent or dishonest acts committed by an Employee ... Provided always that ... (2) Such fraudulent or dishonest acts ... shall mean only fraudulent or dishonest acts committed by an employee with manifest intent: (a) to cause the Insured to sustain such loss; and (b) to obtain financial benefit for the Employee, or for any other person or organisation intended by the Employee to receive such

---

[11] *cf. Courtaulds plc and Courtaulds (Belgium) S.A. v. Lissenden* [1986] 1 Lloyd's Rep. 368 where the insured was covered for loss sustained on account of forgery or fabrication, and moneys were abstracted from a bank account by an employee who forged bank transfers and who concealed how the money had been spent, thus causing additional sums to be expended on lawful objects. The moneys abstracted were within the cover, but a claim for loss of use and extra overdraft interest failed, although it would have succeeded if want of fidelity had been covered, *per* Saville J. at 371. It is not unreasonable for the Solicitors Compensation Fund to compensate a claimant for his actual loss and not for any consequential loss—*R. v. Law Society, ex parte Reigate Projects* [1993] 1 W.L.R. 1531.

[12] See, *e.g. Kenney v. Employers' Liability Assurance Corporation* [1901] 1 I.R. 301.

[13] See, *e.g. American Surety Co. of New York v. Wrightson* (1910) 103 L.T. 663; *Pawle & Co. v. Bussell* (1916) 114 L.T. 805; *Citizens Ins. Co. v. Grand Trunk Rail Co.* (1880) 25 L.C.J. 163; *Colonial Bank of Australasia v. European Ins. and Guarantee Society* (1864) 1 W.W. & A.B. 15.

[14] *Crown Bank v. London Guarantee and Accident Co.* (1908) 17 O.L.R. 95. *Cf. United States Fidelity and Guaranty Co. v. Des Moines National Bank*, 145 Fed.Rep. 273 (1906).

[15] *Walker v. British Guarantee Association* (1852) 18 Q.B. 277.

[16] *Goddard and Smith v. Frew* [1939] 4 All E.R. 358; although some liability policies do now include such a form of cover: see further paras 28–62, *et seq.*, *ante*.

[17] [1999] Lloyd's Rep. I.R. 66.

benefit, other than salaries, commissions, fees, bonuses, promotions, awards, profit sharing, pensions or other employee benefits earned in the normal course of employment."

One division of the assured sold ballasts (regulators for fluorescent tubes). The assured claimed for losses as a result of the fraud of the president of that division. He had supplied defective goods, which the company had been obliged to replace, causing loss, and fraudulently obtained bonuses by means of sales of defective goods and manipulation of the division's books. It was held that there was no loss in respect of the defective ballasts as there had been no loss of property. However the assured was able to recover in respect of the fraudulently obtained bonuses (subject to proof of the requisite intent). There had been a loss of monies standing to the account of the assured, which it would otherwise have retained and used for its own purposes. The exception in clause 2(b) for bonuses applied only to bonuses earned in the ordinary course of employment.[18]

31–30 Obligation of disclosure. Provided that the relationship of the parties is that of insurer and insured,[19] the insured is under the normal duty of disclosure and is bound to disclose any knowledge of previous defalcations on the part of the employee whose integrity is insured.[20] He may even be required to disclose his suspicions, if well-founded.[21]

31–31 Statements in proposal forms. Statements made by the insured in the proposal form with respect to the checks to be made on the employees' honesty may be either warranties as to the future,[22] breach of which will discharge insurers from liability under the policy, or statements of present fact or intention[23]; as such they may be true or false and, if they are false, the insurer will be entitled to avoid the policy for misrepresentation.[24] Answers to questions relating to the duties of an employee cannot be warranties that the employee will perform those duties, for failure to perform such duties is precisely what is being insured against; such answers merely relate to the office system of the employer.[25]

31–32 Alteration in terms of service. A policy which covers the fidelity of a person when acting in one capacity does not cover him if he acts in a different

---

[18] Following the Ontario Court of Appeal in *Crown Life Ins. Co. v. American Home Ins. Co.* (1989) 36 C.C.L.I. 31.

[19] Where *e.g.* a father gives a fidelity bond on behalf of a son, he is probably not to be considered an insurer. *cf. Byrne v. Muzio* (1881) 8 L.R.Ir. 396.

[20] See *Smith v. Bank of Scotland* (1813) 1 Dow. 272; *London General Omnibus Co. v. Holloway* [1912] 2 K.B. 72; *Allis-Chalmers Co. v. Maryland Fidelity and Deposit Co.* (1916) 114 L.T. 433 where the point seems to have been conceded by the insured; and *Mayfield Rural Municipality v. London and Lancashire Guaranty and Accident Co. of Canada* [1927] 1 W.W.R. 67.

[21] *Fertile Valley (Municipality) v. Union Casualty Co.* (1921) 14 Sask.L.R. 413.

[22] *Towle v. National Guardian Assurance Society* (1861) 30 L.J.Ch. 900; *Haworth & Co. v. Sickness and Accident Assurance Society* (1891) 38 Sc.L.R. 394; *Dougharty v. London Guarantee and Accident Co.* (1880) 6 Vict.L.R. 376 (Law). *Cf. Elgin Loan and Savings Co. v. London Guarantee and Accident Co.* (1906) 11 O.L.R. 330; and *Globe Savings and Loan Co. v. Employers' Liability Assurance Corporation* (1901) 13 Man.L.R. 531.

[23] *Benham v. United Guarantee and Life Assurance Co.* (1852) 7 Exch. 744; *R. v. National Ins. Co.* (1887) 13 Vict.L.R. 914; *Att.-Gen. v. Adelaide Life Ins. Co.* (1888) 22 S.Aust.L.R. 5; *Hearts of Oak Building Society v. Law Union and Rock Ins. Co. Ltd* [1936] 2 All E.R. 619.

[24] *McCammon v. Alliance Ass. Co. Ltd* [1931] 4 D.L.R. 811.

[25] *Hearts of Oak Building Society v. Law Union and Rock Ins. Co. Ltd* [1936] 2 All E.R. 619.

capacity[26] or if he is required to perform different duties.[27] Likewise, where an employee was stated to be engaged at a fixed salary of £100 but, during the currency of the policy, the method of remuneration was altered so that the employee was paid by commission, the insurer was held not to be liable under the policy, because there had been a material alteration in the risk.[28]

Not every alteration of the terms on which the servant is employed will, however, discharge the insurers[29] and an increase in the burden of the duties performed will not entitle the insurers to deny liability when the new duties are all within the scope of his employment as it existed when the insurance was effected.[30]

31–33 Time of loss. It is not enough for a loss to be discovered during the currency of the policy; the misappropriation must have been committed after the policy comes into force and before it expires.[31] Provided that the misappropriation took place while the policy was valid, it does not matter that the loss is not discovered until the policy has expired.[32] It is possible, but unusual, for a policy expressly to provide cover in respect of any loss discovered during its currency.[33] It is more usual to provide for losses committed and discovered during the currency of the policy.[34]

31–34 Notice of loss. There is almost invariably a condition in fidelity policies that notice of any breach of duty on the part of the employee must be given to the insurer. If there is such a clause, the assured is bound to notify a breach of duty only when he becomes aware of it; he is not bound to notify mere suspicions.[35] In *European Assurance Society v. Bank of Toronto,*[36] in

---

[26] *Cosford Union v. Poor Law and Local Government Officers' Mutual Guarantee Ass. Ltd* (1910) 103 L.T. 463 (assistant overseer not insured while acting as clerk to the parish council); *Hay v. Employers' Liability Assurance Corpn.* (1905) 6 O.W.R. 459.

[27] *Wembley U.D.C. v. Poor Law and Local Government Officers' Mutual Guarantee Assn. Ltd* (1901) 17 T.L.R. 516. The insurers will not be liable even if the loss occurs in connection with the servant's original duties, *Pybus v. Gibbs* (1856) 6 F. & B. 902.

[28] *North Western Ry v. Whinray* (1854) 10 Exch. 77 (where the remuneration was set out in the recital to the contract).

[29] *Sanderson v. Aston* (1873) L.R. 8 Ex. 73 (where no reference was made in the contract to the terms of the employment).

[30] See *Skillet v. Fletcher* (1867) L.R. 2 C.P. 469.

[31] *Allis-Chalmers Ltd v. Maryland Fidelity and Deposit Co.* (1916) 114 L.T. 433; *University of New Zealand v. Standard Fire and Marine Ins. Co. Ltd* [1916] N.Z.L.R. 509.

[32] Usually there will be a provision that notice is to be given within a specified time of the loss or the discovery of the loss—see, *e.g. Ward v. Law Property Assurance and Trust Society* (1856) 4 W.R. 605, or that the loss is to occur within a specified time before discovery—see, *e.g. Fidelity and Casualty Co. v. Bank of Timmonsville* 139 Fed.Rep. 101 (1905) and *London Guarantee and Accident Co. Ltd v. City of Halifax* [1927] Can.S.C. 165. In *Universities Superannuation Scheme Ltd v. Royal Ins. (UK) Ltd.* [2000] 1 All E.R. (Comm.) 266, fidelity insurance covered, *inter alia,* fraud discovered not later than 24 months after termination of the policy, or resignation of a relevant employee. It was held that the reference to discoverability qualified the acts to which the indemnity applied. It did not delay the accrual of the insured's cause of action from date of loss to date of discovery.

[33] *Pennsylvania Co. for Insurance on Lives & Granting Annuities v. Mumford* [1920] 2 K.B. 537.

[34] *Fanning v. London Guarantee and Accident Co.* (1884) 10 Vict.L.R. 8; *Commercial Mutual Building Society v. London Guarantee and Accident Co.* (1891) M.L.R.Q.B. 307.

[35] *Ward v. Law Property Assurance and Trust Society* (1856) 4 W.R. 605; *American Surety Co. v. Pauly,* 72 Fed.Rep. 470 (1896); *Aetna Indemnity Co. v. Crowe Coal & Mining Co.,* 154 Fed.Rep. 545 (1907).

[36] (1875) 7 Rev.Leg. 57.

which the employee had *mala fide* allowed a client to obtain an excessive overdraft, the policy provided for notice to be given if the assured had a claim by reason of some act or omission of the employee. The Judicial Committee held this to mean that notice must be given when the bank became aware of the infidelity, not when they became aware that the overdraft had been given. Sometimes the policy expressly provides that the insurer is to be under no liability unless he is notified of the loss within a specified time of its occurrence; in such cases the assured cannot make a claim unless he has given notice, even if he is unaware of the loss until the specified time has expired.[37]

31–35 Notice of breach of duty. A clause requiring notification of any breach of duty on the part of the employee is an important protection for the insurer; once such notice is given, he will be entitled to require the insured either to dismiss the employee or to discharge the insurer from his obligations.[38] The question arises whether there is any duty on the insured to give such notice, in the absence of any express term. It has been held that a guarantor is entitled to be informed of any dishonest conduct on the part of the employee which would entitle the employer to dismiss him.[39] This principle would probably be applied in a case of fidelity insurance, because it would be most inequitable that an insured could conceal dishonest conduct on the part of his employee from an insurer who might be under a continuing obligation to indemnify the insured for all losses over a period of time and who might want to trace the delinquent employee as rapidly as possible.[40] It seems that this principle applies to any conduct on the part of the employee which would entitle the employer to dismiss him, whether or not it gives rise to any claim against the surety under the contract,[41] but in a case where the fidelity bond expressly required notification of any fraud or dishonesty, this was held to refer to such fraud or dishonesty as gave rise to a cause of action under the bond.[42]

31–36 Negligence of assured. In accordance with the general law of insurance, it is no defence that the assured has been negligent in supervising the employee.[43] Thus it has been held in Canada that failure by a city corporation to comply with the statutory requirements as to supervision of its employees is not a defence.[44] A statement in answer to a question in an

---

[37] *T. H. Adamson & Sons v. Liverpool and London and Globe Ins. Co. Ltd* [1953] 2 Lloyd's Rep. 355.

[38] If this is not expressly stated, it may well be implied—see *Phillips v. Foxall* (1872) L.R. 7 Q.B. 666, *per* Blackburn J. and *Snaddon v. London, Edinburgh and Glasgow Ins. Co. Ltd* (1902) 5 F. 182, 186 *per* Lord Young.

[39] *Phillips v. Foxall* (1872) L.R. 7 Q.B. 666; *Burgess v. Eve* (1872) L.R. 13 Eq. 450. The principle does not apply if there is no power to dismiss: *Lawder v. Lawder* (1873) Ir.R. 7 C.L. 57; *Byrne v. Muzio* (1881) 8 L.R.Ir. 396; *Caxton and Arrington Union v. Dew* (1899) 68 L.J.Q.B. 380.

[40] *Snaddon v. London, Edinburgh and Glasgow Ins. Co. Ltd* (1902) 5 F. 182.

[41] *Sanderson v. Aston* (1873) L.R. 8 Ex. 73, 76–77 *per* Kelly C.B. But see the comments on this case made in *Durham Corporation v. Fowler* (1889) 22 Q.B.D. 394.

[42] *Byrne v. Muzio* (1881) 8 L.R.Ir. 396.

[43] *Shepherd v. Beecher* (1725) 2 P.Wms. 288. *cf. Guardians of Mansfield Union v. Wright* (1882) 9 Q.B.D. 683. The position might be different if there has been gross negligence or recklessness (see *Harbour Commissioners of Montreal v. Guarantee Co. of North America* (1894) 22 Can.S.C. 542) because it could then be argued that the cause of the loss was the conduct of the insured rather than the peril insured against.

[44] *London Guarantee and Accident Co. v. City of Halifax* [1927] Can.S.C.R. 165.

application form, that the employee's books had been examined and found correct was held to be true when it was proved that an examination had been made and the examiners believed the books to be correct but that errors had been overlooked owing to the carelessness of the examination.[45]

31–37 Policy procured by employee. Where an employer requires an applicant for employment to procure a fidelity bond and the applicant goes to an insurance company and it issues a policy in favour of the employer upon the application of the applicant, the latter is not the agent of the employer for the purpose of procuring the insurance so as to fix the employer with responsibility for non-disclosure of facts known to the applicant but not known to the employer. The applicant is, in fact, procuring the policy in his own interest because he is desirous of obtaining employment, and although the policy insures the employer there is no relationship of principal and agent in the transaction.[46]

31–38 Money due to defaulting employee. The policy may provide for the deduction from the amount otherwise payable under it of all moneys due by the employer to the employee. In one case where the loss was greater than the sum insured, this was held to mean that such moneys should be deducted from the loss and not from the sum insured, and where the insured company was in liquidation and it was uncertain what sum would ultimately be found to be due to the employee, the insured company was held entitled to recover the full sum insured upon the footing that if and when it was settled what sum was due by it to the employee, it should hold that for the insurers.[47]

31–39 Prosecution of defaulter. Where there is a condition to the effect that the insured when called upon shall use all diligence in prosecuting the defaulting employee to conviction, and there is also a condition in general terms that the policy is issued subject to the conditions, which shall be conditions precedent to the right on the part of the employer to recover, the insured cannot recover if he fails to prosecute.[48]

4. INSURANCE DISTINGUISHED FROM SURETYSHIP

31–40 Importance of distinction. A contract of guarantee is a contract whereby one person (the surety) undertakes to a second person (the

---

[45] *Guarantee Co. of North America v. Mechanics' Savings Bank and Trust Co.*, 80 Fed.Rep. 766 (1896).

[46] *Comptoire Nationale v. Law Car and General Ins. Co.* (1909) C.A. 10th June. See the 1st edition of this work at 353. See para. 18–21, *ante.*

[47] *Fifth Liverpool Starr-Bowkett Building Society v. Travellers Accident Ins. Co.* (1892) 9 T.L.R. 221; but see *Board of Trade v. Guarantee Society* (1896) [1910] 1 K.B. 408n. and *Board of Trade v. Employers' Liability Ass. Co.* [1910] 1 K.B. 401. The same principle applies if any money is recovered from the servant, *cf. London Guarantee and Accident Co. v. Hochelage Bank* (1893) 3 Q.R.Q.B. 25.

[48] *London Guarantee Co. v. Fearnley* (1880) 5 App.Cas. 911; *Canada Life Assurance Co. v. London Guarantee and Accident Co.* (1900) 9 Q.R.Q.B. 183. This condition may not perhaps require the insured to extradite a servant who has fled the jurisdiction; *Dougharty v. London Guarantee and Accident Co.* (1880) 6 Vict.L.R. 376 (Law). If the insurers require the employer to prosecute, they are probably liable for the costs because the insured will have incurred expense at their request and will therefore be entitled to an indemnity, *cf. Globe Savings and Loan Co. v. Employers' Liability Assurance Corporation* (1901) 13 Man.L.R. 531.

creditor) that he will answer for the debt, default or miscarriage of a third (the principal debtor).[49] In modern legal parlance "to answer for" means that the guarantor promises to see that the debtor's obligation is performed, whereas an insurer promises to indemnify the insured creditor in the event that it is not.[50] A contract for fidelity, credit or guarantee insurance has obvious affinities with such a contract inasmuch as the insurer undertakes to indemnify the insured in respect of any loss he incurs as a result of the infidelity or insolvency of a third person. Usually it does not matter whether a contract is held to be a contract of insurance or of guarantee[51] but it is sometimes essential to distinguish them. The most important reasons for determining the nature of such a contract are as follows:

(1) A guarantee must be evidenced by a note or memorandum in writing pursuant to section 4 of the Statute of Frauds 1677[52]; a contract of non-marine insurance is fully effective even if made orally.

(2) A contract of guarantee is void if the principal debt is for any reason void[53]; such a consideration is irrelevant to any contract of insurance.

(3) If the principal debtor in a contract of guarantee is discharged, the surety is also discharged[54]; this is not necessarily the case in a contract of insurance.

(4) A contract of insurance is a contract of utmost good faith, requiring full disclosure by the insured; a contract of guarantee is not such a contract and the duty of disclosure, to the extent it exists, is less specific.[55]

(5) A surety who has paid the creditor has a right of action against the debtor in his own name,[56] an insurer is merely entitled, after payment, to be subrogated to the rights of the insured.

(6) Insurers of a debt already guaranteed are not co-sureties with the guarantor; they can therefore exercise the creditors' rights in full by way of subrogation against the principal debtor and the guarantor rather than claiming a rateable proportion by way of contribution.[57]

(7) The issuing of contracts of guarantee does not amount to the carrying on of insurance business for the purposes of the Financial Services and Markets Act 2000.[58]

31–41 Difficulty of distinction. It is difficult to tell whether a court will decide that a particular agreement is a contract of insurance or a contract of

---

[49] See Chitty, *Contracts* (28th ed., 1999), Vol. II, Ch. 44.

[50] *Moschi v. Lep Air Services Ltd* [1973] A.C. 331, 347, *per* Lord Diplock.

[51] *Dane v. Mortgage Ins. Corpn.* [1894] 1 Q.B. 54, 62, *per* Kay L.J.; *Re Law Guarantee Trust and Accident Soc. Ltd, Liverpool Mortgage Insurance Co. Ltd's Case* [1914] 2 Ch. 617, 636, *per* Warrington L.J.; *Seaton v. Heath* [1899] 1 Q.B. 782, 792 *per* Romer L.J.

[52] Chitty, *op. cit.* paras 44–038, *et seq.*

[53] Chitty, *op. cit.* para. 44–037.

[54] Chitty, *op. cit.* paras. 44–064, *et seq. Cf.* the argument advanced in *Dane v. Mortgage Ins. Corpn* [1894] 1 Q.B. 54.

[55] Chitty, *op. cit.* para. 44–032. *Cf. Lee v. Jones* (1864) 17 C.B.(N.S.) 482; *Phillips v. Foxall* (1872) L.R. 7 Q.B. 666; *Workington Harbour and Dock Board v. Trade Indemnity Co. Ltd* (1934) 49 Ll.L.R. 430 especially, *per* Scrutton L.J. whose judgment was particularly commended by Lord Atkin in the House of Lords [1937] A.C. 1, 14; *Credit Lyonnais v. E.C.G.D.* [1996] 1 Lloyd's Rep. 200, 225–7; *Royal Bank of Scotland v. Etridge* [2002] Lloyd's Rep. 343, 387.

[56] Chitty, *op. cit.* para. 44–098.

[57] *Parr's Bank Ltd v. Albert Mines Syndicate Ltd* (1900) 5 Com.Cas. 116. *Cf. Re Denton's Estate* [1904] 2 Ch. 178.

[58] See Ch. 34, *post.*

guarantee. The traditional approach is to be found in the judgment of Romer L.J. in *Seaton v. Heath*,[59] which concentrates on the circumstances in which the agreement is made. He points out that there is no magic in the use of words such as "insurance" or "guarantee" and that the status of the contract depends on "its substantial character and how it came to be effected".[60] If a document is called a "policy", that is, of course, an indication that it is intended to be a contract of insurance,[61] but the form of the contract is by no means conclusive.[62] Thus a document guaranteeing the repayment of a deposit made with a bank, if the bank defaults,[63] a document guaranteeing payment of money secured by a debenture,[64] a document guaranteeing the solvency of a surety[65] or the solvency of a society which has guaranteed debentures issued by a company[66] and a document guaranteeing perform-ance of a contract of sale by the vendors[67] have all been held to be contracts of insurance; but a document entitled "mortgage insurance policy" promis-ing payment to a mortgagee after he had become entitled to exercise his power of sale,[68] a performance bond guaranteeing the performance of his contract by a building contractor,[69] and a document procured by a finance company by which an insurance company promised to indemnify a depositor if his deposit was not repaid[70] have been held to be contracts of guarantee rather than contracts of insurance.

Romer L.J. then says:

> "Contracts of insurance are generally matters of speculation, where the person desiring to be insured has means of knowledge as to the risk, and the insurer has not the means or not the same means. The insured generally puts the risk before the insurer as a business transaction, and the insurer on the risk stated fixes a proper price to remunerate him for the risk to be undertaken. ... On the other hand in ... contracts of guarantee ... the creditor does not himself go to the surety or represent, or explain to the surety, the risk to be run. The surety often takes the position from motives of friendship to the debtor, and generally not as the result of any direct bargaining between him and the creditor, or in

---

[59] [1899] 1 Q.B. 782, 792–793. The decision of the Court of Appeal was reversed in the House of Lords ([1900] A.C. 135) but no doubt was cast on Romer L.J.'s judgment: *Re Denton's Estate* [1904] 2 Ch. 178, 188, *per* Vaughan Williams L.J. Followed in *International Commercial Bank v. Ins. Corp. of Ireland* [1991] I.R.L.M. 726, H.C.

[60] *cf.* "The true effect of the contract is to be ascertained, I think, not upon a scrutiny of the terms used but upon an examination of its effect", *Re Law Guarantee Trust and Accident Society Ltd, Liverpool Mortgage Insurance Co. Ltd's Case* [1914] 2 Ch. 617, 631 *per* Buckley L.J.

[61] *Dane v. Mortgage Ins. Corpn* [1894] 1 Q.B. 54; *Finlay v. Mexican Investment Corpn* [1897] 1 Q.B. 517.

[62] *Trade Indemnity Co. v. Workington Harbour and Dock Board* [1937] A.C. 1, 16–17; *Re Australian and Overseas Ins. Co. Ltd* [1966] 1 N.S.W.R. 558, 565, *per* McLelland C.J.

[63] *Dane v. Mortgage Ins. Corpn* [1894] 1 Q.B. 54; *Laird v. Securities Ins. Co.* (1895) 22 R. 452.

[64] *Finlay v. Mexican Investment Corpn* [1897] 1 Q.B. 517; *Shaw v. Royce Ltd* [1911] 1 Ch. 138; *Re Law Guarantee Trust and Accident Society Ltd, Liverpool Mortgage Insurance Co. Ltd's Case* [1914] 2 Ch. 617.

[65] *Seaton v. Heath* [1899] 1 Q.B. 782; *Parr's Bank Ltd v. Albert Mines Syndicate Ltd* (1900) 5 Com.Cas. 116.

[66] *Re Law Guarantee Trust and Accident Society Ltd, Liverpool Mortgage Insurance Co. Ltd's Case* [1914] 2 Ch. 617.

[67] *Kreglinger and Fernau Ltd v. Irish National Ins. Co. Ltd* [1956] I.R. 116, noted (1975) 38 M.L.R. 212.

[68] *Re Denton's Estate* [1904] 2 Ch. 178.

[69] *Trade Indemnity Co. v. Workington Harbour and Dock Board* [1937] A.C. 1.

[70] *Re Australian and Overseas Ins. Co. Ltd* [1966] 1 N.S.W.R. 558.

consideration of any remuneration passing to him from the creditor. The risk undertaken is generally known to the surety, and the circumstances generally point to the view that as between the creditor and surety it was contemplated and intended that the surety should take upon himself to ascertain what risk he was taking upon himself."

31–42 Three elements. There are three elements of distinction between contracts of guarantee and insurance in this passage. First, the motive of the parties; an insurer takes business for money,[71] while a surety undertakes responsibility as a friend perhaps for no consideration.[72] Secondly, the manner of dealing; an insurer usually receives his business by dealing with the insured (often through a broker) not by dealing with the person whose fidelity or solvency he is insuring, while a surety will usually be approached by the principal debtor. Thirdly, the means of knowledge; an insurer has no means of acquainting himself with the nature of the risk and must rely on the insured to disclose all material facts, while the surety is usually fully aware of the risks he is being asked to assume or is, at least, in as good a position as the creditor to discover the true nature of the risk.[73] If, therefore, there is evidence that the "guarantor" relied on the creditor to inform him about the risk, this will support the conclusion that the contract is one of insurance[74]; if, however, he is sought by the principal debtor who explains the risk to him or leaves him to make his own inquiries, the contract is more likely to be held to be one of guarantee.[75] This approach was followed in *Re Sentinel Securities Plc*[76] in which a company had issued guarantees that in the event that suppliers and installers of home improvements to domestic dwellings, especially double-glazing, should cease to trade owing to insolvency, it would itself or by its sub-contractor honour the original supplier's warranty of its workmanship and product, and complete or repair the defective work of which the customer complained. Notwithstanding that the company was promising to ensure that the supplier's obligation was performed, rather than to pay compensation to the customer, the court held in reliance on *Seaton v. Heath* that it was a contract of insurance in which the benefit was payable in kind.[77]

31–43 There is one further consideration which may be important in distinguishing a contract of guarantee from a contract of insurance. A surety promises to pay the original debt of the principal debtor, while an insurer promises to pay a sum of money in a certain event[78]; this is an independent obligation to pay a new debt and may differ from the original debt in amount and with respect to the time of payment. If, therefore, there is such a

[71] *Re Law Guarantee Trust and Accident Society Ltd, Liverpool Mortgage Insurance Co. Ltd's Case* [1914] 2 Ch. 617, 631, *per* Buckley L.J.; *Parr's Bank Ltd v. Albert Mines Syndicate Ltd* (1900) 5 Com.Cas. 116; *Tebbets v. Mercantile Credit Guarantee Co. of New York*, 73 Fed.Rep. 95, 97 (1896).

[72] *Lee v. Jones* (1864) 17 C.B.(N.S.) 482, 503, *per* Blackburn J.

[73] *Re Denton's Estate* [1904] 2 Ch. 178, 188–189, *per* Vaughan Williams L.J.

[74] *Kreglinger and Fernau Ltd v. Irish National Ins. Co. Ltd* [1956] I.R. 116, 147–149, *per* Davitt J.

[75] *Workington Harbour and Dock Board v. Trade Indemnity Co.* (1934) 49 Ll.L.R. 430, 432, *per* Scrutton L.J.; affirmed [1937] A.C. 1.

[76] [1996] 1 W.L.R. 316.

[77] The *Moschi* decision, [1973] A.C. 331, was not cited, and the facts in *Sentinel* appear to have gone beyond the mere provision of a benefit in kind to indemnify the assured against a loss.

[78] *Dane v. Mortgage Ins. Corpn* [1894] 1 Q.B. 54.

difference it will be an indication that the contract is one of insurance rather than guarantee.[79]

31–44 Hybrid contracts. Contracts of guarantee and contracts of insurance are not, however, mutually exclusive, and a contract may have the attributes of a contract of insurance in so far as the relationship between insurer and insured and the duty of utmost good faith concerned, and at the same time the attributes of a contract of guarantee in so far as the insurer's obligation to pay and his rights over against third parties are concerned.[80]

31–45 Legal expenses insurance. Over the past decade the use of this type of cover has increased substantially. The description embraces cover of differing character, some in the nature of liability insurance and some in the nature of pecuniary loss insurance. The first "LEI" to become established was cover against the costs of bringing a legal claim against a defendant who had caused injury to the assured or damage to the assured's property.[81] It is most frequently sold as an addition to motor or household policies, and is offered as a collateral benefit to a contract of employment or trades union membership, and is known as "BTE" (before the event) insurance. The cover entitles the assured to the services of a solicitor and sometimes to claims management and handling services provided by a separate company, whether or not its service duplicates what solicitors may do. Premiums have been generally low. It has been necessary to make regulations to preclude or settle potential conflicts of interest.[82] The cover may also grant an indemnity against the risk of becoming liable to pay the legal costs of a successful defendant.

31–46 Another more recent type of LEI is "ATE" (after the event) cover, which, as its name suggests, is taken out by the assured after he sees that he will be involved in a particular piece of litigation. There are two principal types of ATE, (i) conditional fee insurance ("CFI") and (ii) both sides' costs insurance ("BSC"). Each category is capable of great variation. Essentially, CFI commonly provides cover for the opponent's costs and the assured's solicitors' disbursements excluding counsel's fees. There are hybrid insurances incorporating elements of both types. Cover is available for claimants and defendants in respect of a particular piece of litigation. The extent to which a successful assured can recover the costs of the ATE premium from his opponent has been the subject of rulings in the Court of Appeal.[83]

[79] *Finlay v. Mexican Investment Corpn* [1897] 1 Q.B. 517; *Re Law Guarantee Trust and Accident Society Ltd, Liverpool Mortgage Insurance Co. Ltd's Case* [1914] 2 Ch. 617, 629–630, *per* Buckley L.J.

[80] *Shaw v. Royce Ltd* [1911] 1 Ch. 138 where it was held that although the contract was probably one of insurance and that the disappearance of the original debt would not, *ex hypothesi*, destroy the guarantee, the guarantee was nevertheless destroyed by the binding arrangements made between the parties. *Cf. Re Law Guarantee Trust and Accident Society Ltd, Liverpool Mortgage Insurance Co. Ltd's Case* [1914] 2 Ch. 617. For the converse case, where it was held that the contract was one of guarantee but that the "insurer" was not a co-surety by reason of the documents made between the parties, see *Re Denton's Estate* [1904] 2 Ch. 178.

[81] For a description of Before the Event cover of this type see *Sarwar v. Alam* [2002] 1 W.L.R. 125.

[82] Insurance Companies (Legal Expenses Insurance) Regulations 1990 (S.I. 1990 No. 1159).

[83] *Callery v. Gray (No. 2)* [2001] 1 W.L.R. 2142.

CHAPTER 32

CONTRACTORS' RISKS POLICIES

32–1 Contractors' risks. Although there are many different risks against which contractors may wish to insure, such risks broadly fall under two heads:

(a) insurance against damage to the contract works, to which may or may not be added, loss of or damage to plant, machinery, and other equipment on the site occupied by the builder or the repairer or other contractor, and

(b) insurance against liability which may be incurred by the contractor in the course of his operations.

Both these types of risks may be covered in one "contractors' all risks" policy[1] or they may be covered separately. As will be seen the term "all risks" is something of a misnomer in as much as the contractor seldom, if ever, gets cover against literally all the risks involved. It has been held that a project manager engaged for a construction project owes a duty of care to the employer to ensure that insurance required to be effected by the contractors was in place.[2]

32–2 Parties. A striking feature of contractors' risks insurance is the appearance of many parties as named assureds in one policy. This is perfectly understandable. Policies are often taken out by a main contractor pursuant to provisions in the contract with the employer, and, even if the contract does not expressly require all interests in the project to be covered in one insurance, it often makes good sense to procure cover not only in the name of the contractor, but also in the joint names of the employer, sub-contractors, and other interested parties. In such cases it is usually provided that each party is insured in respect of his respective rights and interests, and it is unnecessary for any party other than the interested party to be joined in any action against the insurer on the policy. Where there are

---

[1] As in *Petrofina Ltd v. Magnaload Ltd* [1984] Q.B. 127, 131–132. Note that there is in practice no "standard" form of contractors' "all risks" policy. With most major construction contracts the conditions and wording of the policy designed to protect the contract works is a matter of negotiation in each case between the brokers representing the various classes of proposed assureds, and the insurer to whom the proposal is made. The more truly "comprehensive" the policy, the higher the premium.

[2] *Pozzolanic Lytag Ltd v. Bryan Hobson Associates, The Times*, December 3, 1998.

no words of severance to that effect, and where the policy is on contractors' property, a main contractor may cover the entire contract works in his own name and in the names of all the sub-contractors with an interest in them, so that either he or any one of them will be entitled to sue the insurers for loss of or damage to the insured property. In consequence each contractor is entitled to recover for a loss in excess of his own proprietary interest, holding that excess on trust for the others involved.[3] A second consequence of this entitlement is that the insurers are not normally entitled to recover sums paid to one co-assured under the policy by pursuing a subrogated action in the name of that assured against other assureds, even in the absence of specific clauses waiving subrogation rights against co-assureds.[4]

Where the policy covers "contractors" and "sub-contractors", this means persons whose work involves or at least includes physical construction work, and consulting engineers are not included within the cover, so subrogation rights can be pursued against them.[5] In *British Telecommunications Plc v. James Thomson and Sons (Engineers) Ltd*[6] the contract, which was in JCT form with modifications, distinguished between "nominated sub-contractors" and "domestic sub-contractors", and provided only that insurance effected by the employer should enure for the benefit of nominated sub-contractors. It was held by the House of Lords that this distinction was crucial. The insurer was not precluded from exercising subrogation rights against a domestic sub-contractor. There were no reasons for not imposing a duty of care to the employer on the domestic sub-contractor.

32–3 Classification of risks. Modern forms of policy almost invariably make a clear distinction between the two types of risk referred to in paragraph 32–1 above by having one section on property and another on

---

[3] *Petrofina Ltd v. Magnaload Ltd, supra,* at 136. For sub-contractors' insurable interest, see paras 1–54 to 1–58, *ante.*

[4] *Petrofina Ltd v. Magnaload Ltd, supra,* following *Commonwealth Construction Co. Ltd v. Imperial Oil Ltd* (1977) 69 D.L.R. (3d) 558; *Stone Vickers v. Appledore Ferguson Shipbuilders* [1991] 2 Lloyd's Rep. 288, reversed on other grounds [1992] 2 Lloyd's Rep. 578. It appears that the same result would follow if the defendant sub-contractor was not a party to the insurance policy but that, by the terms of a contract with the particular plaintiff, the insurance was expressed to be taken out for his benefit: *Mark Rowlands Ltd v. Berni Inns Ltd* [1986] 1 Q.B. 211. See Ch. 20, *ante.* The JCT form of building contract has been held to mean that the employer's insurance does not inure to the benefit of a negligent contractor: *Barking L.B.C. v. Stanford Asphalt* [1997] C.L.C. 929. In *Petrofina* the reason for the inability to pursue subrogation rights against a co-assured was said to be the principle of circuity. In *Co-operative Retail Services v. Taylor Young Partnership and Others* [2002] 1 All E.R. (Comm.) 918, Lord Hope suggested that the language of circuity should be jettisoned. (This echoed the approach taken by the Court of Appeal: [2001] Lloyd's Rep.I.R. 122 at 137.) Instead the analysis should focus on whether the contractual scheme between the parties meant that they would look to the joint insurance to meet the relevant loss, without recourse to litigation between each other. It was further held that such a contractual scheme would preclude a claim for contribution for damages payable to another party covered by the scheme. In relation to subrogation—see paras 22–98 to 22–102, *supra.*

[5] *Hopewell Project Management Ltd v. Ewbank Preece Ltd* [1998] 1 Lloyd's Rep. 448. See also para. 1–152. A reference to a class such as "contractors" may be construed to mean any party who becomes a contractor during the currency of the policy—*cf. Trident General Ins. Co. Ltd v. Mc Neice Bros Pty Ltd* (1988) 165 CLR 107. If a contractor is not a party to the insurance, it may be able to enforce the insurance under the Contracts (Rights of Third Parties) Act 1999, if the requirements of the Act are satisfied, in particular as to whether the contract purports to confer a benefit on the third party and as to the identification of the third party.

[6] [1999] Lloyd's Rep.I.R. 105.

liability. Where the policy is not so drafted, it can sometimes be a difficult question to decide whether a policy covers the insured for damage to property or only for his liability to third parties. In *American Shipbuilding Company v. Orion Insurance Co. Ltd and Boag*[7] the plaintiffs were ship repairers who were insured under a policy incorporating the Institute Builders' Risks Clauses. While a ship was in dry-dock she slipped from her position and both the hull and the dry-dock were damaged. The insurers contended that the policy only covered liability to third parties and they accordingly paid for the damage to the ship but not for the damage to the dry-dock which was owned by the plaintiffs. This was upheld by the District Judge who decided that "the thrust" of the policy was to provide liability insurance for the plaintiffs and that the only clause providing cover for the plaintiff's own interest was expressed too narrowly to apply to damage to the plaintiff's dry-dock.

32–4 Contractors' all risks. The name given to this type of insurance is usually "contractors' all risks." The policy often includes cover for liability to third parties, but, even where it does not do so, the policy is still sometimes described, albeit inaccurately, as a "contractors' all risks policy". The policy will afford a wide cover on property involved in the assured's work. Thus, after specifying the total sum insured, an ordinary contractors' risks policy relating to a specific construction contract may provide cover in some such terms as:

> "On the works temporary or permanent including Plant, Materials, Buildings completed or in course of erection, and all property brought onto the site including motor vehicles ...., the property of the insured or for which they are responsible all whilst on site of the construction ... and whilst in transit from the ports of unloading of materials."[8]

A contractors' policy may, however, be drafted to cover contractors' risks not merely with regard to one specific project but in respect of a number of building or construction contracts over a stated period. A policy of this sort indemnifying a building contractor in respect of "loss or damage ... to the permanent and temporary works at the site of any Contract" was held to apply not only to ordinary building contracts incorporating I.C.E. or R.I.B.A. standard conditions but also to an agreement whereby the contractor was to take a lease of a site in Manchester and build six "industrial units" on it.[9] It was further held in that case that a retaining wall which the contractor was bound by the agreement to "maintain repair and renew" was not part of the "permanent works" at the site because the contractor had no intention to rebuild it.[10]

The operative clause of a ship-building insurance policy will often be on the following lines:

---

[7] [1969] 2 Lloyd's Rep. 251. *Sed quaere*. It was held that clause 1 of the policy was wide enough to cover the claim but for the fact that it was qualified by clause 2. There is, however, no indication in the report of any express limitation or qualification in either cl. 1 or cl. 2, which latter clause began "This insurance also ..." thus implying an addition rather than a qualification.

[8] See *Jones Construction Co. v. Alliance Ins. Co.* [1961] 1 Lloyd's Rep. 121.

[9] *Rowlinson Construction Ltd v. Ins. Company of North America (U.K.) Ltd* [1981] 1 Lloyd's Rep. 332.

[10] [1981] 1 Lloyd's Rep. 332, 336, *per* Lloyd J.

"This insurance to cover all risks, including fire, while under construction and/or fitting out, except in buildings or workshops, but including materials in yards and docks of the assured, or on quays, pontoons, craft, etc., and all risks while in transit to and from the works and/or the vessel wherever she may be lying, also all risks of loss or damage through collapse of supports or ways from any cause whatever, and all risks of launching and breakage of the ways."[11]

32–5 Duration of the policy. The policy will usually specify a period for which the insurers accept liability. When the policy relates to one particular construction contract only, that period will be the period allowed to the contractor in the building contract and may include a period of maintenance after completion. Invariably building contracts become delayed and extensions of time often have to be sought by the contractor. In such cases he will require an extension of his insurance. Sometimes policies will provide for automatic extensions at an increased premium or a premium to be arranged, but if they do not contain such provisions, the whole insurance contract may have to be renegotiated and fresh insurance may have to be obtained. In *Jones Construction Co. v. Alliance Insurance Co.*[12] the period of insurance was expressed to be "from 8th January 1956 to 30th September 1959, plus 12 months' maintenance". By a subsequent endorsement the period was extended to March 1, 1960. The building contract had, however, to be extended beyond that date and the insurers declined to provide further cover. The plaintiffs claimed that the insurers were bound to extend the policy and contended that no contractor would undertake a building project unless he had cover for the whole period of the contract. The policy provided that the insurers would indemnify the insured "for loss arising during the period stated in the Schedule or any subsequent period in respect of which the Insured shall have paid and the Insurers accepted the premium required for this extension of the term of the Policy". Pearson J. held[13] that, in the face of this express term, it was impossible to imply a term binding the insurers to extend the period of the risk. The provision requiring payment by the insured of a premium and acceptance by the insurers implied that the insurers were free not to accept if they wished to do so. In the Court of Appeal, the plaintiff relied on other terms of the policy to show that the intention of the parties was that the policy should continue for the whole building period. These terms provided for adjustment of the premium having regard to the final contract price and any material alteration in the contract. But the court held that no implication from these provisions could override the clear words of the contract requiring an acceptance of premium for an extended period by the insurers and they dismissed the appeal.

32–6 Defective or faulty material, workmanship or design. The modern form of policy almost invariably contains an express exclusion of cover in respect of loss caused by "defective or faulty material workmanship or

---

[11] See *American Shipbuilding Co. v. Orion Ins. Co.* [1969] 2 Lloyd's Rep. 251.

[12] [1961] 1 Lloyd's Rep. 121. *Cf. Solvency Guarantee Society v. York* (1858) 3 H. & N. 588 where there was an express term as to renewal.

[13] [1960] 1 Lloyd's Rep. 264. For a case where the expiry of an "all risks" extraneous damage policy on a gantry crane in course of erection was agreed to coincide with the issue of a certificate passing it for commercial use—see *Linden Alimak v. British Engine Insurance Ltd* [1984] 1 Lloyd's Rep. 416.

design", thereby affording support for the contention that "all risks" is a misnomer. In *Mitchell Conveyor and Transporter Co. Ltd v. Pulbrook*,[14] however, such cover was included in the policy. In that case the plaintiff contractors had agreed to construct the foundation of an electricity generating station for Birmingham Corporation. The contract, which was not finally agreed until some time after the plaintiffs had taken out an insurance policy with the defendant, provided for certain floors to be finished with an artificial stone, known as granolithic. This granolithic buckled and failed to adhere to the underlying concrete and, although there were various reasons for this, it arose mainly because (a) the granolithic had been mixed in the proportion of two parts of granite chippings to one of cement when three parts of granite chippings would have been preferable, and (b) the granolithic was laid not on fresh concrete but on concrete which had already been laid some time. The plaintiffs paid a sum by way of compensation to the Birmingham Corporation and then claimed to recover that sum from their insurance policy which covered "any loss for the cost of replacing any defective and/or faulty material or workmanship and/or design or imperfections in the original or substituted construction of the plant insured ... together with contingent charges".

The insurers argued that the payment to Birmingham Corporation had to be made because of an inherent vice or defect in the granolithic mixture and that the policy, like an ordinary marine policy, did not cover loss from inherent defect of the subject matter insured. Roche J. held, however, that the plaintiffs were responsible for the designing and planning of the station and, in that capacity, had accepted the Corporation's recommendation as to how the granolithic should be mixed. In these circumstances, the loss fell within the wording of the policy and the insurers were liable, presumably on the basis that the material was defective or that the design (including the granolithic mixed as it was) was faulty.

32–7 A different situation might arise if the proportions of granite chippings and cement had been specified by the Corporation before the policy was made. If the Corporation had specified a mixture of two to one and the contractors had in fact used a mixture of three to one, the insurers would presumably not have been liable since the contractors would have broken their contract instead of performing it.[15] If there had been a subsequent variation by the agreement to use a mixture of three to one, the plaintiffs would presumably succeed, provided that the variation was not so fundamental as to avoid the policy or free the insurers from liability.[16] If the Corporation had specified a mixture of three to one originally, and the contractors had adhered to the specification, the Corporation would not be entitled to have the work redone at the contractors' expense and there would be no claim under the policy since the contractors would have suffered no loss.[17]

32–8 Faulty design. In *Queensland Government Railways v. Manufacturers' Mutual Insurance*[18] there were exceptions in a contractors' all risks

[14] (1933) 45 Ll.L.R. 239.
[15] See the argument of Sir Robert Aske as set out by Roche J. at 244.
[16] (1933) 45 Ll.L.R. 239, 245. There will usually be an express clause in the policy covering variations in the building contract.
[17] *ibid.* at 243–244.
[18] [1969] 1 Lloyd's Rep. 214.

policy for (a) cost of making good faulty workmanship or construction, and (b) loss or damage arising from faulty design and liabilities resulting therefrom. Contractors erected prismatic piers in the course of constructing a railway bridge but the piers were washed away by flood waters. The arbitrator found that the design of the piers was satisfactory in the light of the engineering knowledge in existence at the time when they were constructed, that the contractors had therefore not been negligent in any way and that the loss was not due to faulty design. The Supreme Court of Queensland upheld his award.[19] The High Court of Australia, however, reversed this decision and held that there was faulty design inasmuch as the piers had not been built in such a way as to withstand flood waters. The fact that no one had been negligent did not mean that the design was not faulty. The majority opinion puts the distinction neatly:[20]

> "To design something that will not work simply because at the time of the designing insufficient is known about the problems involved and their solution to achieve a successful outcome is a common enough instance of faulty design. The distinction which is relevant is that between 'faulty' *i.e.* defective design and design free from defect."

However, the words "faulty workmanship" did, at any rate for one member of the court, imply a personal default for which a workman or workmen were to blame.[21] In the event the insurers successfully denied liability. This distinction between faulty design as a state of affairs and faulty workmanship as a personal activity has been used to decide that an exclusion for "increased costs due to redesigning property which has been defectively designed" (in a policy which covered "loss arising out of any fault defect or error in design") is only apt to exclude costs incurred by reason of an originally negligent design, since in such a context it was personal activity to which the exclusion referred.[22]

32–9 A frequent provision in the modern form of all risks policy is a proviso to the exclusion of insurers' liability for faulty materials or workmanship which includes cover for the costs of repair or reinstatement of parts of the contract works other than those directly affected by the faulty workmanship or containing the faulty material, which may themselves have been damaged or destroyed in consequence of the initial damage to, or collapse of, the affected portions. It is not always easy to determine the particular loss or damage which falls into each category.[23]

32–10 Latent defects. Builders' or repairers' policies may often make

---

[19] [1968] 1 Lloyd's Rep. 403.

[20] [1969] 1 Lloyd's Rep. 214, 217.

[21] [1969] 1 Lloyd's Rep. 214, 219, *per* Windeyer J. *Cf. Pentagon Construction (1969) Co. Ltd v. U.S. Fidelity & Guaranty Co.* [1978] 1 Lloyd's Rep. 93, where a concrete tank in a sewage treatment plant was tested before steel struts, which were to be laid across the top of the tank, had been welded to a plate beneath the top. The Court of Appeal of British Columbia held that there was no faulty or improper design, but there had been faulty or improper workmanship in testing the tank before the struts had been welded in place. "Workmanship" comprehended all the skills to be directed to the erection of the tank, not merely manual operations, and the presence or absence of culpable fault was irrelevant.

[22] *Hitchens v. Prudential Assurance* [1991] 2 Lloyd's Rep. 580.

[23] An analogous problem arose under the Liner Negligence Clause inserted into marine hull policies. The current Inchmaree clause is contained in clause 6.2 Institute Time Clauses (Hulls) 1995—see Arnould's *Law of Marine Insurance and Average* (16th ed., 1981), vol. 3 at paras 81–83.

provision for damage due to or arising from a latent defect in machinery or materials. Such provisions clearly cover loss or damage occurring in other parts of the property insured but it is not always clear whether they extend to the cost of repairing the latent defect itself or the cost of any necessary replacement. In marine insurance, the clause known as the Inchmaree clause, covered "loss of or damage to hull through any latent defect in the hull"[24] and it has been held that the existence or discovery of a latent defect is not a casualty and the cost of replacing part of the ship's hull or machinery in substitution for the part which has the latent defect is not recoverable under the clause.[25] Presumably, a clause in the same words in a contractors' policy would be given the same interpretation.

32–11 In *McColl & Pollock Ltd v. Indemnity Mutual Marine Assurance Co. Ltd*[26] the plaintiffs insured were ship repairers and agreed to take the existing cylinders out of a ship and replace them with a new set. The castings for the new cylinders were supplied by sub-contractors and when the new cylinders were inserted in the ship and subjected to steam pressure, it was discovered that there was a crack in one of the cylinders due to a latent defect in the castings. The sub-contractors supplied a new casting free of charge and the plaintiffs machined and finished off the second cylinder but this was found to be leaking and had to be scrapped. A third casting was provided free of charge and was likewise machined and finished by the plaintiffs and was satisfactory. The plaintiffs incurred the cost of taking out the first defective cylinder, machining, fitting and taking out the second defective cylinder and machining and fitting the third satisfactory cylinder. In an action on their insurance policy, it was admitted by the insurers that the trouble arose from a latent defect, but it was argued that the policy only covered damage done by a latent defect not the cost of replacing the machinery subject to the defect. The policy afforded cover for "cost of repairs and/or loss or damage to the interest . . . through any latent defect in the thing insured". Wright J. held that, apart from the words "cost of repairs", the words were indistinguishable from the Inchmaree clause and that the words "cost of repairs" were not appropriate for taking away a cylinder which was inherently defective and replacing it with a satisfactory one. Presumably, if the original cylinder had been repaired, the cost of such repair would have fallen within the clause of the policy, although it would have fallen outside the standard Inchmaree clause. Wright J. further held that the cost of replacement was not a risk "incidental to the testing, fitting and trials of the machinery or the thing insured" because the testing and trials did not cause the latent defect; it merely became obvious at the time when the ship was performing her trials.[27]

32–12 Sometimes a policy will specifically exclude the cost of repair or

---

[24] The current clause is clause 6.2 ITC (Hulls) 1995.
[25] *Oceanic S.S. Co. v. Faber* (1908) 13 Com.Cas. 28; *Hutchins Bros v. Royal Exchange Assurance Corp.* [1911] 2 K.B. 398. The question whether a crack is a latent defect or damage caused by a latent defect is a question of fact: *Promet Engineering v. Sturge* [1997] 2 Lloyd's Rep. 146, CA.
[26] (1930) 38 Ll.L.R. 79.
[27] (1930) 38 Ll.L.R. 79, 83.

renewal of a faultily designed part of the subject matter of the insurance and further exclude any cost or expense incurred by reason of alteration in the design. In such a case the cost of modifying a ship's propeller and of the consequent re-running of sea-trials and maintenance of the vessel while repairs were done and sea-trials were re-run was held not to be recoverable.[28] But similar words in a liability policy, excluding the cost of making good defective materials or goods, do not prevent the insured from recovering where he is liable for the value of damaged goods.[29] Moreover, an indemnity in respect of loss and damage to property insured excluding the costs of rectifying defects in design will cover the cost of remedying physical defects in the property where the defect in design results in damage to the property and rectification does not produce a structure better than that originally designed.[30]

32–13 Surveyors' or experts' fees. If a contractor employs a surveyor or expert in a dispute with his employer and incurs a liability for his fees, it is doubtful whether such fees will be recoverable under the policy in the absence of an express term to that effect. It is submitted that such fees should be recoverable if it was reasonable to retain such services and the charge is reasonable but an expert's fee has been held to be irrecoverable under the heard of "contingent charges."[31]

32–14 Contractors' liability. Building contractors may render themselves liable to a large number of third parties in the course of a building operation and insurance against the consequences of such liability is vital in the interests of both the contractor himself and, indeed, the third parties.[32] Apart from the general public, third parties can of course include others associated with the construction, owners, employers, engineers, subcontractors and all their employees. The general principles of liability insurance have already been discussed[33] and it is only necessary here to consider the meaning of terms and exceptions most commonly found in contractors' liability policies.

32–15 Contractors' officials and employees. In the vast majority of Contractors' All Risk policies, and almost invariably if the contractor is a limited liability company, the liability section will contain a clause extending the indemnity to officers and employees of the contractor and the other co-insureds.

32–16 Liability imposed by law or assumed by contract. Contractors'

[28] *Stone Vickers v. Appledore Ferguson Shipbuilders* [1991] 2 Lloyd's Rep. 288, 303.

[29] *Aswan Engineering v. Iron Trades Mutual* [1989] 1 Lloyd's Rep. 289.

[30] *Cementation Piling Ltd v. Aegon Insurance Ltd* [1995] 1 Lloyd's Rep. 97. *Contrast James Langley v. Forest Giles* [2002] Lloyd's Rep. I.R. 421.

[31] See *Mitchell Conveyor and Transporter Co. Ltd v. Pulbrook* (1933) 45 Ll.L.R. 239, 242. In *Summers v. Congreve Horner, The Times*, July 22, 1991, the insured warranted that a qualified surveyor would be in attendance while an unqualified person was doing an inspection.

[32] Cover against claims made against an insured sub-contractor by "independent third parties" does not embrace third party proceedings against him by the head contractor—*Cook v. Haydon* [1987] 2 Lloyd's Rep. 579.

[33] See Ch. 28, *ante*.

liability policies including the "Public Liability Section" of a contractor's "All Risk" policy may entitle the insured to recover from the insurer in respect of any liability incurred by him arising from his presence or activities upon the contract site. More usually the ambit of the policy will be more restricted, for example, to "compensation which the insured shall become legally liable to pay for accidental damage happening in the course of the construction of the works" and "costs and expenses of litigation"[34] or "all sums which the insured shall become obligated to pay by reason of the liability imposed upon the insured by law[35] for damages because of injury to or destruction of property caused by accident". This last clause was used in a Canadian policy, which went on to exclude "liability assumed by the insured under any contract", and which was considered in *Dominion Bridge Co. Ltd v. Toronto General Insurance Co.*[36] In this case the insured contracted to erect the steelwork for a bridge in British Columbia and, as a result of their negligence the steelwork collapsed and the masonry foundations of the bridge were damaged. By their contract with the Bridge Authority, the insured were obliged to correct or replace any faults in the structure and they accordingly repaired the masonry foundations, and claimed the cost of the repair from their insurers, who denied liability on the ground that the insured's liability was assumed by them under their contract with the Bridge Authority and was excluded by the policy. The insured argued that they would, in any event, have been liable to the Authority in tort for the cost of the repairs and that their claim fell within the general wording of the policy as "liability imposed by law". The Court of Appeal of British Columbia[37] and the Supreme Court of Canada[38] both upheld the insurers' contention and decided that, if a liability could arise both in tort and in contract, it is not covered by a policy which excludes "liability assumed under any contract".

32–17 A recent refinement in relation to liability of this nature is a clause which excludes any liability arising out of contract unless such liability would in any event have arisen in tort. The wording of such clauses does not always make it clear whether the test is liability in tort as if no contract between the assured and the claimant had existed, or liability in tort assuming the existence of a contract. A contractor may be liable in tort as well as in contract,[39] and the existence of the contract could be a factor in establishing the necessary proximity between the parties to found the tortious duty of care.[40] It is submitted that the former test is correct. The purpose of the exception must surely be to relieve the insurer of liability which the assured has incurred directly or by reason of the conclusion of a contract between himself and the claimant.

[34] *Howard Farrow Ltd v. Ocean Accident Guarantee Corp. Ltd* (1940) 67 Ll.L.R. 27. *Cf. Century Indemnity Co. v. Northwestern Utilities Ltd* (1935) 3 D.L.R. 35.
[35] The phrase "at law" has been held to include contractual liability—*Aswan Engineering v. Iron Trades Mutual* [1989] 1 Lloyd's Rep. 289.
[36] [1964] 1 Lloyd's Rep. 194, following *Canadian Indemnity Co. v. Andrews & George Co. Ltd* [1953] 1 S.C.R. 19, and overruling *Featherstone v. Canadian General Ins. Co.* (1959) 18 D.L.R. (2d) 227.
[37] [1962] 2 Lloyd's Rep. 159. *Cf. Foundation of Canada v. Canadian Indemnity Co.* [1977] 2 W.W.R. 75.
[38] [1964] 1 Lloyd's Rep. 194.
[39] *Batty v. Metropolitan Realisations Ltd* [1978] Q.B. 554; *Henderson v. Merrett Syndicates Ltd* [1995] 2 A.C. 145, 184–194.
[40] *Henderson v. Merrett Syndicates Ltd* [1995] 2 A.C. 145, 178–181.

32–18 Damage to property used by the insured. Another exception found in contractors' liability policies is for damage to property used by the insured. This exception was contained in the *Dominion Bridge*[41] case and it was argued by the insurer that the contractor in erecting the steelwork had "used" the masonry foundations which had been damaged and that the contractor could therefore not recover under the policy. This contention provoked a difference of opinion in the Court of Appeal of British Columbia,[42] Des-Brisay C.J. saying that a contractor, performing his obligations to erect on the foundations something that will become part of the complete structure, could not be said to be "using" the foundations.[43] Sheppard J., however, held that the contractor had to incorporate the masonry foundations into his method of construction and that he did therefore "use" the foundations.[44] Neither the third judge of the Court of Appeal nor the Supreme Court expressed any view on this.[45] It is submitted that the opinion of the Chief Justice of British Columbia is the more appropriate in the context of a policy which, as in that case, is expressed to cover the contractor's liability for accidental damage to property resulting from the work performed by him, or otherwise the exclusion would strike at the very basis of his potential liability to the employer.

32–19 Deductibles. Deductibles can give rise to problems in contractors' risks insurance since there may be many ways in which faulty design, material or workmanship can manifest themselves on a large site. When Minster Court in the City of London was being built, 94 identical toilet modules were manufactured off site and then installed into the building as it rose floor by floor. Each toilet module had tiles fixed to a cementitious board which was defective and caused bowing of the tiles in each of the modules. The deductible specified in the building insurance was "the first £250,000 of each and every loss in respect of any component part which is defective in design, materials or workmanship". Insurers argued that the relevant component part was the toilet module and that the deductible applied 94 times but the Court of Appeal took the view that the component part was the cementitious board and that there was only one loss and only one deductible to be applied to the claim.[46]

32–20 Other exceptions and negligence of the insured. It is often said that, in general, the negligence of the insured is no bar to recovery under an insurance policy since this is often precisely what an insured will wish to insure himself against.[47] It is therefore necessary to look at exceptions in policies with some care and courts try to avoid giving to exceptions a meaning which will preclude the insured from recovering, if he has been merely negligent.[48] Liability policies are, moreover, a somewhat special case and often no liability can arise on the part of the insured unless he has been

---

[41] [1964] 1 Lloyd's Rep. 194.

[42] [1962] 2 Lloyd's Rep. 159. *Cf. Foundation of Canada v. Canadian Indemnity Co.* [1977] 2 W.W.R. 75.

[43] [1962] 2 Lloyd's Rep. 159, 162.

[44] *ibid.* at 171–173.

[45] [1964] 1 Lloyd's Rep. 194, 197, *per* Judson J.

[46] *Mitsubishi Electric v. Royal London Insurance* [1994] 2 Lloyd's Rep. 249.

[47] See para. 26–27, *ante*. The insured may also require cover in the event of negligence by a sub-contractor: see *State of Netherlands v. Youell* [1998] 1 Lloyd's Rep. 236.

[48] See para. 28–52, *ante*.

negligent and likewise the only way in which an excepted cause could give rise to liability on the part of the insured will be when it arises by reason of a negligent act on the part of the insured. If, therefore, a contractors' liability policy excludes liability for loss or damage caused by, *e.g.* flood, the insured cannot argue that a flood caused by negligence of himself or his servants is outside the exception, since the exception applies to any flood, however caused.[49] If the flood arose from an act of God or a third party there would be no liability on the insured at all and he would not be seeking to recover under his liability policy.

---

[49] *Howard Farrow Ltd v. Ocean Accident & Guarantee Corp. Ltd* (1940) 67 Ll.L.R. 27.

CHAPTER 33

REINSURANCE

33–1 Definition. The English authorities do not provide a satisfactory definition of reinsurance, and the evolution of reinsurance in its various forms has made it difficult to achieve a comprehensive definition.[1] It was stated in Lord Mansfield's time that:

> "A reassurance is a contract of indemnity between the original and a collateral insurer, by which the first is indemnified by the latter from the risk he has undertaken in respect of the subject insured."[2]

In *Delver v. Barnes*[3] Mansfield C.J. held that a transaction between two underwriters, whereby one allowed the other to be substituted for him on a marine cargo insurance at an increased premium entered in account between them, was not a reinsurance. He said:

> "This contract, although it much resembles, yet does not fully amount to a reassurance, which consists of a new assurance, effected by a new policy on the same risk that was before insured, in order to indemnify the underwriters from their previous subscription: and both parties are in existence at the same time."[4]

33–2 In these early descriptions of reinsurance certain accepted characteristics of modern reinsurance contracts can be perceived. The object of the reinsurance is to indemnify the reinsured against liability which may arise on the primary insurance.[5] The reinsurance is a separate contract from the original insurance,[6] so that there is no privity of contract between the insured

---

[1] This sentence was cited with approval in the judgment of the Court of Appeal in *Toomey v. Eagle Star* [1994] 1 Lloyd's Rep. 516 at 522, and in *Skandia International Corp. v. NRG Victory Reins. Ltd* [1998] Lloyd's Rep. I.R. 439 at 455.

[2] *Andree v. Fletcher* (1787) 2 T.R. 161, 162–163 by Counsel for the defendant. *Cf.* the cynical definition in Park, *Marine Insurance* (8th ed.) vol. 2, p. 595 that "Reassurance, as understood by the law of England, may be said to be a contract, which the first insurer enters into, in order to relieve himself from those risks which he has incautiously undertaken, by throwing them upon other underwriters who are called reassurers". Perhaps the modern aggregate excess of loss policy comes closest to this description of reinsurance.

[3] (1807) 1 Taunt. 48.

[4] (1807) 1 Taunt. 48, 51.

[5] *South British Fire and Marine Ins. Co. of New Zealand v. Da Costa* [1906] 1 K.B. 456, 460, *per* Bigham J.

[6] *British Dominions General Ins. Co. Ltd v. Duder* [1915] 2 K.B. 394, 400, 405. The two contracts may be subject to different systems of law—*Citadel Ins. Co. v. Atlantic Union Ins. Co.* [1982] 2 Lloyd's Rep. 543; in *Forsikrings Vesta v. Butcher* it was suggested by Hobhouse J. that certain clauses in a reinsurance contract were subject to the law of the underlying insurance contract: [1986] 2 Lloyd's Rep. 179. This hybrid approach was not adopted by the House of Lords: [1989] A.C. 852 (see para. 33–56, *post*).

original insurance,[6] so that there is no privity of contract between the insured and the reinsurer.[7] This distinguishes it from double insurance and solvency insurance.[8] It is neither an assignment nor transfer of the original insurance business from one insurer to another,[9] nor is it a relationship of partnership or agency between insurers.[10] It is essentially an independent contract of insurance whereby the reinsurer engages to indemnify the reinsured wholly or partially against losses for which the latter is liable to the insured under the primary contract of insurance.[11] Accordingly it is subject to the general principles and rules of law applying to insurance contracts, such as the principles of utmost good faith[12] and subrogation, and the rules relating to insurable interest and illegality.

33–3 The early definitions are, however, unsatisfactory in certain respects. Lord Mansfield's definition implies that the primary insurance is in force before the reinsurance is placed. This is true of a simple facultative transaction, but it is perfectly possible for the reinsurance contract to come into existence before the original contract of insurance. This will frequently happen in the case of open cover reinsurance.[13] Even a facultative reinsurance may apparently come into being before the original insurance is

---

[6] *British Dominions General Ins. Co. Ltd v. Duder* [1915] 2 K.B. 394, 400, 405. The two contracts may be subject to different systems of law—*Citadel Ins. Co. v. Atlantic Union Ins. Co.* [1982] 2 Lloyd's Rep. 543; in *Forsikrings Vesta v. Butcher* it was suggested by Hobhouse J. that certain clauses in a reinsurance contract were subject to the law of the underlying insurance contract: [1986] 2 Lloyd's Rep. 179. This hybrid approach was not adopted by the House of Lords: [1989] A.C. 852 (see para. 33–56, *post*).

[7] *Re Norwich Equitable Fire Ass. Soc.* (1887) 3 T.L.R. 781; 57 L.T. 241; *Re Law Guarantee Trust and Accident Soc. Ltd* [1914] 2 Ch. 617, 647–648; *English Ins. Co. v. National Benefit Ass. Co.* [1929] A.C. 114, 124; *Versicherungs und Transport AG Daugava v. Henderson* (1934) 39 Com.Cas. 312, 316; *Phoenix General Ins. Co. v. Halvanon Ins. Co.* [1985] 2 Lloyd's Rep. 599, 614. The privity rule has given rise to difficulty in the enforcement of "cut-through" clauses, which provide for circumstances in which direct payments are to be made by a reinsurer to an original insured. However, enforcement of contractual rights by third party beneficiaries is possible in specified circumstances, under the Contracts (Rights of Third Parties) Act 1999. In summary, the beneficiary must be identifiable when the contract is made, and the contractual term must be intended to benefit a party seeking to enforce it. If the conditions in the Act are satisfied, lack of privity will not prevent the insured from making a claim against a reinsurer pursuant to a "cut through" clause (provided that, where the re-insured is insolvent, the clause is enforceable in accordance with any relevant insolvency rules).

[8] Park, *Marine Insurance* (8th ed.) vol. 2, pp. 599–600.

[9] *Re Lancs. Plate Glass Fire and Burglary Ins. Ltd* [1912] 1 Ch. 35.

[10] *Re Norwich Equitable Fire Ass. Soc.* (1887) 3 T.L.R. 781; *English Ins. Co. v. National Benefit Ass. Co.* [1929] A.C. 114; *Motor Union Ins. Co. v. Mannheimer Versicherungs Gesellschaft* [1933] 1 K.B. 812; *Phoenix General Ins. Co. v. Halvanon Ins. Co.* [1985] 2 Lloyd's Rep. 599, 614.

[11] *Versicherungs und Transport AG Daugava v. Henderson* (1934) 39 Com.Cas. 312, 316; *Home Insurance Co. of New York v. Victoria Montreal Fire Ins. Co.* [1907] A.C. 59, 63. However, a contract to indemnify in respect of liabilities assumed under contracts of insurance will not necessarily be a contract of reinsurance: *GMA v. Storebrand & Kansa* [1995] L.R.L.R. 333.

[12] This is to be distinguished from a fiduciary relationship which is not created under a reinsurance treaty—*Law Guarantee Trust and Accident Soc. Ltd v. Munich Reinsurance Co.* [1914] 31 T.L.R. 572.

[13] *Glasgow Ass. Corp. v. Symondson* (1911) 16 Com.Cas. 109, 112.

placed,[14] or before all its terms are agreed.[15] It is also questionable whether all forms of reinsurance are necessarily contracts of insurance. A treaty may represent no more than a standing offer to reinsure if and when business is ceded, and it seems more accurate to classify such an agreement as a contract for insurance rather than of insurance.[16]

33–4 Working definition. American authorities contain a number of attempts to define reinsurance. These differ considerably in their formulation.[17] A useful definition is that a reinsurance contract is one whereby for a consideration one agrees to indemnify another wholly or partially against loss or liability by reason of a risk the latter has assumed under a separate and distinct contract as the insurer of a third person.[18] In *Forsikringsaktieselskapet Vesta v. Butcher (No. 1)* a similar definition was formulated: "Reinsurance is prima facie a contract of indemnity under which the reinsurer indemnifies the original insurer against the whole or against a specified amount or proportion of the risk which the latter has himself insured."[19]

33–5 It is difficult to define further the characteristics of reinsurance. The term "reinsurance" may be used, in a broad sense, to describe any contract of, or for, insurance which is made by an insurer. The term may also be used in a narrower sense to describe an insurance of an insurable interest in the subject matter of an original insurance.[20] It has been pointed out that reinsurance in this latter sense is not a type of liability insurance.[21]

33–6 No statutory definition. Parliament has legislated on reinsurance for nearly 250 years, but the statutes have tended to assume the existence of a definition rather than to provide one. Section 4 of the Marine Insurance Act 1745[22] prohibited reinsurance unless the primary insurer became insolvent or bankrupt, or died, in which case the insurer, or his executors administrators or assignees, were permitted to effect a reinsurance of the interest to the amount of his liability. This prohibition remained in force until the Revenue No. 2 Act of 1864[23] provided that marine reinsurance was lawful, subject to a provision for stamp duty, and the Stamp Act of 1867 repealed the relevant section of the 1745 Act,[24] including "reinsurance" in the expression

---

[14] *General Accident Fire & Life Ass. Co. v. Tanter* [1984] 1 Lloyd's Rep. 58. This is "normal market practice"—*C.T. Bowring Reinsurance Ltd v. Baxter* [1987] 2 Lloyd's Rep. 416, 419, *per* Hirst J.

[15] *South British Fire and Marine Ins. Co. v. Da Costa* [1906] 1 K.B. 456, 459; *Phillips and Stratton v. Dorintal Ins. Ltd* [1987] 1 Lloyd's Rep. 482, 483.

[16] As to treaty reinsurance see para. 33–17, *post*. The distinction between contracts of insurance and contracts for insurance is now well-established. See, for example, in the case of original insurance: *HIH Casualty and General Ins. Co. Ltd v. Chase Manhattan Bank* [2001] Lloyd's Rep. I.R. 703.

[17] *Words and Phrases* (1962), vol. 36A, p. 367 (West Publishing).

[18] *Stickel v. Excess Ins. Co. of America* 23 N.E. (2d) 839, 841 (Ohio 1939) See also *Board of Insurance Commissioners v. Kansas City Title Ins. Co.* 217 S.W. (2d) 695, 697 (Tex. Civ. App. 1949).

[19] [1989] A.C. 852, 908.

[20] *Toomey v. Eagle Star* [1994] 1 Lloyd's Rep. 516, 523.

[21] *Ibid.* at 522. For further discussion of the subject-matter of reinsurance, see para. 33–23, *post*.

[22] 19 Geo. 2 c. 37.

[23] 27 & 28 Vict. c. 56 s.l.

[24] 30 & 31 Vict. c. 23 Schedule D, confirmed in the Statute Law Revision Act 1865.

"sea insurance".[25] Thus for over 100 years reinsurance in England was severely restricted and the courts were principally concerned with deciding whether particular arrangements were or were not reinsurances prohibited by the 1745 Act.[26] Reinsurance was then subject to the Stamp Acts' requirements for valid policies of insurance, and the difficulty of creating marine reinsurance treaties which complied with them led to decisions in this century in which the courts had to determine whether agreements which wore the appearance of reinsurance treaties could be described as agency agreements to take them outside the Stamp Acts.[27]

33–7 Other statutory references. The Marine Insurance Act 1906[28] recognised that an insurer under a contract of marine insurance has an insurable interest in his risk and may reinsure in respect of it.[29] The Act further provided that unless a policy otherwise provides, the original assured has no right or interest in respect of the reinsurance.[30] The Third Parties (Rights Against Insurers) Act 1930[31] does not expressly refer to reinsurance, but does provide that liabilities to third parties will not include a liability as an insurer under a separate contract of insurance.[32] This appears to prevent the Act operating to transfer to an original assured a reinsured's rights against a reinsurer.

33–8 In so far as contracts of reinsurance are contracts of insurance, they have in the past attracted the authorisation requirements of the Insurance Companies Act 1982.[33] The effect of unauthorised original contracts of insurance upon reinsurance is dealt with in section 132 of the Financial Services Act 1986.[34] Reinsurance business is insurance business within the meaning of the Insurance Companies Act 1982 and is subject to the provisions of that Act relating to transfers of insurance business as is retrocession business.[35] Regulation will in future be governed by the Financial Services and Markets Act 2000.[36]

33–9 Reinsurance terminology and categories. Difficulties are apt to arise in determining the precise meaning of reinsurance terminology. Different opinions can persist in the London market concerning the meaning of a particular term or description of business, albeit one in common use.[37] In the

[25] 30 & 31 Vict. c. 23 s.4.

[26] *Andree v. Fletcher* (1787) 2 T.R. 161 and *Delver v. Barnes* (1807) 1 Taunt. 48 were such cases. The policy behind the prohibition was that reinsurance provided a way for an insurer who was gambling on a risk in which his insured had no insurable interest to hedge his bet and cover himself at a lower premium—see (1787) 2 T.R. 161, 165.

[27] *English Ins. Co. Ltd v. National Benefit Ass. Co.* [1929] A.C. 114; *Motor Union Ins. Co. Ltd v. Mannheimer Versicherungs Gesellschaft* [1933] 1 K.B. 812.

[28] 6 Edw. 7 c. 41.

[29] s.9(1).

[30] s.9(2).

[31] 20 & 21 Geo. 5 c. 25.

[32] s.1(5).The Law Commission has proposed that reinsurance should remain excluded under reforms to the 1930 Act: Law Com No. 272, July 2001.

[33] 1982 c. 50.

[34] 1986 c. 60.

[35] *Re N.R.G. Victory Reinsurance Ltd* [1995] 1 W.L.R. 239; *Re Friends Provident Life Office* [1999] Lloyd's Rep.I.R. 547, 551–552.

[36] 2000 c.8. For regulatory requirements under the FSMA 2000, see para. 33–45, *post*.

[37] *e.g. Irish National Ins. Co. Ltd v. Oman Ins. Co. Ltd* [1983] 2 Lloyd's Rep. 453 ("first loss" and "excess of loss" policies).

following paragraphs consideration is given to the fundamental categories of reinsurance and to its basic terminology. Reference should be made to specialist works for a more detailed treatment of market practice and wordings.[38]

33–10 Insurance, reassurance and reinsurance. "Reassurance" and "reassured" are used less commonly than "reinsurance" and "reinsured". They appear to possess the same meaning. "Reassurance" and "reassured" represent the old usage, although while eminent judges still use them the usage cannot yet be said to be archaic.[39] Reinsurance is, generally speaking, a form of insurance[40] but the terms are not synonymous.[41]

33–11 Reinsurance and retrocession. Reinsurance is properly limited to describe reinsurance of original insurance, while retrocession refers to reinsurance of a contract of reinsurance. The reinsurer is the "retrocedant" who cedes his liability to another reinsurer called the "retrocessionaire". The distinction is not always observed in practice. In *Commonwealth Insurance Co. of Vancouver v. Sprinks* Lloyd J. commented:[42]

> "It may be that a retrocession agreement is sometimes described as a reinsurance; in so far as it is a reinsurance of a reinsurer, the use of the word is accurate. But I have never heard a reinsurance of an original insurer described as a retrocession."

33–12 Cession, acceptance and retention. Risks are frequently described as being "ceded" by the reinsured and "accepted" by the reinsurer. Risks which have been ceded are described as "cessions". A portion of a risk which is ceded is sometimes described as a "line", particularly when ceded under a proportional reinsurance. A reinsured may be described as a "cedant". "Cession" has a meaning distinct from its general meaning as a form of assignment. The reinsured will commonly retain an interest for his own account in a risk which he reinsures only partially, and this is referred to as his "retention".[43] The retention provides a measure of the reinsured's

---

[38] Kiln, *Reinsurance in Practice* (3rd ed., 1991); Golding, *The Law and Practice of Reinsurance* (5th ed., 1987); Carter, *Reinsurance* (2nd ed., 1983); Butler & Merkin, *Reinsurance Law*; Barlow Lyde & Gilbert, *Reinsurance Practice and the Law*.

[39] *e.g. Phoenix General Ins. Co. of Greece v. Halvanon Ins. Co. Ltd* [1985] 2 Lloyd's Rep. 599, 603, *per* Hobhouse J. ("reassured"); *Ins. Co. of Africa v. Scor (U.K.) Reinsurance* [1985] 1 Lloyd's Rep. 312, 329–330 ("assured", "reassured"), *per* Robert Goff L.J. No doubt an insurer prefers his reinsurance to provide just that rather than mere reassurance in its colloquial sense, but "reassured" is often found in printed slips.

[40] *Re N.R.G. Victory Reinsurance* [1995] 1 W.L.R. 239.

[41] In the sense that a reinsurance contract will not always be a contract of insurance. See para, 33–20, *post.*

[42] [1983] 1 Lloyd's Rep. 67, 87. *Cf.* the use of a slip headed "Excess Loss Reinsurance" for a first loss retrocession in *Phillips v. Dorintal* [1987] 1 Lloyd's Rep. 482, and the definition of retrocession in *Transcontinental Underwriting Agency S.L.R. v. Grand Union Ins. Co. and P. T. Reasuransi Umum Indonesia* [1987] 2 Lloyd's Rep. 409, 409–410.

[43] For scaling down of retention, see *Great Atlantic Ins. Co. v. Home Ins.* [1981] 2 Lloyd's Rep. 219. For the relationship between retention and the Full Reinsurance Clause, see *Phoenix General Ins. Co. v. Halvanon Ins. Co.* [1985] 2 Lloyd's Rep. 599; and on appeal *sub nom. Phoenix v. ADAS* [1986] 2 Lloyd's Rep. 552. A retention is sometimes reinsured separately, and there may be a term that it will not be the subject of reinsurance. In *Great Atlantic Ins. Co. v. Home Ins. Co.* [1981] 2 Lloyd's Rep. 219, the relevant term was construed not to be a warranty, requiring a fixed retention, but it was recognised that in other contracts provision for a net retention percentage could have this effect. For the materiality of retention, see para. 33–35, *post.* For implied terms and retention, see para. 33–68, *post.*

confidence in the business reinsured, and an incentive to underwrite responsibly.[44]

33–13 Proportional and non-proportional reinsurance. Reinsurance transactions are commonly described as being proportional or non-proportional. In the former the reinsurer contracts for a given proportion of risk and premium, in the latter he does not. Proportional business is subdivided into Quota Share and Surplus business. Quota Share involves the cession by the reinsured of a fixed proportion of business within the scope of the reinsurance contract to the reinsurer. Surplus business involves cession by the reinsured to the reinsurer of a surplus of business over that for which he is prepared to accept liability.

33–14 Non-proportional reinsurance is subdivided into Excess of Loss and Stop Loss business. In Excess of Loss reinsurance the reinsurer agrees to indemnify the reinsured for losses within a particular class which exceed an agreed minimum figure, and then only for the amount of such loss above that minimum figure.[45] Reinsurance of an insurer who is answerable only when a loss exceeds a substantial deductible is not excess of loss reinsurance.[46] In Stop Loss reinsurance the reinsurer becomes liable when the reinsured's aggregated losses exceed an agreed level. This is an accepted device for covering "long tail" liability insurance business. Stop Loss and analogous contracts are reinsurance contracts in the broad sense of insurances entered into by insurers. However, they will not necessarily be reinsurance contracts in the narrow sense of insurances of an insurable interest in the subject matter of an original insurance.[47]

33–15 Attempts are sometimes made to use different terminology in order to describe the mechanics of proportional and non-proportional business. However, the distinction is not clearly observed in practice and no attempt is made to uphold it in this chapter. According to this distinction references to cessions and ceding are inapt in the context of proportional business.[48]

33–16 Facultative reinsurance. The method by which reinsurance may be placed is facultative or by treaty. In its simplest form facultative reinsurance involves the reinsurance of one sole risk, as on a single ship or building, but it could involve reinsurance of a series of related original policies.[49] The

---

[44] *Kingscroft v. Nissan Fire and Marine Ins. Co. (No. 2)* [1999] Lloyd's Rep. I. R. 603, 622. Where the reinsured is underwriting a substantial account, it is common to take out excess of loss protection for the retained risk. In *Kingscroft* a term requiring a percentage retention did not preclude such protection.

[45] *Balfour v. Beaumont* [1982] 2 Lloyd's Rep. 493, 496.

[46] *Irish National Ins. Co. Ltd v. Oman Ins. Co. Ltd* [1983] 2 Lloyd's Rep. 453, where the presence of a large deductible did not convert a first loss fire policy into an excess of loss insurance. A first loss insurance is one where the sum insured is less than the full value of the interest at risk—[1983] 2 Lloyd's Rep. 453, 461. In *Sphere Drake v. Denby* [1995] L.R.L.R. 1 the terms of an oral contract for unlimited excess of loss reinsurance were held to be too uncertain to be enforced at law.

[47] *Toomey v. Eagle Star* [1994] 1 Lloyd's Rep. 516. (For descriptions of personal stop loss insurance at Lloyd's, see *Society of Lloyd's v. Robinson* [1999] 1 W.L.R. 756; *Avon Ins. Plc v. Swire Fraser* [2000] Lloyd's Rep. I. R. 535.)

[48] But cf. per Kerr L.J. in *Citadel Ins. Co. v. Atlantic Union Ins. Co.* [1982] 2 Lloyd's Rep. 543, 546.

[49] *Balfour v. Beaumont* [1982] 2 Lloyd's Rep. 493, 496.

essential characteristic is that both the reinsured and reinsurer are free to choose whether to cede and accept, respectively, any particular risk.[50] It has been described as insurance placed with and written by each underwriter individually rather than under a pre-existing arrangement such as a line slip.[51]

33–17 Treaty reinsurance. The treaty method of reinsurance proceeds by an agreement, or treaty, between reinsured and reinsurer that all risks of the class of business specified by the treaty which are accepted by the reinsured will be ceded to the reinsurer and duly accepted by him. Thus the reinsured binds himself in advance to cede business of the relevant kind, and the reinsurer binds himself to take it, contrary to the freedom of choice allowed to each in facultative transactions. An early treaty to be adjudicated upon was the quota share fire reinsurance treaty considered in *Re Norwich Equitable Fire Assurance Society*.[52] Treaties can cover either proportional or non-proportional business. In the absence of contractual provision to the contrary, cessions of risks to a treaty can occur without notice at the time of each cession to the reinsurer.[53]

33–18 Facultative obligatory reinsurance. In "fac./oblig." (facultative/ obligatory) business the reinsured retains a choice as to what risks he will cede and the reinsurer binds himself to take whatever is ceded, by way of declaration or otherwise.[54] It is as if the reinsurer had made a standing offer to the reinsured to take such business as might be ceded to him at the reinsured's option, and it renders him dependent upon the good judgement of the reinsured in accepting and ceding sound and appropriate risks. He is vulnerable to abuse of the treaty by the reinsured.[55]

33–19 Open Cover Reinsurance. This is an example of fac./oblig. reinsurance, whereby the reinsurer binds himself to accept such risks as the reinsured may cede within a class of business defined by the cover. Typically the arrangement is set up by a reinsurance broker or intermediary so that he is able to cede business on behalf of client reinsured. A contract is created

[50] *Lincoln National Life Ins. Co. v. State Tax Commission* 16 So. 2d (1944 Miss.) 369.

[51] *Balfour v. Beaumont* [1982] 2 Lloyd's Rep. 493 496, where the distinction between horizontal and vertical risk sharing is explained. See also *Insurance Co. of the State of Pennsylvania v. Grand Union Ins. Co.* [1990] 1 Lloyd's Rep. 208, 209 for a discussion of horizontal and vertical reinsurance, and layering of cover.

[52] (1887) 3 T.L.R. 781. The court referred to it as an agreement of agency, although it was accepted that the insured had no contractual relationship with the reinsurer.

[53] *Baker v. Black Sea & Baltic General Ins. Co.* [1995] L.R.L.R. 261, 274; affirmed on different grounds [1996] L.R.L.R. 353 (C.A.); [1998] Lloyd's Rep. I. R. 327 (HL). In *"The Beursgracht" (No. 1)* [2001] 2 Lloyd's Rep. 602 risks attached to the insurance prior to making of a declaration. It was held that declarations were essential contractual machinery in declaring, potentially retrospectively, what risks were being covered. It was subsequently held that the implied obligation to make a declaration within a reasonable time was an innominate term—*The Beursgracht (No. 2)* [2001] 2 Lloyd's Rep. 608. This reasoning was upheld by the Court of Appeal: [2002] 1 Lloyd's Rep. 574.

[54] *Citadel Insurance Co. v. Atlantic Union Ins. Co.* [1982] 2 Lloyd's Rep. 543, 545 (hull open cover); *Phoenix General Ins. Co. v. Halvanon Ins. Co.* [1985] 2 Lloyd's Rep. 599, 602.

[55] As to the implication of terms for protection of the reinsurer, see para. 33–60 & ff. The fac/oblig nature of a contract is almost certain to be material to disclose in seeking reinsurance, and may make it difficult or impossible for reinsurance to be obtained: *Aneco Reins. Underwriting v. Johnson & Higgins* [1998] 1 Lloyd's Rep. 565, reversed on appeal in relation to damages: [2000] Lloyd's Rep. I. R. 12 (C.A.); [2001] UKHL 51.

between reinsured and reinsurer by the act of the broker in declaring the particular risk to be covered, together with his client's name, to the reinsurers.[56] The open cover is perhaps an adaptation to reinsurance of the traditional floating policy of marine insurance.[57] It provides a means for a reinsurer to enter the market and for a reinsured to be certain of his reinsurance cover before entering into original contracts of insurance. These commercial considerations and a readiness to trust the integrity and judgement of a reinsured, or class of reinsured, explain why reinsurers are prepared to overlook the disadvantage of the absence of control over the risks ceded to them.[58] This type of contract can take many forms. The term "open cover" is commonly used to refer to contracts by which a reinsurer is obliged from the outset to accept risks of a specified class or classes; other types of arrangement may provide for further negotiation of particular terms when a risk is declared to the cover, or may do no more than establish a procedural mechanism pursuant to which risks may later be offered by brokers and accepted or rejected by reinsurers.[59] In each case it is necessary to ascertain if the arrangement constitutes a contract, and (if so) with whom.

33–20 In so far as open covers and facultative/obligatory treaties consist of undertakings as to how risks may be ceded, and accepted, in the future, they are arguably not themselves contracts of insurance, but are agreements which create individual contracts of insurance when the reinsured, or intermediary, makes use of the facility available to him for reinsurance, and when declarations are made and individual policies issued.[60] This suggested analysis is consistent with certain decisions holding that marine reinsurance treaties were "contracts for sea insurance" within the Stamp Acts,[61] although it has to be said that the courts did not directly address themselves to the distinction between contracts "of" and "for" reinsurance, and these

---

[56] *Citadel Ins. Co. v. Atlantic Union Ins. Co.* [1982] 2 Lloyd's Rep. 543, 547–548 *per* Kerr L.J.: *Sedgwick Tomenson v. PT Reasuransi Umum* [1990] 2 Lloyd's Rep. 334, 340; *SAIL v. Farex* [1995] L.R.L.R. 116. The description in the text of treaties, fac/oblig business and open covers was adopted in *Trans-Pacific Ins. Co. (Australia) v. Grand Union Ins. Co.* (1989) 18 N.S.W.L.R. 675 at 696–699.

[57] Marine Insurance Act 1906, s.29(1). For an early case in which a floating policy form was used for reinsurance of marine fire risks—see *Imperial Marine Ins. v. Fire Ins. Corp. Ltd* (1879) 4 C.P.D. 116.

[58] *Glasgow Ass. Corp. v. Symondson* (1911) 16 Com.Cas. 109, 111, *per* Scrutton J. For an example of the construction of a marine open cover, with discussion of the range of hull risks which could be reinsured and of factors which might affect rating, see *Abrahams v. Mediterranean Ins. and Reins. Co.* [1991] 1 Lloyd's Rep. 216.

[59] *cf.* the discussion of lineslips at para. 33–26. For an open cover which bound insurers prior to the making of a declaration, see *The Beursgracht (No. 1)* 2 Lloyd's Rep. 602; [2002] 1 Lloyd's Rep. 574, (C.A.).

[60] *Forsikrings. National of Copenhagen v. Att.-Gen.* [1925] A.C. 639, 642, a decision under the Assurance Companies Act 1909. In *SAIL v. Farex* [1995] L.R.L.R. 116, it was held that particular lineslips were not contracts, merely a procedural mechanism for making contracts by means of declarations. In *Mander v. Commercial Union Ass. Co.* [1998] Lloyd's Rep. I. R. 93, the open covers provided in terms for the reinsurer to agree subsequent declarations and premium.

[61] *Home Marine Ins. Co. v. Smith* [1898] 2 Q.B. 351; *Empress Ass. Corp. v. Bowring* (1905) 11 Com.Cas. 107. Cf. *Trans-Pacific Ins. Co. v. Grand Union Ins. Co.* (1989) 18 N.S.W.L.R. 675, 698–699.

decisions offer little guidance on the point.[62] The distinction now appears to be well-established.[63]

33–21 Fronting. Insurer A may be willing to accept a risk but be unable to do so, for example because he is not licensed or is unacceptable to the insured. In this event another insurer, B, may act as a "front" by entering into a contract of insurance with the insured and reinsuring part or all of the risk with insurer A. Ordinarily insurer B will be liable in full to the insured under the contract of insurance but will be entitled to an indemnity from insurer A under the contract of reinsurance, and will receive a commission from insurer A for acting as a front.[64] When the transaction is arranged through an agent it is necessary to establish whether the agent was authorised to bind its principals in this manner, and whether any unauthorised acts have been ratified.[65]

33–22 Pool reinsurance. Pool reinsurance occurs where a number of reinsurers carry on reinsurance through a common underwriting agent. The agent will generally accept and administer business on behalf of pool members, who participate in agreed shares, and act in many respects as a single underwriting unit.[66] The detailed arrangements governing the operation will vary. Typically, incoming insurance risks will be accepted by one or more pool members as insurers; part or all of the risks will be reinsured by other pool members, and part or all of the risks will be retroceded under outward contracts of retrocession. Each pool member will have a management agreement with the underwriting agent relating to the administration of the pool. In this situation, there is a distinction between the liability of the pool member to insureds (or reinsureds) under contracts of insurance to which it is a party, and the liability of the pool member to the underwriting agent under the management agreement.[67] Where the underwriting agent signs a reinsurance contract without qualification as to its agency role, it will personally become a party unless a contrary intention appears in the contract.[68] The agent will be entitled to sue on a contract made in its own

---

[62] A submission that a reinsurance open cover was a "contract relating to sea insurance" rather than a "contract for sea insurance", because the contract was to enter into contract of insurance *in futuro*, was rejected in *Home Marine Ins. Co. v. Smith* [1898] 2 Q.B. 351. The Stamp Act 1891 did not assist clarification by requiring a contract for sea insurance to be embodied in a policy of insurance, ss.93(1), 93(3). For discussion of the limited value of the old authorities— see *Trans-Pacific Ins. Co. v. Grand Union Ins. Co.* (1989) 18 N.S.W.L.R. 675, 697. The distinction between contracts of, and for, reinsurance has been noted in *Pioneer Life Ins. Co. v. Alliance Life Ins. Co.* 30 N.E. 2d 66 (1940 Ill.); *Mauver v. International Reinsurance Corp.*, 74 A 2d 822 (1950 Del.).

[63] See, for example, *HIH Casualty and General Ins. Co. Ltd v. Chase Manhattan Bank* [2001] Lloyd's Rep. I.R. 703.

[64] *Sedgwick Tomenson Inc. v. P.T. Reasuransi Umum Indonesia* [1990] 2 Lloyd's Rep. 334, 341.

[65] *Suncorp Ins. v. Milano Ass. S.p.A.* [1993] 2 Lloyd's Rep. 225; *Deutsche Ruck A.G. v. La Fondiara S.p.A.* [2001] 2 Lloyd's Rep. 621.

[66] *Kingscroft v. Nissan Fire and Marine Ins. Co. (No. 2)* [1999] Lloyd's Rep. I. R. 603, 615.

[67] *GMA v. Storebrand & Kansa* [1995] L.R.L.R. 333. Under pool management arrangements the agent is likely to hold pool records jointly on behalf of all members: *Home Ins. Co. v. Rutty* [1996] L.R.L.R. 415. Where a pool member was by agreement replaced by another insurance company in substitution, the pool manager was held to owe duties in a run-off only to the substitute—*Württenbergische Akt. Versichs. v. Home Ins. Co.* [1997] L.R.L.R. 86.

[68] *Transcontinental Underwriting Agency S.L.R. v. Grand Union Ins. Co.* [1987] 2 Lloyd's Rep. 409.

name for the benefit of its principals.[69] The agent's authority to bind pool members will depend upon the scope of its actual or ostensible authority.[70] Where the agent acts contrary to the agreements governing the pool, the primary remedies are likely to be for breach of contract, or breach of duty in tort. A claim for breach of fiduciary duty may be available in some circumstances, but it will be subject to the same time limits for bringing proceedings as any overlapping contractual or tort claims.[71] Where members of a pool have a common interest, for example in claiming under a contract of retrocession, it may be possible for some members to sue in a representative capacity or on the basis of fiduciary trusteeship on behalf of the others.[72] The composition of pool members may well change over time. A retrocession of the liabilities of pool members is likely to be intended to take effect (subject to its specific wording) so as to provide cover for all members who participate in the pool during the period of the retrocession, including members who join after the date of the contract of retrocession.[73] If there is a retrocession of liabilities arising out of risks underwritten by the agent, it will not (absent clear wording) cover the additional losses which arise from the insolvency of one or more pool members.[74]

33–23 Subject matter and interest. The subject matter of a contract of reinsurance is in many cases the subject matter of the underlying contract of insurance, and the insurable interest of the reinsured in it is his potential liability to pay an indemnity under the primary contract of insurance if the subject matter is lost or damaged by an insured peril.[75] This distinction has been recognised in facultative marine reinsurances[76] and treaty reinsu-

---

[69] *ibid.*

[70] *Yona International Ltd v. La Reunion Francaise Societe Annonyme D'Assurances et De Reassurances* [1996] 2 Lloyd's Rep. 84, 108–109.

[71] *Companhia de Seguros Imperio v. Heath (Rebx) Ltd* [2001] Lloyd's Rep. I. R. 109.

[72] *Pan Atlantic Ins. Co. and Republic Insurance v. Pine Top Ins. Co.* [1988] 2 Lloyd's Rep. 505. However, it seems that this principle cannot be invoked to permit a claim by a party which, at the time of contracting, was not acting as an agent for a party with an insurable interest and which itself had no insurable interest: *Anthony John Sharp and Roarer Investments v. Sphere Drake ("The Moonacre")* [1992] 2 Lloyd's Rep. 501. On the use of representative proceedings generally, see *"The Irish Rowan"* [1989] 2 Lloyd's Rep. 144; *Bank of America National Trust and Savings Association v. Taylor* [1992] 1 Lloyd's Rep. 484.

[73] *Kingscroft v. Nissan Fire and Marine Ins. Co. (No. 2)* [1999] Lloyd's Rep. I. R. 603, 619.

[74] *Wurttembergische Aktiengesellschaft v. Home Ins. Co. (No.3)* [1999] Lloyd's Rep. I. R. 397.

[76] *Uzielli v. Boston Marine Ins. Co.* (1884) 15 Q.B.D. 11, 16, 18; *British Dominions General Ins. Co. Ltd v. Duder* [1915] 2 K.B. 394, 400, 406, 412. The distinction has also been recognised in the context of reinsurance of contingency risks: *CAN Int. Reins. Co. Ltd v. Companhia de Seguros S.A.* [1999] Lloyd's Rep. I. R. 289, 299–300.

[75] *Mackenzie v. Whitworth* (1875) 1 Ex.D. 36; *Dunlop Bros. v. Townend* [1919] 2 K.B. 127; *Phoenix General Ins. Co. v. Halvanon Ins. Co.* [1985] 2 Lloyd's Rep. 599, 607; [1986] 2 Lloyd's Rep. 552, 563. In *Toomey v. Eagle Star* [1994] 1 Lloyd's Rep. 516, the Court of Appeal emphasised these characteristics of reinsurance as properly defined. A similar approach was taken by Lord Hoffmann in *Charter Reinsurance Co. Ltd v. Fagan* [1996] 2 Lloyd's Rep. 113 at 122, but Lord Mustill preferred not to express a final view as to whether reinsurance is always to be regarded as an insurance of the original subject-matter (*ibid.*, 117). In *Skandia International Corp. v. NRG Victory Reins. Ltd* [1998] Lloyd's Rep. I.R. 439, at 454–457 Potter L.J. indicated, taking account of *Fagan*, that it would be rare for a contract of reinsurance to be regarded as liability insurance, rather than reinsurance of the original subject matter. In *Skandia* the reinsurance contract provided that it was a condition precedent to liability that settlement by the reinsured should be in accord with the terms of the original insurance. While the language of indemnity was used, it was still in effect an indemnity against risks falling within the original insurance (at 456). For the statutory and contractual requirements for insurable interest, see Ch. 1, *ante.*

rance.[77] But in determining what is the subject matter of an insurance, and what the precise interest is which is covered by it, the governing consideration is how these are expressed in the contract.[78] It may be that the subject matter and insurable interest are sometimes for practical purposes identical, as in the case of reinsurance of a professional indemnity or public liability insurer, or that the subject matter of the reinsurance cannot readily be equated with the subject matter of the original insurance, as in the case of non-proportional reinsurance.

33–24 The distinction between subject matter and insurable interest is relevant in two respects. First, the reinsured interest need not be specified provided that the subject matter is properly described.[79] Secondly, it is the subject matter of the reinsurance, and so of the primary insurance, which is relevant for the purposes of classification of insurance business for statutory regulation.[80]

33–25 Formation of the contract of reinsurance. The formation of the reinsurance contract is occasionally difficult to analyse, but this will not deter a court from recognising the creation of a contractual relationship where there is a clear intent to create legal relations and the transaction is clearly of a commercial character.[81] Market practices may be relevant to the analysis.[82] But if the reinsurance constitutes a contract of marine insurance the court cannot dispense with the requirement of the Marine Insurance Act 1906 that a contract of marine insurance be embodied in a policy.[83]

33–26 The slip. While reinsurance contracts may be formed by a conventional offer and acceptance in correspondence, they are frequently formed by the reinsurer initialling a slip presented to him by a broker acting for the reinsured. Unless the slip is qualified[84] or is expressly circulated to obtain a quotation,[85] it then contains the contract of reinsurance in the same way as with original insurance.[86] Usually the slip will stipulate for the production of a policy or a full wording. Sometimes it does not, and is then

---

[77] *Forsikringsakt National v. Att.-Gen.* [1925] A.C. 639, 642.

[78] *Phoenix General Ins. Co. of Greece v. ADAS* [1986] 2 Lloyd's Rep. 552, 563.

[79] *Mackenzie v. Whitworth* (1875) L.R. 10 Ex. 142; (1875) 1 Ex.D. 36.

[80] *Glasgow Ass. Corp. (Liquidators) v. Welsh Ins. Corp.* 1914 S.C. 320; *Forsikringsakt National v. Att.-Gen.* [1925] AC. 639; *Phoenix General Ins. Co. v. ADAS* [1986] 2 Lloyd's Rep. 552; *Re N.R.G. Victory Reinsurance* [1995] 1 W.L.R. 239. Where the subject-matter of reinsurance cannot be equated with that of the original insurance, it may be appropriate to regard the reinsurance as falling within the statutory classes for general liability business, or miscellaneous financial loss business: *D.R. Ins. Co. v. Seguros America Banamex* [1993] 1 Lloyd's Rep. 120, 129; *Stronghold Ins. Co. Ltd v. Overseas Union Ins. Ltd* [1996] L.R.L.R. 13, 16. For a similar approach to classification not involving reinsurance, see *Re Cavalier Ins. Co.* [1989] 2 Lloyd's Rep. 430.

[81] *General Accident Fire and Life Ass. Corp. v. Tanter* [1984] 1 Lloyd's Rep. 58, 71–72, *per* Hobhouse J.

[82] A summary of the operation of the London Market is given in *Insurance Co. of the State of Pennsylvania v. Grand Union Ins. Co.* [1990] 1 Lloyd's Rep. 208 at 209–210.

[83] Sections 22 to 24; *Commonwealth Ins. Co. v. Groupe Sprinks* [1983] 1 Lloyd's Rep. 67, 83.

[84] *e.g.* by being initialled "W.P."—*Eagle Star Insurance Co. Ltd v. Spratt* [1971] 2 Lloyd's Rep. 116, 124. See also *SAIL v. Farex* [1995] L.R.L.R. 116, 121 (pencilled "subject to reinsurance" was a qualification of acceptance, not a contractual term).

[85] *General Reinsurance Corp. v. Forsakrings. Fennia Patria* [1983] Q.B. 856, 873.

[86] *General Accident Fire and Life Ass. Corp. v. Tanter* [1984] 1 Lloyd's Rep. 58, 69; [1985] 2 Lloyd's Rep. 529, 533; *General Reinsurance Corp. v. Forsakrings. Fennia Patria* [1983] Q.B. 856, 864.

referred to as a reinsurance slip policy.[87] Sometimes a dispute arises before the policy or wording has been produced, and the resulting lack of documentation impedes resolution of the dispute.[88] The procedure is more complicated where the reinsured has subscribed to a "line slip". This term normally refers to a facility whereby a group of underwriters give a leading underwriter authority to accept proposals for insurance of risks within a defined class on their behalf. These underwriters will obtain reinsurance in advance against their liability on insurances to be concluded on their behalf by the leading underwriter. Those insurances will be concluded on "off-slips", which will indicate that the primary insured is covered subject to the provisions of the line slip, and that the reinsured underwriters in turn are covered by the reinsurance concluded earlier.[89] Where a policy has been issued, the relevance of, and utility of reference to, the terms of the slip will depend on the circumstances. It seems that there is no conclusive rule that renders the slip inadmissible in order to construe the policy wording. However, it will commonly be intended that the slip should be superseded by the policy wording, so that the former cannot assist in interpreting the latter. Further, the use of shorthand in the slip will often make it unhelpful as a guide to the construction of more detailed policy wording.[90]

33–27 Characteristics of reinsurance slips. In general a slip is treated in the same way in both insurance and reinsurance transactions, but there are at least two respects in which reinsurance slips may differ from many primary insurance slips. First, a reinsurance slip frequently creates contractual relations between a number of reinsureds and a number of reinsurers, so that in a composite transaction each reinsured is put in privity of contract with each reinsurer.[91] Secondly, the reinsurance slip may be initialled before conclusion of the primary insurance contract, so that the reinsurer does not then know who will be the reinsured. In *General Accident Fire and Life Assurance Corporation v. Tanter*[92] Hobhouse J. held, expressing a London market usage in legal analysis, that reinsurance resulted from:

---

[87] *e.g. Balfour v. Beaumont* [1984] 1 Lloyd's Rep. 272, 273; *General Accident Fire and Life Ass. Corp. v. Tanter* [1984] 1 Lloyd's Rep. 58, 61; *Phillips v. Dorintal* [1987] 1 Lloyd's Rep. 482, 483.

[88] *Phoenix General Ins. Co. v. Halvanon Ins. Co.* [1985] 2 Lloyd's Rep. 599, 602.

[89] *Balfour v. Beaumont* [1982] 2 Lloyd's Rep. 493, 494–495; [1984] 1 Lloyd's Rep. 272, 273. As to the contractual significance of lineslips and similar arrangements see *SAIL v. Farex* [1995] L.R.L.R. 116, 135–136 and *Denby v. Marchant* [1996] L.R.L.R. 301, 305. The decision in *Denby* was reversed, *sub nom. Denby v. English and Scottish Ins. Co. Ltd*, at [1998] Lloyd's Rep. I.R. 343, where it was emphasised (at 354–356) that the line slip imposed no obligation on the broker to present risks or on the leading underwriter to accept risks. *Cf.* the discussion of open covers in paras. 33–19, *et seq, ante.*

[90] These propositions are derived from a review, *obiter*, of the relevant authorities and principles by Rix L.J. in *HIH Casualty and General Ins. Co. Ltd v. New Hampshire Ins. Co.* [2001] Lloyd's Rep. I.R. 596 at 616–622. Previous authorities which discuss the point include *Youell v. Bland Welch* [1992] 2 Lloyd's Rep. 127 and *Punjab National Bank v. De Boinville* [1992] 1 Lloyd's Rep. 7. In *New Hampshire Ins. Co. v. MGN Ltd* [1997] L.R.L.R. 24 the issuing of policy wording did not preclude reference to the slip in order to determine whether or not the policy wording had been agreed.

[91] *General Accident Fire and Life Ass. Corp. v. Tanter* [1984] 1 Lloyd's Rep. 58, 71. Notwithstanding this diversity of parties, the normal expectation is that the terms of composite reinsurance contained in the same, or materially similar, contractual documents will have the same meaning for all participants: *Kingscroft v. Nissan Fire and Marine Ins. Co. (No.2)* [1999] Lloyd's Rep. I. R. 603, 618.

[92] *ibid.* The learned judge held, following *Glasgow Ass. Co. v. Symondson* (1911) 16 Com.Cas. 109, that the broker was not the agent of the reinsurer to offer reinsurance to the reinsureds, because that would be a reversal of normal market practice—[1984] 1 Lloyd's Rep. 58, 80–81,

(a) initialling by the reinsurer of a reinsurance slip naming the reinsured as "Lloyd's &/or Co.'s",
(b) the notification to a potential reinsured by the broker who had presented the slip that reinsurance was available and
(c) the giving to, and acceptance by, the broker of an order for reinsurance.

In this respect the early definitions of reinsurance referred to above[93] are now outmoded. The fact that the reinsurance contract is made before the primary insurance contract may assist in cases of ambiguity in determining precisely what risk has been accepted by the reinsurer.[94]

33–28 The broker's role. The broker may act in a number of roles in relation to a reinsurance contract. In placing primary insurance the broker will be acting for the insured. In investigating the availability of reinsurance, he will generally be acting either on his own account or (if so instructed by the insurer) on behalf of the insurer. In approaching the insurer with an offer of reinsurance, he will probably be offering to act as an agent of the insurer in obtaining the reinsurance. In approaching the insurer with an offer of reinsurance he will most probably be offering to act as an agent of the insurer in obtaining it, and therefore in the absence of special authority from the assured act on behalf of the insurer and not the assured in arranging it. Consequently his knowledge of facts material to the reinsurance will not be imputed to the assured, and he owes no duty to disclose them to the insurer in his capacity as agent of the assured, while as a general proposition the status of the reinsurance is not a material circumstance in relation to the primary insurance.[95]

33–29 Duty of good faith. The duty to act with the utmost good faith applies to reinsurance contracts because a reinsurance is in the nature of a contract of insurance and because the reinsurer has available to him the same defences to liability as are available to the reinsured in his capacity of primary insurer.[96] The duties of the reinsured to the reinsurer ought to be measured by the same standard expected of the original insured.[97] The duty is therefore based upon the same rules as those applying to original insurance, but its application takes account of features peculiar to reinsurance contracts, particularly treaties.

not reversed. on this point on appeal [1985] 2 Lloyd's Rep. 529. Similar analyses have been adopted to deal with other, complex reinsurance transactions. In *Mander v. Commercial Union Ass. Co.* [1998] Lloyd's Rep. I. R. 93, a declaration of an open cover was analysed in terms of a standing offer of reinsurance to participants in the underlying open covers. In *Kingscroft v. Nissan Fire and Marine Ins. Co. (No.2)* [1999] Lloyd's Rep. I. R. 603 it was held that reinsurers of a pool made a standing offer to provide cover to any pool member who joined the pool after the date of the contract during the period of cover, and waived communication of acceptance of the offer.

[93] See para. 33–1, *ante*.
[94] *Phillips v. Dorintal* [1987] 1 Lloyd's Rep. 482; *Insurance Co. of the State of Pennsylvania v. Grand Union Ins. Co.* [1990] 1 Lloyd's Rep. 208.
[95] *Youell v. Bland Welch (No. 2)* [1990] 2 Lloyd's Rep. 431, 445–446; *Trinity Ins. Co. v. Singapore Avn. & General Ins. Co.* [1993] 2 Re. L.R. 111; *SAIL v. Farex* [1995] L.R.L.R 116.
[96] *China Trades' Ins. Co. v. Royal Exchange Ass. Corp.* [1898] 2 Q.B. 187.
[97] *Equitable Life Ass. Society v. General Accident Ass. Corp.* (1904) 12 S.L.T. 348, 349 *per* Lord Pearson. For discussion of non-disclosure and misrepresentation generally, see Chs. 16 and 17.

33–30 Duty of disclosure. The duty of disclosure in reinsurance is the same as in primary insurance, whether the contract be one of marine or non-marine insurance.[98] The reinsured must disclose to the reinsurer all facts known, or deemed in law to be known, to him and which are not known or deemed to be known to the reinsurer, which are material to the risk in the sense that a prudent insurer would take them into account when deciding whether or not to take the risk and if so on what terms he should do so.[99] The duty has been reformulated in market terms as an obligation to ensure that the presentation of the risk proposed is fair and substantially accurate.[1] However, a reinsurer will only be able to avoid a reinsurance contract on grounds of breach of the duty, or of misrepresentation, when the reinsurer was actually induced by the non-disclosure or misrepresentation to enter into the contract.[2] It may be that in practice reinsurance business is often offered to reinsurers on the basis of limited information in the expectation that the reinsurers will either accept the business on the faith of the summary, or will ask further questions,[3] but the reinsurer is entitled to assume that the summary is fair and accurate, and he will be held to have waived further disclosure only if a prudent insurer would be sufficiently put on notice by the summary that the picture presented was incomplete and could well be altered by further information.[4] Whereas a reinsurer may be expected to be aware of the general course of losses affecting the market in which he operates, he is not to be expected to know particular circumstances affecting limited groups of insured within the overall market.[5] Nor will he be required to carry in his head information which had no interest for him at the time at which he acquired it.[6] However, he will waive disclosure of information which he knows is available and material but decides not to examine.[7]

33–31 The extent to which knowledge is imputed to the reinsured is governed by the same principles as apply to original insurance.[8] The application of these principles may be complicated by the use of agents to manage the business of the reinsured, and by the fact (discussed above) that in complex transactions a broker may have a number of different roles. The imputation of knowledge to the reinsured is limited to those circumstances

---

[98] *Highlands Ins. Co. v. Continental Ins. Co.* [1987] 1 Lloyd's Rep. 109; *CTI v. Oceanus Mutual Underwriting Assoc. (Bermuda) Ltd* [1984] 1 Lloyd's Rep. 476; *Lambert v. Co-operative Ins. Soc. Ltd* [1975] 2 Lloyd's Rep. 485.

[99] *Pan Atlantic Ins. Co. v. Pine Top Ins. Co.* [1995] 1 A.C. 501; *CTI v. Oceanus Mutual Underwriting Assoc. (Bermuda) Ltd* [1984] 1 Lloyd's Rep. 476. For examples of the right to avoid being limited by the terms of the reinsurance see *Toomey v. Eagle Star (No. 2)* [1995] 2 Lloyd's Rep. 88, and *HIH Casualty and General Ins.Co. Ltd v. New Hampshire Ins. Co.* [2001] Lloyd's Rep. I.R. 596.

[1] *CTI v. Oceanus* [1984] 1 Lloyd's Rep. 476 at 497–497, *per* Kerr L.J.

[2] *Pan Atlantic Ins. Co. v. Pine Top Ins. Co.* [1995] 1 A.C. 501.

[3] *Everett v. Hogg Robinson* [1973] 2 Lloyd's Rep. 217, 224; *Commonwealth Ins. v. Groupe Sprinks* [1983] 1 Lloyd's Rep. 67, 79; *CTI v. Oceanus Mutual Underwriting Assoc. (Bermuda) Ltd* [1984] 1 Lloyd's Rep. 476, 496.

[4] *CTI v. Oceanus Mutual Underwriting Assoc. (Bermuda) Ltd* [1984] 1 Lloyd's Rep. 476, 511–512.

[5] *North British Fishing Boat Ins. Co. v. Starr* (1922) 13 Ll.L.R. 206, 210.

[6] *London General Ins. Co. v. General Marine Underwriters Assoc.* [1921] 1 K.B. 104.

[7] *Pan Atlantic v. Pine Top* [1995] 1 A.C. 501. *Cf. GMA v. Storebrand & Kansa* [1995] L.R.L.R. 333—*obiter* observations as to waiver in failing to ascertain the nature of a "mixed bag" of insurance contracts.

[8] See Ch. 17, *ante*.

which, in the ordinary course of business, ought to be known by it.[9] The reinsured will not be deemed to know in the ordinary course of business that it is being defrauded by a managing agent.[10] The reinsured's agent to insure owes a separate duty of disclosure to reinsurers[11]; for this purpose the relevant person is the agent who actually places the reinsurance.[12]

33–32 Disclosure in treaty reinsurance. In so far as a reinsurance treaty is not a contract of insurance the application of the duty of disclosure to it might be thought to be in doubt. However, in *Glasgow Assurance v. Symondson*[13] Scrutton J. rejected the submission that it was inapplicable to the open cover reinsurance before him, while not giving reasons. In *Berger v. Pollock*[14] Kerr J. rejected a similar submission in respect of an open cover for primary marine insurance. It is submitted that the rationale of the doctrine of utmost good faith, which underlies the duty of disclosure, is equally as applicable to reinsurance treaties as to facultative reinsurances. The reinsurer subscribing a treaty is binding himself to offer an indemnity in the future in respect of such risks of the particular kind covered by the treaty as may, or must, be ceded to him thereunder. The contract is an insurance contract in a broad sense and it seems only right that he should be entitled to the benefit of full disclosure before committing himself.[15]

33–33 Duration of duty. In the case of facultative reinsurance, the duty exists up to the time that the reinsurer has bound himself to take the risk. In treaty reinsurance it is clear that the duty exists up to the conclusion of the treaty, but it is submitted that it does not persist in relation to cessions thereunder in cases where the reinsurer is bound to take the risks so ceded, since there is no occasion for him to exercise his judgement upon the risks being ceded.[16] Insofar as an open cover or treaty gives the reinsurer a right to query and refuse risks declared under it, the answer must be different.[17] The extent of a post-contractual duty of utmost good faith is discussed

---

[9] Marine Insurance Act 1906, s.18(1). On the knowledge of agents in reinsurance, see *SAIL v. Farex* [1995] L.R.L.R. 116; *Simner v. New India Ass.* [1995] L.R.L.R. 240; *PCW Syndicates v. PCW Reinsurers* [1996] 1 W.L.R. 1136; *Group Josi Re v. Walbrook Ins. Co. Ltd* [1996] 1 W.L.R. 1152, and Ch. 18, *ante*.

[10] *PCW Syndicates v. PCW Reinsurers* [1996] 1 W.L.R. 1136; *Group Josi Re v. Walbrook Ins. Co. Ltd* [1996] 1 W.L.R. 1152.

[11] Marine Insurance Act 1906, s.19.

[12] *PCW Syndicates v. PCW Reinsurers* [1996] 1 W.L.R. 1136; *Group Josi Re v. Walbrook Ins. Co. Ltd* [1996] 1 W.L.R. 1152 (although in these cases Staughton L.J. preferred to express no view on this point).

[13] (1911) 16 Com.Cas. 109, 120–121.

[14] [1973] 2 Lloyd's Rep. 442, 459–460.

[15] With regard to other types of contract (which are not contracts of or for reinsurance), it is unlikely that new categories of contracts of utmost good faith will be created. But a party may still be obliged not to suppress unusual features of the transaction, by reason of the general principles of misrepresentation: *GMA v. Storebrand & Kansa* [1995] L.R.L.R. 333, 349; *HIH Casualty and General Ins. Co. Ltd v. Chase Manhattan Bank* [2001] Lloyd's Rep. I.R. 703.

[16] It is submitted that this analysis is supported by comments of Kerr L.J. in *Citadel Ins. Co. v. Atlantic Union Ins. Co.* [1982] 2 Lloyd's Rep. 543, 548. See also *CCR Fishing v. Tomenson* [1986] 2 Lloyd's Rep. 513, not reversed on this point on appeal: [1989] 2 Lloyd's Rep. 536; 72 D.L.R. (4th) 478 (1990).

[17] It is submitted that the open cover considered by Kerr J. in *Berger v. Pollock* [1973] 2 Lloyd's Rep. 442, 460 was of this kind, since the voyage proposed for insurance appears to have been outside the ambit of the standard cover and required the premium to be specially

elsewhere.[18] For the purpose of this chapter, it is sufficient to point out that the scope of the post-contractual duty is limited, with remedies for breach likely to be assimilated with contractual remedies.[19]

33–34 Materiality. The test of materiality in cases of non-disclosure and reinsurance will follow the guidelines set down in authorities on original insurance. One special factor may be the inability of the reinsurer to adjust premium rates in respect of business placed under a quota share treaty, so that the effect on premium would not be a relevant constituent of materiality. The point has not been canvassed in detail in English authorities[20] and would, it is submitted, depend upon the terms and operation of any particular treaty.

33–35 The materiality of particular facts depends upon the nature of the business. In a facultative reinsurance those facts relating to the subject matter which are material to the reinsured will be equally material to the reinsurer, such as the absence of a sprinkler system in buildings insured against fire.[21] Where the reinsurer is asked to reinsure an existing portfolio of business, or to subscribe to an aggregate excess of loss cover, then the loss ratio or record for past years will be material, as will any fact bearing upon the profitability or loss-making potential of the business reinsured.[22] It may be material in such a case that the reinsured's maintenance of data is so inadequate that the loss potential of the business cannot be properly judged. The absence of a significant retention is likely to be material. However, the presence or absence of retention is often a matter of such importance that, in circumstances where nothing is disclosed on the point, it may be that the reasonable assumption is that the reinsured has no retention (or the underwriter may have waived the need for further disclosure).[23] Similarly, it is likely to be within the reasonable contemplation of the reinsurer that the reinsured has its own excess of loss insurance programme, so that the existence of such a programme (unless unusual in a material respect) would not be a matter for disclosure.[24] Clauses in the primary insurance which are

rated. If the reinsurance facility involves no binding contract "of" insurance or "for" insurance, and is merely a procedural mechanism to enable subsequent declarations to be made, no duty of disclosure will arise when the facility is agreed: *SAIL v. Farex* [1995] L.R.L.R. 116, 135–136. See also *Mander v. Commercial Union Ass. Co. Plc* [1998] Lloyd's Rep. I.R. 93, 136–137

[18] See Ch. 17, *ante*, in particular para. 17–2, *ante*.

[19] *K/S Merc-Scandia XXXXII v. Certain Lloyd's Underwriters* [2001] 2 Lloyd's Rep 563, C.A.

[20] It is mentioned in passing in *Commonwealth Ins. v. Groupe Sprinks* [1983] 1 Lloyd's Rep. 67, 78, *per* Lloyd J.

[21] *Highlands Ins. Co. v. Continental Ins. Co.* [1987] 1 Lloyd's Rep. 109, 114–116.

[22] *Pan Atlantic Ins. Co. v. Pine Top Ins. Co.* [1995] 1 A.C. 501; *General Accident Fire and Life Assurance v. Campbell* (1925) 21 Ll.L. Rep. 151; *Commonwealth Insurance v. Groupe Sprinks* [1983] 1 Lloyd's Rep. 67. That is not to say that the statistical variation between the actual loss ratio and the ratio misrepresented to the reinsurer will itself necessarily be material in the context of a misrepresentation—[1983] 1 Lloyd's Rep. 67, 78.

[23] *SAIL v. Farex* [1995] L.R.L.R 116, 137 (not challenged on appeal). Cf. *Traill v. Baring* (1864) 4 De G.J. & S.318, although that was a case involving a continuing representation.

[24] *Trinity Ins. Co. v. Singapore Avn. & General Ins. Co.* [1993] 2 Re. L.R. 111; *Kingscroft v. Nissan Fire and Marine Ins. Co. (No.2)* [1999] Lloyd's Rep. I. R. 603. However, a misrepresentation as to the cost of excess of loss protection would be likely to entitle the reinsurer to avoid the contract: *Hill v. Citadel Ins. Co.* [1997] L.R.L.R. 167. The status of the reinsurer's own retrocession arrangements will ordinarily not be material as between the reinsured and the reinsurer: *SAIL v. Farex* [1995] L.R.L.R. 116, 143, 149, 156.

so unusual as to be unexpected should be disclosed.[25] It has been held that the facts that a treaty must result in a loss to the reinsurer, that the reinsured was deprived of the chance to select the risks to be reinsured, and that the risks were laid off at a higher premium than that charged by the reinsured, were not material facts in the context of a proposed open cover reinsurance.[26] However, no expert evidence was tendered as to their materiality in that case,[27] and it is submitted that the same result would not necessarily be reached today, with the assistance of such evidence. In the context of retrocession, it is material to disclose that the underlying reinsurance is of the facultative obligatory type (ie which allows the insured to choose which risks to cede to the reinsurer, and obliges the reinsurer to accept such risks).[28]

33–36 Misrepresentation. Misrepresentation can arise in a number of ways in the formation of reinsurance. It may result from a misrepresentation by the primary insured which is passed on by the reinsured, either expressly or by means of an incorporating clause in the reinsurance contract which adopts a warranty of certain facts given in the primary insurance contract.[29] Alternatively, the reinsured may fail to pass on to the reinsurer material information received from the insured,[30] or may fail to check false information received from the insured.[31] It frequently happens that a proposal for reinsurance contains estimates or opinions, for instance on the nature of the primary insurance[32] or the future scale of claims thereunder in long tail business. In such cases there is an implied representation that there are reasonable grounds for the belief expressed.[33] As with original insurance, material misrepresentation can arise from the manner in which the broker presents the risk. For example, if the broker misrepresents that the risk has already been agreed, or that it is not necessary for the reinsurer to study documents attached to the slip.[34]

33–37 Illegality. In order that the reinsurance contract shall be valid and enforceable it must satisfy the general requirements of lawful insurable

---

[25] *Property Ins. Co. v. National Protector Ins. Co.* (1913) 108 L.T. 104, 106. Presumably the absence of a clause invariably present would be material. In the *Property Insurance* case a clause allowing navigation of the Canadian lakes was held to be unusual, but disclosure was waived by a term in the reinsurance contract that the reinsurer would be bound without notice of original clauses.

[26] *Glasgow Ass. Co. v. Symondson* (1911) 16 Com. Cas. 109.

[27] *ibid.* at 119.

[28] *Aneco Reins. Underwriting Ltd. v. Johnson & Higgins Ltd* [1998] 1 Lloyd's Rep. 565—appealed in relation to damages: [2000] Lloyd's Rep. I.R. 12, C.A.; [2001] UKHL 51, HL.

[29] *Australian Widows Fund Life Ass. v. National Mutual Life Assoc. of Australasia* [1914] A.C. 615.

[30] *Equitable Life Ass. Soc. v. General Accident Ins. Corp.* (1904) 12 S.L.T. 348.

[31] *Highland Ins. Co. v. Continental Ins. Co.* [1987] 1 Lloyd's Rep. 109, where the relevant representation was, in the absence of appropriate qualification, held to be a statement of fact rather than a statement of the reinsured's belief about the actual position. A similar approach was taken in *Sirius Int. Ins. Corp. v. Oriental Ass. Corp.* [1999] Lloyd's Rep. I. R. 342, at 350.

[32] *Irish National Ins. Co. v. Oman Ins. Co.* [1983] 2 Lloyd's Rep. 453. Such an opinion verges upon being a representation of law, *ibid.* at 461.

[33] *Irish National Ins. Co. v. Oman Ins. Co.* [1983] 2 Lloyd's Rep. 453, 461; *Highlands Ins. Co. v. Continental Ins. Co.* [1987] 1 Lloyd's Rep. 109, 113. But note the decision of the Court of Appeal in *Economides v. Commercial Union Ass. Plc* [1998] Q.B. 587, discussed at para. 16–13.

[34] *Mander v. Commercial Union Ass. Co. Plc* [1998] Lloyd's Rep. I.R. 93.

interest and legality. The general principles of illegality[35] apply with equal force to reinsurance as to primary insurance. Thus where reinsurances were effected for the benefit of reinsureds on policies which were illegal and void under section 1 of the Life Assurance Act 1774,[36] the reinsurances were themselves tainted with that illegality and were adjudged illegal and void.[37] The reinsureds could recover neither the amounts insured, despite their own payments made on the primary insurances, nor the premiums paid to the reinsurers.

33-38 Authorisation of business. Difficult issues have arisen as to the effect of contravention of the authorisation requirements of section 2 of the Insurance Companies Act 1982 and of its predecessors. Reinsurance business will in future be regulated under the Financial Services and Markets Act 2000.[38] The regulatory regime is dealt with elsewhere.[39] Reinsurance business falls within the scope of both Acts insofar as it involves the effecting and carrying out of contracts of insurance.[40]

33-39 It will be appreciated that illegality may occur either at the level of the original contract of insurance, or at the level of the reinsurance contract or both. In every case it will be important to consider what enforceable rights exist between the original assured and the insurer and between the reinsured and the reinsurer. This involves an analysis of whether unauthorised insurance and reinsurance contracts are prohibited by statute, and of the extent of any such prohibition. The relevant principles were explored in a series of decisions[41] which examined different aspects of the problem. The combined effect of those decisions has now been overtaken, and radically modified, by statute.[42]

33-40 In the *Bedford* Case,[43] reinsurers denied liability under their reinsurance contract on the basis that the reinsured's original contracts of

---

[35] See Ch. 14. For a case where a plea of illegality based on foreign law was run unsuccessfully, see *Great Atlantic Ins. Co. v. Home Ins. Co.* [1981] 2 Lloyd's Rep. 219.

[36] 14 Geo. 3.

[37] *Re London County Commercial Reinsurance Office Ltd* [1922] 2 Ch. 67.

[38] 2000 c.8.

[39] See Ch. 34, *post*.

[40] *D.R. Ins. Co. v. Seguros America Banamex* [1993] 1 Lloyd's Rep. 120, 126–129. *Cf. Forsikrings. National of Copenhagen v. A.-G.* (1925) 22 Lloyd's Rep. 4; [1925] A.C. 639; *Re N.R.G. Victory Reinsurance Ltd* [1995] 1 W.L.R. 239. Note that under s.3(2) of the 1982 Act authorisation may be restricted to reinsurance business. In relation to the Financial Services and Markets Act 2000 (FSMA), authorisation to carry out a regulated activity is required under s.19. Regulated activity (specified by order) includes activity relating to contracts of insurance: FSMA 2000 s.22; Sch. 2, para. 20. The Financial Services and Markets Act 2000 (Regulated Activities) Order 2001 (S.I. 2001 No. 544) includes amongst regulated activities the effecting, and the carrying out, of a contract of insurance as principal (art. 10). Some insurers are excluded from the requirement of authorisation, including EEA insurers when operating in defined circumstances other than through a UK branch, pursuant to a Community co-insurance scheme, otherwise than as the leading insurer: S.I. 2001 No.544, art.11.

[41] *Bedford Ins. v. Instituto de Resseguros do Brasil* [1985] Q.B. 966; *Stewart v. Oriental Fire and Marine Ins. Co.* [1985] Q.B. 988; *Phoenix General Ins. Co. v. Halvanon Ins. Co. Ltd* [1985] 2 Lloyd's Rep. 599; on appeal *sub nom. Phoenix v. ADAS* [1986] 2 Lloyd's Rep. 552; *Re Cavalier Ins. Co.* [1989] 2 Lloyd's Rep. 430; *D.R. Ins. Co. v. Seguros America Banamex* [1993] 1 Lloyd's Rep. 120.

[42] Financial Services Act 1986, s.132, see para. 33–43, *post* and the Financial Services and Markets Act 2000, (see para. 33–45, *post*).

[43] [1985] Q.B. 966.

insurance were unauthorised. Parker J. upheld this defence. He held that the original contracts of insurance were prohibited by section 2(1) of the Insurance Companies Act 1974 and were void, giving no enforceable contractual rights to insured or to insurer. This meant that the insurer could not claim on his policy of reinsurance since his claim would be in respect of original contracts of insurance which were void *ab initio*. Alternatively, the insurer would be precluded from claiming (even if the original contracts were not void *ab initio*) because he could only advance a claim on the reinsurance contract by setting up and relying upon the unauthorised original contracts of insurance.

33–41 In the *Stewart*[44] Case, Leggatt J. dealt with a different question, namely, whether a reinsurance contract was itself enforceable when the reinsurer was unauthorised under the 1974 Act. It was implicit in Leggatt J.'s judgment that the statutory requirements for authorisation applied to reinsurance just as to insurance. However, he held that the Act did not prohibit individual contracts of insurance or reinsurance.

33–42 *Phoenix General Insurance Co. v. Halvanon Insurance Co.* involved reliance by reinsurers upon allegedly unauthorised contracts of original insurance, just as in the *Bedford* case. The Court of Appeal held,[45] reversing the judgment of Hobhouse J.,[46] that the contracts were not unauthorised. The Court did, however, go on to consider, obiter, the effect of lack of authorisation so as to resolve the difficulties arising from the inconsistency between the decisions in *Bedford*[47] and *Stewart*.[48] The Court upheld the *Bedford* view that unauthorised insurance contracts were void.[49] This meant that if the original contracts of insurance were void, the reinsured would be unable to recover from the reinsurer in respect of reinsurance of such contracts.[50] The reasoning in *Phoenix* was followed in respect of original insurance in *Re Cavalier Insurance Co.*,[51] and in respect of reinsurance in *D.R. Insurance Co. v. Seguros America Banamex*.[52] However, a defence of illegality must be proved to a high degree of probability, involving factual evidence as to the conduct of the relevant reinsurance business.[53] Furthermore, the illegality defence is likely to be of considerably less significance in the future because of the effect of section 132 of the

---

[44] [1985] Q.B. 988.
[45] [1986] 2 Lloyd's Rep. 552. The decision was based on statutory transitional provisions which had not been relied on before Hobhouse J.
[46] [1985] 2 Lloyd's Rep. 599.
[47] [1985] Q.B. 966.
[48] [1985] Q.B. 988.
[49] This was the opinion expressed in para. 424 of the 7th edition of this work.
[50] Where the reinsurer is authorised, the inability to recover under the reinsurance will be due to the voidness of the underlying insurance; the reinsurance itself is likely to be unenforceable but not void *ab initio*—*cf. Harbour Ass. Co. v. Kansa General International Ins. Co.* [1993] 1 Lloyd's Rep. 455, 463, 467 (where the point was discussed but not decided).
[51] [1989] 2 Lloyd's Rep. 430. *Re Cavalier*, innocent consumer insureds were held to be entitled to a return of premium. It is possible that reinsureds might be in a different position, for example if they ought to have been aware of the need for authorisation.
[52] [1993] 1 Lloyd's Rep, 120. This decision was followed in *GMA v. Storebrand & Kansa* [1995] L.R.L.R. 333. However, in the latter case a party which assumed responsibility for the liabilities of an unauthorised insurer, but which was not thereby carrying on prohibited insurance business, would not have been precluded on grounds of public policy from recovering under a contract to indemnify against such liabilities.
[53] *Overseas Union Ins. Ltd v. Incorporated General Ins. Ltd* [1992] 1 Lloyd's Rep. 439.

Financial Services Act 1986, and of the relevant provisions of the Financial Services and Markets Act 2000.

33–43 Section 132 of the Financial Services Act 1986.[54] This section limited significantly the effects of contravention of the authorisation requirements of the Insurance Companies Act 1982.[55] Sections 132(1) and (4) provide, in conjunction with section 132(6), that a contract of insurance effected in breach of section 2 of the 1982 Act is enforceable by the insured against the insurer, although not vice-versa,[56] unless the insured elects to take no benefit under it and to recover premiums paid. Section 132(6) further provides that:

> "a contravention of [s.2] shall not make a contract of insurance illegal or invalid to any greater extent than is provided in this section; and a contravention of [s.2] in respect of a contract of insurance shall not affect the validity of any reinsurance contract entered into in respect of that contract".

Accordingly, the enforceability of the primary contract of insurance removes the objections taken in *Bedford*[57] and in *Phoenix*,[58] namely, that the reinsured could not recover because there was no liability to be reinsured, and because he could not pray in aid the conclusion of the unauthorised contract.[59] Insofar as a contract of reinsurance is concluded with a reinsurer who is carrying on unauthorised business, it is submitted that sections 132(1) and (6) apply to it, so that it is, as a "contract of insurance", enforceable against the reinsurer by the reinsured, although not vice versa, unless the reinsured elects to abandon the contract.

33–44 Differing conclusions were reached in first instance decisions as to whether section 132 took effect retrospectively in relation to contracts entered into before 12 January 1987, when it came into force.[60] Uncertainty as to the scope of the section was resolved by the Court of Appeal in *Group Josi Re v. Walbrook Ins. Co. Ltd.*[61] The Court of Appeal held that the prohibition, arising from section 2 of the Insurance Companies Act 1982, of carrying out contracts which were illegal under the Insurance Companies Act 1974 had been modified by section 132(6). That section limited and defined the extent of the illegality. Any contracts which were illegal under

---

[54] 1986 c. 60.
[55] 1982 c. 50. This re-enacts s.2(1) of the 1974 Act.
[56] Subject to the discretion of the court s.132(3).
[57] [1985] Q.B. 966.
[58] [1986] 2 Lloyd's Rep. 552.
[59] Since s.132(6) provides that the primary contract of insurance is not illegal or invalid to any greater degree than provided in the section, it is not void, it is only unenforceable by the insurer.
[60] In *D.R. Ins. Co. v. Seguros America Banamex* [1993] 1 Lloyd's Rep. 120, at pp. 131–132 the view was expressed that the section did not have retrospective effect. It was conceded in *GMA v. Storebrand & Kansa* [1995] L.R.L.R. 333 that this view was correct. The contrary conclusion was reached in *Bates v. Barrow* [1995] 1 Lloyd's Rep. 680, influenced by the approach taken by the House of Lords to the presumption against statutory retrospectivity in *L'Office Cherifien v. Yamashita-Shinnikon Steamship Co. ("The Boucraa")* [1994] 1 A.C. 486. In *Bates v. Barrow* it was further held that s.132 validated contracts made in contravention of legislation prior to the 1982 Act.
[61] [1996] 1 W.L.R. 1152, 1165–1167, 1172–1174.

the 1974 Act could therefore be carried out (i.e. enforced) in accordance with the terms of section 132 after that section came into force. This reasoning suggests that any contract, whenever made, can be enforced in accordance with section 132 if the carrying out of the contract would otherwise involve a contravention of section 2 of the Insurance Companies Act 1982.

33–45 The Financial Services and Markets Act 2000.[62] The relevant provisions of this Act apply to contracts made after section 26 (which deals with agreements made by unauthorised persons) came into force.[63] The consequences of lack of authorisation differ, depending upon whether the insurer carries on business outside the scope of authorisation obtained pursuant to the Act, or whether the insurer lacks any authorisation at all. If an insurer authorised under the Act carries on a class of business otherwise than in accordance with its authorisation, transactions entered into in course of the unauthorised business are enforceable.[64] The insurer is not guilty of an offence.[65] Whether there is any liability for breach of statutory duty will depend upon whether secondary legislation provides a basis for such liability.[66] If the insurer is not authorised at all, the situation is different. The carrying on of unauthorised insurance will give rise to a contravention of the general prohibition in the Act,[67] and (subject to any defence available under the Act) will give rise to a criminal offence.[68] The unauthorised insurance will (subject to an order allowing enforcement) be unenforceable by the insurer against the insured.[69] It seems that it will be enforceable by the insured, although the insured may elect to receive back premium paid, and compensation for any relevant loss suffered.[70] The court may permit the insurer to enforce the contract, if satisfied that it would be just and equitable to do so.[71] Unlike section 132 of the 1986 Act, section 27 of the 2000 Act does not refer in terms to the enforcement of reinsurance. However, since primary contracts of insurance are apparently enforceable at the suit of the insured, reinsurers could not refuse to pay claims on the basis of a lack of liability of the reinsured to the original assured. Further, a contract of reinsurance would appear to be enforceable by the reassured against an unauthorised reinsurer.

33–46 Construction of reinsurance contracts. It has rightly been observed[72] that the genius of the London market is to set out the elements of a complex transaction involving large sums of money in one short

---

[62] 2000 c.8.

[63] FSMA 2000, s.26(3). Section 26 came into force on 1 December 2001, together with the general prohibition of unauthorised regulated activity in s.19, as a result of the Financial Services and Markets Act 2000 (Commencement No.7) Order 2001, (S.I. 2001 No. 3538). For the type of activity regulated by the Act, see notes to para. 33–38, *ante*. See Ch. 34 for the regulatory regime generally.

[64] s.20(2)(b).

[65] s.20(2)(a).

[66] s.20(3).

[67] s.19

[68] s.23

[69] s.26(1).

[70] s.26(2).

[71] s.28(3).

[72] By Mr John Thomas, Q.C., as he then was, in *Insurance & Reinsurance Law International*, vol. 3, pp. 96–97.

document—the slip. Usually the slip is worded with care by persons experienced in the terms used by the market.[73] Sometimes, however, it is difficult to ascertain the parties' intention from the wording of the slip. Difficulties are caused by the use of abbreviations and delay in producing the detailed wording to set out their meaning in full,[74] by the use of standard wordings of acknowledged pedigree[75] but not always appropriate to the particular transaction[76] and creating either repugnancy or surplusage, and by the practice of incorporation by reference. Expert evidence is often adduced to assist the Court in construing a reinsurance contract, even when no customary usage is contended for.[77] Presumably the evidence is admissible in order to set out the market background against which the relevant documents fall to be interpreted.[78]

33–47 Express terms of reinsurance contracts. It is beyond the scope of this chapter to list all the usual categories of clauses which are to be found in facultative and treaty wordings, and recourse should be had to specialist works on the subject. Reference will be made, however, to particular terms which have engaged the attention of the English courts.

33–48 Incorporation of terms. Reinsurance contracts are frequently expressed in abbreviated form and incorporate by reference the provisions of standard market wordings and the terms of other contracts between different parties. Two different types of incorporating provisions may be distinguished in the authorities, namely, (i) the incorporation of standard terms into the particular contract and (ii) the incorporation into a reinsurance of the terms of the underlying contract of insurance. The principles governing these situations overlap, and are discussed below.

33–49 Incorporation of standard terms. A set of standard terms may be appended, or referred to, in order to complete a summary of the reinsurance provisions. Sometimes these are terms intended for primary insurances. This appears to have been used as an early device for creating reinsurance wordings and it can still create confusion.[79]

33–50 In determining whether a particular term is to be incorporated the courts will enquire first whether there is a clear intention that it is to be incorporated. If so, it will be incorporated to the extent that it is not repugnant to the reinsurance contract and inconsistent with its terms. The

---

[73] *Balfour v. Beaumont* [1982] 2 Lloyd's Rep. 493, 496, *per* Webster J.

[74] *Phoenix General Ins. Co. v. Halvanon Ins. Co.* [1985] 2 Lloyd's Rep. 599, 602.

[75] *Law Guarantee Trust Accident Soc. Ltd v. Munich Reinsurance Co.* (1914) 31 T.L.R. 572, 574.

[76] *South British Fire and Marine Ins. Co. v. Da Costa* [1906] 1 K.B. 456, 460–461; *Great Atlantic Ins. Co. v. Home Ins. Co.* [1981] 2 Lloyd's Rep. 219, 229.

[77] The admissibility of such evidence has been doubted in *Barlee Marine Corp. v. Mountain* [1987] 1 Lloyd's Rep. 471, 475, *per* Hirst J. and in *Baker v. Black Sea & Baltic Gen. Ins. Co.* [1996] L.R.L.R. 353, 356, *per* Staughton L.J. In *Phillips v. Dorintal Ins. Co.* [1987] 1 Lloyd's Rep. 482, 486, a customary usage was proved in relation to terms used in a retrocession slip and confirmation. While factual evidence as to the broking of the risk is also sometimes adduced on issues of construction, its relevance is likely to be limited: *New Hampshire Ins. Co. v. MGN* [1997] L.R.L.R. 24, 55.

[78] *Kingscroft v. Nissan Fire and Marine Ins. Co. (No.2)* [1999] Lloyd's Rep. I. R. 603, 622.

[79] *e.g. Forsikrings. Vesta v. Butcher* [1989] A.C. 852, where "Aquacultural" terms intended for primary insurance were annexed to and incorporated into the reinsurance slip. They were also terms of the underlying insurance.

overall approach is discussed in greater detail below, in relation to the incorporation of terms of an underlying contract. In *Home Insurance Company of New York v. Victoria Montreal Fire Insurance Company*,[80] the Privy Council held that a clause barring claims 12 months from the occurrence of a fire, contained in a policy of original fire insurance attached to, and stated to form part of a contract of reinsurance, was not incorporated. Compliance with the clause by the reinsured might be impossible, since he would be dependent upon the speed at which the primary assured advanced a claim under the underlying contract of insurance. The Privy Council held that it could not have been intended to incorporate the clause because it was inapplicable to a reinsurance, and that the annexure of the printed fire insurance must have been merely to indicate the origin of the liability on the original fire policy which would indirectly lead to a liability on the reinsurance.[81]

33–51 By contrast in *Forsikringsaktieselskabet Vesta v. Butcher*[82] annexed standardised terms of primary insurance were clearly expressed to be incorporated into the contract of reinsurance. It was submitted that certain of those terms which related to obligations to be performed by the primary insured could not be incorporated into a contract between reinsured and reinsurer. Hobhouse J. refused an amendment to raise the point and rejected the submission, saying that it was unsound to argue that because a provision requires, or relates to, an act to be performed by another party, the contracting party cannot be held to promise that the act will be performed. Although the reinsured was dependent on the assured for compliance with the particular provision, he was protected, if wise, by a similar provision in the primary contract of insurance.[83] The case was thereafter dealt with on the footing that the terms of the primary insurance were incorporated, although doubts were expressed in the House of Lords about whether this approach was correct.[84]

33–52 Incorporation of terms of underlying insurance. This is a common feature of reinsurance contracts (although some recent wordings have departed from it). It may be achieved by a provision such as "All terms, clauses and conditions as original".[85] Alternatively, there may be a warranty by the reinsured that the terms and conditions of the insurance and the reinsurance are the same.[86] Broadly, the intended effect appears to be to

---

[80] [1907] A.C. 59.
[81] [1907] A.C. 59, 64. Contrast *CNA Int. Reins Co. Ltd v. Companhia de Seguros Tranquilidade SA* [1999] Lloyd's Rep. I.R. 289, where specific incorporating words could in principle apply to a notice clause, but the lack of a schedule identifying the recipient of the notice, as provided for in the clause, prevented incorporation. For further discussion of the relevant principles, see para. 33–55, *post*.
[82] [1986] 2 Lloyd's Rep. 179, affirmed. [1988] 1 Lloyd's Rep. 19 (C.A.) and [1989] A.C. 852, (H.L.).
[83] [1986] 2 Lloyd's Rep. 179, 186.
[84] [1989] A.C. 852, 895–897, *per* Lord Griffiths.
[85] *Pine Top Ins. Co. Ltd v. Unione Italiana Anglo-Saxon Reins. Co. Ltd.* [1987] 1 Lloyd's Rep. 476. There are variants—*e.g.* terms "as original"—*Citadel Ins. v. Atlantic Union Ins.* [1982] 2 Lloyd's Rep. 543, or "subject to the same clauses and conditions as original policy"—*Charlesworth v. Faber* (1900) 5 Com. Cas. 408, or "conditions as underlying"—*Municipal Mutual Ins. Ltd v. Sea Ins. Co.* [1996] L.R.L.R. 265 (appealed on other grounds: [1998] Lloyd's Rep. I.R. 421).
[86] *Forskrings. Vesta v. Butcher* [1989] 1 A.C. 852.

ensure that the terms and scope of the reinsurance cover are the same as those of the original insurance cover.[87] However, a literal application of the incorporation provision may produce inconsistency or ambiguity or terms which could not have been intended as relating to the reinsurance.

33–53 The terms to be incorporated. The starting point will be to seek to identify the term or terms to which the incorporating words relate; if the words are insufficiently clear, it may be impossible to identify any terms to be incorporated.[88] Difficulty can also arise from use of the phrase "as original" in a retrocession contract. It may be unclear whether this relates to terms of the reinsurance directly underlying the retrocession, or to terms of the original insurance further down the contractual chain. In *Pine Top Insurance Co. Ltd. v. Unione Italiana Anglo-Saxon Reinsurance Co. Ltd* it was held to refer to the original contracts of insurance, and not to the intermediate reinsurance.[89]

33–54 Intention as to incorporation. The essential question will then be whether the parties to the reinsurance contract intended that their contract should include the particular term; this is a question as to the construction of the reinsurance contract in its context, and the answer will depend upon the language of the relevant clauses and the surrounding circumstances.[90] However, there are various criteria which provide assistance in answering the question. They are as follows:

> (a) whether the term makes sense in the reinsurance contract, without undue manipulation; (b) whether the term is germane to the reinsurance, or merely collateral; (c) whether the term is consistent with the other terms of the reinsurance, and (d) whether the term is apposite for inclusion in the reinsurance.[91]

In considering these criteria, and incorporation generally, it is important to take account of whether the insurance and reinsurance were intended to operate on a back-to-back basis. To an extent, this begs the question as to incorporation. Nevertheless, it is relevant that, at least in proportional reinsurance, there is likely to be a presumption that the contracts should provide cover on a back-to-back basis.[92] In deciding whether a clause is

---

[87] *Citadel Ins. v. Atlantic Union Ins.* [1982] 2 Lloyd's Rep. 543, 546; *Forskrings. Vesta v. Butcher* [1988] 1 Lloyd's Rep. 19, 34.

[88] *HIH Casualty & General Ins. Ltd v. New Hampshire Ins. Co.* [2001] Lloyd's Rep. I.R. 596 (reference to incorporation of a "Cancellation Clause" did not incorporate a clause waiving defences arising from breach of the duty of utmost good faith); *Cigna Life Ins. Co. v. Intercaser SA de Seguros Y Reaseguros* [2001] Lloyd's Rep. I.R. 821(contract to which reference made not clearly identified). *Cf. Pine Top Ins. Co. Ltd v. Unione Italiana Anglo-Saxon Reins. Co. Ltd* [1987] 1 Lloyd's Rep. 476 (requirement to identify the terms, conditions and clauses referred to in the incorporating words).

[89] [1987] 1 Lloyd's Rep. 476. Similarly in *Bowring Reins. Ltd v. Baxter* [1987] 2 Lloyd's Rep. 416, "amount as original" in loss of hire reinsurance was held to refer to the hire payable to the insured.

[90] *AIG Europe (UK) Ltd. v. Ethniki* [2000] Lloyd's Rep. I.R. 343, 351; *CNA Int. Reins. Co. Ltd. v. Companhia de Seguros Tranquilidade SA* [1999] Lloyd's Rep. I.R. 289, 299; *Groupama Navigation et Transports v. Catatumbo CA Seguros* [2001] Lloyd's Rep. I.R. 141, 146.

[91] The criteria are identified and discussed in *HIH Casualty & General Ins. Ltd v. New Hampshire Ins. Co.* [2001] Lloyd's Rep. I.R. 596.

[92] *HIH Casualty & General Ins. Ltd v. New Hampshire Ins. Co.* [2001] Lloyd's Rep. I.R. 596, 632–633; *Groupama Navigation et Transports v. Catatumbo CA Seguros* [2001] Lloyd's Rep. I.R. 141, 145, 147. The presumption will not, however, always be appropriate, particularly when

incorporated, it is also necessary to keep in mind its effect as part of the terms of the reinsurance; this is discussed separately below.

33–55 Manipulation of language. So far as manipulation of language is concerned, there is some divergence in the authorities as to the extent to which linguistic massage is proper. Some straightforward manipulation[93] will often be appropriate (such as reading "assured" as "reassured"), provided that this does not involve major rewriting of the clause, and provided that other factors support incorporation.[94] In *CNA International Reinsurance Co. v. Companhia de Seguros Tranquilidade SA*[95] a facultative reinsurance slip referred to standard Lloyd's primary insurance wordings. Clarke J. held that the wordings were incorporated as terms of the reinsurance, although some terms might be inapplicable and others might require manipulation. Thus, a condition that the assured declared that information in a proposal form was true, and based on diligent enquiries, was incorporated into the reinsurance, with alterations to reflect the fact it was the reinsured making the declaration, and that there was no proposal form for the reinsurance. A condition that the assured was not to admit liability was similarly incorporated into the reinsurance. By contrast, a condition as to the giving of notice of loss was not incorporated. In principle incorporation posed no difficulty, but the particular wordings referred to notice being given to parties identified in a schedule. The absence of a schedule in the reinsurance led to the conclusion that the condition was not incorporated.

33–56 Germane to reinsurance. The requirement that the incorporated clause must be germane to the reinsurance has been adapted from authorities dealing with bills of lading and charterparties. These provide some useful general guidance, but they also involve features peculiar to contracts of carriage, which are not necessarily applicable to reinsurance.[96] A clause is germane to the reinsurance if it relates to its subject-matter (including terms of and exceptions to coverage), as opposed to collateral matters such as dispute resolution machinery. Arbitration clauses are likely

---

dealing with non-proportional reinsurance: *Axa Reins. (U.K) Plc v. Field* [1996] 1 W.L.R. 1026; *American Centennial Ins. Co. v. INSCO Ltd* [1996] L.R.L.R 407, 411. It may also be inapposite if the risk as presented to reinsurers differs materially from the risk as assumed by the reinsured: *Gan Ins. Co. v. Tai Ping Ins. Co. Ltd* [1999] Lloyd's Rep. I.R. 472.

[93] *i.e.* which can be done "simply and deftly as a matter of language"—*per* Rix L.J. in *HIH Casualty and General Ins. Co. Ltd v. New Hampshire Ins. Co.* [2001] Lloyd's Rep. I.R. 596 at 633.

[94] *HIH Casualty & General Ins. Ltd v. New Hampshire Ins. Co.* [2001] Lloyd's Rep. I.R. 596, 633 (excessive manipulation required of a waiver of defences clause if all references to reassured were to be read as meaning the reinsurers). See also *Pine Top Ins. Co. Ltd v. Unione Italiana Anglo-Saxon Reins. Co. Ltd* [1987] 1 Lloyd's Rep. 476 (arbitration clause not incorporated); *Highlands Ins. Co. v. Continental Ins. Co.* [1987] 1 Lloyd's Rep. 109 (errors & omissions clause not incorporated); *Municipal Mutual Ins. Ltd v. Sea Ins Co* [1996] L.R.L.R. 265 (notice clause not incorporated—appealed on other grounds: [1998] Lloyd's Rep. I.R. 421).

[95] [1999] Lloyd's Rep. I.R. 289.

[96] *AIG Europe (UK) Ltd v. Ethniki* [2000] Lloyd's Rep. I.R. 343, 351.

to be regarded as collateral, and so not incorporated by general words;[97] as are jurisdiction clauses,[98] and choice of law clauses.[99]

33–57 Unusual clauses. Difficulties can arise where the original insurance contract contains an unusual term about which the reinsurer is unaware when incorporation is agreed. It appears that reinsurers will be bound by terms which are usual.[1] In the case of a clause which is onerous and unusual, it may be relevant to consider whether the reinsurer has been given sufficient notice of the clause to make it fair that it should apply.[2] However, this enquiry will overlap with the question whether there has been a fair presentation of the risk generally. Whether or not the usualness of the term affects incorporation, this factor is relevant to the question whether the term ought to have been disclosed to the reinsurer when the risk was placed. Thus in *Protector Insurance Co. v. National Protector Insurance,*[3] the unusual nature of an option for a voyage to the Great Lakes was treated as a matter relevant to disclosure. In that case, Scrutton J. held that the option was sufficiently unusual to merit disclosure, but that disclosure was waived by an equally unusual incorporating clause which incorporated clauses and conditions "without notice". Questions of incorporation and disclosure may thus substantially overlap in practice.

33–58 No conflict with terms. The fact that a clause will conflict with other terms of the reinsurance, or with standard common law duties,[4] which would otherwise be applicable, is a factor which weighs against incorporation.[5] However, the fact that the reinsurance contains terms which are similar to those in the original insurance does not necessarily mean that the latter are to be ignored.[6]

33–59 Effect of incorporation. If incorporated, a clause may give rise to an

---

[97] *Pine Top Ins. Co. Ltd v. Unione Italiana Anglo-Saxon Reins. Co. Ltd* [1987] 1 Lloyd's Rep. 476; *Hong Kong Borneo Services v. Pilcher* [1992] 2 Lloyd's Rep. 593 (not a reinsurance case); *Excess Ins. Co. v. Mander* [1997] 2 Lloyd's Rep. 119; *Trygg Hansa Ins. Co. Ltd v. Equitas Ltd* [1998] 2 Lloyd's Rep. 439 (principles not altered by the Arbitration Act 1996); *Cigna Life Ins. Co. v. Intercaser SA de Seguros Y Reaseguros* [2001] Lloyd's Rep. I.R. 821.

[98] *AIG Europe (UK) Ltd v. Ethniki* [2000] Lloyd's Rep. I.R. 343; *AIG Europe SA v. QBE International Ins. Ltd* [2001] 2 Lloyd's Rep. 268; *Ass Gen SpA v. Ege Sigorta AS* [2002] Lloyds Rep. I.R. 480.

[99] *Gan Ins. Co. Ltd v. Tai Ping Ins. Co. Ltd* [1999] Lloyd's Rep. I.R. 472.

[1] *Marten v. Nippon Sea and Land Ins. Co.* (1893) 3 Com. Cas. 164 (reinsurer should have realised that a common warehouse-to-warehouse provision was in the original policy); *Charlesworth v. Faber* (1900) 5 Com. Cas. 408 (held covered clause was a usual clause which was incorporated). These authorities are discussed in *HIH Casualty & General Ins. Ltd v. New Hampshire Ins. Co.* [2001] Lloyd's Rep. I.R. 596 at 638–639, where it was held that they do not support a broader proposition (contained in a previous edition of this work) that a reinsurer is not bound by the incorporation of terms unless they are well known and in common use.

[2] In accordance with the general principle adumbrated in *Interfoto Picture Library Ltd v. Stiletto Visual Programmes Ltd* [1989] Q.B. 433.

[3] (1913) 108 L.T. 104. In *HIH Casualty & General Ins. Ltd v. New Hampshire Ins. Co., supra*, the Court of Appeal decided that an issue as to the effect of a clause being unusual could not be decided separately from issues as to the overall presentation: see para. 33–61 *post*.

[4] *HIH Casualty & General Ins. Ltd v. New Hampshire Ins. Co.* [2001] Lloyd's Rep. I.R. 596, 635.

[5] *Australian Widows v. National Mutual Life* [1914] A.C. 634, 642.

[6] *Groupama Navigation et Transports v. Catatumbo CA Seguros* [2001] Lloyd's Rep. I.R. 141 (a term as to maintenance of class in original insurance was incorporated into the reinsurance, and had the same effect under both contracts, notwithstanding the fact that the reinsurance had its own similar term).

independent obligation as between reinsurer and reinsured, separate from the similar obligation as between original insured and the reinsured under the original contract of insurance. While this effectively produces an identity of terms in the two contracts, it will not necessarily lead to back-to-back coverage. Recovery under the reinsurance may be precluded by a breach of the incorporated obligation by the reinsured, even if there has been no similar breach under the original insurance by the original insured. Another possibility is that the incorporated term does not create independent rights or obligations in the reinsurance contract, but is a form of "follow settlements" provision. Incorporation of a clause in this sense means that the clause relates essentially to the performance of the original contract of insurance, and identifies circumstances in which the reinsurers will be liable to the reinsured.[7]

33–60 These principles are discussed in, and illustrated by, *HIH Casualty & General Ins. Ltd v. New Hampshire Ins. Co.*[8] The original insurance was to cover a shortfall in profits arising from the making of films. It included a term (clause 8) under which insurers waived various defences, including defences of mis-representation and non-disclosure. In a determination of preliminary issues, it was held on appeal that a term in the reinsurance referring to the incorporation of a "Cancellation Clause" was not sufficiently clear to incorporate clause 8. However, clause 8 was incorporated into the reinsurance by other general words of incorporation. The clause could not legitimately be manipulated linguistically in order to change references to the reinsured as insurer into references to the reinsurer. Furthermore, it was held that the reinsurers could not have intended to waive potentially independent defences against the reinsured arising, for example, from non-disclosures by the reinsured which might be quite separate and different from any breach in relation to the original insurance contract. These considerations did not prevent incorporation of the clause into the reinsurance in unmanipulated form. If incorporated in that manner, the clause was germane to the cover afforded by the reinsurance. It had two related functions in the reinsurance context. First, it excluded any argument by reinsurers that the reinsured was not liable to the original insured in circumstances where the reinsured might otherwise have had a defence of non-disclosure or misrepresentation. Secondly, if any complaints of non-disclosure or misrepresentation in the placing of the reinsurance were identical to possible complaints about the placing of the original insurance, because the presentations of the risk were effectively the same, the incorporated clause meant that reinsurers could not rely at the level of the reinsurance on defences which had also been waived at the level of the original insurance. It was held that it was not possible to determine by way of preliminary issue whether incorporation was precluded on the ground that insufficient notice was given of an unusual term. That question could not be divorced from the broader question whether the relevant presentation was unfair.

33–61 Significance of incorporating words. The purpose of a provision

---

[7] *HIH Casualty & General Ins. Ltd v. New Hampshire Ins. Co.* [2001] Lloyd's Rep. I.R. 596, 631–632, 640–641 where incorporation operated in the latter sense.
[8] [2001] Lloyd's Rep. I.R. 596.

making the reinsurance contract "subject to" the terms of the underlying contract is not limited to the function of supplementing terms expressly agreed upon through a process of incorporation. Such a provision is essential in a reinsurance contract, designed to cover the risks written under the primary insurance contract so as to achieve an identical standard of liability on the two contracts.[9] It therefore identifies the risk underwritten by the reinsured in respect of which the reinsurer promises indemnity. In a reinsurance subject to original terms the reinsured is not permitted to alter the foundation of the contract by substituting different policies of original insurance on different terms from those in existence when it was concluded,[10] or by varying the terms of the original insurance without the approval of the reinsurer.[11]

33–62 Similar interpretation. Where parties define the scope of the reinsurance cover by reference to the terms of the underlying contract, it follows that they intend the effect of these terms to be the same for each contract. Regardless of the incorporation of terms from the primary insurance, the court may accordingly be led to give them the same interpretation in both contracts.[12] Similarly, where it is held that the parties to the original contract intended that a clause should have a particular definition in that contract, the same clause will be likely to bear the same "dictionary" definition when it appears in the reinsurance contract.[13] However, the assumption that the parties intend a contract of reinsurance to cover the same risks on the same conditions as the original contract of insurance may only be made in the absence of an indication of contrary intention. If, for example, the reinsurance contract contains a term as to the period of cover which differs from the original insurance, a court will give effect to that term notwithstanding the fact that the result will be that the two contracts cannot provide "back to back" coverage.[14] Similarly, where the reinsurance is non-proportional and subject to different underwriting considerations to those applicable to the underlying insurance, it should not be assumed that terms defining how losses are to be aggregated are necessarily intended to operate in the same way in both contracts.[15]

33–63 Choice of law. Besides being an aid to interpretation an incorporation provision may bear upon the selection of the proper law to ensure uniformity of interpretation. In *Citadel Insurance Co. v. Atlantic Union Insurance*[16] Kerr L.J. rejected a submission that a reference to reinsurance terms "as original" meant that the reinsurance was to be governed by the law

[9] *Lower Rhine and Würtemberg Ins. Assoc. v. Sedgwick* [1899] 1 Q.B. 179, 190, *per* Collins L.J.
[10] *Lower Rhine and Würtemberg Ins. Assoc. v. Sedgwick* [1899] 1 Q.B. 179.
[11] *Norwich Union Fire Ins. v. Colonial Mutual Fire Ins. Co.* [1922] 2 K.B. 461. *HIH Casualty and General Ins.Co. Ltd v. New Hampshire Ins. Co.* [2001] Lloyd's Rep. I.R. 596, 623.
[12] *Joyce v. Realm Marine Ins. Co.* (1872) L.R. 7 Q.B. 580, where the court did not expressly refer to incorporation but held that "loading" was to receive the same meaning in the contracts of insurance and of reinsurance in view of the fact that the latter was said to be subject to the terms of the former.
[13] *Forsikrings. Vesta v. Butcher* [1989] A.C. 852, 911.
[14] *Youell v. Bland Welch* [1992] 2 Lloyd's Rep. 127. Contrast *Groupama Navigation et Transports v. Catatumbo CA Seguros* [2001] Lloyd's Rep. I.R. 141, where it was held that terms in the reinsurance were to the same effect as those in the original insurance, so that the latter were incorporated and were to be construed so as to provide back to back cover.
[15] *Axa Reins. (U.K.) plc v. Field* [1996] 1 W.L.R. 1026, 1033–1034.
[16] [1982] 2 Lloyd's Rep. 543, 548.

of the underlying insurance contracts.[17] It follows that contracts of reinsurance and insurance may be intended to apply to the same risk on the same terms, but be governed by different systems of law. In *Forsikrings. Vesta v. Butcher*[18] the reinsurance contract, which was most closely connected with English law, incorporated a number of important clauses from the underlying insurance contract which was impliedly governed by Norwegian law. Certain of them would be construed differently according to the two legal systems. Hobhouse J. held that the terms incorporated into the English law reinsurance contract from the Norwegian law contract of insurance remained subject to Norwegian law, so that in effect the reinsurance contract would have had two governing laws. In the Court of Appeal and House of Lords the matter was regarded as one of the construction of the reinsurance contract and not one of imputed choice of law. Questions of applicable law will now have to be determined by reference to the Rome Convention.[19]

33–64 "Errors and omissions" clauses. These clauses are to be found in all types of reinsurance treaties, with varying wording. Their basic purpose is to protect the reinsured against oversights and mistakes in the administration of a treaty and in particular the declaration or cession of business under it. In *Highlands Insurance Co. v. Continental Insurance Co.*[20] it was submitted that an errors and omission clause in the primary insurance was incorporated into the facultative reinsurance, and had the effect of relieving the reinsured from the consequences of a misrepresentation of the state of the insured buildings. Steyn J. held[21] that it did not apply to pre-contractual material misrepresentations, noting that there was no provision for payment of an additional premium on correction of the error. A similar point arose in *Pan Atlantic Insurance Co. v. Pine Top Insurance Co.*[22] and it was emphasised that such a clause would have to evince a clear intention to exclude the right of avoidance in order to protect the reinsured against the consequences of non-disclosure.

33–65 Period of cover. One basis on which reinsurance cover is conferred is the "risks attaching" basis, whereby the reinsurer agrees to reinsure risks attaching to one or more particular primary insurances. In such a case the reinsurance is co-extensive in time with the original insurances, subject to an express expiry date ante-dating the expiry of those insurances. Another basis of cover is called the "losses occurring" basis, whereby the reinsurer undertakes to indemnify the reinsured in respect of his liability arising out of losses occurring within a specified period, in which case the term of the underlying policy or policies is irrelevant. Sometimes it is unclear which basis of cover is adopted,[23] but it appears from *Balfour v. Beaumont* that a

[17] See also *Gan Ins. Co. v. Tai Ping Ins. Co.* [1999] Lloyd's Rep. I. R. 472 (Taiwanese choice of law in original contract not incorporated into reinsurance).
[18] [1986] 2 Lloyd's Rep. 179; affirmed in C.A., [1988] 1 Lloyd's Rep. 19; affirmed in H.L., [1989] A.C. 852.
[19] See Ch. 13, *ante*, particularly paras. 13–63 to 13–65.
[20] [1987] 1 Lloyd's Rep. 109.
[21] *ibid.* at 117.
[22] [1993] 1 Lloyd's Rep. 496, 502. The point was not pursued on appeal to the House of Lords: [1995] 1 A.C. 501. Contrast *Toomey v. Eagle Star (No. 2)* [1995] 1 Lloyd's Rep. 88, where a contractual clause dealt specifically with the right to avoid. For further discussion, see paras. 16–59 and 17–91, *ante*.
[23] In *Youell v. Bland Welch* [1992] 2 Lloyd's Rep. 127, the reinsurance was of a hybrid nature, operating in part on a risks attaching basis and in part on a loss occurring basis.

stipulation that losses occurring within a defined period are covered points to the "losses occurring" basis.[24] In this formulation the "loss" referred to is usually that in respect of which a claim is made against the primary insurer. In the case of an event causing instantaneous injury or death, such as the airliner crash in *Balfour v. Beaumont*, the loss and the event which causes it are for practical purposes simultaneous, and indeed the court appears to have treated the crash as the loss in question. That would not be appropriate in a case in which, for instance, a defect is incorporated in a product during manufacture and a loss is thereby caused months or even years later, and the distinction will be very relevant in determining whether a loss has occurred within the period of cover. Some treaties, indeed, are written on an "events occurring" basis, whereby it is the event which must occur within the policy period to attract the reinsurance cover. In some excess of loss reinsurance covers written by reference to the reinsured's ultimate net loss, the distinction between a loss and the event causing it is obscured by the use of a clause defining "event" in terms of the losses arising out of an occurrence, or series of occurrences, arising out of one event. In view of these ambiguities in the use of "loss" and "event", it may be hoped that reinsurers' liability will come to be defined by reference to claims made against the reinsured within a particular period, as is the case in primary professional indemnity cover.[25] It has been emphasised that where reinsurance cover is written on a "losses occurring" basis, the stated period of time is of fundamental importance, and that the reinsured must be able to establish that the relevant loss fell within the relevant period.[26]

33–66 "Event" clauses and aggregation. The definition of an "event", or similar criterion for the aggregation of losses, is relevant not only to the period of cover but also to clauses dealing with the aggregates or limits which trigger or circumscribe the provision of indemnity under the reinsurance contract. The problems which can arise in relation to such clauses are illustrated by *Caudle v. Sharp*.[27] The definition of loss in the reinsurance contract included a series of occurrences arising out of one event. Claims arose relating to negligent underwriting of a large number of reinsurance contracts. Clarke J. held, affirming an award of arbitrators, that the relevant "event" was the underwriter's failure to inform himself properly as to the nature of the risks involved, and not the subsequent making of each contract. The Court of Appeal rejected this approach. It held that, in order for a series of losses to arise from one event, it is necessary to identify a common factor which can properly be regarded as an "event", which both causes the losses and is not too remote from them. The underwriter's state of ignorance was not an "event" in this sense. The scope of permissible aggregation depends on the breadth of the language used in the particular contract. Thus in *Axa*

---

[24] *Balfour v. Beaumont* [1984] 1 Lloyd's Rep. 272, affirming [1982] 2 Lloyd's Rep. 493.

[25] In *Caudle v. Sharp* [1995] L.R.L.R. 433 an issue arose as to which terms governed the extension of cover under a reinsurance contract. Evans L.J. expressed the view, *obiter*, that a "claims made" clause was the relevant provision, in the case of an underlying professional indemnity risk. The clause extended cover to all loss arising from claims made in the policy period. It did not extend cover to separate claims made outside the period.

[26] *Municipal Mutual Ins. Ltd v. Sea Ins. Co. Ltd* [1998] Lloyd's Rep. I.R. 421, 436.

[27] [1995] L.R.L.R. 433.

Reinsurance (U.K.) Plc v. Field[28] the House of Lords held that an "originating cause" was a much wider unifying factor for the purpose of aggregation than an "event", and cautioned against an assumption that aggregation would operate in the same way in a contract of original insurance and an excess of loss reinsurance contract. It seems that (absent contrary indications in the contract) an "occurrence" is, for the purposes of aggregation, not materially different from an "event".[29] Where an assured was held liable to pay damages for damage inflicted on property over several months by vandals, owing to lax security, this was compensation paid "in respect of all occurrences of a series consequent to one original cause".[30] In *Brown v. GIO Insurance Ltd*[31] the terms of the reinsurance gave the reinsured the power to decide what constituted an event. It was held that the reinsured could reasonably treat the overall underwriting of an underwriter, caused by his negligent approach, as an "event". The Court of Appeal treated *Axa* as deciding that an "originating cause" is not necessarily an "event", but not as deciding that they could never be the same thing for the purpose of aggregation. Thus, the meaning of a term such as "occurrence" must be derived from the surrounding terms of the policy, and the object of the transaction. There is a presumption in proportional reinsurance that aggregation clauses are likely to be intended to operate in a similar manner at each level of cover (absent clear wording to the contrary). Applying this presumption, it was held in *Mann v. Lexington Ins. Co.*[32] that losses due to riots occurring at different locations and different times constituted more than one occurrence for the purpose of aggregation.

33–67 Aggregate Extension Clause. This form of clause is used particularly in reinsurances of liability and professional indemnity insurances. In *Denby v. English and Scottish Maritime Ins. Co. Ltd*[33] its primary purpose was expressed to be the provision of effective reinsurance where the reinsured is covering aggregated losses exceeding certain limits. It was held that the particular clause only operated if the primary cover was provided on an aggregate basis. It was not enough that there was an aggregate retention or excess in the primary cover. The fact that an excess and limit on recovery was imposed on every loss or claim demonstrated that the primary cover was not provided on an aggregate basis. The decision highlights the difficulties which can arise in attempting to construe the labyrinthine wording of many aggregate extension clauses.

---

[28] [1996] 1 W.L.R. 1026. The decision in this case related to a narrowly defined preliminary issue, which precluded consideration of broader issues by the House of Lords (*ibid.* at 1033, *per* Lord Mustill).

[29] *Kuwait Airways Corp. v. Kuwait Ins. Co. S.A.K.* [1996] 1 Lloyd's Rep. 664. In *American Centennial Ins. Co. v. INSCO Ltd* [1996] L.R.L.R 407 an event or occurrence which "affects" more than one policy was held to mean one which gives rise to a liability under more than one policy.

[30] *Municipal Mutual Ins. Ltd v. Sea Ins. Co.* [1996] L.R.L.R. 265, 271. This aspect of the decision was upheld in the Court of Appeal: [1998] Lloyd's Rep. I.R. 421 at 433–434.

[31] [1998] Lloyd's Rep. I.R. 201.

[32] [2001] Lloyd's Rep. I. R. 179. Contrast *Lloyds TSB v. Lloyds Bank Group Ins. Co. Ltd* [2001] Lloyd's Rep. I. R. 237; decision upheld but with different reasoning by the Court of Appeal [2002] 1 All E.R. (Comm.) 42: an underlying management failure to train staff justified the aggregation of pension mis-selling claims as a related series of acts or omissions.

[33] [1998] Lloyd's Rep. I.R. 343, 359. For further discussion of this type of clause, and the decision in *Denby*, see Butler, "The use of aggregate extension clauses in excess of loss reinsurance agreements" [1999] LMCLQ 380.

33–68 Implied terms—retention. In *Phoenix General Insurance Co. v. Halvanon Insurance Co.*[34] it was submitted that a term should be implied into a facultative/obligatory aviation reinsurance treaty that the reinsured should retain a certain retention for its own account. The submission was rejected. The court remarked that retentions were invariably the subject of express provision, and there was nothing inconsistent between the idea of reinsurance and a nil retention. By leaving blank the space provided in the "full reinsurance clause"[35] for the insertion of an agreed retention percentage, the parties had demonstrated an intention not to insist on a retention. It would appear that if a reinsurer wishes to have the benefit of a retention warranty, he will be expected to insert a clear stipulation into the contract.[36]

33–69 Implied term—exercise of reasonable care and skill. In *Phoenix General Insurance Co. v. Halvanon Insurance Co.* the court accepted that the facultative/obligatory nature of the treaty necessitated the implication of a term obliging the reinsured to conduct its business with reasonable care and skill, and adopted with some modifications a formulation of the term pleaded by the reinsurers in their amended points of defence.[37] This obliged the reinsured:

(a) to keep full and proper records and accounts of all risks accepted, and premiums and claims arising from them;
(b) to investigate all claims and confirm they were within the cover and properly payable before accepting them;
(c) to investigate properly all risks offered to them;
(d) to keep full and accurate accounts to show the accounting position under the treaty;
(e) to ensure the prompt collection of premiums and the prompt payment of premiums to the reinsurers; and
(f) to obtain, file or otherwise properly keep all the relevant documentation and make it reasonably available to the reinsurers.

This represents a significant and useful development in reinsurance law. Item (b) should apply wherever there is a "follow the settlements" clause,[38] and items (a), (d), (e) and (f) must be appropriate to most treaty relationships. Item (c) should apply to any treaty in which the reinsurer has bound himself to take business as ceded to him, and there is little or no restriction on the selection of cessions by the reinsured. The term was held to be innominate, so that the consequences of a breach must depend upon the nature and gravity of the breach itself.

33–70 Reinsurance accounting. Parties to reinsurance contracts will frequently adopt accounting procedures intended to minimise the burden of

---

[34] [1985] 2 Lloyd's Rep. 599; [1986] 2 Lloyd's Rep. 552, 573–574.
[35] This is a standard composite clause containing three separate elements, (i) a "terms as original" clause, (ii) a "follow-the-settlements" clause, and (iii) a retention stipulation. As to whether the last of these would be a warranty, see *Great Atlantic Ins. Co. v. Home Ins. Co.* [1981] 2 Lloyd's Rep. 219.
[36] *Iron Trades Mutual v. Compania de Seguros Imperio* [1991] 1 Re. L.R. 213. For further discussion of retention see paras. 33–12 and 33–35, *ante*.
[37] [1985] 2 Lloyd's Rep. 599, 613–614, not contested on appeal at [1986] 2 Lloyd's Rep. 552.
[38] See para. 33–82, *post*.

dealing with premium and claims. It is not intended in this chapter to discuss such procedures in detail, but a number of aspects of reinsurance accounting have been considered by the English courts. Where the contract provides for premium and claims to be settled on account, a reinsured may be able to "pay" premium by rendering an account showing claims in excess of premium.[39] A premium payment warranty will enable the reinsurer to terminate the contract in the event of late payment, but the parties' dealings with regard to accounting may involve an election in which the right is lost.[40] Commonly, particularly in quota share treaty reinsurance, the reinsurer allows the reinsured to retain a percentage of premium, referred to as "overriding commission" or "overrider". Ordinarily the reinsured incurs no obligation to the reinsurer as to use of overriding commission.[41] The parties may agree upon a mechanism to provide security for the payment of claims, such as the issue of letters of credit in favour of the reinsured. Funds paid by the reinsured in connection with such a mechanism may become subject to a trust in favour of the reinsured.[42]

33–71 Whilst brokers commonly account on a net basis, a broker's principal is (absent contrary agreement) entitled to require payments to be made to it on a gross basis.[43] Difficulties may arise where a broker "funds" claims or premium, *i.e.* pays out sums prior to their receipt from the reinsurer or the reinsured. It is necessary to consider the circumstances in each case in order to ascertain if the receipt of third-party funding has any impact on the reinsured's right to an indemnity from the reinsurer. It will not do so if the payment is voluntary, not relating to a legal liability in respect of the insured loss, and not made in order to diminish the insured loss.[44]

33–72 It is quite common for contracts to contain specific terms regarding the timing of provision of accounting documents and the effecting of payment; in the absence of such terms the relevant obligations will have to be performed in a reasonable time, defined by reference to the circumstances of the particular case.[45] However, delays in reinsurance accounting are common, and in such circumstances it will be difficult to infer an intention to repudiate a contract merely from delay in payment of balances.[46] Delays complicate the task of collection of claims. The broker

---

[39] *Cia Tirrena v. Grand Union Ins. Co.* [1991] 2 Lloyd's Rep. 143.
[40] *ibid.*
[41] *Kingscroft v. Nissan Fire and Marine Ins. Co. (No.2)* [1999] Lloyd's Rep. I. R. 603, 633–634.
[42] *Hurst Bannister v. New Cap Reins. Co* [2000] Lloyd's Rep. I. R. 166.
[43] *AA Mutual Ins. Co. Ltd v. Bradstock Blunt & Crawley* [1996] L.R.L.R. 161.
[44] *Merrett v. Capitol Indemnity Corp.* [1991] 1 Lloyd's Rep. 169 (funded payments by the broker in respect of claims held not to have been made in diminution of the loss arising from the reinsurance). *Cf. Colonia Versicherung AG v. Amoco Oil Co. ("The Wind Star")* [1997] 1 Lloyd's Rep. 261. If the broker makes a payment of premium which is not authorised by the reassured, and in respect of which he is not personally liable, the reassured's liability in respect of premium is not discharged: *Pacific & General (in liquidation) v. Hazell and Minet* [1997] L.R.L.R. 65, 79–81.
[45] *Phoenix General Ins. Co. v. Halvanon Ins. Co.* [1985] 2 Lloyd's Rep. 599, 614–615, where the system of issuing closings and effecting settlement is explained. Absent specific wording to the contrary, the cause of action for an indemnity under a reinsurance contract is not postponed pending the rendering of an account: *Halvanon Ins. Co. v. Comp. de Seguros do Estado de Sao Paolo* [1995] L.R.L.R. 303, 306.
[46] *Fenton Ins. Co. v. Gothaer* [1991] 1 Lloyd's Rep. 172; *Figre Ltd v. Mander* [1999] Lloyd's Rep. I. R. 193. But if the reassured clearly refuses to pay, repudiation can be inferred: *Pacific & General (in liquidation) v. Hazell and Minet* [1997] L.R.L.R. 65.

will generally owe a duty to the reinsured to exercise reasonable skill and care in the collection of claims. This will include a duty to maintain records for as long as a claim could reasonably be regarded as possible.[47] As a means of settling and simplifying accounting issues, reinsureds and reinsurers sometimes enter into "commutation agreements", particularly in relation to old accounts or when one party is in run-off. Such agreements generally release the parties from accrued and future liabilities in consideration of the payment of agreed sums. A suitably-drafted agreement can, in the event of default, permit the parties either to enforce its obligations, or to enforce the underlying obligations arising from the reinsurance.[48]

33–73 Termination: NCAD. Some reinsurance contracts are expressed to be permanent in duration and have no express provision for cancellation. Underwriters sometimes qualify their signature of such contracts with the abbreviation "NCAD", meaning "notice of cancellation at anniversary date", or they may give "provisional" notice of cancellation. Such qualifications have given rise to disputes as to their precise effect.[49] The general intention is often to provide the underwriter with an opportunity to review the operation of the contract prior to its anniversary date, but, in the absence of contrary agreement, if the underwriter purports to give notice of cancellation, one would expect the notice to take effect by terminating the contract at the relevant anniversary date.[50] Where "120 days NCAD" was used in a contract with a fixed duration, it was held that the contract took effect for the fixed period with a renewal to occur in the absence of a timely notice of cancellation.[51]

33–74 Claims—timing and extent of reinsurers' liability: when right to indemnity arises. A contract of reinsurance is a contract of indemnity,[52] the object of which is to indemnify the reinsured against loss. Unless a contrary provision is made in the contract, the ordinary rule applicable to contracts of indemnity since the Judicature Acts will govern the accrual of the reinsured's right to an indemnity, namely, that a loss is established once the liability of the person entitled to indemnity has been ascertained in legal proceedings or by admission or agreement.[53] Accordingly, the right of the reinsured to seek an indemnity arises once his own liability to his insured has been so ascertained and quantified.[54] It is not necessary (subject to specific

---

[47] *Johnston v. Leslie & Godwin* [1995] L.R.L.R. 472.

[48] *Korea Foreign Ins. Co. v. Omne Re S.A.* [1999] Lloyd's Rep. I. R. 509. In relation to reopening settlements generally, see *B.C.C.I v. Ali & Khan* [2001] 1 All E.R. 961.

[49] It is understood that Lloyd's has since 1988 sought to curb the use of "N.C.A.D." terms.

[50] *Kingscroft v. Nissan Fire and Marine Ins. Co. (No.2)* [1999] Lloyd's Rep. I. R. 603, 636–637

[51] *Commercial Union v. Sun Alliance* [1992] 1 Lloyd's Rep. 475.

[52] *Versicherungs und Transport Aktiengesellschaft Davgava v. Henderson* (1934) 39 Com.Cas. 312, 316–317; *British Dominions General Ins. Co. Ltd v. Duder* [1915] 2 K.B. 394, 401, 405, 410; *Merrett v. Capitol Indemnity Corp.* [1991] 1 Lloyd's Rep. 169, 171.

[53] *County & District Properties Ltd v. C. Jenner & Son Ltd* [1976] 2 Lloyd's Rep. 728; *R. & H. Green & Silley Weir Ltd v. British Railways Board* [1985] 1 W.L.R. 570; *Telfair Shipping Corp. v. Intersea SA* [1985] 1 W.L.R. 553, 568.

[54] *Versicherungs und Transport Aktiengesellschaft Daugava v. Henderson* (1934) 39 Com.Cas. 312. The reinsured may be able to obtain an interim payment although the reinsurers' liability is being appealed, at any rate where quantum is not disputed—*Halvanon Ins. Co. v. Central Reinsurance Corp.* [1984] 2 Lloyd's Rep. 420. On the running of limitation periods, see *Baker v. Black Sea & Baltic Gen. Ins. Co.* [1995] L.R.L.R. 261, 286, affirmed on different grounds [1996] L.R.L.R. 353 (C.A.); [1998] Lloyd's Rep. I. R. 327, (H.L.); *Halvanon Ins. Co. v. Comp. de Seguros do Estado de Sao Paolo* [1995] L.R.L.R. 303, 306.

terms discussed below) that he shall have paid the insured.[55] Nor does a right to indemnity arise on the occurrence of an insured peril under the primary insurance.[56]

33–75 Liability of reinsurer co-extensive with liability of reinsured.[57] The key to the extent of the reinsurer's liability is that the contract of reinsurance is one of indemnity against specified liabilities of the reinsured. Consequently, in the absence of special provisions, the reinsured is not entitled to recover more than the amount for which he has compromised his liability to the insured, or else he would profit from the indemnity.[58] Another consequence is that, in the absence of a specific clause concerning recovery of costs, the reinsured has no entitlement to recover the costs incurred by him in defeating a claim brought by the insured, since there is no liability towards the insured to form the subject matter of an indemnity.[59] In the event of the reinsured compromising the insured's claim and then seeking an indemnity from the reinsurer, the latter is entitled to refuse to pay if he demonstrates that the reinsured was under no liability to make an payment, whether or not payment has been made.[60] If he fails to establish that there was no liability, he may defend the reinsured's claim on the ground that the quantum of the settlement was unreasonably large,[61] presumably because, if this is so, the reinsured's loss does not reflect the true measure of his liability to the insured. These general principles are subject to qualifications, as discussed below.

33–76 Where the reinsurance provides world-wide cover, the liability of

---

[55] *Re Eddystone Marine Ins. Co.* [1892] 2 Ch. 423; *Re Law Guarantee Trust and Accident Soc. Ltd* [1914] 2 Ch. 617; *Re Same, Godson's Claim* [1915] 1 Ch. 340. Dicta of Bateson J. in *Firemen's Fund Ins. Co. v. Western Australian Ins. Co. Ltd* (1928) 138 L.T. 108, 112, to the contrary effect cannot stand with these decisions. Similarly, in *North Atlantic Ins. Co. Ltd v. Bishopsgate Ins. Ltd* [1998] 1 Lloyd's Rep. 459, in an excess of loss reinsurance, the reaching of the excess point was determined by reference to the date that the reinsured's liability to pay over the excess was established. A provision for the excess to increase if net premium received by the reinsured increased did not postpone the reinsurer's liability to the reinsured. See further discussion in paras. 33–79 to 33–80, *ante*.

[56] *Versicherungs und Transport Aktiengesellschaft Davgava v. Henderson* (1934) 39 Com.Cas. 312.

[57] This paragraph was cited with approval in *Baker v. Black Sea & Baltic Gen. Ins. Co.* [1995] L.R.L.R. 261, 281; affirmed by C.A.: [1996] L.R.L.R. 353. It was also cited with approval by the House of Lords: [1998] Lloyd's Rep. I.R. 327 at 337. A provision that the liability of the reinsurer is to follow that of the reassured may prevent the reassured from aggregating claims for which he is severally liable—*American Centennial Ins. Co. v. INSCO* [1996] L.R.L.R. 407, 412.

[58] *British Dominions General Ins. Co. Ltd v. Duder* [1915] 2 K.B. 394.

[59] *Scottish Metropolitan Assurance Co. v. Groom* (1924) 20 Ll.L.R. 44, affirming (1924) 19 Ll.L.R. 131. See para. 33–78, *post*.

[60] *Re London County Commercial Reinsurance Office* [1922] 2 Ch. 67, 80, where the reinsured had paid under "honour" policies without legal liability. This is consistent with decisions concerning the recovery of settlement monies by way of damages for breach of contract—*Kiddle v. Lovett* (1885) 16 Q.B.D. 605; *Biggin & Co. Ltd v. Permanite Ltd* [1951] 2 K.B. 314. The onus of proving the absence of liability is on the defendant, alleging, for instance, that the loss was not caused by a peril insured against—*Traders & General Ins. Assoc. v. Bankers & General Ins. Co.* (1921) 9 Ll.L.R. 223, 224, applying these principles to a claim by a retrocedant.

[61] *Traders & General Ins. Assoc. v. Bankers & General Ins. Co.* (1921) 9 Ll.L. Rep. 223. See also *Hong Kong Borneo Services Co. v. Pilcher* [1992] 2 Lloyd's Rep. 593, 598 (not a reinsurance case) and *Toomey v. Eagle Star Ins. Co.* [1993] 1 Lloyd's Rep. 429, 441–442 (where this paragraph was cited with approval, but in the context of a construction of the contract which did not arise on the approach adopted by the Court of Appeal: [1994] 1 Lloyd's Rep. 516).

the reinsured may be determined by foreign courts applying the law applicable to the original insurance, which may differ from the law governing the reinsurance contract. It has been pointed out by the Court of Appeal in *Skandia International Corporation v. NRG Victory Reinsurance Ltd*[62] that an English Court will treat a judgment of the foreign court as to the reinsured's liability as binding, subject to certain qualifications. The qualifications are that:

(a) the foreign court was a court of competent jurisdiction;
(b) the judgment was not obtained in breach of an exclusive jurisdiction clause or similar provision;
(c) the reinsured took all proper defences, and
(d) the decision was not manifestly perverse.

In the *Skandia* Case, the reinsured had settled a claim brought in Texas, and sought to justify its reinsurance claim by reference to advice from a Texas attorney that a jury in Texas instinctively sympathetic to assureds, and directed by a judge without specialist knowledge of insurance law, would be most likely to find for the assured without giving proper consideration to the persuasive argument that the claim fell outside the cover. It was held by the Court of Appeal that the reassured failed to establish that it was liable to its assured. In the absence of a "follow settlements" clause, it was not enough for the reinsured to establish that the settlement was businesslike and reasonable. The reinsured had to demonstrate liability to the insured.

33–77 Qualification—liability of reinsured in addition to liability on policy. The principle that the liability of the reinsurer is co-extensive with that of the reinsured must yield to policy wording which specifies that the reinsured is to be indemnified against liability incurred under contracts of insurance subscribed by it, and which disentitles the reinsured from claiming an indemnity for sums which it has become liable to pay under the general law. For instance, it may be a characteristic of foreign jurisdictions that the insured is entitled to damages from the reinsured for tardiness in settling a claim[63] or in reinstating insured property damaged by fire.[64] Whether an indemnity could then be recovered from reinsurers would depend upon the width of the wording of the contract of reinsurance, and whether the maximum sum covered by the reinsurance was already exhausted by the claim for an indemnity for liability under the primary insurance itself. In *Insurance Company of Africa v. Scor (U.K.) Reinsurance Co. Ltd*[65] the reinsured sought to recover in respect of general damages of US$600,000 and costs of US$58,000 awarded to the insured by a Liberian court for delay in settling the insured's claim under a fire policy. The reinsurance policy contained no express cover for such a head of loss. The reinsured contended that a term was to be implied into the policy permitting recovery of losses sustained by it in consequence of the reinsurers' withholding approval of a

[62] [1998] Lloyd's Rep. I.R. 439.

[63] *Ins. Co. of Africa v. Scor (U.K.) Reins. Co. Ltd* [1985] 1 Lloyd's Rep. 312 (damages awarded by Liberian jury in favour of insured against primary insurer for failure to settle loss within a 60 day period provided in policy).

[64] *Davidson v. Guardian Royal Exchange* [1979] 1 Lloyd's Rep. 406 (award of damages by the Aberdeen Sheriff's Court upheld in the Court of Session for delay in procuring repairs to insured motorcar).

[65] [1985] 1 Lloyd's Rep. 312.

proposed settlement under a "claims co-operation clause". A majority of the Court of Appeal refused to imply such a term into the policy, on the grounds that it was inconsistent with the claims co-operation clause and the limit of indemnity contained in it.[66] The claim would have taken the indemnity beyond the policy limit.[67]

33–78 Costs. Many reinsurance policies contain express provisions governing the reinsurers' liability for costs incurred by, or awarded against, the reinsured. Where recovery of costs is made subject to particular conditions there can be no general right to recovery of costs in the event that these are not fulfilled.[68] In the absence of an express provision there is no indemnity for costs incurred in successfully resisting the insured claim.[69] When costs were incurred by a reinsured in compromising the assured's total loss claim at 66 per cent of the claim figure, the court directed an inquiry as to their amount on the assumption that these costs would be recoverable from reinsurers in addition to an indemnity against the compromised claim itself.[70] The Court of Appeal has refused to imply a term into a reinsurance policy that the reinsurer should indemnify the reinsured for all costs and expenses incurred in contesting the assured's claim after the reinsurer had declined to approve a payment to the assured under the primary insurance.[71]

33–79 Special provisions governing reinsurers' liability: "to pay as may be paid thereon". This clause was introduced with the intention that it should oblige a reinsurer to indemnify the reinsured against honest settlement of a bona fide claim, whether or not the reinsured was legally liable to pay it.[72] It was already described in 1914 as a clause usually found in marine reinsurance policies.[73] However, the original intention had been by then nullified by the construction placed upon the clause by Matthew J. in *Chippendale v. Holt*,[74] namely, that the reinsurer must pay only if there was

---

[66] Robert Goff and Fox L.JJ.; Stephenson L.J. dissenting on this point.

[67] Butler & Merkin, *Reinsurance Law*, suggest at para. C.1.6–08 that such an implied term might be upheld where (a) there was no claims co-operation clause and (b) the claim did not exceed the limit of indemnity. But there could remain a problem of inconsistency with an express promise of indemnity in more limited terms, and the risk that the reinsurer might find himself writing an unauthorised class of business as a result.

[68] *British General Ins. Co. Ltd v. Mountain* (1919) 1 Ll.L.R. 605.

[69] *Scottish Metropolitan Ass. Co. v. Groom* (1924) 20 Ll.L.R. 44, holding that there was no recovery under the marine sue and labour clause. In *Baker v. Black Sea & Baltic Gen. Ins. Co.* [1995] L.R.L.R. 261, 281–282, it was held that a "follow settlements and agreements" clause did not expand coverage to include such costs, affirmed: [1996] L.R.L.R. 353, 363, C.A. The House of Lords in *Baker*, [1998] Lloyd's Rep. I.R. 327, affirmed the decision that there was no basis for an implication by law as to an entitlement to costs, citing this paragraph (at 337). However, the case was remitted to the Commercial Court for consideration of whether the custom and practice of the market was for reinsurers to pay a proportion of costs.

[70] *British Dominions General Ins. Co. Ltd v. Duder* [1915] 2 K.B. 394. The report does not disclose whether the policy contained an express term permitting recovery of costs. Since there seems to have been no argument about it, the successful appellants may well have conceded the point in order to reinforce their submissions based upon the principle of indemnity.

[71] *Insurance Co. of Africa v. Scor (U.K.) Reins. Co. Ltd* [1985] 1 Lloyd's Rep. 312, discussed in the previous paragraph.

[72] *Gurney v. Grimmer* (1932) 38 Com.Cas. 7, 10, *per* Scrutton L.J., and 22–23 *per* Greer L.J. The history of the clause is recounted by Lord Hoffmann in *Charter Reins. Co. Ltd v. Fagan* [1997] A.C. 313 at 393.

[73] *British Dominions General Ins. Co. Ltd v. Duder* [1914] 3 K.B. 835, 839, *per* Bailhache J.; reversed [1915] 2 K.B. 394.

[74] (1895) 1 Com.Cas. 197.

legal liability, proved or admitted, of the reinsured to the assured. The effect of this interpretation was to give the reinsurer the right to take all the defences which were available to the reinsured,[75] and in subsequent cases reinsurers who had subscribed to reinsurance policies containing the clause were held entitled to rely upon defences to liability which they said had been available to the reinsured.[76] Where the reinsured has compromised his liability to the assured the reinsurer cannot dispute quantum unless the settlement was dishonest or was arrived at without the exercise of due diligence by the reinsured.[77] It is clear that the inclusion of the words "to pay as may be paid thereon" neither entitles the reinsured to recover for gratuitous payments to the assured nor to recover for losses for which he was liable on the original insurance but which lie outside the legal ambit of the reinsurance.[78]

33–80 Payment as a precondition to recovery by the reinsured. Under a "pay as may be paid thereon" clause actual payment by the reinsured to the assured is not a condition precedent to the liability of the reinsurer.[79] The question has arisen whether payment is a condition precedent in other forms of clause, for example a clause defining ultimate nett loss for the purpose of indemnification as "the sum actually paid by the reassured in settlement of losses or liability".[80] The question turns on the construction of the particular contract. A court is likely to lean against holding that the reinsurer's liability is a liability to indemnify only against actual payment by the reinsured, because this would deny an indemnity just when it is most likely to be needed, *i.e.* when the reinsured is insolvent, or would risk insolvency if prior payment was required. However, there is no reason why a payment

[75] *China Traders Ins. Co. v. Royal Exchange Ass. Corp.* [1898] 2 Q.B. 187, 191–192, *per* A. L. Smith and Chitty L.JJ. The court allowed an appeal from Mathew J. who, it seems, had not appreciated the ramifications of his decision in *Chippendale v. Holt* (1895) 1 Com.Cas. 197, and the decision is coincidentally an authoritative source for the history of the order for ship's papers.
[76] *St Paul Fire and Marine Ins. Co. v. Morice* (1906) 22 T.L.R. 449 (loss not caused by peril insured against); *Marten v. Steamship Owners' Underwriting Assoc.* (1902) 7 Com.Cas. 195 and *Western Ass. of Toronto v. Poole* [1903] 1 K.B. 376 (whether insured ship a constructive total loss); *Fireman's Fund Ins. Co. Ltd v. Western Australia Ins. Co. Ltd* (1927) 33 Com.Cas. 36 (breach of warranty of seaworthiness); *Merchants' Marine Ins. Co. v. Liverpool Marine and General Ins. Co. Ltd* (1928) 31 Ll.L.R. 45 (causation of loss).
[77] *Western Ass. Co. of Toronto v. Poole* [1903] 1 K.B. 376, 386, *per* Bigham J. In *Gurney v. Grimmer* (1932) 38 Com.Cas. 7, 12 Scrutton L.J. questioned this distinction between liability, which required proof, and quantum, which did not, but it is submitted that Bigham J. was doing no more than apply the ordinary law relating to settlements made by the reinsured—see para. 33–76. See also the comments by Robert Goff L.J. in *Ins. Co. of Africa v. Scor (U.K.) Reins. Co. Ltd* [1985] 1 Lloyd's Rep. 312, 329, and by Stephenson L.J. at 321, and the further comments of Scrutton L.J. in *Davgava v. Henderson* (1934) 39 Com. Cas. 312, 316.
[78] *Uzielli & Co. v. Boston Marine Ins. Co.* (1884) 15 Q.B.D. 11 might seem to contradict this proposition, but it is very doubtful whether this decision is of any authority on the clause in view of the criticisms by the Court of Appeal in the *Duder* case [1915] 2 K.B. 394, and the absence of express reliance on it in a majority of the judgments. It may be that concern at the odd outcome in Uzielli played some part in the development of ultimate net loss clauses in reinsurance contracts, but the historical background is not clear: *Charter Reins. Co. Ltd v. Fagan* [1997] A.C. 313, 393–394. In *Baker v. Black Sea & Baltic General Ins. Co* [1998] Lloyd's Rep. I.R. 327 Lord Lloyd of Berwick commented that *Uzielli* was difficult to understand.
[79] *Re Eddystone Marine Ins. Co.* [1892] 2 Ch. 423; *Re Law Guarantee Trust and Accident Soc.* [1914] 2 Ch. 617.
[80] *Home & Overseas Ins. Co. v. Mentor Ins. Co.* [1989] 1 Lloyd's Rep. 473; *Re A Company No. 0013734* [1992] 2 Lloyd's Rep. 415; *Charter Reins. Co. Ltd v. Fagan* [1997] A.C. 313.

precondition should not be imposed if the language used is sufficiently clear.[81] In *Charter Reinsurance Company Ltd v. Fagan*[82] the House of Lords considered the meaning of an ultimate nett loss clause which referred to "the sum actually paid" by the reinsured. It was held that these words did not impose a precondition of prior payment. They were intended, when analysed in their contractual context, to emphasise that the ultimate liability of reinsurers was to be ascertained by reference to the net liability of the reinsured. On this basis "paid" was construed as meaning "exposed to liability" and "actually" was construed as meaning "when finally ascertained". This construction was far from the ordinary meaning of the words used,[83] but was justified by reference to the specialised form of contract in which they appeared. The decision demonstrates how reluctant courts will be to impose a condition of prior payment in the absence of the clearest of language, and the need to construe reinsurance terms with regard to the overall commercial scheme of the contract.

33–81 "Arranged total loss." Where a facultative marine reinsurance was expressed to cover "total loss only and/or constructive total loss and/or arranged total loss", it was contended that the reinsured could recover for a claim settled artificially with the assured on the basis of a total loss even if in reality it was a partial loss.[84] Rowlatt J. dismissed the argument, and held that reinsurers were entitled to proof that there was a strongly arguable total loss. "Arranged" meant "compromised", not "deemed".[85] Where, however, the reinsurance was against "total constructive compromised and/or arranged total loss", the Court of Appeal held that the context gave the word "arranged" the meaning of "agreed", so that the reinsured was entitled to recover the amount of a genuine settlement of the assured's claims without proof of the occurrence of a constructive total loss.[86]

33–82 "Follow the settlements." This formulation has been used with the intention of obliging reinsurers to indemnify their reinsured against compromises of the assured's claim without proof of liability being required.[87] In *Excess Insurance Co. Ltd v. Matthews*[88] the clause obliged

---

[81] Thus, in the different context of Protection & Indemnity Club mutual insurance, prior payment has been held to operate as a condition precedent to recovery: *Firma C-Trade SA v. Newcastle P&I Assoc. ("The Fanti")* [1991] 2 A.C. 1.

[82] [1997] A.C. 313.

[83] *ibid.* at 386, *per* Lord Mustill. Contrast the interpretation of the same phrase in *The Equitable Fire & Accident Office v. Ching Ho Wong* [1907] A.C. 96.

[84] *Bergens Dampskibs Ass. Fovening v. Sun Ins. Office Ltd* (1930) 37 Ll.L.R. 175.

[85] Butler & Merkin, *Reinsurance Law*, para. C.1.2–12, suggests that the reinsured was required by the judgment to prove a constructive total loss after settlement of a claim so formulated, but it appears that the court contemplated that it would suffice if the claim had appeared to be a genuine total loss claim even if afterwards it was shown not to be—(1930) 37 Ll.L.R. 175, 177.

[86] *Gurney v. Grimmer* (1932) 38 Com.Cas. 7, also following *Street v. Royal Exchange Ass. Co.* (1914) 19 Com.Cas. 339 on the meaning of "compromise". Where a number of separate claims are settled in one transaction but it is not possible to say whether a particular claim has or has not been admitted, there is a compromise of each claim. Equally, if two claims are compromised together on the basis that claim one succeeds in full but claim two is appreciably discounted, there has been a compromise of both claims for the purpose of this wording—Scrutton L.J. at 15 and Greer L.J. at 21. Lawrence L.J. preferred to rest his decision upon "arranged".

[87] The genesis of the clause is noted by Lord Hoffmann in *Charter Reins. Co. Ltd v. Fagan* [1997] A.C. 313, at 393.

[88] (1925) 31 Com.Cas. 43.

reinsurers "to pay as may be paid thereon and to follow their settlements". Branson J. held that the words "to follow their settlements" bound the reinsurers to accept a compromise of both liability and quantum when reached between the reinsured and the assured so long as the compromise was neither dishonest nor made without due care and skill.

33–83 In *Insurance Company of Africa v. Scor (U.K.) Reinsurance Ltd* the reinsurance policy was expressed to be "a Reinsurance of and warranted same ... terms and conditions as and to follow the settlements of the Insurance Company of Africa". It was stated[89] that the effect of the follow settlements clause was to bind reinsurers to indemnify their reinsured in the event that the latter settle a claim by the assured, either by payment or a promise of payment, whether by reason of admission or compromise, provided that:

(a) the claim so accepted falls within the risks covered by the reinsurance policy as a matter of law and
(b) in settling the claim, the reinsured has acted honestly and has taken all proper and businesslike steps in making the settlement.

Consequently, provided that the reinsured has settled a claim acting honestly and in a proper and businesslike manner, subsequent proof that the assured's claim was fraudulent will not release reinsurers from their obligation to follow that settlement.[90]

33–84 A further complication arose in the *Scor* Case[91] by the inclusion in the policy of a "claims co-operation" clause providing that the reinsured would co-operate with the reinsurers in settling claims and that they would not reach a settlement without the prior approval of the reinsurers. A majority of the Court of Appeal held that the combined effect of these inconsistent clauses was to bind reinsurers to follow only such settlements by the reinsured as had been approved by them, whether the claim in question was settled in agreement or by adjudication.[92] Since the reinsurers had not approved the reinsured's satisfaction of a Liberian court judgment obtained against it by the assured, the reinsured was unable to rely upon the "follow settlements" provision, and had to prove its liability to the insured in the usual way, which it did successfully. Stephenson L.J. held,[93] following the decision of Leggatt J. in the Commercial Court,[94] that the reinsured was entitled to recover under the "follow settlements" clause either because the reinsurers were deemed to approve a settlement by judgment of the court or

[89] [1985] 1 Lloyd's Rep. 312, 330, *per* Robert Goff L.J. with whom Fox L.J. agreed at 334. Stephenson L.J. agreed with the second limb of the proviso, but did not mention the first. It is clear that the comments by Scrutton L.J. that a "follow settlements" clause added nothing to a "pay as may be paid" clause do not represent the law—*Sir William Garthwaite (Ins.) Ltd v. Port of Manchester Ins. Co. Ltd* (1930) 37 Ll.L.R. 194, 195; *Daugava v. Henderson* (1934) 39 Com.Cas. 312, 316, where Scrutton L.J. seems to have believed at *Western Ass. Co. of Toronto v. Poole* [1903] 1 K.B. 376 concerned a "follow settlements" clause, which it did not.
[90] [1985] 1 Lloyd's Rep. 312, 322, 330, 334.
[91] [1985] 1 Lloyd's Rep. 312.
[92] *Per* Robert Goff and Fox L.J.J. [1985] 1 Lloyd's Rep. 312, 330–331, 334.
[93] [1985] 1 Lloyd's Rep. 312, 323–324.
[94] [1983] 1 Lloyd's Rep. 541, 557.

because a settlement by adjudication fell outside the scope of the claims co-operation clause and did not require the reinsurers' approval.

33–85 The scope of the obligations arising from "follow settlements" clauses has been considered further since *Scor*. Absent contrary provision, the reinsured will bear the burden of establishing that it has made payment of the claim and that the claim falls within the risks covered by the policy.[95] The reinsured may act prudently in entering into a settlement but the reinsurer will nonetheless not be liable for payments in respect of claims outside the scope of the reinsurance contract.[96] The burden of establishing a breach of the obligation to take proper and businesslike steps in making a settlement ("the businesslike obligation") rests on the reinsurer.[97] It is likely to remain on the reinsurer in circumstances where the reinsured is in breach of an implied obligation to maintain proper records.[98] The information which the reinsurer is entitled to demand from the reinsured concerning a settlement will vary with the circumstances of each case; however, the reinsurer is likely to be entitled to information showing how the claim was dealt with, but not information as to the exact reasons underlying a settlement.[99] The reinsured does not satisfy the businesslike obligation merely by appointing competent loss adjusters or other agents; the reinsured is to be identified with such agents, who must themselves act in a businesslike way.[1]

33–86 The House of Lords considered the operation of "follow settlement" clauses in *Hill v. Mercantile and General Reinsurance Co. Plc*,[2] which was concerned with claims relating to aircraft lost or damaged as a result of the Iraqi invasion of Kuwait in August 1990. Provisional settlements were made as between the original assured and insurers,[3] and formed the basis for claims passed up a chain of reinsurances. The relevant reinsurance contract contained a "follow settlements" clause which expressly required settlements to be within the terms and conditions of original policies and to be within the terms and conditions of the reinsurance. The reinsured issued an application for summary judgment against reinsurers, contending that reinsurers were bound by the settlements. The House of Lords held that reinsurers had arguable defences to the claims. Two basic rules were

---

[95] *Charman v. Guardian Royal Exchange* [1992] 2 Lloyd's Rep. 607, 613.
[96] *Hiscox v. Outhwaite (No. 3)* [1991] 2 Lloyd's Rep. 524.
[97] *Charman v. Guardian Royal Exchange* [1992] 2 Lloyd's Rep. 607; *Baker v. Black Sea & Baltic Gen. Ins. Co.* [1995] L.R.L.R. 261; affirmed on other grounds: [1996] L.R.L.R. 353, CA; [1998] Lloyd's Rep. I. R. 327, HL.
[98] *Baker v. Black Sea & Baltic Gen. Ins. Co.* [1995] L.R.L.R. 261; affirmed on other grounds: [1996] L.R.L.R. 353, C.A.; [1998] Lloyd's Rep. I. R. 327, H.L.
[99] *Charman v. Guardian Royal Exchange* [1992] 2 Lloyd's Rep. 607, 614; *Baker v. Baltic Gen. Ins. Co.* [1995] L.R.L.R. 261, affirmed on other grounds: [1996] L.R.L.R. 353, C.A.; [1998] Lloyd's Rep. I. R. 327, H.L. In *Wurttemburgische v. Home Ins. Co.* [1993] 2 Re. L.R. 253 Evans J. pointed out that it was relevant to consider any inspection rights or course of dealing, and suggested in that case that it would be sufficient for the reinsured to produce documents such as claims records in proper form.
[1] *Charman v. Guardian Royal Exchange* [1992] 2 Lloyd's Rep. 607, 612; *Baker v. Black Sea & Baltic Gen. Ins. Co.* [1995] L.R.L.R. 261, affirmed on other grounds: [1996] L.R.L.R. 353; [1998] Lloyd's Rep. I. R. 327.
[2] [1996] 1 W.L.R. 1239.
[3] The remaining dispute between the original insured and insurers was dealt with in *Kuwait Airways Corp. v. Kuwait Ins. Co. S.A.K.* [1996] 1 Lloyd's Rep. 664. For the final determination of this aspect of the matter, see the judgment of the House of Lords: [1999] 1 Lloyd's Rep. 803.

identified: first, that the reinsurer cannot be held liable unless a loss falls within the cover of the policy reinsured and within the cover created by the reinsurance; secondly, that the parties are free to agree on ways of proving whether these requirements are satisfied.[4] Therefore it was unfruitful to rely on previous authorities (such as *Scor*) based on different clauses and different facts.[5] Under the terms of the particular clause reinsurers were not to be made liable for losses which properly fell outside the legal extent of the risks covered by the contract of reinsurance and the underlying, reinsured contract. The reinsurers were therefore entitled to raise defences as to the number and timing of losses, which were relevant to the periods and limits covered by the reinsurance. The House of Lords also pointed out that the relevant "settlement" had to be a settlement made by the reinsured (as opposed to parties further down the chain of contracts), and held that reinsurers had an arguable defence as to whether there had been any such settlement. The decision emphasises the importance of the construction of the particular clause in its commercial context, taking account of matters such as whether the reinsurance and underlying contract are on the same terms and whether the reinsurance stands at one or more remove from the direct insurance.[6]

33–87 "Follow the fortunes." Various types of "follow the fortunes" clause occur in reinsurance contracts, derived from treaty wordings. Such clauses are sometimes linked with provisions relating to errors and omissions; it should not be assumed that they are necessarily analogous to "follow settlements" clauses. In *Hayter v. Nelson*[7] Saville J. referred to uncertainty as to the effect of such clauses and was not prepared to decide on a summary basis that such a clause meant that a reinsurer is bound by all judgments or awards where the reinsured had taken reasonable steps to defend the proceedings.

33–88 Claims co-operation clause. In the *Scor* Case, the claims co-operation clause provided:

> "It is a condition precedent to liability that all claims be notified immediately to the Underwriters subscribing to this policy, and the Reassured hereby undertake in arriving at the settlement of any claim they will co-operate with the reassured Underwriters, and that no settlement shall be made without the approval of the Underwriters subscribing to this Policy."

It was held that such a clause imposed two distinct obligations on the reinsured. The first obligation was one to notify claims promptly, and compliance with that duty was a condition precedent to liability,[8] as indeed it often is in primary liability insurance policies.[9] The second obligation was to co-operate with the reinsurers in arranging to settle a claim by the insured. Fulfilment of that duty was not a condition precedent to liability.[10] Nor was the duty broken by a failure to co-operate with the reinsurers' investigations

[4] [1996] 1 W.L.R. 1239, 1251.
[5] *ibid.*, 1252.
[6] *ibid.* at 1251–1252.
[7] [1990] 2 Lloyd's Rep. 265, 272.
[8] [1983] 1 Lloyd's Rep. 541, 553.
[9] See Ch. 10 for general discussion of policy terms, and Ch. 19 for notice clauses.
[10] [1983] 1 Lloyd's Rep. 541, 553; [1985] 1 Lloyd's Rep. 312, 318, 326, 330.

into the conduct of the reinsured's own employees, as opposed to an investigation into the basis of the insured's claim.[11] Claims co-operation clauses can take a number of different forms: the parties to a reinsurance contract should take care to specify which is intended to apply.[12]

33–89 Since *Scor* some claims co-operation clauses have been drafted which expressly state that compliance is a condition precedent to liability. In *Gan Insurance Co. Ltd. v. Tai Ping Insurance Co. Ltd. (2 & 3)*[13] the clause provided that "it is a condition precedent to any liability under this policy" that:

(a) the reinsured should give notice of circumstances which might give rise to a claim;
(b) the reinsured should co-operate with reinsurers in the investigation of losses, and
(c) "no settlement and/or compromise shall be made and liability admitted without the prior approval of Reinsurers".

In the Court of Appeal the obligation under (c) was construed disjunctively as meaning that the reinsurers' prior approval was required both prior to entry into settlements and prior to the making of admissions. It was held that the clause meant what it said: compliance was a condition precedent to any recovery under the policy. The reinsured could not, therefore, make a settlement without reinsurers' approval and then seek to recover on the basis that it had in fact been liable to the insured. This result effectively nullifies the "follow settlements" obligation when the reinsurer's consent to the settlement is not obtained. The Court of Appeal held that there was no implied term that the reinsurers could not withhold approval of a settlement unless there were reasonable grounds to do so. However, it was held by a majority in the Court of Appeal that any withholding of approval had to take place in good faith, on the basis of facts relevant to the claim, and not by reference to wholly extraneous considerations.[14]

33–90 Claims control clause.[15] The claims co-operation clause is to be distinguished from a claims control clause. An example of the latter was given in the *Scor* Case as follows:[16]

"It is a condition precedent to any liability under this Policy that the Reinsured shall furnish the Underwriters with all the information available respecting such loss or losses, and the Underwriters shall have the right to appoint adjusters, assessors and/or surveyors and to control

[11] [1983] 1 Lloyd's Rep. 541, 553; [1985] 1 Lloyd's Rep. 312, 318, 326, 330.
[12] *Trans-Pacific Ins. Co. v. Grand Union Ins. Co.* (1989) 18 N.S.W.L.R. 675 where it was impossible to determine which specific clause was intended by an unadorned reference to "claims co-operation clause" in a slip.
[13] [2001] Lloyd's Rep. I. R. 667.
[14] Staughton LJ did not adopt this reasoning, and expressed doubts about the implication of any such term. It remains to be seen if the qualification of reinsurers' right to withhold approval will have any practical significance.
[15] This paragraph was referred to in *CNA International Reinsurance Co. v. Companhia de Seguros Tranquilidade SA* [1999] Lloyd's Rep. I.R. 289 at 303.
[16] [1983] 1 Lloyd's Rep. 541, 553.

all negotiations, adjustments and settlements in connection with such loss or losses."

The claims control clause, as its name implies, is directed at giving reinsurers the right to handle and investigate claims made on the reinsured. While the clause appears not to make the cession of control over claims to the reinsurer an express condition precedent to liability, there is little doubt that the reinsured could not invoke a "follow settlements" clause in the same policy if it had refused to surrender control over a settlement to the reinsurers when requested.[17] If the reinsured was to pay a claim in defiance of the reinsurers, presumably the reinsured could recover an indemnity upon proof of its liability to the insured, but it would be liable in damages for such loss, if any, as had been caused to the reinsurer by its breach of contract. It cannot have been intended that the reinsurers could exercise their right of control unreasonably and to the prejudice of the reinsured, and yet escape paying an indemnity against a valid claim.[18]

33–91 Claims—procedure and disputes: duties of reinsured. The reinsured who wishes to make a claim on the reinsurance contract must comply with such provisions of the contract as prescribe the procedure for bringing claims. It has already been seen that express clauses in the contract may require notice of the insured's claim to be given within certain time limits, and that the reinsured may have to accept supervision by, or consultation with, reinsurers under claims control or claim co-operation clauses. The contract may also require claims to be collected through particular intermediaries. Where a policy provided "All claims to be collected through C.D.L. Ltd", it was held that these words constituted notice to the insurer that C.D.L. were authorised to collect claims, in cash and not in account.[19] A reinsurer and reinsured are likely to have a common interest in the investigation of claims. The community of interest may create common interest privilege for documents dealing with legal advice or litigation.[20]

33–92 The reinsured is obliged, like any insured, to put forward his claim honestly and truthfully. Fraud in the making of a claim will cause the reinsured to forfeit the claim and all benefit under the policy.[21]

33–93 Inspection rights. Reinsurance contracts commonly contain clauses permitting the reinsurer to inspect documents of the reinsured. The reinsured is not (absent contrary provision in the contract) entitled to refuse

---

[17] *Forsikrings Vesta v. Butcher* [1986] 2 Lloyd's Rep. 179, 187, affirmed in C.A.: [1988] 1 Lloyd's Rep. 19. This aspect was not dealt with in detail in the speeches of the House of Lords: [1989] 1 A.C. 852. Lord Templeman expressed disapproval of "insurance jargon" on the point (at 892).
[18] *Forsikrings. Vesta v. Butcher* [1986] 2 Lloyd's Rep. 179, 184, 187–188, in which the claims control clause was in a shorter form than that cited above, and was construed not to be a warranty by Hobhouse J.
[19] *Stolos Cia. SA v. Ajax Insurance Co. Ltd* [1981] 1 Lloyd's Rep. 9; *Cantieri Navali Riuniti SpA v. N.V. Omne Justitia* [1985] 2 Lloyd's Rep. 428, 436.
[20] *Svenska Handelsbanken v. Sun Alliance & London Ins. plc.* [1995] 1 Lloyd's Rep. 84. But the community of interest may not survive avoidance of the reinsurance contract by the reinsurer: *Commercial Union Ass. Co. v. Mander* [1996] 2 Lloyd's Rep. 640.
[21] For detailed discussion of the developing law as to fraudulent claims, see paras 19–54 to 19–65, *ante*. The consequences depend upon the inclusion and wording of any forfeiture clause in the contract.

inspection until after outstanding claims have been paid by the reinsurer.[22] A court will, however, be wary of a tactical request for inspection, made in response to an application by the reinsured for summary judgment. It may be prepared to stay the application so as to permit inspection if the background circumstances indicate that the request is made reasonably, on substantial grounds.[23] The exercise of a contractual right of inspection may result in affirmation of the reinsurance contract;[24] this result will follow if the inspection involves the assertion of a contractual right and amounts to unequivocal conduct consistent only with an intention not to treat the contract as at an end.[25]

33–94 Arbitration clauses. Reinsurance agreements very often provide for resolution of disputed claims by arbitration.[26] It has long been customary for parties to reinsurance agreements to insert wording to the effect that the arbitrators are not to be bound by strict rules of law but are at liberty to resolve disputes referred to them according to equitable principles and interpretation.[27] Sometimes it is provided that the reinsurance is to be interpreted as an honourable engagement or agreement, as opposed to a legal obligation.[28] The English courts have on one occasion held that an arbitration clause in these terms is unenforceable and invalid,[29] but the tendency was to construe them as merely permitting to the arbitrators a certain latitude to depart from "technical" or "strict" rules of law or construction.[30] It was uncertain how wide this freedom extended, but it must be right that such clauses did not confer a general power to come to "a fair result" by departing from fundamental rules of law or from the express words of the agreement.[31] Section 46 of the Arbitration Act 1996[32] provides that an arbitral tribunal may decide a dispute either in accordance with the law chosen by the parties or, if the parties so agree, in accordance with such other considerations as are agreed by them or determined by the tribunal. The validity of honourable engagement clauses has thus been given implicit statutory recognition. When a claim is pursued either by arbitration or by

---

[22] *Re A Company Nos. 008725/91 and 00872/91* [1991] 1 Re. L.R. 288.

[23] No stay was granted in *Trinity Ins. Co. v. Overseas Union Ins. Ltd* [1996] L.R.L.R. 156, nor in *Aetna Reins. Co. (U.K.) Ltd v. Central Reins. Corp. Ltd* [1996] L.R.L.R. 165. A stay was granted in *Pacific & General Ins. Co. Ltd v. Baltica Ins. Co. Ltd* [1996] L.R.L.R. 8.

[24] *Iron Trades Mutual v. Compania de Seguros Imperio* [1991] 1 Re. L.R. 213.

[25] *Pan Atlantic Ins. Co. v. Pine Top Ins. Co.* [1992] 1 Lloyd's Rep. 101, 106–108. This point was not pursued on appeal: [1993] 1 Lloyd's Rep. 496, C.A.; [1995] 1 A.C. 501, H.L.

[26] Where the reinsurance agreement is made on behalf of a Lloyd's syndicate, individual names are not treated separately for the purpose of appointment of an arbitrator and implementation of the arbitration clause: *Hume v. AA Mutual International Ins. Co. Ltd* [1996] L.R.L.R. 19.

[27] *Maritime Ins. Co. v. Assecuranz Union von 1865* (1935) 52 Ll.L. Rep. 16; *Orion Cia Espanola de Seguros v. Belfort Maatshappij Voor Algemena Verzekringeen* [1962] 2 Lloyd's Rep. 257.

[28] *Home Insurance Co. v. Administratia Asigurarilor de Stat* [1983] 2 Lloyd's Rep. 674.

[29] *Orion Cia. Espanola de Seguros v. Belfort* [1962] 2 Lloyd's Rep. 257.

[30] *Eagle Star Ins. Co. v. Yuval* [1978] 1 Lloyd's Rep. 357; *Home Insurance Co. v. ADAS* [1983] 2 Lloyd's Rep. 674; *American Centennial Ins. Co. v. INSCO Ltd* [1996] L.R.L.R. 407, 410.

[31] Mustill & Boyd, *Commercial Arbitration* (2nd ed., 1989), pp. 74–86; *American Centennial Ins. Co. v. INSCO Ltd* [1996] L.R.L.R. 407.

[32] 1996 c. 23. In Scotland the UNCITRAL Model Law on International Commercial Arbitration applies: Law Reform (Miscellaneous Provisions) (Scotland) Act 1990 (c. 40), s.66 and Sch. 7.

litigation in England, the reinsured will be entitled to an award of interest upon sums paid prior to judgment, even where the claim is paid in full after issue of a writ, provided that the money is not accepted in full and final settlement.[33]

33–95 Reinsurance contracts frequently contain terms designed to ensure that arbitrators have commercial experience. A stipulation requiring an arbitrator to be an executive official of an insurance or reinsurance company has been held to be directed to the time of appointment; retirement from an executive post after appointment did not render the arbitrator ineligible.[34] Once an arbitration award has been made, one party may wish to disclose it to others, particularly in circumstances of complex reinsurance disputes. The obligation of confidentiality in respect of the arbitration proceedings will be qualified so as to permit such disclosure if it is reasonably necessary for the establishment or protection of an arbitrating party's rights against a third party.[35]

33–96 Jurisdiction.[36] Council Regulation 44/2001,[37] the EC Regulation which allocates jurisdiction between Member States (with the exception of Denmark), does not apply to matters concerning arbitration,[38] and so is inapplicable to the many reinsurance contracts which provide for disputes to be arbitrated. Section 3 of the Regulation, which sets out special jurisdictional rules for insurance, does not apply to reinsurance.[39] In other respects reinsurance disputes will be subject to the provisions of the Regulation.[40]

33–97 Contracts (Applicable Law) Act 1990.[41] Article 1(3) of the Rome Convention (set out in Schedule 1 of the 1990 Act) provides that the rules of the Convention do not apply to contracts of insurance which cover risks situated in the territories of Member States. This exclusion does not, however, apply to contracts of reinsurance. Thus the uniform rules in the

---

[33] *Edmunds v. Lloyd Italico & L'Ancora Compagnia di Assicurazioni SpA* [1986] 1 Lloyd's Rep. 326. For discussion of principles relating to the award of interest generally, see paras 19–61 to 19–63, *ante*.

[34] *Pan Atlantic Ins. Co. v. Hassneh* [1992] 2 Lloyd's Rep. 120.

[35] *Hassneh v. Mew* [1993] 2 Lloyd's Rep. 243.

[36] For detailed discussion of this topic, see Ch. 13, *ante*.

[37] [2001] O.J. L12/1, 16.1.2001. It came into force on 1 March 2001. Consequential legislative changes were effected by the Civil Jurisdiction and Judgments Order 2001 (S.I. 2001 No. 3929). Procedural changes were effected by the Civil Procedure (Amendment No.5) Rules 2001, (S.I. 2001 No. 4015).

[38] Art. 1(2)(d) of the Regulation. For the scope of the arbitration exclusion, see *The Atlantic Emperor (No. 2)* [1992] 1 Lloyd's Rep. 624; *Part. M/S Heidberg v. Grovesnor Grain & Feed Co. Ltd* [1994] 2 Lloyd's Rep. 287; *Toepfer International GmbH v. Molino Boschi* [1996] 1 Lloyd's Rep. 510; *Toepfer International GmbH v. Soc. Cargill France* [1997] 2 Lloyd's Rep. 98.

[39] Schlosser Report, O.J. vol. 22, No. C 59/117, para. 151.3; Case C-412/98, *Group Josi Reins. Co. S.A. v. Universal General Ins. Co.* [2001] Lloyd's Rep. I. R. 483. See also: *Arkwright Mutual v. Bryanston Inc. Ltd* [1990] 2 Q.B. 649; *Overseas Union Ltd v. New Hampshire* [1992] Q.B. 434; *New Hampshire v. Strabag Bau* [1992] 1 Lloyd's Rep. 361; *Trade Indemnity plc v. Forsakrings Njord* [1995] 1 A.E.R. 796; *Agnew v. Lansforsakringsbolagens AB* [2001] 1 A.C. 223.

[40] See, for example, *AGF v. Chiyoda* [1992] 1 Lloyd's Rep. 325 (Arts. 21 & 22); *New England Reinsurance v. Messoghios Ins. Co.* [1992] 2 Lloyd's Rep. 251, C.A.

[41] 1990 c. 36; Rome Convention: O.J. [1980] L266/1. For discussion of the Convention, see Ch. 13, *ante*. On the Convention generally, see Plender, *The European Contracts Convention* (2001).

Convention apply to reinsurance contracts.[42] In *Gan Insurance Co. Ltd v. Tai Ping Insurance Co. Ltd*[43] a Taiwanese insurer covered risks relating to a factory in Taiwan. The insurance was governed by Taiwanese law. Reinsurance was placed in London. It provided for terms "as original". It was held that this did not import Taiwanese law into the reinsurance. There was an implied choice of English law to govern the reinsurance, pursuant to Article 3 of the Rome Convention, as a result of the use of clauses commonly found in reinsurance placed in London, and as a result of the procedure of placing in the London market, using London brokers.

---

[42] Giuliano-Lagarde Report, O.J. 1980 C282/1, para. 11. For an example of a reinsurer's defence of limitation being decided by reference to foreign law pursuant to s.1 of the Foreign Limitation Periods Act 1984 see *Assitalia-Le Assic. D'Italia v. Overseas Union Ins. Ltd* [1995] L.R.L.R. 76.

[43] [1999] Lloyd's Rep. I.R. 472.

SECTION 3

PARTIES

CHAPTER 34

INSURANCE COMPANIES

1. BACKGROUND

34–1 Introduction. This chapter is concerned to give a general introduction to the principal aspects of the legislation controlling insurance companies and protecting the policyholders of such companies. However, the principal legislation is now the Financial Services and Markets Act 2000, which has implemented a single regulatory structure, under the Financial Services Authority (hereafter the Authority), across the whole of the financial services industry.[1] Therefore, as much of the legislation is no longer particular to insurance companies, the chapter does not seek to cover it exhaustively or to cover the detail so far as it concerns the internal workings of an insurance company.[2] Earlier editions of this work should be consulted for the history before the introduction of modern companies legislation[3] or concerning the introduction of the legislation particular to insurance companies.[4]

34–2 Legal form of insurance companies. As far as the legal form of an insurance company is concerned, since the passing of the first modern Companies Act, the Companies Act 1862, a company or association consisting of more than 20 members and carrying on insurance business must have been constituted in one or other of the following ways, and if constituted otherwise is an illegal company incapable of suing; its contracts cannot be enforced against it by persons having knowledge of the illegality, and it cannot be wound up on its own petition or on the petition of anyone who knowingly took part in the illegal enterprise[5]:

(1) Incorporated by charter.
(2) Incorporated by special Act of Parliament.

---

[1] The new scheme took effect from December 1, 2001. For detailed accounts, see Perry (ed.), *The Financial Services & Markets Act: A Practical Legal Guide* (Sweet & Maxwell, 2001); McMeel and Virgo, *Financial Advice and Financial Products: Law and Liability* (OUP, 2001).
[2] The chapter is also not concerned with the specialised law regarding friendly societies conducting industrial assurance business, although much of that has been brought within the framework established by the 2000 Act.
[3] As to this, see paras 2234–2238 of the 7th edition of this work.
[4] As to this, see paras 2239–2242 of the 7th edition of this work.
[5] *Re Padstow Total Loss* (1882) 20 Ch.D. 137; *Jennings v. Hammond* (1882) 9 Q.B.D. 225; *Shaw v. Benson* (1883) 11 Q.B.D. 563; *Re Ilfracombe Permanent Mutual* [1901] 1 Ch. 102; *Re South Wales Atlantic S.S. Co.* (1876) 2 Ch.D. 763.

(3) Unincorporated but authorised by letters patent under the Chartered Companies Act 1837.[6]

(4) Formed before 1844 as a common law partnership or mutual association and formally registered under section 58 of the Act of that year.[7]

(5) Formed between July 14, 1856 and August 25, 1857 as a common law partnership or association.[8]

(6) Formed under the Act of 1844 and re-registered under the Companies Act 1862.[9]

(7) Formed as a friendly society and registered under the Friendly Societies Acts.[10]

(8) Formed as a trade union.[11]

(9) Formed after 1862 under one of the Companies Acts.[12]

34–3 Insurance companies legislation. The particular legislation that was formerly applicable to insurance companies originated in 1870 and the basic requirement of the Life Assurance Companies Act of that year,[13] of a deposit in court by way of security by any company engaged in life assurance business, was extended successively to other classes of insurance business, culminating in the Insurance Companies Act 1958. New principles were introduced by Part II of the Companies Act 1967, in particular a requirement of authorisation and control based on the personal suitability of officers and controllers, and the 1958 and 1967 Acts, together with amendments made by the Insurance Companies Amendment Act 1973, were consolidated in the Insurance Companies Act 1974. This Act applied only to Great Britain but was extended to Northern Ireland by the Insurance Companies Act 1980.

34–4 The E.C. directives on freedom of establishment. The Act of 1974 was obsolescent at the time when it was passed, because the Council of Ministers of the European Economic Community had already notified a directive[14] on the control of insurance other than life assurance.

This directive, generally known as the "first non-life insurance directive", introduced a uniform system of solvency margins calculated as a percentage of annual premiums or claims (whichever gave the higher result)[15] and prescribed a procedure to be followed in the event that an insurer failed to

---

[6] 7 Will. 4 & 1 Vict. c. 73.

[7] 7 & 8 Vict. c. 110.

[8] The Joint Stock Companies Act 1856 (19 & 20 Vict. c. 47), which replaced the 1844 Act, did not apply to insurance companies until the passing of the Joint Stock Companies Act (Insurance Companies) 1857 (20 & 21 Vict. c. 80).

[9] 25 & 26 Vict. c. 89.

[10] See now the Friendly Societies Acts 1974 and 1992.

[11] The principal relevant legislation is now the Trade Union and Labour Relations (Consolidation) Act 1992. See s.1 of that Act for a definition of "trade union".

[12] See now the Companies Act 1985.

[13] 33 & 34 Vict. c. 61.

[14] No. 73/239 of July 23, 1973 ([1973] O.J. L228/3).

[15] Art. 16.

show possession of the necessary margin.[16] It gave insurers from one E.C. state the right to establish branches or agencies in other E.C. states and prescribed, in broad outline, the authorisation procedure to be followed in such cases.[17] There were also provisions[18] as to the regime to be applied to branches and agencies of insurers with their head offices outside the E.C. (the authorisation of such insurers remaining discretionary). The provisions of the directive were introduced into United Kingdom legislation by statutory instrument, which extensively amended the provisions of the 1974 Act in its application to non-life insurance, while leaving it to apply as originally enacted to life business.

34–5 A directive[19] governing life assurance—the "first life insurance directive"—was subsequently notified. Its provisions were in many ways similar to those of the non-life directive. The principle of a solvency margin was again introduced, though in this case the insurer's mathematical reserves are the basis of the calculation.[20] The most difficult problem to be resolved in the negotiations leading to this directive was the existence of "composite" life and non-life insurers in the United Kingdom, whereas the majority of E.C. states required life assurance to be carried on by "specialist" life companies not involved in any other class of business. The outcome was that no new "composites" could be authorised in the United Kingdom. Existing "composites" could continue and may set up branches or agencies in other E.C. states for the conduct of non-life business. If, however, they wish to do life business elsewhere in the Community, they must set up subsidiaries.[21]

34–6 The first life insurance directive was implemented by the Insurance Companies Act 1981 and almost immediately the whole of the legislation was consolidated in the Insurance Companies Act 1982, which was heavily amended by subsequent regulations[22] to implement further directives on freedom of services.

34–7 E.C. directives on freedom of services. The second non-life insurance directive[23] gave non-life insurers licensed to write insurance business in any E.C. Member State the right to offer "large risks"[24] across national frontiers without the need for authorisation. This was followed by the second life insurance directive.[25] These were quickly superseded when in July 1992, the Council of Ministers adopted the third non-life[26] and the third life directives.[27] These took freedom of services to its logical conclusion by

---

[16] Arts 20, 22.
[17] Arts 10–12.
[18] Arts 23–29.
[19] No. 79/267/EEC of March 5, 1979 ([1979] O.J. L63/1).
[20] See art. 18
[21] Art. 13.
[22] Now repealed and replaced by provisions of and under the 2000 Act.
[23] 88/357.
[24] There were three type of large risks, namely (1) broadly, marine, aviation and transit business, (2) credit and suretyship insurance where the policyholder carried on business, and (3) property, pecuniary and liability insurances relating to a business carried on by the insured where the business met two out of three criteria: (a) 250 employees, (b) an annual turnover of 12 million ECU, (c) a balance sheet total of 6.2 million ECU.
[25] 90/619.
[26] 92/49.
[27] 92/96.

introducing the single European licence. An insurer authorised in any Member State is automatically allowed to sell most types of insurance anywhere else in the European Economic Area, either through a branch or agency in the host state or via direct selling in the host state. The home state controls all its activities and its solvency.[28] The directives also require that no new system of what is called "material control", that is any system for the prior approval of policy terms and premium rates, can be introduced. States that previously had such a system can retain it, but insurers authorised in a Member State that does not exercise such control will not be required to submit policy terms and premium rates to the authorities of any host state that does exercise such control.

34-8 These insurance directives have their equivalent in terms of banking and investment services, and all the directives are now implemented together by the Financial Services and Markets Act 2000[29] and the Financial Services and Markets Act 2000 (EEA Passport Rights) Regulations 2001.[30] The rights conferred thereby are described as "EEA Passport Rights" and are briefly described in the following paragraphs.

34-9 EEA insurer carrying on direct insurance business in the U.K. An EEA insurer wishing to carry on direct insurance business in the U.K.[31] must be authorised in its home state in accordance with the relevant provisions of the first insurance directives, and its supervisory authority must provide the Authority with a notice containing details of it and a certificate attesting to its margin of solvency and indicating the classes of business for which it is authorised. The details required are the name of the company and its authorised agent, the address of its U.K. branch, a scheme of operations prepared in accordance with any requirements of its supervisory authority and, in the case of a motor insurer, confirmation that it has become a member of the Motor Insurers' Bureau.[32] In addition, either the Authority must have informed the supervisory authority of the conditions which, in the general good, must be complied with by the company in carrying on insurance business through the branch or two months must have lapsed from the date of receipt of the notice and certificate.

34-10 EEA insurer providing insurance in the U.K. EEA insurers wishing to provide insurance in the U.K. must similarly be authorised to provide the relevant class or classes of business in their home state and are subject to generally similar conditions. So, their supervisory authority must provide a notice and a certificate, the only material difference being that in this case there will be no branch details or authorised agent.[33]

---

[28] Although there is provision for the host state to take action where the home state defaults in so doing.

[29] ss.31 and 37, and Schs 3 and 4.

[30] S.I. 2001 No. 2511.

[31] The requirements for insurers wishing to effect reinsurance business are similar.

[32] As to the M.I.B., see para. 29–39, *ante.*

[33] Motor insurers must have a claims representative whose details are supplied and be a member of the M.I.B.

2. REGULATION UNDER THE FINANCIAL SERVICES AND MARKETS ACT 2000

(a) *The Regulatory Structure*

34–11 The 2000 Act itself provides only the broad structure under which the Financial Services Authority regulates the financial services industry. It has been augmented by a large volume of secondary legislation and by *The Authority's Handbook*, made under Part X, Chapter 1 of the Act. "The Handbook" is divided into a number of blocks. Those relevant to the regulation of insurance companies under the Act, and the individual components that are also relevant, are as follows. Some more detailed reference is made in subsequent paragraphs.

High Level Standards. This block contains the rules relating to Principles for Businesses; Senior Management Arrangements, Systems and Controls; Threshold Conditions; Statements of Principle and Code of Practice for Approved Persons; The Fit and Proper Test for Approved Persons.

Business Standards. This block contains the Interim Prudential Sourcebook for Insurers[34] and rules relating to Conduct of Business.

Regulatory Processes. This block contains the rules relating to Authorisation, Supervision, Enforcement and Decision making.

(b) *Scope of the Legislation as it Applies to Insurance*

34–12 Classes of insurance business. There is no definition of "insurance" in the legislation, which must therefore be interpreted in accordance with the principles described at the beginning of this work.[35] The classes of insurance business are defined in Schedule 1 of the Financial Services and Markets Act 2000 (Regulated Activities) Order 2001,[36] distinguishing between contracts of general insurance and contracts of long-term insurance and implementing the appropriate provisions in the first non-life and life directives. They also appear in *The Interim Prudential Sourcebook for Insurers.*[37]

34–13 General business. There are 18 classes of general business defined in Part 1 of Schedule 1 as follows:

1. Accident, which may include cover against accidental death but excludes contracts falling within the definition of permanent health business[38];
2. Sickness (again excluding permanent health business);

---

[34] There are separate sourcebooks for banks, building societies, friendly societies and investment businesses. It is intended that ultimately the various *Prudential Sourcebooks* will be merged into one.

[35] See paras 1–1 to 1–10, *ante.*

[36] S.I. 2001 No. 544.

[37] Annex 11.1 (long-term classes); annex 11.2 (general classes).

[38] See para. 34–14, *post.*

3. Land vehicles (excluding railway rolling stock)[39];
4. Railway rolling stock[40];
5. Aircraft[41];
6. Ships (including inland waterway craft)[42];
7. Goods in transit, irrespective of the form of transport, including passengers' baggage;
8. Fire and natural forces, that is, insurance of any kind of property not covered by classes 3 to 7 against damage by fire, explosion, storm or other natural forces, nuclear energy or land subsidence;
9. Damage to property not falling under classes 3 to 8 (this includes theft);
10. Motor vehicle liability[43];
11. Aircraft liability[44];
12. Liability for ships[45];
13. General liability, that is, all third-party liability insurance not falling under classes 10 to 12;
14. Credit;
15. Suretyship[46];
16. Miscellaneous financial loss, which is so defined as to include any kind of insurance not falling within any other class;
17. Legal expenses;
18. Assistance, which means either or both assistance[47] for persons who get into difficulties while travelling, while away from home or their permanent residence, and assistance for persons who get into difficulties otherwise.[48]

34–14 Long-term business. There are nine classes of long-term business, defined in Part II of Schedule 1. Four of these are of no practical importance in the United Kingdom market and are included only because the E.C. directive requires their inclusion. These are tontines, contracts to provide a

---

[39] This comprises only insurance against loss of, or damage to, such vehicles. Class 10 covers the corresponding third-party liability insurance.

[40] This comprises only insurance against loss of, or damage to, such rolling stock. Class 13 covers the corresponding third-party liability insurance.

[41] This comprises only insurance against loss of, or damage to, aircraft. Class 11 covers the corresponding third-party liability insurance.

[42] This comprises only insurance against loss of, or damage to, ships. Class 12 covers the corresponding third-party liability insurance.

[43] Including both carrier's liability and general third-party liability.

[44] Including both carrier's liability and general third-party liability.

[45] Including both carrier's liability and general third-party liability.

[46] The distinction between credit insurance and suretyship is discussed in Ch. 31, paras 31–40 to 31–42, *ante*.

[47] Whether in cash or kind.

[48] Note, though, that vehicle breakdown insurance is not an activity that requires authorisation under the 2000 Act—see art. 12 of the Regulated Activities Order.

sum on marriage or on the birth of a child,[49] collective insurance[50] and social insurance.[51] The other five long-term classes are:

I. *Life and annuity business*, comprising contracts of insurance on human life or contracts to pay annuities on human life, excluding those within class III below;

III. *Linked long-term business*, being life and annuity business in which the benefits are wholly or partly to be determined by reference to the value of property or the fluctuation of an index of property values;

IV. *Permanent health business*, which is insurance against sickness or accident where the contract is not as a general rule terminable by the insurer and is expressed to be in effect for a period of not less than five years, or until the retirement age of the insured or without limit of time[52];

VI. *Capital redemption business*;

VII. *Pension fund management business*

34–15 Groups of classes. So as to enable authorisations to be granted conveniently in respect of classes that are in practice usually carried on together, *The Interim Prudential Sourcebook for Insurers*,[53] though not the legislation, recognises certain groups of classes. Thus, for example, the "motor" group comprises classes 3, 7 and 10, together with class 1 to the extent that it relates to the risk of accidental death or injury as the result of travelling as a passenger, and the "marine and transport" group comprises classes 4, 6, 7 and 12, together with class 1 limited in the same way.

(c) *Authorisation*

34–16 Regulated activities. As indicated earlier, the 2000 Act brings together the regulation of all manner of financial services including insurance. There is a general prohibition, in section 19, on carrying on a regulated activity in the U.K. unless the person in question is an authorised or exempt person.[54] By section 22, an activity is a regulated activity if it is an activity of a kind specified by the Treasury, which is carried on by way of business and relates to an investment of a specified kind. Schedule 2 of the Act includes "rights under a contract of insurance" as an indicative regulated activity and this is confirmed by article 75 of the Regulated Activities Order.

---

[49] These are long-term business only when expressed to be in effect for a period of more than one year. The normal contract insuring against the birth of twins, which is entered into only after pregnancy has commenced and is therefore always of a duration of less than one year, is not included here and accordingly falls within general business class 16 (see para. 34–13, *ante*).

[50] Defined as effecting and carrying out contracts of a kind referred to in article 1(2)(e) of the first long term insurance directive, which itself refers to provisions in the French Code des Assurances.

[51] Defined as effecting and carrying out contracts of a kind referred to in article 1(3) of the first long term insurance directive; these are "operations relating to the length of human life which are prescribed by or provided in social insurance legislation, when they are effected or managed at their own risk by assurance undertakings in accordance with the laws of a Member State".

[52] Sickness and accident policies not fulfilling these requirements fall within general business classes 1 and 2 (see above).

[53] Annex 11.2, Pt II.

[54] For the consequences of acting without permission, see ss.20 and 23; no transaction is void or unenforceable, but there is a limited right to compensation for anyone who suffers loss as a result of the contravention. Contravening the general prohibition is a criminal offence.

Article 10 of the Order amplifies this by separately specifying "effecting a contract of insurance as principal" and "carrying out a contract of insurance as principal" as regulated activities.

34–17 Carrying on business. One question that arises from this is what constitutes "carrying on insurance business"? The words connote some element of continuity, as opposed to mere isolated transactions,[55] but it has been held on the construction of a similar statutory prohibition that a single transaction may afford sufficient evidence of "carrying on business."[56] Further, it was held that the equivalent prohibition in section 2 of the Insurance Companies Act 1982 was contravened by the negotiation of a prospective insurance contract without authorisation.[57]

34–18 Effecting and carrying out as principal. The separate specification, in article 10 of the Regulated Activities Order, of "effecting" and "carrying out" contracts of insurance reflects the fact that insurance business contains two principal elements, first, the negotiation and conclusion of contracts and, secondly, the execution of those contracts by, in particular, paying claims. It also makes it clear that if either or both these activities take place in the United Kingdom, business is being carried on here.[58] On the other hand, if neither activity takes place here, business is not carried on here and the fact that insured property or insured persons may be located in the United Kingdom is irrelevant.[59] In this respect, U.K. law is sharply distinguished from that of most other countries, where it ambit is determined by the "situs of the risk"—a concept unknown to our law.

Activities in the United Kingdom that are customarily those undertaken by insurance brokers acting as such were held not to be evidence of the carrying on of insurance business in a decision under the former legislation.[60] The specific inclusion of the phrase "as principal" in the current legislation reinforces this.

34–19 Authorisation. As far as insurance business is concerned, a person is authorised under the 2000 Act if he has a Part IV permission, is an EEA firm with passport rights or is otherwise authorised by or under the Act. There are two general exemptions. The first relates to trades unions and employers' organisations providing provident or strike benefits exclusively for their own members.[61] The second exempts a former Lloyd's underwriter

[55] *cf. Smith v. Anderson* (1880) 15 Ch.D. 247, 277.

[56] *Cornelius v. Phillips* [1918] A.C. 199

[57] *R. v. Wilson* [1997] 1 All E.R. 119.

[58] In the earlier insurance companies legislation, "effecting and carrying out" appeared as one phrase, although this was interpreted disjunctively: *Bedford Ins. Co. Ltd v. Instituto de Resseguros do Brasil* [1985] Q.B. 966; *Stewart v. Oriental Fire & Marine Ins. Co. Ltd* [1985] Q.B. 988; *Phoenix General Ins. Co. of Greece SA v. Administration Asiguraliror de Stat* [1988] Q.B. 216. See also Lord Goff of Chieveley in *Scher v. Policyholders Protection Board* [1994] 2 A.C. 57, at 99, see also Lord Donaldson M.R. in the Court of Appeal in the latter case at 70.

[59] *cf. Re United General Commercial Ins. Corp.* [1927] 2 Ch. 51.

[60] *Re A Company (No. 007816 of 1994) [1995]* 2 B.C.L.C. 539. It would clearly be otherwise if the brokers were authorised to take all effective decisions, including underwriting decisions: see *Re A Company (No. 007923 of 1994) (No. 2)* [1995] 1 B.C.L.C. 594 and *Secretary of State for Trade and Industry v. Great Western Assurance Co. SA* [1997] 2 B.C.L.C. 685, on appeal from the first-mentioned decision.

[61] The Financial Services and Markets Act 2000 (Exemption) Order 2001 (S.I. 2001 No. 1201), made under s. 38 of the 2000 Act, Sch., para. 43.

who ceased to be an underwriting member of Lloyd's before December 24, 1996 from needing authorisation to carry out contracts of insurance.[62] The Society of Lloyd's is an authorised person under the Act.[63] Insurers who were authorised under section 3 or 4 of the 1982 Act continue to be authorised under the 2000 Act.[64] This category includes insurers who were carrying on business immediately before November 3, 1966, as well as those who obtained authorisation under the Companies Act 1967, the Insurance Companies Act 1974, the Insurance Companies Act 1981 or the 1982 Act itself. Vehicle breakdown insurance does not require authorisation.[65]

34–20 Applications for authorisation. Application for Part IV permission to carry on a regulated activity, including insurance, under section 40 of the 2000 Act must be made in accordance with the "Applications Manual" in *The Authority's Handbook*. An application may not cover both long-term and general business unless the applicant's business will be restricted to reinsurance or the general business is restricted to accident and/or health insurance, and it must specify the classes of business to be carried on.[66] An applicant must be an incorporated company[67] other than a limited liability partnership, a registered friendly society or a registered industrial and provident society.[68]

34–21 Threshold conditions. Schedule 6 of the 2000 Act specifies the threshold conditions that, under section 41, the Authority must ensure that an applicant will satisfy. As they apply to insurance business, they are as follows:

1. The applicant must be a body corporate, a registered friendly society or a member of Lloyd's.
2. The insurer's head office[69] and registered office must be within the United Kingdom.
3. If the insurer has close links with another person, being either a parent or subsidiary of another[70] or where there is a 20 per cent shareholding by one company in the other, the Authority must be satisfied that these links are not likely to prevent effective supervision of the insurer.
4. The resources of the insurer must be adequate in relation to the regulated activities in question.
5. The applicant must be a fit and proper person, having regard to his connection with any other person, the nature of the regulated activity and the need to ensure that its affairs are conducted soundly and prudently. Enquiries by the Authority will be on a case-by-case basis and relevant issues include whether the insurer conducts its business

---

[62] *ibid.* at para. 46.

[63] s.315(1). As to the application of the 2000 Act to Lloyd's, see Ch. 35, *post*.

[64] The Financial Services and Markets Act 2000 (Transitional Provisions) (Authorised Persons, Etc) Order 2001 (S.I. 2001 No. 2636), art. 14.

[65] Regulated Activities Order, art. 12.

[66] Including that to be carried on on an ancillary or supplementary basis as described in para. 34–22, post.

[67] Defined in the "Glossary" to *The Handbook* as any body corporate.

[68] See Sch. 6, para. 1 of the 2000 Act.

[69] This is not defined, but refers to the place from where management decisions are made and central administrative functions are exercised.

[70] As defined in the Companies Act 1985, Pt VIII—see s.420(1) of the 2000 Act.

with integrity and in compliance with proper standards, has a competent and prudent management and conducts its affairs with the exercise of due care, skill and diligence.

34–22 Ancillary and supplementary contracts. Permission given under Part IV of the 2000 Act may include permission to carry out certain other classes of insurance business on an ancillary or supplementary basis.[71] Permission to effect or carry out life and annuity business includes permission to effect or carry out accident and/or sickness business on a supplementary basis. Permission to effect or carry out any class of general insurance includes permission to carry out any other class of general business on an ancillary basis other than credit, suretyship or, except as described below, legal expenses insurance. Effecting or carrying out business on an ancillary business means where the business is the subject of the same contract as the principal business and concerns the same object, and the risks covered are connected to the principal risk. Legal expenses insurance can be effected in an ancillary way if the main risk relates solely to the provision of assistance provided for persons who fall into difficulties while travelling or away from home or away from their permanent residence, or where it concerns disputes or risk arising out of or in connection with the use of sea-going vessels.

(d) *Supervision of Authorised Insurers*

34–23 Continuing duties. Insurance companies are subject to continuing duties under the rules made by the Authority regarding the carrying on of regulated activities (Part X of the 2000 Act). These rules are contained in the *Interim Prudential Sourcebook for Insurers*[72] and, briefly, they relate to the preparation and filing of accounts and statements of business, the separation of assets and liabilities attributable to long-term business, the maintenance of a prescribed solvency margin, and the localisation and matching of assets. There are two provisions specific to insurance rules in Part X. Section 141(1) allows the Authority to make rules prohibiting an authorised insurer from carrying on a specified activity including an activity that is not a regulated activity.[73] Section 141(3) also allows the Authority to make rules in relation to contracts entered into by an authorised long-term insurer, which may (1) restrict the descriptions of property or indices of the value of property by reference to which the benefits under such contracts may be determined and (2) provide, in the interests of the protection of policyholders, for the substitution of one description of property, or index of value, by reference to which the benefits are to be determined for another such description of property or index. Section 142(1) allows the Treasury to make regulations to prevent a parent undertaking of an authorised insurer that falls within a prescribed class from doing anything to lessen the effectiveness of asset identification rules,[74] and to provide that charges created in contravention of asset identification rules are void.[75]

---

[71] See section 3.12 of the "Authorisation Manual" in *The Authority's Handbook*.
[72] These do not apply to EEA insurers exercising passport rights nor, in general, to Lloyd's, which has its own set of rules (see 35–02, post).
[73] s.141(2).
[74] Defined in s.142(2) and see Ch. 3 of the *Interim Prudential Sourcebook for Insurers*.
[75] s.142(3).

34–24 Prohibition. There is an important prohibition made by virtue of the power in section 141(1) in *The Sourcebook*. Rule 1.3 states that an insurer must not carry on any commercial business in the United Kingdom or elsewhere other than insurance business and activities directly arising from that business. However, contravention of rules made by the Authority is not an offence[76] nor does it make any transaction void or unenforceable.[77] This clarifies a point that was uncertain under the statutory provision replaced by rule 1(3).[78]

34–25 Changes in control. There are detailed provisions in Part XII of the 2000 Act laying down the procedures to be followed when someone acquires, increases or reduces their control of an authorised person including an insurer.

(e) *Transfers of Business and Winding Up*

34–26 General. Specific provisions relating to transfers of insurance business and the winding up of insurance companies are retained under the 2000 Act.

34–27 Transfers of business. The provisions on the transfer of insurance business were first recast following implementation of the third insurance directives. They are now contained in Part VII of the 2000 Act and regulations made thereunder,[79] which, in contrast to the previous law, make no fundamental distinctions between a transfer of long-term business and a transfer of general business. Any insurance business transfer scheme within Part VII requires court consent.[80] However, where the transferor is an insurer with its head office in another Member State proposing to transfer its business to an insurer with its head office in the United Kingdom, responsibility for approving the transfer rests with the supervisory authorities of the other Member State; the only obligations in U.K. law are that the Authority issues a certificate as to the solvency of the transferee,[81] and appropriate notice of the execution of the instrument effecting the transfer is published.[82]

---

[76] s.151(1).

[77] s.151(2). A private person who suffers loss as a result of a contravention may have an action for damages for breach of statutory duty: s.150.

[78] The provision was s.16 of the Insurance Companies Act 1982, which made no provision for the effect of breach. In *Fuji Finance Inc. v. Aetna Life Insurance Co. Ltd* [1997] Ch. 173, reversing [1995] Ch. 122, differing views were expressed as to whether or not a contract entered into in breach of s.16 was unlawful and unenforceable on public policy grounds. See para. 34–24 of the ninth edition of this work.

[79] S.I. 2001 No. 3625. Part VII also applies to transfers of banking business.

[80] s.104. A scheme is a transfer of business and within this Part of the Act even if it is designed in effect only to transfer, and ultimately discharge, the liabilities under a reinsurance policy: *Re Friends Provident Life Office* [2000] 2 B.C.L.C. 203.

[81] s.115 and Pt 3 of Sch. 12.

[82] s.116.

34-28 Insurance business transfer scheme. Under section 105, this is a scheme that results in the business transferred being carried on from an establishment of the transferee in an EEA state, which is not an excluded scheme, and where prior to the transfer all or part of the business is one of the following:

1) Business carried on, wholly or in part, in the EEA by a U.K. authorised person[83]; or

2) reinsurance business carried on in the U.K. branch of an EEA firm[84]; or

3) business carried on, wholly or in part, in the United Kingdom by an authorised person who is neither a U.K. authorised person nor an EEA firm.

The excluded schemes[85] are:

Case 1— where the transferor is a friendly society.[86]

Case 2— transfers of reinsurance business by U.K. authorised persons that have been approved by a court in another EEA state or by the relevant regulator in the country or territory in which it is carried on.

Case 3— transfers of business carried on outside the EEA that do not include policies (other than reinsurance policies) against risks arising in the EEA, and which have been approved by the court or regulator in a non-EEA state.

Case 4— transfers of the whole of the business of an authorised person where that is solely reinsurance or captive insurance where all of the policyholders affected have consented to them.[87]

34-29 Either or both the transferor and transferee may apply to the court.[88] Notice of the application must be published in the London, Edinburgh and Belfast Gazettes and in two national newspapers, and sent to every policyholder of the transferor and transferee.[89] The notice must be approved by the Authority prior to publication and sending and contain the address from which the report and statement described below may be obtained.[90] An application must be accompanied by a scheme report in a form approved by the Authority, which can be made only by a person appearing to the Authority to have the necessary skills and nominated or approved by the Authority[91] A copy of the report and a statement setting out the terms of the scheme and containing a summary of the report must be given free of charge to any person who requests them,[92] and a copy of the application and the report and statement must be given free of charge to the

---

[83] An authorised person incorporated in the U.K. or an unincorporated association formed under the law of any part of the U.K.: s.105(8).

[84] Under Sch. 3.

[85] s.105(3).

[86] These are governed by the Friendly Societies Act 1992.

[87] The parties to a scheme falling within cases 2, 3 and 4 have the option of applying to the court for an order sanctioning the scheme: s.105(4).

[88] s.107; the High Court or, in Scotland, the Court of Session.

[89] S.I. 2001 No. 3625, reg. 3(2).There is provision for publication in two newspapers in other Member States where appropriate.

[90] S.I. 2001 No. 3625, reg. 3(3).

[91] s.109.

[92] S.I. 2001 No. 3625, reg. 3(4).

Authority.[93] The Authority and any person (including an employee of either transferor or transferee) who alleges that he would be adversely affected by the transfer are entitled to be heard.[94]

34–30 Before making an order sanctioning an insurance business transfer scheme, the court must be satisfied that the appropriate certificates have been obtained and that, if appropriate, the transferee has or will have the necessary authorisation to carry on the transferred business.[95] It must also consider that, in all the circumstances of the case, it is appropriate to sanction the scheme.[96] The appropriate certificates are specified in Schedule 12 and are essentially a certificate from the appropriate regulator that the transferee possesses the necessary margin of solvency and a certificate, in cases involving risks or firms located in another EEA state, that the host state regulator has consented to the transfer or failed to object to it within three months of being notified. The principles to be applied by the court in deciding whether or not to sanction a transfer are that it should take account of the fact that the board of the transferor company has exercised a commercial judgment that the transfer is beneficial and must consider whether any policyholders, employees or others may be adversely affected, although, even if they are, it does not follow that the scheme must be rejected. The most important criterion is the fairness of the scheme as between the different classes of affected persons and in deciding that, the most important material is the report of the actuary.[97]

34–31 The effects of a court order are specified in section 112. It may deal with a variety of matters, namely the transfer of the whole or any part of the transferor's undertaking and any property[98] or liabilities, [99] the allotment or appropriation by the transferee of any shares, debentures, policies or other similar interests in the transferee which under the scheme are to be allotted or appropriated to or for any other person, the continuation by or against the transferee of any legal proceedings pending by or against the transferor and

[93] S.I. 2001 No. 3625, reg. 3(5). See reg. 4 for effect of failure to comply with these requirements and for the court's power to waive some of them. The discretion of the court to dispense with individual notice to policyholders under equivalent provisions of earlier legislation was exercised in *City of Glasgow Life Ass. Co. and Scottish Union and National Ins. Co., Petitioners* (1913) 50 S.L.R. 787 and *Re Hearts of Oak and General Ass. Co. Ltd* (1914) 58 S.J 433. It was held in *Re Universal Life Ass. Society* (1901) 18 T.L.R 198, that there was no need to give notice to holders of policies issued after the date of the petition.
[94] s.110.
[95] s.111(2).
[96] s.111(3).
[97] *Re Hill Samuel Life Assurance Ltd* [1998] 3 All E.R. 176; *Re AXA Equity and Law Life Assurance Society Plc* [2001] 2 B.C.L.C. 447 (following the unreported decision of Hoffmann J. in *Re London Life Association Ltd*, February 21, 1989). Where not all policies issued by the transferor are the subject of the proposed transfer, for example because they have been issued to non-U.K. residents and it is not clear that the regulatory authorities in the appropriate jurisdiction will consent, the court must take account of this as it is an inherent and essential part of the scheme. Under similar provisions of former legislation it has been held that the court must consider whether there are objections to the proposal even if none has been raised by persons appearing before it (*Re Hearts of Oak and General Ass. Co. Ltd* (1914) 30 T.L.R 436) and that a transfer to a company outside the jurisdiction cannot be sanctioned (*Re Prudential Ass. Co. Ltd* [1939] Ch. 878), although the latter cannot now be an objection where the company is a properly authorised EEA insurer.
[98] Property, rights and powers of any description: s.112(12).
[99] And duties: s.112(13).

any incidental, consequential and supplementary matters necessary to secure that the scheme is fully and effectively carried out.[1] The order will pass the property in assets (free of any mortgage or charge if the order so provides) and transfer liabilities, and is to be treated as an instrument of transfer where that is required for purposes of registration.[2] The court may make such provision as it thinks fit for dealing with the interests of any person who objects to the scheme,[3] for the dissolution, without winding up, of the transferor and for the reduction, on such terms and subject to such conditions as it thinks fit, of the benefits payable under any description of policy or policies generally issued by the transferor and transferred as a result of the scheme.[4] The transferee must deposit two office copies of the order with the Authority within 10 days after it is made.[5]

34–32 The court may, on the application of the Authority, appoint an independent actuary to investigate the business transferred under the scheme and to report to the Authority on any reduction in benefits payable under policies issued by the transferor that, in the opinion of the actuary, ought to be made.[6] Provision is made for EEA policyholders whose local law permits them to cancel a policy in the event of a transfer to have the opportunity to exercise that right.[7]

34–33 Application to Lloyd's. Provision is also made for the application of the procedures for transfer of business to transfers from Lloyd's underwriters.[8] The scheme must result in the business transferred being carried on from an establishment of the transferee in an EEA state, the Council of Lloyd's must by resolution authorise one person to act in connection with the transfer and a copy of the resolution must be given to the Authority.[9] The procedures described in the foregoing paragraphs are then applicable, anything done by the authorised person being deemed to be done by the underwriters for whom he acted.[10]

34–34 Winding up of insurance companies. The provisions of the Insolvency Act 1986 as to the winding up of companies are generally applicable to insurance companies,[10a] but there are a number of special provisions in Part XXIV of the 2000 Act relating to the insolvency of authorised persons and a

---

[1] s.122(1). See also ss.(2). For an example of this, see *Re Hill Samuel Life Assurance Ltd* [1998] 3 All E.R. 176. For these purposes, other than in connection with the allotment or appropriation of shares etc, and for certain other purposes of s.112, where the transferee is not an EEA firm, it is immaterial that the law applicable to any of the contracts of insurance included in the transfer is the law of an EEA state other than the U.K.: s.112(9).

[2] s.122(3) to (6).

[3] Within such time and in such manner as it may direct.

[4] s.112(8).

[5] s.122(10), although the Authority may extend that period: s.122(11).

[6] s.113.

[7] s.114. The U.K. has not taken up the option in the third life directive to allow U.K. policyholders to cancel a policy transferred under a scheme.

[8] The Financial Services and Markets Act 2000 (Control of Transfers of Business Done at Lloyd's) Order 2001 (S.I. 2001 No. 3626). This includes transfers from former underwriting members of Lloyd's as defined in s.324 of the Act. There is no provision for transfers within Lloyd's from one syndicate of underwriters to another.

[9] reg. 4.

[10] reg. 5(2).

[10a] Note that the provisions of the 1986 Act relating to administration have been extended to insurance companies: Financial Services and Markets Act 2000 (Administration Orders Relating to Insurers) Order 2002 (S.I. 2000 No. 1242).

number relating only to insurers.[11] As regards an insurance company carrying out general business which is being wound up voluntarily, the Authority may apply to the court in respect of the company and is entitled to be heard at any hearing of the court in relation to the voluntary winding up.[12] The Authority may present a petition for winding up any authorised person,[13] and the court may order winding up on the grounds that it is unable to pay its debts,[14] or that it is just and equitable that it should be wound up.[15] If any other person presents a petition to wind up an authorised insurer, the petitioner must serve a copy of the petition on the Authority,[16] which is entitled to be heard.[17]

34–35 Special provisions as to long-term business. An insurer that carries on long-term business may not be wound up voluntarily without the consent of the Authority, which must receive notice of the intention to propose the resolution for winding up.[18] Unless the court otherwise directs, the liquidator must carry on the insurer's business so far as it consists of carrying out the insurer's contracts of long-term with a view to its being transferred as a going concern to a person who may lawfully carry out those contracts.[19] For this purpose the liquidator may agree to the variation of any existing contracts of insurance but may not effect new contracts.[20] A special manager of the long-term business may be appointed by the court on the application of the liquidator[21] and an independent actuary may be appointed to investigate the long-term business on the application of the liquidator, the special manager or the Authority.[22] The court has power to reduce, subject to such conditions (if any) as it may determine, the value of one or more of the long-term

[11] For the purpose of Pt XXIV, insurer means anyone effecting and carrying out contracts of insurance who is not a friendly society, an exempt person or a person who carries out certain contracts of insurance (classes 14 to 18 described in para. 34–13, *ante*) only in the course of, or for the purposes of, a banking business: The Financial Services and Markets Act 2000 (Insolvency) (Definition of "Insurer") Order 2001 (S.I. 2001 No. 2634). In addition to the provisions described below, there are the provisions of the Insurers (Winding-up) Rules 2001 (S.I. 2001 No. 3635), made under s.379 of the 2000 Act and s.411 of the Insolvency Act 1986 These rules provide for the proof and valuation of claims under long-term and general policies—see paras. 34–37 to 34–38, *post*. Pt XXIV applies to insolvency proceedings in general, and not just winding up, but no detail relating to the other proceedings is given here.

[12] s.365. The Authority is also entitled to receive all notices and documents sent to creditors and to attend relevant meetings. The voluntary winding up does not bar the right of the Authority to have the company wound up by the court.

[13] And a body carrying on a regulated activity without being authorised.

[14] The provisions of the Insolvency Act 1986, s.123, as to the cases in which a company is deemed to be unable to pay its debts, are applicable, with the addition of the case where a body is in default of an obligation to pay a sum due and payable under an agreement: s.367(4).

[15] s.367. The Authority cannot petition in respect of an EEA insurer unless it has been asked to do so by the home state regulator: s.368.

[16] s.369.

[17] s.371 (applicable generally)

[18] s.366; the copy of the resolution forwarded to the registrar of companies (under s.360 of the Companies Act 1985) must be accompanied by a certificate issued by the Authority stating its consent (subs. (5)); if this is not complied with, the resolution has no effect (subs. (7)).

[19] s.376(2).

[20] s.376(3).

[21] s.376(4), (5). The powers of the special manager and the duration of his appointment are to be determined by the court: s.376(6). The Insolvency Act 1986, s.177(5) (security to be given by special manager) is applied by the 2000 Act, s.376(7).

[22] s.376(10).

insurance contracts effected by the insurer.[23] This power is confined to contracts due and payable on or before the date of presentation of the winding-up petition.[24]

34–36 Where an insurer is being wound up, the assets representing the fund or funds in respect of any long-term business are, as a general rule, available on winding up only for meeting the liabilities of the company attributable to that business, and the other assets of the company are available only for meeting the liabilities of the company attributable to its other business.[25] Separate general meetings of creditors in respect of the two classes of liabilities must be held, and each general meeting has power to give directions concerning only the assets falling within the corresponding category.[26] The respective assets and liabilities must be treated as though they were the assets and liabilities of a separate company.[27]

34–37 Valuation of claims in a winding up. Special provision is made in the Insurers (Winding Up) Rules 2001[28] for the valuation of the claims of policyholders against an insurer in liquidation, depending upon whether the policy is:

(1) a general business policy
(2) a long term policy granted by a company against which no stop order has been made, or
(3) a long term policy granted by a company against which a stop order has been made.[29]

In relation to a claim which has fallen due for payment under a long term policy before the date of the winding up order, or of the stop order if one is made, the policyholder is admitted as a creditor without proof for the amount which appears to be due in respect of the claim.[30] The policyholder under a long term policy is also entitled to claim for the value of his policy in accordance with detailed rules based upon actuarial principles.[31]

34–38 Claims under general business policies. When a claim has fallen due for payment before the date of the winding up order the policyholder submits his proof under the general Insolvency Rules.[32] When his claim is in respect of periodic payments which fall due for payment after the liquidation

---

[23] s.376(8), (9). This power must not be confused with the power under s.377 (see para. 34–39, *post*), to reduce contracts as an alternative to winding up.

[24] *Re Capital Annuities Ltd* [1979] 1 W.L.R. 170.

[25] The Financial Services and Markets Act 2000 (Treatment of Assets of Insurers on Winding up) Regulations 2001 (S.I. 2001 No. 2968), made under ss.378 and 428(3) of the 2000 Act, reg. 3(1). If the assets relating to either category of business exceed the corresponding liabilities, this restriction does not apply to the excess: reg. 3(2).

[26] *ibid.* reg. 4.

[27] The Insurers (Winding Up) Rules 2001 (S.I. 2001 No. 3635), r. 5.

[28] Made under s.379 of the 2000 Act and s. 411 of the Insolvency Act 1986 and replacing, with minor amendments, rules made under earlier legislation. An illuminating historical account of the genesis of the present law is given by Hoffmann J. in *Transit Casualty Co. v. Policyholders Protection Board* [1992] 2 Lloyd's Rep. 358.

[29] For classes of long-term business see para. 34–13, *ante*. A general business policy is for practical purposes any non-life policy.

[30] r. 7(2) (no stop order); r. 8(2) (stop order).

[31] r. 7, schs 2, 3 and 4 (no stop order); r. 8, Sch. 5 (stop order).

[32] S.I. 1986 No. 1925; *Transit Casualty Co. v. Policyholders Protection Board* [1992] 2 Lloyd's Rep. 358, 362; *Scher v. P.P.B. (No. 2)* [1994] 2 A.C. 57, 77.

date where event giving rise to the liability of the company to make them occurred before that date, he is entitled to the value of such payments determined on such actuarial principles and assumptions in regard to all relevant factors as the court shall direct.[33] The same principle applies in relation to liabilities which arise from events that occurred before the liquidation date but which have not fallen due for payment or been notified to the company before that date.[34] Other liabilities are dealt with by Schedule 1, paragraph 3. If the terms of the policy provide for a repayment of premium upon the early termination of the policy or the policy is expressed to run from one definite date to another or the policy may be terminated by any of the parties with effect from a definite date, the value is the greater of (a) the amount (if any) which under the terms of the policy would have been repayable on the early termination of the policy had it terminated on the liquidation date, or (b) the proportionate part of the premium representing the unexpired portion of the period of the policy after liquidation.[35] Paragraph 3(2)(b) provides that in any other case the relevant value is a "just estimate" of the value of the policy. In addition the policyholder may claim under this paragraph for the value of liabilities arising from events occurring before the liquidation, whether under a policy still current at the commencement of the liquidation or under one which has expired before that time.[36]

34–39 Reduction of contracts. The court, in the case of an insurer that has been proved to be unable to pay its debts, may, if it thinks fit, in place of making a winding-up order, reduce the amount of the insurer's contracts on such terms and subject to such conditions as the court thinks fit.[37] A scheme under that provision is a substitute for a winding-up order. Such scheme may make provision for immediate payment, either in full or in part, of policies which have matured, and for the formation of a trust fund into which future premiums will be paid and out of which future claims will be paid on the reduced scale. The provision is not intended to enable an insolvent company to continue to carry on business by relieving it of part of its present and future liabilities. Such a scheme would not be entertained by the court.[38] Where a scheme provided that policyholders whose claims had matured should be paid in full and that other policies should be reduced, the court held that the crucial time was the date of the presentation of the petition, and that no policy maturing after that date should be paid in full.[39] The power of

---

[33] r. 6 and sch. 1, para. 1.

[34] *ibid.* para. 2.

[35] Sch. 1, para. 3, applying the principle derived from *Re Law Car and General Ins. Corp.* [1913] 2 Ch. 103.

[36] *Transit Casualty Co. v. Policyholders Protection Board* [1992] 2 Lloyd's Rep. 358, 364; approved in *Scher v. P.P.B.* [1994] 2 A.C. 57, 77, 86. These "contingent claims" include claims under liability policies where an act or event has triggered the liability of the insured before the liquidation and is covered by the policy, but the claim by the third party has not yet been notified—see [1992] 2 Lloyd's Rep. 358, 361. No doubt events subsequent to the winding up may be used to ascertain the value of the insurer's liability at the date of the liquidation following the principle from *Re Northern Counties of England Fire Ins. Co., MacFarlane's Claim* (1880) 17 Ch. D. 337. As to the valuation of claims under prize indemnity policies see *Re Continental Assurance Co. of London Plc* [1999] 1 B.C.L.C. 751.

[37] s.377.

[38] *Reconstruction Case* (1872) Alb.Arb. Reilly 150; *Re Nelson & Co.* [1905] 1 Ch. 551.

[39] *Re Great Britain Mutual Life* (1882) 20 Ch.D. 351.

approving a scheme under the above provision cannot be exercised so long as there is a winding-up order in existence, and if, after the making of a winding-up order, the policyholders desire to present a scheme for the approval of the court, the winding-up order ought to be discharged and meetings of policyholders and shareholders summoned in order to ascertain their wishes.[40]

34–40 If, upon the hearing of a petition for a winding up, it is suggested that a scheme for reduction of contracts might be arranged, the petition may be ordered to stand over in order to enable meetings to be summoned, and the matter will be referred to chambers.[41]

A scheme for reduction of contracts, when sanctioned by the court, is binding on the company and all policyholders. In a case before the Industrial Assurance Commissioner a scheme for the reduction of the contracts of an industrial assurance company had, by order of the court, been advertised in the local press, direct notice to all the policyholders having been dispensed with. The scheme provided that on its becoming binding all policyholders should be bound on demand to produce their existing policies for endorsement and that the company should indorse the policies of all policyholders, whose contracts were modified, with a statement showing the benefits under the policies as modified by the scheme. The Commissioner held that the company was under no obligation to inform policyholders of the reduction so that they might decide whether they would continue to pay their premiums, and that a policyholder who continued to pay his premium in ignorance of the scheme was not entitled to have his premiums returned.[42]

(f) Compensation and Continuity of Cover

34–41 General. Part XV of the Financial Services and Markets Act 2000, and the rules made thereunder, establishes a scheme for compensating persons who have suffered as a result of the failure of an authorised insurer and for seeking to ensure continuity of cover for persons insured by insurers in financial difficulties. The scheme applies to all investments covered by the 2000 Act, but this account will concentrate upon those aspects of relevance to insurance business. It has replaced the special scheme for the protection of policyholders under the Policyholders Protection Acts 1975 and 1997.[43]

34–42 The scheme manager. Section 212 requires the Financial Services Authority to establish a body corporate to exercise the functions under Part XV; this body, described in the Act as the "scheme manager", is Financial Services Compensation Scheme Ltd (FSCS).[44] Section 213 requires the

---

[40] *Re Great Britain Mutual Life* (1880) 16 Ch.D. 246.
[41] *Re Briton Medical and General* (1886) 54 L.T. 14; *Re Clarke (John) & Co.* [1912] Ir.R 24.
[42] *Rea v. Hearts of Oak Ass. Co.* [1927] I.A.C.Rep. 50.
[43] Although as will be seen, some references to the old scheme are retained, and in many respects the scheme follows that under those Acts. The latter were described in paras. 34–60 to 34–68 of the 9th edition of this work. As to the transitional provisions governing claims made before commencement of the 2000 Act, see the Financial Services and Markets Act 2000 (Transitional Provisions, Repeals and Savings) (Financial Services Compensation Scheme) Order 2001 (S.I. 2001 No. 2967).
[44] The scheme manager has statutory powers, particularly with regard to the obtaining of information, under ss. 219, 220 and 224. It has other duties specified in Ch. 2 of the "Compensation Rules".

Authority to establish the scheme where "relevant persons", including authorised insurers,[45] are unable, or are likely to be unable, to satisfy claims against them. Sections 214–217 indicate the rules that may be made to give effect to the scheme, and these are contained in the "Compensation" part of *The Authority Handbook*.[46] The scheme is funded by levies on authorised firms in accordance with the detailed rules in chapter 13 of "The Compensation Rules".

34–43 Continuity of cover. As far as insurance business is concerned, a person is entitled to compensation where an insurer has failed, described in these paragraphs as an "insurer in default," only where continuation of cover cannot be secured. With respect to long-term insurance, FSCS must make arrangements to secure continuity of such insurance where it is reasonably practicable to do so and one of the following has occurred:

(a) the insurer has passed a resolution for a creditors' voluntary winding up;

(b) the insurer's home state regulator has determined that it appears unable to meet claims and has no early prospect of being able to do so;

(c) a liquidator or administrator, or provisional liquidator or interim manager has been appointed;

(d) the court has made an order for winding up or administration;

(e) a voluntary arrangement has been approved.[47]

The arrangements contemplated may be securing or facilitating the transfer of the long-term business to another insurer or securing the issue of substitute policies by another insurer.[48]

Different rules apply as regards any type of insurance issued by an insurer in financial difficulties. This is defined as where an insurer is in provisional liquidation, has been proved in winding up proceedings to be unable to pay its debts or is the subject of an application under section 425 of the Companies Act 1985 for a compromise or arrangement to reduce or defer payment of the liabilities or benefits under its policies, or where the authority determines that it is unlikely to be able to satisfy claims protected under the scheme.[49] Here, FSCS must take such measures to safeguard insureds on such terms (including terms reducing or deferring payment of any liabilities or benefits) as it considers appropriate if, in its opinion, the cost is likely to be less than the cost of paying compensation.[50] These measures may amount to transferring the insurance business to another insurer or assisting the insurer in difficulties to enable it to continue to effect or carry out contracts of insurance. However, before taking these measures in respect of a long-term insurance contract, FSCS must reduce the insured's interest in the contract to 90 per cent of what would otherwise have been payable and similarly reduce the amount of future premiums.[51]

34–44 Eligible claimants. The persons who may benefit from compensation or continuity of cover under the scheme are called "eligible

---

[45] As to relevant persons, see further para. 34–50, *post*.

[46] Referred to in these paragraphs as the "Compensation Rules".

[47] r. 3.3.1.

[48] r. 3.3.2.

[49] r. 3.3.6.

[50] r. 3.3.3.

[51] r. 3.3.5.

claimants". As far as long-term insurance is concerned, this category[52] comprises any person (including a body corporate and an unincorporated body such as a partnership) other than the following:

(a) directors or managers of the insurer in default[53];

(b) close relatives of the above;

(c) bodies corporate in the same group as the insurer in default;

(d) persons holding 5 per cent or more of the capital of the insurer in default or of any body corporate in the same group;

(e) the auditors of the insurer in default or of any body corporate in the same group or the appointed actuary of insurer in default;

(f) persons who in the opinion of the FSCS are responsible or have contributed to the insurer's default;

(g) persons whose claim arises from transactions in connection with which they have been convicted of an offence of money laundering.

As far as general insurance is concerned, claims under any of the following are totally excluded[54]:

(i) a reinsurance contract;

(ii) a Lloyd's policy;

(iii) an insurance contract relating to aircraft, ships, goods in transit, aircraft liability, liability of ships or credit.

Subject to this, eligible claimants are the following:

(1) Private persons and any business qualifying as small at the date of commencement of the contract within the following categories[55]; a small business is a partnership, body corporate, unincorporated association or mutual association with an annual turnover of less than £1 million[56]:

(a) persons authorised under the Act, other than a sole trader firm or a small business whose claim arises out of an activity regulated under the Act for which they do not have permission;

(b) overseas financial services institutions[57];

(c) collective investment schemes[58] and the operator or trustee of such a scheme;

(d) pension and retirement funds[59] and a trustee of such a fund[60];

(2) A large partnership in respect of a relevant general insurance contract entered into before December 1, 2001.[61]

(3) A third party whose claim arises under the Third Parties (Rights against Insurers) Act 1930,[62] provided that the assured would have been an eligible claimant at the time that his rights against the insurer were transferred to the third party, or the liability transferred was

---

[52] r. 4.2.1 read with r. 4.2.2 and r. 4.3.2.

[53] Except for non-remunerated directors or managers of a non-large mutual association.

[54] See the definition of "relevant general insurance contract" in the "Glossary" to "The Handbook".

[55] r. 4.3.3 read with r. 4.2.2.

[56] See the definition of "small business" in the "Glossary" to "The Handbook".

[57] A firm authorised by an overseas financial services regulator.

[58] Defined in the "Glossary".

[59] Defined in the "Glossary".

[60] With the exceptions in r. 4.2.2(4).

[61] r. 4.3.4.

[62] See Ch. 28, *ante*.

under a contract of employer's liability insurance and it would have been compulsory to insure against it if the contract had been entered into after 1 January 1972,[63] or the amount of the liability of the assured has been agreed in writing by the insurer or determined by a court or arbitrator before the date on which the insurer is in default.[64]

(4) Any person in respect of a liability subject to compulsory insurance,[65] that is under the Riding Establishments Act 1964,[66] the Employers' Liability (Compulsory Insurance) Act 1969[67] and the Road Traffic Act 1988.[68]

34–45 Protected claim. A person is eligible for compensation or continuity of cover in respect of a protected claim, which is a claim under a protected contract of insurance.[69] It is irrelevant that a policy evidencing the contract has not been issued, if the FSCS is satisfied that a person is insured under a contract with an insurance undertaking.[70] Section 5.4 of the Compensation Rules distinguishes between contracts issued after and before December 1, 2001.[71]

34–46 Protected contracts of insurance issued after December 1, 2001. Contracts issued after this date must be of long-term insurance or relevant general insurance,[72] and must relate to a protected risk or commitment under one of the following three types of contract. The first is a contract issued by an insurer in default through an establishment in the United Kingdom where the risk or commitment is situated in an EEA state, the Channel Islands or the Isle of Man. The second is a contract issued by an authorised insurance company through an establishment in another EEA state where the risk or commitment is situated in the United Kingdom. The third is a contract issued through an establishment in the Channel Islands or the Isle of Man where the risk or commitment is situated in the United Kingdom, the Channel Islands or the Isle of Man.

For these purposes, the situation of a risk or commitment is determined as follows. In the case of insurance relating to buildings or to buildings and their contents (in so far as the contents are covered by the same contract), the risk or commitment is treated as situated where the building is situated. In the case of insurance relating to vehicles of any type, the risk or commitment is treated as situated where the vehicle is registered. In the case of policies of a duration of four months or less covering travel or holiday risks (whatever the class concerned), the risk is treated as situated where the policyholder took out the contract of insurance. In any other case, where the policyholder is an individual, the risk or commitment is situated where he has his habitual

---

[63] The date the Employer's Liability (Compulsory Insurance) Act 1969 came into force—see para. 28–71, *ante*. For Northern Ireland the relevant date is December 29, 1975.

[64] r. 3.3.5.

[65] r. 4.3.6.

[66] Or any corresponding enactment for the time being in force in Northern Ireland.

[67] Or the Employers' Liability Order (Defective Equipment and Compulsory Insurance) (Northern Ireland) Order 1972.

[68] Or Pt VIII of the Road Traffic (Northern Ireland) Order 1981.

[69] r. 5.2.1.

[70] r. 5.4.6.

[71] The date when the 2000 Act was brought into force.

[72] That is, excluding those mentioned at (text at note 54).

residence at the date when the contract of insurance commenced, and where the policyholder is not an individual, the risk or commitment is situated where the establishment to which the risk or commitment relates is situated at that date.

34–47 Protected contracts of insurance issued before December 1, 2001. Where a contract was issued before this date but the insurer defaults thereafter, it qualifies for protection if:

(1) it was a relevant general insurance contract,[73] a contract of credit insurance or a long-term insurance contract and

(2) either (a) it was a "United Kingdom policy at the beginning of the liquidation" for the purposes of the Policyholders Protection Act 1975 or (b), if it is a contract of employer's liability insurance entered into before January 1, 1972[74] and the claim was agreed after the default of the insurer, the risk or commitment was situated in the United Kingdom.

34–48 United Kingdom policies under the 1975 Act. These are policies under which at any time the performance by the insurer of any of his obligations under the contract evidenced by the policy would constitute the carrying on by the insurer of insurance business of any class in the United Kingdom.[75] These words bear the same construction as the equivalent words in the repealed Insurance Companies Act 1982,[76] and mean that a policy is a United Kingdom policy if, had any of the obligations under the contract evidenced by the policy been performed at the relevant time, such performance would have formed part of an insurance business which the insurer was authorised to carry on in the United Kingdom, whether or not such obligation(s) would have been performed in the United Kingdom.[77] Thus, in *Scher v. Policyholders Protection Board*,[78] it was held that professional indemnity policies issued to doctors, dentists and lawyers in North America, which were placed and administered in the United Kingdom, were United Kingdom policies, even though the indemnities thereunder were payable in North America. The performance of the contract had to be looked at as a whole and it was not possible to separate the payment of proceeds from the other obligations of the insurers.

34–49 Further liabilities. The FSCS is obliged to treat the following liabilities of an insurance undertaking as giving rise to claims under a protected contract of insurance:

(a) if the contract has not commenced, premiums paid to the insurance undertaking;

---

[73] That is, excluding those mentioned at (text at note 54).

[74] The date the Employer's Liability (Compulsory Insurance) Act 1969 came into force; see para. 28–87, *ante*. For Northern Ireland the relevant date is December 29, 1975.

[75] See s.4(2) of the 1975 Act and see subs. (3) regarding policies issued by friendly societies. Even though the 1975 Act has been repealed, this is clearly still relevant for the purposes of *The Compensation Rules*.

[76] s.96.

[77] *Scher v. Policyholders Protection Board (No. 2)* [1994] 2 A.C. 57.

[78] *Scher v. Policyholders Protection Board (No. 2)*, *ante*.

(b) proceeds of a long-term insurance contract that has matured or been surrendered but which have not yet been passed to the claimant;

(c) the unexpired portion of any premium in relation to relevant general insurance contracts;[79]

(d) claims by persons entitled to the benefit of a judgment under section 151 of the Road Traffic Act 1988.[80]

34–50 Relevant persons. Section 6 of *The Compensation Handbook* defines in detail the persons against whom someone must have a claim in order to qualify for compensation. A "relevant person" is defined as person who at the time the claim against it was made was a participant firm or authorised representative thereof. For insurance purposes, the principal omission from the definition of "participant firm"[81] is members of Lloyd's. Such a person is in default for the purposes of the "Compensation Rules" if it is, in the opinion of the FSCS unable to satisfy protected claims against it or likely to be unable to satisfy protected claims against it. For this purpose the FSCS may so determine if the person is the subject of any of the insolvency proceedings listed in rule 6.3.3 or there is a determination by its Home State regulator that it appears unable to meet claims and has no early prospect of being able to do so. For the purpose of insurance claims, the FSCS must treat any term in the insurer's constitution or in its contracts of insurance, limiting its liabilities under a long-term contract of insurance to the amount of its assets, as limiting its liabilities to any claimant to an amount which is not less than its gross assets.[82]

34–51 Assignment and procedure. Chapter 7 of *The Compensation Handbook* allows the FSCS to make an offer of compensation conditional on the assignment to it of the rights of the claimant against the insurer in default. Section 8.2 allows for the rejection of an application containing any material inaccuracy or omission or one outside the limitation period. Section 8.3 allows the withdrawal of an offer of compensation if it is not accepted or disputed within 90 days and requires the FSCS to seek to recover compensation that should not have been paid. Chapter 9 requires, *inter alia*, the payment of compensation as soon as reasonably possible after it is satisfied as to eligibility and has calculated the amount due, and in any event within three months of that date. It may postpone payment if it considers that the claim is covered by another contract of insurance with a solvent insurance undertaking or where it appears that a person other than the liquidator may make payment or take such action to continue the continuity of cover as the FSCS would undertake.

34–52 Amount of Compensation. Chapter 10 of the *Compensation Rules* determines the amount of compensation.[83] In respect of a relevant general contract of insurance, 100 per cent of the whole claim must be paid in respect of a liability subject to compulsory insurance.[84] As regards claims under the Third Parties (Rights against Insurers) Act in respect of employer's liability

---

[79] In this context disapplying the general principle described in para. 8–1, *ante*.

[80] Or art. 98 of the Road Traffic (Northern Ireland) Order 1981. See para. 29–24, *ante*.

[81] In the "Glossary" to "The Handbook".

[82] r. 6.3.5.

[83] For further detail on paying and calculating compensation, see Chs 11 and 12 of *The Compensation Rules*.

[84] See para. 34–44, *ante*.

insurance before it was compulsory,[85] 90 per cent of the claim must be paid. In all other cases of general insurance, 100 per cent of the first £2,000 and 90 per cent of the remainder of the claim must be paid.

In respect of long-term insurance, 100 per cent of the first £2,000 must be paid together with at least 90 per cent of the remaining value of the policy, including future benefits declared before the date of the insurer's default. The same principle applies to cases where continuity of insurance cover[86] is secured.

(g) *Dispute Resolution and Complaints*

34–53 General. For just over twenty years, many and, ultimately, the vast majority of, insurers transacting personal lines insurance business to individual assureds participated in a voluntary scheme, the Insurance Ombudsman Bureau, for the resolution of complaints by such assureds.[87] This scheme, together with others operating in the financial services sector, was incorporated, with effect from December 1, 2001, in the Financial Ombudsman Service governed by Part XVI and Schedule 17 of the Financial Services and Markets Act 2000.[88] The Financial Services Authority has made detailed rules under the Act that are contained in the "Disputes Resolution: Complaints" part of "The Handbook".[89] Section 225(1) of the Act refers to the scheme as one "under which certain disputes may be resolved quickly and with minimum formality by an independent person." The scheme is free to complainants and is financed by a levy on authorised firms and others within the jurisdiction.[90]

34–54 Financial Ombudsman Service. Formally, the body established to run the scheme is Financial Ombudsman Service Ltd (hereafter FOS). In practice, the work of the Ombudsman is divided into sections, including an Insurance Ombudsman section. It seems clear that the statutory scheme will adopt the same sort of approach to resolving complaints as that followed by the Insurance Ombudsman Bureau, as the relevant statutory provisions and rules closely follow those that governed the operation of the IOB.[91] The following paragraphs describe the salient features of the scheme as they affect insurers.

34–55 Internal complaint handling. As well as providing for dispute

---

[85] See note 74, *ante*.

[86] See para. 34–34, *ante*.

[87] Initially three large insurance companies set up the scheme, but it grew to cover over 90 per cent of private assureds, including those insured by members of Lloyd's. A minority of insurers belonged to the rival Personal Insurances Arbitration Service. For a brief account, see Birds and Hird, *Birds' Modern Insurance Law*, 5th ed., pp. 5–7. Decisions of the Insurance Ombudsman were not subject to judicial review: *R. v. Insurance Ombudsman Bureau, ex p. Aegon Insurance* [1994] C.L.C. 88.

[88] There are detailed transitional provisions covering complaints and disputes arising before December 1, 2001 but not dealt with by then by the IOB or other former dispute resolution system. These are not considered here.

[89] This is referred to here as the "Dispute Resolution Rules".

[90] See s.234.

[91] As well as being set out formally in the IOB's terms of reference etc, the approach of the IOB can be seen from the Annual Reports and case digests issued by the it, most of which are available electronically at *http://www.theiob.org.uk*.

resolution by FOS, the Dispute Resolution Rules[92] require firms, including insurers,[93] in respects of activities carried on from an establishment in the United Kingdom, to have in place and operate appropriate and effective internal complaint handling procedures.[94] These must provide for receiving complaints, responding to complaints, the appropriate investigation of complaints and notifying complainants of their right to go to the FOS where relevant.[95] Insurers must also refer in writing, at or immediately after the point of sale, to the availability of the procedures, publish and supply copies of the details and display in offices to which complainants have access a notice indicating that they are covered by the FOS.[96] There are also detailed provisions regarding time limits for dealing with complaints[97] and record keeping.[98] Firms are obliged to co-operate fully with the Ombudsman in the handling of complaints against them.[99]

34–56 Jurisdiction of the FOS. The Act divides the jurisdiction of the FOS into compulsory and voluntary jurisdiction. Section 226 provides that a complaint must be dealt with under the scheme if the complainant is eligible and willing, the respondent was an authorised person at the time of the act or omission to which the complaint relates and that act or omission occurred after the appropriate rules were in force. All complaints against insurers by eligible complainants are within the compulsory jurisdiction of the FOS. Section 227 essentially allows for firms that are not authorised persons under the Act to participate in the scheme.[1] In the context of insurance business, this will include brokers and other intermediaries selling general insurance who decide to join the scheme. Both jurisdictions cover complaints in relation to activities carried on from an establishment in the United Kingdom.[2] While this covers complaints from persons living abroad who dealt with a U.K.-based insurer, it does not cover, inter alia, complaints against E.U. insurers providing insurance on a services basis without a U.K. establishment.

34–57 Eligible Complainants. There are detailed rules determining who can complain to FOS. As far as insurance business is concerned, the essential requirements are that the respondent must have failed to resolve the complaint to the satisfaction of the complainant within eight weeks of receiving it[3] and that the complainant is a private individual, a business[4] with

---

[92] See Ch. 1.

[93] Note that Lloyd's is separately required by Ch. 1.7 of "The Rules" to establish appropriate procedures.

[94] These rules are required by para. 13 of Sch. 17 to the Act.

[95] r. 1.2.4.

[96] r. 1.2.9.

[97] Ch. 1.4.

[98] Ch. 1.5.

[99] Ch. 1.6.

[1] Referred to in "The Rules" as a "VJ participant". The standard terms applicable to firms participating in the voluntary jurisdiction are contained in Ch. 4 of the Dispute Resolution Rules.

[2] r. 2.7.

[3] r. 2.2.1 (5). The Ombudsman cannot consider a complaint before eight weeks have elapsed from its receipt by a respondent (r. 2.3.1) and there are limitation periods in the same rule.

[4] Including a sole trader, a company, and unincorporated body and a partnership carrying on any trade or business.

a group annual turnover of less than £1 million, a charity with an annual income of less than £1 million or a trustee of a trust with a net asset value of less than £1 million.[5] This is a significant change from the jurisdiction of the former IOB, which, as indicated earlier, covered only complaints from private assureds. Potential, as well as actual, customers may be eligible to complain.[6] In the insurance context this could be relevant, for example, to a complaint against a general insurance broker who has agreed to be subject to the voluntary jurisdiction, as well as a long-term insurance broker, who will be subject to the compulsory jurisdiction, for failure properly to effect insurance on behalf of the complainant. Further complaints may be brought by a person with no actual or potential relationship themselves with the respondent, but who is a person for whose benefit a contract of insurance was taken out or was intended to be taken out or is a person on whom the legal right to benefit from a claim under a contract of insurance has been devolved by contract, statute or subrogation.[7] The first category clearly includes, for example, a beneficiary under a group life insurance policy and a person named or described as entitled to benefit under a household insurance policy effected by their spouse or parent. The second would appear to include someone who has obtained rights under the Third Parties (Rights Against Insurers) Act 1930[8] or Part IV of the Road Traffic Act 1988.[9]

34–58 Determination of complaints. Chapter 3 of the Dispute Resolution Rules makes detailed provision for the procedures for the FOS to determine complaints; no detail is given here. Section 228 of the 2000 Act, which applies only to the compulsory jurisdiction, provides that a complaint must be determined by reference to what is, in the opinion of the ombudsman, fair and reasonable in all the circumstances of the case. This is repeated and amplified in the Rules, which also provide for the same basis to apply to firms submitting to the voluntary jurisdiction. Rule 3.8.1(2) states that in considering what is fair and reasonable in all the circumstances of the case, the Ombudsman will take into account the relevant law, regulations, regulators' codes and guidance and standards, relevant codes of practice and, where appropriate, what he considers to have been good industry practice at the relevant time. Thus the Ombudsman will take account, where relevant, of the Statements of Insurance Practice[10] and the codes issued by the General Insurance Standards Council.[11]

34–59 Awards and costs. Under section 229 of the Act,[12] if he determines in favour of a complainant, the Ombudsman may make a money award and/or direct that the respondent takes such steps in relation to the complainant as he considers just and appropriate (whether or not a court could order those steps to be taken).[13] A money award may compensate for

---

[5] r. 2.4.3(1), subject to the exemptions in para. (2).
[6] See r. 2.4.8.
[7] r. 2.4.10–12.
[8] See paras. 28–9, *et seq., ante.*
[9] See para. 29–24, *ante.*
[10] See paras 17–102 to 17–104, *ante.*
[11] See 36–75, *post.*
[12] Although this applies only to the compulsory jurisdiction, the same principles will apply under "The Rules" to a person submitting to the voluntary jurisdiction.
[13] This enforceable by injunction or, in Scotland, by an order under section 45 of the Court of Session Act 1998: s.229(9).

financial loss and for pain and suffering, damage to reputation or distress and inconvenience.[14] The maximum money award is £100,000, but the ombudsman may recommend that the respondent pay more if he considers that fair compensation requires this.[15] The ombudsman can also award costs reasonably incurred by the complainant.[16]

34–60 Information. The ombudsman has the statutory right to demand information from any party to a complaint that is necessary for the determination of the complaint[17] and a failure to comply with such a demand may be referred to the court[18] and treated as a contempt of court.[19]

---

[14] s.229(3) and r. 3.9.2. Interest may be added (r. 3.9.7) and if so, does not count towards the maximum.
[15] s.229(5).
[16] s.230 and r. 3.9.10.
[17] s.231.
[18] The High Court or, in Scotland, the Court of Session.
[19] s.232.

CHAPTER 35

THE COURSE OF BUSINESS AT LLOYD'S

35–1 Introduction. To chronicle the history of how Lloyd's of London evolved from a small unincorporated association of underwriters and merchants meeting at Lloyd's coffee house into the corporate society of the present day would be beyond the legitimate scope of a work on the current law of insurance, and it has been well recounted by others.[1] However, it should be noted that severe problems in the Lloyd's market in the late 20th century have tarnished its reputation and led to organisational and regulatory changes.[2]

The history of Lloyd's, however, until very recently impressed upon it two characteristics which merit attention. One was the traditional organisation of Lloyd's as a society of individual underwriters which was largely self regulating, and accordingly exempt from the general statutory system of regulation to which insurance companies were subject.[3] This, however, has changed to some extent and may change further in the future. At least three factors should be mentioned here. First, Lloyd's is to a much greater extent than previously under statutory control.[4] In particular, underwriting agents are now regulated in so far as they advise underwriters who invest in the Lloyd's market.[5] Secondly, the European Commission is taking action to determine whether or not the freedom from regulation previously accorded to Lloyd, and still operational to some extent, is compatible with the Insurance Directives.[6] Thirdly, Lloyd's now admits corporate members as underwriters, with limited liability, and it has been suggested that individual underwriting membership should be phased out.

The second characteristic is the development of Lloyd's own internal market usages and practice in the transaction of insurance business, which affect the legal relationship between the assured and Lloyd's brokers and underwriters. In this chapter we will consider first the relationships between Lloyd's underwriters and their agents and with the Corporation of Lloyd's

---

[1] See Gibb, *Lloyd's of London*, (2nd ed., 1972) and Wright & Fayle, *A History of Lloyd's, From the Founding of Lloyd's Coffee House To The Present Day* (1928).

[2] These problems are evident from much of the litigation surrounding in Lloyd's adverted to in subsequent paragraphs. For a detailed account, see the unreported judgment of Creswell J. in *Society of Lloyd's v. Jaffray*, November 3, 2000, [2000] W.L. 1629463.

[3] See Ch. 34, *ante*.

[4] Under the Financial Services and Markets Act 2000. For a useful description, see Ch. 15 of Perry (ed.), *The Financial Services and Markets Act: A Practical Guide* (Sweet and Maxwell, 2001).

[5] This regulation is effected jointly with the Society of Lloyd's.

[6] As to these, see paras 34–4 to 34–9, *ante*.

itself, and secondly, the relevance of Lloyd's usages and practice towards (1) the obtaining of insurance cover at Lloyd's and (2) bringing a claim upon a Lloyd's insurance policy.

1. REGULATION OF THE LLOYD'S MARKET

35-2 The role of the Society and the Financial Services Authority. Insurance cover is not provided by the Society of Lloyd's but by individual Lloyd's underwriters who are grouped into insuring syndicates consisting of anything from two or three to hundreds of members, or "Names" as they are known, as well now as corporate members. The role of the Society is to manage and regulate the Lloyd's insurance market, acting by its elected Council and committees, but, as indicated earlier, this is now effected jointly with the Financial Services Authority. The power and responsibilities of these bodies are set out in the Financial Services and Markets Act 2000 and the Lloyd's Handbook issued by the Authority under the Act, as well as in the Lloyd's Act 1982, which gives the Society the power to make bye-laws. The various rules impose a much stricter regime than that which applied previously.[7] The Authority is under a duty to keep itself informed about the way in which the Council supervises and regulates the market at Lloyd's and the way in which regulated activities are being carried on in that market.[8] However, the Society itself is directly authorised by the Act, with permission to arrange deals in contracts of insurance written at Lloyd's, to arrange deals in participation in Lloyd's syndicates and to carry on activities in connection with or for the purpose of both of these.[9] The Authority, though, has a reserve power under which it can apply various provisions of the Act to Lloyd's underwriters.[10]Alternatively, it can use a direction to the Society or the Council of Lloyd's to impose obligations on members, for example by the making of bye-laws under the 1982 Act.[11] The general provisions relating to transfers of business are applicable, with modifications, to transfers at Lloyd's.[12]

35-3 Before joining a syndicate, a person desiring to be a Lloyd's Name must give undertakings to, and be accepted for membership of, the Society, but no duty is owed by it to an individual Name either to take care in the exercise of its statutory functions to avoid loss being sustained by him or to take steps to alert him to the discovery of matters which may cause him loss.[13] The Council has power to pass bye-laws "requisite or expedient to the proper and better execution of the Lloyd's Acts 1871 to 1982 and for the furtherance of the objects of the Society."[14] This gave the Council authority

---

[7] Lloyd's underwriters were generally exempt from the requirements of the former insurance companies legislation—see *Society of Lloyd's v. Clementson* [1995] L.R.L.R. 307, 323–324. As to former underwriting members see ss.320–322 of the 2000 Act.

[8] Financial Services and Markets Act 2000, s.314.

[9] s.315.

[10] s.316. These provisions are described as the "core provisions" and are detailed in s.317.

[11] s.318, provided that it has consulted as provided for in s.319.

[12] s.323 and The Financial Services and Markets Act 2000 (Control of Transfers of Business Done at Lloyd's) Order 2001 (S.I. 2001 No. 3626).

[13] *Ashmore v. Corporation of Lloyd's (No. 2)* [1992] 2 Lloyd's Rep. 620; *Price v. Society of Lloyd's* [2000] Lloyd's Rep.I.R. 453.

[14] Lloyd's Act 1982, s.6(2).

to introduce a power to compel Names to join a complex scheme of reconstruction,[15] when disastrous losses and "an avalanche of litigation"[16] had threatened the market, which provided, inter alia, that any claims by Names against the Society could not be used to set off the their liabilities under the scheme.[17] The relevant claims by members, which involved allegations that they had been fraudulently induced to become members, were ultimately dismissed.[18]

35–4 Role of underwriting agents. A Name can underwrite insurances at Lloyd's only through an underwriting agent.[19] In practice underwriting agents act in one of three different capacities:

(1) There are members' agents who advise Names on their choice of syndicates and place them on syndicates so chosen.
(2) There are managing agents who conduct the active underwriting of contracts of insurance at Lloyd's on behalf of the members of the syndicates which they manage, and who obtain reinsurances and pay claims.
(3) There are combined agents who perform both the role of members' agents and the role of managing agents in respect of the syndicates under their management.[20]

Prior to 1990 it was usual for a Name to have an agency agreement with a members' agent which would conclude a sub-agency agreement with the managing agents of a syndicate on which the Name was placed, but new standard forms of agency agreement were introduced[21] for the 1990 and subsequent years of account under which a Name would conclude an agency agreement with both types of underwriting agent. Under the new agency agreements both members' and managing agents expressly undertake duties of care and skill and fiduciary obligations towards Names,[22] but it was held that agents appointed on the preceding agency terms already impliedly owed duties of care to Names in the performance of their obligations as agents, both in contract and tort (members' agents) or in tort alone (managing agents).[23]

---

[15] Known as "Equitas" after the group of companies with this name formed to effect the scheme. For a detailed account of the scheme see *Society of Lloyd's v. Leighs* [1997] C.L.C. 759. A summary of the litigation to which it gave rise appears in the Court of Appeal judgment in *Society of Lloyd's v. Fraser* [1999] Lloyd's Rep.I.R. 156 and the unreported judgment of Creswell J in *Society of Lloyd's v. Jaffray*, November 3, 2000, [2000] W.L. 1629463. See also *Manning v. Society of Lloyd's* [1997] CLC 1411 regarding the application of various points of basic contract law to the scheme.

[16] *Society of Lloyd's v. Leighs*]1997] C.L.C. 1398, 1399.

[17] *Society of Lloyd's v. Leighs, supra, Society of Lloyd's v. Fraser, supra.*

[18] *Society of Lloyd's v. Jaffray*, November 3, 2000, [2000] W.L. 1629463. Previously, though, an application by the Society to stay the claims was rejected (*Society of Lloyd's v. Jaffray* [1999] Lloyd's Rep.I.R. 182) and a statutory demand made on a member was set aside (*Garrow v. Society of Lloyd's* [2000] Lloyd's Rep.I.R. 38).

[19] Lloyd's Act 1982, s.8(2), unless the name is himself an underwriting agent.

[20] Members' agents in this sense are now subject to regulation under the Financial Services and Markets Act 2000.

[21] Byelaw No. 8 of 1988. Where more than one members' agent is needed to act for a Name, a co-ordinating agent is appointed to co-ordinate the overall administration of his affairs, para. 1.

[22] Standard Members' Agent's Agreement, para. 6.2; Standard Managing Agent's Agreement, para. 4.2.

[23] *Henderson v. Merrett Syndicates Ltd* [1995] 2 A.C. 145.

35–5 Responsibilities of members' agents. One of the obligations expressly undertaken by a members' agent under the Standard Members' Agents' Agreement[24] is to advise the Name as to which syndicates he should join and the appropriate allocation of his premium income between them. This requires the agent to explain to the Name the type of business written by the relevant syndicates, bearing in mind the underwriting philosophy believed suitable for his needs and the need to maintain a balanced overall portfolio, and in particular to warn the Name of the risks inherent in the high risk business written by some syndicates, such as London Market Excess of Loss business.[25] The Name is required to keep the agent in funds for the purpose of meeting his underwriting liabilities, and the agent is given a complete discretion as to the amounts needed from time to time.[26] The Name agrees not to make any deduction from calls made by the agent and not to make any legal challenge to the agent's calculation of the sums required, provided that the agent is acting in good faith.[27] The agent is not required to investigate and check calls for funds by managing agents of syndicates on which the Name is placed.[28] But the Name is not precluded from bringing legal proceedings for negligent conduct of his underwriting business.[29]

35–6 Responsibilities of managing agents. Under the Standard Managing Agent's Agreement the Name empowers the agent to conduct the underwriting of the syndicate managed by it in its complete discretion and without interference by him,[30] but the agent agrees to use reasonable skill care and diligence in so doing and to act in accord with the perceived interests of the Name.[31] In practice there will be an "active" underwriter for each syndicate who conducts the syndicate's underwriting business from his box in the underwriting room at Lloyd's, at which risks are presented to him. In determining whether reasonable skill and care has been exercised by the underwriter the court will make allowances for the nature of the difficult decisions which underwriting entails, because professional men are not to be made liable for errors of judgment.[32] But prudent underwriting requires the underwriter to exercise care in assembling the data needed for the formation of a judgment and in observing such fundamental principles of underwriting as are reasonably to be followed in the particular business to which he is committing the syndicate. A Name may reasonably expect his managing agent to exercise reasonable care to prevent him from suffering losses and to warn him if he intends deliberately to expose the syndicate to sustaining

---

[24] Std. Memb. Agent's Agreement, para. 4.
[25] *Brown v. KMR Services Ltd* [1995] 2 Lloyd's Rep. 513. "LMX" business is described in *Deeny v. Gooda Walker Ltd. (No. 2)* [1996] L.R.L.R. 183, 188–190.
[26] Standard Members' Agent's Agreement, para. 9.
[27] *Arbuthnott v. Fagan* [1996] L.R.L.R. 135; *Boobyer v. Holman & Co (No. 2).* [1993] 1 Lloyd's Rep. 96, 98.
[28] *Boobyer v. Holman & Co.* [1993] 1 Lloyd's Rep. 96, 97.
[29] *Arbuthnott v. Fagan* [1996] L.R.L.R. 135. Such a claim might be arbitrated under Lloyd's Arbitration Scheme Rules—*Cohen v. Holman & Co.* [1996] L.R.L.R. 387.
[30] See para. 5(a) of the 1988 Form of Managing Agent's Agreemeent.
[31] See para. 4, *supra.*
[32] *Saif Ali v. Mitchell* [1980] A.C. 198, 220, applied in *Deeny v. Gooda Walker Ltd* [1996] L.R.L.R. 183, 207, and *Wynniatt-Husey v. Bromley* [1996] L.R.L.R. 310, 313. See also *Berriman v. Rose Thomson Young* [1996] L.R.L.R. 426, 443, to the same effect.

losses. In *Deeny v. Gooda Walker Ltd (No. 2)*[33] it was held that underwriters acted negligently in writing London Market Excess of Loss business in circumstances where they were unable to make satisfactory assessments of exposure to loss, of premium commensurate with the risk run, and of adequate reinsurance protection. A managing agent owes a duty to Names on his syndicate to exercise care in considering what facts are material to be disclosed to prospective reinsurers of syndicate liabilities, and how the business to be reinsured should properly be described. If his failure to do so results in subsequent avoidance of the reinsurance cover, he will be liable in damages to Names on the syndicate at the time it was placed and also to Names on subsequent years of account who have to bear the unreinsured losses.[34]

35–7 Liability of Name. When a syndicate takes a line on a risk each Name incurs a several liability to the assured, so that he is liable only for his proportion and not for his fellow syndicate members.[35] It follows that each syndicate is not answerable for the lines taken by other syndicates or insurance companies on the same risk. It frequently happens, however, that syndicates, by their active underwriters, delegate to a third party the power to enter into contracts on behalf of their members, and authorise the active underwriter of the leading syndicate to bind them by agreeing variations or extensions of the policy cover. Once a line is taken by a syndicate it results in the conclusion of individual contracts between each Name and the assured, identical save as to the individual proportions subscribed by each Name.[36] Traditionally each Name is personally liable to the limit of his assets for all underwriting written on his behalf.[37] The receipt of premiums and other monies payable to him in connection with his underwriting is governed by the standard Lloyd's Premium Trust Deed into which each Name enters. Such monies include damages recovered in litigation against his agents for negligent underwriting[38] but under previous the wording of the Deed did not include damages payable by his members agent for negligence in regard to his stop loss insurances and selection of syndicates.[39] An amendment made in 1995 includes the latter.[40]

---

[33] [1996] L.R.L.R. 183. Subsequent decisions upon the assessment of damages and the awarding of interest upon them are reported at [1996] L.R.L.R. 176. and 168 respectively. A similar decision was reached in *Wynniatt-Husey v. Bromley* [1996] L.R.L.R. 310 and *Berriman v. Rose Thomson Young* [1996] L.R.L.R. 426.

[34] *Aiken v. Stewart Wrightson Agency* [1995] 1 W.L.R. 1281.

[35] Lloyd's Act 1982 s.8(1). See para. 35–30, *post*, and the description of the Lloyd's market given in *Napier and Ettrick v. Kershaw* [1997] L.R.L.R. 1, 7–8. This description was approved by the House of Lords in *Society of Lloyd's v. Robinson* [1999] 1 W.L.R. 756 at 760.

[36] *Touche Ross v. Baker* [1992] Lloyd's Rep. 207, 209–210.

[37] *Ashmore v. Corporation of Lloyd's* [1992] 2 Lloyd's Rep. 1, 3.

[38] *Napier and Ettrick v. Kershaw* [1997] L.R.L.R. 1, affirmed *sub nom. Society of Lloyd's v. Robinson* [1999] 1 W.L.R. 756.

[39] *Lloyd's (Society of) v. Woodard* [1997] L.R.L.R. 1; *Lloyd's (Society of) v. Morris* [1993] 2 Re. L.R. 217; *Society of Lloyd's v. Robinson, supra.*

[40] The validity of the amendment was upheld in *Society of Lloyd's v. Robinson, supra.*

2. Placing Insurance at Lloyd's

35–8 Insurance risks have to be placed with Lloyd's underwriters by brokers who are approved by the Committee of Lloyd's and who possess the right of access to "the Room", and are described accordingly as "Lloyd's brokers".[41]

35–9 The applicant for a Lloyd's policy must consequently act through a Lloyd's broker.[42] Since he will often instruct his own insurance broker who is not a Lloyd's broker in the first instance, there will frequently be at least two brokers intervening between the assured and the underwriters who subscribe his policy. There may well be more than two,[43] as where, for instance, the applicant is resident abroad and his brokers prefer to instruct agents in London who are not Lloyd's brokers. There is no privity between the assured and the placing broker where the assured effects insurance through a producing broker who then approaches the placing broker.[44]

35–10 The Lloyd's broker writes down the details of the cover which the applicant wishes to obtain on a document known as a "slip", using accepted abbreviations in order to condense the terms of the insurance onto one or two sheets of paper. He then carries the slip round the underwriters' boxes in the Room inviting subscriptions, and negotiating terms and proportions with the various syndicates. He probably does not know which syndicates will subscribe the slip when he starts to invite subscriptions, and the applicant whom he represents certainly has no idea, unless special negotiations have been held beforehand in the case of a risk of special interest or size. In negotiating with underwriters and placing the risk, the Lloyd's broker acts as the agent of the assured,[45] and not of the underwriter, with one important exception that will be mentioned later.[46] Consequently he is under the same obligation to keep within his instructions and to make full disclosure to the underwriter as is an ordinary insurance broker dealing with an insurance company.[47]

---

[41] Lloyd's Act 1982, s.8(3).

[42] *Praet v. Poland* [1960] 1 Lloyd's Rep. 416, 433–434; Lloyd's Act 1982, s.8(3).

[43] In *Anglo-African Merchants v. Bayley* [1970] 1 Q.B. 311, for example, there were three brokers involved. For the authority of an agent for a syndicate see *Hambro v. Burnard* [1903] 2 K.B. 399; [1904] 2 K.B. 10. For the "umbrella arrangement" whereby a Lloyd's broker permits a non-Lloyd's broker to transact business in its name in order to avoid the expense of sub-agency see *Johns v. Kelly* [1986] 1 Lloyd's Rep. 468; *Callaghan and Hedges v. Thompson* [2000] Lloyd's Rep.I.R. 125.

[44] *Prentis Donegan & Partners Ltd v. Leeds & Leeds Co. Inc.* [1998] 2 Lloyd's Rep. 326. With respect, this seems a better view than the contrary seemingly taken in *Velos Group Ltd v. Harbour Insurance Services Ltd* [1997] 2 Lloyd's Rep. 465, although Rix J. in *Prentis Donegan, supra*, was able to distinguish the earlier case on the grounds, *inter alia*, that important authorities were not cited and there were special facts in that case.

[45] *Rozanes v. Bowen* (1928) 32 Ll.L.R. 98, 101; *Anglo-African Merchants v. Bayley* [1970] 1 Q.B. 311, 322; *North and South Trust v. Berkeley* [1971] 1 W.L.R. 471; *Minett v. Forrester* (1811) 4 Taunt. 541n., 544; *American Airlines v. Hope* [1974] 2 Lloyd's Rep. 301, 304, *per* Lord Diplock.

[46] This concerns payment of premium. The Lloyd's broker is personally liable to the underwriter for the premium regardless of whether he receives it from the assured. See para. 35–12, *post*. The Lloyd's placing broker has no ostensible authority to cancel a policy negotiated by him—*Xenos v. Wickham* (1867) L.R. 2 H.L. 296.

[47] Disclosure of a material fact to the Lloyd's broker is therefore not disclosure to the underwriter—*Rozanes v. Bowen* (1928) 32 Ll.L.R. 98, 101; *Empress Assurance Corporation v. Bowring & Co.* (1905) 11 Com.Cas. 107, 112.

35–11 If the underwriter finds the terms on the slip acceptable he initials the slip, thereby binding his syndicate to give cover on the terms of the slip.[48] A Lloyd's slip is more than an engagement of honour. It is a binding contract of insurance in itself from which the underwriters cannot resile.[49] A policy is then prepared and issued in conformity with the slip. The policy is not signed by each syndicate according to post-war Lloyd's practice, but is signed in the names of the syndicates, which initialled the slip, by the Lloyd's Policy Signing Office.[50] The Policy Signing Office executes the policy pursuant to an actual authority bestowed on it by each syndicate, at some stage in the past, and, if in the Office's judgment the policy submitted to it by the broker is in conformity with the slip, it will sign and issue the policy on behalf of the syndicates concerned, binding them just as if the underwriters had executed it themselves.[51]

35–12 The above description of the practice according to which insurance risks are typically placed at Lloyd's will serve as the background to the points discussed in detail in the following paragraphs. It must, however, be appreciated that Lloyd's procedures are far from being inflexible, and variations in the usual practice must be anticipated in particular types of insurance. Thus, for instance, in motor insurance business underwriters have, through Lloyd's brokers, empowered local brokers and insurance agents to issue temporary cover notes in the names of particular syndicates in order to satisfy the motorist's demand for instant cover and to make Lloyd's competitive with other insurers. In that case there is a binding interim insurance agreement preceding any initialled slip, and the insurance agent who issues the cover note in these circumstances is acting as an agent of underwriters with authority bestowed on him through a Lloyd's broker.[52] The main cover is, however, granted after receipt of a proposal in the usual manner described above. There are also cases in which the contract negotiated in the underwriting room, in accordance with the established procedure, is an authority permitting an agent, either in the United Kingdom or elsewhere, to conclude insurance contracts of a specified kind, on behalf of the underwriters granting the authority. In such a case, the agent will usually issue certificates to the insured. It is not unknown for such authorities to be granted by a list of co-insurers including both Lloyd's underwriters and insurance companies.

35–13 Payment of the premium. By reason of a long established custom or

---

[48] Unless the initialling is expressed to be qualified or conditional—*Eagle Star Insurance Co. v. Spratt* [1971] 2 Lloyd's Rep. 116, 124.

[49] *Thompson v. Adams* (1889) 23 Q.B.D. 361; *Grover & Grover v. Mathews* [1910] 2 K.B. 401; *General Reinsurance Corp. v. Forsakr. Fennia Patria* [1983] Q.B. 856. The legal status of a partially subscribed slip is examined below at para. 35–17. For an unsuccessful attempt to set up an oral contract of reinsurance at Lloyd's, see *Sphere Drake Ins. plc v. Denby* [1995] L.R.L.R. 1.

[50] The authority and functions of the Lloyd's Policy Signing Office are analysed in the *Eagle Star* Case, *supra*. For a summary of Lloyd's procedures when a risk is first placed and on renewal see *American Airlines v. Hope* [1974] 2 Lloyd's Rep. 301, 304–305, *per* Lord Diplock. For an account of the practice of "signing down" and of the procedure whereby reinsurance is bound in advance of the primary insurance in the Lloyd's marine market see *General Accident Fire & Life Ass. Corp. v. Tanter* [1984] 1 Lloyd's Rep. 58, 65–73; [1985] 2 Lloyd's Rep. 529, 531–532, C.A. As to allocating business to a particular year of account see *Mander v. Equitas Ltd* [2000] Lloyd's Rep.I.R. 520.

[51] Unless the agreement is for a "slip policy", in which case the slip remains the record of the contract. See note 68, *post*.

[52] *Praet v. Poland* [1960] 1 Lloyd's Rep. 416, 428.

usage of Lloyd's, the underwriter does not claim the premium from the assured but from the Lloyd's broker, and the broker in turn looks to the assured for payment. The custom is founded in the ancient usages of the marine underwriting business in London, and the courts have had it proved a sufficient number of times to accord it judicial notice.[53] So far as the Lloyd's broker and the underwriter are concerned, the premium is treated as a debt due from the broker alone, so that the broker is the principal debtor to the underwriter for it in addition to being an agent of the assured to negotiate the insurance cover.[54] The broker and underwriter maintain a running account showing premiums due from the broker and losses payable on policies for which the underwriter is liable. In order to avoid a multiplicity of dealings from day to day, the account is settled under the Lloyd's central accounting procedure, and payment is made from the one to the other depending on which side the balance falls, traditionally at quarterly intervals.

35–14 The usage is sufficiently old to have been recognised in the days of Lord Ellenborough,[55] and may have been intended to bestow a degree of security upon the underwriters by allowing them to look for payment to a broker known to them, rather than an assured whose reputation was unknown to them.[56] The legal rationale for this course of business is that the broker is considered in law as having paid the premium to the underwriter in place of the assured, and that it has then been lent to the broker by the underwriter, as evidenced by the credit item entered in his accounts in favour of the latter.[57]

35–15 So far as the assured is concerned, he is considered as having agreed to allow the broker to discharge his liability to the underwriter for a premium, and the underwriter cannot come on him for payment. It was established in the 18th century that the broker accordingly could sue the assured for the premium, as money paid to the defendant's use, although no actual payment had been made by him.[58] This precedent troubled at least one eminent judge thereafter as a matter of legal principle,[59] but there is undoubted justice in it, seeing that the assured cannot be sued by the underwriter for the premium which the broker is liable to pay,[60] and the underwriter cannot refuse to pay a loss on the ground that the broker has not accounted to him for the premium.[61] Moreover the assured can sue the

---

[53] *Universo Insurance Co. of Milan v. Merchants' Marine Insurance Co.* [1897] 2 Q.B. 93, 95, 101. It is now codified in s.53 of the Marine Insurance Act 1906 for marine insurance. In *Pacific & General Ins. Co. v. Hazell* [1997] L.R.L.R. 65 the usage was held to be inapplicable to the London non-marine market.

[54] *Universo Insurance Co. v. Merchants' Marine Insurance Co., supra; Praet v. Poland* [1960] 1 Lloyd's Rep. 416, 420; *Scott v. Irving* (1830) 1 B. & Ad. 605; *Grover & Grover v. Mathews* (1910) 102 L.T. 650, 654 (reported less fully in [1910] 2 K.B. 401).

[55] *Edgar v. Fowler* (1803) 1 East. 222; *Dalzell v. Mair* (1808) 1 Camp. 532; *Shee v. Clarkson* (1810) 12 East. 507; *Minett v. Forrester* (1811) 4 Taunt. 541n.

[56] *Universo Insurance Co. v. Merchants' Marine Co.* [1897] 2 Q.B. 93, 99.

[57] *Power v. Butcher* (1829) 10 B. & C. 329, 347, per Parke J., approved in *Xenos v. Wickham* (1863) 14 C.B.(N.S.) 435, and in the *Universo Insurance Co.* case, *supra*.

[58] *Airy v. Bland* (1774) 2 Park's Insurance 811 (8th ed.); *Dalzell v. Mair* (1808) 1 Camp. 532, 534.

[59] *Power v. Butcher* (1829) 10 B. & C. 329, 344, per Littledale J.

[60] *Dalzell v. Mair* (1808) 1 Camp. 532, 534; *Power v. Butcher, supra; Universo Insurance Co. v. Merchants' Marine Co.* [1897] 2 Q.B. 93.

[61] *Scott v. Irving* (1830) 1 B. & Ad. 605; *Sweeting v. Pearce* (1861) 9 C.B.(N.S.) 534.

underwriter for return of the premium where the risk is not run, as where a vessel never sets out on an insured voyage.[62]

35–16 The earlier decisions of the courts holding that the assured is considered as having paid the underwriter appear to have attached some importance to the formal acknowledgment in a policy that the underwriter has received a premium from the assured,[63] but it is clear now that the assured derives his protection from the existence of the usage itself, and not by reason of the acknowledgment that money has been received.[64] The acknowledgment is important to this extent, however; the parties are free to contract out of observing the usage by using clear words to that effect, and the absence of acknowledgment might be a factor in establishing such an agreement.[65]

35–17 Conclusion of the contract. It is well established that once a slip has been fully subscribed up to 100 per cent of the risk, there is a binding contract of insurance between the assured and each underwriter who has initialled it for the proportion which each has subscribed.[66] Neither the assured nor the underwriters may resile from it. Where a slip is oversubscribed, it is a recognised and binding custom of the London marine and non-marine markets that all lines are to be proportionately "written down" to 100 per cent upon the ultimate closing of the risk.[67] This is a qualification of the general rule that an underwriter is bound to the line for which he has subscribed the slip presented to him for initialling. In some cases the slip is never superseded by a full policy insurance wording, the document then being called a "slip policy".[68]

35–18 There used to be doubt as to the legal status of a partially subscribed slip. It was suggested obiter in *Jaglom v. Excess Insurance Co.*[69] that the underwriter's initialling of the slip was an offer to be bound for his proportion of the risk, which the assured was free to accept or reject at a later stage. In this way an assured would be free to resile from an incompletely subscribed slip, and different underwriters need not become bound on different terms. However, this view ran counter to market practice and

---

[62] *Dalzell v. Mair* (1808) 1 Camp. 532.

[63] *Power v. Butcher* (1829) 10 B. & C. 329; *De Gaminde v. Pigou* (1812) 4 Taunt. 246, 247; *Dalzell v. Mair* (1808) 1 Camp. 532, 533, where Lord Ellenborough said: "I should completely knock up the insurance business if I were to allow this acknowledgement to be impeached." Mansfield C.J. would permit such an impeachment if fraud was involved—*Minett v. Forrester* (1811) 4 Taunt. 541n, 544.

[64] *Universo Insurance Co. v. Merchants' Marine Insurance Co.* [1897] 2 Q.B. 93.

[65] *Power v. Butcher* (1830) 10 B. & C. 329, 347.

[66] *Thompson v. Adams* (1889) 23 Q.B.D. 361; *Grover & Grover v. Matthews* [1910] 2 K.B. 401; *Re Yager & Guardian Assurance Co.* (1912) 108 L.T. 38, 43. "The contract is the slip"—"*The Zephyr*" [1984] 1 Lloyd's Rep. 58, 69, *per* Hobhouse J.

[67] *General Reinsurance Corporation v. Forsakringsaktiebolaget Fennia Patria* [1983] Q.B. 856, 865, approving [1982] Q.B. 1022, 1037–1038; "*The Zephyr*" [1984] 1 Lloyd's Rep. 58; [1985] 2 Lloyd's Rep. 529, 531.

[68] See, *e.g.* "*The Leegas*" [1987] 1 Lloyd's Rep. 471; *Philips v. Dorintal Ins. Co.* [1987] 1 Lloyd's Rep. 482; "*The Zephyr*" [1984] 1 Lloyd's Rep. 58; *HIH Casualty & General Ins. Ltd v. New Hampshire Ins. Co.* [2001] 2 All E.R.(Comm) 39.

[69] [1972] 2 Q.B. 250, 257–258.

authority[70] and in *General Reinsurance Corporation v. Forsakringsaktiebolaget Fennia Patria* both Staughton J.[71] and the Court of Appeal[72] disapproved it[73] and upheld the traditional rule that each underwriter is bound on the terms for which he has subscribed the slip whether or not it is fully subscribed, subject only to the custom of "writing-down" described above. The same rule applies whether the slip is for a new risk, or for renewal or variation of an existing risk. Accordingly if a loss occurs before the slip is fully subscribed each underwriter is bound to pay the proportion of it that his line represents[74] even if, had the slip been fully subscribed, that line would have been written down to a smaller proportion subsequently.[75] The Court of Appeal refused to find a custom of the market, or imply a term, to the effect that the assured possesses the option to withdraw from the contract by cancelling the slip at any time until it is fully subscribed.[76]

35–19 Terms to be agreed. It is frequently the case that the slip will record that certain terms are to be agreed after conclusion of the contract, such as the commencement date[77] or the premium.[78] An abbreviation commonly used is "t.b.a." (to be agreed), and a frequent refinement is "t.b.a. l/u", meaning "to be agreed with the leading underwriter".[79] So far as the rate of premium is concerned, it is a common practice for underwriters to take certain risks at a rate to be agreed. The parties thereby agree to leave the rate open for future settlement, and, if a loss occurs before settlement the loss becomes payable subject to deduction of a reasonable premium. In default of agreement between the parties, the amount of the premium will be settled by the court or, if the parties agree, an arbitrator.[80] Insurance at a rate to be agreed is not usual in fire, life, and accident risks, but it is not unknown.

35–20 The phrase "t.b.a." does not, however, invariably mean as a matter of law that the parties have concluded a binding contract pending agreement on the term or terms which are so marked, and the context in which they are used may show that the parties meant that there was to be no binding agreement until the term or terms to be agreed were settled. In *Banque*

---

[70] *Eagle Star Insurance Co. v. Spratt* [1971] 2 Lloyd's Rep. 116, 124, 132; *Thompson v. Adams* (1889) 23 Q.B.D. 361, 364–365; *Grover & Grover v. Mathews* (1910) 102 L.T. 650, 652; 15 Com.Cas. 249, 256 (not cited in the report at [1910] 2 K.B. 401).

[71] [1982] Q.B. 1022, 1038.

[72] [1983] Q.B. 856, 866–867.

[73] Following the opinion expressed in paras 2202–2204 of the 7th edition of this work.

[74] *Morrison v. Universal Marine Insurance Co.* (1872) L.R. 8 Exch. 40; (1873) L.R. 8 Ex. 197.

[75] *"The Zephyr"* [1984] 1 Lloyd's Rep. 58, 86.

[76] [1983] Q.B. 856, reversing Staughton J. [1982] Q.B. 1022, 1038–1039.

[77] *e.g. Jaglom v. Excess Insurance Co.* [1972] 2 Q.B. 250, 267.

[78] *e.g. Banque Sabbag SARL v. Hope* [1972] 1 Lloyd's Rep. 253, 256, where it was said "t.b.a." might also mean "to be advised".

[79] *Touche Ross v. Baker* [1992] 2 Lloyd's Rep. 207, 210.

[80] *Greenock S.S. Co. v. Maritime Insurance Co.* [1903] 2 K.B. 657; *Banque Sabbag S.A.L. v. Hope* [1972] 1 Lloyd's Rep. 253, 260–261, disapproving *Christie v. North British Ins. Co.* (1852) 3 S. & D. (Ct of Sess.) 519 and approving the corresponding paragraph (661) in MacGillivray (5th ed.); affirmed in C.A. on grounds not affecting this statement of the law—[1973] 1 Lloyd's Rep. 233; the decision was affirmed in the House of Lords on a different ground not affecting this point—[1974] 2 Lloyd's Rep. 301.

Sabbag SARL v. Hope,[81] underwriters granted aviation risks cover on a slip which made available additional war risks cover "only at AP and Geographical Limits t.b.a. L/U" (only at an additional premium and geographical limits to be agreed with leading underwriters). Two months after the slip was initialled, but before a policy was issued and before either geographical limits or the extra premium had been settled, three aircraft covered by the policy were destroyed while on the ground at a Middle Eastern airport in circumstances which made them losses by perils covered under the additional war risks cover. The underwriters, however, argued that the war risks cover was not effective until the geographical limits and additional premium were settled, and the Court of Appeal upheld their contention.

It is submitted that the decision turned on two important factors concerning this particular slip. First, the war risks cover required agreement not only on premium but also on the geographical limits of the cover, and there was a logical difficulty in asserting that the cover could be effective before it could be said where it was effective, a point which particularly impressed Phillimore L.J. Secondly, the words "held covered" appeared elsewhere on the slip in relation to other terms concerning geographical limits, but were absent in the context of the war risks cover. This prompted the conclusion, on orthodox principles of construction, that the parties did not intend to provide war risks cover pending agreement on premium and limits because they would then have inserted the letters "h.c." (held covered) in the war risks clause also, and Roskill L.J. reached his decision primarily on these grounds. Lord Denning M.R., however, considered the slip sufficiently ambiguous to permit him to look at the prior correspondence between the parties and he thereupon resolved the ambiguity in favour of the underwriters.

35-21 It is submitted that this case does not displace the usual presumption that, where only the rate of premium is left to be agreed, the cover is effective pending such agreement, especially when more than merely additional cover is involved.[82] The intention to grant cover pending agreement of one or more terms of the insurance is made clearer if the words "held covered" are employed, especially in a renewal. But the phrase will not assist if there is ambiguity as to the extent and duration of the cover so maintained.[83]

35-22 Rectification of policy and slip. If the policy that emanates from the Policy Signing Office does not accord with the slip, the parties are entitled to rectification of the policy to record the terms agreed on the slip. If the slip

---

[81] [1972] 1 Lloyd's Rep. 253; on appeal—[1973] 1 Lloyd's Rep. 233; [1974] 2 Lloyd's Rep. 301. There was no appeal from this part of the Court of Appeal's decision.

[82] This appears especially from Lord Denning's judgment at [1973] 1 Lloyd's Rep. 233, 241, citing Marine Insurance Act 1906, s.31(2).

[83] As there was in *Re Yager and the Guardian Assurance Co.* (1912) 108 L.T. 38 where the phrase applied only to a limited and temporary cover. Sometimes the phrase "held covered as expiring" is used, *i.e.* held covered on same terms as the expiring cover on the subject-matter insured—*Hope*'s Case at [1974] 2 Lloyd's Rep. 301, 305.

itself was defective and failed to record the real agreement between the Lloyd's broker and the underwriter, it also may be rectified if clear evidence of intention is adduced. If rectification is not sought, and it is subsequently necessary to determine what the terms of the cover were, as where cover is renewed "as expiring", the slip is to be regarded as the dominant document in the case of conflict with the policy, as it is more than merely a temporary cover note.[84]

> "This accords with the evidence given generally, which is in fact well known, that business at Lloyd's is done on slips, the leading underwriter does not keep a copy of the policy and may not himself ever see it, and when the time comes for renewal it is the previous year's slip and not the policy that is brought to the leading underwriter together with the new slip."[85]

3. PAYMENT OF LOSSES UNDER LLOYD'S POLICIES

35–23 Lloyd's practice not binding in law. When a Lloyd's broker is instructed by or on behalf of the assured to recover a loss payable under a Lloyd's policy, the practice at Lloyd's is for the underwriter to discharge his liability on the policy by entering a credit for the sum payable in favour of the broker in their running account, after which it is left to the broker to pay the loss to the assured in cash or the equivalent.[86] If the assured is bound by this practice, he is obliged to look to the broker for payment, and cannot claim the sum due in cash from the underwriter in the event of the broker becoming insolvent or refusing to pay him.[87]

The assured, however, is not bound to abide by the act of his broker in receiving payment of the loss in this manner simply because the broker has acted according to the established usage at Lloyd's. Although, as we have seen, the courts accord judicial recognition to the usage of Lloyd's in regard to the payment of premiums,[88] they do not do so with regard to the payment of losses. In law, the crediting of the account in favour of the broker is not recognised as discharging the underwriter's liability to the assured under the contract of insurance because for more than 150 years the usage has been criticised as an unreasonable one which does not bind the assured unless he consents to abide by it.[89]

---

[84] *Banque Sabbag S.A.L. v. Hope* [1972] 1 Lloyd's Rep. 253, 263, *per* Mocatta J., unaffected on this point by the decisions of the appellate courts at [1973] 1 Lloyd's Rep. 233 and [1974] 2 Lloyd's Rep. 301.

[85] *ibid.*

[86] The practice was described in 1821 as one which had already existed for many years—*Todd v. Reid* (1821) 4 B. & Ald. 210, 211.

[87] Drawing a bill of exchange on the broker does not amount to an election releasing the underwriter—*Bartlett v. Pentland* (1830) 10 B. & C. 760, 773, *per* Bayley J.

[88] See para. 35–12, *ante.*

[89] *Todd v. Reid* (1821) 4 B. & Ald. 210; *Bartlett v. Pentland* (1830) 10 B. & C. 760; *Scott v. Irving* (1830) 1 B. & Ad.; *Sweeting v. Pearce* (1859) 7 C.B.(N.S.) 449, explaining *Stewart v. Aberdein* (1838) 4 M. & W. 211, affirmed at (1861) 9 C.B.(N.S.) 534; *Legge v. Byas, Mosley & Co.* (1901) 7 Com.Cas. 16. The matter is now settled by precedent—*Matvieff v. Crosfield* (1903) 8 Com.Cas. 120, where Kennedy J. refused to apply the custom without expressly deciding it was unreasonable.

35–24 At first the usage was stigmatised as "illegal",[90] but the courts were not slow in giving more precise reasons for their disapproval of it. In the first place it offends against the rule implied by common law into the mandate of any agent instructed to collect payment of a sum of money, that he has authority only to receive payment from the debtor in cash or the equivalent,[91] with the further consequence that the debtor must see that the mode of payment adopted by him enables the agent to comply with that rule.[92] Therefore, as Bramwell B. said in *Sweeting v. Pearce*,[93] the custom is unreasonable if only because it empowers the broker and underwriter not to do what the law implies they should do. Secondly, the custom is unreasonable because it substitutes a new debtor for the principal debtor, the underwriter,[94] and especially so in that the assured is deprived of the security of Lloyd's syndicates and is driven instead to rely upon the credit of a particular broker or firm of brokers who are not properly insurers at all.[95] Thirdly, fears have been expressed that to recognise such a custom would tend to promote collusion or fraud between the broker and underwriter.[96] For these reasons the assured is not obliged to abide by the custom unless he gives his consent to his agent acting under it,[97] the agent's action otherwise being regarded in law as unauthorised and invalid.

35–25 Consent of assured. If it is contended that the assured is bound by the Lloyd's usage on grounds of his prior consent, it must be shown that he knew of the usage and consented to be bound by it.

35–26 It is for the underwriter to establish that the assured was acquainted with the custom, and this will be very hard where the assured denies knowledge of it, particularly where he is transacting business in a place remote from the London insurance market,[98] or is not in the sort of occupation where he might be expected to acquire such knowledge.[99] Even where the assured has transacted insurances at Lloyd's before, it cannot be assumed, in the face of his denial, that he must have acquired knowledge of the custom and its effect on him.[1] Even the fact that an assured has collected

---

[90] *Todd v. Reid* (1821) 4 B. & Ald. 210 (headnote). Note the criticisms of the report of this case by Parke B. in *Stewart v. Aberdein* (1838) 4 M. & W. 211, 224.

[91] *Bartlett v. Pentland* (1830) 10 B. & C. 760; *Scott v. Irving* (1830) 1 B. & Ad. 605; *Russell v. Bangley* (1821) 4 B. & Ald. 395, as explained in these two decisions; *Sweeting v. Pearce* (1859) 7 C.B.(N.S.) 449, 484–485; affirmed at (1861) 9 C.B.(N.S.) 534; *Stewart v. Aberdein* (1838) 4 M. & W. 211, 223; *Pearson v. Scott* (1878) 9 Ch.D. 198, 205; approved in *Pape v. Westacott* [1894] 1 Q.B. 272; *Legge v. Byas* (1901) 7 Com.Cas. 16, 19. See also the general statement in *Bowstead & Reynolds on Agency* (17th ed., 2001) Art. 28.

[92] *Barker v. Greenwood* (1837) 2 Y. & C. (Ex.) 414, 419; *Pearson v. Scott* (1878) 9 Ch.D. 198, 205–206; *Bartlett v. Pentland* (1830) 10 B. & C. 760, 773.

[93] (1861) 9 C.B.(N.S.) 534, 541.

[94] *Scott v. Irving* (1830) 1 B. & Ad. 605, 612; *Sweeting v. Pearce* (1861) 9 C.B.(N.S.) 534.

[95] *Stewart v. Aberdein* (1838) 4 M. & W. 211, 224, *per* Cresswell *arguendo*.

[96] *Bartlett v. Pentland* (1830) 10 B. & C. 760, 769.

[97] *Scott v. Irving* (1830) 1 B. & Ad. 605, 612, 614; *Bartlett v. Pentland* (1830) 10 B. & C. 760, 770; *Sweeting v. Pearce* (1859) 7 C.B.(N.S.) 449, 483.

[98] *Bartlett v. Pentland* (1830) 10 B. & C. 760, 774; *Scott v. Irving* (1830) 1 B. & Ad. 605; *McGowin Lumber and Export Co. v. Pacific Marine Ins. Co.* (1922) 12 Ll.L.R. 496.

[99] *Legge v. Byas* (1901) 7 Com.Cas. 16.

[1] *Matvieff v. Crosfield* (1903) 8 Com.Cas. 120; *Pollard, Ashby & Co. v. Franco-British Marine Ins. Co.* (1920) 5 Ll.L.R. 286.

a loss on a previous policy does not mean that, simply because a cheque was paid to him by the broker, he is fixed with knowledge of the practice by which the broker came to pay him. Since Lloyd's usage is restricted to a particular insurance market, it is not of such general notoriety that any assured instructing an agent to deal in it for his account must be taken to know of and acquiesce in its practices.[2]

In *Stewart v. Aberdein*[3] it appears to have been contemplated by the Court of Exchequer Chamber that, if the insured transacted business in a business community where, according to the evidence of insurance brokers, the usage at Lloyd's was well known, he might be taken to share that community's general knowledge, but the evidence of knowledge in that case was unsatisfactory (as noted by Cockburn C.J. in *Sweeting v. Pearce*),[4] and the tendency in that decision to ease the task of the underwriter in proving knowledge on the part of the assured has not been followed. A more typical illustration of the stand taken by the courts appears in *McGowin Lumber and Export Co. v. Pacific Marine Insurance Co.*,[5] where the policy contained the following clause:

> "This policy being issued in England, all losses and claims arising hereon are to be recoverable only according to the customs and usages of Lloyd's unless otherwise stipulated by the terms of the policy."

It was argued by the insurers that the effect of this clause was to bind the assured to accept payment of claims according to the usages at Lloyds, but the assured, an Alabama company, successfully argued that it put them in the same position as an English assured insuring at Lloyd's, so that, in the absence of evidence of actual knowledge, they need not recognise the usage.

35–27 If the assured knows of the usage at Lloyd's and forbids his broker to settle a loss in this way, his express withdrawal of authority from the broker overrides the effect of the usage, since the express term of the agency forbidding the broker to follow it negatives any implication of authority from the usage itself. If, however, knowing that the broker intends to settle a claim in account, he stands by and permits the broker to do so, he may be held to have acquiesced in the practice, although it is submitted that nothing short of tacit encouragement would suffice. It may be also that an express authority may be derived from a special agreement or the particular wording of the instructions to the broker.[6]

---

[2] *Gabay v. Lloyd* (1825) 3 B. & C. 793; *Sweeting v. Pearce* (1859) 7 C.B.(N.S.) 449, 485; affirmed (1861) 9 C.B.(N.S.) 534; *Matvieff v. Crosfield, supra,* deciding that the *Sweeting* Case was not overruled by *Robinson v. Mollett* (1875) L.R. 7 H.L. 802. The *dicta* of Bruce J. in *Acme Wood Flooring Co. v. Marten* (1904) 9 Com.Cas. 157, 162 seem unnecessarily cautious.

[3] (1838) 4 M. & W. 211, following a hint from Lord Tenterden in *Bartlett v. Pentland* (1830) 10 B. & C. 760, 770.

[4] (1859) 7 C.B.(N.S.) 449, 482.

[5] (1922) 12 Ll.L.R. 496.

[6] *De Gaminde v. Pigou* (1812) 4 Taunt. 246; see the discussions in *Scott v. Irving* and *Bartlett v. Pentland, supra.* In *Stolos Cia S.A. v. Ajax Insurance Co. Ltd* [1981] 1 Lloyd's Rep. 9 the clause "All claims ... to be collected through C.D.L. Ltd" was held to mean that all claims were to be collected in cash by C.D.L., and did not constitute an agreement to have claims settled in account between C.D.L. and the insurers.

35–28 Even if the assured does not agree in advance to be bound by the usage under discussion, he will come to be so bound if, after discovering how the broker has acted, he acts in a manner consistent only with approval and adoption of the settlement between his agent and the underwriter. Thus, in *Gibson v. Winter*,[7] the assured adopted the broker's act by suing the underwriters on their settlement in the name of the broker. The principle underlying this rule is simply that of ratification of the unauthorised act of an agent by the assured as the broker's principal. It has been held that, where the assured takes a bill accepted by the broker rather than claim from the underwriter before the broker is seen to be insolvent, that does not amount to an election to sue the broker alone.[8]

35–29 Part payment in cash. If the broker is instructed to collect a payment due under the policy, and the underwriter deducts a part of the total in settlement of his account with the broker and pays over the balance in cash to the latter, the assured has a claim against the underwriter only for the part deducted by him, assuming of course, that he is not bound to recognise their settlement.[9] This accords with the general rules of agency governing cases where an agent accepts part of the sum due in an unauthorised manner,[10] and, it is submitted, is sensible in principle. The decision in *Legge v. Byas, Mosley & Co.*[11] is not an authority against the application of the general rule to part-payments by Lloyd's underwriters. In that case the plaintiff instructed a local agent to collect a loss payable on a livestock policy. The local agent instructed Lloyd's brokers to recover it from underwriters. The Lloyd's brokers collected the amount in full, but deducted a sum from it in purported settlement of a debt allegedly due from the local agent to themselves. The local agent disputed this settlement, and did not pay the balance received by him to the assured, but sent a banker's draft for a lesser amount to the assured's solicitors. They, on behalf of the assured, received it only upon the condition that the assured reserved the right to sue the Lloyd's brokers for the whole sum due. It was held that the assured could sue the Lloyd's brokers for the entire amount, less agreed commission. It must be noted, however, that the local agent was said by the court to have authority to receive payment "by cash and by cash only",[12] and that the Lloyd's brokers had not paid any sum in cash, but by cheque. Moreover, the assured had never accepted the banker's draft in part-payment. It is submitted, therefore, that the learned judge was correct in saying that there was no authority to pay the local agent in the way adopted, but not, with respect, simply because there was a prior settlement. The decision does not, therefore, upset the general rule regarding part-payment in cash.

35–30 Liability of the Lloyd's broker. The broker is liable to be sued by the assured for payment of the loss to him once the underwriter has paid him

---

[7] (1833) 5 B. & Ad. 96.

[8] *Bartlett v. Pentland* (1830) 10 B. & C. 760, 773. *A fortiori* if the underwriter makes no payment or settlement with the broker, and the assured takes a credit note from the broker without the underwriter knowing anything of it—*Macfarlane v. Giannacopulo* (1853) 3 H. & N. 860.

[9] *Scott v. Irving* (1830) 1 B. & Ad. 605.

[10] *Williams v. Evans* (1866) L.R. 1 Q.B. 352.

[11] (1901) 7 Com.Cas. 16.

[12] *ibid.* at 19.

out in cash[13] or has entered a credit to his favour in their mutual accounts.[14] He is also liable to be sued by the underwriter for the return of moneys paid to him in settlement of a loss when payment was made under a mistake of fact for which the assured was responsible, unless he has paid the assured or has allowed for the debt due to the assured in mutual accounting for premiums.[15]

35–31 Liability of individual underwriters. As we have seen a Lloyd's policy is subscribed to by one or more syndicates, each composed of many "names".[16] Each name is liable only for his own subscription, and not for the sums underwritten by his fellow names in the syndicate.[17] Moreover, if one underwriter defaults in payment, the Corporation of Lloyd's is under no liability to make good his default, although in fact a fund is maintained at Lloyd's for the protection of policy holders.[18]

35–32 The practice at Lloyd's when liability is disputed. So far we have considered the effect of the usages of Lloyd's upon the claim made by the assured in circumstances where the underwriters do not dispute liability, and the only question is what sum of money shall eventually be paid to the assured himself. Other factors arise for consideration when underwriters decide to contest the claim presented to them by a Lloyd's broker on behalf of the assured, because the practice adopted for the investigation of the claim and of all facts relevant to liability under the policy in question is apt to place the Lloyd's broker in a position in which there might be a conflict between his duties as agent for the assured and any obligations assumed on underwriters' behalf.

35–33 The practice in question was considered by the Commercial Court in *North and South Trust Co. v. Berkeley.*[19] In that case the plaintiffs were insured under a Lloyd's marine policy on goods, and made a claim on account of an alleged shortage on arrival at destination. The underwriters, acting by the leading underwriter, were not satisfied with the evidence adduced to show the extent of the shortage of the goods, and they instructed the Lloyd's brokers who had made the claim for the assured to instruct an assessor to investigate the circumstances of the loss. This was done, and the

---

[13] *Legge v. Byas, supra.*

[14] *Andrew v. Robinson* (1812) 3 Camp. 199; *Wilkinson v. Clay* (1815) 6 Taunt. 110. Lord Ellenborough's remark that the striking out of the name of the underwriter deprived the assured of all remedies against him is too wide in the light of later decisions such as *Scott v. Irving* (1830) 1 B. & Ad. 605.

[15] *Buller v. Harrison* (1777) 2 Cowp. 565. If the broker has paid the assured, the underwriters must sue the latter; *Holland v. Russell* (1863) 4 B. & S. 14; *Norwich Union Fire Ins. Soc. v. Price* [1934] A.C. 455. The broker cannot claim the loss back from the assured on the ground that he did not know that the underwriter was insolvent when he paid the assured—*Edgar v. Bumstead* (1808) 1 Camp. 411, 420, in which Lord Ellenborough referred to "the well-known course of dealing".

[16] *Thompson v. Adams* (1889) 23 Q.B.D. 361.

[17] *Tyser v. The Shipowners' Syndicate (Reassured)* [1896] 1 Q.B. 135; *Rozanes v. Bowen* (1928) 32 Ll.L.R. 98 101; Lloyd's Act 1982, s.8(1); *Napier and Ettrick v. Kershaw* [1997] L.R.L.R. 1, 8, affirmed, *sub nom., Society of Lloyd's v. Robinson* [1999] 1 W.L.R. 756.

[18] *Industrial Guarantee Corporation v. Lloyd's Corporation* (1924) 19 Ll.L.R. 78. When a defaulting Name's proportion is paid out of the Central Fund, the society has a right of reimbursement against the Name under the Central Fund Byelaws—*Society of Lloyd's v. Clementson* [1995] L.R.L.R. 307.

[19] [1971] 1 W.L.R. 471.

report of the assessor was handed to the brokers. The underwriters, who saw a copy of it, refused to pay the claim, and the assured brought proceedings to obtain payment. In the course of these proceedings they sought to obtain the assessor's report from their brokers, but were refused it on the ground that, in so far as the obtaining of the report was concerned, their brokers were acting on behalf of the underwriters, who had instructed them to obtain one. Consequently the brokers were unable to show it to the plaintiffs, since it would involve them in a breach of their instructions from the underwriters.

Evidence was given by the underwriters to the effect that their instructions to assessors were usually made through the brokers acting for the assured, who therefore acted in a dual role, and were expected not to release any information obtained to the assured. In the same way, it seems, the brokers would be involved in the instructions sent to solicitors by underwriters to obtain a legal opinion, and they might receive the opinion to forward it to the underwriters.

35–34 Following earlier criticism of the practice,[20] Donaldson J. had no hesitation in describing it as an unreasonable custom which could not of itself bind the assured to acquiesce in the dual role of the broker instructed by him.[21] It was unreasonable because it authorised the broker to do what an agent is forbidden by law to do—to accept instructions from a third party which are inconsistent with those he has received from his principal.[22] Only if the principal is fully informed of the broker's wish to do so and what it will entail, and then gives his consent to the agent acting on behalf of another, will he be bound to acquiesce in the second agency.[23]

In the instant case, there had been no such consent, and the brokers were in breach of their agents' duties owed to the assured. The assured, however, were unable to obtain possession of the assessor's report in detinue proceedings or by seeking declarations of their entitlement to possession of it, since the brokers had received it as agents of the underwriters, and the assured had no title in it, the document being commissioned by the underwriters.[24]

35–35 If follows that, if the brokers had possessed documents belonging to the assured, they would have been obliged to deliver them up to the assured if requested to do so, regardless of contrary instructions from the underwriters, and that, if the brokers do succumb to the persuasion of the underwriters and take steps contrary to the interests of the assured, the underwriters could well be guilty of inducing a breach of contract between the assured and the Lloyd's broker.

35–36 By the usage of Lloyd's the Lloyd's placing broker impliedly agrees that, if called upon, he will collect claims arising on the insurance that he places on behalf of the assured. No additional commission is payable, and the broker will be liable to the assured for any loss sustained in consequence of his negligent failure to safeguard the policy documents which are needed

---

[20] *Anglo-African Merchants Ltd v. Bayley* [1970] 1 Q.B. 311, 321–324, *per* Megaw J.
[21] [1971] W.L.R. 471, 482.
[22] [1970] 1 Q.B. 311, 323–324; *Fullwood v. Hurley* [1928] 1 K.B. 498, 502; *Eagle Star Insurance Co. v. Spratt* [1971] 2 Lloyd's Rep. 116, 133; *Callaghan and Hedges v. Thompson* [2000] Lloyd's Rep.I.R. 125, 132; *Bowstead & Reynolds on Agency* (17th ed., 2001) p. 189.
[23] [1971] 1 W.L.R. 471, 484–485.
[24] *ibid.* at 486.

to support a claim.[25] The assured is entitled, of course, to instruct another broker to collect claims on existing business.[26] If Lloyd's brokers wish to accept instructions from underwriters as well as from the assured, they must obtain the assured's consent beforehand. Otherwise unless the assured knows of the existence of the custom and his acquiescence can safely be presumed, the broker acts at his peril in following the usual practice.

35–37 A dispute arose out of a claim for cargo allegedly damaged by fire on board the motor vessel Savonita. The broker became suspicious about the bona fides of the claim and took it upon himself to urge his suspicions upon the leading underwriter and encourage him to repudiate the claim. The assured thereupon instructed another broker, who eventually succeeded in obtaining payment. A board of inquiry appointed by the Committee of Lloyd's expressed the view that the primary duty of the broker is to the assured and that the first broker had erred in taking up a position of opposition to his principal's claim.[27]

35–38 Proceedings outside United Kingdom. Lloyd's underwriters are authorised insurers under the laws of a number of countries outside the United Kingdom. Many of these laws require the appointment of a local representative[28] whose powers include the acceptance of service of suit on behalf of underwriters. It is also common practice for Lloyd's agents to be nominated in particular policies to accept service of suit in proceedings arising out of those policies. Process served upon any of these representatives is transmitted to London for the attention of the underwriters concerned, one of whom will appear as a representative defendant if the proceedings are contested. Under certain of the laws mentioned above, it is theoretically possible (though it is never necessary in practice) to conduct proceedings entirely against the local representative and to execute judgment against him.[29]

---

[25] *Johnston v. Leslie & Godwin Financial Services Ltd* [1995] L.R.L.R. 472.

[26] *ibid.* at p. 477; *Minett v. Forrester* (1811) 4 Taunt. 541n, 543, *per* Lord Mansfield C.J. *arguendo.*

[27] The report of the inquiry was published in Lloyd's List of December 8, 1978.

[28] Known as "Attorney in Fact" in Canada, Illinois and Kentucky, as "General Representative" in Australia and the Republic of Ireland; and as "Mandataire Général" in Belgium, France and Switzerland.

[29] See Belgium, *Arrêté Royal* of March 12, 1976, art. 6(2), (3); France, *Code des Assurances*, art. R321–10; and Kentucky Insurance Code –304. 28–070.

CHAPTER 36

THE ROLE OF AGENTS IN INSURANCE BUSINESS

1. PRINCIPLES OF AGENCY

36–1 Introduction. Most insurance business is in practice transacted through agents, and for good reason. Insurers, for their part, are almost always incorporated companies, which can only act by their agents, from the directors down to a local agent soliciting proposals for insurance. In insurance business transacted at Lloyd's the assured is always represented by a broker. In company business also, the assured is often assisted by retaining a broker or other intermediary to obtain the best possible terms available and to represent him in negotiations with the insurers. Moreover, it is often the case that agency enters into insurance transactions regardless of the role of brokers, because the course of business may demand that one party shall effect an insurance on property on behalf of another. Thus in c.i.f. export sales it is usual for the seller to take out an insurance on the buyer's behalf to cover all or part of the transit of the goods,[1] and it is frequently the case that parties to a building or construction contract, for example, will arrange for a single contractors' risks policy to be taken out by one of them to cover the interests of all.

36–2 When the agents for each party carry out their instructions properly no complication arises and the acts of the agents are imputed to, and bind, their respective principals. Complications arise, however, when an agent makes a mistake and fails to follow his instructions with the result that his principal, on discovering the fact, seeks to avoid responsibility for what the agent has done. Whether he can do so depends upon whether the agent acted within the scope of his authority or not. If he did, the principal is bound by the acts of his agent regardless of the agent's mistake and its prejudice to himself. So where the assured's brokers were authorised to nominate an airport in France to which the assured was to travel for the purposes of a travel insurance cover, and mistakenly nominated Paris in place of Nice, the assured was bound to accept an insurance in that form and to pay the

---

[1] e.g. *Yuill & Co. v. Scott-Robson* [1908] 1 K.B. 270; *Smith v. Lascelles* (1788) 2 T.R. 187 and *Xenos v. Wickham* (1867) L.R. 2 H.L. 296 are examples of factors acting as agents to procure insurance for merchants abroad.

premium.[2] The principles of agency law concerning the authority of agents are therefore of great importance.

36-3 Agents' implied authority. An agent possesses not only the authority expressly bestowed upon him by his principal, but also, by implication, the further authority to do all things necessary in the ordinary course of business for the efficient and proper performance of his duties.[3] Besides possessing an implied authority to take steps necessary to perform his express instructions, a broker[4] or agent[5] may derive an authority from the powers which either practice or usage regards as usually attaching to the position which he occupies in a particular market, where that is established by evidence or judicial knowledge be taken of it. Thus it was held that an insurance broker authorised to subscribe a policy for an underwriter has implied authority to adjust a loss arising under it and to refer a dispute over the loss to arbitration.[6] A broker who subscribes a policy in his own name has power to sue in his own name in an action to enforce it for the benefit of the assured.[7]

36-4 Ostensible authority. The acts of an agent will bind his principal not only to the extent of his actual authority, whether express or implied, but also to the further extent to which he possesses an "ostensible" (or "apparent") authority to commit the acts in question.[8] This ostensible authority is the authority ordinarily attaching to the position or office in which the principal has placed the agent or to the credentials which he has permitted him to hold, regardless of any special limitations imposed on the agent by the principal as a term of the agency relationship. A third party is entitled to assume that the agent's actual authority is commensurate with his ostensible authority unless he knows or has reason to suspect that, in the dealings in question, the agent is exceeding his actual authority by disregarding limitations imposed on him by the principal. The principal cannot subsequently disavow the acts of his agent on the ground that the latter exceeded his actual authority and instructions when doing business with the third party.[9] The basis of this rule is therefore an estoppel against the principal. A representation by the agent that he himself has a particular authority does not bind the principal unless, exceptionally, the latter has

[2] *Zurich General Accident & Liability Ins. Co. v. Rowberry* [1954] 2 Lloyd's Rep. 55. A converse case in which the assured's agent knowingly departed from his instructions in what he thought to be the best interests of his client is *Sedgwick, Collins & Co. v. Highton* (1929) 34 Ll.L.R. 448. Here the assured was not bound by the contract made by his agent, although it is likely that the insurers might have obtained relief if certain amendments had been allowed—see at 458.

[3] See *Bowstead & Reynolds on Agency* (16th ed., 1996) arts 27 to 32, for the different ways in which authority may be implied from status, course of dealing and usage.

[4] *Stockton v. Mason* [1978] 2 Lloyd's Rep. 430. See the discussion of this decision at paras 4–26 to 4–27, *ante.*

[5] *Hambro v. Burnand* [1904] 2 K.B. 10.

[6] *Richardson v. Anderson* (1805) 1 Camp. 43n; *Goodson v. Brooke* (1815) 4 Camp. 163.

[7] *Transcontinental Underwriting Agency v. Grand Union Ins. Co.* [1987] 2 Lloyd's Rep. 409; *Pan Atlantic Ins. Co. and Republic Insurance v. Pine Top Ins. Co.* [1988] 2 Lloyd's Rep. 505, 511; *"The Moonacre"* [1992] 2 Lloyd's Rep. 501, 516.

[8] For a comprehensive study of the law see *Bowstead & Reynolds on Agency* (16th ed., 1996), arts 74 to 75.

[9] *Houldsworth v. City of Glasgow Bank* (1880) 5 App. Cas. 317, 327; *Scarf v. Jardine* (1882) 7 App. Cas. 345, 356–357; *Rainbow v. Howkins* [1904] 2 K.B. 322; *Willis, Faber & Co. v. Joyce* (1911) 27 T.L.R. 388; *Freeman & Lockyer v. Buckhurst Park Properties (Mangal) Ltd* [1964] 2 Q.B. 480; *Eagle Star Ins. Co. v. Spratt* [1971] 2 Lloyd's Rep. 116.

authorised the agent so to represent.[10] Express representation by the principal is not necessary. It suffices for him to allow the agent to hold a position in which he might ordinarily be expected by outsiders to have authority to perform the acts in question,[11] or alternatively to acquiesce in the agent representing himself to have an authority which he did not in truth possess.[12]

36–5 Most cases of ostensible authority concern the activities of agents acting for insurers, and these are considered below,[13] but a few examples may suffice to illustrate the general principle. Where a broker's authority had expired but no notice of the fact had been given by the underwriter for whom he had been acting for two years, either to those with whom the agent had been doing business or at Lloyd's generally, the underwriter, in an action on policies effected by the agent was estopped from contending that the policies were concluded without his authority.[14] An agent in possession of temporary cover notes issued by insurers has ostensible authority to bind the insurers to grant interim cover to an applicant for insurance (even if he is not actually empowered to do more than forward the application to the insurers for approval or rejection)[15] since his possession of the cover notes indicates prima facie the insurers' authorisation of his granting cover. Although there is no English authority directly in point, it is reasonable to assume that a general agent or branch manager who has actual authority to conclude a contract on the insurers' usual terms and conditions would be held to have ostensible authority to dispense with the requirement for pre-payment of the premium or to allow a longer time for its payment than was permitted in the policy.[16] A plea that an agent underwriting for a reinsurance pool in the London market possessed ostensible authority to place one or more pool members as a front for the others failed because it was not the universal practice that such agents had, or were assumed to have, that authority.[17] A plea that an agent underwriting on behalf of a political risks insurance pool in the French market possessed ostensible authority to write CEND risks on fixed assets failed in the absence of expert evidence of the usual powers of such an agent.[18]

36–6 Notice of restricted authority. If the third party dealing with an agent has notice that the latter is exceeding his actual authority, he cannot rely upon the agent's ostensible authority as it might appear to others.[19] The

---

[10] *Armagas v. Mundogas* [1986] 1 A.C. 717.
[11] *Eagle Star Ins. Co. v. Spratt* [1971] 2 Lloyd's Rep. 116; *Suncorp Ins. v. Milano Assicurazioni* [1993] 2 Lloyd's Rep. 225, 231; *Gurtner v. Beaton* [1993] 2 Lloyd's Rep. 369, 379.
[12] *Murfitt v. Royal Ins. Co.* (1922) 38 T.L.R. 334; *Eagle Star Ins. Co. v. Spratt* [1971] 2 Lloyd's Rep. 116, 127–128.
[13] See paras 36–55, *et seq., post.*
[14] *Willis, Faber & Co. v. Joyce* (1911) 27 T.L.R. 388.
[15] *Mackie v. European Assurance Society* (1869) 21 L.T. 102; *Cockburn v. British American Assurance Co.* (1890) 19 Ont.R. 245; *World Marine & General Ins. Co. v. Leger* [1952] 1 D.L.R. 755; *Dicks v. S.A. Mutual Fire & General Ins. Co. Ltd* [1963] 4 S.A. 501 (N).
[16] Gordon, *The South African Law of Insurance* (2nd ed.) p. 134, following Vance, *Handbook on the Law of Insurance* (3rd ed., 1951) pp. 438–439.
[17] *Suncorp Ins. v. Milano Assicurazioni* [1993] 2 Lloyd's Rep. 225, 232–233.
[18] *Yona International v. La Reunion Francaise* [1996] 2 Lloyd's Rep. 84, 108.
[19] *Wilkinson v. General Accident Fire & Life Assurance Corp. Ltd* [1967] 2 Lloyd's Rep. 182; *Baines v. Ewing* (1866) L.R. 1 Ex. 320, where the third party was put on notice as to an excess of authority but did not inquire.

applicant for insurance may well be held to have notice of the agent's excess of authority from a caveat or condition contained in the temporary cover note, receipt,[20] proposal form[21] or policy[22] which he is handed by the agent. In the case of *Henry v. Agricultural Mutual Assurance Association*[23] the insurance association's agent agreed to insure the applicant's property, including certain stocks of grain. The application form filled in by the applicant stated quite clearly, however, that the association did not grant insurances on that type of property, so that the applicant ought reasonably to have realised by inference that this particular agent was exceeding his actual authority, and the association was not bound. The fact that the applicant had not read the proposal form sufficiently carefully to realise this fact made no difference. As a general rule, applicants for insurance are under a duty to read documents that are completed by themselves or in their names, and they will be fixed with knowledge of the matters recited therein.[24] As was said in a Scottish decision: "Every presumption in law is in favour of holding that a man knows what he is putting his subscription to, and, if he did not read what he was signing, *sibi imputet*."[25]

36–7 Where an insurer relies upon the contents of such documents, they must be clearly and unambiguously worded so that a reasonable applicant will know what is meant.[26] By analogy with the authorities concerning exempting conditions in contracts of carriage and storage, it is for the insurers to show that reasonable steps were taken to bring the restrictions to the notice of the applicant, so that, if the wording is printed on the reverse without attention being drawn to it, or if it is in such small print than an ordinary prudent man could not be expected to see it, the insurers will not be able to rely on the restriction of the agent's authority.[27]

36–8 Even when the applicant has notice of restrictive clauses in the proposal form or elsewhere, it may be held that these have been waived by a persistent disregard of the restriction by the agent, acquiesced in by the insurers.[28] Prima facie, however, an agent has no authority to waive the formalities required by insurers as a condition precedent to the making of a binding contract.[29]

---

[20] *Acey v. Fernie* (1840) 7 M & W 151, 153; *Linford v. Provincial Horse & Cattle Ins. Co.* (1864) 10 Jur., N.S. 1066.

[21] *Levy v. Scottish Employers Ins. Association* (1901) 17 T.L.R. 229; *Henry v. Agricultural Mutual Assurance* (1865) 11 Grant 125.

[22] *Horncastle v. Equitable Life Assurance Soc. of USA* (1906) 22 T.L.R. 735; *Comerford v. Britannic Assurance Co. Ltd* (1908) 24 T.L.R. 593; *Feldman v. British Aviation Ins. Co.* [1949] (3) S.A. 1078, S.R.

[23] (1865) 11 Grant 125.

[24] *Biggar v. Rock Life Assurance Co.* [1902] 1 K.B. 516; *McMillan v. Accident Ins. Co.* 1907 S.C. 484; *O'Connor v. Kirby & Co.* [1972] 1 Q.B. 90.

[25] *McMillan v. Accident Ins. Co.* [1907] S.C. 484, 491.

[26] *Ireland v. Livingstone* (1872) L.R. 5 H.L. 395; *Henry v. Agricultual Mutual Assurance Association* (1865) 11 Gr. 125.

[27] *Henderson v. Stevenson* (1875) L.R. 2 Sc. & Div. 470; *Parker v. South Eastern Ry* (1877) 2 C.P.D. 416; *Watkins v. Rymill* (1883) 10 Q.B.D. 178; *Richardson Spence & Co. v. Rowntree* [1894] A.C. 217; *Hood v. Anchor Line* [1918] A.C. 837; *Thornton v. Shoe Lane Parking Ltd* [1971] 2 Q.B. 163.

[28] *Cockburn v. British American Ass. Co.* (1890) 19 Ont. R. 245; *World Marine v. St Leger* [1952] 1 D.L.R. 755; *Post v. Aetna Life Ins. Co.* 43 Barb. 351 (N.Y.S.C. 1864); and *Knickerbocker Life Ins. Co. v. Norton*, 96 U.S. 234, 240 (1877).

[29] *Vaughan v. Hearts of Oak Assurance* [1926] I.A.C. Rep. 77.

36–9 Restrictions on an agent's authority contained in the policy itself will be of no effect if the applicant has not seen the policy or been told of what it says before the contract of insurance is concluded, and the restriction relied upon relates to the making of the contract.[30]

36–10 Ratification. Where acts committed by an agent are not within even his ostensible authority, they will only bind the principal if he thereafter ratifies them. Thus, if a contract is made by an agent without any authority, the insurers may ratify it if it was professed to be made on their behalf and they possessed power to enter into it at the time the agent made it.[31] Ratification may be express or implied. It will be implied wherever the conduct of the principal, or that of his duly authorised agents, is such as to show that he adopts the transaction in whole or in part, regardless of his subjective intention, so long as he, or his agent as the case may be, has full knowledge of the material circumstances in which the un-authorised agent acted.[32] Ratification does not automatically relieve the agent from personal liability to his principal for his excess of authority.[33]

36–11 A contract made in the name of a principal without his authority may be ratified by the principal even though the agent making the contract intended to make it for his own benefit,[34] but in order to found ratification a contract made without authority must be professedly made on behalf of some principal either named or un-named. It appears to be established in marine insurance that a principal may ratify an insurance purporting to be made by an agent on behalf of a class of persons to which that principal belongs, provided that the agent's intention was to protect all persons having the interest possessed by the principal, and that the principal was in existence and capable of being ascertained as a member of that class at the time of contract or subsequently.[35] These principles have been held to apply to non-marine insurance so far as concerns a principal who was ascertainable as a member of that class at the date of contract.[36] If the agent makes the contract without stating that he is acting as an agent, his intention to make it on behalf of a particular principal is immaterial, and does not entitle the principal to ratify it.[37]

36–12 A principal cannot ratify a contract which he could not in the first instance have made[38] and an agent cannot on behalf of the principal ratify a contract made by another agent or a sub-agent unless the agent purporting to ratify has either authority to make the contract or authority to ratify it.[39]

---

[30] *Re Coleman's Depositories & Life & Health Assurance Association* [1907] 2 K.B. 798; *Wood v. American Fire Ins. Co.* 149 N.Y. 382 (1896), and see on this point generally Richards, *Insurance* (5th ed.) para. 4485.

[31] *Re Tiedemann and Ledermann* [1899] 2 Q.B. 66; contrast the situation where the agent contracts "subject to ratification"—*Warehousing & Forwarding Co. of E. Africa v. Jafferali & Sons Ltd* [1964] A.C. 1.

[32] *Suncorp. Ins. v. Milano Assicurazioni* [1993] 2 Lloyd's Rep. 225, 234–235; *Bedford Ins. Co. v. I.R.B.* [1985] Q.B. 966, 987; *Yona International v. L.R.F.* [1996] 2 Lloyd's Rep. 84, 103.

[33] *Suncorp. Ins. v. Milano Assicurazioni, supra.*

[34] *Re Tiedemann and Ledermann* [1899] 2 Q.B. 66.

[35] Arnould, *Law of Marine Insurance* (16th ed., 1981) para. 243.

[36] *National Oilwell Ltd v. Davy Offshore Ltd* [1993] 2 Lloyd's Rep. 582, 593–597.

[37] *Keighley, Maxstead & Co. v. Durant* [1901] A.C. 240.

[38] *La Banque Jacques-Cartier v. La Banque d'Epargne* (1887) 13 App. Cas. 111.

[39] *Re Portuguese Consolidated Mines* (1890) 45 Ch.D. 16; *Suncorp Ins. v. Milano Assicurazioni* [1993] 2 Lloyd's Rep. 225, 235.

36–13 The right to ratify a contract must be exercised within a reasonable time, the right by its nature being an election to confirm and not one to repudiate.[40] The principal may ratify the contract even after it has been repudiated by the third party,[41] but, if the agent and third party agree to rescind a contract made by the agent on behalf of his principal, the latter cannot ratify it.[42]

36–14 A policy of marine insurance effected by an agent without authority may be ratified by his principal even after a loss has occurred.[43] Whether non-marine policies can be ratified after loss in the same way is not clear. In *Waters v. Monarch Fire and Life Assurance Co.*[44] Lord Campbell, in considering a policy on goods effected by a bailee, cited the decisions on marine policies and appeared to think that they applied to the policy before the court, but in *Grover & Grover Limited v. Matthews*[45] it was held that the rule permitting ratification after loss was anomalous and deserved to be confined to marine insurance, and the *Waters* decision[46] was not cited. The Canadian,[47] Australian[48] and U.S.[49] courts have permitted ratification after loss on non-marine risks. The submission in paragraph 370 of the 8th edition of this work that the decision in the Grover case should not be followed has been approved obiter by Colman J. in *National Oilwell (UK) Ltd v. Davy Offshore Ltd.*[50]

36–15 Ratification can be express or it can be implied from knowledge of, and acquiescence in, the contract made by the agent, but in either case it can be achieved only with full knowledge of the character of the act to be ratified, or with an intention to adopt it under any circumstances.[51] Thus if a contract

[40] *Re Portuguese Consolidated Mines* (1890) 45 Ch.D. 16. In *Bedford Ins. Co. v. I.R.B.* [1985] Q.B. 966, 987, Parker J. refused to accept that a reasonable time could not extend beyond the time at which performance of the un-authorised contract was to begin.

[41] *Bolton Partners v. Lambert* (1888) 41 Ch.D. 295.

[42] *Walter v. James* (1871) L.R. 6 Ex. 124.

[43] *Routh v. Thompson* (1811) 13 East 274; *Hagedorn v. Oliverson* (1814) 2 M. & S. 485; *Williams v. North China Ins. Co.* (1876) 1 C.P.D. 757; Marine Insurance Act 1906, s.86.

[44] (1856) 5 E. & B. 870; followed in *London and North Western Ry v. Glyn* (1859) 1 E. & E. 652, Lord Campbell treated the bailee as an agent concluding insurance without authority, but after the decision in *Tomlinson v. Hepburn* [1966] A.C. 451 it is no longer right to speak of him as an agent, and he is in fact someone with a limited insurable interest who can insure in excess of it for another's benefit. See Ch. 1, *ante*.

[45] [1910] 2 K.B. 401.

[46] See n. 44, *ante*.

[47] *Ogden v. Montreal Fire Ins. Co.* (1853) 3 U.C.C.P. 497; *Giffard v. Queen Ins. Co.* (1869) 1 Hannay (N.Br.) 432; *Goulding v. Norwich Union Fire Ins. Soc.* [1947] 4 D.L.R. 236; affirmed [1948] 1 D.L.R. 526; *Goldschlager v. Royal Insurance Co.* (1978) 84 D.L.R. (3d.) 355.

[48] *Trident General Ins. Co. v. McNeice Bros. Pty* (1987) 8 N.S.W.L.R. 270; (1988) 165 C.L.R. 107.

[49] *Snow v. Carr*, 32 Am. Rep. 3 (Ala., 1878); *Home Ins. Co. v. Baltimore Warehouse Co.* 93 U.S. 527 (1876); *Marqusee v. Hartford Fire Ins. Co.* 198 F. 475 (C.C.A. 2, 1912) expressly disapproving the *Grover* Case; *Automobile Ins. Co. v. Barnes-Manley Wet Wash Laundry*, 168 F.2d 381 (C.C.A. 10,1948).

[50] [1993] 2 Lloyd's Rep. 582, 606–608. See also *Graham v. W. Australian Ins. Co.* (1931) 40 Ll.L.R. 64; *Portavon Cinemas v. Price* [1939] 4 All E.R. 601; Clarke, *Law of Insurance Contracts*, (2nd ed., 1994) para. 7–4Dl.

[51] *French v. Backhouse* (1771) 5 Burr. 2727; *Robinson v. Gleadow* (1835) 2 Bing. N.C. 156 (virtually silent acquiescence); *Phosphate of Lime Co. v. Green* (1871) L.R. 7 C.P. 43, 56–57, *per* Willes J. obiter. Admittedly a *dictum*, but in *Petersen v. Ronaasen* (1926) 31 Com.Cas. 347, Mackinnon J. opined that a mere *dictum* of Willes J. was "better than the considered judgment of ten judges today".

of insurance is made on behalf of a company in an unauthorised form, the company's subsequent conduct can ratify it,[52] but its mere recognition of the contract does not amount to ratification unless it has notice of the irregularity, or acts in such a way as to warrant the inference that it intends to waive any issue as to the form of the contract being irregular.[53]

36-16 Warranty of authority. If directors of a company or any persons purporting to act as agents for insurers exceed their powers, they may be personally liable to an assured for a breach of warranty of authority. Similarly, an agent claiming to be instructed to effect an insurance on behalf of the prospective assured will be liable for breach of such a warranty if he has in fact no such instructions and the assured does not adopt the insurance subsequently by ratification. This is because a person purporting to contract on behalf of another impliedly warrants that he has the authority of that other to make the contract, and, if he has not, he must compensate the other contracting party for any damage resulting from the breach of warranty.[54]

36-17 An agent's liability under this warranty is strict and not dependent on negligence. Thus, if a broker renews a contract of insurance on behalf of an assured who has in fact died prior to the renewal, there is a prima facie breach of warranty even if the broker had no means of knowing this.[55] An agent may not disavow his authority after the conclusion of a contract and seek to set up his own breach of the warranty of authority to obtain a benefit. In *Tomison v. City of Glasgow Friendly Society*,[56] a member of a friendly society, acting in accordance with its rules, made a proposal and declaration on behalf of his uncle and aunt for a policy to be issued to them on their own lives and on their own behalf. He had in fact no authority from his uncle and aunt to effect an insurance on their behalf, and, after paying the premiums on the policy for some time in the mistaken belief that he could recover the policy money for his own benefit, he applied for a return of the premiums so paid on the ground that he had acted without authority and that the policy was accordingly void. The Industrial Assurance Commissioner held that the applicant had impliedly warranted the authority bestowed on him by his uncle and aunt and could not therefore be heard to deny it, or say that he had acted without their authority.

36-18 The fact that the third party could have ascertained the absence of authority by making inquiry does not affect the agent's liability, and therefore directors of a company entering into a contract ultra vires the company or outside the scope of their own authority may be liable for breach of warranty of authority, and that notwithstanding that the want of power or

---

[52] *Reuter v. Electric Telegraph Co.* (1856) 6 E. & B. 349.

[53] *Lewis v. Reed* (1845) 13 M. & W. 834; *Freeman v. Rosher* (1849) 13 Q.B. 780.

[54] *Collen v. Wright* (1857) 8 E. & B. 647; *Godwin v. Francis* (1870) L.R. 5 C.P. 295; *Weeks v. Propert* (1873) L.R. 8 C.P. 427; *Harris v. McRobert* (1924) 19 Ll.L.R. 135; *Kaufmann v. British Surety Ins. Co.* (1929) 33 Ll.L.R. 315. If the principal ratified, the damages would be nominal in amount.

[55] This illustration follows from the decision in *Yong v. Toynbee* [1910] 1 K.B. 215 (solicitor representing dead client). The underwriters would have had a claim in, e.g. *Warwick v. Slade* (1811) 3 Camp. 127.

[56] [1931] I.A.C. Rep. 88.

authority was patent in the company's act, deed of settlement, memorandum, or articles.[57]

36–19 Directors or other agents of a company may become personally liable by representing that a sub-agent has greater or other authority from the company than he has in fact,[58] or if they permit a sub-agent to hold himself out as having such authority.

36–20 Where a party dealing with the directors or other agents of an insurance company has actual notice of an express limitation upon their authority, and the parties then enter into a contract under a mutual mistake of law as to the meaning or effect of that limitation, it has been said that there is no implied warranty on either side that the view the parties have taken is the correct one.[59] There seems, however, no reason why, if agents have represented that the effect of the restriction is to give them authority to act, the assured should not hold them liable for breach of that assurance.[60]

36–21 Agent acting in own interest. If an agent has authority, or is held out by his principal as having authority, to make any contract or do any act on behalf of his principal, he will bind his principal by making such a contract or performing that act, even though in fact he is acting for his own interest entirely, and with intent to defraud his principal.[61] If the person dealing with the agent acts in good faith, he can, as against the principal, enforce a contract so made.[62] Thus an agent who issues cover notes and fraudulently appropriates the premiums to his own use will bind the insurers to the contract made under the cover note.[63] For this rule to apply, it is essential that the agent should appear ostensibly to be performing his ordinary duties, since if it is apparent that he is contracting on his own behalf and not inside the scope of his employment at all, there can be no ostensible authority to bind the principal.[64]

2. The Assured's Agent

36–22 Introductory. The agent owes to his client a duty to exercise reasonable skill and care in the performance of whatever instructions he has accepted. This duty of care arises not only out of the contract between them,

---

[57] *W. London Commercial Bank v. Kitson* (1884) 13 Q.B.D. 360; *Chapleo v. Brunswick Building Society* (1881) 6 Q.B.D. 696; *Firbank's Executors v. Humphreys* (1886)18 Q.B.D. 54; *Richardson v. Williamson* (1871) L.R. 6 Q.B. 276.

[58] *Cherry & McDougall v. Colonial Bank of Australasia* (1869) L.R. 3 P.C. 24.

[59] *Beattie v. Lord Edbury* (1872) L.R. 7 Ch. App. 777; affirmed (1874) L.R. 7 H.L. 102; *Rashdall v. Ford* (1866) L.R. 2 Eq. 750.

[60] The distinction between a statement or representation as to law and one as to fact is a capricious one, and the former may often be reformulated as the latter—see, *inter alia*, *Eaglesfield v. Marquis of Londonderry* (1876) 4 Ch.D. 693, 703; affirmed (1878) 38 L.T. 303; *Cooper v. Phibbs* (1867) L.R. 2 H.L. 149; *Solle v. Butcher* [1950]1 K.B. 671.

[61] *Lloyd v. Grace, Smith & Co.* [1912] A.C. 716; *Chatt v. Prudential Ass. Co.* [1926] I.A.C. Rep. 24.

[62] *Hambro v. Burnand* [1904] 2 K.B. 10.

[63] *Hawke v. Niagara District Mutual Fire Ins. Co.* (1876) 23 Grant 139; *Patterson v. The Royal Ins. Co.* (1867) 14 Grant 169.

[64] *McGowan & Co. v. Dyer* (1873) L.R. 8 Q.B. 141, 145.

but also in tort out of his professional status, so that there are parallel rights of action for breach of duty in contract and in tort.[65] Three qualifications to this general principle need to be noted.[66] First, a person may come under a strict contractual liability to procure an insurance for another as the result of a contract between them, as for example in certain mercantile transactions, in which case he will be responsible for breach of duty regardless of negligence.[67] Secondly, the limitation period for bringing actions for breach of either the contractual or tortious duty of care is generally six years from the date of accrual of a cause of action,[68] but a claimant suing an agent for negligence in tort[69] will have the benefit in an appropriate case of the limitation period set by section 14A of the Limitation Act 1980, namely, three years from the date at which he first became aware that the agent had caused him a loss which justified seeking legal redress and that he had a cause of action to pursue against the agent.[70] The six year limitation period applies by analogy[71] to a claim framed as one for equitable damages.[72] Thirdly, the agent may be held to owe a duty of care in tort towards not only his client but to someone who was intended to benefit from the insurance he was employed by the client to arrange, such as a prospective assignee of the policy who had participated in giving the agent instructions.[73] Whether a duty of care is owed to third parties depends upon the circumstances in which it will be held to exist under rules developed by the courts in the law of tort.[74]

36-23 Duty of agent to client. The precise extent of the agent's duties will depend upon the circumstances of each client, but the unifying principle is

---

[65] *Macmillan v. Knott Becker Scott* [1990] 1 Lloyd's Rep. 98,100–101; *The "Superhulls Cover" Case (No. 2)* [1990] 2 Lloyd's Rep. 431, 459; *Punjab National Bank v. De Boinville* [1992] 1 W.L.R. 1138, 1152; *Forsikr. Vesta v. Butcher (No. 1)* [1989] A.C. 852, 860; *Osman v. Moss* [1970] 1 Lloyd's Rep. 313, 317; *Henderson v. Merrett Syndicates Ltd* [1995] 2 A.C. 145, 182. The agent is answerable for the default of sub-agents—"*Superhulls*", at 445; "*The Okeanis*" [1986] 1 Lloyd's Rep. 195, 201—subject to express or implied agreement to the contrary—*Henderson v. Merrett Syndicates* [1995] 2 A.C. 145, 197–203.

[66] In rare cases where an agent may be party to a contract, *e.g.* a line-slip, there may also be a claim under the Misrepresentation Act 1967: see *Avon Insurance Plc v. Swire Fraser Ltd* [2000] Lloyd's Rep.I.R. 535.

[67] *e.g.* the duty of the c.i.f. seller to procure transit insurance for his buyer as in *Yuill v. Robson* [1908] 1 K.B. 270. In *Hood v. West End Motor Car Packing Co.* [1917] 2 K.B. 38 it was held, exceptionally, that the defendant had undertaken an absolute responsibility to procure an effective cargo insurance.

[68] Limitation Act 1980, ss.2 and 5. As to the application of the limitation period in an action against an agent, see *Knapp v. Ecclesiastical Group Plc* [1999] Lloyd's Rep.I.R. 390—the cause of action accrues when the negligence becomes actionable and it is immaterial that the damage becomes more serious or is capable of more precise qualification at a later time.

[69] *Iron Trades Mutual Ins. Co. v. Buckenham* [1990] 1 All E.R. 808; *The ERAS EIL Actions* [1992] 1 Lloyd's Rep. 570, 602.

[70] This is a bare summary only, and the reader is referred to section 14A of the 1980 Act for its detailed application.

[71] Under Limitation Act 1980, s. 36.

[72] *Cia de Seguros Imperio v. Heath (REBX) Ltd* [2001] 1 W.L.R. 112.

[73] *Punjab National Bank v. de Boinville* [1992] 1 W.L.R. 1138.

[74] See, for their application in insurance intermediary cases, the *Punjab National Bank* Case, *supra*; *Macmillan v. Knott Becker Scott* [1990] 1 Lloyd's Rep. 98; *Verderame v. Commercial Union Ass. Co.* [1992] B.C.L.C. 793; *Pryke v. Gibbs Hartley Cooper Ltd* [1991] 1 Lloyd's Rep. 602; "*The Zephyr*" [1985] 2 Lloyd's Rep. 529; *Henderson v. Merrett Syndicates Ltd* [1995] 2 A.C. 145; *Pangood Ltd v. Barclay Brown & Co. Ltd* [1999] Lloyd's Rep.I.R. 405.

that he must exercise reasonable skill and care in performing the duties that he has undertaken, and he will accordingly be answerable for loss caused by his negligence.[75] In this context negligence means a failure to display a reasonable standard of skill and diligence in transacting the business in question. The requisite standard is to be stated objectively by the court.[76] The law does not expect an extraordinary degree of skill,[77] but the standard of skill and diligence ordinarily to be expected of other persons of average capacity and ordinary ability in his position.[78] In order to be acquainted with professional standards the court will receive expert evidence of professional practice[79] and of any code of practice governing the agent's work.[80]

36–24 Obtaining instructions. At the outset the agent's responsibility towards his client requires him to ascertain the client's needs, either by instruction or otherwise.[81] He may need to advise the client of the options open to him and to obtain competitive quotations so that the client can make an informed choice of the exact cover to be obtained. When the agent is insufficiently familiar with the particular market to give advice unaided, it is negligent to give advice without seeking assistance. So where insurance brokers who were engaged to procure an insurance on timber against damage from enemy action replied that it was uninsurable when this was not the case, it was held that they were negligent in giving their legal opinion of the effect of the relevant wartime legislation without taking reasonable precautions to see that it was correct, such as consulting their solicitors.[82]

36–25 Liability for failure to effect insurance. The agent must use reasonable skill and care to procure the cover that his client has requested either expressly or by necessary implication.[83] If he negligently fails to effect a valid insurance in accordance with his instructions, he will be liable to his client for loss so caused and will forfeit his rights against the client in consequence. An agent who has come under an obligation to procure an insurance does not normally warrant to get it at all events.[84] The undertaking is that he will exercise due diligence and skill in getting it if it is possible.

---

[75] *The "Superhulls Cover" Case (No. 2)* [1990] 2 Lloyd's Rep. 431, 446; *Harvest Trucking Co. v. Davis* [1991] 2 Lloyd's Rep. 638, 643.

[76] *Park v. Hammond* (1816) 6 Taunt. 495; *Mallough v. Barber* (1815) 4 Camp. 150.

[77] *Chapman v. Walton* (1833) 10 Bing. 57, 63.

[78] *Harvest Trucking Co. v. Davis* [1991] 2 Lloyd's Rep. 638, 643. It is assumed that the agent has a general knowledge of the type of insurance he agrees to place—"*The Moonacre*" [1992] 2 Lloyd's Rep. 501, 523. In *Henderson v. Merrett Syndicates Ltd* [1994] 2 Lloyd's Rep. 468, 474 Sir Thomas Bingham M.R. defined the duty as: "the standard of skill and care reasonably to be expected of such an agent at the time and with the knowledge that he had or should have had." This was applied by Potter J. in *Aiken v. Stewart Wrightson Agency* [1995] 1 W.L.R. 1281, 1313, to the case of a Lloyd's underwriting agent.

[79] *Harvest Trucking Co. v. Davis, supra*; "*The Moonacre*" [1992] 2 Lloyd's Rep. 501, 525; *Chapman v. Walton* (1833) 10 Bing. 57, 63.

[80] *Harvest Trucking Co. v. Davis, supra.*

[81] *The "Superhulls Cover" Case (No. 2)* [1990] 2 Lloyd's Rep. 431, 445; *Harvest Trucking Co. v. Davis* [1991] 2 Lloyd's Rep. 638, 643; "*The Moonacre*" [1992] 2 Lloyd's Rep. 501, 523; *O'Brien v. Hughes-Gibb & Co.* [1995] L.R.L.R. 90, 99.

[82] *Sarginson Brothers v. Keith Moulton & Co.* (1942) 73 Ll.L.R. 104.

[83] *The "Superhulls Cover" Case (No. 2)* [1990] 2 Lloyd's Rep. 431, 445; *Harvest Trucking Co. v. Davis* [1991] 2 Lloyd's Rep. 638, 643; "*The Moonacre*" [1992] 2 Lloyd's Rep. 501, 523; *Mander v. Commercial Union Assurance Co. Plc* [1998] Lloyd's Rep.I.R. 93; *National Insurance and Guarantee Corp. v. Imperio Reinsurance Co. (UK) Ltd* [1999] Lloyd's Rep.I.R. 249.

[84] *Smith v. Cologhan* (1788) 2 T.R. 188n, *per* Buller J.

36–26 Obligation to insure. The client alleging a breach of duty by his agent in failing to arrange the desired insurance cover must first establish that the agent was obliged to effect an insurance for him.[85] The obligation may arise by implication from a course of dealings or the usage of merchants and businessmen in a particular trade.[86] If it is alleged that the agent failed to carry out his instructions, then the client should show what instructions were given and that the agent has failed to comply with them, either in failing to procure a policy or renewal at all, or in procuring it on the wrong terms.

36–27 Compliance with instructions. The general rule is that the agent departs from his instructions at his peril.[87] He has in general no right to substitute his own judgment, such as deciding a maximum acceptable level of premium.[88] If, however, his instructions are silent on a particular matter that is clearly covered by insurance or other relevant market usage, he may transact the business in accordance therewith.[89] The principal will not succeed in showing that the agent has departed from his instructions if these were ambiguously worded, with the result that the agent has reasonably understood them in a contrary sense to that intended,[90] since such conduct is consistent with the exercise of reasonable skill and care. In determining whether or not the agent's interpretation was reasonable, the court will bear in mind the relationship between the parties that created the obligation to insure and the risks that the parties must fairly be taken to have intended to cover.[91]

36–28 Completion of proposal form. The agent owes his client a duty to take reasonable skill and care in assisting him to complete a proposal form where that is required.[92] If the agent himself fills in the form he must be careful to check with the proposer that the answers are correct.[93] The fact that the proposer should check the answers before signing the proposal form does not necessarily relieve the agent of responsibility for misstatements due to his negligence in completing the form, provided that the proposer's own conduct was not the sole and effective cause of the loss.[94] The agent should

---

[85] *United Marketing Co. v. Hasham Kara* [1963] 1 Lloyd's Rep. 331.
[86] *Smith v. Lascelles* (1788) 2 T.R. 187; *Hurrell v. Bullard* (1863) 3 F. & F. 445; *Callender v. Oelrichs* (1838) 5 Bing.(N.C.) 58.
[87] *Barron v. Fitzgerald* (1840) 6 Bing.(N.C.) 201.
[88] *Wallace v. Tellfair* (1786) 2 T.R. 188n.
[89] *Mallough v. Barber* (1815) 4 Camp. 150; *Smith v. Cologhan* (1788) 2 T.R. 188n; *Vale v. Van Oppen* (1921) 37 T.L.R. 367; *Pacific & General Ins. Co. v. Hazell* [1997] L.R.L.R. 65, 71.
[90] *Fomin v. Oswell* (1813) 3 Camp. 357; *Ireland v. Livingstone* (1872) L.R. 5 H.L. 395; *Provincial Ass. Co. v. Roy* (1879) 10 R.L.O.S. 643; *Vale v. Van Oppen* (1921) 37 T.L.R. 367; "*The Moonacre*" [1992] 2 Lloyd's Rep. 501, 524–525.
[91] *Enlayde v. Roberts* [1917] 1 Ch. 109, 121; *Yuill & Co. v. Robson* [1907] 1 K.B. 685; affirmed [1908]1 K.B. 270.
[92] "*The Moonacre*" [1992] 2 Lloyd's Rep. 501, 523; *O'Connor v. Kirby & Co.* [1972] 1 Q.B. 90; *McNealy v. Pennine Ins. Co.* [1978] 2 Lloyd's Rep. 18.
[93] *Dunbar v. A & B Painters* [1985] 2 Lloyd's Rep. 616, affirmed [1986] 2 Lloyd's Rep. 38.
[94] *Kapur v. J W Francis & Co.* [2000] Lloyd's Rep.I.R. 361, explaining the decision in *O'Connor v. Kirby & Co.* [1972] 1 Q.B. 90 on this ground and disapproving the ratio of Davies L.J. that it was the duty of the proposer only to check that the form was accurate. See also *Dunbar v. A. & B. Painters* [1985] 2 Lloyd's Rep. 616 in which *O'Connor v. Kirby* was not cited, but which itself was not cited in *Kapur v. J W Francis & Co.* In an appropriate case, the court would today be likely to reduce the client's damages for contributory negligence.

also explain to his client the duty to volunteer material circumstances to the insurers.

36–29 Expedition. An agent should exercise reasonable diligence in taking steps to effect an insurance or a renewal of cover, and will be liable to the assured for loss suffered as a result of unreasonable delay.[95] Whether the agent should treat it as a matter of urgency depends upon his knowledge of the need for expedition.[96] So where a broker was instructed on a Friday afternoon to procure cover on a cargo which arrived in London on the following Monday and failed to do so in time, it was held that he was not negligent. He did not know the anticipated date of arrival and hence the reason for urgency, and was not bound to try to get cover before close of business on the Friday.[97] It has been held that a broker is not obliged in law to notify his client as soon as cover is effected, although it is good practice to do so and to permit him to check the terms of the insurance obtained.[98]

36–30 Obtaining satisfactory cover. The agent must take all reasonable care to see that his client is properly covered, such as checking that none of the particular insurance company's categories of unacceptable risks apply to the client,[99] and disclosing and not misrepresenting material facts.[1] Where the owners of a vessel told their brokers that they would be living on board and using a petrol engine, the brokers were negligent in obtaining a standard "lying-up" policy which excluded residence on board and warranted that petrol was not used,[2] and where the cover obtained excluded use of the vessel as a houseboat, the broker was negligent in failing to advise his client about the houseboat exclusion.[3] If the broker is unclear about the meaning of the policy he should seek assistance from the insurers or others.[4] When the broker knows the scope of cover required, he should draw to the attention of his client the presence of any clause in the insurance cover that contains a significant exclusion or limitation and seek instructions upon it.[5] He must ensure that the policy contains any appropriate special clauses normally available in the market to protect his client from unnecessary risks including the risk of litigation.[6] He must take reasonable steps to ensure that his client understands the basis on which the insurance was written and the consequences of underinsurance, especially in a property insurance written on a reinstatement or replacement basis.[7]

---

[95] *Turpin v. Bilton* (1843) 5 M & G 455; *London Borough of Bromley v. Ellis* [1971] 1 Lloyd's Rep. 97.
[96] *United Mills v. Bray & Co.* [1951] 2 Lloyd's Rep. 631.
[97] *Cock, Russell & Co. v. Bray Gibb & Co.* (1920) 3 Ll.L.R. 71.
[98] *United Mills v. Harvey Bray & Co.* [1951] 2 Lloyd's Rep. 631.
[99] *McNealy v. Pennine Ins. Co.* [1978] 2 Lloyd's Rep. 18.
[1] *Aneco Reinsurance Underwriting Ltd v. Johnson & Higgins Ltd* [1998] 1 Lloyd's Rep.I.R. 565, affirmed [2001] UKHL 51, [2002] Lloyd's Rep.I.R. 91; see para. 36–44, *post.*
[2] *Strong & Pearl v. S. Allison & Co.* (1926) 25 Ll.L.R. 504.
[3] *"The Moonacre"* [1992] 2 Lloyd's Rep. 501, 523–525.
[4] *ibid.*
[5] *Harvest Trucking Co. v. Davis* [1991] 2 Lloyd's Rep. 638; *The "Superhulls Cover" Case (No. 2)* [1990] 2 Lloyd's Rep. 431, 445–446; *Tudor Jones v. Crowley Colosso* [1996] 2 Lloyd's Rep. 619.
[6] *FNCB Ltd v. Barnet Devanney (Harrow) Ltd* [1999] Lloyd's Rep.I.R. 459.
[7] *J.W. Bollom & Co. Ltd v. Byas Mosley & Co. Ltd* [2000] Lloyd's Rep.I.R. 136, distinguished in *William Jackson & Sons Ltd v. Oughtred & Harrison (Insurance) Ltd* [2002] Lloyd's Rep.I.R. 230.

36–31 If the broker has negligently failed to take the necessary steps to make the nature of the risk clear to the insurer, he will be answerable for it.[8] If he procures a policy from insurers who, as he ought to know, are in danger of going out of business, he will be responsible for the client obtaining a worthless policy in consequence.[9] If he is asked to transfer cover from one insurer to another he must take care to ensure that the client is not inadvertently left uninsured for a time.[10]

36–32 When a broker has negligently procured inadequate insurance cover for his client, it is generally speaking no defence that the client could have perceived his error from the insurance documents sent to him. The client is entitled to assume that the broker has employed skill and care in obtaining the insurance and is not under a duty towards his agent to vet the cover documents.[11] There are two qualifications to this general rule. First, if the broker's error and its consequences were so blindingly obvious from even a quick reading of the important terms of the cover that the client must have realised that his instructions had not been followed, he may well be held to have ratified, and acquiesced in, the broker's unauthorised conduct.[12] Secondly, if the client's failure to study the insurance documents sent to him can fairly be described as a culpable neglect of his own interests that contributes to his subsequent loss, the damages payable by the broker may be reduced to reflect his contributory negligence and its consequences.[13]

36–33 Where an agent is given a discretion as to the sort of policy he should obtain, or the insurance company which he should approach, he cannot be accused of negligence if he exercises his judgment in a manner disadvantageous to his principal unless it can be said against him that he adopted a course of action which no reasonable agent would have taken.[14] Thus an agent with a choice of insurers is not bound to go to the company offering the lowest premium or the most satisfactory terms.[15] If, moreover, he is ordered to effect renewal of a policy, he is not automatically negligent in not procuring an identical policy to the expiring one.[16]

36–34 Agent's duty to keep principal informed. As has been said earlier, the agent is not accountable for failing to obtain the insurance cover

---

[8] *Warren v. Sutton* [1976] 2 Lloyd's Rep. 276; *British Citizens' Ass. Co. v. Woolland & Co.* (1921) 8 Ll.L.R. 89; *Maydew v. Forrester* (1814) 5 Taunt. 615; *General Accident Fire & Life Ass. Corp. v. Minet* (1942) 74 Ll.L.R. 1; *Coolee v. Wing, Heath & Co.* (1930) 47 T.L.R. 78.

[9] *Osman v. Moss* [1970] 1 Lloyd's Rep. 313.

[10] *Cherry v. Allied Insurance Brokers* [1978] 1 Lloyd's Rep. 274.

[11] *Dickson & Co. v. Devitt* (1916) 21 Com.Cas. 291; *British Citizen's Ass. Co. v. Woolland* (1921) 8 Ll.L.R. 89; *General Accident Fire & Life Ass. Corp. v. Minet* (1942) 74 Ll.L.R. 1; *The "Superhulls Cover" Case (No. 2.)* [1990] 2 Lloyd's Rep. 431, 453–454; "*The Moonacre*" [1992] 2 Lloyd's Rep. 501, 527; *Elliott v. Ron Dawson & Assoc.* (1983) 139 D.L.R. (3d) 323.

[12] *General Accident Fire & Life Ass. Corp. v. Minet* (1942) 72 Ll.L.R. 48, 62; (1942) 74 Ll.L.R. 1, 9; *The "Superhulls Cover" Case (No. 2)* [1990] 2 Lloyd's Rep. 431, 454.

[13] *The "Superhulls Cover" Case (No. 2), supra,* at 461–464; *Forsik Vesta v. Butcher (No. 1)* [1989] A.C. 852, 859; *Tudor Jones v. Crowley Colosso* [1996] 2 Lloyd's Rep. 619, 636–639.

[14] *Cumber v. Anderson* (1808) 1 Camp. 523; *Tasker v. Scott* (1815) 6 Taunt. 234.

[15] *Moore v. Mourgue* (1776) 2 Cowp. 479; *Dixon v. Hovill* (1828) 4 Bing. 665. An agent employed to obtain insurance without a premium limit is not entitled to omit to insure on the ground that he believes all the premiums quoted are excessive—*Wallace v. Tellfair* (1786) 2 T.R. 188n.

[16] *Michaels v. Valentine* (1923) 16 Ll.L.R. 244. A broker should check to see that renewal conditions set out in the expiring policy are fulfilled—*Wilkinson v. Coverdale* (1793) 1 Esp. 74.

requested unless the failure is due to negligence on his part. He will, however, be answerable to his principal if he allows the latter to suffer loss because he has not been informed that cover cannot be effected on the terms required.[17] As long ago as 1788 it was decided in *Smith v. Lascelles* that a merchant who was accustomed to procuring insurance on goods which were the subject of transactions between himself and another merchant, was answerable to the latter when he failed to notify him that he could not or would not effect cover on a particular consignment "because he deprives the other of the opportunity of applying elsewhere to procure the insurance".[18] This decision was followed in *Callander v. Oelrichs*,[19] where it was said that the obligation of notification arose from the relationship of the parties, and that, even if there was no other choice of insurers, the principal ought to be given the chance to amend the terms sought if he thought it advisable.

36–35 If temporary cover has been obtained, a broker who has obtained it for the assured must warn the assured if the insurers refuse to issue a policy,[20] and, if the insurers go out of business to the broker's knowledge, he must warn the assured for whom he placed cover with that firm that he is about to become uninsured.[21] Similarly, brokers have been held liable for not warning a client that he should not move his yacht from her present moorings until the underwriters had agreed to a change of anchorage.[22]

36–36 Measure of damages payable by negligent agent. When an agent has failed to effect or renew a valid insurance in accordance with his instructions and is liable to his client as a result of the principles of law set out in the preceding paragraphs, the basic measure of such damages in the event of a loss is the amount necessary to place the client in the same position as if the insurance had been made or renewed as instructed. This is the amount that the client would have been able to recover from the insurers for his loss.[23] If the policy that the client instructed the agent to obtain would not have covered the loss in any event, damages must be nominal.[24]

---

[17] *The "Superhulls Cover" Case (No. 2)* [1990] 2 Lloyd's Rep. 431, 445, approving this paragraph in the 8th edition of this work; *Harvest Trucking v. Davis* [1991] 2 Lloyd's Rep. 638, 643; *"The Moonacre"* [1992] 2 Lloyd's Rep. 501, 523.

[18] (1788) 2 T.R. 187, 188.

[19] (1838) 5 Bing. (N.C.) 58.

[20] *London Borough of Bromley v. Ellis* [1971] 1 Lloyd's Rep. 97.

[21] *Osman v. Moss* [1970] 1 Lloyd's Rep. 313.

[22] *Strong & Pearl v. S. Allison & Co.* (1926) 25 Ll.L.R. 504. See *McNeill v. Millen & Co* [1907] 2 Ir.R. 328, where the broker incorrectly said that an insurance was effected when it was not, and *Hurrell v. Bullard* (1863) 3 F. & F. 445.

[23] *Harvest Trucking v. Davis* [1991] 2 Lloyd's Rep. 638, 646; *"The Moonacre"* [1992] 2 Lloyd's Rep. 501, 527; *Coolee v. Wing, Heath & Co.* (1930) 47 T.L.R. 78; *Strong & Pearl v. S. Allison & Co.* (1926) 25 Ll.L.R. 504, 508; *Turpin v. Bilton* (1843) 5 M. & G. 455; *Harding v. Carter* (1781), cited in Park, *A System of the Law of Marine Insurance* (8th ed., 1842) Vol. 1, p. 4; *Beattie v. Furness-Houlder* [1976] S.L.T. (Notes) 60. For a similar assessment of loss when a broker failed to report the results of an investigation as promised see *Pryke v. Gibbs Hartley Cooper* [1991] 1 Lloyd's Rep. 602, 620. It may be necessary to make allowance for a higher premium that would have been charged if proper disclosure had been made—*Aiken v. Stewart Wrightson Agency* [1995] 1 W.L.R. 1281, 1317.

[24] *Waterkeyn v. Eagle Star & British Dominions Ins. Co.* (1920) 4 Ll.L.R. 178, 5 Ll.L.R. 42; see also *Fomin v. Oswell* (1813) 3 Camp. 357, 359. In *Ramwade v. W.J. Emson & Co.* [1987] R.T.R. 72, damages were not recoverable as regards the cost of hiring a replacement vehicle that would not have been insured under the motor policy that the brokers should have obtained.

36–37 The position is more complicated where the policy that the agent has negligently failed to effect could have been avoided by the insurers for a breach of condition or warranty prior to the date of the loss. The court must then consider what were the chances of the particular insurers repudiating their liability in the ordinary course of business or, if no particular insurer was in contemplation, what were the chances of a typical reputable insurer of the risks in question doing so.[25] This approach was followed in a case where the loss for which the assured wished to claim fell inside an exclusion from cover.[26] It is for the assured to adduce evidence that the insurers would not have exercised their legal right if the policy had been validly concluded, but would have paid the claim. The court may draw inferences in the absence of evidence from the insurers.[27] Having assessed the chances that the insurers would not have exercised their rights of defence to payment the court then awards to the assured a corresponding proportion of their claim for damages.

36–38 In *Fraser v. Furman*[28] the defendant company had employed insurance brokers to renew their employers' liability policy, which covered them against claims made by employees injured at work owing to a breach of duty by the defendants. The brokers failed to do so. The plaintiff was injured as the result of a breach of statutory duty by the defendants and claimed compensation from them. They in turn sought an indemnity from the brokers because they were not covered by insurance in relation to the claim. The brokers countered by asserting that the insurers contemplated would rightly have repudiated liability under the renewed policy, because the defendants were in breach of a condition in it requiring them to take reasonable precautions to prevent such accidents as that in question, so that only nominal damages could be recovered from them for their failure to renew it. The Court of Appeal held that the quantum of damages did not depend upon whether the assured's claim would have been legally unassailable or not, but upon whether the insurance company in question would actually have run the defence to the claim. In this instance the insurance company possessed a high reputation, and in any case, since the defence was unlikely to succeed, whatever the brokers alleged, the point would not have been taken.[29] Consequently the defendants' claim would have been paid, and they were entitled to a full indemnity from the brokers in damages.

36–39 In *Everett v. Hogg Robinson and Gardner Mountain Insurance Ltd*[30] Kerr J. stated that it was the task of the court to decide what would have been most likely to happen if a claim had been pressed against the insurers, in a similar way to evaluating the loss of a chance, and express its conclusions by way of a discount from the full loss sustained by the assured. He therefore deducted 33⅓ per cent from the assured's claim on the basis of the facts

---

[25] *Fraser v. Furman, Miller Smith & Partners Third Party* [1967] 1 W.L.R. 898.
[26] *Dunbar v. A. & B. Painters* [1986] 2 Lloyd's Rep. 38.
[27] In a case where the claim for damages against the brokers is brought in the same proceedings in which insurers are seeking to avoid the policy the insurers' witnesses are available to give the evidence—see *March Cabaret Club v. The London Assurance* [1975] 1 Lloyd's Rep. 169 concerning the same principles in respect of assessors.
[28] [1967] 1 W.L.R. 898.
[29] [1967] 1 W.L.R. 898, 909.
[30] [1973] 2 Lloyd's Rep. 217, 225.

before him in that case, the balance representing the approximate figure for which the assured and insurer in all probability would have settled.[31]

36–40 What, then, is the position if a broker fails to effect a policy which would in practice have been rendered unenforceable by statute because, for instance, the assured lacked the requisite insurable interest? It would seem to follow from the decision in *Fraser v. Furman*[32] that, if the assured were able to satisfy the court that the insurance company in question would certainly have waived this objection and honoured a claim made under the policy, he ought to recover a full indemnity from the agent in order to be placed in the same position as if the agent had taken it out on his behalf, but unfortunately a previous decision of the Court of Appeal itself has decided that this is not the case.

36–41 In *Thomas Cheshire & Co. v. Vaughan Brothers & Co.*[33] brokers who were instructed to effect a p.p.i. marine policy on the plaintiffs' anticipated profits to be made from the arrival of cargo in England from South America, failed to obtain cover against the risk of the cargo being diverted by a Government order, with the result that the policy obtained did not cover loss of profit when a diversion occurred.[34] The plaintiffs sued the brokers for negligently failing to effect the full cover requested. The brokers contended that, since the p.p.i. policy was rendered null and void by section 4 of the Marine Insurance Act 1906, the plaintiffs would never have had any legally enforceable rights under it against the underwriters. The plaintiffs obtained evidence from the underwriter in question that he would have paid on the policy if the risk had been covered by it, notwithstanding that it was legally unenforceable,[35] and this evidence was apparently accepted by the trial judge, McCardie J. Nonetheless it was held that this was irrelevant, and a principal has no right at all to damages against an agent who has failed to effect a policy which would itself be void and unenforceable at law.

36–42 The ground for this decision given by Banks and Atkin L.JJ. following the earlier authority of *Cohen v. Kittell*[36] was that the plaintiff's action was not maintainable because the plaintiff would never have had any legally enforceable rights under the policy against the underwriter, and the court ought not to speculate upon what advantages the plaintiff might have possessed from this "honour" policy.[37] It was formerly thought that this was indeed the ratio decidendi of the decision, and, consequently, that a principal could never recover damages against an agent for failing to take out a policy under which the insurer would have had a legal defence to payment, as was stated in the fifth edition of this work.[38]

---

[31] See also *O. & R. Jewellers v. Terry* [1999] Lloyd's Rep.I.R. 436 (plaintiffs lost a 30 per cent chance of recovering their full claim from the insurers because of the brokers' breach).

[32] [1967] 1 W.L.R. 898.

[33] [1920] 3 K.B. 240.

[34] The report refers to "non-disclosure". This is misleading. The brokers had failed to obtain as wide a cover as instructed—see, *per* Scrutton L.J. at 253. For the action against the underwriters see *Cheshire & Co. v. Thompson* (1919) 24 Com.Cas. 114, 198.

[35] [1920] 3 K.B. 240, 243. This was not unusual in contemporary practice—see *Maritime Ins. Co. v. Assecuranz Union von 1865* (1935) 52 Ll.L.R. 16, 19.

[36] (1889) 22 Q.B.D. 680.

[37] [1920] 3 K.B. 240, 250, 258.

[38] At para. 615.

36–43 In *Fraser v. Furman*,[39] however, the case was distinguished by Diplock L.J. on the basis that its ratio was confined to instances where the hypothetical policy would have been null and void, and did not apply to a policy that the insurers had a right to avoid. With respect, this seems an unreal distinction. The assured's legal rights under a policy liable to be avoided for some breach or non-disclosure are ultimately as unenforceable as his rights under a p.p.i. insurance, and it seems curious that the assured in *Cheshire v. Vaughan* should fail to obtain damages when the underwriter had said he would have paid, while the assured in *Fraser v. Furman* succeeded without any such intimation being obtained from the insurers. It is submitted that in order to reconcile *Cheshire v. Vaughan* with *Fraser v. Furman*, it should be interpreted as having been decided upon the ground relied upon by Scrutton L.J. namely, that the court ought not to give any effect, directly or indirectly, to a type of policy that Parliament has declared shall be entirely null and void.[40] Put that way, the decision turns upon the grounds of public policy, and the true distinction lies between policies that are liable to be avoided by the insurer's election, and policies that are rendered null and void or illegal[41] by statute or the public policy of the common law. In the case of the latter the court is in reality denying the plaintiff an action rather than enquiring whether he would have been paid.

36–44 Other instances. The guiding principle must be to assess the client's loss by reference to his financial position if his agent had performed his duties towards him. So where it was established that insurers would have written smaller lines on a risk if their brokers had told them that they could not obtain a back-to-back excess of loss reinsurance cover, but the brokers negligently represented that the cover desired had been obtained, the measure of damages was based on the insurers' losses over and above the amount for which they would have been liable on the smaller lines which they would have written.[42]

36–45 Reassured's agent. If the broker or intermediary acting for a reassured performs the task of drafting the wording for the reinsurance he owes a duty to exercise reasonable skill and care in preparing it, so that it shall correctly set forth the terms agreed in negotiations.[43] If the broker in breach of duty fails properly to advise on the availability of reinsurance rather than merely to obtain reinsurance cover for an agreed amount, the

---

[39] [1967] 1 W.L.R. 898, 909.

[40] [1920] 3 K.B. 240, 255–256.

[41] *Webster v. De Tastet* (1797) 7 T.R. 157, a decision concerning an insurance which was to have covered slaves, is an early instance of a contract of insurance which was actually illegal owing to the prohibition on insuring slaves and so aiding a banned trade. Its authority today was doubted by Diplock L.J. in *Fraser v. Furman* [1967] 1 W.L.R. 898, 908. If the policy which the agent is instructed to take out is not only void but actually illegal and prohibited, then the contract of agency becomes ipso facto a contract to achieve an unlawful purpose and hence illegal and unenforceable by either party to it as an instruction to commit a crime: *Harry Parker v. Mason* [1940] 2 K.B. 590. The distinction between void and illegal policies was emphasised in *Cheshire v. Vaughan*.

[42] *The "Superhulls Cover" Case (No. 2)* [1990] 2 Lloyd's Rep. 431, approved by the House of Lords in *Aneco Reinsurance Underwriting Ltd v. Johnson & Higgins Ltd* [2001] UKHL 51, [2002] Lloyd's Rep.I.R. 91.

[43] *ibid.* at 446.

reassured's loss is not limited to the latter sum, but is the whole loss resulting from their providing insurance when no reinsurance was available.[44]

36–46 Agent's rights against principal. On ordinary rules of agency law, the agent's right to commission and an indemnity from his principal depend upon the proper fulfilment of his duties. At common law, the agent's right to commission depends upon his being the effective cause of the insurance being placed and it is not necessary that all the formalities should be concluded through him once he has arranged an introduction between the parties to the contract of insurance.[45] The broker earns the entirety of his commission when the risk is successfully placed, and his right is not affected by a subsequently agreed cancellation of the insurance and return of a proportion of the premium by the insurers to the assured.[46] There is nothing to prevent an agent agreeing more favourable terms for payment of commission, but the court will not give effect to them in the absence of clear evidence.[47] If no rate of commission is agreed, the court will award a reasonable sum.[48] If the agent's default is the cause of the policy procured being unenforceable against the insurer, he loses his rights to commission[49] and indemnities.[50] When the agent takes a secret commission from the insurers, his principal need not pay him one, and can recover it if already paid in ignorance,[51] and the agent is liable to be summarily dismissed under any long term agency contract made with the principal.[52]

3. THE INSURERS' AGENTS

36–47 Directors. Unless restrained by specific provisions in the insurance company's articles, deed or act, as the case may be, the directors of a company have implied authority to do everything necessary to carry on the

---

[44] *Aneco Reinsurance Underwriting Ltd v. Johnson & Higgins Ltd* [2001] UKHL 51, [2002] Lloyd's Rep.I.R. 91.

[45] *McNeil v. Law Union & Rock Ins. Co* (1925) 23 Ll.L.R. 314, following *Nightingale v. Parsons* [1914] 2 K.B. 621. More emphasis should be placed on the word "effective" rather than discussion of whether the agent was "the" or "an" effective cause: *Harding Maughan Hambly Ltd v. Compagnie Europeenne de Courtage d'Assurances et de Reassurances* [2000] Lloyd's I.R. 293, 311, referring to the equivalent paragraph in the 9th edition of this work. The broker has a lien over the policy documents to secure payment—*Fisher v. Smith* (1878) L.R. 4 App.Cas; Marine Insurance Act 1906, s.53(1). The broker is also entitled to apply proceeds collected under the policy to satisfy the debt secured by the lien, but neither the lien under s. 53(2) nor this right applies when the insurance is composite: *Eide UK Ltd v. Lowndes Lambert Group Ltd* [1999] Q.B. 199.

[46] *Velos Group Ltd v. Harbour Insurance Services Ltd* [1997] 2 Lloyd's Rep. 461.

[47] *McNeil, Riley & Co. v. The Steamship Mutual* (1940) 67 Ll.L.R. 142.

[48] *Hugh Allen v. Holmes* [1969] 1 Lloyd's Rep. 348 (assessor).

[49] *Denew v. Daverell* (1813) 3 Camp. 451.

[50] *Barron v. Fitzgerald* (1840) 6 Bing. (N.C.) 201.

[51] *Andrews v. Ramsay* [1903] 2 K.B. 635; *Taylor v. Walker* [1958] 1 Lloyd's Rep. 490. The agent may take a commission from insurers if it is disclosed—*Leete v. Wallace* (1888) 58 L.T. 577. Usage permits a broker to deduct commission from the gross premium. The assured must allow the ordinary amount if it is not the subject of express agreement—*Baring v. Stanton* (1876) 3 Ch.D. 502; *Great Western Ins. Co. v. Cunliffe* (1874) L.R.9 Ch. App. 525. Chapter 5 of the Conduct of Business Rules made by the Financial Services Authority require the disclosure of commission in many circumstances.

[52] *Swale v. Ipswich Tannery Co.* (1906) 11 Com.Cas. 88.

business of the company in a customary and proper manner.[53] In addition, there is no doubt that directors and high-ranking executives have authority, for example, to waive breaches of contract by insured persons in the interests of encouraging custom, even if these acts are not strictly necessary for the execution of business. Such acts of indulgence fall within the apparent or ostensible authority of these agents, but their authority, however wide, is not unlimited.[54] They do not have authority to enter into contracts that the assured knows, or ought to know, exceed their power.[55]

36–48 The law does not prescribe the duties or powers of a managing director. They may be defined by the instrument appointing him, or be such as are from time to time assigned to or vested in him by the board of directors.[56]

36–49 At common law persons dealing with a company were deemed to have notice of the company's powers and of any limitation upon the directors' authority contained in the articles, deed, or act, and when the directors exceeded their authority as therein defined they did not bind the company[57] unless their authority was extended or their unauthorised act was ratified. A qualification on this rule was that, if persons were acting *de facto* as directors and performed acts apparently within the scope of a director's authority, there being nothing external to indicate a failure to observe due formalities, the company was bound by such acts.[58] Thus an applicant receiving a policy of insurance from persons acting *de facto* as directors was not prejudiced by any irregularity in the internal management of the company's affairs, whether it was a failure to appoint a director by proper procedures or an improper exercise of their powers.[59]

36–50 The common law has been altered by what are now sections 35,

---

[53] *Smith v. Hull Glass Co.* (1849) 8 C.B. 670; *Charles v. National Guardian* (1857) 5 W.R. 694; *Re Norwich Equitable Fire* (1887) 57 L.T. 241. The Financial Services and Markets Act 2000 and the rules made thereunder contain important restrictions on the appointment of persons as directors, executives or "controllers" of insurance companies (see Ch. 34, *ante*). There is no express provision in the Act, and no decided case, on the effect of acts done by directors or executives appointed in contravention of these restrictions. It may well be that contracts concluded by such persons on behalf of the company would be unenforceable by the company but enforceable against it, on the grounds of their ostensible authority.

[54] *Small v. Smith* (1884) 10 App.Cas. 119. *Re Security Mutual Life* (1858) 6 W.R. 431.

[55] *Hambro v. Hull & London Fire Insurance Co.* (1858) 3 H. & N. 789; *Montreal Assurance Co. v. Dame Elizabeth Macgillivray* (1859) 13 Moo.P.C. 87, 124; *Re Arthur Average Association* (1875) L.R. 10 Ch.App. 542, 545n.; *Baines v. Ewing* (1866) L.R. 1 Ex. 320. To the extent that these cases deal with the doctrine of *ultra vires*, they are now to be read subject to para. 36–50, *post*.

[56] *Harold Holdsworth & Co. (Wakefield) v. Caddies* [1955] 1 All E.R. 725.

[57] *Re Athenaeum Life Ass. Co.* (1858) 4 K. & J. 549; *Ex p. Wood* (1853) 17 Jur. 813; *Lawe's Case* (1852) 1 De G.M. & G. 421; *Featherstonehaugh v. Lee Moor Porcelain Co.* (1865) L.R. 1 Eq. 318; *Ernest v. Nichols* (1857) 6 H.L.Cas. 401, 417–419; *Montreal Ass. Co. v. Dame Elizabeth Macgillivray* (1859) 13 Moo.P.C. 87; *Re Arthur Average Association* (1875) L.R. 10 Ch.App. 542, 545n., 551.

[58] *Ruben v. Great Fingall Consolidated* [1906] A.C. 439, 443; *Freeman & Lockyer v. Buckhurst Park Properties (Mangal) Ltd* [1964] 2 Q.B. 480; *Hely-Hutchinson v. Brayhead Ltd* [1968] 1 Q.B. 549.

[59] *Re Country Life Insurance* (1870) L.R. 5 Ch.App. 288; *Mahony v. East Holyford Mining* (1875) L.R. 7, H.L. 869; *Prince of Wales Assurance Co. v. Harding* (1858) El.B. & E. 183.

35A and 35B of the Companies Act 1985 as inserted by section 108(1) of the Companies Act 1989. In summary, while directors still owe a duty to the company to act *intra vires*,[60] a party to a transaction with it is not bound to enquire whether the transaction is authorised by the memorandum or is otherwise within the powers of the board.[61] If he deals with the company in good faith the power of the board to bind the company or to authorise others to do so is deemed, in his favour, to be free of any limitation under the company's constitution.[62] He is presumed to have acted in good faith unless the contrary is proved, and even an awareness that the transaction is beyond the constitutional powers of the directors does not establish bad faith.[63]

36–51 The authority of the directors may be extended by the company. A company registered under the Companies Act is absolute master of its own internal regulation, and by altering the articles of association it may extend the directors' authority. This may be done by passing a special resolution to that effect.[64] The articles cannot be altered by an ordinary resolution, and an ordinary resolution does not authorise the directors to act beyond the authority conferred by the articles. But when an act within the power of the company has been done by the directors without authority it may be ratified by an ordinary resolution.[65]

36–52 Ratification by shareholders. The whole body of shareholders in any company may, by general consent and without any formality, either sanction beforehand, or subsequently ratify, an act of the directors otherwise outside their authority.[66] The shareholders may, further, by acquiescence in a course of conduct on the part of the directors, enlarge their authority beyond the limits defined in the articles, act or deed of settlement. The company is not, however, bound by the informal concurrence of some of the shareholders, unless the acquiescence of each shareholder is to be presumed.

36–53 What facts may ground an inference of acquiesence is uncertain. In *Re Athenaeum Life Assurance Co., ex p. Eagle Insurance Co.*[67] Page-Wood V.-C. said that if the form of a policy were not authorised by the deed of settlement, it would be very doubtful whether the shareholders could be said to have acquiesced in its being executed unless notice distinct and clear had been brought home to them in the shape of a report that the policy had been executed on their behalf. In *Phosphate of Lime Co. v. Green*[68] it was held that it was unnecessary to prove conclusively that each shareholder had knowledge of the facts, and consented. It is sufficient to show that the facts were made known to the body of shareholders as a whole, and, if they did not object at the time it must be supposed that they did not intend to refuse to sanction the directors' acts. If there is evidence of consent in that sense, it question of fact whether there was consent or not.

---

[60] s.35(3).
[61] s.35B.
[62] s.35A(1).
[63] s.35(2)(b), (c).
[64] Companies Act 1985, s.9.
[65] *Grant v. United Kingdom Switchback Railway* (1888) 40 Ch.D. 135.
[66] *Ashbury Railway Carriage Co. v. Riche* (1875) L.R. 7 H.L. 653, 675, *per* Lord Cairns.
[67] (1858) 4 K. & J. 549.
[68] (1871) L.R. 7 C.P. 43; *Houldsworth v. Evans* (1868) L.R. 3 H.L. 263, 276. *cf.* Lord Cranworth's stricter views in the *Riche* Case, *supra*, at 680.

36–54 Local agents. The term "local agent" is imprecise since it is apt to describe all agents ranking downwards from the manager of an insurance company's branch office to the part-time commission agent soliciting proposals for insurance from door to door. The cases concerning the authority of local agents do not form a very coherent pattern. This is because the question of the actual or ostensible authority of a particular agent is an issue of fact for the court to decide on the evidence presented to it in each case. Again, the reported cases span more than a century and many jurisdictions. Those collected here are accordingly selected primarily by way of illustration, although we have endeavoured, where possible, to identify principles and factors which influence the courts' thinking.

36–55 The courts have readily assumed that an agent who is given a specific responsibility has ostensible authority to perform other simple duties that do not involve him in contradicting the terms of the company's standard policy or usurping the discretion of senior management. Thus a district agent with authority to enter into contracts of insurance on the insurers' behalf, and take the premiums, has ostensible authority to receive notice from the assured to terminate the cover,[69] and an agent empowered to negotiate the terms of cover and receive premiums for the company has ostensible authority to receive notice of a loss which has occurred.[70] Similarly, a broker with actual authority to subscribe policies for an underwriter and to settle losses thereon, has an ostensible authority to agree to a disputed claim being referred to arbitration.[71] It must also be the case that a local agent above the rank of a canvasser has implied authority to delegate ministerial duties in order to perform his work efficiently,[72] although he could not delegate that part of his work involving an exercise of judgment resulting in the surrender of rights by insurers.[73] In all these cases the agent merely assists the ordinary conduct of existing insurance business without necessarily involving the insurers in a loss of their rights against the assured or committing them to new insurance business.

36–56 Authority to enter into contracts. An agent whose primary function is to introduce new business, and forward proposals to the directors for approval, does not without more possess implied or ostensible authority to contract on behalf of the company,[74] presumably because it is not within the usual responsibility of such agents to decide upon the acceptability of risks presented for approval. Neither does such an agent have power to bind the insurers to the type of policy that is to be issued.[75]

The insurers may, however, clothe their agent with a greater ostensible

---

[69] *Re Solvency Mutual Guarantee Society* (1862) 6 L.T. 574

[70] *Marsden v. City & County Ass. Co.* (1865) L.R. 1 C.P. 232.

[71] *Goodson v. Brooke* (1815) 4 Camp. 163. The report says "implied" but the ground of the decision seems to be that he had ostensible authority.

[72] *Rossiter v. Trafalgar Life Ass. Association* (1859) 27 Beav. 377.

[73] *Summers v. Commercial Union Ins. Co.* (1881) 6 S.C.R. 18; *Canadian Fire Ins. Co. v. Robinson* (1901) 31 S.C.R. 488. These cases were decided upon a Roman law concept of "mandatum," and, in the latter one, under the special provisions of the Quebec Civil Code.

[74] *Linford v. Provincial Horse and Cattle Ins. Co.* (1864) 34 Beav. 291; *Dicks v. S.A. Mutual Fire & General Ins. Co. Ltd* [1963] 4 S.A. 501 (N.); *World Marine & General Ins. Co. v. Leger* [1952] 1 D.L.R. 755; *McElroy v. London Ass. Association* (1897) 24 R. 287; *Bawden v. London Edinburgh & Glasgow Ass. Co.* [1892] 2 Q.B. 534; *Levy v. Scottish Employers' Ins. Co.* (1901) 17 T.L.R. 229.

[75] *Zurich General and Liability Insurance Co. v. Buck* (1939) 64 Ll.L.R. 115.

authority through their own conduct. If he is in possession of interim cover notes ready for issue by him, he has ostensible authority to grant temporary insurances.[76] If, moreover, the insurers know that the agent is making contracts on their behalf, and acquiesce in this practice, they will be estopped from denying his apparent authority to do this later.[77]

36–57 The agent's ostensible authority to enter into contracts, which he derives from possession of the company's cover notes or blank policies, will be lost if these make it clear to an assured prior to contract that the agent in question did not have power to make the contract.[78]

Senior local agents, such as district office managers, may have at least ostensible authority to accept certain sorts of risks on behalf of the company. It would not be normal business practice for an applicant to require such people to produce proof of their authority, and this would be unrealistic where cover was obtained through the post and the assured would have to accept the official's view of his own powers. It is doubtful, however, whether such a manager could make a valid contract of insurance over the telephone, which was never put into writing, since parol insurance cover is not part of the usual course of insurance business.[79] Further, it seems that, by virtue of standard administrative arrangements in the life assurance industry, the above proposition does not apply to senior local agents of life assurance companies, including branch managers, who do not have actual authority to give final approval to applications for life insurance and who would have ostensible authority only if there was some clear representation to that effect by head office.[80]

36–58 Authority to vary terms of policy. An agent who does not possess full authority to accept new risks for the insurer does not as a rule possess any sort of authority to alter the terms or conditions of a written insurance, whether set out in a policy or cover notes, and whether he purports to do so orally or by endorsing the instrument.[81] Thus, in *Comerford v. The Britannic*

---

[76] *Mackie v. European Ass. Society* (1869) 21 L.T. 102; *Dicks v. S.A. Mutual Fire Co. Ltd, supra; Cockburn v. British American Ass. Co.* (1890) 19 Ont.R. 245; *Grimmer v. Merchants' & Manufacturers' Fire Ins. Co.* [1932] 2 D.L.R. 621; *World Marine & General Ins. Co. v. Leger, supra; Haughton v. Ewbank* (1814) 4 Camp. 88. See also paras 4–23 to 4–24, *ante.*

[77] *Cockburn v. British American Ass. Co.* (1890) 19 Ont.Rep. 245; *Murfitt v. Royal Ins. Co.* (1922) 38 T.L.R. 334. McCardie J. used the term "implied authority" but that is apt only for that part of his judgment deciding that the agent necessarily had power to grant cover orally in order to carry on fire insurance business properly.

[78] *Acey v. Fernie* (1840) 7 M. & W. 151; *Walkerville Match Co. v. Scottish Union & National Ins. Co.* (1903) 6 Ont.L.R. 674.

[79] *Davies v. National Fire & Marine Ins. Co. of New Zealand* [1891] A.C 485, 496. In *Murfitt's Case, supra,* the insurers had extended their agent's authority by habitually allowing him to make parol contracts of fire insurance.

[80] *British Bank of the Middle East v. Sun Life Ass. Co. of Canada (U.K.) Ltd* [1983] 2 Lloyd's Rep. 9. This case was concerned with the effect of a guarantee purportedly given by a "unit manager", whose authority was "confirmed" by a branch manager on behalf of the defendant insurance company. The House of Lords accepted unchallenged evidence to the effect that under the common structure of the United Kingdom life assurance industry no agent outside a company's head office had authority to accept a life insurance proposal on behalf of the company.

[81] *Comerford v. Britannic Ass. Co.* (1908) 24 T.L.R. 593; *Horncastle v. Equitable Life Ass. Soc. of U.S.A.* (1906) 22 T.L.R. 735; *Fowler v. Scottish Equitable Life Ins. Society* (1858) 28 L.J.Ch. 225; *Levy v. Scottish Employers' Ins. Co.* (1901) 17 T.L.R. 229; *Wilkinson v. General Accident Fire & Life Ass. Corp. Ltd* [1967] 2 Lloyd's Rep. 182; *Ayrey v. British Legal & United Provident*

Assurance Co.[82] the sum assured by a life policy was stated in the policy. An agent of the company promised the assured a greater sum in a certain event, and it was held he had no ostensible authority to do so. In *Horncastle v. Equitable Life Assurance Society of the U.S.A.*[83] the policy (a semi-tontine life policy) stated that the contract was completely set forth therein, and that no modification could be made to it except by an agreement signed by one of certain officers. An agent, who was not one of such officers, made an oral representation as to the future value of the policy after a certain period, which contradicted the terms of the policy. It was held that, even if the agent had any kind of authority to do this, which was doubtful, the fact that the alleged agreement was at variance with the terms of a written contract made it in any event inadmissible against the society.

36–59   These authorities were followed by the High Court of Southern Rhodesia in *Feldman v. British Aviation Insurance Co.*[84] where the terms of the contract referred only to aircraft flown by pilots in the employ of the assured and holding a "B" Licence. The plaintiff alleged that a branch manager of the company had agreed to extend the cover to any licensed pilot whether or not in the assured's employ. The court held that the branch manager had no ostensible authority to alter the scope of the cover laid down in a written contract. Where, however, the agent misrepresents to a proposer the meaning or effect of a term in the policy which is not easy to interpret and the proposer relies on his explanation in concluding the insurance, the insurer will be estopped from disputing the agent's interpretation if it was reasonable for the proposer to rely on it, and the agent had ostensible authority to explain the policy.[85]

36–60   In a case before the Industrial Assurance Commissioner[86] the proposal form signed by the proposer for life assurance contained a declaration that she agreed there would be no liability upon the society until a policy had been issued and delivered to her. The Commissioner held that the society's agent had no ostensible authority to vary the terms of the contract by telling her that on her signing the proposal and paying the first premium she would be entitled to benefit.

36–61   If the insurers have acquiesced in their agent's habit of altering their policies, they will be estopped as against an assured who has witnessed this fact from denying the agent's apparent authority to do it. Thus, in *Brockelbank v. Sugrue*[87] an overseas agent whose chief function it was to

---

Ass. Co. [1918] 1 K.B. 136, 141; *Boyd v. Colonial Mutual Life Ass. Society Ltd* (1910) 29 N.Z.L.R. 41; *McKinlay v. Life & Health Ass. Association* (1905) 13 S.L.T. 102 (where the point was not properly pleaded); *Pigott v. Employers' Liability Ass. Corporation* (1900) 31 Ont.R. 666.
[82] (1908) 24 T.L.R. 593.
[83] (1906) 22 T.L.R. 735.
[84] [1949] (3) S.A. 1078 (S.R.).
[85] *Kaufmann v. British Surety Ins. Co.* (1929) 33 Ll.L.R. 315, 319; *Hiscox v. Outhwaite (No. 3.)* [1991] 2 Lloyd's Rep. 524, 535.
[86] *Shields v. Co-operative Ins. Soc.* [1949] I.A.C.Rep. (1938–49) 73; *Chatt v. Prudential Ass. Co.* illustrates the same rule [1926] I.A.C.Rep. 24.
[87] (1831) 5 C. & P. 21.

receive proposals and forward them to the insurers was held to have ostensible authority to endorse memoranda on policies issued by them, altering the cover provided, because they had in each case been notified and had done nothing to object.

36–62 Waiver of assured's breach of condition. A local agent acting in the ordinary course of his employment usually has ostensible authority to excuse a breach of condition on the part of the assured, so long as his action does not involve him in entering into a new contract for the insurers,[88] and so long as the assured is not put on notice by the policy or by any document issued by the agent that his action is unauthorised.[89]

36–63 In *Ayrey v. British Legal & United Provident Assurance Co. Ltd*[90] the assured described himself in a life insurance proposal as a fisherman. The company's district office manager for that area was then told that he was in addition a member of the Royal Naval Reserve, which exposed him to increased risks at sea. The manager permitted the insurance to proceed without taking any action, and it was held that he had authority to receive the information and to condone the assured's concealment of his naval duties. It was pointed out that the manager's action did not necessitate his varying the terms of the contract of insurance or entering into a new contract, for which he would not have had authority.[91]

Similarly the district agent of a company, who was empowered to solicit insurances, take the premiums and forward proposals to the insurers, was held to have authority to waive disclosure of the precise age of the life assured in a life assurance proposal when he said that the company could determine it themselves.[92] A similar agent in another case was held to have authority to condone breach of a residence condition in a life policy when receiving renewal premiums to keep the policy on foot.[93]

36–64 In *Acey v. Fernie*[94] it was held that a "country agent", employed to collect renewal premiums and issue receipts for them, had no authority to give a receipt for a premium tendered after the due date named in the policy. The policy was expressed to be at an end if the premium were not paid by a certain time, so that by implication the agent was purporting to make a new contract on behalf of the insurers on the terms of the old policy save as to the date of payment of premiums. The receipt, moreover, which was handed to the assured, contained a warning that the insurance would be cancelled, despite the issue of the receipt, after a certain number of days had elapsed

---

[88] *Acey v. Fernie* (1840) 7 M. & W. 151; *Ayrey v. British Legal & United Provident Ass. Co.* [1918] 1 K.B. 136, 141; *Scott v. Accident Association of New Zealand* (1888) 6 N.Z.L.R. 263.

[89] *Towle v. National Guardian Ass. Soc.* (1861) 30 L.J.Ch. 900, 916; *Acey v. Fernie* (1840) 7 M. & W. 151, 153; *British Industry Life Ass. v. Ward* (1856) 17 C.B. 644; *M'Millan v. Accident Ins. Co.* 1907 S.C. 484; *Commercial Union Ass. Co. v. Margeson* (1899) 29 S.C.R. 601; *Hyde v. Lefaivre* (1902) 32 S.C.R. 474; *Knickerbocker Life Ins. Co. v. Norton* 96 U.S. 234 (1887).

[90] [1918] 1 K.B. 136.

[91] [1918] 1 K.B. 136, 141.

[92] *Splents v. Lefevre* (1864) 11 L.T. 114.

[93] *Wing v. Harvey* (1854) 5 De G., M. & G. 265.

[94] (1840) 7 M. & W. 151 followed in *Jenkins v. Deane* (1933) 47 Ll.L.R. 342, 347, and approved in *London & Lancashire Life Ass. Co. v. Fleming* [1897] A.C. 499.

from the due date.[95] Neither an assessor[96] nor a local agent[97] has authority to waive compliance with a condition requiring full proof of loss to be submitted, when it is clear from the policy that the only manner in which proof can be dispensed with is by dispensation from the head office itself. It is, indeed, probable that, wherever the policy states that notice of loss must be given in writing to the head office of the insurance company, the assured is put on notice that any waiver of that requirement must, by implication, come from head office itself, if the insurers are to be bound by it.[98]

Where an agent was expressly empowered by insurers not only to negotiate terms of cover and take premiums, but also to enter into new contracts of insurance on their behalf, it was held by a New Zealand court, in accordance with the principles suggested above, that he had authority to receive premiums after the due date so as to bind the insurers to revive the policy.[99] The receipt given to the assured contained nothing in it to warn the assured that the agent was exceeding his authority.

36–65 Payment of premiums. By the usual practice of insurance business, premiums are payable in cash or by cheque, independently of payment provisions in the policy. A local agent usually has, therefore, no authority to take a note in lieu of immediate payment or otherwise give credit for the premium.[1] He would, however, possess ostensible authority to do this if he were entrusted with premium receipts which on their face showed that they were intended to be handed over against a promissory note,[2] or where by the parties' previous course of dealings the insurers could be said to have represented the agent as having such authority.[3]

36–66 We have seen that if an agent has authority to do a particular act such as take premiums and issue receipts for them, his principal will be bound by such acts even if the agent intends to cheat the principal and take a benefit for himself.[4] Thus, an agent who fraudulently issues the insurance company's cover notes and appropriates the premiums himself will bind the company to honour the terms of the cover note, so long as the assured is not privy to the fraud.[5] Re *Economic Fire Office Ltd*[6] provides a further illustration. It was arranged that the premiums on a fidelity policy should be paid by the employee in respect of whom the assured, his employer, had taken out the policy. When renewal was due, the employee went to the

---

[95] (1840) 7 M. & W. 151, 153. The decision is probably best explained on this second ground. Unless explained in this way *Acey v. Fernie* is difficult to reconcile with *Wing v. Harvey, supra*, unless *Wing v. Harvey* is, alternatively, explained as a case where the directors themselves acquiesced in the breach of the condition as Knight Bruce L.J. evidently believed (1854) 5 De G., M. & G. 265, 270.

[96] *Atlas Ass. Co. v. Brownell* (1899) 29 S.C.R. 537.

[97] *Commercial Union Ass. Co. v. Margeson* (1899) 29 S.C.R. 601.

[98] *Brook v. Trafalgar Ins. Co.* (1946) 79 Ll.L.R. 365, which might alternatively be explained with reference to the extremely low position of the agent concerned in that case.

[99] *Scott v. Accident Association of New Zealand* (1888) 6 N.Z.L.R. 263.

[1] *Montreal Ass. Co. v. Dame Elizabeth Macgillivray* (1859) 13 Moo.P.C. 87; *Legge v. Byas, Mosley & Co.* (1901) 7 Com.Cas. 16, 18. The authorities concerning waiver of conditions relating to premiums are set out in Ch. 6, *ante*.

[2] *London & Lancashire Life Ass. Co. v. Fleming* [1897] A.C. 499.

[3] e.g. *Globe Mutual Ins. Co. v. Wolff*, 95 U.S. 326 (1877).

[4] See para. 36–21, *ante*.

[5] *Hawke v. Niagara District Mutual Fire Ins. Co.* (1876) 23 Grant 139; *Patterson v. The Royal Ins. Co.* (1867) 14 Grant 169.

[6] (1896) 12 T.L.R. 142.

insurance company's local agent, who was empowered to receive premiums and issue receipts therefor, and told him he could not pay the renewal premium. The company's agent said that he himself would pay the premium, as a favour, to keep the policy on foot, and he issued a receipt saying that the premium had been paid. Had the receipt not been issued to the employee, the assured would have dismissed him. The company's agent, however, failed to pay a premium. It was held that the insurance company were estopped from denying the authority of their agent and were bound by the receipt issued. Had the assured known of the deal made between his employee and the agent, he could not have bound the company to honour the receipt.

36–67 Ministerial acts. Where an agent is held out not as having authority to contract, but only as having authority to perform some purely ministerial act, such as the affixing of a seal or countersigning of a policy otherwise duly executed by the directors, the company is not estopped from denying that the policy to which he affixed the seal, or which he countersigned, was executed by the directors.[7] If an agent is held out as having authority only to communicate the decision of the directors to a person who has made a proposal for insurance, such agent does not bind the company by stating that the directors have accepted the proposal, whereas they have in fact declined it.[8]

36–68 Fraudulent misrepresentation by agent. We have seen that an agent generally has no ostensible authority to contradict the written terms of cover in a policy or interim cover note,[9] so that his representations inconsistent with such written terms do not directly bind the company to the terms stated by the agent. In an appropriate case the assured may seek rescission of the contract of insurance for fraudulent misrepresentation,[10] with return of premiums paid, and the agent may also be criminally liable.[11]

36–69 In *Parker v. Co-operative Insurance Society*[12] the Industrial Assurance Commissioner held that the assured might also recover damages for fraud from the company. There the agent falsely informed the proposer for a policy on the life of her son that it would cover war risks for the full sum assured and in reliance on this representation she signed a proposal in which

---

[7] *Ruben v. Great Fingall Consolidated Co.* [1906] A.C. 439.

[8] *Russo-Chinese Bank v. Li Yau Sam* [1910] A.C. 174; *Att.-Gen. for Ceylon v. A. D. Silva* [1953] A.C. 461; *More v. New York Bowery Ins. Co.*, 130 N.Y. 537 (1892). *Penley v. Beacon Ass. Co.* (1859) 7 Grant 130 contradicts this proposition, but it is clear that the court believed that the directors' subsequent conduct indicated that they had, after all, accepted the risk initially, so that the decision could be explained on that ground.

[9] See para. 36–58, *ante.*

[10] *Kettlewell v. Refuge Ass. Co.* [1908] 1 K.B. 545, affirmed [1909] A.C. 243.

[11] The Financial Services and Markets Act 2000, s.397(1) and (2), makes it an offence to induce or attempt to induce any person to enter into or offer to enter into a relevant agreement (which includes all types of insurance contract) or to exercise, or refrain from exercising, any rights conferred by such an agreement by means of any statement, promise or forecast known to be misleading, false or deceptive or in respect of which he is reckless as to whether it is misleading, false or deceptive or by means of his dishonestly concealing any material fact. The section is only domestic in scope (s.397(7)). As to the penalty, see s.397(8).

[12] [1945] I.A.C.Rep. (1938–1949), 52.

the full sum to be assured was stated without qualification. The policy issued contained a "war-risk clause" limiting the sum payable in the event of the death of the life assured resulting from the existence of a state of war. The son was killed in action against the enemy. The society in accordance with the war-risks clause offered the reduced sum of £2 14s. 6d. instead of £37 16s. 0d., which was the full sum assured. The assured claimed the full sum. The Commissioner held that she could not do so, as the agent had no authority to promise a war-risk policy for the premium quoted, but that she was entitled to recover any damage that she had suffered from the agent's fraudulent misrepresentation. The measure of her loss was the amount that she would have recovered on a war-risks policy (£37 16s.) less the increased premium she would have had to pay for it (£4 2s. 5d.).

This decision, however, is questionable, since it is hard to see how the company could be vicariously liable for the statements of their agent as made in the scope of his employment when he had no authority whatsoever to make them. Moreover, when the assured accepted the counter-offer of the insurers contained in the policy issued to her, she surely did so with notice of the contents thereof, making it difficult to contend that she was induced to contract by representations to a different effect.

36–70 Dual role of agent. It must not be assumed that an agent of the insurers necessarily acts on their behalf for the whole of the time while he is working on insurance business. An agent employed to solicit proposals is not ordinarily the insurers' agent to fill up the proposal form, and, if he does so, he becomes the agent of the assured for that purpose.[13] A broker acting for the proposer for insurance may be the agent of the insurers to grant interim cover.[14] A commission agent paid by the insurers to solicit proposals may be the agent of the proposer to secure a policy and to forward the premium of the insurers.[15]

Similarly a local agent of the insurers may be a solicitor instructed by the assured to effect an assignment of a policy, and, if so, he may receive notice of the assignment in his capacity as the insurers' agent when the assured instructs him in his other capacity to carry out the assignment.[16] The practice of acting for both parties is, however, to be avoided if there is any possibility of a conflict of interests arising.[17]

36–71 While an agent of an insurance company may lawfully insure with them in his private capacity, he cannot, even if he has authority to make contracts, accept his own proposal on the company's behalf.[18] In one case in

[13] *Newsholme Bros. Ltd v. Road Transport & General Ass. Co.* [1929] 2 K.B. 356; *aliter* if the insurers have instructed him to complete the form: *Stone v. Reliance Mutual Ins. Soc. Ltd* [1972] 1 Lloyd's Rep. 469.
[14] *Stockton v. Mason* [1978] 2 Lloyd's Rep. 430.
[15] *Hofmann v. Economic Ins. Co.* [1956] 4 S.A. 380 (W).
[16] *Gale v. Lewis* (1846) 9 Q.B. 730, 744, applied in *Kingscroft Ins. Co. Ltd v. Nissan Fire & Marine Ins. Co. Ltd* [1999] Lloyd's Rep.I.R. 603, 635.
[17] The general rule is that an agent should not accept instructions from a second principal inconsistent with his duty to his first principal unless, after full disclosure of this position, both agree to this—*Fullwood v. Hurley* [1928] 1 K.B. 498, 502; *North & South Trust v. Berkeley* [1970] 2 Lloyd's Rep. 467; *Eagle Star Ins. Co. v. Spratt* [1971] 2 Lloyd's Rep. 116, 133; *Excess Life Ass. Co. Ltd v. Firemen's Ins. Co. of Newark New Jersey* [1982] 2 Lloyd's Rep. 599, 619. See further, para. 35–9, *ante*.
[18] *Pratt v. Dwelling House Mutual Ins. Co.*, 130 N.Y. 206 (1892); *White v. Lancashire Ins. Co.* (1879) 27 Grant 61.

the US[19] where A was secretary of X company and general agent of Y company, and in these capacities concluded a contract of reinsurance between the two companies, it was held that the policy was voidable in equity at the election of either company, but was valid unless avoided. It was contended that A exceeded his authority as agent of the Y company in reinsuring the X company, but it was held that it was within the general scope of his apparent authority, and that the fact that he was secretary of the insured company did not affect it with notice of his want of authority. The rule that the knowledge of an agent is the knowledge of his principal is confined to cases where the knowledge comes to the agent in the course of the transaction in question.

If the assured wishes to say that an agent instructed by him is for some purposes the insurers' agent, it is for him to establish that fact, and the fact that the agent takes a fee out of premiums forwarded to the insurers does not without more make him the agent of the latter.[20]

4. STATUTORY AND PROFESSIONAL REGULATION

36–72 Insurance intermediaries have become subject to a plethora of regulations in the last thirty years. Until recently, these were made pursuant to powers contained in the Insurance Companies Act 1982, the Insurance Brokers (Registration) Act 1977 and the Financial Services Act 1986. Now, the regime under the Financial Services and Markets Act 2000 has replaced both the 1982 and 1986 Acts,[21] and the system of registration under the 1977 Act has been repealed[22] and, as regards general insurance business, for the present replaced by a system of self-regulation operating under the auspices of the General Insurance Standards Council.[23] There is no longer any control of the use of the term "insurance broker". However, it should be noted that HM Treasury and the Financial Services Authority have announced that this self-regulatory scheme will be replaced by a statutory scheme in 2004, which will also implement the proposed EU Directive on Insurance Mediation.

36–73 Long-term insurance intermediaries. Independent intermediaries selling most forms of long-term insurance must be authorised by the Financial Services Authority. An insurer is directly liable for the acts and omissions of one of its appointed representatives.[24] The Authority has made rules that replace those previously made under the 1982 Act, which are contained in the Conduct of Business part of the Authority's Handbook.[25] These have the effect described briefly in the following paragraph.[26]

36–74 Chapter 2 of the COB Rules provides, *inter alia*, that an insurer

---

[19] *New York Central Ins. Co. v. National Protection Ins. Co.* 20 Barb. 468 (N.Y.S.C., 1854); 14 N.Y. 85 (N.Y.C.A.).

[20] *Bancroft v. Heath* (1900) 5 Com.Cas. 110; affirmed (1901) 6 Com.Cas. 137.

[21] See generally, Ch. 34, *ante*.

[22] By the Financial Services and Markets Act 2000, ss. 416(1)(c), 432(3), Sch. 22, as from April 30, 2001.

[23] See para 36–75, *post*.

[24] Financial Services and Markets Act 2000, s.39(3).

[25] Hereafter the "COB Rules".

[26] These rules of course have a wider effect than simply applying to long-term insurance investments.

may not offer to agents inducements which conflict with its duty to the customer, and may not offer commission to an independent intermediary, which is in excess of that disclosed to the customer by the agent. The principal rules relating to intermediaries advising on long-term insurance are contained in chapter 5 of the COB Rules. Insurers must ensure that representatives are in a position to give appropriate advice, and are not influenced by their remuneration to do otherwise. Any independent intermediary must act in the best interests of its customers when giving advice and customers must be informed whether the advice is independent or restricted to the products of one supplier.[27] They must take reasonable steps to ensure that they are in possession of sufficient personal and financial information about the customer relevant to the services in question, and must not make a recommendation unless the transaction is suitable for the customer. They must also take reasonable steps to ensure that the customer understands the risk. A decision to buy a policy must be followed by a "suitability letter."[28] The intermediary must disclose to the customer basic information, including its identity and address, and a statement of authorisation by the Authority. Charges to private customer must not be excessive.

36–75 The General Insurance Standards Council. As mentioned above, a self-regulatory scheme has been introduced under the auspices of the General Insurance Standards Council.[29] However, as indicated earlier, it will be replaced by a scheme under the 2000 Act in 2004. The G.I.S.C. scheme has in fact a wider coverage than simply intermediaries, and under the Financial Services and Markets Act, all organisations, including insurers, involved in general insurance activities are required to join. The Council has rules that incorporate two codes of conduct, one for dealing with private customers and the other covering commercial customers, and procedures to enforce the rules by way of disciplinary procedures. There are also rules governing financial and solvency requirements. Members must have complaints procedures and tell customers what these are. As well as promising, among other things, that members will act fairly and reasonably, provide clear and sufficient information, deal with claims promptly and avoid undisclosed conflicts of interest, both codes require members to explain the duty of disclosure to their customers, both at inception and on renewal of a policy.[30] They must also, if asked, tell customers the commission they will receive. The Code for Private Customers also gives consumers a cooling-off period and imposes a duty to notify consumers that a policy is due for renewal or has expired.[31]

---

[27] The principle of polarisation that was applied under the 1986 Act regime.

[28] Except where the premium is less than £50 per annum.

[29] Further information, including the texts of the G.I.S.C. Codes, can be found on their web site: http://www.gisc.co.uk.

[30] The previous self-regulatory code, which applied to non-broker intermediaries (General Insurance Business—Code of Practice for all Intermediaries (Including Employees of Insurance Companies) other than Registered Insurance Brokers, promulgated by the Association of British Insurers in 1989) was referred to in the judgment in *Harvest Trading Co. Ltd v. P.B. Davis Services* [1991] 2 Lloyd's Rep. 638 as providing useful guidance as to the standard of care expected of an unregistered insurance intermediary. There seems little doubt that the new Codes will afford similar guidance.

[31] It should be noted that the E.C. Commission has presented a proposal for a Directive on Insurance Mediation (Com (2000) 511, September 20, 2000), which would require a scheme for the registration of intermediaries. Existing E.C. law is in the form of a Recommendation (92/48/E.E.C), which is not binding in any way. If the Directive is adopted, it may be possible to comply with it by some form of formal recognition of the G.I.S.C. scheme.

INDEX